D0031799

KOBBÉ'S COMPLETE OPERA BOOK

Kobbé's Complete Opera Book

EDITED
AND REVISED BY

The Earl of Harewood

PUTNAM AND COMPANY

LONDON

CONTENTS

PART I: Before 1800

1 OPERA BEFORE GLUCK

Claudio Monteverdi   (1567-1643)   *La Favola d'Orfeo*, 4
Arianna, 9 · *Il Combattimento di Tancredi e Clorinda*, 10 · *Il Ritorno d'Ulisse in Patria*, 12 · *L'Incoronazione di Poppea*, 15
Henry Purcell (1658-1695) *Dido and Aeneas*, 23
The Beggar's Opera, 28
George Frideric Handel   (1685-1759)   *Giulio Cesare*, 39
Rodelinda, 44 · *Alcina*, 48 · *Semele*, 52
Giovanni Pergolesi (1710-1736) *La Serva Padrona*, 56

2 CHRISTOPH WILLIBALD GLUCK (1714-1787)
Orfeo ed Euridice, 61 · *Alceste*, 66 · *Iphigénie en Aulide*, 71
Iphigénie en Tauride, 75

3 WOLFGANG AMADEUS MOZART (1756-1791)
Idomeneo, 78 · *Die Entführung aus dem Serail*, 84 · *Der Schauspieldirektor*, 90 · *Le Nozze di Figaro*, 90 · *Don Giovanni*, 102 · *Così fan tutte*, 115 · *La Clemenza di Tito*, 126 · *Die Zauberflöte*, 129

PART II: The Nineteenth Century

4 GERMAN OPERA
Ludwig van Beethoven (1770-1827) *Fidelio*, 145
Carl Maria von Weber   (1786-1826)   *Der Freischütz*, 152
Euryanthe, 157 · *Oberon*, 160
Albert Lortzing   (1801-1851)   *Zar und Zimmermann*, 169
Der Wildschütz, 171
Otto Nicolai (1810-1849) *Die lustigen Weiber von Windsor*, 173
Friedrich von Flotow (1812-1883) *Martha*, 176

5 RICHARD WAGNER (1813-1883)
Rienzi, 185 · *Der fliegende Holländer*, 188 · *Tannhäuser*, 195
Lohengrin, 202 · *Tristan und Isolde*, 216 · *Die Meistersinger von Nürnberg*, 232 · *Der Ring des Nibelungen*, 253: *Das Rheingold*, 260, *Die Walküre*, 273, *Siegfried*, 290, *Götterdämmerung*, 301 · *Parsifal*, 316

6 GERMAN OPERA CONTINUED

Franz von Suppé (1819–1895) *Boccaccio*, 333
Peter Cornelius (1824–1874) *Der Barbier von Baghdad*, 337
Johann Strauss (1825–1899) *Die Fledermaus*, 342 • *Eine Nacht in Venedig*, 350 • *Der Zigeunerbaron*, 354 • *Wienerblut*, 358
Karl Goldmark (1830–1915) *Die Königin von Saba*, 362
Hermann Goetz (1840–1876) *Der Widerspänstigen Zähmung*, 365
Karl Millöcker (1842–1899) *Der Bettelstudent*, 368
Engelbert Humperdinck (1854–1921) *Hänsel und Gretel*, 371
Hugo Wolf (1860–1903) *Der Corregidor*, 374

7 ITALIAN OPERA

Domenico Cimarosa (1749–1801) *Il Matrimonio Segreto*, 377
Luigi Cherubini (1760–1842) *Médée*, 380
Gasparo Spontini (1774–1851) *La Vestale*, 385
Gioacchino Antonio Rossini (1792–1868) *L'Italiana in Algeri*, 388 • *Il Turco in Italia*, 393 • *Elisabetta, Regina d'Inghilterra*, 397 • *Il Barbiere di Siviglia*, 400 • *La Cenerentola*, 410 • *La Gazza Ladra*, 414 • *Mosè in Egitto*, 419 • *La Donna del Lago*, 424 • *Semiramide*, 428 • *Le Comte Ory*, 431 • *Guillaume Tell*, 434
Gaetano Donizetti (1797–1848) *Anna Bolena*, 438 • *L'Elisir d'Amore*, 443 • *Lucrezia Borgia*, 447 • *Maria Stuarda*, 450 *Lucia di Lammermoor*, 453 • *Roberto Devereux*, 462 • *La Fille du Régiment*, 465 • *La Favorita*, 468 • *Linda di Chamounix*, 474 • *Don Pasquale*, 478
Vincenzo Bellini (1801–1835) *Il Pirata*, 482 • *La Straniera*, 485 • *La Sonnambula*, 489 • *Norma*, 494 • *Beatrice di Tenda*, 499 • *I Puritani*, 502

8 GIUSEPPE VERDI (1813–1901)

Un Giorno di Regno, 507 • *Nabucco*, 512 • *I Lombardi*, 516 *Ernani*, 521 • *I due Foscari*, 528 • *Attila*, 531 • *Macbeth*, 534 *La Battaglia di Legnano*, 543 • *Luisa Miller*, 546 • *Rigoletto*, 548 • *Il Trovatore*, 561 • *La Traviata*, 570 • *Les Vêpres Siciliennes*, 579 • *Aroldo*, 586 • *Simon Boccanegra*, 590 • *Un*

Ballo in Maschera, 602 · *La Forza del Destino*, 609 · *Don Carlos*, 617 · *Aida*, 629 · *Otello*, 645 · *Falstaff*, 653

9 ITALIAN OPERA CONTINUED

Amilcare Ponchielli (1834–1886) *La Gioconda*, 663
Arrigo Boito (1842–1918) *Mefistofele*, 671 · *Nerone*, 676
Alfredo Catalani (1854–1893) *La Wally*, 680
Ruggiero Leoncavallo (1858–1919) *I Pagliacci*, 683
Pietro Mascagni   (1863–1945)   *Cavalleria Rusticana*, 690
L'Amico Fritz, 695 · *Iris*, 698
Umberto Giordano (1867–1948) *Andrea Chénier*, 701 · *Fedora*, 706

10 FRENCH OPERA

François Adrien Boïeldieu   (1775–1834)   *La Dame Blanche*, 711
Daniel François Auber   (1782–1871)   *La Muette de Portici*, 714 · *Fra Diavolo*, 718
Giacomo Meyerbeer (1791–1864) *Robert le Diable*, 723 · *Les Huguenots*, 725   ·   *Le Prophète*, 734   ·   *Dinorah*, 741
L'Africaine, 743
Jacques François Halévy (1799–1862) *La Juive*, 749
Adolphe Adam (1803–1856) *Le Postillon de Longjumeau*, 755
Hector Berlioz   (1803–1869)   *Benvenuto Cellini*, 757 · *La Damnation de Faust*, 760 · *Les Troyens*, 764 · *Béatrice et Bénédict*, 774
Ambroise Thomas (1811–1896) *Mignon*, 778
Charles François Gounod (1818–1893) *Faust*, 782 · *Mireille*, 790 · *Roméo et Juliette*, 792
Jacques Offenbach (1819–1880) *Orphée aux Enfers*, 797 · *La Belle Hélène*, 801   ·   *La Périchole*, 805   ·   *Les Contes d'Hoffmann*, 809
Edouard Lalo (1823–1892) *Le Roi d'Ys*, 816
Camille Saint-Saëns (1835–1921) *Samson et Dalila*, 819
Léo Delibes (1836–1891) *Lakmé*, 821
Georges Bizet (1838–1875) *Les Pêcheurs de Perles*, 826 · *La Jolie Fille de Perth*, 830 · *Djamileh*, 833 · *Carmen*, 834

Alexis Emmanuel Chabrier (1841–1894) *L'Étoile*, 848 · *Le
Roi malgré lui*, 852
Jules Massenet (1842–1912) *Manon*, 858 · *Werther*, 864
Thaïs, 869 · *Le Jongleur de Notre Dame*, 873 · *Don Quichotte*,
875

11 RUSSIAN OPERA
Michael Ivanovich Glinka (1804–1857) *A Life for the Tsar*,
877 · *Russlan and Ludmila*, 879
Aleksandr Porfyrevich Borodin (1834–1887) *Prince Igor*, 881
Modest Petrovich Moussorgsky (1839–1881) *Boris Godounov*,
888 · *Khovanshchina*, 900 · *The Fair at Sorochintsy*, 904
Peter Ilitsch Tchaikovsky (1840–1893) *Yevgeny Onyegin*, 908
The Maid of Orleans, 917 · *Mazeppa*, 920 · *The Queen of
Spades*, 926 · *Iolanta*, 932
Nikolai Andreevich Rimsky-Korsakov (1844–1908) *Ivan
the Terrible (Pskovityanka)*, 934 · *Maiskaya Noch*, 937
Snegurochka, 941 · *Sadko*, 944 · *Le Coq d'Or*, 947

12 ENGLISH OPERA
Michael William Balfe (1803–1870) *The Bohemian Girl*, 954
Julius Benedict (1804–1885) *The Lily of Killarney*, 957
Vincent Wallace (1814–1865) *Maritana*, 959

13 CZECH OPERA
Bedřich Smetana (1824–1884) *The Bartered Bride (Prodaná
Nevěsta)*, 963 · *Dalibor*, 969 · *The Two Widows (Dvě Vdovy)*,
973 · *The Kiss (Hubička)*, 976 · *The Secret (Tajemství)*, 979
Libuše, 981
Antonín Dvořák (1841–1904) *Rusalka*, 987

PART III: The Twentieth Century

14 GERMAN OPERA
Eugen d'Albert (1864–1932) *Tiefland*, 993
Richard Strauss (1864–1949) *Salome*, 997 · *Elektra*, 1002
Der Rosenkavalier, 1008 · *Ariadne auf Naxos*, 1018 · *Die Frau
ohne Schatten*, 1024 · *Intermezzo*, 1029 · *Die Aegyptische*

Helena, 1033 · *Arabella*, 1036 · *Die schweigsame Frau*, 1041
Friedenstag, 1045 · *Daphne*, 1048 · *Die Liebe der Danae*,
1050 · *Capriccio*, 1054
Hans Pfitzner (1869-1949) *Palestrina*, 1059
Arnold Schoenberg (1874-1951) *Erwartung*, 1065 · *Von
Heute auf Morgen*, 1066 · *Moses und Aron*, 1068
Alban Berg (1885-1935) *Wozzeck*, 1073 · *Lulu*, 1082
Paul Hindemith (1895-1963) *Cardillac*, 1088 · *Mathis der
Maler*, 1093
Kurt Weill (1900-1950) *Aufstieg und Fall der Stadt
Mahagonny*, 1100
Gottfried von Einem (b. 1918) *Dantons Tod*, 1108
Bernd Alois Zimmermann (1918-1971) *Die Soldaten*, 1112
Hans Werner Henze (b. 1926) *Boulevard Solitude*, 1121
König Hirsch (Il Re Cervo), 1125 · *Der Prinz von Homburg*,
1130 · *Elegy for Young Lovers*, 1134 · *The Bassarids*, 1140
Der junge Lord, 1148

15 ITALIAN OPERA

Giacomo Puccini (1858-1924) *Manon Lescaut*, 1154 · *La
Bohème*, 1157 · *Tosca*, 1165 · *Madama Butterfly*, 1175 · *La
Fanciulla del West*, 1182 · *La Rondine*, 1187 · *Il Tabarro*,
1190 · *Suor Angelica*, 1194 · *Gianni Schicchi*, 1195
Turandot, 1200
Francesco Cilea (1866-1950) *Adriana Lecouvreur*, 1205
Ferruccio Busoni (1866-1924) *Turandot*, 1209 · *Arlecchino*,
1213 · *Doktor Faust*, 1216
Italo Montemezzi (1875-1952) *L'Amore dei Tre Re*, 1223
Ermanno Wolf-Ferrari (1876-1948) *I Quattro Rusteghi*, 1229
Il Segreto di Susanna, 1233 · *I Giojelli della Madonna*, 1235
Riccardo Zandonai (1883-1944) *Francesca da Rimini*, 1239
Luigi Dallapiccola (1904-1975) *Il Prigioniero*, 1243

16 FRENCH OPERA

Gabriel Fauré (1845-1924) *Pénélope*, 1249
Gustave Charpentier (1860-1956) *Louise*, 1252
Claude Debussy (1862-1918) *Pelléas et Mélisande*, 1258
Paul Dukas (1865-1935) *Ariane et Barbe-bleue*, 1264

Albert Roussel (1869–1937) *Padmâvatî*, 1267
Henri Rabaud (1875–1949) *Marouf*, 1273
Maurice Ravel   (1875–1937)   *L'Heure Espagnole*, 1275
L'Enfant et les Sortilèges, 1277
Darius Milhaud (1892–1975) *Le Pauvre Matelot*, 1283 · *Opéras-
Minutes*, 1285: *L'Enlèvement d'Europe*, 1286, *L'Abandon
d'Ariane*, 1287, *La Délivrance de Thésée*, 1288 · *Christophe
Colomb*, 1289
Francis Poulenc (1899–1963) *Les Mamelles de Tirésias*, 1294
Dialogues des Carmélites, 1299

17 RUSSIAN OPERA

Igor Fedorovich Stravinsky (1882–1971) *Le Rossignol*, 1308
L'Histoire d'un Soldat, 1311 · *Renard*, 1313 · *Mavra*, 1316
Oedipus Rex, 1318 · *The Rake's Progress*, 1322
Sergei Sergyeevich Prokofiev (1891–1953) *The Gambler*, 1329
The Love for Three Oranges, 1334 · *The Fiery Angel*, 1340
Betrothal in a Monastery, 1348 · *War and Peace*, 1353
Dmitri Dmitrevich Shostakovich   (1906–1975)   *Katerina
Ismailova*, 1371

18 ENGLISH OPERA

Ethel Smyth   (1858–1944)   *The Wreckers*, 1378 · *The
Boatswain's Mate*, 1381
Frederick Delius (1862–1934)   *A Village Romeo and Juliet*,
1383
Ralph Vaughan Williams (1872–1958) *Hugh the Drover*, 1387
The Poisoned Kiss, 1390 · *Riders to the Sea*, 1393 · *The
Pilgrim's Progress*, 1395
Gustav Holst (1874–1934) *Sāvitri*, 1400
Rutland Boughton (1878–1960) *The Immortal Hour*, 1402
William Walton (b. 1902)   *Troilus and Cressida*, 1405 · *The
Bear*, 1410
Michael Tippett (b. 1905)   *The Midsummer Marriage*, 1412
King Priam, 1423 · *The Knot Garden*, 1428
Benjamin Britten (1913–1977) *Peter Grimes*, 1434 · *The Rape
of Lucretia*, 1445 · *Albert Herring*, 1452 · *Let's Make an
Opera!*, 1459 · *Billy Budd*, 1464 · *Gloriana*, 1477 · *The Turn

of the Screw, 1487 · Noye's Fludde, 1500 · A Midsummer
Night's Dream, 1502 · Parables for Church Performance,
1514: Curlew River, 1515, The Burning Fiery Furnace, 1520,
The Prodigal Son, 1523 · Owen Wingrave, 1525 · Death in
Venice, 1532

19 CZECH OPERA
Leoš Janáček (1854–1928) Jenůfa, 1542 · The Adventures
of Mr Brouček, 1550 · Katya Kabanova, 1560 · The Cunning
Little Vixen, 1567 · The Makropulos Affair, 1577 · From
the House of the Dead, 1584
Jaromir Weinberger (1896–1967) Schwanda the Bagpiper,
1590

20 POLISH OPERA
Karol Szymanowski (1882–1937) King Roger, 1594
Krzysztof Penderecki (b. 1933) The Devils of Loudun, 1598

21 HUNGARIAN OPERA
Béla Bartók (1881–1945) Duke Bluebeard's Castle, 1607
Zoltán Kodály (1882–1967) Háry János, 1609

22 SPANISH OPERA
Enrique Granados (1867–1916) Goyescas, 1616
Manuel de Falla (1876–1946) La Vida Breve, 1618 · El Retablo
de Maese Pedro, 1620

23 AMERICAN OPERA
Virgil Thomson (b. 1896) Four Saints in Three Acts, 1623
George Gershwin (1898–1937) Porgy and Bess, 1626
Gian Carlo Menotti (b. 1911) Amelia al Ballo, 1634 · The
Medium, 1636 · The Telephone, 1640 · The Consul, 1641
Amahl and the Night Visitors, 1647 · The Saint of Bleecker
Street, 1650

24 ARGENTINIAN OPERA
Alberto Ginastera (b. 1916) Bomarzo, 1654

25 DANISH OPERA
Carl August Nielsen (1865–1931) Saul and David, 1662
Maskarade, 1665

INDEX, 1671

ILLUSTRATIONS

1 *Alcina* with Joan Sutherland at Covent Garden, 1962. *Photo : Houston Rogers,* FACING PAGE 46
2 *Alceste* at la Scala, 1954. Maria Callas in the title role. *Photo : Piccagliani,* 47
3 Tito Gobbi and Mirella Freni in Mozart's *Le Nozze di Figaro* at Covent Garden. *Photo : Donald Southern,* 78
4 *Don Giovanni:* Ezio Pinza sings the Champagne Aria at Salzburg, 1937. *Photo : Ellinger,* 79
5 *Così fan tutte:* a scene from Act I of Rennert's famous production at Salzburg. *Photo : Salzburger Festspiele,* 174
6 Lotte Lehmann in *Fidelio,* Salzburg, 1935. *Photo : Ellinger,* 175
7 *Tannhäuser* at Bayreuth in Wieland Wagner's production, 1955. *Photo : Festspiele Bayreuth,* 206
8 *Tristan und Isolde:* Brangäne offers Isolde the Love Potion, Bayreuth, 1886, and in the 1974 production. *Photo : Festspiele Bayreuth,* 207
9 *Tristan und Isolde:* the lovers—1865 (*Stuart-Liff Collection*), and nearly a hundred years later, *Photo : Festespiele Bayreuth,* 270
10 Leo Slezak as Walter in *Die Meistersinger,* Vienna, 1905, 271
11 *Das Rheingold:* Valhalla, about 1900 and 1973. *Photo : Helga Wallmüller,* 302
12 *Parsifal:* 1888 and 1965. *Photos : Festspiele Bayreuth,* 303
13 Johann Strauss's *Die Fledermaus* in Vienna. *Photo : Franz Hausmann,* 462
14 Donizetti: Joan Sutherland in *Lucia* at Covent Garden, 1959. *Photo : Houston Rogers,* 463
Monserrat Caballé in *Roberto Devereux. Photo : Aldo Negro,* 463
15 Rosa Ponselle in *Norma* at the Metropolitan, New York, 494
16 *La Traviata* at la Scala, 1955, with Maria Callas. *Photo : Piccagliani,* 495
17 Verdi's *Falstaff* at Covent Garden with Regina Resnik and Geraint Evans. *Photo : Donald Southern,* 718
18 Martinelli as Otello. Caruso as Canio in *I Pagliacci. Stuart-Liff Collection,* 719
19 *Les Troyens* at Covent Garden. *Photo : Houston Rogers,* 750
20 Melba as Lakmé, about 1890. *Stuart-Liff Collection,* 751
21 *Carmen:* The original Carmen, Galli Marié in 1873; Grace Bumbry and Franco Corelli, Chicago, 1964 (*Photo : David*

H. *Fishman*). Wieland Wagner's production, Hamburg, 1965, *Photo* : *Fritz Peyer*, FACING PAGE 846

22 Geraldine Farrar as Manon in Massenet's opera, 847

23 Chaliapin as Boris Godounov, 878

24 *Salome*: Josephine Barstow (Salome) and Emile Belcourt (Herod), English National Opera, 1975. *Photo* : *John Garner*, 879

25 Rose Pauly and Hilde Konetzni in *Elektra*, 1038

26 Lotte Lehmann as the Marschallin in *Der Rosenkavalier*. *Photo* : *Ellinger*, 1039

27 Schoenberg's *Moses and Aaron* in Peter Hall's production at Covent Garden. *Photo* : *Houston Rogers*, 1070

28 Anya Silja and Carlos Alexander in Alban Berg's *Lulu*. *Photo* : *Madeline Winkler-Betzendahl*, 1071

29 Henze: *Elegy for Young Lovers* with Fischer-Dieskau. *Photo* : *Rudolf Betz*, 1134
The *Bassarids* at English National Opera, 1974. *Photo* : *Donald Southern*, 1134

30 Act V of *Pelléas et Mélisande* at Covent Garden. *Photo* : *Reg Wilson*, 1135

31 Callas and Gobbi in Act I of *Tosca* at Covent Garden. *Photo* : *Reg Wilson*, 1166

32 Eva Turner as Turandot in Puccini's opera. *Photo* : *Maurice Seymour*, 1167

33 Stravinsky's *The Rake's Progress* with Jenny Tourel, Tom Rounseville and Elisabeth Schwarzkopf. *Photo* : *Piccagliani*, 1326

34 Prokofiev's *War and Peace*: Norman Bailey as Kutuzov (*above*); Raymond Myers as Napoleon (*below*). *Photos* : *John Garner*, 1327

35 The kiss in Michael Tippett's *The Knot Garden*. *Photo* : *Stuart Robinson*, 1358

36 Geraint Evans, Heather Harper, Jon Vickers in Act III of *Peter Grimes*, 1975. *Photo* : *Donald Southern*, 1359

37 Joan Cross as Queen Elizabeth in *Gloriana*, 1953. *Photo* : *Roger Wood*, 1518

38 *Turn of the Screw*: The ghost of Peter Quint. *Photo* : *Denis de Marney*, 1519

39 Janáček's *Katya Kabanova* at English National Opera. *Photo* : *Donald Southern*. The *Cunning Little Vixen* at the Berlin Komische Oper. *Photo* : *Jürgen Simon*, 1550

40 Marie Collier as Emilia Marty in *The Makropulos Affair*, Sadler's Wells, 1964. *Photo* : *Reg Wilson*, 1551

PREFACE

Gustave Kobbé was born in New York in 1857. He received his musical education in that city and at Wiesbaden in Germany. He began his career as co-editor of the *Musical Review*, and in 1882 was sent as correspondent to Bayreuth by the *New York World* for the first performance of *Parsifal*. He contributed many articles on music to the leading American magazines of his day—*The Century, Scribners, The Forum, North American Review*, etc.—and became music critic of the *New York Herald* when that newspaper was owned by James Gordon Bennett, remaining with it for eighteen years. His hobby was sailing, and it was while he was out in the Great South Bay, Long Island, New York, in July 1918, that a seaplane, coming down for a landing, struck his boat and killed him instantly.

At the time he died, Kobbé was on the point of completing the book which was published after his death as *The Complete Opera Book*. Various additions to it were made before publication and also in subsequent editions with a view to fulfilling the claims of the title, although these must necessarily remain largely illusory. In the early 1950's, I was asked to bring Kobbé up to date and in the 1954 edition an attempt was made to reflect some of the changes which had taken place in the repertory between 1918 and that date.

When preparing that edition I remembered my own reliance on Kobbé when, as a boy at school in the 1930's, I heard broadcasts from British and Continental Opera Houses and often did not know the stories or backgrounds of the works I was listening to. Kobbé was invaluable in giving me an idea of what to expect; but I remember too my chagrin at finding that, for instance, *La Forza del Destino* had the barest of mentions, and it was small consolation, when this opera was being broadcast almost weekly from Italy, to know that it owed its exclusion from Kobbé to the accident that it was little known in America at the time the book was being written.

So in 1954 quite a number of works, ancient as well as modern, were added to what Kobbé himself had prepared and others removed to make way for them—after the new edition had appeared, I was taken to task by no lesser person than that operatic luminary Mary Garden for insufficient attention to 'modern French opera', by which she meant those she had 'created' in the early years of the century. The 1954 Kobbé, though much bigger than the previous edition, still omitted a fair number of works which experience gained during the past twenty years suggests should be included and the present edition is therefore both substantially revised and considerably enlarged. As in 1954, the entry for each opera is signed with an initial, 'K' standing for the material left by Mr. Kobbé; 'K.W.' for the operas added after Kobbé's death by Katherine Wright, who put together the material he left; 'F.B.' for Ferruccio Bonavia; and 'H' for the present editor.

One of the features of operatic life in the 1950's and 1960's (and I can see no reason why it should not continue through the 1970's and further) has been the wholesale revival of works which at one time seemed to have fallen by the wayside: Monteverdi is almost more often played now than Gluck; Mozart's *Idomeneo* became as much the connoisseur's piece of the 1950's and 1960's as *Così* had been for pre-1939 opera-goers; the lesser works of Rossini, Bellini, Donizetti have recently found almost as much favour as those of Verdi; Prokofiev is recognised as an opera composer, and even the problem products of inter-war Germany now emerge as sage examples for the present generation.

This widening of the repertory, in itself a stimulating influence on operatic experience, is perhaps a natural corollary of the one really melancholy feature of operatic life in the middle of the twentieth century: the lack of interest, that was once automatic and widespread, in contemporary works. It is true that the decline applies almost as much to music heard outside the theatre as inside, but if it continues, it must gradually eliminate the production of new works and in the end bring about the extinction of the operatic form through its sheer inability to reproduce itself. Contemporary composers complain about the rigid outlook of managements, the high cost of productions (and therefore limited opportunity) in big opera houses, the non-co-operation of singers, the lack of interest on the part of audiences—such a view would not have impressed Mozart or Verdi (though it might Wagner).

For my own part, while recognising that a blind faith in the future of opera would be totally out of place—it has too many influential detractors crying that it is out of date to make *that* view tenable—I cannot forget that the original notion behind opera is still valid: *dramma per musica*, drama through music. We may come to impatience with the conventions of

Handel, the elegance of the eighteenth century, the lofty passions of the nineteenth, *bel canto*, Wagnerism, Puccini's romanticism, the big apparatus of *Oedipus Rex* and *Peter Grimes* and *War and Peace*; but so long as man has time for the performing arts, he will want to combine music and drama in an effort to make the amalgam amount to something not quite the same as either on its own—and the result will be a candidate for a future edition of Kobbé.

Acknowledgements for the use of musical quotations where the scores are still under copyright are due to:

Messrs Boosey & Hawkes Music Publishers Limited (Rimsky-Korsakov, Strauss, Stravinsky, Prokofiev, Britten, Weinberger, Kodály); Messrs Chappell & Co. Ltd (Granados); Messrs J. & W. Chester Ltd (Falla); Messrs Durand & Cie (Ravel, Roussel, Debussy); Messrs Faber Music Ltd (Britten's Church Operas, 'Owen Wingrave' and 'Death in Venice'); Messrs Heugel (Massenet, Charpentier); Novello & Co. Ltd (Rimsky-Korsakov); G. Ricordi & Co. Ltd (Boito, Puccini, Montemezzi, Zandonai); Messrs Schott & Co. Ltd (Tippett); Messrs Sonzogno (Leoncavallo, Giordano, Cilea, Mascagni); Messrs Stainer & Bell Ltd (Boughton); Messrs Edizione Suvini Zerboni (Dallapiccola); Messrs Universal Edition (Alfred A. Kalmus) Ltd (Berg, Janáček, Weill); Messrs Joseph Weinberger Ltd (Ravel).

My thanks are due to Mr. Harold Rosenthal, who laboured for the 1954 edition to provide the details of premières and performances recorded at the head of each opera and who has revised his work for each succeeding edition including the latest. Also to Mr. Herbert Rees, who is not only the most assiduous of proof-readers but also a mine of knowledge, operatic and otherwise.

January 1976   HAREWOOD

PART I

BEFORE 1800

1
Opera Before Gluck

CLAUDIO MONTEVERDI
(1567–1643)

OPERA is usually and conveniently thought to have begun in 1600, the date of Peri's *Euridice*, the first surviving opera (his *Dafne*, 1597, has been lost). But before then, there was a good deal of stage music of one sort or another—Miracle plays and Mysteries, Moralities and Sacred Dramas, and, perhaps most important, Masques—and all these played their part in the complicated development of opera, a form which is itself to this day in a constant state of evolution.

At the end of the sixteenth century a small group of aristocratic intelligentsia, known collectively to musical history as 'the Camerata', was meeting in Florence. Under the auspices of a certain Count Giovanni Bardi di Vernio, and later of Jacopo Corsi, it included composers such as Vincenzo Galilei (father of the astronomer), Emilio de' Cavalieri, Jacopo Peri, and Giulio Caccini, and the avowed intention was to reproduce as far as possible the combination of words and music which together made up the Greek theatre. With this restorative aim in view, the members laid down that the text must at all times be understood, that the words must be sung with a scrupulously correct and natural declamation, and that above all the music must interpret the spirit of the whole, not concentrate on details of incidents and words or even individual syllables. In a word, taking the Greeks as their authorities, the composers and poets concerned were anxious to end the distortion of the words which was inevitable in polyphonic music; in its place they were responsible for putting monody (or solo song) in something like the form we know to-day.

3

Claudio Monteverdi, already highly successful in polyphonic style, was the composer who was able to build on the foundations which had been laid by the Florentine 'Camerata' and his first opera, *Orfeo*, has been described by Professor Westrup as a landmark 'not because it broke new ground but because in it imagination took control of theory'. Opera was perhaps lucky that there should appear so soon a composer whose outlook was essentially dramatic, and certainly Monteverdi's *Orfeo* makes the *Euridice* of Peri and Caccini (both set Rinuccini's libretto in the same year, 1600) appear pale and monotonous by comparison.

Monteverdi's working career is conveniently divided into two sections: during the first, 1590–1612, he was in the service of the Mantuan court and during the second, 1613–1643, he worked in Venice, as Maestro di Capella of San Marco and as a composer for the theatre. During the first period he wrote three of the twenty-one dramatic (or semi-dramatic) pieces to his credit (*Orfeo* and *Il Ballo delle Ingrate* survive complete, but only a few fragments of *Arianna* exist to-day); of the remaining eighteen, all but four have disappeared (*Tirsi e Clori*, a ballet-opera; *Il Combattimento di Tancredi e Clorinda*, a dramatic cantata; and the operas *Il Ritorno d'Ulisse in Patria* and *L'Incoronazione di Poppea* survive).

The recent tendency is to regard Monteverdi not so much as a great revolutionary but as the culmination of a period of change, as the composer who was thoroughly at home in both the polyphonic and the monodic styles.

LA FAVOLA D'ORFEO
The Legend of Orpheus

Opera in a prologue and five acts. Music by Claudio Monteverdi, text by Alessandro Striggio. First produced privately at the Accademia degl' Invaghiti, Mantua, February 1607, with Giovanni Gualberto[1] as Orfeo, and on February 24 of the same year at the Court Theatre, Mantua. In August 1607 the opera was given in Monteverdi's native town of Cremona, and it is likely that there were stage productions in Turin, Florence, and Milan.

Orfeo was revived in 1904 in a concert version in Paris (arranged Vincent d'Indy); in 1909 in Milan and other Italian cities (arranged

---

[1] A castrato, the first to create an important operatic role.

Giacomo Orefice); in 1910 in Brussels. The first modern stage performance was given at the Théâtre Réjane, Paris, in 1911, in d'Indy's version.

The opera was first heard in America in concert form at the Metropolitan, New York, in 1912 (arranged Orefice), when Hermann Weil was Orfeo and the cast included Rita Fornia, Anna Case, and Herbert Witherspoon. In 1913 Chicago heard a concert version, conducted by Campanini and with Sammarco in the title role. There was a stage performance in Breslau in 1913 arranged by Erdmann-Guckel, and a new realisation by Carl Orff was heard at Mannheim in 1925. Malipiero's arrangement was first performed in Leningrad in 1929. The first American stage performance took place in 1929 at Northampton, Massachusetts, under the auspices of Smith College (in Malipiero's version) with Charles Kullman as Orfeo and Werner Josten conducting.

In England, the first performance (in concert form, arranged d'Indy) took place under the auspices of the Institut Français in 1924, and a stage version (arranged J. A. Westrup and W. H. Harris) was seen in Oxford in 1925 and in London in 1929. Italian revivals have been at the Rome Opera, 1934 (arranged Benvenuti), with Franci (Orfeo), Gabriella Gatti, Giuseppina Cobelli, and Cloe Elmo, conductor Serafin; at la Scala, Milan, 1935 (arranged Respighi), under Marinuzzi and with Carlo Galeffi (Orfeo), Stignani, Carla Segrera, Palombini; at the Florence Festival, 1949 (arranged Frazzi), with Fedora Barbieri (Orfeo), Rizzieri, Corsi, conductor Guarnieri, 1957 with Giuseppe Valdengo. Cesare Brero's version was performed by the Opera Camera of Milan at Versailles in 1964 and at the Aix-en-Provence Festival, 1965. Another realisation is by Maderna who conducted the 1967 production at the Holland Festival with Barry McDaniel. *Orfeo* was produced in Budapest in 1936 (in Respighi's version) and remained in the regular repertory for a number of years. Revived, New York City Center, 1960, with Souzay, conductor Stokowski; Sadler's Wells Opera (realised by Raymond Leppard) 1965, with John Wakefield.

CHARACTERS

Music (Prologue) .... Soprano
Orfeo, *a poet* .... Tenor or Baritone
Euridice, *his wife* .... Soprano
A Nymph .... Soprano
Four Shepherds .... Three Tenors, Bass
Messenger .... Soprano
Hope .... Soprano
Charon .... Bass
Proserpine, *Queen of the Underworld* .... Soprano
Pluto, *King of the Underworld* .... Bass

Apollo ....Tenor or Baritone
Nymphs, Shepherds, Spirits of the Underworld

It is perhaps worth while to give a list[1] of the instruments called for at the beginning of Monteverdi's score of *Orfeo*, and of the additional ones mentioned in the inner pages of the score:

Fundament instruments (i.e. chord-playing)
  2 clavicembalos
  1 double harp (one more needed in performance?)
  2 chitarrones (one more called for in score)
  2 bass cithers (not listed but mentioned in score)
  3 bass gambas
  2 organs with wood (flute) pipes (*Organi di Legno*)
  1 organ with reed pipes (*Regale*)
Stringed instruments
  2 small violins (*alla francese*)
  10 viole da braccio (i.e. a string ensemble, possibly 4 violins, 4 violas, 2 violoncellos)
  2 contrabass viols
Wind instruments
  4 trombones (one more called for in score)
  2 cornetts
  1 flautino alla Vigesima Seconda (i.e. a high recorder; one more (?) called for in score)
  1 high trumpet (*clarino*; possibly referring to use of high range of ordinary trumpet)
  3 soft trumpets (*trombe sordine*)

It seems likely that many of the players doubled, and of course not all the instruments were used at once, apart that is to say from the opening *toccata*, some of the *sinfonie*, and the accompaniments of a few of the choruses. Monteverdi indicated what combination of instruments he required, and he used the contrast of orchestral colour for dramatic purposes.

The opera begins with a *toccata* in C major—'shattering', Redlich calls it—played three times by the whole orchestra before the rise of the curtain. The Prologue consists of a recitation by La Musica of her powers; there are five verses, composed on a bass, each introduced by a *ritornello* which is

[1] The list is quoted in Donald Grout's *A Short History of Opera* (O.U.P.).

played for the sixth time after the last verse. The same *ritornello* recurs for the seventh and eighth times at the end of Act II and at the beginning of Act V. These *ritornelli* are employed throughout the opera to create appropriate atmosphere for the various scenes.

Act I. Shepherds and Nymphs are rejoicing over the wedding of Orfeo and Euridice. The two Shepherds and the Nymph have solo verses in between the choruses, and Orfeo himself sings the first of his big solos, 'Rosa del ciel'. This is followed by a stanza for Euridice, and the choruses are repeated. The act ends with a beautiful chorus praying that their happy state may bring no misfortune on the lovers.

Act II is dominated by the great scene for the Messenger, and by Orfeo's lament, but it begins with a long, beautiful pastoral episode. Orfeo sings first, and his short solo is followed by a strophic song for the second Shepherd, and a duet for two Shepherds; each of these has two verses, and each verse is preceded by its *ritornello*. The Shepherds have a third verse, which is preceded and followed by a different *ritornello*, and the scene is rounded off by a short chorus, in which the Shepherds beg Orfeo to sing. Orfeo sings a strophic song 'Vi ricordo o boschi ombrosi', each of the four verses being preceded by a *ritornello* played by five viole da braccio, one contrabass viol, two clavicembalos, and three chitarroes. It is a simple, carefree aria, and perfectly establishes the mood of contentment and happiness which, after the Shepherd has praised Orfeo's song, is so suddenly broken by the advent of the Messenger with the news of Euridice's death. The unclouded happiness and serenity which have seemed to be Orfeo's have aroused the envy of the gods; the chorus is immediately apprehensive of the nature of the Messenger's errand and Orfeo alone is unaware of the approach of tragedy. 'Ahi, caso acerbo' sings the Messenger to a phrase which is later repeated by the Shepherds, and the chorus. The solo is one of great emotional and dramatic import, and the few phrases of dialogue with Orfeo at the beginning, ending with his stunned 'Ohimè', produce an extraordinary intensity by the simplest means. The Messenger's narration over, the first reaction of horror comes (to the words 'Ahi, caso acerbo') from the Shepherds. A moment later Orfeo (as if repeating the last words he heard, suggests Leo Schrade[1])

---

[1] Leo Schrade: *Monteverdi* (Gollancz).

begins his lament, 'Tu se' morta, se' morta mia vita'. It is short, the feeling is restrained, even classical, but the evocative power of the music is unsurpassed, and the simplicity and passion of the ending 'A dio terra, a dio cielo, e Sole, a Dio', is most moving. The chorus and the Shepherds sing an elaborate threnody to the words 'Ahi, caso acerbo', and mourn the tragedies of Euridice bitten by the Serpent, and of Orfeo transfixed by grief.

Act III.   In impressively solemn declamation, Orfeo is confronted by Hope. He resolves to seek Euridice in Hades. The use of trombones is a feature of the orchestration. Charon's sombre utterance is followed by Orfeo's attempt by means of his powers as a singer to gain admission to Hades. The song with its elaborate ornamentation is a great test of virtuosity, and, as if to emphasise this characteristic, each verse and *ritornello* has a different combination of instruments. It is perhaps surprising that Monteverdi should print an alternative and wholly simple version for the use, one supposes, of singers who were not able to do justice to the more elaborate writing. Charon admits that he has listened to the song with intense pleasure, but it is only after Orfeo has renewed his pleading in the simplest recitative that he yields; who could resist the rising semitones of the impassioned 'Rendetemi il mio ben, Tartarei Numi' with which he ends his plea? Preceded and followed by a solemn *sinfonia*, the act ends with a most lovely, madrigalesque chorus of Spirits.

Act IV.   Proserpine and Pluto discuss Orfeo's plight, and, prompted by his wife and urged by the captive spirits singly and in chorus, the King of the Underworld agrees to release Euridice to her husband. Orfeo is triumphant but his song of rejoicing is interrupted as he looks back to see if Euridice is following. The spirits lament that her short-lived freedom should be snatched from her by her husband's transgression of Pluto's stipulation.

Act V.   Orfeo, wandering on the plains of Thrace, laments his broken heart, and summons nature itself, which has so often benefited from his singing, to join him in his mourning. The *ritornello*, which begins the act, is the same as that used in the Prologue; during the course of the scene, Monteverdi makes use of an echo device. Apollo, Orfeo's father, descends from Heaven and tells his son that he will be translated to divine immortality, and amongst the stars will be able to see his Euridice again. Father and son ascend to Heaven singing together music full of coloratura ornament.

The chorus sings its valediction in a gay 'Moresca'. (It should be noted that Striggio's original libretto brought the legend to an end in accordance with tradition, Orfeo being torn to pieces at a Bacchanalian orgy by the Thracian women, maddened by his unceasing laments for a woman he would not see again.)

'*Orfeo*', says Professor Westrup,[1] 'is curiously representative of its time. We find in it the new recitative already practised by Peri and Caccini, the rhythmical subtlety of the French *chanson*, the traditional polyphony of motet and madrigal, the conventional practice of embellishing a vocal line with *fioriture*, the chromatic devices of the madrigal transferred to monody. . . . *Orfeo* is hardly an experimental work; it is rather a successful attempt to combine into a single whole the varied methods of musical expression current at the time.'   H.

ARIANNA

Opera in a prologue and eight scenes, music by Monteverdi, text by Rinuccini. First performed at the Teatro della Corte, Mantua, May 28, 1608, as part of the festivities connected with the wedding of Francesco Gonzaga with Margherita di Savoia. Virginia Andreini was the original Arianna. The score is now lost, apart from the famous lament and a few other fragments, but stage revivals were presented at Karlsruhe in 1926, and in Paris 1931.

Arianna seems to have been enormously successful when first performed, and the great lament of Arianna, 'Lasciatemi morire', became immediately the most popular piece of music of the day. It began a long line of *lamenti*, and Monteverdi himself transformed it into a five-part madrigal (in 1610) and into a sacred 'Pianto della Madonna' (published 1640).   H.

[1] In his essay on the composer in *The Heritage of Music*, vol. III (O.U.P.).

IL COMBATTIMENTO DI TANCREDI
E CLORINDA

The Fight between Tancredi and Clorinda

Dramatic cantata, music by Monteverdi, text by Tasso: verses 52–68 of Canto XII of *Gerusalemme liberata*.

Il Combattimento was published in 1638, fourteen years after it was written for performance in the Palazzo of Girolamo Mocenigo. In his introduction to the score, Monteverdi describes the first performance. After some madrigals had been sung as an introduction, Clorinda appeared, armed and on foot, followed by Tancredi, also armed but on a *Cavallo Mariano*.[1] The Narrator began his song, and Clorinda and Tancredi acted, or danced, the story in a way suggested by the words. All details of expression were to be observed by singers, actors, and instrumentalists, and the action, half ballet, half acting, was strictly in time with the words and music. The Narrator is instructed to sing clearly and firmly and to articulate well; only in the stanza to Night may he employ decoration; for the rest, he must narrate *a similitudine delle passioni dell' oratione*. At the end, says Monteverdi, the audience was moved to tears and applause at this new sort of entertainment.

Before the action begins, Tancredi, a Christian knight, has fallen in love with Clorinda, a Saracen maiden. She is a brave and skilful warrior and, dressed in man's armour, has assaulted and burnt, with one companion, a Christian fortification. As she is returning from this victory, she is seen and

---

[1] Raymond Leppard has suggested an interesting explanation of the significance of this mysterious term. 'By the time *Combattimento* was published in Book VIII, the circumstances of performance were being *described* and not *prescribed*. The Mocenigo Palace is not large and the courtyard has no place for anyone to sit so it must have been performed on the *piano nobile*, which is also not large. No question then of a real horse. A hobby-horse would seem the most likely and since almost life-size puppets had long been (and still are) a feature of Italian popular theatre, there is the possibility that it was performed by puppets and sung by singers at the side. "Mariano" doesn't exist except in religious or seasonal usage but it is very close to the stem "marionette" (which I believe has a religious origin itself) and I believe that this is the true origin.'

pursued by Tancredi. He thinks her a man and challenges her to mortal combat.

The Narrator (Testo), who remains outside the action but comments upon it, begins by announcing the theme of the story, and straightaway we have, in 6/8 time, a representation of the horseback pursuit. Clorinda and Tancredi defy one another, and Tancredi dismounts for the combat. The Narrator begins his description of the phases of the fight, and before the *sinfonia* which introduces the Invocation of Night, we hear for the first time the string *tremolo*, or *stile concitato*, about which more later. The stanza in praise of Night is a beautiful inspiration; it gives way to a graphic account of the battle, whose musical phases change as often as the various stages of the duel. Not only does Monteverdi use the new device of rapidly repeated notes in the orchestra but he makes the Narrator imitate the device by setting some lines at breakneck speed.

In the middle of the battle, the combatants rest, and their exhaustion is faithfully reflected in the music. Tancredi says that whatever the issue he would like to know the name of his opponent, but Clorinda answers proudly that the warrior who opposes him is one of the two responsible for burning the Christian tower. The music is headed 'Guerra' as they return to fight with renewed zeal. Soon Clorinda is beaten and, transfixed by the sword of her opponent, falls dying at his feet. She forgives him and asks him to mark his forgiveness of her by bestowing Christian baptism on her. He fetches water from a stream which runs nearby, raises her visor and in a moment of horror recognises that his opponent was the Saracen maid he loved so well. He baptises her, and as he does so, she sings a last, rising phrase in which one can feel her soul leaving her earthly body for the heaven which she can see open to receive it: 'S'apre il ciel; io vado in pace.'

In his preface Monteverdi recognises three principal human passions: wrath (*Ira*), temperance (*Temperanza*), and humility or prayer (*Humiltà* or *Supplicazione*). Music, he says, has represented the soft, *molle*, and the temperate, but not the *concitato*, the excited. By means of his invention of the string *tremolo* and by applying it to an appropriate text, he hopes to remedy this defect; with the new device is associated for the first time the string *pizzicato*, like the *tremolo* a commonplace to-day.

The opera is scored for a quartet of strings (written out in

full) supported by contrabass and harpsichord, and it is in
Monteverdi's invention of this combination of sound to fit
action that the unique quality of this fascinating work lies. H.

IL RITORNO D'ULISSE IN PATRIA

Ulysses' Return Home

Opera in a prologue and five acts, text by G. Badoaro. First performed
in Venice, February 1641. Some doubt has been cast on the authenticity
of the ascription to Monteverdi since the score was first published in
Vienna in 1923. However, agreement by now seems fairly general that
the music is in fact by Monteverdi, and Luigi Dallapiccola, the Italian
composer who was responsible for an authoritative arrangement of the
opera (1942), does not hesitate to describe the work as a masterpiece.
The opera was revived in concert form in Brussels 1925 (fragments
only); in Paris (arranged by d'Indy) in 1925 and 1927; and it was broadcast from London in 1928 (in d'Indy's arrangement, English version by
D. Millar Craig). The opera was performed on the stage in Dallapiccola's
arrangement, Florence Festival, 1942, conducted by Mario Rossi and
with Jolanda Magnoni, Cloe Elmo, Fedora Barbieri, Giovanni Voyer,
and Tancredi Pasero; at la Scala, Milan, 1943, with virtually the same
cast; Holland Festival 1962, with de Bossy, Ghitti, van der Zalm, van
der Bilt, conductor Dorati; Piccola Scala, Milan, 1964, with Boyer,
Companeez, Casoni, Zaccaria. Erich Kraack's adaptation was given in
Wupperthal, 1959, and elsewhere in Germany, including Hamburg 1965,
with Häfliger and Kerstin Meyer; Raymond Leppard's at Glyndebourne
in 1972 with Janet Baker and Benjamin Luxon.

CHARACTERS

Giove	Tenor
Nettuno	Basso profondo
Minerva	Soprano
Giunone	Soprano
Mercurio	Baritone
Ulisse	Tenor
Penelope, *wife of Ulisse*	Contralto
Telemaco, *son of Ulisse*	Mezzo-soprano
Antinoo	Basso profondo
Pisandro { *Penelope's suitors* }	Tenor
Anfinomo	Tenor
Eurimaco, *lover of Melanto*	Tenor
Melanto, *Penelope's attendant*	Mezzo-soprano
Eumete, *Ulisse's swineherd*	Tenor

Iro, *suitors' Jester* . . . . Buffo tenor
Ericlea, *Ulisse's nurse* . . . . Mezzo-soprano
           Naiads, Sailors, Sirens, Nereids

The above distribution is that required for Dallapiccola's arrangement of the score; in d'Indy's version, Ulisse, Eurimaco, and Anfinomo were baritones, Telemaco a tenor, and Penelope herself a soprano. In both versions, Monteverdi's five acts are reduced to three (as they are in the Vienna MS. of the score), and this arrangement is being followed here.

Act I. (In Dallapiccola's edition, as in d'Indy's, the prologue, with its allegorical figures—Human Fragility, Time, Fortune, Love—is omitted.) The curtain rises on a room in the royal palace. Penelope, Ulisse's wife, is attended by her nurse, Ericlea, as she bemoans her state of loneliness with her husband still not returned from the war. It is a magnificent lament, proof in its own right that *Ulisse* is by the composer of the *Arianna* lament, say its admirers; 'Torna, torna, deh torna Ulisse' is its poignant refrain. A duet follows between the amorous Melanto and her lover Eurimaco.

The second scene is a discussion between Jove and Neptune on the subject of the gods' punishment of men's sins. The scene changes, and we are with Ulisse on board a Phaeacian ship off the coast of Ithaca. The Phaeacians lay the sleeping Ulisse on the shore. He wakes up, thinks he has been deposited in an unknown land, and laments the fate to whose devices for keeping him from his native country there appears to be no end. Ulisse's lament is not so highly organised as Penelope's in the first scene, but it is one of the most effective moments in the opera. There follows a long scene between Ulisse and Minerva, who appears disguised as a shepherd to comfort Ulisse and spur him on to return home to his wife and his throne. Ulisse eventually recognises Minerva, who tells him that he will not be recognised by anyone—she will disguise him—but will return home to rout the suitors who have taken possession of his palace. The scene ends with Ulisse rejoicing at the turn in his fortunes: 'O fortunato Ulisse'.

Act II. Eumete, Ulisse's old herdsman, is discovered alone. He sings of the contrast between his own contented lot and that of princes, who have possessions but often no happiness. The ridiculous Iro breaks in on his reverie, and smacks his lips over the pampered life *he* leads, contrasting the shepherd's life unfavourably with it. Eumete sends him about his business: 'Corri, corri a mangiar, a crepar' (Haste thee, go and eat, stuff thyself). Ulisse comes in and hears Eumete lament his master's absence; he tells him that Ulisse will not fail his country, and the two go off together, Eumete full of joy at the prospect of Ulisse's return, Ulisse no less happy at having found a guide.

The scene changes to Telemaco's ship, where Telemaco rejoices at the voyage and, joined by Minerva, at the favourable wind. Again there is a change of scene, this time to the grove in which we originally found Eumete. Minerva cautions Telemaco against disregarding her advice now that he is safely landed in his native country. Eumete recognises him and greets him, saying that the old man he has with him (in reality Telemaco's father but not known to either of them) has encouraged him to think Ulisse himself may be on his way to Ithaca. There is a short duet for Ulisse and Eumete on the subject of hope, and Telemaco bids Eumete go to the Queen and warn her that her son has come home to her, and that moreover she should not give up hope of seeing Ulisse himself. No sooner has he gone than Ulisse changes into his own shape and reveals himself to his son. There is a rapturous duet of rejoicing for father and son and the scene ends with Ulisse telling his son to go to Penelope and warn her that Ulisse himself will return before long.

We are in the palace of Penelope, where she is surrounded by her suitors. They beg her, first together then singly, to return their love, but she will have none of them. Into the palace rushes Eumete, bringing the news that Ulisse may be amongst them before long. Penelope leaves the four suitors together, and they agree that come what may they must press their claims on the Queen before it is too late.

Act III. The Palace. Antinoo mocks the poor beggar (in reality Ulisse), who should, he says, be with Eumete looking after the hogs, not in the palace watching them sup. Iro joins in, stuttering as usual (he is Vašek's forerunner), but is challenged to a wrestling match by Ulisse, and soundly beaten. Penelope compliments the old man on his victory. In a moment the other suitors return to her, and she consents to set them a test: the one who can draw Ulisse's bow shall become her husband. Each in turn fails, but Ulisse asks to be allowed to try his strength; he renounces the prize, and says he is anxious only to join in the trial. He draws the bow, amidst exclamations of surprise from the bystanders; then, to the accompaniment of war-like music, transfixes each of the suitors in turn with an arrow. His triumph is complete.

Iro is found alone. His aria, marked *parte ridicola*, is a masterpiece of parody, with the elevated style Monteverdi had done so much to establish as its object. Even the *ciaccona* bass of his own madrigal, 'Zefiro torna', is pressed into service to do justice to the spectacle of Iro lamenting the horror which has come upon him: now that all his patrons are dead, he has an empty belly. He can think of no solution to the difficulty of filling it, and resolves on suicide.

Telemaco and Eumete try to convince Penelope that the old man who successfully drew the bow was Ulisse himself, but even the appearance of her husband in his proper form does not convince her that she is not still the victim of a cruel deception. It is not until Ericlea affirms that she has recognised him by the scar on his shoulder that Penelope allows caution to be replaced by love. Penelope rejoices in an aria before she and Ulisse join in a final duet to celebrate their reunion.   H.

L'INCORONAZIONE DI POPPEA
The Coronation of Poppaea

Opera in a prologue and three acts by Claudio Monteverdi, text by G. F. Busenello. Première at Teatro di Santi Giovanni e Paolo (sometimes called *Teatro Grimani a San Giovanni Crisostema*), in Venice 1642. Performed in Naples 1651. It was revived in concert form in Vincent d'Indy's arrangement by the Schola Cantorum in Paris in 1905; and in 1913 given a stage production there at the Théâtre des Arts with Claire Croiza, Hélène Demellier, M. A. Coulomb, conductor d'Indy. In 1926 it was produced at Smith College, Northampton, Mass., and the following year at Oxford by the University Opera Club in an English translation by R. L. Stuart. Performed at the Florence Festival of 1937 in the Boboli Gardens in a version by G. Benvenuti, with Gina Cigna, Giuseppina Cobelli, Giovanni Voyer and Tancredi Pasero, conductor Gino Marinuzzi; and in the same year at both the Vienna Volksoper in a German version by Křenek, and at the Opéra-Comique, Paris, in Malipiero's version, with Renée Gilly, Madeleine Sibille, Georges Jouatte, André Gaudin, Etcheverry, conductor Gustave Cloez. Malipiero's realisation was revived at the Teatro Olimpico, Vicenza, and in Venice in 1949, with Hilde Gueden, Elsa Cavelti, Giovanni Voyer and Boris Christoff, conductor Erede. A new version by Ghedini was heard at la Scala, Milan, in 1953, with Clara Petrella, Marianna Radev, Renato Gavarini and Mario Petri, conductor Carlo Maria Giulini. Yet another realisation, by Walter Goehr, was first given at the Hamburg Opera in 1959 (having been recorded some years previously), with Anneliese Rothenberger, Ernst Häfliger, Ernst Wiemann, conductor Ernest Bour. Raymond Leppard's realisation was first performed at Glyndebourne in 1962, with Magda Laszlo, Frances Bible, Oralia Dominguez, Richard Lewis, Carlo Cava, conductor John Pritchard, and at the Coliseum, London, in 1971, with Janet Baker, Katherine Pring, Robert Ferguson, Clifford Grant, conductor Leppard. Roger Norrington in 1974 prepared and conducted a version generally thought nearer to the original than perhaps any other since Monteverdi's time, with Kent Opera, with Sandra Browne as Poppaea and Anne Pashley (soprano) as Nero.

CHARACTERS

Goddess of Fortune . . . . Soprano
Goddess of Virtue . . . . Soprano
Goddess of Love . . . . Soprano
Ottone, *Poppaea's former lover* . . . . Soprano[1]
Two soldiers of the Emperor's Bodyguard . . . . . . Tenor
Poppaea. . . . . Soprano
Nero, *Emperor of Rome* . . . . Soprano[2]
Arnalta, *Poppaea's old nurse* . . . . Contralto[3]
Octavia, *Empress of Rome* . . . . .Mezzo-Soprano
Octavia's nurse .Mezzo-Soprano
Drusilla, *Octavia's lady-in-waiting* . . . . Soprano
Seneca, *philosopher, Nero's former tutor* . . . . Bass
Valletto, *a young attendant on Octavia* . . . . Tenor[4]
Damigella, *a maid in Octavia's service* . . . . Soprano
Liberto, *Captain of the Guard* . . . . Baritone
Pallas, *Goddess of Wisdom* . . . . Soprano
Lucano, *Nero's friend* . . . . Tenor
Lictor . . . . Bass
Mercury . . . . .Bass[5]
Venus . . . . Soprano

Soldiers, Disciples of Seneca, Servants,
Consuls, Tribunes, Senators, etc.

Time: About 55 A.D.   *Place*: Rome

L'Incoronazione di Poppea is Monteverdi's last opera, written when he was seventy-five and, according to most critics, his finest achievement. Its circumstances are very

[1] originally male soprano; often a baritone in modern versions [2] originally male soprano; mostly a tenor in modern realisations [3] may have been a tenor originally [4] originally a male soprano [5] originally probably a high tenor.

different from those of *Orfeo*, the composer's first opera inevitably reflecting the splendours of the Mantuan court where he was working; his last, written for the much simpler circumstances of a Venetian public theatre, concentrating directly on character rather than on grandiose surroundings. Monteverdi's pupil, Cavalli, had brought about a meeting with the poet Francesco Busenello, a Venetian lawyer and one-time ambassador to the court of Mantua. Busenello, every commentator agrees, was the first great librettist, and the result of the collaboration is a work unique in its own and indeed in succeeding centuries. Throughout, the focus is on dramatic truth and real-life emotions and their expression; illicit (but passionate) love triumphs over 'right', and in the course of the action injustice is more or less manifestly done to Octavia, Seneca and Ottone.

As far as musical material is concerned, 'all we have is a manuscript written in several hands, a sort of rehearsal or continuo copy ... consisting of a single bass-line, very occasional sketches in parts for *ritornelli*, and a vocal line. Fortunately it has the stamp of authenticity about it since remarks, directions and cuts appear throughout in the composer's hand. This manuscript is preserved in Venice and, except for a later copy to be found in Naples, it is the only music we have of the opera, the rest has to be reconstructed.' So writes Raymond Leppard, whose edition of the opera scored a big success at Glyndebourne in 1962. All modern performances have been based on two ingredients: this manuscript, together with the editor's point of view over matters such as orchestration and cuts (the original has some three-and-a-half hours of music).

In Monteverdi's time, music in the theatre was accompanied by strings and continuo, and wind instruments were more or less restricted to church music, being imported into the opera house almost exclusively for representational purposes—horns for hunting scenes, trumpets and drums for a battle, and so on. Arguments rage over realisation of such scores as this whenever a new one is made or an old revived. For my own part, I tend to believe that, like operatic translations, the realisation which is still viable a generation after it was introduced is so much of an exception as to amount to a piece of re-creation bordering on genius. The reconciliation of claims of scholarship (which takes in everything from grammar to punctilious re-creation of original conditions) with presentation to the public (which must consider an audience's theatrical outlook) is the basis of the scholar's work on his edition at any given time. He must remember that a seventeenth-century composer knew nothing of nineteenth-century practice, but he will forget at his peril that the twentieth-century audience has its sense of climax conditioned by Wagner and Verdi, and is ignorant of the sound of the castrato, expecting rather that the hero will look like a virile man than a transvestite soprano. If scholarship wins at the expense of effect, the new edition will be a desiccated falsification of the *effect* the composer intended, if colour and climax swamp authenticity, it will be laughed out of court by the pundits. And yet, without new realisations, without their editors' various convictions and prejudices and sense of the *immediate*, the public would not have these 'historical' works at all, and would be greatly the poorer for it.

After the overture, in a Prologue (omitted in some versions, including Walter Goehr's and Glyndebourne's 1962 production of Leppard's), the goddesses of Fortune and Virtue flaunt their own successes and mock the shortcomings of the other, until the goddess of Love in her turn vaunts her pre-eminence; against her, the others are as nothing, a position neither seems able or indeed anxious to refute.

Act I.   It is just before dawn and, outside Poppaea's house, two of Nero's guards lie asleep. Ottone her lover, returning from serving abroad, sings lovingly of the house and of Poppaea, until he notices the soldiers and realises that he has been supplanted by no lesser person than the Emperor. His world is in ruins around him. The soldiers wake up, gossip about the love of Poppaea and Nero, and grumble tunefully about their lot and the miseries of soldiering in Rome, with its rebellions, its rapacious philosophers, its corruption. Suddenly they realise that Nero is approaching and are heard no more.

We meet Poppaea and Nero in one of the great love scenes of opera, the first of several in the score. After a night in her arms, Nero is anxious to leave, but cannot drag himself away. She, spurred on by her ambition as well as her evident love for him, employs every delaying tactic known to woman, and by the time he has gone has obtained a half promise that he will put aside the Empress Octavia to marry her. Her reiterated 'Tornerai?' has far more tenderness than urgency, and it is this ability to portray the contradictory elements of real-life emotions which distinguishes composer and librettist from most others who have tackled similar scenes in the history of opera; here, without hiding underlying motives, they catch the freshness and beauty of passion, which has no regard for conventional ideas of right or wrong.

With Nero gone but his promise very much in her mind, Poppaea seems triumphant and expresses her feelings in an aria, 'Speranza, tu mi vai il core accarezzando' (Hope, you caress my heart). Her old nurse, Arnalta, tries to warn her against the snare in which ambition may catch her—the Empress may seek revenge or Nero's love may cool—but Poppaea believes that Love is on her side: 'Non temo di noia alcuna. Per me guerreggia Amor.' (I fear no obstacle. Love and Fortune are my allies.)

In her palace, Octavia laments her humiliation and misery, denouncing in a noble utterance the infidelity of Nero and calling on Jove to punish her erring spouse: 'Disprezzata regina' (Scorned Empress). Her old nurse (in Leppard's version, Drusilla) tries vainly to comfort her, until Seneca is ushered in by Valletto, the Empress's page. Gently but firmly he urges that tears and lamentation are unfit for an Empress, who must find refuge in stoicism; so will she be persuaded that beneath fortune's blows she grows ever more glorious herself. But Octavia objects that to promise greater glory from the torments she undergoes is specious and empty comfort, and Valletto impetuously but melodiously tries to defend his Empress by attacking the old philosopher for his platitudes, ending by threatening to burn his books and his gown.

Alone, Seneca has a vision of Pallas, goddess of Wisdom, who warns him that to interfere in the imperial quarrel will result in his own death. Seneca welcomes the idea of death and claims to have conquered human fear and, as if to reinforce his presentiment, he receives a visit from Nero, who tells him that he plans to set aside Octavia and marry Poppaea. Seneca warns him that the heart is often a bad counsellor, hating law and despising justice, and begs his erstwhile pupil to avoid arousing the resentment of the people and the Senate, and, if nothing else, to have regard for his own good name. Passions mount on both sides, Nero announces his decision to marry Poppaea and leaves Seneca in a fury.

Nero returns to Poppaea and their extended love duet ends with her denunciation of Seneca who, she says, has maintained publicly that Nero's ability to rule depends on Seneca's counsel. Nero, to whom providence denied the quality of dispassionate wisdom, in a single sentence orders one of the guards to carry a message immediately to Seneca to the effect that he must that very day die. Then, in lyrical phrases, he reassures Poppaea that she will see what true love can do, a power in which recent events must have reinforced her belief.

Ottone makes a last attempt at reconciliation with Poppaea but she spurns him and flaunts in his face the fact that she now belongs to Nero. Ottone is overwhelmed by the disaster which has overtaken him and realises that, though his heart contains nothing but love for Poppaea, his pride prompts him to plot her murder. In his misery, he turns quickly to Drusilla, who is in love with him and comes to bring him comfort. Ottone tries to assure her that he now belongs to her, but his protestations ring just short of true and when, in answer to her repeated 'You love me? You love me?', he answers 'Ti bramo' (I want you) we are once again confronted by the dispassionate desire for realism which characterises Busenello.

Act II begins with one of the great scenes of the score, the death of Seneca. First, heralded by Mercury and welcomed by the old philosopher, Nero's sentence of death is communicated by Liberto, Captain of the Praetorian Guard, and Seneca announces to his pupils that the time has come to prove in deed the stoic virtues he has so long preached in theory. In passionate chorus—a madrigal of high and moving quality—they urge him to live, but he bids them prepare the bath in which his guiltless blood will flow away. The next scene, in which figured Virtue, Seneca and 'Un Choro di Virtù', has been lost, but Busenello and Monteverdi follow it with two in the strongest possible contrast with those leading up to and portraying the death of Seneca. In the first, we have an almost literal precursor of the Intermezzos with which composers were in the habit a century later of adorning the intervals of their serious operas. Valletto ('Sento un certo non so che': I have a feeling I can't describe) tells Damigella, a pretty maid, that he has a pain in his heart that he's never known before. Will she help him cure it? As the music flows its spirited way, it is perfectly obvious that she will.

There follows a scene in equally strong contrast, as Nero,

elated at the news of Seneca's death, carouses with his friend Lucano: 'Hor che Seneca è morto, cantiam' (Now that Seneca is dead, let us sing).[1] The macabre situation is stressed rather than played down when Nero left alone sings with the utmost conviction of his love for Poppaea.

A scene between Nero and Poppaea has been lost and we next see Ottone making up his mind in a soliloquy that his former hatred for Poppaea has gone and he must now languish in a state of unrequited love. He cannot kill her, he decides, but it is not long before Octavia at her most domineering arrives and persuades him, not without threats to slander him to Nero, that it is his duty to kill Poppaea. His hesitations and evasions are beautifully characterised in the libretto.

Drusilla rejoices in her love for Ottone, and Valletto asks Octavia's old nurse what she would give for a day of happy youth such as is Drusilla's. 'Everything' is the answer. The arrival of Ottone brings about a change of mood, but Drusilla rises to the occasion, and, when he confides to her that he has in mind to commit a terrible crime for which he must disguise himself in her clothes, she is happy to offer garments and indeed her life's blood for him.

The scene changes to Poppaea's garden, where Poppaea opens her dialogue with Arnalta with the same words to which Nero rejoiced at the news of the death of Seneca: 'Hor che Seneca è morto'. She demands that Love shall guide her ship safe to harbour. Arnalta sings what has perhaps always been the only number known apart from the score, a lullaby of great beauty: 'Oblivion soave'. It has the desired effect and the goddess of Love herself descends while Poppaea sleeps and in an aria promises to watch over her as she lies defenceless. Ottone enters in disguise and with murder in his heart, but the goddess intervenes, Poppaea wakes up and she and Arnalta think to recognise Drusilla, who runs away with Arnalta organising pursuit. The goddess of Love is triumphant: having defended Poppaea, that very day she will see that she becomes Empress!

[1] At Glyndebourne, where Raymond Leppard's version was first heard, this scene, with perhaps unconscious irony, followed the dinner interval and began the second part of the opera. The first part had ended with the death of Seneca, which was preceded by the duet between Valletto and Damigella, so that the message that he must die was separated from his farewell to his disciples by the light-hearted Intermezzo duet.

Act III. Drusilla is at first found singing happily to herself of her love for Ottone, but it is not long before she is identified by Arnalta and arrested for the attempt on Poppaea's life. She protests her innocence, and not all the threats of Nero, who is quickly on the scene, can make her change her story. As she is about to be taken off to torture and death, Ottone himself appears to claim, in spite of Drusilla's protestations, that it was he who was responsible for the attempted crime. A short duet between them leaves Nero in no doubt of Ottone's guilt and he pronounces sentence of banishment on him. Drusilla says she will share in his exile, and Ottone recognises the good fortune which has suddenly overtaken him in what might have proved his most evil hour. Nero finishes the scene by announcing his resolve to divorce Octavia and send her in her turn into exile.

The action has reached a stage where one of the four principal characters has already been disposed of, together with his appropriate coupling. It only remains for the lonely Octavia on the one hand and the far from lonely Poppaea and Nero on the other to meet their fates. Poppaea, announcing her re-birth, learns that it was Ottone and not Drusilla who attempted to murder her, and Nero reveals that he thinks Octavia was behind the plot. She will be exiled and Poppaea that very day will become Empress! In grave, confident music, which only later develops into coloratura flourishes, the couple privately hymn their love.

Arnalta celebrates her own involvement in Poppaea's triumph by recalling in an aria past indignities as a servant and exulting over the prospect of future grandeur.

Octavia, alone as befits her isolated but still imperial state, bids an unhappy but dignified farewell to Rome, her native land, her friends. She claims, quite inaccurately, that she is innocent, but her lament is in the great tradition started by Monteverdi himself.

Poppaea is triumphant, and is greeted first by Nero, who bids her ascend to the apex of sovereignty, then by the consuls and tribunes of Rome itself who hymn her coronation, invoking the three known continents to bow down before her. There is a short intervention by the goddess of Love and Venus (marked in the manuscript as a candidate for a cut, a hint usually taken by subsequent editors), and the opera ends with the idyllic celebration by the two protagonists of their love and their triumph: 'Pur ti miro' (I behold thee).   H.

HENRY PURCELL

(1658–1695)

DIDO AND AENEAS

OPERA in a prologue and three acts by Henry Purcell, text by Nahum Tate. Première at Mr. Josias Priest's Boarding School for Girls, Chelsea, London, 1689. Revived by the Royal College of Music under Stanford at the Lyceum Theatre, London, 1895; in New York, Hotel Plaza, 1923, and Town Hall (in a version by Bodanzky) 1924; at the Scala Theatre, London, 1929; at Sadler's Wells, 1931, with Joan Cross, Sumner Austin, and Frances Geraldi; at the Florence Festival, 1940, conducted by Vittorio Gui with Gianna Pederzini, Ettore Parmeggiani, Dolores Ottani, and Edmea Limberti; at Teatro dell' Opera, Rome, 1949, with Giulietta Simionato and Mario Borriello, conducted by Santini and with sets by Clerici. The 1951 Festival of Britain brought three productions in London: at the Lyric Theatre, Hammersmith, by the English Opera Group in Benjamin Britten's new realisation, with Nancy Evans and Bruce Boyce (later Joan Cross and Peter Pears); at Sadler's Wells, with Eleanor Houston and John Probyn; at the Mermaid Theatre, London, with Kirsten Flagstad and Thomas Hemsley. 1962, English Opera Group with Janet Baker, conducted by Benjamin Britten, at Aldeburgh and Göteborg. There were several productions in Germany and Austria during the 1950's and 1960's, including Schwetzingen, 1966, with Irmgard Seefried; in Italy at Como, 1958, with Gloria Davy; at the Piccola Scala, Milan, 1963, with Teresa Berganza; at the 1960 Aix-en-Provence Festival, also with Berganza.

CHARACTERS

Dido, or Elissa, Queen of Carthage .... Soprano
Belinda, a lady in waiting .... Soprano
First Woman .... Soprano
Second Woman .... Mezzo-Soprano
Sorceress .... Mezzo-Soprano
First Witch .... Soprano
Second Witch .... Soprano
Spirit .... Soprano (or Tenor)
Aeneas, a Trojan prince ..... Tenor (or high Baritone)
A Sailor .... Soprano (or Tenor)
Chorus of Courtiers, People, Witches, Sailors

The prologue, which is included in the libretto, appears never to have been set by Purcell, or, at all events, to have been lost.

23

The overture has the traditional slow and quick sections, and is unmistakably tragic in feeling.

Act I.   Dido is discovered surrounded by her court and attended by her lady-in-waiting, Belinda. Belinda's exhortation, 'Shake the cloud from off your brow', is echoed by the chorus, and is in sharp contrast with the grief-laden aria for Dido which follows, 'Ah, Belinda, I am prest with torment'. This is a magnificent expression of sorrow, dignified and restrained as befits the Queen of Carthage, but worthy of the tragedy it foreshadows and at no point belying the conflict implied in its final words: 'Peace and I are strangers grown'. Belinda does not hesitate to diagnose that it is the presence of the 'Trojan guest' which is at the root of the Queen's unhappiness, and the chorus supports her implied suggestion, that a marriage between the two would solve Carthage's troubles. In the dialogue between Dido and Belinda which ensues, we have a taste of Purcell's extraordinary gift for compressing the most complex emotions into a few bars, and then relieving the tension and crystallising the situation in a set piece for chorus (in this case a *chaconne*) here introduced by a duet for Belinda and an Attendant. Again, her court attempts to encourage her— 'the hero loves as well as you'—and, after Aeneas's entrance and Dido's cold reply to his opening sentence, the chorus, then Belinda, and finally the chorus again support his suit in music of surpassing freshness. The scene ends with a Triumphing Dance, and Dido's acceptance of Aeneas is celebrated by the whole court to gay and simple music.

This opening scene is short, but Purcell does not rely on understatement and implication so much as on an extraordinary clarity and economy of expression. He says more in a couple of long meaningful phrases than many a lesser composer in a whole aria, and his compression never for a moment gives the listener the feeling either that the music is overcharged with emotional content or that the issues have been no more than partially stated. Every shade of feeling is there, though it may require more than usual interpretative insight and musical accuracy if it is to be brought out to the full.

The scene changes to a cave, where lives the Sorceress. She invokes her evil companions to join her in plotting the destruction of Dido and of Carthage. The whole scene, with its laughing choruses, its reference (in the strings) to the horn calls of the hunt now in progress, its echo chorus and its echo dance (phrase and echo are differently harmonised), amounts to an illustration of the insidious beauty of movement which can attend the course of evil just as surely as that of good.

Act II. The Grove. Dido and Aeneas, attended by Belinda and their train, pause in the grove in the middle of the hunt. Belinda and the chorus and later the Second Woman sing of the peculiar delights of the spot they have reached, of its attractions for the goddess Diana and of how it was the scene of Actaeon's death, torn to pieces by his own hounds. Meanwhile, the scene is one of activity, a picnic may be in progress, the attendants moving about, some trophies of the chase carried on, and, in the midst of all, Dido and her husband-to-be, Aeneas. The idyll comes to an end as Dido hears the distant thunder, and Belinda, always ready to take a hint from her mistress, warns the company to repair as soon as it can to shelter; 'Haste, haste to town,' she sings to a rapid, decorated tune which will show up any technical deficiencies in the singer of this role. All leave the stage, but Aeneas is stopped by the appearance of Mercury—in reality, the Sorceress's 'trusty elf' in disguise. He tells Aeneas that he brings Jove's command that the hero shall put off no longer the task which has been allotted him of founding the new Troy on Latin soil. Aeneas replies in a magnificent recitative —one of the highlights of the score. The decision is easily arrived at—it is the gods' command—but to reconcile himself to leaving Dido is something than which, he says, he 'with more ease could die'.

The published versions of the score make Act II end with this recitative, although the oldest version of the libretto has six further lines after the recitative (for the Sorceress and her Attendants) as well as a dance with which to end the act. When his new realisation of the opera was produced during the Festival of Britain, 1951, Benjamin Britten wrote as follows: 'Anyone who has taken part in, or indeed heard a concert or stage performance, must have been struck by the very peculiar and most unsatisfactory end of this Act II as it stands; Aeneas sings his very beautiful recitative in A minor and disappears without any curtain music or chorus (such as occurs in all the other acts). The drama cries out for some strong dramatic music, and the whole key system of the opera (very carefully adhered to in each of the other scenes) demands a return to the key of the beginning of the act or its relative major (D minor or F major). What is more, the contemporary printed libretto (a copy of which is preserved in the library of the Royal College of Music) has perfectly clear indications for a scene with the Sorceress and her Enchantresses, consisting of six lines of verse, and a dance to end the act. It is my considered opinion that music was certainly composed to this scene and has been lost . . . and so I have supplied other music of Purcell's to fit the six lines of the libretto, and a dance to end in the appropriate key.' A proof of the suitable nature of what he chose was its success in performance, and there was appropriateness in the added emphasis this threw on Purcell's careful key scheme as a means of obtaining musical unity and contrast for his opera.

Act III. The scene is set in the harbour of Carthage, with the ships as background. All is preparation for the Trojan fleet's departure, and the orchestra introduces the sailor's song: 'Come away, fellow sailors, come away'. The tune is briskly compelling, the words cynical, as the singer urges his companions to 'take a boozy short leave of your nymphs on the shore'. The chorus repeats the tune after him, and follows it up with a hearty dance. Suddenly, the Sorceress is there with her supernatural band, and the first and second Witches sing a lively duet, whose burden is 'Our plot has took, the Queen's forsook' and which ends with peals of highly organised demoniac laughter. The Sorceress has a short solo in which she plans the destruction of Aeneas as well, and the chorus (whether it consists entirely of supernatural elements or includes some sailors and dockside riff-raff as well is not made clear) underlines her intentions. There is a dance in three sections for the Witches and Sailors, and the stage clears as Dido and Belinda come down to the harbour to look for Aeneas.

Dido is full of foreboding before Aeneas even appears, and his first words confirm her worst fears. With 'Thus on the fatal banks of Nile weeps the deceitful crocodile' she taunts his attempt at explanation, and, when he announces his determination to defy the gods and stay, she will have none of a lover who had once a thought of leaving her. 'Away, away,' she reiterates at the end of their duet; and it is not until his departure that she admits 'Death must come when he is gone'. The chorus sums up the gravity of the situation and prepares the way for Dido's great farewell to life. The recitative is movingly simple, and the aria, 'When I am laid in earth', one of the greatest moments in all opera. Built up on a ground bass,[1] which is first heard as the introduction to the aria after the end of the recitative, this is a piece of controlled vocal writing that is unsurpassed. 'Remember me,' sings the Queen, 'but ah! forget my fate'; and the sense of deep tragedy is increased rather than diminished by the succeeding chorus, 'With drooping wings, ye cupids come, and scatter roses on her tomb'. It is the longest sustained number in the score, and in it Purcell shifts the emphasis of the tragedy from the particular to the universal at the same time as he provides a uniquely beautiful ending to his opera.

Purcell wrote much other music for the stage, but *Dido and Aeneas* must be accounted his only opera proper. *King Arthur* and *The Fairy Queen*, the former with words by Dryden, the latter founded on *A Midsummer Night's Dream*, are included by Dr. Alfred Loewenberg in his monumental *Annals of Opera*; but though they contain magnificent music, this is more in the nature of incidental music to a play than of opera, although the masques in these and other works (such as *The Tempest*) offered Purcell a chance of writing in more extended forms. As a writer for the voice, Purcell was supreme, and his output includes an enormous quantity of songs, many of them connected with the stage, and all of the greatest beauty. His great mastery is universally admitted, and many of the most gifted of contemporary English composers are glad to acknowledge their indebtedness to him not only for his inspiration and example but also for the practical lessons they have learned from his music. It is opera's eternal loss that *Dido* should be the only true opera he has left behind him; the feeling for dramatic expression, which it shows to have been his, only emphasises what was removed by his death at less than forty years of age.   H.

---

[1] In each act there is an aria constructed on this principle: Dido's 'Ah, Belinda' in Act I, the Attendant's 'Oft she visits' in Act II, and Dido's lament in Act III.

THE BEGGAR'S OPERA

BALLAD opera in three acts; words by John Gay, music collected and arranged by Pepusch. Première, Lincoln's Inn Fields, February 9, 1728, with Mr. Walker as Macheath and Lavinia Fenton (later Duchess of Bolton) as Polly. First performed Covent Garden, 1732; New York, 1750. Revived at Covent Garden in an abridged, two-act version in 1813 with Miss Stephens, Mrs. Davenport, Incledon; 1878, with Sims Reeves as Macheath. In a new version by Frederic Austin, revived Lyric, Hammersmith, 1920, where it ran for 1,463 consecutive nights, with Frederick Ranalow as Macheath, Sylvia Nelis, and Frederic Austin; revived there 1925, 1926, 1928, 1929, 1930; at Criterion Theatre, London, 1935; at Brighton, 1940 (under Glyndebourne auspices), with Mildmay, Michael Redgrave, Roy Henderson. New version by Benjamin Britten produced Cambridge, 1948, and subsequently at Sadler's Wells, with Nancy Evans, Rose Hill, Peter Pears, Otakar Kraus, conductor Britten; Vienna, 1949, with Rohs, Funk, Liewehr, conductor Zallinger; Hamburg, 1950, with Enck, Rothenberger, Schütte, conductor Schmidt-Isserstedt. The English Opera Group mounted a new production at Aldeburgh in 1963 with Janet Baker, Harper, Pears, Bryan Drake, and Kelly, which was subsequently heard (with various cast changes) in Edinburgh, London, Montreal and other centres.

CHARACTERS

Beggar . . . . Speaking Role
Mrs. Peachum . . . . .Mezzo-Soprano
Mr. Peachum, *a 'fence'* . . . . Bass
Polly, *their daughter* . . . . Soprano
Captain Macheath, *a highwayman* . . . . .Tenor
Filch, *in Peachum's employment* . . . . .Tenor
Lockit, *the gaoler* . . . . Baritone
Lucy Lockit, *his daughter* . . . . Soprano
Mrs. Vixen
Suky Tawdry
Mrs. Coaxer
Dolly Trull   *ladies of the*   Sopranos, Mezzos, and
Mrs. Slammekin   *town*   Contraltos
Molly Brazen
Jenny Diver
Betty Doxy

28

Harry Paddington		
Ben Budge		
Wat Dreary	*gentlemen of the*	Tenors, Baritones,
Mat of the Mint	*road*	and Basses
Jemmy Twitcher		
Nimming Ned		

Mrs. Trapes, *the 'tally woman'* . . . . .Mezzo-Soprano
Time: Early Eighteenth Century   *Place:* London

Opera in the early part of the eighteenth century meant, for England as for the rest of Europe, Italian opera. Such works as Clayton's *Rosamond* (with libretto by Addison) were freaks, and more important, failures as well. It was not until 1728 that an English opera that may be said to have been a popular success was written, and then, ironically enough, some of the tunes were taken from Italian-operatic and French sources. *The Beggar's Opera* is a ballad opera— earlier examples of the type were Allan Ramsay's pastoral play *The Gentle Shepherd* (revived at the Edinburgh Festival in 1949), and, according to Burney, Durfey's *Wonders in the Sun*. The music is a compilation of tunes drawn from every imaginable source—contemporary opera, ballads, and folk songs—and arranged so as to form a whole connected by dialogue. The arrangers did the same with 'serious' music as was done in England for years by those who collected the music for a Christmas pantomime; everything was laid under contribution, provided only that it was tuneful and popular.

The origin of this particular ballad opera is thought to have been in Swift's often-quoted remark to Gay: 'A Newgate Pastoral might make an odd, pretty sort of thing.' The opera aims partly at satire, partly at parody. Fun is poked at the fashionable opera of the day: '. . . I have a Prison-scene, which the Ladies always reckon charmingly pathetic. As to the parts, I have observed such a nice impartiality to our two Ladies, that it is impossible for either of them to take offence. . . . I hope I may be forgiven, that I have not made my Opera throughout unnatural, like those in vogue; for I have no recitative.' There is also political and social satire, aimed at the Prime Minister, Sir Robert Walpole, and everyone in a position of authority and able to give and receive bribes. Corruption in all its forms is the stuff out of which the dramatic side of the opera is made.

The success of *The Beggar's Opera* was a serious blow to the prestige and the financial standing of the Italian opera, at whose head was Handel; it also of course made the fortunes of those connected with it—as the wits of the time had it, 'it made Rich gay, and Gay rich' (Rich was the manager of the Lincoln's Inn Fields Theatre and later of Covent Garden). Its success was such that the objects of its political satire were seriously worried at the effect it made, and the sequel, *Polly* (1729), was in fact banned and did not reach the stage until 1777 (although Gay made a good deal of money out of the sale of copies). *The Beggar's Opera* did not lack imitators, quite apart from its author's own sequel, but none of them has succeeded in holding public interest to anything like the extent of the original. This seems to have retained a flavour of its own long after the topical allusions have receded to nothing, and it has inspired composers of the twentieth century to attempt forms of modernisation, working from the assumption that the satire and the tunes are so strong in themselves, that they only need to be dressed in suitable clothing for the audience to react to them as enthusiastically as the original spectators did in 1728.

To a great extent, this contention has been borne out in practice. Austin's arrangement of the tunes (he himself was a well-known singer and played Peachum) took London by storm in 1920 and ran for two and a half years. It concentrated on pointing up the undeniable prettiness of the tunes, and provided them with an elegant framework that was distinctly at odds with the satirical intentions of the eighteenth century. Quite different but no less successful was Bertold Brecht's adaptation (*Die Dreigroschenoper*) which appeared in Berlin two hundred years plus a few months after the original had been first heard in London. The composer Kurt Weill used hardly any of the old tunes, and Brecht modernised the setting to conform with his own political ideas rather than those of Gay. No German who was in Berlin at the end of the nineteen-twenties seems to have escaped the spell of this curious piece which was hardly less influential than had been Gay's opera in its own day.

The most recent composer to have been inspired by the old ballad opera is Benjamin Britten. He kept more of the original melodies than Austin (sixty-six out of sixty-nine), dispensed with the 'pretty' introductions and postludes, and re-set the tunes with the aim of producing something like the same effect in 1948 as they had done in 1728. He was anxious to rediscover something of the original contrast between the sweetness of the tunes and the bitterness of the words, and the production purposely emphasised the sordid side of the eighteenth century, not its airs and graces. This re-creation is in its way a masterpiece.

There is a Prologue, spoken by a Beggar and a Player and explaining that the piece is written 'for the celebrating the marriage of James Chaunter and Moll Lay, two most excellent Ballad-Singers'.

Act I. The curtain goes up to reveal a room in Peachum's house; the owner is sitting at a table, before a book of accounts. He sings 'Through all the employments of life, Each Neighbour abuses his brother'. Filch comes in to report on the fates of various members of Peachum's gang, who are up before the courts. He sings the smoothly-flowing ''Tis Woman that seduces all mankind' before being sent off to deliver Peachum's messages to the various prisoners.

Peachum goes through a register of his gang, commenting on the earning (i.e. pick-pocket) capacities of each. Some, he thinks, he will give up at the next sessions and take the money offered for their apprehension. He reaches the name of Bob Booty, when his wife interrupts to enquire why he should mention that name; women, she admits, are notoriously bad judges of a man, whom they love primarily for his courage: 'If any wench Venus' girdle wear'. They exchange words on the subject of murder, a crime Mrs. Peachum seems to fancy less than her husband, and fall to talking about Captain Macheath. It appears that Polly, their daughter, 'thinks him a very pretty man'. 'If love the virgin's heart invade', sings Mrs. Peachum; if she does not marry, 'she's—what I dare not name'. But Peachum is still worried: '. . . I would indulge the girl as far as prudently we can. In anything but marriage.' Leaving his wife to take the coronets out of some handkerchiefs, he goes off to 'terrify her from it, by the example of our neighbours'.

Mrs. Peachum is philosophical—'Why must Polly's marriage, contrary to all observations, make her the less followed by other men?'—and she sings 'A maid is like the golden ore'. Filch comes in; Mrs. Peachum owns herself very partial to his company, but questions him on the relations of Captain Macheath and Polly. He seems embarrassed, and she takes him off to tell her more in private.

Enter Polly and her father. She urges her ability to look after herself, 'Virgins are like the fair flower in its lustre'. Peachum utters a stern warning against her marrying, when 'enter Mrs. Peachum, in a very great passion'. She has found out the worst; 'Our Polly is a sad slut' she sings in her fury, and proclaims for all to hear that Polly has got herself married. 'Can Love be control'd by advice?' asks Polly, but Mrs. Peachum in a delicious tune objects, 'O Polly, you might have toy'd and kiss'd'. Polly tries to keep her end up ('I, like a ship in storms, was tossed'), but is sent off to deal with customers in the front room. When she has gone, Peachum and his wife plot to turn the whole affair to their advantage, not forgetting that a lawyer may get his hands into the business and take all profit out of it: 'A fox may steal your hens, sir'. Polly returns and is told she must straightaway make plans to become a widow; in a word, Macheath must be delivered up to the law in time for the next session! 'O ponder well! be not severe', objects Polly; as a widow, she would cry her heart out: 'The turtle thus with plaintive crying'.

Polly goes, but hides to hear her parents continue their plot, which even gets to the stage when the Old Bailey is mentioned. She is in despair, but the scene changes and she is shown with Macheath; they sing a love duet:

> Pretty Polly, say,
> When I was away,
> Did your fancy never stray
> To some newer lover?

Macheath protests his own constancy: 'My heart was so free, It rov'd like the Bee, 'Till Polly my passion requited', and they swear mutual adoration in 'Were I laid on Greenland's coast', with its refrain of 'Over the hills and far away'. But Polly remembers that Macheath's life is not now safe; her father is plotting against him. 'Oh what pain it is to part' she sings. Their love scene reaches its climax with 'The miser thus a shilling sees', a superb and entirely appropriate ending which is unaccountably omitted from Austin's published score.

The scene changes to a Tavern near Newgate. Macheath's gang discuss their profession and its hazards, but forget their sorrows in a drink: 'Fill every glass'. Macheath comes to tell them that he cannot go with them that night, owing to his

Let us take the road, Hark I hear the sound of coa-ches.

'difference' with Peachum. He wishes them luck and they go off singing 'Let us take the road', to the tune of the march from Handel's *Rinaldo*.

Macheath, alone, muses on the delights to be had from women—he is emphatic about the plural. His romance, 'If the heart of a man', is set to one of the most delightful tunes of the whole score. He does not have to wait long; the women of the town begin to arrive in answer to his invitations previously sent out. He welcomes them and leads them in a dance, 'Youth's the season made for joys'. After some dalliance, Jenny Diver sings suggestively 'Before the Barn-door crowing', and, while the ladies sing 'The gamesters and lawyers are jugglers alike', manages to secure one of his pistols, Suky Tawdry getting hold of the other. They signal to Peachum, who is waiting outside, and he comes in with constables and arrests the Captain. Macheath turns furiously on the women ('At the tree I shall suffer with pleasure'), and is led away, leaving them to dispute about the division of the reward for their work.

The scene changes to Newgate Gaol. Macheath is received by the sinister Lockit, who reminds him that nothing can be had in prison free of charge; 'garnish' is the custom. Macheath is left alone, and reflects that it is Woman that has brought him to his present condition: 'Man may escape from rope and gun'. The tune marvellously combines the lyrical with the dramatic.

Man may escape from rope and gun, nay some have out lived the doctor's pill

Enter Lucy, daughter of Lockit. She loses no time in referring to the 'load of infamy' which she carries, and does not hesitate to blame her pregnancy on Macheath. Revenge is what she is after, she tells him, 'Thus when a good housewife sees a rat'. Macheath pleads with her, and refers to himself as her husband. Lucy is not so quickly taken in ('How cruel are the traitors'), but Macheath works on her to good purpose, and explains away Polly's report of their marriage as mere vanity on her part: 'The first time at the looking-glass'. Lucy takes Macheath off in search of the priest attached to the prison.

Enter Peachum and Lockit, intent on the record of their mutual transactions. Working for the law and at the same time helping to organise crime, they are in a position to make the best of both worlds. Peachum refers openly to the betrayal of friends, and Lockit cautions him to be more careful in his use of words: 'When you censure the age'. Peachum goes further, and questions Lockit's honest dealing. There is a row and the two men are at each other's throats until more moderate counsels prevail, and Peachum eventually leaves, with them in seeming agreement.

It is Lucy's turn to have a disagreement with her father; she begs for mercy for Macheath: 'Is then his fate decreed, sir?' Lockit rejoins with rough comfort—be grateful for release, like other widows: 'You'll think ere many days ensue' (Britten combines the two tunes in an effective duet). Macheath rejoins Lucy, and speculates on his chance of bribing his way out of prison: 'If you at an office solicit your due'. Lucy promises to do what she can to help him—but at that moment Polly herself appears and throws herself about Macheath's neck—'my dear husband'. Seeing him thus languishing she makes an ornithological comparison: 'Thus when the swallow seeking prey'.

Macheath's situation seems desperate: 'How happy could I be with either, Were t'other dear charmer away!' he sings in one of the best known airs of the opera. The two 'wives' come back at him with a duet, 'I'm bubbled. I'm bubbled. O how I am troubled'. (Britten follows the air with the duet and combines the two to make a trio.) Things look black for Macheath, but at last the two women begin to take notice of one another. Polly addresses Lucy, 'Cease your funning', and presently they have at one another, 'Why how now, Madam Flirt'. Peachum enters in search of Polly, but she resists his efforts to take her away: 'No power on earth can e'er divide', set to the 'Irish Howl'. Peachum eventually prises her away

No pow'r on earth can e'er di-vide the knot which sa-cred love hath tied.

from Macheath, and it is left to Lucy, after comparing herself to a fox's mate ('I like the fox shall grieve'), to release him from his chains and guide him from the prison.

Both Austin and Britten have omitted the short final scene for Lucy and Macheath, and have taken the eminently suitable tune of 'No power on earth', set it as an ensemble, and used it as a finale.

Act III takes us again to Newgate, where Lockit is admonishing Lucy for her part in Macheath's escape. She explains that it was not through bribes but from love that she was impelled to help him, and blames Lockit for teaching her to be promiscuous with her kisses—Macheath's naturally tasted so sweet after what she had been through that she lost her heart to him: 'When young at the bar' (the tune is Purcell's). Her mood changes from one of regret for her lost lover to one of recrimination, 'My love is all madness and folly', and Lockit sends her out to repent where he cannot hear her caterwauling. He sums up the whole matter; Peachum is evidently trying to outwit him in the affair of the Captain, and he must at all costs get even with him. 'Of all animals of prey', he reflects, 'Man is the only sociable one.' The aria, 'Thus gamesters united in friendship are found', is bitingly satirical, and in Britten's setting makes a tremendous effect.

The scene changes to a gaming-house, where are assembled ladies and gentlemen, together with Macheath, who there meets Ben Budge and Matt of the Mint, and gives them money. They discuss their affairs, but the scene is dominated by the singing of 'The modes of the court so common are grown', set to the magnificent tune of 'Lillibulero'.

Peachum's House. Peachum and Lockit are again making an attempt to arrive at a settlement of their intricate accounts. They give it up and fall to drinking, agreeing at the same time that it will not be long before Macheath is in their hands again, if they keep a careful watch on Polly: 'What gudgeons are we men'. Mrs. Diana Trapes calls on them, and, before getting down to the business of her visit, toasts them in a fascinating tune, 'In the days of my youth I could bill like a dove'. They join in the refrain. She has come, she says, to see what they have got for her in the way of 'Blacks of any kind. . . . Mantoes—velvet scarfs—petticoats . . .'. In the course of conversation she lets on that she has seen Captain Macheath that very day. Immediately they are all over her, and bid her name her own price for the goods, provided she lead them to the Captain forthwith.

The scene returns to Newgate. Lucy, although still bemoaning her fate ('I'm like a skiff on the ocean tossed'), is planning to even her account with Miss Polly Peachum, whom she is expecting and against whose coming she has the rat's-bane handy. Polly is announced by Filch, and Lucy receives her graciously: 'When a wife's in her pout'. She tries to get her to drink the gin she pours out, but nothing will induce Polly to let a drop pass her lips. They are outwardly all affection: 'A curse attends that woman's love' is not the quarrel the words might suggest, and Polly could not be more affable ('Among the men, coquets we find') nor Lucy more pressing ('Come sweet lass') as she presses her guest to accept her offer of a drink. The scene is brought to an abrupt conclusion by the precipitate entrance of Macheath, again in chains.

The quarrel is almost forgotten in the duet of commiseration which Lucy and Polly sing together, 'Hither dear husband, turn your eyes', but Macheath seems to take a rather different view of events: 'Which way shall I turn me'. Both Polly and Lucy plead with their respective fathers ('When my hero in court appears', and 'When he holds up his head arraign'd for his life'). Peachum and Lockit remain adamant ('Ourselves like the great'), and order Macheath to prepare himself to be conducted to the Old Bailey. He sings 'The charge is prepared', which, in Britten's version, leads to an extensive ensemble.

The condemned hold. Macheath, in a melancholy posture, laments his fate, and fortifies himself with copious draughts of liquor for the ordeal of hanging. He sings snatches of tune, culminating in an outburst against the injustice of the times, set to the tune of 'Greensleeves'. Austin uses only four of the ten tunes specified for this scene, and omits Greensleeves. Britten makes it into a *scena* on the lines of Purcell's Mad Scenes—it is the climax of the opera—and binds it together on a bass derived from 'Greensleeves' itself. The result is impressive, and lends real dignity, not only to the figure of Macheath, but to the ideals for which the satire was battling —and satire is mere bitterness unless reared on an ideal and a truth.

Ben Budge and Matt of the Mint come to say farewell to Macheath; his last request is that they should revenge him upon Peachum and Lockit before they themselves come to the sorry pass in which he finds himself. Lucy and Polly appear, protesting that they would gladly take his place: 'Would I might be hanged'. Macheath joins in and the piece takes on the character of a dirge, more particularly when the sound of the passing-bell is heard (Britten uses this with effect). Four more wives appear claiming Macheath as husband, until he protests that he is ready to go with the Sheriff's officers to execution.

Would I might be hanged! And I would so too To be

hanged with you. My dear with you.

At this point, the Player protests to the Beggar that, if Macheath is hanged, the piece will be downright tragedy. The Beggar is persuaded to allow a reprieve, and Macheath returns to lead the finale, 'Thus I stand like the Turk, with his doxies around'. H.

GEORGE FRIDERIC HANDEL
(1685–1759)

THE music of Handel's operas represents one of the high points of the first half of the eighteenth century, and such obstacle as there is between us and them lies in the conventions which they respect and from which we are totally removed. This was a period of consolidation in operatic history, whose course has always tended to veer from reform or innovation on the one hand (which has mostly meant stress on dramatic expression) to reaction and consolidation on the other (which has often meant emphasis on 'pure' music with arias and singing for their own hedonistic sake). Without benefit of either extreme, opera would not have the force or fascination it has; caught at the top of the pendulum's swing in either direction, opera has produced 'sports' (like Handel's operas or their opposite, Dargomizhsky's recitativic *Stone Guest*), which are very far from typical specimens of the genre.

In Handel's day, therefore, convention was entrenched, with the aria, and more particularly the 'aria da capo' with its obligatory repeat, reigning supreme; with an exit following each aria, itself a purely individual expression; with virtually no ensembles and no chorus, so that even the final number tended to be sung by the principals together; with libretti geared to provide opportunities for 'typical' arias (expressing pity, sorrow, amorous intention, regret, despair, determination, martial ardour, etc.) rather than for character development and surprise. Castrati were the rage of the day, and such heroes as Julius Caesar and Hercules were written for vocal virtuosi whose breath control and volume were apparently sufficient to compensate for a physique which was often obese, sometimes comic and almost invariably unmanly.

Small wonder then that the revival of interest in Handel's operas which came in the early 1920's brought with it much revision, sometimes of musical detail in the interest of musico-dramatic continuity, almost always in the *tessitura* of the voices, so as to preserve an attempt at physical verisimilitude. In a word, castrati heroes became baritones or basses. In the 1960's, during the period of Handel revival loosely associated with the singing of Joan Sutherland, a more scholarly attitude tended to prevail, so that more or less strapping mezzos tackled the great heroes of antiquity, with results which were frequently comic to look at and far from heroic vocally, but which at least allowed Handel's orchestration to be retained and such anomalies avoided as for instance the changing of an obbligato for flute to one for oboe, in order to cut out the solecism of matching the higher instrument to a baritone when Handel had intended it to be in double harness with a mezzo. Each solution has its snags, as has the more obviously reprehensible (but, in view of length, tempting) practice of truncating 'da capo' arias, which when cut often sound either pointless or too long, sometimes paradoxically both.

The plain fact is that Handel himself made changes to suit the exigencies of each situation, altering a soprano part for tenor, importing a number from another work (and another situation) for a new prima donna, adding or subtracting as seemed to him best in each new set of circumstances. To be insistently purist may deprive us of the very real pleasures which can derive from these operas in good performance, to assume that without changes the operas are not viable would prevent a periodic assessment of the works' *Ur*-text, which is surely appropriate to the product of one of opera's few composers of unquestioned genius.   H.

GIULIO CESARE

Opera in three acts by George Frideric Handel, libretto by Nicola Haym. Première March 2, 1724, at Haymarket Theatre, London, with Cuzzoni as Cleopatra, Durastanti as Sesto,[1] Mrs. Robinson as Cornelia, Senesino as Caesar, Berenstadt as Tolomeo.[2] First performed in Germany, Brunswick, 1725; Hamburg, 1725; Vienna, 1731. First performed in Oskar Hagen's revision, 1922, Göttingen, with Wilhelm Guttmann as Caesar, Hagen-Leisner as Cleopatra, G. A. Walter as Sesto, Eleanor Reynolds as Cornelia. First performed Northampton, Mass., U.S.A., 1927; London, Scala Theatre, 1930. In the post-war period, heard at Leipzig, 1950; Düsseldorf, 1953; Vienna, 1954 with Seefried, Höngen, Schoeffler, Berry; Munich, 1955, with della Casa, Malaniuk, Metternich, conductor Jochum; Rome, 1956, with Fineschi, Barbieri, Christoff, Petri; la Scala, 1956, with Zeani, Simionato, Rossi-Lemeni; New York, 1956 (concert version), with Leontyne Price and the counter-tenor Russell Oberlin; and on several German stages during the Handel bi-centenary celebrations in 1959. By Handel Opera Society at Sadler's Wells, 1963, with Joan Sutherland and Margreta Elkins.

CHARACTERS

Julius Caesar . . . . .Contralto (Baritone)[3]
Curio, *a Roman tribune* . . . . Bass
Cornelia, *Pompey's widow* . . . . Contralto
Sesto Pompeo, *son to Cornelia and Pompey* . . Soprano[1]
                                                    (Tenor)
Cleopatra, *Queen of Egypt* . . . . Soprano
Tolomeo (Ptolemy), *King of Egypt* . . Contralto[2] (Bass)

[1] Margherita Durastanti was a soprano, but when the opera was revived in 1725, Sesto Pompeo was sung by the tenor Borosini.
[2] Grove's Dictionary and Deutsch's *Handel, a Documentary Biography* both refer to Berenstadt as a bass, presumably, suggests Winton Dean, because a German castrato (which he *was*) seemed like a contradiction in terms.
[3] The brackets refer to Hagen's 1922 version, in which many modern revivals have been sung.
[1,2] See p. 39.

Achilla, *General and counsellor to Ptolemy* ...... Bass
Nireno, *Cleopatra's confidant* .... Contralto (Bass)
Time: 48 A.D.   *Place:* Egypt

Undoubtedly, the historical overtones and associations of *Julius Caesar* had something to do with the immediate reaction of audiences in the early days of the Handel revival in Germany in the 1920's. But that accounts for only part of its success. Few other scores contain so many numbers which have made their way with the public out of context—and it is generally admitted that Handel's arias, static though they are, are far more effective when surrounded by the dramatic circumstances which provide for the situation and the emotion they are intended to express, than without them. It is in fact one of his most completely satisfactory works for the stage.

Act I.   The scene is Egypt after Caesar's victory over his rival Pompey, at Pharsalus in 48 B.C.

After a short overture the curtain rises to show a broad plain by the Nile with a bridge over the river. The Egyptians in chorus greet the victorious Roman legions, who fill the scene until Julius Caesar himself enters to celebrate his triumph ('Presti omai l'Egizia terra'). To him come Cornelia and her son Sesto to beg him show clemency in his hour of victory, only for Achilla in the same moment to offer Caesar the hospitality of Ptolemy (whose military help Pompey had invoked) and to show him the severed head of Pompey as proof of Ptolemy's change of heart. Caesar condemns the senseless cruelty ('Empio, dirò, tu sei, togliti') and leaves Cornelia to attempt suicide, to dismiss the proffered love of Curio, the Roman tribune, and to lament her wretched loneliness in a beautiful slow aria ('Priva son d'ogni conforto'). Her son Sesto in his turn excitedly vows vengeance on the criminals ('Svegliatevi nel core').

The scene changes to the palace of Ptolemy, where Cleopatra resolves to pit her celebrated beauty against her brother's gift of Pompey's head in a bid for Caesar's favour ('Non disperar'). Now Achilla tells Ptolemy of Caesar's fury at the murder of Pompey and himself offers to kill Caesar and so stabilise Ptolemy's throne if the king will grant him in reward the hand of the beautiful Cornelia. Ptolemy agrees and proudly inveighs against Caesar ('L'empio, sleale, indegno').

In his camp, Caesar in an expressive recitative contemplates the monument he has raised to Pompey's memory and reflects on the transience of fame. To him comes Cleopatra, describing herself as Lidia, one of the Queen's women. Caesar is completely captivated by her beauty ('Non è si vago e bello') and Cleopatra celebrates her success ('Tutto può donna vezzosa') and then with Nireno hides to watch Cornelia dressed in mourning kneel before the monument of her dead husband and movingly apostrophise the urn which contains all that she adored ('Nel tuo seno, amico sasso'). When she vows vengeance on her husband's murderer, her son takes the burden upon himself. Cleopatra, still calling herself Lidia, offers her help, Sesto rejoices because his dream of justice may now come true ('Cara speme'), and the scene ends as Cleopatra exults at the prospect of victory over Ptolemy, then sings an aria ('Tu la mia stella sei'), whose melodious and lovelorn accents to some degree contradict the uncompromising nature of the sentiments contained in her recitative.

The scene changes to the palace of Ptolemy, where the king greets Caesar effusively, offering him entertainment but in no way deceiving the Roman, who in a fine aria with (uniquely in Handel) a horn obbligato, invokes a hunting simile ('Va tacito e nascosto') to describe the relationship of Egyptian king and Roman general. Caesar and the Romans leave Ptolemy and his Egyptian courtiers, and Achilla points out Cornelia to Ptolemy, who is no less struck by her beauty than is his general. When the Roman lady and Sesto advance and challenge Ptolemy to mortal combat, guards are ordered to take the youth to prison, Cornelia to the king's harem, where Achilla may visit her at the king's pleasure. When the king has gone, Cornelia scorns Achilla's offer of freedom in return for marriage, and the act ends with a fine duet of farewell for mother and son.

Act II. Cleopatra has planned to have Caesar brought to her Palace, where she can ravish his senses with the sight of Virtue enthroned on Mount Parnassus. The orchestral *sinfonia* which accompanies his entrance and the revelation of the goddess starts a process of seduction which is fully accomplished when Cleopatra herself, in the guise of the goddess, sings the delectable 'V'adoro pupille', an aria of a tender, sensual beauty that puts it in the class of 'Lascia ch'io pianga', 'Rend' il sereno al ciglio', 'Where'er you walk' or 'Love in her eyes sits playing'—amongst Handel's greatest melodic inspirations. Though the vision of his beloved is removed from him when the mountain closes, Caesar's growing passion is evident in his aria 'Se in fiorito ameno prato'.

The scene changes to the garden of the harem where Cornelia sings sadly of her departed happiness ('Deh piangete, oh mesti lumi'), and resists the blandishments successively of Achilla and Ptolemy, who, unbeknownst to Achilla, is his rival for her favours. Ptolemy's determination is well portrayed in his aria 'Si spietata, il tuo rigore sveglia'. Cornelia is now joined by Sesto, bent on avenging his father's death, to which end Nireno contributes by offering to take him secretly to the king's presence. Cornelia urges him onward ('Cessa omai di sospirare') and Sesto proclaims his resolve in a splendid martial aria, 'L'angue offeso mai riposa'.

The scene returns to Cleopatra, who waits in the guise of Lidia for Caesar. As they are about to declare their love, Curio announces an imminent attempt by Ptolemy's soldiers on Caesar's life, whereupon Cleopatra declares herself in her true identity and, announcing she will quell the conspirators herself, leaves the scene. In a moment she is back urging Caesar to flee the danger, a solution he scorns ('Al lampo dell' armi'). He rushes out and the conspirators can be heard shouting for his death. In a splendidly realised scene of accompanied recitative and aria ('Se pietà di me non senti'), the music depicts the queen's conflicting emotions—her desire for revenge on her enemies and her self-pity, set against her fears for the safety of the man whose love she now craves more than the political favour she once sought.

The scene changes again to Ptolemy's harem where the king sits surrounded by his favourites, amongst them Cornelia, and sings of his amorous feelings: 'Belle dee di questo core'. Sesto rushes in and attempts to stab him, but is prevented by Achilla, who brings news that Caesar defended himself against the attacking soldiers and succeeded in jumping from the palace window into the harbour, where he was presumably drowned. Cleopatra is now bringing her troops against Ptolemy to avenge Caesar's death. As Ptolemy leaves, Achilla asks for the promised reward of Cornelia's hand in marriage, is sharply turned down by Ptolemy, and, as the king departs for battle, goes off muttering of the revenge that will be his. Sesto in despair tries to kill himself, but Cornelia again nerves him to the task in hand and the act ends with a renewal of resolve ('L'aure che spira').

Oskar Hagen in his 1922 revision of score and libretto simplifies the layout of this act into two clear-cut scenes: first, Cleopatra's palace, where the *sinfonia* and 'V'adoro pupille' are followed by the account of the conspirators' attack and Caesar's 'Al lampo dell'armi', the episode ending with Cleopatra's great scene; and next, Ptolemy's harem, where Cornelia's 'Deh piangete' is followed by Ptolemy's 'Si spietata' (in Hagen's score 'Belle dee' precedes his reception of Caesar in the previous act), the unsuccessful attempt on his life by Sesto, the refusal of Achilla's request for Cornelia's hand, and finally Sesto's 'L'angue offeso'. There is something to be said for simplification and concentration on these lines and it is possible to support it by arguing that Handel himself continually altered his works, moreover primarily to suit conditions of performance rather than in the interests of musico-dramatic coherence.

Act III. In a wood near Alexandria, Achilla, with a band of soldiers, prepares to defect to Cleopatra's side, in revenge for Ptolemy's treachery towards him in the matter of his love for Cornelia ('Dal fulgor di questa spada').

A Battle Symphony describes the conflict, from which Ptolemy's supporters emerge victorious. The king orders his sister to prison ('Domerò la tua fierezza') and the scene ends with her great lament at the turn her fortunes have taken ('Piangerò la sorte mia'), a beautiful *largo* aria with a vocal line of the greatest possible simplicity and containing, as contrasting middle section, a vision of herself returning as a ghost to haunt her wicked brother.

By the side of the harbour, and to *andante* music that breathes the very spirit of consolation, Caesar reappears to describe his escape from death by drowning ('Dall'ondoso periglio') and to pray for comfort in his loneliness ('Aure, deh, per pietà') in music that is as touchingly simple and as memorable as the famous 'Ombra mai fu'. Also to the harbour side come Sesto and Achilla, the latter mortally wounded in the battle which, he explains, he joined to revenge himself on the treacherous Ptolemy. Caesar sees him give Sesto the signet ring which will gain them the instant

obedience of his troops, who know a subterranean approach
to the palace where they may overthrow Ptolemy. Caesar
takes charge of the situation and his determination is
displayed in his comparison of his progress to that of a
waterfall ('Quel torrente che cade dal monte'). With Achilla's
death and Caesar's departure to organise the final assault,
Sesto feels that the processes of justice are nearing completion ('La giustizia ha già sull'arco').

The scene changes to Cleopatra's apartments where her sad
farewell to her attendant women is interrupted by the
precipitate and victorious arrival of Caesar to free her.
Immediately, Cleopatra's mood is one of jubilation and she
celebrates the prospect of victory ('Da tempeste il legno
infranto').

Ptolemy meanwhile makes a last attempt to persuade
Cornelia of his love for her, is threatened by her with a
dagger, and eventually falls dead after a duel with Sesto,
whose entry saves his mother from herself avenging her
murdered husband, a deed she nevertheless greets with proper
enthusiasm ('Non ha più che temere').

The harbour at Alexandria is the scene of the final triumph
of Caesar and Cleopatra, which is celebrated with a march, a
duet for the happy couple ('Caro! Bella! più amabile beltà')
and a final chorus of rejoicing.   H.

RODELINDA

Opera in three acts by George Frideric Handel, libretto by A. Salvi
(originally written for Perti's opera of 1710), revised by Nicola Haym.
Completed in January 1725, première at King's Theatre, Haymarket,
February 13 (or 24), 1725, with Cuzzoni, Senesino, Dotti, Paccini,
Boschi, Borosini. First performed in Germany in Hamburg 1734.
Revived Göttingen, 1925 (the beginning of the German Handel revival)
in a new German version by O. Hagen; Smith College, Northampton,
Mass., 1931; Old Vic, London, 1939. More recently Göttingen, 1953;
Leipzig, 1955; Sadler's Wells, London, by Handel Opera Society, 1959,
with Sutherland, Elkins, Janet Baker, Hallett, Herincx, conductor
Farncombe.

CHARACTERS

Rodelinda, *Queen of Lombardy, wife to Bertarido*
Soprano
Bertarido, *King of Lombardy* . . . . Contralto
Grimoaldo, *usurper of Bertarido's throne* . . . . . . Tenor
Eduige, *sister of Bertarido* . . . . Contralto
Unulfo, *a young nobleman, adviser to Grimoaldo, but secretly loyal to Bertarido* . . . . Contralto
Garibaldo, Duke of Turin, *friend to Grimoaldo* . . . Bass
Flavio, *Rodelinda's son* . . . . Silent

Place: The Royal Palace, Milan

Rodelinda has always been one of Handel's most successful operas,[1] revived many times during his lifetime and frequently in the twentieth century. It is unusual in that it casts a tenor in the villain's role—there are few important tenor parts in Handel's operas, the heroic roles which the 19th century might have assigned to tenors being customarily taken by castrati. The opera's one really famous air, 'Dove sei', is well known in England as 'Art thou troubled', but has also been given biblical words and sung as 'Holy, Holy, Holy, Lord God Almighty'—a curious example of the English 19th century's tendency to turn all music into oratorio.

After a *maestoso* opening, the overture is brilliant and florid.

Act I. A room in Rodelinda's apartments. The curtain rises as Rodelinda, alone, mourns the death of her husband, Bertarido ('Ho perduto il caro sposo'), little knowing that he is alive and awaiting his opportunity for revenge on the treacherous Grimoaldo, who has deposed him. Grimoaldo proposes marriage to Rodelinda, but she furiously rejects him ('L'empio rigor del fato vile non potrà farmi').

Grimoaldo consults his friend Garibaldo as to the best method of ridding himself of Bertarido's sister, Eduige, to whom he is betrothed, and of winning Rodelinda. Garibaldo promises to help him, and, when Eduige enters and reproaches Grimoaldo with his fickleness, Grimoaldo vigorously tells her that he is going to find a more worthy consort than she ('Io già t'amai'). When he has gone, the despised Eduige castigates him in her aria 'Lo farò, dirò

[1] Not only was its initial success quite out of the ordinary, but Cuzzoni's brown and silver dress became the rage for the rest of the London season!

spietato', leaving Garibaldo in a recitative and aria to sing of
his aspiration to her hand and so to the throne itself ('Di
Cupido impiego i vanni').

The second scene is set in a cypress wood, where the kings
of Lombardy are traditionally buried. We discover Bertarido
in disguise, contemplating his own tomb which has lately
been erected by Grimoaldo, and giving vent to his longing for
his beloved Rodelinda in the chaste and very famous 'Dove
sei'. When Rodelinda and her son Flavio approach to lay a
wreath, Bertarido is prevented from speaking to them by his
friend Unulfo, and the two men conceal themselves behind
the tomb as Rodelinda mourns her husband in a *largo* aria,
hardly less beautiful than its predecessor ('Ombre, piante,
urne funeste').

Garibaldo appears and, to the fury and despair of the
hidden Bertarido, tells Rodelinda that unless she marries
Grimoaldo her son will be killed. She agrees, but in a
tempestuous *allegro* ('Morrai sì, l'empia tua testa') swears to
have Garibaldo's head as forfeit. Garibaldo tells Grimoaldo
the outcome of his efforts, not forgetting his fear of
Rodelinda's revenge once she is queen. Grimoaldo promises
to protect him ('Se per te giungo a godere').

Unulfo tries to comfort the distraught Bertarido in an aria
('Sono i colpi della sorte'), and Bertarido is forced to admit
that Rodelinda does believe him dead. The act ends with his
aria, 'Confusa si miri l'infida consorte'.

Act II.　A room in Grimoaldo's palace. Eduige swears to
be revenged on Grimoaldo ('De' miei scherni per far le
vendette'). Rodelinda refuses to marry Grimoaldo until he
has killed her son—in this way he will appear in the sight of
the world as a monster ('Spietati, io vi giurai'). Grimoaldo
hesitates, but Garibaldo urges him to agree to what
Rodelinda exacts. Grimoaldo sings of his willing enslavement
to Rodelinda ('Prigioniera hò l'alma in pena'), after which
Garibaldo expounds his Machiavellian theories to Unulfo in
his aria, 'Tirannia gli diede il regno', and leaves the grief-
stricken young man to reflect on the horror of the situation
('Frà tempeste funeste a quest'alma').

The scene changes to 'a delightful place' where Bertarido
in a *larghetto* aria ('Con rauco mormorio piangono') calls
upon the brooks and fountains to share his sorrow, convinced
that Rodelinda has betrayed him. Eduige enters and after

1 *Alcina* with Joan Sutherland in the title role in Zeffirelli's 1962 production at Covent Garden.

2 *Alceste* at la Scala in Margherita Wallmann's production with designs by Pietro Zuffi, 1954. Maria Callas in the title role.

recovering from her amazement at finding her brother alive, assures him that Rodelinda is faithfulness itself. Unulfo supports her, and Bertarido rejoices at this sign of a change in his fortunes ('Scacciata dal suo nido').

Rodelinda in her apartment is told by Unulfo that her husband lives and sings of her happiness ('Ritorna, oh caro e dolce mio tesoro'). Husband and wife are united, but Grimoaldo bursts in and tells Bertarido to say farewell to Rodelinda as prison and death await him. He sings to Rodelinda of his hatred for her husband and leaves ('Tuo drudo è mio rivale'). Bertarido comforts Rodelinda and the act ends with a duet of great tenderness for husband and wife ('Io t'abbraccio, e più che morte').

Act III.   Eduige gives Unulfo a spare key to Bertarido's dungeon and they plan to rescue him (Unulfo: 'Un zeffiro spirò'). Eduige reflects on the danger of their enterprise: 'Quanto più fiera tempesta freme'.

Garibaldo and Grimoaldo are agitated at the possible effect of the death of Bertarido on their respective ambitions and Grimoaldo expresses his fears in an aria: 'Trà sospetti, affetti, e timori'.

The scene changes to a dark dungeon where Bertarido sings of the cruelty of love: 'Chi di voi fù più infedele, cieco Amor'. He is interrupted as a sword thrown through the window by Unulfo crashes to the ground. In the darkness and confusion, Bertarido slightly wounds his friend as he enters but the two escape by way of a secret passage.

Rodelinda and Eduige, also bent on rescue, find Bertarido's bloodstained cloak and jump to the conclusion that he has been murdered—Rodelinda demands movingly, with the force of a cry from the heart, why such pain must be endured: 'Ahi perchè, giusto ciel, tanta pena a questo cor', and 'Se'l mio duol non è si forte'.

In the palace garden Bertarido binds Unulfo's wound and sings of freedom ('Se fiera belva ha cinto frà le catene'). Grimoaldo meanwhile in a fine *scena* is troubled by conscience ('Fatto inferno è il mio petto') and finds consolation only in the idea of changing places with a simple shepherd (a charming Siciliana: 'Pastorello d'un povero armento'). He falls asleep after his reverie, and Garibaldo attempts to kill him with his own sword but is himself slain by Bertarido. Grimoaldo in gratitude renounces the throne and returns

Rodelinda to her husband. The happy Queen sings joyfully 'Mio caro bene', and the opera ends with a triumphant chorus, sung originally of course by the principals plus a small number of extra men on the bass line.   H.

ALCINA

Opera in three acts by George Frideric Handel, text by A. Marchi from Ariosto's *Orlando Furioso* (originally set by Albinoni, 1725). Première Covent Garden, London, April 16, 1735, with Anna Strada[1], Signora Negri, Carestini, Beard, Waltz. First performed in Germany, Brunswick, 1738. Revived Leipzig, 1928 (German version by H. Roth); Halle, 1952; London, St. Pancras Town Hall, 1957, by Handel Opera Society with Sutherland, Monica Sinclair, John Carvalho, conductor Farncombe; Venice, 1960, with Sutherland, Dominguez, Monica Sinclair, in Zeffirelli's production, which was later seen in Dallas, Texas, with Sutherland; Covent Garden, 1960, by Stockholm Opera, with Hallin, Söderström, Meyer, Wixell, and in 1962 in Zeffirelli's production, with Sutherland.

CHARACTERS

Alcina, *a sorceress* .... Soprano
Ruggiero, *a knight* .... Soprano
Morgana, *sister of Alcina* .... Soprano
Bradamante, *betrothed to Ruggiero* .... Contralto
Oronte, *commander of Alcina's troops* .... Tenor
Melisso, *Bradamante's guardian* .... Bass
Oberto, *a young nobleman* .... Soprano
Place: An enchanted island

Handel wrote his operas in the style expected by the audiences of the day, paying little attention to any sort of realism but providing unequalled vehicles for his singers. However dire the situation, he would stop the action so that the characters might embark on arias, which are not only long and elaborate but also very frequently of wonderful and expressive beauty. Plots were a secondary consideration and those of most of Handel's operas strike a remote, even a ludicrous note today. If *Alcina* is no exception to this rule

[1] One of the most celebrated sopranos of the day, Strada is quoted by Čapek and Janáček in *The Makropulos Affair* (see page 1577) at the same time as an example of renowned vocalism and proof of the heroine's longevity.

and presents a startling tangle of disguises and complications, the power and invention of the music is undeniable; in fact it was among the most popular of his later works and was much performed from 1735 to 1737, since when it has been unaccountably neglected, the next performance in England not taking place before 1957! Then the cause of the revival was the suitability of the as yet uncelebrated Joan Sutherland to the title role, and what she has subsequently accomplished in terms of a genuine revival of interest in Handel's operas may almost be compared to what Maria Callas did for Italian operas of the early and middle nineteenth century.

Alcina's original performances were not without set-back and incident. It is related that the famous castrato Carestini refused at first to have anything to do with what became his most celebrated aria 'Verdi prati', on the grounds that it did not suit his voice, and it took a severe dose of spleen from the irascible composer to convince him of his mistake. Marie Sallé, the popular French dancer, was associated with Handel's company during 1735, not always successfully if Prévost is to be believed. He writes in his *Le Pour et le Contre*[1]: 'Mlle Sallé, who had at first been as favourably received by the English as Farinelli (however, in due proportion to her talents), found herself afterwards bitterly attacked both in verse and in prose, without anyone knowing the reasons which might justify this change . . . The opera *Alcine* was given, the story of which is taken from Ariosto. Mlle. Sallé had composed a ballet, in which she cast herself for the role of Cupid and took it on herself to dance it in male attire. This, it is said, suits her very ill and was apparently the cause of her disgrace.'

Act I. The enchantress Alcina lives with her sister Morgana and her General Oronte, on a magic island, which she rules. Many a brave knight has come to woo her but at her hands has suffered transformation into alien form, animal, vegetable or even mineral. Her latest captive is Ruggiero, who still retains human form but in his infatuation for the beautiful sorceress has entirely forgotten Bradamante, to whom he is betrothed. Bradamante, disguised as her own brother Ricciardo, sets off in search of her lover with her guardian, Melisso, and the two are shipwrecked on the very island ruled over by Alcina.

[1] *Handel, a Documentary Biography*, by Otto Erich Deutsch; A. & C. Black, London, 1955.

When the action begins, Bradamante and Melisso are discovered by Morgana who is distinctly attracted by 'Ricciardo' and after a short andante aria ('O s'apre al riso'), leads them off to Alcina's court, where they meet the still bedazzled Ruggiero and Oberto, a young nobleman searching for his father ('Chi m'insegna il caro padre?'). Ruggiero, really believing that he speaks to Ricciardo, announces that he is now in love with Alcina ('Di te mi rido, semplice stolto'). Morgana rejects Oronte, who pays court to her, and announces that she will protect Bradamante, who sings a florid aria on the perils of jealousy ('È gelosia'). The infuriated Oronte tries to revenge himself by telling Ruggiero that Alcina has fallen in love with Ricciardo, and sings a spirited 12/8 aria in which he mocks Ruggiero for having believed in Alcina ('Semplicetto! A donna credi?').

Bradamante and Melisso vainly attempt to convince Ruggiero that his supposed rival is really his betrothed, but he will not listen and rushes off to plead with Alcina to do away with Ricciardo. Morgana begs Bradamante to leave the island, and the act ends with Alcina's brilliant aria 'Tornami a vagheggiar', which has recently become one of the most spectacular vehicles of Miss Sutherland's talents.[1]

Act II. Melisso, in the form of Ruggiero's old tutor Atlante, rebukes him for his behaviour and gives him a magic ring which has the power to remove the spell Alcina has cast over him. Ruggiero at once recovers from his infatuation, and thoughts of his beloved Bradamante come flooding back to him. Melisso concludes his lecture to Ruggiero with a *larghetto andante* aria ('Pensa a chi geme d'amor piagata'). The plot takes another twist when Bradamante reveals her true identity to Ruggiero, only to have him conclude that this is another of Alcina's spells and rebuff her angrily. Bradamante in a bravura aria renews her efforts to convince him ('Vorrei vendicarmi') and eventually he believes her. In order to escape from Alcina he asks her to allow him to go hunting, and sings an aria promising to be faithful to the one he loves ('Mio bel tesoro').

[1] Anna Strada, the original Alcina, was very jealous of the success of Mrs. Young, who sang Morgana, and it has been surmised that, to placate Strada, Handel gave her 'Tornami a vagheggiar', which was originally Morgana's.

Oberto comes to beg Alcina to help him discover his father's whereabouts; she promises, not intending to keep her word, and he sings of his anxiety ('Trà speme e timore').

Oronte tells Alcina that Ruggiero has fled, taking with him the sword and shield which she had hidden because of their magic powers, and in a glorious and extended aria Alcina calls on the gods to witness her distress ('Ah! mio cor! '). Oronte taunts Morgana with the loss of her new lover, but she refuses to believe him and leaves him to sing his *allegro* aria, 'È un folle, è un vile affetto'. However, she comes upon the lovers and confronts them with accusations of treachery. At this point, Ruggiero sings the justly famous 'Verdi prati', and the act ends with a scene in the subterranean cave, where Alcina weaves her spells; in a dramatic accompanied recitative ('Ah, Ruggiero crudel, tu non mi amasti') she bewails her betrayal, then in an aria ('Ombre pallide') invokes the spirits from whom proceeds her power. This is Handel's operatic genius working at the top of its bent—richly melodious writing, at the same time grateful to the singer and expressive of the dramatic situation, and the familiarity it has gained through Sutherland's performance is no more than a just reflection of its quality.

Act III. Morgana with some difficulty persuades Oronte to forgive her fickleness ('Credete al mio dolore'). Alcina, meeting Ruggiero unexpectedly, makes a last desperate attempt to hold him, but without success ('Ma quando tornerai'). Ruggiero sings a triumphant aria ('Stà nell'Ircana pietrosa tana'), and Bradamante rejoices at the happy outcome of her efforts ('All'alma fedel'). Alcina for her part realises the futility of her love for Ruggiero and in downcast mood sings 'Mi restano le lagrime', whose tender cast of melody seems to suggest unexpected depths in the sorceress.

An invisible chorus foretells that the marriage of Ruggiero and Bradamante will found a great family. The unfortunate Oberto, still pleading with Alcina for the release of his father, is ordered by her to kill a lion which she causes to enter, but he realises just in time that it is in fact his father, transformed by Alcina. He sings angrily of the wickedness of the sorceress ('Barbara! Io ben lo sò').

Alcina tries once more to part Ruggiero and Bradamante (a beautiful and expressive trio: 'Non è amor, nè gelosia') and once more fails. Ruggiero now smashes the urn in which rest all Alcina's magical gifts, and immediately all the knights, including Oberto's father, are restored to human shape. All ends happily in a lively chorus and dance, familiar to British ears by its inclusion in the ballet 'The Gods go a-begging'. H.

SEMELE

Opera in three acts by George Frideric Handel, libretto by William Congreve. The music was written between June 3 and July 4, 1743, but the work was not performed (and then in oratorio form) until February 10, 1744, when it was put on at Covent Garden with the French soprano Elisabeth Duparc (better known as La Francesina) as Semele and John Beard as Jupiter. Six performances in this and the following season, always in oratorio form, preceded a century and a half of neglect, until in 1925 the work was first performed on the stage, at Cambridge, in a version prepared by Dennis Arundell. First stage performance in USA at North Western University, Evanston, 1959, conductor Thor Johnson; New York, Empire State Music Festival, 1959, with Elaine Malbin, André Turp, conductor Arnold Gamson. First London stage performance, Sadler's Wells by Handel Opera Society, 1959, with Heather Harper, Monica Sinclair, John Mitchinson, Owen Brannigan, conductor Charles Farncombe; revived, 1961, with Elizabeth Harwood, and Mitchinson; 1960, Edinburgh, by Edinburgh Opera Company with Dorothy Roberts and Andrew Downie; Caramoor Festival, New York, 1969, with Beverly Sills, Elaine Bonassi, Leopold Simoneau, conductor Julius Rudel; Sadler's Wells, 1970, with Lois McDonall, Alexander Young, conductor Charles Mackerras.

CHARACTERS

Jupiter, *King of the Gods* . . . . Tenor
Juno, *his wife* . . . . Contralto
Iris, *her sister* . . . . Soprano
Cadmus, *King of Thebes* . . . . Bass
Semele, *his daughter* . . . . Soprano
Ino, *his other daughter* . . . . Contralto
Athamas, *a Prince of Boeotia* . . . . Alto
Somnus, *God of sleep* . . . . Bass
Apollo . . . . Tenor
Cupid . . . . Soprano
Chief priest of Juno . . . . Bass
Priests and Augurs, Zephyrs, Nymphs and Swains,
Attendants

The Novello vocal score (about 1878) of Handel's *Semele* carries the following introduction: 'The libretto was originally written as an opera-book by Congreve *but, being found unsuitable for the stage*, was converted by some slight alteration into an Oratorio.' What that unsuitability was and why stage performances in England had exclusively been given by amateurs until the summer of 1959—the bicentenary year of Handel's death—remains a matter of very considerable mystery. To decide which is the best of Handel's mature operatic works involves recourse to individual preference, but the music of *Semele* is so full of variety, the recitative so expressive, the orchestration so inventive, the characterisation so apt, the general level of invention so high—in a word, the piece as a whole is so suited to the operatic stage—that one can only suppose its neglect to have been due to an act of abnegation on the part of opera companies, unless of course it is caused by sheer ignorance. The operatic parodist may care to find a parallel between Congreve's characters and those of Wagner—the whole story might in fact be an episode occurring between *Rheingold* and *Walküre*. There is an obvious Wotan and Fricka, Somnus is the equivalent of Erda (albeit appealed to by Fricka rather than Wotan), and Semele herself, though the god's paramour, shares characteristics of Brünnhilde and of Elsa. Only when trying to see in the alto Athamas a parallel with Hunding does one sense the intrusion of an element of the far-fetched.

Act I. There is an Overture, *maestoso* followed by an *allegro* of no less consequence. A stately gavotte sets the scene—the Temple of Juno at Thebes, where religious ceremonies are in progress. Semele, the daughter of King Cadmus, is betrothed to Athamas, Prince of neighbouring Boeotia, but is secretly in love with Jupiter, who has appeared to her in disguise. The priest proclaims the acceptance by Juno of a sacrifice, and the assembled people rejoice: 'Lucky omens bless our rites'. Her father and her fiancé ask Semele to delay the wedding ceremony no longer, and she begs the deity to help her in her predicament: 'Oh Jove, in pity teach me which to choose.'

In a scene, which could in performance be omitted, Semele describes her mournful state ('The morning lark') and Athamas urges his love for Semele ('Hymen, haste, thy torch prepare!'). Ino is afraid Semele will yield to Athamas's pleas, and seems about to admit her own passion for Athamas; Semele urges her to tell all her thoughts. Cadmus admonishes Ino ('Why dost thou thus untimely grieve?'), and her comments on the situation, together with those of Semele and Athamas, turn what seems to begin as a bass aria into a magnificent quartet. The fire on the altar dies down and this sign of godly displeasure is received with dismay by the populace: 'Avert these omens, all ye powers'. Again the flames rise, but when they die down again, it is clear that it is Jupiter's displeasure they have incurred. The people are alarmed ('Cease your vows, 'tis impious to proceed') and rush out of the Temple. There is a scene for Ino and Athamas, by the end of which the latter has understood Ino's love for him. Cadmus returns with his followers, and tells of having seen Semele snatched aloft by an eagle. The others are left lamenting her disappearance, until the priests hail Cadmus and tell him that Jove's favour has lit on his family, an explanation of events which brooks no contradiction, as Semele from a cloud appears to reassure them in a beautiful aria: 'Endless pleasure, endless love Semele enjoys above'.

Act II. A purposeful *sinfonia* leads to a scene between Juno and her sister Iris, who has been sent to discover Semele's whereabouts. Juno inveighs against Semele and vows vengeance. Iris tells her of the protective obstacles with which Jupiter has surrounded his new favourite; they include two fierce dragons. In a vigorous aria full of resolution ('Hence, hence, Iris hence away') Juno tells her sister they will together persuade Somnus, the God of sleep, to 'seal with sleep the wakeful dragons' eyes', so that she may wreak her vengeance on her rival.

The scene changes and we find Semele asleep in her palace, surrounded by Loves and Zephyrs. Cupid sings an aria ('Come, Zephyrs, come while Cupid sings') which is omitted from the vocal scores, as in the arrangement of Congreve's libretto the character of Cupid was cut out altogether—in fact Handel used the first half of the aria in *Hercules* as 'How blest the maid!'

Semele wakes and sings one of the most famous of Handel's inspirations, 'Oh sleep, why dost thou leave me?', an aria of chaste and immaculate beauty, much admired away from the opera but doubly effective in context. Jupiter comes to her side and lyrically reassures her of his love: 'Lay your doubts and fears aside'. The love scene continues with Semele's florid aria ('With hope desiring'), to which the Chorus provides refrain. Pressed to say whether she has any wish Jupiter may gratify, Semele refers to the fact that she is mortal and he a god, and Jupiter, alarmed at the way her thoughts are inclining, hastens to provide distraction: 'I must with speed amuse her'. As they draw apart from the rest of the throng, the Chorus comments: 'Now Love, that ever-lasting boy, invites to revel'. Jupiter returns and announces his intention of bringing Ino to provide company for Semele, in an Arcadian setting to which he will transport them. If his serene aria ('Where'er you walk'[1]) is any indication of the bliss that should obtain there, the sisters' lot will indeed be a fortunate one. It is one of Handel's best-known tunes, but its perennial freshness resists a frequency of amateur performance rivalled amongst classical vocal music perhaps only by Schubert's Serenade.

Ino understands that she has come at Jove's express command to a hallowed spot ('But hark! the Heavenly sphere turns round'), and together she and Semele sing 'Prepare, then, ye immortal choir', leaving the final comment to the Chorus: 'Bless the glad earth with heavenly lays'.

Act III.   Rocking quavers introduce the Cave of Sleep where Somnus lies in slumber. Music that is suddenly energetic accompanies the entrance of Juno and Iris, intent on enlisting Somnus's help to remove the barricade Jupiter has set up around Semele. Somnus's slow aria, 'Leave me loathsome light'—perfect characterisation and a wonderfully beautiful piece of music—ends with the evocative line 'Oh murmur me again to peace'. Juno knows how to rouse him—at the mention of Pasithea's name he springs to life: 'More sweet is that name than a soft purling stream'. Juno gives her orders: Jupiter is to be distracted by dreams of Semele, the dragons are to be soothed by Somnus's leaden rod, and Ino must sleep so that Juno may appear to Semele in her guise. In a duet ('Obey my will') the amorous Somnus, in return for the promise of Pasithea, agrees to all her demands.

Juno disguised as Ino appears to Semele, comments on her beauty and asks if this is a sign that Jupiter has already made her immortal. She holds up a magic mirror and Semele is overcome with admiration of herself. Her bravura aria ('Myself I shall adore'), with its echo effects, shows how miraculously Handel could transform a frivolous idea into music of surpassing grace and loveliness. Juno, still in Ino's shape, urges her to refuse her favours to Jupiter until he

[1] Words by Alexander Pope.

promises her immortality and himself appears, not as mortal, but in his own godly shape—Juno knows that at sight of the god, Semele will be destroyed. Semele is gullible and embraces her: 'Thus let my thanks be paid'. Juno retires as Jupiter approaches.

Jupiter tells Semele that he has had a dream in which she repulsed him, but in spite of the ardour of his aria ('Come to my arms, my lovely fair') she keeps to her resolve: 'I ever am granting, you always complain'. Jupiter solemnly swears to grant her desire, whatever it may be, and immediately Semele asks him to appear in all his godly splendour. Jupiter cannot conceal his consternation, which shows in agitated ornamentation ('Ah, take heed what you press'), but Semele, in coloratura which is no less emphatic, insists: 'No, no, I'll take no less'. In a moving recitative, Jupiter, alone, laments his oath and its inevitable consequence. Juno celebrates her forthcoming triumph ('Above measure is the pleasure'). What the libretto describes as 'a mournful symphony' accompanies Jupiter as he appears to Semele, who realises too late that the vision will scorch her to death. She dies.

At Cadmus's court, the people comment on the story they have heard Ino tell of Semele's love and death: 'Oh terror and astonishment, Nature to each allots his proper sphere'. Ino reveals that it has been prophesied she shall marry Athamas and he rejoices conventionally at the prospect ('Despair no more shall wound me'). A *sinfonia* heralds the appearance on a cloud of Apollo, who announces that a phoenix will arise from Semele's ashes, and the people rejoice: 'Happy shall we be'.   H.

GIOVANNI PERGOLESI

(1710–1736)

LA SERVA PADRONA

The Maidservant turned Mistress

INTERMEZZO in two parts by Giovanni Battista Pergolesi, text by G. A. Federico. First performed August 28, 1733, at the Teatro di S.

Bartolomeo in Naples, with Laura Monti and Gioacchino Corrado. The *Intermezzo* was played in between the three acts of Pergolesi's serious opera *Il Prigioniero Superbo*. First performed in London, 1750; in Baltimore, 1790. Revivals: Lyric, Hammersmith, 1919; Mercury Theatre, London, 1939; Metropolitan, New York, 1935, with Editha Fleischer and Louis d'Angelo, and 1942, with Bidu Sayao and Salvatore Baccaloni; Paris, 1957, with Elena Rizzieri, Paolo Pedani; Royal Festival Hall, London, 1959, with Rizzieri and Bruscantini; Piccola Scala, Milan, 1961, with Mariella Adani and Montarsolo.

CHARACTERS

Uberto .... Bass
Serpina, *his servant* .... Soprano
Vespone, *another servant* .... Mute

Pergolesi was born near Ancona in January 1710, and died near Naples, March 1736. He was a prolific composer of chamber music, sacred music (including the well-known *Stabat Mater*), and operas both serious and comic. *La Serva Padrona* is his only regularly performed stage work, and the freshness of the music takes on added interest when it is remembered that the opera was at the very centre of the famous 'Guerre des Bouffons' in Paris. The production of *La Serva Padrona* by an Italian company in 1752 confirmed the division of all French musicians and intellectuals into two camps, the one favouring Italian opera, the other French. The Nationalists were known as the 'King's Corner' party, their opponents, who included Rousseau and the Encyclopedists, as the 'Queen's Corner' party. The Nationalists admired Lully and the ageing Rameau, the Bouffonists hated what they thought of as the out-moded complexity of French composers. *La Serva Padrona* had one hundred performances at the Opéra before, in 1753, it was transferred to the Comédie Française, where it had ninety-six more.

La Serva Padrona is on a small scale, the orchestra consisting only of a quartet of strings. The piece comprises an overture, and two separate *intermezzi*, each of which includes an aria for both characters and a duet. The overture is a gay piece, and the curtain rises to find Uberto dressing to go out and lamenting that he has had to wait three hours for his chocolate, which has still not arrived. His energetic complaints at the time he is kept waiting are expressed in an aria of a less formal type than the others in the score, each of which is in *da capo* form. His reproaches are directed more specifically at Serpina his maid in the ensuing recitative. However, when it comes to complaints he is no match for her, and after she has finished with her master, she turns on Vespone and sends him briskly about his business. Uberto's aria, 'Sempre in contrasti', is a fresh sort of tune, typical of the score, and demanding more than a little agility from the singer. Serpina tells Uberto that it is much too late for him to go out, and lectures him again in her *allegretto* aria, 'Stizzoso, mio stizzoso'. Uberto can bear the tyranny no longer, and asks Vespone to go and find him a wife. An excellent idea, says Serpina: take me! In a duet, she protests her eligibility and he his intention of, if possible, ridding himself of her altogether (but he confesses to himself that the situation looks like becoming too much for him).

The second *Intermezzo* opens with recitative in which Serpina plans a trick to frighten or cajole Uberto into marrying her. Vespone shall help, and she tells Uberto that she has found a husband for herself, a soldier, by name Captain Tempest. She describes his bad temper and his unreasonable nature, and then in a pathetic aria, 'A Serpina penserete', expresses her hope that she will not be entirely forgotten when she has gone. She seems a different woman, but the moment she sees a change come over her employer's face, the tempo of the music changes too, and we see that it is with the same old Serpina that we have to deal. By the end of the aria, Uberto has taken her by the hand, and she feels her plan is working well. Uberto is in a thorough muddle, and does not know what to think. His E flat aria, 'Son imbrogliato io già', makes clear that he cannot make up his mind whether he is sorry for Serpina or in love with her. It is a mixture of *buffo* and mock serious, and its slow refrain, 'Uberto, pensa a te', indicates a very different mood from that we saw at the beginning of the opera. Serpina returns, bringing with her Vespone dressed up as the gallant captain, and looking as though he would blow up at the least provocation but still, as hitherto, without a word to say to anyone. Uberto is horrified by his disagreeable exterior and by his no less alarming behaviour. Is this a suitable husband for Serpina? She says that the Captain demands a substantial dowry; if it is not forthcoming, he will under no circumstances marry her, but he will insist that Uberto himself takes his place. No sooner is the betrothal between master and maid concluded, than Vespone whips off his moustaches and military disguise. Uberto's protests are in vain, and in the concluding duet, he admits that he is in love, and all seems set for the future, with Serpina happily installed as prospective mistress of the house.   H.

2
Gluck

=============================

CHRISTOPH WILLIBALD GLUCK

(1714–1787)

FOR nearly a century after *Orfeo*'s revival in Berlioz's edition, Gluck was the earliest opera composer regularly represented in the repertory of the modern opera house.

The composer combined with the poet and diplomat Calzabigi in an attempt to reform opera and *Orfeo* was the first product of the partnership. The libretto of Calzabigi was, for its day, charged with a vast amount of human interest, passion, and dramatic intensity, in which particulars, in fact, it was as novel as Gluck's score. Gluck had been a composer of operas in the florid vocal style, which sacrificed the dramatic verities to the whims, fancies, and ambitions of the singers who sought only to show off their voices, but he began, with his *Orfeo*, to pay due regard to true dramatic expression. His great merit is that he accomplished this without ignoring the beauty and importance of the voice, but by striking a balance between the vocal and instrumental portions of the score.

Simple as his operas appear to us to-day, they aroused a strife comparable only with that which convulsed musical circles during the progress of Wagner's career. The opposition to his reforms reached its height in Paris, whither he went in 1773. His opponents invited Nicola Piccinni, at that time famous as a composer of comic operas in the Neapolitan style, to compete with him. The two composers seem to have remained entirely unaffected, but so fierce was the war between their followers that duels were fought and lives sacrificed over their respective merits.

ORFEO ED EURIDICE

Orpheus and Eurydice

Opera in three acts. Music by Christoph Willibald Gluck; libretto by Ranieri da Calzabigi. Productions and revivals: Vienna, October 5, 1762, with Guadagni as Orfeo; Paris, as *Orphée et Eurydice*, with Legros, the tenor, as Orphée, 1774; London, 1770, with Guadagni. Berlioz's revision of the opera was first heard in 1859 in Paris, with Pauline Viardot-Garcia in the title role; New York, 1863 (in English).

Famous revivals: Covent Garden, 1890, with Giulia and Sofia Ravogli; Metropolitan, New York, 1909, with Homer (later Delna) and Gadski under Toscanini; Covent Garden, 1920, with Clara Butt and Miriam Licette under Beecham; 1953, with Kathleen Ferrier; Metropolitan, 1938 and 1941, with Thorborg and Jessner (later Novotna) under Bodanzky (later Walter); Glyndebourne, 1947, with Kathleen Ferrier; Salzburg Festival, 1948, with Höngen, 1959, with Simionato, both conducted by Karajan.

CHARACTERS

Orfeo .... Contralto
Euridice .... Soprano
Amor, *God of Love* .... Soprano
A Happy Shade .... Soprano
Shepherds and Shepherdesses, Furies and Demons,
Heroes and Heroines in Hades

Following a brief and solemn prelude, the curtain rises on Act I, showing a grotto with a tomb of Euridice. The beautiful bride of Orfeo has died. Her husband and friends are mourning at her tomb. During an affecting aria and chorus ('Chiamo il mio ben così') funeral honours are paid to the dead bride. A second orchestra, behind the scenes, echoes, with moving effect, the distracted husband's cries to his bride, until, in answer to the piercing cries of Orfeo, Amor appears. He tells the bereaved husband that Zeus has taken pity on him. He shall have permission to go down into Hades and endeavour to propitiate Pluto and his minions solely through the power of his music. But, should he rescue Euridice, he must on no account look back at her until he has crossed the Styx.

Upon that condition, so difficult to fulfil because of the love of Orfeo for his bride, turns the whole story. For should he, in answer to her pleading, look back, or explain to her why he cannot do so, she will immediately die. But Orfeo, confident in his power of song and in his ability to stand the test imposed by Zeus and bring his beloved Euridice back to earth, receives the message with great joy.

'Fulfil with joy the will of the gods,' sings Amor, and Orfeo, having implored the aid of the deities, departs for the Nether World.

Act. II.   Entrance to Hades. When Orfeo appears, he is greeted with threats by the Furies. The scene, beginning with the Chorus, 'Chi mai dell' Erebo?' is a masterpiece of dramatic music. The Furies call upon Cerberus, the triple-headed dog monster that guards the entrance to the Nether World, to tear in pieces the mortal who so daringly approaches, and the bark of the monster is reproduced in the score. What lifts the scene to its thrilling climax is the infuriated 'No!' which is hurled at Orfeo by the dwellers at the entrance to Hades, when, having recourse to song, he tells of his love for Euridice and his grief over her death and begs to be allowed to seek her. The sweetness of his music wins the sympathy of the Furies. They allow him to enter the Valley of the Blest, a beautiful spot where the good spirits in Hades find rest, a state that is uniquely expressed in their slow dance with its famous flute solo. Euridice (or a Happy Spirit)[1] and her companions sing of their bliss in the Elysian Fields: 'E quest' asilo ameno e grato' (In this tranquil and lovely abode of the blest). Orfeo comes seeking Euridice. His peaceful aria (with its oboe obbligato) 'Che puro ciel' (What pure light) is answered by a chorus of Happy Shades. To him they bring the lovely Euridice. Orfeo, beside himself with joy, but remembering the warning of Amor, takes his bride by the hand and, with averted gaze, leads her from the vale.

Act III.   She cannot understand his action. He seeks to soothe her injured feelings. (Duet: 'Sù, e con me vieni, o cara'.) But his efforts are vain; nor can he offer her any explanation, for he has also been forbidden to make known to her the reason for his apparent indifference. She cannot comprehend why he does not even cast a glance upon her and protests in a passionate aria and duet, 'Che fiero momento', that without his love she prefers to die.

[1] As to whether Euridice or another singer should be entrusted with this aria, Edward Dent has written: 'Managers never realise that Euridice in Act III is a highly sexed person, and wants conjugal rights at once, whereas the Happy Spirit is clearly quite devoid of all human instincts. It is almost impossible to find one singer who can express both these things.'

Orfeo, no longer able to resist the appeal of his beloved bride, forgets the warning of Amor. He turns and passionately clasps Euridice in his arms. Immediately she dies. It is then that Orfeo intones the lament, 'Che farò senza Euridice' (I have lost my Euridice), that air in the score which has truly become immortal:

'All forms of language have been exhausted to praise the stupor of grief, the passion, the despair expressed in this sublime number,' says a writer in the Clément and Larousse *Dictionnaire des Opéras*. It is equalled only by the lines of Vergil:

> Vox ipsa et frigida lingua,
> 'Ah! miseram Eurydicen,' anima fugiente, vocabat;
> Eurydicen,' toto referebant flumine ripae.

> [E'en then his trembling tongue invok'd his bride;
> With his last voice, 'Eurydice,' he cried,
> 'Eurydice,' the rocks and river banks replied.
>   DRYDEN]

In fact it is so beautiful that Amor, affected by the grief of Orfeo, appears to him, touches Euridice and restores her to life and to her husband's arms.

The legend of Orpheus and Eurydice as related in Vergil's *Georgics*, from which are the lines just quoted, is one of the classics of antiquity. In *Orfeo ed Euridice* Gluck has preserved the chaste classicism of the original, in spite of the passion and drama which he successfully attempted to get into his music.

The role of Orfeo was written for the celebrated male contralto Guadagni. For the Paris production the composer added three bars to the most famous number of the score, the 'Che farò senza Euridice', illustrated above. These presumably were the three last bars, the concluding phrases of the peroration of the immortal air. He also transposed the part of Orfeo for the tenor Legros, for whom he introduced a vocal number entirely out of keeping with the role—a bravura aria which for a long while was erroneously ascribed to the obscure Italian composer Ferdinando Bertoni. It is believed that the tenor importuned Gluck for something that would show off his voice, whereupon the composer handed him the air. Legros introduced it at the end of the first act, where to this day it remains in the printed score. When the tenor Nourrit sang the role many years later, he substituted the far more appropriate aria, 'O transport, ô désordre extrême' (O transport, O ecstasy extreme), from Gluck's own *Echo et Narcisse*. It may be of interest to note that, for the revival which he conducted at the Metropolitan in 1910, Toscanini introduced the aria 'Divinités du Styx' (from Gluck's *Alceste*) into the scene in Hades.

Some reconciliation between the Vienna and the Paris versions[1] has, to this day, to be made for each and every production, but that the opera, as it came from Gluck's pen, required nothing more, appeared in the notable revival at the Théâtre Lyrique, Paris, November, 1859, under Berlioz's direction, when that distinguished composer restored the role

[1] A summary of the different versions of *Orfeo* (and some comment on them) may be useful. In effect, Gluck composed the opera twice: for Vienna in 1762, and for Paris in 1774. Each version was written for a male hero, in Vienna for the contralto castrato Guadagni, in Paris for the tenor Legros. The 1762 version is short (about 90 minutes) and dates from *before* Gluck's conscious attempt at reforming opera (the famous manifesto forms the preface to the 1769 printing of *Alceste*, whose première in 1767 provided the first hearing of a reform opera); the 1774 recomposition retains the old material while adding much that is new, and gives Orfeo himself bravura music ranging up to a D. The 1762 version was produced recently at Drottningholm and brought by that company with Kerstin Meyer in the title role to the 1972 Brighton Festival, but most modern revivals which claim to be of the original version in fact retain the 1762 score, recitatives and all, but slyly incorporate the most famous of the 1774 additions. The 1774 Paris version has been frequently revived, usually with some discreet transposition, notably at Sadler's Wells in 1967, and at the Paris Opéra in 1973 to inaugurate the Liebermann régime. The first attempt at a compromise between the two versions was made by Berlioz (with the help of Saint-Saëns) in 1859 for Pauline Viardot. Then, the 1774 version was used, but the tenor role of Orfeo was transposed to fit a female alto voice. (One example of the transmogrification of key and therefore *tessitura*: 'Che farò' in 1762 was in C major, in 1774 in F, in 1859 in C, and at Sadler's Wells in 1967 in E flat!).   H.

of Orfeo to its original form[2] and for a hundred and fifty nights the celebrated contralto, Pauline Viardot-Garcia, sang it to enthusiastic houses.

The opera has been the object of unstinted praise. Of the second act the same French authority quoted above says that from the first note to the last, it is 'a complete masterpiece and one of the most astonishing productions of the human mind. The chorus of demons in turn questions, becomes wrathful, bursts into turmoil of threats, gradually becomes tranquil and is hushed, as if subdued and conquered by the music of Orfeo's lyre. What is more moving than the phrase 'Laissez-vous toucher par mes pleurs'? (A thousand griefs, threatening shades.) Seeing a large audience captivated by this mythological subject; an audience mixed, frivolous and unthinking, transported and swayed by this scene, one recognises the real power of music. The composer conquered his hearers as his Orfeo succeeded in subduing the Furies. Nowhere, in no work, is the effect more gripping.'

Gaetano Guadagni, who created the role of Orfeo, was one of the most famous male contralti of the eighteenth century. Handel assigned to him contralto parts in *Messiah* and *Samson*, and it was Gluck himself who procured his engagement at Vienna. The French production of the opera was preceded by an act of homage, which showed the interest of the French in Gluck's work. Though it had its first performance in Vienna, the score was first printed in Paris and at the expense of Count Durazzo. The success of the Paris production was so great that Gluck's former pupil, Marie Antoinette, granted him a pension of 6,000 francs with an addition of the same sum for every fresh work he should produce on the French stage.

Einstein sums up the work: '*Orfeo ed Euridice* marked an epoch not only in Gluck's work, but in the whole of operatic history. Here for the first time is an opera without *recitativo secco* ... here for the first time was a work so closely grown together with its text that it was unique and could not be composed again. ... An opera at last whose manner of performance required the composer's supervision, the first opera that culminated in the musician's labour!' K.

[2] In so far as a female contralto is the equivalent of a male castrato voice (which it is not). Berlioz of course retained the considerable attractions and additions of the French 1774 version, while transposing the title role from tenor to contralto keys. H.

ALCESTE
Alcestis

Opera in three acts by Christoph Willibald Gluck, text by Ranieri da Calzabigi. Première at the Burgtheater, Vienna, December 26, 1767, with Antonia Bernasconi (Alcestis), Giuseppe Tibaldi (Admetus), Laschi (High Priest and Voice of Apollo). Produced in Paris in a revised version, April 23, 1776, with Mlle Levasseur as Alcestis, and sung in French. First performance in London, King's Theatre, 1795 (in Italian). Important revivals include Florence Festival, 1935 (in Italian) under Vittorio Gui, with Gina Cigna, Nicola Rakowski and Benvenuto Franci; at Covent Garden, 1937, in French, under Philippe Gaubert, with Germaine Lubin, Georges Jouatte and Martial Singher; at the Metropolitan, New York, 1941 (in French), under Ettore Panizza, with Marjorie Lawrence, René Maison and Leonard Warren, and, in 1952 (in English), with Kirsten Flagstad; at Glyndebourne, 1953, with Laszlo; at la Scala, Milan, 1954, with Callas, conductor Giulini; 1974 at Edinburgh Festival with Julia Varady, conductor Alexander Gibson.

CHARACTERS

Admetus .... Tenor
Alcestis .... Soprano
High Priest .... Baritone
Hercules .... Baritone
Evander .... Tenor
Thanatos .... Baritone
Voice of Apollo .... Baritone
Herald .... Baritone
Leaders of the People
                      Soprano, Mezzo-soprano, Baritone
A woman .... Soprano

Gluck goes down to history as a reformer, whose battle against the contemporary abuses of opera proved a turning point in the history of the art. Einstein has suggested that the normal eighteenth-century method of reform being by means of satire and parody, and Gluck being constitutionally unfitted to this medium or to that of *opera buffa*, he was obliged to become the first critical creator in opera's history if he was to express his thoughts on the subject; he had no other 'safety valve'. Be that as it may, his preface to *Alceste* is one of the most famous documents in the annals of opera, and it is reproduced here in the translation of Eric Blom (which occurs in his translation of Einstein's biography of Gluck in Dent's 'Master Musicians' Series):

'When I undertook to write the music for *Alceste*, I resolved to divest it entirely of all those abuses, introduced into it either by the mistaken vanity of singers or by the too great complaisance of composers, which have so long disfigured Italian opera and made of the most splendid and most beautiful of spectacles the most ridiculous and wearisome. I have striven to restrict music to its true office of serving poetry by means of expression and by following the situations of the story, without interrupting the action or stifling it with a useless superfluity of ornaments; and I believed that it should do this in the same way as telling colours affect a correct and well-ordered drawing, by a well-assorted contrast of light and shade, which serves to animate the figures without altering their contours. Thus I did not wish to arrest an actor in the greatest heat of dialogue in order to wait for a tiresome *ritornello*, nor to hold him up in the middle of a word on a vowel favourable to his voice, nor to make display of the agility of his fine voice in some long-drawn passage, nor to wait while the orchestra gives him time to recover his breath for a cadenza. I did not think it my duty to pass quickly over the second section of an aria of which the words are perhaps the most impassioned and important, in order to repeat regularly four times over those of the first part, and to finish the aria where its sense may perhaps not end for the convenience of the singer who wishes to show that he can capriciously vary a passage in a number of guises; in short, I have sought to abolish all the abuses against which good sense and reason have long cried out in vain.

'I have felt that the overture ought to apprise the spectators of the nature of the action that is to be represented and to form, so to speak, its argument; that the concerted instruments should be introduced in proportion to the interest and intensity of the words, and not leave that sharp contrast between the aria and the recitative in the dialogue, so as not to break a period unreasonably nor wantonly disturb the force and heat of the action.

'Furthermore, I believed that my greatest labour should be devoted to seeking a beautiful simplicity, and I have avoided making displays of difficulty at the expense of clearness; nor did I judge it desirable to discover novelties if it was not naturally suggested by the situation and the expression; and there is no rule which I have not thought it right to set aside willingly for the sake of an intended effect.

'Such are my principles. By good fortune my designs were wonderfully furthered by the libretto, in which the celebrated author, devising a new dramatic scheme, had substituted for florid descriptions, unnatural paragons and sententious, cold morality, heartfelt language, strong passions, interesting situations and an endlessly varied spectacle. The success of the work justified my maxims, and the universal approbation of so enlightened a city has made it clearly evident that simplicity, truth and naturalness are the great principles of beauty in all artistic manifestations. For all that, in spite of repeated urgings on the part of some most eminent persons to decide upon the publication of this opera of mine in print, I was well aware of all the risk run in combating such firmly and profoundly rooted prejudices, and I thus felt the necessity of fortifying myself with the most powerful patronage of Your Royal Highness[1] whose August Name I beg you may have the grace to prefix to this my opera, a name which with so much justice enjoys the suffrages of an enlightened Europe. The great protector of the fine arts, who reigns over a nation that had the glory of making them arise again from universal oppression and which itself has produced the greatest models, in a city that was always the first to shake off the yoke of vulgar prejudices in order to clear a path for perfection, may alone undertake the reform of that noble spectacle in which all the fine arts take so great a share. If this should succeed, the glory of having moved the first stone will remain for me, and in this public testimonial of Your Highness's furtherance of the same, I have the honour to subscribe myself, with the most humble respect,

'Your Royal Highness's

'Most humble, most devoted and most obliged servant,
        'CHRISTOFORO GLUCK.'

Calzabigi has not followed the lines of Euripides's tragedy, where the role of Admetus is an inglorious one, and the intervention of Hercules due to his desire to vindicate the laws of hospitality, not to any motive of pity for the sorry plight of Alcestis and Admetus.

Act I.   A magnificently sombre overture fully vindicates Gluck's avowed intention as set forth in the preface; here

[1] Leopold, Duke of Tuscany, who, on the death of Joseph II, was to become Emperor Leopold II.

indeed is the argument of the action. The scene represents a great court in front of the palace of Admetus; at the back can be seen the temple of Apollo. The people crowd into the courtyard and mourn the illness of their King, which, the Herald tells them, is likely to prove fatal. Evander announces the entrance of Alcestis, and the Queen appears flanked by her two children. She laments the prospect in front of her children, soon to be fatherless, and bids the crowd come with her to the temple, there to offer sacrifice to the gods.

In the temple of Apollo, we hear first a simple tune, designated 'Pantomime' in the score, which may serve as background for a dance as well as for the entrance of Alcestis. The High Priest and the chorus call upon the god to avert the fate which is about to overtake Admetus, and, through him, his wife and his people. Alcestis adds her prayer, and a sacrifice is prepared, to the music of another 'Pantomime'. The High Priest, in music that grows more and more awe-inspiring, invokes the god and commands the people to be silent to hear the Oracle's judgement. When it comes, it is more terrible than they had expected: Admetus must die, unless a friend can be found to die in his stead. The people lament the harsh pronouncement and rush from the temple in fear, leaving Alcestis and the High Priest alone. Alcestis awakes to the reality of the situation and resolves to die for her husband, without whom she cannot live. 'Non, ce n'est point un sacrifice', she sings in an aria of noble simplicity. The High Priest tells her that her prayer is granted and she has the rest of the day to prepare herself for the advent of death.

In an aria which has become the most famous of the opera, Alcestis invokes the gods of the underworld and defies them to do their worst; what dread has she of dying for what she loves best in the world? 'Divinités du Styx' is Gluck at his most intense, justifying his own maxims as regards the situation, but with a result that is no less impressive as music than as drama.

Act II.   In a great hall of his palace, Admetus stands to receive the congratulations of his people, headed by Evander, on his apparently miraculous recovery. Dances are performed in his honour. The King enquires what brought about his recovery, and Evander tells him the condition imposed by the Oracle but does not name the victim. The King is horror-stricken and refuses to accept such a sacrifice. Alcestis joins him and shares his joy that they are re-united. The chorus of praise and rejoicing continues, but Alcestis is quite unable to hide the grief she feels as the moment draws near when she must leave her husband and her children for ever. Admetus tries to comfort her in a *da capo* aria of great beauty, 'Bannis la crainte et les alarmes', but to no avail. The Queen avows her love, but finally admits that it is she the gods are taking in place of Admetus. Dramatically, he refuses to accept the sacrifice: 'Non, sans toi, je ne puis vivre'. Alcestis is left alone with the people, and, as they mourn for her grief, sings 'Ah, malgré moi, mon faible cœur partage vos tendres pleurs'.

Act III.   The courtyard of the palace. The people are mourning the deaths of both Alcestis and of Admetus, who has followed her. Hercules arrives, rejoicing that his labours are over, but Evander informs him of the death of his friend Admetus, and of the circumstances surrounding it, and he swears to restore their King and Queen to the people of Greece.

The scene changes to the gates of Hell. Alcestis pleads with the gods of Hell (who remain invisible) that her torment be not prolonged, that she be received at once. Admetus joins her, asking only to be re-united with her in death. He reminds her of her duty to their children, but their duet is interrupted by the voice of Thanatos announcing that the time has come for one of them to offer themselves to Death; the choice is left to Alcestis as to which of the two it shall be. Alcestis will not renounce her right to die for her husband, and the choice appears to have been made, much to the grief of Admetus, when Hercules appears on the scene, determined to deprive the underworld of its prey. He and Admetus defy Hell and its rulers and fight to rescue Alcestis. At the moment of their success, Apollo appears, and announces to Hercules that his action has won him the right to a place amongst the gods themselves, while Admetus and Alcestis are to be restored to earth, there to serve as a universal example of the power of conjugal love.

The scene changes to the palace court, and Apollo bids the people rejoice that their King and Queen are restored to them. Alcestis, Admetus, and Hercules take part in a trio, and the opera ends in general rejoicing.

More than perhaps any other of the operas of his maturity, *Alceste* illustrates the ideal of 'beautiful simplicity' which Gluck tells us in his preface is his aim. Berlioz's admiration for the temple scene is well known, and Ernest Newman further quotes this composer's detailed objection to the changes made in what we now know as 'Divinités du Styx' when the opera was translated from Italian, changes which ruined the beginning of the aria, according to Berlioz. Ironically, when an Italian soprano now sings this aria, she will use an Italian translation of the French translation of the original Italian, and of course employ the musical form of the French version! It should be noted that the original score included a scene in a gloomy forest near Pherae at the beginning of the second act; this is omitted in the French version, which begins with the festivities attending the recovery of Admetus. The third act, while employing much of the music of the original, is entirely altered dramatically, and, says Ernest Newman, distinctly for the worse. Du Roullet's[1] introduction of Hercules has, according to Newman, a vulgarising effect, and only the new scene at the gates of Hell (the entire act originally took place in the courtyard of the palace, where Alceste died, Admetus tried to commit suicide, and a happy ending was provided by the appearance of Apollo) constitutes a worth-while addition to the score as it stood. As with *Orfeo*, a modern performance of *Alceste* entails the preparation of an edition comprising the best elements of the original and the Paris versions.   H.

IPHIGÉNIE EN AULIDE
Iphigenia in Aulis

Opera in three acts by Christoph Willibald Gluck, text by Ranieri da Calzabigi. First performed at the Académie de Musique, Paris, April 19, 1774, with Sophie Arnould (Iphigénie), du Plant (Clytemnestra), Legros (Achilles), Larrivée (Agamemnon).

In 1846 Wagner revised the opera, changing the orchestration, re-writing some of the recitatives. This version, produced at Dresden in 1847, was given on many German stages. There was a famous revival under Mahler in Vienna in 1904 with Gutheil-Schoder, Mildenburg, Schmedes and Demuth. The opera was heard in England for the first time as late as 1933 (at Oxford) and in 1937 (in Glasgow). The first American performance occurred in 1935, in Philadelphia, conducted by Alexander Smallens, and sung by Rosa Tentoni, Cyrena van Gordon, Joseph Bentonelli, and George Baklanoff. It was revived at the Florence Festival of 1950 (in the Boboli Gardens), with Guerrini, Nicolai, Penno, and Christoff; and at la Scala, Milan, in 1959, with Simionato,

---

[1] Lebland du Roullet was responsible for French translation and some adjustments in 1776.

Lazzarini, Pier Miranda Ferraro, Christoff; New York (concert performance), 1962, with Gorr, Marilyn Horne, Simoneau, Bacquier; Salzburg, 1962, with Christa Ludwig, Borkh, King, Berry, conductor Böhm; Drottningholm (Sweden), 1965, with Elisabeth Söderström in the title role.

CHARACTERS

Agamemnon, *King of Mycenae* .... Bass-Baritone
Clytemnestra, *his wife* .... Soprano
Iphigenia, *their daughter* .... Soprano
Achilles, *a Greek hero* .... Tenor
Patroclus .... Bass
Calchas, *the High Priest* .... Bass
Arcas .... Bass
Artemis .... Soprano

Chorus of Priests, People

Time: The beginning of the Trojan War

Place: The island of Aulis

Act I.   Agamemnon, after consulting the oracle, has vowed to sacrifice his daughter, Iphigénie, to Diana in return for a favourable wind to take him and his army safely to Troy. He is persuaded to send for his daughter, on the pretext that her marriage to Achilles shall be solemnised in Aulis. He however secretly sends word to his wife, Clytemnestra, telling her to delay the voyage as the marriage has been postponed. When the opera opens, Agamemnon is seen a prey to agonising remorse, and torn by the conflicting claims of duty and love. The Greeks demand to know the reason of the gods' continued displeasure, and Calchas, the high priest, is filled with sorrow at the thought of the sacrifice that is demanded. He prays to the goddess to find another victim, Agamemnon joins him in prayer, and the Greeks demand the name of the victim that they may immediately make the sacrifice the goddess demands. Calchas assures them that the victim shall be found that very day.

Calchas reasons with Agamemnon in an effort to persuade him to agree to the sacrifice, but the Greek King breaks out into an agonised expression of his overwhelming sorrow. Is it possible that the gods wish him to commit so dreadful a crime? Calchas asks him if his intention is to go against his oath, but Agamemnon replies that he has sworn to sacrifice Iphigénie only if she sets foot on the soil of Aulis. At that very moment, and in the midst of Calchas's denunciation of the King's duplicity, they hear the cries of the Greeks as they welcome Clytemnestra and Iphigénie, newly arrived on the island. As the King and the high priest comment on the possible results of the arrival, the Greeks sing the praises of the Queen and her daughter. Agamemnon secretly informs his wife that Achilles has proved unworthy of Iphigénie and that she and her daughter are therefore to return immediately on their journey. She denounces Achilles to Iphigénie, who is ready to believe her until Achilles himself appears on the scene, overjoyed at her unexpected arrival. Iphigénie is at first cold and unwelcoming, but explanations follow and the act ends with a duet of reconciliation.

Act II.   In spite of the chorus's attempts at reassurance and congratulation on her forthcoming marriage, Iphigénie is filled with foreboding at the prospect of a meeting between Agamemnon and Achilles who by now knows that his prospective father-in-law was responsible for the rumour of his infidelity to Iphigénie. Clytemnestra bids her daughter rejoice, Achilles, after introducing the warrior Patroclus to her, leads a chorus in her praise, and songs and dances are offered in honour of the happy couple. As Achilles is about to lead his bride to the Altar, Arcas, Agamemnon's messenger, intervenes and protests that Agamemnon waits at the altar to sacrifice her in fulfilment of his sacred vow. Clytemnestra begs Achilles to protect his young bride from the consequences of her father's rash action. Achilles impulsively swears to defend her, but Iphigénie reminds him that Agamemnon is her father, and that she loves him in spite of the terrible situation in which fate has placed him.

Agamemnon and Achilles meet, and, in answer to Achilles's reproaches, Agamemnon reminds him that he is supreme commander of the Greek forces and that all owe allegiance to him and obedience to his decisions. Achilles defies him and says that whoever means to lay hands on Iphigénie will have to overcome him first. Agamemnon is left alone with his conscience and the necessity to decide between his duty to the gods and his love for his daughter. In the end he decides to send Clytemnestra and Iphigénie straight away to Mycenae, and by this means he hopes to avoid the consequences of his oath.

Act III.   The Greeks demand that the vow shall be fulfilled as the only means by which the present wrath of the gods may be averted. Achilles begs Iphigénie to fly with him, but she protests her willingness to die, he insists on his determination to save her. Clytemnestra is left alone with her daughter, and tries every means to save her, but the Greeks are implacable in their demand that the sacrifice shall take place. Clytemnestra calls down the fury of Jove on the cruel hosts of the Greeks.

All is ready for the sacrifice and the Greeks beg for an answer to their prayer which will accompany it. The ceremony is interrupted by the arrival of Achilles at the head of the Thessalians, who fall on the assembled Greek troops. A pitched battle is averted by Calchas, who announces that the gods are appeased and prepared to grant fair weather even though Agamemnon's oath is not fulfilled. Husband and wife, parent and child, lover and beloved are reconciled and re-united and the opera ends with rejoicings as the Greeks prepare to set sail for Troy.

Although *Iphigénie en Aulide* has not quite the unity of style and construction that is so marked a feature of the later *Iphigénie en Tauride*, it is full of remarkable music. The leading figures are strongly characterised. Agamemnon is never less than a heroic figure, and the conflict which is the result of his vow makes him the most interesting character in the drama. His arias are magnificently expressive, that of the first act immediately establishing his commanding stature and essential nobility as well as the appalling dilemma he sees before him, the great *scena* at the end of the second act (after the scene with Achilles) even more impressively dramatic. Clytemnestra is less positively involved in the drama, but her intense reaction to its events is expressed in wonderfully dramatic music. In her solo scenes, she passes from straight-forward fury when she hears from Agamemnon of Achilles's supposed unfaithfulness to Iphigénie, through the extremes of grief when she pleads with Achilles to save her daughter, until in the third act she collapses altogether when her pleas to the Greeks go unheeded. Even nowadays the intensity of her emotions is immediately apparent, and one can imagine that such musical expressiveness must have made an extraordinary effect in Gluck's time. Like Ilia in *Idomeneo*, Iphigénie is the victim rather than the agent of the tragedy but her resignation and acceptance of her cruel fate gives rise to music of remarkable beauty. Achilles is the ancestor of Radames and a whole line of heroic tenors, uncomplicated as a person and accustomed to express himself vigorously and uncompromisingly, with a wealth of top notes to emphasise his determination. His aria in Act III when he resolves to save Iphigénie by force of arms made an effect at the first performance comparable to that felt by Italian audiences hearing Verdi's music at the time of the Risorgimento. We are told that the gentlemen in the theatre could hardly refrain from drawing their swords and joining him on the stage in his attempt to rescue his Princess.   H.

IPHIGÉNIE EN TAURIDE

Iphigenia in Tauris

Opera in four acts by Gluck, words by François Guillard.

Produced in the Académie de Musique, Paris, May 18, 1779, with Levasseur, Legros, Larrivée; London (in da Ponte's Italian translation), 1796; Metropolitan Opera House, New York, November 25, 1916, with Kurt, Sembach, Weil, Braun, and Rappold (in German, arranged Richard Strauss). Revived la Scala, 1937, with Caniglia, Parmeggiani, Armando Borgioli, Maugeri, conducted by de Sabata; Berlin 1941, with Müller, Svanholm, Domgraf-Fassbänder, Ahlersmeyer; Aix 1952, with Neway, Simoneau, Mollet, Massard, conductor Giulini; la Scala, 1957, with Callas; Edinburgh Festival and Covent Garden, 1961, with Gorr, conductor Solti; Holland Festival, 1964, with Brouwenstijn, Ilosfalvy, Přibyl,[1] conductor Erede; Opéra, Paris, 1965, with Crespin, Chauvet, Massard.

CHARACTERS

Iphigénie, *Priestess of Diana* .... Soprano
Oreste, *her Brother* .... Baritone
Pylade, *his Friend* .... Tenor
Thoas, *King of Scythia* .... Bass
Diana .... Soprano
Scythians, Priestesses of Diana, Greeks
Time: After the Trojan War   *Place:* Tauris

Iphigénie is the daughter of Agamemnon, King of Mycenae. Agamemnon was slain by his wife, Clytemnestra, who, in

---

[1] In 1780-1, Gluck revised his opera for its performance in German in Vienna, giving the role of Oreste to Josef Valentin Adamberger (like Vilem Přibyl in Holland in 1964, a tenor). Antonia Bernasconi, Josef Souter and Ludwig Fischer made up the remainder of the cast. Fischer, like Adamberger, was to sing the first performance of Mozart's *Entführung* the following year.   H.

turn, was killed by her son, Oreste. Iphigénie is ignorant of
these happenings. She has become a priestess of Diana on the
island of Tauris and has not seen Oreste for many years.

Act I.   Before the atrium of the temple of Diana. To
priestesses and Greek maidens, Iphigénie tells of her dream
that misfortune has come to her family in the distant country
of her birth. Thoas, entering, calls for a human sacrifice to
ward off danger that has been foretold to him. Some of his
people, hastily coming upon the scene, bring with them as
captives Oreste and Pylade, Greek youths who have landed
upon the coast. They report that Oreste constantly speaks of
having committed a crime and of being pursued by Furies.

Act II. Temple of Diana. Oreste bewails his fate. Pylade
sings of his undying friendship for him. Pylade is separated
from Oreste, who temporarily loses his mind. Iphigénie
questions him. Oreste, under her influence, becomes calmer,
but refrains from disclosing his identity. He tells her, however, that he is from Mycenae, that Agamemnon (their father'
has been slain by his wife, that Clytemnestra's son, Oreste,
has slain her in revenge, and is himself dead. Of the once
great family only a daughter, Electra, remains.

Act III.   Iphigénie is struck with the resemblance of the
stranger to her brother and, in order to save him from the
sacrifice demanded by Thoas, charges him to deliver a letter
to Electra. He declines to leave Pylade; nor, until Oreste
affirms that he will commit suicide rather than accept
freedom at the price of his friend's life, does Pylade agree to
take the letter, and then only because he hopes to bring
succour to Oreste.

Act IV.   All is ready for the sacrifice. Iphigénie has the
knife poised for the fatal thrust, when, through an exclamation uttered by Oreste, she recognises him as her brother
The priestesses offer him obeisance as king. Thoas, however
enters and demands the sacrifice. Iphigénie declares that she
will die with her brother. At that moment Pylade at the head
of a rescue party enters the temple. A combat ensues in
which Thoas is killed. Diana herself appears, pardons Oreste
and returns to the Greeks her likeness which the Scythian
had stolen and over which they had built the temple.

Gluck was sixty-five when he brought out *Iphigénie en
Tauride*. A contemporary remarked that there were many
fine passages in the opera. 'There is only one,' said the Abbé
Arnaud. 'Which?'—'The entire work.'

The mad scene for Oreste, in the second act, has been called Gluck's greatest single achievement. Mention should also be made of Iphigénie's 'O toi, qui prolongeas nos jours', the dances of the Scythians, the air of Thoas, 'De noirs pressentiments mon âme intimidée'; the airs of Pylade, 'Unis dès la plus tendre enfance' and 'O mon ami'; Iphigénie's 'O malheureuse Iphigénie', and 'Je t'implore et je tremble'; and the hymn to Diana, 'Chaste fille de Latone' (Chaste daughter of the crescent moon).

Here may be related an incident at the rehearsal of the work which indicates the dramatic significance Gluck sought to impart to his music. In the second act, while Oreste is singing, 'Le calme rentre dans mon cœur', the orchestral accompaniment continues to express the agitation of his thoughts. During the rehearsal the members of the orchestra, not understanding the passage, came to a stop. 'Go on all the same,' cried Gluck. 'He lies. He has killed his mother!'

Gluck's enemies prevailed upon his rival, Piccinni, to write an *Iphigénie en Tauride* in opposition. It was produced in January 1781, met with failure, and put a definite stop to Piccinni's rivalry with Gluck. At the performance the prima donna was intoxicated. This caused a spectator to shout: '*Iphigénie en Tauride!* allons donc, c'est *Iphigénie en Champagne!*'

The laugh that followed sealed the doom of the work.

The version used at the Metropolitan was that made by Richard Strauss, which involves changes in the finales of the first and last acts. Ballet music from *Orfeo* and *Armide* was also introduced.   **K.**

There is much to support the argument that this is Gluck's best opera. Here he comes nearest to a complete reconciliation of his dramatic style with his lyrical, and the extremes represented by *Alceste* and *Armide* are to some extent amalgamated. The dramatic and the sensuous meet in *Iphigénie en Tauride* to form a whole that is more consistent and more expressive than anything Gluck had previously written. Nowhere else did he achieve such homogeneity of style, with whole scenes dominated by a single idea expressed in music of the greatest power, and seldom before had he displayed such invention in the individual arias.   **H.**

3
Mozart

WOLFGANG AMADEUS MOZART
(1756–1791)

IDOMENEO

OPERA in three acts by Mozart. Text by Abbé Varesco, after a French
opera by Campra and Danchet. First performed at Munich, January 29,
1781, with Anton Raaff as Idomeneo, del Prato as Idamante, Dorothea
Wendling as Ilia, Elisabeth Wendling as Electra, Panzacchi as Arbace.
Revived at Karlsruhe, 1917; Dresden, 1925; Vienna, 1931 (revised by
Strauss, new text by Lothar Wallerstein, and with Maria Nemeth,
Elisabeth Schumann, Josef Kalenberg, Eva Hadrabova, Richard Mayr in
the cast); Munich, 1931 (revised by Wolf-Ferrari). The first British
performance was at Glasgow in 1934, and the first English professional
performance at Glyndebourne in 1951, when Fritz Busch conducted a
cast including Sena Jurinac (Ilia), Birgit Nilsson (Electra), Richard
Lewis (Idomeneo), and Leopold Simoneau (Idamante). The first New
York performance was at Town Hall, 1951, with Camilla Williams,
Mariquita Moll, Brenda Lewis, William Hess. Recent revivals include
Salzburg, 1956, with Scheyrer, Goltz, Schock, Kmentt, conductor
Böhm; Sadler's Wells, 1962, with Morison, Woodland, Dowd, McAlpine,
conductor Colin Davis; la Scala, Milan, 1968, with Rinaldi, Gencer,
Kmentt, Schreier, conductor Sawallisch.

CHARACTERS

Idomeneo, *King of Crete* .... Tenor
Idamante, *his son* .... Soprano
Ilia, *a Trojan Princess* .... Soprano
Electra, *a Greek Princess* .... Soprano
Arbace, *confidant of Idomeneo* .... Tenor

3 *Le Nozze di Figaro* with Tito Gobbi and Mirella Freni as Count and
Susanna in Act III at Covent Garden.

4 *Don Giovanni:* Ezio Pinza sings the Champagne aria at Salzburg in 1937. Virgilio Lazzari was Leporello and Bruno Walter the conductor.

High Priest of Neptune .... Tenor
Voice of Neptune .... Bass
People of Crete, Trojan Prisoners, Sailors, Soldiers,
Priests of Neptune, Dancers
The action takes place on the island of Crete

Mozart's third and greatest essay in the form of *opera seria* (his first two, *Mitridate* and *Lucio Silla*, were written respectively ten and nine years earlier) was first performed in 1781 at Munich, for which Opera it was commissioned. Revived only once in the composer's lifetime (for a private performance in Vienna in 1786), it was fairly frequently heard in Germany and Austria after his death but not performed in Britain until 1934, and never on the English professional stage until its production at Glyndebourne in 1951. It was not heard in America until 1947 when performed at the Berkshire Festival, Tanglewood. Why this neglect? First, by its very nature, *Idomeneo* has never been a repertory opera. Secondly and more important, it is an example of an operatic convention whose popularity was nearing its end at the time of the first performance, and with which we have now almost no first-hand acquaintance at all. A castrato ('mio molto amato castrato del Prato', as Mozart called him) was a prominent member of the original cast, and the opera was conceived during the period of vocal virtuosity which is associated with that breed. This is important to an understanding of the whole scheme of *Idomeneo*, as the composer aimed to give the fullest possible scope to his singers and the idiom is dependent for its full effect on singing of considerable stature. But let it not be thought that the opera is just a series of display pieces and formal movements; it is far more than that—Einstein in fact describes it as 'one of those works that even a genius of the highest rank, like Mozart, could write only once in his life'. He was at the height of his powers when it was composed, and the arias are superbly expressive, though on a more rarefied plane than the later comedies have accustomed us to. If drama consists of the interplay of motives and emotions, and tragedy of the ordering of men's destinies by a fate their own actions have provoked, *Idomeneo* is both tragic (in spite of its happy ending) and dramatic. The four main characters, whose conflict reaches its climax with the great quartet in the last act, are sharply defined, and what might well have turned out no more than four stock figures emerge in the course of the musical action as personages no less real, if on an idealised plane, than for instance Susanna or Pamina. In fact we may take Ilia, with the gradual development of her personality through the trials she has to undergo, as a sketch, musically speaking at any rate, for Pamina, Mozart's maturest essay in what one must think of as his conception of the 'perfect' feminine type. It is hardly more fanciful to see in Idamante, her lover, the forerunner of Tamino, even more forceful and generous and dignified for all that he was originally sung by a castrato.

Act I. Idomeneo, King of Crete, has taken part in the Trojan war, and it is many years since he left home. Amongst the prisoners he has sent home is Ilia, daughter of King Priam, who has fallen in love with Idamante, the son of Idomeneo. The overture immediately establishes the character of an opera whose music, without exception, never relaxes its intense seriousness throughout its length; from it, without the need of external evidence as to the conduct of *opera seria*, we may deduce the dignity and stature of the characters involved. Calmly the drama unfolds. In an aria, 'Padre, germani, addio', Ilia reveals that her hatred for the conquerors of her country is as nothing to her love for Idamante. He enters at its conclusion and in veiled terms states his love for Ilia, at the same time announcing that, in honour of his father's imminent return to Crete, the Trojan prisoners are to be set free. A chorus of rejoicing at this news precedes the entrance of Arbace to say that Idomeneo's ship has been sunk; the general consternation is given particular expression by Electra, who fears that his death will remove all obstacles to the marriage of Ilia and Idamante, with whom she is herself in love. Seldom if ever before can passionate fury have been given so illuminating an expression as in her aria. She leaves the stage and, at the end of a chorus of intercession, Idomeneo enters with his followers, whom he dismisses before explaining in an aria the nature of the vow which secured Neptune's intervention in quieting the storm: that he will sacrifice the first living creature he meets in return for deliverance from death. It is, of course, Idamante whom he sees, and their dialogue is made the more poignant because it is some time before Idomeneo recognises his son, whom he has not seen since infancy. In horror, the father orders the son from his presence, and Idamante laments his father's apparent displeasure in an aria 'Il padre adorato ritrovo e lo perdo'. The act ends with a brilliant march and choral *ciaccona* in honour of Neptune.

Act II. The King tells his secret to his counsellor Arbace, who advises that Idamante be sent to a distant country. The whole scene, which was originally included to provide an aria for the tenor Panzacchi, who created the role of Arbace, is usually omitted in modern performance, the act thus beginning with the scene between Idomeneo and Ilia whose aria 'Se il padre perdei' is touchingly beautiful. Idomeneo understands that his vow now involves not only disaster for himself and Idamante but for Ilia as well, but he faces the tragedy with courage and dignity in his great aria 'Fuor del mar ho un mar in seno'. This was written as a show piece for Raaff, the 66-year-old tenor who created the title role in Munich; whatever may be thought about his musical taste (he wanted an aria for himself substituted for the Act III quartet), his technique must have been very considerable indeed.[1] As Edward Dent said: 'Coloratura for men has gone out of fashion, thanks to Wagner, and, thanks to the late Madame Patti, coloratura for women has been associated with the frail type of heroine rather than the heroic. In the eighteenth century and especially in the early half of it, the grand period of *opera seria*, coloratura was almost invariably heroic in character. . . . Donizetti's Lucia is paired off with a flute, Handel's heroes compete with a trumpet.' If the reader doubts whether any twentieth-century singer can overcome the difficulties of such music, I would refer him to a record made by Hermann Jadlowker about the time of the 1914-18 war, in which this aria is sung with extraordinary fluency and power.

A beautiful, lyrical aria for Electra, whom the prospect of requited love has turned into a happy woman, leads into a march, and thence to the famous barcarolle chorus of embarkation, 'Placido è il mar, andiamo'. Idamante and Electra take leave of Idomeneo in a superb trio 'Pria di

[1] A simplified version from Mozart's pen also exists, twenty-two bars shorter and shorn of much of the embellishments. It has often been assumed that the lesser version dates from Mozart's preparation of the score in 1786 for Vienna, but Daniel Heartz and Stanley Sadie have suggested that it is likelier to represent an acknowledgement of the elderly Raaff's diminished capacity and that it was probably sung at the première.   H.

partir', but the music quickens and a storm breaks over the harbour heralding Neptune's vengeance at this attempt to evade the consequences of the vow made to him. Idomeneo admits his guilt but accuses the god of injustice, and the act ends as the crowd disperses in terror.

Act III.   Ilia can think only of her love for Idamante, and her expression of it in her soliloquy 'Zeffiretti lusinghieri' is one of the most perfect moments of the opera. To her comes Idamante; he is going out to fight the monster Neptune has sent to plague the island, and he may not return. Involuntarily, she confesses her love, which leads to a duet. Idomeneo and Electra interrupt the lovers. Idomeneo still cannot bring himself to explain the exact cause of the disaster which is overtaking them all, and Idamante sadly takes his farewell in the noble quartet 'Andrò ramingo e solo'. Einstein calls it 'the first really great ensemble in the history of the *opera seria*' and Edward Dent does not try to disguise his enthusiasm for it when he describes it as 'perhaps the most beautiful ensemble ever composed for the stage'. In truth, one has no cause to complain that either is exaggerating; it shows Mozart at his noblest and most expressive,

and is the moment in the opera when the spirit of tragedy
most completely dominates the music. The scene customarily
and appropriately ends with the quartet, Arbace's elaborate
aria being cut.

After an introduction, the High Priest exhorts the King to
confess his sin to Neptune, and the people are duly horrified
to hear that the sacrifice of Idamante is the price they and he
will have to pay for deliverance from the god's displeasure.
The people are gathered in the Temple of Neptune to witness
the sacrifice, the priests enter to a march and Idomeneo
begins the ceremony with a solemn prayer which is answered
by the priests. A shout of triumph is heard outside and
Arbace announces that Idamante has met the monster in
combat and killed it. However, a moment later Idamante,
who by now knows the story of his father's vow, enters and
offers himself for sacrifice, and Idomeneo cannot but accept
him. The ceremony is about to reach its climax when Ilia
interrupts and demands to be sacrificed in Idamante's place.
The whole situation is resolved by an oracular pronouncement from Neptune, to the effect that the crime can
be expiated, the vow fulfilled, if Idomeneo will renounce the
throne in favour of his son. In the general rejoicing, only
Electra is left with her worst fears realised; in the most
furious of her violent utterances, she gives vent to her despair
and rushes from the stage, or, as some versions have it, falls
dead or commits suicide.

The atmosphere changes to one of peace and fulfilment as
Idomeneo in a last recitative and aria, 'Torna la pace al core',
presents Idamante to the people as their new ruler, and takes
his farewell. At the first performance, this aria had to be cut,
much apparently to Mozart's regret, as anyone who hears it
nowadays will readily understand. The opera ends with the
people celebrating the accession of Idamante in dance and
chorus.

When *Idomeneo* was performed privately in Vienna by
amateur singers, Mozart added two numbers, transposed the
role of Idamante for a tenor, removed most of Arbace's
music, and made certain modifications in the rest of the
opera. That he gave the role of Idamante to a tenor has been
taken by some modern editors to indicate a change of mind
as far as the vocal colour of this role was concerned, but this
is surely to attach too little importance to the practical
conditions of a performance which was after all mostly in the
hands of amateur singers; rather few of these would have

been likely to have been castrati. In any case, however far the colour of the castrato voice must have been from that of a modern soprano, it is hard to believe that it was nearer to a tenor's.

Modern conductors have not surprisingly shown an ambivalent attitude towards the problem of sacrificing either vocal colour, if a tenor sings Idamante, or dramatic verisimilitude, if they choose a soprano. No lesser Mozartian than Colin Davis chose a tenor for his Sadler's Wells revival and his recording, only a year or two after the recording to revert (in my view with positive musical gain) to soprano for a broadcast.   H.

DIE ENTFÜHRUNG AUS DEM SERAIL

The Abduction from the Seraglio

Opera in three acts by Mozart. Text by Gottlieb Stephanie from a play by Bretzner. First performed at the Burgtheater, Vienna, July 16, 1782, with Katharina Cavalieri (Constanze), Therese Teyber (Blonde), Valentin Ademberger (Belmonte), Ludwig Fischer (Osmin), and conducted by Mozart. During the first six years of its existence, there were thirty-four performances in Vienna. First performed in London, Covent Garden, 1827, in English, with additional airs by J. B. Cramer, and sung by Madame Vestris, Miss Hughes, Mr. Sapio, Mr. Benson, Mr. Wrenn. The first performance in New York was in 1860. Other performances in London include those at Drury Lane, 1841 (in German), Her Majesty's, 1866 (in Italian, with recitatives by Arditi). Revived Covent Garden, 1927, with Ivogün, Schumann, Erb, Bender, and conducted by Bruno Walter; 1938, with Berger, Beilke, Tauber, Weber, conducted by Beecham. Produced for the first time at Glyndebourne in 1935, with Noel Eadie, Eisinger, Ludwig, Andresen, and Heddle Nash (Pedrillo), conducted by Fritz Busch. The first performance in Italy did not take place until 1935, at the Florence Festival when Bruno Walter conducted a cast including Perras, Schöne, Kullman, and Sterneck; and the opera was first heard at the Metropolitan, New York, in 1946 in English, with Steber, Alarie, Kullman, Carter, Ernster, conductor Cooper.

CHARACTERS

Constanze, *a Spanish lady* .... Soprano
Blonde, *her English maid* .... Soprano
Belmonte, *a Spanish nobleman* .... Tenor

Pedrillo, *his servant* . . . . Tenor
Pasha Selim . . . . Speaking Part
Osmin, *overseer of his harem* . . . . Bass
     Turkish Soldiers, Guards, Turkish women

A curious 'springboard' (as Einstein calls it in his *Mozart; his Character, his Work*) exists for *Die Entführung*. In 1779 Mozart began the music for a *Singspiel*, perhaps in desperation at the small prospects for operatic composition and performance which Salzburg offered. It was abandoned, probably owing to the arrival of the commission for *Idomeneo*, was only published in 1838 under the title of *Zaïde*, and did not reach the stage until 1866. The reasons are not far to seek: it was conceived on a modest scale—too modest for Mozart's real requirements—and its subject and style were 'Turkish' and very close to those of the opera he undertook a little later, *Die Entführung*, whose story reads like an amplification of *Zaïde*. *Zaïde* contains some attractive music, and the aria 'Ruhe sanft, mein holdes Leben' is of the greatest simplicity and beauty.

Die Entführung (1782) itself is important amongst Mozart's works not least because of the ambitious and extended view he takes in it of the hitherto modest German *Singspiel*. The drama is carried on almost exclusively in speech and it is only in moments of high emotion that the characters have recourse to song—but on what a sublimated level is that song when it comes! To expect in a *Singspiel* the extended finales that are a characteristic of *opera buffa* is to wish for something which would have been out of character with the convention and which Mozart was not trying to provide. Nevertheless, the music is highly expressive. Constanze and Belmonte, the latter at any rate, are perhaps loftier in their musical aspirations than they are in the field of human behaviour, where they lay themselves open to charges of ingratitude and deception. Blonde and Pedrillo, though entertaining, are little more than stock comedy figures. Osmin, however, is one of the composer's great dramatic creations, genuinely and consistently comic in music as in action, yet no mere figure of fun, and as potentially dangerous as he is laughable.

Act I.   The overture is mainly concerned with establishing the 'Turkish' atmosphere of the piece; Mozart also introduces a reference in the minor to Belmonte's aria, 'Hier soll' ich

dich denn sehen, Constanze', which is heard in C major when
the curtain goes up. Belmonte is outside the Pasha Selim's
house, where he believes his beloved Constanze, who has
been carried off by pirates, is a captive. Osmin, in charge of
the Pasha's harem and also, it seems, of his garden, appears
singing a doleful sort of love song, 'Wer ein Liebchen hat
gefunden', one of the delights of the score. He is questioned
by Belmonte: is this not the Pasha Selim's house? It is, and
he works for the Pasha, but an enquiry for Pedrillo produces
an even surlier answer, as this is his *bête noire*, his rival in love
for Blondchen; Pedrillo should, he says, without delay, be
hanged, drawn, and quartered. He chases Belmonte away, but
is immediately confronted with Pedrillo in person, saucier
and more impudent than ever. The situation calls for music
and he relieves his pent-up feelings with an aria that is a
virtuoso expression of rage and also, in good hands, of the
comic bass's art: 'Solche hergelauf'ne Laffen'.

Belmonte returns to find his former servant; each is
delighted at the other's news, Belmonte to hear that
Constanze has remained true to him in spite of the Pasha's
persuasive powers, Pedrillo that there is a boat waiting to
take them all to safety if they can only spirit the women out
of the harem. Belmonte sings a song of love for his absent
Constanze: 'O wie ängstlich, o wie feurig'. It is filled with a
romantic feeling that derives in part, we may suppose, from
Mozart's own love for his Constanze, whom he married a few
weeks after the production of the opera. The orchestral
accompaniment, Mozart tells his father in a letter, represents
the throbbing of the lover's heart, the heaving of his breast,
his sighs and whispers.

Belmonte leaves the stage as Constanze and the Pasha land
from a boat to be greeted in a chorus that is very much in the
Turkish style. The Pasha once again assures Constanze of his
love and of his determination to win hers in return. She sings
of the love that she knew before her captivity and protests
that she will be true to this memory: 'Ach, ich liebte, war so
glücklich'. It is a coloratura aria, but full of sadness for her
past happiness and of determination to resist temptation. She
leaves the stage, and Pedrillo takes this opportunity to
introduce Belmonte to the Pasha as an architect of high
standing. The Pasha intimates that he will not withhold his
favour from him, but after he has gone Osmin remains
unimpressed and tries to bar their way. It is only after a lively

trio, 'Marsch, marsch, marsch', that they contrive to out-
manoeuvre him and enter the palace.

Act II.   Osmin is no match for Blonde in a battle of wits,
as she demonstrates in her aria, 'Durch Zärtlichkeit und
Schmeicheln', and the duet which follows. He knows she will
come off best and can do no more than complain at the folly
of the English in allowing their women so much liberty (in
this story, Blonde is supposed to be English). Constanze
unburdens herself to Blonde: 'Traurigkeit ward mir zum Loose'.

It is perhaps the most deeply felt number of the score, and
one of Mozart's most sublime expressions of grief (like 'Ach,
ich fühl's', in the key of G minor). Blonde retires as the Pasha
comes once more to urge his suit. Constanze is adamant and
launches into one of the most considerable arias Mozart ever
wrote for soprano voice: 'Martern aller Arten'. Laid out on
concerto lines, with four solo instruments and a lengthy
orchestral introduction, it is the one moment in the opera

where Mozart definitely sacrifices the stage situation—the Pasha and Constanze can do little more than glare at each other during the introduction—to the possibilities inherent in his singers, of whom Katharina Cavalieri, the Constanze, was perhaps the most eminent. But the aria that results is musically such a masterpiece that few people will feel disposed to agree with the purists who maintain that it should be cut in performance (unless, that is to say, the singer is going to make a mess of it).

Blonde is wondering if the empty stage signifies that the entreaties of the Pasha have at last been successful when Pedrillo rushes in to tell her that Belmonte is here and a plan afoot for their escape. Osmin is to be drugged to make way for the double elopement. Blonde's joyful song, 'Welche Wonne, welche Lust', contrasts with Pedrillo's definitely nervous reaction to the prospect of dealing with Osmin single-handed ('Frisch zum Kampfe'). However, he tackles as to the manner born the business of persuading Osmin that the Mohammedan doctrine of teetotalism is better honoured in the breach than in the observance, and he soon has him tippling with the best and praising wine in one of Mozart's most exquisite inspirations, the duet 'Vivat Bacchus'. Osmin sinks into a stupor and Pedrillo is able to drag him out of the way and leave the coast clear for a reunion between Belmonte and Constanze. Belmonte in his aria, 'Wenn der Freude Thränen fliessen', is less passionate than Constanze as she begins the quartet which is to end the act. It is a noble piece in spite of the crisis which is contrived to keep it alive—the men ask to be assured again that their lovers were true during captivity—and the musical integrity is unaffected by the dramatic artificiality.

Act III. With much comic pantomime, Pedrillo organises the disposal of the ladders with the help of the captain of the ship which is to take them to freedom. Belmonte enters and is instructed to sing so that no one will notice that he, Pedrillo, is not serenading his Blonde as usual ('Ich baue ganz auf deine Stärke'). A moment later, Pedrillo is back, and ready to give the signal for escape with his enchanting serenade 'Im Mohrenland gefangen war':

Romanze

Im Moh-ren-land ge-fan-gen war - - ein Mädchen hübsch und fein

Nothing in the score is more immediately appealing than this graceful piece, which must be the plum of the whole 'second tenor' repertory. Belmonte and Constanze disappear into the darkness, and Pedrillo rushes up the ladder to fetch his Blonde, unaware that his singing has woken up a guard, a mute, who suspects the worst and dashes off to summon Osmin. The latter arrives as the second pair of lovers is on the point of leaving the house, and his suspicions that a double elopement has been planned are confirmed when Constanze and Belmonte are brought back by the guard which has surprised their escape. 'Ha! wie will ich triumphieren' he sings in his joy that at last he is to have the chance of settling a hundred and one old scores with Pedrillo, and several new ones as well with Belmonte. Never has one operatic character gloated so convincingly over the misfortunes of others, and Osmin parades his vengeful notions in an orgy of triumph, touching a top E and sustaining a bottom D in his highly satisfactory efforts to give them adequate musical expression.

The Pasha is informed of the intended escape and arrives to question the prisoners. Constanze pleads her love for Belmonte as justification for the attempted escape, and her lover assures the Pasha that his father, a rich Spaniard by the name of Lostados, will pay a high ransom for his freedom. Lostados! exclaims the Pasha: you are the son of my greatest enemy, the man who stole from me my love, my career, and my right to live in my native country. Belmonte and Constanze are face to face with death and perhaps torture, and their extensive duet, 'Welch' ein Geschick', reveals a serious approach to their imminent tragedy. The Pasha returns, and announces that he scorns to return evil for evil, that they are free to return to their native Spain whenever they like. The happy couples return thanks in the form of a *vaudeville*, which Belmonte begins, the others singing a verse each and all joining in the refrain:

Vaudeville

Wer so viel Huld ver-ges-sen kann, den seh man mit Ver-ach-tung an

Blonde cannot resist a final dig at the discomfited Osmin, whose rage overcomes him so that he disrupts the harmony of the ensemble with another furious outburst before rushing defeated from the stage, leaving the others to finish on a note of suitable gratitude. They take their leave while the chorus sings the praises of the Pasha and his clemency.   H.

DER SCHAUSPIELDIREKTOR
The Impresario

Another comedy opera, produced 1786, introduces that clever rogue, Schikaneder, at whose entreaty *The Magic Flute* was composed. The other characters include Mozart himself, and Mme. Hofer, his sister-in-law, who was the Queen of the Night in the original cast of *The Magic Flute*. The story deals with the troubles of an impresario due to the jealousy of prima donnas. 'Before they are engaged, opera singers are very engaging, except when they are engaged in singing.' This line is from H. E. Krehbiel's translation of the libretto, produced, with *Bastien and Bastienne* (translated by Alice Matullah, as a 'lyric pastoral'), at the Empire Theatre, New York, October 26, 1916. These charming productions were made by the Society of American Singers with a company including David Bispham (Schikaneder and Colas), Albert Reiss (Mozart and Bastien), Mabel Garrison, and Lucy Gates; the direction that of Mr. Reiss.   K.

LE NOZZE DI FIGARO
The Marriage of Figaro

Opera buffa in four acts by Mozart; text by Lorenzo da Ponte, after Beaumarchais. First performed at the Burgtheater, Vienna, May 1, 1786, with Mmes. Laschi (Countess), Storace (Susanna), Bussani (Cherubino), Gottlieb (Barbarina), Mandini (Marcellina), Messrs. Mandini (Count Almaviva), Benucci (Figaro), Kelly (Basilio and Curzio), Bussani (Bartolo and Antonio), and conducted by Mozart. First performed in England (in Italian) at Haymarket Theatre, London, 1812, and (in English) Covent Garden, 1819, with Mrs. Dickens, Miss Stephens, Miss Beaumont, Messrs. Jones, Liston, Isaacs. The first performance in New York took place in 1824. Revived at Old Vic Theatre, London (Edward Dent's translation), 1920; and first performed at Glyndebourne Festival in 1934, conducted by Fritz Busch, produced by Carl Ebert, and with Aulikki Rautawaara, Audrey Mildmay, Luise Helletsgruber, Willi Domgraf-Fassbänder, Roy Henderson, Norman Allin in the cast.

CHARACTERS

Count Almaviva .... Baritone
Figaro, *his valet* .... Baritone

Doctor Bartolo .... Bass
Don Basilio, *a music-master* .... Tenor
Cherubino, *a page* .... Soprano
Antonio, *a gardener* .... Bass
Don Curzio, *counsellor at law* .... Tenor
Countess Almaviva .... Soprano
Susanna, *her personal maid, engaged to Figaro* . Soprano
Marcellina, *a duenna* .... Soprano
Barbarina, *Antonio's niece* .... Soprano
Time: Eighteenth Century   *Place:* The Count's château of
Aguas Frescas, near Seville

Probably the two perfect 'popular' operas are *Figaro* and
Aida—'popular' in the sense that both are very frequently
performed and neither public nor musicians show signs of
getting tired of listening to them, 'perfect' in the sense that
they combine a sensitivity and delicacy in their musical
construction and workmanship with the all-important
common touch. It is an easy commonplace—perhaps fatally
easy—to pile on superlatives when describing Mozart's operas,
and particularly when talking about *Figaro, Don Giovanni,
Così fan tutte*, and *The Magic Flute*, but it is a fault which is
very difficult to avoid; the plain fact is that an enormous
number of opera-goers would proclaim *Figaro* the most
entertaining operatic comedy they had ever heard.

Figaro was Mozart's first venture with his most famous
librettist, Lorenzo da Ponte (who incidentally provided the
libretti for no less than four operas which had their first
performance during 1786, the year of *Figaro*'s debut).
Although he had had no Italian comic opera produced since
La Finta Giardiniera in 1775, Mozart had in the meanwhile
worked on *L'Oca del Cairo* and *Lo Sposo Deluso*, each of
which he abandoned. He had also composed the music for
Der Schauspieldirektor, a slight piece but sufficient evidence
of the continuing development of his theatrical and musical
craftsmanship. It is surprising in retrospect to note that, in
spite of the brilliant libretto and even more brilliant music,
Figaro made only a moderate success when it was produced
in Vienna, where it had to wait until after the triumph in
Prague before being received into popular affection. It was
incidentally the success of *Figaro* in Prague which led to the
commission to compose *Don Giovanni* for that city.

Act I. The overture is extremely well known, and

nothing could make a better prelude to this marriage day of
feverish activity than the short *presto* movement. When the
curtain rises, Susanna is discovered before the looking-glass.
Figaro is measuring out a space on the floor ('Cinque, dieci').
The room, Figaro explains, is to be theirs—'the most convenient room in the castle, just between milord and milady'.
(Not all stage designers have been prepared to admit that, in
eighteenth-century castle geography, this is likely to have
been a box room or a curtained-off portion of a passage, not a
grand room with a veranda and a view of the Park.) Susanna
astounds him by peremptorily refusing to accept it, but,
when he remonstrates ('Se a caso Madama'—Supposing one
evening my lady should want you[1]), explains that the
position may make it easy for her to go to the Countess, it
also makes it easy for the Count to get to her. The Countess
rings, and Figaro is left alone to contemplate a situation that
is by no means to his liking. In the two movements of his
duet with Susanna, the mood has been one of gaiety and
light-heartedness, which is hardly interrupted by the hint of
intrigue, as Susanna is obviously unperturbed by a situation
she feels herself quite capable of dealing with. But 'Se vuol
ballare' (If you are after a little amusement) shows Figaro in
a state of mind in which determination cannot altogether
eliminate apprehension.

No sooner has he left the stage than we are shown another
aspect of the worry which is to plague him on his wedding-
day. Marcellina comes in with Don Bartolo, the pair of them
hatching a plot which shall compel Figaro to marry
Marcellina as he has defaulted on a debt he owes her. He,
Doctor Bartolo, with his legal knowledge will ensure that
there is no escape for the rascal ('La vendetta'—Now for
vengeance)—a splendid example of what such an aria for
basso buffo can become in the hands of a composer of
genius. As he goes out of one door, Susanna enters by
another and she and Marcellina meet as they attempt to
follow Bartolo; their duet as each offers the other precedence
ends in Marcellina's complete discomfiture. Susanna stays
behind and is immediately confronted with a disconsolate
Cherubino, who wants to enlist her help in getting the Count
to reinstate him as the Countess's page. No one takes him
seriously except himself. He is just at the wrong age: young

---

[1]   Edward Dent's translation, here and later.

enough to be allowed liberties, old enough to take advantage of them (as has happened over his latest exploit with Barbarina, for which he has been dismissed) in a way that cannot be tolerated. He is in love with every woman he comes across, and pours out his adolescent aspirations to Susanna in an aria, 'Non sò più cosa son, cosa faccio' (Is it pain, is it pleasure that fills me?). No sooner has he finished than voices are heard outside and he has only just time to conceal himself before the Count comes into Susanna's room and starts to protest his affections. It is not her lucky day, as the Count is followed a moment or two later by Basilio; in the scramble for concealment, Cherubino nips into the chair behind which the Count takes refuge. Basilio teases Susanna with gossip about Cherubino and when she will not listen, presses her about the page and the Countess—an intrigue which he says everyone is talking about. The Count can bear it no longer and emerges from his hiding-place to demand that the gossip-mongers shall be found and punished. In the ensuing trio—since 'Non sò più cosa son' the action has been carried on in recitative—Susanna faints, but revives in time to plead the cause of the unhappy Cherubino, a mere boy she says. Not so young as you think, says the Count, and describes how he caught him the previous day hiding in Barbarina's room. Suiting the action to the word, he draws the cover from the chair—and there is Cherubino again. Only Cherubino's admission that he had heard what passed between the Count and Susanna ('I did all I could *not* to hear, my lord') stays the penalty that would otherwise be his.

Led by Figaro, a band of peasants comes in to sing the Count's praises, and, at its end, the Count yields to the general entreaties, but only to the extent of giving Cherubino a commission in his Regiment, for which he must leave immediately. Figaro speeds him on his way with a spirited description of what his future life has in store for him. Michael Kelly, the Irish tenor who was the Basilio and Curzio in the original production, tells in his memoirs of the splendid sonority with which Benucci, the Figaro, sang the martial air 'Non più andrai' (Say good-bye now to pastime and play, lad) at the first orchestral rehearsal. Mozart, who was on the stage in a crimson pelisse and cocked hat trimmed with gold lace, kept repeating 'Bravo, bravo, Benucci! ' In truth, it is a stirring finale to an act.

Act II. We are introduced to the Countess in a soliloquy,

'Porgi amor' (God of Love). In this aria, whose simplicity
makes it one of the most taxing entrances for any soprano,
we are made aware of her intense longing for her husband's
love, and also of the reticence which her breeding makes
natural to her. Susanna explains the situation to her and

opens the door to Figaro; his plan is that the Count shall be
given an assignation with Susanna, whose place shall be taken
by Cherubino, and that at the same time he shall be told in
an anonymous letter that the Countess in her turn has made a
rendezvous with an unknown man. Cherubino comes in to
see if he can be dressed for the part, but first sings the song
he has just composed, 'Voi che sapete' (Tell me, fair ladies).
Not only has Mozart got round the difficulty of introducing a
song ('words and music by Cherubino') into a milieu where
singing is the natural means of expression, but he has done so
in such a way that this piece has become one of the world's
most popular tunes. Cherubino tries on the dress to the
accompaniment of a song with action, Susanna's 'Venite
inginocchiatevi' (Come here and kneel before me now). No
sooner is it ended and Cherubino safely buttoned up than a
knock is heard at the door. It is the Count. Consternation.
Cherubino dashes into the Countess's bedroom and Susanna
hides behind a curtain. The Count is suspicious of his wife's
all too obvious nervousness, and suspicion that something is

being hidden from him becomes certainty when he hears a noise and finds the door of her room locked ('Susanna, or via sortite'—Come out, come out, Susanna). He takes his wife with him as he goes off to get tools to break it down with. While he is away Cherubino slips out of hiding and jumps from the window, leaving Susanna to take his place. The little *allegro assai* duet for Susanna and Cherubino is a comedy interlude of the greatest dexterity amidst the ranting and raging of the Count, which redoubles in fury when the Countess tries to explain that Cherubino is in her room without much on because he was being fitted for a charade.

The great finale is begun by the Count to all intents and purposes in a towering passion: 'Esci omai, garzon malnato' (Out you come, no more concealment). The Countess's pleading seems to be in vain, but both are struck dumb with amazement when, at the height of the storm, Susanna emerges coolly from the inner room. It is one of those incomparable musico-dramatic strokes which no listener who knows the opera ever fails to look forward to, and which comes as an anti-climax only in the worst of performances. The Count rushes in to see if Cherubino is not still there, but, finding he is not, can do nothing but sue for pardon. With Susanna's aid, this is obtained, but with it the Count's suspicions begin to take possession of him again. The anonymous letter? Written by Figaro, delivered by Basilio. He thinks he has found someone he can safely be angry with, but is told he must forgive everyone if he himself is to be forgiven for his jealousy. There is a moment of peace and relaxation which ends as Figaro bounds in to summon his master and mistress to the wedding dance which is about to begin. But the Count sees a chance of getting his own back and questions Figaro about the anonymous letter. In spite of hints from the Countess and Susanna, Figaro denies all

knowledge of it, and has almost turned the Count's suspicions when Antonio, the gardener, bursts in, protesting that his life is a perpetual trial but that to-day they have thrown a man out of the window on to his flower-beds, and that is too much. Figaro says that it was he who jumped out, but Antonio thinks it looked more like the page. Figaro sticks to his story until the Count catechises him about a paper Antonio says was dropped near the flower-bed. Figaro searches his pockets and racks his brains, and in the nick of time the Countess recognises it and whispers to Figaro that it is the page's commission. Why was it left? Again, it is only just in time that the Countess remembers that it had not been sealed. Figaro's triumph is short-lived, as Marcellina comes in, supported by Bartolo and Basilio, to lodge formal complaint before the Count against Figaro for breach of promise. The act comes to an end in pandemonium.

The finale is one of the greatest single sections in all Mozart's operas. For variety of motive, tempo, and texture it is unrivalled; the characterisation is consistent and credible and at no time subordinated to more general musical needs; the level of invention is extremely high; and the whole thing is carried on with resources that make use of the nine principals but involve no chorus or scenic display. It is a marvel of ingenuity, and at the same time a model of simplicity.

Act III. The Count has not yet given up hope of Susanna, and when she comes to borrow smelling salts for her mistress he seems within reach of his prize. She agrees to meet him that night in the garden. Their duet, 'Crudel, perchè finora' (Oh, why are you so cruel), reveals the Count as an ardent lover, Susanna as an inattentive beloved, but the result is a masterpiece. As Susanna leaves the room, she meets Figaro and assures him, just a little too loudly, that he is sure now of winning his case against Marcellina. Sure of winning his case? repeats the Count, and launches into a superb recitative and aria, 'Vedrò mentr'io sospiro, felice un servo mio?' (Must I forgo my pleasure, whilst serf of mine rejoices?) Edward Dent has observed that the Count, a man of intense energy, is shown first of all in ensemble, only later in aria, because, one might almost say, he has not time to sing an aria until the moment when he has to take stock of his position. It is an extraordinary piece of self-revelation when it does come, and takes the Count right out of the category

of the unsuccessful lover and erring husband into something much more sinister. But the balance is redressed when it is discovered, after he has given judgment for Marcellina, that that lady is in fact none other than Figaro's mother. In the great sextet which follows, the Count is reduced to expressions of impotent fury: what can he do when confronted with this wholly unexpected development? The sextet is one of the most satisfactory instances in all opera of pure comedy purveyed in terms of straight-faced music.

The scene is empty for a moment, and the Countess comes in to sing the most extended and most moving of her utterances in the opera. 'Dove sono' (I remember days long departed) consists of a lengthy recitative followed by a restrained but highly expressive aria in two sections, *andantino* and later *allegro*. It is her moment of greatest self-revelation, just as his aria was the Count's; if his thoughts were of revenge that his desires are not to be satisfied, hers are of the love he once bore her but which she seems to have lost. His aria grew out of the situation created by his duet with Susanna, the Countess's gives audible expression to a situation which can only be resolved with Susanna's aid and therefore leads to a duet between the two. Between them they arrange where Susanna is to meet the Count that evening. The letter duet, 'Che soave zeffiretto' (How delightful 'tis to wander, by the breath of evening fann'd), is one of the most famous numbers in the score; the mistress dictates a letter to the Count, the maid takes it down, and the voices of both blend as they read it back together. But

the wedding festivities are about to begin and a crowd of village girls presents flowers to the Countess, who is astonished a moment later, when the Count comes in with Antonio, to see one of them unmasked as Cherubino. A tense situation is saved by Barbarina: 'My lord, when you kiss me and tell me you love me, you often say you will give me whatever I want. Give me Cherubino for a husband.' Figaro announces the beginning of the wedding march, the so-called Fandango, the one Spanish element in the score. Like the

march in *Idomeneo* and the minuet in *Don Giovanni* it begins as it were in the middle, and returns to what should properly be the opening section later on. There is a chorus in praise of

the generosity and right-mindedness of the Count in having abolished the *droit de seigneur*, and the happy couples— Bartolo and Marcellina as well as Figaro and Susanna—receive their wedding wreaths from the Count and Countess, Susanna taking the opportunity to give the Count the letter she and her mistress have concocted for him. He opens it, pricking his finger on the pin—a comedy which is watched all unknowingly by Figaro and commented on with some relish. The Count announces general festivity—song, dance, feasting, and fireworks—and the act ends with a repetition of the chorus in his honour.

Act IV. The last act is mainly devoted to clearing up the various situations which have arisen in the course of Figaro's wedding day, but there is one more complication to be added before the process can begin. The atmosphere is highly charged with an almost sinister feeling of foreboding; more perhaps than can be put down to the fact that it is night by the time the act begins. The action takes place in a part of the garden which contains arbours and sheltered walks. Barbarina begins it with a little half-finished cavatina; she has been given the pin which sealed the letter to return to Susanna, but has lost it. She tells the story to Figaro, who comes in with Marcellina and is overcome with distress at this apparent indication of his wife's unfaithfulness.

Arias for Marcellina and Basilio occur at this point, but both are usually omitted. Before Basilio's, Figaro watches Barbarina hide in one of the arbours (where she is to meet Cherubino), and tells Bartolo and Basilio that they are to stay near at hand to witness the seduction of his wife by the Count. Now occurs Figaro's recitative and aria, 'Tutto è disposto' (Everything's ready) and 'Aprite un po' quegli occhi' (Yes, fools you are and will be, fools till your eyes are opened), at the same time his most serious moment (the recitative is tragic in the extreme) and his most comic (the horns at the end are surely intended to be illustrative as well as musical). Susanna asks the Countess (they have by now changed clothes) to be allowed to walk a little apart from her, and sings an aria of exquisite sensibility, ostensibly to the lover she is waiting for, but in reality knowing full well that Figaro is listening to her; 'Deh vieni non tardar' (Then come, my heart's delight). The comedy of mistaken identity begins. Cherubino attempts to flirt with what he thinks is Susanna, in reality of course the Countess. Susanna, the Count, and Figaro observe, and the Count interrupts and starts to make love on his own account to his wife in disguise. Figaro does not know about the change of clothes and it is his turn to interrupt; with the stage empty he invokes the names of the gods to avenge his honour. Susanna (still disguised as the Countess) calls to him and he starts to tell her of the Count's escapade when he recognises that it is in fact Susanna he is talking to. The dramatic tension which may lead to tragedy is shattered, and we are once more safely in comedy. Figaro makes love to her as if she were the Countess, and then laughs at her attempt to disguise herself from him as much as at her indignation. All is forgiven—Susanna does not mind the joke against herself—and the two combine to make the Count think their extravagant love-making is in

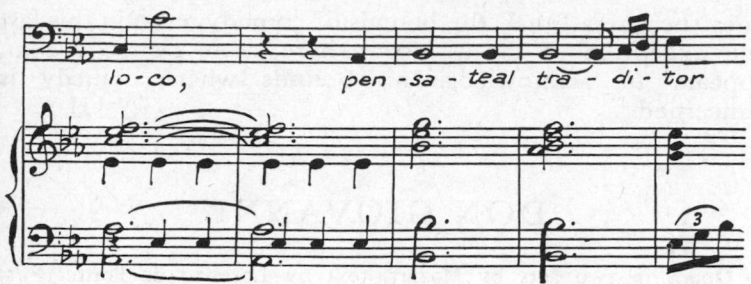

reality that of mistress and valet. The ruse succeeds, the Count summons anyone within hearing to bear witness to the unfaithfulness of his wife, and in succession hauls Cherubino, Barbarina, Marcellina, and the supposed culprit from the arbour in which they have taken refuge. All pleading is in vain, until the voice of the Countess herself is heard behind them all: 'Almeno io per loro perdono otterrò?' (May I then for pardon at last intercede?) The dramatic suddenness of her entry combines with the Count's noble phrase of contrition to make this a moment that can be set beside that of the emergence of Susanna from the Countess's room in Act II. The Count begs forgiveness in a swelling phrase, receives it, and the opera ends in general rejoicing, voiced though by the principals alone and unsupported by the chorus.

Le Nozze di Figaro is an incomparable masterpiece, one moreover that has been praised throughout its history for a variety of reasons. If it was once the brilliant tunes of the solo songs which attracted audience and performers alike, it would probably nowadays be claimed that the ensembles are the main glories of the work. Nothing, one is inclined to think, could be more perfect than the finale to the second act. Such amazing invention and such dexterity cannot be excelled. Maybe it cannot, but in the last act Mozart has achieved something almost more remarkable in the feeling of anxiety which pervades music and situation alike. It is as though the tapestry of the comedy has been reversed and, instead of dazzling with its brilliance, it is shot through with flashes, not of light but of darkness; it is not so much that the garden has a thundercloud hanging over it, but that there is lightning in the air. I know I always have something akin to a feeling of relief when Figaro's little B flat tune arrives to prove that once again we have come through the web of intrigue to the safety and happiness beyond it. At no time

does the opera break the bounds of comedy, even in this last
act, except in so far as Mozart here, as in *Don Giovanni*,
appears to acknowledge no bounds where comedy is
concerned.   H.

DON GIOVANNI

Opera in two acts by Mozart, text by Lorenzo da Ponte. First
performed at the National Theatre, Prague, October 29, 1787, with
Teresa Saporiti, Micelli, Bondini, Luigi Bassi as Don Giovanni, Ponziani,
Baglioni, Lolli. In Vienna, 1788, with Aloysia Lange as Donna Anna,
Cavalieri, Mombelli, Francesco Albertarelli as Don Giovanni, Morella
and Benucci. The English première took place in London at Her
Majesty's Theatre, April 12, 1817, with Mmes. Camporese, Hughes,
Fodor, and Messrs. Ambrogetti, Nedli, Crivelli, and Agrisani. The opera
was given at Covent Garden (in English) on May 30, 1817, and for the
first time in America (as *The Libertine*) in Philadelphia in 1818. It was
presented at the Park Theatre, New York, in 1826 with da Ponte
present, Manuel Garcia senior as Don Giovanni, Manuel Garcia junior as
Leporello, Mme. Garcia as Donna Elvira, and Signorina Maria Garcia
(afterwards the famous Malibran) as Zerlina. Recent revivals: Covent
Garden, 1926, conducted by Bruno Walter, and with Frida Leider,
Lotte Lehmann, Elisabeth Schumann, Mariano Stabile, Fritz Krauss,
and Aquistapace in the cast; 1939 in the same theatre with Elisabeth
Rethberg, Hilde Konetzni, Mafalda Favero, Ezio Pinza, Richard Tauber,
Virgilio Lazzari and conducted by Sir Thomas Beecham. The first
performance at Glyndebourne was in 1936, when Ina Souez, Luise
Helletsgruber, Audrey Mildmay, John Brownlee, Koloman von Pataky,
Salvatore Baccaloni were conducted by Fritz Busch.

Faure and Maurel were great Don Giovannis, Jean de Reszke sang the
role while he was still a baritone, and Scotti made his debut at the
Metropolitan in the role. Renaud appeared as Don Giovanni at the
Manhattan Opera House, and recent exponents of the title role have
included John Forsell, Mariano Stabile, Ezio Pinza, Cesare Siepi, Tito
Gobbi, Fischer-Dieskau and Nicolai Ghiaurov. Lablache was accounted
the greatest of Leporellos, but earlier in his career he had sung Don
Giovanni. The role of Don Ottavio has been sung by Rubini, Mario,
John McCormack, and Schipa; Lilli Lehmann and Ljuba Welitsch have
been renowned in the role of Donna Anna; and Zerlina has been sung
by aspiring *prime donne* from Adelina Patti to Geraldine Farrar,
including some mezzos such as Maria Gay and (at Covent Garden) Anne
Howells.

A curious aside in the history of the work was an adaptation by
Kalkbrenner which was produced in Paris in 1805. How greatly this

differed from the original may be judged from the fact that the trio of
the masks was sung by three policemen!

CHARACTERS

The Commendatore .... Bass
Donna Anna, *his daughter* .... Soprano
Don Ottavio, *her betrothed* .... Tenor
Don Giovanni, *a young nobleman* .... Baritone
Leporello, *his servant* .... Bass
Donna Elvira, *a lady of Burgos* .... Soprano
Zerlina, *a country girl* .... Soprano
Masetto, *betrothed to Zerlina* .... Baritone
Time: Seventeenth Century   *Place:* Seville

For years *Don Giovanni* has been, if not the most popular,
at all events the most frequently praised of operas. Beethoven
is said to have named *The Magic Flute* as his favourite opera,
not, as one might have expected, because of the wide range
of its ideas and its musical level, but because it contained
almost all musical forms, from the fugue to the *Lied*. In the
same sort of way, perhaps *Don Giovanni* owes part of its
success to the almost unique blending of the irresistibly
comic and the tragically serious as much as to the speed of its
dramatic and musical action, and to the quality of the music.
The other decisive factor in its popularity is the fascinating
figure of the Don himself, the libertine and the blasphemer,
whose courage endears him to the men and his scandalous
reputation to the women.

It has even been asserted that Don Juan Tenorio was a
historical personage, but there is little evidence to support
this view. His first recorded appearance in literature is in the
play *El Burlador de Sevilla* written by Tirso de Molina
(1571–1641). Molière's *Le Festin de Pierre* (1665) has little
to do with the Spanish play, but introduces an important
character, Donna Elvira; Shadwell's *The Libertine* appeared
in England in 1676, by which time the story is described as
'famous all over Spain, Italy and France'; Goldoni in 1736
wrote a verse-play, *Don Giovanni Tenorio o sia il Dissoluto*;
but it was in 1787 that there appeared the most important of
the various sources from which da Ponte's libretto derives.
This was Bertati's libretto with music by Giuseppe Gazzaniga.

Da Ponte, Edward Dent suggests, may even have proposed the subject to Mozart knowing that he had a convenient source to hand, and certainly he drew copiously on Bertati's book for his own libretto, which is notwithstanding one of his best.

Don Giovanni was commissioned for the opera in Prague, where *Figaro* had just been a sensational success. It was performed by the same company, Bondini's, and many of the singers were the same as those who had sung the earlier opera when it was presented in Prague, amongst them Bassi, the 22-year-old Don Giovanni, who had already sung the Count. Besides Bassi, the cast consisted of Teresa Saporiti (Donna Anna), Catarina Micelli (Donna Elvira), Teresa Bondini, wife of the manager (Zerlina), Antonio Baglioni (Don Ottavio), Felice Ponziani (Leporello), and Giuseppe Lolli (the Commendatore and Masetto).

There are many stories about the first performance, few of them supported by any reliable evidence. The overture, for instance, is supposed to have been written almost on the eve of the première (and this may well have been the case). Mozart passed a gay evening with some friends. One of them said to him: 'Tomorrow the first performance of *Don Giovanni* will take place, and you have not yet composed the overture!' Mozart pretended to get nervous about it and withdrew to his room, where he found music-paper, pens, and ink. He began to compose about midnight. Whenever he grew sleepy, his wife, who was by his side, entertained him with stories to keep him awake. It is said that it took him but three hours to produce this overture.

At the first rehearsal, not being satisfied with the way in which Signora Bondini gave Zerlina's cry of terror from behind the scenes when the Don is supposed to attempt her ruin, Mozart left the orchestra and went up on the stage. Ordering the first act finale to be repeated from the minuet on, he concealed himself in the wings. When Zerlina's cue came, he quickly reached out a hand from his place of concealment and pinched her leg. She gave a piercing shriek. 'There! That is how I want it,' he said, emerging from the wings, while Signora Bondini, not knowing whether to laugh or blush, did both.

The overture consists of an *andante* introduction which reproduces the scene of the banquet at which the statue appears. It is followed by an *allegro* which characterises the

impetuous, pleasure-seeking Don. Without pause, Mozart
links up the overture with the song of Leporello; wrapped in
his cloak and seated in the garden of a house in Seville, which
Don Giovanni on amorous adventure bent has entered
secretly during the night, he is complaining of the fate which
makes him a servant to such a restless and dangerous master.
'Notte e giorno faticar' (That's the life a servant leads—who
cares when he sleeps or feeds?[1]) runs his song; the music,
like all that Leporello subsequently sings, is in the Italian
buffo tradition, differing in degree of expressiveness but not
in kind of expression from that of other contemporary *buffo*
creations. Don Giovanni hurriedly issues from the house,
pursued by Donna Anna. There follows a trio in which the
wrath of the insulted woman, the annoyance of the libertine,
and the comments of the watching Leporello are expressed
simultaneously. The Commendatore hears the noise, finds his
daughter struggling with an unknown man, and draws his
sword. In spite of the protests of Don Giovanni, who is
reluctant to fight so old an opponent, a duel ensues and in it
the Commendatore receives a mortal wound. The trio which
follows between Don Giovanni, the dying Commendatore,
and Leporello is a unique passage in the history of musical
art. The genius of Mozart, tender, profound, pathetic, is
revealed in its entirety. Written in a solemn rhythm and in
the key of F minor, this trio, which fills only eighteen
measures, contains in a restricted outline but in master
strokes the seeds of the serious side of the drama, just as the
recitative which follows—Don Giovanni makes light of the
whole affair—re-establishes the opera on a basis of comedy,
only to return to seriousness with Anna's grief over the body
of her father. In a duet Don Ottavio, her fiancé, tries to
comfort her and swears to avenge the dead man.

The scene changes and Don Giovanni and Leporello are on
the prowl again; they perceive a woman—or rather, Don
Giovanni does—who appears to be inveighing against a lost
lover. It is Donna Elvira, whom they do not recognise as yet,
but who has been another of the Don's victims. There are in
the tears of this woman not only the grief of one who has
been loved and now implores heaven for comfort, but also
the indignation of one who has been deserted and betrayed.
When she cries with emotion 'Ah, chi mi dice mai quel

[1] English translation throughout by Edward J. Dent (published by
O.U.P.).

barbaro dov' è?' (Where shall I find the traitor who stole my heart away?) one feels that in spite of her anger, she is ready to forgive, if only a regretful smile shall recall her to the man who was able to charm her. The character of her music is seen straightaway in this aria. It is more pliable than Donna Anna's, but perhaps it is the persistent nature it seems to reveal that makes Don Giovanni run quite so fast from her.

As she finishes her outburst, she turns to find that the stranger who is attempting to console her is none other than Don Giovanni himself. Leaving Leporello to explain the reasons why he deserted her, Don Giovanni makes his escape, and Elvira is obliged to listen while the servant runs through a catalogue—grossly exaggerated we may be sure—of his master's conquests. 'Madamina' is a perfect passage of its kind and one of the most famous arias in the repertory of the *basso buffo*. It is an exquisite mixture of grace and finish, of irony and sentiment, of comic declamation and melody, the whole enhanced by the poetry and skill of the accessories. Every word is illustrated by the composer's imagination without his many brilliant sallies injuring the general effect. According to Leporello's catalogue, his master's adventures in love have numbered 2,065—640 in Italy, 231 in Germany, 100 in France, 91 in Turkey, and in Spain no less than 1,003. All sorts and conditions of women have contributed to this formidable total, and it is small wonder that Elvira leaves the stage vowing vengeance upon her betrayer.

The scene changes to the countryside near Don Giovanni's palace not far from Seville. A troop of gay peasants is seen arriving. The young and pretty Zerlina with Masetto, her fiancé, and their friends are singing and dancing in honour of their approaching marriage. Don Giovanni and Leporello join this gathering of light-hearted and simple young people. Having cast covetous eyes upon Zerlina, and having aroused her vanity and her spirit of coquetry by polished words of gallantry, the Don orders Leporello to get rid of the jealous Masetto by taking the entire gathering—except, of course, Zerlina—to his château. Leporello complies, but Masetto, while submitting to be removed, makes it clear to Don Giovanni—and to Zerlina as well—that he is not the fool he may look. This aria 'Ho capito, Signor, si' (You're the master, I'm the man) shows Masetto as a sort of Figaro, duller of wit and in miniature, but an embryonic revolutionary none the less. Don Giovanni, left alone with Zerlina, sings a duet with her which is one of the gems not alone of this opera but

f opera in general. 'Là ci darem la mano' (You'll lay your
hand in mine, dear) provides ample musical evidence, which
is later supported by the Serenade, that though the Don may
be unsuccessful in each of the love affairs on which he
mbarks during the course of the opera, his reputation is still
well deserved.

As they are going off arm in arm, Donna Elvira reappears
nd by her denunciation of Don Giovanni—'Ah, fuggi il
raditor!' (Be warned in time, my child)—makes clear to
Zerlina that there can be two opinions concerning the
haracter of her fascinating admirer. She takes Zerlina with
er as Donna Anna and Don Ottavio come on to the stage,
ut no sooner is Don Giovanni in conversation with the two
han Elvira is back again òn the scene—a true comedy stroke.
n a quartet, she again denounces Don Giovanni as a heartless
eceiver, while he for his part says that she is mad; Anna and
Ottavio are at a loss to know which to believe. Elvira goes

ut, followed a moment later by Don Giovanni, but in the
ew sentences he speaks Donna Anna recognises the voice of
er father's assassin and her own betrayer. Her narrative of
he events of that night is a declamatory recitative 'in style as
old and as tragic as the finest recitatives of Gluck'. The aria
hich follows, 'Or sai chi l'onore' (You know now for
ertain), is no less grandiose, and its implacable vengefulness
nd implacable *tessitura*) presents a problem for the singer
ntrusted with the role of Donna Anna. Never elsewhere

perhaps did Mozart write music for the soprano voice which
is so extremely heavy and taxing.

It is usually at the end of this aria—where it can never fail
to come as an anti-climax—that Ottavio's interpolated aria
'Dalla sua pace' (Mine be her burden, bravely to bear it) is
sung.[1] No change of scene is indicated, but in the opera
house one is often made at this point to allow Don Giovanni
to give his orders for the festivity inside his house rather than
outside in the garden. However, the exuberant 'Fin ch' han
dal vino' (Song, wine, and women) demands not so much an
indoor setting as a baritone with an immaculate technique
and sufficient musical sense to sing it as part of the opera and
not just as a sample of his vocal dexterity.

Scene 4 takes us to the garden outside Don Giovanni's
palace. Masetto reproaches Zerlina for her flirtation, but she
begs his forgiveness in an ingratiating air 'Batti, batti, o bel
Masetto'. This has always been one of the most popular
moments in the opera, and it is true that in the quicker 6/8
section you can almost hear Zerlina twiddling her
unfortunate admirer round her little finger. But, the aria
ended, Masetto's suspicions return when she seems distinctly
nervous at the sound of the Don's voice in the distance.

Now begins the finale, one of the great masterpieces of
dramatic music. From a hiding place Masetto hears Don
Giovanni order his retainers to spare no pains to make the
evening a success, and he is able to confront Zerlina and Don
Giovanni as the latter attempts to lead her off into an alcove.
The situation is well within the Don's compass; he chides
Masetto for leaving his bride-to-be alone, and takes them

[1] Written for the Vienna première of the opera, when the tenor
preferred not to sing 'Il mio tesoro', in place of which Mozart
introduced the duet for Zerlina and Leporello referred to on page 115 in
which she threatens to castrate him with a razor.   H.

both into the house where the dancing is about to begin. Elvira, Anna, and Ottavio appear, all of them masked. Leporello opens a window to let the fresh evening air into the palace and the violins of a small orchestra within can be heard in the middle of a graceful minuet. He sees the three maskers, and in accordance with tradition, they are bidden to enter. After a moment of hesitation, they decide to accept the invitation, and to carry out their undertaking at all cost and to whatever end. Before entering the château, they pause on the threshold and, their souls moved by a holy fear, they address heaven in one of the most remarkable prayers written by the hand of man:

Inside the ballroom, the festivities are in full swing. Don Giovanni and Leporello manoeuvre to keep Masetto from Zerlina, but there is a diversion at the entry of the unknown maskers, who are welcomed by Don Giovanni. The dancing begins with the minuet we have already heard. Its graceful rhythm is prolonged indefinitely as a fundamental idea, while in succession two small orchestras on the stage take up, one a rustic quadrille, the other a waltz. Only the ladies and gentlemen should engage in the minuet, the peasants in the quadrille; and before Don Giovanni leads off Zerlina into an adjoining room he should have taken part with her in this dance, while Leporello seeks to divert the jealous Masetto's attention by seizing him in an apparent exuberance of spirits and insisting on dancing the waltz with him.

Masetto's suspicions, however, are not without justification. He breaks away from Leporello, who hurries to warn his master. But just as he has passed through the door,

Zerlina's piercing shriek for help is heard from within. Don
Giovanni rushes out, sword in hand, dragging with him none
other than the luckless Leporello, whom he has opportunely
seized in the entrance, and whom, under pretext that he is
the guilty party, he threatens to kill. But this ruse fails to
deceive anyone. Anna, Elvira, and Ottavio unmask and accuse
Don Giovanni of the murder of the Commendatore: 'Tutto,
tutto già si sa' (All your guilt is now made clear). Taken
aback at first, Don Giovanni soon recovers himself. Turning
at bay, he defies the threatening crowd. A storm sweeps over
the orchestra. Thunder growls in the basses, lightning plays on
the fiddles. Don Giovanni, cool and intrepid, dashes through
the crowd, which falls back in front of him, and makes his
escape.

Act II.   A street, with Donna Elvira's house in the back
ground. The beginning of Act II furnishes proof—and proof is
needed—that *Don Giovanni* is the *dramma giocoso* of its title.
The duet with which it opens, 'Eh via, buffone' (Now then
you rascal), is in purest *buffo* style, and it is followed by a
trio for Elvira, Don Giovanni, and Leporello which points the
moral even more sharply. Donna Elvira, leaning sadly on her
balcony, gives voice to her melancholy regrets in a tune of
exquisite beauty. In spite of the scene which she has recently
witnessed, in spite of the wrongs she herself has endured, she
cannot hate Don Giovanni or efface his image from her heart.
Her reward is that her recreant lover changes clothes with his
servant in the darkness below, and, while Leporello disguised
as the Don attracts Donna Elvira into the garden, the Don
himself mocks her with exaggerated protestations of love
which she takes at their face value. If the scene is to be taken
seriously—and the music of 'Ah, taci, ingiusto core' (Ah, why
do I remember) is of a quality to support such an attitude—
the way in which sport is made of her pathetic faithfulness
would indicate a revolting callousness on the part not only of
the man who has loved and left her, but of the composer as
well; but if it can be approached by the audience in a spirit of
frivolity, of *opera buffa*, this callousness is less in evidence.

Elvira descends, and Don Giovanni sings, to his own
mandolin accompaniment (too often played *pizzicato* on a
violin), a serenade to Elvira's maid, to whom he has taken a
fancy. 'Deh, vieni alla finestra' (Look down from out your
window) is one of the most famous numbers of the opera,
partly perhaps because of the stress laid on its performance

by eminent singers of the title role. Don Giovanni thinks he sees the object of his affections, but, before he can follow up his advantage, round the corner comes Masetto with a band of peasants bent on finding and murdering no less a person than Don Giovanni. They think they are addressing Leporello, and the disguised Don divides them up into parties and sends them off to the four points of the compass in an effective aria, 'Metà di voi qua vadano' (Let half of you go down the road). Masetto, the ringleader, he keeps with him and, having ascertained exactly what weapons he has with him, proceeds to give him a good drubbing and leaves him groaning on the ground. Zerlina, while by no means in-different to the attentions of the dashing Don, is at heart faithful to Masetto and she comes tripping round the corner when she hears his cries and consoles the poor fellow with the graceful measures of 'Vedrai, carino, se sei buonino' (If you will promise not to mistrust me).

The scene changes to the courtyard of a palace in which Elvira and Leporello take refuge. It turns out to be Donna Anna's, and she is on the point of returning home, escorted by the inevitable Don Ottavio and a band of servants bearing torches. Elvira and Leporello make for the door, but are intercepted by Masetto and Zerlina, who are lurking in it. Everyone takes Leporello for his master and demands his death, demands they seem rather reluctant to withdraw when they find out that it is the servant they have caught after all.

The sextet is a fine ensemble, with its variety of action and of musical sections. It is plainly intended, says Edward Dent, as the finale of an act, not as a movement in the middle of one.[1] It was you then who beat Masetto? asks Zerlina; You who so deceived me? continues Elvira. 'Ah, pietà! Signori miei' (Spare me, spare my life I pray), counters Leporello in an aria which dies away while Leporello holds their attention as he creeps to the door and disappears.

Now comes Don Ottavio's famous aria, the solo number which makes the role coveted by tenors the world over, 'Il

---

[1] This is on the hypothesis that the opera was intended to be in four acts, but was changed to two in the course of rehearsal.   H.

mio tesoro intanto' (Speak for me to my lady). Upon this air praise has been exhausted. It has been called the 'pietra di paragone' of tenors—the touchstone, the supreme test of classical song. In spite of its rather obscure dramatic value, its musical beauty is as undeniable as its difficulty of execution. At this point, it is customary to insert the superb recitative and aria for Elvira, which Mozart composed for Katharina Cavalieri, who sang the role at the Viennese première. She had complained to Mozart that the Viennese public did not appreciate her as did audiences of other cities and begged him for something which would give her voice full scope. The result was 'Mi tradì quell' alma ingrata' (All my love on him I lavished). Again its dramatic justification is slight, but in it Elvira rises to her full height.

After the escapade of the serenade and the beating of Masetto, the Don makes off and chances to meet in the churchyard—which he reaches after some other adventure, we may be sure—with none other than Leporello, who for his part is thankful to have got rid of Elvira; Leporello finds it little to his taste that his master's newest conquest has been someone on whom he—Leporello—has made an impression. Don Giovanni is prepared to laugh the whole thing off when he hears a solemn voice which he is not long in tracing to the statue of the Commendatore, whose death is laid at his own door:

Leporello is ordered to invite the statue—'O vecchio buffonissimo' is Don Giovanni's greeting for him—to supper. This he does in a duet, 'O statua gentilissima', his courage, which fails him at every sentence, being kept at the sticking point by the vigorous encouragement of his master. The statue's utterances in the recitative part of the scene are accompanied by trombones, connected in the opera exclusively with the appearance of the statue and not used, even in the overture, when it is not visible on the stage.

The scene changes once again, this time to a room in Donna Anna's house. Ottavio enters, and she reproaches him when he hints at their forthcoming marriage; at such a time, how could she think of anything but her murdered father? The scene exists solely to give Anna another aria to sing, and 'Non mi dir' (Say no more), beautiful and famous though it is, contributes little to the dramatic development of the opera. The coloratura section, which is included in the *allegretto* with which the aria ends, was once adversely criticised—amongst other critics, by Berlioz—as having no place in music written for Donna Anna, but we may agree with Edward Dent who says severely that 'Mozart without coloratura is only a very mutilated Mozart'.

The scene changes to Don Giovanni's palace. During the brilliant introduction, he seats himself at table and sings of the pleasures of life. An orchestra (on the stage in many modern performances, but probably not at the première) plays airs from Vicente Martin's *Una Cosa Rara*[1] and Sarti's *Fra due Litiganti*, and 'Non più andrai' from Mozart's own *Figaro*—the last-named selection greeted by Leporello with the observation that it is a bit stale. The music is a wonderful picture of the exuberant and devil-may-care nature of Don Giovanni, and is in the gay, debonair style which has all along been characteristic of his music, not least the recitative. At this point Elvira enters and begs the man who has betrayed her to mend his ways. Her plea falls on deaf ears. She goes to the door, but her shriek is heard from the corridor and she re-enters to flee the palace by another door. Don Giovanni sends Leporello to find out what has frightened her, but he echoes her scream and babbles that the statue is outside. Seizing a candle and drawing his sword, Don Giovanni boldly goes into the corridor. A moment later, he backs into the room, receding before the statue of the Commendatore. The lights go out. All is dark save for the flame of the candle in Don Giovanni's hand. Slowly, with heavy footsteps that re-echo in the orchestra, the statue enters. It speaks.

'Don Giovanni, you did invite me here to supper, so bid me welcome.' Don Giovanni nonchalantly orders Leporello to serve supper. 'Nay, do not go,' commands the statue. 'They who taste of the food of the angels eat no more the corrupt food of mortals ... Will you come with me to supper?' Don Giovanni accepts and gives his hand to the

[1] Revived at Ledlanet in Scotland in 1967.

statue in pledge; it is seized in a grip that is icy cold. 'Think on your sins, repent them'—'No.' A fiery pit opens. Demons seize him, unrepentant to the end, and drag him down. The music of the scene is gripping, yet accomplished without other addition than the trombones to the ordinary orchestra of Mozart's day, without straining after effect, without any means save those commonly to his hand.

In the nineteenth century and in the early years of the twentieth, the curtain used to fall at this point, but there is an epilogue in which the characters moralise upon Don Giovanni's end—an important feature of all the plays dealing with the legend. For the Vienna performance of 1788 Mozart cut it out and this was held by the nineteenth century to justify a tragic or at all events a romantic interpretation of the opera; such a view depends on the convenient forgetting of the ludicrously comic duet for Leporello and Zerlina which Mozart wrote specially for this same performance and which is still printed at the end of the vocal score though never performed. The comedy device of the moralising finale has been used as recently as Stravinsky's *The Rake's Progress* (q.v.), and Alexander Goehr's *Arden must die.*

Quite apart from the brilliant speed at which the music of *Don Giovanni* proceeds, quite apart from the juxtaposition of stark tragedy and high comedy in the one work, the opera is distinguished by the fascination attached to its central character. He is a brilliant, irresponsible figure, with a dash of philosophy—sometime, somewhere, in the course of his amours, he will discover the perfect woman, from whose lips he will be able to draw the sweetness of all women. He is a villain with a keen sense of humour; inexcusable in real life, possible only in comedy and represented at the first performance, one should not forget, by a youth no more than twenty-two years old! Leporello is a typical *basso buffo*, except that the quality of the music he has to sing is far higher than customary in this type of role. This is not to say that he is not well characterised, only that there is little new in the conception. At the Viennese première, the singer was Benucci, who had created the role of Figaro there. Ottavio very nearly re-creates the function of the confidant of *opera seria*, so little part does he play in the stage proceedings. The musical side of the role of course is a very different matter; in spite of its difficulty, the part is very much sought after, and not uncommonly a tenor with style and a stage personality astonishes the audience with the positive impression he makes in this basically negative role.

More interesting than the lesser figures amongst the men are the three female members of the cast. Zerlina is often played as if butter would not melt in her mouth, but for the Vienna performance Mozart added a duet for her and Leporello in which she attacks him with a razor but finally, in spite of her threats, contents herself with tying him up. Elvira, though frequently touching in her faithfulness to the memory of the man who has betrayed her (not least in her resolve in the finale that she will finish her days in a convent), is not without a touch of the scold in her make-up. It is perhaps Anna who is the most diversely interpreted of the three female roles. At one extreme, she has been represented as cold and incapable of love, at the other— notably by the German romantic poet E. T. W. Hoffmann—as consumed with passion for Don Giovanni. Einstein finds another solution to the problem: at the rise of the curtain Don Giovanni has in fact succeeded in seducing her, disguised as Don Ottavio. To support this view, he instances the recitative before 'Or sai chi l'onore', Don Giovanni's indifference to Anna (for the same reason as he is indifferent to Elvira), her insistence that Ottavio should revenge her father's murder himself without recourse to the law, and finally her refusal to marry Ottavio until some length of time has elapsed. K., H.

COSÌ FAN TUTTE

Opera buffa in two acts by Wolfgang Amadeus Mozart. Text by Lorenzo da Ponte. First performed at the Burgtheater, Vienna, January 26, 1790, with Ferrarese del Bene, Villeneuve (they were also sisters in real life), Dorotea Bussani, Calvesi, Benucci, Signor Bussani. First performed in London, Haymarket Theatre, 1811. Revived by Sir Thomas Beecham at His Majesty's Theatre, London, 1911, with Ruth Vincent, Lena Maitland, Beatrice La Palme, Walter Hyde, Frederic Austin and Lewys James; Metropolitan, New York, 1922, with Florence Easton, Frances Peralta, Lucrezia Bori, George Meader, Giuseppe de Luca, Adamo Didur, conductor Artur Bodanzky; Glyndebourne, 1934, with Ina Souez, Luise Helletsgruber, Irene Eisinger, Heddle Nash, Willi Domgraf-Fassbänder, Vincenzo Bettoni, conductor Fritz Busch. Recent revivals include, Sadler's Wells, 1944, with Joan Cross, Margaret Ritchie, Rose Hill, Peter Pears, John

Hargreaves, and Owen Brannigan, conductor Lawrance Collingwood; Glyndebourne Opera at the Edinburgh Festival, 1948, with Suzanne Danco, Eugenia Zareska, Hilde Güden, Petre Munteanu, Erich Kunz, Mariano Stabile, conductor Vittorio Gui; at Glyndebourne, 1950, with Sena Jurinac, Blanche Thebom, Alda Noni, Richard Lewis, Erich Kunz, Mario Borriello, conductor Fritz Busch; at Salzburg, 1960, with Schwarzkopf, Ludwig, Sciutti, Kmentt, Prey, Dönch, conductor Böhm. First performance at Covent Garden, 1947, by Vienna State Opera, with Seefried, Höngen, Loose, Dermota, Kunz, Schoeffler, conductor Krips; 1968, with Lorengar, Veasey, Popp, Alva, Ganzarolli, Engen, conductor Solti.

CHARACTERS

Fiordiligi .... Soprano
Dorabella, *her sister* .... Soprano
Ferrando, *her fiancé* .... Tenor
Guglielmo, *engaged to Fiordiligi* .... Bass
Don Alfonso .... Baritone
Despina, *maid to Fiordiligi and Dorabella* .... Soprano
Time: Eighteenth Century   *Place:* Naples

Così fan tutte, ossia La Scuola degli Amanti was written by Mozart to a commission from the Emperor Joseph II; the story is said to have been based on a real-life incident which was the talk of Vienna at the time of its occurrence. Two young officers, confident of the constancy of the sisters to whom they are engaged, enter a bet with an old bachelor friend of theirs, who maintains that a woman's memory is shorter than they think. At his direction, they put on disguises, and start to make love to each other's fiancée, having already taken the precaution of securing the aid of Despina, maid to the two sisters. After a short resistance, the sisters succumb to their wooing, but at the wedding party the two young men disappear to emerge a moment later in their uniforms and confront the inconstant sisters with their original lovers.

The story is slight, but one of da Ponte's neatest, and its symmetrical cast—two pairs of lovers, a third of worldly-wise cynics—and equally symmetrical construction provide Mozart with opportunities for some incomparable music. He was at the very summit of his creative powers, and anyone who knows the opera cannot help being surprised at the nineteenth-century suggestion that he in any way disliked the plot he was to use. The truth is inescapable: in *Così fan tutte* Mozart surpassed even himself in the richness and variety of his invention, in the impeccable skill with which the slenderest drama is adorned with music, in the creation of beauty. The idea is as light as a feather, and yet the music which clothes it suggests not only the comedy which is on the surface and which remains the most important part of the opera, but also the heartbreak which is behind the joke that goes too far and occasionally takes a serious turn. All the odder then that various attempts were made in the nineteenth century and later to provide the music with a new libretto, all of them short-lived—and small wonder in view of the quality of the original, which, as Edward Dent has emphasised, cannot be judged from a summary but must be seen in all its details. The opera 'plays' slower than either *Figaro* or *Don Giovanni*, and it is by no means short, but the stage action is as full of life as the music, and the opera is the ideal piece for a musically sophisticated audience.

The short overture has eight bars of slow introduction before the theme of the title is enunciated (see page 124). Most of the rest of it is quick, until just before the end when the motto theme recurs.

Act I.   The curtain rises on a café where are seated the three men, in the middle apparently of a heated argument, or so one assumes from the vigorous defence of Dorabella, his fiancée, that Ferrando is making as the music begins. There are three trios, the first with the two lovers answering the sceptical Alfonso, the second in the form of an accompanied solo for Alfonso:

the third consisting of jubilation on the part of the lovers at the prospect of winning the bet which they enter upon with Alfonso. It is a scene of the purest comedy and the music matches the artificiality of the mood, culminating in a tune of bubbling, infectious gaiety such as even Mozart himself could not duplicate:

The scene changes, the clarinets play in thirds over the strings,[1] and we can be sure we are with Fiordiligi and Dorabella, the paragons of faithfulness on whose constancy so much has just been wagered. They are discussing the respective merits of their young men as evinced in their portraits, and their sentimental rapture at what they see is conveyed in music of exquisitely exaggerated cast, which

dissolves in the middle into a cadenza in thirds on the word 'Amore'. This day-dreaming is interrupted by the precipitate arrival of Don Alfonso, who makes obvious his distress at the news he is only too anxious to break to the two young ladies: their lovers are ordered to the wars and are to leave

[1] The richness of the wind writing is unusual, even for Mozart, and there is more than a hint here and elsewhere of the great B flat major Serenade (K.361) for thirteen instruments.

immediately. It is Alfonso's nearest approach to an aria in the whole opera—is in fact described as one in the score; its *allegro agitato* perfectly reflects the breathless agitation he counterfeits so well. The situation is admirably summed up in two quintets, which are separated by a short duet for the two officers and a military chorus. In 'Sento, oh Dio' (Courage fails me)[1] the ladies are inconsolable, Don Alfonso builds up the situation, while Guglielmo is inclined to leave specific consolation to Ferrando and himself joins with Alfonso in a more general comment. Twice the two men cannot help nudging the sceptic ('There, you see now'), but he remains quite unconvinced. Ferrando and Guglielmo say good-bye, soldiers march across the stage singing of the joys of a military existence, but the farewells are not complete until all four have sung a protracted and beautiful farewell, to pungent comment from Alfonso ('Di scrivermi ogni giorno': You'll write long letters often).

Their lovers departed, Fiordiligi and Dorabella show real feeling so that even Alfonso joins them in a wonderfully evocative trio, 'Soave sia il vento', as they pray for calm sea and gentle breezes for the travellers. The idyllic mood does not for one bar survive their joint exit. Alfonso muses in *secco* recitative on his plans, but as he grows animated at the thought of woman's changeability he launches into an accompanied tirade against the whole sex, the one inescapably bitter moment of the score.

The scene changes, and we meet the chattering Despina, maid to the two sisters, who soon show that their loss has left them in no mood for chocolate or any other such consolation. Dorabella is the first to give vent to her feelings, in an aria of exaggeratedly tragic order, 'Smanie implacabili', a parody one may think of the self-consciously tragic Donna Elvira or even of the wholly serious Electra in *Idomeneo*. Despina advises a more moderate line; she is the female counterpart of Don Alfonso, and in her philosophy lover's absence affords an opportunity for sport, not for lamentation: 'In uomini, in soldati.' The ladies go out in disgust, and Alfonso seizes the opportunity to enlist Despina as an ally in his attempt to win the wager. Enter the two supposedly departed officers, disguised as Albanians; they are introduced to Despina, who laughs at them but does not recognise them, and is quite prepared to help them in their attempt to win

[1] Translations throughout by the Rev. Marmaduke Browne.

the affections of her mistresses. In a moment, the two are back on the stage, indignant at finding two strange men in their house and demanding their withdrawal. Alfonso stays in hiding but comments on the situation, and emerges to embrace the Albanians as old friends of his; will the ladies not be kind to them—for his sake? Fiordiligi makes it quite clear that their protestations of love are entirely unavailing: she and her sister are each of them 'firm as a rock' ('Come scoglio'). The aria is parodistic in tone, and, with its wide intervals and absurd jumps from the top to the bottom of the soprano range, seems likely to have been at any rate partly intended to poke fun at the phenomenal range and technique of Ferrarese del Bene, the original singer of Fiordiligi, who was da Ponte's mistress at the time of the première but seems to have been no favourite of Mozart's either artistically or personally. Guglielmo answers for Ferrando as well as himself

con·tra i venti e la tem·pe·sta, e la tem·pe· sta

and is given music of such delicacy and charm—'Non siate ritrosi'[1] (O vision so charming)—that one cannot but be surprised that the objects of the two young men's affections turn on their respective heels and leave the room before he has had time to finish the aria, which dissolves in laughter. The rapid laughing trio is charming, but Don Alfonso has his work cut out to persuade his young friends that he has by no means lost his bet at this early juncture. Let them be ready to meet him in the garden in a few minutes' time. Ferrando is left alone to sing of his love in a beautiful aria, in type romantic or even sentimental but hardly comic ('Un' aura amorosa': Her eyes so alluring). Alfonso and Despina reassure themselves that this is only a pair of women, and that there is as yet no danger of losing the bet.

For the finale we are back in the garden, under the blue Neapolitan sky and with the bay of Naples as background. Small wonder that Fiordiligi and Dorabella reflect jointly on the mutability of pleasure in music of exquisite tenderness,

---

[1] A magnificent *buffo* aria, 'Rivolgete a lui lo sguardo' (K.584), was originally planned here, but the slighter piece was substituted, one may imagine, as being more in keeping with this situation.

whose end is hardly reached before Ferrando and Guglielmo rush on to the stage brandishing bottles of poison which Alfonso is unable to prevent them drinking. The situation is sufficiently complicated to provide Mozart with exactly what he wanted for an extended finale. As the Albanians sink into a coma, pandemonium breaks loose, and when Alfonso and Despina rush for the doctor, there is even an opportunity for Ferrando and Guglielmo to join in the ensemble. Alfonso returns with a doctor (Despina in disguise) who proceeds to give the corpses the benefit of the most recent scientific discovery, Mesmerism—as much the latest thing in 1790 one may imagine as Psychiatry was in the 1940's and as likely to raise a laugh, particularly when compressed, as here, into the outward form of an oversize, all-healing magnet. The corpses revive, think at first they are in the Elysian Fields, and demand a kiss from the goddesses to set the seal on their cure. In spite of the promptings of Alfonso and Despina this is denied them, and the curtain falls with the sisters defending what they appear to regard as nothing less than honour itself, to a background of derisive exclamations from Despina and Alfonso, and approving comments of 'Great would be my indignation were they not to answer No' from the Albanians themselves. The music of the finale ranges from the purest beauty—the opening, for instance—to sheer farce—Despina in disguise and her trilling, omnipotent magnet. If there is in this finale less incident than in, for instance, that of Act II of *Le Nozze di Figaro*, there is none the less a musical variety and invention which places it in the very highest company.

Act II. Despina loses her patience with her virtuous employers. Make hay while the sun shines, she says, and behave like normal women when men are around; she rounds off her point in an aria, 'Una donna a quindici anni'. The process of persuasion so well begun is completed by the ladies themselves, who agree that there can be no harm in something so innocent as talk with the strangers. Their minds made up, each selects the appropriate partner—'Prenderò quel brunettino' (Give me then the gentle dark one)—in typically melodious fashion, to find at the end of the duet that they are invited to the garden where an entertainment is planned for their delectation. In truth, Alfonso has not exaggerated: nature has never so well imitated art—not even in the case of Cosima Wagner and the 'Siegfried Idyll'—as to serenade a

loved one with music as entrancing as the duet and chorus,
'Secondate aurette amiche' (Gentle zephyr, softly sighing),
which Ferrando and Guglielmo now combine to sing to them.
I have seen it made the subject of a producer's whims—the
singers exchanging copies of the music, dropping them,
fumbling; doing in fact everything except sing—but nothing
was hindrance enough to stand in the way of the entrancing,
seductive melody. If this is Mozart's most hedonistically
inclined opera, no other number so perfectly illustrates its
prevailing characteristic.

But, the serenade over, neither Albanian seems able to
pursue the advantage gained, and, in disgust, Alfonso and
Despina enact the scene for them. Neither seems a very apt
pupil, but the teachers steal away at the end of their duet
(the few phrases from Ferrando and Guglielmo make it
technically into a quartet), leaving two rather embarrassed
couples behind them talking animatedly about the weather.
Ferrando is led off by Fiordiligi, and, after some tentative
compliments, Guglielmo succeeds in giving Dorabella a heart-
shaped locket, in return for which he removes the medallion
(with its portrait of Ferrando) from her neck. Their duet, 'Il
core vi dono' (This heart that I give you), is charmingly light
in texture and sentiment, and particularly delightful are the
references to the pit-a-pat of their hearts.

The outer defences of Dorabella's constancy have been
rather easily breached; Fiordiligi's are to prove much harder
to carry. She turns a deaf ear to Ferrando's advances, and he
is given a magnificent aria, 'Ah, lo veggio, quell' anima bella'
(Well I knew that a maid so enchanting), in which he
alternately expresses doubts and confidence as to the
eventual outcome of his suit. Although it is one of the
highest pieces Mozart wrote for tenor voice, perhaps it owes
its frequent omission from contemporary performances not
only to this high *tessitura* and its extended form, but also to
the fact that it is immediately followed by an even longer aria
for Fiordiligi which is much too well known to be omitted

under any circumstances. Still, Ferrando's aria is far too good to be neglected as is present practice. Fiordiligi's great rondo, 'Per pietà, ben mio, perdona' (Ah, my love, forgive my madness), is the principal show-piece of the opera; the extensive range, sudden and precipitous leaps from high soprano to contralto and back again, the passages of exacting coloratura, the taxing length—all combine to show off the singer's technique, which is mocked at the same time as it is used to express the turmoil of conflicting emotions in Fiordiligi's mind. A horn obbligato adds to the effect.

Ferrando and Guglielmo meet to compare notes on their progress to date. Guglielmo is suitably smug about the apparent constancy of Fiordiligi, but Ferrando is furiously indignant when he hears of Dorabella's conduct and sees the proof in the shape of the locket he himself had given her. He will have revenge; but, he asks Guglielmo, in what form? Don't take it so much to heart, replies his friend: 'Ladies have such variations, permutations, combinations' ('Donne mie, la fate a tanti'). It is a wonderful example of an *opera buffa* aria, and one of the most delightful moments in the score, as light of touch and delicate in style as the best of Mozart's own chamber music. Symmetry being the thing it is, there follows an aria for Ferrando, less formidable and shorter than 'Ah, lo veggio', although by no means easy to sing; it is sometimes omitted, as is too frequently the aria for Dorabella, 'E' Amore un ladroncello' (Young love is unrelenting), in the next scene.

Fiordiligi resolves to make a last effort to extricate herself and maybe Dorabella as well from the intolerable situation in which they find themselves. She sends for a couple of old suits of uniform belonging to Ferrando and Guglielmo which happen to be conveniently in the house, and announces her intention of going off to the wars taking her equally disguised sister. She launches into the opening measures of a big aria, but she has hardly started to express her determination to reach her lover's side when she is interrupted by Ferrando, still in his Albanian disguise and protesting that before she leave him she should run her sword through his heart and end his agony for ever. Once more he protests his love, and, in response to a meltingly beautiful tune, resistance crumbles and she falls into his arms: they sing of their future happiness. Is it Mozart or the romantic Ferrando who has overreached himself in this love duet? There is a school of

thought which denies to genius the subtleties which are
incidental to the main issue—there is no indication that he
ever actually thought of *that*, they say, choosing to ignore
the part played by the instinctive and the subconscious in the
creative process. If Ferrando is in love with love as well as
with Dorabella, he will be no less shattered by his new and
involuntary success with her sister than he was by news of
her own infidelity. The joke in fact has gone too far, and has
involved too many emotional ties, old and new, for detachment to be any more a possibility—which is exactly what is
conveyed by the uneasiness of the music. Granted that the
lovers who began as puppets have suddenly become warm
and real; perhaps it is one of music's (and therefore opera's)
fascinations that such a transformation is possible, and, when
achieved, so moving.

The whole scene is watched by Guglielmo from the side,
and Alfonso has his work cut out to keep him quiet until it is
over. 'What about your fond Fiordiligi now?' asks Ferrando;
'Fior di Diavolo!' answers the discomfited Guglielmo. They
are no worse than all the other women, affirms Alfonso:
'Tutti accusan le donne' (Everyone berates the ladies), and at
the end of his short solo, he makes the crestfallen lovers
repeat the motto with him: 'Così fan tutte'. Despina brings
the news that her mistresses have made up their minds to make
their Albanian suitors happy and marry them on the spot.

The finale carries the plot one stage further and provides
the expected dénouement. Servants make ready for the
wedding under the direction of Despina, and hail the bridal
couples when they appear. The lovers' toast is introduced by
one of those unforgettable tunes such as Mozart has a habit
of producing at just the moment when abundance has seemed
to be sated, and the toast itself is an enchanting canon, led by
Fiordiligi, which goes harmoniously on its way until it is the
turn of Guglielmo to take up the tune. He contents himself
with an angry aside to the effect that nothing would please
him more than that the wine should turn to poison on their

lips. It has been suggested that the device, which helps to lend variety to the quartet, was dictated to Mozart for the obvious reason that the tune which goes up to A flat was too high for the bass Guglielmo to sing. Alfonso brings in a notary (Despina in yet another costume) who is to take care of the legal side of the weddings, and with much vocal disguise and a spate of pseudo-legal patter (including a punning reference to these 'dame Ferraresi'), the contract is prepared and signed.

This is the signal for a burst of military music from outside, which is immediately recognised by the female signatories as the march to which Ferrando and Guglielmo went off to the wars. Their suspicion turns to consternation when Alfonso confirms that Ferrando and Guglielmo are on their way up to the house at that very moment. The Albanians are bundled out, the sisters try to compose themselves, and their military lovers make an entrance to music which refers back unmistakably to the early part of Act I. Despina is discovered in an ante-room, Alfonso conveniently lets the marriage contracts fall where the young men cannot fail to see them, and they are told that proof of the inconstancy can be found in the next-door room. In a moment they re-appear, bringing with them bits of the Albanian costumes, and moreover singing snatches of the music that helped to bring the wooing to its successful conclusion. Here is a curious anomaly, which I have never yet seen explained. Guglielmo quotes from 'Il core vi dono' and he and Ferrando sing the music associated with Despina's mesmerism in the finale to Act I; but before either of these, Ferrando has quoted something which he in fact never sings at any moment during the opera. Was one of Ferrando's arias changed at rehearsal and did the second thoughts never get as far as this finale, or is there some deeper explanation?

Everything is forgiven, the four lovers are reunited—

whether in the original or Albanian combination we are not told—and the six characters sing a valedictory in praise of him who is able to take the rough with the smooth and who can fall back on reason however the world treats him.

Così fan tutte demands sensitive and beautiful performing, from singers, orchestra, and conductor of course, but no less from producer and designer. It is not the work for the producer who knows nothing in between solemnity and horseplay, nor for the designer who cannot by means of imagination re-create the Mediterranean atmosphere at the same time as he is solving the all-important problem of maintaining continuity, which, here as in Mozart's other operas, is as vital a consideration as it has become in modern Shakespearean production. *Così fan tutte* is a comedy pure and simple, and, like every comedy of genius, it comments profoundly and movingly and above all naturally on human life and manners during the course of its action.

LA CLEMENZA DI TITO
The Clemency of Titus

Opera in two acts by Wolfgang Amadeus Mozart. Text by Mazzolà, adapted from Metastasio. First performed at the National Theatre, Prague, September 6, 1791. First performed in London, King's Theatre, March 27, 1806; revived by the City Opera Club, London, 1949; at the Salzburg Festival, 1949, under Josef Krips, with Hilde Zadek, Wilma Lipp, Marta Rohs, Julius Patzak, Richard Holm, and Otto Edelmann (in an arrangement by Bernhard Paumgartner, which included much music from other sources, notably *Idomeneo*). First performances in English, Falmouth, 1930, London, 1931. U.S. première NBC radio, 1940; first stage performance, Tanglewood, 1952. La Scala, Milan, 1966, with Gordoni, Simionato (her farewell stage performance), Renzo Casellato, Alva, conductor Sanzogno; BBC (Festival Hall), 1969, with Harper, Margaret Price, Kern, Dowd, conductor Colin Davis; Covent Garden, 1974, with Janet Baker as Vitellia, Yvonne Minton as Sextus, Eric Tappy as Titus, conductor Colin Davis.

CHARACTERS

Titus, *Roman Emperor* ....Tenor
Vitellia, *daughter of the deposed Emperor, Vitellius*
....Soprano

Sextus ⎫ *young Roman patricians* ..⎫   Contralto
Annius ⎭   ..⎭   Mezzo-Soprano[1]
Servilia, *sister of Sextus* .... Soprano
Publius, *Captain of the Praetorian Guard* .... Bass
Time: 79–81 A.D.   *Place:* Rome

All his life, Mozart had a longing to write *opera seria*; his attempts begin with *Mitridate,* written during his years in Italy (1770), reached their height in *Idomeneo* (1781) and culminated in *La Clemenza di Tito* (1791). Even though *opera seria* was already in 1781 an out of date form, it was Mozart not Gluck who was in *Idomeneo* to say the final word on the subject. *La Clemenza di Tito* is a rather different matter. Mazzolà's revised version of Metastasio's libretto, though dramatically a great improvement on its model, may not, with its conventional glorification of benevolent despotism, have been particularly congenial material for Mozart. The opera was commissioned to celebrate the coronation in Prague in 1791 of the Emperor Leopold II as King of Bohemia. Mozart had not even finished *The Magic Flute* and was engaged on the *Requiem,* yet *Tito* was written and performed within eighteen days of receipt of the commission, during part of which period the composer was travelling from Vienna to Prague. Small wonder that Mozart had to entrust the composition of the *secco* recitatives to his pupil Süssmayer! Three weeks after the première, *The Magic Flute* was brought out in Vienna; nine weeks later still, Mozart was dead. It only remains to add that the work seems to have failed at its first performance, but within a month had turned into a considerable success. It was performed in most German-speaking theatres (in translation of course) before the end of the first decade of the nineteenth century, and was actually the first of Mozart's operas to be heard in London, in 1806, when it was given in Italian for Mrs. Billington's benefit.

The story is dominated by two considerations: the determination of Vitellia, who is in love with Titus, to have revenge on him when he seems disposed to marry another; and the inclination of Titus to show clemency no matter what the provocation.

Vitellia knows of Titus's plan to marry Berenice, daughter of Agrippa I of Judaea, and she urges Sextus, who is madly in

[1] In some modern versions sung by a tenor.

love with her, to fall in with her plans and lead a conspiracy against Titus. No sooner has he agreed than she hears that Berenice has been sent home and that Titus now plans to marry a Roman. Annius asks his friend Sextus to intercede with the Emperor in the matter of his (Annius's) marriage to Servilia, Sextus's sister, but Sextus is forestalled in his plan when Titus tells him that he has chosen none other than Servilia to be Empress. Servilia herself tells the Emperor that she is in love with Annius, and he renounces her, deciding instead to take Vitellia to wife. Vitellia has no knowledge of this change of plans, and sends Sextus off to set fire to the Capitol and murder Titus, only to hear, the moment he is gone, that she is now the destined bride of Titus. Sextus succeeds in the first part of his plan, but the conspiracy against Titus's life fails when someone else, wearing his mantle, is killed in his stead. The act ends in general confusion.

It is known at the beginning of Act II that Titus has escaped death, and moreover that the details of the plot have been revealed to him. Annius advises Sextus to throw himself on the mercy of the Emperor and to show renewed zeal in his cause. Vitellia in contrast is anxious to avoid any risk that her connection with the plot may be discovered, and she urges Sextus to fly the country. Publius, however, settles the matter by arriving to arrest Sextus, who is tried by the Senate and condemned to death. Titus confronts him with proof of his guilt, but when Sextus has left him, tears up the death sentence he has just signed. As Sextus and the other conspirators are about to be thrown to the wild beasts in the arena, Vitellia can bear the load of guilt no longer and confesses her share in the plot, only in her turn to be forgiven by the clement Emperor.

For years, critical opinion was agreed that the music of *La Clemenza di Tito* was written in a hurry at a time when Mozart was exhausted by illness and overwork, and is therefore of little value. Anyone hearing it again (or maybe for the first time) will find it hard to agree that it is uninspired, although certainly written against time and in an outmoded form. There is almost no dramatic impetus behind the plot of the opera, and few of the arias have powerful situations behind them. But plot was never the strong point of *opera seria*, which aimed rather at providing a dignified and apt frame for the noble music and virtuoso singing which the aristocracy wanted to hear. Mozart and Mazzolà have between them upset some of the static nature of Metastasio's

original libretto but even so they have not succeeded in
altering the essentially conventional nature of the entertainment; on the other hand, Mozart has succeeded in providing a
very superior example of the sort of music which went with
these eighteenth-century occasions—that he did not write
another *Don Giovanni* is logical. He was being asked to write
something entirely different.

Of the twenty-six numbers in the score, only eleven are in
act arias—which shows how much alteration was made in
Metastasio's original, which made provision for no ensembles
of any sort or kind. They range from a simple arietta such as
that for Servilia ('S'altro che lagrime') to the great show
pieces for Sextus ('Parto, parto') and Vitellia ('Non più di
fiori'). These latter have elaborate instrumental obbligati, for
respectively clarinet and basset horn, and Stadler[1] went
specially to Prague to play them. The vocal writing is no less
elaborate, and, in this combination of virtuoso styles for
voice and instrument, the arias look back to 'Martern aller
Arten' (or even 'Possente spirto' from Monteverdi's *Orfeo*),
and forward to such different pieces as Schubert's song 'Der
Hirt auf dem Felsen' and the Mad scene in *Lucia*. The duets
for Sextus and Annius and for Servilia and Annius are
particularly attractive, and there is a fine trio for Vitellia,
Sextus, and Publius in the second act just before the arrest of
Sextus. But the most notable section of the score is the finale
to Act I, after the Capitol has been set on fire by Sextus. An
agitated crowd off stage adds to the terror of the characters
on stage, and Mozart builds up the whole ensemble antiphonally to imposing dimensions. It is genuine dramatic
music, and is the only time the composer makes simultaneous
use of soloists and chorus together in an extended finale. H.

DIE ZAUBERFLÖTE
The Magic Flute

Opera in two acts by Mozart, text by Emanuel Schikaneder. First
performed at the Theater an der Wien, Vienna, September 30, 1791,
with Nanetta Gottlieb (Pamina), Josefa Hofer (Queen of Night), Schack
(Tamino), Gerl (Sarastro), Schikaneder (Papageno). Its first
performances in England were at the Haymarket Theatre, London,
1811, and at Covent Garden, 1833 (in German). The opera was revived

[1] Anton Stadler, virtuoso clarinet player, for whom Mozart's *Quintet*
was also written.

in 1911 by the Cambridge University Music Society in Edward Dent's translation, with Victoria Hopper, Mrs. Fletcher, Steuart Wilson, H. G. Hiller, Clive Carey; in 1914 at Drury Lane under Sir Thomas Beecham, with Claire Dux, Margarete Siems, Kirchner, Knüpfer, Hans Bechstein; in 1938 at Covent Garden under Beecham, with Lemnitz, Berger, Tauber, Strienz, and Hüsch. It has been regularly in the Old Vic and Sadler's Wells repertory since 1921. First performed at Glyndebourne in 1935, with Rautawaara, Kocova, Ludwig, Andresen, Domgraf-Fassbänder and conducted by Fritz Busch. Revived at Salzburg under Toscanini, 1937, with Novotna, Osvath, Roswaenge, Kipnis, Domgraf-Fassbänder; and under Furtwängler in 1949, with Seefried, Lipp, Ludwig, Greindl, and Schmitt-Walter; Covent Garden, 1962, with Carlyle, Sutherland, Richard Lewis, Kelly, Geraint Evans, conductor Klemperer.

CHARACTERS

Tamino, *an Egyptian Prince* . . . . Tenor
Three Ladies, *in attendance on the Queen of Night* . . . .
. . . . .Two Sopranos and Mezzo-Soprano
Papageno, *a bird-catcher* . . . . Baritone
The Queen of Night . . . . Soprano
Monostatos, *a Moor in the service of Sarastro* . . . Tenor
Pamina, *daughter of the Queen of Night* . . . . . Soprano
Three Genii . . . . . . .Two Sopranos and Mezzo-Soprano
The Speaker . . . . Bass
Sarastro, *High Priest of Isis and Osiris* . . . . Bass
Two Priests . . . . .Tenor and Bass
Papagena . . . . Soprano
Two men in armour . . . . Tenor and Bass
Slaves, Priests, People, etc.
Place: Egypt

Emanuel Johann Schikaneder, who wrote the libretto with the aid of a chorister named Gieseke, was a friend of Mozart and a member of the same Masonic Lodge. He was also the manager of a theatrical company and a successful actor,[1] and had persuaded Mozart to compose the music to a puppet show for him. He had selected for this show the story of 'Lulu' by Liebeskind, which had appeared in a volume of Oriental tales brought out by Wieland under the title of *Dschinnistan*. In the original tale a wicked sorcerer has stolen the daughter of the Queen of Night, who is restored by a

[1] According to Einstein, in his youth one of the first German Hamlets.

Prince by means of magic. While Schikaneder was busy on his libretto, a fairy story by Perinet, music by Wenzel Müller, and treating of the same subject, was given at another Viennese theatre. Its great success interfered with Schikaneder's original plan.

At that time, however, freemasonry was a much discussed subject. It had been interdicted by Maria Theresa and armed forces were employed to break up the lodges. As a practical man Schikaneder saw his chance to exploit the forbidden rites on the stage. Out of the wicked sorcerer he made Sarastro, the sage priest of Isis. The ordeals of Tamino and Pamina became copies of the ceremonials of freemasonry. He also laid the scene of the opera in Egypt, where freemasonry believes its rites to have originated. In addition to all this Mozart's beautiful music ennobled the libretto and lent to the whole the force of the mysterious and sacred.

Because of the opera's relationship to freemasonry, commentators[1] have identified Tamino with the Emperor Joseph II, Pamina with the Austrian people, Sarastro with Ignaz von Born, a freemason and a scientist of great eminence; the vengeful Queen of Night was the Empress Maria Theresa, and Monostatos the clergy[2] especially the Jesuits and the religious orders.

Mozart was engaged on *The Magic Flute* from March until July 1791, and again in September of that year. On September 30, two months before his death, the first performance was given.

In the overture, the heavy reiterated chords represent, it has been suggested, the knocking at the door of the lodge room, especially as they are heard again in the temple scene, when the novitiate of Tamino is about to begin. The brilliance of the fugal *allegro* has been commented upon as well as the resemblance of its theme to that of Clementi's sonata in B flat.

Act I. The story opens with Tamino endeavouring to escape from a huge snake. He falls unconscious. Hearing his cries, three black-garbed Ladies-in-Waiting of the Queen of Night appear and kill the serpent with their spears. The opening *allegro* leads to an extended trio for the Ladies, in which they rejoice that they have been able to foil the

[1] Beginning with Moritz Zille, 1866.
[2] And he was portrayed accordingly in Michael Geliot's ingenious production for the Welsh National Opera in 1971.   H.

serpent and comment on the good looks of the youth they
have rescued. Quite unwillingly they leave the handsome
youth, who, on recovering consciousness, sees dancing to
wards him an odd-looking man entirely covered with
feathers. It is Papageno, the Queen's bird-catcher. His song
'Der Vogelfänger bin ich ja' (I am the jolly bird-catcher[1]), is

punctuated with runs on his pipe and shows us at once that
he is a jovial, not to say a popular, type of comedian. He tell
the astonished Tamino that this is the realm of the Queen o
Night. Nor, seeing that the snake is dead, does he hesitate to
boast that it was he who killed the monster. For this lie he is
immediately punished by the three Ladies, who reappear and
place a padlock on his mouth. Then they show Tamino the
miniature of a maiden, whose beauty at once fills his hear
with an ardent love, which he expresses in one of the mos
beautiful of Mozart's tenor arias, 'Dies Bildnis ist bezaubernd
schön' (O loveliness beyond compare). The Ladies tell him
that she is a prisoner in Sarastro's hands, and he has no
sooner sworn to deliver her than the Queen hersel
materialises from the clouds to reinforce his determination
with a description of her desolation now that she has lost her
daughter, and a promise that Pamina shall be his once she is
free. 'O zittre nicht, mein lieber Sohn' (Be not afraid, C
noble youth), she sings, and her *scena* develops into a display
of coloratura fireworks designed primarily, we may be sure
to display the agile technique of the original Queen, Josef;
Hofer, the composer's sister-in-law, but expressive also of her
blind and passionate nature. The Ladies come back, take the
padlock from Papageno's mouth and give him a set of chime
and Tamino a golden flute; by means of these magica
instruments they will be able to escape the perils of their
journey, on which they will be accompanied by three youth

[1] Translation by Edward J. Dent (published by O.U.P.).

or genii. The quintet, 'Hm, hm, hm! Der Arme kann von
Strafe sagen' ('Tis hard such punishment to suffer), apart
from being enchanting in itself, serves also to introduce the
music associated later with the Genii, which has a curious
quality of its own, which one can only ascribe to the lesser
supernatural and call 'magical' (in just the sense Tippett used
the term in *The Midsummer Marriage*).

The scene changes, and a richly furnished apartment in
Sarastro's palace is disclosed. A brutal Moor, Monostatos, is
pursuing Pamina with unwelcome attentions. Even in this
duet, whose basis is surely in comedy, something of the
depth which is to be Pamina's can be discerned; compare her
feminine warmth with the lack of that quality in the Queen
and the three Ladies. The appearance of Papageno puts him
to flight. The Bird-catcher recognises Pamina as the daughter
of the Queen of the Night and assures her that she will soon
be rescued, and, what is more, by someone who has fallen in
love with her without even seeing her—not the sort of thing,
he laments, that ever seems to happen to him. Pamina
consoles him in an exquisitely simple E flat tune and assures
him that love will yet be his: 'Bei Männern, welche Liebe
fühlen, fehlt auch ein gutes Herze nicht' (The kindly voice of
mother Nature wakes love in bird and beast and flower).

The finale takes place in a grove on three sides of which
stand three Temples, dedicated to Wisdom, Reason, and
Nature. Thither the three Genii lead Tamino, and leave him
with the advice that he 'be silent, patient, persevering'. In a
recitative which admirably expresses the dawning of understanding in his mind, Tamino decides to enter the Temples,
but at the first two he is refused admittance, and from the
third emerges a priest who informs him that Sarastro is no
tyrant, no wicked sorcerer as the Queen had warned him, but
a man of wisdom and of noble character. The solemn
atmosphere of their dialogue—an extraordinary example of a
musical argument reinforcing words with logic—serves to
awaken still further Tamino's desire for knowledge (see page
134), and his recitative 'O ew'ge Nacht' (O endless night), takes
the form of question and answer, the answer being supplied
by a hidden and encouraging chorus. He takes his flute and
plays and sings to its accompaniment: 'Wie stark is nicht dein
Zauberton' (O voice of magic melody). The wild animals
come out from their lairs and lie at his feet, but before the
end of the aria he hears Papageno's pan-pipe and at its end he

rushes off to find him. Papageno comes on from the opposite side of the stage leading Pamina whom he intends to unite with Tamino. Their duet, 'Schnelle Füsse, rascher Mut' (Let us hasten, quick as thought) is punctuated with calls on the pipes and answers from the flute but becomes a trio when they are overtaken by Monostatos, who sends for chains with which to complete their capture.

Disaster seems near, but Papageno remembers that he has a last remedy and sets the Moor and his slaves dancing by playing on his magic chimes. He and Pamina rejoice at their escape, but are interrupted by a flourish of trumpets and the sound of a chorus of praise to Sarastro. Papageno wonders what they are going to say to him. 'Die Wahrheit!' (The truth, friend) proudly answers Pamina, and the phrase serves to end the comedy of the escape and to initiate the solemnity of Sarastro's procession. She kneels at Sarastro's feet and explains that she was trying to escape the unwelcome attentions of the Moor. Sarastro comforts her and assures her that he understands her predicament and that the Gods aim to provide a remedy. Monostatos drags Tamino in, and in phrases whose origin is surely in Mozart's 'Turkish' style (see *Entführung*), denounces him to Sarastro, but, instead of the reward he expects, he is sentenced to a sound flogging. Woven into the structure of this section of the finale is the rapturous moment of the first meeting of Pamina and Tamino. By command of Sarastro, the two of them are brought into the Temple of Ordeal, where they must prove that they are worthy of the higher happiness.

Act II. A solemn *andante* sets the scene, which is laid in a grove of palms outside the Temple. Sarastro informs the Priests of the plans which he has laid. The gods have decided that Pamina shall become the wife of the noble youth Tamino. Tamino, however, must prove by his own power that he is worthy of admission to the Temple. Therefore, Sarastro has taken under his protection Pamina, daughter of the Queen of Night, to whom is due all darkness and superstition. But the couple must go through severe ordeals in order to be worthy of entering the Temple of Light, and thus of thwarting the sinister machinations of the Queen. In between his pronouncements the Priests blow their trumpets, repeating the chords which were heard in the overture. Sarastro prays to Isis and Osiris that strength may be granted to the two aspirants after the goal of wisdom: 'O Isis und Osiris'. This solemn prayer is of so noble a nature that it has been described as the only music which could without fear of blasphemy be put into the mouth of God. It certainly belongs in quite another category from that in which is often to be found the music associated in opera with High Priests.

The Porch of the Temple. The ordeals of Tamino and Papageno are about to begin. They are warned by the Priests that they may perish in their search for the Truth, and then enjoined to silence as the first step in their probation. Two Priests warn them in a duet of what will happen if they fail to keep their vow of silence ('Bewahret euch vor Weibertücken': Beware of the wiles of woman's weaving), but no sooner are they left alone and in darkness than they are confronted by the three Ladies of the Queen of Night. In the quintet which follows, the Ladies try to persuade them to abandon their quest, but Tamino, and even, with some prompting, Papageno, maintain a rigid silence in the face of the questioning women. The Priests reappear and congratulate them on having passed their first test.

The scene changes to a garden. Pamina is discovered lying asleep. Towards her steals the Moor, and indulges in what Einstein describes as a 'grotesque, phallic dance' and an aria which is not far behind in that quality: 'Alles fühlt der Liebe Freuden' (All with passion's fever tingle). The accompaniment to the aria is 'to be sung and played very softly, as if the music was a very long way off'—so runs Mozart's own direction. Monostatos comes up to Pamina but a cry of 'Zurück' causes him to start back: it is the Queen of Night. She flings her daughter a dagger with the command that she take it and kill Sarastro. In 'Der Hölle Rache kocht in meinen Herzen' (I'll have revenge, no longer can I bear it) one can feel the fires of fury boiling in the music, with its passionate staccato coloratura, its four top F's, and its headlong impetus. Monostatos returns and, threatening that he will reveal the plot (to which Pamina has never agreed to be a party), demands her love as the price of his silence. Sarastro enters just in time to hurl Monostatos from the defenceless

Pamina, but the Moor departs promising to try if he will have better luck with the mother than with the daughter. Pamina pleads for her mother, but Sarastro assures her that vengeance is not in his thoughts: 'In diesen heil'gen Hallen kennt man die Rache nicht' (We know no thought of vengeance within these temple walls). Again, the nobility of the music's expression equals, perhaps even surpasses, that of 'O Isis und Osiris'. The bass who can sing these two arias evenly throughout their compass, with the flowing *cantilena* they demand and with the necessary expression of their content, will find himself with few rivals.

Hal - len Kennt man die Ra - che nicht

A Hall. Enjoined once more to keep silent, Tamino and Papageno are again left by the attendant Priests. Papageno still chatters to himself, and soon enters into a long conversation with an old crone who introduces herself to him as his yet unknown sweetheart, Papagena. A clap of thunder and she departs, to be replaced by the three Genii who appear bringing with them the flute and magic bells, carrying a table spread with food and drink, and singing in strains similar to those we heard at their first entrance. To the two aspirants comes Pamina, unaware of their vow of silence, but overjoyed to have found Tamino at last. But her delight is short-lived and she suspends belief in human constancy when she can get no answer from her beloved. 'Ach, ich fühl's, es ist verschwunden' (Ah, 'tis gone, 'tis gone for ever) run the words of her G minor aria, in which that mixture of maturity and innocence which she has consistently shown reaches its highest level of expression. Nowhere else in the repertory of the lyric soprano is the grief which passes all bounds given musical expression of such poignant simplicity, nor, one may

Andante.

Ach, ich fühl's, es ist ver-

add, a setting which is so exceptionally difficult to realise in terms of practical performance; this aria stands in the same relationship to the soprano as Sarastro's arias do to the bass.

The scene changes to a vault. The Priests sing a solemn *adagio* chorus of praise to Isis and Osiris, after which Sarastro confronts Pamina with Tamino and tells them to take their last farewell of each other: 'Soll ich dich, Teurer, nicht mehr seh'n?' (And shall I never see thee more?). As throughout the opera, the characterisation is preserved in every phrase, and is most marked when the three singers express the same idea by means of imitation:

muss nun wirk - lich   fort

fort,   wirk - lich fort.

fort!   Die Stunde schlägt

We return to Papageno, who is told he can have one wish granted but is left vaguely dissatisfied when he has drunk the wine he asks for. What is missing? 'Ein Mädchen oder Weibchen wünscht Papageno sich' ('Tis love they say, love only, that makes the world go round). There are three *andante* verses, each with its *allegro* refrain, the *Glockenspiel ritornelli* growing successively more complicated. At the end of the song, the old woman comes back to him and, threatening him with dire penalties if he does not swear to be true to her, when he does so, reveals herself as a young and attractively feathered mate—but poor Papageno is warned off her by a Priest who pronounces him not yet worthy of her.

The three Genii are discovered in a garden singing of the symbolical joys of the rising sun, whose rays drive away the fears of night and herald the reign of light and love: 'Bald prangt, den Morgen zu verkünden' (The rosy flush that greets us yonder). Nothing more suitable for the beginning of the finale of the opera could be found than these sentiments and the disembodied agents through whom they are expressed. None of the music in the opera stands further away from the conventions of *opera buffa* or *Singspiel* or even *opera seria*—the forms known in Mozart's day—than the conception

of this trio of voices, and the hushed beauty of their music seems to convey that sense of being 'different', dedicated even, that characterises the serious side of the music of *The Magic Flute*, and sets it apart from other operas. Not knowing she is observed, Pamina contemplates suicide ('Du also bist mein Bräutigam? Durch dich vollend' ich meinen Gram': No other way but this remains to make an end of all my pains), but is restrained and comforted by the Genii in music of extraordinary tenderness. Two Men in Armour are seen standing at each side of a doorway, and Tamino is brought in by the Priests for the last stage of his initiation. The test of fire and water is heralded by the Men in Armour, whose scene is constructed in the form of a chorale prelude, the orchestra weaving a *fugato* round the chorale 'Ach Gott vom Himmel sieh' darein'. Tamino proclaims his resolution, but is joined by Pamina for these final ordeals. His joy at being not only reunited with her but even allowed to speak to her freely is expressed in an ardent phrase which prepares us for the moving simplicity of their meeting and the duet which follows, and becomes a quartet with the musical entrance of the two guardians of the gates.

Pamina's sufferings appear to have produced an astonishing serenity and even wisdom in her, and she is in a sense Tamino's guide as, to the accompaniment of an *adagio* for the solo flute, they undergo successively the ordeals by fire and by water. At the end they are welcomed into the temple by Sarastro and the Priests.

At this point occurs Papageno's great scene of mock suicide, a parallel trial in comic terms perhaps to the serious trials Tamino and Pamina are expected to surmount. 'Papagena! Papagena!' is a song of a more serious cut than the other two Schikaneder had to himself, but, after an appeal to someone in the audience to volunteer to save him and the subsequent intervention of the Genii, the *scena* ends happily with a jingle of bells, and is followed by an irresistible patter duet for Papageno and Papagena.

Before the Temple, Monostatos leads on the Queen and her Ladies, who are making a last bid for revenge on Sarastro. But their appearance coincides with the stage being flooded with light, and the forces of night disappear before the short chorus extolling the new initiates and the magic flute which was their faithful companion brings the opera to an end.

Nothing is so simple as to be absolutely clear-cut, and in life the serious and the comic are intermingled in a way that is frequently disconcerting but is none the less inevitable. Mozart, who was far from scorning the operatic conventions of his day, seems to have had no qualms about attempting

this mixture in his operas in spite of the lack of preceden
Though both *Figaro* and *Così fan tutte* partake of thi
mixture, they are nevertheless comedies pure though by nc
means simple: the one a comedy of action, the other o:
conversation; but the remaining two out of his four greatest
operas present a more complicated problem. In each of them
the close relationship of the comic and the serious is treated
in art as in life as the natural and inevitable thing we know i
to be. *Don Giovanni*, comic in theme and predominantly
comic in treatment, yet continually takes a turn towards the
serious considerations which arise out of the comedy; *The
Magic Flute*, serious in its presentation of the urge towards ar
understanding of truth, none the less mingles the digressions o
Papageno with the aspirations of Tamino and Pamina. A
refusal to take the story of *The Magic Flute* seriously is tc
turn a blind eye to the impeccable skill of the librettist (o:
librettists) and also to deny to the genius of Mozart the
power of discrimination and choice. To what extent the
fortuitous circumstances surrounding the commission of *The
Magic Flute*—the fact that Schikaneder was an accomplishec
and popular comedian and that freemasonry was a con
troversial topic of the day—may have influenced Mozart in ar
unexpected direction, is likely to be a matter for speculatior
as long as opera is played, but it is in the end almost
irrelevant. His terms of reference and his plans are fas
cinating, but far more important is the work of art which
resulted from them; in the cases of *The Magic Flute* and *Dor
Giovanni* he succeeded in combining the two elements which
go to make up everyday life in a way which may occasionally
have been approached since his day, but which had hardly
before been attempted and has never been surpassed.

K., H.

PART II

THE
NINETEENTH
CENTURY

4
German Opera

LUDWIG
VAN BEETHOVEN
(1770–1827)

FIDELIO

OPERA in two acts by Ludwig van Beethoven. Text by Joseph
Sonnleithner and Georg Friedrich Sonnleithner after the drama by
Jean Nicolas Bouilly. First produced at the Theater an der Wien,
Vienna, November 20, 1805 (in three acts), with Anna Milder, Louise
Müller, Demmer, Meier, Rothe, Weinkopf, and Cache, conducted by
Beethoven; given in two acts on March 29, 1806. First given in its final
form at the Kärnthnerthor Theatre, Vienna, 1814. First performed in
London at the Haymarket (in German) 1832, at Covent Garden (in
English) 1835, with Malibran; New York (in English) 1839, (in
German) 1856; at the Metropolitan, New York, 1884, with Marianne
Brandt, Auguste Kraus, Anton Schott, Adolf Robinson, Josef Miller,
Josef Staudigl, and Otto Kemlitz, conductor Leopold Damrosch. First
performed at Sadler's Wells in Edward Dent's English translation,
1937, with Molly de Gunst, Hamilton-Smith, Tudor Davies, Redvers
Llewellyn, Ronald Stear. Revivals at Covent Garden include those of
1927, with Wildbrunn, Krauss, and Bender, conductor Walter; 1934,
with Lotte Lehmann, Völker, and Kipnis, conductor Beecham; 1938,
with Pauly, Roswaenge, Weber, conductor Beecham; 1948, with Sylvia
Fisher, Hannesson, Franklin, conductor Karl Rankl; 1951, with
Flagstad and Patzak; 1961, with Jurinac, Vickers, Hotter, Frick,
conductor Klemperer. Salzburg, 1927–36, with Lotte Lehmann, and in
1927 Schumann, Piccaver, Jerger, Mayr, conductor Schalk; 1932,
Völker, Rode, Manowarda, conductor R. Strauss; 1936, Pataky,
Jerger, Baumann, conductor Toscanini; Salzburg, 1948–50, with
Schlüter and Flagstad, Patzak, Frantz and Schöffler, Alsen and Greindl,
conductor Furtwängler.

CHARACTERS

Florestan, *a Spanish Nobleman* .... Tenor
Leonora, *his wife, in male attire as Fidelio* .... Soprano
Don Fernando, *the King's Minister* .... Bass
Don Pizarro, *Governor of the prison* .... Baritone
Rocco, *chief jailer* .... Bass
Marcellina, *daughter of Rocco* .... Soprano
Jacquino, *assistant to Rocco* .... Tenor
Soldiers, Prisoners, People
Time: Eighteenth Century   *Place:* A fortress, near Seville

The libretto, which appealed to the composer by reason of its pure and idealistic motive, was not written for Beethoven. It was a French book by Bouilly and had been used by three composers: Pierre Gaveaux (1798); Simone Mayr, Donizetti's teacher and the composer of more than seventy operas (1805); and Paer (1804).

It was Schikaneder, the librettist and producer of Mozart's *Magic Flute*, who commissioned Beethoven to compose an opera. But it was finally executed for Baron von Braun, who had succeeded to the management of the Theater an der Wien.

Beethoven's heart was bound up in the work. Conscientious to the last detail in everything he did, there are no less than sixteen sketches for the opening of Florestan's first air and 346 pages of sketches for the opera. Nor did his labour in it cease when the opera was completed and performed.

Bouilly's libretto was translated and made over for Beethoven by Schubert's friend Joseph Sonnleithner. The opera was brought out November 20 and repeated November 21 and 22, 1805. It was a failure. The French were in occupation of Vienna, which the emperor of Austria and the court had abandoned, and conditions generally were upset. But even Beethoven's friends did not blame the non-success of the opera upon these untoward circumstances. It had inherent defects, as was apparent even a century later, when at the *Fidelio* centennial celebration in Berlin, the original version was restored and performed.

To remedy these, Beethoven's friend, Stephen von Breuning, condensed the three acts to two and the composer made changes in the score. This second version was brought forward to March 29, 1806, with better success, but a quarrel with von Braun led Beethoven to withdraw it. It seems to have required seven years for the *entente cordiale* between composer and manager to become re-established. Then Baron von Braun had the book taken in hand by a practical librettist, Georg Friedrich Treitschke. Upon receiving the revision, which greatly pleased him, Beethoven in his turn re-revised the score. In this form *Fidelio* was brought out May 23, 1814, in the Theater am Kärnthnerthor. There was no question of failure this time. The opera took its place in the repertoire and when, eight years later, Mme. Schröder-Devrient sang the title role, her success in it was sensational.

There are four overtures to the work, three entitled *Leonore* (Nos. 1, 2, and 3) and one *Fidelio*. The *Leonore* overtures are incorrectly numbered. The No. 2 was given at the original performance and is, therefore, No. 1. The greatest and justly the most famous, the No. 3, is really No. 2. The so-called No. 1 was composed for a projected performance at Prague, which never came off. The score and parts, in a copyist's hand, but with corrections by Beethoven, were discovered after the composer's death. When it was recognised as an overture to the opera, the conclusion that it was the earliest one, which he probably had laid aside, was not unnaturally arrived at. The *Fidelio* overture was intended for the second revision, but was not ready in time. The overture to *The Ruins of Athens* was substituted. The overture to *Fidelio* usually is played before the opera and the *Leonore*, No. 3, is frequently inserted between the two scenes of Act II.[1]

In the story of the opera, Florestan, a noble Spaniard, has aroused the enmity of Pizarro, governor of a gloomy mediaeval fortress, used as a place of confinement for political prisoners. Pizarro has been enabled secretly to seize

---

[1] But this practice is by no means universally approved (except, maybe, among conductors, since it gives them a solo opportunity). *Leonore* 3 repeats much of the material of the scene it follows; sacrifices the effect of sunshine and of solution which the C major of the final scene can produce when *not* preceded by music in the same key; and entirely destroys the dramatic balance of the whole act. Edward Dent has pointed out in addition that the careful balance of the instrumentation of the opera is upset (compare the dynamic ranges of the *Fidelio* overture and *Leonore* 3) and once suggested that the piece be played at the end of the whole opera for the benefit of those who must have it and of the prima donna conductors who must play it! H.

Florestan and cast him into the darkest dungeon of the fortress, at the same time spreading a report of his death.

One person, however, suspects the truth—Leonora, the wife of Florestan. Her faithfulness, the danger she runs in order to save her husband, and the final triumph of conjugal love over the sinister machinations of Pizarro, form the motive of the story of *Fidelio*, a title derived from the name assumed by Leonora, when, disguised as a man, she obtains employment as assistant to Rocco, the chief jailer of the prison. Fidelio has been at work and has become a great favourite with Rocco, as well as with Marcellina, the jailer's daughter. The latter, in fact, much prefers the gentle, comely youth, Fidelio, to Jacquino, the turnkey, who, before Fidelio's appearance upon the scene, believed himself to be her accepted lover. Leonora cannot make her sex known to the girl. It would ruin her plans to save her husband. Such is the situation when the curtain rises on the first act, which is laid in the courtyard of the prison.

Act I. The opera opens with a brisk duet between Jacquino and Marcellina, in which he urges her definitely to accept him and she cleverly puts him off. Left alone, she expresses her compassion for Jacquino, but wishes she were united with Fidelio. ('O wär' ich schon mit dir vereint'—O, were I but with you united.)

Later she is joined by her father. Then Leonora (as Fidelio) enters the courtyard. Marcellina, seeing how weary Fidelio is, hastens to relieve the supposed youth of his burden. Rocco hints not only tolerantly but even encouragingly at what he believes to be the fancy Fidelio and Marcellina have taken to each other. This leads up to the quartet in canon form, one of the notable vocal numbers of the opera, 'Mir ist so wunderbar' (How wondrous the emotion). Being a canon, the theme enunciated by each of

the four characters is the same, but if the difference in the sentiments of each character is indicated by subtle nuance of expression on the part of the singers, and the intonation be correct, the beauty of this quartet points the tragic implications of much of the rest of the opera. The participants are

Leonora, Marcellina, Rocco, and Jacquino, who appears toward the close. 'After this canon,' say the stage directions, so clearly is the form of the quartet recognised, 'Jacquino goes back to his lodge.'

Rocco sings a song in praise of money and the need of it for young people about to marry. ('Hat man nicht auch Gold beineben': Life is nothing without money.) Its jocular, vulgar character is curiously at variance with the style of the quartet it follows. The situation is awkward for Leonora, but the rescue of her husband demands that she continue to masquerade as a man. Moreover there is an excuse in the palpable fact that before she entered Rocco's service, Jacquino was in high favour with Marcellina and probably will have no difficulty in re-establishing himself therein when the comely youth Fidelio turns out to be Leonora, the faithful wife of Florestan.

Through a description which Rocco gives of the prisoners, Leonora now suspects what she had not been sure of before: her husband is confined in this fortress and in its deepest dungeon. The scene ends with a trio dominated by Leonora's 'Ich habe Muth'.

A short march, with a pronounced and characteristic rhythm covers the change of scene and announces the approach of Pizarro. He looks over his despatches. One of them warns him that Fernando, the Minister of State, is about to inspect the fortress, representations having been made to him that Pizarro has used his power as governor to wreak vengeance upon his private enemies. A man of quick decision, Pizarro determines to do away with Florestan at once. His aria, 'Ha! welch' ein Augenblick!' (Ah! the great moment!), is one of the heaviest and most difficult solos for bass voice in the dramatic repertory, but its effectiveness is undeniable.

Pizarro posts a trumpeter on the ramparts with a sentry to watch the road from Seville. As soon as a state equipage with outriders is sighted, the trumpeter is to blow a signal. Having thus made sure of being warned of the approach of the Minister, he tosses a well-filled purse to Rocco, and bids him 'for the safety of the State' to make away with the most dangerous of the prisoners—meaning Florestan. Rocco declines to commit murder, but when Pizarro takes it upon himself to do the deed, Rocco consents to dig a grave in an old cistern in the vaults, so that all traces of the crime will be hidden from the expected visitor. The music of this duet, effective enough to begin with, is later subjected to repetition in a way which brings it perilously out of line with the dramatic situation—it provides evidence for those who doubt the existence in Beethoven of a sense of the stage.

Leonora, who has overheard the plot, now gives vent to her feelings in the highly dramatic: 'Abscheulicher! wo eilst du hin?' (Accursed one! Where hasten'st thou?); a deeply moving expression of confidence that her love and faith will enable her, with the aid of Providence, to save her husband's life. The recitative, *andante* air, and quick final section is on the pattern made familiar by Mozart's 'Dove sono', and, later, in the operas of Weber. 'Abscheulicher' is one of the most famous examples of such a *scena*. Soon afterwards she learns that, as Rocco's assistant, she is to help him in digging the grave. She will be near her husband and either able to aid him or at least die with him.

The prisoners from the upper tiers are now, on Leonora's intercession and because it is the King's birthday, permitted a brief opportunity to breathe the open air. The cells are unlocked and they are allowed to stroll in the garden of the fortress, until Pizarro, hearing of this, angrily puts an end to it. The chorus of the prisoners, subdued like the half-suppressed joy of fearsome beings, is one of the significant passages of the score.

Act II.   The scene is in the dark dungeon where Florestan is in heavy chains. The act opens with Florestan's recitative and air, a fit companion piece to Leonora's 'Komm, Hoffnung' in Act I:

The whispered duet between Leonora and Rocco as they dig the grave and the orchestral accompaniment impress one with the gruesome significance of the scene, and with Beethoven's delicate juxtaposition of melodrama and accompanied song.

Leonora thinks she recognises her husband and obtains Rocco's permission to give him some food and drink. His heartfelt thanks for the unexpected kindness, her anguished recognition, and Rocco's premonition that the prisoner is beyond human aid combine in a trio of wonderful beauty.

Pizarro enters the vault, makes himself known to his enemy, and draws his dagger for the fatal thrust. Leonora throws herself in his way. Pushed aside, she again interposes herself between the would-be murderer and his victim, and, pointing at him a loaded pistol, which she has had concealed about her person, cries out: 'First slay his wife!'

At this moment, in itself so tense, a trumpet call rings out from the direction of the fortress wall. Jacquino appears at the head of the stone stairway leading down into the dungeon and announces (in spoken dialogue) that the Minister of State is at the gate. Florestan is saved and the quartet ends with Pizarro's discomfiture. There is a rapturous duet, 'O namenlose Freude' (Joy inexpressible), for him and the devoted wife to whom he owes his life.

In Florestan the Minister of State recognises his friend, whom he believed to have died, according to the reports set afloat by Pizarro, who himself is now apprehended. To Leonora is assigned the joyful task of unlocking and loosening her husband's fetters and freeing him from his chains. A chorus of rejoicing: 'Wer ein solches Weib errungen' (He whom such a wife has cherished) brings the opera to a close.

It is well said in George P. Upton's book, *The Standard Operas*, that 'as a drama and as an opera, *Fidelio* stands almost alone in its perfect purity, in the moral grandeur of its subject, and in the resplendent ideality of its music.' Even those who do not appreciate the beauty of such a work, and unfortunately their number is considerable, cannot fail to agree with me that the trumpet call, and, still more, the immaculate timing with which it brings the prison scene to a climax, is one of the most dramatic moments in opera. I was a boy when I first heard *Fidelio* in Wiesbaden, but I still remember the thrill, when that trumpet call split the air with the message that the Minister of State was in sight and that Leonora had saved her husband:

When *Fidelio* had its first American performance (New York, Park Theatre, September 9, 1839) the opera did not

fill the entire evening. The entertainment as a whole was a
curiosity according to present-day standards. First came
Beethoven's opera, with Mrs. Martyn as Leonora. Then a *pas
seul* was danced by Mme. Araline; the whole concluding with
The Deep, Deep Sea, in which Mr Placide appeared as The
Great American Sea Serpent. This seems incredible. But I
have searched for and found the advertisement in the New
York *Evening Post*, and the facts are as stated.

Under Dr. Leopold Damrosch, *Fidelio* was performed at
the Metropolitan Opera House in the season of 1884–85;
under Anton Seidl, during the season of 1886–87, with
Brandt and Niemann, as well as with Lehmann and Niemann
as Leonora and Florestan. A curiosity in the history of the
opera at the Metropolitan is that for a generation the
audience knew it only with the recitatives composed by the
conductor Bodanzky to replace most of the spoken dialogue.

K.

CARL
MARIA VON WEBER
(1786–1826)
DER FREISCHÜTZ

OPERA in three acts by Carl Maria von Weber, text by Johann
Friedrich Kind. First produced at the Schauspielhaus, Berlin, June 18
1821, with Mmes. Seidler, Eunicke, Messrs. Stümer and Blume. First
performed in London, at the English Opera House, 1824, with Miss
Noel, Miss Povey, Mr. Braham, Mr. Baker, Mr. Bartley, and Mr. Bennet
in German at Her Majesty's Theatre, 1832. First performance in New
York (in English), 1825; (in German) 1845; at Metropolitan Opera
1884. For the performance in Italian at Covent Garden in 1825, Cost
wrote recitatives to replace the spoken dialogue, as did Berlioz for th
production at the Opéra, Paris, 1841. Revived at Metropolitan Opera
1923, with Rethberg, Taucher, and Bohnen, and conducted by
Bodanzky; 1971 with Lorengar, Mathis, Konya, Feldhoff, conducto
Ludwig; at Covent Garden, 1935 (in English), with Eva Turner, Walte

Widdop, Arthur Fear, and conducted by Beecham; 1954 with Fisher and Sutherland, Adèle Leigh, James Johnston and Edgar Evans, Otakar Kraus and Frederick Dalberg, conductor Edward Downes; at Salzburg, 1954, with Grümmer, Streich, Hopf, Böhme, conductor Furtwängler; at la Scala 1955, with de los Angeles, Ratti, Francesco Albanese, Rossi-Lemeni, conductor Giulini.

CHARACTERS

Prince Ottokar . . . . Baritone
Cuno, *the head ranger* . . . . Bass
Max, *a forester* . . . . Tenor
Caspar, *a forester* . . . . Bass
Kilian, *a rich peasant* . . . . Tenor
A Hermit . . . . Bass
Samiel, *the wild huntsman* . . . . Speaking Part
Agathe, *Cuno's daughter* . . . . Soprano
Aennchen, *her cousin* . . . . Soprano
Time: Middle of Seventeenth Century   *Place:* Bohemia

The overture to *Der Freischütz* is the first in which an operatic composer unreservedly has made use of melodies from the opera itself. Beethoven, in the *Leonora* overtures, utilises the theme of Florestan's air and the trumpet call. Weber has used not merely thematic material but complete melodies. Following the beautiful passage for horns at the beginning of the overture is the music of Max's outcry when, in the opera, he senses rather than sees the passage of Samiel across the stage, after which comes the sombre music of Max's 'Hat denn Himmel mich verlassen?' (Am I then by heaven forsaken?) This leads up to the music of Agathe's outburst of joy when she sees her lover approaching.

Act I.   At the target range. Kilian, a peasant, has defeated Max, the forester, at a prize shooting, a *Schützenfest* maybe. Max, of course, as a forester accustomed to use of fire-arms, should have won, and it is disgraceful for him to have been defeated by a peasant. Kilian rubs it in and the men and girls of the village join in the mocking of Max—a clever bit of teasing in music which establishes at the very start the originality of melody, style, and character of the opera.

The hereditary forester, Cuno, is worried over the poor showing Max has made not only that day but for some time past. There is to be a shoot on the morrow before Prince Ottokar. In order to win the hand in marriage of Agathe, Cuno's daughter, and the eventual succession as hereditary forester, Max must carry off the honours in the competition now so near at hand. There is an expressive trio for Max, Caspar, and Cuno with chorus ('O diese Sonne!'), which is followed by a short waltz as the peasants bring the competition to a suitable end. Max is in despair; life will be worthless to him without Agathe, yet he seems to have lost all his cunning as a shot, and without it he cannot win her hand. The first part of this *scena*, 'Durch die Wälder, durch die Auen' (Through the forest and o'er the meadows), is a melody of great beauty, but the music takes on a more sinister character as Samiel, unseen of course by Max, hovers, a threatening shadow, in the background. It is now, when the others have gone, that his comrade Caspar, another forester of dark visage and of morose and forbidding character, approaches him. He hands him his gun, points to an eagle circling far above, and tells him to fire at it. Max shoots, and from its dizzy height the bird falls dead at his feet. It is a wonderful shot, but Caspar explains to him that he has shot with a charmed bullet and that such bullets always hit what the marksman wills them to (*Der Freischütz* can only be translated as 'the free-shooter', i.e. someone who shoots with magic bullets). If Max will meet him in the Wolf's Glen at midnight, they will mould bullets with one of which, on the morrow, he will be able to win Agathe's hand and the hereditary office of forester. Max, to whom victory means all that is dear to him, consents. Caspar's effective drinking song, which precedes his tempting of Max, is forced in its hilarity and ends in grotesque laughter, Caspar being the familiar of Samiel, the wild huntsman. The act ends with an aria for Caspar, whose wide range and rapid passages are taxing for the singer, but which is in keeping with Caspar's sinister character.

Act II.   Agathe's room in the head ranger's house. The music opens with a delightful duet for Agathe and Aennchen and a charmingly coquettish little air for the latter ('Kommt ein schlanker Bursch gegangen'; Comes a comely youth a-wooing). But Agathe has gloomy forebodings, and even her sprightly relative is unable to cheer her up. Left alone, she opens the window and, as the moonlight floods the room, intones the prayer so simple, so exquisite, so expressive: 'Leise, leise, fromme Weise' (Softly sighing, day is dying).

This is followed after a recitative by a rapturous passage
leading into an ecstatic melody as she sees her lover
approaching. It is one of the best known tunes in all opera,
but gains immeasurably from being heard in its context as
part of one of the greatest scenes for solo soprano:

Max comes in and is quickly followed by Aennchen. Very
soon, however, he says he must leave, because he has shot a
deer in the Wolf's Glen and must go after it. The scene ends
with a trio in which the girls try vainly to warn him against
the locality, which is said to be haunted.

The scene changes to the Wolf's Glen, the haunt of Samiel
the wild huntsman (otherwise the devil), to whom Caspar has
sold himself, and to whom he now plans to turn over Max as
a victim, in order to gain for himself a brief respite on earth,
his time to Samiel being up. The younger forester joins him
in the Wolf's Glen and together they mould seven magic
bullets, six of which go true to the mark, the seventh
wherever Samiel wills it. The music has long been considered
the most expressive rendering of the gruesome that is to be
found in a musical score—its power is undiminished to-day
whatever may be thought of the naïveté of the stage
apparatus which goes with it. The ghost of Max's mother
appears to him and strives to warn him away. Cadaverous,
spooky-looking animals crawl out from caves in the rocks and
spit flames and sparks. But the music is a fascinating essay in
the grotesque—nothing comparable had been tried before—
and the way in which it avoids the excessive but yet
cunningly mixes the speaking voice and singing, the purely
musical effect of Max's entrance with the atmospheric climax
of the moulding of the bullets, is entirely admirable. The
music remarkably anticipates Wagner, who got more than one
hint from this scene—but its merits are particular and far
beyond any prophetic qualities it may incidentally possess.

Act III.   After a brief introduction, with suggestions of the hunting chorus later in the action, the act opens with Agathe's lovely cavatina 'Und ob die Wolke' (And though a cloud the sun obscure), a melody of such pure and expressive beauty that even Weber was never able to surpass it. Agathe is attired for the shooting test, which will make her Max's bride if he is successful. Aennchen sings a solo (composed after the rest of the opera), and then comes the enchanting chorus of bridesmaids who enter and wind the bridal garland. This is the piece which Richard Wagner, then seven years old, was playing in a room adjoining that in which his stepfather, Ludwig Geyer, lay in his last illness. As he listened to him playing the bridesmaids' chorus, Geyer turned to his wife, Wagner's mother, and said: 'What if he should have a talent for music!'

The concluding scene—the shooting test—begins with the spirited hunting chorus. Only the seventh bullet, the one which Samiel controls, remains to Max, the others having been used up during the hunt. Caspar, who expects Max to be Samiel's victim, climbs a tree to watch the proceedings from a safe place of concealment. Before the whole village and Prince Ottokar himself the test shot is to be fired. The Prince points to a flying dove and Max raises his gun. At that moment Agathe appears, accompanied by a Hermit, and calls out to Max not to shoot, that she is the dove. But Max has already pulled the trigger; Agathe falls—but only in a swoon—and it is Caspar who tumbles from the tree and rolls, fatally wounded, on the turf. Samiel has had no power over Max, for the young forester had not come to the Wolf's Glen of his own free will, but only after being tempted by Caspar; therefore Caspar had himself to be the victim of the seventh bullet. There is general uproar, Agathe is seen to be alive and Caspar dying, but Max's confession results in a sentence of banishment from the Prince. Only through the intercession (in a chorale-like aria) of the Hermit, a holy man revered by the whole district, is disaster for Max averted and the Prince's forgiveness obtained. The opera ends with the jubilant melody from Agathe's second act scene.

No less notable as portent than as music, Der Freischütz holds an important position in the logical development of music and particularly of opera. If anyone can be said to qualify for such a title, Weber was the founder of the German romantic school—a school which reached its climax with Wagner, its culmination perhaps with Richard Strauss.

The structure of the overture to this opera is much like that to Wagner's *Tannhäuser*. There is also a resemblance in contour between the music of Agathe's jubilation and that of Tannhäuser's hymn of Venus—Wagner worshipped Weber. Without a suggestion of plagiarism, the contour of Wagner's melodic idiom is that of Weber's. The resemblance to Weber in the general structure of the finales to the first acts of both *Tannhäuser* and *Lohengrin* is obvious, and even in some of the leading motives of the Wagner music dramas, the student will find hints of Weber still persisting.

But Weber is much more than just Wagner's forerunner— just as Bellini has importance of his own beyond being the predecessor of Verdi. He is one of the great melodists of musical history, and perhaps no other composer of the romantic movement so completely preserved musical freshness at the same time as he introduced the literary element into music.

K., H.

EURYANTHE

Opera in three acts by Weber. Book, by Helmine von Chezy, adapted from *L'Historie de Gérard de Nevers et de la belle et vertueuse Euryanthe, sa mie*. This is Weber's only 'Grand Opera', i.e. without spoken dialogue. Produced, Vienna, Kärnthnerthor Theatre, October 25, 1823 with Henriette Sontag; London, Covent Garden (in German), 1833; Dury Lane (in German), 1882, with Mmes. Sucher, Peschka-Leutner, Messrs. Nachbaur, Gura, Conductor Hans Richter. Probable American première, Metropolitan, New York, 1887, with Lilli Lehmann, Marianne Brandt, Max Alvary, Emil Fischer, conductor Anton Seidl. Revived Salzburg Festival, 1937, with Maria Reining, Kerstin Thorborg, Karl Friedrich, Alexander Sved, conductor Bruno Walter; Edinburgh Festival, 1958, with Wissmann, Borkh, Traxel, Neidlinger; Florence Festival, 1954, with Wilfert, Borkh, Howard Vandenburg, Alexander Welitsch, conductor Giulini.

CHARACTERS

Euryanthe of Savoy .... Soprano
Eglantine of Puiset .... Mezzo-Soprano
Count Lysiart of Forêt .... Baritone
Count Adolar of Nevers .... Tenor
Louis VII .... Bass

Rudolph, *a knight* .... Tenor
Bertha .... Soprano
Time: Beginning of the Twelfth Century   *Place:* France

Act I. The Palace of the King. Count Adolar chants the
beauty and virtue of his betrothed, Euryanthe. Count Lysiart
sneers and boasts that he can lead her astray. The two
noblemen stake their possessions upon the result.

Garden of the Palace of Nevers. Euryanthe sings of her
longing for Adolar. Eglantine, the daughter of a rebellious
subject who, made a prisoner, has, on Euryanthe's plea, been
allowed the freedom of the domain, is in love with Adolar.
She has sensed that Euryanthe and her lover guard a secret.
Hoping to estrange Adolar from her, she seeks to gain
Euryanthe's confidence and only too successfully. For
Euryanthe confides to her that Adolar's dead sister, who lies
in the lonely tomb in the garden, has appeared to Adolar and
herself and confessed that, her lover having been slain in
battle, she has killed herself by drinking poison from her ring;
nor can her soul find rest until someone, innocently accused,
shall wet the ring with tears. To hold this secret inviolate has
been imposed upon Euryanthe by Adolar as a sacred duty.
Too late she repents of having communicated it to Eglantine
who, on her part, is filled with malicious glee. Lysiart arrives
to conduct Adolar's betrothed to the royal palace.

Act II.   Lysiart despairs of accomplishing his fell purpose,
when Eglantine emerges from the tomb with the ring and
reveals to him its secret. In the royal palace, before a brilliant
assembly, Lysiart claims to have won his wager, and, in
proof, produces the ring, the secret of which he claims
Euryanthe has communicated to him. She protests her
innocence, but in vain. Adolar renounces his rank and estates
and, dragging Euryanthe after him, rushes into the forest
where he intends to kill her and then himself.

Act III.   In a rocky mountain gorge Adolar draws his
sword and is about to slay Euryanthe, who in vain protests
her innocence. At that moment a huge serpent appears.
Euryanthe throws herself between it and Adolar in order to
save him. He fights the serpent and kills it; then, although
Euryanthe vows she would rather he slew her than not love
her, he goes his way leaving her to heaven's protection. She is
discovered by the King, who credits her story and promises
to vindicate her when she tells him that it was through

Eglantine, to whom she disclosed the secret of the tomb, that Lysiart obtained possession of the ring.

Gardens of Nevers, where preparations are being made for the wedding of Lysiart and Eglantine. Adolar enters in black armour with visor down. Eglantine, still madly in love with him and dreading her union with Lysiart, is so affected by the significance of the complete silence with which the assembled villagers and others watch her pass, that, half out of her mind, she raves about the unjust degradation she has brought upon Euryanthe.

Adolar, disclosing his identity, challenges Lysiart to combat. But before they can draw, the King appears. In order to punish Adolar for his lack of faith in Euryanthe, he tells him that she is dead. Savagely triumphant over her rival's end, Eglantine now makes known the entire plot and is slain by Lysiart. At that moment Euryanthe rushes into Adolar's arms, Lysiart is led off a captive. Adolar's sister finds eternal rest in her tomb because the ring has been bedewed by the tears of the innocent Euryanthe.

Apart from its overture *Euryanthe* has never been popular. The overture consists of two vigorous, stirringly dramatic sections separated by the weird tomb motif. The opening chorus in the King's palace is sonorous and effective. There is a very beautiful romanza for Adolar (''Neath almond trees in blossom'). In the challenge of the knights to the test of Euryanthe's virtue occurs the vigorous phrase with which the overture opens. Euryanthe has an exquisite cavatina ('Chimes in the valley'); there is an effective duet for Euryanthe and Eglantine ('Threatful gather clouds about me'). A scene for Eglantine is followed by the finale—a chorus with solo for Euryanthe.

Lysiart's recitative and aria ('Where seek to hide?'), expressive of hatred and defiance—a powerfully dramatic number—opens the second act. There is a darkly premonitory duet for Lysiart and Eglantine. Adolar has a tranquil aria ('When zephyrs waft me peace') with a beautiful woodwind introduction; its fine *allegro* melody is prominent in the overture. There is a duet full of abandon with Euryanthe ('To you my soul I give'). The finale is a quartet with chorus. The hunting chorus in the last act, previous to the King's discovery of Euryanthe, has been called Weber's finest inspiration.

Many efforts have been made by means of a new libretto

or by re-editing to give *Euryanthe* the position it deserves in
the modern operatic repertory. An attempt at a new libretto
was made in Paris in 1857, at the Théâtre Lyrique. It failed.
Having read a synopsis of that libretto, I can readily understand why. It is, if possible, more absurd than the original.
Shakespeare's *Cymbeline* is derived from the same source as
Euryanthe, which shows that, after all, something could be
made of the story.   K.

OBERON

Opera in three acts, by Carl Maria von Weber. Text, in English by
James Robertson Planché. The original story appeared in *La Bibliothèque Bleue* under the title of *Huon de Bordeaux*. Wieland adapted
this story to form his poem *Oberon*, and Planché took his libretto
from Sotheby's translation of Wieland. First performed at Covent
Garden, April 12, 1826, with Miss Paton as Reiza (Rezia only in
German versions), Mme. Vestris as Fatima, Braham as Huon and Bland
as Oberon, the composer conducting. First performance in New York,
1828. Revived, Metropolitan Opera, 1918, with Ponselle, Alice Gentle,
Martinelli, Althouse, conducted by Bodanzky (with recitatives
composed by Bodanzky, instead of spoken dialogue); Salzburg, in
German under Walter, with, in 1932, Maria Müller, Lotte Schoene,
Helge Roswaenge, and, in 1934, Anny Konetzni, Anday, Kullman;
Holland Festival, 1950, with Gré Brouwenstijn, Anna Pollak, Frans
Vroons, conducted by Monteux (in German); Florence Festival, 1952,
in the Boboli Gardens in a production by Herbert Graf, with Doris
Doree, Gianna Pederzini, Tyge Tygesen, Gino Penno, conducted by
Fritz Stiedry (in Italian); Opéra, Paris, 1953, with Araujo, Gedda,
conducted by Cluytens, producer Maurice Lehmann; London 1970
(BBC, in concert) with Joan Carlyle, Alberto Remedios, conductor
Pritchard.

CHARACTERS

Sir Huon of Bordeaux .... Tenor
Sherasmin, *his squire* .... Baritone
Oberon, *King of the Fairies* .... Tenor
Puck .... Soprano
Reiza, *daughter of Haroun el Rashid* .... Soprano
Fatima, *her attendant* ....Mezzo-Soprano
A Sea Nymph .... Soprano

Charlemagne, *Emperor of the Franks*
Haroun el Rashid, *Calif*
Babekan, *a Saracen Prince*
Almanzor, *Emir of Tunis*
Abdullah, *a Corsair*   } Speaking Parts
Titania, *Oberon's wife*
Roshana, *wife of Almanzor*
Namouna, *Fatima's grandmother*
Nadina, *a female of Almanzor's Harem*

The overture, which is one of the best known and most popular of concert pieces, is made up entirely of music which is employed elsewhere in the opera. The horn call (ex. 1) with which it opens, plays a prominent part throughout and is used in rather the same way as the magic instruments in *The Magic Flute*. It is followed by a figure of soft, quickly

descending woodwind chords (ex. 2), which at once suggests the atmosphere of fairyland; its light, airy quality sets the scene for the opening fairy chorus. Two themes follow, still played softly and mysteriously; they are heard again at the end of the opera, as a triumphant march. Atmosphere and tempo change and we hear a stormy figure in the strings (ex. 3); this returns as an accompanying figure to the quartet in

Act II, when the four lovers escape to the ship. The fairy chords have the effect of calming down the violent *allegro* section, and a theme of great beauty (ex. 4), which Huon later sings in the big *scena*, is heard on the clarinet and is then taken over by the strings. This leads straight into an exultant tune (ex. 5), which is typically and unmistakably Weber—

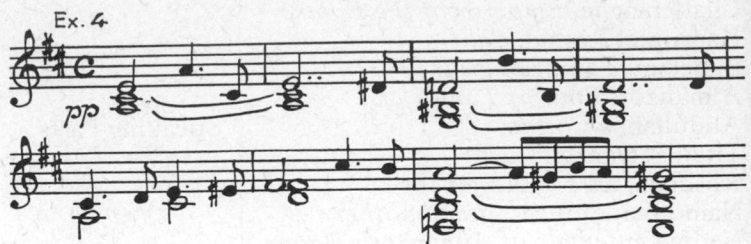

most people will recognise it as from the closing section of Reiza's great aria 'Ocean, thou mighty monster'. As is so often his way with his triumphant themes, Weber first

introduces it quietly and unpretentiously, and it is not till after a recapitulation of the existing material and the introduction of a new, strong theme (later associated with Puck, ex. 6), that he allows us to feel the full force of this

exhilarating tune. It brings the overture to an exciting close.

Act I. The curtain rises to reveal Oberon's bower, where a group of fairies sing over their sleeping King a chorus which breathes the very atmosphere of enchantment. Example punctuates the various sentences, and the composer's marking is *Andante quasi allegretto* (sempre tutto pianissimo possibile). Puck appears and explains that Oberon, having quarrelled with his fairy partner Titania, has vowed never to be reconciled to her until he shall have found two lovers constant through every peril and temptation. To seek such a pair, Puck, his 'tricksy spirit', has ranged through the world in vain. Oberon wakes and, in an aria which fulfils the implications of its *agitato* introduction, laments the 'fatal oath' he has sworn. He learns that Puck has heard sentence passed on Sir Huon of Bordeaux, a young knight, who, having been insulted by the son of Charlemagne, has killed him in single combat and for this has been condemned by the Emperor to proceed to Bagdad, slay him who sits on the Caliph's right hand, and claim the Caliph's daughter as his bride.

Oberon instantly resolves to make this pair the instrument of his reunion with his Queen, and for this purpose he conjures up Huon and Sherasmin asleep before him, and enamours the knight by showing him Reiza, daughter of the Caliph, in a vision. Introduced by the horn call of the overture (ex. 1) she begs for help. (Reiza is the original form, as found in the libretto and in the first English edition of the score. It appears as Rezia in the earliest German score, where Huon is spelled Hüon.)

Oberon wakes Huon to the sound of fairy music, Huon promises to be faithful to his mission, and Oberon with a wave of his wand transports him and his squire to Bagdad. The contrast between the utterances of the mortal Huon and the immortal Oberon is most marked, and the transformation (an enharmonic change from F minor to D major) makes as lovely an effect musically as it should when staged. Huon rejoices at the prospect before him in music of florid cast accompanied by the chorus, and prepares, with the help of the magic horn Oberon has given him, to fulfil his mission.

Two non-musical episodes follow. In the first, Huon and Sherasmin rescue Prince Babekan from a lion. He turns out to be the betrothed of Reiza, but his evil disposition is soon apparent when he and his followers set on their rescuers; they are, however, put to flight. The knight next learns from an old woman, Namouna, that Reiza is to be married next day, but the Princess has been influenced, like her lover, by a vision and is resolved to be his alone. She believes that fate will protect her from her nuptials with Babekan.

Huon exults in his chivalrous role in a great *scena*, whose music exactly fits his youthful heroic character. The magnificent flourish of the opening section is succeeded by a lovely *andante* for the cello which later expresses Huon's sentiments as opposed to his heroic resolves. The *scena* returns to the *Allegro energico* of the beginning and the close is strenuous and forthright. It has been said with more than a little truth that to do justice to this music the singer requires the voice of a Wagnerian tenor and the technique of a coloratura soprano. The combination, if it ever existed, is by no means easy to find in the twentieth century.

The scene changes to the palace of Haroun el Rashid, where Reiza tells Fatima that nothing will induce her to marry anyone other than her destined knight; better death than union with the hated Babekan. The finale begins with a big solo for Reiza, in which she swears to be true to the knight she has as yet seen only in a vision. Fatima tells Reiza that her deliverer is at hand, and mistress and maid contemplate their coming bliss in a simple duettino. The sound of a march is heard and Reiza sings jubilantly above a soft chorus of palace guards and eunuchs.

Act II. We are at the court of Haroun el Rashid. A chorus of attendants and slaves sings the praises of the mighty Caliph, who sits serenely in their midst with Prince Babekan at his right. The Prince asks that there shall be no more delay before he is married to his promised Reiza, and Haroun orders that she be led into his presence. Preceded by dancing girls (to a short orchestral *allegretto grazioso*) she comes in. No sooner is the music ended than the clash of swords is heard outside and in a moment Reiza is in the arms of her rescuer. Huon fights Babekan and vanquishes him, and having spellbound the rest by a blast of the magic horn he and Sherasmin carry off Reiza and Fatima.

A scene without music serves to establish the flight of the four fugitives (they are set on by palace guards, but frighten them off with the help of the horn); it also gives them an opportunity to lose the horn in the course of the fight. Later we find Fatima and Sherasmin together, and, in the course of a love scene, Fatima finds occasion to sing a song of nostalgic import. 'A lonely Arab maid', marked by the composer *Andante amoroso*. The four lovers take ship to the sound of a quartet, the two women answering the two men, all four later joining in a rapturous ensemble to the accompaniment of the string figure of the overture (Ex. 3).

The scene changes to a rocky seashore. Puck calls together his spirits and instructs them to bring about the wreck of the ship in which Reiza and Huon are crossing the sea; the music ends with the rousing of the storm. No sooner are they gone about their work than Huon appears supporting the fainting figure of Reiza. His short *adagio* prayer for her recovery is one of the most beautiful passages in the score and reveals a tender, poetic side to Huon's character which is hitherto unsuspected. His prayer is answered, Reiza revives, and Huon goes off to see if there are other survivors of the wreck.

Reiza is alone. She apostrophises the sea, whose very repose carries menace but whose fury is terrible indeed. 'Ocean, thou mighty monster' is a justly famous aria for dramatic soprano, and, with the overture, it is the one number of *Oberon* which will be familiar to everybody. It is an extended *scena*, modelled on the lines of Agathe's big solo in *Freischütz*, but more dramatic in content. It opens with a grand recitativic introduction, continues with a swelling *allegro con moto* section describing the storm which is still in progress, sinks to the comparative calm of the *maestoso assai*, but rises again steeply as Reiza catches sight of something moving, reaching a climax of excitement as she realises it is a ship; the concluding *Presto con fuoco* is one of the most thrilling passages in opera and is familiar to everyone as the final section of the overture (Ex. 5).

But the ship Reiza has seen turns out to be manned by pirates, who pause only to make her prisoner, and leave Huon, who attempts to rescue her, senseless on the shore.

For the finale, we are back in an atmosphere which is Weber at his most idyllic. The sensuously graceful song of the Sea Nymphs in 6/8 has a magic of its own, but the whole scene, with its short duet for Oberon and Puck and its extended and mostly *pianissimo* chorus of fairies, is wonderfully beautiful. This is pure fairy music, such as even such a specialist as Mendelssohn never excelled (*Midsummer Night's Dream*, like *Oberon*, was written in 1826), and its delicacy and soft charm can never fail to astonish an unsuspecting listener and ravish his musical susceptibilities.

Act III. Fatima, saved with Sherasmin from the wreck but now like him a slave in Tunis, laments her changed fortune in a song with pronounced character-flavour, 'O Araby, dear Araby, my own native land'. But she cannot prevent her natural cheerfulness breaking into the refrain with its repeated 'Al, al, al, al, al, al'. Sherasmin, who works in the same establishment for one Ibrahim, joins her and together they reflect sadly on the distance each of them has come since childhood; again, they finish by looking on the bright side—at least they are together in their slavery, and have a kind master. But a surprise is round the corner and Puck brings in Huon. There is a great recognition, and Fatima says she has even heard that Reiza is in Tunis, but where she does not know. They plan to dress Huon up and get him employment with Ibrahim.

The scene changes to the palace of the Emir of Tunis, where Reiza lies a captive, and has become, like Mozart's Constanze before her, the principal object of a noble master's affections. She grieves for her lost love in an F minor aria of pure and mournful beauty, the counterpart of Huon's prayer in the previous act, 'Mourn thou poor heart'. Like the Pasha Selim, Almanzor respects the grief of his prisoner and tells her he will not use force to compel her to yield to his love.

Huon receives a message, conveyed in the symbolic language of the East by means of flowers. Fatima interprets it for him and tells him it is from Reiza; he is to go at once to her. Huon's rondo, 'I revel in hope and joy again', is likely to test the agility of the tenor but is of comparatively conventional musical value. He is led to the Emir's palace where, in fact, Reiza is incarcerated, but is confronted instead with the Emir's wife, Roshana, thirsting for revenge on the husband who has discarded her in favour of the beautiful captive. She assures Huon that he will have earned her love and the throne of Tunis if he will help her dispose of her erring husband. Neither the prospect of power nor of her love can turn the hero from his purpose, which is to free Reiza, and he has little difficulty in resisting the efforts which Roshana employs to seduce him; his musical answers to the vocal and balletic blandishments of Roshana's attendants are nothing if not firm.

As Huon is rushing from her presence he is surprised and seized by Almanzor and his guard; Roshana tries to stab her husband and is arrested in her turn and led off by negro attendants. Almanzor commands that a pyre be erected and Huon burnt within the hour, and the efforts of Reiza to obtain his pardon only succeed in gaining for her a similar sentence. At this juncture, Sherasmin, who has contrived entrance to the palace, has the magic horn miraculously restored to him, and with its help he is able to change the situation completely.

The sound of music has an exactly similar effect on Almanzor's court as it had on Monostatos's slaves; they no

onger have a desire to do anything but dance, and the four
overs, now reunited, resolve to summon the aid of Oberon in
an effort not only to suspend but to dissolve completely the
nightmare situation in which they find themselves. The god
appears in answer to the horn's blast, and in a short but
beautiful aria hails the faithful, loving pair and tells them that
their prayers are answered and he will restore them to safety
and happiness. They are transported to the court of
Charlemagne, who takes his place with his entourage to the
sound of a march. Huon tells him his commands have been
fulfilled, and he is here with Reiza to claim the promised
pardon. This is granted and the opera ends with a chorus of
praise and thanksgiving.

Oberon has always resisted the efforts which have from
time to time been made to fit it neatly into the category of
German romantic opera. Its pattern is undeniably unconventional, and the signs are that Weber himself was disturbed
by several aspects of the dramatic plan. Various attempts
have been made to adapt the opera for performance, and it is
safe to say that it has been heard far less often in the form in
which Weber left it than in the various arrangements to which
it has been subjected.

Bodanzky composed recitatives in place of the spoken
dialogue for the production at the Metropolitan in 1918, but
otherwise left the score intact. More important is the version
prepared by Mahler in conjunction with the scenic designer
Alfred Roller, with a new German translation by Gustav
Brecher. Mahler arranged a number of musical sections,
usually (but not always) in conjunction with spoken dialogue
as opposed to singing, which he designated 'Melodram'; these
are not given separate numbers in his edition but are clearly
indicated as 13a and 13b in the score. There are eight of
these additions, and they have the effect of connecting
certain sections of the music very closely with the dramatic
action, most particularly of course the horn call, which is
heard at the beginning of the overture, and which in Mahler's
arrangement assumes a musical status comparable to that of
Papageno's pipes. A section of music is introduced to lead
up to the vision of Reiza in Act I, and another to reinforce
the giving of the magic horn by Oberon to Sherasmin before
the ensemble during which takes place the transformation
from France to Bagdad. In Act II, the bewitching of Haroun's

court is made more plausible by means of musical accom
paniment, and the flight of the two pairs of lovers ha
orchestral accompaniment from the moment the hor
invokes Oberon's aid, Oberon and Reiza later betwee
them singing the short aria of Oberon which occurs i
the finale of the third act (in Mahler's version it is th
heard twice). After Reiza has been carried away by th
pirates (which occurs immediately after she has sung 'Ocear
thou mighty monster'), Oberon laments the hard nature c
their trials in a shortened version of his first aria, and Puc
anticipates the fairy music of the finale by singing
reminiscence (shortened, and in C instead of F) of the fair
chorus at the opening of Act I. In Act III, Huon's return jus
before the trio with Fatima and Sherasmin is heralded by
melodrama for Puck, and Mahler omits entirely the rondo fc
Huon which should follow Reiza's F minor aria. The pre
parations for the public burning of Huon are made to th
sound of the march which, later in the finale, reintroduce
Huon to the court of Charlemagne.

The fact that arrangements of the score have been mad
should not influence one to think that *Oberon* is im
practicable; it is unconventional in much the same way a
The Magic Flute is unconventional, with of course th
important difference that Mozart was increasing the statur
of a form—*Singspiel*—which he understood exceedingly wel
whereas Weber, with whom drama and continuity were neve
the strongest points, was attempting a form—Englis
pantomime in its original state (Planché founded pantomime
—which he found completely strange. There is no need t
elevate Weber to Mozart's level: *Oberon* is musically stron
enough to stand on its own merits. No one would deny tha
it would be extremely difficult to achieve a perfect pe
formance nowadays; it is not easy to find a singer for Reiz
almost impossible to think of one to do justice to Huon. Th
production would have to give the impression of being lavis
as well as imaginative. On the other hand the intrinsic meri
of the opera are so great that attempts to stage it are likely t
increase in frequency rather than the reverse; one wonde
how long the country for which Weber originally wrote th
work will continue to ignore it.   H.

ALBERT LORTZING
(1801–1851)
ZAR UND ZIMMERMANN
Tsar and Carpenter

COMIC opera in three acts by Albert Lortzing. Text by the composer, founded on a French play by J. T. Merle. First produced, Leipzig, December 22, 1837; New York, 1851; London, Gaiety Theatre, 1871 (in English, as *Peter the Shipwright*), with Santley and Blanche Cole. Still popular in German-speaking theatres which during 1958–9 played 565 operas by 290 composers. Lortzing with 1,044 performances in 62 theatres came fourth in the list of composers, after Verdi, Mozart and Puccini. *Der Wildschütz* was the second most popular individual opera!

CHARACTERS

Peter I, *Tsar of Russia* .... Baritone
Peter Ivanov, *a runaway Soldier* .... Tenor
van Bett, *Burgomaster of Saardam* .... Bass
Marie, *his niece* .... Soprano
Admiral Lefort, *Russian Ambassador* .... Bass
Lord Syndham, *English Ambassador* .... Bass
Marquis de Chateauneuf, *French Ambassador* .... Tenor
Witwe Browe .... Contralto

Time: 1698   *Place:* Saardam, in Holland

Act I.   Peter the Great of Russia, under the name of Peter Michaelov, is working in the ship-building yards at Saardam, in Holland, with a view to gaining experience and knowledge such as he could never find in Russia itself. He has become friends with Peter Ivanov, another Russian and a deserter from the armed forces. Peter Ivanov has fallen in love with Marie, the Burgomaster's niece, a coquette who cannot resist showing him that he is not the only attractive man about the place. Van Bett, the comically self-opinionated Burgomaster, has been approached by the Ambassadors of England and France to find out if the Tsar is secretly working in Saardam. He calls together the ship-workers, and finding many are called Peter, determines on a subtle and, he thinks, foolproof

stratagem: which of them, he asks, is a foreigner? To his
consternation, two step forward—Peter Ivanov and Peter
Michaelov. He needs time to fathom it all out; let everyone
go back to work—he has all the information he requires. He
decides that Peter Ivanov is the man he is looking for, and
accordingly offers him whatever he chooses, even the hand of
his niece in marriage, if he will admit his identity to the
foreign gentleman he will presently introduce him to. At the
end of the act, the French Ambassador has recognised the
Tsar and even made contact with him, while Syndham and
van Bett, thinking Ivanov is the man they are looking for,
start to pay court to him.

Act II.   A local festivity is in progress. All the principals
of the opera watch the dancing and listen to the singing, and
the French Ambassador even sings a song in praise of
Flemish beauty, much to the chagrin of Peter Ivanov, who
takes it to be aimed at Marie. The principal characters divide
into two groups: Peter Michaelov, the French and Russian
Ambassadors on one side, Peter Ivanov, van Bett, and Lord
Syndham on the other, and negotiations proceed. Van Bett
has had a good deal to drink, and he thinks the time has
come for him to solve his problem in his own way. He
demands, with more forthrightness than manners, the name
and identification of the three Ambassadors present in the
inn. Somewhat taken aback by their answers, he announces
he will arrest the two Peters, and is only prevented from
carrying out his design—in spite of the remonstrance of all
present—when the Tsar draws his sword and announces he
will not be taken alive.

Act III.   Van Bett prepares to send 'the Tsar' on his way
with full musical honours. He rehearses his choir and tells
them that he himself will sing the solo part; nothing is too
much trouble if it will honour their noble visitor. The Tsar
himself has in the meanwhile found the means to provide
himself with a ship in which to sail home, promising before
he leaves a safe conduct for Peter Ivanov. Van Bett starts off
his anthem (which he directs at Ivanov, still thinking him the
Tsar), but is interrupted by the sound of a cannon shot; the
real Tsar is about to leave the harbour. He pauses for a
moment to take leave of his friends, and is gone to the
acclamation of the crowd.

The music of *Zar und Zimmermann* is anything but
complicated, and its square-cut choruses and straightforward

olos revealed little unusual in the imagination of their
omposer. The best role is for van Bett, whose entrance aria
n Act I, with its catch phrase, 'Oh, ich bin klug und weise', is
favourite with German comic basses. Perhaps the most
njoyable moment in the opera is his rehearsal in the last act;
his is capital fun, with van Bett's 'diddle-dum, diddle-dum,
iddle-dum' to show when the orchestra plays alone, and his
elish of the excellence of his own words. In Act II, the
rench Ambassador has a charming solo, 'Lebewohl mein
landrisch' Mädchen', and in the last act occur the Tsar's
ong, 'Sonst spielt' ich mit Szepter und Kron' and the Clog
ance, the latter a direct forerunner of Wagner's apprentices.

H.

DER WILDSCHÜTZ
The Poacher

Opera in three acts by Albert Lortzing. Text by the composer based
n a play by A. von Kotzebue. First produced at Leipzig, December 31,
842. First performance in England, Drury Lane, 1895 (in German);
Jew York, 1856. Edinburgh Festival, 1958, by Stuttgart Opera, with
.ore Wissmann, Plümacher, Wunderlich, Schmitt-Walter, Fritz Linke,
onductor Leitner.

CHARACTERS

Count of Eberbach .... Baritone
The Countess, *his wife* .... Contralto
Baron Kronthal, *her brother* .... Tenor
Baroness Freimann, *a young widow, sister of the Count*
.... Soprano
Nanette, *her maid* .... Soprano
Baculus, *a schoolmaster on the Count's estate* Buffo-Bass
Gretchen, *his fiancée* .... Soprano
Pancratius, *majordomo to the Count* .... Speaking Part
        Servants, Huntsmen, Peasants, Schoolboys

Der Wildschütz is probably, with *Zar und Zimmermann*,
.ortzing's most popular opera; the story is amusing, and the
xcellent comic role of Baculus has the additional merit of

being unique—there can be no other poaching schoolmaster in operatic annals. His 'Fünftausend Thaler' aria is one of the most celebrated solos in the repertory of the German bass. In addition, the score contains another unique feature, a fine comedy quintet—at the billiard table!

Act I.   Baculus has accidentally shot a buck in a wood belonging to Count Eberbach, on whose estate he is employed as schoolmaster. He is filled with consternation when he receives a summons to the castle to account for his poaching. Gretchen, his bride-to-be, says she will intercede for him, but Baculus mistrusts this offer and will not allow her to go. A young student offers to help them in their dilemma and go dressed as Gretchen to ask for the Count's pardon (the student is in reality the Baroness Freimann in disguise; accompanied by her maid Nanette—also dressed as a boy—she wishes, unknown to him, to observe her betrothed, Baron Kronthal). Count Eberbach and the Baron arrive at the school and the Count, taking an instant liking to the supposed Gretchen, invites her and her friends to his birthday celebrations next day.

Act II.   Baculus accompanies the disguised Baroness to the castle. Here everybody is enchanted by her country airs, the Count tries to make love to her on the sly, Baron Kronthal even goes so far as to contemplate matrimony. To save the situation, the Countess takes the 'village girl' into her own room for the night. Meanwhile the Baron offers Baculus no less than 5,000 thalers if he will give up his bride. It is more than the schoolmaster can resist.

Act III.   Baculus sets about persuading Gretchen to fall in with the new situation, only to find to his consternation that the Baron is interested in the Gretchen he first met, not in the real bearer of that name. Baculus's admission that this was a student in disguise has unforeseen consequences: Baron Kronthal is furious that a man should have passed the night in his sister's room—for the Countess, it appears, is his sister. The discovery that the supposed Gretchen is really a student who is really Baroness Freimann solves all problems: the Count, who has been caught kissing her, is able to pass it off as only natural that he should kiss his sister, and the Countess is cleared of all blame.

As for the unhappy Baculus, he receives a full pardon from the Count, and he is even reconciled to Gretchen.   H.

OTTO NICOLAI

(1810–1849)

DIE LUSTIGEN WEIBER VON WINDSOR

The Merry Wives of Windsor

?ERA in three acts by Otto Nicolai. Text by Hermann von Mosenthal, ter Shakespeare's play. First produced at the Berlin Hofoper, March 1849 (the composer died in May), with Zschiesche as Falstaff and e composer conducting. First produced, Philadelphia, 1863; London, r Majesty's 1864 (in Italian), with Tietjens, Vitali, Jura, Santley; lelphi Theatre, London, 1878 (in English); Metropolitan, New York, 00 (in German), with Sembrich, Friedrichs, Dippel, conducted by nil Paur; Covent Garden, 1907 (in German), with Jenny Fischer, nnie Nast, Max Lohfing, Franz Naval. Revived by the Carl Rosa mpany, 1943, with Ruth Packer, Gladys Parr, Norman Allin, Robert dney, conductor Charles Webber; hundredth anniversary production Berlin, Staatsoper, 1949, with Irma Beilke, Margarete Klose, Otto pf, Helmut Krebs, conductor Johannes Schüler.

CHARACTERS

Sir John Falstaff	Bass
Herr Fluth (*Mr. Ford*)	Baritone
Herr Reich (*Mr. Page*)	Bass
Fenton	Tenor
Junker Spärlich (*Slender*)	Tenor
Dr. Caius	Bass
Frau Fluth (*Mistress Ford*)	Soprano
Frau Reich (*Mistress Page*)	Mezzo-Soprano
Jungfer Anna Reich (*Anne Page*)	Soprano
First Citizen	Tenor

me: Reign of Henry IV   *Place:* Windsor

Nicolai, who died before he was thirty-nine, had a busy life professional music-making, and his career embraced such verse activities as organist at the Prussian Embassy in ome, Kapellmeister in Vienna, composer in Italy, founder d conductor of the Berlin Philharmonic, and head of the era in that city. He composed a number of operas, of

which *Die lustigen Weiber von Windsor* is by far the mos
successful, as is hardly surprising in view of the wit, neatness
of construction, and light-hearted gaiety for which it is
distinguished.

Act I.   After an overture which is one of the mos
popular in the concert repertory, we find ourselves in the
garden between the houses of Messrs. Ford and Page (to give
them their Shakespearean names), where their respective
spouses are comparing notes on the love-letters they have
each received that day from no lesser person than Sir John
Falstaff. They leave the stage to the men. Page has promised
the hand of his daughter in marriage to Slender, whom he
prefers to her other suitors, Caius and Fenton, in spite of the
impassioned pleading of the last-named; Fenton is told Ann is
not for a have-not like himself.

Inside Ford's house, his wife waits for the promised visit
from Falstaff. She is furious with all men, and rehearses
what she shall say to this particular specimen. She will make
as if to give in to him—woman's heart is weak, she observes
he will be taken in and believe her. This is a big-scale
coloratura aria, 'Nun eilt herbei', with an elaborate recitative
and much exacting passage work for the singer.

Falstaff duly arrives, his love scene is interrupted by loud
knocking, he hides in the linen basket, and Ford storms in
announcing he has caught his wife at last and bringing a
crowd of witnesses to watch the proceedings. The search
begins and the women laugh at the way their well-planned
joke is taking shape—Falstaff is to be dumped into the river
The light touch of the duet contrasts well with Mistress
Ford's scolding of Ford for his base, unworthy suspicion of
her. The act ends with a general ensemble.

Act II.   We meet Falstaff on home ground for a change
and he leads a drinking song at the 'Gasthaus zum
Hosenbande'—The Garter Inn. 'Als Büblein klein' has always
been popular and it is still a war-horse in the repertory of the
German operatic bass; it is in fact an admirably simple and
highly effective piece. Ford, calling himself Brook (or 'Bach'
in the German), comes to pump Falstaff on the subject of his
relations with Mistress Ford. Their comic duet is admirable
Falstaff's patter being interspersed with horrified inter
jections from Ford. 'Wie freu' ich mich' each sings in turn
the one rejoicing at the prospect of his rendezvous, the other
at the possibility of catching Falstaff in the act. The audience

5 *Così fan tutte*: Hermann Prey, Waldemar Kmentt, Carl Dönch, Graziella Sciutti, Elisabeth Schwarzkopf and Christa Ludwig in Act I of Rennert's famous production at Salzburg.

6 *Fidelio:* Lotte Lehmann, Salzburg, 1935.

too should have the chance of rejoicing at the opportunity
for the competition the music gives to the two singers, an
opportunity not missed in Vienna in the early years of this
century when the richly endowed Leopold Demuth and
Wilhelm Hesch poured their great voices into the roles of
Ford and Falstaff; a splendid gramophone recording exists to
prove the point.

The scene changes to Page's garden, where no less than
three suitors are preparing to serenade Anne. Two of them,
Slender and Caius, make a decidedly comic effect, the other,
Fenton, is distinctly romantic; in fact his 'Horch, die Lerche
singt im Hain' is a deliciously pretty tune. There follows a
pleasant little love duet for Anne and Fenton and a most
ingenious 'quartettino' (as Nicolai calls it) for Anne and the
three lovers, the comic pair overhearing what the other two
are saying to each other, and handing the tune, which was
first sung by Anne, backwards and forwards from one to
another until all four are engaged on it. The whole of this
garden scene is controlled by the lightest of hands and its
delicacy is quite unusual amongst German comic operas of
the period—by comparison it makes Lortzing sound the
clodhopper he unfortunately so often turns out to be.

We are back in Ford's house, as in Act I. Ford tells his wife
she will be found out this time; nothing will prevent him
catching her lover. He is furious—he even examines the
laundry basket which the servants happen to bring through
the room at this moment—and his wife laughs at him. Caius,
Slender, Page knock at the door saying they are there, as
Ford instructed them. Falstaff is smuggled through dressed as
an old woman and guided by Mistress Page. He pretends not
to be able to hear Ford's questions and is got rid of to general
acclamation. There is another unsuccessful search, and the
act ends with an ensemble.

Act III.   The first scene is laid in Mistress Page's house,
and there she sings her ballad of Herne the Hunter, an
agreeable 6/8 tune. Later Anne delivers herself of the aria
which alone makes the role worth a prima donna's while.

The last scene is laid in Windsor Forest, near what the
score describes as 'die Eiche des Jägers Herne', or Herne the
Hunter's Oak—an English description of *Freischütz* probably
sounds just as odd to a German. Here the music we know so
well from the overture comes into its own, and is deployed in
a succession of choruses and dance movements associated

with the preparation and tormenting of Falstaff by the disguised company. Falstaff himself has a trio with the wives of Ford and Page—he makes advances to them both—Anne and Fenton, disguised as Titania and Oberon, have a short duet between ballet movements, and finally the big tune of the overture makes its presence felt. All is resolved and the opera ends with a short trio with chorus.   H.

FRIEDRICH
von FLOTOW
(1812–1883)
MARTHA

OPERA in five acts by Friedrich von Flotow; text by W. Friedrich after a ballet-pantomime, *Lady Henriette, ou La Servante de Greenwich*, by St.-Georges, for which Flotow wrote part of the music. Première at the Kärnthnerthor Theater, Vienna, on November 25, 1847, with Anna Zerr, Alois Ander, Formes. First performed New York, 1852, with Anna Bishop; London, Drury Lane, 1849 (in German), 1858 (in English), Covent Garden, 1858, with Bosio, Didiée, Mario, Graziani; Paris, Théâtre-Lyrique, December 16, 1865, when was interpolated the famous air 'M'Appari', from Flotow's two-act opera, *L'Ame en Peine*, produced at the Opéra, Paris, June, 1846; Metropolitan, New York, 1884, with Sembrich, Trebelli, Stagno, Novara; 1905, with Sembrich, Walker, Caruso, Plançon; 1923, with Alda, Howard, Gigli, de Luca; 1961, with de los Angeles, Elias, Tucker, Tozzi. Revived Covent Garden, 1930, with Edith Mason, Gigli; la Scala, 1931, with Favero, Pederzini, Pertile, Stabile; 1938, with Favero, Elmo, Gigli, Maugeri; Wexford Festival, 1956, with Vivarelli, Shacklock, Traxel, Rothmüller.

CHARACTERS
Lady Harriet Durham, *Maid of Honour to Queen Anne*
.... Soprano
Sir Tristram Mickleford, *her cousin*............ Bass
Plunkett, *a young farmer* .... Bass
Lionel, *his foster-brother; afterwards Earl of Derby*Tenor
Nancy, *waiting-maid to Lady Harriet* .... Contralto

Sheriff .... Bass
Three Man Servants .... ⎰   Tenor and two Basses
Three Maid Servants .... ⎱ Soprano and Mezzo-Soprano
Courtiers, Pages, Ladies, Hunters and Huntresses, Farmers
Time: About 1710   *Place:* In and near Richmond

The first act opens in Lady Harriet's boudoir. The second
scene of this act is the fair at Richmond. The scene of the
second act is laid in Plunkett's farm-house; that of the third
in a forest near Richmond. The fourth act opens in the
farm-house and changes to Lady Harriet's park.

Act I. Scene i.   The Lady Harriet yawned. It was dull
even at the court of Queen Anne. The simple fact is that
Lady Harriet, like many others whose pleasures come so
easily that they lack zest, was bored. Even the resourceful
Nancy was at last driven to exclaim: 'If your ladyship only
would fall in love!'

But herein, too, Lady Harriet had the surfeit that creates
indifference. She had bewitched every man at court only to
remain unmoved by their protestations of passion. Even as
Nancy spoke, a footman announced the most persistent of
her ladyship's suitors, Sir Tristram Mickleford, an elderly
cousin who presumed upon his relationship to ignore the
rebuffs with which she met his suit.

'Most respected cousin, Lady-in-Waiting to Her Most
Gracious Majesty,' he began sententiously, and would have
added all her titles had she not cut him short with an
impatient gesture, 'will your ladyship seek diversion by
viewing the donkey races with me to-day?'

'I wonder,' Nancy whispered, 'if he is going to run in the
races himself?' which evoked from the Lady Harriet the first
smile that had played around her lips that day.

Likely enough Sir Tristram's fair cousin would soon have
sent him on some errand that would have taken him out of
her presence. But when he opened the window, in came the
strains of a merry chorus sung by fresh, happy voices of
young women who, evidently, were walking along the
highway. The Lady Harriet's curiosity was piqued. Who were
these women over whose lives ennui never seemed to have
hung like a pall? Nancy knew all about them. There were
servants on the way to Richmond fair to hire themselves out
to the farmers, according to time-honoured custom.

The Richmond fair! To her ladyship's jaded sense it
conveyed a suggestion of something new and frolicsome.

'Nancy,' she cried, carried away with the novelty of the idea, 'let us go to the fair dressed as peasant girls and mingle with the crowd! Who knows, someone might want to hire us! I will call myself Martha, you can be Julia, and you, cousin, can drop your title for the nonce and go along with us as plain Bob!'

Scene ii.   Meanwhile Richmond fair was at its height. From a large parchment the pompous Sheriff had read the law by which all contracts for service made at the fair were binding for at least one year as soon as money had passed. Among those who had come to bid were a sturdy young farmer, Plunkett, and his foster-brother Lionel. The latter evidently was of a gentler birth, but his parentage was shrouded in mystery. As a child he had been left with Plunkett's mother by a fugitive, an aged man who, dying from exposure and exhaustion, had confided the boy to her care, first, however, handing her a ring with the injunction, if misfortune ever threatened the boy, to show the ring to the Queen.

One after another the girls proclaimed their deftness at cooking, sewing, gardening, poultry tending, and other domestic and rural accomplishments, the Sheriff crying out, 'Four guineas! Who'll have her?—Five guineas! Who'll try her?'

Just then they heard a young woman's voice behind them call out, 'No, I won't go with you!' and, turning, they saw two sprightly young women arguing with a testy-looking old man. Lionel and Plunkett nudged each other. Never had they seen such attractive-looking girls. And when they heard one of them call out again to the old man, 'No, we won't go with you!'—for Sir Tristram was urging the Lady Harriet and Nancy to leave the fair—the young men hurried over to the group.

'Can't you hear her say she won't go with you?' asked Lionel, while Plunkett called out to the girls near the Sheriff's stand, 'Here, girls, is a bidder with lots of money!' A moment later the absurd old man was the centre of a rioting, shouting crowd of girls, who followed him when he tried to retreat, so that finally 'Martha' and 'Julia' were left quite alone with the two men. The young women were in high spirits. They had sallied forth in quest of adventure and here it was. After a few slyly reassuring glances from them, Plunkett overcame his hesitancy and spoke up:

'You're our choice, girls!'

'Done!' cried the girls, who thought it all a great lark, and a moment later the Lady Harriet had placed her hand in Lionel's and Nancy hers in Plunkett's and money had passed to bind the bargain.

The escapade seemed to have gone far enough and the two girls looked about for Sir Tristram to take them away. 'None of that,' said the two farmers, and, when the crowd again gathered about Sir Tristram, they hurried off the girls and drove away, while the crowd blocked the blustering knight and jeered as he vainly tried to break away in pursuit.

Act II.   The adventure of the Lady Harriet and her maid Nancy, so lightly entered upon, was carrying them further than they had expected. To find themselves set down in a humble farm-house, and to be told to go into the kitchen and prepare supper, was more than they had bargained for.

Lionel suggested as a substitute for the kitchen that they be allowed to try their hands at the spinning-wheels. But they were so awkward at these that the men sat down to show them how to spin, until Nancy brought the lesson to an abrupt close by saucily overturning Plunkett's wheel and dashing away with the young farmer in pursuit, leaving Lionel and 'Martha' alone.

It was an awkward moment for her ladyship; to relieve the situation she began to hum and finally to sing, choosing her favourite air, 'The Last Rose of Summer'. But it had the very opposite effect of what she had planned. Lionel, completely carried away, exclaimed: 'Ah, Martha, if you were to marry me, you no longer would be a servant, for I would raise you to my own station!'

Just then fortunately Plunkett dragged in Nancy, whom he had pursued into the kitchen, where she had upset things generally before he had been able to seize her; and a distant tower clock striking midnight, the young farmers allowed their servants, whose accomplishments as such, if they had any, so far remained undiscovered, to retire to their room, while they sought theirs, but not before Lionel had whispered:

'Perchance by the morrow, Martha, you will think differently of what I have said and not treat it so lightly.'

Act III.   But when morning came the birds had flown the cage. There was neither a Martha nor a Julia in the little farm-house, while at the court of Queen Anne a certain Lady Harriet and her maid Nancy were congratulating themselves that, after all, an old fop named Sir Tristram Mickleford had had sense enough to be in waiting with a carriage near the farm-house at midnight and help them escape through the window. The Lady Harriet was no longer bored; and even Nancy had lost her sprightliness. The simple fact is that the Lady Harriet and Nancy, without being certain of it them-selves, were in love.

It chanced that Lionel, in much the same state of mind and heart as her ladyship, was wandering, when suddenly looking up, he saw a young huntress in whom, in spite of her different costume, he recognised the 'Martha' over whose disappearance he had been grieving. But she was torn by conflicting feelings. However her heart might go out toward Lionel, her pride of birth still rebelled against permitting a peasant to address words of love to her. 'You are mistaken. I do not know you!' she exclaimed. And when he in anger began to upbraid her for denying her identity to him who was by law her master, she cried out for help bringing not only Sir Tristram but the entire hunting train to her side. Noting the deference with which she was treated and hearing her called 'My Lady', Lionel now perceived the trick that had been played upon himself and Plunkett at the fair.

Act IV.   Before very long, however, there was a material change in the situation. In his extremity, Lionel remembered about his ring and he asked Plunkett to show it to the Queen and plead his cause. The ring proved to have been the property of the Earl of Derby. It was that nobleman who, after the failure of a plot to recall James II from France and restore him to the throne, had died a fugitive and confided his son to the care of Plunkett's mother, and that son was none other than Lionel, now discovered to be the rightful heir to the title and estates.

Despite his new honours, however, Lionel was miserably unhappy. He was deeply in love with the Lady Harriet. Yet he hardly could bring himself to speak to her, let alone appear so much as even to notice the advances which she, in her contrition, so plainly made toward him.

This sad state of affairs might have continued indefinitely had not Nancy's nimble wit come to the rescue. She and Plunkett, after meeting again, had been quick in coming to an understanding, and now the first thing they did was to plan how to bring together Lionel and the Lady Harriet. One afternoon Plunkett joined Lionel in his lonely walk and, unknown to him, gradually guided him into her ladyship's garden. A sudden turn in the path brought them in view of a bustling scene. Then above it Lionel heard a sweet, familiar voice singing "Tis the last rose of summer'. A moment later, he held his 'Martha' in his arms.

Martha teems with melody. The best known airs are 'The Last Rose of Summer' and Lionel's 'Ach, so fromm' ('M'apparì'[1]: Like a dream). The best ensemble piece, a quintet with chorus, occurs near the close of Act III—'Mag der Himmel euch vergeben' ('Ah! che a voi perdoni Iddio': Heaven alone may grant you pardon). The spinning-wheel quartet in Act II is most sprightly. But, as indicated, there is a steady flow of light and graceful melody in this opera. Almost at the very opening of Act I, Lady Harriet and Nancy have a duet, 'Von den edlen Kavalieren' ('Questo duol che si v'affana': Sure, some noble lord attending). Bright, clever music abounds in the Richmond fair scene, and Lionel and Plunkett express their devotion to each other in 'Ja, seit früher Kindheit Tagen' ('Solo, profugo, reietto': Lost, proscribed, a friendless wanderer). Then there is the gay quartet when the two girls leave the fair with their masters, while the crowd surrounds Sir Tristram and prevents him from breaking through and interfering. It was in this scene that the bass singer Castelmary, the Sir Tristram of a performance of *Martha* at the Metropolitan Opera House, February 10, 1897, was striken with heart failure and dropped dead upon the stage.

A capital quartet opens Act II, in the farm-house, and leads to the spinning-wheel quartet, 'Was soll ich dazu sagen?' ('Che vuol dir ciò?': I know not what to say). There is a duet between Lady Harriet and Lionel, in which their growing attraction for each other finds expression, 'Blickt sein Aug' ('Il suo sguardo è dolce tanto': To his eye, mine gently meeting). Then follows 'Letzte Rose' ('Qui sola, vergin rosa': 'Tis the last rose of summer), the words of a poem by Tom Moore, the music an old Irish air, 'The Groves of Blarney', to which Moore adapted 'The Last Rose of Summer'. A new and effective touch is given to the old song by Flotow in having

---

[1] Internationally, the Italian words are better known than the original German and are here kept in brackets throughout.   H.

the tenor join with the soprano at the close. Moreover, the words and music fit so perfectly into the situation on the stage that for Flotow to have 'lifted' and interpolated them into his opera was a master-stroke. To it *Martha* owed much of its one-time popularity.

'Tis the last rose of sum-mer, Left bloom-ing a - lone

The scene ends with another quartet, one of the most beautiful numbers of the score, and known as the 'Good Night Quartet', 'Schlafe wohl! Und mag Dich reuen' ('Dormi pur, ma il mio riposo': Cruel one, may dreams transport thee).

Act III, played in a hunting park in Richmond forest, on the left a small inn, opens with a song in praise of beer, the 'Porterlied' by Plunkett, 'Lass mich euch fragen' ('Chi mi dirà': Will you tell me). The *pièces de résistance* of this act are the 'Ach, so fromm' ('M'apparì'):

a solo for Nancy, 'Jägerin, schlau im Sinn' ('Il tuo stral nel lanciar': Huntress fair, hastens where); Martha's song, written for Nantier Didiée; 'Quì tranquilla almen poss'io' ('Hier in stillen Schattengründen'; Here in deepest forest shadows); and the stirring quintet with chorus:

In Act IV there is a solo for Plunkett, 'Il mio Lionel perira' (Soon my Lionel will perish), and a repetition of some of the sprightly music of the fair scene.   K.

In the original article, Gustave Kobbé went so far as to group *Martha* with the French repertory on stylistic grounds. I have returned it to its rightful place amongst German works—oddly enough, it was as an Italian (rather than French or German) opera that it made its way in the international repertory, but in the latter half of the twentieth century it has held its position mainly in Germany. Although I cannot agree with Kobbé's view of *Martha* as a French opera, his reasoning is interesting and this is what he wrote:

'It is not without considerable hesitation that I have classed *Martha* as a French opera. For Flotow was born in Teutendorf, April 27, 1812, and died in Darmstadt, January 24, 1883. Moreover, *Martha* was produced in Vienna, and his next best known work, *Alessandro Stradella,* in Hamburg (1844).

'The music of *Martha*, however, has an elegance that not only is quite unlike any music that has come out of Germany, but is typically French. Flotow, in fact, was French in his musical training, and both the plot and score of *Martha* were French in origin. The composer studied composition in Paris under Reicha, 1827–30, leaving Paris solely on account of the July revolution, and returning in 1835, to remain until the revolution in March 1848 once more drove him away. After living in Paris again, 1863–8, he settled near Vienna, making, however, frequent visits to that city, the French capital, and Italy.

'During his second stay in Paris he composed for the Grand Opera the first act of a ballet, *Henriette, ou La Servante de Greenwich.* This ballet, the text by Vernoy de St.-Georges, was for Adele Dumilâtre. The reason Flotow was entrusted with only one of the three acts was the short time in which it was necessary to complete the score. The other acts were assigned, one each, to Robert Bergmüller and Edouard Deldevez. Of this ballet, written and composed for a French dancer and a French audience, *Martha* is an adaptation. This accounts for its being so typically French and not in the slightest degree German.' H.

5
Wagner

WEBER TO WAGNER

IN the evolution of opera from Weber to Wagner what might
otherwise be a gap is filled by composers whose reputations
endure, but whose music is seldom heard to-day. Heinrich
Marschner (1795–1861) composed in *Hans Heiling*, Berlin,
1883, an opera based on legendary material. Its success may
have confirmed Wagner's bent towards dramatic sources of
this kind already aroused by his admiration for Weber. *Hans
Heiling, Der Vampyr* (The Vampire), and *Der Templer und
Die Judin* (Templar and Jewess, a version of *Ivanhoe*) long
held an important place in the operatic repertory of their
composer's native land. On the other hand *Faust* (1818) and
Jessonda (1823), by Ludwig Spohr (1784–1859), have
completely disappeared. Spohr, however, deserves mention as
being one of the first professional musicians of prominence
to encourage Wagner. Incapable of appreciating either
Beethoven or Weber, strange to say, he at once recognised the
merits of *The Flying Dutchman* and *Tannhäuser*, and even of
Lohengrin—a the time sealed volumes to most musicians and
music lovers. As court conductor at Kassel, he brought out
the first two Wagner operas mentioned respectively in 1842
and 1853; and was eager to produce *Lohengrin*, but was
prevented by opposition from the court.

Meyerbeer and his principal operas will be considered at
length in the chapters in this book devoted to French opera.
There is no doubt, however, that what may be called the
'largeness' of Meyerbeer's style and the effectiveness of his
instrumentation had their influence on Wagner.

Gasparo Spontini (1774–1851) was an Italian by birth, but
I believe can be said to have made absolutely no impression
on the development of Italian opera. His principal works, *La
Vestale* (The Vestal Vergin), *Olimpia* and *Fernando Cortez*,

were brought out in Paris and later in Berlin, where he was general music director, 1820–1841. His operas were heavily scored, especially for brass, but the three works mentioned have all been successfully revived, *La Vestale* for Rosa Ponselle at the Florence Festival and at the Metropolitan, *Olimpia* in Florence in 1950, and *Fernando Cortez* in Naples in 1951 (the last two productions with Renata Tebaldi).

RICHARD WAGNER
(1813–1883)
RIENZI

OPERA in five acts by Richard Wagner. Text by the composer after Bulwer Lytton's novel of the same name. First performed at the Hofoper, Dresden, October 20, 1842, with Mmes. Schröder-Devrient, Wüst, Thiele, Messrs. Tichatscheck, Dettmer, Wächter, Vestri, Reinhold, Risse; New York, 1878; London, Her Majesty's (in English), 1879, with Helene Crosmond, Mme. Vanzini, and Joseph Maas, conductor Carl Rosa; Metropolitan, New York, 1886, with Lilli Lehmann, Marianne Brandt, Eloi Sylva, Emil Fischer, conductor Anton Seidl; revived Berlin, 1933, with de Strozzi, Klose, Lorenz, Helgers, List, conductor Blech; Berlin 1941 with Scheppan, Klose, Lorenz, Prohaska; Stuttgart, 1957, with Windgassen, producer Wieland Wagner.

CHARACTERS

Cola Rienzi, *Roman Tribune and Papal Notary* . . Tenor
Irene, *his sister* . . . . Soprano
Stefano Colonna . . . . Bass
Adriano, *his son* . . . . .Mezzo-Soprano
Paolo Orsini . . . . Bass
Raimondo, *Papal Legate* . . . . Bass
Baroncelli ⎫ *Roman citizens* . . . . ⎧ Tenor
Cecco del Vecchio ⎭ . . . . ⎩ Bass
Messenger of Peace . . . . Soprano
Ambassadors, Nobles, Priests, Monks, Soldiers,
Messengers, and Populace
Time: Middle of the Fourteenth Century   *Place:* Rome

The overture of *Rienzi* gives a vivid idea of the action of the opera. Soon after the beginning there is heard the broad and stately melody of Rienzi's prayer, and then the Rienzi motif, a typical phrase, which is used with great effect later in the opera. It is followed in the overture by the lively melody heard in the concluding portion of the finale of the second act. These are the three most conspicuous portions of the overture, in which there are, however, numerous tumultuous passages reflecting the dramatic excitement which pervades many scenes.

Orsini, a Roman patrician, attempts to abduct Irene, the sister of Rienzi, a papal notary, but is opposed at the critical moment by Colonna, another patrician. A fight ensues between the two factions, in the midst of which Adriano, Colonna's son, who is in love with Irene, appears in her defence. A crowd is attracted by the tumult, and among others Rienzi comes upon the scene. Enraged at the insult offered his sister, and stirred on by Cardinal Raimondo, he urges the people to resist the outrages of the nobles. Adriano is impelled by his love for Irene to cast in his lot with her brother. The nobles are overpowered, and appear at the capitol to swear allegiance to Rienzi, but during the festal proceedings Adriano warns him that the nobles have plotted to kill him. An attempt which Orsini makes to murder him is foiled by the steel breastplate which Rienzi wears under his robe.

The nobles are seized and condemned to death, but on Adriano's pleading they are spared. However, when they violate their oath of submission, the people under Rienzi's leadership rise and exterminate them, in spite of Adriano's pleas. In the end the people prove fickle. The popular tide turns against Rienzi, especially in consequence of the report that he is in league with the German emperor, and intends to restore the Roman pontiff to power. As a festive procession is escorting him to church, Adriano, infuriated at the slaughter of his family, rushes upon him with a drawn dagger, but again the blow is averted. Instead of the 'Te Deum', with which Rienzi expected to be greeted on his entrance to the church, he hears the malediction and sees the ecclesiastical dignitaries placing the ban of excommunication against him upon the doors. Adriano hurries to Irene to warn her of her brother's danger, and urges her to seek safety with him in flight. She, however, repels him, and seeks her brother, determined if

ed be to die with him. She finds him at prayer in the
capitol, but rejects his counsel to save herself with Adriano.
Rienzi appeals to the infuriated populace which has gathered
around the capitol, but they do not heed him. They fire the
capitol with their torches, and hurl stones at Rienzi and
Irene. As Adriano sees his beloved one and her brother
doomed to death in the flames, he throws away his sword,
rushes into the capitol, and perishes with them.

The opening of the first act is full of animation, the
orchestra depicting the tumult which prevails during the
struggle between the nobles. Rienzi's brief recitative is a
masterpiece of declamatory music, and his call to arms is
spirited. It is followed by a trio between Irene, Rienzi, and
Adriano, and this in turn by a duet for the two last-named
which is full of fire. The finale opens with a double chorus
for the populace and monks in the Lateran, accompanied by
the organ. Then there is a broad and energetic appeal to the
people from Rienzi, and amid the shouts of the populace and
the ringing tones of the trumpets the act closes.

The insurrection of the people against the nobles is
successful, and Rienzi, in the second act, awaits at the capitol
the patricians who are to pledge him their submission. The
act opens with a broad and stately march, to which the
messengers of peace enter. They sing a graceful chorus. This
is followed by a chorus for the senators, and the nobles then
tender their submission. There is a terzetto, between
Adriano, Colonna, and Orsini, in which the nobles express
their contempt for the young patrician. The finale which
then begins is highly spectacular. There is a march for the
ambassadors, and a grand ballet, historical in character, and
supposed to be symbolical of the triumphs of ancient Rome.
In the midst of this occurs the assault upon Rienzi. Rienzi's
pardon of the nobles is conveyed in a broadly beautiful
melody, and this is succeeded by the animated passage heard
in the overture. With it are mingled the chants of the monks,
the shouts of the people who are opposed to the cardinal and
nobles, and the tolling of bells.

The third act opens tumultuously. The people have been
aroused by fresh outrages on the part of the nobles. Rienzi's
emissaries disperse, after a furious chorus, to rouse the
populace to vengeance. After they have left, Adriano has his
great air, a number which can never fail of effect when sung
with all the expression of which it is capable. The rest of the

act is a grand accumulation of martial music, and includes t.
stupendous battle hymn, which is accompanied by th
clashing of sword and shields, the ringing of bells, and all the
tumult incidental to a riot. After Adriano has pleaded in vain
with Rienzi for the nobles, and the various bands of armed
citizens have dispersed, there is a duet between Adriano and
Irene, in which Adriano takes farewell of her. The victorious
populace appears and the act closes with their triumphan·
shouts. The fourth act is brief and, beyond the description
given in the synopsis of the plot, requires no further comment
    The fifth act opens with the beautiful prayer of Rienzi,
already familiar from the overture. There is a tender duet
between Rienzi and Irene, an impassioned aria for Rienzi, a
duet for Irene and Adriano, and then the finale, which is
chiefly choral.   K.

DER FLIEGENDE HOLLÄNDER
The Flying Dutchman

Opera in three acts by Richard Wagner. Text by the composer
founded on an episode in Heine's *Memoirs of Herr von*
Schnabelewopski. Performed at the Hofoper, Dresden, January 2, 1843
with Mmes. Schröder-Devrient, J. M. Wachter, Messrs. Wächter
Reinhold, Risse, Bielezizky, conductor Wagner; Drury Lane, 1870 (in
Italian; first Wagner opera to be performed in London), with Ilma di
Murska, Mme. Corsi, Messrs. Santley, Perotti, Foli, Rinaldini, conductor
Arditi; Lyceum, 1876 (in English), by Carl Rosa Company
Philadelphia, 1876 (in Italian); Metropolitan, 1889, with Sophie
Weisner, Charlotte Huhn, Reichmann, Kalisch, Fischer, Mittelhauser
conductor Seidl. Interpreters of the title role have included Theodor
Bertram, Anton van Rooy, Friedrich Schoor, Rudolf Bockelmann
Herbert Janssen, Joel Berglund, and Hans Hotter; famous Sentas have
included Emmy Destinn, Maria Müller, Frida Leider, Kristen Flagstad
and Anya Silja.

CHARACTERS

Daland, *a Norwegian sea captain* .... Bass
Senta, *his daughter* .... Soprano
Eric, *a huntsman* .... Tenor
Mary, *Senta's nurse* .... Contralto
Daland's Steersman .... Tenor
The Dutchman .... Baritone
                Sailors, Maidens, Hunters, etc.
Time: Eighteenth century   *Place:* A Norwegian Fishing Village

From *Rienzi* Wagner took a great stride forward to *The Flying Dutchman*. This is the first milestone on his road from opera to music-drama. Of his *Rienzi* the composer was in after years ashamed, writing to Liszt: 'I, as an artist and man, have not the heart for the reconstruction of that, to my taste, superannuated work, which, in consequence of its immoderate dimensions, I have had to remodel more than once. I have no longer the heart for it, and desire from all my soul to do something new instead.' He spoke of it as a youthful error, but in *The Flying Dutchman* there is little, if anything, which could have troubled his artistic conscience.

One can hardly imagine the legend more effective dramatically and musically than it is in Wagner's libretto and score. It is a work of wild and sombre beauty, relieved only occasionally by touches of light and grace, and has all the interest attaching to a work in which for the first time a genius feels himself conscious of his greatness. If it is not as impressive as *Tannhäuser* or *Lohengrin*, nor as tremendous as the music-dramas, that is because the subject of the work is lighter. As his genius developed, his choice of subjects and his treatment of them passed through as complete an evolution as his musical theory, so that when he finally abandoned the operatic form and adopted his system of leading motifs, he conceived, for the dramatic bases of his scores, dramas which it would be difficult to fancy set to music of any other type than that which is so characteristic of his music-dramas.

Wagner's present libretto is based upon the picturesque legend of the Flying Dutchman—the Wandering Jew of the ocean. A Dutch sea-captain, who, we are told, tried to double the Cape of Good Hope in the teeth of a furious gale, swore that he would accomplish his purpose even if he kept on sailing forever. The devil, hearing the oath, condemned the captain to sail the sea until Judgment Day, without hope of release, unless he should find a woman who would love him faithfully until death. Once in every seven years he is allowed to go ashore in search of a woman who will redeem him through her faithful love.

The opera opens just as a term of seven years has elapsed. The Dutchman's ship comes to anchor in a bay of the coast of Norway, in which the ship of Daland, a Norwegian sea-captain, has sought shelter from the storm. Daland's home is not far from the bay, and the Dutchman, learning he has a daughter, asks permission to woo her, offering him in return all his treasures. Daland readily consents. His daughter, Senta, is a romantic maiden upon whom the legend of the Flying Dutchman has made a deep impression. As Daland ushers the Dutchman into his home Senta is gazing dreamily upon a picture representing the unhappy hero of the legend. The resemblance of the stranger to the face in this picture is so striking that the emotional girl is at once attracted to him and pledges him her faith, deeming it her mission to save him. Later on, Eric, a young huntsman, who is in love with her, pleads his cause with her, and the Dutchman, overhearing them and thinking himself again forsaken, rushes off to his vessel. Senta cries out that she is faithful to him but is held back by Eric, Daland, and her friends. The Dutchman, who really loves Senta, then proclaims who he is, thinking to terrify her, and at once puts to sea. But she, undismayed by his words, and truly faithful unto death, breaks away from those who are holding her, and rushing to the edge of a cliff casts herself into the ocean, with her arms outstretched toward him. The phantom ship sinks, the sea rises high and falls back into a seething whirlpool. In the sunset glow the forms of Senta and the Dutchman are seen rising in each other's embrace from the sea and floating upward.

In *The Flying Dutchman* Wagner employs several leading motifs, not indeed with the resource which he displays in his music-dramas, but with considerably greater freedom of treatment than in *Rienzi*. There we had but one leading motif, which never varied in form. The overture, which may be said to be an eloquent and beautiful musical narrative of the whole opera, contains all these leading motifs. It opens with a stormy passage out of which there bursts the strong but sombre Motif of the Flying Dutchman himself, the dark hero of the legend. The orchestra fairly seethes and rages like the sea roaring under the lash of a terrific storm. And through all this furious orchestration there is heard again and again the motif of the Dutchman, as if his figure could be seen amid all the gloom and fury of the elements. There he stands, hoping for death, yet indestructible. As the excited music gradually dies away there is heard a calm, somewhat undulating phrase which occurs in the opera when the Dutchman's vessel puts into the quiet Norwegian harbour. Then, also, there occurs again the motif of the Dutchman, but this time played softly as if the storm-driven wretch had at last found a moment's peace.

We at once recognise to whom it is due that he has found this moment of repose, for we hear like prophetic measures the strains of the beautiful ballad which is sung by Senta in the second act of the opera, in which she relates the legend of The Flying Dutchman and tells of his unhappy fate. She is the one whom he is to meet when he goes ashore. The entire ballad is not heard at this point, only the opening of the second part, which may be taken as indicating in this overture the simplicity and beauty of Senta's character. In fact, it would not be too much to call this opening phrase the Senta Motif. It is followed by the phrase which indicates the coming to anchor of the Dutchman's vessel; then we hear the Motif of the Dutchman himself, dying away with the faintest possible effect. With sudden energy the orchestra dashes into the surging ocean music, introducing this time the wild, pathetic plaint sung by the Dutchman in the first act of the opera. Again we hear his motif, and again the music seems to represent the surging, swirling ocean when aroused by a furious tempest. Even when we hear the measures of the sailors' chorus the orchestra continues its furious pace, making it appear as if the sailors were shouting above the storm.

Characteristic in this overture, and also throughout the opera, especially in Senta's ballad, is what may be called the Ocean Motif, which most graphically depicts the wild and terrible aspect of the ocean during a storm. It is varied from time to time, but never loses its characteristic force and weirdness. The overture ends with an impassioned burst of melody based upon a portion of the concluding phrases of Senta's ballad; phrases which we hear once more at the end of the opera when she sacrifices herself in order to save her lover.

A wild and stormy scene is disclosed when the curtain rises upon the first act. The sea occupies the greater part of the scene, and stretches itself out far toward the horizon. A storm is raging. Daland's ship has sought shelter in a little cove formed by the cliffs. The orchestra, chiefly with the wild ocean music heard in the overture, depicts the raging of the storm, and above it are heard the shouts of the sailors at work: 'Ho-jo-he! Hal-lo-jo!'

As the storm seems to be abating the sailors descend into the hold and Daland goes down into the cabin to rest, leaving his Steersman in charge of the deck. The Steersman, as if to force himself to remain awake, intones a sailor song, but sleep overcomes him and the phrases become more and more detached, until at last he falls asleep.

The storm begins to rage again and it grows darker. Suddenly the ship of the Flying Dutchman, with blood-red sails and black mast, enters the harbour over against the ship of the Norwegian; then silently and without the least noise the spectral crew furl the sails. The Dutchman goes on shore.

Here now occur the weird, dramatic recitative and aria: 'Die Frist is um' (The term is passed, and once again are ended seven long years). Daland perceives the Dutchman and going ashore questions him. It is then that the Dutchman, after relating a mariner's story of ill luck and disaster, asks Daland to take him to his home and allow him to woo his daughter, offering him his treasures. At this point we have a graceful and pretty duet, Daland readily consenting that the Dutchman accompany him. The storm having subsided and the wind being fair, the crews of the vessels hoist sail to leave port, Daland's vessel disappearing just as the Dutchman goes on board his ship.

Act II.   After an introduction in which we hear a portion of the Steersman's song, and also that phrase which denotes the appearance of the Dutchman's vessel in the harbour, the curtain rises upon a room in Daland's house. On the walls are pictures of vessels, charts, and on the farther wall the portrait of a pale man with a dark beard. Senta, leaning back in an armchair, is absorbed in dreamy contemplation of the portrait. Her old nurse, Mary, and her young friends are sitting in various parts of the room, spinning. Here we have that charming musical number famous all the musical world over, partly through Liszt's admirable piano arrangement of it, the 'Spinning Chorus'. It may be cited as a striking instance of Wagner's gift of melody, should anybody at this late day be foolish enough to require proof of his genius in that respect. The girls tease Senta for gazing so dreamily at the portrait of the Flying Dutchman, and finally ask her if she will not sing his ballad.

This ballad is a masterpiece of composition, vocally and instrumentally. It begins with the storm music familiar from the overture, and with the weird measures of the Flying Dutchman's motif which sound like a voice calling in distress across the sea.

Senta repeats the measures of this motif, and then we have the simple phrases beginning: 'A ship the restless ocean sweeps'. Throughout this portion of the ballad the orchestra depicts the surging and heaving of the ocean, Senta's voice ringing out dramatically above the accompaniment. She then tells how he can be delivered from his curse, this portion being set to the measures which were heard in the overture, Senta finally proclaiming, in the broadly delivered, yet rapturous phrases with which the overture ends, that she is

the woman who will save him by being faithful to him unto death. The girls about her spring up in terror and Eric, who has just entered the door and heard her outcry, hastens to her side. He brings news of the arrival of Daland's vessel, and Mary and the girls hasten forth to meet the sailors. Senta wishes to follow, but Eric restrains her and pleads his love for her in melodious measures. Senta, however, will not give him an answer at this time. He then tells her of a dream he has had, in which he saw a weird vessel from which two men, one her father, the other a ghastly-looking stranger, made their way. Her he saw going to the stranger and entreating him for his regard.

Senta, worked up to the highest pitch of excitement by Eric's words, exclaims: 'He seeks for me and I for him.' and Eric, full of despair and horror, rushes away. The door opens and the Dutchman and Daland appear. Senta turns from the picture to him, and, uttering a loud cry of wonder, remains standing as if transfixed without removing her eyes from the Dutchman. Daland in an aria tells her of the stranger's request, and leaves them alone. There follows a duet for Senta and the Dutchman, with its broad, smoothly flowing melody and its many phrases of dramatic power, in which Senta gives herself up unreservedly to the hero of her romantic attachment, Daland finally entering and adding his congratulations to their betrothal. This scene closes the act.

Act III. The music of it re-echoes through the introduction of the next act and goes over into a vigorous sailors' chorus and dance. The scene shows a bay with a rocky shore, with Daland's house in the foreground on one side, and the background occupied by his and the Dutchman's ships. The sailors and the girls in their merry-making call loudly toward the Dutch ship to join them, but no reply is heard from the weird vessel. Finally the sailors call louder and louder and taunt the crew of the other ship. Suddenly the sea, which has been quite calm, begins to rise. The storm wind whistles through the cordage of the strange vessel, and as dark bluish flames flare up in the rigging, the weird crew show themselves and sing a wild chorus, which strikes terror into all the merrymakers. The girls have fled, and the Norwegian sailors quit their deck, making the sign of the cross. The crew of the Flying Dutchman observing this, disappear with shrill laughter.

Senta now comes with trembling steps out of the house. She is followed by Eric. He pleads with her and entreats her to remember his love for her, and speaks also of the encouragement which she once gave him. The Dutchman has entered unperceived and has been listening. Eric, seeing him, at once recognises the man of ghastly mien whom he saw in his vision. When the Flying Dutchman bids her farewell, because he deems himself abandoned, and Senta endeavours to follow him, Eric holds her and summons others to his aid. But, in spite of all resistance, Senta seeks to tear herself loose. Then it is that the Flying Dutchman proclaims who he is and puts to sea. Senta, however, freeing herself, rushes to a cliff overhanging the sea, and calling out,

> 'Praise thou thine angel for what he saith;
> Here stand I faithful, yea, to death,'

casts herself into the sea. The work ends with the portion of the ballad which brought the overture and spinning scene to a close.

Wagner intended *The Flying Dutchman* to be played in a single act—another example of his efforts to break with tradition—and at Bayreuth in 1901 his original design was adhered to. For this purpose, Ernest Newman tells us in his invaluable *Wagner Nights*, cuts were made from bar 26 before the end of the orchestral postlude to Act I to bar 19 of the prelude to Act II, and a dozen bars were omitted at the end of Act II.   K.

TANNHÄUSER

Und der Sängerkrieg auf dem Wartburg
(and the Song Contest at the Wartburg)

Opera in three acts by Richard Wagner, text by the composer.
Première, Dresden, October 19, 1845, with Johanna Wagner, Schröder-
Devrient, Tichatschek, Mitterwurzer, Dettmer, conductor Wagner.
Revised and performed (in what is now known as the 'Paris version')
Opéra, Paris, 1861, with Marie Saxe, Fortunata Tedesco, Niemann,
Morelli, Cazaux, conductor Dietsch. First performed New York 1859;
Covent Garden 1876 (in Italian) with Albani, d'Angeri, Carpi, Maurel,
Capponi, conductor Vianesi; Her Majesty's London, 1882 (in English)
with Valleria, Burns, Schott, Ludwig, Pope, conductor Randegger;
Metropolitan, New York, 1884, with Seidl-Kraus, Slach, Schott, Adolf
Robinson; Covent Garden (in French, in 'Paris version') 1896, with
Eames, Adini, Alvarez, Ancona, Plançon, conductor, Mancinelli. Famous
Tannhäusers include Max Alvary, Winkelmann, Urlus, Slezak, Schmedes,
Melchior.

CHARACTERS

Hermann, *Landgrave of Thuringia*		Bass
Tannhäuser		Tenor
Wolfram von Eschenbach		Baritone
Walter von der Vogelweide	*Knights and*	Tenor
Biterolf	*Minnesinger*	Bass
Heinrich der Schreiber		Tenor
Reinmar von Zweter		Bass
Elisabeth, *niece of the Landgrave*		Soprano
Venus		Soprano
A Young Shepherd		Soprano
Four Noble Pages		Soprano and Alto

Nobles, Knights, Ladies, elder and younger Pilgrims,
Sirens, Naiads, Nymphs, Bacchantes

Time: Early Thirteenth Century   *Place:* Near Eisenach

The story of *Tannhäuser* is laid in and near the Wartburg,
where, during the thirteenth century, the Landgraves of the
Thuringian Valley held sway. They were lovers of art,
especially of poetry and music, and at the Wartburg many
peaceful contests between the famous minnesingers took
place. Near this castle rises the Venusberg. According to
tradition the interior of this mountain was inhabited by
Holda, the Goddess of Spring, who, however, in time became
identified with the Goddess of Love. Her court was filled

195

with nymphs and sirens, and it was her greatest joy to entice into the mountain the knights of the Wartburg and hold them captive to her beauty.

Among those whom she had thus lured into the rosy recesses of the Venusberg is Tannhäuser. In spite of her beauty, however, he is weary of her charms and longs for a glimpse of the world. With the cry that his hope rests in the Virgin, he tears himself away from her. The court of Venus disappears and in a moment we see Tannhäuser prostrate before a cross in a valley upon which the Wartburg peacefully looks down. Pilgrims on their way to Rome pass him by and Tannhäuser thinks of joining them in order that at Rome he may obtain forgiveness for his crime in allowing himself to be enticed into the Venusberg. But at that moment the Landgrave and a number of minnesingers on their return from the chase come upon him and, recognising him, endeavour to persuade him to return to the Wartburg with them. Their pleas, however, are vain, until one of them, Wolfram von Eschenbach, tells him that since he has left the Wartburg a great sadness has come over the niece of the Landgrave, Elisabeth. It is evident that Tannhäuser has been in love with her, and that it is because of her beauty and virtue that he regrets so deeply having been lured into the Venusberg. For Wolfram's words stir him profoundly. To the great joy of all, he agrees to return to the Wartburg, the scene of his many triumphs as a minnesinger in the contests of song.

The Landgrave, feeling sure that Tannhäuser will win the prize at the contest of song soon to be held, offers the hand of his niece to the winner. The minnesingers sing tamely of the beauty of virtuous love, but Tannhäuser, suddenly remembering the seductive and magical beauties of the Venusberg, cannot control himself, and bursts out into a reckless hymn in praise of Venus. Horrified at his words, the knights draw their swords and would slay him, but Elisabeth throws herself between him and them. Crushed and penitent, Tannhäuser stands behind her, and the Landgrave, moved by her willingness to sacrifice herself for her sinful lover, announces that he will be allowed to join a second band of pilgrims who are going to Rome and to plead with the Pope for forgiveness.

Elisabeth prayerfully awaits his return; but, as she is kneeling by the crucifix in front of the Wartburg, the pilgrims

ɔass her by and in the band she does not see her lover. Slowly
and sadly she returns to the castle to die. When the pilgrims'
voices have died away, and Elisabeth has returned to the
castle, leaving only Wolfram, who is also deeply enamoured
of her, upon the scene, Tannhäuser appears, weary and
dejected. He has sought to obtain forgiveness in vain. The
Pope has cast him out forever, proclaiming that no more than
his staff can put forth leaves can he expect forgiveness. He
has come back to re-enter the Venusberg. Wolfram seeks to
restrain him, but it is not until he invokes the name of
Elisabeth that Tannhäuser is saved. A cortège approaches,
and, as Tannhäuser recognises the form of Elisabeth on the
bier, he sinks down on her coffin and dies. Just then the
second band of pilgrims arrive, bearing Tannhäuser's staff,
which has put forth blossoms, thus showing that his sins have
been forgiven.

The overture of the opera has long been a favourite piece
on concert programmes. Like that of *The Flying Dutchman* it
is the story of the whole opera told in music. It certainly is
one of the most brilliant and effective pieces of orchestral
music and its popularity is easily understood. It opens with
the melody of the pilgrims' chorus, beginning softly as if
coming from a distance and gradually increasing in power
until it is heard in all its grandeur.

Having reached a climax, this chorus gradually dies away,
and suddenly, and with intense dramatic contrast, we have all
the seductive spells of the Venusberg displayed before us—
that is, musically displayed; but then the music is so wonderfully vivid, it depicts with such marvellous clearness the
many-coloured alluring scene at the court of the unholy
goddess, it gives vent so freely to the sinful excitement which
pervades the Venusberg, that we actually seem to see what
we hear. This passes over in turn to the impassioned burst of
song in which Tannhäuser hymns Venus's praise, and
immediately after we have the boisterous and vigorous music
which accompanies the threatening action of the Landgrave
and minnesingers when they draw their swords upon
Tannhäuser in order to take vengeance upon him for his
crimes. Upon these three episodes of the drama, which so

characteristically give insight into its plot and action, th‹
overture is based, and it very naturally concludes with the
pilgrims' chorus which seems to voice the final forgiveness of
Tannhäuser.

The curtain rises, disclosing all the seductive spells of the
Venusberg. Tannhäuser lies in the arms of Venus, who
reclines upon a flowery couch. Nymphs, sirens, and satyrs are
dancing about them and in the distance are grottoes alive
with amorous figures. Various mythological amours, such as
that of Leda and the swan, are supposed to be in progress.

Much of the music familiar from the overture is heard
during this scene, but it gains in effect from the distant voices

of the sirens and, of course, from the dances of the denizens
of Venus's court. Very dramatic is the scene between Venus
and Tannhäuser, when the latter sings his hymn in her praise,
but at the same time proclaims that he desires to return to
the world. In alluring strains she endeavours to tempt him to
remain with her, but when she discovers that he is bound
upon going, she vehemently warns him of the misfortunes
which await him upon earth and prophesies that he will some
day return to her and penitently ask to be taken back into
her realm.

Dramatic and effective as this scene is in the original score
it has gained immensely in power by the additions which
Wagner made for the production of the work in Paris, in
1861. The overture does not, in this version, come to a
formal close, but after the manner of Wagner's later works
the transition is made directly from it to the scene of the
Venusberg. The dances have been elaborated and laid out
upon a more careful allegorical basis and the music of Venus
has been greatly strengthened from a dramatic point of view.

so that now the scene in which she pleads with him to remain and afterwards warns him against the sorrows to which he will be exposed, are among the finest of Wagner's compositions, rivalling in dramatic power his ripest work.

Wagner's knowledge of the stage is shown in the wonderfully dramatic effect in the change of scene from the Venusberg to the landscape in the valley of the Wartburg. One moment we have the variegated allures of the court of the Goddess of Love, with its dancing nymphs, sirens, and satyrs, its beautiful grottoes and groups; the next all this has disappeared and we are transported to a peaceful scene whose influence upon us is deepened by the crucifix in the foreground, before which Tannhäuser kneels in penitence. The peacefulness of the scene is further enhanced by the appearance upon a rocky eminence to the left of a young Shepherd who pipes a pastoral strain. Before he has finished piping his lay the voices of the pilgrims are heard in the distance, their solemn measures being interrupted by little phrases piped by the Shepherd. As the pilgrims approach, the chorus becomes louder, and as they pass over the stage and bow before the crucifix, their praise swells into an eloquent psalm of devotion.

Tannhäuser is deeply affected and gives way to his feelings in a lament, against which are heard the voices of the pilgrims as they recede in the distance. This whole scene is one of marvellous beauty, the contrast between it and the preceding episode being enhanced by the religiously tranquil nature of what transpires and of the accompanying music. Upon this peaceful scene the notes of hunting-horns now break in, and gradually the Landgrave and his hunters gather about Tannhäuser. Wolfram recognises him and tells the others who he is. They greet him in an expressive septet, and Wolfram, finding he is bent upon following the pilgrims to Rome, asks permission of the Landgrave to inform him of the impression which he seems to have made upon Elisabeth. This he does in a melodious solo, and Tannhäuser, overcome by his love for Elisabeth, consents to return to the halls which have missed him so long. Exclamations of joy greet his decision, and the act closes with an enthusiastic *ensemble* which is a glorious piece of concerted music and never fails of brilliant effect when it is well executed, especially if the representative of Tannhäuser has a voice that can soar above the others.

The scene of the second act is laid in the singers' hall of

the Wartburg. The introduction depicts Elisabeth's joy at Tannhäuser's return, and when the curtain rises she at once enters and joyfully greets the scenes of Tannhäuser's former triumphs in broad phrases. Wolfram then appears, conducting Tannhäuser to her. Elisabeth seems overjoyed to see him, but then checks herself, and her maidenly modesty, which veils her transport at meeting him, again finds expression in a number of hesitating but exceedingly beautiful phrases. She asks Tannhäuser where he has been, but he, of course, gives misleading answers. Finally, however, he tells her she is the one who has attracted him back to the castle. Their love finds expression in a swift and rapidly flowing dramatic duet, which unfortunately is rarely given in its entirety, although as a glorious outburst of emotional music it certainly deserves to be heard in the exact form and length in which the composer wrote it.

There is then a scene of much tender feeling between the Landgrave and Elisabeth in which the former tells her that he will offer her hand as prize to the singer whom she shall crown as winner. The first strains of the brilliantly effective grand march are then heard. After an address by the Landgrave, which can hardly be called remarkably interesting, the singers draw lots to decide who among them shall begin. This prize singing is, unfortunately, not so great in musical value as the rest of the score, and, unless a person understands the words, it is decidedly long drawn out. What, however, redeems it is a gradually growing dramatic excitement as Tannhäuser voices his contempt for what seem to him the tame tributes paid to love by the minnesingers, an excitement which reaches its climax when, no longer able to restrain himself, he bursts forth into his hymn in praise of the unholy charms of Venus.

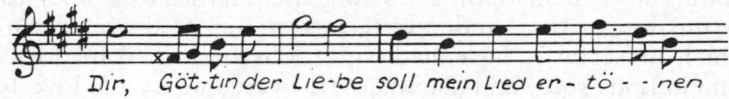

Dir, Göt-tin der Lie-be soll mein Lied er-tö--nen

The women cry out in horror and rush from the hall and the men, drawing their swords, attack him. This brings us to the great dramatic moment, when, with a shriek, Elisabeth, in spite of his betrayal of her love, throws herself protectingly before him, and thus appears a second time as his saving angel. In short and excited phrases the men pour forth their

rath at Tannhäuser's crime in having sojourned with Venus,
nd he, realising its enormity, seems crushed with a con-
ciousness of his guilt. Of great beauty is the septet, 'An angel
as from heaven descended', which rises to a magnificent
limax and is one of the finest pieces of dramatic writing in
Wagner's scores, though all too often execrably sung. The
oices of young pilgrims are heard in the valley. The
Landgrave then announces the conditions upon which
Tannhäuser can again obtain forgiveness, and Tannhäuser
oins the pilgrims on their way to Rome.

The third act displays once more the valley of the
Wartburg, the same scene as that to which the Venusberg
changed in the first act. Elisabeth, arrayed in white, is
kneeling, in deep prayer, before the crucifix. At one side, and
watching her tenderly, stands Wolfram. After a sad recitative
rom Wolfram, the chorus of returning pilgrims is heard in
he distance. They sing the melody heard in the overture and
n the first act; and the same effect of gradual approach is
produced by a superb *crescendo* as they reach and cross the
cene. With anxiety and grief Elisabeth scans them as they go
by to see if Tannhäuser is among them, and when the last one
has passed and she realises that he has not returned, she sinks
again upon her knees before the crucifix and sings the prayer,
'Almighty Virgin, hear my sorrow', music in which there is
most beautifully combined the expression of poignant grief
with trust in the will of the Almighty. As she rises and turns
oward the castle, Wolfram, by his gesture, seems to ask her if
he cannot accompany her, but she declines his offer and
lowly goes her way up the mountain.

Meanwhile night has fallen upon the scene and the evening
tar glows softly above the castle. It is then that Wolfram,
accompanying himself on his lyre, intones the tender and
beautiful 'Song to the Evening Star', confessing therein his
ove for the saintly Elisabeth.

Then Tannhäuser, dejected, footsore, and weary, appears
and in broken accents asks Wolfram to show him the way
back to the Venusberg. Wolfram bids him stay his steps and
persuades him to tell the story of his pilgrimage. In fierce,

dramatic accents, Tannhäuser relates all that he has suffer
on his way to Rome and the terrible judgement pronounce
upon him by the Pope. This is a highly impressive episode
clearly foreshadowing Wagner's dramatic use of musica
recitative in his later music-dramas. Only a singer of th
highest rank can do justice to it.

Tannhäuser proclaims that, having lost all chance o
salvation, he will once more give himself up to the delights o
the Venusberg. A roseate light illumines the recesses of th
mountain and the unholy company of the Venusberg again i
seen, Venus stretching out her arms for. Tannhäuser, t
welcome him. But at last, when Tannhäuser seems unable t
resist Venus's enticing voice any longer, Wolfram conjure
him by the memory of the sainted Elisabeth. The light die
away and the magic charms of the Venusberg disappea
Amid tolling of bells and mournful voices a funeral pro
cession comes down the mountain. Recognising the feature
of Elisabeth, the dying Tannhäuser falls upon her corpse. Th
younger pilgrims arrive with the staff, which has again pu
forth leaves, and amid the hallelujahs of the pilgrims th
opera closes.   K.

LOHENGRIN

Opera in three acts, by Richard Wagner, text by the composer
Première, Weimar, August 28, 1850, with Agthe, Fasztlinger, Beck, vo
Milde, Hoder, conductor Liszt. First performed Covent Garden, 187
(in Italian), with Albani, d'Angeri, Nicolini, Maurel, Seiderman, con
ductor Vianesi; Her Majesty's, London, 1880 (in English); Drury Lane
1882 (in German), with Sucher, Dily, Winkelmann, Kraus, Koege
conductor Richter; New York, 1871; Academy of Music, New York
1874 (in Italian), with Nilsson, Cary, Campanini, Del Puente
Metropolitan (in German), 1885, with Seidl-Kraus, Brandt, Stritt
Robinson, Fischer, conducted by Seidl. Famous interpreters of the titl
role have included Jean de Reszke, van Dyck, Dalmores, Urlus, Slezak
Völker.

CHARACTERS

Henry the Fowler, *King of Germany* . . . . Bass
Lohengrin . . . . Tenor
Elsa of Brabant . . . . Soprano
Duke Godfrey, *her brother*
Frederick of Telramund, *Count of Brabant* . . . Baritone

Ortrud, *his wife* .... Mezzo-Soprano
The King's Herald .... Baritone
Saxon, Thuringian, and Brabantian Counts and Nobles,
   Ladies of Honour, Pages, Attendants
ime: First half of the Tenth Century *Scene:* Antwerp

Lohengrin, at the time of its composition so novel and so
trange, yet filled with beauties of orchestration and
armony that are now quoted as leading examples in books
n these subjects, was composed in less than a year. The acts
vere finished almost, if not quite, in reversed order. For
Vagner wrote the third act first, beginning it in September
846, and completing it March 5, 1847. The first act
ccupied him from May 12 to June 8, less than a month; the
econd act from June 18 to August 2.

Wagner's music, however, was so little understood at the
.me that, even before *Lohengrin* was produced and not a
ote of it had been heard, people made fun of it. A
.thographer named Meser had issued Wagner's previous three
cores, but the enterprise had not been a success. People said
hat before publishing *Rienzi* Meser had lived on the first
loor. *Rienzi* had driven him to the second; *The Flying
Jutchman* and *Tannhäuser* to the third; and now *Lohengrin*
vould drive him to the garret—a prophecy that didn't come
rue, because he refused to publish it.

In 1849, *Lohengrin* still not having been accepted by the
Presden Opera, Wagner took part in the May revolution,
vhich, apparently successful for a very short time, was
uickly suppressed by the military. The composer is said to
ave made his escape from Dresden in the disguise of a
oachman. Occasionally there turns up in sales as a great
urity a copy of the warrant for Wagner's arrest issued by the
Presden police. As it gives a description of him at the time
vhen he had but recently composed *Lohengrin*, I will quote
:

 'Wagner is thirty-seven to thirty-eight years of age, of
medium stature, has brown hair, an open forehead;
eyebrows, brown; eyes, greyish blue; nose and mouth,
proportioned; chin, round, and wears spectacles. Special
characteristics: rapid in movements and speech. Dress:
coat of dark green buckskin, trousers of black cloth,
velvet vest, silk neckerchief, ordinary felt hat and
boots.'

Much fun has been made of the expression 'chin, round and wears spectacles'. Wagner got out of Dresden on the pass of a Dr. Widmann, whom he resembled. It has been suggested that he made the resemblance still closer by discontinuing the habit of wearing spectacles on his chin.

I saw Wagner several times in Bayreuth in the summer of 1882, when I attended the first performance of *Parsifal*, a correspondent by cable and letter for one of the large New York dailies. Except that his hair was grey (and that he no longer wore his spectacles on his chin) the description in the warrant still held good, especially as regards his rapidity of movement and speech, to which I may add a marked vivacity of gesture. There, too, I saw the friend, who had helped him over so many rough places in his early career, Franz Liszt, his hair white with age, but framing a face as strong and keen as an eagle's. I saw them seated at a banquet, and with them Cosima, Liszt's daughter, who was Wagner's second wife, and their son, Siegfried Wagner; Cosima the image of her father and Siegfried a miniature replica of the composer to whom we owe *Lohengrin* and the music-dramas that followed it. The following summer one of the four was missing. I have the *Parsifal* programme with mourning border signifying that the performances of the work were in memory of its creator.

In April 1850, Wagner, then an exile in Zurich, wrote to Liszt: 'Bring out my *Lohengrin*! You are the only one to whom I would put this request; to no one but you would I entrust the production of this opera; but to you I surrender it with the fullest, most joyous confidence.'

Wagner himself describes the appeal and the result, by saying that at a time when he was ill, unhappy, and in despair, his eye fell on the score of *Lohengrin* which he had almost forgotten. 'A pitiful feeling overcame me that these tones would never resound from the deathly-pale paper; two words I wrote to Liszt, the answer to which was nothing else than the information that, as far as the resources of the Weimar Opera permitted, the most elaborate preparations were being made for the production of *Lohengrin*.'

Liszt's reply to which Wagner refers, and which gives some details regarding 'the elaborate preparations', while testifying to his full comprehension of Wagner's genius and the importance of his new score as a work of art, may well cause us to smile to-day at the small scale on which things were done in 1850.

'Your *Lohengrin*,' he wrote, 'will be given under conditions that are most unusual and most favourable for its
success. The direction will spend on this occasion almost
2,000 thalers [about $1,500]—a sum unprecedented at
Weimar within memory of man . . . the bass clarinet has been
bought,' etc. Ten times fifteen hundred dollars might well be
required to-day for a properly elaborate production of
Lohengrin, and the opera orchestra that had to send out and
buy a bass clarinet would be a curiosity. But Weimar had
what no other opera house could boast of—Franz Liszt as
conductor.

Under his brilliant direction *Lohengrin* had at Weimar its
first performance on any stage, August 28, 1850. This was
the anniversary of Goethe's birth, the date of the dedication
of the Weimar monument to the poet, Herder, and, by a
coincidence that does not appear to have struck either
Wagner or Liszt, the third anniversary of the completion of
Lohengrin. The work was performed without cuts and before
an audience which included some of the leading musical and
literary men in Germany. The performance made a deep
impression. The circumstance that Liszt added the charm of
his personality to it and that the weight of his influence had
been thrown in its favour alone gave vast importance to the
event.

On May 15, 1861, when, through the intervention of
Princess Metternich, he had been permitted to return to
Germany, fourteen years after he had finished *Lohengrin* and
eleven years after its production at Weimar, Wagner himself
heard it for the first time at Vienna. A tragedy of fourteen
years—to create a masterpiece of the lyric stage, and be
forced to wait that long to hear it!

Before proceeding to a complete descriptive account of the
Lohengrin story and music I will give a brief summary of the
plot and a similar characterisation of the score.

The story of *Lohengrin* is briefly as follows: The
Hungarians have invaded Germany, and King Henry I visits
Antwerp for the purpose of raising a force to combat them.
He finds the country in a condition of anarchy. The dukedom is claimed by Frederick, who has married Ortrud, a
daughter of the Prince of Friesland. The legitimate heir,
Godfrey, has mysteriously disappeared, and his sister, Elsa, is
charged by Frederick and Ortrud with having done away with
him in order that she might obtain the sovereignty. The King

summons her before him so that the cause may be tried by
the ordeal of single combat between Frederick and a
champion who may be willing to appear for Elsa. None of the
knights will defend her cause. She then describes a champion
whose form has appeared to her in a vision, and she proclaims
that he shall be her champion. Her pretence is derided by
Frederick and his followers, who think that she is out of her
mind; but after a triple summons by the Herald, there is seen
in the distance on the river a boat drawn by a swan, and in it
a knight clad in silver armour. He comes to champion Elsa's
cause, and before the combat betroths himself to her, but
makes a strict condition that she shall never question him as
to his name or birthplace, for should she do so, he would be
obliged to depart. She assents to the conditions, and the
combat which ensues results in Frederick's ignominious
defeat. Judgment of exile is pronounced on him.

Instead, however, of leaving the country he lingers in the
neighbourhood of Brabant, plotting with Ortrud how they
may compass the ruin of Lohengrin and Elsa. Ortrud by her
entreaties moves Elsa to pity, and persuades her to seek a
reprieve for Frederick, at the same time, however, using every
opportunity to instil doubts in Elsa's mind regarding her
champion, and rousing her to such a pitch of nervous
curiosity that she is on the point of asking him the forbidden
question. After the bridal ceremonies and in the bridal
chamber, the distrust which Ortrud and Frederick have
engendered in Elsa's mind so overcomes her faith that she
vehemently puts the forbidden question to her champion.
Almost at the same moment Frederick and four of his
followers force their way into the apartment, intending to
take the knight's life. A single blow of his sword, however,
stretches Frederick lifeless, and his followers bear his corpse
away. Placing Elsa in the charge of her ladies-in-waiting, and
ordering them to take her to the presence of the King, he
repairs thither himself.

The Brabantian hosts are gathering, and he is expected to
lead them to battle, but owing to Elsa's question he is now
obliged to disclose who he is and to take his departure. He
proclaims that he is Lohengrin, son of Parsifal, Knight of the
Holy Grail, and that he can stay no longer in Brabant, but
must return to the place of his coming. The swan has once
more appeared, drawing the boat down the river; bidding Elsa
farewell he steps into the little shell-like craft. Then Ortrud,

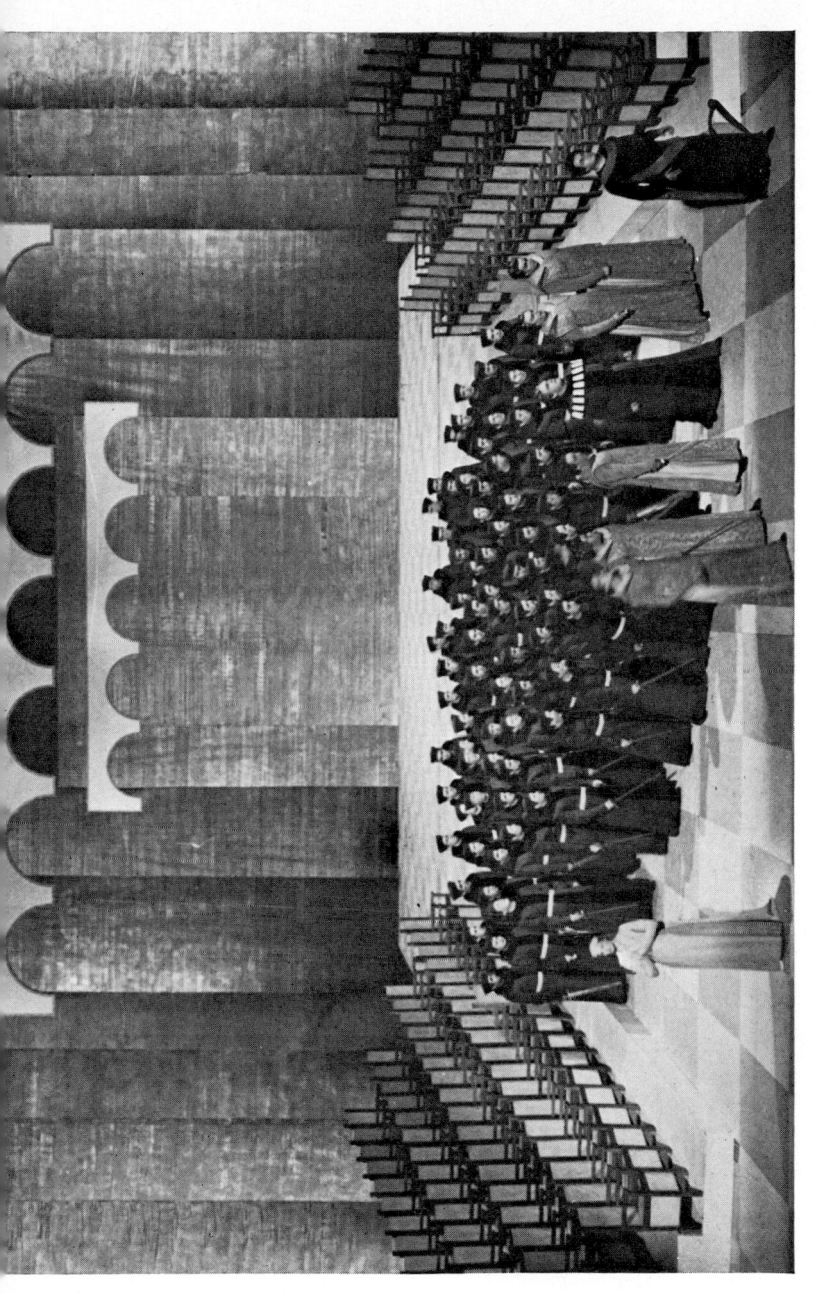

7 *Tannhäuser* at Bayreuth in Wieland Wagner's production, 1955. Gré Brouwenstijn is Elisabeth and Ramon Vinay Tannhäuser.

8 *Tristan und Isolde*: Brangäne offers Isolde the Love Potion—Bayreuth 1886 (Rosa Sucher as Isolde, Gisela Staudigl as Brangäne) and 1974 (Caterina Ligendza and Yvonne Minton).

with malicious glee, declares that the swan is none other than Elsa's brother, whom she, Ortrud, bewitched into this form, and that he would have been changed back again to his human shape had it not been for Elsa's rashness. But Lohengrin, through his supernatural powers, is able to undo Ortrud's work, and at a word from him the swan disappears and Godfrey stands in its place. A dove now descends, and, hovering in front of the boat, draws it away with Lohengrin, while Elsa expires in her brother's arms.

Owing to the lyric character of the story upon which *Lohengrin* is based, the opera, while not at all lacking in strong dramatic situations, is characterised by a subtler and more subdued melodiousness than *Tannhäuser*, is more exquisitely lyrical in fact than any Wagnerian work except *Parsifal*.

There are typical themes in the score, but they are hardly handled with the varied effect that entitles them to be called leading motifs. On the other hand there are fascinating details of orchestration. He uses the brass chiefly to accompany the King, and, of course, the martial choruses; the plaintive, yet spiritual high woodwind for Elsa; the English horn and sombre bass clarinet—the instrument that had to be bought— for Ortrud; the violins, especially in high harmonic positions, to indicate the Grail and its representative, for Lohengrin is a Knight of the Holy Grail. Even the keys employed are distinctive. The Herald's trumpets blow in C and greet the King's arrival in that bright key. F sharp minor is the dark, threatful key that indicates Ortrud's appearance. The key of A, which is the purest for strings and the most ethereal in effect, on account of the greater ease of using 'harmonics', announces the approach of Lohengrin and the subtle influence of the Grail.

The Prelude is based entirely upon one theme, a beautiful one and expressive of the sanctity of the Grail, of which Lohengrin is one of the knights. Violins and flutes with long-drawn-out, ethereal chords open the Prelude. Then is heard on the violins, so divided as to heighten the delicacy of the effect, the Motif of the Grail, the cup in which the Saviour's blood is supposed to have been caught as it flowed from the wound in His side, while He was on the Cross. No modern book on orchestration is considered complete unless it quotes this passage from the score, which is at once the earliest and, after seventy years, still the most perfect example of the effect of celestial harmony produced on the high notes of the divided violin choir. This interesting passage in the score is as follows:

Although this is the only motif that occurs in the Prelude, the ear never wearies of it. Its effectiveness is due to the wonderful skill with which Wagner handles the theme, working it up through a crescendo to a magnificent climax, with all the splendours of Wagnerian orchestration, after which it dies away again to the ethereal harmonies with which it first greeted the listener.

Act I.   The curtain, on rising, discloses a scene of unwonted life on the plain near the River Scheldt, where the stream winds toward Antwerp. On an elevated seat under a huge oak sits King Henry I. On either side are his Saxon and Thuringian nobles. Facing him with the knights of Brabant are Count Frederick of Telramund and his wife, Ortrud, of dark, almost forbidding beauty, and with a treacherous mingling of haughtiness and humility in her carriage.

It is a strange tale the King has just heard fall from Frederick of Telramund's lips. Henry has assembled the Brabantians on the plain by the Scheldt in order to summon them to join his army and aid in checking the threatened invasion of Germany by the Hungarians. But he has found the Brabantians themselves torn by factional strife, some supporting, others opposing Frederick in his claim to the ducal succession of Brabant.

'Sire,' says Frederick, when called upon by the King to explain the cause of the discord that has come upon the land, 'the late Duke of Brabant upon his death-bed confided to me, his kinsman, the care of his two children, Elsa and her young brother Godfrey, with the right to claim the maid as my wife. But one day Elsa led the boy into the forest and returned alone. From her pale face and faltering lips I judged only too well of what had happened, and I now publicly accuse Elsa of having made away with her brother that she might be sole heir to Brabant and reject my right to her hand. Her hand! Horrified, I shrank from her and took a wife whom I could truly love. Now as nearest kinsman of the duke I claim this land as my own, my wife, too, being of the race that once gave a line of princes to Brabant.'

So saying, he leads Ortrud forward, and she, lowering her dark visage, makes a deep obeisance to the King. To the latter but one course is open. A terrible accusation has been uttered, and an appeal must be made to the immediate judgment of God in trial by combat between Frederick and whoever may appear as champion for Elsa. Solemnly the King hangs his shield on the oak, the Saxons and Thuringians thrust the points of their swords into the ground, while the Brabantians lay theirs before them. The royal Herald steps forward. 'Elsa, without delay appear!' he calls in a loud voice.

A sudden hush falls upon the scene, as a slender figure robed in white slowly advances toward the King. It is Elsa. With her fair brow, gentle mien, and timid footsteps it seems impossible that she can be the object of Frederick's dire charge. But there are dark forces conspiring against her, of which none knows save her accuser and the wife he has chosen from the remoter North. In Friesland the weird rites of Odin and the ancient gods still had many secret adherents, Ortrud among them, and it is the hope of this heathenish woman, through the undoing of Elsa and the accession of Frederick whom she has completely under her influence, to check the spread of the Christian faith toward the North and restore the rites of Odin in Brabant. To this end she is ready to bring into play all the black magic of which she secretly is mistress. What wonder that Elsa, as she encounters her malevolent gaze, lowers her eyes with a shudder!

Up to the moment of Elsa's entrance, the music is harsh and vigorous, reflecting Frederick's excitement as, incited by Ortrud, he brings forward his charge against Elsa. With her appearance a change immediately comes over the music. It is soft, gentle, and plaintive; not, however, entirely hopeless, as if the maiden, being conscious of her innocence, does not despair of her fate.

'Elsa,' gently asks the King, 'whom name you as your champion?' She answers as if in a trance; and it is at this point that the music of 'Elsa's Dream' is heard. In the course of this, violins whisper the Grail Motif and in dreamy rapture

Elsa sings, 'I see, in splendour shining, a knight of glorious mien. His eyes rest upon me with tranquil gaze. He stands amid clouds beside a house of gold, and resting on his sword. Heaven has sent him to save me. He shall my champion be!'

The men regard each other in wonder. But a sneer curls around Ortrud's lips, and Frederick again proclaims his readiness to prove his accusation in trial by combat for life and death. 'Elsa,' the King asks once more, 'whom have you chosen as your champion?' 'Him whom Heaven shall send me; and to him, whatever he shall ask of me, I freely will give, e'en though it be myself as bride!' Again there is heard the lovely, broad, and flowing melody of which I have already spoken and which may be designated as the Elsa Motif (Ex. 2).

The Herald now stations his trumpeters at the corners of the plain and bids them blow a blast toward the four points of the compass. When the last echo has died away he calls aloud:

'He who in right of Heaven comes here to fight for Elsa of Brabant, let him step forth!'

The deep silence that follows is broken by Frederick' voice. 'No one appears to repel my charge. 'Tis proven.'

Again the trumpeters blow toward the four points of the compass, again the Herald cries his call, again there is the fateful silence. Suddenly there is a commotion among the men nearest the river bank.

'A wonder!' they cry. 'A swan—drawing a boat by a golden chain! In the boat stands a knight!'

There is a rush toward the bank and a great shout of acclaim, as the swan brings the shell-like boat, in which stands a knight in dazzling armour and of noble bearing, up to the shore. Not daring to trust her senses and turn to behold the wondrous spectacle, Elsa gazes in rapture heavenward, while Ortrud and Telramund, their fell intrigue suddenly halted by a marvel that surpasses their comprehension, regard each other with mingled amazement and alarm.

Lohengrin bids farewell to the swan, which gently inclines its head and then glides away with the boat, vanishing as it had come. The men fall back and the Knight of the Swan, for a silver swan surmounts his helmet and is blazoned upon his shield, having made due obeisance to the King, advances to where Elsa stands and, resting his eyes upon her pure and radiant beauty, questions her.

'Elsa,' he says slowly, as if wishing her to weigh every word, 'if I champion your cause and take you to wife, there is one promise I must exact: Never must you ask me whence I come or what my name.' 'I promise,' she answers, serenely meeting his warning look.

'Elsa, I love you!' he exclaims, as he clasps her in his arms. Then addressing the King he proclaims his readiness to defend her innocence in trial by combat.

In this scene occurs one of the significant themes of the opera, the Motif of Warning—for it is Elsa's disregard of it and the breaking of her promise that brings her happiness to an end.

Three Saxons for the Knight and three Brabantians for Frederick solemnly pace off the circle within which the comabtants are to fight. The King, drawing his sword, strikes three resounding blows with it on his shield. At the first stroke the Knight and Frederick take their positions. At the second they draw their swords. At the third they advance to the encounter. Frederick is no coward. His willingness to meet the Knight whose coming had been so strange proves that. But his blows are skilfully warded off until the Swan Knight, finding an opening, fells him with a powerful stroke.

Frederick's life is forfeited, but his conquerer, perhaps knowing that he has been nothing but a tool in the hands of a woman leagued with the powers of evil, spares it and bids his fallen foe rise. The King leads Elsa to the victor, while all hail him as her deliverer and betrothed.

The scenes here described are most stirring. Before the combat begins, the King intones a prayer, in which first the principals and then the chorus join with noble effect, while the music of rejoicing over the Knight's victory has an irresistible onsweep.

Act II. That night in the fortress of Antwerp, the palace where the knights live is brilliantly illuminated and sounds of revelry issue from it. But in the shadow of the walls sit two figures, a man and a woman; the man, his head bowed in despair, the woman looking vindictively toward the palace. They are Frederick and Ortrud, who have been condemned to banishment, he utterly dejected, she still trusting in the power of her heathenish gods. Not knowing that Ortrud still darkly schemes to ruin Elsa and restore him to power, Frederick denounces her in an outburst of rage and despair.

As another burst of revelry, another flash of light, causes Frederick to bow his head in deeper gloom, Ortrud begins to unfold her plot to him. Let Frederick conceal himself within the minster and, when the bridal procession reaches the steps come forth and, accusing the Knight of treachery and deceit, demand that he be compelled to disclose his name and origin. He will refuse, and thus, even before Elsa enters the minster, she will begin to be beset by doubts. She herself meanwhile will seek to enter the *Kemenate* and play upon her credulousness. 'She is for me; her champion is for you. Soon the daughter of Odin will teach you all the joys of vengeance!' is Ortrud's sinister exclamation as she finishes.

Indeed it seems as if Fate were playing into her hand. For at that very moment Elsa comes out upon the balcony and breathes out upon the night air her rapture at the thought of what bliss the coming day has in store for her. As she lets her gaze rest on the calm night she hears a piteous voice calling her name, and looking down sees Ortrud, her hands raised in supplication to her. Moved by the spectacle of one but a short time before so proud and now apparently in such utter dejection, the guileless maid descends and gently leads her in while Ortrud pours doubts regarding her champion into Elsa's mind. The whole closes with a beautiful duet, which is repeated by the orchestra, as Ortrud is conducted by Elsa into the apartment.

It is early morn. People begin to gather in the open place before the minster and, by the time the sun is high, the space is crowded with folk eager to view the bridal procession. They sing a fine and spirited chorus.

A great shout, 'Hail! Elsa of Brabant!' goes up, as the bride herself appears followed by her ladies-in-waiting. For the moment Ortrud's presence in the train is unnoticed, but as Elsa approaches the minster, Frederick's wife suddenly throws herself in her path.

'Back, Elsa!' she cries. 'I am not a menial, born to follow you! Although your Knight has overthrown my husband, you cannot boast of who he is—his very name, the place whence he came, are unknown. Strong must be his motives to forbid you to question him. To what foul disgrace would he be brought were he compelled to answer!'

Fortunately, the King, the bridegroom, and the nobles approaching from the palace, Elsa shrinks from Ortrud to her champion's side and hides her face against his breast. At that moment Frederick of Telramund, taking his cue from Ortrud, comes out upon the minster steps and repeats his wife's accusation. Then, profiting by the confusion, he slips away in the crowd. The insidious poison, however, has already begun to take effect. For even as the King, taking the Knight on his right and Elsa on his left, conducts them up the minster steps, the trembling bride catches sight of Ortrud whose hand is raised in threat and warning; and it is clinging to her champion, in love indeed, but love mingled with doubt and fear, that she passes through the portal and into the edifice.

Act III. The wedding festivities are described in the brilliant Introduction. This is followed in the opera by the 'Bridal Chorus', which, whenever heard—on stage or in church—falls with renewed freshness and significance upon the ear. The King ceremonially embraces the couple and then the procession makes its way out, until, as the last strains of the chorus die away, Elsa and her champion are for the first time alone.

The love duet is exquisite—one of the sweetest and tenderest passages of which the lyric stage can boast.

It should be a moment of supreme happiness for both, and, indeed, Elsa exclaims as her bridegroom takes her into his arms that words cannot give expression to all its hidden sweetness. Yet, when he tenderly breathes her name, it serves only to remind her that she cannot respond by uttering his 'How sweetly sounds my name when spoken by you, while I, alas, cannot reply with yours. Surely, some day, you will tell me, all in secret, and I shall be able to whisper it when none but you is near!'

In her words the Knight perceives but too clearly the seeds of the fatal mistrust sown by Ortrud and Frederick. Gently he leaves her side and, throwing open the casement, points to the flowery close below, softly illumined by the moon, and sings to an accompaniment of what might be called musical moonbeams, 'Say, dost thou breathe the incense sweet of flowers?' The same subtle magic that can conjure up this scene from the night has brought him to her, made him love her and give unshakeable credence to her vow never to question his name or origin. Will she now wantonly destroy the wondrous spell of moonlight and love?

In spite of the tender warning which he conveys to her, she begins to question him, but he turns toward her and in a passionate musical phrase begs her to trust him and abide with him in loving faith. Her dread that the memory of the delightful place from which he has come will wean him from her; the wild vision in which she imagines she sees the swan approaching to bear him away from her, and when she puts to him the forbidden questions, are details expressed with wonderful vividness in the music.

After the attack by Frederick and his death, there is a dramatic silence during which Elsa sinks on her husband's breast and faints. When I say silence I do not mean that there is a total cessation of sound, for silence can be more impressively expressed in music than by actual silence itself. It is done by Wagner in this case by long drawn-out chords followed by faint taps on the tympani. When the Knight bends down to Elsa, raises her, and gently places her on a couch, echoes of the love duet add to the mournfulness of the music. The scene closes with the Motif of Warning, which resounds with dread meaning.

The second scene takes place on the banks of the Scheldt on the very spot where he had disembarked, the Knight elects to make reply to Elsa's questions. There the King, the nobles, and the Brabantians, whom he was to lead, are awaiting him, and as their leader they hail him when he appears. This scene, 'Promise of Victory', is in the form of a brilliant march and chorus, during which the Counts of Brabant, followed by their vassals, enter on horseback from various directions. In the average performance of the opera, however, much of it is sacrificed in order to shorten the representation.

The Knight answers their hail by telling them that he has come to bid them farewell, that Elsa has been lured to break her vow and ask the forbidden questions which he now is there to answer. From distant lands he came, from Montsalvat, where stands the temple of the Holy Grail, his father, Parsifal, its King, and he, Lohengrin, its Knight. And now, his name and lineage known, he must return, for the Grail gives strength to its knights to right wrong and protect the innocent only so long as the secret of their power remains unrevealed.

Even while he speaks the swan is seen floating down the river. Sadly Lohengrin bids Elsa farewell. Sadly all, save one, look on. For Ortrud, who now pushes her way through the spectators, it is a moment of triumph.

'Depart in all your glory,' she calls out. 'The swan that draws you away is none other than Elsa's brother Godfrey, changed by my magic into his present form. Had she kept her vow, had you been allowed to tarry, you would have freed him from my spell. The ancient gods, whom faithfully I serve, thus punish human faithlessness!'

By the river bank Lohengrin falls upon his knees and prays in silence. Suddenly a white dove descends over the boat; the swan vanishes; in its place Godfrey stands upon the bank, and Lohengrin, entering the boat, is drawn away by the dove. At sight of the young Duke, Ortrud falls with a shriek, while the Brabantian nobles kneel before him as he advances and bow to the King. Elsa gazes on him in rapture until, remembering her own sorrow, as the boat in which Lohengrin stands vanishes around the upper bend of the river, she cries out, 'My husband! My husband!' and falls back in death in her brother's arms.

Lohengrin's narrative of his origin is beautifully set to music familiar from the Prelude; but when he proclaims his name we hear the same measures which Elsa sang in the second part of her dream in the first act. Very beautiful and tender is the music which he sings when he hands Elsa his horn, his sword, and his ring to give to her brother, should he return, and also his greeting to the swan when it comes to bear him back. The work is brought to a close with a repetition of the music of the second portion of Elsa's dream, followed by a superb climax with the Motif of the Grail. K.

TRISTAN UND ISOLDE
Tristan and Isolde

Opera in three acts, by Richard Wagner, text by the composer. Première, Munich, June 10, 1865, with Malvina Schnorr von Carolsfeld, Anne Deinet, Ludwig Schnorr von Carolsfeld (the Tristan was thus in real life the husband of the Isolde), Zottmayer, Mitterwurzer, Heinrich, conductor Hans von Bülow. Bülow it will be remembered was still married to Cosima at the time of the première of *Tristan* and did not in fact divorce her until a year later. First performed Drury Lane, London, 1882, with Rose Sucher, Brandt, Winkelmann, Gura, Landau, conductor Richter; Bayreuth 1886, with Malten, Gisela, Staudigl, Gudehus, Gura, Plank, conductor Mottl; Metropolitan New York, 1886, with Lilli Lehmann, Brandt, Niemann, Robinson, Fischer, conductor Seidl; Covent Garden, 1892, with Rosa Sucher, Schumann-Heink, Alvary, Knapp, conductor Mahler. Jean de Reszke is generally accounted the greatest Tristan heard at the Metropolitan. Others famous in this role were Schmedes, Vogel, Urlus, Melchior, Vinay and Windgassen. Famous Isoldes have included Nordica, Ternina, Fremstad, Mildenburg, Wittich, Gadski, Litvinne, Kappel, Leider, Larsen-Todsen, Marta Fuchs, Flagstad, Lubin, Traubel, Varnay, Mödl, Birgit Nilsson; Bispham, van Rooy, and Hotter were famous Kurwenals and Edouard de Reszke, Mayr, Bohnen, Kipnis, and Weber as King Marke. Amongst Italian singers, Giuseppe Borgatti and Giuseppina Cobelli were particularly well-known exponents of the title roles.

CHARACTERS
Tristan, *a Cornish knight, nephew to King Marke* . Tenor
King Marke, *of Cornwall* . . . . Bass
Isolde, *an Irish princess* . . . . Soprano
Kurwenal, *one of Tristan's retainers* . . . . Baritone
Melot, *a courtier* . . . . Tenor
Brangäne, *Isolde's attendant* . . . . .Mezzo-Soprano
A Shepherd . . . . Tenor
A Sailor . . . . Tenor
A Helmsman . . . . Baritone
Sailors, Knights, Esquires, and Men-at-Arms
Time: Legendary   *Place:* A ship at sea; outside King
Marke's palace, Cornwall; Tristan's
castle at Kareol

Wagner remodelled the *Tristan* legend thoroughly before turning it into a music-drama.[1] He has shorn it of all unnecessary incidents and worked the main episodes into a concise, vigorous, swiftly moving drama, admirably adapted for the stage. He shows keen dramatic insight in the manner in which he adapts the love-potion of the legends to his purpose. In the legends the love of Tristan and Isolde is merely 'chemical'—entirely the result of the love-philtre. Wagner, however, presents them from the outset as enamoured of one another, so that the potion simply quickens a passion already active.

To the courtesy of G. Schirmer, Inc., publishers of my *Wagner's Music-Dramas Analysed*, I am indebted, as I have already stated elsewhere, for permission to use material from that book. I have there placed a brief summary of the story of *Tristan and Isolde* before the descriptive account of the 'book' and music, and accordingly do so here.

In the Wagnerian version the plot is briefly as follows: Tristan, having lost his parents in infancy, has been reared at the court of his uncle, Marke, King of Cornwall. He has slain in combat Morold, an Irish knight, who had come to Cornwall to collect the tribute that country had been paying to Ireland. Morold was betrothed to his cousin Isolde, daughter of the Irish King. Tristan, having been dangerously wounded in the combat, places himself, without disclosing his identity, under the care of Isolde, who comes of a race skilled in magic arts. She discerns who he is; but, although she is aware that she is harbouring the slayer of her intended husband, she spares him and carefully tends him, for she has conceived a deep passion for him. Tristan in his turn falls in love with her, but both believe their love unrequited. Soon after Tristan's return to Cornwall, he is dispatched to Ireland by Marke, that he may win Isolde as Queen for the Cornish King.

The music-drama opens on board the vessel in which Tristan bears Isolde to Cornwall. Thinking that Tristan does not love her, she determines to end her sorrow by quaffing a death-potion; and Tristan, feeling that the woman he loves is about to be wedded to another, readily consents to share it with her. But Brangäne, Isolde's companion, substitutes a

[1] Cf. Frank Martin's *Le Vin Herbé* based on Bédier's version of the legend.

love-potion for the death-draught, and this rouses their love to irresistible passion. Not long after they reach Cornwall, they are surprised in the castle garden by the King and his suite, and Tristan is severely wounded by Melot, one of Marke's knights. Kurwenal, Tristan's faithful retainer, bears him to his native place, Kareol. Isolde follows him, arriving in time to fold him in her arms as he expires. She breathes her last over his corpse.

All who have made a study of opera, and do not regard it merely as a form of amusement, are agreed that the score of *Tristan and Isolde* is the greatest setting of a love-story for the lyric stage. It is a tale of tragic passion, culminating in death, unfolded in the surge and palpitation of immortal music.

This passion smouldered in the heart of the man and woman of this epic of love. It could not burst into clear flame because over it lay the pall of duty—a knight's to his king, a wife's to her husband. They elected to die; drank, as they thought, a death potion. Instead it was a magic love-philtre, craftily substituted by the woman's confidante. Then love, no longer vague and hesitating, but roused by sorcerous means to the highest rapture, found expression in the complete abandonment of the lovers to their ecstasy—and their fate.

What precedes the draught of the potion in the drama, is narrative, explanatory, and prefatorial. Once Tristan and Isolde have shared the goblet, passion is unleashed. The goal is death.

The magic love-philtre is the excitant in this story of rapture and gloom. The Vorspiel therefore opens most fittingly with a motive which expresses the incipient effect of the potion upon Tristan and Isolde. It clearly can be divided into two parts, one descending, the other ascending chromatically. The potion overcomes the restraining influence of duty in two beings and leaves them at the mercy of their passions. The first part, with its descending chromatics, is pervaded by a certain sadness of mood, as if Tristan were still vaguely forewarned by his conscience of the impending tragedy. The second soars ecstatically upward. It is the woman yielding unquestioningly to the rapture of requited love. Therefore, while the phrase may be called the

Motif of the Love-Potion, or, as Wolzogen calls it, of Yearning, it seems best to divide it into the Tristan and Isolde Motifs (A and B).

The two motifs having been twice repeated, there is a *fermata*. Then the Isolde Motif alone is heard, so that the attention of the hearer is fixed upon it. For in this tragedy, as in that of Eden, it is the woman who takes the first decisive step. After another *fermata*, the last two notes of the Isolde Motif are twice repeated, dying away to *pp*. Then a variation of the Isolde Motif leads with an impassioned upward sweep

into another version, full of sensuous yearning, and distinct enough to form a new motif, the Motif of the Love Glance.

This occurs again and again in the course of the Vorspiel. Though readily recognised, it is sufficiently varied with each repetition never to allow the emotional excitement to subside. In fact, the Vorspiel gathers impetus as it proceeds, until, with an inversion of the Love Glance Motif, borne to a higher and higher level of exaltation by upward rushing runs, it reaches its climax in a paroxysm of love, to die away with

repetitions of the Tristan, the Isolde, and the Love Glance Motifs.

In the themes it employs this prelude tells, in music, the story of the love of Tristan and Isolde. We have the motifs of the hero and heroine of the drama, and the Motif of the Love Glance. When, as is the case in concerts, the finale of the work, 'Liebestod',[1] is linked to the Vorspiel, we hear the beginning and the end of the music-drama, forming an eloquent epitome of the tragic story.

Act I.   Wagner refrains from actually placing before us on the stage the events that transpired in Ireland before Tristan was despatched thither to bring Isolde as a bride to King Marke. The events, which led to the two meetings between Tristan and Isolde, are told in Isolde's narrative, which forms an important part of the first act. This act opens aboard the vessel in which Tristan is conveying Isolde to Cornwall.

The scene shows Isolde reclining on a couch, her face hid in soft pillows, in a tent-like apartment on the forward deck of a vessel. It is hung with rich tapestries, which hide the rest of the ship from view. Brangäne has partially drawn aside one of the hangings and is gazing out upon the sea. From above, as though from the rigging, is heard the voice of a young Sailor singing a farewell song to his 'Irish maid'. It has a wild charm and is a capital example of Wagner's skill in giving local colouring to his music. The words, 'Frisch weht der Wind der Heimath zu' (The wind blows freshly toward our home), are sung to a phrase which occurs frequently in the course of this scene. It represents most graphically the heaving of the sea and may be appropriately termed the Ocean Motif. It undulates gracefully through Brangäne's reply to Isolde's question as to the vessel's course, surges wildly around Isolde's outburst of impotent anger when she learns that Cornwall's shore is not far distant, and breaks itself in savage fury against her despairing wrath as she

---

[1] But the word, now customarily applied to the music of Isolde's death, was intended by Wagner to characterise the Prelude, which contains the seeds of Death through Love.

invokes the elements to destroy the ship and all upon it.
Ocean Motif:

It is her hopeless passion for Tristan which has prostrated
Isolde, for the Motif of the Love Glance accompanies her
first exclamation as she starts up excitedly.

Isolde calls upon Brangäne to throw aside the hangings,
that she may have air. Brangäne obeys. The deck of the ship,
and beyond it, the ocean, are disclosed. Around the
mainmast sailors are busy splicing ropes. Beyond them, on
the after deck, are knights and esquires. A little aside from
them stands Tristan, gazing out upon the sea. At his feet
reclines Kurwenal, his esquire. The young Sailor's voice is
again heard.

Isolde beholds Tristan. Her wrath at the thought that he
whom she loves is bearing her as bride to another vents itself
in an angry phrase. She invokes death upon him. This phrase
is the Motif of Death. The Motif of the Love Glance is
heard—and gives away Isolde's secret—as she asks Brangäne in
what estimation she holds Tristan. It develops into a
triumphant strain as Brangäne sings his praises. Isolde then
bids her command Tristan to come into her presence. This
command is given with the Motif of Death, for it is their
mutual death Isolde wishes to encompass. As Brangäne goes
to do her mistress's bidding, a graceful variation of the Ocean

Motif is heard, the bass marking the rhythmic motions of the
sailors at the ropes. Tristan refuses to leave the helm and
when Brangäne repeats Isolde's command, Kurwenal answers
with a song in praise of Tristan. Knights, esquires, and sailors
repeat the refrain. The boisterous measures—'Hail to our
brave Tristan!'—form the Tristan Call.

Heil un-ser Held Tris - tan,

Isolde's wrath at Kurwenal's taunts find vent in a narrative
in which she tells Brangäne that once a wounded knight
calling himself Tantris landed on Ireland's shore to seek her
healing art. Into a nick in his sword she fitted a sword
splinter she had found imbedded in the head of Morold,
which had been sent to her in mockery after he had been
slain in a combat with the Cornish foe. She brandished the
sword over the knight, whom thus by his weapon she knew
to be Tristan, her betrothed's slayer. But Tristan's glance fell
upon her. Under its spell she was powerless. She nursed him
back to health, and he vowed eternal gratitude as he left her.
The chief theme of this narrative is derived from the Tristan
Motif.

> 'What of the boat, so bare, so frail,
> That drifted to our shore?
> What of the sorely stricken man feebly extended there?
> Isolde's art he humbly sought;
> With balsam, herbs, and healing salves,
> From wounds that laid him low,
> She nursed him back to strength.'

etc.

Exquisite is the transition of the phrase 'His eyes in mine were gazing' to the Isolde and Love Glance Motifs. The passage beginning: 'Who silently his life had spared', is followed by the Tristan Call, Isolde seeming to compare sarcastically what she considers his betrayal of her with his fame as a hero. Her outburst of wrath, as she inveighs against his treachery in now bearing her as bride to King Marke, carries the narrative to a superb climax. Brangäne seeks to comfort Isolde, but the latter, looking fixedly before her, confides, almost involuntarily, her love for Tristan.

It is clear, even from this brief description, with what constantly varying expression the narrative of Isolde is treated. Wrath, desire for vengeance, rapturous memories that cannot be dissembled, finally a confession of love to Brangäne—such are the emotions that surge to the surface.

They lead Brangäne to exclaim: 'Where lives the man who would not love you?' Then she weirdly whispers of the love-potion and takes a phial from a golden casket. The motifs of the Love Glance and of the Love-Potion accompany her words and action. But Isolde seizes another phial, which she holds up triumphantly. It is the death-potion. Here is heard an ominous phrase of three notes—the Motif of Fate.

A forceful orchestral climax, in which the demons of despairing wrath seem unleashed, is followed by the cries of the sailors greeting the sight of the land, where she is to be married to King Marke. Isolde hears them with growing terror. Kurwenal brusquely calls to her and Brangäne to prepare soon to go ashore. Isolde orders Kurwenal that he command Tristan to come into her presence; then bids Brangäne prepare the death-potion. The Death Motif accompanies her final commands to Kurwenal and Brangäne, and the Fate Motif also drones threateningly through the weird measures. But Brangäne artfully substitutes the love-potion for the death-draught.

Kurwenal announces Tristan's approach. Isolde, seeking to control her agitation, strides to the couch, and, supporting herself by it, gazes fixedly at the entrance where Tristan remains standing. The motif which announces his appearance is full of tragic defiance, as if Tristan felt that he stood upon the threshold of death, yet was ready to meet his fate unflinchingly. It alternates effectively with the Fate Motif, and is used most dramatically throughout the succeeding scene between Tristan and Isolde. Isolde claims that she wants to drink to their reconciliation. Sombrely impressive is the passage when he bids Isolde slay him with the sword she once held over him.

Shouts of the sailors announce the proximity of land. In a variant of her narrative theme Isolde mockingly anticipates Tristan's praise of her as he leads her into King Marke's presence. At the same time she hands him the goblet which contains, as she thinks, the death-potion and invites him to quaff it. Again the shouts of the sailors are heard, and Tristan, seizing the goblet, raises it to his lips with the ecstasy of one from whose soul a great sorrow is about to be lifted. When he has half emptied it, Isolde wrests it from him and drains it.

The tremor that passes over Isolde loosens her grasp upon the goblet. It falls from her hand. She faces Tristan.

Is the light in their eyes the last upflare of passion before the final darkness? What does the music answer as it enfolds them in its wondrous harmonies? The Isolde Motif;—then what? Not the glassy stare of death; the Love Glance, like a swift shaft of light penetrating the gloom. The spell is broken. Isolde sinks into Tristan's embrace.

Voices! They hear them not. Sailors are shouting with joy that the voyage is over. Upon the lovers all sounds are lost, save their own short, quick interchange of phrases, in which the rapture of their passion, at last uncovered, finds speech. Music surges about them. But for Brangäne they would be lost. It is she who parts them, as the hangings are thrust aside.

Knights, esquires, sailors crowd the deck. From a rocky height King Marke's castle looks down upon the ship, now riding at anchor in the harbour. Peace and joy everywhere save in the lovers' breasts! Isolde faints in Tristan's arms. Yet it is a triumphant climax of the Isolde Motif that is heard above the jubilation of the ship-folk, as the act comes to a close.

Act II. This act also has an introduction which, together with the first scene between Isolde and Brangäne, constitutes a wonderful mood picture in music. Even Wagner's bitterest critic, Eduard Hanslick, of Vienna, was disposed to compare

t with the loveliest creations of Schubert, in which that
:omposer steeps the senses in dreams of night and love.

And so, this introduction of the second act opens with a
notif of peculiar significance. During the love scene in the
)revious act, Tristan and Isolde have inveighed against the
lay which jealously keeps them apart. They may meet only
inder the veil of darkness. Even then their joy is embittered
)y the thought that the blissful night will soon be succeeded
)y day. With them, therefore, the day stands for all that is
nimical, night for all that is friendly. This simile is elaborated
vith considerable metaphysical subtlety, the lovers even
eproaching the day with Tristan's willingness to lead Isolde
o King Marke, Tristan charging that in the broad light of the
ealous day his duty to win Isolde for his King stood forth so
:learly as to overpower the passion for her which he had
iurtured during the silent watches of the night. The phrase,
herefore, which begins the act as with an agonised cry is the
)ay Motif.

The Day Motif is followed by a phrase whose eager,

estless measures graphically reflect the impatience with
vhich Isolde awaits the coming of Tristan—the Motif of
mpatience.

Over this there hovers a dulcet, seductive strain, the Motif
)f the Love Call, which is developed into the rapturous
neasures of the Motif of Ecstasy (top of page 226).

When the curtain rises, the scene it discloses is the palace
;arden, into which Isolde's apartments open. It is a summer
iight, balmy and with a moon. The King and his suite have
leparted on a hunt. With them is Melot, a knight who
)rofesses devotion to Tristan, but whom Brangäne suspects.

Brangäne stands upon the steps leading to Isolde's apartment. She is looking down a wooded clearing in the direction taken by the hunt. She fears the hunt is but a trap and that its quarry is not the wild deer, but her mistress, and the knight who conveyed her for bride to King Marke. Meanwhile against the open door of Isolde's apartment is a burning torch. Its flare through the night is to be the signal to Tristan that all is well, and that Isolde waits.

The first episode of the act is one of those exquisite tone-paintings in the creation of which Wagner is supreme. The notes of the hunting-horns become more distant. Isolde comes from her apartment into the garden. She asks Brangäne if she cannot now signal for Tristan. Brangäne answers that the hunt is still within hearing. Isolde chides her—is it not some lovely, prattling rill she hears? The music is deliciously idyllic—conjuring up a dream-picture of a sylvan spring night bathed in liquescent moonlight. Brangäne warns Isolde against Melot; but Isolde laughs at her fears. In vain Brangäne entreats her mistress not to signal for Tristan. The seductive measures of the Love Call and of the Motif of Ecstasy tell throughout this scene of the yearning in Isolde's breast. When Brangäne informs Isolde that she substituted the love-potion for the death-draught, Isolde scorns the suggestion that her guilty love for Tristan is the result of her quaffing the potion. This simply intensified the passion already in her breast. She proclaims this in the rapturous phrases of the Isolde Motif; and then, when she declares her fate to be in the hands of the goddess of love, there are heard the tender accents of the Love Motif.

In vain Brangäne warns once more against possible treachery from Melot. The Love Motif rises with ever increasing passion until Isolde's emotional exaltation finds expression in the Motif of Ecstasy as she bids Brangäne hie to the lookout, and proclaims that she will give Tristan the signal by extinguishing the torch, though in doing so she were to extinguish the light of her life. The Motif of the Love Call ringing out triumphantly accompanies her action, and dies away into the Motif of Impatience as she gazes in the direction from which she seems to expect Tristan to come to her. Then the Motif of Ecstasy and Isolde's rapturous gesture tell that she has discerned her lover; and, as this motif reaches a fiercely impassioned climax, Tristan and Isolde rush into each other's arms.

The music seethes with passion as the lovers greet one another, and the Love Motif and the Motif of Ecstasy vying in the excitement of this rapturous meeting. Then begins the exchange of phrases in which the lovers pour forth their love for one another. This is the scene dominated by the Motif of the Day, which, however, as the day sinks into the soft night, is softened into the Night Motif, which soothes the senses with its ravishing caress. This motif throbs through the rapturous harmonies of the duet: 'Oh, sink upon us, Night of Love', and there is nothing in the realms of music or poetry to compare in suggestiveness with these caressing, pulsating phrases.

The duet is broken in upon by Brangäne's voice warning the lovers that night will soon be over. The arpeggios accompanying her warning are like the first grey streaks of dawn. But the lovers heed her not. In a smooth, soft melody—the Motif of Love's Peace—whose sensuous grace is simply entrancing, they whisper their love.

It is at such a moment, enveloped by night and love, that death should have come to them; and, indeed, it is for such a love-death they yearn. Hence we have here, over a quivering accompaniment, the Motif of the Love-Death.

Once more Brangäne calls. Once more Tristan and Isolde heed her not.

'Night will shield us for aye!'

Thus exclaims Isolde in defiance of the approach of dawn, while the Motif of Ecstasy, introduced by a rapturous mordant, soars ever higher.

A cry from Brangäne, Kurwenal rushing upon the scene calling to Tristan to save himself—and the lovers' ravishing dream is ended. Surrounded by the King and his suite, with the treacherous Melot, they gradually awaken to the terror of the situation. Almost automatically Isolde hides her head among the flowers, and Tristan spreads out his cloak to conceal her from view while phrases reminiscent of the love scene rise like mournful memories.

Now follows a soliloquy for the King, whose sword instead should have leapt from its scabbard and buried itself in Tristan's breast. For it seems inexplicable that the monarch, instead of slaying the betrayer of his honour, should indulge in a philosophical discourse, ending:

> 'The unexplained,
> Unpenetrated
> Cause of all these woes,
> Who will to us disclose?'

Tristan turns to Isolde. Will she follow him to the bleak land of his birth? Her reply is that his home shall be hers. Then Melot draws his sword. Tristan rushes upon him but, as Melot thrusts, allows his guard to fall and receives the blade. Isolde throws herself on her wounded lover's breast.

Act III. The introduction to this act opens with a variation of the Isolde Motif, sadly prophetic of the desolation which broods over the scene to be disclosed when the curtain rises. On its third repetition it is continued in a long-drawn-out ascending phrase, which seems to represent musically the broad waste of ocean upon which Tristan's castle looks down from its craggy height.

The whole passage appears to represent Tristan hopelessly yearning for Isolde, letting his fancy travel back over the watery waste to the last night of love, and then giving himself up wholly to his grief.

The curtain rises upon the desolate grounds of Kareol, between the outer walls of Tristan's castle and the main structure, which stands upon a rocky eminence overlooking the sea. Tristan is stretched, apparently lifeless, under a huge lime-tree. Over him, in deep sorrow, bends the faithful Kurwenal. A Shepherd is heard piping a strain, whose plaintive notes harmonise most beautifully with the despairing desolation and sadness of the scene. It is the Lay of Sorrow, and by it the Shepherd, who scans the sea, conveys to Kurwenal information that the ship he has dispatched to Cornwall to bear Isolde to Kareol has not yet hove in sight.

The Lay of Sorrow is a strain of mournful beauty, with the simplicity and indescribable charm of a folk-song. Its plaintive notes cling like ivy to the grey and crumbling ruins of love and joy.

The Shepherd peers over the wall and asks if Tristan has shown any signs of life. Kurwenal gloomily replies in the negative. The Shepherd departs to continue his lookout piping the sad refrain. Tristan slowly opens his eyes. 'The old refrain; why wakes it me? Where am I?' he murmurs Kurwenal is beside himself with joy at these signs of returning life. His replies to Tristan's feeble and wandering questions are mostly couched in a motif which beautifully expresses the sterling nature of this faithful retainer, one of the noblest characters Wagner has drawn.

When Tristan loses himself in sad memories of Isolde Kurwenal seeks to comfort him with the news that he has sent a trusty man to Cornwall to bear Isolde to him that she may heal the wound inflicted by Melot as she once healed that dealt Tristan by Morold. In Tristan's jubilant reply during which he draws Kurwenal to his breast, the Isolde Motif assumes a form in which it becomes a theme of joy.

But it is soon succeeded by the Motif of Anguish, when

Tristan raves of his yearning for Isolde. 'The ship! the ship! he exclaims. 'Kurwenal, can you not see it?' The Lay of Sorrow, piped by the Shepherd, gives the sad answer. I pervades his sad reverie until, when his mind wanders to Isolde's tender nursing of his wound in Ireland, the theme of Isolde's Narrative is heard again. Finally his excitement grow upon him, and in a paroxysm of anguish bordering on insanity he even curses love.

Tristan sinks back apparently dead. But no—as Kurwenal bends over him and the Isolde Motif is breathed by the orchestra, he again whispers of Isolde. In ravishing beauty the Motif of Love's Peace caressingly follows his vision as he seems to see Isolde gliding toward him o'er the waves. With ever-growing excitement he orders Kurwenal to the lookout to watch the ship's coming. What he sees so clearly canno

Kurwenal also see? Suddenly the music changes in character. The ship is in sight, for the Shepherd is heard piping a joyous lay. It pervades the music of Tristan's excited questions and

Kurwenal's answers as to the vessel's movements. The faithful retainer rushes down toward the shore to meet Isolde and lead her to Tristan. The latter, his strength sapped by his wound, his mind inflamed to insanity by his passionate yearning, struggles to rise. He raises himself a little. The Motif of Love's Peace, no longer tranquil, but with frenzied rapidity, accompanies his actions as, in his delirium, he tears the bandage from his wounds and rises from his couch.

Isolde's voice! Into her arms, outstretched to receive him, staggers Tristan. Gently she lets him down upon his couch, where he has lain in the anguish of expectancy.

'Tristan!'

'Isolde!' he answers in broken accents. This last look resting rapturously upon her, while in mournful beauty the Love Glance Motif rises from the orchestra, he expires.

In all music there is no scene more deeply shaken with sorrow.

Tumultuous sounds are heard. A second ship has arrived. Marke and his suite have landed. Kurwenal and his men, thinking the King has come in pursuit of Isolde, attack the newcomers but are overpowered, and Kurwenal, having avenged Tristan by slaying Melot, sinks, himself mortally wounded, and dies by Tristan's side. He reaches out for his dead master's hand, and his last words are: 'Tristan, chide me not that faithfully I follow you.'

When Brangäne rushes in and hurriedly announces that she has informed the King of the love-potion and that he comes bringing forgiveness, Isolde heeds her not. As the Love-Death Motif rises softly over the orchestra and slowly swells into the impassioned Motif of Ecstasy, to reach its climax with a stupendous crash of instrumental forces, she gazes with growing transport upon her dead lover, until, with rapture in her last glance, she sinks upon his corpse and expires.

In the Wagnerian version of the legend this love-death, for which Tristan and Isolde prayed and in which they are united, is more than a mere farewell together to life. It is

tinged with Oriental philosophy, and symbolises the taking
up into and the absorption by nature of all that is
spiritual, and hence immortal, in lives rendered beautiful by
love.   K.

DIE MEISTERSINGER VON NÜRNBERG
The Mastersingers of Nuremberg

Opera in three acts by Richard Wagner. Text by the composer.
Première at the Royal Court Theatre, Munich, June 21, 1868, with
Mathilde Mallinger, Sophie Dietz, Franz Betz, Bausewein, Gustav
Hölzel, Fischer, Nachbauer, Schloser, conductor Hans von Bülow. First
performed Theatre Royal, Drury Lane, 1882, with Rose Sucher,
Schefsky, Gura, Koegel, Ehrke, Landau, Winkelmann, Kraus, conductor
Richter; Metropolitan, New York, 1886, with Seidl-Kraus, Marianne
Brandt, Emil Fischer, Josef Staudigl, Kemlitz, Stritt, Krämer,
conductor Anton Seidl; Covent Garden, 1889 (in Italian), with Albani,
Miranda, Lassalle, Isnardon, Abramoff, Winagradow, Jean de Reszke,
Montariol, conductor Mancinelli. Famous interpreters of the part of
Hans Sachs have included Reichmann, van Rooy, Whitehill, Weil,
Soomer, Schorr, Bockelmann, Nissen, Rode, Prohaska, Schöffler,
Berglund, Hotter, Edelmann, and Norman Bailey.

CHARACTERS

Hans Sachs, *Cobbler*	⎫	Bass
Veit Pogner, *Goldsmith*		Bass
Kunz Vogelgesang, *Furrier*		Tenor
Konrad Nachtigall, *Buckle-Maker*		Bass
Sixtus Beckmesser, *Town Clerk*		Bass
Fritz Kothner, *Baker*	⎬ *Mastersingers* ⎨	Bass
Balthasar Zorn, *Pewterer*		Tenor
Ulrich Eisslinger, *Grocer*		Tenor
Augustin Moser, *Tailor*		Tenor
Hermann Ortel, *Soap-Boiler*		Bass
Hans Schwarz, *Stocking-Weaver*		Bass
Hans Foltz, *Coppersmith*	⎭	Bass
Walther von Stolzing, *a young Franconian knight*		Tenor
David, *apprentice to Hans Sachs*		Tenor
A Night Watchman		Bass
Eva, *daughter of Pogner*		Soprano
Magdalena, *Eva's nurse*		Mezzo-Soprano

Burghers of the Guilds, Journeymen, Apprentices, Girls
Time: Middle of the Sixteenth Century   *Place:* Nuremberg

Walther von Stolzing is in love with Eva. Her father having promised her to the singer to whom at the coming mid-summer festival the Mastersingers shall award the prize, it becomes necessary for Walther to seek admission to their art union. He is, however, rejected, his song violating the rules to which the Mastersingers slavishly adhere. Beckmesser, the town clerk who is the 'marker' of the union, is instrumental in securing Walther's rejection. His duty is to mark all violations of the rules against a candidate, and since he is a suitor for Eva's hand, he naturally makes the most of every chance to put down a mark against Walther, whom he recognises as a rival.

Sachs alone among the Mastersingers has recognised the beauty of Walther's song. Its very freedom from rule and rote charms him, and he discovers in the young knight's un-trammelled genius the power which, if properly directed, will lead art from the beaten path of tradition toward a new and loftier ideal.

After Walther's failure before the Mastersingers the impetuous young knight persuades Eva to elope with him. But at night as they are preparing to escape, Beckmesser comes upon the scene to serenade Eva. Sachs, whose house is opposite Pogner's, has meanwhile brought his work-bench out into the street and insists on 'marking' what he considers Beckmesser's mistakes by bringing his hammer down upon his last with a resounding whack. The louder Beckmesser sings, the louder Sachs bangs. Finally the neighbours are aroused. David, who is in love with Magdalena and thinks Beckmesser is serenading her, falls upon him with a cudgel. The whole neighbourhood turns out and a general *mêlée* ensues, during which Sachs separates Eva and Walther and draws the latter into his home.

The following morning Walther sings to Sachs a song which has come to him in a dream; Sachs transcribes the words and passes friendly criticism upon them and the music. The midsummer festival is to take place that afternoon, and through a ruse Sachs manages to get Walther's poem into Beckmesser's possession, who, thinking the words are by the popular cobbler-poet, feels sure he will be the chosen master. Eva, coming into the workshop to have her shoes fitted, finds Walther, and the lovers depart with Sachs, David, and Magdalena for the festival. Here Beckmesser, as Sachs had anticipated, makes a wretched failure, as he has utterly missed the spirit of the poem, and Walther, being called upon by Sachs to reveal its beauty in music, sings his prize song, winning at once the approbation of Mastersingers and populace. After a momentary hesitation on his part he is received into their art union and at the same time wins Eva as his bride.

The Mastersingers were of burgher extraction. They flourished in Germany, chiefly in the imperial cities, during the fourteenth, fifteenth, and sixteenth centuries. They did much to generate and preserve a love of art among the middle classes. Their musical competitions were judged according to a code of rules which distinguished by particular names thirty-two faults to be avoided. Scriptural or devotional subjects were usually selected and the judges or Markers were, in Nuremberg, four in number, the first comparing the words with the Biblical text, the second criticising the prosody, the third the rhymes, and the fourth the tune. He who had the fewest marks against him received the prize.

Hans Sachs, the most famous of the Mastersingers, born November 5, 1494, died January 1576, in Nuremberg, is said to have been the author of some six thousand poems. He was a cobbler by trade—

> *'Hans Sachs war ein Schuh-*
> *macher und Poet dazu.'*

A monument was erected to him in the city of his birth in 1874.

The Mastersingers is a parable of art told in terms of a simple, human love story, with many touches of humour to enliven it, and its interest enhanced by highly picturesque, historical surroundings. As a drama it conveys also a perfect picture of the life and customs of Nuremberg of the time in which the story plays. Wagner must have made careful historical researches, but his book lore is not thrust upon us. The work is so spontaneous that the method and manner of its art are lost sight of in admiration of the result. Hans Sachs himself could not have left a more faithful portrait of life in Nuremberg in the middle of the sixteenth century.

The Mastersingers has a peculiarly Wagnerian interest. It is Wagner's protest against the narrow-minded critics and the prejudiced public who so long refused him recognition Eduard Hanslick, the bitterest[1] of Wagner's critics, regarded

---

[1] But not so bitter that he could not recognise beauty when he heard it, nor give reasons for his likes and dislikes.   H.

the libretto as a personal insult to himself. Being present by invitation at a private reading of the libretto—at this stage, Beckmesser was called Hans Lick—Hanslick rose abruptly and left after the first act. Walther von Stolzing is the incarnation of new aspirations in art; the champion of a new art ideal, and continually chafing under the restraints imposed by traditional rules and methods. Hans Sachs is a conservative. But, while preserving what is best in art traditions, he is able to recognise the beautiful in what is new. He represents enlightened public opinion. Beckmesser and the other Master-singers are the embodiment of rank prejudice—the critics. Walther's triumph is also Wagner's. Few of Wagner's dramatic creations equal in life-like interest the character of Sachs. It is drawn with a loving, firm hand, and filled in with many delicate touches.

The Vorspiel gives a complete musical epitome of the story. It is full of life and action—pompous, impassioned, and jocose in turn, and without a suggestion of the overwrought or morbid. Its sentiment and its fun are purely human. In its technical construction it has long been recognised as a masterpiece.

In the sense that it precedes the rise of the curtain, this orchestral composition is a Vorspiel, or prelude. As a work, however, it is a fully-fledged overture, rich in thematic material. These themes are Leading Motifs heard many times, and in wonderful variety in the three acts of *The Master-singers*. To a great extent an analysis of this overture forecasts the work itself. Accordingly, again through the courtesy of G. Schirmer Inc., I avail myself of my *Wagner's Music-Dramas Analysed*, in the account of the Vorspiel and of the action and music that follow it.

The pompous Motif of the Mastersingers opens the Vorspiel. This theme gives capital musical expression to the

characteristics of these dignitaries; eminently worthy but self-sufficient citizens who are slow to receive new impressions and do not take kindly to innovations. Our term of 'old fogy' describes them imperfectly, as it does not allow for their many excellent qualities. They are slow to act, but if they are once aroused their ponderous influence bears down all opposition. At first an obstacle to genuine reform, they are in the end the force which pushes it to success. Thus there is in the Motif of the Mastersingers a certain ponderous dignity which well emphasises the idea of conservative power.

In great contrast to this is the Lyric Motif, which seems to

express the striving after a poetic ideal untrammelled by old-fashioned restrictions, such as the rules of the Master-singers impose.

But the sturdy conservative forces are still unwilling to be persuaded of the worth of this new ideal. Hence the Lyric Motif is suddenly checked by the sonorous measures of the Mastersingers' March.

In this the majesty of law and order finds expression. It is followed by a phrase of noble breadth and beauty, obviously developed from portions of the Motif of the Mastersingers and so typical of the goodwill which should exist among the members of a fraternity that it may be called the Motif of the Art Brotherhood.

It reaches an eloquent climax in the Motif of the Ideal.

Opposed, however, to this guild of conservative masters is the restless spirit of progress. Hence, though stately, the strains of the Mastersingers' March and of the Guild Motif soon yield to a theme full of emotional energy and much like the Lyric Motif. Walther is the champion of this new

deal—not, however, from a purely artistic impulse, but rather
through his love for Eva. Being ignorant of the rules and rote
of the Mastersingers, when he presents himself for admission
to the fraternity, he sings measures which soar untrammelled
into realms of beauty beyond the imagination of the masters.
But it was his love for Eva which impelled him to seek
admission to the brotherhood, and love inspired his song. He
is therefore a reformer only by accident; it is not his love of
art but his passion for Eva which really brings about
through his Prize Song a great musical reform. This is one of
Wagner's finest dramatic touches—the love story is the mainspring of the action, the moral is pointed only incidentally.
Hence all the motifs in which the restless striving after a new
ideal, or the struggles of a new art form to break through the
barriers of conservative prejudice, find expression, are so
many love motifs, Eva being the incarnation of Walther's
ideal. Therefore the motif which breaks in upon the Mastersingers' March and Guild Motif with such emotional energy
expresses Walther's desire to possess Eva more than his
yearning for a new ideal in art. So I call it the Motif of
Longing.

A portion of 'Walther's Prize Song', like a swiftly

whispered declaration of love, leads to a variation of one of
the most beautiful themes of the work—the Motif of Spring.

And now Wagner has a fling at the old fogyism which wa
so long an obstacle to his success. He holds the masters up t
ridicule in a delightfully humorous passage which parodie
the Mastersingers' and Art Brotherhood Motifs, while th
Spring Motif vainly strives to assert itself. In the bass, th
following quotation is the Motif of Ridicule, the treble bein
a variant of the Art Brotherhood Motif (associated with th
Apprentices):

The passage is followed by the Motif of the Mastersingers
which in turn leads to an imposing combination of phrases
We hear the portion of the Prize Song already quoted—th
Motif of the Mastersingers as bass—and in the middle voice
portions of the Mastersingers' March; a little later the Moti
of the Art Brotherhood and the Motif of Ridicule are added
this grand massing of orchestral forces reaching a powerfu
climax, with the Motif of the Ideal, while the Motif of th
Mastersingers brings the Vorspiel to a fitting close. In thi
noble passage, in which the 'Prize Song' soars above th
various themes typical of the masters, the new ideal seems t
be borne to its triumph upon the shoulders of the con
servative forces which, won over at last, have espoused it
cause with all their sturdy energy.

This concluding passage in the Vorspiel thus brings ou
with great eloquence the inner significance of *Die Meister
singer*. In whatever the great author and composer of thi
work wrote for the stage, there always was an ethica
meaning at the back of the words and music. Thus we draw
our conclusion of the meaning of *Die Meistersinger* story
from the wonderful combination of leading motives in th
peroration of its Vorspiel.

In his fine book, *The Orchestra and Orchestral Music*, W. J
Henderson relates this anecdote: 'A professional musiciar
was engaged in a discussion of Wagner in the corridor of th
Metropolitan Opera House, while inside the orchestra wa

playing the *Meistersinger* overture. "It is a pity," said this wise man, in a condescending manner, "but Wagner knows absolutely nothing about counterpoint."

'At that instant the orchestra was singing five different melodies at once; and, as Anton Seidl was the conductor, they were all audible.'

In a rare book by J. C. Wagenseil, printed in Nuremberg in 1697, are given four 'Prize Master Tones'. Two of these Wagner has reproduced in modern garb, the former in the Mastersingers' March, the latter in the Motif of the Art Brotherhood.

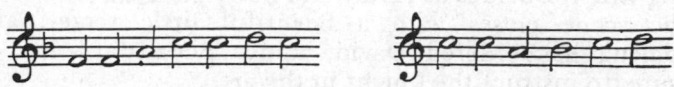

Act I.   The scene of this act is laid in the Church of St. Catherine, Nuremberg. The congregation is singing the final chorale of the service. Among the worshippers are Eva and Magdalena. Walther stands at the side, and, by means of nods and gestures, communicates with Eva. This mimic conversation is expressively accompanied by interludes between the verses of the chorale, interludes based on the Lyric, Spring, and Prize Song Motifs, and contrasting with the strains of the chorale.

The service over, the Motif of Spring, with an impetuous upward rush, seems to express the lovers' joy that the restraint is removed, and the Lyric Motif resounds exultingly as the congregation departs, leaving Eva, Magdalena, and Walther behind.

Eva, in order to gain a few words with Walther, sends Magdalena back to the pew to look for a kerchief and hymn-book she has purposely left there. Magdalena urges Eva to return home, but just then David appears in the background and begins putting things to rights for the meeting of the Mastersingers. Magdalena is therefore only too glad to linger. The Mastersinger and Guild Motifs, which naturally accompany David's activity, contrast soberly with the ardent phrases of the lovers. Magdalena explains to Walther that Eva is already affianced, though she herself does not know to whom. Her father wishes her to marry the singer to whom at the coming contest the Mastersingers shall award the prize;

and, while she shall be at liberty to decline him, she may marry none but a master. Eva exclaims: 'I will choose no one but my knight!' Very pretty and gay is the theme heard when David joins the group—the Apprentice Motif.

How capitally this motif expresses the light-heartedness of gay young people, in this case the youthful apprentices, among whom David is as lovely and buoyant as any.

The scene closes with a beautiful little terzet, after Magdalena has ordered David, under penalty of her displeasure, to instruct the knight in the art.

When the apprentices enter, they proceed to erect the marker's platform, but stop at times to annoy the somewhat self-sufficient David, while he is endeavouring to instruct Walther in the rules of the Mastersingers. The merry Apprentice Motif runs through the scene and brings it to a close as the apprentices sing and dance around the marker's box, suddenly, however, breaking off, when the Mastersingers appear.

Pogner and Beckmesser lead the way, and the latter is established straightaway as a suitor for the hand of Eva, and, musically, as a cantankerous and prickly figure. Pogner renews his acquaintance with Walther, and is surprised to hear that the knight means to present himself as a candidate for the Masters' Guild.

The other Masters enter, there is a roll-call and Beckmesser is chosen as marker. Pogner rises and, in a fine passage for bass voice, offers Eva's hand in marriage to the winner of the coming song contest—with the proviso that Eva adds her consent. The passage is known on concert programmes as 'Pogner's Address'.

Hans Sachs proposes an amendment: let the voice of the people be heard as well as Eva's before a decision is given. This will not only widen the basis of the competition but will also serve as a corrective to the very rules by which the singer is judged and will prevent them becoming stereotyped. But all are against the suggestion, and Pogner proposes that the extra innovation be postponed at any rate for a year.

Walther is introduced by Pogner. The Knight Motif:

The prospective candidate is questioned as to his qualifications and answers in the three verses of 'Am stillen Herd'. Finally Beckmesser, jealous of a prospective rival for Eva's hand and determined that Walther shall fail, enters the marker's box.

Kothner now begins reading off the rules of singing established by the masters; his music is a capital take-off of old-fashioned forms of composition but, if it is not to fail in its humour, requires to be delivered with precision as well as considerable pomposity and unction. Unwillingly enough Walther takes his seat in the candidate's chair. Beckmesser shouts from the marker's box: 'Fanget an!' (Now begin!). After a brilliant chord, followed by an ascending run on the violins, Walther, in ringing tones, enforced by a broad and noble chord, repeats Beckmesser's words. But such a change has come over the music that it seems as if that upward rushing run had swept away all restraint of ancient rule and rote, just as the spring wind whirling through the forest tears up the spread of dry, dead leaves, thus giving air and sun to the yearning mosses and flowers. In Walther's song the Spring Motif forms an ever-surging, swelling accompaniment, finally joining in the vocal melody and bearing it higher and higher to an impassioned climax. He is, however, interrupted by the scratching made by Beckmesser as he chalks the singer's violations of the rules on the slate, and Walther, who is singing of love and spring, changes his theme to winter, which, lingering behind a thorny hedge, is plotting how it can mar the joy of the vernal season. The knight then rises from the chair—another breach of the rules—and sings a second stanza with defiant enthusiasm. As he concludes it Beckmesser tears open the curtains which concealed him in the marker's box, and exhibits his board completely covered with chalk marks. Walther protests, but the masters, with the exception of Sachs and Pogner, refuse to listen further, and deride his singing. We have here the Motif of Derision.

Sachs protests that, while he found the knight's artistic method new, he did not find it formless. The Sachs Motif is here introduced.

It betokens the genial nature of this sturdy, yet gentle man—the master spirit of the drama. He combines the tolerance of a conservative character with the force of a progressive one, and is thus the incarnation of the idea which Wagner is working out in this drama, in which the union of a proper degree of conservative caution with progressive energy produces a new ideal in art. To Sachs's innuendo that Beckmesser's marking hardly could be considered just, as he is a candidate for Eva's hand, Beckmesser, by way of reply, chides Sachs for having delayed so long in finishing a pair of shoes for him, and as Sachs makes a humorously apologetic answer, the Cobbler Motif is heard.

The sturdy burgher calls to Walther to finish his song in spite of the masters. And now a finale of masterful construction begins. In short, excited phrases the masters chaff and deride Walther. His song, however, soars above all the hubbub. The apprentices see their opportunity in the confusion, and joining hands they dance around the marker's box, singing as they do so. We now have combined with astounding skill Walther's song, the apprentices' chorus, and the exclamation of the masters. The latter finally shout their verdict: 'Rejected and outsung!' The knight, with a proud gesture of contempt, leaves the church. The apprentices put the seats and benches back in their proper places, and in doing so greatly obstruct the masters as they crowd toward the doors. Sachs, who has lingered behind, gazes thoughtfully at the singer's empty chair, then, with a humorous gesture of annoyance, turns away.

Act II. The scene of this act represents a street in Nuremberg. There are two corner houses—on the right corner of the alley Pogner's, on the left Sachs's. Before the former is a lime-tree, before the latter an elder. It is a lovely summer evening.

The opening scene is a merry one. David and the apprentices are closing shop. After a brisk introduction based on the Midsummer Festival Motif the apprentices quiz David on his love affair with Magdalena. The latter appears with a basket of dainties for her lover, but on learning that the knight has been rejected, she snatches the basket away from David and hurries back to the house. David is now mockingly congratulated on his successful wooing. He loses his temper and shows fight, but Sachs, coming upon the scene, sends the apprentices on their way and then enters his workshop with David. The music of this episode, especially the chorus, is bright and graceful.

Pogner and Eva, returning from an evening stroll, come down the alley. Before retiring into the house the father, obviously disturbed by the events of the day, questions the daughter as to her feelings concerning the duty she is to perform at the Mastersinging on the morrow. Her replies are discreetly evasive. The music beautifully reflects the affectionate relations between Pogner and Eva. When Pogner, his daughter seated beside him under the lime-tree, speaks of the morrow's festival and Eva's part in it in awarding the prize to the master of her choice before the assembled burghers of Nuremberg, the stately Nuremberg Motif is ushered in.

Magdalena appears at the door and signals to Eva. The latter persuades her father that it is too cool to remain outdoors and, as they enter the house, Eva learns from

Magdalena of Walther's failure before the masters. Magdalena suggests she seek the advice of Sachs.

The Cobbler Motif shows us Sachs and David in the former's workshop. When the master has dismissed his apprentice till morning, he yields to his poetic love of the balmy midsummer night and, laying down his work, leans over the half-door of his shop lost in reverie. The Cobbler Motif dies away to *pp*, and then there is wafted from the orchestra, like the sweet scent of the elder, the Spring Motif, while tender notes on the horn blossom beneath a nebulous veil of tremolo violins into memories of Walther's song. Its measures run through Sachs's head until, angered at the stupid conservatism of his associates, he resumes his work to the brusque measures of the Cobbler's Motif. As his ill humour yields again to the beauties of the night, this motif yields once more to that of spring, which, with reminiscences of Walther's first song before the masters, imbues this masterful monologue, 'Wie duftet doch der Flieder', with poetic beauty of the highest order. The last words in praise of Walther ('The bird who sang to-day', etc.) are sung to a broad and expressive melody.

Eva now comes out into the street and, shyly approaching the shop, stands at the door unnoticed by Sachs until she speaks to him. The theme which pervades this scene seems to breathe forth the very spirit of lovely maidenhood which springs from the union of romantic aspirations, feminine reserve, and rare physical graces. It is the Eva Motif, which, with the delicate touch of a master, Wagner so varies that it follows the many subtle dramatic suggestions of the scene. The Eva Motif in its original form, is as follows:

When at Eva's first words Sachs looks up, there is this elegant variation of the Eva Motif:

Then, the scene being now fully ushered in, we have the Eva Motif itself. Eva leads the talk up to the morrow's festival, and when Sachs mentions Beckmesser as her chief wooer, roguishly hints, with evident reference to Sachs himself, that she might prefer a widower to a bachelor of such disagreeable characteristics as the marker. There are sufficient indications that the sturdy master is not indifferent to Eva's charms, but, whole-souled, genuine friend that he is, his one idea is to further the love affair between his fair neighbour and Walther. The music of this passage is very expressive. The melodic leading of the upper voice in the accompaniment, when Eva asks: 'Could not a widower hope to win me?', is identical with a variation of the Isolde Motif in *Tristan and Isolde*, while the Eva Motif, shyly *pp*, seems to indicate the artfulness of Eva's question. The reminiscence from *Tristan* can hardly be regarded as accidental, for Sachs afterwards boasts that he does not care to share the fate of poor King Marke. Eva now endeavours to glean particulars of Walther's experience in the morning, and we have the Motif of Envy, the Knight Motif, and the Motif of Ridicule. Eva does not appreciate the fine satire in Sachs's severe strictures on Walther's singing—he re-echoes not his own views, but those of the other masters, for whom, not for the knight, his strictures are really intended—and she leaves him in anger. This shows Sachs which way the wind blows, and he forthwith resolves to do all in his power to bring Eva's and Walther's love affair to a successful conclusion. While Eva is engaged with Magdalena, who has come out to call her, he busies himself in closing the upper half of his shop door so far that only a gleam of light is visible, he himself being completely hidden. Eva learns from Magdalena of Beckmesser's intended serenade, and it is agreed that the maid shall impersonate Eva at the window.

Steps are heard coming down the alley. Eva recognises Walther and flies to his arms, Magdalena discreetly hurrying into the house. The ensuing ardent scene between Eva and Walther brings familiar motifs. The knight's excitement is comically broken in upon by the Night Watchman's cow-horn, and, as Eva lays her hand soothingly upon his arm and counsels that they retreat within the shadow of the lime-tree, there steals over the orchestra, like the fragrance of the summer night, a delicate variant of the Eva Motif—the Summer Night Motif.

Eva vanishes into the house to prepare to elope with

Walther. The Night Watchman crosses the stage intoning a mediaeval chant, which makes a quaint effect in the middle of music of such different character.

As Eva reappears and she and the knight are about to make their escape, Sachs, to prevent this precipitate and foolish step, throws open his shutters and allows his lamp to shed a streak of brilliant light across the street.

The lovers hesitate; and now Beckmesser sneaks in after the Night Watchman and, leaning against Sachs's house, begins to tune his lute, the peculiar twang of which, contrasted with the rich orchestration, sounds irresistibly ridiculous.

Meanwhile, Eva and Walther have once more retreated into the shade of the lime-tree, and Sachs, who has placed his work bench in front of his door, begins hammering at the last and intones a song which is one of the rough diamonds of musical invention, for it is purposely brusque and rough, just such a song as a hearty, happy artisan might sing over his work. It is aptly introduced by the Cobbler Motif. Beckmesser, greatly disturbed lest his serenade be ruined, entreats Sachs to stop singing. Sachs argues that he must finish Beckmesser's shoes, or else he will again publicly blame him for neglecting his work in favour of his poetry. In the end, he agrees, but with the proviso that he shall 'mark' each of Beckmesser's mistakes with a hammer stroke. As if to bring out as sharply as possible the ridiculous character of the serenade, the orchestra breathes forth once more the summer night's music before Beckmesser begins his song, and this is set to a parody of the Lyric motif. Wagner, with keen satire, seems to want to show how a beautiful melody may become absurd through old-fogy methods. Beckmesser has hardly begun before Sachs's hammer comes down on the last with a resounding whack, which makes the town clerk fairly jump with anger. He resumes, but soon is rudely interrupted again by a blow of Sachs's hammer. The whacks come faster and faster. Beckmesser, in order to make himself heard above them, sings louder and louder. Some of the neighbours are awakened by the noise and coming to their windows bid

:kmesser hold his peace. David, stung by jealousy as he
:s Magdalena listening to the serenade, leaps from his room
.1d falls upon the town clerk with a cudgel. The neighbours,
nale and female, run out into the street and a general *mêlée*
·nsues, the masters, who hurry upon the scene, seeking to
estore quiet, while the apprentices vent their high spirits by
loing all in their power to add to the hubbub. All is now
loise and disorder, pandemonium let loose upon the
lignified old town.

Musically this tumult finds expression in a fugue whose
:hief theme is the Cudgel Motif.

From beneath the hubbub of voices—those of the
lpprentices and journeymen, delighted to take part in the
·hindy, of the women who are terrified at it, and of the
nasters who strive to stop it—is heard the theme of
3eckmesser's song, the real cause of the row.

Sachs finally succeeds in shoving the apprentices and
·ourneymen out of the way. The street is cleared, but not
)efore the cobbler-poet has pushed Eva, who was about to
·lope with Walther, into her father's arms and drawn Walther
.fter him into his shop.

The street is quiet. And now, the rumpus subsided and all
:oncerned in it gone, the Night Watchman appears, rubs his
·yes and chants his mediaeval call. The street is flooded with
noonlight. The Watchman with his clumsy halbert lunges at
.is own shadow, then goes up the alley.

We have had hubbub, we have had humour, and now we
iave a musical ending elfish, roguish, and yet exquisite in
·entiment. The effect is produced by the Cudgel Motif played
vith the utmost delicacy on the flute, while the theme of
3eckmesser's serenade merrily runs after itself on clarinet and
·assoon, and the muted violins softly breathe the Midsummer
·estival Motif.

Act III. During this act the tender strain in Sachs's
·turdy character is brought out in bold relief. Hence the

prelude develops what may be called three Sachs themes, t
of them expressive of his twofold nature as poet and cobbl
the third standing for the love which his fellow burghers be؟
him.

The prelude opens with the 'Wahn' Motif or Motif c
Poetic Illusion. This reflects the deep thought and poeti
aspirations of Sachs the poet. It is followed by the theme o
the beautiful chorus, sung later in the act, in praise of Sachs
'Awake! draws nigh the break of day'. This theme, amon
the three heard in the prelude, points to Sachs's popularity
The third consists of portions of the cobbler's song in th
second act. This prelude has long been considered one c
Wagner's masterpieces. The themes are treated with th
utmost delicacy, so that we recognise through them both th
tender, poetic side of Sachs's nature and his good-humoure
brusqueness. The Motif of Poetic Illusion is deeply reflective
and it might be preferable to name it the Motif of Poeti
Thought, were it not that it is better to preserve th
significance of the term Wahn Motif, which, there is ampl
reason to believe, originated with Wagner himself. Th
prelude is, in fact, a subtle analysis of character expressed i
music.

How peaceful the scene on which the curtain rises. Sachs ؟
sitting in an arm-chair in his sunny workshop, reading a larg
folio. The Illusion Motif has not yet died away in th
prelude, so that it seems to reflect the thoughts awakened i
Sachs by what he is reading. David, dressed for the festiva
enters just as the prelude ends. He is at first afraid of Sachs'
anger, but sings his song (by a slip of the tongue, he starts of
with the tune of Beckmesser's serenade, but corrects him
self). At the end he realises that it is Sachs's name-day. Whe
David has withdrawn, Sachs is lost in thought
'Wahn! Wahn! Ueberall Wahn!' (Fools, fools, all of then
fools).

While the Illusion Motif seems to weave a poetic atmo
sphere about him, Sachs, buried in thought, rests his hea
upon his arm over the folio. The Illusion Motif is followed b؟

the Spring Motif, which in turn yields to the Nuremberg Motif as Sachs sings the praises of the stately old town. At his reference to the tumult of the night before there are in the score corresponding allusions to the music of that episode. 'A glowworm could not find its mate,' he sings, referring to Walther and Eva. The Midsummer Festival, Lyric, and Nuremberg Motifs in union foreshadow the triumph of true art through love on Nuremberg soil, and thus bring the monologue to a stately conclusion.

Walther now enters from the chamber, which opens upon a gallery, and, descending into the workshop, is heartily greeted by Sachs with the Sachs Motif, which dominates the immediately ensuing scene. Very beautiful is the theme in which Sachs protests against Walther's derision of the masters; for they are, in spite of their many old-fogyish notions, the conservators of much that is true and beautiful in art.

Walther tells Sachs of a song which came to him in a dream during the night, and sings two stanzas of this *Prize Song*, Sachs making friendly critical comments as he writes down the words. The Nuremberg Motif in sonorous and festive instrumentation closes this melodious episode.

When Sachs and Walther have retired Beckmesser is seen peeping into the shop. Observing that it is empty he enters hastily. He is ridiculously overdressed for the approaching festival, limps, and occasionally rubs his muscles as if he were still stiff and sore from his drubbing. By chance his glance falls on the manuscript of the *Prize Song* in Sachs's handwriting on the table, when he breaks forth in wrathful exclamations, thinking now that he has in the popular master a rival for Eva's hand. Hearing the chamber door opening he hastily grabs the manuscript and thrusts it into his pocket. Sachs enters. Beckmesser accuses him of being a secret candidate for Eva's hand; his behaviour of the night before is now plain. Observing that the manuscript is no longer on the table, Sachs realises that Beckmesser has stolen it, and conceives the idea of allowing him to keep it, knowing that the marker will fail most wretchedly in attempting to give musical expression to Walther's inspiration.

The scene places Sachs in a new light. A fascinating trait of his character is the dash of scapegrace with which it is seasoned. Hence, when he thinks of allowing Beckmesser to use the poem the Sachs Motif takes on a somewhat facetious, roguish grace. There now ensues a charming dialogue between Sachs and Eva, who enters when Beckmesser has departed. This is accompanied by a transformation of the Eva Motif, which now reflects her shyness and hesitancy in taking Sachs into her confidence.

With it is joined the Cobbler Motif when Eva places her foot upon the stool while Sachs tries on the shoes she is to wear at the festival. When, with a cry of joy, she recognises her lover as he appears upon the gallery, and remains motionless, gazing upon him as if spellbound, the lovely Summer Night Motif enhances the beauty of the tableau. While Sachs cobbles and chats away, pretending not to observe the lovers, the Motif of Maidenly Reserve passes through many modulations until there is heard a phrase from *Tristan and Isolde* (the Isolde Motif), an allusion which is explained below. The Lyric Motif introduces the third stanza of Walther's *Prize Song*, with which he now greets Eva, while she, overcome with joy at seeing her lover, sinks upon Sachs's breast. The Illusion Motif rhapsodises the praises of the generous cobbler-poet, who seeks relief from his emotions in bantering remarks, until Eva glorifies him in a noble burst of love and gratitude ('O Sachs, mein Freund') in a melody derived from the Isolde Motif.

It is after this that Sachs, alluding to his own love of Eva, exclaims that he will have none of King Marke's sad experience; and the use of the King Marke Motif at this point shows that the previous echoes of the Isolde Motif were premeditated rather than accidental.

Magdalena and David now enter, and Sachs gives to Walther's *Prize Song* its musical baptism, utilising chiefly the first and second lines of the chorale which opens the first act. David then kneels down and, according to the custom of the day, receives from Sachs a box on the ear in token that he is advanced from apprentice to journeyman. Then follows the beautiful quintet, in which the *Prize Song*, as a thematic germ, puts forth its loveliest blossoms. This is but one of the many instances in which Wagner proved that when the dramatic situation called for it he could conceive and develop a melody of most exquisite fibre.

After the quintet the orchestra resumes the Nuremberg Motif and all depart for the festival. The stage is now shut off by a curtain behind which the scene is changed from Sachs's workshop to a meadow on the banks of the Pegnitz, near Nuremberg. After a tumultuous orchestral interlude, which

portrays by means of motifs already familiar, with the addition of the fanfare of the town musicians, the noise and bustle incidental to preparations for a great festival, the curtain rises upon a lively scene. Boats decked out in flags and bunting and full of festively clad members of the various guilds and their wives and children are constantly arriving. To the right is a platform decorated with the flags of the guilds which have already gathered. People are making merry under tents and awnings where refreshments are served. The apprentices are having a jolly time of it heralding and marshalling the guilds who disperse and mingle with the merrymakers after the standard-bearers have planted their banners near the platform.

Soon after the curtain rises the cobblers arrive, and as they march down the meadow, conducted by the apprentices, they sing in honour of St. Crispin, their patron saint, a chorus, based on the Cobbler Motif, to which a melody in popular style is added. The town watchmen, with trumpets and drums, the town pipers, lute makers, etc., and then the journeymen, with comical sounding toy instruments, march past, and are succeeded by the tailors, who sing a humorous chorus, telling how Nuremberg was saved from its ancient enemies by a tailor, who sewed a goatskin around him and pranced around on the town walls, to the terror of the hostile army, which took him for the devil. The bleating of a goat is imitated in this chorus.

With the last chord of the tailors' chorus the bakers strike up their song and are greeted in turn by cobblers and tailors with their respective refrains. A boatful of young peasant girls in gay costumes now arrives, and the apprentices make a rush for the bank. A charming dance in waltz time is struck up. The apprentices with the girls dance down toward the journeymen, but as soon as these try to get hold of the girls, the apprentices veer off with them in another direction. David joins in. This veering should be timed to fall at the beginning of those periods of the dance to which Wagner has given, instead of eight measures, seven and nine, in order by this irregularity to emphasise the ruse of the apprentices.

The dance is interrupted by the arrival of the masters, the apprentices falling in to receive, the others making room for the procession. The Mastersingers and Eva advance to the stately strains of the Mastersinger Motif, which, when Kothner appears bearing their standard with the figure of King David playing on his harp, goes over into the sturdy measures of the Mastersingers' March. Sachs rises and advances. At sight of him the populace intone the noblest of the choruses: 'Awake! draws nigh the break of day', its words a poem by the real Hans Sachs.

At its conclusion the populace break into shouts of praise of Sachs, who modestly yet most feelingly gives them thanks. When Beckmesser is led to the little mound of turf upon which the singer is obliged to stand, we have the humorous variation of the Mastersinger Motif from the Prelude. Beckmesser's attempt to sing Walther's poem ends, as Sachs had anticipated, in utter failure. His attempts at the words is as muddled as his efforts at a tune. The town clerk's effort is received with jeers. Before he rushes away, infuriated but utterly discomfited, he proclaims that Sachs is the author of the song they have derided. The cobbler-poet declares to the people that it is not by him; that it is a beautiful poem if sung to the proper melody and that he will show them the author of the poem, who will in song disclose its beauties. He then introduces Walther. The knight easily succeeds in winning over people and masters, who repeat the closing melody of his *Prize Song* in token of their joyous appreciation of his new and wondrous art. Eva crowns him to the accompaniment of a beautiful vocal phrase—and Sachs's rejected suggestion of letting the people help in the judging is thus brought about.

In more ways than one the *Prize Song* is a mainstay of *Die Meistersinger*. It has been heard in the previous scene of the third act, not only when Walther rehearses it for Sachs, but also in the quintet. Moreover, versions of it occur in the

overture and indeed throughout the work, adding greatly to
the romantic sentiment of the score. For *Die Meistersinger* is
a comedy of romance.

Pogner advances to decorate Walther with the insignia of
the Masters' Guild, but, with an impulsive gesture, the knight
rejects the honour. It is a moment of embarrassment but
Sachs saves the situation. In measures easily recognised from
the Prelude, to which the Nuremberg Motif is added, he
praises the masters and explains their noble purpose as
conservators of art. Eva takes the wreath with which Walther
has been crowned, and with it crowns Sachs, who has
meanwhile decorated the knight with the insignia. Pogner
kneels, as if in homage, before Sachs, the masters point to the
cobbler as to their chief, and Walther and Eva remain on
either side of him, leaning gratefully upon his shoulders. The
chorus repeats Sachs's final admonition to the closing
measures of the Prelude.   K.

DER RING DES NIBELUNGEN

The Ring of the Nibelung

A stage-festival play for three days and a preliminary evening (Ein
Bühnenfestspiel für drei Tage und einen Vorabend), words and music
by Richard Wagner.

The first performance of the entire cycle took place in August 1876
at Bayreuth (for details, see below). The first complete cycle in London
was given at Her Majesty's Theatre, May 5, 6, 8, 9, 1882, conducted by
Anton Seidl and sung in German. The first complete New York cycle
was given at the Metropolitan, March 4, 5, 8, 11, 1889, under Seidl;
previously, there had been performances of the cycle apart from *Das
Rheingold* in 1887–8 also under Seidl. The first cycle at Covent Garden
took place in June 1892, but the four operas were given in the wrong
order so that Alvary could make his debut as the young Siegfried—and
this in spite of the fact that Mahler was the conductor! The first
complete cycle in English was at Covent Garden in 1908, under
Richter.

In 1863, while working upon *Die Meistersinger*, at Penzing near Vienna, Wagner published his *Nibelung* dramas expressing his hope that through the bounty of one of the German rulers the completion and performance of *The Ring of the Nibelung* would be made possible. But in the spring of 1864, worn out by his struggle with poverty and almost broken in spirit by his contest with public and critics, he actually determined to give up his public career, and eagerly grasped the opportunity to visit a private country seat in Switzerland. Just at this very moment, when despair had settled upon him, the long wished-for help came. King Ludwig II of Bavaria, bade him come to Munich, where he settled in 1864. *Tristan* was produced there June 10, 1865. June 21, 1868, a model performance of *Die Meistersinger* which he had finished in 1867, was given at Munich under the direction of von Bülow, Richter acting as chorus master and Wagner supervising all the details. Wagner also worked steadily at the unfinished portion of the *Ring*, completing the instrumentation of the third act of *Siegfried* in 1869 and the introduction and first act of *The Twilight of the Gods* in June 1870.

On August 25, 1870, his first wife having died January 25, 1866, after five years' separation from him, he married the divorced wife of von Bülow, Cosima Liszt. In 1869 and 1870, respectively, *The Rhine Gold* and *The Valkyrie* were performed at the Court Theatre in Munich.

Bayreuth having been determined upon as the place where a theatre for the special production of his *Ring* should be built, Wagner settled there in April 1872. By November 1874, *The Twilight of the Gods* received its finishing touches, and rehearsals had already been held at Bayreuth. During the summer of 1875, under Wagner's supervision, Hans Richter held full rehearsals there, and at last, twenty-eight years after its first conception, on August 13, 14, 16, and 17, again from August 20 to 23, and from August 27 to 30, 1876, *The Ring of the Nibelung* was performed at Bayreuth with the following cast: Wotan, Betz; Loge, Vogel; Alberich, Hill; Mime, Schlosser; Fricka, Frau Grün; Donner and Gunther, Gura; Erda and Waltraute, Frau Jaide; Siegmund, Niemann; Sieglinde, Frl. Schefsky; Brünnhilde, Frau Materna; Siegfried, Unger; Hagen, Siehr; Gutrune, Frl. Weckerin; Rhinedaughters, Lilli and Marie Lehmann, and Frl. Lammert. First violin, Wilhelmj; conductor, Hans Richter. The first Rhine-daughter was the same Lilli Lehmann who, in later years, at the Metropolitan Opera House, New York, became one of the greatest of prima donnas and, as regards the Wagnerian repertory, set a standard for all time. Materna appeared at that house in the *Walküre* production under Dr. Damrosch, in January 1885, and Niemann was heard there later.

The *Ring of the Nibelung* consists of four music-dramas— *Das Rheingold* (The Rhine Gold), *Die Walküre* (The Valkyrie), *Siegfried*, and *Götterdämmerung* (Twilight of the Gods). The books of these were written in inverse order. Wagner made a dramatic sketch of the Nibelung myth as early as the autumn of 1848, and between then and the autumn of 1850 he wrote the *Death of Siegfried*. This subsequently became *The Twilight of the Gods*. Meanwhile Wagner's ideas as to the proper treatment of the myth seem to have undergone a change. *Siegfried's Death* ended with Brünnhilde leading Siegfried to Valhalla—dramatic, but without the deeper ethical significance of the later version, when Wagner evidently conceived the purpose of connecting the final catastrophe of his trilogy with *The Twilight of the Gods*, or End of All Things, in Northern mythology, and of embodying a profound truth in the action of the music-dramas. This metaphysical significance of the work is believed to be sufficiently explained in the brief synopsis of the plot of the trilogy and in the descriptive musical and dramatic analyses below.

In the autumn of 1850 when Wagner was on the point of sketching out the music of *Siegfried's Death*, he recognised that he must lead up to it with another drama, and *Young Siegfried*, afterwards *Siegfried*, was the result. This in turn he found incomplete, and finally decided to supplement it with *The Valkyrie* and *The Rhine Gold*.

Of the principal characters in *The Ring of the Nibelung*, Alberich, the Nibelung, and Wotan, the chief of the gods, are symbolic of greed for wealth and power. This lust leads Alberich to renounce love—the most sacred of emotions—in order that he may rob the Rhinedaughters of the Rhine gold, which they guard, and forge from it the ring which is to make him all-powerful. Wotan by strategy obtains the ring, but instead of returning it to the Rhinedaughters, he gives it to the giants, Fafner and Fasolt, as ransom for Freia, the goddess of youth and beauty, whom he had promised to the giants as a reward for building Valhalla. Alberich has cursed the ring and all into whose possession it may come. The giants no sooner obtain it than they fall to quarrelling over it. Fafner slays Fasolt and then retires to a cave in the heart of a forest where, in the form of a dragon, he guards the ring and the rest of the treasure which Wotan wrested from Alberich and also gave to the giants as ransom for Freia. This treasure includes the Tarn helmet, whose wearer can assume any guise.

Wotan, having witnessed the slaying of Fasolt, is filled with dread lest the curse of Alberich be visited upon the gods. To defend Valhalla against the assaults of Alberich and the host of Nibelungs, he begets in union with Erda, the goddess of wisdom, the Valkyries (chief among them Brünnhilde), wild maidens who course through the air on superb chargers and bear the bodies of departed heroes to Valhalla, where they revive and aid the gods in warding off the attacks of the Nibelungs. But it is also necessary that the curse-laden ring should be wrested from Fafner and restored through purely unselfish motives to the Rhinedaughters, and the curse thus lifted from the race of the gods. None of the gods can do this because their motive in doing so would not be unselfish. Hence Wotan, for a time, casts off his divinity, and, disguised as Wälse, begets in union with a human woman the Wälsung twins, Siegmund and Sieglinde. Siegmund he hopes will be the hero who will slay Fafner and restore the ring to the Rhinedaughters. To nerve him for this task, Wotan surrounds the Wälsungs with numerous hardships. Sieglinde is seized and forced to become the wife of Hunding. Siegmund, storm-driven, seeks shelter in Hunding's hut, but he and his sister recognise one another and flee into the night together. Hunding overtakes them and Wotan, as Siegmund has been guilty of a crime against the marriage vow, is obliged, in response to the urging of his spouse Fricka, the Juno of Northern mythology, to give victory to Hunding. Brünnhilde, contrary to Wotan's command, takes pity on Siegmund, and seeks to shield him against Hunding. As punishment for this, Wotan causes her to fall into a profound slumber. The hero who will penetrate the barrier of fire with which Wotan has surrounded the rock upon which she slumbers can claim her as his bride.

After Siegmund's death Sieglinde gives birth to Siegfried, the son of their illicit union, who is reared by one of the Nibelungs, Mime, in the forest where Fafner guards the Nibelung treasure. Mime is seeking to weld the pieces of

Siegmund's sword (*Nothung*, or Needful) in order that Siegfried may slay Fafner, Mime hoping then to kill the youth and to possess himself of the treasure. But he cannot weld the sword. At last Siegfried, learning that it was his father's weapon, welds the pieces and slays Fafner. His lips having come in contact with the dragon's blood which is on his fingers, he is enabled, through its magic power, to understand the language of the birds, one of which warns him of Mime's treachery. Siegfried slays the dwarf and is then guided to the fiery barrier around the Valkyrie rock. Penetrating this, he comes upon Brünnhilde, and enraptured with her beauty, awakens her and claims her as his bride. She, the virgin pride of the goddess yielding to the love of the woman, gives herself up to him. He plights his troth with the curse-laden ring which he has wrested from Fafner.

Siegfried goes forth in quest of adventure. On the Rhine lives the Gibichung Gunther, his sister Gutrune, and their half-brother Hagen, none other than the son of the Nibelung Alberich. Hagen, knowing of Siegfried's coming, plans his destruction in order to regain the ring for the Nibelungs. Therefore, craftily concealing the relationship of Brünnhilde and Siegfried from Gunther, he incites a longing in the latter to possess Brünnhilde as his bride. Carrying out a plot evolved by Hagen, Gutrune on Siegfried's arrival presents to him a drinking-horn filled with a love-potion. Siegfried drinks, is led through the effect of the potion to forget that Brünnhilde is his bride, and, becoming enamoured of Gutrune, asks her in marriage of Gunther. The latter consents, provided Siegfried will disguise himself in the Tarn helmet as Gunther and lead Brünnhilde to him as bride. Siegfried readily agrees, and in the guise of Gunther overcomes Brünnhilde and delivers her to the Gibichung. But Brünnhilde, recognising on Siegfried's finger the ring which her conqueror had taken from her, accuses him of treachery in delivering her, his own bride, to Gunther. The latter, unmasked and also suspicious of Siegfried, conspires with Hagen and Brünnhilde, who, knowing naught of the love-potion, is roused to a frenzy of hate and jealousy by Siegfried's seeming treachery, to compass the young hero's death. Hagen slays Siegfried during a hunt, and then, in a quarrel with Gunther over the ring, also kills the Gibichung.

Meanwhile Brünnhilde has learned through the Rhine-daughters of the treachery of which she and Siegfried have been the victims. All her jealous hatred of Siegfried yields to

her old love for him and a passionate yearning to join him in
death. She draws the ring from his finger and places it on her
own, then hurls a torch upon the pyre. Mounting her steed,
she plunges into the flames. One of the Rhinedaughters,
swimming in on the rising waters, seizes the curse-laden ring.
Hagen rushes into the flooding Rhine hoping to regain it, but
the other Rhinedaughters grasp him and draw him down into
the flood. Not only the flames of the pyre, but a glow which
pervades the whole horizon illumine the scene. It is Valhalla
being consumed by fire. Through love—the very emotion
Alberich renounced in order to gain wealth and power—
Brünnhilde has caused the old order of things to pass away
and a human era to dawn in place of the old mythological
one of the gods.

The sum of all that has been written concerning the book
of *The Ring of the Nibelung* is probably larger than the sum
of all that has been written concerning the librettos used by
all other composers. *The Ring of the Nibelung* produced
vehement discussion. It was attacked and defended, praised
and ridiculed, extolled and condemned. And it survived all
the discussion it called forth. It is the outstanding fact in
Wagner's career that he always triumphed. He threw his lance
into the midst of his enemies and fought his way up to it. No
matter how much opposition his music-dramas excited, they
gradually found their way into the repertory.

It was contended on many sides that a book like *The Ring
of the Nibelung* could not be set to music. Certainly it could
not be after the fashion of an ordinary opera. Perhaps people
were so accustomed to the books of nonsense which figured
as opera librettos that they thought *The Ring of the Nibelung*
was so great a work that its action and climaxes were beyond
the scope of musical expression. For such, Wagner has placed
music on a higher level. He has shown that music makes a
great drama greater.

One of the most remarkable features of Wagner's works is
the author's complete absorption of the times of which he
wrote. He seems to have gone back to the very period in
which the scenes of his music-dramas are laid and to have
himself lived through the events in his plots. One cannot
imagine Hans Sachs leaving a more faithful portrayal of life in
the Nuremberg of his day than Wagner has given us in *Die
Meistersinger*. In *The Ring of the Nibelung* he has done
more—he has absorbed an imaginary epoch; lived over the

days of gods and demigods; infused life into mythological figures. *The Rhine Gold*, which is full of varied interest from its first note to its last, deals entirely with beings of mythology. They are presented true to life—if that expression may be used in connection with beings that never lived—that is to say, they are so vividly drawn that we forget such beings never lived, and take as much interest in their doings and sayings as if they were lifelike reproductions of historical characters. Was there ever a love scene more thrilling than that between Siegmund and Sieglinde? It represents the gradations of the love of two souls from its first awakening to its rapturous greeting in full self-consciousness. No one stops to think during that impassioned scene that the close relationship between Siegmund and Sieglinde is in fact incestuous. It has been said that we could not be interested in mythological beings—that *The Ring of the Nibelung* lacked human interest. In reply, I say that, wonderful as is the first act of *The Valkyrie*, there is nothing in it to compare in wild and lofty beauty with the last act of that music-drama—especially the scene between Brünnhilde and Wotan.

Brünnhilde is Wagner's noblest creation. She takes upon herself the sins of the gods and by her expiation frees the world from the curse of lust for wealth and power. She is a perfect dramatic incarnation of the profound and beautiful metaphysical motif upon which the plot of *The Ring of the Nibelung* is based.

That there are faults of dramatic construction in *The Ring of the Nibelung* I admit. In what follows I have not hesitated to point them out. But there are faults of construction in Shakespeare. With all its faults of dramatic construction *The Ring of the Nibelung* is a remarkable drama, full of life and action and logically developed, the events leading up to superb climaxes. Wagner was doubly inspired. He was both a great dramatist and a great musician.

The chief faults of dramatic construction of which Wagner was guilty in *The Ring of the Nibelung* are certain unduly prolonged scenes which are merely episodic—that is, unnecessary to the development of the plot, so that they delay the action and weary the audience to a point which endangers the success of the really sublime portions of the score. In several of these scenes there is a great amount of narrative, the story of events with which we have become familiar being retold in detail with the addition of some incidents which connect the plot of the particular music-drama with that of the preceding one. But, as narrative on the stage makes little impression, and when it is sung perhaps none at all, because it cannot be well understood, it would seem as if prefaces to the dramas could have taken the place of these narratives. Certain it is that these long drawn-out scenes did more to retard the popular recognition of Wagner's genius than the activity of hostile critics and musicians. Still, it should be remembered that these music-dramas were composed for performance under the circumstances which prevail at Bayreuth, where the performances begin in the afternoon and there are long waits between the acts, during which you can refresh yourself by a stroll or by the more mundane pleasures of the table. Then, after an hour's relaxation of the mind and of the sense of hearing, you are ready to hear another act. Under these agreeable conditions one remains sufficiently fresh to enjoy the music even of the dramatically faulty scenes.   K.

DAS RHEINGOLD

The Rhine Gold

Prologue (in four scenes) to the trilogy *Der Ring des Nibelungen* by Richard Wagner, text by the composer. First performed at Munich, September 22 1869, with August Kindermann, Nachbar, Vogel, Fischer, Schlosser, Polzer, Bausewein, Sophie Stehle, Frau Müller, Frau Seehofer, Frau Kaufmann, Therese Vogel, Frau Ritte, conductor Franz Wüllner. First performed Her Majesty's Theatre, London, 1882, with Emil Scaria, Vogel, Schelper, Schlosser, Reicher-Kindermann, Schreiber, Riegler, Krauss, Klafsky, Schulze, Eilers, Wiegand, Bürgen, conductor Seidl; Metropolitan, New York, 1889, with Fischer, Grienauer, Mittelhauser, Alvary, Beck, Sedlmayer, Mödlinger, Weiss, Moran-Oldern, Bettaque, Reill, Traubmann, Koschoska, conductor Seidl; Covent Garden, 1892, with Grengg, Alvary, Lissman, Lieban, Ende-Andriessen, Bettaque, Fröhlich, Traubman, Ralph, Schumann-Heink, Dome, Simon, Wiegand, Litter, conductor Mahler; in English, 1908, with Whitehill, Hedmont, Meux, Bechstein, Borghyld Bryhn, Walter Hyde, Radford, Thornton, conductor Richter.

CHARACTERS

Wotan		Bass-Baritone
Donner	*Gods*	Bass-Baritone
Froh		Tenor
Loge		Tenor

Fasolt	Giants	Bass-Baritone
Fafner		Bass
Alberich	Nibelungs	Bass-Baritone
Mime		Tenor
Fricka		Mezzo-Soprano
Freia	Goddesses	Soprano
Erda		Contralto
Woglinde		Soprano
Wellgunde	Rhinedaughters	Soprano
Flosshilde		Mezzo-Soprano

Time: Legendary   *Place:* The bed of the Rhine; a moun-
tainous district near the Rhine; the
subterranean caverns of Nibelheim

In *The Rhine Gold* we meet with supernatural beings
of German mythology—the Rhinedaughters, Woglinde, Well-
gunde, and Flosshilde, whose duty it is to guard the pre-
cious Rhine gold; Wotan, the chief of the gods; his spouse
Fricka; Loge, the God of Fire (the diplomat of Valhalla);
Freia, the Goddess of Youth and Beauty; her brothers
Donner and Froh; Erda, the all-wise woman; the giants
Fafner and Fasolt; Alberich and Mime of the race of
Nibelungs, cunning, treacherous gnomes who dwell in the
bowels of the earth.

The first scene of *The Rhine Gold* is laid in the Rhine, at
the bottom of the river, where the Rhinedaughters guard the
Rhine gold.

The work opens with a wonderfully descriptive Prelude,
which depicts with marvellous art (marvellous because so
simple) the transition from the quiet of the water-depths to
the wavy life of the Rhinedaughters. The double basses
intone E flat. Only this note is heard during four bars. Then
three contra bassoons add a B flat. The chord thus formed
sounds until the 136th bar. With the sixteenth bar there
flows over this seemingly immovable bass, as the current of a
river flows over its immovable bed, the Motif of the Rhine
(quoted in a later manifestation):

A horn intones this motif. Then one horn after another takes it up until its wave-like tones are heard on the eight horns. On the flowing accompaniment of the 'cellos the motif is carried to the woodwind. It rises higher and higher, the other strings successively joining in the accompaniment, which now flows on in gentle undulations until the motif is heard on the high notes of the woodwind.

The scene shows the bed and flowing waters of the Rhine, the light of day reaching the depths only as a greenish twilight. The current flows on over rugged rocks and through dark chasms.

Woglinde is circling gracefully around the central ridge of rock. To an accompaniment as wavy as the waters through which she swims, she sings to the Motif of the Rhine-daughters:

Weia   wa-ga! Wo-ge du Wel-le, walle zur Wie-ge!
Wa-ga-la-wei-a! Wal-la-la, wei-la-la wei - - a!....

Meanwhile Alberich has clambered from the depths up to one of the cliffs, and watches the gambols of the Rhine-daughters. As he speaks to them there is a momentary harshness in the music, whose flowing rhythm is broken. He inveighs against the 'slippery slime' which causes him to lose his foothold.

Woglinde, Wellgunde, and Flosshilde in turn gambol almost within his reach, only to dart away again. He curses his own weakness in the Motif of the Nibelungs' Servitude:

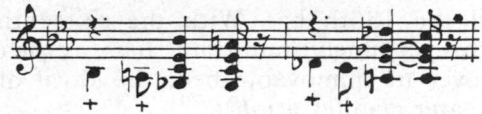

Swimming high above him the Rhinedaughters incite him to chase them. Alberich tries to ascend, but always slips and falls. Then his gaze is attracted and held by a glow which suddenly pervades the water above him and increases until from the highest point of the central cliff a bright, golden ray shoots through the water. Amid the shimmering accompani-

nent of the violins is heard on the horn the Rhine Gold
Motif:

With shouts of triumph the Rhinedaughters swim around
he rock:

As the river glitters with golden light the Rhine Gold Motif
ings out brilliantly on the trumpet. The Rhinedaughters
;ossip with one another, and Alberich thus learns that the
ight is that of the Rhine gold, and that whoever shall shape
. ring from this gold will become invested with great power.
Ve hear the Ring Motif:

Flosshilde bids her sisters be silent, in case some enemy
hould overhear them. Wellgunde and Woglinde ridicule their
ister's anxiety, saying that no one would care to filch the
old, because it would give power only to him who renounces
ove. At this point is heard the darkly prophetic Motif of the
Renunciation of Love:

Alberich reflects on the words of the Rhinedaughters. The
Ring Motif occurs both in voice and orchestra in mysterious
ianissimo (like an echo of Alberich's sinister thoughts), and
s followed by the Motif of Renunciation. Then is heard the
harp, decisive rhythm of the Nibelung Motif. Alberich
iercely springs over to the central rock. The Rhinedaughters
cream and dart away in different directions. Alberich has
eached the summit of the highest cliff.

'Hark, ye floods! Love I renounce for ever!' he cries, an
amid the crash of the Rhine Gold Motif he seizes the gol
and disappears in the depths. With screams of terror th
Rhinedaughters dive after the robber through the darkene
water, guided by Alberich's mocking laugh.

There is a transformation. Waters and rocks sink. As the
disappear, the billowy accompaniment sinks lower and lowe
in the orchestra. Above it rises once more the Motif o
Renunciation. The Ring Motif is heard, and then, as th
waves change into nebulous clouds, the billowy accompan
ment rises *pianissimo* until, with a repetition of the Rin
Motif, the action passes to the second scene. One crime ha
already been committed—the theft of the Rhine gold b
Alberich. How that crime and the ring which he shapes fror
the gold inspire other crimes is told in the course of th
following scenes of *The Rhine Gold*. Hence the significanc
of the Ring Motif as a connecting link between the first an
second scenes.

Scene II.   Dawn illumines a castle with glittering turret
on a rocky height at the back. Through a deep valley betwee
this and the foreground flows the Rhine.

The Valhalla Motif greets us again and again in *The Rhin
Gold* and frequently in the later music-dramas of the cycle
Valhalla is the abode of gods and heroes, and its theme i
divinely, heroically beautiful. Though essentially broad an
stately, it often assumes a tender mood, like the chivalri
gentleness which every hero feels toward woman:

Fricka lies asleep at Wotan's side. As she awakens, her eye
fall on the castle. In her surprise she calls to her spouse
Wotan dreams on, the Ring Motif and later the Valhalla Moti
being heard in the orchestra, for it is with the ring that Wota
is planning to compensate the giants for building Valhalla
instead of rewarding them by presenting Freia to them as h
has promised. As he opens his eyes and sees the castle yo
hear the Spear Motif, which is a characteristic variation of th
Motif of Compact. For Wotan should enforce, if necessary
the compacts of the gods with his spear.

Wotan sings of the glory of Valhalla, Fricka reminds hir

)f his compact with the giants to deliver over to them, for
heir work in building Valhalla, Freia, the Goddess of Youth
ınd Beauty. This introduces on the 'cellos and double basses
he Motif of Compact, a theme expressive of the binding
orce of law and with the inherent dignity and power of the
ense of justice:

Wotan reminds Fricka that she was as anxious as he to
ıave Valhalla built. Fricka answers that this was in order to
persuade him to lead a more domestic life. At Fricka's words,

'Halls, bright and gleaming,'

he Fricka Motif is heard, a caressing motif of much grace
ınd beauty:

It is also prominent in Wotan's reply immediately follow-
ng. Wotan tells Fricka that he never really intended to give
ıp Freia to the giants. Chromatics, like little tongues of
lame, appear in the accompaniment. They are suggestive of
he Loge Motif, for, with the aid of Loge the God of Fire,
Wotan hopes to trick the giants and save Freia.
'Then save her at once!' calls Fricka, as Freia enters in
ıasty flight. The following is the Freia Motif:

With Freia's exclamations that the giants are pursuing her,
he first suggestion of the Giant Motif appears and, as these
great hulking fellows enter, the heavy, clumsy Giant Motif is
ıeard in its entirety:

The giants, Fasolt and Fafner, have come for Freia. In the
ensuing scene, the Giant Motif, the Valhalla Motif, the Motif
of the Compact, and the first bar of the Freia Motif figure
until Fasolt's threatening words,

> 'Peace wane when you break your compact,'

when there is heard a version of the Motif of Compact
characteristic enough to be distinguished as the Motif of
Compact with the Giants:

The Valhalla, Giant, and Freia Motifs again are heard until
Fafner speaks of the golden apples which grow in Freia's
garden. These golden apples are the fruit of which the gods
partake in order to enjoy eternal youth. The Motif of Eternal
Youth, which now appears, is one of the loveliest in the
cycle. It seems as though age could not wither it, nor custom
stale its infinite variety. Its first bar is reminiscent of the Ring
Motif, for there is subtle relationship between the Golden
Apples of Freia and the Rhine gold. Here is the Motif of
Eternal Youth:

It is finely combined with the Giant Motif at Fafner's
words:

> 'Let her forthwith be torn from them all.'

Froh and Donner, Freia's brothers, enter hastily to save their
sister. Froh clasps her in his arms, and, while Donner
confronts the giants, the Motif of Eternal Youth rings out
triumphantly on the horns and woodwind. But Freia's hope
is short-lived. For though Wotan desires to keep Freia in
Valhalla, he dare not offend the giants. At this critical
moment, however, he sees his cunning adviser, Loge,
approaching. These are Loge's characteristic Motifs:

Wotan upbraids Loge for not having discovered something
which the giants would be willing to accept as a substitute for
Freia. Loge says he has travelled the world over without
finding anything to compensate man for the renunciation of
lovely woman. This leads to Loge's narrative of his
wanderings. With great cunning he tells Wotan of the theft of
the Rhine gold and of the wondrous worth of a ring shaped
from the gold. Thus he incites the listening giants to ask for it
as a compensation for giving up Freia. Hence Wagner, as Loge
begins his narrative, has blended, with a marvellous sense of
musical beauty and dramatic fitness, two phrases: the Freia
Motif and the accompaniment to the Rhinedaughters' Shout
of Triumph in the first scene. This music continues until
Loge says that he discovered but one person (Alberich) who
was willing to renounce love. Then the Rhine Gold Motif is
sounded in a minor key and immediately afterward is heard
the Motif of Renunciation.

Loge next tells how Alberich stole the gold. He has already
excited the curiosity of the giants, and when Fafner asks him
what power Alberich will gain through the possession of the
gold, he dwells upon the magical attributes of the ring shaped
from Rhine gold.

Loge's diplomacy is beginning to bear results. Fafner tell
Fasolt that he considers the possession of the gold mor
important than Freia. Notice here how the Freia Motif, s
prominent when the giants insisted on her as their compen
sation, is relegated to the bass and how the Rhine Gold Moti
breaks in upon the Motif of Eternal Youth, as Fafner an
Fasolt again advance toward Wotan, and bid him wrest th
gold from Alberich and give it to them as ransom for Freia
Wotan refuses, for he himself now lusts for the ring made o
Rhine gold. The giants, having proclaimed that they will giv
Wotan until evening to determine upon his course, seize Frei
and drag her away. Pallor now settles upon the faces of th
gods; they seem to have grown older. They are affected by
the absence of Freia, the Goddess of Youth, whose motifs ar
but palely reflected by the orchestra. At last Wotan proclaim
that he will go with Loge to Nibelheim and wrest the entir
treasure of Rhine gold from Alberich as ransom for Freia.

Loge disappears down a crevice in the side of the rock
From it a sulphurous vapour at once issues. When Wotan ha
followed Loge into the cleft the vapour fills the stage and
conceals the remaining characters. The vapours thicken to a
black cloud, continually rising upward until rocky chasms are
seen. These have an upward motion, so that the stage appear
to be sinking deeper and deeper. With a *molto vivace* the
orchestra dashes into the Motif of Flight. From variou
distant points ruddy gleams of light illumine the chasms, and
when the Flight Motif has died away, only the increasing
clangour of the smithies is heard from all directions. This i
the typical Nibelung Motif, characteristic of Alberich'

Nibelungs toiling at the anvil for him. Gradually the sound
grow fainter. Then as the Ring Motif resounds like a shout o
malicious triumph (expressive of Alberich's malign joy at hi
possession of power), there is seen a subterranean caver
apparently of illimitable depth, from which narrow shaft
lead in all directions.

Scene III.   Alberich enters from a side cleft dragging afte
him the shrieking Mime. The latter lets fall a helmet whic
Alberich at once seizes. It is the Tarn helmet, made of Rhin
gold, the wearing of which enables the wearer to becom

▲visible or assume any shape. As Alberich closely examines
▐e helmet the Motif of the Tarn helmet is heard.

It is mysterious, uncanny. To test its power Alberich puts
on and changes into a column of vapour. He asks Mime if
▮ is visible, and when Mime answers in the negative Alberich
▮ies out shrilly, 'Then feel me instead,' at the same time
▮aking poor Mime writhe under the blows of an invisible
▮ourge. Alberich then departs—still in the form of a
▮porous column—to announce to the Nibelungs that they
▮e henceforth his slavish subjects. Mime cowers down with
▮ar and pain.
    Wotan and Loge enter from one of the upper shafts. Mime
▮lls them how Alberich has become all-powerful through the
▮ng and the Tarn helmet made of the Rhine gold. Then
▮lberich, who has taken off the Tarn helmet and hung it
▮om his girdle, is seen in the distance, driving a crowd of
▮ibelungs before him from the caves below. They are laden
▮ith gold and silver, which he forces them to pile up in one
▮ace and so form a hoard. He suddenly perceives Wotan and
▮oge. After abusing Mime for permitting strangers to enter
▮ibelheim, he commands the Nibelungs to descend again into
▮e cavern in search of new treasure for him. They hesitate.
▮ou hear the Ring Motif. Alberich draws the ring from his
▮nger, stretches it threateningly towards the Nibelungs and
▮mmands them to obey their master.
    They disperse in headlong flight, with Mime, into the
▮vernous recesses. Alberich looks with mistrust upon Wotan
▮d Loge. Wotan tells him they have heard report of his
▮ealth and power and have come to ascertain if it is true. The
▮ibelung points to the hoard. He boasts that the whole world
▮ill come under his sway (Ring Motif), that the gods who
▮ow laugh and love in the enjoyment of youth and beauty
▮ill become subject to him (Freia Motif); for he has abjured
▮ve (Motif of Renunciation). Hence, even the gods in
▮alhalla shall dread him (Valhalla Motif) and he bids them
▮eware of the time when the night-begotten host of the
▮ibelungs shall rise from Nibelheim into the realm of day-
▮ht. (Rhine Gold Motif followed by Valhalla Motif, for it is

through the power gained by the Rhine gold that Alberic
hopes to possess himself of Valhalla.) Loge cunningly flatter
Alberich, and when the latter tells him of the Tarn helme
feigns disbelief of Alberich's statements. Alberich, to prov
their truth, puts on the helmet and transforms himself into
huge serpent. The Serpent Motif expresses the windings an
writhings of the monster. The serpent vanishes and Alberic
reappears. When Loge doubts if Alberich can transform
himself into something very small, the Nibelung changes int
a toad. Now is Loge's chance. He calls Wotan to set his foo
on the toad. As Wotan does so, Loge puts his hand to its hea
and seizes the Tarn helmet. Alberich is seen writhing unde
Wotan's foot. Loge binds Alberich; both seize him, drag hir
to the shaft from which they descended and disappear.

Accompanied by the orchestra, the scene changes in th
reverse direction to that in which it changed when Wotan an
Loge were descending to Nibelheim. The Ring Motif die
away from crashing *fortissimo* to *piano*, to be succeeded b
the dark Motif of Renunciation. Then is heard the clangou
of the Nibelung smithies. The Giant, Valhalla, Loge, an
Servitude Motifs follow with crushing force as Wotan an
Loge emerge from the cleft, dragging the pinioned Alberic
with them. His lease of power was brief. He is again in
condition of servitude.

Scene IV.   A pale mist still veils the prospect as at the en
of the second scene. Loge and Wotan place Alberich on th
ground and Loge dances around the pinioned Nibelun
mockingly snapping his fingers at the prisoner. Wotan joir
Loge in his mockery of Alberich. The Nibelung asks what h
must give for his freedom. 'Your hoard and your glitterin
gold,' is Wotan's answer. Alberich assents to the ransom an
Loge frees the gnome's right hand. Alberich raises the ring t
his lips and murmurs a secret behest. The Nibelungs emerg
from the cleft and heap up the hoard. Then, as Alberic
stretches out the ring toward them, they rush in terro
toward the cleft, into which they disappear. Alberich no
asks for his freedom, but Loge throws the Tarn helmet on t
the heap. Wotan demands that Alberich also give up the rin
At these words dismay and terror are depicted on th
Nibelung's face. He had hoped to save the ring, but in vai
Wotan tears it from the gnome's finger. Then Alberich
impelled by hate and rage, curses the ring. The Motif of th
Curse:

9 *Tristan und Isolde:* the lovers—Ludwig and Malwina Schnorr von Carolsfeld, 1865; and Birgit Nilsson and Wolfgang Windgassen at Bayreuth nearly one hundred years later.

10 Leo Slezak as Walter in *Die Meistersinger*, Vienna, 1905.

To it should be added the syncopated measures expressive of the ever-threatening and ever-active Nibelung's Hate:

Amid heavy thuds of the Motif of Servitude Alberich vanishes in the cleft.

The mist begins to rise. It grows lighter. The Giant Motif and the Motif of Eternal Youth are heard, for the giants are approaching with Freia. Donner, Froh, and Fricka hasten to greet Wotan. Fasolt and Fafner enter with Freia. It has grown clear except that the mist still hides the distant castle. Freia's presence seems to have restored youth to the gods. Fasolt asks for the ransom for Freia. Wotan points to the hoard. With staves the giants measure off a space the height and width of Freia. That space must be filled out with treasure. Loge and Froh pile up the hoard, but the giants are not satisfied even when the Tarn helmet has been added. They wish also the ring to fill out a crevice. Wotan turns in anger away from them.

A bluish light glimmers in the rocky cleft to the right, and through it Erda rises. She warns Wotan against retaining possession of the ring. The Erda Motif bears a strong resemblance to the Rhine Motif. The syncopated notes of the Nibelung's Hate, so threateningly indicative of the harm which Alberich is plotting, are also heard in Erda's warning.

Wotan, heeding her words, throws the ring upon the pile. The giants release Freia, who rushes joyfully towards the gods. Here the Freia Motif combined with the Flight Motif, now no longer agitated but joyful, rings out gleefully. Soon, however, these motifs are interrupted by the Giant and Nibelung Motifs, and later the Nibelung's Hate and Ring Motifs. For Alberich's curse already is beginning its dread work. The giants dispute over the spoils, their dispute waxes to strife, and at last Fafner slays Fasolt and snatches the ring from the dying giant, while, as the gods gaze horror-stricken upon the scene, the Curse Motif resounds with crushing force.

Loge congratulates Wotan on having given up the curse-laden ring. But even Fricka's caresses, as she asks Wotan to lead her into Valhalla, cannot divert the god's mind from dark thoughts, and the Curse Motif accompanies his gloomy reflections—for the ring has passed through his hands. It was he who wrested it from Alberich—and its curse rests on all who have touched it.

Donner ascends to the top of a lofty rock. He gathers the mists around him until he is enveloped by a black cloud. He swings his hammer. There is a flash of lightning, a crash of thunder, and lo! the cloud vanishes. A rainbow bridge spans the valley to Valhalla, which is illumined by the setting sun. Wotan eloquently greets Valhalla ('Abendlich strahlt'), and then, taking Fricka by the hand, leads the procession of the gods into the castle.

The music of this scene is of wondrous eloquence and beauty. Six harps are added to the ordinary orchestral instruments, and as the variegated bridge is seen their arpeggios shimmer like the colours of the rainbow around the broad, majestic Rainbow Motif:

Then the stately Valhalla Motif resounds as the gods gaze, lost in admiration, at Valhalla. It gives way to the Ring Motif as Wotan speaks of the day's ills; and then, as he is inspired by the idea of begetting a race of demigods to conquer the Nibelungs, there is heard for the first time the Sword Motif:

The cries of the Rhinedaughters greet Wotan. They beg him to restore the ring to them. But Wotan must remain deaf to their entreaties. He gave the ring, which he should have restored to the Rhinedaughters, to the giants, as ransom for Freia.

The Valhalla Motif swells to a majestic climax and the gods enter the castle. Amid shimmering arpeggios the Rainbow Motif resounds. The gods have attained the height of their glory—but the Nibelung's curse is still potent, and it will bring woe upon all who have possessed or will possess the ring until it is restored to the Rhinedaughters. Fasolt was only the first victim of Alberich's curse.   K.

DIE WALKÜRE
The Valkyrie

Music-drama in three acts, words and music by Richard Wagner. Première, Munich, June 26, 1870, with Sophie Stehle, Therese Thoma, Frau Kaufmann, Heinrich Vogel, August Kindermann, Bausewein, conductor Franz Wüllner. First performed Bayreuth, 1876, with Materna, Schafsky, Niemann, Betz, conductor Richter; Academy of Music, New York, in an incomplete and inadequate performance with Pappenheim, Canissa, Bischoff, Preusser, conductor Neuendorff; Her Majesty's, London, 1882, with Frau Vogel, Sachse-Hofmeir, Reicher-Kindermann, Niemann, Scaria, Wiegand, conductor Seidl; Metropolitan, New York, 1885, with Materna, Seidl-Kraus, Brandt, Schott, Staudigl, Koegl, conductor Damrosch; Covent Garden, 1892, with Ende-Andriessen, Bettaque, Schumann-Heink, Alvary, Reichmann, Weigand, conductor Mahler; 1895 (in English), with Lillian Tree, Susan Strong, Rose Olitzka, Charles Hedmont, Bispham, Alexander Bevan, conductor George Henschel. Famous Brünnhildes have included Ellen Gulbranson, Saltzmann-Stevens, Litvinne, Mildenburg, Kappel, Leider, Larsen-Todsen, Ohms, Flagstad, Marta Fuchs, Traubel, Varnay, Birgit Nilsson; Sieglindes: Marie Wittich, Fremstad, Lotte Lehmann, Rethberg, Marie Müller, Lemnitz; Siegmunds: Jacques Urlus, Melchior, Schmedes, Völker, Lorenz, Vickers; Wotans: van Rooy, Reichmann, Schorr, Bockelmann, Rode, Hotter, Berglund.

CHARACTERS

Siegmund .... Tenor
Hunding .... Bass
Wotan .... Bass-Baritone
Sieglinde .... Soprano
Brünnhilde .... Soprano
Fricka .... Mezzo-Soprano
Valkyries:
    Gerhilde ⎫
    Helmvige ⎬ .... Soprano
    Ortlinde ⎭
    Waltraute ⎫
    Rossweisse ⎪
    Siegrune ⎬ .... Mezzo-Soprano and Contralto
    Grimgerde ⎪
    Schwertleite ⎭

Time: Legendary   *Place:* Interior of Hunding's hut; a
rocky height; the peak of a rocky
mountain (the Brünnhilde rock)

The action of *Die Walküre* begins after the forced marriage of
Sieglinde to Hunding. The Wälsungs are in ignorance of the
divinity of their father, they know him only as Wälse.

Act I.   In the introduction to *Das Rheingold*, we saw the
Rhine flowing peacefully toward the sea and the innocent
gambols of the Rhinedaughters. But *Die Walküre* opens in
storm and stress. The peace and happiness of the first scene
of the cycle seem to have vanished from the earth with
Alberich's abjuration of love, his theft of the gold, and
Wotan's equally treacherous acts.

This *Walküre* Vorspiel is a masterly representation in music
of a storm gathering for its last infuriated onslaught. The
elements are unleashed. The wind sweeps through the forest.
Lightning flashes in jagged streaks across the black heavens.

The two leading motifs are employed in this introduction.
They are the Storm Motif and the Donner Motif. The Storm
Motif is as follows:

These themes are elemental. From them Wagner has
composed storm music of convincing power.

The storm gradually dies away, and the curtain rises to
reveal Hunding's dwelling, built around a huge ash-tree,
whose trunk and branches pierce the roof. In the right
foreground is a large open hearth; in the background a large
door. A few steps in the left foreground lead up to the door
of an inner room.

The door in the background is opened from without.
Siegmund, like a fugitive who has reached the limits of his
powers of endurance, staggers toward the hearth and sinks
down before it.

Wagner's treatment of this scene is masterly. As Siegmund
stands in the entrance we hear the Siegmund Motif on 'cellos
and basses. It seems the wearier for the burden of an
accompanying figure on the horns, beneath which it seems to
stagger as Siegmund staggers toward the hearth.

The Siegmund Motif is followed by the Storm Motif, *pp*—and the storm has died away. The door of the room to the left opens and a young woman—Sieglinde—appears. She has heard someone enter, and, thinking her husband returned, has come to meet him—not impelled to this by love, but by fear. For Hunding had, while her father and kinsmen were away on the hunt, laid waste their dwelling and abducted her and forcibly married her. Ill-fated herself, she is moved to compassion at sight of the storm-driven fugitive before the hearth, and bends over him.

Her compassionate action is accompanied by a new motif, which by Wagner's commentators has been entitled the Motif of Compassion. But it seems to me to have a further meaning as expressing the sympathy between two souls, a tie so subtle that it is at first invisible even to those whom it unites. Siegmund and Sieglinde, it will be remembered, belong to the same race; and though they are at this point of the action unknown to one another, yet, as Sieglinde bends over the hunted, storm-beaten Siegmund, that subtle sympathy causes her to regard him with more solicitude than would be awakened by any other unfortunate stranger. Hence I have called this motif the Motif of Sympathy—taking sympathy in its double meaning of compassion and affinity of feeling:

The beauty of this brief phrase is enhanced by its unpretentiousness. As it is Siegmund who has awakened these feelings in Sieglinde, the Motif of Sympathy is heard simultaneously with the Siegmund Motif.

Siegmund, suddenly raising his head, gasps, 'Water, water!' Sieglinde hastily snatches up a drinking-horn and hands it to Siegmund. As though new hope were engendered in his breast by Sieglinde's gentle ministration, the Siegmund Motif rises higher and higher, gathering passion in its upward sweep and then, combined again with the Motif of Sympathy, sinks to an expression of heartfelt gratitude. This passage is scored entirely for strings.

Having drunk from the proffered cup the stranger lifts a searching gaze to her features, as if they awakened within him memories whose significance he himself cannot fathom. She, too, is strangely affected by his gaze.

Here occurs the Love Motif played throughout as a violoncello solo, with accompaniment of eight violoncellos and two double basses; exquisite in tone colour and one of the most tenderly expressive phrases ever penned.

The Love Motif is the mainspring of this act.

Siegmund asks with whom he has found shelter. Sieglinde replies that the house is Hunding's, and she his wife, and requests Siegmund to await her husband's return.

> 'Weaponless am I:
> The wounded guest
> He will surely give shelter,'

is Siegmund's reply. Sieglinde asks him to show her his wounds, but, refreshed by the draught of cool spring water and with hope revived by her sympathetic presence, he gathers force and, raising himself to a sitting posture, exclaims that his wounds are but slight; his frame is still firm and, had sword and shield held half so well, he would not have fled from his foes. His strength was spent in flight through the storm, but the night that sank on his vision has yielded again to the sunshine of Sieglinde's presence. At these words the Motif of Sympathy rises like a sweet hope. Sieglinde fills the drinking-horn with mead and offers it to Siegmund. He asks her to take the first sip. She does so and then hands it to him. His eyes rest upon her while he drinks. As he returns the drinking-horn to her there are traces of deep emotion in his mien. He sighs and gloomily bows his head. The action at this point is most expressively accompanied by the orchestra. Specially noteworthy is an impassioned upward sweep of the Motif of Sympathy as Siegmund regards Sieglinde.

In a voice that trembles with emotion, he says: 'You have harboured one whom misfortune follows wherever he directs his footsteps. Lest through me misfortune enter this house, I will depart.' With determined strides he has already reached the door, when she, forgetting all in the emotions his presence has stirred within her, calls after him:

'Tarry! You cannot bring sorrow to a house where sorrow already reigns!'

Her words are followed by a phrase weighted with sorrow, the Wälsung Motif:

Siegmund returns to the hearth, while she, as if shamed by her outburst of feeling, allows her eyes to sink toward the ground. They gaze into each other's eyes with deep emotion until Sieglinde's attention is suddenly distracted. The woman is the first to start. She hears Hunding, and soon afterward he stands upon the threshold looking darkly upon his wife and the stranger.

With the approach of Hunding there is a sudden change in the character of the music. We hear the Hunding Motif, *pp*. Then as he stands upon the threshold, this motif resounds with powerful presentiment on the tubas:

The woman, anticipating her husband's inquiry, explains that she discovered the stranger lying exhausted at the hearth and gave him shelter. With an assumed graciousness that makes him if anything more forbidding, Hunding orders her prepare the meal.

'Your name and story?' he asks, after they have seated themselves in front of the ash-tree. Slowly, as if oppressed by heavy memories, Siegmund begins his story, carefully however continuing to conceal his name, since, for all he knows, Hunding may be one of the enemies of his race. Surrounded by enemies against whom he and his kin were constantly obliged to defend themselves, he grew up in the forest. He and his father returned from one of their hunts to find the hut in ashes, his mother a corpse, and no trace of his twin sister. In one of the combats with their foes he became separated from his father.

At this point you hear the Valhalla Motif, for Siegmund's

father was none other than Wotan, known to his human
descendants, however, only as Wälse. In Wotan's narrative in
the next act it will be discovered that Wotan purposely
created these misfortunes for Siegmund, in order to
strengthen him for his task.

Continuing his narrative Siegmund says that, since losing
track of his father, he has wandered from place to place, ever
with misfortune in his wake. That very day he has defended a
maid whom her brothers wished to force into marriage. But
when, in the combat that ensued, he had slain her brothers,
she turned upon him and denounced him as a murderer,
while the kinsmen of the slain, summoned to vengeance,
attacked him from all quarters.

Those whom Siegmund slew were Hunding's kinsmen.
Thus Siegmund's dark fate has driven him to seek shelter in
the house of the very man who is the arch-enemy of his race
and is bound by the laws of kinship to avenge on Siegmund
the death of kinsmen.

As Siegmund concludes his narrative the Wälsung Motif is
heard. Gazing with ardent longing toward Sieglinde, he says:

> 'Now know'st thou, questioning wife,
> Why "Peaceful" is not my name.'

These words are sung to a lovely phrase. Then, as
Siegmund rises and Sieglinde, pale and deeply affected by his
tale, bows her head, there is heard on the horns, bassoons,
violas, and 'cellos a motif expressive of the heroic fortitude
of the Wälsungs in struggling against their fate. It is the Motif
of the Wälsung's Heroism:

The sombre visage at the head of the table has grown even
darker and more threatening. Hunding rises. 'I know a
ruthless race to whom nothing is sacred, and hated of all,' he
says. 'Mine were the kinsmen you slew. I, too, was
summoned from my home to take blood vengeance upon the
slayer. Returning, I find him here. You have been offered
shelter for the night, and for the night you are safe. But
to-morrow be prepared to defend yourself.'

Left alone, Siegmund's gloomy thoughts are accompanied

by the threatening rhythm of the Hunding Motif and the Sword Motif in a minor key, for Siegmund is still weaponless.

'A sword my father did promise

. . . .

Wälse! Wälse! Where is thy sword!'

The Sword Motif rings out like a shout of triumph. As the embers of the fire collapse, there is seen in the glare that for a moment falls upon the ash-tree, the hilt of a sword whose blade is buried in the trunk of the tree at the point upon which Sieglinde's look last rested. While the Motif of the Sword gently rises and falls, like the coming and going of a lovely memory, Siegmund apostrophises the sheen as the reflection of Sieglinde's glance. And although the embers die out, and night falls upon the scene, in Siegmund's thoughts the memory of that pitying, loving look glimmers on.

A moment later, Sieglinde is by his side. She has given Hunding a sleeping-potion. She will point out a weapon to Siegmund—a sword. If he can wield it she will call him the greatest hero, for only the mightiest can wield it. The music quickens with the subdued excitement in the breasts of the two Wälsungs. You hear the Sword Motif and above it, on horns, clarinet, and oboe, a new motif—that of the Wälsung's Call to Victory:

for Sieglinde hopes that with the sword the stranger, who has so quickly awakened love in her breast, will overcome Hunding. This motif has an irresistible, onward sweep. Sieglinde, amid the strains of the stately Valhalla Motif, followed by the Sword Motif, narrates the story of the sword. While Hunding and his kinsmen were feasting in honour of her forced marriage with him, an aged stranger entered the hall. The men knew him not and shrank from his fiery glance. But upon her his look rested with tender compassion. With a mighty thrust he buried a sword up to its hilt in the trunk of the ash-tree. Whoever drew it from its sheath to him it should belong. The stranger went his way. One after another the strong men tugged at the hilt—but in vain. Then she knew who the aged stranger was and for whom the sword was destined.

The Sword Motif rings out like a joyous shout, and Sieglinde's voice mingles with the triumphant notes of the Wälsung's Call to Victory as she turns to Siegmund:

> 'O, found I in thee
> The friend in need!'

Then is heard the Motif of the Wälsung's Heroism, now no longer full of tragic import, but forceful and defiant—and Siegmund holds Sieglinde in his embrace.

There is a rush of wind. The woven hangings flap and fall. As the lovers turn, a glorious sight greets their eyes. The landscape is illumined by the moon. All nature seems to be throbbing in unison with the hearts of the lovers, and, turning to the woman, Siegmund greets her with the Love Song:

The Love Motif, impassioned, irresistible, sweeps through the harmonies—and Love and Spring are united. The Love Motif also pulsates through Sieglinde's ecstatic reply after she has given herself fully up to Siegmund in the Flight Motif—for before his coming her woes have fled as winter flies before the coming of spring. With Siegmund's exclamation

> 'Oh, wondrous vision!
> Rapturous woman!'

there rises from the orchestra like a vision of loveliness the Motif of Freia, the Venus of German mythology. In its embrace it folds this pulsating theme:

It throbs on like a love-kiss until it seemingly yields to the blandishments of this caressing phrase:

This throbbing, pulsating, caressing music is succeeded by a moment of repose. The woman again gazes searchingly into the man's features. She has seen his face before. It was when she saw her own reflection in a brook! And his voice? It seems to her like an echo of her own. And his glance; has it never before rested on her? She is sure it has; it was when the stranger thrust the sword into the ash-tree.

He who thrust the sword into the tree was of her own race, the Wälsungs. Who is he?

'I, too, have seen that light, but in your eyes!' exclaimed the fugitive. 'I, too, am of your race. I, too, am a Wälsung, my father none other than Wälse himself.'

'Was Wälse your father?' she cries ecstatically. 'For you, then, this sword was thrust in the tree! Let me name you, as I recall you from far back in my childhood, Siegmund!'

'Yes, I am Siegmund; and you, too, I now know well. You are Sieglinde. Fate has willed that we two of our unhappy race shall meet again and save each other or perish together.'

Then, leaping upon the table, he draws the sword from the tree as a blade from its scabbard. Brandishing it in triumph, he leaps to the floor and, clasping Sieglinde, rushes forth with her into the night.

And the music? It fairly seethes with excitement. As Siegmund leaps upon the table, the Motif of the Wälsung's Heroism rings out as if in defiance of the enemies of the race. The Sword Motif—and he has grasped the hilt; the Motif of Compact, ominous of the fatality which hangs over the Wälsungs; the Motif of Renunciation, with its threatening import; then the Sword Motif—brilliant like the glitter of refulgent steel—and Siegmund has unsheathed the sword. The Wälsung's Call to Victory, like a song of triumph; a superb upward sweep of the Sword Motif; the Love Motif, now rushing onward in the very ecstasy of passion, and Siegmund holds in his embrace Sieglinde, his bride—of the same doomed race as himself!

Act II.   In the Vorspiel the orchestra dashes into the Motif of Flight. The Sword Motif in 9—8 rhythm closely resembles the Motif of the Valkyries' Ride, and the Flight Motif in the version in which it appears is much like the Valkyries' Shout. The Ride and the Shout are heard in the course of the Vorspiel, the former with tremendous force on trumpets and trombones as the curtain rises on a wild, rocky mountain pass, at the back of which, through a natural rock-formed arch, a gorge slopes downward.

In the foreground stands Wotan, armed with spear, shield,
and helmet. Before him is Brünnhilde in the costume of the
Valkyrie. The stormy spirit of the Vorspiel pervades the
music of Wotan's command to Brünnhilde that she bridle her
steed for battle and spur it to the fray to do combat for
Siegmund against Hunding. Brünnhilde greets Wotan's
command with the joyous Shout of the Valkyries:

The accompanying figure is based on the Motif of the Ride
of the Valkyries:

Brünnhilde faces Wotan, and calls to him that Fricka is
approaching in her ram-drawn chariot. Fricka advances toward Wotan, Brünnhilde having meanwhile disappeared
behind the mountain height. Fricka is the protector of the
marriage vow, and as such she has come in anger to demand
from Wotan vengeance on behalf of Hunding. Her angry,
passionate demeanour is reflected by the orchestra, and this
effective musical expression of Fricka's ire is often heard in
the course of the scene. Wotan, though knowing well what
has brought Fricka upon the scene, feigns ignorance of the
cause of her agitation and asks what it is that harasses her.
Her reply is preceded by the stern Hunding Motif. She tells
Wotan that she, as the protectress of the sanctity of the
marriage vow, has heard Hunding's voice calling for
vengeance upon the Wälsung twins. Her words, 'His voice for
vengeance is raised,' are set to a phrase strongly suggestive of
Alberich's curse. It seems as though the avenging Nibelung
were pursuing Wotan's children and thus striking a blow at
Wotan himself through Fricka. The Love Motif breathes
through at Wotan's protest that Siegmund and Sieglinde only
yielded to the music of the spring night. Wotan argues that
Siegmund and Sieglinde are true lovers, and Fricka should
smile instead of venting her wrath on them. The Motif of the
Love Song, the Love Motif, and the caressing phrase heard in
the love scene are beautifully blended with Wotan's words. In

strong contrast to these motifs is the music in Fricka's outburst of wrath, introduced by the phrase reflecting her ire, which is repeated several times in the course of this episode. Wotan explains to her why he begat the Wälsung race and the hopes he has founded upon it. But Fricka mistrusts him. What can mortals accomplish that the gods, who are far mightier than mortals, cannot accomplish? Hunding must be avenged on Siegmund and Sieglinde. Wotan must withdraw his protection from Siegmund. Now appears a phrase which expresses Wotan's impotent wrath—impotent because Fricka brings forward the unanswerable argument that if the Wälsungs go unpunished by her, as guardian of the marriage vow, she, the Queen of the gods, will be held up to the scorn of mankind.

Wotan would save the Wälsungs, but Fricka's argument is conclusive. He cannot protect Siegmund and Sieglinde, because their escape from punishment would bring degradation upon the Queen-goddess and the whole race of the gods, and result in their immediate fall. Wotan's wrath rises at the thought of sacrificing his beloved children to the vengeance of Hunding, but he is impotent. His far-reaching plans are brought to nought. He sees the hope of having the ring restored to the Rhinedaughters by the voluntary act of a hero of the Wälsung race vanish. The curse of Alberich hangs over him like a dark, threatening cloud. The Motif of Wotan's Wrath is as follows:

Brünnhilde's joyous shouts are heard from the height. Wotan exclaims that he had summoned the Valkyrie to do battle for Siegmund. In broad, stately measures, Fricka proclaims that her honour shall be guarded by Brünnhilde's shield and demands of Wotan an oath that in the coming combat the Wälsung shall fall. Wotan takes the oath and throws himself dejectedly down upon a rocky seat. Fricka strides toward the back.

In this scene we have witnessed the specacle of a mighty god vainly struggling to avert ruin from his race. That it is due to irresistible fate and not merely to Fricka that Wotan's plans succumb, is made clear by the darkly ominous notes of Alberich's Curse, which resound as Wotan, wrapt in gloomy brooding, leans back against the rocky seat, and also when, in a paroxysm of despair, he gives vent to his feelings, a passage which, for overpowering intensity of expression, stands out even from among Wagner's writings. The final words of this outburst of grief:

'The saddest I among all men,'

are set to this variant of the Motif of Renunciation; the meaning of this phrase having been expanded from the renunciation of love by Alberich to cover the renunciation of happiness which is forced upon Wotan by avenging fate:

Brünnhilde casts away shield, spear, and helmet, and sinking down at Wotan's feet looks up to him with affectionate anxiety. Here we see in the Valkyrie the touch of tenderness, without which a truly heroic character is never complete.

Musically it is beautifully expressed by the Love Motif, which, when Wotan, as if awakening from a reverie, fondly strokes her hair, goes over into the Siegmund Motif. It is over the fate of his beloved Wälsungs that Wotan has been brooding. There is a wonderfully soft yet rich melody on four horns. It is one of those beautiful details in which Wagner's works abound.

In Wotan's narrative, which now follows, the chief of the gods tells Brünnhilde of the events which have brought this sorrow upon him. The motifs heard in Wotan's narrative will be recognised, except one, which is new. This is expressive of the stress to which the gods are subjected through Wotan's crime. It is first heard when Wotan tells of the hero who alone can regain the ring. It is the Motif of the God's Stress.

Excited by remorse and despair Wotan bids farewell to the glory of the gods. Then he in terrible mockery blesses the Nibelung's heir—for Alberich has wedded and to him has been born a son, upon whom the Nibelung depends to continue his death struggle with the gods. Terrified by this outburst of wrath, Brünnhilde asks what her duty shall be in the approaching combat. Wotan commands her to do Fricka's bidding and withdraw protection from Siegmund. In vain Brünnhilde pleads for the Wälsung whom she knows Wotan loves. But her pleading is in vain. Wotan is no longer the all-powerful chief of the gods—through his breach of faith he has become the slave of fate.

Slowly and sadly Brünnhilde bends down for her weapons, her actions being accompanied by the Valkyrie Motif. Bereft of its stormy impetuosity it is as sad as her thoughts. Lost in these reflections, which find beautiful expression in the orchestra, she turns toward the background.

Suddenly the sadly expressive phrases are interrupted by the Motif of Flight. Looking down into the valley Brünnhilde perceives Siegmund and Sieglinde approaching in hasty flight. For hours they have toiled forward, yet never have the fugitives been able to shake off the dread sound of Hunding's horn as he calls upon his kinsmen to redouble their efforts to overtake the two Wälsungs. Terror has begun to unsettle Sieglinde's reason. When Siegmund bids her rest she stares wildly before her, then gazes with growing rapture into his eyes and throws her arms around his neck, only to shriek suddenly: 'Away, away!' as she hears the distant horn-calls, then to grow rigid and stare vacantly before her as Siegmund announces to her that here he proposes to end their flight, here await Hunding, and test the temper of Wälse's sword. At last, utterly overcome by the strain of flight, she faints. Slowly Siegmund lets himself down on a rocky seat, drawing her with him, so that when he is seated her head rests on his lap. Tenderly he looks down upon the companion of his flight, and like a mournful memory, the orchestra intones the Love Motif. As he looks up from Sieglinde he sees standing on the rock above them Brünnhilde.

The Motif of Fate—so full of solemn import—is heard:

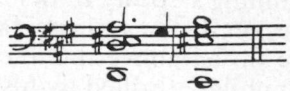

While her earnest look rests upon him, there is heard the Motif of the Death-Song, a prophetic strain:

Brünnhilde gazes upon Siegmund. Then there rises from the orchestra, in strains of rich, soft, alluring beauty, an inversion of the Valhalla Motif. The Fate, Death-Song, and Valhalla Motifs recur, and Siegmund, raising his eyes and meeting Brünnhilde's look, questions her and receives her answers. The episode is so fraught with solemnity that the shadow of death seems to have fallen upon the scene. The solemn beauty of the music impresses itself the more upon the listener, because of the agitated, agonised scene which preceded it.

To the Wälsung, who meets her gaze so calmly, Brünnhilde speaks in solemn tones: 'Siegmund, look on me. I am she whom soon you must prepare to follow.' Then she paints for him in glowing colours the joys of Valhalla, where Wälse, his father, is awaiting him and where he will have heroes for his companions, himself the hero of many valiant deeds. Siegmund listens unmoved. In reply he frames but one question: 'When I enter Valhalla, will Sieglinde be there to greet me?'

When Brünnhilde answers that in Valhalla he will be attended by valkyries and wishmaidens, but that Sieglinde will not be there to meet him, he scorns the delights she has held out. Let her greet Wotan from him, and Wälse, his father, too, as well as the wishmaidens. He will remain with Sieglinde.

Then the radiant Valkyrie, moved by Siegmund's calm determination to sacrifice even a place among the heroes for the woman he loves, makes known to him the fate to which he has been doomed by Wotan. Let Siegmund therefore prepare for Valhalla, but let him leave Sieglinde in her care. She will protect her.

'No other living being but I shall touch her,' exclaims the Wälsung, as he draws his sword. 'If the Wälsung sword is to be shattered on Hunding's spear, it first shall bury itself in her breast and save her from a worse fate!' He poises the sword ready for the thrust above the unconscious Sieglinde.

'Hold!' cries Brünnhilde, thrilled by his heroic love. 'Whatever the consequences which Wotan, in his wrath, shall visit upon me, to-day, for the first time I disobey him. Sieglinde shall live, and with her Siegmund!'

Hunding's horn-calls sound nearer and nearer. With a last look and a last kiss for Sieglinde, Siegmund gently lays her down and begins to ascend toward the peak. Slowly Sieglinde regains her senses. She looks for Siegmund. Instead of seeing him bending over her she hears Hunding's voice as if from among the clouds, calling him to combat; then Siegmund's accepting the challenge. Suddenly a bright light pierces the clouds. Above her she sees the men fighting, Brünnhilde protecting Siegmund who is aiming a deadly stroke at Hunding.

At that moment, however, the light is diffused with a reddish glow. In it Wotan appears. As Siegmund's sword cuts the air on its errand of death, the god interposes his spear, the sword breaks in two and Hunding thrusts his spear into the defenceless Wälsung's breast. The second victim of Alberich's curse has met his fate.

With a wild shriek, Sieglinde falls to the ground, to be caught up by Brünnhilde in headlong flight for the Valkyrie rock.

Act III.   The third act opens with the famous 'Ride of the Valkyries'. The wild maidens of Valhalla coursing upon winged steeds through storm-clouds, their weapons flashing in the gleam of lightening, their weird laughter mingling with the crash of thunder, have come to hold tryst upon the Valkyrie rock.

When eight of the Valkyries have gathered upon the rocky summit of the mountain, they espy Brünnhilde approaching. Instead of a slain hero across her pommel, Brünnhilde bears a woman.

In frantic haste the Valkyrie tells her sisters what has transpired, and how Wotan is pursuing her to punish her for her disobedience. One of the Valkyries ascends the rock and, looking in the direction from which Brünnhilde has come, calls out that even now she can descry the red glow behind the storm-clouds that denotes Wotan's approach. Quickly Brünnhilde bids Sieglinde seek refuge in the forest beyond the Valkyrie rock. The latter, who has been lost in gloomy brooding, starts at her rescuer's supplication and in strains replete with mournful beauty begs that she may be left to her fate and follow Siegmund in death. The glorious prophecy in which Brünnhilde now foretells to Sieglinde that she is to become the mother of Siegfried, is based upon the Siegfried Motif:

Sieglinde, in joyous frenzy, blesses Brünnhilde and hastens to find safety in a dense forest to the eastward, the same forest in which Fafner, in the form of a serpent, guards the Rhine gold treasures.

Wotan, in hot pursuit of Brünnhilde, reaches the mountain summit. In vain her sisters entreat him to spare her. He threatens them harshly, and with wild cries of fear they depart.

Brünnhilde is Wotan's favourite daughter, but his features are dark with anger at her disobedience of his command. Throwing herself at her father's feet, she pleads that he himself had intended to save Siegmund and had been turned from his purpose only by Fricka's interference. But Wotan is obdurate: she must be punished. He will cause her to fall into a deep sleep upon the Valkyrie rock, which shall become the Brünnhilde rock, and to the first man who finds her and awakens her, she, no longer a Valkyrie, but a mere woman, shall fall prey.

This great scene between Wotan and Brünnhilde is introduced by an orchestral passage. The Valkyrie lies in penitence at her father's feet. In the expressive orchestral measures the Motif of Wotan's Wrath mingles with that of Brünnhilde's Pleading. The motifs thus form a prelude to the scene in which the Valkyrie seeks to appease her father's anger, not through a specious plea, but by laying bare the promptings of a noble heart, which forced her, against the chief god's command, to intervene for Siegmund. The Motif of Brünnhilde's Pleading is heard in its simplest form at Brünnhilde's words: 'Was it so shameful what I have done?' and it may be noticed that as she proceeds the Motif of Wotan's Wrath, heard in the accompaniment, grows less stern, until with her plea, 'Soften thy wrath', it assumes a tone of regretful sorrow.

Wotan's feelings toward Brünnhilde have softened from anger at her disobedience to grief that he must mete out punishment. In his reply excitement subsides to gloom. It would be difficult to point to other music more touchingly expressive of deep contrition than the phrase in which

Brünnhilde pleads that Wotan himself taught her to love Siegmund, known as the Motif of Brünnhilde's Pleading:

Then we hear from Wotan that he had abandoned Siegemund to his fate, because he had lost hope in the cause of the gods and wished to end his woe in the wreck of the world.

Brünnhilde makes her last appeal. She tells her father that Sieglinde has found refuge in the forest, and that there she will give birth to a son, Siegfried—the hero for whom the gods have been waiting to overthrow their enemies. If she must suffer for her disobedience, let Wotan surround her sleeping form with a fiery circle which only such a hero will dare penetrate. The Motif of Brünnhilde's Pleading and the Siegfried Motif vie with each other in giving expression to the beauty, tenderness, and majesty of this scene.

Gently the god raises her and tenderly kisses her brow; and thus bids farewell to the best beloved of his daughters. Slowly she sinks upon the rock. He closes her helmet and covers her with her shield. Then, with his spear, he invokes the god of fire. Tongues of flame leap from the crevices of the rock. The forest beyond glows like a furnace, as Wotan, with a last look at the sleeping form of Brünnhilde, vanishes beyond the fiery circle.

A majestic orchestral passage opens Wotan's farewell to Brünnhilde. In all Wagner's music this scene has no peer. Such tender, mournful beauty has never found expression in music—and this, whether we include the vocal part or the orchestral accompaniment in which figures the lovely Slumber Motif:

The Slumber Motif, the Magic Fire Motif, and the Siegfried Motif combine in a masterly scene, towards whose close we hear again the ominous muttering of the Motif of Fate. Brünnhilde may be saved from ignominy, Siegfried may be born to Sieglinde—but the crushing weight of Alberich's curse still rests upon the race of the gods.   K.

SIEGFRIED

Music-drama in three acts, words and music by Richard Wagner
Première, Bayreuth, August 16, 1876, with Unger, Schlosser, Betz, Hill
von Reichenberg, Materna, conductor Richter. First performed He
Majesty's Theatre, London, 1882, with Scaria, Vogel, Schlosser
Schelper, Frau Vogel, Reigler, Schreiber, conductor Seidl; Metropolitan
New York, 1887, with Fischer, Alvary, von Milde, Fererczy, Elmbald
Lilli Lehmann, Brandt, Seidl-Krauss, conductor Seidl; Covent Garden
1892, with Grengg, Alvary, Lieban, Lorent, Wiegand, Rosa Sucher
Schumann-Heink, Traubmann, conductor Mahler; Manchester (in
English), 1901; Covent Garden (in English), 1908, with Clarence
Whitehill, Cornelius, Meux, Bechstein, Agnes Nicholls, Thornton,
Hatchard, conductor Richter.

CHARACTERS

Siegfried .... Tenor
Mime .... Tenor
Wotan (*disguised as the Wanderer*) ...... Bass-Baritone
Alberich .... Bass-Baritone
Fafner (*disguised as a Dragon*) .... Bass
Erda .... Contralto
Forest Bird .... Soprano
Brünnhilde .... Soprano

Time: Legendary   *Place:* A rocky cave in the forest; deep
in the forest; wild region at foot of a
rocky mount; the Brünnhilde Rock

The Nibelungs were not present in the dramatic action of
The Valkyrie, though the sinister influence of Alberich
shaped the tragedy of Siegmund's death. In *Siegfried* several
characters of *Das Rheingold*, who do not take part in *Die
Walküre*, reappear. These are the Nibelungs, Alberich and
Mime; the giant Fafner, who in the guise of a serpent guards
the Nibelung hoard in a cavern, and Erda.

Siegfried has been born of Sieglinde, who died in giving
birth to him. This scion of the Wälsung race has been reared
by Mime, who found him in the forest by his dead mother's
side. Mime is plotting to obtain possession of the ring and of
Fafner's other treasures, and hopes to be aided in his designs
by the young hero. Wotan, disguised as a Wanderer, is
watching the course of events, again hopeful that a hero of
the Wälsung race will free the gods from Alberich's curse.
Surrounded by magic fire, Brünnhilde still lies in deep
slumber on the Brünnhilde Rock.

The Vorspiel of *Siegfried* is expressive of Mime's planning and plotting. It begins with music of a mysterious brooding character. Mingling with this is the Motif of the Hoard, familiar from *The Rhine Gold*. Then is heard the Nibelung Motif. After reaching a forceful climax it passes over to the Motif of the Ring, which rises from *pianissimo* to a crashing climax. The ring is to be the prize of all Mime's plotting.

The opening scene shows Mime forging a sword at a natural forge formed in a rocky cave. In a soliloquy he discloses the purpose of his labours and laments that Siegfried shivers every sword which has been forged for him. Could he (Mime) but unite the pieces of Siegmund's sword! At this thought the Sword Motif rings out brilliantly, and is jubilantly repeated, accompanied by a variant of the Valhalla Motif. For if the pieces of the sword were welded together, and Siegfried were with it to slay Fafner, Mime could surreptitiously obtain possession of the ring, slay Siegfried, rule over the gods in Valhalla, and circumvent Alberich's plans for regaining the hoard.

Mime is still at work when Siegfried enters, leading a bear by a rope, with which he gives it full play so that it can make a dash at Mime. As the latter flees terrified behind the forge, Siegfried shouts with laughter. Musically his buoyant nature is expressed in a theme inspired by the fresh, joyful spirit of a wild, woodland life. It may be called, to distinguish it from the Siegfried Motif, the Motif of Siegfried the Fearless:

In a pretty, graceful phrase Siegfried tells how he blew his horn, hoping it would be answered by a pleasanter companion than Mime. Then he examines the sword which Mime has been forging. The Siegfried Motif resounds as he inveighs against the weapon's weakness, then shivers it on the anvil. The orchestra, with a rush, takes up the Motif of Siegfried the Impetuous:

Mime tells Siegfried how he tenderly reared him from infancy. Mime's reminiscences of Siegfried's infancy are set

to a charming melody, as though Mime were recalling to
Siegfried's memory a cradle song. But Siegfried grows
impatient. If Mime really tended him out of pure affection,
why should Mime be so repulsive to him; and yet why should
he, in spite of Mime's repulsiveness, always return to the
cave? The dwarf explains that he is to Siegfried what the
father is to the fledgling. This leads to a beautiful lyric
episode. Siegfried says that he saw the birds mating, the deer
pairing, the she-wolf nursing her cubs. Whom shall he call
Mother? Who is Mime's wife? This episode is pervaded by the
lovely Motif of Love-Life:

Mime endeavours to persuade Siegfried that he is his father
and mother in one. But Siegfried has noticed that the young
of birds and deer and wolves look like the parents. He has
seen his features reflected in the brook, and knows he does
not resemble the hideous Mime. The notes of the Love-Life
Motif pervade this episode. When Siegfried speaks of seeing
his own likeness, we also hear the Siegfried Motif. Mime
forced by Siegfried to speak the truth, tells of Sieglinde's
death while giving birth to Siegfried. Throughout this scene
we find reminiscences of the first act of *The Valkyrie*, the
Wälsung Motif, the Motif of Sympathy, and the Love Motif.
Finally, when Mime produces as evidence of the truth of his
words the two pieces of Siegmund's sword, the Sword Motif
rings out brilliantly. Siegfried exclaims that Mime must weld
the pieces into a trusty weapon. Then follows Siegfried's
'Wander Song', so full of joyous abandon:

Once the sword is welded, he will leave the hated Mime for
ever. As the fish darts through the water, as the bird flies so
free, he will flee from the repulsive dwarf. With joyous
exclamations he runs from the cave into the forest.

Mime starts a gloomy soliloquy, interrupted by the entrance of Wotan, disguised as a Wanderer. At the moment Mime is in despair because he cannot weld the pieces of Siegmund's sword. When the Wanderer departs, he has prophesied that only he who does not know what fear is—only a fearless hero—can weld the fragments, and that through this fearless hero Mime shall lose his life. This prophecy is reached through a somewhat curious process which must be unintelligible to anyone who has not made a study of the libretto. The Wanderer, seating himself, wagers his head that he can correctly answer any three questions which Mime may put to him. Mime then asks: 'What is the race born in the earth's deep bowels?' The Wanderer answers: 'The Nibelungs.' Mime's second question is: 'What race dwells on the earth's back?' The Wanderer replies: 'The race of giants.' Mime finally asks: 'What race dwells on cloudy heights?' The Wanderer answers: 'The race of the gods.' The Wanderer, having thus answered correctly Mime's three questions, now puts three questions to Mime: 'What is that noble race which Wotan ruthlessly dealt with, and yet which he deemeth most dear?' Mime answers correctly: 'The Wälsungs.' Then the Wanderer asks: 'What sword must Siegfried then strike with, dealing to Fafner death?' Mime answers correctly: 'With Siegmund's sword.' 'Who,' asks the Wanderer, 'can weld its fragments?' Mime is terrified, for he cannot answer. Then Wotan utters the prophecy of the fearless hero.

Several motifs familiar from *The Rhine Gold* and *The Valkyrie* are heard here. The Motif of Compact so powerfully expressive of the binding force of law, the Nibelung and Valhalla Motifs from *The Rhine Gold*, and the Wälsung's Heroism Motif from the first act of *The Valkyrie*, are among these.

When the Wanderer has vanished in the forest Mime sinks back on his stool in despair. We hear the Loge Motif familiar from *The Rhine Gold* and the finale of *The Valkyrie*. At last Mime rises to his feet in terror. He seems to see Fafner in his serpent's guise approaching to devour him, and in a paroxysm of fear he falls with a shriek behind the anvil, just as Siegfried bursts out of the thicket, and with the fresh, buoyant 'Wander Song' and the Motif of Siegfried the Fearless, the foreboding which hung over the former scene is dispelled. Siegfried looks about him for Mime until he sees the dwarf crouching behind the anvil.

Laughingly the young Wälsung asks the dwarf if he ha
thus been welding the sword. 'The sword? The sword?
repeats Mime confusedly, as he advances, and his mind
wanders back to Wotan's prophecy of the fearless hero.
Regaining his senses he tells Siegfried there is one thing he has
yet to learn, namely, to be afraid; Siegfried's mother charged
Mime to teach him fear. Mime asks Siegfried if he has never
felt his heart beating when in the gloaming he heard strange
sounds and saw glimmering lights in the forest. Siegfried
replies that he never has. If it is necessary before he goes
forth in quest of adventure to learn what fear is, he would
like to be taught. But how can Mime teach him?

The Magic Fire Motif and Brünnhilde's Slumber Motif,
familiar from Wotan's Farewell and the Magic Fire scene, are
heard here, the former depicting the weird lights with which
Mime has sought to infuse dread into Siegfried's breast, the
latter prophesying that, penetrating fearlessly the fiery circle,
Siegfried will reach Brünnhilde. Then Mime tells Siegfried of
Fafner, thinking thus to strike terror into the young
Wälsung's breast. But far from it! Siegfried is incited by
Mime's words to meet Fafner in combat. Has Mime welded
the fragments of Siegmund's sword, asks Siegfried. The dwarf
confesses his impotence. Siegfried siezes the fragments. He
will forge his own sword. Here begins the great scene of the
forging of the sword. Like a shout of victory the Motif of
Siegfried the Fearless rings out and the orchestra fairly glows
as Siegfried heaps a great mass of coal on the forge-hearth,
and, fanning the heat, begins to file away at the fragments of
the sword.

The roar of the fire, the sudden intensity of the fierce
white heat to which the young Wälsung fans the glow—these
we would respectively hear and see were the music given
without scenery or action, so graphic is Wagner's score. The
Sword Motif leaps like a brilliant tongue of flame over the
heavy ends of a forceful variant of the Motif of Compact, the
music flows and hisses like a fiery flood as Siegfried pours the
molten contents of the crucible into a mould and then
plunges the latter into water. The glowing steel lies on the

No - thung! No - thung! Neid - li - ches Schwert!

nvil and Siegfried swings the hammer. With every stroke his
oyous excitement is intensified. At last the work is done.
Vith the crash of the Sword Motif, united with the Motif of
iegfried the Fearless, the orchestra dashes into a furious
restissimo, and Siegfried, shouting with glee, holds aloft the
word, then in an exultant gesture, splits the anvil in two—a
erilous moment for all but the strongest-nerved of helden-
enors!

Act II.   The second act opens with a darkly portentous
Vorspiel. On the very threshold of it we meet Fafner in his
notif, which is so clearly based on the Giant Motif that there
s no necessity for quoting it. Through themes which are
amiliar from earlier portions of the work, the Vorspiel rises
o a crashing *fortissimo*.

The curtain rises on a thick forest. At the back is the
ntrance to Fafner's cave. In the darkness the outlines of a
igure are dimly discerned. It is the Nibelung, Alberich,
aunting the cave which hides the treasures of which he was
lespoiled. A bluish light gleams from the forest. Wotan, still
n the guise of a Wanderer, enters.

The ensuing scene between Alberich and the Wanderer is,
rom a dramatic point of view, episodical. Suffice it to say
hat the fine self-poise of Wotan and the maliciously restless
haracter of Alberich are strongly contrasted. When Wotan
1as departed the Nibelung slips into a rocky crevice, where he
emains hidden when Siegfried and Mime enter. Mime
ndeavours to awaken dread in Siegfried's heart by describing
'afner's terrible form and powers. But Siegfried's courage is
1ot weakened. On the contrary, with heroic impetuosity, he
sks to be at once confronted with Fafner. Mime, well
nowing that Fafner will soon awaken and issue from his cave
o meet Siegfried in mortal combat, lingers on in the hope
hat both may fall, until the young Wälsung drives him away.

Now begins a beautiful lyric episode. Siegfried reclines
nder a lime-tree, and looks up through the branches. The
ustling of the trees is heard. Over the tremulous whispers of
he orchestra—known from concert programmes as the
Waldweben' (Forest Murmurs)—rises a lovely variant of the
Välsung Motif. Siegfried is asking himself how his mother
1ay have looked, and this variant of the theme which was
irst heard in *The Valkyrie*, when Sieglinde told Siegmund
hat her home was the home of woe, rises like a memory of
1er image. Serenely the sweet strains of the Love-Life Motif

soothe his sad thoughts. Siegfried, once more entranced b'
forest sounds, listens intently. Birds' voices greet him.

The forest voices—the humming of insects, the piping o
the birds, the quiver of the branches—quicken his half
defined aspirations. He listens, but cannot catch the meanin
of the song. Perhaps, if he can imitate it, he may understan
it. He cuts a reed with his sword and quickly fashions a pip
from it. He blows on it, but it sounds shrill. Perhaps his hor
will serve him better. Putting it to his lips he makes the fores
ring with its notes.

The sound of the horn has awakened Fafner who now, i
the guise of a huge dragon, crawls toward Siegfried. Th
music is highly dramatic. The exultant force of the Motif o
Siegfried the Fearless, which rings out as Siegfried rushe
upon Fafner, the crashing chord as the serpent roars whe
Siegfried buries the sword in its heart, the rearing, plungin
music as the monster writhes in agony—these are graphi
features of the score.

Siegfried raises his fingers to his lips and licks the bloo
from them. Immediately he seems to understand the bird
which has again begun its song, while the forest voices onc
more weave their tremulous melody. The bird tells Siegfrie
of the ring and helmet and of the other treasures in Fafner'
cave, and Siegfried enters it in quest of them. With hi
disappearance the forest murmurs suddenly change to th
harsh, scolding notes heard in the beginning of the Nibelhein
scene in *The Rhine Gold*. Mime slinks in and timidly look
about him to make sure of Fafner's death. At the same tim
Alberich issues forth from the crevice in which he wa
concealed. The scene, in which the two Nibelungs berate eacl
other, is capitally treated, and its humour affords a strikin
contrast to the preceding scenes.

As Siegfried comes out of the cave and brings the ring an
helmet from darkness to the light of day, there are heard th
Ring Motif, the Motif of the Rhinedaughters' Shout o
Triumph, and the Rhine Gold Motif. The forest-weaving agai
begins, and the bird bids the young Wälsung beware of Mim
The dwarf now approaches Siegfried with repulsiv
sycophancy. But under a smiling face lurks a plotting heart
Siegfried is enabled through the supernatural gifts with whicl
he has become endowed to fathom the purpose of the dwarf
who inadvertently discloses his scheme to poison Siegfried
The young Wälsung slays Mime, who, as he dies, hear

Alberich's mocking laugh. Though the Motif of Siegfried the Fearless predominates at this point, we also hear the Nibelung Motif and the Motif of the Curse—indicating Alberich's evil intent towards Siegfried.

Siegfried again reclines under the lime-tree. His soul is uneasy with an undefined longing. As he gazes in almost painful emotion up to the branches and asks if the bird can tell him where he can find a friend, his being seems stirred by awakening passion.

The music quickens with an impetuous phrase, which seems to define the first joyous thrill of passion in the youthful hero. It is the Motif of Love's Joy:

It is interrupted by a beautiful variant of the Motif of Love-Life, which continues until, above the murmuring of the forest, the bird again thrills him with its tale of a glorious maid who has so long slumbered upon the fire-guarded rock. With the Motif of Love's Joy coursing through the orchestra, the bird flutters from the lime-tree's branch, hovers over Siegfried, and hesitatingly flies before him until it takes a definite course towards the background. Siegfried follows, the Motif of Love's Joy, succeeded by that of Siegfried the Fearless, bringing the act to a close.

Act III.   The third act opens with a stormy introduction in which the Motif of the Ride of the Valkyries accompanies the Motif of the Gods' Stress, the Compact, and the Erda motifs.

Then to the sombre, questioning phase of the Motif of Fate, the action begins to disclose the significance of this Vorspiel. A wild region at the foot of a rocky mountain is seen. It is night. In dire distress and fearful that through Siegfried and Brünnhilde the rulership of the world may pass from the gods to the human race, Wotan summons Erda from her subterranean dwelling. But Erda has no counsel for the storm-driven, conscience-stricken god.

The scene reaches its climax in Wotan's noble renunciation of the empire of the world. Weary of strife, weary of struggling against the decree of fate, he renounces his sway. Let the era of human love supplant this dynasty, sweeping away the gods and the Nibelungs in its mighty current; perhaps the twilight of the gods will be the dawn of a more glorious epoch. A phrase of great dignity gives force to Wotan's utterances. It is the Motif of the World's Heritage:

Siegfried enters, guided to the spot by the bird; Wotan checks his progress with the same spear which shivered Siegmund's sword. Siegfried must fight his way to Brünnhilde. With a mighty blow the young Wälsung shatters the spear and Wotan disappears amid the crash of the Motif of Compact—for the spear with which it was the chief god's duty to enforce compacts is shattered. Siegfried stands at the rim of the magic cicle. Winding his horn he plunges into the seething flames. Around the Motif of Siegfried the Fearless and the Siegfried Motif flash the Magic Fire and Loge Motifs.

The flames, having flashed forth with dazzling brilliancy gradually pale before the red glow of dawn till a rosy mist envelops the scene. When it rises, the rock and Brünnhilde in deep slumber under the fir-tree, as in the finale of *The Valkyrie*, are seen. Siegfried appears on the height in the background. As he gazes upon the scene there are heard the Fate and Slumber Motifs and then the orchestra weaves a lovely variant of the Freia Motif. This is followed by the softly caressing strains of the Fricka Motif. Fricka sought to

1ake Wotan faithful to her by bonds of love, and hence the
ricka Motif in this scene does not reflect her personality
ut rather the awakening of the love which is to thrill
iegfried when he has beheld Brünnhilde's features. As
iegfried sees Brünnhilde's charger slumbering in the grove,
ve hear the Motif of the Valkyries' Ride, and, when his gaze
 attracted by the sheen of Brünnhilde's armour, the theme
f Wotan's Farewell. Siegfried raises the shield and discloses
he face of the sleeper, the face being almost hidden by the
elmet.

Carefully he loosens the helmet. As he takes it off
rünnhilde's face is disclosed and her long curls flow down
ver her bosom. Siegfried gazes upon her enraptured.
Drawing his sword he cuts the rings of mail on both sides,
ently lifts off the corselet and greaves, and Brünnhilde, in
oft female drapery, lies before him. He starts back in
vonder. The Motif of Love's Joy expresses the feelings that
vell up from his heart as for the first time he beholds a
voman. The fearless hero is filled with awe by a slumbering
voman. The Wälsung Motif, afterwards beautifully varied
vith the Motif of Love's Joy, accompanies his utterances, the
limax of his emotional excitement being expressed in a
najestic *crescendo* of the Freia Motif. With the Motif of Fate
e faces his destiny; and then, while the Freia Motif rises like
 vision of loveliness, he sinks over Brünnhilde, and with
losed eyes presses his lips to hers.

Brünnhilde awakens, and with a noble gesture greets in
najestic accents her return to the sight of earth. Strains of
oftier eloquence than those of her greeting have never been
omposed. Brünnhilde rises from her magic slumbers in the
najesty of womanhood:

With the Motif of Fate she asks who is the hero who has
wakened her. The superb Siegfried Motif gives back the
roud answer. In rapturous phrases they greet one another. It
 the Motif of Love's Greeting,

which unites their voices in impassioned accents until, as i
this motif no longer sufficed to express their ecstasy, it i
followed by the Motif of Love's Passion,

which, with the Siegfried Motif, rises and falls with the
heaving of Brünnhilde's bosom.

These motifs course impetuously through this scene. Here
and there we have others recalling former portions of the
cycle—the Wälsung Motif, when Brünnhilde refers to
Siegfried's mother, Sieglinde; the Motif of Brünnhilde's
Pleading, when she tells him of her defiance of Wotan's
behest; a variant of the Valhalla Motif when she speaks of
herself in Valhalla; and the Motif of the World's Heritage
with which Siegfried claims her, this last leading over to a
forceful climax of the Motif of Brünnhilde's Pleading, which
is followed by a lovely tranquil episode introduced by the
Motif of Love's Peace,

succeeded by a Motif, ardent yet tender—the Motif of
Siegfried the Protector:

These motifs accompany the action most expressively.
ünnhilde still hesitates to cast off for ever the supernatural
aracteristics of the Valkyrie and give herself up entirely to
egfried. The young hero's growing ecstasy finds expression
the Motif of Love's Joy. At last it awakens a responsive
te of purely human passion in Brünnhilde and, answering
e proud Siegfried Motif with the jubilant Shout of the
alkyries and the ecstatic measures of Love's Passion, she
oclaims herself his.

With the love duet the music-drama comes to a close.
egfried, a scion of the Wälsung race, has won Brünnhilde
r his bride, and upon her finger has placed the ring
shioned of Rhine gold.   K.

GÖTTERDÄMMERUNG

Twilight of the Gods

Music-drama in a prologue and three acts, words and music by
ichard Wagner. First performed Bayreuth, August 17, 1876, with
nger, Gura, Seihr, Hill, Materna, conductor Richter. First performed
er Majesty's, London, 1882, with Vogel, Wiegand, Schelper, Biberti,
au Vogel, Schreiber, Reicher-Kindermann, conductor Seidl;
etropolitan, New York, 1888, with Niemann, Robinson, Fischer, von
ilde, Seidl-Krauss, Brandt, Lilli Lehmann, conductor Seidl; Covent
arden, 1892, with Alvary, Knapp, Wiegand, Lissmann, Klafsky,
ettaque, Schumann-Heink, conductor Mahler; 1908 (in English), with
ornelius, Frederick Austin, Meux, Knowles, Perceval Allen, Edith
vans, conductor Richter.

CHARACTERS

Siegfried . . . . Tenor
Gunther . . . . Baritone
Alberich . . . . Bass-Baritone
Hagen . . . . Bass
Brünnhilde . . . . Soprano
Gutrune . . . . Soprano
Waltraute . . . . .Mezzo-Soprano

First, Second, and Third Norn ....Contralto,
              Mezzo-Soprano, and Soprano
Woglinde, Wellgunde, and Flosshilde .... Sopranos
                and Mezzo-Soprano
          Vassals and Women
Time: Legendary   *Place*: On the Brünnhilde Roc
               Gunther's castle on the Rhin
               wooded district by the Rhine

THE PROLOGUE

The first scene of the prologue is a weird conference of t
three grey sisters of fate—the Norns who wind the skein
life. They have met on the Valkyries' rock and their wor
forebode the end of the gods. At last the skein they ha
been winding breaks—the final catastrophe is impending.

An orchestral interlude depicts the transition from t
unearthly gloom of the Norn scene to break of day, t
climax being reached in a majestic burst of music as Siegfri
and Brünnhilde issue forth from the rocky cavern in t
background. This climax owes its eloquence to three moti
—that of the Ride of the Valkyries and two new motifs, t
one as lovely as the other is heroic, the Brünnhilde Motif,

and the Motif of Siegfried the Hero:

The Brünnhilde Motif expresses the strain of pure, tenc
womanhood in the nature of the former Valkyrie, a
proclaims her womanly ecstasy over wholly requited lov
The Motif of Siegfried the Hero is clearly developed from t
Motif of Siegfried the Fearless. Fearless youth has develop
into heroic man. In this scene Brünnhilde and Siegfried plig
their troth, and Siegfried having given to Brünnhilde the fat
ring and having received from her the steed Grane, whic
once bore her in her wild course through the storm-cloud
bids her farewell and sets forth in quest of further adventu

11 *Das Rheingold:* Valhalla, about 1900 and 1973. Wotan, Freia and the Giants are clearly visible. The 1973 production was in Leipzig by Joachim Herz.

12 *Parsifal:* Parsifal with Kundry and Gurnemanz—1888 Bayreuth
with Rosa Sucher, van Dyck and Heinrich Wiegand; and 1965 with
Jess Thomas, Astrid Varnay, Hans Hotter.

Here occur the two new motifs already quoted, and a third—the Motif of Heroic Love:

Siegfried disappears with the steed behind the rocks and Brünnhilde stands upon the cliff looking down the valley after him; his horn is heard from below and Brünnhilde with rapturous gesture waves him farewell. The orchestra accompanies the action with the Brünnhilde Motif, the Motif of Siegfried the Fearless, and finally with the theme of the love-duet with which *Siegfried* closed.

The curtain then falls, and between the prologue and the first act an orchestral interlude describes Siegfried's voyage down the Rhine to the castle of the Gibichungs where dwell Gunther, his sister Gutrune, and their half-brother Hagen, the son of Alberich. Through Hagen the curse hurled by Alberich in *The Rhine Gold* at all into whose possession the ring shall come, is to be worked out to the end of its fell purpose— Siegfried betrayed and destroyed and the rule of the gods brought to an end by Brünnhilde's expiation.

In the interlude between the prologue and the first act we first hear the brilliant Motif of Siegfried the Fearless and then the gracefully flowing Motifs of the Rhine, and of the Rhinedaughters' Shout of Triumph with the Motifs of the Rhine Gold and Ring. Hagen's malevolent plotting, of which we are soon to learn in the first act, is foreshadowed by the sombre harmonies which suddenly pervade the music.

Act I. On the river lies the hall of the Gibichungs, where live Gunther, his sister Gutrune, and Hagen, their half-brother. Gutrune is a maiden of fair mien, Gunther a man of average strength and courage, Hagen a sinister plotter, large of stature and sombre of visage. Long he has planned to possess himself of the ring fashioned of Rhine gold. He is aware that it was guarded by the dragon, has been taken from the hoard by Siegfried, and by him given to Brünnhilde.

A descendant, through his father, Alberich, the Nibelung, of a race which practised the black art, Hagen plots to make Siegfried forget Brünnhilde through a love-potion to be administered to him by Gutrune. When, under the fiery

influence of the potion and all forgetful of Brünnhilde
Siegfried demands Gutrune to wife, the price demanded will
be that he win Brünnhilde as bride for Gunther. Before
Siegfried comes in sight, before Gunther and Gutrune so
much as even know that he is nearing the hall of the
Gibichungs, Hagen begins to lay the foundation for this
seemingly impossible plot. For it is at this opportune
moment Gunther chances to address him:

'Hark, Hagen, and let your answer be true. Do I head the
race of the Gibichungs with honour?'

'Aye,' replies Hagen, 'and yet, Gunther, you remain unwed
while Gutrune still lacks a husband.' Then he tells Gunther of
Brünnhilde—'a circle of flame surrounds the rock on which
she dwells, but he who can brave that fire may win her for
wife. If Siegfried does this in your stead, and brings her to
you as bride, will she not be yours?' Hagen craftily conceals
from his half-brother and from Gutrune the fact that
Siegfried already has won Brünnhilde for himself; but having
aroused in Gunther the desire to possess her, he forthwith
unfolds his plan and reminds Gutrune of the magic love-
potion which it is in her power to administer to Siegfried.

At the very beginning of this act the Hagen Motif is heard.
Particularly noticeable in it are the first two sharp, decisive
chords. They recur with dramatic force in the third act when
Hagen slays Siegfried. The Hagen Motif is as follows:

This is followed by the Gibichung Motif, the two motifs
being frequently heard in the opening scene.

Added to these is the Motif of the Love-Potion which is to cause Siegfried to forget Brünnhilde, and conceive a violent passion for Gutrune:

Whatever hesitation may have been in Gutrune's mind, because of the trick which is involved in the plot, vanishes when soon afterwards Siegfried's horn-call announces his approach from the river, and, as he brings his boat up to the bank, she sees this hero among men in all his youthful strength and beauty. She hastily withdraws, to carry out her part in the plot that is to bind him to her.

The three men remain to parley. Hagen skilfully questions Siegfried regarding his combat with the dragon. Has he taken nothing from the hoard?

'Only a ring, which I have left in a woman's keep,' answers Siegfried; 'and this.' He points to a steel network that hangs from his girdle.

'Ha,' exclaims Hagen, 'the Tarn helmet! I recognise it as the artful work of the Nibelungs. Place it on your head and it enables you to assume any guise.' He then flings open a door and on the platform of a short flight of steps that leads up to it, stands Gutrune, in her hand a drinking-horn which she extends toward Siegfried.

'Welcome, guest, to the house of the Gibichungs. A daughter of the race extends to you this greeting.' And so, while Hagen looks grimly on, the fair Gutrune offers Siegfried the draught that is to transform his whole nature. Courteously, but without regarding her with more than friendly interest, Siegfried takes the horn from her hands and drains it. As if a new element coursed through his veins, there is a sudden change in his manner. Handing the horn back to her he regards her with fiery glances, while she blushingly lowers her eyes and withdraws to the inner apartment. New in this scene is the Gutrune Motif:

'Gunther, your sister's name? Have you a wife?' Siegfried asks excitedly.

'I have set my heart on a woman,' replies Gunther, 'but may not win her. A far-off rock, fire-encircled, is her home.'

'A far-off rock, fire encircled,' repeats Siegfried, as if striving to remember something long forgotten; and when Gunther utters Brünnhilde's name, Siegfried shows by his mien and gesture that it no longer signifies aught to him. The love-potion has caused him to forget her.

'I will press through the circle of flame,' he exclaims. 'I will seize her and bring her to you—if you will give me Gutrune for wife.'

And so the unhallowed bargain is struck and sealed with the oath of blood-brotherhood, and Siegfried departs with Gunther to capture Brünnhilde as bride for the Gibichung. The compact of blood-brotherhood is a most sacred one. Siegfried and Gunther each with his sword draws blood from his arm, which he allows to mingle with wine in a drinking-horn held by Hagen; each lays two fingers upon the horn, and then, having pledged blood-brotherhood, drinks the blood and wine. This ceremony is significantly introduced by the Motif of the Curse followed by the Motif of Compact. Phrases of Siegfried's and Gunther's pledge are set to a new motif whose forceful simplicity effectively expresses the idea of truth. It is the Motif of the Vow:

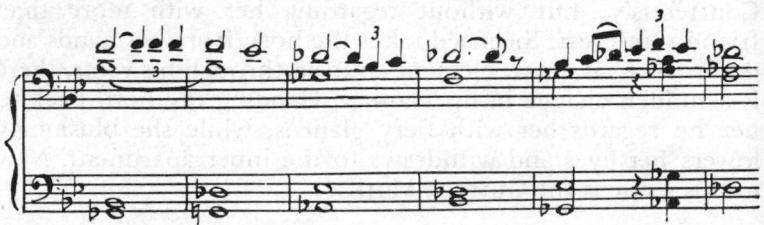

Abruptly following Siegfried's pledge:

'Thus I drink thee troth,'

are those two chords of the Hagen Motif which are heard
again in the third act when the Nibelung has slain Siegfried. It
should perhaps be repeated here that Gunther is not aware of
the union which existed between Brünnhilde and Siegfried,
Hagen having concealed this from his half-brother, who
believes that he will receive the Valkyrie in all her goddess-
like virginity.

When Siegfried and Gunther have departed and Gutrune,
having sighed her farewell after her lover, has retired, Hagen
broods with wicked glee over the successful inauguration of
his plot. During a brief orchestral interlude a drop-curtain
conceals the scene which, when the curtain again rises, has
changed to the Valkyrie's rock, where sits Brünnhilde, lost in
contemplation of the ring, while the Motif of Siegfried the
Protector is heard on the orchestra like a blissful memory of
the love scene.

Her rapturous reminiscences are interrupted by the sounds
of an approaching storm and from the dark cloud there issues
one of the Valkyries, Waltraute, who comes to ask of
Brünnhilde that she cast back the ring Siegfried has given
her—the ring cursed by Alberich—into the Rhine, and thus
lift the curse from the race of gods. But Brünnhilde refuses.

It is dusk. The magic fire rising from the valley throws a
glow over the landscape. The notes of Siegfried's horn are
heard. Brünnhilde joyously prepares to meet him. Suddenly
she sees a stranger leap through the flames. It is Siegfried, but
through the Tarn helmet (the motif of which, followed by
the Gunther Motif, dominates the first part of the scene) he
has assumed the guise of the Gibichung. In vain Brünnhilde
seeks to defend herself with the might which the ring
imparts. She is powerless against the intruder. As he tears the
ring from her finger, the Motif of the Curse resounds with
tragic import, followed by echoes of the Motif of Siegfried
the Protector and of the Brünnhilde Motif, the last being
succeeded by the Tarn helmet Motif expressive of the evil
magic which has wrought this change in Siegfried.
Brünnhilde, in abject recognition of her impotence, enters
the cavern. Before Siegfried follows her he draws his sword
Nothung (Needful) and exclaims:

'Now, Nothung, witness thou, that chaste my wooing is;
To keep my faith with my brother, separate me from his
bride.'

Phrases of the pledge of Brotherhood followed by the
Brünnhilde, Gutrune, and Sword Motifs accompany his
words. The thuds of the typical Nibelung rhythm resound,
and lead to the last crashing chord of this eventful act.

Act II. The ominous Motif of the Nibelung's Hate
introduces the second act. The curtain rises upon the exterior
of the hall of the Gibichungs. It is night. Hagen, spear in hand
and shield at side, leans in sleep against a pillar of the hall.
Alberich appears to urge Hagen to murder Siegfried and to
seize the ring from his finger. After hearing Hagen's oath that
he will be faithful to the hate he has inherited, Alberich
disappears. The weirdness of the surroundings, the monotony
of Hagen's answers, uttered seemingly in sleep, as if, even
when the Nibelung slumbered, his mind remained active,
imbue this scene with mystery.

A charming orchestral interlude depicts the break of day.
Its serene beauty is, however, broken in upon by the Motif of
Hagen's Wicked Glee, which I quote, as it frequently occurs
in the course of succeeding events.

All night Hagen has watched by the bank of the river for
the return of the men from the quest. It is daylight when
Siegfried returns, tells him of his success, and bids him
prepare to receive Gunther and Brünnhilde. On his finger he
wears the ring—the ring made of Rhine gold, and cursed by
Alberich—the same with which he pledged his troth to
Brünnhilde, but which in the struggle of the night, and
disguised by the Tarn helmet as Gunther, he has torn from
her finger—the very ring the possession of which Hagen
craves, and for which he is plotting. Gutrune has joined them.
Siegfried leads her into the hall.

Hagen, placing an ox-horn to his lips, blows a loud call
toward the four points of the compass, summoning the
Gibichung vassals to the festivities attending the double
wedding—Siegfried and Gutrune, Gunther and Brünnhilde;
and when the Gibichung brings his boat up to the bank, the

hore is crowded with men who greet him boisterously, while
Brünnhilde stands there pale and with downcast eyes. But as
Siegfried leads Gutrune forward to meet Gunther and his
bride, and Gunther calls Siegfried by name, Brünnhilde starts,
raises her eyes, stares at Siegfried in amazement, drops
Gunther's hand, advances, as if by sudden impulse, a step
toward the man who awakened her from her magic slumber
on the rock, then recoils in horror, her eyes fixed upon him,
while all look on in wonder. The Motif of Siegfried the Hero,
he Sword Motif, and the chords of the Hagen Motif
emphasise with a tumultuous crash the dramatic significance
of the situation. There is a sudden hush—Brünnhilde
astounded and dumb, Siegfried unconscious of guilt quietly
self-possessed, Gunther, Gutrune, and the vassals silent with
amazement—it is during this moment of tension that we hear
he motif which expresses the thought uppermost in
Brünnhilde, the thought which would find expression in a
burst of frenzy were not her wrath held in check by her
inability to grasp the meaning of the situation or to fathom
the depth of the treachery of which she has been the victim.
This is the Motif of Vengeance:

'What troubles Brünnhilde?' composedly asks Siegfried,
from whom all memory of his first meeting with the rock
maiden and his love for her have been effaced by the potion.
Then, observing that she sways and is about to fall, he
supports her with his arm.

'Siegfried knows me not!' she whispers faintly, as she
looks up into his face.

'There stands your husband,' is Siegfried's reply, as he
points to Gunther. The gesture discloses to Brünnhilde's sight
he ring upon his finger, the ring he gave her, and which to
her horror Gunther, as she supposed, had wrested from her.
In the flash of its precious metal she sees the whole
significance of the wretched situation in which she finds
herself, and discovers the intrigue, the trick, of which she has
been the victim. She knows nothing, however, of the

treachery Hagen is plotting, or of the love-potion that ha
aroused in Siegfried an uncontrollable passion to posses
Gutrune, has caused him to forget her, and led him to win
her for Gunther. There at Gutrune's side, and about to wed
her, stands the man she loves. To Brünnhilde, infuriated with
jealousy, her pride wounded to the quick, Siegfried appears
simply to have betrayed her to Gunther through infatuation
for another woman.

'The ring,' she cries out, 'was taken from me by that man,
pointing to Gunther. 'How came it on your finger? Or, if it i
not the ring'—again she addresses Gunther—'where is the one
you tore from my hand?'

Gunther, knowing nothing about the ring, plainly i
perplexed. 'Ha,' cries out Brünnhilde in uncontrollable rage
'then it was Siegfried disguised as you and not you yoursel
who won it from me! Know then, Gunther, that you, too
have been betrayed by him. For this man who would wed
your sister, and as part of the price bring me to you as bride
was wedded to me!'

In all but Hagen and Siegfried, Brünnhilde's words arous
consternation. Hagen, noting their effect on Gunther, sees i
the episode an added opportunity to mould the Gibichung t
his plan to do away with Siegfried. The latter, through th
effect of the potion, is rendered wholly unconscious of th
truth of what Brünnhilde has said. He even has forgotten tha
he ever has parted with the ring, and, when the men, jealou
of Gunther's honour, crowd about him, and Gunther an
Gutrune in intense excitement wait on his reply, he calmly
proclaims that he found it among the dragon's treasure and
never has parted with it. To the truth of this assertion, to
denial of all Brünnhilde has accused him of, he announce
himself ready to swear at the point of any spear which i
offered for the oath, the strongest manner in which th
assertion can be made and, in the belief of the time
rendering his death certain at the point of that very spea
should he swear falsely.

How eloquent the music of these excitin
scenes!—Crashing chords of the Ring Motif followed by tha
of the Curse, as Brünnhilde recognises the ring on Siegfried'
finger, the Motif of Vengeance, the Valhalla Motif, as sh
invokes the gods to witness her humiliation, the touchingl
pathetic Motif of Brünnhilde's Pleading, as she vainly strive
to awaken memories in Siegfried; then again the Motif o

Vengeance, as the oath is about to be taken, the Murder Motif and the Hagen Motif at the taking of the oath, for the spear is Hagen's; and in Brünnhilde's asseveration, the Valkyrie music coursing through the orchestra.

It is Hagen who offers his weapon for the oath. 'Guardian of honour, hallowed weapon,' swears Siegfried, 'where steel can pierce me, here pierce me; where death can be dealt me, there deal it me, if ever I was wed to Brünnhilde, if ever I have wronged Gutrune's brother.'

At his words, Brünnhilde, livid with rage, strides into the circle of men, and thrusting Siegfried's fingers away from the spearhead, lays her own upon it.

'Guardian of honour, hallowed weapon,' she cries, 'I dedicate your steel to his destruction. I bless your point that it may blight him. For broken are all his oaths, and perjured now he proves himself.'

Siegfried shrugs his shoulders. To him Brünnhilde's imprecations are but the ravings of an overwrought brain. 'Gunther, look to your lady. Give the tameless mountain maid time to rest and recover,' he calls out to Gutrune's brother. 'And now, men, follow us to table, and make merry at our wedding feast!' Then with a laugh and in highest spirits, he throws his arm about Gutrune and draws her after him into the hall, the vassals and women following them.

But Brünnhilde, Hagen, and Gunther remain behind; Brünnhilde half stunned at sight of the man with whom she has exchanged troth, gaily leading another to marriage, as though his vows had been mere chaff; Gunther, suspicious that his honour wittingly has been betrayed by Siegfried, and that Brünnhilde's words are true; Hagen, in whose hands Gunther is like clay, waiting the opportunity to prompt both Brünnhilde and his half-brother to vengeance.

'Coward,' cries Brünnhilde to Gunther, 'to hide behind another in order to undo me! Has the race of the Gibichungs fallen so low in prowess?'

'Deceiver, and yet deceived! Betrayer, and yet myself betrayed,' wails Gunther. 'Hagen, wise one, have you no counsel?'

'No counsel,' grimly answers Hagen, 'save Siegfried's death.'

'His death!'

'Aye, all these things demand his death.'

'But, Gutrune, to whom I gave him, how would we stand

with her if we so avenged ourselves?' For even in his injured
pride Gunther feels that he has had a share in what Siegfried
has done.

But Hagen is prepared with a plan that will free Gunther
and himself of all accusation. 'To-morrow,' he suggests, 'we
will go on a great hunt. As Siegfried boldly rushes ahead we
will fell him from the rear, and give out that he was killed by
a wild boar.'

'So be it,' exclaims Brünnhilde; 'let his death atone for the
shame he has wrought me. He has violated his oath; he shall
die!'

At that moment as they turn toward the hall, he whose
death they have decreed, a wreath of oak on his brow and
leading Gutrune, whose hair is bedecked with flowers, steps
out on the threshold as though wondering at their delay and
urges them to enter. Gunther, taking Brünnhilde by the hand,
follows him in. Hagen alone remains behind, and with a look
of triumph watches them as they disappear within. And so,
although the valley of the Rhine re-echoes with glad sounds,
it is the Murder Motif that brings the act to a close.

Act III.   One of the loveliest scenes of the cycle now
ensues. The Rhinedaughters swim up to the bank of the
Rhine and, circling gracefully in the current of the river,
endeavour to coax from Siegfried the ring of Rhine gold. It is
an episode full of whimsical badinage and more charming
even than the opening of *The Rhine Gold.*

Siegfried refuses to give up the ring. The Rhinedaughters
swim off leaving him to his fate.

Here is the principal theme of their song in this scene:

Distant hunting-horns are heard. Gunther, Hagen, and their
attendants gradually assemble and encamp themselves. Hagen
fills a drinking-horn and hands it to Siegfried whom he
persuades to relate the story of his life. This he does, from his
first memories of Mime ('Mime heiss ein mürrischer Zwerg'),
through the various stages of his growth to maturity—always
recalling the music with which we have become familiar—

ıntil he feels the need to refresh himself by a draught from
he drinking horn, into which Hagen meanwhile has pressed
the juice of a herb. Through this the effect of the love-potion
s so far counteracted that tender memories of Brünnhilde
well up within him and he tells with artless enthusiasm how
ıe penetrated the circle of flame about the Valkyrie, found
Brünnhilde slumbering there, awoke her with his kiss, and
won her. Gunther springs up aghast at this revelation. Now he
knows that Brünnhilde's accusation is true.

Two ravens fly overhead. As Siegfried turns to look after
them the Motif of the Curse resounds and Hagen plunges his
spear into the young hero's back. The Siegfried Motif, cut
short with a crashing chord, the two murderous chords of
the Hagen Motif forming the bass—and Siegfried, who with a
last effort has heaved his shield aloft to hurl it at Hagen, lets
it fall, and, collapsing, drops upon it. So overpowered are the
witnesses—even Gunther—by the suddenness and enormity of
the crime that, after a few disjointed exclamations, they
gather, bowed with grief, around Siegfried. Hagen, with stony
indifference, turns away and disappears over the height.

With the fall of the last scion of the Wälsung race we hear a
new theme, simple yet indescribably fraught with sorrow, the
Death Motif:

Siegfried rises to a sitting posture, and with a strange
rapture gleaming in his glance, intones his death-song. It is an
ecstatic greeting to Brünnhilde. 'Brünnhilde!' he exclaims,
'thy wakener comes to wake thee with his kiss.' The ethereal
harmonies of the Motif of Brünnhilde's Awakening, the Motif
of Fate, the Siegfried Motif swelling into the Motif of Love's
Greeting and dying away through the Motif of Love's Passion
to Siegfried's last whispered accents—'Brünnhilde beckons to
me'—in the Motif of Fate—and Siegfried sinks back in death.

Full of pathos though this episode be, it but brings us to
the threshold of a scene of such overwhelming power that it
may without exaggeration be singled out as the supreme
musico-dramatic climax of all that Wagner wrote. Siegfried's

last ecstatic greeting to his Valkyrie bride has made us realise the blackness of the treachery which tore the young hero and Brünnhilde asunder and led to his death; and now as we are bowed down with a grief too deep for utterance—like the grief with which a nation gathers at the grave of its noblest hero—Wagner voices for us, in music of overwhelmingly tragic power, feelings which are beyond expression in human speech.

Motionless with grief the men gather around Siegfried's corpse. Night falls. The moon casts a pale, sad light over the scene. At the silent bidding of Gunther the vassals raise the body and bear it in solemn procession over the rocky height. Meanwhile with majestic solemnity the orchestra voices the funeral oration of the 'world's greatest hero'. One by one but tragically interrupted by the Motif of Death, we hear the motifs which tell the story of the Wälsung's futile struggle with destiny—the Wälsung Motif, the Motif of the Wälsung's Heroism, the Motif of Sympathy, and the Love Motif, the Sword Motif, the Siegfried Motif, and the Motif of Siegfried the Hero, around which the Death Motif swirls and crashes like a black, death-dealing, all-wrecking flood, forming an overwhelmingly powerful climax that dies away into the Brünnhilde Motif with which, as with a heart-broken sigh, the heroic dirge is brought to a close.

Meanwhile the scene has changed to the Hall of the Gibichungs as in the first act. Gutrune is listening through the night for some sound which may announce the return of the hunt.

Men and women bearing torches precede in great agitation the funeral train. Hagen grimly announces to Gutrune that Siegfried is dead. Wild with grief she overwhelms Gunther with violent accusations. He points to Hagen whose sole reply is to demand the ring as spoil. Gunther refuses. Hagen draws his sword and after a brief combat slays Gunther. He is about to snatch the ring from Siegfried's finger, when the corpse's hand suddenly raises itself threateningly, and all—even Hagen —fall back in consternation.

Brünnhilde advances solemnly from the back. While watching on the bank of the Rhine she has learned from the Rhinedaughters the treachery of which she and Siegfried have been the victims. Her mien is ennobled by a look of tragic exaltation. To her the grief of Gutrune is but the whining of a child. When the latter realises that it was Brünnhilde whom she caused Siegfried to forget through the love-potion, she

lls fainting over Gunther's body. Hagen leaning on his spear
s lost in gloomy brooding.

Brünnhilde turns solemnly to the men and women and
bids them erect a funeral pyre. The orchestral harmonies
shimmer with the Magic Fire Motif through which courses
the Motif of the Ride of the Valkyries. Then, her
countenance transfigured by love, she gazes upon her dead
hero and apostrophises his memory in the Motif of Love's
Greeting. From him she looks upward and in the Valhalla
Motif and the Motif of Brünnhilde's Pleading passionately
inveighs against the injustice of the gods. The Curse Motif is
followed by a wonderfully beautiful combination of the
Valhalla Motif and the Motif of the Gods' Stress at
Brünnhilde's words:

'Rest thee! Rest thee! O God!

For with the fading away of Valhalla and the inauguration
of the reign of human love in place of that of lust and
greed—a change to be wrought by the approaching expiation
of Brünnhilde for the crimes which began with the wresting
of the Rhine gold from the Rhinedaughters—Wotan's stress
will be at an end. Brünnhilde, having told in the graceful,
rippling Rhine music how she learned of Hagen's treachery
through the Rhinedaughters, places upon her finger the ring.
Then turning toward the pyre upon which Siegfried's body
rests, she snatches a firebrand from one of the men, and
flings it upon the pyre, which kindles brightly. As the
moment of her immolation approaches the Motif of
Expiation begins to dominate the scene.

Brünnhilde mounts her Valkyrie charger, Grane, who oft
bore her through the clouds, while lightning flashed and
thunder reverberated. With one leap the steed bears her into
the blazing pyre.

The Rhine overflows. Borne on the flood, the Rhinedaughters swim to the pyre and draw, from Brünnhilde's
finger, the ring. Hagen, seeing the object of all his plotting in
their possession, plunges after them. Two of them encircle
him with their arms and draw him down with them into the
flood. The third holds up the ring in triumph.

In the heavens is perceived a deep glow. It is Götterdämmerung—the twilight of the gods. An epoch has come to a
close. Valhalla is in flames. Once more its stately motif
resounds, only to crumble, like a ruin, before the onsweeping
power of the Motif of Expiation. The Siegfried Motif with a

crash in the orchestra; once more then the Motif of
Expiation. The sordid empire of the gods has passed away. A
new era, that of human love, has dawned through the
expiation of Brünnhilde. As in *The Flying Dutchman* and
Tannhäuser, it is through woman that comes redemption. K.

PARSIFAL

Stage Dedication Festival Play (Bühnenweihfestpiel) in three acts,
words and music by Richard Wagner. Produced Bayreuth, July 26,
1882. Save in concert form, the work was not given elsewhere until
December 24, 1903, when it was produced at the Metropolitan Opera
House at that time under the direction of Heinrich Conried.

At the Bayreuth performances there were alternating casts.
Winkelmann was the Parsifal of the première, Gudehus of the second
performance, Jäger of the third. The alternating Kundrys were Materna,
Marianne Brandt, and Malten; Gurnemanz: Scaria and Siehr; Amfortas:
Reichmann; Klingsor: Hill and Fuchs. Hermann Levi conducted.

In the New York cast Ternina was Kundry, and others in the cast
were Burgstaller (Parsifal), van Rooy (Amfortas), Blass (Gurnemanz),
Goritz (Klingsor), Journet (Titurel); Hertz conducted. First performed
in England, Covent Garden, February 2, 1914, with von der Osten,
Heinrich Hensel, Bender, Knüpfer, August Kiess, Murray Davey, con-
ductor Bodanzky; Covent Garden, 1919 (in English), with Gladys
Ancrum, Mullings, Heming, Allin, Hubert Langley, Foster Richardson,
conductor Albert Coates. Famous Kundrys have included Sucher,
Brema, Mildenburg, Wittich, Gulbranson, Edyth Walker, Saltzmann-
Stevens, Fremstad, Kurt, Matzenauer, Kemp, Leider, Marta Fuchs,
Thorborg, Lubin, Mödl, Varnay, Lammers. In the title role, in addition
to the above: van Dyck, Schmedes, Burrian, Sembach, Urlus, Hutt,
Laubenthal, Melchior, Fritz Wolff, Windgassen, Vickers; as Gurnemanz
Karl Grengg, Felix von Krauss, Karl Braun, Mayr, Andresen, Bohnen,
Kipnis, von Manowarda, Weber, Frick; as Amfortas: Eugen Gura,
Scheidemantel, Karl Perron, Whitehill, Hermann Weil, Plaschke,
Scheidl, Janssen, Schlusnus, Schorr, George London, Fischer-Dieskau.

CHARACTERS

Amfortas, *son of Titurel and ruler of the*
    Kingdom of the Grail .... Bass-Baritone
Titurel, *former ruler* .... Bass
Gurnemanz, *a veteran Knight of the Grail* .... Bass
Klingsor, *a Magician* .... Bass
Parsifal .... Tenor
Kundry .... Soprano
First and Second Knights .... Tenor and Bass
Four Esquires .... Sopranos and Tenors

Six of Klingsor's Flower Maidens . . . . Sopranos
Brotherhood of the Knights of the Grail; Youths and Boys;
  Flower Maidens (two choruses of sopranos and altos)
Time: The Middle Ages   *Place:* Spain, near and in the
                                    Castle of the Holy Grail; in
                                    Klingsor's enchanted castle;
                                    and in the garden of his castle

Parsifal is a familiar name to those who have heard
Lohengrin. Lohengrin, it will be remembered, tells Elsa that
he is Parsifal's son and one of the knights of the Holy Grail.
The name is written Percival in Tennyson's *Idylls of the King.*
Wagner, however, returns to the quainter and more Teutonic
form of spelling. *Parsifal* deals with an earlier period in the
history of the Grail knighthood than *Lohengrin.* But there is
a resemblance between the Grail music in *Parsifal* and the
Lohengrin music—a resemblance not in melody, nor even in
outline, but merely in the purity and spirituality that breathe
through both.

Three legends supplied Wagner with the principal
characters in this music-drama. They were *Percival le Galois;
or Contes de Grail,* by Chrétien de Troyes (1190); *Parsifal,* by
Wolfram von Eschenbach, and a manuscript of the fourteenth
century called by scholars the *Mabinogion.* As usual, Wagner
has not held himself strictly to any one of these, but has
combined them all, and revived them through the alchemy of
his own genius.

Into the keeping of Titurel and his band of Christian
knights has been given the Holy Grail, the vessel from which
the Saviour drank when He instituted the Last Supper. Into
their hands, too, has been placed, as a weapon of defence
against the ungodly, the Sacred Spear, the arm with which
the Roman soldier wounded the Saviour's side. The better to
guard these sanctified relics Titurel, as King of the Grail
knighthood, has reared a castle, Montsalvat, which, from its
forest-clad height facing Arabian Spain, forms a bulwark of
Christendom against the pagan world and especially against
Klingsor, a sorcerer and an enemy of good. Yet time and
again this Klingsor, whose stronghold is near-by, has
succeeded in enticing champions of the Grail into his magic
garden, with its lure of flower-maidens and its arch-
enchantress Kundry, a rarely beautiful woman, and in making
them his servitors against their one-time brothers-in-arms.

Even Amfortas, Titurel's son, to whom Titurel, grown old

in service and honour, has confided his reign and wardship, has not escaped the thrall of Klingsor's sorcery. Eager to begin his reign by destroying Klingsor's power at one stroke, he penetrated into the garden to attack and slay him. But he failed to reckon with human frailty. Yielding to the snare so skilfully laid by the sorcerer and forgetting, at the feet of the enchantress Kundry, the mission upon which he had sallied forth, he allowed the Sacred Spear to drop from his hand. It was seized by the evil-doer he had come to destroy, and he himself was grievously wounded with it before the knights who rushed to his rescue could bear him off.

This wound no skill has sufficed to heal. It is sapping Amfortas's strength. Indecision, gloom, have come over the once valiant brotherhood. Only the touch of the Sacred Spear that made the wound will avail to close it, but there is only one who can regain it from Klingsor. For to Amfortas, prostrate in supplication for a sign, a mystic voice from the sanctuary of the Grail replied that only through a youth 'guileless' and wholly ignorant of sin could the King's salvation be wrought. Instead of succumbing to the temptations of Klingsor's magic garden, he would become, through resisting them, cognisant of Amfortas's guilt, and, stirred by pity for him, make his redemption the mission of his life, regain the Spear and heal him with it. And so the Grail warders are waiting for the coming of the 'guileless fool'.

The working out of this prophecy forms the absorbing subject of the story of *Parsifal*. The plot is allegorical. Parsifal is the personification of Christianity, Klingsor of Paganism, and the triumph of Parsifal over Klingsor is the triumph of Christianity over Paganism.

The character of Kundry is one of Wagner's most striking creations. She is a sort of female Ahasuerus—a wandering Jewess. In the *Mabinogion* manuscript she is no other than Herodias, condemned to wander for ever because she laughed at the head of John the Baptist. Here Wagner makes another change. According to him she is condemned for laughing in the face of the Saviour as He was bearing the cross. She seeks forgiveness by serving the Grail knights as messenger on her swift horse, but ever and anon she is driven by the curse hanging over her back to Klingsor, who changes her to a beautiful woman and places her in his garden to lure the Knights of the Grail to destruction. She can be freed only by

ne who resists her temptations. Finally, she is freed by
Parsifal and is baptised. In her character of Grail messenger
he has much in common with the wild messengers of
Valhalla, the Valkyries. Indeed, in the Edda Saga, her name
appears in the first part of the compound Gundryggja, which
denotes the office of the Valkyries.

THE VORSPIEL

The Vorspiel to *Parsifal* is based on three of the most
deeply religious motifs in the entire work. It opens with the
Motif of the Sacrament, over which, when it is repeated,
arpeggios hover, as in the religious paintings of old masters
angel forms float above the figure of virgin or saint.

Through this motif we gain insight into the office of the
Knights of the Grail, who from time to time strengthen
themselves for their spiritual duties by partaking of the
Communion, on which occasions the Grail itself is uncovered.
This motif leads to the Grail Motif (the so-called 'Dresden
Amen'), effectively swelling to *forte* and then dying away in
ethereal harmonies, like the soft light with which the Grail
illumines the hall in which the knights gather to worship.

The trumpets then announce the Motif of Faith, severe but
sturdy:

The Grail Motif is heard again and then the Motif of Faith is
repeated, its severity exquisitely softened, so that it conveys
a sense of peace which 'passeth all understanding'.

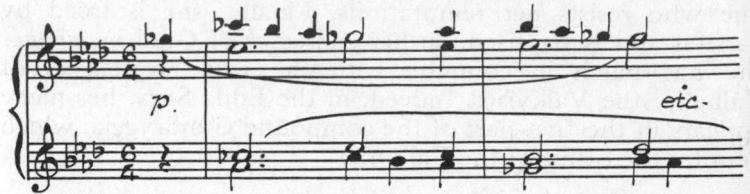

The rest of the Vorspiel is agitated. That portion of the Motif of the Sacrament which appears later as the Spear Motif here assumes through a slight change a deeply sad character, and becomes typical throughout the work of the sorrow wrought by Amfortas's crime. I call it the Elegiac Motif.

Thus the Vorspiel depicts both the religious duties which play so prominent a part in the drama, and the unhappiness which Amfortas's sinful forgetfulness of these duties has brought upon himself and his knights.

Act I. One of the sturdiest of the knights, the aged Gurnemanz, grey of head and beard, watches near the outskirts of the forest. One dawn finds him seated under a majestic tree. Two young Esquires lie in slumber at his feet. Far off, from the direction of the castle, sounds a solemn reveille.

'Hey! Ho!' Gurnemanz calls with brusque humour to the Esquires. 'Not forest, but sleep warders I deem you!' The youths leap to their feet; then, hearing the solemn reveille, kneel in prayer. The Motif of Peace echoes their devotional thoughts. A wondrous peace seems to rest upon the scene. But the transgression of the King ever breaks the tranquil spell. For soon two knights come in the van of the train that thus early bears the King from a bed of suffering to the forest lake near-by, in whose waters he would bathe his wound. They pause to parley with Gurnemanz, but are interrupted by outcries from the youths and sounds of rushing through air.

'Mark the wild horsewoman!'—'The mane of the devil's mare flies madly!'—'Aye, 'tis Kundry!'—'She has swung herself off,' cry the Esquires as they watch the approach of the strange creature that now rushes in. Precipitately she thrusts a small crystal flask into Gurnemanz's hand.

'Balsam—for the King!' There is a savagery in her manner
that seems designed to ward off thanks, when Gurnemanz
asks her whence she has brought the flask, and she replies:
'From farther away than your thought can travel. If it fail,
Arabia bears naught else that can ease the pain. Ask no
further. I am weary.'

Throwing herself upon the ground and resting her face on
her hands, she watches the King borne in, replies to his
thanks for the balsam with a wild, mocking laugh, and
follows him with her eyes as they bear him on his litter
toward the lake, while Gurnemanz and four Esquires remain
behind.

Kundry's rapid approach on her wild horse is accompanied
by a furious gallop in the orchestra. Then, as she rushes upon

the stage, the Kundry Motif—a headlong descent of the string
instruments through four octaves—is heard.

Kundry's action in seeking balsam for the King's wound
gives us insight into the two contradictory natures represented by her character. For here is the woman who has
brought all his suffering upon Amfortas striving to ease it
when she is free from the evil sway of Klingsor. She is at
times the faithful messenger of the Grail; at times the evil
genius of its defenders.

When Amfortas is borne in upon a litter there is heard the
Motif of Amfortas's Suffering, expressive of his physical and
mental agony. It has a peculiar heavy, dragging rhythm, as if
his wound slowly were sapping his life.

A beautiful idyll is played by the orchestra when the knights bear Amfortas to the forest lake.

One of the youths, who has remained with Gurnemanz, noting that Kundry still lies where she had flung herself upon the ground, calls out scornfully, 'Why do you lie there like a savage beast?'

'Are not even the beasts here sacred?' she retorts, but harshly, and not as if pleading for sufferance. The other Esquires would have joined in harassing her had not Gurnemanz stayed them.

'Never has she done you harm. She serves the Grail, and only when she remains long away, none knows in what distant lands, does harm come to us.' Then, turning to where she lies, he asks: 'Where were you wandering when our leader lost the Sacred Spear? Why were you not here to help us then?'

'I never help!' is her sullen retort, although a tremor, as if caused by a pang of bitter reproach, passes over her frame.

'If she wants to serve the Grail, why not send her to recover the Sacred Spear!' exclaims one of the Esquires sarcastically; and the youths doubtless would have resumed their nagging of Kundry, had not mention of the holy weapon caused Gurnemanz to give voice to memories of the events that have led to its capture by Klingsor. Then, yielding

to the pressing of the youths who gather at his feet beneath
the tree, he tells them of Klingsor—how the sorcerer had sued
for admission to the Grail brotherhood, which was denied
him by Titurel, how in revenge he has sought its destruction
and now, through possession of the Sacred Spear, hopes to
compass it.

Prominent with other motifs already heard is a new one,
the Klingsor Motif:

During this recital Kundry still lies upon the ground, a
sullen, forbidding-looking creature. At the point where
Gurnemanz tells of the sorcerer's magic garden and of the
enchantress who has lured Amfortas to his downfall, she
turns in quick, angry unrest, as if she would away, but is held
to the spot by some dark and compelling power.

Gurnemanz concludes by telling the Esquires that while
Amfortas was praying for a sign as to who could heal him,
phantom lips pronounced these words:

> 'By pity lightened
>   The guileless fool;
> Wait for him,
>   My chosen tool.'

This introduces an important motif, that of the Prophecy,
a phrase of simple beauty, as befits the significance of the
words to which it is sung. Gurnemanz sings the entire motif
and then the Esquires take it up. They have sung only the
first two lines when suddenly their prayerful voices are

interrupted by shouts of dismay from the direction of the lake. A moment later a wounded swan, one of the sacred birds of the Grail brotherhood, flutters over the stage and falls dead near Gurnemanz. The knights follow in consternation. Two of them bring Parsifal, whom they have seized and accuse of murdering the sacred bird. As he appears the magnificent Parsifal Motif rings out on the horns:

It is a buoyant and joyous motif, full of the wild spirit and freedom of this child of nature, who knows nothing of the Grail and its brotherhood or the sacredness of the swan, and freely boasts of his skilful marksmanship. During this episode the Swan Motif from *Lohengrin* is effectively introduced. Then follows Gurnemanz's noble reproof, sung to a broad and expressive melody. Even the animals are sacred in the region of the Grail and are protected from harm. Parsifal's gradual awakening to a sense of wrong is one of the most touching scenes of the music-drama. His childlike grief when he becomes conscious of the pain he has caused is so simple and pathetic that one cannot but be deeply affected.

After Gurnemanz has ascertained that Parsifal knows nothing of the wrong he committed in killing the swan he plies him with questions concerning his parentage. Parsifal is now gentle and tranquil. He tells of growing up in the woods, of running away from his mother to follow a cavalcade of knights who passed along the edge of the forest and of never having seen her since. In vain he endeavours to recall the many pet names she gave him. These memories of his early days introduce the sad motif of his mother, Herzeleide (Heart's Sorrow), who has died in grief.

'I do not know,' is the youth's invariable answer to all
questions. His ignorance, coupled, however, with his naïve
nobility of bearing and the fact that he has made his way to
the Grail domain, engender in Gurnemanz the hope that here
at last is the 'guileless fool' for whom prayerfully they have
been waiting, and, the King having been borne from the lake
toward the castle where the holy rite of unveiling the Grail is
to be celebrated that day, thither Gurnemanz in kindly
accents bids the youth follow him.

Then occurs a dramatically effective change of scene. The
scenery becomes a panorama drawn off toward the right, and
as Parsifal and Gurnemanz face toward the left they appear
to be walking in that direction. The forest disappears; a cave
opens in rocky cliffs and conceals the two; they are then seen
again in sloping passages which they appear to ascend. Long
sustained trombone notes softly swell; approaching peals of
bells are heard. At last they arrive at a mighty hall which
loses itself overhead in a high vaulted dome, down from
which alone the light streams in.

The change of scene is ushered in by the solemn Bell
Motif, which is the basis of the powerful orchestral interlude
accompanying the panorama, and also of the scene in the hall
of the Grail Castle.

As the Communion, which is soon to be celebrated, is broken
in upon by the violent grief and contrition of Amfortas, so
the majestic sweep of this symphony is interrupted by the
agonised Motif of Contrition, which graphically portrays the
spiritual suffering of the King.

This subtly suggests the Elegiac Motif and the Motif of
Amfortas's Suffering, but in greatly intensified degrees. For it
is like an outcry of torture that affects both body and soul.

With the Motif of the Sacrament resounding upon the
trombones, followed by the sonorous Bell Motif, Gurnemanz

and Parsifal enter the hall, the old knight giving the youth a position from which he can observe the proceedings. From the deep colonnades on either side the knights march with stately tread, and arrange themselves at the horseshoe-shaped table, which encloses a raised couch. Then, while the orchestra plays a solemn processional based on the Bell Motif, they intone the chorus: 'To the last love feast'. After the first verse a line of pages crosses the stage and ascends into the dome. The graceful interlude here is based on the Bell Motif.

The chorus of knights closes with a glorious outburst of the Grail Motif as Amfortas is borne in, preceded by pages who bear the covered Grail. The King is lifted upon the couch and the holy vessel is placed upon the stone table in front of it. When the Grail Movement has died away amid the pealing of the bells, the youths in the gallery below the dome sing a chorus of penitence based upon the Motif of Contrition. Then the Motif of Faith floats down from the dome as an unaccompanied chorus for boys' voices—a passage of ethereal beauty—the orchestra whispering a brief postludium like a faint echo. This is, when sung as it was at Bayreuth where I heard the first performance of *Parsifal* in 1882, the most exquisite effect of the whole score. For spirituality it is unsurpassed. It is an absolutely perfect example of religious music—a beautiful melody without the slightest worldly taint.

Titurel now summons Amfortas to perform his sacred office—to uncover the Grail. At first, tortured by contrition for his sin, of which the agony from his wound is a constant reminder, he refuses to obey his aged father's summons. In anguish he cries out that he is unworthy of the sacred office. But again ethereal voices float down from the dome. They now chant the prophecy of the 'guileless fool' and, as if comforted by the hope of ultimate redemption, Amfortas uncovers the Grail. Dusk seems to spread over the hall. Then a ray of brilliant light darts down upon the sacred vessel.

which shines with a soft purple radiance that diffuses itself through the hall. All are on their knees save the youth, who has stood motionless and obtuse to the significance of all he has heard and seen save that during Amfortas's anguish he has clutched his heart as if he too felt the pang. But when the rite is over—when the knights have partaken of Communion—and the glow has faded, and the King, followed by his knights, has been borne out, the youth remains behind, vigorous, handsome, but to all appearances a dolt.

'Do you know what you have witnessed?' Gurnemanz asks harshly, for he is grievously disappointed.

For answer the youth shakes his head.

'Just a fool, after all,' exclaims the old knight, as he opens a side door to the hall. 'Begone, but take my advice. In future leave our swans alone, and seek yourself a gander, goose!' And with these harsh words he pushes the youth out and angrily slams the door behind him.

This jarring break upon the religious feeling awakened by the scene would be a rude ending for the act, but Wagner, with exquisite tact, allows the voices in the dome to be heard once more, and so the curtains close, amid the spiritual harmonies of the Prophecy of the Guileless Fool and of the Grail Motif.

Act II. This act plays in Klingsor's magic castle and garden. The Vorspiel opens with the threatful Klingsor motif, which is followed by the Magic and Contrition Motifs, the wild Kundry Motif leading over to the first scene.

In the inner keep of his tower, stone steps leading up to the battlemented parapet and down into a deep pit at the back, stands Klingsor, looking into a metal mirror, whose surface, through his necromancy, reflects all that transpires within the environs of the fastness from which he ever threatens the warders of the Grail. Of all that has just happened in the Grail's domain it has made him aware; and he knows that of which Gurnemanz is ignorant—that the youth, whose approach the mirror divulges, once in his power, vain will be the prophecy of the 'guileless fool' and his own triumph will be assured. For it is that same 'guileless fool' the old knight impatiently has thrust out.

Klingsor turns toward the pit and imperiously waves his hand. A bluish vapour rises from the abyss and in it floats the form of a beauteous woman—Kundry, not the Kundry of a few hours before, dishevelled and in coarse garb girdled with snake-skin; but a houri, her dark hair smooth and lustrous, her robe soft, rich Oriental draperies. Yet even as she floats she strives as though she would descend to where she has come from, while the sorcerer's harsh laugh greets her vain efforts. This then is the secret of her strange actions and her long disappearances from the Grail domain, during which so many of its warders have fallen into Klingsor's power! She is the snare he sets, she the arch-enchantress of his magic garden. Striving, as he hints while he mocks her impotence, to expiate some sin committed by her during a previous existence in the dim past by serving the brotherhood of the Grail knights, the sorcerer's power over her is such that at any moment he can summon her to aid him in their destruction.

Well she knows what the present summons means. Approaching the tower at this very moment is the youth whom she has seen in the Grail forest, and in whom she, like Klingsor, has recognised the only possible redeemer of Amfortas and of—herself. And now she must lure him to his doom and with it lose her last hope of salvation, now, aye, now—for even as he mocks her, Klingsor once more waves his hand, castle and keep vanish as if swallowed up by the earth, and in its place a garden heavy with the scent of gorgeous flowers fills the landscape.

The orchestra, with the Parsifal Motif, gives a spirited description of the brief combat between Parsifal and Klingsor's knights. It is amid the dark harmonies of the Klingsor Motif that the keep sinks out of sight and the magic garden, spreading out in all directions, with Parsifal standing on the wall and gazing with astonishment upon the brilliant scene, is disclosed.

The Flower Maidens in great trepidation for the fate of their lover knights rush in from all sides with cries of sorrow, their confused exclamations and orchestral accompaniment admirably enforcing their tumultuous actions.

The Parsifal Motif again introduces the next episode, as Parsifal, attracted by the grace and beauty of the girls, leaps down into the garden and seeks to mingle with them. It is repeated several times in the course of the scene. The girls, seeing that he does not seek to harm them, bedeck themselves with flowers and crowd about him with alluring gestures, finally circling around him as they sing this caressing melody:

The effect is enchanting, the music of this episode being a marvel of sensuous grace. Parsifal regards them with childlike, innocent joy. Then they seek to impress him more deeply with their charms, at the same time quarrelling among themselves over him. When their rivalry has reached its height, Kundry's voice—'Parsifal, tarry!'—is wafted from a flowery nook near-by.

'Parsifal!' In all the years of his wandering none has called him by his name; and now it floats toward him as if borne on the scent of roses. A beautiful woman, her arms stretched out to him, welcomes him from her couch of brilliant flowers. Irresistibly drawn toward her, he approaches and kneels by her side; and she, whispering to him in tender accents, leans over him and presses a long kiss upon his lips. It is the lure that has sealed the fate of many a knight of the Grail. But in the youth it inspires a sudden change. The perilous subtlety of it, that is intended to destroy, transforms the 'guileless fool' into a conscious man, and that man conscious of a mission. The scenes he has witnessed in the Grail castle, the stricken King whose wound ever bled afresh, the part he is to play, the peril of the temptation that has been placed in his path—all these things became revealed to him in the rapture of that unhallowed kiss. In vain the enchantress seeks to draw him towards her. He thrusts her from him. Maddened by the repulse, compelled through Klingsor's arts to see in the handsome youth her lawful prey, she calls upon the sorcerer to aid her. At her outcry Klingsor appears on the castle wall, in his hand the Spear taken from Amfortas, and, as Parsifal

faces him, hurls it full at him. But lo, it rises in its flight an
remains suspended in the air over the head of him it wa
aimed to slay.

Reaching out and seizing it, Parsifal makes with it the sig
of the Cross. Castle and garden wall crumble into ruins, th
garden shrivels away, leaving in its place a sere wildernes
through which Parsifal, leaving Kundry as one dead upon th
ground, sets forth in search of the castle of the Grail, there t
fulfil the mission with which now he knows himself charge

Act III. Not until after long wanderings through th
wilderness, however, is it that Parsifal once more find
himself on the outskirts of the Grail forest. Clad from hea
to foot in black armour, his visor closed, the Holy Spear i
his hand, he approaches the spot where Gurnemanz, no
grown very old, still holds watch, while Kundry, again i
coarse garb, but grown strangely pale and gentle, humbl
serves the brotherhood. It is Good Friday morn, and peac
rests upon the forest.

Kundry is the first to discern the approach of the blac
knight. From the tender exaltation of her mien, as she draw
Gurnemanz's look toward the silent figure, it is apparent tha
she divines who it is and why he comes. To Gurnemanz
however, he is but an armed intruder on sanctified groun
and upon a holy day, and, as the black knight seats himsel
on a little knoll near a spring and remains silent, the ol
warder chides him for his offence. Tranquilly the knight rise
thrusts the Spear he bears into the ground before him, lay
down his sword and shield before it, opens his helmet, an
removing it from his head, places it with the other arms, an
then himself kneels in silent prayer before the Spea
Surprise, recognition of man and weapon, and deep emotio
succeed each other on Gurnemanz's face. Gently he raise
Parsifal from his kneeling posture, once more seats him o
the knoll by the spring, loosens his greaves and corselet, an
then places upon him the coat of mail and mantle of th
knights of the Grail, while Kundry, drawing a golden flas
from her bosom anoints his feet and dries them with he
loosened hair. Then Gurnemanz takes from her the flask
and, pouring its contents upon Parsifal's head, anoints hir
king of the knights of the Grail. The new king performs hi
first office by taking up water from the spring in the hollo
of his hand and baptising Kundry, whose eyes, suffused wit
tears, are raised to him in gentle rapture.

ere is heard the stately Motif of Baptism:

The 'Good Friday Spell', one of Wagner's most beautiful
nood paintings in tone colour, is the most prominent episode
n these scenes.

Once more Gurnemanz, Kundry now following, leads the
vay toward the castle of the Grail. Amfortas's aged father,
Fiturel, uncomforted by the vision of the Grail, which
Amfortas, in his passionate contrition, deems himself too
sullied to unveil, has died and, the knights having gathered in
he great hall, Titurel's bier is borne in solemn procession and
placed upon a catafalque before Amfortas's couch.

'Uncover the Grail!' shout the knights, pressing upon
Amfortas. For answer, and in a paroxysm of despair, he
springs up, tears his garments asunder and shows his open
wound. 'Slay me!' he cries. 'Take up your weapons! Bury
your sword blades deep—deep in me, to the hilts! Kill me,
and so kill the pain that tortures me!'

As Amfortas stands there in an ecstasy of pain, Pars
enters, and, quietly advancing, touches the wound with t
point of the Spear.

'One weapon only serves to staunch your wounded side—
the one that struck it.'

Amfortas's torture changes to highest rapture. The shrin
is opened and Parsifal, taking the Grail, which again radiate
with light, waves it gently to and fro, as Amfortas and all th
knights kneel in homage to him, while Kundry, gazing up t
him in gratitude, sinks gently into the sleep of death an
forgiveness for which she has longed.

The music of this entire scene floats upon etherea
arpeggios. The Motif of Faith especially is exquisitel
accompanied, its spiritual harmonies finally appearing in thi
form:

There are also heard the Motifs of Prophecy and of th
Sacrament, as the knights on the stage and the youths an
boys in the dome chant. The Grail Motif, which is prominen
throughout the scene, rises as if in a spirit of gentle religiou
triumph and brings, with the Sacrament Motif, the work to
close.   K.

6
German Opera Continued

FRANZ von SUPPÉ
(1819–1895)

BOCCACCIO

OPERA in three acts by Franz von Suppé, libretto by F. Zell and R. Genée. Première at Carl Theatre, Vienna, February 1, 1879, with Fräulein Link as Boccaccio, and Fräulein Streitmann as Fiametta. First performed New York, Thalia Theatre, 1880; London, Royal Comedy Theatre, 1882. Revived New York, Metropolitan (with recitatives by Bodanzky), 1931, with Jeritza as Boccaccio, and Fleischer, Telva, Kirchoff, Meader, Gustav Schützendorf, conductor Bodanzky; Vienna, Volksoper, 1951, with Liewehr as Boccacio and Réthy, Lorna Sidney, Carl Dönch, Szemere, conductor Paulik.

CHARACTERS

Fiametta, *foster-daughter of Lambertuccio* ... Soprano
Boccaccio, *a writer* .... Tenor[1]
Lambertuccio, *a citizen of Florence* .... Tenor
Beatrice, *wife of Scalza* .... Soprano
Peronella, *wife of Lambertuccio* .... Contralto
Pietro, *Prince of Palermo* .... Tenor
Scalza, *a merchant* .... Baritone
Leonetto, *a student* .... Tenor
Isabella, *Lotteringhi's wife* .... Mezzo-Soprano
Lotteringhi, *a cooper of Florence* .... Tenor
Checco, *a beggar* .... Bass
Kolporteur .... Baritone
Majordomo .... Baritone
Time: 1331   *Place:* Florence

[1] Sometimes, as at the première, sung by a Soprano.

Act I.   The scene is the square in front of the Church of Santa Maria Novella, where a crowd of beggars, led by Checco, is preparing to make the best possible use of the opportunities offered by a public holiday. Leonetto takes advantage of the hubbub to slip unnoticed into the house of Scalza, whose wife Beatrice has thoughtfully provided him with a key. Students and townspeople celebrate the holiday with a tarantella, and when a bookseller comes by plying his trade they are eager to be impressed, until the offer of some of Boccaccio's stories, with the recommendation that they breathe the very scandal of Florence, incenses the worthy citizenry and the bookseller is driven off, in spite of protests from the students.

When Scalza returns home, his wife is by no means alone, as it is Boccaccio as well as his friend Leonetto who look out in alarm at the appearance of her husband. Beatrice decides to save herself embarrassment by calling for help against the two men who have 'invaded' the house, Boccaccio and Leonetto emerge and stage a mock duel, which Scalza tries to stop and which is aggravated when the townspeople take sides and join in the fun. Scalza is fearful of the possible outcome, and he drags his wife indoors, leaving the others to discuss the ethics of love, a subject Boccaccio takes up in a lively song ('Ich sehe einen jungen Mann dort stehn')—it may become one of his tales, he explains.

It is time for the service and the crowd goes into the church. Boccaccio hides to listen to Fiametta and Peronella talking of Fiametta's forthcoming marriage to a man of high position. Fiametta sings a romance ('Hab' ich nur deine Liebe'): love without faithfulness has made many a maiden happy, fidelity without love has brought joy to none. Boccaccio joins enthusiastically in the refrain, but the women follow the crowd to church.

Boccaccio devises a scheme to approach Fiametta again dresses himself up as a beggar and waits for her to come out. Meanwhile Pietro is mistaken by Lambertuccio and Lotteringhi for Boccaccio, whose writings they all fear, but he evades them and leaves the coast clear for the disguised Boccaccio to beg for alms from Fiametta. She immediately recognises his voice, and it is clear from their charming duet that what starts as a flirtation is likely to become, at least on her side, something more.

Lotteringhi and Lambertuccio lead the older citizens o

Florence—particularly the married men—in the hunt for
Boccaccio; they enlist the help of Scalza, and it is he who
prevents them venting their spite on Pietro, who has been
captured in error but who is quickly recognised by Scalza as
the Prince of Palermo. There is nothing left for it but to turn
on the offending books themselves; they seize them from the
bookseller, build a fire and burn them, while the students, led
by Boccaccio, cry to be avenged on stupidity. Truth and
honour will survive, they maintain, will rise in fact like a
phoenix from the ashes. In spite of its dramatic action, the
music of this finale remains gay and charming.

Act II. Boccaccio, Pietro and Leonetto join together in
serenading their loved ones, Fiametta, Isabella and Peronella,
and hide when Lotteringhi makes his appearance. His wife,
Isabella, scolds him for the row he's making with his
assistants, and in revenge he sings the Cooper's Song: his wife
has got so used to nagging that it has become her favourite
pastime and he can get his own back only by banging away
at his barrels. Boccacio meanwhile has taken advantage of the
interruption to write love letters to each of the three
recipients of the recent serenades, and their delighted
reaction to the letters produces one of the most attractive
numbers in the score, a trio ('Wie pocht mein Herz so
ungestüm') with an enchanting waltz refrain—a tune good
enough to make the fortune of any operetta:

Peronella and Leonetto, Isabella and Pietro, meet and declare
their love for each other, but are interrupted by the return of
Lotteringhi.

There ensues a ludicrous scene, as Boccaccio, again in
disguise to be near Fiametta, tells Lambertuccio that there is
a magic tree in his garden, whose property is to make anyone
who sits in its branches believe that the couple beneath is
making love—he proves his point with Fiametta. Meanwhile,

Isabella entices her husband Lotteringhi into an empty wine cask, while she and Pietro, Leonetto and Peronella add to the demonstration of the tree's unusual qualities, and musically the sextet of lovers is turned into an octet by the addition of one husband up a tree and another in a barrel.

The idyllic scene is interrupted by Scalza bringing news that Boccaccio has been seen entering the house. Positions are reversed, the lovers hide, the husbands emerge to join in the hunt, but the women are able to reveal that the supposed culprit the crowd has caught is not so much Boccaccio as the man who brings the money to pay for Fiametta's board and lodging! He has now come to take her away, much to her consternation. Boccaccio and his two friends have therefore not only to make their own escape but also to contrive the release of Fiametta as well. Fiametta greets the news of his plan with a reprise of the waltz tune, and as she is borne off in her sedan chair, Boccaccio springs out, dressed as the devil, and scares the crowd away.

Act III.   In the garden of the Duke's Palace, Pietro admits to Boccaccio that he is the mysterious nobleman to whom Fiametta is due to be married; she is the Duke's natural daughter and has now been granted the title of Princess. Fiametta for her part discovers that her lover is none other than Boccaccio and not at all the humble student she had taken him to be. Their misunderstandings are made up in a charming 6/8 duet ('Mia bella fiorentina').

Boccaccio next has to defend himself against the attacks on his writings by Lotteringhi, Lambertuccio and Scalza (who of course do not know him by sight). The women support his contention that it is a writer's job to fight with wit, humour and honesty against the folly of the world. He even counsels the men to do all in their power to prevent their wives becoming bored—therein will lie their undoing.

It remains only for Boccaccio to persuade Prince Pietro to give up Fiametta, and this he succeeds in doing during a theatrical entertainment given in the Duke's house. With a reprise of his motto—wit, humour and honesty are sharp-edged weapons; victory is to him who uses them well—comes to an end a Viennese operetta which must be amongst the half-dozen best specimens of the kind not written by Johann Strauss.   H.

PETER CORNELIUS
(1824–1874)

DER BARBIER VON BAGHDAD
The Barber of Baghdad

OPERA in two acts by Peter Cornelius (1824–1874); text, based on a story from the *Arabian Nights*, by the composer. First performed at Weimar, conducted by Liszt on December 15, 1858. As a result of the feud between Liszt, Weimar's head of music, and Dingelstedt, the manager of the theatre, the first night was made the occasion of a showdown on the part of their rival adherents, and the opera was a fiasco; Liszt resigned his position, and the opera was not given again during the composer's lifetime. Revived Hanover, 1877, and again a failure. Revised and re-orchestrated by Felix Mottl, produced at Karlsruhe, 1885, and in many other German theatres. Metropolitan, New York, 1890, with Sophie Traubmann, Kalisch and Fischer, conducted by Damrosch; Savoy Theatre, London, 1891, by students of the Royal College of Music; Covent Garden, 1906, with Burchardt, Jörn, Knüpfer, and conducted by Richter. Revived Metropolitan, 1925, with Rethberg, Laubenthal, and Bender; London Opera Club, 1949, with Victoria Sladen, Owen Brannigan; Vienna Volksoper, 1949, with Jurinac, Dermota and Edelmann; Edinburgh Festival, 1956, by Hamburg Opera, with Muszely, Konya, van Mill.

CHARACTERS

The Caliph .... Baritone
Baba Mustapha, *a Cadi* .... Tenor
Margiana, *his daughter* .... Soprano
Bostana, *a servant of the Cadi* .... Mezzo-Soprano
Nureddin .... Tenor
Abul Hassan Ali Ebn Bekar, *a Barber* .... Bass
Nureddin's Servants, Friends of the Cadi, People of Baghdad,
Wailing Women, the Caliph's entourage
Place: Baghdad

When he was twenty-five, Cornelius wrote that he was clear in his mind that his natural bent was towards operatic comedy. Considering the success which he achieved in his one attempt at this genre (a posthumous success unfortunately, as the opera had only a single performance in his lifetime), it seems a pity that his two other operas should have been on serious subjects; neither has had anything like the number of performances *Der Barbier* has collected since the composer's death.

Originally Cornelius planned *Der Barbier* in one act, with an extended final scene occupying something like a third of the whole work (see Ernest Newman's *Opera Nights*). Later, he decided on two acts of equal length, and it was in this form that the opera was given in Weimar. After the unsuccessful première, Liszt (who liked the opera but would, apparently, have preferred it to have been a serious rather than a comic work!) persuaded the composer to re-write his overture, and instead of the comedy prelude to substitute something based on the themes of the opera itself. Cornelius died before he could orchestrate the new overture, and this was done after his death by Liszt. For the revivals they conducted, both Mottl and Levi made a number of changes in the orchestration, and it was not until 1904 that the opera was given in the form (and orchestral dress) Cornelius had intended.

The D major overture—that is to say the one written at Liszt's suggestion—is based on references to the Barber's theme, his patter song, Nureddin's appeal to the absent Margiana, the assignation duet between Nureddin and Bostana, and the chorus of Nureddin's servants.

Act I.   Nureddin is lying on a couch at his house, nursing his apparently hopeless love for Margiana. He and his servants, scorning the more scientific forms of diagnosis, fear that his life is in danger. The servants' chorus and Nureddin's love song are delightfully sentimental, and he repeats the name Margiana in the apparent hope that it will ameliorate his sufferings. Left alone, Nureddin again conjures up a vision of his beloved, 'Vor deinem Fenster die Blumen versengte der Sonne Strahl', a song of charmingly romantic character.

To assuage his sufferings comes Bostana, an aged relation of Margiana's father, the Cadi. She tells him that Margiana will receive him that very day when her father goes to the mosque at noon. Bostana gives him his instructions and he repeats them in a quick, canonic duet. Before she goes, she prescribes a bath and a shave for him; he agrees, and again they go over the plan they have formulated. With a last 'Don't forget the Barber' (she has recommended her own favourite to him), she leaves the lover to contemplate his prospective bliss, which he does in an ecstatic *allegro*, 'Ach, das Leid hab' ich getragen, wie ertrag' ich nun mein Glück?'

He is far too much occupied with his daydreams to notice the entrance of the Barber, Abul Hassan Ali Ebn Bekar, carrying with him his towel, his basin, a looking-glass, and other apparatus of his calling, and, in addition, an astrolabe, with which he is accustomed to foretell his clients' futures. Nureddin is anxious to be shaved straight away, but he has to do with the most garrulous man in Baghdad, and the Barber tells him at length and in a series of ingenious multiple rhymes exactly how fortunate it is that Nureddin should have chosen him to perform the necessary offices.

Nureddin tries to stop him and make him get on with the shaving, but Abul must first cast his horoscope. This he does to the accompaniment of Nureddin's rapidly rising impatience, and having finished, once again puts forward his own qualifications in a brilliant patter song. Nureddin, not without justification by now, tells him he is nothing but a chatterbox. This fills the Barber with righteous indignation; his brothers it is true were talkative, but he, the youngest of the family, has always been known for his virtue and his taciturnity. Things seem to be out of hand, and Nureddin yells for his servants to come and deliver him from this plague of a Barber. Their attempts are successful up to a point, but, just as they get him to the door, the Barber flourishes his razor and succeeds in turning them out.

Nureddin resorts to tact, and the Barber is soon ready to begin operations, ready that is to say until his client lets fall the word 'Margiana' from his lips. This starts a flood of reminiscence; the Barber himself was once in love with a Margiana—and this is the song he used to sing to her. As a lover, he is more philosophical than Osmin would be, and one cannot imagine that worthy favouring the object of his affections with the elaborate and apparently endless cadenza with which Abul rounds off his song. He is delighted that Nureddin is in love, but horrified to hear that his Margiana is the daughter of Cadi Baba Mustapha, a villain, he says, who shaves himself. There is no hope unless he accompanies his new-made friend to the assignation.

Nureddin advises him to go back to his doubtless innumerable other customers, but the Barber soliloquises in his absence on the disastrous effect women can have on a man's life: 'So schwärmet Jugend'. What was the ruin of all his six brothers? Love—and the catalogue of their respective misfortunes is punctuated by references to the word 'Lieben'.

Cornelius's ingenuity in varying this repetition is no less to be admired than the old man's ability to find a topic to suit every occasion and, having found it, to dilate upon it endlessly.

Nureddin returns, and is horrified to find the Barber still there and fully purposing to accompany him to Margiana's house. He calls his servants again, and instructs them to minister to the Barber, who, he tells them, is very ill; let them put him to bed and keep him there, sparing no remedy whatsoever. The servants are delighted at the prospect of getting their own back, and they succeed in catching the elusive Abul, whom they deposit on the couch, covering him with cushions and preparing razors and lancets as they sing. The last we hear of them is their recital of the Barber's names in five-part harmony.

Act II.   The Intermezzo is based on the figure associated with the Muezzin's call to prayer. The melody is varied throughout and the effect is a delightful anticipation in music of the moment when Nureddin can meet his Margiana for the first time. When the curtain rises, we are for the first time in the Cadi's house, in that part of it reserved for the women. Margiana expresses her delight at the prospect of Nureddin's arrival: 'Er kommt, er kommt, o Wonne meiner Brust!' No sooner has she finished the long phrase than Bostana rushes in and expresses the same sentiment in an identical melody, only to be joined some moments later by the Cadi, whose sentiments are made known in exactly similar terms, but of course for very different reasons. The women rejoice that Nureddin is coming, the Cadi is excited at the thought of his rich friend Selim's arrival from Damascus, bringing with him splendid presents and a request for the hand of Margiana in marriage. The trio is one of the most beautiful numbers in the score. A chest arrives from Damascus full of the expected treasures, and Margiana is dutifully pleased that her father is happy. Into the general rejoicings comes the sound of the Muezzin, sung offstage by a bass and two tenors; the chant is taken up by the three characters onstage, and the Cadi goes off to the mosque.

In a moment Nureddin is in the room, and he launches into a declaration of his love, which is taken up by Margiana: 'O holdes Bild in Engelschöne'. The alternating triple and quadruple time gives way to a decided 3/4 for the second half of the duet sung in octaves throughout. The duet has a cool,

almost innocent feel about it, as is suitable for a first, almost
formal declaration of love. The idyllic scene is interrupted by
the sound of the Barber's voice from down below. He assures
Nureddin that he is safe with so faithful a watchdog, and
starts to sing his own love song. The lovers make little
progress with so much distraction outside, and to Abul's song
are added a moment later the howls of a slave who has
broken the Cadi's favourite vase and is being punished out of
hand by his master immediately on his return from the
mosque.

The situation is a tricky one for Nureddin, and it takes a
turn for the worse when Abul, hearing the screams of the
slave, construes them as meaning the Cadi is murdering
Nureddin, and yells for help. The sound of a crowd shouting
hostile remarks about the Cadi can be heard below, as
Nureddin is bundled into the treasure chest, which is quickly
emptied. When Abul bursts into the room, bringing with him
some of Nureddin's servants, Bostana tries to tell him that
the unlucky lover has been hidden in the chest, but he takes
it into his head that the box contains nothing but his friend's
corpse. The servants are on the point of carrying out the
chest when the Cadi returns and thinks they are stealing his
treasure. The ensuing alliterative abuse is thought by Ernest
Newman to have been intended as a parody of Wagner's
alliterative methods in *The Ring*: Cornelius was Liszt's
secretary and must certainly have seen the printed copy of
the libretto which Liszt had as early as 1853. A misunderstanding occurs over the word 'Schatz', which the Cadi uses
in its literal sense of 'treasure', and which the Barber
understands as meaning more colloquially 'darling'.

The Cadi, the Barber, the Cadi's friends and retainers,
Nureddin's servants, women already in mourning for him,
and a mixed crowd of inhabitants of Baghdad join in an
ensemble of accusation and counter-accusation, during
which the chest is turned upside down. It is only brought to
an end by the arrival of the Caliph, suitably attended by
magnificently uniformed soldiers. The Cadi explains that
Abul is a thief who is stealing his daughter's treasure. Abul,
after contrasting his silent habits with his brothers' loquacity
and after running through a list of his own accomplishments, denies that he is a thief but accuses the Cadi of having
murdered his friend and hidden the body in the chest.
Margiana and Bostana return, and the Caliph tells Margiana to

open the chest and show him what her father persists in describing as her treasure.

Nobody's consternation could be more genuine than the Cadi's when the senseless body of Nureddin is disclosed in the chest. 'He! Mustapha!' he exclaims, and the cry is taken up by the Caliph and Abul in an ensemble, which is later joined by Margiana and Bostana, who lament the untimely death of the young man. Abul has been bending over the 'dead' body and he brings the lamentation to an end by announcing that Nureddin is not dead after all, but only unconscious. The Caliph suggests that this is the moment when the Barber's miraculous healing powers can suitably be brought into use. Abul starts off with a line from his love song to Margiana but with no result; he tweaks Nureddin's nose and ears and tries smelling salts on him. But the simultaneous application to his nose of the rose Margiana has given him, and to his ears of the second line of the love song, works the trick: Nureddin opens his eyes and gets up.

The Cadi joins the lovers' hands and tells his soldiers to arrest the Barber—merely, he assures him, in order that he may benefit from his advice and his story-telling which have been denied him so long. Abul leads the assembly in a song of praise to the Caliph: 'Heil diesem Hause' and everyone repeats the refrain, 'Salamaleikum'.   H.

JOHANN STRAUSS
(1825–1899)

DIE FLEDERMAUS
The Bat

OPERA in three acts by Johann Strauss. Text by Haffner and Genée, from a French vaudeville 'Le Reveillon' by Meilhac and Halévy. First performed at the Theater an der Wien, Vienna, April 5, 1874, with Marie Geistinger, Mme. Charles Hirsch, Mme. Nittingwe, Herr Szika, Herr Rudinger, Herr Lebrecht, Herr Rott and conducted by the composer. First performed in London, Alhambra Theatre, 1876, with Mlle. Cabella, Miss Chambers, Loredan, Rosenthal, Jarvis, Shaw, conducted by M. G. Jacobi; New York, 1879; Vienna Opera, 1894; Metropolitan Opera, New York, 1905, with Sembrich, Alten, Edyth Walker, Dippel, Reiss, Greder, Goritz, conducted by Nathan Franko. Revived in London at His Majesty's Theatre, 1910, with Carrie Tubb,

Beatrice de la Palme, Muriel Terry, Joseph O'Mara, John Bardsley, Frederick Ranalow, Arthur Royd, conducted by Hamish McCunn; Covent Garden, 1930, with Lotte Lehmann, Schumann, Olszewska, Willi Wörle, Karl Jöken, Hüsch, Habich, conducted by Bruno Walter; Sadler's Wells, 1934, with Joan Cross, Ruth Naylor, Gladys Parr, Tudor Davies, Arthur Cox, Redvers Llewelyn, Percy Heming, conducted by Warwick Braithwaite. Revived at Metropolitan, New York, 1950, with Welitsch, Munsel, Stevens, Svanholm, Tucker, Brownlee, Hugh Thompson, conducted by Eugene Ormandy. A successful film in English, 'O Rosalinde!' (1955-6), starred Michael Redgrave as Eisenstein and Anneliese Rothenberger as Adele, each singing and acting; Ludmilla Tcherina acted Rosalinde while Sari Barabas sang, and Anton Walbrook was Falke.

CHARACTERS

Gabriel von Eisenstein .... Tenor
Rosalinda, *his wife* .... Soprano
Frank, *the governor of the prison* .... Baritone
Prince Orlofsky, *a rich Russian* .... Mezzo-Soprano
Alfred, *a singer* .... Tenor
Dr. Falke, *a friend of Eisenstein* .... Baritone
Dr. Blind, *Eisenstein's attorney* .... Tenor
Adele, *the Eisensteins' maid* .... Soprano
Frosch, *the gaoler* .... Speaking Part
Time: Late Nineteenth Century   *Place:* Vienna

Johann Strauss the younger was already famous as a composer of Viennese dance music before he turned his hand to operetta, his first being *Indigo* (1871), his second *Der Karneval in Rom* (1873), his third *Die Fledermaus*. Whether the spirited action and the predominance of dialogue make it preferable to cast the main roles in *Fledermaus* with actors who can sing, or whether the difficult nature of the vocal music suggests rather singers who can act, has never been settled once and for all. There are disadvantages in either solution: few actresses have the singing technique to encompass the music of Rosalinda and Adele adequately, few singers have the lightness of touch, vocal and dramatic, which is so essential if the spirited nature of the whole entertainment is not to suffer. And the point of course is that the work as a whole—plot as well as score—is a masterpiece, the finest product of the Viennese operetta school, and a cornucopia of fresh, witty, pointed, memorable melody.

The overture, a potpourri, is one of the most popular ever written. The first three tunes are from the prison scene in the last act, the third being associated with the dénouement.

Then comes the famous waltz with its lilting refrain, followed after a short interlude by a mournful tune on the oboe (also in 3/4), with a contrasting section (the tunes associated with Eisenstein's mock-serious farewell before going to prison). The material is repeated, the overture as a whole being dominated by its waltz.

Act I.   We are in Eisenstein's house. The stage is empty, but outside can be heard the sound of Alfred's voice, as he serenades Rosalinda. He is, it appears, an old flame of hers, and he addresses her fittingly as his dove. Adele, the Eisensteins' maid, makes her entrance on a cadenza and proceeds to read a letter from her sister, Ida. The Ballet, of which Ida is a member, has been invited *en bloc* that night to a party[1] which is being given by Prince Orlofsky, a rich young Russian eccentric who is Vienna's latest host; if Adele can get hold of a dress, Ida can take her along—the orchestra fairly bubbles with Adele's excitement. But Rosalinda, who has heard Alfred's serenade and suspects who it is, is far too preoccupied to pay much attention to Adele's plea that she be allowed to go and look after her sick aunt. With Eisenstein due that night at the prison for the start of a five-day prison sentence, she cannot possibly think of sparing anybody; he must have a good supper before he leaves. Alfred waits until Adele has gone and then tells Rosalinda he has heard that Eisenstein will be away for a few days; he will call again that evening. Rosalinda is beside herself: as long as he doesn't sing she is all right—but he is a tenor and who could resist the sound of his top A?

Eisenstein storms in with his advocate, Dr. Blind, who, says Eisenstein, is to blame for the whole affair of the prison sentence, most of all that he is now being sent down for eight days, not five. There is a lively trio for Rosalinda, Eisenstein, and Blind, in which Rosalinda protests her grief—perhaps a shade too much—Eisenstein rages at Blind, and the lawyer

---

[1] The 1870's saw a period of considerable moral permissiveness, in Vienna as elsewhere, even though the rules of conduct were outwardly strict. 'Pleasure' as represented by escape from the 'rule' and the family, was mainly a masculine preserve, and the dancers at Prince Orlofsky's party show the *demi-monde* in contact with society, whose pleasure-ground it was and off whom it lived. Masks covered so wide a multitude of sins that some 'respectable' ladies with their help might hope for a little discreet adventure on their own account. It is sometimes forgotten that *Fledermaus* is Strauss's only opera set in Vienna itself.

runs through a list of legal expedients he will call into play
once he has a chance of appealing against the sentence.

The lawyer leaves, Adele, still in tears about her mythical
aunt, is sent off to order a delicious supper for the master,
and Rosalinda goes to look out some old clothes for him to
go to prison in. Enter Dr. Falke, a friend of Eisenstein, who
has, we should know, been secretly nursing a grievance
against him ever since Carnival. It seems that Falke, dressed
as a bat (hence the title), was left asleep by Eisenstein to find
his way home in broad daylight and in his unconventional
costume. He has a plan, though Eisenstein has not the least
suspicion of it, for revenge. Why, he says, should Eisenstein
not accept the invitation from Prince Orlofsky which Falke
brings him, and go in disguise to the ball, giving himself up to
the prison authorities next morning? Rosalinda need never
know—nor need Eisenstein guess that Rosalinda is also being
asked to the party, at which she will wear a mask. The Bat's
revenge is taking shape, and Eisenstein receives the invitation
to the strains of the same polka which accompanied Adele's
reading of the letter from her sister earlier on. He accepts it
with a minimum of shilly-shallying.

Rosalinda is astonished to hear that her husband is going
off to prison in style, in evening dress in fact, but she is so
pre-occupied with the prospects of Alfred's disturbing
promise to come back at supper-time that she accepts a
flimsy excuse. All is prepared; Rosalinda, Adele (who has
after all been given the night off, in preparation for Alfred's
expected visit), and Eisenstein sing a farewell trio, which is
one of the most delicious moments of the score. Rosalinda
still grieves in exaggerated fashion in the *moderato espressivo*,
but none of the three can keep these long faces for ever, and
the refrain to each of Rosalinda's utterances glitters and
sparkles as gaily as the parties they each of them enjoy in
anticipation. Rosalinda ends with a ringing top C, and
Eisenstein bustles off.

Alfred keeps his promise, and Eisenstein is hardly out of
the house before his wife's admirer is eating the supper that
was originally prepared for him. 'Trinke, Liebchen, trinke
schnell', sings the tenor, and Rosalinda joins in the refrain,
although she cannot help noticing that her companion is
beginning to show the effects of the wine he so melodiously
urges her to drink. The drinking song is interrupted by the
sound of voices below and Frank, the new prison governor,

appears, with the information that he has come to escort
Herr von Eisenstein, who is to be his guest for the next eight
days, to prison. Alfred ropes him in to sing the chorus of his
song, but denies hotly that he is Eisenstein when Frank
addresses him by name. The situation looks compromising,
but Rosalinda carries it off with impressive bravado: does the
governor think she would be at supper as late as this with
someone who is not her husband? 'Mein Herr, was dächten
sie von mir?' (What inferences would you draw?) she sings,
and reconciles Frank to the delay and Alfred to his probable
fate in the enchanting slow waltz refrain to her song.
Rosalinda fears the worst—Alfred and her husband will
almost certainly meet in prison—but what can she do? A
farewell kiss, and Frank, who is also going to Orlofsky's party,
hurries Alfred off, a brisk trio bringing the act to its end.

Act II.   The party at Prince Orlofsky's is in full swing,
and the opening chorus leaves us in no doubt as to its
successful nature. Although he is too blasé to enjoy them
himself, Prince Orlofsky likes his parties to go well—but woe
betide anyone who refuses to drink with him; he will get a
bottle thrown at his head. His song, 'Ich lade gern mir Gäste
ein', a mixture of languid nonchalance and adolescent
gaucherie, is perfect characterisation. With its repeated A
flats, it is not exactly the easiest music for a mezzo-soprano
to sing, requiring as it does a rich lower register if the refrain
(ending with a reiterated 'Chacun à son goût') is to make its
full effect.

Eisenstein, who is introduced as Marquis Renard, feels
sure that he can recognise in one of the guests his wife's
maid, Adele, but Orlofsky and the rest laugh at him for his
curious mistake and Adele herself sings a delightful soubrette
song, 'Mein Herr Marquis', in whose laughing refrain she is
able to make fun of her employer to her heart's content.
Apart from the famous waltz, this is possibly the best-known
number of the score.

Eisenstein has recognised his maid, although he is
persuaded to the contrary, but he does not know his wife
when she comes in masked and is announced as a Hungarian
Countess. She excites his curiosity straightaway, and it is not
long before he is showing her his chiming watch, a bait which
has worked the trick on many an unsuspecting Miss. This time,
though all seems to be beginning well and Eisenstein is soon
timing his Countess's heart-beats, something goes wrong, and

the lady ends up with the watch, which is not at all according to plan. It is a delicious moment, this seduction duet, as anyone who has heard Julius Patzak and Hilde Gueden sing it in the recording of the opera will know, just as those who know this recording and that by Richard Tauber and Vera Schwarz will have a shrewd idea of the contrasting styles of Vienna and Berlin in this kind of music. We hear the watch chime before the singers launch into a gallop, and Rosalinda ends with peals of triumphant coloratura.

Rosalinda will not unmask and it is suggested by Adele that the reason for this is that she is not a Hungarian at all. 'I will prove it,' says Rosalinda; 'the music of my native country shall speak for me.' It is a flimsy enough pretext for the Czardas and Frischka which follows, but once it starts the music is exhilarating enough to make us forget why it began in the first place. If there were no other reason—and there are, in fact, plenty of reasons—this Czardas would make it certain that nobody but a really capable soprano could do justice to the role of Rosalinda. It is not only a display piece of a high order, but it demands something unusual in the way of a dramatic technique. Ernest Newman has written that the Czardas 'shows what depths of expression there were in Strauss had he chosen to explore them more consistently. No genuine Hungarian could sing more movingly of the pain of separation from the beloved homeland, or of the fire in the Hungarian breast that drives them to the dance . . .'

The finale begins. It opens with a short section in praise of champagne, *allegro con brio*. First Orlofsky, then Adele and finally Eisenstein leads the company, which joins in the chorus after three verses. Eisenstein and Frank (who has been introduced as the Chevalier Chagrin) toast each other, and Falke, looking round at the assembled couples, proposes in a slow waltz tune that they shall pledge each other in eternal brother- and sisterhood. Coherent expression seems out of place, and, in their efforts to do justice to the toast, they resort to 'Duidu' and 'la, la, la', relapsing before long into silence for the ballet which, with its dancers, has been mentioned all along as one of the attractions of the party. At the end of the ballet, Orlofsky suggests that the professional dancers should have a rest, and that the guests should show that they are no less adept at the waltz themselves. It is the famous *Fledermaus* waltz, heard first in the overture but now unmistakably staking a claim as rival to 'The Blue Danube'. It

takes the foreground for most of the time, but also serves as
background for the continued flirtation of Eisenstein and
Rosalinda and for much comic byplay between Eisenstein
and Governor Frank. Finally, the clock strikes six, Eisenstein
remembers it is high time for him to go to prison, and the
curtain comes down as he and Frank help each other from
the ballroom.

Act III.   An entr'acte, part march, part waltz, introduces
us to the prison, where Frosch the gaoler (a speaking part)
has been doing his best to emulate in his own quiet way the
grander drinking exploits of Governor Frank; in a word, he is
drunk, a situation of which full advantage is taken by the
professional comic engaged to play the role. His inebriated
gambollings are interrupted from time to time by snatches of
song from cell No. 12, where Alfred is relieving the tedium
of prison life with reminiscences of his serenade to Rosalinda
and with snatches of tunes from other operas as well, if the
truth be known. Frosch staggers off to make another attempt
to curb this nuisance, and no sooner has he gone than Frank
comes in, no less the worse for wear than his underling. He
makes his entrance to musical accompaniment, whistles the
tune of the ball-room waltz, sings a bit of the champagne
song, and soon falls asleep to reminiscences of the waltz.

But his is not to be the sleep of the just, for Frosch has
pulled himself together sufficiently to be able to make his
morning report in the usual way. Nothing untoward has
happened, he says, except that Herr von Eisenstein has been
restless and, having asked for a lawyer, is to see Dr. Blind
almost immediately. The door-bell rings, and Frosch
announces the two young ladies who have so taken Frank's
fancy at the ball, to wit Adele and her sister. Adele, it is
explained, is not yet an artist in fact, only one by nature.
Cannot Frank help her to start a stage career? She sings to
him of her versatility ('Spiel' ich die Unschuld vom Lande'
and says there is nothing she cannot do on the stage, from
country wench to Queen—to say nothing of a flirtatious
French Marquise. There is another ring at the door, and the
Marquis Renard is admitted. When he hears that the Chevalier
Chagrin (whom he at first assumes to have been arrested for
insobriety) is none other than the prison governor, he laughs
aloud at what he thinks is a particularly good jest. Frank for
his part cannot take seriously the announcement that his
friend from the ball is Herr von Eisenstein; did he not himsel

escort that gentleman from his home to the prison, and is he not at this moment incarcerated within twenty feet of where they sit?

Frosch announces that another lady is without (the first two have been shown into cell No. 13, the only empty room), and Frank goes to greet her, leaving Eisenstein to waylay Blind and borrow his wig, glasses and legal paraphernalia in the hope that he may discover who it was who was arrested in his place the previous night.

Rosalinda (it was she who rang just now) has come to see what can be done about getting Alfred out of prison, with the help maybe of the lawyer who is waiting for them. Eisenstein comes in in place of Blind and proceeds to cross-question the two with a vigour more becoming to a prosecuting counsel than to someone engaged for the defence, and they begin to wonder why he is so very strict. He demands the unvarnished truth, which he gets from Alfred in an agreeable tune, punctuated by his own frequent bursts of indignation as the story unfolds. After one of them, Rosalinda defends herself as the victim of a husband who is himself a monster of deceitfulness. Eventually, unable to bear the insults any longer—Alfred asks how they can between them throw dust in the husband's eyes—Eisenstein rises in fury and denounces (in the tune which opens the overture) what he describes as their treachery to him.

The explanation is not long in forthcoming. No sooner is the lively trio between Rosalinda, Eisenstein and Alfred over, than the rest of the company at last night's ball appears as if summoned by magic, all that is to say apart from Adele and her sister—and news of them is quickly forthcoming when Frosch complains to Frank that the two ladies in No. 13 are proving obstructive and have refused to let him give them their regulation bath! Falke explains that Eisenstein's predicament is of his engineering, is in fact his vengeance for the shabby trick played on him a year ago. Alfred and Rosalinda are quick to take advantage of the situation and add that their supper was also an invention designed as part of the joke. Eisenstein is delighted at the way things have turned out, and Rosalinda sings the only possible moral: let all join with her in praising the sovereign reconciling power of King Champagne!   H.

EINE NACHT IN VENEDIG

A Night in Venice

Opera in three acts by Johann Strauss. Libretto by F. Zell and Richard Genée. Première, Friedrich-Wilhelm Städtische Theater, Berlin, October 3, 1883, for whose opening it was commissioned. First produced in Vienna at Theater an der Wien a week later; New York, 1884. Revived Volksoper, Vienna, 1948, with Esther Réthy, Helge Roswaenge, Kunz, Fritz Krenn, conductor Paulik; Komische Oper, Berlin, 1954, with new libretto by Walter Felsenstein, who produced.

CHARACTERS

The Duke of Urbino . . . . Tenor
Caramello, *a barber* . . . . Tenor (or Baritone)
Delacqua, *a Senator* . . . . Baritone
Barbara, *his wife* . . . . Mezzo-Soprano
Barbaruccio, *a Senator* . . . . Speaking Part
Pappacoda, *a cook* . . . . Tenor
Annina, *a young fish-seller* . . . . Soprano
Ciboletta, *Barbara's maid* . . . . Soprano
Agricola . . . . Soprano
Enrico Piselli . . . . Speaking Part
Senators, Senators' Wives, Fishermen, Gondoliers,
Citizens of Venice

Time: Late Eighteenth Century   *Place:* Venice

The overture is a gay compilation of tunes from the opera, in which waltzes play their accustomed part—this is eighteenth-century Venice observed through the eyes and ears of late nineteenth-century Vienna. The famous 'Lagunen-waltzer' is a particularly delectable component:

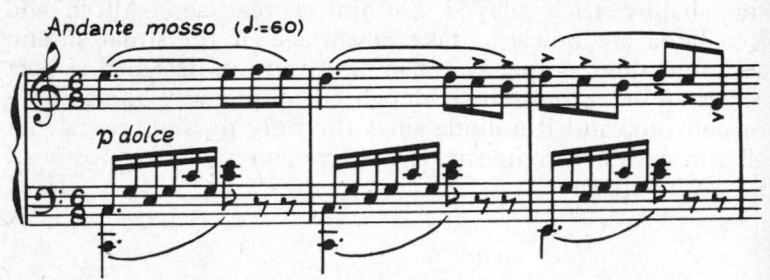

Act I. A crowd of Venetians are rejoicing in the splendour of their city, when Pappacoda congratulates them in a song on having acquired what they have hitherto lacked, a real maker of macaroni—from Naples of course. Young Enrico Piselli, nephew of Senator Delacqua and admirer of the Senator's young wife Barbara, finds in Pappacoda a convenient messenger for the note he means to send to Barbara telling her he will meet her that night. Along comes Ciboletta, Pappacoda's own sweetheart and Barbara's maid, to engage Pappacoda in a duet that is gay enough in spite of Ciboletta's insistence that the duplicity of men will always defeat their urge towards straight dealing.

Enter Annina, crying her wares to a delicious slow waltz: 'Frutta di mare'. Annina has a suitor, Caramello, who works for the Duke of Urbino as barber and general factotum, and Pappacoda loses no time in teasing her about him. The beautiful Barbara Delacqua now appears, and Pappacoda delivers the message from Enrico.

It is the turn of the older generation, and on to the scene come Delacqua himself and another Senator, Barbaruccio, discussing the carnival festivities and the invitation to a masked ball which the Duke has as usual extended to them and their wives. Delacqua is concerned to gain the vacant position of steward to the Duke. Unfortunately, the Duke is a well-known libertine, and Delacqua has thought it prudent to send Barbara by gondola on a visit to the island of Murano.

Now appears Caramello, the Duke's barber and factotum, and in his own view the very devil of a fellow. He hears from Pappacoda of Delacqua's plot to have Barbara safely out of harm's way at carnival time and immediately decides that he himself will take the gondolier's place and convey her to the palace of the Duke who, he knows, was captivated by her beauty during last year's carnival. Barbara for her part has been told that she is to spend a little time at Murano, but, anxious not to miss her rendezvous with Enrico, she hastily arranges for Annina to take her place in the gondola.

In a brilliant duet with Caramello, Annina keeps him at arm's length and compares him to the migratory swallow, which by its very nature denies constancy—'Pellegrina rondinella'. Not everyone is so lighthearted; Ciboletta is in tears because Pappacoda has no money to take her dancing. The problem is solved by Caramello handing out invitations to his master's masked ball and all is happiness again—the four lovers rejoice in a quartet at the prospect of the dance, although Ciboletta, in spite of her transports of delight, feels the need to make it clear that dancing is what she is going for and nothing else.

At last it is the turn of the Duke to appear from his gondola and apostrophise his favourite city: 'Sei mir gegrüsst, du holdes Venezia'.[1] When he encounters the Senators, they tell him that unfortunately their wives cannot accept his kind invitation to the dance. As Delacqua makes his excuse, Caramello whispers to the Duke that it is all a plot to keep the fair Barbara from him but that he, Caramello, is taking care of the whole problem. Delacqua thinks that the coveted stewardship may be brought a little nearer if he can somehow dangle Barbara in front of the Duke's nose, and he therefore sets about procuring someone to take her place in his scheme. He bids a fond farewell to his wife—'Goodbye, you old donkey' says Barbara when his back is turned—and a typically Straussian intrigue is under way. Caramello loses no time in confiding to the Duke that he has arranged to identify himself to Barbara by a particular song. From now on almost nobody will ever again appear as him- or herself.

The Duke's song breathes the very spirit of joyful anticipation, and it is wholly appropriate in the circumstances

[1] Imported by Erich Wolfgang Korngold, for his successful 1923 edition of the operetta, from Johann Strauss's *Simplizius* (1887). H.

that, as he sings it, his voice should be joined by those of Annina, Ciboletta, Barbara, and Pappacoda. It is not long before the voice of Caramello (or it could be that of the Duke himself) can be heard singing the pre-arranged gondolier's song ('Komm' in die Gondel'), a richly swaying waltz. Annina waves to Delacqua, who smiles as he sees (as he thinks) his wife off to Murano. Delacqua's attention is attracted to a party of serenaders, who greet him in terms of exaggerated praise: 'O Delacqua, qua, qua, qua, qua'. It is typical of Strauss's prodigal tunefulness that it is not easy to decide whether the mock serenade to the old cuckold or the romantic serenade of the mock gondolier is the more attractive! The ruse is entirely successful and the 'Ho-a-ho' of the gondolier's song is heard from the distance as the act comes to an end.

Act II.   The entr'acte is a reprise of the gondolier's song and the curtain rises on the ballroom of the Duke's palace. Agricola leads the ladies in greeting the Duke, whom she describes as 'the man of a hundred love affairs'. But that nobleman wants to pursue his latest adventure, with the beautiful Barbara. Annina seems delighted at the predicament her substitution has led her into ('Was mir der Zufall gab') and nothing Caramello can say (duet: 'Hör mich, Annina') will divert her from her intention of extracting as much enjoyment as she can from the situation. The Duke pursues his advantage with reminders of what she said to him last year ('Sie sagten meinem Liebesfleh'n').

But the complications are by no means over. Pappacoda cannot find Ciboletta and is beside himself with worry. His friends from all over the town are on the other hand delighted with the party that the invitations passed out by Caramello have brought them to. Now Delacqua introduces his 'wife', and the Duke, for all that Annina points out that it is Ciboletta in disguise, greets her with studied elegance. Here a snag ensues, because Delacqua's drilling of Ciboletta hopelessly misfires, and instead of asking the Duke for the position of steward for her husband, she begs him, with Pappacoda in mind, for that of chief cook! The Duke now takes Annina and Ciboletta to supper and pays compliments quite indiscriminately to each, much to the dismay of Caramello and Pappacoda, who are waiting at table. The announcement that at midnight by custom all must repair to the Piazza San Marco, precipitates a lively end to the act.

Act III takes place in the Piazza San Marco, with, as the opening chorus proclaims, the carnival spirit still very much in evidence. The pigeons are extolled as symbols of love (in some productions by the chorus, in others by Annina, Ciboletta and the Duke). But while it is given to some to enjoy the fun, others are inevitably roused to jealousy, though few give vent to their feelings in music of such hypnotically melodious a cast as does Caramello when he sees Annina on the Duke's arm: 'Ach, wie so herrlich zu schau'n' he sings to the music of the *Lagunenwalzer*, and only the refrain (purely verbal!) of 'La donna è mobile' suggests the feeling he says he has.

It is time for the general disentanglement. From Ciboletta, Delacqua finds out that Barbara is by no means on Murano as he had thought. Pappacoda is easily consoled for anything he may have suffered when Ciboletta gives him the news of his appointment as the Duke's chef, and he celebrates in a brisk little song in which, rather generously, he lets Ciboletta join. Ciboletta it is who tells the Duke that what he thought was Barbara was Annina all the time, but he takes the news with aristocratic equanimity. To Delacqua's extreme gratification, Barbara explains that she took the wrong gondola and Enrico was kind enough to look after her. To Caramello's delight, he is made the Duke's steward—and, no doubt to the Duke's, his intended wife Annina will never be far away. All ends with suitable carnival rejoicing.   H.

DER ZIGEUNERBARON

The Gipsy Baron

Operetta in three acts by Johann Strauss, text by J. Schnitzer, adapted from a libretto by M. Jokai, based on her story *Saffi*. First performed at the Theater an der Wien, Vienna, October 24, 1885; at the Staatsoper, Vienna, 1910; New York, 1886; London, Rudolf Steiner Theatre, 1935 (amateur production). Revived, New York City Center, 1944; Volksoper, Vienna, 1948, with Esther Réthy, Laszlo Szemere, Walter Höfermayer, Alfred Jerger, conducted by Anton Paulik; Metropolitan, 1959, with Della Casa, Gedda, conductor Leinsdorf; Sadler's Wells, 1964, with June Bronhill, Nigel Douglas, conductor Vilem Tausky.

CHARACTERS

Graf Peter Homonay .... Baritone
Conte Carnero .... Baritone
Sandor Barinkay .... Tenor
Kalman Zsupan, *a pig-farmer* .... Baritone
Arsena, *his daughter* .... Soprano
Mirabella, *her governess* .... Contralto
Ottokar .... Tenor
Czipra, *a gipsy leader* .... Mezzo-Soprano
Saffi, *her foster-daughter* .... Soprano
Pali, *a gipsy* .... Bass

Time: Eighteenth Century   *Place:* Hungary

Act I. The overture, as is Strauss's custom, is based on
tunes from the opera. We are in Hungary in the middle of the
eighteenth century. The scene is the edge of a village, where
stands a deserted and partly ruined castle and a small peasant
house. Nearby is a gipsy's hut. Rustic noises in the orchestra
introduce a lazy, typically Straussian tune in 6/8 rhythm
which is sung by the chorus. Ottokar, a young peasant, comes
in vigorously cursing his continued lack of success in finding
the treasure which is supposed to be hidden in the castle.
Czipra, an old gipsy woman, taunts him for his love of Arsena,
daughter of the rich pig-farmer, Zsupan, who lives nearby.

On to the scene comes a little group, headed by Sandor
Barinkay, to whom by rightful inheritance belongs the castle;
he is about to get it back with the help of Conte Carnero,
Commissioner of Morals, who accompanies him. Barinkay
gives a vivid account of his experiences in a song ('Als flotter
Geist') which has a swinging waltz refrain in which the chorus
joins and which is familiar to anyone who has ever seen a
Strauss film. Carnero wants witnesses for the official reinstatement, but Czipra, pressed into service, says she cannot
write and proceeds to read the hands of Barinkay and
Carnero. Barinkay will find both happiness and fortune
through a faithful wife, who will tell him through a dream
how he can discover hidden treasure. Carnero too will find a
treasure, now much increased in size, which he had thought
lost years before. This mystifies the Commissioner, who
cannot remember any such loss.

Zsupan is to be the other witness, and he appears,
explaining in the thickest of country accents and the most

comical of tunes ('Ja, das Schreiben und das Lesen') that reading and writing have never come his way; he is content with his pigs, and their products. When he hears that Barinkay is to be his neighbour, he warns him to expect some litigation in the matter of property; Barinkay suggests that a match with Zsupan's daughter would prevent any such unpleasantness, and Zsupan calls his daughter from the house. It is not Arsena who answers his summons but Mirabella, her governess, who turns out to be no other than Carnero's long-lost wife (Schatz = darling, as well as treasure). She explains in a song that she had thought him lost these twenty-four years. Czipra's first prophecy is fulfilled.

Arsena eventually makes her appearance, veiled and by no means overjoyed at the prospect of another suitor, as she makes quite clear in a charming song with interjections from the chorus. In spite of Barinkay's graceful proposal of marriage, in spite of the charm of her song, Arsena has fully made up her mind not to marry Barinkay, for the very good reason that she already has a lover; she says she requires a noble suitor and warns Barinkay not, moth-like, to singe his wings at the candle flame.

Barinkay is left alone, disconsolate at his failure. He overhears Saffi, Czipra's daughter, sing a gipsy song in praise of the loyalty the gipsy prides himself on showing to his friend ('So elend und so treu'); it ends with an impassioned *allegretto*. Barinkay is not slow to accept the invitation of the beautiful gipsy girl and her mother and joins them for supper.

It turns out to be Ottokar with whom Arsena is in love, and their after-dark flirtation is observed and overheard by Barinkay, Saffi, and Czipra, the former swearing to be revenged on Arsena for her cavalier treatment of him. The gipsies can be heard in the distance singing the song Saffi has already made known to us, and when they appear Czipra tells them that Barinkay is the true owner of the castle. They make him their chief, and he loses no time in knocking on Zsupan's door and telling him that he now has the title on which Arsena insisted: he is a Gipsy Baron. 'Er ist Baron' sings the ensemble, and Saffi welcomes him to the land of his childhood in a tune already familiar from the overture. Zsupan starts to tell Barinkay he is not the right sort of Baron, but Barinkay makes it quite clear that his ideas have changed; he does not want to marry Arsena, but Saffi! Zsupan is furious, but all join in the big tune of the overture which comes as it were as the coda of the finale.

Act II. The entr'acte, made up of the tune of the opening chorus of Act I, introduces the dawn. Barinkay has spent the night in the ruins of the castle, with Czipra and Saffi, and the three greet the day in a trio ('Mein Aug' bewacht') which ends in something more like a love duet for the two young people. Czipra tells of a dream she has had in which she found the treasure which legend has always associated with the castle; Barinkay laughs at the idea, but agrees to look where she directs—what's the harm? Czipra and Saffi have a little tune in which they mock his scepticism, and all three join in the rapturous treasure waltz ('Ha, seht es winkt') when they uncover the treasure itself. This is one of Strauss's most charming inspirations, and a comparison between it and the ensemble at the end of the previous act shows how much more at home he is writing a simple tune, simply harmonised, than trying to devise something more complicated.

The gipsies arrive to start work at their forge. They sing as they come, and the skit on the anvil chorus from *Trovatore* is unmistakable; the chorus finishes in a gallop. Zsupan appears with the object of getting help for a wagon which has stuck in the mud, but he insults the gipsies who get their own back by stealing his money and his watch. His cries of fury bring Carnero, Mirabella, Ottokar, and Arsena on to the scene, and they are followed by Barinkay and Saffi. Barinkay is by now dressed as a Gipsy Baron, and he greets them with the information that he and Saffi are man and wife. Carnero starts to ask certain questions about the legal side of the affair, and Saffi and Barinkay answer him in a duet which has become the most famous number of the opera: 'Wer uns getraut?' (Who married us?) The birds have performed the ceremony and acted as witness, says Barinkay, and he joins Saffi in the slow refrain.

This is too much for Carnero, who leads Mirabella and Zsupan in a comic ode to morality, the so-called 'Sittencommissions Couplets'.

There is a diversion when Ottokar finds a few pieces of gold and thinks he is on the track of the treasure at last, but Barinkay disillusions him, and the next moment the stage is full of a recruiting party, headed by Barinkay's old friend, Graf Peter Homonay. Led by Homonay, they sing a recruiting song and follow it up with a stirring Csardas.

Homonay refuses to be shocked at Barinkay and Saffi and ir spite of the protestations of Carnero congratulates them on the match.

During the course of the finale, Czipra makes it knowr that Saffi is not really her daughter but a Princess whom she has brought up, and who is descended from the last Pasha of Hungary—she even has documentary proof. 'Ein Fürstenkind', sings the whole company to the music of a gallop, and Saffi joins in with a couple of top C's. Barinkay alone cannot play his part in the rejoicing: Saffi is now unapproachably above him, and he will join Ottokar and Zsupan, who have been impressed as soldiers, and go off to the wars. His regret is touchingly shown, but the Act ends with the 'Werberlied" repeated by the whole company topped by repeated B's and C's from Saffi.

Act III.   The entr'acte makes use of the treasure waltz and the scene is laid in Vienna, where all are assembled to welcome the victorious army, among which are Barinkay Ottokar, and Zsupan. Arsena sings a little song about the incompatibility of courtship and propriety, but the little group is soon joined by the returning heroes. Zsupan sings to them of his exploits, which are hardly of the most military nature but which seem to have been entirely successful. Again, this is an opportunity for the comedian. The rest of the army comes marching on, and we are soon told of the distinguished service of both Barinkay and Ottokar, each of whom is to be rewarded with a title of nobility. In the finale all difficulties are resolved, Arsena flies into Ottokar's arms and Saffi appears from nowhere to greet Barinkay, who lead the full company in a final statement of the waltz refrain of his opening song.   H.

WIENERBLUT

The Viennese Spirit

Operetta in three acts by Johann Stauss, libretto by Viktor Leon and Leo Stein. Première, Carl Theatre, Vienna, October 25, 1899 (a failure) revived with great success Theater an der Wien, Vienna, 1905. Revived Volksoper, Vienna, 1946; Stoll Theatre, London, 1954, with voi Widmann, Eleanore Bauer, Franzi Wachmann, Karl Terkal, Fritz Imhoff conductor Schönherr.

CHARACTERS

Prince Ypsheim-Gindelbach, *Prime Minister of Reuss-*
  Schleiz-Greiz . . . . Baritone
Balduin, Graf Zedlau, *Ambassador of Reuss-Schleiz-*
  Greiz in Vienna . . . . Tenor
Gabriele, Gräfin Zedlau, *his wife* . . . . Soprano
Graf Bitowski
Demoiselle Franziska Cagliari, *a Viennese dancer,*
  Zedlau's mistress . . . . Soprano
Kagler, *her father, a circus manager* . . . . .Comic
Marquis de la Fassade ⎫
Lord Percy ⎬ *diplomats*
Principe de Lugando ⎭
Pepi Pleininger, *a mannequin* . . . . Soprano
Josef, *Graf Zedlau's valet* . . . . Baritone
Anna, *Demoiselle Cagliari's maid*
Time: The Congress of Vienna, 1814–5   *Place:* Vienna

The project for a new operetta, with music from various
earlier works of Strauss's, and to a libretto of the time of the
Congress of Vienna by Leon and Stein (who six years later
wrote *The Merry Widow*), was handed over by Strauss
himself before his death to Adolf Müller, a leading Viennese
theatrical conductor. The result is a compilation, not a newly
minted work, but it has obtained a popularity after Strauss's
death won by only a few of his own original stage works.

Act I. The scene is the villa of Count Zedlau,
Ambassador to Vienna of Reuss-Schleiz-Greiz, a small (and
mythical) state whose Prime Minister is also in Vienna for the
Congress. At the villa, where Count Zedlau whiles away the
time with the dancer Franziska Cagliari, the intrigue is
introduced by Josef, the Count's valet, who has secret papers
for his master's perusal but who can't find him anywhere.
Josef's urgent calls for Anna, the maid, produce instead
Franzi, who is also anxious to know where the Count is; after
all he has been away for five whole days. Her father, Kagler, a
richly comic figure of impeccably Viennese background, now
calls at the villa to make sure that his daughter is to perform
that night at the ball at Count Bitowski's house. He disappears when Count Zedlau is announced.

At first, Franzi is a little cool; hasn't the Count been with
another woman? Only with his wife, for appearance's sake,
he replies to a caressing waltz tune that would melt harder

hearts than Franzi's. When Franzi has gone, the Count tell
the faithful Josef that he and the Countess were seer
together by the Prime Minister, who appears to have taker
her for his mistress, not his wife. Anyhow, he (the Count) ha
discovered a most attractive mannequin, with whom he want
to arrange a rendezvous as soon as possible. Why not the fête
at Hietzing that very evening, suggests Josef, and the Coun
insists, in a charming duet, that Josef should write her the
letter making an assignation ('O komm, zum Stelldichein').

When the Count has gone, there enters Josef's girl friend
Pepi, the model—it is she, of course, for whom the Count ha
fallen and to whom Josef has just unsuspectingly written the
letter. She is going to Hietzing that night, but unfortunately
Josef cannot take her as he will be on duty—their Polka due
('Leichter Blut') is most fetching. Pepi has come about the
dress Franzi is to wear at Count Bitowski's party, and she
finishes her business just as the Prime Minister arrives, askin;
to see his ambassador. Josef tries to gain time by saying tha
neither the Count nor the Countess is at home, but Kagler
who chooses this moment to reappear and thinks th
reference is to his daughter, contradicts him roundly. Wher
therefore Franzi comes in a moment later (finale), it is hardly
surprising that the Prime Minister thinks she is Countes
Zedlau, and starts to sympathise with her husband's wayward
behaviour. Nothing Franzi can say makes him understand th
true situation, but when she goes out in a huff, he lament
the *faux pas* he seems obviously to have made.

It is the moment for a new complication, and the rea
Countess makes her entrance; to the charming tune o
'Morgenblätter' she greets the room she knows so wel
When the Prime Minister returns, he takes the Countess fo
the Count's mistress and seizes the opportunity of upbraidin
the Count for his lack of taste in bringing his mistress to th
villa. Appropriately Franzi comes in, and the Count is face
with his wife and his mistress each asking 'Who is the lady?
and with his Prime Minister mistaking the one for the othe
and treating each—as he thinks—appropriately. The Count ha
a brainwave: to save the situation, will the Prime Ministe
help him by introducing 'the lady' as *his* wife? No sooner sai
than done; unfortunately the Prime Minister chooses th
wrong lady, and it is the Countess whom he presents to Fran.
as his wife. The ensemble ends with doubts distinctly ur
resolved.

Act II.   Count Bitowski's ball starts with a Polonaise sung
by the guests, but soon the Count and Countess are discussing their marriage, which went wrong, they agree, because
of his lack in its early stages of the Viennese spirit—at the
word 'Wienerblut' there is the obvious musical reference.
Now, he agrees in a song, he seems to have substituted the
attitude of a Viennese Don Juan for the serious temperament
natural to Reuss-Schleiz-Greiz. The Count is in danger of
falling in love again with his own wife and is only mildly
disconcerted when Franzi tells him she thinks the woman the
Prime Minister introduced as his wife was in fact a mistress of
the Count's. Suddenly, however, he sees Pepi in the crowd
and takes the chance of slipping the note of assignation into
her hand; to a reprise of the waltz tune, she reads it,
recognises the writing as Josef's and takes it as having come
from him. When Josef appears, seeming preoccupied with his
duties, he consoles her in a languorous tune and explains that
he cannot take her to Hietzing. She is at first vexed with him,
but later realises that the note must have been from the
Count. The invitation is one she feels she can delightedly
accept.
    The comedy of mistaken identity becomes rapidly more
involved. First, pointing to the Countess, the Prime Minister
warns Kagler (the father, as he thinks, of the Countess) that
his daughter has a rival. Next, the Countess, seeing her
husband confirming the rendezvous with Pepi, assumes that
Pepi is his mistress Franzi, of whom she has heard. When the
Countess asks her husband to take her that night to Hietzing,
he refuses on the grounds that he has business with the Prime
Minister, repeating the excuse to Franzi when she makes a
similar request. The Prime Minister tells Franzi that he will
prevent the Count taking his mistress (in reality the
Countess) to Hietzing, but, as the finale begins, is persuaded
by the Countess (whom he still thinks is the mistress) to take
her there himself.
    A further twist: when Franzi and the Countess meet, the
Prime Minister introduces them as each other. They burst out
laughing and the Countess indicates Pepi, who she thinks is
Franzi. Pepi will have none of it, and points to Franzi. When
Josef is appealed to, he simplifies matters by denying that
any of the three is the real Franzi. The Count laughs the
whole matter off and leads the company in a song in praise of
the Viennese waltz. This finale contains sections from both

'Wine, Women and Song' and 'The Blue Danube', as well a 'Wienerblut'.

Act III. The fête at Hietzing. Three couples hav arranged rendezvous: the Countess and the Prime Ministe Franzi and Josef, the Count and Pepi, and their individu duos, interrupted by the popping of three champagne cork become a sextet when the Count from his arbour leads drinking song ('Wine, Women and Song'). One after the othe emerges from seclusion—the Prime Minister unfortunatel falls asleep—and discovers one or more of the complicatioi around them. In the end everyone knows who everyone els is, the Count vouches for Pepi's innocence, and the motto supplied when the Prime Minister gives it as his opinion tha it is all due to—'Wienerblut!' H.

KARL GOLDMARK
(1830–1915)
DIE KÖNIGIN VON SABA
The Queen of Sheba

OPERA in four acts by Karl Goldmark, text by Hermann vo Mosenthal. Première at the Hofoper, Vienna, March 10, 1875, wit Materna, Wild, and Beck. First performance Metropolitan, New Yor! 1885, with Lilli Lehmann (Sulamith; in 1889 at the same house, sh sang the Queen of Sheba), Krämer-Wiedl, Marianne Brandt, Albe Stritt, Adolf Robinson, Emil Fischer, conducted by Anton Seid Metropolitan, 1905, with Rappold (Sulamith), Walker, Alten, Knot van Rooy, Blass, and conducted by Hertz; Manchester, 1910; Londo: Kennington Theatre, 1910. The opera was in the repertory of th Vienna Staatsoper continuously from 1875 to 1938. Revived New Yo: in concert, 1970, with Kubiak, Alpha Floyd, Arley Reece.

CHARACTERS

King Solomon .... Baritone
Baal Hanan, *the Palace overseer* .... Baritone

Assad .... Tenor
The High Priest .... Bass
Sulamith, *his daughter* .... Soprano
The Queen of Sheba .... .Mezzo-Soprano
Astaroth, *her slave* .... Soprano
Voice of the Temple-Watchman .... Bass
me: Tenth Century B.C.   *Place:* Jerusalem

Act I.   In Solomon's magnificent palace everybody is
͏eparing for the reception of the Queen of Sheba. But
ɔbody is more delighted than Sulamith, the daughter of the
igh Priest, for Assad, whom she is to marry and who had
ɔne to meet the foreign queen, will return with her. Here he
ɔmes already into the hall. But Assad, growing pale, draws
ɪck before his betrothed. He confesses to King Solomon
ɪat he has not yet seen the Queen of Sheba, but at a cedar
ɔve in Lebanon a wonderful woman favoured him with her
͏ve and since then his mind has been confused. The King
lls the young man that God will restore his peace of mind
ɪrough marriage to Sulamith. Now the Queen's train
ɔproaches; she greets Solomon and unveils herself. Assad
ɪshes toward her; this was the woman of the cedar
͏ove! What does the young man want of her? She does not
ɪow him.
Act II.   The Queen did not want to recognise Assad but
ɪe woman in her is consumed with longing for him. He
ɔmes and happy love unites them. The scene changes and
ɪows the interior of the Temple, where the wedding of
ssad and Sulamith is about to be solemnised. At a decisive
ɔoment the Queen appears, and Assad throws the ring on the
ɔor and hurries to the Queen, who, for her part, declares a
ɔcond time that she has never seen him; she came only to
͏ing a wedding gift for Sulamith. Assad, who has offended
ɪe Almighty, has incurred the penalty of death.
Act III.   Solomon is alone with the Queen. She has one
quest to make of him, that he shall release Assad. Why? He
nothing to her but she wants to see whether the King has
gard for his guest. However, Solomon understands his
ɪest's scheme and refuses her request; the Queen, breathing
ɪngeance, strides out of the palace. Sulamith is in the depths
ɪ despair but Solomon consoles her; Assad will shake off the
ɪworthy chains. Far away on the borders of the desert, she
ill find peace with him.

Act IV.   Again the scene changes. On the border of th
desert stands the asylum of the young woman consecrated t
God in which Sulamith has found rest from the deceitf
world. Assad staggers thither, a weary, banished man. Agai
the Queen of Sheba appears before him offering him her lov
but he flees from the false woman for whom he ha
sacrificed the noble Sulamith. A desert storm arises, buryin
Assad in the sand. When the sky becomes clear agai
Sulamith, taking a walk with her maidens, finds her lover. Sh
pardons the dying man and sings of the eternal joys whic
they will taste together.

Die Königin von Saba belongs in the category of oper;
whose music is basically conventional and which require
lavish scenic display if they are to be seen at their best. Muc
of the music in its day must have sounded agreeably exoti
on the other hand, such a section as Assad's narration t
Solomon (Act I) reaches an almost Wagnerian length withou
displaying quite Wagnerian expressiveness. The beginning (
the second act, however, with the big *scena* for the Quee
followed by Astaroth's luring song (marvellously effective i
the hands of a great artist), Assad's well-known 'Magisch
Töne' and the big love duet for him and the Queen i
musically speaking, of considerable appeal. Sulamith's tw
great scenes with the chorus ('Der Freund ist dein' in th
opening scene, and the wailing lament in Act III) have
passionate, exotic colouring and demand considerable powe
of execution on the part of the singer. The Queen has
striking duet with Solomon at the beginning of Act III, whe
she attempts to seduce him from the path of duty and t
obtain Assad for herself.   K.W., H.

HERMANN GOETZ
(1840–1876)
DER WIDERSPÄNSTIGEN ZÄHMUNG
The Taming of the Shrew

COMIC opera in four acts by Hermann Goetz, Libretto from Shakespeare's comedy by Joseph Viktor Widmann. Première, Mannheim, October 11, 1874, with Ottilie Ottiker and Eduard Schlosser. First performed Vienna, 1875; London, Drury Lane, 1879; New York, 1886. Revived Metropolitan, New York, 1916, with Ober and Goritz, conductor Bodanzky; Berlin, 1952, with Gudrun Wuestemann and Kurt Rehm; London, City Opera Club, 1959.

CHARACTERS

Baptista, *a rich gentleman of Padua* .... Bass
Bianca ⎫
Katharina ⎬ *his daughters* .... ⎰ Soprano
 ⎱ Soprano
Hortensio ⎫
Lucentio ⎬ *Bianca's suitors* .... ⎰ Bass
 ⎱ Tenor
Petruchio, *a gentleman of Verona* .... Baritone
Grumio, *Petruchio's servant* .... Bass
A tailor .... Tenor
Hortensio's wife .... Mezzo-Soprano
Baptista's and Petruchio's Servants, Wedding Guests, Neighbours, etc.

Place: Acts I, II, III in Padua; Act IV in Petruchio's house in the country

Goetz, a pupil in Berlin of Ulrich and Hans von Bülow, spent much of his life in Switzerland as organist in Winterthur and Zürich. Apart from *The Taming of the Shrew*, he wrote one other opera, *Francesca da Rimini*, which was much less successful than the first, some songs, piano and chamber music, a symphony, concertos for piano and for violin, and some works for chorus and orchestra. *The Taming of the Shrew* is his unquestioned masterpiece, and one wonders why its sound construction and strong lyrical quality, to say nothing of the lively drama contained in the music, have not kept it more firmly in the repertory.

The overture, for the most part vigorous and forthright, suggests the changes of mood of the opera itself and its underlying lyricism.

Act I. Outside Baptista's house in Padua, at night
Introduced by the clarinet, Lucentio sings an ardent an
beautiful serenade to Bianca ('Klinget, klinget, liebe Töne'
Haste ye sounds of love and longing), until he is interrupte
by the noise of Baptista's servants, about to leave hi
employment because of the scolding ways of his daughter
Kate, whose fury at her father's attempts to pacify ther
seems warrant enough for their decision. Bianca appears an
there follows a charming love duet for her and Lucentio ('C
wende dich nicht ab': O turn thou not away). The arrival o
Bianca's grey-beard suitor, Hortensio, with a band o
musicians, puts a stop to the tender scene, and the quarrel o
Hortensio and Lucentio eventually wakes up Baptista, t
whom Lucentio, as explanation of his presence outside th
house, reveals his love for Bianca. None shall pay suit t
Bianca, declares Baptista, until her elder sister is married
meanwhile, Bianca shall study with the best masters in Italy
In their *allegretto* duet, Lucentio and Hortensio offe
Katherine to one another, until each is struck by the brigh
idea of disguising himself as a teacher and so gainin
admittance to Bianca's presence. Petruchio arrives with hi
servant, Grumio, complaining that he is bored with his wealth
he would like nothing better than to share it with a woma
worthy of his metal. Hortensio immediately suggests Kate
Petruchio falls for the idea and in a vigorous aria proclaim
his determination to marry her ('Sie ist ein Weib, für solche
Mann geschaffen': She is a wife, for such a man created).

Act II. A room in Baptista's house, where Kate an
Bianca are dressing. Kate mocks Bianca about the previou
night's serenades; her sister's supine behaviour, she say
shows why men call women the weaker sex. She make
Bianca accompany her on the lute while she sings 'Ich wi
mich Keinem geben' (I'll give myself to no one). Petruchi
comes in with Lucentio and Hortensio and immediately ask
Baptista for Kate's hand in marriage; he will listen to n
warning about her character, and only laughs whe
Hortensio, who has gone disguised as a teacher into th
house, emerges with his lute broken over his head. In
soliloquy Petruchio resolves that nothing will stop hir
winning her as his wife, and their first exchange leaves Kat
wondering whether she has not at last met her match, in bot
senses of the word. The extended duet is excellentl
contrasted, with graceful music for the mocking of Kate, an

n effective quarrel. At the end of the duet, Kate sings of her dawning tenderness for Petruchio to music derived from her defiance of men at the beginning of the act.

Baptista has several times peeped round the door and now comes in to be told by Petruchio that he and Kate are to be married, by Kate that nothing could be further from the truth. Petruchio dominates the quintet which follows Hortensio and Lucentio have come in as well), and at its end Kate agrees to marry him, more apparently to pay him out than for any other reason.

Act III. Baptista, with Katherine and Bianca, Lucentio and Hortensio (still disguised as teachers) are waiting to welcome the wedding guests, to whom shortly Baptista has to make excuses for the absence of Petruchio. Bianca resumes her lessons, and, under guise of translating the *Aeneid*, Lucentio makes himself known. Hortensio, once he has succeeded in tuning his lute, joins them to turn the duet into a trio, one moreover in the best traditions of German comic opera. Baptista bursts in to say that Petruchio has arrived. Deaf to remonstrance about his lateness or the untidiness of his dress, he leads the procession to church, while the servants prepare the wedding breakfast. It is not long before they are back, Hortensio describing Petruchio's disgraceful behaviour during the ceremony, the guests delighted at the prospect of the feast, and Petruchio himself announcing that he and Kate have no time to stay for the party but must be off at once. He will listen to no pleas, but extricates himself from the surrounding guests and carries Kate off with him.

Act IV. At Petruchio's house, the servants' demeanour clearly suggests that tempers are flying, and when the newly married couple comes in, Kate is pale, Petruchio flourishing a riding whip and complaining about everything in sight. The food is whisked away untouched, and Kate is left to soliloquise on her troubles and admit that her spirit is broken: 'Die Kraft versagt' (My strength is spent). Not only is she defeated but she finds she is in love.

Grumio announces a tailor, who urges the qualities of his wares. Kate likes them, but Petruchio finds fault as usual, and in the ensemble which ensues pays for the goods and tramples them underfoot. Next he plays tricks with the times of day; at first, according to Petruchio it is moonlight, then, when Kate agrees with him, mid-day. She owns she is beaten; she is now his loving wife. Immediately, Petruchio

consoles her, and, reconciled, they hear Grumio announce
the arrival of Baptista with the newly married Bianca and
Lucentio, and also Hortensio and his wife. They rejoice to
hear of the taming of the shrew (in the last century, when
Minnie Hauck sang Kate, this excellent septet was omitted
and a waltz for Kate substituted), and the opera ends with a
chorus of wedding guests congratulating Petruchio and Kate.

H.

KARL MILLÖCKER
(1842–1899)
DER BETTELSTUDENT
The Beggar Student

COMIC opera in three acts by Karl Millöcker. Text by Zell and
Genée. First performed at the Theater an der Wien, Vienna, December 6,
1882; New York, 1883; London, Alhambra Theatre, 1884 (in English),
Royalty Theatre, 1895 (in German). Revived at Vienna, Staatsoper,
1936, with Margit Bokor, Dora Komarek, Richard Sallaba, Alfred
Jerger, Frederick Gynrod, conductor Josef Krips; Volksoper, 1949,
with Maria Cebotari, Lorna Sidney, Fred Liewehr, Kurt Preger, Walter
Höfermayer, conductor Anton Paulik.

CHARACTERS

Palmatica, *Countess Nowalska* . . . . .Mezzo-Soprano
Countess Laura, *her daughter* . . . . Soprano
Countess Bronislawa, *Laura's sister* . . . . Soprano
Simon, *the Beggar Student* . . . . Tenor
Jan Janitzky, *Simon's friend* . . . . Tenor
Colonel Ollendorf . . . . Bass
Enterich, *Prison Governor* . . . . Baritone
Richthofen ⎫
Wangenheim ⎬ *Saxon officers*
Henrici ⎭

Time: 1704   *Place:* Cracow

Colonel Ollendorf, Cracow's irascible governor, has been
badly hurt: he was just starting to make advances to Countess

Laura, a proud Polish beauty, when she struck him in the face with her fan—in public, and at an official ball! Honour must be satisfied and he will have his revenge.

Act I. We are in the prison; the prisoners' wives try to persuade Enterich, the prison governor, to let them see their husbands. He is disposed to grant their request, but he confiscates the various delicacies which are intended to cheer the prisoners' lot. To the prison comes Ollendorf, complaining loudly at the treatment meted out to him the night before. His entrance song, with its waltz refrain 'Ach, ich hab' sie ja nur auf die Schulter geküsst', gives an excellent opportunity to a comic bass. The object of Ollendorf's visit is to find two young prisoners and persuade them in return for their freedom to aid him in his scheme of revenge: they are to make love to Countess Laura and her sister, and he will then be able to expose the joke and so avenge the insult to his honour. The two Poles he chooses—political prisoners, both of them—seem light-hearted enough to judge by their duet; they agree to fall in with the scheme, and promise to say nothing about its origin. Ollendorf will fit them out as Prince Wibicky and his secretary—and they will be free.

The scene changes to a fair in the Rathausplatz in Cracow, which is ushered in with a brisk 6/8 chorus and a march. Palmatica and her daughters are there, too poor to buy anything, but doing their best in their 3/8 trio to disguise this painful fact by sneering at what is exposed for sale. Ollendorf introduces the Prince Wibicky and his companion to the Countess and her daughters, and Simon proceeds to tell them of his wanderings over the earth; the flirtations he has indulged in wherever he has been have only proved to him how far superior Polish girls are to those in the rest of the world. His romance, 'Ich knüpfte manche zarte Bände' (Full many a tender knot I've tied), is an excellent example of the unpretentiousness and graceful charm which is to be found in Millöcker at his best. Simon proposes to Laura, and all sit down to table to celebrate the betrothal with—since Ollendorf has to pay—the best mine host can bring them. Laura sings a Polish song—joy and grief, she says, are closely allied; its solemn *andante* opening soon gives way to a sparkling *allegretto*. The town band puts in an appearance with a march which takes its cue from Schubert rather than Sousa, and the act comes to an end with general rejoicing.

Act II. Laura is at home trying on her wedding dress,

assisted by her mother and her sister. She repeats the advice
her mother has given her, that husbands can and should be
dominated by their wives—not by direct precept but by
persuasion, by tears not threats. The Prince's secretary is
announced, and Jan makes up to Bronislawa in a charming
duet.

Jan reminds Simon that plans are afoot to restore Cracow
to the Poles, that the King's nephew, Duke Adam, is
preparing a coup, and that only money is wanting. It looks as
though their schemes are coming to fruition. Simon is alone
with Laura; would she still love him, he asks, if he were poor,
untitled, even an impostor? She tells him her love is proof
against any such change in his status, and asks him whether
he would love her if someone prettier came along, rich and
well-born. Simon reassures her in his turn. The music of the
second part of this duet ('Ich setz' den Fall') is the same as
that of the first, the only difference being that Laura in the
second half sings what Simon had sung in the first, and he
takes over what she had originally sung. Taking courage from
what Laura has told him, Simon writes her a note telling her
the truth about his deception; he is astonished when he sees
later that its reception seems to have made no difference in
her attitude towards him, but he does not know that
Ollendorf has had it intercepted. The marriage is performed
and Ollendorf waits to savour his triumph, which will not be
long delayed. The happy couple are congratulated, their
healths drunk in the bride's shoe, the mazurka is danced,
when suddenly the sound of rowdy singing is heard outside.
Simon's fellow-prisoners have come to join in the fun. All
must come out. Ollendorf explains that the joke was his
revenge: after all, he only kissed her on the shoulder, but she
slapped his face in public. She may repent now at her leisure.

Act III.   The aftermath of Ollendorf's disclosure is still to
be reckoned with. People comment on Simon's dastardly
behaviour and on the punishment which they cannot help
thinking Laura has earned by her behaviour. Bronislaw
confesses that she is still secure in her love, and that the day's
tragedy has not had the effect of removing her appetite
which she had hoped would be assuaged at the wedding feast.

Simon is disconsolate, but Jan explains to him that all will
yet be well. He seems disgraced but he has yet a part to play
in the freeing of Cracow. Ollendorf has approached Jan and
bribed him—with the 200,000 of money they need to finance

Duke Adam's insurrection—if he will give the patriot away.
He for his part has promised to do so after the wedding feast,
and Simon must pretend, for the sake of Poland, to be the
Duke; only by this means can enough time be gained to
enable the Duke himself to get inside the gates with his
troops. Simon confesses that the game is up for him in his
best known aria, 'Ich hab' kein Geld, bin vogelfrei' (I'm
quite cleaned out, my money's gone), with its refrain
challenging Dame Fortune to another game of chance.

Palmatica takes to abusing poor Simon, in spite of the
comment of Ollendorf and Jan, and much to the Beggar
Student's rage. Eventually, Ollendorf reveals what he
describes as the fact of the matter: he has discovered that
Simon is none other than Duke Adam, and he must take him
off to prison and there chop off his head. Consternation is
general, not least as far as Simon is concerned; Palmatica says
she suspected he was noble all along and is delighted to have
him as son-in-law, Laura frantically announces she will die
with him, and Jan trembles in case Simon should not play his
part adequately. All is well, however; a cannon shot is heard,
and the news arrives that Duke Adam has won control of the
city. Ollendorf admits there is nothing more for him to do
but give himself up—whereupon Bronislawa says *she* has
already surrendered herself, to the Secretary. Laura says she
has done no less, to the Beggar Student, but Jan hastens to
correct her: in future he will be known as Count Simon
Rymanowitsch. The opera ends in rejoicing.   H.

ENGELBERT
HUMPERDINCK
(1854–1921)

HÄNSEL UND GRETEL

OPERA in three acts by Engelbert Humperdinck; text by Adelheid
Wette (the composer's sister). First performed at the Hoftheater,
Weimar, December 23, 1893; Daly's Theatre, London, 1894 (in

English), with Marie Elba, Jeanne Douste, Edith Miller, Julia Lennox, Charles Copland, conductor Arditi: Drury Lane, 1895 (in German), by the Ducal Court Company of Saxe-Coburg and Gotha; Covent Garden, 1896, with Marie Elba, Jessie Huddleston, Lilian Tree, Luise Meisslinger, David Bispham, conductor Mancinelli; New York, Daly's Theatre, 1895 (in English); Metropolitan, 1905 (in German), with Lina Abarbanell, Bella Alten, Louise Homer, Marion Weed, Otto Goritz, conductor Alfred Hertz; Covent Garden, by B.N.O.C., January 1923 (first broadcast of a complete opera from an opera house in Europe), with Doris Lemon, Lillian Stanford, Sydney Russell, Richard Collins.

CHARACTERS

Hänsel ....Mezzo-Soprano
Gretel, *his sister* ....Soprano
The Witch.....................Mezzo-Soprano[1]
Gertrude, *mother of Hänsel and Gretel* ......Soprano
Peter, *their father, a broom-maker* ....Baritone
Sandman ....Soprano
Dew Fairy ....Soprano

The opera has established itself in the repertory and is played in almost every town at Christmas.

The first act represents the hut of a broom-maker. Hänsel is binding brooms and Gretel is knitting. The children romp, quarrel, and make up. When their mother, Gertrude, enters she is angry to see them idle, and trying to smack them she upsets a pitcher of milk instead. With all hope of supper vanished she sends the children out into the woods with little baskets to look for strawberries, while she herself, bemoaning their poverty, sinks exhausted upon a chair and falls asleep. A riotous song announces the approach of her husband, drunk as usual. She is about to reproach him when she notices that he has brought sausages, bread and butter, coffee—enough for a feast. He tells her that he has had good luck at the Fair and bids her prepare supper. When he asks for the children he is horrified to hear that they have been sent into the woods, for a wicked fairy lives near the Ilsenstein who entices children to bake them in her oven and devour them. Both parents rush off in search of Hänsel and Gretel.

The second act takes place near the Ilsenstein. Hänsel has filled his basket with berries and Gretel has made a wreath

---

[1] Occasionally sung by a character tenor.

with which her brother crowns her. Before they realise what they are doing the children eat all the berries. Then they see that it is too dark to look for any more or to find their way home. Gretel weeps with fear and Hänsel comforts her. They grow sleepy. The Sandman sprinkles sand into their eyes, but before going to sleep the children are careful not to forget their evening prayer. Fourteen guardian angels are seen descending the heavenly ladder to protect them.

Morning comes with the third act. The Dew Fairy sprinkles dew on the children. Suddenly they notice a little house made of cake and sugar. They start to break off little bits when a voice cries out from within and the witch opens the door. She throws a rope around Hänsel's throat, and tells them both to come in. Frightened, they try to escape, but after binding them with a magic spell she imprisons Hänsel in a kennel, and forces Gretel to go into the house.

When she believes Hänsel to be asleep she turns her attention to the oven, then rides around the house on her broomstick. When she alights she orders Hänsel to show her his finger. But he pokes a stick through the bars and, thinking it is still thin, the witch orders more food for him. While she turns her back, Gretel seizes the juniper bough with which the old woman makes her spells, speaks the magic words and breaks her brother's enchantment. Then the witch tells Gretel to get into the oven and see if the honey cakes are done. But Gretel pretends to be stupid and asks her to show her how to get in. Together the children push the old witch into the oven and slam the door. The oven soon falls to pieces. The children then see a row of boys and girls standing stiffly against the house. Gretel breaks the spell for them as she had done for Hänsel. There is general rejoicing, Gertrude and Peter appear, the old witch is pulled out of the ruined oven as a gigantic honey cake and everyone on the stage joins in a hymn of thanksgiving.

The overture, based on motives from the opera, is very well known. In Act I, there is a long duet for the two children, culminating in their dance, and the rollicking 'Tra-la-la-la' entrance song of the father. Act II begins with the Witch's Ride, and contains the Sandman's song, the children's evening prayer, and the Wagnerian Angels' pantomime. Act III has the Dew Fairy's song, the Witch's big solo, and the Witch waltz in which Hänsel and Gretel celebrate their triumph. K.W.

HUGO WOLF
(1860–1903)
DER CORREGIDOR
The Magistrate

OPERA in four acts by Hugo Wolf; text by Rosa Mayreder-Obermayer founded on P. de Alarcon's story *El sombrero de tres picos*. Première in Mannheim, June, 1896. First performed in Vienna, under Mahler, 1904, with Förster-Lauterer (Frasquita), Breuer (Corregidor), Demuth (Tio Lucas), and Hesch (Repela); London, Royal Academy of Music, 1934; Salzburg Festival 1936, with Novotna (Frasquita), Thorborg (Mercedes), Bella Paalen, Gunnar Graarud, Jerger, Zec, Ludwig Hoffmann, conductor Bruno Walter; London, 1955, by City Opera Club; New York, 1959, in concert form; Wiesbaden, 1960; Zürich, 1972.

CHARACTERS

Don Eugenio de Zuniga, *the Corregidor*
(*magistrate*) .... Buffo Tenor
Doña Mercedes, *his wife* .... Soprano
Repela, *his valet* .... Buffo Bass
Tio Lucas, *a miller* .... Baritone
Frasquita, *his wife* .... Mezzo-Soprano
Juan Lopez, *the alcalde* (*mayor*) .... Bass
Pedro, *his secretary* .... Tenor
Manuela, *a maid* .... Mezzo-Soprano
Tonuelo, *a court messenger* .... Bass
A Neighbour .... Tenor
A Duenna, *employed by the Corregidora* Mezzo-Soprano

Act I. The miller, Tio Lucas, is living a happy life with his beautiful wife, Frasquita. Her love is so true that jealousy, to which he is inclined, cannot thrive. Jealous? Yes, he has a bump of jealousy. True, the Corregidor, who is keenly interested in the Miller's pretty wife, has one too. But no matter, he is a high, very influential functionary. Meanwhile Frasquita loves her Tio Lucas so truly that she can even allow herself a dance with the Corregidor. Perhaps she will cure him so, perhaps she will obtain in addition the wished-for official place for her nephew. The Corregidor too does not keep her waiting long and Frasquita makes him so much in love with her that he becomes very impetuous. Thereupon he loses his balance and the worthy official falls in the dust, out of which the miller, without suspecting anything, raises him up. But the Corregidor swears revenge.

Act II. The opportunity for this comes very quickly. As the miller one evening is sitting with his wife in their cosy room, there comes a knock at the door. It is a drunken court messenger, Tonuelo, who produces a warrant of arrest. Tio Lucas must follow him without delay to the alcalde who has lent himself as a willing instrument to the Corregidor's scheme. Frasquita is trying to calm her anxiety with a song when outside there is a cry for help. She opens the door and before it stands the Corregidor dripping with water. He has fallen in the brook. Now he begs admission from Frasquita, who is raging with anger. He has even brought with him the appointment of the nephew. But the angry woman will pay no attention and sends the Corregidor away from her threshold. Then he falls in a swoon. His own servant now comes along. Frasquita admits both of them to the house and herself goes into town to look for her Tio Lucas. When the Corregidor, awakened out of his swoon, hears this, full of anxiety, he sends his valet after her; he himself, however, hangs his wet clothes before the fire and goes to bed in the miller's bedroom.

(Change of scene.) In the meantime Tio Lucas drinks the alcalde and his fine comrades under the table and seizes the occasion to flee.

Act III. In the darkness of the night, Tio Lucas and Frasquita pass by without seeing each other. The miller comes to his mill. (Change of scene.) Everything is open. In the dust lies the deed of appointment for the nephew; before the fire hang the Corregidor's clothes. A frightful suspicion arises in Tio Lucas's mind which becomes a certainty when through the keyhole he sees the Corregidor in his own bed. He is already groping for his rifle to shoot the seducer and the faithless woman, when another thought strikes him. The Corregidor also has a wife, a beautiful wife. Here the Corregidor's clothes are hanging close at hand. He quickly slips into them and goes back to town. In the meantime the Corregidor has awakened. He wants to go back home now. But he does not find his clothes and so he crawls into those of the miller, and in them is almost arrested by the alcalde who now enters with his companions and Frasquita. When the misunderstanding is cleared up, they all go with different feelings into the town after the miller.

Act IV.   Now comes the explanation and the punishment of the Corregidor, at least in so far as he receives a sound thrashing and becomes really humbled. In reality the miller also has not yet had his 'revenge', but he is recognised and is likewise beaten black and blue—*that* he must suffer in reparation for his churlish doubt of the faithful Frasquita.

The comedy of *Der Corregidor* is *durchkomponiert*. The overture opens with the Corregidor theme (later played on the trombones), and makes play also with the E major love music, which is later heard in the first scene of the second act. Two of Wolf's songs are worked into the libretto of the work, the first, 'In dem Schatten meiner Locken', sung by Frasquita to the Corregidor, the second to words by Heine, 'Herz, verzage nicht geschwind', sung by the Corregidor at the end of the first scene of Act II.   K.W.

7
Italian Opera

DOMENICO CIMAROSA
(1749–1801)

IL MATRIMONIO SEGRETO
The Secret Marriage

OPERA buffa in two acts by Domenico Cimarosa. Text by Giovanni Bertati after Colman's *The Clandestine Marriage*. First performed at the Burgtheater, Vienna, February 7, 1792; la Scala, Milan, 1793; London, 1794; New York, 1834; Her Majesty's, 1842; Covent Garden, 1849. Revivals include Metropolitan, 1937, with Natalie Bodanya, Muriel Dickson, Ira Petina, George Rasely, Julius Huehn and Louis D'Angelo; Rome, 1948, with Alda Noni, Angela Tuccari, Palmira Vitali-Marini, Cesare Valletti, Antonio Cassinelli and Vito de Taranto; la Scala, Milan, 1949, with Alda Noni, Hilde Gueden, Fedora Barbieri, Tito Schipa, Boris Christoff, and Sesto Bruscantini; Fortune Theatre, London, by the London Opera Club, 1949, with Maureen Springer, Pamela Woolmore, Bruna Maclean, Richard Lewis, Bruce Boyce, and Owen Brannigan; Edinburgh, by Piccola Scala, 1957, with Sciutti, Ratti, Alva, conductor Sanzogno; Glyndebourne, 1965, with Margherita Rinaldi, Alberta Valentini, Laghezza, Bottazzo, Davià, Badioli.

CHARACTERS

Geronimo . . . . Buffo
Elisetta, *his daughter* . . . . Soprano
Carolina, *another daughter* . . . . Soprano
Fidalma, *Geronimo's sister* . . . . .Mezzo-Soprano
Count Robinson, *an English milord* . . . . Bass
Paolino . . . . Tenor

Time: Eighteenth Century   *Place:* Bologna

Cimarosa's most famous opera has the distinction of being reputedly the only work ever encored *in toto* on the occasion

377

of its first performance. History has it that the Emperor Leopold II, for whom Mozart wrote *La Clemenza di Tito* a few months earlier, so enjoyed the work that he invited all the participants to supper, after which the performance was repeated!

The story is concerned with events at the house of one Geronimo, a wealthy citizen of Bologna, whose sister Fidalma is installed as mistress of his house, and who has two daughters, Elisetta and Carolina. At the opening of the first act we meet Carolina and Paolino, the latter a junior business associate of Geronimo's and secretly married to Carolina. In their first duet she urges him to hide the secret of their marriage no longer but to reveal it to everyone. There is another duet in lighter vein as Carolina says 'Goodbye' to her husband. Geronimo appears, inclined to deafness and definitely afflicted by the golden malady of the *nouveau riche*. He learns from Paolino that the latter's friend, the English Count Robinson, is on his way to Bologna with the firm intention of arranging a match with no other than Elisetta, Geronimo's daughter. Nothing will please him but to recount the news with all its imports to his family, which he does in a *buffo* aria. The sisters immediately find cause to quarrel, much to Fidalma's annoyance; a trio brings the quarrel to a musical climax.

Fidalma admits to Elisetta that she herself is in love—she underlines it in a song—but she will not admit with whom, though she whispers in an aside to the audience that it is Paolino.

Geronimo cannot wait for the Count's arrival. The English nobleman duly appears and proceeds to address everyone with a maximum of words and a minimum of content—he hates a man who cannot be brief, he says. The situation develops until it becomes, musically speaking, a sextet, and the Count mistakes both the other ladies in turn for the Elisetta who is his bride-to-be. In conversation with Paolino shortly afterwards he reveals that the prospect of marriage with Elisetta fills him with consternation, while he looks with nothing but favour on union with Carolina—a fact which causes Paolino not a little consternation. He proposes to Carolina, but is told as politely as possible that she is not disposed to welcome his proposal; she even lists in her aria the faults which she says she possesses.

Preparations are being made for the banquet which is to be

given in the Count's honour, when that worthy himself enters, protesting his love to Carolina. Elisetta interrupts and upbraids them for their conduct, but Fidalma manages to silence the quarrel which ensues by warning them that Geronimo approaches. He does his best to discover what is the cause of all the fuss, but his deafness, Paolino's unwillingness to let him find out that the Count wishes to marry Carolina, Fidalma's preoccupation with avoiding a family quarrel, and the fact that everyone talks at once, prevent him from carrying out his intention.

At the beginning of the second act Geronimo is still trying to find out what it is all about, and he is found alone with the Count. After some misunderstanding, he gathers that his prospective son-in-law has not taken kindly to his bride-to-be. After voicing their mutual dissatisfaction, the two parties come to an agreement when the Count suggests that he relinquish half the dowry he has been promised if Geronimo will allow him to marry the younger of his two daughters. This arrangement suits Geronimo admirably, and their duet ends in complete accord.

Paolino is told of the new arrangement, and in his desperation is just going to throw himself on Fidalma's mercy, when she, encouraged by what she takes to be glances and sighs directed at her, says that she will accept his proposal and marry him! Paolino can stand the strain no longer and faints away. It is while Fidalma is trying to revive him that Carolina comes on the scene. Fidalma goes to fetch some smelling-salts, and the wretched Paolino tries to explain the situation to Carolina, but it is not until the trio is over and he is able to embark on an aria that he manages to convince her that his protestations of love are not mere deceit.

The Count now tries, by depicting himself as an ogre and a monster of iniquity, to persuade Elisetta to break off the marriage. He fails in his object, and Elisetta and Fidalma (who has revealed that Carolina, though the object of the Count's affections, is herself in love with Paolino) plot to rid themselves of their rival and send her to a convent. Geronimo agrees, and tells her himself of his decision. Poor Carolina is broken-hearted, and her music takes on a moving character as she thinks of the future without her husband. The Count offers his help in her distress, and she is just about to tell him the whole truth when her sister, her aunt, and her father jump out on them declaring that there can be no further doubt since they have caught them in the act. Geronimo sends Paolino off at once with a letter to the Mother Superior of the convent.

The finale begins. The Count is out of his room, although it is night, and muses on the possibility of helping Carolina, when he is surprised by the watchful Elisetta; they say good-night to each other and depart, to be succeeded by Paolino and Carolina planning an elopement. Disturbed by a noise, they quickly hide in Carolina's room, and in a moment the suspicious Elisetta is on the scene. She listens at the door, hears whispers, and rouses the house to come and catch the Count in her sister's room. Everyone rushes to the spot and together they demand that the Count shall come forth and reveal his perfidy. He does—but from his own room, where he has been asleep until woken up by the din. A moment later, Carolina and Paolino come out of the room and admit that they were married two months ago. Eventually, all is forgiven, the Count agrees to marry Elisetta, and happiness reigns supreme.

Cimarosa's main disadvantage *vis-à-vis* a modern audience is that his music reminds them, now of Mozart, now of Rossini, and that in each case they are inclined to compare him unfavourably with the more familiar master. But there is a great deal of excellent music in this opera, and the two finales are models of their kind, as are the arias for Carolina and Paolino, and the comedy duet between Geronimo and the Count.   H.

LUIGI CHERUBINI
(1760–1842)

MÉDÉE

Medea

OPERA in three acts by Luigi Cherubini; text (in French) by François Benoit Hoffmann, after Euripides. Première at Théâtre Feydeau, Paris,

March 13, 1797, with Scio, Gaveaux, Dessaules. First performed in Berlin, 1800, with Schick; Vienna, 1814, with Milder-Hauptmann; London, 1865, at Her Majesty's, with Tietjens, Günz, Santley; 1870, at Covent Garden with Tietjens. The spoken dialogue of the original was set to music by Franz Lachner in 1854 and by Arditi for the London production of 1865 (Lachner's recitatives have been used for most modern presentations). The opera was heard at la Scala in 1909 with Mazzoleni, Cannetti, Frascani, Isabelli, de Angelis, conductor Vitale, but not subsequently revived until in 1953 at the Florence Festival Callas sang it for the first time with Tucci, Barbieri, Picchi, Petri, conductor Gui (subsequently Callas was responsible for revivals at la Scala, Venice, Rome, and in 1958 at Dallas, Texas). Revived, 1958, Cassel with Gerda Lammers; 1959, Covent Garden, with Callas, Carlyle, Cossotto, Vickers, Zaccaria; 1962, Paris Opéra with Rita Gorr; 1968, Venice, with Gencer, Mazzuccato, Bottion, Ruggiero Raimondi, conductor Franci; 1969, Buenos Aires, with Jones, Lerer, Cossutta, Diaz, conductor Previtali; 1970, Holland Festival (concert) with Olivero; 1971, Frankfurt, with Silja; 1971, Mantua, with Olivero; 1972, Vienna, with Rysanek, Lilowa, Prevedi, Ghiuselev, conductor Stein. First performance in England of original Cherubini score, Durham, by the Palatine Group, 1967; and first in the U.S.A. of same version, University of Hartford, Connecticut, 1970, with Lee Venora.

CHARACTERS

Medea, *former wife of Jason* .... Soprano
Jason, *leader of the Argonauts* .... Tenor
Glauce (Dirce), *daughter of Creon* .... Soprano
Creon, *King of Corinth* .... Bass
Neris, *servant of Medea* .... Mezzo-Soprano
1st maidservant .... Soprano
2nd maidservant .... Soprano
Captain of the Guard .... Baritone
Two Children of Medea, Servants of Glauce, Argonauts,
Priests, Soldiers, People of Corinth
Time: Antiquity   *Place:* Corinth

Gluck's so-called 'reform' operas produced a crop of successors, but no more elevated or serious rival than Cherubini's *Medea*, in spite of the fact that in its original version the flow of the music is interrupted by spoken dialogue (this is noted as a circumstance differentiating *Medea* from for instance *Alceste*, not advanced as criticism). Not only is *Medea* a serious work of art but it contains a splendid title role. Madame Scio, the original protagonist, was generally supposed by her contemporaries to have died of a consumption brought on by the strenuous nature of the part only eight years after the première. Teresa Tietjens made it her most famous impersonation in the 1870's and '80's, and indeed it is one of the several operas of the classical epoch revived in the middle of the twentieth century for Maria Callas. Her dramatic intensity and magnificently constructive musical gifts were peculiarly well suited to this role, and she, a Greek, was assisted in the London revival of 1959 by a Greek producer, Alexis Minotis, a Greek designer, John Tsarouchis, and a Greek Bass, Nicola Zaccaria.

Jason, rightful heir to the throne of Thessaly, at his coming of age was set the task of recovering the Golden Fleece by his uncle, the usurper, Pelias. In the Argo he sailed to Colchis, where with the help of the King's daughter Medea he accomplished his mission and ended by eloping with her. King Aeetes followed the Argo, but Medea, to delay the pursuit, had her young brother Absyrtus cut up and thrown into the sea, knowing that Aeetes would collect the pieces in order that they might be decently buried. Arrived safely in Thessaly, Medea caused the death of Pelias, but Jason eventually abandoned her, and with his two sons fled to Corinth.

The overture's format, content and style perhaps explain why Beethoven held Cherubini in such esteem—it is a piece of high seriousness and a fitting precursor of an operatic version of Greek tragedy by one of the composers who most benefited from Gluck's theories. The curtain rises on the royal court of Creon at Corinth. The Argo can be seen riding at anchor in the background. Glauce, Creon's daughter, is surrounded by her women, two of whom lead the others in a graceful serenade to their mistress, whose marriage to Jason is planned for the next day. Eventually their pleas seem to allay most of her forebodings and she sings an aria, praying the God of Love to help her against Medea: 'Hymen, viens dissiper' ('O Amore, vieni a me!')—a rewarding solo of considerable technical difficulty and built on an ample scale.

Creon enters with Jason and assures him of his support, even when the people, incensed against Medea, demand the lives of her children in default of her own. Jason announces that his sailors wish to offer the Golden Fleece in homage to Glauce. They enter to a march, which in its day was much admired by such as *The Times* critic, Chorley. Glauce still fears that Medea will disrupt her happiness, but Jason in an

aria does his best to reassure her: 'Eloigné pour jamais d'une
épouse cruelle' ('Or che più non vedrò quella sposa crudele').
In a beautiful solo, to which Glauce, Jason and the Chorus
later add their voices, Creon invokes the blessings of the Gods
on the forthcoming marriage: 'Dieux et Déesses tutélaires'
('Pronube Dive, Dei custodi').

This trio is the end of tranquillity throughout the opera.
The Captain of the Guard announces that an unknown
woman demands admittance, she enters and unveils herself to
reveal Medea. The citizens and Argonauts retire, fearful of
what may result from Medea's presence. Creon threatens her
with imprisonment if the next day dawns to find her still in
Corinth, and then all retire, leaving her face to face with
Jason.

Medea is confident that the new and the old love struggle
in his breast for supremacy: he can never forget his love for
her nor what she has done for him. In a great aria, 'Vous
voyez de vos fils la mère infortunée' ('Dei tuoi figli la madre
tu vedi'), she pleads her love for him—she, who has never
before abased herself in front of anyone, begs for his pity and
his love. Her repeated cries of 'Ingrat!' ('Crudel!') would
melt the heart of a stronger man than Jason, and it is quite
clear from the succeeding duet that his resistance will not
stand up unaided against Medea's wiles. Together they curse
the fatal Golden Fleece, and he bids her go. She rounds on
him: 'Si tel est son malheur ton épouse en fuyant te percera
le coeur! ingrat!' ('Medea col suo fuggir il cor strap-
perà! Crudel!')—'As she leaves, Medea will transfix your
heart! Cruel man!'. The whole scene between Medea and
Jason—her aria and the extended duet—is a splendid example
of classical music drama.

Act II. The scene represents Creon's palace on one side
of the stage, the Temple of Hera on the other, and the drama
begins straightaway in the orchestra. Medea inveighs against
an injustice that would teach her children to hate their
mother. Neris, her confidante, tells her that the mob is
gathering and demands her blood, but Medea does not
hesitate. She will stay. At that moment, Creon comes out,
urging her to fly the country—if she remain, even he will not
be able to save her. In a scene of some power Medea pleads
her cause with Creon; let his love for his own children
influence him to be merciful to her and grant her a resting
place. He is adamant, supported by his warriors, as Neris joins

her voice to the pleas of Medea. Suddenly Medea seems to realise that her case is hopeless; she begs for one day to be added to the total she may stay in Corinth and Creon has not the heart to refuse her. As Creon and his retinue retire to the Palace, Medea collapses on the steps. Neris dare not interrupt her brooding silence; she will weep with her mistress and be faithful until death. It is a beautiful, mournful aria ('Ah, nos peines': 'Solo un pianto') that Neris sings with bassoon obbligato, the only moment of repose that the drama allows between the entrance of Medea and the final catastrophe.

Medea is implacable—Creon has granted her a day's grace, she will know how to use it! Her rival must die. More—is Jason not a father? As her thoughts begin to appal even her, Jason enters. Medea asks to see her children and rejoices at his evident love for them. In the course of their duet, Medea pretends that her heart will break if she never sees them again and Jason agrees to let them stay with her until her departure from Corinth. While Jason is obviously moved by memories of their love, Medea swears revenge for the sighs he has forced her to feign.

Medea orders Neris to bring her children to her, moreover to fetch as a wedding-present for Glauce the diadem and mantle once blessed by Phoebus Apollo. Neris is astonished at such generosity but leaves to fulfil her mistress's command as the wedding music is heard. Creon, Jason, Glauce, priests, warriors and citizens go in procession to the Temple of Hera, while Medea curses the wedding hymns to which she is listening. As the procession emerges from the temple, Medea hurls herself at the altar, seizes a burning brand and runs with it out of sight.

Act III. A hill, surmounted by a temple, on one side of which can be seen Creon's Palace. It is night and there is thunder. A short orchestral prelude of considerable power leads to the appearance of Medea before the temple. For the first time we see the sorceress in her true colours as she invokes the Infernal Gods to aid her purpose, the more so as she feels her resolve weaken at the sight of the children brought to her by Neris. She cannot bring herself to plunge a dagger into their defenceless breasts, and laments the power they still have over her: 'Du trouble affreux' ('Del fiero duol'), but ends the aria with a renewed threat of vengeance on Jason.

Neris tells of Glauce's grateful reception of Medea's gift

and Medea gloats over the fate that will be hers once she places the poisoned jewels on her forehead. Neris begs her to be content with this revenge and spare her children. At her mistress's command she takes them into the temple, and Medea is a prey to indecision; she must have a full revenge but they are her children as well as Jason's. At last all pity is purged from her heart. The cry can be heard from those in the temple who are witnesses to Glauce's horrible death, and Medea sets off like a wild beast to complete her vengeance. Jason appears with the crowd, Neris reveals Medea's purpose, but before he can reach the entrance of the temple, Medea emerges, flanked by the three Furies and brandishing in her hand the knife with which she has killed the children. As Jason, Neris and the crowd scatter, the temple bursts into flames. It is Medea's ultimate revenge.   H.

GASPARO SPONTINI
(1774–1851)
LA VESTALE
The Vestal Virgin

OPERA in three acts by Gasparo Spontini, libretto by Etienne de Jouy, originally written for Boieldieu, later refused by Méhul. Première, Paris Opéra, December 15, 1807, with Branchu, Maillard, Lainé, Dérivis. Given at the Opéra 213 times by 1857. First produced la Scala, 1824, with Ferron; King's Theatre, Haymarket, London, 1826, with Biagnoli; Philadelphia, 1828. Revived Covent Garden in German, 1842, with Schodl; la Scala, 1908, with Mazzoleni, Micucci-Anelli, Emilio de Marchi, Stracciari, de Angelis, conductor Toscanini; Buenos Aires, 1910, with Mazzoleni, Cuccini, Rousselière, Cirino; Metropolitan, 1925, with Ponselle, Matzenauer, Edward Johnson, de Luca, Mardones, conductor Serafin; Florence Festival, 1933, with Ponselle, Stignani, Melandri, Biasini, Pasero, conductor Gui; la Scala, 1955, with Callas, Stignani, Corelli, Sordello, Rossi-Lemeni.

CHARACTERS

Licinio, *a Roman General* .... Tenor
Giulia, *a young Vestal virgin* .... Soprano

Cinna, *a centurion*................. Tenor/Baritone
The Pontifex Maximus .... Bass
The Chief Priestess ....Mezzo-Soprano
A Consul................................. Bass
Vestals, Priests, People, Matrons, Young Women, Senators
Consuls, Lictors, Warriors, Gladiators, Dancers, Children
Prisoners
Place: Rome

After a spacious overture, the scene is set in the Forum in
Rome, in front of the Temple of Vesta. Preparations for the
triumph of the Roman leader Licinio are in progress. Licinio
admits to his friend Cinna that he still loves one of the Vestal
priestesses, Giulia by name, who was once affianced to him
but whom he finds on his return from the wars vowed to the
service of Vesta. Licinio and Cinna join their voices in a duet

The Chief Priestess and Giulia lead the Vestals in
processional hymn towards the temple, and instruct them
that their duties will consist of crowning the hero of the
triumph. They withdraw, and Giulia and the High Priestess
are left alone, for the latter to attempt in a recitative and aria
that is Gluck-like in its intensity ('E l'amore un mostro') to
strengthen the resolve of the former to keep her vows of
chastity. Giulia prays for help and begs that she may not be
in the Temple to receive the victor of the wars, but the High
Priestess insists that she fulfil her duties. Giulia left alone
sings of her guilty love.

A vast procession comes towards the temple and the
people hymn the victorious general; Licinio plots with Cinna
the abduction of Giulia, but in a moment it is time for Giulia
to crown him with a golden laurel wreath. An ensemble
develops during which Licinio tries to tell Giulia of his plan
for her elopement with him that very night. Licinio is
congratulated on his victory, and, in a tune which might have
come from *Tannhäuser* or *Rienzi*, all praise his valour which
has brought them peace. The act ends with extended
triumphal dances.

Act II. Night. In the Temple of Vesta, the virgin
priestesses worship the goddess and the High Priestess con
signs to Giulia the duty of tending the sacred flame, which
must never be extinguished. Alone, Giulia, in the best known
scene of the opera, prays for the goddess's intervention to
release her from the profane love which torments her. The

weeping phrases, the classical shape, the underlying drama of his *scena* convincingly argue Spontini's claim (made in conversation with Wagner) to be recognised as the natural successor of Gluck, rather than just the contemporary and rival of Cherubini, as we today might think of him. The intense lyricism of the prayer ('Tu che invoco con orrore') is succeeded by a very dramatic section ('Su questo sacro altare') in which Giulia admits to herself that her love for Licinio is all-powerful, and the aria ends with an impassioned avowal of her betrayal of trust as a priestess ('Sospendete qual che istante').

Licinio enters and declares the strength of his love. Soon their voices are joined in passionate duet, and they do not notice until too late that the flame has died out. Cinna warns them to fly while there is still time, but voices can be heard approaching and Licinio rushes off to get help. The Pontifex Maximus denounces Giulia for the neglect of her sacred duties, and she begs for death as the just reward of her impiety. In a beautiful aria ('O nume tutelar'), Giulia prays to the gods, not for herself but that Licinio may not be involved in her fate. She refuses to reveal his name to the Pontifex Maximus, who curses her and orders that she be first divested of the veil and ornaments of her priestly office and then buried alive.

Act III. Near where Giulia's tomb lies open and waiting for her, Licinio inveighs against the cruelty of her impending fate. His friend Cinna begs him not to resort to force but to try to persuade the Pontifex Maximus to clemency. Licinio's efforts to this end meet with a blank refusal from the priest, until in despair he declares himself Giulia's accomplice and in a duet denounces the cruelty the Pontifex Maximus dispenses in the name of religion.

In spite of a warning from the Augurer, the Pontifex Maximus intends to carry through his plan, and Giulia is led in conducted by lictors and surrounded by Vestals, wearing the black veil of her shame. Giulia bids farewell to her companions and to the High Priestess. Her veil is placed on the altar; if the goddess pardons her, then she will cause the veil to burn with sacred fire as a sign of forgiveness. The Vestals pray, the Pontifex Maximus orders Giulia to descend to her tomb and she tenderly bids farewell to her lover ('Caro oggetto'). Even the precipitate arrival of Licinio cannot change the course of events; Giulia denies that she even

knows him, and descends into the tomb. Suddenly the s⸱
darkens, and a shaft of lightning ignites the veil on the alta⸱
Vesta has forgiven, Giulia is released, and the opera ends with
choral and balletic rejoicings, dedicated to the glory of Venus.

H.

GIOACCHINO ANTONIO ROSSINI

(1792–1868)

L'ITALIANA IN ALGERI

The Italian Girl in Algiers

OPERA in two acts by Gioacchino Rossini; text by A. Anelli (originally written for L. Mosca and performed at la Scala in 1808). Première on May 22, 1813, at Teatro San Benedetto, Venice. First performed in London, Haymarket Theatre, 1819 (in Italian); Princess's Theatre, 1844 (in English); New York, 1832 (in Italian). Revived Metropolitan, New York, 1919, with Besanzoni, Hackett, Didur, de Luca, conductor Papi; Turin, 1925, with Supervia, conductor Gui; Rome, 1927, with Supervia, Folgar, Bettoni, Scattola; Paris, 1933; la Scala, Milan, 1933, with Castagna; Covent Garden, 1935, with Supervia, Ederle, Bettoni, Scattola, conductor Bellezza; Colon, Buenos Aires, 1938, with Pederzini, conductor Serafin; Basle, 1938, with Else Böttcher; Florence Festival, 1941, with Pederzini; la Fenice, Venice, 1946, with Danco; Rome Opera, 1948, with Pederzini, Sinimberghi, Bettoni, Ghirardini, conductor Gui; la Scala, 1953, with Simionato, Dobbs, Valletti, Petri, Bruscantini; Glyndebourne, 1957, with Dominguez, Oncina, Montarsolo, Cortis, conductor Gui; Sadler's Wells at London Coliseum, 1968, with Patricia Kern as Isabella, conductor Mario Bernardi; Metropolitan, New York, 1974, with Marilyn Horne.

CHARACTERS

Mustafa, *Bey of Algiers* .... Bass
Elvira, *his wife* .... Soprano
Zulma, *her confidante* .... Contralto
Haly, *in the service of the Bey* .... Bass
Lindoro, *an Italian in love with Isabella* .... Tenor
Isabella .... Contralto
Taddeo, *an old Italian* .... Baritone

Rossini's *L'Italiana in Algeri* is *commedia dell'arte* set to music. The plot and the words are less those of a well-constructed play, rather the situations used by the actors of the *commedia dell'arte* for their free invention. The nearest parallel to it is the modern music hall, where the comedian was accustomed to 'gag' at will, and in fact relied very largely on his method to hold his audience's attention. Improvisation was out of the question the moment music entered into partnership, but the plot provides plenty of evidence as to its origin.

On its first performance, the opera was immediately successful. 'When Rossini wrote *L'Italiana*', notes Stendhal, 'his youthful genius was bursting into flower.' And the brilliant character of the work shows clearly the spirit, optimism, and geniality of youth (Rossini was only twenty-one at the time). The whole work was written in twenty-seven days.

Act I. The overture, one of the composer's most famous, begins with a strong feeling of latent drama, but this soon gives way to an enchanting *allegro*. The interplay of the woodwind, and in fact the writing for this section of the orchestra throughout the opera, is particularly attractive.

We are in the palace of the Bey of Algiers. A chorus of the eunuchs of the harem (tenors and basses, surprisingly enough) laments the sad lot of women, while Elvira, the Bey's wife, assisted by her confidante, Zulma, bemoans her own tragedy —her husband no longer loves her. Enter the Bey in person. With a multitude of roulades he inveighs against the arrogance of women, and, the moment Elvira speaks directly to him, protests that his eardrums are broken. A lively ensemble ensues (it is a quartet, Haly, the captain of the Bey's corsairs, having joined the family quarrel), and at its end Haly is told by the Bey that he must go off and find him an Italian wife—nothing else will satisfy him. (Haly's name will impress the Englishman as more apt to the context if he imagines it without the initial 'H'.)

The Bey has in his service an Italian, now one of the slaves, by name Lindoro. In a slow cavatina, 'Languir per una bella', he laments the absence of his beloved. It is a particularly attractive example of Rossini's highly decorated lyric style, and is followed by a vigorous *cabaletta*, no less full of coloratura and, with its high C's, B naturals, and B flats, calculated to try the technique of any but the most agile of

tenors. The Bey asks Lindoro whether he would like to get
married. Not unless he was in love, is Lindoro's reply. A
charming duet ensues between the two. The subject is
marriage, with particular reference to the qualifications
necessary in the prospective partner, and in style it is not
unlike that between Almaviva and Figaro in the first act of *Il
Barbiere*.

The scene changes. Isabella, who has been roaming the seas
in search of her lost lover Lindoro, is involved in a shipwreck,
conveniently on the shore of Algeria. Haly's men exclaim on
the beauty of the slaves, and on Mustafa's good fortune in
securing so many additions to his harem. 'Cruda sorte!'
(Cruel fate) sings Isabella; she is in this danger only because
of her faithfulness to Lindoro—but the *cabaletta* leaves us in
no doubt whatsoever as to her confidence in her own ability
to look after herself. All are made prisoner, and Haly is
overjoyed to find that Isabella and Taddeo, an ageing and
comic admirer she has brought with her for company on the
voyage, are indeed Italians; they shall go to the Bey. Left
alone with Taddeo, Isabella seems less dismayed than he at
the indication that she is destined for the Bey's Seraglio.
They quarrel and argue about the situation in their duet, 'Ai
capricci della sorte', but all is made up in a charming *allegro
vivace*, in which they agree that the status of uncle and niece
(which they have decided shall be their official relationship)
has its advantages. The tune is enchantingly silly, and an
excellent example of Rossini's ability to write music that is
genuinely comic as well as being, in the right hands, extremely pretty.

We return to the palace. Elvira and Zulma remonstrate
with Lindoro because he seems disinclined to marry the
former, even though the Bey has offered him freedom (and
money) if he will take her off his hands. Haly brings the news
of Isabella's capture, and the Bey rejoices at his good fortune
in an aria whose coloratura difficulties rival those of a Handel
bass aria: 'Già d'insolito ardore'. After he has gone, Elvira
admits she still loves her inconstant husband, but Lindoro
comforts her: if she comes to Italy with him, she will find
husbands and lovers as she pleases.

The finale begins with the eunuchs singing the praises of
'Mustafa the scourge of women, who changes them from
tigresses to lambs'. Isabella is led in and cannot contain her
amusement at the sight of Mustafa; her tune is irresistibly

ɔmic, and the duet as she makes up to the bemused Mustafa
s very funny. Taddeo pushes himself forward: is he not her
ıncle? A quartet follows between Isabella, Taddeo, Haly, and
Mustafa, and at its end, Elvira, Zulma, and Lindoro enter the
ıall. Isabella and Lindoro recognise each other, and the
ʃuartet becomes a septet, dominated by a florid figure for
Lindoro and Mustafa. Isabella makes a fuss when she dis-
:overs that Elvira is the Bey's wife whom he is discarding,
ınd the complications mount until the end of the act.

Act II. The eunuchs comment on Mustafa's love-lorn
:ondition. Haly advises Elvira and Zulma to keep on the right
ide of Mustafa; he may change his mind again. At the
noment, there appears no prospect of this, for, no sooner has
ıe come in, than he sends his wife and her slave to tell the
talian girl he wishes to drink coffee with her later. Isabella,
ılone with Lindoro, reproaches him because of his forth-
:oming marriage to Elvira, but eventually accepts his pro-
estations of unchanging affection for herself, and together
hey plan an escape, the prospect of which spurs Lindoro to
ın even more exuberant expression of devotion than here-
ofore. Mustafa tells Taddeo that he will make him, in
ıonour of his niece, Grand Kaimakan of Algeria. The chorus
ing his praises, and Taddeo follows with an amusing aria, 'Ho
ın gran peso sulla testa'.

Isabella is in front of her looking-glass, finishing dressing.
Ilvira and Zulma come to deliver the Bey's message, and
sabella orders coffee for three from her slave, Lindoro, saying
he would not dream of excluding the Bey's wife from the
ɔarty. She will in fact, as woman to woman, give her a much
ıeeded lesson in man-management. Sitting in front of her
ɔoking-glass and watched from behind by Lindoro, Haly and
Mustafa, she sings 'Per lui, che adoro', which is in effect an
ria with comments and later accompaniment from the three
nen. Mustafa cannot wait to be alone with Isabella and tells
'addeo that it is his duty as Kaimakan to conduct her to his
ɔresence and leave them alone together. At the beginning of
he quintet, Mustafa makes formal and florid presentation to
sabella of Taddeo, Grand Kaimakan; this over, he sets about
etting rid of the men, but with little success. Coffee comes
ı, and, after a moment, so does Elvira, and what has begun
s a quartet becomes a quintet. Mustafa becomes enraged,
ınd the ensemble ends in a *crescendo* of pandemonium.

Haly is found alone; in a pleasantly straightforward aria,

'Le femine d'Italia', he praises the wiles of Italian women an
the way in which they insinuate themselves into men's
affections. No sooner has he left the stage than Taddeo and
Lindoro appear, the former telling the latter in confidence
that he loves Isabella, who he once thought loved a certain
Lindoro, but who he finds loves him (Taddeo) truly after
all. Lindoro is suitably impressed by the announcement, but
privately finds time to express pleasure that his rival should
be so obviously insignificant. As Mustafa comes in, Lindoro
whispers to his compatriot to back him up in the plan he is
about to put forward. Mustafa seems disposed to complain of
the treatment he has received at Isabella's hands, but he is
reassured, and told she waits only until he joins that ancient
and noble Italian order of the 'Pappatacci' (literally 'eat and be
silent', but having the significance of a complacent husband).
Mustafa, who is quite unaware of what it implies, consents to
be enrolled, and the trio which ensues, known as the trio of
the 'Pappatacci', once sent the public raving with delight—
indeed, it might well do so again. Lindoro has a flowing, high
tune and he is supported by the two lower voices to make a
very comic effect. It is a charming piece and one of the gems
of the score. Haly meanwhile is suspicious: why, he asks
Zulma, does Isabella give too much to drink to the eunuchs
and the Moors? For fun, she tells him, and to make it into a
true holiday.

In preparation for the ceremony to enrol Mustafa in the
inglorious ranks, Isabella gathers together all the Italians in
the Bey's service and appeals to their patriotism to help her
carry out her plans, which include escape for them all during
the course of the initiation ceremony. They greet her in a
chorus, and she sings her recitative ('Amici, in ogni evento'
and rondo ('Pensa alla patria'), taking the chance of having a
dig at Taddeo and a kind word for Lindoro. This is a big-scale
bravura aria, and contains in its first words one of Rossini'
few overt references to patriotism (that is to say, before the
time of *Guillaume Tell*).

Announced by Lindoro, the 'Pappatacci' chorus comes on
with horns blowing. Mustafa, prompted by Isabella, swears to
obey all the rules of the order, which he then repeats after
Taddeo; what it amounts to is that the duty of the model
husband is to eat and sleep soundly—nothing else. Isabella
and Lindoro indulge in a display of affection as a 'test' for
Mustafa—he fails, but is prompted by Taddeo, and swears he

will not offend against the rules again. A chorus of European slaves can be heard from outside, where the boat Isabella has chartered to take them all home is waiting in full sight of the Bey's palace. Isabella and Lindoro prepare to go on board, and Mustafa treats it all as part of his initiation, although Taddeo is worried at the turn events are taking. In an *allegro*, Mustafa discovers his mistake through the intervention of Elvira, Zulma, and Haly, who convince him he has been hoodwinked. He turns to Elvira as his true love—Italians were only a passing fancy. Isabella and her party are still within sight of the palace, and the opera ends with mutual congratulations from both parties, escapers, and erstwhile captors as well.   H.

IL TURCO IN ITALIA
The Turk in Italy

Opera in two (now customarily three) acts by Gioacchino Rossini, libretto by Felice Romani. Première, la Scala, Milan, August 14, 1814, with Maffei-Festa, Giovanni David, Filippo Galli, Luigi Pacini. First performed, King's Theatre, London, 1821, with Giuseppina and Giuseppe Ronzi de Regnis (their London debuts); New York, 1826; Edinburgh, 1827. In Italy, not given between 1855 and its revival at the Teatro Eliseo, Rome, in 1950, with Callas, Valletti, Stabile, Bruscantini, conductor Gavazzeni; la Scala, 1955, with virtually the same cast; Edinburgh Festival, 1957, by Piccola Scala, with Ratti, Cossotto, Alva, Corena, Bruscantini, conductor Gavazzeni: Glyndebourne, 1970, with Sciutti, Benelli, Roux, Montarsolo, conductor Pritchard.

CHARACTERS

Selim, *the Turk* .... Bass
Fiorilla, *a young Neapolitan wife* .... Soprano
Geronio, *her husband* .... Bass
Narciso, *in love with Fiorilla* .... Tenor
Zaida, *a Turk* .... Mezzo-Soprano
Albazar, *a Turk* .... Tenor
Prosdocimo, *a poet* .... Baritone
Time: Eighteenth Century   *Place:* In and around Naples

Act I.   After a witty and typical overture, of which more than one version exists, the first scene shows a gypsy encamp-

ment on the outskirts of Naples. Members of the crowd are
having their fortunes told, and amongst the most active
fortune-tellers are two runaway Turks, Zaida and Albazar by
name. Zaida is unhappy: a slave in Turkey, she loved her
master and despairs of ever seeing him again.

To the camp in search of inspiration comes Prosdocimo, a
poet, ordered by his patron to produce a stage comedy. He is
unable to believe that yet another piece on the theme of
flirtatious wife and ridiculous husband—as are in real life
Donna Fiorilla and Don Geronio—would be found acceptable. Just then, none other than Don Geronio appears,
looking for a gypsy to read his palm and advise him how to
cope with his high-mettled wife. It appears that the stars are
not propitious, and he is thoroughly disgruntled at the
gypsy's predictions. The scene concludes (although this
section is usually omitted) with the questioning of Zaida by
Prosdocimo. She reveals that she was driven away from her
master, Selim Damelec of Erzerum, by the intrigues of her
rivals, and Prosdocimo comforts her with the news that a
Turkish Pasha is due to sail into Naples at any moment;
perhaps he would intercede for her with her master.

The harbour-side. Donna Fiorilla is introduced in a
bravura aria ('Non si dà follia maggiore'): she discourses to the
bystanders on the agreeable complications of her love life,
but quickly turns her attention to a ship flying the Turkish
flag which nears the quayside. Announced in the minor, as
befits a late-eighteenth or early-nineteenth century musical
Turk, Selim's cavatina ('Bella Italia') is in the florid style
Rossini favoured for his comic basses. Fiorilla is obviously
ripe for a flirtation, and Selim abruptly diverts his praises
from the country to its inhabitants, particularly those of the
female sex. Fiorilla joins in the concluding phrases of the
aria, there is an exchange of compliments, and the scene ends
with a quick duet for her and Selim.

As well as an ageing husband, Fiorilla is blessed with a
young lover, Narciso, and he gives vent to his feelings in an
aria ('Un vago sembiante di gioia'). But the conclusion of the
scene in the harbour is dominated by the Pirandellian
Prosdocimo, who sees in the way events are shaping a perfect
theme for his comedy. As he reflects on the subject—a stupid
husband, a flighty wife, a lover supplanted by a handsome
and amorous Turk; what more can one ask for?—he is
overheard by the husband and the lover he refers to, and the

soliloquy becomes a trio. To the ingredients he mentions, they wish to add another, a poet quickened by immediate physical chastisement, but Prosdocimo eludes them and their discomfiture is complete.

The scene changes to an apartment in Fiorilla's house. Fiorilla is entertaining Selim to coffee—a pastime, judging from this opera and *L'Italiana*, that librettists seem to have thought particularly suitable when Italian women flirt with Turks. When he protests his devotion, she makes some sly remarks about the hundred women of his harem, and the fine quartet (which in most modern versions ends Act I) begins with their amorous fencing. When Geronio enters, Selim flies at him in a passion, but Fiorilla turns the whole incident in her favour, has Geronio paying compliments to Selim, and only Narciso is put out by her handling of events. The quartet bubbles along, and before it is over Selim has managed to make an assignation with Fiorilla for that night at the harbour.

The penultimate scene of Act I (or nowadays usually the first of Act II) takes place in Geronio's house. He is full of regrets for his marriage to someone so much younger than himself, whom he moreover cannot control. Firmness and decision are necessary, suggests Prosdocimo, but, alone with Fiorilla, Geronio has no sort of success with the new formula. Once more, Fiorilla dominates him completely. At the start of their duet ('Per piacere alla Signora, che ho da far') he is already apologetic, by the middle she is feigning love and (in a graphic musical phrase) imitating weeping, and telling him that it is *he* who has caused *her* such sorrow; by the end he is eating out of her hand.

The finale moves to the gypsy quarter, to which comes Selim to find out if the omens are good for his planned elopment with Fiorilla. Zaida recognises him and a reconciliation seems likely, much to the discomfiture of Prosdocimo, since this is the last turn he wants events to take if his story is to come up to scratch. The arrival of Narciso in obvious distress does little to rectify the situation, but the appearance of an apparently love-lorn Fiorilla is a distinct improvement—better still, she is pursued by her irate husband. As Fiorilla and Zaida confront one another, all is ready for an ensemble of misunderstanding, with everyone pulling apparently in different directions. The fight of the two women finally convinces Prosdocimo that nature has

imitated art to perfection: he could not wish for a bette
finale.

Act II (Act III more often). Prosdocimo, intent on the
development of his plot, urges Geronio to catch Fiorilla and
Selim together that night and so put an end to the intrigue
No sooner has the poet left than Selim appears, proposing a
solution that would resolve the present difficulties: why
should Geronio not follow Turkish custom and sell him
Fiorilla—after six years of marriage to one woman he must be
a bit tired of her! Their duet, with its extended *crescendo* in
the final section, is one of Rossini's masterpieces and the
equal of that for Dandini and Don Magnifico in *Cenerentola.*

Fiorilla has an aria with chorus of a delicacy that can only
be described as Mozartian ('Se il zefiro si posa'), after which
she proclaims her intention of worsting anyone who dares set
herself up as a rival. When she is joined by Zaida, Selim is
bidden to choose between them, but before he can make up
his mind, Zaida renounces a claim that she does not want to
press in such circumstances. The field is apparently free for a
clearing up of misunderstandings between Fiorilla and Selim,
and their duet ('Credete alle femine') with its florid writing is
a moment of near-seriousness. It is left to Prosdocimo to
re-introduce the note of comedy—at a masked ball planned for
that evening Selim is to carry off Fiorilla, he tells Geronio
and Narciso. Why should Zaida not dress up as Fiorilla, and
Geronio disguise himself as Selim? The plot thickens when
Narciso, beside himself with unhappiness, decides to take
advantage of the scheme and appear as a third Selim.

At the ball, a festal chorus and a waltz set the scene for the
comedy of errors which is worked out in a splendid quintet
('Oh guardate, che accidente, non conosco più mia moglie').
All the conspirators in their present predicaments express
consternation about their respective futures; the early part of
the ensemble, partly unaccompanied, brings to mind nothing
so much as *Così fan tutte*, but the *allegro* is full of high
spirits that are pure Rossini—he even, at one point, adds a
trumpet to the voices for good measure.

The upshot is that Fiorilla's escapade is unmasked, and in an
aria she laments her disgrace and the loss at one and the
same time of honour, husband and peace of mind. In the end,
all is well; Selim bids farewell to Italy in order to return to
Turkey with Zaida; Fiorilla remains 'faithful' to Geronio;
Narciso decides to profit from the examples before him; and

Prosdocimo has the ending for his play. All join in the moral:
'Restate contenti, felici vivete'.   H.

ELISABETTA, REGINA D'INGHILTERRA

Elizabeth, Queen of England

Opera in two acts by Gioacchino Rossini, libretto by Giovanni
Schmidt. Première at San Carlo, Naples, October 4, 1815, with Isabella
Colbran, Dardanelli, Nozzari, Garcia the elder. First performed
Dresden, 1818; London, 1818, with Fodor, Corri, Crivelli, Garcia; Paris,
1822. Revived by Radio Italiana for Coronation of Queen Elizabeth II,
1953, with Maria Vitale, Lina Pagliughi, Campora, Pirino. No stage
performance can be traced from 1841 to 1968, when the opera was
revived at the Camden Festival, London. Revived Palermo, 1971 (and
Edinburgh Festival 1972), with Leyla Gencèr, Margherita Guglielmi,
Umberto Grilli, Pietro Bottazzo, conductors Gavazzeni and Sanzogno.

CHARACTERS

Elizabeth I, *Queen of England* . . . . Soprano
The Earl of Leicester, *Commander of the army* . . Tenor
Matilda, *his secret wife* . . . . Soprano
The Duke of Norfolk . . . . Tenor
Henry (Enrico), *Matilda's brother* . . . . . Mezzo-Soprano
Fitzwilliam (Guglielmo), *Captain of the Royal Guard*
. . . . Tenor
Courtiers, Soldiers and People
Place: London   *Time:* Late Sixteenth Century

After his successes in the North of Italy, Rossini was in
1815 engaged by the famous impresario Domenica Barbaia to
work for the San Carlo in Naples.[1] Barbaia, who had recently
rebuilt the theatre after it had burnt down and was in high
favour with King Ferdinand, is one of the most extraordinary
figures in the history of opera. He started life as a waiter, was
the first to think of mixing whipped cream with coffee or

---

[1] Between 1815 and 1822, Rossini wrote nine serious operas and one
comic for Barbaia. Andrew Porter, in an article for the Edinburgh
Festival in 1972, has suggested that it was only later in Paris that the
composer had his chance to realise to the full the ideals he had
adumbrated in the Neapolitan operas of 1815-22.

chocolate, speculated in army contracts during the
Napoleonic Wars, and made a fortune at the gambling rooms
in Milan. He is traditionally supposed to have been illiterate,
but there is no doubt at all as to his brilliant success as an
impresario—no contradiction involved, maybe, either.

The libretto of Rossini's first opera for Barbaia was
adapted from a contemporary play, which had been taken
from an English novel called *The Recess* written by a certain
Sophia Lee in 1785. Rossini wrote it for Isabella Colbran,
Barbaia's mistress and later to become the composer's wife. It
has two noteworthy musico-historical features: for the first
time Rossini gave his recitatives orchestral accompaniment
throughout, and, also for the first time, he wrote out all the
vocal ornaments in full—he had heard the castrato Velluti
indulge in such prodigality of ornamentation in *Aureliano in
Palmira* that he became alarmed at what a less musical singer
might do in comparable circumstances. In a single word,
Rossini was writing for a new audience and he would leave
nothing to chance in his efforts to conquer it.

Act I.   For the overture Rossini borrowed from his own
less successful opera *Aureliano*, a trick he was to repeat less
than two years later when he used exactly the same piece of
music for *Il Barbiere di Siviglia*, the one overture thus doing
duty for no less than three operas.

Leicester's military triumph in Scotland is being celebrated
at the Palace of Whitehall in London, where Norfolk makes
no attempt to hide his jealousy. The Courtiers salute the
Queen, who greets them in dignified (and florid) music and
gives vent to her feelings of joy in music hardly
distinguishable from 'Io sono docile' (*Barbiere*)—there are a
few, but a very few, differences between the two arias,
written only eighteen months apart. Leicester is announced,
proclaims the defeat of the Scots and is welcomed by the
Queen, to the chagrin of Norfolk. Leicester says he has
brought the sons of the nobility as hostages from Scotland,
but, in an aside, cannot hide his surprise at seeing amongst
them, disguised as a boy, his secretly married wife, Matilda.
The Queen takes them all into her service as pages. Alone,
Leicester reproaches Matilda with her foolhardy behaviour—
as a relation of Mary, Queen of Scots, she is in great
danger—in a duet ('Incauta, che festi?'), an immediate success
at the première according to Stendhal. Matilda, who has
revealed her knowledge of Elizabeth's love for Leicester, is

eft with her brother Henry, one of the hostages, to bewail
her ill fortune in a mellifluous aria ('Sento un intorna voce').

The false Norfolk, under the pledge of friendship, learns
from Leicester the secret of his marriage. Norfolk hastens to
tell the news to the Queen, who herself has planned to marry
Leicester, and whose reaction to the news is expressed with a
mixture of fury and dignity in the beautiful duet which ensues for her and Norfolk ('Perche mai, destin crudele'). Its vigorous quick section foreshadows *William Tell* or even early Verdi.

In a few bars before the finale begins, Elizabeth orders
Fitzwilliam, who already suspects Norfolk's perfidy, to have
the guard stand by and sends for Leicester and the Scottish
hostages. Matilda she quickly recognises from her obviously
anxious manner, and she proceeds to confront Leicester as
her principal adviser and the hero of the moment. When she
offers to make him her Consort, he is thrown into complete
confusion and tries to refuse. The Queen flies into a passion,
denounces the unhappy pair and summons the guard to
arrest them. The finale, described by Stendhal as
'magnificent', is an impressive piece, at one moment full of
sound and fury, at the next reminiscent of Mozart.

Act II. Elizabeth sends for Matilda and demands, in
what is perhaps the finest scene of the opera, that she sign a
paper renouncing all claim to Leicester in return for the
safety of her husband and her brother ('Pensa che sol per
poco sospendo l'ira mia'). Stendhal describes at some length
the great success in this scene of Colbran for whom (or for
her Royalist connections) he usually reserves little but scorn.
Bellini may well have taken the duet, particularly its slow
second section, as a model for his famous 'Mira, o Norma'.
Enter Leicester to read the document, to defy the Queen by
tearing it up, and to turn the splendid duet into a no less
notable trio. They are led off under arrest, but the Queen in a
moment of revulsion and understanding orders the banishment
of the false Norfolk, whose duplicity she has now seen through.

Outside the Tower of London, people lament the
impending fate of Leicester, and there follows a scene in
which Norfolk, now under sentence of exile, tries, in an aria
with chorus, to act the part of rabble-raiser.

An evocative prelude leads us to a dungeon in the Tower,
where Leicester laments his fate. Flute and cor anglais
continue the tale of his uneasy, half-voiced dreams. The false
Norfolk brings him promises of help; and their florid duet,

'Deh, scusa i trasporti', is something of a rarity, an extended movement for two tenors. To the prison comes the Queen, anxious to see her favourite before his execution. Norfolk has meanwhile concealed himself, and Matilda and Henry have managed to insinuate themselves into the dungeon. Leicester hears that it was Norfolk who accused him, the Queen comes to understand the extent of Norfolk's treachery, and Norfolk himself draws his dagger and is about to stab the Queen when Matilda throws herself in between them.

In the splendid and (Stendhal tells us) in its day much admired finale, the Queen denounces Norfolk and condemns him to death, then, in a slow[1] and increasingly decorated section in triple time ('Bell'alme generose'), turns to Matilda and Leicester and, in gratitude for their loyalty, extends her mercy to them and grants them their freedom. The voices of the people pleading Leicester's cause can be heard from outside, Elizabeth shows them their liberated hero, and the opera comes to an end with roulades from the Queen, who is acclaimed by the crowd.   H.

IL BARBIERE DI SIVIGLIA
The Barber of Seville

Opera in two acts by Rossini; text by Sterbini founded on Beaumarchais. Première on February 20, 1816, at the Teatro Argentina, Rome, with Giorgi-Righetti, M. Garcia, L. Zamboni, Vitanelli Botticelli, conductor Rossini (as *Almaviva, ossia l'Inutile Precauzione*, title of *Il Barbiere* first used at Bologna, 1816). Haymarket, London, 1818, with Fodor, Garcia, Naldi, Angrisani, Ambrogetti; Covent Garden, 1818, with Mrs Dickons, Mr. Jones, Mr. Liston, Mr. Fawcett, Mr. Isaacs; New York, 1819 (in English), with Thomas Phillips and Miss Leesugg; 1825 (in Italian), with Garcia the Elder as Almaviva, Garcia the Younger as Figaro, Malibran as Rosina; Metropolitan, 1883, with Sembrich, Stagno, del Puente, Mirabella, Corsini, conductor Vianesi. Revived Covent Garden, 1919, with Borghi-Zerni, Tom Burke, Sammarco, Cotreuil, Malatesta, conductor Mugnone; 1925, with dal Monte, Borgioli, Franci, Cotreuil, Malatesta, conductor Votto; 1926, with Capsir, Hackett, Badini, Chaliapin, Malatesta; 1935, with Pons, Dino Borgioli, de Luca, Pinza, Scattola, conductor Bellezza; 1946, with Carosio, Infantino, Franci; 1960, with Berganza, Alva, Panerai, Vinco,

[1] Familiar to English ballet audiences as Lisa's flute tune in *La Fille Mal Gardée*.

Corena, conductor Giulini; at la Scala, Milan, 1952, with Simionato, Tagliavini, Bechi, Rossi-Lemeni, Luise, conductor de Sabata, and 1956 with Callas, Alva, Gobbi, Rossi-Lemeni, Luise, conductor Giulini.

CHARACTERS

Count Almaviva . . . . Tenor
Doctor Bartolo . . . . Basso-Comico
Don Basilio, *A singing teacher* . . . . Bass
Figaro, *a barber* . . . . Baritone
Fiorello, *servant to the count* . . . . Bass
Ambrogio, *servant to the doctor* . . . . Bass
Rosina, *the doctor's ward* . . . . Mezzo-Soprano
Berta, *Rosina's governess* . . . . Soprano
 Notary, Constable, Musicians, and Soldiers
Time: Seventeenth Century   *Place:* Seville, Spain

Upon episodes in Beaumarchais's trilogy of *Figaro* comedies, two composers, Mozart and Rossini, based operas that have long maintained their hold upon the repertory. The three Beaumarchais comedies are *Le Barbier de Séville, Le Mariage de Figaro*, and *La Mère Coupable*. Mozart selected the second of these, Rossini the first; so that although in point of composition Mozart's *Figaro* (May 1786) antedates Rossini's *Barbiere* (February 1816) by nearly thirty years, *Il Barbiere di Siviglia* precedes *Le Nozze di Figaro* in point of action. In both operas Figaro is a prominent character, and, while the composers were of wholly different nationality and race, their music is genuinely and equally sparkling and witty.

There is much to say about the first performance of *Il Barbiere di Siviglia*; also about the overture, the origin of Almaviva's graceful solo, 'Ecco ridente in cielo', and the music selected by prima donnas to sing in the 'lesson scene' in the second act. But these details are better preceded by some information regarding the story and the music.

Act I, Scene i. A street by Dr. Bartolo's house. Count Almaviva, a Grandee of Spain, is desperately in love with Rosina, the ward of Doctor Bartolo. Accompanied by his servant Fiorello and a band of musicians, he serenades her with the smooth, flowing measures of 'Ecco ridente in cielo' (Lo, smiling in the eastern sky):

Ec - co ri - den - te in cie - - lo

He pays off the musicians and tells them to go away quietly, but his generosity provokes a hubbub as they crowd round him to say 'thank you'.

Just then Figaro, the barber, the general factotum and busybody of the town, dances in, singing the famous patter air, 'Largo al factotum della città' (Room for the city's factotum):

Lar - go al fac - to - tum del - la cit - tà   lar - go

As a bravura aria for high baritone it is perhaps unequalled and certainly it has no rival in point of popularity for voices of this type.

Figaro is Dr. Bartolo's barber, and, learning from the Count of his heart's desire, immediately plots with him to bring about an introduction to Rosina.

Rosina is strictly watched by her guardian, Doctor Bartolo who himself plans to marry his ward, since she has both beauty and money. In this he is assisted by Basilio, a music-master. Rosina, however, returns the affection of the Count although she has never met him, and, in spite of the watchfulness of her guardian, she contrives to drop a letter from the balcony to Almaviva, declaring her passion, and at the same time requesting to know her lover's name. He tells her in an aria that it is Lindoro.

A clever duet between Figaro and the Count brings the scene to a close — in the first section Almaviva promises money to the Barber, the second is in praise of love and pleasure, and Figaro's skill in providing them.

Scene ii.   A room in Dr. Bartolo's house. Rosina enters. She sings the brilliant 'Una voce poco fa' (A little voice I

U - na vo - ce po - co fà   qui nel cor mi ri - suo - no

heard just now), followed by 'Io sono docile' (With mild and docile air).

Meanwhile Bartolo has made known to Basilio his suspicions that Count Almaviva is in town and moreover in love with Rosina. Basilio advises to start a scandal about the Count and, in an aria ('La calunnia') remarkable for its descriptive *crescendo*, depicts how calumny may spread from the first breath to a tempest of scandal.

Figaro, who has left Almaviva, tells Rosina that Signor Lindoro is his cousin, and adds that the young man is deeply in love with her. Rosina is delighted. She gives him a note to convey to the supposed Signor Lindoro. (Duet, Rosina and Figaro: 'Dunque io son, tu non m'inganni?'—Am I his love, or dost thou mock me?)

Bartolo taxes Rosina with having dropped a note from the balcony, and, even though she has a ready answer to all his questions, he continues to disbelieve her excuses and reads her a lecture on the futility of trying to deceive him. His aria, 'A un dottor della mia sorte' is a fine *buffo* piece, and superior to 'Manca un foglio', which was often sung in its place and is anyhow not by Rossini at all.

To obtain an interview with Rosina, the Count disguises himself as a drunken soldier, and forces his way into Bartolo's house. The disguise of Almaviva is penetrated by the guardian, and the pretended soldier is placed under arrest, but is at once released upon secretly showing the officer his order as a Grandee of Spain. There is an irresistibly comic sextet for Rosina, Almaviva, Bartolo, Berta, Figaro, and Basilio—'Fredda ed immobile' (Awestruck and immovable), and the act ends in a general finale.

Act II. The Count again enters Bartolo's house. He is now disguised as a music-teacher, and pretends that he has been sent by Basilio to give a lesson in music, on account of the illness of the latter. He obtains the confidence of Bartolo by producing Rosina's letter to himself, and offering to persuade Rosina that the letter has been given him by a mistress of the Count. In this manner he obtains the desired

opportunity, under the guise of a music lesson—the 'music
lesson' scene, which is discussed below—to hold a whispered
conversation with Rosina. Figaro also manages to obtain the
keys of the balcony, an escape is determined on at midnight,
and a private marriage arranged. Now, however, Basilio makes
his appearance. The lovers are disconcerted, but manage, by
persuading the music-master that he really is ill—an illness
accelerated by a full purse slipped into his hand by Almaviva
—to get rid of him. He departs after the quintet, 'Buona sera,
mio Signore' (Fare you well then, good Signore):

Figaro starts to shave the Doctor, while Almaviva and
Rosina plan an elopement. But Bartolo becomes suspicious,
gets out of his chair when no one is looking, and catches the
lovers in compromising conversation.

When the Count and Figaro have gone, Bartolo, who
possesses the letter Rosina wrote to Almaviva, succeeds, by
producing it, and telling her he secured it from another
lady-love of the Count, in exciting the jealousy of his ward.
In her anger she discloses the plan of escape and agrees to
marry her guardian. At the appointed time, however, Figaro
and the Count make their appearance—the lovers are
reconciled, and a notary, procured by Bartolo for his own
marriage to Rosina, celebrates the marriage of the loving pair.
When the guardian enters, with officers of justice into whose
hands he is about to consign Figaro and the Count, he is too
late, but is reconciled by a promise that he shall receive the
equivalent of his ward's dowry.

Just before Almaviva and Figaro enter for the elopement
there is a storm. The delicate trio for Almaviva, Rosina, and
Figaro, 'Zitti, zitti, piano' (Softly, softly and in silence),
bears, probably without intention, a resemblance to a passage
in Haydn's *Seasons*:

The first performance of *Il Barbiere di Siviglia*, an opera that has held its own for over a century, was a scandalous failure, which, however, was not without its amusing incidents. Castil-Blaze, Giuseppe Carpani in his *Rossiniane* and Stendhal in *Vie de Rossini* (a lot of it 'cribbed' from Carpani) have told the story. Moreover the Rosina of the evening, Mme. Giorgi-Righetti, who was both pretty and popular, has communicated her reminiscences.

On December 26, 1815, Duke Cesarini, manager of the Argentine Theatre, Rome, for whom Rossini had contracted to write two operas, brought out the first of these, *Torvaldo e Dorliska*, which was poorly received. Thereupon Cesarini handed to the composer the libretto of *Il Barbiere di Siviglia*, which Paisiello, who was still living, had set to music more than a quarter of a century before. A pleasant memory of the old master's work still lingered with the Roman public. The honorarium was 400 Roman crowns (about $400) and Rossini also was called upon to preside over the orchestra at the pianoforte at the first three performances. It is said that Rossini composed his score in a fortnight. Even if not strictly true, from December 26 to the February 5 following is but little more than a month. The young composer had too much sense not to honour Paisiello, or, at least, to appear to. He hastened to write to the old composer. The latter, although reported to have been intensely jealous of the young maestro (Rossini was only twenty-five) since the sensational success of the latter's *Elisabetta, Regina d'Inghilterra* (Elizabeth, Queen of England), Naples, 1815, replied that he had no objection to another musician dealing with the subject of his opera. In reality, it is said, he counted on Rossini's making a glaring failure of the attempt. The libretto was rearranged by Sterbini, and Rossini wrote a preface, modest in tone, yet without a hint that he considered the older score out of date. But he took the precaution to show Paisiello's letter to all the music lovers of Rome, and insisted on changing the title of the opera to *Almaviva, ossia l'Inutile Precauzione* (Almaviva, or the Useless Precaution).

Mme. Giorgi-Righetti reports that 'hot-headed enemies' assembled at their posts as soon as the theatre opened, while Rossini's friends, disappointed by the recent ill luck of *Torvaldo e Dorliska*, were timid in their support of the new work. Furthermore, according to Mme. Giorgi-Righetti,

Rossini weakly yielded to a suggestion from Garcia, and permitted that artist, the Almaviva of the première, to substitute for the air which is sung under Rosina's balcony, a Spanish melody with guitar accompaniment. The scene being laid in Spain, this would aid in giving local colour to the work—such was the idea. But it went wrong. By an unfortunate oversight no one had tuned the guitar with which Almaviva was to accompany himself, and Garcia was obliged to do this on the stage. A string broke. The singer had to replace it, to an accompaniment of laughter and whistling. This was followed by Figaro's entrance air. The audience had settled down for this. But when they saw Zamboni, as Figaro, come on the stage with another guitar, another fit of laughing and whistling seized them, and the racket rendered the solo completely inaudible. Rosina appeared on the balcony. The public greatly admired Mme. Giorgi-Righetti and was disposed to applaud her. But, as if to cap the climax of absurdity, she sang: 'Segui, o caro, deh, segui così' (Continue, my dear, do always so). Naturally the audience immediately thought of the two guitars, and went on laughing, whistling, and hissing during the entire duet between Almaviva and Figaro. The work seemed doomed. Finally Rosina came on the stage and sang the 'Una voce poco fa' (A little voice I heard just now) which had been awaited with impatience (and which to-day is still considered an operatic *tour de force* for soprano). The youthful charm of Mme. Giorgi-Righetti, the beauty of her voice, and the favour with which the public regarded her, 'won her a sort of ovation' in this number. A triple round of prolonged applause raised hopes for the fate of the work. Rossini rose from his seat at the pianoforte, and bowed. But realising that the applause was chiefly meant for the singer, he called to her in a whisper, 'Oh, natura!' (Oh, human nature!)

'Give her thanks,' replied the artist, 'since without her you would not have had occasion to rise from your seat.'

What seemed a favourable turn of affairs did not, however, last long. The whistling was resumed louder than ever at the duet between Figaro and Rosina. 'All the whistlers of Italy,' says Castil-Blaze, 'seemed to have given themselves a rendezvous for this performance.' Finally, a stentorian voice shouted: 'This is the funeral of Don Pollione,' words which doubtless had much spice for Roman ears, since the cries, the hisses, the stamping, continued with increased vehemence.

When the curtain fell on the first act Rossini turned toward the audience, slightly shrugged his shoulders, and clapped his hands. The audience, though greatly offended by this show of contemptuous disregard for its opinion, reserved its revenge for the second act, not a note of which it allowed to be heard.

For the second performance of *Il Barbiere* Rossini replaced the unlucky air introduced by Garcia with the 'Ecco ridente in cielo', as it now stands. This cavatina he borrowed from an earlier opera of his own, *Aureliano in Palmira* (Aurelian in Palmyra). It also had figured in a cantata (not an opera) by Rossini, *Ciro in Babilonia* (Cyrus in Babylon)—so that measures first sung by a Persian king in the ancient capital of Nebuchadnezzar, and then by a Roman emperor and his followers in the city which flourished in an oasis in the Syrian desert, were found suitable to be intoned by a love-sick Spanish count of the seventeenth century as a serenade to his lady of Seville! It is amusing to note in tracing this air to its original source, that 'Ecco ridente in cielo' figured in *Aureliano in Palmira* as an address to Isis—'Sposa del grande Osirde' (Spouse of the great Osiris).

Equally curious is the relation of the overture to the opera. The original is said to have been lost. The present one has nothing to do with the ever-ready Figaro, the coquettish Rosina, or the sentimental Almaviva, although there have been writers who have dilated upon it as reflecting the spirit of the opera and its characters. It came from the same source as 'Lo, smiles the morning in the sky'—from *Aureliano*, and in between had figured as the overture to *Elisabetta, Regina d'Inghilterra.*

It is a singular fact that the reception of *Il Barbiere* in Paris was much the same as in Rome. The first performance in the Salle Louvois was coldly received. Newspapers compared Rossini's *Barber* unfavourably with that of Paisiello. Fortunately the opposition demanded a revival of Paisiello's work. Paer, musical director at the Théâtre Italien, not unwilling to spike Rossini's guns, pretended to yield to a public demand, and brought out the earlier opera. But the opposite of what had been expected happened. The work was found to be superannuated. It was voted a bore, and Rossini triumphed. The elder Garcia, the Almaviva of the production in Rome, played the role in Paris, as he also did in London, and at the first Italian performance of the work in New York.

Rossini had the reputation of being indolent in the extreme
—when he had nothing to do. We have seen that when the
overture to *Il Barbiere di Siviglia* was lost (if he really ever
composed one), he did not take the trouble to compose
another, but replaced it with an earlier one. A similar legend
exists in connection with the lesson Almaviva is supposed to
give Rosina in Dr. Bartolo's house. This is said to have been
lost with the overture—quite erroneously; it exists and is now
usually sung in performance. As with the overture, according
to the legend, Rossini did not attempt to recompose this
number either. He simply let his prima donna sing anything
she wanted to. 'Rosina sings an air, ad libitum, for the
occasion,' reads the direction in the libretto. Perhaps it was
Giorgi-Righetti who first selected 'La Biondina in
gondoletta', which was frequently sung in the lesson scene by
Italian prima donnas. Later there was substituted the air 'Di
tanti palpiti' from the opera *Tancredi*, which is known as the
'aria dei rizzi', or 'rice aria', because Rossini, who was a great
gourmet, composed it while cooking his rice. Pauline
Viardot-Garcia (Garcia's daughter), like her father in the
unhappy première of the opera, sang a Spanish song. This
may have been 'La Calesera', which Adelina Patti also sang in
Paris about 1867. Patti's other selections at this time included the laughing song, the so-called 'L'Eclat de Rire'
(Burst of Laughter) from Auber's *Manon Lescaut*, as highly
esteemed in Paris in years gone by as Massenet's *Manon* now
is. In New York I have heard Patti sing in this scene the
Arditi waltz, 'Il Bacio' (The Kiss); the bolero of Hélène, from
Les Vêpres Siciliennes (The Sicilian Vespers), by Verdi; the
'Shadow Dance' from Meyerbeer's *Dinorah*, and, in
concluding the scene, 'Home, Sweet Home', which never
failed to bring down the house, although the naïveté with
which she sang it was more affected than affecting.

Among prima donnas much earlier than Patti there were at
least two, Grisi and Alboni (after whom boxes were named at
the Academy of Music), who adapted a brilliant violin piece,
Rode's 'Air and Variations', to their powers of vocalisation
and sang it in the lesson scene. I mention this because the
habit of singing an air with variations persisted until Mme.
Sembrich's time. She sang those by Proch, a teacher of many
prima donnas, among them Tietjens and Peschka-Leutner,
who sang at the Peace Jubilee in Boston (1872) and was the
first to make famous her teacher's coloratura variations, with
'flauto concertante'. Besides these variations, Mme. Sembrich

ang Strauss's 'Voce di Primavera' waltz, 'Ah! non giunge' from *La Sonnambula*, the bolero from *The Sicilian Vespers*, and 'O luce di quest' anima' from *Linda di Chamounix*. The scene was charmingly brought to an end by her seating herself at the pianoforte and singing, to her own accompaniment, Chopin's 'Maiden's Wish'. Mme. Melba sang Arditi's waltz, 'Se Saran Rose', Massenet's 'Sevillana', and the mad scene from *Lucia*, ending, like Mme. Sembrich, with a song to which she played her own accompaniment, her choice being Tosti's 'Mattinata'. Mme. Galli-Curci was apt to begin with the brilliant vengeance air from *The Magic Flute*, her encores being 'L'Eclat de Rire' by Auber and 'Charmant Oiseau' (Pretty Bird) from David's *La Perle du Brésil* (The Pearl of Brazil). 'Home, Sweet Home' and 'The Last Rose of Summer', both sung by her to her own accompaniment, conclude this interesting 'lesson', in which every Rosina, although supposedly a pupil receiving a lesson, must be a most brilliant and accomplished prima donna.

Readers familiar with the history of opera, therefore aware that Alboni was a contralto, will wonder at her having appeared as Rosina, when that rôle is associated with prima donnas whose voices are extremely high and flexible.[1] But the rôle was written for low voice. Giorgi-Righetti, the first Rosina, was a contralto. As it is now sung by high sopranos, the music of the rôle is transposed from the original to higher keys in order to give full scope for brilliant vocalisation on high notes.

Many liberties have been taken by prima donnas in the way of vocal flourishes and a general decking out of the score of *Il Barbiere* with embellishments. The story goes that Patti once sang 'Una voce poco fa', with her own frills added, to Rossini in Paris.

'A very pretty song! Whose is it?' is said to have been the composer's cutting comment.

There is another anecdote about *Il Barbiere* which brings in Donizetti, who was asked if he believed that Rossini really had composed the opera in thirteen days.

'Why not? He's so lazy,' is the reported reply.

If the story is true, Donizetti was a very forward young

---

[1] The comment was wholly apt in the early part of this century, the move to return to a mezzo-soprano Rosina having come, oddly enough, since the end of the war in 1945. Many younger readers will never have heard the high soprano Rosina, except on early gramophone records.

H.

man. He was only nineteen when *Il Barbiere* was produced and had not yet brought out his first opera.

The first performance in America of *The Barber of Seville* was in English at the Park Theatre, New York, May 3, 1819. (May 17, cited by some authorities, was the date of the third performance, and is so announced in the advertisements.' Thomas Phillips was Almaviva and Miss Leesugg, Rosina 'Report speaks in loud terms of the new opera called *The Barber of Seville* which is announced for this evening. The music is said to be very splendid and is expected to be most effective.' This primitive bit of 'publicity', remarkable for its day, appeared in *The Evening Post*, New York, Monday, May 3, 1819. The second performance took place May 7. Much music was interpolated. Phillips, as Almaviva, introduced 'The Soldier's Bride', 'Robin Adair', 'Pomposo, or a Receipt for an Italian Song', and 'the favourite duet with Miss Leesugg, of "I love thee" '. (One wonders what was left of Rossini's score.) In 1821 he appeared again with Miss Holman as Rosina.

That Phillips should have sung Figaro, a baritone rôle in *Le Nozze di Figaro*, and Almaviva, a tenor part, in *Il Barbiere* may seem odd. But in the Mozart opera he appeared in Bishop's adaption, in which the Figaro rôle is neither too high for a baritone, nor too low for a tenor. In fact the liberties Bishop took with Mozart's score were so great (and so outrageous) that Phillips need have hesitated at nothing.

On Tuesday, November 22, 1825, Manuel Garcia, the elder, issued the preliminary announcement of his season of Italian opera at the Park Theatre, New York. The printers appear to have had a struggle with the Italian titles of operas and names of Italian composers. For *Evening Post* announces that 'The Opera of H. *Barbiora di Seviglia*, by Rosina, is now in rehearsal and will be given as soon as possible.' That 'soon as possible' was the evening of November 29, and is regarded as the date of the first performance in America of opera in Italian.
K.

LA CENERENTOLA
Cinderella

Opera in two acts by Gioacchino Rossini, text by Jacopo Ferretti (founded on Etienne's French libretto for Isouard's *Cendrillon*, 1810). Première at the Teatro Valle, Rome, January 25, 1817, with Giorgi-

Righetti in the title rôle. First performed in London, Haymarket Theatre, 1820 (in Italian); New York, 1826 (in Italian); Covent Garden, 1830 (in English), with Paton. Revived Pesaro, 1920, with Fanny Anitua; Rome, 1920; Paris, 1929, with Supervia, Ederle, Bettoni; Vienna, 1930, with Kern, von Pataky; Berlin, 1931, with Schoene, Hüsch, Kandl; Florence Festival, 1933, with Supervia, conductor Serafin; Covent Garden, 1934, with Supervia, Dino Borgioli, Ghirardini, Pinza, conductor Marinuzzi; la Scala, 1937, with Pederzini, conductor Marinuzzi; Buenos Aires, 1939, with Pederzini; Florence Festival, 1942, with Barbieri; la Scala, 1946, with Barbieri, Infantino, Maugeri, Tajo, conductor Serafin; Trieste, 1951, with Simionato; Glyndebourne, 1952, with de Gabarain, Oncina, Bruscantini, Ian Wallace, conductor Gui; Sadler's Wells, London, 1959, with Kern, Alexander Young, Dowling, Glynne, conductor Balkwill.

CHARACTERS

Don Ramiro, *Prince of Salerno* . . . . Tenor
Dandini, *his valet* . . . . Bass
Don Magnifico, *Baron of Mountflagon* . . . . . Buffo-Bass
Clorinda⎱
Thisbe ⎰ *his daughters* . . . . {Soprano / Mezzo-Soprano}
Angelina, *known as Cinderella, his step-daughter*
                                                              Contralto
Alidoro, *a philosoper* . . . . Bass

The action takes place partly in the house of Don Magnifico, partly in the palace of the Prince.

Act I. Cenerentola is, of course, Cinderella, and as the curtain rises she is seen making coffee for her half-sisters, singing a pathetic little song the while. The friend and counsellor of the Prince, Alidoro, enters disguised as a beggar. The two sisters curtly dismiss him; Cinderella pities him and offers him refreshment, to the intense annoyance of her sisters. The quarrel is interrupted by the entrance of the Prince's followers. Clorinda and Thisbe feel convinced that he must fall an easy victim to their charms. They listen rather reluctantly while their father tells them at length of a dream he has had, and then go to make ready for the Prince, who arrives disguised as his valet, Dandini, to find Cinderella alone.

Cinderella and the Prince fall in love at first sight and express their feelings in a love duet which has all the wit and melodiousness characteristic of its composer: (*see page 412*).

Cinderella must go to the sisters, who clamour for her services. The Prince, left alone, does not know what to think

of his charmer. His musings are interrupted by the arrival of Dandini (masquerading as the Prince).

While Dandini misquotes Latin to give himself an air, the voice of Cinderella is heard begging the Baron to allow her to go to the ball. Neither the Baron nor her sisters will listen to her; the third daughter is dead, they tell the Prince, and Cinderella is only a servant. They leave, but Alidoro promises to help Cinderella.

The next scene takes place in the Prince's palace. The Baron has been appointed chief butler to the Prince and is busy tasting the wines. The disguised Prince has seen enough of Clorinda and Thisbe by this time to know that neither could make him happy. The girls, for their part, set about capturing Dandini, and when the arrival of a distinguished but unknown lady is announced, their jealousy is up in arms. The unknown, however, looks too much like Cinderella to arouse their alarm.

Act II.   Clorinda and Thisbe are no longer on friendly terms, as each believes she has made a conquest of the Prince, but Dandini is himself in love with Cinderella and asks her to marry him. Cinderella refuses and confesses her love for his 'valet'. The Prince overhears her, comes forward, and himself proposes to her. Cinderella admits that she loves him, but before consenting to be his bride the Prince must find out who she is. She gives him a bracelet which matches another she is wearing and departs.

The Baron enters and asks Dandini whether it would be possible to speed up the wedding. Dandini has a secret; but first, if he were to marry one of the Baron's daughters, he asks, how should she be treated? The Baron tells him: thirty lackeys always at hand; sixteen horses; a dozen dukes, a coach with six footmen and 'dinners with ices' always ready. Dandini thereupon confesses that he is but a valet and that marriage with a daughter of the Baron is unthinkable.

The next scene is at the Baron's house, where Clorinda and

Thisbe scowl at Cinderella, who resembles the hateful
stranger of the ball. A storm rages outside—brought about by
the incantations of the philosopher, Alidoro. The Prince and
Dandini seek refuge while another coach is got ready; the
Baron orders Cinderella to bring the best chair forward for
the Prince. Cinderella, trying to hide herself, puts her hands
up to cover her face, and the Prince notices the bracelet, the
companion of which he holds. All the knots are gradually
unravelled. The Baron, Clorinda, and Thisbe, unable to
understand, rudely order Cinderella away. The Prince grows
angry and threatens them with his displeasure. The scene
changes to the palace, where the intercession of Cinderella
results in the pardon of the Baron and his daughters, and all
ends merrily.   F. B.

Not the least reason for the comparative lack of popularity
of Rossini's operas in the earlier twentieth century—only *The
Barber* survived in the repertory—was the florid nature of the
vocal writing; *Cenerentola* is no exception to this rule, in fact
it emphasises it, since the title rôle, like that of *L'Italiana*, is
written for that *rara avis* a coloratura contralto. Though
attempts have been made to arrange the music for a soprano
(as has been done with Rosina), the opera generally has to
wait for revival until a low voice with phenomenal agility
comes along. When it does, we have an opportunity of
hearing the brilliant rondo, 'Nacqui all'affanno, al pianto',
with which the opera ends, in its proper context and not on a
gramophone record or (more rarely) concert platform; and
the unmatched ensembles for which Rossini is renowned
show a modern audience the stuff a comic opera was made of
in the days when every singer was a master of the bravura
coloratura style, and most of them brilliant actors and
actresses as well. Nobody has surpassed Rossini in the surface
brilliance of his comic invention, and only Mozart and (in one
opera) Verdi have added to it a depth of feeling of which
Rossini was seemingly incapable but which turns comedy
from the most artificial of media into the truest. In
Cenerentola, it is not the motives of the characters which
matter—apart from the charming duet early in Act I, the love
of Prince Ramiro for Cinderella plays little part in the
music—nor even primarily their reactions to their own and
other people's motives, but the situations these motives get
them into. And situations with Rossini lead not so much to
arias as to ensembles. Rossini's ability to catch hold of the

verbal rhythm of a chance phrase and turn it into music (e.g. the ensemble after Alidoro's announcement of Cinderella's arrival at the ball), his dexterity with patter, his astonishing manipulation of the simplest material until it becomes a towering invention of quicksilver sound—these qualities are heard at their best in the quintet which begins 'Signore, una parola', in the finale of Act I, which ends with the *crescendo* first heard in the overture, in the brilliantly comic duet of Dandini and Magnifico in Act II. The climax of the opera comes, not with the rondo at the end, good though it is, but with the great E flat ensemble of stupefaction after the Prince and Dandini have taken refuge from the storm in the astonished Don Magnifico's house. This sextet is built up on a slow, *staccato* tune (marked *maestoso*: majestically) from which each singer in turn breaks away with a florid phrase, the others meanwhile keeping up the steady rhythm with a constant repetition of the tune and a maximum use of the words and particularly of the opportunities given by the rolled Italian 'r'. This is an ensemble to set beside the Barber's matchless 'fredda ed immobile' as high-water marks of comedy in music.   H.

LA GAZZA LADRA

The Thieving Magpie

Opera in three acts by Gioacchino Rossini, libretto by Gherardini. Première, la Scala, Milan, May 31, 1817, with Teresa Belloc, Savino Monelli, Filippo Galli, Antonio Ambrosi. First performed London, King's Theatre, 1821, with Violante Camporese and Vestris in the cast; Covent Garden, 1830 (in English, as *Ninetta; or The Maid of Palaiseau*; music adapted by Bishop), with Mary Anne Paton; Covent Garden, 1847, with Grisi, Alboni, Mario, Tamburini; 1863, with Patti, Didiée, Neri-Baraldi, Faure, Ronconi; and 1883, with Patti, Scalchi, Frappoli, Cotogni; New York, 1830 (in French), 1833 (in Italian). Revived Pesaro, 1941, in new edition arranged by Zandonai with Lina Aimaro, Cloe Elmo, Luigi Fort, Carmelo Maugeri, Luciano Neroni, conducted by Zandonai. Subsequently heard in this version in Rome, 1942; Wexford, 1959, with Mariella Adani, Janet Baker, Nicola Monti, Paolo Pedani, Giorgio Tadeo, conductor Pritchard; and at Florence, 1965, with Nicoletta Panni, Anna Maria Rota, Cesare Valletti, Paolo Montarsolo, Paolo Washington, conductor Bartoletti. Première at Sadler's Wells, London, 1966, the score reconstructed from the manuscript in the Bibliothèque Nationale, Paris, and new English version by Tom Hammond, with Catherine Wilson, Patricia Kern, Donald Pilley, Denis Dowling, Harold Blackburn, Don Garrard, conductor Balkwill.

CHARACTERS

Fabrizio Vingradito, *a rich farmer* . . . . Bass
Lucia, *his wife* .Mezzo-Soprano
Giannetto, *his son, a soldier* . . . . Tenor
Ninetta, *a servant in their house* . . . . Soprano
Fernando Villabella, *Ninetta's father, a soldier*   Baritone
Gottardo, *the village mayor* . . . . Bass
Pippo, *a young peasant in Fabrizio's service* . . Contralto
Isaac, *a wandering pedlar* . . . . Tenor
Antonio, *the gaoler* . . . . Tenor
Giorgio, *the mayor's servant* . . . . Bass
Ernesto, *friend of Fernando, a soldier* . . . . Bass
A Magpie . . . .
An Usher, Armed men, Villagers, Fabrizio's employees
Place: A big village not far from Paris

Immediately after the success of *La Cenerentola* in Rome in January 1817, Rossini went via Bologna to Milan, where he had a contract to write an opera for la Scala. This commission he approached with some circumspection as the Milanese audience had not, according to Stendhal, taken kindly to his earlier operas and their suspicion of the composer would have been anything but assuaged by his recent successes in Rome and Naples. Since he was already in Milan at the beginning of March, ready to start work on whatever libretto the management might provide him with and the première did not take place until the end of May, it was for Rossini an unusually long period for the writing and preparation of an opera.

In the event, the composer achieved one of the greatest triumphs of his career, and Stendhal describes the first night as the most successful he had ever attended. Perhaps because the score contained something for everyone—pathos, comedy, tragedy, gaiety—perhaps because, as Toye says, things of startling originality were presented in a manner that anybody could follow and understand', nothing in the opera failed to please. The overture, with its opening drum roll (two of the main characters are soldiers returning from

the wars), is one of Rossini's most lively and splendid, one
moreover whose music has considerably more connection
with the rest of the opera than is customary with Rossini.

The curtain rises on the courtyard of the house o.
Fabrizio, a rich merchant. A magpie is sitting by an open
cage. The people of the village, amongst them Pippo, who
works for Fabrizio, are rejoicing at the prospect of the return
of Giannetto, the son of the house, who is expected back
from the wars. Everything is going with a swing when
suddenly Pippo's name is called. The disembodied voice turns
out to be the magpie's and the bird, in answer to Lucia's
question as to whom Giannetto shall marry, answers pertly
'Ninetta!' Lucia clearly finds such a match unthinkable
though Fabrizio and the others approve the bird's choice, and
in fact she seems inclined to pick on Ninetta for anything
even blaming her because one of the silver forks is missing
When all leave to make further preparations for the arrival o
Giannetto, the stage is empty for the entry of Ninetta
carrying a basket of strawberries. She sings of her happines.
at the prospect of the return of Giannetto, with whom she i
secretly in love ('Di piacer mi balza il cor'), an attractive aria
whose layout and even the cast of whose music reminds the
listener of 'Una voce poco fa'. Fabrizio, who hints that he
would not oppose a match with Giannetto, and Lucia, who
charges Ninetta to look after the silver canteen with specia
care, go off to wait for Giannetto, and the old pedlar Isaac
starts to hawk his wares in a cracked and nasal voice.

At last Giannetto arrives, and immediately it is apparen
that he has eyes only for Ninetta, to whom he sings an aria
full of love: 'Ma quel piacer che adesso, o mia Ninetta'. In ;
spirited brindisi led by Pippo all rejoice and then leave th
courtyard empty.

As Ninetta says a temporary goodbye to her beloved, ;
man enters, whom she does not at first recognise as her fathe
but whom she greets rapturously once he makes himsel
known. He has infringed military law and is in fact even nov
condemned to death. A long duet ensues between father and
daughter ('Come frenar il pianto') but Ninetta's efforts a
consolation turn to fear as she sees the mayor coming
towards them.

The mayor makes his entry with a big buffo aria 'Il mio
piano è preparato', and he soon makes it plain that Ninetta i
the objective his plan is designed to achieve. The mayor start

o pay court to her when to his indignation a message is
brought to him. As he tries to decipher it, Ninetta tells her
father to make his escape, but he says he has no money and
asks her to sell on his behalf a silver spoon, which is all he has
left, and bring him the money to a hiding place he designates.
As he is about to go, the mayor stops him and insists that
Ninetta read the message aloud as he cannot make it out
without his spectacles. As soon as it becomes plain to her
that the letter describes her father as a deserter and asks the
mayor to help bring him to justice, she changes name and
description and there occurs the famous trio 'Oh Nume
benefico', Fernando hiding behind the doorway and joining
his voice with Ninetta's in thanking heaven for its intervention, the mayor calling down a benediction on his
amatory designs.

Once he thinks himself alone with Ninetta, the mayor
makes a proposition to her, but she withstands him so firmly
that even an old roué could be forgiven for thinking her a
spitfire in ingénue's clothing. Fernando can bear the scene no
longer and interrupts with a vigorous protest: 'Uom maturo e
magistrato'. The scene ends with a lively *stretta*, as each of
the three characters realises he or she has gone a good deal
further than originally intended. As the mayor retreats and
Ninetta's father also makes good his escape, the magpie
snatches up the silver spoon and flies away with it.

The scene changes to a room in Fabrizio's house. Isaac's
voice is heard outside and Ninetta sells him the silver spoon
which her father has entrusted to her. As she is about to take
him the money, Giannetto appears, closely followed by his
father, who makes to join the hands of the two lovers. The
mayor greets the returned Giannetto, while Lucia goes to
count the silver. When she reports a spoon missing, the
mayor, with maximum pomposity, sits down to make a legal
report. 'Who can the thief be?' asks Giannetto. 'Ninetta,'
answers the magpie.

A sextet develops as the mayor takes down the evidence
and when he asks Ninetta her father's name and gets the
answer 'Fernando Villabella' he suddenly realizes that the
deserter in the official despatch was her father and that she
was shielding him when she read it out. Things look black
when Ninetta pulls out her handkerchief and some money
tumbles to the ground. Lucia asks where it comes from, and
all Ninetta's protestations are insufficient to divert suspicion,

even Pippo's testimony that it came from Isaac only elicitin
from the old pedlar himself the information that she sold hir
a spoon, moreover with the initials F.V. on them—since Isaa
has now sold it, it cannot be compared with those i
Fabrizio's canteen. Even Giannetto now starts to believe he
guilty, and, at the lowest ebb of her fortunes, Ninett
movingly leads the ensemble: 'Mi sento opprimere'. Th
arrival of an armed escort triggers off a frenzied stretta to th
finale, a typically brilliant, typically solid Rossinian edifice
Nothing will soften the mayor's wrath and apparent zeal fo
justice, and Ninetta is marched off as a criminal.

Act II.   Outside the prison cells of the Town Hal
Antonio, the gaoler, tries to comfort Ninetta, then brings i
Giannetto, who is intent on persuading her to prove he
innocence. She assures him in a beautiful duet ('Forse un c
conoscerete') that though her lips are now sealed, one da
her innocence will be apparent to all. Giannetto leaves as th
mayor approaches and that worthy makes a determine
effort to suggest that nothing but altruism motivates h
actions: let her just for a moment trust him (that he happen
to adore her is coincidental, he explains) and she may yet b
saved. Unfortunately for the mayor, the judicial tribun;
arrives and his presence is necessary to greet it (the inter
ruption is accompanied by the crescendo from the overture
Pippo is Ninetta's next visitor and she asks him to take th
three crowns she got for the silver to her father's hidin
place. Pippo himself is to keep her cross as a sign of th
affection that was between them. They sing sadly in duet o
joint memories of which Ninetta's gift must in future serve a
sole souvenir, and finally, to the allegro of the overturc
Ninetta gives Pippo her ring to deliver to Giannetto i
memory of her.

The scene changes to Fabrizio's house where Lucia is a pre
to doubts about Ninetta's guilt, doubts which are resolved i
favour of the accused when Fernando enters and proclaim
his passionate conviction of his daughter's innocence.

The great hall in the Town Hall. The Tribunal assemble
and, in a scene which has been much admired ever since
was written, sings imposingly of its powers and th
inexorable manner in which it exercises them. The judg
reads out Ninetta's conviction, sentences her to death, an
when not even the pleas of Giannetto and Fabrizio persuad
her to bring evidence to prove her innocence, the sentence

confirmed. At this point Fernando rushes in and demands in a dramatic *scena* that his innocent daughter be freed. He is overpowered by the guards, but continues to hurl defiance at the Tribunal, which reiterates its decision. A solemn ensemble develops during whose course Giannetto joins Ninetta in leading a chorus of protest, but all is in vain, and at the end of the scene, Fernando is taken to the cells and Ninetta towards the place of execution.

The scene changes to the village square, where Lucia laments the tragic turn events have taken. Pippo is counting his money, and when he puts it down for a moment to talk to the mayor's servant, Giorgio, the magpie flies down and steels a coin. They pursue it out of sight.

Ninetta, surrounded by armed men, is taken towards the scaffold amidst the lamentations of the bystanders. Her last thought is of her father ('Deh tu reggi in tal memento'). Suddenly Pippo and Antonio rush in shouting to Giorgio that they have discovered the real thief: the magpie. Everything has been found in a secret hiding place and Ninetta is innocent after all. To mounting orchestral excitement, Ninetta is freed, the mayor thwarted, and general rejoicing released. Ninetta returns thanks in a tune of delightful innocence, but admits her joy is not complete until she knows what is to happen to her father. At this very moment he appears, released from prison by an order signed by the king himself. Since the mayor has already expressed his profound sorrow at the turn events seemed likely logically to take, it remains only for Lucia to join the hands of Ninetta and Giannetto in token of recognition of the happiness so long delayed, happiness which now seems to have overtaken one and all and which Rossini loses no time in expressing in music.   H.

MOSÈ IN EGITTO
Moses in Egypt

Opera in four acts (originally three) by Gioacchino Rossini, libretto by A. L. Tottola. Première at San Carlo, Naples, March 5, 1818, with Benedetti as Mosè, Isabella Colbran and Nozzari. First performed in Budapest, 1820 (in German); Vienna, 1821 (in German); London, 1822 (in Italian, as *Pietro l'Eremita*), and in 1833 at Covent Garden (in English under the title *The Israelites in Egypt* and with additions from Handel's oratorio); Paris, 1822; New York, 1832. Rossini very substantially revised the opera for Paris (as *Moïse et Pharaon*), where it was first given in the new version in 1827, with a new libretto by Jouy, with Levasseur as Moïse, Ciniti as Anaïse, and Nourrit the younger as Aménophis (its hundredth performance in Paris in this version was in 1838). First performed in second version in Perugia, 1829; Covent Garden, 1850 (as *Zora*), with Zelger as Mosè, Castellan as Anaide, Tamberlik and Tamburini; New York, 1860. Revived la Scala, 1918, with Nazzareno de Angelis, Giannina Russ, Dolci, Merli, conductor Serafin; 1937, with Tancredi Pasero, Cigna, Pagliughi, Elmo, Tafuro, Lo Giudice, Armando Borgioli, conductor Marinuzzi; 1950, with Pasero; 1959, with Christoff; 1965, with Ghiaurov. At Florence Festival, 1935, with Pasero, Arangi-Lombardi, Scuderi, Stignani, conductor Gui; Rome, 1948, with Rossi-Lemeni; Falmouth, 1953 (first performance in England since 1850); Welsh National Opera (also in London), 1965, with Michael Langdon, Pauline Tinsley, Stuart Burrows; concert performances in Los Angeles in 1965 with Jerome Hines and in New York in 1966 with Ghiaurov; Rome, 1971, with Christoff.

CHARACTERS

Moses/Moïse/Mosè, *leader of the Israelites* . . . . Bass
Aaron/Eliezer/Elisero, *his brother* . . . . Tenor
Pharaoh/Pharaon/Faraone, *King of Egypt* . . . . . Baritone
Aménophis/Aménofi, *his son* . . . . Tenor
Auphis/Ophide/Aufide, *An Egyptian officer* . . . . Tenor
Osiris/Oziride/Osiride, *high priest of Isis* . . . . Bass
Miriam/Marie/Maria, *Moses's sister* . . . . .Mezzo-Soprano
Anais/Anaï/Anaide, *her daughter* . . . . Soprano
Sinais/Sinaïde/Sinaide, *Pharaoh's wife* . . . . Soprano
A mysterious voice . . . . Bass
Hebrews, Egyptians, Priests, Guards, Soldiers, Dancers

Before 1820, Rossini was in the habit of finishing as many as four operas in a single year, and 1818, when the first version of *Mosè* was written for Naples, saw three operas written though only two performed. Like others commissioned for the San Carlo by Barbaia at this time, it was written for Isabella Colbran, once Barbaia's mistress and soon to be Rossini's wife, and the librettist achieved something of a feat in making the female role of Moses's niece the pivot round which the antagonism of Moses and Pharaoh revolved.

The opera's initial success was surpassed at the revival a year later—a rare enough honour in itself at that date—when Rossini added the famous prayer in the last act, purely and simply to divert the audience's attention from the inadequacies of the San Carlo's staging of the Red

Sea! Stendhal tells us that it was the work of a few minutes to write the piece out, but the story is apocryphal and we know from Rossini's own correspondence that he wrote the tune first and had Tottola fit words to it after it was complete. It was this number which had the Italian ladies literally in paroxysms after its first performances—doctors were called in to deal with them—and it is the only one now known separately, not surprisingly since in the second version this is an opera of duets and ensembles and not at all of arias, but it is appropriate that it was this prayer which was sung on the steps of Santa Croce in Florence when in 1887 the body of Rossini was removed from Paris, where he had died almost twenty years before, and was re-buried in the great Florentine cathedral. Appropriate, too, that on this occasion the vast crowd insisted on a repeat!

It was the work of two months, Francis Toye tells us in his biography of the composer, to turn *Mosè* into *Moïse*, on which later version modern revivals have been based, although usually in Italian rather than the French which was heard in Paris in 1827. The second version involved extensive re-writing, with a new first act; for all that it embodies certain episodes of the Neapolitan version, there is much other new music and much earlier music omitted. Its success was instantaneous, even Balzac praising the opera as 'an immense musical poem', and saying that in this opera he seemed to be watching the liberation of Italy.

Act I. The camp of the Israelites in Egypt is suggested atmospherically in the short *andante* Prelude, an *allegro* leading straight into the first scene. In a fine chorus, the Israelites pray for relief from their bondage and to be allowed to return to their fatherland. Moses appears and demands that his followers cease their lamentations; if they had faith in Him, God would reward them by leading them home. Moses's brother, Aaron, has gone to Pharaoh to plead the Israelite cause and he now returns, together with Moses's sister Miriam, and her daughter Anaïs, who was kept hostage by the Egyptians but whom Pharaoh, influenced by Queen Sinais, has now restored to the Israelites as an earnest of his good faith and decision to set the people free. Pharaoh's son Aménophis has, according to Miriam, fallen in love with Anaïs.

Moses feels that God is about to reward their faith, and a rainbow appears in the sky at the same time as a mysterious voice can be heard reminding Moses and the Israelites that

God has kept His promises to them and ordering him to receive God's laws. All swear in an *a capella* ensemble to observe these laws. Moses leads the people as they give thanks to God and urges them to hasten their preparations to leave Egypt and return home.

All depart except Anaïs, who loves the Egyptian prince Aménophis, who himself presently appears and begs her to stay with him, abandoning her mother and the Israelite people. Aménophis is a passionate lover, but Anaïs seems proof against his pleas, even when he threatens to influence Pharaoh to revoke the order for the liberation of the Israelites, who must now by command of his father bow to Aménophis's edicts. Stendhal esteemed this duet beyond anything in the opera except perhaps the introduction (then to Act I and now to Act II) and the two prayers. 'This is not a piece of music of the moment; it must last as long as powerful feeling itself shall endure.' Aménophis leaves, and Aaron and Miriam lead the company in a thanksgiving hymn. Only Anaïs cannot associate herself with the rejoicing and in a duet of charmingly intimate character she admits her predicament to her mother.

Aménophis is as good as his threat and, as the finale starts, he tells Moses that Pharaoh has reversed his decree and that the Israelites are to return to captivity. Anaïs attempts unsuccessfully to intercede, and Moses threatens God's vengeance on Egypt if His people's departure is put off. For this threat, Aménophis orders his soldiers to slay Moses, but the crime is prevented by the appearance of Pharaoh and Sinais. A great ensemble develops, and Pharaoh announces that Aménophis has spoken the truth and that he has withdrawn his original promise to allow the Israelites to depart. A splendid finale reaches its climax as Moses raises his staff to heaven, the sun is eclipsed and the plague of darkness descends upon Egypt.

Act II.   Pharaoh's palace.[1]   Darkness lies over Egypt and Sinais, Pharaoh and Aménophis lament the apparently eternal night in a magnificent trio with chorus, whose quality explains Stendhal's comment that, at the première, in spite of his inherent suspicion of such Biblical scenes as a representation of the plagues of Egypt, he found himself surrendering completely and almost instantly to the music (One must not forget that, in the original version, this was

[1] Introduced in *Moïse*, as in *Mosè*, by three reiterated C's.

he opera's opening scene.) Pharaoh summons Moses, who
arrives with his brother and is faced with Pharaoh's demand
hat the curse of darkness be lifted from his kingdom; with
he return of light, the Israelites may depart. In a splendid
prayer ('Arbitre suprême du Ciel et de la Terre';
Eterno! immenso! incomprensibil Dio!'),[1] Moses asks God
o restore light to the land and, as he waves his staff, light
eturns. Reaction to the new situation is in the form of a
most expressive canon, enunciated by solo horn, led by
Moses and taken up in succession by Aaron, Sinais,
Aménophis and Pharaoh. Aaron is optimistic that this light
will pierce to the heart of Pharaoh, who is now disposed to
allow the Israelites out of captivity, in spite of the efforts of
Aménophis to restrain him. Throughout the *stretta*, Aménophis
opposes his will to that of the otherwise rejoicing Israelites.

The act often ends with the scene between Pharaoh and
Aménophis in which the King tells his son that he is to marry
he daughter of the King of Assyria, much to the despair of
Aménophis, who still loves Anaïs. There is, however, an
additional scene for Aménophis and his mother Sinais in
which the Queen, although she had earlier supported the
Israelites' efforts to obtain liberation, laments in an attractive
aria the impending departure of Anaïs, Moses and the
Hebrews, while Aménophis works himself into such a passion
at the idea of losing Anaïs that he declares, to his mother's
consternation, that he himself will kill Moses.

Act III. The Temple of Isis. Egyptians are worshipping
the goddess, whose High Priest, Osiris, joins Pharaoh in
making offerings to the deity. There follows a three-
movement ballet, written of course for the Paris version and
attractive in invention. Moses comes to claim the fulfilment
of Pharaoh's promise, but the High Priest insists that the
Hebrews should first render homage to Isis, to Moses's
considerable indignation. Auphis, an Egyptian officer, reports
a series of new plagues, the Nile's waters having turned red,
earthquakes shaking the land, and the air being filled with
insects. The High Priest tries to prevail on Pharaoh to punish
Moses for these new disasters, while Sinais's voice urges her
husband to keep his original promise. Again Moses lifts his
staff, and this time the altar fire is extinguished. The fraught
nature of the situation is celebrated in a fine ensemble, after

[1] 'This entrance of Moses recalls everything that is sublime in
Haydn . . .' writes Stendhal.

which Moses and Osiris in turn demand justice from Pharaoh. The Egyptian King decrees that the Israelites shall be expelled from Memphis in chains and the finale ends as impressively as it began.

Act IV. The desert, in the distance the Red Sea. Aménophis renews his pleading with Anaïs, telling her he is prepared to renounce his claim to the throne of Egypt if she will marry him. He urges his devotion, but Anaïs is torn between her loyalty to the Israelites and her love for the prince who is their enemy; the situation is unresolved and they hide when a march announces the arrival of Moses and the Israelites, guarded and chained. This is the day on which they shall return to the Promised Land, Moses announces, but Miriam is sad that her daughter has stayed behind. Suddenly, Anaïs reappears to the joy of all, and announces that her freedom she owes to Aménophis who himself stands before them to demand her hand in marriage. When Moses bids her make her choice, Anaïs, torn as she is, decides in an aria to follow the Israelites in spite of her love for Aménophis. The Prince warns Moses that Pharaoh plans a treacherous assault on them as they march undefended, and admits that he himself will join this Egyptian army.

The scene changes to the shore of the Red Sea. Faced with an impossible crossing in front of him and an implacable army behind him, Moses prays to God in the most famous passage of the score, the prayer, added for the revival in Naples the season following the première, 'Des cieux où tu résides, grand Dieu' ('Dal tuo stellato soglio'), in which he is joined by the voices of Anaïs, Aaron and Miriam.

Anaïs sees the Egyptians about to attack, but Moses leads the Israelites into the sea, which miraculously parts leaving a passage for them to pass through. As the Egyptians follow, with Pharaoh and Aménophis in the vanguard, the waters close upon them, there is an orchestral depiction of the catastrophe which befalls the Egyptian army and the opera ends with a *Cantique* of thanksgiving for the Israelite leaders (cut in the Italian score of the French version).　　　H.

LA DONNA DEL LAGO
The Lady of the Lake

Opera in two acts by Gioacchino Rossini, text by A. L. Tottola, after Sir Walter Scott's narrative poem *The Lady of the Lake.*

remière, San Carlo, Naples, September 24, 1819, with Isabella Colbran, Rosanna Pisaroni, Giovanni Davide. First produced London, King's Theatre, Haymarket, 1823, with Giuseppina Ronzi de Begnis, Vestris, Curioni; New York, 1829 (in French). Performed regularly in London in the 1840's and 1850's with Grisi and Mario. Revived Florence Festival, 1958, with Rosanna Carteri, Irene Companeez, Cesare Valletti, conductor Serafin; London, 1969, Camden Festival with Kiri Te Kanawa, Gillian Knight, Maurice Arthur, John Serge, conductor Gerald Gover; Italian Radio, 1970, with Caballe, Julia Hamari, Pietro Bottazzo, Franco Bonisolli, Paolo Washington, conductor Piero Bellugi.

CHARACTERS

Ellen (Elena) . . . . Soprano
Hubert (James V of Scotland) . . . . Tenor
Roderick Dhu (Roderigo) . . . . Tenor
Malcolm Groem . . . . .Mezzo-Soprano
Archibald Douglas, Earl of Angus . . . . Bass
Serano, *Douglas's retainer* . . . . Bass
Albina, *Ellen's confidante* . . . . .Mezzo-Soprano
Clansmen, Huntsmen, Pages, Ladies and
Gentlemen of the Court
Place: Scotland   *Time:* First half of the sixteenth Century

Between the beginning of December 1818 and the end of December the following year, Rossini had no fewer than four operas put on the stage—two at the San Carlo in Naples, one in Venice and one at la Scala.[1] Of the four, the only one likely to be known even by name nowadays is *La Donna del Lago*, taken from Scott's romantic poem *The Lady of the Lake*. The opera swiftly went the international rounds, was heard 32 times in its first season at la Scala, remained popular in London until 1851 but seems not to have been revived between 1860 and 1958, when the Maggio Musicale Fiorentino mounted it with Tullio Serafin conducting. It is full of graceful, expressive music and amounts to one of Rossini's most attractively lyrical scores. That it suffered a century of neglect may perhaps be attributed to three factors: the role of Ellen was written for Colbran and is lyrical until the taxingly brilliant final aria[2] which puts it out of consideration for most sopranos or mezzos; the two principal tenor roles bristle with high notes, cascade with

[1] Though he was under contract to Barbaia as musical director and principal composer, he had frequent leave of absence.
[2] In Florence in 1958 it was apparently omitted.

runs and roulades, and yet demand to be sung with a consistent smoothness out of reach of most singers for the past hundred years or so; and—most important—the story is concerned with characters of a much lower voltage than the Normas, Lucias, or early Verdi heroines who supplanted them in the imagination of a later generation.

Rossini's opera, like Scott's poem, relates a romantic story of the young King James V of Scotland (born 1512, died 1542). For two years from 1526, Archibald Douglas, Earl of Angus, kept the King imprisoned, until he escaped in 1528. Douglas fled to England, and the King took revenge on his relations. At the start of the opera, Douglas has returned to Scotland and is living under the protection of Roderick Dhu, who belongs to a faction opposing the young King. In gratitude for shelter, Douglas has promised the hand of his daughter Ellen in marriage to Roderick.

Act I, scene i: the shores of Lake Katrine, with the Ben Ledi mountains in the background. A hunting party greets the dawn and Ellen comes into view in a boat. In a flowing, 6/8 cavatina, 'Oh mattutini albori' (O morning dawn), she expresses her hopes that her young lover Malcolm may be with the hunting party, but she is surprised by Hubert, who is impressed by her beauty and tells her that he has lost the remainder of the hunters. She offers him shelter, their voices join in the melody of Ellen's cavatina, and they leave together, just as Hubert's companions return.

Scene ii: Douglas's cottage. Ellen reveals to Hubert that she is the daughter of the famous Douglas who has been exiled from the Court, a decision which Hubert in an aside says the King much regrets. It is obvious that Hubert is attracted towards Ellen, and when her friends refer to the love her father's friend, Roderick, feels for her and she openly admits in duet that she loves not Roderick but another, Hubert mistakenly dares to hope that it may be he.

All leave, and Malcolm, the object of Ellen's affections, enters and reveals his hopes and fears in a soliloquy. Serano, Douglas's servant, announces that Roderick and some soldiers are already in the valley, news which Douglas receives with joy. Ellen dares to oppose his wish that she may be united with Roderick, to Malcolm's joy and her father's displeasure. In an aria he commands her obedience, but when he leaves Ellen and Malcolm sing of their love in a slow movement of great charm.

Scene iii: an open field surrounded by high mountains. Roderick is greeted by his clansmen and responds in a brilliantly florid aria. Tenderly, he declares his love for Ellen, who herself tries to hide her apprehension, while her father begins to wonder whether her heart is given to another.

Malcolm at the head of his followers has arrived to join Roderick, and Douglas begins to understand who it is that his daughter loves. Roderick refers to Ellen as his consort-to-be, and Malcolm is about to give himself away when Ellen restrains him, and the four protagonists of the drama, together with Albina and the chorus, comment on the situation. With the announcement by Serano that they are threatened by the enemy, patriotism replaces private emotions, and the act ends with a warlike ensemble of defiance and determination.

Act II, scene i: a cave by the lake. Hubert has returned to seek out the girl with whom he has fallen in love and he sings of his passion: 'Oh fiamma soave' (Oh sweet flame). Ellen appears and he bares his heart, but she admits she loves another and offers him only her friendship. He gives her a ring, telling her that he had it from the King of Scotland, whose life he saved; if any member of her family is in danger, she should take it to the King, who will grant any wish she may ask. Their extended duet is overheard by Roderick, whose voice joins with theirs (the music demands high C's from both tenors and a pair of D's from Hubert) before he surprises them and challenges Hubert to reveal his identity. He says he does not fear the King's enemies but, at a cry from Roderick, the side of the lake is covered with his followers, who have been hiding in the undergrowth. Ellen stops them falling on Hubert without more ado, and a scene of splendid effect ends as Hubert and Roderick prepare to fight, much to Ellen's dismay.

Scene ii: a great room in Stirling Castle. Ellen was born in the castle and she returns to it to ask the King to help her father, who is in prison. Her feelings as she beholds the place of her birth are by no means unmixed, as here she found nothing but misfortune, in contrast to the humble cottage where she has been happy. She enquires for the King and is amazed to find that he and Hubert are one and the same person. When she pleads for her father, he is restored to her arms and eventually a pardon granted to Malcolm. (The quartet, 'Cielo il mio labbro inspira', for Ellen, Malcolm,

Hubert/James and Douglas was taken, with Rossini's sanction, from his opera *Bianca e Falliero* and even printed in scores and libretti of the 1830's and 1840's.) The opera ends with a brilliant and very appealing finale, 'Tanti affetti in tal momento' (So many feelings in one moment), dominated by Ellen, and, it appears, the one passage to find favour at the San Carlo première.   H.

SEMIRAMIDE

Opera in two acts by Gioacchino Rossini; text by Gaetano Rossi, founded on Voltaire's tragedy. First performed on February 3, 1823, at the Fenice Theatre, Venice; London, Haymarket, 1824; Covent Garden, 1842 (in English), with Adelaide Kemble, Mrs. Shaw, Mr. Giubilei, Mr. Leffler; opened the Royal Italian Opera, Covent Garden, 1847, with Grisi, Alboni, Tamburini, Lavia, Tagliafico, conductor Costa; New York, 1845; Metropolitan, New York, 1893, with Melba, Scalchi, Guetary, Castelmary, E. de Reszke; Florence Festival, 1940, with Gatti, Stignani, Tagliavini, Pasero, conductor Serafin. Revived at la Scala, Milan, 1962, with Sutherland, Simionato, Raimondi, Ganzarolli, conductor Santini.

CHARACTERS

Semiramide, *Queen of Babylon* . . . . Soprano
Arsace, *Commander of the Assyrian Army* . . . Contralto
Ghost of Nino . . . . Bass
Oroe, *High Priest of the Magi* . . . . Bass
Assur, *a Prince* . . . . Baritone
Azema, *a Princess* . . . . Soprano
Idreno, *an Indian Prince* . . . . Tenor
Mitrane, *Captain of the Guard* . . . . Tenor
Magi, Guards, Satraps, Slaves
Time: Antiquity   *Place:* Babylon

Semiramide seems to have had its day. Yet, were a soprano and a contralto, capable of doing justice to the rôles of Semiramide and Arsace, to appear in conjunction in the operatic firmament, the opera might be successfully revived, as it was for Patti and Scalchi.[1] The latter, in her prime when she first appeared in America, was one of the greatest of contraltos. I think that all who, like myself, had the good fortune to hear the revival of *Semiramide*, still consider the

[1] And was for Joan Sutherland and Giulietta Simionato.   H.

singing by Patti and Scalchi of the duet, 'Giorno d'orrore' (Day of horror), the finest example of *bel canto* it has been their privilege to listen to. For beauty and purity of tone, smoothness of phrasing, elegance, and synchronisation of embellishment it has not been equalled here since.

In the first act of the opera is a brilliant aria for Semiramide, 'Bel raggio lusinghier' (Bright ray of hope),—the one piece that has kept the opera in the gramophone repertory.

A priests' march and chorus, which leads up to the finale of the first act, is accompanied not only by orchestra, but also by full military band on the stage, the first instance of the employment of the latter in Italian opera. The duet, 'Giorno d'orrore,' is in the second act.

For many years the overture to *Semiramide* was a favourite at popular concerts. It was admired for the broad, hymnlike air in the introduction, which in the opera becomes an effective chorus,

and for the graceful, lively melody, which is first announced on the clarinet. I call it 'graceful' and 'lively', and so it would

be considered to-day. But in the opera it accompanies the
cautious entrance of priests into a darkened temple where a

deep mystery is impending, and, at the time the opera was
produced, this music, which now we would describe as above,
was supposed to be 'shivery' and 'gruesome'. In fact the scene
was objected to by audiences of that now seemingly remote
period, on the ground that the orchestra was too prominent
and that, in the treatment of the instrumental score to his
operas, Rossini was leaning too heavily toward German
models! But this, remember, was in 1823.

The story of *Semiramide* can be briefly told. Semiramide,
Queen of Babylon, has murdered her husband, Nino, the
King. In this deed she was assisted by Prince Assur, who
expects to win her hand and the succession to the throne.

Semiramide, however, is enamoured of a comely youth,
Arsace, victorious commander of her army, and supposedly a
Scythian, but in reality her own son, of which relationship
only Oroe, the chief priest of the temple, is aware. Arsace
himself is in love with the royal Princess Azema.

At a gathering in the temple, the gates of the tomb of Nino
are opened as if by invisible hands. The shade of Nino
announces that Arsace shall be his successor; and summons
him to come to the tomb at midnight there to learn the
secret of his assassination.

Enraged at the prophecy of the succession of Arsace and
knowing of his coming visit to the tomb of Nino, Assur
contrives to enter it; while Semiramide, who now knows that
the young warrior is her son, comes to the tomb to warn him
against Assur. The three principal personages in the drama are
thus brought together at its climax. Arsace makes what
would be a fatal thrust at Assur. Semiramide interposes
herself between the two men and receives the death wound.
Arsace is proclaimed king and the avenger of his father's
murder.

According to legend, Semiramis, when a babe, was fed by
doves; and, after reigning for forty-two years, disappeared or
was changed into a dove and flew away. For the first New York
performance Garcia announced the work as *La Figlia
dell'Aria, or Semiramide.*   K.

LE COMTE ORY

Count Ory

Opera in two acts by Gioacchino Rossini, libretto in French by Scribe and Delestre-Poirson. Première, Académie Royale, Paris, August 20, 1828, with Cinti-Damoreau, Javureck, Nourrit, Levasseur, Dabadie. Outstandingly successful in Paris, where 400 performances by 1884. First performed King's Theatre, London, 1829; Covent Garden, 1854, with Bosio, Marai, Lucchesi, Tagliafico, Zelger. Revived Florence Festival, 1952, with Barabas, Monti, Capecchi, Petri, conductor Gui; Glyndebourne at Edinburgh Festival, 1954, with Barabas, Oncina, Bruscantini, Wallace, conductor Gui; Berlin, Städtische Oper, 1957, with Barabas, Häfliger, Krukowski, Kohn, conductor Richard Kraus; Piccola Scala, Milan, 1958, with Sciutti, Berganza, Oncina, Panerai, Calabrese, conductor Sanzogno; Sadler's Wells, 1963, with Elizabeth Harwood, Patricia Kern, Alexander Young, Dowling; 1972, with Valerie Masterson and John Brecknock.

CHARACTERS

Raimbaud, *friend to Comte Ory* .... Baritone
Alice, *a peasant girl* .... Soprano
Comte Ory, *a young and profligate nobleman* ... Tenor
Ragonde, *companion to Comtesse Adèle* .... Contralto
The tutor .... Bass
Isolier, *page to Comte Ory* .... Mezzo-Soprano
A young nobleman, *friend to Comte Ory* .... Tenor
Comtesse Adèle .... Soprano

Time: The Crusades   *Place:* Touraine

Following the great success of *Moïse* in Paris, Rossini set to work on a light-hearted comedy in French style—this in spite of the fact that his mother, to whom he was devoted, had recently died. Scribe and Delestre-Poirson reworked a vaudeville they had written a dozen years before, doubling its length by adding an additional act (the first), and Rossini set it, using four numbers from *Il Viaggio a Reims*. The result has been very much admired, particularly in France, where composers as different as Berlioz and Milhaud have praised it warmly, and its recent revivals have been widespread and successful.

The story is of the dissolute young Comte Ory and his efforts (as unsuccessful as Don Giovanni's) to win the favours of a lady. The Comte de Formoutiers is away on the Crusades, leaving his sister, Adèle, and her companions

431

without male protection in the castle. Determined to reach her, Comte Ory and a young scapegrace friend, Raimbaud, have dressed themselves up as hermits and are hanging about the gate of Adèle's castle, waiting for a chance to get in. When the curtain rises on Act I after a mainly martial introduction, Raimbaud is summoning the peasantry to the hermit's presence: in a moment he will appear—let them put their offerings over on the bank, and a truce to ribaldry. Ragonde comes to rebuke the crowd for its levity at a time when Countess Adèle is mourning her brother's absence; she and her mistress mean to consult the hermit with a view to alleviating their present distress.

Just then the Count appears: the *tessitura* of his cavatina ('Que les destins prospères') is high, like the rest of the role, and in it he offers his help to all and sundry, particularly those of the fair sex who want for husbands. In a typical *crescendo* ensemble, all ask for benefits which he confers. Ragonde, whom he has earlier addressed as 'dame trop respectable', tells him that the Countess and the other ladies of the castle have made vows Lysistrata-like to shun the society of men until the Comte de Formoutiers is back from the Crusades. Now she is lonely and depressed and, to the Count's delight, wants his advice.

On to the empty stage come the Count's tutor and his page, Isolier; the former looking for his elusive charge, the latter suggesting that he may find his lordship in this vicinity, for no better reason than that Isolier himself is in love with his cousin Adèle and sees a chance of being near her. In an aria the tutor complains of his unhappy lot, but he starts to smell a rat when he hears some girls singing the praises of a hermit who arrived eight days before—exactly the time the Count has been gone. Isolier in contrast suspects nothing: he sings a delightful, sprightly duet with his master, whom he does not recognise, and to whom (in search of spiritual advice) he unwittingly reveals his love for Adèle and his plan to gain admission to the castle disguised as a pilgrim. Ory resolves to adopt the plan himself.

Adèle now emerges to consult the hermit, and in an agitated aria ('En proie à la tristesse') admits that her self-denying vow has induced a fit of melancholy. The cure is simple, says the Count; she must fall in love—and forthwith he absolves her from her vow. In her cabaletta she accepts his advice and seems likely to fix her affections on her cousin

Isolier until the hermit warns her against the machinations of the page of the notorious Comte Ory. At that moment the tutor arrives, recognises his charge and gives the show away. From different points of view all express horror at such a turn of events in a beautiful unaccompanied septet, at whose end the Countess receives news that her brother and his companions are likely to return home within a day. Reflecting on the short time he now has in which to accomplish his design, the Count leads off a brilliant *allegro spiritoso* ensemble, which brings the act to an end.

Act II is set inside the castle, where Adèle and her companions—not forgetting Ragonde—are waiting for the return of the crusaders. Surrounded by the women, they sing a duet 'Dans ce sèjour calme et tranquille' and congratulate themselves on their recent escape from the wiles of Comte Ory. Through the noise of a storm can be heard the sound of pilgrims intoning their chant. The Countess cannot refuse hospitality to the travellers and sends Ragonde, who comes back to say that they are nuns fleeing from the wicked Comte Ory. She brings with her the Mother Superior, who is of course the Count in disguise.

The Mother Superior protests the gratitude of all the nuns in a duet ('Ah, quel respect, madame') and slyly confides to the Countess that rumour has it that the Count loves her—which news causes that lady much indignation. Food is provided for the weary travellers and once they are alone their delight in their situation is expressed in a rollicking chorus. Only one thing is missing—and Raimbaud comes in to tell them in an aria that he has found it: wine! The drinking chorus is gay and infectious, but it changes quickly to the pilgrims' plaint when a footstep is heard approaching. It is the Countess to tell them that their accommodation for the night is prepared.

Isolier brings Adèle news of the imminent arrival of her brother, and when he hears of the nuns lodged within the walls he is overcome with suspicion. He warns Adèle that she may be sheltering the Count himself, and, when they hear someone coming, volunteers to save her from the fate which seems to be in store for her. The Count attempts to make love to Adèle, but his advances are intercepted in the dark by Isolier, who loses no time in passing them on, one might say with interest, to his beautiful cousin. The trio ('A la faveur de cette nuit obscure') is the most celebrated number in the score; says Francis Toye: 'for loveliness of melody, originality of harmony, charm of part-writing, it is beyond praise, worthy of Mozart at his best. Berlioz, who cannot be suspected of undue tenderness towards Rossini, writes . . . that this particular trio was, in his opinion, the composer's absolute masterpiece.'[1]

Suddenly, trumpets are heard signalling the return of the crusaders. Ory is discovered, Isolier reveals himself, counters his master's fury with the threat to disclose all to his father, but relents to help him escape. The opera ends with the anticipated arrival of the returning warriors.   H.

GUILLAUME TELL
William Tell

Opera in four acts by Gioacchino Rossini; text by V. J. Etienne de Jouy and H. L. F. Bis after Schiller. Première on August 3, 1829, at the Opéra, Paris, with Nourrit as Arnold; the four acts were reduced to three in June 1831. First performed in London, Drury Lane, 1830 (in English); Her Majesty's, 1839 (in Italian); Covent Garden, 1845 (in French); New York, 1831 (in English), 1845 (in French), 1855 (in Italian). Revived, London Opera House, 1911, with Victoria Fer, Orville Harrold, conductor Ernaldy; at Metropolitan, New York, 1923, with Ponselle, Martinelli, and 1931, with Lauri-Volpi; Colon, Buenos Aires, 1923, with Spani, Sullivan, Galeffi; la Scala, Milan, 1930, with Bruna Rasa, Lauri-Volpi, Franci; Rome Opera, 1930, with Arangi-Lombardi; Paris Opéra, 1932, with Norena, O'Sullivan, Huberty, Journet; Berlin, 1934, with Heidersbach, Roswaenge, Bockelmann, Bohnen, Kipnis, conductor Heger; Florence Festival, 1939, with Gatti, Mazaroff, Sved, Pasero, conductor Marinuzzi; Rome, 1950, with Gatti, Filippeschi, Silveri; Florence Festival, 1952, with Rossi-Lemeni (Tell), Tebaldi, Baum, and Serafin conducting; Drury Lane, London, 1958, with Bechi and Filippeschi. Revived la Scala, Milan, 1965, with Ilva Ligabue, Gianni Raimondi, Giangiacomo Guelfi, conductor Molinari-Pradelli.

CHARACTERS

Guillaume Tell . . . . Baritone
Hedwige, *Tell's wife* . . . . Soprano
Jemmy, *Tell's son* . . . . Soprano
Arnold, *suitor of Mathilde* . . . . Tenor
Melcthal, *Arnold's father* . . . . Bass
Gessler, *governor of Schwitz and Uri* . . . . Bass
Mathilde, *Gessler's sister* . . . . Soprano

[1] *Rossini: a study in tragi-comedy* by Francis Toye, Heinemann, 1934.

Rudolph, *captain in Gessler's guard* . . . . Tenor
Walter Furst . . . . Bass
Leuthold, *a shepherd* . . . . Bass
Ruedi, *a fisherman* . . . . Tenor

Peasants, Knights, Pages, Ladies, Hunters, Soldiers,
Guards, and three Bridal Couples

Time: Thirteenth Century   *Place:* Switzerland

Arnold, a Swiss patriot and son of the venerable Swiss
leader, Melcthal, has saved from drowning Mathilde, sister of
the Austrian tyrant Gessler, whom the Swiss abhor. Arnold
and Mathilde have fallen in love with each other.

Act I.   A beautiful May morning has dawned over the
Lake of Lucerne, on which Tell's house is situated. It is the
day of the Shepherd Festival. According to ancient custom
the grey-haired Melcthal blesses the loving couples among
them. But his own son, Arnold, does not ask a blessing of the
old man; although he loves Mathilde, his heart belongs to his
native land. The festival is interrupted by the sound of horns.
It is the train of Gessler, the hated tyrant. Leuthold rushes in,
breathless. In order to protect his daughter from dishonour,
he has been obliged to kill one of Gessler's soldiers. He is
pursued. To cross the lake is his only means of escape. But
who will take him in the face of the storm that is coming
up? Tell wastes no time in thinking. He acts. It is the last
possible moment. Gessler's guards are already in sight,
Rudolph at their head. With Tell's aid the fugitive escapes
them, but they turn to the country folk, and sieze and carry
off old Melcthal.

Act II.   In a valley by a lake Arnold and Mathilde meet
and again pledge their love. Arnold learns from Tell and
Walter that his father has been slain by Gessler's order. His
thoughts turn to vengeance. The three men bind themselves
by oath to free Switzerland. The cantons gather and swear to
throw off the Austrian yoke.

Act III.   The market-place in Altdorf. It is the hundredth
anniversary of Austrian rule in Switzerland. Fittingly to
celebrate the day Gessler has ordered his hat to be placed on
top of a pole, and the Swiss are commanded to make obeisance
to it. Tell comes along holding his son Jemmy by the hand.
He refuses to pay homage to the hat. As in him is also
recognised the man who saved Leuthold, he must be
punished. Gessler cynically orders him to shoot an apple

from Jemmy's head. The shot succeeds. Fearless, as before, Tell informs Gessler that the second arrow was intended for him, had the first missed its mark. Tell's arrest is ordered, but the armed Swiss, who have risen against Austria, approach. Gessler falls by Tell's shot; the fight ends with complete victory for the Swiss. Mathilde who still loves Arnold finds refuge in his arms.

Guillaume Tell is the only opera by an Italian of which it can be said that the overture has gained world-wide fame, and justly so, while the opera itself is so rarely heard that it may almost be said to have passed out of the repertory. Occasionally it is revived for the benefit of a high tenor like Tamagno.[1] In point of fact, however, it is too good a work to be made the vehicle of a single operatic star. It is quite likely that, with a fine ensemble, *Guillaume Tell* could be restored to the list of operas regularly given.

The care which Rossini bestowed on this work is seen in the layout and composition of the overture, which as an instrumental number is as fine a *tour de force* as his 'Una voce poco fa', 'Bel raggio', or 'Giorno d'orrore' are for voice. The slow introduction denotes Alpine calm. There is a beautiful passage for violoncellos, which has been quoted in books on instrumentation. In it Rossini may well have harked back to his student years, when he was a pupil in violoncello playing at the conservatory in Bologna. The calm is followed by a storm and this, in turn, by a 'Ranz des Vaches'. The final section consists of a trumpet call, followed by a fast movement, which can be played so as to leave the hearer quite breathless. It is supposed to represent the call to arms and the uprising of the Swiss against their Austrian oppressors, whose yoke they threw off.

The most striking musical number in the first act of the opera is Arnold's 'Ah, Mathilde':

Ah, Ma-thil-de, je t'ai - - me et je t'a-dore.

A tenor with powerful high tones in his voice can always render this with great effect. In fact it is so effective that its

---

[1] or Lauri-Volpi, Mazaroff, Filippeschi.   H.

coming so early in the work is a fault of construction which in my opinion has been a factor in the non-success of the opera as a whole. Even a tenor like Mierzwinski, 'a natural singer of short-lived celebrity', with remarkable high notes, could in this number rouse to a high pitch of enthusiasm an audience that remained comparatively calm the rest of the evening.

The climax of the second act is the trio between Arnold, Tell, and Walter, followed by the assembly of the cantons and the taking of the oath to conquer or die (May glory our hearts with courage exalt).

Its most effective passage begins as follows:

Another striking musical number is Arnold's solo in the last act, at sight of his ruined home, 'Asile héréditaire' (O, silent abode).

At the initial performance of *Guillaume Tell* in Paris, there was no indication that the opera was not destined to remain for many years in the repertory. It was given fifty-six times. Then, because of the great length of the opera, only the second act was performed in connection with some other work, until the sensational success of Duprez, in 1837, led to a revival.

Guillaume Tell, given in full, would last nearly five hours. The poor quality of the original libretto by de Jouy led to the revision by Bis, but even after that there had to be cuts.

'Ah, Maestro,' exclaimed an enthusiastic admirer of Rossini to that master, 'I heard Act II of your *William Tell* at the Opera last night!'

'What!' asked Rossini. 'The whole of it?'

Clever; but by his question Rossini unconsciously put his finger on the weak spot of the opera he intended to be his masterpiece. Be it never so well given, it is long-winded.

K.

GAETANO DONIZETTI

(1797–1848)

DONIZETTI, like Rossini and Verdi, unlike Beethoven and Wagner, was a practitioner not a questioner. He could invent music that was original, but he accepted the aesthetic conventions of his day and sought inspiration within them and seldom attempted to break new ground. By this time, Beethoven and romantic striving had burst the moulds of symphonic form but Italian opera in the first half of the nineteenth century was nonetheless a period of certainty. Viable forms (different for tragedy and comedy) had been forged by Rossini and his contemporaries and were being exploited by Bellini, Donizetti, and even (for his first twenty creative years) Verdi. This process satisfied audiences, who knew what to expect and delighted in re-discovering the pleasures of past performances; singers, whose status it enshrined and whose prowess it displayed; and composers, whose formal problems were largely solved and who had merely to find the notes to express the situations which were to hand.

In Donizetti's tragedies, you will find the expected introductory chorus of the heroine's opening cavatina, the meetings and partings of lovers and would-be lovers, the confrontations of rivals, the mistakes of identity, and of course the mad scenes (sometimes masquerading as death scenes, but mad scenes nonetheless, with their jumps through time and space so that a quotation of earlier music may poignantly recall earlier bliss). A Donizetti subject, whether from Schiller or Scott, whether concerned with a Scottish queen or an Amazonian heroine, will follow the same well-trodden path. Ocassionally a great scene will emerge—the sextet in *Lucia*, or the pathetic end of *Anna Bolena*—but the form will be predictable throughout, which need be no more than to say that some Haydn symphonies are better than others, that a choice is permissible even among the many examples of Madonna and Child by Giovanni Bellini. H.

ANNA BOLENA
Anne Boleyn

Opera in two acts by Gaetano Donizetti, libretto by Felice Romani. Première, Teatro Carcano, Milan, Dec. 20, 1830, with Giuditta Pasta,

Elisa Orlandi, Rubini, Galli. First performed at la Scala, 1832, with Pasta (later Grisi), Deval and Negrini. London, King's Theatre, 1831, with Pasta, Rubini, Lablache; New York, 1843 (in French). Revived Covent Garden, 1847, with Giulia Grisi, Alboni, Mario, Tamburini; Drury Lane, London, 1871, with Tietjens, Sinico, Agnesi; Bergamo, 1956 (after 113 years absence from Italy) with Marina Cucchio, Maria Minetto, Gianni Iaia, Algorta; la Scala, 1957, with Callas, Simionato, Raimondi, Rossi-Lemeni in a production by Luchino Visconti, conductor Gavazzeni; New York (in concert) 1957, with Gloria Davy, Simionato, Kenneth Smith, conductor Arnold Gamson; Glyndebourne, 1965, with Gencer, Patricia Johnston, Oncina, Cava, conductor Gavazzeni; New York (in concert) 1967, with Suliotis, Horne and Domingo.

CHARACTERS

Enrico VIII, *King of England* . . . . Bass
Anna Bolena, *his second wife* . . . . Soprano
Giovanna Seymour, *her lady-in-waiting* . . . . . . Soprano
Lord Rochefort, *Anne Boleyn's brother* . . . . Bass
Lord Riccardo Percy . . . . Tenor
Smeaton, *the Queen's page* . . . . Contralto
Hervey, *Official at the Court* . . . . Tenor

Courtiers, Officials, Lords, Huntsmen, Soldiers, etc.

Time: 1536   *Place:* England—Acts I and II Windsor;
Act III London

Operatic legend once had it that in the autumn of 1830—whose beginning saw the première in Paris of that source of the romantic movement, Victor Hugo's *Hernani*— both Bellini and Donizetti were working at Lake Como on operatic commissions from the impresario of the Teatro Carcano, Milan, Bellini staying at Moltrasio with Giuditta Turina on one side, Donizetti on the other at Blevio with Giuditta Pasta. Each composer had a libretto from the celebrated Felice Romani and each was determined to outdo the other. Like most legends, the facts are a little different; Donizetti's libretto for *Anna Bolena* was in his hands on November 10th (the composition was finished by December 10th), Bellini's for *La Sonnambula* only in December.

At the time of Donizetti's death, the critic of the *Revue des deux Mondes* pointed to five of his operas as most likely to survive: *Lucia, Favorita, L'Elisir, Don Pasquale* and *Anna Bolena*, and certainly the opera was in as high favour with the public as with prima donnas, who found a perfect vehicle for their gifts in Anna's 'Piangete voi?' and 'Al dolce guidami', a mad scene to vie with those from *Sonnambula* and *Puritani, Lucia* and *Linda*. In the 1950's, *Anna Bolena* was one of the most successful of the several operas to benefit from the revival of interest in *bel canto* that owed its impulse mainly to the sovereign interpretative powers of Maria Callas, but which in Italy at any rate had sufficient impetus to carry through even with lesser singers.

It was with Callas in the title role and in a magnificent production by Visconti that the opera triumphed at la Scala in 1957, and it was in this role a year later that Callas returned to the Italian stage after the most resounding scandal of her career. She had inaugurated the 1957–8 season in Rome in *Norma* and, with the President of the Republic in the house, withdrew after the first act, at which point the performance came to an unscheduled end. The storm which broke about her head next day[1] accused her amongst other things of insulting the head of State, and quite ignored the fact that she was ill and had asked for a substitute (two other members of the cast had already withdrawn with the same virus) but had mistakenly yielded to the pleas of the management to sing. She did not appear in Italy again until nearly four months later, at the time of the Milan Fair, at which time la Scala's Gala for the President was rather ostentatiously changed from the originally scheduled *Anna Bolena* with Callas to something less controversial. I was present when a few days later *Anna Bolena* had its seasonal première. The atmosphere in the house was full of nervous expectancy and not until the finale of Act I (by which time the action had already been interrupted by an interval, as in most other modern stagings) did the hostility abruptly change, but then it would have taken a more solidly hostile audience than la Scala's to ignore Callas's 'Giudici, ad Anna! Ad Anna! Giudici!', a less than Italianate reaction to operatic drama to resist her impassioned attack in the *stretta* and her ability at the repeat to cap the intensity of the first section. That hundreds of enthusiastic Milanese waited two

[1] Occasioned, said cynics, less by indignation on behalf of the President than by chagrin on the part of Roman grandees, who not only lacked cars to take them home unexpectedly early but arrived to find their retainers uninhibitedly celebrating the New Year in their absence!

nours at the stage door to escort the exhausted prima donna
to supper at three in the morning seemed no more than a
fitting tribute to an evening that had begun with assassination
somehow round every corner and had ended in triumph.

Act I.   The first scene of the opera shows the great
staircase at Windsor Castle, where a crowd of courtiers
discuss the King's growing love for Jane Seymour, who
presently appears, troubled that the Queen should show such
solicitude to one whom she does not recognise as her rival.
To solemn music, the Queen enters, full of forebodings which
are only increased by the sad little song with which her page
Smeaton tries to beguile her mood. The Queen's slow
cavatina ('Come, innocente giovane') is followed by a
cabaletta, after which she and the Court withdraw. Jane
Seymour alone gives voice to her anxiety, but the appearance
of the King and his ardent wooing soon remove her doubts
and the scene ends with a big-scale duet, in whose course the
King reveals that he intends to expose the unfaithfulness of
his wife and marry Jane.

A courtyard in the castle. The Queen's brother Rochefort
is astonished to see Percy, whom the King has recalled from
exile in the hope that he will provide the evidence against the
Queen. Percy admits that the love he felt for Anne Boleyn as
a girl is not dead because she is now Queen (Cavatina: 'Da
quel dì che lei perduta'). Preparations are in train for the
Court to go hunting, and when the King and Queen appear,
Percy's hopes are encouraged by the Queen's obvious confusion. The scene ends with an impressive quintet ('Io senti i
sulla mia mano'), during whose course the King instructs
Hervey to watch Percy's behaviour with the Queen,
Rochefort laments Percy's lack of discretion, and the
courtiers are filled with apprehension at the new turn of
events.

Scene iii.[1]   In a corridor leading to the Queen's private
apartments, Smeaton is gazing enraptured at a miniature of
the Queen, which he kisses as he sings of his love for her
('Ah, parea che per incanto'). He hides when the Queen
comes into view with her brother, who is trying to persuade
her to grant an audience to Percy. When Percy appears, the
Queen remains adamant: she is a wife and a Queen and will

[1] Now, usually Act II.

not listen to his protestations. At the end of their duet, the Queen refuses to see him again and Percy draws his sword to kill himself, only for Smeaton to rush from his hiding place. The Queen faints as Rochefort runs to warn her that the King is on his way, and Henry arrives to catch her in what he purports to find a compromising situation: 'Tace ognuno è ognun tremante!' Smeaton's protestation of her innocence is rendered less credible by the discovery of the portrait he wears round his neck, and, as Jane Seymour comes in, the King renews his accusations and threats. He condemns the conspirators to separate cells and orders the Queen to make her defence before the judges, not to him. 'Giudici, ad Anna' comes her despairing cry; 'Ah, segnata è la mia sorte' (My fate is sealed) she leads the *stretta* to what with a Callas can be extraordinary effect.

The second act shows the Queen in custody and then face to face with the scaffold. In the first scene, her ladies-in-waiting try to comfort her as she waits for trial, but Hervey announces that the King has decided to deprive her of even their support. Jane Seymour comes to advise her to try to save her life with a plea of guilty, then confesses that she is the one the King has designated to take the Queen's place. In the course of a grandiose duet, Anne generously forgives her.

The second scene takes place in a vestibule before the Council Chamber, where Hervey tells the assembled courtiers that Smeaton has confessed and implicated the Queen. The King passes through and the Queen proudly refutes the accusations which are about to be levelled at her, at the same time admitting that before becoming Queen she had loved Percy. The King's rage and determination to be revenged ('Ambo morrete'), Percy's ecstatic proclamation of his love, the Queen's regret that no hope now is left her, are combined in a noble trio, after whose *stretta*, as the Queen and Percy are led off by guards, Jane Seymour herself comes to intercede for the unfortunate Queen she both loves and rivals ('Per questa fiamma indomita'). Her plea avails nothing since Hervey comes to announce the Council's unanimous sentence of death on the Queen and her accomplices.

In the Tower of London lie the conspirators. When Hervey comes to convey the King's clemency to Percy and Rochefort, each indignantly refuses to live while the guiltless Queen must die. (This scene, which contains a beautiful lyrical aria for Percy, 'Vivi tu, te ne scongiuro', was omitted in la Scala's revival.)

The last scene is one of Donizetti's great masterpieces of melodic and dramatic inspiration. In the Tower of London the Queen waits for death. She has lost her senses and chides her ladies for weeping (in a fine preludial chorus) on her wedding day when the King awaits her. Her mood shifts from terror to joy and, when she thinks she sees Percy smile at her, she sings ecstatically 'Al dolce guidami', movingly preluded by cor anglais solo. Hervey comes to order the Queen and the three condemned with her to proceed to the scaffold, and Smeaton admits that the false confession he made, hoping to save his own life, has contributed to her downfall. Anne again loses her reason, orders Smeaton to tune his harp and sing to her, then intones a prayer ('Cielo, a miei lunghi spasimi')[1] while Smeaton, Percy and Rochefort join their voices to hers. The firing of a cannon and ringing of bells are heard acclaiming the new Queen, and the opera ends with an impassioned outburst of denunciation from Anne Boleyn ('Coppia iniqua').   H.

L'ELISIR D'AMORE

The Elixir of Love

Opera in two acts by Gaetano Donizetti; text by Felice Romani. Première at the Teatro della Canobbiana, Milan, May 12, 1832, with Sabina Heinefetter, Genero, Dabadie, Frezzolini. First performed in London, Lyceum Theatre, 1836; New York, 1838; Metropolitan, New York, 1904, with Sembrich, Caruso, Scotti, Rossi, conductor Vigna; 1916, with Hempel, Caruso, Scotti, Didur, conductor Papi; revived 1941, with Sayao, Landi, Valentino, Baccaloni, conductor Panizza; Covent Garden, 1950, with Carosio, Tagliavini, Gobbi, Tajo, conductor Capuana; Glyndebourne, 1961, with Ratti, Alva, Sordello, Badioli, conductor Cillario. Famous Nemorinos of this generation also include Schipa, Gigli and di Stefano.

CHARACTERS

Nemorino, *a young peasant* . . . . Tenor
Adina, *wealthy, and owner of a farm* . . . . Soprano

[1] The tune is a decorated version of 'Home Sweet Home' (from Bishop's opera *Clari*, 1823), which enjoyed enormous popularity at the time.

Belcore, *a sergeant* .... Baritone
Dulcamara, *a quack doctor* .... Bass
Giannetta, *a peasant girl* .... Soprano
Time: Nineteenth Century   *Place:* A small Italian village

Act I.   Beauty and riches have made the youthful Adina
exacting. She laughs at the embarrassed courting of the
true-hearted peasant lad, Nemorino, mocks at the story of
Tristan and Isolde, rejoices that there are now no more
elixirs to bring the merry heart of woman into slavish
dependence on love. Yet she does not seem so much
indifferent to Nemorino as piqued over his lack of courage to
come to the point.

Sergeant Belcore arrives in the village at the head of a
troop of soldiers. He seeks to win Adina's heart by storm.
The villagers tease Nemorino about his soldier rival, and he is
driven almost to despair by their raillery. Enter the
peripatetic quack, Dr. Dulcamara. For a ducat Nemorino
eagerly buys of him a flask of cheap Bordeaux, which the
quack assures him is an elixir of love that within twenty-four
hours will enable him to win Adina. Nemorino empties the
flask at a draught. A certain effect shows itself at once.
Under the influence of the Bordeaux he falls into extravagant
mirth, sings, dances—and grieves no more about Adina, who
becomes piqued and, to vex Nemorino, engages herself to
marry Sergeant Belcore. An order comes to the troops to
move. The Sergeant presses for an immediate marriage. To
this Adina, still under the influence of pique, consents.
Nemorino seeks to console himself by louder singing and
livelier dancing.

Act II.   The village is assembled on Adina's farm to
celebrate her marriage with the Sergeant. But it is noticeable
that she keeps putting off signing the marriage contract.
Nemorino awaits the effect of the elixir. To make sure of it, he
buys from Dulcamara a second bottle. Not having the money
to pay for it, and Belcore being on the look-out for recruits,
Nemorino enlists and, with the money he receives, pays
Dulcamara. The fresh dose of the supposed elixir makes
Nemorino livelier than ever. He pictures to himself the glory
of a soldier's career. He also finds himself greatly admired by
the village girls for enlisting. Adina also realises that he has
joined the army out of devotion to her, and indicates that she
favours him rather than Belcore. But he now has the exalted

pleasure of treating her with indifference, so that she goes away very sad. He attributes his luck to the elixir.

The villagers have learned that his rich uncle is dead and has left a will making him his heir. But because this news has not yet been communicated to him, he thinks their attentions due to the love philtre, and believes the more firmly in its efficacy. In any event, Adina has perceived, upon the Sergeant's pressing her to sign the marriage contract, that she really prefers Nemorino. Like a shrewd little woman, she takes matters into her own hands, and buys back from Sergeant Belcore her lover's enlistment paper. Having thus set him free, she behaves so coyly that Nemorino threatens to seek death in battle, whereupon she faints right into his arms. The Sergeant bears this unlucky turn of affairs with the bravery of a soldier, while Dulcamara's fame becomes such that he can sell the villagers his entire stock of Bordeaux at a price that makes him rich.

The elixir of life of this *Elixir of Love* is the romance for tenor in the second act, 'Una furtiva lagrima' (A furtive tear), which Nemorino sings as Adina sadly leaves him, when she thinks that he has become indifferent to her. It was because of Caruso's admirable rendition of this beautiful romance that the opera was revived at the Metropolitan Opera House, New York, in 1904. Even the instrumental introduction to it, in which the bassoons carry the air, is captivating.

U-na fur-ti-va la-gri-ma   Negl'oc-chi suoi spun-to,

Act I is laid on Adina's farm. Nemorino sings a charming song, 'Quanto è bella', and Adina has a florid air, 'Chiedi all'aura lusinghiera' (Go, demand of yon light zephyr), with which she turns aside from Nemorino's attentions.

Chie-di all'au-ra lu - sin-ghie - - - - ra,

The scene then changes to a square in the village. Here Dr. Dulcamara makes his entry, singing his *buffo* air, 'Udite, udite, o rustici' (Give ear, now, ye rustic ones). There are two attractive duets in this scene. One is for Nemorino and Dr.

Dulcamara, 'Obbligato! obbligato!' (Thank you kindly! thank you kindly!)

The other, for Adina and Nemorino, is 'Esulti pur la barbara per poco alle mie pene' (Tho' now th' exalting cruel one can thus deride my bitter pain).

Act II, which shows a room in Adina's farm house, opens with a bright chorus of rejoicing at her approaching wedding. Dulcamara brings out a piece of music, which he says is the latest thing from Venice, a barcarole for two voices. He and Adina sing it; a dainty duet, 'Io son ricco, e tu sei bella' (I have riches, thou hast beauty) which figures in all the old potpourris of the opera.

Io son ric-co, e tu sei bel-la; Io du-ca-ti, e vezzi hai tu

There is a scene for Nemorino, Giannetta, and the peasants, in which Nemorino praises the elixir, 'Dell'elisir mirabile' (Of this most potent elixir). Later comes another duet for Adina and Dulcamara, 'Quanto amore!' (What affection!) in which Adina expresses her realisation of the death of Nemorino's affection for her.

'The score of *Elisir d'Amore*,' says the *Dictionnaire des Opéras*, 'is one of the most pleasing that the Bergamo composer has written in the comic vein. It abounds in charming motifs and graceful melodies. In the first act the duet for tenor and bass between the younger villager and Dr. Dulcamara is a little masterpiece of animation, the accompaniment of which is as interesting as the vocal parts. The most striking passages of the second act are the chorus, "Cantiamo, facciam brindisi"; the barcarole for two voices, "Io son ricco, e tu sei bella"; the quartet, "Dell'elisir mirabile"; the duet between Adina and Dulcamara, "Quanto amore"; and finally the lovely and smoothly flowing romance of Nemorino, "Una furtiva lagrima", which is one of the most remarkable inspirations of Donizetti.'

To these one may add the melodious passage in which Adina makes her peace with Nemorino: 'Prendi, per me sei libero'.   K.

LUCREZIA BORGIA

Opera in a prologue and two acts by Gaetano Donizetti; text by Felice Romani (after Victor Hugo). Première at la Scala, Milan, on December 26, 1833, with Lalande, M. Brambilla, Pedrazzi, Mariani, Spiaggi; Her Majesty's Theatre, London, 1839, with Grisi, Ernesta Grisi, Mario, Tamburini; New York, 1844; Covent Garden, 1847, with Grisi, Alboni, Mario, Tamburini; Metropolitan, 1904, with de Macchi, Edyth Walker, Caruso, Scotti, conductor Vigna. Revived Colon, Buenos Aires, 1919, with Mazzoleni, Gigli; Florence, 1933, with Arangi-Lombardi, Pederzini, Gigli, Pasero, conductor Marinuzzi; la Scala, 1951, with Mancini, Pirazzini, Picchi, Rossi-Lemeni, conductor Capuana; revived Naples, 1966, with Gencer, Rota, Aragall, Petri. Teresa Tietjens in the last century and Montserrat Caballe in the 1960's have been two of the most famous exponents of the title role.

CHARACTERS

Alfonso d'Este, *Duke of Ferrara* . . . . Baritone
Lucrezia Borgia . . . . Soprano
Maffio Orsini . . . . Contralto
Gennaro ⎧ *Young noblemen in* ⎫ . . . . Tenor
Liverotto ⎨ *the service of the* ⎬ . . . . Tenor
Vitellozzo ⎩ *Venetian Republic* ⎭ . . . . Bass
Gazella . . . . Bass
Rustighello, *in the service of Don Alfonso* . . . . . . Tenor
Gubetta ⎫ *in the service of Lucrezia* . . . . ⎧ Bass
Astolfo ⎭ ⎩ Bass
Gentleman-at-Arms, Officers, Nobles and Ladies of the Venetian Republic; same, attached to court of Alfonso.

Time: Early Sixteenth Century   *Place:* Venice and Ferrara

When an opera, without actually maintaining itself in the repertory, nevertheless is an object of occasional revival, it is sure to contain striking passages that seem to justify the experiment of bringing it forward again. *Lucrezia Borgia* has a male character, Maffio Orsini, sung by a contralto. Orsini's ballata, 'Il segreto per esser felici' (O the secret of bliss is perfection), is a famous contralto air which Ernestine Schumann-Heink, with her voice of extraordinary range, made well known all over the United States.

The music has all the dash and abandon that the words suggest. Orsini sings it at a banquet in Ferrara. Suddenly from a neighbouring room comes the sound of monks' voices chanting a dirge. A door opens. The penitents, still chanting, enter. The lights grow dim and one by one go out. The

central doors swing back. Lucrezia Borgia appears in the
entrance. The banqueters are her enemies. She has poisoned
the wine they have just quaffed to Orsini's song. They are
doomed. The dirge is for them. But—and this she did not
know—among them is Gennaro, her illegitimate son, whom
she dearly loves. She offers him an antidote, but in vain. He
will not save himself while his friends die. She then discloses
the fact that she is his mother. But, even then, instead of
accepting her proffered aid to save his life, he repulses her.
Lucrezia herself then drains the poisoned cup from which he
has quaffed, and sinks, dying, upon his prostrate form. Such
is the sombre setting for the Brindisi when heard in the
opera.

Il se-gre-to-to peres-ser fe-li · · ·ci s o per prova el'inseg-noagliami-ce

The tenor rôle of Gennaro has also been responsible for
occasional revivals of the work. Mario introduced for this
character, as a substitute for a scene in the second act,
recitative and air by Lillo, 'Com' è soave quest' ora di
silenzio' (Oh! how delightful this pleasing hour of silence).

Prologue. Terrace of the Grimani palace, Venice. Festival
by night. Gennaro, weary, separates from his friends and falls
asleep on a stone bench of the terrace. Here he is discovered
by Lucrezia, who is masked. She regards him with deep
affection. 'Com' è bello! quale incanto' (Holy beauty, child of
nature) she sings.

Com' è bel - lo quale in - can - to

Gennaro awakens. In answer to her question he tells her
that he has been brought up by a poor fisherman, 'Di
pescatore ignobile' (Deem'd of a fisher's lowly race).

Larghetto

Di pes - ca - to - re i - gno - bi - le.

The youth's friends come upon the scene. Maffio Orsini tears the mask from Lucrezia's face, and in a dramatic concerted number he and his friends remind Lucrezia, for the benefit of Gennaro, who has been struck by her beauty and was unaware that she was the hated Borgia, how each has lost a brother or other relative through her. 'Maffio Orsini, signora, son' io cui svenaste il dormente fratello' (Madam, I am Orsini. My brother you did poison, the while he was sleeping). And so each one in order.

Gennaro turns from her in loathing. She faints.

Act I. A public place in Ferrara. On one side a palace. Alfonso, who, incidentally, is Lucrezia's fourth husband, she having done away with his predecessors by poison or other murderous means, is jealous of Gennaro. Like the youth himself, he is ignorant that Lucrezia is Gennaro's mother, and is persuaded that he is her paramour. He has a full-scale solo: 'Vieni, la mia vendetta' (Haste then to glut a vengeance), with its *cabaletta*, 'Qualunque sia l'evento' (On this I stake my fortune).

Qua-lun-que sia l'e - ven-to, che può re-car for-tu-na.

Gennaro and his friends come into the Plaza. They see the letters BORGIA under the escutcheon of the palace. Gennaro, to show his detestation of Lucrezia's crimes, rushes up the steps and with his sword hacks away the first letter of the name, leaving only ORGIA. At the command of the Duke he is arrested.

Lucrezia, not knowing who has committed the outrage, demands of her husband that its perpetrator be put to death. Alfonso, with cynical readiness, consents. Gennaro is led in. Lucrezia now pleads for his life. The Duke is firm, even though Lucrezia quite casually reminds him that he is her fourth husband and may share the fate of the other three. His comment is the command that Gennaro shall meet death by quaffing a goblet of poisoned wine handed to him by Lucrezia herself. There is here a strong trio for Lucrezia, Gennaro, and Alfonso, as Alfonso pours wine for himself and Lucrezia from a silver flagon, while he empties the poisoned contents of a gold vessel, 'the Borgia wine', into Gennaro's cup. But Lucrezia has the antidote; and, the Duke having left her with Gennaro in order that she shall have the pleasure of watching the death of the man of whom he suspects her to be enamoured, she gives it to Gennaro, and bids him flee from Ferrara.

Act II is laid in the Negroni palace, and is the scene of the banquet, which has already been described.   K.

MARIA STUARDA
Mary Stuart

Opera in three acts by Gaetano Donizetti. Text by Giuseppe Bardari. First performed under the name of *Buondelmonte* at the Teatro San Carlo, Naples, October 18, 1834, with Ronzi de Begnis, del Sarre, Francesco Pedrazzi, Carlo Ottolini Porto, Achille Balestracci. Produced under its original title at la Scala, Milan, December 30, 1835, with Maria Malibran, Giacinta Puzzi-Tosso, Domenico Reina, Ignazio Marini, Pietro Novelli. Revived Bergamo, 1958, with Renata Heredia Capnist, Dina Soresi, Nicola Tagger, Antonio Zerbini, conductor Olivero de Fabritiis; Stuttgart, 1958, with Maria Kouba, Grace Hoffman, Josef Traxel, Marcel Cordes, Gustav Grefe; New York (concert performance), 1964, with Irene Jordan, Hoffman, Traxel; London, St. Pancras Festival, 1966, with Maria Landis, Cynthia Jolly, David Hillman, Bryan Drake; Florence Festival, 1967, with Leyla Gencer, Shirley Verrett, Franco Tagliavini, Giulio Fioravanti, Agostino Ferrin, conductor Francesco Molinari-Pradelli (Edinburgh Festival, 1969, with the same cast, but conducted by Nino Sanzogno); Barcelona, 1968, with Montserrat Caballe, Ina del Campo, Pierre Duval, John Darenkamp, Raimundo Torres. Rome, 1970, with Caballe, Reynolds, Oncina, Fioravanti, Gaetani, conductor Bartoletti; la Scala, 1971, with Caballe, Verrett, Garavanta, Fioravanti, Washington, conductor Cillario; London (concert), 1971, with Caballe, Verrett; San Francisco, 1971, with Sutherland, Tourangeau, Burrows, Opthof, Berberian, conductor Bonynge; New York, City Opera, 1972, with Sills, Tinsley, conductor Rudel; London Coliseum, 1973, with Baker, Tinsley, Erwen, Garrard, conductor Mackerras.

CHARACTERS

Elisabetta (Elizabeth, Queen of England) . . . . . Soprano
Maria Stuarda (Mary, Queen of Scots) . . . . Soprano
Anna (Hannah Kennedy) . . . . .Mezzo-Soprano
Leicester (Robert Dudley, Earl of Leicester) . . . . Tenor
Talbot (Earl of Shrewsbury) . . . . Baritone
Cecil (Lord Burleigh) . . . . Bass
A Herald . . . . Bass

Time: 1567   *Place:* The Palace of Westminster, London; Fotheringay Castle, Northamptonshire

Maria Stuarda dates from 1834, after *Anna Bolena*, *L'Elisir d'Amore* and *Lucrezia Borgia*, and before *Lucia* (1835), *Campanello* and *Betly* (1836). Its early history is stormy, involving censorship troubles in Naples and a first night with a new libretto under the title of *Buondelmonte*; rivalry between prima donnas ending in fisticuffs on the stage; and a rehabilitation in Milan for which Malibran (in the title rôle) was wretchedly out of voice but refused to give up the part because of the fees involved.

In the second half of the twentieth century this second of the three operas Donizetti wrote involving Queen Elizabeth (*Elisabetta al Castello di Kenilworth* is the first and *Roberto Devereux* the third) seems very definitely representative of the composer at his best as well as at his most typical.

At the start of the opera Mary, Queen of Scots, has fled from her subjects and been imprisoned in Fotheringay Castle by her cousin, Elizabeth, Queen of England. We do not meet her until Act II of Donizetti's opera, which is modelled on Schiller's play and includes the famous scene of the encounter between the two Queens, a dramatically effective falsification of history on Schiller's part.

Act I. In the Palace of Westminster, courtiers await with some excitement the arrival of Queen Elizabeth, rumoured to be about to unite by marriage the thrones of England and France. The Queen, however, has inclinations towards another and less exalted man, as she reveals in her graceful cavatina 'Ah, quando all'ara scorgemi'. The court and Talbot urge clemency in her dealings with her cousin Mary Stuart, Cecil reminds her of the untrustworthiness of her rival, while the Queen remains firm in her path of indecisiveness. When Leicester enters, she appoints him her ambassador to France, notices his reluctance to accept, raises suspicions in the minds of the bystanders that this may be the man whom she secretly loves, and leaves the stage.

Talbot reveals to Leicester that he has been to Fotheringay and that Mary Stuart (referred to throughout the opera indiscriminately as 'Maria' and 'Stuarda') has asked by letter for Leicester's help in her predicament. Leicester, impressed again by the beauty of her portrait ('Ah, rimiro il bel sembiante') and the poignancy of her situation, longs to free her but promises Talbot not further to jeopardise her safety by any impetuous action. When the Queen returns and demands to see the letter he is holding, she realises from it that Mary has at one time or another had designs both on the throne which she herself occupies and the man whom she at present favours. In the course of their duet, Leicester pleads successfully that the Queen agree to visit Mary in prison at Fotheringay ('Era d'amor l'immagine', and 'Sul crin la rivale').

Act II.   In the Park at Fotheringay, Mary recalls with her companion Anna the soft, far-off days of her happy life at the French court ('Oh nube! che lieve per l'aria ti aggiri'). Her reminiscences turn to agitation at the approach of the Queen's hunting party and the prospect of the meeting which she has yearned for and now dreads. Leicester is first on the scene, to counsel her to adopt a submissive attitude towards Elizabeth, to swear himself to exact vengeance if the Queen remain obdurate, and, at the end of their duet, to ask for Mary's hand in marriage.

When Elizabeth appears, she brings with her an atmosphere of suspicion (egged on by Cecil), mistrust (because of her doubts of Leicester's motives), and apprehension (because she and her imprisoned cousin are to meet face to face for the first time). The confrontation is preceded by one of those moments of frozen drama that are peculiar to opera, a sextet in the composer's best vein, which opens with Elizabeth's reaction to her first sight of Mary: 'E sempre la stessa, superba, orgogliosa' (Unchanged she remains, proud and haughty). Mary forces herself to kneel before her cousin and beg for forgiveness, only to hear herself accused of treachery and in effect of murdering her husband, Darnley. In furious reaction, she insults the Queen, addressing her as 'Figlia impura di Bolena' and 'bastarda'. Her cause is all too evidently lost as the Queen summons the guards, and the act ends with Elizabeth in impassioned tones condemning her rival and cousin to death.

Act III.   The first scene plays at the Palace of Westminster, where Queen Elizabeth waits to sign the death warrant ('Quella vita a me funesta'). The appearance of Leicester, whom she suspects of an amorous involvement with her cousin, and the persistent promptings of Cecil combine to resolve her doubts and she signs, to start a fine trio of mutual recrimination, during whose course she orders Leicester to witness the execution.

At Fotheringay, Mary hears of the sentence from Cecil and is offered and refuses the services of an Anglican priest. There

follows the great scene of the confession by the loyal Talbot,
which so moved Queen Maria Cristina of the Two Sicilies
when she saw it at the dress rehearsal in 1834 that she fainted
and which, with its linked chain of expressive melodic sections,
seems to look forward to Verdi and the series of similarly constructed scenes, such as Gilda's in the first act of *Rigoletto* and
Leonora's with Padre Guardiano in the second of *Forza*.
Mary at one moment seems to see, and we and Talbot
through Donizetti's trombones to perceive, the ghost of her
second husband, Henry Darnley, whom the librettist makes
her refer to as Arrigo ('Delle mie colpe lo squallido
fantasma'). She poignantly remembers the murdered Rizzio,
but, as she clears her conscience ('Quando di luce rosea'),
denies all complicity in her husband's death, which she claims
was the direct result of Elizabeth's jealousy of their mutual
love. Schiller's play leaves this issue unresolved, but there is
no doubt that Donizetti's music demands that, though she
admits to complicity in the Babington plot, Mary be judged
innocent of murder.

In a room next to the scene of the impending execution,
Mary's supporters protest what they think of as a crime
against an innocent woman. Anna tries to stop them disturbing the last hours of her mistress, who enters, sees them
for the first time since her condemnation and prays calmly
and movingly to God ('Deh! tu di un umile preghiera'). We
hear the first of the three cannon shots which are to
announce the moment of the execution, and Cecil brings the
Queen's offer of a last wish. Mary asks that Anna may go
with her to the steps of the scaffold. She continues in a mood
approaching resignation ('Di un cor che more') until the
appearance of the distraught Leicester and the sound of the
second cannon shot precipitate a last protest of innocence
('Ah, se un giorno da queste ritorte'). The third cannon shot
sounds and Mary walks upright and dignified to her death.

H.

LUCIA DI LAMMERMOOR

Opera in three acts by Gaetano Donizetti; text by Salvatore
Cammarano after Sir Walter Scott's novel. Première at Teatro San
Carlo, Naples, September 26, 1835, with Persiani, Duprez, Cosselli,
Porto; Her Majesty's, 1838; New Orleans, 1841; New York, 1843;
Metropolitan, New York, 1883, with Sembrich, Campanini,

Kaschmann, Augier. Revived Covent Garden, 1925, with Toti da
Monte, Dino Borgioli, Badini; 1959, with Sutherland, conductor
Serafin; la Scala, Milan, 1923, with dal Monte, Pertile, Stracciari, Pinza
conductor Toscanini; 1936, with dal Monte, Schipa; 1938, with
Pagliughi, Gigli, conductor Marinuzzi; 1947, with Pagliughi, Gigli,
Savarese, Siepi, conductor Panizza; 1954, with Callas, di Stefano
Panerai, Modesti, under Karajan. Other celebrated Lucias have been
Lucca, Patti, Gerster, Melba, Tetrazzini, Galli-Curci, Barrientos, Pacini,
Pareto, Scotto.

CHARACTERS

Lord Henry Ashton, *of Lammermoor* . . . . Baritone
Lucy, *his sister* . . . . Soprano
Edgar, *Master of Ravenswood* . . . . Tenor
Lord Arthur Bucklaw . . . . Tenor
Raymond, *chaplain at Lammermoor* . . . . Bass
Alice, *companion to Lucy* . . . . Mezzo-Soprano
Norman, *follower of Ashton* . . . . Tenor

Relatives, Retainers, and Friends of the House of
Lammermore

Time: About 1700   *Place:* Scotland

(Note. The characters in Italian are Enrico, Lucia, Edgardo,
Arturo, Raimondo, Alisa and Normanno.)

Lucia di Lammermoor is generally held to be Donizetti's
finest work, apart perhaps from *Don Pasquale*. 'In it the vein
of melody—now sparkling, now sentimental, now tragic—
which embodies Donizetti's best claim on originality and
immortality, finds, perhaps, freest and broadest development.' These words are quoted from Baker's *Biographical
Dictionary of Musicians*, a volume that rarely pauses to
comment on an individual work. The melodies of *Lucia* are
many and beautiful, and, even when ornate in passages, are
basically expressive of the part of the tragic story to which
they relate. Moreover, the sextet at the end of the second act
when Edgar of Ravenswood appears upon the scene just as
Lucy with trembling hand has affixed her signature to the
contract of marriage between Lord Bucklaw and herself,
ranks as one of the finest pieces of dramatic music in all
opera, and for popularity is rivalled, in Italian opera, by only
one other composition, the quartet in *Rigoletto*.

Another number, the mad scene in the third act, gives
coloratura sopranos an opportunity for technical display

qual to that afforded by the lesson scene in *Il Barbiere di
iviglia*; and, unlike the latter, the music does not consist of
nterpolated selections, but of a complete *scena* with
ffective recitatives and brilliant solos, that belong to the
core.

In the story of *Lucia* the heroine's brother, Lord Henry
Ashton of Lammermoor, in order to retrieve his fallen
ortunes and extricate himself from a perilous situation in
which his participation in political movement directed against
he King has placed him, arranges a marriage between his
ister and Lord Arthur Bucklaw. Lucy herself knows nothing
f this arrangement. Henry, on the other hand, is equally
gnorant of an attachment which exists between Lucy and
dgar of Ravenswood, between whose family and his own
here has long been a deadly feud. When he discovers it, he
ses the most underhand methods to break it off.

Edgar of Ravenswood is the last of his race. While he is
bsent on a mission to France in the interests of Scotland, he
ispatches many letters to Lucy. These letters are inter-
epted by Henry, who also arranges that a forged paper,
ending to prove the infidelity of Edgar, is shown to Lucy.
Urged by the importunity of her brother, and believing
erself deserted by her lover, Lucy unwillingly consents to
ecome the bride of Lord Arthur Bucklaw. But, just as she
as signed the marriage contract, Edgar of Ravenswood
uddenly appears. He has returned from France, and now
omes to claim the hand of Lucy—but too late. Convinced
hat Lucy has betrayed his love, he casts the ring she gave
im at her feet and invokes imprecations upon her and his
ncient enemies, the House of Lammermoor.

At night he is sought out in his gloomy castle by Henry.
They agree upon a duel to be fought near the tombs of the
Ravenswoods, on the ensuing morning, when Edgar, weary of
fe, and the last of a doomed race, intends to throw himself
n his adversary's weapon. But the burden of woe has proved
oo much for Lucy to bear. At night, after retiring, she goes
ut of her mind, slays her husband, and dies of her sorrows.

Edgar awaits his enemy in the churchyard of Ravenswood.
ut Ashton has fled. Instead, Edgar's solitude is interrupted
y a train of mourners coming from the Castle of
Lammermoor. Upon hearing of Lucy's death he plunges his
agger into his breast, and sinks down lifeless in the
hurchyard where repose the remains of his ancestors.

On the stage this story is developed so that shortly after

the curtain rises on Act I, showing a grove near the Castle o
Lammermoor, Henry learns from Norman the latter'
suspicions that Lucy and Edgar have been meeting secretly i
the park of Lammermoor. Norman has dispatched his hunt:
men to discover, if they can, whether or not his suspicion
are correct. 'Cruda, funesta smania' (Each nerve with fur
trembleth), sings Henry.

Returning, the hunters relate, in a brisk chorus, that

>Long they wander'd o'er the mountain,
>Search'd each cleft around the fountain,

finally to learn by questioning a falconer that the intrude
upon the domain of Lammermoor was none other than Edga
of Ravenswood. Rage and the spirit of revenge are expressec
in Henry's vigorous *cabaletta*, 'La pietade in suo favore
(From my breast I mercy banish).

The scene changes to the park near a fountain. What nov
occurs is usually as follows. The curtain rises, and shows the
scene—evening and moonlight. There is played a beautifu
harp solo, an unusual and charming effect in opera. Havin;
prepared the mood for the scene which is to follow, it i
promptly encored and played all over again. Then Lucy
appears with her companion, Alice. To her she relates the
legend of the fountain, 'Regnava nel silenzio' (Silence o'er al
was reigning):

Reg - na - va nel si - len - zio

(This is generally sung in D but was written in E)

This number gives an idea of the characteristics of Lucy':
principal solos. It is brilliant in passages, yet its melody i
dreamy and reflective. Lucy's solo, following the legend o
the fountain, dispels the dark forebodings it had inspired
This second solo for Lucy, one of the best known operatic
numbers for soprano, is the 'Quando rapita' (Then swift a
thought):

Quando rapita in es - ta - si del più co-cen-te ardo - re

Another beautiful and familiar number is the duet between Lucy and Edgar, who has come to tell her of his impending departure for France and to bid her farewell: 'Verranno a te sull' aure' (My sighs shall on the balmy breeze).

Act II. Apartment in the Castle of Lammermoor. In a sad tune Lucy protests to her brother against the marriage which he has arranged for her with Bucklaw. Henry then shows her the forged letter, which leads her to believe that she has been betrayed by her lover. 'Soffriva nel pianto languia nel dolore' (My sufferings and sorrow I've borne without repining) begins the duet between Lucy and Henry with an especially effective cadenza—a dramatic number.

Though believing herself deserted by Edgar, Lucy still holds back from the thought of marriage with another, and yields only to save her brother from a traitor's death, and even then not until she has sought counsel from Raymond, the Chaplain of Lammermoor, who adds his persuasions to Henry's.

The scene of the signing of the contract opens with a quick, bright chorus of guests who have assembled for the ceremony. There is an interchange of courtesies between Henry and Arthur; and then Lucy enters. The sadness of her mien is explained by her brother to Arthur on the ground that she is still mourning the death of her mother. Desperate, yet reluctant, Lucy signs the contracts of dower; and at that moment, Edgar, a sombre figure, but labouring under evident tension, appears at the head of the broad flight of steps in the background, and slowly comes forward.

The orchestra preludes briefly, and the great sextet has begun. Edgar and Henry: 'Chi mi frena in tal momento? Chi troncò dell'ire il corso?' (What restrains me at this moment? Why my sword do I not straightway draw?):

Because he sees Lucy 'as a rose 'mid tempest bending'

even Henry is moved to exclaim, 'To my own blood I am traitor':

The chorus swells the volume of sound, but Lucy's voic soars despairingly above all:

Lucy and Edgar—they are the victims of Henry's treachery as will soon transpire.

Act III.   The first scene is laid in Edgar's gloomy castl

whither at night comes Henry to challenge him to a duel at morn.[1]

The scene then changes back to Lammermoor, where the wedding guests are still feasting. Their revels are halted by Raymond, who, horror-stricken, announces to them that Lucy has gone mad and slain her husband; and soon the unhappy bride herself appears. Then follows the mad scene, one of the greatest show numbers for soprano, with the further merit that it fits perfectly into the scheme of the work.

This is an elaborate *scena*. In an earlier part of the opera Donizetti made effective use of a harp. In the mad scene he introduces a flute obbligato, which plays around the voice, joins with it, touches it with sharp, brilliant accentuations, and glides with it up and down the scale in mellifluous companionship.

In a brief article in *The Musician*, Thomas Tapper writes that 'to perform the mad scene has been an inspiration and incentive to attainment for many singers. Its demands are severe. There must be the "mood", that is, the characterisation of the mental state of Lucy must be evidenced both in vocal tone and physical movement. The aria requires an unusual degree of facility. Its transparency demands adherence to pitch that must not vary a shade from the truth (note the passage where voice and flute are in unison). The coloratura soprano is here afforded unusual opportunity to display fluency and flexibility of voice, to portray the character that is "as Ophelia was"; the dramatic intensity is paramount and must be sustained at a lofty eminence. In brief, the aria is truly a *tour de force*.'

One of the best things in the above is its insistence on the 'mood', the emotional situation that underlies the music. However brilliant the singing of the prima donna, something in her performance must yet convey to her hearers a sense of the sad fortunes of Lucy of Lammermoor.

To the accomplishment of this Donizetti lends a helping hand by introducing, as a mournful reminiscence, the theme of the first act love duet for Lucy and Edgar ('My sighs shall on the balmy breeze'); also by the dreaminess of the two melodies, 'Alfin son tua' (Thine am I ever):

---

[1] Often, though not invariably, omitted in performance.

and 'Spargi d'amaro pianto' (Shed thou a tear of sorrow):

The *scena* ends with a *stretto*, a concluding passage taken in more rapid tempo in order to enhance the effect.

There is a point in the mad scene where it is easy to modulate into the key of G major. Donizetti has written in that key the aria 'Perchè non ho del vento' (Oh, for an eagle's pinions) which sopranos sometimes introduce during the scene, since it was composed for that purpose.

Probably the air is unfamiliar to opera-goers in this country. Lionel Mapleson, once the librarian of the Metropolitan Opera House, never heard it sung there, and was interested to know where I had found it. As it is a florid, brilliant piece of music, and well suited to the scene, I quote a line of it, as a possible hint to some prima donna.

During the finale of the opera, laid near the churchyard

where lie the bones of Edgar's ancestors, Lucy's lover holds the stage. His final aria, 'Tu che a Dio spiegasti l'ali' (Tho' from earth thou'st flown before me), is a passage of mournful beauty, which has few equals in Italian opera.

Tu che a Dio spie-gas-ti l'a-li o bell' alma in-na-mo-ra-ta

Of the singers of former days who have been heard as Lucia, Adelina Patti interpreted the rôle with the least effort and the greatest brilliancy. Hers was a pure flexible soprano, which seemed to flow forth spontaneously from an inexhaustible reservoir of song. Unfortunately she was heard by many long after her days had passed. She had too many 'farewells'. But those who heard her at her best will always remember her as the possessor of a naturally beautiful voice, exquisitely trained.

Italo Campanini, a tenor who was in his prime when Mapleson was impresario at the Academy of Music, was one of the great Edgars. He was an elder brother of Cleofonte Campanini, orchestral conductor and director of the Chicago Opera Company.

As for Caruso, rarely have I witnessed such excitement as followed the singing of the sextet the evening of his first appearance as Edgar at the Metropolitan Opera House. It is a fact that the policeman in the lobby, thinking a riot of some sort had broken loose in the auditorium, grabbed his night stick and pushed through the swinging doors—only to find an audience vociferously demanding an encore. Even granted that some of the excitement was 'worked up', it was, nevertheless, a remarkable demonstration.

The rôle of Henry, though, of course, of less importance than Edgar, can be made very effective by a baritone of the first rank. Such, for example, was Antonio Galassi, who, like Campanini, was one of Mapleson's singers. He was a tall, well-set-up man; and when, in the sextet, at the words 'E mio rosa inaridita' (Of thine own blood thou'rt the betrayer), he came forward in one stride, and projected his voice into the proceedings, it seemed as if, no matter what happened to the others, he could take the entire affair on his broad shoulders and carry it through to success.   K.

ROBERTO DEVEREUX

Robert Devereux

Opera in three acts by Gaetano Donizetti. Libretto by Salvator
Cammarano after Ancelot's *Elisabeth d'Angleterre*. Première, Naple
October 29, 1837, with Giuseppina Ronzi de Begnis, Almerind
Granchi, Giovanni Basadonna, Paul Barroilhet. First performed i
Venice in 1838 with Carolina Ungher and Moriani; Paris, 1838, wit
Grisi, Rubini, Tamburini; la Scala, 1839, with Armenia, Mazzarell
Salvi, Marini; London, 1841, with Grisi and Rubini; New York, 184!
After 1882, when it was given in Pavia, there is no record o
performance until it was revived in 1964 at the San Carlo, Naples, wit'
Leyla Gencer, Anna Maria Rota, Ruggero Bondini, Piero Cappuccill
Revived in concert form, 1965, Carnegie Hall, New York, wit!
Montserrat Caba   Lili Chookasian, Juan Oncina, Walter Albert:
conductor Cillario; Barcelona, 1968, with Caballe Marti, Cappuccill
Bonn, 1969, with Sonja Poot, Gunnar Drago; London (in concert'
1970, with Caball(Troyanos, Marti, Sardinero; New York City Opera
1970, with Sills, Beverly Wolff, Domingo, Quilico.

CHARACTERS

Elizabeth, *Queen of England* .... Soprano
Duke of Nottingham .... Baritone
Sara, Duchess of Nottingham .... Mezzo-Soprano
Roberto Devereux, Earl of Essex .... Tenor
Lord Cecil .... Tenor
Sir Walter Raleigh .... Bass
A Page .... Bass
Nottingham's servant .... Bass
Ladies of the Royal Court, Courtiers, Pages, Royal Guards,
Nottingham's Attendants

Time: 1598   *Place:* Englan(

Roberto Devereux is the fifty-seventh of Donizetti'
seventy operas, and it was written only nineteen years afte
his first, under circumstances about as unpropitious as can b(
imagined. In 1836, he lost his father and his mother within :
few weeks of each other and his wife died in July 1837
Roberto Devereux was commissioned for Naples, which city
while he was struggling to complete the opera, was in the gri|
of a disastrous cholera epidemic. The opera was nonetheless :
success at its première, though it was not long befor(
Donizetti was speaking of a jinx on the work, both th(
baritone and the prima donna falling ill during the first run o

13 *Die Fledermaus* in Vienna, with Hilde Güden, Eberhard Wächter, Rita Streich.

14 (*Above*) Joan Sutherland in *Lucia* at Covent Garden 1959.
(*Below*) Monserrat Caballé in *Roberto Devereux*.

performances and the opera being performed elsewhere in a pirated edition, a disaster more from the point of view of his pocket than his pride.

The overture, written for the Paris première, includes anachronistically a woodwind variant of *God Save the Queen*, its principal merit perhaps and one which may have led to its inclusion in the 1970's in programmes conducted by Richard Bonynge, husband of Joan Sutherland.

The opera has only a slender basis in historical fact, but it is convenient to place it in 1598, the year of Essex's rebellion and execution. As a background to the story it is important to know only that Essex is back from his military mission to Ireland and is about to stand trial. Sara,[1] Duchess of Nottingham, pines with love for Roberto[1] Devereux, Earl of Essex, and cannot hide her tears from the other ladies of the Court as she reads the story of fair Rosamond (the heroine incidentally of Donizetti's opera *Rosamunda d'Inghilterra*): All' afflitto è dolce il pianto' (Weeping is sweet to one who sorrows). The Queen enters and reveals to Sara that she has consented to see Essex without whom her life has no meaning and whom she suspects, not of the treason of which he is accused but of infidelity to her: 'L'amor suo mi fe' beata' (His love is a blessing to me). Cecil comes to demand the Queen's approval of his Peers' judgement on Essex, but she asks for further proof of treason and says she will see him, her *cabaletta* revealing her unabated feelings for her subject.

Essex proclaims his fidelity to his Sovereign but, in the course of a grandiose *scena* during which she refers to the ring she once gave him and which he has only to produce for her to guarantee his safety, so far forgets himself as to fancy for a moment that the Queen knows of his secret passion for Sara. No amount of protestation can allay the suspicion he has created and the unhappy Essex is left alone to lament the turn fate has taken against him. His friend Nottingham, come to assure him of his support in the Council, reveals in a cavatina ('Forse in quel cor sensibile': Perhaps in that sensitive heart) that his wife Sara, a prey to grief and weeping, has even aroused his own jealous suspicions. Cecil summons Nottingham to the Council and he goes reiterating his devotion to Essex.

---

[1] Italian names preferred throughout.

Scene ii.   To Sara's apartments in Nottingham House
Essex comes to upbraid her that she married another and to
bid her farewell. She pleads that her father's sudden death
while Essex was abroad precipitated her into a loveless
marriage and urges him to turn towards the Queen. Protesting
that his heart is dead to love, he tears the Queen's ring from
his finger and throws it on the table. In the course of their
duet, Sara gives him a blue scarf she has embroidered and he
swears to wear it near his heart.

Act II.   The Hall at the Palace of Westminister (as Act I
Scene i). Lords and Ladies of the Court brood on Essex's
likely fate; without the Queen's aid, he is lost—and her
present mood suggests this will not be forthcoming. Cecil
enters to tell the Queen that the Council, in spite of
Nottingham's defence of his friend, has brought in a sentence
of death, which now awaits only her approval. Cecil leaves
and Raleigh comes to tell Elizabeth that when Essex was
arrested and searched a silk scarf was found next to his
heart. No sooner has the Queen recognised it as Lady
Nottingham's than Nottingham himself comes in to plead in a
duet for Essex's life. Essex himself is brought in under guard
and the Queen confronts him with the scarf, proof that he
lied to her once when he denied being in love. Nottingham,
too, recognises his wife's scarf and calls down the vengeance
of Heaven on his faithless friend. The trio ('Un perfido, un
vile, un mentitore tu sei') runs the gamut of emotions of the
betrayed friend, the discovered and anxious lover, and above
all the scorned woman before, with the summoning of the
Courtiers, it becomes a finale in which all voices join for their
different reasons in condemning Essex's treachery.

Act III opens in Sara Nottingham's apartments. She
receives news of Essex's condemnation, plans immediately to
take the ring Essex has left with her to the Queen in token of
his plea for mercy, only to look up into the unforgiving eyes
of her husband. In the course of their duet, he denounces
Essex and, when sounds of a procession taking the
condemned man to prison are heard in the distance, makes
clear his intention of preventing her conveying the ring to the
Queen.

The scene changes to the Tower of London, where Essex
waits for news of the pardon which he believes will certainly
follow delivery of the ring to the Queen. He pictures offering
himself to the sword of Nottingham and with his dying

breath assuring his friend that Sara has remained chaste in
spite of all temptation ('Come uno spirto angelico', 'Like an
angelic spirit'). But ... the anticipated pardon does not
arrive, rather are heard the funeral sounds of the guard
approaching to take him to his death. In spite of the urgency
of the situation, it is easy to see in Donizetti's reaction to it,
both in march and *cabaletta*, the sort of operatic cliché on
which Sullivan in his comic operas seized with such relish.

The last scene shows the Queen in the Great Hall
surrounded by her ladies and anxiously awaiting the arrival of
the trusted Sara to comfort her, as well as a sight of the ring
which she believes Essex will send her (she does not of course
connect the two events). Her beautiful aria ('Vivi ingrato')
shows a forgiving side to her nature not before revealed in the
opera, but the sight of the distraught Sara bringing the ring,
and her immediate recognition of a hated rival does not sway
her from her purpose. She orders a stay of execution at the
very moment when a cannon shot is heard giving the signal to
the headsman. The Queen turns in misery to blame Sara until
Nottingham himself reveals his guilt in preventing the ring
reaching the Queen. The opera ends as Elizabeth, beside
herself with grief, sees visions of the Crown bathed in blood,
of a man running through the Palace corridors carrying his
own head, of a tomb opening for her where once stood her
throne. It must be the only *cabaletta* in opera to be marked
maestoso for most of its course, and only in the last few
seconds is it superseded by the more conventional *allegro*.

H.

LA FILLE DU RÉGIMENT
La Figlia del Reggimento—The Daughter of the Regiment

Opera in two acts by Gaetano Donizetti; text by J. H. Vernoy de
Saint-Georges and F. Bayard. Première at the Opéra-Comique, Paris,
February 11, 1840. First performed in Milan, 1840; New York, 1843
(in French); London, Her Majesty's, 1847; Metropolitan, New York,
1902, with Sembrich, Salignac, Gilibert; revived 1917, with Hempel,
Carpi, Scotti, and 1940, with Pons, Jobin, Baccaloni. Heard at la Scala,
Milan, 1928, with dal Monte, Lomanto, di Lelio; Covent Garden, 1966,
with Sutherland, Pavarotti, Malas; la Scala, Milan, 1968, with Freni,
Pavarotti, Ganzarolli. Famous Maries have also included Lind, Sontag,
Lucca, Patti, Tetrazzini.

CHARACTERS

Marie, *the 'Daughter of the Regiment'* . . . . Soprano
Sulpice, *sergeant of French Grenadiers* . . . . Bass
Tonio, *a Tyrolese peasant in love with Marie* . . . . Tenor
Marquise de Birkenfeld . . . . Soprano
Hortensio, *steward to the Marquise* . . . . Bass
Corporal . . . . Bass
A Peasant . . . . Tenor
Duchesse de Krakenthorp . . . . Soprano
       Soldiers, Peasants, Friends of the Marquise, etc.
Time: 1815   *Place:* Mountains of the Swiss Tyrol

Act I.   A valley in the Tyrolese mountains. On the right is a cottage, on the left the first house of a village. Heights in the background. Tyrolese peasants are grouped on rising ground, as if on the lookout. Their wives and daughters kneel before a shrine to the Virgin. The Marquise de Birkenfeld is seated on a rustic bench. Beside her stands Hortensio, her steward. They have been caught in the eddy of the war. An engagement is in progress not far away. The Tyrolese chorus sings valiantly, the women pray: the French are victorious. And why not? Is not the unbeaten Twenty-first Regiment of Grenadiers among them?

One of them is coming now, Sergeant Sulpice, an old grumbler. After him comes a pretty girl in uniform, a vivandière—Marie, the daughter of the regiment, found on the field of battle when she was a mere child, and brought up by a whole regiment of fathers, the spoiled darling of the grenadiers. She sings 'Au bruit de la guerre j'ai reçu le jour'

('Apparvi alla luce, sul campo guerrier'): (I first saw the light in the camp of my brave grenadiers), which ends in a brilliant cadenza.

The Sergeant puts her through a drill. Then they have a 'Rataplan' duet, which may be called a repetition of Marie's solo with an accompaniment of rataplans. The drum is the music that is sweetest to her; and, indeed, Marie's manipulation of the drum-sticks is a feature of the rôle.

But for a few days Marie has not been as cheerful as formerly. She has been seen with a young man. Sulpice asks her about him. She tells the Sergeant that this young man saved her life by preventing her from falling over a precipice. That, however, establishes no claim upon her. The regiment has decreed that only a grenadier shall have her for wife.

There is a commotion. Some soldiers drag in Tonio, whom they charge as a spy. They have discovered him sneaking about the camp. His would have been short shrift had not Marie pleaded for him, for he is none other than her rescuer. As he wants to remain near Marie, he decides to become a soldier. The grenadiers celebrate his decision by drinking his health and calling upon Marie to sing the 'Song of the Regiment', a dapper tune, which is about the best known number of the score: 'Chacun le sait, chacun le dit' ('Ciascun lo dice, ciascun lo sà!'

(All men confess it, go where we will!
Our gallant Regiment is welcome still.)

There is then a love scene for Marie and Tonio, followed by a duet for them, De cet aveu si tendre ('A voti cosi ardente'): (No longer can I doubt it).

Afterwards the grenadiers sing a 'Rataplan' chorus. But alas, the Sergeant has been informed that the Marquise de Birkenfeld desires safe conduct. Birkenfeld! That is the very name to which were addressed certain papers found on Marie when she was discovered as a baby on the battlefield. The Marquise examines the papers, declares that Marie is her niece and henceforth must live with her in the castle. Poor Tonio has become a grenadier in vain. The regiment cannot help him. It can only lament with him that their daughter is lost to them. She herself is none too happy. She sings a sad farewell, 'Il faut partir, mes bons compagnons d'armes' ('Convien partir! o miei compagni d'arme'): (Farewell, a long farewell, my dear companions).

Act II. In the castle of the Marquise. Marie is learning to dance the minuet and to sing classical airs. But in the midst of her singing she and Sulpice, whom the Marquise also has brought to the castle, break out into the 'Song of the Regiment' and stirring 'rataplans'. The liveliness, however, is only temporary, for poor Marie is to wed, at her aunt's command, a scion of the ducal house of Krakenthorp. The march of the grenadiers is heard. They come in, led by Tonio who has been made a captain for valour. Sulpice can now see no reason why Marie should not marry him instead of the nobleman selected by her aunt. And, indeed, Marie and Tonio decide to elope. But the Marquise confesses to the Sergeant, in order to win his aid in influencing Marie, that the girl is really her daughter, born out of wedlock. Sulpice informs Marie, who now feels that she cannot go against her mother's wishes.

In the end, however, it is Marie herself who saves the situation. The guests have assembled for the signing of the wedding contract, when Marie, before them all, sings fondly of her childhood with the regiment, and of her life as a vivandière.

The society people are scandalised. But the Marquise is so touched that she leads Tonio to Marie and places the girl's hand in that of her lover. The opera ends with an ensemble, 'Salute to France!'   K.

LA FAVORITA

The Favourite

Opera in four acts by Gaetano Donizetti; text by Alphonse Royer and Gustav Vaez after a drama *Le Comte de Comminges* by Baculard d'Arnaud. Première at the Paris Opéra, December 2, 1840. First performed in London, Drury Lane, 1843 (in English); New Orleans, 1843 (in French); Covent Garden, 1845 (in French); Her Majesty's, 1847 (in Italian); Metropolitan, New York, 1895, with Mantelli, Cremonini, Ancona, Plançon; 1905, with Edyth Walker, Caruso, Scotti, Plançon. Last London performance, 1912, at London Opera House, with Augusta Doria, Orville Harrold. Recent revivals: la Scala, 1934, with Stignani, Pertile; Rome, 1935, with Cobelli, Gigli; la Scala, 1939, with Stignani, Malipiero, Tagliabue, Pasero; Rome, 1946, with Stignani, Lauri-Volpi, Bechi; la Scala, 1949, with Stignani, Poggi, Silveri, Siepi; Rome, 1951, with Barbieri, Lauri-Volpi; la Scala, 1962, with Simionato, Raimondi; Chicago, 1964, with Cossotto, Alfredo Kraus, Bruscantini, and Florence, 1966, with same cast.

CHARACTERS

Alfonso XI, *King of Castile* .... Baritone
Ferdinand, *a young novice of the Monastery of St. James
    of Compostella* (Fernando) .... Tenor
Don Gaspare, *the King's Minister* .... Tenor
Balthazar, *Superior of the Monastery of St. James*
    (Baldassare) .... Bass
Leonora di Gusman...................... Soprano
Inez, *her confidante* .... Soprano
Courtiers, Guards, Monks, Ladies of the Court, Attendants
Time: About 1340   *Place:* Castile, Spain

With Campanini as her Ferdinand, Leonora was, for a number of seasons, one of the principal roles of Annie Louise Cary at the Academy of Music.

There is in *La Favorita* a strong, dramatic scene at the end of the third Act. As if to work up to this as gradually as possible, the opera opens quietly.

Ferdinand, a novice in the Monastery of St. James of Compostella, has chanced to see and has fallen in love with Leonora, the mistress of Alfonso, King of Castile. He neither knows her name, nor is he aware of her equivocal position. So deeply conceived is his passion, it causes him to renounce his novitiate and seek out its object.

Act I. The interior of the monastery. Ferdinand makes known to Balthazar, the Superior, that he desires to renounce his novitiate, because he has fallen in love, and cannot banish the woman of his affections from his thoughts. He describes her to the priest as 'Una vergine, un angiol di Dio' (A virgin, an angel of God).

Although this air bears no resemblance to 'Celeste Aida' its flowing measures and melodious beauty, combined with its position so early in the opera, recall the Verdi aria—and prepare for it the same fate—which is to be marred by the disturbance caused by late-comers and to remain unheard by those who come still later.

Balthazar's questions elicit from Ferdinand that his only

knowledge of the woman, whose praises he has sung, is of her youth and beauty. Name and station are unknown to him although he believes her to be of high rank. Balthazar, who had hoped that in time Ferdinand would become his successor as superior of the monastery, releases him reluctantly from his obligations, and prophesies, as the novice turns away from the peaceful shades of the cloister, that he will retrace his steps, disappointed and heart-broken, to seek refuge once more within the monastery's walls.

The scene changes to an idyllic prospect on the island of St. Leon, where Leonora lives in splendour. She, for her part, is deeply enamoured of Ferdinand, yet is convinced that, because of her relations with King Alfonso, he will despise her once he discovers who she is. But so great is her love for him, that, without letting him learn her name or station, she has arranged that he shall be brought blindfolded to the island.

'Bei raggi lucenti' (Bright sunbeams, lightly dancing), a graceful solo and chorus for Inez, Leonora's confidante, and her woman companions, opens the scene. It is followed by 'Dolce zeffiro il seconda' (Gentle zephyr, lightly wafted), which is sung by the chorus of women, as the boat conveying Ferdinand touches the island and he, after disembarking, has the bandage withdrawn from over his eyes, and looks in amazement upon the charming surroundings amid which he stands. He questions Inez regarding the name and station of her who holds gentle sway over the island, but in vain. Inez and her companions retire, as Leonora enters. She interrupts Ferdinand's delight at seeing her by telling him—but without giving her reasons—that their love can lead only to sorrow, that they must part. He protests vehemently. She, however, cannot be moved from her determination that he shall not be sacrificed to their love, and hands him a parchment, which she tells him will lead him to a career of honour.

He still protests. But at that moment Inez, entering hurriedly, announces the approach of the King. Leonora bids Ferdinand farewell and goes hastily to meet Alfonso. Ferdinand now believes that the woman with whom he has fallen in love is of rank so high that she cannot stoop to wed him, yet expresses her love for him by seeking to advance him. This is confirmed when, on reading the scroll she has given him, he discovers that it gratifies his highest ambition and confers upon him a commission in the army. The act closes with his martial air, 'Si, che un tuo solo accento' (Oh, fame, thy voice inspiring).

He sees the path to glory open up before him, and with it the hope that some great deed may yet make him worthy to claim the hand of the woman he loves.

Act II. Gardens of the Palace of the Alcazar. Ferdinand's dream of glory has come true. We learn, through a brief colloquy between Alfonso and Don Gaspare, his minister, that the young officer has led the Spanish army to victory against the Moors. Indeed, this very palace of the Alcazar has been wrested from the enemy by the young hero.

Gaspare having retired, the King, who has no knowledge of the love between Ferdinand and Leonora, sings of his own passion for her in the expressive air, 'Vien, Leonora, a' piedi tuoi' (Come, Leonora, before thee kneeling).

The object of his love enters, accompanied by her confidante. The King has prepared a fête in celebration of Ferdinand's victory, but Leonora, while rejoicing in the honours destined to be his, is filled with foreboding because of the illicit relations between herself and the King, when she truly loves another. Moreover, these fears find justification in the return of Gaspare with a letter in Ferdinand's handwriting, and intended for Leonora, but which the minister has intercepted in the hand of Inez. The King's angry questions regarding the identity of the writer are interrupted by confused sounds from without. There enters Balthazar, preceded by a priest bearing a scroll with the Papal seal. He faces the King and Leonora while the lords and ladies, who have gathered for the fête, look on in apprehension, though not wholly without knowledge of what is impending.

For there is at the Court of Alfonso a strong party that condemns the King's illicit passion for Leonora, so openly shown. This party has appealed to the Papal throne against the King. The Pope has sent a Bull to Balthazar, in which the Superior of the Monastery of St. James is authorised to pronounce the interdict on the King if the latter refuses to dismiss his favourite from the Court and restore his legitimate wife to her rights. It is with this commission Balthazar has now appeared before the King, who at first is inclined to refuse obedience to the Papal summons. He wavers. Balthazar gives him time till the morrow, and until then witholds his anathema.

Balthazar's vigorous yet dignified denunciation of the

King, 'Ah paventa il furor d'un Dio vendicatore' (Do not call down the wrath of God, the avenger, upon thee), forms a broadly sonorous foundation for the finale of the act.

Ah paven-ta ilfu·rar d'un Di - o ven-di-ca-to - re

Act III.   A salon in the Palace of the Alcazar. In a brief scene the King informs his minister that he has decided to heed the behest of the Church and refrain from braving the Papal malediction. He bids Gaspare send Leonora to him, but, at the first opportunity, to arrest Inez, her accomplice.

It is at this juncture, as Gaspare departs, that Ferdinand appears at court, returning from the war, in which he has not only distinguished himself by his valour but actually has saved the kingdom. Alfonso asks him to name the prize which he desires as recompense for his services. Leonora enters. Ferdinand, seeing her, at once asks for the bestowal of her hand upon him in marriage. The King, who loves her deeply, and has nearly risked the wrath of the Pope for her sake, nevertheless, because immediately aware of the passion betweeen the two, gives his assent, but with reluctance, as indeed appears from the 'irony that pervades his impressive solo, 'A tanto amor' (Thou flow'r belov'd).

He then retires with Ferdinand.

Leonora, touched by the King's magnanimity, inspired by her love for Ferdinand, yet shaken by doubts and fears, because aware that he knows nothing of her past, now expresses these conflicting feelings in her principal air, 'O, mio Fernando,' one of the great Italian airs for mezzo-soprano.

O, mio Fer-nan-do, del - la ter-ra il tro - no

She considers that their future happiness depends upon Ferdinand's being truthfully informed of what her relations have been with the King, thus giving him full opportunity to decide whether, with this knowledge of her guilt, he will marry her, or not. Accordingly she despatches Inez with a letter to him. Inez, as she is on her way to deliver this letter, s intercepted by Gaspare, who carries out the King's command and orders her arrest. She is therefore unable to place in Ferdinand's hands the letter from Leonora.

Into the presence of the assembled nobles the King now brings Ferdinand, decorates him with a rich chain, and announces that he has created him Count of Zamora. The zealous lords whisper among themselves about the scandal of Ferdinand's coming marriage with the mistress of the King; but Leonora, who enters in bridal attire, finds Ferdinand eagerly awaiting her, and ready to wed her, notwithstanding, as she believes, his receipt of her communication and complete knowledge of her past.

While the ceremony is being performed in another apartment, the nobles discuss further the disgrace to Ferdinand in his marriage. That Leonora was the mistress of the King is, of course, a familiar fact at court, and the nobles regard Ferdinand's elevation to the rank of nobility as a reward not only for his defeat of the Moors, but also for accommodatingly taking Leonora off the hands of the King, when the latter is threatened with the malediction of Rome. They cannot imagine that the young officer is ignorant of the relations that existed between his bride and the King.

Ferdinand re-enters. In high spirits he approaches the courtiers, offers them his hand, which they refuse. Balthazar now comes to learn the decision of the King. Ferdinand, confused by the taunting words and actions of the courtiers, hastens to greet Balthazar, who, not having seen him since he has returned victorious and loaded with honours, embraces him, until he hears Gaspare's ironical exclamation, 'Leonora's bridegroom!' Balthazar starts back, and it is then Ferdinand learns that he has just been wedded 'alla bella del Re'—to the mistress of the King.

At this moment, when Ferdinand has but just been informed of what he can only interpret as his betrayal by the King and the royal favourite, Alfonso enters, leading Leonora, followed by her attendants. In a stirring scene, the dramatic climax of the opera, Ferdinand tears from his neck the chain Alfonso has bestowed upon him, and throws it contemptuously upon the floor, breaks his sword and casts it at the King's feet, then departs with Balthazar, the nobles now making a passage for them.

Act IV. The cloisters of the Monastery of St. James. Ceremony of Ferdinand's entry into the order. 'Splendon più

belle in ciel le stelle' (Behold the stars in splendour celestial`
a distinguished solo and chorus for Balthazar and the monk;

Left alone, Ferdinand gives vent to his sorrow, which sti
persists, in the romance, 'Spirto gentil' (Spirit of Light), on
of the most exquisite tenor solos in the Italian repertory.

Spir-to gen-til ne'so-gni mie - i bril-las-ti un di ma ti per-de-i

Balthazar and the monks return. With them Ferdinanc
enters the chapel. Leonora, disguised as a novice, comes upo
the scene. She hears the chanting of the monks, Ferdinand'
voice enunciating his vows. He comes out from the chapel
recognises Leonora, bids her be gone. 'Ah! va, t'invola
questa terra' (These cloisters fly).

She, however, tells him of her unsuccessful effort to le
him know of her past, and craves his forgiveness for th
seeming wrong she has wrought upon him. 'Pietoso al par de
Nume' (Forgiveness through God I crave of thee).

All of Ferdinand's former love for her returns. 'Vieni
ah! vieni' (Joy once more fills my breast).

He would bear her away to other climes and there happil
pass his days with her. But it is too late. Leonora dies in hi
arms. 'By to-morrow my soul, too, will want your prayers'
are Ferdinand's words to Balthazar, who, approaching, ha
drawn Leonora's cowl over her dishevelled hair. He calls upo
the monks to pray for a departed soul.   K.

LINDA DI CHAMOUNIX

Linda of Chamounix

Opera in three acts by Gaetano Donizetti; text by Gaetano Ross
Première at the Kärnthnerthor Theater, Vienna, May 19, 1842. Firs
performed London, Her Majesty's Theatre, 1843; New York, 1847
with Clothilda Barili; last London performance, 1888, with Fursch
Madi, Trebelli, Navarini. Revived Metropolitan, New York, 1934, wit
Pons, Swarthout, Crooks, de Luca, Pinza, conductor Serafin; San Carlo
Naples, 1934, with dal Monte, Kovaceva, Manuritta, Montesanto
Badini, conductor Baroni; la Scala, Milan, 1939, with dal Monte, Elmo
Malipiero, Basiola, Pasero, conductor Marinuzzi; Trieste, 1949, wit
Carosio, Palombini, Valletti, Taddei, Mongelli.

CHARACTERS

Marquis de Boisfleury . . . . Baritone
Carlo, *Vicomte de Sirval* . . . . Tenor
Prefect . . . . Bass
Pierotto. . . . . Contralto
Linda . . . . Soprano
Antonio . . . . Baritone
Maddalena . . . . Soprano
Intendant . . . . Tenor
Peasant men and women, Savoyards, etc.
Time: 1760, during the reign of Louis XV
Place: Chamounix and Paris

Claiming pride of place amongst Donizetti's pastoral
operas, and belonging to a line that includes such works as
Bellini's *La Sonnambula* and Meyerbeer's *Dinorah* and of
which Mascagni's *L'Amico Fritz* is a late representative,
Linda is still the subject of occasional revival, as a repository
of several admirable singing roles and much highly agreeable
music, including one of Donizetti's most famous soprano arias.

An overture typical of its period and excellent of its kind
leads at the rise of the curtain to a chorus of villagers on their
way to church. The scene is Chamounix, a village of Savoy,
the period about 1760, and the time of day is dawn.
Maddalena awaits with some trepidation the return of her
husband Antonio from a visit to the Marchesa, who owns
their farm and the mortgage which has been raised on it.
Antonio returns, says they have the Marchesa's brother, the
Marquis de Boisfleury, speaking for them, and then sings
melodiously of the valley they have both known all their lives
as their home: 'Ambo nati in questa valle' (Both of us born in
this valley).

The shout of the villagers outside heralds the arrival of the
Marquis de Boisfleury himself, a man by no means averse to
self-congratulation and unquestionably on the prowl for
Linda, Antonio's daughter, of whose charms he has received
excellent reports—hence his supposed support in the matter
of the mortgage. He is disappointed at her non-appearance—
she is in church—but promises for them his protection in the
future and for Linda a position at the castle.

All leave, and Linda comes out of the house. She has been
to an assignation with her lover, a young and penniless
painter named Carlo, but has arrived late and found only the

flowers he left for her. There is no doubt she is in love and
hopes to see him again in the very near future–'O luce di
quest' anima' she sings in the best known aria of the score, a
delightful *allegretto* piece, near the heart of the repertory of
the coloratura soprano:

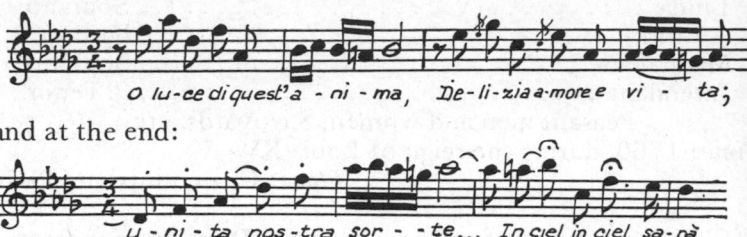

O lu-ce di quest'a - ni - ma, De-li-zia a-more e vi - ta;

and at the end:

u - ni - ta nos-tra sor - - te,.. In ciel, in ciel sa- rà

A group of young men and women from the village are on
their way to France, amongst them Pierotto, the village poet
and a childhood friend of Linda's. All beg him to sing his
latest song and he obliges with a sentimental ditty ('Per sua
madre andò una figlia'), about a young girl who leaves her
native village to earn money for her mother, loves, is
betrayed, and dies.

On to the empty village scene comes Carlo to find Linda
plunged by the ballad into sombre thoughts, from which his
ardent protestations lead her into an impassioned love duet.

They leave and the Prefect comes to see Antonio, warning
him that the Marquis, so full of protestations, has sinister
designs on Linda. In an extended and beautiful duet,
Antonio protests to heaven against such a fate for Linda, the
Prefect goes on to suggest more practically that she be sent
away with the band of Savoyards. Antonio agrees, and the
Prefect stays to warn Linda of the danger that treatens her.
Linda accepts to go and for the finale the Prefect bestows a
blessing on the departing group.

Act II.   On arrival in Paris, Linda has found that the
brother of the Prefect, to whom she was given a letter of
introduction, has died. In the meanwhile her beloved Carlo
has caught up with her, made known his real identity as the
Vicomte de Sirval, son of the Marchesa, and installed her in
style preparatory to their marriage. She hears Pierotto's tune
outside and has him brought in to her. He is astonished to
find her in these circumstances, but she explains her forthcoming marriage to Carlo. In a florid duet Linda and Pierotto
declare their devotion to one another and Pierotto leaves.

No sooner has Pierotto gone than the old Marquis bursts into the room, to Linda's surprise and dismay: what if Carlo return? In a buffo duet, the old man offers to better in every respect the comparative splendour in which she now lives. Linda protests and in a charming *andante mosso* tune, the Marquis wonders if he has got himself in too deep, and Linda (in the accents of *Don Pasquale*'s Norina) worries in case Carlo were to come in unexpectedly. Finally, amidst much ado, Linda sends him packing.

Linda retires, and Carlo has the stage to himself in which to lament in a beautiful aria his inability either to combat his mother's decision that he shall make a rich marriage or to communicate this thoroughly unwelcome news to Linda ('Se tanto in ira'). Linda returns and their duet ('Ah! dimmi, dimmi io t'amo') is full of passion, but Linda refuses a kiss when she hears the sound of Pierotto's hurdy-gurdy which reminds her of childhood and innocence.

Carlo leaves, and this time it is the turn of her own father to elude vigilance and penetrate to Linda's apartment. He has come to plead with the son of the owner of his farm and he urges his suit with what he takes to be the Vicomte's mistress ('Un buon servo del Visconte di Sirval'). Linda hides her identity from him at first, but inevitably he discovers who she is. At the height of their scene Pierotto bursts in. He has seen a wedding feast in progress at Carlo's house! The news and her father's repeated curses carry Linda over the border-line of sanity, a state of mind so ardently coveted by the nineteenth-century soprano. In the beautiful and expressive duet which ends the act, she takes Pierotto for Carlo, demands to be taken by him to the altar, and ends singing with Pierotto for all the world as heartrendingly mad as Lucia.

Act III. The village square at Chamounix. A scene of rejoicing as the Savoyards return home, considerably richer than when they set out. Only Antonio, says the Prefect, is denied the pleasure of welcoming home his child. At that moment, there rushes in the young Vicomte de Sirval. His mother has relented and he may now marry the girl of his choice: Linda. She is dead, replies the Prefect. Carlo tells the story of their life together in Paris, but the Prefect, in a duet of considerable warmth, can do no more, in spite of Carlo's broken-hearted protestations, than beg him to trust in the mercy of heaven.

The square fills again as the Marquis is heard returning

from his Parisian jaunts. The teasing of the Savoyards—some of them saw his flirtations in Paris—disconcerts him not at all, and he expatiates in a *buffo* aria on the forthcoming marriage between his nephew and a beautiful and virtuous girl.

But a happy ending is in store. Pierotto leads Linda into the village, playing his hurdy-gurdy to remind her of home and so bring her step by step nearer Chamounix, her family and friends. Carlo, bringing the deed of Antonio's farm, is appalled to see Linda in so parlous a condition. Suddenly she recognises her mother and seems to know Carlo's voice. His aria ('E la voce che primiera') half convinces her that it is he, and after a repetition of their first act duet, her reason returns and she recognises everyone gathered compassionately round her. Only the Marquis has to create some diversion until Linda addresses him as 'Uncle'. The opera ends with a short and joyful duet for Linda and Carlo.   H.

DON PASQUALE

Opera in three acts by Gaetano Donizetti; text by Giovanni Ruffini and the composer. Première at the Théâtre-Italien, Paris, January 3, 1843, with Grisi, Mario, Tamburini, Lablache. First performed, la Scala, Milan, 1843; Her Majesty's, London, 1843; New Orleans, 1845; New York, 1846. Revived Metropolitan, 1899, with Sembrich, Salignac, Scotti, Pini-Corsi, conductor Mancinelli; 1935, with Bori, Schipa, de Luca, Pinza, conductor Panizza; 1940, with Sayao, Martini, Valentino, Baccaloni, conductor Papi (1945, conductor Busch); Covent Garden, 1920, with Pareto, Govoni, Paterna, Badini, conductor Bavagnoli; 1937, with Favero, Dino Borgioli, Biasini, di Lelio, conductor Salfi; Glydebourne, 1938, with Mildmay, Dino Borgioli, Stabile, Baccaloni, conductor Busch; Cambridge Theatre, London, 1946, with Noni, MacPherson, Stabile, Lawrence, conductor Erede. Revived la Scala, Milan, 1930, with dal Monte, Lomanto, Stabile, Autori, conductor Calusio; 1936, with Carosio, Schipa, de Luca, Badini, conductor Marinuzzi; 1950, with Noni, Prandelli, Taddei, Pasero, conductor Capuana. Revived Vienna, 1944, with Noni, Dermota, Kunz, Vogel, conductor Paulik; Piccola Scala, Milan, 1959, with Sciutti, Alva, Panerai, Bruscantini, conductor Sanzogno; Edinburgh Festival, 1963 (by San Carlo Opera, Naples), with D'Angelo, Alfredo Kraus, Capecchi, Corena, conductor Erede.

CHARACTERS

Don Pasquale, *an old bachelor* .... Bass
Dr. Malatesta, *his friend* .... Baritone
Ernesto, *nephew of Don Pasquale* .... Tenor

Norina, *a young widow* .... Soprano
A Notary .... Baritone
'ime: Early Nineteenth Century   *Place:* Rome

The overture is mainly concerned with Ernesto's serenade
rom the last act, and Norina's aria from the first. It
admirably suggests the lively tone of the opera.

Act I.   The first scene is set in Don Pasquale's room. The
wealthy Don Pasquale is about to marry. Though determined
imself to have a wife, he is very angry with his nephew
Ernesto for wishing to do likewise, and threatens to disinherit
im on that account. Ernesto is greatly disturbed by these
hreats, and so is his lady-love, the sprightly young widow
Norina, when he reports them to her.

When the curtain rises, Don Pasquale is impatiently waiting
or Malatesta, who, not being able to dissuade his friend from
marriage and still less able to influence him to allow his
nephew to follow the dictates of his heart, pretends to
acquiesce in the madcap scheme. He proposes that his 'sister'
hall be the bride (Don Pasquale has no one in particular in
mind), and describes her in a graceful aria, 'Bella siccome un'
ingelo', as a timid, naïve, ingenuous girl, brought up, he says,
n a convent. She is, however, none other than Norina, who is
n no way related to Malatesta. At this description, Don
'asquale is quite unable to contain his delight, in spite of
Malatesta's attempts to restrain him, and when he is alone, he
breaks into a gay cavatina, 'Ah, un foco insolito'.

Don Pasquale prepares to give his nephew a lecture on the
subject of his future conduct, and tells him in the course of it
hat he is proposing to take a wife himself. This arouses
Ernesto's incredulity, and his uncle is obliged to repeat it
several times before he can take it in. When he does, it is to
ealise that it finally cuts him off from the marriage he
imself proposed to enter into. 'Sogno soave e casto' (Fond
dream of love thou hast perished) he sings, in one of
Donizetti's soaring inspirations, while the old uncle grumbles
away in the bass. When Don Pasquale says he has already
consulted Malatesta, Ernesto's last remaining hope vanishes;
here is no one now to dissuade the old fool.

The scene changes to Norina's room, where she is reading.
Quel guardo il cavaliere' (Glances so soft and bright) begins
her recitative—but she is only reading a novel aloud; her aria,
So anch'io la virtù magica' (I know what spells a glance can

dart), shows her sprightly nature in an enchanting tune

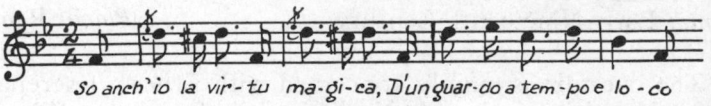

So anch'io la vir-tu ma-gi-ca, D'un guar-do a tem-po e lo-co

A letter is brought to her, and when Malatesta comes to tell her
that Ernesto's old uncle has fallen for the scheme which shall
finally make him agree to his nephew's marriage, she is
anything but pleased with the way things have gone; they
have not had time to tell Ernesto about their scheme and he
has written that he is furious. However, Malatesta is
convinced all is going well, and he and Norina rehearse how
they shall behave with Don Pasquale when finally he meets
his convent-bred bride. The music is pure effervescence, with
its sparkling coloratura and its gaily changing tunes, and no
one who heard Mariano Stabile sing it with Alda Noni in
London during the revival in 1946–8 will ever forget the
effect it made.

Act II. We are in Ernesto's lodgings. The owner is in
despair at the prospect of losing his bride and his home (Don
Pasquale has told him to clear out of the house). A long horn
prelude ushers in the recitative and aria, 'Cercherò lontana
terra', one of the most famous of the opera.

At home, Don Pasquale receives his prospective bride and
her sponsor, his friend, Malatesta. She is shy, he urges her on
and the husband-to-be watches every manoeuvre enraptured.
Norina is eventually persuaded to speak to Pasquale, and
assures him that she is only interested in the things of the
household—sewing, making clothes, and looking after the
kitchen. A notary has been sent for, and Malatesta dictates
the terms of the marriage, the others, including the notary
repeating his words after him. A witness is needed, but none
seems forthcoming until Ernesto rushes in proclaiming his
betrayal to anyone who chooses to listen. Malatesta has his
work cut out to explain the situation to him, without letting
Don Pasquale know the way the wind is blowing.

The moment the contract is signed, Norina's temper seems
to change, and she spits fire at every one of Don Pasquale's
attempts at either conciliation or authority. He is con-
founded at the contrast, and dumb with horror when she says
that Ernesto is just the person to take her out walking,
something that is plainly beyond the capacity of a man of his

years—or girth, for that matter. The quartet redoubles in
vigour, and Norina and Ernesto have a charming lyrical aside
which leaves no one in any doubt as to their mutual feelings.
When Norina calls together the servants, and, finding there
are only three in all, laughingly directs that more be engaged
and that the wages of those at present in service be doubled,
Don Pasquale can bear it no more. 'Son tradito, son tradito'
(I'm a victim of collusion) he shouts in his rage, and the
stretta of the quartet brings the act to a spirited conclusion.

Act III.   The room is the same as that of the previous
scene. Servants are rushing hither and thither executing
Norina's commands, and disposing of what she has ordered
for the house. Don Pasquale sees her dressed up to the nines
and about to go out of the house; may he ask where? To the
theatre she says—without him. Their duet works the quarrel
up until Norina finds occasion to box her 'husband's' ears. As
far as Don Pasquale is concerned, it is the end of his hopes
and pretensions as well as his hateful marriage, and even
Norina is sorry that she has had to go so far to bring the
foolish old man to what is, from her and Ernesto's point of
view, a reasonable frame of mind. She rushes from the room,
but takes care to drop a note as she goes. It purports to be
from Ernesto, and makes an assignation for that very evening
in the garden. Don Pasquale reads it, and sees in it his chance
of getting quit of the whole affair; he will send for Malatesta.

When he has left the room, the servants flock back into it,
and comment on the happenings in the house in a charming
chorus. Malatesta arrives and proceeds to give Don Pasquale
the benefit of his advice. The two men confer in a famous
comic duet, whose every performance has reduced an
audience somewhere to helpless laughter. Its *buffo* 6/8 finish
is one of the funniest pieces of music in the post-Rossinian
repertory.

The scene changes to the garden, where Ernesto sings to
Norina the beautiful serenade, 'Com' è gentil'. The story is

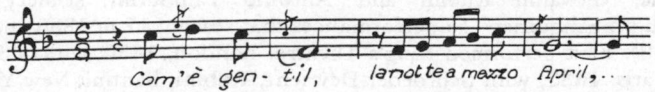

Com' è gen-til,   la notte a mezzo April,...

that after one of the rehearsals Donizetti asked the music
publisher, Dormoy, to go with him to his lodgings. There he
rummaged among a lot of manuscripts until, finding what he
was looking for, he handed it to Dormoy. 'There,' he said,

'give this to Mario and tell him to sing it in the last scene in the garden as a serenade to Norina.' When the opera was performed, Mario sang it, while Lablache, behind the scenes, played an accompaniment on the lute. It was the serenade. It is in truth the very essence of a light-handed nocturnal piece, and most of the great lyric tenors of history, from Mario to Schipa, have tried at one time or another to prove that never before has it been so stylishly sung.

It is immediately followed by a duet that is no less charming and hardly less well known, 'Tornami a dir'. This is all thirds and sixths for the two voices, but the effect is entrancing. Don Pasquale and Malatesta surprise the lovers, Ernesto escapes, but Norina stays as if to brave it out. Malatesta twists everything round to everyone's satisfaction, and soon Ernesto and Norina are waiting to be married, and moreover with the full approval of Don Pasquale. Suitably, Malatesta leads off the *Rondo finale* with which the work ends.   K., H.

VINCENZO BELLINI
(1801–1835)
IL PIRATA
The Pirate

OPERA in two acts by Vincenzo Bellini; libretto (from the French translation of a five-act tragedy by the Irish writer, the Rev. R. C. Maturin, *Bertram, or The Castle of St Aldobrando*) by Felice Romani. Première, la Scala, Milan, October 27, 1827, with Henriette Méric-Lalande, Giovanni Rubini and Antonio Tamburini; scenery by Alessandro Sanquirico (15 performances that season, 12 in 1830 and 12 in 1840). First performed King's Theatre, London, 1830, with la Scala cast; Paris, 1832, with Schroeder-Devrient, Rubini, Santini; New York, 1832. Revived Rome, 1935, with Iva Pacetti, Gigli, Mario Basiola, conductor Serafin; Catania, 1951, with Lucy Kelston, Renzo Pigni, Gian Giacomo Guelfi; Palermo, 1958, with Kelston, Picchi, Taddei; la Scala, 1958, with Callas, Corelli, Bastianini; New York (both times in concert), 1959 with Callas, 1966 with Montserrat Caballé; Florence,

1967, with Caballe, Flaviano Labò, Piero Cappuccilli; Philadelphia, 1968, with Caballe, Bernabe Marti, John Reardon; London (in concert), 1969, with Caballe, Marti, Vicente Sardinero; Wexford, 1972, and York Festival, 1973, with Christiane Eda-Pierre.

CHARACTERS

Ernesto, *Duke of Caldora* . . . . Baritone
Imogene, *his wife* . . . . Soprano
Gualtiero, *former Count of Montalto* . . . . Tenor
Itulbo, *Gualtiero's lieutenant* . . . . Tenor
Goffredo, *a hermit, once tutor to Gualtiero* . . . . . . Bass
Adele, *Imogene's companion* . . . . Soprano
A little boy, *son to Imogene and Ernesto*
Fishermen and women, Pirates, Knights, Ladies
Time: Thirteenth Century   *Place:* The castle of Caldora
and its neighbourhood, in Sicily

Bellini came of a musical family in Sicily, and his early experience was in church music in his native country. Six years in Naples ended in 1826 with a successful operatic première (his second work for the stage), *Bianca e Gernando* (*sic* in earlier version), and a resulting commission for la Scala. *Il Pirata* was the first libretto written for him by Felice Romani, henceforth (apart from *I Puritani*) his invariable collaborator, and with it he emerged as a major operatic force.

The background of the Sicilian story has Ernesto, Duke of Caldora, and Gualtiero, Count of Montalto, as rivals in politics as well as for the hand of the fair Imogene, Gualtiero and Imogene's father following the cause of King Manfred, Ernesto that of Charles of Anjou. Imogene loves Gualtiero, who is however banished following the death of King Manfred and the defeat of his followers by the Anjou party. In exile, he leads a band of pirates from Aragon to ravage the shores of Sicily, in the hope of revenge and recovering Imogene. She, however, has been forced through threats to her father's life to marry the Duke of Caldora, who has recently commanded the fleet which defeated the Aragonese pirates, their leader escaping from battle only to be overtaken by a storm and shipwrecked on the coast not far from Caldora.

Act I.   After a conventional overture, the curtain rises to agitated music to show the anguished populace watching the shipwreck. The storm over, survivors come on shore, and the

hermit Goffredo recognises Gualtiero, who vigorously proclaims that nothing but his continuing love for Imogene has
supported him through his trials ('Nel furor delle tempeste':
'Through the fury of the storm').

Honouring old custom, it is the Duchess herself who comes
to offer hospitality to the strangers, for whom Itulbo acts as
spokesman. Horrified at the idea that their leader may be
dead, Imogene in a beautiful aria ('Lo sognai ferito') confides
her fears to Adele, telling her also of a dream she has had in
which she saw her husband kill her one-time lover. At sight of
Imogene, Gualtiero can barely restrain himself and the sound
of his involuntary but still anonymous cry awakes poignant
memories for Imogene.

At night, the pirates, drinking rousingly on the castle
terrace, are warned by Itulbo not to give away their as yet
undisclosed identity. Imogene is still troubled by thoughts of
the stranger who has taken refuge with the hermit Goffredo,
and it does not take long after his arrival at the castle before
he reveals to her who he is. The story of Imogene's coercion
by Ernesto comes out, and Gualtiero's stupefaction,
expressed in one of Bellini's most melting cantilenas ('Pietosa
al padre'), turns, when he sees Imogene's small son, to
thoughts of revenge.

Imogene, left alone in her grief, hears the sounds of
carousal within, and the scene changes to the great hall of the
castle, where the Duke's men celebrate victory. Ernesto
himself rejoices in an aria (to the accompaniment of strings
and three trombones, *piano*) and reproaches Imogene that
she alone remains outside the general festivities. For himself,
the sole shadow on his joy is the doubt about the fate of the
hated Gualtiero. He will question the fugitives and their
leader who seems to have found shelter with the hermit.
Itulbo poses as the pirate chief, Ernesto threatens imprisonment, Imogene pleads the general cause, the hermit restrains
the frantic Gualtiero, who emulates Ernesto in his willingness
to breathe fire and slaughter at every opportunity. A quintet
(and soon a sextet) develops with comments from the chorus,
and the act ends in a *stretta* but without public disclosure of
Gualtiero's identity.

Act II. In the ante-chamber to Imogene's apartments,
Adele tries to reassure her entourage as to Imogene's health.
She tells her mistress that Gualtiero will not leave without
seeing her, but it is the Duke who now confronts her squarely

with accusations of infidelity. She defends herself by saying that it is true she still loves Gualtiero but as someone she knew in the past; Ernesto must be content that she is his wife and the mother of his son. The slow music of their fine duet suggests a degree of acceptance of the situation, but Ernesto's fury is unleashed when he gets a message to the effect that Gualtiero is even now sheltering in the castle.

On the terrace, Itulbo unsuccessfully tries to persuade Gualtiero to forgo his meeting with Imogene. The tone of the lovers' scene is one of passion as well as resignation, and towards its end they are watched by Ernesto, who remains in hiding to add his voice to a trio of finest inspiration. Ernesto is discovered, and he and Gualtiero go off to end their rivalry in mortal combat.

To the great hall of the castle come the Duke's retainers to mourn his death and to swear vengeance on his killer. To their amazement, Gualtiero surrenders voluntarily and is handed over to the Council of Knights, bidding farewell in an aria ('Tu vedrai la sventurata') to the absent Imogene and asking her forgiveness.

In Bellini's operas, it is the woman who is customarily protagonist and *Il Pirata* is no exception, in spite of its title and the unusual robustness of much of the music. Imogene's reason and strength of will have collapsed under the strain of events, and her last scene is introduced by a plaintive and beautiful *cor anglais* solo, which movingly expresses her anguished state. She thinks she sees Ernesto, and later their son, who pleads with his father for the life of Gualtiero who once spared Ernesto's. Musically, Bellini already inhabits the world of 'Casta diva' of four years later, and the slow 'Col sorriso d'innocenza' is a beautiful inspiration, with a worthy pendant in the *cabaletta* 'Oh sole, ti vela di tenebre oscure'; together, and after Imogene hears that the Council has condemned Gualtiero to death, they bring the opera to an impressive conclusion.   H.

LA STRANIERA
The Stranger

Opera in two acts by Vincenzo Bellini; text by Felice Romani based on Vicomte d'Arlincourt's novel *L'Etrangère*. Première, la Scala, Milan February 14, 1829, with Henriette Méric-Lalande, Caroline Unger,

Domenico Reina, Antonio Tamburini. First produced London, King
Theatre, 1832, with Giuditta Grisi, Rubini, Tamburini; New York, Parl
Theatre, 1834. Revived Catania, 1954, with Adriana Guerrini, Adriana
Lazzarini, Pier Miranda Ferraro, Ugo Savarese; Palermo, 1968, with
Renata Scotto, Elena Zilio, Renato Cioni, Domenico Trimarchi
conductor Sanzogno; New York (concert performance), 1969, with
Montserrat Caballe, Bianca Maria Casoni, Amedeo Zambon, Vicente
Sardinero; Edinburgh Festival, 1972, by Palermo Company with
Scotto, Zilio, Ottavio Garaventa, Trimarchi, conductor Sanzogno.

CHARACTERS

Alaide (la Straniera) .... Soprano
Il Signore di Montolino .... Bass
Isoletta, his daughter .... Mezzo-Soprano
Arturo, Count of Ravenstal .... Tenor
Baron Valdeburgo .... Baritone
The Prior of the Templars .... Bass
Osburgo, confidant of Arturo .... Tenor

Place: Brittany

La Straniera was written in 1829 for la Scala, Bellini's
second opera with Felice Romani, who was to be his librettist
for all the remaining operas except the last, I Puritani. Like
the first with Romani, Il Pirata, La Straniera shows a more
vigorous approach to drama than the later Bellini operas
where elegiac melody is as much in evidence as romantic
passion. Leslie Orrey in his book about Bellini lays great
stress on the fine quality of the choral writing in La
Straniera.

All these operas once came newly minted from the
composer's pen, written like Handel's to display the ability in
brilliance or pathos of the great prima donnas of the day and
to show off their skill and dexterity. In our own time, Callas
for a few short unforgettable years at la Scala made works of
this period her own, recreating perhaps three operas every
two years. More recently, newer claimants with a modicum
of technique but less imagination have attempted to emulate
her, but with them one revival is hardly to be distinguished
from the other, thus suggesting that the effort of imagination
involved in recreation is of a very particular and rare order.
Instant Bellini or Donizetti is not at all what Callas made.

Act I, scene i.　Near the castle of Montolino, peasants and
members of Lord Montolino's entourage celebrate in a

barcarole chorus the forthcoming marriage of Isoletta, his daughter, to Arturo, Count of Ravenstal. Only Isoletta cannot share in the rejoicing because, as she confides to her friend Baron Valdeburgo, she has detected a change in the attitude of her fiancé towards her. She fears he is in love with an unknown woman who lives across the lake—*la Straniera*. Valdeburgo, and later Isoletta's father and Arturo's friend Osburgo, do their best to comfort her, and in the distance they hear the voices of the crowd who are inveighing against *la Straniera* as a witch.

Scene ii. *La Straniera*'s hut in the woods. Arturo has come to seek her out. Alaide, the Stranger, enters (introduced by harp) and muses on the sadness which can result from a love which trusts too much ('Ah! Sventurato il cor che fida'). She reproaches Arturo for having sought out her hiding place, and, in answer to a passionate declaration of love, assures him that Heaven has put an insurmountable barrier between them.

Scene iii. Osburgo is near the dwelling of the dreaded *Straniera* with a hunting party. Valdeburgo tries to persuade Arturo to return to his proper place at the heart of the wedding festivities. When he refers to the Stranger as unworthy of Arturo, the latter begs him at least to see her and to judge whether he can then still condemn her. As soon as he sees Alaide, Valdeburgo gives a cry of recognition. Alaide is equally delighted, and Arturo's suspicions are first aroused and then, when Valdeburgo tells him that for reasons he cannot reveal Arturo must renounce his love, as he thinks, confirmed. Only the intervention of Alaide prevents him falling upon his erstwhile friend with his sword. Arturo leaves only when Alaide reluctantly agrees to see him again.

Scene iv. A gloomy prelude brings us to the shore of the lake near the castle. Arturo learns from Osburgo and his friends that they have heard Alaide and Valdeburgo planning to elope. He himself believes he knows the worst when he overhears Alaide address Valdeburgo as Leopoldo, whereupon he attacks and wounds him so that he falls into the lake. Alaide in her horror reveals that he is her brother. Arturo jumps in after him and a group of countrymen, led by Osburgo, surprise her alone with a bloodstained sword and accuse her of murder.

Act II, scene i.   In a room in the castle, the Prior of the

Order of the Hospitallers is hearing the evidence of Osburgo against *la Straniera*. When she appears, he seems for a moment to recognise her voice, but recalls himself to reality. Arturo rushes in to say that it is he who is guilty of the murder of Valdeburgo, but the problem is resolved with the re-appearance of Valdeburgo to announce that neither Arturo nor Alaide is guilty. Valdeburgo offers to protect Alaide and, when the members of the court demand that she shall unveil, she consents to do so only to the Prior himself. He is astonished at what he sees and announces that she is free to depart.

Scene ii.   Arturo makes for Alaide's hut, but in a vigorous duet Valdeburgo heads him off. Arturo is persuaded to go back to Isoletta, after Valdeburgo has conceded that he will bring Alaide to the wedding.

Scene iii.   The church. Isoletta is full of foreboding and in an aria, 'Ah! se non m'ami più' (flute obbligato) reveals her sorrow.[1]

A wedding hymn starts the proceedings, but Arturo is obviously distraught and Isoletta threatens to abandon the ceremony. Suddenly Alaide intervenes, and insists that Isoletta and Arturo shall go towards the altar, Alaide herself rushing outside to pray movingly for God's forgiveness ('Pago, o ciel tremendo'). Arturo, with drawn sword, tries to order her to follow him, but the Prior announces that she must take her rightful place as Queen of France.[2] Arturo reacts by throwing himself on his sword, Isoletta falls on his dead body and *la Straniera* fulfils the prophecy contained in her opening words, to dwell in the sadness of a love which trusted too well.

It has been suggested—reasonably I think—that the impossibly violent loves of the romantics were less erotic in origin than manifestations of rebellion against the norms of society. By these canons, both Arturo and *la Straniera* are romantic figures sacrificed on the altars of self-fulfilment.

H.

[1] In the Palermo revival of 1968 transferred quite appropriately to the first scene of Act I.

[2] The King of France fled on his wedding night from his bride Isamberga of Denmark, and later married Agnese of Pomerania, the opera's heroine. The Pope ordered the King to return to his first wife, Agnese going into exile. With the death of Isamberga, Agnese may now return to the King.

LA SONNAMBULA
The Sleepwalker

Opera in two acts by Vincenzo Bellini; text by Felice Romani. ˥remière at the Teatro Carcano, Milan, on March 6, 1831, with Pasta, ˥ubini, Mariani. First performed in London, Haymarket, 1831, with ˥asta, Rubini, Santini; Drury Lane, 1833 (in English), with Malibran ˥er début), Templeton, Seguin; Covent Garden, 1835, with same cast; ˥ew York, 1835 (in English); 1844 (in Italian). Performed at Covent ˥arden, 1910, with Tetrazzini, McCormack, Edmund Burke; revived ˥letropolitan, New York, 1932, with Pons, Bourskaya, Gigli, Pinza, ˥nductor Serafin; la Scala, Milan, 1935, with dal Monte, Schipa, ˥asero, conductor Guarnieri; 1939, with Carosio, Malipiero, Pasero, ˥nductor Marinuzzi; Rome Opera, 1951, with Carosio, Valletti, ˥hristoff; la Scala, 1955, with Callas, Monti, Zaccaria in Visconti's ˥roduction (also Edinburgh, 1957, with Callas and later Scotto); ˥ovent Garden, 1960, with Sutherland, conductor Serafin; ˥letropolitan, New York, 1963, with Sutherland, Gedda, Tozzi.

CHARACTERS

Count Rodolpho, *lord of the castle* .... Bass
Teresa, *proprietress of the mill* .... Mezzo-Soprano
Amina, *her foster-daughter* .... Soprano
Lisa, *proprietress of the village inn* .... Soprano
Elvino, *a young farmer* .... Tenor
Alessio, *a villager* .... Bass

Notary, Villagers, etc.

˥ime: Early Nineteenth Century   *Place:* A Village in
                                                Switzerland

Act I. The village green. On one side an inn, in the ˥ackground a water mill, in the distance mountains. As the ˥urtain rises the villagers are making merry, for they are ˥out to celebrate a nuptial contract between Amina, an ˥rphan brought up as the foster child of Teresa, the mistress ˥f the village mill, and Elvino, a young landowner of the ˥eighbourhood. These preparations, however, fill with ˥alousy the heart of Lisa, the proprietress of the inn, for she ˥ in love with Elvino. Nor do Alessio's ill-timed attentions ˥ease her. Amina enters under the care of Teresa, and ˥turns her thanks to her neighbours for their good wishes. ˥he has two attractive solos; these are 'Come per me sereno' ˥low, for me brightly shining) and the cabaletta 'Sovra il sen

489

la man mi posa' (With this heart its joy revealing). Both a
replete with grace and charm.

When the village notary and Elvino appear, the contract
signed and attested, and Elvino places a ring on Amina
finger. Duet: 'Prendi, l'anel ti dono' (Take now the ring I giv
you), a composition in long-flowing expressive measures.

The village is startled by the crack of whips and the rumb
of wheels. A handsome stranger in officer's fatigue unifor
appears, and desires to have his horses watered and fe
before he proceeds to the castle. The road is bad, night
approaching. Counselled by the villagers, and urged by Lis
the officer consents to remain the night at the inn.

The villagers know it not at this time, but the officer
Rodolpho, the lord of the castle. He looks about him an
recalls the scenes of his youth: 'Vi ravviso' (As I view).

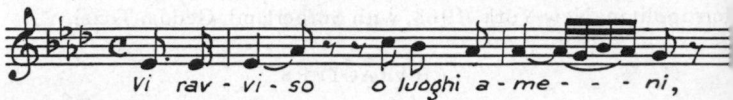

He then gallantly addresses himself to Amina in a charmii
cabaletta, 'Tu non sai in quei begli occhi' (Maid, those brig]
eyes my heart impressing).

Elvino is piqued at the stranger's attentions to his brid
but Teresa warns all present to retire, for the village is said t
be haunted by a phantom. The stranger treats the supe
stition lightly, and, ushered in by Lisa, retires to the villa
inn. All then wend their several ways homeward. Elvin
however, finds time to upbraid Amina for seemingly havir
found much pleasure in the stranger's gallant speeches, bt
before they part there are mutual concessions and forgivene
('Son geloso del Zefiro errante').

Rodolpho's sleeping apartment at the inn. He enter
conducted by Lisa. She is coquettish, he quite willing to me
her halfway in taking liberties with her. He learns from h
that his identity as the lord of the castle has now bee
discovered by the villagers, and that they will shortly come t
the inn to offer their congratulations.

He is annoyed, but quite willing that Lisa's attractior
shall atone for the discovery. At that moment, however, the
is a noise without, and Lisa escapes into an adjoining roon
in her haste dropping her handkerchief, which Rodolph
picks up and hangs over the bedpost. A few moments later h

amazed to see Amina, all in white, raise his window and
nter his room. He realises almost immediately that she is
alking in her sleep, and that it is her somnambulism
which has given rise to the superstition of the village
hantom. In her sleep Amina speaks of her approaching
marriage, of Elvino's jealousy, of their quarrel and recon-
liation. Rodolpho, not wishing to embarrass her by his
resence should she suddenly awaken, extinguishes the
andles, steps out of the window and closes it lightly after
im. Still asleep Amina sinks down upon the bed.

The villagers enter to greet Rodolpho. As the room is
arkened, and, to their amusement, they see the figure of a
oman on the bed, they are about to withdraw discreetly,
hen Lisa, who knows what has happened, enters with a light,
rings in Elvino, and points out Amina to him. The light, the
unds, awaken her. Her natural confusion at the situation in
which she finds herself is mistaken by Elvino for evidence of
uilt. He casts her off. The others, save Teresa, share his
suspicions. Teresa, in a simple natural way, takes the
handkerchief hanging over the bedpost and places it around
mina's neck, and when the poor, grief-stricken girl swoons,
Elvino turns away from her, her foster-mother catches her
n her arms.

In this scene, indeed in this act, the most striking musical
umber is the duet near the end. It is feelingly composed,
nd is almost wholly devoid of vocal embellishment. It begins
ith Amina's protestations of innocence: 'D'un pensiero,
d'un accento' (Not in thought's remotest region).

When Elvino's voice joins hers there is no comfort for her
n his words. He is still haunted by dark suspicions.

An unusual and beautiful effect is the closing of the duet
ith an expressive phrase for tenor alone: 'Questo pianto del
io cor' (With what grief my heart is torn).

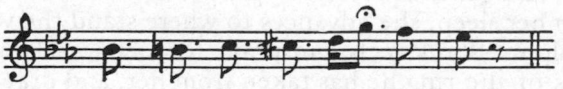

Act II.   A shady valley between the village and the castle
The villagers are proceeding to the castle to beg Rodolpho to
intercede with Elvino for Amina. Elvino meets Amina. Still
enraged at what he considers her perfidy, he snatches from
her finger the ring he gave her. Amina still loves him. He
expresses his feelings in the air: 'Ah! perchè non posso
odiarti' (Ah! Why is it I cannot hate you).

Scene ii.   The village, near Teresa's mill. Water runs
through the race and the wheel turns rapidly. A slender
wooden bridge, spanning the wheel, gives access from some
dormer lights in the mill roof to an old stone flight of steps
leading down to the foreground.

Lisa has been making hay while the sun shines. She has
induced Elvino to promise to marry her. Preparations for the
wedding are on foot. The villagers have assembled. Rodolpho
endeavours to dissuade Elvino from the step he is about to
take. He explains that Amina is a somnambulist. But Elvino
has never heard of somnambulism. He remains utterly
incredulous.

Teresa begs the villagers to make less disturbance as poor
Amina is asleep in the mill. The girl's foster-mother learns of
Elvino's intention of marrying Lisa. Straightway she takes
from her bosom Lisa's handkerchief, which she found
hanging over Rodolpho's bedpost. Lisa is confused. Elvino
feels that she, too, has betrayed him. Rodolpho again urges
upon Elvino that Amina never was false to him—that she is
the innocent victim of sleepwalking.

'Who can prove it?' Elvino asks in agonised tones.

'Who? She herself!—See there!' exclaims Rodolpho.

For at that very moment Amina, in her nightdress, lamp in
hand, emerges from a window in the mill roof. She passes
along, still asleep, to the lightly built bridge spanning the mill
wheel, which is still turning round quickly. Now she sets foot
on the narrow, insecure bridge. The villagers fall on their
knees in prayer that she may cross safely. Rodolpho stands
among them, head uncovered. As Amina crosses the bridge a
rotting plank breaks under her footsteps. The lamp falls from
her hand into the torrent beneath. She, however, reaches the
other side, and gains the stone steps, which she descends. Still
walking in her sleep, she advances to where stand the villagers
and Rodolpho. She kneels and prays for Elvino. Then rising
she speaks of the ring he has taken from her, and draws from
her bosom the flowers given to her by him on the previous

lay. 'Ah! non credea mirarti, si presto estinto, o fiore'
'Scarcely could I believe it that so soon thou would'st wither,
O blossoms).

Gently Elvino replaces the ring upon her finger, and kneels
before her. 'Viva Amina!' cry the villagers. She awakens.
Instead of sorrow, she sees joy all around her, and Elvino,
with arms outstretched, waiting to beg her forgiveness and
lead her to the altar:

It ends with this brilliant passage:

The 'Ah! non giunge' is one of the show pieces of Italian
opera. Nor is its brilliance hard and glittering. It is the
brightness of a tender soul rejoicing at being enabled to cast
off sorrow. Indeed, there is about the entire opera a sweetness and a gentle charm, that go far to account for its having
endured so long in the repertory, out of which so many
works far more ambitious have been dropped.

Opera-goers of the old Academy of Music days recalled the
bell-like tones of Etelka Gerster's voice in 'Ah! non giunge';
nor were they ever able to forget the bird-like, spontaneous
singing in this rôle of Adelina Patti, gifted with a voice and an
art such as those who had the privilege of hearing her in her
prime did not hear since, nor are likely to hear again.
Admirers of Mme. Sembrich's art also were justly numerous,
and it was fortunate for habitués of the Metropolitan that she
was so long in the company singing at that house. She was a
charming Amina. Tetrazzini was brilliant in *La Sonnambula*.

The story of *La Sonnambula* is simple and thoroughly intelligible. The mainspring of the action is the interesting psycho-physical manifestation of somnambulism. This is effectively worked out, and the crossing of the bridge in the last scene is a tense moment in the simple story. It calls for an interesting stage 'property'—the plank that breaks without precipitating Amina, who sometimes may have more embonpoint than voice, into the mill-race. All these elements contribute to the success of *La Sonnambula*, which, produced in 1831, is still a good evening's entertainment.

K.

NORMA

Opera in two acts by Vincenzo Bellini; text by Felice Romani, founded on L. A. Soumet's tragedy. Première on December 26, 1831, at la Scala, Milan, with Pasta, Grisi, Donzelli, Negrini; London, Haymarket, 1833, with Pasta, de Meric, Donzelli, Galli; Drury Lane, 1837; Covent Garden, 1841, with Adelaide Kemble, Rainforth, Harrison, Leffler; New Orleans, 1836; New York, 1841 (in English); 1843 (in Italian); Metropolitan, New York, 1891, with Lilli Lehmann, 1927, with Ponselle, Telva, Lauri-Volpi, Pinza, conductor Serafin; Covent Garden, 1929, with Ponselle, Cattaneo, Fusati, Manfrini, conductor Bellezza; Metropolitan, New York, 1936, with Cigna, Castagna, Martinelli, Pinza, conductor Panizza; 1943, with Milanov, Castagna, Jagel, Cordon, conductor Sodero; la Scala, 1952, with Callas, Stignani, Penno, Rossi-Lemeni, conductor Ghione; Covent Garden, 1952, with Callas, Stignani, conductor Gui; 1967, with Sutherland, Marilyn Horne, Franco Tagliavini, Rouleau, conductor Bonynge.

CHARACTERS

Pollione, *Roman Pro-consul in Gaul* . . . . Tenor
Oroveso, *Archdruid, father of Norma* . . . . Bass
Norma, *High priestess of the druidical temple* . Soprano
Adalgisa, *a virgin of the temple* . . . . Soprano
Clotilda, *Norma's confidante* . . . . Soprano
Flavio, *a centurion* . . . . Tenor
Priests, Officers of the Temple, Gallic Warriors,
Priestesses and Virgins of the Temple
Time: Roman Occupation, about 50 B.C.   *Place:* Gaul

Act I. Sacred grove of the Druids. The high priest Oroveso comes with the Druids to the sacred grove to beg of the gods to rouse the people to war and aid them to

15 Rosa Ponselle in *Norma* at the Metropolitan, New York.

16 *La Traviata* at la Scala, 1955, with Callas in Visconti's production.

accomplish the destruction of the Romans. Scarcely have they gone than the Roman Pro-consul Pollione appears and confides to his Centurion, Flavio, that he no longer loves Norma, although she has broken her vows of chastity for him and has borne him two sons. He has seen Adalgisa and his heart is now hers.

At the sound of the sacred instrument of bronze that calls the Druids to the temple, the Romans disappear. The priests and priestesses approach the altar, and Norma, the high priestess, daughter of Oroveso, ascends the steps. No one suspects her intimacy with the Roman enemy. But she loves Pollione and seeks to avert the danger that would threaten him, should Gaul rise against the Romans, by prophesying that Rome will fall through its own weakness, and declaring that it is not yet the will of the gods that Gaul shall go to war. She also prays to the goddess for the return of the Roman leader, who has left her.

In the next scene, which also takes place in the sacred grove, Adalgisa is shown waiting for Pollione, who joins her and begs her to fly with him to Rome, where their happiness would be secure. After some hesitation, she agrees to go with him.

The scene changes and shows Norma's dwelling. The priestess is steeped in deep sadness, for she knows that Pollione plans to desert her and their offspring, although she is not yet aware of her rival's identity. Adalgisa comes to unburden her heart to her superior. She confesses that she has become untrue to her faith through love—and, moreover, love for a Roman. Norma, thinking of her own unfaithfulness to her vows, is about to free Adalgisa from hers, when Pollione appears. For the first time Norma learns the identity of the Roman Adalgisa loves. When she learns the truth the latter turns from Pollione; she loves Norma too well to go away with the betrayer of the high priestess.

Act II. Norma, filled with despair, is beside the cradle of her little ones. An impulse to kill them comes over her, but motherhood triumphs over unrequited love. She will renounce her lover, and Adalgisa shall become the happy spouse of Pollione, but shall promise to take the place of mother to her children. Adalgisa, however, will not hear of treachery to Norma. She will go to Pollione, but only to remind him of his duty.

The scene changes again to a wooded region of the temple

in which the warriors of Gaul have gathered. Norma awaits
the result of Adalgisa's plea to Pollione; then learns that she
has failed and has come back to the grove to pass her life as
a priestess. Norma's wrath is now beyond control. She strikes
the brazen shield, and, when the warriors have gathered,
joyfully proclaims her message: War against the Romans! But
with the deep war song now mingles the sound of tumult
from the temple. A Roman has broken into the sacred
edifice and has been captured. It is Pollione, who Norma
knows has attempted to carry off Adalgisa. The penalty for
his intrusion is death. But Norma, moved by love to pity and
still hoping to save her recreant lover, submits a new victim
to the enraged Gauls—a perjured virgin of the priesthood.

'Speak, then, and name her!' they cry.

To their amazement she utters her own name, then
confesses all to her father, and to his care confides her
children.

A pyre has been erected. She mounts it, but not alone.
Pollione, his love rekindled at the spectacle of her greatness
of soul, joins her. In the flames he, too, will atone for their
offences before God.   K.

Norma is a work of great lyrical beauty and considerable
dramatic tension—the combination which Bellini only this
once succeeded in achieving. The music unfolds in long
scenes, but the listener never loses the feeling that the threads
are drawing gradually and inevitably together towards the
final tragic dénouement.

The overture is in the nature of a dramatic prelude. The
Druids are shown first in a solemn introduction (in which
occurs a haunting wood-wind phrase), followed by an
inflammatory pronouncement by Oroveso, which leads to a
typical early nineteenth-century Italian march. Next we are

introduced to the Romans, in the persons of Pollione and his
friend Flavio; Pollione has a cavatina, 'Meco all' altar di
Venere', whose ending is interrupted by the sounds of the
Druids gathering for their ceremony, but he has time for a
cabaletta before he disappears from view. The introduction

to the great scene of Druidical rites is in the form of a march which is later used for the quick section of Norma's great and justly famous 'Casta diva', which forms the centre-piece of this scene and indeed of the whole opera. This prayer to the 'chaste goddess' is one of the most celebrated of soprano

Ca - - - sta Di - - va,

arias, and its form and melodic contour are said (with other pieces of the same kind in Bellini's works) to have had the strongest influence on the character and mood of Chopin's Nocturnes, a view which is easy to understand when one hears the aria well sung. Even transposed, the fioriture ornaments are taxing to the average soprano—but the truth is that the average soprano cannot (and never could) tackle the title rôle.

Adalgisa is the fourth character to be presented musically; her impressive recitative, 'Sgombra è la sacra selva', is her only solo opportunity, but it leads to a big-scale duet with Pollione, 'Va crudele, al dio spietato', and is followed by an extensive scene with Norma herself as she confesses her guilt, and a trio which ends the Act. Better known and even more

Oh! di qual sei tu vit - ti-ma

beautiful is the great scene for the two sopranos in Act II, 'Mira, o Norma' after Norma has begged Adalgisa to marry Pollione and to look after the two children Norma has had by

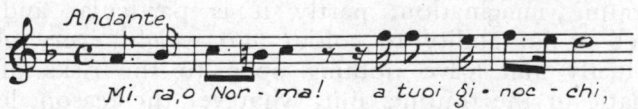

Mi. ra,o Nor - ma! a tuoi gi - noc - chi,

him. Adalgisa's devotion is touchingly and beautifully shown in this duet, which contains one of Bellini's finest melodies. Norma and Adalgisa sing in thirds together in the slow section and again in the decorated quick section, with which it ends.

The last part of the opera begins with Oroveso's solo, 'Ah, del Tebro' (marked 'con ferocia' in the score), gathers momentum when Norma summons the Druids and with them sings a determined chorus, 'Guerra!' and reaches its climax when Pollione is left alone with Norma. Their two great duets, of which 'In mia man alfin tu sei' takes place in private, 'Qual cor tradisti' in public and with choral support, form the climax of the opera. Bellini's vocal writing is at its most expressive, and the drama is hardly less intense than in, for instance, the duet between Radames and Amneris in the last act of *Aida*. The opera ends fittingly with a beautiful trio, 'Deh, non volerli vittime', for Norma, Pollione, Oroveso and the chorus.

'Bellini's and Romani's *Norma*,' wrote Andrew Porter in *The New Yorker* in 1973, 'remains one of the most demanding parts in opera, both vocally and dramatically. It calls for power; grace in slow cantilena; pure, fluent coloratura; stamina; tones both tender and violent; force and intensity of verbal declamation; and a commanding stage presence. Only a soprano who has all these things can sustain the role. There have not been many such sopranos. The critics of the nineteenth century delighted to describe and compare the fine points of the performances by Giulia Grisi, Malibran, Adelaide Kemble, and, later, Lilli Lehmann.'

In the two periods before and after the 1939–45 war, *Norma* acquired two great protagonists: Rosa Ponselle and Maria Callas, something I know from first-hand knowledge in the one case and from reliable hearsay and gramophone records in the other. With such exponents, *Norma*, above all Bellini's operas, flowers, gains in expressiveness and dramatic impact and the music grows to full stature as it cannot when the performance is in lesser hands. Partly, this gain is general and the result of technical attainments, of superior, more penetrating imagination; partly it is particular and the product of an ability to colour and weight every phrase individually and leave nothing open to the risks of the automatic or the routine. But, whatever the reason, let no one imagine he has genuinely heard *Norma* without a truly great singer in the title role. Not to have one is as dire in its consequences as a performance of *Götterdämmerung* with an inadequate Brünnhilde. The trouble as far as Bellini is concerned is that, in the twentieth century, there have been fewer great Normas than fine Brünnhildes.   H.

BEATRICE DI TENDA

Opera in two acts by Vincenzo Bellini, text by Felice Romani. Première at la Fenice, Venice, March 16, 1833, with Giuditta Pasta, Anna dal Serre, Alberico Curioni, Orazio Cartagenova. First performed Palermo, 1833; Naples, 1834, with Persiani; London, 1836; Vienna, 1837; Paris, 1841; New Orleans, 1842; New York, 1844. Revived Palermo, 1959, with Rubio, Ligabue, Oncina, Taddei, conductor Gui; New York (American Opera Society), 1961, with Sutherland, Horne, Cassilly, Sordello, conductor Rescigno; la Scala, 1961, with Sutherland, Kabaivanska, Campora, Dondi, conductor Gavazzeni; Naples, 1962, with Sutherland; Venice, 1964, with Gencer, Sgourda, Oncina, Zanasi, conductor Gui.

CHARACTERS

Filippo Maria Visconti, *Duke of Milan* .... Baritone
Beatrice di Tenda, *his wife* .... Soprano
Agnese del Maino, *beloved of Filippo* ... .Mezzo-Soprano
Orombello, *lord of Ventimiglia* .... Tenor
Anichino, *friend of Orombello and formerly minister to Facino, Duke of Milan* .... Tenor
Rizzardo del Maino, *Agnese's brother* .... Tenor
Courtiers, Judges, Officials, Soldiers, Women-in-waiting

Time: 1418   *Place:* The Castle of Binasco

Beatrice di Tenda is the composer's penultimate opera, first performed just over a year after *Norma* and nearly two before *I Puritani*. It was commissioned by Lanari, impresario of the Fenice Opera in Venice, for the Carnival of 1833, and, by October 1832, Bellini and Romani had decided on a subject to do with Queen Christina of Sweden. A month later, composer and librettist had dropped Queen Christina and, in agreement with the great singer Pasta, settled on *Beatrice di Tenda*; by mid-December, Bellini, in Venice to produce *Norma*, had received nothing from Romani and by the end of the month police action had been invoked to persuade Romani to leave Milan to fulfil his contract with Venice. Between the beginning of January and March 16, 1833, the normally slow-working Bellini received his verses, set them, rehearsed the performers and produced the opera—to finish up with something of a failure with the audience[1] and to have Romani apologising to the public for

[1] '*Beatrice* is musically speaking one of Bellini's richest operas', wrote that considerable authority, Vittorio Gui.

the haste with which he had been constrained to work! The similarity of the story to that of *Anna Bolena* (Romani's libretto was set by Donizetti in 1830) is too marked to be disregarded.

The story is based on an event in Italian history. Filippo Visconti, after the death of his brother and of their father Gian Galeazzo, joined with the general Facino Cane to restore order, and, Facino himself being dead, married his widow Beatrice di Tenda, through whom he inherited army and possessions. When the opera begins, Filippo is bored with Beatrice and has fallen in love with Agnese del Maino.

The overture, which features Beatrice's fourth scene 'Deh! se mi amasti', brings us to the courtyard of the castle of Binasco. Bystanding courtiers are amazed that Duke Filippo has left the festivities so early and hear from him that it is because of his lack of sympathy with his wife, who presides over them. The voice of Agnese can be heard singing from the castle ('Ah, non pensar che pieno sia'), and Filippo, encouraged by his sycophantic entourage, mellifluously admits his love for her ('Come t'adoro').

In her own apartments, Agnese awaits the result of an anonymous letter of assignation she has sent Orombello, lord of Ventimiglia, with whom she is secretly in love. In the course of their duet, Agnese comes to understand that Orombello is in love with Beatrice, and her furious reaction presages danger for the Duchess.

Beatrice, strolling in the grounds of the ducal palace with her maids of honour, laments in a beautiful cavatina ('Ma la sola, ohimé, son' io') and cabaletta ('Ah! la pena in lor piombò') her husband's oppressive treatment of her subjects as well as his present spurning of her love, which in the past had raised him to his present position as Duke. As she leaves, Agnese's brother, Rizzardo, brings to the scene Filippo, who longs for an excuse to rid himself of Beatrice but, now that he suspects her (falsely, as it turns out) of an amorous intrigue, finds himself furious at the discovery. Their confrontation, mildness itself at first on her side, is composed of insults and accusations on his, culminating in his claim to possess proof that she is plotting with their subjects to remove him.

The fourth scene of the act takes place in a remote part of the castle. Armed soldiers discuss the Duke's behaviour—love or anger, they say, will soon force him to show his hand.

When they have gone, Beatrice enters and kneels in front of a statue of Facino, her first husband, from whom she begs forgiveness ('Deh! se mi amasti un giorno') that she so soon forgot his memory in marriage with another. She is, she says, by all forsaken—by all, cries Orombello, but not by him! He knows her plight, knows too that her subjects venerate her still and will with him at their head come to her aid. But Beatrice knows she can accept no aid from Orombello, aware as she is that gossip ascribes to him a hopeless love for her and wishing to avoid all danger of compromising herself. As Orombello kneels at her feet, Filippo with his entourage appears on the scene to accuse her of furnishing him with proof of all his suspicions. A great ensemble, Verdian in its thrust and directness, builds up as each character protests his or her emotions, and the act comes to an end with Filippo, enraged at Orombello's protestations of Beatrice's innocence, ordering them both to prison.

Act II. A tribunal court inside the castle. A vigorous orchestral prelude leads to the revelation by the Gentlemen of the Court that Orombello has succumbed to the pressure of torture and confessed. Filippo is deaf to the pleas of Anichino, and at the appearance of the judges he demands an exemplary sentence for the guilty woman. When confronted with Orombello and the news that he has confessed, Beatrice berates him for what she can only think is a futile effort to buy his life, until, in a burst of revulsion, he proclaims that his confession was made under duress and is false. An ensemble develops, with Beatrice voicing her thanks to Orombello and to heaven, Orombello his new-found stead-fastness, Agnese her doubts and remorse, Anichino his certainty of their joint innocence, Filippo his increased determination to make the charge stick, if necessary through further torture. There is a moment of pathos as Beatrice warns her husband that heaven is watching his actions, then Filippo baldly states his conviction that the law must run its course with maximum severity.

Filippo is face to face with his conscience, on which alone, he maintains in answer to Agnese's plea for mercy, rests the responsibility for punishing the guilty pair. At first he cannot understand how others can feel remorse where he cannot, then, as he fancies he hears Beatrice's voice under torture, wonders whether he himself is as obdurate as he tries to make out, finally discovering the truth about his feelings as

he learns from Anichino that, in spite of Beatrice's refusal to
confess under torture, the judges have agreed on her death
warrant, which now lacks only his signature. He cannot sign
and so send to the block the woman who saved him once
from the life of a wandering fugitive ('Qui m'accolse
oppresso, errante')—it is the one moment of humanity in a
character otherwise drawn too black for credibility. But
Filippo's clemency is short-lived, and the news that the
people and elements of Facino's army are massing against
him causes him to sign the decree, insisting that it is not he
but Beatrice's own villainy which condemns her ('Non son io
che la condanno').

The last scene takes place in a hall leading to the castle
dungeons. Her maids of honour have left Beatrice at prayer in
her cell, but soon she emerges to tell them that heaven has
helped her triumph over the pain of her ordeal, that she will
die wrapped in virtue's mantle, while Filippo and her enemies
await God's punishment for their crimes against truth and
justice. The appearance of Agnese to confess her part in
Beatrice's torment—it was she who stole her letters, and with
her own honour bought the death of Beatrice—leads to a
change of heart in Beatrice as, in a beautiful trio initiated by
Orombello from his near-by cell ('Angiol di pace'), she grants
Agnese her pardon.

A funeral dirge announces the guards who are to escort
Beatrice to the scaffold, and, as Agnese faints in anguish,
Beatrice poignantly asks for prayers for Filippo and Agnese
and not for herself ('Ah!. se un'urna'), then in a brilliant
cabaletta ('Ah! la morte a cui m'appresso') appears to
welcome the prospect of death as amounting to victory over
the sorrows of earth.   H.

I PURITANI

The Puritans

Opera in three acts, by Vincenzo Bellini; words by Count Pepoli.
Produced, Paris, Théâtre des Italiens, January 25, 1835, with Grisi as
Elvira, Rubini as Arturo, Tamburini as Riccardo, and Lablache as
Giorgio. London, King's Theatre, May 21, 1835 (in Italian); la Scala,
Milan, 1835; Philadelphia, 1843; New York, February 3, 1844;
Academy of Music, 1883, with Gerster. Revived, Manhattan Opera
House, December 3, 1906, with Bonci as Arturo, and Pinkert as Elvira;
and in 1909 with Tetrazzini as Elvira; Metropolitan, 1918, with

Barrientos, Lazaro, de Luca, Mardones; Florence, 1933, with Capsir, Lauri-Volpi, Basiola, Pinza, conductor Serafin; la Scala, Milan, 1942, with Carosio, Salvarezza, Pasero; Rome Opera, 1948, with Pagliughi, Filippeschi, Tagliabue, Neroni; la Scala, 1949, with Carosio, Conley, Tagliabue, Siepi, conductor Capuana; Fenice, Venice, 1949, with Callas, Perino, Savarese, Christoff, conductor Serafin; Glyndebourne, 1960, with Sutherland, Filacuridi, Blanc, Modesti, conductor Gui; Covent Garden, 1964, with Sutherland, Craig, Bacquier, Rouleau.

CHARACTERS

Lord Walton, *of the Puritans* .... Bass
Sir George Walton, *his brother, of the Puritans* ... Bass
Lord Arthur Talbot, *of the Cavaliers* .... Tenor
Sir Richard Forth, *of the Puritans* .... Baritone
Sir Benno Robertson, *of the Puritans* .... Tenor
Queen Henrietta, *widow of Charles I* .... Soprano
Elvira, *daughter of Lord Walton* .... Soprano
Puritans, Soldiers of the Commonwealth, Men-at-Arms,
Women, Pages, etc.

Time: English Civil War   *Place:* Near Plymouth, England
(The leading characters are customarily called Enrichetta, Arturo, Riccardo, and Giorgio in Italian.)

Act I is laid in a fortress, near Plymouth, held by Lord Walton for Cromwell. Lord Walton's daughter, Elvira, is in love with Lord Arthur Talbot, a cavalier and adherent of the Stuarts, but her father has promised her hand to Sir Richard Forth, like himself a follower of Cromwell. He relents, however, and Elvira is bidden by her uncle, Sir George Walton, to prepare for her nuptials with Arthur, for whom a safe conduct to the fortress has been provided.

Queen Henrietta, widow of Charles I, is a prisoner in the fortress. On discovering that she is under sentence of death, Arthur, loyal to the Stuarts, enables her to escape by draping her in Elvira's bridal veil and conducting her past the guards, as if she were the bride. There is one critical moment. They are met by Sir Richard, who had hoped to marry Elvira. The men draw their swords, but a disarrangement of the veil shows Sir Richard that the woman he supposes to be Lord Arthur's bride is not Elvira. He permits them to pass. When the escape is discovered, Elvira, believing herself deserted, loses her reason. Those who had gathered for the nuptials, now, in a stirring chorus, invoke maledictions upon Arthur's head.

Act II plays in another part of the fortress. It concerns itself chiefly with the exhibition of Elvira's madness. But it has also the famous martial duet, 'Suoni la tromba' (Sound the trumpet), in which Sir George and Sir Richard announce their readiness to meet Arthur in battle and strive to avenge Elvira's sad plight.

Act III is laid in a grove near the fortress. Arthur, although proscribed, seeks out Elvira. Her joy at seeing him again temporarily lifts the clouds from her mind, but renewed evidence of her disturbed mental state alarms her lover. He hears men, whom he knows to be in pursuit of him, approaching, and is aware that capture means death, but he will not leave Elvira. He is apprehended and is about to be executed when a messenger arrives with the news of the defeat of the Stuarts and a pardon for all prisoners. Arthur is freed. The sudden shock of joy restores Elvira's reason. The lovers are united.

As an opera *I Puritani* lacks the naïveté of *La Sonnambula*, nor has it any one number of the celebrity of 'Casta diva' in *Norma*. Occasionally, however, it is revived for a tenor like Bonci, whose elegance of phrasing finds exceptional opportunity in the rôle of Arthur; or for some renowned prima donna of the brilliant coloratura type, for whom Elvira is a grateful part.

The principal musical numbers are, in Act I, Sir Richard Forth's cavatina, 'Ah! per sempre io ti perdei' (Ah! forever have I lost thee); Arthur's romance, 'A te o cara' (To thee, beloved);

and Elvira's sparkling polacca, 'Son vergin vezzosa' (I am a blithesome maiden).

In Act II we have Sir George's romance, 'Cinta di fiori', and Elvira's mad scene, 'Qui la voce sua soave' (It was here in sweetest accents).

This is a *legato* melody of infinite pathos and beauty—one of Bellini's finest inspirations and perhaps the loveliest and most purely musical of all nineteenth-century mad scenes. It is followed by a beautiful cabaletta, 'Vien, diletto' (Come, dearest love).

The act closes with the duet for baritone and bass, between Sir Richard and Sir George, 'Suoni la tromba', a fine sonorous proclamation of martial ardour.

It was in this duet, on the occasion of the opera's revival for Gerster, that I heard break and go to pieces the voice of Antonio Galassi, the great baritone of the heyday of Italian opera at the Academy of Music. 'Suoni la tromba!'—he could sound it no more. The career of a great artist was at an end.

'A una fonte afflitto e solo' (Sad and lonely by a fountain), a beautiful number for Elvira, occurs at the beginning of the third act. There is also in this act the impassioned 'Vieni fra queste braccia' (Come to these arms) for Arthur and Elvira, with its two top D's for the tenor. It is followed by a big ensemble, 'Credeasi, misera', dominated by the tenor's part, in which occurs what must be the only example of a top F written for the tenor.   K.

Bellini's simplicity of style amounts at its best to genius, but it is too often companioned by his fatal dramatic naïveté. There are fine dramatic strokes in *Puritani*—the sound of Elvira's voice offstage as she interrupts the stage action with the beginning of 'Son vergin vezzosa' is one of them—but even such scenes as this, or the exquisite 'Qui la voce', require to be integrated to the drama if they are to achieve a genuine dramatic as well as musical effect.

The inventive genius of Bellini puts him, to my way of thinking, in a higher category than that occupied by Donizetti, but in a work like *I Puritani* one would sometimes sacrifice a little of the music's lyrical beauty for an extra helping of the dramatic talent and expertise of Bellini's in other respects less gifted contemporary.   H.

8
Verdi

GIUSEPPE VERDI
(1813–1901)

UN GIORNO DI REGNO
King for a Day

OPERA in two acts by Giuseppe Verdi; text by Felice Romani (subtitle: *Il finto Stanislao*—first set in 1818 by Gyrowetz). Première, la Scala, Milan, September 5, 1840, with Marini, Abbaddia, Salvi, Ferlotti, Scalese, Rovere. Not revived after the 1840's until broadcast by Radio Italiana during the Verdi celebrations of 1951, with Pagliughi, Laura Cozzi, Oncina, Capecchi, Bruscantini, Dalamangas, conductor Simonetto. Performed New York, Amato Opera Theatre, 1960; London, St. Pancras, 1961, with Cynthia Jolly, Bettina Jonic, Alfred Hallett, James Atkins, Eric Garrett, conductor Hans Ucko.

CHARACTERS

Cavalier di Belfiore,[1] *a French officer impersonating
Stanislao of Poland* .... Baritone
Baron di Kelbar .... Basso Buffo
The Marchesa del Poggio, *a young widow, the Baron's
niece, in love with Belfiore* .... Soprano
Giulietta di Kelbar, *the Baron's daughter* Mezzo-Soprano
Edoardo di Sanval, *a young official*,
la Rocca's nephew .... Tenor
La Rocca, *Treasurer to the Estates of Brittany*
Basso Buffo
Count Ivrea, *Commander of Brest, engaged
to the Marchesa* .... Tenor
Delmonte, *esquire to the false Stanislao* .... Bass

Time: August 1733 *Place:* Baron di Kelbar's castle near Brest

[1] The Italian spelling has been retained throughout.

After the favourable reception of Verdi's first opera *Oberto* at la Scala in 1839, the impresario Merelli commissioned the young composer to write him three operas in the next two years, to be produced either at la Scala or the Imperial Theatre in Vienna. The first of these was to be an *opera buffa,* and the circumstances of its composition and première have become famous—the illness of the composer, the death of his wife, an inadequate performance, a disastrous public reception and the withdrawal of the opera to Verdi's intense chagrin. The composer never forgave the Milanese public for what he thought an act of cruelty to a young composer badly in need of encouragement, and years later, when congratulated by a friend on a recent success, refused to show satisfaction at the public's favourable reaction, which he thought as capricious and lacking in seriousness as its former disapproval. Revivals of *Un Giorno di Regno* have never been successful, but in 1951 a carefully prepared Italian broadcast showed it, in spite of obvious indebtedness to Rossini and Donizetti, to be musically delightful.

The story is taken from an incident which took place during the wars of Polish succession in the 18th century, when Stanislas Leszczynski, whose right to the throne had been challenged and who had been hiding in France, made his way secretly back to Poland and reappeared with dramatic suddenness at a service in Warsaw Cathedral, to be recognised as the rightful claimant. There is, however, little historical basis for the actual incidents which form the subject of Romani's libretto.

After a gay and brilliant overture referring to the opening and closing scenes of the opera, the first scene takes place in a hall in the castle where servants are excitedly making preparations for the double wedding of the Baron's daughter Giulietta to the rich old Treasurer, la Rocca, and of his niece, the Marchesa, to Count Ivrea. In point of fact, rejoicing is slightly out of place as Giulietta is in love with young Edoardo di Sanval and the Marchesa is marrying the Count in a fit of temper, having been, she thinks, jilted by Cavalier di Belfiore. The Baron and the Treasurer congratulate one another on the great honour which may be accorded them in having the King of Poland as witness to the double ceremony. Delmonte announces the arrival of his master and in comes the 'King', in reality the Cavalier di Belfiore, disguised (Il finto Stanislao—The false Stanislas) in order to distract attention from the real Stanislao's bid for power. In a lyrical aside ('Compagnoni di Parigi') he sings of his wish that his companions in Paris could see him, the wildest drinker of them all, playing so dignified a role, then in the cabaletta reiterates his desire that the company should treat him not as a king but as a friend.

The Baron invites him to the double wedding and Belfiore is most disturbed to hear that one of the brides is to be the Marchesa, with whom he is in love. Demanding to be left alone, he writes urgently to the Polish Court in hope that Stanislao has by now been enthroned and that he may therefore be released from his impersonation. In his turn Edoardo di Sanval, who is in despair at the prospect of Giulietta's marriage, begs, now that life for him is over, to be enlisted in the service of Poland ('Proverò che digno io sono'—I shall prove that I am worthy). Belfiore accepts him, determined, even if his spurious court goes up in smoke, to get the better of the Baron. To a martial air the two sing of glory and heroism, but as they go off together, the Marchesa enters unseen and recognises Belfiore. She is puzzled by his behaviour, and wonders if he will reveal himself when he hears of her approaching marriage. In a beautiful cavatina ('Grave a core innamorato') she sings of the impossibility of hiding her love and hopes to gain her uncle's forgiveness.

Scene ii.   The garden of the castle. While the peasant girls surround her with gifts of fruit and flowers, Giulietta reflects that it is a young man she wants to marry, not an old one. Her father the Baron, in company with her elderly fiancé, comes in and reproaches her for hiding at a moment when she is about to meet a king and her future husband is nearby. The Treasurer comforts her—it is her innocence which makes her melancholy, and she will be much gayer in the morning. Belfiore enters and presents Edoardo as his new squire. In order to give the thwarted lovers an opportunity to talk, he says he requires the advice respectively of the Baron in military and the Treasurer in political problems. Edoardo is to entertain his future aunt, while the important discussion takes place, and Belfiore keeps the two old men with their backs to the young people by means of an enormous map which he asks them to scrutinise. That Edoardo makes the most of his chance does not go unnoticed by his jealous uncle, who is so infuriated that he interrupts the strategical discussion and has to be admonished by the 'King'.

Belfiore finally calls a halt, much to the Treasurer's relief, but at this point the Marchesa arrives, whispering to Giulietta that she has come only because of her. When the Baron makes haste to rebuke her for her rudeness to the noble visitor, she apologises to Belfiore and each wonders what the other is thinking. After an *allegro* sextet, Belfiore, the Baron and the Treasurer depart, but Edoardo and Giulietta are disappointed to find the Marchesa at first so disinclined to discuss their problems. She apologises and, because she too knows love, promises to help them. The scene ends with a spirited trio ('Noi siamo amanti e giovani'—We are young and in love).

Scene iii: the same as scene i.   Belfiore tells la Rocca that, if he were not about to be married, he would, because of his brilliant financial brain, give him a ministry in the government, and the hand of a rich Polish Princess into the bargain. La Rocca finds this prospect irresistible, agrees to it and, when the Baron comes in to discuss the marriage contract, timidly suggests that he is unworthy of Giulietta. The Baron, incredulous and scandalised by turns, challenges the terrified Treasurer to draw his sword. The latter shouts for help, everyone runs in and the Baron tells them his daughter has been insulted; Giulietta of course is delighted and the Marchesa cunningly puts forward the idea to the Baron of avenging his honour and humiliating the Treasurer by marrying Giulietta to Edoardo. Belfiore's entrance causes general embarrassment and the Baron apologises for their behaviour. Each participant hopes to enlist the King's aid, and accordingly all together begin to explain the situation, until Belfiore demands they speak one at a time. But it is no use: they are too anxious and upset to obey and the act ends with all begging the King for pardon and agreeing to accept his decision.

Act II, scene i.   The menservants of the Baron are undecided whether any wedding will ever take place, as these aristocrats seem to change their minds every five minutes. Their perplexity is not allayed by Edoardo, who in an ecstasy of happiness tells them that love has at last come to him and that he is to marry Giulietta. The servants leave and Belfiore, Giulietta and la Rocca enter, the 'King' questioning his squire and his newly-appointed 'minister' as to why the Baron is adamant in refusing to allow the marriage of Edoardo to Giulietta. When told it is because he is penniless, Belfiore promptly orders the luckless Treasurer to endow Edoardo with one of his several castles and an income for life. The poor Treasurer asks for time, but the 'King' demands an instant answer, and la Rocca is left alone to weigh the pros and cons of his situation. He is interrupted by the still furious Baron, demanding an explanation. The exasperated Treasurer says that if the Baron is after a fight he can have one, and goes on to advise his adversary to select his last resting place. The two apoplectic old men rush off, hurling insults at one another.

Scene ii.   A conservatory overlooking the garden. The Marchesa and Belfiore enter separately, the latter unseen by his beloved. The Marchesa is angry and puzzled at Belfiore's attitude and vows to force an explanation. Belfiore, still disguised as the King, discloses his presence and says it is easy to see she is thinking of the Cavalier. 'Yes,' says the Marchesa, 'I am trying to think how to punish him for his faithlessness and have decided not to marry him.' Belfiore does not believe her and each thinks the other's cunning quite transparent. The Baron rushes in to say that the Count will be arriving at any moment. Good, says the Marchesa, she is eager to marry him. 'What about the Cavalier?' asks Belfiore. 'Why is he not here?' she asks. In an *andante cantabile* aria, she sings sadly that all she wants is for him to appear to the one who adores him and ask her forgiveness. The servants announce the arrival of the Count, and the Marchesa goes to meet her bridegroom, vowing to forget her faithless lover.

Giulietta comes in, delighted that her father has consented to her marriage with Edoardo and overcome with gratitude to the King, who is responsible for this change of heart. When Edoardo enters and tells her that he must leave with Belfiore, Giulietta insists that as her future husband his place is with her. Edoardo pleads the vow he has taken to follow the King, but Giulietta interrupts to say that she knows nothing about war, only that she should be the most important thing in his life. The two, in an *allegro* duet, are eventually reunited and convinced that all will yet be well.

The Marchesa's fiancé, Count Ivrea, has now arrived, and the Baron is assuring the Count that his beloved has no longer any thought of the Cavalier. The Marchesa promises to marry the Count, provided the Cavalier does not appear within an hour. Belfiore enters with Giulietta and Edoardo, and announces that he must leave at once on urgent business. The Marchesa says she hopes he will stay for her wedding but is mortified when he tells her that the Count must accompany him. Belfiore is delighted to observe her dismay, but the rest of the company is taken aback by this sudden, apparently churlish act.

Delmonte now brings a message from the Polish Court; Belfiore is excited but will only reveal the news after Giulietta has been safely betrothed to Edoardo with himself and la Rocca as witnesses. Once this is accomplished, Belfiore announces that Stanislao has been accepted in Warsaw, that if he himself is no longer a King he has at least been made a Marshal and can now resume his identity as Belfiore. He embraces the delighted Marchesa, and the Baron, the Count and the Treasurer give in to the inevitable, for the opera to end with general rejoicing at the restoration of Stanislao and at the happiness of the reunited lovers.   H.

NABUCCO

Opera in four acts by Giuseppe Verdi; text by Temistocle Solera (refused by Nicolai). Première at la Scala, Milan, March 9, 1842, with Giuseppina Strepponi (who, years later, became Verdi's wife), Bellinzaghi, Miraglia, Ronconi, Dervis. First performed in London, Her Majesty's Theatre, 1846, as *Nino* (in Italian): Covent Garden, 1850, as *Anato*, with Castellan, Costi, Tamberlik, Ronconi, Tagliafico, conductor Costa; New York, 1848. Revived Florence Festival and la Scala, 1933, with Cigna, Stignani, Dolci (in Milan, Voyer), Galeffi, Pasero, conducted by Gui and produced by Ebert; Verona Arena, 1938, with Jacobo, Stignani, Voyer, Tagliabue, Pasero, conductor Capuana; la Scala, 1946, for the reopening of the rebuilt theatre, with Pedrini, Barbieri, Binci, Bechi, Siepi, conductor Serafin; Rome, 1951, with Caniglia, Pirazzini, Francesco Albanese, Bechi, Rossi-Lemeni, conductor Gui; Welsh Nat. Op. Co., 1952, with di Leo, Tom Williams; and at Sadler's Wells, London, 1955, with Packer, Ronald Jackson, Hervey Alan, conductor Groves; New York, Metropolitan Opera, 1960, with Rysanek, MacNiel, Siepi, conductor Schippers; la Scala, Milan, 1966, with Suliotis, Giangiacomo Guelfi, Ghiaurov.

CHARACTERS

Abigaille, *a slave, believed to be the elder daughter of Nabucco* .... Soprano
Fenena, *daughter of Nabucco* .... Soprano
Ismaele, *nephew of the King of Jerusalem* ...... Tenor
Nabucco, *King of Babylon* .... Baritone
Zaccaria, *High Priest of Jerusalem* .... Bass

High Priest of Babylon .... Bass
Abdallo, *an old officer in Nabucco's service* ..... Tenor
Anna, *sister of Zaccaria* .... Soprano
Time: 586 B.C.   *Place:* Jerusalem, Babylon

Nabucco was Verdi's first great success, the opera that established him as one of the leading composers of Italy, the theme which identified him for the first time publicly with his country's political aspirations. Its success was huge, mainly because of its musical quality but also to some extent because of the vivid way in which the composer gave expression to his countrymen's aspirations towards the liberty and self-government which had never yet been theirs. No Italian who heard 'Va, pensiero' could fail to identify himself with the chorus of exiles who were singing it, and it soon become one of the most popular tunes of the day. Franz Werfel, in his collection of Verdi's letters, has described the scene of Verdi's second funeral in Milan a few months after his death (the first, as directed in his will, was very simple): '... then came one of the great and rare moments when people and music become one. Without any preconcerted plan, by some inexplicable inspiration, there suddenly rose out of the monstrous soul of the multitude the chorus from *Nabucco* with which Giuseppe Verdi had become the voice of consolation and hope for his people, sixty years before. "Va, pensiero sull' ali dorate!" '

The rather conventional overture makes use of various tunes from the opera, notably the big choral themes.

Act I.   In passionate choruses, the priests and people of Jerusalem lament their defeat at the hands of Nabucodonosor, King of Babylon (hereinafter, as in the opera, called Nabucco'), and beg Jehovah to prevent the capture of the Temple. In an impressive solo, 'Sperate, o figli', Zaccaria exhorts them to have faith in God, but the news that Nabucco is advancing on the Temple itself throws them once more into consternation.

Ismaele, who brought the news of the enemy's further

advance, is left alone with Fenena, a hostage in the hands of
the Jews, whom he has loved ever since she rescued him
when, as Jewish envoy in Babylon, he had been thrown into
prison. Their colloquy is interrupted by the appearance of
Abigaille, Fenena's supposed sister, at the head of a band of
Babylonian soldiers. She threatens the two lovers with instant
death, but admits to Ismaele that she loves him and says she
has it in her power to save him if he were disposed to return
her love. The trio which follows has the mixture of intensity
and suave vocal writing which distinguishes similar moments
in *Norma* (though the dramatic situation is by no means
similar). Zaccaria rushes in saying he has seen the King riding
towards the Temple itself; in a moment Babylonian troops
fill the Temple, and Nabucco himself rides to the door.
Zaccaria threatens to kill Fenena, Nabucco's daughter, if he
desecrate the holy place, but Nabucco taunts the defeated
Jews ('Tremin gl'insani'), and Zaccaria's attempt on Fenena's
life is frustrated by Ismaele. Nabucco's anger now flows
unrestrained, and he orders the sacking of the Temple.

Act II.   The Jews have been carried captive into Babylon,
and Nabucco, away at the wars, has left Fenena as Regent in
his stead. Abigaille, jealous of her sister's position and burning
to know whether or not she is Nabucco's daughter or, as
rumour has it, only a slave, finds a document which proves
that the latter estimation of her birth is the true one. Her
fury is unbridled, but she remembers her love for Ismaele,
and the first part of her great aria is smooth and expressive.
The High Priest of Bel informs her that Fenena is setting free
the Jewish prisoners; he urges her to seize power, and says he
has already spread the report that Nabucco has been killed in
battle. Abigaille's reaction to this situation is expressed in a
cabaletta suitably vigorous and determined.

The Hebrews are gathered together in a room of the
palace, and, in a noble example of Verdian prayer ('Tu sul
labbro'), Zaccaria invokes the guidance of God. The people
curse Ismaele, but Zaccaria reminds them that Fenena, for
whose sake he committed the act of treachery, has become a
convert to their faith.

Abdallo rushes in to tell them that the popular cry goes up
that the King is dead, and Abigaille plans Fenena's death. In a
moment Abigaille, surrounded by court officials, comes to
demand the crown from Fenena. It is, however, Nabucco
who steps between them, seizes it, and places it on his own
head, defying Abigaille to take it from him. Nabucco

predicting that the incident will have dire consequences, leads off an ensemble[1] which is extraordinarily effective and notable for its excellent contrasting of soloists and chorus. Nabucco proclaims himself God, and commands the protesting Zaccaria and Fenena to bow down before him. There is a clap of thunder, and the crown is torn from his head by a supernatural force. When the crowd has recovered from its consternation, the King is seen to be mad, babbling of persecution and complaining that not even his daughter will help him. Zaccaria proclaims the punishment of heaven on the blasphemer, but Abigaille snatches up the crown crying that the glory of Babylon is not yet departed.

Act III. Abigaille has been installed as Regent, with the support of the priests, who demand the death of the captive Jews, amongst them Fenena. Nabucco is led into Abigaille's presence by his faithful Abdallo, and the rest of the first scene consists of an extended duet between the King and his supposed daughter. At first, he is enraged at finding someone else on his throne, but Abigaille taunts him into sealing the death sentence of the Jews, and, when she tells him he is a prisoner in her hands, his mood changes to one of supplication and desperation. Throughout his career, Verdi was to entrust crucial scenes of his operas to these lengthy, highly developed duets. Already in *Oberto*, there is a long scene of reconciliation between Oberto (bass) and his estranged daughter (soprano), and these two examples from his first and third operas are the forerunners, in manner if not in shape, of that great line which was to include the scene for Macbeth and his wife after the murder, the first act duet for Rigoletto and Gilda, the meeting between Violetta and Germont, the two great duets for Simon Boccanegra and Fiesco, the love duet from *Ballo*, Leonora's scene with Padre Guardiano in *Forza*, Philip's interviews with Posa and the Grand Inquisitor in *Don Carlos*, the two examples in the third act of *Aida*, the love duet in *Otello* and the second act scene between Otello and Iago, and Falstaff's conversation with Ford.

The second scene of the act takes place on the banks of the Euphrates, where the enslaved Jews sing the psalms of their lost fatherland. 'Va, pensiero' is the first of Verdi's patriotic choruses, and its poignant melody is typical of the composer's writing in this vein. Zaccaria upbraids the Jews

[1] The section beginning 'le folgoi intorno' must have been suggested by the sextet in Donizetti's *Maria Stuarda*.

for their defeatist attitude and tries to galvanise them into life and resistance by prophesying the imminent fall of Babylon.

Act IV. Nabucco in prison wakens from a nightmare (suggested in the prelude) to hear the crowd down below crying 'Death to Fenena'. He sees her being led to execution, and prays movingly to Jehovah to pardon him his sin of pride and spare her life: 'Dio di Giuda'. Abdallo appears at the head of the guard and frees his master, who rushes out to rescue his daughter.

The scene changes to the place of execution. A funeral march is heard and Fenena has a beautiful prayer as she and the Jews prepare for death. The arrival of Nabucco and his followers arrests the sacrifice, the false idol is thrown down as if by magic, and all join in a prayer of thanksgiving to Jehovah. The general rejoicing is interrupted by the arrival of Abigaille, who in her remorse has taken poison and presently dies, calling on God for forgiveness. Zaccaria promises glory to his convert, Nabucco.

There is no doubt that *Nabucco* represents a significant advance on Verdi's two earlier operas, *Oberto*, a story of the struggle for power in Northern Italy in the thirteenth century, and *Un Giorno di Regno* (King for a Day), his ill-fated comedy, but it is difficult to agree with those commentators who find in it the most satisfactory of the operas written before *Rigoletto*. The frequent and highly successful revivals which it has enjoyed in recent years prove that it is still a living force, but few people who have heard *Macbeth* would be inclined to estimate it above that near-masterpiece, and there would be many (the present writer amongst them) to prefer *Ernani* to the earlier work. *Nabucco*, however, represents something important in Verdi's output: it was his first success, and in it he can be seen making a serious attempt at the musical portrayal of character.   H.

I LOMBARDI
The Lombards

Opera in four acts by Giuseppe Verdi; text by T. Solera. Première, la Scala Milan, February 11, 1843, with Erminia Frezzolini, Guasco, Derivis. First produced London, Her Majesty's Theatre, 1846, with Grisi, Mario, Fornasari; New York, 1847 (first Verdi opera to be performed there); Paris Opéra, 1847 (as *Jérusalem*, in a revised version)

with Frezzolini, Duprez, Alizard. Retranslated into Italian as
Gerusalemme and produced la Scala, Milan, 1850. Revived London, Her
Majesty's, 1867, with Tietjens, Mongini, Santley; Turin, 1926; la Scala,
Milan, 1931, with Scacciati, Merli, Vaghi, conductor Panizza; Florence
Festival, 1948, with Mancini, Gustavo Gallo, Pasero, conductor Ettore
Gracis; Birmingham, 1935 (by the Midland Music Makers); Berne,
1954, in a new version by Stephen Beinl; London, Sadler's Wells, 1956,
by the Welsh National Opera Company.

CHARACTERS

Arvino ⎱ *sons of Folco* . . . . ⎰ Tenor
Pagano ⎰   ⎱ Bass
Viclinda, *wife of Arvino* . . . . Soprano
Giselda, *her daughter* . . . . Soprano
Pirro, *Pagano's henchman* . . . . Bass
Prior of the city of Milan . . . . Tenor
Acciano, *tyrant of Antioch* . . . . Bass
Oronte, *son of Acciano* . . . . Tenor
Sofia, *wife of Acciano*. . . . . Soprano
Priests, People of Milan, Retainers of Folco,
Muslim Envoys, Crusader Knights and Soldiers,
Pilgrims, Muslim Women, Lombard Ladies
Time: 1099   *Place:* Milan, Antioch,
the country near Jerusalem

The commission to write *I Lombardi* for la Scala was the
direct result of the success of *Nabucco* a year earlier. As soon
as the opera was announced, the Archbishop of Milan drew
the attention of the police to religious references in the
libretto—a baptism and the like—which could cause offence if
represented on the stage. Artistic considerations finally
prevailed over the scruples of the Chief of Police, and the
opera was given with only one minor alteration, the words
'Ave Maria' changed to 'Salve Maria'. In the event the
authorities are likely to have been more worried by the
patriotic demonstrations which were, in the Italy of the time,
the natural result of such a subject.

Act I, scene i. A short prelude full of foreboding leads to
the curtain rising on the Piazza di Sant'Ambrogio, Milan.
Sounds of rejoicing come from within the Cathedral, and the
crowd outside comments on the strange turn of events. Many
years ago the brothers Arvino and Pagano loved Viclinda,
who favoured Arvino. As the young couple was one day
going to church, Pagano struck and wounded his brother and
was in consequence banished to the Holy Land, where it was

hoped he might repent of his crime. Now, his offence
expiated, he has been forgiven and has returned home; but
comments the crowd, there is still the glint of evil in his eye
As they emerge from the Cathedral, Pagano ostensibly prays
for Heaven's forgiveness, and an ensemble develops ('T'assale
un tremito!'). Giselda and Viclinda are apprehensive, Arvino is
seized with sudden foreboding, Pagano and his henchman
Pirro plot revenge, and the crowd worries whether to take
outward signs of peace at their face value. The Prior proclaims the appointment of Arvino as Leader of a Crusade
and all call down anathema on anyone who shakes the
solidarity of the holy enterprise.

All leave except Pagano and Pirro. A group of nuns prays
within as Pagano broods outside, advancing disappointmen
in love as the reason for wandering from the paths of virtue
('Sciagurata! hai tu creduto'). Pirro says that Pagano's
followers are assembled, and in his cabaletta Pagano rejoices
at the prospect of revenge.

Scene ii.   A room in the Palace of Folco, the father of
Pagano and Arvino. Viclinda, Giselda and Arvino believe that
Pagano's repentance is feigned, and in a lovely passage,
Giselda prays to Heaven ('Salve Maria—di grazie il petto').
The Gallery is empty as Pirro leads Pagano towards Arvino's
room. A moment later the interior of the Palace is lit up by
flames. Pagano tries to carry off Viclinda, but, hearing the
voice of Arvino, finds that he has killed his own father
and not his brother. The scene fills, all curse Pagano for his
crime and in his horror he joins in the general execration. His
attempt at suicide is prevented; he must end his days in
solitary exile.

Act II, scene i.   Acciano's Palace in Antioch. Acciano on
his throne receives a group of Muslim ambassadors, who call
down Allah's vengeance on the invading army of Crusaders.
They depart at the entrance of Oronte and Sofia, Acciano's
son and wife. Sofia, who is veiled, is secretly a Christian.
Oronte reveals his love for Giselda, now a captive in Antioch,
in an aria ('La mia letizia infondere') whose lyrical beauty
rivals in Verdi's early output the equally inspired 'Quando le
sere al placido' (*Luisa Miller*). As he shows in the cabaletta
(two versions of which exist), Oronte is so persuaded of the
perfection of his beloved that he is convinced that her God
must be the true God.

Scene ii.   A cave on a mountain overlooking Antioch. A

Hermit, Pagano as will be revealed much later, prays in a fine aria ('Ma quando un suon terribile') that he may soon have a chance of aiding the crusading army to capture Antioch from the Saracens. To the Hermit comes Pirro, now a converted Muslim, to ask for spiritual guidance. Their colloquy is interrupted by the sound of the invading crusaders; they disappear into the cave and the Hermit emerges in military array just as Arvino, the leader of the Crusaders, appears. Arvino approaches the Hermit, little knowing it is his own brother and most deadly enemy from whom he is asking prayers for the safety of his daughter, now a prisoner. The Hermit gives comfort and the scene ends with an *allegro vivace* hymn of hate against the Saracens.

Scene iii.   The Harem in Acciano's Palace. Taunted by the other women, Giselda prays to Heaven ('Oh madre, dal cielo soccorri al mio pianto'). Suddenly women flee through the harem pursued by soldiers, and Queen Sofia reveals that her husband and her son have been killed by the attacking Crusaders—she points to Arvino as their ferocious leader. In music of considerable conviction ('No, Dio nol vuole'), Giselda denounces her father for the blood he has shed.

Act III, scene i. The Valley of Jehoshaphat; the Mount of Olives and Jerusalem in the distance. A procession of pilgrims sings a devotional chorus of typically *Risorgimento* cut. They go on their way, and Giselda appears, desolate at the loss of her lover Oronte, whom she presumes dead in the slaughter which followed the capture of the city. But the man who now appears in Lombard clothing is none other than Oronte himself, lamenting that his love for Giselda has caused him to take on a coward's disguise in the hope of seeing her again. Their duet reveals their mutual determination to give up everything for their love, and Oronte even says he means to adopt Giselda's faith. Warlike shouts from the Crusaders' camp make Giselda afraid for Oronte's life and they flee together.

Scene ii.   Arvino's tent. He inveighs against the treachery of his daughter's flight, but his thoughts are interrupted as his men tell him of a rumour that Pagano has been recognized in the camp. Arvino's anger turns against this wicked brother.

Scene iii.   A cave on the banks of the River Jordan. The prelude is in the form of a violin solo with orchestral accompaniment, so elaborate in the writing that it might be the end of a movement of a concerto. Oronte has been mortally wounded in the attempt to escape, and Giselda, beside herself with grief at this new blow, cries out at the injustice of God's ways, only to be rebuked by the Hermit who appears in the entrance to the cave. The extended trio, 'Qual volutà trascorrere',

always with the violin obbligato in the background and with Oronte's interrupted cantilena as he gasps for breath, is one of the most famous of Verdian death-scenes. The Hermit baptises Oronte as he dies in Giselda's arms.

Act IV, scene i. A cave near Jerusalem. Giselda asleep sees a vision of Oronte amongst the blessed and even hears his voice. She expresses her perturbation in an agitated quick solo ('Qual prodigio'), curiously known on old records as 'the Polonaise from *I Lombardi*' although in common time.

Scene ii. The Crusader camp near the Tomb of Rachel. The scene opens with a great chorus of longing, which, as a hymn of the *Risorgimento*, ranks as companion-piece to, and in its own day achieved comparable popularity with, 'Va pensiero' from *Nabucco* (this line of patriotic music culminates as late as 1865 in the chorus in the last act of *Macbeth*). The Crusaders are preparing an assault on Jerusalem, and Arvino and the Hermit lead them to battle.

An orchestral interlude takes us to scene iii, set in another part of Arvino's Camp. Arvino and Giselda attend the Hermit who has been carried in wounded. At mention of Arvino's name, the Hermit comes out of his delirium to mutter of parricide. It is not long before he reveals his name and, in a moving death-scene, Giselda joins her voice to his in begging Arvino to forgive his past wrongs. The opera ends as Pagano begs for a last sight of the Holy City, over whose walls the banner of the Cross can be seen flying.   H.

ERNANI

Opera in four acts by Giuseppe Verdi; text by Francesco Maria Piave, after the drama by Victor Hugo. Première at the Fenice Theatre, Venice, March 9, 1844, with Löwe, Guasco, Superchi, Selva. First performed at Her Majesty's Theatre, London, 1845; New York, 1847; Metropolitan, 1903, with Sembrich, de Marchi, Scotti, Edouard de Reszke, conductor Mancinelli; 1921, with Ponselle, Martinelli, Danise, Mardones, conductor Papi; 1928, with Ponselle, Martinelli, Ruffo, Pinza, conductor Bellezza; 1956, with Milanov, del Monaco, Warren, Siepi; revived la Scala, 1935, with Cigna, Merli, Armando Borgioli, Pasero, conductor Marinuzzi; Berlin, 1935, with Lemnitz, Wittrisch, Janssen, Bohnen, conductor Blech; la Scala, 1941, with Castellani, Merli, Bechi, Pasero, conductor Marinuzzi; Rome, 1951, with Mancini, Penno, Silveri, Christoff, conductor Santini; Florence Festival, 1957, with Cerquetti, del Monaco, Bastianini, Christoff, conductor Mitropoulos; la Scala, Milan, 1960, with Margherita Roberti, del Monaco, Bastianini, Rossi-Lemeni; London, Sadler's Wells, 1967, with Tinsley, Donald Smith, Bickerstaff, Clifford Grant, conductor Bryan Balkwill.

CHARACTERS

Don Carlos, *King of Castile* .... Baritone
Don Ruy Gomez de Silva, *Grandee of Spain* ...... Bass
Ernani, or John of Aragon, *a bandit chief* ...... Tenor
Don Riccardo, *esquire to the King* .... Tenor
Jago, *esquire to Silva* .... Bass
Elvira, *kinswoman to Silva* .... Soprano
Giovanna, *in Elvira's service* .... Soprano
Mountaineers and Bandits, Followers of Silva, Ladies of Elvira, Followers of Don Carlos, Electors and Pages

Time: Early Sixteenth Century   *Place:* Spain

His father, the Duke of Segovia, having been slain by order of Don Carlos's father, John of Aragon has become a bandit. Proscribed and pursued by the emissaries of the King, he has taken refuge in the fastnesses of the mountains of Aragon, where, under the name of Ernani, he is leader of a large band of rebel mountaineers. Ernani is in love with Donna Elvira, who, although she is about to be united to her relative, the aged Ruy Gomez di Silva, a grandee of Spain, is deeply enamoured of the handsome, chivalrous bandit chief.

Don Carlos, afterwards the Emperor Charles V, also has fallen violently in love with Elvira. By watching her windows he has discovered that at dead of night a young cavalier

522   THE COMPLETE OPERA BOOK

(Ernani) gains admission to her apartments. He imitates h
lover's signal, gains admission to her chamber, and declare
his passion. Being repulsed, he is about to drag her off by
force, when a secret panel opens, and he finds himsel:
confronted by Ernani. In the midst of a violent scene Silva
enters. To allay his jealousy and anger at finding two men
apparently rival suitors, in the apartment of his affianced, the
King, whom Silva does not recognise, reveals himself, and
pretends to have come in disguise to consult him about his
approaching election to the empire, and a conspiracy that is
on foot against his life. Then the King, pointing to Ernani, says
to Silva, 'It doth please us that this, our follower, depart,
thus insuring Ernani's temporary safety—for a Spaniard does
not hand an enemy over to the vengeance of another.

Believing a rumour that Ernani has been hunted down and
killed by the King's soldiers, Elvira at last consents to give her
hand in marriage to Silva. On the eve of the wedding however
Ernani, pursued by the King with a detachment of troops,
seeks refuge in Silva's castle in the disguise of a pilgrim
Although not known to Silva, he is under Spanish tradition
his guest, and from that moment entitled to his protection

Elvira enters in her bridal attire. Ernani is thus made aware
that her nuptials with Don Silva are to be celebrated on the
morrow. Tearing off his disguise, he reveals himself to Silva.
and demands to be delivered up to the King, preferring death
to life without Elvira. But true to his honour as a Spanish
host, Silva refuses. Even his enemy, Ernani, is safe in his
castle. Indeed he goes so far as to order his guards to man the
towers and prepare to defend the castle, should the King seek
forcible entry. He leaves the apartment to make sure his
orders are being carried out. The lovers find themselves alone.
When Silva returns they are in each other's arms. But as the
King is at the castle gates, he has no time to give vent to his
wrath. He gives orders to admit the King and his men, bids
Elvira retire, and hides Ernani in a secret cabinet. The King
demands that Silva give up the bandit. The grandee proudly
refuses. Ernani is his guest. The King's wrath then turns
against Silva. He demands the surrender of his sword and
threatens him with death, when Elvira interposes. The King
pardons Silva, but bears away Elvira as hostage for the
loyalty of her kinsman.

The King has gone. From the wall Silva takes down two
swords, releases his guest from his hiding-place, and bids him

cross swords with him to the death. Ernani refuses. His host has just protected his life at the danger of his own. But, if Silva insists upon vengeance, let grandee and bandit first unite against the King, with whom the honour of Elvira is unsafe. Elvira rescued, Ernani will give himself up to Silva, to whom, handing him his hunting-horn, he avows himself ready to die, whenever a blast upon it shall be sounded from the lips of the implacable grandee. Silva, who has been in entire ignorance of the King's passion for Elvira, grants the reprieve, and summons his men to horse.

He sets on foot a conspiracy against the King. A meeting of the conspirators is held in the Cathedral of Aix-la-Chapelle, in the vault, within which stands the tomb of Charlemagne. It is resolved to murder the King. A ballot decides who shall do the deed. Ernani's name is drawn.

The King, however, has received information of the time and place of this meeting. From the tomb he has been an unobserved witness of the meeting and purpose of the conspirators. Booming of cannon outside tells him of his choice as head of the Holy Roman Empire. Emerging from the tomb, he shows himself to the awed conspirators, who imagine they see Charlemagne issuing forth to combat them. At the same moment the doors open. The electors of the Empire enter to pay homage to Charles V.

'The common herd to the dungeon, the nobles to the headsman,' he commands.

Ernani advances, discovers himself as John of Aragon, and claims the right to die with the nobles—'to fall, covered, before the King'. But upon Elvira's fervent plea, the King, now also Emperor, commences his reign with an act of grace. He pardons the conspirators, restores to Ernani his titles and estates, and unites him with Elvira.

Silva, thwarted in his desire to marry Elvira, waits to sound the fateful horn until Ernani and Elvira, after their nuptials, are upon the terrace of Ernani's castle in Aragon. Ernani, too chivalrous to evade his promise, stabs himself in the presence of the grim avenger and of Elvira, who falls prostrate upon his lifeless body.

In the opera, this plot develops as follows: Act I opens in the camp of the bandits in the mountains of Aragon. In the distance is seen the Moorish castle of Silva. The time is near sunset. Ernani's followers sing, 'Allegri, beviamo' (Haste! Clink we our glasses).

Ernani sings Elvira's praises in the air 'Come rugiada al cespite' (Balmier than dew to drooping bud)

Co - me ru - gia - da al ce - spi - te

This expressive number is followed by one in faster time, 'O tu, che l'alma adora' (O thou toward whom, adoring soul)

O tu, che l'al - maa - do - ra Vien, vien, la mia vi - ta in - fio - - ra,

Enthusiastically volunteering to share any danger Ernani may incur in seeking to carry off Elvira, the bandits, with their chief at their head, go off in the direction of Silva's castle.

The scene changes to Elvira's apartment in the castle. It is night. She is meditating upon Ernani. When she thinks of Silva, 'the frozen, withered spectre', and contrasts with him Ernani, who 'in her heart ever reigneth', she voices her thoughts in that famous air for sopranos, one of Verdi's loveliest inspirations, 'Ernani! involami' (Ernani! fly with me):

Er - na - ni! Er - na - - ni l'in - vo - la - mi All' ab - borri - to am - ples - so

It ends with a brilliant cadenza, 'Un Eden quegli antri a me' (An Eden those caverns to me).

Young maidens bearing wedding gifts enter. They sing a chorus of congratulation. To this Elvira responds with a graceful cabaletta, the sentiment of which however is expressed as an aside, since it refers to her longing for her young, handsome, and chivalrous lover. 'Tutto sprezzo che d'Ernani' (Words that breathe thy name Ernani):

Tut - to sprez - zo, che d'Er - na - ni

The young women go. Enter Don Carlos, the King. There
s a colloquy, in which Elvira protests against his presence;
nd then a duet, which the King begins, 'Da quel dì che t'ho
veduta' (From the day, when first thy beauty).

A secret panel opens. The King is confronted by Ernani,
nd by Elvira, who has snatched a dagger from his belt. She
nterposes between the two men. Silva enters. What he
oeholds draws from him the melancholy reflections—
Infelice! e tuo credevi' (Unhappy me! and I believed thee), an

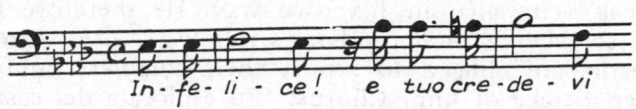

xceptionally fine bass solo. He follows it with the vindictive
Infin, che un brando vindice' (In fine a swift, unerring
olade).

Men and women of the castle and the King's suite have
come on. The monarch makes himself known to Silva, who
does him obeisance and, at the King's command, is obliged to
et Ernani depart. An ensemble brings the act to a close.

Act II. Grand hall in Silva's castle. Doors lead to various
apartments. Portraits of the Silva family, surmounted by
ducal coronets and coats-of-arms, are hung on the walls. Near
each portrait is a complete suit of equestrian armour, corresponding in period to that in which lived the ancestor
represented in the portrait.

The persistent chorus of ladies, though doubtless aware
that Elvira is not thrilled at the prospect of marriage with her
'frosty' kinsman and has consented to marry him only
because she believes Ernani dead, enters and sings
'Esultiamo!' (Exultation!), then pays tribute to the many
virtues and graces of the bride.

To Silva, in the full costume of a Grandee of Spain, and
seated in the ducal chair, is brought in Ernani, disguised as a
monk. He is welcomed as a guest; but, upon the appearance
of Elvira in bridal array, throws off his disguise and offers his
life, a sacrifice to Silva's vengeance, as the first gift for the
wedding. Silva, however, learning that he is pursued by the
King, offers him the protection due to a guest under the roof
of a Spaniard.

'Ah, morir potessi adesso' (Ah, to die would be a blessing)

is the impassioned duet sung by Elvira and Ernani, when Silva
leaves them together.

Ah, mo-rir po-tes-sia-des-so O mio Er-na-ni sul tuo pet-to

Silva, even when he returns and discovers Elvira in Ernani's
arms, will not break the law of Spanish hospitality, preferring
to wreak vengeance in his own way. He therefore hides
Ernani so securely that the King's followers, after searching
the castle, are obliged to report their complete failure to
discover a trace of him. Chorus: 'Fu esplorata del castello'
(We have now explored the castle).

Then come the important episodes described—the King's
demand for the surrender of Silva's sword and threat to
execute him; Elvira's interposition; and the King's sinister
action in carrying her off as a hostage, after he has sung the
significant air 'Vieni meco, sol di rose' (Come with me, a
brighter dawning waits for thee).

Vie - ni me-co, sol di ro - se

Ernani's handing of his hunting horn to Silva and his
arousal of the grandee to an understanding of the danger that
threatens Elvira from the King, are followed by the finale, a
spirited call to arms by Silva, Ernani, and chorus, 'In arcione,
in arcione, cavalieri!' (To horse, to horse, cavaliers!).

Act III. The scene is a sepulchral vault, enclosing the
tomb of Charlemagne in the Cathedral of Aix-la-Chapelle.
The tomb is entered by a heavy door of bronze, upon which
is carved in large characters the word 'Charlemagne'. Steps
lead to the great door of the vault.

It is to this sombre but grandiose place that the King has
come in order to overhear, from within the tomb of his
greatest ancestor, the plotting of the conspirators. His
soliloquy, 'Oh, de' verd' anni miei' (Oh, for my youthful
years once more), derives impressiveness both from the
solemnity of the situation and the music's flowing measure:

Oh de' verd'an - ni mie - - i

The principal episode in the meeting of the conspirators is their chorus, 'Si ridesti il Leon di Castiglia' (Let the lion awake in Castilia). Dramatically effective too in the midst of the plotting is the sudden booming of distant cannon. It startles the conspirators. Cannon boom again. The bronze door of the tomb swings open and the King presents himself at its entrance. Three times he strikes the door of bronze with the hilt of his dagger. The principal entrance to the vault opens. To the sound of trumpets electors enter, dressed in cloth of gold. They are followed by pages carrying, upon velvet cushions, the sceptre, crown, and other imperial insignia. Courtiers surround the Emperor. Elvira approaches. The banners of the Empire are displayed. Many torches borne by soldiers illuminate the scene. The act closes with the pardon granted by the King, and the stirring finale, 'Oh, sommo Carlo!' (O noble Charles!).

Act IV, on the terrace of Ernani's castle, is brief, and there is nothing to add to what has been said of its action. Ernani asks Silva to spare him till his lips have tasted the chalice filled by love. He recounts his sad life: 'Solingo, errante misero' (To linger in exiled misery).

Silva's grim reply is to offer him his choice between a cup of poison and a dagger. He takes the latter. 'Ferma, crudele, estinguere' (Stay thee, my lord, for me at least) cries Elvira, wishing to share his fate. In the end there is left only the implacable avenger, to gloat over Ernani, dead, and Elvira prostrate upon his form.

Ernani, brought out in 1844, is, with *Nabucco*, the earliest work by Verdi that maintains a foothold in the modern repertory, though by no means a firm one. Hanslick, the Viennese critic, pointed out that whereas in Victor Hugo's drama the mournful blast upon the hunting horn, when heard in the last act, thrills the listener with tragic foreboding, in the opera, after listening to solos, choruses, and a full orchestra all the evening, the audience is but little impressed by the sounding of a note upon a single instrument. That

comment, however, presupposes considerable subtlety, so far
undiscovered, on the part of operatic audiences.

Early in its career the opera experienced various
vicissitudes. The conspiracy scene had to be toned down for
political reasons before the production of the work was
permitted. Even then the chorus, 'Let the lion awake in
Castilia', caused a political demonstration. In Paris, Victor
Hugo, as author of the drama on which the libretto is based
raised objections to its representation, and it was produced in
the French capital as *Il Proscritto* (The Proscribed) with the
characters changed to Italians. Victor Hugo's *Hernani* was a
famous play in Sarah Bernhardt's repertory during her early
engagements in America, and her Doña Sol (Elvira in the
opera) was one of her finest achievements.   K.

Ernani is in many respects a fine opera. Since 1844, the
whirligig of fashion has made one, two, three, perhaps four
revolutions, and now, most of a hundred and fifty years since
the first performance and after a period when it was looked
upon as crude and empty, the opera is once again, in
adequate performances and with singers who can do justice
to the music, accepted by audiences as a thrilling and
rewarding experience. Its whipcrack melodies have the energy
of youth, and, for all its frequent lack of subtlety, the genius
of the composer is very much in evidence.   H.

I DUE FOSCARI

The Two Foscari

Opera in three acts by Giuseppe Verdi, libretto by Piave after the
play by Byron. Première, Rome, November 3, 1844, with Barbieri-Nini
Roppa, de Bassini. First produced London, Her Majesty's, 1847, with
Grisi, Mario, Ronconi: New York, 1847. Revived Halle, 1927; Stuttgart
1956 (as *Der Doge von Venedig*) with Kinas, Traxel, Czubok
conductor Leitner; Venice, 1957, with Gencer, Picchi, Giangiacomo
Guelfi, conductor Serafin; Wexford Festival, 1958, with Angioletti, de
Monte, Pedani, conductor Balkwill.

CHARACTERS

Francesco Foscari, *octogenarian Doge of*
 Venice .... Baritone
Jacopo Foscari, *his son* .... Tenor
Lucrezia Contarini, *wife to Jacopo* .... Soprano

Jacopo Loredano, *member of the Council of Ten* .   Bass
Barbarigo, *Senator, member of the Council* . . . . . Tenor
Pisana, *friend and confidante of Lucrezia* . . . . . Soprano
Attendant on the Council of Ten . . . . Tenor
Servant of the Doge . . . . Bass
Members of the Council of Ten and of the 'Giunta';
Lucrezia's Maids; Venetian Ladies;
Maskers and Venetians of both sexes; Gaolers, Gondoliers,
Pages, two Sons of Jacopo Foscari

Time: 1457   *Place:* Venice

There is a short prelude, whose *adagio* theme is associated
with the despair of the opera's hero, Jacopo Foscari. The
curtain rises on a room in the Doge's Palace in Venice, where
the Council of Ten sings in a solemn chorus of the implacable
nature of its deliberations, and then leaves for the Council
Chamber. Jacopo Foscari is brought in and left to wait while
the Council decides his fate. He is the son of the aged Doge
and has been exiled after an accusation of murder. Now he
has illegally returned in order to see his family and his
beloved native city, and it is this transgression of the law that
the Council is at present considering (Byron's play has him
accused by his enemies of conspiring with the Milanese
against the Venetians, but this complication is virtually
absent from the opera). In a beautiful aria ('Brezza del suol
natio') he sings of his love for Venice and, in the brisk
cabaletta, of his determination to prove his innocence.

The scene changes to a room in the Palazzo Foscari.
Jacopo's wife, Lucrezia, eludes her female attendants and
rushes into the room to plead with the Doge for clemency for
Jacopo. In a cavatina ('Tu al cui sguardo onnipossente') she
prays for heaven's help in her misery. Lucrezia's companion
Pisana tells her that the Council has decided again to
condemn Jacopo to exile, and Lucrezia rails against the
injustice of the sentence.

In his private apartments, the old Doge laments the fate
which opposes in him the judge's duty to a father's love for
his son. The dilemma is expressed in an aria of great dignity
and pathos, 'O vecchio cor che batti', the only moment of
the score known out of context (Pasquale Amato's pre-Great
War gramophone record was for many years a best-seller).
Lucrezia is announced and pleads vehemently that the Doge
publicly recognise what the father instinctively knows, that

Jacopo is guiltless. In tender music, the old man makes it clear that he is convinced his son is innocent, but equally clear that he feels himself powerless, caught between paternal feeling and the obligations of his position.

Act II.   The State Prison. In the darkness of the dungeon, Jacopo laments his misfortunes in a state of mounting delirium. One moment he thinks he sees the man he is accused of murdering, Carmagnola by name, and a little later he fails at her entrance to recognise his wife. The scene between husband and wife maintains the intensity of Jacopo's monologue, and, when singing is heard outside, Jacopo bursts into furious condemnation of those who are tearing his loved ones from him. The Doge comes to bid farewell to his son. In a fine trio ('Nel tuo paterno amplesso') Jacopo takes comfort in his father's embrace and affirms his innocence, the Doge describes himself as a dying man, and Lucrezia asks for heaven's vengeance on the authors of their misfortunes. Loredano, a member of the Council of Ten who has sworn vengeance on the Foscari family for their responsibility, as he maintains, for the death of his father and uncle, comes into the prison to conduct Jacopo to hear the judgement of the Council of Ten, and the impressive scene ends with a *presto* quartet.

In the great hall, the Council waits for Jacopo and discusses the crime for which he was once sentenced to exile; its re-affirmation of the sentence now confirms the incorruptible nature of Venetian justice. When the Doge is seated, Loredano announces the 'clemency' of the Council, but Jacopo protests and asks them to believe in his original innocence. The Doge confirms the sentence as Lucrezia brings in her children to reinforce the plea. Jacopo now pleads for pardon, kneeling with his children at the Doge's feet, and the act ends in a grandiose finale, during whose course Lucrezia begs in vain to be allowed to accompany her husband into exile.

Act III.   It is carnival, and the Square of St Mark's fills with masked revellers. Gondoliers sing a barcarole. Jacopo is escorted from the Doge's Palace to the state barge, which waits to take him into exile. His mournful song of farewell turns into a cry of despair when he recognises his enemy Loredano.

In his private rooms, the Doge sings movingly of the fate which has deprived him of three sons in infancy and now banishes a fourth, leaving him to die alone. Barbarigo brings news that another has confessed to the murder of which

Jacopo was accused, but Lucrezia is not far behind him to assure them that this cannot avert the inevitable tragedy, as Jacopo breathed his last the moment the barge left the confines of the lagoon. The vigour of the Foscari family has passed to Lucrezia, who alone has the strength to proclaim retribution for their enemies.

The Doge receives the Council of Ten, which, through the mouth of Loredano, demands his abdication on grounds of age and the bereavement he has recently suffered. The Doge at first refuses—when he for his part asked to abdicate years ago, was he not constrained to swear to remain in office until death?—but they press their demands with threats. The Doge at first defies them ('Questa dunque e l'iniqua mercede'), and turns on them for removing his last hope of happiness ('Ah, rendete il figlio a me'). Eventually he takes the ring off his finger, the cap off his head, but summons up a last gesture of defiance to order Loredano away from the ducal emblems. Lucrezia arrives in time to hear the great bell toll for the election of a Malipiero as Doge. Old Foscari sinks down exhausted and broken, and sobs out his life, watched by the Council, amongst them the exultant Loredano.   H.

ATTILA

Opera in a prologue and three acts by Giuseppe Verdi, libretto by Temistocle Solera. Première, Venice, March 17, 1846, with Sophie Loewe, Guasco, Constantini, Marini. First produced London, Her Majesty's, 1848, with Sophie Cruvelli, Italo Gardoni, Velletti, Cuzzoni; New York, 1850. Revived Venice Festival, 1951 (concert performance), with Mancini, Penno, Giangiacomo Guelfi, Italo Tajo, conductor Giulini; Sadler's Wells, London, 1963, in English with Rae Woodland, Donald Smith, Mossfield, Donald McIntyre, conductor John Matheson. Rome, 1964, with Roberti, Limarilli, Zanasi, Arie, conductor Previtali; Trieste, 1965, with Christoff; Buenos Aires, 1966, with Tatum, Cossutta, Glossop, Hines, conductor Pritchard; Berlin, 1971, with Janowitz, Franco Tagliavini, Wixell, van Dam, conductor Patane; Edinburgh Festival, 1972, with Maragliano, Prevedi, Bruson, Ruggiero Raimondi, conductor Patane; Florence, 1972, with Gencer, Luchetti, Mittelmann, Ghiaurov, conductor Muti.

CHARACTERS

Attila, *King of the Huns* . . . . Bass
Uldino, *a Breton slave of Attila's* . . . . Tenor
Odabella, *daughter of the Lord of Aquileia* . . . Soprano
Ezio, *a Roman general* . . . . Baritone

Foresto, *a knight of Aquileia* ....Tenor
Pope Leo I ....Bass
Time: Fifth Century A.D.   *Place:* Italy

After a short prelude, the curtain rises on the Prologue to show a piazza in Aquileia. Attila's army has sacked the city and is celebrating victory, with invocations to Wodan and praise of their general, who presently appears amongst his troops and takes his seat on the throne. He is angry to see that, in spite of his strict orders, some of the enemy women have been saved. In an aria, Odabella, who leads them, proclaims the invincible spirit of the Italian women, who fought alongside their men, unlike the women who have accompanied his army. The spitfire coloratura of her music is as full of venom as that of Lady Macbeth, and Attila in admiration offers her any gift she wants—she settles for a sword, and he gives her his own. In a cabaletta, she swears to herself that with it she will exact vengeance for all that she has lost.

Ezio, the emissary of the Roman Emperor, is announced. In an extended duet, he offers Attila the hegemony of the world—the Emperor of the East is old, the ruler of the West a mere boy, he himself requires only that Italy shall be left to

A-vrai tu l'u - ni - ver - - so, re-sti l'I- -ta - lia, re - - sti l'I - ta - lia a me

him. At the climax of the duet come the words 'Avrai tu
l'universo, resti l'Italia a me', and one can guess at the effect
both words and the proud and challenging musical phrase to
which they are sung must have had in *Risorgimento* Italy.
Attila reacts against this apparent act of treachery; how can
Italy, whose most valiant leader is a traitor, ever hope to defy
him? Ezio reminds him of his defeat at Châlons and
announces the defiance of Rome.

The scene changes. Foresto, once one of the leaders of
Aquileia, has led a band of refugees out to the lagoons, where
they have built a sad little group of huts, miserable now, but
later to become the proud city of Venice. They salute the
dawn, and Foresto comes to greet them, still in his aria
mourning his beloved Odabella, but proclaiming to the
undisguised satisfaction of his followers their determination
to raise from the lonely lagoon a city no less splendid than
the one they have left—a compliment to Venice by Verdi's
librettist, Solera, not likely to be missed by the Fenice
audience in 1846.

Act I. A wood near Attila's camp. In heartfelt phrases
over *cor anglais* and then full woodwind accompaniment,
Odabella laments the death of her father. To her comes
Foresto, at first and in spite of her joy at seeing him, full of
reproaches that she has betrayed him with the slayer of her
family. She justifies herself and reminds him of Judith who
saved Israel.

The second scene takes place in Attila's tent, where the
conqueror lies asleep, covered by a tiger skin. He wakes,
clearly under the influence of a dream, and tells his
attendant, Uldino, that he has been visited in his sleep by a
vision of an old man, who warned him solemnly against
continuing his march on Rome. Shaking off his forebodings,
Attila calls together the priests and the army and orders that
the march be resumed. From a distance a group can be heard
approaching, and, when it turns out to be children and virgins
headed by the old man he saw in his dream, Attila's
resolution is no longer proof against his superstitions, least of
all when the old man (described in the score as Saint Leo)
repeats the very words we have just heard Attila recount to
Uldino. The act ends with a great ensemble, not unlike the
finale to the banqueting scene in *Macbeth*, in which Attila
decides to bow to what is evidently the will of heaven.

Act II. In his camp, Ezio reads a letter from the Emperor
Valentinian, commanding him to return to Rome. Such a boy

to *command* him! In a beautiful aria ('Dagli immortal vertici'), he gives expression to his love of his country, then urged by Foresto to join the forces resisting Attila, resolve to die if need be in defence of his country.

Attila's camp as in Act I. The troops are feasting in honou of the truce, and Attila, in spite of the warnings of the priests, entertains Ezio. The sudden extinguishing of the torches by a squall of wind appals the guests, but Attila refuses to be diverted even by so ill an omen from his purpose. When Uldino gives Attila a cup in which to pledge the guests, Odabella, who knows it is poisoned, warns Attila against drinking it. Foresto proudly acknowledges that he was responsible for the attempt on Attila's life, but, when Odabella demands his safety as the price of her warning Attila consents to spare him, announcing at the same time that Odabella shall be his bride. Suspicious again of her motives, Foresto bitterly reproaches Odabella and leaves.

Act III. A wood dividing Attila's camp from Ezio's. Foresto and Ezio are still determined to carry out their plan and Foresto in a fine aria laments the faithlessness of Odabella. Ezio joins him, and they proclaim their common resolve, but even the arrival of Odabella does not quieten Foresto's suspicions of her conduct, exacerbated as they have been by the sound of what he takes—rightly—for her wedding chorus. In a beautiful trio ('Te sol quest'anima') she tries to convince him that her heart has always been his and his alone.

Attila comes to claim his bride and is astonished to find her in the arms of Foresto. He bitterly reproaches all three—the slave he was to marry, the criminal whose life he spared, the Roman with whom he has a truce—but they defy him and his threats in a lively quartet. As the Roman soldiers who have been organised by Ezio and Foresto rush in to kill Attila Odabella stabs him to the heart: 'E tu pure, Odabella?'.   H.

MACBETH

Opera in four acts by Giuseppe Verdi; text by Francesco Maria Piave. Première in Florence, March 14, 1847, with Barbieri-Nini, Varesi. First performed in New York, 1850; Dublin, 1859, with Pauline Viardot-Garcia as Lady Macbeth and Arditi conducting. Revised for Paris and first performed there in the new version, April 21, 1865, with Rey

Balla, Ismael. Revived Dresden, 1928, with Eugenie Burckhardt, Robert Burg, Willy Bader, conductor Kutzchbach; Berlin, 1931, with Binder-nagel and Onegin (Lady Macbeth), Reinmar, Andresen; Rome, 1932, with Scacciati, Franci, conductor Guarnieri; Vienna, 1933, with Rose Pauly; Glyndebourne, 1938 (for the first time in England, though productions had been scheduled for seasons of 1861 and 1870 but abandoned), with Vera Schwarz (in 1939, Grandi), Valentino, Franklin, David Lloyd, conductor Busch, producer Ebert; la Scala, Milan, 1938, with Cigna and Jacobo, Sved, Pasero, Parmeggiani, conductor Marinuzzi; Buenos Aires, 1939, with Spani, Sved, Vaghi, conductor Panizza; Edinburgh Festival, 1947, with Grandi, Valentino, Tajo, Midgley, conductor Goldschmidt (Glyndebourne production); Zürich, 1949, with Malaniuk and Dow; Berlin, 1950, with Mödl, Metternich, conductor Keilberth; la Scala, 1952, with Callas, Mascherini, conductor de Sabata; Metropolitan, 1958, with Rysanek, Warren; Covent Garden, 1960, with Shuard, Gobbi; la Scala, Milan, 1964, with Birgit Nilsson, Giangiacomo Guelfi, conductor Scherchen.

CHARACTERS

Lady Macbeth .... Soprano
Macbeth, *a general* .... Baritone
Banquo, *a general* .... Bass
Macduff, *a Scottish nobleman* .... Tenor
Duncan, *King of Scotland* .... Mute
Lady-in-waiting to Lady Macbeth .... Soprano
Malcolm, *son of Duncan* .... Tenor
Fleance, *son of Banquo* .... Mute
Doctor .... Bass

Time: 1040   *Place:* Scotland

After the première in Paris of the revised version of *Macbeth* (1865), Verdi was accused amongst other things of not knowing Shakespeare. The accusation moved him to fury, and he, the most modest of composers, wrote: 'I may not have rendered *Macbeth* well, but that I do not know, do not understand and feel Shakespeare, no, by heavens, no! He is one of my very special poets, and I have had him in my hands from my earliest youth, and I read and re-read him continually.'

Macbeth remained a favourite of Verdi's amongst his own works. He spent a considerable time revising it, and its comparative lack of success in his lifetime was a constant source of irritation to him. Piave the librettist was provided with a detailed scenario by the composer before he was allowed to put pen to paper, so that the dramatic construction is Verdi's. Faced with the difficulty of putting a fairly

long play on to the operatic stage, Verdi concentrated on
three principals: Lady Macbeth, Macbeth, and the Witches—
he was emphatic on this last point. Lady Macbeth is explicitly (as in Shakespeare implicitly) the dominating figure,
although her husband remains at the centre of the tragedy;
Macduff is reduced to little more than a member of the
ensemble (even his solitary aria forms part of the moment of
stillness before the turning point in the action); and Banquo,
a considerable figure until his murder, disappears well before
the half-way mark. Malcolm is almost entirely eliminated,
and the Doctor and the Gentlewoman are retained mainly for
the sleep-walking scene.

Act I, which takes the action up to the end of Shakespeare's Act II, scene iii, begins with Macbeth's first
encounter with the Witches, then moves to Lady Macbeth's
reading of the letter, the message from her husband, and

> '. . . come you spirits
> That tend on mortal thoughts, unsex me here'.

There follow the arrival of Macbeth and Duncan, the murder,
Macbeth's horror, and finally the discovery of the crime.

Act II begins with the decision that Banquo now threatens
Macbeth's position, and proceeds to his murder, finishing
with the banquet scene and the appearance of the ghost.

In Act III, Macbeth again goes to the Witches for reassurance, is found by his wife in a state of collapse after the
various apparitions, and, with her, vows Macduff's death.

The last act opens with a group of Scottish refugees,
among them Macduff, singing of Macbeth's reign of terror in
Scotland; their gloom is dispelled by the arrival of Malcolm
with the relieving army. The scene changes to Dunsinane for
the sleep-walking episode, Macbeth's reception of the news
that Birnam Wood is on the march, and the final triumph of
Malcolm and death of Macbeth. Only essentials are preserved,
but they form the core of Shakespeare's drama, and might
have been the framework from which he produced the play,
as they were to be the framework of Verdi's opera.

The prelude concentrates on material later used in the
sleep-walking scene. The first scene takes place on the heath,
where the Witches sing a fantastic chorus while waiting for
Macbeth, and then prophesy his future in awesome tones. A
messenger arrives to announce that Macbeth has been granted
the title and estates of the rebel Cawdor, and Macbeth and

anquo meditate in a duet on the implications of the prophecy, half of which has already come true. The scene concludes with a chorus and dance for the Witches.

Lady Macbeth reads the letter from her husband in which he tells her of the meeting with the weird band, and launches into a determined recitative. 'Vieni, t'affretta' has been described by some as an inadequate setting of the great soliloquy of Act I, but it is strikingly effective in its context, and anyone who heard Margherita Grandi sing it at Glyndebourne or Edinburgh knows that it can, with its cabaletta, 'Or tutti, sorgete, ministri infernali', produce an effect of tigerish ferocity, and it is not unreasonable to assume that this is what Verdi had in mind and could obtain in his own day—not unreasonable either to think that retention of both verses of the cabaletta (exceptional then in modern performances of Verdi's operas) had something to do with the effect on the audience of the scene as a whole.

Macbeth arrives and in a few pregnant sentences, and with hardly a direct word spoken, the murder is decided upon, as the march which announces the King's arrival is heard offstage. The march itself is commonplace enough, but by no means unsuitable to accompany the pantomime which goes with the King's procession—no word is spoken throughout his passage across the stage.

Macbeth, alone, sees a dagger in front of him, and with his solioquy, in itself highly expressive, begins the great duet between the two principal characters. The murder done, Macbeth staggers down the stairs with the dagger still in his hands: 'Fatal mia donna! un murmure, com' io, non

Allegro con voce soffocata

Fa-tal mia donna! un murmure, com' io non in-ten-de - sti?

intendesti?' He describes the scene and the murmuring of the grooms in the ante-chamber, and the way 'Amen' stuck in his throat, and in the end it is Lady Macbeth who has to take the dagger back into the King's chamber.

Characteristically, this duet is marked to be sung 'sotto voce, e cupa', that is to say in a half voice and with dark, stifled tone. Only a few phrases, such as Macbeth's outburst of agonised horror when he catches sight of his blood-stained hands, 'Oh, vista orribile', are to be sung out, and they are

specifically marked 'a voce aperta'. The original Lady Ma
beth records that there were 151 rehearsals of this duet befor
the composer was satisfied, and that the sleep-walking scene—
Verdi always maintained that these were the opera's two
crucial moments—cost her three months of ceaseless worry
before her movements and singing were judged to be satisfactory.

Banquo and Macduff arrive to accompany the King on his
way, and Banquo broods impressively in C minor on the
horrid portents of the night, while his companion goes to
rouse the King. The murder is discovered, and all gather
together for the magnificently sonorous and excitingly
written finale, one of the most splendid (and, for the
principal female singer, one of the most exacting) in any of
Verdi's earlier operas.

Act II. Macbeth is discovered on stage (the orchestral
prelude is a reminiscence of 'Fatal mia donna'), where he is
quickly joined by Lady Macbeth, who accuses him of
avoiding her. They decide that the death of Banquo is
necessary to their schemes, and Lady Macbeth is left alone to
sing an expressive aria, 'La luce langue', whose ferocious
determination (it dates from 1865) puts it into quite another
class from the much tamer piece it replaces, and whose
layout reminds us that 'O don fatale' (*Don Carlos*) was
written less than two years after the revision of *Macbeth*.

The scene changes to a park, where a band of assassins is
waiting for Banquo. Their chorus is a particularly fortunate
example of the conventional music given to bands of
murderers in Italian opera of the period (or indeed to any
felonious nocturnal gathering for that matter; cf. the chorus
near the end of Act I of *Rigoletto*). Banquo's aria which
follows is a beautiful example of Verdi's writing for bass
voice; at its end, the murderers fall upon him, but his son
escapes.

The opening music of the banquet scene has a feverish,
spurious gaiety, which it may be going too far to ascribe
solely to the composer's sense of dramatic character (as if it
were the inn scene in *Wozzeck*) but which is uncannily apt in

its context. The same quality is evident in the graceless, nerve-ridden *Brindisi*, which Lady Macbeth sings to the assembled guests; the close relationship of its tune to the flowing 6/8 *Brindisi* in *Traviata* and the strong contrast of mood between the two has been pointed out by Desmond Shawe-Taylor, writing in the *New Statesman*. In between verses, Macbeth has a conference with a representative of the band charged to murder Banquo and learns that Fleance, Banquo's son, has escaped. Returning to his guests, he complains that Banquo's absence detracts from the pleasure of the occasion and says he himself will sit for a moment in his place. As he goes to the chair, he sees the ghost of the murdered man, and bursts into an agonised denial of his guilt, to the astonishment of the company, which naturally sees nothing. Lady Macbeth's remonstrances finally nerve him to face his guests again, which he does with an attempt at making light of the lapse. Lady Macbeth sings another verse of the *Brindisi*, but Macbeth's frenzy breaks out again as the ghost makes another appearance. His nerve has gone, and the assembly draws away from him, sensing the guilt he makes little attempt any longer to conceal. His sombre tune, 'Sangue a me', begins the finale, which is musically and dramatically no less effective than that to Act I.

Act III. The Witches sit round their cauldron in a dark cave. Their chorus is in the same vein as that of the first act, and is succeeded by a ballet, written of course for Paris (1865) and interrupted in the middle by the appearance of Hecate to instruct her followers as to their conduct when they are visited, as they will shortly be, by Macbeth. The dance continues and at its end Macbeth appears and demands to know his future destiny. The music is extraordinarily suggestive and Verdi has perhaps nowhere else so successfully evoked the supernatural as in the scene of the apparitions, which is punctuated by the distraught comments of Macbeth himself. The King loses consciousness, and the Witches dance and sing round him before disappearing.

The mood changes, Lady Macbeth appears searching for her husband, and asks what he has learnt from the Witches. He tells her and finishes by revealing that he has seen foretold the line of kings which Banquo will sire. The energy of Lady Macbeth's denial that this shall come to pass communicates itself to her husband and arouses something of his old military spirit, so that their short but vigorous duet makes a very striking end to the act.

Act IV. We are at the turning-point in the drama, the zenith of the ambitious career of the Macbeths, and the nadir of the fortunes of the people of Scotland. As we might expect from the Verdi of 1847, the force opposed to Macbeth's tyranny is not only retribution but the less tragic and more immediately topical one of patriotism, which is implied throughout and personified in Macduff, Banquo, the Chorus, and, of course, in the minor figure of Malcolm. 'Patria oppressa', the chorus of the Scottish exiles in Act IV, is in direct line from 'Va, pensiero' in *Nabucco*, with its wailing minor second in the accompaniment, sometimes ascending, sometimes descending (it appears again in the sleep-walking scene) and its wonderfully evocative contours.

Macduff's beautiful aria completes the still moment at the centre of the dramatic action, and is succeeded by a quick movement as Malcolm's army crosses the stage; Malcolm and Macduff sing a duet with the chorus.

Nothing in the score of *Macbeth* is more worthy of admiration that the sleep-walking scene, which is cast in the form of the old soprano 'mad scene', but has a freedom of movement and an expressiveness that Verdi was not to excel in a similar set piece, one is tempted to say, until Aida's arias nearly twenty-five years later. Much of the preliminary orchestral music has been heard in the prelude, but the expressive quality of the vocal writing is quite extraordinary, and the scene itself very exacting for the singer, comprising as it does every shade of expression, and a very wide compass, from C flat at the bottom to top D flat in the last phrase of all (marked 'un fil di voce').

Macbeth is at bay, furious that Malcolm is marching on him with an army reinforced by English troops but confident in his knowledge that the Witches have prophesied for him immunity from death at the hands of anyone 'born of woman'. He curses the low friendless state which his way of life has brought him, but leads his men defiantly to war when he hears that his wife is dead. The battle is accompanied by a fugue, which persists through the short encounter of Macbeth and Macduff and eventually gives way to a general chorus of rejoicing at the defeat of the tyrant.

Apart from the ballet, which was written specially for Paris, four pieces were inserted in 1865 in place of material which now finds no place in the revised opera: in Act II, Lady Macbeth's aria, 'La luce langue'; in Act III the final duet; in Act IV the chorus of exiles (replacing one similar in feeling and with the same words), and the whole of the battle scene (i.e. after Macbeth's aria). Originally, the opera ended with a short *scena* for Macbeth and this has in fact always been used in Glyndebourne's production of the opera, Busch and Ebert inserting it after the fugue and before the entrance of Macduff and Malcolm. Even with the inclusion of this material, which the composer himself had discarded, there is no doubt that the last section of the opera, with its brilliantly descriptive fugue and firm, 'national' final chorus, is a vast improvement on the rather ordinary ending of the original version.

There are quite a number of changes in the rest of the opera, notably in the *presto* section of the big duet of Act I, Macbeth's reaction to the first appearance of the ghost in the banquet scene, the E major section of the first chorus of Act III, and the apparitions scene. These are usually designed to give more prominence to climaxes and moments of extreme

intensity, and the composer has been so successful in his
tidying up of his score that one must be grateful that he did
not decide to re-write the whole opera, as some commentators, notably Francis Toye, have suggested would have been
his best course.

All his life, Verdi strove towards an expression of character, and nowhere previously had he been so successful in its
portrayal as in *Macbeth*. Macbeth himself is shown as dominated, even more than in the play, by the other two main
characters, his wife and the Witches; that is to say, his own
personality plays proportionately a lesser part in determining
events, and he is shown often at his worst and most
susceptible, hardly ever at his best as poet or soldier. All the
same, the working of remorse on his conscience—Verdi, like
Shakespeare, obviously thinks of him as a better man than his
actions—is excellently shown, and the long duet after the
murder subtly and admirably expresses his terror at his deed
and its inevitable consequences, and constitutes, with the
sleep-walking scene, the most complete musical expression of
the element of tragedy and destiny in the composition of the
two leading figures.

Macbeth's loss—if loss it can be called—is, of course, Lady
Macbeth's gain, and she dominates music and action alike.
Judged purely as a role for a singing actress, it is one of the
finest Verdi ever wrote, but its significance goes further than
that and it is perhaps the earliest Verdian role in which a
complete musical development can be traced along with the
dramatic and psychological growth in a character. The progress from the aria in the first act, 'Vieni, t'affretta', which is
in form a conventional aria with cabaletta (although a most
exciting and successful one), through the increasingly un-
nerving events of the intermediate scenes, to the final, long,
wailing curve of the sleep-walking scene is a remarkable
musical study of gradual disintegration under the influence of
conscience.

Macbeth may be said to sum up, better perhaps than any
other opera, this period of Verdi's career; for the first time he
had achieved a combination of the three characteristics which
dominate his music: the theatre, patriotism, and character.

                                                    H.

LA BATTAGLIA DI LEGNANO

The Battle at Legnano

Opera in three acts by Giuseppe Verdi, libretto by Salvatore
Cammarano. Première, Teatro Argentina, Rome, January 27, 1849,
with Teresa de Giuli-Borsi, Gaetano Fraschini, Filippo Colini. First
performance in Great Britain, 1960, by Welsh National Opera (in a
World War II setting, libretto by John and Mary Moody under the title
of *The Battle*), with Heather Harper, Ronald Dowd, Ronald Lewis,
Hervey Alan, conductor Charles Groves; London, Sadler's Wells
Theatre (by Welsh National Opera), 1961. Revived la Scala, Milan,
1916, with Rosa Raisa, Giulio Crimi, Giuseppe Danise, Giulio Cirino;
Parma, 1951, with Adriana Guerrini, Gino Penno, Ugo Savarese, Andrea
Mongelli; Florence Festival, 1959, with Leyla Gencer, Gastone
Limarilli, Giuseppe Taddei, Paolo Washington, conductor Vittorio Gui;
la Scala, Milan, 1961, with Antonietta Stella, Franco Corelli, Ettore
Bastianini, Marco Stefanoni, conductor Gavazzeni.

CHARACTERS

Frederick Barbarossa	Bass
First Consul of Milan	Bass
Second Consul of Milan	Bass
The Mayor of Como	Bass
Rolando, *Duke of Milan*	Baritone
Lida, *his wife*	Soprano
Arrigo, *a warrior from Verona*	Tenor
Marcovaldo, *a German prisoner*	Baritone
Imelda, *Lida's servant*	Mezzo-Soprano
A Herald	Tenor

Time: Twelfth Century   *Place:* Como and Milan

The theme for this opera was suggested to Verdi by the
poet Cammarano, at a time when the composer was uneasy at
the way the liberal and nationalist revolution was going
and anxious to express his patriotism. He was able to embark
on the work at once through the lapse of a previous contract
with the San Carlo in Naples and devoted himself to it
throughout the summer of 1848, finishing it at the end of the
year. The première took place in Rome on January 27, 1849,
the production being supervised by Verdi himself. It was
received with such delirious excitement—partly because the
theme of the victory of the Lombard League over Frederick
Barbarossa was so topical—that the entire fourth act was

repeated. A little later the opera was suppressed by th
Austrian censorship, but it was revived in 1861 in Milan, th
title being changed to *L'Assedio di Haarlem*, the Emperor t
a Spanish duke and the Italian patriots to Dutchmen; on thi
occasion however it was a failure. As recently as 1960, th
opera was revived by the Welsh National Opera with a furthe
change of scene, this time to modern dress and with the titl
The Battle.

Act I.   An overture of distinctly military flavour intro
duces the first scene, set in Milan, where a League, compose
of contingents from the various cities of Lombardy, i
forming to repulse the imminent invasion by Frederic
Barbarossa. Rolando, leader of the Milanese troops, discover
that the group from Verona is led by his beloved friend
Arrigo, whom he had long believed killed in battle. Arrig
explains that he was taken prisoner and the two comrade
rejoice at their happy reunion. In a chorus of great fervour a
the patriots vow to die if necessary for their cause.

Scene ii opens in a shady place where we find Lida and he
ladies. After a gentle chorus, Lida's lyrical and highly orna
mented aria is interrupted by Marcovaldo, who is a captiv
and has fallen in love with Lida. She repulses him angrily.

Arrigo and Rolando arrive, and the embittered Marco
valdo, noticing Lida's agitation at the sight of Arrigo, jump
at once to the conclusion that she is secretly in love wit
him. Lida and Arrigo are left alone, and in a highly emotiona
duet we learn that they had indeed been betrothed year
before. Arrigo reproaches Lida for her marriage to Rolando
even her eminently valid excuse that she thought he was dea
does not seem to satisfy him and he leaves her angrily.

Act II.   Arrigo and Rolando are in Como to persuade th
local leaders to join forces with them against Barbarossa. Th
Mayor's refusal on the grounds that he has a treaty wit
Barbarossa infuriates Rolando and Arrigo, who argue that th
whole future of Italy is at stake and beg him to reconsider
'What answer are we to take back?' they ask. They are soo
answered by the sudden and startling appearance o
Frederick Barbarossa himself, who tells the two envoys t
return with the news of imminent and inescapable disaste
and shows them a great German camp outside the city. I
spite of this show of Barbarossa's power, Arrigo and Roland
retain their confidence in eventual victory, and the act end
with a rousing chorus in which all the Lombards swear t
fight to the death.

Act III. In the crypt of Milan Cathedral, Arrigo is initiated into the ranks of the Death Riders (*Cavalieri della Morte*), a band of warriors all of whom have taken a solemn and terrible oath to rid their country of the invaders or die in the attempt.

The second scene takes place in Lida's rooms. Convinced he is going to be killed in battle, she has written a letter to Arrigo which her maid is to deliver, and she sings of her grief in phrases which cast distinct foreshadows of *Traviata*.

Rolando has premonitions of death as he says goodbye to his wife and child, and when Arrigo enters, he draws him aside to tell him that he, Rolando, has been made leader of the Death Riders, an honour which will almost certainly result in his death. Arrigo promises that if Rolando is killed he will look after his family, and the men leave separately. At this point the treacherous Marcovaldo intercepts Rolando and gives him Lida's letter to Arrigo, which he has bought from her servant Imelda—the letter in which Lida implores Arrigo, for the sake of what they once meant to each other, to see her before the battle. Rolando swears to be revenged on them both.

The third scene finds Arrigo in his room writing to his mother. Lida comes to him, saying that she still loves him but that they must never meet again. She is on the point of explaining that she has come to see him because he has ignored her letter when Rolando is heard at the door. Arrigo hastily conceals Lida on the balcony, but Rolando, pretending to see if it is time to set off for the battle, discovers her. He is about to kill Arrigo without more ado, but, on hearing the trumpets sounding the call to arms, he realises that a far greater punishment would be to bring dishonour on Arrigo by preventing him from joining the patriot army; he locks him in his room. The thought of the shame which he will suffer spurs Arrigo to leap from the balcony with a cry of 'Viva Italia!' Franz Werfel, in his edition of Verdi's letters,[1] illustrates the inflammatory effect that Verdi's music had on the patriotic Italians of his day. 'At this very point a sergeant of dragoons in the gallery of the Teatro Costanzi did the same thing that the tenor was doing on the stage. Deprived of his reason by the irresistibly tempestuous rhythm of the music, he tore off his tunic, and leapt from the

---

[1] *Verdi: The Man in his Letters* (edited Franz Werfel and Paul Stefan: translated by Edward Downes. L. B. Fisher, New York, 1942).

parapet of the gallery into the orchestra, where, surprisingly enough, he neither broke his back nor seriously injured anyone else.'

Act IV.   In the Cathedral, the people of Milan amongst them Lida, are waiting to hear news of the battle which will have been joined at Legnano. News comes of the complete rout of the Austrian army. Arrigo himself has dragged the Emperor from his horse but has been mortally wounded and is being brought, as he wishes, to die in the Cathedral. He is carried in by the Death Riders and swears to Rolando that he and Lida are innocent. Rolando believes him, forgives him and embraces Lida. Arrigo kisses the flag and dies while the citizens of Milan rejoice at the victory.   H.

LUISA MILLER

Opera in three acts by Giuseppe Verdi; text by S. Cammarano from Schiller's play *Kabale und Liebe*. Première at the Teatro San Carlo, Naples, December 8, 1849, with Gazzaniga, Salandri, Malvezzi, Selva, de Bassini. First performed in Philadelphia, 1852; London, Her Majesty's Theatre, 1858, with Piccolomini, Giuglini, Vialetti Beneventaro. Revived Berlin, 1927; Metropolitan, 1929, with Ponselle Lauri-Volpi, de Luca, Pasero, Ludikar, conductor Serafin; Florence Festival, 1937, with Caniglia, Lauri-Volpi, Armando Borgioli, Pasero, conductor Gui; Rome, 1949, with Caniglia, Pirazzini, Lauri-Volpi Silveri, Baronti, conductor Santini; Florence Festival, 1966, with Suliotis, Enzo Tei, MacNeil, Cava, conductor Sanzogno; Metropolitan New York, 1968, with Caballe, Tucker, Sherrill Milnes, Tozzi, conductor Schippers.

CHARACTERS

Count Walter .... Bass
Rodolfo, *his son* .... Tenor
Miller, *an old soldier* .... Baritone
Luisa, *his daughter* .... Soprano
Federica, Duchess of Ostheim, *Walter's niece* . Contralto
Laura, *a peasant girl* .... Contralto
Wurm .... Bass

Ladies attending the Duchess, Pages, servants,
and Villagers

Time: First half of the Eighteenth Century. *Place:* The Tyrol

Act I.   A village in the Tyrol. Luisa is the daughter of Miller, an old soldier. There is ardent love between her and

Rodolfo, the son of Count Walter, who has concealed his real name and rank from her and her father and is known to them as a peasant named Carlo. Old Miller, however, has a presentiment that evil will result from their attachment. This is confirmed in his mind on his being informed by Wurm that Carlo is Rodolfo, his master's son. Wurm is himself in love with Luisa.

The Duchess Federica, Count Walter's niece, arrives at the castle. She had been brought up there with Rodolfo, and has from childhood cherished a deep affection for him; but, compelled by her father to marry the Duke d'Ostheim, has not seen Rodolfo for some years. The Duke, however, having died, she is now a widow, and, on the invitation of Count Walter, who has, unknown to Rodolfo, made proposals of marriage to her on his son's behalf, she arrives at the castle, expecting to marry at once the love of her childhood. The Count, having been informed by Wurm of his son's love for Luisa, resolves to break off their intimacy. Rodolfo reveals to the Duchess that he loves another. He also discloses his real name and position to Luisa and her father. The Count interrupts this interview between the lovers. Enraged at his son's persistence in preferring a union with Luisa, he calls in the guard and is about to consign her and her father to prison, when he is, for the moment, deterred and appalled by Rodolfo's threat to reveal that the Count, aided by Wurm, assassinated his predecessor in order to obtain possession of the title and estates.

Act II.   Luisa's father has been seized and imprisoned by the Count's order. She, to save his life, consents, at the instigation of Wurm, to write a letter in which she states that she had never really loved Rodolfo, but only encouraged him on account of his rank and fortune, of which she was always aware; and finally offers to fly with Wurm. She even manages to convince the Duchess that her love for Rodolfo was never more than pretence. The letter, as the Count and his steward have arranged, falls into the hands of Rodolfo, who, enraged by the supposed treachery of the woman he loves, consents to marry the Duchess, but ultimately resolves to kill Luisa and himself.

Act III.   Luisa also has determined to put an end to her existence. Rodolfo enters her home in the absence of Miller, and, after extracting from Luisa's own lips the avowal that she did write the letter, he pours poison into a cup, from

which they both drink. She had sworn to Wurm that she
would never reveal the fact of the compulsion under which
she had written the letter, but feeling herself released from
her oath by fast approaching death, she confesses the truth to
Rodolfo. The lovers die in the presence of their horror-
stricken parents, but not before Rodolfo has summoned the
strength to draw his sword and run Wurm through the body
with it.

The overture has been much praised, the finale to Act I is
excellent, and earlier in the act there are three effective arias
for Luisa, Miller, and Walter. The duet between Wurm and
Walter and Rodolfo's aria are the best passages in Act II: the
latter, 'Quando le sere al placido', is one of the most

beautiful arias Verdi ever wrote, and its wistful loveliness is
unsurpassed in his music. Francis Toye describes Act III as
the best of the opera because of its uncommon dramatic
fitness. Luisa's 'Piangi, piangi' in the scene with Rodolfo, and
the final trio are singled out for particular praise.   K.

RIGOLETTO

Opera in three Acts by Giuseppe Verdi; text by Francesco Maria
Piave after Victor Hugo's *Le Roi s'amuse*. Première at the Teatro la
Fenice, Venice, March 11, 1851, with Brambilla, Casaloni, Mirate,
Varesi, Ponz, Damini. First performed Covent Garden, 1853, with
Bosio, Mario, Ronconi; New York, 1855, with Frezzolini, Bignardi;
Covent Garden (in English), 1909, with Beatrice Miranda, Wheatley, L.
Turner; Sadler's Wells (Dent's translation), 1937, with Ruth Naylor,
Edith Coates, Francis Russell, Redvers Llewellyn. Famous Gildas of this
century include Melba, Tetrazzini, Galli-Curci, dal Monte, Norena,
Pagliughi, Pons, Sayao, Berger; in the role of the Duke, Caruso, Bonci,
Hislop, Piccaver, Dino Borgioli, Gigli, Schipa, Björling; of Rigoletto,
Scotti, Ruffo, de Luca, Sammarco, Formichi, Joseph Schwarz, Franci,
Stabile, Basiola, Warren.

CHARACTERS

The Duke of Mantua .... Tenor
Rigoletto, *his jester, a hunchback* .... Baritone
Count Ceprano   ⎱ *Nobles* .... ⎰   Bass
Count Monterone ⎰   ⎱ Baritone
Sparafucile, *a bravo* .... Bass
Matteo Borsa, *a courtier* .... Tenor
Cavaliere Marullo, *a courtier* .... Baritone
Countess Ceprano .... Mezzo-Soprano
Gilda, *daughter of Rigoletto* .... Soprano
Giovanna, *her duenna* .... Mezzo-Soprano
Maddalena, *sister to Sparafucile* .... Contralto
Courtiers, Nobles, Pages, Servants
Time: Sixteenth Century   *Place:* Mantua

Rigoletto is a distinguished opera. Composed in forty days in 1851, it still retains its vitality. Twenty years, with all they imply in experience and artistic growth, lie between *Rigoletto* and *Aida.* Yet the earlier opera, composed so rapidly as to constitute a *tour de force* of musical creation, seems destined to remain a close second in popularity to the more mature work of its great composer.

There are several reasons for the public's abiding interest in *Rigoletto.* It is based upon a most effective play by Victor Hugo, *Le Roi s'amuse,*[1] known to English play-goers in Tom Taylor's adaptation as *The Fool's Revenge* (the jester was one of Edwin Booth's great rôles). Rigoletto, the hunchback, has been vividly characterised by Verdi in his music, and it is a rôle which has appealed to many famous artists. Ronconi (who taught singing in New York for a few years, beginning in 1867) was a notable Rigoletto; so was Galassi, whose intensely dramatic performance was once vividly recalled by the older opera-goers; Renaud at the Manhattan Opera House, Titta Ruffo at the Metropolitan Opera House, Philadelphia, both made their American débuts as Rigoletto.

But the opera offers other rôles of distinction. Mario was a famous Duke in other days. Caruso made his sensational début at the Metropolitan in the character of the volatile Duke of Mantua, November 23, 1903. We have had as Gilda, Adelina Patti, Melba, and Tetrazzini, to mention but a few;

[1] Whose hero was of course François I of France, a circumstance which explains the grandiose court life, hardly credible even in luxurious Mantua, whither the censor transferred the story.   H.

and the heroine of the opera was one of the rôles o
Galli-Curci, who appeared in it in Chicago, November 18
1916. No coloratura soprano can, so to speak, afford to be
without it.[1]

Thus the opera has plot, a central character of vita
dramatic importance, and at least two other characters o
strong interest. But there is even more to be said in its behalf
For, with the sextet in *Lucia*, the quartet in the last act of
Rigoletto is the finest piece of concerted music in Italiar
opera.

The argument of *Rigoletto* deals with the amatory esca
pades of the Duke of Mantua, in which he is aided by
Rigoletto, his jester, a hunchback. Rigoletto, both by his
caustic wit and unscrupulous conduct, has made many
enemies at court. Count Monterone, who comes to the court
to demand the restoration of his daughter, who has beer
dishonoured by the Duke, is met by the jester with laughter
and derision. The Count curses Rigoletto, who is stricker
with superstitious terror.

Rigoletto has a daughter, Gilda, whom he keeps in stric
seclusion. But the Duke, without being aware who she is, ha
seen her, unknown to her father, and fallen in love with her
Count Ceprano, who many times has suffered under
Rigoletto's biting tongue, knowing that she is in some way
connected with the jester (in fact believing her to be his
mistress, and glad of any opportunity of doing him ar
injury), forms a plan to carry off the young girl, and so
arranges it that Rigoletto unwittingly assists in her abduction
When he finds that it is his own daughter whom he has aidec
to place in the power of the Duke, he determines to murder
his master, and engages Sparafucile, a bravo, to do so. Thi
man has a sister, Maddalena, who entices the Duke to a
lonely inn. She becomes fascinated with him, however, and
begs her brother to spare his life. This he consents to do in
before midnight anyone shall arrive at the inn whom he car
kill and pass off as the murdered Duke. Rigoletto, who ha
recovered his daughter, brings her to the inn so that, by being
a witness of the Duke's inconstancy, she may be cured of her
unhappy love. She overhears the plot to murder her lover
and Sparafucile's promise to his sister. Determined to save

---

[1] Although Verdi never looked upon it as anything but a lyrical rôle
and Toscanini even cast it (in a concert performance) with a dramatic
soprano, Zinka Milanov.   H.

the Duke, she knocks for admittance, and is stabbed on entering. Rigoletto comes at the appointed time for the body. Sparafucile brings it out in a sack. The jester is about to throw it into the water, sack and all, when he hears the Duke singing. He tears open the sack, only to find his own daughter, at the point of death.

The prelude sets forth the music associated with the curse. Act I opens in a salon in the Duke's palace. A suite of other apartments is seen extending into the background. All are brilliantly lighted for the fête that is in progress. Courtiers and ladies are moving about in all directions. Pages are passing to and fro. From an adjoining salon music is heard and bursts of merriment.

There is effervescent gaiety in the orchestral accompaniment to the scene. The Duke and Borsa enter from the back. They are conversing about an 'unknown charmer'—none other than Gilda—whom the Duke has seen at church. He says that he will pursue the adventure to the end, although a mysterious man visits her nightly.

Among a group of guests the Duke sees the Countess Ceprano, whom he has been wooing quite openly, in spite of the Count's visible annoyance. The dashing gallant cares nothing about what anyone may think of his escapades, least of all the husbands or other relatives of the ladies. 'Questa o quella per me pari sono' (This one, or that one, to me 'tis the same).

The music floats on air. It gives at once the cue to the Duke's character. Like Don Giovanni he is indifferent to fate, flits from one affair to another, and is found as fascinating as he is dangerous by all women, of whatever degree, upon whom he confers his doubtful favours. The Duke dances with Countess Ceprano to the strains of a minuet that is curiously reminiscent of the one in *Don Giovanni.*

Rigoletto, hunchbacked but agile, sidles in. He is in cap and bells, and carries the jester's bauble. The immediate object of his satire is Count Ceprano, who is watching his wife, as she is being led off on the Duke's arm. Rigoletto then goes out looking for other victims. Marullo joins the nobles. He tells them that Rigoletto, despite his hump, has an

inamorata. The statement makes a visible impression upon
Count Ceprano, and when the nobles, after another sally
from the jester, who has returned with the Duke, inveigh
against his bitter tongue, the Count bids them meet him at
night on the morrow and he will guarantee them revenge
upon the hunchback for the gibes they have been obliged to
endure from him.

The gay music, which forms a restless background to the
scene of which I give the gist, trips buoyantly along, to be
suddenly broken in upon by the voice of one struggling

without, and who, having freed himself from those evidently
striving to hold him back, bursts in upon the scene. It is the
aged Count Monterone. His daughter has been dishonoured
by the Duke, and he denounces the ruler of Mantua before
the whole assembly. His arrest is ordered. Rigoletto mocks
him until, drawing himself up to his full height, the old noble
not only denounces him, but calls down upon him a father's
curse.

Rigoletto is strangely affrighted. He cowers before
Monterone's malediction. It is the first time since he has
appeared at the gathering that he is not gibing at someone. Not
only is he subdued; he is terror-stricken.[1]

Monterone is led off between halberdiers. The gay music
again breaks in. The crowd follows the Duke. But Rigoletto?

The scene changes to the street outside his house. It is
secluded in a courtyard, from which a door leads into the
street. In the courtyard are a tall tree and a marble seat.
There is also seen at the end of the street, which has no
thoroughfare, the gable end of Count Ceprano's palace. It is
night.

As Rigoletto enters, he remembers Monterone's curse. His
entrance to the house is interrupted by the appearance of

[1] Monterone's cursing of Rigoletto supplies a main motivation of the
opera, constantly referred to by its victim, who recognises in it and its
implications the 'tragic flaw' of his own nature: here, in the one decent
side to him, he can be mortally hurt. All the more reason to cast a fine
singer of dominant personality in the role of Monterone.   H.

Sparafucile, an assassin for hire. In a colloquy, to which the orchestra supplies a subtly contrived 'nocturne' accompaniment, he offers to Rigoletto his services, should they be needed, in putting enemies out of the way—and his charges are reasonable.

(The scoring is for muted solo cello and double bass, accompanied by *pizzicato* strings.)

Rigoletto has no immediate need of him, but ascertains where he can be found.

Sparafucile goes. Rigoletto has a soliloquy, 'Pari siamo'; 'How like are we!—the tongue, my weapon, the dagger his! to make others laugh is my vocation—his to make them weep! ... Tears, the common solace of humanity, are to me denied.... "Amuse me, buffoon"—and I must obey.' His mind still dwells on the curse—a father's curse, pronounced upon him, a father to whom his daughter is a jewel. He refers to it, even as he unlocks the door that leads to his house, and also to his daughter, who, as he enters, throws herself into his arms.

He cautions her about going out. She says she never ventures beyond the courtyard save to go to church. He grieves over the death of his wife—Gilda's mother—that left her to his care while she was still an infant. 'Deh non parlare al misero' (Speak not of one whose loss to me.).

Deh non par-la-re al mi-se-ro

He charges her attendant, Giovanna, carefully to guard her. Gilda endeavours to dispel his fears. The result is the tender duet for Rigoletto and Gilda, beginning with his words to Giovanna, 'Veglia, o donna, questo fiore' (Ah, watch I pray this tender flower), a duet considerably improved when given in its entirety and not with the cut which has become customary in Italy.

Rigoletto hears footsteps in the street and rushes ou
through the door of the courtyard to see who may be there
As the door swings out, the Duke, for it is he, in the guise o:
a student, whose stealthy footsteps have been heard by the
jester, conceals himself behind it, then slips into the court
yard, tosses a purse to Giovanna, and hides in the shadow o:
the tree. Rigoletto reappears for a brief moment to say
good-bye to Gilda and once more to warn Giovanna to guard
her carefully.

When he has gone Gilda worries because fear drove her to
refrain from revealing to her father that a handsome youth
has several times followed her from church. This youth's
image is installed in her heart. 'I long to say to him "I lo'—"'

The Duke steps out of the tree's shadow, motions to
Giovanna to retire and, throwing himself at Gilda's feet, takes
the words out of her mouth, exclaiming, 'I love thee!'

No doubt taken by surprise, yet also thrilled with joy, she
hearkens to him rapturously as he declares, 'È il so.
dell'anima, la vita è amore' (Love is the sun by which passioi
is kindled).

E il sol dell'a- ni- ma, la vi-ta è a- mo - re,

The meeting is brief, for again there are footsteps outside.
But their farewell is an impassioned duet, 'Addio speranza ed
anima' (Farewell, my hope, my soul, farewell).

He has told her that he is a student, by name Walter Maldè.
When he has gone, she muses upon the name, and, when she
has lighted a candle and is ascending the steps to her room,
she sings the enchanting air, 'Caro nome che il mio cor' (Dear
name, my heart enshrines).

Ca-ro no-me che il mio cor Fes-ti pri-mo pal-pi-tar,

If the Gilda be reasonably slender and pretty, the scene,
with the courtyard, the steps leading up to the room, and the
young maiden gracefully and tenderly expressing her heart's
first romance, is charming, and in itself sufficient to account
for the attraction which the rôle holds for prima donnas.

Tiptoeing through the darkness outside come Marullo, Ceprano, Borsa, and other nobles and courtiers, intent upon seeking revenge for the gibes Rigoletto at various times has aimed at them, by carrying off the damsel, whom they assume to be his *inamorata*. At that moment, however, the jester himself appears. They tell him they have come to abduct the Countess Ceprano and bear her to the ducal palace. To substantiate this statement Marullo quickly has the keys to Ceprano's house passed to him by the Count, and in the darkness holds them out to Rigoletto, who, his suspicions allayed because he can feel the Ceprano crest in bas-relief on the keys, volunteers to aid in the escapade. Marullo gives him a mask and, as if to fasten it securely, ties it with a handkerchief, which he passes over the piercings for his eyes. Rigoletto, confused, holds a ladder against what he believes to be the wall of Ceprano's house. By it, the abductors climb his own wall, enter his house, gag, seize, and carry away Gilda, making their exit from the courtyard, but in their hurry failing to observe a scarf that has fluttered from their precious burden.

Rigoletto is left alone in the darkness and silence. He tears off his mask. The door to his courtyard is open. Before him lies Gilda's scarf. He rushes into the house, into her room, reappears, staggering under the weight of the disaster, which, through his own unwitting connivance, has befallen him.

'Ah! La maledizione!' he cries out. It is Monterone's curse.

Act II has its scene laid in a salon of the ducal palace.

The Duke is disconsolate. He has returned to Rigoletto's house, found it empty, the bird flown. The scamp mourns his loss—in affecting language and music, 'Parmi veder le lagrime' (Fair maid, each tear of mine that flows).

In a capital chorus he is told by Marullo and the others that they have abducted Rigoletto's *inamorata*.

Scor-ren-do u-ni - ti re-mo - ta vi - - a

The Duke well knows that she is the very one whose charms are the latest that have enraptured him: 'Possente amor mi chiama' (To her I love with rapture)—the cabaletta is often omitted in performance.

He learns from the courtiers that they have brought her to

the palace. He hastens to her, 'to console her', in his own
way. It is at this moment Rigoletto enters. He knows his
daughter is in the palace, and has come to search for her.
Aware that he is in the presence of those who took advantage
of him and thus secured his aid in the abduction of the night
before, he yet, in order to accomplish his purpose, must
appear light-hearted, question craftily, and be diplomatic,
although at times he cannot prevent his real feelings breaking
through. It is the ability of Verdi to give expression to such
varied emotions which makes this scene one of the most
remarkable in his early operas. It is dominated by an
orchestral motive, that of the clown who jests while his heart
is breaking.

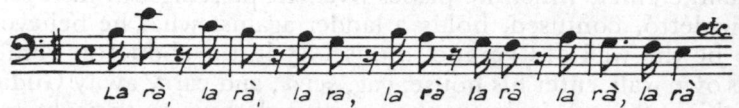

La rà,   la rà,   la ra,   la rà   la rà   la rà,   la rà

Finally he turns upon the crowd that taunts him and hurls
invective upon them—'Cortigiani, vil razza dannata' (Ah, ye
courtiers, vile race accursed). When a door opens and Gilda,
whose story can be read in her aspect of despair, rushes into
his arms, he orders the courtiers out of sight with a sense of
outrage so justified that, in spite of the flippant words with
which they comment upon his command, they obey it.

Father and daughter are alone. She tells him her story—of
the handsome youth, who followed her from church—'Tutte
le feste al tempio' (On every festal morning).

Then follows her account of their meeting, his pretence
that he was a poor student, when, in reality, he was the
Duke—to whose chamber she was borne after her abduction.
It is from there she has just come. Her father strives to
comfort her—'Piangi, fanciulla' (Weep, my child)—in one of
Verdi's loveliest duets.

At this moment he is again reminded of the curse
pronounced upon him by the father he had mocked. Count
Monterone, between guards, is conducted through the apartment to the prison where he is to be executed for denouncing
the Duke. Rigoletto vows vengeance upon the betrayer of
Gilda: 'Sì, vendetta, tremenda vendetta.'

It was a corrupt, care-free age. Victor Hugo created a
debonair character—a libertine who took life lightly and
flitted from pleasure to pleasure. And so Verdi lets him flit

rom tune to tune—gay, melodious, sentimental. There still
are plenty of men like the Duke, and plenty of women like
Gilda to love them; and other women, be it recalled, as
discreet as the Duchess, who does not appear in this opera
save as a portrait on the wall from which she calmly looks
down upon a jester invoking vengeance upon her husband,
because of the wrong he has done the girl, who weeps on the
breast of her hunchback father.

To Act III might be given as a sub-title, 'The Fool's
Revenge', the title of Tom Taylor's adaptation into English
of Victor Hugo's play. The scene shows a desolate spot on
the banks of the Mincio. On the right, with its front to the
audience, is a house two storeys high, in a very dilapidated
state, but still used as an inn. The doors and walls are so full
of crevices that whatever is going on within can be seen from
without. In front are the road and the river; in the distance is
the city of Mantua. It is night.

The house is that of Sparafucile. With him lives his sister
Maddalena, a handsome young gipsy woman, who lures men
to the inn, there to be robbed—or killed, if there is more
money to be had for murder than for robbery. Sparafucile is
seen within, cleaning his belt and sharpening his sword.

Outside are Rigoletto and Gilda. She cannot banish the
image of her despoiler from her heart. Hither the hunchback
has brought her to prove to her the faithlessness of the Duke.
She sees him in the garb of a soldier coming along the city
wall. He descends, enters the inn, and calls for wine and a
room for the night. Shuffling a pack of cards, which he finds
on the table, and pouring out the wine, he sings of woman.
This is the famous 'La donna è mobile' (Fickle is woman
fair).

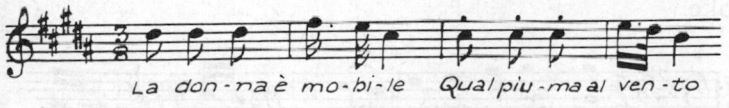

La don-na è mo-bi-le   Qual piu-ma al ven-to

It has been highly praised and violently criticised; and
usually gets as many encores as the singer cares to give. As for
the criticisms, the cadenzas so ostentatiously introduced by
singers for the sake of catching applause are no more Verdi's
than is the high C in *Il Trovatore*. The song is perfectly in
keeping with the Duke's character. It has grace, verve, and
buoyancy; and, what is an essential point in the development

of the action from this point on, it is easily remembered. In any event I am glad that among my operatic experiences I can count having heard 'La donna è mobile' sung by such great artists as Campanini, Caruso, and Bonci, the last two upon their first appearances in the rôle in America.

At a signal from Sparafucile, Maddalena joins the Duke. He presses his love upon her. With professional coyness she pretends to repulse him. This leads to the quartet, with its dramatic interpretation of the different emotions of the four participants. The Duke is gallantly urgent and pleading: 'Bella figlia dell'amore' (Fairest daughter of the graces).

Maddalena laughingly resists his advances: 'I am proof, my gentle wooer, 'gainst your vain and empty nothings'.

Gilda is moved to despair: 'Ah, thus to me of love he spoke.'

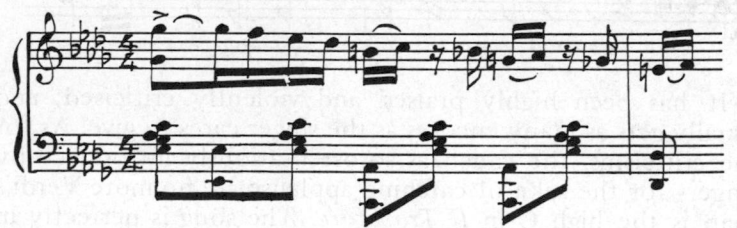

Rigoletto mutters of vengeance.

They continue so to the end. Gilda's voice, in brief cries of grief, rising twice to the effective climaxes, then becoming even more poignant through the syncopation of the rhythm.

This quartet is usually sung as the *pièce de résistance* of the opera, and is supposed to be the great event of the performance. I cannot recall a representation of the work with Nilsson and Campanini in which this was not the case, and it was so at the Manhattan when *Rigoletto* was sung there by Melba and Bonci. But at the Metropolitan, after Caruso's advent, *Rigoletto* became a 'Caruso opera', and the stress was laid on 'La donna è mobile', for which numerous encores were demanded, while with the quartet the encore was deliberately side-stepped—a most interesting process for the initiated to watch.

After the quartet, Sparafucile comes out and receives from Rigoletto half of his fee to murder the Duke, the balance to be paid when the body, in a sack, is delivered to the hunchback. Sparafucile offers to throw the sack into the river, but that does not suit the jester's desire for revenge. He wants the grim satisfaction of doing so himself. Satisfied that Gilda has seen enough of the Duke's perfidy, he sends her home, where, for safety, she is to don male attire and start on the way to Verona, where he will join her. He himself also goes out.

A storm now gathers. There are flashes of lightning; distant rumblings of thunder. The wind moans (indicated by the chorus, *à bouche fermée*, behind the scenes). The Duke has gone to his room, after whispering a few words to Maddalena. He lays down his hat and sword, throws himself on the bed, sings a few snatches of his song, and in a short time falls asleep. Maddalena, below, stands by the table. Sparafucile finishes the contents of the bottle left by the Duke. Both remain silent for a while.

Maddalena, fascinated by the Duke, begins to plead for his life. The storm is now at its height. Lightning plays vividly across the sky, thunder crashes, wind howls, rain falls in torrents. Through his uproar of the elements, to which night adds its terrors, comes Gilda, drawn as by a magnet to the spot where she knows her false lover to be. Through the crevices in the wall of the house she can hear Maddalena pleading with Sparafucile to spare the Duke's life. 'Kill the hunchback', she counsels, 'when he comes with the balance of the money.' But there is honour even among assassins as among thieves. The bravo will not betray a customer.

Maddalena pleads yet more urgently. Well—Sparafucile will give the handsome youth one desperate chance for life: should any other man arrive at the inn before midnight, that man will he kill and put in the sack to be thrown into the river, in place of Maddalena's temporary favourite. A clock strikes the half-hour. Gilda is in male attire. She determines to save the Duke's life—to sacrifice hers for his. She knocks. There is a moment of surprised suspense within. Then everything is made ready. Maddalena opens the door, and runs forward to close the outer one. Gilda enters. For a moment one senses her form in the darkness. A half-stifled cry; then all is buried in silence and gloom.

The storm is abating. The rain has ceased; the lightning becomes fitful, the thunder distant and intermittent. Rigoletto returns. 'At last the hour of my vengeance is nigh.' A bell tolls midnight. He knocks at the door. Sparafucile brings out the sack, receives the balance of his money, and retires into the house. 'This sack his winding sheet!' exclaims the hunchback, as he gloats over it. The night has cleared. He must hurry and throw it into the river.

Out of the second storey of the house and on to the wall steps the figure of a man and proceeds toward the city. Rigoletto starts to drag the sack with the body towards the stream. Lightly upon the night fall the notes of a familiar voice singing:

> La donn' è mobile
> Qual piuma al vento;
> Muta d'accento,
> E di pensiero.
>
> (Fickle is woman fair,
> Like feather wafted;
> Changeable ever,
> Constant, ah, never.)

It is the Duke. Furiously the hunchback tears open the sack. In it he beholds his daughter. Not yet quite dead, she is able to whisper, 'Too much I loved him—now I die for him.' There is a duet: 'Lassu—in cielo' (From yonder sky).

'Maledizione!' The music of Monterone's curse upon the ribald jester, now bending over the corpse of his own despoiled daughter, resounds from the orchestra. The fool has had his revenge.   K.

IL TROVATORE
The Troubadour

Opera in four acts by Giuseppe Verdi; text by S. Cammarano, from the Spanish drama of the same title by Antonio Garcia Gutiérrez. Première at the Teatro Apollo, Rome, January 19, 1853, with Penco, Goggi, Baucardé, Guicciardi, Balderi. First performed Paris, 1854 and 1857[1] (in French); New York, 1855, with Steffanone, Vestvali, Brignoli, Amodio; Covent Garden, 1855, with Ney, Viardot, Tamberlik, Tagliafico; Drury Lane, 1856 (in English), with Louisa Pyne, Susan Pyne, Harrison, Good; Metropolitan, 1883, with Valleria, Trebelli, Stagno, Kaschmann. Revived Covent Garden, 1927, with Leider, Olszewska, Pertile, A. Borgioli; Sadler's Wells, 1939 (Dent's translation), with Jeanne Dusseau, Edith Coates, Henry Wendon, Redvers Llewellyn; Covent Garden, 1939, with Cigna, Wettergren, Björling, Basiola, conductor Gui; Florence Festival, 1939, with Caniglia, Stignani, Lauri-Volpi, A. Borgioli, conductor Gui; Covent Garden, 1964, with Gwyneth Jones, Simionato, Prevedi, Glossop, conductor Giulini. Famous Manricos also include Caruso, Zenatello, Slezak, Martinelli, Bergonzi, Corelli.

CHARACTERS

Count di Luna, *a young noble of Aragon* ..... Baritone
Ferrando, *di Luna's captain of the guard* .... Bass
Manrico, *a chieftain under the Prince of Biscay, and reputed son of Azucena* .... Tenor
Ruiz, *a soldier in Manrico's service* .... Tenor
An Old Gypsy .... Baritone
Duchess Leonora, *lady-in-waiting to the Princess of Aragon* .... Soprano
Inez, *confidante of Leonora* .... Soprano
Azucena, *a Biscayan gypsy woman* .... .Mezzo-Soprano
Followers of Count di Luna and of Manrico; Messenger, Gaoler, Soldiers, Nuns, Gypsies

Time: Fifteenth Century   *Place:* Biscay and Aragon

For many years *Il Trovatore* has been an opera of world-wide popularity, and for a long time could be accounted the most popular work in the operatic repertory of practically

[1] For the French production of 1857, Verdi wrote some fifteen minutes of ballet music (part of which was performed in Sadler's Wells's revival at the Coliseum in 1972), and slightly expanded the finale of the opera, re-introducing the 'Miserere' at the end (I heard it in Paris when the opera was revived there for the first time since 1923(!) in 1973, Charles Mackerras conducting).   H.

every land. The libretto of *Il Trovatore* is considered in certain circles the acme of absurdity.

While it is true that the story of this opera seems to be a good deal of a mix-up, it is also a fact that, under the spur of Verdi's music, even a person who has not a clear grasp of the plot can sense the dramatic power of most of the scenes. It is an opera of immense verve, of temperament almost unbridled, of genius for the melodramatic so unerring that its composer has taken dance rhythms, like those of mazurka and waltz, and on them developed melodies most passionate in expression and dramatic in effect. The music of *Il Trovatore* is swift, spontaneous, and stirring. Absurdities, complexities, unintelligibilities of story are swept away in its unrelenting progress. *Il Trovatore* is the Verdi of forty working at white heat.

One reason why the plot of *Il Trovatore* seems such a jumbled-up affair is that a considerable part of the story is supposed to have transpired before the curtain goes up. These events are narrated by Ferrando, the Count di Luna's captain of the guard, soon after the opera begins. Could the audience be sure of knowing what Ferrando is singing about, the subsequent proceedings would not appear so hopelessly involved, or appeal so strongly to humorous rhymesters, who usually being their parodies on the opera with, 'This is the story of *Il Trovatore*'.

What happened before the curtain goes up on the opera is as follows: The old Count di Luna, some time deceased, had two sons nearly the same age. One night, when they still were infants and asleep in a nurse's charge in an apartment in the old Count's castle, a gypsy hag, having gained stealthy entrance into the chamber, was discovered leaning over the cradle of the younger child, Garzia. Though she was instantly driven away, the child's health began to fail and she was believed to have bewitched it. She was pursued, apprehended, and burned alive at the stake.

Her daughter, Azucena, at that time a young gypsy woman with a child of her own in her arms, was a witness to the death of her mother, which she swore to avenge. During the following night she stole into the castle, snatched the younger child of the Count di Luna from its cradle, and hurried back to the scene of execution, intending to throw the baby boy into the flames that still raged over the spot where they had consumed her mother. Almost bereft of her senses, however, by her memory of the horrible scene she had witnessed, she seized and hurled into the flames her own child, instead of the young Count (thus preserving, with an almost supernatural instinct for opera, the baby that was destined to grow up into a tenor with a voice high enough to sing 'Di quella pira').

Thwarted for the moment in her vengance, Azucena was not to be completely baffled. With the infant Count in her arms she fled and rejoined her tribe, entrusting her secret to no one, but bringing him up—Manrico, the Troubadour—as her own son; and always with the thought that through him she might wreak vengeance upon his kindred.

When the opera opens, Manrico has grown up; Azucena has become old and wrinkled, but is still unrelenting in her quest for vengeance. The old Count has died, leaving the elder son, Count di Luna of the opera, sole heir to his title and possessions, but always doubting the death of the younger, despite the heap of infant's bones found among the ashes about the stake.

Each of the four acts of this opera has a title: Act I, 'Il Duello' (The Duel); Act II, 'La Gitana' (The Gypsy); Act III, 'Il Figlio della Zingara' (The Gypsy's Son); Act IV, Il Supplizio' (The Penalty).

Act I. Atrium of the palace of Aliaferia, with a door leading to the apartments of the Count di Luna. Ferrando, the captain of the guard, and retainers, are reclining near the door. Armed men are standing guard in the background. It is night. The men are on guard because Count di Luna desires to apprehend a ministrel knight, a troubadour, who has been heard on several occasions serenading the Duchess Leonora, for whom a deep but unrequited passion sways the Count.

Weary of the watch, the retainers beg Ferrando to tell them the story of the Count's brother, the stolen child. This Ferrando proceeds to do in the ballad, 'Abbietta zingara' (Sat there a gypsy hag).

Ferrando's gruesome ballad and the comments of the horror-stricken chorus dominate the opening of the opera. The scene is an unusually effective one for a subordinate character like Ferrando, but in Il Trovatore Verdi is lavish with his melodies—more so, perhaps, than in any of his other operas.

The scene changes to the gardens of the palace. On one side a flight of marble steps leads to Leonora's apartment. Heavy clouds obscure the moon. Leonora and Inez are in the garden. From the confidante's questions and Leonora's answers it is gathered that Leonora is enamoured of an unknown but valiant knight who, lately entering a tourney, won all contests and was crowned victor by her hand. She knows her love is requited, for at night she has heard her Troubadour singing below her window. In the course of this narrative Leonora has two solos. The first of these is the romantic 'Tacea la notte placida' (The night calmly and peacefully in beauty seemed reposing).

It is followed by the graceful and engaging 'Di tale amor che dirsi' (Of such a love how vainly),

with its brilliant cadenza.

Leonora and Inez then ascend the steps and retire into the palace. The Count di Luna now comes into the garden. He has hardly entered before the voice of the Troubadour, accompanied on a lute, is heard from a nearby thicket singing the familiar romanza, 'Deserto sulla terra' (Lonely on earth abiding).

From the palace comes Leonora. Mistaking the Count in the shadow of the trees for her Troubadour, she hastens toward him. The moon emerges from a cloud, she sees the figure of a masked cavalier, and recognizing it as that of her lover, turns from the Count toward the Troubadour. The Troubadour discloses his identity as Manrico, one who as a follower of the Prince of Biscay is proscribed in Aragon. The men draw their swords. There is a trio that fairly seethes with passion—'Di geloso amor sprezzato' (Fires of jealous, despised affection).

The men rush off to fight their duel. Leonora faints.

Act II.   An encampment of gypsies. There is a ruined house at the foot of a mountain in Biscay, the interior partly exposed to view; within, a great fire is lighted. Day begins to dawn.

Azucena is seated near the fire. Manrico, enveloped in his mantle, is lying upon a mattress; his helmet is at his feet; in his hand he holds a sword, which he regards fixedly. A band of gypsies are sitting in scattered groups around them.

Since an almost unbroken sequence of melodies is a characteristic of *Il Trovatore*, it is not surprising to find at the opening of this act two famous numbers in quick succession—the famous Anvil Chorus,

in which the gypsies, working at the forges, swing their hammers and bring them down on clanking metal in rhythm with the music; and Azucena's equally well-known 'Stride la vampa' (Upwards the flames roll).

In this air, which the old gypsy woman sings as a weird but impassioned outpuring of memories and hatreds, she relates the story of her mother's death. 'Avenge thou me!' she murmurs to Manrico, when she has concluded.

Swept along by the emotional stress under which she labours, Azucena concludes her narrative of the tragic events at the pyre, voice and orchestral accompaniment uniting in a vivid musical setting of her memories. Naturally, her words arouse doubts in Manrico's mind as to whether he really is her son. She hastens to dispel these; they were but wandering thoughts she uttered. Moreover, after the recent battle of

Petilla, between the forces of Biscay and Aragon, when he was reported slain, did she not search for and find him, and has she not been tenderly nursing him back to strength?

The forces of Aragon were led by Count di Luna, who but a short time before had been overcome by Manrico in a duel in the palace garden; why, on that occasion, asks the gypsy, did he spare the Count's life?

Manrico's reply is couched in a bold, martial air, 'Mal reggendo all'aspro assalto' (Ill sustaining the furious encounter). But at the end it dies away to *pp*, when he tells how, with the Count's life his for a thrust, a voice, as if from heaven, bade him spare it—a suggestion, of course, that although neither Manrico nor the Count know that they are brothers, Manrico unconsciously was swayed by the relationship.

Enter now Ruiz, a messenger from the Prince of Biscay, who orders Manrico to take command of the forces defending the stronghold of Castellor, and at the same time informs him that Leonora, believing reports of his death at Petilla, is about to take the veil in a convent near the castle.

The scene changes to the cloister of this convent. It is night. The Count and his followers, led by Ferrando, and heavily cloaked, advance cautiously. It is the Count's plan to carry off Leonora before she becomes a nun. He sings of his love for her in the air, 'Il balen del suo sorriso' (Bright her smiles, as when bright morning), which is justly regarded as one of the most chaste and beautiful baritone solos in Italian opera.

It is followed by an air *alla marcia*, also for the Count, 'Per me ora fatale' (Oh, fatal hour impending).

A chorus of nuns is heard from within the convent, and Leonora, with Inez, and her ladies, comes upon the scene. They are about to proceed from the cloister into the convent when the Count interposes, but before he can seize Leonora, another figure stands between them It is Manrico, with him Ruiz and his followers. The Count is foiled.

'E deggio!—e posso crederlo?' (And can I still my eyes believe?) exclaims Leonora, as she beholds before her Manrico, whom she had thought dead. It is here that begins the impassioned finale, an ensemble consisting of a quartet for Leonora, Manrico, the Count di Luna and Ferrando, with chorus.

Act III. The camp of Count di Luna, who is laying siege to Castellor, whither Manrico has safely borne Leonora. There is a stirring chorus for Ferrando and the soldiers.

The Count comes from his tent. There is a commotion. Soldiers have captured a gypsy woman found prowling about the camp. They drag her in; it is Azucena. Questioned, she sings that she is a poor wanderer who means no harm. 'Giorni poveri vivea' (I was poor, yet uncomplaining).

But Ferrando, though she thought herself masked by the grey hairs and wrinkles of age, recognises her as the gypsy who, to avenge her mother, threw the infant brother of the Count to the flames. In the vehemence of her denials, she cries out to Manrico, whom she names as her son, to come to her rescue. This still further enrages the Count, who orders that she be cast into prison and then burned at the stake. She is dragged away.

The scene changes to a hall adjoining the chapel in the stronghold of Castellor. Leonora is about to become the bride of Manrico, who sings the beautiful lyric, 'Ah sì, ben mio, coll'essere' (Ah yes, thou art my spouse by right).

Its serenity makes all the more effective the tumultuous scene that follows, and it assists in giving to that episode, one of the most famous in Italian opera, its true significance as a dramatic climax.

Just as Manrico takes Leonora's hand to lead her to the altar of the chapel, Ruiz rushes in with word that Azucena has been captured by the besiegers and is about to be burned to death. Already through the windows of Castellor the glow of flames can be seen. Her peril would render delay fatal. Dropping the hand of his bride, Manrico draws his sword, and, as his men gather, sings 'Di quella pira' (See the pyre blazing), and rushes forth at the head of his soldiers to attempt to save Azucena. The line 'O teco almeno corro a morir' (Or, all else failing, to die with thee), contains the famous high C.

o te-co al -me - - no cor - ro a mor - ir

This is a *tour de force*, which has been condemned as vulgar and ostentatious, but which undoubtedly adds to the effectiveness of the number. There is, it should be remarked, no high C in the score of 'Di quella pira'. It was introduced by a tenor, who saw a chance to make an effect with it, and succeeded so well that it became a fixture.

Dr. Frank E. Miller, author of *The Voice* and *Vocal Art Science*, the latter the most complete exposition of the psycho-physical functions involved in voice-production, informed me that a series of photographs were made (by an apparatus too complicated to describe) of the vibrations of Caruso's voice as he takes and holds the high C in 'Di quella pira'. The record measured fifty-eight feet. While it might not be correct to say that Caruso's high C is fifty-eight feet long, the record is evidence of its being superbly taken and held.

Not infrequently the high C in 'Di quella pira' is faked for tenors who cannot reach it, yet have to sing the rôle of Manrico, or who, having been able to reach it in their younger days and at the height of their prime, still wish to maintain their fame as robust tenors. For such the number is transposed. The tenor, instead of singing high C, sings B flat, a tone lower, and much easier to take. By flourishing his sword and looking very fierce he usually manages to get away with it. Transpositions of operatic airs requiring unusually high voices are not infrequently made for singers, both male and female, no longer in their prime, but still good for two or more 'farewell' tours. All they have to do is to step up to the footlights with an air of perfect confidence, which indicates that the great moment in the performance has arrived, deliver, with a certain assumption of effort—the semblance of a real *tour de force*—the note which has conveniently been transposed, and receive the enthusiastic plaudits of their devoted admirers. But the assumption of effort must not be omitted. The tenor who sings the high C in 'Di quella pira' without getting red in the face will hardly be credited with having sung it at all.

Act IV.   Manrico's sortie to rescue his supposed mother has failed. His men have been repulsed, and he himself captured and thrown into the dungeon tower of Aliaferia, where Azucena is already enchained. The scene shows a wing of the palace of Aliaferia. In the angle is a tower with window secured by iron bars. It is night, dark and clouded.

Leonora enters with Ruiz, who points out to her the place of Manrico's confinement and retires. That she has conceived a desperate plan to save her lover appears from the fact that she wears a poison ring, a ring with a swift poison concealed under the jewel, so that she can take her own life, if driven thereto.

Unknown to Manrico, she is near him. Her thoughts wander to him 'D'amor sull'ali rosee' (On rosy wings of love depart).

It is followed by the 'Miserere', which was for many years the most popular of all melodies from opera.

The 'Miserere' is chanted by a chorus within. Against this as a sombre background are projected the heart-broken ejaculations of Leonora. Then Manrico's voice in the tower intones 'Ah! che la morte ognora' (Ah! how death still delayeth).

Familiarity may breed contempt, and nothing could well be more familiar than the 'Miserere' from *Il Trovatore*. Yet, well sung, it never fails of effect. Leonora, sure only that Manrico is alive if under sentence of death, sings an impassioned *stretta*, to the scene: 'Tu vedrai che amore in terra'.

The Count enters, to be confronted by Leonora. She promises to become his wife if he will free Manrico. Di Luna's passion for her is so intense that he agrees. There is a solo for Leonora, 'Mira, d'acerbe lagrime' (Witness the tears

of agony), followed by a duet between her and the Count
who little suspects that, Manrico once freed, she will escape a
hated union with himself by taking the poison in her ring.

The scene changes to the interior of the tower. Manrico
and Azucena sing a duet of mournful beauty, 'Ai nostri
monti' (Back to our mountains).

Leonora enters and bids him escape. But he suspects the
price she has paid; and his suspicions are confirmed by
herself, when the poison she has drained from beneath the
jewel in her ring begins to take effect and she feels herself
sinking in death, while Azucena, in her sleep, sings dreamily,
'Back to our mountains'.

The Count di Luna, coming upon the scene, finds Leonora
dead in her lover's arms. He orders Manrico to be led to the
block at once and drags Azucena to the window to witness
the death of her supposed son.

'It is over!' exclaims di Luna, when the executioner has
done his work.

'The victim was thy brother!' shrieks the gypsy hag.
'Thou art avenged, O mother!' She falls near the window.

'And I still live!' exclaims the Count.   K.

LA TRAVIATA
Fallen Woman

Opera in three acts by Giuseppe Verdi; text by Francesco Maria
Piave, after Alexandre Dumas's play *La Dame aux Camélias*. Première at
Teatro la Fenice, Venice, March 6, 1853, with Salvini-Donatelli,
Graziani, Varesi. First performed at Her Majesty's Theatre, London,
1856, with Piccolomini, Calzolari, Beneventato; New York, 1856, with
La Grange, Brignoli, Amodio; Covent Garden, 1858, with Bosio, Mario;
Metropolitan, 1883, with Sembrich, Capoul, del Puente, conductor
Vianesi. Revivals at Covent Garden include 1930, with Ponselle, Gigli,
Noble; 1939, with Caniglia, Gigli, Basiola, conductor Gui; 1946, with
Carosio, Gallo, Tagliabue, conductor Capuana; 1948, with
Schwarzkopf, Neate, Silveri; 1958, with Callas, Valletti, Zanasi; 1966,
with Freni, Cioni, Cappuccilli, under Giulini; la Scala, 1955, with Callas,
di Stefano, Bastianini, in Visconti's production, conductor Giulini.
Famous Violettas have also included Patti, Nilsson, Bellincioni, Melba,
Tetrazzini, Galli-Curci, Selma Kurz, Muzio, Sayao, Albanese.

CHARACTERS

Alfredo[1] Germont, *lover of Violetta* .... Tenor
Giorgio Germont, *his father* .... Baritone
Gastone de Letorières, *a young man about town* . Tenor
Baron Douphol, *a rival of Alfredo* .... Baritone
Marchese d'Obigny .... Bass
Doctor Grenvil .... Bass
Giuseppe, *servant to Violetta* .... Tenor
Violetta Valery, *a courtesan* .... Soprano
Flora Bervoix, *her friend* .... Mezzo-Soprano
Annina, *Violetta's confidante and maid* ..... Soprano
Ladies and Gentlemen; Servants and masks; Dancers and Guests.

Time: 1850   *Place:* Paris and vicinity

At its production in Venice in 1853 *La Traviata* was a failure, for which various reasons can be advanced. The younger Dumas's play, *La Dame aux Camélias*, familiar to English playgoers under the incorrect title of *Camille*, was a study of modern life and played in modern costume. When Piave reduced his *Traviata* libretto from the play, he retained the contemporary period. This is said to have nonplussed an audience accustomed to operas laid in the past and given in 'costume'.[2] But the chief blame for the fiasco appears to have rested with the singers. Graziani, the Alfredo, was hoarse. Salvini-Donatelli, the Violetta, was inordinately stout. The result was that the scene of her death as a consumptive was received with derision. Varesi, the baritone, who sang Giorgio Germont, considered the rôle beneath his reputation—notwithstanding Germont's beautiful solo, 'Di Provenza'—and was none too cheerful over it. There is evidence in Verdi's correspondence that the composer had complete confidence in the merits of his score, and attributed its failure to its interpreters and its audience.

When the opera was brought forward again a year later, the same city which had decried it as a failure acclaimed it a success. On this occasion, however, the period of the action

[1] The opera is occasionally revived with the French names of the play—Armand, Marguerite and so on—replacing the more familiar Italian of Piave.   H.

[2] So commentators have frequently said, but the truth is that, though the modern setting was one of the aspects of *Traviata* which most attracted Verdi, the first performances in Venice were given with an early 18th century setting.   H.

was set back to the time of Louis XIV, and costumed
accordingly. There is, however, no other opera to-day in which
this matter of costume is 'so much a go-as-you-please affair
for the principals, as it is in *La Traviata*. I do not recall
whether Christine Nilsson dressed Violetta according to the
Louis XIV period, or not; but certainly Adelina Patti and
Marcella Sembrich, both of whom I heard many times in the
rôle (and each of them the first time they sang it in America),
wore the conventional evening gown of modern times. To do
this has become entirely permissible for prima donnas in this
character.[1] Meanwhile the Alfredo may dress according to
the Louis XIV period, or wear the swallow-tail costume of
Victorian times, or compromise, as some do, and wear the
swallow-tail coat and modern waistcoat with knee-breeches
and black silk stockings. As if even this diversity were not yet
quite enough, one of the most notable Germonts of the
twentieth century, Renaud, who at the Manhattan Opera
House sang the rôle with the most exquisite refinement,
giving a portrayal as finished as a genre painting by
Meissonier, wore the costume of a gentleman of Provence
of, perhaps, the middle of the last century.

Act I. A salon in the house of Violetta. In the back scene
is a door, which opens into another salon. In the centre of
the apartment is a dining-table, elegantly laid. Violetta is
conversing with Dr. Grenvil and some friends. Others are
receiving the guests who arrive, among whom are Baron
Douphol and Flora on the arm of the Marquis.

The opera opens with a brisk ensemble. Violetta is a
courtesan (*traviata* = the fallen woman). Her house is the scene
of a revel. Early in the festivities Gaston, who has come in
with Alfredo, informs Violetta that his friend is seriously in
love with her. She treats the matter with outward levity, but
it is apparent that she is touched by Alfredo's devotion.
Already, too, in this scene, there are slight indications, more
emphasised as the opera progresses, that consumption has
undermined Violetta's health.

First in the order of solos in this act is a spirited drinking
song for Alfredo, which is repeated by Violetta. After each
measure the chorus joins in. This is the 'Libiamo ne' lieti
calici' (Let us quaff from the wine-cup o'erflowing).

[1] Visconti's famous production at la Scala in 1955 set the opera with
great effect in the 1870's, with Maria Callas and the other ladies of the
cast in bustles.   H.

Li - bia . . . mo li - bia - mo ne' lie - - ti ca - - li - ci

Music is heard from an adjoining salon, toward which the
guests proceed. Violetta is about to follow, but is seized with
a coughing spell and sinks upon a sofa to recover. Alfredo has
remained behind. She asks him why he has not joined the
others. He protests his love for her. At first answering his
words with banter, she becomes more serious, as she begins
to realise the depth of his affection for her. How long has he
loved her? A year, he answers—'Un dì felice, eterea' (One day
a rapture ethereal) he sings.

In this the words 'Di quell'amor ch'è palpito' (Ah, 'tis with
love that palpitates) are set to a phrase which Violetta repeats
in the famous 'Ah, fors'è lui', just as she had previously
repeated the drinking song.

Con espansione

Di quell' a - mor, quell'a - 'mor   ch'è   pal - pi - to

Verdi thus seems to intend to indicate in his score the
effect upon her of Alfredo's genuine affection. She repeated
his drinking song; now she repeats, like an echo of heart-
beats, his tribute to a love of which she is the object.

It is when Alfredo and the other guests have retired that
Violetta, lost in contemplation, her heart touched for the
first time, sings 'Ah fors'è lui che l'anima' (For him, perchance, my longing soul).

Ah fors' è   lui che l'a - ni - ma   so - lin - ga ne' tu -

- mul - ti, so - lin - ga ne' tu - mul - ti

Then she repeats, in the nature of a refrain, the measures
already sung by Alfredo. Suddenly she changes, as if there
were no hope of lasting love for a woman of her character,

and dashes into the brilliant 'Sempre libera' (Ever free shall I
still hasten madly on from pleasure to pleasure).

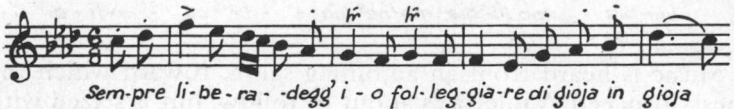

Sem-pre li-be-ra--degg' i - o fol-leg-gia-re di gioja in   gioja

Alfredo's voice can be heard outside with the refrain, 'Di
quell' amor'.

Act II.   Salon on the ground floor of a country house
near Paris, occupied by Alfredo and Violetta, who for him
has deserted the allurements of her former life. Alfredo
enters in sporting costume. He sings of his joy in possessing
Violetta: 'De' miei bollenti spiriti' (Wild my dream of
ecstasy).

From Annina, the maid of Violetta, he hears that the
expenses of keeping up the country house are much greater
than Violetta has told him, and that, in order to meet the
cost, which is beyond her own means, she has been selling her
jewels. He immediately leaves for Paris, his intention being to
try to raise money there so that he may be able to reimburse
her.

After he has gone, Violetta comes in. She has a note from
Flora inviting her to some festivities at her house that night.
She smiles at the absurdity of the idea that she should return,
even for an evening, to the scenes of her former life. Just
then a visitor is announced. She supposes he is her business
agent, whom she is expecting. But, instead, the man who
enters announces that he is Alfredo's father. His dignity, his
aloof yet restrained manner, at once fill her with apprehension. She has foreseen separation from the man she loves, and
now senses that the dread moment is impending.

The elder Germont's plea that she leave Alfredo is based
both upon the blight which threatens his career by his liaison
with her, and upon another misfortune that will result to the
family. There is not only the son; there is a daughter—'Pura
siccome un angelo' (Pure as an angel) sings Germont, in the
familiar air.

Allegro moderato

Pu - ra sic-co-me un an - ge-lo

Should the scandal of Alfredo's liaison with Violetta continue, the family of a youth, whom the daughter is to marry, threaten to break off the match. Therefore it is not only on behalf of his son, it is also for the future of his daughter, that the elder Germont pleads. As in the play, so in the opera, the reason why the role of the heroine so strongly appeals to us is that she makes the sacrifice demanded of her—though she is aware that, among other unhappy consequences to her, it may aggravate the disease of which she is a victim and hasten her death, wherein, indeed, she even sees a solace. She cannot yield at once. She prays, as it were, for mercy: 'Non sapete' (Ah, you know not).

Finally she yields in a tune of infinite beauty: 'Dite alla giovine' (Say to thy daughter);

then 'Imponete' (Now command me); and, after that, 'Morrò—la mia memoria' (I shall die—but may my memory).

Germont retires. Violetta writes a note, rings for Annina, and hands it her. From the maid's surprise as she reads the address, it can be judged to be for Flora, and, presumably, an acceptance of her invitation. When Annina has gone, she writes to Alfredo informing him that she is returning to her old life, and that she will look to Baron Douphol to maintain her. Alfredo enters. She conceals the letter about her person. He tells her that he has received word from his father that the latter is coming to see him in an attempt to separate him from her. Pretending that she leaves so as not to be present during the interview, she bids him farewell: 'Amami, Alfredo'— for the soprano, one of the opera's emotional touchstones.

Alfredo is left alone. He picks up a book and reads listlessly. A messenger enters and hands him a note. The address is in Violetta's handwriting. He breaks the seal, begins to read, staggers as he realises the import, and would collapse, but that his father, who has quietly entered from the garden, holds out his arms, in which the youth, believing himself betrayed by the woman he loves, finds refuge.

'Di Provenza il mar, il suol chi dal cor ti cancellò' (From fair Provence's sea and soil, who hath won thy heart away), sings the elder Germont, in an effort to soften the blow that has fallen upon his son.

Di Pro - ven -za il mar, il suol

Alfredo rouses himself.[1] Looking about vaguely, he sees Flora's letter, glances at the contents, and at once concludes that Violetta's first plunge into the vortex of gaiety, to return to which she has, as he supposes, abandoned him, will be at Flora's fête.

'Thither will I hasten, and avenge myself!' he exclaims, and departs precipitately, followed by his father.

The scene changes to a richly furnished and brilliantly lighted salon in Flora's house. The fête is in full swing. There is a ballet of women gypsies, who sing as they dance 'Noi siamo zingarelle' (We're gypsies gay and youthful).

Gaston and his friends appear as matadors and others as picadors. Gaston sings, while the others dance, 'E Piquillo, un bel gagliardo' ('Twas Piquillo, so young and so daring).

It is a lively scene, upon which there enters Alfredo, to be followed soon by Baron Douphol with Violetta on his arm. Alfredo is seated at a card table. He is steadily winning. 'Unlucky in love, lucky in gambling!' he exclaims. Violetta winces. The Baron shows evidence of anger at Alfredo's words and is with difficulty restrained by Violetta. The Baron, with assumed nonchalance, goes to the gaming table and stakes against Alfredo. Again the latter's winnings are large. A servant's announcement that the banquet is ready is an evident relief to the Baron. All retire to an adjoining salon. For a brief moment the stage is empty.

Violetta enters. She has asked Alfredo to come and speak to her. He joins her. She begs him to leave. She fears the Baron's anger will lead him to challenge Alfredo to a duel. The latter sneers at her apprehensions and suggests that it is the Baron she fears for. Violetta's emotions almost betray her, but she remembers her promise to the elder Germont, and exclaims that she does indeed love the Baron.

[1] There is a *cabaletta* to the aria, mostly but not invariably omitted in performance, in which Germont repeats his plea to become his son's refuge.   H.

Alfredo tears open the doors to the salon where the banquet is in progress. 'Come hither, all!' he shouts.

They crowd upon the scene. Violetta, almost fainting, leans against the table for support. Facing her, Alfredo hurls at her invective after invective. Finally, in payment of what she has spent to help him maintain the house near Paris in which they have lived together, he throws in her face all his winnings at the gaming table. She faints in the arms of Flora and Dr. Grenvil.

The elder Germont enters in search of his son. He alone knows the real significance of the scene, but for the sake of his son and daughter cannot disclose it. A dramatic ensemble, in which Violetta sings, 'Alfredo, Alfredo, di questo core non puoi comprendere tutto l'amore' (Alfred, Alfred, little canst thou fathom the love within my heart for thee) brings the act to a close.

Act III.   Violetta's bedroom. At the back is a bed with the curtains partly drawn. The prelude to this act, like that to Act I, is a notably beautiful piece.

Violetta awakens. In a weak voice she calls Annina, who, waking up confusedly, opens the shutters and looks down into the street, which is gay with carnival preparations. Dr. Grenvil is at the door. Violetta endeavours to rise, but falls back again. Then, supported by Annina, she walks slowly toward the settee. The doctor enters in time to assist her. Annina places cushions about her. To Violetta the physician cheerfully holds out hope of recovery, but to Annina he whispers, as he is leaving, that her mistress has but a few hours more to live.

Violetta has received a letter from the elder Germont telling her that Alfredo has been told by him of her sacrifice and has been sent for to come to her bedside as quickly as possible. But she has little hope that he will arrive in time. She senses the near approach of death. 'Addio del passato' (Farewell to bright visions) is more like a sigh from the

depths of a once frail but purified soul than an aria.

A bacchanalian chorus of carnival revellers floats up from the street. Annina, who had gone out with some money which Violetta had given to distribute as alms, returns. Her manner is excited. Violetta is quick to perceive it and divine its significance. Annina has seen Alfredo. The dying woman bids Annina hasten to admit him. A moment later he holds Violetta in his arms. Approaching death is forgotten; nothing again shall part them. They will leave Paris for some quiet retreat. 'Parigi, o cara, noi lasceremo' (We shall fly from Paris, beloved), they sing.

But it is too late. The hand of death is upon the woman's brow. 'Gran Dio! morir sì giovane' (O, God! to die so young).

The elder Germont and Dr. Grenvil have come in. There is nothing to be done. The cough that racked the poor frail body has ceased. La Traviata is dead.

Not only were *Il Trovatore* and *La Traviata* produced in the same year, but *La Traviata* was written between the date of *Trovatore*'s première at Rome (January 19) and March 6. Only four weeks in all are said to have been devoted to it, and part of the time Verdi was working on *Trovatore* as well. Nothing could better illustrate the fecundity of his genius, the facility with which he composed. But it was not the fatal facility that sacrifices real merit for temporary success. There are few echoes of *Trovatore* in *Traviata*; but the remarkable achievement of Verdi is not only in having written so beautiful an opera as *La Traviata* in so short a time, but in having produced in it a work in style wholly different from *Il Trovatore*. The latter palpitates with the passions of love, hatred, and vengeance. The setting of the action encourages these, consisting as it does of palace gardens, castles, dungeons. *La Traviata* in contrast plays in drawing-rooms. The music corresponds with these surroundings, and is vivacious, graceful, gentle. When it palpitates, it is with sorrow.[1]

[1] The listener in the late twentieth century may wonder in effect if in any other opera the subtleties of its characters' hopes and setbacks have been so eloquently and poignantly conveyed by means of expressive melody as here.   H.

Oddly enough, although *Il Trovatore* is by far the more robust and at one time was, as I have stated, the most popular opera in the world, I believe that to-day the advantage lies with *La Traviata*, and that, as between the two, there belongs to that opera the ultimate chance of survival. I explain this on the ground that, in *Il Trovatore*, the hero and heroine are purely musical creations, the real character drawing, dramatically and musically, being in the rôle of Azucena, which, while a principal rôle, has not the prominence of Leonora or Manrico. In *La Traviata*, on the other hand, we have in the original of Violetta—the Marguerite Gauthier of Alexandre Dumas, *fils*, the Marie Duplessis of real life—one of the great creations of nineteenth-century drama, the 'frail' woman redeemed by the touch of an artist. Piave, in his libretto, preserves the character. In the opera, as in the play, one comprehends the injunction, 'Let him who is not guilty throw the first stone'. For Verdi has clothed Violetta in music that brings out the character so vividly and so beautifully that whenever I see *Traviata* I recall the first performance in America of the Dumas play by Bernhardt, then in her slender and supple prime, and the first American appearance in it of Duse, with her exquisite intonation and restraint of gesture.

In fact, operas survive because the librettist has known how to create a character and the composer how to match it with his musical genius. Recall the dashing Don Giovanni; the resourceful Figaro, both in the Mozart and the Rossini operas; the real interpretative quality of a mild and gracious order in the heroine of *La Sonnambula*—innocence personified; the gloomy figure of Edgar stalking through *Lucia di Lammermoor*; the hunchback and the titled gallant in *Rigoletto*, and you can understand why these very old operas have lived so long. They are not make-believe; they are real.

K.

LES VÊPRES SICILIENNES

I Vespri Siciliani — The Sicilian Vespers

Opera in five acts by Giuseppe Verdi; text in French by Scribe and Charles Duveyrier. Première at the Opéra, Paris, with Cruvelli as Hélène, June 13, 1855. First performed in Italy, Parma, 1855; at la Scala, Milan, 1856 (as *Giovanna de Guzman*); at San Carlo, Naples, 1857 (as *Batilde di Turenna*); Drury Lane, London, 1859; New York, 1859. Revived

Stuttgart, 1929 (in a new German version by G. Bundi); Berlin, 1932, with Anni Konetzni, Roswaenge, Schlusnus, List, conductor Kleiber; Palermo, 1937, with Arangi-Lombardi, Franco lo Giudice, Guicciardi, Vaghi, conductor Capuana; Genoa, 1939, with Scacciati, Olivato, Armando Borgioli, Pasero, conductor Gui; Florence Festival, 1951, with Callas, Kokolios, Mascherini, Christoff, conductor Kleiber; la Scala, Milan, 1951, with substantially the same cast, conductor de Sabata; Cardiff 1954, by Welsh Nat. Op. Co. Successful modern revivals in productions by John Dexter with sets by Josef Svoboda have been in Hamburg, 1969, with Felicia Weathers, Wieslaw Ockman, David Ohanesian, Hans Sotin; Metropolitan, 1974, with Caballe, Gedda, Milnes, Diaz, conductor James Levine; Paris, 1974 (in Italian), with Arroyo, Domingo, Ohanesian and Glossop, Roger Soyer.

CHARACTERS

Elena (Hélène), *sister of Frederick of Austria* . . Soprano
Arrígo (Henri), *a young Sicilian* . . . . Tenor
Guido di Monforte (Montfort),
    Governor of Sicily . . . . Baritone
Giovanni da Procida, *Sicilian doctor* . . . . Bass
de Béthune, *a French officer* . . . . Bass
Count Vaudemont, *a French officer* . . . . Bass
Ninetta, *in attendance on Elena* . . . . Soprano
Danieli, *a young Sicilian* . . . . Tenor
Tebaldo (Thibault), *a French soldier* . . . . Tenor
Roberto (Robert), *a French soldier* . . . . Bass
Manfredo, *A Sicilian* . . . . Tenor

Time: 1282   *Place:* Palermo

Les Vêpres Siciliennes as it was originally called was commissioned for the Great Exhibition of 1855. Much as Verdi disliked the conditions of work in Paris, he could not but find it an honour to be asked to write music for so great an occasion in the artistic capital of the world. In the event, he disliked the libretto, as offending the French because of the massacre at the end, and the Italians because of the treacherous behaviour of the Sicilian patriots, and his relations with Scribe were even the subject of comment in the newspapers. As if Verdi had not enough to bear, Cruvelli, the admirable soprano entrusted with the rôle of Elena, elected to disappear without a word to anyone during rehearsals. 'She seems to have gone', says Francis Toye, 'on a kind of anticipatory honeymoon with one Baron Vigier, whom she married shortly afterwards'.

The opera is concerned with the occupation of Sicily by French troops during the thirteenth century, and the efforts of the Sicilians to dislodge them. The overture is one of Verdi's best, and is dominated by the long cello tune, taken from the duet in Act III between Arrigo and Monforte.

Act I.   A detachment of French troops is in the great square at Palermo, some of them drinking, others watching the crowd of Sicilians which eyes them sullenly from the other side of the square. The French sing of their enforced absence from their native land, the Sicilians of their hatred of their oppressors. An exchange between de Béthune, Roberto, and Tebaldo (I have used the Italian names throughout, as the opera is almost always nowadays given in that language) indicates that there is nothing new about the proprietary attitude of occupying troops towards the women of the country.

At this moment the French notice Elena crossing the square. She has been praying for her brother, who was executed by order of Monforte for his patriotic activities. A drunken soldier is struck by her beauty and orders her to sing to entertain the French conquerors. Somewhat to his surprise she consents, but her song is not at all what it was expected to be. The loosely knit opening phrases and the long *cantabile* line lead to a sudden and inflammatory *allegro giusto*, which whips up the courage of the downcast Sicilians. It is a scene of considerable theatrical power and makes a great effect when sung by a soprano of the calibre of Maria Callas, who was in the revival at the Florence Festival in 1951. No one who heard her will forget her repeated 'il vostro fato è in vostra man' (Votre salut est dans vos mains), nor the brilliant effect of her coloratura and top notes in the *cabaletta* itself.

The Sicilians rush at the French, but the abortive rising is quelled by the appearance of Monforte, alone and unarmed, at the door of his palace. The square clears as if by magic, and Elena, supported by her attendants Ninetta and Danieli, is left alone with Monforte. Their quartet is mostly unaccompanied, and at its end Arrigo, who has been imprisoned, rushes up to Elena with the news of his release. He does not notice Monforte but, in spite of his openly expressed patriotic sentiments, is ordered by him to remain behind. The act ends with a duet between the two, in which Monforte offers Arrigo fame in the service of the French. His offer is indignantly spurned, as is his command that Arrigo associate no more with the rebel Elena, into whose palace without more ado Arrigo betakes himself.

Act II takes place outside the city, in a valley, to which comes Procida, until his banishment leader of the Sicilian patriots and now returned secretly to stir up resistance. He salutes his beloved native land in a recitative and aria which has become perhaps the most famous number of the opera, 'O tu Palermo' (O toi, Palerme). In a *cabaletta*, he exhorts the

small band of chosen patriots to prepare with him the deliverance of Sicily.

Elena and Arrigo have been bidden to meet the exiled patriot, and he leaves them together while he goes off to set plans afoot, but not before he has enrolled Arrigo as one of the leaders of the projected revolt. Arrigo declares his love to Elena and swears to avenge the death of her beloved brother. A messenger arrives from Monforte bringing an invitation to Arrigo to attend a ball. He indignantly refuses it, and is immediately surrounded by soldiers and led away.

Procida returns to learn of this new mishap, but he sees an opportunity of stirring up feeling against the French in the betrothal festivity which is about to take place, and for which a crowd can be seen approaching. He will suggest to the French that they carry off the young women, an outrage which may perhaps rouse the Sicilians from their apathy. Couples in festive attire dance a *tarantella*, but Procida's plan works all too well, and in a moment the French soldiers have fallen on the women, carried off some and put the rest to flight.

Only a few patriots are left behind with Procida and Elena, and together in half-strangled sentences they give vent to their feelings, which are further exacerbated by the sound of a complacent barcarole being sung at sea by a boat-load of French pleasure-seekers. The two choruses combine most effectively as the act comes to an end.

Act III. Monforte is found alone in his palace. He reflects on the injustice he did years ago to the woman who became

the mother of his son, but escaped from him and brought up
that son to hate his father as the oppressor of the Sicilians.
Now, on her death-bed, she has written to him that the son
he has not seen for eighteen years is no other than Arrigo, his
sworn enemy. Monforte's soliloquy 'In braccio alle dovizie'
(Au sein de la puissance) gives effective expression to his

In braccio a-lle do - vi - zie, nel se - no de-glio - nor

indecision and agony of mind, and is in many ways more
satisfactory than the big duet between Monforte and his
newly found son which immediately follows it. Here occurs
the tune first heard on the celli in the overture, which,
memorable though it no doubt is, has more than a little
complacency about it when heard in its proper context—and
complacency is the last thing felt by either father or son in
their peculiar predicament.

The scene ends with Arrigo calling on his mother's
memory, but at the beginning of the ballroom scene he is
apparently sufficiently reconciled, at any rate temporarily, to
accompany his father to the great hall, where together they
watch the lengthy ballet of the seasons, which Monforte has
planned for the entertainment of his guests. This is a French
ballet on a grand scale and, whatever its importance to the
devotees of Grand Opera in its heyday, it tends nowadays to
impress listeners mostly with its length—it lasts for half an
hour—and the way it holds up the dramatic action at a crucial
point. On the other hand to leave it out is no solution, as the
ball is then left as it were without its core[1]. Perhaps its salvation would be to incorporate it in a separate ballet, as did
Constant Lambert with the ballet music from *Le Prophète*,
and to give only one of the four sections when the opera is
revived.

Amongst the invited guests are to be seen a number of
masked figures with silk ribbons fastened to their cloaks.
These are the Sicilian conspirators, led by Procida and Elena.
The tension of Arrigo's predicament—whether to allow his
father to be murdered, or to betray his friends—is skilfully

[1] But it *was* successfully omitted in John Dexter's austerely impressive
production (1974) at the Metropolitan.

suggested by the snatched conversations he has with Elena
and Procida in the midst of the general festivity. Finally, he
makes an attempt to warn Monforte that his life is in danger
but the governor refuses to leave the ball. When Procida
advances upon him, Arrigo steps in between, the conspirators
are arrested, and the act ends with an impressive concerted
piece, in which the Sicillians unite in cursing the treachery of
Arrigo.

Act IV takes place in the great courtyard of the fortress
whither Arrigo has come, armed with a pass from Monforte
to see the prisoners. In a sombre E minor aria, 'Giorno di
pianto' (O jour de peine), he reflects on the situation he is in
when his dearest friends are likely to look upon him as their
worst enemy. The thought of Elena's hate is too much for
him, he thinks he hears her coming up from her cell, and in
an ecstasy he prays for her forgiveness. When Elena appears
she does in fact greet him as a traitor, and repeats his words
'Non son reo' (Malheureux et non coupable), after him
ironically, until he admits to her that their enemy is his own
father. Her tone changes to one of pity, and later she admits
in a ravishing Bellini-like *cantilena* that her greatest sorrow in
prison was the necessity to think of the man she loves as a
traitor. Their music takes on the character of a love duet
before Procida is led out of the prison by the guards. He sees
Arrigo, but ascribes his apparent repentance to yet another
treacherous trick.

Monforte enters and orders that the preparations for the
double execution shall go forward straightaway, in spite of
the pleading of Arrigo, who demands to die with them—such
an honour, says Procida, is too great for so notorious a
traitor. Monforte bids Arrigo pay no attention to the insults
of his erstwhile comrades; let him but remember that he is his
son. Procida is stupefied at this totally unexpected revelation
and in a few moving phrases bids farewell to the country for
whose ideals he has fought. His phrases lead to a quartet
(with Elena, Arrigo, Monforte) of considerable beauty, which
in its turn gives way to the execution music, heard already in
the overture but now assuming considerable poignancy, with
Monforte urging that pardon will only be given if Arrigo will
address him as Father; Arrigo is hesitant, Elena and Procida
emphatic that death is preferable to dishonour, and all the
time the sound of the funeral hymn accompanies the victims
as they draw nearer to the block and the headman's axe.

At last Arrigo gives in to Monforte's dearest wish, pardon is forthwith granted and with it a general amnesty. The troth of Elena and Arrigo is announced, and the curtain falls on a general ensemble.

Act V is set in the gardens of Monforte's palace, where the wedding of Elena and Arrigo is about to be celebrated. After a chorus, Elena sings her well-known *Bolero*, 'Merce, dilette amiche' (Merci, jeunes amies), a lively and appropriate display piece. Arrigo joins her and sings a charming air, 'La brezza aleggia intorno a carrezzarmi il viso' (La brise souffle au loin plus légère et plus pure), an entirely lyrical interlude in what is by no means otherwise a predominantly lyrical score.

Arrigo disappears and Elena is joined by Procida, now more than ever the plotter with a dagger ever conveniently to hand, for whose over-simplified drawing Verdi so much reproached Scribe. He congratulates Elena on having provided with her wedding the opportunity for the Sicilian patriots to fall on the unarmed French, and tells her that the ringing of the bells will be the signal for the massacre. Nothing she can say will deflect the fanatic from his purpose and he defies her to denounce him to the French and so prevent the carrying out of his plan. Elena's only reply is to refuse to go through with the wedding, much to Arrigo's consternation. There is an impressive and extended trio for Elena, Arrigo, and Procida, which is one of the best numbers in the opera and which dominates the finale. Monforte enters, sweeps aside Elena's objections, the cause of which has not been revealed to him, and himself pronounces the betrothal, at the same time ordering the bells to ring out. The Sicilians rush from their hiding-places, and Procida's revenge is complete.

Les Vêpres Siciliennes has been much criticised as being one of Verdi's weakest pieces, and it is true that it does not reach the heights of *Don Carlos* or *Simon Boccanegra*. On the other hand, recent revivals have been attended by a good deal of success, and the unfamiliar music is in the habit of striking its listeners as vastly better than the commentators have made out. In fact, the least satisfactory thing about *Vêpres* is its unwieldy shape: Verdi himself complained about the enormous length of the five acts required for a French Grand Opera, and the spectacular nature of the work makes it difficult (though I think not impossible) to combine two acts

in one. There is, of course, a further difficulty, not peculia
to this score but none the less potent: the role of Elen:
requires a coloratura dramatic soprano of a very high order
When one can be found, the opera seems likely to be revivec
for many years to come.

It would be a pity if it were not, as there is much music o
fine quality in this score. In the first act, Elena's aria and the
unaccompanied quartet are brilliantly successful numbers
and in the second, 'O tu Palermo' is one of Verdi's mos
famous bass arias. Monforte's monologue at the beginning o
Act III is of an expressive quality worthy of Philip himself
and the choral finale after the attempted murder is mos
effective. The whole of the fourth act seems to me on Verdi'
highest level, the solo for Arrigo and that for Elena in the
middle of the duet being outstandingly successful, and the
moment of suspense before the execution most movingl
done. The fifth act can seem rather long in performance, bu
Arrigo's lyrical tune and the large-scale trio are first-rate

H.

AROLDO

Opera in four acts by Giuseppe Verdi; text by Francesco Mari
Piave, based on his libretto for *Stiffelio* (1850), which was in three acts
Première Rimini, August 16, 1857, with Marcellina Lotti (later know
as Lotti della Santa), Giovanni Pancani, Carlo Poggiali, Cornago
Gaetano Ferri. First produced New York, Academy of Music, 1863
London, St. Pancras Town Hall, 1964, with Anne Edwards, Nasc
Petroff, Michael Maurel, Noel Mangin, conductor Gerald Gover
Revived Florence Festival, 1953, with Antonietta Stella, Gino Penno
Aldo Protti, Ugo Novelli, conductor Tullio Serafin; Hamburg, 1954
with Anne Bollinger, Peter Anders, Josef Metternich, James Pease
Trieste, 1954, with Anna Maria Rovere, Roberto Turrini, Ugo Savarese
Ugo Novelli, conductor Franco Capuana; Wexford Festival, 1959, wit
Mariella Angioletti, Nicola Nikolov, Aldo Protti, conductor Charle
Mackerras; New York, 1961, Amato Opera Company, with Georg
Shirley in the title-role. (*Stiffelio* was successfully revived in Parma i
1968, with Angeles Gulin, Gastone Limarilli, Walter Alberti, Zerbini.

CHARACTERS

Aroldo, *a Saxon Knight* (Stiffelio[1]) .... Tenor
Mina, *his wife* (Lina) .... Soprano

[1] The names of the corresponding characters in *Stiffelio* are i
brackets.

Egberto, *Mina's father* (Stankar) . . . . Baritone
Godvino, *a knight* (Raffaele) . . . . Tenor
Briano, *a holy man* (Jorg) . . . . Bass
Enrico, *Mina's cousin* (Federico) . . . . Tenor
Elena, *Mina's cousin* (Dorothea) . . . . . . Mezzo-Soprano
Time: About 1200   *Place:* England and Scotland
        Stiffelio was set in Germany at the beginning
                   of the nineteenth century

Verdi was already interested in the French and Spanish
plays which were to become *Rigoletto* and *Il Trovatore* when
he accepted Piave's suggestion of a French play less than two
years old whose subject was the curious one, for a Catholic
country, of a Protestant clergyman whose wife has
committed adultery and whom he finds it in his heart, after
her father has killed her lover, to forgive. This became
Stiffelio which was reasonably successful in its early
performances and which Verdi in a letter of 1854 mentions
as one of two operas which had not taken the public's fancy
but which he would not like to see forgotten. The other is *La
Battaglia di Legnano*. In 1856, he worked with Piave to revise
the libretto, which he now found unsatisfactory at least for
an Italian audience, and in 1857 the revised work was
produced as the inaugural production of a new opera house
in Rimini. The outline of the story has stayed the same,
except that time and place have been moved from early 19th
century Germany to England and Scotland around 1200,
with the principal figures Crusaders rather than Protestant
clergymen and their colleagues. Much of the music remains
the same, although alterations are frequent, and one or two
numbers have been re-written. The main difference comes in
the final scenes of the two operas, *Stiffelio*'s Act III scene ii
being set in a church where the congregation first prays and
Stiffelio later preaches on the gospel story of the woman
taken in adultery before publicly forgiving his wife. *Aroldo*'s
Act IV, as will be seen later, provides quite a different ending
for the opera.

After an effective overture whose slow opening section is
dominated by a horn solo, the curtain rises on Act I to show
a great hall in Egberto's castle. It is empty, but sounds of
rejoicing come from within, the half-heard music making in
the empty space a curious effect of foreboding, an impression
not belied at the entrance of Mina, who in her soliloquy

reveals the torment of a conscience labouring under a guilty
secret: during her husband's absence, she has been unfaithful
to him with Godvino, a guest in her father's castle. Her
anguished recitative and heartfelt prayer could hardly be in
stronger contrast with the bravura writing frequently heard in
an introductory aria for a nineteenth-century opera's heroine.

Aroldo enters with Briano, who has campaigned with him
on the crusade and is now acting as a kind of spiritual adviser.
Aroldo immediately notices his wife's perturbed condition,
but Briano leaves them alone together and there is tenderness
in Aroldo's cavatina, 'Sotto il sol di Siria', in which he
describes his longing for Mina while he was abroad. Mina
punctuates his cavatina with exclamations of remorse, and
Aroldo finally demands a smile of welcome instead of the
tears with which she has greeted him. He notices that the ring
his mother had given her has gone, and in a cabaletta he
denounces its loss.

Briano returns and takes Aroldo off to join in the celebrations for his return, while Mina, observed by her father,
who begins to suspect Godvino's role, resolves to confess all
to Aroldo in a letter. Egberto interrupts, reads what she has
written, and succeeds in persuading her not to confess her
adultery to Aroldo in case the shock of learning of the
family's shame should kill him.

The second scene takes place in a big hall in the castle.
When it is left momentarily deserted by the knights and their
ladies, Godvino, observed by Briano, comes with a letter he
has written to Mina and leaves it in a huge locked book which
lies on the table and of which he carries the key. Briano does
not recognise Godvino except as a friend of Aroldo's, and,
when Egberto and his daughter and then his son-in-law and
the other guests re-appear, Briano describes what he has seen
to Aroldo, but by mistake points out the man who hid the
letter as Enrico, Mina's cousin. Aroldo is asked to describe
the crusade to the guests, but instead he starts to talk about
the book and the letter and then, in music which to some
extent presages *Otello*, demands that Mina unlock the book
that he may see what is inside. He breaks the lock and the
letter falls out, but Egberto retrieves it and, denying it to
Aroldo, himself destroys it. Aroldo's rage knows no bounds,
but it is Egberto who orders Godvino to meet him later in the
graveyard for a duel.

Act II.   The ancient graveyard of the castle, with a church visible on one side and the castle on the other. The music is darkly suggestive, as Mina in a splendid aria prays at her mother's tomb, comparing the purity of her mother with her own guilt ('Ah! dagli scanni eterei'). Godvino comes to plead his love, but she orders him not to profane the place where her mother is buried, then demands that he give her back the ring she gave him at the time of their mutual love. He refuses and insists that he will defend her in her predicament, but she makes it quite clear in her cabaletta that she will have no more to do with him.

Egberto arrives to confront them and challenges Godvino to fight to the death. Godvino at first refuses to fight a man so much older than himself, but Egberto goads him, and they are separated only by the arrival of Aroldo. Aroldo greets Godvino warmly, but this is too much for Egberto who denounces Godvino as the man who has betrayed Aroldo's honour. Mina appears, cannot deny Aroldo's charge, and Aroldo's impassioned outburst of jealous fury is not unworthy of the Verdi of thirty years later. A most impressive quartet follows, at the end of which Aroldo challenges Godvino to fight him. Sounds of prayer come from the church, and Briano attempts to persuade Aroldo to temper his rage and, as a Christian who has recently fought for his faith, to forgive his enemies. Aroldo is still beside himself with fury, and the act ends as, in his emotion, he collapses unconscious.

Act III.   An ante-chamber of the castle. Egberto, planning vengeance, finds that Godvino has escaped and in a fine aria bemoans the dishonour which has fallen on him and his family. He contemplates suicide, but Briano intervenes with the news that Godvino is back in the castle. One of them must die, says Egberto, and celebrates the prospect in a cabaletta of splendid impact, marked, most unusually, *pianissimo*, a direction Verdi underlines by the unusual expedient of a footnote in the vocal score enjoining the singer to sing it 'extremely quietly apart from the last phrase'.

Aroldo enters with Godvino and, demanding that he choose whether he values his own freedom more or the future of the woman he has betrayed, sends him to wait in a neighbouring room. Then he confronts Mina with the news that he himself will leave that very night and, so that she may be free to join the man she truly loves, he offers her a divorce. The duet is in Verdi's extended manner, and at its end Mina signs the paper he offers her. Egberto rushes in with a blood-stained sword in his hand, having killed Godvino, and Mina stays behind to pray forgiveness while Aroldo goes into the church.

Act IV takes place on the banks of Loch Lomond (*sic*), some time later. In the introduction, imitation bagpipes are followed by a huntsmen's chorus, and, as the sun sets, there is even a hint of 'The Campbells are Coming'—could Verdi have known it? In a rustic hut, Aroldo and Briano have retired from the world, and Aroldo admits to himself that he still loves Mina; as the sound of the angelus is heard, he and Briano join in the evening prayer.

A storm breaks out, stunningly portrayed in the music with pre-echoes of *Otello*, and from the boat which is driven up on the shore emerge Egberto and Mina. They go to the hut for shelter, and Aroldo immediately recognises Mina. Aroldo tries to repulse her, but Egberto urges that her trials in exile have brought her to a state of repentance, and Briano quotes the scriptures so that finally, after a short but impressive quartet, love triumphs—unexpectedly, in this quasi-tragedy.

Modern revivals suggest that *Stiffelio* is just as viable as *Aroldo* and that each has claims to figure amongst Verdi's unjustly neglected works. It is interesting that the story of *Stiffelio*, which was once widely accepted as impossibly stilted and unlikely, could in the 1970's seem a far more interesting dramatic situation than the over-conventional world of the crusades which, to the romantics, made the perfect setting for any grouping of high-minded dramatic sentiments.   H.

SIMON BOCCANEGRA

Opera in three acts and a prologue by Giuseppe Verdi; text by Francesco Maria Piave, from a play by Gutiérrez. Première at the Teatro la Fenice, Venice, March 12, 1857, with Bendazzi, Negrini, Giraldoni, Echeverria, Vercellini. First performed in revised version (alterations by Boito), la Scala, Milan, 1881, with d'Angeri, Tamagno, Maurel, Edouard de Reszke, conductor Faccio. Revived Vienna (in Werfel's version), 1930, with Nemeth, von Pataky, Rode, Manowarda, conductor Krauss; Berlin, 1930, with Reinmar; Metropolitan, New York, 1932, with Müller, Martinelli, Tibbett, Pinza, conductor Serafin; la Scala, 1933, with Caniglia, Bagnariol, Galeffi, de Angelis, conductor Gui; Florence Festival, 1938, with Caniglia, Civil, Sved, Pasero, conductor Gui; Sadler's Wells, 1948, with Gartside, Johnston, Matters, Glynne, conductor Mudie; Metropolitan, New York, 1949, with Varnay, Tucker, Warren, Szekely, conductor Stiedry; Rome, 1949, with Fineschi, Picchi, Gobbi, Siepi, conductor Serafin; Venice, 1950, with Mancini, Penno, Tagliabue, Christoff; Covent Garden, 1965, with Santunione, Cioni, Gobbi, Rouleau, conductor de Fabritiis. Revived la Scala, Milan, 1965, with Tucci, Prevedi, Giangiacomo Guelfi, Ghiaurov, conductor Gavazzeni; Berlin, German Opera, 1969, with Janowitz, Cossutta, Wixell, Talvela, conductor Maazel; Vienna, 1969, with Janowitz, Cossutta, Wächter, Ghiaurov, conductor Krips.

CHARACTERS

Amelia Boccanegra (*sometimes called Maria, and under the name of Amelia Grimaldi during Act I*) . Soprano
Gabriele Adorno, *a patrician* . . . . Tenor
Simon Boccanegra, *a plebeian, later Doge* . . . . Baritone
Jacopo Fiesco, *a patrician* . . . . Bass
Paolo Albiani, *a plebeian* . . . . Baritone
Pietro, *a plebeian* . . . . Bass
A Captain . . . . Tenor

Time: Fourteenth Century   *Place:* In and near Genoa

Simon Boccanegra was unsuccessful when first performed in Venice, and indeed Verdi himself referred to this first version as 'monotonous and cold', so that it is not surprising that he chose to revise the opera over twenty years after the first performance. At this time he had written *Aida* and the *Requiem* and plans for *Otello* already existed in his mind, and it was to Boito, as his prospective collaborator in the greater enterprise of *Otello*, that he entrusted the revision. In this version the opera has gradually won its way into the international repertory, but one is bound to admit that Boito's contribution, while it included the insertion of a scene nothing short of genius, stopped short of clarifying the complications of the plot. This small but important task has been attempted with a very fair measure of success by Franz Werfel, working in Germany in the 1920's, and by Norman Tucker in his English translation of 1948.

Genoa in the fourteenth century was ruled by an elected Doge, who had hitherto always been chosen from the ranks of the patricians. Fiesco, who is in office when the story begins, has a daughter, Maria, who has fallen in love with a plebeian, Simon Boccanegra, and borne him a daughter. His seafaring exploits, in the course of which he cleared the seas of the African pirates who so impeded the smooth course of Genoa's trade, have won him considerable fame but not the right to treat the Doge's daughter as his equal. Their child was looked after at Pisa by an old woman while he was at sea, until one day on his return home he found her dead, and his daughter vanished. Since then, he has sought her in vain, and he does not know that she was found wandering on the sea shore by Count Grimaldi, a patrician, and brought up by him as his own child.

Prologue. Paolo, political leader of the plebeians, and Pietro, an influential member of the movement, are in conversation, the latter proposing that Lorenzino shall be the plebeian choice for Doge, the former suggesting that Boccanegra would be a better candidate. Pietro agrees to organise the people's vote for Boccanegra in return for honour and riches for himself. (Tucker simplifies the plot, omitting all mention of Lorenzino, a nebulous figure who plays an important part in the drama but never appears on the stage, and making Paolo renounce the honour for himself, before suggesting Boccanegra's name.) Boccanegra has been specially called to Genoa by Paolo, and agrees to accept the position, which should win him permission to marry his beloved Maria. The people are called together, and Paolo announces to them that Boccanegra is to be their candidate; they unite in cursing Fiesco, in whose palace they see mysterious lights.

The whole of this section is set to music that is extraordinarily suggestive of underground movement and conspiracy under the cover of darkness, from the mysterious prelude to Paolo's cursing of the haughty patricians and his *sotto voce* working up of the crowd in fear of the nameless doings in Fiesco's palace.

The square empties, and Fiesco leaves his home, lamenting the loss of his daughter, from whose death-bed he has just come. His noble, restrained cry of grief, 'Il lacerato spirito' (Weary and worn with suffering[1]), with its moving orchestral postlude, establishes him straightaway as a flesh-and-blood personality whose emotions may be subdued to his sense of rank, but who is none the less anything but an insensitive, cardboard figure:

[1] English translation by Norman Tucker.

He sees Boccanegra enter the square and confronts him again with an accusation of the wrong he has done Maria. It is the first of the two great duets between the adversaries, Fiesco's fury contrasting well with Boccanegra's pleading as he tells the story of the loss of the little daughter, which has robbed one of them of his only child, the other of the grand-daughter he has never seen.

Fiesco leaves Boccanegra, telling him that only the sight of his grand-daughter can bring peace between them. He watches from a distance as the distracted man knocks on the palace door, then, finding it open, goes up, only to find that his Maria is dead. Boccanegra reappears to hear the plaudits of the mob, as they crowd into the square (to a most democratic-sounding march) and salute their new Doge.

Act I.   Twenty-five years have passed. Amelia, Boccanegra's daughter, is standing in the garden of the Grimaldi palace, near the sea. It is dawn, and she salutes the beauty of the scene and memories of her childhood in a lovely aria, 'Come in quest' ora bruna' (See how sky and ocean), whose shimmering accompaniment might have been sketched by a French Impressionist painter. She hears the voice of Gabriele, her lover, serenading her from a distance, and when he appears, tells him of her fears for his safety and that of Andrea (in reality, Fiesco in disguise), who she knows is plotting against the Doge. Her warning, and Gabriele's answer, turn to thoughts of their mutual love, which take on a greater urgency when Pietro comes to announce that the Doge asks to be received by Amelia on his way back from hunting, for no other purpose, as she well knows, than that of asking her hand in marriage for his henchman, Paolo. Gabriele resolves immediately to ask the blessing of Andrea, Amelia's guardian now that Count Grimaldi has been banished from Genoa for political intrigue, on their marriage. When he does so, Fiesco tells him the story of Amelia's adoption (he has, of course, no idea of her actual identity), Gabriele swears eternal love to her, and Fiesco blesses Gabriele in his affection for Amelia and his patriotic love of Genoa.

The Doge greets Amelia, shows her the pardon he is granting to Count Grimaldi, and asks her if she is content with her life of seclusion. She answers that she has a lover, and is pursued by one she hates—Paolo. In any case she confides to the Doge that she is not Grimaldi's daughter, but an orphan, whose only clue to her identity is a locket containing the portrait of her mother. With great emotion, Boccanegra recognises it as that of Maria, and knows he has found his daughter at last. Their duet mounts in intensity, through Simon's lyrical reaction to the possibility of having

Fig-lia! atal no-me io pal-pi-to qual se m'ap-ris-se i cie-li

found his daughter, until uncertainty gives way to proof, and he gratefully acknowledges her. The direct expression of the latter part of the duet gives way to unique tenderness as it comes to an end, and the orchestral postlude, with Boccanegra's final, ecstatic 'Figlia!' (Daughter) on a high F, makes a fitting end to a remarkable scene. It remains only for Boccanegra to deny any hope of Amelia to the waiting Paolo and for Paolo to plot her abduction with his crony Pietro, before the scene changes and we return to the political struggle.

The finale of Act I, which plays in the Council Chamber of the Doge, dates entirely from Boito's revision, and amounts to fifty pages of vocal score, or almost one half of the entire act. It is one of the finest scenes in all Verdi, and an extraordinary and entirely worthy anticipation of the work of the composer and librettist in *Otello*; it has been not inaccurately said that if Otello had ever been shown in council, this is how it might have sounded.

We find the Doge, surrounded by the plebeian and patrician members of his Council (the former in the majority), receiving emissaries from the King of Tartary, who pledges himself to keep his waters open to the ships of Genoa. He goes on to read and support a message from Petrarch, which urges that peace should immediately be made with Venice, which, like Genoa, acknowledges a common fatherland, Italy. (In Tucker's version, the message is from the Pope, and concerns the internal strife of patrician and plebeian, rather than that of the rival sea powers of Genoa and Venice.) A noise of rioting is heard in the distance, and Paolo sees through the window that the crowd is dragging Adorno to the palace; the words 'Morte ai patrizi' (Death to the nobles) can now be distinguished. In a moment, the Council has divided itself into patricians and plebeians, each group with swords drawn. Simon hears the cry 'Morte al Doge', and sends his herald to open the doors of the palace and say to the crowd that he awaits them in his Council Chamber, if they wish to find him. The sound of the trumpet can be heard calling them to silence, but the herald's words cannot be distinguished, only the sound of the yell of 'Evviva il Doge' as he ends.

It is a scene of breathless drama achieved by the simplest means, and the domination of Boccanegra is nowhere better shown than in his efforts to keep peace, not only in the city but within his own Council as well.

The mob rushes in, crying for vengeance on Gabriele Adorno and Andrea (or Fiesco), whom they drag into the Doge's presence. It seems from Adorno's own account that he has slain Lorenzino, who had abducted Amelia, and that before he died, the villain admitted he was the agent of a mightier man than he, 'a man of high position'. He is about to stab Boccanegra for the crime which he supposes to be his when Amelia, who has entered through the crowd, throws herself between the two men. Her story corroborates Gabriele's, but before she can name the offender, patrician and plebeian accuse and counter-accuse each other of the crime. Only Boccanegra's intervention prevents further bloodshed.

His great plea for peace and unity, 'Piango su voi, sul placido raggio del vostro clivo' (Sadly I see the sweet bloom of spring on our native hillsides), leads to an extended ensemble, led by Amelia, who echoes the prayer (see page 597) that peace may return to all their hearts. (In Tucker's

version, it is not Lorenzino who abducts Amelia at Paolo's
behest, but Pietro, who is thus absent from the Council
Chamber scene, where his part is slight.)

Adorno surrenders his sword to Boccanegra, who accepts
it, before turning 'con forza terribile' to Paolo. He speaks
with ever-increasing intensity of his determination to find the
traitor who raised his hand against Amelia, and in a terrible
voice calls on Paolo to join with him in cursing the villain.
This Paolo cannot avoid doing, and his curse is taken up by
the bystanders, in whom the scene seems to induce something approaching hysteria, to judge from their first *forte* cry

of 'Sia maledetto! !' (He is accursed), and the subsequent and
ever softer repetitions. The crowd disperses, Paolo rushes out
and only Boccanegra and his daughter are left alone at the
end of a scene whose atmosphere has been at any rate partly
induced by the uncanny nature of the principal motif, played
by cello and double-bassoon.

Act II. Paolo is alone, a prey to acute fear of the

consequences of his action and of the curse he was obliged by
the implacable Boccanegra to deliver against himself. He sees
himself as rejected by all, patricians and plebeians alike, but
rears himself like a snake to threaten the absent Doge with
the most terrible and the most secret vengeance at his
command—poison. Fiesco and Adorno are brought in, and he
offers the former his liberty if he will perform one vital
action: kill the Doge. If he refuse, the details of the patrician
plot, as well as the names of the men who lead them, both of
which are known to him, shall go forthwith to the Doge
himself. Fiesco indignantly refuses the offer, but Paolo has
one weapon left; as Adorno prepares to leave with Fiesco, he
asks him if he knows that Amelia is here in the palace, as
Boccanegra's mistress? (Tucker has changed the order of
events: the interview with Fiesco, who enters alone, begins
the act, is followed by Paolo's soliloquy, at the end of which
Adorno is brought in alone.)

Adorno accepts Paolo's slander all too easily, and launches
into a magnificent tirade in A minor against the Doge, who
once ordered his father's execution and has now ravished the
girl he loves. He prays, in the dominant major, that his fears
may be groundless and that Amelia's love may still be his.
Amelia comes in and he confronts her with the accusation,
which she indignantly denies. She attempts to persuade him to
leave, but the Doge can be heard approaching, and Adorno
hides, still breathing threats of revenge.

Boccanegra notices that his daughter has tears in her eyes,
and tells her that he knows the reason, which she has already
revealed to him: she is in love. When he hears the name of
Adorno, his worst fears are realised; Adorno is a traitor and a
plotter against the state. She entreats him to pardon Gabriele,
with whom she would rather die than live on alone. The Doge
tells her to leave him, and wonders whether it is strength or
weakness which prompts him to pardon an enemy. He pours
water from the jug which Paolo has poisoned, drinks from it,
and, in a sad phrase, reflects on the melancholy destiny of
those who wear a crown. He feels himself falling asleep, and
murmurs Amelia's name while the orchestra softly
adumbrates the theme of their duet in Act I.

Adorno steps from concealment; the man who murdered
his father and who is now his rival is at his mercy! But
Amelia steps between the two men, Boccanegra awakes, takes
in the situation and defies Adorno to kill a defenceless man.

Gabriele says Boccanegra's life is forfeit in return for his
father's. Boccanegra replies that his revenge is already
complete since he has taken from him the thing in life that he
values most, his daughter. Adorno is overcome at the news,
and begs for forgiveness from Amelia, whom he says he has
pursued with too jealous a love. He begs for death at the
Doge's hands, in music whose virility and youthful, heroic
quality is as good as anything of the kind Verdi ever wrote.
Boccanegra's humanity does not desert him and he pardons
his would-be murderer in a phrase whose nobility dominates
the latter part of the splendid trio:

Warlike sounds are heard outside, and Boccanegra,
remembering the conspiracy, orders Adorno to join his
friends, whose rebellion has evidently started. But Adorno
swears loyalty to the Doge and the act ends as he promises to
do what he can to put an end to the fighting.

Act III. The scene changes from Simon's private apartments to a great hall, whose window reveals a view of Genoa
harbour. The city is lit up with torches in honour of the
crushing of the revolt. Fiesco's sword is returned to him and
he is released. As he turns to go, he sees Paolo with an escort
of guards, and learns that he took part in the rebellion and,
when captured, was immediately condemned to death by
Boccanegra—but Paolo can exult in the knowledge that the
Doge will follow him quickly to the grave, slain by the slow
poison he has prepared for him. The sound of the wedding

hymn of Gabriele and Amelia can be heard, and Paolo is conducted to the scaffold with its sound ringing in his ears, leaving Fiesco full of regret that Boccanegra's end should be brought about in so treacherous and dishonourable a manner but still determined to see him again.

A proclamation is read from the balcony, ordering that the lights be extinguished in honour of the valiant dead. The Doge himself enters the hall, already affected by the poison he has taken. The sight of the sea and the feel of the salt wind on his brow restores his confidence, and brings back to him memories of the life he once led as a free man on the sea he loved and understood so well. It is a moving, expansive moment, one of those pieces of unforced self-revelation in which this opera abounds, and whose beauty is so intense that one finds oneself waiting for them at every performance one hears. Why, asks Boccanegra, did he not find death at this early, happy stage of his career? As if in answer to his question comes an echo from the concealed Fiesco. The Doge makes an effort to summon his guards, but Fiesco reveals himself as the ancient enemy long thought dead. It is the moment, not of Fiesco's revenge, but of Boccanegra's atonement, and he proudly announces that there can be peace between them now that in Amelia he has found the daughter he had lost. Fiesco's hate turns to pity for the man he knows has only a short time to live. As is appropriate the second of the two great duets is on an even more generous scale than that of the prologue, when Fiesco first imposed his conditions for reconciliation on the unfortunate Boccanegra. The passionate declamation of the bass is matched here by the mature, conciliatory tone of Boccanegra's music.

Boccanegra summons up strength to tell Amelia of her descent, and to appoint Adorno as his successor before he dies in the arms of his children and surrounded by his friends and counsellors. Fiesco goes to the balcony and announces to the assembled crowd that Gabriele Adorno is their new Doge: when they shout for Boccanegra, he reveals to them that he is dead.

Much has been made of the complication of the original libretto, and of the difficulty Boito apparently had in tidying it up, but the truth is that very little more is needed to make the story entirely comprehensible, even easy to follow, provided it is heard by an audience in its own language; at any rate, that was the common experience at Sadler's Wells.

Apart from a general tidying up of the dialogue, Boito was responsible for the finale of Act I, generally conceded to be the finest section of the opera. Verdi's revision was even more thorough. Details of the orchestration, of the vocal line, and of the harmony are altered all over the place, in much the same way as they had been in *Macbeth* but on a far more extensive scale. Entirely new is the opening scene of the prologue up to Fiesco's aria (apart from Paolo's 'L'altra magion'); the introduction to Act I, the duet for Gabriele and Fiesco, the climax of the recognition duet, and of course the Council Chamber scene; Boccanegra's short solo in Act II and Paolo's *Credo*-like soliloquy which precedes it; the opening of Act III up to the entrance of Boccanegra and to a large extent the final quartet with chorus.

That Verdi entertained such high regard for the opera is perhaps to some extent due to his love for Genoa itself. Certainly his music communicates this love as well as the city's dependence for life on the sea. But the most remarkable thing about the opera is its central figure, a puissant character and amongst Verdi's greatest creations; all the way through, one cannot help but be impressed by the amazing consistency of the characterisation. Never before perhaps had a composer succeeded in putting the unspectacular quality of statesmanship on to the stage, although quite a number had tried, e.g. Mozart in *La Clemenza di Tito*. Boccanegra is a mature creation, whose insight and integrity are expressed in music as well as in the drama. It is not only that Verdi has been provided with striking situations for his main character—the sudden recognition of a long-lost daughter, the cursing of the abductor, the falling asleep and waking to find his daughter's prospective bridegroom standing over him with a dagger, the confronting by his ancient enemy apparently risen from the dead—but that the music shows exactly the same consistent understanding that we are asked to believe was Boccanegra's. Not a bar of recitative, not a note in the great solos and ensembles in which he takes part but contributes to this picture of the central figure, which is in addition perhaps the most exacting baritone part Verdi ever wrote, certainly one of the most rewarding. H.

UN BALLO IN MASCHERA
A Masked Ball

Opera in three acts, by Giuseppe Verdi; text by Somma, based on Scribe's libretto for Auber's opera *Gustave III, ou Le Bal Masqué*. Première at Apollo Theatre, Rome, February 17, 1859, with Julienne-Dejean, Scotti, Sbriscia, Fraschini, Giraldoni. First performed New York, 1861; London, Lyceum Theatre, 1861, with Tietjens, Lemaire, Gussier, Giuglini, Sedie; Metropolitan, 1889 (in German), with Lilli Lehmann, Perotti, Reichmann, conductor Seidl. Revived Metropolitan, 1903, with Jean de Reszke; 1905, with Caruso, Eames, Homer, Scotti, Plançon, Journet; Covent Garden, 1919, with Destinn, Martinelli, Dinh Gilly; 1935, with Eva Turner, Dino Borgioli, Fear, conductor Raybould; Florence Festival, 1935, with Cigna, Grani, Buades, Lauri-Volpi, Armando Borgioli, conductor Serafin; 1941, with Caniglia, Grani, Stignani, Gigli, Bechi; Metropolitan, 1940, with Milanov, Thorborg, Björling, Sved, conductor Panizza; 1949, Edinburgh Festival, with Welitsch and Grandi, Noni, Picchi, Silveri, conductor Gui; la Scala, Milan, 1958, with Callas, Ratti, Simionato, di Stefano, Bastianini. Bonci was one of the most famous exponents of the role of Riccardo, and Selma Kurz's trill was apparently never heard to better advantage than as Oscar.

CHARACTERS

Riccardo, *Count of Warwick* (Gustavus III) . . . . . Tenor
Amelia . . . . Soprano
Renato, *Secretary to the Governor* (Anckarstroem)
　　　　　　　　　　　　　　　　　　　　　　　　Baritone
Samuele (Count Ribbing) ⎱ *enemies of the* ⎰ 　　Bass
Tomaso (Count Horn) 　　⎰ *Governor* 　⎱ · · · · Bass
Silvano, *a sailor* (Cristian) . . . . Baritone
Oscar, *a page* . . . . Soprano
Ulrica, *a fortune-teller* (Arvidson) . . . . Contralto

A Judge, a Servant of Amelia, Populace, Guards, Courtiers, etc. (The names used when the opera is set in Boston appear first, those when it is restored to its Swedish setting are added in brackets.)

The English libretto of *Un Ballo in Maschera* has the following note:

'The scene of Verdi's *Ballo in Maschera* was, by the author of the libretto, originally laid in one of the European cities. But the government censors objected to this, probably because the plot contained the record of a successful conspiracy against an established prince or governor. By a change of scene to the distant and, to the author, little-known city of Boston, in America, this difficulty seems to have been obviated. The fact should be borne in mind by Bostonians and others, who may be somewhat astonished at the events which are supposed to have taken place in the old Puritan city.'

Certainly the events in *The Masked Ball* are amazing for the Boston of Puritan or any other time, and the reason is not far to seek.

Auber produced, in 1833, an opera on a libretto by Scribe, entitled *Gustave III, ou Le Bal Masqué*, and it is upon this Scribe libretto that the book of *Un Ballo in Maschera* is based. Verdi's opera was originally called *Gustavo III*, and, like the Scribe-Auber work, was written around the assassination of the liberal Gustavus III, of Sweden, who, March 16, 1792, was shot in the back during a masked ball at Stockholm.

Verdi composed the work for the San Carlo Theatre, Naples, where it was to have been produced for the carnival of 1858. But on January 14 of that year, while the rehearsals were in progress, Felice Orsini, an Italian revolutionist, made his attempt on the life of Napoleon III. In consequence the authorities forbade the performance of a work dealing with the assassination of a king. The suggestion that Verdi adapt his music to an entirely different libretto was put aside by the composer, and the work was withdrawn, with the result that a revolution nearly broke out in Naples. People paraded the street, and by shouting 'Viva Verdi!' proclaimed, under guise of the initials of the popular composer's name, that they favoured the cause of a united Italy, with Victor Emanuel as King; viz. Vittorio Emmanuele Re D'Italia (Victor Emanuel, King of Italy). Finally the censor in Rome suggested, as a way out of the difficulty, that the title of the opera be changed to *Un Ballo in Maschera* and the scene transferred to Boston— for, however nervous the authorities were about having a king murdered on the stage, they regarded the assassination of an English governor in far-off America as a quite harmless diversion. So, indeed, it proved to be, the only excitement evinced by the audience of the Apollo Theatre, Rome, on the evening of February 17, 1859, being the result of its enthusiasm over the various musical numbers of the work, this enthusiasm not being at all reduced by the fact that, with the transfer to Boston, two of the conspirators, Samuel and Tom, became negroes, and the astrologer who figures in the opera, a negress!

The change of scene from Boston to Naples (where the

scene has often been laid) is said to have been initiated in
Paris upon the instance of Mario, who 'would never have
consented to sing his ballad in the second act in short
pantaloons, silk stockings, red dress, and big epaulettes of
gold lace. He would never have been satisfied with the title of
Earl of Warwick and the office of governor. He preferred to
be a grandee of Spain, to call himself the Duke of Olivares,
and to disguise himself as a Neapolitan fisherman, besides
paying little attention to the strict accuracy of the role, but
rather adapting it to his own gifts as an artist.' The ballad
referred to in this quotation undoubtedly is Riccardo's
barcarolle, 'Di' tu se fedele il flutto m'aspetta' (Declare if the
waves will faithfully bear me).

Far more sensible is it to put the setting back to the
original Sweden,[1] and so restore the correct historical background to a set of happenings that is substantially based on
historical fact. Gustavus III was a monarch distinguished for
his liberal views, Richard, Count of Warwick, is a librettist's
makeshift. Similarly, Anckarstroem, Horn, and Ribbing were
sincere fighters for a reactionary, aristocratic cause—which
we can understand even if we do not sympathise with it—and
they bear little resemblance to the ludicrous Tom and Sam,
or the implausible half-breed Renato. If the change from the
negress Ulrica to the society go-between Mam'zelle Arvidson
is rather more difficult to reconcile with the music, the
enormous gain to the other characters surely affords ample
compensation. It is not that the change affects the music, only
that the motivation of the action becomes immediately much
stronger.

Act I.   Reception hall in the Governor's house. Riccardo
is giving an audience. Oscar, his page, brings him the list of
guests invited to a masked ball. Riccardo is especially
delighted at seeing on it the name of Amelia, the wife of his
secretary, Renato, although his conscience bitterly

[1] As was done in Stockholm in the late 1950's in a production of
startling brilliance by Göran Gentele, whose much lamented death
occurred in 1972 shortly before the start of his term as General
Manager of the Metropolitan Opera, New York. This production did
not attempt to hide the known homosexuality of Gustavus III—Oscar
was only one of several shapely pages—and effectively emphasised such
physical characteristics as his very quick movements and the whole
Swedish background. The production was seen at the Edinburgh
Festival in 1959.   H.

reproaches him for loving Amelia, for Renato is his most faithful friend, ever ready to defend him. The secretary has recently discovered a conspiracy against his master, but as yet has been unable to learn the names of the conspirators.

At the audience a judge is announced, who brings for signature the sentence of banishment against an old fortune-teller, by name Ulrica. Oscar, however, intercedes for the old woman. Riccardo decides to visit her in disguise and test her powers of divination.

The scene changes to Ulrica's hut, which Riccardo enters disguised as a fisherman. Without his knowledge, Amelia also comes to consult the sorceress. Concealed by a curtain he hears her ask for a magic herb to cure her of the love which she, a married woman, bears for Riccardo. The old woman tells her of such a herb, but Amelia must gather it herself at midnight in the place where stands the gibbet. Riccardo thus learns for the first time that she loves him, and of her purpose to be at the place of the gibbet at midnight. When she has gone he comes out of his concealment and has his fortune told. Ulrica predicts that he will die by the hand of a friend. The conspirators, who are in his retinue, whisper among themselves that they are discovered. 'Who will be the slayer?' asks Riccardo. The answer is, 'Whoever first shall shake your hand.' At this moment Renato enters, greets his friend with a vigorous shake of the hand, and Riccardo laughs at the evil prophecy. His retinue and the populace rejoice with him.

Act II. Midnight, beside the gallows. Amelia, heavily veiled, comes to pluck the magic herb. Riccardo arrives to protect her. Amelia is unable to conceal her love for him. But who comes there? It is Renato. Concern for his master has called him to the spot. The conspirators are lying in wait for him nearby. Riccardo exacts from Renato a promise to escort back to the city the deeply veiled woman, without making an attempt to learn who she is, while he himself returns by an unfrequented path. Renato and his companion fall into the hands of the conspirators. The latter do not harm the secretary, but want at least to learn who the Governor's sweetheart is. They lift the veil. Renato sees his own wife. Rage grips his heart. He bids the leaders of the conspiracy meet with him at his house in the morning.

Act III. A room in Renato's dwelling. For the disgrace he has suffered he intends to kill Amelia. Upon her plea she is allowed to embrace her son once more. He reflects that, after all, Riccardo is much the more guilty of the two. He refrains from killing her, but when he and the conspirators draw lots to determine who shall kill Riccardo, he calls her in, and, at his command, she draws a piece of paper from an urn. It bears her husband's name, drawn unwittingly by her to indicate the person who is to slay the man she loves. Partly to remove Amelia's suspicions, Renato accepts the invitation to the masked ball which Oscar brings him, Riccardo, of course, knowing nothing of what has transpired.

In the brilliant crowd of maskers, the scene having changed to that of the masked ball, Renato learns from Oscar what disguise is worn by Riccardo. Amelia, who, with the eyes of apprehensive love, has also recognised Riccardo, implores him to flee the danger that threatens him. But Riccardo knows no fear. In order that the honour of his friend shall remain secure, he has determined to send him as an envoy to England, accompanied by his wife. Her, he tells Amelia, he will never see again. 'Once more I bid thee farewell, for the last time, farewell.'

'And thus receive thou my farewell!' exclaims Renato shooting him in the back.

With his last words Riccardo assures Renato of the guilt-lessness of Amelia, and admonishes all to seek to avenge his death on no one.   K.

Un Ballo in Maschera was able to triumph over early vicissitudes of censorship, so that d'Annunzio, fifty years after its première and in no spirit of tongue in cheek, could call it the most operatic of operas. More than half a century later still, during which time it has moved from popular to highbrow acceptance, it strikes me as little short of flawless among the operas of this period of Verdi's output: better shaped than *Forza del Destino*, more exuberant than *Simon Boccanegra*, more Italian and less discursive than the even greater *Don Carlos*. Above all, the listener in the second half of the twentieth century will admire the exquisite balance between the romantic and tragic elements of the music on the one hand and its strongly ironic characteristics on the other, evidenced not only in what Oscar and the conspirators sing, but most of all in the rounded musical picture of the tenor hero. His characterisation ranges from the unreserved romanticism of the haunting 'La rivedrà', the love duet and the last act aria, through the exuberance of his lead of the *stretta* to the finale of the first scene, to his amused, even witty rejection of the portentous in his reaction to Oscar's plea for Ulrica, above all in 'E scherzo od è follia'.

Out of all this, Verdi has fabricated a unique atmosphere, a subtler, more believable portrayal of a closed community than that of *Rigoletto*, as evocative of a Court cultivated and liberal-minded, about which most of us have read little, as is *Don Carlos*'s music of one with which we are tolerably familiar.

Ballo is rare among Verdi's operas in providing a longer, richer, more rewarding part for tenor than for baritone. Though the subtleties of the role provide scope for maximum artistry, the music's high spirits also seem to me to call for vocal youth and brilliance. Early in the first act comes Riccardo's 'La rivedrà nell'estasi' (I shall again her face behold), a beautiful lyrical solo which also forms the main theme of the Prelude:

This is followed by the faithful Renato's 'Alla vita che t'arride' (To our life with joy abounding), more of a muscle-flexer than a big statement and peculiar in that its fine recitative is given to the tenor and not to the baritone at all.

Oscar is the gadfly of the score, the dispenser of musical spice and, logically in view of the historical Gustavus III's known predilections, the agent to bring out the most buoyant side of the hero's character. In 'Volta la terrea', he vouches for the fortune teller:

The scene in Ulrica's hut begins with her effective invocation to the spirits of the underworld and there follows a trio for Amelia, Ulrica and Riccardo, during which the latter overhears Amelia's welcome confession of love for himself and which has as its climax a great welling phrase for Amelia:

Riccardo's charming barcarolle is addressed to the sorceress, a Neapolitan-type melody, 'Di' tu se fedele il flutto m'aspetta', but the highlight of the scene is the quintet which expresses Riccardo's disbelief in Ulrica's prophecy regarding his death:

It was in Florence in 1898 that Alessandro Bonci, then only 28 years old, first inserted a cascade of laughs to fill in the rests, and articulated his invention with such grace and dexterity that the old composer wrote to congratulate him on the innovation, which he perceived to be wholly in character. Bonci made an elegant recording of it 28 years later and virtually every tenor since (with a handful of exceptions, including oddly enough Björling) has followed his example in including the so-called 'risata'.

Amelia's great recitative and aria which starts the Gallows scene is as taxing as anything in operatic literature, and the *scena* demands singing on the biggest possible scale: 'Ma dall'arido stelo divulsa'. At the end of the solo, with its near-hysterical second section culminating in a top C, Riccardo enters and there ensues the most expansive love duet Verdi wrote before *Otello*. At its end, Renato comes to save Riccardo, there is a short, agitated trio as they discuss escape, and the finale is concerned with the unsuccessful efforts of Renato to get his disguised wife past the conspirators, her unmasking, and the consequent rage of the one and remorse of the other. With the mocking laughter of the conspirators, this is one of Verdi's most fascinating scenes, foreshadowing the music of Fra Melitone in *Forza* and of course *Falstaff*.

The last act starts with an aria for Amelia, 'Morrò, ma prima in grazia', as she pleads to be allowed to see her son again. It is, however, primarily Renato's scene and he must stand like a Colossus over it. The dramatic recitative and tremendously taxing aria, 'Eri tu', which follows Amelia's aria, requires in the first half of the aria proper scarcely less dramatic intensity than Iago's 'Credo', a lyricism worthy of Germont père in the concluding section, and throughout it makes supreme demands on the sustaining qualities of a baritone voice as well as on its power. There follows the scene in which Renato receives the two leaders of the conspiracy and agrees to make common cause with them, Amelia's drawing of the lots, and finally a brilliant solo for Oscar, 'Ah! di che fulgor' which turns into a quintet as Amelia, Renato and the conspirators react to the news that Riccardo is to give a masked ball that very night.

The last scene is preceded by a solo for Riccardo, introspective in the recitative 'Forse la soglia attinse' and full of romantic stress in the aria 'Ma se m'è forza perderti', in which he decides to send Amelia and her husband on a foreign mission.

Finally, the masked ball, where early on occurs Oscar's brilliant solo, beginning, in reply to Renato's question about Riccardo's disguise, 'Saper vorreste'. Selma Kurz was famous for her performance of this role, not least at Covent Garden between 1904 and 1907, and her recordings preserve not only an individual, limpid sound and an incomparable trill, but also those cadenzas and top notes with which she decorated music and situation alike, a trilling and waltzing around the stage which caused her to fall foul of the conductor Mancinelli at Covent Garden in 1904 but which succeeded Bonci's 'risata' as a public attraction early in the century. Most of the scene is carried on over dance music, and the farewell duet between Riccardo and Amelia is particularly moving, as is Riccardo's death scene. A shot rings out, Riccardo falls into the arms of Oscar, Amelia rushes to him, the dance music stops, he forgives his enemies and dies.

K., H.

LA FORZA DEL DESTINO
The Force of Destiny

Opera in four acts by Giuseppe Verdi; text by Francesco Maria Piave, founded on a Spanish drama by the Duke of Rivas, *Don Alvaro o La Fuerza de Sino*. Première at St. Petersburg on November 10, 1862, with Barbot, Didiée, Tamberlik, Graziani, Angelini. First performed, New York, 1865; London, Her Majesty's Theatre, 1867, with Tietjens, Trebelli, Mongini, Santley, Gassie, conductor Arditi. Revived Metropolitan, 1918, with Ponselle, Caruso, de Luca, Mardones, conductor Papi; 1942, with Milanov, Baum, Tibbett, Pinza, conductor Walter; Dresden, 1926, with Seinemeyer, Pattiera, Burg, Plaschke, conductor Busch; Vienna, 1926, with Angerer, Piccaver, Schipper, Mayr; la Scala, 1928, with Scacciati, Merli, Franci, Pasero, conductor

Toscanini; Covent Garden, 1931, with Ponselle, Pertile, Franci, Pasero, conductor Serafin; Buenos Aires, 1933, with Muzio, Gigli, conductor Marinuzzi; la Scala, 1940, with Cigna, Gigli, A. Borgioli, Pasero, conductor Marinuzzi; 1949, with Barbato, Filippeschi, Silveri, Christoff, conductor de Sabata; Edinburgh Festival, 1951, with Wegner, Poleri, Rothmüller, Dargavel, conductor Busch; Metropolitan, New York, 1952, with Milanov, Tucker, Warren, Siepi; Covent Garden, 1962, with Cavalli, Bergonzi, John Shaw, Ghiaurov, conductor Solti.

CHARACTERS

Donna Leonora di Vargas .... Soprano
Preziosilla, *a gypsy* .... Mezzo-Soprano
Don Alvaro .... Tenor
Don Carlo di Vargas, *Leonora's brother* ..... Baritone
Padre Guardiano, *a Franciscan monk* .... Bass
Marchese di Calatrava, *Leonora's father* .... Bass
Fra Melitone, *a Franciscan monk* .... Baritone
Curra, *Leonora's maid* .... Mezzo-Soprano
The Mayor of Hornachuelos .... Bass
Trabuco, *a muleteer* .... Tenor
A Surgeon .... Tenor
Time: Middle of Eighteenth Century   *Place:* Spain and Italy

Forza is customarily criticised for its rambling libretto, and because the destiny which is proclaimed in the title tends to be replaced in the story by the less compelling factor of coincidence. Francis Toye is at some pains to point out that Rivas's play, *Don Alvaro*, is dominated by the principle of the blood-feud, in which facts were more important than intentions, and that to understand the original significance of the play entails an imaginative reconstruction of this outmoded attitude. He also suggests that Rivas, a liberal, may have intended to show that life should be influenced by other considerations than that of the honour of noble Spanish families—in any case, his scenes of popular life were particularly successful.

The overture is a vividly exciting affair, dominated by Leonora's aria from Act II, and the music concerned with 'fate':

Reference is also made to Alvaro's *cantabile con espressione* tune (in A minor) from the fourth act duet, and to themes from the duet between Leonora and Padre Guardiano.

Act I takes place in Leonora's room. She says good night to her father and is then overcome with remorse at the idea of leaving him so suddenly—for she has arranged that very night to elope with her lover, Don Alvaro. In an aria, 'Me pellegrina ed orfana' (As wanderer and orphan), she pictures her friendless lot in a foreign country, for which even the prospect of marriage with her lover cannot console her. It is late; he surely cannot come now—but no sooner are the words spoken than the sound of his horses is heard and he has bounded in through the window, protesting his eternal love for her. His passionate description of the preparations for their elopement evokes, after some hesitation, an equally demonstrative response from Leonora, but the delay proves disastrous, and, before they can escape, the Marchese is in the room, denouncing his daughter's seducer. Alvaro protests his and her innocence, and throws down his pistol in token of his surrender to the mercy of the Marchese. It goes off and fatally wounds the old man, who curses Leonora as he dies.

Act II. Leonora has been separated from Alvaro in their flight; each believes the other dead, but Don Carlo, Leonora's brother, knows that they are alive and scours the land to revenge himself on the murderer of his father and on the sister who has brought dishonour to his family.

The first scene is laid in the inn at the village of Hornachuelos, where are gathered various village worthies, muleteers, servants and a mysterious student, who is no other than Don Carlo in diguise. The company sings and dances until the meal is announced; Leonora appears for a moment at the door seeking shelter, just as the student says grace, but she recognises in him her brother and withdraws. Presently Preziosilla, a gypsy, enters, telling the guests that war has broken out and that all should lose no time in going to Italy to fight the Germans. She sings a song in praise of war and its delights, and proceeds to tell the fortunes of the assembled company, incidentally informing the student that his being in disguise cannot be hidden from her.

Pilgrims can be heard outside, and all join in their prayer, not least Leonora, who observes from the door and prays to be delivered from her brother's vengeance. It is a splendid example of choral writing. Don Carlo plies the muleteer with questions about the traveller he brought to the inn, and is asked in his turn, since he is so curious about others, to tell the company his own story. This he does in a ballad; he is Pereda, a young student, who has followed his friend Vargas in his quest for the murderer of his father. The murderer it appears has escaped to South America, and the sister of Vargas, whom the murderer seduced, is dead. The mayor says it is late, all bid each other good night, and, after a final dance, the scene comes to an end.

Leonora continues on her way and at the opening of the next scene we find her outside the monastery of the 'Madonna degli Angeli', near Hornachuelos, whither she has been sent for sanctuary. In the most extended aria of the opera, she prays for forgiveness for her sin, and takes courage from the sound of the hymn which can be heard coming from the church. At the beginning of the scene can be heard the 'fate' motif familiar from the overture, then, after a dramatic recitative, the aria, 'Madre, pietosa Vergine' (Holy Mother, hear my prayer), whose climax comes with the great phrase (in the major) of which such use has already been made in the overture: 'Deh, non m'abbandonar':

Leonora rings the bell, and a window in the door opens to reveal the head of Fra Melitone, who is impressed to hear that Father Cleto sent her and agrees to inform the Father Superior of her presence. He receives her kindly, and knows immediately who she is when she tells him who sent her. He warns her of the extreme loneliness of the solitary life she proposes to lead in the cave where once before a female penitent lived out her life, but she is determined to go through with her plan, and he, convinced of her steadfastness of purpose, agrees to allow her request. He himself will bring her food daily and in case of urgent danger or the approach of death she can ring a bell to summon help; otherwise, she will never again set eyes on a human being. He gathers the monks together and tells them that once again the cave will be occupied; no one is to approach it or make any attempt to discover the identity of the penitent.

Leonora's scene with the Padre Guardiano is one of the finest in all Verdi, and belongs to the line of great duets to which reference has been made earlier in these pages. The expressive vocal line is enhanced by the contrasting nature of the various sections, whether it be the loose-limbed tune in which Leonora first tells of the gradual awakening of peace in her soul, or the closely knit E major duet in which Padre Guardiano immediately afterwards warns her of the danger she runs in living alone, the long sentences in which Padre Guardiano urges her to draw closer to God, or the passionate phrases she employs to voice her thanks to the salvation she feels she has found. The finale (the short service in which the Father Superior blesses Leonora and warns the monks in future not to approach her solitary cell) is the perfect pendant to a great scene. Padre Guardiano leads them in pronouncing a curse on anyone who violates the sanctity of the cell, and then the sound of Leonora's voice floats out over the male voices of the monks in the prayer to the Virgin, 'La Vergine degli angeli'. It would be difficult to imagine music that more perfectly combined simplicity of means and beauty of effect.

Act III.   The scene changes to Italy, near Velletri, where the fighting referred to at the beginning of the previous act is taking place. Don Alvaro and Don Carlo di Vargas, each under assumed names and unknown to the other, have enlisted in the Spanish contingent which is taking part in the fighting. The sound of gambling is heard as Alvaro comes forward to sing his long recitative and aria, 'O tu che in seno agli angeli' (O sainted soul, in rest above), a fitting expression of the torture his lonely soul has suffered since the death of the Marchese di Calatrava, and before that when his father, related to the last of the Incas, tried to free his country from foreign rule only to meet death on the scaffold.

In response to a cry for help, he rushes offstage, to reappear with none other than his old enemy Don Carlo, whom he has saved from death at the hands of a gang of ruffians. Having exchanged false names, they swear friendship and go off together in answer to an urgent call to arms.

The scene changes, and we see a military surgeon surrounded by soldiers watching the battle from a distance. Victory is to the Italians and the Spaniards, but Don Carlo brings in Alvaro grievously wounded. When Carlo seeks to give his friend the military decoration of the order of Calatrava, he shudders at the name, but a moment later he entrusts Carlo with his last instructions. He has a small casket which contains a letter and which must be burnt unopened after his death; will his friend do this for him? Carlo swears to carry out the commission faithfully. The duet, 'Solenne in quest' ora' (In this solemn hour), has become world-famous, partly, perhaps, because of the celebrity of the gramophone record made of it by Caruso and Scotti, but also because of its graceful tune and remarkably apt relationship to the situation (an appropriateness which would be the more frequently noticed if the tenor singing Alvaro paid more attention to the portrayal of a dying man and less to the display of his own voice):

Alvaro is carried away by the surgeon, and Carlo reflects on the secret which lies hidden in the fateful box. His friend trembled at the name of Calatrava; could it be his enemy in disguise? He soliloquises on the temptation the casket presents even to a man of honour, 'Urna fatale del mio destino' (Fatal urn of my destiny), but finds a portrait inside which no oath prevents him from inspecting. It is Leonora's! The secret is out, and his newly found friend is recognised as his old enemy! At this moment a messenger tells him that Alvaro's life is saved; in an *allegro* he rejoices at the prospect of revenge.

The scene changes to a military camp near Velletri. A military patrol passes, and as dawn approaches Don Alvaro can be seen crossing the camp. Carlo calls him, and asks him if he is strong enough to fight a duel. With whom? Has he had no message lately from Don Alvaro, the Indian? Alvaro's protests and offers of friendship are in vain; Carlo insults him until he has provoked the duel he is seeking, only to be interrupted by the patrol on its way home. Alvaro, left alone, resolves to seek sanctuary in a monastery. The scene is in the splendid tradition of duets for tenor and baritone which Verdi did so incomparably, and it is to be regretted that recent custom in Italy is to omit it altogether, either with a view to shortening the long opera, or else to save the tenor in what is anyhow a role of considerable weight. In any case, the duet is in a false position, as Toye points out, and was originally designed to end the act.

It is dawn. Soldiers polish their equipment, pedlars offer their wares, food and drink is for sale, and Preziosilla offers to tell fortunes until the appearance of a band of recruits gives her an opportunity of leading a tarantella in an effort to dispel their gloom. Mixed up in the dance is Fra Melitone, who extricates himself and treats the company to a discourse on its several vices, the whole thing dressed up in a series of outrageous puns. The soldiers make an attempt to give him a drubbing, but Preziosilla interrupts them and sings a spirited though hardly imaginative 'Rataplan', which ends the act.

Act IV.   The scene shows the cloister of the Convent of the 'Madonna degli Angeli', where a crowd of beggars is assembling to collect the free soup which the monks dole out regularly. Fra Melitone is in charge, and his marked lack of patience and his intense annoyance at being compared unfavourably by the crowd with Padre Raffaello (in reality Alvaro in disguise) make him more than usually short with his customers. Finally, he can bear their torments and their importunities no longer, and he kicks over the cauldron with what remains of the soup inside. The Father Superior, who has been watching, reproaches him gently for lack of patience, and bids him not complain if Raffaello be preferred to him. Melitone says he likes Raffaello but cannot understand his odd, haunted look—caused, says the Father Superior, by his frequent fasts and his concentration on his duty.

The music of Melitone is always cited as amongst the most interesting in *Forza*, as giving a foretaste of the methods Verdi was to employ years later when writing *Falstaff*. There is a good deal of truth in this view; the rhythms and orchestral accompaniment as well as the shape of the vocal line certainly suggest an entirely new type of character for Verdi.

The monastery door-bell rings violently, and Meliton
admits Don Carlo himself, asking for Padre Raffaello
Melitone says there are two of that name in the monastery
but from the description he easily knows which is meant. H
goes off to fetch him, while Don Carlo muses on how hi
hatred for Alvaro was sufficient to penetrate the mos
unlikely of hiding-places. Alvaro comes in, Carlo disclose
himself and immediately challenges him to a duel, producin
two swords as he does so from under his cloak. Alvaro plead
with him to renounce his thoughts of vengeance, and believ
what he now hears from the mouth of a priest, that his siste
Leonora was never dishonoured, that he has nought to aveng
but the misfortune which has dogged them both. Alvaro wil
even do what he says he has never before done, kneel at Do
Carlo's feet. Carlo says this act proclaims the baseness of hi
birth and for a moment Alvaro's feelings threaten to get th
better of his self-control, but he chokes down his anger unti
Carlo strikes him across the face, branding him a coward wit
the blow. Alvaro's vows are forgotten and he proclaims tha
he is ready to fight him. They rush off to expiate th
blood-feud which has followed them for so long.

The duet is a magnificent passage, perhaps the finest an
most expressive for tenor and baritone which Verdi achieve
before the days of *Otello*. It is immediately followed by
quick change of scene; the 'fate' motif sounds, and Leonor
is seen outside her grotto. In great long phrases of suppli
cation she prays for the peace which she has never know
since the day she first secluded herself from the world: 'Pace
pace, mio Dio' (Peace, grant me peace, O Lord). She sees th
bread which has been left for her and which serves only t
prolong, as she says, a wretched life. Suddenly, the sounds o
fighting can be heard, and, calling down a curse on whoeve
dares to profane her solitude, she returns to her cell.

In a moment, the voice of Carlo can be heard begging fo
absolution; he is dying, and Alvaro, distracted that he ha
once again the blood of a Vargas on his hands, bangs on th
door of Leonora's cell and begs for help for the dying man
Leonora rings the bell in her alarm but a moment late
appears and is recognised by Alvaro, who tells her what ha
happened. She goes to the spot where her brother lies dyin
and a few seconds later her cry is heard as Carlo stabs her
revenge uppermost in his mind even at his last moment
Alvaro can restrain his anger no longer when he sees Leonor

supported by Padre Guardiano, and he curses the fate which
has brought so much misery on them all. The old Father
Superior in music of great nobility bids him not to curse but
to prostrate himself before the might of Heaven, whither the
angel, who now lies dying, is going. In the presence of her
lover and of the old priest who brought her such salvation as
earth can offer, Leonora dies, and so expiates the curse which
fell on them all with the death of her father.

H.

DON CARLOS

Opera in five acts by Giuseppe Verdi; text by G. Méry and C. du
Locle (in French), after Schiller. Première at Opéra, Paris, March 11,
1867, with Marie Sass, Gueymard, Morère, Jean Baptiste Faure, Obin,
David, conductor Emil Perrin. First performed at Covent Garden,
1867,[1] with Pauline Lucca, Fricci, Naudin, Grazziani; New York, 1877.
Produced in revised version at la Scala, Milan, 1884, with Bruschi-
Chiatti, Pasqua, Tamagno, Lhérie, Silvestri, Navarrini. Revived
Metropolitan, 1920, with Ponselle, Matzenauer, Martinelli, de Luca,
Didur, conductor Papi; la Scala, 1926, with Scacciati, Cobelli, Trantoul,
conductor Toscanini; Vienna, 1932 (in revised version by Werfel), with
Ursuleac, Rünger, Völker, Schipper, Manowarda, conductor Krauss;
Covent Garden, 1933, with Cigna, Giani, Lappas, Rimini, Autori,
Tomei, conductor Beecham; Venice, 1938, with Grandi, Merli,
Valentino, conductor Gui; Sadler's Wells, 1938, with Dusseau, Coates,
Tudor Davies; Florence Festival, 1950, with Caniglia, Stignani, Picchi,
Silveri, Christoff, Neri, conductor Serafin (5 acts)[2]; Metropolitan,
1950, with Delia Rigal, Barbieri, Björling, Merrill, Siepi, Hines,
conductor Stiedry (4 Acts); Covent Garden, 1958, with Brouwenstijn,
Barbieri, Vickers, Gobbi, Christoff, conductor Giulini, producer

[1] Escudier for this production removed Act I and the ballet
reinstating Carlos's aria in the Garden scene of what then became Act II.

H.

[2] First performance *in this version* at Modena in 1886. Andrew
Porter describes this as 'a scissor-and-paste job, in which Act I as
published in 1867 was joined to the four revised acts of 1883'. This was
Florence's version of 1950, Covent Garden's of 1958, but there is no
evidence that Verdi had anything to do with it, though he must have
allowed it.

H.

Visconti (5 Acts)[1]; Salzburg Festival, 1958, with Jurinac, Christa Ludwig, Fernandi, Bastianini, Siepi, under Karajan (4 Acts).

CHARACTERS

Elisabeth de Valois, *later Queen of Spain* ..... Soprano
Princess Eboli, *her lady-in-waiting* .....Mezzo-Soprano
Don Carlos, *heir to the Spanish throne* .... Tenor
Rodrigo, *Marquess of Posa* .... Baritone
Philip II, *King of Spain* .... Bass
The Grand Inquisitor .... Bass
A Monk .... Bass
Tebaldo, *Elisabeth's page* .... Soprano
Count Lerma .... Tenor
The Royal Herald .... Tenor
A heavenly voice .... Soprano

Time: Mid-Sixteenth Century   *Place:* France and Spain

Don Carlos has always suffered from an inherent dis advantage; it was written for Paris, in the five-act, display conscious tradition which Meyerbeer did so much to establish at that house, and it is therefore too long for modern tastes In 1882-3 Verdi undertook, with Ghislanzoni, his librettis for *Aida*, to produce a shorter version, but this entailed, a well as the omission of the ballet music, the jettisoning o most of the important first act, which it is hard to justify artistically. Since then, the most satisfactory revivals of the opera have usually made an attempt at including the first act whatever they may have cut later on.[2]

Spain is nearing the end of a war with France, and one o the conditions of peace is that the heir to the throne o Spain, Don Carlos (in reality an epileptic and a monster, bu represented in Verdi as well as in Schiller as a brilliant young man), would marry Elisabeth the daughter of the King o France.

[1] And has therefore French characteristics. Modern scholarshi favours use of the French libretto, but after some heart-searching, I hav here retained the more familiar Italian.   H.

[2] In 1866, writing to Tito Ricordi, Verdi had insisted that *Don Carlos* be given complete; in 1874 he was angry at cuts made fo Reggio; in 1875 he said that cuts for the Vienna production would b difficult. In 1882-3, Verdi himself removed Act I and the ballet salvaging only the tenor's aria.   H.

Act I.   Don Carlos has come secretly to France to see the
bride who has been chosen for him. A hunt is in progress near
Fontainebleau (there is no prelude to the opera) and
Elisabeth and her page Tebaldo are separated from the main
body of riders. They disappear in search of their companions
and Carlos, alone, sings of the love which the sight of his
bride has awakened in his heart. His romance was salvaged in
an altered version when Verdi discarded Act I in his attempt
at revision. Elisabeth reappears and Don Carlos offers to
escort her home, saying he is a member of the staff of the
Spanish envoy. He lights a fire and is questioned by the
Princess about the young Spanish Prince to whom she is
betrothed but whom she has never met. She fears for her
marriage if love does not enter into it. Carlos tells her she
need have no fear; the Prince will love her—and he shows her
a portrait, which she naturally recognises as his. He declares
his love, which she admits she returns. Their duet, which was
omitted in the 1884 version, is a particularly lovely inspi-
ation, and the delicate beauty of Elisabeth's phrase, 'Di qual
amor, di quant' ardor' (Ah yes, 'tis love), as she recognises the
love in her heart, is something that can ill be spared, not only
for its own sake but because it is used later in the opera in
something approaching the manner of a motif:

Tebaldo returns and warns Elisabeth that the Spanish
envoy is approaching to make a formal request for her hand
in marriage for his master, the King of Spain himself, not for
Don Carlos as had originally been arranged. The two lovers
are filled with consternation, but Elisabeth accedes to the
prayers of the crowd of courtiers who beg her to acquiesce
and so put an end to the war. The acclamations of the crowd
mingle with the agonised regrets of Elisabeth and Carlos as
the curtain falls.
    Act II.   In an effort to forget the misery of the world,
Carlos has taken refuge in the Convent of San Yuste, where
his grandfather, Charles V, before him had gone to end his

days. Monks are praying before the tomb of the great
Emperor, and one of them proclaims the uselessness of
expecting peace in this life. Don Carlos remembers the
curious stories to the effect that Charles V is not really dead
at all but still living peacefully as a forgotten monk, and
fancies he sees and hears a resemblance to his grandfather.
The bass solo with the chorus is highly impressive, the more
particularly since this is the first contact we have with the
influence of the Church, which is to be one of the
dominating features of the opera. In the four-act version,
here occurs Don Carlos's romance.

Carlos is overjoyed to see Rodrigo, Marquess of Posa, his
greatest friend, lately returned from Flanders. Carlos confides
to him that he loves none other than his own stepmother—
will his friend turn from him at the news? Rodrigo expresses
his determination to help him, and bids him devote himself
to the cause of the oppressed people of Flanders, and forget
his own troubles in his efforts to right their wrongs. They
swear eternal friendship, 'Dio, che nell'alma infondere amor'
(God, who has filled our hearts), to a theme which is heard
frequently throughout the opera. It has always seemed to me
a noble expression of feeling, but has sometimes been
criticised for its supposed banality:

A procession passes in front of the tomb, and the King
himself is seen leading his Queen by the hand. The sight is
almost too much for Carlos, but he is sustained by Rodrigo,
and by the voice of the mysterious monk, who leads the
chanting. The scene ends with a reiteration of the friendship
theme.

The scene changes to a garden outside the monastery. The
Queen's entourage wait for their mistress, and Princess Eboli,
supported by the irrepressible Tebaldo, wiles away the time
by singing the song of the veil, a Moorish love-romance. With

s ambitious cadenzas and rapid coloratura, it is a fine
isplay piece for the mezzo-soprano who sings Eboli.[1]

The Queen leaves the church and makes her way to where
er ladies are waiting for her. Rodrigo is announced, and
ives her a letter he has brought from her mother in Paris, at
he same time slipping a note from Carlos into her hand. She
eads the message, while Rodrigo takes Eboli aside to tell her
he latest news from Paris. The conversation between the two
nd the asides from Elisabeth are carried on to the
ccompaniment of a graceful dance rhythm, which most
uccessfully suggests the elegant court atmosphere. Elisabeth
hanks Rodrigo and bids him ask some favour. He will, but
ot for himself. In a short aria ('Carlo ch'è sol il nostro
more') he asks for her help and influence with the King in
cquiring for Carlos what he most desires, an interview with
is father. Eboli, who is in love with Carlos, is struck with the
hought that the agitation she has noticed in him when she
as been in attendance on the Queen may be due to
ndeclared love for herself. Elisabeth signifies to Rodrigo
hat she will see her son, and he contrives to manoeuvre the
adies out of hearing so that the interview takes place in
rivate.

Carlos enters and greets his mother formally, asking for her
nfluence in persuading the King to send him to Flanders. But
is outward calm is not proof against contact with the person
e loves, and he bitterly reproaches her for her seeming in-
lifference, which, she tells him, is no more than the duty she
wes his father. In music of melting tenderness, Carlos shows
hat he understands her meaning, but it is clear that love for
er still dominates his thoughts (example page 622).

Suddenly, he passes into a mood of exaltation and falls
enseless at Elisabeth's feet (the only reference in the opera to
he fits which appear to have been so common with the real
)on Carlos). Elisabeth for a moment fears he is dying, but in his
lelirium he once again proclaims his love for her. Coming to

[1] According to Andrew Porter (Proceedings of Royal Musical
Association, 15 · iv · 72) originally written in G when Eboli was cast
efore the Paris première with a young French mezzo-soprano; the aria
vas transposed up a tone by the composer when Pauline Gueymard, a
oprano hardly less celebrated than Marie Sass herself, was given the
ole. This accounts, says Andrew Porter, for the role of Eboli—begun
or an Azucena and completed for a Leonora—still proving so difficult
or a single mezzo (or a soprano) to compass.   H.

himself, he takes her in his arms, but she tears herself away demanding whether he means to murder his father and then lead his mother to the altar. With a cry of grief, Carlos rushes from her presence, and she is left asking for Heaven's assistance in her predicament.

The King leaves the church to find that his orders have been disobeyed and that the Queen is unattended. He dismisses the offending lady-in-waiting. Elisabeth ignores the affront to herself, and does her best to console the unhappy woman in a tender aria ('Non pianger mia compagna').

Philip watches until the Queen withdraws, followed by her ladies, but bids the Marquess of Posa remain behind. Why, he asks, has so tried and trusted a servant of Spain never asked him for a favour—preferment, or even an audience? Rodrigo answers that service is his reward; but there is a favour he would like to ask, not for himself, but for others. He pleads for a relaxation of the measures being taken against the people of Flanders, who are even now dying by the sword and starvation. Only severity, answers the King, can cure such infidels and rebels of their heresies; and he cites the contentment and peace of the people of Spain as an example of what he hopes to bring to the Flemish. It is the peace of desolation that he brings, replies Rodrigo. Let the King beware lest history say of him: 'This man was Nero!' Let him instead build an empire founded on freedom. The King tells him his dreams are those of youth; but let him have no fear of the throne, rather beware of the Grand Inquisitor, not only for his own sake but because the King wants him as counsellor. He confides his fear over Elisabeth and Carlos to Rodrigo, who takes this confidence in him as a sign that happier times may be at hand for all whom he loves. With a last warning to beware the Inquisition, the King dismisses Rodrigo from his presence.

The second act is dominated by the two duets. That for Elisabeth and Don Carlos is a most moving affair, with its wonderful characterisation of Carlos's hopeless love for Elisabeth and the suggestive description of of his delirium. The interview between Philip and Rodrigo shows Verdi's mastery in setting to music not only the clash involved between differing personalities but also the logical type of argument which takes place when the personalities involved are what we would call reasonable, intelligent beings.

Act III. A masked ball is in progress at the palace in Madrid (it was here that the ballet music originally occurred), and Carlos waits in the Queen's gardens in response to an anonymous note which he has received making the assignation. He sees what he thinks is Elisabeth, and pours out his love to her, until she unmasks and reveals that it is Eboli. He cannot conceal his dismay, and she accuses him of loving the Queen just as the watchful Rodrigo comes upon them. Carlos, he says, is not well and can be held responsible for neither his words nor his actions; but Eboli is not deceived, and in spite of Rodrigo's threat against her life, she promises to exert her power in bringing about their downfall. Rodrigo persuades Carlos to give him any incriminating papers he may have in his possession in case Eboli carries out her threats, and the curtain falls on a *fortissimo* statement in the orchestra of the theme of the oath of friendship.

The second scene is placed in the square in Madrid, where preparations are afoot for an *auto-da-fé*, the ceremonial punishment of heretics at the stake. The people rejoice in the might of Spain as a procession of monks precedes the mournful band of victims of the Inquisition. The members of the court, headed by the Queen, enter in procession, and, to the acclamation of the crowd and announced by a herald, Philip himself comes ceremonially through the door of the Cathedral, the Crown of Spain on his head. He repeats the oath which he swore before his coronation, to wage war against the enemies of the Faith. Led by Carlos, six deputies from Flanders fling themselves at his feet protesting their own loyalty and that of his Flemish subjects but begging for relief from their suffering. The King is adamant in his attitude toward them, and an ensemble develops in which some of the court and part of the crowd join in begging for mercy, others, led by the priests, demand death for the traitors and heretics.

Don Carlos stands before his father and asks that he may begin his training for the Crown which will one day adorn his brow by being put as the King's deputy at the head of his Flemish subjects. The King refuses a demand which would create a weapon which might one day be used against Spain itself. Carlos in desperation draws his sword and announces that he will save Flanders; consternation fills the bystanders that he should have dared to draw his sword in the presence of the King. Philip orders that he be disarmed, but no one dare obey, until Rodrigo, who sees that he is otherwise lost, quietly asks for his sword and gives it to the King. The procession advances, the sound of the monks singing the death-knell of the heretics can be heard, and over all a voice from heaven promises peace in the next world to those who are suffering so much in this.

Act IV.   The first scene takes place in Philip's own room, where, for the first time in the opera, we see him alone, as a man and not only as a king. In his monologue he betrays his anxiety, more, his acute misery over the failure of his marriage, his loneliness not only as a king, because his state demands it, but as a man, because his wife has no love for him in her heart. The Grand Inquisitor is announced, an old man, ninety years of age, blind but walking erect with the aid of a stick.

He has been sent for; may he know why? The King explains that his son has offended grievously and has publicly taken the part of the heretic Flemish; he intends to exact no penalty from him at all, or else to punish him with nothing less than death. If he decides on the latter alternative, has he the support of Holy Church in so extreme a measure? The Inquisitor says that God was not afraid to give His only Son that the world might be saved. Has the King nothing more to ask of him? No. Then it is his duty, as Inquisitor, to speak to him as the King. The fault of the impetuous Carlos is as nothing to that committed by the man he wishes to denounce: the Marquess of Posa. The King will not agree to this sacrifice, and is castigated by the Inquisitor as a man whose heart is not wholly given to God. Refusing to make any concession whatsoever, the Inquisitor goes his way, leaving behind him a sadder man.

No sooner has the Inquisitor left than Elisabeth rushes into Philip's presence, demanding the King's help in regaining her casket of jewels, which has disappeared from her room. He asks her coldly if what she seeks is the casket on his table; she opens it to reveal a portrait of Carlos. Philip denounces what he describes as her adultery in phrases of ever mounting tension, and Elisabeth faints. Eboli and Rodrigo answer the King's call for help, and Philip himself expresses his bitter regret at his rash and cruel suspicion. Eboli is stricken with conscience at what her jealousy of Carlos and Elisabeth have brought about—it was she who suggested the King look in the jewel case—and Rodrigo sees in the crisis a situation from which he can only rescue Carlos by taking his place as offering on the altar of liberty. The Queen revives and voices her loneliness and desolation. The two men leave the room and Eboli throws herself at the feet of the Queen to confess a double fault: that she has excited the King's suspicions because of her own jealousy, and that she herself has been guilty of the adultery of which she suspected Elisabeth—she has in fact been the King's mistress. Elisabeth's dignity remains unshaken, but she orders Eboli to leave her presence for ever and choose exile or life in a nunnery if she is to expiate her crime. Left alone, Eboli pours forth her grief and misery at what her fatal beauty has brought about; one thing only remains for her to do before she leaves the court for the last time—she must do whatever is in her power to save Carlos from the threat of death which hangs over him.

The first scene of Act IV of *Don Carlos* is one of the finest in all Verdi's operas. A mere catalogue of what it contains is

perhaps enough to give some idea of its varied, many-sided
nature, and yet to suggest the strong dramatic line which runs
through it all. It begins with the greatest of all Verdi's bass
arias, the *scena* 'Ella giammai m'amò' (She has no love for
me), a remarkable portrayal of the King's anguish and
loneliness (example on page 625).

There follows the duet between the two basses, a uniquely
varied piece of writing, whose strength is unsurpassed, one
makes bold to say, in any operatic music. The clash of
personalities is extraordinary, the King, bigot though he is,
still relying on logic and reason for his argument, the
Inquisitor, impregnable in his privileged stronghold, carrying
logic and argument before him in his religious conviction.

At the end, after the King has twice made unsuccessful
attempts at reconciliation or at any rate at a kind of working
peace, his reserve breaks down, and in a mighty two-octave
phrase spanning the bass's top and bottom F's he demands
rhetorically whether the throne must always bow the knee to
the altar. The short scene between Philip and Elisabeth,
particularly the King's measured cursing of his wife's
infidelity, is excellent, as is the equally brief but no less
expressive scene between Eboli and Elisabeth, and the
quartet which divides the two is equally remarkable. It is

dominated by Philip's rising phrase, but the Queen's revival from her swoon is marvellously done, and the whole quartet is a splendid example of Verdi's ensemble writing. To crown an act of almost unmatched richness, we have 'O don fatale' (O fatal beauty), a superb, economical piece of construction, which brings the act to an appropriate close and ends Eboli's appearances in a blaze of musical glory.

Scene ii is set in Carlos's prison. To him comes Rodrigo, knowing that the letters from Flanders which were originally addressed to Carlos have been found in his possession and that his days are therefore numbered. He bids farewell to his friend in an expressive aria, 'Per me giunto è il dì supremo' (The last day for me has dawned). A shot rings out and he falls mortally wounded by an assassin who has crept into the prison after him and discharged his arquebus into his back. He tells Carlos ('O Carlo ascolta') that the Queen will wait for him on the following day outside the Convent of San Yuste and will see him for the last time. He dies happy, he says, at the thought that in Carlos a champion of liberty survives him. The act often ends here.

Philip makes an attempt to give back his sword to his son, but Carlos spurns him as the murderer of his friend. A noise can be heard; it is a mob which has gained entrance to the prison building, crying for liberty and the release of Don Carlos. Eboli herself is with them, making a last effort to save Carlos from the results of his folly. The people demand that Carlos be given up to them, but at this moment the Inquisitor appears as if from nowhere and castigates the crowd which has dared to raise its hand against the Lord's anointed; let them go down on their knees before him. Once more, the Church has come to the rescue of the throne.

Act V. The scene is the cloister of San Yuste. Elisabeth kneels at the tomb of Charles V. She sings sadly of the joys she once knew, of her native France and her love for the youthful Don Carlos, and of the sorrow she now has in parting from him for ever: 'Tu che le vanità conoscesti del mondo' (Thou who knowest the hearts and the frailty of mortals). The wide-ranging melody shows Elisabeth at

S'an-cor si pian-ge in cie - - lo,

full stature as a mature person, and does something to give the lie to those who look upon this as one of Verdi's less interesting heroines.

The exquisite phrase, originally heard in the duet in Act I and since then associated with her youth in France, recurs as she remembers her past happiness (example on p. 619). The aria finishes with a renewal of her prayer for peace, ending exquisitely *ppp*.

Elisabeth and Carlos meet for a last farewell, and recall the happiness that might have been theirs, turning their attention however from the past and present toward the future, which holds for Carlos a career devoted to the liberal causes that Rodrigo loved so well. It is the last of their three extensive duets, and worthy of the richness of the two that went before. As they take their leave of one another, Philip comes from his hiding-place, seizes Elisabeth, and demands that the Grand Inquisitor, who is with him, shall do his duty towards Carlos. The old priest orders his guards to seize the prince, but Carlos defends himself and backs toward the tomb of Charles V at the rear of the cloister. Suddenly, a voice can be heard coming from it, and the Emperor himself (or a monk in his guise) appears and takes his grandson into the safety of the cloister. The ending has been much criticised as a weakened version of Schiller, where Philip hands his son over to the mercy of the Inquisition, and in some productions an attempt has been made to return to Schiller's original.

Don Carlos is in almost every respect a magnificent opera, weakened only by one less than first-class scene (the spectacular *auto-da-fé*, which refuses to touch the heights, unlike the triumph scene in *Aida*), and by its excessive length—the five-act production in Florence in 1950, even with some cuts, played with intervals for over five hours! It contains Verdi's greatest bass role and one of the greatest of his mezzo-soprano roles; two superb singing roles in Elisabeth and Carlos; and an opportunity for a notable baritone to re-create out of the slightly reduced figure of Posa the great liberal of Schiller's play. It also contains one of the most perfect climactic scenes in all Verdi, the first of the fourth act, in which the diverse threads of the drama, which have been developed in the five preceding scenes, are drawn together. The two scenes which follow resolve the conflicts which it has brought to a head—in Act IV, scene ii, Catholic Spain *v.* Protestant Flanders, liberal Rodrigo *v.* established authority

(Crown and Church), Church *v.* State; in Act V, Elisabeth *v.* Eboli (over Carlos), and Philip *v.* Carlos (over Elisabeth and Flanders). With these five major issues at stake, it is hardly surprising that the opera is a long one, any more than it is surprising that the subject elicited some of Verdi's most memorable music. H.

AIDA

Opera in four acts by Giuseppe Verdi; text by Antonio Ghislanzoni from the French prose of Camille du Locle, plot by Mariette Bey. Première at Cairo on December 24, 1871, with Pozzoni, Grossi, Mongini, Steller, Medini, Costa, Bottardi, conductor Bottesini. First performed at la Scala, Milan, February 8, 1872, with Stolz, Waldmann, Fancelli, Pandolfini, Maini, conductor Verdi; New York, 1873; Covent Garden, 1876, with Patti, Gindele, Nicolini, Graziani, Capponi, Feitlinger, conductor Bevignani; Her Majesty's Theatre, 1880 (in English), with Minnie Hauk, J. Yorke, Maas, Ludwig, Conly, conductor Randegger. Continuously in the repertories of all leading opera houses. Famous as Aida have been Lilli Lehmann, Nordica, Eames, Gadski, Destinn, Russ, Boninsegna, Raisa, Muzio, Rethberg, Giannini, Ponselle, Arangi-Lombardi, Turner, Cigna, Caniglia, Milanov, Welitsch, Leontyne Price; as Radames: Tamagno, Caruso, Zenatello, Slezak, Martinelli, Pertile, Lauri-Volpi, Merli, Vinay, del Monaco; as Amneris: Mantelli, Homer, Kirkby Lunn, Mildenburg, Edyth Walker, Matzenauer, Onegin, Minghini-Cattaneo, Stignani, Castagna, Wettergren, Simionato.

CHARACTERS

Aida, *Amneris's Ethiopian slave* . . . . Soprano
Amneris, *Daughter of the King of Egypt* Mezzo-Soprano
Amonasro, *King of Ethiopia, father of Aida* . . . Baritone
Radames, *Captain of the Egyptian Guard* . . . . Tenor
Ramphis, *High Priest of Egypt* . . . . Bass
The King of Egypt . . . . Bass
Messenger . . . . Tenor
Priests, Soldiers, Ethiopian Slaves, Prisoners,
Egyptians, etc.
Time: Epoch of the Pharaohs   *Place:* Memphis and Thebes

Aida was commissioned by Ismail Pasha, Khedive of Egypt, for the Italian Theatre in Cairo, which opened in November, 1869. The opera was produced there December 24, 1871, not at the opening of the house, as is sometimes erroneously stated. Its success was sensational.

Equally enthusiastic was its reception when brought out at la Scala, Milan, February 8, 1872, under the direction of Verdi himself, who was recalled thirty-two times and presented with an ivory baton and diamond star with the name of Aida in rubies and his own in other precious stones.[1]

It is an interesting fact that *Aida* reached New York before it did any of the great European opera houses save la Scala. It was produced at the Academy of Music under the direction of Max Strakosch, November 26, 1873. I am glad to have heard that performance and several other performances of it that season. For the artists who appeared in it gave a representation that for brilliancy has not been surpassed if, indeed, it has been equalled. In support of this statement it is only necessary to say that Italo Campanini was Radames, Victor Maurel Amonasro, and Annie Louise Cary Amneris. No greater artists have appeared in these rôles in America. Mlle. Torriani, the Aida, while not so distinguished, was entirely adequate. Nanneti as Ramphis, the high priest, Scolara as the King, and Boy as the Messenger, completed the cast.

I recall some of the early comment on the opera. It was said to be Wagnerian. In point of fact *Aida* is Wagnerian only as compared with Verdi's earlier operas. Compared with Wagner himself, it is Verdian—purely Italian. It was said that the fine melody for the trumpets on the stage in the pageant scene was plagiarised from a theme in the Coronation March of Meyerbeer's *Prophète*. Slightly reminiscent the passage is, and, of course, stylistically the entire scene is on Meyerbeerian lines; but these resemblances are no longer of importance.

Paris failed to hear *Aida* until April 1876, and then at the Théâtre Italien, instead of at the Grand Opéra, where it was not heard until March 1880, when Maurel was the Amonasro and Edouard de Reszke, later a favourite basso at the Metropolitan Opera House, the King. In 1855 Verdi's opera, *Les Vêpres Siciliennes* (The Sicilian Vespers) had been produced at the Grand Opéra and occurrences at the rehearsals had greatly angered the composer. The orchestra clearly showed a disinclination to follow the composer's minute directions regarding the manner in which he wished his work interpreted. When, after a conversation with the chef d'orchestre, the only result was plainly an attempt to

---

[1] It is now in the museum of la Scala, Milan.   H.

annoy him, he put on his hat, left the theatre, and did not return. In 1867 his *Don Carlos* met only with a *succès d'estime* at the Opéra. He had not forgotten these circumstances, when the Opéra wanted to give *Aida*. He withheld permission until 1880. But when at last this was given, he assisted at the production, and the public authorities vied in atoning for the slights put upon him so many years before. The President of France gave a banquet in his honour and he was created a Grand Officer of the National Order of the Legion of Honour.

When the Khedive asked Verdi to compose a new opera especially for the new opera house at Cairo, and inquired what the composer's terms would be, Verdi demanded $20,000. This was agreed upon and he was then given the subject he was to treat, *Aida*, which had been suggested to the Khedive by Mariette Bey, the great French Egyptologist. The composer received the rough draft of the story. From this Camille du Locle, a former director of the Opéra Comique, who happened to be visiting Verdi at Busseto, wrote a libretto in French prose, 'scene by scene, sentence by sentence', as he has said, adding that the composer showed the liveliest interest in the work and himself suggested the double scene in the finale of the opera. The French prose libretto was translated into Italian verse by Antonio Ghislanzoni, who wrote more than sixty opera librettos, *Aida* being the most famous. Mariette Bey brought his archaeological knowledge to bear upon the production. 'He revived Egyptian life of the time of the Pharaohs; he rebuilt ancient Thebes, Memphis, the Temple of Phtah; he designed the costumes and arranged the scenery. And under these exceptional circumstances, Verdi's new opera was produced.'

Verdi's score was ready a year before the work had its première, the production being delayed by force of circumstances. Scenery and costumes were made by French artists, but before these accessories could be shipped to Cairo, the Franco-Prussian war broke out. They could not be got out of Paris, and their delivery was delayed accordingly

Does the score of *Aida* owe any of its charm, passion, and dramatic stress to the opportunity thus afforded Verdi of going over it and carefully revising it, after he had considered it finished? Quite possibly. For we know that he made changes, eliminating, for instance, a chorus in the style of Palestrina, which he did not consider suitable to the priesthood of Isis. Even this one change resulted in condensation, a valuable quality, and in leaving the exotic music of the temple scene entirely free to exert to the full its fascination of local colour and atmosphere.

The story is unfolded in four acts and seven scenes.

Act I, scene i.   After a very brief but beautiful prelude, based on the theme associated with Aida (heard at the outset) and a descending figure later connected with the priests, the curtain rises on a hall in the King's palace at Memphis. Through a high gateway at the back are seen the temples and palaces of Memphis and the pyramids.

It has been supposed that, after the invasion of Ethiopia by the Egyptians, the Ethiopians would be a long time in recovering from their defeat. But Amonasro, their king, has swiftly rallied the remnants of his defeated army, gathered new levies to his standard, and crossed the frontier—all this with such extraordinary rapidity that the first news of it has reached the Egyptian court in Memphis through a messenger hot-foot from Thebes with the startling word that the sacred city itself is threatened.

While the priests are sacrificing to Isis in order to learn from the goddess whom she chooses as leader of the Egyptian forces, Radames, a young warrior, indulges in the hope that he may be the choice. To this hope he joins the further one that, returning victorious, he may ask the hand in marriage of Aida, an Ethiopian slave of the Egyptian King's daughter, Amneris. To these aspirations he gives expression in the romance, 'Celeste Aida' (Radiant Aida).

Ce - leste A - i - da

It ends effectively with the following phrase:

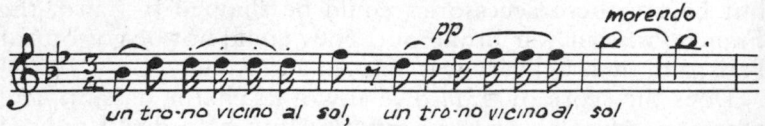

un tro-no vicino al sol,   un tro-no vicino al sol

He little knows that Aida is of royal birth or that Amneris herself, the King's daughter, is in love with him and, having noted the glances he has cast upon Aida, is fiercely jealous of her—a jealousy that forms the mainspring of the story and leads to its tragic dénouement.

A premonition of the emotional forces at work in the plot is given in the 'Vieni, o diletta' (Come dearest friend), beginning as a duet between Amneris and Aida and later becoming a trio for them and Radames. In this the Princess feigns friendship for Aida, but, in asides, discloses her jealous hatred of her.

Meanwhile the Egyptian hosts have gathered before the temple. There the King anounces that the priests of Isis have learned from the lips of that goddess the name of the warrior who is to lead the army—Radames! It is the Princess herself who, at this great moment in his career, places the royal standard in his hands. But amid the acclaims that follow, as Radames, to the strains of march and chorus, is conducted by the priests to the temple of Phtah to be invested with the consecrated armour, Amneris notes the fiery look he casts upon Aida. Is this the reason Radames, young, handsome, brave, has failed to respond to her own guarded advances? Is she, a princess, to find a successful rival in her own slave?

Meanwhile Aida herself is torn by conflicting emotions. She loves Radames. When the multitude shouts 'Ritorna vincitor!' (Victorious return!) she joins in the acclamation. Yet it is against her own people he is going to give battle, and the Ethiopians are led by the king, Amonasro, her father. For she, too, is a princess, as proud a princess in her own land as Amneris herself, and it is because she is a captive and a slave that her father has so swiftly rallied his army and invaded Egypt in a desperate effort to rescue her, facts which for obvious reasons she has carefully concealed from her captors.

It is easy to imagine Aida's agonised feelings since Radames has been chosen head of the Egyptian army. If she prays to her gods for the triumph of the Ethiopian arms, she is betraying her lover. If she asks the gods of victory to smile upon Radames, she is a traitress to her father, who has taken up arms to free her, and to her own people. Small wonder if she exclaims, as she contemplates her own wretched state:

'Never on earth was heart torn by more cruel agonies. The sacred names of father, lover, I can neither utter nor remember. For the one—for the other—I would weep, I would pray!'

The lines to which Aida's aria is set have been highly praised. They furnished the composer with opportunity, of which he made full use, to express conflicting emotions in music of dramatic force and the concluding passage, 'Numi pietà' (Pity, kind heaven), is of extraordinary beauty:

Nu-mi pie-tà Del mio sof-frir! Spe-me non v'ha del mio do lor

Scene ii.   Ramphis, the high priest, at the foot of the altar; priests and priestesses; and afterwards Radames are shown in the Temple of Vulcan at Memphis. A mysterious light descends from above. A long row of columns, one behind the other, is lost in the darkness; statues of various deities are visible; in the middle of the scene, above a platform rises the altar, surmounted by sacred emblems. From golden tripods comes the smoke of incense.

A chant of the priestesses, accompanied by harps, is heard from the interior. Radames enters unarmed. While he approaches the altar, the priestesses execute a sacred dance. On the head of Radames is placed a silver veil. He is invested with consecrated armour, while the priests and priestesses resume the religious chant and dance.

The entire scene is saturated with local colour—piquant, exotic, it is as Egyptian to the ear as to the eye. You see the temple, you hear the music of its devotees, and that music sounds as distinctively Egyptian as if Mariette Bey had unearthed two examples of ancient Egyptian temple music and placed them at the composer's disposal. It is more likely, however, that the themes are original with Verdi and the Oriental tone colour, which makes the music of the scene so fascinating, is due to his employment of certain intervals peculiar to the music of Eastern people. The interval, which, falling upon Western ears, gives an Oriental sound to the scale, consists of three semi-tones. In the very Eastern sounding themes in the temple scenes in *Aida*, these intervals are G to F flat, and D to C flat.

The sacred chant

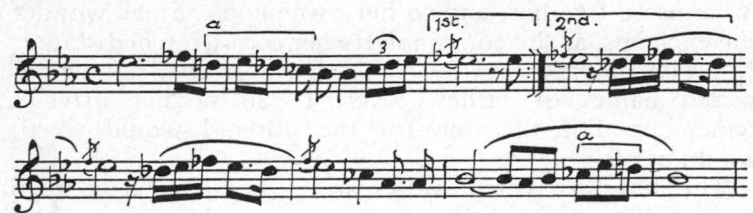

twice employs the interval between D and C flat, the first time descending, the second time ascending, in which latter it sounds more characteristic to us, because we regard the scale as having an upward tendency, whereas in Oriental systems the scale seems to have been regarded as tending downward.

In the sacred dance

the interval is from G to F flat. The intervals, where employed in the two music examples just cited, are bracketed. The interval of three semi-tones—the characteristic of the Oriental scale—could not be more clearly shown than it is under the second bracket of the sacred dance.

Act II, scene i.   In this scene, which takes place in a hall in the apartments of Amneris, the Princess adopts strategy to discover if Aida returns the passion which she suspects in Radames. Messengers have arrived from the front with news that Radames has put the Ethiopians to utter rout and is returning with many trophies and captives. Naturally Aida is distraught. Is her lover safe? Was her father slain? It is while Aida's mind and heart are agitated by these questions that Amneris chooses the moment to test her feelings and wrest from her the secret she longs yet dreads to fathom.

The Princess is reclining on a couch in her apartment in the palace at Thebes, whither the court has repaired to welcome the triumphant Egyptian army. Slaves are adorning her for the festival or agitating the air with large feather fans. Moorish slave boys dance for her delectation and her attendants sing:

> While on thy tresses rain
> Laurels and flowers interwoven,
> Let songs of glory mingle
> With strains of tender love.

In the midst of these festive preparations Aida enters, and Amneris, craftily feigning sympathy for her lest she be grieving over the defeat of her people and the possible loss in battle of someone dear to her, affects to console her by telling her that Radames, the leader of the Egyptians, has been slain.

It is not necessary for the Princess to watch the girl intently in order to note the effect upon her of the sudden and cruelly contrived announcement. Almost as suddenly, having feasted her eyes on the slave girl's grief, the Princess exclaims: 'I have deceived you; Radames lives!'

'He lives!' Tears of gratitude instead of despair now moisten Aida's eyes as she raises them to Heaven.

'You love him; you cannot deny it!' cries Amneris, forgetting in her furious jealousy her dignity as a Princess. 'But know, you have a rival. Yes—in me. You, my slave, have a rival in your mistress, a daughter of the Pharaohs!'

Having fathomed her slave's secret, she vents the refined cruelty of her jealous nature upon the unfortunate girl by commanding her to be present at the approaching triumphant entry of Radames and the Egyptian army:

'Come, follow me, and you shall learn if you can contend with me—you, prostrate in the dust, I on the throne beside the king!'

What has just been described is formulated by Verdi in a duet for Amneris and Aida, 'Fu la sorte dell'armi a' tuoi funesta' ('Neath the chances of battle succumb thy people), which expresses the craftiness and subtlety of the Egyptian Princess, the conflicting emotions of Aida, and the dramatic stress of the whole episode.

This phrase especially expresses the combined haughtiness and jealousy in the attitude of Amneris toward Aida:

Scene ii.   Brilliant indeed is the spectacle to which Aida is compelled to proceed with the Princess. It is near a group of palms at the entrance to the city of Thebes that the King has elected to give Radames his triumph. Here stands the temple of Ammon. Beyond it a triumphal gate has been erected. When the King enters to the cheers of the multitude and followed by his gaudily clad court, he takes his seat on the throne surmounted by a purple canopy. To his left sits Amneris, singling out for her disdainful glances the most unhappy of her slaves.

A blast of trumpets, and the victorious army begins its defile past the throne. After the foot-soldiers come the chariots of war; then the bearers of the sacred vases and statues of the gods, and a troupe of dancing girls carrying the loot of victory. A great flourish of trumpets, an outburst of acclaim, and Radames, proudly standing under a canopy borne high on the shoulders of twelve of his officers, is carried through the triumphal gate and into the presence of his King. As the young hero descends from the canopy, the monarch, too, comes down from the throne and embracing him exclaims:

'Saviour of your country, I salute you. My daughter with her own hand shall place the crown of laurels upon your brow.' And when Amneris, suiting her action to her father's words, crowns Radames, the King continues: 'Now ask of me whatever you most desire. I swear by my crown and by the sacred gods that nothing shall be denied to you this day!'

But although no wish is nearer the heart of Radames than to obtain freedom for Aida, he does not consider the moment as yet opportune. Therefore he requests that first the prisoners of war be brought before the King. When they enter, one of them, by his proud mien and spirited carriage, easily stands forth from the rest. Hardly has Aida set eyes upon him that she utters the startled exclamation, 'My father!'

It is indeed none other than Amonasro, the Ethiopian king, who, his identity unknown to the Egyptians, has been made captive by them. Swiftly gliding over to where Aida stands, he whispers to her not to betray his rank to his captors. Then, turning to the Egyptian monarch, he craftily describes how he has seen the king of Ethiopia dead at his feet from many wounds, and concludes by entreating clemency for the conquered. Not only do the other captives and Aida join in his prayer, but the people, moved by his words and by his noble aspect, beg their king to spare the prisoners. The priests, however, protest. The gods have delivered these enemies into the hands of Egypt; let them be put to death lest, emboldened by a pardon so easily obtained, they should rush to arms again.

Meanwhile Radames has had eyes only for Aida, while Amneris notes with rising jealousy the glances he turns upon her hated slave. At last Radames, carried away by his feelings, himself joins in the appeal for clemency. 'Oh, King,' he exclaims, 'by the sacred gods and by the splendour of your crown, you swore to grant my wish this day! Let it be life and liberty for the Ethiopian prisoners.' But the high priest urges that, even if freedom is granted to the others, Aida and

her father be detained as hostages and this is agreed upon.
Then the King, as a crowning act of glory for Radames, leads
Amneris forth, and addressing the young warrior, says:

'Radames, the country owes everything to you. Your
reward shall be the hand of Amneris. With her one day you
shall reign over Egypt.'

A great shout goes up from the multitude. Unexpectedly
Amneris sees herself triumphant over her rival, the dream of
her heart fulfilled, and Aida bereft of hope, since for
Radames to refuse the hand of his king's daughter would
mean treason and death. And so while all seemingly are
rejoicing, two hearts are sad and bewildered. For Aida, the
man she adores appears lost to her for ever, and all that is left
to her are the tears of hopeless love; while to Radames the
heart of Aida is worth more than the throne of Egypt, and its
gift, with the hand of Amneris, is like the unjust vengeance of
the gods descending upon his head.

This is the finale of the second act. It has been well said
that not only is it the greatest effort in this style of the
composer, but also one of the grandest conceptions of
modern musical and specifically operatic art. The
importance of the staging, the magnificence of the spectacle,
the diversity of characterisation, and the strength of action
of the drama all conspire to keep at an unusually high level
the inspiration of the composer.

The triumphal chorus, 'Gloria all'Egitto' (Glory to Egypt),
is sonorous and can be rendered with splendid effect. It is
preceded by a march.

Then comes the chorus of triumph.

Voices of women join in the acclaim.

The priests sound a warning note.

Del - la vit - to - ria a - gliarbi-tri su - pre-mi

The trumpets of the Egyptian troops execute a most brilliant modulation from A flat to B natural. The reference here is to the long, straight trumpets with three valves (only one of which, however, is used). These trumpets, in groups of three, precede the divisions of the Egyptian troops. The trumpets of the first group are tuned in A flat.

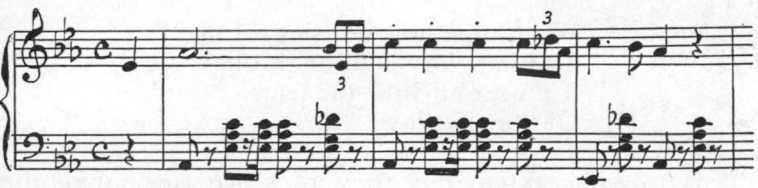

When a second group enters and intones the same stirring march theme in B natural,[1] the enharmonic modulation to a tone higher gives an immediate and vastly effective 'lift' to the music and the scene.

The entrance of Radames, borne on high under a canopy by twelve officers, is a dramatic climax to the spectacle. But a more emotional one is to follow.

The recognition of King Amonasro by his daughter; the supplication of the captives; the plea of Radames and the people in their favour; the vehement protests of the priests who, in the name of the gods of Egypt, demand their death;

---

[1] The conductor Edward Downes pointed out to me that when in 1925 Tutankhamen's tomb was opened, two trumpets were found inside, one tuned in A flat, the other in B natural, a coincidence, it is true, but a remarkable one!　　　　　　　　　　　　　　H.

the diverse passions which agitate Radames, Aida, and Amneris; the hope of vengeance that Amonasro cherishes—all these conflicting feelings are musically expressed with complete success. The structure is reared upon Amonasro's plea to the King for mercy for the Ethiopian captives, 'Ma tu, Re, tu signore possente' (But thou, O king, thou puissant lord).

Ma tu, Re, tu sig-no-re pos-sen-te

When the singer who takes the role of Amonasro is also a good actor, he will know how to convey, between the lines of this supplication, his secret thoughts and unavowed hope for the reconquest of his freedom and his country. After the Egyptian King has bestowed upon Radames the hand of Amneris, the chorus, 'Gloria all'Egitto', is heard again, and, above its sonorous measures, Aida's cry:

> What hope now remains for me?
> To him, glory and the throne:
> To me, oblivion—the tears
> Of hopeless love.

It is to some extent due to Verdi's management of the score to this elaborate scene that *Aida* not only has superseded all spectacular operas that came before it, but has held its own against and survived all those that have come since. Its predecessors were merely spectacular; in *Aida* the surface radiates and glows because beneath it seethe the fires of conflicting human passion. In other operas spectacle is merely spectacle; in *Aida* it clothes in brilliant habiliments the forces of impending tragedy.

Act III.   That tragedy further advances towards its consummation in the present act.

It is a beautiful moonlight night on the banks of the Nile—moonlight whose silvery rays are no more exquisite than the music that seems steeped in them. Half concealed in the foliage is the temple of Isis, from which issues the sound of women's voices, softly chanting. A boat approaches the shore and out of it steps Amneris and the high priest, with a train of closely veiled women and several guards. The Princess is about to enter upon a vigil in the temple to implore the favour of the goddess before her nuptials with Radames.

For a while after they have entered the temple, the shore
seems deserted. But from the shadow of a grove of palms
Aida cautiously emerges into the moonlight. In song she
breathes forth memories of her native land: 'Oh, patria mia,
mai più ti rivedrò' (Oh, native land, I ne'er shall see thee
more).

It is an aria whose freedom of form and richly expressive
melodies have won it admirers ever since the first performance, and there is no better known aria in the repertory
of the Italian dramatic soprano. Here Radames has asked
Aida to meet him. Is it for a last farewell? If so, the Nile shall
be her grave. She hears a swift footfall, and turning, in
expectation of seeing Radames, beholds her father. He has
fathomed her secret and divined that she is here to meet
Radames—the betrothed of Amneris! Cunningly Amonasro
works upon her feelings. Would she triumph over her rival? The
Ethiopians again are in arms. Again Radames is to lead the
Egyptians against them. Let her discover from him the path
which he intends to take with his army and that path shall be
converted into a fatal ambush.

At first the thought is abhorrent to Aida, but her father by
craftily inciting her love of country, and no less her jealousy
and despair, at last is able to wrest consent from her; then
draws back into the shadow as he hears Radames approaching.

It is difficult to bring Aida to make the designs of her
father agree with her love for the young Egyptian chief. But
the subtlety of the score, its warmth, its varied and ably
managed expression, make plausible the submission of the
young girl to the adjurations of Amonasro, and excusable a
decision of which she does not foresee the consequences. To
restore the crown to her father, to view again her own
country, to escape an ignominious servitude, to prevent her
lover becoming the husband of Amneris, her rival,—such are
the thoughts which assail her during this duet, and they are
quite capable of disturbing for a moment her better reason.

As she is still reluctant to lure from her lover the secret of
the route by which, in the newly planned invasion of her
country, the Egyptians expect to enter Ethiopia, Amonasro

changes his tactics and conjures up for her in music a vision o
the carnage among her people, and finally invokes he
mother's ghost, until, in *pianissimo*, dramatically contrasting
with the force of her father's savage imprecation, sh
whispers, 'O patria! quanto mi costi!' (Oh, native land! how
much thou demandest of me!).

This duet of Aida and Amonasro is in the line of Verdi'
most famous duets. Its dramatic effectiveness is enormou
and nowhere is there a better example of his skill i
advancing the drama in purely musical terms. Amonasr
clinches his ascendancy over Aida in a great phrase which is
close descendant of Leonora's in *Forza*.

Amonasro leaves. Aida awaits her lover. When she some
what coldly meets Radames's renewed declaration of love
with the bitter protest that the rites of another love are
awaiting him, he unfolds his plan to her. He will lead the
Egyptians to victory, and on returning with these fresh
laurels, he will prostrate himself before the King, lay bare his
heart to him, and ask for the hand of Aida as a reward for his
services to his country. But Aida is well aware of the power
of Amneris and that her vengeance would swiftly fall upon
them both. She can see but one course to safety—that
Radames join her in flight to her native land, where, amid
forest groves and the scent of flowers, and all forgetful of the
world, they will dream away their lives in love. This is the
beginning of the dreamy yet impassioned love duet—
'Fuggiam gli ardori inospiti' (Ah, fly from where these
burning skies). She implores him in passionate accents to
escape with her. Enthralled by the rapture in her voice,
thrilled by the vision of happiness she conjures up before
him, he forgets for the moment country, duty, all else save
love; and exclaiming, 'Love shall be our guide!' turns to fly
with her.

This duet, charged with exotic rapture, opens with
recitativo phrases for Aida. I have selected two passages for
quotation: 'Là tra foreste vergini' (There 'mid the virgin

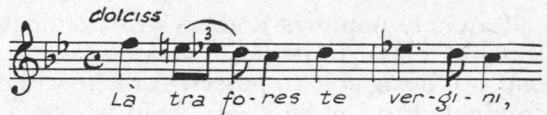

orest groves) and 'In estasi la terra scorderem' (In ecstasy the world forgotten).

But Aida, feigning alarm, asks:

'By what road shall we avoid the Egyptian host?'

'The path by which our troops plan to fall upon the enemy will be deserted until to-morrow.'

'And that path?'

'The pass of Napata.'

A voice echoes his words, 'The pass of Napata.'

'Who hears us?' exclaims Radames.

'The father of Aida and king of the Ethiopians,' and Amonasro issues forth from his hiding-place. He has uncovered the plan of the Egyptian invasion, but the delay has been fatal. For at the same moment there is a cry of 'Traitor!' from the temple.

It is the voice of Amneris, who with the high priest has overheard all. Amonasro, baring a dagger, would throw himself upon his daughter's rival, but Radames places himself between them and bids the Ethiopian king fly with Aida. Amonasro, drawing his daughter away with him, disappears in the darkness; while Radames, with the words, 'Priest of Isis, I remain with you,' delivers himself a prisoner into his hands.

Act IV, scene i. In a hall of the Royal Palace Amneris awaits the passage, under guard, of Radames to the dungeon where the priests are to sit in judgment upon him. She now bitterly repents the doom her jealousy is about to bring upon the man she loves and calls to the guard to bring Radames to her. Their duet is a magnificently dramatic passage as

Amneris alternately implores Radames to exculpate himself
and rages at his refusal to do so. Radames's world has fallen
around him: not being able to possess Aida he will die.

He is conducted to the dungeon, from where, as from the
bowels of the earth, she hears the sombre voices of the
priests.

Three times Ramphis accuses Radames of treason, and
three times Radames is silent in face of the accusation.

The dramatically condemnatory 'Traditor!' is a death-knell
for her lover in the ears of Amneris. And after each
accusation silence from Radames, and a cry from the priest
of 'Traitor!' Amneris realises only too well that his approaching doom is to be entombed alive. Her revulsions of feeling
from hatred to love and despair find vent in highly dramatic
musical phrases. In fact Amneris dominates this scene, which
with its frenzied curse of the cold-hearted priests, is one of
the most powerful passages for mezzo-soprano in all opera.

Scene ii. This is the famous double scene. The stage
setting is divided into two floors. The upper floor represents
the interior of the Temple of Vulcan, resplendent with light
and gold; the lower floor a subterranean hall and long rows of
arcades which are lost in the darkness. A colossal statue of
Osiris, with the hands crossed, sustains the pilasters of the
vault.

In the temple Amneris and the priestesses kneel in prayer.
And Radames? Immured in the dungeon and, as he thinks
doomed to perish alone, he sees a form slowly take shape in
the darkness, and his own name, uttered by the tender
accents of a familiar voice, falls upon his ear. It is Aida.
Anticipating the death to which he will be sentenced, she has
secretly made her way into the dungeon before his trial and
there hidden herself to find reunion with him in death. And
so, while in the temple above them the unhappy Amneris
kneels and implores the gods to vouchsafe Heaven to him
whose death she has compassed, Radames and Aida, blissful
in their mutual sacrifice, await the end.

From 'Celeste Aida', Radames's apostrophe to his beloved
with which the opera opens, to the muted passion and
unearthly stillness of 'O, terra, addio' (Oh, earth, farewell!)

O terra ad-dio; ad-di-o val-le di pian-ti

which is the swan song of Radames and Aida, united in death
in the stone-sealed vault—such is the tragic fate of love, as set
forth in this beautiful and eloquent score by Giuseppe Verdi.

K.

OTELLO

Opera in four acts by Giuseppe Verdi; text by Arrigo Boito, after
Shakespeare's play. Première at la Scala, Milan, February 5, 1887, with
Pantaleoni, Tamagno, Maurel, conductor Faccio. First performed in
New York, 1888, with Eva Tetrazzini, Marconi (later Campanini),
Galassi; Lyceum Theatre, London, 1889, with Cataneo, Tamagno,
Maurel, conductor Faccio; Covent Garden, 1891, with Albani, Jean de
Reszke, Maurel; Metropolitan, New York, 1894, with Albani, Tamagno,
Maurel. Revived Covent Garden, 1926, with Lehmann, Zenatello,
Stabile; 1928, with Sheridan, Zanelli, Inghilleri; 1933, with Pampanini,
Melchior, Rimini; 1937, with Ciani (later Norena), Martinelli, Formichi
(later Tibbett), conductor Beecham; 1950, by Company of la Scala,
Milan, with Tebaldi, Vinay, Bechi, conductor de Sabata; 1955, with
Brouwenstijn, Vinay, Otakar Kraus, under Kubelik. Revived at Metro-
politan, 1902, with Eames, Alvarez, Scotti; 1937, with Rethberg,
Martinelli, Tibbett, conductor Panizza. Revived at la Scala, 1927, with
Scacciati, Trantoul, Stabile, conductor Toscanini; 1935, with Caniglia,
Merli, Stabile, conductor Marinuzzi; 1938, with Caniglia, Merli, Biasini,
conductor de Sabata; 1942, with Caniglia, Lauri-Volpi, Stabile, con-
ductor Marinuzzi; 1947, with Caniglia, Vinay, Bechi, conductor de
Sabata. After Tamagno's death, Zenatello and Slezak became the
leading international exponents of the title role, to be followed by
Zanelli and later Martinelli, and (after 1945) by Vinay and del Monaco.
Other famous singers of the title role have included Pertile, Vickers,
McCracken and (in England) Frank Mullings.

CHARACTERS

Otello, *a Moor, general in the Venetian army* . . . . Tenor
Iago, *his ensign* . . . . Baritone
Cassio, *his lieutenant* . . . . Tenor
Roderigo, *a Venetian gentleman* . . . . Tenor
Lodovico, *ambassador of the Venetian republic* . . . Bass
Montano, *predecessor of Otello in Cyprus* . . . . Bass
A Herald . . . . Baritone
Desdemona, *wife to Otello* . . . . Soprano
Emilia, *Iago's wife and Desdemona's lady* Mezzo-Soprano
Soldiers and Sailors of the Republic, Venetian ladies and
gentlemen, Cypriot men and women

Time: End of the Fifteenth Century   *Place:* A seaport in Cyprus

Otello has been described as the 'perfect' opera. It first appeared nearly sixteen years after *Aida*, after which only the composition of the *Manzoni Requiem* (1884), itself a work on the very highest level, had shown the public that the ageing composer had not actually given up composition. In *Otello* Verdi was working with one of Italy's foremost poets, Boito, who was in his own right a composer of rank, to produce an opera at the very height of his powers. The enthusiasm engendered by its first performances gave way to something closer to respect as the years went by, but by now a performance of *Otello* which is not sold out is a rarity, and the opera is as much a part of the repertory—in spite of the difficulty of casting the title rôle—as *Don Giovanni* or *Tristan*.

In *Otello* as in *Macbeth*, his previous Shakespearean opera, Verdi had a hand in the construction of the libretto, although Boito must have the credit for the remarkable feat of compression which has gone toward it. In Shakespeare's play there are nearly 3,500 lines; in the opera under 800. The Venetian scenes have been cut out, and each of the four acts plays without a break with (in the modern, not the Shakespearean sense) no more than a single change of scene (in Act III).

In Act I, the chorus waits for the arrival of the victorious Otello's ship out of the storm. Iago meanwhile plots with Roderigo and succeeds later in making Cassio drunk; there is a fight which is interrupted by Otello, who deprives Cassio of his office. Desdemona enters and the act ends with a duet.

In Act II, Iago advises Cassio to look for reinstatement as Otello's lieutenant through Desdemona's influence, and, left alone, soliloquises on the futility of life and the glory of evil (the 'Credo'). There follows the first phase of the planting of the seed of jealousy in Otello's heart, an interruption from women of the island who come to serenade Desdemona, her pleading of Cassio's cause, the offer of the handkerchief to bind Otello's head and Iago's theft of it as it falls. Iago presses his advantage and Otello's peace is gone. The account of Cassio's dream leads to the joint oath of vengeance which ends the act.

The Venetian ambassadors are announced as in harbour at the beginning of Act III, when Otello asks Desdemona for the handkerchief, is put off, and finishes by insulting her. Iago stations him behind a column to see Cassio play unwittingly with the handkerchief, and the two plot Desdemona's death

n half a dozen sentences as the ambassadors enter. Their
reception, the striking of Desdemona, and a general ensemble
lead to Otello's frantic dismissal of the assembly; he lies
prostrate as the curtain falls.

Act IV, in Desdemona's bedroom, consists of the Willow
Song and prayer, the murder of Desdemona and the death of
Otello.

Act I.   In the background, a quay and the sea; a tavern
with an arbour; it is evening. After the crashing opening
chord, Otello's ship can be seen making for port through a
heavy storm. Among the crowd of watchers who exclaim
upon the danger to the vessel, are Iago and Roderigo. The
storm prepares vividly for our first encounter with Otello,
who is, as it is obvious he must be, the dominating figure of
the opera. His opening shout of triumph, 'Esultate! l'orgoglio
musulmano sepolto è in mar' (Hear glad tidings. Our wars are
done. The ocean has whelmed the Turk), makes a splendid
entrance, and shows the warrior in all his glory, unhurried
and unrivalled, in a way that perhaps Shakespeare without
the help of music never quite achieves.

Otello ascends the steps to the quay, is acclaimed by the
crowd, and proceeds to the castle followed by Cassio,
Montano, and soldiers. The people start a wood fire and
gather about it dancing and singing: 'Fuoco di gioia' (Flame
brightly burning). It transpires in talk between Iago and
Roderigo that Iago hates Otello, to whom he is outwardly so
devoted, because he has advanced Cassio over him, and that
Roderigo is in love with Desdemona.

The fire dies out, the storm has ceased. Now comes the
scene in which Iago purposely makes Cassio drunk, in order
to cause his undoing, He sings a drinking song, 'Inaffia
l'ugola' (Then let me the canakin clink), which Cassio tries
unsuccessfully to repeat after him; under the influence of the
liquor Cassio resents the taunts of Roderigo, which Iago has

instigated. Montano tries to quiet them, Cassio draws, and i
the fight that follows Montano is wounded. The tumul
brings Otello to the scene, and, with an imperious call, h
brings the brawl to an end (Boito's use of 'Keep up you
bright swords'—'Abbasso le spade'—at this point is evidence o
his care for detail). Cassio is dismissed from the Moor'
service and Iago has scored his first triumph.

The people disperse, quiet settles upon the scene, an
Otello and Desdemona are alone. At her first musica
entrance, Desdemona is to some extent characterised by he
very isolation, far more so than if she had been shown on th
quayside to welcome her husband. Her presence brings fort
an entirely new aspect of Otello's character. So far, we hav
seen only the man of authority, but in the love duet Otell
the poet is put forward with a persuasiveness that is to kee
this side of him fresh in the minds of the audience, howeve
low he may fall for the rest of the drama. For the duet Boit

has used lines from the Senate scene of Shakespeare's Act I
and also from Othello's welcome to Desdemona in Cyprus.

This is Verdi's only full-scale love duet in which there is n
sense of urgency or restriction; all the previous examples
however beautiful, have been either illicit or liable to inter
ruption at every moment. In his music, the composer encom
passes the sensitivity of both lovers, the mature ye
impetuous Otello, the serene but passionate Desdemona
frequently giving them the same phrases to sing, yet alway
differentiating the one from the other with the surest an
most delicate touch imaginable. Just before the close of th
act, Otello embraces Desdemona; the musical phrase is use
again before the end of the opera:

The music is in the form of one of those long, quasi-conversational duets which the composer made so peculiarly his own, and which, from his very earliest operas to this one, are to be the vehicles of some of his most subtle expression. There would be many to support the claim that this is the most beautiful love music ever written.

Act II. A hall on the ground floor of the castle. Iago, planning to make Otello jealous of Desdemona, counsels Cassio to induce the Moor's wife to plead for his reinstatement. When he is alone, Iago sings his famous Credo: 'Credo in un Dio crudel che m'ha creato simile a sè' (I believe in a cruel God, who has fashioned me in his own image). Though this is generally looked on as a masterpiece of invective, it could be regarded as a simplification of Shakespeare's Iago, the lines and the sentiments being original to Boito. Declamatory trumpets are conspicuous in the accompaniment.

Iago, seeing Otello approach, leans against a column and looks fixedly in the direction of Desdemona and Cassio, exclaiming, as Otello enters, 'Ha! I like not that.' As in the corresponding scene in the play, this leads up to the questioning of him by Otello and to Iago's crafty answers, which not only apply the match to, but later fan the flame of Otello's jealousy. The temptation of Otello by Iago is set to music that is suggestive and fluid to a marked degree. Every word has due weight, and the rising temperature of the music throughout the act is exactly calculated to fit the growing and unremitting intensity of the play at this point.

Now comes the interruption of the madrigal; by its end, Otello is once more under the spell of Desdemona's beauty and transparent innocence, and is prepared to put suspicion behind him. But in a moment she has asked him to pardon Cassio, has asked again when he refuses gently to consider the subject at such a juncture, and then accused him of ill-temper in his answer. In the quartet which follows, between Desdemona, Emilia, Otello and Iago, the poison works, and

at its end Otello dismisses Desdemona, but not before Iago
has had the opportunity to steal the handkerchief round
which so much of the rest of the plot is to turn.

Otello and Iago are left alone again, and Otello voices his
grief at the loss of his peace of mind in his present wretched
and suspicious state: 'Ora e per sempre addio' (Now and for
ever, farewell). It is the equivalent of the farewell to arms in
the play, and the type of musical expression used here is far
more straightforward than in the earlier part of the act, as
befits Otello decided as compared with Otello perplexed.

Iago makes pretence of calming him, but to such a fury is
the Moor aroused that he seizes Iago, hurls him to the
ground, and threatens to kill him should his accusations
against Desdemona prove false. Iago ventures on yet another
and bolder step, and describes a dream he says Cassio has had
while sharing a room with him. He talked openly in his sleep
of his love for Desdemona, and Iago describes what ensued in
wonderfully suggestive music:

He caps it all by telling Otello that he has even seen the
handkerchief, which Otello gave his wife when they were
married, in the hands of Cassio.

Otello's rage knows no limits, and in music of relentless
fury, he pledges himself to prove Desdemona's guilt and to
avenge it; Iago joins him in his oath: 'Sì, pel ciel marmoreo
giuro' (Witness yon marble heaven):

Act III.   The great hall of the castle; at the back a terrace.
After a brief scene in which the approach of the ambassadors
is announced, Desdemona enters. Wholly unaware of the cause
of Otello's strange actions towards her, she again begins to
plead for Cassio's restoration to favour:

Allegro moderato

Dio ti gio-con-dyospo-so del-l'alma mi-a so-vra - - no

Boito has used Otello's insistence on the handkerchief while Desdemona urges Cassio's reinstatement, and combined it with part of the so-called 'brothel' scene. Upon her knees, Desdemona vows her constancy: 'Esterrefatta fisso' (Upon my knees before thee), but Otello's mixture of fury, irony and hysteria proves too much for her, and she rushes from his presence.

Left alone, Otello soliloquises in the introspective mood of the temptation scenes ('Had it pleased Heaven to try me with affliction'), and there is nothing of the character of the outburst at the end of Act II about his monologue until its close, when Iago re-enters and tells him that Cassio is at hand, and the music rises suddenly to a strident climax.

Otello hides and Iago brings in Cassio, who is led into banter about Bianca, which Otello half hears and takes to refer to Desdemona. During the course of the trio, Iago contrives that Cassio shall reveal the handkerchief so that Otello may see it (Iago has conveyed it to Cassio's chambers, after stealing it from Emilia). Cassio disappears when the trumpets are heard announcing the arrival of the Venetian ambassadors, and, in a few bars of music and with the acclamation of the crowd as background, Otello plots with Iago that Desdemona shall die that very night in the bed she has fouled.

The Venetian ambassadors arrive. There follows the scene in which the recall of Otello to Venice and the appointment of Cassio as Governor of Cyprus in his stead are announced. In the presence of the ambassadors, the Moor strikes down Desdemona, and all join her in a plea for mercy, at the end of which ensemble Otello orders them to leave the hall. Overcome by his rage and emotion, Otello falls in a swoon, while the people, believing that their deliverer is to return to Venice to receive new honours at the hands of the Republic, shout his praises from outside. Iago reaches the heights of his power with his triumphant 'Ecco il Leon!' over the prostrate body of the general who trusts him and has just granted him promotion, but whom he hates so much.

Act IV.   The scene is Desdemona's bedchamber. There is

an orchestral introduction of great beauty; then, as in the play, comes the brief dialogue between Desdemona and Emilia. Desdemona sings the pathetic Willow song: 'Piangea cantando'. Her singing is interrupted as she talks to Emilia, and at its end she says good-night, the song dying away into

silence as Emilia goes out, only to be called back by Desdemona's heartrending cry of 'Ah! Emilia, Emilia, addio!' It is the most moving moment of a moving scene.

Emilia leaves, and Desdemona kneels down before the image of the Virgin and intones an exquisite 'Ave Maria', beginning and ending in pathetic monotone. The violins end Desdemona's prayer on a high A flat, and the double basses herald Otello's entrance with a *pianissimo* bottom E, five octaves and a half below. He moves toward Desdemona's bed, hesitates, and then kisses her three times. He vainly tries to force her to admit the crime he thinks she has committed, and then smothers her in spite of her pleas for mercy. The sound of knocking is heard and Emilia runs into the room crying that Cassio has killed Roderigo. She hears a dying gasp from Desdemona, and rushes from the room screaming that her mistress has been murdered. Cassio, Iago, and Lodovico answer her summons, and Emilia reveals Iago's villainy, which is confirmed by Montano, who has heard the confession of the dying Roderigo. Iago escapes, and Otello seizes his sword from the table, defying anyone present to require it of him. 'Niun mi tema' (Let no one fear me) he sings before addressing himself to the dead Desdemona in music whose pathos is doubled by its contrast with what has gone before. He stabs himself, and the music associated in the Love Duet with his kiss is heard: 'Un bacio, un bacio ancora, un altro bacio', before he lies dead beside his wife. In his last utterance he has resumed the nobility of the earlier part of the opera, and his death scene musically has much of the quality of the great closing speech of the last act of Shakespeare's play.   K., H.

FALSTAFF

Opera in three acts by Giuseppe Verdi; text by Arrigo Boito. Première at la Scala, Milan, February 9, 1893, with Stehle, Zilli, Pasqua, Garbin, Maurel, Pini-Corsi, Paroli, Arimondi, conductor Mascheroni. First performed Opéra-Comique, Paris, 1894; Covent Garden, 1894, with Ravogli, de Lussan, Olgina, Pessina, Arimondi; Metropolitan, New York, 1895, with Eames, de Lussan, Schalchi, Russitano, Maurel, Campanari, conductor Mancinelli. Revived at la Scala, 1921, with Canetti, Marmora, Casazza, de Paolis, Stabile, Badini, conductor Toscanini; 1926, with Raisa, Rimini, conductor Panizza; 1931, with Dalla Rizza, Stabile, conductor Panizza; 1936, with Caniglia, Favero, Casazza, Landi, Stabile, Badini, Bettoni, conductor de Sabata; 1950, with Tebaldi, Noni, Barbieri, Francesco Albanese, Stabile, Silveri, Siepi, conductor de Sabata. Covent Garden, 1926, with Stabile; 1937, with Caniglia, Albanese, Cravcenco, Fort, Formichi, Biasini, conductor Beecham; Sadler's Wells, 1938, with Parry, Cross, Matters; Cambridge Theatre, 1948, with Stabile, conductor Erede; Covent Garden, 1950, by a Scala company. Metropolitan, 1925, with Bori, Alda, Telva, Gigli, Scotti, Tibbett, conductor Serafin; 1938, with Tibbett, conductor Panizza. Salzburg, 1935, with Caniglia, Mason, Cravcenco, Dino Borgioli, Stabile, Biasini, conductor Toscanini; Covent Garden, 1961, with Angioletti, Freni, Resnik, Geraint Evans, Shaw, conductor Giulini; Florence Festival, 1955, with Tebaldi, Barbieri, Campora, Gobbi and Stabile, Capecchi, conductor Votto.

CHARACTERS

Sir John Falstaff	Baritone
Fenton, *a young gentleman*	Tenor
Ford, *a wealthy burgher*	Baritone
Dr. Caius	Tenor
Bardolph ⎱ *followers of Falstaff*	⎰ Tenor
Pistol ⎰	⎱ Bass
Alice Ford, *Ford's wife*	Soprano
Nanetta, *her daughter*	Soprano
Mistress Page	Mezzo-Soprano
Dame Quickly	Contralto

Burghers and Street-folk, Ford's servants, etc.

Time: Reign of Henry IV   *Place:* Windsor

If Verdi surrounded the writing of *Otello* with mystery, this was as nothing compared with the secrecy which shrouded its successor, which Verdi insisted, almost until it was finished, was being written purely for his own pleasure and with no thought or intention of public performance. The aged composer seems to have laid down the score with a

feeling of real regret and a conviction that his life's work wa
ended with its completion. As far as opera was concerned
this turned out to be true, but the anything but negligibl
'Quattro Pezzi Sacri' testify to his continued energy as
musical creator.

Shakespeare's comedy, *The Merry Wives of Windsor*, did
not by any means have its first lyric adaptation when Verd
penned the score of his last work for the stage. *Falstaff* by
Salieri was produced in Vienna in 1798; another *Falstaff* by
Balfe came out in London in 1838, and Otto Nicolai's *The
Merry Wives of Windsor* is mentioned on pages 173-176 o
this book. The character of Falstaff also appears in *Le Songe
d'une Nuit d'Eté* (Midsummer Night's Dream) by Ambroise
Thomas (who also wrote a *Hamlet*), which came out at Pari
in 1850; 'the type is treated with an adept's hand, especially
in the first act, which is a masterpiece of pure comedy in
music'—so says a contemporary. A one-act piece, *Falstaff*
by Adolphe Adam, was produced at the Théâtre Lyrique in
1856. Since Verdi, only Vaughan Williams seems to have
attempted to set *Falstaff* to music, his *Sir John in Love*
having appeared for the first time in 1935. Holst's shor
opera, *At the Boar's Head*, sets the tavern scenes of *Henry IV*

In both *Otello* and *Macbeth*, Verdi and his librettists had
kept as close to Shakespeare as operatic form would allow
them; and that, in essentials, as I have tried to indicate, wa
very close. But in *Falstaff*, they contrived to inject a
considerable measure of the great Falstaff of *Henry IV* into
the veins of the Falstaff of *The Merry Wives of Windsor*
and so the operatic adaptation is in many ways an improve
ment on the original.

Act I.   A room at the Garter Inn—the 'Giarrettiera', as the
Italian has it. Dr. Caius comes to complain that Falstaff has
beaten his servants, and that Bardolph (Bardolfo) and Pisto
(Pistola) made him drunk and then robbed him. Falstaff
laughs and talks him out of countenance, and he swears that
he will never get drunk again, save in the society of honest
sober people, noted for their piety. As he leaves after this
grandiloquent statement, Pistol and Bardolph, beating time as
they do so, sing an antiphonal 'Amen', until Falstaff stops
them with his complaint that they sing out of time.

He looks at his bill, compares the total with what is left
in his purse, and starts to complain that the prodigal living of
his two cronies is reducing him to a state of beggary, and

what is worse, is bringing him perilously close to reducing his weight—and Falstaff, as he rightly says, without his corporation would be a shadow of his real self. The others applaud such self-revelation—'Falstaff immenso! enorme Falstaff!'—and Falstaff proceeds to tell them that he is currently enamoured of no less than two ladies, the wives of Ford and Page. He has written two love letters, and Bardolph and Pistol are to bear them to their destinations. But this the two worthies refuse to do; their honour will not allow them to take part in such a transaction. Cursing them, Falstaff sends the notes off by a page, and rounds on the pair of them. What right have they to talk of honour, ruffians that they are? Boito has transplanted the Honour monologue, and here Verdi sets it with incomparable aptness and relish: 'L'onore! Ladri!' At its end, Falstaff picks up a broom and chases Bardolph and Pistol out of the room.

The scene changes to the garden of Ford's house, and the orchestra tells us clearly we are in presence of the merry wives, Alice Ford, Meg Page, and Mistress Quickly. With them is Anne Ford[1] (Nanetta). In company with Quickly, Meg has come to pay a visit to Alice Ford to show her a letter which she has just received from Falstaff. Alice matches Meg's with one she also has received from him, and the four read the two letters which, save for the change of address, are exactly alike. The women are half amused, half annoyed at the presumption of the fat knight, and plan to avenge themselves upon him.

Meanwhile Ford goes walking before his house together

---

[1] Anne Page in Shakespeare, with a new patronym.

with Caius, young Fenton (who is in love with Nanetta, but frowned on as a suitor by Ford), Bardolph and Pistol. The last two have betrayed their master, and from them Ford has learned that Falstaff is after his wife. He too meditates revenge, and the female quartet and the male quintet sometimes mingle, sometimes are heard on their own. Fenton and Nanetta remain behind for a fleeting kiss, and sing a miniature love duet together, ending with a phrase of melting beauty:

The women return, but quickly disappear when they think they are being overheard, and once again the two young lovers are alone and can indulge in their battle of kisses. The men reappear, so do the women, and separately they put the finishing touches to their schemes of revenge. This is the famous ensemble in which Verdi combines what was previously sung separately by the men and the women; that the men are singing *alla breve* and the women in 6/8 makes it notoriously difficult to perform:

Act II reverts to the Garter Inn, where Falstaff is still at table. Beating their breasts in mock penitence, Bardolph and Pistol beg to be forgiven for their previous infidelity, and tell Falstaff that an old woman is outside asking to be admitted to his presence. Dame Quickly comes in, and, with the orchestra, makes deep obeisance to the knight: 'Reverenza' is set characteristically to a musical representation of a curtsey. Falstaff is all condescension and affability—'Buon giorno, buona donna':

nd Quickly delivers her messages, one from each of the
adies, to the effect that Alice will receive the knight, but
hat Meg's husband guards her too jealously ever to leave her
lone. Alice can see him from two till three ('Dalle due alle
re') when her husband is always out. Falstaff repeats the
vords with evident delight, and assures Quickly that he will
ot default on the assignation. Quickly starts to leave, and is
ipped by Falstaff as he dismisses her, again with a magnifi-
ent sense of the appropriate gesture. He is left alone with
houghts of his impending success: 'Alice è mia' (Alice is
nine) he sings (orchestrally this is the epitome of Falstaff's
lelight and anticipation):

nd has time for a little strutting march of self-satisfied
riumph ('Va, vecchio John') before his next visitor is
nnounced.

It is Ford. He introduces himself to Falstaff under the
iame of Master Brook (Signor Fontana), presents the knight
vith a purse of silver as a bait, then tells him that he is in love
vith Mistress Ford, whose chastity he cannot conquer, and
iegs Falstaff to lay siege to her and so make the way easier
or him. Falstaff catches up the suggestion of music from
iim, and breaks mockingly into a little song of delicious
riumph:

L'a-mor, l'a-mor che non ci dà mai tre-gue Fin-chè la vi-ta strug-ge.

Falstaff gleefully tells him that he has a rendezvous with her that very afternoon, and that he (Master Brook) may be quite sure that he will be able eventually to attain what he so much desires. When Ford asks if Falstaff knows the husband of Alice, he hears himself described with contumelious abuse. The comedy is rich and never underlined and this duet stands as the last of the long line of similarly conceived scenes which occur all through Verdi's work.

Falstaff goes out for a moment to change his clothes, and Ford is left alone, a prey to jealousy in its most tormenting form. His soliloquy in praise of jealousy might be expected to put Verdi in a dangerous position after his completely successful creation of a tragic jealous passion in *Otello*, but peril is circumvented, and this is one of the great moments of the opera, and moreover a complete re-creation of the Elizabethan delight in the comedy of the enraged cuckold. Falstaff returns, and, after some argument as to who shall go through the door first, they go off arm in arm.

The scene changes to Ford's house, where the four women get ready to give Falstaff the reception he deserves. We learn quite casually from talk between Mistress Ford and Nanetta that Ford wants to marry off the girl to the aged pedant, Dr Caius, while she of course will marry none but Fenton, with whom she is in love. Her mother promises to aid her plans. Alice leads an ensemble with a *staccato* melody, and Quickly gives warning of Falstaff's approach.

Alice sits herself down and starts to play on the lute, to whose accompaniment Falstaff begins to sing her praises in extravagant terms. He sings a little song of irresistible melody 'Quand' ero paggio del Duca di Norfolk' (When I was page to the Duke of Norfolk's grace), in which he describes his own slender and comely build when he was a boy. They are interrupted by Quickly, who announces that Ford can be seen approaching. The fat lover must be concealed. This is accomplished by getting him behind a screen, just before

Ford enters with his followers, hoping to surprise the man who has invaded his home. They begin a search of the rooms. While they are off exploring another part of the house, the women hurry Falstaff into a big washbasket, pile the soiled linen over him, and fasten it down. Scarcely has this been done when Ford comes back and hears the sound of kissing behind the screen. No longer any doubt! Falstaff is hidden there with his wife. He gathers everyone together and knocks down the screen—to find behind it Nanetta and Fenton, who have used to their own purpose the diversion of attention from them by the hunt for Falstaff. Ford, more furious than ever, rushes out, while his wife and her friends call in the servants, who lift the basket and empty it out of the window into the Thames below. When Ford comes back, his wife leads him to the window and shows him Falstaff striking out for the shore.

Act III. Falstaff is sitting recovering at the Garter. His thoughts are gloomy and he calls for more wine, but even that prospect does not seem to make him more cheerful. The world is in a sorry state, he reflects, when such a pearl of knighthood as himself can be bundled unceremoniously into a basket full of dirty linen and dropped into the water. Everything is going to the dogs—even a subdued memory of the little march only reminds him that he is the last of the old brigade. Suddenly, the host appears with a bottle of wine, and Falstaff's mood alters perceptibly at the prospect of swamping some of the Thames water inside him with some good wine. The scene has begun as invective against an ungrateful world, but it finishes as a panegyric in praise of wine, with the full orchestra trilling in sympathy as the wine mounts to colour his view of humanity.

Once more Quickly curtseys to him (considerably, it must be admitted, to his dismay), and offers him a rendezvous with Alice. Falstaff wants to hear no more of such things, and it takes all Quickly's powers of persuasion to get him even to listen, much less to agree to a meeting-place. However, in the end, he cannot resist the temptation which is being dangled in front of him, and settles for midnight at Herne the Hunter's Oak in Windsor forest, where he is to appear (as we learn a moment later from the concealed Alice and her friends) disguised as the black huntsman himself, who, according to legend, hanged himself from the oak, with the result that the spot is haunted by witches and sprites.

The scene ends with an ensemble as the women an
Fenton arrange the details of the evening's fun, and Ford an
Caius plot that Caius's betrothal to Nanetta shall b
announced that very night. The women call to each othe
offstage and the strings offer fifteen bars of idyllic com
mentary as darkness falls.

The last scene takes place by moonlight under Herne'
Oak. Horn-calls and references to the love music form th
basis for the prelude to Fenton's aria, which begins the act. I
is filled with the same sweetness as can be found in the lov

music and it ends with their love motifs. Disguises are hastil
donned, and in a moment Falstaff is heard arriving. He i
wearing a brace of antlers on his head and is wrapped in
heavy cloak. Midnight strikes, echoed at each stroke b
Falstaff, who consoles himself for the incongruity of hi
disguise by remembering that Jove disguised himself as a bul
for love of Europa. For a moment he is alone with Alice, bu

they are immediately interrupted by noises, and Alice disappears into the darkness leaving Falstaff to fend for himself.

Nanetta, who is disguised as Queen of the Fairies, calls her followers around her, and they pirouette until she begins to sing. Verdi has given them music of exquisite delicacy and the choral writing is as delicious as that for the soloist: 'Sul fil d'un soffio etesio' (From secret caves and bowers).

Bardolph in disguise stumbles on the recumbent figure of Falstaff (who has hidden his face so as not to see the fairies), and calls everyone to him. The merry women, Ford's entourage, and about a hundred others, all disguised and masked, unite in mystifying, taunting, and belabouring Falstaff, until the knight at last recognises Bardolph amongst his tormentors. Everyone unmasks in turn, and Falstaff's enormity and folly is brought to light for his discomfiture. He makes a valiant attempt to recapture the initiative by complaining that without his participation a joke seems to have no wit in it, and all—even Ford—agree that his wit alone is sufficient to redeem him, in spite of his egregious faults.

Ford takes Nanetta by the hand and announces her betrothal to Caius, and does the same to another disguised young couple whom Alice leads up to him. He bids them all unmask—to find that Bardolph has been dressed up in Nanetta's clothes and is now therefore betrothed to Caius, and that the other couple were Nanetta and Fenton in disguise. Falstaff cannot resist the temptation to turn Ford's question back on him: who is the dupe now? But Alice will not let him get away with it; he is to be placed beside Ford and Caius; if they are dupes, so is he. Ford is induced to bless his daughter and her sweetheart, and Falstaff leads the company in a final fugue: 'Tutto nel mondo è burla. L'uom è nato burlone' (Jesting is man's vocation. Wise is he who is jolly):

Tutt·o nel mondo è bur-la. L'uom   è na-to bur-lo·ne, bur-lo·ne, bur-lo·ne

For the second time in his career[1], Verdi, who despised academicism with unabating scorn, finished a Shakespearean

---

[1] *Macbeth* was the first.

opera with what is traditionally the most academic of forms, a fugue.

It would take most of a book to describe *Falstaff* in sufficient detail to do anything like justice to the kaleidoscopic variety of the score. There is a sparkle, a rapidity of utterance, a speed of movement, an economy of means in the ensemble writing that has no equal in music written since Mozart, and every bar is endowed with a refinement of expression and a restraint that it would be difficult to imagine in the composer of the operas written before *Macbeth*. The music is even more fluid than in *Otello* and rhythmic ideas are caught up, dropped, and used again with a dexterity which Shakespeare himself never excelled in his own medium. It is all as light as air, and yet out of it has been fashioned Shakespeare's Falstaff drawn (without intending any pun) completely in the round, speaking Italian but more English at heart than in any English musical re-creation of him.   H.

9
Italian Opera Continued

AMILCARE PONCHIELLI
(1834–1886)

LA GIOCONDA
The Ballad Singer

OPERA in four acts by Amilcare Ponchielli; text by Arrigo Boito. Première at la Scala, Milan, April 8, 1876, with Mariani, Biancolini-Rodriguez, Barlani-Dini, Gayarre, Aldighieri, Maini. First performed Covent Garden, 1883, with Maria Durand, Stahl, Tremelli, Marconi, Cotogni, Edouard de Reszke; Metropolitan, 1883, with Nilsson, Fursch-Madi, Stagno, del Puente, Novarre. Revived Metropolitan, 1904, with Nordica, Homer, Walker, Caruso, Giraldoni, Plançon; Covent Garden, 1907, with Destinn, Kirkby Lunn, Thornton, Bassi, Sammarco, Journet, conductor Campanini; Metropolitan, 1925, with Ponselle, Telva, Gigli, Danise, Mardones, conductor Serafin; la Scala, Milan, 1927, with Arangi-Lombardi, Stignani, Merli, Franci, Pasero, conductor Toscanini; Covent Garden, 1929, with Ponselle, Minghini-Cattaneo, Merli, Inghilleri, conductor Bellezza; la Scala, Milan, 1934, with Cigna, Stignani, Ziliani, Galeffi; Metropolitan, 1937, with Cigna, Castagna, Martinelli, Morelli; 1939, with Milanov; 1943, with Roman, Castagna, Tucker, Bonelli. Revived la Scala, Milan, 1952, with Callas,[1] Stignani, di Stefano, Tagliabue, Tajo, conductor Votto.

CHARACTERS
La Gioconda, *a ballad singer* . . . . Soprano
La Cieca, *her blind mother* . . . . Contralto

[1] Whose Italian debut was in the title role at the Arena di Verona in August 1947. H.

Alvise Badoero, *one of the heads of the State
Inquisition* .... Bass
Laura, *his wife* .... .Mezzo-Soprano
Enzo Grimaldo, *a Genoese nobleman* .... Tenor
Barnaba, *a spy of the Inquisition* .... Baritone
Zuane, *a boatman* .... Bass
Isèpo, *a public letter-writer* .... Tenor
A Pilot .... Bass
Monks, senators, sailors, shipwrights, ladies, gentlemen,
populace, masquers, guards, etc.
Time: Seventeenth Century   *Place:* Venice

Twenty-one years elapsed between the production of *La
Gioconda* at the Metropolitan Opera House and its revival
After its reawakening, it took good hold on the repertory
which made it difficult to explain why it should have been
allowed to sleep so long. It may be that possibilities of
casting it did not suggest themselves; not always does 'Cielo e
mar' flow as suavely as it did from the throat of Caruso
Then, too, managers are superstitious, and may have
hesitated to make re-trial of anything that had been
attempted at that first season of opera at the Metropolitan
one of the most disastrous on record. Even Praxede
Marcelline Kochanska (in other words Marcella Sembrich)
who was a member of Henry E. Abbey's troupe, was no
re-engaged, and did not reappear at the Metropolitan unti
fourteen years later.

There was in the course of the first Metropolitan per
formance of the opera in 1883 an unusual occurrence and
one that is interesting to hark back to. Nilsson had a voice of
great beauty—pure, limpid, flexible—but not one conditioned
to a severe dramatic strain. Fursch-Madi, on the other hand
had a large, powerful voice and a singularly dramatic tem
perament. When La Gioconda and Laura appeared in the
great duet in the second act, 'L'amo come il fulgor del creato
(I love him as the light of creation), Fursch-Madi, without
great effort, 'took away' this number from Mme. Nilsson, and
completely eclipsed her. When the two singers came out in
answer to the recalls, Mme. Nilsson, as etiquette demanded
was slightly in advance of the mezzo-soprano, for whom
however, most of the applause was intended.

Each act of *La Gioconda* has its separate title: Act I, 'The
Lion's Mouth'; Act II, 'The Rosary'; Act III, 'The House of

Gold'; Act IV, 'The Orfano Canal'. The title of the opera can
be translated as 'The Ballad Singer', but the Italian title
appears invariably to be used.

Act I. Grand courtyard of the Ducal palace, decorated
for festivities. At back, the Giant's Stairway, and the Portico
della Carta, with doorway leading to the interior of the
Church of St. Mark. On the left, the writing-table of a public
letter-writer. On one side of the courtyard one of the historic
Lions' Mouths, with the following inscription cut in black
letters into the wall:

FOR SECRET DENUNCIATIONS
TO THE INQUISITION
AGAINST ANY PERSON,
WITH IMPUNITY, SECRECY, AND
BENEFIT TO THE STATE.

It is a splendid afternoon in spring. The stage is filled with
holiday-makers, monks, sailors, shipwrights, masquers, etc.,
and amidst the busy crowd are seen some Dalmatians and
Moors.

Barnaba, leaning his back against a column, is watching the
people. He has a small guitar, slung around his neck.

The populace gaily sings, 'Feste e pane' (Sports and
feasting). They dash away to watch the regatta, when
Barnaba announces that it is about to begin. He watches
them disdainfully. 'Above their graves they are dancing!' he
exclaims. Gioconda leads in La Cieca, her blind mother.
There is a scene of much tenderness between them: 'Figlia,
che reggi il tremulo piè' (Daughter, in thee my faltering
steps).

Barnaba is in love with the ballad singer, who has several
times repulsed him. She is in love with Enzo, a nobleman,
who has been proscribed by the Venetian authorities but is in
the city in the disguise of a sea captain. His ship lies in the
Fusina Lagoon.

Barnaba again presses his love upon the girl. She escapes
from his grasp and runs away, leaving her mother seated by
the church door. Barnaba is eager to get La Cieca into his
power in order to compel Gioconda to yield to his sinister
desires. Opportunity soon offers. For now the regatta is
over, the crowd returns bearing in triumph the victor in the
contest. With them enter Zuàne, the defeated contestant,
Gioconda, and Enzo. Barnaba subtly insinuates to Zuàne that
La Cieca is a witch, who has caused his defeat by sorcery.

The report quickly spreads among the defeated boatman's friends. The populace becomes excited, La Cieca is seized and dragged from the church steps. Enzo calls upon his sailors, who are in the crowd, to aid him in saving her.

At the moment of greatest commotion the palace doors swing open. From the head of the stairway where stand Alvise and his wife, Laura, who is masked, Alvise sternly commands an end to the rioting, then descends with Laura.

Barnaba, with the keenness that is his as chief spy of the Inquisition, is quick to observe that, through her mask, Laura is gazing intently at Enzo, and that Enzo, in spite of Laura's mask, appears to have recognised her and to be deeply affected by her presence. Gioconda kneels before Alvise and prays for mercy for her mother. When Laura also intercedes for La Cieca, Alvise immediately orders her freed. In one of the most expressive airs of the opera, 'Voce di donna, o d'angelo' (Voice thine of woman, or angel fair), La Cieca thanks Laura and gives to her a rosary, at the same time extending her hands over her in blessing.

She also asks her name. Alvise's wife, still masked, and looking significantly in the direction of Enzo, answers, 'Laura!' ''Tis she!' exclaims Enzo.

The episode has been observed by Barnaba, who, when all the others save Enzo have entered the church, goes up to him and, despite his disguise as a sea captain, addresses him by his name and title, 'Enzo Grimaldo, Prince of Santa Fior'. The spy knows the whole story. Enzo and Laura were betrothed. Although they were separated and she obliged to wed Alvise, and neither had seen the other since then until the meeting a few moments before, their passion is still as strong as ever. Barnaba, cynically explaining that, in order to obtain Gioconda for himself, he wishes to show her how false Enzo is, promises him that he will arrange for Laura, that very night, to be aboard Enzo's vessel, ready to escape with him to sea. The duet is justly famous.

Enzo departs. Barnaba summons one of his tools, Isèpo, the public letter-writer, whose stand is near the Lion's Mouth. At that moment Gioconda and La Cieca emerge from the church, and Gioconda, seeing Barnaba, swiftly draws her mother behind a column, where they are hidden from view. The girl hears the spy dictate to Isèpo a letter, for whom intended she does not know, informing someone that his wife plans to elope that evening with Enzo. Having thus learned that Enzo no longer loves her, she vanishes with her mother into the church. Barnaba drops the letter into the Lion's Mouth. Isèpo goes. The spy addresses in soliloquy the Doge's palace. 'O monumento! Regia e bolgia dogale!' (O mighty monument, palace and den of the Doges).

The masquers and populace return, singing. They dance *La Furlana*. In the church a monk and then the chorus chant. Gioconda and her mother come out. Gioconda laments that Enzo should have forsaken her. La Cieca seeks to comfort her. In the church the chanting continues.

Act II. Night. A brigantine, showing its starboard side. In front, the deserted bank of an uninhabited island in the Fusina Lagoon. In front, a smaller altar of the Virgin, lighted by a red lamp.

At the rise of the curtain sailors are discovered; some seated on the deck, others standing in groups, each with a speaking trumpet. They sing a Marinaresca, in part a sailors' shanty, in part a regular melody.

In a boat Barnaba appears with Isèpo. They are disguised as fishermen. Barnaba sings a fisherman's ballad, 'Ah! Pescator affonda l'esca' (Fisher-boy, thy net now lower).

He has set his net for Enzo and Laura, as well as for Gioconda, as his words, 'Some sweet siren, while you're drifting, in your net will coyly hide', imply. The scene is full of 'atmosphere'.

Enzo comes up on deck, gives a few orders; the crew go below. He then sings the famous 'Cielo e mar!' (O sky, and sea)—an impassioned voicing of his love for her whom he awaits. The scene, the moon having emerged from behind a bank of clouds, is of great beauty.

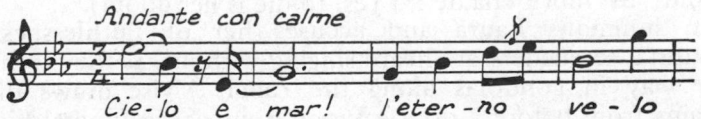

A boat approaches. In it Barnaba brings Laura to Enzo. There is a rapturous greeting and a passionate love duet: 'Laggiù, nelle nebbie remote'. They are to sail away as soon as the setting of the moon will enable the ship to depart undetected. There is distant singing. Enzo goes below. Laura kneels before the shrine and prays, 'Stella del marinar! Vergine Santa!' (Star of the mariner! Virgin most holy).

Gioconda steals on board and confronts her rival. The duet between the two women, who love Enzo, and in which each defies the other, 'L'amo come il fulgor del creato' (I adore him as the light of creation), is the most dramatic number in the score.

Gioconda is about to stab Laura, but stops suddenly and, seizing her with one hand, points with the other out over the lagoon, where a boat bearing Alvise and his armed followers is seen approaching. Laura implores the Virgin for aid. In doing so she lifts up the rosary given to her by La Cieca. Through it Gioconda recognises in Laura the masked lady who saved her mother from the vengeance of the mob. Swiftly the girl summons the boat of two friendly boatmen who have brought her thither, and bids Laura make good her escape. When Barnaba enters, his prey has evaded him; Gioconda has saved her. Barnaba hurries back to Alvise's galley, and, pointing to the fugitive boat in the distance, bids the galley start in pursuit.

Enzo comes on deck. Instead of Laura he finds Gioconda. There is a dramatic scene between them. Venetian galleys are seen approaching. Rather than that his vessel shall be captured by them, Enzo sets fire to it.

Act III.   A room in Alvise's house. Alvise sings of the vengeance he will wreak upon Laura for her betrayal of his honour. 'Sì! morir ella de'!' (Yes, to die is her doom).

He summons Laura and accuses her of faithlessness. Nocturnal serenaders are heard singing without, as they wend their way in gondolas along the canal. Alvise draws the curtains from before a doorway and points to a funeral bier erected in the chamber beyond. To Laura he hands a phial of swift poison. She must drain it before the last note of the serenade they now hear has died away. He will leave her; the chorus ended, he will return to find her dead.

When he has gone, Gioconda, who, anticipating the fate that might befall the woman who has saved her mother, has been in hiding in the palace, hastens to Laura, and hands her a flask containing a narcotic that will create the semblançe of death. Laura drinks it, and disappears through the curtains into the funeral chamber. Gioconda pours the poison from the phial into her own flask, and leaves the empty phial on the table.

The serenade ceases. Alvise, re-entering, sees the empty phial on the table. He enters the funeral apartment for a brief moment. Laura is lying as one dead upon the bier. He believes that he has been obeyed and that Laura has drained the phial of poison.

The scene changes to a great hall in Alvise's house, where he is receiving his guests. Here occurs the immensely popular 'Dance of the Hours', a ballet suite which, in costume changes, light effects and choreography represents the hours of dawn, day, evening, and night. It is also intended to symbolise, in its mimic action, the eternal struggle between the powers of darkness and light. (A more satirical, and extremely funny, interpretation was put on it by Walt Disney in his film *Fantasia*.)

Barnaba enters, dragging in with him La Cieca, whom he has found concealed in the house. Enzo also has managed to gain admittance. La Cieca, questioned as to her purpose in the House of Gold, answers, 'For her, just dead, I prayed'. A hush falls upon the fête. The passing bell for the dead is heard slowly tolling. 'For whom?' asks Enzo of Barnaba. 'For Laura', is the reply. The guests shudder. 'D'un vampiro fatal l'ala fredda passò' (As if over our brows a vampire's wing had passed), chants the chorus. 'Già ti veggo immota e smorta' (I behold thee motionless and pallid), sings Enzo. Barnaba, Gioconda, La Cieca, and Alvise add their voices to an ensemble of great power. Alvise draws back the curtains of the funeral chamber, which also gives upon the festival hall. He points to Laura, extended upon the bier. Enzo, brandishing a dagger, rushes upon Alvise, but is seized by guards.

Act IV. The vestibule of a ruined palace on the island of

Giudecca. In the right-hand corner an opened screen, behind which is a bed. On a couch are various articles of mock jewellery belonging to Gioconda.

On the right of the scene a long, dimly lighted street. From the end two men advance, carrying in their arms Laura, who is enveloped in a black cloak. The two *cantori* (street singers) knock at the door. It is opened by Gioconda, who motions them to place their burden upon the couch behind the screen. As they go, she pleads with them to search for her mother, whom she had not been able to find since the scene in the House of Gold.

She is alone. Her love for Enzo, greater than her jealousy of Laura, has prompted her to promise Barnaba that she will give herself to him, if he will aid Enzo to escape from prison and guide him to the Orfano Canal. Now, however, despair seizes her. In a dramatic soliloquy—a 'terrible song', it has been called—she invokes suicide. 'Suicidio! . . . in questi fieri momenti tu sol mi resti' (Ay, suicide, the sole resource now left me). For a moment she even thinks of carrying out Alvise's vengeance by stabbing Laura and throwing her body into the water—'for deep is yon lagoon'.

Through the night a gondolier's voice calls in the distance over the water: 'Ho! gondolier! hast thou any fresh tidings?' Another voice, also distant: 'In the Orfano Canal there are corpses.'

In despair Gioconda throws herself down weeping near the table. Enzo enters. In a tense scene Gioconda excites his rage by telling him that she has had Laura's body removed from the burial vault and that he will not find it there. He seizes her. His dagger is already poised for the thrust. Hers—so she hopes—is to be the ecstasy of dying by his hand!

At that moment, however, the voice of Laura, who is coming out of the narcotic, calls, 'Enzo!' He rushes to her, and embraces her. In the distance is heard a chorus singing a serenade. It is the same song, before the end of which Alvise had bidden Laura drain the poison. Both Laura and Enzo now pour out words of gratitude to Gioconda, who has provided everything for flight. A boat, propelled by two of her friends, is ready to convey them to a barque which awaits them. What a blessing, after all, has proved to be the rosary, bestowed upon the queenly Laura by an old blind woman. Enzo and Laura voice their thanks: 'Sulle tue mani l'anima tutta stempriamo in pianto' (Upon thy hands thy generous tears of sympathy are falling), and the scene works up to a powerful climax.

Once more Gioconda is alone. The thought of her compact with Barnaba comes over her. She starts to flee the spot, when the spy himself appears in the doorway. Pretending that she wishes to adorn herself for him, she begins putting on the mock jewellery, and, utilising the opportunity that brings her near the table, seizes the dagger that is lying on it. 'Gioconda is thine!' she cries, facing Barnaba, then stabs herself to the heart.

Bending over the prostrate form, the spy furiously shouts into her ear, 'Last night thy mother did offend me. I have strangled her!' but no one hears him. La Gioconda is dead. With a cry of rage, he rushes from the spot.   K.

ARRIGO BOITO
(1842–1918)
MEFISTOFELE

OPERA in four acts by Arrigo Boito, words by the composer. Première at la Scala, Milan, March 5, 1868, with Reboux, Flory, Spallazzi Junca (not a success). In a revised version, produced at Bologna, 1875, with Borghi-Mamo, Campanini, Nannetti, with great success. First performed Her Majesty's Theatre, London, 1880, with Nilsson, Trebelli, Campanini, Nannetti, Grazzi, conductor Arditi; New York, Academy of Music, 1880, with Valleria, Cary, Campanini, Novara; Metropolitan, 1883, with Nilsson, Trebelli, Campanini, Mirabella. Revived Metropolitan, 1889 (Lehmann), 1896 (Calvé), 1907 (Farrar, Martin, Chaliapin); Covent Garden, 1914, with Muzio, Raisa, McCormack, Didur; 1926, with Scacciati, Merli, Chaliapin; la Scala, 1918, with Cannetti, Gigli, de Angelis, conductor Toscanini; 1924, with Spani, Arangi-Lombardi, Pertile, de Angelis; 1934, with Caniglia, Bruna Rasa, Masini, Pinza; 1936, with Tassinari, Bruna Rasa, Pertile, Pasero; 1952, with Tebaldi, Martinis, Tagliavini, Rossi-Lemeni, conductor de Sabata; Metropolitan, 1920, with Alda, Easton, Gigli, Didur; San Francisco, 1952, with Sayao, Fenn, Tagliavini, Rossi-Lemeni; Chicago, 1961, with Ligabue, Christa Ludwig, Bergonzi, Christoff, conductor Votto; London, Sadler's Wells (by Welsh National Opera), 1957, with Raimund Herincx.

CHARACTERS

Mefistofele .... Bass
Faust .... Tenor
Margherita .... Soprano
Martha .... Contralto
Wagner .... Tenor
Elena .... Soprano
Pantalis .... Contralto
Nereo .... Tenor

Mystic choir, celestial phalanxes, cherubs, penitents, wayfarers, men-at-arms, huntsmen, students, citizens, populace, townsmen, witches, wizards, Greek chorus, sirens, naiads, dancers, warriors

Time: Middle Ages   *Place:* Heaven; Frankfurt, Germany; Vale of Tempe, Ancient Greece

Mefistofele is in a prologue, four acts, and epilogue. In Gounod's *Faust*, the librettists were circumspect, and limited the book of the opera to the first part of Goethe's *Faust*, the story of Faust and Marguerite—succinct, dramatic, and absorbing. Only for the ballet did they reach into the second part of Goethe's play and appropriate the scene on the Brocken, which, however, is frequently omitted.

Boito, himself a poet, based his libretto on both parts of Goethe's work, and endeavoured to give it the substratum of philosophy upon which the German master reared his dramatic structure. This, however, resulted in making *Mefistofele* two operas in one. Wherever the work touches on the familiar story of Faust and Marguerite, it is absorbingly interesting, and this in spite of the similarity between some of its scenes and those of Gounod's *Faust*. When it strays into Part II of Goethe's drama, the main thread of the action suddenly seems broken. That is why one of the most profound works for the lyric stage, one of the most beautiful scores that has come out of Italy, figures comparatively rarely in programmes outside its native country.

The Prologue opens in the nebulous regions of space, in which float the invisible legions of angels, cherubs, and seraphs. These lift their voices in a hymn of praise to the Supreme Ruler of the universe. Mefistofele comes on the scene at the close of the anthem, and, standing erect amid the clouds, with his feet upon the border of his cloak, mockingly addresses the Deity: 'Ave Signor'. In answer to the question from the mystic choir, 'Knowest thou Faust?', he replies ontemptuously, and offers to wager that he will be able to entice Faust to evil, and thus gain a victory over the powers of good. The wager is accepted, and the spirits resume their chorus of praise.

Musically the Prologue is full of interest.[1] There are five distinct periods of music, varied in character, so that a scene in which there is but little stage action has the necessary movement. There is the prelude with mystic choir; the sardonic scherzo foreshadowing the entry of Mefistofele; his scornful address, in which he engages to bring about the destruction of Faust's soul; a vivacious chorus of cherubs (impersonated by twenty-four boys); a psalmody of penitents and spirits.

Act I. The drama opens on Easter Sunday, at Frankfurt on Main. Crowds of people of all conditions move in and out of the city gates. Among them appears a grey friar, an object of both reverence and dread to those near him. The aged Dr. Faust and his pupil Wagner descend from a height and enter upon the scene, shadowed by the friar, whose actions they discuss. Faust returns to his laboratory, still at his heels the friar, who, unheeded, enters with him, and conceals himself in an alcove. Faust gives himself to meditation, and upon opening the sacred volume is startled by a shriek from the friar as he rushes from his place of concealment. Faust makes the all-potent 'sign of Solomon', which compels Mefistofele to throw off his friar's disguise and to appear in his own person in the garb of a cavalier, with a black cloak upon his arm. In reply to Faust's questionings, he declares himself the spirit that denieth all things, desiring only the complete ruin of the world, and a return to chaos and night. He offers to make Faust the companion of his wanderings, upon certain conditions, to which the latter agrees, saying: 'If thou wilt bring me one hour of peace, in which my soul may rest—if thou wilt unveil the world and myself before me—if I may find cause to say to some flying moment, "Stay, for thou art blissful", then let me die, and let hell's depths engulf me'. The contract agreed, Mefistofele spreads his cloak, and both disappear through the air.

The first scene of this act gains its interest from the

[1] And a favourite of Toscanini's, who performed it often in concert and chose it, together with Act III of the same opera and an act of *Nerone* for his solitary post-war operatic appearance at la Scala in June 1948.   H.

reflection in the music of the bustle and animation of th
Easter festival. The score plastically follows the man
changing incidents of the scene upon the stage. Conspicuou
in the episodes in Faust's laboratory are Faust's beautiful ai
'Dai campi, dai prati' (From the fields and from th
meadows); Mefistofele's proclamation of his identity, 'Son l
spirito che nega sempre tutto' (I am the spirit that denieth
and the duet beginning 'Se tu mi doni un'ora'.

Act II opens with the garden scene. Faust (rejuvenated
and under the name of Henry), Margaret, Mefistofele, an
Martha stroll here and there in couples, chatting and lov
making. Thence Mefistofele takes Faust to the heights of th
Brocken, where he witnesses the orgies of the Witche
Sabbath. The fiend is welcomed and saluted as their kin;
Faust, benumbed and stupefied, gazes into the murky sk\
and experiences there a vision of Margaret, pale, sad, an
fettered with chains.

In this act the garden scene is of entrancing grace.
contains Faust's 'Colma il tuo cor d'un palpito' (Flood tho
thy heart with all the bliss), and the quartet of farewell, wit
which the scene ends, Margaret, with a gay and reckless laug
of ineffable bliss, exclaiming to Faust that she loves him. Th
scene on the Brocken, besides the whirl of the witches' org\
has a solo for Mefistofele, when the weird sisters present t
him a glass globe, reflected in which he sees the earth: 'Ecc
il mondo' (Behold the earth).

Act III.   The scene is a prison. Margaret lies extende
upon a heap of straw, mentally wandering, and singing t
herself. Mefistofele and Faust appear outside the gratin;
They converse hurriedly, and Faust begs for the life c
Margaret. Mefistofele promises to do what he can, and bic
him haste, for the infernal steeds are ready for flight. H
opens the cell, and Faust enters it. Margaret thinks the jailo\
have come to release her, but at length recognises her love\
She describes what followed his desertion of her, and beg
him to lay her in death beside her loved ones—her bab
whom she drowned, her mother whom she is accused c
having poisoned. Faust entreats her to fly with him, and sh
finally consents, saying that in some far distant isle they ma
yet be happy. But the voice of Mefistofele in the backgroun
recalls her to the reality of the situation. She shrinks awa
from Faust, prays to Heaven for mercy, and dies. Voices c
the celestial choir are singing softly 'She's saved!' Faust an

Mefistofele escape as the executioner and his escort appear in the background.

The act opens with Margaret's lament, 'L'altra notte in fondo al mare' (To the sea, one night in sadness), in which she tells of the drowning of her babe.

There is an exquisite duet, for Margaret and Faust, Lontano, sui flutti d'un ampio oceano' (Far away, o'er the waves of a far-spreading ocean), and a fine passage for Margaret, 'Spunta l'aurora pallida', before her death.

Act IV. Mefistofele takes Faust to the shores of the Vale of Tempe. Faust is ravished with the beauty of the scene while Mefistofele finds that the orgies of the Brocken were more to his taste.

It is the night of the classic Sabbath. A band of young maidens appear, singing and dancing. Mefistofele, annoyed and confused, retires. Helen enters with chorus, and, absorbed by a terrible vision, rehearses the story of Troy's destruction. Faust enters, richly clad in the costume of a knight of the fifteenth century, followed by Mefistofele, Nereo, Pantalis, and others. Kneeling before Helen, he addresses her as his ideal of beauty and purity. Thus pledging to each other their love and devotion, they wander through the bowers and are lost to sight.

Helen's ode, 'La luna immobile innonda l'etere' (Motionless floating, the moon floods the dome of night); her dream of the destruction of Troy; the love duet for Helen and Faust,

'Forma ideal purissima' and 'Ah! Amore! misterio celeste
('Tis love, a mystery celestial); and the dexterous weaving o
a musical background by orchestra and chorus, are the chief
features in the score to this act.

In the Epilogue, we find Faust in his laboratory once
more—an old man, with death fast approaching, mourning
over his past life, with the holy volume open before him
Fearing that Faust may yet escape him, Mefistofele spread
his cloak, and urges Faust to fly with him through the air
Appealing to Heaven, Faust is strengthened by the sound o
angelic songs, and resists. Foiled in his efforts, Mefistofel
conjures up a vision of beautiful sirens. Faust hesitates
moment, flies to the sacred volume, and cries, 'Here at last
find salvation'; then falling on his knees in prayer, effectuall
overcomes the temptations of the evil one. He dies amid
shower of rosy petals, and to the triumphant song of
celestial choir. Mefistofele has lost his wager, and hol
influences have prevailed.

We have here Faust's lament, 'Giunto sul passo estremo
(Nearing the utmost limit); his prayer, and the choir'
message of salvation.   K.

NERONE

Nero

Opera in four acts by Arrigo Boito; text by the composer. Première
May 1, 1924, at la Scala, Milan, with Raisa, Bertana, Pertile[1], Galeff
Journet, Pinza, conductor Toscanini. First performed Rome, 1928
with Scacciati, Bertana, Lauri-Volpi, Franci, Maugeri, conducto
Marinuzzi; Buenos Aires, 1926, with Arangi-Lombardi, Bertana, Pertile
Franci, Formichi, Pinza, conductor Marinuzzi. Revived la Scala, 1939
with Cigna, Stignani, Voyer, Sved, Baronti, conductor Marinuzzi
Rome, 1950, with Laszlo, Minarchi, Annaloro, Tagliabue, Mongelli
conductor Santini.

CHARACTERS

Nerone, *Emperor of Rome* .... Tenor
Simon Mago, *a sorcerer* .... Baritone
Fanuèl, *a Christian leader* .... Baritone
Asteria .... Soprano
Rubria, *a Vestal Virgin* .... Mezzo-Soprano

[1] Martinelli was invited but prevented from going by Gatti-Casazz
who was pursuing his feud with Toscanini.

Tigellino, *follower of Nerone* .... Bass
Gobrias, *follower of Simon Mago* .... Tenor
Dositèo, *a Roman* .... Baritone
Pèrside, *a Christian* .... Soprano
Cerinto .... Contralto
Time: About 60 A.D.   *Place:* Rome and nearby

In *Mefistofele* Boito sought to express, in words and music, the conflict between good and evil; in *Nerone* the contrast is between the dying pagan world and Christianity. On the one hand decay and luxury and power; on the other faith, simplicity and a new idea.

Act I. The Appian Way. Simon Mago and Tigellino are waiting for Nero, who comes to bury the ashes of his mother, Agrippina, whom he has murdered. He arrives fearful and trembling and almost penitent but for the fact that in the Oresteia he finds a precedent for matricide. He has heard an unearthly voice saying 'I am Orestes', and he finds comfort in the thought that he is the reincarnation of Orestes. Tigellino has dug a deep trench where the ashes of Agrippina, which Nero carries, must be buried. He apostrophises the grave: 'Queste ad un lido fatal'. When this is accomplished Simon Mago gives him absolution. Just as the rite is ending the figure of a woman, whose neck is encircled by snakes, seems to rise from the ground. Nero flies, followed by Tigellino. Simon stays and boldly challenges her.

The newcomer is Asteria, who loves Nero and follows him everywhere. Simon believes she may be of use to him and promises to bring her to Nero if she will do his bidding. Simon descends to the crypt where the Christians are wont to gather, while two Christians, Rubria and Fanuèl, meet above. Rubria loves Fanuèl, but Fanuèl has no other thought than his mission. Rubria recites the Lord's Prayer, watched by Asteria. When the two Christians see their arch-enemy, Simon, issuing from the crypt, Rubria is sent to warn the Christians, while Fanuèl remains to face whatever danger there is. But Simon has no hostile intentions. He sees the old world going to ruin and now offers power and wealth to Fanuèl if Fanuèl will but teach him how to work miracles. The music at this point works in the traditional 'intonation' of the 'Credo'. Fanuèl, dreaming of a world in which neither power nor wealth has a share, indignantly refuses. The two must henceforth be enemies.

The news of Nero's return has reached Rome and a great procession comes to meet him. A scene of triumph closes the act.

Act II.   The temple of Simon Mago. The stage is divided into two by the altar where Simon pretends to work a miracle. Before the altar are the faithful; behind, Simon's adepts. The faithful worship and pray; the adepts laugh and count their gains. When the mock ceremony is over, Simon prepares the temple for the expected visit of Nero. The Emperor must be made to believe that Simon can work miracles. Asteria will therefore pretend to be a goddess; echoes must be arranged to give the voice of god or goddess an awful timbre; mirrors must be placed so as to make it appear that phantoms visit the temple. Nero appears and addresses the supposed goddess: 'Oh, come viene a errar'; everything follows the appointed course until Nero touches Asteria and the goddess reveals herself as a woman. In vain the metallic voice of the oracle is heard warning Nero. The emperor no longer fears these gods. He snatches a torch and throws it in the mouth of the bronze shell in which an adept of Simon plays the part of the oracle. He calls to his guards, who arrest Simon and his followers, and sets about destroying the temple. Simon has boasted that he could fly; on the next festival he will be thrown from a tower of the circus and fly—if he can. Then, standing over the ruins, Nero takes a cithara and sings.

Act III.   In an orchard away from the noise of Rome the Christians meet. Solemnly their leader, Fanuèl, expounds to them the Beatitudes; Rubria tells the parable of the foolish virgins in music of utmost suavity. The lesson is interrupted by the arrival of Asteria who has escaped from her prison house to warn them that Simon has tried to purchase freedom by betraying the Christians to Nero. Rubria urges Fanuèl to fly but he refuses. Two beggars come to them in the darkness; they are Simon and Gobrias, one of his assistants disguised, who come to spy. Discovering Fanuèl, Simon sends to warn the guards; there is a short scene of considerable power between Fanuèl and Simon Mago. When the guards arrive, the Christians would attack Simon, but Fanuèl orders them to submit. He turns to his followers and tells them his journey is ended. As he goes the women make a path of flowers before him. Rubria is left alone while the Christians' hymn dies away in the distance. The whole passage, with its mixture of Christian serenity and dramatic power, is most impressive.

Act IV. The first scene takes place in the 'Oppidum', where the mob attending the games in the circus has gathered to applaud the victors and abuse the vanquished. Here are Simon, closely followed by two guards, and Gobrias. They are plotting to burn Rome and escape the punishment which awaits Simon. The conspiracy is made known by Tigellino to Nero, who refuses to interfere. He has planned the games; he is determined to succeed and to please the mob; if the mob demands victims it shall have them. Fanuèl is brought in together with other Christians, who go to their martyrdom in the circus. A vestal appears, preceded by a lictor, and demands their pardon. Nero angrily orders the veil to be torn from her. It is Rubria, who has come to help Fanuèl. Her efforts are in vain. She too is condemned. The Christians go to their death; Simon follows, and then the light of the flames which are consuming the city are seen in the distance.

The second scene takes us to the 'spoliarium', where those who died in the circus are thrown. Asteria and Fanuèl, who, thanks to the fire, have escaped, have come to seek Rubria. They find her wounded to death. Before dying she confesses her sin. She was a vestal; she worshipped with the Christians and then returned every day to Vesta. Now she would kneel and beg forgiveness; she cannot move. There is time for another confession; she loves Fanuèl. He too loves and now calls her his bride, his beloved. As Rubria feels life ebbing, she asks Fanuèl to tell her once more of Galilee and of the sea on whose strand Christ prayed. Fanuèl obeys, and with that image in her eyes and in her mind, Rubria dies.

The scene of Rubria's death is one of the most successful of the opera, and Boito achieves a moving effect without even momentary recourse to the tear-jerking methods which were so much in evidence in Italy in the early twentieth century.

Nerone was planned originally in five acts. It is known that Boito worked at the opera all his life, adding and cancelling and improving till old age made him desist. When he had finally revised the fourth act he wrote on the last page: 'The End: Arrigo Boito and Kronos'.

Nerone was never produced in the author's lifetime. It aims, perhaps, too high. Boito obviously meant to give the three arts of the music drama equal importance. The first and

the fourth act exploit in superb fashion the resources of
theatrical presentation; the libretto is a masterpiece of
learning leavened by a true poet's emotion; but the music has
lost some of the easy charm that was the great merit of
Boito's first opera, *Mefistofele.*

If it lacks lyrical force, *Nerone* has nevertheless pages of
great beauty, and is still the subject of occasional revival.

F. B.

ALFREDO CATALANI
(1854–1893)
LA WALLY

OPERA in four acts by Alfredo Catalani, text by Luigi Illica. Première
at la Scala, Milan, on January 20, 1892, with Darclée, Stehle, Guerrini,
Suagnes, Pessina, Cesari, Brancaleoni, conductor Mascheroni. First
performed Metropolitan, 1909, with Emmy Destinn, Riccardo Martin,
Amato, Campanari, conductor Toscanini; Manchester, 1919. Revived la
Scala, 1922, with Sheridan, de Voltri, Bertana, Piccaluga, Noto, di
Lelio, conductor Panizza; 1936, with Cigna, Carosio, Palombini, Merli,
Armando Borglio; Rome, 1944, with Caniglia, Renato Gigli; 1946, with
Caniglia, Ziliani, Silveri; Venice, 1951, with Guerrini, Voyer, Panerai,
Baronti, conductor Votto; la Scala, 1953, with Tebaldi, Scotto, del
Monaco, Giangiacomo Guelfi, conductor Giulini.

CHARACTERS

Wally .... Soprano
Stromminger, *her father* .... Bass
Afra, *a landlady* .... Contralto
Walter, *a strolling minstrel* .... Soprano
Giuseppe Hagenbach, *of Sölden* .... Tenor
Vincenzo Gellner, *of Hochstoff* .... Baritone
The Messenger of Schnals .... Tenor

Time: 1800   *Place:* Tyrol

Act I.   Stromminger is celebrating his seventieth birthday.
There is shooting, and Gellner hits the target. Hagenbach of

Sölden would not have thought much of that, says Stromminger, adding that he cares little for the boasts of this individual, who is anyhow the son of his greatest enemy. While Stromminger and Gellner drink, Walter sings a song, which, he says, has been written by Wally. Hagenbach enters, flushed with triumph and holding the skin of a bear he has shot. Stromminger mocks his skill, then insults his father, so that Hagenbach throws Stromminger to the ground.

Wally rushes to protect her father, and recognises Hagenbach, who does not know her, as the youth she has been secretly in love with for some time. Gellner, who himself is in love with Wally, warns Stromminger that his daughter has fallen for his enemy, and Stromminger tells Wally that she must marry Gellner within the month. Wally tries to persuade Gellner to give her up, but becomes indignant when he seems determined to carry out her father's scheme. Stromminger threatens to throw her out of his house if she does not agree to his suggestion, and Wally retorts that if he does she will go off alone into the snow.

Act II. The Eagle Tavern at Sölden. The landlady Afra is engaged to Hagenbach. Stromminger is now dead, and Wally has inherited a fortune. Gellner is no longer gay and care-free, but taciturn and even sinister. A festival is in progress, to which Wally is sure to come, they say, particularly since she will there meet her adored Hagenbach. He comes in, and seems to have little regard for Wally, whom he thinks of as better able to hate than to love. He is bet that he will not succeed in snatching a kiss from Wally, and, in spite of the warnings of Afra that you cannot play with love, he accepts the challenge.

When Wally comes in, someone suggests the kissing game, but Wally says that this is not the sort of thing that amuses her, as it does the other village girls, who use it as an excuse for what they cannot otherwise have. The people go in to Mass, and Wally, who has not seen Gellner since she left home on his account, offers him money if he will go away. He protests that he still loves her madly, and that in any case there is no use her setting her cap at Hagenbach as he is engaged to Afra. Wally is furious, and insults Afra; Hagenbach tells her that he will avenge her.

The dance starts. Hagenbach has turned the eagle's wing in his hat upside down, which means that any promise made has no value. Only Gellner notices, but Wally dances all the same

with Hagenbach. In the end, he finds her passionate fascination is too much for him, and what has started as a game has
gone rather further. He kisses her, but is then dragged away
amid shouts of 'Hagenbach has won his bet and Afra is
revenged'. Wally turns to Gellner, asks if he still wants her,
and then says that Hagenbach, for what he has done to her,
must die.

Act III.   Hochstoff. Wally's bedroom can be seen on one
side, on the other is the bridge over the Ache. Wally returns
from the dance, dismisses Walter who had accompanied her,
and retires to her room, not however before hearing that
Hagenbach has started for Hochstoff on some unidentified
mission. Wally laments her broken dream of love, but finds
enough forgiveness in her heart to wonder whether she
should tell Gellner that he must not do her bidding and rid
the world of Hagenbach. Suddenly there is a knock at the
door; Gellner tells her he has taken advantage of the dark and
has just pushed Hagenbach into the abyss below.

Wally is horror-stricken, and drags Gellner out. A crowd
collects in answer to her cries for help. Wally promises Afra
that Giuseppe shall be hers if he survives, and herself goes
down with a rope to rescue him. He is brought up unconscious. Wally tells Afra that he has been restored to her
by the grace of God. She kisses him, and says that Afra
should tell him she has returned the kiss he gave her at the
dance.

Act IV.   Tired and hopeless, Wally contemplates the
glacier near her house. Walter comes by and tells her that she
is in danger from the avalanches which are prevalent at that
time of the year—it is Christmas; why does she not come
down to celebrate with them? She says good-bye to Walter,
asking him only that he will pause on his way down and sing
for her the song of the Edelweiss which was heard earlier in
the opera.

He leaves her sadly, and she prepares to die like the girl in
the song. Suddenly, she hears another voice, not Walter's. She
thinks at first that it is the elves of the glacier who are
coming to fetch her, but soon understands that it is Hagenbach, recovered from his injuries and come to confess his love
for her. Wally does not like to believe him, even when he tells
her that his accident occurred when he was on his way to tell
her he loved her. She admits her share in his 'accident', and
he embraces her and tells her that it makes no difference to

his love. The sky is overcast, and a fog comes up. Hagenbach
goes to look for the path down. He shouts up to Wally, but
the sound of an avalanche is heard. Wally calls anxiously to
him, but all is silent. Opening her arms wide, she throws
herself after the avalanche.   H.

RUGGIERO LEONCAVALLO

(1858–1919)

I PAGLIACCI

The Strolling Players

OPERA in two acts, words and music by Ruggiero Leoncavallo.
Première, Teatro dal Verme, Milan, May 21, 1892, with Stehle, Giraud,
Maurel, Ancona, Daddi, conductor Toscanini. First performed Covent
Garden, May 1893, with Melba, de Lucia, Ancona; Grand Opera House,
New York, June 1893, under the direction of Gustav Hinrichs, with
Selma Kronold, Montegriffo, and Campanari; Metropolitan later the
same year, with Melba, de Lucia, and Ancona. Constantly performed
at all opera houses. Famous Canios have included Caruso, Martinelli,
Zenatello, Gigli.

CHARACTERS

Canio (*in the play 'Pagliaccio'*), *head of a troupe of*
   strolling players ....Tenor
Nedda (*in the play 'Columbine'*), *wife of Canio* Soprano
Tonio (*in the play 'Taddeo'*), *a clown* ....Baritone
Beppe (*in the play 'Harlequin'*) ....Tenor
Silvio, *a villager* ....Baritone
               Villagers
Time: The Feast of the Assumption, about 1865-70
               Place: Montalto, in Calabria

Pagliacci opens with a prologue. There is an instrumental
introduction. Then Tonio pokes his head through the

curtains,—'Si può? Signore, Signori' (By your leave, Ladies
and Gentlemen)—comes out, and sings. The prologue
rehearses, or at least hints at, the story of the opera, and does
so in musical phrases, which we shall hear again as the work
progresses—the bustle of the players as they make ready for
the performance; Canio's lament that he must be merry
before his audiences, though his heart be breaking; part of
the lovemaking music between Nedda and Silvio; and the
theme of the intermezzo, to the broad measures of which
Tonio sings, 'E voi, piuttosto che le nostre povere gabbane'
(Ah, think then, sweet people, when you behold us clad in
our motley):

The prologue, in spite of ancient prototypes, was a bold
stroke on the part of Leoncavallo, and, as the result proved, a
successful one. Besides its effectiveness in the opera, it has
made a favourite concert number.

Act I.   The edge of the village of Montalto, Calabria.
People are celebrating the Feast of the Assumption. In the
background is the tent of the strolling players. These players,
Canio, Nedda, Tonio, and Beppe, in the costume of the
characters in the play they are to enact, are parading through
the village.

The opening chorus, 'Son qua' (They're here), proclaims
the innocent joy with which the village hails the arrival of the
players, who, having finished their parade through the village,
are returning to their tent. Beppe, in his Harlequin costume,
enters leading a donkey drawing a gaudily painted cart, in
which Nedda is reclining. Behind her, in his Pagliaccio
costume, is Canio, beating the big drum and blowing the
trumpet. Tonio, dressed as Taddeo, the clown, brings up the
rear. The scene is full of life and gaiety.

Men, women, and boys, singing sometimes in separate
groups, sometimes together, form the chorus. The rising
inflection in their oft-repeated greeting to Canio as 'il
principe se dei pagliacci' (the prince of players), adds
materially to the lilt of joy in their greeting to the players
whose coming performance they evidently regard as the
climax to the festival.

Canio addresses the crowd. At seven o'clock the play will begin. They will witness the troubles of poor Pagliaccio, and the vengeance he wreaked on the Clown, a treacherous fellow. 'Twill be a strange combination of love and of hate. Again the crowd acclaims its joy at the prospect of seeing the players on the stage.

Tonio comes forward to help Nedda out of the cart. Canio boxes his ears, and lifts Nedda down himself. Tonio, jeered at by the women and boys, angrily shakes his fists at the youngsters, and goes off muttering that Canio will have to pay high for what he has done. Beppe leads off the donkey with the cart, comes back, and throws down his whip in front of the tent. A villager asks Canio to drink at the tavern. Beppe joins them. Canio calls to Tonio. Is he coming with them? Tonio replies that he must stay behind to groom the donkey. A villager suggests that Tonio is remaining in order to make love to Nedda. Canio takes the intended humour of this sally rather grimly: 'Un tal gioco, credetemi' (Such a game, believe me, friends). He says that in the play, when he interferes with Tonio's lovemaking, he lays himself open to a beating. But in real life—let anyone, who would try to rob him of Nedda's love, beware. The emphasis with which he speaks causes comment.

'What can he mean?' asks Nedda in an aside.

'Surely you don't suspect her?' question the villagers of Canio. 'Of course not,' protests Canio, kissing Nedda on the forehead.

Just then the bagpipers from a neighbouring village are heard approaching. The musicians, followed by the people of their village, arrive to join in the festival. All are made welcome, and the villagers, save a few who are waiting for Canio and Beppe, go off down the road toward the village. The church bells ring. The villagers sing the pretty chorus, 'Din, don—suona vespero' (Ding, dong—the vespers bell). Canio nods good-bye to Nedda. He and Beppe go toward the village.

Nedda is alone. Canio's words and manner worry her. 'How fierce he looked and watched me! Heavens, if he should suspect me!' But the birds are singing, the birds, whose voices her mother understood. Her thoughts go back to her childhood. She sings, 'Oh! che volo d'augelli' (Ah, ye beautiful song-birds), which leads up to her vivacious *ballatella*, 'Stridono lassù' (Forever flying through the boundless sky).

Tonio comes out from behind the theatre. He protests his love for Nedda. The more passionately the clown pleads, the more she mocks him, and the more angry he grows. He seeks forcibly to grasp and kiss her. She backs away from him. Spying the whip where Beppe threw it down, she seizes it and with it strikes Tonio across the face. Infuriated, he threatens, as he leaves her, that he will yet be avenged on her.

A man leans over the wall. He calls in a low voice, 'Nedda!' 'Silvio!' she cries. 'At this hour . . . what madness!'

He assures her that it is safe for them to meet. He has just left Canio drinking at the tavern. She cautions him that, if he had been a few moments earlier, his presence would have been discovered by Tonio. He laughs at the suggestion of danger from a clown.

Silvio has come to secure the promise of the woman he loves, and who has pledged her love to him, that she will run away with him after the performance that night. She does not consent at once, not because of any moral scruples, but because she is afraid. After a little persuasion, however, she yields. The scene reaches its climax in an impassioned love duet, 'E allor perchè, di', tu m'hai stregato' (Why hast thou taught me Love's magic story). The lovers prepare to separate, and agree not to see each other again until after the play, when they are to meet and elope.

But the jealous and vengeful Tonio has overheard them, and has run to the tavern to bring back Canio. He comes just in time to hear Nedda call after Silvio, who has climbed the wall, 'Tonight, love, and forever I am thine.'

Canio, with drawn dagger, makes a rush to overtake and stay the man, who was with his wife. Nedda places herself between him and the wall, but he thrusts her violently aside, leaps the wall, and starts in pursuit. 'May Heaven protect him now,' prays Nedda for her lover, while Tonio chuckles.

The fugitive has been too swift for Canio. The latter returns. 'His name!' he demands of Nedda, for he does not know who her lover is. Nedda refuses to give it. Silvio is safe! What matter what happens to her. Canio rushes at her to kill her. Tonio and Beppe restrain him, and Tonio whispers to him to wait: Nedda's lover surely will be at the play—a look, or gesture from her will betray him. Then Canio can wreak vengeance. Canio thinks well of Tonio's ruse. Nedda escapes into the theatre.

It is time to prepare for the performance. Beppe and Tonio
retire to do so.

Canio's grief over his betrayal by Nedda finds expression in
one of the most famous numbers in Italian opera, 'Vesti la
giubba' (On with the motley), with its tragic 'Ridi Pagliaccio'
(Laugh then, Pagliaccio), as Canio goes toward the tent, and
enters it. It is the old and ever effective story of the buffoon
who must laugh, and make others laugh, while his heart is
breaking.

Act II.   The scene is the same as that of the preceding act.
Tonio with the big drum takes his position at the left angle of
the theatre. Beppe places benches for the spectators, who
begin to assemble, while Tonio beats the drum. Silvio arrives
and nods to friends. Nedda, dressed as Columbine, goes about
with a plate and collects money. As she approaches Silvio,
she pauses to speak a few words of warning to him, then goes
on, and re-enters the theatre with Beppe. The brisk chorus
becomes more insistent that the play begin. Most of the
women are seated. Others stand with the men on slightly
rising ground.

A bell rings loudly. The curtain of the tent theatre on the
stage rises. The scene represents a small room with two side
doors and a practicable window at the back. Nedda, as
Columbine, is walking about expectantly and anxiously. Her
husband, Pagliaccio, has gone away till morning; Taddeo is at
the market; she awaits her lover, Harlequin. A dainty minuet
forms the musical background.

A guitar is heard outside. Columbine runs to the window
with signs of love and impatience. Harlequin, outside, sings
his pretty serenade to his Columbine, 'O Colombina, il tenero
fido Arlecchin' (O Columbine, unbar to me thy lattice high).

The ditty over, she returns to the front of the mimic stage, seats herself, back to the door, through which Tonio, as Taddeo, a basket on his arm, now enters. He makes exaggerated advances to Columbine, who, disgusted with his boldness, goes to the window, opens it, and signals. Beppe, as Harlequin, enters by the window. He makes light of Taddeo, whom he takes by the ear and turns out of the room, to the accompaniment of a few kicks. All the while the minuet has tripped its pretty measure and the village audience has found plenty to amuse it.

Harlequin has brought a bottle of wine, also a phial with a sleeping potion which she is to give her husband when opportunity offers, so that, while he sleeps, she and Harlequin may fly together. Love appears to prosper, till suddenly, Taddeo bursts in. Columbine's husband, Pagliaccio, is approaching. He suspects her and is stamping with anger. 'Pour the philtre in his wine, love!' admonishes Harlequin, and hurriedly gets out through the window.

Columbine calls after him, just as Canio, in the character of Pagliaccio, appears in the door. 'To-night, love, and forever, I am thine!'—the same words Canio had heard his wife call after her lover a few hours before.

Columbine parries Pagliaccio's questions. He has returned too early. He has been drinking. No one was with her, save the harmless Taddeo, who has become alarmed and has sought safety in the closet. From within, Taddeo expostulates with Pagliaccio. His wife is true, her pious lips would ne'er deceive her husband. The audience laughs.

But now it is no longer Pagliaccio but Canio who calls out threateningly, not to Columbine, but to Nedda, 'His name!'

'Pagliaccio! Pagliaccio!' protests Nedda, still trying to keep up the play, 'No!' cries out her husband—in a passage dramatically almost as effective as 'Ridi Pagliaccio!'—'I am Pagliaccio no more! I am a man again, with anguish deep and human!' The audience thinks his intensity is wonderful acting—all save Silvio, who shows some signs of anxiety.

'Thou had'st my love,' concludes Canio, 'but now thou hast my hate and scorn.'

'If you doubt me,' argues Nedda, 'why not let me leave you?'

'And go to your lover!—his name! Declare it!'

Still desperately striving to keep up appearances, and avert the inevitable, Nedda, as if she were Columbine, sings a chic gavotte, 'Suvvia, così terribile' (I never knew, my dear, that you were such a tragic fellow).

She ends with a laugh, but stops short, at the fury in Canio's look, as he takes a knife from the table.

'His name!' 'No!'—Save her lover she will, at whatever cost to herself.

The audience is beginning to suspect that this is no longer acting. The women draw back frightened, overturning the benches. Silvio is trying to push his way through to the stage.

Nedda makes a dash to escape into the audience Canio pursues and catches up with her.

'Take that—and—that!' (He stabs her in the back.) 'Soccorso . . . Silvio!' (Help! Help!—Silvio!)

A voice from the audience cries, 'Nedda!' A man has nearly reached the spot where she lies dead. Canio turns savagely, leaps at him. A steel blade flashes. Silvio falls dead beside Nedda.

'Gesummaria!' shriek the women; 'Ridi Pagliaccio!' sob the instruments of the orchestra. Canio stands stupefied. The knife falls from his hand:

'La commedia è finita' (The comedy is ended).

There are plays and stories in which, as in *Pagliacci*, the drama on a mimic stage suddenly becomes real life, so that the tragedy of the play changes to the life-tragedy of one or more of the characters. *Yorick's Love,* in which I saw Lawrence Barrett act, and of which I wrote a review for *Harper's Weekly*, was adapted by William D. Howells from *Drama Nuevo* by Estebanez, which is at least fifty years older than *Pagliacci*. In it the actor Yorick really murders the actor whom, in character, he is supposed to kill in the play. In the plot, as in real life, this actor had won away the love of Yorick's wife, before whose eyes he is slain by the wronged husband. About 1883, I should say, I wrote a story, *A Performance of Othello*, for a periodical published by students of Columbia University, in which the player of Othello, impelled by jealousy, actually kills his wife, who is the Desdemona, and then, as in the play, slays himself. Yet, although the *motif* is an old one, this did not prevent Catulle

Mendès (who himself had been charged with plagiarising, in
La Femme de Tabarin, Paul Ferrier's earlier play, *Tabarin*)
from accusing Leoncavallo of plagiarising *Pagliacci* from *La
Femme de Tabarin*, and from instituting legal proceedings to
enjoin the performance of the opera in Brussels. Thereupon
Leoncavallo, in a letter to his publisher, stated that during his
childhood at Montalto a jealous player killed his wife after a
performance, that his father was the judge at the criminal's
trial—circumstances which so impressed the occurrence on his
mind that he was led to adapt the episode for his opera.
Catulle Mendès accepted the explanation and withdrew his
suit.   K.

PIETRO MASCAGNI
(1863–1945)
CAVALLERIA RUSTICANA
Rustic Chivalry

OPERA in one act by Pietro Mascagni; text by G. Menasci and G.
Targioni-Tozzetti, based on the story of G. Verga. Première on May 17,
1890, at Teatro Costanzi, Rome, with Bellincioni, Stagno, Salasso,
conductor Mugnone. First performed Philadelphia, 1891, with Kronold,
Guille, del Puente; Metropolitan, New York, 1891, with Eames, Valero;
Shaftesbury Theatre, London, 1891, with Musiani, Brema, Damian,
Vignas, Brombara, conductor Arditi; Covent Garden, 1892, with Calvé,
de Lucia. Special fiftieth anniversary performances under the direction
of the composer took place in Italy in 1940, including Rome, with
Bruna Rasa, Masini, Franci.

CHARACTERS

Turiddu, *a young soldier* . . . . Tenor
Alfio, *the village teamster* . . . . Baritone
Lola, *his wife* . . . . Mezzo-Soprano
Mamma Lucia, *Turiddu's mother* . . . . Contralto
Santuzza, *a village girl* . . . . Soprano
Villagers, Peasants, Boys
Time: The present, on Easter day   *Place:* A village in Sicily

Cavalleria Rusticana in its original form is a short story, compact and tense, by Giovanni Verga. From it was made the stage tragedy, in which Eleonora Duse displayed her great powers as an actress. It is a drama of swift action and intense emotion; of passion, betrayal, and retribution. Much has been made of the role played by the 'book' in contributing to the success of the opera. It is a first-rate libretto—one of the best ever put forth. It inspired the composer to what has remained his only significant achievement. But only in that respect is it responsible for the success of *Cavalleria Rusticana* as an opera. The hot blood of the story courses through the music of Mascagni, who in his score also has quieter passages, that make the cries of passion the more poignant. Like practically every enduring success, that of *Cavalleria Rusticana* rests upon merit. From beginning to end it is an inspiration. In it, in 1890, Mascagni, at the age of twenty-six, 'found himself', and ever afterwards was trying, unsuccessfully, to find himself again.

The prelude contains three passages of significance in the development of the story. The first of these is the phrase of the despairing Santuzza, in which she cries out to Turiddu that, despite his betrayal and desertion of her, she still loves and pardons him. The second is the melody of the duet between Santuzza and Turiddu, in which she implores him to remain with her and not to follow Lola into the church. The third is the air in Sicilian style, the *Siciliana*, which, as part of the prelude, Turiddu sings behind the curtain, in the manner of a serenade to Lola: 'O Lola, ch'ai di latti' (O Lola, fair as a smiling flower).

With the end of the *Siciliana* the curtain rises. It discloses a public square in a Sicilian village. On one side, in the background, is a church, on the other Mamma Lucia's wineshop and dwelling. It is Easter morning. Peasants, men, women, and children cross or move about the stage. The church bells ring, the church doors swing open, people enter. A chorus, in which, mingled with gladness over the mild beauty of the day, there is also the lilt of religious ecstasy, follows. Like a refrain the women voice and repeat 'Gli aranci olezzano sui verdi margini' (Sweet is the air with the blossoms of oranges). The men meanwhile, pay a tribute to the industry and charm of women. Those who have not entered the church go off singing. Their voices die away in the distance.

Santuzza, sad of mien, approaches Mamma Lucia's hou
just as her false lover's mother comes out. There is a bri
colloquy between the two women. Santuzza asks fo
Turiddu. His mother answers that he has gone to Francofonte
to fetch some wine. Santuzza tells her that he was see
during the night in the village. The girl's evident distress
touches Mamma Lucia. She bids her enter the house.

'I may not step across your threshold,' exclaims Santuzza
'I cannot pass it, I, most unhappy excommunicated outcast!

Mamma Lucia may have her suspicions of Santuzza'
plight. 'What of my son?' she asks. 'What have you to tel
me?'

But at that moment the cracking of a whip and the jingling
of bells are heard from off-stage. Alfio, the teamster, comes
upon the scene. He is accompanied by the villagers. Cheer
fully he sings the praises of a teamster's life, also of Lola's
his wife's, beauty. The villagers join him in chorus, 'Il cavallc
scalpita' (Gaily moves the tramping horse).

Alfio asks Mamma Lucia if she still has on hand some o
her fine old wine. She tells him it has given out; Turiddu has
gone away to buy a fresh supply of it.

'No,' says Alfio. 'He is here. I saw him this morning
standing not far from my cottage.' Mamma Lucia is about tc
express great surprise. Santuzza is quick to check her.

Alfio goes his way. A choir in the church intones the
'Regina Coeli'. The people in the square join in with
'Allelujas'. Then they kneel and, led by Santuzza's voice, sing
the Resurrection hymn, 'Inneggiamo, il Signor non è morto'
(Let us sing of the Lord now victorious).

Mamma Lucia asks the girl why she signalled her to remain
silent when Alfio spoke of Turiddu's presence in the village
'Voi lo sapete' (Now you shall know), exclaims Santuzza, and
in one of the most impassioned numbers of the score, pours
into the ears of her lover's mother the story of her betrayal.
Before Turiddu left to serve his time in the army, he and Lola
were in love with each other. But, tiring of awaiting his
return, the fickle Lola married Alfio. Turiddu, after he had
come back, made love to Santuzza and betrayed her; now,
lured by Lola, he has taken advantage of Alfio's frequent
absences, and has gone back to his first love. Mamma Lucia
pities the girl, who begs that she go into church and pray for
her.

Turiddu comes, a handsome fellow. Santuzza upbraids him

for pretending to have gone away, when instead he has surreptitiously been visiting Lola. It is a scene of vehemence. But when Turiddu intimates that his life would be in danger were Alfio to know of his visits to Lola, the girl is terrified: 'Battimi, insultami, t'amo e perdono' (Beat me, insult me, I still love and forgive you).

Such is her mood—despairing, yet relenting. But Lola's voice is heard off-stage. Her song is carefree, a key to her character, which is fickle and selfish, with a touch of the cruel. 'Fior di giaggiolo' (O gentle flower of gold) runs her song. It conveys in its melody, its pauses, and inflections, a quick sketch in music of the heartless coquette, who, to gratify a whim, has stolen Turiddu from Santuzza. She mocks the girl, then enters the church. Only a few minutes has she been on the stage, but Mascagni has let us know all about her.

A highly dramatic scene, one of the most impassioned outbursts of the score, occurs at this point. Turiddu turns to follow Lola into the church. Santuzza begs him to stay. 'No, no, Turiddu, rimani, rimani ancora—Abbandonarmi dunque tu vuoi?' (No, no, Turiddu! Remain with me now and forever! Love me again! How can you forsake me?).

A highly dramatic phrase, already heard in the prelude, occurs at 'La tua Santuzza piange e t'implora' (Lo! here thy Santuzza, weeping, implores thee).

Turiddu repulses her. She clings to him. He loosens her hold and casts her from him to the ground. When she rises, he has followed Lola into the church.

But the avenger is nigh. Before Santuzza has time to think, Alfio comes upon the scene. He is looking for Lola. To him in the fewest possible words, and in the white voice of suppressed passion, Santuzza tells him that his wife has been unfaithful with Turiddu. His outburst has real strength. In the brevity of its recitatives, the tense summing up in melody of each dramatic situation as it develops in the inexorably swift unfolding of the tragic story, lies the strength of *Cavalleria Rusticana*.

Santuzza and Alfio leave. The square is empty. But the

action goes on in the orchestra. For the *intermezzo*—the famous *intermezzo*—which follows, recapitulates, in its forty-eight bars, what has gone before, and foreshadows the tragedy that is impending. There is no restating here of leading motives. The effect is accomplished by means of terse, vibrant melodic progression. It is melody and yet it is drama. Therein lies its merit. For no piece of serious music can achieve the world-wide popularity of this *intermezzo* and not possess merit.

What is to follow in the opera is quickly accomplished. The people come out of church. Turiddu, in high spirits, because he is with Lola and because Santuzza no longer is hanging around to reproach him, invites his friends over to his mother's wineshop. Their glasses are filled. Turiddu dashes off a drinking song, 'Viva il vino spumeggiante' (Hail! the ruby wine now flowing).

Alfio joins them. Turiddu offers him wine. He refuses it. The women leave, taking Lola with them. In a brief exchange of words Alfio gives the challenge. In Sicilian fashion the two men embrace, and Turiddu, in token of acceptance, bites Alfio's ear. Alfio goes off in the direction of the place where they are to test their skill with the stiletto.

Turiddu calls for Mamma Lucia. He is going away, he tells her. At home the wine cup passes too freely. 'Mamma, quel vino è generoso' (Mother, the red wine burns me like fire). He must leave. If he should not come back she must be like a kindly mother to Santuzza—'Santa, whom I have promised to lead to the altar'.

He goes. Mamma Lucia wanders aimlessly to the back of the stage. She is weeping. Santuzza comes on, throws her arms around the poor woman's neck. People crowd upon the scene. All is suppressed excitement. There is a murmur of distant voices. A woman is heard calling from afar: 'They have murdered neighbour Turiddu!'

Several women enter hastily. One of them, the one whose voice was heard in the distance, repeats, but now in a shriek, 'Hanno ammazzato compare Turiddu!'—(They have murdered neighbour Turiddu!).

Santuzza falls in a swoon. Mamma Lucia is supported by some of the women.

A tragedy of Sicily, hot in the blood, is over.

K.

Verismo in Grove's Dictionary (1954) is 'a term used to

...assify Italian opera of a sensational, supposedly "realistic" kind, including the works of Mascagni, Leoncavallo, Puccini, Giordano etc.' Other works of reference, less tendentiously, allow that the essential difference between *verismo* operas and their predecessors lies in the libretti, which deal with everyday situations as opposed to costume plays and historical episodes or legends.

But whatever definition may be preferred, the average opera-goer understands from the word a distinct comment on the music, and expects something demanding first and foremost power and attack from the singer and only secondarily a smooth legato or any relevance to the art of *bel canto*. This is very far from being the whole truth, and it is the more unfortunate that the *verismo* school is often (in dictionary or history) held to have started with *Cavalleria Rusticana*, whose subject is sensational in that it deals with a story contemporary to the 1880's but whose composer at that time wrote as an instinctive successor to Bellini.

For my own part, I have for many years believed that *Cavalleria Rusticana* is both undervalued and misinterpreted. At least at this stage of his career (which embraces also *L'Amico Fritz*) Mascagni wrote a lyrical and expressive vocal line and only occasionally in *Cavalleria* (notably in the duet for Alfio and Santuzza) is the score touched by the violence we have come wrongly to think of as *verismo*. To interpret him otherwise is to do him an injustice, as will I believe be apparent to those who have heard his own magnificent recording of the opera, with Lina Bruna Rasa, Gigli and Gino Bechi, made in 1940. As to the opera's motivation, it seems to me not only tragic but steeped in the ritual of a primitive, believing people. Turiddu knows that, if Alfio challenges him, he cannot refuse to fight and he knows too that in justice he will be killed. In comparison, *I Pagliacci*, with which *Cavalleria* is usually teamed, is effective but no more than a lurid newspaper anecdote of a *crime passionel*.   H.

L'AMICO FRITZ
Friend Fritz

Opera in three acts by Pietro Mascagni; text by P. Suardon (N. Daspuro), founded on Erckmann-Chatrian's novel. Première on November 1, 1891, at Teatro Costanzi, Rome, with Calvé, Synnemberg, de Lucia, Lhérie, conductor Ferrari. First performed Covent Garden, 1892, with Calvé, Ravogli, de Lucia, Dufriche; Philadelphia, 1892, Metropolitan, New York, 1893, with Calvé, Scalchi, de Lucia, Ancona. Revived Metropolitan, 1923, with Bori, Fleta, Danise; la Scala, Milan, 1930, with Marengo, Dino Borgioli, Ghirardini, conductor Mascagni; 1937, with Favero, Schipa, Danise; Florence Festival, 1941, with Magnoni, Tagliavini, Poli, conductor Mascagni; London, Drury Lane, 1958, with Panni, Misciano, Pedani; la Scala, Milan, 1963, with Freni, Raimondi, Panerai, conductor Gavazzeni.

CHARACTERS

Fritz Kobus, *a rich bachelor landowner* .... Tenor
Suzel, *a farmer's daughter* .... Soprano
Beppe, *a gypsy* .... Mezzo-Soprano
David, *a Rabbi* .... Baritone
Hanezò ⎱ *friends of Fritz* .... ⎰ Bass
Federico ⎰   ⎱ Tenor
Caterina, *Fritz's housekeeper* .... Soprano
Time: 'The present'   *Place:* Alsace

Act I.   The dining-room of Fritz's house. He complains to his friend David that he has once again been asked to provide the dowry for two neighbours who want to get married. He himself cannot understand this business of falling in love and sighing for a woman. Two friends, Hanezò and Federico, come in with Caterina his housekeeper to wish him luck on his fortieth birthday. They are all coming to sup with him, but David must leave them to give the good news to the young lovers. Fritz laughs at him, but he prophesies that within a year Fritz himself will be married.

Caterina brings in Suzel, the daughter of one of Fritz's tenants, who gives him flowers as a present: 'Son pochi fiori' she sings, a pretty little aria. Fritz makes her sit beside him; before long they hear the sound of Beppe's fiddle outside. There is general admiration for his music-making, and, when he comes in, he is asked to sing for the company. This he does, and at the same time contrives to pay Fritz a graceful compliment on the subject of his charitable disposition: 'Laceri, miseri.'

Suzel leaves to rejoin her family, and all exclaim on her attractiveness now that she is nearly grown-up. David comments that he is likely soon to be marrying her off to someone or other, and Fritz protests that she is only a girl. David says he is prepared to bet Fritz that he will soon be married himself, and they agree that Fritz's vineyard shall be the subject of their wager. A party of orphans who have been befriended by Fritz come in to the sound of a march, and the act ends in general rejoicing.

Act II.   An orchard near a farm. Suzel is picking cherries; she sings a little ditty to express her happiness and the whole scene is full of pastoral charm. Fritz comes in ('Suzel, buon dì'), compliments Suzel on her singing, and thanks her for the flowers she has picked him; she tells him the cherries are already ripe.

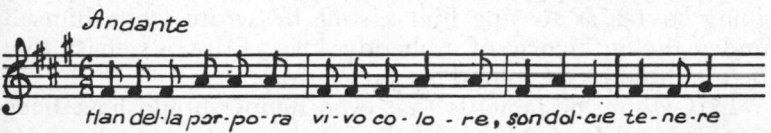

hlan del·la por·po·ra   vi·vo co·lo - re, son dol·cie te·ne·re

She mounts a ladder, picks the cherries and throws them down to Fritz, who is charmed and captivated by her youth and freshness. Where else can he find such peace and innocence ('Tutto tace'); when but in spring ('Tu sei bella, o stagion primaverile')?

Tu sei bel - la, o ..... sta·gion pri·ma·ve - ri - le! Rin -no- vel - la fiori e amor il dol·ce a·pri - le!

It is doubtful whether Mascagni ever elsewhere wrote music of such delicacy and inspiration.

The sound of bells and cracking whips heralds the arrival of David, Beppe, Hanezò, and Federico. They suggest a drive round the countryside, but David pleads fatigue and stays behind. When Suzel offers him some water to drink, he tells her the scene reminds him of the story of Isaac and Rebecca, and makes her read the appropriate passage from the Bible. This she does, David thinks, with evident understanding of its relevance to her situation. When Fritz and the others return, David determines to test Fritz's reaction and tells him that he has found a suitable husband for Suzel and that her father approves. Fritz is horrified at the idea, and when David has left him, he admits to himself that he must be in love, but immediately determines to evade the consequences and return with his friends to town. David does his best to comfort the unhappy Suzel, who watches him go—he has not even said good-bye—with a sad heart.

Act III. The *intermezzo* which begins the Act has attained considerable popularity with Italian audiences, and is nearly as often encored as the famous vocal numbers of the score. The scene is the same as that of the first act. Fritz is distracted with the worry that the discovery of love has brought him. Beppe comes in and tries to comfort him, even going so far as to sing him a song he wrote while himself under the influence of unhappy love. Fritz is aghast that Beppe should have joined his persecutors.

Left alone, he laments that even Beppe should have been troubled with love; what hope, he implies, is there for him? He launches into a full-scale aria on the subject of the fatal passion: 'O amore, o bella luce del core.' David comes to him and tells him that all is arranged for Suzel's wedding; only his consent is now needed. Fritz distractedly refuses it, and rushes from the room. David calls in Suzel, who has brought fruit for Fritz. Why does she look so sad, he asks? She sings plaintively of her love for Fritz: 'Non mi resta che il pianto.'

Fritz himself comes in and asks her if it is true that she is going to be married. She begs him to save her from a match she does not want. He finally admits that he loves her himself, and they sing happily of their future bliss. David wins his bet, and all congratulate Fritz on his new-found happiness.

L'Amico Fritz is still frequently played in Italy. If there is nothing else in it to equal the Cherry duet, it has a consistent gentleness and charm. It also contains one of the few roles in which a tenor has the chance to impersonate a middle-aged lover; perhaps on that account, and for the Cherry duet, it will not fail of revival for many years to come.

H.

IRIS

Opera in three acts by Pietro Mascagni, text by Luigi Illica. Première on November 27, 1898, at the Teatro Costanzi, Rome, with Darclée, de Lucia, conductor Mascagni; revised version performed at la Scala, Milan, 1899, with the same singers. First performed Philadelphia, 1902, conductor Mascagni; New York, 1902, with Farneti; Metropolitan,

907, with Eames, Caruso, Scotti, Journet; Covent Garden, 1919, with Sheridan, Capuzzo, Couzinou, Huberdeau, conductor Mugnone. Revived Metropolitan, 1915, with Bori; Chicago, 1929, with Mason, Cortis; Metropolitan, 1931, with Rethberg, Gigli, de Luca, Pinza; la Scala, 1924, with Vigano, Pertile, Badini, conductor Toscanini; 1936, with Pampanini, Bertelli; 1944, with Carbone, conductor Guarnieri. Revived London, Opera Viva, 1967, with Victoria Elliott and Robert Thomas.

CHARACTERS

Il Cieco, *the blind man* .... Bass
Iris, *his daughter* .... Soprano
Osaka, *a rich young man* .... Tenor
Kyoto, *a takiomati* .... Baritone
Ragpickers, Shopkeepers, Geishas, Mousmés (laundry girls), Samurai, Citizens, Strolling Players, Three Women representing Beauty, Death, and the Vampire; a Young Girl

Time: Nineteenth Century   *Place:* Japan

Act I.   The home of Iris near the city. The hour is before dawn. The music depicts the passage from night into day. It rises to a crashing climax—the instrumentation including tamtams, cymbals, drums, and bells—while voices reiterate, 'Calore! Luce! Amor!' (Warmth! Light! Love!). In warmth and light there are love and life. A naturalistic philosophy, to which this opening 'Hymn to the Sun' gives the key, runs through *Iris*.

Fujiyama glows in the early morning light, as Iris, who loves only her blind father, comes to the door of her cottage. She has dreamed that monsters sought to injure her doll, asleep under a rosebush. With the coming of the sun the monsters have fled.

Iris is young and beautiful. She is desired by Osaka, a wealthy rake, and Kyoto, keeper of a questionable resort, plots to obtain her for him. While her father prays and *mousmés* sing on the bank of the stream, Iris tends her flowers: 'In pure stille.' Osaka and Kyoto come to her cottage with a marionette show. The play starts, and after a while Osaka, in the person of Jor, son of the sun god, sings a serenade: 'Apri la tua finestra.' While Iris is intent upon the performance, three geisha girls, representing Beauty, Death, and the Vampire, dance about her. They conceal her from view by spreading their skirts. She is seized and carried off.

Osaka, by leaving money for the blind old father, makes the abduction legal. When Il Cieco returns, he is led to believe that his daughter has gone voluntarily to the Yoshiwara. In a rage he starts out to find her.

Act II.   Interior of the 'Green House' in the Yoshiwara. Kyoto and Osaka regard the sleeping Iris, who awakens. At first she thinks it is an awakening after death. But death brings paradise, while she is unhappy. Osaka, who has placed jewels beside her, comes to woo, but vainly seeks to arouse her passions. In her purity she remains unconscious of the significance of his words and caresses. His brilliant attire leads her to mistake him for Jor, the sun god, but he tells her he is Pleasure. That frightens her. For, as she narrates to him, one day, in the temple, a priest told her that pleasure and death were one: 'Un dì (ero piccina) al tempio.'

Osaka embraces her in a last effort to win her love ('Or dammi il braccio tuo'), then wearies of her innocence and leaves her. But Kyoto, wishing to lure him back, attires her in transparent garments and places her upon a balcony. The crowd in the street cries out in amazement over her beauty. Again Osaka wishes to buy her. She hears her father's voice, and joyously makes her presence known to him. He, ignorant of her abduction and believing her a voluntary inmate of the 'Green House', takes a handful of mud from the street, flings it at her, and curses her. In terror, she leaps from a window into the sewer below.

Act III.   Ragpickers and scavengers are dragging the sewer before daylight. In song they mock the moon. A flash of light from the mystic mountain awakens what is like an answering gleam in the muck. They discover and drag out the body of Iris. They begin to strip her of her jewels. She shows signs of life. The sordid men and women flee. The rosy light from Fujiyama spreads over the sky. Warmth and light come once more. Iris regains consciousness. Spirit voices whisper of earthly existence and its selfish aspirations typified symbolically by the knavery of Kyoto, the lust of Osaka, the desire of Iris's father, Il Cieco, for the comforts of life through her ministrations.

Enough strength comes back to her for her to acclaim the sanctity of the sun. In its warmth and light—the expression of Nature's love—she sinks, as if to be absorbed by nature into the blossoming field that spreads about her. Again, as in the beginning, there is the choired tribute to warmth, light, love—the sun!   K.

UMBERTO GIORDANO
(1867–1948)

ANDREA CHÉNIER

OPERA in four acts by Umberto Giordano; text by Luigi Illica. Première at la Scala, Milan, on March 28, 1896, with Carrera, Borgatti, Sammarco. First performed New York, 1896; Manchester, 1903 (in English); Camden Town Theatre, London, 1903 (in English); Covent Garden, 1905, with Strakosch, Zenatello, Sammarco, conductor Mugnone; Metropolitan, New York, 1921, with Muzio, Gigli, Danise, conductor Moranzoni. Revived Covent Garden, 1925, with Sheridan, Lauri-Volpi, Franci; 1930, with Sheridan, Gigli, Inghilleri; la Scala, fiftieth anniversary performance in 1946, with Caniglia, Beval, Piero Guelfi, conductor Giordano; 1949, Giordano Commemoration performance, with Tebaldi, del Monaco, Silveri, conductor de Sabata; Metropolitan, New York, 1954, with Milanov, del Monaco, Warren; 1962, with Eileen Farrell, Corelli, Merrill; London, Drury Lane, 1958, with Luciana Serafini, Annaloro (replaced after 1st act by Giuseppe Savio), Giangiacomo Guelfi, conductor Bellezza; London, Sadler's Wells, 1959, with Victoria Elliott, Craig, Glossop.

CHARACTERS

A Major-domo . . . . Baritone
Charles Gérard . . . . Baritone
Madeleine de Coigny . . . . Soprano
Countess de Coigny, *her mother* . . . . Mezzo-Soprano
Bersi, *Madeleine's mulatto maid* . . . . Mezzo-Soprano
Fléville, *a cavalier ('Romanziere')* . . . . Baritone
The Abbé . . . . Tenor
Andrea Chénier, *a poet* . . . . Tenor
Mathieu, *a waiter* . . . . Baritone
Incredibile[1], *a spy* . . . . Tenor
Roucher, *a friend of Chénier's* . . . . Bass
Madelon, *an old woman* . . . . Mezzo-Soprano
Dumas, *president of the tribunal* . . . . Baritone
Fouquier-Tinville, *attorney-general* . . . . Baritone
Schmidt, *gaoler at St. Lazare prison* . . . . Baritone
Courtiers and ladies, citizens of France, soldiers, servants,
peasants, prisoners, members of revolutionary tribunal
Time: Before and after French Revolution   *Place:* Paris

[1] 'Incroyable' = a beau of the French Directoire period. This one is an informer, or spy.

701

Historical as a character though André Chénier was, Giordano's librettist, Luigi Illica, has turned his life into fiction. Chénier was a poet, dreamer, and patriot; he was born in Constantinople, but returned to Paris for his education, and there became a participant in the Revolution, and later a victim of it.

Act I.   Ballroom in a chateau. Preparations are in train for a big party, and Gérard is amongst the servants setting the room to rights. He mocks at the falsities and conventions of aristocratic life, but his words take on a more menacing character when, provoked by the sight of his old father carrying in some furniture, he launches forth into a denunciation of the masters he works for and the system which keeps them in their unearned luxury: 'Son sessant' anni.' The Countess, her daughter Madeleine, and Bersi come to see that the last-minute preparations for the party are going well. The Countess checks up on endless details, Madeleine discusses with her maid what she shall wear, and Gérard comments on the beauty of the daughter of the house, with whom he is secretly in love.

The guests arrive, notable amongst them the Abbé and Fléville, the latter of whom introduces an Italian musician, and the poet Chénier. The Abbé wants to talk politics, but with some graceful phrases Fléville bids the guests turn their minds to the serious business of the Pastoral they are about to see and hear. There is a pastoral chorus, and then Chénier, who has declined the Countess's request that he read a poem, agrees to recite at Madeleine's invitation.

He sings the well-known *Improvviso di Chénier*, 'Un dì, all' azzurro spazio', in which he contrasts the beauty of nature with the misery man makes around him; he denounces the selfishness of those in authority—priests, politicians, aristocrats—and his extremist sentiments find little favour with the guests (though the aria itself has become enormously popular since first sung).

Madeleine apologies to him for the situation her request has put him in, but the Countess quickly gets the band to strike up a gavotte. Even that is interrupted when Gérard bursts in at the head of a band of beggars, announcing, butler-like, 'His Lordship, Misery!'. The major-domo gets them to leave, but not before Gérard has torn his coat from his back, and denounced it as a sign of slavery. The gaiety recommences and amusement goes on as if nothing has happened.

Act II. The Café Hottot in Paris. The first phase of the Revolution is over, and at one side of the stage is an altar-like affair, on which stands a bust of Marat. Chénier sits alone at a table, and at another are Bersi and Incredibile, the spy. Bersi asks whether it is true that there are spies about and remarks that she herself has nothing to fear; is she not a true daughter of the Revolution, who thoroughly enjoys the new freedom, the drinking, and even watching a tumbril go by? Incredibile reads aloud from the note he is making about Bersi and about Chénier, each of whom he thinks a suspicious character.

Roucher appears and goes up to Chénier with a passport which he has been influential in getting for him. It is important he should flee at once, as he has powerful enemies. Chénier rejects such counsel of despair, and sings of his confidence in his own destiny: 'Credo a una possanza arcana.' Chénier moreover has received several anonymous letters from a woman, whose image has been built up in his mind until she is the most beautiful creature he has ever imagined. Chénier is about to leave, when Robespierre and several other leading Revolutionaries appear, followed by a cheering crowd. Gérard is one of the leaders, and Incredibile stops him to enquire more details about the woman he is trying to find. Gérard gives him a lyrical description of the beauty of Madeleine. Roucher is approached by Bersi, who tells him that someone wishes to see Chénier, someone who is in danger.

Madeleine arrives at the meeting-place and is soon joined by Chénier. It is some minutes before he recognises her and discovers that it was she who wrote the letters he has been receiving; at the same time, Incredibile looks from his hiding-place, makes up his mind that this is the woman Gérard is looking for, and goes off to tell him where she is. Madeleine asks Chénier for help in her loneliness, and he avows his love in a passionate duet. They are about to rush away together, when Gérard appears in their path, closely followed by the spy and by Roucher. Chénier shouts to his friend Roucher to take Madeleine into his charge, and he and Gérard draw their swords, neither having recognised the other. They fight, Gérard falls wounded, and recognises his opponent; he murmurs to him to be on his guard—he is on Fouquier-Tinville's list as a counter-revolutionary.

Incredibile returns with police, a crowd collects and demands vengeance on the assailant of a leader of the people; but Gérard says he did not recognise his attacker.

Act III.   The Revolutionary Tribunal. Mathieu speaks to
the crowd which has assembled to watch the proceedings and
tries to get them to contribute money and valuables to the
common fund. The response is listless, until Gérard comes in
and makes an impassioned speech. Immediately, all are ready
to give, not least amongst them an old woman (Madelon),
who says that she has already lost two sons fighting for
France, but now offers the youngest, a boy of about fifteen.
The crowd disperses singing the revolutionary song, *La
Carmagnole*.

Gérard asks Incredibile, who has appeared, whether there
is news of either Chénier or Madeleine—as to the former, a
newsboy can be heard crying that he is arrested, and the
latter, says the spy, will not be long in coming to look for her
lover. Gérard is shocked by the spy's cynicism, still more so
when Incredibile urges him to write out the indictment
against Chénier; it will be needed for the forthcoming session
of the Tribunal.

Gérard is haunted by conscience and memory of his
former patriotic enthusiasm. Can he denounce Chénier as 'an
enemy of his country' ('Nemico della patria')? His
revolutionary zeal, which formerly fed on such ideals as
brotherly love, is now kept alive by jealousy and lust. It is an
effective outburst. Swayed by his desire for Madeleine, he
impulsively signs the indictment and gives it to Incredibile.

Madeleine is brought in by Mathieu, and Gérard explains
that Chénier has been arrested by his orders and because of
his own passion for her. She turns from him, but then offers
her love in exchange for Chénier's freedom. She tells Gérard
the story of her mother's horrible death, in the flames of her
house as it was burned by the mob: 'La mamma morta.' The
tribunal is ready to sit and people crowd into the court.
Gérard tells her he will do what he can for Chénier, and
writes a note to the President.

The Tribunal is in session. Several prisoners are summarily
condemned, to the applause of the crowd, and when
Chénier's turn comes, he is refused permission by the court
to answer the charge. On Gérard's insistence, he is finally
allowed to defend himself. He has fought for his country and
his ideals with sword and with pen; let them now take his
life, but leave his honour unstained: 'Sì, fui soldato.' Gérard
raises his voice in Chénier's defence; the indictment was false,
he says. But all is in vain, and the death sentence is duly
passed and acclaimed.

Act IV. In the courtyard of the Prison of St. Lazare,
Chénier waits for the tumbril. Roucher is with him, and when
he finishes writing, his friend asks him to read the poem he
has written. 'Come un bel dì di Maggio' he sings in a beautiful
aria which describes his feelings as a poet in the face of
death:

Roucher bids him farewell and leaves him to return to his
cell.

Gérard appears at the outer gate, with Madeleine, and the
gaoler lets them in. He agrees to allow Madeleine to take the
place of a female prisoner condemned to death, and so to die
with Chénier. Gérard leaves, determined to make a last effort
in their defence, and Chénier is brought in. Their duet is on a
grand scale; they exult in their love and rejoice that death
will unite them for ever: 'Vicino a te.' In an opera in which
Giordano has indulged to the full his gift for passionate,

lyrical melody, it is fitting that the most lyrical and the most passionate moments should come in the short last act, in the shape of Chénier's aria and the great duet.

Andrea Chénier is by far Giordano's most popular opera, and also his best; it is still in the regular Italian repertory.

H.

FEDORA

Opera in three acts by Umberto Giordano; text by A. Colautti from the play by Sardou. Première on November 17, 1898, at the Teatro Lirico, Milan, with Bellincioni, Caruso, Delfino Menotti, conductor Giordano. First performed Covent Garden, 1906, with Giachetti, Zenatello, Sammarco, conductor Mugnone; New York, Metropolitan, 1906, with Cavalieri, Caruso, Scotti, conductor Vigna. Revived Metropolitan, 1923, with Jeritza, Martinelli, Scotti, conductor Papi; Covent Garden, 1925, with Jeritza, Lappas, Badini, conductor Failoni; la Scala, Milan, 1932, with Cobelli, Pertile, Stabile, conductor de Sabata; 1939, with Pacetti, Gigli, Manacchini, conductor Marinuzzi; 1941, with Pederzini, Pigni, Gobbi, conductor Ghione; 1948, with Caniglia, Prandelli, Mascherini, conductor de Sabata; 1956, with Callas, Corelli, Colzani, conductor Gavazzeni.

CHARACTERS

Princess Fedora Romanov	Soprano
Count Loris Ipanov	Tenor
De Siriex, *a French diplomat*	Baritone
Countess Olga Sukarev	Soprano
Grech, *a police officer*	Bass
Cirillo, *a coachman*	Baritone
Dmitri, *a groom*	Contralto
A little Savoyard	Mezzo-Soprano
Désiré, *a valet*	Tenor
Baron Rouvel	Tenor
Lorek, *a surgeon*	Baritone
Borov, *a doctor*	Baritone
Nicola ⎱ *footmen*	⎰ Tenor
Sergio ⎰	⎱ Baritone
Boleslao Lazinski, *a pianist*	Mime

Time: Late Nineteenth Century   *Place:* St. Petersburg, Paris, Switzerland

Fedora is, after *Andrea Chénier*, Giordano's most successful opera, and it is still popular in Italy. It is written in the composer's familiar style—a mixture of the mellifluous and the stressful.

Act I plays in St. Petersburg, at the house of Count Vladimir Andrejevich; the time is 'the present'. The Count's servants are waiting for his return home, playing dominoes and gossiping about his way of life—gambling, drinking, and women are his diversions, which, they say, will have to stop now that he is marrying the rich widow, Princess Fedora. A bell rings; it is the Princess herself, asking where her fiancé is.

The sound of a sledge is heard, and Grech enters quickly, asking where the Count's room is. The Count is carried to it, gravely wounded; doctors arrive, and we catch a glimpse of the end of the bed before the doctors close the door. No one knows who has wounded him, and Grech, the police officer in charge of the case, questions everyone present, beginning with Dmitri, Désiré, and Cirillo. The coachman gives his evidence dramatically and with emotion as he thinks about his master. He drove him to the shooting gallery, he said, and, a quarter of an hour after arriving, he heard two shots. Someone rushed out, leaving bloody footprints on the snow, and disappeared into the darkness. He (Cirillo) hailed a passing cab (in which was de Siriex) and together they went into the house, to find the Count upstairs covered in blood. It comes to light that the Count received a letter that very morning, brought by an old woman—and the building in which he was found wounded was let to an old woman. Was anyone else seen in the house during the morning? Yes, a young man, who sat down without giving his name, and eventually rushed out.

Suddenly, one of the servants remembers that it was Count Loris Ipanov who was there that morning—and Fedora jumps at the idea that it must have been he who committed the murder. Grech goes to his rooms—he lives just opposite—but returns to say that their quarry has escaped them. In the meanwhile the doctor summons Fedora, whose shriek of consternation tells us conclusively that Vladimir is dead.

Act II. Fedora has determined to devote herself to the pursuit and capture of the man she presumes is her fiancé's murderer, Count Loris Ipanov, and to extract a confession of his guilt from him. A reception is in progress at her house in Paris, and Countess Olga introduces her friend the pianist, Boleslao Lazinski, to the guests. Fedora comes up to de Siriex, now French Foreign Secretary, and says to him with peculiar emphasis: 'I may need your help. You are an old friend, this is a newer one—Count Loris Ipanov.' De Siriex is astonished at the speed with which Fedora has caught up with Loris.

Fedora is alone with Loris, and he declares his love in the passionate *arioso*, 'Amor ti vieta' (Love doth forbid you not to love). This flowing *cantilena* is one of the best-known songs in the repertory of the Italian tenor, and its performance customarily sends an Italian audience into a delirium of delight.

Fedora tells Borov, who asks her if she would like to give him a message for any Russian friend, that she too is going back to Russia almost immediately. She has been pardoned and her possessions restored to her. Loris is disconsolate, and admits that he cannot go. Fedora says she will intercede for him, but he tells her that in itself is unlikely to prove sufficient to have his sentence revoked. While Lazinski, with much comic pantomime, starts to play for the guests, Loris confesses to Fedora that he was in fact responsible for the death of Count Vladimir, but that he is innocent of his murder. Fedora can hardly contain her triumph. Loris says he can bring proof of his innocence, and she bids him return that very night with his documents.

Fedora, alone, sits down at her writing table. She calls to Grech and confirms that he and his men are to kidnap Loris once he has given her proof of his guilt and convey him on board a Russian ship. She has written to General Jarischkin in St. Petersburg to inform him of the way events have been moving, and has added the names of Loris's brother and of his friend Sokolev, who have been, she says, accomplices in his crime.

Loris arrives, and Fedora immediately accuses him of being a Nihilist and implicated in the plot against the Tsar's life, as well as guilty of the murder of Count Vladimir. He denies that this act was murder, and tells her the story of the Count's duplicity in carrying on a clandestine affair with Loris's wife, Wanda. He discovered the liaison by chance, and found proof in the shape of a letter from Wanda to Vladimir, which he took from a drawer in Vladimir's house the day of the murder. He shows Fedora letters from Vladimir to Wanda, and she knows that he is speaking the truth. Loris's confession, 'Mia madre, la mia vecchia madre' is one of the best-known passages in the score. He continues his story: he went to the place of assignation and caught the guilty pair together, was shot at by Vladimir and wounded, and, when he fired in his turn, inflicted a mortal wound on his enemy. Wanda escaped, only to die later.

Fedora is overcome at the story, but Loris tells her he is still pursued by an unknown adversary, who sets spies on him and will not let him live out his exile in peace. 'Vedi, io piango' (See, I am weeping) he sings, thinking of the mother and the native land he cannot see again. The signal is heard, and Fedora with difficulty prevents Loris from rushing out to meet his accusers. Only when she admits she loves him and will keep him with her, does he succumb to her persuasion.

Act III.   Fedora's villa in Switzerland. Mountaineers sing a Swiss song as a prelude to a short but passionate interchange between Fedora and Loris, who are now married and living happily together. Olga interrupts the idyllic scene, and is prepared to be enthusiastic about everything—even the bicycle she sees propped up against the wall. Loris recommends a tandem as better suited to her amatory purposes. Loris goes to collect his mail as de Siriex enters. He cannot resist telling Olga that her Polish pianist was in reality a spy, set on her trail to pump information from her.

When they are alone, de Siriex tells Fedora that Jarischkin had pursued his vengeful career until his dismissal by the new Tsar. Two young men, accomplices so it was said in the murder of Count Vladimir, were arrested; one disappeared, the other was shut up in a prison on the banks of the Neva, where, the tide rising suddenly, he was slowly drowned in his dungeon. It was Valerian, Loris's brother. The news of his death proved such a shock to his aged mother that she fell ill and died.

Fedora is left alone, and prays that Loris may be saved from the net she has unwittingly drawn around him: 'Dio di giustizia' (O God of justice). Loris enters and finds a telegram telling him he has been pardoned and is free to return to Russia. His joy knows no bounds. But he has a letter from his friend Borov, who also sent the telegram, in which he indicates that a woman's accusation has been the means of prolonging his exile, and has even caused the deaths of his supposed 'accomplices', Valerian and Sokolev, which in their turn have broken the heart of his mother, who has died of shock.

Loris will not listen to Fedora's attempt to suggest that the woman in question may have done what she did believing him to have been guilty of a monstrous crime, but a renewal of her pleading shows him that his enemy has been none other than Fedora herself. He rushes at her in fury, but she drinks the poison she has carried concealed in the Byzantine crucifix she wore, and Borov arrives to find her dying. Loris's grief knows no bounds, and to the tune of 'Amor ti vieta', he forgives the woman who has brought such hate and such love into his life.   H.

10
French Opera

FRANÇOIS ADRIEN BOÏELDIEU
(1775–1834)

LA DAME BLANCHE
The White Lady

Opera in three acts by Boïeldieu, text by Scribe, founded on Scott's *Guy Mannering* and *The Monastery*. Première at the Opéra-Comique, Paris, December 10, 1825, with Mmes. Rigaut, Boulanger, MM. Ponchard, Henri. First performed Drury Lane, London, 1826 (in English); Haymarket, 1834 (in German); New York, 1827 (in French). Revived Metropolitan, 1904, with Gadski, Naval, Blass, conductor Mottl; Paris, 1926, with Féraldy, Faroche, Villabella, Marrio; Brussels, 1936; London, Philopera Circle, 1955; Toulouse, 1961; Ghent and Bordeaux, 1963, the latter with Michel Sénéchal.

CHARACTERS

Gaveston, *steward to the late Comte d'Avenel* . . . . Bass
Anna, *his ward* . . . . Soprano
Georges Brown, *a young English officer* . . . . Tenor
Dickson, *tenant on the estate* . . . . Tenor
Jenny, *his wife* . . . . Soprano
Marguerite, *old servant of the Comte d'Avenel* . Soprano
Gabriel, *employed by Dickson* . . . . Bass
MacIrton, *Justice of the Peace* . . . . Bass

Time: 1759   *Place:* Scotland

La Dame Blanche had one of the most successful premiéres in all operatic history, and still stands as one of the most notable hits in the history of opéra-comique. The 1,000th

performance at the Opéra-Comique in Paris was in 1862, the
1,675th in 1914. The score is full of delightful and skilfully
written music, and the work still appears to have a sparkle
and lightness of touch which distinguish it from its many less
praiseworthy successors.

Act I takes place in front of Dickson's house. Dancing and
singing are in progress in honour of the christening of
Dickson's small child. Georges Brown arrives, makes himself
known as an officer in the King's service, and accepts to take
the place of the child's missing godfather. He enquires about
the history of the castle of Avenel, which dominates the
countryside, and is told that, amongst other things, it boasts
a ghost, not a malicious one as is so often the case, but a
female, known as 'the White Lady', whose special office is to
protect her sex from their false-hearted suitors. Everyone
believes in her, and most are firmly convinced that at one
time or another they have seen her. Dickson is summoned to
meet her that very night, and, in spite of his very definite
fears, he dare not disobey. Georges offers to go in his stead,
and the offer is gratefully accepted. They wish him god-
speed.

Act II.   A Gothic room in the Castle. It is only half-lit
and Marguerite is sitting there spinning. Anna comes in and
Marguerite hears from her something of the story of the old
Count's missing heir, whom Gaveston is thought to have
spirited away so as to obtain the castle and the Count's lands
for himself. Gaveston enters and tries unsuccessfully to
discover from Anna where the Countess hid the treasure
before she died. Someone rings the door-bell and Gaveston
says he will not allow anyone to enter; but Anna pleads with
him—has he not enemies enough without making any
more? She knows that it is Dickson, come at the order of the
'white lady' (for it is Anna who appears as the ghost, and
who has summoned Dickson, hoping to be able through him
to prevent the castle falling into Gaveston's hands). Anna
tells Gaveston that she will the next day reveal the Countess's
secret if he will allow the traveller in. Anna disappears and
Marguerite goes to open the doors.

Georges Brown, who has come in Dickson's place, says
that he has heard that the castle has a ghost, and he would
like to have the opportunity of seeing it. When the other two
go to bed, he is left alone in the great room. He stokes up the
fire, and sings a serenade, hoping to entice the ghost to

appear. She does, in the person of Anna, who believes at first that it is Dickson come to meet her as she had ordered. She discovers that it is Georges Brown and recognises him as a wounded officer she had once tended and nursed and grown fond of. He is astonished that the ghost should know such details of his past as that he was wounded—he has been trying ever since to find his benefactress, whom he loves—and promises, as she asks, that he will perform whatever she orders on the morrow.

She disappears and Gaveston comes in, and, after some talk, invites Georges to stay for the auction which is just about to begin. Jenny and Dickson ply him with questions, but he reveals nothing of what he has seen.

Dickson has been charged by his fellow farmers to bid as high as he dare in order to prevent the castle falling into Gaveston's hands. The bidding advances, Dickson is obliged to drop out, but then Georges Brown comes into the reckoning. He is about to give in when the sight of Anna spurs him on to greater efforts, and eventually the castle is knocked down to Georges. He must pay, says the justice, by midday. Gaveston is besides himself with fury.

Act III. The same room. Anna and Marguerite discuss the whereabouts of a certain statue of the 'white lady' in which, says Anna, all the family money was once hidden. Marguerite remembers a secret passage, and they go off to explore it. The crowd meanwhile assembles to do honour to the new owner, and sings to him a version of the old Scottish tune 'Robin Adair', which he recognises and is able to finish.

Gaveston asks Georges for some explanation of his extraordinary behaviour of that morning; has he the money to pay for the castle? No, says Georges, but the 'white lady' will provide it. Georges leaves and his place is taken by MacIrton, a friend of Gaveston's who warns him that the once lost son of the house has turned up in England and now goes under the name of Georges Brown. Anna, in hiding, overhears.

Just before midday, MacIrton comes with representatives of the law to collect the money; Georges asks for time to communicate with the white lady, who is financing the whole transaction, he says. Anna appears in the guise of the white lady, bringing the treasure chest with her—she has found it after all. Moreover she declares that Georges Brown is the missing heir to the estates of Avenel.

The freshness of the tunes, the gaiety of the personalities

at work in it—these qualities seem to survive the passing of years as far as *La Dame Blanche* is concerned. Such passages as Georges' invigorating 'Ah, quel plaisir d'être soldat', the agreeable ballad of 'la dame blanche' sung by Jenny and Dickson, and the charming *allegretto* section of the duet in Act II for Anna and Georges—these have the lightness of touch and distinction that even now is implied by the expression 'opéra-comique'. Anna's aria at the beginning of Act III has an almost Weber-like feeling about it, and several of the tunes are cut in his style. The figure of Georges Brown himself (the combination of the French spelling of the Christian name with this surname is irresistible) is particularly attractive. His part in the action is romantic, debonair and devil-may-care and yet it never for a moment goes against the logic of the drama; he does not behave like a hero without good reason. Highly successful are his two romantic solos, the one when he is waiting for the ghost to appear ('Viens gentille dame'), the other equally charming when he tries to catch the tune of 'Robin Adair' as the chorus starts to sing it in Act III.   H.

DANIEL
FRANÇOIS AUBER

(1782–1871)

LA MUETTE DE PORTICI

The Dumb Girl of Portici

OPERA in five acts by Auber, text by Scribe and Delavigne. Première at the Opéra, Paris, February 29, 1828, with Mlles. Noblet, Cinti-Damoreau, MM. Nourrit, Dabadie. First performed at Drury Lane, London (in English), 1829; New York, 1829 (in English); Covent Garden, 1845 (in French); 1849 (in Italian), with Grisi and Mario; Metropolitan, 1884, with Bely, Schott, Kögel, conductor Damrosch. Braham was a noted Masaniello. Revived with explicit revolutionary overtones, Berlin, Staatsoper, 1953, with Stolze.

CHARACTERS

Alfonso d'Arcos, *son of the Spanish Viceroy of*
  Naples .... Tenor
Lorenzo, *his confidant* .... Tenor
Selva, *an officer of the Viceroy's guard* .... Bass
Masaniello, *a fisherman of Naples* .... Tenor
Pietro, *his friend* .... Baritone
Fenella, *Masaniello's sister* .... Dancer
Borella ⎱ *fisherman* .... ⎰ Bass
Moreno ⎰   ⎱ Bass
Elvira, *a Spanish Princess* .... Soprano
A Maid of Honour to the Princess ..... Mezzo-Soprano
Time: 1647   *Place:* Naples

The story of *La Muette de Portici* is based on the historical
happenings of the year 1647, when the people of Naples rose
against their Spanish oppressors. The opera is perhaps the
most successful Auber ever wrote; within twelve years of the
first performance, there had been 100 representations at the
Paris Opéra, and the 500th occurred in 1880. 'It is well
known', says Loewenberg, 'that a performance (not the first
performance though as sometimes stated) at Brussels, August
25, 1830, gave the signal to the outbreak of the Belgian
revolution, which led to the independence of the country.'

The overture has an almost Rossinian animation, and its
popularity is still considerable. Act I takes place in the
gardens next to the palace of the Duke of Arcos, Spanish
Viceroy of Naples. A chapel can be seen. Against a chorus of
rejoicing, the Viceroy's son, Alfonso, laments his conduct in
seducing an innocent and poor Neapolitan maid, Fenella,
who loved him but whom he has had to cast off in view of his
approaching marriage with Elvira, the Spanish Princess whom
he loves. Fenella, who is dumb, has disappeared, and for a
month there has been no sign of her. In a big aria, Elvira
proclaims her happiness to the young girls who are attending
her to the altar. Dances are performed for her entertainment,
but Elvira is informed that a fishermaid, pursued by soldiers,
is asking for her protection. Elvira questions Fenella, who
tells her story in dumb show.

The Princess with her attendants goes into the chapel.
When she emerges with her bridegroom, Alfonso recognises
Fenella, whom Elvira beckons towards them. Fenella
indicates that it is Alfonso who has betrayed her. Elvira is

horrified, and the act ends in general consternation at the turn events have taken.

Act II.   Portici, on the seashore between Naples and Mount Vesuvius. Fishermen are assembling, and greet their leader, Masaniello. He sings a barcarole ('Amis la matinée est belle'), which is fuller of foreboding than of the joy of living. As yet only Pietro, Masaniello's friend, knows of the sad fate of Fenella, but he now reports that he has been unable to find her anywhere, or indeed to gather any news of her whereabouts. The two friends swear vengeance on the tyrants, who have oppressed their people for so long and who have now done so grievous an injury to the most defenceless of their subjects; 'Amour sacré de la patrie' runs the refrain of the famous patriotic duet, which history says was the signal for the start of the Belgian revolution.

Fenella comes to seek Masaniello, and tells him her story. She will not admit her lover's name, but signifies that he is married and so cannot redeem her shame. Masaniello swears to be revenged, and calls the fishermen to arms. They swear perdition to the enemies of the country.

Act III.   A public square in Naples. Alfonso tries to persuade Elvira that he loves her, and that his penitence for the wrong he did the fishergirl is sincere. She yields to his entreaty, and he commands the guards to find Fenella and bring her before Elvira. The market is in full swing, and people buy and sell; a *tarantella* is danced. The guards think they see Fenella and attempt to arrest her. Masaniello intervenes and, when the guards would arrest him too, calls on the people to rise. The soldiers are driven off, but before leading his improvised army off to further conquests, Masaniello calls on them to pray for God's guidance in their just enterprise. The act comes to an end as they prepare to subdue the city.

Act IV.   Portici; the hut of Masaniello. Masaniello laments that the battle for liberty should have bred licence and destructiveness amongst the conquering rabble he led to victory. Fenella appears, pale and with faltering steps, and her brother gently sings her to sleep. Pietro and his companions come to incite Masaniello once more to place himself at their head and lead them to victory and revenge. He pleads for moderation, and for a cessation of bloodshed.

They go to the back of the house, and shortly afterwards a knock is heard. Alfonso and Elvira come to seek shelter from the bloodthirsty mob, little knowing from whom they are asking it. At first Fenella does not want to save Elvira, whom she thinks of as her rival, but Elvira's pleading wins her pity, and she vows to save them or die with them in the attempt. Much to Fenella's joy, Masaniello agrees to shelter the two fugitives.

Pietro appears with representatives of the people to ask Masaniello to take the keys of government and rule over them. Pietro recognises Alfonso, and an ensemble ensues between the two Spanish fugitives, Masaniello, Pietro, and the chorus. Pietro wishes to put them straightway to death, Masaniello urges that his oath of hospitality is binding. In the end Masaniello gives the Spaniards safe-conduct and threatens to slay anyone who makes a move against them. Pietro and his followers swear that Masaniello shall be the next to fall—their words are spoken against a background of praise for Masaniello as victor of the day.

Act V. In front of the Viceroy's palace at Naples. Pietro sings a barcarole with the chorus; in between the two verses he confides to a friend that he has already administered poison to Masaniello, who bade fair to become a greater tyrant than those they deposed in his favour. Even as he sings, the 'king of the day' is lying dying, and no human power can save him.

News comes that Alfonso is marching against them at the head of troops, and, almost as bad, that Vesuvius is in eruption; the credulous peasants think that the wrath of heaven is being visited on the rebels. Only Masaniello can save them, cry the people, but Pietro and his friends reveal that the poison has made the hero the victim of hallucinations. Masaniello himself comes out of the palace, and is obviously not in his right mind. All appeal to him as their only hope; but he takes no notice and sings the barcarole we heard in the first act. Not until Fenella appears can he grasp the import of the situation, but then he places himself at the head of the rebels and marches off with them.

Fenella prays for his safe return. A moment later Elvira appears, explaining that Masaniello has saved her life from the murderous stroke of one of his followers; Alfonso, who follows her, continues the story—Masaniello himself was struck down in revenge for his saving of Elvira. Fenella is overcome by the news and commits suicide.

H.

FRA DIAVOLO

Opera in three acts by Auber, text by Scribe. Première at Opéra Comique, Paris, January 28, 1830, with Mmes. Prévost, Boulanger, M Chollet. First performed Drury Lane, 1831; New York, 1831; Lyceum 1857 (in Italian), with Borsio, Gardoni, Ronconi, Tagliafico. Las performance at Covent Garden, 1896, with Engle, de Lucia, Pini-Corsi Arimondi, Bispham. Revived Metropolitan, 1910, with Alten anc Clément, conductor Hertz; Berlin, 1934, with Eisinger, Pattiera Schützendorf, Hüsch, conductor Blech; la Scala, Milan, 1934, with Carosio, Pertile, Autori, Bettoni, Nessi, conductor Santini; Sadler's Wells, 1935 (in English), with Naylor, Arthur Cox (Carron), Matters. Stear, Lloyd; Berlin, 1936, with Berger, Völker, Eugen Fuchs, Helgers Stockholm, 1948; Naples, 1962, with Vicenzi, Lazzari, Valdengo, Ercolani; Wexford Festival, 1966, with Valentini, Anna Reynolds, Benelli, Nigel Douglas, Antonio Boyer; Marseilles, 1966, with Mady Mesplé and Michel Sénéchal; San Francisco, 1968, with Mary Costa, Sylvia Anderson, Nicolai Gedda. Fra Diavolo was a favourite role of many famous tenors, amongst them, Bonci and Schipa.

CHARACTERS

Fra Diavolo, *a bandit chief* . . . . Tenor
Lord Cockburn, *an English tourist* . . . . Tenor
Lady Pamela, *his wife* . . . . Mezzo-Soprano
Lorenzo, *an officer of carabiniers* . . . . Tenor
Matteo, *an innkeeper* . . . . Bass
Zerlina, *his daughter* . . . . Soprano
Giacomo, *a bandit* . . . . Bass
Beppo, *a bandit* . . . . Tenor
Time: Eighteenth Century   *Place:* Near Naples

Fra Diavolo, one of the most popular of all opéras-comique, is now remembered chiefly through its overture. All the same, its admirable music and excellent story seem to entitle it to more frequent revival than in fact, outside Germany, it seems to receive.

The story is concerned with Fra Diavolo, a famous bandit leader in the district round Naples. His reputation is to some extent that of a Robin Hood, his chivalry being above question and his tendency to give generously to the poor out of what he has taken from the rich. At the time of the story, he is travelling under the name of the Marquis of San Marco.

Act I. Matteo's tavern. A reward of 10,000 *piastres* has been offered for the apprehension of the bandit Fra Diavolo. Lorenzo and his troop of carabiniers are drinking at the inn,

17 *Falstaff* at Covent Garden: with Regina Resnik and Geraint Evans.

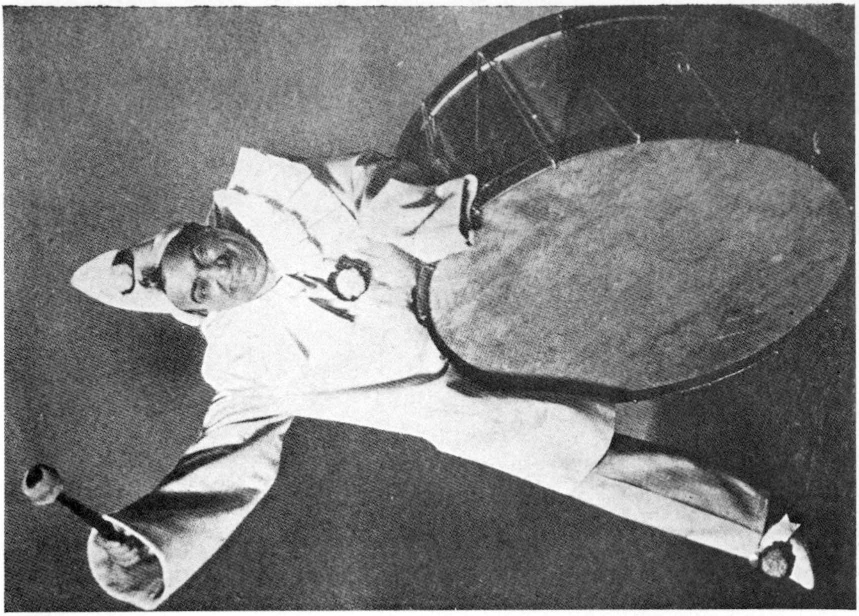

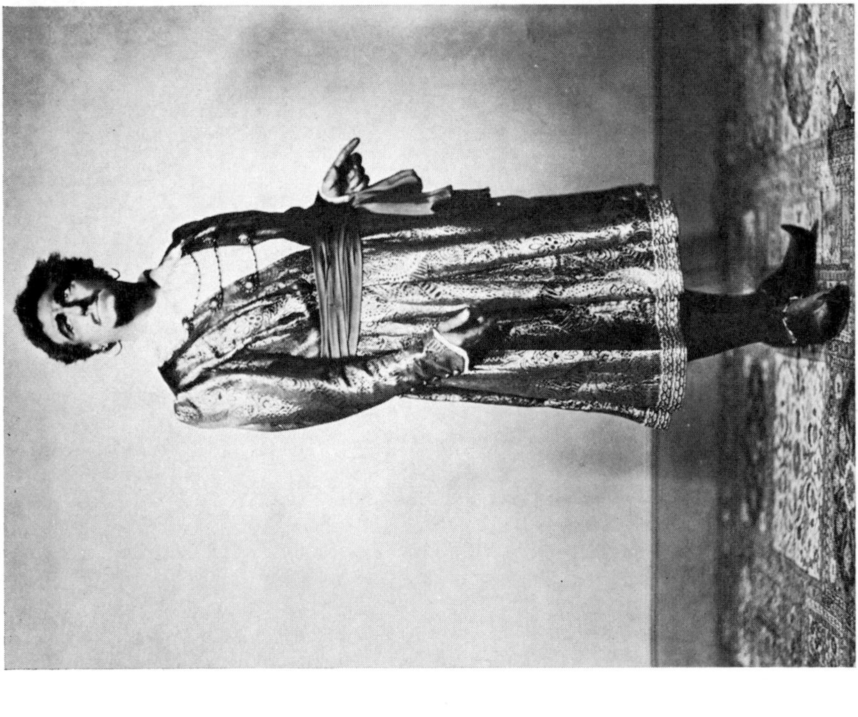

but the brigadier seems unusually preoccupied. It soon turns out that he is full of sadness at the prospect of losing his sweetheart, Zerlina, the innkeeper's daughter, whom her father has destined for a wealthier suitor, the farmer Francesco. The party is interrupted by the precipitate arrival of Lord Cockburn, wealthy English traveller, and his wife, Lady Pamela, complaining loudly that they have been set upon and robbed, only escaping with their lives because they had the presence of mind to abandon their coach. Lorenzo starts off to look for the brigand, after hearing that Lord Cockburn means to offer a reward of 6,000 *scudi* for the return of his wife's jewels.

The English couple have only just finished an altercation on the subject of the attentions of a certain Marquis of San Marco to her ladyship—in one case welcome, in the other not so welcome—when a carriage draws up at the door, and the Marquis himself is announced. He seems delighted to see Pamela, and says that he is going to stay the night. Matteo hastens to see that he is suitably provided with food, and then bids his daughter look after the Marquis well while he himself is away for the night making the final arrangements for her wedding to Francesco.

The Marquis asks why the English lord seems in such a bad temper and is told that he has just been robbed by the notorious Fra Diavolo. The Marquis expresses incredulity at the idea that there should be bandits in such civilised parts of the country, but Zerlina is told to sing him the local ballad of Fra Diavolo. He joins in the last verse. A couple of beggars come in, and the Marquis says he will pay for their board and lodging. When the innkeeper and his daughter have gone out, these turn out to be Giacomo and Beppo, two members of Fra Diavolo's band, and they discuss the affair of the English nobleman with him, admitting that they were unable to find the gold he was reputed to have with him. Fra Diavolo says he will try to find out its whereabouts from Lady Pamela, whom at that moment he spies coming towards them. He dismisses his retainers, and starts to pay compliments to the lady, turning their emotional duet into a barcarole when he catches sight of her husband. The Marquis flatters Milord into giving away the secret hiding-place of his money; he boasts that it is in bills, sewn into his cloak and his wife's gown.

There is a noise outside; it is the troop of carabiniers returning after a most successful sortie against the bandits.

They report that they have killed at least twenty and recaptured the stolen property. Lady Pamela insists that Lorenzo be given his reward straightaway, so that he can convince Matteo that he is wealthy enough to marry Zerlina. The act ends with Lorenzo and the soldiers announcing their intention to capture the bandit chief himself, Fra Diavolo swearing to be revenged for the loss of his followers.

Act II. The curtain rises to show Zerlina's bedroom. Lord Cockburn and wife are sleeping next door, and the only way into their room is through hers. Zerlina prepares the rooms, singing a brilliant aria the while. Their occupants come up to bed, quarrelling as they do so sufficiently for Zerlina to remark that she and her husband will not be like that a year after their wedding day. Zerlina goes with them to their room to help Lady Pamela undress and to see if there is anything they need.

Enter Fra Diavolo, who has discovered that Zerlina's room is next to that of the English travellers, and who means to hide there himself, with his two followers, so as to relieve them for the second time of their valuables. He sings a barcarole to attract the attention of Giacomo and Beppo, and lets them in through the window. They hear Zerlina's voice and all go to hide, Beppo and Giacomo going through some glass doors from which the bedroom is in full view. Zerlina undresses and pauses for a moment to admire her face and figure in the looking-glass; this is too much for the watchers who cannot restrain their laughter. Zerlina says her prayers and goes to bed, soon to fall asleep. It is the moment for Diavolo and his two followers to make their way towards Milord's rooms. Giacomo is about to stab Zerlina—might she not give them away if there were to be any noise? — but she murmurs a prayer in her sleep and he cannot bring himself to do the deed.

Suddenly, there is a noise downstairs; Zerlina wakes up to hear Lorenzo calling for her. He and his men have not found Fra Diavolo and would like food and shelter for the rest of the night. She admits them; Lord Cockburn makes an appearance to complain about the noise but that is forgotten when Beppo knocks something over in the cupboard in which he is hidden. All is not lost however, Fra Diavolo taking it upon himself to step out and confront the brigadier and the Englishman. He had, he confesses to each of them separately, a rendezvous; he whispers the names of Zerlina and Lady

Pamela into the appropriate ear. He is challenged by Lorenzo, and accepts. When Zerlina and Lady Pamela appear, they are met with nothing but coldness by respectively the lover and the husband on whom they were counting for comfort.

Act III. The mountains, not far from Matteo's inn. Fra Diavolo has laid his plans carefully. He means to be revenged on Lorenzo for what he and his soldiers have done to the rest of his band. Meanwhile, he sings of the charms of a bandit's life. The Easter procession is about to start out from the inn, watched by Beppo and Giacomo, who have orders to wait until Lorenzo and his soldiers have moved off, then ring the church bell to indicate to Fra Diavolo that the way is clear. Lorenzo, in a romance, sings sadly of the love he had thought faithful but has found to be false. Suddenly, he remembers that he has a debt of honour to pay at exactly this hour. He reproaches Zerlina for her unfaithfulness, which she indignantly denies. Just then Beppo and Giacomo catch sight of her and recognise her as the girl they watched going to bed the previous night. They laugh at the memory and repeat some of her phrases, just a little too loudly it appears, for she hears them and demands that someone find out the truth about how they overheard her when she was alone in her own bedroom. A paper giving Fra Diavolo's plan is found on one of them and the plot is revealed.

Lorenzo orders that Giacomo be taken to ring the bell, and that when Fra Diavolo appears Beppo tell him the way is clear. He will then fall into their hands. All goes as he has hoped. Diavolo appears and descends to the square, where he is surrounded by carabiniers and made prisoner. All is explained and forgiven. (In an alternative ending to the opera, Fra Diavolo is shot by the soldiery in the ambush.)

H.

GIACOMO MEYERBEER

(1791–1864)

ALTHOUGH he was born in Berlin (September 5, 1791), studied pianoforte and theory in Germany, and attained in that country a reputation as a brilliant pianist as well as producing several operas there, Meyerbeer is regarded as the founder[1] of what is generally understood as French Grand Opera. It has been said of him that 'he joined to the flowing melody of the Italians the solid harmony of the Germans, the poignant declamation and varied, piquant rhythm of the French'; which is a good description of the opera that flourished on the stage of the Académie or Grand Opéra, Paris. The elaborately spectacular scenes and finales in Meyerbeer's operas were the models for many of his successors, Italian as well as French and German. He understood how to write effectively for the voice, and he was an opera composer who made a point of striving for tone colour in the instrumental accompaniment. Sometimes the effect may be too calculated, too cunningly contrived, too obviously sought for. But what he accomplished had decided influence on the enrichment of the instrumental score in operatic composition.

Much criticism has been directed at Meyerbeer, and much of his music has disappeared from the stage. Meyerbeer had the pick of the great artists of his day. His works were written for and produced with brilliant casts, and had better not be sung at all than indifferently.

Meyerbeer came of a Jewish family. His real name was Jakob Liebmann Beer. He prefixed 'Meyer' to his patronymic at the request of a wealthy relative who made him his heir. He was a pupil in pianoforte of Clementi; also studied under Abbé Vogler, being a fellow pupil of C. M. von Weber. His first operas were German. In 1815 he went to Italy and composed a series of operas in the style of Rossini. Going to Paris in 1826, he became 'immersed in the study of French opera, from Lully onward'. The first result was *Robert le Diable* (Robert the Devil), Grand Opéra, Paris, 1831. Much of the music of *L'Etoile du Nord* came from an earlier score, *Ein Feldlager in Schlesien* (The Camp in Silesia), Berlin, 1843.

---

[1] Or at least the grandest exploiter of the form. But just as it was Mozart with *Idomeneo* rather than Gluck who wrote the greatest *opera seria*, so it is arguable that the finest example of French Grand Opera was not by Meyerbeer at all but is to be found in Verdi's *Don Carlos*.
                                                                              H.

ROBERT LE DIABLE
Robert the Devil

Opera in five acts by Meyerbeer; words by Scribe and Delavigne. Première Grand Opéra, Paris, November 22, 1831, with Mmes. Dorus-Gras, Cinti-Damoreau, MM. Nourrit, Levasseur. First performed Drury Lane, London, 1832 (in English), as *The Demon, or the Mystic Branch*; Covent Garden, 1832 (in English), as *The Fiend Father, or Robert of Normandy*; Her Majesty's Theatre, 1847 (in Italian), with Jenny Lind (her London début); New York, 1834 (in English), with Mrs. Wood as Isobel and Wood as Robert, the opera being followed by a *pas seul* by Miss Wheatley, and a farce, *My Uncle John*; Astor Place Opera House, 1851, with Steffanone, Bosio, Bettini, Marini; Academy of Music, 1857, with Formes as Bertram; Metropolitan, 1883, with Fursch-Madi, Valleria, Stagno, Mirabella. Last Covent Garden performance, 1890, with Fanny Moody, Stromfield, Charles Manners, Guetray, conductor Arditi. Revived Florence Festival, 1968, with Scotto, Merighi, Christoff.

CHARACTERS

Alice, *foster-sister of Robert* .... Soprano
Isabella, *Princess of Sicily* .... Soprano
The Abbess . . . . Dancer
Robert, *Duke of Normandy* .... Tenor
Bertram, *the Unknown* .... Bass
Raimbaut, *a minstrel* .... Tenor
Time: Thirteenth Century   *Place:* Sicily

The production of *Robert le Diable* in Paris was such a sensational success that it made the fortune of the Grand Opéra. Whatever criticism may now be directed against this opera, it was a remarkable creation for its day. Meyerbeer's score not only saved the libretto, in which the grotesque is carried to the point of absurdity, but actually made a brilliant success of the production as a whole.

The story is legendary. Robert is the son of the arch-fiend by a human woman. Robert's father, known as Bertram, but really the devil, ever follows him about, and seeks to lure him to destruction. The strain of purity in the drama is supplied by Robert's foster-sister, Alice, who, if Bertram is the prototype of Mephistopheles in *Faust*, may be regarded as the original of Micaela in *Carmen*.

Robert, because of his evil deeds (inspired by Bertram), has been banished from Normandy, and has come to Sicily. He has fallen in love with Isabella, she with him. He is to attend a tournament at which she is to award the prizes. Tempted by Bertram, he gambles and loses all his possessions, including even his armour. These facts are disclosed in the first act. This contains a song by Raimbaut, the minstrel, in which he tells of Robert's misdeeds; he is saved from the latter's fury by Alice, who is betrothed to Raimbaut, and who, in an expressive air, pleads vainly with Robert to mend his ways and especially to avoid Bertram, from whom she instinctively shrinks. In the second act Robert and Isabella meet in the palace. She bestows upon him a suit of armour to wear in the tournament. But, misled by Bertram, he seeks his rival elsewhere than in the lists, and, by his failure to appear there, loses his honour as a knight. In the next act, laid in the cavern of St. Irene, occurs an orgy of evil spirits, to whose number Bertram promises to add Robert. Next comes a scene that verges upon the grotesque, but which is converted by Meyerbeer's genius into something highly fantastic. This is in the ruined convent of St. Rosalie. In a big solo ('Nonnes, qui reposez') Bertram summons from their graves the nuns who, in life, were unfaithful to their vows. The fiend has promised Robert that if he will but seize a mystic cypress branch from over the grave of St. Rosalie, and bear it away, whatever he wishes for will become his. The ghostly nuns, led by their Abbess (Taglioni at the Paris première), dance about him. They seek to inveigle him with gambling, drink, and love, until, dazed by their enticements, he seizes the branch. Besides the ballet of the nuns, there is a scene for Raimbaut and Bertram—'Du rendezvous' (Our meeting place), and 'Le bonheur est dans l'inconstance' (Our pleasure lies in constant change).

The first use Robert makes of the branch is to effect entrance into Isabella's chamber. He threatens to seize her and bear her away, but yields to her entreaties, breaks the branch, and destroys the spell. In this act—the fourth—occurs the famous air for Isabella, 'Robert, toi que j'aime' (Robert, whom I love).

Once more Bertram seeks to make a compact with Robert, the price for which shall be paid with his soul. But Alice, by repeating to him the last warning words of his mother, delays the signing of the compact until the clock strikes twelve. The spell is broken. Bertram disappears. The cathedral doors swing open disclosing Isabella, who, in her bridal robes, awaits

Robert. The finale contains a trio for Alice, Robert and Bertram, which is considered one of Meyerbeer's finest inspirations.   K.

LES HUGUENOTS
The Huguenots

Opera in five acts by Giacomo Meyerbeer; text by A. E. Scribe after Deschamps. Première at the Opéra, Paris, February 29, 1836, with Mmes. Falcon, Dorus-Gras, Nourrit, Levasseur, Serda. First performed Covent Garden, 1841 (in German); 1845 (in French); 1848 (in Italian); New Orleans, 1839; New York, 1845 (in French). Revived Metropolitan, 1883, with Nilsson, Sembrich, Campanini, Mirabella, Kaschmann, conductor Vianesi; performed frequently at Covent Garden in the 1900's with Destinn, Tetrazzini, Caruso, Scotti, Journet; revived Buenos Aires, 1916, with Raisa, Clasenti, Martinelli, Crabbé, Journet, conductor Panizza; Rome, 1923, with Llacer, Pasini, O'Sullivan, Parvis, Donaggio, conductor Gui; Covent Garden, 1927, with Scacciati, Guglielmetti, O'Sullivan, Stabile, Kipnis, conductor Bellezza; Verona Arena, 1933, with Raisa, Saraceni, Lauri-Volpi, Rimini, Pasero, conductor Votto; Paris, 1936, with Hoerner, Delmas, Thill, Huberty, Pernet; la Scala, 1962, with Simionato, Sutherland, Cossotto, Corelli, Ganzarolli, Ghiaurov, Tozzi.

CHARACTERS

Valentine, *daughter of St. Bris and betrothed to de Nevers* .... Soprano
Marguerite de Valois, *betrothed to Henry IV, of Navarre* .... Soprano
Urbain, *page to Marguerite de Valois*. . .Mezzo-Soprano[1]

Count de St. Bris	*Catholic noblemen*	Baritone
Count de Nevers		Baritone
Cossé		Tenor
Méru		Baritone
Thoré	*Catholic gentlemen*	Baritone
Tavannes		Tenor
de Retz		Baritone

Raoul de Nangis, *a Huguenot nobleman* .... Tenor
Marcel, *a Huguenot soldier, servant to Raoul* ..... Bass
Bois-Rosé, *a Huguenot soldier* .... Tenor

----

[1] Originally for Soprano.   H.

Maurevert, *a Catholic nobleman* .... Bass
Catholic and Huguenot Ladies and Gentlemen of the Court;
Soldiers, Pages, Citizens, and Populace; Night Watch,
Monks, and Students.
Time: August 1572   *Place:* Touraine and Paris

It has been said that, because Meyerbeer was a Jew, he chose for two of his operas, *Les Huguenots* and *Le Prophète*, subjects dealing with bloody uprisings due to religious differences among Christians. *Les Huguenots* is written around the massacre of the Huguenots by the Catholics, on the night of St. Bartholomew's, Paris, August 24, 1572; *Le Prophète* around the seizure and occupation of Münster, in 1555, by the Anabaptists, led by John of Leyden. Even the ballet of the spectral nuns, in *Robert le Diable*, has been suggested as due to Meyerbeer's racial origin and a tendency covertly to attack the Christian religion. Far-fetched, I think. Most likely his famous librettist was chiefly responsible for choice of subjects and Meyerbeer accepted them because of the effective manner in which they were worked out. Even so, he was not wholly satisfied with Scribe's libretto of *Les Huguenots*. He had the scene of the benediction of the swords enlarged, and it was upon his insistence that Deschamps wrote in the love duet in Act IV. As it stands, the story has been handled with keen appreciation of its dramatic possibilities.

Act I. Touraine. Count de Nevers, one of the leaders of the Catholic party and a great lady-killer, has invited friends to a banquet at his château. Among these is Raoul de Nangis, a Huguenot. He is accompanied by an old retainer, the Huguenot soldier, Marcel. In the course of the fête it is proposed that everyone shall toast his love in a song. Raoul is the first to be called upon. The name of the beauty whom he pledges in his toast is unknown to him. He had come to her assistance while she was being molested by a party of students. She thanked him most graciously, and he lives in the hope of meeting her again.

Marcel is a fanatic Huguenot. Having followed his master to the banquet, he finds him surrounded by leaders of the party belonging to the opposite faith. He fears for the consequences. In strange contrast to the glamour and gaiety of the festive proceedings, he intones Luther's hymn 'Ein' feste Burg' (A Stronghold sure). The noblemen of the

Catholic party instead of becoming angry are amused. Marcel repays their levity by singing a fierce Huguenot battle song. That also amuses them.

At this point the Count de Nevers is informed that a lady is in the garden and wishes to speak with him. He leaves his guests who, through an open window, watch the meeting. Raoul, to his surprise and consternation, recognises in the lady none other than the fair creature whom he saved from the molestations of the students and with whom he has fallen in love. Naturally, however, from the circumstances of her meeting with de Nevers he cannot but conclude that a liaison exists between them.

De Nevers returns, rejoins his guests. Urbain, the page of Queen Marguerite de Valois, enters. He is in search of Raoul, having come to conduct him to a meeting with a gracious and noble lady whose name, however, is not disclosed. Raoul's eyes having been bandaged, he is conducted to a carriage and departs with Urbain, wondering what his next adventure will be.

Act II. In the Garden of Chenonceaux, Queen Marguerite de Valois receives Valentine, daughter of the Count de St. Bris. The Queen knows of her rescue from the students by Raoul. Desiring to put an end to the differences between Huguenots and Catholics which have already led to bloodshed, she has conceived the idea of uniting Valentine, daughter of one of the great Catholic leaders, to Raoul. Valentine, however, was already pledged to de Nevers. It was at the Queen's suggestion that she visited de Nevers and had him summoned from the banquet in order to ask him to release her from her engagement to him—a request which, however reluctantly, he granted.

Here, in the Gardens of Chenonceaux, Valentine and Raoul are, according to the Queen's plan, to meet again, but she intends first to receive him alone. He is brought in, the bandage is removed from his eyes, he does homage to the Queen, and when, in the presence of the leaders of the Catholic party, Marguerite de Valois explains her purpose and her plan through this union of two great houses to end the religious differences which have disturbed her reign, all consent.

Valentine is led in. Raoul at once recognises her as the woman of his adventure but also, alas, as the woman whom de Nevers met in the garden during the banquet (he has, as

yet, no knowledge of the purpose of this meeting). Believing
her to be unchaste, he refuses her hand. General consternation. St. Bris, his followers, all draw their swords. Raoul's
flashes from its sheath. Only the Queen's intervention
prevents bloodshed.

Act III.   The scene is an open place in Paris before a
chapel, where de Nevers, who has renewed his engagement
with Valentine, is to take her in marriage. The nuptial cortège
enters the building. The populace is restless, excited.
Religious differences still are the cause of enmity. The
presence of Royalist and Huguenot soldiers adds to the
restlessness of the people. De Nevers, St. Bris, and another
Catholic nobleman, Maurevert, come out from the chapel,
where Valentine has desired to linger in prayer. The men are
still incensed over what appears to them the shameful
conduct of Raoul toward Valentine. Marcel at that moment
delivers to St. Bris a challenge from Raoul to fight a duel.
When the old Huguenot soldier has retired, the noblemen
conspire together to lead Raoul into an ambush. During the
duel, followers of St. Bris, who have been placed in hiding,
are suddenly to issue forth and murder the young Huguenot
nobleman.

From a position in the vestibule of the chapel, Valentine
has overheard the plot. She still loves Raoul and him alone.
How shall she warn him of the certain death in store for
him? She sees Marcel and counsels him that his master must
not come here to fight the duel unless he is accompanied by a
strong guard. As a result, when Raoul and his antagonist
meet, and St. Bris's soldiers are about to attack the
Huguenot, Marcel summons the latter's followers from a
nearby inn. A street fight between the two bodies of soldiers
is imminent, when the Queen and her suite enter. A gaily
bedecked barge comes up the river and lays to at the bank. It
bears de Nevers and his friends. He has come to convey his
bride from the chapel to his home. And now Raoul learns,
from the Queen, and to his great grief, that he has refused the
hand of the woman who loved him and who had gone to de
Nevers in order to ask him to release her from her engagement to him.

Act IV.   Raoul seeks Valentine, who has become the wife
of de Nevers, in her home. He wishes to be assured of the
truth of what he has heard from the Queen. During their
meeting footsteps are heard approaching and Valentine

barely has time to hide Raoul in an adjoining room when de Nevers, St. Bris, and other noblemen of the Catholic party enter, and discuss a plan to be carried out that very night—the night of St. Bartholomew—to massacre the Huguenots. Only de Nevers refuses to take part in the conspiracy. Rather than do so, he yields his sword to St. Bris and is led away a prisoner. The priests bless the swords, St. Bris and his followers swear loyalty to the bloody cause in which they are enlisted, and depart to await the signal to put it into effect, the tolling of the great bell from St. Germain.

Raoul comes out from his place of concealment, his one thought to hurry away and notify his brethren of their peril. Valentine seeks to detain him, entreats him not to go, since it will be to certain death. As the greatest and final argument to him to remain, she proclaims that she loves him. But already the deep-voiced bell tolls the signal. Flames, blood-red, flare through the windows. Nothing can restrain Raoul from doing his duty. Valentine stands before the closed door to block his egress. Rushing to a casement, he throws back the window and leaps to the street.

Act V. Covered with blood, Raoul rushes into the ball-room of the Hotel de Nesle, where the Huguenot leaders, ignorant of the massacre that has begun, are assembled to celebrate the marriage of Marguerite de Valois and Henry IV, and summons them to battle. Already Coligny, their great commander, has fallen. Their followers are being massacred.

The scene changes to a Huguenot churchyard, where Raoul and Marcel have found temporary refuge. Valentine hurries in. She wishes to save Raoul, and adjures him to adopt her faith. De Nevers has met a noble death and she is free—free to marry Raoul. But he refuses to marry her at the sacrifice of his religion. Now she decides that she will die with him and that they will both die as Huguenots and united. Marcel blesses them. The enemy has stormed the churchyard and begins the massacre of those who have sought safety in the edifice itself. Again the scene changes, this time to a square in Paris. Raoul who has been severely wounded, is supported by Marcel and Valentine. St. Bris and his followers approach. In answer to St. Bris's summons, 'Who goes there?' Raoul, calling to his aid all the strength he has left, cries out, 'Huguenots'. There is a volley. Raoul, Valentine, Marcel lie dead on the ground. Too late St. Bris discovers that he has been the murderer of his own daughter.

Originally in five acts, the version of *Les Huguenots* usually performed contains but three. The first two acts are drawn into one by converting the second act into a scene and adding it to the first. The fifth act (or in the usual version the fourth) is nearly always omitted.[1] This is due to the length of the opera. The audience takes it for granted that, when Raoul leaves Valentine, he goes to his death. I have seen a performance of *Les Huguenots* with the last act. So far as an understanding of the work is concerned, it is unnecessary. It also involves as much noise and smell of gunpowder as Massenet's opera, *La Navarraise*—and that is saying a good deal.

The performances of *Les Huguenots*, during the most brilliant revivals of that work at the Metropolitan Opera House, New York, under Maurice Grau, were known as 'les Nuits de sept étoiles' (the nights of the seven stars). A manager, in order to put *Les Huguenots* satisfactorily upon the stage, should be able to give it with seven first-rate principals, trained as nearly as possible in the same school of opera. The work should be sung preferably in French and by singers who know something of the traditions of the Grand Opéra, Paris. Mixed casts of Latin and Teutonic singers mar a performance of this work. That *Les Huguenots* has lost almost all its former popularity since 'the nights of the seven stars', is due to the dearth of singers of the necessary calibre almost as much as to the change in public taste. What would have been Meyerbeer singers now concentrate on Wagner, and Meyerbeer is given no more.

After a brief overture, in which 'Ein' feste Burg' is prominent, the first act opens with a sonorous chorus for the diners in the salon of de Nevers's castle. Raoul, called upon to propose in song a toast to a lady, does so in the romance, 'Plus blanche que la blanche hermine' (Whiter than the whitest ermine). The accompaniment to the melodious measures with which the romance opens is supplied by a viola solo, the effective employment of which in this passage shows Meyerbeer's knowledge of the instrument and its possibilities. This romance is a perfect example of a certain phase of Meyerbeer's art—a suave and elegant melody for voice, accompanied in a highly original manner, part of the time, in this instance, by a single instrument in the orchestra,

---

[1] But not at la Scala in 1962.   H.

which however, in spite of its effectiveness, leaves an impression of simplicity not wholly uncalculated.

Raoul's romance is followed by the entrance of Marcel, and the scene for that bluff, sturdy old Huguenot campaigner and loyal servant of Raoul, a splendidly drawn character, dramatically and musically. Marcel tries to drown the festive sounds by intoning the stern phrases of Luther's hymn. This he follows with the Huguenot battle song, with its 'Piff, paff, piff', which has been rendered famous by the great bassos who have sung it, not least Edouard de Reszke.

De Nevers is then called away and upon his rejoining his guests there enters Urbain, the page of Marguerite de Valois, to greet the assembly with the brilliant recitative, 'Nobles Seigneurs, salut!' This is followed by a charming cavatina, 'Une dame noble et sage' (A wise and noble lady). Originally this was a soprano number, Urbain having been composed as a soprano role, which it remained for twelve years. Then, in 1844, when *Les Huguenots* was produced in London with Alboni as Urbain, Meyerbeer transposed it, and a contralto, or mezzo-soprano, part it has remained ever since, its interpreters having included Annie Louise Cary, Trebelli, Scalchi, and Homer.

The letter brought by Urbain is recognised by the Catholic noblemen as being in the handwriting of Marguerite de Valois. As it is addressed to Raoul, they show by their obsequious demeanour toward him the importance they attach to the invitation. In accordance with its terms Raoul allows himself to be blindfolded and led away by Urbain.

Following the original score and regarding what is now the second scene of Act I as the second act, this opens with Marguerite de Valois's apostrophe to the fair land of Touraine ('O beau pays de la Touraine'), which, with the *cabaletta* immediately following, 'A ce mot tout s'anime et renaît la nature' (At this word everything revives and Nature renews itself), constitutes an animated and brilliant scene for coloratura soprano.

There is a brief colloquy between Marguerite and Valentine, then the graceful female chorus, sung on the bank of the Seine and known as the 'bathers' chorus', this being followed by the entrance of Urbain and his engaging song— the rondeau composed for Alboni—'Non! — non, non, non, non, non! Vous n'avez jamais, je gage' (No! — no, no, no, no, no! You have never heard, I wager).

Raoul enters, the bandage is removed from his eyes, and there follows a duet, 'Beauté divine, enchantresse' (Beauty brightly divine, enchantress), between him and Marguerite, all graciousness on her side and courtly admiration on his. The nobles and their followers come upon the scene. Marguerite de Valois's plan to end the religious strife that has distracted the realm meets with their approbation. The finale of the act begins with the swelling chorus in which they take oath to abide by it. There is the brief episode in which Valentine is led in by St. Bris, presented to Raoul, and indignantly spurned by him. The act closes with a turbulent ensemble. Strife and bloodshed, then and there, are averted only by the interposition of Marguerite.

Act III opens with the famous chorus of the Huguenot soldiers in which, while they imitate with their hands the beating of drums, they sing their spirited 'Rataplan'. By contrast the Catholic maidens, who accompany the bridal cortège of Valentine and de Nevers to the chapel, intone a litany, while Catholic citizens, students, and women protest against the song of the Huguenot soldiers. These several choral elements are skilfully worked out in the score. Marcel, coming upon the scene, manages to have St. Bris summoned from the chapel, and presents Raoul's challenge to a duel. The Catholics form their plot to assassinate Raoul, of which Valentine finds opportunity to notify Marcel, in a long duet which is one of the most striking scenes of the opera. The duel scene is preceded by a stirring septet, a really great passage, 'En mon bon droit j'ai confiance' (On my good cause relying). The music, when the ambuscade is uncovered and Marcel summons the Huguenots to Raoul's aid and a street combat is threatened, reaches an effective climax in a double chorus. The excitement subsides with the arrival of Marguerite de Valois, and of a barge containing de Nevers and his retinue. A brilliant chorus, supported by the orchestra and by a military band on the stage, with ballet to add to the spectacle forms the finale, as de Nevers conducts Valentine to the barge, and is followed on board by St. Bris and the nuptial cortège.

The fourth act opens with a romance for Valentine, 'Parmi les pleurs' (Amid my tears, by dreams once more o'ertaken). The scene of the consecration of the swords is one of the greatest in the opera; but for it to have its full effect St. Bris must be an artist like Plançon, who, besides being endowed with a powerful and beautifully managed voice, was superb in appearance and as St. Bris had the bearing of the dignified, commanding yet fanatic nobleman of old France. Musically and dramatically the scene rests on St. Bris's shoulders, and broad they must be, since his is the most conspicuous part in song and action, from the intonation of his solo, 'pour cette cause sainte, obéisses sans crainte' (With sacred zeal and ardour let now your soul be burning),

to the end of the savage *stretta*, when the conspirators, having tiptoed almost to the door, in order to disperse for their mission, suddenly turn, once more uplift sword hilts, poignards, and crucifixes, and, after a frenzied adjuration of loyalty to a cause that demands the massacre of an unsuspecting foe, steal forth into the shades of fateful night.

Powerful as this scene is, Meyerbeer has made the love duet which follows even more gripping. For now he interprets the conflicting emotions of love and loyalty in two hearts. It begins with Valentine's exclamation, 'Oh, ciel! Où courez-vous?' and reaches its climax in a *cantilena* of supreme beauty, 'Tu l'as dit, oui tu m'aimes' (Thou hast said it; aye, thou lov'st me),

Andante amoroso

which is broken in upon by the sinister tolling of a distant bell—the signal for the massacre to begin. An air for Valentine, an impassioned *stretta* for the lovers, Raoul's leap from the window, followed by a discharge of musketry, from which, in the curtailed version, he is supposed to meet his death, and this act, still an amazing achievement in opera, is at an end.

In the fifth act, there is the fine scene of the blessing by Marcel of Raoul and Valentine, during which strains of Luther's hymn are heard, intoned by Huguenots, who have crowded into their church for a last refuge.

Les Huguenots has been the subject of violent attacks, beginning with Robert Schumann's essay indited as far back as 1837, and starting off with the assertion, 'I feel to-day like the young warrior who draws his sword for the first time in a holy cause'. Schumann's most particular 'holy cause' was, in this instance, to praise Mendelssohn's oratorio, *St. Paul*, at the expense of Meyerbeer's opera *Les Huguenots*, notwithstanding the utter dissimilarity of purpose in the two works. On the other hand, Hanslick remarks that a person who cannot appreciate that dramatic power of this Meyerbeer opera must be lacking in certain elements of the critical faculty. Even Wagner, one of Meyerbeer's bitterest detractors, found words of the highest praise for the passage from the love duet which is quoted immediately above. The composer of *The Ring of the Nibelung* had a much broader outlook upon the world than Schumann, in whose genius there was, after all, a good deal of the *bourgeois*.

Pro or con, when *Les Huguenots* is sung with a fully adequate cast, it cannot fail to make a deep impression—as witness 'les nuits de sept étoiles'.

A typical night of the seven stars at the Metropolitan Opera House, New York, was that of December 26, 1894, when the prices for the first time were raised to $7.

The *sept étoiles* were Nordica (Valentine), Scalchi (Urbain), Melba (Marguerite de Valois), Jean de Reszke (Raoul), Plançon (St. Bris), Maurel (de Nevers), and Edouard de Reszke (Marcel). Two Academy of Music casts are worth referring to. April 30, 1872, Parepa-Rosa, for her last appearance in America, sang Valentine, Wachtel was Raoul and Santley St. Bris. The other Academy cast was a 'Night of six stars', and is noteworthy as including Maurel twenty years, almost to the night, before he appeared in the Metropolitan cast. The date was December 24, 1874. Nilsson was Valentine; Cary, Urbain; Maresi, Marguerite de Valois; Campanini, Raoul; del Puente, St. Bris; Maurel, de Nevers; and Nanneti, Marcel. With a more distinguished Marguerite de Valois, this performance would have anticipated the 'nuits de sept étoiles'.

K.

LE PROPHÈTE

The Prophet

Opera in five acts by Meyerbeer; words by Scribe. Première Grand Opéra, Paris, April 16, 1849, with Pauline Viardot and Roger. First

performed London, Covent Garden, July 24, 1849, with Mario,
Viardot-Garcia, Miss Hayes, and Tagliafico; New Orleans, April 2, 1850;
New York, Niblo's Garden, November 25, 1853, with Salvi (John of
Leyden), Steffanone and Mme. Maretzek. Revived in German,
Metropolitan Opera House, by Dr. Leopold Damrosch. December 17,
1884, with Anton Schott as John of Leyden, Marianne Brandt as Fides
and Schroeder-Hanfstaengl as Bertha. It was given ten times during the
season, in which it was equalled only by *Tannhäuser* and *Lohengrin*.
Revived Covent Garden, 1890 (in French), with Richard, Jean de
Reszke, Edouard de Reszke; last performed there 1895, with Ravogli,
Tamagno. Also, Metropolitan Opera House, 1898–99, with Jean de
Reszke, Brema (Fides), Lehmann (Bertha); January 22, 1900, Alvarez,
Schumann-Heink, Suzanne Adams, Plançon and Edouard de Reszke; by
Gatti-Casazza, February 7, 1918, with Caruso, Matzenauer, Muzio,
Didur, and Mardones; and 1927, with Corona, Matzenauer, Martinelli.
Modern revivals have included those in Zürich, 1962, with Gordoni,
Warfield, McCracken, conductor Krachmalnick; Turin Radio, 1963,
with Rinaldi Horne, Gedda; Berlin, German Opera, 1966, with
Annabelle Bernard, Warfield, McCracken, conductor Hollreiser.
Schumann-Heink was a celebrated Fides.

CHARACTERS

John of Leyden	Tenor
Fides, *his mother*	Mezzo-Soprano
Bertha, *his bride*	Soprano
Jonas ⎱	⎰ Tenor
Matthisen ⎬ Anabaptists	⎨ Bass
Zacharias ⎰	⎱ Bass
Count Oberthal	Baritone

Nobles, Citizens, Anabaptists, Peasants, Soldiers,
Prisoners, Children

Time: 1534–35   *Place:* Dordrecht, Holland, and Münster

Act I. At the foot of Count Oberthal's castle, near
Dordrecht, Holland, peasants and mill hands are assembled.
Bertha and Fides draw near. The latter is bringing to Bertha a
betrothal ring from her son John, who is to marry Bertha on
the morrow. But permission must first be obtained from Count
Oberthal as lord of the domain. The women are here to seek
it.

There arrive three sombre-looking men, who strive to rouse
the people to revolt against tyranny. They are the
Anabaptists, Jonas, Matthisen, and Zacharias. The Count,
however, who chances to come out of the castle with his
followers, recognises in Jonas a steward who was discharged

from his employment. He orders his soldiers to beat the three men with the flat of their swords. John's mother and Bertha make their plea to Oberthal. John and Bertha have loved ever since he rescued her from drowning in the Meuse. Admiring Bertha's beauty, Oberthal refuses to give permission for her to marry John, but, instead, orders her seized and borne to the castle for his own diversion. The people are greatly agitated and, when the three Anabaptists reappear, throw themselves at their feet, and on rising make threatening gestures toward the castle.

Act II. In John's inn at Leyden are the three Anabaptists and a throng of merrymaking peasants. Full of longing for Bertha, John is thinking of the morrow. The Anabaptists discover that he bears a remarkable resemblance to the picture of King David in the Cathedral of Münster. They believe this resemblance can be made of service to their plans. John tells them of a strange dream he has had, in which he found himself standing under the dome of a temple with people prostrate before him. They interpret it for him as evidence that he will mount a throne, and urge him to follow them. But for him there is but one throne—that of the kingdom of love with Bertha.

At that moment, however, she rushes in and begs him quickly to hide her. She has escaped from Oberthal, who is in pursuit. Oberthal and his soldiers enter. The Count threatens that if John does not deliver over Bertha to him, his mother, whom the soldiers have captured on the way to the inn, shall die. She is brought in and forced to her knees. A soldier with a battle-axe stands over her. After a brief struggle of conscience, John's love for his mother conquers. He hands over Bertha to Oberthal. She is led away. Fides is released.

The three Anabaptists return. Now John is ready to join them, if only to wreak vengeance on Oberthal. They insist that he come at once, without even saying farewell to his mother, who must be kept in ignorance of their plans. John consents and hurries off with them.

Act III. The winter camp of the Anabaptists in a forest of Westphalia, before Münster. On a frozen lake people are skating. The people have risen against their oppressors. John has been proclaimed a prophet of God. At the head of the Anabaptists he is besieging Münster.

The act develops in three scenes. The first reveals the psychological medley of fanaticism and sensuality of the

nabaptists and their followers. In the second John enters.
berthal is delivered into his hands. From him John learns
hat Bertha again has escaped from the castle and is in
Münster. The three Anabaptist leaders wish to put the Count
o death. But John, saying that Bertha shall be his judge, puts
ff the execution, much to the disgust of the three fanatics,
who find John assuming more authority than is agreeable to
hem. This scene, the second of the act, takes place in
Zacharias's tent. The third scene shows again the camp of the
Anabaptists. The leaders, fearing John's usurpation of power,
ave themselves headed an attack by their followers on
Münster and met with defeat. The rabble they led is furious
nd ready to turn even against John. He however by sheer
orce of personality coupled with his assumption of superhuman inspiration, rallies the crowd to his standard, and
eads it to victory.

Act IV. A public place in Münster. The city is in
possession of the Anabaptists. John, once a plain innkeeper
f Leyden, has been swept along on the high tide of success
nd decides to have himself proclaimed Emperor. Meanwhile
Fides has been reduced to beggary. The Anabaptists, in order
o make her believe that John is dead—so as to reduce to a
minimum the chance of her suspecting that the new Prophet
nd her son are one and the same—left in the inn a bundle of
ohn's clothes stained with blood, together with a script
tating that he had been murdered by the Prophet and his
ollowers.

The poor woman has come to Münster to beg. There she
meets Bertha, who, when Fides tells her that John has been
murdered, vows vengeance upon the Prophet.

Fides follows the crowd into the cathedral, to which the
scene changes. When, during the coronation scene, John
peaks, and announces that he is the elect of God, the poor
beggar woman starts at the sound of his voice. She cries out,
'My son!' John's cause is thus threatened and his life at stake.
He has claimed divine origin. If the woman is his mother, the
people, whom he rules with an iron hand, will denounce and
kill him. With quick wit he meets the emergency and even
makes use of it to enhance his authority by improvising an
affirmative scene. He bids his followers draw their swords and
thrust them into his breast, if the beggar woman again affirms
hat he is her son. Seeing the swords held ready to pierce
him, Fides, in order to save him, now declares that he is not

her son—that her eyes, dimmed by age, have deceived her.

Act V. The three Anabaptists, Jonas, Matthisen, and Zacharias, had intended to use John only as an instrument to attain power for themselves. The German Emperor, who is moving on Münster with a large force, has promised them pardon if they will betray the Prophet and usurper into his hands. To this they have agreed, and are ready on his coronation day to betray him.

At John's secret command Fides has been brought to the palace. Here her son meets her. He, whom she has seen in the hour of his triumph and who still is all-powerful, implores her pardon, but in vain, until she, in the belief that he has been impelled to his usurpation of power and bloody deeds only by thirst for vengeance for Bertha's wrongs, forgives him on condition that he return to Leyden. This he promises in full repentance.

They are joined by Bertha. She has sworn to kill the Prophet whom she blames for the supposed murder of her lover. To accomplish her purpose, she has set a slow fire to the palace. It will blaze up near the powder magazine, when the Prophet and his henchmen are at banquet in the great hall of the palace, and blow up the edifice.

She recognises her lover. Her joy, however, is short-lived for at that moment a captain comes to John with the announcement that he has been betrayed and that the Emperor's forces are at the palace gates. Thus Bertha learns that her lover and the bloodstained Prophet are one Horrified, she plunges a dagger into her heart.

John determines to die, a victim to the catastrophe which Bertha has planned, and which is impending. He joins the banqueters at their orgy. At the moment when all his open and secret enemies are at the table and pledge him in a riotous bacchanale, smoke rises from the floor. Tongues of fire shoot up. Fides, in the general uproar and confusion calmly joins her son, to die with him, as the powder magazine blows up, and with a fearful crash the edifice collapses in smoke and flame.

John of Leyden's name was Jan Beuckelszoon. He was born in 1509. In business he was successively a tailor, a small merchant, and an innkeeper. After he had had himself crowned in Münster, that city became a scene of orgy and cruelty. It was captured by the imperial forces June 24 1535. The following January the 'prophet' was put to death by torture. The same fate was meted out to Knipperdölling, his henchman, who had conveniently rid him of one of his wives by cutting off her head.

The music of the first act of Le Prophète contains a cheerful chorus for peasants, a cavatina for Bertha, 'Mon cœur s'élance' (My heart throbs wildly), in which she voices her joy over her expected union with John; the Latin chant of the three Anabaptists, gloomy yet stirring; the music of the brief revolt of the peasantry against Oberthal; the plea of Fides and Bertha to Oberthal for his sanction of Bertha's marriage to John, 'Un jour, dans les flots de la Meuse' (One day in the waves of the Meuse); Oberthal's refusal, and his abduction of Bertha; the reappearance of the three Anabaptists and the renewal of their efforts to impress the people with a sense of the tyranny by which they are oppressed.

Opening the second act, in John's tavern, in the suburbs of Leyden, are the chorus and dance of John's friends, who are rejoicing over his prospective wedding. When the three Anabaptists have recognised his resemblance to the picture of David in the cathedral at Münster, John, observing their sombre yet impressive bearing, tells them of his dream, and asks them to interpret it: 'Sous les vastes arceaux d'un temple magnifique' (Under the great dome of a splendid temple). They promise him a throne. But he knows a sweeter empire than the one they promise, that which will be created by his coming union with Bertha: 'Pour Berthe moi, je soupire'. Her arrival in flight from Oberthal and John's sacrifice of her in order to save his mother from death, lead to Fides's solo, 'Ah, Mon fils' (Ah, my son), one of the great airs for mezzo-soprano.

Most attractive in the next act is the ballet of the skaters on the frozen lake near the camp of the Anabaptists.[1] The scene is brilliant in conception, the music delightfully rhythmic and graceful. There is a stirring battle song for Zacharias, in which he sings of the enemy 'as numerous as the stars', yet defeated. Another striking number is the fantastic trio for Jonas, Zacharias, and Oberthal, especially in the descriptive passage in which in rhythm with the music, Jonas strikes flint and steel, ignites a lantern and by its light

[1] Now frequently heard as the music for Les Patineurs, Frederick Ashton's successful ballet for Sadler's Wells. H.

recognises Oberthal. When John rallies the Anabaptists, who have been driven back from under the walls of Münster, and promises to lead them to victory, the act reaches a superb climax in a 'Hymne Triomphal' for John and chorus: 'Roi du Ciel et des Anges' (Ruler of Heaven and the Angels):

At the most stirring moment of this finale, as John is being acclaimed by his followers, mists that have been hanging over the lake are dispelled. The sun bursts forth in glory.

In the next act there is a scene for Fides in the streets of Münster, in which, reduced to penury, she begs for alms. There also is the scene at the meeting of Fides and Bertha. The latter believing, like Fides, that John has been slain by the Anabaptists, vows vengeance upon the Prophet.

The great procession in the cathedral with its march and chorus has been, since the production of Le Prophète in 1849, a model of construction for spectacular scenes in opera. The march is famous. Highly dramatic is the scene in which Fides first proclaims and then denies that John is her son. The fifth contains a striking solo for Fides ('O Prêtres de Baal') and a duet for her and John. The climax, however, comes with the drinking song, 'Versez, que tout respire l'ivresse et le délire' (Quaff, quaff, in joyous measure; breathe, breathe delirious pleasure), in the midst of which the building is blown up, and John perishes with those who would betray him.

During the season of opera which Dr. Leopold Damrosch conducted at the Metropolitan Opera House, 1884–85, when this work of Meyerbeer's led the repertory in number of performances, the stage management produced a fine effect in the scene at the end of Act III, when the Prophet rallies his followers. Instead of soldiers tamely marching past, as John chanted his battle hymn, he was acclaimed by a rabble, wrought up to a high pitch of excitement, and brandishing cudgels, scythes, pitchforks, and other implements that would serve as weapons. The following season, another stage-manager, wishing to outdo his predecessor, brought with him an electric sun from Germany, a horrid thing that almost blinded the audience when it was turned on.   K.

DINORAH

ou

LE PARDON DE PLOËRMEL

Opera in three acts by Giacomo Meyerbeer, words by Barbier and Carré. Première Opéra-Comique, Paris, April 4, 1859, with Mme. Cabel, MM. St. Foy, Faure. First performed Covent Garden, 1859 (in Italian), with Miolan-Carvalho, Gardoni, Graziani; New Orleans, 1861; New York, 1862; Metropolitan, 1892, with van Zandt, Giannini, Lassalle. Revived Paris, 1912, with Vauchelet, Capitaine, Albers; Metropolitan, 1925, with Galli-Curci, Tokatyan, de Luca; Brussels, 1939. Apart from Galli-Curci, famous in the title role were Ilma di Murska, Patti, Tetrazzini.

CHARACTERS

Dinorah, *a peasant girl* .... Soprano
Hoël, *a goat-herd* .... Baritone
Corentino, *a bagpiper* .... Tenor
Huntsman .... Bass
Harvester .... Tenor
Goat-herds .... Soprano and Contralto
Time: Nineteenth Century   *Place:* A village in Brittany

Dinorah is betrothed to Hoël. Her cottage has been destroyed in a storm. Hoël, in order to rebuild it, goes into a region haunted by evil spirits, in search of hidden treasure. Dinorah, believing herself deserted, loses her reason and, with her goat, whose tinkling bell is heard, wanders through the mountains in search of Hoël.

The opera is in three acts. It is preceded by an overture during which there is sung by the villagers behind the curtain the hymn to Our Lady of the Pardon. The scene of the first act is a rough mountain passage near Corentino's hut. Dinorah finds her goat asleep and sings to it a graceful lullaby, 'Dors, petite, dors tranquille' (Little one, sleep; calmly rest). Corentino, in his cottage, sings of the fear that comes over him in this lonely region. To dispel it, he plays on his cornemuse. Dinorah enters the hut, and makes him dance with her, while she sings.

When someone is heard approaching she jumps out of the window. It is Hoël. Both he and Corentino think she is a sprite. Hoël sings of the gold he expects to find, and offers

Corentino a share in the treasure if he will aid him lift it.
According to the legend, however, the first one to touch the
treasure must die, and Hoël's seeming generosity is a ruse to
make Corentino the victim of the discovery. The tinkle of the
goat's bell is heard. Hoël advises that they follow the sound
as it may lead to the treasure. The act closes with a trio, 'Ce
tintement que l'on entend' (The tinkling tones that greet the
ear). Dinorah stands among the high rocks, while Hoël and
Corentino, the latter reluctantly, make ready to follow the
tinkle of the bell.

A wood of birches by moonlight is the opening scene of
the second act. It is here Dinorah sings of 'Le vieux sorcier de
la montagne' (The ancient wizard of the mountain),
following it with the 'Shadow Song', 'Ombre légère qui suis
mes pas' (Fleet shadow that pursues my steps)—'Ombra
leggiera' is the more familiar Italian version:

This is a passage so graceful and, when sung and acted by an
Adelina Patti, was so appealing, that I am frank to confess it
suggested to me the chapter entitled 'Shadows of the Stage',
in my novel of opera behind the scenes, *All-of-a-Sudden
Carmen*.

The scene changes to a wild landscape. A ravine bridged by
an uprooted tree. A pond, with a sluiceway which, when
opened, gives on the ravine. The moon has set. A storm is
rising.

Hoël and Corentino enter; later Dinorah. Through the
night, that is growing wilder, she sings the legend of the
treasure, 'Sombre destinée, âme condamnée' (O'ershadowing
fate, soul lost for aye).

Her words recall the tragic story of the treasure to
Corentino, who now sees through Hoël's ruse, and seeks to
persuade the girl to go after the treasure. She sings gaily, in
strange contrast to the gathering storm. Lightning flashes
show her goat crossing the ravine by the fallen tree. She runs
after her pet. As she is crossing the tree, a thunderbolt
crashes. The sluice bursts, the tree is carried away by the
flood, which seizes Dinorah in its swirl. Hoël plunges into the
wild water to save her.

Not enough of the actual story remains to make a third act. But as there has to be one, the opening of the act is filled with a song for a Hunter (bass), another for a Reaper (tenor), and a duet for Goat-herds (soprano and contralto). Hoël enters bearing Dinorah, who is in a swoon. Hoël here has his principal air, 'Ah! mon remords te venge' (Ah, my remorse avenges you). Dinorah comes to. Her reason is restored when she finds herself in her lover's arms. The villagers chant the 'Hymn of the Pardon'. A procession forms for the wedding, which is to make happy Dinorah and Hoël, everyone in fact, including the goat. K.

L'AFRICAINE
The African Maid

Opera in five acts by Meyerbeer; words by Scribe. Première Grand Opéra, Paris, April 28, 1865, with Marie Sasse, Battu, Naudin, Faure. First performed in London (in Italian), Covent Garden, July 22, 1865, with Lucca, Fioretti, Wachtel, Graziani; (in English) Covent Garden, October 21, 1865; New York, Academy of Music, December 1, 1865, with Mazzoleni as Vasco, and Zucchi as Selika; September 30, 1872, with Lucca as Selika; Metropolitan Opera House, January 15, 1892, with Nordica, Pettigiani, Jean de Reszke, Edouard de Reszke, Lassalle. Revived Arena, Verona, 1932, with Bruna Rasa, Gigli, Armando Borgioli, Righetti; Metropolitan, 1933, with Ponselle, Martinelli, Armando Borgioli, Lazzari, conductor Serafin; Rome, 1937, with Caniglia, Licia Albanese, Gigli, Basiola, Vaghi, conductor Serafin; Vienna, 1937, with Anny Konetzni, Gerhart, Piccaver, Jerger, Zec, conductor Alwin; Berlin, 1951, with Wasserthal, Beilke, Beirer, Metternich, Greindl, conductor Ludwig; Munich, 1962, with Ingrid Bjoner, Fahberg, Jess Thomas, Imdahl, Engen; Naples, 1963, with Stella, Rinaldi, Nicola Nikolov, Protti, Ivo Vinco, conductor Capuana; Florence, 1971, with Jessye Norman, Sighele, Veriano Luchetti, Giangiacomo Guelfi; San Francisco, 1972, with Verrett, Domingo.

CHARACTERS

Selika, *a slave* .... Soprano
Inez, *daughter of Don Diego* .... Soprano
Anna, *her attendant* .... Mezzo-Soprano
Vasco da Gama, *an officer in the Portuguese Navy* Tenor
Nelusko, *a slave* .... Baritone
Don Pedro, *President of the Royal Council* ...... Bass
Don Diego, *Member of the Council* .... Bass

Don Alvar, *Member of the Council* . . . . Tenor
Grand Inquisitor . . . . Bass
High Priest of Brahma . . . . Baritone
Priests, Inquisitors, Councillors, Sailors, Indians,
Attendants, Ladies, Soldiers
Time: Early Sixteenth Century   *Place:* Lisbon; on a ship
at sea; and India

In 1838 Scribe submitted to Meyerbeer two librettos: that
of *Le Prophète* and that of *L'Africaine*. For the purposes of
immediate composition he gave *Le Prophète* the preference,
but worked simultaneously on the scores of both. As a result,
in 1849, soon after the production of *Le Prophète*, a score of
L'Africaine was finished.

The libretto, however, had never been entirely satisfactory
to the composer. Scribe was asked to retouch it. In 1852 he
delivered an amended version to Meyerbeer who, so far as his
score had gone, adapted it to the revised book, and finished
the entire work in 1860. 'Thus,' says the *Dictionaire des
Opéras*, 'the process of creating *L'Africaine* lasted some
twenty years and its birth appears to have cost the life of its
composer, for he died, in the midst of preparations for its
production, on Monday, May 2, 1864, the day after a copy
of his score was finished in his own house in the Rue
Montaigne and under his eyes.'

Act I.   Lisbon. The Royal Council Chamber of Portugal.
Nothing has been heard of the ship of Bartholomew Diaz, the
explorer. Among his officers was Vasco da Gama, the
affianced of Inez, daughter of the powerful nobleman, Don
Diego. Vasco is supposed to have been lost with the ship and
her father now wishes Inez to pledge her hand to Don Pedro,
head of the Royal Council of Portugal.

During a session of the Council, it is announced that the
King wishes to send an expedition to search for Diaz, but one
of the councillors, Don Alvar, informs the meeting that an
officer and two captives, the only survivors from the wreck
of Diaz's vessel, have arrived. The officer is brought in. He is
Vasco da Gama, whom all have believed to be dead. Nothing
daunted by the perils he has been through, he has formed a
new plan to discover the new land that, he believes, lies
beyond Africa. In proof of his conviction that such a land
exists, he brings in the captives, Selika and Nelusko, natives
apparently of a country still unknown to Europe. Vasco then

retires to give the Council opportunity to discuss his enterprise.

In his absence Don Pedro, who desires to win Inez for himself (he knows that she loves Vasco) and to head a voyage of discovery, surreptitiously gains possession of an important chart from among Vasco's papers. He then, in spite of Don Alvar's efforts, persuades the Grand Inquisitor and the Council that the young navigator's plans are futile. Through his persuasion they are rejected. Vasco, who has again come before the meeting, when informed that his proposal has been set aside, insults the Council by charging it with ignorance and bias. Don Pedro, utilising the opportunity to get him out of the way, has him seized and thrown into prison.

Act II. Vasco has fallen asleep in his cell. Beside him watches Selika. In her native land she is a queen. Now she is a captive and a slave, her rank of course unknown to her captor, since she and Nelusko have carefully kept it from the knowledge of all. Selika is deeply in love with Vasco and is broken-hearted over his passion for Inez, of which she has become aware. But the love of this supposedly savage slave is greater than her jealousy. She protects the slumbering Vasco from the thrust of Nelusko's dagger. For her companion in captivity is deeply in love with her and desperately jealous of the Portuguese navigator for whom she has conceived so ardent a desire. Not only does she save Vasco's life, but on a map hanging on the prison wall she points out to him a route known only to herself and Nelusko, by which he can reach the land of which he has been in search.

Inez, Don Pedro, and their suite enter the prison. Vasco is free. Inez has purchased his freedom through her own sacrifice in marrying Don Pedro. Vasco, through the information received from Selika, now hopes to undertake another voyage of discovery and thus seek to make up in glory what he has lost in love. But he learns that Don Pedro has been appointed commander of an expedition and has chosen Nelusko as pilot. Vasco sees his hopes shattered.

Act III. The scene is on Don Pedro's ship at sea. Don Alvar, the leader of the faction in the Royal Council which supported da Gama's claim to head the expedition, has become suspicious of Nelusko. Two ships of the squadron have already been lost; Don Alvar fears for the safety of the flagship. At that moment a Portuguese vessel is seen

approaching. It is under command of Vasco da Gama, who has
fitted it out at his own expense. Although Don Pedro is his
enemy, he comes aboard the admiral's ship to warn him that
the vessel is on a wrong course and likely to meet with
disaster. Don Pedro, however, accuses him of desiring only to
see Inez, who is on the vessel, and charges that his attempted
warning is nothing more than a ruse with that purpose in
view. At his command, Vasco is seized and bound. A few
moments later, however, a violent storm breaks over the ship.
It is driven upon a reef. Savages, for whom Nelusko has
signalled, clamber up the sides of the vessel and massacre all
save a few whom they take captive.

Act IV.   On the left, the entrance to a Hindu temple; on
the right, a palace. Tropical landscape. Selika is welcomed
back as Queen and takes the sacred oath. Among those saved
from the massacre is Vasco. He finds himself in the land
which he has sought to discover—a tropical paradise. He is
threatened with death by the natives, but Selika, in order to
save him, protests to her subjects that he is her husband. The
marriage is now celebrated according to East Indian rites.
Vasco, deeply touched by Selika's fidelity, is almost determined to abide by his nuptial vow and remain here as Selika's
spouse, when suddenly he hears the voice of Inez. His passion
for her revives.

Act V.   The gardens of Selika's palace. Again Selika
makes a sacrifice of love. How easily she could compass the
death of Vasco and Inez! But she forgives. She persuades
Nelusko to provide the lovers with a ship and bids him meet
her, after the ship has sailed, on a high promontory overlooking the sea.

To this the scene changes. On the promontory stands a
large mancanilla tree. The perfume of its blossoms is deadly
to anyone who breathes it in from under the deep shadow of
its branches. From here Selika watches the ship set sail. It
bears from her the man she loves. Breathing in the poison-
laden odour from the tree from under which she has watched
the ship depart, she dies. Nelusko seeks her, finds her dead,
and himself seeks death beside her under the fatal branches
of the mancanilla.

Meyerbeer considered *L'Africaine* his masterpiece, and
believed that through it he was bequeathing to posterity an
immortal monument to his fame. But although he had

worked over the music for many years and produced a wonderfully well-contrived score, his labour upon it was more careful and self-exacting than inspired; and this despite moments of intense interest in the opera. Not *L'Africaine*, but *Les Huguenots*, is considered his most striking work.

L'Africaine calls for one of the most elaborate stage-settings in opera. This is the ship scene, which gives a lengthwise section of a vessel, so that its between-decks and cabin interiors are seen—like the compartments of a huge but neatly partitioned box laid on its oblong side; in fact an amazing piece of stage architecture.

Scribe's libretto has been criticised, and not unjustly, on account of the vacillating character which he gives Vasco da Gama. In the first act this operatic hero is in love with Inez. In the prison scene, in the second act, when Selika points out on the map the true course to India, he is so impressed with her as a teacher of geography that he clasps the supposed slave-girl to his breast and addresses her in impassioned song. Selika, being enamoured of her pupil, naturally is elated over his progress. Unfortunately Inez enters the prison at this critical moment to announce to Vasco that she has secured his freedom. To prove to Inez that he still loves her Vasco glibly makes her a present of Selika and Nelusko. Selika, so to speak, is no longer on the map so far as Vasco is concerned, until in the fourth act she saves his life by pretending he is her husband. Rapturously he pledges his love to her. Then Inez's voice is heard—and Selika again finds herself deserted. There is nothing for her to do but to die under the mancanilla tree.

'Is the shadow of this tree so fatal?' asks a French authority. 'Monsieur Scribe says yes, the naturalists say no.'[1] With this question and answer *L'Africaine* may be left to its future fate upon the stage, save that it seems proper to remark that, although the opera is called *The African Maid*, Selika appears to have been an East Indian (but the name is Arabian).

---

[1] A ludicrous invention, it has always been thought, of Scribe's, no tree's ambience having such a power. In the Caribbean, however, the manchineel tree is notorious for its noxious properties, the drip from its leaves after rain causing burns and blisters on the skin of whoever sits beneath it. Death might well be the reward for anyone foolish enough to eat its fruit.　　　　　　　　　　　　　　　　　　　　　　H.

Early in the first act of the opera occurs Inez's ballad, 'Adieu, mon beau rivage' (Farewell, beloved shores). It is gracefully accompanied by flute and oboe. This is the ballad to the river Tagus, which Vasco hears her sing in the fourth act and which revives his love for her. The finale of the first act—the scene in which Vasco defies the Royal Council—is a powerful ensemble. The slumber song for Selika in the second act, as she watches over Vasco, 'Sur mes genoux, fils du soleil' (On my knees, offspring of the sun) is charming and entirely original, with many exotic and fascinating touches. Nelusko's air of homage, 'Fille des rois, à toi l'hommage' (Daughter of Kings, my homage thine), expresses a sombre loyalty characteristic of the savage whose passion for his queen amounts to fanaticism. The finale of the act is an impressive unaccompanied septet for Inez, Selika, Anna, Vasco, Alvar, Nelusko, and Don Pedro.

In the act which plays aboard ship, are the graceful chorus of women, 'Le rapide et léger navire' (The swiftly gliding ship), the prayer of the sailors, 'O grand Saint Dominique', and Nelusko's song, 'Adamastor, roi des vagues profondes' (Adamastor, monarch of the trackless deep), a savage invocation of sea and storm, chanted to the rising of a hurricane by the most dramatic figure among the characters in the opera. For like Marcel in *Les Huguenots* and Fides in *Le Prophète*, Nelusko is a genuine dramatic creation.

The Indian march and the ballet, which accompanies the ceremony of the crowning of Selika, open the fourth act. The music is exotic, piquant, and in every way effective. The scene is a masterpiece of its kind. There follow the lovely measures of the principal tenor solo of the opera, Vasco's 'O Paradis, sorti de l'onde' (Paradise, lulled by the lisping sea). Nelusko sings movingly of his love for Selika: 'L'avoir tant aimée' (To have loved her so much). Then comes the love duet between Vasco and Selika, 'O transport, ô douce extase' (Oh transport, oh sweet ecstasy). One authority says of it that 'rarely have the tender passion, the ecstasy of love been expressed with such force'. Now it would be set down simply as a tip-top love duet of the old-fashioned operatic kind.

The scene of Selika's death under the mancanilla tree is preceded by a famous prelude for strings in unison supported by clarinets and bassoons, a brief instrumental recital of grief that makes a powerful appeal. The opera ends dramatically with a soliloquy for Selika—'D'ici je vois la mer immense' (From here I gaze upon the boundless deep).   K.

JACQUES
FRANÇOIS HALÉVY
(1799–1862)
LA JUIVE
The Jewess

OPERA in five acts by Halévy, text by Scribe. Première at the Opéra, Paris, February 23, 1835, with Mmes. Falcon, Dorus-Gras, Nourrit, Levasseur. First performed New Orleans, 1844; Drury Lane, London, 1846; Covent Garden, 1850 (in Italian), with Pauline Viardot, Tamberlik, Pololini; Metropolitan, 1885, with Materna, Udvardy, Kögel, conductor Damrosch. Revived Metropolitan, 1887, with Lilli Lehmann, Niemann, Fischer; 1919, with Ponselle, Caruso, Rothier, conductor Bodanzky; 1924, with Easton, Martinelli, Rothier; 1936, with Rethberg, Martinelli, Pinza; Paris, 1933, with Hoerner, Franz, Huberty; Brussels, 1938; New York, 1944, with Doree, Carron; Karlsruhe, 1952; Ghent, 1964, with Geri Brunin and Tony Poncet; London (in concert), 1973, with Richard Tucker. Rosa Raisa was famous in the role of Rachel, and Duprez one of Nourrit's most famous successors in the role of Eléazar.

CHARACTERS

Princess Eudoxia, *niece of the Emperor* . . . . . . Soprano
Rachel, *daughter of Eléazar* . . . . Soprano
Eléazar, *Jewish goldsmith* . . . . Tenor
Léopold, *prince of the Empire; employed by Eléazar
    under the name of Samuel* . . . . Tenor
Ruggiero, *provost of the city of Constance* . . . . Baritone
Albert, *sergeant in the army of the Emperor* . . . . . Bass
Cardinal de Brogni, *president of the Council* . . . . . Bass
Time: 1414   *Place:* Constance, in Switzerland

Halévy was thirty-five at the time of the first performance of *La Juive*; later he wrote a number of other operas, and many of them were most successful, but *La Juive* remains the work by which his name goes down to posterity. Wagner had more than a little admiration for his work, and it seems likely that he was, apart from Verdi and Berlioz, the most talented of the composers who tackled the specifically French form of 'grand opera'—more so on the evidence of *La Juive* than

Meyerbeer, but unfortunately quite without Meyerbeer's drive and energy.

The original plan was to give the rôle of Eléazar, one of the greatest in the nineteenth-century tenor repertory, to a high bass, and to place the scene of the opera in Spain at the time of the Inquisition's greatest power, but in the end the chief role was written for the great tenor Nourrit, who himself, if tradition is to be believed, had a hand in the writing of certain portions of the opera, notably the famous aria, 'Rachel, quand du Seigneur'.

Before the opera opens, various relevant events have taken place. De Brogni was once chief magistrate of Rome. During one of his periodical absences from the city, Rome was captured by the besieging Neapolitans, and considerable portions of the city burnt. Amongst the houses pillaged and destroyed was Brogni's own; he returned to find his wife dead and his child vanished, and therefore presumably dead too. In his agony, Brogni gave up his civic dignities and joined the Church, later rising to become the Cardinal who is one of the principal figures of the story.

Act I.   The overture is concerned with contrasting the themes representing the Jewish and the Christian elements of the story, and the curtain goes up to reveal a square in the city of Constance, in Switzerland (the action takes place throughout in this city). On one side of the square can be seen the great door of a church; on the other, amongst other shops, the house and workroom of Eléazar, the Jewish goldsmith and jeweller. Inside the church, the choir is chanting a *Te Deum*, outside a bystander resents the fact that some Jew seems to be working on a Christian feast-day. Léopold, the young general who has just triumphantly led his armies to victory over the Hussites, is in Constance in disguise—on a previous visit he had met and fallen in love with Eléazar's daughter, Rachel, and he wishes to resume the acquaintance. He is recognised by one of his own soldiers, but enjoins the fellow to silence, at the same time enquiring the cause of the festivity he seems to have stumbled upon. Albert tells him that it is in honour of the state visit of the Emperor, who has called a great council with a view to uniting all the Christians of the world into one solid faith, an undertaking only envisaged since Léopold's own victories over the dissident Hussites.

A great choral 'Hosanna' resounds from the church, and the congregation pours out, to listen to the proclamation in

19 *Les Troyens* at Covent Garden with Jon Vickers as Aeneas.

20 Melba as Lakmé, Brussels, about 1890.

the Emperor's name of a public holiday by Ruggiero, the
provost of the town. Nothing could suit the temper of the
people better, but no sooner have they voiced their
enthusiastic reaction than Ruggiero hears the sound of work
going on in Eléazar's shop and orders the occupants to be
brought before him. Eléazar is dragged out with his daughter
by his side. He answers Ruggiero's questions with defiance;
did he not watch his own sons burned by Christians? Why
should he bow to their laws? Ruggiero threatens him with a
similar death, but intervention comes from an unexpected
source. Cardinal Brogni is passing with his retinue, and asks
what is the cause of the noise. He recognises Eléazar, and the
jeweller reminds him that it was in Rome that they formerly
knew each other, in the days before the Cardinal had entered
the service of the Church (there is no mention of it in the
opera, but in Scribe's original story it is made clear that
Brogni had banished Eléazar from Rome, thus saving his life
after he had been condemned to death as an usurer). Brogni
sings a calmly flowing *cavatina*, 'Si la rigeur et la vengeance',

in which he prays that enlightenment may come to the
Jewish unbelievers; the aria develops into an ensemble, after
which the stage clears.

Only Léopold is left behind. He takes up a position outside
Eléazar's house (he has been taken on there as a workman,
under the name of Samuel, and they believe him to be Jewish),
and proceeds to serenade Rachel. It is a charming, high-lying
melody, and it is not long before Rachel answers it from
inside. She bids him come that very evening, when her father
and his fellow-believers will be celebrating the feast of the
Passover. Léopold is about to object when a crowd
rushes into the square, intent on making the most of the
Emperor's largesse. The choruses pile up on one another,
there is a brisk dance, and the drinking is general. Eléazar and
Rachel, trying to cross the square, are recognised as Jews by
Ruggiero and set upon by the mob. Eléazar confronts them
with dignity, but they are for throwing him in the lake, when
salvation comes in the person of Léopold who, though still
disguised, is immediately recognised by Albert, who causes

the crowd to leave the Jewish pair alone. Rachel is astonished
at the effect Samuel has on the Christians and at first tries to
restrain him from intervening. Rachel is left wondering at
Léopold's inexplicable power; Eléazar continues to pour
scorn on the hated Christians.

Act II.   A room in Eléazar's house, where the feast of the
Passover is being celebrated. Eléazar leads the chant ('O Dieu
Dieu de nos pères'), which the others, together with Rachel
repeat after him. Eléazar pronounces a curse upon anyone
who dares profane the holy feast ('Si trahison ou perfidie'),
and then distributes the unleavened bread, Samuel being the
last to receive it. He thinks he has escaped notice when he
drops it without tasting it, but Rachel has seen his gesture,
and is worried by what it may import. The scene is
immensely impressive, and the measured incantation of the
opening is one of the most remarkable moments in the opera:

Eléazar's supplication to God ('Dieu, que ma voix
tremblante') is barely finished when there is a knock at the
door. He commands the Jews to put away the ritual vessels
and candles, and the table is removed, the Jews themselves
going out through a back door. Léopold is about to depart,
when Eléazar commands him to stay with him. The door is
opened, and in comes the Princess Eudoxia. She makes
herself known, and Eléazar kneels before her. Her object is to
buy from him a fine chain which she hears he has; it once
belonged, Eléazar tells her, to the Emperor Constantine
himself. She wishes to buy it for her husband Léopold, whom
that day she expects back from the wars, where he has
defeated the Hussites. Léopold overhears the conversation,
and is filled with remorse at his deceit. Eudoxia orders that the
chain be brought the next day to her palace.

While Eléazar sees Eudoxia to the door, Rachel returns and
asks Samuel to explain his conduct when saving them from
the mob, and also, that evening, at the Passover service. He
protests that he must see her in great privacy.

Rachel comes back to keep her rendezvous with Léopold. Her heart is full of foreboding, even fear: 'Il va venir! et d'effroi je me sens frémir'. The aria admirably expresses the mixture of feelings of which she is conscious, and is full of the apprehension with which she awaits their meeting. Léopold admits to her that he has deceived her, and is in fact a Christian. Rachel bitterly reproaches him for his deception; he can but defend himself by saying that there was no thought in his mind but love of her. Léopold's pleading is so passionate (the music expresses it most convincingly) that Rachel is on the point of yielding, when her father confronts them.

Eléazar declares that their offence is such that they shall not escape punishment. In a trio they admit their guilt and express terror at the wrath of Eléazar, who tells them that only the fact that Samuel is a Jew prevents him from striking him dead on the spot for his falsity. Léopold bids him strike; he is a Christian. Rachel intercepts the blow, and pleads distractedly for her lover; she also is guilty. Eléazar declares himself willing to agree to the marriage, but his wrath knows no bounds when Léopold says that he is unable to marry Rachel.

Act III in some versions begins with a scene for Eudoxia and Rachel, who asks to be allowed to serve as a slave in her palace for one day only; she has trailed Léopold to the palace, but does not yet know his real identity, although she believes that such a position would make revenge possible. Eudoxia agrees to her request.

When this scene is omitted, the act begins in the gardens of the Emperor's palace, where a festival in honour of Léopold is in progress. The Emperor himself is seated at the high table, together with Brogni, Léopold and Eudoxia. A ballet is performed for their entertainment, and at its end, Eléazar and Rachel come to bring Eudoxia the chain she has bought for Léopold. When she is about to place it round her husband's neck, Rachel snatches it from her and announces that Léopold has committed the heinous crime of consorting with a Jewess, and that she herself is the Jewess in question.

There is a moment of stupefied horror. When Eléazar asks if the Christian laws are directed only against Jews or apply equally to themselves—Léopold has silently admitted the charge—Cardinal Brogni rises to his feet and pronounces a terrible anathema on all three, who have dared to break the laws of heaven: 'Vous, qui du Dieu vivant'.

Act IV.   All have been condemned to death, but Eudoxia
resolves to risk humiliation in order to save Léopold, whom
she still loves. She begs Rachel to retract her charge against
Léopold. Rachel at first proudly refuses, then says she will do
as she has been asked, saying to herself that a Jewess can outdo
a Christian in magnanimity. The scene is highly dramatic and
is succeeded by one hardly less compelling when the Cardinal
confronts Rachel and begs her to abjure her faith and so save
herself from death. She refuses.

Brogni resolves to send for Eléazar in a last effort to save
Rachel's life. He pleads with him to renounce his faith, and in
so doing to save her life; but the old man is resolute in the
face of temptation, and refuses to deny his father's creed. He
reminds Brogni of the time when his house and family
perished in the conflagration; his daughter was saved by a
Jew who came to fight the flames, and she is alive now. But
though her whereabouts are known to him, he will take his
revenge by carrying the secret with him to death. Brogni
implores him to reveal what he knows, but he will say no
more.

Eléazar is torn with doubts; can he bear, by his orthodoxy
and his own uncompromising hatred of Christians, to send his
daughter to her death? The thought tortures him, and resolves itself into a great expression of emotion: 'Rachel,
quand du Seigneur'. This is the climax of the opera, and
Eléazar is at one and the same time at his noblest and his

most human. He hears the savage cries: 'Au bûcher, les Juifs'
from outside, and is strengthened in his decision; Rachel shall
die a victim of their hate. The end of the act is hardly less
moving than the great aria a little earlier.

Act V.   From a tent, a view is to be had of the ground on
which the scaffold is erected for the martyrdom of the two
Jews—Léopold's sentence has been commuted to one of
banishment. The people howl for the death of the Jews, and
presently Eléazar and Rachel are seen coming slowly towards
the scaffold. Just as he is about to mount the scaffold.
Eléazar asks Rachel if she would like at the last moment to

abjure her faith and adopt Christianity, but she proudly
disdains any such idea. She is thrown into the cauldron by
the executioners, at the very moment when Brogni is told by
Eléazar, 'Your daughter perished in those flames'.   H.

ADOLPHE ADAM
(1803–1856)
LE POSTILLON DE LONGJUMEAU
The Coachman of Longjumeau

OPERA in three acts by Adolphe Adam, text by A. de Leuven and
L. L. Brunswick. Première at Opéra-Comique, Paris, October 13, 1836,
with Mme. Roy, MM. Chollet, Henri. First performed St. James's
Theatre, London, 1837 (in English); Drury Lane, 1845 (in French);
New York, 1840 (in English). Revived Berlin, 1930, with de Garmo,
Roswaenge, Helgers, conducted by Blech; Vienna Volksoper, 1964,
with Murray Dickie; still performed in German opera houses. The most
famous of all Chappelous was Theodor Wachtel, who himself began life
as a stableman.

CHARACTERS

Madeleine, *Chappelou's wife* . . . . Soprano
Rose . . . . Soprano
Chappelou, *a coachman* . . . . Tenor
Le Marquis de Corcy, *head of the Paris Opéra* . . . Tenor
Bijou, *Chappelou's friend* . . . . Baritone
Bourdon . . . . Bass
Time: Early Nineteenth Century   *Place:* Longjumeau; Paris

Act I. Chappelou, the coach-driver of Longjumeau, is
about to be married to the young mistress of the post-house,
Madeleine. The wedding over, his friends make him stay
behind—as is the custom—to sing. He says he has no heart for
it, but in response to their urging chooses a favourite song, on
the subject of the Postillion of Longjumeau, who wins the
love of a beautiful princess, mainly, one gathers from the

music, because of his exquisitely beautiful post-horn playing. This is the song which has made the opera famous, and the tenor who can imitate the post-horn when it comes to the top D's is sure of a success.

The effect of the song is further-reaching than either singer or those who asked for it could have guessed. Chappelou is heard by the Marquis de Corcy, who is head of the Opéra in Paris, and who urges Chappelou to come with him to augment the sadly depleted ranks of the tenors of his company. Chappelou tries to postpone his departure, but the Marquis is adamant; if he wants to come to Paris, he must leave straight away. Chappelou charges his friend Bijou, who also has a voice, to tell Madeleine he will be back to-morrow, or next week, but that he has had to leave hurriedly, to meet the King in Paris and to make his fortune. Madeleine is broken-hearted and furious with her inconstant lover, but Bijou makes up his mind to follow Chappelou the next day, so that his voice may be given to the world as well.

Act II.   Madeleine is now in Paris under the assumed name of Madame de Latour. Having inherited a fortune from an old aunt who had died, she passes as a rich and noble lady, but the whole object of her expedition is to find her errant husband and punish him for what he has done to her. These sentiments she puts forward in an aria at the beginning of the act; but it is clear that in spite of the ten years of absence she still loves her husband.

A rehearsal is in progress at the Opéra, where Chappelou, under the name of St. Phar, has become principal tenor, and where his friend Bijou (called Alcindor) is leader of the chorus. St. Phar protests that they are all asked to sing too much, and he at any rate has a sore throat. The Marquis is in despair; the performance they are rehearsing is to be given in honour of Madame Latour, and the Marquis is in love with her. Immediately, St. Phar seems better—he too is violently in love with the lady—and he is able to sing his song, top C, top D, and all.

There is an interview between St. Phar and Madame Latour in which the tenor lays bare his heart and Madame eventually agrees to marry him. He is congratulated by his comrades and invites them all to the wedding. St. Phar, it should be mentioned, unwilling to commit bigamy, has persuaded his friend Bijou to dress up as a priest and take the wedding ceremony, but Madame has somehow got to know about this and has locked Bijou up, together with the second leader of the chorus, so that the ceremony is perfomed by a real priest.

Act III.   The Marquis remembers that St. Phar has a wife at home and so is fully conscious that bigamy is being committed; however, since he is himself in love with the beautiful Madame Latour, he does nothing to prevent the marriage going through, but he rejoices to himself that to-morrow he will be able to bring the police to arrest his rival. St. Phar is full of happiness in his marriage, but it is short-lived. Bijou escapes, and reveals the horrid truth to him; it was not he but a priest who officiated at the wedding, which is thus not mock, but real.

Madelcine has not yet finished with her husband, but comes to him in her original country clothes, and with Madeleine's voice. Then, blowing out the candle, she proceeds to hold a conversation with herself, altering her voice from that of Madeleine to that of Madame Latour and back again. Chappelou does not know what to say, and his despair is complete when the police are heard knocking at the door. Headed by the Marquis, they prepare to take him away—to be hanged, says the Marquis. Madeleine demands to be allowed to go with him—and then suddenly puts on her 'grand' voice, saying that there are two witnesses to the crime. She reveals the truth, and all is forgiven.   H.

HECTOR BERLIOZ
(1803–1869)
BENVENUTO CELLINI

OPERA in three acts by Berlioz. Words by de Wailly and Barbier. Première Grand Opéra, Paris,[1] September 10, 1838, with Dorus-Gras,

[1] The importance of a Paris production dominates French operatic history until late in the nineteenth century, and Berlioz, much as he despised the standards of the Opéra, moved heaven though not invariably earth in his efforts to get his work performed there. H.

Stolz, Duprez, Derivis; there were twenty-nine rehearsals, seven per
formances. First performed London, Covent Garden, 1853, unde
Berlioz's own direction, with Julienne, Tamberlik, Tagliafico (in
Italian); by Liszt, at Weimar, 1852; by von Bülow, Hanover, 1879
Revived Vienna, 1911; Théâtre des Champs-Elysées, Paris, 1912, con
ducted by Weingartner; Dresden, 1929; Glasgow, 1939 (in English); Car
Rosa in London, 1957, with Craig, cond. Hammond; Amsterdam, 1961
with Gedda, conductor Prêtre; Geneva, 1964, with Esposito, Gedda
New York (concert performance), 1965; London, Covent Garden,
1966, with Elizabeth Vaughan, Minton, Gedda, Massard, conductor
Pritchard; San Carlo, Naples (Italian première), 1967, with Kabaivanska,
Anna Maria Rota, Nicola Tagger, conductor Previtali.

CHARACTERS

Cardinal Salviati[1] .... Bass
Balducci, *Papal treasurer* .... Bass
Teresa, *his daughter* .... Soprano
Benvenuto Cellini, *a goldsmith* .... Tenor
Ascanio, *his apprentice* .... Mezzo-Soprano
Francesco ⎱ *artisans in Cellini's workshop* ... ⎱ Tenor
Bernardino ⎰ ... ⎰ Bass
Fieramosca, *sculptor to the Pope* .... Baritone
Pompeo, *a bravo* .... Baritone
Time: 1532   *Place:* Rome

The overture, which makes use of material from the opera,
is one of Berlioz's best-known.

Act I. The carnival of 1532. Shrove Monday. We are in
the house of the Papal treasurer, Balducci, who has scolded
his daughter Teresa for having looked out of the window.
The old man is quite vexed, because the Pope has summoned
the Florentine goldsmith Cellini to Rome.

Balducci's daughter Teresa, however, thinks quite otherwise and is happy. For she has found a note from Cellini in a
bouquet that was thrown to her from the street by a
mask—Cellini, of course. She sings of her pleasure and delight
in an attractive cavatina, followed by an *allegro con fuoco*. A
few moments later Cellini appears at her side. There is a
gloriously broad, *andante* tune for them both to sing (it is
later used for the *Carnaval Romain* overture). Cellini pro-

---

[1] The part of Cardinal Salviati was originally allotted by Berlioz to
Pope Clement VII. The Paris censorship forbade the representation of a
Pope on the stage; but the part was restored in the Covent Garden
production of 1966.

O Te - re - sa,   vous que j'aime   plus que ma vi - e

poses a plan of elopement. In the morning, during the carnival mask, he will wear a white monk's hood, his apprentice Ascanio a brown one. They will join her and they will flee together. But a listener has sneaked in—Fieramosca, the Pope's sculptor and no less Cellini's rival in love than in art. He overhears the plot and also the unusually rude remarks made about him by Teresa and Cellini. Unexpectedly, too, Teresa's father, Balducci, comes back. His daughter still up? In her anxiety to find an excuse, she says she heard a man sneak in. During the search Cellini disappears, and Fieramosca is apprehended. Before he can explain his presence, women neighbours, who have hurried in, drag him off to the public bath house and treat him to a ducking.

Act II.   In the courtyard of a tavern Cellini is seated, with his assistants. In a romance, he sings that he is happy in his love, for he places it even higher than fame, which alone heretofore he has courted. He must pledge his love in wine. Unfortunately the host will no longer give him credit. Just then Ascanio brings some money from the Papal treasurer, but in return Cellini must promise to complete his *Perseus* by morning. He promises, although the avaricious Balducci has profited by his necessity and has sent too little money. Ascanio is informed by Cellini of the disguises they are to wear at the carnival, and of his plan that Teresa shall flee with him. Again Fieramosca has been spying and overhears the plot. Accordingly he hires the bravo Pompeo to assist him in carrying off Teresa.

A change of scene shows the crowd of maskers on the Piazza di Colonna. It is carnival time and the music is a brilliant representation of the gaiety and spirit of the scene. Balducci comes along with Teresa and together they see the play in which, in revenge for his niggardly payment to them, Cellini and his friends have arranged that the snoring Midas shall look like Balducci. Cellini takes advantage of the confusion caused by Balducci's protests to approach Teresa with Ascanio. At the same time, from the other side come two more monks, also in the disguise she and her lover agreed upon. Which is the right couple? Soon the two couples fall upon each other. A scream, and one of the brown-hooded monks (Pompeo) falls mortally wounded to the ground. A white-hooded monk (Cellini) has stabbed him. The crowd hurls itself upon Cellini. But at that moment the boom of a cannon gives notice that the carnival celebration is over. In the first shock of surprise Cellini escapes, and in his place the other white-hooded monk, Fieramosca, is seized.

Act III. Before Cellini's house, in the background of which, through a curtain, is seen the foundry, the anxious Teresa is assured by Ascanio that her lover is safe. Soon he comes along himself, and describes his escape. With his white habit he was able to join a procession of monks similarly garbed and so make his way safely home. While Ascanio prepares for their flight, Cellini and Teresa have a duet; the beautiful line of the tune makes this one of the most magnificent episodes of the score.

Balducci and Fieramosca rush in. Balducci wants to force his daughter to become Fieramosca's bride. The scene is interrupted by the arrival of Cardinal Salviati to see the completed *Perseus*. Poor Cellini! Accused of murder and the attempted kidnapping of a girl, the *Perseus* unfinished, the money received for it spent! Heavy punishment awaits him, and another shall receive the commission to finish the *Perseus*.

The artist flies into a passion. Another finish his masterpiece! Never! The casting shall be done on the spot! He is left alone and sings a beautiful 6/8 *andante* aria. Then the casting begins. Not metal enough? He seizes his completed works and throws them into the molten mass. Eventually, the master shatters the mould. The *Perseus* in all its glory appears before the eyes of the astonished onlookers—a potent plea for the inspired master. Once more have Art and her faithful servant triumphed over all rivals. K., H.

LA DAMNATION DE FAUST
The Damnation of Faust

In its original form a 'dramatic legend' in four parts for the concert stage. Music by Hector Berlioz. Words, after Gérald de Nerval's version of Goethe's play by Berlioz, Gérard, and Gandonnière. Produced in its original form as a concert piece at the Opéra-Comique, Paris, December 6, 1846; London, two parts of the work, under Berlioz's direction,

Drury Lane, February 7, 1848; first complete performance in England, Free Trade Hall, Manchester. February 5, 1880; New York, February 12, 1880, by Dr. Leopold Damrosch. Adapted for the operatic stage by Raoul Gunsbourg, and produced by him at Monte Carlo, February 18, 1893, with Jean de Reszke as Faust; Liverpool, 1894. Revived Monte Carlo, March 1902, with Melba, Jean de Reszke, and Maurice Renaud. Given in Paris with Calvé, Alvarez, and Renaud, to celebrate the centennial of Berlioz's birth, December 11, 1903. New York, Metropolitan, 1906, with Farrar, Rousselière, Plançon; Manhattan Opera House, 1907, with Dalmores and Renaud. Revived la Scala, Milan, 1929, with Cobelli, Merli, Galeffi, conductor de Sabata; Covent Garden, 1933, with Cigna, Voyer, Formichi, conductor Beecham; Buenos Aires, 1941, with Djanel, Maison, Romito; la Scala, 1947, with Gatti, Binci, Gobbi, conductor Serafin; Paris Opéra (in Béjart's production), 1964, with Denise Monteil, Guy Chauvet, Jacques Mars, conductor Markevitch; San Carlo, Naples, 1964, with Simionato, Ruggero Bondino, Bastianini, conductor Maag; Sadler's Wells, 1969, with Curphey (later Janet Baker), Alberto Remedios, Herincx, conductor Charles Mackerras.

CHARACTERS

Marguérite .... Soprano
Faust .... Tenor
Méphistophélès .... Bass
Brander .... Bass
Students, Soldiers, Citizens, Men and Women,
Fairies, etc.

In the first part of Berlioz's dramatic legend Faust is supposed to be on the plains of Hungary. Introspectively he sings of nature and solitude. There are a chorus and dance of peasants and a recitative. Soldiers march past to the stirring measures of the *Rákóczi March*, the national air of Hungary.

This splendid march Berlioz orchestrated in Vienna, during his tour of 1845, and conducted it at a concert in Pest, when it created the greatest enthusiasm. It was in order to justify the interpolation of this march that he laid the first scene of his dramatic legend on the plains of Hungary.

The next part of the dramatic legend only required a stage setting to make it operatic. Faust is in his study, lamenting his joyless existence. He is about to quaff poison, when the walls part and disclose a church interior. The congregation, kneeling, sings the Easter canticle, 'Christ is Risen', and Faust is comforted by their singing. Méphistophélès however appears and offers to show Faust all that his soul can desire.

The two start off together to sample what joy and pleasure can be had on earth. Change of scene to Auerbach's cellar, Leipzig. Revel of students and soldiers. Brander sings the 'Song of the Rat', whose death is mockingly grieved over by a 'Requiescat in pace' and a fugue on the word 'Amen', sung by the roistering crowd. Méphistophélès follows this up with the 'Song of the Flea', in which the skipping about of the elusive insect is depicted in the accompaniment.

In the next scene in the dramatic legend, Faust is supposed to be asleep on the banks of the Elbe. Méphistophélès sings the beautiful 'Voici des roses', after which comes the most exquisite effect of the score, the 'Dance of the Sylphs', a masterpiece of delicate and airy illustration. Violoncellos, *con sordini*, hold a single note as a pedal point, over which is woven a gossamer fabric of melody and harmony, ending with the faintest possible *pianissimo* from drum and harps. Gunsbourg employed here, with admirable results, the aerial ballet, and gave a rich and beautiful setting to the scene, including a vision of Marguérite. The ballet is followed by a chorus of soldiers and a students' song in Latin.

Part III.   The scenic directions of Gounod's *Faust* call Marguérite's house—so much of it as is projected into the garden scene—a pavilion. Gunsbourg made it more like an arbour, into which the audience could see through the elimination of a supposedly existing wall, the same as in Sparafucile's house in the last act of *Rigoletto*. Soldiers and students are strolling and singing in the street. Faust sings 'Merci doux crépuscule', and rejoices to be in Marguérite's room. He hides; Marguérite comes in and sings the ballad of the King of Thule. Berlioz's setting of the song is primitive, and he aptly characterises the number as a *Chanson Gothique*. It is a marvellously effective re-creation of the mediaeval spirit. The Invocation of Méphistophélès is followed by the 'Minuet of Will-o'-the-Wisps':

Then comes Méphistophélès' serenade, 'Devant la maison', a brilliant, elusive, piece of mockery.

Faust enters Marguérite's house. There is a love duet, 'Ange adorable', which becomes a trio when Méphistophélès joins the lovers and urges Faust's departure.

Part IV. Marguérite is alone. Berlioz, instead of using Goethe's song, 'Meine Ruh ist hin' (My peace is gone), the setting of which by Schubert is famous, substitutes a poem of his own. Introduced by the sad strains of the cor anglais, the unhappy Marguérite sings 'D'Amour, l'ardente flamme' (Love, devouring fire), an aria of extraordinary beauty:

The singing of the students and the soldiers grows fainter. The 'retreat'—the call to which the flag is lowered at sunset—is sounded by the drums and trumpets. Marguérite, overcome by remorse, swoons at the window.

A mountain gorge. The scene begins with Faust's soliloquy, 'Nature, immense, impénétrable et fière' (Nature, vast, unfathomable and proud), an invocation to nature that is enormously impressive. The *Ride to the Abyss*; moving panorama; pandemonium; redemption of Marguérite, whom angels are seen welcoming in the softly illumined heavens far above the town, in which the action is supposed to have transpired.

The production by Dr. Leopold Damrosch of *La Damnation de Faust* in its original concert form in New York, was one of the sensational events in the concert history of America. As an opera, however, the work has failed outside France to make the impression that might have been expected from its effects on concert audiences.   K.

Berlioz's *Faust* is in fact an extraordinarily imaginative work. Every opera-lover who knows it will be filled with regret that Berlioz wrote it in cantata form; the result is a mixture which is, like the same composer's *Roméo et Juliette*, too dramatic for the concert hall, insufficiently stage-worthy for the opera house.   H.

LES TROYENS
The Trojans

Opera in five acts by Hector Berlioz, text by the composer after Vergil. The work was not produced in its entirety until twenty-one years after the composer's death. Part II (*Les Troyens à Carthage:* see below for details of the division) was first performed at the Théâtre-Lyrique, Paris, November 4, 1863, with Charton-Demeur as Dido and Monjauze as Aeneas. Between that date and December 20, 1863, there were twenty-one performances of the opera, which was then dropped. The entire work was given at Carlsruhe on December 5 and 6, 1890, in a German version by O. Neitzel, with Reuss-Belce (Cassandre), Mailhac (Didon), conducted by Mottl (Part I, known separately as *La Prise de Troie*, thus had its world première on December 5, 1890). Concert performances in U.S.: Part I, New York, 1877; Part II, 1887. Part I was first performed in French at Nice, 1891; in Paris, Opéra, 1899, with Mme. Delna, MM. Lucas, Renaud, conducted by Traffanel; it was revived in Geneva, 1932. Part II was revived Opéra, Paris, 1892, with Delna, Laffarge; first performed Liverpool (in concert form), 1897; first performed in Italy, Naples, 1951, with Cavelti, Tygesen, Tajo, conductor Cluytens. Both parts (i.e. *Les Troyens* as Berlioz conceived it) were performed in Cologne, 1898 (in German); Stuttgart, 1913 (arr. Schillings); Opéra, Paris, 1921 (in a reduced version), with Gozategui, Isnardon, Franz, Rouard and revived there 1939, with Anduran, Ferrer, de Trévi,[1] Singher; 1961, with Crespin, Serres, Chauvet, Massard; first performed Berlin, 1930 (in four acts), with Leider, Roswaenge, conductor Blech; Glasgow 1935 (English translation by E. J. Dent), conductor Erik Chisholm; Oxford (reduced version), 1950, with Arda Mandikian and John Kentish, conductor Westrup; Covent Garden (virtually complete, in English) 1957, with Thebom, Shuard, Vickers, cond. Kubelik; la Scala (extensively cut), 1960, with Simionato, del Monaco, conductor Kubelik; Boston, 1955, with Mariquita Moll, Arthur Schoep, conductor Goldovsky; Buenos Aires, Teatro Colón,

---

[1] Georges Thill, the maker of a famous record of the great tenor *scena*, sang Aeneas in a revival in 1930 at the Paris Opéra of part ii.

1964, with Crespin (as Cassandra and Dido), Chauvet; San Francisco, 1966, with Crespin (in both roles), Vickers; Stuttgart, 1967, with Grace Hoffman, Hillebrecht, del Monaco; Scottish Opera, 1969, with Janet Baker, Dowd, conductor Gibson, (uncut, in English).

CHARACTERS

Part I: *La Prise de Troie*

Cassandre, a Trojan prophetess . . . . Soprano
Ascagne, son of Aeneas . . . . Soprano
Hécube, wife of Priam . . . . Mezzo-Soprano
Polyxéne, daughter of Priam . . . . Soprano
Enée (Aeneas), a Trojan hero . . . . Tenor
Chorèbe, fiancé of Cassandre . . . . Baritone
Panthée, a Trojan priest . . . . Bass
Ghost of Hector . . . . Bass
Priam, King of Troy . . . . Bass
A Trojan soldier . . . . Baritone
A Greek Captain . . . . Bass
Hélénus, son of Priam . . . . Tenor
Andromaque, widow of Hector . . . . Mime
Astyanax, her son . . . . Mime
     Soldiers of Greece and Troy, Citizens, Women, Children

Part II: *Les Troyens à Carthage*

Didon (Dido), Queen of Carthage . . . . . . Mezzo-Soprano
Anna, her sister . . . . Contralto
Ascagne . . . . Soprano
Enée . . . . Tenor
Iopas, a Carthaginian poet . . . . Tenor
Hylas, a young Phrygian sailor . . . . Tenor
Narbal, Dido's minister . . . . Bass
Panthée . . . . Bass
First soldier . . . . Baritone
Second soldier . . . . Bass
Two Trojan Captains . . . . Baritone, Bass
The Ghost of Cassandre . . . . Mezzo-Soprano
The Ghost of Chorèbe . . . . Baritone
The Ghost of Hector . . . . Bass
The Ghost of Priam . . . . Bass
The God Mercury . . . . Bass
     Trojan Captains, Courtiers, Hunters, Carthaginians,
     Invisible Ghosts, Workmen, Sailors, Labourers, Naiads,
            Fauns, Satyrs, Wood Nymphs

Les Troyens is Berlioz's greatest opera, and in many respects his greatest achievement. In it he unites his yearning for the classicism of Gluck, for design and form, with his own passion for what is expressive and vivid. The work is on the grandest scale, and Berlioz himself noted the timings which the five acts would require: Act I, 52 minutes; Act II, 22 minutes; Act III, 40 minutes; Act IV, 47 minutes; Act V, 45 minutes—a total of 206 minutes.[1] With four intervals, each lasting a quarter of an hour (*if* the elaborate sets did not require more), the performance would thus take four hours and twenty-six minutes, he calculated. But he was fated never to hear his opera in the form in which he conceived it; when it was performed at the Théâtre-Lyrique, the first two acts were removed, and only the second part—known in vocal scores, and in most performances for that matter, as *Les Troyens à Carthage*—was given. The scale was too exacting for most managements to tackle, and so it has proved until most recent times.

Les Troyens is in fact one of the few neglected masterpieces of opera from the past which remains to be rediscovered. On this subject, Donald Grout, in his *A Short History of Opera* (O.U.P), has written: '. . . *Les Troyens* is the most important French opera of the nineteenth century, the masterpiece of one of France's greatest composers, the Latin counterpart of Wagner's Teutonic *Ring*; its strange fate is paralleled by nothing in the history of music unless it be the century-long neglect of Bach's *Passion according to St. Matthew* . . . in a country properly appreciative of its cultural monuments it would seem that *Les Troyens* ought to be produced regularly at state expense until singers, conductors and public are brought to realise its greatness. Of all the works of the French grand-opera school in the nineteenth century, this is the one most worthy of being so preserved.'

The difficulties in the way of performance are many, and Berlioz had neither a Ludwig of Bavaria to start him off with ideal, or nearly ideal productions, nor subsequently a Bayreuth Festival at which to produce works requiring more than the normal time, both for rehearsal and performance. The staging is prodigiously exacting, with its frequent changes of

[1] But these timings are usually exceeded in performance. Scottish Opera's had just over four hours of music, and the performance, with a dinner interval of one hour, lasted five hours 48 minutes. The acts were timed as 60 minutes; 25 minutes; 60 minutes; 45 minutes; 53 minutes.

scene, its huge chorus, its several ballets—including the inordinately difficult-to-stage *Chasse royale*—and its unusually large scale. The principal singing roles are formidable, those of Dido and Aeneas particularly so, and moreover two of them disappear after two acts—Cassandra and Chorèbe (though the latter can, if need be, double Narbal). There is no doubt that Berlioz has put many obstacles in between his score and the public, some of them probably unavoidable. There is equally little doubt that the work ranks amongst the masterpieces of opera.

Berlioz's life-long enthusiasm for Vergil was second only to his love for Shakespeare; in point of fact, both contribute to the libretto of *Les Troyens*, the former for the narrative of the love of Dido for Aeneas as told in the first, second and fourth books of the *Aeneid*, the latter for the interpolation of the scene for Jessica and Lorenzo from *The Merchant of Venice*, which provides words for the great love duet between Dido and Aeneas in Act IV.

Les Troyens begins at the point in the Trojan war when the Trojans have lost Hector, the Greeks Achilles and Patroclus, and the Trojans have reason to believe that their enemies have had enough. The war has gone on for over nine years already, and the Greeks have retired, leaving behind them the wooden horse.

PART I

Act I.   The scene is the abandoned camp of the Greeks on the wooded plain in front of Troy. On one side stands a throne, on the other an altar, at the back the tomb of Achilles, on which sit three shepherds playing the double-flute. The people rejoice that their ten years of confinement are over: 'Quel bonheur de respirer l'air pur des champs'. There is talk of the wooden horse, and everyone rushes off to see this curiosity, everyone except Cassandra, who remains behind prophesying the doom of Troy: 'Malheureux roi!' Even Chorèbe, her lover, believes that her mind is deranged. He tries to console her, but she continues to predict the fall of the city and his death. She is unable to persuade him to leave Troy, but resigns herself to death on the morrow.

The character of Cassandra is splendidly depicted in the opening scene, Cassandra of whom Berlioz exclaimed when he finally gave up hope of hearing the first part of his opera:

'Ah, my noble Cassandra, my heroic virgin, I must needs
resign myself to never hearing thee'. The classical feeling of
the opening aria shows Berlioz's affinity to his beloved
Gluck, and the duet between her and Chorèbe is full of
feeling.

The second scene is set in front of the Citadel, again with
an altar on one side, a throne on the other. The Trojans
celebrate their deliverance from the Greeks with a procession
and public games. The music is a great hymn of thanksgiving.
Hector's widow and her son Astyanax, dressed in white
clothes of mourning, place flowers at the foot of the altar,
while Cassandra foretells for them an even greater sorrow
than they have yet known.

The scene is broken in upon by the precipitate arrival of
Aeneas who distractedly describes the terrible scene he has
just witnessed on the seashore. The priest, Laocoön, suspecting some hidden design of the Greeks, threw a javelin
into the side of the wooden horse, whereupon two serpents
came up out of the sea and devoured him before the eyes of
the Trojans. All assembled express their horror and fear at
this phenomenon in a magnificent octet with chorus:
'Châtiment effroyable'. Aeneas suggests that the disaster may
have been brought upon them by Pallas, outraged at the
insult to the horse, which has been dedicated to her. They
should placate her by bringing the image within the walls and
taking it to her temple. Cassandra alone remains behind as
they leave to give effect to Aeneas's suggestion. She laments
the step they are taking, which, she predicts, will lead to sure
disaster.

To the sound of a march, the horse is dragged inside the
city walls (this is the 'Trojan March' often heard in concerts).

In spite of the rumour that the sound of arms has been heard
coming from inside the horse, the people persist in greeting

its arrival with joy, and the sound of their song grows gradually in volume until it fills the whole city. Only Cassandra dissents from the rejoicing, but her suggestion that the horse should be destroyed forthwith meets with no favourable response from the crowd.

Act II. The first scene plays in Aeneas's palace. Aeneas's son, Ascagne, comes in, but seeing his father asleep, dare not wake him, and leaves the room. The ghost of Hector appears and marches slowly across the room.[1] Aeneas wakes, greets the hero, and hears from him that Troy has fallen. He is instructed to take his son and the images of the gods and to take ship across the seas, there—in Italy—to found a new empire. Hector's speech is set to a descending chromatic octave, each sentence delivered on one note, a semitone below the previous one. It is an impressive scene. At its end, Panthée comes to Aeneas bringing the images of the Trojan gods. He tells Aeneas of the happenings in the centre of the town; in the middle of the night, the horse opened to disgorge a troop of well-armed Greek soldiers. Priam is dead, and the town sacked and on fire. Aeneas rushes off to lead his men into battle.

The second scene takes place in the Temple of Vesta, where the Trojan women are gathered together, lamenting the fall of Troy. To them comes Cassandra, announcing the escape of Aeneas. For herself nothing remains, she says, since Chorèbe is dead. She urges the women to take their own lives rather than fall as slaves into the hands of the Greeks, and drives out the few who are not willing to die rather than go to certain dishonour, herself staying as leader of those who are resolved on death. The tension mounts, some Greeks come in and demand to know where the treasure is hidden. Cassandra answers by stabbing herself. Some of the women throw themselves from the gallery of the temple, others follow her example, and as they die all cry 'Italie!'

When this first section of *Les Troyens* is played as a separate opera (under the title of *La Prise de Troie*), it is divided into three acts; the first comprises the opening chorus, Cassandra's aria and her duet with Chorèbe, the

---

[1] Patrick J. Smith in *The Tenth Muse* points out that this strikingly dramatic scene is a quite straightforward descendant of the *ombra* scene of the 17th century operas, itself often allied to the slumber scene (*cf.* the play in *Hamlet*).

second opens with the rejoicings and continues until the end of Act I proper, the third consists of Berlioz's Act II.

PART II

The rest of the opera takes place in Carthage. Originally, there was no prelude to the opera (which of course was designed to begin with the episodes in Troy itself), but when it was decided to give the second part alone, Berlioz composed a prelude to it, which is now printed in the vocal scores (although not in the one Berlioz prepared). At the first performance he made up his mind that it was essential for the audience to know the events that should have taken place in the first half, and of which they were necessarily ignorant; he therefore had the story recited by a speaker in Greek costume, and followed this with a performance of the Trojan march together with the chorus which accompanies the entrance of the wooden horse within the walls of Troy. This he felt was essential, since the march plays so important a role in the second part of the opera, and much of its significance would be lost upon an audience which had never heard it before in their lives.

Act III.   An amphitheatre in the garden of Dido's palace at Carthage. A festival is taking place to celebrate the progress which has been made in building the city. Dido herself is greeted with a rapturous chorus, 'Gloire à Didon', when she takes her place on the throne. In a majestic aria ('Chers Tyriens'), she speaks of the work required to raise the city from nothing, and of what still remains to be done. The people for their part swear to protect her and her kingdom against Iarbas, who has demanded her hand in marriage and is now daring to invade their territory.

A sort of harvest festival now takes place. Each section of national life files past the Queen, and is rewarded for its industry. Singing 'Gloire à Didon', the people march out. leaving Dido alone with her sister, Anna. A conversation ensues, in which it is made clear that Anna thinks Dido is badly in need of a husband (she is a widow), and that Carthage needs a king just as much. Dido thinks sadly of her dead husband, and Anna does not press the point, which she feels is already gained.

Iopas comes in to tell the Queen that a foreign fleet has anchored in their harbour, driven apparently by the recent storm, the leaders are asking to see the Queen. She gives orders that they be informed she will receive them, then recalls her own experiences on the sea as a fugitive from Tyre. The Trojan march is heard (this time in the minor), and the survivors are led in by Ascagne, Aeneas having assumed a disguise and allowing his son to speak for the whole company. Dido welcomes them, and says that Aeneas, the noble warrior and friend of the great Hector, cannot be anything but an honoured guest at her court. At that moment, Narbal enters in great perturbation; Iarbas at the head of a horde of Numidian troops has advanced into their territory, laying waste the country, and even now threatening Carthage itself. Instantly Aeneas proclaims himself leader of the Trojans and offers his services and theirs to help repel the Queen's enemies. His offer is accepted, and at the head of the army he marches out to repel the invader, leaving his son in Dido's hands.

In Berlioz's original plan, the third act ended with the great symphonic intermezzo, the *Chasse royale et orage*. In modern scores this appears at the end of the following act, where it is perhaps less happily placed, although a self-contained episode, supplying its own context.

The scene is a virgin forest near Carthage. Naiads cross the glade and swim in the stream. The sound of the hunt can be heard in the distance; the naiads listen anxiously, then disappear. Huntsmen cross the stage; there are signs that a storm is approaching, and one of them takes shelter under a tree. Ascagne is seen, and after him come Dido and Aeneas, the former dressed as Diana, the latter as a warrior, and both take shelter. Naiads dash off, fauns and satyrs dance, and cries of 'Italie!' are heard. A tree falls struck by lightning and bursts into flames; the fauns pick up its burning branches and dance off. The scene is covered with thick clouds, the storm dies down, and gradually peace returns. Ernest Newman[1] has described this scene as 'the finest and most sustained piece of nature painting in all music; it is like some noble landscape of Claude come to life in sound'. Later on he adds: 'The reader who knows his Vergil will not make the mistake, however, of seeing in *the Royal Hunt and Storm* only a piece of nature painting in music, dragged in for its own pictorial sake. He will listen imaginatively to it, as Berlioz certainly intended him to do, as the passionate climax to the realisation by Dido and Aeneas of their love for each other.'

[1] In *Opera Nights*: Putnam.

Act IV. Dido's gardens, by the sea. Everything is
decorated to celebrate Aeneas's victorious return. Narbal
confides to Anna his fear that Aeneas's coming will not be
for Carthage's or for Dido's good. Already she neglects
affairs of state. Anna asks him if he cannot see that Dido is in
love with her guest; where else could Carthage find a better
king? But Narbal's forebodings are by no means quietened by
this thought.

To an orchestral reminiscence of the crowd's greeting early
in the previous act, Dido comes in with her royal guest. A
ballet is danced for their entertainment. At its end, Dido asks
Iopas to sing; he does so, charmingly, to the accompaniment
of a harp and various instruments: 'O blonde Cérès'. But
Dido can find no pleasure in anything that keeps her
attention from Aeneas. She asks him to continue his recital
of the fate of Troy. What happened to Andromaque, she
asks. Though at first determined to die, in the end she
submitted to love's urgings and married her captor Pyrrhus.
'O pudeur', sings Dido, 'Tout conspire à vaincre mes

remords'. Ascagne removes her ring, and Anna comments on
his likeness to Cupid. Aeneas's voice has already been heard,
but now Iopas and Narbal add theirs to make up the quintet.
It is one of the loveliest moments in the score, and the
ensemble is built up like one of Verdi's on the individual
reactions to the now apparent love of Dido for Aeneas. It is
followed by a septet (Dido, Aeneas, Anna, Ascagne, Iopas,
Narbal, Panthée, and the chorus) which is no less beautiful:
'Tout n'est que paix et charme'.

Everyone leaves the stage except Dido and Aeneas, who
are alone in the garden: 'Nuit d'ivresse et d'extase infinie'. It

s the beginning of the incomparable Shakespearean love
duet, one of the finest in all opera: 'Par une telle nuit' (In
such a night as this). Idea succeeds idea, and a reference to
their own names brings the duet to an idyllic close. They go
off with Dido leaning on Aeneas's shoulder, just as a shaft of
moonlight reveals a statue of the god Mercury which comes
to life and reiterates the knell of their hopes: 'Italie!'

Act V. The harbour at night. The Trojan ships are lying
at anchor, and the tents of the Trojans cover the beach. A
young sailor, Hylas, sings sadly of his homeland: 'Vallon
sonore'. Panthée and the Trojan chiefs direct that preparations be made for the fleet's departure, which is only delayed
because of Aeneas's love for Dido; every moment wasted is
likely to bring down the anger of the gods—even now the
disembodied cry of 'Italie' can be heard again. Two soldiers
on sentry duty have little use for what they undoubtedly
think of as the high-falutin' talk about 'Italie'. They are
perfectly content in Carthage, where the food and the
women are entirely to their liking. This new voyage is likely
to lead to nothing but inconvenience for them—but they break
off as they see Aeneas coming towards them.

Aeneas is torn between his overwhelming love for Dido, to
whom he has broken the news that he must leave, and his
sense of duty and of destiny: 'Inutiles regrets. Je dois quitter
Carthage'. But he thinks longingly of Dido, and cannot bear
the thought of their farewell: 'Ah, quand viendra l'instant des
suprêmes adieux?' His initial agitation returns: 'En un dernier
naufrage'. Once again he hears the voices, and now sees the
spectre of his father Priam, followed by those of Chorèbe,
Cassandra, and Hector; each in turn orders him to follow his
destiny. His mind is made up and he orders the Trojans to
their boats: 'Debout, Troyens', ending with a sad, slow
farewell to the absent Dido. The *scena* is one of the most
magnificent in the tenor repertory.

Dido has followed Aeneas, and a short scene takes place
between them, Dido reproaching, weeping, begging him to
stay, Aeneas almost prepared to give way until the sound of
the Trojan march is heard in the distance. Then, with a cry of
'Italie', Aeneas rushes on to one of his vessels.

The second scene takes place in Dido's palace. Dido tries
to persuade her sister Anna to go to the harbour to intercede
for her. Anna says Aeneas's departure had become inevitable,
if the gods were to be obeyed; but she maintains that, in spite

of the gods, he still loves her. Dido says this is impossible; if *her* love would compel her to disobey Jove himself. When Iopas describes the ships putting out to sea, Dido bursts out in fury, ordering the Carthaginians to pursue and destroy the traitorous Trojans. She herself has done wrong by not from the start treating the Trojans as they have finished by treating her. Why did she not serve up the body of Ascagne to Aeneas at a feast? One thing only is left her: to raise an awful pyre to the god of the underworld, and on it burn everything that was ever connected with the traitorous Aeneas.

Anna and Narbal leave her, and Dido's grief overflows; she tears her hair and beats her breast in her anguish: 'Ah, je vais mourir'. She will burn on the pyre, and perhaps from his ship Aeneas will catch sight of the flames which will signal her terrible end. She bids farewell to the great city: 'Adieu, fière cité'.

The last scene takes place on a terrace overlooking the sea. A funeral pyre is presided over by priests of Pluto. Dido, preceded by Anna and Narbal, comes slowly in. Anna and Narbal solemnly curse the Trojans, after which Dido prepares to mount the steps of the pyre. She looks sadly at Aeneas's accoutrements on it; then, taking his sword, stands with it while she prophesies that her people will one day produce a warrior to avenge on his descendants the shame now brought by Aeneas. Then she plunges the sword into her breast. Anna tries to help her, but Dido revives only long enough to communicate her further vision, in which she sees Rome triumphant. She dies as the Carthaginians hurl further curses at the Trojans. But the Trojan March contradicts them, and a vision of eternal Rome rises behind Dido's pyre.   H.

BÉATRICE ET BÉNÉDICT

Opera in two acts by Hector Berlioz. Words by the composer, after Shakespeare's *Much Ado about Nothing*. Produced at Baden-Baden, August 9, 1862, with Charton-Demeur, Monrose, Montaubry. First performed Weimar, 1863; Carlsruhe, 1888, conducted by Mottl; Vienna, 1890; Opéra-Comique, Paris, 1890; Glasgow (in English), 1936; New York, Carnegie Hall, 1960; Festival Hall, London, 1962, with Cantelo, Veasey, Watts, Mitchinson, conductor Colin Davis; Paris, Opéra-Comique, 1966, with Hélia T'Hézan, Monique de Pondeau, Voli, conductor Dervaux; Manhattan School of Music, New York, 1965; Cambridge, 1967, with Anne Howells, Kenneth Bowen, conductor David Atherton.

CHARACTERS

Don Pedro, *a general* .... Bass
Leonato, *governor of Messina* .... Bass
Hero, *his daughter* .... Soprano
Béatrice, *his niece* .... .Mezzo-Soprano
Claudio, *an officer*....................... Baritone
Bénédict, *an officer* .... Tenor
Ursula, *Hero's companion* .... Contralto
Somarone, *orchestral conductor* .... Bass

Place: Messina, Sicily

The story is an adaptation of a shortened version of Shakespeare's play, which preserves the spirit of the comedy, but omits the saturnine intrigue of Don John against Claudio and Hero. The gist of the comedy is the gradual reaction of the brilliant but captious Béatrice from pique and partially feigned indifference toward the witty and gallant Bénédict, to love. Both have tempers. In fact they reach an agreement to marry as a result of a spirited quarrel.

The overture, like that for *Benvenuto Cellini*, is made up from tunes used elsewhere in the opera. Thus the opening *allegretto scherzando* later accompanies the duet at the end of the opera, and the *andante* tune is Béatrice's 'Il m'en

souvient'. The overture is a brilliant and gay piece of music, and it has become very popular in the concert hall, where, probably, many of its admirers are entirely ignorant of the fact that it belong to an opera.

Act I. The action takes place in the garden of Leonato, the governor of Messina. There is general rejoicing that the town is no longer in danger from the besieging army of Moors, which has finally been driven off. After some dialogue—this is an opéra-comique, with much of the action

carried on in ordinary speech—the chorus starts to repeat its
praises of the victorious general and his troops, much to
Béatrice's dissatisfaction. There is a dance, a Sicilienne in 6/8
time, of charming individuality, and the stage empties.

Hero has a splendid aria in which she looks forward to
seeing Claudio again. The lovely, calm tune of the opening
larghetto section, 'Je vais le voir', is a good example of that
stylistic refinement and purity which is a feature of Berlioz's
music, and the quick section, 'Il me revient fidèle', makes an
exhilarating finish. Bénédict and Claudio arrive, and the
skirmishing of the protagonists begins. 'Comment le dédain
pourrait-il mourir?' (Is it possible disdain should die?), begins
their duet, a true inspiration. It is followed by a trio for the
three men, Bénédict, Claudio, and Don Pedro: 'Me
marier? Dieu me pardonne', a 3/8 *allegretto*, in which
Bénédict makes furious answer when he is twitted on the
subject of marriage. It is dominated by long musical
sentences for Bénédict, upon which the others comment.

Berlioz introduces a non-Shakespearean character,
Somarone, a *maître de chapelle*, who rehearses his chorus and
orchestra in an *Epithalame grotesque*, a choral fugue on the
subject of love. Gradually Bénédict is brought to realise that
all is not well with his plans for perpetual bachelordom. He
sings a spirited *rondo* 'Ah, je vais l'aimer', a charming and
original piece of the greatest vitality.

It is evening, and Hero and Ursula close the act with a slow
duet—a Nocturne, 'a marvel of indescribable lyrical beauty in
which Berlioz's feeling for nature is wonderfully expressed'
(so says W. J. Turner). One has to turn to *Così fan tutte* to
find idyllic writing for combined female voices of comparable
beauty:

Act II opens with a version of the *Sicilienne* already heard. There is a dialogue between the servants, and Somarone starts up a drinking song, whose accompaniment is provided by guitars, trumpets, and tambourines (the guitar was the instrument on which Berlioz most enjoyed performing). The stage empties, and Béatrice comes in. Bénédict loves her; how to overcome her own increasing feeling for him? She has an aria on the grand scale, 'Il m'en souvient', whose tune has already been heard in the overture. The impressive *scena* finishes with an *allegro agitato*, 'Je l'aime donc?'

There is a flowing, 6/8 trio of great beauty for Hero, Béatrice and Ursula, in which Béatrice reveals that her feelings have undergone a considerable change since we first met her. She positively welcomes the tenderness which she earlier despised: 'Et ton époux restera ton amant'. This and the succeeding number, an offstage chorus with guitar accompaniment, Berlioz added to the score after returning from Baden-Baden, where the opera was first produced.

Béatrice and Bénédict both try to conceal their mutual love, but it is in vain. After a general *Marche nuptiale*, the two marriage contracts are signed between Béatrice and Bénédict, and Hero and Claudio—and the opera finishes with a brilliant duet for Béatrice and Bénédict: 'L'amour est un flambeau'. This, called a *scherzo-duettino* by the composer, is accompanied by the opening figure of the overture, and its sparkle and gaiety make the perfect comedy ending. That it is a love duet is never concealed, but it is informed with a spirit of liveliness and wit which give it a quality hardly realised otherwise in opera outside Verdi's *Falstaff*.

Béatrice et Bénédict not only reflects Berlioz's love of Shakespeare but also a mid-nineteenth century view of the playwright. The 'serious' side of the story has gone, but in its place is a rich warmth of invention such as virtually no other composer has brought to Shakespeare. To try to re-interpret Berlioz's interpretation of his favourite poet—by for instance introducing Shakespearean elements Berlioz omitted—has no other effect than to distort (particularly since *Much Ado* can still be performed without Berlioz) an operatic masterpiece.

H.

AMBROISE THOMAS
(1811–1896)
MIGNON

OPERA in three acts by Ambroise Thomas, words, based on Goethe's *Wilhelm Meister*, by Barbier and Carré. Produced, Opéra-Comique, Paris, November 17, 1866, with Galli-Marié. London, Drury Lane, July 5, 1870, with Nilsson, Volpini, Bettini, Faure. New York, Academy of Music, November 22, 1871, with Nilsson, Duval (Philine), Mlle. Ronconi (Frédéric), and Capoul; Metropolitan Opera House, October 21, 1883, with Nilsson, Capoul, and Scalchi (Frédéric). Revived Metropolitan, 1926, with Bori, Gigli; Sadler's Wells, 1932, with Rose Morris, Tudor Davies; la Scala, Milan, 1933, with Besanzoni, Schipa; Metropolitan, 1938, with Risë Stevens; la Scala, 1945, with Pederzini, Schipa; 1947, with Simionato, di Stefano. Frédéric, since Trebelli appeared in the role in London, has become a contralto instead of a buffo tenor part. The 'Rondo Gavotte' in Act II, composed for Trebelli by Thomas, has since then been a fixture in the score.

CHARACTERS

Mignon, *stolen in childhood from an Italian castle* ....Mezzo-Soprano
Philine, *an actress* ....Soprano
Frédéric, *a young nobleman* ..Buffo Tenor or Contralto
Wilhelm Meister, *a student on his travels* ....Tenor
Laerte, *an actor*..........................Tenor
Lothario .... Bass
Jarno, *a gypsy*............................. Bass

Antonio, *a servant* .... Bass
    Townspeople, Gypsies, Actors and Actresses,
            Servants, etc.
Time: Late Eighteenth Century *Place:* Acts I and II,
                        Germany; Act III, Italy

Notwithstanding the popularity of two airs in *Mignon*—
'Connais-tu le pays?' and the Polonaise—the opera has lost
much of its hold on the repertory. It is a work of delicate
texture, of charm rather than passion, with a story that is,
perhaps, too ingenuous to appeal to the sophisticated
audience of the modern opera house. Moreover, the
'Connais-tu pays?' was at one time done to death, both by
concert singers and amateurs. Italian composers are fortunate
in having written music so difficult technically that none but
the most accomplished singers can risk it.

    Act I.   Courtyard of a German inn. Chorus of towns-
people and travellers. Lothario, a wandering minstrel, sings,
accompanying himself on his harp, 'Fugitif et tremblant' (A
lonely wanderer). Philine and Laerte, on the way with their
troupe to give a theatrical performance in a neighbouring
castle, appear on a balcony. Mignon is sleeping on straw in
the back of a gypsy cart. Jarno, chief of the gypsy band,
rouses her. She refuses to dance. He threatens her with a
stick. Lothario and Wilhelm protect her. Mignon divides a
bouquet of wild flowers between them.

    Laerte, who has come down from the balcony, engages
Wilhelm in conversation. Philine joins them. Wilhelm is greatly
impressed with her blonde beauty. He does not protest when
Laerte takes from him the wild flowers he has received from
Mignon and hands them to Philine.

    When Philine and Laerte have gone, there is a scene
between Wilhelm and Mignon. The girl tells him of dim
memories of her childhood—the land from which she was
abducted. It is at this point she sings 'Connais-tu le pays?'
(Knowest thou the land?). Wilhelm decides to purchase her
freedom, and enters the inn with Jarno to conclude the
negotiations. Lothario, who is about to wander on, has been
attracted to her, and, before leaving, bids her farewell. They
have the charming duet, 'Légères hirondelles' (O swallows,
lightly gliding). There is a scene for Philine and Frédéric, a
young boy, who is in love with her. Philine is after better
game. She is setting her cap at Wilhelm. Lothario wishes to

take Mignon with him, but Wilhelm fears for her safety with
the old man, whose mind sometimes appears to wander.
Moreover Mignon ardently desires to remain in the service of
Wilhelm who has freed her from bondage to the gypsies, and
when Wilhelm declines to let her go with Lothario, is
enraptured, until she sees her wild flowers in Philine's hand.
Already she is passionately in love with Wilhelm, and jealous
when Philine invites him to attend the theatricals at the
castle. Wilhelm waves adieu to Philine, as she drives away.
Lothario, pensive, remains seated. Mignon's gaze is directed
toward Wilhelm.

Act II.   The entr'acte is the tune of the famous gavotte.
Philine's boudoir at the castle. The actress sings of her
pleasure in these elegant surroundings, and of Wilhelm.
Laerte is heard off-stage, singing a madrigal to Philine. 'Belle
ayez pitié de nous' (Fair one, pity take on us).

He ushers in Wilhelm and Mignon, then withdraws.
Mignon, pretending to fall asleep, watches Wilhelm and
Philine. While Wilhelm hands to the actress various toilet
accessories, they sing a graceful duet, 'Je crois entendre les
doux compliments' (Pray, let me hear now the sweetest of
phrases). Meanwhile Mignon's heart is tormented with
jealousy. When Wilhelm and Philine leave the boudoir the girl
dons one of Philine's costumes, seats herself at the mirror and
puts on rouge and other cosmetics, as she has seen Philine do.
In a spirit of abandon she sings a brilliant *Styrienne*, 'Je
connais un pauvre enfant' (A gypsy lad I well do know). She
then withdraws into an adjoining room. Frédéric enters the
boudoir in search of Philine. He sings the gavotte, 'Me voici
dans son boudoir' (Here am I in her boudoir). Wilhelm comes
in, in search of Mignon. The men meet. There is an exchange
of jealous accusations. They are about to fight, when Mignon
rushes between them. Frédéric recognises Philine's costume on
her, and goes off laughing. Wilhelm, realising the awkward
situation that may arise from the girl's following him about,
tells her they must part. 'Adieu, Mignon, courage' (Farewell
Mignon, have courage). She bids him a sad farewell. Philine
re-enters. Her sarcastic references to Mignon's attire wound
the girl to the quick. When Wilhelm leads out the actress on
his arm, Mignon exclaims: 'That woman! I loathe her!'

The second scene of this act is laid in the castle park.
Mignon, driven to distraction, sings a *scena* of real dramatic
power: 'Elle est là, près de lui?' She is about to throw herself

into the lake, when she hears the strains of a harp. Lothario, who has wandered into the park, is playing. There is an exchange of affection, almost paternal on his part, almost filial on hers, in their duet, 'As-tu souffert? As-tu pleuré?' (Hast thou known sorrow? Hast thou wept?). Mignon hears applause and acclaim from the conservatory for Philine's acting. In jealous rage she cries out that she wishes the building might be struck by lightning and destroyed by fire; then runs off and disappears among the trees. Lothario vaguely repeats her words. 'Fire,' she said! 'Ah, fire! fire!' Through the trees he wanders off in the direction of the conservatory, just as its doors are thrown open and the guests and actors issue forth.

They have been playing *A Midsummer Night's Dream*, and Philine, flushed with success, sings the brilliant *Polonaise*, 'Je suis Titania' (Behold Titania, fair and gay). Mignon appears. Wilhelm, who has sadly missed her, greets her with so much joy that Philine sends her into the conservatory in search of the wild flowers given to Wilhelm the day before. Soon after Mignon has entered the conservatory it is seen to be in flames. Lothario, obedient to her jealous wish, has set it on fire. At the risk of his life Wilhelm rushes into the burning building and reappears with Mignon's fainting form in his arms. He places her on a grassy bank. Her hands still holds a bunch of withered flowers.

Act III.   Gallery in an Italian castle, to which Wilhelm has brought Mignon and Lothario. Mignon has been dangerously ill. A boating chorus is heard from the direction of a lake below. Lothario, standing by the door of Mignon's sick-room, sings a lullaby, 'De son cœur j'ai calmé la fièvre' (I've soothed the throbbing of her aching heart). Wilhelm tells Lothario that they are in the Cipriani castle, which he intends to buy for Mignon. At the name of the castle Lothario is strangely agitated.

Wilhelm has heard Mignon utter his own name in her delirium during her illness. He sings, 'Elle ne croyait pas' (She does not know). When she enters the gallery from her sick-room and looks out on the landscape, she is haunted by memories. There is a duet for Mignon and Wilhelm, 'Je suis heureuse, l'air m'enivre' (Now I rejoice, life reawakens). Philine's voice is heard outside. The girl is violently agitated. But Wilhelm reassures her.

In the scenes that follow, Lothario, his reason restored by being again in familiar surroundings, recognises in the place his own castle and in Mignon his daughter, whose loss had unsettled his mind and sent him, in minstrel's disguise, wandering in search of her. The opera closes with a trio for Mignon, Wilhelm, and Lothario. In it is heard the refrain of 'Connais-tu le pays?'   K.

CHARLES FRANÇOIS GOUNOD

(1818–1893)

FAUST

OPERA in five acts by Gounod; words by Barbier and Carré. Produced Théâtre-Lyrique, Paris, March 19, 1859, with Miolan-Carvalho, Faivre, Duclos, Barbot, Reynald, Balanque. Opéra, Paris, March 3, 1869, with Christine Nilsson, Colin, and Faure. London, Her Majesty's Theatre, June 11, 1863, with Tietjens, Trebelli, Giuglini, Santley, Gassier; Covent Garden, July 2, 1863 (in Italian), with Miolan-Carvalho, Tamberlik, Faure; Her Majesty's Theatre, January 23, 1864, in an English version by Chorley, for which, Santley being the Valentine, Gounod composed what was destined to become one of the most popular numbers of the opera, 'Even bravest heart may swell'. New York, Academy of Music, November 26, 1863 (in Italian), with Clara Louise Kellogg, Henrietta Sulzer, Francesco Mazzoleni, Hannibal Biachi. Metropolitan Opera House, opening night, October 22, 1883, with Nilsson, Scalchi, Lablache, Campanini, Novara, Del Puente. Famous interpreters have included—Marguérite: Patti, Melba, Eames, Nordica, Suzanne Adams, Calvé, Farrar, Sayao, de los Angeles; Faust: Jean de Reszke, Capoul, Campanini, Caruso, Muratore, Dalmorès, Bjoerling, Gedda; Méphistophélès: Edouard de Reszke, Plançon, Delmas, Journet, Vanni-Marcoux, Chaliapin, Pinza.

CHARACTERS

Faust, *a learned doctor* .... Tenor
Méphistophélès .... Bass
Marguérite .... Soprano
Valentin, *a soldier, brother to Marguérite* ..... Baritone

Siebel, *a village youth, in love with*
Marguérite .... .Mezzo-Soprano
Wagner, *a student* .... Baritone
Martha Schwerlein, *neighbour to*
Marguérite .... .Mezzo-Soprano
Students, Soldiers, Villagers, Angels, Demons,
Cleopatra, Lais, Helen of Troy, and others
Time: Sixteenth Century   *Place:* Germany

Gounod's librettists, Michel Carré and Jules Barbier, with a
true Gallic gift for practicable stage effect, did not seek to
utilise the whole of Goethe's *Faust* for their book, but
contented themselves with the love story of Faust and
Marguérite, which also happens to have been entirely original
with the author of the play, since it does not occur in the
legends. But because the opera does not deal with the whole
of *Faust*, Germany, where Gounod's work enjoys great
popularity, refuses to accept it under the same title as the
play, and calls it *Margarethe* after the heroine.

As reconstructed for the Opéra, where it was brought out
ten years after its production at the Théâtre-Lyrique, *Faust*
develops as follows:

There is a brief prelude. A *ff* on a single note, then
mysterious, chromatic chords, and then the melody which
Gounod composed for Santley.

Act I.   Faust's study. The philosopher is discovered alone,
seated at a table on which an open tome lies before him. His
candle flickers in its socket. Night is about to turn to dawn.

Faust despairs of solving the riddle of the universe. Aged,
his pursuit of science vain, he seizes a flask of poison, pours it
into a crystal goblet, and is about to drain it, when, day
having dawned, the cheerful song of young women on their
way to work arrests him. The song dies away. Again he raises
the goblet, only to pause once more, as he hears a chorus of
labourers, with whose voices those of the women unite.
Faust, beside himself at these sounds of joy and youth, curses
life and advancing age, and calls upon Satan to aid him.

There is a flash of red light and out of it, up through the
floor, rises Méphistophélès, garbed as a cavalier, in vivid red.
Alternately suave, satirical, and demoniacal in bearing, he
offers to Faust wealth and power. The philosopher, however,
wants neither, unless with the gift also is granted youth: 'Je
veux la jeunesse' (What I long for is youth). That is easy for

his tempter, if the aged philosopher, with pen dipped in his blood, will but sign away his soul. Faust hesitates. At a gesture from Méphistophélès the scene at the back opens and discloses Marguérite seated at her spinning wheel, her long blonde hair falling down her back. 'O Merveille!' (A miracle!) exclaims Faust, at once signs the parchment, and drains to the vision of Marguérite a goblet proffered him by Méphistophélès. The scene fades away, the philosopher's garb drops off Faust. The grey beard and all other marks of old age vanish. He stands revealed a youthful gallant, eager for adventure, instead of the disappointed scholar weary of life. There is an impetuous duet for Faust and Méphistophélès: 'A moi les plaisirs' ('Tis pleasure I covet). They dash out of the cell-like study in which Faust has vainly devoted himself to science.

Act II.   Outside one of the city gates. To the left is an inn, bearing as a sign a carved image of Bacchus astride a keg. It is kermesse time. There are students, among them Wagner, burghers old and young, soldiers, maidens, and matrons.

The act opens with a chorus. *Faust* has been given so often that this chorus probably is accepted by most people as a common-place. In point of fact it is an admirable piece of characterisation. The groups of people are effectively differentiated in the score. The toothless chatter of the old men (in high falsetto) is an especially amusing detail. In the end the choral groups are deftly united.

Valentin and Siebel join the throng. The former is examining a medallion which his sister, Marguérite, has given him as a charm against harm in battle. He sings the number which Gounod composed for Santley, 'Even bravest heart may swell' (Avant de quitter ces lieux).

Wagner mounts a table and starts the 'Song of the Rat'. After a few lines he is interrupted by the sudden appearance of Méphistophélès, who, after a brief parley, sings 'Le veau d'or' (The golden calf), a cynical dissertation on man's worship of mammon. He reads the hands of those about him. To Siebel he prophesies that every flower he touches shall wither. Rejecting the wine proffered him by Wagner, he strikes with his sword the sign of the inn, the keg, astride of which sits Bacchus. Like a stream of wine fire flows from the keg into the goblet held under the spout by Méphistophélès, who, raising the vessel, pledges the health of Marguérite.

This angers Valentin and leads to the 'Scène des épées'.

Valentin unsheathes his blade. Méphistophélès, with his sword, describes a circle about himself. Valentin makes a pass at his foe. As the thrust carries his sword into the magic circle, the blade breaks. He stands in impotent rage, while Méphistophélès mocks him. At last, realising who his opponent is, Valentin grasps his sword by its broken end, and extends the cruciform hilt toward the red cavalier. The other soldiers follow their leader's example. Méphistophélès, no longer mocking, cowers before the cross-shaped sword hilts held toward him, and slinks away. A sonorous chorus, 'Puisque tu brises le fer' (Since you have broken the blade) for Valentin and his followers distinguishes this scene.

The crowd gathers for the kermesse dance—'the waltz from *Faust*', familiar the world round, and undulating through the score to the end of the gay scene, which also concludes the act. While the crowd is dancing and singing, Méphistophélès enters with Faust. Marguérite approaches, on her way from church, prayer-book in hand. Siebel seeks to join her. But every time the youth steps toward her he meets the grinning yet sinister Méphistophélès, who dexterously manages to get in his way. Meanwhile Faust has joined her. There is a brief colloquy, he offers his arm to conduct her through the crowd, but she modestly declines. The episode, though short, is charmingly melodious. The phrases for Marguérite can be made to express coyness, yet also show that she is not wholly displeased with the attention paid her by the handsome stranger. She goes her way. The dance continues: 'Valsons toujours' (Waltz away!).

Act III. Marguérite's garden. At the back a wall with a wicket door. To the left a bower. On the right Marguérite's house, with a bow window facing the audience. Trees, shrubs, flower beds, etc.

Siebel enters by the wicket. Stopping at one of the flower beds and about to pluck a nosegay, he sings the graceful 'Faites-lui mes aveux' (Bear my avowal to her). But when he picks a flower, it shrivels in his hand, as Méphistophélès had predicted. The boy is much perturbed. Seeing, however, a little font with holy water suspended by the wall of the house, he dips his fingers in it. Now the flowers no longer shrivel as he touches them. He arranges them in a bouquet, which he lays on the house step, where he hopes Marguérite will see it, and leaves.

Faust enters with Méphistophélès, but bids the latter

withdraw, as if he sensed the incongruity of his presence near the home of a maiden so pure as Marguérite. The tempter having gone, Faust proceeds to apostrophise Marguérite's dwelling in the exquisite romance, 'Salut! demeure chaste et pure'.

Méphistophélès returns. With him he brings a casket of jewels and a handsome bouquet. With these he replaces Siebel's flowers. The two men then withdraw into a shadowy recess of the garden to await Marguérite's return.

She enters by the wicket. Her thoughts are with the handsome stranger—above her in station, therefore the more flattering and fascinating in her eyes—who addressed her at the fair. Pensively she seats herself at her spinning wheel and, while turning it, without much concentration of mind on her work sings 'Il était un roi de Thulé', the ballad of the King of Thule, her thoughts, however, returning to Faust before she finishes the number, which is set in the simple fashion of a folk-song.

Approaching the house, and about to enter, she sees the flowers, stops to admire them, and to bestow a thought of compassion upon Siebel for his unrequited devotion, then sees and hesitatingly opens the casket of jewels. Their appeal to her feminine vanity is too great to permit her to return them at once to the casket. Decking herself out in them, she regards herself and the sparkling gems in the handglass that came with them, then bursts into the brilliant 'Air des Bijoux' (Jewel Song):

one of the most brilliant airs for coloratura soprano, affording the greatest contrast to the folklike ballad which preceded it, and making with it one of the most effective scenes in opera for a soprano who can rise to its demands, the chaste simplicity required for the ballad, the joyous abandon and faultless execution of elaborate embellishments involved in the 'Air des Bijoux'. When well done, the scene is brilliantly successful; for, added to its own conspicuous merit, is the fact that, save for the very brief episode in Act II, this is the first time in two and a half acts that the limpid and grateful tones of a solo high soprano have fallen upon the ear.

Martha, the neighbour and companion of Marguérite, joins her. In the manner of the average duenna, whose chief duty in opera is to encourage love affairs however fraught with peril to her charge, she is not at all disturbed by the gift of the jewels or by the entrance upon the scene of Faust and Méphistophélès. Nor, when the latter tells her that her husband has been killed in the wars, does she hesitate, after a few exclamations of rather forced grief, to seek consolation on the arm of the flatterer in red, who leads her off into the garden, leaving Faust with Marguérite. During the scene immediately ensuing the two couples are sometimes in view, sometimes lost to sight in the garden. The music is a quartet, beginning with Faust's 'Prenez mon bras un moment' (Pray lean upon mine arm). It is artistically individualised. The couples and each member thereof are neatly characterised in Gounod's score.

For a moment Méphistophélès holds the stage alone. Standing by a bed of flowers in an attitude of benediction, he invokes their subtle perfume to lull Marguérite into a false sense of security. 'Il était temps!' (It was the hour) begins the soliloquy. For a moment, as it ends, the flowers glow. Méphistophélès withdraws into the shadows. Faust and Marguérite appear. Marguérite plucks the petals of a flower: 'He loves me—he loves me not—he loves!' There are two ravishing duets for the lovers, 'Laisse-moi contempler ton visage' (Let me gaze upon thy beauty), and 'O nuit

Andante.

Laisse moi, Laisse moi contempler ton vi-sa-ge.

d'amour . . . ciel radieux!' (Oh, night of love! oh, starlit sky!). The music fairly enmeshes the listener in its enchanting measures.

Faust and Marguérite part, agreeing to meet on the morrow. She enters the house. Faust turns to leave the garden. He is confronted by Méphistophélès, who points to the window. The casement is opened by Marguérite, who believes she is alone. Kneeling in the window, she gazes out upon the night flooded with moonlight. 'Il m'aime; . . . Ah! presse ton retour, cher bien-aimé! Viens!' (He loves me; ah! haste your return, dearly beloved! Come!)

With a cry, Faust rushes to the open casement, sinks upon his knees. Marguérite, with an ecstatic exclamation, leans out of the embrasure and allows him to take her into his arms. Her head rests upon his shoulder.

At the wicket gate is Méphistophélès, shaking with laughter.

Act IV. The first scene in this act takes place in Marguérite's room. No wonder Méphistophélès laughed when he saw her in Faust's arms. She has been betrayed and deserted. The faithful Siebel, however, still offers her his love—'Si la bonheur à sourire t'invite' (When all was young and pleasant, May was blooming)—but Marguérite still loves the man who betrayed her, and hopes against hope that he will return.

This episode is followed by the cathedral scene. Marguérite has entered the edifice and knelt to pray. But, invisible to her, Méphistophélès stands beside her and reminds her of her guilt. A chorus of invisible demons calls to her accusingly. Méphistophélès foretells her doom. The 'Dies iræ', accompanied on the organ, is heard. Marguérite's voice joins with those of the worshippers. But Méphistophélès, when the chant is ended, calls out that for her, a lost one, there yawns the abyss. She flees in terror. This is one of the most significant episodes of the work.

Now comes a scene in the street, in front of Marguérite's

...se. The soldiers return from war and sing their familiar ...orus, 'Gloire immortelle' (Glory immortal). Valentin, fore-...arned by Siebel's troubled mien that all is not well with Marguérite, goes into the house. Faust and Méphistophélès come upon the scene. Facing the house, and accompanying himself on his guitar, the red gallant sings an offensive serenade: 'Vous qui faites l'endormie'. Valentin, aroused by the insult, which he correctly interprets as aimed at his sister, rushes out. There is a spirited trio, 'Allons, messieurs'. Valentin smashes the guitar with his sword, then attacks Faust, whose sword-thrust, guided by Méphistophélès, mortally wounds Marguérite's brother. Marguérite comes into the street, throws herself over Valentin's body. With his dying breath her brother curses her.

Sometimes the order of the scenes in this act is changed. It may open with the street scene, where the girls at the fountain hold themselves aloof from Marguérite. Here the brief meeting between the girl and Siebel takes place. Marguérite then goes into the house; the soldiers return, etc. The act then ends with the cathedral scene.

Act V. When Gounod revised *Faust* for the Grand Opéra, Paris, the traditions of that house demanded a more elaborate ballet than the dance in the Fair scene afforded. Consequently the authors reached beyond the love story of Faust and Marguérite into the second part of Goethe's drama and utilised the legendary levels of Walpurgis Night (eve of May 1st) on the Brocken, and highest point of the Hartz mountains. Here Faust meets the courtesans of antiquity— Laïs, Cleopatra, Helen of Troy, Phryne. *Les Nubiennes, Cléopatra et la Coupe d'Or* (Cleopatra and the Goblet of Gold), *Les Troyennes* (The Trojan Women), *Variation*, and *Danse de Phryné* are the dances in this ballet. Elsewhere more frequently than not the scene is omitted. To connect it with the main story, there comes to Faust, in the midst of the revels, a vision of Marguérite. Around her neck he beholds a red line, 'like the cut of an axe'. He commands Méphistophélès to take him to her.

They find her in prison, condemned to death for killing her child. There is an impassioned duet for Faust and Marguérite. He begs her to make her escape with him. But her mind is wandering. In snatches of melody from preceding scenes, she recalls the episode at the fair, the night in the garden. She sees Méphistophélès, senses his identity with the arch-fiend. There is a superb trio, in which Marguérite

ecstatically calls upon angels to intervene and save he
'Anges purs! Anges radieux!' (Angles pure, radiant, brigh
The voices mount higher and higher, Marguérite's soaring to

splendid climax. She dies.
'Condemned!' cries Méphistophélès.
'Saved,' chant ethereal voices.
The rear wall of the prison opens. Angels are seen bearing
Marguérite heavenward. Faust falls on his knees in prayer.
Méphistophélès turns away, 'barred by the shining sword of
an archangel'.   K.

MIREILLE

Opera in three acts (originally five) by Charles Gounod, text by Carré
after Frédéric Mistral's poem *Mireio*. Première at the Théâtre-Lyrique,
Paris, March 19, 1864, with Miolan-Carvalho and Michot. The revised
version, which involved substantial changes in the music as well as a
pastoral ending substituted for the original tragedy, was made later in
1864. First performed at Her Majesty's, London, 1864, with Tietjens,
Giuglini, Santley; Philadelphia, 1864; Covent Garden, 1891, with
Eames, Lubert, Ceste. Revived at Metropolitan, 1919, with Barrientos,
Hackett, Whitehill, conductor Monteux. In open air at the Val d'Enfer
Les Baux, 1954, with Vivaldi, Gedda, Dens, conductor Cluytens.

CHARACTERS

Mireille . . . . Soprano
Vincent, *her lover* . . . . Tenor
Ourrias, *a bull-tender* . . . . Baritone
Maître Ramon, *father of Mireille* . . . . Bass
Taven, *an old woman, thought to be a
    witch* . . . . Mezzo-Soprano
Andreloux, *a shepherd* . . . . Mezzo-Soprano
Maître Ambroise, *father of Vincent* . . . . Bass
Clémence . . . . Soprano
Time: Mid-Nineteenth Century   *Place:* In and near Arles

Act I.   The overture sets the Provençal atmosphere, with
its *cornemuse* tunes. The scene is a mulberry plantation.
After a pastoral chorus, Mireille confesses that she is in love

with Vincent, who returns her affection. Her song, 'O légère hirondelle', in the waltz rhythm in which Gounod liked to introduce his heroines, is attractively ingenuous. In spite of the warning of Taven that a girl should not give her heart away so openly, least of all when there is little possibility of parental approval for the proposed match, Mireille makes no pretence of hiding her feelings when Vincent comes towards her. In an agreeable duet they repeat their vows, and pledge each other to meet in a particular sanctuary if ever trouble should threaten their lives.

Act II. A festival is in progress at Arles. A *farandole* chorus makes a vigorous introduction to the act. Mireille and Vincent are there together and, when asked by the company to sing, they perform the graceful *Chanson de Magali*: 'La brise est douce'. Taven warns Mireille that Vincent has a rival, Ourrias, who has admitted his love for her. Mireille is indignant at the idea that she might prove unfaithful to Vincent: 'Trahir Vincent!' She will be true to him all her days: 'Non, jamais, jamais! A toi mon âme'.

Mireille's graceful avowal of her love is followed by the entrance of Ourrias, 'Si les filles d'Arles', a typically bucolic song. Before the act ends, Ourrias has asked for Mireille's hand and been refused, Vincent's father, Ambroise, has likewise pleaded for his son and been told that his reasons were nothing short of mercenary, and Mireille has emphasised the firmness of her attachment for Vincent, in spite of her father's preference for Ourrias.

Act III. The scene is a desert in the region of Crau, where little has a chance to grow before being burnt up by the heat of the sun. A *Musette* is succeeded by a charming shepherd's song: 'Le jour se lève', sung by Andreloux. Mireille, on her way to the sanctuary she and Vincent agreed upon in Act I, pauses to envy the carefree shepherd: 'Heureux petit berger'. Taven succeeds in catching her up and informing her of an unsuccessful attack made upon Vincent's life by Ourrias; Mireille hurries on towards the sanctuary.

The scene changes to the sanctuary itself, the church of Les Saintes Maries. There is a march and chorus for the pilgrims, after which Vincent appears, vainly searching for Mireille. In an effective, high-lying tenor aria, 'Anges du Paradis', he prays that she may win her way to their meeting-place, in spite of the torrid heat of the Provençal sun. Mireille arrives in a state of collapse, but, at sight of her lover waiting for her, she revives, and together they rejoice in their happiness in a charming duet, 'La foi de son flambeau divin'. There is another moment of anxiety when Mireille again appears to lose control of her senses, but the presence of her father blessing her union with Vincent restores her strength.

The alternative ending develops the plot by Ourrias to kill Vincent. There is a short fight between the two rivals which ends in Ourrias stabbing Vincent with his murderous trident, and Ourrias tries to escape across the Val d'enfer, only to be confronted by the reproaching voices of conscience in the shape of the spirits of deceived lovers which haunt the place. Even the boatman who comes to his aid seems to know of his crime, and he drowns making his escape.

Mireille herself dies of exhaustion on her way across the desert of Crau to the appointed meeting-place with Vincent. Her big scene, beginning 'Voici la vaste plaine et le désert de feu' is one of the best bits of the score, and it impressively combines the lyrical qualities of Gounod's music with something considerably more dramatic.

Mireille is a romantic love story set in Provence, and there is nothing realistic about the way Gounod has approached it; but the music's genuinely lyrical quality and charm should ensure it at least a toehold on the repertory for years to come. It would be opera's, and particularly French opera's, loss if this was not so.   H.

ROMÉO ET JULIETTE
Romeo and Juliet

Opera in five acts by Gounod; words by Barbier and Carré, after the tragedy by Shakespeare. Produced Paris, Théâtre-Lyrique, April 27, 1867, with Miolan-Carvalho, Michot, Barre, Cazaux; January 1873, taken over by the Opéra-Comique; Opéra, November 28, 1888, with Patti, Jean and Edouard de Reszke, Delmas. London, Covent Garden (in Italian), July 11, 1867, with Patti, Mario, Cotogni, Tagliafico. New York, Academy of Music, November 15, 1867, with Minnie Hauck; Metropolitan Opera House, December 14, 1891, with Eames, Jean and Edouard de Reszke. Chicago, December 15, 1916, with Muratore and Galli-Curci. Revived Covent Garden, 1919, with Melba, Ansseau; Metropolitan, 1922, with Bori, Gigli; Covent Garden, 1930, with Edith Mason, Burdino, Brownlee, Pinza, conductor Barbirolli; Covent Garden

Company's Tour, 1937, with Lisa Perli, Nash, Brownlee, Allin, conductor Beecham; Metropolitan, 1937, with Sayao, Crooks, Brownlee, Pinza, conductor d'Abravanel; 1945, with Munsel, Jobin, Singher, Pinza; 1968, with Mirella Freni and Franco Corelli.

CHARACTERS

The Duke of Verona . . . . Bass
Count Paris . . . . Baritone
Count Capulet . . . . Bass
Juliet, *his daughter* . . . . Soprano
Gertrude, *her nurse* . . . . .Mezzo-Soprano
Tybalt, *Capulet's nephew* . . . . Tenor
Romeo, *a Montague* . . . . Tenor
Mercutio . . . . Baritone
Stephano, *Romeo's page* . . . . Soprano
Gregory, *a Capulet retainer* . . . . Baritone
Friar Lawrence . . . . Bass
Benvolio, *retainer to the Montagues* . . . . Tenor
Friar Jean . . . . Bass
Nobles and Ladies of Verona, Citizens, Soldiers, Monks, and Pages

Time: Fourteenth Century　　　　　　　*Place:* Verona

Having gone to Goethe for *Faust*, Gounod's librettists, Barbier and Carré, went to Shakespeare for *Roméo et Juliette*, which like *Faust*, reached the Paris Grand Opéra by way of the Théâtre-Lyrique.

Roméo et Juliette has been esteemed more highly in France than elsewhere. In England it has never enjoyed much popularity, apart from the period when Patti and after her Melba used to star in the rôle of Juliet. In America, save for performances in New Orleans, it was only during the Grau régime at the Metropolitan Opera House, when it was given in French with casts familiar with the traditions of the Opéra, that it can be said regularly to have held a place in the repertory. Eames is remembered as a singularly beautiful Juliet, vocally and personally; Capoul, Jean de Reszke, and Saléza, as Romeos; Édouard de Reszke as Frère Laurent.

Nicolini, who became Adelina Patti's second husband, sang Romeo at the Opéra to her Juliet. She was then the Marquise de Caux, her marriage to the Marquis having been brought about by the Empress Eugénie. But that this marriage was not to last long, and that the Romeo and Juliet were as much in love with each other in actual life as on the stage, was revealed one night to an Opéra audience, when, during the balcony scene, prima donna and tenor—so the record says— imprinted twenty-nine real kisses on each other's lips.

The libretto is in five acts and follows closely, often even to the text, Shakespeare's tragedy. There is a prologue in which the characters and chorus briefly rehearse the story that is to unfold itself.

Act I.   The grand hall in the palace of the Capulets. A masked ball is in progress. The chorus sings gay measures. Tybalt speaks to Paris of Juliet, to whom Paris is engaged and who at that moment appears with her father. Capulet bids the guests welcome and to be of good cheer—'Soyez les bienvenus, amis' (Be ye welcome, friends), and 'Allons! jeunes gens! Allons! belles dames!' (Bestir ye, young nobles! And ye, too, fair ladies!)

Romeo, Mercutio, Benvolio, and half-a-dozen followers come masked. Despite the deadly feud between the two houses, they, Montagues, have ventured to come as maskers to the fête of the Capulets. Mercutio sings of Queen Mab, a number as gossamer-like in the opera as the monologue is in the play; hardly ever sung as it should be, because the role of Mercutio is rarely assigned to a baritone capable of doing justice to the airy measures of 'Mab, la reine des mensonges' (Mab, Queen Mab, the fairies' midwife).

The Montagues withdraw to another part of the palace. Juliet returns with Gertrude, her nurse. Full of high spirits, she sings the graceful and animated waltz, 'Je veux vivre dans ce rêve, qui m'enivre' (Fair is the tender dream of youth). The nurse is called away. Romeo, wandering in, meets Juliet. Their love, as in the play, is instantaneous. Romeo addresses her in passionate accents, 'Ange adorable' (Angel! adored one). His addresses, Juliet's replies, make a charming duo.

Upon the re-entry of Tybalt, Romeo, who had removed his mask, again adjusts it, but Tybalt suspects who he is, and from the utterance of his suspicions Juliet learns that the handsome youth, to whom her heart has gone out, is none other than Romeo, scion of the Montagues, the sworn enemies of her house. The fiery Tybalt is for attacking Romeo and his followers then and there. But old Capulet, respecting the laws of hospitality, orders that the fête proceed.

Act II. The garden of the Capulets. The window of
Juliet's apartment, and the balcony, upon which it gives.
Romeo's page, Stephano, a character introduced by the
librettists, holds a ladder by which Romeo ascends to the
balcony. Stephano leaves, taking the ladder with him.

Romeo sings, in one of Gounod's loveliest tenor arias,
'Ah! léve-toi soleil' (Ah! fairest dawn arise). The window
opens, Juliet comes out upon the balcony. Romeo conceals
himself. From her soliloquy he learns that, although he is a
Montague, she loves him. He discloses his presence. The
interchange of pledges is exquisite. Lest the sweetness of so
much love music becomes too cloying, the librettists interrupt it with an episode. The Capulet retainer, Gregory, and
servants of the house, suspecting that an intruder is in the
garden (they have seen Stephano speeding away), search
unsuccessfully and depart.

The nurse calls. Juliet re-enters her apartment. Romeo
sings, 'O nuit divine' (Oh, night divine). Juliet again steals out
upon the balcony. 'Ah! je te l'ai dit, je t'adore!' (Ah, I have
told you that I adore you), sings Romeo. There is a beautiful
duet, 'Ah! ne fuis pas encore!' (Ah, do not flee again), a
brief farewell, and the curtain falls upon the balcony scene.

Act III, part i. Friar Lawrence's cell. Here takes place the
wedding of Romeo and Juliet, the good friar hoping that
their union may lead to peace between the two great
Veronese houses of Montague and Capulet. There are in this
part of the act Friar Lawrence's prayer, 'Dieu, qui fis
l'homme à ton image' (God, who made man in Thine image);
a trio, in which the friar chants the rubric, and the pair
respond; and an effective final quartet for Juliet, Gertrude,
Romeo, and Friar Lawrence ('O pur bonheur').

Part ii. A street near Capulet's house. Stephano, having
vainly sought Romeo, and thinking he still may be hiding in
Capulet's garden, sings a ditty likely to rouse the temper of
the Capulet household, and brings its retainers into the street,
thus affording Romeo a chance to get away. The ditty is 'Que
fais-tu, blanche tourterelle' (Gentle dove, why art thou
clinging?). Gregory and Stephano draw and fight. The scene
develops, as in the play. Friends of the two rival houses
appear. Mercutio fights Tybalt and is slain, and is avenged by
Romeo, who kills Tybalt, Juliet's kinsman, and, in consequence, is banished from Verona by the Duke, who appears
as the fighting reaches its climax.

Act IV. It is the room of Juliet, to which Romeo has gone in order to bid her farewell, before he goes into exile. The lingering *adieux*, the impassioned accents in which the despair of parting is expressed—these find eloquent utterance in the music. There is the duet, 'Nuit d'hyménée, O douce nuit d'amour' (Night hymeneal, sweetest night of love). Romeo hears the lark, sure sign of approaching day, but Juliet protests 'Non, non, ce n'est pas le jour' (No, no! 'Tis not yet the day). Yet the parting time cannot be put off longer. Romeo: 'Ah! reste! reste encore dans mes bras enlacés' (Ah! rest! rest once more within mine entwining arms); then both, 'Il faut partir, hélas' (Now we must part, alas).

Hardly has Romeo gone when Gertrude runs in to warn Juliet that her father is approaching with Friar Lawrence. Tybalt's dying wish, whispered into old Capulet's ear, was that the marriage between Juliet and the noble whom Capulet has chosen for her husband, Count Paris, be speeded. Juliet's father comes to bid her prepare for her marriage. Neither she, the friar, nor the nurse dare tell Capulet of her secret nuptials with Romeo. This gives significance to the quartet, 'Ne crains rien' (Fear no more). Capulet withdraws, leaving, as he supposes, Friar Lawrence to explain to Juliet the details of the ceremony. It is then that the friar, in the dramatic 'Buvez donc ce breuvage' (Drink then of this philtre), gives her the potion, upon drinking which she shall appear as dead.

The scene changes to the grand hall of the palace. Guests arrive for the nuptials. There is occasion for the ballet, so essential for a production at the Opéra. Juliet drains the phial, falls as if dead. (This scene, written in 1888, is often omitted.)

Act V. The tomb of the Capulets. Romeo, having heard in his exile that his beloved is no more, breaks into the tomb. She, recovering from the effects of the philtre, finds him dying, plunges a dagger into her breast, and expires with him.

In the music there is an effective prelude. Romeo salutes the tomb, 'Salut, tombeau sombre et silencieux', and sings, to his beloved, apparently lying dead, 'O ma femme! ô ma bien aimée' (O wife, dearly beloved). Juliet, not yet aware that Romeo has taken poison, and Romeo forgetting for the moment that death's cold hand already is reaching out for him, they sing, 'Viens, fuyons au bout du monde' (Come, let us fly to the ends of the earth). Then Romeo begins to feel the effect of the poison, and tells Juliet what he has done. 'Console-toi, pauvre âme' (Console thyself, sad heart). But Juliet will not live without him, and while he in his wandering mind hears the lark, as at their last parting, she stabs herself. K.

JACQUES OFFENBACH
(1819–1880)

ORPHÉE AUX ENFERS
Orpheus in the Underworld

OPERA in two acts by Jacques Offenbach, text by Hector Crémieux and Halévy. Première at the Bouffes-Parisiens, October 21, 1858, with Mme. Tautin, MM. Léonce, Tayau, Désiré. First performed New York, 1861 (in German); London, Haymarket Theatre, 1865; St. James's Theatre, London, 1869, with Hortense Schneider. Revived Sadler's Wells, 1960, with June Bronhill; Kansas City, 1968, with Sciutti, Monica Sinclair, Driscoll, Cuénod, conductor Rescigno.

CHARACTERS

Pluto, *god of the underworld* . . . . Tenor
Jupiter, *king of the gods* . . . . Baritone
Orpheus, *a violinist* . . . . Tenor
John Styx, *a fool* . . . . Baritone
Mercury . . . . Tenor
Bacchus . . . . Speaking role
Mars . . . . Bass
Morpheus . . . . Tenor
Eurydice, *Orpheus's wife* . . . . Soprano
Diana . . . . Soprano
Public Opinion[1] . . . . Mezzo-Soprano
Venus . . . . Contralto
Cupid . . . . Soprano
Juno . . . . Mezzo-Soprano
Minerva . . . . Soprano

[1] In the Sadler's Wells production, Calliope, Orpheus's mother.

Offenbach's parody of the story of Orpheus originally obtained something of a *succès de scandale*; he was accused of blaspheming antiquity, and of satirising the government and prevailing social conditions. Since he was at the time in rather trying financial straits as manager of the Bouffes-Parisiens, success in whatever form it came was by no means unwelcome. History suggests that the role of John Styx was an afterthought and designed especially for the actor Bache, an excellent musician who had just left the Comédie Française. At a revival of *Orphée* (1867), the notorious courtesan Cora Pearl sang Cupid, relinquishing the role, however, after only twelve days. On this occasion, Madame Ugalde, later the first Nicklausse, was Eurydice.

The overture as we know it from concert performances is not by a long chalk what Offenbach designed to precede his opera, but was compiled by a certain Carl Binder for the first performance in Vienna; he made use of the overture which Offenbach wrote (an introduction, minuet, and embryonic canon) and added to it the famous violin solo and the Can-Can.

Act I.   First tableau.   Public Opinion introduces the characters. Eurydice sings lightly and prettily of the extra-marital love she feels in her heart, while the flutes bill and coo around the vocal line: 'La femme dont le cœur rêve, N'a pas de sommeil'. Orpheus sees her with flowers in her hand; who are they for? It appears that each has lost his or her heart to someone else, and neither intends to renounce the new-found love in favour of connubial bliss. They quarrel and it transpires that Eurydice has a morbid dislike of Orpheus as an artist, hating his fiddle-playing above everything. This is the crowning insult. Orpheus announces he will play for her his latest violin concerto (it lasts one and a quarter hours, he says), and the famous violin tune starts. The duet which it initiates is charming, and it is not long before the fiddle tune influences the vocal parts.

Eurydice's lover is Pluto, who appears on earth in the guise of a shepherd and bee-keeper under the name of Aristeus. He charms Eurydice with a Chanson Pastorale, but admits to her that love for him involves transporting her to the underworld. She says good-bye to life most attractively, and leaves a note behind for Orpheus, telling him that she is dead. This he finds, but his discreet rejoicings are broken in upon by Public Opinion, who threatens him with scandal if he does not follow his wife to Hades; the fact that he does not want to get her back means that his reclamatory action will be even more virtuous than if he did! They start off on their journey, Orpheus complaining at the way he is treated, Public Opinion urging him on in a delightful *marziale* duettino.

The scene changes to Mount Olympus, where the gods are sleeping peacefully. They introduce themselves one by one, Cupid being followed by Venus, a wordless chorus dividing their verses. Jupiter is woken up by Diana's horn. Diana is unhappy, and admits it is because she could not that morning any longer find Actaeon on earth in his accustomed place. Jupiter reveals that he took it upon himself to change Actaeon into a stag, as he was worried that Diana seemed to be compromising herself rather badly with him. All the gods complain about Jupiter's high-handed, tyrannical ways, but they are interrupted when news comes that Eurydice has arrived amongst them. Pluto makes his entrance and is rebuked by Jupiter for having carried off the delightful Eurydice. He defends himself, and soon the gods join in chorus to announce that they are rebelling against the intolerable domination of Jupiter—to say nothing of the eternal monotony of their diet of nectar and ambrosia. In turn, Minerva, Cupid, Venus, and Diana remind Jupiter of the disguises he has in the past assumed for his earthly amours, and, in charming and witty 'Couplets', they mock him for his obvious interest in the case of Eurydice: 'Ne prends plus l'air patelin, on te connaît Jupin'. Pluto adds insult to injury by saying that in his view the disguises were necessary because Jupiter was so villainously ugly that he would have got nowhere with the girls without them.

At this juncture, Orpheus and Public Opinion are announced, and Jupiter exhorts the gods to be on their best behaviour when he gives audience to the strangers. Pluto leads off the finale to the first act and continues to deny that he has had anything to do with hiding Eurydice. Orpheus starts to ask for Eurydice back, but he has only got as far as the first phrase of 'J'ai perdu mon Eurydice' when the gods and goddesses take up the tune and sing it for him; his demands are obviously granted in advance, since the appeal of his song has penetrated even to Mount Olympus. Much to Orpheus's dismay, Jupiter orders Pluto to return Eurydice to her husband, and says that he will himself come down to Hades to look for her. Won't he take them too, please, ask

the other gods and goddesses, and, when he grants their
request, they all join in a hymn of praise which soon becomes
a gay gallop tune.

Act II. Tableau iii.   A sparkling *allegretto* entr'acte intro
duces the scene in the underworld. Eurydice is being looked
after by John Styx, a complete fool on earth and now
charged with prison duties in Hades. In a song, with an
enchantingly silly melody, he explains that he was once king
of Boeotia: 'Quand j'étais roi de Béotie'. Once he is out of
the way, Jupiter comes looking for Eurydice, in whom he is
considerably interested. He disguises himself as a fly, and
imitates its buzzing. Eurydice quickly takes a liking to the fly
('Bel insecte à l'aile dorée'), and they sing and buzz a duet
together. At the end, Jupiter in his own voice rejoices at the
capture that he seems to have made, and he eventually admits
his identity. The scene ends as John Styx repeats his song and
is mocked and imitated by Pluto.

Tableau iv.   A splendid *Chœur infernal* opens the scene.
Eurydice has by now been turned by Jupiter into a
Bacchante, and she is persuaded by Cupid to sing a Bacchic
Hymn for their delight. Jupiter proposes a minuet, and all
comment on his admirable dancing of it. Then begins the
famous Can-Can tune, probably the best-known piece in the
opera. Jupiter is about to go off with Eurydice when Pluto
stops him, just at the moment when they can hear the sound
of Orpheus's fiddle playing 'J'ai perdu mon Eurydice' for all
it is worth. He is warned that he must walk in front of his
wife, and that even to glance back at her will lead to a
revocation of his permission to take her back with him to
earth. Public Opinion urges him to obey the god's injunction,
but Jupiter has an unexpected card up his sleeve; he hurls a
thunderbolt and the noise gives Orpheus such a shock that he
involuntarily looks round to see what made it, and so forfeits
his right to his bride. Everyone is delighted, Eurydice stays
on as a Bacchante, and all join in a final version of the
Can-Can to express their pleasure at the turn events have
taken.

It is a little hard to explain why in England Johann Strauss
was for so long more popular than Offenbach. Is it that the
touch of sentimentality which is to be found in almost all
Strauss's tunes, even the best, is almost completely absent
from Offenbach's, at any rate until the time of the
barcarole? Or is Offenbach's satire too pointedly local for

vival a hundred years after its time? It is difficult to give a
conclusive answer; Offenbach wrote startlingly good comic
music, full of excellent tunes and humorous invention, and it
seems likely to please almost anyone who is at all interested
in the best sort of 'light' music (what else can one call it?).
Orphée itself is a most accomplished and stylish bit of
fooling, at its broadest in the spoofing of Gluck's 'J'ai perdu
mon Eurydice', at its most hilarious and catching in the
famous Can-Can.   H.

LA BELLE HÉLÈNE
The Fair Helen

Opera in three acts by Jacques Offenbach, libretto by Meilhac and
Halévy. Première December 17, 1864, at Théâtre des Variétés, Paris,
with Hortense Schneider as Hélène, Mlle Sully as Oreste, Dupuis as
Paris. First performed London, 1866, with Hortense Schneider; New
York, 1867 (in German). Revived Paris, 1890, with Jeanne Granier,
1899, with Simon-Girard; 1919, with Marguerite Carré; 1960, with
Géori Boué; London, Adelphi Theatre, 1932, in a new version by A. P
Herbert with Evelyn Laye; Sadler's Wells, 1963, with Joyce Blackham.

CHARACTERS

Paris, *son of Priam, King of Troy* . . . . Tenor
Menelaus, *King of Sparta* . . . . Tenor
Agamemnon, *King of Argos* . . . . Baritone
Calchas, *High Priest of Jupiter* . . . . Bass
Achilles, *King of Phthiotis* . . . . Tenor
Orestes, *son of Agamemnon* . . . . Soprano
Ajax I, *King of Salamis* . . . . Tenor
Ajax II, *King of Locris* . . . . Baritone
Helen, *Queen of Sparta* . . . . Soprano
Bacchis, *Helen's attendant* . . . . .Mezzo-Soprano
Leoena, *a courtesan* . . . . Soprano
Parthoenis, *a courtesan* . . . . Soprano
Guards, Slaves, People, Princes, Princesses, Mourners
for Adonis, Helen's Entourage

Time: Antiquity   *Place:* Greece

Act I.   The introduction consists of the Marche des Rois,

and Paris's song played on the oboe. In front of the temple, a
chorus pays mock homage to Jupiter ('Jupin' in French)
during a festivity in honour of Venus. Helen leads the women
in their devotions. She sings a mellifluous air in 6/8 ('Amours
divins'), then reveals in a conversation with Calchas that she
is obsessed with the promise Venus has made to Paris, that he
shall win the most beautiful woman in the world. This is
clearly a delicate situation for her, as who else can lay claim
to such a title? To a comic march there enters Orestes,
Agamemnon's precocious son, with Leoena and Parthoenis,
the courtesans. He has an extremely skittish song, in whose
refrain Calchas joins:

> 'C'est avec ces dames qu'Oreste
> Fait danser l'argent à papa;
> Papa s'en fiche bien au reste,
> Car c'est la Grèce qui paiera.'

Calchas is embarrassed at Orestes's insistence on bringing the
two ladies into the temple and Orestes accommodatingly
leaves, singing his refrain as he goes.

Enter a shepherd asking peremptorily whether a message
has yet come from Venus. Even as he speaks the messenger
dove arrives, a little out of breath, and Calchas reads Venus's
command—that the shepherd shall win the most beautiful
woman in the world, clearly Helen. Calchas realises it is Paris,
agrees obsequiously to help, and asks rather knowingly for a

t-hand impression of Venus. This Paris gives him in his
nous song ('Au mont Ida'), perhaps the best known, cer-
inly one of the most attractive of Offenbach's lyrical tunes.
To the accompaniment of a very graceful piece of music,
Helen and the women process from the temple, and Helen
interrogates Calchas about the handsome young shepherd.
Calchas leaves them together, but they have time for only a
few words before the Kings of Greece enter in procession.
The two Ajaxes, followed by Achilles, announce themselves
and their attributes in comic fashion (No. 1). Next it is the
turn of Menelaus, hymning his expectation of imminent
cuckoldry, and finally of Agamemnon, King of Kings. The
whole episode is Offenbach at his best; memorable and
devastatingly comic. It is said that the composer once
intended at this point to have a parody of the tournament of
song in *Tannhäuser*, but he gave up the idea and we have
instead a game of charades, whose winner is to receive his
prize from Helen herself. The Kings are bad at the competition, which is won by Paris, still disguised as a shepherd. He
announces his identity and, amidst general acclamation
('C'est l'homme à la pomme'), Helen crowns him victor, and
invites him to supper. On the side Calchas agrees to try to
arrange for Menelaus to be absent. There is a clap of thunder,
and Calchas takes the opportunity of announcing a decree
from Jupiter: Menelaus must go to Crete ('What the devil to
do?' is that worthy's aside). The finale gets under way as they
all, led by Helen, admonish Menelaus 'Pars pour la Crète', to
the urgent tune of No. 1.

Act II. An entr'acte based on the ripe waltz tune of the
Act's finale takes us to Helen's apartments, where she sits,
surrounded by her women, who urge her to make a specially
fine toilet on this day of all days. Helen for once seems
virtuously inclined and chooses a sober dress; let fate not
have it *all* its own way. A message comes from Paris, asking
Helen to receive him. She tries to refuse, but sighs:
'Pourquoi, ô déesse, as-tu toujours choisi notre famille pour
faire tes expériences?' In a song that is a gem of wit and
beauty, Helen laments (if that is the right word) her fatal
gift:

> Dis moi, Vénus,
> Quel plaisir trouves-tu,
> A faire ainsi cascader
> La vertu?

Example No. 1

Dis-moi, Vé-nus, Quel plaisir trou-ves-tu, A faire ain-

-si cas-ca-der, cas-ca-der, La ver-tu?

When one hears it, it is hard to imagine that even Offenbach ever wrote anything more mouth-wateringly appetising. It sums up a whole generation which lived hedonistically but retained the ability to mock itself while doing so.

Paris comes in unannounced, finds her determinedly resistant to love and to threats, and bids her beware of trickery. The music announces the gambling-game of Goose (Snakes and Ladders). The Kings bet, Calchas is caught cheating and treated in an ensemble as if he were a welshing bookmaker.

Helen sends for Calchas and asks him by prayer to cause her to dream a rendezvous with Paris. She sleeps, Paris enters disguised as a slave, sends Calchas packing, and is alone with Helen. Orestes and the girls can be heard singing outside and soon Helen wakes up. She takes the reality of Paris for the dream she so much wanted, and their extended love duet rivals Gounod in its melodic innocence ('Oui, c'est un rêve'). Their bliss is interrupted by the wholly unexpected arrival of Menelaus, who raises the alarm and summons the Kings who are having supper next door. Orestes with his perpetual song arrives first, but the others are not far behind. Menelaus asks what sort of a show they have made of looking after his honour in his absence. Paris vocalises (like Jupiter as the fly in *Orpheus*—does this have an amorous connotation for the composer?), but Menelaus is more taken aback by the suggestion, quickly seized on by Helen, that he is really the most to blame; it is customary for husbands to send warning of their return, is the burden of Helen's delightful song! Agamemnon tries to send Paris away—but, Paris rejoins, in that case he will have to return. To the tune of the waltz of the entr'acte, now with a mocking onomatopoeic verbal accompaniment, they urge him on his way.

Act III. The seaside resort of Nauplia. The entr'acte
makes use of Orestes's tune and the curtain goes up to show
the Spartans in holiday mood, singing the praises of Venus.
Orestes is inclined to think that Menelaus's insistence on the
departure of Paris has offended Venus, who seems to have
taken revenge on the women of Greece by making them more
susceptible than usual to the dictates of the heart. The Kings
complain about the crowd now to be found at the seaside—
there is no room for decent bathing any more.

Enter Helen and Menelaus quarrelling. Why had Helen said,
'Oh, then it *wasn't* a dream'? Helen explains that Venus had a
hand in it, and Paris *is* very attractive. Agamemnon is
dissatisfied—Greece is in a sorry moral state due to Venus's
displeasure at Paris's departure. It's all Menelaus's fault; if his
behaviour could pass as exemplary for a man, it is nothing
short of idiotic for a King. In a famous trio, satirising at the
same time patriotic moments in *William Tell* and *La Muette
de Portici*, Agamemnon and Calchas try to persuade Menelaus
to give up Helen to Paris—in order that Greece may be saved
from moral chaos!

Menelaus has a better idea. He has invited the High Priest
of Venus from Cythera to exorcise their troubles, and at that
moment he appears in a great ship accompanied by his
retinue. The Greeks welcome him and pray for help in their
predicament. He (it is Paris all the time) chides them for their
melancholy reception—Venus's cult is a gay one—and breaks
into a *Tyrolienne*, complete with yodelling effects. The High
Priest promises them pardon in Venus's name, provided
Menelaus allows Helen to embark forthwith for Cythera to
make sacrifice to Venus. Helen appears, agrees after some
persuasion to go, and embarks, whereupon Paris reveals
himself: Menelaus will not see Helen again—but the implied
threat is lost in the final chorus of good wishes for the voyage
to Cythera (No. 1).   H.

LA PÉRICHOLE

Operetta in three acts by Jacques Offenbach; libretto by Meilhac and
Halévy, based on Mérimée's play *La Carosse du Saint-Sacrement*.
Première (in two acts) at the Variétés, Paris, October 6, 1868, with
Hortense Schneider. A third act was added for the revival at the same
theatre in 1874. First performed New York, 1869; London, 1870. Most
recent revivals include those at the Metropolitan, New York, 1957 (in
English), with Patrice Munsel, Theodor Uppman, Ralph Herbert,

Lorenzo Alvary, conductor Jean Morel; London, John Lewis Partnership, 1961.

CHARACTERS

La Périchole, *a street singer* .... Soprano
Piquillo, *another street singer, in love with her* ... Tenor
Don Andres de Ribeira, *Viceroy of Peru* ..... Baritone
Don Pedro de Hinoyosa, *Governor of Lima* ... Baritone
Comte Miguel de Panatellas, *lord-in-waiting to
    the Viceroy* .... Tenor
Le Marquis de Santarem .... Baritone
Le Marquis de Tarapote .... Bass
Two Notaries .... Tenor, Baritone
The old prisoner

Guadalena ⎫ *joint proprietresses of the* ⎧ Soprano
Berginella ⎬ *"Three Cousins" tavern* ⎨ Soprano
Mastrilla ⎭ ⎩ Mezzo-Soprano

Manuelita, Ninetta ⎫ *Ladies of* ⎧ Sopranos
Brambilla ⎬ *the Court . . .* ⎨ Mezzo-Soprano
Frasquinella ⎭ ⎩ Contralto

Courtiers, Citizens, Pages, Guards, etc.

Time: Late Eighteenth Century   *Place:* Lima, capital of Peru

The story of *La Périchole* is taken supposedly from Prosper Mérimée's play *La Carosse du Saint-Sacrement*,[1] but the adaptation is a very long way indeed after the original. Offenbach's librettists have abandoned even the bones of the original plot and instead have developed the idea of the situation to make a satire on the Second Empire.

Act I.   There is a lively prelude—a march and two airs from the first act—and the curtain goes up on the public square in Lima in front of the café of the 'Three Cousins'. It is the Viceroy's birthday, and he has the habit of roaming round the streets, as he thinks incognito, to find out exactly what is being said and thought about him. Wine is free, and the people of Lima, prompted by the Governor, are perfectly prepared to humour the Viceroy in his masquerade. The three proprietresses of the 'Three Cousins' make themselves known in an attractive trio, and then the crowd hears the signal warning them of the Viceroy's approach. His entrance song proclaims his confidence in the impenetrable nature of

[1] Mérimée's drama was played in London in 1957 with Edwige Feuillère, and it was from it, too, that derived Jean Renoir's beautiful film 'The Golden Coach', starring Anna Magnani.

⎯s disguise, and it is accompanied by the chorus agreeing to ⎯⎯⎯spect the incognito of which he is so proud. Across the ⎯quare come two street singers, la Périchole and Piquillo, her lover. They announce the title of their ballad as 'The Soldier and the Indian Maid' and a very catchy ballad it is that they sing in duet. The song finished, they take a collection, not very successfully because Piquillo looks so fierce that he frightens off all the men who want to give la Périchole money, and they are obliged to try another number, a 'séguedille pour soirée'. This time the collection is spoiled by a circus procession, and la Périchole and Piquillo are left hungry, tired and penniless.

Piquillo leaves the stage, and Don Andres can resist the attractions of la Périchole no longer. He asks her if she wouldn't like to be one of the Viceroy's Ladies-in-Waiting—his wife is dead, but he thinks it nice to carry on old customs. She is hungry and she accepts, but first she must write a letter to tell Piquillo what has happened and say goodbye to him. Her attractive song of farewell ('O mon cher amant'), a genuinely touching piece, is in unusually serious vein for Offenbach and his public. She arranges for her letter to be given to Piquillo, but in the meanwhile Don Andres has discovered a snag: nobody but a married woman can become Lady-in-Waiting to the Viceroy, and la Périchole is single. There is a simple solution: he orders Panatellas, his Lord-in-Waiting, to find the lady a husband, and Don Pedro, as Governor of Lima, to collect a notary to perform the marriage ceremony.

In the meanwhile Piquillo receives the letter and in despair is about to hang himself when a diversion occurs. He is selected by Panatellas as the prospective husband of the Viceroy's new lady friend, and in return for money he agrees to come along to the Palace.

The finale takes place in an atmosphere of considerable well-being. Both prospective parties to the marriage and the two notaries who are to perform it have had their consciences eased with alcohol. La Périchole in fact sings a charmingly tipsy waltz song ('Ah, quel dîner') as she waits to sign the wedding agreement. She is delighted to recognise Piquillo as the bridegroom, but he is too drunk to have any idea who she is and takes care to explain that he is in love with someone else. The marriage duly takes place and the Chorus works up so much enthusiasm that it seems certain at any moment to break into a can-can. La Périchole and Piquillo, more from

force of habit than anything else, sing a snatch of the ball.
we heard earlier, and on this note the act comes to an end.

Act II.   An elaborate entr'acte takes us to a grand room
in the Palace. The situation is complex. The newly created
Countess of Tabago must be presented officially by her
husband to the Viceroy, but it proves by no means easy to
persuade Piquillo to fall in with this scheme, particularly as
he now has only one thought in the world and that is to
return to la Périchole, wherever she may be. The ladies of the
Court are not only jealous of the new arrival but also
contemptuous of her lowly birth. When la Périchole appears,
Piquillo of course recognises her and loses his temper to such
a degree that none of her efforts (even the famous air 'Mon
Dieu, que les hommes sont bêtes') serves to calm him. He
proceeds to denounce her, for all the world like Alfredo in *La
Traviata,* as a heartless and wicked jade, so that the Viceroy
has little option but to order him off to prison. There he is
to be confined with all other husbands who have proved
recalcitrant—to a most seductive waltz tune, great play is
made with the individual syllables of the word 'recalcitrant',
which comes as the climax to one of Offenbach's most
splendid finales.

Act III, scene i.   A dungeon in the prison. The court
officials conduct Piquillo to his jail, congratulate him on his
honourable conduct, and leave him, not however before
singing a brilliant trio with him in the form of a bolero. While
Piquillo, in a charming song, wonders if his 'wife' is going to
do anything about his predicament, la Périchole for her part
has procured the Viceroy's permission to visit her husband in
prison and, after some mutual recriminations, his heart is
melted—as whose wouldn't be? — by her slow waltz song 'Tu
n'es pas beau', and its refrain 'je t'adore, brigand'. All is made
up between them, and they resolve to bribe the jailor and
procure Piquillo's escape—unfortunately the jailor turns out
to be Don Andres in another of his disguises, this time a
successful one. He gets his own back by ordering la Périchole
to be chained to the wall opposite Piquillo, but in a delightful
trio whispers to her as he leaves the dungeon that she will be
released the moment she gives the sign that she loves him.

The lovers are not long together before an old prisoner
burrows his way like a mole through the wall. He has been in
prison for years, nobody quite knows why, but at last he
seems within reach of escape. He helps to free them from

their shackles, and they agree that la Périchole shall make the signal to the Viceroy. When he comes in full of ardour, they capture him, tie him up and make their way safely out of the jail.

The second scene is again set in the public square. The soldiers are out and searching the town for the runaways, who for their part have taken refuge in the café of the 'Three Cousins'. There is a very agreeable trio for the cousins and, once the soldiers have left the square, the three escaped prisoners make their appearance. They decide to give themselves up, and la Périchole urges a final appeal to the Viceroy's good nature in the form of a ballad 'La Clémence d'Auguste'. It is completely successful, he grants them their freedom, says they are to keep their titles and la Périchole anything he has given her, and the operetta ends with a repetition of the ballad heard in the first act.   H.

LES CONTES D'HOFFMANN

The Tales of Hoffmann

Opera in three acts by Jacques Offenbach, text by Barbier and Carré. Première Opéra-Comique, Paris, February 10, 1881, with Adèle Isaac (Stella, Olympia, Antonia), Ugalde, Talazac, Taskin. First performed New York, 1882; London, Adelphi Theatre, 1907; His Majesty's, 1910; Covent Garden, 1910, with Teyte, Nevada, de Lussan, Hyde, conductor Beecham; Metropolitan, New York, 1913, with Hempel, Fremstad, Bori, Macnez, Gilly, conductor Polacco. Revived Metropolitan, 1924, with Morgana, Bori, Fleta, de Luca; Covent Garden, 1936, with Andreva, Delprat, Dino Borgioli, Pinza, conductor Beecham; Florence Festival, 1938, with Menotti, Favero, Novotna, Lomanto, Ghirardini, conductor Gui; Metropolitan, 1943, with Munsel, Djanel, Novotna, Jobin, Pinza, Singher, conductor Beecham; Vienna State Opera, 1947, with Lipp, Welitsch, Jurinac, Patzak, Schöffler; Berlin, Komische Oper, 1958, in production and arrangement by Felsenstein with Muszely, Nocker, Asmus, conductor Václav Neumann; Sadler's Wells, 1970, with Anne Evans, William McAlpine, Geoffrey Chard, conductor Nicholas Braithwaite.

CHARACTERS

Lindorf, *a councillor of Nuremberg* . . . . Bass[1]
Andrès, *Stella's servant* . . . . Tenor

[1] It is customary for the incarnations of Hoffmann's evil genius (Lindorf, Coppelius, Dapertutto and Dr. Miracle) to be undertaken by the same singer, as are, exceptionally, the three soprano roles.

Hermann, *a student* .... Baritone
Nathanael, *a student* .... Tenor
Luther, *innkeeper* .... Bass
Hoffmann, *a poet* .... Tenor
Nicklausse, *his companion* .... Mezzo-Soprano
Spalanzani, *an inventor* .... Tenor
Cochenille, *his servant* .... Tenor
Coppelius, *a scientist and Spalanzani's rival* .. Baritone[1]
Olympia, *a mechanical doll* .... Soprano
Antonia, *a singer* .... Soprano
Crespel, *her father, a councillor of Munich* .... Baritone
Frantz, *his servant* .... Tenor
Dr. Miracle, *a doctor* .... Baritone[1]
The voice of Antonia's mother .... Mezzo-Soprano
Giulietta, *a courtesan* .... Soprano
Schlemil, *her lover* .... Bass
Dapertutto, *a sorcerer* .... Baritone[1]
Pittichinaccio, *an admirer of Giulietta's* .... Tenor
Stella, *an opera singer* .... Soprano
The Muse of Poetry .... Actress

Time: Nineteenth Century   *Place:* Nuremberg,
                                        Munich, Venice

Offenbach died during rehearsals of *Hoffmann*, and Ernest Guiraud orchestrated the piece for its Opéra-Comique première, 'tidying' it up and dropping the Giulietta act in the process (in order to retain the barcarole, he set the Antonia act in Venice!). A dozen years after the first performance Giulietta was brought back, but out of sequence, before Antonia rather than after as Offenbach and his librettists had intended. The episodes of Hoffmann's three loves have little intrinsically in common, and the invention of an evil genius appearing in different disguises to remove the ladies from Hoffmann's grasp (or save his poetic genius from them?) provides continuity rather than a powerful dramatic clash. Editors therefore have seized on the fact that there is no genuinely final version and have cut, added and generally re-worked the opera for almost every revival. Mahler for Vienna scrapped Prologue and Epilogue, but Hans Gregor in Berlin in 1905 restored arias for Coppelius and Dapertutto, taking care however to put Coppelius's tune under Dapertutto's words (the music of the so-called Mirror or Jewel aria was originally written for *Le Voyage dans la Lune*

[1] See p. 809.

nd there is no convincing evidence that Offenbach had finally
ecided to use it in *Hoffmann*). Felsenstein in Berlin in 1958
and Edmund Tracey and Colin Graham for Sadler's Wells in
1970 are examples of recent attempts to restore Offenbach's
intentions as far as they are known or can be deduced. In
either case, as in any remotely 'authentic' performance, the
order is as given hereafter and the opera is in *opéra-comique*
form, with a considerable quantity of spoken dialogue.

Prologue.   Luther's Tavern in Nuremberg, situated next
door to the opera house, where a performance of *Don
Giovanni* is in progress. A drinking chorus can be heard
off-stage. Lindorf comes in with Andrès, the servant of the
prima donna Stella, who is singing in *Don Giovanni*. Lindorf
obtains from him a letter his mistress has written to
Hoffmann, making an assignation for that evening and enclosing the key of her room. Lindorf, who assumes during
the course of the opera and in various forms the role of
Hoffmann's evil genius, in an aria exults over his prospective
victim. A crowd of students enter the tavern and immediately
start to celebrate the prospect of the beer which Luther
brings them.

Enter Hoffmann, with Nicklausse. They sit down with the
students, and Nicklausse, with obvious ironical intent, starts
to hum 'Notte e giorno faticar' from the act of *Don Giovanni*
they have just been listening to. Hoffmann seems out of
humour, and it appears that he is haunted by the sight of
Stella, with whom he was once in love. He is prevailed upon
to sing a song to the assembled company, and strikes up the
Legend of Kleinzach ('Il était une fois à la cour d'Eisenbach').
With the chorus echoing his phrases, he goes briskly through
the description of the little dwarf whose knees clicked
together as he walked, but when he comes to describe his
face, suddenly falls into a reverie and instead starts to
rhapsodise on the features of his lady-love. He is interrupted,
recovers himself, and finishes the song he began.

Hoffmann and the students complain about the quality of
Luther's beer, and a punch bowl is brought and duly greeted
with song. Hoffmann is by no means pleased to see Lindorf,
whom he refers to as haunting his steps and bringing him bad
luck. He offers to tell the story of the three great loves of his
life, and, in spite of Luther's warning that the curtain is going
up on the second act of *Don Giovanni*, all announce their
intention of staying behind to listen. The first, says
Hoffmann, was called Olympia.

Act I (Olympia) is introduced by a mocking minuet. When the curtain goes up, we are in Spalanzani's room. He is waiting for the arrival of guests who have been invited to witness the astonishing feats of which his performing doll, Olympia, is capable. Spalanzani mutters about the fortune he hopes to make from his invention, which will recoup him for the loss he suffered when Elias the banker went broke. If only his rival Coppelius does not try to claim a share of the proceeds!

Hoffmann appears, and is immediately impressed by Olympia, whom he takes for Spalanzani's daughter. He sings ardently to her of his love. His aria, 'Ah, vivre deux', is one of the loveliest expressions of his romantic spirit which is to be found in the whole opera. Nicklausse is not at all surprised to find his master in his usual love-lorn condition, but comments tartly on the improbable nature of the new object of his affections—a mechanical doll indeed!

Coppelius comes in and observes Hoffmann gazing fatuously at the doll. He tries to interest him in his own invention: eyes and spectacles to suit every requirement. 'J'ai des yeux' he sings as he shows off his wares. We may guess that the pair he sells to Hoffmann are rose-tinted; at any rate, they seem to increase his delight in beholding Olympia. Spalanzani sees Coppelius, and is forced to acknowledge the latter's share in Olympia; he supplied her eyes, in consideration of which Spalanzani makes him out a bond for five hundred crowns—drawn on Elias's bank.

The guests start to arrive. To the familiar tune of the minuet, they thank Spalanzani for his hospitality. He produces Olympia, whom he describes as his daughter, for their admiration, and accompanies her on the harp while she sings her famous Doll's song to the assembled company: 'Les oiseaux dans la charmille'. The music perfectly imitates the automaton-like delivery that one might expect from a mechanical toy, and in between whiles Spalanzani winds up the spring which brings his 'daughter' to life. She extends her hand to the guests who crowd round to congratulate her, and is left alone with Hoffmann while the others go in to supper. He sings to her, but, when he touches her shoulder, she suddenly rises from the sofa and goes quickly across the room, brushing through the curtains which divide her room from the main part of the house. Hoffmann follows her, in spite of Nicklausse's warning that Olympia is a lifeless doll.

Coppelius returns having found out that he has been cheated by his rival. The dance begins again, and Hoffmann waltzes with Olympia, who, once she is wound up, goes faster and faster so that the other guests wonder if they can save Hoffmann from breaking his neck. When Spalanzani finally manages to catch up with the doll and stop her, she breaks out into coloratura gyrations over the top of the chorus. Olympia is put away in her room, and all bend over to·see what damage has been done to the exhausted Hoffmann. Suddenly, the noise of smashing machinery is heard. Coppelius emerges from Olympia's room, laughing with triumph, and Hoffmann is left disillusioned at the discovery that his beloved was only a doll.

Act II (Antonia). Munich; a room in Crespel's house. Antonia, his daughter, sits singing: 'Elle a fui, la tourterelle'. Crespel comes into the room, and is distressed to find his daughter in a fainting condition. She has broken her promise not to sing, but she says it was the sight of her mother's portrait that prompted her to it. Crespel has already seen signs of the consumption which carried away her mother, and he blames her overwrought condition on Hoffmann, to escape whose attentions he has brought her to Munich. Crespel shouts for his deaf old servant Frantz, to whom he gives orders that no one is to be admitted to the house on any pretext whatsoever. When he is alone, Frantz protests that his crotchety master would make his life a misery were it not for the consolation he gets from his singing and dancing, both of which he does well, he says. After demonstrating the questionable truth of both these assertions, he falls exhausted into a chair, from which Hoffmann, who comes through the door with Nicklausse, at last manages to rouse him.

Hoffmann looks at the song which is lying open on the harpsichord, and has just begun to sing it when Antonia appears. After an impassioned duet, Antonia hears her father coming, and Hoffmann hides as she leaves the room. Crespel comes in, wishes Hoffmann to the devil, but transfers his spleen to Dr. Miracle, when Frantz tells him the doctor is at the door. He tries to have him kept outside but is too late, and with a burst of laughter, Miracle enters. Hoffmann from hiding sees Miracle's preparations to treat Antonia, and recognises that he is evil; Crespel is in despair at not being able to get rid of the man who, he is certain, killed his wife and means to kill his daughter as well. Although she has not

yet appeared, Miracle pretends to feel Antonia's pulse and
announces his worry at its irregular movement. In response to
his command, she sings a brilliant flourish from her room,
but still does not appear. Crespel begs Miracle to leave her
alone, but he insists that he can cure Antonia, if only he is
allowed to.

Hoffmann is alone, but is soon joined by Antonia, whom
he tries to persuade to renounce her singing for the sake of
her health and their love. She agrees, but no sooner is
Hoffmann safely out of the way than Dr. Miracle is back,
pouring temptation into her ear. Can she bear to waste such
talent by silencing her voice for ever? Before long, Antonia
hears the voice of her mother calling upon her to sing; the
portrait glows with life, and Miracle says that he is only there
to cause her to give effect to her mother's dearest wish. There
is a splendid trio, during whose course Miracle seizes a violin
from the walls and plays wildly on it. Antonia's voice rises
higher and higher until she falls dying to the ground. Miracle
disappears, and Crespel rushes in to hear his daughter's last
words. When Hoffmann comes in, Crespel blames him for
Antonia's death. Hoffmann wants to call a doctor, but, in
answer to his summons, it is Miracle who comes.

Act III (Giulietta).   Venice. The decorated gallery of a
palace overlooking the Grand Canal. The guests of Giulietta
are grouped around, and some of them lie on the sofas.
Nicklausse and Giulietta in a gondola sing the famous
barcarole, 'Belle nuit, ô nuit d'amour', one of the world's
most popular operatic tunes.

Hoffmann objects to its melancholy strains, and responds
with a lively song, whose refrain is taken up by the chorus.
Giulietta introduces her guests and takes them off for a game
of cards, Nicklausse taking the opportunity of telling
Hoffmann that he means to take him away the moment he
shows the least sign of falling in love with Giulietta.
Hoffmann swears that he will not succumb to her charms—
may his soul be forfeit to the devil if he does!

Dapertutto watches him and, when he has gone out,
produces a great diamond, with which, he says, he will
persuade Giulietta to capture the soul of Hoffmann for him
as she has done with that of Schlemil. They have only to look
into his magic mirror, and their souls stay with their
reflections. He is given a powerful aria, 'Scintille diamant',
which admirably displays a strong bass voice.

Giulietta agrees to do Dapertutto's command, and

upbraids Hoffmann for wishing to leave just because he has lost his money gambling. Hoffmann is quite unable to resist her, and he sings lovingly of the passion which overwhelms him in her presence: 'O Dieu de quelle ivresse'. Like his song to Olympia, this is lyrical expression of a high order.

O Dieu de quelle i - vresse em - brasses-tu mon â - me

There is an ecstatic duet for them, 'Si ta présence m'est ravie', during whose course she obtains the reflection which Dapertutto covets. Then, Schlemil rushes in and furiously denounces Giulietta's unfaithfulness. Hoffmann discovers that he has no reflection when he looks into a mirror, but still he will not leave Giulietta, whom he loves madly, he says. A septet[1] begins, in which Hoffmann declares his love, Dapertutto and Pittichinaccio their contempt for the poet; Giulietta admits that she found the diamond irresistible, Schlemil furiously anticipates revenge, and Nicklausse and the chorus look with pity at Hoffmann's predicament.

Giulietta saves the situation by suggesting an excursion on the canal, but Hoffmann and Schlemil fight, the former, using Dapertutto's sword, succeeding in killing his rival and removing from a chain round his neck the key of Giulietta's room. The sound of the barcarole can be heard, but, when Hoffmann rushes away to find his Giulietta, it is to see her float away in the gondola, in the arms of Pittichinaccio.

There is an intermezzo based on the barcarole, and in the epilogue we are back in Luther's tavern. Hoffmann's story is finished; so too is the performance of *Don Giovanni* in which Stella has been taking part. She is doubtless, as Nicklausse observes, the personification of the three types of womanhood that Hoffmann has idealised in his stories. But Hoffmann is too drunk to care—Lindorf is perfectly confident on that score—and, as the students eddy round him singing the drinking song from the prologue, the Muse of Poetry appears by his side claiming him for her own. Hoffmann seems to be in a stupor. As Lindorf leads Stella from the room, she turns and throws a flower from her bouquet to him. He looks blankly in her direction. There is no doubt that he is dead drunk.   H.

[1] Usually found here but by Sadler's Wells restored to its allegedly correct position in the Epilogue.

EDOUARD LALO

(1823–1892)

LE ROI D'YS

The King of Ys

OPERA in three acts by Edouard Lalo, text by Edouard Blau. Première at the Opéra-Comique, Paris, May 7, 1888, with Deschamps-Jéhin, Simonnet, Talazac, conductor Danbé. First performed New Orleans, 1890; Covent Garden, 1901, with Paquot, Adams, Jerome, Plançon; Metropolitan, 1922, with Ponselle, Alda, Gigli, Danise, Rothier, conductor Wolff.

CHARACTERS

Le Roi d'Ys .... Bass
Margared ⎱ *his daughters* .... ⎧ Soprano
Rozenn ⎰ .... ⎩ Soprano
Mylio .... Tenor
Karnac .... Baritone
Saint Corentin .... Bass
Jahel .... Baritone

Nobles, Warriors, Soldiers, People

The story is founded upon a Breton legend.

The impressive overture uses themes from the opera, prominent amongst them the duet 'En silence pourquoi souffrir?', which occurs as a cello solo, and Margared's aria in the second act.

Act I. Outside the palace of Ys. The people rejoice that the war in which they have recently been engaged is at an end, and that peace has been brought to them through the betrothal of the King's daughter Margared to the enemy leader, Karnac. As the crowd leaves the stage, the two sisters appear. Rozenn asks Margared why her looks are sad on the day on which her engagement is announced: 'En silence pourquoi souffrir?' At first Margared will not share her grief with anyone else, but eventually she admits that her heart was secretly given to a man, and that man was in the ship on which sailed the soldier Mylio, whom nobody has seen since the cessation of hostilities. She hates Karnac with a double loathing; he takes her away from the man she loves, and he is the enemy of her country. Rozenn tries to comfort her; she must lose no time in admitting her repugnance for Karnac, before it is too late and the marriage contract signed and sealed.

Alone, Rozenn in an aria avows her own love for Mylio himself. He appears suddenly at her side, and they pledge eternal faith to each other. Mylio disappears, and the King leads out Margared to meet Karnac, who appears with his followers. The people rejoice at the marriage which will put an end to their sufferings. During the course of the ceremony, Rozenn whispers to Margared that not only has Mylio returned—she has seen him—but his companions too, and amongst them must be the man for whom Margared languishes. Margared turns impulsively to her father, and repudiates Karnac; she cannot marry, she says, a man she does not love. The general consternation grows when Karnac pledges himself in revenge to carry the war through until Ys is totally destroyed. But at this moment, Mylio pushes his way through the crowd and swears to fight for Ys until the war is brought to a victorious conclusion. The people acclaim their champion.

Act II.   The great hall of the palace. Margared looks from the window at Karnac's troops assembling on the plain below. Mylio will lead the armies of Ys, and Margared is filled with turbulent feelings on his account, which she expresses in a splendid aria: 'Lorsque je t'ai vu soudain'. She suspects that Mylio loves Rozenn; if it is so, her love for her sister and Mylio would turn to implacable hate.

No sooner are the words out of her mouth than Rozenn and the King enter with Mylio. Margared hides, and hears Mylio reassure Rozenn—Saint Corentin has blessed the battle on which he is embarking—and, a moment later, her sister proclaim her love for the valiant general. The King gives his blessing to them, and then leaves with Mylio. Margared confronts Rozenn as her rival for the love of Mylio. May he die rather than be united with Rozenn! Rozenn is horror-stricken at her sister's words and tries to defend herself; were she in Margared's place, her heart might break, but she would not give way to hate: 'Tais-toi, Margared!' But Margared is not to be appeased; she curses her sister and vows vengeance on her for having stolen Mylio.

The scene changes to the great plain in front of the castle

of Ys. Mylio is proclaimed victorious, but ascribes the enemy's defeat to the intervention of Saint Corentin, the patron saint of Ys. The stage empties, and Karnac appears, dishevelled and worn after his unsuccessful fight. Margared stands before him, and offers him revenge for his defeat; she will, with his help, open the flood-gates and let in the sea to drown the town. As they go off together past the chapel of Saint Corentin, Margared challenges the Saint to avert the disaster she will bring on Ys. The sky darkens, the statue of the Saint comes to life and calls on her to repent.

Act III.   Gallery in the palace. On one side is the door to Rozenn's apartments. In accordance with Breton marriage custom, it is protected by young girls against the efforts of the friends of the bridegroom to force an entrance. Mylio himself joins his retainers and pleads his own cause. He sings the famous *Aubade*, 'Vainement, ma bien-aimée', a tune of delicious fragrance, accompanied by the female chorus. It accomplishes its purpose, and Rozenn to a Breton tune says she will grant his request. The procession forms up, and makes its way into the chapel opposite. As the sound of the *Te Deum* can be heard from the chapel, Margared and Karnac make their way into the castle. Karnac demands that Margared fulfil her promise, and when she seems reluctant to bring disaster on her relations and her countrymen, he taunts her until she is mad with jealousy.

Karnac and Margared leave together, and Mylio and Rozenn emerge from the ceremony, and sing of their love: 'A l'autel j'allais rayonnant'. Margared reappears and overhears Rozenn and her father pray for her return. She is overcome with remorse and, when cries of alarm are heard outside, hastens forward to warn them of their impending fate. She tells them that Karnac has thrown open the gates which keep the sea from drowning the city, but that she herself has killed him for his deed.

The scene changes to the highest point of the city, where the people have taken refuge to escape the fate which threatens them all. The noise of the angry sea can be heard, and the crowd comments on the situation and prays for deliverance from death. The water still mounts, and the King laments that half the city has already disappeared, carrying away most of his subjects. Suddenly Margared, as if in a trance, reflects that the waters will not recede until they have claimed their required victim. She herself is that victim, she of her own choice has brought this disaster on them, it was her hand that opened the gates. She will die in expiation of her crime. She throws herself into the sea, which immediately grows calmer, and the people thank Saint Corentin for their deliverance.   H.

CAMILLE SAINT-SAËNS
(1835–1921)
SAMSON ET DALILA

OPERA in three acts by Camille Saint-Saëns, text by Ferdinand Lemaire. Première at the Hoftheater, Weimar, December 2, 1877, with Müller, Ferenczy, Milde, conductor Lassen. First performed in France, Rouen, 1890, with Bossy; Paris, Eden Theatre, 1890, with Bloch, Talazac, Bouhy; Opéra, Paris, 1892, with Deschamps-Jéhin, Vergnet, Lassalle, Fournets, conductor Colonne; Covent Garden, 1893 (concert); New Orleans, 1893; Metropolitan, 1895, with Mantelli, Tamagno, Campanari, Plançon, conductor Mancinelli. Revived Covent Garden, 1909, with Kirkby Lunn, Fontaine; Metropolitan, 1915, with Matzenauer, Caruso, Amato; Berlin, 1929, with Onegin, Oehmann; Sadler's Wells, 1932, with Willis, Cox; la Scala, Milan, 1936, with Stignani, Merli, Beuf, conductor de Sabata; Metropolitan, 1936, with Wettergren, Maison, Pinza; 1940, with Stevens; 1964, with Gorr, Jess Thomas, Bacquier; la Scala, Milan, 1947, with Stignani, Tasso; 1950, with Barbieri, Vinay, conductor de Sabata; 1961, with Simionato, del Monaco, conductor Gavazzeni.

CHARACTERS

Dalila ....Mezzo-Soprano
Samson ....Tenor
High Priest of Dagon ....Baritone
Abimelech, *satrap of Gaza* ....Bass
An old Hebrew ....Bass
The Philistines' Messenger ....Tenor
Hebrews, Philistines
Time: B.C.   *Place:* Gaza

Act I.   Before the curtain rises we hear of the Philistines at Gaza forcing the Israelites to work. When the curtain is raised we see in the background the temple of Dagon, god of the Philistines. The Jews give voice to their despair, but Samson addresses them in an effort to rouse them from their depressed condition ('Arrêtez, ô mes frères', and 'L'as-tu donc oublié?'). At the third attempt, he succeeds to such effect that the new defiance in their voices attracts the attention of Abimelech, who comes in with his guards and pours scorn on the God who so signally fails to come to their aid in their plight. Samson slays Abimelech with the sword he has snatched from him and Israel's champion starts out to complete the work. Dagon's high priest may curse ('Maudite à jamais soit la race'), but the Philistines are not able to offer resistance to the onslaught of the enemy. Already the Hebrews are in a position to rejoice and gratefully praise God, when the Philistines' most seductive maidens, Dalila at their head, appear to do homage to the victorious Samson ('Je viens célébrer la victoire'). Of what use is the warning of an old Hebrew? The memory of the love which she gave him when 'the sun laughed, the spring awoke and kissed the ground', the sight of her ensnaring beauty, the tempting dances, bewitch the champion anew. Dalila completes her victory in the languorous aria 'Printemps qui commence'.

Act II.   The beautiful seductress waits in her house in the valley of Sorek for her victim. She summons love to her aid in a splendid aria, 'Amour, viens aider ma faiblesse', cast in the same voluptuous mould as the rest of her music. Dalila has never loved the enemy of her country, and she hates him since he left her. Thus, when the high priest comes to her, his exhortation to revenge is not needed, although it has the effect of strengthening her resolve to obtain from Samson the secret on which depends his superhuman strength.

Dalila begins to despair of his coming, but not long after she has gone into the house, he appears, torn by doubt and irresolution, and determined that he is only going to say farewell to Dalila. Her blandishments however gradually break down his resolve, and 'Mon cœur s'ouvre à ta voix' (the most famous number of the score) seems to leave him powerless in her hands. But he summons up reserves of resistance, and refuses to tell her his secret when she demands it of him. She rushes alone into her house, but after a further moment of indecision, Samson follows her in. Their destiny is fulfilled. Dalila's cry of triumph summons the Philistines. Deprived of his hair, the betrayed champion is overcome.

Act III. In a dungeon the blinded giant languishes. But more tormenting than the corporal disgrace or the laments of his companions are the reproaches in his own breast. He sings 'Vois ma misère, hélas', and his voice mingles with the reproaches of the Hebrews, who blame him and his weakness for their plight. Now the doors rattle. Soldiers come in to drag him to the Philistines' celebration of their victory. The scene changes. In Dagon's temple the Philistine people are rejoicing. Bitter scorn is poured on Samson whom the high priest insultingly invites to sing a love song to Dalila. The false woman herself mocks the powerless man. A Bacchanale is danced. Samson prays to his God: just once again may he have strength! And while the intoxication of the festival seizes on everybody, he has himself led between the two pillars which support the temple. He clasps them. A terrible crash—the fragments of the temple with a roar bury the Philistine people and their conqueror. K.W., H.

LÉO DELIBES
(1836–1891)
LAKMÉ

OPERA in three acts by Léo Delibes, text by Edmond Gondinet and Philippe Gille, after Pierre Loti's *Le Mariage de Loti*. Première at the Opéra-Comique, Paris, on April 14, 1883, with van Zandt, Frandin, Talazac, Barré, Cobalet, conductor Danbé. First performed London, Gaiety Theatre, 1885, with van Zandt, Dupuy, Carroul, conductor Bevignani; New York, 1886, with Pauline L'Allemand: Metropolitan, 1892, with van Zandt, Montariol, Edouard de Reszke; Covent Garden, 1910, with Tetrazzini, McCormack, Edmund Burke. Revived Metropolitan, 1916, with Barrientos, Martinelli, Rothier; 1931, with Pons, Thill; 1938, with Pons, Jagel, Pinza; 1946, with Pons, Jobin, Vaghi, conductor Fourestier; Seattle, 1967, with Sutherland; Wexford, 1970, with Christiane Eda-Pierre, John Stewart, Jacques Mars.

CHARACTERS

Lakmé .... Soprano
Mallika, *her slave* .... Mezzo-Soprano
Ellen ⎫
      ⎬ *English ladies* .... ⎰ Soprano
Rose ⎭   ⎱ Soprano
Mistress Bentson, *their governess* ..... Mezzo-Soprano
Gérald, *an English officer* .... Tenor
Nilakantha, *a Brahmin priest* .... Bass-Baritone
Frédéric, *an English officer* .... Baritone
Hadji, *servant of Nilakantha* .... Tenor

Time: Nineteenth Century   *Place:* India

Act I. Lakmé is the daughter of Nilakantha, a fanatical Brahmin priest. While he nurses his hatred of the British invaders who have forbidden him to practise his religion, his daughter and other devotees of his cult sing an invocation to the gods: 'Blanche Dourga, Pâle Siva, Puissant Ganeça'. Lakmé's vocal embroidery over the top of the chorus is full of coloratura work. Nilakantha goes to another gathering of the faithful, and leaves Lakmé alone with her companions in the idyllic garden which surrounds the temple he has built for the practice of his religion. Lakmé and Mallika sing together a most attractive barcarole as they prepare to bathe in the stream: 'Dôme épais, le jasmin'. The rippling theme of the

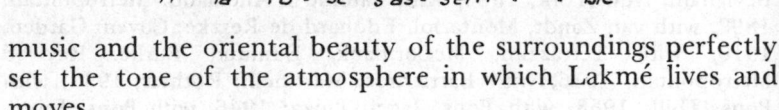

music and the oriental beauty of the surroundings perfectly set the tone of the atmosphere in which Lakmé lives and moves.

Lakmé removes her jewellery, placing it on a stone bench, and she and Mallika get into a boat and are quickly lost to sight.

We are next introduced to the English figures of the opera, two army officers, a couple of young girls, and their ineffably comic governess, Mistress Bentson. They are all in varying degrees suspicious of the Orient and its mystery, which they profess to find very queer indeed. They break through the bamboo fence which surrounds the temple, and exclaim with delight at what they can see inside. Frédéric warns them that several of the flowers are poisonous (even some of those which are quite harmless in Europe); he also says that the hut belongs to a dangerous and implacable Brahmin, whose one delight is in his beautiful daugher. In a quintet they speculate on the feelings of such a girl, who is shut off by her priestly vocation from contact with the outside world: 'Quand une femme est si jolie'.

The women want a sketch done of Lakmé's jewels, and Gérald, who is something of an artist, says he will stay behind and do one, if they will go back to the town. Left alone, he is fascinated by the jewels, and he speculates on the beauty and youth of their owner. Gérald's aria, 'Fantaisie aux divins mensonges', is one of the gems of the score; in aptness, melodic freshness and unpretentious charm it is one of the most attractive arias in the French repertory.

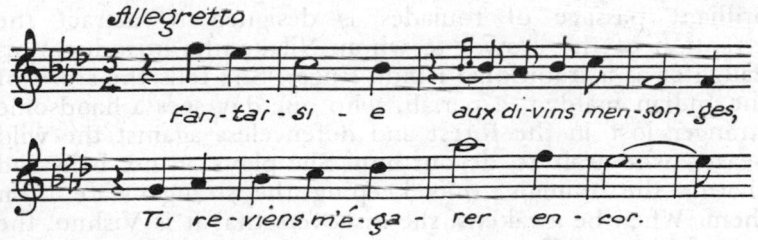

He sees Lakmé and Mallika returning, and hides. Lakmé dismisses Mallika and wonders to herself why she should feel so oddly sad and happy at the same time: 'Pourquoi dans les grands bois'. She sees Gérald, and, filled with alarm, cries for help. But, when Mallika and Hadji come to her aid, she sends them off to look for her father. Alone with Gérald, she tells him that a word from her could have brought about his death; he must leave and forget he ever saw her. But Gérald is obviously infatuated, and he sings passionately of love: 'C'est le dieu de la jeunesse, c'est le dieu du printemps'. Lakmé's voice joins his, until the sound of her father returning brings her back to reality. She begs Gérald to leave, but as he disappears through the gap in the bamboo, Nilakantha appears, and cries for vengeance on whoever has dared profane his temple precincts.

Act II. The scene is a bazaar, with a temple in the background. The stage is crowded with soldiers, sailors, and tourists, who mingle with the street-sellers and natives. Mistress Bentson is surrounded by beggars and sellers, who, in the course of conversation, relieve her of her watch and handkerchief, before she is rescued by Frédéric. A bell rings to signal the closing of the market, and the festival begins. Girls perform various exotic dances, and Nilakantha appears, disguised as an old Hindu penitent and accompanied by his daughter. By now Gérald and his fiancée Ellen have appeared on the scene, and Gérald, out of earshot of the girls, has been told by Frédéric that their regiment leaves before dawn to move against a party of rebellious natives. Lakmé hints to her father that Brahma might not be averse to pardoning an offence by a stranger, but her father indignantly denies any such possibility. He sings tenderly of his love for Lakmé: 'Lakmé, ton doux regard se voile'.

Nilakantha demands that his daughter shall sing to attract the man who has dared to venture on to sacred ground—drawn, Nilakantha is sure, by the beauty of Lakmé herself. A brilliant passage of roulades is designed to attract the attention of the crowd, to whom Nilakantha introduces his daughter as a traditional Hindu singer. She tells the story of the Indian maiden, a pariah, who one day sees a handsome stranger lost in the forest and defenceless against the wild beasts, who wait to devour him. She plays on her bells and charms the animals, thus keeping the stranger safe from them. When he awakens, she discovers that it is Vishnu, the son of Brahma. He transports her with him to the skies, and ever since that day the traveller has heard the sound of bells in that particular part of the forest. This is the famous Bell Song ('Où va la jeune Hindoue?'), to which more than to anything else the opera owes its continued popularity. Its bell

effects and seductive melody have been instrumental in making it a favourite of all sopranos with any pretensions to vocal agility, but frequent bad performance should not influence the opera lover against it. In the hands of a coloratura soprano who is also musically inclined its effect is still considerable.

To Nilakantha's fury, nobody appears in answer to Lakmé's singing, and he is still ignorant of the identity of the stranger who braved his anger by polluting the temple grounds. He bids his daughter continue her singing, which she reluctantly does, until, seeing Gérald, she utters a cry of anguish and faints in his arms. Nilakantha is convinced that he knows his enemy, and plots to isolate and destroy him during the course of the procession of the goddess which takes place later that night. The stage has meanwhile emptied as soldiers cross the square, and are watched by the gaping crowds.

Lakmé is left alone with the faithful Hadji, who tries to console her, and promises to do whatever she asks him; whether to help a friend or dispose of an enemy, she has only to command him. Hardly has he finished speaking when Gérald returns and rushes to Lakmé's side. There is a love duet for them ('Dans le vague d'un rêve'), during whose course Lakmé admits her love for the young officer whose religion is not her own. Lakmé plans a new life for them, far away in a part of the forest known only to her and where she has a little hut: 'Dans la forêt près de nous'.

The procession comes into sight, and the English ladies and their escort, Frédéric, watch it as it goes by, the priests chanting their hymn to Dourga. Frédéric comments ironically on Gérald's infatuation for the Hindu 'goddess', and says that he would be really worried were it not that they have to leave that very night, and that Gérald is therefore unlikely to have an opportunity of seeing her again. As the procession passes, Nilakantha's plan is put into operation, and Gérald falls stabbed. Lakmé rushes despairingly to him, but finds that he is only slightly injured. Hadji will help her to remove him to her secret hiding-place, and he will be hers.

Act III. The entr'acte suggests a lullaby, and when the curtain goes up, we are in the hut in the forest, where Gérald is lying on a couch, while Lakmé sings to him: 'Sous le ciel tout étoilé'. When he wakes up, he is at first not sure what has happened to him, but Lakmé reminds him that it was Hadji who carried him to the forest. In one of the happiest pieces of the score, 'Ah, viens dans la forêt profonde', Gérald gives lyrical expression to his happiness far from the world with Lakmé as his only companion.

From afar off can be heard the sound of singing, and

Lakmé tells Gérald that it is a band of lovers come to drink of the sacred spring whose waters confer the gift of eternal love on whoever drinks them. She herself will fetch water from the spring in which they may pledge their love. As she goes, Frédéric, who has been watching, appears at Gérald's side. He has followed the traces of blood which were left as Hadji carried the wounded man through the woods to safety. Frédéric reminds Gérald that he is due to go with his regiment that very night, but Gérald is intoxicated with his love for Lakmé. He can forget Ellen, to whom he was engaged, but can he, asks Frédéric, forget his honour as a soldier. As he leaves, Frédéric knows he has triumphed over Gérald's infatuation, and Gérald himself knows it when, a moment after Lakmé's return, he hears in the distance the sound of soldiers marching.

Lakmé notices the change which has come about in her lover during her short absence, and, while his attention is concentrated on the sound of the march, she tears off a leaf of the fatal *datura* tree, and bites it. 'Tu m'as donné le plus doux rêve', she tells Gérald when he again becomes conscious of her existence. Together they drink the water from the cup, and swear to love each other through all eternity. Lakmé admits to Gérald that she thinks he is in no danger of breaking his oath, since she is at that very moment dying. Their voices join again in a duet, but Lakmé dies a moment later, though not before she has had time to tell Nilakantha, who discovers them, that she and her lover have together drunk of the sacred spring. As Gérald cries out in despair, Nilakantha thinks of Lakmé transported to eternal life, and is content.　　　　　　　　　　　　　　　　　　　　H.

GEORGES BIZET

(1833–1875)

LES PÊCHEURS DE PERLES

The Pearl Fishers

OPERA in three acts by Georges Bizet, text by Carré and Cormon. Première at the Théâtre-Lyrique, Paris, on September 30, 1863, with

lle. de Maesen, Morini, Ismaël, Guyot. First performed Covent
Garden, 1887, as *Leïla*, with Fohström, Garulli, Lhérie, Miranda;
Philadelphia, 1893; Opéra-Comique, Paris, April 21, 1893, with Calvé,
Delmas, Soulacroix, Challet, conductor Danbé; Metropolitan, 1896
(two acts only, in combination with *La Navarraise*), with Calvé,
Cremonini, Ancona, Arimondi. Revived Metropolitan, 1916, with
Hempel, Caruso, de Luca, Rothier, conductor Polacco; Covent Garden,
1920, with Pareto, Tom Burke, Badini, Edmund Burke, conductor
Beecham; Berlin, 1934, with Berger, Wittrisch, Schlusnus, conductor
Blech; la Scala, Milan, 1938, with Carosio, Lugo, Biasini, Baronti,
conductor Capuana: 1948, with Fineschi, Infantino, Guarrera, Modesti,
conductor Capuana.

CHARACTERS

Leïla, *priestess of Brahma*	Soprano
Nadir, *a fisherman*	Tenor
Zurga, *king of the fishermen*	Baritone
Nourabad, *high priest of Brahma*	Bass

Time: Antiquity   *Place:* Ceylon

Act I.   The scene is the seashore, where the fishermen are
holding fête preparatory to choosing a chief. They sing and
dance, and eventually select Zurga as king; he accepts their
confidence. Nadir appears, is greeted after his long absence,
and describes his adventures in the jungle. There is a fond
reunion between Zurga and Nadir. They were formerly
friends, but recall their rivalry for the hand of the beautiful
priestess, Leïla, whom they had seen together in the Brahmin
temple of Candy. Their love for her had brought enmity
between them, but they recall that the oath of friendship
which they swore has never since been broken. Their duet,
'Au fond du temple saint' (In the depths of the temple), is an
example of Bizet's melodic inspiration at its finest, and is one
of the most beautiful tenor-baritone duets in all French
opera. Its theme is used throughout the opera as a friendship
motto:

News is brought that a boat has arrived, bringing with i
the unknown virgin whose duty is to pray during the time the
fishermen are at sea, so as to ward off evil spirits. Zurga tells
Nadir that she is veiled and must not be approached or seen
by anyone during the time of her vigil. She is brought in by
the old priest Nourabad, and welcomed by the fisherfolk.
Zurga swears her in as the inviolate virgin protectress of the
fishermen, and threatens her with death if she prove false to
her oath.

Leïla and Nadir recognise each other, and he stands
watching as if in a dream as she ascends the cliff. In an aria of
great beauty he reflects on his love, which has never been
dimmed by the passing of time: 'Je crois entendre encore' (I
hear as in a dream):

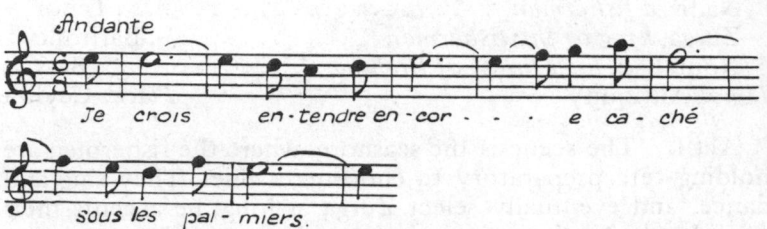

This is the best-known section of the score, not least in its
Italian translation, 'Mi par d'udir ancora'. Leïla reappears,
and sings an invocation to Brahma, echoed by the chorus,
before she is left alone on her rock for her vigil. Before the
end of the act, Nadir, gazing up at Leïla, sings ardently of his
love for her and swears to protect her from danger.

Act II. In a ruined temple, the high priest, Nourabad,
warns Leïla on pain of death to be faithful to her religious
vows. She will be alone but well guarded. Leïla tells him he
need have no fear; she never breaks her promise. The
necklace she wears was given her by a fugitive, whose
hiding-place she refused to reveal although the daggers of his
pursuers were pointed at her heart; she had promised not to
betray him.

Nourabad leaves her, and she sings of the love which fills
her heart: 'Comme autrefois dans la nuit sombre'. Suddenly,
not far away, she hears the voice of Nadir singing a serenade:
'De mon amie fleur endormie'. A moment later he is with
her, and a passionate duet of almost Verdian character
develops: 'Ton cœur n'a pas compris le mien'. Leila begs

Nadir to leave her, and they agree to meet again the next day; but Nourabad has seen Nadir's escape, and he calls down anathema on both their heads, while the chorus mutter that they can see a storm arising. Nadir is captured by the guards, Nourabad accuses the lovers of sacrilege, the crowd take up his cry for vengeance. Zurga claims the right, as chief and therefore judge, to settle the case himself, and he inclines to be merciful for the sake of his friend. But Nourabad ·tears the veil from Leïla's head, and Zurga, recognising Leïla, swears to be revenged on Nadir for his treachery. Leïla and Nadir pray to Brahma for help, while the crowd call on him to avenge the sacrilege.

Act III. Zurga's tent. The chief contrasts his own restless state of mind with the abated storm, which for a time threatened destruction of the fishing fleet: 'L'orage s'est calmé'. He laments the breaking of his friendship with Nadir: 'O Nadir, tendre ami de mon cœur'. It is a fine lyrical *scena* of considerable power. Leïla appears before him, and expresses her willingness to die, but pleads for Nadir. Zurga eventually gives in to jealousy at the idea of losing Leïla to Nadir, and is cursed by Leïla for his jealous cruelty. Just before leaving him, she asks that a last favour may be granted her; she has a necklace which she would like to have sent to her mother far away. This she puts into Zurga's hands as she leaves him.

The second scene of Act III is set at the place of execution, where a funeral pyre has been erected. There are savage dances and choruses, the sopranos reiterating 'Brahma!' on a high G, before Nourabad leads Leïla out into the middle of the populace. Just as the guilty lovers are to meet death, a distant glow is seen. Zurga dashes in crying that the camp is on fire, and the people rush out to fight the flames. Zurga tells Leïla and Nadir that it was he who set fire to the camp; the necklace she gave him was once his, and he the fugitive she saved from death long ago. He unfastens their chains and bids them flee; there is a solemn trio 'O lumière sainte'. Zurga impedes their pursuers, but is denounced by Nourabad, who had stayed behind in hiding when the others left. Zurga is stabbed from behind by one of his subjects. The music of 'Au fond du temple saint' is heard in the orchestra, and the top line is sung by Leïla and Nadir in octaves as they appear on the top of the rock, at whose foot far below Zurga lies dying.   K., H.

LA JOLIE FILLE DE PERTH

The Fair Maid of Perth

Opera in four acts by Georges Bizet; text by J. H. Vernoy de Saint-Georges and J. Adenis, founded on Scott's novel *The Fair Maid of Perth*. Première Théâtre-Lyrique, Paris, 26 December, 1867, with Mlles Devriès, Ducasse, and Messrs. Massy, Barré, Lutz. First produced Manchester, 1917, by the Beecham Opera Company with Sylvia Nelis, Edith Clegg, Walter Hyde, Webster Millar, Powell Edwards, and in London at Drury Lane, 1917, by the same cast; Covent Garden, 1919. Revived Oxford, 1955; B.B.C. (in concert, English), 1956, with Mattiwilda Dobbs, Anna Pollak, Alexander Young, Nevin Miller, David Ward, Owen Brannigan, conductor Beecham.

CHARACTERS

Simon Glover, *glove maker* .... Bass
Catherine Glover, *his daughter* .... Soprano
Mab, *Queen of the Gypsies* . Soprano or Mezzo-Soprano
Henry Smith, *the armourer* .... Tenor
The Duke of Rothsay .... Baritone or Tenor
Ralph, *Glover's apprentice* .... Bass or Baritone
A Lord in the service of Rothsay .... Tenor
The Duke's major-domo .... Bass
Place: Scotland

Bizet signed a contract with Carvalho for *La Jolie Fille de Perth* in July 1866 when he was 27 and finished it in December of the same year; Winton Dean in his book about the composer describes the libretto as the worst Bizet ever had to set. Certainly it is far from Walter Scott, and the libretto's naive treatment of the novel's characters has probably led to the opera's under-valuation. The part of Catherine was intended for Christine Nilsson, but that great prima donna preferred to create Ophelia in Ambroise Thomas's *Hamlet* at the Opéra. *La Jolie Fille de Perth* was well received at its first performance, better than any other opera of Bizet's during his lifetime, but it had a mere 18 performances and was not heard again in Paris until 1890, and it is a historical oddity that it has never been performed at the Opéra-Comique.

Act I. After a bout of communal singing in his work-p, Smith laments the absence of his beloved Catherine over, but his thoughts are interrupted by sounds from utside. He opens the door to give shelter to the gypsy Mab, vho is being molested by a group of young men. She hides as Catherine comes in with her father and the apprentice Ralph, Ralph making little attempt throughout the scene to hide his jealousy of the sympathy between Smith and Catherine. Glover has brought provisions for a wedding feast, venison, pâté, pudding and whisky amongst them—his gourmand tendencies are recognised throughout the opera, not least in the first act finale—and Catherine celebrates the holiday in a brilliant and rapid polonaise:[1] 'Ah! le carnaval apporte encore des plaisirs'. Glover prefers Smith to Ralph as a suitor for Catherine's hand, and Smith and Catherine are left to sing sweetly in duet together. Will she be his Valentine? As token of his devotion, he gives her a gold-enamelled flower.

Enter the Duke of Rothsay, arrogant and at first unrecognised. He asks for Smith's professional services, but his interest is in Catherine and, in the course of a trio, he invites her to his castle at night, much to the rage of Smith, who seems at one point to be out-hammering Sachs in his effort to drown the words of a rival far more dangerous than any Beckmesser—all this to the most mellifluous music imaginable. The quarrel is about to blaze into a fight when Mab emerges from her hiding-place, to Catherine's considerable dismay and everybody else's embarrassment. The lively trio becomes a livelier quartet, and in the course of the finale, after her father's entry and recognition of the Duke, Catherine quarrels with Smith, throws down the flower which he had earlier given her—Mab picks it up—and flounces out.

A nocturnal march introduces Act II. But it is not a night for sleep and carnival is in full swing, the Duke dispensing hospitality and all watching the gypsies dance to a musical number of real fame, which was encored at the first performance. The Duke enlists the help of Mab in his scheme to abduct Catherine, Mab (who was once his mistress) seeming in a charming song to fall in with the scheme but in fact determined to substitute herself for Catherine.

Smith sings a most attractive serenade in 6/8 outside

[1] Bizet wrote a more lyrical aria as an alternative for the singer of Catherine, and it appears in an appendix to the vocal score.

Catherine's window ('A la voix d'un amant fidèle'),[1] one the four numbers known outside performance, and it followed immediately by the splendid, if lugubrious, drinking song of the bibulous Ralph, 'Quand la flamme de l'amour', hardly less well-known and perhaps even better.

Ralph collapses out of breath, and it is unfortunate that the Duke's major-domo chooses to ask him the way to Catherine's house, even more so that he watches a masked female figure, to a reminiscence of Smith's serenade, accompany the major-domo towards the castle. Ralph is indignant at the turn of events and rouses both Glover and Smith, who rush off, leaving Ralph in his befuddled state to observe the real Catherine lean out of her window in an attempt to answer Smith's serenade.

Act III. Introduced by a graceful minuet entr'acte, familiar from its introduction into the second *L'Arlésienne* suite, the Duke of Rothsay in his castle is gaming with the gentlemen of his house and describes in a cavatina the effect his new love has had on him before starting to woo her (it is of course Mab unrecognisably masked). Mab is suitably cynical about the Duke's sincerity as he uses much the same words to his supposed Catherine as he had once upon a time used to her (and Bizet the tune of his entr'acte minuet). The Duke takes Catherine's rose, which Mab is wearing, and eventually Mab makes her escape pursued by the Duke, to be succeeded by Smith, who, albeit rather gently, voices his despair and determination to be revenged. Smith hides and is indignant when Glover accompanied by Catherine asks the Duke to give his permission for her to marry Smith. In the course of the extended finale—the score's most ambitious section—the unfortunate Catherine finds herself at first forgiven for her supposed infidelity, then apparently sharing a guilty secret with a lord of the manor whom she hardly knows, finally rejected by a lover whose fury knows no bounds when he sees the golden flower pinned to the Duke's tunic.

Act IV. It is the morning of St. Valentine's Day, and Smith and Ralph quarrel when the latter defends Catherine's honour. They arrange to fight a duel. Catherine appears, and she and Smith sadly recall past love. Smith is aware that

[1] Its popularity in England is due to Heddle Nash's celebrated recording and it is comparatively far less known in France. Bizet originally wrote it for *Don Procopio* (1859).

Ralph is likely to kill him in the duel, and Catherine collapses. The chorus greets St. Valentine's Day, Mab enters to relate that the Duke at her insistence has stopped the duel, and all now turn their attention to Catherine, whose wits have conveniently, at least from the nineteenth-century operatic point of view (though in defiance of Sir Walter Scott), deserted her. Her Ballade is a graceful example of the mad scene—for all that Winton Dean in his splendid book on Bizet says it 'raises a critical blush'—but the situation is apparently resolved when Smith serenades under Catherine's window, and Mab acts her part. Smith greets her as his Valentine, and all ends happily.

'The development shown in *La Jolie Fille de Perth* is in some ways negative rather than positive: Bizet has eliminated many of the weaknesses of the two previous operas, but not pursued his advances, particularly in the harmonic sphere. It is a less arresting and a less uneven opera, and consequently has been underrated. For much of its apparent tameness the libretto is responsible'.[1] That it is a step on Bizet's road from graceful melody to major achievement (in *Carmen*) of the perfect *opéra-comique* is undeniable, as witness the serenade, Ralph's drinking song, the skilful even ironic use of the music associated with the Duke's wooing of Catherine, notably in the finale of Act II and in Act III. And yet the opera, like *Pêcheurs de Perles*, is more than just a signpost on a road to a great capital city, and one hopes revivals—they will be no more than that—will continue while the tradition of *opéra-comique* (to which it belongs in spirit if not in literal fact) continues. H.

DJAMILEH

Opera in one act by Georges Bizet, text by Louis Gallet. Première at the Opéra-Comique, Paris, May 22, 1872, with Mme. Prelly ('the voiceless Venus' as Gauthier-Villars called her), MM. Duchesne, Potel. First performed Covent Garden, 1893, with Bonnard, Coatellier, Gherlsen; Boston, 1913; Covent Garden, 1919, with Gladys Ancrum, Webstar Millar, Walter Hyde, conductor Pitt; Berlin, 1927; Vienna, 1938, with Brems and Dermota. Revived Paris, 1938, with Tourel, Arnoult, Bourdin.

[1] Winton Dean: *Bizet, His Life and Works* (Dent).

CHARACTERS

Djamileh, *a slave* . . . . .Mezzo-Soprano
Haroun, *a prince* . . . . Tenor
Splendiano, *his secretary* . . . . Tenor (or Baritone)
A slave merchant

Djamileh, a beautiful slave, is in love with her master, Prince Haroun, a Turkish nobleman, who is tired of her and is about to sell her. She persuades his secretary, Splendiano, who is in love with her, to aid her in regaining her master's affections. She will marry Splendiano if she fails.

Accordingly, with the secretary's aid, when the slave dealer arrives, she is, in disguise, among the slaves offered to Haroun. She dances. Haroun is entranced, and immediately buys her. When she discloses her identity, and pleads that her ruse was prompted by her love for him, he receives her back into his affections.

Djamileh is for mezzo-soprano, the men's roles for tenor. Besides the dance, there are a duet for the men, 'Que l'esclave soit brune ou blonde' (Let the slave be dark or fair); a trio, 'Je voyais, au loin la mer s'étendre' (The distant sea have I beheld extending); and the chorus, 'Quelle est cette belle?' (Who is the charmer?).   K.

CARMEN

Opera in four acts by Georges Bizet; words by Henri Meilhac and Ludovic Halévy, founded on the novel by Prosper Mérimée. Première, Opéra-Comique, Paris, March 3, 1875, the title rôle being created by Galli-Marié with Chapuy, Lhérie, Bouhy. Her Majesty's Theatre, London (in Italian), June 22, 1878, with Minnie Hauck; same theatre, February 5, 1879 (in English); same theatre, November 8, 1886 (in French), with Galli-Marié. Covent Garden, 1882, with Pauline Lucca, Valleria, Lestellier, Bouhy. Minnie Hauck, who created Carmen in London, also created the role in America, October 23, 1879, at the Academy of Music, New York, with Campanini, del Puente. The first New Orleans *Carmen*, January 14, 1881, with Mme. Ambré. Calvé made her New York début as Carmen at the Metropolitan Opera House, December 20, 1893, with Jean de Reszke and Eames. Campanini, Jean de Reszke, Caruso, Clément, Saléza, Dalmores, Muratore, Martinelli, Ansseau, Thill, Maison, Vickers have been celebrated as José; Eames and Melba have been unapproached as Micaela; del Puente, Galassi, Campanari, Plançon, Amato, and Journet were famous as Escamillo.

Covent Garden Carmens have included de Lussan, Calvé, ourguignon, Olszewska, Supervia, Renée Gilly, Coates, Shacklock, Brems, Mödl, Resnik, Veasey, Cortez, Troyanos, Verrett. Other famous interpreters of the title role have been Bressler-Gianoli, Maria Gay, Gutheil-Schoder, Farrar, Mary Garden, Besanzoni, Jeritza, Ponselle, Giannini, Bruna Castagna, Risë Stevens, Swarthout, Djanel, Pederzini, Bumbry.

CHARACTERS

Don José, *a corporal of dragoons* . . . . Tenor
Escamillo, *a toreador* . . . . Baritone
El Dancairo   } *smugglers* . . . . { Tenor
El Remendado   }   { Tenor
Zuniga, *a captain* . . . . Bass
Morales, *an officer* . . . . Baritone
Micaela, *a peasant girl* . . . . Soprano
Frasquita } *gypsies, friends of Carmen* . . . . . . { Soprano
Mercédès }   { Soprano
Carmen, *a cigarette girl and gypsy* . . . . Soprano

Innkeeper, Guide, Officers, Dragoons, Boys,
Cigarette Girls, Gypsies, Smugglers, etc.

Time: About 1820   *Place:* Seville, Spain

Act I. A square in Seville. On the right the gate of a cigarette factory. At the back, facing the audience, is a practicable bridge. In front, on the left, is a guard-house. Above it three steps lead to a covered passage. In a rack, close to the door, are the lances of the dragoons of Almanza, with their little red and yellow flags.

The prelude, one of the most famous orchestral pieces in all opera, begins with an exhilarating *presto*, but contains a brooding, apprehensive section in the middle. At the end of the work, this music turns out to be connected with the idea of fate.

Morales and soldiers are near the guard-house. People are coming and going. There is a brisk chorus, 'Sur la place' (O'er this square). Micaela comes forward, as if looking for someone.

'And for whom are you looking?' Morales asks of the pretty girl, who has shyly approached the soldiers lounging outside the guard-house.

'I am looking for a corporal,' she answers.

'I am one,' Morales says, gallantly.

'But not *the* one. His name is José.'

The soldiers, scenting amusement in trying to flirt with a pretty creature, whose innocence is as apparent as her charm, urge her to remain until Don José comes at change of guard. But, saying she will return later, she runs away like a frightened deer, past the cigarette factory, across the square, and down one of the side streets.

A fascinating little march of fifes and trumpets is heard, at first in the distance, then gradually nearer.

The change of guard arrives, preceded by a band of street lads, imitating the step of the dragoons. After the lads come Captain Zuniga and Corporal José; then dragoons, armed with lances. The ceremony of changing the guard takes place to the accompaniment of a chorus of gamins and grown-up spectators. It is a lively scene.

'It must have been Micaela,' says Don José, when they tell him of the girl with tresses of fair hair and dress of blue, who was looking for him. 'Nor do I mind saying,' he adds, 'that I love her.' And indeed, although there are some sprightly girls in the crowd that has gathered in the square to see the guard changed, he has no eyes for them, but, straddling a chair out in the open, busies himself trying to join the links of a small chain that has come apart.

The bell of the cigarette factory strikes the work hour, and the cigarette girls push their way through the crowd, stopping to make eyes at the soldiers and young men, or lingering to laugh and chat, before passing through the factory gates.

A shout goes up:

'Carmen!'

A girl, dark as a gypsy and lithe as a panther, darts across the bridge and down the steps into the square, the crowd parting and making way for her.

'Love you?' she cries insolently to the men who press around her and ply her with their attentions. 'Perhaps to-morrow. Anyhow not to-day.' Then, a dangerous fire kindling in her eyes, she sways slowly to and fro to the rhythm of a *Habanera*, singing the while, 'L'amour est un oiseau rebelle',

> 'Love is a gypsy boy, 'tis true,
>   He ever was and ever will be free;
> Love you not me, then I love you,
>   Yet, if I love you, beware of me!'

Often she glances toward José, often dances so close to him that she almost touches him, and by subtle inflections in her voice seeks to attract his attention. But he seems unaware of her presence. Whether he is thinking of Micaela, or has steeled himself against the gypsy, in whose every glance, step, and song lurks peril, the handsome dragoon could not be busying himself more obstinately with the broken chain in his hand.

'Yet, if I love you, beware of me!'

Tearing from her bodice a blood-red cassia flower, she flings it at him point-blank. He springs to his feet, as if he would rush at her. But he meets her look, and stops where he stands. Then, with a toss of the head and a mocking laugh, she runs into the factory, followed by the other girls, while the crowd, having had its sport, disperses.

The librettists have constructed an admirable scene. The composer has taken full advantage of it. The *Habanera* establishes Carmen in the minds of the audience—the gypsy girl, passionate yet fickle, quick to love and quick to tire. Hers the dash of fatalism that flirts with death.

At José's feet lies the cassia flower thrown by Carmen, the glance of whose dark eyes had checked him. Hesitatingly, yet as if in spite of himself, he stoops and picks it up, presses it to his nostrils and draws in its subtle perfume in a long breath. Then, still as if involuntarily, or as if a magic spell lies in its odour, he thrusts the flower under his blouse and over his heart.

He has no more than concealed it there, when Micaela again enters the square—and hurries to him with joyful exclamations. She brings him tidings from home, and some money from his mother's savings, with which to eke out his small pay. They have a charming duet, 'Parle-moi de ma mère' (Speak to me of my mother).

It is evident that Micaela's coming gives him a welcome change of thought, and that, although she cannot remain long, her sweet, pure presence has for the time being lifted the spell the gypsy has cast over him. For, when Micaela has gone, José grasps the flower under his blouse, evidently intending to draw it out and cast it away.

Just then, however, there are cries of terror from the cigarette factory and, in a moment, the square is filled with screaming girls, soldiers, and others. From the excited utterances of the cigarette girls it is evident that there has been a quarrel between Carmen and another girl, and that Carmen has wounded the latter with a knife. Zuniga promptly orders José to take two dragoons with him into the factory and arrest her. Not the least abashed, and smirking, she comes out with them. When the captain begins questioning her, she answers with a gay 'Tra la la, tra la la', pitching her voice on a higher note after each question with an indescribable effect of mockery, that makes her dark beauty the more fascinating.

Losing patience, the officer orders her hands tied behind her back, while he makes out the warrant for her imprisonment. The soldiers have driven away the crowd, Don José is left to guard Carmen.

Pacing up and down the square, he appears to be avoiding her. But she, as if speaking to herself, or thinking aloud, and casting furtive glances at him, tells of a handsome young dragoon with whom she has fallen in love.

'He is not a captain, nor even a lieutenant—only a corporal. But he will do what I ask—because he is in love with me!'

'I? — I love you?' José pauses beside her.

With a coquettish toss of the head and a significant glance she asks, 'Where is the flower I threw you? What have you done with it?' Then, softly, she sings another alluring melody in typical Spanish dance measure, a *Seguidilla*, 'Près des remparts de Séville'.

'Carmen!' cries José, 'you have bewitched me' . . .

'Near by the ramparts of Seville' . . . 'And the dance with my lover I'll share!' she murmurs insinuatingly, and at the same time she holds back her bound wrists towards him. Quickly he undoes the knot, but leaves the rope about her wrists so that she still appears to be a captive, when the

aptain comes from the guard-house with the warrant. He is
followed by the soldiers, and the crowd, drawn by curiosity
to see Carmen led off to prison, again fills the square.

José places her between two dragoons, and the party starts
for the bridge. When they reach the steps, Carmen quickly
draws her hands free of the rope, shoves the soldiers aside,
and, before they know what has happened, dashes up to the
bridge and across it, tossing the rope into the square as she
disappears from sight, while the crowd, hindering pursuit by
blocking the steps, jeers at the discomfited soldiers.

Act II.   The tavern of Lillas Pastia.

Frasquita, Mercédès, and Morales are with Carmen; also
other officers, gypsies, etc. The officers are smoking. Two
gypsies in a corner play the guitar and two others dance.
Carmen looks at them. Zuniga speaks to her; she does not
listen to him, but suddenly rises and sings, 'Les tringles des
sistres tintaient' (Ah, when of gay guitars the sound).

Frasquita and Mercédès join in the 'Tra la la la' of the
refrain. While Carmen clicks the castanets, the dance, in
which she and others have joined the two gypsies, becomes
more rapid and violent.

There are shouts outside, 'Long live the torero! Long live
Escamillo!' The famous bull-fighter, the victor of the bull
ring at Granada, is approaching. He sings the famous
'Couplets du Toréador', a rousing song with refrain and
chorus. 'Votre toast je peux vous le rendre' (To your toast I
drink with pleasure) begins the number. The refrain with
chorus, is 'Toréador, en garde' (Toreador, e'er watchful be).

Tor - e - a - dor   en   gar - - de

Escamillo's debonair manner, his glittering uniform, his
reputation for prowess, make him a brilliant and striking
figure. In his turn he is much struck with Carmen. She is
impressed by him, but her fancy is still for the handsome
dragoon, who has been under arrest since he allowed her to
escape, and has been freed only that day. The Toreador,
followed by the crowd, which includes Zuniga, departs.

It is late. The tavern keeper closes the shutters and leaves
the room. Carmen, Frasquita, and Mercédès are quickly
joined by the smugglers, El Dancairo and El Remendado. The

men need the aid of the three girls in wheedling the
coastguard, and possibly others, into neglect of duty. Their
sentiments, 'Quand il s'agit de tromperie' (When it comes to a
matter of cheating... let women in on the deal), are
expressed in a quintet that is full of spontaneous
merriment—in fact, nowhere in *Carmen*, not even in the most
dramatic passages, is the music forced.

The men want the girls to depart with them at once.
Carmen insists on waiting for José. The men suggest that she
win him over to become one of their band. Not a bad idea,
she thinks. They leave it to her to carry out the plan.

Even now José is heard singing, as he approaches the
tavern, 'Halte là! Qui va là? Dragon d'Alcala!' (Halt
there! Who goes there? Dragoon of Alcala!). He comes in.
Soon she has made him jealous by telling him that she was
obliged to dance for Zuniga and the officers. But now she
will dance for him.

She begins to dance. His eyes are fastened on her. From
the distant barracks a bugle call is heard. It is the 'retreat',
the summons to quarters. The dance, the bugle call, which
comes nearer, passes by the lithe, swaying figure, the wholly
obsessed look of José. José starts to obey the summons to
quarters. Carmen taunts him with placing duty above his love
for her. He draws from his breast the flower she gave him,
and, showing it to her in proof of his passion, sings the
famous 'La fleur que tu m'avais jetée' (The flower that once
to me you gave).

La fleur que tu m'a-vais je - té - e

Carmen tries to persuade him to stay with her and later
join the band, 'Là-bas, là-bas, dans la montagne', but he
hesitates to become a deserter and follow her to the
mountains. At that moment Zuniga, thinking to find Carmen
alone, bursts open the tavern door. There is an angry scene
between Zuniga and José. They draw their sabres. The whole
band of smugglers comes in at Carmen's call. El Dancairo and
El Remendado cover Zuniga with their pistols, and lead him
off.

'And you? Will you now come with us?' asks Carmen of
Don José.

He, a corporal who has drawn his sabre against an officer, an act of insubordination for which severe punishment awaits him, has no choice left but to follow his temptress to the mountains.

Act III.   A rocky picturesque spot among rocks on a mountain. At the rising of the curtain there is complete solitude. After a few moments a smuggler appears on the summit of a rock, then two, then the whole band, descending and scrambling down the mass of rocks. Among them are Carmen, Don José, El Dancairo, El Remendado, Frasquita, and Mercédès.

The opening chorus has a peculiarly attractive lilt.

Don José is unhappy. Carmen's absorbing passion for him has been a brief duration. A creature of impulse, she is fickle and wayward. Don José, a soldier bred, but now a deserter, is ill at ease among the smugglers, and finds cause to reproach himself for sacrificing everything to a fierce and capricious beauty, in whose veins courses the blood of a lawless race. Yet he still loves her to distraction, and is insanely jealous of her—for which she gives him ample cause. It is quite apparent that the impression made upon her by Escamillo is deepening. Escamillo has been caught in the lure of her dangerous beauty, but he does not risk annoying her by sulking in her presence, like Don José, but goes on adding to his laurels by winning fresh victories in the bull ring.

Now that Don José is more than usually morose, she says, with a sarcastic inflection in her voice: 'If you don't like our mode of life here, why don't you leave?' 'And go far from you! Carmen! If you say that again, it will be your death!' He half draws his knife from his belt.

With a shrug of her shoulders Carmen replies: 'What matter—I shall die as fate wills'. And, indeed, she plays with fate as with men's hearts. For whatever else this gypsy may be, she is fearless.

While Don José wanders moodily about the camp, she joins Frasquita and Mercédès, who are telling their fortunes by cards. The superstitious creatures are merry because the cards favour them. Carmen takes the pack and draws.

'Spades! — A grave!' she mutters darkly, and for a moment it seems as if she is drawing back from a shadow that has crossed her path. But the bravado of the fatalist does not long desert her.

'What matters it?' she calls to the two girls. 'If you are to die, try the cards a hundred times, they will fall the same—spades, a grave!' Then, glancing in the direction where Don José stands, she adds, in a low voice, 'First I, then he!'

The Card Trio, 'Mêlons! Coupons!' (Shuffle! Throw!) is a brilliant passage of the score, broken in upon by Carmen's fatalistic soliloquy: 'En vain pour éviter'.

A moment later, when the leader of the smugglers announces that it is an opportune time to attempt to convey their contraband through the mountain pass, she is all on the alert and aids in making ready for the departure. Don José is posted behind a screen of rocks above the camp, to guard against a surprise from the rear, while the smugglers make their way through the pass.

Unseen by him, a guide comes out on the rocks, and, making a gesture in the direction of the camp, hastily withdraws. Into this wild passage of nature, where desperate characters but a few moments before were encamped, and where Carmen had darkly hinted at fate, there descends Micaela, the emblem of sweetness and purity in this tragedy of the passions. She is seeking Don José, in hopes of reclaiming him. Her romance, 'Je dis que rien ne m'épouvante' (I try not to own that I tremble), is characterised by Mr. Upton as 'the most effective and beautiful number in the whole work'—a verdict that is a trifle unkind to Carmen and Don José, and might not have pleased Bizet. The introduction for horns is an exquisite passage, and the expectations it awakens are fully met by the melodious measures of the romance.

Je dis que rien ne m'é-pou-vante

Having looked about her, and failing to find Don José, she withdraws. Meanwhile Don José, from the place where he stands guard, has caught sight of a man approaching the camp. A shot rings out; it is Don José who has fired at the man coming up the defile. He is about to fire again, but the nonchalant manner in which the stranger comes on, and, waving his hat, calls out, 'An inch lower and it would have been all over with me!' causes him to lower his gun and advance to meet him.

'I am Escamillo and I am here to see Carmen,' he says gaily. 'She has a lover here, a dragoon, who deserted from his troop for her. She adored him, but that, I understand, is all over with now. The loves of Carmen never last long.'

'Slowly, my friend,' replies Don José. 'Before anyone can take our gypsy girls away, he must pay the price.'

'So, so. And what is it?'

'It is paid with the knife,' grimly answers José, as he draws his blade.

'Ah,' laughs the Toreador, 'then you are the dragoon of whom Carmen has wearied. I am in luck to have met you so soon.'

He, too, draws. The knives clash, as the men, the one a soldier, the other a bullfighter, skilfully thrust and parry. But Don José's is the better weapon, for, as he catches one of Escamillo's thrusts on his blade, the Toreador's knife snaps short. It would be a fatal mishap for Escamillo, did not at that moment the gypsies and smugglers, recalled by the shot, hurry in and separate the combatants. Unruffled by his misadventure, especially as his ardent glances meet an answering gleam in Carmen's eyes, the Toreador invites the entire band to the coming bullfight in Seville, in which he is to figure. With a glad shout they accept.

'Don't be angry, dragoon', he adds tauntingly. 'We may meet again.'

For answer Don José seeks to rush at him, but some of the smugglers hold him back, while the Toreador leisurely goes his way.

The smugglers make ready to depart again. One of them, however, spies Micaela. She is led down. Don José is reluctant to comply with her pleas to go away with her. The fact that Carmen urges him to do what the girl says only arouses his jealousy. He bursts out tragically that he will not leave her, should his refusal cost him his life. This is one of the most dramatic moments of the whole score.

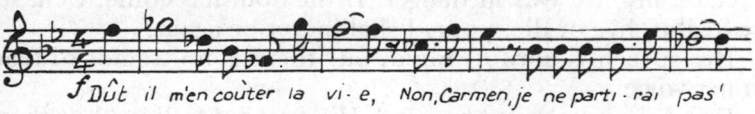

Dût il m'en coûter la vi - e, Non, Carmen, je ne parti - rai pas'

But when at last Micaela tells him that his mother is dying of a broken heart for him, he makes ready to go.

In the distance Escamillo is heard singing the refrain of his song. Carmen listens, as if enraptured, and starts to run after him. Don José with bared knife bars the way; then leaves with Micaela.

Act IV.   A square in Seville. At the back the entrance to the arena. It is the day of the bullfight. The square is animated. Watersellers, others with oranges, fans, and other articles. Chorus. Ballet.

Gay the crowd that fills the square outside the arena where the bullfights are held. It cheers the first strains of music heard as the festival procession approaches, and it shouts and applauds as the various divisions go by and pass into the arena: 'The Alguacil on horseback!'—'The chulos with their pretty little flags!'—'Look! The banderilleros, all clad in green and spangles, and waving the crimson cloths!'—'The picadors with the pointed lances!'—'The cuadrilla of toreros!'—'Now! Vivo, vivo! Escamillo!' And a great shout goes up, as the Toreador enters, with Carmen on his arm.

There is a brief but beautiful duet for Escamillo and Carmen, 'Si tu m'aimes, Carmen' (If you love me, Carmen), before he goes into the building to make ready for the bullfight, while she waits to be joined by some of the smugglers and gypsies, whom Escamillo has invited to be witnesses, with her, of his prowess.

As the Alcade crosses the square and enters the arena, and the crowd pours in after him, one of the gypsy girls from the smugglers' band whispers to Carmen:

'If you value your life, Carmen, don't stay here. He is lurking in the crowd and watching you.'

'He? — José? — I am no coward.—I fear no one.—If he is here, we will have it over with now,' she answers, defiantly, motioning to the girl to pass on into the arena into which the square is rapidly emptying itself. Carmen lingers until she is the only one left, then, with a shrug of contempt, turns to enter—but finds herself facing Don José, who has slunk out from one of the side streets to intercept her.

'I was told you were here. I was even warned to leave here, because my life was in danger. If the hour has come, well, so be it. But, live or die, yours I shall never be again.'

Her speech is abrupt, rapid, but there is no tremor of fear in her voice.

Don José is pale and haggard. His eyes are hollow, but they glow with a dangerous light. His plight has passed from the pitiable to the desperate stage.

'Carmen,' he says hoarsely, 'leave with me. Begin life over again with me under another sky. I will adore you so, it will make you love me.'

'You never can make me love you again. No one can *make* me do anything. Free I was born, free I die.'

The band in the arena strikes up a fanfare. There are loud vivos for Escamillo. Carmen starts to rush for the entrance. Driven to the fury of despair, his knife drawn, as it had been when he barred her way in the smugglers' camp, Don José confronts her. He laughs grimly.

'The man for whom they are shouting—he is the one for whom you have deserted me!'

'Let me pass!' is her defiant answer.

'That you may tell him how you have spurned me, and laugh with him over my misery!'

Again the crowd in the arena shouts: 'Victory! Victory! Vivo, vivo, Escamillo, the toreador of Granada!'

A cry of triumph escapes Carmen.

'You love him!' hisses Don José.

'Yes, I love him! If I must die for it, I love him! Victory for Escamillo, victory! I go to the victor in the arena!'

She makes a dash for the entrance. Somehow she manages to get past the desperate man who has stood between her and the gates. She reaches the steps, her foot already touches the landing above them, when he overtakes her, and madly plunges his knife into her back. With a shriek heard above the shouts of the crowd within, she staggers, falls, and rolls lifeless down the steps into the square.

The doors of the arena swing open. Acclaiming the prowess of Escamillo, out pours the crowd, suddenly to halt, hushed and horror-striken, at the body of a woman dead at the foot of the steps.

'I am your prisoner,' says Don José to an officer. 'I killed her.' Then, throwing herself over the body, he cries: 'O Carmen, my beloved Carmen!'

At its production at the Opéra-Comique, *Carmen* was a failure. In view of the world-wide popularity the work was to achieve, that failure has become historic. It had, however, one lamentable result, in that it was a contributory cause of Bizet's death exactly three months after the production, and before he could have had so much as an inkling of the success *Carmen* was to obtain. It was not until four months after his death that the opera, produced in Vienna, celebrated its first triumph. Then came Brussels, London, New York. At last, in 1883, *Carmen* was brought back to Paris for what Pierre

Berton calls 'the brilliant reparation'. But Bizet, seriously ill
with *angina pectoris*, and mortally wounded in his pride as an
artist, had died disconsolate. The 'reparation' was to the
public, not to him.

Whoever will take the trouble to read extracts from the
reviews in the Paris press of the first performance of *Carmen*
will find that the score of this opera, so full of well rounded,
individual, and distinctive melodies—ensemble, concerted,
and solo—was considered too Wagnerian. More than one trace
of this curious attitude toward an opera, in which the
melodies crowd upon each other almost as closely as in *Il
Trovatore* and certainly are as numerous as in *Aida*, was still
to be found in the article on *Carmen* in the *Dictionnaire des
Opéras*, one of the most unsatisfactory essays in that work.
Nor, speaking with the authority of Berton, who saw the
second performance, was the failure due to defects in the
cast. He speaks of Galli-Marié (Carmen), Chapuy (Micaela),
Lhérie (Don José), and Bouhy (Escamillo), as 'equal to their
tasks . . . an admirable quartet'.

America has had its Carmen periods. Minnie Hauck
established an individuality in the role, which remained
potent until the appearance of Calvé. When Grau wanted to
fill the house, all he had to do was to announce Calvé as
Carmen. She so dominated the character with her beauty,
charm, *diablerie*, and vocal art that, after she left the
Metropolitan Opera House, it became impossible to revive the
opera there with success, until Farrar made her appearance in
it, November 19, 1914, with Alda as Micaela, Caruso as Don
José, and Amato as Escamillo.

A season or two before Oscar Hammerstein gave *Carmen* at
the Manhattan Opera House, a French company, which was
on its last legs when it struck New York, appeared in a
performance of *Carmen* at the Casino, and the next day went
into bankruptcy. The Carmen was Bressler-Gianoli. Her
interpretation brought out the coarse fibre in the character,
and was so much the opposite of Calvé's that it was interesting
by contrast. It seemed that had the company been able to
survive, *Carmen* could have been featured in its repertory, by
reason of Bressler-Gianoli's grasp of the character as Mérimée
had drawn it in his novel, where Carmen is a much coarser
personality than in the opera. The day after the performance
I went to see Heinrich Conried, then director of the
Metropolitan Opera House, and told him of the impression

21 *Carmen*: the original Carmen, Galli Marié in 1873; Grace Bumbry and Franco Corelli in Chicago, 1964; Kjerstin Meyer and Rudolf Schock in Wieland Wagner's production, Hamburg, 1965.

22 Geraldine Farrar as Manon in Massenet's opera.

she had made, but he did not engage her. The Carmen of Bressler-Gianoli (with Dalmores, Trentini, Ancona, and Gilibert) was one of the principal successes of the Manhattan Opera House. It was first given December 14, 1906, and scored the record for the season with nineteen performances, *Aida* coming next with twelve, and *Rigoletto* with eleven.

Mary Garden's Carmen was distinctive and highly individualised on the acting side. It lacked however the lusciousness of voice, the vocal allure, that a singer must lavish upon the role to make it a complete success.

One of the curiosities of opera in America was the appearance at the Metropolitan Opera House, November 25, 1885, of Lilli Lehmann as Carmen.

A word is due to Bizet's authors for the admirable libretto they have made from Mérimée's novel. The character of Carmen is, of course, the creation of the novelist. But in his book the Toreador is not introduced until almost the very end, and is but one of a succession of lovers whom Carmen has had since she ensnared Don José. In the opera the Toreador is made a principal character, and figures prominently from the second act on. Micaela, so essential for contrast in the opera, both as regards plot and music, is a creation of the librettists. But their master-stroke is the placing of the scene of the murder just outside the arena where the bullfight is in progress, and in having Carmen killed by Don José at the moment Escamillo is acclaimed victor by the crowd within. In the book he slays her on a lonely road outside the city of Cordova the day after the bullfight.   K.

ALEXIS
EMMANUEL CHABRIER
(1841–1894)

L'ÉTOILE
The Star

OPERA bouffe in three acts by Emmanuel Chabrier, libretto by E. Leterrier and A. Vanloo. Première at Bouffes Parisiennes, Paris, November 28, 1877, with Paola-Marie, Berthe Stuart, Luce, Messrs Daubray, Joly, Scipion, Jannin, conductor Leon Rocques. First produced in New York (as *The Merry Monarch*) 1890, adapted by J. C. Goodwin and W. Morse, with the music arranged by J. P. Sousa. This version was given at the Savoy Theatre, London, in 1899, with new dialogue and lyrics and additional music by I. Caryll, the whole retaining little of Chabrier's original. Revived Paris, 1925; 1941, first given at Opéra-Comique, with Fanély Revoil, Lilie Grandval, Madeleine Grandval, Madeleine Mathieu, René Hérent, Balbon, Derroja, conductor Roger Desormière.

CHARACTERS

King Ouf I . . . . Tenor
Siroco, *Court Astronomer* . . . . Bass
Hérisson de Porc Épic . . . . Tenor
Tapioca, *his Private Secretary* . . . . Baritone
The Chief of Police . . . . .Speaking
The Mayor . . . . .Speaking
Lazuli, *a Pedlar* . . . . .Mezzo-Soprano
Princess Laoula . . . . Soprano
Aloès, *wife of Hérisson* . . . . Soprano
Ladies and Gentlemen of the Court, People, Guards

After a bracing, unpretentious overture, the curtain rises on a public square; on the right is some form of observatory, on the left a small hotel. Rumour has it that King Ouf in disguise is prowling round the town, and the citizens warn each other to be on the watch. Why? The appearance of a cloaked figure, which proceeds to ask leading questions of individuals about King and Government, soon answers the question. The King must provoke one of his too law-abiding subjects into subversive talk if the rest of them are not be to cheated of their main pleasure at his birthday celebrations—a public execution. Nobody obliges with an anti-Ouf remark, so he vents his disappointment on Siroco, the Astronomer Royal, who descends opportunely from his observatory. The King explains a clause in his will under which Siroco must die a quarter of an hour after his employer, then orders Siroco to look into the omens which surround Ouf's projected marriage with Princess Laoula, the daughter of his neighbour, King Mataquin, by which he proposes to bring peace between the two countries and provide his own with an heir to the throne.

On to the empty stage come four cloaked figures, respectively Hérisson de Porc Épic, King Mataquin's Ambassador, Tapioca, his confidential secretary, Princess Laoula, and Aloès, wife of Hérisson. In chorus they announce their intention of remaining incognito under the guise of shopkeepers, and each in turn sings of the joys and beauties of commerce. For reasons that he says are diplomatic, like those for their incognito, Hérisson has been passing Laoula off as his wife—a complicated manoeuvre, but where would diplomacy (and diplomats) be without complications?

They all go into the hotel as Lazuli, a pedlar, comes on singing gracefully of the power of cosmetics in the female world ('Je suis Lazuli')—an undoubted 'hit' number. As he unpacks his gear, Lazuli admits to himself that he has fallen in love with one of four travellers he has just met, and he gives his last golden piece to Siroco in return for a promise to consult the stars about his future. While his horoscope is being cast, Lazuli prepares to sleep and sings a touching romance to the star on which so much appears to depend.

No sooner have Hérisson and Tapioca left the inn, than Aloès and Laoula come out too, resolved on adventure. They catch sight of the recumbent Lazuli and decide to wake him up. The obvious way is to tickle him, and this method is graphically illustrated in the music ('Il faut le chatouiller pour le mieux réveiller'). Lazuli pretends to be asleep until he has the chance of seizing hold of his tormentors, who tell him that they are unmarried shop assistants. He declares his love for Laoula and gives practical proof of it in the form of a kiss, but the return of Hérisson and Tapioca spoils a promising scene. Lazuli is desolate to hear that Laoula is the wife of Hérisson, and when King Ouf, still on the look out for a victim for the public holiday, approaches him, he is understandably out of humour, speaks ill of the Government and finishes by boxing the ears of his interrogator. Beside himself with joy, Ouf summons his guards and reveals to Lazuli that the ears he has just boxed are the King's. For his offence he must die—and the King sends for the instruments of torture whose praises he sings in the 'Couplets du Pal'. As Lazuli is about to be ceremonially impaled, Siroco interrupts to say that the stars reveal that Lazuli's destiny is intimately connected with that of the King himself, and that the King's death will closely follow Lazuli's. There is a quick change of plans, Lazuli is pardoned, and the King countermands the order for the *pal* and instead sends for his *palanquin* and announces that he will instal Lazuli in the Royal Palace.

Act II.   The Throne Room in the King's Palace; at the back, windows giving a view on to a lake. Lazuli, now richly caparisoned and waited on by Maids of Honour, whom he thanks in a Brindisi, is visited by the King and Siroco, who have come to satisfy themselves about his health, on which so much depends for each of them. Their solicitude leaves him a prey to considerable misgivings, and, exclaiming that nothing shall keep him a prisoner shut away from his lady-love, he escapes with the aid of a tablecloth through the window. Ouf and Siroco return, are seized with consternation at what they see, promise to grant Lazuli his liberty and so persuade him to climb back again. He tells them he is in love with a married woman but, in a lively song, rejoices that husbands have never bothered him much—at worst he challenges them to a duel. When Hérisson the new ambassador is announced and recognised by Lazuli as the husband of his *innamorata*, King Ouf, much to Hérisson's fury, cannot give him his full attention. He is very little concerned with the details of Hérisson's mission as an ambassador, very much with his skill as a duellist, so much so that he unwittingly almost provokes Hérisson to deliver the ultimatum he always carries in his pocket against emergencies. The crisis however is averted when Hérisson goes off to fetch Princess Laoula.

So that Lazuli may be assisted to win Hérisson's wife, Hérisson when he reappears is arrested and removed by Siroco, leaving the way clear for the lovers. At this point there is a charming quartet for Lazuli and Laoula, Tapioca and Aloès, which becomes a sort of double love duet as it is clear that Tapioca means to practise on Aloès all the attentions which Lazuli lavishes on Laoula. Ouf not unnaturally takes Aloès for the Princess he is betrothed to. Nobody disillusions him, but Tapioca takes it upon himself to escort Aloès to her room. Ouf offers Lazuli freedom and money, Laoula expresses gratitude in a charming song ('Moi, je n'ai pas une âme ingrate') and, in a trio, Ouf speeds them on their way—none too soon as Hérisson, who has escaped, at this moment charges into the room. Ouf calms him and everything is prepared for a ceremonial welcome to the Princess, when Hérisson returns, leading in Aloès and Tapioca, furious not only that Princess Laoula has disappeared but that he has found his wife and Tapioca in a highly compromising situation. The embroilment soon becomes plain even to Ouf, whose consternation mounts as Hérisson reveals that he has sent the guards off in pursuit of the eloping lovers, and explodes at the sound of a shot. Laoula is led in alone, and sadly starts to tell her story. When she describes how Lazuli suddenly disappeared to the bottom of the lake, her tune becomes brilliant and gay ('Et puis crac! Tout changea dans une minute'). It is the finale of the act and everyone thankfully joins in.

Act III. An entr'acte based on the tickling trio brings up the curtain on another room in the Palace. Even surreptitiously putting the clock back cannot disguise from Ouf and Siroco the unhappy fact that they are waiting for death, which seems to become even more certain when the Chief of Police tells them that the finding of Lazuli's hat and coat seems to confirm his demise. It is plain to them that only a glass of cordial can restore their spirits, and they go off to find comfort.

Lazuli now emerges from hiding. Confident of his own prowess as a swimmer (we heard about it when he was escaping earlier on) he had dived from the boat and so evaded his pursuers. The trouble is, as we learn in a song ('Enfin je me sens mieux'), that his ducking has given him a horrible cold and he sneezes throughout his number. He hides as Ouf and Siroco reappear. Even a glass of yellow chartreuse has not completely restored the King's morale and wits, and Lazuli from his hiding place sees him inadvertently insult Hérisson, receive the ever-ready ultimatum, but successfully evade the consequences by pleading that it is Hérisson's fault that Lazuli is dead and that the King must therefore shortly die. Hérisson is touched at the situation and offers condolences which Ouf delightedly accepts.

The scene, with its references to his impending end, has tired Ouf, and Siroco timidly suggests that the remedy is another glass of cordial—this time perhaps some green chartreuse, at double the strength. There ensues the *Duetto de la chartreuse verte*, a hilarious parody of an early nineteenth-century Italian piece and a strong candidate for an encore. Ouf and Siroco leave together, and Lazuli comes out of hiding a good deal clearer in his understanding of the situation than before. He listens while Aloès tries to console Laoula, who is clearly very unhappy at his (Lazuli's) death, then he himself joins in to make the duet a trio. There is a grand reunion, and Lazuli tries to explain to Laoula that it is because he is officially dead that he will eventually marry her—she will make as if to return to her father's Court, but he will wait for her outside the city.

Re-enter Ouf, clear in his mind about only one thing, that on the whole he prefers green to yellow chartreuse, because green is stronger. He has another look at Laoula then decides on a quick wedding, urging the joys of widowhood on the disconsolate Princess, who in a sweetly pretty song in 6/8 compares herself with a rose that once picked starts to wither and die. Just in time for Laoula, Ouf is reminded by the observatory clock that he has been tampering with the one in the Palace, and seeing that the hour is at hand, renounces the proposed wedding. When the clock strikes and he remains alive, he finds time amidst his relief to assure Siroco of impending punishment, but regains his good humour in time to pardon Lazuli, who has been arrested by the diligent Chief of Police, and, to the tune of 'Le Pal', to bless Laoula and Lazuli and provide the necessary happy ending.   H.

LE ROI MALGRÉ LUI
King in Spite of Himself

Opéra-Comique in 3 acts by Emmanuel Chabrier. Libretto by Emile de Najac and Paul Burani. Première, May 18, 1887, Opéra-Comique, Paris, with Adèle Isaac, Cécile Mézéray, Max Bouvet, Delaguerrière, Lucien Fugère, conductor Danbé. Revived in a new dramatic version by Albert Carré, at Opéra-Comique, 1929, with Brothier, Guyla, Bourdin, Musy; 1946, with Turba-Rabier, Vina Bovy, Bourdin, Musy; 1959, with Micheau, Castelli, Clément, Musy.

CHARACTERS

Henri de Valois, *King of Poland* . . . . Baritone
Comte de Nangis, *a member of his suite* . . . . Tenor

Duc de Fritelli .... Buffo Baritone
Count Laski, *a Polish patriot* .... Bass
Basile, *an innkeeper* .... Tenor
Villequier ⎫   ⎧ Bass
Liancourt ⎪   Tenor
Elbeuf ⎬ *French noblemen* ....⎨ Tenor
Maugiron ⎪   Baritone
Quélus ⎭   ⎩ Baritone
A soldier .... Bass
Minka, *one of Count Laski's serfs* .... Soprano
Alexina, *Duchess of Fritelli* .... Soprano
Six Serfs, Pages, French Noblemen, Polish Noblemen,
Soldiers, Polish Ladies, People
Place: Poland

Henri de Valois is King of Poland but he is bored with
position and surroundings alike and nothing, he thinks,
would please him better than to be rid permanently of both.
When the curtain rises, the French nobles of his Court are
gathered together in the castle near Cracow, playing cards
and chess, fencing and generally whiling away the tedium of
life in a Court far from home. Nangis sings of the penance of
existence in a barbarous capital, relieved only by the
possibilities of a diverting love affair, then takes credit for the
new soldiers he has succeeded in recruiting. The King enters,
is acclaimed, reviews disinterestedly the soldiers drawn up for
him, and receives in reply to an enquiry the answer that a
bodyguard is necessary for him as many Poles opposed his
election as their King—Villequier suspects a plot against his
life. The post from France is brought ceremonially to the
King, who in a beautiful romance hymns the praises of his
longed-for native land. He is depressed at the unreality of his
position: his senior French advisers fear he will rush off to
France, his Polish subjects, led by Count Laski, dread his
staying in Poland. He decides he must go incognito, even
though the Poles do not know him by sight, amongst his
subjects to discover their views.
Enter Duke Fritelli, an Italian attached to the Court but
married to a Polish wife, niece moreover to the suspect Count
Laski. With his conceit and cowardice and his lack of
physical attraction, he is a recognised figure of fun, but the
King asks him for his interpretation of the Polish character—
this he gives in a remarkable and brilliantly characterised
song, 'Le Polonais est triste et grave'. The King insists on the

attractions of Italian women, instancing an adventure he recently had with a masked Venetian in her native city. The Duke goes to fetch his wife, whom the King wishes presented, and the King discovers from Nangis that he is in love with Minka, a slave in the household of Count Laski. She regularly passes on information of her master's plots against the King. The King tells Nangis that they will go together in disguise to Cracow to spy out the land.

No sooner have the King and his attendants gone than sounds of a scuffle are heard, and Nangis has to rescue Minka from a soldier who is attacking her with a whip. She is safe with him, and in tender music they celebrate at the same time her escape and the love they feel for one another. The courtiers return, admire the object of Nangis's affections, and leave the lovers alone together. In conversation, Minka reveals that there is to be a ball that night at Count Laski's, then again protests her love for Nangis, this time in a graceful romance ('L'amour, ce divin maître'). The King sends for Nangis, who makes a date with Minka later in the park—she will sing and so he will be able to find her in the dark. Minka hides at the approach of the Duke and Duchess of Fritelli, intent on making obeisance to the King.

Thinking themselves alone, Alexina, the Duchess, reveals to her husband, who is also in the plot, that the Polish opponents of Henri de Valois meet that night at her uncle's house. When Fritelli suggests that she is made for romance and that he, her husband, should be the object of her passion, she bursts out laughing, and in a rapid duet advises her husband to concentrate on ambition, while he urges on her the claims of love. She starts to tell him of an adventure she had in Venice when Fritelli realises that, for all the innocent slant she gives it, it is complementary to the one the King has just told; *she* was the Italian under whose spell he fell! When news comes that the King is too busy to receive the Duchess, Fritelli is overjoyed and announces to her his convinced adherence to the plot to drive out the foreign ruler.

Fritelli and his wife depart, and Minka is about to tell Nangis of the plot against the King's life, when the King himself comes from his room. He makes a sign to Nangis, whom he dismisses, and Minka, believing him like Nangis a member of the King's entourage, in a duet tells him about the plot, about her love for Nangis, and about the Polish gossip about the King they do not want. She points out Fritelli as

one of the conspirators and leaves. The King immediately
confronts Fritelli with the accusation, then pardons him on
condition that Fritelli takes him (the King) to the ball at
Laski's that very night. The King looks for a pretext for a
Frenchman to present himself as a prospective conspirator,
then, finding the guard turned out to accompany him on his
ride, pretends to lose his temper with Nangis (on the grounds
that he must have given away his intended journey) and
sentences him to immediate imprisonment. The Finale works
up to a fine ensemble of perplexity à la Rossini ('Qu'a-t-il
fait? En effet qu'a-t-il pu commettre?') and the King departs
as Nangis is led off by the guards.

Fritelli starts to explain to his wife that the King cannot
now receive her, when he appears unannounced. It is
immediately clear that each recognises the other as the
nameless lover from Venice, but that neither has an inkling of
the identity of the other. Fritelli is made to introduce the
King as Nangis, who as a result of his unjust treatment is
anxious to join the conspirators. The trio ('Quelle surprise,
ma beauté de Venise') makes a brilliant effect but is
interrupted by the voice of Minka, singing in the park as she
waits for her rendezvous with Nangis. The night watch goes
by singing, challenges and recognises Fritelli, and Henri de
Valois brings the act to a close: 'Conspirons tous trois contre
Henri de Valois'.

The second act takes place in the great hall of Count
Laski's Palace at the start of the Ball. The music—the well-
known *Fête Polonaise*—is a choral dance, brilliantly
orchestrated and altogether in the tradition of Berlioz (*cf.*
scene of the Roman Carnival in *Benvenuto Cellini*). The Ball
is an excuse for Count Laski to gather together the conspirators. Alexina introduces as a sympathiser the Comte de
Nangis (the King in disguise) but a complication is introduced
when the ubiquitous Minka overhears the introduction and
knows that some deception is afoot. During the course of a
choral ensemble of conspirators, which rivals Meyerbeer for
massive effect and far outdoes him for musical excitement,
the *soi-disant* Nangis swears with the others to do all possible
to remove the King from Poland, and Fritelli, in spite of
efforts at evasion, is charged with abducting his master and
placing him in a closed carriage bound for the border.
However, when most have gone, the disguised King takes pity
on Fritelli and says he has a more subtle plan to effect the

removal of the King—who was once, Alexina points out, his
greatest friend. 'Rien n'est aussi près de la haine que l'amitié'
is the burden of a witty and exquisite quartet, in which
Alexina and the King are joined by Fritelli and Laski.

There follows an interlude, the Sextuor des Serves and
the Chanson tzigane, dramatically superfluous but musically
very much to the point, with its sensuous writing for
concerted female voices and its exceptionally brilliant solo
for Minka, who relates the story of her happy love to her
fellow serfs until such time as she hears the voice of her
lover—gratification at his release from prison is however
short-lived as the serfs are all summoned to dance again for
new arrivals.

The King enters, followed by Alexina, who is still ignorant
of his identity but knows him as the man who swore eternal
faith in Venice and then disappeared; 'Oui, je vous hais', she
sings, but the duet turns to a barcarole reminiscence of their
rapturous experience—it might be a precursor of Reynaldo
Hahn's operetta style. Alexina is clearly in love, and when she
leaves, the King asks Fritelli whose wife she may be, is put
off with vague hints of six children, false teeth and a wooden
leg, but has the last word when he says he will ask Laski to
release him from his promise. The reason: he is in love with a
Pole!

Fritelli starts to ask Minka to inform the Count her master
that the King is at the ball in disguise, then decides to tell
Laski himself and goes off. Minka alone sings to attract her
lover who appears just long enough to be told about the
King's supposed presence at the ball before hiding. The news
passes round until Laski has the doors shut and guarded.
When Nangis does not remove his mask, Laski assumes that
he is the King and an ensemble begins, Offenbachian in spirit
and culminating in Nangis's spritely song (prompted by the
real King), 'Je suis le roi'. The Poles demand his signature to
an act of abdication, the King orders him to sign, but
prompted by Minka he refuses, and is promptly put gently
but firmly under lock and key while his captors deliberate
the method of getting rid of him. When his death is voted as
alternative to abdication, the real King proposes himself as
the true victim.

Consternation is general, led by Alexina, who vouches for
his *bona fides* as a mere member of the Court. When the
conspirators draw lots for the man to deal the fatal blow,
each puts the name of Nangis on a paper, but when the King

makes as if to enter and deal a death blow to himself, Minka appears and admits she has helped Nangis escape. The conspirators realise that vengeance may at any moment overtake them, and, the King promising to keep his oath, they agree to leave the house, to a thundering reprise of the *ensemble de la conjuration.*

Act III.   The complications must be resolved, which they are, though not before some fairly extensive and choice red-herrings have been found, chased, pickled and discarded. The scene is the hall of an inn on the Polish frontier; numbered doors give off on either side and the hall is full of decorations, most of them bearing the letter H. A crowd sings of its joy at the prospect of a new King for Poland, but Fritelli, who casts his eye over the decorations, has to explain that the new King is Archduke Ernest, not Henri de Valois! The music is a vivid *allegro tempo mazurka,* chorus and ensemble in the style of the opening of the last act of *Carmen,* spiced with ingredients peculiar to the composer of *España.* In the course of a not too satisfactory conversation with Basile, the innkeeper, who has no particular use for kings, still less for the business of changing them—unless this involves increased drinking—Fritelli learns that a distinguished-looking traveller arrived at the inn the night before and is now lodged in room eight. Obviously, thinks Fritelli, Archduke Ernest. Immediately bouquets are handed out, the peasants bidden to be on their best behaviour, and Fritelli steps forward with a smile, the first to greet the Archduke— only to see Henri de Valois step with a grin through the door.

The explanation is simple: horses were prepared to take him to the frontier but no further, and the coachman deposited him here—will the Duke please order a carriage to take him a stage further? More than that, will he convey his infinite regrets to the charming niece of Count Laski that he had to leave without saying goodbye? The Duke does not know whether to be angry or relieved, but goes off to do the King's bidding, leaving the field clear for the entrance of Alexina and Minka, who has been allowed to accompany her in her carriage. Together they lament the precipitate departure of the men they love (the sentiments are genuine enough, even if by now the names have got thoroughly mixed up); their slow 6/8 *nocturne,* with its mellifluous writing for two female voices, inevitably evokes the Berlioz of *Béatrice et Bénédict.*

At this moment Fritelli comes in carrying the hot water

the King has demanded, delivers it, intimates to the despair
of Alexina and Minka that the King and Nangis have both left
for France, and then explodes at Alexina's complaint at his
cavalier dismissal of her: 'Nous ne sommes plus à Venise,
Madame!' He rates her for her indiscretions in a comic song:
'Je suis du pays des gondoles' (what is the reference to
Berlioz's *Marche Hongroise* as refrain at end of each verse?),
explains that he is on an errand for the Archduke, and enters
room number eight. Alexina for her part goes through the
performance of collecting the peasants and preparing to
salute the new King, only to see her lover come out.

All is explained, his identity as King and hers as the Duke's
wife, but there is an interruption as Minka runs in, crying
that Count Laski is at hand; she will be taken back to
Cracow, the King will be slain. Henri consents to leave, saying
that he has kept his word and the King is no more; Minka
believes he has killed her lover and runs after him, vowing
revenge; and Laski is told 'Le roi n'est plus'. But an
important change has taken place that morning, when news
was received that the Archduke had renounced the throne
and the Polish nobles, impressed by Henri's chivalrous
conduct the night before, had decided to renounce their
opposition. He must be stopped before it is too late!

It remains to resolve Minka's dilemma, expressed in a
despairing aria. Nangis appears to explain the deception and
claim her in a love duet, before the sound of the March of the
King's guard is heard outside, and Henri returns in something
like triumph. He extends grace to everyone present, and the
opera ends with the shields bearing the royal H once more to
the front, and a general acclamation for 'Le Roi malgré lui'.

H.

JULES MASSENET

(1842–1912)

MANON

OPERA in five acts by Jules Massenet, text by Meilhac and Gille, based
on the story by the Abbé Prévost. Première, Opéra-Comique, Paris,
January 19, 1884, with Marie Heilbronn, Talazac, Taskin, Cobalet,

conductor Danbé. First performed in England, Liverpool, 1885, with
Marie Roze; Drury Lane, (in English), with Roze, Maas, Ludwig,
conductor Eugene Goossens (Snr.); Covent Garden, 1891, with Sybil
Sanderson, van Dyck, Isnardon; New York, Academy of Music, 1885,
with Minnie Hauck, Giannini, del Puente; 1895 (in Italian), with Sybil
Sanderson, Jean de Reszke, Ancona, Plançon. Covent Garden revivals
include 1919, with Edvina and Ansseau, conductor Beecham; 1926,
with Heldy and Ansseau; since 1947, McWatters, Schwarzkopf, de los
Angeles, Leigh, Scotto have sung the title role in London. Famous
interpreters of Manon include also Mary Garden, Farrar, Bori, Grace
Moore, Favero, Sayao. Famous des Grieux: Clément, Caruso, Gigli,
Schipa, Tagliavini, di Stefano.

CHARACTERS

Chevalier des Grieux . . . . Tenor
Comte des Grieux, *his father* . . . . Bass
Lescaut, *of the Royal Guard, cousin to Manon* . Baritone
Guillot de Morfontaine, *Minister of Finance, an*
    old roué . . . . Tenor
De Brétigny, *a nobleman* . . . . Baritone
Manon Lescaut . . . . Soprano
Pousette, Javotte, Rosette, *actresses* . . . . Sopranos
    Students, Innkeeper, a Sergeant, a Soldier,
    Gamblers, Merchants and their Wives, Croupiers,
    Sharpers, Guards, Travellers, Ladies, Gentlemen,
    Porters, Postilions, an attendant at the Monastery
    of St. Sulpice, the People

Time: 1721   *Place:* Amiens, Paris, Havre

Act I. Courtyard of the inn at Amiens. Guillot and de
Brétigny, who have just arrived with the actresses Pousette,
Javotte, and Rosette, are shouting for the innkeeper. Townspeople crowd about the entrance to the inn. They descry a
coach approaching. Lescaut, who has alighted from it, enters
followed by two guardsmen. Other travellers appear amid
much commotion, amusement, and shouting on the part of
the townspeople. Lescaut is awaiting his cousin Manon,
whom he is to conduct to a convent school, and who presently
appears and gives a sample of her character, which is a
mixture of demureness and vivacity, of serious affection and
meretricious self-seeking, in her opening song, 'Je suis encore
tout étourdie' (A simple maiden fresh from home), in which
she tells how, having left home for the first time to travel to
Amiens, she sometimes wept and sometimes laughed. It is a
chic little song.

Lescaut goes out to find her luggage. From the balcony of the inn the old roué Guillot sees her. She is not shocked, but laughs at his hints that he is rich and can give her whatever she wants. De Brétigny, who, accompanied by the actresses, comes out on the balcony in search of Guillot, also is much struck with her beauty. Guillot, before withdrawing with the others from the balcony, softly calls down to her that his carriage is at her disposal, if she will but enter it and await him. Lescaut returns but at the same time his two guardsmen come after him. They want him to join with them in gambling and drinking. He pretends to Manon that he is obliged to go to his barracks for a short time. Before leaving her, however, he warns her to be careful of her actions. 'Regardez-moi bien dans les yeux' (Now give good heed to what I say).

Left alone, Manon expresses admiration for the jewels and finery worn by the actresses. She wishes such gems and dresses might belong to her: 'Voyons Manon, plus de chimères'. The Chevalier des Grieux, young, handsome, ardent, comes upon the scene. He falls in love with Manon at first sight. Nor does she long remain unimpressed by the wooing of the Chevalier. Beginning with his words, 'If I knew but your name', and her reply, 'I am called Manon', the music soon becomes an impassioned love-duet. To him she is an enchantress. As for her—'A vous ma vie et mon âme' (To you my life and my soul).

Manon sees Guillot's postilion, who has been told by his master to take his orders from Manon. She communicates to des Grieux that they will run away to Paris in Guillot's conveyance. 'Nous vivrons à Paris tous les deux'. At the duet's climax they shout in triumph, and are off. There is much

confusion when the escape is discovered. Ridicule is heaped upon Guillot, for is it not in his carriage, in which the old roué hoped to find Manon awaiting him, that she has driven off with her young lover!

Act II. The apartment of des Grieux and Manon, Rue Vivienne, Paris. Des Grieux is writing at his desk. Discovering Manon looking over his shoulder, he reads her what he has written—a letter to his father extolling her beauty and asking permission to marry her. Musically, it is a scene of great charm.

The scene is interrupted by knocking and voices without. The maidservant announces that two guardsmen demand admission. She whispers to Manon, 'One of them loves you—the nobleman, who lives near here'. The pair are Lescaut and de Brétigny, the latter masquerading as a soldier in Lescaut's regiment. Lescaut scents more profit for himself and for his cousin Manon in a liaison between her and the wealthy nobleman than in her relations with des Grieux. Purposely he is gruff and demands 'yes' or 'no' to his question as to whether or not des Grieux intends to marry the girl. Des Grieux shows the letter he is about to dispatch to his father. Apparently everything is satisfactory. But de Brétigny manages to convey to Manon the information that the Chevalier's father is incensed at his son's mode of life and has arranged to have him carried off that night. If she will keep quiet about it, he (de Brétigny) will provide for her handsomely and surround her with the wealth and luxury she craves. She protests that she loves des Grieux—but is careful not to warn him of the impending abduction. This lively quartet aptly contrasts the lovesick des Grieux and the practical Lescaut and de Brétigny.

Lescaut and the nobleman depart, after Lescaut, sly fellow, has blessed his 'children', as he calls Manon and des Grieux. Shortly afterwards the latter goes out to dispatch the letter to his father. Manon, approaching the table, which is laid for supper, sings the charming air, 'Adieu, notre petite table' (Farewell, dear little table). This is followed by the exquisite air with harp accompaniment, 'Le Rêve de Manon' (A vision of Manon), which is sung by des Grieux, who has re-entered and describes her as he saw her in a dream: 'En fermant les yeux'. Here is an example of Massenet's graceful talent at its best—sensitive, expressive, and full of that indefinable thing we call 'style'.

There is a disturbance outside. Manon knows that the men who will bear away her lover have arrived. She loves des Grieux, but luxury means more to her than love. An effort is made by her to dissuade the Chevalier from going outside to see who is there—but it is a half-hearted attempt. He goes. The noise of a struggle is heard. Manon, 'overcome with grief', exclaims, 'He has gone'.

Act III. Scene i.   The Cours la Reine, Paris, on the day of a popular fête. Stalls of traders are among the trees. There is a pavilion for dancing. After some lively preliminary episodes between the three actresses and Guillot, Lescaut enters singing sentimentally of a certain Rosalinde. After him comes de Brétigny with Manon. She sings frivolously of her gay life, 'Je marche sur tous les chemins', and follows this up with the famous *Gavotte*: 'Obéissons quand leur voix appelle' (List to the voice of youth when it calleth).[1]

The Comte des Grieux, father of the Chevalier, comes upon the scene. From a conversation between him and de Brétigny, which Manon overhears, she learns that the Chevalier is about to enter the seminary of St. Sulpice and intends to take holy orders. After a duet between Manon and the Comte, one of the most charming of the lesser-known passages of the score and a good example of Massenet's ability to forward the drama in a set-piece, the Comte retires, and Guillot returns, bringing with him the ballet from the Opéra. This luxury, we heard a little earlier, Manon had been refused by de Brétigny on the grounds of expense, and has now been brought by Guillot, who hopes to win her away from her current lover. There is dancing by the ballet, at the end of which Manon, who to Guillot's dismay says she has seen nothing, orders her chair, and bids the amazed Lescaut have her conveyed to the seminary of St. Sulpice.

Scene ii.   Ante-Chapel of St. Sulpice. Nuns and visitors, who have just attended religious service, are praising the sermon delivered by des Grieux, who enters a little later

[1] At the Opéra-Comique, instead of the Gavotte is sung the *Fabliau*, 'Oui, dans les bois'.   H.

.ired in the garb of an abbé. The ladies withdraw, leaving
es Grieux with his father, who has come in unobserved, and
.ow vainly endeavours to dissuade his son from taking holy
orders: 'Epouse quelque brave fille'. Left alone, des Grieux
cannot banish Manon from his thoughts. 'Ah! fuyez douce
image' (Ah! depart, image fair), he sings in an aria which
rises almost to a frenzy; then slowly goes out.

Almost as if in answer to his soliloquy, the woman whose
image he cannot put away enters the chapel. From outside
chanting is heard. Summoned by the porter of the seminary,
des Grieux comes back. He protests to Manon that she has
been faithless and says that he will not turn from the peace
of mind he has sought in religious retreat.

Gradually, however, he yields to the pleading of the
woman he loves: 'N'est-ce plus ma main que cette main
presse? . . .

Ah! regarde moi! N'est-ce plus Manon?' (Is it no longer my
hand, your own now presses? . . . Ah! look upon me! Am I
no longer Manon?) The religious chanting continues, but
now only as a background to an impassioned love duet—
'Ah! Viens, Manon, je t'aime!' (Ah Manon, Manon! I love
thee).

Act IV. Hôtel de Transylvanie, a fashionable gambling
house in Paris. Play is going on. Guillot, Lescaut, Pousette,
Javotte, and Rosette are of the company. Later Manon and
des Grieux comes in, and the latter makes impassioned
declaration of his love for Manon, which alone has brought
him to such a place:

Manon, who has run through her lover's money, counsels the
Chevalier to stake what he has left on the game. Des Grieux
plays with amazing luck against Guillot and gathers in

winning after winning. 'Faites vos jeux, Messieurs', cry t
croupiers, while Manon joyously sings, 'Ce bruit de l'or, ‹
rire, et ces éclats joyeux' (Music of gold, of laughter, an‹
clash of joyous sounds). The upshot of it all, however, is that
Guillot accuses the Chevalier of cheating, and after an angry
scene goes out. Very soon afterwards, the police, whom
Guillot has summoned, break in. Upon Guillot's accusation
they arrest Manon and the Chevalier. 'O douleur, l'avenir
nous sépare' (Oh despair! Our lives are divided for ever), sings
Manon, her accents of grief being echoed by those of her
lover.

Act V, originally given as a second scene to the fourth act,
takes place at a lonely spot on the road to Havre. Des Grieux
has been freed through the intercession of his father. Manon,
however, has been condemned as a prostitute to deportation
to the French colony of Louisiana. Des Grieux and Lescaut
are waiting for the prisoners to pass with their escort of
soldiers. Des Grieux hopes to release Manon by attacking the
convoy, but Lescaut restrains him. The guardsman finds little
difficulty in bribing the sergeant to permit Manon, who is
already nearly dead from exhaustion, to remain behind with
des Grieux, between whom the rest of the opera is a dolorous
duet, ending in Manon's death. Even while dying her dual
nature asserts itself. Feebly opening her eyes, almost at the
last, she imagines she sees jewels and exclaims, 'Oh! what
lovely gems!' She turns to des Grieux: 'I love thee! Take
thou this kiss. 'Tis my farewell for ever.' It is, of course, this
dual nature which makes the character drawn by Abbé
Prévost so interesting.

The last act is original with the librettists. In the story the
final scene is laid in Louisiana (see Puccini's *Manon Lescaut*).
The effective scene in the convent of St. Sulpice was
overlooked by Puccini, as it also was by Scribe, who wrote
the libretto for Auber's *Manon*. This latter work survives in
the laughing song, 'L'Eclat de Rire', which Patti introduced
in the lesson scene in *Il Barbiere di Siviglia*, and which
Galli-Curci later revived for the same purpose.   K.

WERTHER

Opera in four acts by Jules Massenet; text by Edouard Blau, Paul
Milliet, and Georges Hartmann, after Goethe's novel. Première in a

German version at the Vienna Opera, February 16, 1892, with Marie Renard, Forster, van Dyck, Neidl. First performed Opéra-Comique, Paris, January 16, 1893, with Marie Delna, Laisné, Ibos, Bouvet; Chicago, 1894; New York, 1894, and Covent Garden the same year, with Eames, Arnoldson, Jean de Reszke. Revived Metropolitan, 1910, with Farrar, Alma Gluck, Clément, Dinh Gilly; 1971, with Christa Ludwig and Franco Corelli; His Majesty's Theatre, London (in English), 1910; la Scala, Milan, 1939, with Pederzini, Schipa; 1951, with Simionato, Tagliavini; New York, City Centre, 1948, with Heidt and Conley; Sadler's Wells (in English), 1952, with Marion Lowe and Rowland Jones; Glyndebourne, 1966, with Héllia T'Hézan, Jean Brazzi, conductor Cillario; 1969, with Veasey and Brazzi.

CHARACTERS

Werther, *a poet, aged 23* . . . . Tenor
Albert, *a young man, aged 25* . . . . Baritone
The Magistrate, *aged 50* . . . . Bass
Schmidt⎱ *friends of the Magistrate* . . . . ⎱Tenor
Johann ⎰   ⎰Bass
Charlotte, *the Magistrate's daughter,*
    aged 20 . . . . .Mezzo-Soprano
Sophie, *her sister, aged 15* . . . . Soprano
Children, Neighbours of the Magistrate
Time: About 1780   *Place:* Frankfurt

After a prelude consisting of the music associated with the more forceful as well as the idyllic side of Werther's character, the curtain rises on Act I, which takes place in the garden outside the Magistrate's house. The owner is rehearsing his children in a Christmas song; they sing it badly, but his comment—that they would not dare sing like that if their sister Charlotte were there—has the effect simultaneously of introducing Charlotte and improving the singing. Two friends of the Magistrate, Johann and Schmidt, pause to listen to the singing and remind the Magistrate of his promise to meet them later that night at the 'Raisin d'or'. Sophie has come in and mention is made of the dreamer Werther, and the practical Albert; the last-named will make, says Schmidt, a model husband for Charlotte. Schmidt and Johann go off singing 'Vivat Bacchus', and everyone else goes into the house.

Werther appears, asking for the Magistrate's house, and expressing his pleasure in the country atmosphere in a graceful recitative and aria, 'O nature pleine de grâce' (page 866). Charlotte, dressed for the dance which is to take place that

Modéré ... *dim* ... *p*

f O na-tu-re, pleine de grâ-ce Reine du temps et de l'es-pa-ce

night, comes out of the house with the children and takes advantage of the lateness of her escort to cut them their bread and butter. Various guests arrive and are greeted by the Magistrate. Charlotte says good-night to the children, who, the Magistrate says, have been in her charge since their mother's death. Werther's outburst when confronted with the family scene, 'O spectacle idéal', is sufficiently expressive to banish memories of Thackeray's notorious comment on Goethe's novel:

> 'Charlotte, having seen his body
>   Borne before her on a shutter,
> Like a well-conducted person,
>   Went on cutting bread-and-butter.'

Most successful is the way Massenet in a few minutes of music suggests the passage of time while Charlotte and Werther are at the ball: a few sentences for the Magistrate alone and then with Sophie, an empty stage before the entry of Albert, his recognition by Sophie followed by his aria—and night has fallen completely, the moon risen, and the scene is set for the return of the principals.

The music of the 'Clair de lune' is heard in the orchestra as Charlotte and Werther come into the garden, arm in arm.

Lent et soutenu

mf

Their mutual attraction is obvious and Werther declares his passionate love for Charlotte before Massenet interrupts the duet with an effect that is as simple as it is telling: the Magistrate calls out from the house that Albert is back—the idyll is shattered, and we have taken the turn towards tragedy which is to be the eventual outcome. The 'Clair de lune' duet shows many of Massenet's qualities at their best—the elegant simplicity of the vocal line, the economical role of the

:hestra, the shapely, rewarding contours of the tune, the ntle but evocative atmosphere of the whole. It is not ndramatic—the vocal line becomes gradually animated as the ituation develops, and Charlotte's reticence is influenced by Werther's rising passion—but it is still the world of understatement, of the small gesture as opposed to the large, the world which Massenet knew and interpreted best.

A few hasty sentences explain that Albert is the fiancé Charlotte's mother wished for her, and the curtain falls on Werther's desperate cry, 'Un autre! son époux!'

Act II. In front of the church. The two bon-vivants Johann and Schmidt are drinking at the inn. Inside the church the golden wedding of the village pastor is being celebrated. Charlotte and Albert appear, apparently full of happiness after three months of marriage, and go into the church. Werther catches sight of them as they disappear: 'Un autre est son époux'. He soliloquises in music of more vigorous character than we have previously heard from him as he laments that marriage with Charlotte is an impossibility for him: 'J'aurais sur ma poitrine'. He sinks down overcome with unhappiness, and, when he comes out of the church, Albert takes the opportunity of talking to his friend, who, he thinks, is, or has been, in love with Charlotte. After a painful admission, Werther affirms his loyalty to both ('Mais, comme après l'orage'). Sophie, in a little song which might have done duty for the immature Manon ('Le gai soleil'), sings of the happiness which is in her heart. Werther resolves to leave, but the sight of Charlotte is too much for him and he renews his protestations of love. She begs him to go and at all events to stay away until Christmas time. Werther is overcome by the situation; unable to give up his love, he prays at the same time for strength to stay away and for the happiness which his return could bring him: 'Lorsque l'enfant revient d'un voyage'. Seeing Sophie, he tells her he is going away, never to return. She loses no time in informing her sister and brother-in-law of this decision, and Albert comments darkly that this can mean only that Werther is still in love with Charlotte.

Act III. It is Christmas. Charlotte realises that she returns Werther's love; merely to re-read the letters he has written her is enough to bring her to the verge of hysteria (see page 868). Her sister's efforts to cheer her up are in vain, and when Sophie refers to Werther, Charlotte's reserve breaks down and she confesses her love for him: 'Va! laisse couler mes larmes'.

Mais si je ne dois re-pa-raî-tre, Au jour fi-xé de-vant toi, ne m'ac-cu-se pas, pleure moi!

Left alone, she prays for strength: 'Ah! mon courage m'abandonne'. When she is in contact with other people, Charlotte's words and behaviour are as conventional as a Victorian novel (fortunately, this is not by any means always the case with her music), but this can to a large extent be forgiven her for the depth and vehemence of feeling she shows in this scene. Her reading of the letters, the 'Air des larmes', and her prayer for strength together make up a scene which is hardly less powerful and convincing than Tatiana's 'Letter scene' in *Eugene Onegin*. In a moment Charlotte becomes a real and believable person, not the prig we have known in the other two acts.

Suddenly, Werther himself appears, confessing that his reason had urged him to stay away but instinct had proved too strong; he is here on the appointed day of Christmas. They look together at the books they used to read, the harpsichord they used to play, and Charlotte reminds Werther that he was translating Ossian before he went away. The sight of the book awakens memories in Werther's mind, and from it he sings a song of tragic love: 'Pourquoi me réveiller?' This aria has become enormously popular, and in it for the first time in Charlotte's presence Werther uses the directness of musical expression which has hitherto been reserved for soliloquies.

When Charlotte's voice betrays her feelings, Werther's restraint vanishes and he embraces her. The music has a genuine tragic ring about it as Werther becomes more and more excited, and in fact, from the beginning of Act III right

Il brû--le sur ma lèvre. encor i-nas-sou-vi-e

through to the end of the opera, there is a straightforward-ness and a decisiveness that contrasts with the frustration, the continual second thoughts of the first two acts. Werther

draws back and Charlotte rushes from the room, locking the
door behind her. Albert returns and connects his wife's
agitation with Werther's return, of which he has already
learned. Just then the servant comes in with a message from
Werther: 'I am going on a long journey, will you lend me
your pistols?' Albert tells Charlotte to give them to the
servant; she does so mechanically, but realises the significance
of the message a moment after her husband has gone out of
the room.

Act IV. The scene changes to Werther's apartment (Acts
III and IV are played without an interval). Charlotte comes in
to find Werther dying. He prevents her going for help, and is
contented when she tells him she has loved him from the
moment they first met. As he dies, the voices of the children
celebrating Christmas can be heard outside his room. H.

THAÏS

Opera in three acts by Jules Massenet; text by L. Gallet after the
novel of Anatole France. Première at the Opéra, Paris, March 16,
1894, with Sybil Sanderson, Delmas, and Alvarez. First performed New
York, 1907; Covent Garden, 1911, with Edvina, Dinh Gilly, conductor
Panizza; revived 1919, with Edvina, Couzinou, conductor Beecham;
1926, with Jeritza, Servais, conductor Bellezza. Revived Metropolitan,
1917, with Farrar, Amato; 1922, with Jeritza, Whitehill; 1939, with
Jepson, John Charles Thomas; la Scala, Milan, 1942, with Favero,
Bechi, conductor Marinuzzi; Chicago, 1959, with Leontyne Price. After
1945 in the repertory of the Opéra, Paris, with Géori Boué and
Bourdin. Amongst the most famous exponents of the title role has been
Mary Garden.

CHARACTERS

Athanaël, *a young Cenobite monk* . . . . Baritone
Nicias, *a young Alexandrian* . . . . Tenor
Palémon, *an old Cenobite* . . . . Bass
Servant of Nicias . . . . Baritone
Thaïs, *a courtesan* . . . . Soprano
Crobyle, *a slave* . . . . Soprano
Myrtale, *a slave* .Mezzo-Soprano
Albine, *an abbess* . . . . Contralto

Time: Fourth Century A.D.   *Place:* In and near Alexandria

The action of *Thaïs* takes place at the end of the fourth
century. The first act shows us, in a corner of the Theban

plain on the banks of the Nile, a refuge of Cenobites. The good fathers are finishing a modest repast at their common table. One place near them remains empty, that of their comrade Athanaël (Paphnuce in the novel) who has gone to Alexandria. Soon he comes back, greatly scandalised at the sensation caused in the great city by the presence of a shameless courtesan, the famous actress and dancer, Thaïs, who seems to have turned the sceptical and light heads of its inhabitants. Now, in his younger days Athanaël had known this Thaïs, and in Alexandria too, which he left to consecrate himself to the Lord and to take the robe of a religious man.

Athanaël is haunted by the memory of Thaïs. He dreams that it would be a pious and meritorious act to snatch her from her unworthy profession and from a life of debauchery which dishonours her and of which she does not even seem to be conscious. He goes to bed and sleeps under the impress of this thought, which does not cease to confront him, so much so that he sees her in a dream on the stage of the theatre of Alexandria, representing the Loves of Venus. He can refrain no longer and on awaking he goes to search her out, firmly resolved to do everything to bring about her conversion.

Arrived at Alexandria, Athanaël meets an old friend, the beau, Nicias, to whom he makes himself known and who is the lover of Thaïs for a day longer because he has purchased her love for a week which is about to end. Athanaël confides his scheme to Nicias who receives him like a brother and makes him put on clothes which will permit him to attend a fête and banquet which he is to give that very night in honour of Thaïs. Soon he finds himself in the presence of the courtesan who laughs at his first words and who engages him to come to see her at her house if he expects to convert her. He does not fail to accept this invitation and once in Thaïs's house tells her to be ashamed of her disorderly life and with eloquent words reveals to her the heavenly joys and the felicities of religion. Thaïs is very much impressed; she is on the point of yielding to his advice when afar off in a song are heard the voices of her companions in pleasure. She repels the monk, who, without being discouraged, goes away, saying to her: 'At thy threshold until daylight I will await thy coming'.

In fact here we find him at night seated on the front steps of Thaïs's house. Time has done its work and a few hours have sufficed for the young woman to be touched by grace. She goes out of her house, having exchanged her rich

~~~rments for a rough woollen dress, finds the monk, and begs
~~~im to lead her to a convent. The conversion is accomplished.

But Athanaël has deceived himself. It was not love of God
but jealousy which dictated his course without his being
aware of it. When he returns to the Thebaid after having
conducted Thaïs to a convent and thinks he has found peace
again, he perceives with horror that he loves her madly. His
thoughts without ceasing turn to her and in a new dream, a
cruel dream, he seems to see Thaïs, sanctified and purified by
remorse and prayer, on the point of dying in the convent
where she took refuge. On awaking, under the impression of
this sinister vision, he hurries to the convent where Thaïs in
fact is near to breathing her last breath. But he does not wish
that she die; and while she, in ecstasy, is only thinking of
heaven and her purification, he wants to snatch her from
death and only talks to her of his love. Thaïs dies and
Athanaël falls stricken beside her.

This subject, half mystic, half psychological, was it really a
favourable one for theatrical action? Was it even treated in
such a way as to mitigate the defects it might present in this
connection? We may doubt it. Nevertheless M. Massenet has
written on this libretto of *Thaïs* a score which, if it does not
present the firm unity of those of *Manon* and *Werther*,
certainly does not lack either inspiration or colour or
originality and in which moreover are found in all their force
and all their expansion the technical qualities of a master to
whom nothing in his art is foreign. All the music of the first
act, which shows us the retreat of the Cenobites, is of a sober
and severe colour, with which will be contrasted the movement and the gracefulness of the scene at the house of Nicias.
There should be noted the peaceful chorus of monks, the
entrance of Athanaël ('Hélas, enfant encore'), the fine phrase
which follows his dream: 'Toi qui mis la pitié dans nos âmes',
and the very curious effect of the scene where he goes away
again from his companions to return to Alexandria. In the
second act the invocation placed in the mouth of Athanaël,
'Voilà donc la terrible cité', written on a powerful rhythm, is
followed by a charming quartet, a passage with an emphasis
full of grace and the end of which especially is delightful. I
would indicate again in this act the rapid and kindly dialogue
of Nicias and of Thaïs, 'Nous nous sommes aimés une longue
semaine', which seems to conceal under its apparent indifference a sort of sting of melancholy, and the charming air
for Thaïs, 'Qui te fait si sévère'. I pass over the air of Thaïs:

'Dis-moi que je suis belle', an air of bravado solely designe
to display the finish of a singer,[1] to which I much prefer th
whole scene that follows, which is a long duet in which
Athanaël tries to convert Thaïs. The severe and stern accents
of the monk put in opposition to the raillery and the
voluptuous buoyancy of the courtesan produce a striking
contrast which the composer has known how to place in
relief with a rare felicity and a real power. The symphonic
intermezzo which, under the name of '*Méditation*', separates
this act from the following, is nothing but an adorable violin
solo, supported by the harps and the development of which,
on the taking up again of the first motif by the violin, brings
about the entrance of an invisible chorus, the effect of which
is purely exquisite.

The curtain rises on the scene in which Thaïs, who has put
on a rough woollen dress, goes to seek the monk to flee with
him. Here is a duet in complete contrast with the preceding.
Athanaël wants Thaïs to destroy and burn whatever may
preserve the memory of her past. She obeys, demanding
favour only for a little statue of Eros: 'L'amour est une vertu
rare'. It is a sort of invocation to the purity of love, written,
if one may say so, in a sentiment of chaste melancholy and
entirely impressed with gracefulness and poetry. The duet for
Athanaël and Thaïs, sung when they arrive at the oasis with
her in a state of exhaustion, is moving and simple, and it is
the best sustained section of the score. Deserving special
praise is the final scene, that of the death of Thaïs. The
composer knew wonderfully well how to seize the contrast
between the pious thoughts of Thaïs, who at the moment of
quitting life begins to perceive eternal happiness, and the
powerless rage of Athanaël, who, devoured by an impious
love, reveals to her, without her understanding or comprehending it, all the ardour of a passion that death alone
can extinguish in him. The touching phrases of Thaïs, the
despairing accents of Athanaël, interrupted by the desolate
chants of the nuns, companions of the dying woman,
provoke in the hearer a poignant and sincere emotion. That is
one of the finest pages we owe to the pen of M. Massenet. We
must point out especially the return of the beautiful violin
phrase which constitutes the foundation of the intermezzo of
the second act.   K.W.

[1] Nevertheless, most people have since found it, with the duet at the
oasis, the best movement in the score.   H.

LE JONGLEUR DE NOTRE DAME

Our Lady's Tumbler

Opera in three acts by Jules Massenet; text by M. Léna. Première at Monte Carlo, February 18, 1902, with Charles Maréchal, Renaud. First performed at the Opéra-Comique, Paris, 1904, with Maréchal, Allard, Fugère, Huberdeau (shortly afterwards the part of Jean was taken over by Mary Garden); Covent Garden, 1906, with Laffite, Gilibert, Serveilhac, Crabbé; New York, 1908, with Garden, Renaud, Dufranne; London Opera House, 1912, with Fer, Chadal, Combe. Revived Chicago, 1929, with Garden, Formichi, Cotreuil; la Scala, Milan, 1938, with Malipiero, Maugeri, Bettoni, conductor Marinuzzi; Colon, Buenos Aires, 1944, with Marzella, Romito, Damiani; la Fenice, Venice, 1948, with Malipiero.

CHARACTERS

Jean, *a tumbler* . . . . Tenor (Soprano)
Boniface, *cook at the monastery* . . . . Baritone
The Prior . . . . Bass
A poet-monk . . . . Tenor
A painter-monk . . . . Baritone
A musician-monk . . . . Baritone
A sculptor-monk . . . . Bass
Two angels . . . . Soprano, Mezzo-Soprano
Time: Fourteenth Century   *Place:* Cluny

Act I. The square of Cluny in the fourteenth century. The façade of the abbey can be seen. It is market-day, and dancing is going on in the square. A hurdy-gurdy is heard in the distance, and Jean, the tumbler, comes into view. He starts his patter, but is mocked by the crowd, and has no sort of success until in desperation and with a bad conscience he sings the so-called 'Alleluiah du vin', in which the chorus joins happily. They are interrupted by the Prior, furious at the near-sacrilege which has been committed just outside the monastery.

The Prior vents his wrath on Jean, who alone stays behind. When he finds that the blasphemer is disposed to regret his actions, the Prior bids him dedicate himself to the Virgin. Jean is doubtful about renouncing his freedom at so early a stage of his life; he has valued his liberty: 'Liberté! Liberté! c'est elle que mon cœur pour maîtresse a choisie.'

873

Jean's resolve to repent seems to be weakening, but he is
particularly anxious not to have to leave behind the cap and
bells, which have been the symbols of his trade. The Prior
turns on him with some asperity, but decides to make a last
attempt to win him over; he shows him the good things being
taken by Brother Boniface into the monastery; all are
destined for the monks' table. Boniface goes over the
splendid array of provisions which he has brought for the
greater glory of the Virgin and the greater comfort of her
servants: 'Pour la vierge'. The *Benedicite* is heard from inside
the monastery, and all cry 'A table'. Jean follows the others
inside.

Act II.   Interior of the abbey. Monks are at work. A
painter is finishing a statue of the Virgin, a musician is
rehearsing a hymn with the choir, Boniface prepares vegetables. Only Jean has nothing to do. To the Prior, he
confesses that he knows no Latin, and that the songs he used
to sing were all profane and in French. His fellow brethren
mock him for his idleness, and each advises him that his own
profession—be it painting, sculpture, poetry—is the only one
for him. The Prior is obliged to intervene and ask for some
concord in place of the dispute which seems to be growing.
Only Boniface, when the others have gone, tries to comfort
Jean; there are other things in life than art—and think of the
pride which seems to go with it. He tells him a story to
console him—the legend of the humble sage, which opened at
the request of the Virgin to hide the Saviour from the sight
of the soldiers sent to kill him, and in doing so outshone the
rose, which was too proud to perform the service asked of it:
'Fleurissait une rose'. The passage has become the best known
in the whole work.

Boniface reflects before dropping the subject that the sage
is of course extremely valuable in cooking, and he then leaves
to look after his kitchen. Jean is struck with what he has
heard, and begins to believe that even the humblest can serve
the Virgin in a way acceptable to her. Can he not do so
himself?

Act III.   The abbey chapel. The painted figure of the
Virgin, which we saw early in the previous scene, is now set
up, and the monks are singing a hymn. As they leave the
chapel, the painter who was responsible for the statue takes a
last look at his work. He is about to leave when he catches
sight of Jean, coming in with his tumbler's gear. He hides

fore Jean can see him, and watches while Jean prays at the altar. Jean takes off his monkish garb and arrays himself in his old clothes. He plays a few chords on his hurdy-gurdy, just as he had at his first entrance in the square—but the painter-monk waits for no more; Jean is mad, and he must run and tell the Prior.

In the meanwhile, Jean goes through his repertory, not without some lapses of memory, such as when he starts to hand round his begging bowl. He has not got very far before the Prior arrives, led by the monk who had first seen Jean at his strange occupation. Fortunately Boniface has come too, and he restrains the Prior whose immediate reaction is that Jean is committing sacrilege and must be stopped at once. Eventually Jean dances, just as the monks begin to arrive. They are all horrified by what they can see, but they stay out of sight of Jean, who goes on until he falls exhausted at the foot of the statue.

As they are about to rush forward and seize Jean as a malefactor, Boniface stops them and points to the Virgin, whose arm is miraculously extended to bless the man lying at her feet. Jean awakes from his trance to find the Prior and the others bending over him. He expects punishment, and cannot understand their talk of a miracle. With a last song of praise, he falls back dead.   H.

DON QUICHOTTE

Opera in five acts by Jules Massenet; text by Henri Cain, after Le Lorrain's play based on Cervantes's novel. Première Monte Carlo, February 19, 1910, with Lucy Arbell, Chaliapin, Gresse. First performed Paris, 1910, with Arbell, Vanni Marcoux, Fugère; London Opera House, 1912, with Kirlord, Lafont, Danse; New Orleans, 1912; New York, 1914, with Garden, Vanni Marcoux, Dufranne; Metropolitan, 1926, with Easton, Chaliapin, de Luca; Chicago, 1929, with Glade, Vanni Marcoux, Cotreuil. Revived Opéra Comique, 1931; Brussels, 1934; Opéra, Paris, 1947, with Renée Gilly, Vanni Marcoux, Musy, conductor Cluytens; Belgrade, 1956, with Čangalović (subsequently toured all over Europe including 1962 Edinburgh Festival).

CHARACTERS

La Belle Dulcinée .... Contralto
Don Quichotte .... Bass

Sancho .... Baritone
Pedro, *burlesquer* ⎫ *admirers of Dulcinée* .. ⎰ Soprano
Garcias, *burlesquer* ⎭   ⎱ Soprano
Rodriguez ⎫ *admirers of Dulcinée* .... ⎰ Tenor
Juan   ⎭   ⎱ Tenor
Two servants .... Baritone
Tenebrun, Chief, and other Bandits, friends of Dulcinée,
                        and others
Time: The Middle Ages.   *Place:* Spain

Act I.   Square in front of the house of Dulcinée, whose
beauty people praise in song. In the midst of the throng ride
Don Quichotte and his comical companion, Sancho. They
give money to the beggars who flock round them. Night and
moonlight. Don Quichotte serenades Dulcinée ('Quand
apparaissent les étoiles'), arousing the jealousy of Juan, a
lover of the professional beauty, who now appears and
prevents a duel. She is amused by the avowals of Don
Quichotte, and promises to become his beloved if he will
recover a necklace stolen from her by brigands.

Act II.   On the way to the camp of the brigands, Don
Quichotte composes a poem in Dulcinée's honour, much to
Sancho's exasperation. Here occurs the fight with the wind-
mill.

Act III.   Camp of the brigands. Don Quichotte attacks
them. Sancho retreats. The Knight is captured. He expects to
be put to death. But his courage, his grave courtesy, and his
love for his Dulcinée, deeply impress the bandits. They free
him and give him the necklace.

Act IV.   Fête at Dulcinée's. To the astonishment of all
Don Quichotte and Sancho put in an appearance. Dulcinée,
overjoyed at the return of the necklace, embraces the
Knight. He entreats her to marry him at once: 'Marchez dans
mon chemin'. Touched by his devotion, Dulcinée disillusions
him as to the kind of woman she is.

Act V.   A forest. Don Quichotte is dying. He tells Sancho
that he has given him the island he promised him in their
travels; the most beautiful island in the world—the 'Island of
Dreams'. In his delirium he sees and hears Dulcinée. The
lance falls from his hand. The gaunt figure in its rusty suit of
armour—no longer grotesque, but tragic—stiffens in death.

                                                K.W.

11
Russian Opera

MICHAEL
IVANOVICH GLINKA
(1804–1857)

A LIFE FOR THE TSAR[1]
Ivan Susanin

OPERA in four acts and an epilogue by Michael Ivanovich Glinka; text
by G. F. Rozen. Première December 9, 1836, St. Petersburg. This work
opened every new season at St. Petersburg and Moscow until 1917.
First performed la Scala, Milan, 1874; Covent Garden, 1887, with
Albani, Scalchi, Gayerre, Devoyod; Manchester, 1888 (in Russian);
San Francisco, 1936 (in Russian); Stuttgart, 1937; Berlin, Staatsoper,
1940, with Cebotari, Roswaenge, Prohaska; la Scala, 1959, with Scotto,
Raimondi, Christoff; San Carlo, Naples, 1967, with Adriana Maliponte,
Giorgio Casellato, Christoff.

CHARACTERS

Antonida, *Susanin's daughter* .... Soprano
Ivan Susanin, *a peasant* .... Bass
Sobinjin, *Antonida's Bridegroom* .... Tenor
Vanja, *an orphan boy adopted by Susanin* ... Contralto
A Polish Commander .... Baritone

Time: 1613   *Place:* Domnin, Moscow, and a Polish camp

Act I.   A village street at Domnin. The peasants sing a
patriotic song to celebrate the imminent return of Sobinjin
from the wars. Antonida, his fiancée, is no less glad, and in a

[1] Glinka originally called his opera *Ivan Susanin* and changed it
only after prompting from the Imperial Court to *A Life for the Tsar*.
Now in Soviet Russia (though not yet invariably outside) the original
title is used again.

877

cavatina she pours out her happiness at the prospect of seeing
him again. Susanin enters with news that is less to the taste of
the company; a Polish army is advancing on Moscow. The
chorus is alarmed, but their fears lessen when Sobinjin
himself appears and tells them that the Poles have in fact
been repulsed. He is anxious that his marriage with Antonida
should immediately be celebrated, but Susanin is full of
forebodings at the state of the country and will not bless
their union until a Tsar has been elected. Sobinjin finds this
objection easy to overcome; a Tsar has in fact just been
chosen, and it is no other than their own landlord,
Romanoff. Susanin withdraws his objections, and, amidst
general rejoicing, agrees to the wedding.

Act II. The Polish headquarters. A magnificent ball is in
progress, and the Poles are full of confidence that their
forthcoming campaign against the Russians will be crowned
with success. A series of dances follows, including a
Cracoviak and two Mazurkas. A messenger enters and tells
the Polish commander of the Polish defeat and of the
election of Romanoff as Tsar of Russia. The Poles plan to
capture the young Tsar at the monastery where he is at
present living.

Act III. Susanin's house. Vanja sings a song, and Susanin
joins in to comment on Russia's present happy state. He goes
on to say that he hears rumours that the Poles are planning to
capture the young Tsar. Vanja and Susanin look forward to
the day when the boy will be old enough to take his place
amongst Russia's soldiers. Peasants enter to congratulate
Antonida and Sobinjin on their wedding, and a quartet
follows for Antonida, Vanja, Sobinjin, and Susanin.

In the middle of the rejoicing Polish troops enter and try
to force Susanin to tell them the way to the monastery where
the Tsar lives. Susanin at first refuses, but then manages to
convey to Vanja that he must ride ahead to warn the Tsar
while Susanin himself leads the Poles out of their way. He
pretends to accept their bribe, and goes off with them much
to the despair of Antonida, who comes in just in time to see
her father taken off.

She tells Sobinjin of the disaster which has come upon
them; he does his best to console her, and gathers together a
band of peasants with whom he goes off in an attempt to
rescue Susanin.

Act IV. A forest, at night. Sobinjin's men are dis-
heartened by the intense cold, but in a vigorous aria he

23 Chaliapin as Boris Godounov.

24 Josephine Barstow (Salome) and Emile Belcourt (Herod) in
Joachim Herz's production of *Salome* for English National
Opera, 1975.

restores their confidence. Glinka composed an alternative version for this scene, and set it in the forest near the monastery. Vanja, who has ridden his horse to death, rushes in, knocks at the monastery doors and convinces the servants of the danger which threatens the Tsar's life.

The scene changes to another part of the forest. Everything is covered in snow, and the Poles accuse Susanin of having lost the way. He denies it, and they light a fire before settling down to rest for the night. Susanin is left alone, and in a famous scene he makes up his mind that it is his duty to give his life for his country. A storm blows up, the Poles awake, and, as day dawns, Susanin tells them that he has deliberately led them astray into the wildest part of the forest; the Tsar is safe and beyond their reach. They kill him.

Epilogue. A street in Moscow. Everyone is festively dressed and they sing the praises of the Tsar. Antonida, Vanja, and Sobinjin join the crowd. The news of Susanin's death has reached the capital, and the crowd shares the grief of his dependants.

The scene changes to a square in front of the Kremlin. The Tsar's procession can be seen entering the capital.   H.

RUSSLAN AND LUDMILA

Opera in five acts by Michael Ivanovich Glinka, text by V. F. Shirkov and K. A. Bakhturin after Pushkin. Première December 9, 1842, at St. Petersburg. First performed London, Lyceum Theatre, 1931, with Lissitchkina, Rebane, Pozemkovsky, Kaidanoff; Berlin, Staatsoper, 1951, with Keplinger, Müller, Hülgert, Wolfram, conductor Quennet; New York, 1942 (in concert); Hamburg, 1969, with Scovotti, Boese, Judith Beckmann, Schultz, Hubert Hofmann, Mangin, conductor Mackerras.

CHARACTERS

Svietosar, *prince of Kiev* .... Bass
Ludmila, *his daughter* .... Soprano
Russlan, *a knight* .... Baritone
Ratmir, *oriental prince* .... Contralto
Farlaf, *a warrior* .... Bass
Gorislava, *Ratmir's slave* .... Soprano
Finn, *a good fairy* .... Tenor
Naina, *a bad fairy* .... Mezzo-Soprano
Bayan, *a bard* .... Tenor
Tchernomor, *an evil dwarf*

Michael Ivanovich Glinka's second opera is based upon one of Pushkin's earliest poems. The poet had hardly agreed to prepare a dramatic version of his fairy-tale for the composer when he was killed in a duel incurred owing to the supposed infidelity of his wife. As a result of Pushkin's untimely end, Glinka employed the services of no less than five different librettists.

The opera opens with an entertainment held by the Grand Duke of Kiev in honour of his daughter Ludmila's suitors. A bard prophesies wonders in the future in connection with Ludmila and Russlan, and Ludmila herself welcomes her suitors and sings of her reluctance to leave her own home and the music which has been her joy in it. Of the three suitors, Russlan, a knight, Ratmir, an Oriental poet, and Farlaf, a blustering coward, Russlan is the favoured one. A thunderclap followed by sudden darkness interrupts the festivities. When this is over, Ludmila has disappeared. After a canon for Ludmila's father and her three suitors, Svietosar promises her hand in marriage to anyone who will rescue her.

The second act takes place in the cave of Finn, the wizard, to whom Russlan has come for advice. The knight hears that the abduction is the work of Tchernomor the dwarf. Finn warns him against the interference of Naina, a wicked fairy. He then starts out on his search. The next scene shows Farlaf in consultation with Naina. Here occurs Farlaf's famous *Rondo*, a brilliant patter song. The fairy advises him to neglect Ludmila until she is found by Russlan, then carry her off again. The next scene shows Russlan on a battle-field. He muses on the silent field: perhaps death will come as silently, and he will hear no more of the singing in which he delights. In spite of the mist he finds a lance and shield. When the atmosphere grows clearer he discovers a gigantic head, which by its terrific breathing creates a storm. The head is represented musically by a chorus which sings inside it. Russlan subdues the head with a stroke of his lance. Under it is the magic sword which will make him victorious over Tchernomor. The head then explains that its condition is due to its brother, the dwarf, and reveals to Russlan the use to be made of the sword.

Act III. The enchanted palace of Naina. Nymphs sing a chorus of enticement. Gorislava, who loves Ratmir, appears. When the object of her passion appears he slights her for a siren of Naina's court. Russlan, too, is imperilled by the sirens, but he is saved from their fascination by Finn.

The fourth act takes place in the dwelling of Tchernomor. Ludmila, in despair, refuses to be consoled by any distraction. She finally falls asleep, only to be awakened by Tchernomor and his train. The arrival of Russlan interrupts the ensuing ballet. Forcing Ludmila into a trance, Tchernomor meets Russlan in single combat. The knight is victorious, but unable to awaken Ludmila from her sleep. He carries her off.

In the fifth act Russlan, with a magic ring, the gift of Finn, breaks Tchernomor's spell and restores Ludmila to consciousness.   K.W.

ALEKSANDR PORFYREVICH BORODIN
(1834–1887)

PRINCE IGOR

OPERA in a prologue and four acts by Borodin; text by the composer after a play by V. V. Stassov; completed by Rimsky-Korsakov and Glazunov. Première November 4, 1890, at St. Petersburg. First performed London, Drury Lane, 1914, with Kousnetzoff, Petrenko, Andreev, Chaliapin; Metropolitan, New York, 1915, with Alda, Amato, Didur; Covent Garden, 1919 (in English), with Licette, Thornton, Millar, Edmund Burke, Allin, conductor Coates. Revivals include Berlin, 1930, with Branzell, Roswaenge, Schorr, Scheidl, conductor Blech; Covent Garden, 1935, with Rethberg, Branzell, Kullman, Janssen, Kipnis, conductor Beecham; 1937, with Karnika (later Lissitchkina), Renée Gilly, Burdino, Noble, Bernasconi, conductor Goossens; la Scala, 1940, with Scuderi, Alfano, Fratesi, Sved, di Lelio, conductor Capuana; Vienna, 1947, with Hilde Konetzni, Nikolaidi, Rothmüller, Alsen, conductor Krips; la Scala, 1964, by Bolshoi Opera with Victor Nechipailo, Ivan Petrov; Montreal (EXPO 1967), by Bolshoi Company with Kiselyev; New York, City Opera, 1969.

CHARACTERS

Igor Sviatoslavich, *Prince of Seversk* . . . . Baritone
Yaroslavna, *his wife* . . . . Soprano

Vladimir Igorevich, *Igor's son* . . . . Tenor
Vladmir Yaroslavich, *Prince Galitzky, brother
  of Yaroslavna* . . . . Bass
Kontchak ⎱ *Polovtsian Khans* . . . . Bass
Gzak   ⎰
Kontchakovna, *Kontchak's daughter* . . .Mezzo-Soprano
Ovlour, *a Polovtsian* . . . . Tenor
Skoula ⎱ *Gudok players* . . . . ⎰ Bass
Eroshka⎰   ⎱ Tenor
Yaroslavna's Nurse . . . . Soprano
A young Polovtsian Maiden . . . . Soprano
   Russian Princes and Princesses, Boyars and their
   Wives, Old Men, Russian Warriors, Young Women,
   People; Polovtsian Chiefs, Kontchakovna's Women,
   Slaves of Khan Kontchak, Russian Prisoners of War,
   Polovtsian Troops

Time: 1185   *Place:* The town of Poutivl,
                                         the Polovtsian camp

Borodin, who divided his life between science and music,
wrote his opera piece by piece. Rimsky-Korsakov wrote that
he often found him working in his laboratory that communicated directly with his house. 'When he was seated before
his retorts, which were filled with colourless gases of some
kind, forcing them by means of tubes from one vessel to
another, I used to tell him that he was spending his time in
pouring water into a sieve. As soon as he was free he would
take me to his living-rooms and there we occupied ourselves
with music and conversation, in the midst of which Borodin
would rush off to the laboratory to make sure that nothing
was burning or boiling over, making the corridor ring as he
went with some extraordinary passage of ninths or seconds.
Then back again for more music and talk.'

Borodin, himself, wrote: 'In winter I can only compose
when I am too unwell to give my lectures. So my friends,
reversing the usual custom, never say to me, "I hope you are
well" but "I do hope you are ill." At Christmas I had
influenza, so I stayed at home and wrote the Thanksgiving
Chorus in the last act of *Igor*.'

He never finished his opera. It was completed by Rimsky-
Korsakov and his pupil Glazunov, and three years after his
death received its first performance. Borodin never wrote
down the overture, but Glazunov heard him play it so
frequently that it was an easy matter for him to orchestrate it
according to Borodin's wishes. The composer left this note

about his opera: 'It is curious to see how all the members of our set agree in praise of my work. While controversy rages amongst us on every other subject, all, so far, are pleased with *Igor*—Moussorgsky, the ultra-realist, the innovating lyrico-dramatist, Cui, our master, Balakirev, so severe as regards form and tradition, Vladimir Stassov himself, our valiant champion of everything that bears the stamp of novelty or greatness.'

The overture is composed entirely of music heard later. It opens with the music which precedes Igor's great aria in the second act, continues with themes later associated with Khan Kontchak and Kontchakovna, before reaching the impassioned No. 1:

and No. 2:

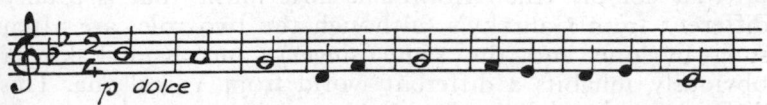

The Prologue takes place in the market-place of Poutivl, where rules Igor, Prince of Seversk. Although implored to postpone his departure because of an eclipse of the sun, which his people regard as an evil omen, Igor with his son Vladimir departs to pursue the Polovtsi, a Tartar tribe, formerly driven to the plains of the Don by Igor's father, Prince Sviatoslav of Kiev.

Act I takes place in the house of Prince Vladimir Galitzky, brother of Igor's wife, Yaroslavna. Galitzky in Igor's absence has been appointed to govern Poutivl and watch over the Princess Yaroslavna. He is popular with the crowd, on account of his easy-going, profligate ways. In an incisive, vigorous aria, which perfectly sets off his irresponsible character, he makes it clear that he is a man of mettle, and one to be reckoned with.

Some young girls venture into Galitzky's presence to appeal for his help and protection against his hangers-on, who have abducted one of them. He refuses to take any steps in the matter. Skula and Eroshka, a pair of drunken *Gudok* players who have deserted from Igor's army, try to stir up the mob against their absent chief. They sing the praises of their patron, Galitzky, and demand rhetorically to know why he should not become their prince and rule over them.

The scene changes to Yaroslavna's room, where the same party of girls as had failed to enlist Galitzky's sympathy comes to ask for aid. This is preceded by a beautiful, warm arioso passage for Yaroslavna alone. That she is a match·for her brother she proves a moment later when he enters her room. She compels him to agree to give up the girl who was abducted.

In the finale, an account is given of the disasters which have befallen Igor—he has been defeated, he and the young prince are prisoners, and the enemy is marching on Poutivl. The alarm bell is sounded, but the act ends on a note of defiance, the loyal boyars swearing to defend Yaroslavna, their princess.

Act II takes place in the camp of the Polovtsi. In this and the next act, Borodin has been highly successful in giving his music (to our western ears at any rate) something of an oriental colour. Khan Kontchak sings music that is totally different from Galitzky's (although the two roles are often sung by one and the same singer), and Kontchakovna obviously inhabits a different world from Yaroslavna. This difference is immediately apparent in the opening scene, when the young Polovtsian maidens sing their languorous song to their mistress. They dance for her, but the day is drawing to an end, and she puts an end to their activities, and herself sings a beautiful nocturne whose languishing, chromatic melody speaks longingly of love: 'Now the day-light dies'.

Kontchakovna sees a group of Russian prisoners coming into the camp, and bids her women give them water to drink. The prisoners sing their thanks, and move on towards captivity, followed by the Polovtsian guards. Prince Vladimir, Igor's son, has already fallen in love with the Khan's daughter, and he expresses his feelings in an aria of exquisite beauty, 'Daylight is fading away'. As Ernest Newman has said, this melody would in itself provide an excuse for the love interest which Borodin has introduced at this point, but the passionate duet which follows is hardly less successful, and the whole episode, by no means central to Igor's story, seems entirely justified by the beautiful music it has caused Borodin to write.

Kontchakovna tells Vladimir that she is confident her father will not oppose their marriage, but Vladimir is sure Igor will not even consider giving his approval to a match with the daughter of his enemy. They leave as Igor approaches, filled with longing for his homeland, and walks through the camp where he is held prisoner. At his approach, we hear the music which began the overture. He sings desperately of his past happiness and present misery (No. 1), and longs for freedom to re-establish his glory and to ensure the safety of his people. There is tenderness in his reference to Yaroslavna (No. 2), but his *scena* dies away in a mood of despair.

To him comes the Tartar traitor Ovlour, and, in music of insinuating character, offers to help him escape. He refuses— honour prevents him taking such a course, however much he may be tempted.

Hardly has Ovlour gone than Khan Kontchak himself appears before Igor. In a great bass *scena*, the Khan offers the Prince anything he may desire to make his captivity less irksome. He looks upon him as an honoured guest, not as a prisoner; will he choose hawks, horses, a finer tent, slaves? Igor answers that nothing in his captivity irks him—only his loss of liberty. Even liberty the Khan will restore him, if he will pledge his word not to make war on him again. Why should they not unite? Together the world would be at their feet. But Igor admits that if he were given his freedom, his first action would be to raise an army and march against the Tartars who threaten the peace of his land. The Khan appears to like his guest's frankness, and gives orders that the dancing slaves should be brought in to perform for their joint entertainment.

Now begin the famous Polovtsian dances, known from frequent performance with or without the chorus (which is in reality an integral part of them), in concert hall, and as a separate ballet. In scope they range from soft enticing melody to harsh vigour, with more than a touch of the barbaric in it. The name of *Prince Igor* is familiar to probably 1,000 people who know the dances to every one who knows the opera. In context, they make a thrilling finale to an act whose varied musical spendours constitute perhaps Borodin's most enduring memorial.

Act III. The prelude is a savage Polovtsian march, occasionally heard in the concert hall. In the theatre it continues, augmented by the chorus, to accompany the entrance of Khan Gzak and his warriors, who like Kontchak, have been victorious over their Russian foes, and who bring in their train a crowd of prisoners. We see the primitive side of Kontchak's character in the vigorous and triumphant aria in which he welcomes his brothers-in arms and rejoices in the slaughter and devastation they have left behind them. The sound of trumpets announces the division of the spoils, as the two Khans go off to make new plans for their campaigns against the Russians. The Tartars keep up the mood of urgency sounded by Kontchak's aria, but the Russians, when they are left alone by their captors, lament the state into which their country has fallen. Is it not the duty of Igor, they ask, to escape from captivity and lead his countrymen to revenge and freedom? Igor is persuaded that he must sacrifice honour to duty.

In celebration of their victory, the Polovtsi guards make merry, and it is not long before they are in a drunken state, though still capable of rolling out another chorus in praise of their invincible leaders. It is Ovlour's chance. He settles the details of the escape with Igor and Vladimir and arranges to meet them with the horses he has in waiting on the other side of the river. But Kontchakovna has had word that an escape is plotted, and she is full of reproaches, not at the treachery which is planned but that Vladimir should be prepared to leave her without so much as an attempt to take her with him. She pleads that the voice of love should be heard as well as that of duty. Vladimir is undecided, but his father hears what Kontchakovna is suggesting, and a fine trio ensues, in which Igor (to the tune of No. 1) opposes his will to Kontchakovna's. The Khan's daughter finally has recourse to a desperate expedient, and rouses the camp. Igor escapes, but Vladimir is left behind in the hands of the Polovtsi.

The Polovtsi pursue Igor, and at first cry for the death of Vladimir, in spite of the pleas of Kontchakovna. However, Kontchak appears on the scene, and admits his admiration for Igor; in his position, he would have followed the same course. In a couple of phrases, he shows both sides of his simple yet complex nature; let them hang the guards who should have prevented Igor's flight, but may Vladimir be spared to live amongst them as Kontchakovna's husband, and their ally. A chorus of praise to Kontchak brings the act to an end.

Act IV. The city walls and public square of Poutivl.

Yaroslavna laments her lost happiness. Her plaintive phrases eventually give way to the passionate theme associated with Igor's love for her (No. 2). After the extensive *scena* for Yaroslavna, who sits absorbed in her gloomy thoughts, some peasants pass by, at least as full of their own woes as she is of hers. There seems no hope in their plight.

But the tide is due to turn for the Russians. Yaroslavna sees in the distance two horsemen riding furiously towards the city; one of them seems arrayed like a prince, the other is evidently from his dress a Polovtsian. Is this a good or evil omen? Dare she hope that this is her husband returned, perhaps with good news? She recognises Igor, and in a moment they are in each other's arms. Their duet is rapturous with delight, and they go off together towards the citadel, pausing however in front of the gate of that building just as Eroshka and Skoula come into sight, slightly drunk as is their habit, and giving vent to disloyal sentiments on the subject of their rightful prince. Igor is the cause of all their woes, they sing—but they are filled with consternation when they recognise the subject of their conversation standing only a few yards from them. What is to be done? Their cause is lost! Shall they go into voluntary exile to escape the penalty that must surely be theirs? No! The thought of enforced wandering is hardly less repugnant than the possibility of death; let them stay, and brave it out.

Borodin was much too fond of his drunken rascals to let them finish the opera with anything but a flourish (cf. Moussorgsky with Varlaam and Missail), and Eroshka and Skoula duly emerge on top when they announce the return of Igor to his as yet unsuspecting subjects. They are hailed as at any rate partially responsible for the joy which has come to the city—were they not the first to notice Igor? — and they are allowed to participate in the finale (marked *allegro marziale*), in which the return of Igor and the imminent fall of Galitzky are jointly celebrated.

Borodin did not 'finish' *Prince Igor* (although he wrote all the music) and the kind of revision to which a composer of an epic of this sort might be expected to subject his work was not available to him. The organisers of modern performances are faced with a dilemma when confronted with an opera which sprawls (as to my mind does *Prince Igor*) and which yet contains music of such evident value. Some have revised it entirely as did Eugene Goossens for Covent Garden in

1937, others have simply omitted Act III entirely, thus bringing the opera within manageable length while omitting little of the drama though much that is of musical value (some was included at the New York City Opera in 1969). A final—even an interim—editorial solution has not yet been reached, hardly even attempted.   K.W., H.

MODEST
PETROVICH
MOUSSORGSKY
(1839–1881)

BORIS GODOUNOV

OPERA in a prologue and four acts by Modest Moussorgsky; text from Pushkin's play of the same name and Karamzin's *History of the Russian State*. There have been no less than four main versions of *Boris*, two by Moussorgsky and two by Rimsky-Korsakov, quite apart from various more recent attempts to prepare performing versions. (A), composed and orchestrated between October 1868 and December 1869, consisted of seven scenes: Courtyard of Novodevichy Monastery; Coronation; Pimen's cell; the inn; the Tsar's apartments; before the Cathedral of St. Basil in Moscow (including the simpleton); death of Boris. This version was submitted to the committee of the Imperial theatres and rejected by them. (B) Moussorgsky immediately started on a second version, accepting the advice of his friends during composition, and finishing by June 1872. In February 1872 the Coronation scene was performed by Napravnik at a concert, and in April Balakirev conducted the Polonaise. This version was also rejected by the committee, but the inn scene and the two scenes of the Polish act were performed publicly in February 1873 at the Marinsky Theatre with Petrov, the most famous Russian bass of his day, as Varlaam, Komissarzhevsky as Dimitri, Platonova as Marina; the rest of the programme consisted of Act I of *Freischütz* and Act II of *Lohengrin*. As a result of the success of this performance, the entire opera (though with a number of important cuts) was performed on January 27/February 8, 1874, with Melnikov as Boris, and Petrov, Komissarzhevsky, and Platonova in the parts they had played in 1873; Napravnik conducted, and the opera was a great success with the public, although damned by the critics. By 1882 it had dropped from the repertory. In 1896 Rimsky-Korsakov revised and re-scored the work, making a large number of cuts and composing some new passages to bridge the gaps caused by the cuts. This (C) was performed in 1896; in 1899 by the Mamontov Company, with Chaliapin in the title role; and in 1904 at the Imperial Theatres, again with Chaliapin in the title role. In 1906–8, Rimsky-Korsakov worked on another edition of the opera (D) in which he restored the cuts he had previously made, and retained his own additions to the score. It is in version (D) that the opera has most often been performed.

(D) First produced Paris Opéra, 1908, and la Scala, Milan, 1909, with Chaliapin; Metropolitan, New York, 1913, with Didur, conductor Toscanini; London, Drury Lane, 1913, with Chaliapin; Aldwych, London (in English), 1916. Revived, Metropolitan, 1921, with Chaliapin; 1939, with Pinza; 1943, with Kipnis; la Scala, 1922, with Vanni Marcoux, conductor Toscanini; 1930, with Chaliapin; 1941, with Pasero; 1949, with Christoff, conductor Dobrowen; Covent Garden, 1928, with Chaliapin. In 1935 Moussorgsky's (A) was performed at Sadler's Wells, London (in English), with Ronald Stear as Boris; in 1948, Moussorgsky's (B) was produced at Covent Garden (in English), with Silveri in the title role; in 1949 Christoff sang the title role, in 1950 (by which time a retrograde step to Rimsky-Korsakov's (D) had been made) Weber was Boris, and in 1952 Rossi-Lemeni sang the title role; in 1958, a reversion to substantially (B) was made under Kubelik and with Christoff, but this included the St. Basil scene as well as the Forest of Kromy, the Idiot's utterances being cut from the latter. In Karajan's spectacular production at Salzburg in 1965, Ghiaurov sang the title role with Jurinac, Uzunov, Stolze, Gyuselev, Diakov.

CHARACTERS

Boris Godounov . . . . Bass
Feodor, *his son* . . . . Mezzo-Soprano
Xenia, *his daughter* . . . . Soprano
The Old Nurse . . . . Contralto
Prince Shouisky . . . . Tenor
Andrey Tchelkalov, *clerk of the Douma* . . . . . . Baritone
Pimen, *monk and chronicler* . . . . Bass
The Pretender Dimitri, *called Grigory* . . . . Tenor
Marina Mnishek, *a Polish Princess* . . . . Soprano
Rangoni, *a Jesuit in disguise* . . . . Bass
Varlaam ⎱ *vagabonds* . . . . ⎰ Bass
Missail ⎰ . . . . ⎱ Tenor
The Hostess of the Inn . . . . Mezzo-Soprano
Nikitich (Michael), *constable* . . . . Bass
The Idiot . . . . Tenor
Two Jesuits . . . . Bass
Time: 1598–1605   *Place:* Russia and Poland

The subject brings to the stage one of the most curious episodes of the history of Russia in the sixteenth and seventeenth centuries. Boris Godounov, the brother-in-law and chief minister of Tsar Feodor, son of Ivan, has caused to be assassinated the young Dimitri, half-brother of the Tsar and his heir. On the death of Feodor, Boris, who has committed his crime with the sole object of seizing power, has himself acclaimed by the people and ascends the throne. But about the same time, a young monk named Grigory escapes from his monastery, discards his habit, and goes to Poland where he passes as the dead Tsarevich Dimitri. The Polish government receives him all the more cordially as it understands the advantage such an event might afford it. Soon the pretended Dimitri, who has married the daughter of the Voyevode of Sandomir, puts himself at the head of the Polish army and marches with it against Russia. Just at this moment they hear of the death of Boris, and the false Dimitri, taking advantage of the circumstances, in turn usurps power.

As a matter of historical fact, Boris's son Feodor was murdered and his daughter Xenia taken by Dimitri as his mistress (Dvořák's opera *Dmitrij* deals with these events). Dimitri's tenure of power was not long, as he was deposed and killed by Shouisky, who reigned in his stead. History has acquitted Boris of the crime of murdering Feodor (although for the purposes of the opera it must of course be accepted as true), but Shouisky goes down as an ambitious and cruel Tsar. Marina seems to have been all that is implied in the opera; after the death of Dimitri, she became the wife of yet another pretender to the throne, whom she claimed to recognise as her lost husband.

Of the poetical drama, a historian of Russian music, himself a composer, César Cui, has written: 'There is no question here of a subject of which the different parts, combined in such a way as to present a necessary sequence of events, one flowing from the other, correspond in their totality to the ideas of a strict dramatic unity. Each scene in it is independent; the roles, for the greater part, are transitory. The episodes that we see follow each other necessarily have a certain connection; they all relate more or less to a general fact, to a common action; but the opera would not suffer from a rearrangement of the scenes nor even from a substitution of certain secondary episodes by others. This depends on the fact that *Boris Godounov* properly speaking

is neither a drama nor an opera, but rather a musical
chronicle after the manner of the historical dramas of
Shakespeare. Each of the acts, taken separately, awakens a
real interest which, however, is not caused by what goes
before and which stops brusquely without connection with
the scene which is going to follow.' Let us add that some of
these scenes are written entirely in prose while others are in
verse and we will have a general idea of the make-up of the
libretto of *Boris Godounov*, which moreover offered the
composer a series of scenes very favourable to music.

K.W.

Prologue.   After a short prelude the curtain goes up to
show the courtyard of the Monastery of Novodevichy, near
Moscow. It is crowded with people, who are ordered by a
police officer to keep up a prayer for guidance. The moment
his back is turned they show clearly by their talk among
themselves that they are in entire ignorance of why they are
there at all. The prayer rises to a frenzy of wailing, but is
interrupted by the appearance of Tchelkalov, the secretary of
the Douma, who informs them that Boris has not yet yielded
to the petitions of the government and people, who urge him
to accept the crown.

The sound of pilgrims nearing the monastery can be heard,
and they distribute alms and relics to the people as they pass
through their midst.

The second scene of the prologue is laid in the courtyard
of the Kremlin in Moscow. Facing the spectators in the
background is the Red Staircase leading to the Tsar's apartments; on the right and near the front, the people on their
knees occupy the space between the two Cathedrals of the
Assumption and the Archangel. The porches of both churches
are in view.

Bells are pealing and a procession of boyars and guards
crosses the stage. Prince Shouisky cries 'Long life to thee,
Tsar Boris Feodorovich', and the people break into a
splendid song in praise of the new Tsar. Boris himself
appears, and, in a mood that is introspective rather than
triumphant, prays for the guidance of Tsar Feodor in his
great task; may he justify the people's confidence during the
reign that is just beginning. He bids the boyars come with

him to pray before the tombs of Russia's departed rulers; after prayer, the people from beggar to prince shall feast as his guests. The people break out again into acclamation, and the curtain falls.

Act I. It is five years since Boris's coronation. The background to the story is one of famine and plague, and the people have deserted the ways of law and order and taken to pillage. For Russia's misfortunes, for the death of his sister, Tsar Feodor's widow, for the death of his prospective son-in-law, Boris is blamed—and this in spite of his efforts to rule wisely and well.

The scene is a cell in the monastery of Chudov, where the old monk, Pimen, is engaged on his chronicle of the history of Russia. It is late at night, but Pimen is satisfied that he has reached the end of his labours. He will be able to leave his history to be continued in the future by some monk, as anonymous and little anxious for personal glory as himself. The sound of chanting can be heard from another part of the monastery, and suddenly Grigory, Pimen's young companion in his cell, wakes up. For the third time he has dreamed that he stood on the top of a high tower from which he could see all Moscow lying at his feet. The crowd below mocked him with their laughter, and he, overcome with shame and terror, fell from the tower and awoke from his dream (the reference is to a version of Dimitri's murder; he is thought to have been thrown down from a high tower).

Pimen tries to comfort him, and persuade him to resign himself to a life of contemplation. He himself, before he became a monk and was still young, had fought in the armies of Tsar Ivan the Terrible and lived a sinful life of fighting and feasting. Grigory continues to lament that his whole life has been spent inside the walls of the monastery, that he has never known action and the world. Pimen reminds him that many of Russia's most famous warriors turned to a solitary existence to end their days in peace, not least of them war-like Ivan himself, who died in this very cell. The last Tsar, Feodor, was a man of peace, but now God has sent to Russia the fierce Tsar Boris, a regicide. At this, Grigory asks Pimen how old would have been Dimitri, brother of Feodor, had he lived. Pimen tells him that he would have been about his own age, nearly twenty (in version (A) Moussorgsky included a passage in which Pimen described the scene after the murder of the young Tsarevich at Uglich, but this was

omitted from version (B)). The orchestra gives out a theme
which is later to be associated both with Grigory's ambition
and the murdered Dimitri, whom he pretends to be:

Pimen expresses his hope that Grigory will carry on his
work of chronicler when he is dead and gone, and, the bell
for matins being heard, he leans on Grigory's arm as he goes
to the door of the cell. Grigory remains behind; Boris shall
not escape the judgment of heaven for his crime, he says.

The second scene is set in an inn on the Lithuanian border
of Russia. The hostess sings a little song, half ribald in
content, half nonsense. She is interrupted by the sound of
singing from outside, and sees that her visitors are monks.
When they enter, they are seen to be as disreputable a pair of
vagabonds as ever took to the road; their names are Varlaam
and Missail, and their time is spent, by their own admission,
mainly in begging and converting the proceeds into good
liquor. With them is Grigory, who has fled from his
monastery, and is even now on his way to Lithuania and
freedom, pursued, owing to an unguarded remark of his own
before leaving the monastery, by the police, who have orders
to apprehend him.

The hostess provides her reverend guests with wine, and,
warmed by it, Varlaam launches into a ferocious song about
his achievements as a soldier in Ivan the Terrible's army at
the battle of Kazan. It is a moment of splendid vigour.
Varlaam curses Grigory for not joining him in either drink or
song, and becomes positively maudlin in his reflections.
Meanwhile, Grigory takes the hostess aside and questions her
on the best route to the Lithuanian border. She tells him that
patrols are out because of some fugitive monk from Moscow,
but confides that there is a safe road by which he may reach
his goal unobserved.

Varlaam continues to sing and he is obviously on the verge
of falling asleep when the room is suddenly full of the guards
of whom the hostess has just been complaining to Grigory
that they never catch their man and serve only to annoy
peaceful citzens like herself. They question Grigory, who
strikes them as harmless enough, then turn their attention to
the vagabond monks, who seem well enough to fit the

description of the man they are after. Varlaam and Missail are perfectly accustomed to such cross-questioning, and their answers have the whine of long experience about them. The captain of the police hands the warrant to Varlaam and orders him to read it, but he pleads lack of practice. Grigory is instructed to read it aloud; he does so, substituting a description of Varlaam for what is written on the paper. When they surround the old monk, he says he will make an effort to decipher the paper, which plainly does not say what Grigory has read out, since he is not the renegade they are after. With much difficulty he spells out the correct sense, and all realise that Grigory is their man. He jumps out of the window and escapes.

Act II. The Tsar's apartments in the Kremlin. The Tsarevich Feodor is sitting reading, while his sister Xenia sings sadly to herself of the husband who died before they were ever married. The Nurse tries to comfort her, then sings a nursery song about a gnat. Feodor complains that it is a very depressing song, and leads another, a clapping game, in which the Nurse joins. As it reaches its climax the Tsar himself appears, the Nurse is overcome with terror and vainly tries to explain to Boris that she is an old woman and easily frightened. Boris comforts his daughter in her sadness, and goes over to where his son is looking at a map of the Russian empire. He bids him take his lessons seriously; the time may soon come when he will be called on to rule over the countries he sees outlined on this map.

In his son's presence Boris pours out his agony of mind, the doubts and torments which his rule over Russia has brought him, the enemies who conspire against him, the remorse which fills his soul when he recalls the murdered Dimitri. This great monologue ('I have attained the highest power') rises to a climax of intensity, then falls away as Boris himself sinks under the weight of conscience. Two themes should be quoted; the first is heard again during the scene of Boris's death:

the second is associated with his guilt in relation to the murdered Dimitri:

A noise is heard outside, and the Tsar sends Feodor to find out its cause. The boyar-in-waiting comes to ask for an audience on behalf of Prince Shouisky. Boris says he will see him. The boyar goes on to warn his master of the rumours that the disaffected nobles have been in touch with the Poles at Cracow, and that Shouisky himself is in league with them. A messenger has even arrived from Cracow . . . let him be arrested, says Boris. As the boyar leaves, Feodor returns, and explains to his father in a charming song that the fuss was about a parrot which escaped and flew at the maids in its panic. Boris is pleased with the way his son tells the story.

Shouisky comes in and is greeted with a storm of abuse from Boris, who accuses him of double-dealing, hypocrisy and treason. Shouisky brushes the accusations aside, but tacitly admits his correspondence with rebels. He has come he says to bring Boris grave news; a pretender has arisen in Poland, and has been publicly acknowledged by the King of Poland, and privately by the Pope. After assuring the Tsar that his throne is inviolate and protected by the love his people bear him, he adds that he is in duty bound to warn him that it is possible that the Russian people themselves might be attracted to the pretender's cause if he were to cross the border calling himself Dimitri and claiming to be the lost Tsarevich.

At mention of Dimitri's name the Tsar dismisses his son (illogically, Ernest Newman once rightly claimed, since he has already in his presence mentioned the death of his rival for the throne), and is alone with Shouisky. He orders him to confirm or deny that Dimitri's was the body which was buried at Uglich; does he now know the story that the dead can walk again? Shouisky makes as if to soothe his fears. The boy was in truth Dimitri, and he himself watched for five days while the bodies of the prince and the men killed by the crowd as his murderers lay on the cathedral steps. The others began to putrefy, but Dimitri's alone was as fresh as when it was killed, in spite of the blood-red circle round his neck. On Dimitri's face, an angelic smile was seen.

Boris can bear the story no more, and signs to Shouisky to leave him. Shouisky looks back as he goes out and sees Boris sink exhausted into a chair. He feels that he is suffocating, as much with terror and remorse as from lack of air. At this very moment a chiming clock (it is known that they were introduced into Russia in Boris's time) begins to strike. The figures begin to move, and Boris takes them for an apparition of the murdered child. His hysteria verges on madness, and he sinks sobbing to the floor as he prays to God for forgiveness. The sinister power of the music is extraordinary, and Ernest Newman has called it 'one of the most tremendous scenes in all opera'.

Act III. The Polish Act. The first scene is laid in the apartments of Marina Mnishek, daughter of the Voyevode of Sandomir. The girls amuse her with their songs, and she in turn sings of her ambition; she is not interested in love songs but in tales of heroic deeds. She dismisses her attendants and sings an air *alla mazurka*, in which she gives further vent to her ambitious plans particularly as they concern the pretender Dimitri, through whom she hopes to ascend the throne of Russia.

Her reveries are interrupted by the sudden appearance of Rangoni, a Jesuit, introduced into the story by Moussorgsky. He exhorts her to remember her duty to her faith when she is paramount ruler in Moscow; her aim must be to convert the heretic Russians to the true religion. Marina's angry objections are silenced when he protests that he is heaven's messenger and so the keeper of her soul.

The second scene is laid by a fountain in the garden of Mnishek at Sandomir; it takes place by moonlight. Dimitri has been given a rendezvous by Marina and as he waits for her, he sings ardently of his love. What has been described as an 'oily, snakelike motive' in the shape of a chromatic scale announces that Rangoni has sidled into view. He tells Dimitri (as Grigory is now known by all) that Marina loves him passionately, in spite of the insults she has had to bear on his account. He will lead Dimitri to his beloved, and in return asks for nothing more than that he shall be allowed to follow the Tsarevich and to watch over his spiritual welfare wherever he goes. Rangoni bids him hide as Mnishek's guests can be seen coming out of the house.

A polonaise is danced, during which the nobles pay court to Marina and plan their march on Moscow. Dimitri watches the scene with jealous eyes, and it stings him to a resolution he has not known before (this to a more heroic version of the

Dimitri theme). When Marina comes out into the garden, she finds him full of tender phrases and protestations, and it takes all her haughtiness and pride to sting him once again into a determined frame of mind, so that he reacts to her insults with a declaration of his intention immediately to lead an army on Moscow. Marina has got from him what she wanted, and she can afford in the famous love duet to fawn on him. Poor Dimitri was not hard to catch, and he takes Marina in his arms as he protests his love for her. At the moment of their embrace, Rangoni can be seen looking from his hiding-place, while the orchestra runs down his chromatic scale to show the triumph is neither Marina's nor Dimitri's, but his and his Church's. (Apart from the Polonaise and the duet, much of this act is often omitted in performance.)

Act IV. Moussorgsky, advised it is said by his friends, in version (B) placed the scene of Boris's death before the so-called revolutionary scene, thus implicitly making the Russian people the real protagonists of his drama. But it is more accurate to refer to (D) as Moussorgsky's latest work on the score, and to think of it as final and testamentary is perhaps an exaggeration. In (C) and (D), Rimsky-Korsakov reversed this order of things, and when his versions have been performed, the death of Boris finishes the opera and is preceded by the revolutionary scene.

In Moussorgsky's latest version then, the first scene of Act IV is set in the Granovitaya Palace in the Kremlin, where a session of the Douma is taking place, expressly summoned to discuss the measures necessary for repelling the invasion which is threatened. They seem more interested in deciding on the pretender's fate once he is in their hands than in suggesting means to catch him, but their deliberations are interrupted by the arrival of Prince Shouisky, just as they were beginning to complain that his absence deprives them of invaluable council. Straightaway he begins to tell them of the curious sight he saw the previous day, when leaving the Tsar's apartments. Boris was muttering to himself, and seemed to be trying to ward off some spectre, crying, as he did so, 'Away, away'.

No sooner has he uttered the word than Boris's own voice is heard outside, and the same word is on his lips. He staggers into the chamber and seems to see none of the boyars who watch him in frightened silence. Shouisky brings him to his senses, and he takes his seat on the throne, and prepares to

listen to the counsel of his boyars. But Shouisky begs to be
allowed to speak, and says that a holy man of great age is
waiting outside and desires to speak to the Tsar. Boris thinks
this may calm his overheated brain and orders that he be
admitted.

It is Pimen, and he tells a strange story. A shepherd, blind
since birth, was told in a dream to go to the tomb of the
Tsarevich Dimitri at Uglich and there to pray beside his
tomb. He did so, and immediately his sight was restored.
Boris is overcome with horror at this mention of Dimitri,
and, calling for light, falls unconscious into the arms of the
boyars. He understands that he is dying, and sends for his son
and for the *skhima* (it was customary for the Tsar to be
received into the Church as a monk before he died).

When Feodor arrives, Boris orders that they be left alone.
He bids farewell to his son, and tells him that he is lawful heir
to the throne of Russia. Let him beware of the nobles and
their plots, and let him care with his life for the Russian
people and for his sister Xenia, who will be under his
protection. He feels the hand of death upon him, and prays
to God that his children may be blessed. The sound of the
passing bell can be heard, and then, softly from behind the
scenes, the chant of monks praying for the repose of the
Tsar's soul. The boyars return to the chamber, and, with a
last cry of 'While I have breath I still am Tsar', Boris falls
dying in their midst.

Perhaps the opera owed its original popularity in the early
years of the twentieth century as much to Chaliapin's
performance of the title role as to anything else, and in
particular to his singing and acting of this death scene. But its
power is such and its effect so moving that it would be wrong
to think that only a Chaliapin can do it justice. It is likely to
stand for many years to come as one of the great scenes of
opera.

The second scene of Act IV is laid in a clearing in the
forest of Kromy. Dimitri has marched into Russia at the head
of his troops, and the country is in a chaotic state of famine
and pillage. It is hard to imagine the disorder and horror,
which are the natural consequences of war, better expressed
than in Moussorgsky's music for this scene. During its course,
the mob baits a landlord who has been a supporter of Boris
and whom they have captured. Children mock an idiot, who
sings a pathetic song:

They steal the few pence he has managed to collect. Varlaam and Missail chant the praises of Dimitri, and, when two Jesuits appear on the scene, denounce them to the crowd, which promptly prepares to string them up on an improvised gallows.

A procession passes across the scene, heralding the approach of Dimitri himself, followed by his troops. He releases the boyar and the Jesuits, and bids the people follow him to Moscow. Then, at the head of his troops and supporters, he leaves the stage. It is empty except for the idiot who has taken no part in welcoming the new Tsar. Seated on his stone, he bewails the fate of Russia; 'Woe and sorrow always, lament, Russian folk, poor hungry folk'.

The controversy over whether to use the Rimsky-Korsakov edition of the score or to return to Moussorgsky's version B—version A was heard at Sadler's Wells before the war—still seems to be unresolved. Though most authorities are agreed that the strength of the original, with its stark scoring, is considerably dissipated by Rimsky-Korsakov's bowdlerisation, managements seem disposed to continue with version D, mostly because singers already know it and are disinclined to re-learn their parts. Audiences which heard the opera when it was produced at Covent Garden in 1948 and 1958 will have some idea of the strength of the work in its original scoring. They will also remember that when a really powerful singing actor was found for the title role, considerable portions of Rimsky-Korsakov's scoring had to be introduced as the singer was unfamiliar with the original scoring. The prejudice in fact has still to be broken down, and there was for instance in 1975 no complete recording of (D).

What has been accepted wherever the work has been performed in virtually whatever version is the extraordinary power of characterisation which Moussorgsky's music possesses. Even as small a role as that of the boyar Tchelkalov (whose entire part consists of some thirty bars of music) appears to be a personality and not just a lay figure. The nurse, Feodor and Xenia are more developed, and such characters as Varlaam and Prince Shouisky are superbly portrayed with real economy. Boris himself is a towerin creation of demonic power, and to sing the role is the summi of ambition of every bass or bass-baritone with Slav tendencies in his make-up. No less remarkable is the way in which the crowd stands out as one of the main influences in the opera. I have never been convinced that it is projected with even greater force than the figure of Boris himself (as some maintain), but the understanding quality of the music Moussorgsky has written for it is extraordinary. *Boris* stands as the greatest operatic product of the Russian school. H.

KHOVANSHCHINA

The Khovansky Rising

Opera in five acts by Modest Moussorgsky; text by the composer and V. V. Stassov. Première February 21, 1886, at St Petersburg. Completed and orchestrated by Rimsky-Korsakov. Official première St. Petersburg, November 7, 1911, with Zbrueva, Lobinsky, Sharonoff, Chaliapin, conductor Coates; Paris, 1913, and London, Drury Lane, 1913, with Petrenko, Damaev, Zaporojetz, Chaliapin, conductor Cooper; Drury Lane, 1917 (in English); Covent Garden, 1919, with Thornton, Millar, Richardson, Allin, conductor Pitt; Paris, 1923, with Charmy, Laval, Journet, Huberty, conductor Koussevitsky; la Scala, Milan, 1926, with Bertana, Dolci, Sdanowsky, Journet; Philadelphia, 1928, with Fedotova, Windheim, Shvetz, Figaniak, conductor Grigaitis; Colon, Buenos Aires, 1933, with Stignani, Ziliani, Morelli, Vaghi; Florence Festival, 1948, with Pini, Parmeggiani, Inghilleri, Christoff, conductor Gui; la Scala, Milan, 1949, with Barbieri, Francesco Albanese, Inghilleri, Christoff, Rossi-Lemeni, conductor Dobrowen; Metropolitan, New York, 1950, with Stevens, Sullivan, Tibbett, Hines, conductor Cooper; Munich, 1956, with Töpper, Hopf, Holm, Metternich, Frick, Engen, cond. Fricsay; Edinburgh Festival, 1962, by Belgrade Company with Bugarinović, Čangalović; Covent Garden, London, 1963, in Shostakovich's version, with Elizabeth Vaughan, Monica Sinclair, Craig, Forbes Robinson, David Ward, Rouleau, conductor Silvestri; and 1972 in Russian in perhaps the first uncut performance anywhere, with Yvonne Minton, Robert Tear, Donald McIntyre, David Ward, Martti Talvela, conductor Edward Downes.

CHARACTERS

Prince Ivan Khovansky, *leader of the Streltsy Musketeers* .... Bass
Prince Andrew Khovansky, *his son* .... Tenor
Prince Vassily Galitsin .... Tenor
The Boyar Shaklovity .... Baritone

Dositheus, *Leader of the Old Believers* . . . . Bass
Martha, *young widow, an Old Believer* . . .Mezzo-Soprano
A Scrivener . . . . Tenor
Emma, *a young girl from the German quarter* . Soprano
Varsonofiev, *attendant upon Galitsin* . . . . Baritone
1st ⎫ *musketeers (Streltsy)* . . . . ⎰ Bass
2nd ⎭   ⎱ Bass
Kouzka, *a musketeer* . . . . Tenor
Streshniev . . . . Tenor
Susanna, *an Old Believer* . . . . Soprano
A Lutheran Pastor . . . . Baritone
Musketeers, Old Believers, Maids-in-Waiting and
Persian Slaves in the suite of Prince Ivan Khovansky,
Bodyguards of Peter the Great (Petrovtsy-Poteshny),
Populace

Time: 1682–9

Acts I, II, and III take place in Moscow; Scene i of Act IV
on the estate of Prince Khovansky; Scene ii in Moscow; Act
V in a wood near Moscow.

Moussorgsky's aim was to picture the struggle between the
old and the new in Russian life at the time of the assumption
of power by Peter the Great (1682– 9 is the period chosen).
On the one hand are the reactionary Princes Khovansky with
their Streltsy followers who engage in political strife with the
Regent (Galitsin's party); on the other, the Old Believers
under Dositheus, who had refused to accept the reforms
imposed as long before as 1654. The 'new' regime of Peter
the Great was victorious in its struggle against both the
Streltsy and the Old Believers, and it is with the outcome of
this clash rather than of those between the nobles and their
followers that *Khovanshchina* is concerned.

Moussorgsky, although he began the opera as early as
1872, did not live to finish it himself, the necessary work of
scoring and piecing together being done by Rimsky-
Korsakov, who also effected a number of changes in his 1883
edition. A more faithful edition by Shostakovich appeared in
1959.

Act I. There is a beautiful prelude beginning *andante
tranquillo*. The Red Square in Moscow at sunrise. Kouzka, a
musketeer,[1] lies half asleep on guard. A passing patrol sees

---

[1] Or *Streltsy*, a band of ill-disciplined troops, who had originally
put the Empress Sophia on the throne, but later led by Prince Ivan
Khovansky. Many of them were 'Old Believers'.

him and from their conversation it appears that the Streltsy were busy during the night 'making short work' of their opponents in the city. The Scrivener (public letter writer) comes to his place in the square where he is soon engaged by the Boyar Shaklovity who dictates a letter to the Tsar and his council warning them of the plots of Prince Khovansky and his son, who, aided by the Old Believers, would become Tsar. The letter must be anonymous and the Scrivener must forget that he wrote it. A mob arrives and forces the Scrivener to read them the proclamation the Streltsy have stuck on the pillar in the middle of the square. The chorus splendidly announces the arrival of Prince Khovansky and causes the Scrivener to quit his place in haste. The Prince arrives and addresses the people, telling them that treason is rife in Russia and that he is determined to crush the enemies of the Tsars. The people end with an invocation of the 'White Swan'. With the assent of the people he orders the Streltsy to patrol the city.

As soon as the procession has departed with the crowd, Emma enters followed by the Prince's son, Andrew Khovansky, who attempts to kiss her in spite of her resistance. Emma's alarm is allayed by the arrival of Martha, whom Andrew Khovansky has loved and left. Martha upbraids Andrew and bids him repent. The angry youth answers by attacking her with a dagger. But Martha is also armed and successfully parries the blow. The arrival of Andrew's father and his Streltsy puts an end to the quarrel. The old Prince likes Emma's looks and orders his guards to take charge of her. His son would rather kill the girl than see her in the hands of the Streltsy, and would do so but for Dositheus, who arrives in time to arrest Andrew's blow. The chief of the Old Believers restores peace. Martha takes Emma in her care and departs with her. Prince Khovansky and his Streltsy return to the Kremlin, while Dositheus and the Old Believers fall to prayer.

Act II. An apartment in the house of Prince Galitsin, councillor and one-time lover of the Tsarevna. The Prince is discovered reading a love-letter from the Tsarevna. His uneasy conscience tells him, however, not to trust to the favour of the ruler. Varsonofiev announces a Lutheran Pastor who complains of the ill-treatment of Emma by the Khovanskys, a private quarrel in which Galitsin says he cannot intervene. He has invited Martha to his house to cast his horoscope. Now she is announced by his attendant Varsonofiev. A bowl of

…ater is brought, and gazing intently at it, Martha in her
ɔ-called 'Divination', a celebrated and impressive passage,
tells of the disgrace and poverty that will be Prince Galitsin's
portion in the time that is coming. He dismisses her angrily
then gives orders that she must be seized and secretly
drowned. Alone he broods on his past services to Russia. His
musing is interrupted by the arrival of Old Prince Khovansky,
who has come to complain of Galitsin's interference in his
capacity as adviser to the Tsarevna, and of a slight put upon
himself. Angry words pass between them until Dositheus
appears and advises that differences be reconciled and a
return made to government based on the ancient books and
customs. The song of the Old Believers heard in the distance
angers Galitsin, while Khovansky sees in them the saviours of
Russia. Martha rushes in suddenly to ask Galitsin's protection
against his servant who attempted to drown her. He was on
the point of doing so but the attempt was foiled by the
arrival of the Petrovtsy, the bodyguard of Peter the Great.
The presence of the Tsar's troops in Moscow, unsuspected
hitherto, alarms the Princes. The Boyar Shaklovity comes to
tell them that the Khovanskys have been denounced to Tsar
Peter as traitors.

Act III. The Streltsy quarter. Martha sits on a mound near
the home of Prince Andrew Khovansky and, to a beautiful
tune, sings of her past love. She is overheard by Susanna who
accuses her of irredeemable sin. Dositheus appears and
comforts Martha. As they retire, Shaklovity comes and in an
aria, whose mood is almost one of prophetic dedication,
expresses the hope that Russia may be freed from a government which oppresses her. The chorus of the Streltsy
approaches and Shaklovity conceals himself. They arrive
singing a drinking song and urging one another to repay theft
or gossip of neighbours by ravage and destruction. Their
women folk now enter and revile them. The uproar is stilled
by the arrival of the Scrivener. He has seen foreign
mercenaries attack women and children on the outskirts of
the Streltsy's own quarters. The Streltsy call in alarm to
Prince Khovansky asking to be led against the mercenaries.
But the Prince advises submission to the will of Tsar Peter.

Act IV, part i. The residence of Prince Ivan Khovansky,
where takes place one of the tautest, most gripping episodes
of the entire epic. As the Prince is listening to the singing of
his serving girls, Varsonofiev comes from Prince Galitsin to
warn him of the danger which threatens him. Khovansky

does not heed the warning and orders his Persian slaves to b
brought to him to dance. As the dancing ends the Boyar
Shaklovity enters to invite Khovansky to the Tsarevna's
council. Khovansky at first refuses to go but later makes
ready to accompany him. As he leaves the room ('White
Swan'), he is stabbed in the back by Shaklovity.

Part ii.   The square in front of the Church of Saint Basil
in Moscow. To the sound of impressively solemn music (in
concerts, often known as 'Entr'acte, Act IV'), the people
watch the departure of Prince Galitsin in a carriage guarded
by troopers. He has been condemned to exile. As they follow
at the tail of the procession, Dositheus enters lamenting the
fall of the two great nobles, Khovansky and Galitsin. After a
short dialogue with Martha he leaves her alone to face Prince
Andrew Khovansky, who angrily demands news of Emma.
Emma, answers Martha, is now safe and perhaps wedded to
the man she loved, from whom she had been separated by
Andrew. He threatens Martha with the death of a sorceress at
the hands of the Archers. Martha defies him and Andrew calls
the Archers. They come, but not in answer to his call—a
mournful procession, carrying blocks on which their heads
soon must fall. Andrew is taken to a secret refuge by Martha.
The crowd asks for the death of the Archers, but the herald
of the Tsar's guards comes to announce that they have been
pardoned. (As a matter of historical fact, the Streltsy were
not pardoned but put to death with the cruellest tortures.)

Act V.   A Pine wood near Moscow. The Old Believers
have come to their hermitage for the last time. Their cause is
lost, their sect persecuted throughout Russia. The quarrels
of princes have brought about their ruin. Rather than yield to
the soldiers who surround their retreat they will perish
together. Dositheus sings a beautiful prayer in which he says
that the world shall see how men can die for its salvation.
The Old Believers, amongst whom are Martha and Andrew,
build a funeral pyre which they ascend carrying a lighted
taper. As the flames rise and overpower them the troops sent
to arrest them arrive and fall back horror-stricken at the sight
of the smoking pyre.   F. B., H.

THE FAIR AT SOROCHINTSY

Opera in three acts by Modest Moussorgsky; text by the composer,
founded on an episode from Gogol's *Evenings on a Farm near Dekanka*.

Left unfinished at the time of the composer's death, without the
greater part of the last act, and unorchestrated. Given at a concert at St.
Petersburg, 1911, semi-publicly at the Comedia Theatre, 1911. Another
version at the Free Theatre, Moscow, November 3, 1913. In 1917 the
opera was produced in a version by César Cui at the Musical Drama
Theatre. This version replaced by yet another for which Tcherepnin was
responsible, Monte Carlo, 1923, with Luart, John McCormack; Buenos
Aires, 1929, with Maria Kouznetzoff, Davidoff, Sdanovsky, conductor
Fitelberg; Metropolitan, New York, 1930, with Müller, Bourskaya,
Jagel, Pinza, conductor Serafin; Fortune Theatre, London, 1934;
Covent Garden, 1936, with Danieli, de Villiers, Russell, Kassen, con-
ductor Coates; Trieste, 1940, with Sani, Pauli, Serpo, Bettoni; Savoy
Theatre, London, 1942, with Bayan, Slobodskaya, Boleslawski, Parry
Jones, Kiriloff, conductor Fistoulari.

CHARACTERS

Tcherevik, *an old countryman* . . . . Bass
Parassia, *his daughter* . . . . Soprano
Khivria, *his wife* . . . . Mezzo-Soprano
Gritzko, *a young countryman* . . . . Tenor
The Priest's Son . . . . Tenor
Tcherevik's Crony . . . . Bass
The Gypsy . . . . Bass
Young Men and Women, Gypsies, Merchants, Cossacks,
Jews, etc.
Place: Sorochintsy, in Little Russia.

Sorochintsy Fair was written at about the same time as
Khovanshchina. The story is one of Gogol's, the scene
Gogol's own birth-place, in the Ukraine. Moussorgsky wrote
the libretto himself, though handicapped in doing so by his
scanty knowledge of Ukrainian dialect. Much of the opera
was unfinished at his death, but it has had more than a little
success outside Russia in Tcherepnin's version.
    The introduction is labelled 'A Hot Day in Little Russia',
and is an attempt to emulate Gogol's description of the
atmosphere in which the story is to take place. The curtain
rises on Act I to reveal a market scene: 'Moussorgsky
constructs' (says Calvocoressi in his 'Master Musicians'
volume on the composer) 'a sort of kaleidoscopic musical
mosaic which conveys, as realistically as an opera chorus can
hope to convey, the confused impression of a country fair'.
Tcherevik has brought his daughter, Parassia, to a fair for the
first time, and she is excited at the bustle, and the quantity

of things which are for sale. An old gypsy raises his voice above the hubbub to wish everyone well, but also to warn them that the ground on which they stand is cursed by the periodic visitation of a devil—taking the form of a pig and looking, according to legend, for the sleeve (or 'red *svitka*') of a garment he had pawned years ago, but of which he has never been able to recover this one portion.

Parassia has found her young lover, Gritzko, with whom she sits while the gypsy is telling his story. Tcherevik suddenly notices that she is not with him, but Gritzko introduces himself, and asks for Parassia's hand in marriage. The old man can see no harm in such an idea, particularly since Gritzko is the son of an old friend of his, and he gives the couple his blessing. Tcherevik disappears, but presently he and his crony reappear from the inn, happily drunk. They are not left long in peace, Khivria, Tcherevik's wife, putting in an appearance, and showing little disposition to acquiesce in the notion of acquiring a son-in-law whom she has not yet even seen, much less approved of.

They leave the stage, and Gritzko laments the turn his affairs have taken. Tcherepnin's version has at this point a beautiful aria, but it was intended by the composer for Act III, not Act I at all, the scene in which Gritzko gives way to his sadness having been indicated in the scenario but not (as far as is known) composed. To Gritzko comes the old gypsy, offering, in return for a reduction in the price of the oxen Gritzko wishes to sell him, to convert Tcherevik (and, through him, Khivria) to the idea of Gritzko's marriage with Parassia. Gritzko gladly accepts the offer and the bargain which goes with it.

The act should end with the *Hopak* (the best-known bit of the score), but in Tcherepnin's version this is transferred to the end of the opera, where it makes an excellent finale. In its place is a duet for Parassia and Gritzko, which brings the act to an end.

Act II. Tcherevik's house. Khivria is busy in the kitchen. Tcherevik is asleep. He wakes up, and there is a short quarrel between husband and wife, during whose course Khivria enquires about the sale of the farm produce. Tcherevik leaves the room, and Khivria waits anxiously for her lover, the priest's son, for whom she has prepared the delicacies he cannot resist. He eventually comes into sight, and makes a splendidly comic figure, his pious utterances contrasting nicely with his evidently un-pious intentions. These he is busy making manifest, when suddenly there is a noise outside. Khivria has only just time to hide her lover before Tcherevik and his cronies return home, making a deal of noise, and scared at the idea of being where the 'red sleeve' is liable to be found.

They all drink, and, to keep their spirits up, Tcherevik sings riotously for their entertainment. The unfortunate priest's son knocks over a tin can but this is accepted as the work of the 'red sleeve', and no one takes it for what it is. In the end the crony recites the story for the company. When he reaches the climax, the window blows open, and the head of a pig is seen—it is in this form that the devil is said to roam the world looking for his lost garment. General consternation. In the exclamation of horror which follows the revelation, the priest's son loses his balance, and falls into the midst of the assembly, covered by Khivria's nightdress. Presently he is revealed, and Tcherevik's friends laugh at the resolute, proud Khivria, who has given herself away so badly.

Act III.   The village square: Tcherevik's house visible in the background. Moussorgsky made a special and elaborated version of his *Night on the Bare Mountain* (1867) to act as a ballet-intermezzo between Acts II and III of *Sorochintsy Fair*. The dramatic situation is that Gritzko, the *parobok* (young peasant), is asleep in the open; to him in his dream appears the whole rigmarole of the kingdom of darkness and black magic, and dances round him.

Parassia, alone, sings sadly of her lover, but, looking into a mirror, regains her spirits and sings a charming *Hopak* (marked *allegretto grazioso*). She dances as she sings. Tcherevik emerges from the house at the same moment as Gritzko appears. Tcherevik loses no time in giving his consent to the marriage—the Gypsy's scheme has worked perfectly— and the two young lovers celebrate their future happiness in a lively duet. The rejoicing becomes more general as the other villagers join in, and even the advent of Khivria, emitting story-book step-mother's disapproval from every pore, cannot put a damper on the jollity; Tcherevik has acquired new authority from the episode of the priest's son, and will brook no contradiction. The opera ends with the exciting *Hopak* designed by Moussorgsky to come at the end of Act I but transferred by Tcherepnin.

It must be emphasised that the version referred to is Tcherepnin's, which does not by any means follow

Moussorgsky's sketch-plan in every particular. However, as the third act, and even the end of the second, exist in no more than fragmentary form, and as Tcherepnin's is the version usually heard, it seemed more practical to concentrate on that, rather than elaborate on the work in its unfinished state.   H.

PETER ILITSCH TCHAIKOVSKY

(1840–1893)

TCHAIKOVSKY wrote no fewer than ten operas, which together constitute a bulky argument to set against the idea that he was primarily an instrumental composer with a dramatic work or two to his credit. Their success has been decidely varied, but eventually two of them have established themselves in the world's restricted operatic repertory— *Eugene Onegin* and *The Queen of Spades*. Desmond Shawe-Taylor wrote in 1950:[1] 'It is insular ignorance to regard them as interesting failures, or even as obscure local successes. In Russia their great popularity has not only survived the Revolution but positively increased: Tatiana is now the beloved heroine of the factory, as formerly of the drawing-room; though gambling and superstition are officially frowned upon, Herman and the ghost of the Countess have lost nothing of their glamour'.

YEVGENY ONYEGIN

Opera in three acts by Peter Ilitsch Tchaikovsky; text by the composer and K. S. Shilovsky, after Pushkin. Première Imperial College of Music, Little Theatre, Moscow, March 29, 1879; publicly Moscow, 1881; Olympic Theatre, London, 1892 (in English); la Scala, Milan, 1900; Covent Garden, 1906, with Destinn, Battistini, Journet, conductor Campanini; Metropolitan, New York, 1920, with Muzio,

[1] In *Opera*.

Martinelli, de Luca, Didur, conductor Bodanzky; revived 1957, with Amara, Tucker, London, cond. Mitropoulos. Sadler's Wells, 1934, with Cross, Wendon, Austin, conductor Collingwood; revived 1952, with Shuard, Rowland Jones, Sharp; Vienna, 1937, with Lehmann, Maikl, Sved, Hofmann, conductor Walter; Berlin, 1945, with Lemnitz, Witte, Domgraf-Fassbaender; New York City Centre, 1947, with Brenda Miller; Vienna, 1950, with Welitsch, Schock, London, Frick; Glyndebourne, 1968, with Söderström, Ochman, Selimsky, Kim Borg, conductor Pritchard; Covent Garden, 1971, with Ileana Cotrubas, Robert Tear, Victor Braun, conductor Georg Solti, producer Peter Hall.

CHARACTERS

Madame Larina, *who owns an estate*	. . .	Mezzo-Soprano
Tatiana \ *her daughters*		Soprano
Olga /		Contralto
Filipievna, *Tatiana's nurse*	. . . .	Mezzo-Soprano
Lenski, *Olga's fiancé*	. . . .	Tenor
Eugen Onegin, *his friend*	. . . .	Baritone
Prince Gremin, *an old general*	. . . .	Bass
A Captain	. . . .	Bass
Zaretski	. . . .	Bass
Monsieur Triquet, *a Frenchman*	. . . .	Tenor

Time: Late Eighteenth Century   *Place:* A country estate;
St. Petersburg

The idea of setting Pushkin's poem, *Eugen Onegin*, as an opera seems to have been suggested to Tchaikovsky in 1877, by which date he had already written four operas. After a short hesitation, he accepted the subject, and with it the risk of being accused of misrepresenting a classic—for Pushkin's poem was already looked upon in Russia as being in that class. He seems to have set the Letter scene straight away, and at the time he wrote that 'he loved Tatiana and was terribly indignant with Onegin, who seemed to him a cold, heartless coxcomb'. It was during the course of work on his opera that he himself received a passionate avowal of love from a girl who had apparently made his acquaintance while he was teaching at the Conservatory in Moscow; his determination not to emulate Onegin was so strong that he took the fatal decision to embark on a loveless marriage. The results were disastrous, and the composer, a homosexual, seems to have been lucky to escape with nothing worse than a severe nervous breakdown before the doctors insisted that the marriage come to an end.

Much of Pushkin's social commentary finds no place in the libretto, but in general the latter follows fairly closely the lines of the poem, apart that is to say from the emphasis thrown on Tatiana as opposed to Onegin, and the ending which has been amplified and slightly romanticised so that there is a short duet between Tatiana and Onegin, before Tatiana leaves Onegin to contemplate a future without her.

Act I.   The short prelude is built up on the phrase (Ex. 1):

it is wonderfully apt to the purpose, and produces a curious effect of anticipation on the listener.

The curtain rises to reveal Madame Larina's garden. Madame Larina and Filipievna are sitting making jam, and through the open window of the house can be heard the voices of Tatiana and Olga as they practise a duet. The two older women listen to the first stanza in silence but start to talk (like all country house audiences, big or small) during the second, and the duet of necessity becomes a quartet. Outside the garden can be heard the sound of a chorus of reapers coming nearer. They present Madame Larina with a decorated sheaf, singing the while an attractive tune of evident folk-song connections. The chorus is followed by a rapid choral dance.

Tatiana timidly says that these country songs take her in imagination to far-off regions, but Olga takes a matter-of-fact line and says she has no time for such dreams; they do nothing but make her want to dance too. In a little song which is not without tenderness, she gives expression to her light-hearted philosophy. Madame Larina congratulates her daughter, and thanks the reapers for their song, she and Filipievna notice that Tatiana looks pale, but she says (and the clarinet plays a theme associated with her) she is only absorbed in her book, with its tale of lovers' troubles. A carriage is heard on the drive; Lenski must be here—and is it not Onegin with him? Tatiana's imagination flies ahead of her and she tries to get away, but is restrained.

Madame Larina greets her guests, but leaves her daughters to entertain them. A quartet begins, the men and the women conversing separately. Finally, Lenski goes towards Olga, Onegin to Tatiana, and the first pair talk of their mutual pleasure in meeting—they are engaged and have not seen each other since yesterday—and the second of the pleasures, or otherwise, of existence in the country. This conversational music is excellently contrived and sounds, provided the producer can match it as he should, wonderfully natural. Lenski has an *arioso* passage of rapturous import, which is both sincere and immature, conventional and poetic—but then the characters in this opera have a tendency to be life-like persons, rather than romantic giants. The scene often ends at this point, but there is properly a short passage during which Onegin and Tatiana return from their stroll down the garden, the former finishing a story; it gives Filipievna the chance of speculating aloud as to the possibility of Tatiana being interested in the young neighbour.

The scene changes to Tatiana's bedroom, where Filipievna is saying good night to her charge. There is delicate, suggestive orchestral writing in the short prelude. Tatiana and her nurse have been talking, but Tatiana cannot get to sleep and asks Filipievna to tell her a story—about her own early life, and her marriage. Tatiana listens for a bit but her thoughts soon wander and the gradually mounting tension in the orchestra shows the way her feelings are rising. Filipievna asks her if she is ill; no, she is not, but she is in love, Tatiana tells her—and Filipievna must keep it a secret.

The moment she is alone, the violence of her emotion is restrained no more, but finds full expression in an orchestral passage which precedes the ecstatic phrase with which she releases her pent-up feelings:

She starts to write and the orchestra with a wealth of detail supplies what she does not say aloud. She makes a fresh start and, as Gerald Abraham[1] has admirably put it, 'the simple oboe line crossed by the dropping fourths and fifths of flute, clarinet and horn and the light splash of the harp magically not only conveys the naive character and romantic mood of the writer but suggests, almost pantomimically, the act of writing in a way comparable with, though not like, the "writing" passages in *Boris Godounov* and *Khovanshchina* (the scene in Pimen's cell and the scene of the public scribe)':

Snatches of recitative are interspersed with the letter writing, and the music is now lyrical and reflective, now impassioned and almost declamatory, the contrasting moods being bound together by the commentary of the orchestra. Could she love another, she asks herself? Never!

Everything she has ever done has been done for him, as if in his presence. The horn answers the voice in an expressive phrase:

Gerald Abraham has called it a motto theme for the whole opera, though an unconscious one, which is particularly apt since the Letter scene is known to have been composed before the rest of the opera, Tchaikovsky having even thought at one time of setting it as a song quite apart from its context.

Each stage of the fateful letter which is to change Tatiana's life is expressed in the music until finally it is finished and nothing is left but to send it. Day is dawning, the sound of a

[1] In the symposium on Tchaikovsky published by Lindsay Drummond.

shepherd's pipes can be heard, and Filipievna comes to waken Tatiana. She is sent to deliver the note to Onegin, and the curtain falls as the orchestra recapitulates Tatiana's longing.

The third tableau of the first act takes place in a different part of the garden which we already saw in the first scene. Girls sing a graceful, folk-like chorus as they gather the crop of berries, and Tatiana comes on the scene in a state of considerable emotion; she has seen Onegin making his way towards her, and in a minute she will know the answer to her letter—would she had never written it! Onegin in his aria expresses himself calmly and collectedly. She has written frankly to him, he will answer her no less frankly, as is her due. He is not cruel, but discouraging within the code of manners. Love and marriage are not for him; he loves her like a brother, no more. The chorus is heard again as Onegin gently leads the humilated Tatiana from the scene.

Act II.   A ball is in progress at Madame Larina's house in honour of Tatiana's birthday. The guests are engaged in an old-fashioned waltz, and they sing of their enjoyment as they dance (my American score mentions a male semi-chorus of 'Elderly Landed Gentry', which is as nice a designation as is to be found in opera, apart perhaps from the full chorus of Hermits in Verdi's *Attila*). Onegin is there dancing with Tatiana, a combination which gives rise to some ill-natured gossip amongst the more senior element of the neighbours, who look upon Onegin with anything but favour. He is bored with the whole business and chooses to direct his spite against Lenski, who insisted he should come, by stealing a dance from Olga that she had promised to her fiancé. Lenski's remonstrances are in vain, and Olga defends her behaviour when he reproaches her with it, giving the Cotillon as well to the persistent and—says Lenski—flirtatious Onegin.

There is a diversion as Triquet, the old French tutor, consents to sing a song, which he dedicates to Tatiana. It is a charming piece of pastiche, as good in its way as the equivalent to be found in *Pique Dame*—how perfectly Tchaikovsky did this kind of thing! The Cotillon begins with a Mazurka, and Onegin and Olga dance, watched angrily by Lenski. Onegin provokes him by asking why he does not join in, and a quarrel slowly works up until Lenski challenges his erstwhile friend to give him satisfaction for his behaviour. Madame Larina is in a great state that this sort of thing should happen in her house. In music of melting tenderness,[1] Lenski recalls the happiness he has known in just this house which he has now made the scene of a quarrel and a scandal. In the ensemble which follows, Onegin bitterly regrets his provocative and thoughtless behaviour, and everyone else, including by now Tatiana, is filled with consternation at the prospect of the duel. Onegin makes up his mind that the affair has gone too far for there to be any possibility of reconciliation, and he and Lenski insult each other, rush together and are separated as the scene comes to an end.

Early next morning the duel is to take place near a mill on the banks of a wooded stream. The melancholy prelude anticipates Lenski's great scene of farewell to life and all he has loved. He and his second, Zaretski, exchange a few words and he is then left alone. He sings of his past, his carefree youth, and contrasts it with his present state, when he cares little whether as a result of the duel he is left alive or dead; the loss of Olga will be his one regret. It is a fine lyrical outpouring, supreme amongst tenor scenes in Russian opera, and unbearably pathetic in its context.

Onegin arrives, rather late—Pushkin describes how he overslept—and Zaretski immediately demands to know where his second is; duels cannot be fought except according to the rules, and he owns that he is a stickler for etiquette. Onegin introduces his servant as his second, and hopes that Zaretski will have no objection; he is a man of the highest character. The two seconds go off to discuss the conditions of the duel, and

[1] When I heard this opera in Moscow in 1961, Lenski was the great Sergei Lemeshev, advertised outside in letters as big as the opera's title and cheered to the echo by the younger element of the audience. His singing of the opening of this great ensemble was unforgettable, the nearest thing I have met in real life to the poetic *bel canto* to be found in the records of, for instance, Fernando de Lucia.

Lenski and Onegin stand apart without looking at one another and sing a canon. I have read that the duel 'seems rather poor and stagey' (Rosa Newmarch's words) after Lenski's aria, but to me the music at this point seems uncannily right. There is no need to labour the point that the form of a canon exactly expresses the relationship—the thoughts of the two men are similar but divided by form and come together only as they regret that etiquette precludes a reconciliation at this late hour. The bleak tune has just that dead-pan nervousness which the situation might be expected to produce, and the repetition of the word 'No' at the end has a chilling finality. The opponents measure up, and Lenski is killed. Students of irony should not forget that Pushkin himself was killed in a duel only six years after writing *Yevgeny Onyegin*.

Act III.   Some years have passed and the end of the story takes place in St. Petersburg. A ball is in progress in a fashionable house—the contrast with the country dance at Madame Larina's cannot be over-emphasised. As the curtain rises, a Polonaise begins (*the* Polonaise often heard in concert performance, just as the Waltz in the previous act was *the* Waltz); it is played through in its entirety with plenty of action but no singing, and a stage production requires presentation in something like ballet form. Onegin is there, just returned at the age of twenty-six to civilisation after the years he has spent in the wilderness to atone for the death of the friend he has killed in a duel. An Ecossaise begins but the tempo changes to a slow waltz in D flat as Prince Gremin and

his wife—Tatiana, no less—come into the ballroom. The guests, Onegin amongst them, comment on her beauty. The Prince goes to talk to his kinsman, Onegin, who questions him as to the identity of the lady with whom he has come to the ball, while Tatiana asks those nearest her who it is her husband is talking to. The beauty of the waltz theme and the skill with which Tchaikovsky uses it as a background for conversation are equally notable here.

In an aria Gremin tells Onegin of the love and beauty Tatiana has brought into his life since their marriage two years ago. The aria is a favourite of very Russian bass, and it has the important effect in the opera of turning Gremin from a lay figure into a thinking, feeling person, part of Tatiana's background it is true, but real enough to make her loyalty entirely plausible. The single aria in fact creates the impression of a truly noble figure.

Gremin introduces his cousin to his wife, and Tatiana asks to be taken home, leaving Onegin to vent his feelings in an impassioned aria, whose final section is the same (a minor third lower) as the opening section to Tatiana's Letter scene. The scene ends with a repeat of the Ecossaise.

The last scene plays in a reception room in Prince Gremin's house. Tatiana has had Onegin's letter and there is no doubt that he is now passionately in love with her, to such an extent that words fail him at his entrance and he sinks on his knees at Tatiana's feet. Tatiana recalls their former meetings—the letter, and his lecture to her on the subject of maidenly reticence—to a tune (derived from Gremin's aria) which is heard played by flute and clarinet in octaves in the orchestral prelude to the scene. She contrives to make some show of indignation at his return; is he only looking for the notoriety of having his name coupled with that of a woman prominent in society? But he is so obviously sincere and in earnest that she cannot restrain her tears for long. For a moment they recall the happiness that could have been theirs long ago, but which, through fate's decree, is now out of their reach. They must part, says Tatiana, since she is Gremin's wife. But Onegin urges his love once more, and Tatiana launches into a big tune in D flat, which is to

dominate the rest of the scene. Characteristically, though it stands for her admission of her love, it is first heard as she admonishes Onegin to remember the path of honour and leave her, and only later as an avowal of love. For a moment they sing this theme together, as Tatiana prays for courage, but suddenly she finds the strength to go out of the room, leaving Onegin distraught behind her as the final curtain falls.

The music of *Onegin* can be said to have grown outwards from the Letter scene, so much of it is derived from that great central episode. This is not surprising, since for the most part the other characters are seen in relation to Tatiana, and therefore naturally take their cue from her great moment of self-revelation (the duel scene is the only one in which Tatiana does not appear at all; otherwise, only the Waltz and the Polonaise may be said to take place without paying much attention to her or her style of music). One must assume that it was Tchaikovsky's extraordinary reaction to Tatiana which prompted him to such subtle development of her music and which enabled him to give the opera its uncommon unity. One expects a nervous response to every stimulus from this composer, but the sensitivity he shows to each contrasting mood, the graded coloration, the concentration on shades and details, all suggest an unusual arousing of his creative spirit. Its subtlety of detail makes *Onegin* extremely hard to perform. The opera is not written in sharply defined lengths (although it is in numbers), and the balance of one section with another, of one tempo with its near but subtly different neighbour, is no less important than the bringing out of the delicate colouring of the orchestration. But the successful performance reveals what is to my mind one of the great romantic masterpieces yet achieved within the operatic form. H.

THE MAID OF ORLEANS
Orleanskaya Dyeva

Opera in four acts by Peter Ilitsch Tchaikovsky, text by the composer, founded on Zhukovsky's Russian version of Schiller's tragedy. Première, St. Petersburg, February 25, 1881, with M. D. Kamenskaya, M. D. Vasiliev, P. E. Stravinsky (Igor Stravinsky's father) as Dunois. First performed Prague, 1882—the first of Tchaikovsky's operas to be heard outside Russia; Moscow, 1899, revived September, 1907. Revived Brno, 1940, conductor Rafael Kubelik; Perugia, 1956, with Marcella Pobbe, David Poleri, Enzo Mascherini, conductor Perlea; Saarbrucken, 1967, with Faith Puleston, Caterina Ligendza; Leipzig, 1970.

CHARACTERS

Joan of Arc .... Mezzo-Soprano or
Soprano[1]
Charles VII, *King of France* .... Tenor
Agnes Sorel, *his mistress* .... Soprano
Thibaut, *Joan's father* .... Bass

[1] The original Joan was a mezzo-soprano and Tchaikovsky modified some sections of the score for her.

Raymond, *a young man in love with Joan* ......Tenor
Dunois, *a French soldier* ....Baritone
Bertrand, *an old peasant* .... Bass
Lionel, *a Burgundian soldier* ....Baritone
The Archbishop............................ Bass
A soldier .... Bass
Lore .... Bass
An angel voice .... Soprano
Time: 1430–1431   *Place:* France

Act I.   An extended prelude introduces immediately a
yearning, compassionate theme, *andante* and very Slav in its
expression. There follows a fiery *allegro vivo* (associated with
the sound of the tocsin and the crowd's fear in face of
English military successes) and an *allegro giusto* (associated
with Joan's hearing of the angel voices at the end of Act I
and her determination to pursue a course of resistance).

In the village of Domrémy, girls sing as they decorate an
ancient oak. Thibaut, Joan's father, comes in with a young
man, Raymond, whom he envisages as the husband Joan will
need to defend her in the troubled times in which they are
living. There is a trio started by Raymond during whose
course Joan is introduced musically to the opera. The mood
changes with the sound of a tocsin and the populace
expresses dread of the successful English invasion (the *allegro
vivo* of the overture). An old peasant Bertrand describes the
incipient diasaster, and Joan alone refuses to react in terms of
despair. In a mood of inspiration, she prophesies an end to
misfortune, the victory of the French troops and the death of
the leader of the enemy forces, Salisbury. No one believes her,
her father tending to think that she is influenced by the
devil; but a soldier comes in to confirm the death of
Salisbury and immediately hope is renewed. In ecstasy, Joan
leads them in prayer, Raymond and Bertrand joining their
voices to the general mood of confidence.

Left alone, Joan expresses her conviction that the time has
come to act, to leave home and join the troops. Her aria of
decision is a splendid and justly famous utterance, simple of
melody, warm and emotional in its appeal.[1] Joan is genuinely
grief-stricken at the prospect of leaving her village, but she
hears a chorus of angels saying that the day of decision has

[1] Popularly known as 'Adieu forêts', and a favourite recording piece
for sopranos and mezzos alike.

arrived, and the act ends as she prophesies victory to the tune of the overture's *allegro giusto*.

Act II. The royal castle at Chinon. A martial entr'acte, based on Joan's rallying of the French in the previous scene, leads us to the King's presence. Minstrels and tumblers entertain the King and his mistress Agnes Sorel, first in a beguiling and gently lyrical tune whose melody is assigned by Tchaikovsky to the chorus but has sometimes been sung by tenor solo, and later in a succession of musically attractive dances. The soldierly Dunois in a duet tries to persuade Charles to place himself at the head of his army and lead the French against the English, but the King is irresolute, and cannot bring himself to leave Agnes. Suddenly, a wounded soldier brings news of further losses in battle and expires before he can even finish his message. The King loses what courage he had, and Dunois indignantly leaves him to the consolation of Agnes, which is gently and effectively accomplished, first in an *arioso* then in duet.

Fanfares are heard and Dunois re-enters to announce a near-miracle, victory snatched from the hands of the English, a fact immediately confirmed to the incredulous King by the Archbishop himself. This dignitary further relates that the instrument of the enemy's discomfiture was an unknown warrior maid. The people rejoice, bells are rung, and Joan enters. Dunois has previously on instruction taken the King's place on the throne, but Joan immediately picks out her sovereign from the surrounding courtiers. To his astonishment, she can tell him the purport of his secret prayers but her finest moment—writing no less expressive than Moussorgsky's for Martha in *Khovanshchina*—comes in an inspired passage when she tells the story of her life. The Archbishop leads a massive general ensemble of approval which mounts to enthusiasm when the King places her at the head of the army.

Act III, scene i. Vigorous introductory music brings the rise of the curtain to show Joan in single combat with Lionel, a Burgundian fighting on the English side. She has him at her mercy but spares his life and, as she sees him face to face, they fall in love. After an extended duet, Lionel prefers to surrender to Dunois as prisoner rather than make his escape, as Joan urges.

A march leads to scene ii, the Coronation of the King as Charles VII at Reims (it was this scene which at the time of the first performance brought critical complaints of the influence of Meyerbeer on the composer). After appropriate ceremonial business, Thibaut and Raymond reappear, the King proclaims Joan the saviour of France, Thibaut denounces her as diabolically inspired, and a splendid ensemble follows. Joan, urged by King and Archbishop to defend herself but believing her sparing of Lionel's life and her love for him to be a sign of inner guilt, remains silent. Dunois throws down a gauntlet, a challenge to someone to pick up as defender of Joan's innocence. Loud claps of thunder are taken as a sign from heaven that she is guilty and all leave except Lionel and Joan herself. When he offers to protect her, she recoils from him in horror as the enemy who has brought destruction upon her. At the end of the act she is left alone to contemplate the King's sentence of banishment upon her.

Act IV, scene i. A wood. Introduced by turbulent music, Joan sits alone torn by thoughts of her love for Lionel, who presently appears by her side. Their impassioned duet is one of the crucial episodes of the score, its course interrupted by sounds of heavenly voices telling her that she will atone for her sins with suffering and death. Enemy soldiers appear and Lionel is killed, Joan taken prisoner.

Scene ii. A square in Rouen. Joan has been condemned to death at the stake and a funeral march ushers in the final scene. The crowd is moved by her imminent fate, Joan's courage momentarily fails but her angel voices bring consolation, and the music moves on inexorably as she is tied to the stake and the fire lit.   H.

MAZEPPA

Opera in three acts by Peter Ilitsch Tchaikovsky, libretto by the composer and V. P. Burenin (founded on Pushkin's *Poltava*). Première Moscow, February 15, 1884, and in St. Petersburg, February 19, 1884. First performed in England, Liverpool, August 6, 1888 (in Russian, by a touring company); in Germany, at Wiesbaden, 1931; in New York, 1933, by a Ukrainian company; in Vienna, 1933, in German, in concert form. Revived Florence, 1954, with Magda Olivero, Marianna Radev, David Poleri, Ettore Bastianini, Boris Christoff, conductor Jonel Perlea; Wiesbaden, 1960; Berlin Festival, 1969 (by Belgrade Opera), with Radmila Bakočević, Svonimir Krnetić, Nikola Mitić, Miroslav Čangalović, conductor Oskar Danon.

CHARACTERS

Mazeppa, *the Cossack Hetman* . . . . Baritone
Kochubey, *a wealthy Cossack* . . . . Bass
Maria, *his daughter* . . . . Soprano
Andrei, *a young Cossack* . . . . Tenor
Orlik, *Mazeppa's henchman* . . . . Bass
Iskra, *Governor of Poltava* . . . . Tenor
Liubov, *Kochubey's wife* . . . . .Mezzo-Soprano
A drunken Cossack . . . . Tenor
Cossacks and their Women, Kochubey's Servants,
Monks
Time: Beginning of Eighteenth Century   *Place:* Little Russia

Tchaikovsky first told his publisher about the project of an opera on the subject of *Mazeppa* in June, 1881, less than four months after the production of *The Maid of Orleans.* He seems to have vacillated in his enthusiasm for the project, writing four numbers, breaking off to sketch out a duet made from the material of the symphonic *Romeo and Juliet* (it was completed and scored by Taneiev after his death), and then embarking on another love duet, inspired by a play by Antropov. Before long this last had become the great duet of Mazeppa and Maria in Act II, and from then on, apart from some disappointment over the time he took over the orchestration, he seems to have been fairly satisfied with progress.

The overture is a brilliant piece, containing a foretaste of the *Hopak*, and a beautiful *andantino con moto* melody. The first scene of Act I takes place in the garden of the rich Cossack, Kochubey. Girls sing a flowing 5/4 chorus as they tell their fortunes by throwing garlands into the river, but Maria, Kochubey's daughter, will not join in their game. She loves the powerful Mazeppa, her father's contemporary and guest, and when the girls have gone, she makes it clear that his grey hair and a wide difference in age seem to her no obstacles to enduring love. Her soliloquy is interrupted by Andrei, a young Cossack madly, but as he knows hopelessly, in love with her. In their lyrical duet, Maria asks for his forgiveness for the pain she causes him, and he recognises that hope no longer remains for him.

Mazeppa comes out and renews his thanks to Kochubey for the extent of his hospitality. To all he wishes every good fortune for the future, and Kochubey orders his retainers to provide entertainment for their honoured guest. This they do, in chorus and a rousing *Hopak*, the latter a particularly attractive piece, sometimes played in the concert hall.

Alone with Kochubey, Mazeppa loses no time in asking for the hand of Maria in marriage. At first his friend, with many protestations of affection, tries to put him off, urging that Mazeppa is the girl's god-father; how could he marry her—he, an old man, her father's contemporary? But Mazeppa insists, until Kochubey gives him a round refusal and demands that he leave the house. The quarrel attracts the attention of the others, and Liubov, Andrei and Iskra, followed by Kochubey's retainers and guests, come to see what is the matter. A great ensemble develops, with Maria torn between duty to her father and love for Mazeppa, who resolves the situation by summoning his followers to carry off Maria by force. Maria makes her choice to go with Mazeppa willingly and, with a last threat to his hosts, Mazeppa takes his bride and his retinue away.

The second scene plays in a room in Kochubey's house. Women, led by Liubov, are lamenting the departure of Maria. Liubov, supported by Iskra and Kochubey's retainers, urges revenge on Mazeppa for the injury he has done them, and Kochubey resolves to unmask what he describes as Mazeppa's false patriotism and to reveal to the Tsar[1] that Mazeppa is secretly intriguing with the Swedes. Andrei's offer to carry the information to the Tsar is accepted by Kochubey in music of grave conviction, and the finale ends with general support for the expedition, the one chance as all see it of overthrowing the tyrant.

Act II, scene i. A dungeon in Mazeppa's Castle of Belotserkovsky. The Tsar, who trusts Mazeppa implicitly, has delivered his accusers into his hands. Kochubey is chained to a pillar. He reflects on the way the Tsar has treated him, and bemoans his fate. Orlik comes specifically to discover where he has hidden his treasure. The old man will give nothing away, and Orlik summons the torturer to add force to his interrogation. The scene is one of Tchaikovsky's finest, packed with conflict, from the sombre and beautiful prelude, through Kochubey's fine and gloomy monologue to the intensely dramatic interview between him and Orlik.

Scene ii. A room in the Castle. Mazeppa is looking out of

[1] Peter the Great; the period is some twenty years later than that of *Khovanshchina*.

the window and Tchaikovsky shows him in very different
light from the tyrant postulated in the previous scene, as he
poetises in a lovely passage over the beauty of the Ukrainian
night. He stills his conscience with reminders of Kochubey's
ambition; he must die, and when Orlik comes to tell him
that torture has wrung nothing from the old man, he gives
orders for his execution in the morning. Left alone, Mazeppa
gives passionate expression in a big arioso in G flat to his love
for Maria, who, he says, has brought spring into an old man's
life (this arioso was interpolated after the opera's initial
production).

With the entrance of Maria we reach the key scene of the
opera, the equivalent of the Letter Scene in *Onegin*, whose
achievement sets the rest of the opera in motion, giving body
to the central dramatic figures, though not quite permeating
the music as in the case of *Onegin*. Maria reproaches Mazeppa
because he has lately seemed cold to her, and he replies with
a warmth that is entirely consistent with that shown in the
preceding arioso:

He goes on to tell her of his plan to set up an independent state in the Ukraine with himself at its head:[1]

Maria does not hide her enthusiasm or her confidence in him, even when he says that the adventure may lead him to a throne or the gallows. Mazeppa tests her to discover whom she would choose to see saved if it came to a question of death for him or for her father. She admits she would sacrifice anyone rather than Mazeppa.

Left alone, Maria starts to think of her parents, but is suddenly joined by her mother who has stolen into the castle unobserved by the guards. Will her daughter use her influence to save her father from the sentence of death under which he lies? Maria does not understand what she is talking about, and Liubov explains that Kochubey's actions against Mazeppa have brought him to his present miserable situation.

[1] 'When Mazeppa is telling Maria of his ideal of a free and independent Ukraine, neither "under the protection of Warsaw" nor "under the despotism of Moscow", Tchaikovsky introduces a modified quotation, or rather allusion, of a kind common enough in literature but exceedingly rare in music: the orchestra underlines Mazeppa's words with a passage marked in the score by square brackets and the letters 'Zh.z.Ts.G.' (*i.e. Zhizn' za Tsarya Glinki*)—compounded of the mazurka from *Life for the Tsar* and the *Slavsya* from the same opera, symbols of Warsaw and Moscow respectively. The point is, of course, far too subtle for an opera audience, perhaps too subtle for any audience'—so writes Gerald Abraham in *Music of the Masters: Tchaikovsky*; Lindsay Drummond, 1945.

Maria is aghast at the news, and both rush out to do what they can to save Kochubey.

Scene iii. A field by the scaffold. People are waiting for the arrival of the executioner's victims. Tchaikovsky describes this as a 'folk scene', and it is punctuated by the song of a drunken Cossack, who sings a ribald song (musical ancestry held in common with the Inn Scene in *Boris*), much to the discomfiture of the crowd—an admirable piece of dramatic irony. The procession comes into sight with Mazeppa on horseback, Kochubey and Iskra heavily guarded. Kochubey prays movingly, and at the moment the axe falls, Maria and her mother rush in to try to save him, but too late.

Act III begins with a symphonic picture 'The Battle of Poltava', sometimes played in the concert hall. As musical symbols of the Russian victory, Tchaikovsky makes use of the famous 'Slava' (used also by Beethoven in his second Rasumovsky quartet, by Moussorgsky in the Coronation scene in *Boris*, and by Rimsky-Korsakov in *The Tsar's Bride*), as well as of a liturgical chant, which he himself had employed earlier in the *1812 Overture*, and, most extensively, of a military march of the period of Peter the Great.

When the curtain rises it is to show the same scene as the first scene of Act I, but now neglected and half ruined. Andrei in an aria vigorously voices his regret that he has not been able to revenge himself on Mazeppa in the battle. He has returned now to the spot which was once the centre of all his thoughts, the place where he was happy in the company of Maria. He hears the sound of horses' hooves and hides. Mazeppa comes in with Orlik. Both are in flight from the Tsar's troops, and Mazeppa turns and abuses Orlik who has addressed him by his title of Hetman—the title he has lost in his vain attempt to win supreme power.

Andrei recognises Mazeppa's voice, and challenges him to answer for his misdeeds in mortal combat. Andrei attacks Mazeppa but is fatally wounded, and lies dying when Maria emerges from the house. Mazeppa calls to her, but she has lost command of her senses, half recognises him only and babbles of her father's death, of which the direct cause has been her own elopement. Orlik drags Mazeppa away, urging him to forget a woman who is mad and who has brought him to his present pitch of disaster.

Maria is left alone in her misery. She takes Andrei's head in her hands and sings softly to him of their happy childhood.

He dies in her arms and an opera, in which blood, battle and ambition have figured large, ends with the gentlest of cradle songs.   H.

THE QUEEN OF SPADES

Pikovaya Dama/Pique Dame

Opera in three acts by Peter Ilitsch Tchaikovsky; text by Modest Tchaikovsky (the composer's brother), based on Pushkin. Première, St. Petersburg, December 19, 1890, with Nicola Figner and Medea Mei. First produced at la Scala, Milan, 1906, with Corsi, D'Alberti, de Cisneros, Zenatello, Stracciari, Didur; Metropolitan, New York, 1910, with Destinn, Meitschek, Slezak, Didur, Forsell, conductor Mahler; London Opera House, 1915, with Rosing; Buenos Aires, 1924, with Koshetz, Zalevsky, Zaporojetz; Zürich, 1940; Berlin, Staatsoper, 1948, with Scheppan, Rünger, Schuffer, Metternich; Vienna State Opera, 1946, with Hilde Konetzni and Welitsch, Hoengen, Lorenz, Schoeffler, conductor Krips; Covent Garden, 1950 (in English), with Zadek, Coates, Edgar Evans, Rothmüller, Walters, conductor Kleiber. Revived Metropolitan, New York, 1965, with Stratas, Resnik, Vickers, conductor Schippers; Glyndebourne, 1971, with Kubiak, Maievsky, conductor John Pritchard.

CHARACTERS

Tchekalinsky } officers		Tenor
Sourin		Bass
Herman, *a young officer*		Tenor
Count Tomsky		Baritone
Prince Yeletsky		Baritone
The Countess		Mezzo-Soprano
Lisa, *her grand-daughter*		Soprano
Pauline, *Lisa's companion*		Contralto
Governess		Mezzo-Soprano
Mascha, *Lisa's maid*		Soprano
Master of Ceremonies		Tenor
Tchaplitsky } gamblers		Tenor
Narumoff		Bass
Chloë		Soprano
Daphnis (Pauline) } *in the interlude*		Contralto
Plutus (Tomsky)		Baritone

Servants, Guests, Gamblers, Children

Time: End of Eighteenth Century   *Place:* St. Petersburg

Quite a number of changes of emphasis as well as of detail were made before Pushkin's poem could become an opera libretto—and these have often come in for hostile criticism. Pushkin's story is cynical in character, with a mixture of the grotesque, and his hero is a cold-blooded, unromantic officer, interested only in the secret of the cards and not in any way concerned with Lisa, except in so far as she brings him into contact with the old Countess. Tchaikovsky and his brother have turned Herman into a romantic, almost Byronic character as much in love with Lisa as with gambling, and they have elevated Lisa to become the Countess's granddaughter, at the same time providing the story with a tragic ending. That they have made something that differs from Pushkin's original story is undeniable; but whether it is much less good, is a moot point.

A short prelude leads to the first scene of Act I, which is laid in an open space in the Summer Garden, St. Petersburg. It is spring, and seated on the benches are nurses and governesses chatting together. Children are playing. After a chorus, in whose course a little group of children play at mounting the guard, Sourin and Tchekalinsky enter, discussing the gambling propensities of Herman; it seems that he was last night at his usual habit of watching the players, silent and never risking a throw.

As they speak, Herman comes in with his friend Tomsky, who is questioning him about the sorrow which seems to hang over his life, and has quite changed him from the spirited boy he once knew. Herman explains the change by saying that he has fallen in love, but does not even know the name of the object of his affections. His *arioso* in praise of the unknown lady has a typical Tchaikovskian freshness. Tomsky suggests that the first thing to do is to learn the lady's name, and then set about wooing her in earnest, but Herman is afraid she is above him in station and will prove beyond his reach. Tomsky is amazed at Herman's mixture of devotion and despair, and they go off together.

The promenade continues, Tomsky and Herman return, and the former greets Prince Yeletsky, who is in the first flush of happiness, having that very morning become engaged. His rejoicings contrast with Herman's bitter despair. A moment later, Yeletsky points out his Lisa to Tomsky, and Herman recognises her as his own beloved. Lisa and her grand-mother, the Countess, exclaim as they catch sight of

Herman; they have noticed his ardent looks, but are unaware of his identity. A short quintet ensues, after which Tomsky greets the Countess, who asks Herman's name, and Yeletsky goes towards Lisa.

Presently the Countess takes her grand-daughter away, accompanied by Yeletsky, and the others speculate as to the rumours which surround the Countess's past. She was a great gambler it seems, but has now renounced cards. Is it possible to believe such stories? Tomsky is surprised that her history is not better known, and proceeds to tell it in a ballad. The Countess was a beauty when she was young, and one of her most ardent admirers was the Count Saint-Germain; but, alas, she preferred gambling to love. One day at the tables she had lost everything; her depression was noticed by the Count, who followed her from the room, and offered to reveal to her the secret of 'three cards', would she but grant him one rendezvous. Her indignation at such a suggestion was quickly overcome, and next morning she was back at the tables, where nothing could stop her winning run. It was whispered that she subsequently passed the secret on to her husband, and years later to a young gallant who had taken her fancy; but in a dream she had been warned that she would die when next anyone tried to win her secret from her.

The recital is not lost on Herman, and Tchekalinsky and Sourin hasten to repeat the refrain mockingly in his ear. A storm is brewing, and all take shelter except Herman, who stays as if in a trance in the middle of the stage. He broods on the story—what use would the secret be to him with Lisa beyond his reach?—and then gives expression to his determination to win Lisa away from the Prince.

Scene ii.   Lisa's room. A balcony can be seen through the open window, and beyond it the garden. Lisa is sitting at the harpsichord, surrounded by girls of her own age. She and Pauline together sing an old-fashioned duet, which, no less than for instance the opening duet of *Eugene Onegin*, shows how much life Tchaikovsky can breathe into what is no more and no less than pastiche. The listeners duly applaud, and then demand more; Lisa asks Pauline to sing alone, and she follows her romance with a lively peasant song, too lively it appears for the peace of the house, for the governess comes in to ask for a little less noise.

Lisa sees her friends to the door, and tries to fob off Pauline's enquiries about her gloomy look. When she is alone, she gives vent to her feelings in a beautiful aria. Is this marriage to which she is contracted the fulfilment of her dreams? Nobody could have better qualifications than the Prince—he is kind, good-looking, clever, well-born, rich—and yet her heart is full of heavy foreboding.

Suddenly Herman appears at the window. Lisa makes as if to rush through the door, but Herman persuades her to stay and listen to him for a moment. In music of passionate tenderness, he declares his love, and it is immediately evident that Lisa is far from indifferent to what he says. Their conversation is interrupted by a loud knocking at the door; it is the Countess, come to see if Lisa is yet asleep. Herman hides, Lisa calms the Countess's fears, while Herman softly echoes the refrain of Tomsky's ballad; can it be true that she will die when a third man 'impelled by despair' demands to know the secret? When they are left alone, Lisa sinks into Herman's arms, and the curtain falls as they embrace.

Act II. A large reception room. A masked ball is taking place at the house of a rich dignitary. Theatrical boxes down the sides of the room between the columns. Dances take place, and the movement is general. The Master of Ceremonies invites the guests into the garden to see the firework display, and Tchekalinsky and Sourin plan to play a trick on Herman, who, they say, is obsessed by the idea of the Countess's 'three cards'. The Prince is there with Lisa, to whom he addresses an aria whose sentiments are both noble and touchingly chivalrous: 'I love you, dear, beyond all reck'ning'. They go off together, and Herman appears reading a note which Lisa has sent him: 'After the performance wait for me in my room. I must speak with you'. Did he but know the secret of the 'three cards', he could be wealthy, and then aspire to Lisa's hand. As if in the echo of his thoughts, he hears Tchekalinsky and Sourin whisper: 'Are you then that third man? . . . three cards?' Herman wonders whether he is hearing the voice of a ghost.

The Master of Ceremonies announces: 'Our host now prays you all to take your seats, to see a pretty pastoral called *The Faithful Shepherdess*'. The masque begins. It is the story of Daphnis, Chloë, and Plutus. A chorus and saraband are followed by a Mozartian duet for Chloë and Daphnis (the latter is played by Pauline). There is an impressive entry for Plutus (Tomsky), riding in a golden chariot, but Chloë spurns his love, even though it is accompanied by untold wealth, and she and Daphnis plight their troth to the tune of their earlier duet. The chorus rejoices in the happiness of the two lovers.

The interlude over, Herman waits for Lisa. She gives him a key and tells him to gain access to their house through her grand-mother's room—the old woman will still be playing cards at midnight—and then with the key open the secret door which is situated behind the portrait of the Countess, and which leads to her own apartments. Herman says he cannot wait until the following day, but will come that very night; Lisa is submissive to his desire. The act ends as the Master of Ceremonies announces the imminent arrival of the Empress herself, and the guests join in welcoming her.

The second scene of Act II is laid in the Countess's bedroom, which is empty. Herman enters, hesitates for a moment, and then hearing the sound of voices conceals himself. The Countess herself, preceded by maids and attendants, comes in. She takes off her evening dress and puts on a night-gown, then stops the sycophantic chorus which has been accompanying her preparations for bed and says she will sit in a chair for a few minutes. Some reflections on the decline of society are followed by reminiscences of 'the old days', when things were done as they should be, when people really could dance, when la Pompadour was queen of Paris, when she herself—the Countess—sang before the King. She sings very softly to herself an air from Grétry's *Richard Cœur de Lion*; then, suddenly aware that the room is still full of servants, their eyes and ears bursting with curiosity, sends them all packing.

She is alone, and again starts to hum the tune which is in her head. But the words die on her lips as she catches sight of Herman in front of her. She does not speak another word, but mouths incoherently as if she had lost the power of speech. Herman begs her not to be frightened; he wants nothing but that she should tell him her secret, the secret of the 'three cards'. In desperation Herman draws his pistol, and the Countess dies of shock at the sight. With a despairing cry that he can now never know the secret, he turns to find Lisa entering the room, alarmed by the noise. She is horrified by the sight which meets her eyes, and no less horrified to learn why it was that Herman was there. So it was for love of gambling not for her sake that he came here at midnight! She bids him leave.

Act III, Scene i. Herman's quarters in the barracks. The

..ound of drums and trumpets, suggestive of a funeral march, can be heard; the wind moans, and Herman sits reading a letter from Lisa, in which she apparently forgives him for the slight she had read into his action, understands that he did not intend to kill her grand-mother, and makes an appointment for midnight by the canal. Herman is overcome by conscience, and obsessed by memories of the Countess's funeral, which he attended. Suddenly, the door opens, the candle is blown out, and the ghost of his victim can be seen in the doorway. She tells Herman that he must marry Lisa, and that the secret of the three cards shall be his: Three! Seven! Ace! He mutters the formula as the curtain falls.

Scene ii.   By the canal. Lisa waits for Herman: 'It is near to midnight'. Can he deceive her, and will she wait in vain? Her nerves are worn with sorrow and waiting. Lisa's aria is particularly fine, and its fame as a concert piece should not blind one to the effect it makes in its original context.

But Lisa's fears are quieted when Herman appears, and sings to her of their future together. All seems well, until Herman tells her they must leave for the gaming-house. Lisa thinks he is mad, but he blurts out his obsession, and, deaf to her pleading, pushes her aside and goes his way. Lisa rushes to the parapet of the canal, and throws herself over the edge.

Scene iii.   The gambling house. Supper is in progress, and a few are playing cards. The praises of wine, youth and merriment are sung. Tomsky greets the Prince with some surprise, since he is no longer a habitual gambler. Yeletsky admits that it is to take his revenge he has come: unlucky in love, lucky at cards. Tomsky is persuaded to sing for their entertainment, which he does to a most lively tune. Herman enters, and asks who will play with him. Tchekalinsky accepts, and Herman stakes hugely and wins twice, on the three and seven. He rejoices in his fortune: 'What is our life? A game!', then challenges anyone to stake once more. No one accepts, until the Prince steps forward and offers to play with him. Herman reluctantly agrees, and turns up a card, announcing an ace without even looking at it. But the Prince calmly rejoins: 'No, 'tis your Queen of Spades'. With a wild cry, Herman sees the ghost of the Countess. Everyone moves away from him, as he gibbers with fear and rage. He stabs himself, and with his dying breath asks for the Prince's pardon for what he has done to him. A prayer goes up for his soul, and Herman dies.   H.

IOLANTA

Opera in one act by Peter Ilitsch Tchaikovsky, libretto by Modest Tchaikovsky, the composer's brother. Première, December 6/18, 1892, St. Petersburg, with Edmea Mey-Figner, Nicola Figner. Revived Leipzig, 1955; Moscow, 1957; London, Camden Festival, 1968, with Josephine Barstow, Adrian de Peyer, Norman Welsby, conductor David Lloyd-Jones.

CHARACTERS

René, *King of Provence* .... Bass
Robert, *Duke of Burgundy* .... Bass-Baritone
Count Vaudémont, *a Burgundian knight* .... Tenor
Ebn-Hakia, *a Moorish doctor* .... Baritone
Almeric, *King René's armour-bearer* .... Tenor
Bertrand, *the gate-keeper* .... Baritone
Iolanta, *the King's daughter* .... Soprano
Martha, *Iolanta's nurse and Bertrand's wife*... Contralto
Brigitte, *Iolanta's friend* .... Soprano
Laura, *Iolanta's friend* .... Mezzo-Soprano
Servants and Friends of Iolanta, Members of the King's
Retinue, the Duke of Burgundy's Retainers

Time: Fifteenth Century   *Place:* Provence

Iolanta was commissioned to be produced in double harness with the famous ballet *Nutcracker*.[1] Tchaikovsky began work on it some six months before the première, but soon after he had finished it, he confessed that 'Medieval Dukes and Knights and Ladies captivate my imagination but not my *heart*'. As so often before, the composer approached the libretto through a crucial scene, here the duet between Iolanta and her lover Vaudémont, and this music permeates the whole score. The libretto has its origins in a story by Hans Andersen.

A sombre prelude perhaps suggests Iolanta's blindness. The curtain rises on a beautiful garden, outside the Palace of René, King of Provence. To the accompaniment of graceful music, Princess Iolanta is picking fruit with her friends. Iolanta is blind but, at the King's express command, she has never been allowed to know that she is different from everyone around her. She finds the fruit by touch and puts it in the basket, but gradually she becomes listless: how do they

[1] *Iolanta*, which is of course played without interval, lasts some 90 minutes.

know she is crying without having *touched* her eyes? In an *arioso* of some feeling, Iolanta contrasts her present mood of unrest, with her former happiness. Martha tries to calm her fears; girls bring in the flowers they have picked, and sing an attractive chorus in 6/8 time, and Martha and Iolanta's friends lull her to sleep in a trio of considerable beauty.

Retainers appear to announce the King's arrival. King René tells the famous Moorish doctor, Ebn-Hakia, that in him rests Iolanta's last hope, and the doctor goes to look at his prospective patient as she lies asleep. When he is alone, the King prays in an aria ('When I, Lord, rouse thy wrath') for God's mercy on his innocent daughter. Ebn-Hakia says he can cure Iolanta's blindness on two conditions: that she be told she is blind, and that she acquire the will to be able to see. The King laments that such a price is more than he is prepared to pay, and even when Ebn-Hakia has (in an *arioso* full of oriental suggestions) emphasised how much the body is dependent on the spirit, he refuses to agree.

The King and the doctor leave and into the garden come Robert, Duke of Burgundy, and Count Vaudémont, who have lost their way. Vaudémont is immediately taken by the beauty of the garden, and Robert is glad of anything that delays his business with the King—he has never seen Iolanta, to whom he is engaged, but he loves another and wants the King to release him from the betrothal. When Vaudémont suggests that Iolanta may be very beautiful, Robert exclaims in a fine quick-moving outburst: 'Who can compare to Mathilde?' Suddenly they come upon the sleeping girl; Vaudémont is overcome by her beauty, but Robert fears the work of a sorcerer and wants to drag him away. When she wakes, Robert leaves to fetch their companions, and Iolanta brings wine to Vaudémont.

The duet which ensues is the central piece of the opera. Love dawns in a G major theme of great tenderness, and the music quickens as Vaudémont asks Iolanta for a red rose to add to the white one she has already picked for him. She brings him another white one and seems not to understand the difference, and suddenly Vaudémont begins to realise that she is blind. He comforts her and sings of the beauties of the world around them. The climax comes at Vaudémont's impassioned description of light, to which Iolanta's response is no less rapturous.

The King, Ebn-Hakia and Iolanta's attendants enter,

expecting to see her asleep, and are astonished instead to find her with a young man, who, she tells them, has given her an idea of the meaning of the word 'light'. The King is overcome with horror, but Ebn-Hakia knows there is now hope of curing Iolanta's blindness. Ebn-Hakia leads a big ensemble as everyone reacts to the situation. The King begins to understand and decrees that the stranger's life shall be forfeit if she does not acquire the power of sight. To the big G major theme (now a semitone higher) Iolanta proclaims her determination to save the life of the Knight with whose voice she has fallen in love. She leaves and the King explains to Vaudémont that his threat was intended solely to provide Iolanta with the incentive to see.

Burgundy returns and admits his secret, the King agrees that Vaudémont shall marry Iolanta, and when news is brought of the success of Ebn-Hakia's ministrations, happiness seems to be within the grasp of everyone. The women come out rejoicing, and Iolanta can hardly believe what meets her eyes. She thanks God for his mercy, for the wonders she can now comprehend, and not least for the love she feels in her heart for Vaudémont.   H.

NIKOLAI ANDREEVICH RIMSKY-KORSAKOV

(1844–1908)

PSKOVITYANKA

The Maid of Pskov, or Ivan the Terrible

OPERA in four acts by Rimsky-Korsakov; text by the composer founded on a play by L. A. Mei. Première, January 13, 1873, at St. Petersburg. Revived Moscow, 1898, with a new prologue. First performed Paris, 1909 (in Russian); Drury Lane, London, 1913, with Brian, Nicolaewa, Petrenko, Andreev, Zaporojetz, Chaliapin, conductor nil Cooper; 1917 (in English); Palermo, 1959, with Zeani, Bertocci, ossi-Lemeni; Trieste, 1967, with Bakocevic, Lajos Kozma, Christoff.

CHARACTERS

Tsar Ivan Vassilievich, the Terrible :. . . . . Bass
Prince Youry Ivanovich Tokmakov, *Tsar's Viceroy*
  and *Mayor of Pskov*. . . . . Bass
Boyar Nikita Matouta . . . . Tenor
Prince Afanasy Viazemsky . . . . Tenor
Bomely . . . . Bass
Michael Andreievich Toucha, *a Burgher's son* . . . Tenor
Yousko Velebin, *messenger* . . . . Bass
Princess Olga Yourievna Tokmakov . . . . Soprano
Boyardin Stephanida Matouta (Stesha), *a companion*
  of Olga . . . . Soprano
Vlassievna ⎱ *old nurses* . . . . ⎰ Alto
Perfilievna ⎰   ⎱ Mezzo-Soprano
A Sentry . . . . Tenor
  Officers, Judges, Boyars of Pskov, Burgher's
  Sons, Oprichniki (Ivan's Bodyguards), Pages in
  Waiting, Muscovite Archers (Streltsy), Serving
      Maidens, Boys, the People, Huntsmen
Time: 1570

The first two acts take place in Pskov. Scene i, Act III, near the Monastery of Pedersk. Scene ii, on the bank of the River Mediedna.

Act I, scene i. The garden of Prince Tokmakov's mansion. Olga and the two old nurses, Vlassievna and Perfilievna, are watching young girls at play. When the game takes the players to a distant part of the garden the two nurses discuss local gossip and a rumour that Olga is not a Boyar's daughter but comes of 'higher stock'. Vlassievna dismisses the subject as nonsense. Much more important is the news that has been received from Novgorod. Tsar Ivan has led his troops there; and they are now punishing the proud city, slaying the guilty and the innocent alike. The players return and, tired of their game, ask Vlassievna for a story. The nurse consents and begins to tell a legend of a fearsome dragon and the Tsarevna Lada. The story is interrupted by a shrill whistle which frightens the girls and sends them indoors. The whistle was to signal the coming of Olga's

lover, Michael Toucha, who climbs over the fence and await
Olga. She comes to him and learns that Michael is determined
to go and seek wealth in distant lands before asking her
father, Prince Tokmakov, for her hand. Olga persuades him
to stay, afraid lest in his absence she should be affianced to
her father's friend, the old Boyar Matouta. The approach of
Prince Tokmakov, with the Boyar Matouta, hastens Michael's
departure while Olga hides in the bushes. Hidden, she hears
the two conversing of Tsar Ivan who is marching on Pskov
from Novgorod. Then the conversation becomes more intimate. Tokmakov will give Olga to Matouta, but he must first
tell him the secret of her birth. She is not his daughter but his
niece. Her mother was his wife's sister. Her father is
unknown. Suddenly the bells are heard calling the citizens to
the market-place and the distant glow of beacon fires is seen
in the sky. The Prince and Matouta hasten to the assembly. A
masterly interlude depicts the atmosphere of terror and
anxiety.

Scene ii. The market-place of Pskov. The people and
Boyars have come to hear the news brought by a messenger
from Novgorod. When all are assembled the messenger
reports that Novgorod is in ruins, destroyed by the order of
the cruel Tsar who with his savage guards is now marching to
Pskov. The people seem inclined to oppose his coming by
force of arms, but Prince Tokmakov persuades the majority
that having done no wrong it will be wiser to meet the Tsar
with humility and kindness. Michael Toucha alone protests
that rather than see Pskov humbled and robbed of her
freedom he will go into exile after striking a blow for the
cause of the city. The bells ring out again as Michael with a
number of followers leaves the market-place singing a martial
hymn.

Act II, scene i. The market-place is thronged with the
crowd awaiting the arrival of the terrible Ivan. At one side of
the stage are tables with the ceremonial bread and salt. In the
crowd is the nurse Vlassievna vainly attempting to comfort
Olga, who grieves over her father's promise to Matouta and
her unknown parentage. The advance guard of the Tsar's
following, the Tartars, arrive on the stage flourishing their
whips; then a procession and finally the ruthless Tsar himself.

Scene ii. An apartment in Prince Tokmakov's house. The
Prince is welcoming the Tsar to his home and trying to avert
the tyrant's anger. The Tsar's words give him little confi-

dence. When, however, Olga goes to offer him a salver and a cup the Tsar becomes suddenly agitated. He demands to know who she is, expresses his intention of taking her to Moscow in his train and, after dismissing all but Prince Tokmakov, learns from him the mystery of Olga's birth. He is deeply moved by the Prince's recital and after a short prayer promises to end all bloodshed and to forgive Pskov.

Act III, scene i. In a dense forest the Tsar and his friends are hunting. The voices of girls are heard singing in the distance. As night falls Olga comes to her tryst with Michael Toucha. He persuades her to leave Pskov and share his fortunes. The lovers are surprised by the servants of Matouta who call their master and capture them. Michael is left senseless on the ground and Olga is carried back to the Tsar.

Scene ii. The Tsar's tent. In a soliloquy Ivan recalls his past and his love for Olga's mother. Olga is his own daughter. Prince Viazemsky comes to announce the arrival of Matouta who wishes to offer Olga to the Tsar. Ivan orders Matouta to be brought to him with Olga. Matouta he dismisses in anger but he forgives Olga, touched by her faith in him and by her simplicity. As they talk together, Michael Toucha is heard outside urging his companions to attack the Tsar and rescue Olga. Ivan, seizing his sword, stands at the entrance of the tent to cut down any who should dare to enter. But Olga, evading his attention, rushes out to her lover and a shot meant for Michael hits her instead. She is brought in dead by the soldiers. The chorus, which has entered the tent, closes the opera, bidding Russians end their quarrels for the sake of one who was sacrificed in the cause of Pskov.   F. B.

MAISKAYA NOCH
A May Night

Opera in three acts by Nikolai Andreevich Rimsky-Korsakov, libretto by the composer founded on a story by Gogol. Première, January 21, 1880, Moscow, conducted by Napravnik. First performed in London, Drury Lane, 1914, with Petrenko, Smirnoff, Belianin. Revived Oxford, in English, 1931; Cardiff, 1959, by Welsh National Opera Company, with Heather Harper, John Kentish, Duncan Robertson, Bryan Drake, Harold Blackburn, conductor Warwick Braithwaite (and at Sadler's Wells, 1961).

CHARACTERS

The Mayor . . . . Bass
Levko, *his son* . . . . Tenor
The Mayor's sister-in-law . . . . .Mezzo-Soprano
Hanna . . . . Mezzo-Soprano
The Mayor's Clerk . . . . Bass
The Distiller . . . . Tenor
Kalenik . . . . Baritone
Pannochka, *a water sprite* . . . . Soprano
Three Water Sprites . . . . . .   Soprano & Mezzo-Soprano
Time: Nineteenth Century   *Place:* A small village in Russia

A May Night was Rimsky-Korsakov's second opera, and, if his output for the stage is divided basically into three categories it belongs with *Christmas Eve Revels* amongst the 'Peasant' group, the others being 'Heroic' (*Ivan the Terrible, The Tsar's Bride, Pan Voyevoda, Servilia*), and 'Fantastic' (*Snow Maiden, Sadko, Tsar Saltan, Katschei the Immortal, Kitezh, Coq d'Or*). Only *Mozart and Salieri* does not fit any of the three categories.

The story is taken from Gogol, and, as well as a very strong nationalist quality, it introduces without any apparent strain a supernatural element which might come straight from *Sadko*. The overture was once well-known from concert performance and was for a long time a favourite of Sir Thomas Beecham.

Act I. In a small village in the heart of Russia, the peasants are celebrating Whitsuntide with dances and games. A game of 'Millet' is going on, while Kalenik, the best dancer in the village, demonstrates his skill. The crowd moves on, and Levko appears to serenade his sweetheart, Hanna. It is an attractive and lively romance that he sings to the accompaniment of his bandura (piano and harp in the orchestra), and it is not long before she comes out to him. Their extended duet suggests that they are very much in love, but Hanna is still worried that Levko's father, the Mayor, may consider it a bad match and forbid their marriage. Levko does his best to reassure her, and she asks him to tell her again the legend of the deserted castle across the lake.

His story is an odd one. Long ago, an old nobleman lived there with his beautiful daughter, Pannochka. When Pannochka discovered her step-mother was a witch, her father drove her out; she drowned herself, and became a

..usalka, or water-spirit. One day she and her companions .eized the witch, and pulled her into the lake, but through her magic powers she turned herself into a Rusalka, indistinguishable from the others. Not until she discovers which of her companions is the witch, can Pannochka free herself of the evil spell.

The lovers say goodnight as they hear the revellers returning. The women of the village sing a little chorus in honour of Pentecost, and Kalenik leads a Hopak, singing as vigorously as he dances. Levko stays behind when they go, and is startled to hear someone call up to Hanna's window. He is furious when he finds it is his own father, the Mayor, who pays court to her and abuses Levko as a fledgling while doing so! Levko attracts the attention of his friends, who drive the old man away with their mockery. He suggests to them that they disguise themselves that night, and teach the Mayor a lesson by singing a mocking song outside his house. This song is the invigorating and justly famous 'Song on the Village Mayor'—to give it the title it has acquired on western gramophone records.

Act II. That night the Mayor, with the aid of his spinster sister-in-law, is entertaining a rich crony who hopes to open a distillery on the site of the old castle. But their jollity is due for interruption, first by Kalenik, who is drunk and difficult to get rid of, then by a stone flung through the window, and finally by the sound of Levko and his friends singing their song at the tops of their voices outside the window. The Mayor grabs Levko, but a gust of wind blows out the candles and in the general confusion Levko escapes and the Mayor instead bundles his protesting sister-in-law into a cell. The Mayor's Clerk, who has heard the ribald singing, enters to say that *he* has caught the principal culprit and has locked him up. Puzzled, they investigate, and out of the first cell bursts the infuriated sister-in-law to run screaming from the house.

Mayor, Clerk and Distiller now investigate the Clerk's prisoner. The Mayor peeps through the keyhole, and reacts to what he sees with impotent cries of 'Satanas', which the others take up when they have had a look in their turn. The solution is clearly to burn the devil—obviously it is he—and only the protestations of the sister-in-law (who has now twice been bundled into a cell, the second time by the mob after they have liberated the Clerk's prisoner, Levko) saves her

from a Witch's fate. Once free, she turns on the Mayor; it
all a plot on his part to prevent her seeing his philanderings
which have become a byword throughout the village. It's
now the turn of the Watch, who bring in a very drunken
Kalenik. The Mayor tries to rescue what is left of his dignity
by ordering them to clear the streets of the band which so
grievously insulted him.

The music of the whole act has a most agreeable *buffo*
character, and the role of the Mayor, which was created by
Stravinsky's father, is rich in comic possibilities. The second
scene has something of the variety and even the flavour of a
Rossini finale, on which it would appear to be modelled.

Act III.   The deserted castle by the lake. Levko sings a
hauntingly beautiful love song ('Sleep my beloved')—to the
Russian tenor what *Cielo e mar* or the *Lamento di Federico*
is to the Italian:

Suddenly, as Levko sings Hanna's praises, a troop of water
nymphs emerges from the lake. There is a delightful 6/8
chorus for them before Pannochka, their Queen, asks Levko if

he will help her spot her wicked step-mother, who is
concealed in their midst. Each in turn pretends to be a raven,
until one does so with such spiteful conviction that Levko
points to her and the others fall on her and drag her down
into the lake. Pannochka in a little duet thanks Levko and
gives him a paper, which she says will settle his father's
opposition to his marriage with Hanna.

No sooner have the water nymphs gone than Levko is
seized by the Watch as the author of the previous night's
disturbances. The Clerk however looks at the paper
Pannochka has given Levko, recognises the Governor's seal,
and proceeds to read out an indictment of the Mayor's
incompetence, and an order for the immediate celebration of
the wedding of Levko and Hanna.

The villagers sing their Whitsuntide song, Hanna is reunited
with Levko, while the Mayor is overjoyed at the official
letter's news that the governor is to dine with him—even the
way his hand has been forced over the matter of Hanna and
Levko, even the muttered threats of his sister-in-law, cannot
spoil that.   H.

SNEGUROCHKA
The Snow Maiden

Opera in a prologue and four acts by Rimsky-Korsakov; text by the
composer from a play by N. Ostrovsky. Première, February 10, 1882,
St. Petersburg. First performed Metropolitan, New York, 1922, with
Bori, Telva, Harrold, Laurenti, conductor Bodanzky (in French);
Buenos Aires, 1929, with Kouznetzoff, conductor Fitelberg; Sadler's
Wells, 1933, with Olive Dyer, Cross, Coates, Tudor Davies, Austin,
conductor Collingwood.

CHARACTERS

Snegurochka	Soprano
Shepherd Lehl	Alto
Coupava	Soprano
Fairy Spring	Mezzo-Soprano
Bobilicka	Mezzo-Soprano
Spirit of the Woods	Tenor
Page	Mezzo-Soprano
Tsar Berendey	Tenor
Misgir	Baritone

King Frost .... Bass
Bobil .... Tenor
Bermate .... Bass

Snegurochka (The Snow Maiden) was written in 1880, and
in his autobiography Rimsky-Korsakov tells us how he
became enamoured of the subject and how he came to write
it in the 'genuine Russian village' of Stlelyovo in the brief
period of three months. The orchestration took longer. The
full score was begun on September 7, 1880, and completed
on May 26 of the following year. When the work was ready,
the composer played it through to his friends Balakirev,
Borodin, and Stassov, and all three were pleased, but each in
his own way. 'Stassov and Balakirev were gratified chiefly
with the folk-like and fantastic portion of the opera.
Borodin, on the other hand, seemed to appreciate it in its
entirety.' Balakirev 'could not curb his passion for meddling',
and suggested the transposition of the Introduction into B
minor. Rimsky-Korsakov declined to do it, because it would
have meant, amongst other things, the transposition of the
theme representing Spring, which was indissolubly linked in
his imagination with the key of A minor. He also tells us
without any false modesty that in writing it he felt 'a
matured musician and operatic composer who had finally
come to stand on his own feet'. This opinion was confirmed
by the public, who found the work more ingenious and
distinguished than anything Rimsky-Korsakov had previously
written.

The action takes place in the fabulous kingdom of Tsar
Berendey in prehistoric times. The scene of the Prologue is
the Red Mountain near the capital. Act I, in the village of
Berendey; Act II, in the Tsar's palace; Act III, in the sacred
forest; and Act IV, in the village of Yarilo.

Prologue. It is early spring, but although the snows are
melting the wind is cold. Flocks of birds arrive from the
south carrying with them the Fairy Spring. Many years ago, in
a whimsical mood she wooed icy Winter, who now treats her
like a slave. Hence the cold which endures and makes the
very birds shiver. Their love is dead, but Spring and Winter
have a bond in the child that was born of their love, the maid
Snegurochka. They fear for her, for she is now sixteen years
old and can no longer be kept hidden and protected as she
must be; for if the sun-god, Yarilo, should get a glimpse of

her she would die. They must go northward now, but before going entrust her to the keeping of the Spirit of the Wood, who promises to guard her from mischance. Snegurochka is free to go into the world.

A carnival rout invades the stage as Spring and Winter depart. Snegurochka goes amongst the people and her beauty makes a deep impression on Bobil and Bobilicka, who adopt her. Particularly to be noted in the prologue is the very beautiful aria given at her entrance to Snegurochka. One of the problems of this opera is to find a soprano with a voice equal to the music she has to sing, and physical attributes that fit the child-like character she has to play.

Act I. Snegurochka begs Lehl, a young shepherd and singer, to perform for her. He sings two charming folk-like songs for her, but her artless advances are little to his liking, and he goes off eagerly enough at the invitation of the other girls. The little daughter of Spring and Winter knows now the pangs of unrequited love. The situation is complicated by the arrival of the wealthy youth, Misgir, who comes to wed Coupava, but seeing Snegurochka, falls in love with her and bluntly refuses to proceed with the marriage ceremony. Even though Snegurochka refuses to take any notice of Misgir's impassioned advances, Coupava is desolate, and only saved from suicide by the large-hearted Lehl.

Act II. In the palace of the Tsar, Coupava comes to claim redress for the affront Misgir has put upon her. The Tsar orders a court of justice to be held and commands the presence of Misgir and Snegurochka. The Tsar, impressed by Snegurochka's beauty, asks her who her lover is. When she replies that she has no lover, the Tsar protests that not to love is a sin against the sun-god, Yarilo, and ends the trial by promising a reward to anyone who succeeds in winning the love of Snegurochka.

The music of this act, with its serene aria for the Tsar, has a unity, and the action an economy and suspense that are not always apparent in the rest of the opera, which often appears rather loosely knit.

Act III. There is feasting and jollity in the Holy Wood. Even the great Tsar sings a cavatina. It is followed by the celebrated Dance of the Tumblers. Lehl is of the company, and, at the command of the Tsar, sings a delicious song. As a reward he is allowed to claim a kiss from any of the girls present. He passes by Snegurochka, who runs away in tears, and chooses Coupava. Snegurochka, broken-hearted, will not listen to Misgir. When the two are left alone and Misgir would urge his love, Snegurochka vanishes and the Spirit of the Wood, faithful to his trust, bars the way and prevents Misgir from following.

Act IV.   Snegurochka in despair appeals to her mother. She wants to love and be loved. Spring grants her wish, and when Misgir returns she greets him lovingly as her hero. The Tsar greets the couples waiting to be married, amongst them Misgir and Snegurochka. But all is not well. The sun-god has warmed Snegurochka's heart with a ray of sunshine and her destiny must be fulfilled; the little daughter of Spring and Winter must die. As the mist rises she melts away. Misgir throws himself into the lake, but the Tsar interprets his death and that of Snegurochka as a removal of the factor which has influenced Yarilo to withhold his blessings from them. From now on, says the Tsar, Yarilo may be expected to pour his bounty on them. A white-clad youth appears on the mountain top bearing a sheaf of corn in his hand, and the opera ends with an invocation to Yarilo, led by Lehl.   F. B., H.

SADKO

Opera in seven scenes (three or five acts) by Rimsky-Korsakov; text by the composer and V. I. Bielsky. Première, Moscow, January 7, 1898; Metropolitan, New York, 1930, with Fleischer, Johnson, Basiola, Ludikar, conductor Serafin (in French); London, Lyceum Theatre, 1931, with Lissitchkina, Sadoven, Pozemkovsky, conductor Goossens; Rome, 1931, with Saraceni, Pederzini, Livi, Damiani, Vaghi, conductor Marinuzzi; la Scala, Milan, 1938, with Carosio, Giani, Parmeggiani, de Franceschi, Sdanowski, conductor Marinuzzi; Staatsoper, Berlin, 1946, with Berger, Klose, Suthaus, Schock, Neumann, Prohaska, conductor Schüler. Currently in repertory of Russian companies.

CHARACTERS

The King of the Ocean . . . . Bass
Volkhova, *his daughter* . . . . Soprano
Sadko, *a singer of Novgorod* . . . . Tenor
Lubava, *his wife* . . . . Mezzo-Soprano
Nejata, *a gousli player from Kiev* . . . . . . Mezzo-Soprano
A Viking Merchant . . . . Bass
A Hindu Merchant . . . . Tenor

A Venetian Merchant . . . . Baritone
Four Buffoons . . Two Mezzo-Sopranos, Tenor and Bass
Two Elders, *merchants of Novgorod*. . . . . Tenor and Bass
Place: Novgorod, and the bottom of the sea

Tableau I. The merchants of Novgorod sit down to a feast, rejoicing in their prosperity. Nejata, singer and *gousli* player who comes from Kiev, sings a song about the heroic days of old. The merchants would like one of their own countrymen to perform the same service for Novgorod, and Sadko, who enters at that moment, is asked if he will oblige. But his song worries them; he suggests that Novgorod is on a lake, and that, if their ships could only reach the ocean, they could bring back fortunes from all over the world. They laugh at him and bid him good-bye. The feast goes on to the accompaniment of song and dance.

Tableau II. On the shores of Lake Ilmen, Sadko sings of his distress and disillusionment: 'Oh, yon dark forest'. Fascinated by Sadko's singing, swans swam towards him, and, as they reach him, become young women, Volkhova, the Sea Princess, amongst them. He sings again for them, they dance, and the Princess tells him that he has won her love. When dawn comes, she parts from Sadko, but tells him that he will catch three golden fish in the lake, that he will make a journey to a foreign land, and that she will wait faithfully for him until he comes to her. She returns to the deep, where her father, the King of the Ocean, holds sway. The sun rises.

Tableau III. Lubava at home laments the absence of her husband Sadko. Has he gone to seek adventure afar off? Yet only yesterday he assured her of his love. She is overjoyed when he comes in, but broken-hearted when he leaves her again, shouting 'Farewell'.

Tableau IV. The quayside at Novgorod, on Lake Ilmen. Ships lie at anchor, and the people of the town crowd round the rich foreign merchants, who come from every land known to man. Soothsayers ply their trade, Nejata sings to the accompaniment of his *gousli*, buffoons sing and dance, the sound of a pilgrim's chant can be heard. Sadko appears and is greeted with laughter, which increases when he tells them he knows a secret: golden fish can be caught in the lake. He bets his head against the wealth of everyone assembled there that he can prove that he speaks the truth. A net is let down, the song of the Sea Princess is heard, and sure enough, when it is drawn up, there are three gold fishes in the net. Sadko invites all the adventurous men of the port to join him in his journey, and they go off to make their preparations.

Nejata sings of the nightingale that became a great merchant. When he returns, Sadko says he will restore the wealth of the merchants, but would take only their ships. He asks three of the merchants, the Viking, the Venetian and the Indian, to sing to him of their native lands, so that he may decide which to visit. The Viking sings first: his country's shores are rugged, the sea rough, and his countrymen fierce fighters. The slow, *pesante* aria is one of the best known in the Russian bass's repertory. Next comes the Indian merchant, with music and story of much more exotic cast. India is a land of gems and mystery, and his song, any hearer would admit, is the stuff of which dreams are made. It is one of the world's famous melodies, known from having been sung by half the sopranos and tenors who have ever appeared on the concert platform, and by its frequent appearance on violin recitalists' programmes. In its original setting it is a tenor melody:

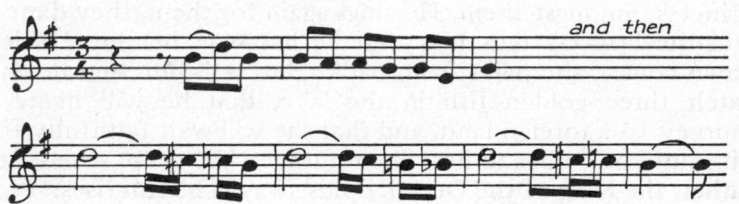

Third representative of the merchants of the world is the Venetian, a baritone, who sings a barcarole. Sadko settles that Venice shall be his destination. He asks the Novgorod people to look after Lubava, and sets sail.

Tableau V. Sadko is on his way home laden with treasure. The ship is becalmed—due to their not having sacrificed to the King of the Ocean all the twelve years they have been away, says Sadko. They pour treasure over the side, but still the ships remains becalmed. Next at Sadko's command they throw wooden logs over the side: Sadko's sinks, and he descends by a ladder to the water's edge, stepping on to a plank which has been thrown overboard. Immediately a breeze gets up, the ship sails away leaving Sadko abandoned, and a mist comes up.

When it clears away (Tableau VI) we are at the bottom of

the sea, at the court of the King of the Ocean. The king and queen sit on thrones, their daughter, Volkhova, sits spinning seaweed. Sadko sings for the king and queen, and is promised the hand of Volkhova in marriage. The wedding guests arrive—every denizen of the deep seems to have been invited—and the marriage is celebrated fittingly. Dances are performed for their entertainment, Sadko sings again and arouses such enthusiasm amongst his hearers that they join in the dance. So fast become the movements of the dancers that the waves are lashed into a fury and ships are sunk. Suddenly an apparition warns them that the reign of the King of the Ocean is at an end. Sadko and Volkhova seated in a shell are drawn away by seagulls.

Tableau VII. It is morning. Sadko sleeps by the side of Lake Ilmen, watched over by Princess Volkhova, who sings a lullaby as she watches. She bids a last farewell to the still-sleeping minstrel, then vanishes in mist, becoming the great river Volkhova and flowing thenceforth from Lake Ilmen to the sea.

Lubava is still distractedly looking for her husband, and she is filled with delight to see him lying by the lake asleep. He thinks he has been asleep ever since he last saw her, and that he has dreamed his voyage. But the sight of his fleet coming up the new river convinces him that it has all taken place, and that he really has become the richest man of Novgorod. All the citizens of that town welcome him, not least the three merchants who sang to him before he left home.   H.

LE COQ D'OR

Zolotoy Pyetushok/The Golden Cockerel

Opera in three acts by Nikolai Rimsky-Korsakov; text by V. Bielsky after Pushkin. Première, Moscow, October 7, 1909. First performed Paris Opéra, 1914; Drury Lane, London, 1914, with Dobrowolska, Petrenko, Petroff, Altchevsky, conductor Emil Cooper; Metropolitan, New York, 1918, with Barrientos, Didur, conductor Monteux (in French). Revived Covent Garden, 1919 (in English), with Nelis, Richardson, conductor Beecham; Buenos Aires, 1937, with Carosio, Melnik; Metropolitan, 1937, with Pons and Pinza, 1942, with Bok and Pinza, 1945, with Munsel and Cordon; Rome, 1940, with Carosio, Pasero, conductor Serafin; Covent Garden, 1954, with Dobbs, Cuénod, Glynne, conductor Markevitch (in English); New York, City Opera, 1967, with Sills, Treigle.

CHARACTERS

King Dodon .... Bass
Prince Guidon .... Tenor
Prince Afron .... Baritone
General Polkan .... Bass
Amelfa, the royal housekeeper .... Contralto
The Astrologer .... Tenor
The Queen of Shemakha .... Soprano
The Golden Cockerel .... Soprano

Le Coq d'Or was Rimsky-Korsakov's last opera. The censor refused to sanction its performance—rather surprisingly, unless he found the references to misconduct of war a little too apt to be pleasant—and it was not until after the composer's death that it was performed. When the work was given in Petersburg, it was thought to be over-taxing for the singers who are obliged to dance, or for the dancers who are obliged to sing. Fokine, the choreographer, ingeniously devised the plan of having all the singers seated at each side of the stage, while the dancers interpreted in pantomime what was sung. In spite of the protests made by the composer's family, this was done in Paris, London, and New York, but the innovation long ago served its purpose in launching the work before the public, and a return has been made to the directions laid down by Rimsky-Korsakov.

The story of *Le Coq d'Or* is taken from Pushkin, who in his turn got it from his nurse. It is quite possible to fill it with symbolical meaning, although the librettist, Bielsky, preferred to think of it as dealing with human passions and weaknesses in their essence and quite apart from any particular context. Of the work as a whole, Ernest Newman (in *Opera Nights*) has written: 'One of the things that constitute the charm of *The Golden Cockerel* for us to-day is the fact that not only are we not sure what it all means but we are not quite sure that it means anything at all, or that it meant anything in particular for either Bielsky or Rimsky-Korsakov beyond opportunity after opportunity for humour, beauty, burlesque, and, occasionally, sincere feeling. And all the ingredients of the pot are so good in themselves that it does not worry us in the least that we cannot find the right name for the strange dish that is the totality of them'.

A muted trumpet gives out the theme associated with the cockerel, Ex. 1:

and it is immediately followed by a descending chromatic melody on the clarinet, which is characteristic of the Queen of Shemakha, Ex. 2:

Much of the music of this short prelude is derived from the Queen's aria of Act II. The thin, *staccato* sound of the xylophone heralds the appearance of the Astrologer before the curtain. By his art, he says, he will conjure up for the audience a tale from long ago; though it is only a fairy story, its moral is excellent. The Astrologer's music is instrumental rather than vocal in character and its *tessitura* abnormally high.

After this short prologue the curtain rises on Act I, which takes place at the court of King Dodon. The council-room is magnificently decorated, and the king is seated in the middle of his ministers and advisers, his two sons, Guidon and Afron, on either side of him. He complains that his neighbours do not treat him fairly; when he was young and vigorous, he used to go out to attack them at the head of his armies; now that he is old, they are inclined to invade him, in spite of the fact that he finds it more and more troublesome to engage in warfare. What advice can his councillors give him to meet the present invasion threat? Guidon, his elder son, is the first to speak. He has naturally given the matter some thought, and his recommendation is that the king withdraw his army inside the capital of his kingdom, and there, supplied with a vast stock of provisions and necessaries, think out the whole problem at leisure. All applaud the suggestion, except old General Polkan, the king's chief minister, who finds the whole notion futile and unpractical. Afron spurns his brother's plan, and advises that the army be disbanded and sent home; once the enemy is past them, they may re-unite and fall upon him from the rear and destroy him. Dodon is delighted, but Polkan demolishes Afron's proposal as quickly as he had Guidon's. There seems no reasonable and practical solution.

Suddenly, preluded by the same music as we had heard in the prologue, the Astrologer appears at the top of the stairs, dressed in a blue robe covered in golden stars, and with a long white astrakhan hat on his head. In music of characteristic cast, he offers the king a magic golden cockerel, which has only to be placed so that it has a view of the surrounding country, and it will crow to give warning of any danger. When it is quiet, the king may rest peacefully and take his ease with no fear of danger to cause him worry. Dodon is delighted, and offers the Astrologer any reward he likes to name, but the old man says he will not take money or honours, but would like to have the king's promise in writing so as to take advantage of his offer at some future date. This request is refused, the king saying in effect that his word is his bond.

The cock (to the sound of Ex. 1) bids the king take his ease heedless of danger. Dodon rejoices at the prospect of never again having to be on his guard against the unknown; he will indulge his pleasures and his desire for sleep from now on for ever. He begins to feel sleepy, and the royal nurse, Amelfa, has his bed brought in by servants. He lies down, eats sweetmeats out of a bowl, and plays with his parrot, which sings to him (in the orchestra). As he goes to sleep, watched by the faithful Amelfa, the orchestra begins the slumber scene (as it is known in the orchestral suite), in which the wood-wind quietly repeat the cockerel's assurance that he can rest undisturbed while the cellos play a gentle lullaby. Even Amelfa falls asleep, and the sound of No. 2 shows that the king in his dreams is anticipating his amorous encounter of the next act.

But the king has not slept for long before he is aroused by the warning cry of the cockerel, which is echoed by the instruments of the orchestra. Polkan manages to wake his master, who gives orders for a general mobilisation of the army, which must proceed to the scene of war and return as soon as it has accomplished its duty. It gets under way to the sound of a march. Soon all is quiet, and Dodon is allowed by his watchful bird to return to his slumbers. He cannot

capture his attractive dream—cannot even remember what
. was about. Amelfa tries to help him and makes one or two
suggestions, finally hitting upon the right one. All go to sleep
once more, only to be awakened by an even more urgent
summons from the cockerel than previously. The crowd
rushes around, and this time Polkan warns the king that he is in
danger himself, and that he must gird himself and lead his
army to victory. With much grumbling, Dodon prepares to
don his armour. It is found to be rusty and dirty, his sword is
too heavy, his cuirass is too tight for him and will hardly
meet round his middle. But in the end, although it still looks
as though nothing fits properly, he is sufficiently arrayed to
go off to the wars, which he does to the acclamation of the
crowd.

Act II. But the war goes badly, and moonlight in a
narrow pass reveals the bodies of the soldiers and the king's
two sons, lying dead and unattended. The march of the
preceding act is now oppressed with gloom, and Dodon
bursts into lamentation when he finds the bodies of his slain
sons. His lament is typically Russian in character; it may be
excessive, but it is certainly not lacking in seriousness.

The mists which have shrouded the pass lift, and reveal a
tent. General consternation. Could it belong to the enemy
general? Reluctantly the soldiers are persuaded to drag a piece
of comic artillery which is trained on the tent, and eventually
with much difficulty fired. But its only effect is that a
beautiful young woman emerges from the tent; the soldiers,
all but Dodon and Polkan, take to their heels and disappear.
The young woman, with nothing but the clarinet phrase of Ex.
2 as prelude, sings the praises of the sun, which gives life and
beauty to her native land. This is the famous 'Hymn to the
Sun', whose sensuously beautiful melody has made it
amongst Rimsky-Korsakov's vocal compositions second in
popularity only to the Song of the Indian Guest from *Sadko*.

When she is questioned, the girl reveals that she is the
Queen of Shemakha, come to subdue Dodon, not by force of
arms but by her own physical beauty. Dodon is shyer than
Polkan, but eventually Polkan's bluntness goes too far and
she asks for him to be sent away. Dodon promptly complies,
and Polkan watches subsequent proceedings from behind the
queen's tent (the bodies of the soldiers have by now been
cleared away, and the scene is bathed in sunlight).

Beginning with a little 6/8 tune in which she describes her

unclothed beauty, the queen proceeds to vamp Dodon
seductive snatches of song. Even an orchestral reference to
the cockerel's warning makes not the slightest difference to
the king, who appears to enjoy the process of becoming
ensnared. The queen tells him he must sing for her, as he no
doubt once did in his youth, and at her orders he starts an
incredibly primitive-sounding melody, much to her glee. The
queen tries new tactics. At home everyone obeys her slightest
whim, and her caprice rules her kingdom; Oh, for
contradiction, even domination! Timidly Dodon offers
himself as dominator, and she asks him to dance for her—as
he must once have danced when he was young. She rigs him
up with a fan and scarf in place of his cumbersome armour,
and has her slaves play a slow melody to accompany him. She
joins him and mocks his efforts, which land him, as the music
gets quicker, on some cushions in a state of collapse.

By now, the king is completely under the queen's spell. He
repeats his offer of his hand, his possessions, his throne, his
kingdom. She accepts, with the proviso that Polkan shall
forthwith be whipped; Dodon offers to go further and behead
him. Preparations are immediately put in hand for a return to
Dodon's kingdom, and, while the queen's slaves mock at her
newest capture, Dodon's army lines up to escort their
monarch and his bride to their capital. The act ends with the
grotesque procession.

Act III.   We are back in Dodon's capital. The crowd is
wondering if and when he will return. Rumours are noised
abroad: he has won a great victory, but lost his two sons, and
is escorting home as his bride a young queen whom he
rescued from a dragon. All must be well, argue the people,
since the cockerel is quiet. Then the cry goes up that the
procession is at hand. It files through the crowd, and
eventually the king and his bride appear, riding in their gilded
chariot, and acclaimed by the crowd.

Suddenly, proceedings are interrupted by the appearance
of the Astrologer, preceded naturally by his characteristic
music. He has come to claim his reward from the king; it shall
be the princess who rides by the king's side! The king angrily
refuses, but the Astrologer persists, emphasising his determination to risk marriage even at his age with a sustained top
E (Rimsky-Korsakov, in his preface to the score, underlines
the fact that the role of the Astrologer requires a tenor with a
highly developed falsetto voice). The king orders his guards

to remove the old man, and when he seems still anxious to continue the dispute, Dodon strikes him on the head with his sceptre, and kills him. The sky darkens, thunder is heard, and Dodon has the grace to appear embarrassed at the turn events have taken; such a bad omen on one's wedding day! The queen laughs at the whole episode, but, when Dodon tries to embrace her, repulses him in disgust. The cockerel suddenly comes to life, utters a piercing cry, flies over the head of the crowd and pecks the king on the head. He falls dead, and the crowd loyally breaks into lamentation for him. The sky becomes completely dark, and when light returns, both queen and cockerel have disappeared.

In the epilogue, the resuscitated Astrologer announces that the story is only a fairy tale and that in Dodon's kingdom only the queen and he himself were mortals.

It seems likely that *Le Coq d'Or* will gradually be accepted as in its way the best of Rimsky-Korsakov's operas. It is more compactly shaped than his other stage works, and here the gorgeous orchestration has a new economy and is treated with a more directly pointed sense of style than elsewhere. The spectacular staging which the work requires, and the hardly less spectacular vocal writing for the coloratura-soprano queen are qualities which have contributed towards the opera's popularity; they also constitute a direct link with Rimsky-Korsakov's most famous pupil, Stravinsky, whose first opera, *Le Rossignol*, begun a year after *Le Coq d'Or*, makes use of exactly the same characteristics.   H.

12
English Opera

MICHAEL WILLIAM BALFE
(1803–1870)

THE BOHEMIAN GIRL

OPERA in three acts by Michael William Balfe; text by Alfred Bunn founded on the ballet-pantomime, *The Gipsy*, by St. Georges. Première, Drury Lane, London, November 27, 1843. First performed New York, 1844; Her Majesty's Theatre (in Italian), 1858. Revived Sadler's Wells, 1932, with Kemp, Coates, Tudor Davies, Kelsey, Austin; Covent Garden Company at Liverpool, 1951, and subsequently at the Royal Opera House, in a new version by Sir Thomas Beecham and Dennis Arundell with Roberta Peters, Coates, Marlowe and Lanigan, Dickie, Walters, Glynne, conductor Beecham. Like *Maritana*, continuously in the repertories of the British touring companies until the 1930's.

CHARACTERS

Arline, *daughter of the Count* . . . . Soprano
Thaddeus, *a proscribed Pole* . . . . Tenor
Queen of the Gypsies . . . . Alto
Devilshoof, *chief of the gypsies* . . . . Bass
Count Arnheim, *Governor of Presburg* . . . . Bass
Florestein, *his nephew* . . . . Tenor
Captain of the Guard . . . . Bass
Officer . . . . Tenor
Buda, *Arline's attendant* . . . . Soprano

The *Bohemian Girl* owes its popularity to the easy melodies which abound in its score and also, partly, to the fact that it embodies elements which commended opera to a certain class of audience a hundred years ago. There are no subtleties in the libretto of Alfred Bunn; in fact it has been held up to ridicule ever since it was written. On the other hand, the action is vigorous and as remote from everyday life as one could well imagine. The chief characters are either noblemen or gypsies—noblemen who have the power of life and death over the people, and gypsies who may rob and cheat but also number amongst their companions beings as innocent and pure as the hero and heroine of the story.

The action takes place at Presburg in Poland.

Act I. Thaddeus, a Polish noble exiled after a rebellion, has sought the company of Devilshoof and his gypsies in order to escape the punishment to which he has been condemned. As a gypsy he saves the life of Arline, the daughter of Count Arnheim, the Austrian governor of the province. The delighted father invites both Thaddeus and Devilshoof to his castle. They go, but refuse to drink the health of the Emperor as loyal subjects should. Devilshoof is cast into prison; Thaddeus, who saved little Arline, is allowed to go free. Devilshoof, however, is the master locksmith for whom locks and bars have no secret. He escapes from prison and, to revenge himself for the slight that has been put on him, steals Arline and hides her amongst the gypsies.

The chief numbers in Act I are Thaddeus's entrance aria, "'Tis sad to leave our fatherland', and, 'In the gypsy's life you read', the gypsy chorus, which recurs often during the course of the action.

Act II. Twelve years have gone by and Arline, grown to womanhood, has fallen in love with her rescuer, Thaddeus, who returns her love and wishes to marry her. There is, however, an obstacle. The Queen of the Gypsies is herself in love with Thaddeus, and the Queen is not a woman to be slighted with impunity.

Devilshoof and his friends have robbed Florestein, nephew of Count Arnheim, of all he possessed while he was returning from a feast. The Queen, fearing the Count's power, orders the booty to be returned. The trinkets are returned accordingly, all but a medallion which Devilshoof has taken as his share, but which the Queen retains with a view to its later uses. When she is forced by gypsy custom to unite Thaddeus and Arline, she begins to plot and plan the girl's downfall, and the opportunity is not long in coming.

The gypsies have mingled with the crowds at the fair and there the Queen presents Arline with the medallion stolen from Florestein. This young nobleman, who was at first attracted by Arline and then piqued by her refusals, on seeing the trinket, accuses her of theft and, in spite of the gypsies' resistance, Arline is taken to the castle to be tried. Count Arnheim would be merciful since the accused woman is just the age of his lost daughter, but the evidence is against her and he is forced to find her guilty. Arline does not know the secret of her birth although she has dreamt, as she confided to Thaddeus earlier on, that she 'dwelt in marble halls with vassals and serfs at my side'. Blood, however, will tell; feeling herself disgraced, she is about to stab herself to the heart when the Count himself stops her and in grasping her hand he notices a scar, similar to that his lost daughter bore, on her arm. Recognition follows, to the great joy of all but Thaddeus, who fears that Arline is lost to him.

This act contains the best-known aria in the score, Arline's 'I dreamt that I dwelt in marble halls', a simple tune which, when well sung as it was by, for instance, Roberta Peters in the Covent Garden revival in 1951, is of truly appealing character.

There are also the Count's, 'The heart bowed down', a duet for Arline and Thaddeus, and of course the inevitable repetition of the gypsies' chorus.

Act III. Arline is faithful to her lover and, in spite of her high station and its advantages, would return to him. The Count, appealed to by the lovers, sternly objects to the marriage of his daughter with a gypsy. Whereupon Thaddeus, stung to the quick, reveals his real identity. The fact that he rebelled against the Austrians is forgotten and forgiven, and a wedding-feast arranged. The Queen alone is angry and disappointed. She aims a shot at Arline, but the bullet ricocheting, kills her that fired it. Thaddeus's aria, 'When other lips and other hearts', occurs early in Act III.

The Bohemian Girl, Maritana and *The Lily of Killarney* were collectively known for many years as 'The English Ring'.   F. B.

JULIUS BENEDICT

(1804–1885)

THE LILY OF KILLARNEY

OPERA in three acts by Julius Benedict, text by J. Oxenford and D. Boucicault, after the latter's play *Colleen Bawn*. Première, Covent Garden, February 8, 1862, with Louise Pyne, Henry Haigh, Charles Santley, William Harrison. First produced New York, 1868; Brunswick, Hamburg and other German cities, 1863, as *Die Rose von Erin*. Revived Covent Garden, 1902, with Fanny Moody, Joseph O'Mara, Charles Macgrath, Charles Manners; Sadler's Wells, 1931, with Jean Kemp, Arthur Cox, Henry Wendon, Harry Brindle.

CHARACTERS

Eily O'Connor (The Colleen Bawn) ....Soprano
Hardress Cregan, *secretly married to Eily* ....Tenor
Mrs. Cregan, *his mother*..................Contralto
Mr. Corrigan, *Holder of a mortage on the Cregan
    lands* .... Bass
Myles na Coppaleen, *in love with Eily* ....Tenor
Danny Mann, *a boatman, devoted to Hardress* .Baritone
Miss Ann Chute, *an heiress* ....Soprano
Sheelah......................................Contralto
Father Tom ....Bass
O'Moore ....Bass

Time: Nineteenth Century   *Place:* Ireland

Act I, scene i.   The hall at Tore Cregan. Hardress Cregan, whose secret marriage to the beautiful peasant girl Eily O'Connor is unknown even to his mother, is entertaining his friends. Two guests squabble about the merits of their horses, and Hardress decides that only a steeplechase can satisfactorily settle the argument. Mrs. Cregan is left alone to be visited by Mr. Corrigan, a vulgarian who holds a mortage on the Cregan property and threatens that, if Hardress does not marry the heiress Ann Chute and so obtain the money, he will demand her own hand in marriage. She is outraged at the suggestion.

At this point Danny Mann is heard singing in the distance, and Corrigan tells Mrs. Cregan that Mann is waiting to take Hardress to visit the Colleen Bawn and forces her to watch

957

the lantern signals as proof of her son's infatuation. They listen as Hardress and Danny sing 'The Moon has raised her lamp above', a duet that is probably the best known piece in the score. In a quartet ('Ah, never was seen') Mrs. Cregan and Corrigan sing of their anger and suspicion, while Danny and Hardress are heard singing on their way to Eily.

Scene ii. Eily's cottage. Corrigan tries to extract information about Hardress from Myles na Coppaleen, a peasant hopelessly in love with Eily, who sings of his unrequited love ('From Inchigela' and 'It is a charming girl'). Eily, with Myles, Sheelah and Father Tom (a good priest who watches over her) is waiting for her husband. She tells the story of her secret marriage in a romance ('In my wild mountain valley'), and the four sing a lively quartet which is interrupted, to the chagrin of Myles, by the sound of Hardress approaching. Father Tom begs Eily to make her marriage public, but when Hardress arrives he tries to induce her to surrender her marriage certificate to him and so conceal the matter altogether. Myles and Father Tom succeed in making Eily promise never to part with the precious document, and Hardress leaves in a passion.

Act II opens with a hunting chorus as Hardress begins to pay court to Ann Chute. She sings a florid air ('The eye of love is keen') which is followed by a duet ('Ah, never may that faithful heart'), in which Hardress is nagged by conscience as he thinks of Eily. Hardress is horrified when Danny Mann suggests that he should murder Eily so as to clear the way for him; if he decides on her death, he has only to send Danny his glove as a signal.

Scene ii. There follows a tempestuous scene with Hardress flying into a passion at Corrigan's attentions to his mother; Mrs. Cregan crying that her son could save her from him if he wished, and Corrigan taunting Hardress with his love for Eily. All this is overheard by Danny Mann, who darkly hints to Mrs. Cregan that if she can persuade Hardress to send him his glove, her troubles will be over. Mrs. Cregan is puzzled but goes off to do as he suggests. She returns with the glove and gives it to Danny, whose momentary pangs at the prospect of his self-imposed task eventually yield to his feelings of loyalty to his master.

Scene iii. At her cottage, Eily sings of her loneliness and longing for her husband. Danny Mann, much the worse for drink, comes to tell her that he will row her across the lake to

Hardress. Myles begs her not to go, but Eily mocks his fears and goes off in Danny's boat.

Scene iv.   To a lonely cave comes Myles, still singing of his hopeless love for Eily. Seeing an otter slither off a rock, he goes to get his gun.

Danny rows Eily into the cave, sets her ashore on a rock and demands her marriage lines or her life. She refuses to give them up and Danny pushes her into the water. A shot is heard and Danny too falls into the sea. Myles comes to look for the otter he thinks he has shot and finds Eily under the water. He plunges in and drags her out, as the song of the boatmen can be heard in the mysterious distance.

Act III.   Myles sings a lullaby to Eily and then he, Eily and Father Tom together thank heaven for her rescue. The scene changes to the town, where Hardress is about to marry Ann Chute. Suddenly, Corrigan arrives with soldiers who arrest Hardress for his part in the murder of Eily, Danny Mann having made a dying confession. Villainy is only kept from triumph by the timely arrival of Myles and Eily to refute the allegation. The truth about the marriage is revealed, Mrs. Cregan allays suspicion about her son by admitting that he knew nothing about Danny Mann and the glove; and all ends in a gay Rondo Finale.   H.

VINCENT WALLACE
(1814–1865)
MARITANA

OPERA in three acts by Vincent Wallace; text by Edward Fitzball, based on the play, *Don César de Bazan*. Première, Drury Lane, London, November 15, 1845. First performed Philadelphia, 1846; New York, 1848; Her Majesty's Theatre, London (in Italian), 1880. Revived Lyceum, London, 1925; Old Vic and Sadler's Wells, 1931, with Kennard (later Cross), Morris, Cox, Austin, Brindle. Continuously in the repertories of the British touring companies until about 1930.

CHARACTERS

Maritana, *a handsome gitana* .... Soprano
Don Caesar de Bazan .... Tenor
Don José de Santarem, *an unscrupulous courtier* Baritone
Lazarillo, *a poor boy* .... .Mezzo-Soprano
The Marchioness of Montefiore ...... .Mezzo-Soprano
Captain of the Guard .... Baritone
Marquis of Montefiore .... Bass
The King .... Bass
The Alcade .... Bass

Soldiers, Gypsies, Populace

Place: Madrid

Maritana deals, like Balfe's *Bohemian Girl*, on the one hand with the very poor and the very rich and powerful on the other. The essential difference is that while there is no humour of any kind in *The Bohemian Girl*, the librettist of *Maritana*, Edward Fitzball, has contrived to invest the character of Don Caesar de Bazan with a lighthearted, whimsical humour which, if it is not wit, is at least an acceptable substitute for it. As regards the music, the soprano aria 'Scenes that are brightest' and the tenor's 'Yes, let me like a soldier fall' make a perfect match to Balfe's 'I dreamt that I dwelt in marble halls'.

Don José, a young and wealthy courtier of Madrid, is enamoured of the Queen of Spain. Don José believes that the Queen would be his if he could only persuade her that the King does not care for her. The King himself is of a roaming, roving disposition and he has been much attracted lately by the simple charms of Maritana, a street singer, whom we meet at the beginning of Act I engaged in her occupation and surrounded by an admiring crowd. Don José naturally determines to do his utmost to further the King's interests in this quarter, although he well knows that Maritana is above the temptations of wealth and position. Since she does not care for the King, José has to wait until chance comes to aid his desires. The opportunity comes with the return to Madrid of Don Caesar de Bazan, a nobleman as poor as a church mouse and as proud as Satan. Don Caesar, the hero of countless duels, when told by Don José that duelling has been forbidden on pain of death, declares his intention never to fight again. He learns that anyone who forfeits his life to the law on this particular day of the year is not going to be shot a clean, soldierly fashion, but hanged. But when Lazarillo, a poor apprentice, is pursued by guards, he does not hesitate to challenge their captain so as to give Lazarillo a chance of escaping. Don Caesar wounds the captain, but is himself apprehended and marched to jail.

Act II. Interior of a fortress. The prospect of dying a felon's death horrifies him and when offered he accepts eagerly a strange proposal from Don José. Don José, believing that if Maritana could be married to a nobleman he could bring her more easily to comply with the King's wishes, proposes a bargain. Don Caesar will be shot and not hanged if he consents to marry before his execution a veiled lady. Don Caesar is ready to do anything if he can escape the rope, and sings one of the best arias of the opera, exalting the advantages of a soldier's death: 'Yes, let me like a soldier fall'. Don José recalls his first sight of the Queen: 'In happy moments day by day', and resolves to go through with his scheme. The marriage takes place there and then and so, apparently, does the execution—apparently, since Lazarillo, to show his devotion to the man who risked death to serve him, had abstracted the bullets from the executioners' rifles. The soldier of the song fell only to rise again. As soon as the firing squad has gone, Don Caesar walks away and goes in search of the unknown lady he has wedded.

Meanwhile, the King, remembering Don Caesar's former services to the State, had pardoned him. But the pardon fell into the hands of Don José, who did not hesitate to hide it and free himself of Don Caesar's presence.

Scene ii. Maritana has now been taken to the castle of the Marquis of Montefiore. There she is introduced to the King: 'Hear me, gentle Maritana'. Her heart has been given to the gallant Don Caesar and she refuses to listen to the advances of her royal master. Don Caesar comes to the Marquis's house, in search of his wife, whom he is sure he will recognise, although he has only seen her once heavily veiled: 'There is a flower that bloometh'. At Don José's instigation, the Marchioness poses as the wife of Don Caesar, who is completely disillusioned when he sees her age. He is about to sign away all claim on her, when he hears and recognises Maritana's voice and suspects that some intrigue is in progress: 'What mystery?' Don José has Don Caesar re-arrested.

Act III. A magnificent apartment. Maritana laments the

loss of her liberty: 'Scenes that are brightest'. The King comes to her pretending to be her husband. Lazarillo, ordered by Don José to guard their privacy and to shoot anyone who attempts to enter, fires on an approaching stranger. His aim is not accurate enough to hit Don Caesar, who climbs in through the window to meet the King, whom Maritana had left to nurse his disappointment alone, 'What are you doing here?' he asks, without recognising the King. 'I am the master here, the Count of Bazan,' replies His Majesty. 'Oh, well', retorts the nobleman, 'I, then, must be the King'. In the course of the wrangle, Don Caesar finds out from the King that he was pardoned and that the execution which nearly cost him his life need never have taken place. The King leaves, and Don Caesar is face to face with Maritana. They recognise each other as husband and wife. The Queen arrives, escorted by Don José, who meant to show her her spouse's infidelity. Explanations ensue (Don Caesar incidentally ran his sword through Don José's body to save the Queen from his importunity) and all ends happily for Don Caesar and his true love, the street singer, Maritana.   F.B.

13
Czech Opera

BEDŘICH SMETANA
(1824–1884)

THE BARTERED BRIDE
Prodaná Nevěsta

OPERA in three acts by Bedřich Smetana; text by Karel Sabina. Première, Prague National Theatre, May 30, 1866; some alterations were made to the work in 1869 and the final version produced, 1870. First performed Chicago, 1893 (in Czech); Drury Lane, London, 1895 (in German); Covent Garden, 1907 (in German), with Bosetti, Nast, Naval, Marx, conductor Schalk; Metropolitan, New York, 1909 (in German), with Destinn, Jörn, Reiss, Didur, conductor Mahler; Sadler's Wells, 1935 (in English), with Cross, Tudor Davies, Powell Lloyd, Matters, conductor Collingwood; la Scala, Milan, 1935, with Oltrabella, Wesselowski, Nessi, Pasero, conductor Ghione. Revivals include Covent Garden, 1931 (in English), with Phillips, Ben Williams, Dua, Heming, conductor Barbirolli; 1939 (in German), with Hilde Konetzni, Tauber, Tessmer, Krenn, conductor Beecham; 1955 (in English), with Morison, Lanigan, Pears, Dalberg, conductor Kubelik; Metropolitan, 1926, with Müller (later Rethberg), Laubenthal, Meader, Bohnen, conductor Bodanzky; 1941, with Novotna, Kullman, Laufkoetter, Pinza, conductor Walter; Sadler's Wells (at the New Theatre), 1943, with Hill (later Sladen), Servent, Pears, Donlevy, conductor Collingwood; Vienna State Opera, 1951, with Jurinac, Dermota, Christ, Edelmann, conductor Ackermann.

CHARACTERS

Krušina,[1] *a peasant* . . . . Baritone
Ludmila, *his wife* . . . . Mezzo-Soprano
Mařenka,[2] *their daughter* . . . . Soprano

[1] š = approximately 'sh'; [2] ř = approximately 'rj' (as in Dvořak);

Micha, *a landlord* .... Bass
Hata, *his wife* .... Mezzo-Soprano
Vašek, *their son*. .... Tenor
Jenik, *Micha's son by his first marriage* .... Tenor
Kečal,[1] *a marriage broker* .... Bass
Ringmaster *of a troupe of circus artists* .... Tenor
Esmeralda, *a dancer* .... Soprano
An 'Indian' .... Bass

The Bartered Bride is so much of a national institution
inside Czechoslovakia, and has more recently been accepted
by the outside world as so typical of the very best type of
'folk opera' that it is surprising to remember that Smetana
was looked upon during his life-time as insufficiently
nationalist in feeling, and his other operas as too strongly
under the influence of Wagner. Yet so it was. *The Bartered
Bride* won him immediate recognition as a musical patriot,
but the public attitude to some of his other works so angered
the composer that he claimed to have written this popular
comedy without either conviction or much enthusiasm.

The Overture, written before the rest of the opera, so great
was Smetana's enthusiasm for the subject he was to tackle, is
immensely and justifiably popular as a concert piece. Its
themes are later used in connection with Kečal and the
marriage contract (in the finale to Act II, the Inn Scene), but
whatever their associations, their dashing quavers, Mozartian
in their gaiety and appropriately marked *vivacissimo*, give the
opera an irresistible start.

Act I. Spring in a Bohemian village. The village inn is on
one side of the stage. It is holiday time, and the villagers are
rejoicing at the prospect of the dancing which will take place
to celebrate it. Only Mařenka and Jenik seem left out of the
general gaiety, and their gloom, we learn, is caused by the
fact that Mařenka has just learned that her parents plan a rich
marriage for her, in spite of her heart having long since been
given to the handsome but impecunious Jenik. The villagers
go off to dance, and Mařenka tells Jenik that her heart would
break were he to desert her; her love is his, even though she
knows so little of his antecedents and background. Their love
duet leaves little doubt of their mutual affection; the lyrical
main section is heard fairly frequently during the course of
the opera as a love motif.

---

[1] č = approximately 'ts'.

Mařenka and Jenik leave the stage and are succeeded by Mařenka's parents, who are being harangued by that typically Czech institution, the marriage broker. He has the gift of the gab, and it is some time before either of his listeners can get a word in past his apparently endless repetitions of his patter. When they do, it is clear that they are prepared to accept his suggestion that Mařenka shall marry the son of Tobias Micha, a rich neighbour. Krušina thinks the contract should be taken up forthwith; he himself knows Micha, but he cannot so much as remember the names of his two sons. Kečal protests that there is only one; the other, by Micha's first marriage, disappeared from home years ago and is now presumed dead. In spite of Kečal's enthusiastic description of the prospective bridegroom, who was only prevented by his natural modesty from meeting them even now, Ludmila still thinks the final decision should be left in Mařenka's hands.

The trio becomes a quartet when Mařenka herself appears on the scene. She has one small objection to the scheme, she says: she has become engaged to Jenik. Kečal refuses to take such objections seriously, Krušina is furious that his permission has not already been asked, and even Ludmila thinks Mařenka might have handled the whole affair more tactfully. Mařenka knocks the contract out of Kečal's hand, and leaves her parents wishing that Kečal had brought the bridegroom along with him; a sight of him might have caused her to change her mind.

The act ends with a spirited polka, danced and sung by the assembled villagers, and watched by their elders from the tables of the hospitable inn.

Act II. The scene changes to the inside of the inn, where the men are busy drinking; in a chorus, they sing the praises of beer. Kečal is there looking for Jenik, who seems sunk in reflection. Both, however, join in the chorus, Kečal vaunting money as the most desirable of possessions, Jenik objecting that he prefers love. Women join the men, and all dance a brilliant and energetic Furiant, known, like the overture, in the concert hall.

All leave the inn, and the coast is clear for a first sight of Vašek, who comes shyly in, stammering out that he has been sent off by his mother to woo his prospective bride, a frightening business, but one that he does not see how to avoid without making himself a laughing stock. He is an enchantingly silly figure, with his stutter and his transparent simplicity. It does not take long before Mařenka, who comes in to find him alone, realises that this is the bridegroom who has been picked out for her. She is horrified, and proceeds to tell him that she, like all the other village girls, is really sorry that so handsome a lad is contracted to Mařenka, a flighty girl who will lead him an awful dance once they are married. Vašek is frightened at what his mother may say, but Mařenka paints a much brighter prospect for him with another girl, prettier than Mařenka and already very much attracted to him from a distance. He eventually agrees to give up Mařenka, and tries to kiss the pretty girl in front of him; she evades him, but he follows her out of the room.

Kečal has the prospect of a sizeable commission if he brings off the matter of Mařenka's betrothal to the son of Tobias Micha, and he does not intend to lose it. Accordingly, he is prepared to invest a proportion of it in buying off the tiresome suitor whom Mařenka appears to favour. He takes Jenik to the inn for a drink, and talks the matter over. Things do not seem to be getting very far, but Kečal is at pains to point out that there are as good fish in the sea as ever came out of it; why worry so much about this particular girl, when there are others only too anxious to get married? He seems to have made some headway as a result of his monologue, and he attempts to clinch the matter by offering Jenik a match in which there would be some money for him. However, even the brilliant and lively tune of their duet, which Jenik repeats after him, is not enough to persuade the young man to give up his sweetheart, and Kečal is eventually reduced to offering him a substantial sum of money if he will renounce his claim on Mařenka. Jenik takes some persuading, but finally agrees to do so—but only to the eldest son of Tobias Micha, the money to be paid to him and to be reclaimable under no circumstances whatsoever.

Kečal goes off well satisfied with the bargain he has made, but he leaves behind him a Jenik who knows quite well that the eldest son of Micha, presumed dead, is none other than himself. He has acquired a marriage contract to his beloved and a dowry from his cheese-paring stepmother at the same time! The plan must succeed! We can have no doubts as to the sincerity of Jenik's love for Mařenka after the beautiful love song which he sings the moment Kečal's back is turned. He has not only outwitted the broker, but he deserves his reward!

But he is not left alone for long. Kečal brings in Krušina and all the villagers to celebrate his successful handling of what turned out to be by no means a simple affair. The finale uses the material already heard in the overture. Kečal calls for silence, as he wants everyone to witness the legality of the document he is now going to have signed in their presence. In legal language, Kečal reads it out; it is to the effect that Jenik has agreed to renounce Mařenka. Krušina and Kečal are delighted, so apparently is Jenik, but the villagers cannot quite understand the position until Kečal adds that the whole thing is in consideration of the sum of three hundred gulden. Then popular fury knows no bounds; even Krušina is shocked that Jenik should abandon Mařenka for money, and Jenik signs amidst a general demonstration of hostility.

Act III has the same set as Act I. Vašek is in stuttering despair that he cannot find the girl who gave him such good advice and whom he found so attractive. His genuinely comic aria is marked *lamentoso*. His thoughts are interrupted by the arrival of a circus troupe, headed by a redoubtable Ringmaster and heralded by the so-called March of the Comedians. The Ringmaster announces that the attractions include the great dancer, Esmeralda, and a real, live, American bear. Let all the bystanders stay and watch a sample of what the company can do! To the accompaniment of the delightfully varied and tuneful Dance of the Comedians, the clowns and dancers go through their paces, watched by an admiring throng.

When all have gone their way, only Vašek is left behind admiring the beautiful Esmeralda. Just then, one of the clowns comes running in to tell the Ringmaster that the man who usually plays the bear is much too drunk to go through with his role. He himself has looked for a suitable substitute, but something is wrong with everyone he has asked, and he is at his wits' end. Esmeralda solves the problem by suggesting that the dimwit who has been gawking at her for some minutes would be just the right build. The Ringmaster asks Vašek if he would like to dance with the beautiful girl, Esmeralda assures him that she will teach him how, and the agreement is completed. He will make his début that night— all this to an enchanting dance tune sung by the two circus professionals, but made into a trio by the prancing if silent Vašek.

Vašek is just practising some steps to himself, when he sees his parents. Hata wants him to come with them to meet his future bride, but he is unwilling, and downright determined when he hears that it is Krušina's Mařenka who is his destined spouse. He does not know who it is he wants to marry, or rather he does not know her name, but he *is* sure that it is not Mařenka. He escapes, and a moment later in comes Mařenka, furious and mortified at the news her father tells her, that Jenik has sold her love for money. The orchestra reminds her of Jenik's protestations of undying affection, and she is inconsolable.

Vašek reappears and is overjoyed to hear that the girl who stands before him, whom he found so attractive, is Mařenka after all. But poor Mařenka asks for time in which to make up her mind, and the parents of the prospective bride and bridegroom join with Kečal in exhorting her to give the matter serious thought. This sextet (Mařenka joins them just before it finishes) is a lovely, contemplative piece. The mood is continued when Mařenka is left alone to lament her unhappy position. Everything around her seems dead, she sings, but her misery gives way to melancholy when she reflects that it is she who has changed, and not the spring, which is as lovely as ever.

To her comes Jenik, apparently in the best of spirits. Mařenka is furious with him, and even more so when he seems to treat the whole affair as an excellent joke. Nothing he can do will reconcile her to hearing him out. The argument is by no means over when Kečal comes up to them, to tell Jenik he can have his money as soon as Mařenka has signed the contract. Jenik urges her to do so, which naturally only increases her fury against him, and gives Kečal an even worse opinion of the type of man with whom he is dealing— these sentiments find expression in a trio.

Everyone in the village comes together for the finale which is to see the betrothal of Mařenka and (as Jenik insists the description shall run) 'the son of Tobias Micha'. Everyone congratulates Mařenka on the match, nobody louder than Jenik, who has no sooner opened his mouth than he is recognised by Hata and Micha as the long-lost son of the latter. He asks Mařenka whether she will have him or Vasek, and her triumphant answer leaves Kečal babbling with fury at having been outwitted. He makes himself so conspicuous in fact that everyone laughs at his discomfiture; he goes out in a real rage.

All is now set for a happy ending, but there is an interruption as a couple of small boys rush in shouting that the bear is loose! He shambles in, but it is not long before the voice of Vašek can be heard inside the skin saying that nobody need be frightened, as the bear is only him. Hata takes him off, and all rejoice at the betrothal of the bartered bride and her faithful lover.   H.

DALIBOR

Opera in three acts by Bedřich Smetana, German text by J. Wenzig, Czech transl. by Špindler. Première at Prague, May 16, 1868, with Benevicová-Miková (Milada), Lukes (Dalibor). First performed in Vienna, 1892; revived 1938, with Hilde Konetzni, Réthy, Mazaroff, Destal, Kipnis, conductor Walter. First performed Chicago, 1924; Berlin, 1940, with Lemnitz, Scheppan, Völker, Bockelmann, von Manowarda; Edinburgh Festival, 1964 (first performance in Great Britain), by Prague Opera with Miková, Domaninská, Přibyl, Bednař, Haken, conductor Jaroslav Krombholc.

CHARACTERS

Vladislav, *King of Bohemia* .... Baritone
Dalibor, *a knight* .... Tenor
Budivoj, *captain of the guard* .... Baritone
Beneš, *the gaoler* .... Bass
Vítek, *Dalibor's squire* .... Tenor
Milada, *sister of the dead Burgrave* .... Soprano
Jitka .... Soprano
Zdeněk's ghost
                    Nobles, soldiers, men and women
Time: Fifteenth Century   *Place:* Prague

The story of *Dalibor* was a legend[1] which symbolised Czech aspirations long before Smetana took it as a subject for

---

[1] The original legend concerns, says Brian Large, 'the rebellious knight, Dalibor, imprisoned in the Daliborka Tower near Hradčany ... in 1498 for leading an uprising for the recognition of peasant brewing rights. During captivity, Dalibor learnt to play the violin so beautifully that people came from all over the city to hear him. Though tortured ... and later executed for his part in inciting serfs to rebel against their tyrannical masters, Dalibor became a symbol of just revolt against royal power.'

an opera. It is hard to believe that his librettist's treatment of the story owed nothing to *Fidelio* and that dramatic resemblances between the two are pure coincidence. After 1919, when Czech independence ceased to be a dream and became reality, the opera took on new significance for the Czech people, and it has since then been looked on, with *The Bartered Bride*, as a national institution, a position which its theme and the splendid music in which it is clothed seem amply to justify.

In her *The Music of Czechoslovakia* (O.U.P.), Rosa Newmarch writes: 'The theme of *Dalibor* seems to have been noted down by the composer as early as 1863. It appears in the opera soon after the opening fanfare, and in this form, *largo maestoso*, probably represents the destiny, rather than the personality, of Dalibor, and is always treated by the orchestra, rather than by an individual voice or instrument. A modified form of it, in F major, depicts Dalibor the proud knight and intrepid hero. Out of this theme grows the melody associated with Dalibor's murdered friend, Zdeněk. It is of a softer type and more suited to its eventual use as a violin solo when the spirit of Zdeněk appears to Dalibor in the dungeon. . . . The motif of deliverance—another derivative—appears as a brilliant little fanfare in G major.'

There is no extensive overture, and the curtain rises after fifteen bars of music on the judgment hall of the King's palace in Prague. Dalibor has been engaged in strife with the Burgrave of Ploskovice; his friend Zdeněk was captured and put to death, and, in revenge, Dalibor has killed the Burgrave. For this he is coming up for judgment in front of the King. The people, amongst them Jitka, an orphan whom Dalibor has befriended, are waiting for the assembly of the court; they praise Dalibor as their friend and protector. The King enters with his judges, and rehearses the charges against Dalibor. He calls Milada, the sister of the dead Burgrave, to substantiate her accusations.

Amidst expressions of sympathy for her bereavement, she tells the dramatic story of Dalibor's entry into the castle, and of how he killed her brother. The King assures her Dalibor will pay for his crime with his life, and he orders that the accused may be brought in. As he enters, murmurs of admiration are heard on all sides, and even Milada is compelled to comment on his fearless, noble appearance. Dalibor does not deny his action; only, it was not murder but vengeance for murder. In an aria he tells of his love for his friend and of his violin playing (the solo violin is throughout associated with Zdeněk). Zdeněk was captured in battle, and when Dalibor asked what ransom was required to redeem him, he was sent his head on the end of a lance. Milada begins to feel pity for her former foe. Dalibor defies the King; he has committed no crime, only revenged the murder of his friend. If now his life is spared, he will continue to exact vengeance; not the King himself shall stand in his way!

The verdict of the court is imprisonment for life; Dalibor invokes the free spirit of Zdeněk—did he hear the sentence? Dalibor is led away, and Milada pleads for his life. But the judges say he has openly threatened the King; even when Milada protests that she herself, whom he has most wronged, is prepared to forgive him, they are unimpressed. Milada, thinking she is alone, admits to herself that she is in love with Dalibor. Jitka overhears her and begs her to exert herself to free Dalibor. In a vigorous concluding duet, they agree together to free him from prison.

Act II. Street below the castle in which Dalibor is imprisoned. From an inn comes the sound of gay singing. Jitka and Vítek, Dalibor's page, greet each other eagerly in a charming duet. They discuss Dalibor's plight and Jitka reveals that Milada is already inside the prison disguised as a boy. They are optimistic that their cause has not received so severe a setback in the imprisonment of Dalibor as might have been feared; he will soon be out, and victory and freedom will be theirs. The music has an exuberance that is positively Weberian in character.

The scene changes to the house of Beneš, the gaoler, inside the castle. Night is falling and sentries patrol up and down. Budivoj warns Beneš that there is a danger of a rising in favour of Dalibor; he, as head gaoler, is answerable for the prisoner's safe-keeping with his life. Budivoj looks at Milada who is standing nearby in disguise, and enquires who it is; Beneš tells him it is his new assistant. The parallel of the whole situation with that of *Fidelio* is too obvious to need pointing out. In music of sombre character, Beneš reflects on the gloomy nature of his calling.

Milada comes to tell Beneš that his meal is ready. The gaoler refers most sympathetically to Dalibor, who, he says, has asked for a fiddle to play in his dungeon. He tells Milada to take the instrument down to the prisoner, and says he himself will go to fetch it. Milada left alone rejoices at the prospect of seeing Dalibor for the first time face to face. Beneš returns and gives Milada instructions on how to find the appropriate dungeon.

The scene changes again, this time to Dalibor's cell. Dalibor has a vision of Zdeněk, who appears to him and plays his violin; when he has gone, Dalibor invokes his reappearance in a beautiful aria. Presently Milada brings him the instrument he has asked for. She admits that she was his accuser at his trial, and that she hated him. She tells of her useless pleas that he should be allowed to go free, and of the preparations which are in hand for his escape. Will he pardon her for what she has done to him; ever since the trial she has loved him from afar. The whole scene is one of extraordinary power, and the lyrical duet itself of haunting beauty. It seems to me no exaggeration to describe this as one of the most beautiful love duets in all opera.

Act III. The throne room of the King, brightly lit. He is surrounded by his councillors. Budivoj and Beneš appear in front of him, the former saying that he has news of a rising which is plotted in Dalibor's favour. Beneš tells his story; he had an apprentice, who suddenly disappeared, leaving behind him some money and a note of thanks. But at least Beneš was in time to prevent Dalibor's escape—the lad had certainly something to do with the preparations he discovered for freeing the prisoner. Beneš pleads for leniency for himself. The King, in spite of misgivings as to the justice of his action (voiced in a beautiful aria), finally accepts the judgement of his Council that Dalibor be condemned to instant death.

Plans are afoot for Dalibor's escape, and he stands in his cell, free of fetters and rejoicing in a brilliant and exciting aria as he thinks of the freedom he can bring to his people when once he has escaped. But Budivoj rushes in with his guards, secures his prisoner and informs him of the court's decision that he shall die. Dalibor muses on his coming death in music of poignant sadness.

During a march interlude, the scene changes to an open square in front of the castle. Milada, clad for war, with Jitka, Vítek, and their armed supporters, wait for the signal. They hear the tolling of a bell and the sound of a chorus of monks, and Milada is afraid that Dalibor is being done to death inside the prison while they wait for his signal to attack it. They prepare to assault the castle.

Women comment on what they can see, and presently
Dalibor comes out of the castle carrying Milada, who is
wounded. She dies in his arms, and, when Budivoj appears
with troops, Dalibor stabs himself and dies with his beloved.
There is an alternative ending to the opera, in which Dalibor
is executed before Milada and the rescue party can reach
him; Milada is killed in the attack.)   H.

DVĚ VDOVY
The Two Widows

Opera in two acts by Bedřich Smetana, libretto by Emmanuel
Züngel founded on a comedy by P. J. F. Malefille. Première, March 27,
1874, in Prague with Marie Sittová, Ema Saková, Antonin Vávra, Karel
Čech, conductor Smetana. New version, with recitatives instead of
spoken dialogue, Prague, 1878. First performed in Germany, Hamburg,
1881; in Vienna by company from Olomouc, 1924; London, Guildhall
School of Music, 1963. Very frequently heard in Czechoslovakia and
fairly often in Germany in the years after 1945.

CHARACTERS

Karolina Záleská, *widow and heir of a rich Colonel*
                                        Soprano
Anežka Miletinskà, *a widow, her cousin* . . . . . . Soprano
Mumlal, *gamekeeper in Karolina's service* . . . . Bass
Ladislav Podhajský, *a neighbouring landowner* . . . Tenor
Toník, *a peasant* . . . . Tenor
Lidka, *a maid* . . . . Soprano
            Villagers, Servants
Time: Late Eighteenth Century   *Place:* Karolina's house

Smetana deliberately set out to write an opera in, as he
himself said, 'a distinguished salon style', with all the
elegance of the drawing room. In his output *The Two
Widows* is, so to speak, the equivalent of *Onegin* or *Traviata*
or *Così fan tutte*, and for us it is peculiar to read that it
succeeded straight away in spite of accusations of being
Wagnerian in style.

A bustling overture leads to a lively chorus as villagers
come to invite Karolina, the lady of the manor, to the harvest
festival. She gently mocks her cousin Anežka for continuing
to wear nothing but black so long after her husband's death.
In a charming aria Karolina explains her philosophy: she is
independent and busy, she runs her estate well, and she finds

it a highly satisfactory existence. Her advice to her cousin is
to marry—and she'd better begin her new regime by going to
the harvest festival dance that very night.

Enter Mumlal, Karolina's game-keeper and general
factotum, and a born grumbler. A trio bubbles away and we
might be in the agreeable world of *Die lustigen Weiber von
Windsor* as Mumlal explains that the bane of his life at the
moment is a poacher who, to add insult to injury, never even
hits what he shoots at. A shot is heard, Mumlal is sure it is his
tormentor, and Karolina sends him off to arrest the culprit.
The two ladies withdraw as Ladislav comes into view. In an
excellent example of the tenor-bass duets which figure largely
in Smetana's operas, Ladislav makes it clear that his one
object is to be taken to the manor, there to meet his beloved
Anežka, and his only complaint is at Mumlal's slowness in
effecting his capture. Karolina insists they put him on trial
straight away, Ladislav is brought in, and all comment on his
capture in a quartet, to which he and Anežka make contributions which are full of feeling. In a fervent solo and with
a plea of unrequited love, Ladislav defends his action to an
audience that is by no means unresponsive. A lively trio for
the ladies and Ladislav leads to the reading out of the
description of the prisoner which Mumlal has been
laboriously concocting: 'Height—average; hair—average . . .
etc.', and then to his sentence to half a day's imprisonment in
the house. The scene ends with an exhilarating reprise of the
trio, this time with Mumlal adding his voice to make it a
quartet.
Mumlal takes Ladislav off, and on his return is surrounded
by the young people of the village, amongst them Toník and
Lidka, all eager to know the story of the arrest he has made.
Has it something to do with love, they ask? Mumlal abuses
the tender passion, only to have Toník and Lidka mock him
for his cynicism, and to find the gentry supporting the
majority opinion as the curtain falls.
Act II. A large hall with a sun porch. A lively prelude
leads to Ladislav's lyrical song in praise of Maytime and love,

sung from his room (off stage). Anežka listens but, in course of conversation with Karolina, agrees to renounce any pretensions to Ladislav's affections in favour of Karolina, who well knows that Anežka is in love with Ladislav and hopes to force her to admit it by making her jealous; the attractive duet is based on Karolina's opening aria.

Anežka alone reads a letter she has received from Ladislav; she goes to burn it, then snuffs the candle and hides the letter as Ladislav appears. In a long scene, Ladislav gently pleads his cause, and recites from memory the letter, which Anežka pretends not to have read. In the end she tells him she can never be more to him than a friend, and they say goodbye. Throughout the scene, Smetana has written music of the utmost tenderness for his lovers, and even when Anežka appears to reject Ladislav's pleading, her real feelings are never in doubt—the music is as touching and genuine as for instance that of Mařenka's aria in *The Bartered Bride*.

The plot thickens as Karolina, dressed for the dance, pretends to appropriate Ladislav herself. Anežka's big *scena* is an extended and shapely aria of considerable beauty—she laments her unhappy and lonely situation. When Mumlal comes in, it is to complain to Anczka at the way his mistress is carrying on, kissing as is the local custom the man with whom she dances. In a comic song, he expounds his philosophy—he thunders with anger on every possible occasion, it seems—but Anežka can stand him no longer and flounces out. Mumlal hides as Lidka, who has been dancing, runs in pursued by Toník, demanding the kiss that is his due. She is coy, Mumlal fulminates from behind a pillar for all the world like a Czech Osmin and interposes himself when Lidka finally grants the kiss—'it tasted like pepper and salt' is the young couple's comment. But they get their own back a minute later and box the old man's ears soundly. The trio is one of the most delightful numbers of the score.

In a scene with Ladislav, Karolina makes him admit that it is love that has brought him to her estate; they are observed together by Anežka, who jumps to obvious but mistaken conclusions. In a quartet (Mumlal comes in too) each admits his or her true reaction to the situation, and finally in a *stretta* three, with Mumlal vigorously dissenting, proclaim their faith in the power of love. Ladislav runs off, Anežka is constrained to admit to Karolina that she loves him after all, he hears the admission from his hiding place, and as the banquet is announced, only Mumlal is left grousing away. A chorus of rejoicing and a polka bring to an end an opera that is one of the most tuneful and delightful of any that has *not* yet been accepted into the world's repertory.   H.

HUBIČKA
The Kiss

Opera in two acts by Bedřich Smetana, text by E. Krasnohorská. Première, Prague, November 7, 1876. First performed in Chicago, 1921; in England, Carl Rosa, 1948, with Packer, Myrrdin, conducted by Tausky (there had been an amateur performance at Liverpool in 1938). Revived Cambridge University, 1969.

CHARACTERS

Paloucký, *a peasant* .... Bass-Baritone
Vendulka, *his daughter* .... Soprano
Lukáš, *a young widower* .... Tenor
Tomeš, *brother-in-law of Lukáš* .... Baritone
Martinka, *Vendulka's old aunt* .... Contralto
Matouš, *an old smuggler* .... Bass
Barče, *a servant girl* .... Soprano
A frontier guard .... Tenor

Place: In the mountains on the borders of Bohemia.

The Kiss is an undemonstrative opera, with the mildest of jokes for subject—the superstitious reluctance of a bride-to-be to give her lover a kiss before their marriage, and their subsequent quarrel (Act I) and reconciliation (Act II, Scene ii). The first scene of Act II is devoted to the frustration of the principal characters, with a band of smugglers (a virtually unexplained interruption) as background. Smetana has provided attractive, melodious and singable music, which may not have quite the point of his *Bartered Bride* score but is full of charm and by no means without tunes that contain all the elements of popularity.

Act I is set in a room in Paloucký's cottage. Through the open window can be seen the village square. Lukáš, a young peasant, was always in love with Vendulka, but, at the wish of his parents, he married another woman. Now she is dead and he is free to marry Vendulka. Martinka is delighted at the way things have worked out, but Vendulka's father has some

misgivings; both Vendulka and Lukáš are headstrong, determined people—she would do better to refuse him, he tells his
daughter. Her unhappiness is so obvious at this piece of
advice, that he relents; but he does not appear to alter his
view that this marriage is a risky affair.

Barče rushes in to say that the wooing party is about to
put in an appearance, and soon Lukáš and Tomeš appear at
the window, followed by a crowd of curious villagers. Tomeš
explains that Lukáš has come a-wooing; Paloucký gives his
consent, but in such a way that Lukáš takes offence that it
was not done more gladly. Paloucký explains that he thinks
the prospective couple are too hot-tempered to keep peace
for long, but he gives them his blessing and all is forgiven and
forgotten in a moment. There is a duet for the two lovers, at
the end of which Lukáš makes as if to kiss Vendulka; she
refuses to allow him to do so. Lukáš insists, she continues to
refuse, and the fat is in the fire as Paloucký predicted. But all
is well again when Tomeš starts up a drinking song, in which
everyone joins, before leaving the happy couple alone together.

They sing of their love, and presently Lukáš's child is
brought in a cradle, much to Vendulka's joy. He tries to kiss
her again—after all, they are alone now—but she will still not
allow him to do so, not until after their wedding. The quarrel
breaks out again, and eventually Vendulka threatens to throw
Lukáš out of the house, to the surprise of everyone except
her father, who had anticipated just such a situation arising.
Lukáš makes a last demand for what he has come to think of
as his right, and, when it is refused, leaves in high dudgeon.

Martinka advises Vendulka to make up the quarrel, and
bids her good night. Vendulka sits herself by the cradle of the
child and sings to it as she rocks it to sleep. She sings two
separate songs, which together make a most appealing aria, at
the end of which Vendulka herself falls asleep. She is woken
up by the sound of a polka outside her window, and she sees
Lukáš dancing merrily in front of the house, and kissing the
girls with whom he dances. She is furious, but even Tomeš's
endeavours are not sufficient to quieten Lukáš, whose blood
is up, and who is determined to get his revenge publicly on
Vendulka. As the curtain falls, Vendulka exclaims that she
must go away from the place where she has been so publicly
humiliated.

Act II. A thick wood near the frontier of Bohemia.

Matouš appears at the head of a band of smugglers, all
carrying heavy bundles. There is a smugglers' chorus, after
which the stage is left empty until the arrival of Lukáš, who
in an aria expresses his despair at the disappearance of
Vendulka, whom he dearly loves in spite of his impetuous
and odious behaviour. Tomeš is looking for him, and
presently appears along the same path, to be overjoyed at the
sight of his brother-in-law, for whose safety he was becoming
really worried. Lukáš is anxious to restore himself in
Vendulka's favour, and Tomeš bids him only have the
courage to admit he was in the wrong, and she will have him
back at once. It is a fine example of Smetana's tenor-baritone
duets, of the type best known from the famous specimen in
The Bartered Bride.

Matouš, who has overheard the conversation between
Lukáš and Tomeš, comes out into the open when they have
left and has a good laugh at Lukáš's expense. He is waiting
for Martinka, who lives nearby and is in league with the
smugglers, but when she comes into sight, she has Vendulka
with her. Vendulka is frightened by the loneliness of the
forest, but Martinka comforts her before giving a signal,
which brings Matouš out of hiding. Vendulka begins to
lament her fate, but Matouš knows that the happy ending to
her story is being prepared by no one else than Lukáš
himself, who is only too anxious to make up their quarrel.

When Matouš goes his way, he gives some of his contraband to Martinka, who shares the burden with Vendulka. A
frontier guard appears but leaves them unmolested. Martinka
continues her efforts to persuade Vendulka to return home,
where she is sure Lukáš will be waiting for her.

Next morning, outside Martinka's cottage. Barče is trying
to find Martinka or Vendulka to tell them the news she has
heard from Matouš. She thinks she can hear them coming—
but it is the sound of a lark. She rejoices in the lark's singing
in an attractive aria, but one so difficult as to be beyond the
capacity of almost any soprano willing to take secondary roles.

Up the path to Martinka's cottage come Matouš, Paloucký,
Lukáš and Tomeš, with a whole crowd of villagers. Barče
wrings her hands in frustration that Martinka and Vendulka
are not there to welcome them and so make the reconciliation possible. Lukáš apologises to Paloucký for his
behaviour, and soon afterwards Vendulka appears. She and
Lukáš are obviously overjoyed to see each other again, but

when Vendulka comes towards him with open arms, Lukáš
refuses to kiss her—until he has openly begged her pardon for
his behaviour towards her.   H.

TAJEMSTVÍ

The Secret

OPERA in three acts by Bedřich Smetana, libretto by Eliska
Krasnohorská. Première at the New Czech Theatre, Prague, September
18, 1878, with Sittová, Fibichová, Mareš, Lev. First performed Vienna
(in German), 1895; Oxford (in English), 1957, with a cast including
Janet Baker as Rose, conductor Jack Westrup.

CHARACTERS

Councillor Malina .... Bass
Councillor Kalina .... Baritone
Miss Rose, *Malina's sister* .... Contralto
Blaženka, *Malina's daughter* .... Soprano
Vítek, *a forester, Kalina's son* .... Tenor
Boniface, *an old soldier, Kalina's nephew* ..... Baritone
Skřivánek, *a ballad singer* .... Tenor
The Builder............................ Baritone
The Innkeeper .... Soprano
Jirka, *the bellringer* .... Tenor
The Ghost of Friar Barnabáš .... Baritone
        Councillors, Neighbours, Boys and Girls,
            Harvesters, Bricklayers
Time: End of Eighteenth Century   *Place:* In and near the
                                          Bezděz Mountain

The Secret was written at a time when the last vestiges of
Smetana's hearing were disappearing, and when he had lost
his job as conductor at the Opera. It was immediately
successful, but soon lost favour with a public which wanted
more than anything else a repeat of *The Bartered Bride*. Its
present popularity in Czechoslovakia dates from its re-
studying by Karel Kovařović in Prague 25 years after the
première.

The overture, on an extended scale, is lively in spite of the
almost foreboding nature of the C minor theme (the secret)
with which it opens. From the rise of the curtain, any lover
of *The Bartered Bride* will feel on safe ground, as chorus and
solo, aria and duet alternate in an open-air setting of village

activity. Rose, Malina's sister, and Kalina were years ago prevented from marrying by her family on the grounds that he was too poor for her. The families have remained rivals and lose no opportunity for insult and recrimination. Now on one side of the street the harvest is being threshed in Malina's barn, on the other the bricklayers and their foreman are rejoicing at the completion of Kalina's new house. Before long the two factions are quarrelling, but the arrival of the musician, Skřivánek, provides a distraction, until each·side bribes him to sing a derogatory song about the other. In a charming piece, he gently mocks each until for a moment it looks as though there will be a reconciliation. But the quarrel breaks out anew, and it is only prevented from becoming a brawl by the intervention of Blaženka and Vít. The rioters disperse, and in a charming *arioso* piece Vít makes an assignation with Blaženka for that evening.

Rose (who is described as 'a little over 30') has earlier mentioned a secret, supposed to have been left after his death by Friar Barnabáš so that Kalina might find a treasure. Kalina denies any knowledge of it, but Boniface has found a piece of old mouldy paper in a bit of wood he picked up to use as a weapon. He gives it to Kalina, who recognises it as Friar Barnabáš's instruction, which must remain his secret. The jealous Boniface, himself a suitor for Rose's hand, tells the builder, who immediately communicates the news to whomever he meets, and the finale to Act I has the news being broadcast to all and sundry by the bell-ringer, while Blaženka and Vít murmur tenderly of love.

Act II. A ruin on Mount Bezděz. The 'secret' motif opens the prelude to an impressive *scena* for Kalina, who has come to look for the treasure, rails against his rejection on the score of poverty, and reveals that his present affluence is all bluff. In music of energetic cast, he wonders if it is money he craves—but why, he asks himself. Because of Rose? Kalina falls asleep, but as he dreams the ghost of Friar Barnabáš spurs him on to find the treasure, and he wakes to watch a procession of maidens and pilgrims on their way to the chapel. He determines to follow them, not sure whether his dream was inspired by heaven or hell.

Blaženka and Vít have arranged to meet here, and their scene is a big-scale love duet, dominated by a solo for Blaženka. Vít protests that he wants her for his wife when Blaženka makes it clear that she wishes their idyll to continue in a series of lovers' meetings. They are about to say good-night, when they are observed by Boniface, who fetches the parents. An ensemble of almost Rossinian brilliance develops as the elders watch the lovers parting. When they are discovered, they plead with their relations, until Rose denounces any Kalina as certain to be untrue. Vít cannot bear to hear his father slandered and says that he and Blaženka would refuse money but will elope together.

At the end of the impressive octet, Rose is left alone to muse longingly on the contrast between this love which knows no hindrance, and her own for Kalina which was so early blighted. Boniface enters stealthily, and in a martial air offers himself as her bridegroom, but before Rose can answer, they see Kalina advancing with his lantern and spade. They watch him start to dig, but suddenly he cries out Rose's name and disappears into the hole, leaving Rose and Boniface aghast behind him.

Act III.   In Malina's house there is rejoicing at the finish of the hop harvest, and Rose encourages Blaženka to ask her father directly if she may get married. She sings a fresh and touching aria in which she compares her love to a stream; let it not dash against the stones and be split up and wasted. A patter ensemble develops as they discuss Kalina's debts, and a loud banging is heard behind the wall, but no one takes much notice as at that moment Vít comes to say goodbye before leaving to seek his fortune. His account of his future moves even Malina to pity, but he says he will give Blaženka's hand in marriage only if Kalina himself comes to beg for it on his son's behalf. Just as Boniface puts himself forward as a suitor for Rose's hand, more knocks are heard, and the general reaction is one of fear of the supernatural. Skřivánek improvises a song in praise of Barnabáš's good nature, and the knocking is heard again. To repetitions of the 'secret' motif, Kalina bursts through the wall by the great stove. He has found Friar Barnabáš's treasure: it is Rose! There is a happy ending, with Kalina asking Malina to bestow the hand of his daughter on Vít and that of Rose on Kalina himself.   H.

LIBUŠE

Opera in three acts by Bedřich Smetana; text (originally in German) by Josef Wenzig, translated into Czech by Erwin Špindler. Première, Prague, for the opening of the Czech National Theatre (Národní Divadlo), June 11, 1881, with Marie Sittová, Irma Reichová, Betty

Fibichová, Josef Lev, Karel Čech, Antonin Vavra, František Hynek, Leopold Stropnicky. The theatre was burnt down two months later, and a new building was inaugurated in 1883, again with *Libuše*. The thousandth performance of operas by Smetana in Prague was celebrated with this work on August 27, 1905. First performed Vienna, 1924, by Olomouc Opera Company; Zagreb, 1933. Frequently revived all over Czechoslovakia. No record of either British or U.S. productions.

CHARACTERS

Libuše, *a Bohemian princess*	Soprano
Přemysl of Stadice	Baritone
Chrudoš from Ottava ⎱ *brothers*	Bass
Šťáhlav from Radbuza ⎰	Tenor
Lutobor, *their uncle*	Bass
Radovan, *head of the Council*	Baritone
Krasava, *Lutobor's daughter*	Soprano
Radmila, *sister of Chrudoš and Šťáhlav*	Contralto
Four reapers	Sopranos / Contralto / Tenor

Elders and Noblemen, Maidens at Libuše's Court,
Přemysl's retinue, People

Time: Pagan era   *Place:* Vyšehrad and Stadice,
in the Bohemian mountains

Smetana had been appointed conductor at the provisional theatre rather over a year before he completed *Dalibor*. He tried to improve every aspect of the theatre but was particularly concerned with a representative repertory, if possible of Czech music. Between 1866 and 1872, 82 different operas were performed, 33 of which were new productions prepared and conducted by Smetana himself. In 1869, he wrote a concert piece called *Libuše's Judgement*, and this seems to have been the seed from which came the fourth of his operas, chronologically speaking, though the penultimate to reach the stage. From the start, he said of *Libuše*, 'I desire it to be used only for festivals which affect the whole Czech nation. *Libuše* is not an opera of the old type, but a festive *tableau*—a form of musical and dramatic sustenance.'

In the event, he had his way, but at a cost. The composition lasted from 1869 to 1872, but it was another nine years before the opera reached the stage, for the simple reason that Smetana refused it performance at the other

Prague theatres and insisted that it should inaugurate the
National Theatre when it was eventually opened. The overture was played before, but by the time the work reached the
stage, Smetana himself was deaf and could hear nothing at
all. Dr. Brian Large in his remarkable biography[1] of Smetana
says: 'Whereas *The Brandenburgers in Bohemia* unfolds like a
historical novel, *The Bartered Bride* reads like an idyll, and
Dalibor develops with epic pathos, it is *Libuše* alone which
has the grandeur of an ode. It is not opera in the traditional
sense but a magnificent pageant, a hymn to the nation, cast
in six tableaux.' He compares it with two other monuments
of the nineteenth century, Wagner's *Die Meistersinger* and
Berlioz's *Les Troyens*, and the last scene, with its prophetic
note, certainly recalls Berlioz's Dido.

The noble overture opens with a splendid fanfare, and is
built up on two further ideas, the first associated throughout
the opera with Libuše and first heard on the oboe Ex. 1:

another associated with Přemysl, first heard on horns Ex. 2:

Act I, scene i.   At Vyšehrad, overlooking the Vltava
valley. Libuše, as her father's only child, is ruler of Bohemia
and now sits surrounded by her maidens. In measured tones,
Radmila introduces the case which she has to try and which
concerns Radmila's two brothers, who are in dispute over

[1] *Smetana* by Dr. Brian Large (Duckworth, London, 1970).

their dead father's estate. From her anguished comments, Krasava, who stands to one side, is plainly concerned with the way matters will turn out. A solemn orchestral introduction leads to Libuše's majestic prayer for enlightenment, 'Eternal Gods'. Libuše leaves for the council chamber, but Krasava and Radmila remain behind, Krasava admitting her guilty involvement but refusing to elaborate on it.

The scene changes to an open space at Vyšehrad. The two litigants, Chrudoš and Šťáhlav, wait for Libuše's arrival, and the music is as urgent as befits the heat of the brothers' quarrel. Chrudoš interrupts the bystanders' conventional regrets at the fraternal strife, and Šťáhlav states his opposition though in more measured terms. Their uncle Lutobor thinks reconciliation most unlikely, and for his part wishes that the princess might decide to take a husband to sustain her in her heavy task.

The sounds of a march introduce Libuše's procession (Ex. 1, now in the violins) and in another big public statement she makes plain the purpose of the meeting and the purport of the brothers' quarrel. Chrudoš angrily proposes that they follow German custom, under which the elder brother inherits all. Šťáhlav adopts a more conciliatory tone and agrees to abide by whatever is decided. Libuše gives judgement that, according to ancient custom, the estate of a father shall be managed jointly by the brothers or, if they prefer, divided between them. Chrudoš dissents, and Libuše turns judgement over to the Council. Radovan affirms the Elders' agreement with Libuše, at which point Chrudoš furiously rejects her as a suitable judge on the grounds that she is a weak woman, and rushes from the spot. His brother and his uncle follow him, but Libuše decides to abdicate her power, bidding the people choose her a husband to whom she may hand over rule. In an ensemble, the choice is referred back to her and, amid general rejoicing, she chooses Přemysl of Stadice, whom she has loved since childhood.

Act II, scene i.   A burial mound in the country. Lutobor bemoans his fate in having fathered a daughter so different in temperament from his. But Krasava, who follows him, plainly wishes to confess her fault—that she loves Chrudoš, having rejected him at first in order to lead him on, and now knows she is the cause of near disaster—and she does so in music of vibrant passion. Šťáhlav and Radmila overhear her confession and join their voices to her plea to her father, who relents to demand that she achieve reconciliation with Chrudoš and ɪerself persuade him to bow the knee to Libuše. Otherwise, he will see her no more.

Chrudoš comes in, his mind full of spleen—against the idea of accepting Libuše's rule, against his beloved Krasava, whom he thinks loves his brother. When Krasava herself appears and admits her fault before pleading her genuine love for him, he at first resists, then, after she has invoked his father's memory, succumbs to the love that has been choking him—to the obvious approval of Radmila, Šťáhlav and Lutobor. The two brothers embrace.

The scene changes to the countryside in the neighbourhood of Stadice. In the background stands Přemysl's beautiful farmhouse, surrounded by lime trees. The atmosphere is of the idyllic countryside, and voices of harvesters off-stage precede Přemysl's famous aria ('Již plane slunce'; The sun is blazing), a monument in Czech operatic literature which runs the gamut of idealised masculine emotions: disciplined if perhaps hopeless love for a good woman, ardour for patriotic duty, the whole tempered by a belief in the solvent qualities of the natural order. The farm workers return home and are greeted by Přemysl (we are near the world of *The Bartered Bride*), but Přemysl himself remains outside and alone, lost in thoughts of Libuše and the deep peace of the countryside—a beautiful lyrical passage.

A crowd of people, led by Radovan and the Elders, comes to bring the news that Přemysl has been chosen as Libuše's consort. Přemysl voices his gratitude towards the people and the circumstances of his life as a farmer, then goes with the Elders, the more willingly when he learns from them the possibility of danger from the dissident Chrudoš. There is a vigorous finale for Přemysl, Radovan and the crowd.

Act III. We are back at Libuše's court. Festively clad, she awaits the arrival of her chosen bridegroom, but first, with Radmila and Lutobor watching, she solemnises the reconciliation of Chrudoš and Šťáhlav, then the betrothal of Chrudoš and Krasava. She promises to intercede on Chrudoš's behalf with Přemysl, to whom in future will her supreme power belong.

As a cry goes up heralding Přemysl's arrival, all hurry out and Libuše is left alone, praying to the spirit of her dead father Krok for blessings on this solemn moment in her life. Her maidens reappear to escort her towards her waiting bridegroom and the scene ends with their bridal chorus.

The scene changes to the second of Act I, a great meeting

place in Vyšehrad. Chrudoš and Lutobor, together with
Šťáhlav, Radmila and Krasava, await the appearance of
Libuše and Přemysl. Chrudoš's rebellious spirit is again in the
ascendant and it takes all the persuasion that Lutobor,
Šťáhlav and Krasava can command before he vows to give
soft answers rather than display the stiff-necked pride which
is his natural instinct.

A ceremonial procession of noblemen and Elders, headed
by Radovan is followed by Libuše and Přemysl. Přemysl
greets the people and promises to serve them to the best of
his ability. He and Libuše sing together to ask for the blessing
of the gods—the nearest Smetana could get, surmises Brian
Large, to finding love music for two heroic leaders of the
Bohemian people. The scene of general rejoicing turns to the
more specific as Přemysl applauds the reconciliation of
Chrudoš and Šťáhlav, then demands that Chrudoš make
amends for his insult to Libuše. As Chrudoš makes to bow
the knee, Přemysl embraces him as a man of spirit and the
onlookers rejoice in an act of generosity which augurs well
for Přemysl's reign.

Libuše meanwhile has been gazing in front of her in a state
of prophetic rapture. She starts to foretell the heroic destiny
of the Czech people and in six 'pictures' (the word is
Smetana's own) we see successively Prince Břetislav, who
united Bohemia and Moravia and secured the western frontier
of the country by defeating a German invasion; Jaroslav of
Sternberk, who defended the country against the Tartars;
King Ottokar II, who increased the Slavonic empire, together
with his granddaughter Elisabeth and her son Charles IV, who
improved the status of Bohemia in Central Europe and
founded the University; then Žižka, Prokop the Great and
the Hussites; the wise King George of Podiebrad, who
consolidated the results of the Hussite revolution; and
ultimately, as Libuše's vision dims into a general conviction
of a great Czech destiny, the royal castle in Prague which
dominates the whole scene. In spite of attempts to illustrate
each tableau, and Smetana's use of the Hussite chorale 'Ye
who are God's warriors' as the basis for the music, this has
more solemnity and grandeur than true drama, but the final
quarter of an hour none the less makes a fitting ending to a
festive work, even though one may think that in general the
score is notable more for lyrical expansiveness than for
economy of means, for Smetana's peculiar—and moving—
expressiveness rather than for urgency or concise dramaturgy.

H.

ANTONÍN DVOŘÁK

(1841–1904)

RUSALKA

OPERA in three Acts by Antonín Dvořák, libretto by S. J. Kvapil. Première, March 31, 1901, National Theatre, Prague, with Maturová, Kabátová, Pták, Kliment, conductor Kovařovic (by 1950, the opera had been performed over six hundred times at the National Theatre in Prague). First performed in London by John Lewis Musical Society in 1950 in an English version by Christopher Hassall; Sadler's Wells, 1959, with Joan Hammond, Joan Stuart, Charles Craig, Howell Glynne, conductor Vilem Tausky.

CHARACTERS

Wood Nymphs . . . . Two Sopranos, Contralto
Water Nymphs . . . . Dancers
The Spirit of the Lake . . . . Bass
Rusalka, *his daughter* . . . . Soprano
Ježibaba, *the Witch* . . . . Mezzo-Soprano
Voice of a Huntsman . . . . Tenor
The Prince . . . . Tenor
The Forester . . . . Baritone
The Kitchen Boy . . . . Mezzo-Soprano
The Foreign Princess . . . . Soprano
Water Nymphs, Courtiers and Wedding Guests

Act I. The short and beautiful prelude admirably suggests the poetical, twilit atmosphere of the opera. In the fourth bar occurs an important melodic phrase associated with Rusalka and her native watery element, Ex. 1:

987

A clearing on the shore of the lake; in the background, a cottage. The good-natured old Spirit of the Lake is tempted out of the lake depths, where he has his abode, by the singing of the Wood Nymphs. When they have gone, Rusalka rises from the water and sadly asks her father for advice. The music has a warmth and tenderness that is Smetana at his finest as she tells him she has fallen in love with a handsome young prince and wants to become human in order to know the bliss of union with him. Her confession fills her father with sadness, but he advises her to visit the old Witch who lives nearby. Rusalka alone confides to the moon the secret of her longing—this passage is justly famous as one of the most touching and yet chaste of operatic love songs, Ex. 2:

and

Rusalka calls to Ježibaba, the Witch, and begs for her help. Ježibaba will grant her human attributes, but she will not be able to speak and, if he prove false to her, both she and her lover will be damned for ever. Together Rusalka and Ježibaba cast the spell. The voice of the Spirit of the Lake is raised in anguish from the depths, but Rusalka's decision is irrevocably taken.

The sound of horns and of a huntsman's singing in the distance sets the scene for the Prince's entrance. He is in pursuit of a white doe, but feels a mysterious attraction when he is by the shores of the lake. He suspects magic but sends his companions back to the palace saying he wants to stay alone with whatever mysterious power rules the place. To the strains of Ex. 1, Rusalka comes out of Ježibaba's hut, and the Prince is immediately enchanted at her appearance. He sings warmly to her, and without a word—in his presence she is dumb—Rusalka falls into his arms. Her sisters and the Spirit of the Lake are filled with alarm but the Prince is enraptured and flinging his cloak round her, takes Rusalka off towards his palace.

Act II. The Palace Grounds. The palace is full of guests invited to the wedding of the Prince and the mysterious Rusalka. In a charming scene, a forester and a boy from the palace kitchen exchange the latest news—the kitchen boy is frankly scared by Rusalka, who gives him the creeps; the forester suspects witchcraft. There is more gossip: the Prince is said already to have begun to tire of his silent beauty and his eyes have turned towards a foreign Princess. They hurry out as the Prince and Rusalka are seen approaching. That she has given him so little sign of her love has begun to baffle him, and he fears for his happiness once they are married. When the foreign Princess comes by, the Prince sends Rusalka into the palace to dress for the Ball and he, himself, goes off with the Princess, who clearly takes it as a personal slight that the Prince is to marry Rusalka. Rusalka goes sadly into the Palace as the melody of Ex. 1 is heard.

The dance music strikes up and a brilliant scene follows as the Ball begins. It is temporarily interrupted by the melodious lament of the Spirit of the Lake, who emerges from the fountain to express his despair at the downfall of his favourite daughter. He continues to mourn while the chorus sings the beautiful 'White flowers are blooming by the way'. Rusalka runs to him and is now able to give passionate voice to her misery that the Prince has all evening paid court to the foreign Princess and not to her. Before long the Prince leads his new lady-love away from the dancing and their fiery

duet contains all the warmth that the Prince had missed in
Rusalka. They embrace, but Rusalka throws herself into her
bridegroom's arms, and the Spirit of the Lake proclaims that
the Prince will now never be free of her. The Prince implores
the foreign Princess's help, but she turns proudly away from
him.

Act III.   A glade by the side of the Lake, as in Act I.
Evening. Rusalka is now the victim of her lover's infidelity
and condemned to wander for ever as a will o' the wisp. In an
aria she longs for death, but Ježibaba comes out of her hut to
say that only the shedding of human blood can now redeem
her from the curse which hangs over her. Rusalka sings
touchingly and resignedly of her fate and, as the Wood
Nymphs comment on her short sojourn in the world, she
sinks alone into the waters.

Now the forester and the kitchen boy come to ask the
Witch to help the Prince, who is, they fear, under supernatural influence. The forester pushes the boy forward, but
neither dares knock at the door. When Ježibaba answers to
the cries of her name, she makes short work of their plea to
help restore the confidence of the Prince, and between them
she and the Spirit of the Lake put the timid pair to flight.

The Wood Nymphs gather at the side of the lake and sing
and dance to music of graceful character until stopped by the
Spirit of the Lake, who reminds them of Rusalka's
melancholy fate. The Prince staggers out of the wood,
muttering about the snow-white doe, which first led him here
to Rusalka. He recognises the place and calls on Rusalka to
return to him. To a magically tender setting of Ex. 1, Rusalka
appears. The Prince begs her if she is a ghost to take his life
too, and he asks her forgiveness for his cruelty towards her.
Tenderly she reproaches him for having lied to her; she was
not able to give him the passion he craved, and now, if she
were to embrace him, he would die at her caress. In ecstatic
phrases he begs for the kiss which will end his life, and he
dies in her arms. Even the Spirit of the Lake's pronouncement that Rusalka's fate will not be mitigated by her lover's
sacrifice, cannot mar the apotheosis of Rusalka and the
Prince through the love that finally they share.   H.

PART III

THE
TWENTIETH
CENTURY

14
German Opera

EUGEN D'ALBERT
(1864–1932)
TIEFLAND
The Lowlands

OPERA in a prologue and two acts by Eugen d'Albert; text by Rudolph Lothar after a Catalonian play *Tierra Baixa*, by Angel Guimerà. Première at the Neues Deutsches Theater, Prague, November 15, 1903. First performed in Berlin, 1907; Vienna, 1908; Metropolitan, 1908, with Destinn, Schmedes, Feinhals, conductor Hertz; Covent Garden, 1910, with Terry, Teyte, John Coates, Frederick Austin, conductor Beecham. Revived Berlin, 1939, with Rünger, Asserson, Völker, Bockelmann, Hiller; Vienna, 1947, with Helena Braun, Schwaiger, Friedrich, Kamann, conductor Loibner.

CHARACTERS

Sebastiano, *a rich land-owner*		Baritone
Tommaso, *the village elder (aged ninety)*		Bass
Moruccio, *a miller*		Baritone
Marta		Soprano
Pepa		Soprano
Antonia	*in Sebastiano's*	Soprano
Rosalia	*employment*	Contralto
Nuri, *a little girl*		Soprano
Pedro, *a shepherd*		Tenor
Nando, *a shepherd*		Tenor
The Priest		Mute

Time: Early Twentieth Century   *Place:* The Pyrenees and the Lowlands of Catalonia

D'Albert, who was born in Glasgow, was not only a pianist of very high attainments, but also a successful composer, whose operas range from comedy to a German form of

verismo; *Tiefland* is an example of the latter aspect of h
style. D'Albert was married and divorced no less than si
times, his second wife being the great pianist Teresa Carreño

Prologue.   A rocky slope high up in the Pyrenees. A
shepherd's hut can be seen. Pedro and Nando greet each
other, Pedro observing that he has not seen anyone for three
months, and has not spoken to a soul for six. He protests that
he finds the shepherd's life perfect, but that he has sometimes in his prayers asked God to send him a wife ('Zwei
Vaterunser bet' ich').

Soon, Sebastiano appears at the top, accompanied by
Marta and Tommaso; he sends Tommaso off to look for
Pedro, and orders Nando to bring them milk, bread and
cheese. He himself explains the object of their errand to
Marta, who has been his mistress for some time. He has
brought her up here to show her to Pedro, whom he has
picked out as a suitable husband for her!

Pedro tells Nando of his good fortune, but the latter
warns him about conditions down there in the valley. Pedro
sings a last greeting to the mountains he knows so well ('Ich
grüss' noch einmal meine Berge') and the curtain falls.

Act I.   The interior of the mill. The millwheel can be
seen, various doors leading to other parts of the house, and in
the background the huge entrance gate, through which, when
it is open, one can see far into the distance. Moruccio is
working, but is interrupted by the arrival and importunate
questioning of Pepa, Antonia, and Rosalia; is it true that
Marta is getting married?

Marta comes in for a moment, but, seeing all the people
there, hurries out again. The three women begin to laugh at
the curious situation which her marriage will create, not least
for the duffer who is going to become her husband. Marta
comes back and drives them out of the gate. But she seems
pleased to see Nuri, and for a moment it looks as though she
will confide in the child.

Nuri goes and Marta reflects on her misery. She is
Sebastiano's property, and had not the courage to free herself
by drowning herself in the stream. Now she is to marry a
mountain lout. . . . She hurries out when she hears what she
thinks may be the noise of the escort bringing her bride-
groom-to-be. Tommaso comes into the mill, and Moruccio
asks him how he came to be a party to the arrangement of
such a wicked marriage.

Darkness falls, cries of 'the bridegroom!' can be heard, and

Pedro arrives, closely followed by Sebastiano, who orders that Marta be brought from her room.

While Pedro is getting dressed outside, Marta and Sebastiano are alone. There is an extensive duet in which Sebastiano claims that Marta's love will be his even after she is married to Pedro. That very night, if she sees a light in her room, it will be the signal that he is there.

Pedro with other villagers come for Marta, and they leave for the church. Tommaso, however, asks to speak to Sebastiano. He hints at the accusation which Moruccio has made against Marta, but Sebastiano says it is false; moreover, he who made it shall remain no longer in his service.

The moon rises, the wedding procession can be heard returning, and Marta comes in, followed by Pedro. He attempts to make love to her, but she will have none of him, and even refuses to accept the wedding present he offers her, a silver Taler. It was hard-earned, he says, and proceeds to tell Marta the story of his fight with a wolf which habitually preyed on the sheep, and which he eventually managed to kill with his knife, receiving as a reward the Taler from Sebastiano's own hands ('Wolfserzählung').

Marta seems impressed by his narrative and touched that he wants to give the piece of silver to her. But she bids him goodnight, and points to a room which she describes as his in exactly the opposite direction from hers. When he protests, she presumes that he has been told what a shameful bargain he made when he married her. But Pedro knows nothing of her past, and speaks of nothing but his love for her. Suddenly, Pedro sees a light in her room. He feels in his pocket for his knife and is about to approach the curtain which covers the door when the light disappears and Marta says that she saw nothing. She resigns herself to spending the night in the main room, and Pedro lies down on the floor, determined to see her vigil through with her.

Act II.   The curtain rises to show Marta and Pedro in the same positions as at the end of Act I. Nuri is heard singing behind the scenes, and Marta gets up and goes out to her room. Nuri wakes up Pedro, who thinks for a moment it is Marta. He says he will not stay any longer; he is sure there was a man in her room last night.

His suspicions are confirmed when Nuri says she is sorry everyone is laughing at him on account of the marriage he has made. He now knows that his dishonour is public property—but at whose hands is he dishonoured?

Marta sees him with Nuri, and has a spasm of jealousy. He goes out with Nuri, and Marta is about to follow them when she meets Tommaso coming to see her. He curses her for what she has let him all unwittingly do to Pedro. In a moving passage ('Ich weiss nicht, wer mein Vater war') she tells him her story, how she was left alone with her mother—she never knew her father—and they earned their living by begging in the streets. One day an old man, a cripple, joined them, and after that he lived with them. Her mother died, and she stayed with the cripple, who would not let her go as she was pretty and her dancing brought them money. Eventually their wanderings led them to this valley, where she was seen by Sebastiano, who spoke the first kind words she had ever heard. The cripple was installed as miller, and she became mistress of Sebastiano, the lord of the manor. She was fourteen years old when she arrived. Now she has been forced into marriage with Pedro; but a wonderful thing happened to her in the chapel when she fancied she heard a voice proclaiming him as her destined mate. Tommaso tells her she must, if she loves Pedro, make up her mind to tell him her secret.

As Tommaso is leaving, the women waylay him and start to question him; what does he know? Nothing, he answers, and goes on his way. Pedro is the next to be cross-questioned. He loses his temper and tries to force them to tell him why they laugh at him, but to no avail. Ask Marta, they tell him. Marta brings him his food, but he tells her that he should kill her, not forgive her, as she asks. He is about to leave her, when she makes a last effort to provoke him. She tells him she was another man's before she was married to him; everyone was laughing at the wedding for that reason, and he was coward enough to sell his honour for money. Beside himself, Pedro stabs her in the arm, and Marta weeps for joy. At last he has punished her for her fault; will he not strike her dead? Pedro is in despair; he admits his love; will she not come with him to the mountains where they can live together in peace, away from these accursed lowlands? Marta joins her voice with his.

They are about to leave arm-in-arm when Sebastiano appears at the gate. Pedro tells him that he must take back his gift of the mill; he and his bride are returning to the mountains—but Sebastiano does not even notice Pedro. He commands Marta to dance for him, as she used to do once

('Hüll in die Mantille'). Peasants support his singing, but Pedro orders Marta to follow him. A quarrel works up, and Pedro is with difficulty restrained from attacking Sebastiano when Marta tells him whose light it was in her room the previous night. But men seize Pedro and drag him away, while Marta falls unconscious.

Tommaso appears and tells Sebastiano that the father of his bride-to-be will not be seeing him that day, as Sebastiano was expecting. He, Tommaso, has made it his business to inform him of the background to the projected marriage, and he will have nothing further to do with Sebastiano. There is a violent duet between Marta and Sebastiano, the latter proclaiming that she is all that is left to him now, Marta objecting that she loves Pedro. At the end Sebastiano defies the absent Pedro to take her from him, only to find that Pedro has gained access to the room and is ready to fight him for Marta.

Sebastiano makes for the gate, but Pedro heads him off, and forces him to stay. Pedro draws his knife, but throws it away, saying that they will fight with bare hands. Sebastiano makes an effort to reach the knife but Pedro forestalls him and seizes him by the throat in a grip of iron, not releasing him until all signs of life are extinct. He drops lifeless to the floor. Pedro goes to the entrance of the mill calling for the villagers. They come in and see the corpse on the floor. Now is the time to laugh, orders Pedro. As for him, he will away into the hills again, taking Marta his wife with him.   H.

RICHARD STRAUSS
(1864–1949)
SALOME

OPERA in one act by Richard Strauss; words after Oscar Wilde's poem of the same title, translated into German by Hedwig Lachmann. Première in Dresden, December 9, 1905, with Wittich, von Chavanne, Burrian, Perron, conductor von Schuch. Sir Arnold Bax in *Farewell my*

Youth wrote that Burrian '... created a quite horrifying Herod, slobbering with lust, and apparently almost decomposing before our disgusted but fascinated eyes'. First performed Berlin, 1906, with Destinn, Goetze, Krauss, Baptist Hoffmann, conductor Strauss; la Scala, Milan, 1906, with Krusceniski, Bruno, Borgatti; Metropolitan, 1907, with Fremstad, Weed, Burrian, van Rooy, conductor Hertz; 1909, Manhattan Opera (in French), with Mary Garden, de Cisneros, Dalmorès, Dufranne; 1910, Covent Garden, with Ackté, Metzger, Ernst Krauss, Whitehill, conductor Beecham. Revivals at Covent Garden: 1924, with Ljüngberg, Olszewska, Kirchhoff, Schipper; 1937, with Ranczak (later Schulz), Kalter, Ralf, Schöffler, conductor Knappertsbusch; 1947, with Welitsch (later Cebotari), Höngen, Patzak, Rothmüller, conductor Clemens Krauss; 1949 (in English), with Welitsch, Shacklock, Lechleitner, Schon, conductor Rankl (décor by Salvador Dali); 1970, with Bumbry, conductor Solti. Revived at Metropolitan, 1933, with Ljüngberg, Lorenz, Schorr, conductor Bodanzky; 1937, with Marjorie Lawrence, Branzell, Maison, Huehn, conductor Panizza; 1942, with Djanel, Branzell, Maison, Janssen, conductor Szell; 1949, with Welitsch, Thorborg, Lorenz, Berglund, conductor Reiner; in Berlin, 1942, with Cebotari, Pölzer, Prohaska; Berlin, German Opera, 1963, in Wieland Wagner's production with Silja, Varnay, Stolze, Grobe, Dooley, conductor Maderna; Metropolitan, New York, 1965, with Nilsson, Dalis, Liebl, Alexander, Dooley, conductor Böhm.

CHARACTERS

Herod Antipas, *Tetrarch of Judea* .... Tenor
Herodias, *wife of Herod* .... Mezzo-Soprano
Salome, *daughter of Herodias* .... Soprano
Jokanaan (*John the Baptist*) .... Baritone
Narraboth, *a young Syrian, Captain of the Guard* Tenor
Herodias's Page .... Alto
Five Jews .... Four Tenors, One Bass
Two Nazarenes .... Tenor, Bass
Two Soldiers .... Bass
A Cappadocian .... Bass
A Slave

Time: About 30 A.D.   *Place:* The palace of Herod
at Tiberias, Galilee

On the great terrace of Herod's palace, off the banquet hall, is his body-guard. The ardent looks of the young captain, Narraboth, a Syrian, are directed toward the banquet hall where Salome is seated. In vain the Page, who is aware of the neurotic taint in the woman, warns him. The young captain is consumed with ardent desires.

The night is sultry. The soldiers' talk is interrupted by the sounds from the hall. Suddenly there is heard a loud and deep voice, as from a tomb. Dread seizes even upon the rough soldiers. He who calls is a madman according to some, a prophet according to others, in either case, a man of indomitable courage who with terrifying directness of speech brings the ruling powers face to face with their sins and bids them repent. This is Jokanaan. His voice sounds so reverberant because it issues from the gloomy cistern in which he is held a captive.

Suddenly Salome, in great commotion, steps out on the terrace. The greedy looks with which Herod, her stepfather, has regarded her, as well as the talk and noisy disputes of the gluttons and degenerates within, have driven her out. In her stirs the sinful blood of her mother, who, in order that she might marry Herod, slew her husband. Depraved surroundings, a court at which the satisfying of all desires is the main theme of the day, have poisoned her thoughts. She seeks new pleasures, as yet untasted enjoyments. Now, as she hears the voice of the Prophet, there arises in her the lust to see this man, whom she has heard her mother curse, because he has stigmatised her shame, and whom she knows the Tetrarch fears, although a captive. What she desires is strictly forbidden, but Narraboth cannot resist her blandishments: 'Du wirst das für mich tun, Narraboth.' The strange, gloomy figure of Jokanaan, fantastically noble in the rags of his captivity, emerges from the well to extended orchestral music (including a mature statement of the figure associated with him): No. 1.

The sight of him stirs Salome's morbid desires. There is a lengthy scene between them. When he appears, Jokanaan denounces Herod and Herodias ('Wo ist er, dessen Sündenbecher jetzt voll ist?'). Salome is fascinated by him and he turns on her ('Wer ist dies Weib, das mich ansieht?'), and rages at her as the daughter of an iniquitous mother. Salome tells him in music of rising intensity of her desire for his body ('Jokanaan, ich bin verliebt in deinen Leib'), his hair ('In dein Haar bin ich verliebt'), and finally his mouth

('Deinen Mund begehre ich'). A significant phrase emerges:
No. 2.

Her arts are brought into full play in her efforts to tempt
him, but with the sole result that he bids her do penance.
This but adds fuel to the flames. When Narraboth, in despair
over her actions, kills himself on his own sword, she does not
so much as notice it. Appalled by the wickedness of the
young woman, the Prophet warns her to seek for the only
one in whom she can find redemption, the Man of Galilee:
'Es lebt nur Einer, der dich retten kann.' But, realising that
his words fall on deaf ears, he curses her and retreats into his
cistern.

Herod, Herodias and their suite come out on to the
terrace: 'Wo ist Salome? Wo ist die Prinzessin?' Herod is
suffering under the weight of his crimes—soon after coming
in, he has an hallucination that the wind is blowing round his
head—but the infamous Herodias is as cold as a serpent.
Herod's sinful desire for his stepdaughter is the only thing
that can stir his blood. He asks Salome to drink from a cup
(No. 3):

and to eat some fruit so that he may have the pleasure of
putting his teeth and lips in the same place; in spite of
Herodias's objections, this he follows up by asking Salome to
sit beside him on his throne in her mother's place.

But Salome is weary and indifferent; Herodias, full of bitter
scorn for him and for her daughter. Against the Prophet,
whose voice terrifies whoever hears it, her hatred is fierce.
But Herod stands in mysterious awe of the Prophet. He
refuses to give him up to the Jews, who clamour to be
allowed to judge him, and insists that the Prophet is a holy
man who has even beheld God. This starts a theological
argument amongst the Jewish guests at the feast, who dispute

in a fugal quintet. No sooner is it finished than two Nazarenes proclaim their conviction that the Messiah is in their midst; he has even raised the dead from their graves. Herod is immediately filled with misgivings, which are not quieted by the Prophet's continued prediction of doom.

It is almost as much because of his dread of the future as for longing for her that Herod asks as a diversion for Salome to dance in order that life may flow warm again in his chilled veins. Salome demurs until he swears that he will grant any request she may make of him. She executes the 'Dance of the seven veils', casting one veil after another from her. The dance is long and an exacting undertaking for any *prima donna* who has still, be it remembered, the most taxing part of her vocal assignment to come. At the first performance, the dance was performed by a dancer, and the soprano emerged from the crowd at its end; but at a later performance history relates that Frau Wittich undertook it herself, much to the distress of the composer, who let it be known that he preferred a Salome with two distinct personalities rather than risk a repetition of what he had seen.

When she has finished, Herod asks Salome what her reward shall be. In part prompted by Herodias, but also by her own mad desire to have vengeance for her rejected passion, she demands the head of the Prophet. Herod offers her every-thing else he can name—precious stones, his unique white peacocks, the mantle of the High Priest, even the Veil of the Temple—but Salome refuses to release him from his promise. At last, almost faint with weariness and fear, he gives in.

The executioner descends into the cistern. Jokanaan is slain (to the eerie sound of a pinched B flat on a solo double-bass) and his severed head presented to Salome upon a silver charger. She is in ecstasy and circles round the head addressing it as though it were still living. Alive he refused her his lips; now, in a frenzy of lust, she presses hers upon them. Even Herod shudders and turns from her revolted. 'Kill that woman!' he commands his guards, who crush her under their shields.

Although *Salome* so far shocked convention at the beginning of the century that it was withdrawn from the Metropolitan after a dress rehearsal and one performance—practically on command, it is said, of the board of directors—it has proved in the long run no exception to the rule of diminishing artistic returns on an investment in the 'shocking'. Certainly it would surprise its early detractors to know that it is now a standard display piece for dramatic soprano, and on the fringe of every repertory.

The passage of time has brought general agreement on the weak points of the score. But, when all is said and done, *Salome* has unusual qualities, not least its unquestioned vitality. What could be more evocative and suggestive of what is to come than the opening music, which so unerringly sets the scene? Strauss's vivid characterisation of persons is equally notable: there are few better musical portrayals of neurasthenia than is to be found in the music of Herod, and his decadence, lust and fear are implicit in every bar he sings. But the best of the character studies is contained in the title role. Each and every change of this emotionally unstable character is reflected in the music, and her final scene with the head of Jokanaan transcends the dramatic implications of the words, and is written, through her eyes as it were, as a sort of psychopathic *Liebestod*.[1]   K., H.

ELEKTRA

Opera in one act by Richard Strauss, text by Hugo von Hofmannsthal, after Sophocles. Première Dresden, January 25, 1909, with Anny Krull, Siems, Schumann-Heink, Sembach, Perron, conductor von Schuch. First performed Berlin, 1909, with Plaichinger, Goetze, Rose, Grüning, Bischof, conductor Blech; Vienna, 1909, with Marie Gutheil-Schoder, Mildenburg, Weidemann; la Scala, Milan, 1909 (in Italian), with Krusceniski, Cannetti, de Cisneros, Gaudenzi, Cirino; New York, Manhattan Opera, 1910 (in French), with Mazarin, Gerville-Réache, Duffault, Huberdeau; Covent Garden, 1910, with Edyth Walker, Rose, Mildenburg, d'Oisly, Weidemann, conductor Beecham; Hull, 1912 (in English), with Florence Easton.

Revived Covent Garden, 1925, with Kappel, Olszewska, Soot, Schorr, conductor Walter; 1938, with Pauly, Hilde Konetzni, Thorborg, Wolff, Janssen, conductor Beecham; 1953, with Schlüter, cond. Kleiber; 1957 with Lammers, cond. Kempe; 1965, with Shuard, Resnik, cond. Kempe; 1969, with Nilsson, Resnik, cond Solti. At Metropolitan, 1938, with Pauly, Thorborg, Althouse, Schorr, conductor Bodanzky; la Scala, 1943, with Rünger, Ursuleac, Höngen; Vienna, 1949, with Anny

---

[1] The first part of the poem, suggested Ernest Newman from internal evidence, which Strauss set, and therefore, like the Letter Scene in *Eugen Onegin*, the source of much of the opera's music. H.

Konetzni, Hilde Konetzni, Höngen, Lorenz, Nissen; Florence Festival, 1950, with Anny Konetzni, Mödl, conductor Mitropoulos; Munich, 1952, with Borkh, Kupper, Fischer, Klarwein, Frantz; Metropolitan, 1952, with Varnay, Wegner, Höngen, Svanholm, Schöffler, conductor Reiner. Gutheil-Schoder was one of the most famous of Elektras.

CHARACTERS

Klytemnestra, *widow of Agamemnon* . . Mezzo-Soprano
Elektra ⎱ *her daughters* . . . . ⎰Soprano
Chrysothemis⎰   ⎱Soprano
Aegisth, *Klytemnestra's paramour* . . . . Tenor
Orest, *son of Klytemnestra and Agamemnon* . . Baritone
Tutor of Orest . . . . Bass
The Confidante of Klytemnestra . . . . Soprano
The Trainbearer of Klytemnestra . . . . Soprano
A Young Servant . . . . Tenor
An Old Servant . . . . Bass
The Overseer . . . . Soprano
Five Maidservants . . . . ⎰ 1, Contralto
                             ⎱ 2, 3, Mezzo-Soprano
                              4, 5, Soprano

Time: Antiquity   *Place:* Mycenae

Elektra is now accepted as one of Strauss's most successful operas, and one of the strongest candidates amongst them for survival; the 'shocking' element is more part and parcel of the drama than the similar element in *Salome*, and the work as a whole is built on a firmer foundation—so might run a consensus of opinion some seventy years after the first performance. But it was not always so. Mme. Schumann-Heink, the Klytemnestra of the original production in Dresden, said: 'I will never sing the role again. It was frightful. We were a set of mad women. . . . There is nothing beyond *Elektra*. We have lived and reached the furthest boundary in dramatic writing for the voice with Wagner. But Richard Strauss goes beyond him. His singing voices are lost. We have come to a full stop. I believe Strauss himself sees it'—and (comments Mr. Kobbé) in his next opera, *Der Rosenkavalier*, the composer shows far more consideration for the voice. Nonetheless, legend has it that at the Dresden dress rehearsal, he called down into the orchestra pit: 'Louder! I can still hear Frau Heink!'

Beyond the fact that Agamemnon was murdered by his

wife, Klytemnestra, and her paramour Aegisthus, it is not essential to know the details of the Greek story, but it is nevertheless against this background that even Hofmannsthal and Strauss, with all their changes of emphasis, have laid their opera. Agamemnon and Menelaus, the sons of King Atreus, married the sisters Klytemnestra and Helen. The latter was carried off by Paris, son of Priam, King of Troy, and it was to procure her return to her husband and to avenge the insult to Greece that the Trojan war began. On their way to Troy, the Greek fleet touched at Aulis and was caught there by the adverse winds, the goddess Artemis being angry with Agamemnon, who had killed one of her sacred hinds. To appease the goddess and to ensure that the fleet reached Troy in safety, Agamemnon sent for his daughter Iphigenia and sacrificed her.[1] The war over, Menelaus and Helen were driven by storms to Egypt, where they stayed for some years (and formed the subjects of Strauss's *Die Aegyptische Helena*[2]), and Agamemnon returned to Mycenae. Here he found that Klytemnestra had installed Aegisthus as her lover. With the excuse of the sacrifice of her daughter to salve her conscience Klytemnestra murdered Agamemnon in his bath and installed Aegisthus as his successor. Three children survived their father: Elektra, who was reduced to menial status, Chrysothemis, and Orestes, who was sent away to safety, according to some versions by a faithful slave, to others by Elektra. Eventually, Orestes returns, gives out that he is dead, gains admittance to the palace, and slays the guilty Klytemnestra and her lover.

The work is in one long act—Strauss was always strongly opposed to having another work given on the same evening— but that act has been divided by analysts into seven sections: (1) Elektra; (2) Chrysothemis; (3) Klytemnestra; (4) Elektra and Chrysothemis; (5) Orestes; (6) the Recognition; (7) the Vengeance.

The curtain rises straight away to show the inner court of the palace of Mycenae. At the back can be seen the palace itself; in the court is a well, from which servants are drawing water as the curtain goes up. They discuss the unpredictable Elektra, who howls like the dogs with whom her mother and stepfather have condemned her to live and eat. Some hate her, others pity her, only the fifth maid reveres and loves her.

[1] See pages 72-5; [2] See pages 1033-6.

For her defence of Elektra she is set upon by the others, and when they have gone inside, the fifth maid can be heard crying out that she is being beaten.

The scene is empty before Elektra comes from the house alone. In a great monologue ('Allein! Weh, ganz allein!') she rehearses the story of her father's murder, calls on his name (No. 1), and looks forward to the time when his death will be

A - ga - mem - - non!

avenged by herself and Orestes. When this is accomplished she will dance in triumph round the corpses of her enemies. The motif associated with the children of Agamemnon (No. 2) is important:

The second stage begins when Chrysothemis joins Elektra. Hofmannsthal designs her as a weaker and more human contrast to the implacable Elektra, and she is little inclined to join her sister in the schemes for revenge which are constantly being urged upon her. Instead, she issues a warning that further horrors are in store for Elektra. Poor Chrysothemis feels the fires of love frustrated within her ('Ich hab's wie Feuer in der Brust') and longs to escape from her hateful prison, to which she is doomed by the fear which her sister's weird hatred inspires in Klytemnestra. The ordeal to which both are subjected is leaving its mark on them, she says.

Noises are heard within of running footsteps, torches can be seen, and Chrysothemis says she will not stay to meet Klytemnestra who must surely be coming out. Elektra, however, is determined to speak to her mother.

Stage three begins as Klytemnestra is seen for the first time through the middle window. She is bloated and decayed, and sleepless nights and debauched days have left her looking as though it were an effort to keep her eyes open. She leans on the arm of her Confidante. Her first words are to mourn the evil workings of fate which have given her such a daughter but presently she comes down to the courtyard, and, dismissing her attendants, is left alone with the daughter she hates and fears so much.

She is tormented by dreams; knows her daughter no remedy for them? Elektra is wise, and alone can help her. She describes her sleepless nights; is there not some sacrifice she can make to the gods to alleviate the torture she suffers? Elektra answers her insinuatingly, and in terms that admit of two meanings. Yes, there is a victim, who is unconsecrated and roams free; it is a woman, married, who can be killed at any time of day or night, with an axe, by a man, a stranger, but of their kin. Klytemnestra becomes impatient, and Elektra asks whether her mother means to call her brother back from exile. Klytemnestra is uneasy at mention of him, and Elektra accuses her of sending money to bribe those who are looking after him to kill him; the trembling of her body at his name proves as much. But Klytemnestra says she fears nobody. She will find means of dragging from Elektra the secret of whose blood must flow to cause her nightmares to abate. Elektra springs at her; it is *her* blood that is required. *She* is the victim the gods have marked down. Elektra describes the chase which will end with Klytemnestra's death. The librettist indicates: 'They stand eye to eye—Elektra in wild intoxication; Klytemnestra breathing in horrible spasms of fear.'

At this moment the Confidante runs out of the palace and whispers in Klytemnestra's ear. A look of triumph comes into the Queen's face, and she goes into the palace, leaving Elektra alone in the courtyard. Stage 4. Not long afterwards, Chrysothemis comes out crying the dread news that Orestes is dead. Elektra at first will not believe it, but Chrysothemis says that two strangers, one old, the other young, brought the news; Orestes was dragged to death by his own horses. A servant comes out of the palace, demanding a horse as quickly as possible so that he may fulfil his mistress's command and carry the news to Aegisthus.

Elektra now demands that Chrysothemis shall help her in her self-appointed task; alone she cannot slay Klytemnestra and Aegisthus but with her sister's help she would be able to accomplish the deed. She flatters Chrysothemis that she is strong, and she promises that she will henceforth look after her as if she were her slave. She holds Chrysothemis fast, but when her sister eventually frees herself and rushes from the courtyard, she hurls a curse after her.

The fifth stage begins as Elektra, left alone, begins to dig like an animal at the side of the courtyard. She looks up twice, and then sees someone standing by the gate. Who is interrupting her thus? He asks her if she works in the palace. She answers bitterly that she does. He tells her that he has business with the Queen; he and another have brought the news of Orestes's death. Elektra's grief at the news is overwhelming; must she look upon him who lives, while someone a thousand times as good as he lies dead? Elektra's utterance takes on the character of a lament for Orestes, whom she will never see again. The stranger asks her if she is of the royal house that she takes Orestes's death as so personal a matter. She reveals her name, and the stranger exclaims in astonishment. He reveals that Orestes is not dead, and, a moment later, servants come in and kiss his hand. Who is he, demands Elektra? Everyone knows him, he answers, except his own sister.

The Recognition Scene (stage 6) is the emotional climax of the opera. Elektra's ferocity drops from her to be replaced by tenderness, and the unremitting tension of the music gives way to lyricism: 'Orest! Orest! Orest!'

Elektra will not allow her brother to embrace her. She contrasts her former beauty with her present state; everything she has renounced in expiation of the murder of her father. Together they exult in the prospect of the righteous revenge which they will exact on Agamemnon's murderers. They are recalled to the reality of the situation by Orestes's tutor.

The seventh and last stage of the drama begins when the Confidante appears and leads Orestes and the tutor inside. Elektra is alone, in horrible excitement, waiting for the sounds which will tell her that the first part of the revenge is over. A shriek tells her that Orestes has found Klytemnestra. By now the palace is aroused, but Elektra bars the entrance with her body.

Aegisthus saunters into the courtyard, and Elektra offers to light him into the palace. Aegisthus wonders at the change that has come over Elektra, who is circling round him in a strange sort of dance. Aegisthus enters the palace, but re-appears a moment later at a window, yelling for help.

Women rush out of the palace, amongst them Chrysothemis, who has discovered that Orestes is back. Their rejoicings are very different in character, and Elektra breaks away from her sister, throwing back her head like a maenad, and dancing about like a demented creature. Her thirst for vengeance is satisfied, and her dance increases to frenzy. Suddenly she collapses dead upon the ground. With a last cry of 'Orest!' Chrysothemis rushes to the door of the palace, and bangs on it. The orchestra continues to give out the motif associated with Agamemnon.   H.

DER ROSENKAVALIER

The Knight of the Rose

Opera in three acts by Richard Strauss; text by Hugo von Hofmannsthal. Première, Dresden, January 26, 1911, with Siems, Nast, von der Osten, Perron, conductor Schuch. First performed Berlin, April 1911, with Hempel, Dux, Lola Artôt de Padilla, Knüpfer, conductor Muck; Vienna, 1911, with Weidt, Förstel, Gutheil-Schoder, Mayr; la Scala, Milan, 1911, with Agostinelli, Ferraris, Bori, Ludikar; Covent Garden, 1913, with Siems, Dux, von der Osten, Knüpfer, conductor Beecham; Metropolitan, 1913, with Hempel, Case, Ober, Goritz, conductor Hertz; Sadler's Wells, 1939 (in English), with Cross, Naylor, McArden, Stear, conductor Collingwood. Covent Garden revivals include 1924, with Lehmann (later Leider), Schumann, Reinhardt, Mayr, conductor Walter; 1933, with Lehmann, Kern, Hadrabova, Kipnis, conductor Beecham; 1936, with Rethberg, Andreva, Lemnitz, List, conductor Reiner; 1936, by Dresden company, with Marta Fuchs, Cebotari, Rohs, Ermold, conductor Böhm; 1938, with Lehmann (later

Hilde Konetzni), Berger, Lemnitz, Krenn, conductor Kleiber; 1947, with Doree, McWatters, Sladen, Franklin, conductor Rankl; 1950, with Fisher, Graf, Shacklock, Glynne, conductor Kleiber; 1953, cond. Kempe; 1966, in Visconti's production, with Jurinac (Marschallin), Carlyle, Veasey, Langdon, conductor Solti. First produced Glyndebourne, 1959, with Crespin, Rothenberger, Söderström, Czerwenka, conductor Ludwig. Revived English National Opera, 1975, with Anne Evans and Lois McDonall, Masterson, Barstow, Warren-Smith, conductor Mackerras.

CHARACTERS

Princess von Werdenberg (*The Feldmarschallin*) Soprano
Baron Ochs von Lerchenau .... Bass
Octavian, *younger brother of Count Rofrano* .. Soprano
Herr von Faninal, *a wealthy parvenu* .... Baritone
Sophie, *his daughter* .... Soprano
Marianne, *her duenna* .... Soprano
Valzacchi, *an Italian intriguer* .... Tenor
Annina, *his partner in crime* .... .Mezzo-Soprano
A Police Commissar .... Bass
The Major-domo to the Marschallin .... Tenor
Faninal's Major-domo .... Tenor
A Notary .... Bass
An Innkeeper .... Tenor
A Singer .... Tenor
A Flute-player ⎫
A Hairdresser ⎬ *silent*
A Scholar ⎪
A Noble Widow ⎭
Three Noble Orphans ......Soprano, Mezzo, Contralto
A Dressmaker .... Soprano
An Animal-Tamer .... Tenor
Four Servants of the Marschallin Two Tenors, Two Basses
Four Waiters .... One Tenor, Three Basses
A Little Negro Page
Time: The reign of the Empress Maria Theresa *Place:* Vienna

Der Rosenkavalier since its first performance has probably been played more often than any other German opera written in the twentieth century. Perhaps its popularity is partly to be accounted for by its plethora of waltz rhythms—it has even been said: 'It is hardly an exaggeration to call the basic conception ... that of an immense concert waltz'—that, and the human figure of the Marschallin.

Rosenkavalier requires an enormous orchestra: an examination of the full orchestral score shows that 112 instruments are needed, 19 of them for an orchestra on the stage in the third act. The composer demands for his main orchestra: 16 first, 16 second violins, 12 violas, 10 violoncellos, 8 double-basses, 3 flutes (3rd also piccolo), 3 oboes (3rd also cor anglais), 1 bass clarinet (also corno di bassetto), 3 bassoons (3rd also contra bassoon), 4 horns, 3 trumpets, 3 trombones, 1 tuba, timpani, celesta, 2 harps, and 3 players for bass drum, cymbals, triangle, tambourin, Glockenspiel, tenor drum, side drum, bells, castanets. The conductor is directed to reduce the number of strings in passages 'where the audibility of the words requires it'.

Act I.   Bedroom in the Princess von Werdenberg's palace. Morning. The curtain rises after an impassioned orchestral introduction, which is explicitly supposed to represent the love-making which immediately precedes the audience's first view of the stage, as suggested by the stage directions which have Octavian kneeling by the side of the bed in which the Marschallin lies; she is hidden but for her arm by the curtain. These directions were not followed in the first production at the Berlin Opera House, due it is said to Court intervention.

The prelude, whose opening bars are quoted below (No. 1), begins with the excitement of the love-making very much

in mind. 1a is the theme of the Rosenkavalier; its continuation perhaps serves to link him with the Marschallin, who is shown in passionate and contemplative moods by Nos. 2

and 3 respectively, the latter bringing the prelude to its end:

When the curtain rises Octavian, a handsome youth just seventeen years old, is in post-coital conversation with the Princess, whose husband, a Field Marshal, is away hunting. Octavian is loath to go, the Princess equally loath to have him depart. For she cannot conceal from herself that in spite of Octavian's present love for her the disparity in their ages will soon cause him to look to women younger than herself for love (she is 32).

There is a commotion beyond the door of the Marschallin's suite of rooms. Taking alarm—they both think it is her husband returned—Octavian escapes behind the bed, where he disguises himself in the attire of a chambermaid. But the alarm is less serious than the Marschallin had feared. One of her relatives, the country-bred Baron Ochs von Lerchenau, wishes to see her. The servants try to persuade him that the hour is much too early, but he forces his way in.

No sooner is he through the door than his attention is distracted from his noble cousin, whom he so confidently proclaimed would be glad to see him, and focussed on the chambermaid, whom he finds very much to his liking. He ogles her and tries to make an early assignation, and it is only reluctantly that he comes to the point of his visit. Has her highness been able to help in the matter which was set out in his recent letter to her? So occupied has she been with Octavian that she has quite forgotten what it was Ochs wanted her to do, but it transpires that the object of his visit is to have her name for him a Knight of the Rose (*Rosenkavalier*) to take the customary symbol on his behalf to a certain Sophie, daughter of the wealthy and recently ennobled Herr von Faninal, whom he has decided to take to wife.

Not only does Ochs want help over the matter of the silver rose, he is also anxious that the Marschallin shall recommend an attorney to him, as the details of the marriage contract have yet to be settled. Let him wait, she suggests, not without reluctance, until her morning levée, which is due to begin at any moment. Her own attorney will be there and can help him. Ochs pursues the supposed Mariandel shamelessly, and a chance remark from the Marschallin, to the effect that he seems to know how to take his pleasures where he finds them, sets him off on his favourite subject: love in all its shapes and forms. His monologue consists partly of reminiscence, partly of anticipation, and partly of pure fancy—would he were like Jupiter who could assume a hundred disguises for the purpose of his amours.

The levée begins. In turn we meet the notary, the chef, an Italian singer, three poor orphans, and two Italian scandalmongers. While the hairdresser attends to the Marschallin's coiffure for the day, the others try to enlist her interest in their various causes. Musically, the most appealing is the Italian singer who demonstrates his art in a *pastiche* aria, 'Di rigori armato il seno', of considerable charm. In the meanwhile, the Marschallin contemptuously rejects the attempts of the Italians to interest her in a scandal-sheet, and Ochs argues with the attorney, his temper spilling over at the suggestion that the dowry is due from him to the bride, not the other way round. In his rage, he bangs the table and shouts—and interrupts the tenor at the climax to the second verse of his song. But calm is restored, and all leave the room, including the down-at-heel servants who have accompanied Ochs to the capital and have handed him the silver rose.

The Marschallin alone is a prey to autumnal thoughts. Was she not herself just such a girl as this poor unsuspecting creature whom Ochs, with all his crudity, is going to marry? 'Kann mich auch an ein Mädel erinnern?' she sings, and even the return of Octavian, booted and spurred and full of chivalrous speeches, cannot change her mood. Whatever his intentions now, it will not be long before he has left her for another, younger woman: 'Die Zeit, die ist ein sonderbar Ding.' Her sad, reflective, almost bitter mood is something Octavian cannot understand. She tells him he may ride beside her carriage in the afternoon, and he leaves her with an approach to formality. No sooner has he left the room than she remembers she did not even kiss him; she rings for the servants and tells them to run after him and bring him back, but they return to say he has galloped away from the door. The Marschallin accepts the inevitable and sends for her little black page, Mahomet, and gives him the silver rose in its case, bidding him take it to Count Octavian; he will know what to do with it.

Act II. Salon in the house of Herr von Faninal. This lately ennobled *nouveau riche* considers it a great distinction that the Baron Ochs von Lerchenau, a member of the old nobility, should apply for the hand of his daughter. That the Baron only does it to mend his broken fortunes does not appear to worry him, although his daughter Sophie is a sweet and modest girl. She and her duenna, Marianne, await her suitor in great agitation, Faninal having been advised by his major-domo that etiquette demands he should be absent at the moment when the bearer of the silver rose arrives in his house.

Marianne comments delightedly on the appearance of Octavian's coach—and on the neighbours who are watching it—and cries of 'Rofrano' are heard from outside. As the music reaches a climax Octavian, escorted by his servants, comes in carrying the silver rose in his right hand (No. 4).

He makes a little formal speech to Sophie, who takes the rose and comments on the scent it gives off, due, Octavian says, to the Persian attar which has been sprinkled on it. In a rapturous, soaring phrase (No. 5), Sophie releases the excitement which has been pent up inside her for so long—

excitement caused, we may surmise, as much by the unexpected sight of Octavian as by the rose or anticipation of
her bridegroom:

There follows a short duet, after which the two young
people sit down and engage in polite conversation, waiting
for the arrival of the Baron. Octavian is smitten with the
charms of the girl, and she for her part is at once attracted to
the handsome young cavalier. So their conversation imperceptibly drifts towards an intimate tone, only to be interrupted when the real suitor enters. His brutal frankness in
letting Sophie comprehend that he is condescending in
courting her and his general lack of manners thoroughly
repel the girl. Only the humming of his favourite waltz (No. 6)

nows a more agreeable side to his character. Octavian
meanwhile is boiling with rage and jealousy, as the girl's aversion to the Baron increases.

As if to save the situation, Ochs is called by the notary
into an adjoining room where the marriage contract is to be
drawn up. Sophie is shocked at what she has just experienced. Never will it be possible for her to marry the detested
Baron, especially since she has met the gallant Octavian. The
two are quick in agreeing. Sophie sinks into his arms.

At that moment there rush out from behind the two large
ornamental stoves which adorn the room the intriguers,
Valzacchi and Annina, anxious to be employed by Ochs as
spies. Their cries bring the Baron from the next room. The
servants rush in. Octavian tells Ochs of Sophie's antipathy,
and adds taunt to taunt, until, however reluctant to fight, the
Baron is forced to draw his sword. In the encounter, Octavian
lightly 'pinks' him. The Baron raises a frightful outcry. There
ensues the greatest commotion, due to the mix-up of the
servants, the doctor, and the rage of Faninal, who orders
Sophie to a convent when she positively refuses to give her hand
to Lerchenau. The latter meanwhile rapidly recovers when his
wound has been dressed and he has drunk some more of
Faninal's good wine.

Octavian is determined to win Sophie. For that purpose he
decides to make use of the two intriguers, who are so
disgusted by the niggardly treatment of the Baron that they
readily fall in with the plans of the young cavalier. After the
crowd has dispersed and the Baron is left alone lying on the
sofa, and humming his favourite waltz tune (No. 6) to
himself, Annina approaches and hands him a note. In this the
Princess's chambermaid promises him a rendezvous. Ochs is
delighted at the new conquest he believes himself to have
made.

The finale of the act is dominated by Ochs's famous waltz
tune, initially heard soon after he meets Sophie for the first
time.

Act III.   After a brilliant orchestral *fugato* the curtain
rises on a room in an inn near Vienna. With the help of
Valzacchi and Annina, who are now in the service of both the
Baron and Octavian, but are more prone to further the
latter's plans because he pays them better, Octavian has hired
a room in an inn. This room is fitted up with trap-doors,
blind windows and the like. Here, at the suggestion of the

intriguers, who have the run of the place and know to wha.
uses the trick room can be put, Ochs has made his rendezvous
for the evening with the pretty chambermaid. Octavian, in his
girl's clothes, is early at the meeting-place.

Between the Baron and the disguised Octavian, as soon as
they are alone, develops a rude scene of courtship, mostly to
the accompaniment of waltz tunes. Octavian is able to hold
him off skilfully, and gradually there is unfolded in all its
details the mad practical joke in which the Baron is involved.
Strange figures appear at the windows. Lerchenau, ignorant
and superstitious, thinks he sees ghosts. Suddenly, what is
supposed to be a blind window bursts open and a woman
dressed in mourning rushes in. It is the disguised Annina, who
claims to be Ochs's deserted wife. Innkeeper and servants
hurry in. The clamour and confusion become more and more
frantic. Finally the Baron himself calls for the police, without
thinking what a 'give away' it may be for himself. When the
Commissary of Police arrives, to save his face he gives out
that his companion is his affianced, Sophie von Faninal.
That, however, only adds to the confusion, for Octavian's
accomplices have sought out Faninal and invited him on
behalf of the Baron to come to the inn. In his amazement,
the Baron can think of no other way out of the dilemma save
to act as if he did not know Faninal at all, at which the latter,
naturally, is greatly angered.

When the confusion is at its height, the Marschallin
suddenly appears. A lackey of the Baron, seeing his master in
such difficulties, has run to her to ask for her powerful
protection. She quickly takes in the whole situation. The
Police Commissary was once her husband's orderly and it is
easy for her to persuade him that the whole matter was just a
joke and no more. Sophie, who has already informed Ochs
that her father never wishes to see him again—nor does she
for that matter—is heart-broken at the idea that the 'joke'
may even have included Octavian and herself, but her anxiety
does not last long. After the Marschallin has got rid of
Ochs—he has long since outstayed his welcome, but even his
going is attended by more farcical complications—she pushes
Octavian towards Sophie. However bitterly Octavian's disaffection grieves her, she is a clever enough woman of the
world to recognise that the time for her to give him up has
come.

The last section of the opera does something to remove the

...mpression of the musical bustle and purposelessness of the earlier part of Act III. It contains the great trio ('Hab' mir's gelobt, ihn lieb zu haben') for the Marschallin, Sophie, and Octavian, in an early example of Strauss's luxuriant writing for combined female voices, always a feature of his scores and here at its finest and most effective:

Octavian and Sophie are forgiven—the stature of the Marschallin can be seen from the great sweep of the first phrase of the trio—and the Marschallin leaves them alone together, saying she will go into the other room to console Faninal for what has happened to him during the day.

There is a little duet for the two lovers ('Ist ein Traum, kann nicht wirklich sein'), set to the simplest tune imaginable and punctuated by No. 4a; their happiness is complete. The Marschallin reappears leaning on Faninal's arm; she says no more than 'Ja, ja', but the orchestra refers gently to music already heard in her monologue at the end of Act I. The lovers are alone again. One more reference to their unexpectedly blissful state, and they go quickly out to the carriage hand in hand. But it is not quite the end of the opera. Sophie has dropped her handkerchief, and Mahomet, the little black page, comes running back to look for it; he finds it, runs out to the carriage, and the curtain falls.

Der Rosenkavalier is a masterpiece of pastiche, an evocation of an unrealistic, fairy-story Vienna of long ago, a brilliant technical tour-de-force. The principal means Strauss and Hofmannsthal employed, for all their attractiveness, are either anachronistic, like the ubiquitous and magical waltzes, which perfectly suggest a period atmosphere of which they were never part, or else invented, like the plausible but unhistorical presentation of a rose to an engaged girl. But if the means defy the purist, the end is phenomenally successful: Strauss's invention is expressive and memorable, Hofmannsthal's elegant and a model of sensibility. One of the finest fruits of their collaboration is a kind of fast-moving musical conversation, always apt to situation, full of character, a unique example of speech heightened by music, which neither descends to banality nor blurs the conversational outline with too lyrical a musical overlay. From this basis grow moments of genuine pathos which give the opera memorability—the Marschallin's reflections on the passing of her youth, the reluctant but genuine magnanimity in giving up Octavian to a younger woman—as well as such traditionally operatic set-pieces, as Ochs's waltz, the glittering entrance of Octavian and his presentation of the rose to Sophie, or, best of all, the great third act trio which provides a splendid and cathartic musical summary of the emotional threads which have gone to make the drama.   K., H.

ARIADNE AUF NAXOS
Ariadne on Naxos

In its original form, opera in one act by Richard Strauss; text by Hugo von Hofmannsthal. The work was designed to follow a condensed version of Molière's *Le Bourgeois Gentilhomme* (translated by Hofmannsthal), for which Strauss provided incidental music. This version was first heard at Stuttgart, October 25, 1912, with Jeritza, Siems, Jadlowker, conductor Strauss. First performed Berlin, 1913, with Hafgren-Waag, Bosetti, Jadlowker, conductor Blech; His Majesty's Theatre, London, 1913, with von der Osten, Bosetti, Marak, conductor Beecham (Tree was Monsieur Jourdain, and the translation was by Somerset Maugham). Revived Edinburgh Festival, 1950 (by Glyndebourne company), with Zadek, Hollweg, Anders, conductor Beecham (Miles Malleson, who translated the play, also played Jourdain). Subsequently, the opera was revised, the Molière play dropped, the new version having its première in Vienna, October 4,

1916, with Jeritza, Selma Kurz, Környey, Duhan, and Lehmann, substituting as the Composer (according to her autobiography) for the indisposed Gutheil-Schoder; conductor Schalk. First performed Berlin, 1916, with Hafgren-Waag, Hansa, Lola Artôt de Padilla, Kirchner, conductor Blech; Covent Garden, 1924, with Lehmann, Ivogün, Schumann, Fischer-Niemann, conductor Alwin; Turin, 1925, with Arangi-Lombardi, Pasini, Tess, Dolci, conductor Gui; Philadelphia, 1928 (the cast included Helen Jepson as Echo and Nelson Eddy as Harlequin; the conductor was Alexander Smallens); New York, 1934; Rome, 1935, with Anny Konetzni, Kern, Hadrabova, Kalenberg, conductor Krips (ensemble from Vienna Opera); City Center, New York, most successfully in 1946, with Ella Flesch, MacWatters, Stoska, Argyris, conductor Halasz (the first professional performance in New York). Revived Berlin, 1932, with Anny Konetzni, Ivogün, Lorenz; Covent Garden, 1936, with Marta Fuchs, Sack, Wieber, Ralf, conductor Strauss (ensemble of Dresden Opera); Vienna, 1947, with Cebotari, Noni, Jurinac, Friedrich; Munich, 1952, with Cunitz, Lipp, Jurinac, Patzak, conductor Keilberth; Glyndebourne, 1953, with Dow, Dobbs, Jurinac, Lewis, conductor Pritchard; Metropolitan, 1962, with Rysanek, d'Angelo, Meyer, Jess Thomas, conductor Böhm.

CHARACTERS

Characters in the Prologue:

The Major-domo	Speaking Role
Music Master	Baritone
The Composer	Soprano
The Tenor (*later Bacchus*)	Tenor
An Officer	Tenor
The Dancing Master	Tenor
The Wig-maker	Bass
A Lackey	Bass
Zerbinetta	Soprano
Prima Donna (*later Ariadne*)	Soprano
Harlequin	Baritone
Scaramuccio	Tenor
Truffaldino	Bass
Brighella	Tenor

Characters in the Opera:

Ariadne		Soprano
Bacchus		Tenor
Naiad		Soprano
Dryad	*three nymphs*	Contralto
Echo		Soprano
Zerbinetta	*characters of Intermezzo*	Soprano
Harlequin		Baritone

Scaramuccio ⎫   ⎧ Tenor
Truffaldino ⎬ *characters of Intermezzo* · · · · ⎨ Bass
Brighella   ⎭   ⎩ Tenor

(The characters in the Opera are the same in both versions; those of the Prologue belong only to the second version, the original conception of the opera calling for the cast of Molière's *Le Bourgeois Gentilhomme* for the first part of the evening.)

One of the first things to strike anyone who reads the correspondence of Strauss and Hofmannsthal is the considerable difference there often is between their first thoughts on the subject of one of their operatic collaborations, and their last. Thus *Rosenkavalier* was thought of as a simple comedy with important roles for a baritone and a soprano in boy's clothes, and in the earlier stages of the correspondence there is no mention of the Marschallin, who was later to become the central figure in the comedy. *Ariadne* went through an even stranger evolution. Originally conceived as a little opera lasting half an hour, and designed as a thank-offering to Max Reinhardt, who produced *Rosenkavalier* in Dresden, it was intended to form the musical divertissement in Molière's *Le Bourgeois Gentilhomme*, taking the place of the Turkish ballet called for by Monsieur Jourdain. In the end the opera became a much more extensive affair than at first envisaged, and lasted about three times as long as projected. Unfortunately, the combination of a theatrical with an operatic company proved beyond the means of most theatres, and the work as it stood was decided to be impracticable. Strauss therefore revised it and substituted a musical prelude (lasting about thirty-five minutes) for the Molière play, making at the same time some alterations in the body of the opera itself (this, however, remains substantially the same as in the first version, although the role of Zerbinetta[1] has been slightly shortened).

Ariadne has usually been performed in its second version, but such an authority on Strauss's music as Sir Thomas Beecham wrote (in his autobiographical *A Mingled Chime*): 'In this, the earlier version of *Ariadne*, I have always considered that the musical accomplishment of Strauss attained

[1] Margarethe Siems was not only the original Zerbinetta but had earlier created Chrisothemis and the Marschallin.

its highest reach, yielding a greater spontaneity and variety of invention, together with a subtler and riper style, than anything that his pen had yet given to the stage ... the Bacchus section of the opera is one of the purple patches in the operatic literature of the twentieth century. ... The later version has not only failed to hold the stage,[1] but has dimmed the public recollection of the far superior and more attractive original.'

The original version of the opera calls for an abbreviated version of *Le Bourgeois Gentilhomme* to form the first part of the evening's entertainment. The theme of this is that Monsieur Jourdain, the bourgeois who is determined to become a gentleman by sheer concentrated hard work and who means to learn to dance, sing, fence, compose, philosophise, is at the same time laying siege to the affections of a certain Marquise Dorimène. She for her part is in love with the shady Count Dorante, who has undertaken to bring her to the lavish dinner party which is given in their honour by Jourdain. The play is garnished with some delightful incidental music by Strauss, and the three principal characters remain at the side of the stage while the opera is performed for their benefit.

In the revised version, the Prologue takes place at the house of a Viennese *nouveau riche* (not in Paris, as in the Molière). We see musicians, singers, actors, carpenters, and stage hands preparing for the first performance of a serious opera which has been specially commissioned by the owner of the house to entertain his guests. There is consternation when the Major-domo announces that after the opera there will be a Harlequinade entertainment; moreover, the two shows must not overrun their allotted span of time, as the fireworks must begin precisely at nine o'clock! Worse is to come, as a little later the Major-domo comes in to inform the two troupes that his master has changed his mind, and now both entertainments will be played simultaneously, the serious opera being punctuated by intervals of dancing from the comedians.

The dominating figure of the prologue is the composer, a creation of the second version and a touching figure which has found admirable exponents almost every time the opera has been performed. He extemporises an aria which he intends for the tenor (this is derived from a little song heard

---

[1] History suggests this judgment was, to put it mildly, premature.

during the course of the play in the first version), he
languishes at the idea of his masterpiece being combined with
a common dancing show, he tries to explain to Zerbinetta
that Ariadne prefers death to the embraces of any man other
than her beloved, and, proving unsuccessful in this, he
indulges in a duet with Zerbinetta in which he comes
perilously close to declaring that he loves her. There is some
trouble with both tenor and prima donna, after which the
composer brings the prologue to a suitable end by declaring
his conviction in the power of music, the most sacred of the
arts.

After an interval, the curtain rises on the opera itself,
which is watched from boxes by the owner of the house and
his guests. The setting, which we have hitherto seen only
from its reverse side, is now seen from in front. At one side
of the set is a cave, in whose entrance Ariadne can be seen
asleep, watched by Naiad, Dryad and Echo. In a trio (of the
type made familiar by Wagner's Rhinemaidens), these
creatures express a certain sympathy with Ariadne's sorrow,
to which however they have become accustomed with the
passage of time.

A great *scena* begins for Ariadne. She is speaking as if in a
dream, and takes no notice when the Harlequinade quartet
and Zerbinetta comment on her distress and try to think of
means of comforting her. Ariadne welcomes the idea of
death, and not even a determined effort by Harlequin to cure
her of her madness—for he thinks it must surely be that
which is wrong with her—can stop her for long. 'Es gibt ein
Reich, wo alles rein ist; es hat auch einen Namen:
Totenreich,' she continues, and at mention of death's
messenger, Hermes, her monologue becomes more urgent.
The last section of the monologue, where Ariadne rejoices in
the idea of the deliverance death will bring to her, is ecstatic
in import, and (from the singer's point of view) Wagnerian in
weight.

The four comedians make another attempt to cheer up the
melancholy Ariadne, but their dancing and singing have not
the slightest effect, even when they are joined by the
sprightly Zerbinetta. Eventually, Zerbinetta bids them leave
her to see what she can do on her own. Her *scena* is one of
the most taxing ever written for coloratura soprano—the
qualification is hardly necessary; it has really no rival. After
a recitative, 'Grossmächtige Prinzessin' (Most gracious

sovereign lady), she appeals to Ariadne as woman to woman. Ariadne is not the first to be abandoned by her lover, and will not be the last. Zerbinetta expounds her own fickle

Als ein Gott Kam Je-der ge-gangen und sein Schritt schon machte mich stumm.

philosophy, and is quite unconcerned when Ariadne disappears inside her cave. She goes into details of her amorous career in an *allegretto scherzando* ('So war es mit Pagliazzo') at which point the vocal writing parts company with what is normally considered advisable to write for a singer and becomes a fantastic display of vocal fireworks (even the transposition into D major from the E of the original leaves something which is technically beyond all but the most accomplished of coloratura sopranos).

Als ein Gott . . . . kam Je - der ge - gan - gen

The section of the opera which begins at her recitative is entirely Zerbinetta's. She is pursued by the four comedians, each of whom seems amorously inclined. Zerbinetta encourages and eludes them all, until only Scaramuccio, Brighella, and Truffaldino are left on the stage. Much to their annoyance, Zerbinetta is immediately heard conversing tenderly with Harlequin, whom they had thought safely out of the way. They rush out to see what they can do about it.

No sooner are they gone than the three attendant nymphs return to the stage, full of the sight they have just seen. A youthful god is coming, Bacchus, fresh from the embraces of Circe, but eager for new adventure. They call to Ariadne, who emerges from the cave in time to hear Bacchus off-stage calling for Circe. The nymphs beg him to continue singing, and Ariadne hails him as the longed-for messenger of death. The opera ends with an extended love duet, Wagnerian in its length and weight if not in its character. In Bacchus's arms, Ariadne finds consolation, and Strauss even allows Zerbinetta to pop in for a moment to comment that all has turned out exactly as she would have expected. Bacchus and Ariadne go together into the cave. (In the first version, soon after Bacchus is first heard off-stage, there is a fairly lengthy interruption by Zerbinetta, during which Ariadne is arrayed in fine clothes; it is only after this that the god is first seen on the stage.)

Ariadne is scored for a small orchestra of thirty-nine players.   H.

DIE FRAU OHNE SCHATTEN

The Woman without a Shadow

Opera in three acts by Richard Strauss; text by Hugo von Hofmannsthal. Première in Vienna, October 10, 1919, with Lehmann, Jeritza, Weidt, Oestvig, Manowarda, Mayr, conductor Schalk. First performed Dresden, 1919, with Rethberg, von der Osten, Metzger, Vogelstrom, Plaschke, cond. Reiner; Berlin, 1920, with Kemp, Hafgren-Dinkela, Branzell, Hutt, Armster; Salzburg, 1932, with Lehmann, Ursuleac, Rünger, Völker, Manowarda, cond. Clemens Krauss; 1932, Zürich; 1934, Venice, with Viennese company; 1938, Rome, with Pauly, Ursuleac, Voyer, Franci, cond. Marinuzzi; la Scala, 1940, with Pacetti, Roman, Voyer, Franci, cond. Marinuzzi; Buenos Aires, 1949, with Hilde Konetzni, Hörner, Höngen, Suthaus, Weber, cond. Kleiber; Munich, 1954, with Schech, Rysanek, Hopf, Metternich, cond. Kempe; 1959, San Francisco, with Schech, Lang, Dalis, Feiersinger, Yahia, cond. Ludwig; Munich's rebuilt opera reopened 1963, with Borkh, Bjoner, Mödl, Jess Thomas, Fischer-Dieskau, cond. Keilberth; 1966, London, by Hamburg company, with Kuchta, Tarres, Kozub, Crass; 1966, Metropolitan, New York, with Christa Ludwig, Rysanek, Dalis, King, Berry, cond. Böhm; 1967, Covent Garden, with Borkh, Hillebrecht, King, McIntyre, cond. Solti; Paris, 1972, with Ludwig, Rysanek, Hesse, King, Berry, conductor Böhm.

CHARACTERS

The Emperor ....Tenor
The Empress, *his wife* ....Soprano
The Nurse (*Die Amme*) ....Mezzo-Soprano
A Spirit-messenger ....Baritone
The Keeper of the Gates of the Temple
...................Soprano or Tenor (falsetto)

Apparition of a Youth .... Tenor
The Voice of the Falcon .... Soprano
A Voice from Above .... Contralto
Barak, *the dyer* .... Bass-Baritone
His Wife .... Soprano
The One-eyed ⎫   ⎧ Bass
The One-armed ⎬ *brothers of Barak* .... ⎨ Bass
The Hunchback ⎭   ⎩ Tenor
Six Children's Voices .. Three Sopranos, Three Contraltos
Voices of the Nightwatchmen .... Three Basses
Servants of the Emperor, Voices of unborn Children, Spirits

The Emperor of the South Eastern Islands is married to a supernatural being, the daughter of Keikobad, king of the spirits. She emerged from a white gazelle which he shot while out hunting. Their love is mutual and ardent, but their marriage is childless; in token of her barren state, the Empress throws no shadow. This is the main theme of the story; to make love complete, the woman must bear children, and of this the shadow is the outward sign.

Act I. The opera, which is by no means short, each of the three acts lasting over an hour, starts when the Emperor and Empress have been married twelve moons. It is dark, and the Nurse is crouching on a flat roof above the Imperial gardens. To her appears a messenger. After reassuring himself that the Empress still throws no shadow, he tells the Nurse that he is from Keikobad and has come to inform her that the Empress may stay only another three days on earth. She must then go back to Keikobad, and the Emperor will be turned into stone.

The messenger disappears and the Emperor comes from the house. He tells the story of how he first saw and won his wife. He tells the Nurse that he is going hunting for three days, and refers to his favourite falcon which he has not seen since the day he met his wife. The Emperor leaves, day dawns, and the Empress comes from her chamber. She too talks of her love, but then catches sight of the falcon, whose voice is heard to say: 'The woman throws no shadow, the Emperor must turn to stone.' The Empress understands that the only way to save him is to acquire a shadow, and she begs the Nurse to help her find one.

The orchestra represents their journey to earth, and the

second scene is set in the hut of the dyer, Barak. It is poorly furnished, and serves at the same time as workshop and bedroom. When the curtain rises, the three deformed brothers of the dyer are fighting.

In the scene which ensues, the contrasting characters of Barak and his wife are made apparent. She nags and complains, he is patient and full of natural goodness. But he upbraids her for not having given him a child in the two and a half years during which they have been married. He goes off to take his goods to market.

No sooner has he gone than the Empress and her Nurse enter the hut, dressed simply as peasants. The Nurse is immediately aware that in the dyer's wife she has found a good subject for her black arts. She praises her for her beauty, and asks if she does not know that she could sell her shadow and get for it all the luxuries and riches she has always desired. The Nurse tempts her with visions, which she summons to aid her in achieving her object.

The dyer's wife agrees to exchange her own prospect of motherhood for the promise of riches. She will deny her bed to her husband. The Empress and the Nurse go out, saying that they will be back next day. When she is alone, the woman has another vision. This time she hears the voices of her unborn children coming from the flames of the fire. She is terrified.

Barak enters to find his bed separated from his wife's. He is sad, but optimistic that this is only a temporary state of affairs. As they lie down, the voices of nightwatchmen can be heard coming from outside.

Act II. In his introduction to the published libretto, Hofmannsthal says: 'The trials continue; all four must be cleansed—the dyer and his wife, the Emperor and the daughter of the spirits. The one pair is too much of the earth earthy, the other too full of pride and remote from the earth.'

The scene is again Barak's hut. The struggle to obtain the shadow continues. The Nurse tempts the woman with the apparition of a handsome youth, who appears each time the dyer is out of the hut. The woman believes she hates her husband and thinks it would be simple to deceive him, and yet does not quite dare to do so. Barak feels the change in her reaction to him, and his simple, good heart grows sad. He invites some beggar children to share in their meal.

The scene changes to the Emperor's falcon house in the forest. The Emperor has found his falcon again, and follows it to the falcon house. There he sees his wife, from whom he has had a letter to the effect that she has been alone and seen no one during his absence hunting. He senses immediately that she has been in contact with the things of the earth.

The scene changes to Barak's hut. It is the third day and the Nurse continues her efforts to gain the shadow of the dyer's wife for the Empress. The Nurse and the dyer's wife go out of the hut together, leaving the Empress and Barak. As the curtain falls, it is obvious that she feels sympathetically towards Barak, and regrets what she is causing to happen to him and his wife.

The Empress's bedroom in the falcon house. She lies on her bed in restless sleep, and the Nurse lies at the foot of the bed. She has a vision of her husband wandering through tomb-like caves, and hears the voice of the falcon: 'The woman throws no shadow; the Emperor must turn to stone.' She is much moved by this, but also touched by Barak's distress, which she is fully aware is caused by her actions.

Back in Barak's hut, the Nurse makes her final attempt to win the woman's shadow from her. Although it is midday, it is growing dark, a storm is brewing, and the three crooked brothers of Barak are howling in terror. The Nurse senses that there are supernatural powers at work over which she has no control, but assures the Empress of their ultimate attainment of their object. The Empress is appalled by the sufferings of men, but grateful that fate has led her to meet Barak, whose integrity has convinced her of the dignity of humanity. The climax of the scene comes when the woman tells Barak that she has been unfaithful to him and sold her shadow and her unborn children with it. To prove the truth of her words, the brothers light a fire and it is seen that she throws no shadow. Barak threatens to kill her, and as if by magic a sword is there to his hand. The Empress refuses to take the shadow at such a price, but the woman, overcome by remorse when she sees the result of her admission, tells Barak that she has not done what she has confessed, but has only wished to do it.

As the Nurse tears the Empress from the scene, the earth opens and swallows up Barak and his hut.

Act III. Subterranean vault, divided by a thick wall in the middle. On one side is Barak, on the other his wife, each however unconscious of the presence of the other. In a famous passage, she wrestles with her conscience ('Schweigt doch, ihr Stimmen'), he tries to find consolation and peace for the two of them ('Mir anvertraut, dass ich sie hege').

Trombone calls summon the Empress to the judgment hall where her father Keikobad presides. The Nurse wants to prevent her from entering, for she fears Keikobad's anger more than death; her purpose now is to persuade the Empress to return to earth to continue her search for the shadow. But the Empress is determined to enter where she knows her husband is being judged. She bids the Nurse farewell for ever; the Nurse does not understand men and their struggles and the price they pay for their guilt. She herself has learned to love them and to understand them in their misery. She enters the Temple. The voices of Barak and his wife are heard calling for each other.

The Empress demands to know her place in the scheme of the universe. A voice from above tells her to drink of the Water of Life and the shadow of the woman will be hers and she will be human. But the voices of Barak and his wife are again heard, and the Empress refuses to drink and be guilty of the crime of their undoing. She feels she belongs to the human race, and yet she refuses to yield to the temptation, which would involve the destruction of innocent beings. She demands to see her father, the judge. The alcove is illuminated, and the Emperor appears, turned to stone except for his eyes, which can be seen pleading with her for life. In her desperation, she wants to rush to her husband's side, and her anguish is increased when she hears a voice call: 'The woman throws no shadow, the Emperor must turn to stone.' She is again urged to drink of the Water of Life, to gain the shadow and save her husband. It is her moment of supreme trial, and she falls to the ground in the agony of her inner struggle. Finally, a cry breaks from her lips: 'I will not.'

As soon as this cry is heard, the water disappears, and the Temple is brightly lit from above. The Empress rises to her feet and it can be seen that she throws a shadow. The Emperor descends from his alcove, the voices of their unborn children are heard singing from above, and in their happiness the Emperor and Empress embrace and fall on their knees to give thanks for deliverance from their trial.

The scene changes to a beautiful landscape, with a water-fall in the middle. The Emperor and Empress stand beside it. Below it can be seen the figures of Barak and his wife, who ᴸave found each other. The voices of unborn children complete the happiness of each couple.   H.

INTERMEZZO

Opera in two acts by Richard Strauss; text by the composer. Première, Dresden, November 4, 1924, with Lotte Lehmann, Joseph Correck, Theo Strack, Hans Lange, Liesl von Schuch, Ludwig Ermold, conductor Fritz Busch. First performed Berlin, 1925, with Hussa, Scheidl, Guszalewicz, Leo Schützendorf, conductor Szell; Vienna, 1927, with Lehmann, Jerger, conductor Strauss; Berlin, 1930, with Reinhardt, Scheidl; Zürich, 1951, with Ebers, Wolff; Cuvelliéstheater, Munich, 1960, with Steffek, Prey; New York, 1963, with Curtin, Donald Bell; Edinburgh Festival, 1965 (Munich company), with Steffek, Prey; Glyndebourne, 1974, with Söderström.

CHARACTERS

Christine . . . . Soprano
Little Franz, *her eight-year-old son*
Hofkapellmeister Robert Storch, *her husband* . Baritone
Anna, *the chambermaid* . . . . Soprano
Baron Lummer . . . . Tenor
The Notary . . . . Baritone
His Wife . . . . Soprano

Kapellmeister Stroh[2]		Tenor
Commercial Councillor	*Storch's skat*	Baritone
Justizrat[3]	*partners*[1]	Baritone
Kammersänger[4]		Bass

Time: The Nineteen-Twenties   *Place:* Grundlsee and Vienna

When the opera was first produced, emphasis was laid in newspaper reports on the fact that the basis of the work was taken from incidents in the composer's private life. The emphasis can hardly be thought to have been misplaced, since

[1] Strauss played regularly; these particular parties were apparently in Berlin at the beginning of the century.
[2] Stroh was the conductor Joseph Stransky who was later associated for a period with the New York Philharmonic.
[3] An honour bestowed on legal dignitaries by the Emperor and perhaps equivalent to the British Q.C., or Queen's Counsel.
[4] The Kammersänger was the heroic Wagnerian tenor Ernst Kraus, a member of the Berlin State Opera from 1896 to 1924 who sang Wagner at Bayreuth and Covent Garden.

Strauss himself took care that the sets were made to corres
pond with his own home at Garmisch, and Joseph Correck, the
creator of the role of Hofkapellmeister Storch, wore a
specially constructed mask to make his resemblance to
Strauss more marked.

Act I. The dressing-room of the house of Kapellmeister
Storch. Seven o'clock in the morning. Open suitcases everywhere indicate that Storch and his wife are busy packing. She
is thoroughly bad-tempered, abusing the servants, complaining incessantly at her husband, and, when he seems
inclined to answer back, reminding him that she comes of a
much better family than he does; who is he, anyway?

After successive exhibitions of her short temper with both
maid and cook, Christine admits to the former that not the
least of her husband's shortcomings in her view is his
incessant kindness and gentleness; if only he would stand up
to her like a man and not give way so much, she would have
far more respect for him. The telephone rings, and Christine
is asked by a neighbour to go skating. She accepts.

An interlude (there are twelve in the course of the opera,
and they constitute the chief means of sustained lyrical
expression) leads us to a new scene: the toboggan track.
Tobogganists cross the stage, but when it is Christine's turn
she runs into a young man on skis. She is furious and abuses
him, complaining that the fall hurt her very much—there is
no word of whether he is injured or not. But when she
discovers that he is the well-connected Baron Lummer, she is
all over him and only too anxious that he should know she is
the wife of the famous composer Storch. She asks him to
come and visit her.

An interlude composed of waltzes and other dances takes
us to an inn at Grundlsee, where Christine and the Baron are
dancing. They converse, and one gathers that he is there for
his health. The whole short scene is brilliantly alive; it is the
music of the third act of *Rosenkavalier* transferred,
shortened, and without any element of farce.

Dining-room in the Storchs' house. Christine reads a letter
which she is writing to her husband, and in which she talks
about the excellent young escort she has acquired for herself.
At that very moment, in comes the Baron. They sit opposite
each other reading the newspaper, and she asks him when he
is going to begin his studies. His family apparently want him
to read law, but he is anxious to take up the study of natural

history, for which, without them, he has not the means. She says that he has only to wait until her husband is back, and he will not lack support.

The wistful music from the moment of the Baron's exit is combined with the interlude which follows it to make a concert excerpt, usually known as 'the Interlude from *Intermezzo*'. When the curtain rises, we are in the Baron's room in the house of the notary. He exclaims with impatience at the demands made upon him by Frau Storch. Can she really expect him to sit about with her in the evenings reading the newspapers! And all that talk about his studies . . . and his ill-health. He is interrupted by a girl-friend, obviously come to keep an appointment; he will join her in a minute. He sits down to write a letter to his patroness (as he refers to her); he must have money.

Another interlude brings us again to the Storchs' diningroom. Christine has had the letter—a thousand marks, he asks for! He must be mad! At this moment the Baron himself puts in an appearance, and is immediately sent outside to wipe his shoes. She tells him that what he asks for is impossible; but she is sure her husband will help him with his studies when he gets back. Let him not spoil their agreeable relationship by insisting.

At this juncture, the maid brings in a note and hands it to her. It is addressed to Kapellmeister Storch, but Christine opens it, and exclaims in horror. She reads aloud: 'My darling. Do send me two tickets for the opera again tomorrow. Afterwards in the bar as usual! Your Mieze Meier.' The Baron is solicitous, but she sends him away, and when he is gone, she writes out a telegram: 'Who is Mieze Meier? Your infidelity discovered. Am leaving you for good.' She hustles the maid to pack all the suitcases: they are leaving the house—for good.

Another interlude. The child's bedroom. Christine sits by the side of his bed, crying. She abuses her husband, but the child will not hear of this: his father is good and kind, and it is she who is horrid and makes scenes. She replies that she is much too good for the man she married; she kneels melodramatically at the foot of the bed and prays.

Act II. The 'skat' game. The scene is a comfortable sitting-room in the house of the Commercial Councillor. Round the 'skat' table sit the Justizrat, the Commercial Councillor, the Kammersänger, and Kapellmeister Stroh. The conversation which accompanies the game centres round the agreeable character of Storch, which contrasts so markedly with his highly disagreeable wife. When he arrives, Storch apologises for being late and then joins the game. They ask after his wife, and he tells them of the letter he has had in which she talks of her new-found friend the Baron. They cannot keep a hint of criticism from their tone when they refer to Christine, but Storch explains that he finds her extremely stimulating—in any case, her bristling exterior conceals the proverbial heart of gold.

A telegram comes for Storch, whose jocularity falls from him as he reads it. He gives it to Stroh and asks him to read it aloud. Stroh's comment is: 'What, do you know her, too?' but Storch hurries out of the room in obvious distress, leaving the others to comment ironically but without malice on the surprising news that such an obviously model husband should turn out to be no better than the rest of them.

The scene changes to the office of the notary. Frau Kapellmeister comes in and demands a divorce. The notary assumes that this is because of the Baron, and is distinctly surprised to hear that Christine is convinced she has evidence against her husband.

A stormy interlude leads to the third scene, in the Prater in Vienna. Storm. Storch is seen wandering about. He has had no answer to his telegrams to Christine, no explanation even of the identity of the mysterious Mieze Meier. He cannot leave Vienna and his work on account of so ridiculous a misunderstanding, but his worry is very real. Stroh finds him and explains that the letter must have been meant for him; the two names are not dissimilar, and probably the volatile Mieze looked up his address in the telephone book, assuming that he—Stroh—was no less a man than the famous Hofkapellmeister. Storch is furious, and demands that Stroh put right the whole ghastly muddle. He must take Christine proof and go at once.

Scene iv.   Christine's dressing-room. Packing and disorder. Christine vents her wrath on everybody and everything in sight. Everyone is against her, she is sure, but she wishes she had not sent the Baron to Vienna to check up on Mieze Meier. Storch's telegrams have caused her to wonder whether there is not some mistake. Another telegram arrives, this time containing the news that Stroh is coming with a full explanation of the whole situation. Stroh is announced and the curtain falls as she goes out to hear what he has to say.

The dining-room, decorated for Storch's return. Christine s wildly excited, she must go and greet him. But she stops herself, and when he rushes in and tries to embrace her, she coldly gives him her hand. She contrives to nag in spite of Storch's obvious delight at seeing her, and seems to think that he must make amends in some way for what has happened. When she tells him she is sick of him and all other men, and he can go and make arrangements for a divorce with the notary, he rounds on her and gives her a long-needed piece of his mind, after which he leaves the stage. She is astonished at his change of attitude, but at this juncture in comes the Baron. It appears from what he says that he has bungled the meeting with Mieze.

Storch comes back and pretends to be jealous of the Baron. Christine says he was quite agreeable for a bit, but rather a bore, particularly when he asked her for a thousand marks. Storch is delighted at this, and thinks it a great joke. All is set for their reconciliation, and when the curtain falls, they have made up all their differences, and Christine has even gone so far as to comment what a happy marriage theirs is.   H.

DIE AEGYPTISCHE HELENA
The Egyptian Helen

Opera in two acts by Richard Strauss; text by Hofmannsthal. Première at Dresden, June 6, 1928, with Rethberg, Rajdl, Taucher, Plaschke, conductor Busch. First performed Vienna, 1928 with Jeritza, Angerer, Graarud, conductor Strauss; Berlin, 1928, with Müller, Alpar, Laubenthal, Schorr, conductor Blech; Metropolitan, 1928, with Jeritza, Fleischer, Laubenthal, Whitehill, conductor Bodanzky; Salzburg Festival, 1933, with Ursuleac, Völker, conductor Krauss. Revived Berlin, 1935, with Ursuleac, Heidersbach, Völker, Prohaska, conductor Krauss; Munich, 1940, with Ursuleac, Ranczak, Hotter, and 1956, with Rysanek, Aldenhoff, Uhde; New York, Philharmonic Hall, 1967, with Bjoner, Elizabeth Carron, Olvis; Vienna, 1970, with Gwyneth Jones, Coertse, Jess Thomas, Glossop, conductor Krips.

CHARACTERS

Helena, *wife of Menelaus* .... Soprano
Menelaus .... Tenor
Hermione, *their child* .... Soprano
Aithra, *the daughter of an Egyptian King; a
  sorceress* .... Soprano

Altair .... Baritone
Da-Ud, *his son* .... Tenor
First and Second Servants of
    Aithra .... Soprano, Mezzo-Soprano
Three Elves .... Two Sopranos, Contralto
The Omniscient Sea-shell .... Contralto
Time: 1193–1184 B.C. (after the Trojan war)   *Place:* Egyp

The Trojan war is over, and Menelaus has killed Paris, the
ravisher of his wife Helena, and is now returning home with
his wife. He has made up his mind that his honour, as well as
the blood of the countless Greeks who died fighting for his
cause, demands that Helena should pay the supreme price for
what has been caused through her beauty, and he is deter
mined to sacrifice her himself, either at sea or when they
reach their native soil. But in a storm his ship is wrecked.

Act I.   A great room in Aithra's palace. The Sea-shel
assures Aithra of Poseidon's love, but conjures up for her a
description of Menelaus's ship, bearing the fairest of women
who is about to be murdered by her husband. Aithra causes a
storm, which wrecks the ship, and it is not long before
Menelaus enters the room, leading a golden-haired woman
behind him. He feels that he must fulfil his vow and slay
Helena, but she tries to entice him to her arms once again
Aithra intervenes and causes Menelaus to think he sees and
hears Paris and the Trojans, whom he has killed, once more
rising against him. He rushes from the room after them, and
Helena is comforted by Aithra, who gives her a potion to
drink, which brings forgetfulness of every ill.

Menelaus returns convinced that he has killed two of the
beings he was pursuing—Paris and Helena. He can see their
blood on his dagger—but what he brandishes is spotless and
shining. Aithra convinces him that for the past ten years he
and the Greeks have been victims of a fantastic delusion; it
was not Helena at all who was in Troy—she has been here
these ten years, lying in a deep sleep, safe from the touch of
man.

Aithra makes a sign, and Helena is visible to Menelaus
waking in all her beauty from her sleep. He is overjoyed, and
cannot resist the happiness which the vision affords him. At
Helena's insistence, Aithra transports them by her magic arts
to a land where the name of Helena means nothing to man or
woman. They go together over the threshold of a sleeping

chamber, and Aithra watches the triumph of her scheme
while she prepares to effect a transformation of their state.

Act II.   A tent opening wide on to a palm grove, behind
which the Atlas Mountains are visible. Helena and Menelaus
awaken after their magic flight. Helena expresses her ecstasy:
Zweite Brautnacht! Zaubernacht, überlange!' But Menelaus
is only half restored to her; for him, she is still a phantom,
conjured up by the magic arts of Aithra, and his conscience is
occupied with the murder—he thinks of it as that—of Helena
which he accomplished outside the palace of Aithra. It is as
he widower of Helena that he thinks of himself.

To visit Helena comes a chieftain of the desert, Altair by
name, with his followers. He salutes the queen reverently,
and then, as Menelaus takes his place behind her with drawn
sword in his hand, commands his followers led by his son,
Da-Ud, to do obeisance before her. Menelaus shows signs of
being jealous of Da-Ud—is he not like Paris?—but Helena tries
to comfort him. Altair invites Menelaus to join the hunt, and
offers him Da-Ud as his guide. As he departs, Altair shows his
contempt for Menelaus, but makes no secret of his open
admiration for Helena.

While Menelaus makes ready for the hunt, Da-Ud throws
himself at Helena's feet and declares his devotion and
adoration of her, but Helena takes no more notice of his
protestations than she has of Altair's. Menelaus departs, but
refuses to give up his sword, which Helena wants to take
from him but which he insists on having with him for the
hunt.

Aithra and attendants come to Helena. Aithra reveals that
she has not only given Helena the draught which brings
eternal forgetfulness of all that is unpleasant, but has also in
error provided her with the antidote. She has come to remove
this from Helena, lest she should accidentally taste of it. But
Helena proclaims that this alone can save her and Menelaus
from the position they are in, this alone can convince
Menelaus that she is Helena and not a nymph conjured up by
Aithra to take Helena's place in his bed. Helena bids her
slaves mix the potion using the remembrance draught.

Altair appears at the entrance of the tent, and declares his
passion for Helena. Slaves describe the progress of the hunt,
but their voices change from excitement to horror as they
perceive that Menelaus and Da-Ud are engaged in deadly
combat. Soon it is evident that Menelaus has triumphed, and

it is not long before Da-Ud's dead body is borne in by th
slaves to the sound of solemn music.

Menelaus appears not to understand that he has slain th
son of his host, but, while the slaves gather to bid him an
Helena to Altair's feast, Helena and her attendants bus
themselves over the mixing of the potion which will restor
his memory to him. When it is finally ready, Helena bids hin
drink, and herself sets the example. Menelaus takes the cup
and, for a moment after he has drunk, it looks as though h
will kill her. Then he drops his sword and gazes at his wife
recognising her and stretching out his arms as though to gras
a shadow.

Altair dashes in as though to take Helena by force an
with the help of his slaves separate her from her husband. Bu
at the same moment appears Aithra at the head of cohorts o
her supernatural followers, and commands Altair not t
presume to raise his hand against her or the woman sh
would protect. In the middle of Aithra's troops stand
Hermione, the daughter of Helena and Menelaus. The oper
comes to an end after she has asked her father: 'Where is m
beautiful mother?' All is forgiven and forgotten, and Helen
and Menelaus enter together upon a new life.   H.

ARABELLA

Opera in three acts by Richard Strauss; text by Hugo vo
Hofmannsthal. Première Dresden, July 1, 1933, with Ursuleac, Boko
Kremer, Jerger, Plaschke, conductor Clemens Krauss. First performe
Vienna, 1933, with Lehmann, Jerger, conductor Krauss; Berlin, 193
with Ursuleac, Heidersbach, Wittrisch, Prohaska, Krenn; Coven
Garden, 1934, with artists of première; Buenos Aires, 1934, wit
Teschemacher, Fleischer, Kipnis, Grossman, conductor Busch; Geno
1936, with dalla Rizza, Jerger, conductor Strauss; Salzburg, 1942, wit
Ursuleac, Eipperle, Taubmann, Reinmar, conductor Krauss; 1947, wit
Reining, della Casa, Taubmann, Hotter, conductor Böhm; Zürich, 194
with Cebotari, della Casa, Schöffler; Vienna, 1952, with della Cas
Felbermayer, Edelmann, conductor Moralt; Covent Garden, 1953, wit
della Casa, Uhde, conductor Kempe; New York, Metropolitan, 195
with Steber, Gueden, London, conductor Kempe; Covent Garden
1965, with della Casa, Carlyle, Fischer-Dieskau, conductor Solti.

CHARACTERS

Graf Waldner .... Bass
Adelaide, *his wife* .... Mezzo-Soprano

Arabella	his daughters	Soprano
Zdenka		Soprano
Mandryka, *a Croatian landowner*		Baritone
Matteo, *an officer*		Tenor
Graf Elemer		Tenor
Graf Dominik	*suitors of Arabella*	Baritone
Graf Lamoral		Bass
The 'Fiakermilli'		Soprano
A Fortune-teller		Soprano

Welko, Servant of Mandryka; Djura, Jankel, Servants
of Mandryka; a Servant, Arabella's Duenna,
Three Card-players, a Doctor, Groom

Time: 1860   *Place:* Vienna

There is no prelude and the curtain rises to show a salon in
an hotel in Vienna; it is richly and newly furnished in the
taste of the 1860's. We soon learn that the fortunes of the
Waldner family are very low indeed. Graf Waldner is a
gambler and has been losing heavily, and the only hope for
the future seems to lie in matching the beautiful Arabella
with a rich suitor. Zdenka, the younger child, has been
brought up as a boy, as her parents always wanted one and
Adelaide insists that they cannot possibly afford to have two
daughters coming out near the same time.

Adelaide is having her fortune told, and Zdenka, dressed in
boy's clothes, is making excuses for her parents to the
tradesmen who call to talk about their unpaid bills. Zdenka is
left alone, and shortly afterwards a young officer, Matteo,
who is desperately in love with Arabella, comes in. He asks
for news of his beloved from Zdenka whom, like everyone
else, he believes to be her brother (and therefore Zdenko).
Arabella has not looked at him for days, and if it were not
for the wonderful letter she wrote him a day or two ago, he
would be in complete despair. He threatens to go away or kill
himself if Arabella continues to ignore him. When he has
gone, Zdenka reveals her perturbation; she is in love with
Matteo herself and it is *she* who wrote him the letter.

There follows a scene between the two sisters. Arabella as
usual has presents from her three noble suitors, and from
Matteo as well, but she has no real interest in any of them,
and Zdenka's pleading for Matteo affects her little. One day
the right man will come along, and she will know him straight
away ('Aber der Richtige, wenn's einen gibt für mich'):

The two voices join in a charming and typically Straussian duet, whose theme[1] is frequently heard in the course of the opera. Arabella is confident in the future, even though it is the end of Carnival and she should decide which suitor she will accept before the night is over.

Elemer, one of the three suitors, comes to take Arabella for a ride in a sleigh; she says she will be ready in half an hour. When Elemer has gone, Arabella asks Zdenka if she has noticed the stranger whom she has seen during the past day or two from her room, and whom she thinks looks extremely attractive. No sooner has she spoken than he appears again in the street but he goes away without so much as looking up at the window.

The parents come back to the hotel and send their daughters out of the room. The Count has been losing again, and is depressed that he finds only bills waiting for him, and no word from any of his regimental cronies, to all of whom he had written for help in his financial embarrassment. There was one in particular, rich and eccentric, Mandryka by name, whom he thought would never fail him. Adelaide tells him she has dreamed all will go well. A servant announces that there is a gentleman to see Graf Waldner. It turns out to be Mandryka, nephew and heir of the Count's old comrade. He has fallen in love with the photograph of Arabella which Waldner sent with his letter, and in a strange mixture of formality and open-heartedness (a musical purple passage) asks for her hand in marriage. To pay for his journey to Vienna he says he sold some woods, and he offers Waldner a couple of thousand-gülden notes. The latter can hardly believe his senses, and when Mandryka has gone, he imitates his tone of voice: 'Teschek, bedien' dich' (Please, help yourself!)

There is a short scene between Zdenka and Matteo, in which the latter shows his desperate anxiety to know

---

[1] Slavonic in origin.

25 Rose Pauly and Hilde Konetzni in *Elektra.*

26 Lotte Lehmann as the Marschallin in *Der Rosenkavalier*.

whether he can yet have the letter from Arabella which Zdenka promised him sh ̍ was writing. He is told he may have it that night at the Fiakerball (a ball to which everyone goes in costume: a 'Fiaker' was a two-horse cab). He leaves, and Arabella comes in ready for her drive with Elemer. Zdenka refers to him as 'dein Elemer' (your Elemer), and the sound of the words has a romantic ring in Arabella's ears as she repeats them. But the idea of the romantic stranger is much more attractive to her, and even the horrid thought that he may be already married is not enough to dampen her enthusiasm.

Act II.   A ballroom. Arabella, very much the queen of the ball, comes downstairs with her mother and several attendant cavaliers, to be introduced by her parents to Mandryka, who is waiting below, and in whom Arabella recognises the stranger she has seen from her window. She is left alone with him, and sits down, refusing a dance to each of her other suitors in turn. His impassioned language astonishes her, but she is completely fascinated and convinced that she has found the right man in him: 'Und du wirst mein Gebieter sein.' Their love duet[1] is impassioned enough to suggest to us that she is right.

She asks to be allowed an hour at the ball to say good-bye to the things which have made up her girlhood. At that moment, the rest of the guests crowd around her, and the Fiakermilli—a pretty girl dolled up to the nines—curtsies and brings her a bouquet. She sings a brilliant coloratura polka song for Arabella's entertainment, after which Arabella goes off to dance with Dominik.

Waldner's reaction to the news of Arabella's engagement is naturally one of delight. Matteo, however, is heart-broken, not at the news (which he has not heard), but because Arabella has not looked in his direction all evening. Zdenka, however, does her best to reassure him, and says that Arabella relies on his love, though she may not find ways of showing it. Mandryka orders champagne for everyone present at the ball; no one shall be without when he is as happy as he now feels himself. Arabella says good-bye to her three suitors, to whom she is grateful but whom she must

---

[1] During its course, Mandryka conveys the information that in his country a glass of water is given by the girl to her prospective fiancé in token of engagement.

relinquish now that she has found the right man. She goes off again to dance.

Zdenka reappears and gives Matteo a letter, which she says is from Arabella. It contains the key of Arabella's room, according to Zdenka, and she insists that if the unbelieving Matteo come to that room in a quarter of an hour, he will receive everything that he most longs for. Mandryka overhears the conversation and cannot believe his ears. He decides there must be another Arabella perhaps in the same hotel, but, when he cannot find his fiancée, is forced to the conclusion that his worst suspicions are justified, and that it must be she who made the assignation. In desperation, Mandryka flirts with the Fiakermilli. A note from Arabella is handed to him: she has gone home but will be his to-morrow. Arabella's parents notice her absence, and they go off to the hotel with Mandryka to find her.

Act III.   A lounge in the hotel, with staircase leading upstairs. Night.

There is a short prelude,[1] and when the curtain goes up Matteo is seen about to come down the stairs. He hides when he hears a bell. Arabella comes in, smiling happily. Music from the ball plays around her as she sings of the happiness which she and Mandryka will enjoy amidst his fields and forests. Matteo reappears and is astonished to see Arabella in the hall. She can make no sense at all of his ardour and his insinuations, and he for his part cannot understand her coldness and apparent heartlessness.

In the middle of their misunderstanding, Arabella's parents arrive with Mandryka, who immediately recognises Matteo as the man he saw receive the key at the ball and is now convinced of the worst. He remains unpersuaded by Arabella's protestations of innocence, tempers rise, and a duel between Mandryka and Matteo is only prevented by the sudden appearance of Zdenka, in a negligée and with her hair down. She rushes down the stairs, and says that she only wants to say good-bye before throwing herself into the Danube. Arabella says she will stand by her whatever her trouble, and Zdenka eventually stammers out that it was she who sent the note to Matteo, and the key inside it was to her room, not Arabella's. The room was dark, and Matteo could not have known that it was not Arabella.

[1] Used as a bridge passage when Acts II and III are played without interval, a Munich innovation by Strauss.

Mandryka tries to put his shame and sorrow into words, but Arabella turns to Zdenka without a glance in his direction and thanks her for teaching her to follow the dictates of her heart. Prompted by Arabella and Mandryka—Arabella bears no malice—Waldner agrees to give Zdenka's hand to Matteo, and the crowd which has been attracted by the noise, begins to disperse. Arabella tells Mandryka that there must be no attempt at explanation between them until morning; she would however be grateful if one of his servants could fetch her a glass of clear, cold water. She would find it refreshing after the tumult of the evening's events. She goes slowly up the stairs without another word.

Mandryka waits dejectedly below, when at the top of the stairs appears Arabella. Holding the glass of water in her hand she makes her way slowly down and offers it to him. The opera ends with their love duet: 'Das war sehr gut, Mandryka.' H.

DIE SCHWEIGSAME FRAU
The Silent Woman

Opera in three acts by Richard Strauss; text by Stefan Zweig, freely adapted from Ben Jonson's comedy *Epicoene, or the Silent Woman*. Première, Dresden, June 24, 1935, with Cebotari, Sack, Kremer, Ahlersmeyer, Plaschke, conductor Böhm. The opera was frowned on by the Nazis,[1] and after very few performances was removed from the Dresden repertory. First performed Zürich, 1936, with Moor, Emmerich, Oeggl, conductor Denzler; la Scala, Milan, 1936, with Carosio, Sinnone, Stabile, Bettoni, conductor Marinuzzi; Zürich, 1942, with Moor, Funk, Chabay, Rothmüller, Rehfuss, conductor Reinshagen; Cologne, 1948, with Eipperle; Munich, 1949, with Ebers, Klarwein, Wieter, Dalberg, Kusche; New York, City Opera, 1955, with Joan Carroll, Alexander, Ukena, Beattie, conductor Peter Hermann Adler; Komische Oper, Berlin, 1956, in Felsenstein's production, with Arnold, Reinmar; Salzburg, 1959, with Gueden, Wunderlich, Prey, Hotter, conductor Böhm; Covent Garden, 1961 (in English), with Holt, MacDonald, David Ward, conductor Kempe; Vienna, 1968, with Coertse, Blankenship, Kerns, Czerwenka, conductor Varviso.

[1] Strauss's letter to the Jewish Stefan Zweig referring to the Nazis as a passing phase in German life has been much quoted: then against him but more recently as expressing his true sentiments *vis-à-vis* Hitler. Zweig committed suicide in 1942.

CHARACTERS

Sir Morosus		Bass
His Housekeeper		Contralto
The Barber		Baritone
Henry Morosus		Tenor
Aminta, *his wife*		Coloratura Soprano
Isotta		Coloratura Soprano
Carlotta	*actors*	Mezzo-Soprano
Morbio		Baritone
Vanuzzi		Bass
Farfallo		Bass

Actors and Neighbours

Time: About 1780   *Place:* A room in Sir Morosus's house in a London suburb

Hofmannsthal had died in 1929, leaving behind him the libretto of *Arabella*, but after his death Strauss had to look round for a new collaborator. His choice fell upon Stefan Zweig, and together they turned to Ben Jonson for inspiration, Zweig having already had considerable success with his German version of *Volpone*.

After an overture, described by the composer as a *Potpourri*, the curtain rises on Act I, to show a room in Sir Morosus's house. It is untidy, and the bric-à-brac about the room indicates that it belongs to a former seaman. We are straightaway introduced to the mainspring of the action, Schneidebart, the barber, who is approached by Sir Morosus's housekeeper with the suggestion that he should implant the idea in Sir Morosus's head that he wants to get married and that she is just the person. Life is impossible in the house, what with his exaggerated notions about eliminating any kind of noise, and anyhow he needs a wife. The barber is properly scornful of her suggestion, but at this moment Morosus himself comes in, fulminating about the noise.

While he is being shaved, he launches forth into a diatribe against the perpetrators of the crime of noise, by which he is surrounded and from which he cannot find any means of escape. He sings sadly of his loneliness; could he only find someone to care for him, his life would acquire the purpose which it lacks. At the end of the opera the melody is developed into a grateful hymn of thanksgiving for peace. The barber suggests he should marry a young and silent wife, and, when told there is no such thing, offers to find one.

Morosus, although objecting that he is too old, is obviously not averse to considering the suggestion.

The noise of someone trying to gain admittance to his room causes a further tantrum, but when the intruder turns out to be his nephew Henry, whom he had thought dead, his displeasure turns to extravagant rejoicing. He must be received with all honour. Henry starts to tell him he has his troupe with him. Morosus misunderstands him and thinks he has said 'troops', and the initial joy turns to fury when he discovers Henry is a member of a theatrical company. He refuses even to accept Aminta, Henry's wife, as his niece, insults them all, disinherits Henry, and orders the barber to find him a wife forthwith, and moreover to bring a priest with him when he brings her to the house.

Consternation follows Sir Morosus's withdrawal, but it soon gives place to a discussion of ways and means of taking revenge on the old curmudgeon for his insults. Henry says he is happy in his love and would not barter it for a house made entirely of gold. The barber reminds him that he is throwing away quite a large fortune, but he and Aminta sing a love duet amidst expressions of admiration from the troupe. The barber sees a possible solution in the task which has been set him; it will not be easy to find a silent woman—why should Aminta, Isotta and Carlotta not be dressed up and produced as candidates next morning? Schneidebart says he will take all arrangements into his own hands, and everyone is delighted, except Aminta, who says she would prefer to move the old man to fall in with the situation rather than trick him into it. But she quickly accepts the suggestion, and the curtain falls as they make their plans.

Act II. The same room, the afternoon of the next day. Morosus is warned by his housekeeper that some sort of intrigue is brewing, but he will not listen to her, and continues to array himself in his smartest clothes. The barber comes in to say that he has brought three girls with him, and takes the opportunity of warning the old man that he should not be too ardent with them. Is he likely to eat them? demands Morosus angrily.

When they present themselves for his inspection, the three actresses impersonate three quite different types: Carlotta is a country girl, Isotta a young lady of fashion, and Aminta is dressed simply and unpretentiously. Their conversation matches their clothes: Carlotta is a hopeless bumpkin with a hideous accent, and Morosus soon dismisses her; Isotta's high-flown, pretentious talk culminates in an effort to read his hand, and she also is sent packing; but Aminta behaves naturally and Morosus is obviously impressed by her demeanour. After listening to her for a bit, Morosus tells the barber that Aminta is the one for him (she calls herself Timida). When they are left alone it becomes apparent that he is genuinely touched by her youth and beauty, and he attempts to apologise for what must look to her a poor bargain, she is so young, and he so old. Aminta also seems to regret the part she has undertaken to play.

But the scheme is well under way, and Schneidebart returns with two members of the company dressed up as a priest and a notary. The mock marriage is concluded, but no sooner is it over than more members of the company come in, proclaiming that they are old shipmates of Sir Morosus and mean to celebrate with him. This they proceed to do and it is some time before his furious protests are successful in getting rid of them.

Morosus and Aminta are alone, and in an aside she reveals that she has no relish for the part she has to play. It is a question of *Don Pasquale* all over again. Aminta makes scene after scene; she is the mistress of the house, and his wishes have no significance at all. Morosus is dumbfounded, until rescued by Henry, who sends Aminta out and consoles his old uncle. The act ends after a short scene between Henry and Aminta, in which she tells him how she disliked ill-treating the old man; but she consoles herself with the thought that it was only done for her husband's sake.

Act III.   The scene is the same. Before the curtain rises, the noise of vigorous hammering is heard, and the scene discloses a troop of workmen redecorating the room under Aminta's orders. Henry, in disguise and with another member of his company as accompanist, gives Aminta a singing lesson. This is the last straw, and Morosus is on the verge of despair when the barber comes in to announce that the Chief Justice of England is on his way to the house, and everything is prepared for a divorce. Aminta rejects the idea out of hand, but the legal party makes its appearance and proceeds to rehearse in dog Latin the grounds on which a divorce can be granted. Isotta and Carlotta witness that Sir Morosus is by no means the first man Timida has known, and Henry, disguised, admits that he has known her intimately. Timida swears she has known but one man—her husband. But the Chief Justice, although agreeing that there is evidence of promiscuity, rules that what took place before marriage is no grounds for divorce. Morosus nears the end of his tether and threatens to commit suicide if he cannot obtain his freedom.

In his misery he throws himself on his bed, and, at a signal from the barber, Henry and Aminta go up to him and explain the truth; it has all been a hoax. He is at first bewildered, then furious, and then bursts out laughing; he may have been close to suicide, but it cannot be denied they put on a wonderful show! He confesses himself willing to hear all their operas if they can make him laugh as much as he has laughed to-day, at himself. The rejoicing is general, and when he, Aminta, and Henry are alone, Morosus sings happily of the peace which he has at last found. He sinks back in his chair, and sighs with contentment.   H.

FRIEDENSTAG
Peace Day

Opera in one act by Richard Strauss; text by Joseph Gregor. Première, Munich, July 24, 1938, with Ursuleac, Patzak, Ostertag, Hotter, Hann, Weber, Wieter, conductor Clemens Krauss (the opera is dedicated to Ursuleac and Krauss). First performed Berlin, 1939, with Ursuleac, Prohaska, Bockelmann, Sinimberghi, conductor Krauss; Zürich, 1939, with Annie Weber, Stig, Emmerich, conductor Denzler; Venice, 1940, with Grandi, Valentino, Rakowski, Cassinelli, conductor Gui. Revived Munich, 1961, with Hillebrecht, Metternich, conductor Keilberth; Los Angeles (University of Southern California), 1967; BBC broadcast (in English), 1971, conductor Edward Downes.

CHARACTERS

Commandant of the Beleaguered Town		Baritone
Maria, *his wife*		Soprano
Sergeant		Bass
Corporal		Baritone
A Private Soldier		Tenor
A Musketeer	*of the Garrison*	Bass
A Bugler		Bass
An Officer		Baritone
A Front-line Officer		Baritone
A Piedmontese		Tenor
The Holsteiner, *commanding the besieging army*		Bass

Burgomaster⎫   ⎧ Tenor
Bishop   ⎬ *of the*   ⎨ Baritone
A Woman of the People⎭ *beleaguered town* ⎩ Soprano

Soldiers of the garrison and of the besieging army,
Elders of the town and women of the deputation to
the Commandant, Townspeople

Time: October 24, 1648   *Place:* The Citadel of a beleaguered
                                    town during the Thirty Years
                                    War.

The scene shows the great circular room in the citadel. A
gallery with loopholes runs round at about a man's height.
One staircase leads to the upper storey of the fortress,
another descends.

The soldiers sing a ditty, but from far off can be heard
the sound of the townspeople, already afoot and crying that
their hunger can no more be borne.

To the sound of a mournful march and with the cries of
'Hunger! Bread!' still sounding from outside, the town elders
enter, led by the Burgomaster and the Bishop. Suddenly, the
musket-butts strike the ground, and the Commandant
appears on the upper stairway. He is a handsome man of
about fifty. He warns the deputation that he will hear them
but that his answer to anything they may say which involves
a cowardly action on his part will be violent—he seizes a
musket from a soldier and throws it down at their feet as he
speaks. Burgomaster and Bishop plead with him to allow the
surrender of the town, but he will not listen to their
arguments.

An officer announces to the Commandant that all the
ammunition is spent; will he give the order that more be
fetched from the secret cellars, where they all know there is a
plentiful supply? The Commandant refuses, but bids them
trust him. He reads aloud the Emperor's message which
reached him only the previous day; it bids them hold out at
all costs. But the cries of the deputation redouble in urgency,
the crowd shouts for peace, and eventually the Commandant
says he is ready to agree to their demands; let them only wait
until midday before the surrender takes effect. He himself
will give the signal, a rousing, flashing sign which all will
recognise.

The deputation departs well content with what it has
achieved, but it is clear a moment later that the

Commandant, rather than surrender, plans to set fire to his arsenal and so blow himself and his garrison sky-high.

The stage is empty for a moment, but from below comes Maria, the Commandant's wife. She is younger than he is, and she muses on the situation in which all find themselves. Her monologue ends with a paean of praise to hope, which has returned with the rising sun, which now shines brightly through the loophole.

Maria tries to persuade her husband, who enters at that moment, to confide in her why he looks so different from usual. He urges her to escape since the citadel and all within it are doomed to die. She thanks the sun for the light it has shed on her life; it has melted the heart she had thought frozen, it has removed the look that worried her so much. She will not be parted from the husband she loves so much, be it in life or in death, in peace or in war.

They embrace. The light has grown dimmer during their duet. The soldiers come one by one into the room, last of all the sergeant, with the fuse in his hand. The Commandant motions him towards the arsenal. Suddenly, the sound of a cannon shot is heard. It is the sign the Commandant has hoped for; it means the enemy is attacking. But no enemy can be seen advancing, and instead bells begin to ring out from the town, one after another, bells which have not been heard since the days of peace, almost longer ago than anyone can remember.

A moment later the Burgomaster is up the stairs and into the room, a changed man from the time when he led the deputation to pray for surrender. Peace has now come. The Commandant protests that he will not surrender, but to the sound of a march the Holsteiner's troops enter the citadel, their commander at their head. His voice can be heard from outside demanding to know where his noble, lion-hearted foe is to be found, that he may embrace him. But the Commandant returns harsh words for kind, and refuses to shake the hand which the Holsteiner proffers him. He draws his sword, and the Holsteiner puts his hand on his, but Maria throws herself between the two men. She begs her husband to acknowledge that at long last love and brotherhood have come into the lives of all of them instead of hatred and strife. He looks at her, and then throws away his sword and embraces the Holsteiner leader. The opera ends with an extended hymn to peace, in which all the soloists join. H.

DAPHNE

Opera in one act by Richard Strauss; text by Joseph Gregor. Première, Dresden, October 15, 1938, with Teschemacher, Jung, Ralf, Kremer, conductor Böhm (given in a double bill with *Friedenstag*). First performed Berlin, 1939, with Cebotari, Focke, Ralf, Anders, conductor Krauss; la Scala, Milan, 1942, with Cigna, Gallo, conductor Marinuzzi; Buenos Aires, 1948, with Bampton, Kindermann, Svanholm, Dermota, Weber, conductor Kleiber. Revived Munich, 1950, with Kupper, Fischer, Fehenberger, Hopf, Hann, conductor Jochum; Vienna, 1950, with Kupper, conductor Moralt; New York, Town Hall, 1960, with Gloria Davy, Crain, Robert Nagy; Munich, 1964, with Bjoner, Madeira, Uhl, conductor Keilberth; Santa Fe (New Mexico), 1964, with Sylvia Stahlmann, Shirley, Glade Peterson, Gramm.

CHARACTERS

Peneios, *a fisherman* .... Bass
Gaea, *his wife* .... Contralto
Daphne, *their daughter* .... Soprano
Leukippos, *a shepherd* .... Tenor
Apollo .... Tenor
Four Shepherds .... Baritone, Tenor, Two Basses
Two Maids .... Soprano
Time: Antiquity   *Place:* Near Peneios's hut

There is a short pastoral introduction, after which the curtain rises to show Peneios's hut and the landscape round it. Heralded by the sound of their flocks, the four shepherds appear in pairs and discuss the forthcoming feast-day in honour of Dionysus, which is traditionally the time for lovers' mating. The last rays of the sun light up the stage as Daphne comes in. In a long monologue she reveals her love of nature and identification of herself with the trees and flowers around her; the prospect of the festivity gives her no pleasure.

Leukippos, her childhood's playmate, tells her how much he loves her, and tries to embrace her. She repulses him and refuses to accompany him to the festival, at the same time, however, telling him that her affection for him is by no means gone although she characterises it as sisterly. Gaea has heard the end of their conversation, and she comes to bid her daughter dress herself for the party. The time will come when she will open her heart to love. Daphne listens to her mother, but will not dress up in the clothes the maids bring for her. Gaea follows Daphne from the stage, and the maids are left to comment on the situation. Soon they hear the sound of Leukippos's lamentations. They determine to help him to win Daphne's love, and offer to dress him up in the clothes she has rejected.

As light dies away, the dignified figure of Peneios appears, accompanied by Gaea and the shepherds. He points to the light which still shines on Mount Olympus; the day will yet come when the gods will return amongst men. In spite of murmurs of protest from the shepherds, he affirms his belief that Apollo will come to them, and suggests they prepare a great feast to receive him worthily. Peneios laughs and is answered by a mysterious echo. A stranger appears—Apollo dressed as a herdsman—and greets the company. He tells them his cattle had run wild, and he has only just succeeded in rounding them up. Gaea and the shepherds laugh at Peneios for this mundane realisation of his prophecy that Apollo would visit them. He answers by sending for Daphne and bidding her look after the stranger.

When Daphne appears, Apollo is amazed at her beauty, and calls her 'Sister'. She is taken aback by the compliments he pays her, but starts to do her parents' bidding, and puts a blue cloak round his shoulders. She feels an affinity with him, and asks him his true identity. In enigmatic language, he explains that he saw her from his chariot. She does not understand who he is, but starts to tell him how she hates to be parted from the sun, whereupon he repeats sentences to her from her opening monologue. She sinks on his breast, and rejoices in his promise that she will never again be parted from the sun. For a time she is hidden in the blue of his cloak, but suddenly tears herself free. Apollo declares that he loves her, and tells her to listen to the distant chanting; it is the voice of lovers. But Daphne is full of fear; Apollo told her he was her brother, and now he talks of love.

A procession, led by Peneios and Gaea, approaches, and Daphne joins the women, Apollo the men. They sing the praises of Dionysus, and the feast begins. Leukippos, who is dressed up amongst the women, invites Daphne to join their dancing. No sooner has she done so than Apollo bursts out in complaint that Peneios and his daughter are the victims of deception. With the sound of a thunderclap, he disrupts the feast, whereupon Leukippos reveals himself as a suitor for

Daphne's hand. In a fiery passage he begs her to follow him. Daphne complains that she is being doubly deceived, both by the playmate of her youth, and by the stranger, who is not what he seems to be. Apollo reveals himself as the sun, and in the dispute which follows Daphne's refusal to bind herself to either of her suitors, Apollo wounds Leukippos with an arrow.

In a scene with the dying man, Daphne discovers that her lover was a god, and blames herself for Leukippos's death. Apollo watches her, spellbound by her beauty and full of regret for his action in killing Leukippos. He asks Dionysus to forgive him for having caused the death of one of his disciples, and, begging Zeus to pardon him that he strayed outside his sphere in interfering with mortals, he asks that he be given Daphne, not in mortal guise but transformed into imperishable form as one of the trees she loves so well. From her branches, men will in future cut the wreaths reserved for those who are best and bravest amongst them. Gradually Daphne changes into a laurel tree, and her voice is heard celebrating her altered state.   H.

DIE LIEBE DER DANAE
The Love of Danae

Opera in three acts by Richard Strauss; text by Joseph Gregor. The opera was in rehearsal during the late summer of 1944, but a Nazi edict closing the theatres as a result of the plot against Hitler's life prevented a public performance. In the event, *Die Liebe der Danae* was heard at a well-attended dress rehearsal (August 16), conducted by Clemens Krauss and with a cast headed by Ursuleac, Taubmann, and Hotter. The official première was at the Salzburg Festival, August 14, 1952, with Kupper, Gostic, Szemere, Schöffler, conductor Krauss. First performed in Vienna, 1952, with Kupper, Gostic, Patzak, Poell, conductor Krauss; Berlin, 1952, with Richter, Beirer, Poell, conductor Ludwig; la Scala, Milan, 1952, with Dow, Gostic, Ego, conductor Krauss; Covent Garden, 1953, with Kupper (later Rysanek), Vandenburg, Frantz, conductor Kempe; Los Angeles, 1964, (in English).

CHARACTERS

Jupiter . . . . Baritone
Mercury . . . . Tenor
Pollux, *King of Eos* . . . . Tenor
Danae, *his daughter* . . . . Soprano

Xanthe, *her servant*		Soprano
Midas, *King of Lydia*		Tenor
Four Kings, *nephews to Pollux*	Two Tenors, Two Basses
Semele ⎫		Soprano
Europa ⎬ *four queens*		Soprano
Alcmene ⎱		Mezzo-Soprano
Leda ⎭		Contralto
Four Watchmen		Four Basses

Chorus of Creditors, Servants and Followers of Pollux
and Danae, People

As early as the spring of 1920, Hofmannsthal sent Strauss a scenario under the title *Danae, or the prudent marriage.* The suggestion had not been taken up by the composer at the time Hofmannsthal died (in 1929), but Strauss's attention was drawn to it later, and he eventually persuaded Gregor to write a text after Hofmannsthal's theme. The composition was finished in June 1940, so that though *Die Liebe der Danae* was the last of Strauss's operas to reach public performance, its composition in fact antedates that of *Capriccio* by some two years.

Act I.   The first scene is laid in the throne-room of King Pollux. It is shabby and there is only part of the golden throne left. One can see the former splendour, but now creditors besiege the hall and demand payment. The King appears and tries to pacify them, telling them that his nieces, the four most beautiful women alive, and their husbands, kings of the islands, have set out to find a husband for Danae, and that Midas, the richest man in the world whose touch turns anything to gold, is on his way to marry her. But the crowd is sceptical and falls on the throne and plunders what is left.

An interlude depicts the Golden Rain. Bedchamber of Danae. She awakes and tells Xanthe, her maid, of her dream, in which she was surrounded and covered with gold. It fell on her lips and on her breasts, and she can hardly believe it was only a dream, so real and wonderful was the sensation of the gold. A march is heard in the distance, and Xanthe announces a new suitor. But Danae says that she will only accept the man who can bring her the gold.

The third scene shows a pillared hall in the palace; in the distance the sea. A large gathering—the King, his councillors, and his creditors—awaits the return of the emissaries. They announce that Midas is the new suitor, whose touch has turned even the portrait of Danae to gold. He sends a golden garland to Danae. A cry is heard—'A ship! A ship of gold!'—and everyone rushes towards the harbour to greet Midas. Only Danae stays behind. It is all like her dream, and she determines that the bringer of gold shall be her bridegroom.

Midas comes in, dressed in simple clothes and saying he is Chrysopher, friend of Midas, come to prepare her to meet the King. She is obviously impressed by him and cannot conceal her disappointment that he is only the forerunner of her suitor. He for his part is reluctant to fulfil his bargain, and hand her over to his master.

The scene changes to the harbour, where the crowd exuberantly welcomes the supposed Midas, in reality none other than Jupiter clothed in golden raiment. Danae recognises him as the master of her golden dreams; but is he the master of her love? She faints, and the curtain falls.

Act II. In a magnificent bed-chamber, the four queens are decorating the bridal bed. Jupiter enters, clothed from head to foot in gold. The four queens know him, for in various guises he has been the lover of each of them—as cloud, bull, Amphitryon, and swan. He warns them not to give his disguise away, but they cannot restrain their jealousy that for Danae he is not content to stay in the form of gold, but has taken the form of a real man—and why the double deception over Midas? He explains that his love for Danae is great, and she is made even more desirable in his eyes because of her coldness and disdain of men. He hopes to find true love at last. As for the impersonation of Midas, that is done to deceive Juno, whose jealousy is stronger than ever, and whose punishments for those he has loved grow ever more severe. As he has taken the outward form of Midas, the real Midas can always take his place should Juno approach in anger. The four queens praise his cunning, and try to entice him back to them.

Midas enters and the women leave the bridal chamber. Jupiter is jealous in case Midas should capture Danae's love, and reminds him that, when he conferred the golden touch upon him, it was with the condition that he should obey his every command. He has been made the richest man on earth, but should he now prove false to his bargain, he will forthwith change back into the donkey-driver Jupiter first knew. Jupiter leaves, a soft march announces the arrival of

Danae, and Midas dons the golden clothes which Jupiter has left behind him.

Danae enters accompanied by the four queens, who tell her that the object of her affections has formerly been the lover of each one of them; when they recognise Midas, they take fright, and disappear. Midas explains as much as he dares; he is the master of the gold, and yet not the suitor on the ship. Danae does not understand the mystery, but it is clear that she wants only him, and, when he turns everything in the room to gold, she knows it must be Midas. They fall into each other's arms. A thunderclap, and Danae is seen turned to a golden statue.

Midas curses himself and his gift. Jupiter appears and claims Danae as his, but Midas objects that she must come to life only for the sake of him whom she truly loves. They both offer her what it is in their power to give: Jupiter—golden dreams, temples, and divine honours; Midas—only his human love and poverty. Her voice is heard as though from afar off, choosing Midas. Danae and Midas disappear, and Jupiter alone laments the loss of what might have been. Danae was offered the fate of the gods, and she has chosen the fate of mortals.

Act III.   An open road in the East. Danae and Midas are seen to wake up. Danae slowly begins to understand what has happened. Midas, the favourite of the god, has renounced riches and power and has returned to be the humble donkey-driver on account of his love for her. She is content.

The scene changes to a sunny forest in the mountains. Mercury, half god, half jester, reports to Jupiter that the episode of Danae has caused mirth amongst the gods, but has thrown everyone on Pollux's island into confusion. Jupiter is confronted by the four queens, who have found their way to him with Mercury's help. They flatter him, and affect to regard the episode as an amusing trick played on Danae and designed to draw Juno's attention to her while he diverts himself with them. But soon Jupiter tires of them, and bids a final farewell to them, to his last and dearest love, and to earth.

Unfortunately for his plans, Pollux and his nephews and creditors have found him, and demand satisfaction for the deception which has been practised on them. On Mercury's advice, Jupiter lets money fall from the skies, and they all rush after it. Mercury recommends that Jupiter should not abandon his pursuit of Danae; now that she is poor, how much more easily will she succumb to the lure of gold than when she dwelt in a palace!

Midas's hut, simply but tidily kept. Danae sings of her love. Jupiter enters, dressed in the manner Midas has described to Danae as affected by the man who first gave him the gift of the golden touch. He tries to discover if Danae is discontented with her lot; he reminds her of her golden dreams, but she is proof against his temptations, and finally convinces him that she loves Midas. Jupiter is moved by her obvious faithfulness, and tells her the story of Maia, who was loved by the god and brought forth Spring. The duet is one of Strauss's most inspired passages. At its end, Jupiter recognises Danae's greatness, and she too is full of gratitude for his understanding. He thanks her and leaves. Danae looks after him. Midas's music is heard in the orchestra and she goes out to meet him. H.

CAPRICCIO

Opera in one act by Richard Strauss; text by Clemens Krauss. Première, Munich, October 28, 1942, with Ursuleac, Ranczak, Taubmann, Hotter, Höfermayer, Hann, conductor Krauss. First performed Zürich, 1944, with Cebotari, Rohs, Dermota, Kunz, Schöffler, conductor Böhm; Salzburg, 1950, with della Casa, Höngen, Dermota, Braun, Wolff, Schöffler, conductor Böhm; Vienna, 1951, with Goltz (later della Casa), Höngen, Wenkoff, Braun, Schöffler, conductor Kempe; Covent Garden, 1953, with Cunitz, Holm, Peter, Kusche, conductor Heger; New York, Juilliard School, 1954, with Gloria Davy, Blankenship, Thomas Stewart; Glyndebourne, 1963, with Söderström, Cervena, Horst Wilhelm, Wolansky, Krause, Kusche, conductor Pritchard.

CHARACTERS

The Countess .... Soprano
Clairon, *an actress* .... Contralto
Flamand, *a musician* .... Tenor
Olivier, *a poet* .... Baritone
The Count, *the Countess's brother* .... Baritone
La Roche, *director of a theatre* .... Bass
Monsieur Taupe .... Tenor
Italian Singers .... Soprano, Tenor
A Young Dancer
The Major-domo .... Bass

Eight Servants .... Four Tenor, Four Bass
Three Musicians .... Violin, 'Cello, Cembalo
Time: About 1775, at the   *Place:* A château near Paris
time of Gluck's operatic reforms

From the earliest times its practitioners have been concerned with the theory and re-shaping of opera. Every opera ever written constitutes an acceptance of an old form or an attempt to introduce a new, and each example is a particular commentary on operatic form in general. But the commentary is customarily implicit in the work and not explicit as in Strauss's last opera *Capriccio*, in which he and Clemens Krauss took opera itself as subject (*Capriccio* was finished in 1942, and, though performed before *Danae*, was in fact the last opera on which the composer worked).

The scene is laid in France, at the time of Gluck's reform. At the house of the charming Countess, a number of people are discussing the theme 'Prima le parole, dopo la musica', led by Flamand, a musician, and Olivier, a poet, who are rivals for the affections of the Countess as well as in their art. Arguing from a different angle is the Countess's brother, whose interest in music or poetry is mild, but whose regard for the stage, and most of all for Clairon a leading actress, is quite the reverse. More professional in his practical attitude than the artists, more knowledgeable in his cynicism than the Count, is La Roche, a theatrical manager, who incidentally emerges as the strongest personality in a cast of types. Each character finds his attitude to opera reflected symbolically in his relationship to the Countess and the other guests.

Originally the opera was intended to be a short, one-act affair, designed to go with *Friedenstag* and *Daphne*, but in its final form it lasts nearly two hours and a half—and there is of course no interval. The opera's main drawback in fact is to be found in that besetting sin of so much German romantic music and not least of Strauss himself: a lack of economy. The attractive string sextet for instance, which acts as overture and which is being played as the curtain rises, lasts over 10 minutes, and even Strauss's least critical audience must suspect a certain discrepancy between the conversational subject and the large orchestra which 'accompanies' it. All the same, the opera has powerful attractions in the skill with which the operatic discussion is argued and the way in which composer and librettist have contrived to diversify the subject—to say nothing of the power of invention Strauss still shows in it—and I think it is likely to gain ground in the repertory as the years go by, particularly if played in the language of the audience.

We are in the salon of a château near Paris where plans are afoot to celebrate the birthday of the young widowed Countess Madeleine. Flamand has written a string sextet for the occasion, and he and Olivier are listening to the music, on whose qualities the theatre director La Roche seems already to have passed judgement by falling asleep in an armchair. He wakes to join in the discussion and they point out that this is the man in whose hands lies the fate of composers. La Roche believes in entertainment—splendid decor, top notes, beautiful women. He is for Italian opera and he cannot resist mentioning that even highbrow creative artists have their foibles: Olivier did not seem to disdain the talent—or the beauty—of the famous Clairon, who by happy chance is not only the object of the Count's admiration but will arrive soon at the château to play opposite the Count in Olivier's play.

The Count and Countess come in from next door and the others quickly disappear. The Count clearly favours the poetic muse, perhaps because of his interest in Clairon. His sister equally obviously inclines towards music—but by no means to the exclusion of words. The Count is in no doubt about his sister's interest in the two artists and wonders aloud which she will eventually choose.

Re-enter La Roche, Flamand and Olivier, the first-named to announce that all is ready for the rehearsal of the birthday entertainment, which will consist of the new music by Flamand, Olivier's drama and finally an *azione teatrale* by his entire company. All discussion stops with the entrance of Clairon, who dominates proceedings as she greets the Countess and then enquires from Olivier if he has yet finished the play.

He has, and Clairon and the Count read the scene, which culminates in the Count's declamation of a sonnet.[1] He is congratulated and La Roche takes them all off into the theatre, leaving Flamand and Olivier with the Countess.

Olivier criticises the way the Count reads the sonnet and recites it to the Countess as a personal utterance. Flamand goes to the harpsichord and begins to improvise and

---

[1] A translation of a sonnet by Ronsard.

eventually leaves the room with Olivier's manuscript. It is Olivier's chance to declare his love, which he does delicately and gently. Flamand returns to sing the sonnet he has just set ('Kein Andres, das mir so im Herzen loht': Naught else there is that flames so in my heart) and the Countess and Olivier join their voices to his to make a trio of extraordinary beauty. Flamand and Olivier seem likely to quarrel about the true authorship of the sonnet, but the Countess decides the issue quite neatly: it is now hers!

La Roche takes Olivier away to rehearsal and Flamand in his turn is able to declare his love. He presses Madeleine to decide between him and Olivier, and she promises that he shall hear her answer next morning at eleven o'clock.

The sounds of rehearsal can be heard from next door (where the Prompter, to general amusement, is found to have fallen asleep) and the Countess orders refreshment to be brought in. She and the Count exchange thoughts on the progress of their affairs of the heart. He must not be too easily carried away by his feelings for Clairon, she advises him, only to have to admit that for her own part she is still undecided between poet and composer, but has already started to wonder whether an opera might not be the collaborative outcome of their interest in her.[1]

Rehearsal is over, and refreshments served while La Roche introduces a dancer for their delectation (*Passepied, Gigue, Gavotte*). During the course of the *Gigue*, Olivier tries unsuccessfully to make up to Clairon, and after the dancing is over the Count comments to Flamand that the dance is an aspect of art where his own contribution is entirely secondary. On the contrary, says Flamand; without music, it would never occur to anyone even to lift a foot.

A fugue ensues, described as 'discussion on the theme "Words or Music"'. Music goes deeper than words; words express thought with greater clarity; music is the art of the sublime; in the theatre, words and music must work together. The Count, Clairon and Olivier are against opera, but the director has a passion for *bel canto*, and at this point introduces two Italian singers who entertain the company with a duet in the Italian style.

The Count offers to take Clairon back to Paris, but the director now takes the opportunity of announcing the form

---

[1] Strauss wrote the opera without interval but at this point a break has been made, notably (but not exclusively) at Glyndebourne.

the entertainment will take for the Countess's birthday. The first part of the act of homage will consist of a sublime allegory: 'The Birth of Pallas Athene'. This revelation and the details of the action provoke a torrent of abuse and disbelief and the assembled company expresses its feelings in the first part of a great octet, subtitled 'Laughing Ensemble'.

The Countess tries to mend matters and asks La Roche for an exposition of the second part of the play. This, he says, shall be heroic and highly dramatic: 'The Fall of Carthage'. He has hardly started to describe the magnificent spectacle in prospect when Olivier and Flamand begin to attack him, and the second part of the octet ensues (titled 'Dispute') But La Roche does not take all this lying down and launches into a most effective defence. Olivier's verse is all right—when Clairon speaks it; Flamand's music will fit the salon, but the theatre needs something of greater moment. For his own part, he serves the eternal art of Theatre itself and he wants drama to show human beings in all their aspects and deal with every problem and possibility of every age. His moving defence ends with his own idea of an epitaph in which he proclaims himself the friend of comedy, a guardian angel of artists, the patron of serious art.

La Roche's declaration has won the day and all congratulate him. The Countess demands a collaboration between Flamand and Olivier, to the dismay of her brother who realises that she has commissioned an opera. In spite of his reservations, they start to discuss a subject— *Ariadne? Daphne?* No, says the Count; choose a theme which describes everyday life; write about today's events as all have lived them! The idea is taken up and in the end La Roche sweeps off poet and musician, actress and her admirer, and the Countess retires to her room, leaving the salon to the care of eight servants, who enter and comment in an extended chorus on the events of the day. No sooner have they left than a voice comes from the darkness: 'Herr Direktor!' It is Monsieur Taupe, the prompter, who has fallen asleep and now wonders how on earth he is to get home. The major-domo is almost ready to take him at his own valuation— without him the theatre could not function at all—and offers to help in his predicament.

The salon is now lit only by the light of the moon and into it comes the Countess, elegantly dressed. The major-domo follows her in, lights the candles and gives her two messages:

that her brother will not be home for supper that evening, and that the poet Oliver will call on her to learn how the opera should end—tomorrow, at eleven. The stage is set for the great final scene, one of Strauss's most splendid perorations and a hymn in praise of the beauty of the high female voice which leaves one in no doubt as to which side engages the composer's sympathy in the argument between words and music. In the course of the scene, the Countess comes to understand that, since the sonnet, these two men are as inextricably bound up in the art that between them they can produce as they are as rivals for her hand. She sings two verses of the sonnet, looks at herself in the looking glass and comes to realise that she cannot make the choice which will give the opera an ending. Either alternative seems trivial.

The major-domo solves the problem by announcing that supper is served.   H.

HANS PFITZNER

(1869–1949)

PALESTRINA

OPERA in three acts by Hans Pfitzner; text by the composer. Première Munich, June 12, 1917, with Karl Erb, Feinhals, Brodersen, Bender, Gustav Schützendorf, Ivogün, conductor Bruno Walter. First performed (by the company from Munich) in Basle, Berne, Zürich, 1917; Vienna, 1919, with Erich Schmedes, Schipper, Duhan, Mayr, Madin, Maikl, Lotte Lehmann, Kittel; Berlin, 1919, with Josef Mann, Armster, Marherr, conductor Pfitzner. Revived Berlin, 1939, with Wittrisch, Bockelmann, Soot, Spletter; Vienna, 1949, with Patzak, Hotter, Poell, Alsen, Jerger, Pölzer, Jurinac, Rohs, conductor Krips; Munich, 1949, with Fehenberger (later Patzak), Kronnenberg (later Hotter), Nentwig, conductor Heger; Salzburg, 1955, with Lorenz, Schoeffler, Frantz, Frick, Söderström, Madeira, conductor Kempe; Vienna, 1965, with Wunderlich, Wiener, Berry, Frick, Jurinac, Christa Ludwig, conductor Heger.

CHARACTERS

I. Singers:
Pope Pius IV . . . . Bass
Giovanni Morone, *Papal legate* . . . . Baritone

Bernardo Novagerio, *Papal legate*. . . . . Tenor
Cardinal Christoph Madruscht . . . . Bass
Carlo Borromeo, *Cardinal from Rome* . . . . Baritone
Cardinal of Lorraine . . . . Bass
Abdisu, *Patriarch of Assyria* . . . . Tenor
Anton Brus von Müglitz, *Archbishop of Prague* . . . Bass
Count Luna, *envoy from the King of Spain* . . . Baritone
Bishop of Budoja ⎫ *Italian Bishops*. . . . . ⎧ Tenor
Theophilus of Imola ⎭ . . . . ⎩ Tenor
Avosmediano, *Bishop of Cadiz* . . . . Bass-Baritone
Giovanni Pierluigi Palestrina . . . . Tenor
Ighino, *his son, aged fifteen* . . . . Soprano
Silla, *his pupil, aged seventeen* . . . . Mezzo-Soprano
Bishop Ercole Severolus, *master-of-ceremonies*
    at Council of Trent . . . . Bass-Baritone
Five singers from Chapel of Santa Maria
    Maggiore in Rome . . . . . . Two Tenors, Three Basses
Singers from Papal Chapel, Archbishops, ⎫
    Bishops, Abbots, Ambassadors, Envoys, ⎬ *Chorus*
    Theologians, Servants, Soldiers, People . . ⎭

II. Silent Characters:
    Two Papal Nuncios, Jesuits, Massarelli, Bishop of Thelesia,
        Secretary of Council, Giuseppe, Old Servant of
        Palestrina

III. Singing Apparitions:
    Apparition of Lucretia, Palestrina's dead wife . . Contralto
    Apparitions of Nine Dead Composers . . ⎧ Tenor
        ⎩ Baritone, Bass
    Three Angelic Voices. Soprano
    Angels . . . . Chorus
Time: November–December 1563, 　　*Place:* Rome; Trent
the year of the end of the Council of Trent

Act I. A solemn prelude leads straight into the action
which is laid in a room in Palestrina's house. Silla, Palestrina's
pupil, is sitting there trying over one of his own compositions
on the viol (in the last bars of the prelude, this is suggested in

he orchestra by two solo violas). Ighino comes in, looking sad. In the course of conversation between the two, it transpires that Ighino is worried by the look of unhappiness he has seen now for so long on his father's face; has Silla not noticed it? Palestrina's pupil admits he can see little wrong with his master, nor can he imagine why he should be unhappy—he, the famous composer. But Ighino pours out his feelings: fame has brought his father little; he has been desperately lonely ever since the loss of his wife, and has written nothing. His life in fact seemed to come to an end with her death.

Palestrina comes into the room with Cardinal Borromeo, and the two boys leave. The Cardinal is astonished at the music he heard when they came in (Silla was practising his song again), and he asks Palestrina whether he likes that kind of thing. It is perhaps the new music, the music of the future, replies the master. Borromeo admits that Palestrina's attitude of world-weariness, of submission to the new tendencies, makes him impatient. Without him, what is church music to become? He goes into further detail: his object in coming secretly to Palestrina's house is practical. The Council of Trent, which has been sitting these eighteen years, is now coming to an end. Pope Pius was originally not content with reforming the abuses of church music, but wished to return to Gregorian chant and consign to the flames all other sacred music. Only he—Borromeo—resisted this reactionary view, but he had an ally in the Emperor, who opposed so drastic a change. The case is now won, but has yet to be proved: this can only be done if a Mass is written by a contemporary composer of such calibre as to convince the Pope and his Council. Such a work would be a model for future composers, and would secure the future of church music. It is Palestrina's task to write it!

But Palestrina regretfully says that he is not the right man for the task. Neither the Cardinal's scorn nor his raging nor his pleas are sufficient; Palestrina still insists that even an artist's powers can grow old. Borromeo's anger overflows, and in the end he accuses the composer of blasphemy. He leaves the room in ungovernable fury. Palestrina is moved by what he has seen and heard: there goes my last friend, is his comment. As he muses on the uncertainty of men's conditions and the mysteries of life, looking sadly at the portrait of his dead wife, and reflects that since her death he has been tired and unable to work, he is surrounded by a vision of the composers of the past. He recognises them as his predecessors, and they remind him of his youth, when he first came to know them. They encourage him, and tell him that his ultimate duty is not yet accomplished.

As Palestrina's aversion to composition seems to weaken, the ghosts of the composers watch with an interest that is almost 'knowing'; these are the growing pains once familiar to them all! With Palestrina's resistance overcome, they gradually disappear, but immediately he starts to hear the voices of angels, which dictate his Mass to him. At the height of his inspiration, Palestrina sees the ghost of his wife, Lucretia, who appears to him as she had in life, bringing a message of peace, the peace for which he has longed ever since her death. This scene of the dictation of the Mass is the crux of the opera. It is perhaps sufficient praise to say that it succeeds in giving an impression of the artist's exaltation at the moment of creation.

It is dawn, the angel voices die away, the bells of Rome can be heard in the distance, and Palestrina sinks down exhausted. The floor of the room is covered with music-paper, and, when Silla and Ighino come for their morning lesson, they are overjoyed to see that the master has spent the night working. They gather up the sheets of music, and gradually realise that an entire Mass has been written in a single night. As the curtain falls, Silla wonders whether anything written so quickly can possibly add to the master's fame.

Act II.   The agitated prelude is in direct contrast to what preceded the first act. The scene is in the great hall in the palace of Cardinal Madruscht at Trent, where preparations are almost complete for renewal of the conference. Cardinal Novagerio makes fun of the farce which always attends the Spanish delegate's efforts to obtain his rightful precedence, and a little later takes the opportunity of warning the servants, who are all of different nationalities, that they will be severely punished if they again start to quarrel in the streets, as has happened recently.

Borromeo arrives, and there is a fairly lengthy political discussion between him and Novagerio. Novagerio congratulates Borromeo on the way he has managed the question of church music, but Borromeo reveals that he has been unsuccessful in getting Palestrina to write the Mass he needs.

He has had him thrown into prison, but doubts whether the work can be ready in time, even if gaol were to break Palestrina's self-imposed silence. Novagerio suggests that there are ways to force men to bend to the will of their masters, but Borromeo starts back in horror at the implication of his remarks.

The other delegates begin to arrive, the Italians suspicious of the Germans, the Spaniards commenting on the Italians who, they say, swarm over the place like ants. Some talk in an indignant way of heretics, others are more concerned over whether or not their expenses to and from the conference will be paid by their diocese. The master-of-ceremonies, Bishop Ercole Severolus, announces that the conference is about to begin and invites the delegates to take their places in proper order of precedence. This done, they are addressed by Morone, the papal legate, who prays that wisdom may attend their deliberations and inform their decisions. He calls down a malediction on all heretics, in which the entire conference joins, apart, that is to say, from the liberal-minded but boorish Bishop of Budoja, who makes the mistake of praying that they may be enlightened rather than destroyed, and gets a number of dirty looks from his fellow delegates.

Discussion begins on the subject of the musical side of the church service. The Pope's approval is dependent on a work being written which satisfies ritual considerations. Borromeo announces that such a Mass is being written, and that Palestrina is the composer. The business of the conference proceeds, but points of order seem to be preferred for discussion to points of doctrine. The Spanish envoy objects to the speed at which business is being transacted, and his quarrelsome attitude brings down upon him the objections of a number of delegates based on precedence and the exalted position he has claimed as his by right. Some sense of responsibility returns when the Bishop of Budoja shouts at the top of his voice that peace is the last thing likely to be obtained by such a conference divided against itself, but the meeting again degenerates into nationalist quarrelling and, after quelling the shouts, Morone decides to end the session. He calls the delegates for the afternoon, but warns them that the co-operation of them all, and not least of the Spanish envoy, will be needed if this last session of the conference is to accomplish the task set before it.

As soon as the delegates have gone, not without some

more sharp remarks, the Spanish servants gather together and mutter that their delegate has been insulted, and it is not long before a free fight develops between the servants. Madruscht appears with soldiers at his back; seeing the disorder, he commands them to open fire and bids them to take any survivors they can catch to the torture chambers. No one shall thus defile the Church's Council with unseemly conduct.

Act III. Palestrina's room as in Act I. The composer is sitting in his chair, barely visible to the audience. Five singers from the chapel stand round him, and Ighino is kneeling by his side. The singers express concern for Palestrina's condition, and when he wakes from his trance, he does not seem to recognise them, though they are from his own choir. He asks Ighino why they are waiting and gazing at him. His son tells him that at that very moment his Mass is being sung at the Pope's Palace. He seems not to grasp the significance of this, but refers to being asked some question about it in prison. The others remind him that they gathered together the pages of the Mass he wrote and that they were subsequently taken away from them.

Suddenly there is a noise from the street, and the people can be heard crying: 'Long life to Palestrina, saviour of music!' People crowd into the room, asking for the master, Palestrina, and saying that the Pope has given it as his opinion that the new Mass is Palestrina's best work. The Pope himself is coming to congratulate him! The Holy Father makes his entrance, followed by his Cardinals, amongst them Borromeo, and tells Palestrina of the enormous impression his Mass has made on them all. He must remain in his service until the end of his life.

The Pope leaves, blessing Palestrina and his singers. The Cardinals follow the Pope, all, that is, except Borromeo, who makes a sign to the singers to leave him alone with Palestrina. They look at each other for a moment, then with a cry Borromeo falls on his knees in front of the composer, who puts his hands gently on the Cardinal's head. Palestrina raises the Cardinal to his feet and they stay for a moment in an embrace, before the Cardinal goes quickly from the room.

Ighino, who has watched the scene from concealment, rushes out to ask his father if he is not the happiest man in the world. Maybe, says his father, but he is old and shows his happiness less demonstratively than Ighino. Where is Silla, he

sks. He guesses he has gone to Florence, and Ighino confirms
his impression. There is more acclamation for Palestrina from
outside, and he bids his son laugh and dance and sing if he
wants to. He himself remains alone in his room. He goes
quietly towards the portrait of his wife, Lucretia, then walks
to his organ and plays softly. The crowd is still below,
shouting praises to his name, and with these sounds in his
ears, the curtain falls.   H.

ARNOLD SCHOENBERG
(1874–1951)
ERWARTUNG
Expectation

MONODRAMA in one act (4 scenes) by Arnold Schoenberg, libretto by
Marie Pappenheim (composed 1909, published 1916). Première, Prague,
June 6, 1924 (during ISCM Festival), with Marie Gutheil-Schoder,
conductor Alexander Zemlinsky. First performed Wiesbaden, 1928;
Berlin, 1930, with Moje Forbach, conductor Klemperer; Zürich, 1949,
with Dorothy Dow; Hamburg, 1955, with Helga Pilarczyk; Holland
Festival, 1958, with Pilarczyk, conductor Hans Rosbaud; Sadler's Wells,
1960, by New Opera Company, with Heather Harper; Covent Garden,
1961, with Amy Shuard, conductor Georg Solti.

CHARACTER
The Woman

Schoenberg completed the enormously complex though
short score (no more than half an hour) in the unbelievably
short space of seventeen days, towards the end of 1909, in
the period when to all intents and purposes he had
abandoned tonality but had not yet evolved the 12-note
system.

Written for a single voice and full orchestra, the opera—
called 'Monodrama' by its composer—is concerned with the
half-demented ravings of a woman searching along a moonlit

path through a forest for her lover (maybe in a nightmare, She sings in broken phrases of 'their' garden, of the night, the forest, the moon, is terrified by imagined pursuit and feared wild beasts and shadows, by a log she mistakes for a body At the end of the third brief scene, she rushes out into the woods leaving the orchestra to give a vivid impression of a thud ding, terror-ridden heart such as is found nowhere else in music

In the fourth and last scene, which amounts to nearly half the work, the woman finds herself near a darkened house and is terrified by the deathly silence. She stumbles over her lover's body, shot dead by her rival, and the rest of the scene consists of hysterical mourning, references to the involve ment of another woman, attempts to revive the dead man and cries for help. Eventually, she rises from the corpse and wanders off, muttering 'I was seeking...' as the orchestra sound evaporates into the air with a cold shiver of ascending semi-quavers as if an icy finger were running down the spine.   H.

VON HEUTE AUF MORGEN
From One Day to the Next

Opera in one act by Arnold Schoenberg, text by 'Max Blonda'.[1] Première, Frankfurt, February 1, 1930, with Else Gentner-Fischer, Benno Ziegler, Elisabeth Friedrich, Anton Maria Töplitz, conductor Wilhelm Steinberg. First performed Naples, 1953, with Lydia Styx, Edith della Pergola, Willy Krämer, Nasco Petroff, conductor Hermann Scherchen; Holland Festival, 1958, with Erika Schmidt, Magda Laszlo, Derrik Olsen, Herbert Schachtschneider, conductor Hans Rosbaud; London, 1963, Royal Festival Hall (concert performance), with Erika Schmidt, Heather Harper, Herbert Schachtschneider, Derrik Olsen, conductor Antal Dorati; Vienna, Theater an der Wien, 1965, (Austrian première); Paris, Théâtre des Champs-Elysées, 1967, with Pilarczyk, Leonard Delaney, conductor Léon Barzin.

CHARACTERS

The wife .... Soprano
The husband .... Bass-Baritone
The friend .... Soprano
The tenor .... Tenor

Time: The Present

[1] The composer's second wife Gertrud Kolisch.

Written in 1928, twenty years after the completion of *Erwartung, Von Heute auf Morgen* is the only genuinely comic work in the composer's output and his choice of subject[1] was influenced, it is said, by his admiration for Hindemith's *Neues vom Tage*. The comedy has however serious overtones, portrayed along almost Aesopian lines, Schoenberg's moral being that 'the so-called modern, the merely modish, exists only "from one day to the next" '. The tale is set in the framework of a domestic scene which is quickly told. A husband and wife return from a party and discuss their fellow guests. He has been particularly taken with a woman, a childhood friend of his wife's, whose elegance and sophistication appeal to him far more than his wife's familiar domesticity, she with a famous tenor who has flattered her. Each ridicules the other's infatuation and they soon quarrel. The wife, nettled by her husband's words, transforms herself into a dazzling figure of fashion. He woos her passionately but she treats him with scorn and even ejects her little boy who has been woken by the argument.

The gasman arrives—much to her husband's astonishment as it is the middle of the night—and demands to be paid. The wife says she has spent all the money on dresses and insists they move to a hotel. She starts to pack. The telephone rings. It is the tenor who, to the husband's disgust, resumes his flattery. He has had a bet with their mutual friend from the party, he maintaining that the light they can see through the window must be from the wife's shining eyes, she that it is an ordinary electric light; if she wins, she must persuade the wife and her husband to accompany them to a nearby bar and if he does, he must get the husband—with his wife of course—to agree to do the same.

The whole thing strikes the wife as eminently reasonable (although her husband does not agree and curses away in the background), and she promises that they will meet in ten minutes. She changes into a cocktail dress, an action which provokes her husband to jealous fury. Her scorn redoubles and he has no alternative but to admit with some reluctance that he really loved her as she was but never realised it. Will she not come back to him? She at once reverts to her real self and in a tender scene they pledge mutual fidelity. They are interrupted by the singer and the friend who, having been

[1] Based on an episode from the life of the composer Franz Schreker.

kept waiting in the bar, have come to fetch them. Each of the visitors tries to woo his or her respective prey but the couple resisting all temptation and attempts to jeer at their old fashioned ideas, see them off and the work ends with the family at breakfast discussing their tempters. 'Mummy what's up-to-date people?' asks the child.

The music, written in clear and easily perceptible forms, is at the same time elaborately textured and extremely expressive, although by the time it was written Schoenberg had evolved the twelve-note system and contained himself firmly within it. It is scored for a wide variety of instruments including, apart from the normal orchestral complement, two saxophones, mandolin, guitar, banjo, celesta, piano and flexatone, and divides itself naturally into short arias and ensembles, very 'vocal' in character, between which are conversational links in a recitative pattern. The characters and their moods and actions are sharply defined by the orchestra and, considering its complexity, the piece is astonishingly accessible.

H.

MOSES UND ARON
Moses and Aaron

Opera in three acts, text and music by Arnold Schoenberg. Première in concert, March 12, 1954, NWDR Hamburg, with Helmut Krebs, Hans Herbert Fiedler, conductor Hans Rosbaud. Stage première, Zürich, June 6, 1957, with Helmut Melchert, Fiedler, conductor Rosbaud. First performed Berlin, 1959, with Melchert, Greindl, conductor Scherchen (the Berlin production was later seen in Vienna in 1960, and in Paris and Milan in 1961); Covent Garden, 1965, with Richard Lewis, Forbes Robinson, conductor Solti, producer Peter Hall; Paris, 1975, in French with Richard Lewis, Raymond Gerome.

CHARACTERS

Moses ....Bass speaking role
Aaron, *his brother* ....Tenor
A young girl ....Soprano
An invalid woman ....Contralto
A young man ....Tenor
A naked youth ....Tenor
Another man ....Baritone
Ephraimite ....Baritone
A priest ....Bass
Four naked virgins .... Two Sopranos, Two Contraltos

The Voice from the   Sopranos, Trebles, Altos, Tenors,
   Burning Bush   Baritones, Basses (3–6 to each part)
Six solo voices in   Soprano, Mezzo-Soprano, Contralto,
   the orchestra   Tenor, Baritone, Bass
Beggars, Elderly Persons, Elders, Tribal Chieftains,
           Israelite People

Schoenberg started work on the music of his last and only full-length opera in 1931 and the second act was finished in Barcelona in 1932—but he seems to have had the opera in mind from the mid-1920's. The circumstances of the third act must remain something of an enigma. The text exists; in 1949 he writes that he has already to a great extent conceived the music and could write it in 'only a few months', in 1950 that he has found 'neither time nor mood for the composing of the third act. . . . that depends upon my nervous eye affliction', later the same year 'it is not entirely impossible that I should finish the third act within a year'. But in the year in which he died: 'Agreed that the third act may simply be spoken, in case I cannot complete the composition.' In the event, most people who have heard the two acts of the opera in performance are agreed that it is in no sense a fragment, but a complete and stage-worthy work, perfectly capable of standing in its two-act form. Scherchen's experiment in Berlin, where he performed the third act with music taken from Act I, met with less approval.

The text is the composer's own and represents his religious and philosophical thoughts. The drama lies in the conflict between Moses the thinker and Aaron the man of action; Aaron's every attempt to give practical expression to Moses's thoughts results in compromise and a debasing of ideals. To realise his conception, Schoenberg uses an orchestra of hardly more than normal size (only in the *Dance before the Golden Calf* does it supplant the voices as the main means of expression), but his demands on the vocal forces at his disposal are very considerable indeed. There are only two long solo parts, Moses and Aaron, but the smaller roles and solo ensembles are complicated and vitally important. The emphasis laid on the chorus is quite out of the ordinary, and there are various semi-chorus groups to be contrasted with the main body. They are asked to speak as well as sing, and often the two methods of expression are combined to remarkable effect. 'The speaking is part of the music and, in the score, written out in musical notation. Within the ensemble of voices its effect is similar to that of the percussion in the orchestra, especially in respect of rhythmic precision; at the same time the notes also indicate the intonation of the spoken phrases, so that spoken melodies are heard; and spoken chords are produced by the different voices of the chorus (though the pitch remains indefinite).'[1]

Act I.   The Calling of Moses. There is no prelude, but soft, slow chords (including six solo voices in the orchestra pit) introduce Moses at prayer. The six solo voices in the orchestra and a spoken semi-chorus answer him from the Burning Bush. He is called to lead the Israelites out of Egyptian bondage, and to his protest that he is old and unable to convince the unbelieving people, the answer comes that Aaron his brother will be his mouthpiece. The singing and speaking choruses proclaim God's promise to the Israelites that they are His chosen people.

Moses meets Aaron in the Wasteland. *Grazioso* music of almost chamber music delicacy, in 6/8 tempo and in strong contrast with what has preceded it, introduces the second scene (it is associated with the character of Aaron). Though Aaron immediately understands the part he must play in fulfilling the destiny of the Israelites, it is apparent that he and Moses approach their task from opposite points of view. 'To Moses, God is pure thought—unimaginable because any attempt at an image distorts the idea. "Thou shalt not make unto thyself any graven image . . . ." The disparity between an idea and its realisation, which Schoenberg symbolises in the figure of Moses and Aaron, penetrates into every field of human affairs. Things are never as they were expected. Any work of art is an inadequate image of the artist's original conception. Religious, political, social ideals become idols in reality. Aaron however is simpler-minded and his views of things dictated by emotions. He greets the mission of liberating his people with great enthusiasm, but does not understand what is implied in Moses's conception of God. He asks: "Invisible? unimaginable? . . . can you love what you dare not imagine?" Moses sternly replies: "Dare not? Unimaginable? . . . Purge your thinking, free it from the trivial, devote it to truth; no other reward will thank your sacrifice".'[2] The duet, with its unique combination of singing tenor and speaking bass, is most impressive.

[1] Erwin Stein, writing in *Opera*, August 1957.   [2] *ibid.*

27 *Moses and Aaron* at Covent Garden in Peter Hall's production.

Moses and Aaron bring God's message to the people. Three young Israelites have seen Aaron in a state of religious exaltation, but others, particularly the priests, are less inclined to believe that a new God will deliver them from Pharaoh. A great chorus, partly singing, partly speaking, develops as Moses and Aaron are seen approaching from the distance. Together they proclaim God and his purpose. When the people demand a God they can understand if they are to follow him, Moses feels that he has failed in the task for which he was chosen, but Aaron snatches his rod and rouses the people to a state of religious mania with his miracles—the turning of the rod into a serpent, the leprous hand, and the transforming of the Nile water into blood. The people express their fervour in a march, Aaron celebrates his moral victory in a big aria—the victory which has at the same time won over the people and betrayed Moses's ideals—and, to the tune of the march, the Israelites prepare to set out on their journey through the desert.

Act II. Between the acts, there is an interlude, sung and spoken in a whisper by the chorus in front of the curtain: 'Wo ist Moses?'—an extraordinary, hushed, mystical *scherzo* of a movement, of the greatest beauty.

Aaron and the Seventy Elders before the Mountain of Revelation. The Israelites are encamped below Mount Sinai and now even the Elders grumble at Moses's continued absence: 'Forty days now, yet we're still waiting.' Aaron tries to pacify them, but the sound of a mob can be heard approaching and in a moment the angry people burst on to the scene, shouting for Moses's blood. The Elders call on Aaron to deal with them, and he starts to explain that Moses's very nearness to God may have caused his removal from the leadership of the people. When they threaten to vent their rage on the priesthood as well as on Moses, Aaron regains command of the situation by promising to give the gods comprehensible form. He sends for gold and the people rejoice in chorus.

The Golden Calf and the Altar. *The Dance before the Golden Calf* is the climax of the opera, as vast a conception musically as it is complicated visually, with its rapid rises and falls in temperature and a gamut running from drunkenness and dancing through the fury of destruction and suicide to the erotic orgy with which it ends. As Aaron announces the casting of the image, processions of camels, asses, horses, porters and wagons come on to the scene and unload their riches, while animals of all sorts are brought in, decorated and finally sacrificed, all this to the accompaniment of the orchestra alone in music of the richest texture. The butchers dance to a vivid rhythm, but the music dies down in a lyrical episode as a sick woman is carried to the image and healed the moment she touches it. Beggars bring their last possessions, old men sacrifice themselves in front of the calf, and the tension mounts again as, to the sound of trombones, the tribal leaders gallop in to worship the calf. A youth tries to break up the idolatry and recall the people to their former state of grace, but he is slaughtered almost casually by an Ephraimite. The rejoicing soon turns to ecstasy, ecstasy to a savage frenzy as four naked virgins (in a contrasting and delicately beautiful vocal quartet) offer themselves for sacrifice upon the altar. Destruction and suicide are followed by an orgy of rape until gradually the people pass into exhaustion and sleep. The music dies down, the fires are extinguished and the stage is in almost complete darkness when a man turns on his side, seems to see something in the distance, and cries: 'Moses is descending from the mountain.'

Moses appears, the tablets of the laws in his hands and commands: 'Begone, thou image of impotence.' The people are terrified as the Golden Calf disintegrates, and they leave Moses alone with Aaron.

Moses and Aaron. In answer to Moses's angry question, Aaron does not so much defend himself as explain that his actions were the logical outcome of Moses's idea; as Moses's mouthpiece he must interpret his ideas in terms which the people can understand. Moses in his fury smashes the tablets of stone, which he sees in their turn as no more than images. The theological argument is dramatic in character, as Moses unswervingly reiterates his faith, and Aaron in music of florid cast defends the integrity of the people. In the background, led by a pillar of fire, the children of Israel can be heard and seen as they resume their march to the promised land (the march from the end of Act I is heard again). Moses is left alone and in despair. 'O Wort, du Wort, das mir fehlt' (O word, thou word that I lack) is his moving last utterance.

Act III, which remains uncomposed, consists for the most part of a dialogue between Moses and Aaron, the latter now a prisoner and in chains. In the presence of the Seventy Elders, Moses restates his conviction of the ideal nature of the

ɔdhead, and of the misrepresentation of His word as Aaron
ɔiced it. Aaron attempts unsuccessfully to defend his
ɑctions, and at the end, when he is given his freedom, he falls
down dead. (Though Schoenberg in a letter had seemed to
give permission for the last act to be spoken, in the Zürich
production, which was supervised by his widow and conducted by Rosbaud, it was omitted. In Berlin, Scherchen had
the third act spoken to musical accompaniment taken from
the first act.)   H.

ALBAN BERG

(1885–1935)

WOZZECK

OPERA in three acts and fifteen scenes by Alban Berg; text adapted by
the composer from Büchner's drama of the same name. Première, Berlin
Staatsoper, December 14, 1925, with Sigrid Johanson, von Scheele-
Müller, Leo Schützendorf, Waldemar Henke, Martin Abendroth, con-
ductor Kleiber. First performed Vienna, 1930, with Pauly, Manowarda,
conductor Krauss; Amsterdam, 1930, with Brünn, Bitterauf, conductor
Pella; Philadelphia, 1931, with Roselle, Ivantzoff, conductor Stokowski;
New York, 1931, same cast; London (Queen's Hall, in concert form),
with Blyth, Bitterauf, conductor Boult; Rome, 1942, with Gatti,
Gobbi, conductor Serafin. Revived Düsseldorf, 1948, with Mödl,
Nillius, conductor Hollreiser; Naples, 1949, with Danco, Gobbi, con-
ductor Böhm; Berne, 1951, with Borkh, Fehr, conductor Aesbacher;
Salzburg Festival, 1951, with Goltz, Josef Herrmann, conductor Böhm;
Covent Garden, 1952, with Goltz, Rothmüller, Parry Jones, Dalberg,
conductor Kleiber; New York, City Centre, 1952, with Neway,
Rothmüller, conductor Rosenstock; la Scala, Milan, 1952, with Dow,
Gobbi, conductor Mitropoulos; Buenos Aires, 1952, with Goltz,
Rothmüller, conductor Böhm; New York, Metropolitan, 1959, with
Steber, Uhde, conductor Böhm; Paris, 1963 and 1966, conductor
Boulez; Edinburgh Festival, 1966 (by Stuttgart Opera), with Seefried,
Stolze (as Wozzeck).

CHARACTERS

Wozzeck, *a soldier* .... Baritone
The Drum-major .... Tenor
Andres, *a soldier* .... Tenor
The Captain .... Tenor
The Doctor .... Bass
First and Second Workmen .... Baritone and Bass
An Idiot .... Tenor
Marie .... Soprano
Margret .... Contralto
Marie's Child .... Treble
Soldiers, Maids, Servants, Children

Conceived in 1914, when Berg saw a performance of *Wozzek*, the stylistically prophetic play by Georg Büchner (1813–1837), *Wozzeck*'s composition was interrupted by the first world war, in which Berg served. The music was completed in 1921, and in 1923 Universal Edition undertook to publish the opera. In the meanwhile, Berg tried to persuade some opera house or other to mount the work (he was helped by the noted pianist, Eduard Steuermann, who played the score to one uninterested Generalmusikdirektor after another). It was eventually accepted by Kleiber for production at the Staatsoper, Berlin, but, eighteen months before the Berlin première, the public had the opportunity of hearing the so-called Fragments from *Wozzeck* (the first half of Act I, Scene iii; Act III, Scene i; and Act III, Scene v and the interlude which precedes it), sung by Sutter-Kottlar and conducted by Scherchen. From that moment *Wozzeck* became a centre of controversy, and musicians and opera-goers alike divided into those who loved and those who loathed the work—in either case, the reaction was often stronger than the reasons which could be found to support the impression.

Wozzeck is in three acts, each of five scenes. The music is continuous and often Berg provides no more than a few seconds of interlude music during which the scene change must be made.

Berg himself has related music and drama in the most succinct way in the following key:

STAGE	Act I	MUSIC
Wozzeck in his relationship to his surroundings		*Five Character-Pieces*
Wozzeck and the Captain	Scene i	Suite
Wozzeck and Andres	Scene ii	Rhapsody
Marie and Wozzeck	Scene iii	Military March and Lullaby
Wozzeck and the Doctor	Scene iv	Passacaglia
Marie and the Drum-major	Scene v	*Andante affettuoso* (*quasi Rondo*)
	Act II	
Dramatic development		*Symphony in Five Movements*
Marie and the Child, later Wozzeck	Scene i	Sonata Movement
Captain and Doctor, later Wozzeck	Scene ii	Fantasy and Fugue
Marie and Wozzeck	Scene iii	*Largo*
Beer-garden	Scene iv	Scherzo
Sleeping quarters in the Barracks	Scene v	*Rondo con introduzione*
	Act III	
Catastrophe and Epilogue		*Six Inventions*
Marie with the Child	Scene i	Invention on a theme
Marie and Wozzeck	Scene ii	Invention on one note
Inn	Scene iii	Invention on a rhythm
Wozzeck's death	Scene iv	Invention on a chord of six notes
	Orchestral Interlude:	Invention on a key
Children at play	Scene v	Invention on quaver figure

However, the composer himself (in an article published in the *Neue Musik-Zeitung*, 1928, and reprinted in Willi Reich's book on Berg) has given a warning to those people who may be tempted to perform a mental analysis of *Wozzeck* during performance: 'However thorough one's knowledge of the musical forms which are to be found within the opera ... from the moment when the curtain rises until it falls for the last time, nobody in the audience ought to notice anything of these various Fugues and Inventions, Suite and Sonata movements, Variations and Passacaglias—everyone should be filled only by the idea of the opera, an idea which far transcends the individual fate of Wozzeck.'

Berg was a pupil of Schoenberg's, and his musical style is influenced by many of his teacher's theoretical and practical ideas. *Wozzeck* is not, however, composed according to Schoenberg's so-called dodecaphonic method, although the theme of the Passacaglia in Act II has twelve notes. Key signatures, except in the Act III Interlude, are discarded, and the composer makes considerable and subtle use of *Sprechstimme*, best known from Schoenberg's employment of it in *Pierrot Lunaire*. *Sprechstimme* is best described as 'musically defined speech'. Rhythm and intonation are exactly prescribed, but 'in the execution each note is only defined in the moment when it is articulated, immediately afterwards the voice drops or rises as in natural speech'.[1] All authorities are agreed that an over-vocal and *cantabile* style in *Sprechstimme* is disastrous, and that the finished result should sound something like the poetic declamation of a good actor.

Act I. The curtain rises in the third bar of the opera on Scene i, which is laid in the Captain's room. It is morning, and the Captain is being shaved by Wozzeck, his soldier-servant. The Captain is a garrulous, digressive individual, and he moralises to the bewildered Wozzeck: if he hurries so much, what will he do with the ten minutes he saves? He puts aside the subject of Eternity, and asks Wozzeck if the wind is not blowing south-north, chortling at the automatic 'Jawohl, Herr Hauptmann' which he gets as answer. The observation that Wozzeck is a good fellow, but without moral sense—witness the fact that he is unmarried but has a child—finally breaks through Wozzeck's preoccupation. Did not the Lord God say 'Suffer little children to come unto me', asks Wozzeck. The Captain's voice rises to a top C in his astonishment at this answer, and Wozzeck explains that only the rich can afford conventional morality (Example 1).

Wozzeck thinks too much, muses the Captain, and he dismisses him with the admonition that he is not to hurry so dreadfully.

Scene ii. Wozzeck and Andres are cutting sticks at sundown in a field from which can be seen the town. Andres sings to himself, but Wozzeck cannot rid his mind of an impression that the place they are in is haunted. He imagines every sort of thing, babbles of the intrigues of the Freemasons, thinks the ground is going to open under his feet,

[1] Erwin Stein's article on *Wozzeck*, in *Opera*, January 1952.

and is convinced the whole world is on fire when the setting
sun colours the horizon red. This short scene contains some
of Berg's most dazzling orchestral invention.

Scene iii.   Marie's room; evening. The sound of a military
march played behind the scenes makes it quite plain that
what Marie is looking at out of the window is the band going
back to barracks. The Drum-major waves to her, and she sings
happily to the band's tune, so happily in fact that her

neighbour Margret cannot resist a malicious comment about
her lively interest in soldiers. After an exchange of abuse
Marie slams the window and shuts out the sound of the band.
She sings a lyrical cradle song to her child, before there is a

knock at the window, and Wozzeck himself is seen standing
there. He cannot come in as it is too late, he has not even
time to look at the child which Marie holds up to him. His
confused talk worries her and, after he is gone, she rushes out
of the door.

Scene iv (the Passacaglia) is laid in the Doctor's study, next
day. Wozzeck, in return for a small pittance, is prepared to
act as a guinea-pig for the doctor's dietetic experiments. The
Doctor complains that Wozzeck does not follow out all his
instructions, and his scientific talk further confuses the
unhappy man, whose outburst causes the Doctor to suggest
that he may well end up in a lunatic asylum. The Doctor is
ecstatic about the fame which will result when his new
theories are published, and the curtain goes down as he
re-examines Wozzeck's tongue.

Scene v.   The street in front of Marie's house, where the
Drum-major is posturing to her evident admiration. He
assures her that his present finery is as nothing to what he

wears on Sundays. Marie repulses him once when he tries to embrace her, but the second time does not resist him, and, with the exclamation 'What does it matter? It's all the same', takes him into her house.

Act II.   In her room, Marie is admiring herself and her new ear-rings in a bit of broken mirror. She tries to get the child to go to sleep, then falls to admiring herself again. Wozzeck comes in, and asks what it is that she is trying to hide. She says she found the ear-rings, and he observes that he has never had the luck to find things like that in pairs. He looks at the sleeping child, then, with a reference to No. 1, reflects that life is nothing but work, and that even in sleep man sweats. He gives Marie the money he has earned from the Captain and the Doctor (to the accompaniment of a string chord of C major) and goes out, leaving her to reflect sadly on her infidelity to him.

Scene ii takes place in the street. The Doctor is hurrying along when he is stopped, in spite of his protests, by his friend the Captain, on whom he revenges himself by giving him details of various fatal cases he has recently seen, ending with a warning that the Captain's own flushed condition may easily be a symptom of an impending apoplectic fit, from which death, or at least paralysis, is likely to result. The Captain becomes lyrical at the thought of his own demise, but consoles himself with thoughts of what nice things people will say of him after he has gone.

His reverie is interrupted when Wozzeck comes rapidly down the street—he cuts through the world like one of his own razor blades, says the Captain in a depressed way. The mention of shaving reminds him of the scandal about Marie and the bearded Drum-major, and he and the Doctor proceed to torment Wozzeck with innuendo (has he not lately found a hair of a beard in his soup?) and even the imitation of a military march. The seriousness with which Wozzeck takes their insinuations quite shocks his tormentors, and he bursts out with a *fortissimo* imprecation at the impossibility of finding satisfaction in life. The Doctor feels his pulse to see if emotion is affecting it, and both he and the Captain exclaim in surprise as their victim rushes off down the street.

Scene iii takes place in the street in front of Marie's house. It is the slow movement of the symphony (*largo*) and is scored for a chamber orchestra of fourteen players, composed according to the distribution of Schoenberg's

Kammersymphonie. Marie is standing in front of her house when Wozzeck comes up to her. She is as beautiful as sin, he says—but how can sin be beautiful? Did *he* stand there? Marie replies that she cannot control who walks in the street, and, when Wozzeck looks as though he will strike her: 'Better a knife blade in my heart than lay a hand on me. . . . My father would never dare when I was little.' Wozzeck repeats her words in a dazed sort of way as she goes into the house.

Scene iv takes us to a beer-garden, where dancing is in progress to a slow Ländler played on the stage by a Heurige orchestra: 2—4 fiddles tuned a tone high, clarinet in C, accordion, several guitars, a Bombardon in F (Bass Tuba). There is general dancing, and a couple of exceedingly drunk workmen sing in a maudlin way of the effect of brandy on the soul. Wozzeck comes in and sees Marie dancing with the Drum-major; his jealousy grows until he is about to rush on to the dance floor and separate them, when the dance stops. The soldiers, with Andres as soloist, begin a lusty hunting song, ending on a sustained C for the soloist. The first workman climbs on to a table and starts a most effective example of one of those wholly logical, wholly nonsensical discourses traditionally associated with the very drunk. It is entirely conducted in *Sprechstimme*, and shows how effective and expressive a medium that can be.

A snatch of the male chorus succeeds the sermon, after which an Idiot appears on the scene, wanders over to where Wozzeck is sitting, and observes 'Lustig, lustig . . . aber es riecht . . . ich riech Blut' (Joyful, joyful . . . and yet it reeks . . . it reeks . . . of blood). The whole role contains only thirteen notes, and yet the tiny scene in which the Idiot appears, to a mainly accordion accompaniment, has an extraordinary fascination and significance. The dancing begins again and Wozzeck's imagination is obsessed with the idea of blood.

Scene v takes place in Wozzeck's barrack room at night. Before the curtain goes up, the sound of snoring can be heard from the sleeping occupants of the room (the chorus in five parts hum wordlessly with half-open mouths), and as soon as the stage can be seen, Wozzeck is heard complaining to Andres that he cannot sleep for memories of the dance hall. The Drum-major staggers into the room, proclaiming his conquest at the top of his voice and demanding that Wozzeck drink with him. The latter turns away and whistles to

himself, whereupon the Drum-major yanks him from where
he stands; they fight for a moment, Wozzeck is knocked to
the ground, and the Drum-major shakes him and threatens to
knock all the breath out of his body. He goes out, leaving
Wozzeck staring in front of him. 'He bleeds,' exclaims
Andres. The suggestion of blood seems to Wozzeck like fate's
prompting: 'One time after another.'

Act III.   Musically, this act is particularly concentrated
and consists of six Inventions (that is Berg's name for them).

Scene i.   Marie's room at night. The solo viola gives out
the theme. Marie is reading the story of Mary Magdalen in the
Bible, and cannot help comparing what she reads with her
own life. She ends with a cry for mercy: 'Saviour . . . as Thou
hadst mercy on her, have mercy now on me, Lord!' The

scene, which is of haunting beauty, has *Sprechstimme* when
Marie reads from the Bible, singing when she comments on
what she has read.

Scene ii.   A pond in the wood, later that night. Wozzeck
appears with Marie, whom he prevents from going home as
she wishes. He reflects on how long they have known each
other, and, when Marie sees the moon rise, draws a knife and
cuts her throat, then bends over her: 'Dead!' the interlude
consists of two long *crescendi* on B natural, beginning with a
ppp solo horn, and continuing through the whole orchestra
until, after a percussive rhythm, the second *crescendo* takes
in the percussion as well. Straightaway the curtain rises on
Scene iii, with the hammering of a quick polka on an
out-of-tune piano. The scene represents an inn. Wozzeck is
amongst the dancers. He takes Margret for partner, and leads
her to a table, where he tries to make love to her. She sings a
short song, but stops when she sees blood on Wozzeck's
hand. He makes some attempt to explain it away by saying
he cut his arm, then pushes through the dancers who have by
now crowded round him, and rushes from the room.

Scene iv is laid, once again, at the pond. Wozzeck searches
for the knife, which he dropped after the murder and which
would incriminate him if found. He finds it, pauses for a
moment to look at the body of Marie, then throws the knife

into the water, into which he watches it sink. The whole world seems to him bathed in blood; he sees spots on his hands and his clothes, and walks hopelessly into the water to wash it off. It rises to his neck, but still he walks further, until he has disappeared from sight. As the Doctor and the Captain come into view and comment on the sound they hear—the sound of a man drowning, hazards the Doctor—the orchestra suggests the waters closing over Wozzeck's head in rising chromatic scales.

The great D minor interlude forms the climax of the opera,

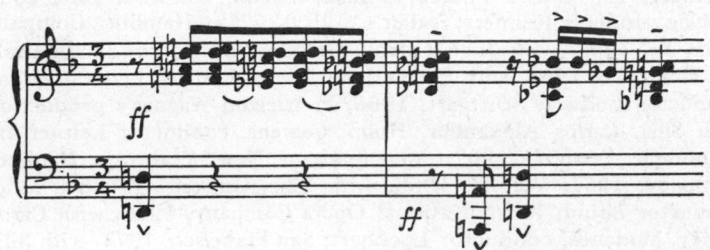

and at the same time a lament for Wozzeck himself, the opera's hero. Reference is made to music from earlier scenes, and the themes most closely connected with Wozzeck himself are heard in ennobled form. 'In this interlude,' says Erwin Stein, 'Berg does not speak through the medium of the drama, but addresses us directly. The change of accent is striking and its sincerity makes us realise why we love Berg's music.'

Scene v takes place in the street outside Marie's house. Children are playing. Apart and playing by himself is Marie's child. Other children come running in, and one of them says that Marie has been found dead. The child cannot take in what it is being told, and goes on playing its game: 'Hopp-hopp, hopp-hopp, hopp-hopp.' The curtain drops slowly.

Wozzeck may not be an exact representation of the 'common man' but he is an artistic projection of one side of his make-up—the side which leads in logical progression from everyday circumstances to the violent consequences which are potentially their outcome. This progression in *Wozzeck* is described in musical language of such potency, in orchestral invention of such overwhelming beauty, and culminates (in the last interlude) in a passage of such compassionate humanity that it is certainly not too early to acclaim the opera as a classic.   H.

LULU

Opera in three acts by Alban Berg; text adapted by the composer from Wedekind's *Erdgeist* and *Die Büchse der Pandora*. Première in the unfinished form in which it was left by the composer at the time of his death in Zürich, June 2, 1937, with Nuri Hadzic as Lulu, Aster Stig (Dr. Schön), Emmerich (Athlete), Peter Baxeranos (Alwa), Maria Bernhard (Geschwitz), Feichtinger (Gymnasiast), Paul Feher (Painter), Honisch (Schigolch), conductor Denzler. First performed Venice, 1949, with Styx, Rehfuss, Demetz, Zareska, conductor Sanzogno; Essen, 1953, with Spletter, Jüllich, Peter Walter, Offermanns, conductor König; Hamburg, 1957, with Pilarczyk, Blankenheim, Ruesche, Litz, cond. Ludwig, producer Rennert; Sadler's Wells, 1962, by Hamburg Company; Santa Fe, 1963, with Joan Carroll, Gramm, Shirley, conductor Craft; San Francisco, 1965, with Evelyn Lear, Vinay, Richard Lewis, Cervena, conductor Ludwig; Stuttgart, 1966, in Wieland Wagner's production, with Silja, Carlos Alexander, Holm, Cervena, conductor Leitner and Edinburgh Festival, 1967; Metropolitan, New York, by Hamburg Company, 1967; Vienna, 1968, with Silja, Gutstein, Kmentt, Mödl, conductor Böhm; Welsh National Opera Company, 1971, with Carole Farley, Modenos, conductor Lockhart; San Francisco, 1971, with Silja, Cervena, Ulfung, Hopferweiser, Alvary, conductor Dohnanyi.

CHARACTERS

Lulu	High Soprano
Gräfin Geschwitz	Dramatic Mezzo-Soprano
A Wardrobe-mistress A Schoolboy ('Der Gymnasiast')	} . . Contralto
The Doctor	Speaking Part
The Painter	Lyric Tenor
Dr. Schön, *a newspaper editor*	Heroic Baritone
Alwa, *Dr. Schön's son, a writer*	Young Heroic Tenor
An Animal-tamer Rodrigo, *an athlete*	} Bass
Schigolch, *an old man*	High Character Bass
The Prince, *a traveller in Africa*	Tenor
The Theatre Director	Buffo Bass

Time: Last quarter of the Nineteenth Century

Place: A German city

Lulu, Berg's second and last opera, is written throughout in the dodecaphonic system. When the composer died, he had finished Acts I and II, and part of Act III, i.e. part of the big ensemble in the opening scene. In addition, he had sketched, in more or less elaborate form, the whole of the

est of the work, which is to say that, except for some lines
in the ensemble, all the words had been set.[1] Some of the
music of this Act was included amongst the five Symphonic
Pieces from the opera, which he completed beforehand. The
Symphonic suite (which requires a singer for performance)
consists of (1) *Rondo* (duet Lulu-Alwa, II, i, and end of II,
ii), (2) *Ostinato* (Interlude II, i-ii), (3) *Song of Lulu* (II, i), (4)
Variations (Interlude III, i-ii), (5) *Adagio* (Interlude I, ii-iii,
and end of opera, including arietta of Geschwitz).

Prologue. An animal-tamer, accompanied by the clown
from his circus, steps in front of the curtain and introduces
his troupe, amongst whom is Lulu, dressed in Pierrot's
costume.

The curtain goes up on scene i of Act I to reveal a painter's
studio, where Lulu, dressed as Pierrot, is being painted. Dr.
Schön, a newspaper editor, watches the proceedings. Schön's
son, Alwa, enters and is surprised to find Lulu there without
her husband. She explains that she expects him at any
moment, and Alwa, who works in the theatre, takes his
father off to his dress rehearsal, leaving Lulu and the Painter
alone. The latter admits he cannot give his mind to his work,
and tries to embrace Lulu. He chases her vigorously round
the room—the two voices are in canon and begin with Lulu's
motif (heard first in the Prologue)—and kisses her hands just

before the sound of her husband's knocking is heard.

He succeeds in forcing the door, only to collapse at their
feet with the shock of finding them in a compromising
position. They gradually come to realise he is dead and Lulu
comments, with more interest than regret, on his death
(*Canzonetta* introduced by saxophone solo). There is a duet
for Lulu and the Painter, in which his questions about her
beliefs receive the unvaried answer 'I don't know', and the

[1] Efforts were made after Berg's death to have the opera finished by
one of his contemporaries sympathetic to his music. But when initial
attempts failed, the composer's widow gradually imposed an embargo on
any work on her late husband's opera, a work moreover which most
experts would accept as one of the great operatic masterpieces of the
twentieth century.

Painter sings an *arioso* when Lulu leaves him alone while she goes to change her clothes.

An interlude leads to scene ii, which takes place in an elegant room in which hangs Lulu's portrait as Pierrot. The Painter, who is now her husband, comes in with the mail, and Lulu reads with amazement a notice of the engagement of Dr. Schön. There follows a light-hearted *Duettino* between her and the Painter, at the end of which the studio bell rings. The Painter looks out and says it is a beggar. He goes off to his studio to work, and Lulu lets in the 'beggar', who turns out to be Schigolch, who is supposed to be her father, but in reality one presumes is a former lover. He expresses admiration of her present surroundings; she has gone a long way since he last saw her.

As he leaves, Schön enters (Sonata movement begins), recognises Schigolch with some surprise, and then proceeds to tell Lulu that she must stop coming to see him now that he is engaged. She retorts that she belongs to him (the slow beginning of the coda of the sonata's exposition has something of the significance of a love theme); he rescued her from the streets as a child, and anyhow her husband is blind to anything she does, and does not think of her as a person but as his 'little darling', and his 'birdy'.

The Painter enters, Lulu leaves, and Schön first urges him to watch Lulu more carefully, then, as the music gains in urgency, gradually reveals something of her past to him. He himself introduced her to Dr. Goll, her previous husband; it was just after the death of his (Schön's) own wife, and Lulu was doing her utmost to take her place. She has been known by a different name to each of her lovers; Schön calls her Mignon, Dr. Goll called her Nelly, and the Painter refers to her as Eva. The Painter makes as if to go out and talk to Lulu, but presently groans are heard and Lulu and Dr. Schön force open a locked door (rhythmical canon of percussion) to find the Painter lying dead.

The bell rings and Alwa comes in full of excitement at the news that revolution has broken out in Paris. Schön fears that the scandal which will inevitably follow discovery of the Painter's suicide will endanger his own engagement, but, editor-wise, hopes the sensation of the news from France may serve to cover it up. The curtain falls to Lulu's words, sung to her motive: 'You will marry me after all.'

An extended Interlude, in which the love theme is developed, leads to a third scene, which takes place in Lulu's dressing-room behind the scenes in a theatre. Alwa waits for Lulu to come off the stage, and reminds her how, as a young man, he wanted to induce his father to marry her after his mother's death. Lulu replies that she knows perfectly well that Dr. Schön put her on the stage so that somebody rich should fall in love with her and take her off his hands.

She goes out for the next part of her act, and Alwa observes that her life history would make a splendid story for an opera. A Prince, who intends to marry her, enters and launches into extravagant praise of Lulu. There is a noise off-stage, and Lulu is carried in after fainting during her act—an accident caused, Lulu explicitly says, because she had to dance in front of Schön's prospective bride.

Lulu and Schön are left alone (development section of the Sonata) and a scene ensues between them, Lulu taunting him for not having already married his innocent bride and for his unavailing attempts to free himself from her own domination. In despair, he tries to tear himself away, but she shows herself the stronger (recapitulation of the Sonata) and forces him to write, word by word to her dictation, a letter to his fiancée, breaking off the engagement. The curtain falls as Schön exclaims 'Now comes my execution' (love music). Lulu prepares to continue the act which was interrupted by her fainting fit.

Act II, scene i, takes place in a palatial hall decorated in the German Renaissance style. Gräfin Geschwitz, dressed in clothes of distinctly masculine cut, is paying a call on Lulu, to whom she is obviously very much attracted. Schön, who is now Lulu's husband, is present, and when Lulu has left with Geschwitz, he shows that jealousy has brought him to the verge of madness. He looks behind the curtains, a loaded revolver in his hand, as if he expected to find some lover there. Lulu returns and she and Schön leave the stage together.

No sooner have they gone than Geschwitz sneaks back into the room and conceals herself, just before Schigolch, an Athlete and a Schoolboy come in (the last-named a 'Hosenrolle', or travesty part). The boy is in love with Lulu and Schigolch has acted as go-between in arranging a meeting. They are drinking and smoking when Lulu comes in, but all hide when Alwa is announced. Alwa with rising excitement declares his love for Lulu. She counters that it was she who was responsible years ago for poisoning his mother. Dr. Schön watches the scene from a hiding-place, and catches sight of the Athlete, who is also hiding. Schön leads Alwa, who is no longer in control of himself, from the room, and returns to launch a tirade against Lulu, offering her the revolver, with which he has been pursuing the Athlete, and telling her to use it against herself.

Next he finds Geschwitz and drags her from the room, all the time continuing to urge Lulu to commit suicide. Here follows Lulu's song (it is dedicated by the composer to Anton von Webern); in it, she justifies herself and says she has never tried to seem other than she is. Schön again attempts to force the revolver against Lulu, there is a cry from the boy, and Lulu fires five shots into Schön's body. The entire scene between Schön and Lulu is built up on an aria of five verses for Schön, the different episodes coming as interruption between the verses.

Lulu is horrified by what she has done; Schön was her only love. Alwa returns, and Schön's last words to him are in the nature of a demand for vengeance. Lulu in an arietta pleads to Alwa for mercy, but the curtain falls as the police appear.

The exciting Interlude between the scenes is designed to accompany a silent and largely symbolical film, showing what happens to Lulu in the time which intervenes. It shows a court scene, during whose course Lulu is condemned for the murder of Schön; her entry into hospital after she has contracted cholera; and the means of escape (about which more later) through the intervention of Geschwitz.

Scene ii takes place in the same set as scene i, the room however looking dirty and ill-kept. Geschwitz, Alwa and the Athlete (dressed as a footman) are together, and from the conversation we gather that Lulu has had cholera, from which Geschwitz has also only just recovered, that Lulu is to be rescued from the prison hospital where Geschwitz will take her place, and that Lulu is going to marry the Athlete. Schigolch takes Geschwitz off to put the plan into execution—we hear that Geschwitz in her passion for Lulu purposely contracted cholera to make the plan of escape possible.

No sooner are Alwa and the Athlete alone than the Schoolboy appears with a plan for Lulu's escape. They try to convince him that she is dead, and hustle him out of the room just before she comes in, supported by Schigolch. The

Athlete is so put out when he sees her looking pale and emaciated that he shouts abuse at her, and leaves the room. Schigolch goes off to collect the tickets for Paris, and Alwa and Lulu are alone. After a passionate love duet, they leave together for Paris.

Act III, scene i.[1] An elegant house in Paris, obviously frequented by characters of the demi-monde. The scene is one of activity, Casti Piani, an elegant white-slave trafficker, who knows of Lulu's past, suggests that she should enter a brothel; he threatens to expose her to the police if she decline his suggestion. She refuses and prepares to escape. She dresses up a manservant in some of her clothes and herself puts on boy's clothes and escapes. The police arrive to find only the servant.

Scene ii. An attic in a London slum. Lulu is now on the streets and with her earnings keeps Alwa and Schigolch. Geschwitz appears from Paris. She has saved Lulu's Pierrot portrait and shows it to them. Several male visitors are brought to the room (one of them takes fright when he sees Geschwitz). Lulu's last pick-up is Jack the Ripper. He murders her and, when Geschwitz tries to come to her aid, kills her as well.

After the first public hearing of the work, Erwin Stein wrote as follows: 'The music itself shows Berg at the height of his musical achievement. It enriches the picture we had already gained of the composer through his original and important achievements and is another confirmation of the fact that twelve-tone compositions are capable of the greatest variety of expression.

'The lyrical passages ... are some of the most beautiful things Berg ever wrote. They belong for the most part to the character of Alwa, the contemplative artist who represents the opposite pole to the impulsive Lulu. Not less effective is the drawing of the other characters. The music surrounds every figure with a special atmosphere, showing up the features and giving weight to their miming and gestures. The comic element, represented by Schigolch and the Athlete, is also depicted with incisive humour. Yet the whole is en-

---

[1] Act III cannot yet be performed in anything like the form Berg planned, although various attempts have been made to patch up some approximation using the published music and the text of the published libretto.

veloped in sound of a unique character. And in spite of occasional powerful *crescendos*, the orchestration of *Lulu* shows a preference for the delicate, gracious colours befitting the heroine.'   H.

PAUL HINDEMITH
(1895–1963)
CARDILLAC

OPERA in three acts by Paul Hindemith, libretto by Ferdinand Lion, from E. T. A. Hoffmann's story *Das Fräulein von Scuderi*. Première in Dresden, November 9, 1926, with Robert Burg, Claire Born, Grete Merrem, Max Hirzel, Ludwig Eybisch, Adolph Schoepfin, Paul Schöffler, conductor Fritz Busch. First performed in Vienna, 1927, with Jerger, Stünzner, Achsel, Hofer, Maikl, conductor Heger; Prague, 1927; Berlin, 1928, with Krenn, Hüni-Mihacsek, de Strozzi, Fidesser, conductor Klemperer; London, 1936, Broadcasting House (concert, in English) with Arthur Fear, Noel Eadie, Miriam Licette, Frank Mullings, John McKenna, conductor Clarence Raybould; Venice, 1948, conductor Sanzogno. New Version: Zürich, 1952, with Herbert Brauer, Hillebrecht, Müller-Bütow, Lechleitner, Lichtegg, conductor Reinshagen; during 1953–4 at Frankfurt, with Willi Wolff, Schlemm, producer Rennert, conductor Solti; Hanover; Nuremberg; in 1961 in Hamburg, with Fliether, conductor Ludwig. Revived (in original version): Wuppertal, 1960, producer Reinhardt, conductor Ratjen (and at Holland Festival); Vienna, 1964, with Wiener, Lipp, Seefried, Nocker, Stolze, conductor Ludwig; la Scala, Milan, 1964, with Ganzarolli, Muszely, Laszlo, Merighi, Aragall, producer Kašlik, conductor Sanzogno; Munich, 1965, with Fischer-Dieskau, Kirschstein, Töpper (as the Lady), Paskuda, Holm, conductor Keilberth; Santa Fe, 1967, with Reardon, conductor Craft (the outdoor opera house was burned out following the first night); London, New Opera Company, 1970, with John Cameron, Pashley, Elizabeth Robson, Irons, Wakefield.

CHARACTERS
The Goldsmith Cardillac . . . . Baritone
His Daughter . . . . Soprano
The Lady . . . . Soprano

The Officer . . . . Tenor
The Cavalier . . . . Tenor
The Gold merchant. . . . . Bass
The Officer of Police . . . . High Bass
The King; Knights and Ladies of the Court; the Police;
the Crowd
Time: The Seventeenth Century   *Place:* Paris

Cardillac was Hindemith's fifth opera, his first of full
length, and written after the one-acters *Mörder, Hoffnung der
Frauen* (to libretto by the painter Kokoschka), *Das Nusch
Nuschi* (like its predecessor, given by Fritz Busch in Dresden
in 1921), *Sancta Susanna* (rejected as obscene by Stuttgart
but given in Frankfurt in 1922) and the Christmas fairy-tale,
Tuttifäntchen. It concerns itself with the relationship between the artist and society, a theme stated here in more
extreme form than in the composer's later operas *Mathis der
Maler* (about the painter Grünewald) and *Die Harmonie der
Welt* (about the astronomer Kepler).
As befits a period of Hindemith's creative life which was
combative and progressivist, the original score of *Cardillac*, if
cool, is muscular and purposeful, and its energy suits a story
which shows the artist insisting on his prerogatives rather
than the philosophical *Mathis* setting the world more
patiently to rights. The music is scored for inflated chamber
orchestra (eighteen strings are specified) and is in style
contrapuntal and linear, in form baroque—Hindemith uses
Aria, Duet, Fugato, Passacaglia, etc., and the tension of the
opera comes less from the drama and inherent moments of
pathos than from the musical impetus of taut, closed forms.
Cardillac expresses a reaction against the German tradition
of through-composed dramatic music, as epitomized by
Wagner and carried on during Hindemith's youth by Strauss.
The more astonishing is it that the composer saw fit in 1952,
nearly a generation after the opera's first performance, to
revise it extensively.[1] An act is added (consisting musically of
Lully's opera *Phaeton*, with the Lady of Act I transformed
into a leading singer), a new and milder text by the composer
himself is substituted for Ferdinand Lion's original adaptation of E. T. A. Hoffmann, there are some cuts and some new

[1] One must not forget that Hindemith had already produced, many
years apart, two quite different versions of *Das Marienleben*, a song
cycle to words by Rainer Maria Rilke.

music, but basically the orchestral part is retained with a new vocal line above it setting new words. As *The Times* critic, William Mann, wrote at the time of the first British performance (of version I): 'This must seem a monumental gesture of artistic insensibility. Why did Hindemith attempt it? I believe he wanted to match his technical mastery against that of Bach, who often used earlier music of his own for quite different purposes. Hindemith believed, I surmise, that good music would sound equally apt whatever dramatic goings-on it accompanied. He was wrong.'

Hindemith's revised version of the opera had its première in Zürich and was generally looked upon as watered-down, even sentimentalised, in comparison with the original. The composer's embargo on the 1926 version was not generally lifted until his death in 1963.

Act I.   An energy-laden prelude takes us into the first scene, a street in the city onto which lead streets from all sides. The Paris mob is in the grip of panic, as we hear when the curtain goes up. A series of murders has been committed and their mysterious perpetrator cannot be found. The mob is looking for a victim to assuage its fear and seizes on one suspect after another, threatening to come to blows within itself, until interrupted by a posse of the King's Guard. Its officer, in an extended declamatory passage (sung at the first performance by the young Paul Schöffler) announces the King's edict: that the murderer shall be slowly burnt alive. The crowd seems satisfied, even appeased at this announcement and starts to disperse, as it goes making way with some reverence for a lone figure, who salutes them and leaves the square. (Cardillac does not sing at this first appearance.)

A Lady asks the Cavalier who it is that is treated with such unusual respect. He explains that it is the goldsmith Cardillac, an artist of unsurpassed skill, whose creations moreover are intimately connected with the recent series of murders; each of the victims is known to have bought an example of Cardillac's work shortly before death. As the Cavalier grows more pressing, the Lady has an idea: she will be his that very night if he bring her the finest piece to be found in Cardillac's workshop! She leaves and the Cavalier's ardent reaction finds expression in an aria, contrasting the possibility of a night of love with a night of death, one of which he feels must within hours be his reward.

The curtain falls quickly and we are taken into the second

scene in an interlude, during whose course the atmosphere of action is exchanged for the languor of the bedchamber. The mood is sustained as the Lady sings a nocturne of considerable lyrical appeal, surrendering sensuously to sleep at the prospect of the arrival of her lover and the great gift he will bring her. There follows a scene which quickly became notorious, a pantomime to the accompaniment of a duet started by two solo flutes. The Cavalier arrives, bringing with him a golden belt of the greatest splendour. The Lady wakes, seems at first about to express surprise at the intrusion but then succumbs to the beauty of Cardillac's creation and the proximity of her lover. Before they can consummate their desire, at the duet's climax (if the word can be used in connection with so cool a structure) a dark figure appears cloaked and masked in the room, stabs the Knight to death and disappears, taking the Belt with him—the action takes place in a moment of complete silence before the curtain music dashes to a conclusion.

Act II takes us to Cardillac's workshop, with the Master in full activity. To the cool, impersonal sound of a tenor saxophone, Cardillac sings an arioso, with gold as his subject ('Mag Sonne leuchten!': 'Let sunlight enter'). A gold merchant, plainly nervous at the prospect of the interview, brings him gold, which he rejects as impure. The gold merchant already suspects that it is more than coincidence that the murder victims have all been customers of Cardillac's. He believes that the great artist's creations possess a beauty beyond the deserts of men, and must be thought of as causes of the crimes rather than their innocent accompaniment. Cardillac's firm 'Was ich erschuf, ist mein' ('What I create is mine') causes the gold merchant to leave the shop, muttering that he will keep a watch on the goldsmith. Cardillac leaves his daughter in charge and goes off with the merchant.

In an aria, cast in the form of a *concerto grosso* movement with violin, oboe and horn *concertante*, the daughter waits in a mood of some trepidation for her lover. He is a young Officer (in Hindemith's 1952 revision, as in Hoffmann's original story, Cardillac's apprentice), and their duet together reveals her as divided between her love for him and their plan to elope, and her duty towards her father.

Cardillac returns, this time with gold that he has passed as unalloyed. His daughter chides him for caressing the metal

with an affection he never shows her, then tells him she is in
love—but that she will nevertheless not leave him! To the
first part of her announcement, Cardillac blandly asserts that
he noticed a change in her weeks ago, but to the second he
retorts that he is no old man but able to renew his hold on
life with each new creation. He will give her to her lover.
Their scene ends with a slow fugato duet, after which the
daughter goes inside.

In a curious episode, Cardillac observes the King and his
Court outside, shows the monarch (who remains silent
throughout) his finest works, and ends by contriving to
rebuff the King when he wishes to buy, and admitting when
he is alone, 'I should have had to murder him! He would have
had to die!' The golden belt, which the Cavalier bought, is
now restored to its place in the collection, to its creator's
unconcealed glee. He notices a spot of blood on the belt and
cleans it with loving care.

Into the shop comes the Officer, announcing that he must
have the most beautiful of all Cardillac's creations. He asks
for his daughter's hand in marriage, much to Cardillac's relief,
shows surprise at the ease with which his request is granted,
then in Cardillac's rejoinder receives a clue to the latter's
obsession: 'Could I ever love what is not entirely mine?' The
Officer tries to buy the golden chain, Cardillac attempts to
dissuade him, but the purchase is completed. The curtain falls
after an aria (saxophone *obbligato* again) in which Cardillac
appears at first to be contemplating the replacement of the
chain he has just sold, only, by its end, to have donned the
black coat and mask in pursuit of his obsession.

Act III.   A street in front of a tavern. The gaiety of
roisterers at night is expressed in the orchestra (including
instruments behind the scenes), and the Officer strolls by
singing an arietta as he goes and wearing the chain round his
neck. Observed by the gold merchant, Cardillac is following
him. He attacks and slightly wounds the Officer, is recognised
and bidden make good his escape, while the gold merchant
raises the alarm at the top of his voice. Guards and members
of the crowd drag in Cardillac, but the Officer says this was
not his assailant and points to the gold merchant as possibly
the criminal. All express various shades of amazement in an
extended and full-blooded quartet in which the original three
voices are joined by that of Cardillac's daughter. There is a
duet between the daughter and her lover in which the former

calls down damnation on the assailant's head only to be rebuked by the Officer, and the crowd celebrates Cardillac's vindication.

In the last section of the opera (a *Passacaglia*), Cardillac has a final confrontation with the mob and ultimately with his conscience. The gold merchant is at most an accomplice, he asserts; he himself understands the workings of the mind of such a criminal, has even been watching him, but he will never give him away. The crowd turns against Cardillac, threatening to destroy his workshop and all it contains if he will not reveal the murderer's identity. To save his works, he cries out that he himself is the murderer, and the mob beats him to death as the Officer fights his way through to put a stop to the riot. He it was against whom Cardillac raised his dagger that very evening; why does the mob set itself up as Cardillac's judge? He is no murderer but the victim of a sacred madness. As his daughter and her lover raise Cardillac's body, a flicker of life runs through him and, catching sight of the chain—*his* chain—with a last despairing effort he raises his head to kiss it, then falls back dead.

The opera finishes with a beautiful threnody over the dead Cardillac, with the high voices of the daughter and the Officer raised above those of the crowd ('Nacht des Todes ... Ein Held starb': 'Night of death ... a hero died'). H.

MATHIS DER MALER
Mathias the Painter

Opera in seven scenes by Paul Hindemith; text by the composer. Première, May 28, 1938, Zürich Stadttheater, with Hellwig, Funk, Stig, Baxevanos, Mossbacher, Honisch, Rothmüller, Emmerich, conductor Denzler. First performed Amsterdam, 1939; London, Queen's Hall (concert version), 1939, with Stiles-Allen, Eadie, Noble, Fullard, Parry Jones, Francis Russell, conductor Raybould; Stuttgart (first performance in Germany), 1946, with Wissmann, Stoll, Czubok, Windgassen, von Rohr, conductor Leitner; Munich, 1948, with Schech, Sommerschuh, Reinmar, Klarwein, Kusche, Kuen, Dalberg, Fehenberger, conductor Solti; Berlin Staatsoper, 1948, with Klein, Beilke, Gonszar, Witte, conductor Schüler; Rome, 1951, by company from Stuttgart; Hamburg, 1952, with Wasserthal, Rothenberger, Ahlersmeyer, Melchert, Theo Herrmann, Bensing, conductor Ludwig; Edinburgh Festival, 1952, by Hamburg ensemble (producer Rennert); Boston University, 1956, in English; 1967 in Montreal and at

Metropolitan, New York, with Tarres, Mathis, Hubert Hoffmann, Cassilly, conductor Schmidt-Isserstedt.

CHARACTERS

Cardinal Albrecht von Brandenburg, *Archbishop of Mainz* .... Tenor
Mathis, *painter in his employment* .... Baritone
Lorenz von Pommersfelden, *Dean of Mainz* ...... Bass
Wolfgang Capito, *the Cardinal's counsellor* ...... Tenor
Riedinger, *a rich citizen of Mainz: a Lutheran* .... Bass
Hans Schwalb, *leader of the peasants' army* ..... Tenor
Truchsess von Waldburg, *leader of the Confederate army* .... Bass
Sylvester von Schaumberg, *one of his officers* ... Tenor
Graf von Helfenstein .... Silent
Gräfin von Helfenstein, *his wife* .... Contralto
Ursula, *Riedinger's daughter* .... Soprano
Regina, *Schwalb's daughter* .... Soprano

Time: The Peasants' War, about 1525   *Place:* In and near Mainz

Hindemith was a native of Mainz, and for his fifth opera he took as his central figure the early sixteenth-century painter, Mathias Grünewald, who spent much of his life in the service of the Archbishop of Mainz, and who is famous for the great altar-piece of Isenheim. He worked on the opera during the early period of the Nazi regime in Germany, and it is not hard to trace a direct relationship between the political circumstances of Germany at that time and the happenings of the opera, whose philosophical argument had to Hindemith as to Mathis a significance that was practical as well as theoretical.

The story takes place against a background of the Reformation and of the Peasants' War in Germany. It is divided into seven scenes, which are not continuous, and it is customary to have an interval after the fourth scene, by which time the opera has already lasted nearer two hours than one.

The prelude to the opera bears the sub-title of 'Engelkonzert' (Concert of Angels) and is inspired by part of the Isenheim polyptych. It is well known in the concert hall from its position as the first movement of the symphony Hindemith arranged from the music of his opera, and its contrapuntal character is typical of the composer's method in this opera as in so many of his other works.

Scene i takes place in the courtyard of St. Anthony's monastery at Mainz, where Mathis is painting a fresco. The seriousness of purpose which distinguishes the opera is immediately shown in Mathis's introspective monologue, in which his rejoicing at the coming of spring cannot be separated from his doubts as to whether he is worthily fulfilling his mission as a painter. His thoughts are interrupted by the breathless arrival of Schwalb and his daughter Regina, who are seeking sanctuary from the pursuing troops of the Fürstenbund. Mathis extends his help to them, and takes pity on Regina, who, in the midst of her misery, sings a sad little folk-song. Mathis gives her a ribbon with which she binds her hair, but their conversation is interrupted by the return of Schwalb, refreshed and with his wounds bound up. He expresses astonishment that Mathis is content to occupy himself with painting instead of taking part in the struggle for freedom. The painter appears convinced by his argument, and their voices join in an expression of conviction in the importance of the peasants' cause.

Regina rushes in to warn her father that their pursuers are in sight, and Mathis gives them his horse, telling Schwalb that he can in future count on his help. The scene ends after Mathis has admitted to Sylvester that he has helped the rebel leader to escape, and has claimed his right to answer for his actions to no one but the Cardinal.

Scene ii.   The hall in the Martinsburg, the Archbishop's palace in Mainz. The rival factions of Papists and Lutherans dispute while waiting for the arrival of the Archbishop. Pommersfelden stands with the Papists, Capito with the Lutherans, amongst whom can be seen Riedinger and his daughter, Ursula. Peace comes momentarily with the Archbishop's entrance, and all leave the hall except Pommersfelden, Capito, Riedinger and his daughter. Mathis comes in after his year of absence to be greeted with an expansive phrase from Ursula, who is in love with him. A quartet ensues in which Mathis and Ursula talk of their pleasure in seeing each other again, while the Cardinal promises Riedinger that the order to burn Lutheran books shall not be executed in Mainz. Pommersfelden objects that the order is from Rome itself, and the Cardinal reluctantly agrees that it must be carried out.

There is some dispute about the suitability or otherwise of Mathis's representation of the saints in his pictures, which turns before long to a discussion of the empty state of the Cardinal's treasury. Sylvester enters and accuses Mathis before the Cardinal of having helped Schwalb's escape. Mathis admits the accusation but pleads strongly for the peasants' cause, and begs the Cardinal not to furnish the Fürstenbund with the money they have just asked for, but instead to support the juster cause of the rebels; in return, he will serve his patron without payment for the rest of his life. The Cardinal replies that his official conduct is bound by treaties; only where art is concerned has he a free hand. Let Mathis not interfere with what he does not understand. Mathis defies his patron and his prince, and the differing points of view of the Cardinal, Mathis, Pommersfelden, Capito, and the warlike Sylvester are combined in a noble quintet. The scene ends with Mathis receiving permission to withdraw from the Cardinal's service.

Scene iii.   A room in Riedinger's house; in the background can be seen the preparations for the public burning of the Lutheran books. Riedinger and his friends attempt to hide their treasured possessions, but soldiers assisted by Capito carry them off. Capito appeases the wrath of the Lutherans by showing them a letter purporting to have come from Luther to the Cardinal in which he urges him strongly to give a lead to the clergy by renouncing his celibacy. Capito's scheme is to persuade the Cardinal, who is in urgent need of money, to make a rich marriage—and with whom more suitable than Riedinger's daughter, Ursula, who at that moment comes into the room. Riedinger himself hints at what is planned for her before he leaves Ursula, to join his fellow-Lutherans as their books are burnt in the market-place, a scene that is suggested by the chorus in the background.

Mathis appears to bid Ursula farewell. She welcomes him exultantly, and tells him how much she has missed him during his year of leave from the Cardinal's service. He answers that his spirit is sick within him and he must leave her and his work to join in the struggle for freedom; only through contact with misery can he recover his own soul. They protest their undying love for each other, but their duet ends with the cry: 'The love, the unity in which we have lived, gives way to suffering.' Mathis embraces Ursula and goes out.

When Riedinger asks her how she can preserve her calm

during the calamity which has befallen those who share her religious beliefs, Ursula says she has made up her mind to accept the sacrifice demanded of her by her faith. Riedinger rejoices and proclaims that the fire lit by their enemies has signalled the beginning of a new period of determination which shall end in victory.

Scene iv. The rebellious peasants have seized a war-ravaged village and are terrorising the local nobility. They drag in Count Helfenstein and his wife, and kill the Count almost before her eyes. Mathis protests against this betrayal of the principles for which they are fighting, and tries to defend the Countess from their molestations, but he is knocked down. Only the advent of Schwalb saves him from further injury. The peasants' leader calls them all to arms to fight the Fürstenbund army, which is even now entering the village. But they are already downhearted at the prospect of meeting trained troops, and soon come back in disorder. Schwalb himself is trapped and falls before the lances of his enemies, who come through the village to the sound of a march. Mathis only escapes with his life through the Countess's intervention, and he comes to understand his own complete failure as a man of action; his lofty ambitions, his efforts to better the lot of the peasants, have ended in this. He sees Regina, overcome with horror at her father's death, and takes her away with him to look for shelter.

Act II, scene v. The Cardinal's study in the Martinsburg in Mainz. Capito has been trying to persuade the Cardinal to renounce his oath of celibacy and to adopt the course Luther advocates, and marry. His most cogent argument is that a rich wife would solve the Cardinal's very considerable financial difficulties; but Albrecht resents Capito's attempt to interfere with his conscience, and to treat him as if he were not capable of making up his own mind. Capito tries flattery, and then introduces Ursula as the prospective bride. The Cardinal is astonished to see her. In music of ever-increasing fervour she explains to him that only her abiding faith in Lutheranism would have driven her to the position in which she now finds herself. Love has grown cold within her, but she is willing to submit to marriage for the sake of the cause she loves.

The Cardinal calls Capito and Riedinger into the room and tells them that he is convinced by Ursula's show of faith: her example has shown him that he too must stand by what he has been taught. He dismisses Capito from his post as adviser, saying he will lead a simpler life in the future; and he gives permission to the Lutherans to declare themselves openly. There is an impressive quartet between the Cardinal, Ursula, Capito, and Riedinger, and at its end Ursula asks the Cardinal to bless her before she goes out again into the world. He consents to do this, and Ursula departs, leaving behind her a man whom she has ennobled by teaching him at one and the same time the meaning of Faith and of Tolerance.

Scene vi.   In the Odenwald, Mathis and Regina pause during their flight. Regina says she still dreams she is pursued by the image of her dead father. Mathis tries to calm her by describing to her his vision of the Concert of Angels, accompanied in the orchestra by the music we originally heard in the prelude. Together they sing the chorale ('Es sungen drei Engel'), also heard in the prelude, until Regina falls asleep and Mathis despairingly contrasts his present spiritual misery with the comparative state of grace in which he painted the picture he has just described.

In the manner of the Temptation of St. Anthony, Mathis is tempted by Luxury, wearing the face of the Countess; by wealth (Pommersfelden); a beggar, a courtesan, and a martyr (Ursula); scholarship (Capito); and a knight in shining armour (Schwalb). They enter successively, Mathis answers each in turn, and the music works up to a climax when the demons appear to torment the Saint. There is a great ensemble, at whose end the Cardinal, in the guise of St. Paul, comes to comfort and advise St. Anthony (part of the Isenheim altar depicts the Conversation between St. Paul and St. Anthony). St. Anthony asks what he has done that he should have reached his present state of uncertainty. St. Paul tells him that he has been untrue to himself. In throwing in his lot with the people, he has denied the gifts he had from God, and has in fact withdrawn from the people he tried to help. Let him return to his art, denying himself but dedicating his work to God. In so doing he will become part of the people. The tree knows nothing of its fruits. At the end of the vision, in which the composer speaks his mind on the subject of the artist, the two voices join together in a paean of praise, ending with a magnificent 'Alleluia'.

It is the crucial scene of the opera (Hindemith has used the themes from it as a basis for the last movement of his Symphony), and it was presumably from the Temptation section of the Isenheim altar and the Conversation of St. Anthony and St. Paul that Hindemith initially drew inspiration for his theme and his central figure.

Scene vii.   Mathis's studio in Mainz. Mathis is lying asleep, exhausted with his work, and Ursula watches alone by the side of the dying Regina. Ursula reflects on the meaning of their lives, and on Mathis's unprecedented inspiration since his return to Mainz and to art. Regina wakes and raves about the memory of her dead father, whose face she can see in Mathis's painting of the Crucifixion. She asks Ursula to give Mathis the ribbon which she originally received from him at their first meeting, and Ursula recognises it as one she herself had given Mathis. Regina sings a couple of sentences of the chorale, before dying with Mathis by her side.

The interlude, marked 'Very slowly', is entitled 'Entombment', and serves as the slow movement of the symphony. At its end, the curtain rises to show the studio empty except for a table, on which lie several objects. The Cardinal comes to say farewell to Mathis, embracing him for the last time. Mathis himself takes a case and puts away materially and symbolically the things which have represented the main efforts of his life. It is in this spirit of utter humility that the opera ends.

Hindemith's concentration on the issues at stake has never blinded him to the necessity for putting them forward dramatically within the framework he has chosen; he makes no concessions, but he works in terms of opera as a medium. One may feel that the text is long, that Hindemith cannot get rid of his tendency to settle down to a busy contrapuntal style the moment he is at a loss for an idea, but no listener who is seriously interested in opera can come away from a performance of the work without having been impressed by Hindemith's lofty conception of the artist's responsibility, and his equally lofty view of what opera can and must accomplish. Intense seriousness of purpose does not by itself secure artistic results, but integrity shines through *Mathis*, and the opera is perhaps strongest in the composer's conviction in his theme and its expression.   H.

KURT WEILL

(1900–1950)

AUFSTIEG UND FALL DER STADT MAHAGONNY

Rise and Fall of the City of Mahagonny

OPERA in three acts by Kurt Weill; libretto by Bertolt Brecht. Première, Leipzig, March 9, 1930, with Mali Trummer, Marga Dannenberg, Paul Beinert, conductor Gustav Brecher, producer Walter Brügmann, designer Casper Neher. First produced Berlin, 1931, with Lotte Lenya, Trude Hesterberg, Harold Paulsen, conductor Alexander von Zemlinsky, producer Ernst Anfricht, after which it was banned in Germany under the Nazis. A Paris production of the *Songspiel* was agreed to by Weill in 1932, and this version was heard in Venice, 1949, with Hilde Gueden; Cologne, 1952; and on the Turin Radio, 1953. First post-war stage performances (in a garbled version) Darmstadt, 1957, and Kiel, 1961. Operatic (Leipzig) version, Heidelberg, 1962; Hamburg, 1962, with Helga Pilarczyk, Gisela Litz, Helmut Melchert, conductor Janos Kulka; London, Sadler's Wells, 1963, with April Cantelo, Patricia Bartlett, Ronald Dowd, conductor Colin Davis.

CHARACTERS

Leokadja Begbick .... Contralto
Fatty, *the book-keeper* .... Tenor
Trinity Moses .... Baritone
Jenny .... Soprano
Jim Mahoney .... Tenor
Jake Schmidt .... Tenor
Alaska Wolf Joe .... Bass
Pennybank Bill .... Baritone
Toby Higgins .... Tenor (can be taken by
the singer of Jake)
Six Women of Mahagonny; the Men of Mahagonny

Brecht's first collaboration with Kurt Weill, a pupil of

Busoni's,[1] was in 1927, when at Baden-Baden a *Songspiel Kleine Mahagonny*, was given on July 17 in the same programme as short operas by Milhaud, Toch and Hindemith. This work consisted of five songs of Brecht's set to music by Weill (it is interesting to note that Brecht himself had earlier set them to music) and it was not until after their collaboration on *Die Dreigroschenoper* (a play with music, 1928), *Der Lindberghflug* (a cantata, 1928) and *Happy End* (a play with music, 1929), that they were able to finish the full length opera which they had straightaway started to develop from the material of the *Songspiel*. Later collaboration was on *Der Jasager* (a children's opera, 1930), *Mann ist Mann* (a play with songs, 1931) and *Die sieben Todsünden* (*The Seven Deadly Sins*: a ballet-opera, 1933).

Whatever else it may be, *The Rise and Fall of the City of Mahagonny* is an opera, written for opera singers (it was not until the Berlin production that Lotte Lenja took over the role of Jenny), and designed in what can only be described as the operatic convention, that is to say with the characters singing not just songs but frequently when in real life they would speak. Brecht on the one hand had the strongest antipathy to what he described as 'culinary' opera—opera with 'a hedonistic approach'—and on the other believed that the theatrical art of the future would make frequent use of music, not least as a means of halting the action and driving home a message; music to his way of thinking even in an opera would be at the service of the dramatist. Most theoreticians believe that in opera, on the contrary, whatever the *content* of the piece, the *form* is dictated by music. Here comes a fundamental clash. After his collaboration with Weill came to an end, Brecht went on to write a series of committed plays (his study of Marx began only in 1927) and to found in East Berlin after the war one of the great theatrical companies of our time. Weill in contrast, after their last and in some ways most attractive work *The Seven Deadly Sins*, never again found a librettist to inspire him to that unique mixture of rag-time, operetta, pop and counterpoint that was all his own and has come, in the minds of most listeners, to be identified in the first place with the singing of

[1] Busoni at one time accused Weill (before the collaboration with Brecht, by which time Busoni was dead) of attempting to become a 'poor man's Verdi'.

his wife Lotte Lenja and in the second with the Berlin of the Weimar Republic.

Mahagonny itself is a baffling work, put forward by some as a kind of masterpiece—but a masterpiece to which, according to them, no kind of justice seems ever to be done in performance—an anti-capitalist satire rejected by official Marxism, whose book by the didactic prophet of the modern theatre seems paradoxically to have dated far more quickly than the music of a composer whom we associate exclusively with a particular period and place. Nevertheless, the première in Leipzig[1] provoked demonstrations by the Nazis, who were later to banish composer and author and ban their works, and every subsequent revival has been attended by controversy, the Hamburg production scheduled for autumn 1961 being postponed until the following year because it was felt unwise to risk such a work in the weeks following the building of the Berlin wall. It remained for Lotte Lenja, the composer's widow, in her notes on the complete recording in which she sang Jenny, to remind readers that the opera, which is now solemnly worked over by the critics, had once—for her and Brecht and Weill—been such fun to create.

As the music[2] dashes energetically into action, a much battered truck comes to stop in a desolate part of America, and from it emerge Leokadja Begbick, Trinity Moses and Fatty the book-keeper, all on the run from the police. If they can't go any further, why not stay here and found a new city, where no one has to work and where there are prize fights every third day—so explains Leokadja in an extended *arioso* ('Sie soll sein wie ein Netz'—it is to be like a net, which is put out to catch edible birds).

And so the city was founded and called Mahagonny, and the first sharks moved in. Enter Jenny, the mulatto from Cuba, and six other girls, who sit on their suitcases and introduce themselves in the famous *Alabama-song*, written originally in Brecht's peculiar pidgin-English[3] and set to one of Weill's most haunting tunes, Ex. 1:

[1] Klemperer refused to do it at the Kroll Oper in Berlin, and years later (in *Conversations with Klemperer*, edited by Peter Heyworth) referred to it as a 'complete failure'.

[2] For a small orchestra with emphasis on saxophone, banjo, bass guitar, piano, zither, accordion.

[3] Brecht thought at one time that a form of pidgin-English would be the world's first universal language!

Moderato assai (♩=69)

Jenny: Oh! Moon_____ _____ of A - la - ba - - ma we now _____ must say good - bye.

The news of the founding of a city of pleasure reaches the big cities, where the inhabitants hymn their misery while Fatty and Moses cry the praises of Mahagonny. In the next few days, all the malcontents of the continent move to Mahagonny, notably the lumberjacks Jim, Jake, Bill and Joe, who sing a quick fox-trot in anticipation of the pleasures to come (including a parodistic phrase from the Bridesmaids' Chorus from *Freischütz*).

The hero of the story is Jim Mahoney, and he and the others are greeted by Mrs. Begbick, Trinity Moses losing no time in proffering pictures of the available girls from whom they may care to choose. Jenny and the six girls are produced, and Jake offers $30 for Jenny, who protests in a song: 'Ach, bedenken Sie, Herr Jakob Schmidt'—just think how little you get for $30. Jim says perhaps he'll take her, and when the others have gone, he and Jenny exchange to a wistful tune such vital information as whether Jenny shall comb her hair forward or back, shall or shan't wear underwear under her skirt.

Disillusion has set in and, says Mrs. Begbick, people are starting to leave town. Fatty counters with the news that the police are catching up with Begbick. Jim comes in, planning to leave because he has just seen a notice 'Forbidden'! Jake, Bill and Joe sing the praises of the city with its everlasting freedom, but Jim's blues come straight from the purposelessness of it all.

In front of the inn, which is known as 'Nothing barred', the men are sitting drinking and listening to the strains of 'The Maiden's Prayer'—eternal art, thinks Jake. Jim's mock ballad of the sufferings he underwent in Alaska in order eventually to reach a haven of rest complains of the inadequacy of what he has found, and it takes a concerted effort to prevent him carving up everything in sight with his famous knife.

The loudspeaker announces a 'typhoon', and a *fugato* introduces an impressive set piece of lamentation.

The next scene is called 'The Night of the Hurricane'. The men sing determinedly in chorus (echoes of the chorale from *Die Zauberflöte*), Jake laments and Jenny sadly repeats the Alabama-song. Jim mockingly expounds his philosophy: what sort of horror is a hurricane when compared to man? The long scena, in whose course we learn that the hurricane is heading straight for Mahagonny and that the police who were pursuing

Mrs. Begbick have been killed, reaches its climax with Jim leading what is perhaps the best (as well as the best-known) of the songs: 'Denn wie man sich bettet, so liegt man' (As you make your bed, you must lie there) Ex. 2:

As the curtain falls, there can be seen a map with an arrow moving slowly across it towards Mahagonny.

Act II. Again the map, with the arrow still moving towards Mahagonny and successive radio announcements indicating the imminence of danger, until 'the hurricane has been diverted past Mahagonny and continues on its way'! The citizens rejoice; if they have learnt anything, it is to enjoy what luck has unexpectedly sent them. From now on the motto is 'nothing barred'. First, gluttony. To a slow parodistic waltz (zither and accordion), Jake sits down to dine and eats three entire calves, expiring as he asks for more.

Next, love. In the room at the back can be seen a girl and a man with Mrs. Begbick between them. She admonishes the man to spit out his gum, wash his hands and behave decently.

The lights go out, the chorus sings the Mandalay-song and urges him to get on with it, but when the lights go up, Jenny and Jim are seen sitting a little way apart, he smoking, she making up. They sing tenderly about two cranes flying in the sky, a duet in which Brecht's lyrical invention is matched by Weill's to form one of the most purely 'operatic' numbers in the whole score. It was placed here in the published score apparently at the behest of Weill's publishers, though intended by author and composer for the third act.

Next, prize fights. Trinity Moses and Alaska Wolf Joe are matched to the astonishment of Fatty and the other men, who predict a walk-over for Trinity Moses. Jim and Joe rather sentimentally remember the seven winters they spent together in Alaska, and Jim puts his money on Joe, who duly fulfils expectations and is knocked out. 'Dead!' says the referee. The crowd laughs, and the men come forward with a reminder that here nothing's barred, that we may now expect the boozing as well.

Jim, Bill and Jenny are playing billiards, and Jim invites everyone to drink with him. Jim finds he has run out of money and asks Jenny to help him. They make a boat out of the billiard table, and Jim, Bill and Jenny climb on it, until Jim announces that they have arrived back in Alaska. Trinity Moses and the widow Begbick demand payment, but Jim has nothing left and everyone except Bill and Jenny move away from him, and even they refuse to come to his financial rescue. As Jim, who has committed the ultimate capitalist crime of running out of money, is bound and led away, Jenny repeats, 'Denn wie man sich bettet, so liegt man.' The act ends with Jim alone in the forest, tied by one foot to a tree and longing in an impressive *scena* (which rises to a 'culinary' top C) for the night to continue and for the day never to arrive.

Act III. Jim is to be tried in what passes for a Court of Justice in Mahagonny—the widow Begbick sits as judge, Fatty is defence counsel and Trinity Moses prosecutes. One Toby Higgins is being tried for murder, and, as Trinity Moses waxes eloquent on the depravity of the crime, the accused can be seen bargaining in mime with the judge. Apparently he offers a big enough bribe because defending counsel is allowed to ask for the injured party to be produced, and nobody coming forward the case goes by default.

It is Jim's turn and he asks his friend Bill to let him have
$100 so that his case can be conducted decently. Again they
remember their seven winters together in Alaska, but
sentiment cannot interfere with financial considerations as
far as Bill is concerned and he refuses the loan. As the
prosecution starts its case, Begbick again bargains, but Jim is
unable to respond and the prosecution gets down to details.
Jim is accused of the seduction of Jenny, of singing
cheerfully during the approach of the 'typhoon', of
corrupting the entire city, of sending his friend to certain
death in a prize fight merely to win his bet, of not being able
to pay for the whisky which he drank and the curtain rod he
broke. Each time the question is, 'Who is the injured party?'

The men demand Jim's acquittal on the grounds that his
behaviour during the typhoon injured nobody, that it
certainly wasn't he who killed Alaska Wolf Joe, but as he is
undoubtedly guilty of the last charge, he is sentenced on all
five, and the penalty becomes increasingly stiff, ending with
death for the failure to pay for the whisky. The verdict is
universally applauded.

People are sitting around in a bar reading a newspaper and
displaying the disillusion which has once again overtaken
Mahagonny. Jointly they long for a change:

> 'Let's go, let's go to Benares,
> to Benares where the sun is shining'.

The loudspeaker announces the impending execution of
Jim Mahoney and suggests that, though many will dislike
seeing the spectacle, most of the spectators in the audience
would be no more willing than have been the inhabitants of
Mahagonny to stump up money for him. A tender farewell
between Jenny and Jim, who consigns her to his best friend
Bill, precedes his walk to the place of execution. Jim in
rather lugubrious music proclaims that he has no regrets, that
his philosophy is unchanged and that life is meant to be
drained in gigantic draughts. Jim is seated on the electric
chair but asks whether they do not know that there is a God.
During his execution the others act out the coming of God to
Mahagonny, Trinity Moses taking the chief role.

The loudspeaker announces that giant processions took
place in protest against the tremendously high cost of living,
and that these heralded the end of the 'City of Nets'. During
the march-finale which is dominated by 'Denn wie man sich

bettet, so liegt man' and the Alabama-song, the processions appear, each of them carrying an appropriate banner, and the opera ends with the line 'Können uns und euch und niemand helfen!' (We can't help ourselves or you or anyone).   H.

GOTTFRIED von EINEM
(b. 1918)

DANTONS TOD
The Death of Danton

OPERA in two parts by Gottfried von Einem; text by the composer and Boris Blacher after Büchner's drama of the same name (1835). First produced at the Salzburg Festival, August 6, 1947, with Maria Cebotari, Julius Patzak, Paul Schoeffler, conductor Ferenc Fricsay. Subsequently produced in Vienna, Hamburg, Berlin and Brussels. Revived Munich, 1956, with Gerda Sommerschuh, Richard Holm, Frans Andersson, conductor Lovro von Matacic; New York City Opera, 1966 (in English), with Sylvia Grant, William Dupree, John Reardon, conductor Ernst Märzendorfer; Berlin, 1967, with Annabelle Bernard, Loren Driscoll, Dietrich Fischer-Dieskau, conductor Heinrich Hollreiser; Vienna, 1967, with Lisa Della Casa, William Blankenship, Eberhard Wächter, conductor Josef Krips; Rome, 1970, with Maria Chiara, Sergio Tedesco, Mario Basiola (jr.), conductor Bruno Bartoletti.

CHARACTERS

Georges Danton ⎫   ⎧Baritone
Camille Desmoulins ⎬ *Deputies* . . . .⎨ Tenor
Hérault de Séchelles ⎭   ⎩ Tenor
Robespierre . . . . Tenor
Saint-Just . . . . Bass
Herrmann, *President of the Revolutionary*
   Tribunal . . . . Baritone
Simon, *a prompter* . . . . Buffo-bass
A Young Man . . . . Tenor
First Executioner . . . . Tenor
Second Executioner . . . . Tenor
Julie, *Danton's wife*. . . . . Mezzo-Soprano
Lucile, *Camille Desmoulins' wife* . . . . Soprano

A Woman .... Soprano
Madam Simon .... Contralto
              Men and Women of the People
Time: 1794   *Place:* Paris

Einem's first opera was written towards the end of the
second world war at the suggestion of his teacher, Boris
Blacher, with whom he collaborated in adapting Büchner's
play for the operatic stage. Few operas of this vintage and of
German or Austrian background have stayed so persistently
in the repertory, a survival due as much to musical strength as
to dramatic excellence.

Act I.   The first scene shows Danton and his friends in
the Gaming Rooms. Hérault de Séchelles and a female friend
play while Danton pays considerable attention to his young
wife Julie. The scene is lively and conversational and there
are spirited and pointed exchanges—it is the year 1794 and
the power of Robespierre is absolute. Most of those who
fought in the struggle for freedom have by now been
liquidated. When Camille Desmoulins, a younger
revolutionary leader and a friend of Danton's, makes his
entrance he loses no time in stating his view that the moment
has now come to call a halt. He is revolted by the ever-
increasing number of executions and urges Danton himself to
oppose Robespierre's reign of terror. Danton however seems
to have grown tired and sceptical and events have caused him
to lose his faith in human virtue. 'The statue of freedom is
not yet cast; the furnace is glowing and we can all burn our
fingers on it.'

An urgently lyrical interlude takes us from the leaders of
the revolution to the people who are led. The theatrical
prompter, Simon, is furious with his wife because, as he
thinks, she has put their daughter on the streets, and the
choruses have a savage note as the crowd masses to listen to
Simon inveigh against the rich who can buy the love of the
poor. They seize a young aristocrat and are about to hang
him from the nearest lamp-post when he catches their fancy
with a cool witticism and to his surprise finds his death
sentence commuted to a round of applause. Robespierre
himself appears before the excited crowd and announces new
death sentences, to popular acclaim. The lonely figure is
chillingly characterised in music and, when the crowd leaves
the square and Danton enters it, the contrast between the

two is very marked. Danton challenges his opponent with, 'You are disgustingly upright', but Robespierre's reaction is completely without heat, though the short scene is one of considerable power. No sooner has Danton departed, to Robespierre's comment that he must clearly be done away with, than St. Just enters with documentary evidence to support Danton's indictment before the tribunal. Camille Desmoulins must also die—Robespierre hesitates for a moment since Camille was his friend, then, as near to passion as his nature can contrive, makes his decision: 'Away with them. Quickly. Only the dead do not return.' The orchestra's *larghetto* coda underlines the dictator's final words, 'They all desert me. All is bare and empty. I am alone.'

Scene iii is set in the house of the Desmoulins. Camille, who is an enthusiastic patriot and humanist, is in conversation with Lucile his wife and Danton his friend. Danton is called out of the room, and immediately the tone of the music becomes lyrical as Camille and Lucile sing of their involvement, only a moment later to be interrupted by Danton's re-entry to tell them that he has been denounced and that the committee has decided on his arrest. His friends beg him to escape but he refuses: 'I shall know how to die courageously. It is easier than living.' Camille, who has no suspicion that his own arrest is impending, wants to talk to Robespierre, but his departure leaves Lucile full of foreboding. In an effective aria she reflects on the horror of the times in which they live, then finds that she can no longer remain in the room and rushes out into the street to look for Camille, their thoughts underlined by a funeral march in the orchestra.

Act II. Arrests have continued and Danton and Camille and many of their friends now lie in prison. The fourth scene shows at the same time the interior of the prison (dark as the curtain rises) and its exterior, where the mob rages. At first their enthusiasm is for the newly arrested leaders, but soldiers are in front of the gaol, and Simon stirs them to hatred with his allegations that Danton has lived in luxury, for all the world like any aristocrat, while Robespierre has trodden the path of virtue and righteousness: 'Long live Robespierre, down with the traitors.'

The interior of the prison now lights up, showing a group of prisoners, amongst them Danton and Camille, who are awaiting trial. Camille is full of thoughts of Lucile and cannot ιccept that his life hangs in the balance. Danton, in contrast, awaits death with sad composure, and his beautiful monologue perfectly expresses his resignation. Lucile appears at the barred window of the prison, driven mad by sorrow but still able to recognise Camille and speak to him. The voices of Danton, Camille and Lucile blend in a beautiful trio which is supported and then interrupted by the shouting of the other prisoners as they rattle the bars of their windows.

The Revolutionary Tribunal. Herrmann presides and the scene begins with the hearing of Danton's case, to constant interruptions from the mob which surrounds the court. Danton passionately denies the charge that he has conspired with the royalists and the aristocrats, and when he reminds the court of his own revolutionary achievements, the power of his oratory starts to win over the crowd. Herrmann announces a recession, and St. Just brings in new evidence against Danton. When the court reassembles, Danton speaks even more boldly than before and in a great prophetic speech the accused becomes the accuser of a bloody regime. The mob starts to turn against Robespierre, and the scene ends in tumult as the prisoners are hustled out by soldiers.

The last scene takes place in the public square, where a mob surrounds the guillotine, dancing and singing the Carmagnole in celebration of the impending executions. Danton's passion may have carried the mob at his trial, but the verdict had already been decided and nothing now will prevent the mob's enjoyment of its favourite form of entertainment. A tumbril brings in Danton, Camille and Hérault who sing bravely: 'Our enemy is the stupidity of the masses which can be pierced only by the sword of the spirit.' The crowd continues to roar the Carmagnole as Danton and his two friends mount the scaffold and after a few words from each to the crowd, the executions proceed.

The heads are in the basket, the show is over, the crowd can leave and night has fallen. Two executioners are tidying up after the day's work, singing a sentimental song as they clean. When they leave, Lucile appears and stands on the steps of the guillotine, singing forlornly of what she and France have lost. Whatever her state of mind, she cannot forget Camille and the last word will inevitably be with the guillotine.   H.

BERND ALOIS ZIMMERMANN

(1918–1971)

DIE SOLDATEN

The Soldiers

OPERA in 4 acts and 15 scenes by Bernd Alois Zimmermann, libretto from the play (1775) by Jakob Michael Lenz. Première in Cologne, February 15, 1965, with Edith Gabry, Liane Synek, Helga Jenckel, Anton de Ridder, Claudio Nicolai and Zoltan Kelemen, conductor Michael Gielen, producer Hans Neugebauer. First performed Cassel, 1968, with Hildegard Urmacher, Regina Fonseca, Margarete Ast, Sigurd Björnsson, Hans Helm, Hans-Georg Knoblich, conductor Gerd Albrecht; Munich, 1969 (after a reported 33 rehearsals for orchestra and no less than 377 for soloists), with Catherine Gayer, Charlotte Berthold, Gudrun Wewezow, de Ridder, Hans Wilbrink, Keith Engen, conductor Gielen, producer Václav Kačlik, designer Josef Svoboda; Düsseldorf, 1971, with Gayer, Faith Puleston, Trudeliese Schmidt, de Ridder, Peter-Christoph Rünge, Marius Rintzler, conductor Günther Wich, and in 1972 at Edinburgh Festival.

CHARACTERS

Wesener, *a fancy goods merchant in Lille* . . . . Bass
Marie ⎱ *his daughters* . . ⎰ High Coloratura Soprano
Charlotte ⎰   ⎱   Mezzo-Soprano
Wesener's old mother . . . . Contralto
Stolzius, *a draper in Armentières* . . . . High Baritone
Stolzius's mother . . . . Contralto
Obrist, *Graf von Spannheim* . . . . Bass
Desportes, *a young nobleman in the French Army* . . . . High Tenor
A young gamekeeper, *in the service of Desportes* . . Actor
Captain Pirzel . . . . High Tenor
Eisenhardt, *an Army chaplain* . . . . Baritone
Major Haudy . . . . Baritone
Major Mary . . . . Baritone
Three young officers . . . High Tenor (or High Soprano)
The Comtesse de la Roche . . . . Mezzo-Soprano
The young Count, *her son* . . . . High Lyric Tenor
An Andalusian waitress . . . . Dancer

Three cadets . . . . Dancers
Madame Roux, *hostess of the coffee house* . . . . . Silent
The servant of Comtesse de la Roche . . . . Actor
The young cadet . . . . Actor
A drunken officer . . . . Actor
Three officers . . . . Actor
Eighteen Officers and Cadets; Ballet, doubles of
the actors and dancers
Time: Yesterday, Today, and Tomorrow
Place: French-speaking Flanders

'What are the requirements for a modern opera?' asked
Zimmermann. 'The answer can be given in one sentence:
opera as total theatre! This is the way to think about opera,
or rather about theatre, by which I mean the concentration
of all theatrical media for the purpose of communication in a
place created specially for this purpose. In other words:
architecture, sculpture, painting, musical theatre, spoken
theatre, ballet, film, microphone, television, tape and sound
techniques, electronic music, concrete music, circus, the
musical, and all forms of motion theatre combine to form the
phenomenon of pluralistic opera. . . . The most urgent
requirement now is finally to concentrate and intellectually
to coordinate the new discoveries of recent years. In my
Soldaten I have attempted to take decisive steps in this
direction. In some scenes of this opera I have employed
speech, singing, screaming, whispering, jazz, Gregorian chant,
dance, film, and the entire modern "technical" theatre to
serve the idea of the pluralistic form of musical theatre.' But
this pluralism of Zimmermann's goes far beyond the
combining of the many factors in the one art-form of opera
and refers just as much to 'the simultaneous occurrence of
past, present and future as *one* complicated cross-relationship
of inseparable factors in our lives, ever-present to each other,
as if they were taking place on the inside surface of a vast
globe with the audience suspended somewhere in the middle
taking in the sweep of cause and effect simultaneously.'[1]
It was presumably because it deliberately ignored the
classical unities of time, place and action in favour of a rapid
cross-cutting of the often very short scenes—which approached
his own notion of a pluralistic scene—that Zimmermann
chose a play by Jakob Michael Lenz, the German dramatist

[1] James Helme Sutcliffe in *Opera*, June 1969.

of the second half of the eighteenth century, whose work exhibited a certain iconoclastic turn of mind (a lesser, though earlier, worker in Büchner's field) and whose play was distinctly anti-establishment. Zimmermann's attraction was not of course to the relatively prosaic events of Lenz's play—the seduction of the middle-class Marie by the upper-class Desportes and her decline from respectability to the miserable existence of a soldiers' whore; rather it sprang from his conviction that Lenz's characters 'inevitably collide with an inescapable situation—innocently rather than guiltily—which directly leads towards rape, murder and suicide and finally towards the destruction of everything existing'.

In the event, Zimmermann's theories and his practice of them did not lead as smoothly and inevitably to performance as the quality of his work would suggest. He started work on the opera in 1957 and in 1958 it was officially commissioned by the Opera of Cologne, his native city. It was not long however before the Opera House's direction, the producer Oscar Fritz Schuh and the conductor Wolfgang Sawallisch, decided that the opera was impossible to perform in its original form. In 1963–4 the composer prepared a simplified score, which had its première in early 1965. What was lost was mainly due to Zimmermann's acceptance, reluctant we may suppose, of standard theatrical architecture instead of a 'theatre of the future' yet to be built and capable of giving more vivid expression to his attempt to show the inevitability of events and the unimportance of the time-order in which they take place—'Kugelgestalt der Zeit' is the expression he used; 'the spherical shape of time', you might translate it. He wanted to surround the audience with action either live or on film, so that in, for instance, scene vi or xiii, the use of twelve surrounding stages, each with its attendant musicians together making up the vast orchestral resources required, would force listeners to focus on either the past, the present or the future, each a candidate for their attention. The score published in 1966 postulates various stage levels and three film screens, and Günther Rennert, Munich's Intendant in 1969, though not the producer of *Die Soldaten* then, publicly gave it as his opinion that the opera gained in power from being confined to normal stage restrictions rather than allowed to run riot over twelve stages so that no audience could possibly catch all that was going on at the same time. For what it is worth, a good judge told me he preferred the simpler, more concentrated performance in Düsseldorf to the multi-faceted Munich production, itself a simplification of the original. Whether the composer's full intentions will ever be realised, only time will tell.

Act I. An extended and violent prelude, dominated by an obsessive drum beat, leads us straight into Scene i (*Strofe*), which plays in Wesener's house in Lille. Marie asks the advice of her sister Charlotte as she writes a bread-and-butter letter to Madame Stolzius in Armentières, where she has recently been staying. What she does not want her sister to know is that she has fallen in love with young Stolzius and hopes to see him again.

Scene ii (*Ciacona I*): Stolzius's house in Armentières. Stolzius is obviously labouring under stress, and it is some time before his mother shows him a letter which turns out to be from Marie, with whom he in his turn has fallen in love. Immediately the clouds lift, for him at least though not for his mother, since she plainly has been less smitten by the girl's charms than has her son.

A short interlude (*Tratto I*) takes us to Scene iii (called *Ricercari I*) again in Lille. Baron Desportes, a young officer in the French army, calls on Marie in her father's house. He opens his courtship of her with a florid, wide-ranging phrase, 'Mein göttliche Mademoiselle' (a kind of modern 'Reverenza!'),[1] which effectively characterises an ardent, not too sincere young man used to expressing himself in formal fashion and which remains typical of his music throughout the opera. He affects to be shocked when Marie tells him that her father has warned her that men are false, and his 'göttliche Mademoiselle' becomes even more fulsome and exaggerated than before. When Wesener comes in, Desportes tries to take advantage of the situation by inviting Marie to the theatre, but Wesener is adamant that she is not used to such diversions and cannot go. Her disappointment is quite apparent, and Wesener tries to read her a lecture on the situation, excusing his severity by assuring her, not without tenderness, that she is his only joy in life.

The music quickens and in a couple of bars we are, for Scene iv (*Toccata I*), back in Armentières, where, in a public place, we meet for the first time the military in force. Haudy, Pirzel, and the chaplain Eisenhardt lead a discussion about the comparative merits of the theatre and the sermon as

[1] Mistress Quickly's greeting to Falstaff in Verdi's opera.

opportunities for moralising, and the others, particularly three young officers, join in spasmodically. 'A whore will always be a whore,' announces Haudy at the top of his voice, only to have the chaplain rebuff his contention with, 'a whore never became a whore without being made one'.

Scene v (*Nocturne I*): in Lille. Marie is alone in her room and her father comes to ask whether Desportes' intentions towards her are honourable. She shows him the letter in the form of a love poem which he has written her, and Wesener reads it over with some satisfaction. Though he advises her not to accept presents from him, it is quite apparent that the prospect of a Baron for a son-in-law is not unattractive to him, but he wants her to hedge her bets by not breaking off with young Stolzius before Desportes has proposed to her formally. Marie left alone reveals in an important *arioso* not only that she still has misgivings but that her love for Stolzius is far from dead. Thunder and lightning outside the window and a comparable turmoil in the orchestra seem to bode no good.

Act II: scene vi (*Toccata II*): in Armentières—the café where Madame Roux holds sway with the Andalusian waitress as one of the principal attractions of her establishment. Hither flock the soldiers, and Zimmermann notates the layout of tables, partly to secure ensemble balance, and partly because he makes provision for the occupants of each one to tap with tea or coffee spoon, fist, open or closed hand, on table or vessel in the course of the action (an exactly notated effect). A drunken young officer announces to all and sundry, 'If I had a wife I should give you permission to sleep with her, if you could persuade her to it.' The chaplain and Pirzel take their places well to the front, as also the young Count de la Roche. After general discussion, an elaborate dance begins, full of jazz complications and led by the Andalusian (it is during this dance that the percussion effects on glass, cup and table-top are most in evidence). Stolzius comes in and is unmercifully teased with insinuations about the behaviour of Marie in Lille. He pretends not to know what they're talking about and certainly not to have heard of their brother officer Desportes. It is not long before he precipitately leaves and an *Intermezzo* with organ, stage music, a variety of percussion takes us to:

Scene vii: in Lille (*Capriccio, Corale and Ciacona II*). Marie sits in tears after reading a reproachful letter from Stolzius, and hands it to Desportes, when he comes in and asks her what is the matter. Desportes starts by being indignant at what he describes as the impertinence of the writer, then he says he will dictate an answer. But the letter is soon lost sight of in the hysteria of coloratura laughter as the physical seduction of Marie begins. At this point the scene, like the means the composer employs throughout, becomes for the first time pluralistic as Zimmermann simultaneously shows the seduction, Stolzius's far-off instinctive reaction to it, and a third party ruminating on the situation. As well as Marie and Desportes, we see Wesener's old mother, perhaps in the centre, foretelling misfortune for her beloved granddaughter and, on the side of the stage opposite to Marie's room in Lille, Stolzius in Armentières miserable at the tone of Marie's letter which has in effect broken off the engagement. He tries to defend Marie to his mother but vows vengeance on Desportes. Meanwhile, the wordless love scene has continued and we have effectively reached the halfway point in the action with Marie's seduction complete and her downfall therefore (in eighteenth-century terms) more or less assured—a musical scene of remarkable complexity and brilliant invention.

A short prelude leads us into Act III, and the first scene (*Rondino*) takes place in Armentières, where, in the principal square, the chaplain and Captain Pirzel are engaged on one of their interminable discussions. The chaplain wants to discuss the implications of Mary's intended move to Lille, but Pirzel insists on philosophising—'Der philosophiert mich zu Tode': 'He'll philosophise me to death,' says his victim. The chaplain observes that you cannot go out of the door without finding a soldier embracing a girl, but this provokes further theoretical stuff from Pirzel, whose lengthy military service seems to have driven him into some kind of private mental corner, as a refuge presumably from the irrationality of much of what has been going on professionally round him.

Scene ix (*Rappresentazione*): Mary's room. A knock at the door heralds the arrival of a stiff and nervous Stolzius, dressed in uniform and applying to become Major Mary's batman. Mary accepts him.

The tenth scene (*Ricercari II*) follows after a single silent bar and takes place in Wesener's house in Lille. Charlotte is scolding her sister for taking up with Major Mary the moment Desportes has left the town. Marie tries to excuse herself—it is all the fault of Desportes for going away, and Mary was

anyhow his best friend—but Charlotte is not to be put off and,
as Marie makes up in the looking glass, hisses 'Soldier's hussy!'
at her back. Major Mary comes in to be greeted by Marie
with a sort of parody of Desportes' greeting in the third
scene, a gallantry he echoes in his turn. All three prepare to
leave, but the girls notice before doing so a resemblance
between Mary's batman, standing discreetly in the background, and 'a certain person'. The interlude is called
Romanza, and is one of the score's most considerable pieces.

Scene xi (*Nocturne II*): in the house of the Comtesse de la
Roche. It is evening, and the Countess is waiting up for the
return of her son, musing that it seems inevitable that
children regularly cause their parents pain from the womb to
the grave. Now her son has started to have secrets from her.
Her thoughts are conveyed in a wide-ranging solo *arioso*,
which becomes with the entrance of her son (the young
Count whom we have already rather unobtrusively met in the
two regimental scenes), an extended and vocally grateful duet
(vociferously and aptly applauded by the audience, the
second time I heard the opera). The burden of their conversation is basically the unsuitability of Fräulein Wesener as
a potential consort for the young Count. Countess de la
Roche herself will take responsibility for the girl's future.

Scene xii (*Tropi*): in Lille, Wesener's house. From the
conversation of Charlotte and Marie, it seems that Major
Mary, like the Count, has in his turn deserted Marie, but their
discussion is interrupted by the arrival of a servant asking on
behalf of the Countess de la Roche if the young ladies are at
home. Flustered, they send down a message that it will be an
honour to be visited by her. With an exactly balanced
mixture of condescension and warmth, the Countess asserts
that she is Marie's best friend, commiserates with her on the
gossip which is rife in the town, bids her in a firm but kindly
way to forget all about the young Count, and offers in order
to repair the blow her honour has suffered to take her as a
companion into her own house. The scene develops into a
splendid trio for female voices and the Countess leaves,
enjoining Marie to think over her offer.

Act IV starts with a scene (*Toccata III*) in the café in
Armentières in which Zimmermann's pluralistic theories are
put most extensively and effectively into practice. The
subject is the various stages of Marie's downfall, represented
simultaneously as if in a kind of dream on different levels on
the stage, one with dancers, another with all the performers,

a third with their doubles, and yet again in film on three screens.[1] The whole thing is conceived as if Marie were on trial. Mixed on the three screens and cross-cut from one to another, the salient events of the action are shown. Major Mary has quickly found out where Marie is to be found, and the Countess has surprised them in a garden rendezvous. Marie has run away from the Countess's house and is not to be found at her father's. At the same time, Desportes, who, the original play tells us, has been trying, even though Wesener has guaranteed debts he left behind him in Lille, to rid himself of his discarded mistress by getting her well and truly involved with Mary, has written to his gamekeeper at home to say he has found a woman for him. Marie, homeless and terrified, is raped by the gamekeeper, and becomes a common prostitute. Stolzius, apprised of events, buys poison with which to effect his revenge. The threads of the very complex scene are drawn together in a great common utterance on the part of all the participants: 'And must those who suffer injustice tremble, and only those who do wrong be happy.'

An interlude (*Tratto II*) leads to scene xiv (*Ciacona III*): in Armentières, Major Mary's room. Desportes is dining with his friend, and Stolzius keeps on fetching them fresh napkins so as to overhear the conversation. Desportes speaks in the most callous manner imaginable of Marie, who wrote to tell him she planned to visit him at home. What if his father had seen her, Desportes demands rhetorically, and goes on to explain that he quickly arranged for his keeper, a strong, masculine sort of chap, to give her the kind of reception she deserved. Mary protests at so revolting a stratagem, but Desportes thinks that Marie would have nothing to complain about if his keeper were to marry her. Major Mary insists that he himself would have married her if the young Count de la Roche had not got in the way. At this point, Stolzius serves soup, into which he has put the poison he bought, and its effect on Desportes is almost immediate. Stolzius seizes Desportes by the ears and yells 'Marie!' in his face, then, as he watches Desportes' agony, drinks poison himself and dies.

The last scene (*Nocturne III*) takes place on the road. To the accompaniment of stylised and amplified vocal noises, a miserable beggar woman—Marie of course—accosts old Wesener and begs for money. At first he refuses but then he

---

[1] And this is the composer's simplified, compromise version!

thinks of the possible plight of his daughter and relents. He does not recognise her. While the end of the tragedy is being played out, various scenes are enacted in contrapuntal contrast, from the sight of groups of officers having recourse to Madame Bischof's establishment in the café to films of soldiers of all ages and all nationalities marching relentlessly over the cobblestones, until the latter idea takes over the scene entirely to the accompaniment of an amplified march on the drums. Marie lies motionless on the stage throughout and it is emphasised that the soldiers are only symbolical of those who are responsible for the misery of others, by no means intended as exclusive perpetrators of those crimes against humanity which Zimmermann so cogently protests.

Zimmermann has written a complicated serial score, involving vast stage and musical resources, but what impresses the listener at the end of a performance is the clarity of organisation, the audibility of text, the subtlety of the sounds he has heard. His vocal line is often angular and complex but also lyrical and expressive, his orchestra is filled with colour as well as weight of sonority. Above all, he has written an opera that is full of compassion and humanity, that speaks to the hearts of audiences which see and hear it.

It is known that Zimmermann planned a second stage work *Medea*, in which he hoped that he could further develop his ideas about simultaneousness and multimedia. For years, he was working on the libretto after a drama by the German poet Hans-Henny Jahnn. As far as is known, he never reached the point of being able to start composing.

H.

HANS
WERNER HENZE
(b. 1926)

HENZE was the first to come to international attention of the musicians associated with Darmstadt, where after 1945 a centre grew up for German composers whose interests lay in the currents of contemporary music banned as decadent by the Nazi regime. He was a pupil of Wolfgang Fortner's and rapidly became the leading composer of his generation and rose 'to be inspiration, and interpreter and prophet for those whose musical understanding was formed after the war. Then, Schoenberg and Stravinsky were the old gods, still speaking; but Henze speaks for, and with, us.'[1]

Henze has contributed to the continuing vitality of the operatic form as much perhaps as anyone else of his generation, and his versatility comes partly from the wealth of practical experience he gained as a conductor for ballet and opera in provincial theatres. The long list of his compositions comprises a number of symphonies and other music with orchestra, chamber music on a considerable scale, a full-length ballet for Covent Garden (*Ondine*) as well as, by 1970, no fewer than six full-length operas, all richly and variously wrought. All the more disconcerting was it to read in the summer of 1970 an interview with the composer which suggested he was disposed to reject the medium altogether. He was quoted (accurately, I am quite sure) as saying: 'My crisis was not so much about opera as about music, music-making and people, and in this context I could see that I would contribute no more new operas, masquerades, charades . . . I feel opera is finished. Of course, the basic idea of putting drama to music is not finished . . . the major musical and technical problem is the disintegration of those traditional means of expression that are essential to the making of an opera. Their decay, heralding the decay of present society, naturally also heralds the decay of its theatre.' He went on to give a more or less Marxist explanation of his current position, but his admirers could take comfort from the reference to 'putting drama to music', which had an encouraging ring to it.

BOULEVARD SOLITUDE

Opera in seven scenes by Hans Werner Henze, text by Grete Weil, after the play by Walter Jockisch, which in its turn is a modern version of *Manon Lescaut*. Première, February 17, 1952, in Hanover, with Sigrid Klaus, Walter Buckow, conductor Johannes Schüler. First produced Düsseldorf, 1953, with Anna Tassopoulos; San Carlo, Naples, 1954, with Lydia Styx, conductor Jonel Perlea; Rome, 1954, with Magda

---

[1] Andrew Porter writing in 1962.

Laszlo, conductor Nino Sanzogno; London, at Sadler's Wells by New
Opera Company, 1962, with April Cantelo, John Carolan, Peter
Glossop.

CHARACTERS

Manon Lescaut . . . . High Soprano
Armand des Grieux, *a student* . . . . Lyric Tenor
Lescaut, *Manon's brother* . . . . Baritone
Francis, *Armand's friend* . . . . Baritone
Lilaque *père, a rich old gentleman* . . . High Tenor Buffo
Lilaque *fils* . . . . Baritone
A prostitute . . . . Dancer
Servant to Lilaque *fils* . . . . Mime
Two drug addicts . . . . Dancers
A cigarette boy . . . . Dancer
Newspaper Sellers, Beggars, Whores, Police,
Students, Travellers

Time: After the end of the 1939–45 war   *Place:* Paris

Henze's first opera (1950–1) is a modern version of the
Manon story and with it he secured an immediate success
with the critics and before long with the public as well.
Henze's style is eclectic, and this thoroughly attractive little
work—small in pretensions and length (less than two hours
including interval), considerably greater in achievement—
invokes some jazz and popular elements as well as Stravinsky
and Berg.

Scene i. The crowded waiting room of a large French
railway station; the music at first entirely timpani and
percussion. When the departure of a train is announced,
Francis claps his friend Armand on the shoulder and leaves.
Manon comes in with her brother who steers her in the
direction of Armand's table and then leaves her to go and
drink at the bar. After a few moments, Manon takes out a
cigarette which Armand lights, asking her if she too is going
to Paris. No, says Manon, to a finishing school in Lausanne.
Armand launches into a sad account of the loneliness of
student life in Paris and the unattainability of the sort of
women he dreams of. Manon joins in but provides the story
with a happy ending, and the two get up and leave together;
the pick-up is effectively completed.

Scene ii. A small attic room in Paris. Armand and
Manon lie in bed in the morning and sing a wistful song.
Manon chatters gaily of a hat which has taken her fancy and

announces her intention of buying it. No, protests Armand;
since he stopped his studies, his father has cut off his
allowance and they have no money. He gets up to dress and
goes off in search of his friend Francis. While he is out of the
room, Lescaut comes in. What does he need—more
money? No, says Lescaut coarsely, just her two ravishing
breasts. He has found her a new admirer, old and fat but rich
as well. Armand comes back and Manon embraces him
tenderly as he goes out. Lescaut in a wild song sardonically
compliments his sister on her cruelty to Armand—the more
brutally she treats her lovers, the higher will she rise—then
leaves, giving her five minutes to make up her mind. Manon
reproaches the absent Armand for leaving her alone and a
prey to the old temptations; but as she sings, she is preparing
to leave him.

    Scene iii.   An elegant boudoir in the house of Lilaque
père. Manon sings an aria as she writes to Armand, reassuring
him that she is happy and treated with every consideration
by the generous Monsieur Lilaque. The only flaw in her
existence is that Armand cannot visit her, and that could
easily be remedied as every day at 5 in her own little carriage
she drives in the Bois de Boulogne. At this point she is
interrupted by Lescaut who is furious that she prefers to
write to her lover instead of looking after Lilaque and
proceeds to tear the letter up. When Manon protests that he
is destroying the only true thing in her life, he retorts that
she is his source of income and he needs more money at
once. He notices a strongbox, forces it and in spite of
Manon's protests steals the money it contains. Lilaque enters,
greets Manon tenderly and Lescaut with courtesy, at once
offering to leave brother and sister alone to finish their talk.
However, as he is about to leave the room he notices the
broken safe and his good humour turns to rage as he throws
the two out. The grotesque (but not by any means
despicable) figure of Lilaque is characterised by very high
tenor writing notably in the lyrical trio which constitutes the
musical form of the scene once Lilaque has joined the
Lescaut pair.

    Scene iv.   A University Library. Armand and Francis,
with other students (who form a choral background to the
entire scene), are studying the poems of Catullus. Francis is
enthralled by his studies, but Armand can think only of
Manon, and when Francis tells him that she and Lescaut have

been chucked out of Lilaque's house for theft, Armand protests that he would believe anything of Lescaut but that Manon could commit no crime. Francis goes off in a huff as Manon enters and sits by Armand. They join in reading a love poem which all too aptly fits their own situation and which gradually becomes an impassioned love duet. The parallel with Massenet's St. Sulpice scene is apt and only the protests of des Grieux are absent.

Scene v.   A dive. The reconciliation has not lasted long, Armand has taken to drugs, and while he sings of the forgetfulness he buys, everyone else dances to music that recalls *Wozzeck* with overtones of Gershwin. Lescaut comes in with Lilaque's son—Manon's latest 'suitor'—and they sit at the bar. Lescaut asks Armand where Manon is, but Armand's only interest is in more cocaine, which he gets from Lescaut.

Manon enters and joins her brother and Lilaque *fils*. Stimulated by the drug, Armand starts to rave and tries to stop Lilaque from touching Manon. Lescaut orders him off and Manon tries to soothe him with promises for the future. Lilaque finally loses patience and goes off with Manon and her brother, leaving Armand sitting alone. A beautiful girl comes in and gives Armand a letter. As he reads it, Manon's voice is heard telling him to come and see her the following night as Lilaque will be away; meanwhile as consolation she sends him one of the prettiest girls in Paris. But Armand is too far gone to notice her and the girl shrugs apathetically and leaves him asleep.

Scene vi.   After a striking interlude, we find ourselves in a room in the apartment of Lilaque *fils*. It is early morning and Manon and Armand are together. Manon gaily remarks on the change in her fortunes from the grimy railway station and the little attic to her present luxury, but Armand reminds her that once they were alone together, a point of view Manon cannot understand. Lescaut, who has been keeping watch, hurries in and tells Armand he must be off in case the servants see him. As he is about to take Armand out, he notices an abstract painting on the wall. Is it a Picasso? No, but all the same beautiful, says Armand. Manon and Lescaut ridicule the picture, but Lescaut, with an eye to the main chance, rips it from its frame and hides it under his coat. At this point they hear the voice of Lilaque *père* who has been called by a suspicious servant. Manon quickly hides the two men behind a curtain and goes out in an attempt to prevent the old man from coming in. He protests that his delight at seeing her quite erases his memories of her past misdeeds, but to her horror he insists they return to the room she has just left, especially because it contains a modern painting which, although he personally finds it incomprehensible, is said by psychiatrists to be most beneficial to the subconscious. All Manon's efforts are in vain and he steers her back the way she has come. The moment he sees the picture has gone he starts to raise the roof with his accusations, in which he includes the two men who he suspects are in hiding behind the curtain. Lilaque shouts to the servant to call the police and himself bars the door. Lescaut draws a revolver and shoots him dead, pressing the gun into Manon's hand as he escapes. Lilaque *fils* enters and sees Manon and Armand standing over his father's body.

Scene vii.   An intermezzo introduces the last scene, which takes place outside a prison on a grey winter's day. Armand waits to catch a last glimpse of Manon as she is taken off to prison and sings an aria of hopelessness. The police herd Manon and some other prisoners away before she and Armand can exchange a word and from this point the action becomes a symbolical pantomime, involving people from the railway station, police, singing children, Lilaque *fils* following the corpse of his father on a barrow, even (in the London production) Lescaut and a bikini-ed girl friend holidaying by the sea on the proceeds of what we have been watching. 'Et c'est là l'histoire de Manon, de Manon Lescaut.'   H.

KÖNIG HIRSCH
Il Re Cervo/King Stag

Opera in three acts by Hans Werner Henze, text by Heinz von Cramer after the story by Carlo Gozzi. Première (as *König Hirsch*), Berlin Städtische Oper, September 23, 1956, with Helga Pilarczyk, Nora Jungwirth, Sandor Konya, Martin Vantin, Helmut Krebs, Tomislav Neralic, conductor Hermann Scherchen. First performed Darmstadt, 1959, with Käthe Maas, George Maran, conductor Hans Zanotelli; Bielefeld, 1960. Revised (as *Il Re Cervo*) 1962, Cassel, conductor Henze; Munich, 1964, with Felicia Weathers, Claude Heater, Hans-Günter Nöcker, conductor Christoph von Dohnanyi; Santa Fé, 1965, with Mildred Allen, George Shirley, Donald Gramm; Helsinki, 1971; B.B.C., 1973 (in English).

CHARACTERS

Leandro, *the King* .... Tenor
Costanza, *his beloved* .... Soprano
Tartaglia, *the Chancellor* .... Bass-Baritone
Scollatella I .... Coloratura-Soprano
Scollatella II .... Soubrette
Scollatella III .... Mezzo-Soprano
Scollatella IV .... Alto
Checco, *a melancholy musician* .... Tenor-Buffo
Coltellino, *an unsuccessful murderer* ..... Tenor-Buffo
Six Alchemists
Two Statues .... Contralto
Cigolotti, *a magician* .... Speaking role
The Stag .... Speaking role

Voices of the Wood, Voices of the People,
Voices of the Wind, Courtiers, Pages, Wild Animals,
People from the City, Soldiers, Huntsmen

Time: Antiquity   *Place:* Near Venice, between
                                            sea and forest

Henze's second opera, *Il Re Cervo*, is an adaptation of one of the fables of Carlo Gozzi, the Venetian contemporary and rival of Goldoni and source of such twentieth-century operas as Busoni's and Puccini's *Turandot*, Casella's *La Donna Serpente* and Prokofiev's *The Love for Three Oranges*. It was the composer's second opera and much of it was written on Ischia, where Henze went to live in 1953, so that the music is perhaps the most influenced by the composer's chosen Italian environment of any opera he has yet written. The first version of the opera would have run for more than five hours, and it was heavily cut for the Berlin première in 1956, according to those who already knew it, to its considerable detriment. By 1962, the composer had decided on a revised version, about half as long, and this was first heard in Cassel.

King Leandro (Deramo in Gozzi's play) has grown up in the forest amongst animals. He succeeds to the throne, returns as an innocent to the complicated world of men, is crowned, chooses a bride, only to abdicate when his Chancellor, Tartaglia, has her arrested. The King abdicates and through a magic spell takes possession of the body of a dead stag, with the result that the Chancellor is able to use the same spell to assume the lifeless form of the King and take control. He reduces the country to ruins until the Stag

King reappears to the joy of the populace. The false king is killed and the true one re-enters his body to general acclamation.

Act I: the King's castle, where preparations are in hand for his coronation. A fearful storm rages (depicted in the *Vivace* orchestral opening) and an early candidate for the role of Queen—Scollatella—emerges to complain of the appalling effect the weather has had on her clothes. She is still not without confidence that she will win the King's hand, but she finds she is frightened at being alone while the thunder rages round the building and she looks into a mirror and summons up a double. Scollatella II comes out of the mirror, also complaining about the weather, and it is not long before Scollatella III and Scollatella IV are also involved in thinking up schemes to win the King's favour, although Scollatella I insists that, if their plans go right, she alone will be called Queen.

The Coronation Procession. Scollatella I hides as Tartaglia, the King's Chancellor, comes in and, obviously up to no good, conceals himself. Celebratory choral music can be heard, and Tartaglia storms about the futility of it all—a boy King being led like a lamb to the slaughter, fawning courtiers all over the place, while he is not accorded his just deserts. He will strike fear into all their hearts, and he even invokes the elements to put a stop to the farcical proceedings. From the attitudes he strikes and the authority which he obviously expects to assert, Scollatella thinks Tartaglia must be King and makes herself known before disappearing into the background.

At this point, Costanza is brought in by two guards. Tartaglia questions her and offers to release her, but she does not want to go. What is the King like? Obviously, judging from her arrest, less kind-hearted than the man she is now face to face with. Tartaglia assures her that the King is a monster and gives her a dagger with which he instructs her to murder him. She demurs but Tartaglia forces her to conceal the weapon and tells her to wait for him outside.

The animals, who have been the King's friends in the forest, form a semi-circle round him as in movingly direct vocal terms he bids them goodbye. The animals leave him alone and the celesta introduces two statues (both contraltos) who warn him of the dangers he faces amongst men. Their music goes some way towards evoking the purity of the world of the boys in *The Magic Flute*, and they assure the King that they will help him by laughing the moment anyone tells him an untruth. Their aid will continue as long as he wants it.

Preceded by a fanfare, Tartaglia makes his entrance and announces to the King that ,the moment to choose the royal bride is at hand. To more fanfares, Scollatella I comes in and makes her obeisance, followed by II, III and IV. They compete for the King's interest, and general quarrelling and tumult ensue in a series of musically interesting and contrasted orchestral sections. The King asks which of them, if married to him, would be saddest if he died and the answer eludes them. Tartaglia in an aside mutters of his intention to spread his net and wait for fish to enter it. The King is keen to get rid of Scollatella I and assures her that no one has given him more pleasure than she. The statues laugh and the King knows that none so far is worthy to be his bride.

Tartaglia introduces Costanza. Her first utterance obviously impresses the King who begs her to go on talking. She admits she is no longer afraid of him and he himself is reassured by the silence of the statues. They sing together in an *adagio* section, the first love duet in the opera, and at its end, Leandro, unable to bear the idea that he may lose Costanza, attacks the statues and breaks them. Immediately Tartaglia is on the spot and shows the King Costanza's concealed weapon. She is arrested by the guards and when the King, broken-hearted and without the statues to advise him, says he will exercise clemency, Tartaglia insists on death for a potential regicide. The King decides he will abdicate and leave for the forest, and Cigolotti (disguised as a parrot) leads him away.

The stage is Tartaglia's; he rejoices that he has set his net and the fishing has been good. Spirits of the Wind dash across the stage, and Coltellino, Tartaglia's hired assassin, and Checco, a musician who follows Cigolotti and carries a guitar on his back, enter after them. Coltellino, who has lost his pistol and dagger to the Spirits of the Wind, does not at all want Checco hanging around him, still less when he is invited to listen to Checco's song. In the end Checco leaves, and Coltellino hastens to Tartaglia's summons. Doesn't he want to be an honest murderer like his father? Let him then follow the King into the forest and murder him! Even the loss of dagger and pistol is not accepted by Tartaglia as excuse, and he hands Coltellino replacements. The act ends with a curious postscript as a group of six alchemists comes in speaking happily and rhythmically to each other and announcing to the furious Tartaglia that they have come to give a party for King Leandro. They are too late, says Tartaglia.

Act II takes place in the wood—a great breathing organism—and we hear the forest sounds as voices call to each other in alarm. There is a stranger present, a voice announces, and soon others proclaim that the wood is full of men. Leandro appears and it is not long before Scollatella's voice joins with his (she is being groomed by her mirror doubles who now act as maids). Scollatella is obsessed with the idea that she is in reality a Queen, and Leandro turns from her. The action is fast and furious but in a way simple. Animals flee from humans; the alchemists reappear disguised as animals and are themselves terrified of the huntsmen, who will try to kill them, and of the other animals, who may find them even easier prey. Tartaglia attempts to murder Leandro with his knife but fails, and both Checco and Coltellino complicate the action with their fears and failures.

Cigolotti plans that Checco alone shall know the secret of the transformation spell, which he shall give only to the King and thus save the King's life. Checco has a beautiful, enigmatic song, nearer perhaps to Britten or Tippett than to most other Italian or German music, and lightly accompanied on guitar. A stag appears and Tartaglia wounds it so that it escapes. Tartaglia's designs are murderous. He tries to get news of the King's whereabouts from Checco. By magical means, they see the stag die and Tartaglia hears the transformation spell from Checco, who intends only to give it to the King. Leandro by its aid changes into the stag and goes off, but Tartaglia in his own turn repeats the spell and assumes the King's body. Checco is beside himself with horror at what he has inadvertently set in motion and Cigolotti laments a turn of events which has Tartaglia and his evil soul inhabiting the King's body. Tartaglia's *credo* follows: he will impose his will on the country, stamp on it if he choose. Meanwhile, he sets in motion a stag hunt which will eliminate Leandro for ever, but, as the act ends, the elements seem to be conspiring against him and a storm breaks over the wood.

Act III plays in the deserted city, where Tartaglia has been exercising absolute rule. Decay has set in, the people are oppressed and their only hope comes from the legend that when a stag appears in the streets, the rule of peace will return. And this is in effect what happens. Quite quietly,

Leandro as the Stag King walks through the streets, finding that no one answers his calls, although Coltellino melodiously laments his lack of prowess as a murderer.

Even the alchemists are persecuted unter Tartaglia's rule, but gradually news of the King's return reaches the city, and Costanza comes to look for the man she was allowed to love for so short a time. The Stag King approaches her, and their second duet confirms their mutual love until her touch makes the stag flee the scene, just in time too, as Tartaglia appears, in the guise of the King and armed to the teeth against the fears and forebodings he finds on every side. He greets Costanza, as if he were the King she loves, but she detects the fraud straightaway and will have none of him. Her disappearance brings on a kind of brainstorm, and Tartaglia calls for his soldiers and defies his enemies.

People start to become conscious of the presence in their midst of the stag, against whom Tartaglia continues to rail, demanding that it be shot the moment it is sighted. Finally, Coltellino, taking straight aim with the assistance of Cigolotti but mistakenly thinking the King he sees is the King whom Tartaglia has retained him to murder, shoots his target—but it is of course Tartaglia who falls dead just as he is about to kill the stag.

Leandro works the transformation spell and is restored to his original shape, so that the opera may end with choral rejoicing, enclosing a short, simple duet for Leandro and Costanza, in which he claims her as his bride.

The plot is said to have been one which Brahms contemplated for an opera and it has obvious affinities with Bartok's *Cantata Profana*. For Henze at the age of 29 it was a fairy story with overtones of the Nazi Germany of his boyhood, and the opera has excited ardent admiration so that William Mann in *The Times*, at the time of the B.B.C.'s English performance in 1973, was able to write: 'in 1955 . . . Henze's head was full of marvellous vocal and orchestral music, longing to be released'.   H.

DER PRINZ VON HOMBURG
The Prince of Homburg

Opera in three acts by Hans Werner Henze, text by Ingeborg Bachmann after the drama by Heinrich von Kleist. Première, Hamburg State Opera May 22, 1960, with Liselotte Fölser, Mimi Aarden, Helmut Melchert, Vladimir Ruzdak, Toni Blankenheim, Herbert Fliether, conductor Leopold Ludwig. First performed London, Sadler's Wells Theatre, 1962, by Hamburg Company (with the première cast except for Colette Lorand and Henze conducting); Paris, Frankfurt Opera, 1962; Düsseldorf, 1964, with the title-role rewritten for tenor and sung by Andor Kaposy.

CHARACTERS

Friedrich Wilhelm, *Elector of Brandenburg*
.... Dramatic Tenor
The Electress, *his wife*.................... Contralto
Princess Natalie von Oranien, *her niece, Colonel-in-Chief of a Dragoon Regiment* .... Soprano
Field Marshal Dörfling.................... Baritone
Prince Friedrich Artur von Homburg, *General of Cavalry* ....High Baritone
Colonel Kottwitz, *of the Princess's Regiment* ..... Bass
Count Hohenzollern, *attached to the Elector* .Lyric Tenor
First Officer .... Tenor
Second Officer .... Baritone
Third Officer .... Bass
First Lady of the Court .... Soprano
Second Lady of the Court ....Mezzo-Soprano
Third Lady of the Court .... Contralto
Sergeant .... Baritone
First and Second Orderly .... Tenor, Baritone
Other Officers ....Tenors and Basses
People of the Court (Pages, Servants, etc.),
Military Personnel (Guards, Cadets, Soldiers)

Time: 1675 *Place:* Fehrbellin, Germany

The libretto by Ingeborg Bachmann, a regular colla-borator of Henze's, is based on Kleist's last play, *Prinz Friedrich von Homburg* (1811). The background is the successful world of Prussian militarism in the seventeenth century, and the hero of the play is a poet and dreamer who nonetheless accepts the values of his environment. It was at a performance by Jean Vilar's Théâtre National Populaire, with Gérard Philippe as the hero, that Ingeborg Bachmann discovered, far from Prussia and outside Germany, that she loved the play. To some degree, composer and librettist have consciously de-Germanised what Kleist wrote, and Andrew Porter in a review pointed out that Kleist's lines for the Elector:

'He will teach you, be assured,
what military discipline and obedience are'

have been changed in the libretto to:

'. . . what freedom and honour are.'

Act I, scene i.   Garden of a castle in Fehrbellin. It is night and the Prince von Homburg is sitting as if in a trance, half awake and half asleep, twining a wreath in his hand. The remainder of the Elector's entourage is killing time before the battle, and they have noticed that their General of Cavalry is missing. They emerge from the castle to find him alone and some wonder whether he is ill. The Elector takes the wreath from his hand, places a silver chain round his neck and gives him the hand of Princess Natalie. They depart and the Prince is left stroking the glove of the Princess. Count Hohenzollern wakes his friend from his dream . . . but the glove remains for him as an unexplained link between dream and reality, with fantasy still to him, in his state of half-trance, the more believable condition.

The whole scene has the softness of a dream but the interlude takes us to a different world, a military conference in a hall in the castle. Field Marshal Dörfling dictates the plan of battle, instructing the Prince von Homburg to hold his attack with his cavalry force until he receives specific orders. The Prince listens dreamily, has to be continually reminded where he is, and is obsessed with the idea that Princess Natalie is looking for the glove she has lost and which he holds in his hand. He lets it fall, she recognises it as hers and he understands the element of reality which his dream contained.

Scene iii.   The battlefield of Fehrbellin. Officers are waiting for the battle to begin and Homburg tries to check with his friend Hohenzollern as to the orders he received yesterday and about which he is unclear in his mind. He is dreaming of Natalie when the first cannon shot is heard and the battle is joined. Officers watch its progress from a hillock, the Swedes are seen to be giving way and suddenly Prince Friedrich, without waiting for his orders, gives the command to attack. No argument will restrain him, he orders a fanfare to be sounded and rushes into battle.

During the interlude with its plaintive saxophone solo, it becomes dark and then gradually lightens to show the scene the following morning. Dead and wounded are being carried away and rumour has it that the Elector has been killed. The Electress and Princess Natalie are overcome with grief and the Prince von Homburg joins them in their mourning. Friedrich and Natalie avow their love for one another. But rumour was false, and the Elector stands before them with the Field Marshal and other officers safe and sound. The Elector declares that victory was endangered because the cavalry attack was started too early and that he will have whoever was responsible court-martialled and condemned to death. When the Prince comes to bring him trophies of victory, he orders his sword taken from him and the act ends after an ensemble with the Prince escorted towards Fehrbellin and prison.

Act II: scene iv. Prison. Prince Friedrich has been condemned to death by the court martial, and he realises the gravity of the situation when he hears from his friend Count Hohenzollern that the Elector has sent for the death warrant in order to sign it.

Scene v. On his way to appeal, he sees with horror the grave which has been dug for him in the courtyard of the castle.

Scene vi. The Electress's room. Homburg begs the Electress to intervene on his behalf but she feels, however great her love for him, that she is powerless in the present situation. Natalie tells him she loves him and will make an attempt to persuade the Elector to change his mind.

Scene vii. The Elector's room. Natalie begs her uncle to pardon Homburg; he is taken aback to find that the young man has so far forgotten his training as to think exclusively of his freedom. Finally, the Elector gives Natalie a letter in which he offers to let Homburg go free if he can find it in his heart and mind to consider the judgement made against him unjust.

Scene viii. Prison. Natalie brings Prince Friedrich the Elector's letter and tells him that he will immediately be free. But Friedrich hesitates, then decides the judgement was just and that he cannot write the Elector the letter which would set him free. Natalie kisses him and says that if he feels it right to follow the dictates of his own heart, she will follow hers—she decides to order her Regiment of Dragoons to free the Prince by force.

Act III: scene ix. The Elector's room. The Field Marshal brings the news that Princess von Oranien's Regiment is in the town intending to free the Prince von Homburg from prison. At the same time, the Elector receives a letter conveying the Prince's decision. Officers come to the Elector to request that the Prince be pardoned and the Elector decides to bring him from prison, saying that he will teach them what freedom and what honour are. The Prince comes in, greets his friends but will not change his decision, holding that death will wash him clean of guilt. The Elector is overjoyed, believes Friedrich has re-established his honour and gives orders that he be conducted back to prison. As he prepares to go, he makes it plain that even in the face of the pleading of Natalie and Count Hohenzollern, he will not change his mind. But the Elector believes he has established a crucial point of principle and can now tear up the death warrant, which he proceeds to do.

Scene x. To the sound of a funeral march, Prince Friedrich is brought blindfold by Count Hohenzollern into the garden. The Prince, who believes he is about to be executed, feels himself already withdrawn from life. Suddenly, the Elector leads in his court, the Prince's blindfold is removed as he stands before the Elector, just as in his dream before the battle. What had been a dream of victory wreath, princely chain and bride becomes reality.   H.

ELEGY FOR YOUNG LOVERS

Opera in five acts by Hans Werner Henze, libretto by W. H. Auden and Chester Kallman. Première (in German), May 20, 1961, at Schwetzingen Festival (Munich Opera), with Eva-Marie Rogner, Ingeborg Bremert, Lilian Benningsen, Friedrich Lenz, Dietrich Fischer-Dieskau, Karl Christian Kohn, producer Henze, conductor Heinrich Bender. First performed in England, Glyndebourne, 1963, (in English), with Dorow, Söderström, Kerstin Meyer, Turp, Carlos Alexander, Hemsley, conductor John Pritchard; Zürich, 1961, by Munich Opera; Berlin, 1962, with Catherine Gayer, Liane Dubin, Martha Mödl, Fischer-Dieskau, Grobe, Hemsley, conductor Reinhard Peters.

CHARACTERS

Gregor Mittenhofer, *a poet* . . . . Baritone
Dr. Wilhelm Reischmann, *a physician* . . . . Bass
Toni Reischmann, *his son* . . . . Lyric Tenor
Elisabeth Zimmer . . . . Soprano
Carolina, *Gräfin von Kirchstetten* . . . . Contralto
Frau Hilda Mack, *a widow* . . . . High Soprano
Josef Mauer, *an alpine guide* . . . . Speaker
Servants at the 'Black Eagle' . . . . Silent

Time: 1910   *Place:* Austrian Alps

29 (*Above*) *Elegy for Young Lovers:* Fischer-Dieskau in the Munich
production.

(*Below*) *The Bassarids* at English National Opera, 1974, with Josephine
Barstow, Norman Welsby, Katherine Pring, Ken Woollam, Gregory
Dempsey, the chorus in background.

It is curious that *Elegy for Young Lovers*, like the other opera of Henze's with an English libretto by W. H. Auden and Chester Kallman, *The Bassarids*, was first performed in German translation. The librettists have told us that Henze asked them late in autumn of 1958 for a libretto with 'a subject and situation which would call for tender, beautiful noises' and the composer planned a 'small, subtle orchestra' as the basis for his chamber opera, in which certain instruments could be associated with various leading characters, a flute for instance with Hilda Mack, the brass with Mittenhofer, violin and viola with the young lovers, cor anglais with Carolina, bassoon or saxophone with Dr. Reischmann.

The story is in outline not complicated, though it is packed with incident, psychological nuance and wit. It is concerned basically with (wrote the composer in 1970) 'the Birth of a Poem that is in process throughout the three acts, from the moment of the first idea to the final public reading. What happens around this process of birth, the hilarious, the wicked, the vulgar, the banal, the murderous, serves mainly to put into question the figure of the *Artist as a Hero* as the nineteenth century created it, as the twentieth century has not yet completely liquidated it.'

'The artist as hero' is the great poet Gregor Mittenhofer, who goes every year to a mountain inn, the Schwarze Adler, in the Austrian Alps. This particular spring he arrives with Carolina von Kirchstetten, his patroness and unpaid secretary, Elisabeth Zimmer, his young mistress, Dr. Reischmann, his doctor. He hopes that as in former years he will get inspiration from the crazy 'visions' of the widow Mack, who has lived at the inn for the past forty years, ever since her bridegroom was killed climbing the Hammerhorn on the first day of their honeymoon. Not all the poet's hopes are realised. The body of the long dead Herr Mack is found preserved in a glacier and his widow's lunacy is replaced by pungent insight into the motives of her neighbours. Elisabeth falls in love with Toni, Dr. Reischmann's son; and Mittenhofer, deprived of one of his sources of inspiration, finds another in the predicament of the two young lovers who have, with his knowledge, ventured up the mountain side, a fact he neglects to mention to a guide who could save them. The opera ends as he reads his new *Elegy for Young Lovers* to a fashionable audience.

ACT I
The emergence of the bridegroom (each Act and each Scene
has been given a title by the librettists)
I. *Forty years past.*   Hilda Mack, still dressed and made
up in the style of a young woman of the 1870's, sings in
eloquent music of wide range (well over two octaves) of the
day her husband went to climb the Hammerhorn and of her
determination to wait for his return.
II. *The order of the day.*   The inside of the inn lights up
to show Carolina at her desk. Dr. Reischmann enters and
watches her sort press cuttings. Each is summoned in turn,
the one to take the Master his second egg, the other to give him
his morning injection, and the doctor feels Carolina's pulse to
diagnose a bout of flu. The fact that Carolina must finance
the poet by hiding coins where he may expect to find them,
elicits from Dr. Reischmann a 'What would poets do without
their nannies?' and in duet they agree that they are essential
to him, however slight the thanks they get for their faithful
service.
III. *A scheduled arrival.*   The doctor is waiting for the
arrival of his son Toni, who is going through a 'phase' and
seems likely to prove poor company. As soon as Toni comes
in, his father starts to question him, offer him diversion of
one sort or another, every remark producing an exasperated
comment from Toni.
IV. *Appearances and visions.*   Carolina entices Frau Mack
inside just as Mittenhofer, his arm round Elisabeth Zimmer,
makes his entrance, 'a tall well-built man of almost 60,
wearing a corduroy jacket and knickerbockers. His high
forehead and Beethoven-like mane of snow-white hair are
impressive, and he is apt to accentuate both by shaking his
head back.' Mittenhofer is introducing the young people
when Frau Mack starts on one of her coloratura visions, to
the intense satisfaction of the poet, who starts to take notes.
The others leave, Toni commenting, 'What a shamelessly low
variety show.' It is a big-scale aria in typically wide-ranging
style that Frau Mack sings, and in it she seems to foretell
what hindsight tells us is the death of the two young lovers.
V. *Worldly business.*   Mittenhofer is delighted at what he
has got, comments crustily on the reviews Carolina attempts
to show him, and then starts to read yesterday's typing,
interrupting it to yell at Carolina about a mistake she has
made and taunting her until she falls in a faint at his feet. Dr.

Reischmann runs in, and he and a maid carry Carolina to a chair.

VI. *Help.* Mittenhofer disappears to his study, but re-appears a moment later to search the room for his money, like a child looking for sweets. He finds what he is looking for, counts it, puts it in his pocket, bows to the flower pot where he found it, and goes back to his room.

VII. *Unworldly weakness.* Poor Carolina is in a state— 'death in fact looks dazzlingly attractive' is her comment.

VII. *Beauty in death.* Josef Mauer, an Alpine guide, comes in to tell them that a body has been found on the Hammerhorn—fresh and young-looking, his skull cracked at the back. It must be Frau Mack's husband!

IX. *Who is to tell her?* Carolina says she is feeling too ill and she and Dr. Reischmann agree that it must be Elisabeth.

X. *Today's weather.* Gently and kindly, Elisabeth breaks the news to Frau Mack, who is full of foreboding for Elisabeth's own future. In the end she succeeds (in a beautiful canonic duet) in telling her the news, which Frau Mack appears to understand. Toni watches the end of the scene and is moved by the unexpected warmth Elisabeth shows.

XI. *A visionary interlude.* Toni sings a song in tender remembrance of his mother, who died long ago; then turns back to stare at the place where Elisabeth was standing. (It is amazing to find this as an optional cut in the vocal score.)

XII. *Tomorrow: two follies cross.* Hilda, who has remained still throughout Toni's song, suddenly rises in a state bordering on ecstasy. To end the act, she joins in climactic duet with Toni, she because 'the crystal is broken', he because he realises he is falling in love with Elisabeth.

ACT II
The emergence of the bride

I. *A passion.* A few days later: mid-afternoon. Elisabeth and Toni are now plainly in love, as witness their joyful duet, and Toni urges her to break with Mittenhofer. Carolina catches them in each other's arms and calls for the doctor to help her settle what she thinks of as nonsense.

II. *Sensible talk.* Dr. Reischmann tries to reason with Toni inside, Carolina with Elisabeth outside; 'what the world needs are warmer hearts, not older poets' is the gist of the discussion.

III. *Each in his place*.   In a duet which is composed of two separate monologues, the two young people express their outrage.

IV. *The Master's time*.   Carolina's line, 'It's time for the Master's tea', precipitates a crisis: as Elisabeth in one room asks Toni to take her away, Mittenhofer in another is told by Carolina that there is a situation between Elisabeth and Toni, and asks Carolina to have Elisabeth join him at tea.

V. *Personal questions*.   Mittenhofer's tack is to criticise himself and play on Elisabeth's guilt feelings. 'I was angry for the sake of an unmade verse crying out to be made . . . once again I'm made to learn that in the end a poet may depend on no one but himself.' He is the best devil's advocate imaginable, and the gist of the scene is an *apologia pro vita sua*. At the monologue's end, Elisabeth leaves, without having told him anything.

VI. *The troubles of others*.   Elisabeth (and later the orchestra) is sad.

VII. *What must be told*.   Elisabeth admits to Toni that she has said nothing, partly because they know nothing about each other, partly because she did not dare. Toni says he will do the job.

VIII. *The wrong time*.   As Toni goes towards Mittenhofer's door, the poet himself emerges, to listen to Toni's protestations of love for Elisabeth. An ensemble of considerable dimensions builds up, involving all four characters, Mittenhofer, Elisabeth (Carolina taking her place at its end), Toni, the doctor.

IX. *The bride*.   Elisabeth bursts into tears, a cow bell rings, and Frau Mack comes into sight, singing tipsily (and higher than ever) and rejoicing in the new situation, which she relishes to the full. Top C's abound, Frau Mack demands 10% of Mittenhofer's future royalties, and after a ringing top E natural, turns to Elisabeth and starts to comfort her. 'Frau Mack, do you think I'm a whore?' Mittenhofer resolves the situation by begging Dr. Reischmann to bless the lovers.

X. *The young lovers*.   In a grandiose ensemble, Mittenhofer explains his new poem, 'The Young Lovers'. The characters seem to breathe life from his words, which perfectly express their different situations for them.

XI. *The flower*.   The doctor blesses the match and Mittenhofer, taking advantage of the moment and the fact that in a day or two's time he will be 60, begs the young couple to stay over a day or two longer and pick him on the slopes of the Hammerhorn an Edelweiss, which he needs if he is to finish his poem. They agree; Frau Mack plans her departure.

XII. *The vision of tomorrow.* The young lovers will stay, Mittenhofer refuses his tonic—to watch young love is enough—and, after a moment of six voices together, the rest leave and Mauer comes in to tell Mittenhofer that tomorrow will be warm and the weather on the slopes of the Hammerhorn propitious enough for them to find the Edelweiss he craves.

XIII. *The end of the day.* The atmosphere changes from one of acquiescence to another of unbridled fury—Mittenhofer's 'shoulders rise, his fists clench. He turns round, his features distorted with rage. He stamps his feet and makes a noise like an enraged ram.' In a furious monologue, he inveighs against all around him, from Frau Mack to the doctor, from Carolina to Elisabeth. 'Why don't they die?' He is about to hurl an inkwell across the room when Frau Mack comes back to confront him, so that he departs with a bellow of rage leaving her in uncontrollable laughter.

ACT III
Man and wife

I. *Echoes.* Hilda is ready to travel, Toni and Elisabeth to ascend the mountain, which they do singing a folk song, while Hilda sings farewell. An ensemble mounts, during whose course Mittenhofer can be heard trying out rhymes and prepositions. Frau Mack feels she is too young—or is it too old?—and the keys of the town house remind Mittenhofer of a prisoner's cell.

II. *Farewells.* It remains for Frau Mack to bow tenderly out of the opera, giving Carolina the colossal scarf she has been knitting for the past 40 years. Mittenhofer comes out to persuade Carolina to laugh, and Frau Mack has a good word even for him.

III. *Scheduled departures.* 'The young in pairs, the old in two proceed'; the music is a quartet.

IV. *Two to go.* Carolina makes some attempt to damp down the fires which still burn within Mittenhofer, but to no great avail. At the end of the scene Mauer hurries in to say that a threatening blizzard is blowing up and that in minutes the mountain will be blanketed in snow. Is anyone still up there? Mittenhofer, without looking at Carolina, denies knowledge of anyone, and Mauer hurries off to ask the question elsewhere.

V. *Mad happenings*.   As the sky darkens, Mittenhofer and Carolina confront each other and the Master slyly suggests that she go away 'for a change of scene'. If she was ever quite sane, she is no longer.

VI. *A change of scene*.   For the first time we are outside the inn, and the Hammerhorn is visible, in a blizzard. An extended orchestral interlude leads us to Toni and Elisabeth in the last stages of exhaustion on the mountain.

VII. *Man and wife*.   (Scenes VII and VIII were omitted at Glyndebourne in 1961.) Their duet takes the form of reminiscences of a long married husband and wife. They discuss the imagined birth and death of children, a love affair in Munich, forgiveness and togetherness.

VIII. *Toni and Elisabeth*.   They have discovered something beyond love: Truth. This will help them to die.

IX. *Elegy for young lovers*.   Mittenhofer is tying his white tie before going on stage to read poetry in Vienna. He goes through a cheer sequence—'One. Two. Three. Four. Whom do we adore?'—then dedicates the poem he is about to read to 'the memory of a brave and beautiful young couple, Toni Reischmann and Elisabeth Zimmer'. He mouths beneath an invisible ensemble of Hilda Mack, Elisabeth, Carolina, Toni and the doctor; the poem is, with the help of others, finished, and the opera therefore at an end.   H.

THE BASSARIDS

Opera seria with Intermezzo in one act by Hans Werner Henze; libretto, based on *The Bacchae* of Euripides, by W. H. Auden and Chester Kallman. Première, Salzburg, August 6, 1966, with Ingeborg Hallstein, Kerstin Meyer, Vera Little, Loren Driscoll, Helmut Melchert, Kostas Paskalis, William Dooley, Peter Lagger, conductor Christoph von Dohnanyi. First produced Deutsche Oper, Berlin, 1966, with the same cast and conductor; la Scala, Milan, 1967, in Italian, with Meneguzzer, Meyer, Driscoll, Picchi, Paskalis, Washington, conductor Sanzogno; Santa Fé, 1967, in English, with Regina Safarty, Driscoll, John Reardon, conductor Henze; B.B.C., 1967 (broadcast only), conductor Downes; English National Opera, 1974, with Barstow, Katherine Pring, Collins, Dempsey, Woollam, Welsby, McDonnell, Wicks, producer and conductor Henze.

CHARACTERS

Dionysus (also Voice and Stranger) .... Tenor
Pentheus, *King of Thebes* .... Baritone
Cadmus, *his grandfather, founder of Thebes* ..... Bass
Tiresias, *an old blind prophet* .... Tenor
Captain of the Royal Guard .... Baritone
Agave, *Cadmus's daughter and mother of Pentheus*
.... Mezzo-Soprano
Autonoe, *her sister* .... Soprano
Beroe, *an old slave, once nurse to Semele*
and later to Pentheus .... Mezzo-Soprano
Young woman, *slave in Agave's household* .... Mute
Child, *her daughter* .... Mute
Bassarids (Maenads and Bacchants),
Citizens of Thebes, Guards, Servants
Time: Antiquity   *Place:* The Royal Palace, Thebes,
and Mount Cythaeron

The Bassarids,[1] Henze's second collaboration with W. H. Auden and Chester Kallman, is a free adaptation of *The Bacchae* of Euripides. The composer asked his librettists to mould the opera in the form of a symphony, and the result is a continuous work, about as long as *Das Rheingold*, cast in four movements—composer and librettists use this title to designate the changes of mood. It was freely said at the time of the opera's première that the writers agreed to provide the tragic libretto of *The Bassarids* provided Henze 'made his peace with Wagner'. Peter Heyworth[2] suggested that this stipulation was very much in the composer's interests. 'In a period when the orchestra has evolved into such a uniquely supple and expressive instrument and the springs of melody have run so low ... there has seemed something almost perverse in Henze's devotion to the closed and essentially melodic forms of the old Italian opera ... in his manner of manipulating material, Henze is deeply indebted to the Schoenbergian dodecaphonic technique, and the most natural means of applying this to opera lies in the quasi-symphonic Wagnerian music drama, if only because both are rooted in the art of variation.'

[1] The title *Bassarids* is an alternative name for *Bacchae*, or worshippers of Dionysus.
[2] Writing in *The Observer* after the Salzburg performance.

The story symbolises 'the terrible revenge taken by the sensual Dionysian side of human nature if its existence is denied and its demands repressed',[1] and the achievement of the librettists is to have not only reflected the brutality of the century in which they write (and during which we watch and listen) but also to have filled the book with a web of psychological motivation. In the process, they have inspired the composer to one of his most important operatic scores.

Thebes was founded by Cadmus, son of Agenor, King of Tyre, and brother of Europa, who had been loved by Zeus in the guise of a bull. Five warriors, known as the Sown Men because they sprang from the dragon's teeth Cadmus sowed, helped him to build the citadel of Thebes and themselves founded the city's noble families, one of their number Echion marrying Cadmus's youngest daughter Agave. Another of Cadmus's daughters was Semele, whom Zeus courted as a mortal. Zeus's wife, Hera, disguised herself as Semele's servant, Beroe, and persuaded her to demand that Zeus should reveal himself in all his divine splendour, a piece of mortal folly whose gratification reduced her to ashes.[2] Zeus, legend goes, succeeded in rescuing her unborn child, Dionysus, and sewing him into his thigh from which eventually the boy was born.

Before the opera starts, Semele's tomb is already a shrine of pilgrimage for devotees of the cult of Dionysus, but some people, including Semele's own sisters, believe that Semele's lover was a mortal and not Zeus at all and consequently view the cult with contempt. Cadmus has abdicated in favour of his grandson Pentheus, who now reigns as King of Thebes. On his shoulders rather than on those of his grandfather lies the momentous responsibility of deciding whether to risk offending the other gods by recognising Dionysus's divinity, or run the consequences of Dionysus's wrath by opting for the theory that Semele's lover was mortal. Pentheus's invidious position is complicated by his absolute belief in reason and conviction that the source of all human blindness and wrongdoing lies in the passions of the flesh.

First movement. The courtyard of the Royal Palace in Thebes, with the Palace on one side and the tomb of Semele on the other; in front of the tomb is an altar on which a flame burns. The citizens of Thebes are gathered in tribute to

---

[1] *The Times* after the première in Salzburg.   [2] See pp. 52–6.

their new king, whom they hymn in chorus. Their theme is the founding of Thebes and its present—they hope auspicious—rule by a Sown Man's son, Pentheus. Suddenly a voice is heard from a distance: 'Ayayalya! the God Dionysus has entered Bœotia!' The musical atmosphere dramatically changes from the matter-of-fact to one of mystery, and the reaction of the people is instantaneous: they take up the chant and go off in the direction from which the singing seems to have come—the populace has turned in a few bars of music into Bassarids.

When Cadmus, Beroe, Agave and Tiresias make their entry, it is to find the space in front of the palace empty. Tiresias, the old blind prophet whose weakness is that he cannot bear to be excluded from the latest movement, longs to join the worshippers of Dionysus and go to Mount Cythaeron. Cadmus urges caution, on the grounds that no one yet knows for sure that Dionysus is a god, and moreover the mere mention of his name seems to infuriate Pentheus the King. When Agave asks Beroe if Semele was loved by Zeus, she can elicit from her no more than, 'I know nothing', which only increases her contempt for Tiresias's enthusiasm.

During the following scene, the Bassarids' hymn continues as background. Cadmus is concerned with the crucial matter of whether Dionysus is divine or not, but Agave's attention is quickly diverted by the sight of the Captain of the Guard, a handsome man no longer in his first youth but sufficiently attractive to appeal to her deprived, widow's eyes. Autonoe comes in behind Agave, and it is plain that she too is attracted by the Captain of the Guard. Beroe tells them that the King wants his most prominent relations to hear the first proclamation of his reign, which the Captain of the Guard now reads; the royal message denounces the idea that Semele was the object of the affections of one of the immortals and therefore that her offspring could be himself a God, and forbids Thebans to subscribe to any such belief.

Before his grandfather, mother, aunt and nurse have had time to do more than begin their comment on his proclamation, Pentheus himself appears. He is a young man, spare, athletic even ascetic in appearance, and immediately starts to dilate on the ignorance which has permitted women to light a flame on Semele's tomb. After a moment's hesitation, he flings his cloak over the flame on the altar and extinguishes it. Only then does the King notice that the people, who had been summoned to listen to his proclamation, are not in the square and, when Agave reveals to him that they danced off to Cythaeron, he departs in a fury, leaving his relations to comment from their various points of view on the course of events. Suddenly the off-stage voice of Dionysus is heard singing mysteriously and beautifully the praises of Cythaeron (usually referred to as his Serenade). Agave and Autonoe are hypnotised by what they hear and dance away so that they are out of sight by the time Pentheus re-appears.

Second movement. Cadmus in his despair reasserts his authority—Pentheus after all rules by his consent. But Pentheus refuses to listen to him, proclaims that in future Thebes will know a harder rule, and, to Cadmus's evident dismay, orders the guards out, instructing them to proceed to Cythaeron and return with what prisoners they can take. The sound of the Bassarids' chant is heard again, and during Pentheus's aria (its burden: Thebes must once again know Truth and spurn what is false) his old nurse Beroe mutters a prayer to herself. When he has finished, Pentheus turns to Beroe, and swears in her presence to 'abstain from wine, from meats, and from woman's bed, live sober and chaste till the day I die'.

The guards return with their prisoners, amongst them Agave, Autonoe, Tiresias, a youthful stranger, who is in fact Dionysus, a few male Bacchants, and a young woman with her child. All are in a state of trance and the Bassarids' chant continues as Pentheus, unable to get any sensible answer from his prisoners, orders the Captain to take them away and question them with torture, leaving behind only Tiresias, the unknown young man, and his own relations to be examined by the King himself.

Agave is the first to be questioned and in an aria she attempts to describe what she saw on Mount Cythaeron—'a kind of Wordsworthian mystical vision of nature', the librettists have called it. Beroe tries to warn Pentheus, but the scene is soon out of his control as each one present pursues his or her own line of thinking. To the King's fury, not only can he himself get nothing out of the prisoners, but the Captain tells him that even under torture the others seemed to feel no pain and gave no information. The King orders Agave and Autonoe to their palace, bids the Captain of the Guard demolish Tiresias's house, and himself starts to question the stranger (whom he imagines a priest of Dionysus), at first casually, but gradually, as he reacts to the answers he gets, with barely suppressed fury. In the course of an aria, the stranger tells him of the curious adventure which befell him in the Aegean, when he hired a ship and crew to take him to the island of Naxos. The sailors turned out to be pirates and altered course, meaning to sell him as a slave. But Dionysus caused a vine to grow from the deck and wild animals to appear on board, so that the seamen leapt overboard in terror at the plague of serpents he conjured up and were turned into dolphins.

Third movement. The Bassarids continue to sing, the Captain returns and waits for orders, and Pentheus's calm finally breaks with the result that he orders the Captain to take the stranger away and 'break that smiling mouth of its lie. Lay whips to his pampered flesh . . .'.

Influences beyond Pentheus's control take over. There is the sound of an earthquake, Pentheus's cloak is plucked from Semele's tomb so that the flame shoots up again, and the prisoners can be heard shouting as they escape towards Cythaeron. The King orders the Captain to take the guard on to the hill and wipe out all the worshippers of Dionysus he can find, but the stranger urges a more cautious course, his words having a curious effect on Pentheus, who seems to agree with the advice he is being given and who welcomes, repelled and fascinated at the same time, the offer which is made to him, that he may by magic see the rites in which his mother and his aunt are engaged. His mother's mirror is fetched and held so that it reflects the flame from Semele's tomb. The audible laughter of the Bassarids serves as a link as the scenery disappears to be replaced by what is described in the score as 'a realistically painted representation of a Boucher-like garden, with statues of mythological groups', where plays the

Intermezzo. In a period, up-dated setting—'Marie Antoinette' is the style—Agave and Autone are breathless with laughter in their reaction to the behaviour of Pentheus. With the Captain of the Guard, whom each thinks of as a kind of sexual plaything, they enact the story of the Judgement of Calliope—as will be seen at the end, in reality Pentheus's repressed fantasies, where sex is far from the robust thing known to Thebes, but, in a decadent world, the subject of giggles.

Cinryas, King of Cyprus, has boasted that his daughter. Smyrna is more beautiful than the goddess Aphrodite. In revenge, Aphrodite has had Smyrna fall in love with her own father by whom, while he is drunk, she becomes pregnant. When Cinryas discovers what has happened, sword in hand he chases his daughter, whom Aphrodite turns into a myrrh tree at the moment Cinryas's sword splits her in two. Out falls the infant Adonis. With an eye to the future, Aphrodite hides him in a chest and entrusts it to Persephone, Queen of the Dead, who herself falls a prey to feminine curiosity and opens the chest, immediately to fall in love with Adonis, whom she takes off to her own palace. Aphrodite appeals to Zeus and he appoints the Muse Calliope to make judgement. The verdict of Calliope is that each of the goddesses has rendered Adonis signal service and therefore has an equal claim on him; his year should therefore be divided into three parts, one for Aphrodite, one for Persephone and one to be spent as he himself chooses. Aphrodite cheats and by her magic contrives that Adonis spends all the year with her, with the result that Persephone, with more than a little justification, goes to Ares (Mars) and tells him that Aphrodite has a mortal lover whom she prefers to him. The god in his jealous rage disguises himself as a boar and gores Adonis to death on Mount Lebanon. As part of the up-dating process (for the modern audience in the theatre rather than the voyeur king) the names of the characters in the story are changed from their Greek equivalents to Mars, Pluto, Jove, Venus, Proserpine.

The story is worked out in semi-formal musical terms and played as a charade by Agave, Autonoe and the Captain, while Tiresias enters dressed as a kind of Bacchant to act as Calliope. A pair of mandolins and a guitar on the stage gives the accompaniment an element of period flavour, and recitatives, arias (usually with a specified *cabaletta*), duets, a round for four voices, a formal trio and a final quartet follow each other in sequence, to music which owes something to the Stravinsky of the 1920's, until all four dissolve in laughter and the Captain starts to make good his escape, averring 'my prospects here are gross and grim: those two will have me limb from limb'. The laughter of the Bassarids ends the Intermezzo as it had begun it and takes us back to

A courtyard of the palace. Pentheus is beside himself with righteous horror and indignation and determines to go off to Mount Cythaeron to learn the worst. The stranger seems to warn him of the perils he will run but insists that he must dress as a woman if he is to have any chance of escaping detection. Pentheus seems again to fall under the stranger's spell and, as he goes off to disguise himself, Beroe enters and begs the stranger to spare him, addressing him as Dionysus. He refuses, and Pentheus emerges tricked out incongruously in one of Agave's dresses. The voices of Dionysus and Pentheus join and by the end of their scene together sound—literally, as they sing together—as one. Dionysus takes Pentheus by the hand and leads him through the lines of the bodyguard towards Cythaeron. Beroe is left alone lamenting the loss of the King whom she fears she will see no more. Cadmus adds his own lament, this time for the prospective fall of Thebes.

With the sound of the Bassarids becoming insidiously audible again, the scene changes, a procession of torches can be seen, the world of the senses has again taken over and through the foliage Pentheus can be observed crouching on a branch of a tree. The Bacchic orgy proceeds, Pentheus temporarily disappears and the voice of Dionysus himself is heard greeting the Maenads and inviting them to hunt down a trespasser who must, he says, be in their midst. The movements of the Bassarids have started as ritual but, as the music mounts in tension, they acquire purpose and the man hunt is on. Suddenly, a shaft of light, which should remind the onlooker of the light from Agave's mirror, falls on Pentheus and he is seen to be surrounded. In a moving final statement, half dignified, half imploring, he begs his mother to recognise him, but in vain, and as the lights go out, nothing but his scream is left of what had once been King of Thebes.

Fourth movement.   The Maenads are heard in a chorus of triumph, and, back in the courtyard of the palace, Cadmus and Beroe are still keeping watch. When they appear, Agave is seen to be carrying the head of Pentheus torn from his body, and, shuddering, Cadmus attempts to introduce an element of the rational into a situation which, he sees clearly, poses the end of the Thebes he himself had created. When Agave demands to see the King, he starts slowly to question her, as to what she can see, what she can remember and finally, what she can recognise in the gory object she carries. She tries to maintain her belief that it is the head of a young lion, but in the end—agonisingly—recognises her own son. As the Captain and the guards carry in the mangled corpse of King Pentheus on a litter, Autonoe and the Chorus disclaim all part in the murder, but Agave understands and asks her father to take Pentheus's sword and slay her with it. An ensemble of lamentation covers the efforts of Agave to move from a state of shock to one where the deepest grief is possible, and she mourns the death of her son in a slow aria, its burden in the final words:

> 'We both did what neither would:
> The strong Gods are not good.'

Suddenly, Dionysus is on the scene, proclaiming, with so little preamble that the effect is one of insensitivity, his godly condition, and banishing Cadmus, Autonoe and Agave from Thebes, and ordering the Captain to set fire to the palace. In a sudden burst of defiance, Agave turns to Dionysus and tells him to remember the fate of Uranus and Chronos.[1] Tartarus waits for them all in the end.

As the stage is bathed in flame, Dionysus sings of his purpose in coming to Thebes—vengeance for what the city and its inhabitants have done to his mother; it remains now only for him to restore Semele to the position from which her enemies tried to remove her. As the opera ends in a soft chorus of the Bassarids, two statues are seen standing on Semele's tomb, representing Dionysus and Thyone (the new name of the translated Semele) and appearing to the eyes of the twentieth-century audience as 'two enormous primitive fertility idols of an African or South Seas type'.

H.

DER JUNGE LORD
The Young Lord

Comic opera in two acts by Hans Werner Henze, libretto by Ingeborg Bachmann, after a fable from *Der Scheik von Alexandria und seine Sklaven* by Wilhelm Hauff. Première, Deutsche Oper, Berlin, April 7, 1965, with Edith Mathis, Patricia Johnson, Loren Driscoll, Donald Grobe, Barry McDaniel, conductor Christoph von Dohnanyi. First performed Stuttgart, 1965, with Liselotte Rebmann, Lilian Benningsen,

---

[1] Uranus in Greek mythology was the personification of Heaven. He hated his children, the Titans, and confined them in Tartarus. But they broke out and his son Chronos dethroned him, only later in his turn to be dethroned by his own son Zeus.

Gerhard Stolze, James Harper, Karlheinz Peters, conductor Ferdinand Leitner; Rome, 1965, with Maria Chiara, Fedora Barbieri, Giuseppe Campora, Aldo Bottion, conductor Henze; Dresden, 1967; San Diego, 1967; London, 1969 (by Cologne company), with Wendy Fine, Cvetka Ahlin, Hubert Mohler, James Harper, Claudio Nicolai, conductor Marek Janowski.

CHARACTERS

Sir Edgar .... Silent
His secretary .... Baritone
Lord Barrat, *Sir Edgar's nephew* .... Tenor
Begonia, *his Jamaican cook* .... Mezzo-Soprano
The Mayor .... Bass-Baritone
Councillor Hasentreffer .... Baritone
Councillor Scharf .... Baritone
Professor von Mucker .... Buffo tenor
Baroness Grünwiesel .... Mezzo-Soprano
Frau von Hufnagel .... Mezzo-Soprano
Frau Hasentreffer .... Soprano
Luise, *the Baroness's ward* .... Soprano
Ida, *her friend* .... Soprano
A maid .... Soprano
Wilhelm, *a student* .... Tenor
Amintore La Rocca, *a circus director* .. Dramatic Tenor
A lamplighter .... Baritone
Monsieur La Truiare, *dancing master* .... Silent
Meadows, *the butler* .... Silent
Jeremy, *a Moor* .... Silent
Circus Performers, a Teacher, a Military Band, a
Dance Band, Ladies and Gentlemen of Society,
Men and Women of the People, Children

Time: 1830　　　　　　　　　*Place:* Hülsdorf-Gotha

Henze's fifth opera written for the stage (as opposed to radio) is a black comedy, based on the German Wilhelm Hauff's parable *Der Affe als Mensch*, written after he had been living for some time in Italy and drawing on his enthusiasm for early nineteenth-century opera composers—Rossini and Bellini for instance. This is the early nineteenth century seen through Henze's musical eyes, just as we have looked at the eighteenth through Stravinsky's. There is lyrical writing in plenty—*Der junge Lord* is a thoroughly 'vocal' opera—but the main expression is through the ensemble as developed by Rossini and the Verdi of *Falstaff*. It all bustles along at a capital pace, easy to listen to, witty, but in no sense a classical comedy with a happy ending. The monkey screams because he is learning the hard way, the rose he gives to Luise has a sharp enough thorn to draw blood.

The action takes place in the German town of Hülsdorf-Gotha in 1830. It is autumn and the leaves are turning yellow.

Act I.   The small but pretty square of the town. Rumour has it that a rich Englishman—a man of learning—is about to arrive in the town, where he has rented a house and where he proposes to spend some time (and doubtless money too). The senior citizens speculate on the possibilities and rehearse their speeches of greeting. Luise, the most eligible girl in the town, is obviously attracted to Wilhelm, a student, and they sing lyrically standing a few yards apart. Schoolchildren are rehearsed in a *cantata* of greeting for the visitor, when the arrival of the first carriage is signalled. The Mayor and the other worthies form up as a welcome committee and watch, with some stupefaction, as emerge one after another, not the grandee they had expected, but his retinue, starting with a collection of animals, continuing with a black page and some other servants, and finishing with Begonia, his black cook from Jamaica, who succeeds in dominating the scene. She takes a swig of rum, lapses occasionally into English, and then joins with the others in expectation of a third, even more splendidly decorated carriage.

From it with much ceremony (including a snatch of Turkish music from *Die Entführung*) emerges Sir Edgar,[1] a little tired from his journey but prepared through his secretary to make a relatively gracious answer to the blandishments of the reception committee. Nonetheless he refuses all invitations and even denies having any particular wishes; he only wants to put the town to no inconvenience whatsoever. The skies grow dark, Begonia puts up her umbrella, and embarrassment if anything increases at the way the weather has added to the general farce and confusion. Only Luise and Wilhelm welcome the distraction.

Scene ii.   Baroness Grünwiesel's salon. Even though Sir

[1] An operatic curiosity was the appearance of Sir Rudolf Bing, longtime General Manager of New York's Metropolitan Opera, in this silent role at New York's City Opera in 1973. Bing, who had retired from the Metropolitan in 1972, had always maintained a lofty hostility towards rival companies particularly those close to home.

Edgar has so far turned down all invitations, Baroness Grünwiesel, as Hülsdorf-Gotha's leader of society, has gathered together its ladies to meet him, hoping that an appropriate exception will be made in her case. Her plans for him and Luise are all too obvious, but everything changes when a message is brought by Jeremy, the black page (who throws the Baroness's servants into confusion), to the effect that Sir Edgar cannot accept her invitation. Such an insult is not to be borne and nothing will calm the Baroness's mounting fury. From now on she has only one aim in life, to make life in the town impossible for their odious visitor! Will she prove a worthy successor to Rossini's Don Basilio? The interlude suggests she may.

Scene iii. The town square. An unpretentious country circus has established itself and its performance is coming to an end; we see the final turns. Its Neapolitan director, Amintore La Rocca, thanks the public just as the door of Sir Edgar's house opens and, preceded by his staff, he emerges to watch the circus. The only gesture of recognition he makes towards the townspeople is at their children, and comments—for instance that he goes to the circus but not to church—are fairly free. The town council attempts to flatter Sir Edgar, his secretary tries to put them off, Wilhelm and Luise indulge in the mildest of flirtations, La Rocca continues to salute the public, until a crisis develops when the councillors decide to deny the circus a licence to perform. Sir Edgar offers to pay their dues and ends by inviting director, dancing girl, fire-eater and 'human monkey' into his house, leaving the citizens outside, the humblest admiring his generosity, the more puffed up complaining at the slight he seems to offer them. Just before the curtain falls, two men creep in to percussive accompaniment and write the word SHAME on the front of Sir Edgar's house.

Act II: scene iv. The scene is the front of Sir Edgar's house on a typical German winter's night with snow on the ground. The sympathy of the townspeople has turned against the Englishman, and children pelt the unfortunate Jeremy with snowballs as he returns from a shopping expedition. A lamplighter is making his rounds and hears from the house bloodcurdling cries and shrieks suggestive of something appalling going on inside. He rushes off, and the scene is clear for Luise and Wilhelm to confess their love to each other, which they do most tenderly in a lyrical duet.

Their idyll is interrupted by more shrieks from the house and then by the arrival of the Mayor and town council, led by the lamplighter to the scene of the supposed crime. The shrieks are heard again and the Mayor demands to be admitted to investigate. Sir Edgar's secretary tells them that the door is open and indeed Sir Edgar appears at it, but leaves the secretary to explain that what they have heard are the sighs and complaints of Sir Edgar's nephew, recently arrived from London and now hard at work learning German, a process he finds thoroughly disagreeable and against which they have heard his protests. As soon as he is proficient, they will all be invited to meet him! They depart in a much better mood.

Scene v.   A reception in the library of Sir Edgar's house. Maps, geological exhibits, skeletons, stuffed animals, antique statues, form part of the extravagant elegance. Final preparations for a party are in hand, and Begonia waltzes across the stage with a vast dish of goodies in either hand. She is on top of the world and breaks into English to inform us (as so often before) of Napoleon's attitude towards these edibles, in this case favourable. The secretary tries to get in a word, Jeremy pinches something from a plate, and all is ready for the entrance of the guests, headed by the Baroness herself, with Luise and Ida and the other worthies of the town, not forgetting Wilhelm. The secretary greets them, tea or punch or champagne is served and there are expressions of general gratification.

The secretary says that Sir Edgar still has reservations about his nephew's ability to speak German, but everyone makes light of the problem and in a moment Sir Edgar becomes visible on a staircase, with the young Lord. Sir Edgar kisses the Baroness's hand, and so after a moment's hesitation does Lord Barrat. He is wearing gloves and spectacles and is very smartly dressed. His conversation is a bit limited but everyone is impressed, not least Luise, whose handbag he seizes, and, after a quick look round, chucks behind him. The Baroness appears by no means nonplussed and tells Luise to offer him a cup of tea. After a moment's hesitation and conversation with Ida, she brings him the cup, which he takes in both hands, empties and then throws behind him. When he starts to kiss in rapid succession the hands of the Baroness and Luise, everyone, after a moment's stupefaction, breathes again.

Nothing goes absolutely right, in spite of the Mayor's

interest in Begonia, and when Lord Barrat puts first one leg and then the other on the table, there is nothing to do for the ladies but comment on the elegance with which he pursues his eccentricities, a point of view with which Wilhelm is not in accord. In spite of his foul mood, Wilhelm goes with Sir Edgar and the secretary to look at the collection, and for the first time finds his interest involved. The Mayor continues to pay court to Begonia, who gives him at least as good as she gets, and the ladies cluster round Lord Barrat. This worthy distinguishes himself by pulling a ribbon off Luise's dress and then starts to dance, imitated by the other young men. He plays with Luise's shawl, and Begonia comments 'Jamaica girls call this *hanky-panky*. Napoleon hated it.' Wilhelm can stand it no longer and faces up to Lord Barrat, to whom Sir Edgar and the secretary make signs to depart. Luise faints, and Wilhelm feels everyone against him.

Scene vi. The great ballroom in the Casino. Luise leaves the scene of activity and comes in by one of the doors to sing of her happiness in an aria. Her love for Lord Barrat has transformed her from the naïve girl who fell in love with Wilhelm to somebody much more knowing. Lord Barrat comes in and moves silently towards her, gives her a rose so that the thorn scratches her hand until the blood flows. Barrat and Luise sing together and after a moment Wilhelm comes in and watches them and soon everyone is a party to the secret of the betrothal.

The room fills up and all start to dance (Debutantes' waltz), Lord Barrat in so exaggerated a manner as to cause everybody else to try at first to copy him (as they have earlier his clothes and manners) until, after a bit, he takes Luise alone on to the floor and the others draw back. After a moment and watched all the time by Sir Edgar's secretary, he seizes an instrument from one of the band and blows it savagely to the mild astonishment of the councillors, who continue to contrive some form of admiration. When he starts to swing from the chandeliers, astonishment gives way to alarm, and even the appearance of Sir Edgar, who greets Wilhelm, does not prevent an element of panic creeping in, as Lord Barrat dances Luise into exhaustion, then proceeds to tear his gloves, tie and clothes off, throwing them in every direction. Before long the monkey is revealed and led from the room at a sign from Sir Edgar. Luise and Wilhelm clutch one another, but the comedy comes to an end in general consternation.   H.

15
Italian Opera

GIACOMO PUCCINI
(1858–1924)

MANON LESCAUT

OPERA in four acts by Giacomo Puccini; text by Praga, Oliva, and Illica. Première on February 1, 1893, at the Teatro Regio, Turin, with Cesira-Ferrani, Cremonini, Moro, Polinini, conductor Pome. First performed at Covent Garden, 1894, with Olgina, Beduchi, Pini-Corsi; Philadelphia, 1894; New York, 1898; Metropolitan, 1907, with Cavalieri, Caruso, Scotti. Revived Covent Garden, 1920, with Quaiatti (later dalla Rizza), Burke, Badini; 1929, with Sheridan (later Pampanini), Pertile, Badini; 1937, with Oltrabella, Menescaldi, Noble; Metropolitan, 1927, with Alda, Gigli, Scotti, Didur, conductor Serafin; 1949, with Kirsten, Björling, Valdengo; la Scala, Milan, 1922, with Carraciolo, Pertile, Badini, conductor Toscanini; 1934, with Pacetti, Ziliani, Biasini; 1941, with Caniglia, Gigli, Poli, conductor Marinuzzi; 1944, with Favero, Beval, Stabile, conductor Marinuzzi; 1949, with Barbato, del Monaco, Colombo; Metropolitan, New York, 1956, with Steber, Tucker, Guarrera, under Mitropoulos; Covent Garden, 1968, with Collier, Ilosfalvy, Massard, conductor Kertesz.

CHARACTERS

Manon Lescaut	Soprano
Lescaut, *sergeant of the King's Guards*	Baritone
Chevalier des Grieux	Tenor
Geronte di Ravoir, *Treasurer-General*	Bass
Edmondo, *a student*	Tenor
The Innkeeper	Bass
A Dancing Master	Tenor
A Musician	Mezzo-Soprano
A Lamp-Lighter	Tenor
A Naval Captain	Bass
A Wig-maker	Mime

A Sergeant of Archers .... Bass

Time: Eighteenth Century   *Place:* Amiens, Paris,
                                         Havre, Louisiana

Act I plays in front of an inn at Amiens. Edmondo has a
solo with chorus of students and girls. Des Grieux is teased
for looking unhappy; perhaps he has had an unsuccessful love
affair? He replies by mockingly serenading them all: 'Tra voi,
belle, brune e bionde.' Lescaut, Geronte, and Manon arrive in
a diligence. Lescaut is taking his sister to a convent to
complete her education, but finding her to be greatly
admired by the wealthy Geronte, is quite willing to play a
negative part and let the old satyr plot with the landlord to
abduct Manon. Des Grieux, however, sees her and asks her
what her name is. 'Donna non vidi mai simile a questa' (Never
did I behold so fair a maiden), he sings in praise of her
beauty:

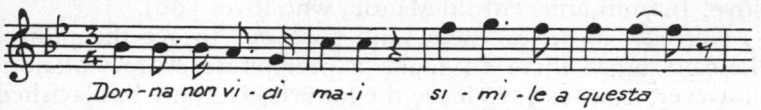

Don-na non vi - di ma-i   si - mi -le a questa

It is the turn of the students to laugh at him.

With Manon, as with des Grieux, it is love at first sight.
When she rejoins him, as she had promised to, they have a
love duet. 'Vedete? Io son fedele alla parola mia' (Behold
me! I have been faithful to my promise), she sings.
Edmondo, who has overheard Geronte's plot to abduct
Manon, informs des Grieux, who has little trouble in inducing
the girl to elope with him. They drive off in the carriage
Geronte had ordered. Lescaut, who has been carousing with
the students, hints that, as des Grieux is not wealthy and
Manon loves luxury, he will soon be able to persuade her to
desert her lover for the rich Treasurer-General.

Such, indeed, is the case, and in Act II she is found
ensconced in luxurious apartments in Geronte's house in Paris.
But to Lescaut, who prides himself on having brought the
business with her wealthy admirer to a successful conclusion,
she complains that in these silken curtains ('In quelle trine
morbide') there is a chill that freezes her. She wishes she
might be back in the humble dwelling where she knew love.
The aria is one of the most beautiful Puccini ever wrote:

A dancing master enters. Manon, Lescaut, Geronte, and old beaux and abbés who have come in with Geronte, form up for the dance, and a lesson in the minuet begins.

Manon is carried away, and expresses her delight in a brilliant aria with chorus: 'L'ora o Tirsi, è vaga e bella.' The soprano who can float a *pianissimo* top C can make a ravishing effect at its end.

Lescaut hurries off to inform des Grieux, who has made money in gambling, where he can find Manon. When the lesson is over and all have gone, her lover appears at the door: 'Tu, tu, amore! Tu?' At first he reproaches her, but soon is won by her beauty. There is an impassioned love duet, 'Vieni! Colle tue braccia stringi Manon che t'ama' (Oh, come love! In your arms enfold Manon, who loves you).

Geronte surprises them, and goes out to get the police. Lescaut urges them to make a precipitate escape. Manon, however, now loath to leave the luxuries Geronte has lavished on her, insists on gathering up her jewels in order to take them with her. Des Grieux reproaches her for her love of luxury, and all the unhappiness she has caused them in the past and will cause them in the future: 'Ah, Manon, mi tradisce il tuo folle pensier', one of Puccini's finest lyrical inspirations. The delay is fatal. The police arrive. She is arrested on the charge made by Geronte that she is an abandoned woman.

Act III. Her sentence is banishment, with other women of loose character, to the then French possession of Louisiana. The journey to Havre for embarkation is represented by an *intermezzo* in the score, and an extract from Abbé Prévost's story in the libretto. The theme of the *intermezzo*, a striking composition, is as follows:

The scene of Act III is laid in a square near the harbour at Havre. Des Grieux and Lescaut have a plan to free Manon rom imprisonment, but are foiled. A lamp-lighter goes across the stage. There is much hubbub when the roll is called of the women who are to be transported. As they step forward, the crowd comments upon their looks. When it is Manon's turn, des Grieux stays at her side. The guard threatens him, but he is distracted with grief at the prospect of losing her and will stand no opposition: 'Ah, non v'avvicinate' (Ah, do not approach me). He appeals to the ship's captain, whose attention has been drawn by the noise, to be taken along with Manon, no matter how lowly the capacity in which he may be required to serve on board: 'Guardate, pazzo son' (Have a care! I'm driven to madness). It is a scene of powerful drama, and can make a splendid effect—must make such an effect, in fact, since the captain is sufficiently impressed to grant his request.

Act IV.   A vast plain on the borders of the territory of New Orleans. The country is bare and undulating, the horizon is far distant, the sky is overcast. Night falls. Thus the stage directions. Manon and des Grieux have left New Orleans—the victims of jealousy and intrigue—and Manon is exhausted with the journey. They sing sadly of the fate which has overtaken them, and Manon begs des Grieux to leave her to die alone. He goes off to look for help and, left alone, she gives expression to her terror and misery in a despairing aria: 'Sola, perduta, abbandonata.' When he returns, she is dying. Des Grieux collapses by her side.   K.

LA BOHÈME
The Bohemians

Opera in four acts by Giacomo Puccini; text by Giacosa and Illica. Première on February 1, 1896, at the Teatro Regio, Turin, with Cesari-Ferrani, Pasini, Gorga, Wilmant, Mazzara, Pini-Corsi, conductor

Toscanini. First performed in England in Manchester, 1897, with Alice
Esty, Robert Cunningham; Covent Garden (in English), 1897, with
Alice Esty, Bessie McDonald, Umberto Salvi, Maggi; 1899 (in Italian),
with Melba, de Lussan, de Lucia, Ancona, Journet, Gilibert, conductor
Mancinelli; Los Angeles, 1897; New York, 1898; Metropolitan, 1900,
with Melba, Occhiolini, Saléza, Campanari, conductor Mancinelli.
Revived at la Scala, Milan, 1924, with Zamboni, Ferraris, Pertile,
Franci, conductor Toscanini; 1947, with Favero, Menotti, Lauri-Volpi.
Tagliabue; 1963, with Freni, Sciutti, Raimondi, Panerai, Vinco under
Karajan (in production by Zeffirelli). Covent Garden revivals include
1935, with Grace Moore, Naylor, Dino Borgioli, Brownlee, Pinza; 1938,
with Perli, Andreva, Gigli, Rossi-Morelli, conductor Gui.

CHARACTERS

Rodolfo, *a poet* .... Tenor
Marcello, *a painter* .... Baritone
Colline, *a philosopher* .... Bass
Schaunard, *a musician* .... Baritone
Benoit, *a landlord* .... Bass
Alcindoro, *a state councillor and admirer of*
    Musetta .... Bass
Parpignol, *an itinerant toy vendor* .... Tenor
Custom-house Sergeant .... Bass
Musetta, *a grisette* .... Soprano
Mimi, *a seamstress* .... Soprano
   Students, Work Girls, Citizens, Shopkeepers, Street
     Vendors, Soldiers, Waiters, Boys, Girls, etc.
Time: About 1830   *Place:* Latin Quarter, Paris

La Bohème is considered by many Puccini's finest score.[1]
Since the opera is laid in the Quartier Latin, the students'
quarter of Paris, where gaiety and pathos elbows, it laughs as
well as weeps. Authors and composers who can tear passion
to tatters are more numerous than those who have the light

---

[1] In *Bohème*, Puccini's melodic invention and its turn to expressive
use is at fullest flood and most apt, and he combines it moreover with
an epigrammatic, conversational conciseness that is unique in his
output. As a kind of Italianate parallel to *Rosenkavalier* in terms of
putting across the conversation concisely and with heightened
expression, it is his masterpiece—but few of the listeners regularly
bowled over by its melodic flow and memorability give pause to
discover that points are made, contrary to the work's reputation,
almost too fast for any but connoisseurs to take in!   H.

touch of comedy. The latter, a rare gift, confers distinction upon many passages in the score of *La Bohème*, which now sparkles with merriment, now is eloquent of love, now is filled with despair.

Act I. The garret in the Latin Quarter, where live the inseparable quartet—Rodolfo, poet; Marcello, painter; Colline, philosopher; Schaunard, musician—who defy hunger with cheerfulness and play pranks upon the landlord of their meagre lodging, when he importunes them for his rent.

When the act opens, Rodolfo is at a table writing, and Marcello is at work on a painting, 'The Passage of the Red Sea'. He remarks that, owing to lack of fuel for the garret stove, the Red Sea is rather cold.

'Questo mar rosso' (This Red Sea) runs the duet, in the course of which Rodolfo says that he will sacrifice the manuscript of his tragedy to the needs of the stove. They tear up the first act, throw it into the stove, and light it. Colline comes in with a bundle of books he has vainly been attempting to pawn. Another act of tragedy goes into the fire, by which, still hungry, they warm themselves.

But relief is nigh. Two boys enter, bringing provisions and fuel. After them comes Schaunard. He tosses money on the table. The boys leave. In vain Schaunard tries to tell his friends the ludicrous details of his three-days' musical engagement to an eccentric Englishman. It is enough for them that it has yielded fuel and food, and that some money is left over for the immediate future. Between their noise in stoking the stove and unpacking the provisions, Schaunard cannot make himself heard.

Rodolfo locks the door. Then all go to the table and pour out wine. It is Christmas Eve. Schaunard suggests that, when they have emptied their glasses, they repair to their favourite resort, the Café Momus, and dine. Agreed. There is a knock. It is Benoit, their landlord, come for the rent. They let him in and invite him to drink with them. The sight of the money on the table reassures him. He joins them. The wine loosens his tongue. He boasts of his conquests of women at shady cafés. The four friends feign indignation. What! He, a married man, engaged in such disreputable proceedings! They seize him and eject him, locking the door after him.

The money on the table was earned by Schaunard, but, according to their custom, they divide it. Now, off to the Café Momus—that is, all but Rodolfo, who will join them soon, when he has finished an article he has to write for a new magazine, the *Beaver*. He stands on the landing with a lighted candle to help the others down the rickety stairs.

With nothing that could be designated as a set piece, there has nevertheless not been a dull moment in the music of these scenes. All has been brisk, merry and sparkling, in keeping with the careless gaiety of the four dwellers in the garret.

Rodolfo sits down to write. Ideas are slow in coming. There comes a timid knock at the door.

'Who's there?' he calls.

It is a woman's voice that says, hesitatingly, 'Excuse me, my candle has gone out.'

Rodolfo runs to the door, and opens it. On the threshold stands a frail, appealing young woman. She has a candle in one hand, in the other a key. Rodolfo bids her come in.

She lights her candle by his, but, as she is about to leave, collapses with a fit of coughing in a chair. When she has recovered, the draught again extinguishes first her candle, then Rodolfo's. The room is dark, save for the moonlight that, over the snow-clad roofs of Paris, steals in through the garret window. Mimi exclaims that she has dropped the key to the door of her room. They search for it. He finds and pockets it. Guided by Mimi's voice and movements, he approaches. As she stoops, his hand meets hers. He clasps it.

'Che gelida manina' (Your tiny hand is frozen), he exclaims with tender solicitude. 'Let me warm it into life.' He then tells her who he is, in what has become known as the *Racconto di Rodolfo* (Rodolfo's Narrative); the gentle and solicitous phrase, 'Che gelida manina', followed by the proud exclamation, 'Sono un poeta' (I am a poet), leads up to an eloquent avowal of his dreams and fancies. Then comes the girl's charming 'Mi chiamano Mimi' (They call me Mimi), in which she tells of her work and how the flowers she embroiders for a living transport her from her narrow room out into the broad fields and meadows.

Her frailty, which one can see is caused by consumption in its early stages, makes her beauty the more appealing to Rodolfo.

His friends call him from the street below. Their voices draw Mimi to the window. In the moonlight she appears even lovelier to Rodolfo. 'O soave fanciulla' (Lovely maid in the moonlight) he exclaims, as he takes her to his arms. This is the beginning of the love duet, which, though it be sung in a garret, is as impassioned as any that has echoed through the corridors of operatic palaces, or the moonlit colonnades of forests by historic rivers. The theme is quoted here in the key in which it occurs, like a premonition, a little earlier in the act:

The theme of the love duet is used by the composer several times in the course of the opera, and always in association with Mimi. Especially in the last act does it recur with poignant effect.

Act II. A meeting of streets, where they form a square, with shops of all sorts, and the Café Momus. The square is filled with a happy Christmas Eve crowd. Somewhat aloof from this are Rodolfo and Mimi. Colline stands near the shop of a clothes dealer. Schaunard is haggling with a tinsmith over the price of a horn. Marcello is chaffing the girls who jostle against him in the crowd.

There are street vendors crying their wares; citizens, students, and work-girls, passing to and fro and calling to each other; people at the café giving orders—a merry whirl, depicted in the music by snatches of chorus, bits of recitative, and an instrumental accompaniment that runs through the scene like a many-coloured thread, and holds the pattern together.

Rodolfo and Mimi enter a bonnet shop. The animation outside continues. When the two lovers come out of the shop, Mimi is wearing a new bonnet trimmed with roses. She looks about.

'What is it?' Rodolfo asks suspiciously.

'Are you jealous?' asks Mimi.

'The man in love is always jealous.'

Rodolfo's friends are at a table outside the café. Rodolfo joins them with Mimi. He introduces her to them as one who will make their party complete, for he 'will play the poet, while she's the muse incarnate'.

Parpignol, the toy vendor, crosses the square and goes off, followed by children, whose mothers try to restrain them. The toy vendor is heard crying his wares in the distance. The quartet of Bohemians, now a quintet through the accession of Mimi, order food and wine.

Shopwomen, who are going away, look down one of the streets and exclaim over someone whom they see approaching.

''Tis Musetta! My, she's gorgeous! — Some stammering old dotard is with her.'

Musetta and Marcello have loved, quarrelled, and parted. She has recently formed a liaison with the aged but wealthy Alcindoro de Mittoneaux, who, when she comes into the square, is out of breath trying to keep up with her.

Despite Musetta's and Marcello's attempt to appear indifferent to each other's presence, it is plain that they are not so. Musetta has a chic waltz song, 'Quando me'n vo' soletta per la via' (As through the streets I wander onward merrily), one of the best-known numbers of the score, which she deliberately sings at Marcello, to make him aware, without arousing her aged gallant's suspicions, that she still loves him. Marcello joins *fortissimo* in the reprise.

Pretending her shoe hurts she makes the ridiculous Alcindoro remove it, and trot off with it to the cobbler's. She and Marcello embrace and she joins the five friends at their table, and the expensive supper ordered by Alcindoro is served to them with their own.

A military tattoo is heard approaching from the distance.

There is a great confusion in the square. A waiter brings the bill for the Bohemians' order. Schaunard looks in vain for his purse. Musetta comes to the rescue. 'Make one bill of the two orders. The gentleman who was with me will pay it.'

The patrol enters, headed by a drum major. Musetta is without her shoe, so Marcello and Colline lift her between them to their shoulders and carry her through the crowd, which, sensing the humour of the situation, gives her an ovation, then swirls around Alcindoro, whose foolish figure, appearing from the direction of the cobbler's shop with a pair of shoes for Musetta, it greets with jeers. For his ladybird has fled with her friends from the *Quartier*, and left him to pay all the bills.

Act III.   A gate to the city of Paris on the Orleans road. A toll house at the gate. To the left a tavern, from which, as a sign-board, hangs Marcello's picture of the Red Sea. Several plane trees. It is February and snow is on the ground. The hour is that of dawn and it is cold (as the open fifths of the orchestra aptly illustrate). Scavengers, milk women, truckmen, peasants with produce, are waiting to be admitted to the city. Custom-house officers are seated, asleep, around a brazier. Sounds of revelry are heard from the tavern.

Into the square comes Mimi from the Rue d'Enfer, which leads from the Latin Quarter. She looks pale, distressed, and frailer than ever. A cough racks her. Now and then she leans against one of the plane trees for support.

A message from her brings Marcello out of the tavern. He tells her he finds it more lucrative to paint signboards than pictures. Musetta gives music lessions. Rodolfo is with them. Will not Mimi join them? She weeps, and tells him that Rodolfo is so jealous of her she fears they must part. The duet has real feeling. When Rodolfo, having missed Marcello, comes out to look for him Mimi hides behind a tree, from where she overhears her lover tell his friends that he wishes to give her up because of their frequent quarrels. 'Mimi è una civetta' (Mimi is a heartless creature) is the burden of his song. Her violent coughing reveals her presence. They decide to part—not angrily, but regretfully. Tenderness runs through Mimi's farewell: 'Donde lieta usci,' with its closing line: 'Addio, senza rancore' (Farewell then, I wish you well).

Meanwhile Marcello, who has re-entered the tavern, has caught Musetta flirting with a stranger. This starts a quarrel, which brings them out into the street. The lovers' joint

farewell thus becomes a quartet: 'Addio, dolce svegliare'
(Farewell, sweet love), sing Rodolfo and Mimi, while

Marcello and Musetta upbraid each other. The temperamental
difference between the two women, Mimi gentle and
melancholy, Musetta aggressive and disputatious, and the
difference in the effect upon the two men, are admirably
brought out by the composer. 'Viper!' 'Toad!' Marcello and
Musetta call out to each other, as they separate; while the
frail Mimi sighs, 'Ah! that our winter night might last
forever', and she and Rodolfo sing, 'Our time for parting's
when the roses blow'.

Act IV. The scene is again the attic of the four
Bohemians. Rodolfo is longing for Mimi, of whom he has
heard nothing, Marcello for Musetta, who, having left him, is
indulging in one of her gay intermezzos with one of her
wealthy patrons. 'Ah, Mimi, tu più non torni' (Ah, Mimi,
fickle-hearted), sings Rodolfo, as he gazes at the little pink
bonnet he bought her at the milliner's shop on Christmas
Eve. Schaunard comes in and thrusts the water bottle into
Colline's hat as if the latter were a champagne cooler. The
four friends seek to forget sorrow and poverty in assuming
mock dignities and then indulging in a frolic about the attic.
When the fun is at its height, the door opens and Musetta
enters. She announces that Mimi is dying and, as a last
request, has asked to be brought back to the attic, where she
had been so happy with Rodolfo. He rushes out to get her
and supports her feeble and faltering footsteps to the bed, or
which he gently lowers her.

She coughs; her hands are very cold. Rodolfo takes them
in his to warm them. Musetta hands her earrings to Marcello
and bids him go out and sell them quickly, then buy a tonic
for the dying girl. There is no coffee, no wine. Colline takes
off his overcoat, and having apostrophised it in the 'Song o:
the Coat', goes out to sell it, so as to be able to replenish the
larder. Musetta runs off to get a muff for Mimi, her hands are
still so cold.

Rodolfo and the dying girl are now alone. This tragic
moment, when their love revives too late, finds expression, a

once passionate and exquisite, in the music. The phrases 'Che
gelida manina' and 'Mi chiamano Mimi', from the love scene
in the first act, recur like mournful memories.

Mimi whispers of incidents from early in their love. 'Te lo
rammenti' (Ah! do you remember).

Musetta and the others return. There are tender touches in
the good offices they would render the dying girl. They are
aware before Rodolfo that she is beyond aid. In their faces he
reads what has happened. With a cry, 'Mimi! Mimi!' he falls
sobbing upon her lifeless form. Musetta kneels weeping at the
foot of the bed. Schaunard, overcome, sinks back into a
chair. Colline stands dazed at the suddenness of the
catastrophe. Marcello turns away to hide his emotion.

'Mi chiamano Mimi'!   K.

TOSCA

Opera in three acts by Giacomo Puccini, text by Giacosa and Illica,
after the play by Sardou. Première on January 14, 1900, at the Teatro
Constanzi, Rome, with Darclée, de Marchi, Giraldoni, conductor
Mugnone. First performed at la Scala, Milan, 1900, with Darclée,
Borgatti, Giraldoni, conductor Mancinelli; Metropolitan, 1901, with
Ternina, Cremonini, Scotti, conductor Mancinelli. Revived la Scala,
1927, with Scacciati, Pertile, Galeffi, conductor Toscanini; Covent
Garden, 1964 (in Zeffirelli's production), with Callas, Cioni, Gobbi,

conductor Cillario. Famous Toscas have included Cavalieri, Destinn, Edvina, Eames, Muzio, Jeritza, Pacetti, Lotte Lehmann, Cobelli, Cigna, Caniglia, Grandi, Welitsch, Crespin. Amongst the best-known singers of Scarpia have been Scotti, Baklanoff, Formichi, Franci, Stabile, Tibbett, Rothmüller, Gobbi, Otakar Kraus.

CHARACTERS

Floria Tosca, *a celebrated singer* . . . . Soprano
Mario Cavaradossi, *a painter* . . . . Tenor
Baron Scarpia, *Chief of Police* . . . . Baritone
Cesare Angelotti, *a political prisoner* . . . . Bass
A Sacristan . . . . Baritone
Spoletta, *a police agent* . . . . Tenor
Sciarrone, *a gendarme* . . . . Bass
A Gaoler . . . . Bass
A Shepherd Boy . . . . Contralto
     Roberti, Executioner; a Cardinal, Judge, Scribe,
     Officer, and Sergeant, Soldiers, Police Agents,
     Ladies, Nobles, Citizens, Artisans, etc.
Time: June 1800   *Place:* Rome

Three chords played *fff, tutta forza,* and denoting the imperious yet sinister and vindictive character of Scarpia—such is the introduction to *Tosca.*

Act I.   The church of Sant' Andrea della Valle.[1] To the right the Attavanti chapel; left a scaffolding, dais.
     Enter Angelotti. He has escaped from prison and is seeking a hiding-place. Looking about, he recognises a pillar shrine containing an image of the Virgin, and surmounting a receptacle for holy water. Beneath the feet of the image he searches for and discovers a key, unlocks the Attavanti chapel and disappears within it. The Sacristan comes in. He has a bunch of brushes that he has been cleaning, and is evidently surprised not to find Cavaradossi at his easel. He looks into the basket, finds the picnic in it untouched, and is now sure he was mistaken in thinking he had seen the painter enter.
     The Angelus is rung. The Sacristan kneels. Cavaradossi enters. He uncovers the painting—a Mary Magdalen with large

[1] Sardou describes the church as 'L'Eglise Saint Andréa des Jésuites à Rome. Architecture du Bernin'. He meant Sant' Andrea al Quirinale, but this being an oval church may account for the librettists having made the transfer.   H.

31 Callas and Gobbi in Act I of *Tosca* at Covent Garden.

32 Eva Turner as Turandot in Puccini's opera.

blue eyes and masses of golden hair. The Sacristan recognises in it the portrait of a lady who has lately come frequently to the church to worship. The good man is scandalised at what he considers a sacrilege. Cavaradossi, however, has other things to think of. He compares the face in the portrait with the features of the woman he loves, the dark-eyed Floria Tosca, famous as a singer. 'Recondita armonia di bellezze diverse' (Strange harmony of contrasts deliciously blending), he sings in a celebrated lyrical passage.

Meanwhile the Sacristan, engaged in cleaning the brushes in a jug of water, continues to growl over the sacrilege of putting frivolous women into religious paintings. Finally, his task with the brushes over, he points to the basket and asks, 'Are you fasting?' 'Nothing for me,' says the painter. The Sacristan casts a greedy look at the basket, as he thinks of the benefit he will derive from the artist's abstemiousness, and leaves.

Angelotti, believing no one to be in the church, comes out of his hiding place. He recognises Cavaradossi as a political sympathiser and explains that he has just escaped from the prison in the Castle of Sant' Angelo. The painter at once offers to help him. Just then, however, Tosca's voice is heard outside. The painter presses the basket with wine and food upon the exhausted fugitive, and urges him back into the chapel, while from without Tosca calls more insistently, 'Mario! Mario!'.

Feigning calm, for the meeting with Angelotti, who had been concerned in the abortive uprising to make Rome a republic, has excited him, Cavaradossi admits Tosca. Jealously she insists that he was whispering with someone, and that she heard footsteps and the swish of skirts. Her lover reassures her, tries to embrace her. Gently she reproves him. She cannot let him kiss her before the Madonna until she has prayed to her image and made an offering. She adorns the Virgin's figure with flowers she has brought with her, kneels in prayer, crosses herself and rises. She tells Cavaradossi to await her at the stage door that night, and they will steal away together to his villa. He is still distrait. When he replies, absent-mindedly, he surely will be there, her comment is, 'You say it badly'. Then, beginning the love duet, 'Non la sospiri la nostra casetta' (Do you not long for our dovecote secluded), she conjures up for him a vision of that 'sweet, sweet nest in which we love-birds hide'.

For the moment Cavaradossi forgets Angelotti; then, however, urges Tosca to leave him, so that he may continue with
his work. She is vexed and, when she recognises in the picture
of Mary Magdalen the fair features of the Marchesa Attavanti,
she becomes jealous to the point of rage. But her lover soon
soothes her; what eyes could be more beautiful than hers
('Qual' occhio al mondo')? The various episodes of the duet
make this one of the most effective passages of its kind
Puccini ever wrote.

Tosca having departed, Cavaradossi lets Angelotti out of
the chapel. He is a brother of the Marchesa Attavanti, of
whom Tosca is so needlessly jealous and who has concealed a
suit of woman's clothing for him under the altar. They talk
with hatred of the man responsible for keeping Angelotti in
prison—Scarpia, 'a bigoted satyr and hypocrite, secretly
steeped in vice, yet most demonstratively pious'—the first
hint we have in the opera of the relentless character, whose
desire to possess Tosca is the mainspring of the drama.

A cannon shot startles them. It is from the direction of the
castle and announces the escape of a prisoner—
Angelotti! Cavaradossi suggests the grounds of his villa as a
place of concealment from Scarpia and his police agents,
especially the old dried-up well from which a secret passage
leads to a dark vault. It can be reached by a rough path just
outside the Attavanti chapel. The painter even offers to guide
the fugitive. They leave hastily.

The Sacristan enters excitedly; he has great news—word has
been received that Bonaparte has been defeated. The old man
now notices, greatly to his surprise, that the painter has
disappeared. Acolytes, penitents, choristers, and pupils of the
chapel crowd in from all directions. There is to be a *Te Deum*
in honour of the victory, and that very evening, in the
Farnese palace, a cantata with Floria Tosca as soloist. It
means extra pay for the choristers. They are jubilant.

Scarpia's sudden entrance immediately quietens the
hubbub. A hush falls upon all. For a while they are motionless, as if spellbound, while he gives his orders. While
preparations are made for the *Te Deum*, Scarpia orders a
search in the Attavanti chapel. He finds a fan which, from the
coat-of-arms on it, he recognises as having been left there by
Angelotti's sister. A police agent also finds a basket. As he
comes out with it, the Sacristan unwittingly exclaims that it
is Cavaradossi's, and empty, although the painter had said
that he would eat nothing. It is plain to Scarpia, who has also

discovered in the Mary Magdalen of the picture the likeness to the Marchesa, that Cavaradossi has given the basket of provisions to Angelotti, and been an accomplice to his escape.

Tosca comes in and quickly approaches the dais. She is greatly surprised not to find Cavaradossi at work on the picture. Scarpia dips his fingers in holy water and ironically extends them to Tosca. Reluctantly she touches them, then crosses herself. Scarpia insinuatingly compliments her on her religious zeal. She comes to church to pray, not, like certain frivolous wantons—he points to the picture—to meet their lovers. He now produces the fan. 'Is this a painter's brush?' he asks, and adds that he found it on the easel. Quickly, jealously, Tosca examines it, sees the arms of the Attavanti. She had come to tell her lover that, because she is obliged to sing in the cantata, she will be unable to meet him that night. Her reward is this evidence, offered by Scarpia, that he has been carrying on a love affair with another woman, with whom he probably has gone to the villa. She gives way to an outburst of jealous rage; then, weeping, leaves the church, to the doors of which Scarpia gallantly escorts her. He beckons to his agent Spoletta, and orders him to trail her and report to him at evening at the Farnese Palace.

Church bells are tolling. Intermittently from the Castle of Sant' Angelo comes the boom of the cannon. A Cardinal has entered and is advancing to the high altar. The *Te Deum* begins. Scarpia soliloquises vindictively: 'Va, Tosca! Nel tuo cuor s'annida Scarpia' (Go, Tosca! There is room in your heart for Scarpia).

He pauses to bow reverently as the Cardinal passes by. Still soliloquising, he exults in his power to send Cavaradossi to execution, while Tosca he will bring to his own arms; for her, he exclaims, he would renounce his hopes of heaven. He kneels and joins in the *Te Deum*.

This finale, with its elaborate apparatus, its complex emotions and the sinister and dominating figure of Scarpia set against a brilliant and constantly shifting background, makes a stirring and effective climax to the act.

Act II. The Farnese Palace. Scarpia's apartments on an upper floor. A large window overlooks the palace courtyard. Scarpia is seated at table supping. At intervals he breaks off to reflect. His manner is anxious. An orchestra is heard from a lower storey of the palace, where Queen Caroline is giving an entertainment in honour of the reported victory over Bonaparte. They are dancing, while waiting for Tosca, who is to sing in the cantata. Scarpia summons Sciarrone and gives him a letter, which is to be handed to the singer upon her arrival. Alone, he exults on the probable outcome of the affair: Tosca will yield to his desires. It is in violent conquests like this that he finds his greatest pleasure: 'Ella verrà' (She will come).

Spoletta returns from his mission. Tosca was followed to a villa almost hidden by foliage. She remained but a short time. When she left it, Spoletta and his men searched the house, but could not find Angelotti. Scarpia is furious, but is appeased when Spoletta tells him that they discovered Cavaradossi, put him in irons, and have brought him with them.

Through the open window there is now heard the beginning of the cantata, showing that Tosca has arrived and is on the floor below, where are the Queen's reception rooms. Upon Scarpia's order there are brought in Cavaradossi, Roberti, the executioner, and a judge with his clerk. Cavaradossi's manner is indignant, defiant, Scarpia's at first suave. Now and then Tosca's voice is heard singing below. Finally Scarpia closes the window, thus shutting out the music. His questions addressed to Cavaradossi are now put in a voice more severe. He has just asked, 'Once more and for the last time, where is Angelotti?', when Tosca, evidently alarmed by the contents of the note received from Scarpia, hurries in and, seeing Cavaradossi, fervently embraces him. Under his breath he manages to warn her against disclosing anything she saw at the villa.

Scarpia orders that Cavaradossi be removed to an adjoining room and his deposition there taken. Tosca is not aware that it is the torture chamber whose door has closed upon her lover. With Tosca Scarpia begins his interview quietly, deferentially. He has deduced from Spoletta's report of her having remained but a short time at the villa that, instead of discovering the Attavanti with her lover, as she jealously had suspected, she had found him making plans to conceal Angelotti. In this conjecture he has just been confirmed by her frankly affectionate manner toward Cavaradossi.

At first she answers Scarpia's questions as to the presence of someone else at the villa lightly; then, when he becomes more insistent, her replies show irritation, until, turning on her with 'ferocious sternness', he tells her that his agents are attempting to wring a confession from Cavaradossi by torture. Even at that moment a groan is heard. Tosca implores mercy for her lover. Yes, if she will disclose the hiding-place of Angelotti. It looks as though she will give in, and Scarpia orders that the pressure be slackened; but the sound of Cavaradossi's voice reassures Tosca and she denies that she knows anything. Scarpia orders that the treatment be started again. Groan after groan escapes from the torture chamber. Tosca, overcome, bursts into convulsive sobs and sinks back upon a sofa. Spoletta kneels and mutters a Latin prayer. Scarpia remains cruelly impassive, silent, until, seeing his opportunity in Tosca's collapse, he steps to the door and signals to the executioner, Roberti, to apply still greater pressure. The air is rent with a prolonged cry of pain. Unable longer to bear her lover's anguish and, in spite of warnings to say nothing which he has called out to her between his spasms, she says hurriedly and in a stifled voice to Scarpia, 'The well . . . in the garden'.

Cavaradossi is borne in from the torture chamber and deposited on the sofa. Kneeling beside him Tosca lavishes tears and kisses upon him. Sciarrone, the judge, Roberti, and the clerk go. In obedience to a sign from Scarpia, Spoletta and the agents remain behind. Still loyal to his friend, Cavaradossi, although racked with pain, asks Tosca if unwittingly in his anguish he has disclosed aught. She reassures him.

In a loud and commanding voice Scarpia says to Spoletta: 'In the well in the garden—go, Spoletta!'

From Scarpia's words Cavaradossi knows that Tosca has betrayed Angelotti's hiding place. He tries to repulse her.

Sciarrone rushes in much perturbed. He brings bad news. The victory they have been celebrating has turned into defeat. Bonaparte has triumphed at Marengo. Cavaradossi is roused to enthusiasm by the tidings. 'Victory! Tremble, Scarpia, you butcherly hypocrite,' he cries.

It is his death warrant. At Scarpia's command Sciarrone and the agents seize him and drag him away to be executed.

Quietly seating himself at table, Scarpia invites Tosca to a chair. Perhaps they can discover a plan by which Cavaradossi may be saved. He carefully polishes a wineglass with a napkin, fills it with wine, and pushes it toward her.

'Your price?' she asks contemptuously.

Imperturbably he fills his glass. 'Già mi dicon venal' (Venal my enemies call me) he sings in a passage of great power (the

Giàmi strug-gea l'a-mor del-la di-va!

Cantabile di Scarpia it used to be called at the time the opera first appeared). *She* is the price that must be paid for Cavaradossi's life. The horror with which she shrinks from the proposal, her unfeigned detestation of the man putting it forward, make her seem the more fascinating to him. There is a sound of distant drums. It is the escort that will conduct Cavaradossi to the scaffold.

Distracted, not knowing whither or to whom to turn, Tosca now utters the famous 'Vissi d'arte, vissi d'amore, non feci mai male ad anima viva'. It is to passages of surpassing eloquence like this that Puccini owes his fame, and his operas are indebted for their strong power of appeal.

Beginning quietly,

Vis-si d'ar-te, vis-si d'a-mo-re

'Vissi d'arte' works up to the impassioned, heart-rending outburst of grief with which it comes to an end:

Per-chè, per-chè se-gnor, ah, ...

perchè me ne ri-mu-ne ri co-si?

A knock at the door. Spoletta comes to announce that Angelotti, on finding himself discovered, swallowed poison. 'The other,' he adds, meaning Cavaradossi, 'awaits your decision.' The life of Tosca's lover is in the hands of the man who has told her how she may save him. Softly Scarpia asks her, 'What say you?' She nods consent; then, weeping for the shame of it, buries her head in the sofa cushions.

Scarpia says it is necessary for a mock execution to be gone through with, before Tosca and Cavaradossi can flee Rome. He directs Spoletta that the execution is to be simulated—'as we did in the case of Palmieri. You understand'.

'*Just* like Palmieri,' Spoletta repeats with emphasis and goes.

Scarpia turns to Tosca. 'I have kept my promise.' She, however, demands safe conduct for Cavaradossi and herself. Scarpia goes to his desk to write the paper. With trembling hand Tosca, standing at the table, raises to her lips the wineglass filled for her by Scarpia. As she does so she sees the sharp, pointed knife with which he peeled and quartered the apple. A rapid glance at the desk assures her that he still is writing. With infinite caution she reaches out, secures possession of the knife, conceals it behind her back. Scarpia has finished writing. He folds up the paper, advances toward Tosca with open arms to embrace her.

'Tosca, at last thou art mine!'

With a swift stroke of the knife, she stabs him full in the breast.

'It is thus that Tosca kisses!'

He staggers, falls. Ineffectually he strives to rise; makes a final effort; falls backward; dies.

Glancing back from time to time at Scarpia's corpse, Tosca goes to the table, where she dips a napkin in water and washes her fingers. She arranges her hair before a looking-glass, then looks on the desk for the safe-conduct. Not finding it there, she searches elsewhere for it, finally discovers it clutched in Scarpia's dead fingers, lifts his arm, draws out the paper from between the fingers, and lets the arm fall back stiff and stark, as she hides the paper in her bosom. For a brief moment she surveys the body, then extinguishes the lights on the supper table.

About to leave, she sees one of the candles on the desk still burning. She lights with it the other candle, places one to the

right, the other to the left of Scarpia's head, takes down a
crucifix from the wall, and, kneeling, places it on the dead
man's breast. There is a roll of distant drums. She rises and
steals out of the room.

In the opera, as in the play, which was one of Sarah
Bernhardt's triumphs, it is a wonderful scene—one of the
greatest in all melodrama. Anyone who has seen it adequately
acted, knows what it has signified in the success of the opera,
even after giving Puccini credit for 'Vissi d'arte' and an
expressive accompaniment to all that transpires on the stage.

Act III.   A platform of the Castle Sant' Angelo. Left, a
casement with a table, a bench, and a stool. On the table are
a lantern, a huge register book, and writing materials. Suspended on one of the walls are a crucifix and a votive lamp.
Right, a trap door opening on a flight of steps that lead to
the platform from below. The Vatican and St. Peter's are
seen in the distance. The clear sky is studded with stars. It is
just before dawn. The jangle of sheep bells is heard, at first
distant, then nearer. A shepherd sings his song. A dim, grey
light heralds the approach of dawn.

The firing party conducting Cavaradossi ascends the steps
through the trap door and is received by a jailer. A bell
strikes. 'You have an hour,' the jailer tells Cavaradossi. The
latter craves a favour of being permitted to write a letter. It
being granted, he begins to write, but soon loses himself in
memories of Tosca. 'E lucevan le stelle ed olezzava la terra'
(When the stars were brightly shining, and faint perfumes the
air pervaded)—a tenor air of great beauty, which reaches its
climax with

O dolce baci, o languide ca-rezze

He buries his face in his hands. Spoletta and the sergeant
conduct Tosca up the steps to the platform, and point out to
her where she will find Cavaradossi. A dim light still envelops
the scene as with mystery. Tosca, seeing her lover, rushes up
to him and, unable to speak for sheer emotion, lifts his hands
and shows him—herself and the safe-conduct.

'At what price?' he asks.

Swiftly she tells him what Scarpia demanded of her and
how, having consented, she thwarted him by slaying him with

her own hand. Lovingly he takes her hands in his: 'O dolci mani mansuete e pure' (Oh! gentle hands, so pitiful and tender).

Their voices join in a love duet that is half wistful, half resolute with determination to forget the past. 'Amaro sol per te m'era il morire' (The sting of death, I only felt for thee, love).

She informs him of the necessity of going through a mock execution. He must fall naturally and lie perfectly still, as if dead, until she calls to him. They laugh over the ruse. It will be amusing. The firing party arrives and the sergeant offers to bandage Cavaradossi's eyes. The latter declines. He stands with his back to the wall as the soldiers take aim. Tosca stops her ears with her hands so that she may not hear the explosion. The officer lowers his sword. The soldiers fire. Cavaradossi falls. 'How well he acts it! ' exclaims Tosca.

A cloth is thrown over Cavaradossi. The firing party marches off. Tosca cautions her lover not to move yet. The footsteps of the firing party die away—'Now get up.' He does not move. Can he not hear? She goes nearer to him. 'Mario! Up quickly! Away!—Up! Up! Mario!'

She raises the cloth. To the last Scarpia has tricked her. He had ordered a real, not a mock execution—just like Palmieri.

There are cries from below the platform. Scarpia's murder has been discovered, and his myrmidons are hastening to apprehend her. She springs upon the parapet and throws herself into space.   K.

MADAMA BUTTERFLY
Madam Butterfly

Opera in three acts by Giacomo Puccini, text by Giacosa and Illica. Première at la Scala, Milan, on February 17, 1904, with Storchio, Giaconia, Zenatello, de Luca, conductor Campanini. The occasion was a fiasco, and there was only one performance, but a revision was hugely successful in May, 1904, at Brescia, with Krusceniski and Zenatello, conducted by Toscanini. First performed Covent Garden, 1905, with Destinn, Lejeune, Caruso, Scotti, conductor Campanini; Washington, 1906 (in English); Metropolitan, 1907, with Farrar, Homer, Caruso, Scotti. Revived la Scala, 1925, with Pampanini, Pertile, Paci, conductor Toscanini; 1938, with Adami-Corradetti, Lugo, de Franceschi, conductor de Sabata; 1940, with Favero, Pigni, Poli, conductor Guarnieri. Famous Butterflies have included Tamaki Miura, Rethberg, Sheridan, dal Monte, Teyte, Joan Cross, Albanese, Cebotari, de los Angeles, Jurinac.

CHARACTERS

Cio-Cio-San, Madam Butterfly. . . . . Soprano
Suzuki, *her servant* . . . . .Mezzo-Soprano
Kate Pinkerton, *Pinkerton's American
     wife*. . . . . Mezzo-Soprano
B. F. Pinkerton, *Lieutenant, U.S. Navy* . . . . Tenor
Sharpless, *U.S. Consul at Nagasaki* . . . . Baritone
Goro, *a marriage broker* . . . . Tenor
Prince Yamadori, *a rich Japanese* . . . . Baritone
The Bonze, *Cio-Cio-San's uncle* . . . . Bass
The Imperial Commissioner . . . . Bass
The Official Registrar . . . . Baritone
Trouble, *Cio-cio-San's Child*
     Cio-Cio-San's relations and friends; servants
Time: Early Twentieth Century   *Place:* Nagasaki

Act I. There is a prelude, based on a Japanese theme. This theme runs through the greater part of the act. It is employed as a background and as a connecting link, with the result that it imparts much exotic tone colour to the scenes. The prelude passes over into the first act without a break.

Lieutenant B. F. Pinkerton, U.S.N., is on the point of contracting a 'Japanese marriage' with Cio-Cio-San, whom her friends call Butterfly. At the rise of the curtain Pinkerton is looking over a little house on a hill facing the harbour. This house he has leased and is about to occupy with his Japanese wife. Goro, the *nakodo* or marriage broker who has arranged the match, has also found the house for him and is showing him over it, enjoying the American's surprise at the clever contrivances found in the Japanese house construction. Three Japanese servants are in the house, one of whom is Suzuki, Butterfly's faithful maid.

Sharpless, the American Consul at Nagasaki, arrives. In the chat which follows between the two men it becomes apparent that Sharpless looks upon the step Pinkerton is about to take with disfavour. He argues that what may be a mere matter of pastime to the American Naval lieutenant, may have been taken seriously by the Japanese girl and, if so, may prove a matter of life or death to her. Pinkerton laughs off his friend's fears and, having poured out drinks for both, recklessly toasts his 'real' American wife of the future. Further discussion is interrupted by the arrival of the bride with her relatives and friends.

After greetings have been exchanged, the Consul on conversing with Butterfly becomes thoroughly convinced that he was correct in cautioning Pinkerton. For he discovers that she is not contemplating the usual Japanese marriage of arrangement, but has fallen in love with Pinkerton and is taking it with complete seriousness. She has even gone to the extent, as she confides to Pinkerton, of secretly renouncing her religious faith, the faith of her forefathers, and embracing his, before entering on her new life with him. This step, if discovered by her relatives, will mean that she has cut herself loose from all her old associations and belongings and entrusted herself and her future entirely to her husband.

Minor officials whose duty it is to see that the marriage contract, even though it be a 'Japanese marriage', is signed with proper ceremony, arrive. In the midst of drinking and merry-making they are startled by fierce yells from a distance, gradually drawing nearer. A weird figure, shouting and cursing wildly, appears upon the scene. It is Butterfly's uncle, the Bonze (a Japanese priest). He has discovered her renunciation of faith, now calls down curses upon her head for it, and insists that all her relatives, even her immediate family, renounce her. Pinkerton, enraged at the disturbance, turns them out of the house. The air shakes with their imprecations as they depart. Butterfly is weeping bitterly, but Pinkerton soon contrives to comfort her and the act closes with a passionate love scene.

The Japanese theme, which I have spoken of as forming the introduction to the act and acting as background to the greater part of it, never becomes monotonous because it is interrupted by several other musical episodes. Such are the short theme to which Pinkerton sings 'Tutto è pronto' (All is ready), and the skippy little theme when Goro tells Pinkerton about those who will be present at the ceremony. When Pinkerton sings 'Dovunque al mondo' (The whole world over, on business or pleasure the Yankee travels), a motif based on the *Star Spangled Banner* is heard for the first time.

In the duet between Pinkerton and Sharpless, which Pinkerton begins with the words, 'Amore o grillo' (Is it love or fancy), Sharpless's serious argument and its suggestion of the possibility of Butterfly's genuine love for Pinkerton are well brought out in the music. When Butterfly and her party arrive, her voice soars above those of the others to the strains of the same theme which occurs as a climax to the love duet at the end of the act and which, in the course of the opera, is heard on other occasions so intimately associated with herself and her emotions that it may be regarded as a motif expressing the love she has conceived for Pinkerton.

Full of feeling is the music of her confession to Pinkerton that she has renounced the faith of her forefathers, in order to be a fit wife for the man she loves: 'Ieri son salita' (Yesterday I crept softly to the Mission). An episode, brief but of great charm, is the chorus 'O Kami! O Kami!' (Let's drink to the newly married couple). Then comes the interruption of the cheerful scene by the appearance of the Bonze, which forms a dramatic contrast.

The love scene between Pinkerton and Butterfly is extended. From its beginning, 'Viene la sera' (Evening is falling, to the end, its interest never flags. It is full of beautiful melody charged with sentiment and passion, yet varied with lighter passages, like Butterfly's 'I am like the moon's little goddess'; 'I used to think if anyone should want me'; and the exquisite, 'Vogliatemi bene' (Ah, love me a little). There is a beautiful melody for Pinkerton, 'Love, what fear holds you trembling'. The climax of the love duet is reached in two impassioned phrases: 'Dolce notte! Quante stelle' (Night of rapture, stars unnumbered),

'Oh! Quanti occhi fisi, attenti' (Oh, kindly heavens).

Act II.   Three years have elapsed. It is a long time since Pinkerton has left Butterfly with the promise to return to her 'when the robins nest'. When the curtain rises, after an introduction, in which another Japanese theme is employed, Suzuki, although convinced that Pinkerton has deserted her mistress, is praying for his return. Butterfly is full of faith and trust. In chiding her devoted maid for doubting that Pinkerton will return, she draws in language and song a vivid picture of his home-coming and of their mutual joy therein: 'Un bel dì vedremo' (One fine day).

In point of fact, Pinkerton really is returning to Nagasaki, but with no idea of resuming relations with his Japanese wife. Indeed, before leaving America he has written to Sharpless asking him to let Butterfly know that he is married to an American wife, who will join him in Nagasaki. Sharpless calls upon Butterfly, and attempts to deliver his message, but is unable to do so because of the emotions aroused in Butterfly by the very sight of a letter from Pinkerton. It throws her into a transport of joy because, unable immediately to grasp its contents, she believes that in writing he has remembered her and must be returning to her. Sharpless endeavours to make the true situation clear to her, but is interrupted by a visit from Yamadori, a wealthy Japanese suitor, whom Goro urges Butterfly to marry. For the money left by Pinkerton with his little Japanese wife has dwindled almost to nothing, and poverty stares her in the face. But she will not hear of an alliance with Yamadori. She protests that she is already married to Pinkerton, and will await his return.

When Yamadori has gone, Sharpless makes one more effort to open her eyes to the truth. They have a duet, 'Ora a noi' (Now at last), in which he again produces the letter, and attempts to persuade her that Pinkerton has been faithless to her and has forgotten her. Her only reply is to fetch in her baby boy, born since Pinkerton's departure. Her argument is that when the boy's father hears what a fine son is waiting for him in Japan, he will hasten back. She sings to Trouble, as the little boy is called: 'Sai cos' ebbe cuore' (Do you hear, my sweet one, what that bad man is saying), and the aria rises to a dramatic climax. Sharpless makes a final effort to disillusion her, but in vain. If Pinkerton does not come back? There are two things, she says, she can do—return to her old life as a Geisha; or die. She sings a touching little lullaby to her baby boy, Suzuki twice interrupting her with the pathetically voiced exclamation, 'Poor Madam Butterfly!'

A salute of cannon from the harbour announces the arrival of a man-of-war. Looking through the telescope, Butterfly and Suzuki discover that it is Pinkerton's ship, the *Abraham Lincoln*. Now Butterfly is convinced that Sharpless is wrong. Her faith is about to be rewarded, and the man she loves is returning to her. The home must be decorated and made cheerful and attractive to greet him. She and Suzuki distribute cherry blossoms where their effect will be most charming. The music accompanying this is the enchanting duet of the flowers, 'Scuoti quella fronda di ciliegio' (Shake that cherry tree till every flower). Most effective is the joint phrase, 'Gettiamo a mani piene mammole e tuberose' (In handfuls let us scatter violets and white roses).

Buterfly adorns herself and the baby boy. Then with her fingers she pierces three holes in the paper wall of the dwelling. She, Suzuki and the baby peer through these, watching for Pinkerton's arrival. Night falls. Suzuki and the boy drop off to sleep. Butterfly rigid, motionless, waits and watches, her faith still unshaken, for the return of the man who has forsaken her. The pathos of the scene is profound; the music, with the hum of voices, borne upon the night from the distant harbour, exquisite.

Act III.   When the curtain rises, night has passed, dawn is breaking. Suzuki and the baby are fast asleep, but Butterfly still is watching. Again Puccini employs a Japanese melody (the 'vigil' theme):

When Suzuki awakes, she persuades the poor little 'wife' to go to rest, which Butterfly does only upon Suzuki's promise to awaken her as soon as Pinkerton arrives. Pinkerton and Sharpless appear. Suzuki at first is full of joyful surprise, which, however, soon gives way to consternation when she learns the truth. Pinkerton himself, seeing about him the proofs of Butterfly's complete loyalty to him, realises the heartlessness of his own conduct. There is a soaring trio for

Pinkerton, Sharpless, and Suzuki: 'Io so che alle sue pene.' Pinkerton, who cannot bear to face the situation, sings a tearful farewell to the house he once knew so well ('Addio fiorito asil'), and rushes away, leaving it to Sharpless to settle matters as best he can.

Butterfly has become aware that people are below. Suzuki tries to prevent her coming in, but she appears, radiantly happy, and expecting to find her husband. The pathos of the scene in which she learns the truth is difficult to describe. She does not burst into lamentations. With a gentleness which has been characteristic of her throughout, she bears the blow. She even expresses the wish to Kate, Pinkerton's real wife, that she may experience all happiness, and sends word to Pinkerton that, if he will come for his son in half an hour, he can have him.

Sharpless and Mrs. Pinkerton withdraw. In a scene of tragic power, Butterfly mortally wounds herself with her father's sword (the blade of which bears the inscription, 'To die with honour when one can no longer live with honour'), drags herself across the floor to where the boy is playing with his toys and waving a little American flag, and expires just as Pinkerton enters to take away her son.

Much was once made of Puccini's use of Japanese tunes as a 'background' to the opera, and he was contrasted favourably with the older composers who cared nothing for 'atmosphere' and relied solely on melody. The 'atmosphere' of *Butterfly* now seems of only secondary importance, and it is in the delineation of character that the opera seems strongest. In this respect, Butterfly dominates.

The use of the *Star Spangled Banner* motif as a personal theme for Pinkerton always has had a disagreeable effect upon me, and from now on should be objected to by all Americans.[1]

I 'did' the first night of David Belasco's play *Madam Butterfly* for the New York *Herald*. The production occurred at the Herald Square Theatre, Broadway, and Thirty-fifth Street, New York, March 5, 1900, with Blanche Bates as Butterfly. It was given with *Naughty Anthony*, a farce-comedy also by Belasco, which had been a failure. The tragedy had been constructed with great rapidity from John Luther Long's story, but its success was even swifter. At the

[1] It has never been, apparently, and seems now to cause no comment after some seventy years of repeated hearings.   H.

Duke of York's Theatre, London, it was seen by Francis
Nielsen, stage-manager of Covent Garden, who immediately
sent word to Puccini urging him to come from Milan to
London to see a play which, in his hands, might well become
a successful opera. Puccini came at once, with the result that
he created a work which has kept its popularity until today.

K.

LA FANCIULLA DEL WEST
The Girl of the Golden West

Opera in three acts by Giacomo Puccini; text by G. Civinini and C.
Zangarini, from the play by David Belasco. Première at Metropolitan,
New York, December 10, 1910, with Destinn, Caruso, Amato, con-
ductor Toscanini. First performed Covent Garden, 1911, with Destinn,
Bassi, Dinh Gilly, conductor Campanini; la Scala, Milan, 1912, with
Poli-Randaccio, Martinelli, Galeffi. Revived Metropolitan, 1929, with
Jeritza, Martinelli, Tibbett; la Scala, 1930, with dalla Rizza, Thill,
Viglione-Borghese, conductor de Sabata; 1937, with Cobelli, Merli,
Armando Borgioli; 1943, with Carbone, Lauri-Volpi, Reali, conductor
Erede; San Francisco, 1943, with Kirk, Jagel, Weede; Rome, 1947, with
di Giulio, Ferrauto, Franci; Buenos Aires, 1951, with Barbato,
Annaloro, Galeffi, conductor Panizza; Rome, 1952, with Caniglia,
Lauri-Volpi, de Falchi; la Scala, 1956, with Corelli; 1957, with del
Monaco; Florence Festival, 1954, with Steber, del Monaco,
Giangiacomo Guelfi, under Mitropoulos; San Carlo, Naples, 1962, with
Magda Olivero; Metropolitan, New York, 1961, with Price, Tucker,
Colzani; Sadler's Wells, 1963, with Fretwell, Donald Smith, Herincx.

CHARACTERS

Minnie, *owner of 'The Polka'*	Soprano
Jack Rance, *the Sheriff*	Baritone
Dick Johnson, *a bandit*	Tenor
Nick, *bar-tender at 'The Polka'*	Tenor

Sonora		Baritone
Trim		Tenor
Sid		Baritone
Handsome	*miners*	Baritone
Harry		Tenor
Joe		Tenor
Happy		Baritone
Larkens		Bass

Ashby, *agent of the Wells Fargo Transport Co.* . . .	Bass
Billy Jackrabbit, *a Red Indian*	Bass

Wowkle, *Billy's squaw* . . . . .Mezzo-Soprano
Jake Wallace, *a travelling minstrel* . . . . Baritone
José Castro, *a 'greaser' from Ramerrez's band* . . . . Bass
A Courier . . . . Tenor
Time: 1849–1850   *Place:* A mining camp

The score is prefaced with a note which quotes from an early history of California: 'In those strange days, people coming from God knows where, joined forces in that far Western land, and, according to the rude custom of the camp, their very names were soon lost and unrecorded, and here they struggled, laughed, gambled, cursed, killed, loved, and worked out their strange destinies in a manner incredible to us to-day. Of one thing only we are sure—they lived.' In such an atmosphere, Puccini designed that his opera should be played.

Act I.   A large room, roughly built in the shape of a triangle, forming the inside of 'The Polka', the inn where the miners come to drink and gamble. It is presided over by Minnie, whom they respect, love and protect, and who in return has even ventured to set up a sort of elementary school for the roughest of the inhabitants. She is looked after by two Red Indian servants, Billy and Wowkle. There is a bar, various trophies of the chase, a notice offering a reward for the arrest of Ramerrez, and a sheet-iron screen to protect a person from pistol shots.

Miners greet each other, and a game of faro starts up. Larkens is observed to be melancholy—he has got gold fever, says Nick. Jake comes through singing a melancholy song, in whose refrain all join. Larkens breaks down, and Sonora takes up a collection for him. Sid is caught cheating, and the miners are for meting out justice to him themselves, but Rance, the Sheriff, who has been in and out of the bar since the beginning, dominates the scene, and tells them rather to pin a card on Sid's chest as a token that he must not play; pass the word round the camp, and string him up if he takes off the mark of shame. Ashby comes in, asks after Minnie, and tells Rance that he is close on the heels of the notorious Ramerrez. Minnie sends in hot whisky and lemon, and they all drink to her, Rance taking the opportunity of mentioning that she is likely soon to become Mrs. Rance. Sonora mocks him, and they fight, but are separated after a moment by a woman's strong arm. It is Minnie. She tells them all off, and they bring one or two small gifts they have got for her. Rance and Ashby talk apart, as Minnie takes down the Bible and starts to teach from it.

The post arrives, and Ashby has a letter from Nina Micheltorena, a cast-off girl-friend of Ramerrez's, indicating where he is to be found that night. He rejoices at the prospect of catching him at last. Everyone reads letters and newspapers and comments on what he finds inside.

A stranger is outside, Nick says, asking for whisky with water. They all laugh at the notion. Rance comes up to Minnie and starts to tell her how much he loves her, but she interrupts and will have none of it. He goes sulkily away, and, when she asks whether he is angry with her, bursts out into an avowal of his passion: 'Minnie della mia casa son partito.' He left everything without regret when his gambler's heart impelled him to come out West, but now he would give a fortune for a kiss from her. Minnie says that love is not like that; she has happy memories of her parents and her home-life, and would not take a husband unless she loved him as they loved each other: 'Laggiù nel Soledad.'

Nick brings in the stranger, Dick Johnson. Rance is rude to him, but Minnie recognises him and talks about the time they first met. Rance comes over and knocks his glass off the counter, saying that he is Sheriff and demanding to know what is the stranger's business. The miners are about to take Rance's part when Minnie says she will vouch for him. Johnson takes Minnie off to dance. While they are away, Castro is brought in; he is a member of Ramerrez's band and has been captured. He says he will lead them to the bandit's camp if they will spare him, then, seeing Johnson's saddle lying on the ground, thinks to himself they have already captured him. A moment later he notices his chief come from the other room. Asking for something to drink, he tells Johnson that he has given nothing away, and that the gang is all round, only waiting until the Sheriff and his men are out of the way before they fall on the defenceless camp and pillage it.

Johnson remains behind with Minnie when the others ride off. He comments on her defenceless state and on the strange fact that she is guarding the miners' gold. She tells him that she loves the life she lives and would have no other. They are interrupted by Nick who says that a bandit has been seen skulking round the camp quite near at hand. Johnson comforts her, and agrees to her suggestion that he should come up later that evening to her cabin to continue the conversation and have a meal. As he goes out, she bursts into tears, but he tells her: 'You've the face of an angel.'

Act II.   Minnie's hut—a single room, above which is a loft. When the curtain goes up, Wowkle is singing a lullaby to her papoose. She and Billy talk for a moment—shall they get married? — before Minnie comes in, sends Billy about his business and tells Wowkle that there will be two for supper. She starts to dress up in what little finery she has, obviously hoping to make a real impression on Johnson when he comes. He knocks at the door and comes in. They sit down to supper, and Johnson comments that the life up here must be lonely. 'Oh, you've no notion how exciting my life is,' says Minnie. The mountains and the wild flowers, and her school for the miners—these keep her very busy: 'Oh, se sapeste.'

They sing of their happiness, and Minnie makes up a bed for herself in front of the fire. She has persuaded Johnson to spend the night there, as he would inevitably get lost in the heavy snow. There is a noise from outside, and voices demand admittance. Minnie hides Johnson behind the curtains of the bed, and lets in Rance, Nick, Ashby, and Sonora. They were worried for her safety—Dick Johnson, they have discovered, is none other than the notorious Ramerrez. They were led by Castro to his hiding-place, where they found his girl, Nina Micheltorena, who showed them a photograph of him—Rance hands it to Minnie, who laughs loudly.

She says good-night to them, then rounds furiously on Johnson. He admits he came to rob, but at sight of her, changed his purpose. In an aria he explains his upbringing: his father was a bandit, and when he died six months ago ('Or son sei mesi') left nothing for him, his mother and his brothers, but the gang of thieves he led. He was fated to take to the road, but from the moment he met Minnie he longed to lead an honest life. He does not expect forgiveness, only understanding.

Johnson rushes out, and a moment later there is the sound of a shot. A body falls against the door; Minnie opens it, and he staggers in, telling her not to shut the door as he will leave again. She cries that she loves him and will help him, and, putting the ladder in place, drags him to concealment in the loft. No sooner is he in hiding than Rance is again at the door. He searches everywhere for his quarry, then, asking Minnie to swear that he is not hidden there, tries to embrace her. She backs away from him; he accuses her of loving the bandit. With a gesture of defiance, Rance swears to Minnie that she shall never be Johnson's. A drop of blood falls on his outstretched hand, then another. Rance calls to Johnson to come out of hiding; he descends the ladder, helped by Minnie, and collapses at the bottom. Minnie tries a last desperate expedient. She suggests to Rance that they should play a game of poker: if she wins, Johnson's life is hers, if she loses, Rance wins her love. He cannot resist the gamble. They play two hands, each winning one, but before the last Minnie shows signs of distress and asks Rance to get her a drink from the bottle in the corner. She has previously secreted some cards in her stocking, and now, unable to bear the thought of losing at one stroke love and honour, she substitutes the cards for the hand she has been dealt. Rance returns, and against his three kings, Minnie is able to show three aces and a pair. He leaves the house, and Minnie is left alone with the lover whose life she has saved.

Act III.   A clearing in the forest. Nick, Rance, and Ashby are resting there round a fire. They are members of a party which is hunting for Ramerrez. They reflect bitterly on the change that Johnson's arrival has brought into their lives. A noise is heard and Ashby shouts that his men seem to have caught up with their quarry. But it is a false alarm, although they are hard on his tracks. Ashby goes off with them, while Rance raises his arms toward Minnie's cabin, and shouts triumphantly that she will not see her lover again, except at the end of a rope. There is another false alarm, and then Sonora gallops in shouting that they have caught him at last. Ashby hands over Johnson to the Sheriff, who suggests that they string him up forthwith. All unite in calling down curses on his head, each ascribing a different crime to him and his gang. He protests that he stopped short of murder, and asks for one thing only, that he be allowed to speak before he dies. He makes an impassioned plea that Minnie shall think he has gone free, that she shall wait for him, but never know the ignominious fate which overtook him: 'Ch'ella mi creda libero e lontano' (Let her believe that I have gained my freedom). It is one of Puccini's most famous arias, and one that is familiar to every Italian that has ever been to the opera, and to most that have not. In the 1914–18 war it was even a favourite song with troops on the march.

Almost before Johnson has finished speaking, Rance rushes up to him and hits him in the face, to sounds of disapproval from the bystanders. They are about to hang their prisoner when Minnie's voice is heard. In a moment she is among them, threatening the first man that takes a step towards Johnson, and defying them all to do their worst. For years she shared their troubles and their dangers—will they deny her the first thing she has ever asked of them? She and Johnson were planning to start a new life together, the bandit having died in her cabin a week before, when the honest man was born. Sonora goes to her side and takes her part; they agree that they owe her too much to deny her this. She and Johnson go off arm-in-arm, to seek a new existence together.

H.

LA RONDINE

The Swallow

Lyric comedy in three acts by Giacomo Puccini; text by G. Adami, from the German libretto by A. M. Willner and H. Reichert. Première at Monte Carlo on March 27, 1917, with dalla Rizza, Ferraris, Schipa, Francesco Dominici, Huberdeau, conductor Marinuzzi. First performed Bologna, 1917; Rome, 1918; Metropolitan, New York, 1928, with Bori, Fleischer, Gigli, Tokatyan, Ludikar, conductor Bellezza. Revived Metropolitan, 1936, with Bori, Martini, conductor Panizza; la Scala, Milan, 1940, with Favero, Malipiero, conductor Marinuzzi; Rome, 1940, with Favero, Gigli, Gobbi, Taddei. First performance in England, 1966, by Opera Viva; English Opera Group, 1974, with June Bronhill.

CHARACTERS

Magda, *Rambaldo's mistress* .... Soprano
Lisette, *her maid* .... Soprano
Ruggero, *a young man* .... Tenor
Prunier, *a poet* .... Tenor[1]
Rambaldo, *a wealthy Parisian* .... Baritone
Périchaud .... Bass-Baritone

Gobin ⎱ *his friends* .... ⎰ Tenor
Crébillon ⎰ ⎱ Bass-Baritone

Yvette ⎱ *ladies of pleasure and* ⎰ Soprano
Bianca ⎬ *friends of Magda* ⎰ Soprano
Suzy ⎰ ⎰ Mezzo-Soprano

A steward .... Bass

Ladies and Gentlemen of the world, Citizens, Students,
Artists, Demi-Mondaines, Dancers, etc.

Time: The Second Empire   *Place:* Paris

[1] Originally baritone, later tenor.

It was while he was in Vienna in 1912 that Puccini was asked by an Austrian publisher to write a light opera in something approaching the Viennese manner. The war prevented fulfilment of the suggested contract, but Puccini decided to set the libretto which had been prepared for him, albeit in a somewhat different form from that originally envisaged. The music is light in character and frequently employs waltz rhythms, but the composer has abandoned any attempt to write an operetta.

Act I.   A luxuriously furnished room in Magda's house in Paris. Magda and Rambaldo are entertaining their friends, amongst whom is Prunier, a poet. He sings his latest song, sitting at the piano. It tells the story of one Doretta, who dreams that the King looked upon her one day. When Prunier says that the end evades him, Magda takes up the tale ('Chi il bel sogno di Doretta'). Rambaldo produces a necklace he has been meaning all evening to give Magda, and she is immediately the centre of an admiring and envious circle. Lisette the maid, about whose cheeky habits Prunier is not slow to complain but whom Magda praises as a ray of sunshine in her life, asks Rambaldo whether he will at last see the young man who has been waiting for nearly two hours to see him. He is the son of an old friend of Rambaldo's.

Magda talks to her friends of the old days when she was still an innocent girl and went to Bullier's café in search of adventure and, maybe, love. The dancing was something that she can never forget, nor the memory of the man she met there, into whose eyes she gazed, but whose name she never knew. 'Ore dolci e divine' (Happy hours, golden hours) she sings, and the music traces every stage of that never-to-be-forgotten experience of her carefree youth.

Ruggero is brought in just as Prunier starts to tell everyone's future from their hands; Magda's is that, like a swallow, she will migrate far away from Paris, perhaps to find love. The conversation turns to where Ruggero shall spend his first evening in Paris; Bullier's is chosen, and Lisette (about whose impertinence Prunier continues to complain) agrees that the choice is an excellent one.

All leave, except Prunier who stays on the verandah. It is Lisette's day off, she reminds Magda, who dismisses her and goes off to her room. The stage is empty for a moment, before Lisette reappears, dressed in an assortment of her mistress's finery. She runs into Prunier, who takes her in his arms with obvious affection—objecting, though, a moment

.ater, that her clothes have been badly chosen and do not match. She rushes out and reappears more suitably dressed and they go off together for the evening. Magda herself comes in, hardly recognisable in that her hair has been re-done and she is dressed simply and as a grisette. She takes a look in the glass, is satisfied, and leaves the room.

Act II.   Chez Bullier; the ballroom. The room is crowded with artists, grisettes, demi-mondaines, men about town, etc. Flower-girls offer their wares for sale. Ruggero is sitting alone at one of the tables, apparently oblivious of the confusion and noise and gaiety around him, and quite unresponsive to the various girls who try to entice him away with them. Magda comes in and has some difficulty in fending off any number of would-be escorts, which she succeeds in doing by saying she is meeting the young man sitting by himself in the corner.

Ruggero is delighted when she sits by him and will not let her go, as she suggests she should the moment her molesters are out of the way. They dance, and Magda is irresistibly reminded of her adventure long ago; they even write their names in pencil on the marble-topped table at which they are sitting. Prunier and Lisette come in, and Lisette thinks she recognises her mistress, but is persuaded by her escort that she is mistaken. They are introduced to each other, and sing a quartet expressing their different views and requirements of love.

Some of the other dancers shower flowers on them, but Magda suddenly sees Rambaldo come in, and Prunier hastens to get Ruggero and Lisette out of the way. Rambaldo comes over to Magda, brushes Prunier aside, and asks her if she is coming home with him. She tells him she has found love and is not leaving with him, now or at any time. In spite of the blow he preserves his dignity, and leaves her sitting where he has found her. Ruggero returns and together they leave the restaurant.

Act III.   A little cottage, near Nice, in which live Magda and Ruggero, secure in their love. The two lovers are having tea, and the sea can be heard in the distance. They are blissfully happy, and Ruggero, who says he has written to ask his father's consent to their marriage, tells her of his confidence that his family will receive her as one of themselves. Magda wonders how best to let him know the details of her past.

Lisette and Prunier can be heard in the distance, and they

appear just after Ruggero and Magda have left the stage. I appears that Prunier tried to make Lisette into a successful actress, only to have to listen to the hisses of the audience at her one and only appearance. Lisette now wants to see if she can get back her old job with Magda. Magda agrees, and Lisette immediately seems more natural in her accustomed surroundings—so too would Magda, hints Prunier, if she were to return to Paris and gaiety, as she surely will, some time, some day. Magda understands that Rambaldo has sent her a message through Prunier, and that she can return to him whenever she wishes.

Prunier prepares to go, saying he has finished with Lisette for ever—but he does not omit to find out when she is going out that night, so as to be ready to meet her. Ruggero comes in with a letter he has had from his mother, and makes Magda read it, which she does with aching heart. She tells him she cannot deceive him any longer; he must know that she has been ready to sell her favours for money, that she has lived in guilty splendour. She can love him, but she cannot marry him and come to meet his mother as if she were a virgin bride. They must part, she insists, and, supported by Lisette and with breaking heart, she goes out, back to her own existence, leaving behind her the one love of her life.   H.

IL TABARRO

The Cloak

Opera in one act by Giacomo Puccini; text by G. Adami, after the play by Didier Gold, *La Houppelande*. Première at Metropolitan, New York, on December 14, 1918, with Muzio, Crimi, Montesanto, Didur, conductor Moranzoni. First performed at Rome, 1919, with Maria Labia, di Giovanni (Edward Johnson), Galeffi, conductor Marinuzzi; Buenos Aires, 1919, with Labia, Grassi, Viglione-Borghese, conductor Serafin; Covent Garden, 1920, with Quaiatti, Burke, Gilly; la Scala, Milan, 1922, with Concato, Piccaluga, Noto, conductor Panizza; Sadler's Wells, 1935 (in English), with Winifred Kennard, Wendon, Matters. Revived la Scala, 1936, with Carbone, Merli, Franci, conductor Marinuzzi; Metropolitan, 1946, with Albanese, Jagel, Tibbett; Covent Garden, 1965, with Collier, Craig, Gobbi, conductor Pritchard.

CHARACTERS

Michele, *owner of a barge, aged fifty* . . . . Baritone
Luigi, *a stevedore, aged twenty* . . . . Tenor
'Tinca', *a stevedore, aged thirty-five* . . . . Tenor

'Talpa', *a stevedore, aged fifty-five* . . . . Bass
Giorgetta, *Michele's wife, aged twenty-five* . . . Soprano
Frugola, *Talpa's wife, aged fifty* . . . . . . .Mezzo-Soprano
Time: Early Twentieth century   *Place:* The Seine, in Paris

Puccini's *Trittico* consists of an example of Grand Guignol,
a piece of sentimentality, and a comedy. *Suor Angelica*,
which came second in the original performances, has never
caught on with either public or managements, but *Gianni
Schicchi*, the comedy, was an immediate success and has
remained one ever since, being frequently played apart from
its companions. *Tabarro*, the melodramatic opening, was
slower to find favour, but recently seems to have come into
its own, and indeed this is hardly surprising. In it the *verismo*
side of Puccini's make-up, which found its best-known
expression in *Tosca*, had a subject to which it was entirely
suited. The rather commonplace ambitions and desires of the
characters are uncomplicated by such ideas as Freedom and
there is no need, as in *Tosca*, to bring in Napoleon and the
Battle of Marengo as what amount to no more than stage
props. From the point of view of directness of expression,
Tabarro is something of a masterpiece.

The action takes place on board a barge, whose master is
Michele. It is moored in the Seine and the imposing shape of
Notre-Dame can be seen in the distance. The barge takes up
most of the stage, but beyond it can be seen the shore, to
which it is connected by a gangway.

The curtain rises before the music begins. A swaying
orchestral figure denotes the gentle movement of a boat tied
up to the shore:

It is the end of the day, and workmen are finishing their
job of loading the barge. Michele and Giorgetta take little
notice of them as they work, but Giorgetta suggests that they

should be offered a drink before they go. Michele goes up to embrace her, but she only offers him her cheek, and he goes discontentedly on shore. The workmen crowd round Giorgetta, and drink to her in a well-defined triple time. An organ-grinder goes by on the shore and Luigi calls to him to play for them. Giorgetta says she only understands one kind of music, that which sets her feet dancing.

The phrase is later considerably developed in her love scene with Luigi.

Tinca is immediately at her side offering himself as a partner. His clumsiness becomes too much for her, and Luigi pushes him aside and takes his place, holding Giorgetta closer than is perhaps necessary. Talpa sees Michele coming and the dancing stops hurriedly, as the workmen disappear. Giorgetta asks Michele about arrangements for the morrow, when they are due to leave for Rouen; he will take the three—Tinca, Talpa, and Luigi—who have been helping him in Paris.

Frugola, Talpa's wife, appears and talks of her curious occupation as a rag-picker. Her one love, it appears, is her cat, for whom she buys the best meat available. Talpa, Tinca and Luigi with other stevedores come up from the hold, and Tinca explains that he drinks to forget his sorrows. Luigi takes up the cue: he is right, their fate is a miserable one ('Hai ben ragione'). The solution, says Tinca, is to follow his example: drink!

Talpa and Frugola prepare to go wearily home, dreaming of the cottage in the country that they have always wanted but are never going to be able to afford. Giorgetta admits that her dream is for something quite different; she was born in the suburbs of Paris, and wishes that Michele might one day give up their nomadic existence and settle down: 'E ben altro il mio sogno.' This is one of the opera's purple passages, and Luigi joins his voice to hers as they agree that this former life was the happiest they have known. 'Ma chi lascia il sobborgo.'

Giorgetta and Luigi are alone. They listen to voices singing ff-stage (to Example 1); then Luigi moves quickly towards Giorgetta, who stops him with a gesture. They are lovers and Luigi complains of the barrier which prevents them being happy together; their duet is founded on Example 2. There is a short interruption as Michele comes up from down below. Luigi asks him to put him ashore next day at Rouen; he means to try his luck there as a labourer. Michele advises strongly against such a course of action, and Luigi agrees to go on working for him. Michele says good-night. Luigi's enthusiasm carries Giorgetta away, and the duet rises to a climax as Luigi agrees to come for Giorgetta in an hour's time; they will use the same signal as last night, a lighted match will mean that all is safe.

Luigi leaves Giorgetta, who reflects sadly on the difficulties in the way of being happy in this life, as Michele comes back and asks her why she has not yet gone to bed. They talk for a moment of their crew, and then Michele comes close to her with an affectionate gesture. Why can they not renew their old love, which seems to have cooled since the death of their child: 'Perchè, perchè non m'ami più?' (Ah, why do you love me no more?'). Why does she no longer come for warmth beneath his cloak? 'Resta vicino a me' (Stay close by my side) he begs; but Giorgetta prosaically explains the cooling of affection between them—they are both getting older.

She goes off to bed, and Michele stays on deck apparently reconciled to what she has told him. But the moment she has gone, he exclaims in fury: 'You whore!' He listens for a moment while two lovers on shore say good-night, and a bugle sounds from the near-by barracks, then peers in at the window to see Giorgetta still dressed and apparently waiting: for what? What has changed her? Who is her lover? He goes through the men with whom he knows her to be in fairly frequent contact, but dismisses each one in turn. Who can it be? Would he could catch him and crush the life out of him between his hands. His monologue is a powerful passage, and as his anger rises, so the orchestra boils with his emotions.

He raises his pipe and lights it with a match, giving as he does so, all unwittingly, the signal agreed upon by Luigi and Giorgetta. Michele sees a movement, and quickly hides himself, then throws himself on the figure which creeps towards the boat. It is Luigi. Michele's hands are round his throat as he demands an admission of guilt. He chokes Luigi,

then, as Giorgetta, roused by the noise, appears, hides the
body under his cloak and stands as if nothing had happened.
Giorgetta comes up to him, and asks him to warm her under
his cloak. With a terrible cry, he opens his cloak and reveals
what is concealed beneath it.   H.

SUOR ANGELICA
Sister Angelica

Opera in one act by Giacomo Puccini; text by G. Forzano. Première
at Metropolitan, New York, on December 14, 1918, with Farrar, Perini
conductor Moranzoni (in conjunction with premières of *Gianni*
Schicchi and *Il Tabarro*). First performed Rome, 1919, with dalla
Rizza, conductor Marinuzzi; Buenos Aires, 1919, with Mazzoleni
conductor Serafin; Covent Garden, 1920, with dalla Rizza; la Scala
Milan, 1922, with Carena, Casazza, conductor Panizza. Revived la Scala
1936, with Oltrabella, Casazza, conductor Marinuzzi; 1944, with
Oltrabella, Palombini, conductor Marinuzzi; Covent Garden, 1965, with
Carlyle, Fisher, conductor Pritchard.

CHARACTERS

Suor Angelica . . . . Soprano
The Princess, *her aunt* . . . . Contralto
The Abbess . . . . Mezzo-Soprano
The Alms Collector . . . . Soprano
Mistress of the Novices . . . . Mezzo-Soprano
Suor Genovieffa . . . . Soprano
Suor Osmina . . . . Soprano
Suor Dolcina . . . . Mezzo-Soprano
Aspirant Sisters . . . . Mezzo-Sopranos
Nursing Sister . . . . Soprano
Novices, Sisters
Time: Seventeenth Century   *Place:* The cloisters of a nunnery

Suor Angelica, the daughter of a noble Florentine family
has taken the veil to expiate the scandal which has over
shadowed her life; she is the unmarried mother of a little
baby. Seven years she has spent in the peace and seclusion of
a convent, in a state of mind that has alternated between
repentance and longing for the child she has never really
known. The Abbess tells her that she has a visitor, her aunt
the Princess, towards whom her attitude must be one of
reverence and humility.
   The Princess has come to obtain from Angelica her

signature to a legal document in connection with her sister's forthcoming marriage. She impresses upon her that her life must be given up now and for ever to atoning for the sin she once committed. When Angelica asks for news of the little child which has had to live its life in the great outside world without its mother, she is told coldly that it died two years ago.

In a frenzy of despair, Angelica resolves on suicide. She gathers herbs and flowers and makes from them a poisonous draught, which she drinks. She prays to the Virgin that she may not die in mortal sin, and, as if in answer to her prayer, sees a vision of the Blessed Virgin leading a little child towards her. An invisible chorus sings of salvation as she dies.

The opera has never been popular, and only Angelica's lament, 'Senza mamma', has attained the fame which has attended some of Puccini's other arias.   H.

GIANNI SCHICCHI

Opera in one act by Giacomo Puccini, text by G. Forzano. Première at Metropolitan New York, on December 14, 1918, with Easton, Crimi, de Luca, conductor Moranzoni. First performed at Rome, 1919, with dalla Rizza, di Giovanni (Edward Johnson), Galeffi, conductor Marinuzzi; Buenos Aires, with Vanni Marcoux, conductor Serafin; Covent Garden, 1920, with dalla Rizza, Tom Burke, Badini, conductor Bavagnoli; a Scala, Milan, 1922, with di Voltri, Marion, Badini, conductor Panizza. Revived Covent Garden, 1926, with Torri, Minghetti, Badini; 1931, with Rettore, Nash, Badini, conductor Barbirolli; 1937, with Ziffado, Nash, Crabbé; la Scala, 1928, with Galeffi; 1944, with Menotti, Malipiero, Stabile, conductor Marinuzzi; 1947, with Forti, Sinimberghi, Stabile, conductor Capuana; Metropolitan, 1936, with Tibbett; 1944, with Albanese, Martini, Baccaloni; Sadler's Wells, 1935 (in English), with Naylor, Tudor Davies, Sumner Austin, conductor Menges; Covent Garden, 1962, with Joan Carlyle, André Turp, Geraint Evans, conductor Solti.

CHARACTERS

Gianni Schicchi, *aged fifty*..............Baritone
Lauretta, *his daughter, aged twenty-one*......Soprano
Relations of Buoso Donati:
    Zita, *called La Vecchia, cousin of Buoso, aged*
      sixty ....Contralto
    Rinuccio, *nephew of Zita, aged twenty-four*...Tenor
    Gherardo, *nephew of Buoso, aged forty*......Tenor
    Nella, *his wife, aged thirty-four*..........Soprano

Gherardino, *their son, aged seven* . . . . Alto
Betto di Signa, *brother-in-law of Buoso, poor and
    badly dressed, of indefinite age* . . . . Bass
Simone, *Buoso's cousin, aged seventy* . . . . Bass
Marco, *his son, aged forty-five.* . . . . Baritone
La Ciesca, *Marco's wife, aged
    thirty-eight* . . . . .Mezzo-Soprano
Maestro Spinelloccio, *doctor.* . . . . Bass
Ser Amantio di Nicolao, *lawyer.* . . . . Baritone
Pinellino, *cobbler.* . . . . Bass
Guccio, *painter* . . . . Bass

Time: 1299   *Place:* Florence

Gianni Schicchi, an historical character, has the honour of
being mentioned by Dante in the 30th Canto of *The Inferno,*
where he appears in company with the incestuous Myrrha of
Cyprus as a 'pallid, naked shape' (the connection between the
two is that both counterfeited the shape of another for their
own ends).

Before the curtain rises, there are a few bars of rapid music,
whose impetus is however tempered to become a lament (in
the minor) by the time the action begins. A chuckling figure,
Ernest Newman suggests, is used to indicate that the shadow
of Gianni Schicchi is already over them:

The opera takes place in a bedroom in the house of Buoso
Donati, who has recently died. The dead man is lying in bed,
and his relations are kneeling round him, behaving with
proper solemnity, that is all except Gherardino, who is
heartily bored by the whole proceedings. A whisper goes
round; 'it is rumoured in Signa' that Buoso's wealth has been
left to the monks, and the agitation of the mourners resolves
itself in a request for the advice of Simone, he having once
been mayor of Fucecchio and therefore of them all the wisest
as well as the oldest. Simone tells them that if the will is
already in the hands of lawyers, there is no hope for them,
but if it is still in the room, something may yet be done
about it.

A search for the will begins, and becomes ever more

feverish as first one, then another thinks he or she has
discovered it, only to find that it is a false alarm. At last
Rinuccio holds it triumphantly aloft, but before giving it up
asks for a reward for having found it, in the shape of
permission to marry Lauretta, Gianni Schicchi's daughter.
Zita is far too much concerned with the will to worry about a
little thing like that, and eventually it is opened (in the
meanwhile, Rinuccio sends Gherardino off to fetch Gianni
Schicchi and his daughter). The will is addressed to Zita and
Simone: expectation runs high, and speculation as to what is
the portion of each even higher. They read the will in silence
and, as they begin to understand its import, mounting horror;
the rumour in Signa was by no means an exaggeration.
Simone speaks for them all, and gradually they collect their
wits sufficiently to be able to utter a rapid curse on the
monks who will grow fat on *their* portions. Who would ever
have thought, reflects Zita broken-heartedly, that they would
ever shed so many genuine tears when Buoso was taken from
them?

A thought seems to strike them all at the same time; if
only it were possible . . . They appeal to Simone but he can
offer them no comfort. Rinuccio suggests that only one man
can help them: Gianni Schicchi. Zita furiously says they have
heard enough of him and his brood for one day, but Rinuccio
is not to be put off, least of all when Gherardino bursts into
the room and says the man they are discussing is on his way.
He praises Schicchi's resourcefulness and cunning, and urges
them to stop their spiteful gossip about his origins and lack
of family tree. Has not majestic Florence herself got her roots
in the countryside? Rinuccio's song, 'Firenze è come un
albero fiorito,' has an antique flavour about it, as if it were a
traditional song. It contains in the middle a broad phrase
which is later to blossom out into Lauretta's well-known
song:

Gianni Schicchi arrives with his daughter, and wonders if
the long faces he can see are to be taken as meaning that
Donati is better. He is told and the sad facts of the will, and
comments that this means they are disinherited. Zita repeats

the word, and snaps out that he can take himself and his daughter back to where they came from; her nephew shall never marry a nobody. Schicchi bursts out into a vivid denunciation of the snobbish money-grabbing old hag, who would sacrifice young people's happiness to her own greed. An ensemble develops, through which runs the lovers' sad plaint that they had hoped (vainly it seems) to be married before midsummer. Rinuccio prevents Schicchi leaving unceremoniously, and begs him at least to look at the will. Schicchi is reluctant, but Lauretta adds her plea to Rinuccio's and he gives way. 'O mio babbino caro' (O my beloved daddy), built up on the phrase from Rinuccio's aria (now in A flat, rather than B flat), has become enormously popular over the years, and is now nearly as well known as 'Un bel dì' or 'Mi chiamano Mimi'. Its lyrical charm must be taken in this context as a masterly piece of tongue-in-cheek writing.

Schicchi walks up and down considering the will; 'it can't be done', he concludes, and immediately there is an outburst of sorrow from the lovers. More consideration, same conclusion, another lament, before finally a ray of hope presents itself to Schicchi's agile mind (the lovers react appropriately). Lauretta is sent out on the balcony to feed the bird, and he asks if anyone apart from themselves yet knows of Buoso's death. No one, comes the answer: then there is hope, he concludes, and immediately gives orders that the funeral ornaments, etc., be removed from the room (to the sound of a muffled funeral march rhythm). Just then, a knock is heard, and in comes the doctor, not however before Schicchi has had time to jump behind the curtains of the bed. Schicchi answers the doctor's queries in what he hopes is Donati's voice, and tells him he is feeling better; they all bid the doctor good-night and breathe a sigh of relief at his departure. Schicchi outlines his plan: let them send for a lawyer, giving out that Buoso has had a relapse and wishes to make his will. Schicchi's monologue is slyness and good humour personified, and at its end the relatives shriek with delight and the ensemble takes on break-neck speed as all congratulate Schicchi (and themselves) on the possibilities of the scheme.

Collectively they tell him to divide the possessions equally amongst them, but each one then asks for the plums for himself. Schicchi laughs at them all, just at the moment the passing bell is heard—but it is for the servant of the mayor, they are told, and heave a sigh of relief. Simone suggests that the division should be left to the sense of justice of their friend, but again, as Schicchi is helped into Buoso's nightclothes, each one in turn offers him some reward if he will leave the particularly coverted things to him. He agrees to each. When he is dressed, Zita, Ciesca, and Nella gather round and admire his get-up, which they say is perfect; they lead a chorus of praise for him.

When all is ready, he says that before going to bed he must warn them of the danger they are collectively running. The law provides penalties for falsifying a will—exile, and the loss of the right hand for the malefactor and his accomplices—and they are each one of them liable to these penalties. With mock solemnity he bids a sad farewell to the Florence they all love, and the relations, seeing the force of his argument, sadly repeat the phrases after him: 'Farewell, dear Florence. . . . I wave good-bye with this poor handless arm.'

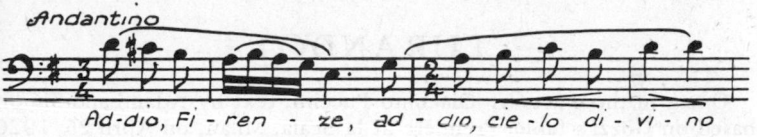

Then, a knock is heard at the door, all is ready, and the lawyer and the two witnesses who are to assist him are admitted. Schicchi answers their questions in a thin, assumed voice, and, with many comic touches, they go through the terms of the new will. The inexpensive funeral which Schicchi orders pleases the relations, and something is left in turn to each of them, until the moment arrives when there remain only the prizes—the villa in Florence, the saw-mills at Signa, and the mule. Amidst protests from the relations he leaves each in turn to 'his devoted friend, Gianni Schicchi', commenting, when they interrupt, that he knows best what is good for Schicchi. When the interruptions look like becoming too violent, he sings a line or two of the farewell to Florence, and they understand only too well that they are caught in their own trap, and that there is nothing they can do. As if to add insult to injury, he directs Zita to give twenty florins to each of the witnesses and a hundred to the lawyer.

As soon as the lawyer has gone, they all rush at Schicchi and tear the night-shirt off his back. He picks up Donati's stick and deals some shrewd blows with it, as he chases them out of the house, which is now his, and which they attempt to pillage before leaving. Lauretta and Rinuccio sing of the happiness they will know together, and Schicchi returns, bringing with him some of the things the relations had carried off. He turns to the audience: 'Could you imagine a better use for Buoso's money? . . . if you have enjoyed yourselves this evening, I trust you will applaud a verdict of "Extenuating Circumstances".'

Puccini owes an obvious debt to Verdi for his example in *Falstaff*, but it would be churlish to deny him his achievement in writing music of such dexterity and brilliance, even if it falls short of the magnitude and humanity of its greater predecessor. *Gianni Schicchi* makes use of a side of the composer's make-up hitherto only revealed in such passages as the interplay of the Bohemians in *Bohème*, the entrance of the Sacristan in *Tosca*: in *Schicchi*, however, the wit is sharper and the tempo of movement faster than anywhere else in his output.   H.

TURANDOT

Opera in three acts by Giacomo Puccini; text by Adami and Simoni based on Gozzi's fable. Première at la Scala, Milan, on April 25, 1926, with Raisa, Zamboni, Fleta, Rimini, Nessi, Palai, Carlo Walter, conductor Toscanini. First performed in Rome, 1926, with Scacciati, Torri, Merli, conductor Vitale; Buenos Aires, 1926, with Muzio, Pampanini, Lauri-Volpi, conductor Marinuzzi; Metropolitan, 1926, with Jeritza, Attwood, Lauri-Volpi, conductor Serafin; Covent Garden, 1927, with Scacciati (later Easton), Schoene, Merli, conductor Bellezza. Revived Covent Garden, 1929, with Eva Turner; 1931, with Nemeth, Norena, Cortis, conductor Barbirolli; 1937, with Turner, Favero, Martinelli; 1946, with Turner, Terry, Midgley, conductor Lambert; 1963, with Shuard, Kabaivanska, Prevedi, conductor Downes; 1967, with Nilsson, McCracken, conductor Mackerras; Metropolitan, New York, 1961, with Nilsson, Moffo, Corelli, conductor Stokowski. Other famous exponents of the title role have included Mafalda Salvatini, Cigna, Grob-Prandl, Borkh, Rysanek.

CHARACTERS

Princess Turandot .... Soprano
The Emperor Altoum .... Tenor
Timur, *exiled King of Tartary* .... Bass
Calaf, *his son* .... Tenor
Liù, *a slave girl* .... Soprano
Ping, *Grand Chancellor of China* .... Baritone
Pang, *supreme lord of provisions* .... Tenor

Pong, *supreme lord of the Imperial Kitchen* . . . . . Tenor
A Mandarin . . . . Baritone
Time: Antiquity   *Place:* Pekin

Turandot is a version of the ancient fairy tale of the cruel
Eastern Princess who slays those who love her. The fame of
Turandot's beauty has spread far and wide; her wooers come
to Pekin from distant lands. But before they can approach
her they must submit to a trial. If they can answer three
riddles they win the bride and, with her, the throne of China.
But if they fail they must accept the penalty—and the
penalty is death.

As the curtain rises on the first act the mob is waiting to
learn the result of a trial which has just taken place in the
Imperial Palace. When they hear from a Mandarin that the
Prince of Persia has failed and must lose his life their joy is
unbounded. They exchange rude jests with the headsman
and look eagerly for the moon whose rising is the signal for
the execution.

In the crowd is also the blind banished King of Tartary,
Timur, accompanied by a faithful slave girl, Liù; the joy of
their meeting with his son Calaf, whom he had thought dead,
has, however, a dark shadow; the plotters who have usurped
the crown of Tartary would not hesitate to slay Calaf if they
knew that he was alone and defenceless. Timur has determined therefore to keep his name and birth a secret. He tells
Calaf the story of his flight, aided only by Liù. Why has she
risked so much, asks the Prince; because he once smiled at
her in the Palace, she tells him.

The crowd urges on the executioner and his assistants to
sharpen the ceremonial sword ('Gira la cote'). This done,
they wait for the rising of the moon, to music subtly
suggestive of half-dark, half-light. The moon rises, but as the
funeral procession, led by the pathetic figure of the victim,
wends its way slowly up the hill leading to the place of
execution there is a change of heart in the mob. Voices are
heard calling for a pardon, and Calaf curses the beauty which
sends to the scaffold noble and innocent lovers. Turandot
herself appears for a moment on the balcony of the Palace.
The clamour for a reprieve rises from all sides. It is answered
by Turandot with a gesture which means death to the
unhappy Prince of Persia, and the halted procession moves on
again.

But the beauty of Turandot has claimed another victim. The sight of her has been enough to stifle in Calaf all feeling other than the desire to win her. He, too, will submit to the test and either win her or end like the Prince of Persia.

In vain his father and Liù (who loves him) implore him to desist. In vain the three ministers of the Imperial Household, Ping, Pang, and Pong, attempt to disuade him with material arguments. They make their entrance to music of characteristic cast:

Liù pathetically begs him in an exquisite passage to relinquish his attempt: 'Signore, ascolta' (My Lord, hear me).

In an aria he comforts her: 'Non piangere, Liù' (Do not weep Liù), but his determination is not to be shaken, and as the curtain descends he gives the signal which announces the arrival of a new claimant to the hand of Turandot.

Act II.   The first scene (a pavilion) shows the three ministers, Ping, Pang, and Pong (a re-incarnation of stock characters of the *Commedia dell'Arte*) lamenting the state of China.

Surely, they say, this is the end of its kingly race of rulers. Heads fall like rotten apples and no one can bring peace to the distracted country. They think longingly of their distant homes. The music is remarkable for the consistent way in which Puccini suggests the kaleidoscopic nature of the three dignitaries. If the scene of the enigmas is the opera's slow movement, this is undoubtedly its *scherzo*.

Drums are heard in the distance; the hour of the trial draws near and they retire meekly 'to enjoy the latest torture'. The sounds of a majestic march are heard; the curtains are drawn apart and disclose the throne room where the trial is to take place.

High above all the others sits the old Emperor, surrounded
by his sages and guards. Calaf is led to the Imperial presence
with noblemen and soldiers who carry strange banners. Last
to come is Turandot. When the loyal acclamations have died
down the Emperor addresses Calaf and asks him to retire
from the contest; the victims of Turandot are too many
already. When Calaf answers with a refusal, Turandot tells, in
her turn, the story of her ancestress who 'thousands and
thousands of years ago' was betrayed by a foreign conqueror
who sacked the city and carried her into exile where she died
of grief: 'In questa reggia' (Within this Palace). It is to avenge
her that Turandot has devised the trial. She, too, tells Calaf
to desist and warns him that while the riddles are three, there
is but one chance of escaping death. Calaf answers her
somewhat rhetorically but with immense confidence, and
their joint voices in their excitement soar thrillingly to a top
C.

Gli e-nig-mi so-no tre, u-na e la vi-ta

The first riddle is no sooner asked than it is answered. The
'phantom that is born every night and dies every day', says
Calaf, 'is what now inspires me: it is Hope.' Turandot,
alarmed by the prompt solution, hastens to ask the second
riddle. 'Tell me,' she asks, 'what is it that at times is like a
fever, yet grows cold when you die; that blazes up if you
think of great deeds?' Calaf hesitates a moment, then gives
the right answer: it is The Blood. His reply arouses the joy of
the courtiers, who encourage him: 'Keep up your heart,
reader of riddles.' It only annoys Turandot. She orders
silence, and then puts the third question: 'What is the ice that
sets you on fire? ' and as Calaf seems at a loss she taunts him:
'You are afraid, death is near.' But after a while Calaf guesses:
'You are the ice that sets me on fire'; the answer to the last
riddle is 'Turandot'. He has won the contest and receives the
praise of the courtiers. But Turandot is not yet won.
Angry and fearful she begs the Emperor not to treat her
like a slave given to the foreign prince, for she would die of
shame. The Emperor objects that his oath is sacred and that
the contest has been fairly won. Magnanimously Calaf him-

self comes to her rescue. 'I have answered three riddles,' he says; 'if before morning you can discover but one secret—the name I bear, and which you do not know, I will die as I would have died if I had never answered your riddles.'

Act III takes us back to the scene of the first. It is night and the voice of the Mandarin is heard: Turandot's orders are that no one shall sleep in Pekin until the name of the strange prince is discovered; the penalty for disregarding her injunction is death. Calaf hears the proclamation, but is unmoved. In a delightful aria ('Nessun dorma': None shall sleep) typical of Puccini's happiest work, he expresses the conviction that he alone will reveal the secret. When the sun is high in the heavens Turandot will be his bride.

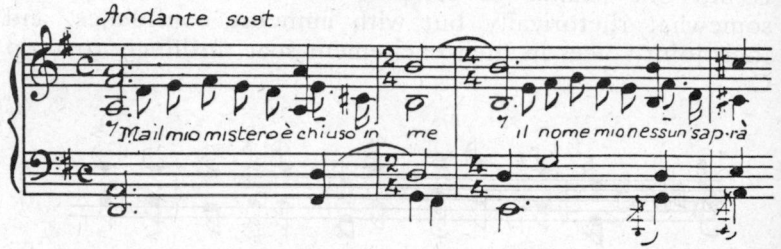

Ping, Pang, and Pong come to him offering any prize he chooses to ask, slaves, riches, power and a safe way out of China, if he will but tell them his name. Neither bribes nor threats can move Calaf. Turandot's guards now come on the scene; they have arrested Timur and Liù, who had been seen speaking to Calaf; they must know his name. Turandot, apprised of the capture, comes to order that torture be applied to Timur to make him reveal the secret. Fearing for the old man's life, Liù boldly steps forward: 'I know the name,' she says, 'and I alone.' She is taken; she is tortured, but refuses to tell. 'What gives you this power of resistance?' asks Turandot; 'Princess, it is love' ('Tanto amore segreto'). The executioner is called for, but Liù says she can bear the pain no longer. She addresses Turandot directly: 'Tu, che di gel sei cinta' (Thou, who with ice art girdled). This aria is the emotional climax of the opera; Liù embodies the female virtues which are so conspicuously lacking in Turandot, and Puccini has perfectly captured the qualities of this last of the 'frail women' he always dealt with so lovingly in his music. At the end of the aria, she snatches the dagger of a soldier and stabs herself to death. There is an outburst of rage from

Timur, then the body is carried away followed by the crowd. Calaf and Turandot are alone.[1]

Calaf upbraids the Princess with her cruelty; then he takes hold of her and boldly kisses her on the mouth. Turandot's strength is gone and with it all thought of revenge, all her fierceness and courage. The dawn comes to herald a new day; she weeps in the arms of Calaf: 'Del primo pianto.' The reign of Turandot is over. She humbly begs Calaf to go and carry away his secret. But Calaf knows that he has won her. 'I have no longer a secret,' he replies. 'I am Calaf, the son of Timur. I give you my name and with it my life.'

Trumpets are heard announcing the meeting of the court. The scene is switched back to the throne room. There Turandot addresses the assembled courtiers and the Emperor: 'I have discovered the stranger's secret and his name is—Love.'

The music of *Turandot* retains much of Puccini's directness with a richer and bolder harmonic structure. The composer's faith in the power of melody was unshaken; his last opera is extremely melodious. Yet he dreamt of something lovelier than anything he had ever written for the last love duet, which was to be the crowning incident of *Turandot*, as the love duet of *Tristan* is the central pivot of that opera. This he did not live to write.   F.B.

FRANCESCO CILEA
(1866–1950)
ADRIANA LECOUVREUR

OPERA in four acts by Francesco Cilea; text by Colautti, from the play by Scribe and Legouvé. Première on November 26, 1902, at the Teatro Lirico, Milan, with Pandolfini, Ghibaudo, Caruso, de Luca, conductor Campanini. First performed Covent Garden, 1904, with Giachetti, Anselmi, Sammarco, conductor Campanini; Metropolitan, New York,

---

[1] Of the concluding duet only some sketches were found at the composer's death. Out of these Signor Alfano has found the material for the last scenes which were added by him.

1907, with Cavalieri, Caruso, Scotti, conductor Ferrari. Revived la Scala, Milan, 1932, with Cobelli, Pederzini, Pertile, Ghirardini, conductor Ghione; 1939, with Oltrabella, Elmo, Voyer, Valentino; 1942, with Cobelli; 1945, with Favero; Rome, 1952, with Caniglia, Benedetti, Campora, Gobbi; Metropolitan, New York, 1963, with Tebaldi, Dalis, Corelli, Colzani; Edinburgh Festival, 1963 (by San Carlo Opera, Naples), with Magda Olivero, Lazzarini, Oncina, Bruscantini. Magda Olivero has been one of the most famous of recent exponents of the title role.

CHARACTERS

Maurizio, *Count of Saxony* ....Tenor
Prince de Bouillon ....Bass
L'Abate di Chazeuil ....Tenor
Michonnet, *stage director of the Comédie-*
    Française ....Baritone
Quinault ⎱ *members of the company* ....⎰ Bass
Poisson ⎰   ⎱ Tenor
Major-domo ....Tenor
Adriana Lecouvreur ....Soprano
Princesse de Bouillon ....Mezzo-Soprano
Mlle. Jouvenot ⎱ *Members of the* ⎰ Soprano
Mlle. Dangeville ⎰ *company*   ⎱ Mezzo-Soprano
A Chamber Maid

Ladies, Gentlemen, Servants

Time: 1730   *Place:* Paris

Act I.   The foyer of the Comédie-Française. Actors and actresses going on to the stage demand their swords, hats, coats from Michonnet, who complains that everyone expects him to do everything at the same time. The Prince de Bouillon comes in with the Abate and greets the actors and actresses. The visitors look through at the stage, and comment on the fullness of the house; hardly surprising, says Michonnet, since both Duclos and Adriana Lecouvreur are playing to-night. Adriana comes in trying over her speech. She acknowledges the cries of admiration modestly, and says that she is only the handmaid of the arts: 'Io son l'umile ancella.' It is one of Cilea's finest inspirations, and the tune is heard frequently throughout the opera as a 'motto' theme for Adriana.

Io son l'u-mil e an-cel-la del Gen - - nio cre-a-tor

Michonnet is her best friend, she tells them all, and the faithful Michonnet bursts into tears of emotion; when all have left he admits the reason—he has been in love with Adriana ever since she joined the company. Dare he tell her now? He starts to, but she tells him that she is in love with an unknown cavalier, attached to the Count of Saxony. Michonnet leaves her alone, and in a moment her as yet unknown lover is at her side. He addresses her in a passionate *arioso*: 'La dolcissima effigie.' Adriana says she will play only for him tonight, and leaves him, giving him before she does so violets for his buttonhole.

The Prince and the Abate come in, and the latter reads a letter which they have intercepted; it is from the Prince's wife, but because it makes an assignation for eleven o'clock in the villa of the Prince's mistress, the actress Duclos, they think it is from her. Their plan to surprise the lovers is overheard by some of the actors and actresses, and a spritely ensemble ensues.

Act II. The Princesse de Bouillon—it is she who has arranged the assignation—is seated, listening to the voices of the night. She reflects agitatedly on the torments of love in a big soliloquy: 'Acerba voluttà.' Maurizio arrives, and excuses his lateness; he was followed. She notices the violets and asks whether they had nothing to do with his lateness; he says it was for her he brought them: 'L'anima ho stanca'.

Their conversation is interrupted by the sound of a carriage outside; it is her husband, exclaims the Princess—she must hide. This she does, and the Prince de Bouillon, accompanied by the Abate, comes in to find Maurizio alone. They taunt him that he is caught, and are astonished when he threatens a duel. Why should he make so much fuss? The Prince is tired of la Duclos; why should not the Count of Saxony take her on as his mistress? Maurizio begins to understand, when, a moment later, Adriana is led in and introduced to him. This time, the astonishment is hers; the man she had thought a retainer turns out to be the Count of Saxony himself. The Prince and the Abate go out to see that they are not kept waiting longer for supper, and Adriana and Maurizio are alone.

In a short duet they renew their passionate vows. Michonnet comes in, asking that he may speak to Duclos, as an important decision has to be made over a new role before morning. She is here, says the Abate; Maurizio tries to silence him, but Michonnet takes the decision into his own hands and goes firmly into the room which Maurizio has tried to bar. Maurizio swears to Adriana that Duclos is not there; his appointment had to do with his political position, not with love. She believes him, and when Michonnet comes out saying it was not the Duclos, and the Abate wishes to discover the lady's identity, it is Adriana who prevents him. She says to Michonnet that she means to keep her word to Maurizio and help whoever it is.

Adriana knocks at the door and says she can save the lady inside with the aid of the key of the garden in which she has in her hand. The Princess plies her with questions, and eventually admits that she loves Maurizio. Adriana proudly claims his love as her own, to the tune of her recent duet with him. The act ends as the Princess escapes just before the Prince and his followers return.

Act III.   A party is being prepared in the house of the Prince de Bouillon. The Princess wonders where she has heard the voice of her rival; she cannot place it. The guests arrive, amongst them Adriana, whom the Princess naturally recognises immediately, and who sings the tune originally heard to the words of 'Io son l'umile ancella'. The Princess mutters something about a duel which she says Maurizio has taken part in, and in which he was gravely wounded—and Adriana shows obvious signs of emotion. Maurizio comes in, and is persuaded to talk about his battle experiences. A ballet entertainment has been arranged, and during its course the conversation continues, developing in the end into a battle of wits between the Princess and Adriana.

Act IV.   The scene is the same as that of Act I. Michonnet waits for Adriana who presently appears in a mood bordering on suicide. Various actors and actresses come in to congratulate her on her birthday, and presently a casket is brought in. Adriana opens it as the others leave, and sees in it violets, the very ones she had given Maurizio the previous evening, but by now shrivelled and old. She sings sadly to the violets, in whose shrivelled appearance she sees the dying of Maurizio's love for her: 'Poveri fiori.' Michonnet tries to comfort her, and smiles when he hears Maurizio's voice outside. Adriana cannot resist Maurizio's protestation of innocence, least of all when he proposes marriage to her, and tells her in the same breath that all his claims have been met and he is once more in possession of his rightful titles.

For a moment she tries to impress him by saying that the stage is the only throne she can ever mount, but her love is too much for her, and she and Maurizio rest happily in each other's arms.

Suddenly, she turns pale and would fall if Maurizio did not catch her. She thinks it has something to do with the flowers which she gave Maurizio and which he returned to her, but he denies having ever done such a thing. Adriana is convulsed with pain, and for a moment does not recognise her lover. Maurizio sends for help, and Michonnet comes in; he thinks the flowers may have been poisoned and suggests that a rival has done it. After a further convulsion, Adriana dies in their arms. The Princess's revenge is complete.   H.

FERRUCCIO BUSONI
(1866–1924)
TURANDOT

A Chinese fable in two acts, after Gozzi; music by Ferruccio Busoni, text by the composer. The music was developed from incidental pieces written for Reinhardt's production of Gozzi's play in Berlin, 1911. Première, Zürich, May 11, 1917. First performed Frankfurt, 1918; Berlin, 1921, with Lola Artôt de Padilla, Ober, conductor Blech. Revived Venice Festival, 1940, with Carbone, Limberti, Ziliani, Colella, conductor Previtali; Hamburg, 1948, with Werth, Melchert, conductor Grüber; la Scala, 1962, with Kabaiwanska, Cioni, conductor Sanzogno; Berlin, German Opera, 1966, with Annabelle Bernard, Haefliger, conductor Patane. New York, Little Orchestra Society, 1967, with Hannelore Kuhse.

CHARACTERS

The Emperor Altoum .... Bass
Turandot, *his daughter* .... Soprano
Adelma, *her confidante*............. Mezzo-Soprano
Calaf, *a young unknown prince*............... Tenor
Barak, *his faithful servant* .... Baritone
The Queen Mother of Samarkand, *a negress* ... Soprano

Truffaldino, *chief eunuch* . . . . High Tenor
Tartaglia   } *Altoum's ministers* . . . . { Bass
Pantalone }   { Bass
Eight Doctors . . . . Tenor, Bass
A Singer . . . . Mezzo-Soprano
     Slaves, Weeping Women, Eunuchs, Soldiers, a Priest,
                              Dancers
Time: Antiquity   *Place:* The Far East

The action follows in the main the course which has become familiar to opera-goers through Puccini's opera of the same name.

Act I.   An introduction in march rhythm leads to the first scene. The stage is empty when the curtain rises, but Calaf dashes through the gates and rapturously greets the city of Peking. His old servant Barak recognises him; not having seen him for so long, he had thought he was dead. Calaf tells him that his father, Timur, is also alive, and that he himself is looking for fortune in Peking. Barak tells him the story of Turandot and the riddles, whereupon Calaf laughs and seems unable to take the riddles too seriously, even though he catches sight of some heads impaled on spears at Turandot's order. Barak points to the procession which is at that moment going by, mourning the Prince of Samarkand, who has been put to death that very day. The lament is led by the Prince's mother, an aged negress. At its end, she curses Turandot, and throws the portrait of the princess from her. Barak comments that even the portrait of Turandot is said to enslave those who gaze upon it. Calaf looks at it, and in an *arioso* proclaims his love for its subject. He determines to try his luck.

Scene ii.   Truffaldino comes in front of the curtain and, in a high piping tenor, summons some slaves.

Slow, solemn music heralds the appearance of the Emperor Altoum, Turandot's father, who is preceded by wise doctors and attendants. The Emperor complains about his daughter's cruel behaviour, while his two comic advisers, Pantalone and the stuttering Tartaglia gather about to flatter him. In a short aria, the Emperor prays to Confucius that he may at long last win a son in the coming trial between the stranger and Turandot. He commands that the unknown suitor be brought before him. Trumpets sound, and Calaf throws himself at the Emperor's feet. The old man is immediately impressed by the stranger's looks; who is he? Calaf answers that he is a prince, but his name must remain unknown for the present. The Emperor bids him retire now if he wants to withdraw from what is likely to prove an unequal conquest, but Calaf's reply is that he desires only death or Turandot; for him there can be no third alternative. Altoum offers him honours and riches if he will renounce the trial. Pantalone and Tartaglia add their voices in an effort to dissuade Calaf, but he is adamant. The brilliant quartet ends as Calaf reaffirms his determination on a series of high A's.

Turandot enters, veiled. She demands to know who dares to match his wisdom with hers, but, when she catches sight of the stranger, admits to herself that she is moved by the sight of him. The chorus softly agrees that he is different from the other suitors, and Adelma, Turandot's confidante, in an aside recognises the prince as the young man she once fell in love with when she was a girl.[1] Calaf again denies that there is any possibility for him but Turandot or death; Turandot's rejoinder is that his death will be her death.

The Emperor suggests that Turandot ask three easy riddles so that the form of the trial may be honoured; after that the wedding between her and her unknown suitor can take place. Turandot refuses, the riddles are laid down by law. Truffaldino rings a bell and announces each riddle in turn. They are on a more metaphysical plane than those in Puccini's opera (see p. 1203), and the answers are respectively Human Understanding, Morals, Art. After Calaf has guessed the second, Turandot offers to let her suitor free and to forgo the last question. He refuses, but when Turandot unveils herself as she asks the third question, it looks as though he is lost. However, he pulls himself together and answers the third as he has the first two.

The Emperor and his entourage are delighted with Calaf's success; he calls for music, and the rejoicing is general. Turandot admits she has lost, but says the shame is more than she can bear; at the altar she will kill herself. Calaf admits that his victory is hollow if she still hates him. He offers her a fourth chance; he will ask her a riddle. What is his name? Calaf reflects that he who reaches his peak of happiness is fuller of sorrow than he was before.

Act II. The chorus and its leader sing before the curtain

[1] From this figure, Puccini and his librettist fabricated the tragic Liù.

goes up showing Turandot's room. Slaves dance and sing for the entertainment of Turandot and Adelma, but Turandot stops them abruptly and sends them away. She cannot make out her own feelings: does she love the victorious stranger after all? She knows that if she were to give way she would soon regret it. Turandot shall die untouched, is her decision. Her big aria is highly dramatic and, in spite of its greater economy, almost as taxing for the singer as the music Puccini wrote for his heroine.

Truffaldino comes in. He had headed the band of Turandot's followers whose duty it was to discover the stranger's name. His aria is exactly calculated for the high, thin voice which has characterised him throughout the opera. When he asked the stranger his name, he says, he got the answer, 'Death or Turandot'.

The Emperor comes to see his daughter. He tells her he knows the stranger's name, but nothing will make him tell her; the stranger is too good for her, and he is glad that she will be humiliated in front of the whole world. Turandot faces him bitterly—he will be sorry for his unjust words to her when she faces the stranger on the following day. She turns in her misery to Adelma. Adelma says the Emperor is not alone in knowing the prince's name. In a pathetic, proud tune, Adelma says that the princess has just addressed her as 'friend', and yet keeps her a slave, in spite of her royal birth; if she will give her her freedom she will in return reveal the stranger's name, which she knows. Turandot starts to protest, but Adelma says that the prince once laughed at her when she was a girl, and she wants revenge more than anything in the world. Turandot greets her as sister, and Adelma whispers into her ear as the curtain falls.

An intermezzo leads to the last scene, which takes place in the throne-room. Drums beat the rhythm of a funeral march, during which Tartaglia and Pantalone lament, asking themselves the while what the sound of mourning can be about. They are answered by the Emperor; it is for Turandot, no one else. Turandot at first agrees that it is for her, and Calaf admits that he is deeply grieved at the misery which his success induces in her. The Emperor thereupon orders gay music, but suddenly Turandot rounds on them and admits that the funeral music was part of her scheme to make her revenge the sweeter. She knows the stranger's name: Calaf! She dismisses Calaf, to the Emperor's obvious sorrow, and her suitor turns to go, saying that he will easily find death in the wars. As he turns to go, however, Turandot herself calls him back by name. She welcomes him as her husband, and the general lamentation is instantly turned to rejoicing, not least for the Emperor, for whom this means an end of sorrow.   H.

ARLECCHINO
Harlequin

Opera in one act by Ferruccio Busoni, text by the composer. Première, Zürich, May 11, 1917, with Alexander Moissi as Arlecchino. First performed Frankfurt, 1918; Berlin, 1921, conducted by Blech; Vienna, 1926; London (B.B.C.), 1939; Venice Festival, 1940, with Tellini, Mazziotti, Gelli, conductor Gui; New York, Carnegie Hall (semi-staged), 1951; Glyndebourne, 1954, with Malbin, Dickie, conductor Pritchard. Revived Berlin Staatsoper, 1946, with Beilke, Witte, conductor Schüler; Berlin, German Opera, 1966, with Johnson, Grobe, McDaniel, Lagger, conductor Patane; Bologna, 1967, with Gatta, Garaventa, Boyer, Monachesi, conductor Ceccato.

CHARACTERS

Ser Matteo del Sarto, *a tailor* . . . . Baritone
Abbate Cospicuo . . . . Baritone
Dottor Bombasto . . . . Bass
Harlequin . . . . Actor
Leandro . . . . Tenor
Annunziata, *Matteo's wife* . . . . Silent
Columbine, *Arlecchino's wife* . . . . .Mezzo-Soprano

Time: Nineteenth Century   *Place:* Bergamo

Busoni called *Arlecchino* 'ein theatralisches Capriccio' (a theatrical caprice), and Edward Dent in his biography of the composer has suggested that it is in the nature of a play for puppets. As if to emphasise this, Harlequin speaks a prologue in which he warns the audience not to take the play too literally; it is all in the spirit of a proverb.

The work is in four parts, each corresponding to an aspect of Harlequin; we see him as rogue, as soldier, as husband, and as conqueror. A quick, lively introduction leads to the first scene. Matteo is sitting in front of his house, sewing at his leather and reading Dante to himself. In a window upstairs, Harlequin can be seen making love to Matteo's wife. Matteo comments on his reading, which reminds him, he says, of opera (the orchestra plays a bit of 'Fin ch'han dal vino' from *Don Giovanni*). Harlequin wonders how he is to get away. In the end he jumps blatantly out of the window, and, when Matteo seems surprised to see him, says to him in an agitated way, 'Don't you know the barbarians are surrounding the town?', which frightens and upsets the good man to such an extent that he forgets where Harlequin came from. In his confusion, Matteo drops the key to his front door, and Harlequin picks it up and locks the door from outside, putting the key into his pocket when he has finished. Harlequin can be heard singing gaily from behind the scenes as he goes off.

The doctor and the abbé come into sight, arguing together rather in the manner of the doctor and the captain in *Wozzeck*. The abbé sings a song in praise of Tuscany and its wine. Their slanging match abates, and they shout to Matteo, who is absent, they notice, from his usual place in front of his house. In a trio in which a march theme is prominent, he explains about the barbarians who are surrounding the town—all their daughters will be ravished and their friends killed—and asks why they have not taken refuge themselves. They say they will go off and consult the Burgomaster about the invasion, and they disappear laughing in the direction of the tavern.

Harlequin reappears dressed as a recruiting sergeant, with two supporters behind him. The music is a parodistic reference to the march from *La Fille du Régiment*. He tells Matteo he is wanted immediately for the army; there can be no discussion. Matteo asks for permission to take his Dante with him, and then, to the sound of a funeral march, he is marched away by the two stooges.

A minuet starts in the orchestra as Harlequin tries the key he has copied from Matteo's; it fits, but at that moment he is spoken to from behind. He turns to find it is no other than his own wife, Columbine. Why, she demands in an aria, is he so cruel and unfaithful to her? She starts to flatter him—she would do everything for him, if he would only let her—but it is no use, and, distracting her attention for a moment, Harlequin disappears.

Columbine is determined to find out what Harlequin was after in this particular house, but at that moment she hears the tenor voice of Leandro singing a romance, and she is quite unable to resist it. Leandro hears her version of her ory, and immediately offers to revenge her honor. His first song is a parody of romantic German song, his second of a classical Italian equivalent. There is a flowery love scene for the two, which is almost too much for Columbine. At any rate, she enquires whether Leandro is not being just the least little bit sloppy in the aria he is singing; let her wait for the *stretta*, is his answer. Harlequin comes on the scene, announces that Columbine is his wife, leads her off into the tavern, and draws his wooden sword to fight Leandro. He knocks him out with the flat of his sword, and, shouting 'murder' at the top of his voice, disappears into the house of Matteo.

Columbine emerges from the tavern, together with the abbé and the doctor, who are both by now very drunk. They remember that they have to see the Burgomaster about the barbarians who are invading the town, but the subject does not appear to be entirely clear in their minds. Suddenly, the doctor stumbles over the body of Leandro. With a shriek, Columbine recognises it. The other two start to wonder what they are to do at this hour of the night with a body of a dead man. On further investigation, Columbine decides he is not dead after all, which suggestion at first causes consternation in the minds of the other two. However, they eventually come round to her way of thinking, and try to enlist the help of the neighbours; heads appear at the windows, but are immediately withdrawn when it becomes known what is wanted of them. The doctor and the abbé are sad but philosophical about the whole affair. Suddenly a donkey appears, hitched to a cart. It is the work of providence, is the comment. In a quartet, the abbé prays, Leandro returns to consciousness, the doctor comments on the medico-philosophical aspects of the affair, and Columbine pours scorn on all men impartially. In the end, all get into the donkey cart, and drive off.

Harlequin looks down from the window of Matteo's house and waves to them as they go, rejoicing in his freedom. He comes out, bringing Matteo's wife with him and they go off together. Matteo is seen coming towards his house. He has been deserted by his companions, presumes that peace has been concluded, and is returning home. He finds his wife has left the house, and so philosophically gets out his Dante and his sewing as before, and starts to read where he left off. The passage has to do with infidelity. . . .

A drop-curtain falls. In pairs, the various character including the donkey and his driver, come to make their bows to the audience. Last come Harlequin and Annunziata, Matteo's wife; Harlequin speaks an epilogue: he introduces Annunziata to them—they have not been lucky enough to see much of her during the evening—and then asks what the moral of the story is to be. Everything is new, everything goes on as before, is his conclusion; but his advice to the audience is that they should make up their own minds.

The stage directions suggest that if a second curtain call is needed, the drop should be raised to reveal Matteo still sitting and sewing and reading and waiting.

'Few of Busoni's compositions gave him so much satisfaction as *Arlecchino*,' says Edward Dent in his biography (O.U.P. 1933). 'Both from a literary and musical point of view he regarded it as his most individual and personal work. One reason for its lack of popularity up to the present is that it demands an unusual alertness of mind on the part of the spectator. The libretto is extremely terse in style, and was considerably reduced in the process of setting it to music, for Busoni was always determined to make the musical form the deciding factor in his works for the stage. With the older composers this principle led to the expansion of the libretto by frequent repetition of the words; with Busoni it led to compression.'   H.

DOKTOR FAUST

Opera in six tableaux (two prologues, one scenic interlude, and three scenes); text by the composer. Première, Dresden, May 21, 1925, with Meta Seinemeyer, Theo Strack, Robert Burg, conductor Fritz Busch. First performed Berlin, 1927, with Leider, Soot, Schorr; London, Queen's Hall (concert), in English translation by E. J. Dent, 1937, conducted by Boult, with Blyth, Parry Jones, Noble, Wendon; Florence Festival, 1942, with Oltrabella, Renato Gigli, Manacchini, conductor Previtali; Berlin, 1954, with Fischer-Dieskau; London, 1959 (concert) with Harper, Richard Lewis, Fischer-Dieskau, conductor Boult; la Scala 1960, with Roberti, Bertocci, Dondi; Holland Festival, 1962, by Wupperthal Opera; New York, Carnegie Hall, 1964 (concert), with Bjoner, Shirley, Fischer-Dieskau; Florence Festival, 1964, with Maragliano, Handt, Cesari; Stockholm, 1969, with Söderström, Erik Saeden.

CHARACTERS

Doctor Faust		Baritone
Wagner, *his famulus, later Rector of Wittenberg University*		Baritone
A Man Dressed in Black		
A Monk		
A Herald	*Mephistopheles in his various disguises*	Tenor
A Chaplain		
A Courier		
A Night-watchman		
The Duke of Parma		Tenor
The Duchess of Parma		Soprano
The Master of Ceremonies		Bass
The Girl's Brother, *a soldier*		Baritone
A Lieutenant		Tenor
Three Students from Cracow.		Tenor, Two Basses
A Theologian		Bass
A Jurist		Bass
A Doctor of Natural History		Baritone
Four Students from Wittenberg		Four Tenors
Gravis		Bass
Levis		Bass
Asmodus	*spirit voices*	Baritone
Beelzebub		Tenor
Megärus		Tenor
Sixth Voice (Mephistopheles)		Tenor

Church-goers, Soldiers, Courtiers, Students

Time: Sixteenth Century   *Place:* Wittenberg, Parma

Busoni drew his text from the old puppet-play of *Faust*, and he is indebted to Goethe only for the richness and nobility of the language in which he has expressed his conception—he was a life-long student and devotee of Goethe. *Doktor Faust* represents the summing-up of his life's work.

The orchestral prelude is in the nature of an impressionistic study of distant bells'.[1] Towards the end of he prelude the chorus behind the scenes can be heard singing the single word 'Pax' (Edward Dent has aptly pointed out hat this part of the work was written at Zürich in 1917). The curtain goes up and an actor steps out in front of a

[1] E. J. Dent, *Ferruccio Busoni* (O.U.P.).

drop-curtain to recite the verse prologue, in which Busoni
explains how the subject came to be chosen.

He disappears and the first scene is revealed: Faust's study
in Wittenberg, where he is superintending some alchemical
process. Wagner tells him that three students are asking to see
him, and, when Faust seems reluctant to receive them,
explains that they have with them a remarkable book, called
'Clavis Astartis Magica'. Faust is excited; this is perhaps the
book which will give him the magic power he has so long
sought. The three young men, dressed in black, enter Faust's
room, and announce themselves as students from Cracow.
Faust is reminded of his youth, with its hopes and its dreams
and its plans. The students give him the book, a key with
which to unlock it, and a letter which makes it his property.
He offers them hospitality, but they decline it, and take their
leave. Will he see them again? 'Perhaps' is their only answer.
Wagner returns, and Faust wonders why he does not show
the visitors out. He saw no one, says Wagner, and Faust
begins to understand the identity of the strangers. The pots
on the hearth begin to hiss and crackle.

When the curtain rises on the second prologue, the scene is
unchanged. It is night. With the key in hand which the
students have given him, Faust loosens his girdle and with it
draws a magic circle. Standing inside it, he calls upon Lucifer
to send down his servant. Six tongues of flame appear
hovering in the air. Each of them represents one of Lucifer's
intimates: Faust questions the first five—how fast is each?—
and dismisses each with contempt at the answer he gets. He
steps out of the circle and seems reluctant to question the
last spirit in case it too should disappoint him. A voice
addresses him by name, and proclaims that it is as fast as
human thought. 'The scene with six flames,' says Edward
Dent, 'is conceived musically as a set of variations on a
theme; the first spirit is a deep bass, and the voices rise
progressively, so that the last—Mephistopheles—is a high
tenor'. Mephistopheles's musical entrance is cruelly exacting
as he is asked to sustain successively a high A natural, a B
flat, and a B natural, and the phrase in which he boasts of the
speed ends on a sustained C natural.

Faust appears satisfied by the answer of the sixth voice
and he summons him to appear in physical shape. O
Mephistopheles, Faust makes an unusual demand: 'Give me
for the rest of my life the unconditional fulfilment of every
wish; let me embrace the world, the East and the South that

...ll me; let me understand the actions of mankind and extend them; give me Genius! give me its pain too, that I may be happy like no other—make me *free*.[1] But Faust has stepped outside the magic circle, and Mephistopheles will only agree to serve him at a price: after he has done Faust's bidding, Faust must agree to serve him for ever. Faust says he will serve no one, and is about to dismiss him like the others, when Mephistopheles reminds him that his creditors are at the door, that the brother of the girl he has seduced is searching for him to kill him, and that no help but the devil's will suffice to extricate him from his predicament.

Faust reluctantly agrees to Mephistopheles's bargain, and the scene ends as he signs the agreement. During the later part of the scene, an unseen chorus sings the 'Credo' and the 'Gloria' and the curtain falls as an 'Alleluiah' is heard.

The Intermezzo takes place in the Romanesque side-chapel of a great cathedral. The whole scene is dominated by the sound of the cathedral organ—Dent says that Busoni 'wanted the organ to be no mere background; it was to fill the whole theatre with its reverberation. Unfortunately there are few theatres which possess organs of sufficient power to carry out the composer's design.' A soldier, described as the 'girl's brother', is praying that he may be enabled to avenge her seduction. Mephistopheles points him out to Faust and then sets about the task of removing him. He takes on the aspect of a monk and kneels beside the soldier, who does his best to get rid of him. Suddenly, soldiers appear in the doorway and point out the soldier as the man who killed their captain. They fall upon him and kill him, leaving Mephistopheles triumphant; sacrilege and murder—and both laid to Faust's account—seems pretty good going for one day.

The main part of the action now begins. The scene is laid at the court of the Duke of Parma who has just married a beautiful wife. The celebrations are suggested by the orchestral Cortège with which the scene starts (this in an extended form constitutes the second part of the 'Sarabande and Cortège from *Doktor Faust*', which is sometimes heard in the concert hall). Having regard to the end of this scene (when Faust elopes with the Duchess), it is hardly surprising that the music for all its brilliance has a sinister tang to it. The pageant and ballet which introduces the rejoicing also make use of Busoni's *Tanzwalzer*, a work dating from 1920 and dedicated to the memory of Johann Strauss; this is a separate

[1] E. J. Dent, *Ferruccio Busoni* (O.U.P.).

composition, unlike the Sarabande and Cortège which da
from the same year but were always intended as sketches fo
Doktor Faust.

The master of ceremonies proposes that the Duke and his
newly wed Duchess shall receive Faust, by now famous
throughout the world for his learning, and reputedly a man
of sinister reputation. Mephistopheles is on hand as Faust's
herald, and he announces his master, who makes a distinguished appearance, with (according to the stage directions) either black boys or monkeys carrying his train. The
chorus welcomes him and expresses open admiration; the
Duchess whole-heartedly concurs but the Duke has misgivings
lest the rumours about him prove true.

Faust is greeted by the Duke, and proceeds to show his
powers by turning light into darkness. He asks the Duchess
what he shall do for her delectation; ask for something
impossible, suggests the Duke. She would like to see
Solomon, she declares; in a moment he appears before them,
with the Queen of Sheba at his side. The Duke is quick to
notice that the Queen has a look of the Duchess about her,
and that Solomon closely resembles Faust. For her next wish,
the Duchess insists that Faust shall not only perform it but
divine beforehand what it is. Samson and Delilah appear
under Delilah's bed hides a black slave holding the fatal
shears ready to her mistress's hand. Once again the visions
wear the features of the Duchess and Faust. The third
apparition is conjured up by Faust of his own accord; Salome
and John the Baptist stand before the court, and near them
the executioner. Again, the protagonists seem to have
borrowed the masks of Faust and his noble hostess, and this
time the executioner resembles the Duke. 'At a word from
Salome, his head falls,' comments Faust. 'He must not die,'
answers the Duchess eagerly. Faust is confident that the
Duchess loves him.

The Duke makes an end of the performance by inviting
Faust to the ducal table, but Mephistopheles dissuades his
master, warning him that the food is poisoned, and together
they leave the stage. For a moment, no one is visible, but
presently the Duchess comes into sight once more, convinced
that Faust is calling her. She sings rapturously of her love for
him, then goes slowly out. Her voice can be heard calling
off-stage.

It is suddenly daylight. The Duke of Parma is in excited

conversation with his Chaplain, who tells him that the
Duchess has eloped with Faust; he saw them disappear
together on winged horses. It would be best to hush everything up and marry the sister of the Duke of Ferrara, who
otherwise threatens war. The Duke accepts his Chaplain's
counsel, and as the curtain falls, we see the hand raised in
blessing turn to a claw.

The Sarabande, an extended and solemn orchestral piece
described as a symphonic intermezzo, ushers in the last act.
The scene is an inn at Wittenberg, where Faust sits drinking
and discussing philosophy with his students. The discussion
soon approaches a quarrel, and Faust does his best to calm
things down: nothing can be proved, he says; let them follow
Luther's example. ... He has not even time to get out
Luther's name when the company divides into Catholics and
Protestants, and a Latin *Te Deum* is heard in violent
opposition to 'Ein' feste Burg'.

Faust sits pensively aside until one of the students asks
him to tell them of his amorous adventures with women. The
orchestra *sotto voce* remembers the cortège, and Faust starts
to tell them of the most beautiful woman he ever loved, a
Duchess, on her wedding day, only a year ago. Does she ever
think of him now, he wonders. At that moment, in comes
Mephistopheles in the guise of a messenger. The Duchess of
Parma, who has just died, sends something to Faust for a
remembrance. At Faust's feet he places the corpse of a
new-born baby, to the general horror of the company. He
proceeds to tell Faust's story in unromantic terms, and caps
it by setting fire to the bundle, which was only straw. From
the smoke he summons Helen of Troy.

At this point Mephistopheles leaves Faust alone. Faust
raves of his dream of beauty but, just as he seems about to
grasp the vision, it disappears into nothing, and he is alone
once more. He turns to see three dark figures standing in the
shadow, and demanding the return of the book, the key and
the letter which went with them. Faust motions them away:
he has destroyed what they are demanding from him. They
tell him his hour has come, but he has nothing but contempt
for them, and welcomes the end of his life.

The scene changes to a street in Wittenberg. It is winter,
snow is on the ground, the Night-watchman's voice informs
the citizens that ten has struck (it is Mephistopheles in the
last of his disguises). Students congratulate Wagner on his

opening speech as Rector of the University, where he has succeeded Faust.

Faust comes in, recognises Wagner's house as once his, listens as the *Dies Irae* is sung in the church, and sees a beggar woman opposite, a child in her arms. He gives her some money, but as soon as he sees her, knows her as the Duchess. She gives him the child saying that she has already tried twice to do so. It is dead. She disappears. Faust tries to get into the church to pray, but his way is barred by the soldier who was killed in the Romanesque chapel. Faust removes him—his power still extends to spirits—and tries to pray before a crucifix at the side of the church door. But he cannot find words, and, when the light from the Night-watchman's lantern shines on the crucifix, he sees the form of Helen of Troy upon it.

With a cry of horror he turns away, then masters himself for a supreme trial of strength. (At this point Busoni's score ends; the rest of the opera is finished by Jarnach.[1]) Faust lays the dead body of the child on the ground and covers it with his cloak. He throws his girdle on the ground, and steps within the circle. He exerts his will in a final effort to project his personality into the body of the child. May his faults be rectified in this child, and may it accomplish what he has failed to do. He dies, and as the Watchman announces midnight, a naked youth with arms uplifted and bearing a green twig in his hand, rises from Faust's body and walks unconcernedly through the snow. The Night-watchman lifts his lamp and looks down at the dead body. Has this man had an accident, he asks?

H.

---

[1] Philipp Jarnach was Busoni's pupil. At one time, there was talk of asking Schoenberg to undertake the completion.

ITALO MONTEMEZZI
(1875–1952)

L'AMORE DEI TRE RE
The Love of Three Kings

OPERA in three acts by Italo Montemezzi; text by Sem Benelli, from his play of the same name. Première, la Scala, Milan, April 10, 1913, with Villani, Ferrari-Fontana, Galeffi, de Angelis, conductor Serafin. First performed Metropolitan, New York, 1914, with Bori, Ferrari-Fontana, Amato, Didur, conductor Toscanini; Covent Garden, 1914, with Edvina, Crimi, Cigada, Didur, conductor Moranzoni. Revivals include Metropolitan, 1926, with Ponselle, Gigli, Danise, Didur, conductor Serafin; 1939, with Jepson, Tokatyan, Bonelli, Pinza, conductor Papi; 1949, with Kirsten, Kullman, Weede, Lazzari; la Scala, 1926, with Cobelli, Lo Giudice, Morelli, de Angelis, conductor Toscanini; 1932, with dalla Rizza, Piccaluga, Morelli, Lazzari, conductor de Sabata; 1937, with Scuderi, Marcato, Tagliabue, Pasero, conductor Marinuzzi; 1948, with Petrella, Francesco Albanese, Guarrera Rossi-Lemeni, conductor Capuana; 1953, with Araujo, Prandelli, Valdengo, Rossi-Lemeni, conductor de Sabata; Covent Garden, 1930, with Ponselle, Merli, Inghilleri, Autori (later Pinza), conductor Bellezza; Buenos Aires, 1938, with Rethberg, Jagel, Galeffi, Pinza, conductor Serafin; San Francisco, 1941, with Moore, Kullman, Weede, Pinza, conductor Montemezzi, 1966, with Kirsten, Campora, Wolansky, Ghiuselev, conductor Molinari-Pradelli.

CHARACTERS

Archibaldo, *King of Altura* .... Bass
Manfredo, *son of Archibaldo* .... Baritone
Avito, *a former prince of Altura* .... Tenor
Flaminio, *a castle guard* .... Tenor
Fiora, *wife of Manfredo* .... Soprano
A youth, a boy child (voice behind the scenes),
a handmaiden, a young girl, an old woman,
other people of Altura
Time: The Tenth Century   *Place:* A remote castle of Italy,
forty years after a Barbarian
invasion, led by Archibaldo

This opera is one of the most successful products of 20th century Italian music, more popular, it must be admitted, in America, where it has been frequently performed, than in its native Italy. Based upon a powerful tragedy by Sem Benelli, one of the foremost of Italian playwrights, it is a combination of terse, swiftly moving drama with a score which vividly depicts events progressing fatefully toward an inevitable human cataclysm. While there are few set-pieces in Montemezzi's score, nevertheless it is melodious—a succession of musical phrases that clothe the words, the thought behind them, their significance, their most subtle suggestion, in the weft and woof of expressive music. It is a medieval tapestry, the colours of which have not faded, but still glow with their original depth and opulence.

Act I. The scene is a spacious hall open to a terrace. A lantern employed as a signal sheds its reddish light dimly through the gloom before dawn.

From the left enters Archibaldo. He is old with flowing white hair and beard, and he is blind. He is led in by his guide Flaminio, who is in the dress of the castle guard. As if he saw, the old blind king points to the door of a chamber across the hall and bids Flaminio look and tell if it is quite shut. It is slightly open. Archibaldo in a low voice orders him to shut it, but make no noise, then, hastily changing his mind, to leave it as it is.

In the setting of the scene, in the gloom penetrated only by the glow of the red lantern, in the costumes of the men, in the actions of the old King, who cannot see but whose sense of hearing is weirdly acute, and in the subtle suggestion of suspicion that all is not well, indicated in his restlessness, the very opening of this opera immediately casts a spell of the uncanny over the hearer. This is enhanced by the groping character of the theme which accompanies the entrance of Archibaldo with his guide, depicting the searching footsteps of the blind old man.

There is mention of Fiora, the wife of Archibaldo's son, Manfredo, who is in the north, laying siege to an enemy stronghold. There also is mention of Avito, a prince of Altura, to whom Fiora was betrothed before Archibaldo humbled Italy, but whose marriage to Manfredo, notwithstanding her previous betrothal, was one of the conditions of peace. Presumably—as is to be gathered from the brief colloquy—Archibaldo has come into the hall to watch with Flaminio for the possible return of Manfredo, but the restlessness of the old king, his commands regarding the door opposite, and even certain inferences to be drawn from what he says, lead to the conclusion that he suspects his son's wife and Avito. It is also clear—subtly conveyed, without being stated in so many words—that Flaminio, though in the service of Archibaldo, is faithful to Avito, like himself a native of the country which Archibaldo has conquered.

When Flaminio reminds Archibaldo that Avito was to have wedded Fiora, the blind king bids his guide look out into the valley for any sign of Manfredo's approach. 'Nessuno, mio signore! Tutto è pace!' is Flaminio's reply. (No one, my lord! All is quiet!')

Archibaldo, recalling his younger years, tells eloquently of his conquest of Italy, apostrophising the ravishing beauty of the country, when it first met his gaze, before he descended the mountains from which he beheld it. He then bids Flaminio put out the lantern, since Manfredo comes not. Flaminio obeys; then, as there is heard in the distance the sound of a rustic flute, he urges upon Archibaldo that they go. It is nearly dawn, the flute appears to have been a signal which Flaminio understands. He is obviously uneasy, as he leads Archibaldo out of the hall.

Avito and Fiora come out of her room. The woman's hair hangs in disorder around her face, her slender figure is draped

Dam-mi   le   labbra   e   tan-ta   ti   da - ro

in a very fine ivory-white garment. The very quiet that prevails fills Avito with apprehension. It is the woman, confident through love, that seeks to reassure him.

For the moment Avito is reassured. There is a brief but passionate love scene. Then Avito perceives that the lantern has been extinguished. He is sure someone has been there, and they are spied upon. Once more Fiora tries to give him confidence. Then she herself hears someone approaching. Avito escapes from the terrace into the dim light. The door on the left opens and Archibaldo appears alone. He calls 'Fiora! Fiora! Fiora!'

Concealing every movement from the old man's ears, she endeavours to glide back to her chamber. But he hears her.

'I hear thee breathing! Thou'rt breathless and excited! O Fiora, say, with whom hast thou been speaking?'

Deliberately she lies to him. She has been speaking to no one. His keen sense tells him that she lies. For when she sought to escape from him, he heard her 'gliding thro' the shadows like a snowy wing'.

Flaminio comes hurrying in. The gleam of armoured men has been seen in the distance. Manfredo is returning. His trumpet is sounded. Even now he is upon the battlement and embraced by his father. Longing for his wife, Fiora, has led him for a time to forsake the siege. Fiora greets him, but with no more than a semblance of kindness. With cunning, she taunts Archibaldo by telling Manfredo that she had come out upon the terrace at dawn to watch for him, the truth of which assertion Archibaldo can affirm, for he found her there. As they go to their chamber, the old man troubled, suspecting, fearing, thanks God that he is blind.

Act II. The scene is a circular terrace on the high castle walls. A single staircase leads up to the battlements. It is afternoon. The sky is covered with changing, fleeting clouds. Trumpet blasts are heard from the valley. From the left comes Manfredo with his arms around Fiora. He pleads with her for her love. As a last boon before he departs he asks her that she will mount the stairway and, as he departs down the valley, wave to him with her scarf. Sincerely moved to pity by his plea, a request so simple and yet seemingly meaning so much to him, she promises that this shall be done. He bids her farewell, kisses her, and runs off to lead his men back to the siege.

Fiora tries to shake off the sensation of her husband's embrace. She ascends to the battlemented wall. A handmaid

brings her an inlaid casket, from which she draws forth a long
white scarf. The orchestra graphically depicts the departure
of Manfredo at the head of his cavalcade.

Fiora sees the horsemen disappear in the valley. As she
waves the veil her hand drops wearily each time. Avito
comes. He tells her it is to say farewell. At first, still touched
by the pity which she has felt for her husband, Fiora restrains
her passionate longing for her lover, once or twice waves the
scarf, tries to do so again, lets her arms drop, her head droop,
then, coming down the steps, falls into his arms open to
receive her, and they kiss each other as if dying of love.
'Come tremi, diletto' (How thou art trembling, beloved!)
whispers Fiora.

'Guarda in su! Siamo in cielo!' (Look up! We are in
heaven!) responds Avito.

But the avenger is nigh. He is old, he is blind, but he
knows. Avito is about to throw himself upon him with his
drawn dagger, but is stopped by a gesture from Flaminio,
who has followed the king. Avito goes. But Archibaldo has
heard his footsteps. The king orders Flaminio to leave him
with Fiora. Flamino bids him listen to the sound of horses'
hoofs in the valley. Manfredo is returning. Fiora senses that
her husband has suddenly missed the waving of the scarf.
Archibaldo orders Flaminio to go meet the prince.

The old king bluntly accuses Fiora of having been with her
lover. Cowering on a stone bench that runs around the wall,
she denies it. Archibaldo seizes her. Rearing like a serpent,

Fiora, losing all fear, in the virtual certainty of death at the hands of the powerful old man who holds her, boldly vaunts her lover to him. Archibaldo demands his name, that he and his son may be avenged upon him. She refuses to divulge it. He seizes her by the throat, again demands the name, and when she still refuses to betray her lover, throttles her to death. Manfredo arrives. Briefly the old man tells him of Fiora's guilt. Yet Manfredo cannot hate her. He is moved to pity by the great love of which her heart was capable, though it was not for him. He goes out slowly, while Archibaldo hoists the slender body of the dead woman across his chest, and follows him.

Act III. The crypt of the castle, where Fiora lies upon her bier with white flowers all about her, and tapers at her head and feet. Around her, people of her country, young and old, make their moan, while from within the chapel voices of a choir are heard.

Out of the darkness comes Avito. The others depart in order that he may be alone with his beloved dead, for he too is of their country, and they know. 'Fiora! Fiora! – È silenzio!' (Fiora! Fiora! – Silence surrounds us) are his first words, as he gazes upon her.

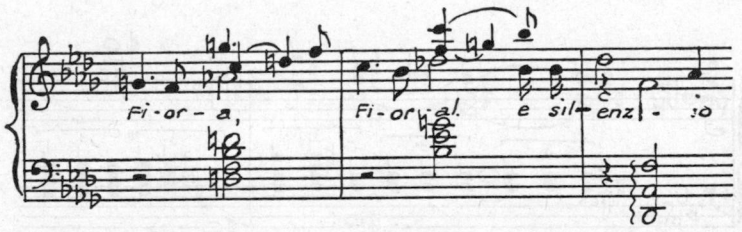

Then, desperately, he throws himself beside her and presses his lips on hers. A sudden chill, as of approaching death, passes through him. He rises, takes a few tottering steps toward the door.

Like a shadow, Manfredo approaches. He has come to seize his wife's lover, whose name his father could not wring from her, but whom at last they have caught. He recognises Avito. Then it was he whom she adored.

'What do you want?' asks Avito. 'Can you not see that I can scarcely speak?'

Scarcely speak? He might as well be dead. Upon Fiora's lips Archibaldo has spread a virulent poison, knowing well that her lover would come into the crypt to kiss her, and in that very act would drain the poison from her lips and die. Thus would they track him.

With his last breath, Avito tells that she loved him as the life that they took from her, aye, even more. Despite the avowal, Manfredo cannot hate him; but rather is he again disposed to wonder at the vast love Fiora was capable of bestowing, yet not upon himself.

Avito is dead. Manfredo, too, throws himself upon Fiora's corpse, and from her lips draws in what remains of the poison, quivers, while death slowly creeps through his veins, then enters eternal darkness, as Archibaldo gropes his way into the crypt. The blind king approaches the bier, feels a body lying by it, believes he has caught Fiora's lover, only to find that the corpse is that of his son.

Such is the love of three kings; of Archibaldo for his son, of Avito for the woman who loved him, of Manfredo for the woman who loved him not.

Or, if deeper meaning is looked for in Sem Benelli's powerful tragedy, the three kings are in love with Italy, represented by Fiora, who hates and scorns the conqueror of her country, Archibaldo; coldly turns aside from Manfredo, his son and heir apparent with whose hand he sought to bribe her; hotly loves, and dies for a prince of her own people, Avito. Tragic is the outcome of the conqueror's effort to win and rule over an unwilling people. Truly, he is blind. K.

ERMANNO
WOLF-FERRARI
(1876–1948)

I QUATTRO RUSTEGHI
The School for Fathers

OPERA in four acts by Ermanno Wolf-Ferrari: text by G. Pizzolato from Goldoni; German text by H. Teibler. Première Munich, March 19,

1906. First performed Teatro Lirico, Milan, 1914; la Scala, Milan, 1922, with Labia, Soster, Fabbri, Azzolini, Scattola, conductor Panizza; Buenos Aires, 1927, with Cobelli, Cravcenco, Marengo, Azzolini, Vanelli, conductor Panizza; Berlin, 1937, with Berger, Heidersbach, Marherr, Spletter, Prohaska, Neumann, Helgers, Fleischer; Sadler's Wells, London, 1946, with Gruhn, Jackson, Hill, Iacopi, Manton, Glynne, Franklin, conductor Robertson; New York City Centre, 1951, with Faull, Yeend, Mayer, Russell, Pease, Scott, conductor Halasz.

CHARACTERS

Lunardo, *merchant* (Mr. Crusty) .... Bass
Margarita, *his second wife* (Margery).... Mezzo-Soprano
Lucieta, *his daughter by his first wife* (Lucinda) . Soprano
Maurizio, *merchant* (Mr. Hardstone)
.... Bass or Bass-Baritone
Filipeto, *his son* (Peter) .... Tenor
Marina, *aunt to Filipeto* (Maria) .... Soprano
Simon, *her husband* (Mr. Gruff) .... Bass-Baritone
Canciano, *a wealthy merchant* (Sir James Pinchbeck)
.... Bass
Felice, *his wife* (Felicia) .... Soprano
Count Riccardo Arcolai, *a visitor to Venice* ..... Tenor
A Young Maid

Time: End of the eighteenth century   *Place:* Venice

(The names given in brackets were those used for the successful Sadler's Wells production, in Edward Dent's translation, when the scene was transferred from Venice to London.)

Ermanno Wolf-Ferrari has set to music more than one of Goldoni's Venetian comedies, which, written mostly in dialect, have a somewhat limited appeal. *I Quattro Rusteghi* is probably the finest of them all. The character-drawing is finished and the action moves quickly to its climax. The provincial colours of the picture have militated against rapid and wide acceptance of the opera, as of the comedy. But Germany has given it a welcome and the London production, whose translator, Edward Dent, transferred the action from Venice to London, has met with success.

The 'rusteghi' (in no sense 'rustics') are the honest, plain-speaking, conservative, domestic tyrants who, believing that woman's place is the home, forbid anything that might enliven the tedium of domestic work. It is on this conflict between old prejudices and a more generous understanding of woman's function in life that the plot of the comedy rests. It has been called a comedy of bad manners.

Act I. Lunardo's wife, Margarita, and her step-daughter, Lucieta, are sitting knitting and embroidering. It is carnival and their thoughts turn to the amusements and gaiety of more fortunate people. Margarita remembers that before marrying Lunardo there were parties at home and occasional visits to the theatre. Lucieta is of marrying age and hopes for a husband and better times. Lunardo enters silently, desiring to speak with his wife yet unwilling to interrupt her occupation. When the two are finally alone he tells her as an important secret that he and his friend Maurizio have arranged to wed Lucieta to Maurizio's son, Filipeto. The fact that the young people have never seen each other is, to them, immaterial. Margarita's very reasonable objections are rudely ignored. Lunardo's will is law. He answers Margarita's arguments with: 'I am the master.' Maurizio is announced and Margarita retires. The two 'rusteghi' now discuss the details of the contract—Lucieta's dowry, her clothes (no silk but good, honest home-spun), jewels which must not be re-set as the fashionable people do who thus pay twice for the gems. The dour, rigid character of the domestic bears is well described in this scene.

The second part of the act takes us to the house of Marina and her husband—even more of a 'rustego' than Lunardo. Marina is singing the tune familiar to everyone from its use as an interlude before Act II. Filipeto enters and begins by asking whether his uncle is in. He is in great dread of his uncle and means to avoid him. The purpose of his visit is to enquire whether his aunt has heard anything about his own wedding. His father has informed him abruptly that he intends to give him a wife and the homely youth is flustered, yet determined not to marry a girl he does not like; he begs his aunt to help him. If having seen the girl he does not like her, he will run away rather than marry her: ('Lucieta! xe un bel nome'; 'Lucinda! her name at least is pretty'). Simon arrives and unceremoniously dismisses Filipeto. Marina has another caller, the talkative Felice, accompanied by her husband and her 'cavalier servente', Count Riccardo. The husband, Canciano, stands mute and disapproving. The two women put their heads together determined that the men shall not be allowed to have it all their own way.

Act II. The act is preceded by the famous intermezzo,

which serves admirably as an example of the composer's light, graceful style:

When the curtain rises, we are back in Lunardo's house. Lucieta has persuaded Margarita to lend her a few trinkets but Lunardo arrives on the scene and orders the girl to take off her borrowed finery. They are joined by Marina and Simon. When the women retire the men rail at them and lament the passing of the good old days when women were women and did as they were told ('What has become of the old sort of women?'). The appearance of Felice is the signal for their departure. The other women join her, and Lucieta is congratulated on her betrothal. 'Shall I see my future husband?' she asks and hears that Felice and her friends have found a way to bring the young people together. It is carnival and Filipeto, escorted by Riccardo, plans to arrive disguised as a girl. If they should be discovered they will pass him off as a distant female relative. He soon arrives, and in a very charming little scene Marina persuades him to take off the mask. Meanwhile the men have settled their business and Filipeto's father, Maurizio, has gone off to bring the youth to the betrothal. Now Lunardo surprises the women who have just time to hide Filipeto in a closet and Riccardo in another. The situation is tense. Maurizio returns very angry with the news that Filipeto is not to be found anywhere. All that is known is that he left the house with Riccardo. Canciano then begins to show himself in his true colours. He dislikes Riccardo; he will have no dealings with him; he must be an imposter. But Riccardo is a man of spirit and, hearing all that Canciano is saying, comes out of hiding and challenges him. Filipeto is found, the whole conspiracy discovered, and a very angry Lunardo orders the callers to leave his house. There will be no wedding for Lucieta.

Act III. The act begins with Lunardo, Simon, and

Canciano considering in gloom the wickedness of the women's conduct. What is the next step to be? Lucieta can be sent away to the country but how can the other women be punished? The plain truth is that the women are necessary to their own comfort and, if they were sent away, the men themselves would suffer. This homely commination is interrupted by the arrival of Felice. She is received with hostility at first, for she is the arch-plotter. But her arguments are unanswerable, and, delivered with the speed and accuracy of aim which she commands, irresistible. What harm has been done? Would it not have been much worse if the young people had *not* liked each other's looks? Slowly, slowly the men begin to relent and finally and not very graciously are won over. The opera ends like a fairy story with wedding bells.

At the time of the first performance of the opera at Sadler's Wells (1946), *The Times* wrote as follows of the music: 'It flows spontaneously; it has a touch of distinction which saves it from the obvious; it is technically modern yet picks up the *opera buffa* tradition of the eighteenth century with the utmost grace and learning; it has a vein of lyrical melody and excels in ensemble.'   F.B.

IL SEGRETO DI SUSANNA
Susanna's Secret

Opera in one act by Ermanno Wolf-Ferrari; text by Enrico Golisciani (German version by Kalbeck). Première, Munich, December 4, 1909 (in German), conductor Mottl. First performed New York (by Chicago company), 1911, with Carolina White and Sammarco; Rome, 1911; Covent Garden, 1911, with Lipkowska, Sammarco; Metropolitan, 1912, with Farrar, Scotti, conductor Polacco. Revived la Scala, Milan, 1917, with Vallin, Parvis, conductor Panizza; Covent Garden, 1919, with Borghi-Zerni, Sammarco, conductor Coates; Metropolitan, 1921, with Bori, Scotti; la Scala, 1934, with Oltrabella, Biasini; Glyndebourne, 1958, with Costa, Roux, conductor Pritchard. The little opera is a direct descendant of the eighteenth-century *Intermezzo*.

CHARACTERS

Count Gil, *aged thirty* . . . . Baritone
Countess Susanna, *his wife, aged twenty* . . . . . . Soprano
Sante, *their servant, aged fifty* . . . . Silent

Time: The present   *Scene:* Piedmont

After a short overture, suitably labelled *vivacissimo*, the curtain rises to show a handsome apartment in the Count's house. Gil in walking clothes enters hurriedly: 'The light grey cloak, pink hat and feather . . . could I be mistaken?' He goes out quickly, and a moment later Susanna comes in wearing a grey cloak, and a pink hat. She gives her coat and hat and a parcel to the servant, and goes out again, having first made sure that her husband is in his room. No sooner has she gone than Gil reappears, and listens at the door of *her* room, seeming relieved to find that she is there. He must be mistaken—and yet: he has distinctly caught a smell of tobacco in his house—and he is a non-smoker. He catches himself out being unmistakably jealous. He questions Sante whether he is a smoker . . . or his mistress? The old servant shakes his head at each question. Who can it be then?

Gil is in even more of a state by the time Susanna comes into the room. He greets her, and comments on having seen someone just like her while he was out walking; it could not be her because he has forbidden her to go out alone. But why does she blush? Only because he is unkind for the first time. Rapturously, Gil assures her of his undying, unswerving devotion: 'Il dolce idillio'; a love duet follows, and at its end Gil is about to embrace his wife, when he smells the hated tobacco smell. She is horrified that he should notice—she knows how much he hates the smell—and he thinks he has turned suspicion that she is visited by an admirer into certainty. In a moment they are at cross purposes: Susanna suspects he knows her secret—'If I'm left at home and you're late at the club, the time goes quicker. . . . Do like other husbands, and shut one eye discreetly to my little secret'; but Gil suspects something quite different, and smashes the vases in his fury. Susanna escapes to her room ('to have a good cry'), and Gil throws himself into a chair in a paroxysm of grief. Sante surveys the room in comic dismay, and proceeds to tidy up the mess.

After an intermezzo, during which Sante gets the room straight again, Susanna comes out and brings Gil his gloves, hat, and umbrella; she is sure he must want to go out. Just before he goes, she sings sweetly to him; will he not give her a word of love, one tender look, before he goes ('Via, così non mi lasciate')? He relents to the extent of kissing her on the forehead, and departs.

Susanna, alone, relaxes and Sante brings her the cigarettes she has been out to buy. No sooner has she lit one than Gil is neard knocking at the door. He hunts everywhere but finds no one, only the smell of tobacco. Beside himself with rage, he goes out again. This time, Susanna has time to sing an aria to the cigarette for whose refreshing perfume she so yearns: 'O gioja, la nube leggera.' But she is not undisturbed for long. Gil suddenly appears through the window, and confronts his wife. She puts her hand behind her back, he snatches to see what she is hiding, and burns himself. The secret is out: she smokes. All is forgiven, and they each light a cigarette, dancing round each other with joy.   H.

I GIOJELLI DELLA MADONNA
The Jewels of the Madonna

Opera in three acts by Ermanno Wolf-Ferrari; text by Golisciani and Zangarini; German version by H. Liebstöckl. Première, Berlin, December 2, 1911; Chicago and New York, 1912, with White Bassi, Sammarco; Covent Garden, 1912, with Edvina, Martinelli, Sammarco; Metropolitan, New York, 1926, with Jeritza, Martinelli, Danise, conductor Papi. Revived Covent Garden, 1925, with Jeritza, Merli, Noto, conductor Bellezza; Chicago, 1940, with Giannini, Jagel, Czaplicki, conductor d'Abravanel. Italian stage première not until 1953, in Rome, with Clara Petrella, Prandelli, Gobbi.

CHARACTERS

Gennaro, *a blacksmith*	Tenor
Maliella, *adopted daughter of Carmela*	Soprano
Rafaele, *leader of the Camorrists*	Baritone
Carmela, *Gennaro's mother*	Mezzo-Soprano
Biaso, *a scribe*	Tenor
Ciccillo, *a Camorrist*	Tenor
Stella ⎫	Soprano
Concetta ⎬ *friends of Camorrists*	Soprano
Serena ⎭	Contralto
Rocco, *a Camorrist*	Bass

Grazia, a dancer; Vendors, Monks, Populace

Time: The present   *Place:* Naples

Act I. A small square in Naples, near the sea. Carmela's house, Gennaro's smithy, an inn, and the little hut of Biaso, the scribe, among many other details. 'It is the gorgeous afternoon of the festival of the Madonna, and the square swarms with a noisy crowd, rejoicing and celebrating the events with that strange mixture of carnival and superstition so characteristic of Southern Italy.' This describes most aptly the gay, crowded scene, and the character of the music with which the opera opens. It is quite kaleidoscopic in its constant shifting of interest. At last many in the crowd follow a band, which has crossed the square.

Gennaro in his blacksmith's shop is seen giving the finishing touches to a candelabrum on which he has been working. He places it on the anvil, as on an altar, kneels before it, and sings a prayer to the Madonna—'Madonna, con sospiri' (Madonna, tears and sighing).

Maliella rushes out of the house pursued by Carmela. She is a restless, wilful girl, possessed of the desire to get away from the restraint of the household and throw herself into the life of the city, however evil—a potential Carmen, from whom opportunity has as yet been withheld. Striking an attitude of bravado, and in spite of Gennaro's protests, she voices her rebellious thoughts in the 'Canzone di Cannetella',—'Diceva Cannetella vedendosi inserata' (Thus sang poor Cannetella, who yearned and sighed for her freedom).

A crowd gathers to hear her. From the direction of the sea comes the chorus of the approaching Camorrists. Maliella and the crowd dance wildly. When Carmela reappears with a pitcher of water on her head, Maliella is dashing along the quay screaming and laughing.

Carmela tells her son the brief story of Maliella. Once when he was ill as a baby, she vowed to the Madonna that she would adopt a baby girl and treat her as her own daughter if only her beloved son were allowed to recover. There is a touching duet for mother and son ('T'eri un giorno ammalato bambino'), in which Carmela bids him go and pray to the Madonna, and Gennaro asks for her blessing before he leaves to do so. Carmela then goes into the house.

Maliella runs in. The Camorrists, Rafaele in the van, are in pursuit of her. Rafaele, the leader of the band, is a handsome, flashy blackguard. When he advances to seize and kiss her, she draws a dagger-like hat-pin. Laughing, he throws off his coat, like a duellist, grasps and holds her tightly. She stabs his hand, making it bleed, then throws away the skewer. Angry at first, he laughs disdainfully, then passionately kisses the wound. While the other Camorrists buy flowers from a passing flower girl and make a carpet of them, Rafaele picks up the hat-pin, kneels before Maliella, and hands it to her. Maliella slowly replaces it in her hair, and then Rafaele, her arms being uplifted, sticks a flower she had previously refused, on her breast, where she permits it to remain. A few moments later she plucks it out and throws it away. Rafaele picks it up, and carefully replaces it in his button-hole. A little later he goes to the inn, looks in her direction, and raises his filled glass to her, just at the moment when, although her back is toward him, a subtle influence compels her to turn and look at him.

Tolling of bells, discharge of mortars, cheers of populace, announce the approach of the procession of the Madonna. While hymns to the Virgin are chanted, Rafaele pours words of passion into Maliella's ears. The image of the Virgin, bedecked with sparkling jewels—the jewels of the Madonna— is borne past. Rafaele asseverates that for love of Maliella he would even rob the sacred image of the jewels and bedeck her with them. The superstitious girl is terrified.

Gennaro, who returns at that moment, warns her against Rafaele as 'the most notorious blackguard in this quarter'; at the same time he orders her into the house. Rafaele's mocking laugh infuriates him. The men seem about to fight. Just then the procession returns, and they are obliged to kneel. Rafaele's looks, however, follow Maliella, who is very deliberately moving toward the house, her eyes constantly turning in the Camorrist's direction. He tosses her the flower she has previously despised. She picks it up, puts it between her lips, and flies indoors.

Act II. The Garden of Carmela's house. On the left wall a wooden staircase. Under this is a gap in the back wall shut in by a railing. It is late evening.

Carmela, having cleared the table, goes into the house. Gennaro starts in to warn Maliella. She says she will have freedom, rushes up the staircase to her room, where she is seen putting her things together, while she hums, 'E ndringhete' (I long for mirth and folly).

She descends with her bundle and is ready to leave. Gennaro pleads with her. As if lost in a reverie, with eyes half-closed, she recalls how Rafaele offered to steal the jewels of the Madonna for her. Gennaro, at first shocked at the sacrilege in the mere suggestion, appears to yield gradually to a desperate intention. He bars the way to Maliella, locks the gate, and stands facing her. Laughing derisively, she reascends the stairs.

Her laugh still ringing in his ears, no longer master of himself, he goes to a cupboard under the stairs, takes out a box, opens it by the light of the lamp at the table, selects from its contents several skeleton keys and files, wraps them in a piece of leather, which he hides under his coat, takes a look at Maliella's window, crosses himself, and sneaks out.

From the direction of the sea a chorus of men's voices is heard. Rafaele appears at the gate with his Camorrist friends. To the accompaniment of their mandolins and guitars he sings to Maliella a lively waltz-like serenade: 'Aprila, o bella, la fenestrella.' The girl, in a white wrapper, a light scarlet shawl over her shoulders descends to the garden. There is a love duet: she promises that on the morrow she will join him. Then Rafaele's comrades signal that someone approaches.

Left to herself, she sees in the moonlight Gennaro's open tool box. As if in answer to her presentiment of what it signifies, he appears with a bundle wrapped in red damask. He is too distracted by his purpose to question her presence in the garden at so late an hour and so lightly clad. Throwing back the folds of damask, he spreads out on the table, for Maliella, the jewels of the Madonna.

Maliella—in an ecstasy, half mystic, half sensual, and apparently seeing in Gennaro the image of the man who promised her the jewels, Rafaele, who has set every chord of passion in her nature vibrating—no longer repulses Gennaro, but, when at the foot of a blossoming orange tree he seizes her, yields herself to his embrace. The scene is described in the libretto with a realism that leaves no doubt as to its meaning.

Act III.   A haunt of the Camorrists on the outskirts of Naples. On the left wall is a rough fresco of the Madonna, whose image was borne in procession the previous day. In front of it is a sort of altar.

The Camorrists gather. They are men and women, all the latter of doubtful character. There is singing with dancing—the 'Apache', the 'Tarantelle'. Stella, Concetta, Serena, and Grazia the dancer, are the principal women. They do not anticipate Maliella's expected arrival with much pleasure. When Rafaele comes in, they ask him what he admires in her. In his answer, 'Non sapete . . . di Maliella la preziosa qualità' (Know you not of Maliella), he tells them her chief charm is that he will be the first man to whom she has yielded herself.

In the midst of an uproar of shouting and dancing, while Rafaele, standing on a table, cracks a whip, Maliella rushes in. In an agony she cries out that, in a trance, she gave herself to Gennaro. The women laugh derisively at Rafaele, who has just sung of her as being inviolable to all but himself. There is not a touch of mysticism about Rafaele. That she should have confused Gennaro with him, and so have yielded herself to the young blacksmith, does not appeal to him at all. For him she is a plucked rose to be left to wither. Furiously he rejects her, flings her to the ground. The jewels of the Madonna fall from her cloak. They are readily recognised, for they are depicted in the rough fresco on the wall.

Gennaro, who has followed her to the haunt of the Camorrists, enters. He is half mad. Maliella, laughing hysterically, flings the jewels at his feet, shrieking that he stole them for her. The crowd, as superstitious as it is criminal, recoils from both intruders. The women fall to their knees. Rafaele curses the girl. At his command, the band disperses. Maliella goes out to drown herself in the sea. 'Madonna dei dolor! Miserere!' prays Gennaro. His thoughts revert to his mother: among the débris he finds a knife and plunges it into his heart.   K.

RICCARDO ZANDONAI
(1883–1944)
FRANCESCA DA RIMINI

OPERA in four acts by Riccardo Zandonai; text by Tito Ricordi after d'Annunzio's play of the same name. Première, Teatro Regio, Turin, February 19, 1914, with Canetti, Crimi, Cigada, Paltrinieri, conductor Panizza. First performed Covent Garden, 1914, with Edvina, Martinelli, Cigada, conductor Panizza; la Scala, Milan, 1916, with Raisa, Pertile, Danise; Metropolitan, 1916, with Alda, Martinelli, Amato, conductor

Polacco; Chicago, 1917, with Raisa, Crimi, Rimini. Revived la Scala, 1929, with dalla Rizza, Pertile, Maugeri, conductor Panizza; 1937, with Cigna, Parmeggiani, Maugeri, conductor Zandonai; 1942, with Somigli, Ziliani, Maugeri, conductor Guarnieri; 1946, with Carbone, Ziliani, Stabile, conductor Guarnieri; 1950, with Caniglia, Prandelli, Biasini, conductor Capuana; 1959, with Olivero, del Monaco, Giangiacomo Guelfi; San Francisco, 1956, with Gencer, Richard Martell, Colzani, conductor de Fabritiis; Newark, U.S.A., 1966, with Floriana Cavalli.

CHARACTERS

Francesca	*the son and daughters of*	Soprano
Samaritana	*Guido Minore of Polenta*	Soprano
Ostasio		Baritone
Giovanni lo Sciancato (the lame)		Baritone
Paolo il Bello (the handsome)	*Sons of Mala-testa of Ver-rucchio*	Tenor
Malatestino dall'occhio (the one-eyed)		Tenor
Biancofiore		Soprano
Garsenda		Soprano
Altichiara	*Francesca's women* . . .	Mezzo-Soprano
Donella		Mezzo-Soprano
The Slave		Contralto

Ser Toldo Berardengo, *a lawyer* . . . . Tenor
A Jester . . . . Bass
An Archer . . . . Tenor
A Torchbearer . . . . Baritone

Archers, Torchbearers, Musicians

Time: End of Thirteenth Century   *Place:* Ravenna; Rimini

Act I.   The scene is a court in the house of the Polentani, in Ravenna, adjacent to a garden, whose bright colours are seen through a pierced marble screen. A colloquy between Francesca's brother Ostasio and the notary Ser Toldo Berardengo informs us that for reasons of state Francesca is to be married to that one of the three sons of Malatesta da Verrucchio, who, although named Giovanni, is known as Gianciotto, the Lamester, because of his deformity and ugliness. As Francesca surely would refuse to marry Gianciotto, a plot has been formed by which she is introduced to his handsome younger brother Paolo, with whom, under the impression that he is her destined bridegroom, she falls deeply in love at first sight, a passion that is fully eciprocated by him, although they have only beheld each other, and not yet exchanged a word.

Act II. The scene is the interior of a round tower in the fortified castle of the Malatestas. The summit of the tower is crowned with engines of war and arms. There are heavy crossbows, ballistas, a catapult, and other medieval machinery of battle. The castle is a stronghold of the Guelfs. In the distance, beyond the city of Rimini, are seen the battlements of the highest Ghibelline Tower. A narrow fortified window looks out on the Adriatic.

Soon after the act opens, an attack takes place. The battle rages. Amid all this distracting and therefore futile tumult, occurs the first meeting between Francesca and Paolo since the marriage into which she was tricked. Their love is obvious enough. Paolo despairingly seeks death, to which Francesca also exposes herself by remaining on the platform of the tower during the combat.

The Malatestas are victorious. The attacking foes are driven off. Gianciotto comes upon the platform and brings news to Paolo of his election as Captain of the people and Commune of Florence, for which city Paolo presently departs. Malatestino is carried in wounded (he has lost the sight of an eye), but he exhibits great courage and wishes to continue the fight.

Act III. The scene is the beautiful apartment of Francesca, where, from an old tome, she is reading to her women the story of Lancelot and Guinevere.

The women dance and sing until, on a whispered word from her slave, Francesca dismisses them. Paolo has returned. The greeting from her to him is simple enough: 'Benvenuto, signore mio cognato' (Welcome my lord and kinsman), but the music is charged with deeper significance.

Even more pronounced is the meaning in the musical phrase at Francesca's words, 'Paolo, datemi pace' (Paolo, give me peace).

Together they read the story which Francesca had begun reading to her women. Their heads come close together over the book. Their white faces bend over it until their cheeks almost touch; and when, in the ancient love tale, the queen and her lover kiss, Francesca's and Paolo's lips meet and linger in an ecstasy of passion.

Act IV. This act is divided into two parts. The scene of the first part is an octagonal hall of grey stone. A grated door leads to a subterranean prison.

Malatestino is desperately in love with Francesca, and even hints that he would go to the length of poisoning Gianciotto. Francesca repulses him. Cries of a prisoner from the dungeon have disturbed Francesca. When she complains of this to Malatestino, he goes down into the prison and kills the captive.

Gianciotto enters the room and Francesca complains to him of Malatestino's cruelty and of his attitude towards her—what it is she does not specify. Francesca has prepared food for her husband before his journey, and he removes his sword and helmet before eating. Suddenly there is a terrible cry from the dungeon; it is evident that Malatestino has carried out his intention of beheading the prisoner. A moment later, knocking is heard at the door through which Malastestino went down to the dungeon; Francesca quickly goes out so as not to have to see him again.

Out of revenge for his slighted passion, Malatestino excites the jealousy of Gianciotto by arousing his suspicions of Paolo and Francesca, pointing out especially that Paolo has returned from Florence much sooner than his duties there would justify him in doing. Gianciotto works himself up into a passion and demands to be shown proof of the accusation. Malatestino bids him wait only until nightfall and he shall have it.

The scene of part two is laid in Francesca's chamber. It is night. Four waxen torches burn in iron candlesticks.

Francesca is lying on the bed. From her sleep she is roused by a wild dream that harm has come to Paolo. Her women try to comfort her. After an exchange of gentle and affectionate phrases, she dismisses them.

A light knocking at the door, and Paolo's voice calling, 'Francesca!' She flings open the door and throws herself into the arms of her lover. There is an interchange of impassioned phrases. Then a violent shock is heard at the door, followed by the voice of Gianciotto, demanding admission. Paolo spies a trap-door in the floor of the apartment, pulls the bolt, and bids Francesca open the door of the room for her husband, while he escapes.

Gianciotto rushes into the room. Paolo's cloak has caught in the bolt of the trap-door. He is still standing head and shoulders above the level of the floor. Seizing him by the hair, the Lamester forces him to come up. Paolo unsheathes his dagger. Gianciotto draws his sword, thrusts at Paolo. Francesca throws herself between the two men, receives the thrust of her husband's sword full in the breast, and falls into Paolo's arms. Mad with rage, her deformed husband with another deadly thrust pierces his brother's side. Paolo and Francesca fall at full length to the floor. With a painful effort, Gianciotto breaks his blood-stained sword over his knee.   K.

LUIGI DALLAPICCOLA
(1904–1975)

IL PRIGIONIERO
The Prisoner

OPERA in a Prologue and one act by Luigi Dallapiccola, text by the composer from *La Torture par l'espérance* by Villiers de l'Isle-Adam and *La Légende d'Ulenspiegel et de Lamme Goedzak* by Charles de Coster. Première, 1949, by Radio Italiana, Turin, in concert with Magda Laszlo, Emilio Renzi, Scipione Colombo, conductor Hermann Scherchen. First staged at Teatre Comunale, Florence, May 20, 1950, with the same principals apart from Mario Binci replacing Renzi. First performed Essen, 1954; London (in concert), 1954, with Laszlo, Krebs, Willy Heyer, conductor Scherchen, and on stage in English, Sadler's Wells (by New Opera Company), 1959, with Rosina Raisbeck, Alexander Young, John Cameron, conductor Leon Lovett; Teatro Colon, Buenos Aires, 1954; City Center, New York, 1960, with Anne McKnight, Richard Cassilly, Norman Treigle, conductor Stokowski; la Scala, Milan, 1962, with Laszlo, Aldo Bertocci, Eberhard Wächter, conductor Sanzogno, producer Rennert. The publisher records that in the first dozen years after its première, there were no fewer than 186 performances of this modern opera on radio, concert platform and stage.

CHARACTERS

The Mother .... Dramatic Soprano
The Prisoner .... Baritone
The Gaoler ⎫
The Grand Inquisitor ⎰ .... Tenor
Two priests .... Tenor and Baritone
A 'Fra Redemptor' (or torturer) .... Silent
Time: Second half of the Sixteenth Century *Place:* Saragossa

In 1955, Roman Vlad, in one[1] of an illuminating series of commentaries on Dallapiccola's music, described the composer's activity to date as having been in three periods: the first, 1930–6, predominantly diatonic; the second, lasting into the war years, 'characterised ... by the constantly increasing number of chromatic threads which Dallapiccola wove into the diatonic fabric of his works. They tended to resemble actual twelve-note rows and ultimately absorbed the diatonic elements.' In the third phase, 'he began to adopt a systematic row-technique', and Vlad describes this as a period 'in which the composer achieves mastery of his own language', an arrival in effect at artistic maturity. *Il Prigioniero* belongs to this period of Dallapiccola's activity, and is the composer's second stage work, its predecessor the successful one-act opera *Volo di Notte* (1937–9 and based on Saint-Exupéry's novel of night-flying, *Vol de Nuit*), its successors the 'sacra rappresentazione', *Job* (1950), and the ambitious *Ulisse*, which occupied Dallapiccola for many years and was first heard in Berlin in 1968.

A follower at remote control of Schoenberg and Berg, an enthusiastic admirer at one end of the scale of Monteverdi (he

[1] Roman Vlad in *The Score.*

made a very successful performing edition of *Il Ritorno d'Ulisse in Patria*) and at the other of Debussy (his private introduction to the music of *Le Martyre de Saint Sébastien* vastly enhanced my first stage experience of this music in 1951), Dallapiccola's earlier exposure of his preoccupation with the humanitarian problems of our time was heard in the masterly *Canti di Prigionia* for chorus and orchestra (1938–41). *Il Prigioniero* develops with intensity, even desperation, another aspect of the subject of liberty, though this time with the crucial difference that the Prisoner, unlike for instance Savonarola in the *Canti*, 'goes to his death with the most atrocious doubt that can torment the human soul: and death then appears not as a supreme act of liberation but as the final annihilation of the existence and wholeness of the human personality. This doubt is at the bottom of the sense of man's tragedy; it is the most profound motivation known to man, and not even saints are immune from its temptation. Previously Dallapiccola had not experienced it, or at least had never expressed it; *Il Prigioniero* is his first tragic opera'.[1]

The opera, in a Prologue and one act, was written between 1944 and 1947 and orchestrated in Spring 1948. I was present at its first, highly successful stage performance at the Maggio Musicale in 1950 and well remember the composer, at the last of many solo curtain calls, bowing ironically to a solitary detractor in the gallery (so enthusiastic as to have brought a whistle with him) as if in sympathy with Shaw's famous curtain speech in a comparable situation: 'You and I may know there's nothing in it, but who are we against so many?'

Dallapiccola took his libretto from *La torture par l'espérance* by Conte Villiers de l'Isle-Adam (1838–89), interpolating a short episode from *La Légende d'Ulenspiegel et de Lamme Goedzak* by the Belgian Charles de Coster (1827–79). He has substituted the anonymous Prisoner for the named hero of Villiers de l'Isle-Adam's story and has added the figure of the Mother. The opera, in which sparing use is made of *Sprechstimme* (see page 1076), is in seven parts and lasts about 50 minutes.

In the Prologue, the Mother is waiting to visit her son in prison, and sings in a *Ballata*[2] of the recurring dreams which

---

[1] Roman Vlad, *ibid.*

[2] This and similar descriptions are quoted from the score.

haunt her sleep and in which she sees at the end of a dark cavern a figure, which terrifies her as it approaches and can be recognised as King Philip II until it changes imperceptibly into the image of Death. 'The Prologue is based', says Vlad, 'on the dodecaphonic combination set out in the impetuous dramatic statement with which the opera opens',[1] Ex. 1:

As the Mother's voice rises to a hysterical B flat, the offstage chorus cuts her short with 'Fiat misericordia tua, Domine, super nos' (Let thy mercy prevail, O Lord) in the first *Intermezzo Corale*.

The curtain rises on a dark cell within the Inquisitor's Prison in Saragossa, where the Prisoner is in process of telling his Mother of the torture he has suffered and of how the Gaoler, addressing him finally as 'Fratello' (Brother), Ex. 2:

<hr>

[1] Roman Vlad: *ibid.*

has led him back to faith and hope and even to want to pray as in childhood, Ex. 3:

This is one of the three fundamental rows on which the whole opera is based (the others, examples 4 and 5).

The conversation is interrupted by the Gaoler who gently encourages the Prisoner to new hope with the news that Flanders is in revolt and the great bell Roelandt, symbol of liberty, about to ring out again. In this section of the opera appear first the two other fundamental rows, Ex. 4:

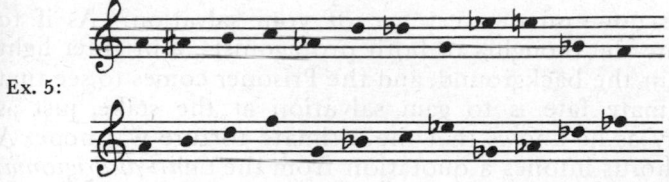

which Dallapiccola has described as 'rows of hope and liberty'. The Gaoler's description of events takes place in an *Aria in tre strofe*, and he leaves the Prisoner with the words 'There is one who watches over you. . . . Have faith, brother. Sleep now . . . and hope.' The Prisoner repeats the words as if he cannot believe them, then notices that the Gaoler has left the cell door slightly ajar and rushes out.

A short orchestral interlude leads to the third scene, which shows the successive stages of the Prisoner's slow and agonised attempt to make his way through the underground passages of the prison to freedom. Musically the scene is divided into three *Ricercari* ('super *Signore, aiutami a camminare*', 'super *Fratello*', and 'super *Roelandt*'), and dramatically the path of the Prisoner's 'escape' is complicated

by the sight of a torturer, who does not see him, the passage
of a couple of monks too engrossed in theological discussion
to notice him, and finally by his perception of a draught of
fresh air which encourages him to think he is nearing safety.
He prays 'Signore, aiutami a salire!', and a moment later
opens the door to hear as he thinks the great bell Roelandt.

A second *Intermezzo Corale* sung as before by offstage
chorus, provides a climax, and indeed in the score the
composer instructs that its 'sonority . . . must be formidable;
every spectator must feel literally swept away and drowned
in the immensity of the sound. Mechanical means (loud-
speakers etc.) should unhesitatingly be used if necessary to
obtain this effect.'

The fourth and last scene finds the Prisoner in a Spring
garden, under a starry sky. 'Alleluja!' he sings at the prospect
of freedom and moves toward a great cedar which dominates
the foreground. In a kind of ecstasy, he spreads his arms
toward the tree in a gesture of love towards all humanity—
only for the choral background to his exuberant cries to shut
off abruptly and to be succeeded by a soft 'Fratello' this time
from the lips of the Grand Inquisitor, whose arms open as if
part of the tree to embrace his captive: 'Why do you want to
leave us now, on the very eve of your salvation?' As if to
underline the thoughts of both protagonists, a brighter light
is seen in the background, and the Prisoner comes to see that
his ultimate fate is to gain salvation at the stake, just as
certainly as he knows that the ultimate torture was hope. A
small chorus intones a quotation from the *Canti di Prigionia*,
almost muffling the last whispered 'La liberta?' ('Freedom?')
of the Prisoner.   H.

16
French Opera

GABRIEL FAURÉ
(1845–1924)

PÉNÉLOPE

OPERA in three acts by Gabriel Fauré, libretto by René Fauchois. Première, March 4, 1913, in Monte Carlo, with Luciene Bréval, Charles Rousselière, conductor Léon Jéhin. First performed in Paris at Th. des Champs-Elysées, 1913, with Bréval, Muratore, conductor Hasselmans; Brussels, 1913, with Croiza, Darmel; Opéra-Comique, 1919, with Germaine Lubin, Rousselière. Revived Opéra, 1943, with Lubin, Jouatte; Bordeaux, 1957, with Régine Crespin, Raoul Jobin; Buenos Aires, 1962, with Crespin, Guy Chauvet.

CHARACTERS

Ulysses, *King of Ithaca*	....	Tenor
Eumaeus, *an old shepherd*	....	Baritone
Antinoös		Tenor
Eurimachus		Baritone
Laertes	*Penelope's suitors*	Tenor
Ctesippos		Baritone
Pisander		Baritone
A shepherd	....	Tenor
Penelope, *Queen of Ithaca*	....	Soprano
Eurycleia, *Ulysses's nurse*	....	Mezzo-Soprano
Cleone		Mezzo-Soprano
Melantho		Soprano
Alkandra	*Servants*	Mezzo-Soprano
Phylo		Soprano
Lydia		Soprano
Eurynome, *the housekeeper*	....	Soprano

Shepherds, Servants, Dancers and Flute Players

Pénélope is Gabriel Fauré's first true opera, compos
when he was 50, 13 years after *Prométhée*, a big-scale dram
which used many operatic ingredients. Its success has beer
spasmodic, Fauré's admirers, such as the composer Koechlin
insisting on it not only as a major work of one of France'
leading composers but also as something of a landmark in th
history of French lyric drama, its detractors finding i
undramatic. It has been the subject of occasional revival bu
has never established itself, even in the French capital.

Act I.   The story starts as Penelope waits for the return o
her husband Ulysses, plagued not only by the pretenders t
his throne and his marriage bed, but also by her own effort
to retain faith in his ultimate return. The first three scenes
playing in an ante-room to Penelope's chamber, serve a
exposition. After a prelude, which aptly sets out the opera'
seriousness of purpose, we meet Penelope's serving maids
who admit that in Penelope's place they would long sinc
have succumbed to the suitors' blandishments. The suitor
suddenly push their way in, demanding to see the Queen, an
opposed by the aged Eurycleia; when Penelope hersel
appears, it is with incomparable dignity of posture, music anc
phrase, and the music is fired to splendour as she protest
that Ulysses, her husband, has bidden her wait for him; ever
day she expects him to return, in all the glory in which h
left. The suitors are cynical—he will never come back—bu
worried that the shroud she has been weaving for old Laertes
the father of Ulysses, is still far from finished, and the Quee
thus protected from their wooing by their promise to respec
her privacy until she has finished preparing the shroud for he
dead father-in-law. In future, they say she must work unde
their supervision.

Eurimachus signs for flute players and dancers to ente
which they do to a most attractive tune in triple time. Dea
to the suitors' blandishments, Penelope, in another momen
of musical inspiration, launches a last appeal: 'Ulysses, prou
husband . . . gentle warrior . . . powerful king . . . come, hel
me in my distress', and outside a voice answers her appeal. I
is Ulysses, disguised as an old beggar. In spite of th
opposition of the suitors, Penelope receives him and promise
him hospitality. As every other night, she refuses a
invitation to the feast, and the suitors go off arm in arm wit
the more amenable of the palace girls.

Penelope is left with the old man and she confides him t

the care of Eurycleia, his old nurse, who is not long in recognising him. When she is alone, Penelope starts, as is her wont every night, to unravel the work on the shroud which she has done during the day, but this time the suitors surprise her and insist that the very next day she choose between them.

The old beggar returns, and his words are of such comfort that Penelope agrees to take him with them when she and Eurycleia mount their nightly vigil on the hill which commands a view of the sea and any approaching ship. Left alone for a moment, Ulysses voices his excitement in exuberant phrases, then accompanies the two women.

At the start of the second act, a shepherd is singing mournfully of his occupation. Penelope comes to the promontory, followed by Eurycleia and Ulysses. Memories of her husband crowd in on her, and in a duet with the old man she is told that the warrior king has lived under his roof in Crete for twelve days. His description of Ulysses convinces Penelope, and before long he is assuring her of Ulysses's innermost feelings. Suddenly the old man proposes a stratagem: let Penelope yield only to the suitor who can bend the great bow Ulysses left behind him! She agrees and goes sadly home, while Ulysses, galvanised to life, calls together the shepherds, makes himself known to them, and enlists their help in the plan he has for the punishment of her suitors.

There is great urgency in the opening of the third act, as Ulysses reveals that he has chosen the great sword of Hercules with which to wreak his vengeance. Eurycleia is overcome by the Queen's distress, but Ulysses reassures her: the stratagem will work and by nightfall she will have seen her mistress smile again. Eumaeus arrives to tell the King that fate has played into their hands in that the shepherds have been ordered by the pretenders to bring beasts to the court for a sacrifice.

The suitors enter and summon Penelope to make her choice. She tells them that the man amongst them who can bend the bow of Ulysses shall remain in the Palace; then, struck by a sudden revulsion of feeling, begs them to leave before her presentiment of death is fulfilled. Each in turn tries his hand and each fails, until Ulysses, still in disguise, asks to be allowed his turn, to the undisguised contempt of the suitors. He bends the bow, shoots an arrow through the twelve rings of axes, the target designated to try the archer's skill, then aims the bow in turn at each of the suitors, and with the aid of Eumaeus and the shepherds, slays the pretenders and their followers. Justice is done and the opera ends in triumph as the Court rejoices in the happiness of the reunited couple.   H.

GUSTAVE CHARPENTIER

(1860–1956)

LOUISE

OPERA in four acts by Gustave Charpentier; text by the composer. Première, Opéra-Comique, Paris, February 2, 1900, with Marthe Rioton, Deschamps-Jéhin, Maréchal, Fugère, conductor Messager. First performed Berlin, 1903, with Destinn, Goetze, Philipp, Baptist Hoffmann; Vienna, 1903, with Gutheil-Schoder, Slezak, Demuth, conductor Mahler; New York, Manhattan Opera House, 1908, with Garden, Bressler-Gianoli, Dalmorès, Gilibert, conductor Campanini; Covent Garden, 1909, with Edvina, Bérat, Dalmorès, Gilibert, conductor Frigara; Metropolitan, 1921, with Farrar, Bérat, Harrold, Whitehill. Revivals include Covent Garden, 1919, with Edvina, Ansseau, Cotreuil, conductor Coates; 1928, with Heldy, Kaisin, Journet; 1936, with Delprat, Verdière (later Maison), Bouilliez, conductor Sargent; Metropolitan, 1930, with Bori, Trantoul, Rothier; 1939, with Moore, Maison, Pinza; 1947, with Dorothy Kirsten, Jobin, Brownlee, conductor Fourestier; la Scala, Milan, 1923, with Heldy, Casazza, Pertile, Journet, conductor Toscanini; 1929, with dalla Rizza; 1934, with Favero, Casazza, Ziliani, Stabile; New York, City Opera, 1962, with Arlene Saunders, Claramae Turner, John Alexander, Treigle, conductor Morel: San Francisco, 1967, with Saunders, Cervena, Alexander, Rossi-Lemeni.

CHARACTERS

Louise . . . . Soprano
Her Mother . . . . Contralto
Irma . . . . Soprano
Camille . . . . Soprano

Gertrude .... Contralto
An Errand Girl .... Soprano
Elise .... Soprano
Blanche .... Soprano
Suzanne .... Contralto
A Street-sweeper ....Mezzo-Soprano
A Young Rag-picker .... Mezzo-Soprano
A Forewoman .... Mezzo-Soprano
A Milk Woman .... Soprano
A Newspaper-girl .... Soprano
A Coal-gatherer ....Mezzo-Soprano
Marguérite .... Soprano
Madeleine .... Contralto
A Dancer
Julien, *a young artist* .... Tenor
Louise's Father .... Bass
A Night-Prowler ('Noctambule') .... Tenor
A Ragman .... Bass
An Old Bohemian .... Baritone
A Song Writer .... Baritone
A Junkman .... Bass
A Painter .... Bass
Two Philosophers ....Tenor, Bass
A Young Poet .... Baritone
A Student .... Tenor
Two Policemen .... Baritone
A Street Arab .... Soprano
A Sculptor .... Baritone
An Old Clothes Man .... Tenor
An Apprentice .... Baritone
The King of Fools .... Tenor
Street Pedlars, Workmen, etc.

Time: The present   *Place:* Paris

The part of Louise was created by Mlle Rioton, who then sang for the first time in an opera house; her fragile appearance and beautiful singing are said to have been ideally suited to the opera.

She was succeeded in the title role by Mary Garden, who was to make Louise into one of her greatest successes.

There is a short prelude, which reiterates a figure used extensively in the course of the opera:

It is associated rather with the call of freedom, which, to
Louise, is inextricably bound up with Julien, than with Julien
himself. Three bars before the end of the prelude is heard a
motif which refers to Louise's father.

A room in a working man's tenement. Through a large
open window can be seen a terrace belonging to an artist's
studio, which is situated opposite the building in which
Louise's parents live. As the curtain goes up, Julien can be
heard and seen serenading Louise: ('O cœur ami! O cœur
primis!') to No. 1. Louise comes into the room in answer to
his summons, and a conversation ensues between them. It
appears that Louise has suggested Julien should write formally
to her parents asking for her hand in marriage; if they refuse
permission, she will run away with him. But this, she insists,
must be a last resort, as she loves her parents and hates the
thought of parting with them on bad terms.

Louise asks Julien to tell her again how he first fell in love
with her. He goes over it in detail—not for the first time we
may imagine—from a description of his dreams (he is a poet)
to the meeting of their realisation—herself—on the staircase:
'Depuis longtemps j'habitais cette chambre.' He becomes
lyrical in his description of his beloved, but, at the climax of
his story, in comes Louise's Mother. She does not
immediately make her presence known (except in the
orchestra), but hides to listen to what is being said. The
tender conversation continues, and is not without its dis-
paraging reference to the Mother, who finally puts an end to
it by dragging Louise away and shutting her in the kitchen,
returning to shout to Julien that if he does not shut up she
will come and pull his ears for him. Louise sneaks in for just
long enough to see the letter to her parents that Julien holds
up to her and then goes back to the kitchen.

The Mother reappears and shuts the window. Louise makes
an effort to keep up appearances and arranges the supper, but
her Mother does not mean to leave her in peace. She imitates
the tone of the conversation she has overheard, and mocks
Louise's love for Julien. Only the sound of the Father coming

up the stairs from work stops her laying her hands on her unfortunate daughter. The Farther comes in, asks whether supper is nearly ready, and proceeds to open the letter which Julien has left for him. Louise and her Father embrace—they are obviously very fond of one another—and the family sits down to table.

Louise takes the letter to her Father, who has left it by his plate, then goes to the kitchen to help wash up. The Father re-reads the letter, and appears to want to give the whole matter his consideration. But the Mother is furious, and, when Louise contradicts a particularly vicious insinuation about Julien, she slaps her face, to the Father's obvious displeasure. The Father asks Louise to read the paper to him. She starts, but mention of spring in Paris is too much for her, and she dissolves in tears as the curtain comes down.

Act II. The prelude is called 'Paris s'éveille'. The scene shows a street at the foot of the hill of Montmartre. Five o'clock in the morning in April. The house where Louise works as a dressmaker is seen on one side of the stage. Various derelict citizens of Paris go about their business, whether it be the setting up of a stall from which to sell milk, or the search for something worth while amongst the rags and refuse of the city. One of the figures in this scene is the Night-Prowler. He is represented as a late reveller returning home, but he is also intended to symbolise the 'Plaisirs de Paris' for which Louise and those like her long so ardently. In his symbolism, Charpentier has made use of a pun on the word 'plaisir', which is also a kind of wafer, and whose street-seller's cry is associated musically with the Night-Prowler.

Julien, accompanied by some Bohemian friends, comes to wait for Louise, in order to find out what the answer to his letter is likely to be. Street cries are heard. The girls who work at the dressmaker's begin to arrive, and they are soon followed by Louise and her Mother. The Mother goes, Louise enters the house, but is soon dragged out of it by Julien, who questions her about the answer to the letter. He is furious at the lack of rebellion in her attitude towards her parents; will she go back on her promise to come away with him?

The scene changes to the work room of the dressmaker's establishment. The girls are sitting round the tables, sewing and chattering. All is bustle and gossip. They notice that Louise has been crying, and suggest that she is in love. She denies it furiously, but Irma launches into a song on the subject of love, and soon the sound of a polka is heard from down below, immediately followed by the voice of Julien serenading Louise: 'Dans la cité lointaine.' The girls are at first pleased, but seeing that his song is addressed apparently to none of them they begin to find it a bore. Louise can bear the situation no longer, and puts on her outdoor things; asking them to explain that she has had to go home, she dashes out, and is later seen going arm in arm with Julien down the street. Peals of laughter from the girls.

Act III. A little garden on the side of Montmartre. A small one-storeyed house on one side. Panorama of Paris. Almost twilight. As the curtain rises, Louise sings her celebrated romance, 'Depuis le jour où je me suis donnée'. Life has changed for her since she came to live with Julien, and a new happiness has come into her existence: 'Ah, je suis heureuse!' 'Depuis le jour' has become a favourite aria, and its soaring lyricism has sufficient fervour to enable it to make a considerable impression even when heard out of its context.

Louise explains that in her workshop no one took trouble about her or appeared to like her; even her father, who loves her, always treated her as a little girl, and her mother beat and scolded her ('Qui aime bien, châtie bien'). Together she and Julien rejoice at the sight of the lights of Paris coming up one after another, together they sing of their freedom: 'Libres!'

There follows the curious episode of the 'Couronnement de la Muse'.[1] Into the garden come Bohemians, who proceed to decorate the front of the house with paper lanterns and streamers. They are followed by a crowd and a procession whose centre-piece turns out to be none other than the Night-Prowler of Act II now dressed up as the King of the Fools. Louise is crowned Queen of Bohemia and Muse of Montmartre. But the jollity is suddenly interrupted when a sad figure is seen standing apart. It is Louise's Mother, who seems a very different person from the fire-eater of Act I. She comes to say that Louise's Father is very ill and desperately anxious to see her again. For a time, they had kept up the

---

[1] The music is drawn from a composition of Charpentier's specially written for just such a ceremony in 1897. The Muse of Montmartre, chosen by popular vote, was to be publicly crowned, but owing to the appalling weather the function had to be put off until two years later.

pretence that she was dead, but she had found him creeping along to Louise's room at night, and crying out her name. Julien is at first suspicious, but he eventually agrees that Louise may go home, the Mother having promised that she shall return to him as soon as she wishes.

Act IV. The scene is the same as that of the first act. Julien's terrace is no longer visible. Louise is still with her family, which has broken the promise to allow her to return to Julien. Her Father is just recovering from the illness which has kept him from work, but he has changed a good deal since we last saw him, and the contented and resourceful man of the first act has become a grumbler: 'Les pauvres gens peuvent-ils être heureux?' Everything is against him now, and he complains of the ingratitude of children, who would throw off the authority of those who love them and are prepared to die for them.

The significance of what he says is not lost on Louise. But she looks longingly through the window at Paris, and when her Mother says that they cannot think of letting her go back to Julien, in spite of their promise, she says wanly that he who laughs last laughs best. She goes to say good night to her Father, who kisses her lovingly and long and takes her in his arms. She draws away unresponsively, but he calls her to him, puts her on his knee as if she were still a child, and sings a 'Berceuse' to her: 'Reste . . . repose-toi . . . comme jadis toute petite'. There is real feeling in this music, and for a moment the Father's self-pity can be forgotten.

But Louise's distress is too poignant to be ignored for long—and that is just what her parents seem to be successfully doing. Louise reminds them of their promise, and then quietly but feelingly asserts her right to be free: 'Tout être a le droit d'être libre.' The sound of a waltz she heard during her brief period of freedom—the voice of Paris itself—calls to Louise. She responds passionately and invokes the name of the city to set her free. All the efforts of her Father are not enough to stifle the feeling which is growing within her. At last her Father loses his temper completely, orders her from the house, and even chases her round the room, until she runs out of the door. His anger spent, the father calls pitiably for Louise. Then he shakes his fist at the city, and the curtain falls on his cry: 'O Paris.'   H.

CLAUDE DEBUSSY

(1862–1918)

PELLÉAS ET MÉLISANDE

OPERA in five acts by Claude Debussy; text from Maeterlinck's play of the same name. Première, Opéra-Comique, Paris, April 30, 1902, with Garden, Gerville-Réache, Périer, Dufranne, Vieuille, conductor Messager. First performed New York, Manhattan Opera House, 1908, with Garden, Gerville-Réache, Périer, Dufranne, Arimondi, Crabbé, conductor Campanini; Covent Garden, 1909, with Féart, Bourgeois, Warnéry, Vanni Marcoux, Bourbon, Crabbé, conductor Campanini; la Scala, Milan, 1908, with Ferrari, Giraud, Amato, Cirino, conductor Toscanini; Metropolitan, New York, 1925, with Bori, Johnson, Whitehill, Rothier. Revivals include Covent Garden, 1920, with Edvina, Maguénat, Huberdeau, Cotreuil, conductor Pitt; 1930, with Teyte, Bourdin, Brownlee, Autori; 1937, with Perli, Gaudin, Vanni Marcoux, Bernasconi; 1949, with Joachim, Jansen, Etcheverry, conductor Désormière; la Scala, 1925, with Heldy, Bertana, Legrand, Journet, conductor Toscanini; 1949, with Boué, Bourdin, Etcheverry, Médus, conductor de Sabata; Metropolitan, 1940, with Jepson, Cathelat; 1943, with Sayao, Singher; 1949, with Dosia, Jansen; Glyndebourne, 1962, with Duval, Henry Gui, Roux, conductor Gui. Revived at Covent Garden, 1969, with Söderström, George Shirley, conductor Pierre Boulez.

CHARACTERS

Arkel, *King of Allemonde* .... Bass
Geneviève, *mother of Pelléas and Golaud* .... Alto
Pelléas ⎱ King Arkel's grandsons .... ⎰ Tenor[1]
Golaud ⎰   ⎱ Baritone
Mélisande .... Soprano
Yniold, *Golaud's son by his first marriage* .... Soprano
A Physician .... Bass

Some works of art sum up the past, some presage the future—amongst operas, one thinks of Mozart's in the first category, of *Tristan* or *Falstaff* or *Wozzeck* in the second. *Pelléas* seems to do neither. Obviously Debussy was anything but a composer insulated from outside influences, but *Pelléas* belongs to no line and (unlike Debussy's piano and orchestral

---

[1] Or high baritone. Jean Périer, the original Pelléas, also sang Scarpia, Colline, Sharpless; Warnéry was Gonzalve in *L'Heure Espagnole*, Mime in *Siegfried*; Bourdin an Onegin, Shirley a celebrated Don Ottavio.

works) has few imitators. However, if the work is something of a dead end, it is anything but sterile; in fact, every time one hears it, one is more convinced than ever that it is a work of outstanding, uncanny beauty, of incredibly perceptive imagination, and its very lack of followers is some indication that what it has to say has been said once and for all.

So much has been written about the tenuous nature of *Pelléas* that it is perhaps worth while emphasising that such a description applies only to the dramatic side of the work. The characters do not reveal the full extent of their feelings in their every utterance—to that limited extent *Pelléas* is a 'realistic' opera—and they prefer to deal in indefinite, non-committal phrases rather than in a grandiose flaunting of feelings. But there is no musical under-emphasis in the ordinary sense of that term; what Debussy was after was surely the exact opposite—a precise, unexaggerated musical statement of the sentiments which are expressed, and an equally precise indication of what the characters concerned clearly feel to lie behind those sentiments. It is sometimes difficult not to believe that, from the point of view of public acceptance of the work, more harm than good has been done by frequent quotation of the climax of the duet in Act IV:

It was not understatement that Debussy was after—as must be clear from the passion of many other moments of the score; it was not even simplification. Gallic precision demanded that a subtle situation should be uncomplicated by formula or convention. And that of course meant that what Debussy wrote was worryingly 'different' for its original audiences.

Each scene is connected to its predecessor by an orchestral

interlude, and the acts are thus musically continuous.

Act I, scene i.   In a forest, Golaud while hunting has lost his way following a wild boar and come to a place unknown to him. There he sees a girl sitting by a spring. She acts like a figure in a fairy tale and behaves like a person strange to and isolated from the world. Finally Golaud succeeds in inducing Mélisande—she at last tells him her name after repeated urging—to follow him out of the dark woods.

Scene ii.   A room in the castle. Geneviève is reading to the aged, almost blind King Arkel a letter which Golaud has written to his half-brother Pelléas: 'Voici ce qu'il écrit à son frère Pelléas'. From this letter we learn that Golaud has already been married for six months to the mysterious Mélisande. He has great love for his wife, about whom, however, he knows no more to-day than he did at first in the woods. So he fears that his grandfather, the King, may not forgive him for this union and asks Pelléas to give him a sign in case the King is ready 'to honour the stranger as his daughter'. Otherwise he will steer his ship to a remote land and return home no more. King Arkel has arrived at that time of life when the wisdom of experience tends to make one forgiving toward everything that happens. So he pardons Golaud and commissions his grandson Pelléas, who has entered the room, to give his brother the sign agreed upon. Pelléas has asked him if he may leave to say farewell to a dying friend, who has written to him; but Arkel reminds him that his duty is to await his brother's return, and tend his father who lies sick above them.

Scene iii.   Before the castle. The queen Geneviève seeks to calm Mélisande's distress at the gloominess of the world into which she has wandered. Pelléas too is there. Together they watch a ship sail away out to sea, accompanied by the sound of an invisible chorus.

Act II, scene i.   A fountain in the park. Pelléas and Mélisande go together to this thickly shaded spot in the heat of the day. Is Mélisande a Melusine-like creature? Water attracts her wonderfully. Pelléas bids her take care: 'Prenez garde de glisser.' She bends over her reflection and her hair falls into the water. Because she cannot reach the water, she is tempted to play with the ring that Golaud sent her. It slips from her hand to the sound of a harp *glissando*, and sinks.

Scene ii.   There must have been some peculiar condition attached to the ring. At the same hour that it fell in the fountain Golaud's horse shied while hunting so that he was hurt and now lies injured in bed. Mélisande is taking care of him. She tells Golaud that she does not feel well here. She is oppressed by a certain foreboding, she does not know what it is. Golaud tries to comfort her; he seizes her hands and sees that the ring is missing. Then he drives her out into the night to look for it. 'Sooner would I give away everything I have, my fortune and goods, rather than have lost the precious ring.' Pelléas will help her find it.

Scene iii.   Before a grotto in the rocks. Mélisande has deceived Golaud by telling him that the ring has slipped from her hand into the sea. So Pelléas must now lead her to this grotto in order that she may know at least the place in which she can claim that she lost the ring—a dreadful place in which the shadow of death stalks. There they see three mysterious bearded beggars, sleeping in what shelter they can find.

Act III, scene i.   A tower in the castle. At the window of the tower Mélisande is standing combing her hair that she has let down: 'Mes longs cheveux.' Then Pelléas comes along the

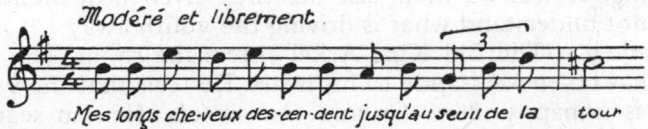

Mes longs che-veux des-cen-dent jusqu'au seuil de la tour

road that winds around under her window. He is coming to say farewell; early the next morning he is going away. So Mélisande will at least once more reach out her hand to him that he may press it to his lips. Love weaves a web about the twain with an ever thicker netting without their noticing it. Their hands do not touch but as Mélisande leans forward so far her long hair falls over Pelléas's head and fills the youth with passionate feelings. Their words become warmer —then Golaud comes near and reproves their 'childishness'. He goes off with Pelléas.

The whole scene, from the ravishing harp sound of the opening until the appearance of Golaud, is no more and no less than a passionate love scene (although no word of love is spoken)—but with what sensitivity has Debussy set it!

Scene ii.   In the vault under the castle. Like a gloomy menace Golaud leads Pelléas into these underground rooms where the breeze of death blows. Seized with shuddering they leave.

Scene iii.   On the terrace at the entrance to the vault
Golaud in earnest words warns Pelléas to keep away from
Mélisande and to refrain from confidential conversations with
her.

Scene iv.   Before the castle. In vain Golaud has sought to
quiet himself by saying that it was all nothing but childishness. Jealousy devours his heart. So now he lifts up his
little son Yniold, offspring of his first marriage, to spy
through a window on the intimacy of Pelléas and Mélisande.
The child cannot tell him of anything improper, yet Golaud
senses that there is something between the couple. And he
feels that he himself is old, much older than Pelléas and
Mélisande. Dramatically, this is one of the tensest scenes of
the whole score, and Golaud's agony and impotence are made
more apparent by the innocence and fright of Yniold as he
reports what he sees.

Act IV, scene i.   In a room in the castle Pelléas and
Mélisande meet. This evening he must see her. She promises
to go to the old fountain in the park where she formerly lost
the ring. It will be their last meeting. Even now Mélisande
does not understand what is driving the youth away.

Scene ii.   The old King Arkel enters the room. The aged
man has taken Mélisande to his heart. He feels that the young
wife is unhappy. Now Golaud also enters. He can scarcely
remain master of his inner commotion. The sight of his wife,
who appears the picture of innocence, irritates him so much
('Une grande innocence') that he finally in a mad rage throws
her on her knees and drags her across the room by her hair.
Only Arkel understands and pities:

Si j'é-tais Dieu,   j'au-rais pi-tié du cœur des hom-mes

Scene iii.   By the old spring in the park. There is an

oppressive feeling of disaster in the air. Only little Yniold does not suffer this gripping burden. He has dropped something behind a stone and is looking for it. Then he catches sight of some sheep being driven past and listens to them as they go. (This scene is often omitted in performance.)

Scene iv.   It is already growing dark when Mélisande goes to Pelléas. And yet in their farewell, perhaps also on account of Golaud's outburst of anger, the couple clearly see what has caused their condition, and there comes over them something like the affirmation of death and the joy of dying. Fate shuts the gates of the castle upon them; like fate they see Golaud coming. They rejoice in the idea of death. Pelléas falls by Golaud's sword, Mélisande flees from her husband's pursuit into the night.

Act V.   A room in the castle. Mélisande lies stretched out in bed. Arkel, Golaud, and the physician are conversing softly in the room. No; Mélisande is not dying from the insignificant wound Golaud has given her. Perhaps her life will be saved. But Golaud's bitter remorse at what he has done cannot be calmed; 'J'ai tué sans raison! . . . Ils s'étaient embrassés comme des petits enfants. . . . Je l'ai fait malgré moi.' Mélisande awakes as if from dreaming. Everything that has happened is like a dream to her. Desperately Golaud rushes to her couch, begs her pardon, and asks her for the truth. He is willing to die too, but before his death he wants to know whether she has betrayed him with Pelléas. She denies it. Golaud presses her so forcibly and makes her suffer so that she is near death. The earthly things fall away from her as if her soul were already free. It is not possible to bring her back now. The aged Arkel brings the child she has borne to her and offers the last services for the dying woman, to make the way free for her soul escaping from earthly pain and the burden of the tears of persons left behind.

K. W., H.

PAUL DUKAS

(1865–1935)

ARIANE ET BARBE-BLEUE

Ariadne and Bluebeard

OPERA in three acts by Paul Dukas; text after Maeterlinck's play of the same name. Première, Opéra-Comique, Paris, May 10, 1907, with Georgette Leblanc (Maeterlinck's wife), Brohly, Vieuille. First performed Metropolitan, New York, 1911, with Farrar, Rothier, conductor Toscanini; la Scala, Milan, 1911, with Pierich, Ludikar, conductor Serafin; Buenos Aires, 1934, with Bunlet, Romito, conductor Panizza; Covent Garden, 1937, with Lubin, Etcheverry, conductor Gaubert; Naples, 1950, with Varenne, Chalude, conductor Wolff; Lisbon, 1963, with Borkh, Depraz.

CHARACTERS

Barbe-Bleue............................... Bass
Ariane ....Mezzo-Soprano
La Nourrice .... Contralto
Sélysette.......................Mezzo-Soprano
Ygraine............................... Soprano
Mélisande .... Soprano
Bellangère .... Soprano
Alladine .... Mime
An Old Peasant .... Bass
Second Peasant .... Tenor
Third Peasant .... Bass

Peasants, Crowd

Place: Bluebeard's castle

Act I.   A vast and sumptuous hall of semi-circular form in Bluebeard's castle. At the back a large door, on either side of which are three small ebony doors. Through the open window, can be heard the sound of an angry crowd. They believe that Bluebeard has murdered his wives one by one, and that the beautiful Ariane is to be the next victim. Can she not be saved? They comment on the arrival of the carriage; it it true that she already knows all that there is to know about the castle? Is it true that the previous five wives are *not* dead, but still alive in a dungeon? Voices are said to have been heard.

The windows of the hall shut, the roar of the crowd recedes to a murmur, and Ariane and her nurse come in by a side door. The nurse starts to lament their fate; they are as good as dead already—the crowd was trying to warn them—he is mad and has already killed five wives. Ariane is calmer; she is convinced that Bluebeard loves her, and that she must win his secret to save them all. He has given her seven keys, six of silver, and one of gold; those of silver she may use to open any door she likes, that of gold she must not touch. It must be that one, then, that guards his secret; she will have nothing to do with the silver keys, only the gold will answer her purpose. Suiting the action to the word, she throws down the silver keys, but the nurse hastens to pick them up; they will unlock his treasure, he told them.

Taking the keys, the nurse unlocks the six doors. They slide open as she turns the keys, and from them in succession pour cascades of amethysts, sapphires, pearls, emeralds, rubies and diamonds. Ariane is not looking for treasures, but she cannot resist the sight of the diamonds: 'O mes clairs diamants!' she sings, in a great lyrical outburst, whose high *tessitura* makes one wonder whether any mezzo-soprano ever negotiated the title role successfully.

Ariane is intent on discovering what is behind the seventh forbidden door. She bids her nurse hide herself, and puts the key into the lock. Nothing can be seen when the doors open, but a sad, subdued sound is heard; it is the sound of the other five wives, says Ariane. The chant grows stronger, and as Ariane is about to enter the vault, Bluebeard himself comes into the hall. He reproaches Ariane for her faithlessness, but she demands to know the truth. He takes her by the arm and bids her follow him. She struggles to free herself, the nurse joins in to help and the sounds of the quarrel penetrate to the crowd waiting outside. A stone is thrown through the windows, and the nurse runs to unbolt the door, through which streams a crowd of peasants. Bluebeard prepares to defend himself, but Ariane goes gently but firmly to the people and assures them that she has not been hurt. She closes the gate.

Act II. A vast subterranean hall. It is nearly dark. Ariane and the nurse appear, the former holding a lamp. Ariane stumbles on the other wives, lying huddled in the middle of the vaulted hall. In her joy that they are alive, she rushes to them and embraces them: 'Ah! Je vous ai trouvées!' When the nurse brings the light, she sees that the captives are ill-clothed, and that their dungeon is unprepossessing; they look dazed and frightened at the unaccustomed light. One by one Ariane calls them to her[1] and reassures them; she has not come to join them as a captive but to free them, has in fact obeyed a higher law than Bluebeard's. Outside the birds are singing and the sun is shining. A drop of water extinguishes Ariane's light, but she shows no signs of fear. The others, who are used to the dark, lead her to the light—they say there is some light in the corner of the dungeon. When she gets there, Ariane finds that there are bars and bolts, which, say the other wives, they have never tried to open. It is the sea which is behind the wall, and to open it would let in the waves. But Ariane throws herself against it, and opens it, like a door, to admit light through what appears to be a great window: 'Ah, ce n'est pas encore la clarté véritable.' She takes a stone and smashes this, and immediately the whole chamber is bathed in brilliant, blinding light, so that Ariane herself can hardly bear its brightness, and the others have to protect themselves as if against fire. Ariane encourages them to look out at the world from which they have been cut off, and she leads them off to freedom, singing joyfully as they go.

Act III. The scene is the same as that of Act I. All the wives are adorning themselves with the jewels which Ariane found with the aid of her six silver keys. They were unable to escape from the castle, since the drawbridges rose when they approached them, the moats filled magically with water. They speculate as to where Bluebeard has gone, but Ariane bids them concentrate on adorning themselves for the freedom which will surely be theirs.

The nurse comes in hurriedly to say that Bluebeard has returned. Soon his carriage can be seen approaching. He descends from it and is attacked by the villagers, who are determined to end what they consider his tyranny. His bodyguard deserts and Bluebeard himself is wounded. The peasants bind him and are about to drown him in the moat. Others crowd into the castle, and, Ariane having opened the great doors of the hall, they appear on the threshold, carrying Bluebeard. They offer him to the wives; let them take what revenge they like—he is securely bound. Ariane thanks them

[1] When Mélisande's name is mentioned, the theme from Debussy's Act I, scene iii, is heard.

and bids them go to their homes to tend their wounds.
When they have left the castle, the women all crowd round
Bluebeard to see what can be done for his wounds. They are
found not to be serious, but the bonds with which he is
secured are so tight as to risk strangling him. Ariane cuts
them with a dagger, and he is able to get up. She herself
departs, although Bluebeard makes a movement as if he
wished her to remain. But when she in turn asks the five
wives to go with her, they decline and she leaves them with
Bluebeard in the castle.   H.

ALBERT ROUSSEL
(1869–1937)
PADMÂVATÎ

OPERA-ballet in two acts. Music by Albert Roussel, libretto by Louis
Laloy. Première at the Opéra, Paris, June 1, 1923, with Ketty
Lapeyrette, Jane Laval, Paul Franz, Eduard Rouard, conductor Philippe
Gaubert. Revived, 1946, with Hélène Bouvier, Renée Mahé, Charles
Fronval, Marcel Clavère. First produced Buenos Aires, 1949, with
Bouvier, Negroni, Tygessen, Filipe Rimito, conductor Calusio; 1968,
with Lyane Dourian, Noémi Souza, Jon Vickers, Angel Mattiello,
conductor Georges Prêtre; Naples, 1952, with Janine Micheau,
Tygessen, Vieuille, conductor Cluytens; Strasburg, 1967, with
Geneviève Marcaux, Guy Chauvet, Franz Pétri; London, Coliseum
(concert performance) 1969, with Rita Gorr, Jane Berbié, Albert
Lance, Gérard Souzay, conductor Jean Martinon.

CHARACTERS

Ratan-Sen, *King of Chitoor* .... Tenor
Padmâvatî, *his wife* .... Contralto
Alauddin, *the Mogul Sultan of Delhi* .... Baritone
The Brahmin .... Tenor
Gora, *steward of the Palace at Chitoor* .... Baritone
Badal, *Ratan-Sen's envoy* .... Tenor
Nakamti, *a young girl* .... Mezzo-Soprano
The sentry .... Tenor
A priest .... Bass

Two women of the palace.........Soprano, Contralto
A woman of the people .... Soprano
A warrior .... Tenor
A merchant .... Tenor
An artisan............................ Baritone
    Warriors, Priests, Women of the palace, Populace

DANCERS

A woman of the palace
A female slave
A warrior
Kali
Durga
Prithivi, Parvati, Uma, Gauri
    Girls of the palace, Female Slaves, Warriors
Time: 1303   *Place:* Chitoor

Roussel first visited the East during his Naval service and
returned there in 1909 on a cruise lasting four months,
visiting amongst other places in India, Bombay, Ellora,
Jaipur, Benares, as well as Ceylon, Singapore and Saigon. On
his return, he wrote his orchestral triptych *Evocations*, in
which his memories of Ellora, Jaipur and Benares live fully
up to the title rather than indulging in any form of Oriental
reminiscence. In 1914, Jacques Rouché became Director of
the Opéra; he had been at the head of the Théâtre des Arts
where in 1913 Roussel's ballet *Le Festin de l'Araignée* was
given, and one of his first actions after his new appointment
was to commission a lyric work from Roussel. The composer
chose a subject which had attracted him during his Indian
journey, and the French orientalist, Louis Laloy, wrote the
libretto. He had finished the vocal score by the outbreak of
war and orchestrated it in 1918, after ill health caused
his retirement from the Navy, to which he had been recalled.
    Much has been made of the Oriental inspiration in
Roussel's music, but it is true to say that he never attempted
to apply Hindu melodic or rhythmic patterns to his music,
except where the works were of directly Oriental character,
and his music remained entirely European. Certain sections
of *Padmâvatî*, particularly those lyrical in character, make
use of Hindu scale forms not usually found in Western music.
The pantomime of the third scene of Act II starts with an
imitation of the *arpeggio*-like sweep down the sympathetic

strings with which sitar recitals customarily begin.

Chitoor has for ruler the noble and just Prince Ratan-Sen, married to the beautiful Padmâvatî, whose name denotes the sacred lotus or Padma. In the past, a Brahmin priest had fallen in love with Padmâvatî and was banished from Chitoor. He has now taken service with the Mogul ruler of Delhi, Alauddin, and to avenge himself on Ratan-Sen, he persuades Alauddin to attack Chitoor.

After a prelude, which starts slowly and atmospherically, the curtain rises to show the people of Chitoor in the public square in front of the palace. They await the arrival of Alauddin and his envoys, who are to discuss peace with Ratan-Sen, and girls garland the sacred images as a watchman announces the approach of the Mogul prince. Gora, steward of the palace, tries to reassure the crowd about their traditional enemies, but his own suspicions are roused when Badal tells him that behind the screen of the peaceful delegation the Mogul army is gathering in the plain.

The music, already full of anticipation of events to come, gathers momentum as Alauddin makes his appearance with the Brahmin priest in his entourage, and is hailed in a wordless chorus. After the sovereigns have greeted each other, Ratan-Sen proposes a pledge to their future alliance. Gora demands that the Brahmin leave them while they confer, but Alauddin insists on his favourite counsellor remaining. At his guest's suggestion, Ratan-Sen orders a display of dancing, first to vigorous 5/4 and 7/4 rhythms by his soldiers, then by the female slaves to a less energetic but still lively 6/8 with a slow central section. Alauddin asks to see the Hindu palace dancers themselves, a right denied to unbelievers, saying that he has been converted to Hinduism by the Brahmin. After a languorous dance in triple time accompanied by wordless chorus, Alauddin makes his request to see Padmâvatî, the fame of whose beauty has travelled far, and the Brahmin in a beautiful aria passionately sings the praises of her charms. Ratan-Sen, in spite of his misgivings, feels that he cannot refuse, and Padmâvatî appears veiled on a balcony among her women, amongst whom Nakamti in a song of considerable allure[1] compares her beauty to the sun, which disperses night and awakens the flowers ('Elle monte au ciel où rêve le printemps'): The opening and often-

[1] And according to Vuillemin, says Basil Deane in his book on Roussel, of Hindu origin.

repeated phrase of Nakamti's aria serves as motif for
Padmâvatî and is unusually successful in that not only is it
associated with her beauty, which Nakamti is specifically
hymning, but it does not exclude the quality of modesty, by
tradition all-important amongst Indian women; that it is
heard only from Nakamti and in the orchestra, and that
Padmâvatî herself never sings it, somehow underlines this
quality. When Ratan-Sen bids Padmâvatî lower her veil,
Alauddin seems overcome by what he has seen and makes
an excuse to leave. He puts off signing the treaty until the
next day when he may bring appropriate gifts.

As the Brahmin is about to follow his master, he is
recognised by one of the guards and challenged. He waits to
hear the watchman report that Alauddin has left the city,
then delivers his master's challenge: if Padmâvatî is not
handed over to Alauddin (reference to Nakamti's song), the
Mogul army already encamped in the plain will sack the city
of Chitoor. Ratan-Sen's refusal is brusque and to the point,
but the crowd lynches the Brahmin, who dies prophesying
death for Ratan-Sen and Padmâvatî and destruction to the
people of Chitoor.

In the final scene of this act, against a background of distant calls to arms, Padmâvatî laments that she should be the innocent occasion of disaster—a sacrilegious death has already occurred—and prays that she may meet death rather than be separated from Ratan-Sen.

The second act, introduced by a solemn prelude, takes place in the Temple of Siva,[1] which contains a gigantic statue of the god, with a door in its base leading to the crypt. It is night. At dawn next day, if Padmâvatî has not been handed over to Alauddin, Chitoor will be sacked. Ratan-Sen is even now leading his warriors in a last desperate sally against the Moguls, and Padmâvatî has come to the temple to add her supplications to those which we hear rising solemnly from the crypt. The priests emerge, chanting a litany to Siva, and Padmâvatî asks them what they have learnt from the god. They tell her that a supreme sacrifice at dawn is required, but when Padmâvatî offers herself to die, she is told that there must be more than one victim.

Ratan-Sen appears in the temple, wounded and with the news that his soldiers are defeated and a truce granted only until dawn. He tries to explain the full horror of the situation to Padmâvatî, but she cannot imagine him allowing more than her dead body to fall into the hands of the Mogul king, and the possibility of Ratan-Sen handing her over alive to Alauddin is something she cannot envisage. He describes the suffering the people of Chitoor will have to undergo if Alauddin is refused, and she at last understands what he means. She sings longingly of her arrival from Singhal, of her happiness at Chitoor, of her readiness to follow him to death; then, to forestall the sacrilege which she sees he is planning to commit, stabs him to the heart in full knowledge that custom demands that she commit suttee[2] on her husband's funeral pyre.

The third scene is a great ritual of death. First, Padmâvatî is prepared for her immolation. As she sings a lament ('O mes

---

[1] Siva: one of the major Gods of the Hindus. 'In the worship of Siva,' says Benjamin Walker's *Hindu World*, 'was centred that element of dread and uncertainty that is associated with the unknown and the unfathomable.' Siva is at the same time destroyer, creator and preserver.

[2] Suttee: the ancient Hindu custom whereby the widow commits suicide (preferably voluntarily) on the funeral pyre of her husband.

soeurs fidèles') she is attired as a bride by the priestesses. Next comes an extended dance sequence. A fire is lit which provides the illumination for a mime-dance by four vampire-like figures. These are succeeded by the two figures presaging death, Kali[1] and Durga, who dance in narrowing circles round Padmâvatî, the chosen victim. The funeral ceremony itself opens with a wordless female chorus, into which the priests' invocations are gradually woven, reaching a climax when they garland first the body of Ratan-Sen, then that of the living Padmâvatî, at the same time as are heard the first lamentations of the crowd outside the palace waiting in mounting fear for dawn.

At the first rays of sunlight, the procession starts to move. The body of Ratan-Sen is carried slowly to the crypt, Padmâvatî following half walking, half carried. The invocations inside the temple and the imprecations of the people outside are expressed in choral writing of some complexity, and, as Ratan-Sen's funeral pyre begins to blaze and Padmâvatî with a supreme gesture of terror is gently carried into the crypt, the music reaches its final climax. There is a great shout as Alauddin bursts through the Temple door, but all that he can see is the smoke slowly drifting up from the crypt, as the orchestra recalls Nakamti's celebration of Padmâvatî's beauty.

The opera, which with 100 minutes of music is by no means long, is Roussel's most ambitious project. It could be argued that he is less than perfectly served by his poet, and certainly there is more urgency in music than libretto. The composer deals in sustained musical shapes, and drama for him lies in the musical expression of the powerful overall theme rather than in portrayal of immediate situation, of clash of motive or will, of violent incident. Characterisation is incidental, but what is notable is the composer's ability to organise, whether the long opening movement with its processions and its messengers, the extended and contrasted dance scenes in both acts, or the quasi-finale of the first act (taking the concluding scene of that act as postlude or reflective comment on its main action). The noble utterances of Padmâvatî herself are worthy, it seems to me, to stand beside those of Berlioz's Dido, and it is a tribute to the

[1] Kali and Durga: Kali, an aboriginal goddess, wife of Siva, and black of visage, is associated with death, as is Durga, a renowned slayer of demons.

composer's powers of organisation that the drama does not seem to suffer in spite of the fact that Alauddin sings no more after the first act, and that the central figure of Padmâvatî herself is a silent participant after her great lament early in Act II. All the same, the musical splendours of the choral funeral procession bring to a most impressive end an opera whose almost complete neglect ever since it was written would be unbelievable even in France were it not for such overwhelming precedent as Berlioz's *Troyens*.   H.

HENRI RABAUD
(1875–1949)
MAROUF

OPERA in five acts by Henri Rabaud; text by Lucien Népoty. Première at Opéra-Comique, Paris, May 15, 1914, with Davelli, Périer, Vieuille, conductor Ruhlmann. First performed at la Scala, Milan, 1917, with Vallin, Macnez, conductor Panizza; 1939, with Favero, Malipiero, Poli, Baccaloni, conductor Marinuzzi; Metropolitan, New York, 1917, with Alda, de Luca, Rothier, conductor Monteux; 1937, with Chamlee; Buenos Aires, 1917, with Vallin, Crabbé; 1923, with similar cast; 1935, with Bovy, Gaudin; 1942, with Denya, Singher; 1946, with Mazella, Jansen; 1966, with Massard; San Francisco, 1931, with Gall, Chamlee. Revived Opéra-Comique, 1949, with Géori Boué, Bourdin, Pernet, conductor Fourestier; Lisbon, 1960, with Michèau, Jansen, Roux.

CHARACTERS

Princess Saamcheddine	Soprano
Fatimah, *wife of Marouf*	Soprano
Marouf, *cobbler of Cairo*	Tenor (or Baritone)
The Sultan of Khaïtan	Bass
The Vizier	Baritone
Ali	Baritone
The Fellah	Tenor
Two Merchants	Tenor, Bass
Chief of the Sailors	Tenor
Two Muezzins	Tenor

The Pastry-cook Ahmad .... Bass
The Cadi .... Bass
Two Mamalik .... Bass
Time: Legendary   *Place:* Cairo, Khaïtan, the desert

Act I.   Cairo, Marouf is unhappy at home. His wife,
Fatimah, is ugly and has a bad disposition. When she asks for
rice cake, sweetened with honey, and, thanks to his friend
the pastry-cook, Marouf brings her cake sweetened with cane
sugar instead, she flies into a rage and runs to tell the Cadi
that her husband beats her. The credulous Cadi orders the
Cobbler thrashed by the police in spite of protesting
neighbours. Marouf, disgusted, decides to disappear. He joins
a party of passing sailors.

Act II.   A tempest wrecks the ship, and Marouf alone is
saved. Ali, his friend, whom he has not seen for twenty years
and who has become rich in the meantime, picks him up on
the shore and takes him to the great city of Khaïtan,
'somewhere between China and Morocco'. Marouf is
presented to the townspeople as the richest merchant in the
world who has a wonderful caravan on the way. He is
accepted everywhere and in spite of the doubting Vizier the
Sultan invites him to his palace.

Act III.   Arrived there, he offers him his beautiful
daughter as a bride, in spite of the warnings of the Vizier,
who advises him that it would be more prudent to await the
arrival of the caravan, before taking any irrevocable step.

Act IV.   For forty days Marouf lives in luxury with the
Princess. He empties the treasury of the Sultan, who consoles
himself with thoughts of the promised caravan which must
soon arrive. At last the Princess questions Marouf who tells
the truth. They decide upon flight, and the Princess disguises
herself as a boy.

Act V.   At an oasis in the desert they are sheltered by a
poor peasant. Marouf seeks to repay his hospitality by a turn
at his plough. The implement strikes an iron ring attached to
the covering of a subterranean chamber. The ring also has
magic power. When the Princess rubs it the poor peasant is
transformed into a genie, who offers his services, and discloses a hidden treasure. When the Sultan and his guards, in
pursuit of the fugitives, appear upon the scene the sounds of
an approaching caravan are also heard in the distance. The
Sultan apologises. Marouf and the Princess triumph. The

doubting Vizier is punished with a hundred lashes.

The music of *Marouf* is attractive, if 'obvious' in character. It is based on the sort of Eastern *pastiche* which has served its turn in everything from *Turandot* and *Hassan* to *Chu Chin Chow*; the difference is that Rabaud has mixed it more skilfully than many of his predecessors and successors. As well as the dances and court episodes, *Marouf* contains a number of effective solos: Marouf's lament ('Il est des Musulmans'), which begins the whole opera and is heard again at intervals throughout the first act, has a haunting melancholy about it; in Act II he boasts the riches of his mythical caravan in an extended aria ('A travers le désert'); in Act IV he reflects in a delicious little air, imitated, says the composer, from an oriental song ('Dans le jardin fleuri').

K. W., H.

MAURICE RAVEL
(1875–1937)
L'HEURE ESPAGNOLE
The Spanish Hour

OPERA in one act by Maurice Ravel; text by Franc-Nohain. Première, Opéra-Comique, Paris, May 19, 1911, with Vix, Périer. First performed at Covent Garden, 1919, with Donalda, André Gilly, Dua, Maguénat, Cotreuil, conductor Pitt; Chicago and New York, 1920, with Gall, Maguénat, Defrère, Warnéry, Cotreuil, conductor Hasselmans; Metropolitan, 1925, with Bori, Errolle, Bada, Tibbett, Didur, conductor Hasselmans; la Scala, Milan, 1929, with Supervia, Menescaldi, Damiani, Baccaloni, conductor Santini. Revived Covent Garden, 1924, with di Lima, Warnéry, Couzinou; 1926, with Heldy; 1962, with Costa, conductor Solti: San Francisco, 1945, with Albanese, Garris, de Paolis, Harrell, Baccaloni, conductor Merola; Netherlands Opera, 1950, with van der Veen, Vroons, Baylé, conductor Monteux; Opéra-Comique, Paris, 1951, with Duval, Giraudeau, Vieuille, conductor Cluytens; Naples, 1952, with Marthe Luccioni, conductor Cluytens; Sadler's Wells, 1961, by New Opera Company with Collier, Alexander Young, Glossop, Glynne; Chicago, 1965, with Berganza, Alfredo Kraus, Bruscantini; Glyndebourne, 1966, with Garcisanz, Sénéchal, Le Hémonet, Cuénod, conductor Pritchard.

CHARACTERS

Concepcion, *wife of Torquemada* . . . . Soprano
Gonzalve, *a poet* . . . . Tenor
Torquemada, *clock-maker* . . . . Tenor
Ramiro, *a muleteer* . . . . Bariton-Martin
Don Inigo Gomez, *a banker* . . . . Bass
Time: Eighteenth Century   *Place:* Toledo

The action passes in the shop of Torquemada, an absent-minded clock-maker of Toledo, in the eighteenth century. It is his day for attending the public clocks in various parts of the town. It is also the one day that his wife Concepcion can enjoy her love affairs with complete freedom. As the clock-maker leaves his house, Ramiro, a muleteer, arrives to have his watch fixed. It is a family heirloom and most important to him. Much to Concepcion's annoyance, Torquemada invites the customer to await his return. In despair Concepcion wonders what to do with the unwelcome visitor. Equally embarrassed, he offers to carry to her room one of the large clocks which her husband has declared too heavy for him to lift.

While he takes the clock to the other room Concepcion's lover Gonzalve appears. During the muleteer's absence he is hidden in a large grandfather clock. There follows an interchange of clocks, and the unsuspecting muleteer carries Gonzalve inside a clock to Concepcion's room. Inigo, a banker, who is another admirer of Concepcion's, enters. He in his turn is hidden in a clock. Another switching of timepieces effects a change in lovers. But neither turns out to be satisfactory, the one perpetually indulging in flights of poetic fancy, the other proving simply ridiculous, and it is the muleteer who by his prowess and strength wins Concepcion's admiration; she transfers her temporary affections to him and takes him up to her room. While they are away, Torquemada returns. He finds two dejected philanderers hidden in his clocks and takes the opportunity of selling one to each of them. Concepcion and Ramiro re-enter. The husband, however, probably believes that there is safety in numbers and the opera ends with a sparkling quintet, whose moral, say the characters, comes from Boccaccio:

Entre tous les amants, seul amant efficace,
Il arrive un moment, dans les déduits d'amour,
Où le muletier a son tour!

From the delightful clock noises of the opening to the Habanera quintet of the end, *L'Heure Espagnole* is full of charming music. One should however mention that it is music designed to point up the witty stage action, and that there are hardly any 'numbers' (Concepcion's exasperated 'Ah, la pitoyable aventure' is the nearest) in the accepted sense—as one might well expect from Ravel's injunction to his singers: '*dire* plutôt que *chanter*.' Gonzalve is the only exception to this rule, and he waxes positively lyrical at times (e.g. his characteristically Spanish opening song). It is all very light, and, since everyone seems to be agreed that the opera will not bear translation, we may for once legitimately call it very French as well.   K. W., H.

L'ENFANT ET LES SORTILÈGES
The Child and the Magic

Opera in two parts by Maurice Ravel; text by Colette. Première Monte Carlo, March 21, 1925, with Gauley, Warnéry, Lafont, conductor de Sabata. First performed Opéra-Comique, Paris, 1926, with Féraldy, Calvet, Sibille, Bourdin, Hérent, Guénot, conductor Wolff; San Francisco, 1930, with Queena Mario, conductor Merola; Florence Festival, 1939, by company from Opéra, Paris (where the work was revived that year), with Micheau, Branèze, Cernay, conductor Previtali; Buenos Aires, 1944, with Oyuela, Kindermann, Negroni, Cesari, conductor Wolff; la Scala, Milan, 1948, with Branèze, Danco, Schenneberg, Gianotti, conductor de Sabata. Revived Opéra-Comique, Paris, 1951, with Angelici, Turba-Rabier, Jourfier, conductor Cluytens; London, Sadler's Wells, 1965, conductor Matheson.

CHARACTERS

The Child	Mezzo-Soprano
His Mother	Contralto
The Louis XV Chair (La Bergère)	Soprano
The Chinese Cup	Mezzo-Contralto
[1] The Fire	Soprano Léger
[1] The Princess	Soprano Léger
The Cat	Mezzo-Soprano
The Dragonfly (La Libellule)	Mezzo-Soprano
[1] The Nightingale (Le Rossignol)	Soprano Léger
The Bat (La Chauve-Souris)	Soprano
The Little Owl (La Chouette)	Soprano

[1] These roles *must* (according to the score) be sung by the same singer.

The Squirrel (L'Ecureuil) . . . . .Mezzo-Soprano
A Shepherd Girl (Une Pastourelle) . . . . Soprano
A Shepherd (Un Pâtre) . . . . Contralto
The Armchair (Le Fauteuil) . . . . Basse Chantante
The Grandfather Clock (L'Horloge Comtoise) . Baritone
The Tea Pot (La Théière) . . . . Tenor
[1] The Little Old Man (Arithmetic) . . . . Tenor
The Tom Cat . . . . Baritone
A Tree . . . . Bass
[1] The Frog (La Rainette) . . . . Tenor
Settle (Le Banc), Sofa (Le Canapé),
    Ottoman (Le Pouf), Wicker Chair . . Children's Chorus
Numbers (Les Chiffres) . . . . .Children's Chorus
Shepherds, Frogs, Animals, Trees . . . . Chorus

Colette's libretto originally began as a scenario for a ballet, which she sent to the director of the Opéra in Paris, who in turn sent it on to Ravel, who was then serving with the French Army at the front. It was not until the summer of 1920 that the composer started work in earnest, by which time the ballet scenario had become an operatic libretto. Ravel interrupted his work more than once in favour of other things, but it was finished towards the end of 1924.

The scene is laid in a room in an old Norman country house, giving on to a garden. Big armchairs, a grandfather clock, wallpaper with shepherds and shepherdesses on it. A round cage with a squirrel in it hangs near the window. Remains of a fire in the grate, kettle singing. The cat also singing. It is afternoon. The Child, aged six or seven, is sitting at his lessons, at the height of a fit of laziness. He bites his penholder, scratches his head and mutters under his breath. Work exasperates him and he only wants to do the things he is not allowed to do.

His mother comes in with his tea, asks him how he is getting on, and is vexed to see that he has done nothing but make a blot on the table-cloth. When she asks him to promise to work, the child puts out his tongue at her. She leaves him saying he will be left alone in the room until supper-time as a punishment. The Child suddenly loses control, and dashes about the room indulging in an orgy of destruction. He

[1] These roles *must* (according to the score) be sung by the same singer.

smashes the cup and teapot, pricks the squirrel with his pen, pulls the cat's tail, flourishes the poker, stirs up the fire, and upsets the kettle into it to produce clouds of steam and ashes. Then, brandishing the poker like a sword, he swoops on the wall-paper and pulls great strips of it off the wall. He opens the grandfather clock, swings on the pendulum and pulls it off, and finally makes a dash at his books and tears them up with a scream of delight. All this takes place in a few seconds and to the accompaniment of suitably vivacious music.

From now until the end of the opera, the child is going to realise the consequences of his destructive actions, and in a way that is likely to astonish him more than any other—from the objects of his temper themselves. He sinks into a chair, but, to his infinite surprise, it moves slowly away from him, to the creaking sound of a double-bassoon, and, bowing gravely to a Louis XV chair, leads her in a stately but grotesque dance. Their conversation, to which the Child listens in amazed silence, is to the effect that they will never again have to put up with the weight and the pranks of the naughty child they have had to stand for so long. They are joined in vigorous expression of this sentiment by Settle, Sofa, Ottoman, and Wicker Chair.

Next comes the mutilated clock, striking uncontrollably and complaining bitterly of the treatment which has deprived him, literally, of his balance. To hide his shame, he goes to the end of the room and stands with his face to the wall. From the floor comes the voices of the Chinese cup and teapot ('Wedgwood noir' says the score): 'How's your mug? Rotten . . . better had . . . come on! . . . I punch, Sir, I punch your nose . . . I boxe you, I marm'lad you.' The words are nonsense, compounded from English and the more nebulous orientalisms such as 'Mah-jong', 'kong-kong', 'Harakiri' and even 'Caskara'; the music is a brilliant parody

of the foxtrot of American jazz (1920's style), and the nostalgic tune is sustained now by the voices, now by the first trombone, who is ordered to "vibrer avec la coulisse'. The foxtrot is justly one of the most famous moments of the score, but it evoked more hostility at the first performances than almost any other passage.

The Child suddenly feels very much alone and goes towards the fire, which however spits in his face and announces to coloratura music that warmth is only for those who are good; bad children will be burnt. The fire pursues the Child round the room until it succumbs quietly to the ashes, which dance with it for a moment and then extinguish it altogether. There is a procession, half comic, half pathetic, of the shepherds and shepherdesses from the torn wall-paper, after which the Fairy Princess rises out of the torn picture book, on which the Child has rested his head. He was half-way through her story, but now that the book is torn he will never know how it will all turn out. The Child tries to hold her back as she sinks through the floor, and his lyrical phrases after she has gone are really moving in their mixture of simplicity and intensity.

There is just a chance that the end of the story may be amongst the pages which lie round his feet, and he looks for it, but in vain. All he can find are the torn sheets of an arithmetic book, from which emerges an old man covered with arithmetical symbols and crowned with a Pi. Without even pausing to look round him, the little old man starts to reel off problems of the sort which begin 'If two taps fill a bath in . . .'. He and the Child catch sight of one another at the same moment, and immediately he and his platoon of figures start to torment the Child with quick-fire arithmetical nonsense. The Child is whirled into the dance, and sinks down exhausted holding his head.

He does not notice the black cat come out from under the armchair, yawn, and start to wash itself. It is playing with a ball when the Child notices it and says wearily that he supposes it too has acquired the habit of speech. The cat signs that it has not, and spits at him, before going off to the window, where a white cat has appeared. Now comes the famous Cats' love duet, which caused such a storm at the first performance. No word is spoken, but the 'Mi-inhou' and 'Mornaou', which Colette has chosen to represent cat's speech, are set to exact notes and marked 'nasal'.

The result is brilliantly real, and the animals work themselves up to a frenzy of excitement before bounding out of the window into the garden.

The Child follows them hesitatingly, and at this point the stage directions require that the room walls fall away, the ceiling disappear, and the Child with the two cats be transported into the garden, which is flooded with moonlight and lit by the last rays of the setting sun. The short and very beautiful orchestral interlude is for strings; piccolo and Swanee whistle imitate bird noises and the whole atmosphere is one of pure moonlight and magic. A chorus of frogs can be heard from behind the scenes, and the Child is delighted to be out in the garden he loves so well.

But even here he is not to escape the accusing voices which have haunted him indoors. The tree complains about the cuts made in his flanks the day before, and the Child leans his cheek against the tree in sympathy. A dragonfly flashes across the scene calling for the mate she has lost, and who is now pinned to the wall in the Child's room. A nightingale is heard against the background of the frogs' chorus (the music soars to a top F), and a bat complains that his mate was killed by the Child, leaving the family helpless. Frogs come out of the water and sit round the edge until the pool is completely ringed with them. They dance. One lays its head on the Child's knee, and is immediately admonished by a squirrel for taking such a risk with so dangerous a creature. She herself was able to escape, but another squirrel was caught and now languishes in a cage in the Child's room. The Child tries to explain that it was so as to be able to gaze for ever into the squirrel's beautiful eyes that he took her captive, but this answer proves anything but satisfactory to the squirrel, who makes a moving plea for the freedom she and her kind love above everything else.

The Child realises that the animals are happy all round him, and begins to feel lonely with no one paying any attention to him. Suddenly he cries out 'Maman'. Immediately the atmosphere of peace is broken. Some animals disappear, but those who stay behind form a menacing chorus, with the Child as the object of their dislike. Each one has a grudge to pay off, and together they rush at the Child, catch hold of him, buffet him, turn him round, shove him, and then forget all about him as, in their anxiety to be the first to down him, they become excited at the battle and turn on each other.

The Child is pushed over into a corner of the stage, when all of a sudden a little squirrel who has been wounded limps over towards him. The Child takes a ribbon and binds up the squirrel's paw, watched by the other animals. Their animosity turns to something quite different as they exclaim in amazement at the Child's kindly action. 'He has stifled the bleeding, he has bound up the wound.' What can they do to help him, now that he looks so helpless and lonely all by himself in the garden? Just now he cried out; what was the word? They try to call 'Maman', thinking that will help the Child, whom they now know to be good and kind. The animals help him up and start to lead him towards the house whose windows have just been lit up. The opera ends as the Child calls simply and confidently 'Maman'.

One can only imagine that the neglect of Ravel's operatic masterpiece is due to the twin difficulties of translation and of fulfilling the exacting stage directions. There can be no other reason, as the music is in many ways the best and most complete that he ever wrote. He is at the very height of his powers, and working well within them to produce a work whose inventiveness appears to be equal to every facet of the situations he has undertaken. Above all, the subject is one that exactly suits his peculiar type of genius; the work brilliantly switches from parody to the most moving lyricism, to onomatopoeic representation of the story. It is hard to imagine the listener who would not be enchanted by its fancy and fantasy, particularly now that several gramophone recordings have made the opera anything but the rarity it used to be.   H.

DARIUS MILHAUD
(1892–1975)

LE PAUVRE MATELOT
The Poor Sailor

OPERA in three acts by Darius Milhaud; text by Jean Cocteau. Première, December 16, 1927, at Opéra-Comique, Paris, with Madeleine Sibille, Legrand, Vieuille, Musy, conductor Lauweryns. First performed Berlin, 1929, with Novotna, conductor Zemlinsky. Revived with new orchestration, Geneva, 1934; Philadelphia, 1937, with Anna Leskaya, Fritz Kreuger; Vienna, 1937; Opéra-Comique, 1938; Berlin, 1947, with Enk, Schuffler, Heinz Nilssen, Schirp; Düsseldorf, 1948, with Teschemacher, Ostertag, conductor Hollreiser; London Opera Club, 1950, with Vyvyan, Servant, Loring, Wallace, conductor Renton; la Scala, Milan, 1950, with Favero, Malipiero, Inghilleri, Beuf, conductor Sanzogno; Hamburg, 1951.

CHARACTERS

The Wife .... Soprano
The Sailor .... Tenor
His Father-in-law .... Bass
His Friend .... Baritone

Time: The present   *Place:* A seaport

The opera, which is dedicated to Henri Sauguet, is divided into three acts, but is played without intervals and in all lasts only some thirty-five minutes. The action takes place in and near a bar kept by the Wife. Also visible are the street and a wine shop kept by the Friend. The Wife and the Friend are dancing. She has waited fifteen years for the return of her husband from abroad, and has steadfastly refused to give up hope of his return, in spite of his long absence. The Friend is disposed to encourage her to hope, and he expresses admiration for the way she has remained faithful; a port like this, he says, is not the sort of place where one would expect to find *that*. She is perfectly candid; she might have deceived her husband if he had been there, but with him away and his photograph still hanging over the bed, how could she do such a thing? Besides, no other man has yet caught her fancy.

Her Father takes a very different view of this chastity of his daughter's; why can't she find herself a man, who could

1283

take over the bar and run it properly? The Friend says that
he himself has proposed to her, but she has always turned
him down. She makes the obvious retort; supposing they did
get married, and one day the bell rang and in walked her
husband—his friend? Her Father still refuses to take the same
view, even when optimistically she imagines him coming back
as rich as Croesus. If he is poor, there is no crime she would
not commit to set him up again properly.

The Friend goes back to his shop. The Father repeats his
suggestion that they would make a fine pair, but the Wife
gives lyrical expression to her resolve to remain true to the
husband she still believes will return to her. Her Father
reminds her that she was twenty-five when he left, and is now
forty. While they are arguing and before they leave the stage,
the Sailor himself appears unobserved in the street, hesitates
in front of their door, and then decides not to open it. What
if his own wife does not recognise him—nobody has so far.
Would it not be best to see first what effect his appearance has
on his Friend? He knocks, and is at first rejected as a
drunkard, until he mentions that he has a wife opposite.
Then his Friend recognises him. The Sailor congratulates
himself that he did not risk going home announced. He has
changed, he knows; in the fierce climates he has known, who
would not have done? He asks after his wife, and is reassured
that she is waiting for him. He has money enough to end all
their troubles.

The Friend is for going over straightaway, but the Sailor
suggests he sleeps in his Friend's house for the night. He
would like to meet his wife as a stranger; his travels have
given him a taste for adventure and this shall be his last.

Act II.   Next day, the Sailor bids his Friend good-bye,
and goes, not without some misgivings, to see what his
reception will be like at the bar. He tells his Wife that he
brings her news of her husband; he has returned, but dare not
come to her until nightfall, as he is pursued by creditors. She
says they cannot help him; they are penniless themselves. The
Sailor is sceptical; since when has a pretty woman gone short
of money? His Father-in-law sneers at the Wife, but she takes
no notice, and leads a short ensemble of strong rhythmical
impulse: 'Cher époux!' She is filled with delight that her
husband is likely to be restored to her, and quite undismayed
to learn that had he accepted the love of a cannibal queen he
might have come home with the treasures which in point of

fact devolved upon his shipmate. The Sailor shows her the pearls which were his reward, he says, for taking her husband's place as the queen's lover.

The Sailor asks if he may stay the night with them, and is told that no one who brings such good news could be refused so small a request. The Friend is full of curiosity to know what has happened, and he thinks of the excuse of returning the heavy hammer he borrowed the previous day from the Wife. She does not tell him that she has had news of her husband, but, as she locks up, she is struck with the resemblance which the weary Sailor, stretched out on a bench, bears to her husband.

Act III. The Sailor lies asleep. The Wife comes in with the hammer in her hand, looks at him for a moment, raises it, then apparently thinks better of her plan. She coughs, but he does not stir. She raises the hammer again and strikes him on the head with it. When he moves convulsively, she strikes him again, then drops the hammer, and rifles his pockets quickly, removing the pearls. The noise arouses her father, whom she instructs to help her carry the body. They will dump it in the rain-water tank, and tell the neighbour that their visitor had to leave early in the morning. There is a knock at the door, but they stay quiet and their neighbour leaves them undisturbed. They prepare to carry the body away, as the Wife sings lyrically of her husband's impending return. II.

OPÉRAS–MINUTES
Instant Operas

Three one-act operas, lasting about eight minutes each, by Darius Milhaud; text by Henri Hoppenot. *L'Enlèvement d'Europe* was first given at Baden-Baden, July 17, 1927, in conjunction with Toch's *Die Prinzessin auf der Erbse*, Hindemith's *Hin und Zurück*, and Weill's *Mahagonny*. The same work was performed for the first time with the other two Opéras-Minutes (*La Délivrance de Thésée* and *L'Abandon d'Ariane*) at Wiesbaden, April 20, 1928. First performed Budapest, 1932, in Hungarian; Minneapolis, 1967; Florence, 1970.

These miniature but highly entertaining operas are nothing if not satirical in intent. Mythology in general, and more particularly the classical French interpretation of it, are spoofed to the limit, alike by librettist (who, like Claudel, once represented his country as ambassador) and composer. Milhaud's *Phèdre* bears the same relationship to Racine's as Offenbach's *Orphée* does to Gluck's. The music itself, spiced with South American rhythms, is very attractive, and Milhaud's quick-fire inventiveness seems peculiarly well suited to the original form he has invented.

L'ENLÈVEMENT D'EUROPE
The Rape of Europa
CHARACTERS

Agénor . . . . Bass
Pergamon, *Europa's suitor* . . . . Baritone
Jupiter, *in the guise of a bull* . . . . Tenor
Europa, *Agénor's daughter* . . . . Soprano

Chorus of 'maîtresses-servantes' . . . . . . {
One Soprano
One Mezzo
One Contralto

Chorus of Soldier-Labourers . . . . {
One Tenor
One Baritone
One Bass

The set represents the front of the palace of King Agénor of Thebes. The chorus of women is hanging about near a well, and that of the men near a field. The Chorus reiterates the name of 'Europa', in alternate rising 7ths and 9ths. Pergamon emerges from the palace, and gives vent to his wrath at the discovery that Europa prefers the society of bulls and cows to that of a hero like himself. Agénor agrees that his daughter has never shown much taste for the company of men of warlike accomplishments. She appears with the bull to which she has taken so evident a fancy, and the chorus makes scornful references to her passion for its bellowings.

Jupiter explains his love for Europa, and pleads passionately for satisfaction of 'cette double ardeur du taureau dans mes reins et du Dieu dans mon cœur'. The chorus mocks the beast, and Pergamon, beside himself, draws his bow and looses an arrow at his rival, much to the consternation of the bystanders. The arrow strikes home, but the bull shakes itself free and the missile speeds back to him who dispatched it, and transfixes him. After Pergamon's death, the chorus sings a valediction, in which the 7ths and 9ths of the beginning are prominent. Europa rides away into the distance with the bull.   H.

L'ABANDON D'ARIANE

Ariadne Deserted

CHARACTERS

Ariane . . . . Soprano
Phèdre, *her sister* . . . . Soprano
Thésée . . . . Tenor
Dionysos, *the god, in disguise* . . . . Baritone

Chorus of Shipwrecked Mariners . . . . . $\left\{\begin{array}{l}\text{One Tenor} \\ \text{One Baritone} \\ \text{One Bass}\end{array}\right.$

Chorus of Gypsy Bacchants . . . . $\left\{\begin{array}{l}\text{One Soprano} \\ \text{One Mezzo} \\ \text{One Contralto}\end{array}\right.$

The scene represents part of the island of Naxos; rocks visible in the background. During the piece, darkness falls, and it is almost night at the end. As the curtain rises, the stranded mariners are grouped left, playing dice, the Bacchants are sitting around a cooking pot, looking like gypsies; Dionysos is amongst the Bacchants, dressed as a beggar. Like a 'Greek chorus', the two groups join to convey the information that it is Ariane's custom to come to that part of the island every night in order to escape the attentions of Thésée, whom she cannot abide. Phèdre meanwhile longs unavailingly for his caresses.

Before long, the two sisters, dressed exactly alike, come into view, and each gives vivid utterance to the sentiment ascribed to her by the chorus, which for its part prays to Dionysos to help each in her different affliction. Dionysos, in his capacity as a beggar, laments his blindness and begs for charity. Each sister gives him money. When the sailors announce that Thésée can be seen coming that way, Ariane says she will hurry away, while Phèdre rejoices at the prospect of seeing her beloved.

Thésée cries aloud the name of Ariane, and tenderly asks if no one can give him information as to her whereabouts. Dionysos offers him a cup of precious wine for which he returns thanks in an exultant musical sentence ending resoundingly on a high B flat. The wine has the effect of making him see double, and when Phèdre comes from her place of concealment he thinks she is the two sisters and goes

1287

out with her. The chorus comments in Tango rhythm, and Dionysos informs Ariane that Thésée will in future regard Phèdre as his consort. She thanks him for his kindness towards her, and a moment later Dionysos and the Bacchants shed their beggar's clothes and are revealed in dazzling white. Ariane and her sister gave alms to a god and his reward is to grant their joint wishes. She has one more request; may she finish her days with Diana in the firmament on high? It becomes darker and Dionysos leads her up the rocks; behind her appears the constellation of Ariadne. The chorus rejoices; the opening chorus is repeated in a different rhythm (alternating 6/8 and 5/8 in a bar), and sung over an instrumental accompaniment that has the flavour of a modernised version of a *toccata* from one of Monteverdi's operas.

H.

LA DÉLIVRANCE DE THÉSÉE

Theseus Redeemed

CHARACTERS

Aricie .... Mezzo-Soprano
Phèdre, *her sister* .... Soprano
Hippolyte, *son of Phèdre* .... Baritone
Théramène, *Hippolyte's friend* .... Baritone
Thésée, *husband of Phèdre* .... Tenor
Chorus of Distant Voices .... Mixed Vocal Quartet

A great hall in the palace of Thésée; a throne in the middle. Hippolyte complains to his friend Théramène of the unwelcome attentions of his mother, Phèdre; he is in love with Aricie, to whom he presently pours out his heart, only to be told that Aricie cannot make a decision either way without the consent of Thésée, Hippolyte's father. Enter Phèdre, whose presence causes Aricie and Théramène to withdraw respectfully. She is overjoyed to find Hippolyte alone, but he repulses her, and the trumpets announce the return of Thésée from yet another successful and hazardous exploit. When Thésée appears, Phèdre turns the tables and asks for his protection against her incestuous son. Thésée promptly banishes him and orders him to go out to do battle with the monster which even now threatens the walls of the city.

The chorus takes up the very attractive rhythm of the

Beguine, which started as Hippolyte left the stage with Théramène; the words are 'Oui, c'est lui! C'est bien lui!' With the chorus as background, Thésée gives an account of his adventure:

> J'arrivai: Ils tremblèrent;
> J'avançai: Ils reculèrent;
> Je dégainai: Ils décampèrent;
> Je les tuai: Ils expirèrent!

Thésée being a tenor, they 'decamp' on a top C, but, by the time his miniature aria has come to an end, the chorus is exclaiming at some new misfortune: 'O douleur! O tristesse!' In spite of the pleas of Phèdre and Aricie, they make no attempt to explain what causes their distress and alarm, but in no time Théramène, who has witnessed all, returns. He takes up his position for 'Le Récit' (a reference to Racine's *Phèdre*) and begins: 'A peine nous sortions,' only to be interrupted by the omniscient Thésée: 'Je connais . . . finis vite.' There is nothing left for Théramène to do (he makes this quite clear) but to revenge the death of Hippolyte. He takes out his sword and stabs Phèdre to the heart, whereupon Thésée orders the guards to hang him from the nearest tree.

Aricie, aided by the wordless chorus, laments the series of disasters which have befallen them in a single day, but consolation for the two survivors is close at hand. Thésée puts his arm round Aricie, and in phrases of exaggeratedly lyrical character invites her to console herself with him. Poor Aricie, who has earlier been referred to as 'craintive' and 'pudique', seems to be the only one of the characters to benefit from the catastrophes, and by the end we find Thésée addressing her more optimistically as 'la timide Aricie'.

H.

CHRISTOPHE COLOMB
Christopher Columbus

Opera in two parts and twenty-seven scenes by Darius Milhaud; text by Paul Claudel. Première, Berlin, May 5, 1930, with Reinhardt, Scheidl, conductor Kleiber. Given in concert form in Paris 1936, London 1937, Antwerp 1940, New York 1952, with Dow, David Lloyd, Harrell, Brownlee, Norman Scott, conductor Mitropoulos. In 1968, a one-act opera *The Discovery of America*, drawn by Gunther Schuller from *Christophe Colomb*, was performed in San Francisco.

CHARACTERS

Isabella, *Queen of Spain* .... Soprano
Christopher Columbus I .... Baritone
Christopher Columbus II .... Baritone
Narrator .... Speaker
Counsel for the Prosecution .... Speaker
The Representative of the Sailors .... Speaker
Major-domo .... Tenor
Master of Ceremonies .... Tenor
The Cook .... Tenor
The King of Spain .... Bass
The Commandant .... Bass
Messenger .... Baritone
Sultan Miramolin .... Tenor
Chorus, officers, counsel, creditors etc., etc.

Christophe Colomb is in the tradition of French operas built on the largest possible scale, a tradition which was carried forward from Lully by Rameau, Spontini, Berlioz, Meyerbeer. Milhaud and Claudel have however rejected the quasi-realistic treatment of their subjects which was adopted by at any rate the more recent of their predecessors (if the word realistic has any validity when applied to stage works), and have concentrated on the symbolical aspects of the story of Columbus. The resulting opera is thus not only highly exacting to stage—it involves a vast apparatus—but anything but easy for the audience to understand. It belongs in fact, as Edward Dent has said in his Pelican *Opera*, to the category of works which one expects to see only once in a lifetime.

Act I. (1) The Narrator and Chorus come on in procession, after which (2) the Narrator announces: 'The Book of the Life and Voyages of Christopher Columbus, who discovered America. In the name of the Father, and of the Son, and of the Holy Ghost.' (3) With the Chorus murmuring in the background, and supported by the percussion, the Narrator prays for light and strength in his endeavour to explain the book. (4) On a cinematic screen at the back of the stage, a globe can be seen spinning round; above it can be made out a dove, glowing with light.

(5) A humble inn at Valladolid. Columbus is seen as an old, broken man, his only possession a mule. (6) Narrator and Chorus call on him to join with posterity in looking at his past life and the results of his actions. The Counsel for the

Prosecution signifies his presence. (7) The Narrator refers to the court of Spain, and the embodiments of Envy, Ignorance, Vanity, and Avarice put in an appearance to the accompaniment of Spanish dance rhythms. Prosecution and Defence argue over the behaviour of the King of Spain towards Columbus, and Columbus himself is eventually stung into entering the discussion. He is accused of lying and exaggeration, but defends himself.

(8) An orchestral passage accompanies the clearing of the stage, which is effected by a cloud of doves ('Colombes' in French). (9) The Court of Isabella the Catholic. The Queen is shown as a child surrounded by a childish court. She receives Sultan Miramolin (also represented by a child), who gives her a dove in a cage. She accepts the gift, puts a ring on its foot, and releases it. The scene is accompanied by a wordless chorus. (10) The dove over the sea. (11) The Narrator continues the story of Columbus. As a boy he read the story of Marco Polo; the screen shows a jumble of incidents in the tale, and when Columbus's mother or his sister comes to look over his shoulder at what he is reading and so enters into his consciousness, she also appears on the screen. There is conflict between the views of the Man at the Window, who urges him to seek adventure, and the Chorus, which tries to prevent him leaving his family. His second self bids him follow the call of adventure, in the name of God. As the scene ends, a dove flies in through the window, with a ring on its foot.

(12) Columbus leaving Genoa says good-bye to his family, and sets out over the seas. He interrogates a dying sailor as to what he has seen in the West. (13) Columbus and his creditors. He glories in the sea he has conquered, but the cries of his creditors will not be silenced; three guitarists add their voices, but the creditors agree that a last voyage, however desperate an undertaking, represents their only chance of payment. (14) Columbus goes to the court of the King of Spain, and tells the Major-domo that he has not come to ask anything of the King, but rather to give him something. He is mocked for his opinions and his pretensions, and the Major-domo tells him to come back to-morrow, taking care however to ask on the sly whether he has gold to offer.

(15) Queen Isabella is seen at prayer. On the screen appear representations of the crowds, the processions, battles which have led to the capture of Granada and the unification of

Spain. A wordless chorus accompanies her prayer to God. She has played her part in the unification of Spain by bringing Aragon to Castile; may she not now lay down her life, her duty accomplished? She sees a mystical vision and hears the voice of Saint James, demanding that she look beyond the seas. Had she not another ring besides that she gave her husband? Yes, she put it on a dove's foot and she saw it again on Christopher Columbus's hand.

(16) Cadiz. Recruiting is going on for the three vessels which are to form Columbus's expedition of discovery. (17) The Master of Ceremonies calls the roll of the demon gods of America. They make reference to the plagues they will inflict on Columbus and his crew. (18) Columbus receives representatives of the crew, who come with complaints that food is short. The men wish to return and give up the expedition which they think is condemned by God from above. Columbus consults his senior officers and men, and all advise him that the expedition is doomed unless he turns back at once. He refuses, and the situation becomes ugly with the threat of mutiny. Columbus speaks up bravely to defend his policy, and is so convinced that he is right in his calculations that he bids the sailors drink the water they have with them and eat the food; sufficient will still remain for their needs. No sooner are the words out of his mouth than a bird appears, and the scene ends with a cry of 'Land!' from the look-out.

(19) America. The ships can be seen approaching, and from them is heard the sound of a 'Te Deum'. The first part ends with the large-scale setting of the 'Sanctus'.

Act II. An interlude shows the effect Columbus's discovery has on the whole world; nobody talks of anything else, but whether the earth is round and the New World possible. The Narrator tells of the difficulties which follow the discovery of America; the cruel treatment of the natives leads to revolt and further repression; the New World does not bring the profit expected of it, and Columbus's enemies are busy in Spain. (1) The King summons three wise men to give him counsel. They give their advice in oblique form, but warn the King against his subject Columbus: 'You must honour him—you must watch him—you must bury him.' (2) Controversy. The orchestra plays quietly while the different groups engage in argument among themselves.

(3) On his fourth voyage, Columbus was put in chains by

the man appointed by the King to take over his command; he is seen lying bound in the hold of the ship, where he is visited by his successor and exhorted to put forth his influence in saving the ship, which has run into dangerous waters. The Commandant is accompanied by the Cook, who begs Columbus to act like Samson pulling the Temple of Dagon about the ears of the Philistines, and destroy the ship. But Columbus prays and three times the ship weathers the crises which come upon it.

(4) Christopher Columbus's conscience. The Cook acts as guide while Columbus looks back at his past actions and their consequences. He sees the inhabitants of America, on whom his discovery of the new continent has brought ruin and destruction: the slaves he sold to pay his debts; the wife and mother he abandoned; himself as he was contented at Genoa, and at Lisbon; and his own ghost. The Cook reminds him that there are other unknown seas beyond the one he has discovered, and tells him that the New World will not be named after him but after an obscure member of his own crew, Amerigo Vespucci, whom he can scarcely remember.

(5) The boat arrives safely, and the scene changes to Spain. A Messenger comes from Queen Isabella. On her bed of suffering, she thought of Columbus and his expedition, and now sends words of comfort to him on his return to Spain. Her funeral procession can be seen crossing the stage. (6) The book is almost finished, says the Narrator. The servant at the inn comes in to demand payment of Columbus's bill. Will the innkeeper not wait three days, asks Columbus; he once asked his sailors to wait three days before killing him, and in those days he discovered a New World. Will the innkeeper not do the same? That worthy answers that he will take the mule unless he is paid by to-morrow, and goes out, leaving Columbus in despair and praying for help.

(7) The Paradise of the Idea. The scene takes on a resemblance to that of Act I, scene ix, the court of Isabella in Mallorca. But it has changed, and everything has become the colour of silver. It is paradise. Isabella greets her friends, and is welcomed by the ladies of her court—all children, as in the previous scene in these surroundings. Sultan Miramolin comes to bring her gifts, and she remembers when he gave a dove long ago, and she put her ring on its foot. How can she enter into the kingdom of heaven without her friend Christopher Columbus, she asks? Let him be fetched. No one has been

able to find him, she is told; he is not to be found in any of the palaces of Spain. But Isabella can see him in the inn at Valladolid, and she is told that he is dying on a bed of straw. She is further told that he does not wish to come at her command, but intends to fulfil his destiny, with her ring on his finger. She may have his mule.

(8) The scene disappears. The image of Saint James appears on the screen; he it was who guided the Queen safely to heaven. Isabella leads a prayer for Columbus. At the final Alleluiah, a dove flies from the globe.   H.

FRANCIS POULENC
(1899–1963)

LES MAMELLES DE TIRÉSIAS
The Breasts of Tiresias

OPÉRA-bouffe in a prologue and two acts; music by Francis Poulenc, text by Guillaume Apollinaire. Première, Opéra-Comique, Paris, June 3, 1947, with Denise Duval, Paul Payen, conductor Albert Wolff. First performed in U.S.A., at Brandeis University, Mass., 1953; New York, 1957, with Duval, Singher, Gramm; in England, at Aldeburgh Festival, 1958, with Jennifer Vyvyan, Peter Pears, Hervey Alan, and Poulenc and Benjamin Britten at two pianos, conductor Charles Mackerras.

CHARACTERS

The Director of the Theatre . . . . Baritone
Thérèse . . . . Soprano
Her Husband . . . . Tenor[1]
Monsieur Lacouf . . . . Tenor
Monsieur Presto . . . . Baritone
The Gendarme . . . . Baritone
The Newspaper Vendor . . . . Mezzo-Soprano
The Reporter from Paris . . . . Tenor

[1] In the printed score and in the Paris performances of 1947 (and some subsequently abroad), the Husband was sung by a baritone; the composer later revised the role for a tenor.

The Son ....Baritone
Members of the audience:
   An Elegant Lady................Mezzo-Soprano
   A Woman ....Mezzo-Soprano
   A Bearded Gentleman .... Bass
              People of Zanzibar
Time: 1910   *Place:* Zanzibar, an imaginary town on the
                      French Riviera, between Nice and
                               Monte Carlo

'Chabrier,' said Francis Poulenc, '... is my true grand-father', and Chabrier, for all his devotion to Wagner, derives much of the flavour of his unique talent from a deliberate cultivation of vulgarity, as evidenced in for instance the overblown music-hall tunes of *España*, a masterpiece and musically a product of some sort of *nostalgie de la boue*. With this musical adherence and his admiration for Guillaume Apollinaire, many of whose poems he had already set, it is not surprising that Poulenc's first opera is a tearaway farce. *Les Mamelles de Tirésias*, says Edward Lockspeiser, 'unites the worlds of surrealism and the music-hall. In his intro-duction to this fantasy on the change of sexes which, incidentally, he wrote for an intensely serious purpose—Apollinaire believed that the French were neglecting the act of love—he has this to say on the origin of the Surrealist movement: "When man wanted to imitate walking, he invented the wheel, which has no connection whatever with a leg. This was an unconscious surrealist example".'

Other early influences on the composer were the eccentric and talented Erik Satie, and the other composers irrationally joined together by contemporary criticism as *Les Six*: Auric, Milhaud, Durey, Tailleferre and Honegger.

Apollinaire's drama was written in 1903 but produced only in 1917. Poulenc finished his first opera in 1945 and it was given at the Opéra-Comique in June 1947, after a preparatory period, the composer used to say, which proved the effectiveness of its motto, 'Français, faites des enfants', since the first two sopranos entrusted with the leading role had to relinquish it on account of pregnancy.

There is a quiet orchestral introduction and the curtain rises to reveal the theatre director, who appeals directly to the audience in calm, measured, serious tones: 'Public,[1]

---

[1] Apollinaire's spelling.

attendez sans impatience, je vous apporte une pièce dont le but est de réformer les mœurs. Il s'agit des enfants dans la famille. . . .' His description of what the audience is going to see touches frenzy before returning to the serious tones of the start and the work's motto: 'Et faites des enfants, vous qui n'en faisiez guère.' It is the opera's most extended musical structure and the music is without a hint of irony.

No sooner has the director disappeared than the curtain rises to reveal the main square of Zanzibar, complete with houses, café, a view of the port. Exoticism is not in question, and Zanzibar appears to lie somewhere between Nice and Monte Carlo. With the entrance of the charming and energetic Thérèse, the musical mood changes completely to one of bustle and farce. She announces herself feminist, refuses to submit to her husband's wishes, wants to be a soldier. His cries from the house—'Donnez-moi du lard'—only inspire her to a denunciation of love and further proclamations of ambition. At this moment her breasts seem anxious to escape from their owner, she opens her blouse (on a top C) and they escape, two children's balloons attached to her now only by the strings. After celebrating their loss and their beauty in a slow waltz, she reflects that they are a cause of sin and so—'Débarrassons-nous de nos mamelles'—the action suited to the words by means of an explosion effected with the aid of a cigarette lighter. She feels her beard sprouting, looks in the looking-glass and turns round to reveal that she is right, congratulating herself on the discovery in a brisk *paso doble*.

The husband emerges, a bouquet of flowers in his hands, assumes that what appears to be a stranger in Thérèse's clothing has murdered his wife, but is disillusioned by Thérèse's announcement that she has ceased to be his wife and will be in future known as Tirésias (in musical accents strongly anticipatory of Blanche de la Force in *Dialogues des Carmélites*). Thérèse-Tirésias disappears into the house and drum rolls accompany the descent from the window of intimate household objects, explained deprecatingly by the husband as 'the piano', 'the violin'.

As the husband returns to his house, a polka starts up and a couple of drunks, Presto the fat one and Lacouf the thin one, come out of the café. They have been gambling and in the friendliest possible way they quarrel, arrange a duel and happily shoot each other (the whole scene owes something to the Chabrier of *L'Étoile* and its 'Duo de la Chartreuse Verte'). It is left to Thérèse, now dressed in the height of masculine fashion, and her husband, disguised as a rather untidy housewife, to mourn the loss of these two worthy citizens, an activity in which the inhabitants of Zanzibar solemnly join, but which husband and wife have discovered only by reading the newspaper with which they have equipped themselves.

Quick music and a drum roll precede the appearance of the husband and the gendarme, the latter of whom theoretically pursues crime but seems to prefer to pay court to the husband, whom he takes for a female, to the latter's undisguised mockery, the whole scene taking place against a background of Woman's Lib. cries from the populace of Zanzibar.

In an arietta, the husband explains to the gendarme, whom he addresses as 'Fameux représentant de tout autorité', that he feels it essential that Zanzibar should have children and, if women refuse to provide them, he will. Somehow, in spite of the farcical nature of the situations in which he invariably finds himself, the husband's solo utterances seem always to have a particular lyrical warmth of their own.

The first half ends with a scene of considerable vivacity, a newspaper-seller denouncing a hoax, the husband assuring the gendarme that if he comes back that night he will show him that he has managed, single-handed as it were, to produce children; even Lacouf and Presto reappear apparently full of life, the chorus meanwhile providing a solemn chorale against which the liveliness of the others produces a suitable contrast. For the rapid *stretta à la Rossini*, the stage direction has the curtain descend until only the singers' legs are visible.

The Ravel-like entr'acte has a solemn opening before six mixed couples from the chorus enter and dance a kind of farcical gavotte in front of the curtain, a manoeuvre interrupted only when strange noises are heard coming from the orchestral pit—the cries of infant children.

The second part begins where the first left off, now with the scene filled with cradles, and in front of them writing material and a gigantic pot of glue. The husband is delighted with his success—Forty thousand new children in a single day! — and the voices of the children echo their father's self-satisfaction. In comes a journalist, demanding to know the husband's secret and presuming that he must be very rich to afford so large a family. Not at all, returns the husband, but they should be able to support him once they are grown up. He already has one called Joseph whose novel has to date sold 600,000 copies. A vast tome descends in front of the journalist who starts, with the greatest possible difficulty, to read it, then, impressed by the evidence of the husband's income, tries to touch him for a small loan. He is immediately—and literally—kicked out.

The husband seems to read (unaccompanied) a moral from the whole affair: the more children you have, the richer you'll be. He will start by making a journalist, but the eighteen-year-old who results from his curious activities starts to blackmail him, so that the boy's departure elicits no more comment than a quick 'That one worked out badly'. He is contemplating further creative activities when he bumps into the gendarme, who holds him by the shoulder and remonstrates about the addition of over 40,000 inhabitants to the population of Zanzibar. How are they to be fed? With ration cards, suggests the husband; these can be obtained at the Cartomancienne's (fortune teller's).

No sooner mentioned than this lady appears, her grandiose cadenzas accompanied on the lyre which she carries. No aria unfortunately eventuates from it, but the fortune teller offers to tell everyone's future, in spite of the gendarme's warning that her trade is against the law. She counsels fecundity, severely condemning the gendarme, who appears to be sterile. His attempt to avenge his honour by attacking her ends in his strangling by the fortune teller, who reveals herself, when the husband tries to restrain her, as none other than Thérèse. The husband is delighted and even the gendarme revives. The only trouble is that her figure seems, much to her husband's dismay, no more ample than it had in her recent masculine manifestation. She makes light of the problem in the charming arietta ('Qu'importe, viens ceuillir la fraise') and, as the sun sinks and the scene lights up for night, the husband joins her in a lazy, amorous waltz. The inhabitants provide them with vocal accompaniment, while the husband goes to buy some balloons at the appropriate shop, an action which quite fails to impress Thérèse who looses them into the night sky. The action[1] ends with a *stretta* and then the moral; 'Ecoutez, O Français, les leçons de la guerre, et faites des enfants, vous qui n'en faisiez guère.' H.

[1] Which lasts a few minutes less than one hour.

DIALOGUES DES CARMÉLITES

Opera in three acts by Francis Poulenc, libretto by Emmet Lavery from the drama by Georges Bernanos, itself inspired by a novel of Gertrude von Le Fort and a scenario of Rev. Fr. Bruckberger and Philippe Agostini. Première, Jan. 26, 1957, at la Scala, Milan, with Virginia Zeani, Leyla Gencer, Gigliola Frazzoni, Eugenia Ratti, Gianna Pederzini, conductor Nino Sanzogno (la Scala had asked Poulenc for a new ballet score but were told the composer was thinking of writing an opera, whose première they immediately secured). First performed at Paris Opéra, 1957, with Denise Duval, Régine Crespin, Rita Gorr, Liliane Berton, Denise Scharley, conductor André Cluytens; Cologne, 1957; San Francisco, 1957, with Dorothy Kirsten, Leontyne Price, Blanche Thebom, Sylvia Stahlman, Claramae Turner, conductor Leinsdorf; London, Covent Garden, 1958, in English with Elsie Morison, Joan Sutherland, Sylvia Fisher, Jeanette Sinclair, Jean Watson, conductor Kubelik; Vienna, 1959, with Seefried, Zadek, Goltz, Rothenberger, Hoengen, conductor Hollreiser.

CHARACTERS

Marquis de la Force .... Baritone
Chevalier de la Force, *his son* .... Tenor
Blanche de la Force, *his daughter* (Sister
    Blanche of the Agony of Christ) .... Soprano
Thierry, *a footman* .... Baritone
Mme. de Croissy, *the Prioress* (Mother
    Henriette of Jesus) .... Contralto
Sister Constance of St. Denis,
    a young novice .... Soprano
Mother Marie of the Incarnation,
    assistant prioress .... Mezzo-Soprano
M. Javelinot, *a doctor* .... Baritone
Madame Lidoine, *the new prioress*
    (Mother Marie of St. Augustine) .... Soprano
Mother Jeanne of the Child Jesus .... Contralto
Sister Mathilde .... Mezzo-Soprano
Father Confessor of the Convent .... Tenor
1st Commissary .... Tenor
2nd Commissary .... Baritone
Officer .... Baritone
Gaoler .... Baritone
Eleven Carmelites .... Soprano, Mezzo-Soprano
                                                 Contralto

Officials of the Municipality, Officers, Policemen,
Prisoners, Guards, Townspeople
Time: Between April 1789   *Place:* The Carmelite Convent
and summer 1792   at Compiègne; Paris

Even though the genesis of Bernanos's *Dialogues des
Carmélites* is a story by a German writer and an idea for a
film scenario by two Frenchmen (it was only the dialogue for
this film that Bernanos was asked to supply), 'the psychology
of fear which is the main theme of the *Dialogues* is treated in
a way entirely characteristic of Bernanos; and the same is true
of the interpretation offered in this play of the Communion of
the Saints: "One does not die alone; one dies for others and
even in the place of others".'[1]

It is the great merit of Poulenc's setting of Bernanos's
Dialogues that he preserves all the essential character of the
original, that all the words are clearly audible, and that the
result is compelling drama, if not invariably compelling
music.

Act I, scene i: the Library in the Paris house of the
Marquis de la Force, April 1789. The Marquis is resting, but
the Chevalier bursts in; rumour has it there is a mob about
and his sister Blanche is out late in the carriage. The Marquis
loses his calm as he remembers a ghastly incident of nearly
twenty years before when his pregnant wife was jolted in her
carriage by a mob and died in giving birth to Blanche. The
Chevalier is particularly worried because of Blanche's
impressionable, not to say morbid, nature, but when she
comes in it is to say that the long and exhausting service that
morning has tired her and she will go to bed. A moment later
her scream is heard from the passage—she has unexpectedly
caught sight of a lamp carried by a servant. It is more than a
momentary fear that the shock releases in Blanche, and she
formally and with no sign of panic asks her father's
permission to join a Carmelite convent; how else is someone
as nervous as she is to find salvation?

Scene ii: the Parlour of the Carmelite Convent at
Compiègne a few weeks later. The aged Prioress on one side
of a screen interviews Blanche who sits on the other. The
Prioress explains that her seated posture is due to her
illness—otherwise sitting is a pleasure she renounced long ago.
When Blanche professes to be attracted even by the

---

[1] *Francis Poulenc,* by Henri Hell (1959).

privations of the Order, the Prioress emphasises that prayer is the sole reason for the Carmelites' existence. Under her questioning Blanche breaks down in tears, but the Prioress softens towards her and asks her whether she has already chosen her religious name in case she is admitted to the Order; Blanche answers 'Sœur Blanche de l'Agonie du Christ'.

Scene iii: in the Convent. Blanche and Constance, now novices, are busy with household work. Constance prattles away about her country upbringing, until Blanche snubs her levity with the reminder that the Prioress is lying near them gravely ill. Constance's reaction is to try to get Blanche to join her in offering their lives to God in place of that of the old Prioress, but Blanche rejects the idea in an agony of fear. Constance artlessly tells her of a dream she has had that she and Blanche will die together.

Scene iv: the cell of the Prioress. The Prioress on her deathbed is obsessed with fear of death, and the Assistant Prioress, Mother Marie of the Incarnation, tries to give her strength. The Prioress entrusts to Mother Marie the care of Blanche, the newest Carmelite to be admitted and one for whom the Prioress feels a special responsibility. Sister Blanche comes in to say goodbye and is admonished to preserve her innocence of character through trust in God. The Doctor enters and the Prioress asks for more drugs, if only to be strong enough to bid a public farewell to her charges. Mother Marie begs her to concern herself only with God, but the Mother Superior reacts violently: 'Who am I, wretched as I am at this moment, to concern myself with Him? Let Him first concern Himself with me!' She sees visions of an altar desecrated, the chapel laid waste and nothing Mother Marie can do will restrain the flood of words that pours from her. Mother Marie sends a message that the Sisters cannot be allowed to see the Prioress, who is powerless any more to impose her will. Blanche returns, the Prioress tries to speak to her, but falls dead.

Act II, scene i: the Chapel of the Convent. The body of the old Prioress lies in State, and when Constance goes to fetch replacements, Blanche by herself makes a half-hearted attempt to pray and then rushes towards the door, where she is met by Mother Marie. She attempts to explain, but Mother Marie leads her towards her cell; let her not talk about her failure—tomorrow it will fill her with sorrow, at present it can only cause her shame.

Blanche and Constance are taking flowers to the grave of the old Prioress. They hope that Mother Marie will be chosen to succeed her and Constance wonders at the difficulty the old Prioress had found in dying; one would have said she had been given the wrong death by mistake, as if it had been someone else's coat in a cloakroom. Perhaps someone when it comes to their turn to die will find a better death than they deserve.

Scene ii: the Hall of the Chapter House. It is not Mother Marie who is chosen Prioress but a certain Madame Lidoine, from outside.[1] She speaks to the nuns in an aria, praising the old Prioress and bidding them at all times to remember their duty, which is to pray. Anything that may lure them from their duty, even the joy of martyrdom, is to be shunned. She leaves Mother Marie to finish the address, after which in a beautiful ensemble the nuns offer up an 'Ave Maria'.

The bell at the side door rings. It is the Chevalier de la Force asking to see his sister before he goes abroad.

Scene iii: the Parlour of the Convent. With a screen between them and with Mother Marie in the background, the Chevalier accuses Blanche of staying in the Convent because of her fear of fear; Blanche forbids him to leave on a note of anger and misunderstanding. It is an impressively tense scene and reveals in music much of the change that has come over Blanche since she joined the Carmelite Order.

Scene iv: the Sacristy of the Convent. The Father Confessor has just finished saying what he tells the nuns is his last Mass. The priesthood has been proscribed and he must go into hiding. When Constance asks rhetorically if there are no men left in France, the Prioress says, 'When there are not priests enough, there will be plenty of martyrs, and the balance of grace will thus be restored.' Mother Marie seizes on her words: it is the duty of the daughters of Carmel to give their lives so that France may once again have priests. The Mother Superior firmly corrects her: it is not for them to decide if their names shall one day be inscribed amongst the martyrs. She leaves and the nuns are left looking in astonishment at Mother Marie.

The bell rings again violently, the nuns rush in all

[1] We are told that, as a matter of history, the inhibited and intense Mother Marie was an illegitimate daughter of the King's, and that the choice of Madame Lidoine, daughter of a local tradesman, may have been considered advisable as a sop to the spirit of the times.

directions and a mob pours in. Two commissars announce the expulsion of the nuns from the Convent. Mother Marie, now in charge, gets into an argument with the first Commissar, who takes her aside and reveals he was once a Sacristan and is at heart a true servant of the Church. He leads the mob out. Blanche carries a statue of the infant Christ in her arms, but, at a sudden shout from the mob, drops it in terror on the floor where it smashes.

Act III, scene i: the ruined Chapel of the Convent. As the Prioress is away, Mother Marie in the presence of the Father Confessor addresses the assembled nuns. She proposes that together they take a vow of martyrdom to save the Order from harm. But, she says firmly, if the vote is not unanimous, the proposal shall be abandoned. The Father Confessor receives their votes, and Mother Marie announces that there is one voice against. Immediately Constance, to save Blanche from embarrassment, says that that vote was hers: she will retract, and thus they will be unanimous. Blanche and Constance as the youngest go first to take the vow, no sooner has Blanche passed the Father Confessor than she takes advantage of the general confusion to escape.

Outside the Convent, an Officer congratulates the nuns, who leave in civilian costume, on their discipline and public spirit, but advises them that they will be watched. The Prioress wants to warn the Father Confessor against coming to celebrate Mass; it would be too dangerous for them all. Mother Marie reacts with smouldering violence: how can they reconcile this caution with their vow? The Prioress says that each is responsible before God as an individual, but she herself must answer for them all and she is old enough to know how to keep her accounts.

Scene ii: the ruined library in the Paris house of the Marquis de la Force. Blanche in peasant costume is cooking when Mother Marie comes in to tell her that she has come to fetch her. Blanche prevaricates and tells Mother Marie that her father was guillotined and she is now alone. Mother Marie gives her an address, where she will be safe and where she (Mother Marie) will wait for her until the following night. Blanche says that she cannot go, but Mother Marie is quietly confident.

In a street near the Bastille, Blanche hears that they have arrested all the members of the Convent at Compiègne.

Scene iii: the prison of the Conciergerie. The Prioress tries to comfort the nuns at the end of their first night in prison; from now on, she will consider herself bound by their vow of martydom, though it was made in her absence. Constance is convinced that Blanche will return, because of a dream she has had. The Gaoler announces the findings of the Tribunal: it is death for each one of them. The Mother Superior places them once more under an oath of obedience and gives them her blessing.

In a dark corner of a street, Mother Marie hears of the death sentence from the Father Confessor. She must die with them, she says, but the Father Confessor suggests that this may not be the will of God.

Scene iv: In the Place de la Révolution the scaffold is prepared and the crowd watches as the Prioress leads in her little band of fourteen Carmelite followers. Singing the 'Salve Regina', one after another they mount the scaffold, and each time the guillotine drops there is one voice the fewer to sustain the singing. When Sister Constance is alone, she sees Blanche in the crowd, stops for an instant, then goes with renewed confidence to her death. Blanche takes up the chant, and with a new serenity follows her sisters to accomplish the vow they swore together.   H.

17

Russian Opera

IGOR FEDOROVICH STRAVINSKY

(1882–1971)

STRAVINSKY is one of the undisputed giants amongst composers of this century, over 60 years of which he strides as a colossus. Above all perhaps is his contribution to musical theatre. In ballet, he is supreme, prolific, various and consistent; his contribution to opera, if you believe as I do that opera is drama conveyed through music and heightened in the process, is less momentous but also telling.

Two quotations: 'Perhaps *The Nightingale* only proves that I was right to compose ballets since I was not yet ready for opera . . .';[1] 'If I live to write another opera, I suspect it will be for the electronic glass tube and the Idiot Box, rather than for the early baroque stages of the world's present-day opera houses'.[2] If the first denotes retrospective uncertainty as to his initial approach to opera, surprising perhaps since he had been an operatic enthusiast in youth and was the son of a celebrated singer, the second is consistent with the search for form which is the history of his operatic endeavour. In over 40 years of fairly consistent approach, he produced eight operas[3] in as many forms, only one of full length, another without singing, two more usually associated with the ballet

---

[1] Stravinsky and Craft: *Expositions and Developments*, Faber 1962.

[2] Stravinsky: 'Working notes for *The Flood*' in *Dialogues and a Diary*, Faber 1968.

[3] *Rossignol, L'Histoire d'un Soldat, Renard, Mavra, Oedipus Rex, Perséphone* (in Loewenberg's *Annals of Opera*), *The Rake's Progress, The Flood*.

1305

than with opera companies, another for television.

Let us from the outset narrow the field. Stravinsky wrote à propos *The Rake's Progress*: 'I believe music drama and opera to be two very, very different things. My life work is a devotion to the latter'. All the same, though he proclaims himself 'in the line of the classical tradition', right from the start he shows an unwillingness to accept a nineteenth-century conception of opera, inherited say from his teacher, Rimsky-Korsakov, for all the latter's influence on *The Nightingale* (1908: 1913–14). His chosen fairy story is quite unheroic in character, and he investigates what one might describe as the more private problems to which it gives rise. In *L'Histoire d'un Soldat*, he has made a virtue out of self-imposed necessity, contriving somehow, while writing a piece whose dimensions by definition are suitable for a village hall, to create something with a far wider relevance, hitting nerve centres unerringly with what the composer himself has described as '. . . characteristic sounds . . . the scrape of the violin and the punctuation of the drums. The violin is the soldier's soul, and the drums are the diablerie'. Though his aim was different, one should perhaps note that Stravinsky with this 'economical' piece no more succeeded in creating a cheaper alternative to the standard repertory than did Britten a generation later with his chamber operas. Each produced good art but neither significantly cut costs.

The aftermath of the war coincided with Stravinsky's 'exile' from Russia, and he continued to tap the vein of Russian fairy tale, exotic and fascinating to non-Russian ears, later more fully exploited in *Les Noces*. *Renard* (1917) and *Mavra* (1921), however different from each other, stand in relation to the latter masterpiece as a kind of *Parergon*. *Mavra*, with its self-conscious evocation of early, Italian-influenced, Russian operas, is almost as dense in texture as *Les Noces* (with of course a quite different vocal idiom), and I remember longing when I first heard it for a pause in the singing, a couple of bars here and there for air. I do not feel that way now, and the two works, together with the greater *Les Noces*, represent important aspects of Stravinsky's search for operatic form.

In *Oedipus Rex* (1926–7) stylisation is carried much further than before, a 'dead' language used, action all but eliminated and allowed only at crucial moments, and the story is mostly in the hands of a non-singing narrator. All the same, the music conveys the theme's agonising inevitability every bit as well as any play on the subject, and new aspects of Stravinsky come into play; the violence of the music's hammer blows at critical moments (Jocasta's entry, the mid-way chorus, the Messenger), as well as an ability to convey pathos which contradicts the composer's published tenets (the listener who hears 'Lux facta est' unmoved has a stony heart indeed).

Perséphone (1933–4), with its curiously conceived dialogue between singer and dancer-narrator, seems to me his least successful stage work, and in fact he did not again attempt musical theatre with words for nearly 15 years. When he did, the result contained elements of throwback, and was so far from *durchkomponiert* as to be nearer Rossini than Wagner or Berg. All the same, *The Rake's Progress* (1948–51) contains its measure of surprises, whether the extraordinary harpsichord-dominated cemetery scene and its incredibly intense postlude, the 10-bar woodwind-accompanied discovery that Nick's revenge is to leave Tom mad, or the wealth of lyrical melody throughout the score, expressive and moving in a different way from anything in Stravinsky's earlier output. (The story that Metropolitan opera-goers' reaction to the music when it was first given there was such that they spat at the box office people has always seemed so hard to believe that I imagined it was a management excuse for pusillanimity.) Here Stravinsky comes nearest to comment on human truth on a domestic level than anywhere else, even *l'Histoire d'un Soldat*: that he did not forge his own new language is more surprising than that here his compassion emerges in such lyrical passages as the trio following Ann's discovery that Tom is married, Baba's Marschallin-like final exit or Ann's cradle song in Bedlam.

All Stravinsky's operas, except for the two greatest, *Oedipus* and *The Rake's Progress*, are direct products of some larger phase of his creative activity, and *The Flood* (1961–2) is representative of a period of serial activity in the composer's life which produced *Movements; A Sermon, A Narrative, A Prayer; Abraham and Isaac*. It is compact to the point of terseness and invariably powerful. Nothing overall could be less like *The Rake* of 11 years before, and, even though it begins and ends with a hark-back to the choral style of *Noces* and contains more than one echo of *The Rake*'s vocal writing, there is something appropriate in the old

innovator finishing, with the first TV opera commissioned
from a great composer, an operatic career for whose output
we must feel gratitude for what it includes, only strengthened
by regret for what we never had—the orchestration and
completion of *Khovanshchina*, above all the planned but
unwritten opera with Dylan Thomas.   H.

LE ROSSIGNOL
The Nightingale

OPERA in three acts by Igor Stravinsky; text by the composer and S.
Mitousoff after Hans Andersen's fairy tale. Première, Paris, Opéra, May
26, 1914; first performed Drury Lane, London, 1914, with
Dobrovolska, Petrenko, Brian, Andreev, Warfolomeiev, conductor
Cooper; Covent Garden, 1919 (in English), with Nelis, Clegg, Moore,
D'Oisly, Richardson, Austin, conductor E. Goossens (snr.); New York,
Metropolitan, 1926, with Talley, Bourskaya, Wakefield, Errolle,
Schützendorf, Didur, conductor Serafin; la Scala, Milan, 1926, with
Pasini, conductor Stravinsky; Buenos Aires, 1927, with Dal Monte,
Tedeschi, conductor Calusio; Berlin (as ballet), 1929. Revived Trieste,
1935, with Menotti, conductor Salfi; Genoa, 1937, with Pagliughi,
Fort, conductor Gui; Palermo, 1950, with Grani, conductor Questa;
Holland, 1952, with Dobbs, conductor Bruck; Sadler's Wells, 1960, by
New Opera Company with Marion Studholme (in English); B.B.C. (in
concert), 1972, with Elizabeth Harwood, conductor Pierre Boulez (in
Russian).

CHARACTERS

The Fisherman .... Tenor
The Nightingale .... Soprano
The Cook .... Mezzo-Soprano
The Chamberlain .... Bass
The Bonze .... Bass
1st Japanese Envoy .... Tenor
2nd Japanese Envoy .... Baritone
3rd Japanese Envoy .... Tenor
The Emperor of China .... Baritone
Death .... Alto

Chorus of Courtiers and Ghosts

Act I.   A forest on the seashore at night. At the back of
the stage a Fisherman in his boat. He is waiting to hear the
Nightingale which delights him every night and causes him to
forget his fishing. After a while the Nightingale begins to sing.

Presently other interested spectators arrive—the Emperor's Chamberlain, a Bonze (priest) and the Emperor's Cook, the latter bringing her confederates and other courtiers to give the Nightingale a formal invitation to court to sing before the Emperor. The Nightingale remarks that her voice is far sweeter in the forest than in the palace. Since, however, the Emperor wills it otherwise, the Emperor shall be obeyed. The bird alights on the hand of the Cook, who takes it to the palace while the Fisherman continues to sing the bird's praises.

Act II. The act opens with an entr'acte (with chorus) during which the stage is hidden by veils. The chorus inquires of the Cook (who has been appointed 'Grand Cordon Bleu') about the Nightingale. The Cook describes the little bird whose songs fill the eye with tears. As the curtain rises the Chamberlain announces the Emperor, who arrives in great state with the Nightingale. At a sign from the Emperor the Nightingale begins to sing and the Emperor is so charmed that he offers the Nightingale the order of the Golden Slipper. But the bird requires no other honour than that of having charmed the great monarch. Three envoys from the Emperor of Japan offer the Emperor a mechanical bird which also sings. As soon as the mechanical nightingale's song begins the real one flies away. The Emperor, affronted, condemns it to perpetual banishment. The voice of the Fisherman is heard again as the curtain descends.

Act III. The Emperor is ill and Death sits at the foot of his bed wearing the imperial crown and grasping his standard. The ghosts of his good and his bad deeds crowd round the bed. The Emperor calls for his musicians. The Nightingale answers the call. It has come to banish ghosts and to sing of the coming dawn. Even Death is persuaded by the loveliness of the song to give back the crown and the standard. The Nightingale's charm has conquered disease, and as the courtiers arrive in solemn procession to salute the ruler whom they expect to find dead, the sun floods the room with light, Death disappears and the Emperor rises from his bed and wishes his courtiers a good morning. The Fisherman bids all acknowledge in the song of the Nightingale the voice of heaven.   F. B.

Le Rossignol was begun in 1908 just before the death of Stravinsky's teacher, Rimsky-Korsakov, but interrupted after the completion of the first act by the commissioning by

Diaghilev of *The Fire Bird*. A request from the newly
founded Free Theatre of Moscow to complete the opera led,
in 1913, to a resumption of work, but now, of course, by a
much maturer composer than the comparative beginner of
1908. The styles of Act I and Acts II and III are, however,
not so sharply contrasted that unity is ruled out, particularly
taking into account the fact that Act I is little more than a
lyrical prologue to the action of the two succeeding Acts; but
some critics have found a discrepancy.

The delightful melody of the Fisherman's song, which is

used to frame each act, the pageantry of the Chinese March,
the delicate, expressive filigree of the Nightingale's exacting

coloratura music—these elements are by no means the whole
story. The music has charm, the orchestration is masterly
without using colour primarily for its own sake, but these
factors hardly account for the lasting qualities of so unpretentious a work. The truth is I think that here, as virtually
throughout his output, the composer knows as few others
how to exercise an iron control over his material; inspiration
never leads to excess, a small gesture never produces an
over-exuberant musical reaction. It is precisely because the
work tells its tale without embellishment, because the
nightingale limits her brilliance and does not try to emulate a
nineteenth-century heroine—in a word because of Stravinsky's
immaculate sense of scale and style—that *Le Rossignol* much
more than half a century after it was written can prove, as
exemplified by the perfectly judged advocacy of Pierre
Boulez in his 1972 London concert, so thoroughly rewarding
an experience.   H.

L'HISTOIRE D'UN SOLDAT

A Soldier's Tale

A tale to be read, played and danced, by Igor Stravinsky, libretto by
C. F. Ramuz. Première, Lausanne, September 28, 1918. First performed
London, in concert at Wigmore Hall, 1920, Arts Theatre Club (staged),
1927; Berlin Volksbühne, 1924; New York, 1926. Revived London,
King George's Hall, 1953, by the Theatre Music Group; Edinburgh
Festival, 1954, with Moira Shearer, Robert Helpman, conductor Hans
Schmidt-Isserstedt, producer Günter Rennert; Sadler's Wells, 1958, by
New Opera Company (in double bill with *Le Rossignol*).

CHARACTERS

Narrator
The Devil
The Soldier
The Princess (dancer)

An *opera* that has no singing, that was designed to be
played in village halls, that has seven instrumentalists accompanying its one dancing and three audible characters? In
1918 Stravinsky was living in Switzerland, short of money
and of a theme on which to compose. He and his friend, the
Swiss writer Ramuz, decided on a collaboration in which the
three elements of music, acting or dancing, and narration,
should be almost equal partners. It would involve the smallest
forces possible and should be possible to play in any hall or
building or even in the open air. The result is a modern
Morality, which makes its not inconsiderable impact as much
by means of the pungent, suggestive music as through an
ironical text. It is difficult to see exactly what category of
musical theatre it fits, but somehow opera seems to be the
nearest. The work has a playing time of about fifty minutes.

Part I.   March of brilliant character (No. 1) sets the scene.
A soldier is on his weary way home from the wars. He stops
and looks through his pack—there's a picture of his girl friend
and, more important, his fiddle, which has been his companion for so long. The fiddle dominates the next section of
music (No. 2: Little tunes beside a brook). The Devil, disguised
as a little old man with a butterfly net, wants to barter the
violin for a book he produces—worth any money, he says, as it
foretells the future. The soldier accepts and when the Devil

1311

finds he cannot play the instrument, the soldier agrees to teach it him.

Off they go together and the soldier lives for two days in great comfort. When he eventually gets home (reprise of the march) he finds that he has been away not three days but three years and that his friends and even his mother and his girl friend take him for a ghost, not a living being at all. Now he understands who was his host for those 'days' of luxury. His dejection and loneliness are shown in a desolate Pastorale (No. 3). He catches sight of his enemy and wants to attack him. But the Devil reminds him of the book he bartered for the fiddle. He starts to read it and its teaching brings him wealth beyond his wildest dreams; only happiness is still out of reach and he starts to long for the good things of the past, symbolised for him by the sound of the fiddle (No. 2). He is rich, but he begins to suspect that he is dead. The Devil comes now in the guise of an old-clothes woman and begs him to buy something, finally producing an ancient violin, *his* old fiddle—again its sound mocks him (No. 2).

Part II.   To the sound of the March (No. 1) the soldier crosses the border to the neighbouring country. In desperation, he has thrown away his possessions and is back as he was at the start, only without his pack. At a frontier inn he hears that the Princess is ill and that the King has promised her hand in marriage to whoever can cure her. Why should he not try his luck? He makes up his mind and to the sound of the Royal march (No. 4: a stylised Spanish *Pasodoble*) he arrives at the Palace Gates and goes inside, only to find the Devil sitting there, disguised as a violin virtuoso. The King receives the Soldier and promises that he may see the Princess next day.

Now the narrator takes a hand in the action and eggs the soldier on to play cards against the Devil—if he loses, he'll have no more of the Devil's money and they will be quits. The ruse works and the soldier finds to his joy that he can play the violin again (No. 5: little concert). Eric White[1] mentions an odd feature of the 'little concert': 'It is curious to find that . . . one of the most memorable themes of *The Soldier's Tale* came to Stravinsky in a dream, during which, according to Schaeffner, he saw a gypsy woman seated on the steps at the back of a caravan, playing a violin with the full

---

[1] In *Stravinsky: a critical survey*, 1947.

length of the bow at the same time as she suckled her child. This haunting minor motif is first heard from the cornet followed by the bassoon in the "little concert"[1] and, later, from the violin in the "tango".[2] Although no very extended use is made of it, its character is so strong that in retrospect it seems to flavour the whole work.'

The music rouses the Princess who is cured during the course of the three dances which follow in sequence (No. 6: tango, waltz and ragtime). Next it is the turn of the Devil, who is obliged to dance till he drops exhausted (No. 7: the Devil's dance). A 'little chorale' (No. 8) celebrates the victory of the lovers, but the Devil in a 'spoken song' (No. 9) swears revenge. There is a 'great chorale' (No. 10) during which the narrator points a moral:

'Il ne faut pas vouloir ajouter à ce qu'on a ce qu'on avait,
On ne peut pas être à la fois qui on est et qui on était.
Il faut savoir choisir; on n'a pas le droit de tout avoir: c'est défendu.
Un bonheur est tout le bonheur; deux, c'est comme s'ils n'existaient.'

There remains but to finish the 'opera'. The Princess suggests that they might visit the soldier's old home and on the way at the frontier the Devil, who has regained the violin, justifies the title of the last piece of music: 'The triumphal march of the Devil' (No. 11). Eric White[3] refers to the role played by the percussion which, he says, 'starts by underlining the violin theme, but gradually develops a more or less independent existence so that, when the other instruments *tacent*, it is left to bring the work to a strange and sombre conclusion. It is as if, once the Devil has finally carried off the soldier, the spirit of the music should abandon its body and only its skeleton remain behind.'[4]

RENARD

A burlesque for the stage, to be sung and acted; based on popular Russian folk tales. Music and words by Igor Stravinsky, French translation by C. F. Ramuz. Première in double-bill with *Mavra* at Paris

[1] Sections 13 to 15, 17 and 18;   [2] Sections 4 and 8.
[3] Op. cit.   [4] Op. cit.

Opéra, June 2, 1922. First produced New York (in concert), 1923; Berlin, 1925; London (B.B.C.), 1935. Revived Edinburgh Festival, 1961, with Murray Dickie, Alfred Hallett, John Lawrenson, Trevor Anthony, conductor Alexander Gibson.

CHARACTERS

The Cock .... Tenor
The Fox .... Tenor
The Goat .... Bass
The Cat .... Bass

Renard was commissioned by Princesse Edmond de Polignac who expressed the view that, after Wagner and Strauss, the time had come to return to works for small and unusual ensembles and suggested that Stravinsky compose a work of this type to be performed in her Paris house. Stravinsky at once proposed *Renard*, which had been germinating in his mind for some time—the duet for the cat and the goat was in fact written some years earlier, while he was working on *Les Noces* in Switzerland. He began work on *Renard* at once and in his enthusiasm he temporarily abandoned the half-finished *Les Noces*.

At this time Stravinsky's friendship with the Swiss writer Ramuz was already well established and, in the course of three years, the two co-operated on the texts of *Les Noces* and *L'Histoire d'un Soldat*, as well as the French translation of *Renard*, whose Russian words Stravinsky himself had already written. This translation took an infinity of time and trouble because of the great importance Stravinsky attached to the relationship of word-sounds and music.

Renard was produced in 1922 for Diaghilev's company by Bronislava Nijinska, the sister of Nijinsky, and the sets were by Larionov, the new work waiting for its première until the completion of *Mavra* (see page 1316).

In a note to the score, Stravinsky says, 'The play is acted by clowns, dancers or acrobats, preferably on a trestle stage placed in front of the orchestra.[1] If performed in a theatre it should be played in front of the curtain. The actors remain on the stage all the time. They come on in view of the audience to the strains of the little march, which serves as an introduction, and make their exit in the same way. The

---

[1] cf. *L'Histoire d'un Soldat*.

actors do not speak. The singers (2 tenors and 2 basses) are placed in the orchestra.' The orchestra is small, containing single woodwind, two horns, trumpet, percussion and single strings, as well as a cembalon, an instrument which had so enchanted Stravinsky when he first heard it in a café in Geneva that he at once bought himself one and learned to play it.

A pompous little *da capo* march introduces the work after which the four singers sing a lively *allegro*, in which they rail against their enemy, the fox. The cock is fidgeting on his perch and we are introduced to him by a broken upward sweep on the cembalon. In a mournful little song he describes his daily life, after which the fox to another cembalon *arpeggio* enters disguised as a nun. He begs the cock to come down and confess his sins, but the cock recognises him and refuses (to a phrase from the first *allegro*). The fox renews his efforts, and reminds the cock of his offensively polygamous domestic arrangements, to such effect that the silly bird hops down from his perch with a resounding crash on cymbal and drums. Renard, of course, grabs him at once and the cock screeches to the cat and the goat to come to his help. They do so and drive the fox away, after which cock, goat and cat dance triumphantly.

The second part begins with the cock climbing complacently on to his perch, to the same cembalon chord as before, and resuming his sad little song which is again interrupted by the fox, this time not in disguise. The fox once more tries to wheedle the cock down to the ground with flattering words and glittering promises, even at one moment—in an attempt at disguise? —using a bass voice. The idiotic cock resists for a time but in the end jumps down again to a resounding bang from the bass drum. The fox pounces and this time things look very black for the poor cock as his friends the cat and the goat take a good deal longer than before in coming to his aid. The fox begins to pull out all his feathers, and the cock, in desperation, sings a *moderato* aria to the fox, begging for mercy. In the end, realising it is all in vain, the cock prays for the welfare of all his surviving relatives and finally passes out.

The cat and the goat enter and sing a jolly *scherzando*, accompanying themselves on the *guzla*. In their song, they pretend to be well disposed towards the fox who becomes momentarily distracted when they suggest that Mrs. Fox is

betraying him; this is their chance and they strangle him. As
he dies the four singers shout triumphantly seven times, after
which the actors dance for joy and in conclusion ask for a
token of gratitude from the audience if they have been
pleased. The opening march is played once more and the
performers leave the stage.   H.

MAVRA

Opera buffa in one act by Igor Stravinsky, text by Boris Kochno
after Pushkin. Première, Paris, June 2, 1922, by Diaghilev company
with Slobodskaya, Sadoven, Rozovska, Skoupevski, conductor Gregor
Fitelberg. First performed Krolloper, Berlin, 1928, London (BBC)
1934, Philadelphia Orchestra, 1934; Rome, 1942, with Iris Adami-
Corradetti, Elvira Casazza, Augusto Ferrauto, conductor Previtali; la
Scala, 1942; Edinburgh Festival, 1958, by Hamburg Opera with Melitta
Muszely, Gisela Litz, Jürgen Förster, conductor Leopold Ludwig.

CHARACTERS

Parasha .... Soprano
The Neighbour .... Mezzo-soprano
The Mother .... Contralto
The Hussar .... Tenor
Time: Charles X   *Place:* Russia

Stravinsky has said that *Mavra* was conceived because the
natural sympathy he had always felt for the melodic
language, vocal style and conventions of the old Russo-Italian
opera induced him to experiment with this style at a time
when it was almost extinct. He thought the form admirably
suitable for the story he had in mind, *The Little House in the
Forest* by Pushkin, and wrote *Mavra* 'in the direct tradition
of Glinka and Dargomijsky'.[1]
   The work was written while the composer was living at
Biarritz but was interrupted by orchestration he had to do
for Diaghilev for the London revival of *The Sleeping Beauty.*
It was completed in March, 1922, except for the overture
which was added later in Paris, and at the première, according
to Diaghilev's plan, *Renard* also received its first performance. The libretto is by Boris Kochno, who later became
Diaghilev's secretary and assistant.

[1] Stravinsky: *Poetics of music: in the form of six lessons* (O.U.P., 1947).

Mavra is totally unlike anything Stravinsky had hitherto attempted; it is indeed the first opera of his which places the *entire responsibility for musical and dramatic effect on the singers* who, for the first time in Stravinsky's output, are permitted to indulge in words, music and action simultaneously. *Le Rossignol*, his first opera, springs to mind as a possible contradiction, but even here the principal singing role is sung from the orchestra pit and not from the stage; *Renard* (see page 1314) has the singers in the pit while the action is mimed on the stage; *Pulcinella* and *Les Noces*, though each has vital singing roles, are none the less pure ballets; *L'Histoire d'un Soldat* is an opera with no singers; in the later *Oedipus Rex* the composer depersonalises his singers with masks and stylized movement until in action they are only just more than puppets; in *Perséphone* he carries the action even further from the singers; in fact, only *The Rake's Progress* apart from *Mavra* has traditional operatic form. In *Mavra* the orchestra rarely takes the attention from the voices except for the infrequent moments when the singers are silent and once during the quartet.

The first performance was directed by Bronislava Nijinska, the sister of Nijinsky, who, Stravinsky says 'had marvellous ideas, which were unfortunately baulked by the inability of the singers to subject themselves to a technique and discipline in the practice of which they were unversed'.[1] One feels a pang of sympathy for these unfortunate artists who, as well as having to cope with Stravinsky's difficult writing, were expected to be able to fulfil the presumably non-vocal ideas of Madame Nijinska.

A Russian Village. The opera opens in the living room of the house occupied by Parasha and her mother. Parasha, in love with the Hussar who lives nearby, sings of her impatience as she sits at her embroidery.[2] Her lover comes to the window and the two sing a duet. The Hussar goes away and the Mother appears, complaining at length of the difficulty of getting a servant now that her old and apparently perfect cook Thecla has died. She urges Parasha to find her a new maid, and Parasha goes off in search of one. The Mother grumbles on and is joined by the Neighbour; the two women

[1] *Stravinsky in the Theatre*; Peter Owen Limited, 1951.
[2] This aria is often heard in Stravinsky's own arrangement for solo violin.

complain happily about the servant problem, the state of the weather and the price of clothes these days.

Parasha comes triumphantly back with a young woman who, she says, will be just right. Her name is Mavra and she used to be in service with old Anna next door. It is, of course, the Hussar in disguise, but the Mother and the Neighbour are both taken in and the four unite in a quartet, the women telling Mavra that the new girl has a lot to live up to after the lamented Thecla, and the Hussar joining in sympathetically. The Neighbour goes home, the Mother upstairs and the scheming lovers sing ecstatically of the success of their plan and the happiness it will bring them.

The Mother reappears, gives Mavra a mass of work to do and takes Parasha off for a walk, saying in an aside that she is going to return early just to make sure the girl is a good worker. Left alone, the Hussar sings of his love for Parasha and the wonderful days which lie ahead, after which he decides to make the most of his solitude and shave himself. In the middle of this operation, complicated as it is by unfamiliar furniture and female attire, the mother comes back and is so shocked at what she sees that she faints. The Neighbour rushes in, and the curtain falls as the Hussar jumps out of the window leaving Parasha calling plaintively after him.   H.

OEDIPUS REX

Opera-oratorio in two acts by Igor Stravinsky; text by Jean Cocteau after Sophocles, translated into Latin by J. Daniélou. Première, Théâtre Sarah Bernhardt, Paris, May 30, 1927 (in concert), conducted by Stravinsky. First performed on the stage in Vienna, 1928; Berlin, 1928, conductor Klemperer; New York (concert), 1928; New York (stage), 1931, conductor Stokowski; Buenos Aires, 1931, with Riavez, conductor Ansermet; London, Queen's Hall (concert), 1936, with Slobodskaya, Widdop, Harold Williams, Norman Walker, conductor Ansermet; Florence Festival, 1937, with Alfano, Malipiero, conductor Molinari; la Scala, Milan, 1948, with Danco, Demetz, conductor Sanzogno; Berlin, 1951, with Ilosvay, Krebs, Frick, conductor Fricsay; Cologne, 1951, with Mödl, Pears, Rehfuss, conductor Stravinsky (concert); Paris, 1952, with Zareska, Simoneau, conductor Stravinsky (staged by Cocteau); Holland Festival, 1952, with Bouvier, Vroons, conductor Bruck; Edinburgh, 1956, by Hamburg Company, with Ilosvay, Melchert; Sadler's Wells, 1960, with Monica Sinclair, Dowd, conductor Colin Davis; New York, City Opera, 1959, with Claramae

Turner, Cassilly, conductor Stokowski; la Scala, Milan, 1969, with
Horne, Lajos Kozma, conductor Abbado.

CHARACTERS

Oedipus, *King of Thebes* . . . . Tenor
Jocasta, *his wife* . . . . .Mezzo-Soprano
[1] Creon, *Jocasta's brother* . . . . Bass-Baritone
Tiresias, *a soothsayer* . . . . Bass
The Shepherd . . . . Tenor
[1] The Messenger . . . . Bass-Baritone
Chorus (Tenors and Basses)

The action is continuous, although divided into two acts.
It is put forward in the shape of six tableaux, with a
minimum of action (the characters are directed to give the
impression of living statues), and that explained beforehand
in the language of the audience by a narrator. The text is in
Latin.

Act I.   1. The Narrator sets the scene for the audience; of
Oedipus he says: 'At the moment of his birth a snare was laid
for him—and you will see the snare closing'. In the opening
chorus, 'Kaedit nos pestis',[2] the men of Thebes lament the
plague which is destroying the inhabitants of the town. They
beg their king, Oedipus, to help them in their affliction. This
he promises to do: 'Liberi, vos liberabo.'

2. Creon, who has been sent to Delphi to consult the
oracle, returns. In an aria, 'Respondit deus', he reports that
the god has revealed that Laius's murderer still lives on in
Thebes, undetected and unpunished. He must be discovered.
Oedipus answers that he himself, with his skill in solving
riddles, will track down the murderer: 'Non reperias vetus
skelus.'

3. The chorus prays to Minerva, Diana and Phoebus (or
Athene, Artemis, and Apollo, as they would be in Greek),
and welcomes Tiresias, whom Oedipus has decided to con-

[1] These roles may be taken by the same singer.

[2] The spelling used is often onomatopoeic, to ensure uniform
pronunciation.

sult. Tiresias is blind, and referred to by the Narrator as 'the
fountain of truth', but at first he refuses to answer the King's
questions. Oedipus taunts him, and he makes it clear that he
will hold nothing more back: the King's assassin is a
king! ('Dikere non possum'). Oedipus is furious at the implication behind the words, and suggests that Creon and Tiresias
are in league to oust him from the throne: 'Stipendarius es'
he snarls at Tiresias. The aria ('Invidia fortunam odit') dies
away in silence, and is succeeded by a magnificent chorus of
greeting and praise to Queen Jocasta; 'Gloria!' This is the end
of the first act.

Act II begins with a reprise of the sonorous 'Gloria'
chorus.

4. Jocasta is now seen on the stage. She has come, says the
Narrator, attracted by the dispute of her husband and her
brother. How can they raise their voices thus in anger in the
stricken city ('Nonn' erubeskite, reges')? Oracles, she says
are accustomed to deceive those who consult them ('Mentita
sunt oracula'); did they not predict that her former husband

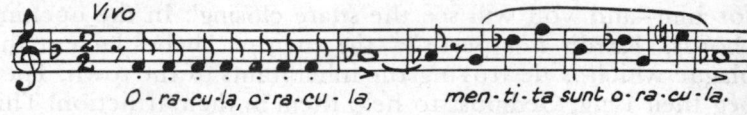

O - ra - cu - la, o - ra - cu - la,   men - ti - ta sunt o - ra - cu - la.

Laius, would be killed by his own son, and was he not in fact
murdered by robbers at the cross-roads ('trivium') between
Daulia and Delphi? The chorus takes up the word 'trivium'
but its repetition has the effect of filling Oedipus with
horror. In a duet with Jocasta ('Pavesco subito, Jocasta') he
explains that on his way from Corinth to Thebes he himself
killed a stranger at that very cross-roads. Jocasta makes an
attempt to reassure him ('Oracula mentiuntur'), but it is of
little avail.

5. The messenger steps forward to inform Oedipus that
King Polybus is dead, and that Oedipus, so far from being his
son, was only adopted by him. The messenger goes on to tell
how Oedipus as a baby was rescued by a shepherd after he
had been abandoned on the mountain side and then handed
over to King Polybus ('Reppereram in monte puerum
Oedipoda'). The shepherd corroborates his evidence, and his
words so overwhelm the Queen that she disappears from the
scene, convinced and horror-stricken by what she has heard.
Oedipus, however, thinks she is merely ashamed of his

apparently lowly birth ('Nonne monstrum reskituri'), and it is only after the messenger and the shepherd unite to accuse him of parricide and incest that he is conscious of his crime and its enormity. The chorus repeats the words of the King's accusers, after which shepherd and messenger withdraw. With a quiet dignity that has not been in evidence in his previous utterances, Oedipus resigns himself to acknowledging the truth. On the words 'Lux facta est', he disappears.[1]

6. The messenger reappears, and the Narrator explains that the audience is about to hear the monologue: 'The divine Jocasta is dead'; he describes how she has hanged herself and how Oedipus has pierced his eyeballs with the golden pin Jocasta wore. He bids farewell to Oedipus—Oedipus whom his people loved.

The great scene in which the messenger and the chorus bewail Jocasta's suicide ('Divum Jocastae caput mortuum!')

brings the work to its emotional climax. As the messenger disappears, and Oedipus is seen with his pierced eyes, the chorus comments gently on his broken condition and bids him a last farewell.

The work is short (it lasts about an hour), and from the opening chorus the expression is direct and, whether Stravinsky liked it or not, emotional. Oedipus himself is a fascinating character study, passing as he does from the heights of power and self-confidence, through arrogance (in his attitude to Creon and Tiresias) and self-pity ('Amiki, amiki' in the aria 'Invidia fortunam odit'), until he reaches a condition of understanding and horror at his position. It is interesting to note that he uses a musical language that is, in its vocal line, curiously like that of Monteverdi's *Orfeo*, particularly in its expressive use of coloratura (e.g. Ex. 1). Oedipus is the central figure, but the climaxes are often associated with his surroundings. Successive heights of intensity are reached with the magnificent 'Gloria' chorus which closes the first act and begins the second, the aria for Jocasta and her duet with Oedipus, and the very powerful section in

---

[1] By means of a trap-door, according to the original stage directions.

which the Messenger and the chorus lament the suicide of Jocasta. The form of the work may seem anti-operatic to those who have not heard it; but the music expresses drama and character in every bar, and even if stylisation had been avoided and movement included at every possible moment, nothing would have been added to the total effect, which, as far as I am concerned, remains shattering.   H.

THE RAKE'S PROGRESS

Opera in three acts and an epilogue by Igor Stravinsky; text by W. H. Auden and Chester Kallman. Première, Venice Festival, September 11, 1951, with Schwarzkopf, Tourel, Tangeman, Rounseville, Otakar Kraus, Cuénod, Arié, conductor Stravinsky. First performed Zürich, 1951, with Harvey, Malaniuk, Lichtegg, Wolff, conductor Reinshagen; Stuttgart, 1951, with Wissmann, Marta Fuchs, Holm, Neidlinger, conductor Leitner; la Scala, Milan, 1951, with Schwarzkopf, Elmo, Picchi, Kraus, Cuénod, conductor Leitner; Vienna, 1952, with Berger, Höngen, Schock, Jerger, conductor Hollreiser; London (B.B.C. broadcast), 1953, with Catley, Pollak, Young, Kraus, conductor Sacher; Metropolitan, New York, 1953, with Güden, Thebom, Conley, Harrell, conductor Reiner; Edinburgh Festival (Glyndebourne Company), 1953, with Elsie Morison, Merriman, Richard Lewis, Hines, conductor Wallenstein; Sadler's Wells, 1962, with Morison, Young, Herincx, conductor Colin Davis; Edinburgh Festival, by Scottish Opera, 1967, with Elizabeth Robson, Cervena, Alexander Young, van der Bilt, conductor Gibson.

CHARACTERS

Trulove	Bass
Anne, *his daughter*	Soprano
Tom Rakewell, *her sweetheart*	Tenor
Nick Shadow	Baritone
Mother Goose, *a brothel-keeper*	Mezzo-Soprano
Baba the Turk, *bearded lady in a circus*	Mezzo-Soprano
Sellem, *the auctioneer*	Tenor
Keeper of the Madhouse	Bass

Whores and Roaring Boys, Servants, Citizens, Madmen

Time: Eighteenth Century   *Place:* England

Act I. After a very short prelude, the scene opens to show the garden of Trulove's house in the country. It is spring. In an arbour, Anne and Tom are seated. A trio develops, Anne and Tom rejoicing in the season which seems made for their love ('The woods are green'), and Trulove in the background expressing the hope that his fears about Tom's future may prove unfounded. Anne goes indoors and Mr. Trulove tells Tom that he has secured for him the offer of a city position. When Tom declines, he comments that his daughter may choose a poor husband, but he will see to it she does not marry a lazy one.

Tom alone is scornful of his prospective father-in-law's attitude; why should he waste his time in an office? He has other plans, and proposes to rely primarily on the goddess of fortune. 'Since it is not by merit we rise or we fall,' is the

Since it is not by merit we rise or we fall

burden of his aria, whose vigorous expression suggests that Tom underestimates his own energies. He breaks off: 'I wish I had money.' Immediately a figure appears at the garden gate, and asks for Tom Rakewell. It is Nick Shadow, the bearer, so he says, of good tidings for Tom and anyone else who wishes him well. Tom calls into the house for Anne and Trulove, and Nick tells all three that Tom has been left a fortune by an unknown uncle.

Tom rejoices in his good luck ('I wished but once, I knew that surely my wish would come true'), and thanks Nick for his tidings. Nick in his turn thanks him that he has found a new master, and Anne and Trulove thank God for the turn in Tom's fortunes. The words 'Be thanked' for each character are set to a dropping minor ninth. For a moment, Tom and Anne sing happily to one another ('O clement love'), but Nick interrupts to say that the inheritance of a fortune entails certain business transactions; they must go up to London immediately. Anne starts to say good-bye to Tom, Nick returns to say the carriage waits, and Tom agrees to reckon up what his services have been worth a year and a day after his engagement. A further farewell, a further warning on the part of Trulove that fortune so easily come by may prove an inducement to idleness, and the stage is clear. Nick turns to the audience: 'The Progress of a Rake begins.'

Scene ii is set in Mother Goose's brothel. It opens with a brilliant introduction and chorus for Whores and Roaring Boys:

Roaring Boys: With air commanding and weapon handy
            We rove in a band through the streets at night,
            Our only notion to make commotion
            And find occasion to provoke a fight.

Whores: With darting glances and bold advances
            We open fire upon young and old;
            Surprised by rapture, their hearts are captured,
            And into our laps they pour their gold.

Nick asks Tom to recite to Mother Goose what he has been taught: 'One aim in all things to pursue: My duty to myself to do.' etc. Only when Nick mentions the word 'love' does Tom falter in his lesson: 'That precious word is like a fiery coal, it burns my lips.' Nick introduces Tom to the company as 'a stranger to our rites', and according to custom, Tom is asked to sing. 'Love, too frequently betrayed' is the theme of his beautiful cavatina, with its rippling clarinet accompaniment.

'How sad a song,' comment the habitués of the brothel; but sorrow is quickly forgotten in such surroundings. Mother Goose claims Tom as hers for the night, the chorus form a lane with the men on one side and the women on the other, as in a children's game, and Mother Goose and Tom walk slowly between them to a door back-stage. The chorus sings away merrily (in a manner not far removed from 'Oranges and Lemons') and their refrain, 'Lanterloo', brings the scene to an end.

The third scene has the same setting as the first. Anne is sad that no word has come from Tom since he left for London. 'Quietly, Night, O find him and caress' she sings in a full-scale aria. There is an interruption as Trulove calls from the house, and Anne makes up her mind that Tom needs her more than her father does. This gives the cue for the cabaletta (Stravinsky actually uses the word in the score— perhaps the only time a composer has ever done this); it is a lively tune punctuated by a brilliant little orchestral *ritornello:* 'I go to him. Love cannot falter.'

Act II, scene i. Morning room of Tom's house in London. Tom is at breakfast. He has not found happiness in London, and he sings of the city's disillusion, which he contrasts with life as it would have been at the side of the one true person he knows and of whom now he dare not even think. The music is in the form of an extended, loosely knit *scena*: 'Vary the song, O London, change!'

At Tom's words 'I wish I were happy', Nick appears and
hows his master an advertisement for a circus, in which is
eatured Baba the Turk, the bearded lady. Let him advise his
naster: marry Baba! If he wants to be free and happy, he
nust be unlike the 'giddy multitude . . driven by the un-
redictable Must of their pleasures and the sober few . . .
ound by the inflexible Ought of their Duty'; he must 'learn
o ignore those twin tyrants of appetite and conscience'. How
etter than by marrying Baba? The music of Nick's aria,
That man alone his fate fulfils', for the first time suggests the
inister purpose behind the façade of bonhomie. Tom looks
ip from the broadsheet and begins to laugh: 'My tale shall be
old, Both by young and by old.' It is agreed that he shall
narry Baba the Turk.

Scene ii.   Outside Tom's house in London. Anne has
rrived and is waiting apprehensively for him to return home.
A procession of servants carries parcels into the house, and
Anne wonders what their significance can be. A sedan chair is
orne in. Tom gets out of it and comes quickly up to Anne.
he must leave London, where 'Virtue is a day coquette', and
orget him; he is not worthy of her. At that moment a head is
oked out of the sedan chair; it is Baba, heavily veiled,
lemanding to know how much longer she is to be kept
vaiting. Tom admits she is his wife. There is a trio in which
Anne and Tom sing of their might-have-beens, and Baba
xpresses her extreme dislike of being kept waiting. Anne
eaves, Tom helps Baba from the chair, and, to the acclama-
ions of a crowd which has gathered to welcome her, she
nters the house. As a climax to the scene, she unveils and
eveals her beard.

Scene iii.   The same room as Act II, scene i, except that it is
now cluttered up with every conceivable kind of object:
tuffed animals and birds, cases of minerals, china, glass, etc.
Tom and Baba are at breakfast. Tom sulks, but Baba chatters
on breathlessly and appears to be in the middle of a detailed
nventory of her possessions, which she has picked up all over
he world in the course of her colourful career. After a bit
he becomes conscious that Tom has not spoken, and turns
ovingly to him. He repulses her, and, losing her temper, she
aces furiously about the room, smashing the more fragile
ut less valuable parts of her collection, and proclaiming
ngrily that Tom must be in love with the girl he met when
hey first came to the house. She embarks on a florid phrase,

but Tom, throwing patience to the winds, seizes his wig which is standing nearby, and shoves it over her face back to front so that she is cut off in mid-note.

His misery is complete, and there is only one remedy: sleep. While he is asleep, Nick comes in, wheeling an object covered with a dust sheet. He removes it and discloses a fantastic baroque machine, into which he puts first a loaf of bread, and then above it a piece of broken china. He turns the handle, out comes the loaf. Tom wakes up with the words 'I wish it were true', and explains to Nick that he has had a dream in which he invented a machine which turned stones to bread, and so relieved the sufferings of mankind. Nick asks him if it was anything like what he sees beside him, and Tom demonstrates it to his own complete satisfaction. Nick encourages Tom to think he may make his fortune with this invention, then suggests he ought to tell his wife. 'My wife?' says Tom with a gesture in her direction, 'I have no wife. I've buried her.'

Act III.   The first scene is laid in Tom's room, as for Act II, scene iii, except that now everything is covered in dust and cobwebs. Baba is still sitting motionless at the table, where she was left with the wig over her face. An auction is about to take place, and the citizens are examining the objects up for sale. From time to time, they comment on the extravagance and false promises which have brought ruin to so many and which have caused this sale. Anne comes in, searching for Tom, but no one can give her any definite news of him. She decides to look for him in the house.

The door is flung open and in comes Sellem, preceded by servants carrying an auctioneer's apparatus. He gets down to business straightaway, and his patter is as resourceful (and as meaningless) as one would expect. It is all carried off with great style, and the waltz tune as Sellem puts up the various items is positively elegant in its inconsequentiality (as anyone will know who heard the incomparable performance of Hugues Cuénod at the première). Finally he comes to Baba, whom he introduces in an awe-struck whisper:

> An unknown object draws us, draws us near.
> A cake? An organ? Golden Apple Tree?

The bidding rises higher and higher, and Sellem, to calm the crowd, snatches off the wig. Baba finishes her phrase, and turns to strike consternation into the bystanders. Each knows

33 *The Rake's Progress*: Jenny Tourel, Tom Rounseville and Elisabeth Schwarzkopf in the Street scene at the 1951 première.

34 *War and Peace* by English National Opera: Norman Bailey as
Kutuzov (*above*); Raymond Myers as Napoleon during the burning of
Moscow (*below*).

her, and she dominates all. Even the sound of the voices of Tom and Nick off-stage (singing a ballad tune which resembles 'Lilliburlero') in no way disconcerts her: 'The pigs of plunder' is her only comment. She comforts Anne: 'You love him, seek to set him right: He's but a shuttle-headed lad'; then, with the greatest dignity announces her intention of returning to the stage and her interrupted career.

Again, the voices of Tom and Nick are heard below, and Anne leads the *stretto-finale*: 'I go to him, I go, I go, I go, I go to him.' Baba tells Sellem to fetch her carriage, and orders the crowd out of her way: 'The next time you see Baba, you shall pay.'

The scene changes to a churchyard. The smell of death is in the music, and Tom's utterances have a new sense of seriousness:

Nick reveals himself in his true colours (to the tune of the ballad):

> A year and a day have passed away
> Since first to you I came . . .

> 'Tis not your money but your soul
> Which I this night require.

The vocal writing for Tom, caught in the trap of his own devising, in some respects recalls that for Oedipus in a similar situation; it is Stravinsky at his most expressive and his most powerful, and the crucial scene of the opera. Nick relents to the extent of inviting Tom to play cards in a last effort to save himself from hell. Tom wins the game, but in his rage Nick condemns him to insanity.

Nick sinks into a nearby grave and the stage remains dark for a moment. When the lights come up again, Tom is sitting on a green mound, putting grass in his hair and singing in a child-like voice: 'With roses crowned, I sit on ground, Adonis is my name' (the ballad-tune again). The scene is very short, but the musical suggestion of madness is achieved with economy of means but extremely moving results:

The scene changes to Bedlam. Tom is surrounded by madmen. In his own mind he is still Adonis, and he exhorts the company to prepare for his wedding with Venus. The sound of a key turning in the lock is heard, and the chorus's reaction is swift:

> Hark! Minos comes who cruel is and strong:
> Beware! Away! His whip is keen and long.

But it is the gaoler bringing with him Anne, who has come to visit Tom. Anne addresses Tom as Adonis, and in a moment he is happy not only that she has come, but that he is proved right in the sight of his fellow madmen, who predicted that no Venus would answer his call. There is a love duet, and at its end Anne helps the exhausted Tom on to the straw pallet, which lies in the middle of the room. She rocks him to sleep with a Lullaby.

Gent - ly,   lit -tle boat, A-cross the o-cean float

The gaoler brings in her father, who leads her gently away. When she has gone, Tom wakes and raves of his Venus, who was with him and has disappeared. The others will not believe that she was ever there, and he sinks back dead on the mattress.

> Mourn for Adonis, ever young, the dear
> Of Venus: weep, tread softly round his bier.

The curtain descends and in front of it step the five principal characters, Anne, Baba, Tom, Nick, and Trulove, to sing an epilogue. The Moral:

> For idle hands
> And hearts and minds
> The Devil finds
> A work to do.

H.

SERGEI SERGYEEVICH PROKOFIEV

(1891–1953)

THE GAMBLER

OPERA in four acts (six scenes), music by Sergei Prokofiev, text (after Dostoievsky's novel, *Igrok*, '*The Gambler*') by the composer. Première, Brussels, April 29, 1929, in a French translation by Paul Spaak, conducted by Corneil de Thoran. First performed in Italy, Naples, 1953, with Barbato, Gardino, Pirazzini, Annaloro, Sinimberghi, Tajo, conductor Scherchen; in Germany, Darmstadt, 1956; Belgrade, 1961, with Heybalova, Starč, Zarko Cvejič, conductor Danon; Edinburgh Festival, 1962, with Belgrade Company.

CHARACTERS

The General, *a retired army officer* (55) . . . . .Bass
Pauline, *the General's step-daughter* . . . . Soprano
Alexey, *tutor to the General's children* (25) . . . . . Tenor
'Babulenka', *the General's rich aunt* (75) .Mezzo-Soprano
The Marquis . . . . Tenor
Mr. Astley, *a rich Englishman* . . . . Baritone
Blanche, *a demi-mondaine* (25) . . . . Contralto
Prince Nilsky . . . . Tenor

Baron Würmerhelm (45) . . . . Bass
Baroness Würmerhelm . . . . .Mute
Potapitsch, *Babulenka's steward* . . . . Baritone
In the Gambling scene:
   The Director . . . . Bass
   The first croupier . . . . Tenor
   The second croupier . . . . Tenor
   The fat Englishman . . . . Bass
   The tall Englishman . . . . Bass
   The florid lady . . . . Soprano
   The pale lady .Mezzo-Soprano
   A respectable old lady . . . . .Mezzo-Soprano
   A suspicious old lady . . . . Contralto
   A heated gambler . . . . Tenor
   A gambler in ill-health . . . . Tenor
   A hunch-backed gambler . . . . Tenor
   An unlucky gambler . . . . Baritone
   An old gambler . . . . Bass

Six gamblers . . . . { 2 Tenors / 2 Baritones / 2 Basses

The Head-waiter, the Page-boy; Babulenka's three servants;
Gamblers, People staying in the hotel, servants, Porters.
Time: 1865   *Place:* The imaginary town of Roulettenburg

Prokofiev was fascinated by the theatre from the time his
parents took him to Moscow when he was eight, and he
wrote some half a dozen operas before the end of his student
days, one of which (*Maddalena*; 1911, revised 1913) nearly
reached the stage. Albert Coates in the early days of the war
was in the process of replacing Nápravník as head of the
Maryinsky Theatre in St. Petersburg, and plans to stage *The
Gambler* in 1917—the first opera on a subject by
Dostoievsky—were only prevented by the Revolution. In
1927-8 Prokofiev revised the orchestration and rewrote
certain passages which he had come to regard as 'mere
padding disguised by monstrous chords', for another projected production (also for Leningrad), but again it came to
nothing and the work received its première in Brussels a year
later, and then languished a further 24 before again coming to
the notice of the European opera houses.

Like Merimée's Don José and the Abbé Prévost's Chevalier
des Grieux, Dostoievsky's Alexey Ivanovich is the teller of

the story of *The Gambler*, here cast in the form of a diary. Unlike Bizet and Massenet, Prokofiev refuses to displace his hero, but keeps Alexey at the centre of the story; the end is changed and Prokofiev chooses not to follow Dostoievsky in showing Alexey the successful gambler declining through a sojourn with Blanche in Paris to become a hopeless gambling addict, borrowing money from the friendly Astley and quite uninterested in the latter's assurance that Pauline still loves him.

The background of the opera is an imaginary German spa by the name of Roulettenburg, in reality Wiesbaden. There a retired Russian General waits for news that a rich relation (always referred to as Babulenka—Grandmama—but in reality his aunt) has died leaving him her fortune. With him are his young children, his step-daughter Pauline, and the children's tutor, Alexey. The General has borrowed large sums of money from the rich French Marquis and has fallen in love with Blanche. Alexey for his part loves Pauline, who has in the past had an affair with the Marquis.

Act I.   The garden of the Grand Hotel in Roulettenburg. In a few short, halting sentences which seem to epitomise the ambivalent relationship between them, Pauline elicits from Alexey that he has staked and lost the money she gave him to gamble with. Blanche, the Marquis and Mr. Astley appear and watch the General open a telegram which to their chagrin still speaks of Babulenka's health, not yet of her death. They advise Alexey to give up gambling, but he reacts vigorously: his Tartar nature forbids something so tame as earning merely in order to save. To Astley, Alexey spits out his dislike of the other's hyprocrisy, then, in a scene with Pauline, explains that to win he must gamble with his own money—when that happens he will pay her debts, he will declare the passion he feels for her.

Re-enter the General, thanking the Marquis for yet another loan and singing an I.O.U. which, to his dismay, is for double what he has received. Alone with Alexey again, Pauline asks if he would live up to his promise to die for her—would he kill if she named the man? Alexey refuses to take her seriously, but when, as climax to their scene together, she orders him almost in a frenzy to insult the fat Baroness Würmerhelm, he reluctantly goes towards his unsuspecting victim, crudely declares himself her slave, and the curtain falls on a scene of general consternation.

Act II.   In the hall of the hotel casino, the General rebukes Alexey for his conduct, but is unprepared for Alexey's vigorous reaction: what right had someone who is neither his father nor his guardian to apologise on his behalf? As Alexey leaves, the General is begging him to behave with restraint.

Alexey returns to find only Mr. Astley, with whom he discusses at first his own predicament, then the General's affair with Blanche, who was originally in Roulettenburg with an Italian Prince and was later barred from the Casino at the request of Baroness Würmerhelm, who saw her making advances to her husband. Now, she has caught the General and, once he inherits, she will become his wife—and Pauline will be snapped up by the money-lending Marquis! At that moment the Marquis himself puts in an appearance and attempts rather clumsily to dissuade Alexey from aggravating the affair with the Germans, supporting his case with a note from Pauline. Alexey mutters to himself that he will eventually square accounts with the Marquis.

As Blanche and the General discuss the imminence of the General's inheritance, Babulenka herself appears on the scene in a wheel chair and attended by her servants, come, she announces, to try her hand at this gambling they all appear to enjoy so much. All salute her in turn, Alexey and Pauline with affection and respect, the General with considerable embarrassment, Blanche and the Marquis somewhat distantly. The old lady tells them that she cured herself by sending the doctors away, that she knows moreover that they have all been waiting for her to die. As Babulenka is carried up to her room to rest before going to the tables, Blanche departs on the arm of Prince Nilsky.

Act III.   A room in the Grand Hotel, outside the gaming rooms. Inside the old lady is gambling away her fortune; outside, the General bemoans the turn of events and fails to enlist either the sympathy of Blanche or the help of Alexey, who alone has any influence on Babulenka. Prince Nilsky's announcement of further losses galvanises the General to make a last effort, and he rushes into the Casino, leaving Blanche to take the Prince's arm and Alexey to reflect that were it not for Pauline he would be laughing at their imminent downfall. Pauline is perpetually in his thoughts, and mention of her name brings her rapidly to the scene, for him to repeat his declaration that he is always at her service.

The old lady reappears; she has lost all the money she brought with her and is leaving immediately. In music of genuine warmth she asks Pauline to accompany her. Pauline hesitates; at least, warns the old woman, let her beware of the Marquis, from whom can come no good. The General wants to get into the old lady's room, but Potapitsch bars the way, and the General in his distraught condition intermittently forgets his immediate purpose and falls to lamenting Blanche's unkindness towards him.

Act IV.   The first scene takes place in Alexey's room, where he finds Pauline waiting for him. The Marquis has written to say that, bearing in mind that Alexey has gambled away her share of the family fortunes, he has ordered his agents to preserve for her the twenty thousand francs from the sale of the General's property. Alexey is indignant at such insulting behaviour, but his suggestion that she borrow from Astley stings Pauline into asking if she should give herself to the Englishman rather than to him. Alexey's astonishment is complete, but with it comes an idea and he runs off.

A frenzied orchestral introduction takes us to the brilliantly lit gambling room. For a moment Alexey watches the play, then it is his turn. He stakes successfully on red, stakes and wins again and eventually in an extraordinary run of luck breaks the bank at the first table. He rushes to the second table, followed by several other gamblers, and repeats his incredible luck; then to a third, always with a winning streak that excites envy and admiration. This is one of Prokofiev's most brilliant scenes, a *Cours à l'abîme* in *scherzo* form, and the voices of the players cross and intermingle without merging into a chorus. The music captures the over-heated atmosphere, the rapt concentration of the players, the almost ritualistic movements of the croupiers with their incantations of 'Les jeux sont faits . . . Rien ne va plus'.

An entr'acte[1] preserves, even enhances, the tension of the previous scene, with the cries of the gamblers coming from behind the lowered curtain, and the last scene returns to Alexey's room. He relives his success, then suddenly remembers Pauline who is watching him, and offers her the money to throw in the Marquis's teeth. She reacts with peals

[1] In the Belgrade production, which was seen in Edinburgh, used as a prologue to the opera (with the curtain up) as well as appearing in its proper place.

of laughter, and it is in a context of hysteria that they declare they will never part, will together take refuge with Babulenka. Now, Pauline insists, where are the fifty thousand francs? He hands the money over, and with all her strength she hurls it back at him. 'Pauline', he cries after her; then his thoughts go back to the casino and the unrepeatable run of luck, and as the curtain falls, he is staring fixedly at an imaginary roulette wheel.   H.

THE LOVE FOR THREE ORANGES
Lyubov k trem Apelsinam

Opera in a prologue and four acts by Sergei Prokofiev; text by the composer after the comedy of Carlo Gozzi. Première, Chicago, December 30, 1921, with Koshetz, Pavlovska, Falco, Dusseau, Mojica, Dua, Defrère, Cotreuil, Dufranne, conductor Prokofiev. First performed New York (Manhattan Opera House), 1922, with Chicago cast; Cologne, 1925, with Elsa Foerster, conductor Szenkar; Berlin, 1926; Leningrad, 1927; la Scala, Milan, 1947, with Gatta, Madonna, Ticozzi, del Signore, Nessi, Colombo, Arié, Dalamangas, conductor Questa; Edinburgh Festival, 1962, Belgrade Opera, with Heybalova, Andrasevič, Zarko Cvejič, conductor Danon; Sadler's Wells, 1963, with Hunter, de Peyer, Garrard, conductor Lovett. Revived with great success, New York City Centre, 1949, with Faull, Mayer, Haskins, Nadell, Rounseville, Gauld, Tyers, Winters, conductor Halasz.

CHARACTERS

The King of Clubs, *ruler of an imaginary kingdom,*
    whose inhabitants are clothed as playing cards .. Bass
The Prince, *his son* .... Tenor
Princess Clarissa, *niece of the King* .... Contralto
Leandro, *his prime minister, dressed as King of*
    Spades .... Baritone
Truffaldino, *jester* .... Tenor
Pantaloon, *friend and adviser of the King* ..... Baritone
The Magician Tchelio, *protector of the King* ...... Bass
Fata Morgana, *a witch, protectress of Leandro* . Soprano
Linetta   ⎱ *the Princesses hidden*   ⎰ Contralto
Nicoletta ⎰ *in oranges*   ⎰ Mezzo-Soprano
Ninetta   ⎰   ⎰ Soprano
The Cook .... Bass
Farfarello, *a devil* .... Bass
Smeraldina, *Fata Morgana's black servant* .Mezzo-Soprano

The Master of Ceremonies .... Tenor
The Herald .... Bass
The Trumpeter .... Bass Trombone
Ten Reasonable Spectators .... Five Tenors, Five Basses
    Monsters, Drunkards, Gluttons, Guards, Servants,
    Soldiers, Jokers, Highbrows, Wits, Romantics,
    Lowbrows, Little Devils, Doctors, Courtiers

The opera is a farcical but entertaining re-working of the
commedia dell'arte atmosphere (itself partly parody) of
Gozzi's play. The prologue shows the dispute between the
protagonists of the various forms of theatrical entertainment.
Each faction insists that nothing other than their favourite
shall be played, but all are put to confusion when ten masked
announcers appear to inform them that, whatever they say,
they are going to see something quite different from what
they are used to, 'The Love for Three Oranges'! The curtain
parts to allow a 'trumpeter' (playing a bass trombone) to
announce the appearance of a herald, who in his turn
announces that the burden of the story is the apparently
incurable hypochondria of the son of the King of Clubs.
    Act I, scene i.   The King's palace. The doctors inform the
King that his son cannot be cured of his illness, and the King
immediately goes into paroxysms of grief; who will succeed
him if his son is removed from him? His odious niece, Clarissa,
presumably. Here there is some anxiety amongst the spectators on the stage in case the King should lose his dignity.
The King makes up his mind that the boy must be made to
laugh, as the physicians allowed that there was a chance of
curing him if that could be achieved. Pantaloon suggests that
the most likely way of doing it would be through feasts and
theatrical performances. He shouts for Truffaldino, who
undertakes to arrange everything, and disappears.
    The King sends for Leandro and orders that plans for
feasts and spectacles be put in train. Leandro, who is not at
all anxious for the Prince's recovery, tries to raise objections
to the scheme, and the scene ends with Leandro and
Pantaloon shouting abuse at each other.
    The stage darkens, a curtain covered with cabalistic signs
descends, and Tchelio and Fata Morgana, surrounded by a
chorus of little devils, proceed to play against each other with
gigantic cards. Behind their chairs, the representations of the
King of Clubs and the King of Spades respectively show that

the game is in effect that of the King's protector against
Leandro's. Tchelio loses. The music occurs in the orchestral
suite[1] as 'Scène infernale'.

The scene returns to the King's palace, where Leandro and
the wicked Clarissa have reached an understanding, whereby
the Princess undertakes to marry Leandro, who must encompass the Prince's death and so clear the way for her accession.
She is not satisfied with the progress so far made, but
Leandro is confident that his method—to fill the Prince full
of tragic prose and boring verse—will yet prove lethal. There
is an interruption as the spectators in the boxes get out of
hand and invade the stage. When Clarissa demands action,
Leandro discovers the negress Smeraldina is eavesdropping.
They threaten to kill her, but she reveals that Tchelio
protects the Prince and may yet succeed in his stratagems to
make him laugh. Only through the intervention of Fata
Morgana, her mistress, can this be avoided. If she comes to the
festivity, all will yet be well. The three voices are raised,
calling for Fata Morgana.

Act II. The Prince's room. He is surrounded with
medicines of all sorts and on his head is a compress. He is ill
and bored, and none of Truffaldino's antics suffices to make
him laugh. In the end, Truffaldino persuades him to dress and
watch the diversions which have been planned for his benefit.
The well-known march begins in the orchestra, and continues

[1] The suite consists of Les ridicules, Scène infernale, Marche,
Scherzo, Le Prince et la Princesse, La Fuite.

as an interlude to the second scene, which takes place in the great hall of the palace. The King is there with Clarissa, and also in evidence are Leandro and Pantaloon. The Prince is dressed in a thick coat and covered in furs lest he catch cold.

Truffaldino stages a comic battle between 'Monsters', and later turns loose a crowd of drunkards and gluttons to fight for food and drink; all to no avail—the Prince does not laugh. In despair, he looks round and catches sight of the witch Fata Morgana. He is horrified that such an old hag should intrude and tries to eject her. In their struggle, she loses her balance, does an involuntary somersault, and achieves the apparently impossible; the Prince starts to laugh. The whole court, and even the spectators, join in, and in their delight, everyone starts to dance—everyone, that is to say, apart from Leandro and Clarissa who are anything but pleased at the turn events have taken.

But Fata Morgana is not long in recovering from her discomfiture. She curses the Prince and, surrounded by her troop of little devils, pronounces his fate; he will fall in love with three oranges, and will pursue them to the ends of the earth. Immediately, the Prince starts to cry out that he will depart forthwith on his journey, accompanied by Truffaldino. Amidst general lamentation, the little devil Farfarello appears and with a pair of bellows wafts the wanderers on their way.

Act III. The desert. Tchelio makes a vain attempt to restrain Farfarello from wafting the Prince and his companion to perdition, but Farfarello tells him that his loss at cards has rendered his magic powers inoperative—and he proves as much by disobeying him. The Prince and Truffaldino appear, and the Magician, having discovered they are seeking the three oranges, advises them, if they ever find them, to cut them open only near water. He also warns them that they are in the keeping of the terrible Creonte, who takes the form of a gigantic cook. In case it may help, he gives Truffaldino a magic ribbon, hoping it may distract the cook's attention while they filch the oranges.

Farfarello appears again with his bellows and like lightning the Prince and Truffaldino are transported towards their destination. This is the *scherzo* of the suite, which, with the March, has become the most popular section of the work.

The two adventurers stand in front of the castle, and are filled with fright at what lies before them. They are about to go into the kitchen, when from it emerges the colossal cook. Both hide, but Truffaldino is quickly discovered and saved from the cook's wrath only because the latter sees and falls hopelessly for the ribbon round his neck. Meanwhile the Prince creeps silently into the kitchen and emerges a moment later with the three oranges, which are of a calibre that befits their vast guardian. The cook asks for the ribbon, is given it as a present, and capers with delight, while, to the music of the *scherzo*, the Prince and Truffaldino make their escape.

We meet them again in the desert, where the oranges they have been carrying have grown to really huge dimensions, big enough one might think to contain a human being. The Prince falls asleep, but Truffaldino is so thirsty he cannot resist cutting open one of the oranges, which, in spite of Tchelio's warning, he hopes may assuage his thirst. He cuts the skin and out steps Princess Linetta. She says that she will die of thirst if she is not immediately given some water, and, when none is forthcoming, demonstrates that she can be as good as her word. The same happens when Princess Nicoletta comes from the second orange. Truffaldino, at his wits' end and unable to wake the Prince, rushes despairingly off into the desert.

The Prince awakes, appears in no way disconcerted by the sight of the two dead girls but orders four soldiers who conveniently appear to bury them with all due honour. Then he addresses himself to the third orange, which he is sure contains all that he has ever dreamed of. He cuts it open with his sword, and a third girl appears, more beautiful than the others; he immediately recognises her as the one being he has waited for since birth. She expresses sentiments that are in no way dissimilar, except that she adds to them a request for water that is no less urgent than that of the other princesses. She sinks into the Prince's arms, and it looks as though she will follow the other ladies to the grave. The spectators however rouse themselves to save what looks likely to develop into an impossible situation. A bucket of water is produced from one of the boxes, and the Princess's life is saved. The Prince and his prospective bride enthuse over each other (and are nearly interrupted from the boxes), but, when the Prince says they must return to his father's palace, she demurs: he must fetch her a suitable dress before she can think of meeting his father.

Princess Ninetta is alone. Towards her glides the figure of

Smeraldina, behind whom looms the shadow of Fata
Morgana. The occupants of the boxes are in a fever-heat of
anxiety, which turns out to be fully justified when
Smeraldina sticks a long magical pin into Ninetta's head. She
groans long and sadly, and is seen to have been turned into a
rat. The spectators quickly regain the boxes they have left,
and Fata Morgana tells Smeraldina that she must take
Ninetta's place when she meets the King.

The sound of the March is heard, and a procession appears,
with the King and the Prince at its head. They come up to
Smeraldina, who proclaims herself the princess, much to the
Prince's dismay. He refuses to marry her, saying this negress
is by no means the girl he left; but his father objects, and he
is forced to give her his arm and lead her back to the palace.

Act IV.   When the curtain rises, the cabalistic curtain of
Act I, scene ii, is seen once more. Fata Morgana and Tchelio
are at it again, abusing one another like pickpockets, and
making accusations of everything from lack of imagination to
being a fake. Fata Morgana seems to be having the better of
the argument, when the spectators get out of their boxes,
surround her, and shove her into a section of the structure
from which they have come, shutting the door firmly behind
her. Smoke and fire can be seen, and for the moment Tchelio
is triumphant.

Scene ii.   The royal throne-room. Leandro and the master
of ceremonies make last-minute adjustments, but it is not
long before the procession is upon them. When the curtains
round the throne are drawn aside, in the Princess's place can
be seen sitting a large rat—Princess Ninetta in her meta-
morphosed state. All are aghast, the King sends for his
guards, but Tchelio does his best to transform the rat into the
princess he knows it to be. All of a sudden his efforts work,
and Princess Ninetta stands before them. The Prince is beside
himself with joy, and Smeraldina's discomfiture is complete.
She is recognised as an accomplice of Leandro, and is accused
with him and Clarissa of treason. For a moment the court
watches the King go through the agonising process of making
up his mind; then he turns to them full of resolve: all the
culprits shall be hanged. In vain does Truffaldino plead for
mercy; the King will grant none.

As the guards move towards them, the guilty crew takes
flight, and soon the scene is covered with parties chasing each
other, all of a dither in case the traitors get away, but none

knowing which way they have gone. Suddenly, Fata Morgana appears in the middle of the stage, a trap-door opens, and her followers disappear down it to safety. The courtiers arrive too late, and there is nothing to do but cry 'God save the King' which the King immediately amends to 'God save the Prince and Princess'. (At the City Centre, there were one or two changes of detail. The last scene took place in the kitchen of the royal palace, where Truffaldino had fallen asleep and burnt the toast. The Princess, changed into a white pigeon, not a rat, suddenly flutters down into the kitchen, and is disenchanted by Tchelio. The traitors are condemned to sweep the kitchen, not to die, but are saved from this fate-worse-than-death by Fata Morgana. The opera ends in this version with a repetition of the March.)   H.

THE FIERY ANGEL

L'Ange de Feu

Opera in five acts and seven tableaux by Sergei Prokofiev. Libretto by the composer from a novel by Valery Briusoff (published in Russia in 1907). First complete performance in concert at the Théâtre des Champs Elysées, Paris, November 25, 1954, with Lucienne Marée, Xavier Depraz, conducted by Charles Bruck (Fr. transl. by André Michel). Stage première, Venice, September 14, 1955, with Dow, Panerai, conductor Sanzogno. First performed la Scala, 1957, with Goltz, Panerai, conductor Sanzogno; Spoleto, 1959, with Gencer, Panerai, conductor Kertesz; Cologne, 1960, with Pilarczyk, Carlos Alexander; Opéra-Comique, Paris, 1964, with Cavalli, Julien Haas, conductor Sebastien; Sadler's Wells, 1965, by New Opera Company with Collier, John Shaw; Frankfurt, 1969 (and Edinburgh Festival, 1970), with Anja Silja, Rudolf Konstantin, conductor Christoph von Dohnanyi (omitting the end of Act II and the whole of Act IV!).[1]

CHARACTERS

Ruprecht, *a knight* . . . . Baritone
The Hostess of the Inn . . . . Contralto
Renata . . . . Soprano

[1] In this misunderstood version, Ruprecht dies in the duel, a curious fate for the narrator of a story.

The Servant at the Inn .... Baritone
The Sorceress .... .Mezzo-Soprano
Jakob Glock .... Tenor
Agrippa von Nettelsheim, *a philosopher* .... Tenor
Count Heinrich .... .Mute
Mathias .... Baritone
The Doctor .... Tenor
Mephistopheles .... Tenor
Faust .... Baritone
The Innkeeper at Cologne .... Baritone
The Mother Superior .... .Mezzo-Soprano
The Inquisitor .... Bass
Two young Nuns .... Sopranos
Time: Sixteenth Century   *Place:* Germany, mainly Cologne

Prokofiev worked on *The Fiery Angel* between 1920 and
1926, beginning it, that is to say, in America after the failure
of *The Love for Three Oranges.*[1] The strongly romantic
subject is in great contrast to the ironic rationalism more
usually associated with him, but he seems to have been
overwhelmed by the possibilities of the story,[2] so that,
without immediate prospects of production, he shut himself
up from March, 1922, for 18 months at Ettal near
Oberammergau, where, as he says, the action might have
'taken place in the back yard'. In the event, the opera seems
to have been accepted by Bruno Walter for Berlin in 1926,
revised then but never performed. Koussevitzky played an
Interlude and the Agrippa scene at a concert in Paris three
years later, and the composer planned but did not carry out
an extensive revision in the early 1930's, including a re-write
of the libretto. The work was then mislaid and its existence
even partially forgotten until it turned up in Paris after the
composer's death. Prokofiev himself had in the meanwhile
used some music from it for his third symphony.[3]

[1] After the Chicago première of this opera, Prokofiev seems to have
hoped that Mary Garden, in her double capacity as Director of the
Chicago Opera and leading *prima donna*, would mount *The Fiery Angel*
and herself sing the title role. But unfortunately, he writes, she resigned
the directorship .

[2] It is hardly a coincidence that an earlier opera, *Maddalena*—his
first—was also concerned with obsession.

[3] First performed in Paris, spring, 1929, under Pierre Monteux.

The Fiery Angel belongs to the epoch of *Wozzeck*, but even that masterpiece amongst products of the post-Freudian era hardly surpasses it in its capacity to evoke and portray neurasthenia. But here a distinction must be made. *Wozzeck* belongs to a different world from the one inhabited by the emigré Prokofiev. His adopted Paris was dominated by Stravinsky's neo-classicism, the ironies of Cocteau and Satie, the new exploits of Les Six; and the Germany, where he retired to write *The Fiery Angel*, by the opulence of Richard Strauss, with apparently at the time no more than minority dissension on the part of Schoenberg and his adherents on the one hand and Hindemith on the other—at first sight, hardly a promising climate one might think in which to conceive an opera totally different from anything Prokofiev had previously written and of a violence unparalleled perhaps in the twentieth century. But in the event it turned out to be his operatic masterpiece.

The work is allegorical on two simultaneous levels. On one plane, Renata symbolises the struggle between good and evil, and the capacity to believe that evil is good and to act on this belief. She is haunted by visions of an Angel, and her passion for him amounts to obsession; to her he is Good, and no one else she meets is of any significance, except as help in her search for the Angel, or his physical embodiment, Heinrich. On another level, this is the account of an all-absorbing (for Briusoff, one supposes, autobiographical), but ultimately unsuccessful love affair, seen through the suffering eyes of the male, but more damaging in the final analysis it would appear for the female protagonist than for him.

Musically, the work is dominated by two themes associated with Renata, which with their derivatives occur throughout:

Ex. 1

RENATA

grâ - - ce

Act I.   A room in a shabby inn. The innkeeper conducts
Ruprecht to his room for the night. No sooner has she left
him than he hears hysterical and terrified imprecations
coming from behind an apparently disused door. He forces it,
and Renata, distraught and dishevelled, throws herself into
his arms for protection, continuing to defend herself against
her unseen attacker even after Ruprecht has drawn his sword
and made the sign of the cross. The music vividly portrays

her exhaustion as Ruprecht prays and her terror abates.

She tells her story in an extended narration of considerable musical splendour. It was when she was eight that an Angel first appeared to her, dressed in white with blue eyes and golden hair and surrounded by flames. His name was Madiel and he appeared to her day and night, eventually announcing to her that her destiny was to be a saint. When she was 17, her urgent desire for carnal love drove him away, to her utter despair, but eventually he told her in a dream that he would return in human form. As soon as she saw Count Heinrich she knew, in spite of his denial, that he was Madiel in human form. Her desires were fulfilled and there ensued with Heinrich a year of happiness such as had never been since Eve was expelled from Paradise. In the end he abandoned her, and now Ruprecht has saved her from the fiend who has pursued her with visions and nightmares ever since.

The noise attracts the attention of the innkeeper and her servant. Renata is a loose woman, the innkeeper explains to Ruprecht; she bewitched the Count and tormented the villagers, and now she must leave the inn. Ruprecht cannot understand what is going on, but he shrugs his shoulders and decides that, once the innkeeper goes, this attractive girl, witch or no witch, shall be his. As she looks out of the window yearning for Heinrich, Ruprecht unsuccessfully tries to seduce her. He quickly abandons the attempt, but from that moment Ruprecht seems to become involved in the search for Heinrich almost as much as Renata herself.

When the innkeeper brings in a fortune-teller, with all her traditional accoutrements including a toad in a cage, the contrast with Renata is intentional; the one is up to all the tricks of the trade which is her livelihood, the other attracted to sorcery only as a means to an end. The act ends with an impressive musical scene, in which the old fortune-teller makes obscure references to Renata's guilt.

Act II takes place in Cologne. The Introduction features the theme of Ruprecht's disappointment:

Renata is alone reading a book of magic when Ruprecht comes in, complaining that the week they have been in the city has been spent only in feverish search for Heinrich; they have looked in every church, in each narrow street, they have tried magic, but all to no avail. Without Heinrich she cannot live, is her answer. Jakob Glock has been commissioned to bring more books of magic, and Renata fastens on them, telling Ruprecht that, despite his uncomplaining love, his declared lack of jealousy, beside Heinrich he is nothing; were she to be walking with Heinrich and to find Ruprecht's body self-slain in the gutter, she would take no more notice than to ask for the removal of such carrion.

Renata burns the magic herbs acquired from the sorceress, and soon a knock is heard on the wall—it is a spirit, she says, announcing the arrival of Heinrich. With some remarkable *divisi* writing for the strings, Prokofiev expresses Renata's obsession in a scene that is musically of very striking quality with, in its total effect, something of the drama and irresistibility of Berlioz's *Cours à l'abîme*.

The door opens, but the music subsides to impotence and Ruprecht finds nothing. Renata collapses weeping, while Ruprecht swears he will compel the spirits to aid her in her search. Glock reappears; he will take Ruprecht to speak with the philosopher–magician, Agrippa von Nettelsheim.

A fine symphonic interlude takes us to Agrippa's studio, where he sits surrounded by books, bottles of medicine, human skeletons, and three black dogs. In a scene whose impressive music supplies a climax even to the feverish excitement of its predecessor, Agrippa reveals himself as a master of the diabolical arts, 'cold and steely, immensely powerful and terribly convincing. Here is damnation'.[1] As a philosopher, however, he refuses to help Ruprecht. The first scene of Act II provided most of the music for the third movement of Prokofiev's third symphony (a *scherzo* 'dénué de gaieté' the composer called it), and the interlude and second scene for the last movement of the same work.

The first scene of Act III shows Renata in despair outside the door of a house. It is Heinrich's; she has seen him and been rejected as a woman possessed by the devil. Ruprecht returns from his encounter with Agrippa and hears the story of Renata's *volte face*—she no longer loves Heinrich, who, she is convinced, was an impostor, not the embodiment of her Madiel. If Ruprecht will kill her seducer, she will be his, and follow him wherever he goes. After a moment's hesitation, Ruprecht demands entrance to Heinrich's house, while Renata offers up a prayer to Madiel for forgiveness that she mistook Heinrich for him and for strength for the future. It has the force of a great aria of dedication.

Ruprecht can be seen at a window as he challenges Heinrich, who himself suddenly becomes visible; in appearance he is the very incarnation of all that Renata has ever ascribed to Madiel, a true angel of fire. Renata is overwhelmed at the sight of him, and when Ruprecht reappears, in another complete change of heart, she forbids him to shed a drop of Heinrich's blood, rather to allow himself to be killed.

An interlude depicts the duel (part of it can be heard in the first movement of the third symphony). At its end, Ruprecht is discovered lying seriously wounded on the banks of the Rhine, where Renata tends him, and in a lyrical aria sings of her love for him, swearing that if he dies she will enter a convent. After Renata's *berceuse*, delirium (Ruprecht's from his wound? Renata's from her obsession?—it is the only moment of the story when Renata and Ruprecht are musically at one) suddenly seizes both in music of uncanny intensity, a chorus of women behind the

---

[1] Hans Swarsenski, in an excellent article on the opera in *Tempo*, 1956.

stage commenting ironically the while on the instability of love. A doctor who has been fetched by Mathias, Ruprecht's friend, pronounces that Ruprecht will live.

In Act IV, in a public garden, Renata tells Ruprecht, who has hardly recovered from his wound, that she must leave him; to accomplish the salvation of her soul, she must take the veil. When Ruprecht protests his love for her, she tries to commit suicide, turning the attack on him as he tries to prevent her. Mephistopheles and Faust have come into the garden and watch the scene. When the pot-boy, in response to their order, only brings wine, Mephistopheles threatens to swallow the child, and a little later at a single gulp makes good his boast, subsequently restoring him to life at the request of the innkeeper. They accost Ruprecht and arrange that he shall next day show them the sights of Cologne.

Act V starts with some beautiful slow music (in Symphony III, the subject of the second movement), chanted by the nuns of the convent of which Renata has become a member. The music is the more welcome by its contrast with the frenzy which has preceded it. The same abstraction from the world is apparent when the Mother Superior asks Renata about her visions: has she seen evil spirits? No, says Renata, she always turned her back on them. The fact remains, the Mother Superior points out, that since she entered the convent, the place has been in an uproar, full of strange noises and the sisters attacked by devils.

The nuns in the meanwhile have filled one side of the crypt, and now the Inquisitor and his followers enter to examine Renata. He asks her to furnish him with proof that her visions have never been inspired by Hell. The spirit who visits her, she tells him, has always spoken of virtue, of the importance of the life to come—are these the words of the devil? Immediately two young sisters cry out in terror, knocks are heard on the wall, and the scene becomes one of pandemonium as one group after another becomes caught up in the general turmoil, a few supporting Renata but most crying out against her. The exorcism proceeds, but finally, as Mephistopheles and Ruprecht appear, the nuns rush frenziedly at the Inquisitor and his supporters, and the opera ends as he pronounces Renata a heretic and sentences her to death. The final scene, with its intricate part-writing for the women against the *cantus firmus* of the Inquisitor, is masterly in its effect and brings the opera to an over-whelming conclusion. H.

BETROTHAL IN A MONASTERY

Opera in four acts by Sergei Prokofiev, text by Mira Mendelson from Sheridan's *The Duenna*. Première planned for 1941 but postponed because of the German invasion of Russia; plans for a 1943 production at the Bolshoi, Moscow, also abandoned. Première, Kirov Theatre, Leningrad, November 30, 1946. First performed New York, Greenwich Mews Playhouse, 1948 (as *The Duenna*), with two-piano accompaniment; Leipzig, 1957; East Berlin, 1958, conductor Lovro von Matacic; Naples, 1959, with Rosetta Noli, Belen Amparan, Agostino Lazzari, Francesco Albanese, Fernando Corena, Guido Mazzini, conductor Fabien Sevitzky; Zagreb Opera, 1960 (and in Paris, 1961); BBC London (tape of performance at the Stanislavsky Theatre, Moscow) 1963; Strasbourg, 1973, with Esther Casas, Jocelyne Taillon, Michel Sénéchal, Frantz Petri.

CHARACTERS

Don Jerome, *a rich man of Seville* . . . . Tenor
Ferdinand ⎱ *his children* . . . . ⎰ Baritone
Louisa ⎰ . . . . ⎱ Soprano
The Duenna (Margaret) . . . . Contralto
Antonio, *in love with Louisa* . . . . Tenor
Clara d'Almanza, *friend of Louisa* . . . . . Mezzo-Soprano
Mendoza, *a rich fish merchant* . . . . Bass
Don Carlos, *an impoverished nobleman, friend
    of Mendoza* . . . . Baritone
Father Augustine, *Father Superior of the
    Monastery* . . . . Baritone
Brother Elixir ⎱ ⎰ Tenor
Brother Chartreuse ⎭ *monks* . . . . ⎱ Baritone
Brother Benedictine⎰ ⎭ Bass
1st Monk . . . . Tenor
2nd Monk . . . . Tenor
Lauretta, *Louisa's maidservant* . . . . Soprano
Rosina, *Clara's maidservant* . . . . Contralto
Lopez, *Ferdinand's servant* . . . . Tenor
Friend of Don Jerome . . . . Non-singing
Servant of Don Jerome . . . . Non-singing

Servants, Maidservants, Monks, Guests, Maskers,
Tradespeople

Time: Eighteenth Century　　　　　　　　　*Place:* Seville

Prokofiev's fifth opera is taken from an English literary subject, *The Duenna* by Sheridan.[1]

An introduction, *moderato ma con brio*, brings us to the house of Don Jerome, a fussy rich old man of Seville, who has a son and a daughter, Ferdinand and Louisa, for the latter of whom he has engaged a duenna. In front of Don Jerome's house, he and the fish merchant Mendoza are discussing a partnership which they plan to form—together they will corner the fish trade of Seville—and they seal the bargain with an agreement for Mendoza to marry Louisa.

They leave and Ferdinand comes in with his servant Lopez to lament with considerable romantic ardour the apparent capriciousness of his lady-love Clara. It has grown dark and Antonio comes in equipped with a guitar obviously about to serenade underneath Louisa's window, something which Ferdinand accepts thinking it would at least keep him from laying siege to the affections of Clara, with whom he is known to have once been in love. Antonio sings, chases away some mocking carnival maskers and has the gratification of seeing Louisa come out on her balcony, obviously delighted at his appearance and prepared to join him in song.

Don Jerome has been woken up by it all, but Louisa hides in time, and he, too, is bamboozled by the maskers, who dance round him to such purpose that he is driven to reflect that Louisa had better marry soon or she will be the prey of some serenading fool. The act ends with extensive and lively dancing by other groups of maskers, some in oriental costume.

Act II. The first scene is set in Louisa's apartment in Don Jerome's house, where she is discussing with her duenna the possibility of marrying the man she has fallen in love with. The duenna has ideas of herself marrying Mendoza and his money, thus leaving Louisa free for Antonio. They plot just as Don Jerome himself appears, berating Ferdinand for his lovesick behaviour. He means to impose his will on Louisa in the matter of the marriage with Mendoza, but both his children argue hotly against the plan. Don Jerome loses his patience and swears he will lock Louisa up until she changes her mind and accepts his will.

Ferdinand advises his father to let his sister marry someone she really loves and is disconcerted at Don Jerome's blank

[1] The subject also of Roberto Gerhard's only opera, unfortunately as yet only performed on radio and never on stage.

refusal, not least as he remembers Antonio's one-time love fo
Clara. His meditations are interrupted by the sound of the
lamentations of the duenna and the insistence of Don
Jerome, who has found the incriminating love letter that she
and Louisa have planned would fall into his hands. Their duet
leaves us uncertain as to which has been the more effective,
the sack he has given her or the notice she has promptly given
him. At all events, she leaves to go to Louisa's room. Enter
Louisa, disguised in the duenna's clothes—cape, hood, veil
and all—and pretending to weep. Don Jerome shows her the
door, covertly watched by the duenna, and shouts angrily
after what is, though he does not know it, his daughter
Louisa.

On the waterfront, fishwives are selling their wares, shortly
to be observed by Don Mendoza and his impoverished friend
Don Carlos. When they leave, Doña Clara and Rosina, her
maidservant, come into view, the former delighted at the idea
that she has left home at last but furious that it is through
the intervention of her lover, who stole at night into her
room and has thus by his presumption mortally affronted
her.

No sooner have they left than Louisa comes in, lamenting
her inability to locate Antonio. Should she look for help
from her friend Clara—but then Clara is such a plaster
saint! At that moment, Clara catches sight of her but fails to
evade her, and they quickly discover that the one is eloping
and the other hiding. In a lyrical aria, Clara tells Louisa the
story: lying awake at night, she heard her lover steal into her
room but felt she must reject him for his over-ardent
behaviour. Louisa attempts to console her but is plainly
disconcerted to hear Clara seem to opt for a convent.
Suddenly, Louisa catches sight of Mendoza, and immediately
decides to ask Clara to allow her to masquerade for a bit as
Doña Clara d'Almanza, which Clara agrees to on condition
that Louisa, if she sees her brother Ferdinand, will swear not
to have seen Clara anywhere, least of all tell him where she
has gone—the Convent of St. Catherine, whose geography
Clara proceeds to describe in some detail in the ostensible hope
that Louisa will mention not so much as the position of the
back door to Ferdinand.

Mendoza and Don Carlos come in and Louisa, pretending
to be Clara, makes up to Mendoza and asks him to carry a
message to her lover Antonio, thus provoking Mendoza's

indignation since, for a moment, he half thought she was attracted to him. All the same, he knows Antonio was Louisa's suitor, and he feels this latest development may suit his purposes. Bidding Don Carlos escort Louisa (whom of course he thinks to be Clara) to Mendoza's house, Mendoza plans himself to visit the house of Don Jerome to see his betrothed.

Back in Don Jerome's house, where he is hearing from Mendoza how Doña Clara has run away from home, Don Jerome cannot refrain from singing his daughter's praises. It soon becomes apparent however that Louisa refuses to put in an appearance if her father is present at her meeting with Mendoza. Eventually he takes his leave, and the duenna enters dressed as Louisa. Mendoza is at first lyrically polite but much taken aback when he contrives to peep at her face. The duenna wins him round with flattery so that he becomes convinced he was mistaken to have found her hideous, and succumbs when she sings him a song. In the end, they are plotting to elope together, and Mendoza is left to face Don Jerome with this romantic prospect in view. Don Jerome and Mendoza finish the act with a drinking song.

Act III. Don Carlos has conducted Louisa to Mendoza's lodgings, whither Mendoza loses no time in bringing Antonio. Antonio smells a rat and cannot believe that it is his old flame Clara who has summoned him, but Mendoza and Don Carlos push him into the room where they say Clara is waiting and then, as the music depicts a tender scene inside, proceed themselves to peer through the keyhole into the room. When Antonio and Louisa re-enter arm-in-arm, Don Carlos is scandalised that Antonio should so lightly steal his friend's beloved, but Mendoza welcomes young love and says that he himself will that very night go to Don Jerome's house in order to abduct Don Jerome's daughter. The scene ends with a quartet, Louisa and Antonio hymning the setting sun while Mendoza and Don Carlos wonder about the compensations available to those of maturer years.

There is jaunty music-making in Don Jerome's house, with the host playing the clarinet, a friend the cornet, and a servant the big drum. Don Jerome cannot understand how it is that his daughter, who yesterday so vehemently refused the bridegroom chosen for her, has now decided to elope with him. Lopez ushers in Don Carlos who has brought Mendoza's letter asking the bride's father for forgiveness. Don Jerome

readily grants it, and Don Carlos agrees to bear the message
back to Mendoza. The music-making continues, but now a
messenger brings a letter from Louisa herself, again asking
Don Jerome to bless the marriage. Again he agrees, inter
rupting the music to instruct Lopez to organise a wedding
banquet, and the scene ends with the music reaching a
climax.

Clara, dressed as a nun, is lamenting her fate in the conven
garden. To her comes Louisa to plead for Ferdinand, and it i
apparent that Clara would give in were he there at tha
moment. Antonio joins them and together he and Louisa
read her father's answer to her plea for recognition of he
marriage. Antonio cannot understand it, but they leave
arm-in-arm and full of delight, only for poor Clara to lamen
the misery of her predicament. It is not long however before
Ferdinand is inside the convent wall, but confusion reign
supreme, and he believes he can see Doña Clara d'Almanza
disappearing with his faithless friend Antonio. Clara is over
joyed at his jealousy, her anger melts and she swears tha
Louisa will not be the only bride that day.

Act IV. In the Monastery, a number of monks are
drinking wine. Their mood is one of hilarity, and they toast
the sisters of the Order of St. Catherine, not forgetting the
little dark-eyed novice. The music bubbles on as the wine
starts to take control, and it is only gradually that those to
whom wine speaks most deeply come to understand that rich
clients have been announced and they must rapidly change
their tune, which they proceed—literally—to do. Antonio and
Mendoza have come to ask the brethren's help in the project
closest to their hearts, which is that they both want to get
married. After the mysterious appearance of a purse, the
monks agree to do their bit. A complication ensues when
Louisa rushes in followed by Ferdinand, who believes that hi
beloved Clara is to be married to Antonio. Antonio and
Ferdinand are about to fight, when Clara enters, minus he
veil but still dressed as a nun, and she and Louisa stop the
fight. Clara was the black-eyed novice, and the monks are
riveted by her appearance. Before long, the lovers' misunder
standings are resolved and the appropriate marriages blessed

In the Ballroom of Don Jerome's house, preparations are
in hand for the celebration of Louisa's wedding. But the
principal guests seem to be absent. Finally, Mendoza come
in calling for his wife, and the duenna makes her firs

pearance as a married woman. Don Jerome is taken aback
ɔ recognise his old employee, the more so when a moment
ater he finds Antonio and Louisa kneeling in front of him
ınd asking for his blessing. Guests arrive as efforts are made
:o clear up the various misconceptions, and soon it is the turn
ɔf Ferdinand and Doña Clara to kneel beside Louisa and
Antonio. Don Jerome starts to work out that his daughter
ıas married a pauper who has at least the grace to be
ıandsome, and his son has married a lady with a princess's
ɟowry. Things haven't turned out quite so badly as he might
ıave expected and rejoicings proceed more or less unclouded
vhile Don Jerome shows his prowess on the musical glasses.

H.

WAR AND PEACE

Voina y Mir

Opera in thirteen scenes by Sergei Prokofiev; libretto by the composer
ınd Mira Mendelson, after Tolstoy. The original version (heavily cut)
ʒiven in concert in Moscow, June 7, 1945,[1] with Nadion (Natasha),
ɪvanov (Andrei), Pirogov (Kutuzov), conductor Samosud. Première
(first eight scenes only) at Maly Theatre, Leningrad, June 12,
1946, with Lavrova, Chishko (Pierre), Shaposhnikov (Andrei),
Andrukovich (Anatol), Juravlenko (Old Prince Bolkonsky), conductor
Samosud. Part II was heard at a closed première in 1947. Première of
so-called 'final' version (eleven scenes only, omitting scenes 7 and 11),
Maly Theatre, Leningrad, April 1, 1955, with Lavrova, Sokolova,
Baskova (Hélène), Gliebov (Pierre), Andrukovich, Shaposhnikov,
Modestov (Napoleon), Butiagin (Kutuzov), conductor Grikurov. First
non-Russian performance, Florence, 1953, with Rosanna Carteri, Franco
Corelli, Ettore Bastianini, Italo Tajo, Fernando Corena, Mirto Picchi,
Renato Capecchi, Anselmo Colzani, conductor Artur Rodzinski. First
ɔerformed Moscow, Nemirovich-Danchenko Theatre, 1957, with
Kaievchenko, Shtavinsky, Radzuevsky, Morozov, Kandielaki, Pirogov,
conductor Shaverdov (13 scenes, with internal cuts); NBC TV, New
York, 1957, with Helena Scott, Davis Cunningham, Morley Meredith,
Kenneth Smith, conductor Peter Herman Alder; Bolshoi Theatre,
Moscow, 1959, with Vishnevskaya, Archipova, Grigoriev, Kipkalo,
Maslennikov, Vedernikov, Lisitsian, conductor Melik-Peshayev; Leipzig,
1961; Zagreb, 1961, with Stilinović, Zunec, Petrušanec (Kutuzov). First
British performance Leeds Festival, 1967, (in concert), with Elizabeth

[1] The same day as the première of *Peter Grimes* in London.

Vaughan, Gregory Dempsey, Hans Wilbrink, Ivo Zidek, Dona
McIntyre, conductor Edward Downes; Sadler's Wells, 1972, wit.
Josephine Barstow, Ann Hood, Kenneth Woollam, Tom McDonnel
John Brecknock, Norman Bailey, Raymond Myers, conductor Davi
Lloyd-Jones, producer Colin Graham; Australia, for opening of Sydne
Opera House, 1973, with Eilene Hannen, Ronald Dowd, McDonnel
Robert Gard, Neil Warren-Smith, Myers, conductor Edward Downes.

CHARACTERS

Prince Andrei Bolkonsky . . . . Baritone
Natalya Rostova (Natasha) . . . . Soprano
Sonya, *Natasha's cousin* . . . . Mezzo-Soprano
Maria Dmitrievna Akhrosimova . . . . Contralto
Count Ilya Rostov, *Natasha's father* . . . . Bass
Count Pyotr Bezukhov (Pierre) . . . . Tenor
Hélène Bezukhova, *his wife* . . . . Mezzo-Soprano
Prince Anatol Kuragin, *her brother* . . . . Tenor
Dolokhov, *an officer* . . . . Baritone
Colonel Vasska Denisov . . . . Baritone
Field-Marshal Prince Mikhail Kutuzov . . . . Bass
Napoleon Bonaparte . . . . Baritone
Platon Karataev, *an old soldier* . . . . Tenor
The Host . . . . Tenor
His Major-domo . . . . Tenor
Madame Peronskaya . . . . Soprano
The Tsar . . . . Silent role
Prince Nikolai Bolkonsky, *Andrei's father*. Bass-Baritone
His Major-domo . . . . Baritone
An old valet . . . . Baritone
A Housemaid. . . . . Soprano
Princess Marya Bolkonskaya, *Andrei's sister*
. . . . Mezzo-Soprano
Balaga, *a troika driver* . . . . Bass
Matriosha, *a gipsy* . . . . Mezzo-Soprano
Dunyasha, *Natasha's maid* . . . . Soprano
Gavrila, *Akhrosimova's butler* . . . . Bass
Metivier, *A French doctor* . . . . Baritone
A French Abbé . . . . Tenor
Tikhon Scherbatsky, *a partisan* . . . . Baritone
Vasilisa . . . . Mezzo-Soprano
Fyodor, *a partisan* . . . . Tenor
Matveyev, *a Muscovite* . . . . Baritone
Two Prussian Generals . . . . Speaking roles

Prince Andrei's Orderly .... Tenor
Two Russian Generals .... Speaking roles
Kaizarov, *Aide-de-camp to Kutuzov* .... Tenor
Adjutant to General Compans................ Tenor
Adjutant to Marshal Murat ....Treble
Marshal Berthier .... Baritone
Marquis de Caulaincourt ....Silent role
General Belliard .... Baritone
Adjutant to Prince Eugène .... Tenor
Aide-de-camp to Napoleon .... Bass
Off-stage Orderly .... Tenor
Monsieur de Beausset .... Tenor
General Bennigsen .... Bass
Prince Mikhail Barclay de Tolly .... Tenor
General Yermolov .... Baritone
General Konovnitsin...................... Tenor
General Rayevsky....................... Baritone
Captain Ramballe .... Bass
Lieutenant Bonnet .... Tenor
Ivanov, a Muscovite .... Tenor
Captain Jacqueau .... Bass
Marshal Berthier's Adjutant .... Tenor
Mavra Kusminitchna, *The Rostovs' Housekeeper*
.... Contralto
Marshal Davout........................... Bass
A French Officer .... Baritone
Three Madmen .... Tenor, Baritone, Actor
Two French Actresses .... Soprano
ime: 1806–1812
lace: Russia—Otradnoye, Petersburg, Moscow, Borodino,
ili, near Smolensk

According to Mira Mendelson, for whom Prokofiev had
eft his Spanish-born wife,[1] the composer was thinking of
vriting an opera on Tolstoy's *Resurrection* when she started
o read *War and Peace* aloud to him. He was immediately
truck by its operatic possibilities, the scene of the meeting
etween Natasha and the wounded Prince Andrei particularly
ppealing to him. In April, 1941,[2] they started to prepare a

[1] Prokofiev and Mira Mendelson met in Spring, 1940, when the
omposer was 51 and she was 25.
[2] I am indebted to Rita McAllister, lecturer in music at Edinburgh
Iniversity, for much valuable information on chronology.

scheme for the libretto, by July the German invasion o Russia had provided him with the spur to tackle it and eleve scenes had been decided upon; on August 15, already evacuated to the Caucasus, he started work on the com position. As a matter of history, he worked at it on and of during the last eleven years of his life and the opera has gone through a number of different versions.

By midsummer 1942,[1] eleven scenes were completed in piano score (two changes from the original eleven), and a this point it was suggested to the composer that there was a lack of heroic quality in the war scenes—not surprising since the original idea had been for something relatively small-scale, with the emphasis on Pierre and the inner struggle of the individual rather than on Kutuzov and the outward struggle of the nation. He had already orchestrated Peace, but he set to work to comply with the Committee's request so that all eleven scenes were finished by April, 1943, to form the definitive First Version, a mimeographed vocal score of which was published at that time (excluding the Epigraph, which was however finished). Plans for a performance at the Bolshoi Theatre in 1943, Samosud conducting and Eisenstein producing, were shelved,[2] but an idea for an enlarged version in two parts emerged, and in June, 1946, the forces of the Maly Theatre, Leningrad, under Samosud gave Part I, consisting of Scenes 1–7 (Scene 2 had been added at Samosud's suggestion to the original scheme) and Scene 8 (the battle of Borodino). Performance of Part II was planned, and during 1946–7 Prokofiev wrote Scene 10 (the Council of War at Fili), only for events to overtake the planners in the shape of the infamous Zhdanov decree of February 10, 1948.

A word of explanation seems necessary. After the première of Muradely's opera The Great Friendship, Andrei Zhdanov, acting it is believed after he and Stalin had both intensely disliked the new work, met the Moscow composers in January, 1948, to initiate a new 'hard line'. Khrennikov became the new General Secretary of the composers

---

[1] In November, 1941, he moved from Nalchik to Tbilisi in Georgia and in May, 1942, to Alma-Ata in Kazakhstan, where he collaborated with Eisenstein on the film Ivan the Terrible.

[2] A private performance of this version with piano accompaniment was given in Moscow in October, 1944, and a public concert in June, 1945.

ne over-riding importance of melody in Soviet music
vas re-emphasised, and war was declared against formalism,
naturalism, modernism, and Westernism.

In December 1948, after Part II had been dropped in
Leningrad at Dress Rehearsal stage, Prokofiev, who according
to his colleague Kabalevsky 'considered the opera the best
thing he had written'[1], started to plan a version suitable for a
single evening and suggestions to this end are contained in the
preface to the published vocal score. In spite of internal
re-arrangements made during the period 1948–52 (Kutuzov's
aria went through many versions, the latest in 1953, a matter
of weeks before the composer's death in March that year),
the 13-scene scheme remains, and it is this, together with
overture and choral Epigraph which is now treated as the
final version—long (more than four hours of music) and
therefore often cut in performance, sometimes only section-
ally, occasionally by as much as two complete scenes (usually
ii and xi; at the Florence première, ii and ix).

Part I. The granite-hard choral movement called Epigraph in the score and often appropriately substituted at the
start of the opera[2] for the much less interesting overture, is a
massive piece of block harmony and, with its emphasis on the
primordial strength of Russia in the face of her enemies,
makes a most effective opening. (The overture itself is
concerned with War rather more than Peace, and is usually
omitted.) The Epigraph contains a sung reference to Ex. 9 as
well as an enunciation of Ex. 8 which symbolises the surge of
optimism which is itself the result of fervent patriotism.

The first scene is set in the garden of Count Rostov's estate
at Otradnoye. It is a moonlit night in May, 1806. The
widower Prince Andrei Bolkonsky, who is visiting the estate
on business, cannot sleep. His idealism, Ex. 1:

[1] Boris Schwarz: *Music and Musical Life in Soviet Russia
1917–1970* (Barrie & Jenkins).
[2] As in the productions at the Bolshoi Theatre in 1959 and by
Sadler's Wells at the London Coliseum in 1972. In Australia, for the
opening of the Sydney Opera House, the conductor Edward Downes
omitted the overture and placed the Epigraph before the scene of the
burning of Moscow (which was itself cut in entirety up to the entry of
Napoleon). Placed at the opening of the opera, it not only makes a
magnificent prelude in itself but suggests a background of world events
against which the private affairs of Part I are played.

passes to thoughts of Spring, Ex. 2:

35 The kiss in *The Knot Garden* at Covent Garden (Thomas Hemsley, Raimund Herincx, Robert Tear, Thomas Carey).

and then gives way to a mood of disillusion. From an upstairs room, Natasha, who is preceded by Ex. 2 and sings to a version of Ex. 1, can be heard complaining to her cousin Sonya that she too cannot sleep. Natasha thinks she has never seen anything so beautiful as their garden bathed in moonlight, and Prince Andrei is moved by the romantic situation and the innocence and charm of the young girl. How could he ever have believed that his life was at an end (Ex. 2)? The mood of the scene is lyrical and expressive—in fact one may doubt if Prokofiev ever elsewhere penned music of such tenderness. It exactly fits the Byronic romanticism of the characters, and its ancestor is clearly Tchaikovsky's writing in the opening scene of *Eugene Onegin*[1]—and what better model could there possibly be?

Scene ii takes place on New Year's Eve, 1810, at a ball in a palace in Petersburg. Guests dance a brilliant polonaise, and are invited to listen to a new cantata. Count Rostov enters with Natasha and Sonya, and they are closely followed by Count and Countess Bezukhov—Madame Akhrosimova makes a complimentary remark to Natasha but she and Madame Peronskaya comment with a certain asperity on the beauty of the celebrated Hélène Bezukhova whose white shoulders they say have been polished by half the male eyes of Petersburg. The Tsar makes his entry, polonaise is succeeded by mazurka, Natasha wonders if no one will ask her to dance (Ex. 1), and then Pierre, rich and unconventional, approaches his friend Prince Andrei and suggests he should ask the young Natasha Rostova to dance. The nostalgic music of the waltz at this point reflects the effect the dance is having on the mind of the impressionable Natasha, whose first ball it is, Ex. 3:

[1] Indeed Rita McAllister in her programme note for the Sadler's Wells 1972 production, tells us: 'Natasha's main theme and the motif of Prince Andrei's love ... were taken over directly from ... the unperformed incidental music written (by Prokofiev) for a dramatic production of *Eugene Onegin* in 1936. Natasha's theme belonged to the young Lensky, Andrei's to Tatiana in her love for Onegin.'

Tempo di Valse

The scene ends on a note of something like ecstasy, with Andrei murmuring to himself after the dance: 'If she first approaches her cousin and then another lady, she will become my wife'.[1] When Natasha goes up to Sonya, Andrei's mood of exultation seems justified, but he is not the only man to have been impressed by Natasha, the glittering and dissolute Prince Anatol Kuragin having earlier asked his sister Hélène Bezukhova to arrange an introduction to the new young beauty. The scene ends with an Écossaise.

Prince Andrei has proposed to Natasha and in the third scene (February, 1812) Count Rostov brings his daughter (Ex. 1) to see old Prince Bolkonsky, Andrei's father, who has insisted meanwhile that Andrei should spend a year abroad. Count Rostov asks if the Prince and the Princess his daughter are at home. He does not relish the prospect of the interview, but Natasha is a good deal more confident. When she sings it, Ex. 1, originally sung by Andrei, seems to stand for the idealism in her character as well as for their mutual love and Ex. 2 for the trust she now feels in Andrei. They are told that the old man cannot see them, but his spinsterish daughter Princess Marya comes in and Count Rostov quickly makes his excuses to her and departs. No sooner has he gone, than the old Prince puts in an appearance, dressed in night-cap and dressing gown. With obvious insincerity, he apologises for his attire to Natasha, mutters threateningly and leaves. Marya starts to excuse his behaviour—he is perpetually in pain—but Natasha understands all too well that he is the obstacle to her marriage. Count Rostov returns and goes to speak with Princess Marya, leaving Natasha alone. She is outraged at the behaviour of the Bolkonskys but this makes her think, and thought conjures up the image of Andrei, whom she realises means everything to her, Ex. 4:

---

[1] Translation by Edward Downes.

Per-haps he'll come, per-haps he'll come to-mor-row

When Princess Marya makes a conscious attempt at conversation, Natasha puts her off with some dignity. The scene gives the opportunity in a fine soliloquy for a considerable musical development of the character of Natasha, and we are conscious of a more mature and determined person than hitherto.

Scene iv takes place in the living room of Pierre Bezukhov's house in May, 1812,—the whole scene amounts to a dance on a less grandiose scale than in Scene ii, built up on yet another waltz, with interpolations in 4/4. Hélène compliments Natasha on not staying at home just because she is engaged, then lets slip the information that the previous night her brother Prince Anatol had admitted to them that he was pining for love of none other than Natasha. Hélène laughs at Natasha's embarrassment and, when a moment later Count Rostov wants to take his family home, insists they stay. In touchingly diffident music, Natasha reflects that neither Hélène nor Pierre seems at all shocked at Prince Anatol having fallen in love with her; she will not be shocked either. The dancing resumes and Anatol proceeds to woo Natasha passionately (this version of the waltz[1] symbolises

[1] From the incidental music to *Eugene Onegin*.

the fascination Anatol holds for Natasha), Ex. 5:

He succeeds in kissing her and gives her a letter of
assignation. Natasha is obviously affected by its fervour—but
she loves Andrei (Ex.2). If only he were here now (Ex.
4)! Count Rostov returns to take Natasha and Sonya home.

Scene v.   June   12,   1812.   Dolokhov's   apartments.
Anatol's elopement with Natasha is arranged, and he is waiting
for the pre-arranged moment. He sings with the conviction of
infatuation, however cynical, and when Dolokhov, who has
made all the detailed arrangements, tries to argue his friend
out of going through with the mad project, shrugs off his
arguments. He likes women young, and anyhow he is in love
(echo of the previous scene's waltz: Ex. 5). Here incongruously occurs Ex. 1, presumably as ironic counterpoint
to Anatol's thoughts. Enter Balaga, with whom Dolokhov has
arranged for a carriage and the fastest horses he can procure.
He seems to have been implicated in Anatol's escapades
before now, and the three of them drink to the adventure as
Anatol says a musically nostalgic goodbye to Moscow and to
his gypsy mistress Matriosha.

Scene vi.   The same night: a room in the house of Maria
Dmitrievna Akhrosimova, where Natasha is staying while her
father is away. Natasha waits alone for Anatol, until her maid
Dunyasha rushes in to say that Sonya has given away the
elopement plans. Anatol appears at the door, but the butler,
Gavrila, bars the way to him, and Anatol escapes with

Dolokhov, Natasha falling in despair on the sofa. Akhrosimova comes in and starts to rate Natasha for her behaviour, but Natasha defies her and begs to be left alone. Suddenly, Akhrosimova softens, the music now in great contrast to her formal denunciation of a moment ago. Can Natasha not think of her father and of Prince Andrei? Natasha runs off sobbing just as Gavrila announces Count Pierre Bezukhov—his theme precedes him, Ex. 6:

Pierre is told of the situation and when Natasha comes back (Ex. 1 swamping Ex. 5), wondering if he is friend or enemy, he starts to console her. In answer to Natasha's repeated questions he assures her that Anatol is already married, then succumbs to pity for her—will she not treat him as a friend? Her reaction is to beg him to explain to Andrei and ask him, though all is over between them, to forgive her for the pain she will have caused him (Ex. 4). Pierre promises, and then in an outburst of frankness, tells her that if he were himself free, he would now be on his knees asking for her hand in marriage. He runs out of the room, and Natasha follows him as Akhrosimova and Sonya come in, Sonya beside herself with worry that Natasha now looks upon her as an enemy and wondering whether she may not do something desperate. Natasha's voice is heard off stage: 'Sonya, help me! Sonya, I'm the worst of all.'

Scene vii.[1]   The same night, Hélène is entertaining guests, amongst them Anatol. Pierre comes in and proceeds to attack his brother-in-law for his infamous conduct, insisting that he leave Moscow immediately. Anatol is taken aback by his vehemence and agrees, leaving Pierre alone to reflect on the pointlessness of his existence, with its unproductive wealth and the worthless friends by whom he is surrounded (the music springs from material already exposed in the previous scene, particularly Ex. 6 and its derivations).

Denisov interrupts his soliloquy to bring the news that Napoleon is about to cross the Russian frontier. It means war.

Part II.   All six scenes of the second part of the opera are concerned with the defence of Russia against the invasion of the French, and the Russian people led by Marshal Kutuzov take the central position. In general, the musical tone, which mainly fluctuates between a representation on the one hand of patriotic fervour and of devastation on the other, is very different from that of the preceding scenes—only when Andrei and Pierre appear on the battlefield of Borodino and in the scene of the death of Andrei do we return to the musical style of Part I—and it is this contrast which has caused some commentators to talk about *War and Peace* as two separate operas on a single evening. I believe it is truer to think of it as combining a tragedy and an epic in one work, the tragedy of Natasha and Prince Andrei, begun in Part I and brought to a climax in Part II, the epic of the Russian people's struggle against the invader, adumbrated in the Epigraph and dominating Part II.

Scene viii.   The music starts with Ex. 7, associated with the horrors of war:

_____

[1] Prokofiev suggested that this scene might be cut if the opera is found too long in performance, but its excision has the unfortunate effect of greatly reducing the musical portrayal of Pierre.

August 25, 1812. Near Borodino, men are at work digging
defences, soldiers and peasants working side by side for the
defence of Moscow and filling the scene with their fervent
working and marching songs. Prince Andrei has raised and
trained his own regiment. Lieutenant-Colonel Denisov asks
him for the whereabouts of Field-Marshal Kutuzov and, on
their way to the Commander-in-Chief, Denisov talks to
Andrei of his idea to make use of partisans against the
French—a mere five hundred men skilfully deployed could
harass Napoleon's lines of communication and ensure his
defeat.

Andrei returns. By sheer coincidence he has just met
Denisov, who was once engaged to the Natasha in whom he
himself thought to realise all his hopes for the future (Exx. 2
and 3). His thoughts are bitter (Ex. 1) when suddenly he
recognises the highly unmilitary figure of Pierre Bezukhov.
He does not want to be further reminded of Natasha, and his
welcome is a little cool. Pierre explains that he has come to
Borodino as a mere onlooker. As they talk, two German
generals pass by, agreeing that since the object is to rout the
enemy one cannot be too concerned with civilian casualties.
Andrei is furious: Russia is being devastated, his father has
been killed (Ex. 7), and these Prussians, who have unsuccessfully fought Napoleon all over Europe, talk of text-book
battles! His orderly tells Andrei that the Regiment is drawn
up and waiting, and Andrei turns to Pierre, in spite of his
presentiments, still patriotically convinced of ultimate
victory, Ex. 8:

hap - pen, we shall win the bat - tle to - mor - row

A cry goes up as the Marshal leaves his tent, and Andrei embraces Pierre, both men convinced they have met for the last time. Pierre departs just as Kutuzov enters with his Aide-de-camp and a group of soldiers. His first appearance to a wisp of flute tone (Ex. 9a) brings Ex. 9 softly in the orchestra:

Andante molto

and his first words as he watches the guerillas at work are sung to this music. He throws each group a well-timed word of commendation, then catches sight of Prince Andrei and sends for him. His intention is to appoint him to his staff, but Andrei declines the position. Kutuzov reacts as do all commanders more at home in field than study, half vexed that he is deprived of a valuable adviser, half delighted to find that the man he chose prefers to serve in the front line (a reference to Ex. 8). The soldiers proclaim their patriotic fervour in a chorus based on Ex. 9, until the sound of a shot heralds the start of the battle (Ex. 7).

Scene ix.   In the Shevardino redoubt the same day, Napoleon directs the battle surrounded by his staff. The music is a sinister sort of *scherzo* in Prokofiev's most sardonic vein, with references to Ex. 9 when allusion is made to Russian heroism. The French commander-in-chief broods on the possible outcome of the battle. Moscow is at his mercy; he will earn history's gratitude by showing clemency. In spite of the urgent requests from the Marshals, he refuses at first to commit his reserves, but eventually gives in. De Beausset tries unsuccessfully to get the Emperor to eat luncheon, and the scene ends with a cannon shot landing almost at their feet. By not succumbing in mid-war to the full temptation of equating Napoleon with Hitler, Prokofiev has achieved the impossible by placing, in the course of a ten-minute scene, one of history's greatest figures convincingly on the musical stage.

Scene x.   In a peasant's hut in the village of Fili, Marshal Kutuzov is two days later holding a Council of War, surrounded by his generals (Ex. 7; later Ex. 9). Two courses are open to them, each potentially disastrous: to defend Moscow puts the army at risk; to retreat would leave the capital at the enemy's mercy. After listening to his generals, it is for Kutuzov to make the momentous decision. He orders a retreat (Ex. 9), confident that only through the sacrifice of Moscow is there a hope of final victory. The generals leave and Kutuzov's faith is expressed in soliloquy to a broad tune,[1] Ex. 10:

---

[1] David Lloyd-Jones demonstrated to me that this great tune was first written for chorus as part of the incidental music to Part 1 of the film *Ivan the Terrible*.

Its immediate appeal and memorability has caused some commentators to mutter patronisingly of music aimed at the masses, but others will remember that it is now not so common for an operatic tune to induce a feeling of genuine patriotic fervour, something which must have been just as firmly in Prokofiev's mind in the period 1941–5 as it was in Verdi's at the time of the Risorgimento.[1]

Scene xi. Moscow's inhabitants have set fire to the great city rather than surrender it to the invader (Ex. 7 frequently throughout the scene). Nothing is as the French expect and the soldiers start to loot. Pierre, who feels he could put an end to the horrors by killing Napoleon, learns that the Rostovs have left Moscow taking with them the wounded

---

[1] An early example of music's patriotic potency, not so intentional perhaps on the part of the composer, occurred on August 25, 1830, when the audience at a performance of Auber's *La Muette de Portici* in Brussels rushed out into the streets after the patriotic duet 'Amour sacré de la patrie' in a state of excitement which led to the beginning of the revolt against the Dutch!

from their house, Natasha still not knowing that Andrei is amongst them. Pierre forcibly prevents some French soldiers from molesting the harassed citizens and, when soldiers drag in a group of Muscovites accused of having started the fires, he is shoved in amongst them. Marshal Davout confirms his order that incendiaries be shot. The veteran Karataev touchingly reassures Pierre of the values to be found in suffering, but most of the incendiaries are reprieved and marched off as prisoners (Ex. 7). French actresses rush into the streets, screaming that the theatre is on fire, and lunatics save themselves as the hospital burns. Introduced by Ex. 7 in the orchestra and surrounded by his staff, Napoleon makes his way through the thick smoke of burning Moscow, defeated by the city's resistance and mightily impressed by the courage of its inhabitants.

Scene xii shows Prokofiev at his most intense and his most dramatic, in this mood, one of the great twentieth-century masters of opera. At the back of a peasant's hut at Mitishi, Prince Andrei is lying wounded. He is delirious and the chorus can be heard singing 'Piti-piti-piti' as the blood pounds in his ears. The music returns to the lyricism of the opera's first part, but as Andrei thinks of Moscow Ex. 10 makes itself felt. He longs to see Natasha again (Ex. 1) and she has in fact found her way to his death-bed, is recognised (Ex. 4), wonders if he has changed towards her, and then starts to beg for forgiveness. Andrei tells her that he loves her more than he ever has before and their voices join to celebrate what he thinks of as new happiness. He asks her if he will live (Ex. 1) and she tries to reassure him. He falls asleep dreaming of their first dance together (Ex. 3). As his last spasm comes, the sound of 'Piti-piti-piti' becomes ever more insistent until it suddenly stops.

Scene xiii.   On the road to Smolensk, November 1812. A storm is raging. French troops are in retreat (a hint of the *scherzo* trumpets of Scene ix), escorting a group of Russian prisoners of war, amongst them Pierre and Karataev. Karataev can go no further and is shot as a straggler. Guerillas attack the French and free the prisoners (Ex. 8), and Pierre is recognised by Denisov, who assures him of victory (Ex. 8 again) and tells him also that Andrei is dead but Natasha safe in Moscow (Ex. 1). In a moment the Russian advance guard appears preceding the Marshal himself (Ex. 8 followed by Ex. 9). He is tired, but he knows that the French are beaten and his work done. All join in a great peroration to the eternal Russian spirit (Ex. 10).

Prokofiev may on the one hand be thought to have attempted the impossible in turning Tolstoy's novel into a one-evening opera, but there is reason on the other for thinking that the epic which has resulted will convey some of the novel's essence to the listener who already knows the book, which is to say three out of every four members of any Russian audience. If he has had a measure of success in evoking Tolstoy, has he written an opera that is valid in its own right? After the work's première in Zagreb in 1961, The Times correspondent had this reaction: 'There is a real problem in how to view the opera to its best advantage. The trouble is that two frames of reference are needed. To see the opera only as a nationalistic exercise is to pass over the many pretty and charming places in the first part. But to disregard entirely political and patriotic matters (and intent) can lead to considerable annoyance at the chest-beating, muscle-flexing, tear-jerking banality of some moments in the second part.' Oddly enough, critics after the British stage première in 1972 were about equally divided in preferring War to Peace and vice versa, and each party held its view to be self-evidently correct. But their concerted opinion was more positive than had been The Times eleven years earlier.

My own position is far less didactic, accepting as I do the echoes of Tchaikovsky in the first part and, in the second, the thrusting choruses and insistently-appealing aria of Kutuzov as equally evocative of the moods Prokofiev wanted to create, pointing to a host of moments which illuminate character and situation, to Prokofiev's rare ability to combine pathos with narrative, and to the unfailing musicality of the whole great epic. In 1972, a quarter of a century distant from the war and in a musical climate when new and (dare I say it?) romantic music had the therapeutic value of water in a desert, to hear as I did rehearsal after rehearsal and half a dozen performances in the space of five weeks was to be convinced all over again—this time from practical experience whereas originally from score, disc and a single Bolshoi performance—that Prokofiev's War and Peace is more or less indistinguishable from a masterpiece.   H.

DMITRI DMITREVICH SHOSTAKOVICH

(1906–1975)

KATERINA ISMAILOVA

Lady Macbeth of Mtsensk

OPERA in four acts (nine scenes) by Dmitri Shostakovich; libretto, after N. Leskov, by A. Preis and D. Shostakovich. Première, Leningrad, January 22, 1934, conducted by Samosud. First Performed Moscow, 1934, produced by Nemirovich-Danchenko; Cleveland (in Russian) 1935, conductor Rodzinski; London, Queen's Hall (in concert), 1936, with Slobodskaya, Hughes Macklin, Harold Williams, conductor Albert Coates. Revived in original version Düsseldorf, 1959, with Erika Wien, Rudolf Francl, Randolph Symonette, conductor Erede. Revised by the composer and first performed in new version Leningrad, January, 1963; outside Russia, Covent Garden, 1963, with Marie Collier, Charles Craig, Otakar Kraus, conductor Edward Downes; San Francisco, 1964, with Marie Collier, Jon Vickers, Chester Ludgin, conductor Leopold Ludwig.

CHARACTERS

Boris Timofeevich Ismailov, *a merchant* . . . . . High Bass
Zinovy Borisovich Ismailov, *his son, a merchant* . . Tenor
Katerina Lvovna Ismailova, *wife of Zinovy*
    Borisovich . . . . Soprano
Sergei, *employed by the Ismailovs* . . . . Tenor
A Drunk . . . . Tenor
Aksinya . . . . Soprano
Mill hand . . . . Baritone
Steward . . . . Bass
Two Workmen . . . . Tenors
Coachman . . . . Tenor
Porter . . . . Bass
A Nihilist . . . . Tenor
Priest . . . . Bass
Police-Sergeant . . . . Baritone
Policeman . . . . Bass
Drunken Guest . . . . Tenor
Sergeant . . . . Bass
Sentry . . . . Bass
Sonyetka, *a convict* . . . . Contralto

Old Convict .... Bass
Female Convict .... Soprano
Workpeople, Foremen, Policemen, Guests, Convicts
Time: Mid-nineteenth Century   *Place:* Kursk Gubernia,
Russia

Leskov's original story, a masterpiece in its way, is dated 1865. Shostakovich and his librettist decided to retain little of its ironical character, choosing instead, with an eye perhaps to political capital, to accentuate the dislikable qualities of the characters of the old regime to the point in some cases of caricature. The exception to this rule is Katerina herself, to whom the composer has given sympathetic characteristics and the lyrical music to go with them.

Act I, scene i.   Katerina's room. She is lying on her bed, bored with the tedium of her life and the loveless marriage she contracted five years ago. Heralded by a bassoon tune, Boris Timofeevich, her disagreeable old father-in-law, comes upstairs to rail at her and complain that she has not yet given his son an heir—no doubt she would like to take a lover, but his watchfulness will prevent any idea of that sort. As he goes out he tells Katerina to get ready the poison for the rats, and she mutters that nothing would please her better than to feed it to him. Boris is back in a moment with his son, Zinovy, and some servants. A dam has been damaged and must be mended and Zinovy himself prepares to set off to superintend the work. The servants set up a mock plea to persuade him not to leave them, but Zinovy pays little attention and introduces to his father Sergei, whom he has just engaged. Boris insists that Zinovy make his wife swear an oath to be faithul to him while he is away and, in spite of Zinovy's protests, crowns the performance by forcing her to kneel. They all go out and Aksinya comments on the saucy looks of Sergei who was dismissed from his last place because the mistress nearly fell for him.

An orchestral interlude leads to scene ii, the Ismailovs' yard. The servants, amongst them Sergei, have caught Aksinya and are pinching and prodding her as if she were a pig ready for market, and her complaints are loud and continuous. Katerina appears and rates them for their unkindness and for wasting time. Sergei insists on shaking her by the hand, and in a moment Katerina is wrestling with him. He throws her just as Boris Timofeevich comes out of the house

d sends them all about their business. He threatens to tell
novy about his wife's behaviour.

Another interlude takes us to Katerina's bedroom. As
usual she is bored, but she is not alone for long before the
voice of her father-in-law is heard outside scolding her for
wasting the candle. When he has gone, she looks out of the
window and sings a beautiful song contrasting her lonely
state with the freedom of the birds she sees outside her
window: 'At my window alone on a summer day.' On the
pretext of wanting to borrow a book, Sergei appears at the
door, reminds her how agreeable their wrestling was just now
and, seizing her, offers to start it again. They embrace, make
passionate love and are only momentarily disconcerted when
the voice of Boris Timofeevich can be heard outside the door
asking if Katerina is safely in bed.

Act II, scene iv.   The Yard. To the accompaniment of
highly suggestive music, Boris Timofeevich is prowling up and
down like a tom cat underneath Katerina's window,
remembering the sexual prowess of his youth and making
comparisons between such joys of the past and his son's
present avoidance of them. He sees a light in Katerina's
window and now cannot resist giving utterance to his
lecherous thoughts. What wouldn't he do if he were ten years
younger—he seems about to show us when Sergei can be seen
at the window kissing Katerina goodbye. During the
rapturous farewell, Boris recognises Sergei and when he
climbs down the drainpipe catches him by the collar. Boris
shouts for help, has Sergei stripped and tied to a post, and
after summoning Katerina to the window to watch, proceeds to flog him. Katerina screams to be let out of her room,
but no one moves, and in the end she slides down the
drainpipe and throws herself at her father-in-law. The
flogging over, Sergei is carried away and Boris Timofeevich
demands supper from his daughter-in-law.

With Sergei safely locked up in the store-room, Boris sends
a message to his son to tell him there is trouble at home. But
Katerina's revenge is not long delayed. She has poisoned the
mushrooms and Boris begins to feel the pain gnawing at his
vitals. He cries for a priest, but Katerina is implacable, takes
the keys from his pockets and leaves him to die alone. Some
workmen coming back from a drink cannot understand his
babbling, but the priest arrives in time to hear him accuse his
daughter-in-law of murder. She for her part mourns so

eloquently that the priest is left to muse, in music of inan
popular style, on the mysteries of dying. As the curtain fal.
an extra battery of brass, not so far heard, lets loose witr
shattering effect a series of discords which lead into the
entr'acte, itself the opera's biggest single movement, a
massive passacaglia which powerfully sums up the overheated
drama.

Scene v. Katerina's bedroom. The lovers are together.
Katerina's passion is reflected in her music, but Sergei is
already more disposed for sleep—an erotic predicament fully
reflected in the music. Sergei worries, he tells Katerina, at the
thought of Zinovy's return, which will inevitably mean the
end of their love. If only he were her husband and not her
lover! The train of thought is not hard to follow, and Sergei
eggs her on until, satisfied, he falls asleep. Her thoughts about
the future are interrupted by the appearance of the ghost of
Boris Timofeevich (bass chorus off-stage), at first unable to
frighten her, but in the end causing her shrieks of terror to
wake up Sergei. Sergei cannot see the ghost and they fall
asleep again, until Katerina thinks she hears someone
stealthily approaching the door. They realise it is Zinovy
Borisovich, and Sergei hides.

Zinovy calls to Katerina who eventually lets him in. How
has she spent her time? Father's death was very sudden. Why
is the bed made up for two—and why is there a man's belt on
it? He knows all about her scandalous behaviour, he says, and
picking up the belt he starts to beat her with it, until Sergei
rushes out from his hiding place. Zinovy scrambles to the
window, but Katerina pulls him back and starts to throttle
him. Sergei helps her and soon Zinovy is dead. To the tune of
a grotesque march, they carry the body down to the cellar,
Katerina lighting the way with a candle. What starts as a
jaunty, light-hearted tune finishes in something sinister and
woe-begone as they bury the body. The curtain comes down
with Katerina and Sergei standing locked in each other's
arms.

Act III, scene vi.   Katerina and Sergei on their wedding
day brood about the crime which lies hidden behind the
cellar door. As they leave to go to the party, a drunk enters
on the prowl for more liquor. In a brilliantly funny scene, he
runs through a whole catalogue of reasons why it is essential
for him to get supplies from the cellar, breaks down the door
but emerges almost immediately holding his nose and com-

plaining about the appalling stink. What can it be? Further investigation convinces him that he has found the decomposing corpse of Zinovy Borisovich.

Scene vii, preceded by an entr'acte drawn from the music of the previous scene, takes place in the local police station, where the Sergeant and his men are sitting, frantically doing nothing. In a parody of an operetta chorus, they hymn their unceasing importance but lament their present unemployment. Things look up when a nihilist teacher is brought in and questioned, but even this cannot compensate for what really riles them—that they have not been invited to the Ismailov wedding feast. When the drunk bursts in with news that he has found a corpse in the Ismailovs' cellar, the Sergeant and his men behave as if they have been expecting some such information and hurry off to make their arrests.

A short and brisk entr'acte takes us to scene viii, where, in the Ismailovs' garden, the wedding feast is in progress. Suddenly Katerina notices that the padlock of the cellar is broken. She tells Sergei the game is up and they must leave immediately. He is just coming back from the house with some money, when the Sergeant and his men enter the garden. His tone is bantering, but Katerina quickly realises there is no point in pretence and holds out her wrists for the handcuffs. Sergei tries to escape but they catch him, beat him and secure him too. Completely happy, the police march their prisoners off to gaol.

Act IV, scene ix. It is evening and a large band of convicts, all of them shackled, has halted temporarily near a bridge. Men and women are in separate groups. In contrast to the grotesque and even farcical happenings of the previous act, this last scene is entirely tragic and mostly lyrical. An old convict, Dostoievskian in his resignation and in his musical utterance taking after Moussorgsky, sings movingly of the long unforgiving road they must travel to Siberia. A subdued Katerina bribes a guard to let her go through to the men and she makes her way to Sergei. His reception of her caresses is thoroughly disagreeable—has she forgotten that it's entirely her fault he is here at all? She goes sadly back to the other women, lamenting (in a beautiful *arioso* with cor anglais obbligato) that, hard as were the sentence and the flogging, harder still is it to know from Sergei's every gesture that he hates her.

Meanwhile Sergei goes up to Sonyetka and in music of

operetta-like banality starts to flirt with her. She is a
mercenary little baggage and insists that her favours must be
paid for. Her stockings are torn; she will be Sergei's if he can
get her another pair—from Katerina for instance. On the
pretext that his legs hurt him, Sergei wheedles her only spare
pair out of Katerina. Immediately he gives them to Sonyetka
and carries her off triumphantly, leaving Katerina in an agony
of jealousy. The women mock her and their noise brings the
sentry running up. Katerina laments slowly and agonisingly,
before the Sergeant in charge wakes everyone up and gets
the column ready to move off. The old convict rouses the
stupefied Katerina, and she gets slowly to her feet, goes up to
Sonyetka who is standing on the bridge, seizes her and jumps
with her into the river. The Sergeant looks after them,
decides there is nothing to be done as the current is too
strong, and orders everybody to move off. With the old convict trying to brace up their morale, they start on their way.

   Katerina Ismailova is undeniably a mixture of styles,
parody jostling lyricism, and farce elbowing tragedy. But, if it
is the creation of a young opera composer, it is also a work of
flair and brilliance and unfailing vitality. Its early success was
very considerable, but in January, 1936, (a few days after
Stalin and Molotov had publicly approved Dzerzhinsky's
opera *And Quiet Flows the Don*, based on Sholokhov's novel)
an article appeared in *Pravda* entitled 'Muddle instead of
Music'. It denounced *Katerina Ismailova* as modernist and
confused, its music 'leftist' and discordant. From then on,
Shostakovich enjoyed an up-and-down career in Soviet
Russia, mostly applauded for his earnest endeavour to live up
to the ideals of Socialist Realism, occasionally disapproved
for palpably falling short of them. The once popular *Lady
Macbeth of Mtsensk* (abroad, the opera usually carried the
name of Leskov's story) became something of a legend, never
performed in its native land and very seldom outside owing
to the tight control kept on orchestral material. Rumours of
work on a new version were current from about 1957 (when
Covent Garden enquired about the possibility of performance) but each winter went by without the projected
première materialising. A thorough revision of a work which
started as something of a patchwork of styles and which was
written nearly a generation earlier was unlikely and indeed
hardly possible; and any attempt to obliterate the 'immoral'
elements of the story seemed doomed to failure.

After the war, there were only two Western productions of
the opera in its original form, in Venice in 1947, and in
Düsseldorf in 1959—and no sooner was permission given for
the second of these than it was withdrawn, but only after a
contract between the publisher and the Düsseldorf theatre
had been signed. Those of us who saw this production could
have been excused for wondering if it would turn out to be
the last performance in our time of a minor contemporary
masterpiece, but the composer's revision, nearly thirty years
after the opera was written, removed the work from the
realms of conjecture and allowed a new generation to make
up its own mind. When it was finally heard, the revision
turned out to consist of no more than some smoothing out of
the extremities of the vocal line, of some changes in the
words and stage directions, and of the composition of new
interludes between scenes i and ii and scenes vii and viii.

H.

18
English Opera

ETHEL SMYTH
(1858–1944)

THE WRECKERS
Standrecht

OPERA in three acts by Dame Ethel Smyth; text by Brewster (in French) from his Cornish drama, *Les Naufrageurs*. Première, Leipzig, November 11, 1906. First performed London (Queen's Hall concert), 1908, conductor Nikisch; His Majesty's Theatre, 1909, conductor Beecham; Covent Garden, 1910, with Edyth Walker, Edith Evans, Booker, Koubitzky, Weidemann, Ranalow, conductor Bruno Walter; Sadler's Wells, 1939, with Coates, Gruhn, Wright, Roderick Lloyd, Hargreaves, conductor Braithwaite.

CHARACTERS

Pascoe, *headman of the village and local
    preacher aged fifty-five* . . . . Bass (Baritone)
Lawrence, *keeper of the lighthouse* . . . . Baritone
Harvey, *Lawrence's brother-in-law* . . . . Bass
Tallan, *landlord of the tavern* . . . . Tenor
Jack, *son of Tallan, aged fifteen* . . . . Mezzo-Soprano
Mark, *a young fisherman* . . . . Tenor
Thirza, *wife of Pascoe, aged twenty-two* Mezzo-Soprano
Avis, *daughter of Lawrence, aged seventeen* . . . Soprano
    A Preacher, Fishermen, Shepherds, Miners and their
            Women; Wreckers and Pietists
Time: Late Eighteenth Century   *Place:* Cornwall

The drama unfolds itself on the Cornish coast, in the second half of the eighteenth century, at the time of the Wesleyan Revival. The Cornish village in which the action takes place is inhabited by a fierce people who believe that wrecks on their coasts are a direct gift from Providence. For a long time ships have passed the dangerous coast in safety and the inhabitants are on the verge of famine. Believing this to be a punishment for their sins, they implore Heaven to deliver into their hands mariners to murder and ships to rob.

Act I. The chapel bells are calling the congregation to prayer, and as the curtain rises a number of people are seen on the way to church singing a hymn. Tallan and Jack, coming from the tavern, profess to believe in wine rather than prayer. A gust of wind, however, is enough to drive all other concerns from their minds. For wind means a bad sea and a bad sea may bring a wreck to their coast. The sight of Pascoe, their chief man and preacher, causes the merry-makers to put down their glasses hastily. Pascoe reproves them, but as soon as he is gone Avis boldly challenges their belief in Pascoe. It is not because of their sins that ships go in safety, she says, but because some traitor has been lighting a beacon to warn sailors off the coast. Her father, Lawrence, keeper of the lighthouse, has himself seen the beacon when on stormy nights he put out the lamp of the lighthouse to lure ships to destruction. Pascoe's wife, Thirza, enters, and while some avoid her, others ask her to join them in prayer. Thirza returns a disdainful answer, and, turning her back on the wreckers, enters her cottage.

As soon as she has gone the others go to chapel, leaving Avis alone. She hides and sees Mark passing and throwing flowers through the window of Thirza's cottage. Avis, who is herself in love with Mark, comes forward and accuses him of neglecting her for Thirza. Mark makes light of Avis's jealousy, and, declaring that she is but a child whose fancies are not to be taken seriously, joins the worshippers in the chapel. Seeing Thirza enter with Mark's flower on her breast, Avis hints at her knowledge that Thirza, enamoured of Mark, has betrayed her husband. Pascoe, returning, sends Avis to chapel, then gently rebukes Thirza for not going there. Thirza answers that to pray for the destruction of ships and sailors in order to enrich the villagers is revolting to her. She abhors the wreckers. Pascoe defends them, pleading ancient customs, but Thirza will not listen. She recalls with horror the awful scenes she has witnessed; Pascoe himself has become hateful in her sight. As she runs away, the people issue from the chapel praising the preacher who 'shouted and thundered' till 'all felt convicted of sin'. After they are gone, Lawrence, Harvey, Tallan, and Jack consult about the steps to be taken to discover who signals to the ships. They decide to watch various parts of the cliffs, and the act ends as the people prepare to attack a barque which has been seen driving on the rocks.

Act II.   The act is ushered in by a prelude describing the 'Cliffs of Cornwall', which has had considerable success as a concert piece. The scene represents a desolate part of the seashore where Avis and Jack are watching for the 'traitor'. Avis at first is very scornful of Jack's efforts, then, thinking that Jack's friendship may be of use to her, allows him to kiss her. As they go to watch elsewhere, Mark enters determined once more to warn ships off that fateful strand. He collects wood for his bonfire and is about to light it when Thirza enters and begs him not to do it as the beach is watched, and should he be discovered he would be killed as a traitor. In a great love scene, the two decide to go to some distant country together, and forgetting all prudent counsel, Thirza herself applies the torch to the fire. It will be their farewell to Cornwall. Pascoe is led thither by the light of its flame and discovers Thirza in the arms of Mark. The latter escapes, but Thirza proudly boasts of having lit the fire, and tells Pascoe that she loves another. Pascoe falls senseless while the crowd gathers around them. He will be taken to the cave where 'traitors' are judged and, if found guilty, condemned to death.

Act III.   The crowd assembles in the cave which opens on the sea through a narrow archway. A path leading to the top of the cliff can be barred by an iron gate. Amongst the crowd are Thirza, Avis, and Jack. A little later Harvey, Tallan, Pascoe, and Lawrence join them. Still later, Mark appears. It is dawn, but torches are necessary to light the dark cave. Lawrence is the accuser. He relates how he and the others saw the fire and, going to it, found Pascoe in a swoon close by the beacon. Pascoe refuses to say whether he himself lit the fire, whereupon Avis, pointing to Thirza, accuses her of having bewitched her husband. Thirza answers contemptuously, but if Pascoe cannot or will not deny the accusation, he must die. Then Mark comes forward and owns that it was he who lit the warning light, at the bidding of 'a voice that we needs must follow'. He demands to be condemned. Thirza then says that if it was Mark who betrayed them, hers was the real guilt. Avis seeks to save Mark by asserting that he passed the night with her, but her stratagem fails. Thirza and Mark are both condemned to death and left in the cave, where the rising tide must drown them. The crowd leaves, locking the gate that leads to the top of the cliff. Their voices outside singing the psalm for the passing of souls mingle with the last song of the lovers as the waves invade the cave. F. B.

THE BOATSWAIN'S MATE

Comedy in one act and two parts. After W. W. Jacobs's story of that name. Dramatised for music and composed by Ethel Smyth. Accepted for performance in Germany, the production was prevented by the outbreak of war in 1914. First performed in London in 1916 at Shaftesbury Theatre, with Townsend, Pounds, Ranalow, conductor Goossens. First performed Old Vic, 1922; Covent Garden, 1923, with Buckman, Sidney Russell, Michael, Allin, conductor Goossens; Sadler's Wells, 1933, with Naylor, Cox, Austin, Brindle, conductor Beecham.

CHARACTERS

Harry Benn, *ex-boatswain* .... Tenor
Ned Travers, *ex-soldier* .... Baritone
Mrs. Waters, *Landlady of 'The Beehive'* ...... Soprano
Mary Ann, *a servant girl* .... Burlesque Actress:
need not sing
Policeman .... Bass
Chorus of Agricultural Labourers. Two Cats
(behind the scenes)

Time: Early Twentieth Century *Place:* England

N.B.—The opera may be played either with a pause between Parts I and II, or straight through. Part I consists of spoken dialogue and music; Part II is wholly music.

Part I. The scene represents the outside of a country inn, 'The Beehive', kept by a buxom widow, Mrs. Waters. The ex-boatswain, Harry Benn, drinks his beer and hopes to put an end to his loneliness by marrying Mrs. Waters. As 'The Beehive' stands alone in a country road he believes that the security afforded by the presence of a man on the premises must be a cogent argument in his favour. That very night the maid, Mary Ann, will be away, and Benn urges his suit. But Mrs. Waters will have none of him. Having tried marriage once, she is of opinion that 'once bitten, twice shy' is a good saying. She has to go to the post office, and she asks Benn to look after any customer who might turn up. Left to himself, Benn recalls his wanderings over the world and the visions which haunted them—visions of 'piling up dollars and choosing a wife'. His reminiscences are cut short by the arrival of the ex-soldier Ned Travers, who mistakes him for the landlord. Benn explains that without being the landlord he is in charge because of the great friendship existing between himself and the landlady. Travers winks knowingly, and the pair get on famously together, Benn promising Travers a job as soon as Mrs. Waters (who has refused him five times in the last fortnight) changes her mind. While Travers sings of his adventures when he was in the Army, Benn has matured a plan in his mind to bring matters to a head and make Mrs. Waters look upon him with a more favourable eye. And this he tactfully suggests to his new friend, whose help is indispensable. In the middle of the night Travers is to effect an entrance into 'The Beehive' and frighten the landlady. When she cries out Benn will rush in, tackle the supposed burglar, win her gratitude and her hand. Travers demurs at first, but two good sovereigns persuade him to undertake the job. To be quite safe he obtains from Benn a written declaration dictated in the style of grand opera recitative to the effect that Travers only pretends to be a burglar and that 'all is above board and ship-shape'. This declaration Benn signs and gives to Travers.

Part II.   The interior of 'The Beehive' at night. The moon shines outside. Benn and Travers appear at the window. They force the catch and Travers enters. After exchanging a few final remarks with Benn he is left alone to fulfil his mission. He takes off his boots, and humming a song, begins to ascend the stairs leading to Mrs. Waters's room. It is not easy to climb in the dark without making a noise. He stumbles, and a light from above announces that the noise has been heard. Mrs. Waters appears, a light in one hand, a gun in the other. Travers hastily hides in a cupboard. Mrs. Waters follows and turns the key, locking him in. Having secured her supposed burglar, she is on the point of rousing the neighbours when Travers begs her to desist, assuring her he is no burglar and giving her Benn's declaration. Mrs. Waters is amazed, but she opens the door of the cupboard on condition that Travers will do exactly as she tells him. A charming duet, 'O dear, if I

▪ad known he was quite a young man, I'd have put on more clothes!' hints at future developments. But Mrs. Waters means to give Benn a lesson. She will fire the gun at a mat and pretend she has killed the burglar. No sooner said than done. Travers hides while Mrs. Waters fires and then calls out 'murder'. The expectant Benn rushes in to find a very different situation from the one he had planned. He is staggered by the new turn of events and horrified when the landlady sings a valse tune to 'The first thing to do is get rid of the body'. He is sent to dig the grave, haunted by the fear of ghosts, but soon returns with a policeman to whom he has given himself up for the murder of Travers at 'The Beehive'. The arrival of the policeman is heralded by the fate motif of Beethoven's C minor symphony. A very lively quartet ensues, for Mrs. Waters has to produce Travers and convince the representative of the law that there has been no murder. Finally the policeman and Benn are driven out of doors by Travers and Mrs. Waters. Travers improves the situation by making love to Mrs. Waters, who at first appears indignant, then softens and finally permits him to return to enquire as to new possible developments. It would be the best joke of all if Benn should find Travers installed as the landlord of 'The Beehive'. Mrs. Waters takes down the handglass and looks at herself with evident satisfaction, while Mary Ann returns to find that 'the missus can kick 'er 'eels' in her delight at the unexpected outcome of the adventure.   F. B.

FREDERICK DELIUS
(1862–1934)

A VILLAGE ROMEO AND JULIET

OPERA in a prologue and three acts by Frederick Delius; text by the composer, based on a story by Gottfried Keller. Première, Berlin, February 21, 1907. First performed Covent Garden, 1910, with Ruth Vincent, Hyde, Dearth, Maitland, conductor Beecham. Revived 1920 with Licette, Hyde, Heming, Michael, conductor Beecham; Royal College of Music, 1934, conductor Beecham; Bradford, 1962, by Sadler's Wells with Morison, Wakefield, conductor Meredith Davies.

American première, Washington, 1972, with Patricia Wells, Joh
Stewart, John Reardon.

CHARACTERS

Manz ⎱
Marti ⎰ *rich farmers* .... ⎰ Baritone
                                          ⎱ Baritone

Sali, *son of Manz* ⎰ *as a child* .... Soprano
                    ⎱ *as a man* .... Tenor

Vreli, *daughter of Marti* .... Soprano
The Dark Fiddler, *rightful heir to the wood* ... Baritone
Two Peasants .... Baritone
Three Women .... Soprano, Mezzo-Soprano
Gingerbread Woman .... Soprano
Wheel-of-Fortune Woman .... Soprano
Cheap Jewellery Woman .... Mezzo-Soprano
Showman .... Tenor
Merry-go-Round Man .... Baritone
The Slim Girl .... Soprano
The Wild Girl .... Mezzo-Soprano
The Poor Horn-Player .... Tenor
The Hunch-backed Bass Fiddler .... Bass

Time: Mid-Nineteenth Century. Six years elapse between the
    first and second scenes
Place: Seldwyla, Switzerland

Professor Arthur Hutchings, author of an authoritative
book on Delius, admonishes the listener: 'Opera-goers who
require the stage properties and dramatic interruptions of
Italian opera, the pageantry and ballet of Russian opera, the
discrimination of character and emotional versatility of
Mozartian opera, cannot fail to be disappointed in *A Village
Romeo and Juliet.* No opera is more musical, because in no
opera has the composer been more certain that by music he
would tell the tale; Cecil Gray has called it "a symphonic
poem with the implicit programme made explicit upon the
stage." ... In this work the opera-goer must expect only
music, and music chiefly of the same kind—sustained, dreamy
beauty, slightly off-set by the sinister strains of the Dark
Fiddler or the litigious quarrels of the farmers.'
    Scene i.   September. A piece of land luxuriously over-
grown on a hill, the broad fields of Manz and Marti lie on
either side, only a small piece of either field being visible.

Manz and Marti are rivals for the strip of wild land which lies
between their fields. They are both ploughing when the
action begins, and each, when the other is not looking, takes
an extra furrow out of the waste land.

Sali and Vreli bring their parents' midday meals, then go
off to play together in the woods. Manz and Marti reappear
to eat their dinners together. The children come out of the
wood at the same time as the Dark Fiddler can be heard in
the distance. Marti recognises him, and knows that the land
should be his, but that, being a bastard, he has no legal right
to it. The Fiddler disappears, watched by the children. Their
parents are no less baffled by his appearance than they are.
They start to discuss the prospective sale of the land, each
criticising the way the other has stolen a furrow here and
there. They quarrel furiously, and forbid their respective
children ever again to play with each other.

Scene ii.   Six years later. Outside Marti's house, which has
a neglected air about it. The children are now grown up, and
ever more closely drawn towards one another. Sali comes
towards the house, from which Vreli presently looks out
longingly. They patch up a quarrel, caused one imagines by
the lawsuit in which their parents have been frittering away
their heritages. They are pessimistic about the situation, but
Sali hopes all may yet come right if they stick together. They
make an appointment for the evening, in the fields.

Scene iii.   The wild land, overgrown with poppies. Sali
waits for Vreli, who comes in and calls him, then hides until
he finds her. Their delight in each other's company is
obvious. The sound of the Dark Fiddler's playing is heard,
and he reminds them that they have played on his land. Now
that they are all beggars, he feels they are equal. Why do they
not come with him and share his vagabond's existence? He
does not seem to expect an answer, but is confident they will
meet again. Vreli remembers that the last time they saw him
was on the dread day when their fathers quarrelled. Sali
reassures her, and they talk happily of their childhood days.
They embrace.

Marti can be seen looking for Vreli. He spies them, and is
dragging Vreli away when Sali fells him with a blow.

Scene iv.   A slow introduction leads to a new scene, the
interior of Marti's house, now quite bare, apart from a bed
and a bench. Vreli is sitting in front of the fire, reminding
herself sadly that this is her last night in her old home. Sali

comes in, and after an ecstatic greeting, they sing of their
love, and pledge their word never to leave each other again
Vreli tells Sali that she has just taken her father away, as he
has lost his mind as a result of Sali's blow. She will have to
leave as the house has been sold. They sit down together in
front of the fire, and fall asleep in each other's arms. The
stage grows dark, and their dream is represented in music
They dream they are being married in the old church of
Seldwyla. Church bells ring, the organ plays, a hymn is sung
and finally the bells ring again merrily.

Dawn breaks, and the lovers awake to understand that i
was all a dream. Can they not have a whole day together, ask
Vreli, in which to wander through the woods, and dance? 'T
Berghald,' exclaims Sali. The sound of yodelling can be hear
in the distance, and together they leave the house.

Scene v.   The Fair. The whole apparatus of a fair, from
merry-go-rounds to shooting galleries, is visible. The variou
sellers cry their wares, and the showman leads some of th
crowd into a tent. Enter Sali and Vreli. They look happy, an
join in the gaiety of the fair until they are recognised by
woman from Seldwyla, with her companions. They bu
everything that attracts them, but suddenly notice that the
are being watched curiously by the crowd. Self-consciousl
they leave the fair, and make for the Paradise Garder
another dancing place.

The interlude during the change of scene is the famou
walk to the Paradise Garden (composed five years later tha
the rest of the opera to themes from it). In the middle of th
interlude, the stage directions indicate that Sali and Vre
should be seen resting on their journey.

Scene vi.   The vagabonds are heard in the distance befor
the curtain rises. When it does, it is to reveal a dilapidate
country house, now used as an inn. The river flows nearby
and a barge full of hay is moored on it. The Dark Fiddler an
his companions the vagabonds sit round a table. It is evening
The Dark Fiddler is evidently telling his friends the story o
the strife between Manz and Marti and its origin.

As he reaches the inconclusive end of his story, Sali an
Vreli come into the garden. The Dark Fiddler strongly advise
them to take to the road and join him and his friends. Th
Dark Fiddler plays while they dance. All join him in trying t
persuade the two young lovers to join them, but they fea
they are too respectable for a vagabond's life. Sali and Vre

gree that they could never take to the new life that is
ıggested to them. Bargemen are heard singing in the dis-
ınce, and gradually it dawns on Sali and Vreli that the only
ʻay out for them is to 'drift down the river' like the
argemen, but with a difference; they can never return.

Watched by the Dark Fiddler and the vagabonds, they get
ıto the barge. Vreli throws her nosegay into the river, and
ali draws the plug from the bottom of the boat and throws
in too. As the boat moves out into the middle of the
tream, Sali and Vreli fall into each other's arms on the bed
f hay. Boatmen can be heard in the distance singing 'Ho,
ʼavellers we a-passing by'. Of the end, Professor Hutchings
as written: 'The orchestra alone then concludes the work
ʼith a perfection unattainable by words; the music can
ıggest the deep and enfolding waters. However much the
athetic emotions have been stirred, we are satisfied and
omforted almost as by the "happy ending" of comedy.'

H.

RALPH VAUGHAN WILLIAMS
(1872–1958)

HUGH THE DROVER

ᵖPERA in two acts by Ralph Vaughan Williams, text by Harold Child.
remière, Royal College of Music, London, July 4, 1924. First per-
ᵒrmed His Majesty's Theatre, 1924, with Mary Lewis, Tudor Davies,
ollier, conductor Sargent; Washington, 1928; Toronto, 1932; R.C.M.,
933; Sadler's Wells, 1937, with Cross, Tudor Davies, Llewellyn,
ᵒnductor Collingwood; New York, 1952. Revived Sadler's Wells, 1950,
ʼith Gartside, Johnston, Roderick Jones, conductor Robertson: R.C.M.
ondon, 1972, for Vaughan Williams's Centenary.

CHARACTERS

A Showman .... High Baritone
Mary, *the constable's daughter* .... Soprano
Aunt Jane, *the constable's sister* .... Contralto
The Turnkey .... Tenor
The Constable .... Bass

```
John the Butcher .................. Bass-Baritone
Hugh the Drover .......................... Tenor
A Cheap-Jack .......................... Baritone
A Shell-fish Seller ........................ Bass
A Primrose-seller ...................... Contralto
A Ballad-seller .......................... Tenor
Susan ................................ Soprano
Nancy .................................. Alto
William ................................ Tenor
Robert ................................. Bass
A Fool ................................. Bass
An Innkeeper ........................... Bass
A Sergeant ............................ Baritone
```

Townspeople, Toy-sellers, Boys, Soldiers, Stall-keeper, Juggler,
Dancing-girl, Trumpeter, etc.

Time: About 1812   *Place:* A small town in the Cotswolds

The composer of *Hugh the Drover* has made extensive use
of English folk songs in his score, giving the music a peculiar
flavour and affecting also the treatment of the story, which
bears a distinctly original stamp. Although all the melodies
seem to bear some resemblance to folk songs, five authentic
traditional tunes ('Cockles', 'Toy Lambs', 'Primroses', 'Maria
Martin', and 'Tuesday Morning') are used in the first act and
one (the psalm-tune 'York') in the second.

Act I.   The scene represents a fair with booths and stalls
amongst which the crowd of sightseers moves slowly
admiring, laughing, jesting with showmen, ballad singers and
Cheap-Jacks. The Showman has a dummy of Napoleon
'Boneyparty', which is to be set on fire to delight the patriots
of Cotsall. The voice of Mary is heard singing 'I'm to be
married on Tuesday morning'. Mary is to marry on the
morrow John the Butcher; but the thought of the wedding
gives her no joy; she does not love John, the strongest and
richest man in the town. Her Aunt Jane persuades her to
accept her fate, when a stranger, Hugh the Drover, comes by
it is love at first sight with both Hugh and Mary. 'Sweet little
linnet' he calls her, and instead of riches he offers her a
roaming life of toil. Hugh's rousing song of the open road
stirs Mary's fancy; she is not afraid; with him and with him
alone can she find peace.

John enters with the crowd and eagerly embraces the
proposal to fight Hugh for Mary. The crowd makes a ring for

he two champions; they fight, and John does not fight fair.
Hugh, undismayed, continues the fight and, in the end, beats
ohn. But John, rather than resign his claims to Mary, accuses
Hugh of being a French spy. Mary is sure that Hugh cannot
·e a traitor; the crowd is not as faithful, and now acclaims
he Constable (Mary's father), who will put Hugh in the
tocks. Hugh is dragged off while the crowd jeers at the
French spy'.

Act II, scene i.   The market-place of the town. After-
.oon. (The composer directs that this scene[1] may be omitted
f the opera is found to be too long; the act then starts with
cene ii.) Hugh, guarded by John and four other men, is
rought in and about to be put in the stocks. The Constable
sks John whether it might not be more prudent to let Hugh
o; how can they prove he is a spy? John shows him money:
hat can prove anything.

Mary comes in, asks her father's pardon, and says she is
ow willing to marry John. The Constable is for taking her at
er word, but John is still suspicious, the more so when she
sks for Hugh to be freed since it is on her account that he is
1 the stocks. The Constable suggests they let him go—they
ave no evidence against him—but John sees through Mary's
tratagem, and urges them to bind Hugh fast lest he should
scape. Mary and Aunt Jane lament the failure of their
cheme, and they leave Hugh alone in the stocks.

Scene ii.   The church bells play the psalm-tune 'York'.
.arly morning the next day. Hugh is in the stocks.

John and his friends have made a night of it. In passing
hey come to taunt and hit Hugh who, of course, cannot
etort. As soon as they go Mary comes to set Hugh free,
aving taken the key of the stocks from her father. The
overs are on the point of running away when voices are
eard. A woman has caught sight of Hugh and Mary and gives
he alarm. Hugh goes back to the stocks and hides Mary
nder his cloak. The Turnkey and the Constable are pacified
t the sight of him, but no sooner have they gone when other
ounds of May festivities come to the lovers' ears. It is John,
vho comes to wake up Mary, bringing a spray of mayflowers.
Mary cannot be found. The Constable, Aunt Jane, and the

[1] Added for the 1933 revival at the R.C.M., London, when Beecham
onducted, the scene never, it would appear, entirely convinced its
omposer, who, however, some reports notwithstanding, did not
pecifically discard it.

Turnkey, coming to inquire into the new mystery, discovers
Mary sitting in the stocks side by side with Hugh. Many
would set Mary free; she refuses to go. The Constable
disowns her; John declares that a trollop from the stocks is
not a fit wife for him, but the crowd sympathises with the
generous girl. There is every likelihood of a fight between
the friends of John and the friends of Mary and Hugh when
the arrival of soldiers called to take away Hugh puts an end
to the dispute.

John is very anxious that Hugh should be instantly
arrested and tried. As soon, however, as the sergeant looks at
Hugh he discovers an old comrade; His Majesty has no better
friend in England than Hugh the Drover. Annoyed at having
come on a wild-goose chase he refuses to go away empty-
handed. He takes John and promises to make a soldier of
him. The Constable apologises to Hugh; their friends beg
them to stay. In a final homily Hugh tells them that he does
not love the smooth, sleek life of the town, and prefers 'the
windy wolds of life', where man has to do and dare or die. It
is a call that he and Mary must obey. They go, followed by the
farewells of their friends.   F. B.

THE POISONED KISS

Opera in three acts. Music by Ralph Vaughan Williams. The libretto
of the opera, by Evelyn Sharp, is derived partly from a tale of Richard
Garnett and partly from Nathaniel Hawthorne's story of Rapaccini'
daughter. *The Poisoned Kiss*, composed during 1927-8, was first
presented at Cambridge on May 12, 1936, and later the same year at
Sadler's Wells Theatre, London; New York, Juilliard School, 1937;
London Opera Centre, 1975.

CHARACTERS

Hob ⎫
Gob ⎬ *assistants to Dipsacus*
Lob ⎭
Dipsacus, *a professional magician* . . . . Bass
Tormentilla, *his daughter* . . . . Soprano
Angelica, *her maid* . . . . Soprano
Amaryllus, *son of the Empress of Golden Town* . Tenor
Gallanthus, *his jester* . . . . Baritone
Three ⎫ *assistants to the Empress* . . ⎰   Soprano,
Mediums ⎭   ⎱ Mezzo-Sopranos
The Empress Persicaria . . . . Contralto

Described as a romantic extravaganza, the opera is really a fairy tale set to characteristic and very charming music, and with spoken dialogue to help along the action.

The overture, compounded of tunes later heard in the opera, is directed to be played with the house lights up.

The first act is set near the house of Dipsacus on the edge of a forest where no man dwells. After the rise of the curtain rival choirs, representing the powers of good and evil, sing of the beauty of day and night respectively, but as soon as they have gone Angelica is left to lament the fate of an attractive young girl whose life passes in complete seclusion. All unknown to her, however, the prince and his jester have been roving in the forest and now the jester, Gallanthus, arrives. Angelica, who has never seen a young man before, falls in love with him; Gallanthus falls in love with her. Their billing and cooing is interrupted by the coming of Dipsacus who is aware that strangers have entered what he considers his own province, and he means to expel them by magic. The stage is emptied, but now Tormentilla arrives followed by Amaryllus. He met her in the forest nursing a cobra and, fearing for her life, has struck the snake a blow with his cane. Tormentilla does not fear snakes. She has been fed on poisons by Dipsacus, who has his own reasons for the strange diet. But Amaryllus does not know it and cannot understand why Tormentilla instead of thanking him weeps over her pet that has been hurt. An understanding is, however, soon reached when youth calls to youth; in their love duet, Amaryllus sings 'Blue larkspur in a garden, White clouds in summer skies', while Tormentilla, reared on poisons, uses the same tune for 'Black henbane in a thicket, Slime of the serpent's trail'. The two are about to go roving in the forest when Dipsacus intervenes. After some questioning Tormentilla whispers the word Love, upon which Dipsacus tells her his plans. When he was young he was scorned by the Empress of Golden Town and has vowed to be revenged. He has fed Tormentilla on poisons solely in order that her kiss should be death to any lover. She will have to meet the Empress's son, make him kiss her and thus kill him. That is Dipsacus's design. But Tormentilla refuses to be a party to such a murderous plot and the angry magician instantly banishes her and her maid. They, for their part, are not unwilling to go, especially as Angelica has abstracted a piece of the philosopher's stone which has the same virtue as Aladdin's lamp. They rub the stone, express a wish and the stage is filled with a host of milliners and dressmakers with their latest creations. As they go, the curtain falls.

Act II. Tormentilla's apartments in Golden Town. The room is filled with flowers sent by Tormentilla's admirers. Her beauty has excited such interest that when abroad she must wear a veil to avoid the unwelcome attentions of Golden Town gallants. She loves the prince whom she believes to be a shepherd boy, for the cunning son of the Empress, wanting to be loved for himself alone, has concealed his identity. Part of the act is taken up with the plots of the three assistants of the Empress and counterplots of three assistants of the magician. The assistants of the Empress have been instructed to poison Tormentilla, for that is the way in which the jealous mother gets rid of any young woman likely to steal her son's affections; the assistants of the magician on the other hand plot to bring the young lovers together so that the prince should kiss Tormentilla and die. The assistants of the Empress fail in their purpose. They present Tormentilla with a box of poisoned chocolates, but she, having been made immune, eats them with relish and without the least harm. The assistants of the magician are more successful. They bring the prince to Tormentilla's apartment; the lovers meet and kiss and the prince falls, apparently dead.

Act III. We are now in the palace of the Empress. The prince is not dead, having been fed on antidotes since childhood, but he is ailing. The doctor, seriously alarmed, bluntly tells the Empress that the only way to cure him is to bring to his side the woman whose name is ever on his lips. The Empress is very angry, but if neither her spells nor the art of the physician will serve, Tormentilla will have to come and stay till the prince is restored to health.

Meanwhile Dipsacus, who knows all that has happened, comes to gloat over the distracted woman who once jilted him. He boldly tells the Empress that he and his magic alone are responsible for the prince's illness. They quarrel at first; but the thoughts of the past crowd on them; the old love is not dead; they grow sentimental and fall into each other's arms. They are found in this position by the prince and Tormentilla. Marriages are arranged—not excluding the marriage of Gallanthus and Angelica. The act which began with a waltz and a tango (the composer's touch is ever light) ends in a glorious hornpipe dance. No magic has power against true love, and love has conquered once more.

F.B.

RIDERS TO THE SEA

Opera in one act by Ralph Vaughan Williams; text by J. M. Synge. Première, London, Royal College of Music, December 1, 1937. Produced Cambridge Arts Theatre, 1938, with Janet Smith-Miller, Margaret Field-Hyde, Olive Hall, Marcus Dods. Revived Wolverhampton, 1950; Sadler's Wells, 1953, with Marjorie Shires, Elizabeth Robinson, Olwen Price, John Faasen, conductor John Matheson; Naples, 1959, with Pina Malagrini, Elena Todeschi, Miriam Pirazzini, Guido Mazzini, conductor Francesco Molinari-Pradelli.

CHARACTERS

Maurya, *an old woman*	Contralto
Bartley, *her son*	Baritone
Cathleen, *her daughter*	Soprano
Nora, *her younger daughter*	Soprano
A Woman	Mezzo-Soprano

Chorus of women

Time: Early Twentieth Century *Place:* An island off the west coast of Ireland

This short music drama, based almost word for word on J. M. Synge's one-act play about a fishing community on the Isle of Arran, is probably the composer's most successful opera. Begun in 1925, it was finished in 1932 and first performed at the Royal College of Music in December, 1937. Its relative neglect by opera companies is due to the difficulty of finding a suitable companion piece, which only makes it the more regrettable that the composer abandoned his original idea of setting Synge's *The Tinker's Wedding* which would have made the appropriate comic contrast.

The opera begins with a short prelude[1] in which we hear the sea swelling from ominous calm to the growing storminess heard as the door opens on scene i to admit Nora to the cottage kitchen where her sister Cathleen sits spinning. Nora has brought with her some clothes taken from a drowned man to discover if they belong to Michael, their

---

[1] Vaughan Williams uses a small orchestra: single woodwind apart from a second flute (the only clarinet is a bass clarinet); brass confined to two horns and one trumpet; and a limited string section.

brother, who, like his father and four other brothers, has been lost at sea. Maurya, their mother, is trying to rest in the next room, and the two younger women, over menacing orchestral sounds of rising wind and sea, quietly talk of their mother's wretchedness and hide the clothes away from her in the loft.

Maurya cannot sleep. She no sooner expresses her anxiety that Bartley, her only remaining son, intends to take the horses in the boat to the Galway Fair than Bartley himself arrives to collect a rope for a halter. In spite of the entreaties of his mother and sisters, he calmly gives them instructions on how to manage during his absence and goes out saying that he will ride the red mare with the grey pony running behind. Cathleen and Nora reproach their mother for not giving Bartley her blessing, and make the excuse that they have forgotten to give him his bread for the journey in order to send her after him. She stands for a moment in the doorway and sings mournfully 'in this place it is the young men do be leaving things behind them for them that do be old', then sets out into the wind, strongly expressed in strings and woodwind.

In Maurya's absence her daughters, at times unaccompanied or over a wandering solo oboe, decide to open the bundle of clothes. They find to their horror that they were certainly Michael's. Their mourning is heartfelt but, on hearing their mother return, they hide the clothes and compose themselves.

Maurya comes in and sits keening to herself. Cathleen tries to discover what has so terribly distressed her and Maurya tells them that she has seen Bartley riding to the sea on the red mare with Michael dressed in fine clothes and new shoes riding behind him on the grey pony. But, Cathleen tells her, they now know Michael is dead. Maurya is adamant and says that this vision means she will lose Bartley as well. Over an off-stage chorus of wailing women she sings of the deaths of all her men one after the other. As she describes the bringing home of the body of Patch, the door opens and behind the old women who come in is carried the dripping corpse of Bartley. He has been knocked into the sea by the grey pony.

Against the keening of the women, Maurya in a majestic aria sings of her resignation, which amounts almost to relief, as the sea has now taken from her everything that it could and is powerless to hurt her further. No longer will she worry

about the wind and the tide; at last she can rest. Over a
sustained F minor background she blesses all her dead one by
one. Then as the music slides into E major she calls on God
to bless the soul of everyone left living in the world. The
sound of orchestra and wailing women surges up as Maurya
sings proudly that Michael has had a clean burial and Bartley
will have a fine coffin and a deep grave, but calm returns as
she says, 'No man at all can be living for ever and we must be
satisfied.' She kneels submissively by the bier. A sudden gust
blows open the cottage door through which we hear the
ceaseless noise of the sea. A soprano voice grows fainter and
fainter in the distance as the stage fades into darkness and we
are left only with the sound of the wind.   H.

THE PILGRIM'S PROGRESS

A morality in a prologue, four acts and an epilogue, founded on
Bunyan's Allegory of the same name; music by Ralph Vaughan
Williams. Première, Covent Garden, April 26, 1951, with Arnold
Matters, Inia Te Wiata, Norman Walker, Edgar Evans, conductor
Leonard Hancock; B.B.C. (in Studio), 1960, with John Noble, Herincx,
conductor Boult.

CHARACTERS

John Bunyan, *the writer* . . . . Bass-Baritone
The Pilgrim . . . . Baritone
Evangelist . . . . Bass
The Four Neighbours:
   Pliable . . . . Tenor
   Obstinate . . . . Bass
   Mistrust . . . . Baritone
   Timorous . . . . Tenor
Three Shining Ones ⎱ *in the House* ⎰ Soprano, Mezzo,
The Interpreter ⎰   *Beautiful* ⎱ Contralto, Tenor
Watchful, *the Porter* . . . . High Baritone
A Herald . . . . High Baritone
Apollyon ⎱   ⎰   Bass
Two Heavenly ⎬ *in the Valley of* ⎨ Soprano,
  Beings ⎰   *Humiliation* ⎱   Contralto

Lord Lechery		Buffo Tenor
A Jester		Dancer
Demas		Baritone
Judas Iscariot		Baritone
Simon Magus		Bass
Worldly Glory		High Baritone
Madam Wanton		Soprano
Madam Bubble	*in Vanity Fair* ...	Mezzo-Soprano
Pontius Pilate		Bass
Usher		Buffo Tenor
Lord Hate-Good		Bass
Malice		Soprano
Pickthank		Contralto
Superstition		Tenor
Envy		Bass

A Woodcutter's Boy .... Soprano or Treble
Mister By-Ends .... Buffo Tenor
Madam By-Ends .... Contralto
Three Shepherds .... Tenor, Baritone, Bass
The Voice of a Bird.................... Soprano
A Celestial Messenger .... Tenor
Chorus of the Men and Women of the House
Beautiful, of 'Certain persons clothed in gold', of
Doleful Creatures, of Traders in Vanity Fair, of
Angels in the Celestial City.

Act I. Prologue.   'Bunyan is sitting in Bedford Gaol and is
writing the last words of *The Pilgrim's Progress*, "So I awoke,
and behold it was a dream." Then he stands and, turning to
his hearers, reads from the beginning. As he reads there
appears a vision of the Pilgrim with a burden on his back,
with his lamentable cry "What shall I do?" A curtain falls
hiding Bunyan, and the Pilgrim is left alone reading his book
and lamenting'—thus the synopsis printed as an introduction
to the piano score.

The Evangelist appears and directs Pilgrim to the Wicket
Gate, encouraging him to bear his burden until he comes 'to
the place of deliverance'. Pilgrim is about to go when four
neighbours, Pliable, Obstinate, Mistrust, and Timorous,
attempt to dissuade him from his perilous undertaking. At
the behest of the Evangelist, he starts again in quest of 'Life,
eternal life!'

The Wicket Gate: behind it, the House Beautiful. Pilgrim

stumbles in and kneels in front of the Cross. He hears the voices of Three Shining Ones, who presently appear, take the burden off his back and lay it on the Sepulchre, then raise him to his feet and lead him to the gate. An Interpreter receives him, and a chorus of men and women welcome him to the house. Pilgrim kneels while the Interpreter places the mark of the seal on his forehead. A procession appears, carrying a white robe, which the Three Shining Ones place on Pilgrim's shoulders. The Interpreter slowly leads Pilgrim into the house.

A Nocturne interlude leads straight to Act II (and should only, says the composer, be included if it is wished to perform Acts I and II without a break). Watchful, the porter of the house, goes his rounds and prays for the blessing of sleep on all that rest within.

An open road stretches out straight from the back of the stage. A Herald steps forward: 'This is the King's highway . . . It is straight as a rule can make it. Who will go on that way?' Pilgrim asks for his name to be set down in the book, and while the scribe enters it and Pilgrim is provided with armour, the chorus sings Bunyan's hymn, 'Who would true valour see, Let him come hither.'

The Valley of Humiliation, a narrow gorge, shut in at the back by a bare grey hill. A Chorus of Doleful Creatures is howling when Pilgrim appears. He is hailed by Apollyon, who proclaims that he is King of the region wherein Pilgrim was born and challenges him to fight for his soul. Pilgrim is victorious in the combat, but sinks down weak with his wounds until revived by two Heavenly Beings, bearing a branch of the Tree of Life and a cup of the Water of Life. The Evangelist appears and announces new trials for Pilgrim; he shall pass through Vanity Fair, where he will be ill-treated by the inhabitants: 'Be thou faithful unto death, and the King shall give thee the Crown of Life.' Pilgrim is invested with the Staff of Salvation, the Roll of the Word and the Key of Promise.

Act III. Vanity Fair. Booths are up against the house walls on each side of the stage. A lane runs up stage between the booths. The Chorus stands round the booths dressed in fantastic dresses of all periods. 'All that the world can provide is for sale. Every age and every nation is represented and among them Lord Lechery offers his particular brand of merchandise. The Pilgrim enters and the crowd surrounds him. "What will ye buy?" But the Pilgrim prays to keep his eyes from vanity. A procession enters of various well-known characters who succumbed to the lure of gold or power, Demas, Judas Iscariot, Simon Magus, Worldly Glory, and Pontius Pilate. Then the mood changes, Madam Bubble, Madam Wanton, and Lord Lechery offer him the lust of the flesh and the pride of life, but the Pilgrim waves them away. "I buy the truth." He defies their Prince Beelzebub, the father of lies. At this moment appears the Lord Hate-Good, who, after hearing the witnesses against the Pilgrim, condemns him to prison and death' (so is the scene described in the synopsis to the score).

The Pilgrim in prison laments his condition. Why has God forsaken him? Suddenly he remembers the Key of Promise which has been entrusted to him. He puts it into the lock and the gates fly open. The moon gradually illuminates the landscape and reveals the Pilgrim's Way, up which Pilgrim strides.

Act IV.   The edge of a wood. The Pilgrim's Way is seen stretching out into the distance with the Delectable Mountains far off. When the curtain rises, a Woodcutter's Boy is sitting and chopping firewood. He sings gaily as he works. Pilgrim asks him how far he still has to go before he reaches the Celestial City. He is told that it is not far from the Delectable Mountains which are visible from where they stand. Enter Mister and Madam By-Ends. They are full of talk, but admit that though some 'are for religion in rags and contempt', they themselves 'are for him when he walks in his golden slippers in the sunshine and with applause'. They refuse to accompany Pilgrim on the terms he proposes, preferring their old principles, 'since they are harmless and profitable'. Pilgrim goes on, leaving the boy alone.

The Delectable Mountains, near the Heavenly City. This is the episode known as *The Shepherds of the Delectable Mountains* and performed separately under that title as early as 1922 and frequently revived since then[1] (though it lasts little more than quarter of an hour, it stands well by itself and achieved considerable popularity in the twenty-nine years between its first performance and its incorporation in the longer work). Three shepherds are kneeling in prayer just before sunset. Pilgrim enters and asks them if he is on the way to the Celestial City. They reassure him and ask him to stay

[1] Première, R.C.M., London, 1922. First performed Sadler's Wells, 1947; Cincinnati, 1949.

with them for a while, to solace himself with the good of the Delectable Mountains. The voice of a bird is heard singing, and the shepherds join in the hymn. But a Celestial Messenger appears to summon Pilgrim to the Celestial City, and, as a symbol of his mission, ceremonially pierces Pilgrim's heart with an arrow. He leads Pilgrim off, and points the way forward. As Pilgrim is seen entering the River of Death, the shepherds raise their voices in song, being joined before the end of the scene by the sound of an invisible chorus.

The stage is quite dark. A distant trumpet sounds, and the voices from the Celestial City are heard a long way off but gradually getting nearer. Men and women on earth join in with them. Darkness gradually gives way to light, and Pilgrim is seen climbing the stairs to the Gates of the City. They open and he is welcomed by angels. His Pilgrimage is over.

Epilogue. The vision fades. Bunyan addresses his hearers and shows them his book. 'O come hither, and lay my book, thy head and heart together.'

It has been rightly said that the key to the work lies in its title: it is a Morality, not an Opera. The composer has been more interested in evoking a half-mystical, half-pastoral atmosphere than in creating dramatic tension through concentration on character and situation. But, even if *The Pilgrim's Progress* eventually attains more success as an oratorio than as an opera, as many people suggested at the time of its first performance, it stands as a monument to the composer's life-long seriousness of purpose (he was seventy-eight when it was first given) and equally long preoccupation with the subject of Bunyan's allegory. In his score, he has not only incorporated the episode of *The Shepherds of the Delectable Mountains* but has also drawn extensively upon material already familiar from the fifth symphony (at the time this work was first performed, it was explicitly stated that the composer had used themes from his then unfinished opera).

H.

GUSTAV HOLST

(1874–1934)

SĀVITRI

AN episode from the Mahā Bhārata. Words and music by Gustav Holst. Première, Wellington Hall, November 5, 1916. First performed Lyric Theatre, 1921; Covent Garden, 1923, with Dorothy Silk, Heseltine, Farrington, conductor Pitt; Chicago, 1934; Sadler's Wells, 1935, with Vowles, Morgan Jones, Roderick Lloyd, conductor Corbett; Oxford, 1937. Cincinnati, 1939; St. Pancras Town Hall, 1952, with Cantelo, Young, Hemsley, conductor Colin Davis; Aldeburgh, 1956, with Mandikian, Pears, Hemsley, conductor Mackerras.

CHARACTERS

Satyavān, *a woodman* .... Tenor
Sāvitri, *his wife* .... Soprano
Death .... Bass

Place: A wood at evening in India

The following note has been added to the score by the composer by way of preface: 'The piece is intended for performance in the open air or in a small building. When performed out of doors there should be a long avenue or path through a wood in the centre of the scene. When a curtain is used, it should be raised before the voice of Death is heard. No curtain, however, is necessary. The orchestra consists of two string quartets, a contra-bass, two flutes and an English horn. There is also a hidden chorus of female voices.'

The play opens on an empty stage. A voice is heard calling to Sāvitri. Death, the Summoner, whose path may not be turned, draws near to carry Satyavān, Sāvitri's husband, through the dark gates that sooner or later open for all. Sāvitri enters, distracted by the awful cry she has heard, unable to realise how or why Satyavān, young, strong, and fearless, should be taken from her. His voice is heard as he approaches on the homeward way after the day's labour, singing of Sāvitri's loveliness. He finds her sick with fear and

1400

trembling. The distant voices of the chorus give an eerie colour to the scene while Sāvitri laments the vanity of all things. Trees and shrubs and all that walks and creeps are unreal. The only reality is Death. It is Sāvitri who feels the coming doom, and her senses, sharpened by poignant grief, hear and see things that are hidden from her husband. Hearing her cry out wildly, 'He comes', Satyavān picks up his axe and boldy challenges the stranger. The brave words die on his lips, the axe falls from his hand, and after an appeal to Sāvitri he sinks to the ground while Death slowly approaches to claim him as his own. Sāvitri gathers the body in her arms and sings softly to weave a spell so that no evil thing may come near. When Death is quite close she is herself overcome for a moment, but conquering her fears, she finds the strength to welcome the 'Just One'. 'I myself,' she sings, 'can almost see the gentle faces and hear the voices of those that are in Death's Abode where the air is holy,' and she asks Death to be taken there together with Satyavān. That may not be, answers Death, but, since Sāvitri, far from shrinking, gave him welcome, he will grant her a boon which, however, must not be Satyavān's life. 'Well then,' says Sāvitri after a while, 'grant me life.' 'But thou hast life now,' objects Death. 'If thou art not a blind spirit,' retorts Sāvitri, 'thou must understand that, for a woman, Life means stalwart sons and bright-eyed daughters: Life is a communion and eternal.' Her passionate pleading succeeds. Death grants her the boon— Satyavān's life, because if Satyavān dies Sāvitri's voice must become mute and she herself but 'an image floating on the waters of memory'. True to his word, Death goes away and Satyavān comes to life again. The opera ends with Sāvitri singing gently to Satyavān as she sang when she held him lifeless in her embrace.

Sāvitri occupies in the works of its composer the place which *The Prodigal Son* occupies amongst the works of Debussy. If in some respects it is not quite a mature product, it contains nevertheless seeds which later came to ripeness in the remarkable later works. In the handling of chorus and orchestra there is already ample evidence of a strong individual bent and the employment of free rhythms is also very characteristic. The chorus is used throughout as part of the orchestra, singing not words but the sound of the vowel 'u' in 'sun'. In this way Holst obtains some novel and very beautiful effects.   F. B.

RUTLAND BOUGHTON

(1878–1960)

THE IMMORTAL HOUR

OPERA in two acts by Rutland Boughton, the libretto being adapted from the play and poems of Fiona Macleod.

On August 26, 1914, *The Immortal Hour* was performed at Glastonbury. It was an immediate success, and Elgar pronounced it a work of genius. The chief interpreters on that occasion were Irene Lemon (Etain), Frederic Austin (Eochaidh), Muriel Boughton (Spirit Voice), Neville Strutt (Manus), Agnes Thomas (Maive), Arthur Trowbridge (Old Bard), Arthur Jordan (Midir), and the composer himself sang the part of Dalua. The war delayed its production in London, and it was only in 1920 that it was given there at the Old Vic Theatre. In 1922 the Birmingham Players brought it to London, where it played at the Regent Theatre for 216 performances, with Gwen Ffrangçon Davies as Etain; Kingsway Theatre, London, 1926; New York, 1926; Royal Academy of Music, 1939; Sadler's Wells, 1953, with Patricia Howard, Lanigan, Hargreaves, Clarkson, conductor James Robertson.

CHARACTERS

Dalua	Baritone
Etain	Soprano
Eochaidh	Baritone
Spirit Voice	Mezzo-Soprano
Manus	Bass
Maive	Contralto
Old Bard	Bass
Midir	Tenor

Chorus of Druids and Warriors

Act I, scene i. A forest. A pool in the background.

Dalua, the Lord of Shadow, a creature of the fairy world, passes wearily through the forest. The spirits of the trees dance around him in the darkness while a ghostly chorus mocks him. Sternly he tells them to be still for he hears the voice of another wanderer in the darkness. The spirits disappear. Dalua hides behind a tree while Etain comes haltingly forward. She comes from the land of the young, where death is only a passing shadow, and there she would return even though she finds fair the moonlight and the woods. Dalua recognises her and, stepping forward, salutes her, 'daughter of Kings and Star among the dreams that are

1402

ves and souls'. She does not know him; she has forgotten
the fairy world to which she belongs and which Dalua seeks
to recall to her. She does not know why she is in the wood.
But Dalua knows. A King of men has wooed the 'Immortal
Hour'. He felt in his heart such a love as the earth could
not appease and has called upon the gods to send him one
fairer than any mortal maid, and the gods sent Etain. Who is
this King? asks Etain. He is coming hither now—answers
Dalua—and he shall have the madness he desires and think it
wisdom. Etain goes out slowly while the sound of the horn
heralds the coming of Eochaidh, the King. Dalua salutes him
and the King recognises in him one whom he has known in
dreams—why is he in this lonely wood? 'I am here,' says
Dalua, 'to drink at the fountain of all dreams.' The scene
ends and the voices of Dalua and Eochaidh are heard receding
in the distance.

Scene ii.   The hut of Manus and Maive. Manus sits before
the pine-log fire. His wife stands at the back, plucking
feathers from a dead cockerel. In a sheltered recess sits Etain.

Manus and Maive are discussing the stranger who has just
visited them and given them three pieces of gold—one for
Etain, one for any stranger who might come, and one for
keeping silence. Etain laments the beauty of her world, lost
to her, and asks the peasants if they know of it. But Manus is
afraid to answer. Just then the horn is heard outside. It is
Eochaidh calling to the people in the hut. He is told to enter
and, exchanging a greeting with his humble host, the King
sees Etain. Manus and Maive retire in the shadow while
Eochaidh and Etain are left to sing their love. The whole
scene is dominated by the beautiful phrase

The King makes himself known to Etain who can only tell
him her name because she is still bewildered by a strange
darkness on her mind. The course of true love runs smooth
enough until voices are heard singing the praise of the lordly
ones 'who dwell in the hills'. The theme has haunting charm:

How   beau-ti-ful they are,   The lord-ly ones

The curtain descends with Eochaidh kneeling by the side
of Etain, who listens spellbound as the voices outside slowly
melt away in the distance.

Act II.   A year has passed and Druids are celebrating the
anniversary of the meeting of their King Eochaidh and his
bride. Etain would like to speak to them and thank them for
their welcome when she is suddenly assailed by strange
thoughts and longings. Wearily she bids them farewell and
would retire, when Eochaidh begs her to remain and not
leave him alone this night. He is full of forebodings, having
heard strange laughter and seen in the gloom ghostly shapes.
Surely Dalua has bewitched his eyes. Etain too has heard the
magic music; she must go. Slowly she descends from her
throne and goes out. The King sends away the bards and the
warriors. As they move to go they are confronted by a
stranger, Midir, who comes to claim a boon. He is himself a
King's son. He wishes the King well; may he obtain his heart's
desire. Eochaidh grants the boon and requests the bards and
Druids to leave him alone with the stranger. As soon as they
are gone the King turns eagerly to Midir whose power he feels
to be more than mortal, and asks: 'Give me my heart's desire.
Tell me there is to be no twilight upon my joy.' Midir
answers him by throwing off his cloak and, clad in pure gold,
tells the story of Aedh the shining god and of Dana; how
they loved and how Oengus was born of their union.
Murmuring 'dreams, dreams', Eochaidh turns to the subject
of Midir's request for a boon. Midir asks to be allowed to kiss
the Queen's hand. Eochaidh has promised, and although he
grieves at the thought of waking the Queen weary with
sadness and dreams, he sends for her. While they are waiting
for Etain an old bard sings of things that have come and
gone and of dreams that have passed silent and swift like
shadows. Etain appears in the doorway dressed as she was when
Eochaidh first saw her in green with the mystic mistletoe in
her hair. She does not recognise Midir but readily allows him,
at the King's request, to kiss her hand and to sing a song he
has made. The song is the one that has been heard at the
close of the first act, exalting the 'lordly ones in the hollow
hills'. Its effect on Etain is that of a spell, and when Eochaidh
would come near her she seems unaware of his presence.
Then Midir sings another more joyous song of the land of
youth where there is no death, of the land of heart's desire,
and Etain feels drawn irresistibly to him. In a strained voice

Eochaidh implores Etain to stay, but Etain no longer hears him. An unseen chorus now takes up the haunting melody and Etain slowly follows Midir as in a trance. The stage grows dark; only a light shines where Midir stands. As he passes out of sight complete darkness falls on the stage. Dalua enters, and rapidly touches Eochaidh, who falls inert to the ground.

F. B.

WILLIAM WALTON
(b. 1902)

TROILUS AND CRESSIDA

OPERA in three acts by William Walton; text by Christopher Hassall. Première, Covent Garden, London, December 3, 1954, with Magda Lazslo, Monica Sinclair, Richard Lewis, Peter Pears, Otakar Kraus, Frederick Dalberg, conductor Sir Malcolm Sargent. First performed San Francisco, 1955, with Dorothy Kirsten, Frances Bible, Richard Lewis, Ernest McChesney, Robert Weede, Giorgio Tozzi, conductor Erich Leinsdorf; New York, City Centre, 1955, with Phyllis Curtin, Gloria Lane, Jon Crain, Norman Kelley, Lawrence Winters, Yi-Kwei-Sze, conductor Joseph Rosenstock; la Scala, Milan, 1956, with Dorothy Dow, David Poleri, Antonio Pirino, Italo Tajo, conductor Sanzogno. Revived Covent Garden, 1963, with Marie Collier, Josephine Veasey, André Turp, John Lanigan, Kraus, Forbes Robinson, conductor Sargent.

CHARACTERS

Calkas, *High Priest of Pallas* .... Bass
Antenor, *Captain of Trojan spears* .... Baritone
Troilus, *Prince of Troy* .... Tenor
Pandarus, *brother of Calkas* .... Tenor Buffo
Cressida, *daughter of Calkas* .... Soprano
Evadne, *her servant* .... Mezzo-Soprano
Horaste, *a friend of Pandarus* . ... Baritone
Diomede, *Prince of Argos* .... Baritone
A woman's voice within the temple
Priests, Soldiers, Trojans, Greeks, etc.
Time: About the Twelfth Century B.C.   *Place:* Troy

Sir William Walton's only full-length opera was commissioned in 1947 by the B.B.C. Its first performance was at Covent Garden towards the end of 1954 and it was an immediate success, its straightforward manner and late romantic style appealing to the London public. It was no more successful in its foreign productions than were other British operas of the period—*Gloriana, The Midsummer Marriage, Billy Budd*—but revival has suggested that the music's strong lyrical impulse, from the same source as that of the composer's Violin Concerto, puts it into a longer-lasting category than that of the 'well-made' opera.

Act I. Before the Temple of Pallas in the citadel of Troy. Quiet timpani and a murmuring chorus of worshippers from within the temple set the scene, but soon the muttering becomes desperate, and it is apparent that the starving population of Troy is liable to riot in protest against conditions. Calkas tries to quieten them and reminds them that the oracle at Delphi has already spoken. His unequivocal if defeatist interpretation is to advise them to parley with the Greeks while there is still time. Antenor, intent on a foray with his warrior companions, overhears him and challenges his right to utter such counsel of despair. He rouses the crowd, and Calkas is obviously in some danger until Troilus appears and restores order. He wishes Antenor luck on his mission and is hardly ruffled when his friend guesses that it is the presence of the beautiful Cressida which draws him to the temple.

In a gently lyrical aria Troilus admits to himself that he loves Cressida, and as the music reaches a climax the temple doors open and Cressida, preceded by two priests, appears in the doorway. Troilus has never spoken to her before and her first musical utterance is subdued: 'Morning and evening I have felt your glance follow me out of sight.' She is a widow and is soon to take her vows as a priestess; in Pallas, she feels, lies her only hope for the future.

Troilus unavailingly protests his love, and as Cressida disappears her place is taken by her uncle Pandarus, whose arrival produces a complete change of musical mood, from the lyrical to something much more volatile. He takes in the situation at a glance and proceeds to win Troilus's confidence, so that the prince departs in high hopes. Pandarus is about to enter the temple in search of Cressida when the doors open and Calkas emerges, followed by Cressida and vadne. Pandarus listens to Calkas admit to his daughter and her companions that he plans to quit the city and desert to the enemy. Cressida's pleas fail and he departs, leaving her to sing of an incident in childhood which she now recognises as representing presentiments of desertion, always connected with her father ('Slowly it all comes back'). Warmth enters the music as she interprets the warrior in her dream of long ago as the Troilus of today—the Troilus they (and the Gods who preside over our destinies at birth) will not allow her to love!

Pandarus and Evadne confirm that Calkas has deserted, and Pandarus prays to Aphrodite to ensure that his tongue has not lost its golden touch; only with its aid can he rescue the family from a crisis. In lively, flexible music, he starts to plead Troilus's cause with Cressida but is interrupted by the arrival of the prince himself. Troilus is met by Antenor's soldiers with the news that their captain has been taken prisoner. Troilus swears that he will be rescued, either by means of an exchange of prisoners, or else by force of arms. As Troilus goes to look for Calkas, Pandarus persuades Cressida to come next day to a supper party at his house, then, before she leaves, prevails upon her to leave her crimson scarf as a token of esteem for Troilus. Troilus for his part has discovered that Calkas, the father of his beloved, is a traitor, but the music returns, as he catches sight of Cressida's scarf, to the ecstatic lyricism of his aria earlier in the scene.

Act II. A room in Pandarus's house the following evening. The music, with its syncopated rhythms, immediately recalls us to the mood induced by Pandarus's arrival in the previous act. Supper is over and the guests are playing chess, Cressida with Horaste. A storm is blowing up and Pandarus, thinking this will suit his book, dispatches a messenger to fetch Troilus. At the first sign of rain, Pandarus urges Cressida and the other guests to stay the night and promptly shows her an alcove furnished with a bed. In gently decorative music, her ladies prepare Cressida for the night. She cannot sleep and in an aria admits to herself that she is in love—her basically cool music (the languor of the beauty long accustomed to admiration?) soon turns to passion as she proclaims 'friend and foe, Troilus my conqueror'.

Pandarus comes in to say that Troilus is in the house, racked with jealousy and begging to see her. 'On jealousy's hot grid he roasts alive,' begins the ensemble which becomes

a trio when Troilus overhears Pandarus's barefaced fabri
cation—one of the liveliest and most successful moments of
the score, cut at Covent Garden's 1963 revival. Troilus
interrupts, denounces the trickster who admits he has made it
all up, and starts to woo Cressida from her tears. A love duet
develops, under the star, as it were, of Aphrodite, whose
protection the lovers invoke. Pandarus looks in, is delighted
at what he sees, snuffs the candles and tiptoes away without
interrupting the lovers.

The storm breaks in an orchestral interlude, which depicts
the love-making within as well as the wind and rain outside
and which might not have been as it is without *Peter Grimes*
but is none the less essentially Walton. It ends with peaceful
dawn and the opening of scene ii as Troilus and Cressida
together watch the sun rise over the roofs of Troy. Like
Pandarus, they are disturbed to hear the sound of
approaching drums, and Pandarus is particularly concerned
for the good name of his family. A military deputation is at
the door and Troilus must not be discovered; Pandarus will
cope with the visitors.

It is Diomede, a young Greek commander, who explains
that Calkas wishes to have his daughter restored to him and
that the commanders of the army have agreed that Cressida
shall go to the Greek camp in exchange for the Trojan
warrior Antenor. When Pandarus claims that Cressida is not
in his house, Diomede searches, discovers her and marvels at
her beauty. Troilus emerges at Diomede's departure and says
he will not rest until the agreement is revoked and Cressida
back in Troy. In the meanwhile, he will send daily messages
and will corrupt the sentries so that he may visit her in the
Greek camp. There is a moving vocal postlude, as it were, to
their grand duet, and, as Cressida leaves, Troilus gives her
back the crimson scarf which she had given him and which
she must now keep as a token of their love.

Act III. The Greek encampment. Early evening ten
weeks later. Calkas's tent can be seen at the side, and at the
back the battlements. A sad cor anglais solo (marked *lugubre*)
introduces the scene and the sound of night watchmen's
voices can be heard. Cressida, whose distraught loneliness is
all too apparent in every bar she sings, implores Evadne to see
if there is a message from Troilus at the palisade. She has not
heard from him since they parted and is beginning to despair.
Evadne knows Cressida's coldness to Diomede jeopardises

...neir safety, and her solo ('Night after night the same') offers ...her mistress no comfort. Cressida for her part is a prey to every kind of fear, most of all that Troilus is already dead, and she prays movingly to the goddess either to allay or confirm her fears. Calkas interrupts her reverie and protests that it is madness to continue to flout Diomede, whom Cressida admits to finding attractive. No sooner has she mentioned his name than Diomede is standing in front of her, demanding her final decision as to whether she will become his wife. Abandoning all hope of seeing Troilus again (return of cor anglais solo), Cressida yields to Diomede's demands, even ceding him the scarf he begs from her as a favour. Evadne overhears and secretly destroys the last of the many messages Troilus has sent Cressida, all of which at Calkas's behest she has concealed from her mistress.

Troilus and Pandarus have gained admittance to the Greek lines in an hour of truce, and they urge Evadne to fetch Cressida, whose ransom has at last been arranged. Cressida comes from her tent, richly dressed to meet Diomede, but her music speaks of heartbreak rather than rejoicing, and only the sound of Troilus's voice brings a quickening of the musical pulse. His pleading is full of tenderness, but, in spite of the many messages he protests he has sent, the news of her ransom obviously perplexes Cressida. Before she can convince Troilus that he has come too late, Greeks can be heard acclaiming her as Diomede's bride.

Diomede himself comes into view wearing the crimson favour on his helmet and in time to hear Troilus claim Cressida as his, body and spirit. Diomede orders Cressida to denounce him, and when she hesitates, he is overcome by the public humiliation and begins an embittered lament which develops into a full-scale and impressive sextet eventually swelled by the chorus. It is broken off by the infuriated Diomede, who stamps on Cressida's scarf. Troilus falls on him with his sword and is getting the better of their fight when Calkas stabs him mortally in the back. Diomede gives orders that the body of the gallant Trojan prince be carried away with due honours, that Calkas be sent in fetters back to Troy, and that Cressida shall stay in the camp of the Greeks for the enjoyment of whoever chooses her. Left alone for a moment, she utters a final lament to the Gods, then, seeing Greek soldiers approach, snatches up Troilus's sword and, binding it with her scarf, kills herself.   H.

THE BEAR

Opera in one act by William Walton, libretto by Paul Dehn. Première, Aldeburgh Festival, June 3, 1967, with Monica Sinclair, John Shaw, Norman Lumsden, conductor James Lockhart (later same year at Sadler's Wells, London, and in Montreal). Première, B.B.C. T.V., 1970, with Regina Resnik, Thomas Hemsley, Hammond-Stroud, conductor Walton.

CHARACTERS

Yeliena Ivanovna Popova, *a young woman* ....Mezzo-Soprano
Grigory Stepanovitch Smirnov, *a middle-aged landowner* ....Baritone
Luka, *Madame Popova's servant* .... Bass

Time: 1888   *Place:* The drawing room of Madame Popova's house in the country in Russia

Commissioned by The Serge Koussevitsky Music Foundation in 1965, the completion of this light-hearted one-acter was interrupted when the composer had to undergo a serious operation, and the opera waited for first performance until the 1967 Aldeburgh Festival.

Written on a framework of Chekhov's short story of the same name, the plot concerns Madame Popova, the pretty young widow of a landowner, who clings, against the strongly proffered advice of her old manservant, Luka, to the idea of a virtuous, life-long widowhood, although, as she well knows, her late husband was no paragon of virtue. It seems that, while he was impervious to her reproaches during his lifetime, she intends, perhaps for this reason, to pursue him with them into the hereafter.

Luka announces that a man has arrived, saying he is determined to see her on what he describes as urgent business. The visitor forces his way in and introduces himself as Grigory Stepanovitch Smirnov, landowner and retired lieutenant of artillery. The late Popov owed him 1,300 roubles for oats. His bank is demanding interest on the loan tomorrow, and, if his estate is not to be forfeit and he himself declared a bankrupt, he must be paid at once. Refusing to listen to Madame Popova's promise that her bailiff will pay, he insists that she alone can help. When his language becomes too strong, Madame Popova sweeps out

1410

slamming the door and leaving the frustrated Smirnov bemoaning the fact that all his debtors vanish when he pursues them while his creditors are all too readily available.

As Smirnov works himself up into a fine state of rage and indignation at his evil fortune and emphasises his total aversion to dealing with women, Luka enters to say that Madame Popova is indisposed and can see no one. Smirnov announces that he will get his own back even if he has to stay for a year and he orders the servant to unharness his horses and bring him a bottle of vodka. Catching sight of his unkempt reflection in the looking-glass, he is temporarily disconcerted at his own boorishness but soon flies again into a passion when reproached by Luka for his behaviour.

Madame Popova returns, eyes modestly cast down! Will Smirnov not wait until the end of the week? He is adamant; unless he is paid at once, he will hang himself! With Smirnov's insistence that he will remain there until he is paid, deadlock seems to have been reached. Their quarrel is lively but capped by a sprightly aria from Madame Popova who, stung by Smirnov's assertion that men are more faithful than women, tells him the dreadful tale of her husband's infidelities and emphasises her own hyper-virtuous conduct and her intention of remaining pure for evermore.

Unconvinced, Smirnov makes the point that her clinging to widow's weeds has not made her forget to powder her face. This is too much for Madame Popova and she orders him out. At the argument's height, Smirnov proposes they settle the quarrel with a duel. Let there be real equality between the sexes! Madame Popova accepts the proposition with alacrity and goes off to fetch her late husband's pistols. Smirnov is full of admiration for her spirit and regrets the need to kill such a splendid creature. Madame Popova returns with the pistols (to the horror of Luka) and asks Smirnov to instruct her in their use as she has never handled them before. By the end of the lesson, Smirnov is head-over-heels in love and says he will fire into the air. She mistakes his infatuation for fear and orders him out. They gaze at each other and Smirnov declares his love for her. She threatens to shoot. He announces that to be shot by her would be a pleasure. She clings rather shakily to her dignity and rings for Luka to show Smirnov out but, by the time the old man arrives, the couple are in a tender embrace.

The charm of the piece is enhanced by its liberal spicing

with parodies of other composers, including Stravinsky and
Britten, and the connoisseur will enjoy picking them out like
sixpences from a Christmas pudding.   H.

MICHAEL TIPPETT
(b. 1905)

THE MIDSUMMER MARRIAGE

OPERA in three acts by Michael Tippett, text by the composer
Première, Covent Garden, January 27, 1955, with Joan Sutherland
Adèle Leigh, Oralia Dominguez, Monica Sinclair, Edith Coates, Richard
Lewis, John Lanigan, Otakar Kraus, Michael Langdon, conductor John
Pritchard. Revived Covent Garden, 1957, with Jeannette Sinclair
Nancy Thomas, Howell Glynne replacing Leigh, Dominguez, Kraus
1968, with Joan Carlyle, Elizabeth Harwood, Helen Watts, Alberto
Remedios, Stuart Burrows, Raimund Herincx, conductor Colin Davis
B.B.C. Studio performance, 1963, with Catherine Gayer, J. Sinclair, Jane
Baker, Richard Lewis, John Dobson, Glynne, conductor Norman de
Mar.

CHARACTERS

Mark, *a young man of unknown*
    parentage.............................. Tenor
Jenifer, *his betrothed* .... Soprano
King Fisher, *Jenifer's father,*
    a businessman .... Baritone
Bella, *King Fisher's secretary* .... Soprano
Jack, *Bella's boyfriend, a mechanic* .... Tenor
Sosostris, *a clairvoyante* .... Contralto
The Ancients, *priest and priestess of*
    the temple .... Bass, Mezzo-Soprano
Strephon, *one of the dancers*
       Chorus of Mark's and Jenifer's friends;
       dancers attendant on the Ancients

Time: The present

'Of its nature opera', wrote Wilfrid Mellers at the start of an article[1] some years ago, 'is to some degree mythical (in which sense it is "universal"), to some degree social (in which sense it is tied to an historical past and an immediate present).' Tippett's 'quest' opera, written consciously under the influence of T. S. Eliot's verse drama (he once corresponded with Eliot with a view to getting the poet to write the libretto or at least the lyrics) is of course a comedy, and it is concerned, as he says,[2] 'with the unexpected hindrances to an eventual marriage', the hindrances basically 'our ignorance or illusion about ourselves'. In it Tippett emphasises myth, investigating the problems of carnal and spiritual union and the nature of self-knowledge. Mark and Jenifer are the young lovers, and we see their misunderstandings, clashes, adjustments of personality, reaction to opposition—the predicament of most young couples in love, though here made explicit and symbolical where usually implicit and matter-of-fact. Like Pamina and Tamino, Mark and Jenifer have the need for a hard, conscious, uncompromising development of the inner being, and they explore the male and female elements of their own personalities, the understanding of which in self as in the other is a basis for a happy relationship between two people. The opera is essentially the story of their inner development. The 'social' element in *The Midsummer Marriage* is one of place rather than time—as one reviewer[3] put it after the 1968 Covent Garden revival, 'the hilltop clearing in the wood, the burgeoning summer, the sense of the past, the presence of England (and in particular of the West country), with which libretto and music are saturated.'

Act I (Morning). 'When fully lighted the stage . . . presents a clearing in a wood, perhaps at the top of a hill, against the sky. At the back of the stage is an architectural group of buildings, a kind of sanctuary, whose centre appears to be an ancient Greek temple.' Steps to the right lead upwards and end abruptly in mid-air; to the left, steps lead down through gates into the hillside itself. It is half light before sunrise on a midsummer day, and the music is of the utmost vigour and brilliance. To keep an assignation with Mark and Jenifer, who plan to marry, come their friends. Caution and purpose are

[1] *New Statesman* March 31, 1967.
[2] Michael Tippett: *Moving into Aquarius*, Routledge & Kegan Paul.
[3] David Cairns in *The Spectator*, April, 1968.

immediately apparent. They greet the rising sun on mid
summer morning, then perceive the temple building[1] and
hear the music coming softly from it, Ex. 1.

Magic is in the air, the magic of the eternal ritual before
which mundanity recedes, the magic which 'seems much
nearer than expected'. The chorus hides as the dancers
emerge, led by Strephon and followed by the Ancients,
Ex. 2:

[1] 'The temple ... is not real but an inheritance, a tradition, to warn
us of natural forces against which we all, at some time, rebel but which
we cannot ever be freed from: when we accept their background
existence they help us.' William Mann, *The Times*, April 19, 1968.

The dance, Ex. 3:

is formal and interrupted by the entrance of Mark calling for
a new dance for his wedding day. He is told to watch, with
the admonition 'change the unchanging ritual, there'll be no
point of rest', but after a few bars of Ex. 3, the He-Ancient
to Mark's indignation trips Strephon with his stick, eventually
ordering the party back into the temple with the warning:
'We do not seek . . . to hold you longer from your dreams;
you shall learn a new dance before you leave this place
today'. They depart to Ex. 2.

In an extended, florid aria, ranging from A natural at the
top to B natural nearly two octaves below, Mark exhorts
them to celebrate his love with him; 'Ah, the summer
morning dances in my heart', he sings, and Tippett's exuberant
music catches the words; a splendid affirmation.

Jenifer appears, dressed much to Mark's surprise for a
journey and not a wedding; their duet (with six-part chorus
beneath it) is rapturous enough, but all Mark's pleading
makes little difference: 'It isn't love I want, but truth,' says

Jenifer (anticipating in her inherited determination the appearance of her headstrong father, King Fisher). Her feminine instinct for chastity and intellectual independence is affronted by Mark's masculine desire and assertion. They have to learn to accommodate each other's point of view—hence the events of the drama.

Jenifer starts to climb up[1] the broken stairs, disappearing suddenly on a *diminuendo* top B flat. Mark is half-laughingly consoled: 'She'll come back', but hearing the voice of Jenifer's businessman father, King Fisher, he decides complementarily to emulate Jenifer and go in search of that element in himself which corresponds with the feminine principles of instinct, fertility and love—the qualities for whose lack he appears temporarily to have lost Jenifer. He goes down through the gates and into the hillside.

Tippett himself in a broadcast has compared King Fisher to Boss Mangan in Shaw's play *Heartbreak House*, and King Fisher stands for all elements, parental and otherwise, which are hostile to Jenifer and Mark and obstructive to their development. He is often associated musically with Ex. 3, which here stands for uncomprehending authority. Summoning his secretary Bella, he proceeds, with her as intermediary, to enlist the help of the Ancients (derivation of Ex. 2) in tracing his daughter who has, he assumes, eloped with Mark. When they refuse to open the gates, he sends Bella for her boy friend Jack, a workman who will do the job for them, and himself turns on the men and women who crowd round: 'So you are Mark's fine brood of friends.' In a vigorous monologue, he suborns the men with money and drives them off, but has less luck with the women, who refuse to work for him.

Enter Jack, who with Bella represents the uncomplicated, Papageno–Papagena, pair of lovers, able to live their lives by means of intuition and needing no deeper knowledge of the currents which lie beneath the surface of human love. Jack agrees to do the job ('My card will tell you who I am and what the wage a week I earn. But it can't tell you what I dream'), spends a moment of wishful thinking in duet with Bella, but is confronted by a warning voice from behind the gates (derivation of Ex. 1). King Fisher wants action, but this

---

[1] In mythology, the upper regions stand broadly speaking for the masculine principle, Mother Earth for the feminine.

time the voice of Sosostris is even more vehement in urging caution. The men cry forward, the women are for restraint, but King Fisher gets his way until at the decisive moment Jenifer reappears at the top of the steps partially transformed.[1]

She has hardly started to explain her experience when Mark too becomes visible, also transfigured, in his case towards Dionysus. In their dangerous exaltation—this is still an early stage of the road they have to travel—they postulate different points of view and the Ancients and the dancers come impressively from the temple and demand that each shall put a case ('Pride has subtle and peculiar power to swell the stomach but not heal the heart. You are contained within the spirit, not the spirit shrunk in you, else it burst the bonds and break you').

First Jenifer in a splendid statement, full of musical embroidery and elaboration and with a magical slow section with soft trumpet *obbligato* (a girl dancer visible playing it), then Mark in a hardly less magnificent aria, 'As stallions stamping' (a boy dancer clashes cymbals behind him), refer in rather oblique terms to their experiences. The dancers and their friends meanwhile force King Fisher further and further away from the protagonists, until Jenifer moves across the stage to confront Mark and show him the animal she feels he has become. The mirror she holds up to him falls from her hand and she starts to descend as he climbs the steps up which she had formerly sought enlightenment, each now attempting to recover the spiritual balance which is tottering with the symbolical reversal of roles. King Fisher fulminates and rushes out, while the friends of Mark and Jenifer understand that 'Mark and Jenifer endure for us', proclaiming themselves 'the laughing children' as the act comes to an end in something close to ecstasy, the orchestra returning to the mood of the act's opening bars.

The second Act (Afternoon) shows the same physical scene from a rather different angle. The magical side of the atmosphere of Act I is immediately heard in enhanced (though musically different) form, Ex. 4:

---

[1] The score tells us: 'The ancient Greek prototype towards which Jenifer's transfiguration is tending would be Athena... no exact imitation of Athena is meant, for the natural Jenifer is still visible behind the supernatural transfiguration.'

Strephon starts to dance below the temple steps, then hides when the chorus is heard off stage, celebrating the longest day. Jack and Bella come on with a few friends, but are soon left alone. Bella brings up the subject of marriage, they look forward to their future bliss in a scene which is full of tenderness, for all that it is the most nearly conventional of the opera.

They go into the wood, Strephon takes up a dancing position and there begins the central section of the act, an elaborate and closely worked out ballet sequence[1] in which the unconscious conflict between the sexes is shown at its most savage,[2] albeit in music of unusual and persuasive richness even for Tippett. The sequence is as follows:

I The Earth in Autumn: the Hound chases the Hare.
II The Waters in Winter: the Otter chases the Fish.
III The Air in Spring: the Hawk chases the Bird.

At the start (Ex. 1) some of the trees of the wood represented by dancers begin to move and take up position to form a kind of racecourse. The course set and announced for the first two dances by the solemn, grand chords of Ex. 5,

round it in succession (and in its differing manifestations for each dance) the hare is pursued by a hound, the fish through the river by an otter, the broken-winged bird in a cornfield by a hawk. The first two with difficulty escape, the fish not

[1] The Ritual Dances (three in Act II, the Fire Dance in Act III) were first publicly performed in February, 1953, in Basle under Paul Sacher, who had offered Tippett a commission and received these dances in return.

[2] '. . . the man dances all the evasive tricks and the woman pursues him with shrewish relentlessness . . . the reconciliation of these dancers in Act III shows us the true union of opposites after Mark and Jenifer have achieved their inner resolution'. Robert Donington in *The Music Review*, May, 1957.

before being pinned to the bank by the otter, but it is apparent that the hawk will catch the bird until Bella, who has been watching with Jack, screams and breaks the spell.

A prelude ushers in the splendid musical sequence, and each of the three sections of the ballet consists of transformation, preparation for the dance, and the dance itself. The movements of pursuer and quarry are graphically depicted, sometimes ritually, sometimes almost naturalistically, and there is strong differentiation between the backgrounds—forest for the hare, water for the fish, air and the cornfield below it for the bird.

Jack comforts Bella, who retrieves the situation with mirror and powder-puff, singing a charming arietta as she refurbishes her make-up ('They say a woman's glory is her hair')[1] before confiding to Jack that King Fisher has plans for both of them in his next move. The act ends with offstage cries in praise of midsummer and Example 4 in the orchestra.

Act III (Evening and Night). The last act is the most problematical for anyone coming new to it. What we have had so far is a look in depth at the problems of one couple—their efforts to get inside the mind of the other, parental opposition, misunderstandings and so on; a glance at the way another couple, instinctively and not bothering about the motives behind their thoughts and actions, solve theirs. We have also sensed (and sometimes seen) the usually unseen forces behind our actions: ritual, tradition, the instinct for what we can only inexactly call 'magic' that resides in all of us. Now, Tippett takes us nearer the magical and ritual forces which influence our actions; we hear the one in the voice of Sosostris, see the other in terms of the ritual fire dance, and gain insight into the power of each as we watch the death of the defiant and obstinately mundane King Fisher, and the symbolical transfiguration of Mark and Jenifer. The opera will end with the triumph of young love in its new-found understanding and a sense that the eternal mysteries go on unchanged.

The scene is as at the opera's start; it is plain that some kind of picnic has taken place and on one side of the stage is dancing. The action is languid until the revitalising influence of King Fisher is felt, announcing that he has brought his

[1] Like the 'Ritual Dances', this section of the score was also heard publicly before the first night when Adèle Leigh, the original Bella, sang it for BBC Television when I interviewed the composer a few days before the première.

own brand of magic to counteract that of the Ancients: Madame Sosostris, a clairvoyante. The crowd is to escort her to the spot, where he will have a confrontation with the Ancients, whom Bella now calls (Ex. 2). In spite of the Ancients' attempts to dissuade him, King Fisher persists, and a procession (Ex. 3 in evidence in a march[1]), comes up the hill bearing a litter, on which is a cloaked figure whom Bella wastes no time in recognising as Jack.

When the fun subsides and the crowd moves, a contraption is seen, of vaguely human form and covered in veils, to which King Fisher explains the situation briefly, calling upon Madame Sosostris to locate his absent daughter. In music of impressive cast, at first slow and measured, Sosostris begins her invocation, 'I am what has been, is and shall be', gradually mounting in tempo and intensity and rising in *tessitura* as she follows it with a divination of the union of Jenifer and Mark, both physical in that they are in love and symbolical in that Jenifer is now ready to accept the masculine in Mark which she has come to understand (and vice versa).[2] It is the most extended vocal movement in a score full of notable vocal writing.

King Fisher interrupts the vision and dashes the bowl to the ground, in the next breath demanding that Jack undertake another role, this time as his agent to unmask Sosostris' imposture. At the end of an ensemble, in which Jack and Bella, the two Ancients, and King Fisher battle for supremacy, Jack throws down belt and holster, his symbols of office, and turns his back on King Fisher who reluctantly picks them up. He moves to unveil Sosostris, and his actions are the subject of comment by the Ancients, and the bystanders, who watch the last veil fall of itself to disclose an incandescent bud, which falls open like huge lotus petals. Inside, transfigured, are Mark and Jenifer.[3] King Fisher threatens, but when Mark and Jenifer turn towards him, he falls dead to the ground. Chorus and She-Ancient antiphonally sing his

[1] Recalling the Turkish music in Beethoven's Ninth Symphony, acutely noted Hugh Wood in an article in 1970.

[2] 'It is the union of masculine and feminine elements in any one of us,' says Robert Donington in *Michael Tippett: A Symposium on his 50th Birthday* (Faber).

[3] 'In Indian mythology, Mark and Jenifer would be transfigured as Siva-Sakti (Siva and Parvati). All the gestures and poses are hieratic.' Ibid.

threnody over a Purcellian bass ('Mourn not the fall of a man that goes down leaving the room for someone beautiful'). It is not only the funeral march of an archetypal villain but of a Priest-King, who must die that life can be re-born.

Introduced by the same music as the other ritual dances, Strephon and a female dancer, with wooden stick and block begin to make ritual fire. The chorus joins in (Ex. 5), and Mark and Jenifer celebrate their vision: 'Sirius rising as the sun's wheel rolls over at the utter zenith', and all including He- and She-Ancient proclaim their belief in carnal love and fertility. As the fire dance proceeds, Mark, Jenifer and Strephon seem to be drawn inside the lotus bud, whose petals close upon them so that finally nothing but the torch lighted at the start of the dance can be seen. Eventually even this is drawn into the veils, which break into flame (Ex. 5), glow, die out and leave the stage dark.

'Was it a vision? Was it a dream?' The light starts to return but the temple is shrouded in dawn mist as at the opening. As warmth pervades the music again, Mark and Jenifer can be heard, and soon they are visible too as their mortal selves, proclaiming that they have found truth, and that 'All things fall and are built again, and those that build them again are gay' (Ex. 2). The curtain falls on an empty stage. 'Were the mists to lift again, it would be seen that the temple and the sanctuary of buildings were only ruins and stones silhouetted against the clear sky'.

It is curious that by Tippett's own account his first concept of his opera was visual ('A stage picture of a wooded hill top with a temple, where a warm and soft young man was being rebuffed by a cold and hard young woman to such a degree that the collective, magical archetypes take charge—Jung's *anima* and *animus*') and not primarily musical. Only later did he hear Mark and Jenifer singing arias, 'the soprano's having coloratura, and the tenor's being rhapsodic'. And yet the score has, rightly in my view, been associated with 'an uplifted, visionary lyricism'.[1]

From the time of the first performance, the opera has divided opinion, most at first fastening on obscurity in the action, clumsiness in the libretto, which they felt invalidated Tippett's musical vision. Others fell immediately under the composer's spell, myself amongst them—I was lucky to be

[1] William Mann in *Michael Tippett: A Symposium on his 60th Birthday*.

working at Covent Garden at the time the opera was, not without controversy, put into rehearsal and first produced. As David Cairns said at the time of the 1968 revival: 'The score has the power to intoxicate the listener, to possess his imagination and to secure his devotion for life, to sweep aside reservations.' It is not hard to believe that it will be one of the works of the mid-twentieth century which will be revived long past its own generation, which has in fact the possibility of becoming a true classic, in the sense that it reveals to its own and succeeding generations a truth which we (and they) need to know—and reveals it in major musical terms. H.

KING PRIAM

Opera in three acts, words and music by Michael Tippett. Première, May 29, 1962, at Coventry (and later at Covent Garden) with Forbes Robinson, Marie Collier, Josephine Veasey, Margreta Elkins, Richard Lewis, conductor John Pritchard. First performed in Germany, Karlsruhe, 1963, with Howard Vandenburg,[1] Ingeborg Felderer, conductor Arthur Grüber. Revived Covent Garden, 1967, with Forbes Robinson, Anna Green, Patricia Johnson, Yvonne Minton, Richard Lewis, conductor Pritchard; 1972, with Robinson, Harper, Johnson, Gillian Knight, Lewis, conductor Colin Davis.

CHARACTERS

Priam, *King of Troy* .... Bass Baritone
Hecuba, *his wife* .... Dramatic Soprano
Hector, *their eldest son* .... Baritone
Andromache, *Hector's wife* ...Lyric Dramatic Soprano
Paris, *Priam's second son* ....Tenor (Boy Soprano in scene ii)
Helen, *wife to King Menelaus of Sparta, then Paris's lover* ....Mezzo-Soprano
Achilles, *a Greek hero* .... Heroic Tenor
Patroclus, *his friend* .... Light Baritone

CHARACTERS AND CHORUS IN THE SCENES AND INTERLUDES

Nurse ....Mezzo-Soprano

[1] Vandenburg started his career in America as a baritone, sang tenor roles in Germany and at Covent Garden (including Radames), and then reverted to baritone to include even this bass role. In 1972, he was enough of a tenor again to audition Siegfried for Sadler's Wells!

Old Man .... Bass
Young Guard .... Lyric Tenor
Hermes, *messenger of the Gods* ..... High Light Tenor
Chorus of Hunters, Wedding Guests, Serving Men,
Warriors etc.

Time: Antiquity   *Place:* Troy

In his second opera, *King Priam*, Tippett breaks almost
entirely with the luxuriant writing of *The Midsummer
Marriage*, something which disturbed the nostalgic admiration
of many lovers of the earlier work. As *Midsummer Marriage*
refers in its musical proliferation to such works as the song
cycle *The Heart's Assurance* (1951) and the Piano Concerto
(1953–5), the isolated orchestral textures and starker lines of
the music of *King Priam* relate to the Concerto for Orchestra
(1962–3).

The composer has prefaced the score with the German
Words 'Es möge uns das *Schicksal* gönnen, dass wir das innere
Ohr von dem Munde der Seele nicht abwenden' (May *Fate*
grant that we never turn our inner ear away from our soul's
lips), and explained at the time of the first performance that
the work was concerned with Choice—Priam's after the
prophecy over the fate of Paris, Paris's after the hunting
episode to go to Troy, Priam's to accept him, Helen's to leave
Sparta with Paris, Paris's between the three Graces, and so on
throughout. But, essentially, it is Tippett's reaction to the
events and circumstances of one of the world's greatest
myths, with its tensions and heroic loves, its themes of
courage and suffering, and public and private trial.

Act I.   Heralds with trumpets in front of the curtain and
a wordless chorus behind it, the latter much used throughout
the opera to express stress and particularly battle, the former
as 'links' between the episodes of the heroic drama, usher in
the action, which starts with discussion of Hecuba's dream—
that her newly-born son Paris will cause his father's death.
Hecuba's reaction to the Old Man's reading of the dream
comes in an aria, 'Then am I no longer mother to this child',
which quickly reveals her forthright, passionate nature.
Priam's reaction is less positive and exposed in a ruminative
soliloquy, whose first words, 'A father and a King', are used
later to pinpoint the moment when choice was available to
him and he allowed heart (typified in this phrase) to rule
head (which insisted on the child's death), and, more
culpably, did not hide this reaction from the Young Guard,

to whom he gave the job of killing the child and who knew Priam's feelings contradicted his words.

A vocal Interlude, involving the Nurse, Old Man and Young Guard—the opera's 'Greek Chorus'—discusses choice in its relation to the particular situation.

Priam's son Hector, attempting to demonstrate his physical prowess by subduing and capturing a wild bull single-handed, is dismayed when a young lad jumps on its back and rides it away. Eventually, the boy comes in, reveals that he loves the bull as his best friend but would like to join the young heroes of Troy. Hector offers to teach him the arts of war, a proposition Priam accepts provided the boy's father agrees and he makes a free choice. This the boy does, saying that his name is Paris, a revelation which startles Priam into a soliloquy. He cannot conceal his joy that the gods have reversed his 'choice' of long ago, and his fear that Hecuba's dream may yet prove inspired; in effect, he accepts the new turn of fate.

Nurse, Old Man and Young Guard witness the decision and comment in a second Interlude on its importance. Guests come rejoicing from the wedding feast of Hector and Andromache, at the same time admitting that the mutual hostility of Hector and Paris has caused Paris to set sail from Troy to the court of Menelaus at Sparta.

We see Helen and Paris, obviously already consumed with passion. Paris insists that Helen must choose between him and Menelaus and at the end of their duet exacts her promise to leave with him if he comes to fetch her. Even Paris in his soliloquy admits to dismay at the prospect their planned elopement opens before him, but turns to wonder whether there is in fact any element of choice in human affairs—do he and Helen 'choose' when, having been apart, their bodies rush together as one? Hermes, as if in answer to his question, comes to tell him he must choose between three Graces: Athene, Hera and Aphrodite (sung by Hecuba, Andromache, Helen). How in choosing one can he escape the wrath of the others? Hermes answers that he will not escape—but he must still choose. Athene offers him courage on the battlefield, Hera satisfaction in marriage, and each curse him when it is obvious he will choose Aphrodite and therefore elope with Helen and plunge Greece and Troy into war.

Act II. Troy is besieged and Hector taunts Paris with having run away in battle from Menelaus. Priam tries to patch up their quarrel, and Paris eventually follows Hector to battle. The first Interlude has the Old Man asking Hermes to let him see Achilles sulking in his tent.

Except in one short crucial scene, it is the private Achilles whom we meet in the opera, and he is found in his tent with Patroclus, singing sadly to the sound of guitar, 'O rich soiled land', a song of longing for peace and beauty quite at variance with the actions for which Achilles, here as in any other version of the legend, is renowned. Patroclus weeps that Achilles should have so taken to heart the loss of a girl, given as booty after the sack of Thebes and then taken away again, as to refuse to join the battle. Together they cook up the idea that Patroclus shall wear Achilles's armour against the Trojans, and Achilles pours a libation to the gods in order that Patroclus may return safely.

The Act's second Interlude has the Old Man begging Hermes to warn the Trojans of their peril at Patroclus's hands. Paris comes to tell Priam that Hector has killed Patroclus in single combat, and Hector to parade before his father in Achilles's armour. A fine trio celebrates the victory and the prospect the Trojans now have of destroying the Greek fleet, but it is interrupted at its climax by the sound of Achilles's war cry. This is the finest *coup de théâtre* the composer has yet achieved (the only one, you might argue, he ever truly attempted), and the blood-curdling challenge has haunted whoever heard the opera since Richard Lewis first superbly delivered it at Coventry in May, 1962, a reaction Tippett undoubtedly anticipated, to judge by the stage direction he allows himself at this point: 'Hector stands as though transfixed!'

Act III.   Cellos alone introduce Andromache, waiting like a fighter pilot's mate for her warrior to return from single combat, knowing that each vigil so far has had a happy ending but aware that the credibility gap is narrowing. In her aria, she remembers her foreboding the day Achilles killed her father and brothers, but she refuses to yield to Hecuba's entreaty to go on to the walls of Troy in order to call Hector back from the field of battle; why does King Priam not end the war by sending Helen back to Sparta? Hecuba retorts that it is not for Helen that the Greeks have gone to war, but to win Troy itself. When Helen appears, Andromache can assuage her nerves with insults about Helen's low priority amongst war objectives, marriage 'vows' to Menelaus, and so on. Helen's answer takes the form of a great aria, its burden:

'women like you, wives and mothers, cannot know what men may feel with me'. The voices of the three women join in perhaps the most inspired section of the score, a fine trio in which each invokes the name and attributes of her mate and predicts death.

The others leave Andromache. Serving women pretend to go about their business in Hector's house, but they have already heard the rumour: '... we could tell the story too, the pathetic story of our masters, viewed from the corridor'. Priam feels alone, isolated by his subjects from some disaster. Only Paris has the courage to tell him that Hector is dead; he cannot accept his father's reproaches and regrets at the result of the choice of twenty and more years ago and proclaims his intention of absenting himself until he has worked out his destiny by killing Achilles.

The last section of the opera begins as Paris leaves and Priam moans to himself: 'A father and a King.' Had the augurs predicted Hector's death and not his own, he would not only have ordered but also willed the killing of the infant Paris. His conscience speaks in the guise of the Young Guard, the Old Man and the Nurse who make him recite the dread chain of events, with vengeance inevitably following military murder, and he gradually accepts the inexorable laws by which men of all ages have lived.

The second Interlude, purely orchestral, ushers in the scene in Achilles's tent, climactic if undemonstrative, in which King Priam begs the body of Hector from the Greek who slew him. Achilles seems to start to urge the law of retribution, but his mention of the name of Patroclus shows the full extent of the wound his friend's death caused him. Priam kisses his hands, 'the hands of him who killed my son', and Achilles grants him the body of Hector. Just as he stood to pour a libation when Patroclus went off to fight, so he stands now to ask his friend's forgiveness for the act of non-hostility which might seem to negate the vengeance he has so bloodily exacted. Achilles and Priam discuss the destiny of each, Achilles's to die at the hands of Paris, Priam's to be killed by Achilles's son Neoptolemus.

The third Interlude has Hermes announcing the deaths of the protagonists and hymning music's all-healing supremacy. Paris offers to fight to defend Priam, who has refused to leave Troy with him. Priam prays and fails to recognise Hecuba. Stress mounts in the chorus, Andromache spurns Paris and his defence of Priam, and Helen takes her place. 'They stand silent together, the beautiful ill-fated pair', and Priam sends Paris on his way to a hero's death, leaving Helen to make her peace with her lover's father. Priam comforts her—and himself—with the idea, which she enunciates, that neither he nor Hector ever reproached her for her part in events. Finally, Helen goes and as the offstage sound of the chorus dies away, Priam sinks inaudibly down before the altar where, as Hermes appears before him and departs, Neoptolemus runs his sword through him to kill him instantly. 'Choice' is at an end.

H.

THE KNOT GARDEN

Opera in three acts; words and music by Michael Tippett. First performed at Covent Garden, December 2, 1970, with Jill Gomez, Josephine Barstow, Yvonne Minton, Robert Tear, Thomas Hemsley, Raymund Herincx, Thomas Carey, producer Peter Hall, conductor Colin Davis.

CHARACTERS

Faber, *a civil engineer, aged about 35* . Robust Baritone[1]
Thea, *his wife, a gardener* . . . . Dramatic Mezzo
Flora, *their ward, an adolescent girl* Light High Soprano
Denise, *Thea's sister, a Freedom-fighter*.Dramatic Soprano
Mel, *a Negro writer in his late twenties*
. . . . .Lyric Bass Baritone
Dov, *his white friend, a musician*. . . . . Lyric Tenor
Mangus, *an analyst* . . . . .High Tenor Baritone
Time: The Present   *Place:* A high-walled house-garden

In a preface to the published score, the composer has written: 'The scene, whether labyrinth or rose garden, changes with the inner situations. If the garden were ever finally visible, it might be a high-walled house-garden shutting out an industrial city. The labyrinth on the other hand can never be actual. It appears, if at all, as a maze which continually shifts and possibly (in Act II) spins.

'Time is the present. Although the duration is obviously within one day, from getting up to bedtime, the dramatic action is discontinuous, more like the cutting of a film. The

---

[1] The composer's own descriptions of the voices required.

term used for these cuts is Dissolve,[1] implying some deliberate break-up and re-formation of the stage picture.'

He has further told us 'Parolles' defiant realism in *All's Well that Ends Well*, "simply the thing I am shall make me live", is the motto of the whole work.'

As an introduction to Act I, which has the sub-title Confrontation, Tippett wrote in the original Covent Garden programme: '*The Knot Garden* is about the loves and hates of seven people in modern England. Mangus, a psychoanalyst, has been invited to stay in the house of Faber and his wife Thea. She hopes that Mangus can help with the problems of their young ward Flora, who is obsessed by the half-real, half-imagined sexual threat of Faber. Mangus discovers that it is not Flora that is sick but the marriage, and engineers a series of confrontations and "games" to resolve the difficulties. He sees himself as a modern Prospero, manipulating the characters. Dov, a musician, and his lover Mel, a young Negro writer, are also staying in the house, but as Thea's guests rather than Faber's. The arrival of Thea's sister Denise, a revolutionary, changes all the relationships.'

Act I. Uncompromising, strenuous, wide-striding music (the storm) introduces Mangus, who at his first appearance is described as 'a still point in a whirling storm'. Straightaway, he alludes to Prospero and seems full of self-confidence. Here occurs the first Dissolve, ten bars of loud *allegro molto* followed by five of *diminuendo* timpani roll and a soft horn call (sometimes on cellos); it is the same each time it occurs in Acts I and II, but varies in Act III. Thea comes slowly from the inner garden stopping occasionally to tend the flowers. Mangus offers to help, but Thea's authority in the garden is absolute. Flora screams off-stage and rushes still screaming into Thea's arms. Faber follows her, but Thea sends Flora away with Mangus and turns harshly to Faber. Flora is their ward, and Thea continues her gardening analogy before saying that, if she may mother her, he—Faber—should father her, not play the lecher. Thea leaves, and Faber, who has been put in the wrong, wonders how this now happens so regularly. As to his relationship with Flora, he says, half to himself and half to Mangus, 'I do not flirt with Flora; Flora screams before I . . . Impossible!', then goes off to work. Mangus is left to muse on the way each withdraws to the refuge of either factory or garden, and again refers to the

---

[1] There are two in Act I, one in Act II, five in Act III.

possibility that, Prospero-like, he may put all to rights. Dissolve (music as before).

Thea recommends flower therapy to Flora—or, more prosaically, tells her to arrange some roses in a bowl—and Flora hums enigmatically to herself before telling Thea that her sister Denise has sent a message that she will be arriving later that day. Flora's desultory and now solitary humming turns more purposefully into 'eeny meeny, miny, moe', but is interrupted by the rumbustious arrival of Dov and Mel in fancy dress, the one tricked out as Ariel, the other as Caliban (jazz drummer's kit in the orchestra). Dov tries to hook Mel, whose Caliban disguise is fish-like, they hold a tableau and Flora stares at them until they suggest that if she thinks they are waxworks, she should pay, and if alive, she should speak. They introduce themselves, Mel as a writer, Dov as a musician, then sing a nonsense rhyme together as Thea and Mangus come from the house.

Mangus is of course delighted at the augmentation of *The Tempest* cast, which now has Ariel, Caliban, Ferdinand and Miranda as well as his Prospero. He takes Flora off to look for costumes and each of the two men who are left takes a glass from Thea's tray until Mel seems hypnotically drawn to Thea, leaving Dov alone to smash his glass to smithereens and start to howl like Ariel's dog. Faber is amazed at what he sees on his return, but Dov's reprise of the ditty he and Mel have already sung leads to an explanation of identities, and Dov moves towards Faber at exactly the moment when Thea and Mel reappear on the opposite side of the stage (the composer explains that the resultant tableau cannot become a vocal ensemble because the tensions are not yet ready for such expression).

Tension builds but is exploded by the sound of Flora's renewed screams as she starts half-hysterically to describe the disconcerting nature of Denise's arrival, explained the moment Denise comes into view and it can be seen that she is disfigured by the torture she has endured in her one-woman efforts to set the world to rights. She knows the effect she will have on them and starts in an extended and passionate aria to explain what she has been through (she is a musical cousin to Queen Hecuba in *King Priam*, although her defiance has occasionally a hint of Achilles's war-cry about it). She wants no pity and her rhetorical question 'How can I turn home again to you, the beautiful and damned?' receives no

direct reply until Mel attempts to relieve the tension by
starting a blues, itself developed into a considerable ensemble
which eventually includes even Mangus and finally Denise
herself, soaring to top C and D flat just before the act comes
to an end with Mel's softly spoken, 'Sure, baby'.

Act II.   Labyrinth. The composer's programme note tells
us all the action of the opera takes place in Thea's garden,
and especially in the Knot Garden of the title. 'Knot gardens
were intricate, formal patterns, made usually of tiny box
hedges in Elizabethan gardens. In reality, such a garden was
very small in scale, but the characters of the opera find that
at times of crisis, the delicate love knot grows to become a
threatening maze in which they cannot find each other. And
when they do, their hates and loves are more naked and
violent.' In the score he goes further, and specifies that 'it
appears as if the centre of the stage had the power to "suck
in" a character at the back of the stage, say, and "eject" him at
the front. During their passage through the maze, characters
meet and play out their scenes. But always one of the
characters in these scenes is about to be ejected while a fresh
character has been sucked in and is whirled to the meeting
point.'
     The music is violent from the outset and the first to be
whirled in are Thea and Denise, aware of each other, not
dissimilar in their sentiments but not properly conversing.
Thea is whirled off and Faber makes some kind of contact
with Denise, who riposts that she is just as tough as Thea
before being herself whirled off and replaced by Flora (her
ditty again), who backs away from Faber with renewed
screams. No amount of reasoning from Faber can change her
attitude towards him, she drops the flowers she has been
carrying and is whirled off as Thea reappears to strike Faber
with a horse-whip. When Thea disappears, Dov, dressed now
as himself, takes her place, still howling like a dog but
prepared to sympathise with Faber's predicament—each of
them, he feels, humiliated by a woman. Faber is obviously
attracted in spite of himself, but his 'Come, I never kissed a
man before' only just precedes his disappearance, as Mel is
whirled on. Mel's very effective scene with Dov, directed to
be played 'like a song and dance number' and with jazz-kit
accompaniment, has as its refrain 'One day we meet together,
brother' and as its burden the discovery that two souls, who
thought they were twin, need to discover their true natures.

Dov is whirled off as the music calms and Denise appears to play on Mel's feelings for oppressed men anywhere (the tune of 'We shall overcome'[1] appears in the orchestra and for a moment in Mel's vocal line). As Mel turns to Denise, Dov is thrown from the labyrinth, Thea returns and so does Faber until Flora and Dov, after the act's first Dissolve, are left together.

'As the sense of nightmare clears away, Dov comes to life first. He sees the plight of Flora and goes to comfort her,' say the stage directions—and he comforts her with music, in an infinitely touching scene, first getting her to sing the opening phrases of Schubert's *Die liebe Farbe*, orchestrated with magical touch (and ending with a direct quotation of the first chord of Beethoven's G major Piano Concerto, a key work in Tippett's musical ancestry). 'But it's a boy's song,' says Dov, which causes Flora to say 'Sometimes I dream I am a boy who dies for love. And then I am a girl again.' Dov riposts with his own song, much less simple in outline: 'I was born in a big town, in a home without a garden' (a most appreciable product of the lyrical side of Tippett's genius which gave us *Boyhood's End* and *The Heart's Assurance*). The magic of love is in the air (perhaps indicated by alternating vibraphone and electric guitar) but, the stage directions tell us, 'as the song ends a shadow enters the garden. It is Mel. He taps the lovers on the shoulder: "Come, I taught you that." ' For all Dov's denial, the spell is broken and the music fades.

Act III. Charade. In his programme note, Tippett says, 'Mangus, continually dreaming of himself as Prospero, has from the start of the opera been cajoling the other characters to play a series of short charades with him on scenes from *The Tempest*.' In the stage directions in the vocal score, he goes further: 'Five of the characters in the opera have roles in the Charade: Mangus-Prospero, Dov-Ariel, Mel-Caliban, Flora-Miranda, Faber-Ferdinand. These roles are never absolute; they are dropped at need. Thea and Denise remain themselves. Anyone may be a spectator when not playing a scene in the Charade.' There is magic in the air as Mangus attempts to set the scene and describes a situation where 'this garden is now an island,' which provokes Thea's ironic 'Where you play Prospero, man of power; to set the world to rights!', and Denise is stung into stepping into Mangus's circle to proclaim

---

[1] The marching song of Martin Luther King's civil rights movement.

'Power is in the will.' But Thea, not to be outdone, steps into the circle herself and cries out, 'Forgiveness. Blood from my breast. Here on this island, I know no god but love.'

In the first Charade, Mangus-Prospero explains the island and its inhabitants to Flora-Miranda, conjuring Mel-Caliban to stand upright, to his daughter's delight, and Dov-Ariel to leave the tree where Sycorax has imprisoned him. But Dov-Ariel flings himself on Mel-Caliban and belabours him, far beyond the calls of the script. Dissolve (with the music this time varied).

There is an exchange between Thea and Denise. The first seems to understand that things go wrong, the second does not accept confusion: 'Before an assignment the mood was dedication and the mind was clear.' Both agree that Mel could be Denise's salvation. Dissolve.

Flora-Miranda is asleep; Dov-Ariel is on guard; Mangus-Prospero watches through a telescope. Mel-Caliban creeps up on the sleeping girl, leaps on her and tries to tear her clothes off (action resulting in 1970 in Covent Garden's first—momentarily—topless soprano). Denise protests and Mel says he is only playing the role he was given and no more. Let Denise lay her head against his pounding heart (where, says Dov, *his* head often lay), and she will understand, but she will not—yet. There is a short duet for Dov and Mel, 'Black earth for white roses?', at the end of which Thea asks Mangus whether he is man of power or voyeur. Mangus's answer is to disclose Faber-Ferdinand and Flora-Miranda playing chess—but not for long, as Flora-Miranda upsets the board. 'That scene went wrong!' says Faber; 'that scene went right!'" says Mangus.

The board is set again, and Thea, left alone, expresses new-found confidence in an *arioso* full of melismas: 'I am no more afraid. So we swing full circle back towards the sanctity of marriage.' Dissolve.

A denouement seems called for, according to Flora-Miranda, and Mangus-Prospero offers to provide it, at least for Dov and Mel. As judge, with Faber-Ferdinand as some sort of jailer, he tries first Dov-Ariel and frees him, then Mel-Caliban. The Charades are at an end, and it is a time for quotation, musical and Shakespearean. Voices off join in with incoherent cries, coalescing at last into the first word of Dov-Ariel's 'Come unto these yellow sands', which words dominate the ensemble. Mel leaves with Denise, Flora goes

off alone in spite of Dov's anxiety to follow her, so that in
the end he follows Mel and Denise. Mangus can see only Thea
and Faber alone in the garden (Dissolve: modified version of
original), and they begin to speak, though not to each other.
'I put away the seed packets. I put away the factory
papers . . . Our enmity's transcended in desire.'

That the problems of each couple, or of each individual,
are resolved is evident; but their catalyst seems to have been
musical rather than explicitly contained in the events of the
drama.

When in 1972 *The Knot Garden* was first revived at Covent
Garden, more than one critic referred to the work as being
'real', *The Times*'s William Mann finishing his notice
'. . . overtly serious scenes, as well as other moments of
comedy, now emerge with new force. One cannot call it
realism. The charm and power of *The Knot Garden* is that it
is a real play, not a fake of real life behaviour.'   H.

BENJAMIN BRITTEN
(1913–1977)
PETER GRIMES

OPERA in a prologue, an epilogue, and three acts by Benjamin Britten;
text by Montagu Slater, after the poem by George Crabbe. Première,
Sadler's Wells, London, June 7, 1945, with Joan Cross, Coates, Iacopi,
Blanche Turner, Bower, Pears, Roderick Jones, Donlevy, Brannigan,
Morgan Jones, Culbert, conductor Goodall. First performed Stockholm,
1945, with Sundström, Svanholm, Sigurd Björling, Jacobsson, Wirén,
Gösta Björling, conductor Sandberg; Berkshire Festival, U.S.A., 1946,
with Manning, Wm. Horne, Pease, conductor Bernstein; Zürich, 1946,
with Cross, Cordy, von Sieben, della Casa, Moor, Pears, Andreas
Boehm, Rehfuss, Vichegonov, Libero de Luca, conductor Denzler;
Basle, 1946, with Annie Weber, Wosniak, Rothmüller, Preger,
Ollendorf, conductor Krannhals; Hamburg, 1947, with Schlüter, Gura,
Rothenberger, de Freitas, Markwort, Broecheler, Pfeifle, Roth,
Göllnitz, conductor Hollreiser; Berlin, 1947, with Grümmer, Witte,
Heinz Nissen, Schirp, conductor Heger; Covent Garden, 1947, with
Cross, Coates, Pears, Tom Williams, Brannigan, Norville, conductor

Rankl; la Scala, Milan, 1947, with Danco, Ticozzi, Prandelli, Colombo, Borriello, conductor Serafin; Metropolitan, New York, 1948, with Resnik (later Stoska), Jagel (later Sullivan), Brownlee, Hines, Garris, conductor Emil Cooper; 1967, with Amara, Vickers, Geraint Evans, conductor Colin Davis.

CHARACTERS

Peter Grimes, *a fisherman* . . . . Tenor
John, *his apprentice* . . . . Silent
Ellen Orford, *a widow, schoolmistress of the*
    Borough . . . . Soprano
Captain Balstrode, *retired merchant skipper* . . . Baritone
Auntie, *landlady of 'The Boar'* . . . . Contralto
Her two 'Nieces', *main attractions of 'The Boar'* . Soprano
Bob Boles, *fisherman and Methodist* . . . . Tenor
Swallow, *a lawyer* . . . . Bass
Mrs. (Nabob) Sedley, *a rentier widow of an*
    East India Company's factor . . . . . . .Mezzo-Soprano
Rev. Horace Adams, *the rector* . . . . Tenor
Ned Keene, *apothecary and quack* . . . . Baritone
Dr. Thorp . . . . Silent
Hobson, *the carrier* . . . . Bass
Chorus of Townspeople and Fisherfolk
Time: Towards 1830   *Place:* The Borough, a fishing village,
East coast of England

The idea of *Peter Grimes* came to Britten in America in 1941 after reading an article by E. M. Forster on the subject of George Crabbe, the poet of England and more particularly of East Anglia. Shortly afterwards, Koussevitzky, the conductor, offered to commission him to write an opera, and, immediately on his return to England (in the spring of 1942), he set to work with Montagu Slater to hammer out the libretto.

This is freely adapted from Crabbe's story, which forms a part of his long poem, *The Borough*. The venue remains Aldeburgh, where Crabbe was born and where Britten, shortly after the première of *Peter Grimes*, made his home, but the character of Peter Grimes is to some extent softened; he is no longer the uncomplicated sadist of Crabbe's poem, but a proud, self-willed misfit, whose uncompromising independence and unwillingness to accept help brings him in the end to disaster.

The immediate success of Britten's first opera is a matter of history. Its first performance came a month after the end of the war in Europe and coincided with the return of the Sadler's Wells Company to its London home; the music has unflagging vitality and invention; the subject was susceptible enough to traditional big-scale operatic treatment to please old opera-goers, and the anti-hero (an early example of the type in popular form) sufficiently 'different' to please the more sophisticated. That it has not since fluctuated much in popular estimation (at least in non-Latin countries) is due perhaps almost as much to Britten's ability to choose a subject which would touch the public's sensitivity as to the superior quality of the resulting opera. One could even argue that *Peter Grimes*'s success has made it curiously hard for later and by no means inferior operas by the same hand to make their way through the opera houses of the world, though such a contention should not be thought to denigrate the sterling qualities of the opera in question.

Prologue.   The Moot Hall of the Borough, where the inquest is being held on Grimes's apprentice who died at sea. As the curtain goes up, we hear in the wood-wind a theme which is associated with Swallow, the Borough lawyer and Coroner (No. 1).

The people of the Borough, who crowd the hall, suspect Grimes of having caused the boy's death, and feeling runs high. When asked to give evidence, Grimes repeats the oath after Swallow in notes an octave higher and of double the time value. He tells a story of distress at sea, how he and the boy, when out fishing, were driven from their course by a change of wind, how they were three days without water, and how the boy died of exposure.

When it comes to confirming the details of what occurred when Grimes landed his boat, Swallow and Grimes refer in turn to Ned Keene, the Rector, Bob Boles, Auntie, Mrs. Sedley, and Ellen Orford, who corroborate the evidence as their names are called. (This device is entirely plausible from the point of view of the drama, and allows in the shortest possible time an exposition of the characters of all the main

figures of the opera.) There is some interruption from the
onlookers, and at the end the Coroner gives his verdict:
'. . . your apprentice died in accidental circumstances. But
that's the kind of thing people are apt to remember', and at
the same time advises Grimes to get a grown-up, not a boy, to
help him in future. Grimes tries to make himself heard above
the growing uproar in the court, but it is impossible, and
Hobson, after vainly shouting for silence, clears the court.

Grimes and Ellen Orford are left alone, and Ellen tries to
give what comfort she can. Their duet begins with Ellen
singing in E major, Peter in F minor, but as Peter gradually
warms to her quiet confidence in his future, he takes up her
key and they finish together: 'here is a friend.'

Britten begins each of his three acts with a so-called
Interlude, and also connects the two scenes of each of them
with a similar orchestral piece. Prologue and Act I (which
takes place on the beach, showing the Moot Hall, Boar Inn,
and the porch of the church) are joined by the first of these
Interludes (2A):

This calm piece seems to express the typical movement of
waves and water (No. 2B):

which so often heralds a new day for the fishermen of the
Borough.

The first part of the scene is in the form of an extended
chorus (No. 3) with interruptions from Auntie, who opens up
for the day; Boles, who protests at anything which comes

into the category of fun; Balstrode, who is concerned with
what the weather has in store; the Rector and Mrs. Sedley,
who wish each other 'Good morning'; and Ned Keene, who
says he is anxious for an assignation with one of Auntie's
'Nieces' that night.

In the meanwhile, the fishermen and their womenfolk go
about their daily business, mending nets and preparing for
the day's work. Grimes's voice is heard off, calling for help
with his boat, which is refused him until Balstrode and Keene
decide to give him a hand.

Keene tells Grimes that he has found him another
apprentice whom he has only to fetch from the workhouse.
When Keene asks him, Carter Hobson refuses to have anything to do with the transaction: the cart's full. 'I have to go
from pub to pub,' sings Hobson, in what Britten describes as
a 'half number'. The chorus supports Hobson's refusal, but
Ellen Orford takes up his tune and offers to help him mind
the boy if he will agree to bring him back. The chorus's
protest rises in vigour until Ellen takes her stand firmly
against them: 'Let her among you without fault cast the first
stone.' Her D minor *arioso* is the first extended solo writing
of the opera, and its mixture of determination not to give
way to the weight of opinion, and of tenderness, well
illustrates the character of her music throughout the opera.
Hobson yields to her pleading, and Mrs. Sedley asks Keene if
he yet has her pills, her laudanum. He says he will not get
them until that night; let her meet him in the pub and collect
them.

Balstrode sees through his glasses that the storm cone has
been hoisted, and he leads a great fugal ensemble, in which
join the voices of Keene, Auntie, the two Nieces, Bob Boles,
the chorus and orchestra (one of the characteristics of the
Nieces is that they nearly—but not quite—always sing together in unison). Bob Boles calls on the Borough to repent,
and the passage ends with the fervent prayer: 'O tide that
waits for no man, spare our coasts.' The storm music is now
firmly established, and it dominates the rest of the act.

Balstrode comments on Grimes's apparently convinced
isolation—even now, he stays out in the storm, instead of
coming into the pub—and suggests that he would be better
off working on a merchantman, away from the gossip of the
Borough. He is 'native, rooted here', replies Grimes: 'By
familiar fields Marsh and sand.' Touched however by the old

captain's kindliness, he tells him in an *arioso* passage the story of his horrifying experience when alone at sea with only the corpse of the dead boy to keep him company in the boat. He plans to stop the gossips with the one thing they listen to—money (a rapid *scherzando* passage). The duet grows in intensity as he refuses to listen to Balstrode's advice. Left alone, he reflects passionately on the peace which could be his were Ellen to become his wife.

The interval of the ninth has been thought to characterise Grimes's maladjustment, and we hear it in its minor form at the beginning of the scene with Balstrode (No. 4A)

and resolved into the major when he thinks of Ellen and his possible salvation (No. 4B).

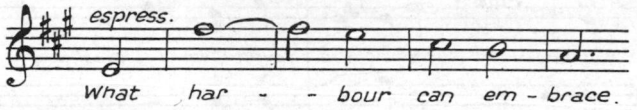

With the fall of the curtain, we hear for the first time the full force of the storm in the orchestral interlude which follows, and which is developed from the storm themes already heard, with a reference in the midde to No. 4B.

Scene ii is placed in the interior of The Boar, where warmth and calm contrasts with the storm which enters each time one or other of the characters opens the door to come in. Mrs. Sedley is an unexpected visitor, but she explains that she is waiting there for Ned Keene.

Two episodes characterise the music: Balstrode complains about the noise the frightened 'Nieces' make, and is rebuked by Auntie in a half-humorous piece; Bob Boles makes drunken advances to one of the Nieces, tries to hit Balstrode, who overpowers him and leads the company in 'We live and let live, and look we keep our hands to ourselves.'

Grimes comes in, and Mrs. Sedley promptly faints. Grimes takes little notice of what has been or is going on inside The Boar but sings introspectively of the mystery of the skies and human destiny: 'Now the Great Bear and Pleiades.' The melody is in the orchestra and in canon, but the effective words, the contrasting *molto animato* in the middle, and the suggestive and reiterated 'Who, who, who, who can turn skies back and begin again' make this into a *scena* of haunting beauty.

The reaction to Grimes's mood is, not unnaturally, one of consternation, and Ned Keene saves the situation by starting off a round: 'Old Joe has gone fishing.' Three distinct tunes are used and combined in the metre of 7/4 (No. 5).

The storm is heard again, and Hobson the carter comes in with Ellen and Grimes's new apprentice. The bridge is down, they almost had to swim, and everyone is chilled to the bone. Auntie offers refreshment, but Grimes wants to be off, taking the boy with him. Ellen tells him gently: 'Peter will take you home,' upon which the chorus comments derisively 'Home! do you call that home!'

Act II opens with a prelude in complete contrast to what has gone before. It is Sunday morning, and the sunlight is reflected off the waves as everyone goes to church. The interlude is made up of a lively and brilliant *toccata* (No. 6)

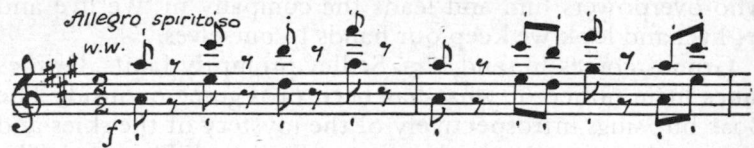

which contrasts with a broad, appealing lyrical tune, heard first on the violas and 'cellos (in unison) and again immediately on the rise of the curtain, sung by Ellen who comes in with John, the new apprentice (No. 7):

con espansione

f Glit-ter of waves and glit-ter of sun-light

Bid us re-joice and lift our hearts on high

The scene which follows takes place within a frame provided by the music of the church service which is heard from time to time off-stage. During the hymn (*maestoso*) Ellen talks to the boy about his life at the workhouse, and her own love of her teacher's life and determination that the new apprentice's life shall be different from that of the old, ending 'Every day I pray it may be so.' The beginning of the Confession and Responses (*Recitativo agitato*) coincides with Ellen's discovery that the boy has a torn coat and—worse—a bruise on his neck. With the Gloria (*Andante con moto*) she tries, in music of aria-like stature, to provide comfort for herself almost as much as for the boy. Peter Grimes comes in quickly as the chorus begins the Benedicite (*Allegro agitato*), and tells the boy they are off to work, answering Ellen roughly when she reminds him that it is Sunday, a day of rest. The chorus starts the Creed (*Adagio*) as Ellen pleads with Peter to adjust his ways to the boy's tender years. 'Were we mistaken when we schemed to solve your life by lonely toil?' she asks him, and concludes: 'Peter! we've failed'—and he cries out in agony and strikes her, matching the chorus's 'Amen' with his own *fortissimo* 'So be it, and God have mercy upon me!' (No. 8).

largamente

ff So be it And God have mer-cy upon me

Grimes drives the boy off in front of him, and leaves Ellen to make her way weepingly home.

Auntie, Bob Boles, and Ned Keene sing a brisk trio based on Grimes's example 8: 'Grimes is at his exercise', and the service comes to an end, spilling its congregation on to the beach. Some of them, Mrs. Sedley naturally amongst them, have heard the noise of the quarrel during the service, and the chorus murmurs in indignation at what it only half understands. Balstrode tries to exert a calming influence, Swallow chips in with a sitting-on-the-fence platitude, but Bob Boles inflames popular sentiment and calls on Ellen Orford, who has come back to collect her things, to tell them what was going on.

She attempts to explain in terms of what they tried to do, but the weight of opinion is too solidly against her—she is now firmly associated in their minds with Grimes and his misdeeds—and though her voice rises higher and higher in her efforts to make herself understood, the ensemble and the chorus cap her efforts, on which they have commented derisively all the time, with a cry of 'Murder!' In spite of Balstrode's protest that they are wasting their time, the Rector and Swallow organise a party to investigate what is going on at Grimes's hut, Carter Hobson beats his drum to call the men together in the emergency, and they march off together to the tune of a vindictive chorus, whose last words are 'Bring the branding iron and knife, what's done now is done for life.'

As their voices die away in the distance, two flutes in seconds introduce a 6/8 'trio' for the two Nieces, Auntie, and Ellen (except in the first and last phrases the Nieces sing in unison), whose calm beauty provides a contemplative ending to a scene which has otherwise been dramatic and even violent. The women reflect on their relationship with men: 'Do we smile or weep, Or wait quietly till they sleep?'.

The interlude joining the first scene of Act II to the second is a Passacaglia, which is the centre-piece of the whole opera. It is built up on example 8, and through it runs a desolate viola solo, which represents the fate of the apprentice caught up in Grimes's destiny.

The curtain rises on scene ii in Grimes's hut, an upturned boat boarded in to afford shelter from the weather, and full of ropes and fisherman's tackle. Until the sound of the chorus off-stage just before its end, the scene consists of an extended monologue for Grimes, the boy's part being confined to a single scream.

The music settles down to an aria, in which Grimes seeks to contrast what he is in reality with what he has always dreamed and planned, with Ellen's help, to be. The florid cast of the music and the idyllic nature of the words eventually gives place to a feverish description of that awful vigil with the dying apprentice in the boat. With the words 'in harbour still and deep' the aria comes to an end, and in the next bar the sound of the investigatory procession from the village can be heard. Grimes reacts violently to it, thinks the boy is the cause of its coming to his hut, and shouts his defiance of what it can do to him. With an admonition to be careful, Grimes hustles the boy down the cliff, turns as he senses the unwelcome visitors nearing his door, and hears the boy scream as he falls down the cliff to his death. Grimes climbs quickly after him. With the scream, the orchestral sound cuts off suddenly and leaves only an eerie echo on the celesta.

The Rector puts his head round the door, and is followed by Swallow, Keene, and Balstrode. They find nothing, but comment on the open door with the precipice almost directly beyond it, and the neatness of the hut, and Swallow sums up the feelings of all when he says that the whole episode seems to have ended by quieting village gossip once and for all.

Act III opens with a Moonlight prelude of great simplicity and beauty, whose rising theme is punctuated now and then by a little figure for flute and harp.

The curtain rises to reveal the same scene as the first of Act I (the Borough street and beach), this time at night. A dance is in progress in the Moot Hall, and there is a steady procession between there and The Boar. The off-stage band plays a rustic jig, and Swallow appears, all dignity discarded, chasing one of the nieces and singing a raffish tune. The first Niece is presently joined by the second—they find safety in numbers—and together they elude Swallow, who angrily goes into The Boar, leaving the orchestra to enjoy his tune. Ned Keene, with intentions that are in no way dissimilar from Swallow's, starts off for the place where the Nieces have gone into hiding, but is waylaid by Mrs. Sedley, who, to the accompaniment of a *Ländler* from the off-stage orchestra, and much to his disgust, tries to enlist his interest in proving Peter Grimes a murderer.

While the orchestra starts up a hornpipe, the older members of the community bid each other good night, the Rector outdoing everyone in affability, a section of extraordinary musical refinement and beauty. Mrs. Sedley, hardly visible, broods in the darkness: 'Crime which my hobby is

sweetens my thinking.' She is still in concealment when Ellen
and Balstrode walk up from the beach, the latter revealing
that Grimes's boat is in but he is nowhere to be found, the
former overcome by recognising the boy's jersey, which she
herself had made him, and which Balstrode has found washed
up by the tide.

Ellen's aria, 'Embroidery in childhood was a luxury of
idleness' (No. 9), is, like the trio at the end of the first scene

of the previous act, a moment of stillness in the drama, which
has been advanced in one way or another by every other
section of the music, but which is here commented upon in
music that is florid and exacting, but whose effect is one of
tranquillity and resignation. It is the most extended aria of
the opera, and also one of its most affecting passages.

Ellen is in despair, but Balstrode says there may yet be
something they can do for him, in his hour of 'unearthly
torment'. Mrs. Sedley now has the clue she needs, and she
goes officiously towards the door of The Boar, and calls for
Mr. Swallow. Auntie protests that her customers come to her
for quiet and peace, but Mrs. Sedley is not to be gainsaid, and
Swallow eventually comes out to find out what all the noise
is about. When he hears that Grimes's boat is back he orders,
as mayor of the Borough, that Hobson take a posse of men
and find Grimes. Hobson summons the men to help him, and
in an atmosphere of hysteria and brutality, which is
horrifyingly reflected in the big ensemble, 'him who despises
us we'll destroy', the inhabitants set out to hunt down the
fellow-citizen they cannot understand. The scene ends with
fortissimo cries of 'Peter Grimes' before the curtain comes
down.

The sixth interlude, a short one, has been described by
Sackville-West as 'one of the strangest and most imaginative
passages in the opera. . . . The music, which transfers us from

the one-track hysteria of the crowd to the echoing limbo of Grimes's mind, is ... bound together by a single chord, a dominant seventh on D—held, *ppp*, throughout the interlude by three muted horns. Figures of nightmare sea-birds fly through the fog uttering fragments of themes which Grimes has sung earlier. . . .'

As the curtain rises, the search-party can be heard crying 'Peter Grimes', and at the same time a fog-horn (tuba off-stage on E flat followed by an appoggiatura D natural) makes itself heard. Grimes drags himself in and has a long mad scene to himself, accompanied only by the off-stage chorus and the fog-horn against the background of the horn chord. He babbles of home, and sings snatches that remind him of the various stages of his tragic story. Ellen comes in with Balstrode and tells him they have come to take him home, but he appears not to recognise her until he sings a reminiscence of example 4B, which represents his aspirations and is now associated with what he has failed to obtain. Balstrode drops into ordinary speech (the chorus and the unvarying foghorn have, for the first time since the interlude, ceased to make themselves heard) to tell Peter to take his boat out to sea and sink her there. He goes off to help Peter with the boat, then returns and leads Ellen away.

Very quietly, three violins begin to play the music of the prelude to Act I (No. 2A), as the stragglers return from the unsuccessful chase. It is morning, and the chorus sings the same tune as at the beginning of Act I. Swallow looks through his glasses to confirm the coastguard's report that a boat has been seen sinking out at sea, but no one is interested. The Borough has forgotten its manhunt and prepares to get on with another day (No. 3).   H.

THE RAPE OF LUCRETIA

Opera in two acts by Benjamin Britten; text by Ronald Duncan, based on André Obey's play, *Le Viol de Lucrèce*. Première at Glyndebourne, July 12, 1946; the work was later toured throughout England with a double cast, the first-named singer in each case having sung at the première: Cross (Nielsen), Ferrier (Evans), Ritchie (Duff), Pollak (Lawson), Pears (Schiøtz), Kraus (Rogier), Donlevy (Sharp), Brannigan (Walker), conductor Ansermet (Goodall). First performed Basle, 1947, with Lorand, von Sieben, Wosniak, Gschwend, conductor

Krannhals; Chicago, 1947, with Resnik, Kibler, Kane, Rogier, conductor Breisach; Mulhouse, 1948, with Sabatier, von Sieben, Bécour, Clément, conductor Krannhals; Paris, 1948, with Mulhouse company; New York, 1949, with Lewis, Kitty Carlisle, Kane, conductor Breisach; Rome, 1949, with Vitali-Marini, Gardino, Manuritta, Franci, conductor Santini; Salzburg Festival, 1950, with Kupper, Höngen, Güden, Dagmar Hermann, Patzak, Uhde, Poell, Böhme, conductor Krips; Munich, 1951, with Schech, Barth, Klarwein, Uhde, conductor Heger; New York, City Opera, 1958, with Frances Bible, conductor Rudel; Edinburgh Festival, 1963, by English Opera Group, with Sylvia Fisher, Kjerstin Meyer, Dowd, Glossop, conductor Meredith Davies; Leningrad and Moscow, 1964, by English Opera Group, with Fisher, Baker, Pears; U.S. tour by National Opera Company, 1967, with Joy Davidson.

CHARACTERS

Male Chorus	Tenor
Female Chorus	Soprano
Lucretia	Contralto
Collatinus, *her husband*	Bass
Lucia, *her attendant*	Soprano
Bianca, *her nurse*	Contralto
Tarquinius, *Prince of Rome*	Baritone
Junius, *a Roman general*	Baritone

Time: 500 B.C.   *Place:* In or near Rome

Although *The Rape of Lucretia* is to date the most lyrical of Britten's operas, its actual organisation is more formal than for instance that of *Peter Grimes*. The two acts, which are divided into two scenes each, take place within a musical and dramatic frame provided by a Male and a Female Chorus. These two commentators assume, together with the orchestra, the duties of preparation, comment, heightening of the tension, and summing-up which, in *Grimes*, were allotted to the orchestra alone, and in fact the interludes in the middle of each act are vocal as opposed to the purely instrumental equivalents in the earlier opera. The function of the Choruses is not only to act as a link between the authors and the audience, but also to give expression to the reactions of both these elements to the story which is being enacted on the stage, and which has evidently assumed a mystical and even religious significance to musician and poet. The opera is scored for chamber orchestra of twelve instruments and piano.

Act I. The Male and Female Choruses are discovered sitting on thrones, one on either side of the stage. They move about hardly at all during the course of the opera, and they are at times (e.g. during the interludes) cut off from the main part of the stage by a back-cloth.

We are *in medias res* straight away as the Male Chorus announces *con forza* in the third bar: 'Rome is now ruled by the Etruscan upstart, Tarquinius Superbus.' In a nervous half *arioso*, half recitative style, he introduces the story by sketching in the historical background against which it is set. The particular situation—the war against Greece—is indicated by the Female Chorus before the two voices join in a lyric statement (No. 1):

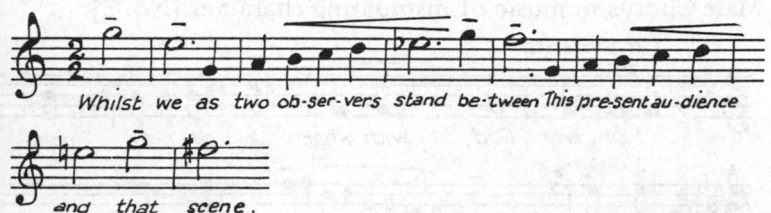

The front-cloth rises, as the orchestra (muted strings and harp) suggests an atmosphere of oppressive heat, a night alive with the noise of crickets and bull-frogs. The scene is a camp outside Rome, with the generals' tent in the foreground. The Male Chorus and the orchestra are interrupted in their description of the lights of distant Rome by an explosive drinking song for the officers.

The officers discuss the outcome of their bet the night before, when they rode home unannounced to see what their wives were doing in their absence. Only Lucretia, Collatinus's wife, was at home, and the others, not excluding Junius's Patricia, were all found in one compromising situation or another. 'And Collatinus has won the bet', shouts Tarquinius, 'And Junius is a cuckold, a cuckold's a cock without a crow. . . .' Tarquinius's motif is heard for the first time at the words 'You forget I am the *Prince of Rome*' (the four descending notes C, B, A, and G sharp).

Tarquinius and Junius quarrel and start to fight but are separated by Collatinus, who suggests they drink a toast together. Tarquinius immediately proposes it (No. 2):

and all join in. This is the Lucretia motif.

At its end, Junius rushes angrily from the tent, pulling the flaps shut behind him; he is furiously jealous of Lucretia's chastity, and repeats her name again and again, easing his agony by abusing her. His aria is developed to a point at which the idea of revenge fills his mind, when for the second time the Male Chorus takes over from him. What Junius might have said aloud, or at any rate what he would have admitted to feeling, is sung by him; the jealousy which causes his anger and the thoughts it suggests to him—things he would *not* have admitted to feeling—are described by the Male Chorus in music of insinuating character (No. 3).

Junius ends his aria with a final explosive 'Lucretia!' (example 2), and Collatinus walks out to him to reason with him and persuade him to take a less directly personal view of the situation. Collatinus's aria, 'Those who love create', replaces one written for the first version of the opera, which had the dramatic disadvantage of involving Collatinus in not understanding that Junius's driving motive is jealousy. The change was made in order to reduce the risk that Collatinus might appear too soft a character to be pitted against Tarquinius—one of nature's cuckolds in fact. Collatinus goes off to bed, leaving Tarquinius and Junius to resolve their differences in a striking duet, which finishes with a canon at the half bar; as they put it,

> It seems we agree,
> But are not of the same opinion!

Junius leaves Tarquinius alone, after suggesting that to prove Lucretia chaste is something even the Prince will not dare to attempt. The Male Chorus to the orchestral accompaniment of the opening of the scene comments on Tarquinius's indecision, until his cry of 'My horse! My horse!' reveals that his mind is now all too firmly made up.

The curtain falls rapidly and immediately the Male Chorus begins a graphic description of Tarquinius's Ride to Rome.

The music's energy mounts until the Ride is brought to a temporary halt by the River Tiber. Tarquinius and his horse take to the water, and the Chorus describes their crossing (No. 3). The slow *crescendo* from the solo flute's *ppp* to the full orchestra's *ff* is extraordinarily evocative, and the Ride culminates in the Chorus's *ff* 'Lucretia' as the curtain goes up to reveal the hall of Lucretia's house.

In Lucretia's house, all is peace. She and her two female companions are spinning, and the Female Chorus's beautiful spinning song, with its flute and harp accompaniment, not only sets the mood but also frames the three solo verses, each with its 'nostalgic ninth', which Lucretia, Bianca, and Lucia sing in turn. Lucretia thinks she hears a knock, but finding it is not Collatinus or his messenger, as she had hoped, sings an *arioso*, 'How cruel men are to teach us love'. The women prepare for bed, and a trio develops between Lucia and Bianca, who vocalise on 'Ah' while folding up the linen, and the Female Chorus who comments on this ubiquitious and calming feminine action.

'How quiet it is to-night', reflects Lucretia; '. . . it must be men who make the noise', retorts Bianca, and immediately we hear a suggestion of Tarquinius's Ride in the orchestra. Lucia continues to muse in the strains of the Linen trio, Male and Female Choruses point to the contrast between the peace within and the man who is coming so fast to disturb it, and a loud knocking announces that Tarquinius has arrived. The rest of the scene is carried on in pantomime, to the expressive comment of the two Choruses, until Lucretia's two companions remark on the strangeness of a visit so late from the Prince whose palace lies only just across the city, but who is asking for Lucretia's hospitality. She cannot refuse it, and there starts a chain of 'Good nights', each one based on Tarquinius's motif but subtly different from the next, and each introduced by one or other of the Choruses. The act ends when all have done suitable obeisance to the Prince.

Act II. As before, the two Choruses introduce the act.

The curtain rises to show Lucretia asleep in bed as the bass flute, muted horn, and bass clarinet introduce the Female Chorus's Lullaby, a tune of exquisite sensitivity (see page 1450). It is marked *piano*, and by the end the composer writes *ppppp* over the score. The hushed atmosphere is continued in the next section, in which the Male Chorus, speaking in a mysterious voice accompanied only by percussion, describes

Tarquinius's approach to Lucretia's room. As Tarquinius reaches the head of the bed, the first phrase of the Female Chorus's Lullaby is heard again. In an extended and impressive aria, Tarquinius sings of his feelings for Lucretia; the middle section is heard against the Female Chorus's Lullaby, and at the end of the aria Tarquinius bends over Lucretia to wake her, as he has planned, with a kiss.

Lucretia wakes (to the sound of the 'whip'—a little used orchestral instrument) and is confronted with the sight of Tarquinius. Immediately the character of the music changes. Lucretia pleads for mercy in music of rapidly rising tension, and Tarquinius does his best to establish that her resistance is diminishing: 'Can you deny your blood's dumb pleading?' The Choruses take Lucretia's part in the quartet which ensues: 'Go, Tarquinius, whilst passion is still proud and before your lust is spent', but it is too late, and Tarquinius pulls the cover from the bed and threatens Lucretia with his sword. The scene ends with a statement by the quartet *a capella* of the music heard originally in Junius's soliloquy (No. 3), and Tarquinius beats out the candle with his sword as the curtain falls rapidly.

The Interlude takes the form of a figured chorale sung by the two commentators, in which they interpret in Christian terms the scene they have just witnessed, while the orchestra depicts the physical events of the rape. The Interlude dies away and the front-drop goes up to show the hall of Lucretia's house as in the second scene of Act I. Everything is flooded with light, and Lucia and Bianca exult in the beauty of the day. Their *aubade* gives them plenty of opportunity for coloratura display before they discuss whether it was Tarquinius they heard gallop out of the courtyard earlier in the morning. Lucia sings a little arietta, 'I often wonder whether Lucretia's love is the flower of her beauty,' before Lucretia is seen coming into the hall.

She is obviously full of foreboding, and her initially quiet behaviour gives way to something like hysteria when she is offered the orchids to arrange: 'How hideous! Take them away!' She bursts into wild activity and orders Lucia to send a messenger to Collatinus, telling him to come home. She laughs hysterically but calms sufficiently to arrange the rest of the flowers, which she does while she sings an aria, a miniature of beauty and pathos, and one of the major inspirations of the score. Bianca's aria is in complete contrast; she remembers when life was still sweet and fresh for all of them before the fatal yesterday.

There is a short interchange between Bianca and Lucia (Lucretia has left the stage) in which the former bids the latter prevent the messenger reaching Collatinus; but it is too late, and in a moment Collatinus and Junius are with them, demanding to know where Lucretia is.

Lucretia herself comes in, dressed in purple mourning, and in eleven bars of orchestral music (cor anglais and strings) the essence of her tragedy is conveyed. It is a passage of incomparable beauty and poignancy. Collatinus addresses his wife in words and music that are calculated to comfort and sustain her, affirming that they must never again be parted. Their voices blend before Lucretia makes her confession to Collatinus, the orchestra punctuating what she has to say with *sotto voce* memories of the music which went with what she is describing. Finally, she sings a modified version of No. 3 ending, 'For me this shame, for you this sorrow'. Collatinus attempts to forgive her, but she is overcome by what has happened to her, and stabs herself, dying in Collatinus's arms.

Her funeral march (marked *alla marcia grave*) takes the form of an extended *chaconne*. It is sung by all the characters in tableau, Collatinus and Junius first, then Bianca and Lucia, and finally the two commentators joining their voices in the magnificent ensemble. The protagonists in the drama kneel round the body of Lucretia, while the commentators continue to discuss the tragedy. The Female Chorus cannot accept the finality with which the story has closed, and ends incredulously 'Is this it all?' to which she receives conclusive answer from her male companion: 'It is not all . . . For now He bears our sin and does not fall . . . In His passion is our hope, Jesus Christ, Saviour, He is all, He is all.' The Christian ethic has been allowed—some commentators have said 'forced'—to draw a moral from the pagan story. The opera ends with a final statement of the lyrical passage heard at the end of the prologue (No. 1).   H.

ALBERT HERRING

Opera in three acts by Benjamin Britten; text by Eric Crozier, adapted from Maupassant's story *Le Rosier de Madame Husson*. Première, Glyndebourne, June 20, 1947, with Joan Cross, Ritchie, Nancy Evans, de la Porte, Parr, Pears, Sharp, Parsons, Lumsden, Roy Ashton, conductor Britten. First performed Tanglewood, U.S.A., 1949; Hanover, 1950, conductor Schüler; Berlin, 1950, with Losch, Krebs, Brauer, Heinz Nissen, conductor Ludwig; New York, 1952, by Opera Futures Workshop; Berlin, Komische Oper, 1958, producer Herz; Moscow, 1960, by Komische Oper, Berlin; Edinburgh Festival by English Opera Group, 1965, with Fisher, Cantelo, Macdonald, Luxon, conductor Tausky; Hamburg, 1966, with Edith Lang, Steiner, Troyanos, Mödl, Wohlfahrt, Blankenburg, conductor Mackerras; New York City Opera, 1971, with Faull, John Stewart, conductor Bernardi.

CHARACTERS

Lady Billows, *an elderly autocrat* . . . . Soprano
Florence Pike, *her housekeeper* . . . . Contralto
Miss Wordsworth, *head teacher* . . . . Soprano
Mr. Gedge, *the Vicar* . . . . Baritone
Mr. Upfold, *the Mayor* . . . . Tenor
Superintendent Budd . . . . Bass
Sid, *a butcher's assistant* . . . . Baritone
Albert Herring, *from the greengrocer's* . . . . Tenor
Nancy, *from the bakery* . . . . .Mezzo-Soprano
Mrs. Herring, *Albert's mother* . . . . .Mezzo-Soprano
Emmie ⎤   ⎧ Soprano
Cis   ⎬ *village children* . . . . ⎨ Soprano
Harry ⎦   ⎩ Treble

Time: April and May of 1900
Place: Loxford, a small market-town in East Suffolk, England.

During a tour of English cities with *Lucretia* in 1946, Britten decided for the future to form his own chamber opera company, the English Opera Group, with the result that, though *Albert Herring* like *Lucretia* was first given at

Glyndebourne, it was presented under the management of the English Opera Group rather than of the Christies themselves. *Albert Herring* kept the chamber opera form of *Lucretia* but, as a comedy, represented a new departure for Britten, a fact only emphasised by his original choice, subsequently discarded, of *Mansfield Park* as the subject of his third opera. Kathleen Ferrier was to have had a leading part in it, but in 1947 at Glyndebourne she sang Gluck's *Orfeo* for the first time.

Act I. The curtain rises after two bars of the busy prelude to show the breakfast room of Lady Billows's house, where Florence, her housekeeper and devoted assistant, is tidying up the room. Lady Billows is half-heard calling instructions from her room (off-stage), and Florence checks off in her notebook what she has to see to that morning; sample: 'Advert in chemist's window . . . indecent . . . tear it up!'. Florence seems about to favour us with some revelation of her private aspirations, when a knock is heard at the door, which Florence opens to admit Miss Wordsworth, the Vicar, the Mayor, and Mr. Budd, the committee which is to decide between the rival candidates for the position of Queen of the May.

An *alla marcia* introduces her Ladyship, who seems at one moment in danger of not noticing her visitors, except to complain that the room stinks of tobacco. But the situation is saved, and, while she greets the committee, the orchestra begins the fugal tune which develops after a bit into a full-blooded quintet: 'We've made our own investigations and bring you our nominees.'

They sit down. Lady Billows rhapsodises on the subject of the position of May Queen, her first four notes constituting a 'Festival motif' (example 1), and grows eloquent as she

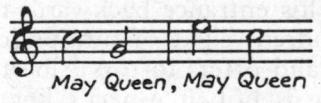

May Queen, May Queen

considers the 'state of complete moral chaos' from which it is expected to retrieve the town. The names are put forward *quasi ballata* by each member of the committee and vetoed with uncommon gusto by Florence. A short quartet, beginning with the Vicar's 'Oh, bitter, bitter is the fruit' and ending with Budd's pregnant 'and darkness has its uses', leads to a furious aria for Lady Billows. She denounces the town as a 'spawning-ground of horror', and Florence takes particular pleasure in repeating her last words—'sty the female sex has soiled'.

It is the moment for a brain-wave, and Superintendent Budd has it: why not a *King* of the May? He launches headlong into an aria: 'Albert Herring's clean as new-mown hay', but the other members hint delicately that he is perhaps an unusually backward boy, and Lady Billows snubs the suggestion as firmly as she can. She calls helplessly on the Vicar for some comfort in an awkward situation; there *are* apparently no virgins in Loxford. The Vicar rises to the occasion with a string of persuasive platitudes and a big *cantabile* tune ('Is Albert virtuous, yes or no?') which is taken up by the others, and eventually repeated drowsily by Lady Billows.

'Right! We'll have him! May King! That'll teach the girls a lesson!' she says, and leads off the fugal finale (No. 1). She leaves the room for a moment and returns to transform the finale into a florid, Purcell-like choral ode, with which the scene ends.

The interlude prepares us for the village children whom we are to meet in the next scene. The rhythm of their song (or rather of the game they are playing) is announced by the percussion, and the curtain goes up to show the interior of Mrs. Herring's grocer's shop, outside which can be seen playing Emmie, Cis, and Harry: 'Bounce me high, bounce me low'. The ball bounces into the shop, and Harry goes in after it, taking the opportunity to pinch some apples for himself and the others. They are interrupted by Sid, who empties Harry's pockets, and, pausing to take an apple for himself, shouts for Albert.

The hero makes his entrance backwards through the door, and carrying a hundredweight of turnips (or so he tells us). Sid gives his order and offers to toss Albert for it, double or quits. But gambling is not in Albert's line: 'Mum wouldn't like it.' Sid tempts him to break the apron strings with a recital of the pleasures of independence: 'Tickling a trout, poaching a hare.' Albert tries not to listen, and Sid is just off, when Nancy, his girl friend, the baker's daughter, comes in, obviously in the middle of her shopping.

Sid buys Nancy a couple of peaches (from the firm's petty

cash, he says), and tells her to bring them that night and meet
him at quarter past eight for a walk together in the moonlight; if she is late, he will whistle under her window. Albert
comments on their duet, which thus becomes a trio, moreover of true lyrical beauty. Sid and Nancy go off together,
Sid of course forgetting to pay for his herbs, and Albert is
left alone to think about what he has seen and heard. His
monologue begins with a rapid passage marked *Risoluto*, in
which he wonders if his mother's strictness really leads to
anything valuable, and continues with flowing phrases as he
reflects on what he misses. It is interrupted by another
customer—Emmie come to buy herbs for a stew—but ends
with a half-defiant 'Golly, it's about time!'.

Florence comes into the shop and sends for Mrs. Herring
to tell her that the Festival Committee is about to pay her a
visit. There is no time for further explanation before Lady
Billows is upon them, announcing (No. 2):

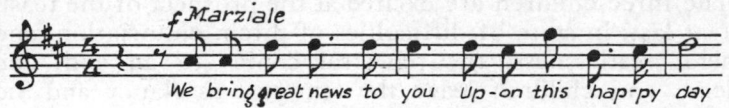

It is a forthright tune, and in its course she conveys, amongst
other things, the information that the prize consists of
twenty-five golden sovereigns.

The visiting party makes its way home, and the winner is
left alone with the jubilant Mrs. Herring, who is only
momentarily put out when Albert says firmly that he intends
to refuse the prize. Mum's firmness is very much to the fore
as she sends him upstairs to repent his abortive rebellion, to
delighted cries of 'Albert's Mum took a stick, Whacked him
on the thingmijig' from the children, who have watched the
scene through the window.

Act II. Horn calls on the Festival motif (No. 1) run
through the short prelude, before the curtain goes up on the
inside of a marquee set up in the vicarage garden. 'There is a
long trestle-table loaded with cakes, jellies, and other good
things. Nancy is bringing in plates of sandwiches.'

Sid tells Nancy what has been going on down at the
church, in an aria that is richly ironical. What of Albert? 'The
poor kid looks on tenterhooks. He's in the mood to escape if
he could.' 'You've got some scheme,' says Nancy, and Sid
takes her outside to tell her what it is.

With the flute twittering away *presto* above the strings (No. 3), Miss Wordsworth brings in the children to run

through the anthem they are going to sing in celebration of Albert's coronation as King of the May.

The three children are excited at the prospect of the feast, but at last, in spite of difficulties of pitch, enunciation, and general restlessness, the rehearsal comes to an end, and teacher and children leave the tent just as Nancy and Sid return to it, the plot having been revealed. Sid pours rum into the lemonade glass in Albert's place (to the accompaniment of the *Tristan* chord) and all is ready for the reception of the official procession.

Miss Wordsworth hurries the children back, and Superintendent Budd, Mrs. Herring, the Mayor, Florence, the Vicar, and Lady Billows come in successively, each singing characteristic music. The anthem goes off quite well, flowers are presented, and the children are thanked for their contribution to the feast. All take their places to a confused burble of conversation (as highly organised as the rest of the music), and the Vicar rises to introduce the first speaker.

This, of course, is Lady Billows, who begins with phrases of an ambitious range that rivals even Fiordiligi's. She loses her notes, but general applause covers the gap and she presents Albert with his prize of twenty-five sovereigns. In turn, and each introduced by the Vicar, come speeches from the Mayor, Miss Wordsworth and Mr. Budd, and finally Albert is called on to make some sort of reply. He can get no further than 'Er . . . er . . . thank you . . . very much', but rejoicing is general, and the Vicar leads off a congratulatory ensemble 'Albert the Good! Long may he reign!' (No. 4):

Albert drinks to the toast, enormously likes what he tastes, and comes round to Nancy for more, reaching her with a resounding hiccup (on a top C flat). He is cured, by drinking from the wrong side of a glass, and the curtain goes down as the feast gets under way, and a fugue starts on the melody of 'Albert the Good'.

The interlude continues with the noise of the feast for a bit, then changes character as May Day turns into May Night and becomes a nocturne. Scene ii takes place inside Mrs. Herring's shop a little later that night. Albert comes back from the feast, enters gaily, and sings exuberant reminiscences of his triumph, punctuating his song by banging the shop door and ringing the bell. In his *scena*, he runs through a variety of subjects, from the necessity of finding some matches, to the charms of Nancy—and at mention of her, Sid's whistle can be heard outside in the street as he attempts to hurry up the keeping of their rendezvous. Outside, Nancy comments sympathetically on Albert's plight and shyness, they sing a short but forceful duet, kiss, and are off, leaving behind a much shaken, even an excited Albert.

Gone are most of Albert's inhibitions, and for the first time he sees himself as others see him, a shy, gawky, mother-ridden boy. He remembers the money in his pocket and decides to toss for it, whether he shall go off on the bust ... or not. It comes down heads 'for yes', and he starts off to find out what he has been missing all this time.

Act III. The *prestissimo* prelude immediately suggests the atmosphere of the man-hunt which follows the discovery of Albert's disappearance. Nancy sings three verses of an aria which has been aptly described as Mahlerian in feeling, before Sid comes wearily into the shop, complaining that one can hear nothing but Albert's name everywhere.

Superintendent Budd asks for Mrs. Herring, and observes to Sid that murder, arson, robbery, rape (*Lucretia* motif) he can deal with, but 'God preserve me from these disappearing cases'. Mrs. Herring comes down, a picture of inconsolable grief. She has only one photograph of Albert, but the Superintendent is welcome to that for identification purposes. Mrs. Herring begins the quartet (*come un lamento*) which ensues; Nancy and later Miss Wordsworth and the Vicar join her.

Harry complicates matters with his shouted: 'There's a Big White Something in Mrs. Williams' well', and Mrs. Herring collapses, just as Lady Billows comes to join in the practical side of the hunt. A procession appears escorting the Mayor, who carries a tray, on which is Albert's orange wreath— 'Found on the road to Campsey Ash, crushed by a cart'.

There ensues the Threnody (No. 5), a great ensemble for nine voices, on an *ostinato*. Each individual has a characteristic verse to himself, the others meanwhile continuing the lament:

The shop bell rings, and Albert pokes his head round the door. 'What's going on?' he asks, and immediately a storm of recrimination and questioning breaks around his head. He must explain everything at once, and only Sid and Nancy take his part and protest against 'prying and poking and probing at him, with your pious old faces delighting in sin'. All the same, Albert starts to tell them a story in which more is hinted at than actually described. All are horrified, and their horror is not diminished when Albert blames it all on the life of repression and mollycoddling he has been forced to lead. At the end of his recital of his doings, Albert sings a tune (No. 6) which is at the same time ridiculously mild and inoffensive, and also warm and curiously full of understanding, even wisdom:

Grazioso

And I'm more than grateful to you 'all for kind-ly pro-vi-ding the where-with-al

Its effect on everyone is electrical; they have met their match and can no longer patronise their innocent May King.

'I didn't lay it on *too* thick, did I?' Albert asks Sid and Nancy; then, seeing the children mocking him from the window, he invites them inside to sample what the shop can offer in the way of fruit. The opera concludes as they all sing example 2, and Albert throws his orange-blossom wreath into the audience. **H.**

LET'S MAKE AN OPERA!

An entertainment for young people, in two parts (and three acts); text by Eric Crozier, music by Benjamin Britten. Première at the Aldeburgh Festival, June 1949, with Gladys Parr, Anne Sharp, Elizabeth Parry, Max Worthley, Norman Lumsden, John Moules, conducted by Norman Del Mar. During 1949, given by the English Opera Group at the Wolverhampton and Cheltenham Festivals, and at the Lyric, Hammersmith, during November, December, 1949, and January, 1950. First performed St. Louis, 1951, and subsequently all over the world.

CHARACTERS

Of the Play	*Of the Opera*	
Gladys Parworthy	Miss Baggott, *the housekeeper* .	Contralto
Norman Chaffinch,	Black Bob, *the sweep-master*, and	
a composer	Tom, *the coachman*	Bass
Max Westleton	Clem, *Black Bob's assistant*, and	
	Alfred, *the gardener*	Tenor
Pamela Wilton	Rowan, *the nursery-maid*	Soprano
Anne Dougall	Juliet Brook (aged fourteen) . .	Soprano
Mr. Harper	The conductor of the Opera	
John	Sam, *the new sweepboy* (eight) . .	Treble
Bruce	Gay Brook (thirteen)	Treble
Monica	Sophie Brook (ten)	Soprano
Peter	John Crome (fifteen)	Treble
Mavis	Tina Crome (eight)	Soprano
Ralph	Hugh Crome (eight)	Treble

Time: 1810   *Place:* Children's nursery of Iken Hall, Suffolk

It is suggested that the names of the actual performers be used for the characters of the play. The accompaniment is for solo string quartet, piano duet (four hands on one piano), and percussion (one player is enough). For the grown-ups, professionals or gifted amateurs are needed, but the children (apart from Juliet) should be played by children. The composer characteristically adds a note to the effect that the boys should not be scared of using their chest voices.

The first two acts of *Let's Make an Opera!* are in the form of a play and illustrate the preparation and rehearsal of *The Little Sweep*, a children's opera which is performed in Act III.

Act I.   The drawing-room of Mrs. Parworthy's house. The various characters are grouped round Mrs. Parworthy as she tells them a story handed down to her by her own grandmother, the Juliet Brook of the opera. All comment on the story as it unfolds, and there is a discussion as to whether it would be better to do it as an opera or as a play, but the decision is never really in doubt, and the main question is whether the opera can be written and rehearsed in time for performance during the Christmas holidays.

The second scene is concerned with some early stages of rehearsal and the successful auditioning of Max Westleton, of the local building office. Snatches of the music which is later to be heard in the opera are introduced here.

Act II represents the stage of the hall or theatre just before the dress rehearsal of *The Little Sweep*. The conductor takes the opportunity of rehearsing the audience in the four songs it is required to sing, first with piano and then with orchestra.

The Little Sweep has no overture but opens with the first of the four songs which require the participation of the audience, the 'Sweep Song'. This song, which is sung with the curtain down, incidentally introduces its performers to the intricacies of 5-in-a-bar. When the curtain rises, the nursery can be seen in all its prettiness, and Clem and Black Bob in their turn are heard singing the 'Sweep Song' as they drag in little Sammy, their apprentice. One of the things attempted earlier in the play is an explanation of 'ensemble'—one of the children wonders in what way it differs from a chorus, and is told each person has his or her own musical line. An ensemble of exactly this type is the second number of the opera, and the definition is made doubly clear, since each character sings his own line as a solo before joining in with it in the ensemble.

Miss Baggott takes Rowan next door to cover everything
up with dust-sheets, leaving the two sweeps to get on with
the job. With horrid relish, they pull Sammy's clothes off, tie
a rope round his waist and send him up the chimney, with
the unambiguous instruction: 'Scrape that flue clean, or I'll
roast you alive.'

For a moment the nursery is empty, but the children can
be heard off-stage organising a game of hide-and-seek. Juliet
runs in, hides under a dust-sheet and is discovered by Jonny,
who promptly hides with her. Before the others arrive, they
hear sounds from the chimney: 'Help! I'm stuck.' They call
the others (in this section the dialogue is spoken) and
together all take hold of the rope and start to pull, at first
gently, then more vigorously when Sammy seems to be very
firmly stuck indeed:

Sammy comes tumbling out of the chimney, there is a
moment of gasped astonishment, and then 'Is he wounded?'
is the question to which all want an answer. The best Sammy
can do is repeat pathetically 'Please don't send me up again'.
The children quickly decide that they must hide Sammy and,
taking him by the hand, lead him across the dust-sheets
towards the window; 'Sooty tracks upon the sheet' they sing
in unison as they lay the false trail. Footsteps can be heard,
and the children bundle Sammy into their toy-cupboard, hide
his clothes, and then themselves disappear under the dust-
sheets. When Miss Baggott and the sweeps come into the
room it is apparently empty. Straightaway they notice the
tell-tale footsteps, and their reaction is expressed in a flabber-
gasted, breathless version of 'Sooty tracks'. Clem and Black
Bob yell for Sam; there is no answer, and, with Miss Baggott,
they launch into a ferocious vengeance trio ('Wait until we
catch him'), at the end of which the sweeps disappear to look
for their apprentice, leaving Miss Baggott shouting
impotently after them: 'Come back.'

Rowan is left in the room, which is still apparently empty,

and she has an agitated recitative, followed by a smooth *cantilena* in which she gives fervent expression to her hope that Sammy will evade his masters. She is interrupted in full song by the sight of the children's heads emerging from under the sheets. They enlist her help, and decide that the first thing to do is to give Sammy a bath. That obviously cannot be done in full view of the audience, so the curtain comes down and Sammy's ablutions are described in the second audience song, 'Sammy's Bath', a syncopated tune in 3/4 time of vigorous character, to whose third verse the fiddles provide a markedly chromatic accompaniment.

The curtain goes up again and Rowan and the children still to the tune of 'Sammy's Bath' and (our eyes tell us) with complete justification, sing: 'O Sammy is whiter than swans as they fly.' Sammy thanks them, and they ask him how he came to be mixed up with his blackguardly employers. Sammy explains that his father broke his hip and had to sell him to find money to support the family. There is a slow, sad ensemble in which Rowan and the children try to offer Sammy comfort ('O why do you weep through the working day?'), only to receive the unvarying reply from the object of

their sympathies: 'How shall I laugh and play?' Jonny suggests that they should take Sammy away with them when they leave next day, and, after some persuasion, Rowan agrees to leave a space in the top of a trunk.

Suddenly, Miss Baggott is heard coming along the passage. To the accompaniment of music marked *presto furioso* Sammy is hidden in the toy-cupboard, the bath and utensils removed, and the toys produced as if by magic. Miss Baggott punctuates her imprecations against the sweeps with frequent references to her extreme fatigue: 'Oh! my poor feet!' The children smother her with compassion, but it is not long before Miss Baggott is at her old games again, criticising the way Rowan has done the room ('Curtains crooked') and expecting to find that the toys have not been properly tidied in the cupboard. She goes towards it to make certain, and is just about to open the door when Juliet saves the situation by collapsing dramatically, with a loud scream. 'Help, help! She's collapsed'; Miss Baggott fusses round her; the children meanwhile carry Juliet from the room, then return to rejoice at the complete success of Juliet's stratagem.

There is another interlude (with the curtain down), and the audience sings 'The Night Song', whose delicious tune

The owl wide-winging thro' the sky In search of mice and lesser fry

well lives up to its description of *andante tenebroso*. The audience divides into four sections to describe the nocturnal habits of owl, heron, turtle-dove and chaffinch (with suitable bird noises at the ends of verses), and all combine for the last two verses. The last scene takes place the following morning. Juliet brings Sammy his breakfast, and sings an aria to him: 'Soon the coach will carry you away.' She gives him three half-crowns, a parting gift from her brother and sister and herself, and then the others come in to say good morning to their departing visitor. After kisses all round, he is packed into the trunk, and the lid fastened down.

Tom, red-faced and permanently short of breath, with the assistance of Alfred, laid low by chronic lumbago, comes to take the trunk downstairs. With a maximum of delay and comic business, they take hold of it, but it won't shift. Miss Baggott makes a great deal of fuss, but Tom and Alfred are adamant: 'Either that there box is unpacked or we leave her where she lies.' Finally a solution is found when Rowan and the children offer to lend a hand, and the trunk is triumphantly transported from the room, Miss Baggott following it with her habitual grumble: 'Don't drop it!'

There remains only the finale—the *envoi* it might be called, Jonny, the Twins and Rowan rush in to say good-bye, Juliet, Gay, and Sophie wave from the window and describe the progress of the carriage down the drive. The percussion imitates the horse's hooves, and the entire cast returns to the stage and sings the verses, with the audience supplying the refrain:

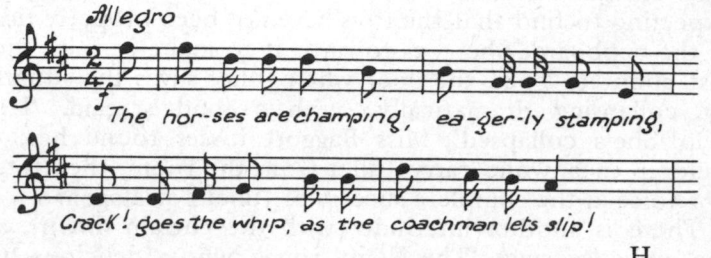

The hor-ses are champing, ea-ger-ly stamping,
Crack! goes the whip, as the coachman lets slip!

H.

BILLY BUDD

Opera in four acts by Benjamin Britten; words by E. M. Forster and Eric Crozier, based on the story by Herman Melville. Première, Covent Garden, December 1, 1951, with Pears, Uppman, Dalberg, Hervey Alan, Geraint Evans, Langdon, Marlowe, Te Wiata, conductor Britten. First performed Wiesbaden, 1952, with Liebl, Gschwend, Stern, Kronenberg, Böhmer, conductor Elmendorff; Paris, 1952, with London cast; N.B.C. Television, New York, 1952; Bloomington, U.S.A., 1952. Revised version B.B.C. broadcast, 1961, with Pears, Joseph Ward, Langdon, conductor Britten; Covent Garden, 1964, with Richard Lewis, Kerns, Forbes Robinson, conductor Solti; Florence Festival, 1965, with Picchi, Alberto Rinaldi, Rossi-Lemeni; Cologne, 1966, with Schachtschneider, Nicolai, Gerd Nienstedt, conductor Kertesz; New York, concert performance, 1966, with Richard Lewis, Kerns, Forbes Robinson, conductor Solti; Hamburg, 1972, with Harald Ek, Richard Stilwell, Louis Hendrikx.

CHARACTERS

Captain Vere, *in command of H.M.S. 'Indomitable'* . Tenor
Billy Budd . . . . Baritone
Claggart, *Master-at-arms* . . . . Bass
Mr. Redburn, *First Lieutenant* . . . . Baritone
Mr. Flint, *Sailing Master* . . . . Baritone
Lieutenant Ratcliffe . . . . Bass

Red Whiskers, *an impressed man* .... Tenor
Donald, *a member of the crew* .... Baritone
Dansker, *an old seaman* .... Bass
Novice .... Tenor
Squeak, *ship's corporal* .... Tenor
Bosun .... Baritone
First and Second Mates .... Baritones
Maintop .... Tenor
The Novice's Friend .... Baritone
Arthur Jones, *an impressed man* .... Baritone
Four Midshipmen .... Boy's Voices
Officers, Sailors, Powder Monkeys, Drummers, Marines

Time: During the French Wars of 1797
Place: On board H.M.S. *Indomitable*, a 'seventy-four'

Britten had already discussed the possibility of collaboration with E. M. Forster, the great novelist, before
deciding on a subject, and the story goes that writer and
musician simultaneously and independently suggested
Herman Melville's last story, *Billy Budd*, to each other. The
co-operation of Eric Crozier was enlisted when Forster
insisted that his own knowledge of stage procedure was
inadequate. The libretto, apart from the shanties and a direct
quotation from Melville's own ballad, 'Billy in the Darbies', is
in prose, and there are no women in the cast.

The background to the story is to be found in the ideas
which were aroused by the philosophical implications of the
French Revolution, and in conditions in the British Navy at
that time. The action is set in 1797, just after the mutinies at
Spithead and the Nore, when memories of 'the floating
Republic' were still very much in people's minds. Fear of
mutiny, and in fact of anything which might be a conceivable
prelude to mutiny, dominated the reactions of the officers,
and conditions on board ship in 1797 were such as to form
an atmosphere which would be, to say the least of it,
conducive to unrest and disaffection.

Act I. For the Prologue, Captain Vere is shown as an old
man. Years after his retirement, he meditates on his career
and what it has taught him, on the mystery of good and evil,
and on the unfathomable ways of Providence which provides
a flaw in every attempt at good. Doubt, expressed musically
by an ambiguity between the keys of B flat major and B
minor, provides the emotional key to the scene. We hear for

the first time the music later associated with Billy's stammer
when Vere refers to 'some imperfection in the divine image'
The Prologue, which is played with Vere standing in isolation
and with the stage in darkness, comes to an end as Vere's
mind goes back to the year 1797.

The lights go up on the first scene, which shows the main
deck and quarter-deck of H.M.S. *Indomitable*. An area of the
main deck is being 'holy-stoned' by some sailors, who are
urged on in their work by the first mate. The music suggests
the ship's calls. At intervals the men sing while they work
and their music has a double significance: it combines the
half-contented, half-dangerous swell of the sea in its motion
and derivations from it are used throughout the opera to
suggest the idea of mutiny. In the last scene of the opera, it
returns with increased emotional effect (No. 1):

Mr. Flint, the Sailing Master, watches the work, pulls a
man up for not taking his full share in it, and gives orders to
the Bosun; a party of young Midshipmen (trebles) try to
show their authority by giving orders in their turn and are
mocked by Donald as they cross the decks; and all the while
the working song continues. One of the men, the Novice,
collides accidentally with the Bosun and is threatened with
the cat; the Bosun organises a working party to hoist a sail.
The Novice slips as he runs off and the Bosun turns savagely
on him and has Squeak, the ship's corporal, list him for
twenty strokes.

To the sound of the working song, the stage empties,
leaving Mr. Flint alone on the quarter-deck. The look-out
spots the guard-boat returning from a press-ganging
expedition, Mr. Redburn comes up on deck, Claggart is sent
for, and preparations are made for the reception of the
recruits, while Mr. Flint grumbles away in a short aria about
the inadequacy of the recruits who come to join the ship's
company: 'We seem to have the devil's own luck.' Mr
Ratcliffe, who has led the party which boarded the
merchantman, *Rights o' Man*, reports that he has returned

vith three recruits. As Claggart steps forward to take charge
of questioning them, he is announced by the tuba and
impani (as already adumbrated during Flint's aria), and his
first utterance (2a) constitutes his motif (No. 2):

Red Whiskers does his best to protest against his enforced
enlistment (in music that is all semi-quavers), Arthur Jones
replies meekly enough, and finally Billy Budd answers confidently and enthusiastically that the sea is his life and his
trade is 'Able Seaman'. When asked about his parents, he is
undismayed: 'Haven't any. They say I was a . . . was a
. .'—and the stammer music is heard as he tries to get out
the word 'foundling'. The officers are delighted with their
new recruit—'He is a king's bargain' is Claggart's sardonic
comment—and place him in the foretop watch. In an
exhilarating passage marked *very lively*, Billy rejoices in his
new life: 'Billy Budd, king of the birds!' He ends with a
farewell to what is past, and to the ship on which he served:
Farewell to you, old comrades, farewell to you for ever. . . .
'arewell, *Rights o' Man*' (No. 1). This brings an immediate
reaction from the officers, who jump to the conclusion that
it has political significance.

The decks are cleared, and Mr. Redburn instructs Claggart
to keep a watch on the new recruit. Claggart waits until the
first Lieutenant has gone below, then vents his spleen: 'Do
they think I am deaf? . . . These officers! They are naught but
dust in the wind.' He summons Squeak, who thinks at first it
is Red Whiskers he is to watch but is told to keep an eye on
Billy Budd, and to provoke him by petty thefts from his
kit-bag. Claggart continues to express his hatred of the life in
which he finds himself, but is interrupted by the arrival of
the Novice's friend to report that the flogging has taken place
and that the offender has collapsed as a result of it; he cannot
walk. 'Let him crawl' is Claggart's cynical reaction; he turns

on his heel and leaves as a sad little procession comes in to a
pathetic tune on the saxophone (the particular colour of this
instrument is associated with the Novice). The Novice is
half-dragged, half-carried in by a little band of men, amongst
them the Novice's Friend. In the subdued ensemble which
follows (a trio, as the semi-chorus sings in unison), the Novice
expresses utter despair—his heart is broken as well as his
body—and the others try to comfort him, in spite of their
conviction 'We're all of us lost for ever on the endless sea'
(No. 3):

As they go out, Billy and Dansker, followed by Donald
and Red Whiskers, emerge from the shadows where they have
been watching. Their *scherzando* quartet is in complete
contrast to what has gone before. The old hands make fun of
Red Whiskers and assure him and Billy that it will be their
turn next. Dansker dubs Billy 'Baby Budd', and Donald
catches hold of Red Whiskers's beard and pulls him around.
The horse-play comes to a sudden end as Claggart appears on
deck, and a moment later Captain's Muster is heard (on the
flutes). Donald has just time to refer to the captain as 'Starry
Vere' (it is Vere's motif, the inversion of the lament, No. 3)
No. 4

before the ship's company comes quickly on deck, and is
ordered by Claggart to fall in without delay.[1]
The officers begin to make their way on to the quarter-

---

[1] In 1961 Britten condensed the opera to two acts, a version which
has found slightly less than universal favour. Act I's finale disappeared
completely, with the consequence that Captain Vere is seen first in
private, and face to face with the ship's company only in Act III; and
that direct contact with Billy Budd is postponed to the second scene of
that act. The music at the opening of Act IV being similar to that at
the end of Act III, the running of those two acts together has the effect
of eliding no more than a few bars of music.

deck, and as the music reaches a climax, Vere himself appears. In language and music that is quite free from bombast, he addresses the ship's company and informs them that they are nearing action. He will do everything he can for them when it comes to battle, and the victory must come from their combined efforts. The men are enthusiastic about what he has to say, and Billy leads a chorus of praise for Vere as the act comes to an end.

Act II. Evening, a week later. Vere, alone in his cabin, sends his cabin boy to ask his officers to take a glass of wine with him. He is reading, but looks up from his book, and in a few beautiful *arioso* phrases prays that he and his company may be allowed grace to emulate the virtues and the courage of the people of ancient times:

Mr. Redburn and Mr. Flint are announced, and together they and Vere drink the King's health, then fall to discussing the prospect of action, which they all think is imminent. Flint takes a bluff seaman's view of the war, and starts a *scherzando* duet, 'Don't like the French', in which Redburn joins with some relish. Vere smiles and admits he shares their sentiments; another toast—'The French, down with them!'

The word 'mutiny' creeps into the conversation, and immediately casts its shadow over the officers' thoughts. In a short aria, marked *pp* and *cantabile*, Redburn takes up Flint's reference to 'Spithead, the Nore, the floating republic' (No. 1). He was there, and he knows what mutiny of that sort can mean. 'O God, preserve us from the Nore' is his prayer. Vere's comment is even firmer, as he denounces the ideas, French in their origin, which gave rise to the scandal of the Nore. 'We must be on our guard' is his conclusion. The others remember 'that young chap who shouted out "Rights o' Man" ', but Vere is of the opinion that there is nothing to fear from that quarter. The sound of singing can be heard

from below, and Vere makes a kindly reference to the loyalty
of their crew, before Mr. Redburn knocks briskly on the door
and announces, 'Land on the port bow. . . . Enemy waters'.
The two officers leave Vere to go to their stations and the
Captain is left alone, first reading, then listening more and
more intently to the sound of the shanty which wells up
from the berth-deck. One of the happiest moments in the
opera comes with the first sound of the singing of the crew,
when Vere's comments seem to radiate confidence and a
sympathetic understanding of the comradeship and mutual
trust which go to make a happy and efficient ship.

Scene ii takes place in the berth-deck. It is preceded by an
orchestral interlude, making use of the shanty which has
already been hinted at in the cabin scene ('Blow her to Hilo'),
going on to a second ('Over the water'), and then returning to
the first to land with overwhelming effect on a great golden
chord of E flat major (chorus and orchestra) as the curtain
rises. The scene is animated and yet contented. The first
shanty drifts slowly to an end and Donald starts another in a
brisker tempo: 'We're off to Samoa, by way of Genoa.' Red
Whiskers and Billy add verses of their own, and the whole
thing works up to an exuberant climax for full orchestra and
chorus.

Billy and Red Whiskers try to persuade Dansker to join in
the fun, but he pleads age and indifference: There's only one
thing in the world that I want and I ain't got it.' Billy offers
to lend him the tobacco he wants and goes off to get it from
his kit-bag. The sound of his stammer is heard, and a moment
later he drags Squeak out into the open, protesting that he
has not been at Billy's kit-bag as Billy seems to think. But
Squeak spoils his case by drawing a knife, and a fight begins
between the two, with everyone taking Billy's side. Billy
floors him in an instant, and next thing Claggart is among
them, demanding to know how the whole thing started. He
turns to Dansker for an explanation, and gets it in the
simplest terms imaginable. Squeak is arrested, clapped in
irons, and, when he threatens to blow the gaff about
Claggart's advice to him, gagged as well. 'As for you . . .', says
Claggart, turning to Billy (2a), 'Handsomely done, my lad.
And handsome is as handsome did it, too' (the words are
Melville's).

The sound of 'Over the water' is heard off-stage, and
Claggart remains motionless, muttering 'Handsomely done,

my lad' to himself. When the lights have receded from the hammocks and all other noise is stilled, he permits himself to give expression to the thoughts which govern his heart: 'O beauty, O handsomeness, goodness, would that I never encountered you!' Claggart recognises in Billy what Iago found in Cassio:

> He hath a daily beauty in his life
> That makes me ugly,

or, as Claggart himself puts it, 'The light shines in the darkness, and the darkness comprehends it and suffers'. His musical denunciation of the power of good with which he finds his own evil face to face is accompanied by a trombone solo, and the sinister power of the aria reaches a climax with its ending: 'I, John Claggart, Master-at-arms upon the *Indomitable*, have you in my power, and I will destroy you.'

Claggart's revelation of his evil purpose is immediately followed by the entrance of the Novice (No. 3). Two curious scenes ensue, both nocturnal in character and marked *pianissimo*. The first is between Claggart and the Novice, whom he has summoned with a view to forcing him, through his fear of future punishment, to obtain evidence against Billy. The Novice, after a moment of revulsion against the scheme, accepts the guineas which Claggart gives him to pass on to Billy. His agonised remorse at the part he is forced to play ('It's fate, I've no choice, everything's fate') nevertheless leads him straight to where Billy lies asleep.

The second nocturne-like scene is between Billy and the Novice, and it is introduced by a tune of uncanny peace, on a solo 'cello over two bass clarinets (the tune is heard again in a far more extended form at the beginning of Act IV) (No. 6):

Billy takes time to wake up, and even longer before he understands the import of what the Novice is driving at, with his talk of pressing and gangs and whether Billy won't lead them. When he tumbles to it, the Novice scampers off as Billy is seized with another fit of stammering, which resolves itself when Dansker appears on the scene, roused by the unusual noise. Billy's nervousness betrays itself in some agitated phrases as he tries to tell Dansker what the fuss is about. But Dansker understands all too well when he hears what Billy has to say about guineas and mutiny. The act ends with a big-scale duet for Billy and Dansker, which is cast in the form of a passacaglia. Dansker enunciates its theme with a variation of Claggart's motif (No. 7):

Billy puts forward the argument that Claggart likes him, that he himself likes the life on board where his ship-mates are his friends, that he is rumoured as a candidate for promotion. Dansker's rejoinder is unvarying: 'Jemmy-legs is down on you'.

Act III[1] brings the action with the French to an unachieved climax, and sees the conclusion of Claggart's efforts to pull down the power for good which he has detected in the ship's company.

The first scene shows the main- and quarter-decks (as for Act I) some days later. Before the curtain goes up, the music is already dominated by the *ostinato* rhythm which is used for the battle. Vere and Redburn are worried by the look of the rapidly increasing mist, but further conversation is prevented by the appearance of the Master-at-arms, who removes his cap as a sign that he wishes to speak to the Captain. Vere's thoughts are still concerned with the effect the weather is likely to have on the prospect of action, but consents to see Claggart. The latter, with frequent reference to his own long and faithful service, starts to formulate a charge against some sailor as yet unnamed, who, he says, is likely to endanger the safety of the ship. Vere grows impatient at Claggart's circumlocution, but the interview is cut short by a yell from the main-top: 'Enemy sail on starboard bow!'

At the same moment the mist lifts and instantly the stage (like the music) hums with activity. Sail is crowded on, Vere orders action stations, and the heartfelt relief of the crew at

---

[1] Act II in the revised version.

he prospect of a reward for the weeks of waiting is expressed
in Example 8:

Gunners run to their guns and start loading, seamen go to
the nettings with lashed hammocks and stow them as a rough
screen against shot, sand is scattered on deck, water-tubs and
matches are made ready, powder monkeys with a high-
pitched and continuous yell scramble to their stations, and
finally the marines march into position. A call for volunteers
for a boarding party is answered by Donald, Red Whiskers,
Dansker, and (from high up in the rigging) Billy. All is ready
and excitement reaches fever-pitch, but the enemy is still out
of range. There is a general prayer for wind to fill the sails, a
moment when it looks as though anticipation will be realised,
the climax when a shot is fired, and then frustration which
amounts almost to despair when the mist returns to render
further pursuit impossible (the music associated with the mist
is used again later). Orders are given to dismiss, and the
officers are depressed about the effect this set-back may have
on discipline.

Claggart is again seen standing cap in hand waiting to be
noticed by the Captain. He seems about to re-open his
preamble ('... nothing but my duty could bring me
back...') but this time Vere makes no attempt to hide his
impatience at the turn events have taken ('Now be brief, man,
for God's sake'), and at the evasive way in which Claggart
starts out to tell his story ('Mutiny? I'm not to be scared by
words'). The Master-at-arms shows the Captain the gold
which was used, he says, by a common seaman to bribe a
comrade. Vere is sceptical; how would a sailor have gold in
his possession? When Claggart brings out the name of Billy
Budd, Vere is frankly incredulous: 'Nay, you're mistaken....

Don't come to me with so foggy a tale.' The Master-at-arms persists in his story, and Vere flares up at him: 'Claggart! Take heed what you say. There's a yard-arm for a false witness.' He sends a boy for Billy and tells Claggart to follow the accused into his room and there confront him with his charge.

As the officers come forward towards Vere, he exclaims vehemently: 'O this cursed mist.' There is a short quartet, one of those moments of tenderness in which the score abounds and which seems to express a sympathy with the aspirations of the crew, as well as (from Vere's point of view) a determination to clear up a mystery which was rapidly becoming inextricably connected with the physical phenomenon of the mist. In the Interlude which follows, the music of the mist surrounds chorale-like statements of No. 5, and the conflict is clearly that going on in the mind of Vere, who is faced with discovering the truth or otherwise of an accusation which, if substantiated, carries the supreme penalty with it.

Fanfares, associated with Billy, bring the interlude to an end, and the curtain goes up to reveal Vere with the mists cleared and his mind made up, as is apparent from his first words: 'Claggart! John Claggart, beware! I'm not so easily deceived . . . .' Billy himself comes in, full of confidence that he has been summoned to hear that he has been promoted, and unable to keep the words off his lips. Vere encourages Billy to talk, which he does enthusiastically, while, to a lyrical tune, Vere reflects 'this is the man I'm told is dangerous'.

Claggart is admitted, and, after Vere has cautioned both men to speak only the truth, proceeds immediately to charge Billy with mutiny (derivation of mutiny motif). Vere orders Billy to make answer to his accuser. He is seized with stammering and suddenly hits out at Claggart, striking him a blow in the middle of the forehead. Claggart falls, and, after a couple of gasps, lies motionless. Vere kneels down by him and quickly realises he is dead. He sends Billy, who has remained motionless since Claggart fell, into his stateroom, and shuts the door after him, then orders his cabin boy to fetch the officers.

Vere is in no doubt as to the predicament he is in. Claggart's evil purpose is clear enough, and yet his innocent victim by his own action has doomed himself, and there is no way of averting the penalty which hangs over his head. Vere's agony is made very apparent in a monologue. The officers enter the cabin and are immediately told the facts. Each reacts differently: Redburn: 'What is the truth? Justice is our duty'; Flint: 'What unheard-of brutality . . . revenge . . .'; Ratcliffe: 'The boy has been provoked . . . let us be merciful.'

Vere summons a drumhead court, which he will attend as witness and over which Redburn will preside. Billy is brought in, the charge read to him, and Vere states the bare facts. Billy agrees that they are true, and can plead nothing but his innocence of what Claggart charged him with. Vere declines to add supposition and opinion to the facts as he has stated them, and, in spite of Billy's agonised 'Captain Vere, save me', he is told to wait in the inner room. The three officers consider their verdict. The penalty Billy's action has made inevitable is clearly laid down in the Mutiny Act, the Articles of War, King's Regulations; there is nothing to discuss. They appeal for guidance to Vere, but he refuses to interfere. Their verdict is 'Guilty', and they pronounce the penalty: 'Death. Hanging from the yard-arm.' Vere accepts the verdict, and orders that it be carried out next morning; the Master-at-arms to be buried with full naval honours.

In *Billy Budd*, the tragedy is seen as it were through the eyes of Vere, and poignant expression of it comes at the end of this act, first in an *arioso* for Vere himself, and then in the extraordinary ending when, after Vere has gone to inform Billy of the verdict and the stage is left empty, Britten writes a succession of thirty-five common chords, whose different dynamics and scoring convey the changes of emotion with which the message is given and received. It is in effect a great cadence in F major, and in the last half-a-dozen bars recurs a suggestion of the 6/8 tune heard when Billy was woken up by the Novice in Act II (No. 6).

The first scene of Act IV shows a bay of the gun deck, shortly before dawn the next morning. Billy is in irons between two cannon. The music continues where Act III left off, and above the gently swaying accompaniment Billy sings a slow, pathetic tune of resignation and farewell (No. 6). The words are Melville's, taken from the poem which he describes as composed by a shipmate after the execution and put posthumously into the mouth of Billy himself ('Billy in the Darbies').

Billy's introspection comes to an end when Dansker steals

in, ignoring the rule which forbids the prisoner to talk to members of the crew while awaiting execution, and brings him a mug of grog. 'All's trouble' he says, 'Some reckon to rescue you . . . they swear you shan't swing.' The notion that his death may precipitate the mutiny the idea of which he abhors fills Billy with new courage. He is vigorous in denunciation of any plan to set him free, and says Dansker's news has jolted him out of 'thinking on what's no use'. What has happened and is going to happen to him he ascribes to the workings of fate: he had to 'strike down that Jemmy-legs', and 'Captain Vere has had to strike me down, fate.' He says good-bye to Dansker, and his new courage finds expression in an ecstatic ballad tune, which is as simple as it is moving (No. 9). The chords with which the previous act ended recur again in the accompaniment.

The interlude is made up from the calls associated with the ship's routine and the music of the verdict, and the curtain goes up to show the main deck and quarter-deck at four o'clock the next morning. Daylight is just beginning to show, and the ship's crew assembles to the sound of a funeral march, which can be described as a fugue on a rhythm of timpani and drums, on which is imposed music characteristic of each group as it enters to watch the grim pageantry of the execution. Vere takes his place and straightaway Billy is led in between a guard of marines. Mr. Redburn reads the sentence, Billy turns to Vere and shouts to him 'Starry Vere, God bless you', and his cry is taken up by the crew. Then he turns about with his escort, and marches smartly out. Vere removes his hat and all eyes turn to follow Billy as he ascends the mast.

The men on the main deck suffer an immediate revulsion of feeling, and turn in revolt to the quarter-deck. This is the moment described in Melville: 'Whoever has heard the freshet-wave of a torrent suddenly swelled by pouring showers in tropical mountains, showers not shared by the plain; whoever has heard the first muffled murmur of its sloping advance through precipitous woods, may form some conception of the sound now heard.'

Britten writes a *presto* fugue on a variation of the mutiny theme (to the sound of 'ur' in 'purple'), but this savage incoherence gradually changes to a passionate echo of the swelling music associated with the routine work in the first act (No. 1). This ending to the drama seems to indicate that this is no theme of disillusionment, but rather carries a message of confidence, if not in Good itself, at least in Man's capacity to understand and be influenced by Good.

The light fades and presently Vere is seen standing alone, an old man as in the Prologue. For a moment it looks as though he finds the memory of what he might have prevented too much for him ('I could have saved him . . . O what have I done?'), but he takes strength from Billy's ballad (No. 9) and this is combined with the 'cadence of comfort' from the end of Act III. The Epilogue comes quietly to an end as the orchestra stops playing, the lights fade, and only Vere's voice is heard rounding out the story.   H.

GLORIANA

Opera in three acts by Benjamin Britten, words by William Plomer. First performed Covent Garden at a Gala in connection with Coronation of Queen Elizabeth II, June 8, 1953, with Cross (later Shacklock), Vyvyan (later Sutherland), Sinclair, Leigh, Pears (later Lanigan), Geraint Evans, Matters, Dalberg, Te Wiata, conductor Pritchard; Cincinnati, 1955, with Borkh, Conley, conductor Krips; London, Royal Festival Hall, 1963, with Fisher, Pears, Hemsley, Forbes Robinson; Sadler's Wells, 1966, with Fisher, Vyvyan, Wakefield, John Cameron, Garrard, conductor Bernardi (by Sadler's Wells Company in Brussels and Lisbon, 1967); Münster, 1968, with Martha Mödl; English National Opera, Munich, 1972, Vienna, 1975, conductor Mackerras.

CHARACTERS

Queen Elizabeth the First . . . . Soprano
Robert Devereux, Earl of Essex . . . . Tenor
Frances, Countess of Essex . . . . .Mezzo-Soprano
Charles Blount, Lord Mountjoy . . . . Baritone
Penelope (Lady Rich), *sister to Essex* . . . . Soprano
Sir Robert Cecil, *Secretary of the Council* . . . . Baritone
Sir Walter Raleigh, *Captain of the Guard* . . . . Bass

Henry Cuffe, *a satellite of Essex* . . . . Baritone
A Lady-in-Waiting . . . . Soprano
A Blind Ballad-Singer . . . . Bass
The Recorder of Norwich . . . . Bass
A Housewife . . . . Mezzo-Soprano
The Spirit of the Masque . . . . Tenor
The Master of Ceremonies . . . . Tenor
The City Crier . . . . Baritone
Chorus, Dancers, Actors, Musicians

Scene: England in the time of Queen Elizabeth I
Time: The later years of her reign, which lasted from 1558 to 1603

Act I, scene i.   The prelude is marked 'very lively', and the rhythm of the brass calls anticipates the chorus's commentary on the events of scene i, which take place outside a tilting ground. A tournament is in progress inside. Cuffe looks through an opening in the wall and reports to Essex that Mountjoy has accepted a challenge, and that the crowd acclaims its favourite: 'Our joy mounts up, our hope, Mountjoy'. Essex is furiously jealous, when, to the evident delight of the crowd, Mountjoy is victorious and receives his prize—a golden chessman—from the Queen herself.

At this point the bustle and excitement of the tournament give way to a hymn-like tune sung by the crowd in praise of the Queen (No. 1):

'Green leaves are we, Red rose our golden Queen,
O crowned rose among the leaves so green.'

The music symbolises the affectionate relationship between the Queen and her subjects, and is one of the opera's dominant themes.

Mountjoy appears and bids his page bind his prize upon his arm. Essex accuses him of arrogance and provokes him to fight. A trumpet fanfare off-stage causes Essex to drop his guard for a moment, and he is slightly wounded in the arm

The trumpets draw nearer, and the Queen emerges from the tilting ground, surrounded by her court and followed by the crowd. She wastes no time in summing up the situation, and upbraids both lords for offending against the rule that no duel may be fought at court. She turns to Raleigh for his view, and he gives it—as one 'of riper age'. In an aside, both Essex and Mountjoy make quite clear that they bitterly resent what they regard as Raleigh's insolence—he is older and more experienced than they are but of far less exalted origin, and they object the more for that.

The Queen summons the two late combatants to her, and tells them she has need of them both; let them come to court, but as friends, not as enemies, and they can count on her support and protection. There is an ensemble, in which the Queen, Essex, Mountjoy, Cuffe, Raleigh and the chorus join, and a trumpet march brings the scene to an end (No. 1).

Scene ii. The Queen's ante-room in Nonesuch Palace. The Queen is closeted alone with Cecil. She refers to the recent duel between the two young lords, and asks Cecil whether he has had news of the reaction of Lady Rich to the fight—'the dark Penelope' who is sister to Essex, mistress to Mountjoy.[1] When she admits her liking for Essex, 'the lordly boy', Cecil (whom she calls by his historical nickname of 'pigmy elf') warns her to be on her guard. In a short lyrical passage the Queen reminds Cecil that she has wedded herself to the realm; she seeks no husband and is content if her people are happy (No. 1)—she has learned from her preceptor, Ascham, that Love is better than Fear. Cecil reminds her of his father's ancient counsel to the sovereign whom he loved and served so long:

> 'There comes a moment when to rule
> Is to be swift and bold:
> Know at last the time to strike:
> It may be when the iron is cold!'

As the Queen and her counsellor turn to affairs of state, a theme is heard which is associated throughout the opera with the cares of government, and often, because his presence betokens preoccupation with them, with Cecil as well.

---

[1] Whom she married after the death of her husband, Lord Rich.

Its optimistic rise in the major and measured fall in the minor is characteristic. At mention of the possibility of a new Armada from Spain, the Queen laments the certain waste of life and money: 'We can but watch and wait' (No. 2).

Essex is announced and Cecil withdraws. Essex's greeting to his sovereign and his cousin[1] is exuberant (No. 3):

and the Queen asks her Robin—as she calls him—to soothe her worries by singing and playing to her. Suiting the tune to the words and accompanying himself on the lute, Essex sings 'Quick music's best when the heart is oppressed', a little lyric whose enchanting, quicksilver grace is too remote from the Queen's mood to afford her the comfort she seeks. Essex sings again, this time quietly, slowly, and with a depth of feeling and sensitivity that affords a complete musical recreation of that quality which one may suppose caused the Queen to pin her faith for the future to her brilliant but unpredictable cousin (No. 4):

[1] His mother, Leicester's widow, was niece to Anne Boleyn, Queen Elizabeth's mother.

The music has a far-reaching significance in the opera and
pitomises their relationship. For Essex it stands for the trust
nd affection which he can give as well as receive in his most
ntimate moments with his sovereign; for Queen Elizabeth it
ymbolises the one link with youth and brilliance which is
eft her in her old age—a link that is as much practical as
entimental, since Essex's prowess is in her mind as
ntimately linked with the fortunes of England as with those
f England's Queen. The words of the poem Britten has set in
ne of his finest inspirations are by Essex himself.[1]

There is an affectionate duet between the two, which is
nterrupted when Elizabeth points to the silhouette of
Raleigh, which can be seen at the entrance. Essex refers to
Raleigh as 'the jackal', and denounces him as his enemy who
s, with Cecil, determined to prevent him going to Ireland,
here to overthrow the Queen's enemy, Tyrone. At this point
ccurs a phrase associated with Essex's fatal ambitions, which
lays a prominent part in the opera (No. 5):

The Queen dismisses Essex and is alone.

The Queen's thoughts run to duty and to love—the claims
f one, the solace of the other, and their mutual incompati-
ility. Her soliloquy begins with a *forte* statement on the
rombones of No. 1, which dominates it. After a triumphant
esolution,

> 'I live and reign a virgin,
> Will die in honour,
> Leave a refulgent crown',

he Queen kneels and prays to God for strength and grace to
ulfil the high office to which she has been called. The
ccompaniment is based on a fourteenth-century setting of
he 'Gloria'.

Act II, scene i.   The Guildhall at Norwich. It was Queen
Elizabeth's custom to make periodic tours of England—
uring which time she was said to be 'On Progress'—and,

[1] Its first phrase is based on the opening of a madrigal by Wilbye,
Happy were he'.

when the curtain rises (in crushed-note chords, the town be‖
peal in the orchestra), she is attended by her court, Esse‖
Cecil, Raleigh, and Mountjoy amongst them, and th
Recorder of the City of Norwich is coming to the end of h
address of welcome. The Queen thanks him and the citizer
for their greetings, is cheered by the assembled populac
and, when the Recorder comes to kneel in homage an
stumbles, helps him solicitously to his feet. The Record‖
asks her if she will see the Masque they have prepared in h‖
honour, an invitation to which the Queen signifies her asser
but which provokes an impatient aside from Essex, chafing ‖
the enforced inactivity (No. 5). Ireland is again uppermost ‖
his mind.

The Masque begins. A chorus is grouped round a fancif‖
leafy bower, with the Spirit of the Masque in the centr‖
After a salute to Gloriana, Time and Concord, represented b
male and female solo dancers, appear and dance togethe
They are followed by troupes of country maidens and rust‖
swains, and finally all unite in homage to Gloriana. The mus‖
is a set of six contrasted dances, introduced by the Spirit ‖
the Masque and set for unaccompanied voices. The Quee
graciously returns thanks to the citizens of Norwich, and th
finale makes great use of No. 1.

The second scene is laid in the garden of Essex's house. ‖
is evening. The fresh, lyrical atmosphere of the early part ‖
the scene is immediately established by an introduction f‖
flutes, celesta, and muted strings *pizzicato*. Mountjoy sings ‖
his love for Penelope Rich, who presently appears and gree‖
him rapturously. Their duet has not run its course before it
interrupted by the voices of Essex and Lady Essex, who d‖
not see them and are discussing the Queen's continued refus‖
to advance Essex to the position of Lord Deputy in Irelan‖
which he considers his due. Mountjoy and Penelope commer
on Essex's displeasure (No. 5), then resume their colloqu‖
But Essex's anger mounts—'In time, I'll break her will, I'
have my way'—and his sister and his friend break off to war
him against talk which others might consider treasonable. ‖
quartet develops, in which Essex's impatience overflow‖
Lady Essex urges caution, and first Penelope, later eve‖
Mountjoy, encourage him to hope for preferment as tim‖
reduces the Queen's grasp on power: 'Ours to decide wh‖
other head will wear the crown. . . . Ourselves to rule th
land.'

The third scene of Act II takes place in the great room in
e Palace of Whitehall during the course of a Ball given by
e Queen. The whole scene is built up on a series of dances
the Elizabethan style, which are played on the stage and
ed to frame a considerable development of the dramatic
uation. A majestic Pavane is taken up by the stage band as
on as the curtain rises; the court is dancing. A buzz of
nversation follows but quietens when the Queen's lady-in-
aiting comments admiringly on the splendour of Lady
sex's dress. 'Will the Queen approve?' is Frances's less
nfident reply as the Master of Ceremonies announces a
alliard, a quick dance to slow music (it is marked *gently
wing*).

The Queen enters (No. 1), catches sight of Lady Essex and
oks her up and down, then orders that 'La Volta' be played.
is is a brilliant piece in 6/4 time; its salient feature was the
ssing of the ladies in the air by their partners (a famous
cture of Queen Elizabeth dancing 'La Volta' exists at
nshurst). The vigorous nature of the dance exhausts even
e apparently inexhaustible Queen, and she commands that
e ladies go to change their linen, as was the custom of the
y, while a Morris dancer performs for the entertainment of
ose who remain. At the end of his dance, Lady Essex
rries in, breathlessly complaining that her new dress has
sappeared while she was changing. The reason is not far to
ek, for the Queen suddenly returns, wearing the missing
ess. It is much too short for her, and she looks grotesque.
r a moment she stalks round, while the court looks on in
nazement, then turns to Lady Essex:

> 'If being too short it becometh not me
> I have it in mind it can ne'er become thee.'[1]

The Queen leaves, and in an ensemble Essex, Mountjoy,
d Penelope attempt to comfort the stricken Frances Essex,
ho for her part is more concerned with the inflammatory
fect the episode may have on her husband than with the
sult offered to herself. Her anxiety is not without founda-
n; to her own conciliatory 'And as the Queen hath her
nditions, Robert, take care!' Essex retorts 'Con-

---

[1] The episode may at first strike a modern audience as too grotesque
be credible, but it is based on an authenticated incident, when the
een humiliated a lady of the court suspected of being Essex's
stress.

ditions! Her conditions are as crooked as her carcase!' S
unguarded and extreme an utterance dismays even Penelope
but as usual the Queen turns out to be unpredictable. Sh
caps her insult to Essex's wife by returning to the stage wit
her Councillors to proclaim formally that Essex is appointe
Lord Deputy in Ireland and charged to subdue the rebelliou
Tyrone (No. 5). The chorus salutes the 'Victor of Cadiz' an
implores him to overcome the foreign threat, while th
Queen and the other principal characters react to th
appointment in their different ways, whether jealous
ambitious, or loving. Essex himself sings of the charg
entrusted to him (No. 5), and the scene comes to an en
when the Queen commands a 'Coranto' which is danced b
the entire court as the curtain comes down, the fu
orchestra, with its intimations of Essex's star in th
ascendant, gradually swamping the stage band with its danc
music.

Act III.   The tragedy of *Gloriana* is first of all that whic
almost inevitably, in some way or other, attends a rulin
prince, and only secondly that of Essex, the individual i
whose fate the sovereign's hopes for the future of th
country are epitomised. The catastrophe which is to brin
about the fall of Essex—the failure in Ireland—has alread
taken place when Act III begins; and it is the Queen we se
take the 'tragic' decision, not Essex. The working out of hi
destiny involves the tragedy of the Queen whose trust h
held.

The prelude is marked *quick and agitated*. When th
curtain goes up we are in the Queen's ante-room at None
such. It is early morning and the maids of honour are i
conversation. The subject is Ireland. The news is of delay
and instead of the defeat of Tyrone, it looks as though the
will soon be talking of the fall of Essex. Suddenly anothe
lady-in-waiting enters in great perturbation to ask if th
Queen is yet dressed. There is a great stir below. . . . She nee
go no further, for Essex himself bursts into the room
demanding to see the Queen. When told she is not yet ready
he sweeps back the curtain behind which she can be see
without her wig at her dressing-table.

She dismisses her attendants, and turns to him (No. 3). A
first the interview is quiet: 'But what must I forgive? Becaus
you catch an ageing woman unadorned,' asks the Quee
There is a moment of sadness ('You see me as I am'), whic

leads to a tender duet ('Because you're here when larks alone have right of audience'), and it is not until Essex mentions the foes which 'beset me now here in England, at home' (No. 5) that the Queen rounds on him and puts her as yet unspoken accusations into words. He has failed in his trust; he is not only unfit but untrue. Essex pleads his devotion to her (No. 3), and her anger quickly changes to sorrow, until he is reduced to memories: 'O put back the clock to the birth of our hope!' The scene grows in intensity as the music gets slower and softer, and anger is replaced by the agony of the might-have-been, until Essex and the Queen together recall the song which has symbolised their relationship (No. 4). 'Go, Robin, Go! Go!' (No. 2).

The Queen is quickly joined by a lady-in-waiting, who in her turn is followed by the others. As the tiring-maids finish the Queen's toilet, the maids-of-honour, led by the lady-in-waiting, sing gently and comfortingly to their mistress. When Cecil arrives, the Queen is majestically arrayed (No. 1). He tells her that Tyrone is still unsubdued, and that Essex has not only failed in his mission but has brought with him a horde of his unruly followers. The Queen makes up her mind without delay and gives orders that Essex be kept under supervision. With the music dominated by No. 5, she comments: 'I have failed to tame my thoroughbred.'

Scene ii is laid in a street in the City of London. The short orchestral prelude is based on No. 6. A blind Ballad-Singer[1] sits outside a tavern surrounded by old men, and relays what he hears to his listeners. He is the medium through which we hear of the progress of Essex's rebellion, from the moment when it is first discovered that the Earl is free, until Essex is publicly proclaimed a traitor by the City Crier. There are interruptions between the Ballad-Singer's verses from a rabble of boys, led by a couple of armed followers of Essex; from Cuffe, who tries to recruit support for his master, and is routed with the aid of a bowl of slops by an angry housewife; and from the City Crier with his dread proclamation. The scene is built up on the Ballad-Singer's tune (No. 6) which is marked *very freely*, and which has a curious, camp-fire,

---

[1] In Elizabethan times, ballad-singers were accustomed to convey the news of the day in their impromptu ballads, which they sang accompanying themselves on the Gittern, a stringed instrument; they were thus a sort of cross between newspaper-seller, news-commentator, and calypso singer.

popular quality about it that is peculiarly appropriate to its position in the opera:

To bind by force, to bolt with bars the wonder of this age

Scene iii. A room in the Palace of Whitehall. The orchestra preludes on No. 7, and the curtain goes up to show Cecil, Raleigh, and other members of the Council waiting to acquaint the Queen with their decision in the case of the Earl of Essex. They are unanimously agreed that he is guilty, but

No. 7

Es -sex is guil-ty and con-demned to die

Cecil warns them that the Queen may yet hesitate to make up her mind, may even pardon him. When she enters they inform her of the verdict and, when Cecil tries to press her to make a quick decision lest the people should doubt Essex's guilt, she forbids him to prate to her of her duty.

She is alone and her dilemma is forcefully portrayed until Raleigh steps in and announces that Lady Essex, Penelope Rich, and Mountjoy have come to intercede for the fallen Essex. After an ensemble, Lady Essex is promised (No. 1) that, whatever happens to her husband, her children will not suffer. It is the turn of Penelope to make her plea, which she does in terms which can only be described as feudal: it is not only Essex's service to his Queen but his rank which entitles him to a pardon. The Queen is roused to fury by her words, and sends for the warrant to sign it in the presence of the woman who has thus opened her eyes to danger. Penelope shrieks with anguish as the orchestra has a *fff* statement of No. 4, which is to dominate the rest of the opera. The short scene is a perfect example of Britten's operatic ability to pin down emotion and situation swiftly and effectively, so that drama and music have inextricably moved forward together.

From the departure of Essex's three supporters, the stage darkens and the action becomes unrealistic—as if to emphasise this, the dialogue is mostly spoken against an orchestral background of No. 4. Various episodes of the end of Queen Elizabeth's life are recalled. Her godson Harington reminds her that he knew Essex in Ireland, Cecil pleads to be allowed to approach James VI of Scotland about his succession, the French Ambassador presents his credentials, the Queen makes her so-called Golden Speech to the House of Commons ('I have ever used to set the last Judgment Day before mine eyes'), the lady-in-waiting goes to fetch some nourishment, and then thinks she has seen the ghost of her mistress. Cecil appears again in an effort to get the Queen to go to bed, and the Archbishop of Canterbury is seen kneeling in prayer (some adjustment to the number and sequence of these episodes was subsequently made). As the Queen's life draws to its close, from behind the scenes can be heard the chorus singing softly to the tune of No. 1.

Gloriana together with its composer was under considerable attack at the time of its Coronation première, some critics, amateur rather than professional, deciding that it was an insult to the young Queen Elizabeth to show her ageing predecessor partly in a human rather than exclusively a regal light, and one celebrated gossip-writer going so far as to aver that he would rather spend a night in a boiler factory than sit through the opera again! And yet the work is a product of the composer's early maturity, full of operatic insight, arguably the most relaxed he had yet written, and a complete vindication, as it seems to me, of his attempt to write at the same time a 'national' opera and for a specifically 'grand' occasion. That it was misunderstood and intensely disliked by a 1953 assemblage of grandees and courtiers provides a rather acid comment on the different standards prevailing in the mid-twentieth and the late sixteenth centuries, when a luminary of the aristocracy could be the author of the words of 'Happy were he'. H.

THE TURN OF THE SCREW

Opera in a prologue and two acts by Benjamin Britten, libretto by Myfanwy Piper, after the story by Henry James. Première by the English Opera Group at the Venice Festival, September 14, 1954, with Jennifer Vyvyan, Joan Cross, Arda Mandikian, Olive Dyer, David Hemmings, Peter Pears, conductor Britten. First performed Sadler's Wells (by English Opera Group) October 6, 1954, by the same cast;

Florence Festival, 1955; Stratford, Ontario, 1957; Berlin, 1957, all by the English Opera Group. First independent production Darmstadt, 1958, with Ursula Lippmann, Martha Geister, Dorothea von Stein, George Maran, conductor Hans Zanotelli; Stockholm, 1959, with Elisabeth Söderström, Eva Prytz, Kjerstin Dellert, Sven-Erik Vickström, conductor Lars af Malmborg; Boston, USA (first professional American performance), 1961, with Patricia Neway, Ruth Kobart, Naomi Farr, Richard Cassilly, conductor Julius Rudel; New York City Opera, 1962, with Neway, Cassilly, conductor Rudel; Scottish Opera, 1970, with Catherine Wilson, Gregory Dempsey, conductor Roderick Brydon.

CHARACTERS

The Prologue .... Tenor
The Governess .... Soprano
Miles ⎫
Flora ⎭ *children in her charge* .... ⎧ Treble
                                         ⎩ Soprano
Mrs. Grose, *the housekeeper* .... Soprano
Miss Jessel, *the former governess* .... Soprano
Peter Quint, *the former manservant* .... Tenor
Time: The middle of the Nineteenth Century
Place: Bly, an English country house

The Turn of the Screw is an operatic adaptation of Henry James's story, preserving almost every detail intact; certain episodes have been run together, but almost nothing has been omitted. The composition of the orchestra is the same as in Britten's other chamber operas,[1] except that a thirteenth player has been added to take care of piano and celesta, which figure largely in the orchestration.

With a view to musical unity in an opera which is continuous and has a prologue and sixteen scenes (with each of which is associated a dominant instrument), the work is based on a Theme:

Each scene is connected to its successor by a musical variation on this Theme, which itself involves the twelve notes of the scale and is built up on alternately rising fourths

[1] Flute (doubling piccolo and bass flute), oboe (doubling English horn), clarinet (doubling bass clarinet), bassoon, horn, percussion, harp, piano (doubling celesta), string quartet, double bass.

and falling minor thirds. It first occurs after the Prologue and before the first scene of Act I. The Theme employs the 12 semitones of the scale, but the music is so far from being dodecaphonic that each variation and its succeeding scene has in fact a definite tonal centre, an exact calculation of key sequence being a principal means of preserving musical unity. One of the features of James's story is a series of reflections on its implications, particularly on the exact states of tension and emotion in his central character, and the variations turn the screw and form musical counterparts to these literary soliloquies, increasing the tension little by little until the final catastrophe is reached.

The opera begins with an explanatory prologue, tenor accompanied by piano alone: 'It is a curious story. I have it written in faded ink—a woman's hand, governess to two children—long ago . . .'. The visit to the children's handsome guardian, the conditions which should govern the engagement (that she must assume complete responsibility and make all decisions, referring nothing to him), her doubts, and her final acceptance influenced by the trust her charming employer was prepared to put in her—these are set out in the prologue, whose music foreshadows the fourths which dominate the opera's Theme.

The Theme is presented on the piano above tremolo strings before the first scene, Ex. 1:

The presentation of the Theme is followed by music illustrating the Governess's journey to Bly. In the first bar is heard the music associated with the main emotional influences on Miles's life, that is to say, Quint and the new

Governess; it occurs a few moments later in more characteristic vocal form, Ex. 2:

Above an accompaniment confined to timpani and insistent
on the interval of the fourth, the Governess voices her
misgivings and wonders what her charges will be like. 'Very
soon I shall know', she concludes, and the variation, beginning with Ex. 1 in a higher position, takes us straight into the
busy, everyday world of Bly.

The children are agog to know what their future governess
will be like, Mrs. Grose is more interested in getting them to
practise their bows and curtseys, which they do to musical
accompaniment, and before either enquiries or rehearsals are
completed, the Governess is there to greet them (immediately, Ex. 2 is heard on solo violin). The children bow and
curtsey and then, while Mrs. Grose chatters unconcernedly
on, the Governess rhapsodises on the beauty of the children
and the grandeur of Bly. The children are going to show her
round the place and she ends lyrically, 'Bly is now my home'.

The second variation (theme in the bass, otherwise music
associated with the children's everyday life) takes us to the
porch at Bly (scene 3). Mrs. Grose brings the Governess a
letter: 'Mrs. Grose! He's dismissed his school.' (Here, for the
first time, occurs the sound of the celesta, later associated
with Quint; Ex. 3.)

The reason? 'An injury to his friends.' Has Mrs. Grose ever
known him bad? Wild, she says, but not bad, and as if to
reinforce her conviction the children are seen and heard in
the background singing together the nursery rhyme
'Lavender's blue'; the grown-ups turn their duet into a
quartet, and the scene ends with the Governess's determined
answer to Mrs. Grose's anxious question: 'I shall do nothing'.

Variation III, an idyllic synthesis of bird-calls on the
wood-wind, creates the atmosphere of a summer evening. The
Governess's lyrical aria (scene iv) shows that the peaceful
environment has quieted her initial fears, but it is just at the
moment when she admits herself 'alone, tranquil, serene' that

chill comes over the evening, Ex. 3:

and she turns to see an unknown male figure high up on one of the towers of the house. The guardian? No! She knows everyone in the house; is it a stranger or some madman locked away?

Variation IV (Ex. 1 again in the bass) marked 'very quick and heavy', anticipates the children's vigorous singing of 'Tom, Tom, the piper's son' (scene v), which rapidly, and in spite of its apparent gaiety, takes on the character of a sinister march. The Governess comes into the room, and, as the children's tune dies away, Ex. 3 is heard again and the enigmatic figure of the tower is visible outside the window. She runs to see who is there, finds nobody, and returns to describe to Mrs. Grose what she has seen: 'His hair was red, close-curling, a long pale face, small eyes . . . . He was tall, clean-shaven, yes, even handsome, but a horror!' Mrs. Grose's reaction is instantaneous: 'Quint! Peter Quint!' (Ex. 3), and her grief and terror are made very evident as she tells the story of his domination of the household and of his eventual death, Ex. 4:

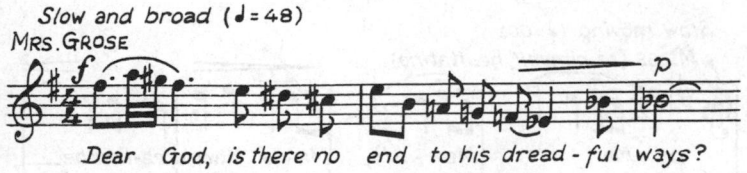

Gradually Mrs. Grose explains her hatred and fear of Quint,

and a new figure emerges, Ex. 5:

indicative of her diffidence. At first mention of Miss Jessel the characteristic sound of low gong is heard, but the music is pervaded by Ex. 4.

The way the colour drains from the orchestra, like blood from the face, as the Governess understands she saw a ghost, is one of Britten's most potent strokes. The Governess thinks she understands. Her peace at Bly is at an end. Quint, in death as in life, returns to dominate the children, and her main charge must henceforth be their protection against influences which, if she cannot withstand their power, will ruin them. The Governess's resolution is expressed to Ex. 2. Mrs. Grose seems to understand nothing clearly, but promises her help.

A brisk double fugue with entries of two themes constituting Ex. 1 introduces and rhythmically prepares the lesson scene. Miles recites the traditional Gender Rhymes to be found in every English schoolboy's Latin Grammar ('Many nouns in -is we find . . .') and Flora's enthusiasm for history is not allowed to divert him from repeating his lesson. What other tags does he know, asks the Governess, and he answers in a curious, haunting melody, Ex. 6:

Ma - lo   Ma - lo in an ap - ple tree___
C. A.

that seems to summarise everything mysterious that may lie
behind his natural childlike gaiety, the only side we have seen
of him so far:

> 'Malo: I would rather be
> Malo: in an apple tree
> Malo: than a naughty boy
> Malo: in adversity.'

It disconcerts the Governess in its strangeness, and there is no
reassurance in Miles's explanation 'I found it, I like it, do
you?'

The seventh scene shows Flora in a not dissimilar light. She
and the Governess are by the lake at Bly, and Flora asks if it
figures in her geography book. The Governess gets her to
repeat the names of the seas she has learnt, and she
announces dramatically that the lake they are standing beside
is called the Dead Sea. She turns from geography to the task
of singing her doll to sleep with a lullaby built up on the
fourths and minor thirds of Ex. 1, while the Governess reads
nearby. She arranges the covers for the doll, and deliberately
turns to face the audience as the ghost of Miss Jessel appears
at the other side of the lake. The Governess looks up from
her reading, sees Miss Jessel (to the sound of her characteristic gong and chords), Ex. 7:

(♩ = 60)

Gong   pp   p   mf

who disappears, and immediately deduces from Flora's unnatural silence that she has seen her too. She hurries Flora
away, and then faces a situation (Ex. 2) rendered doubly
desperate by the certainty that each of the children under her
charge is haunted by a presence from the dead.

Celesta and harp (Ex. 3) usher in the last scene of the first act, while the horn reminds us of Ex. 1 (Variation VII). It is night, and the sound of Quint's voice quietly breaks the silence with a long reiterated coloratura flourish (derived from Ex. 3), Ex. 8:

It is a moment of chilling beauty, made more effective because it is the first time a man's voice has been heard since the Prologue, and it might never have been put in quite these musical terms if the composer had not heard Peter Pears, the original Quint, singing unaccompanied Perotin ('Beata viscera') in Aldeburgh Church a year or so earlier. Quint is eventually made out, high in the tower, as when the Governess first saw him, and Miles can be seen in the garden below him. 'I'm all things strange and bold . . .', he sings to Miles: 'In me secrets, half-formed desires meet.' Miles is fascinated and answers him, and soon Miss Jessel's voice, introduced by the chords and gong of Ex. 7, can be heard calling Flora, who responds in her turn. A *pianissimo* duet in 3/8 time, marked 'quick and lightly' develops for Quint and Miss Jessel, Ex. 9:

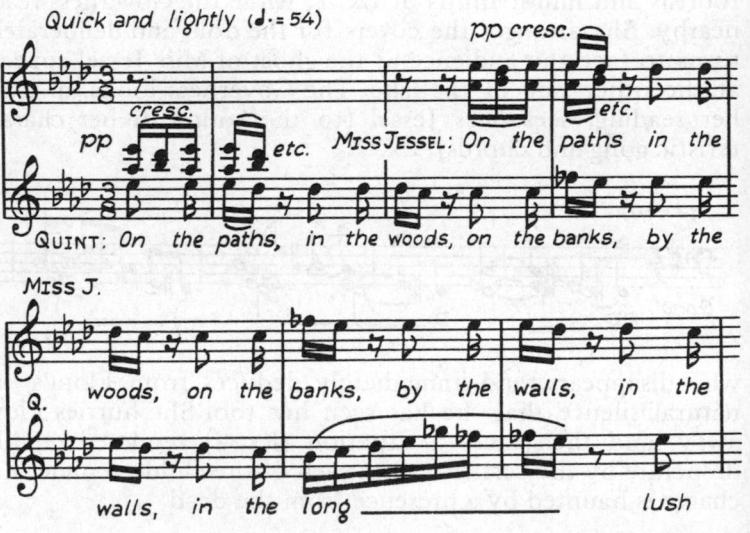

may be thought of as denoting contact between ghosts and children. At its end the voices of the Governess and Mrs. Grose can be heard calling for the children (Ex. 1 in the horn). As soon as they appear, the ghosts vanish, Mrs. Grose hustles Flora indoors, and the Governess is left to hear Miles's enigmatic answers to her question—one of Henry James's unforgettable strokes: 'You see, I am bad, aren't I?'

Act II. Variation VIII begins with the clarinet imitating Quint's opening flourish, Ex. 8, and indeed the whole prelude is composed from music already heard in the previous scene. It introduces a colloquy between Miss Jessel and Quint, whose stage direction reads 'the lights fade in on Quint and Miss Jessel—nowhere'. The dramatic theme of their duet: 'Why did you call me from my schoolroom dreams? I call? not I! You heard the terrible sound of the wild swan's wings.' The duet mounts in urgency as each participant asserts (Ex. 2) that, with his or her peace of mind established, Ex. 10:

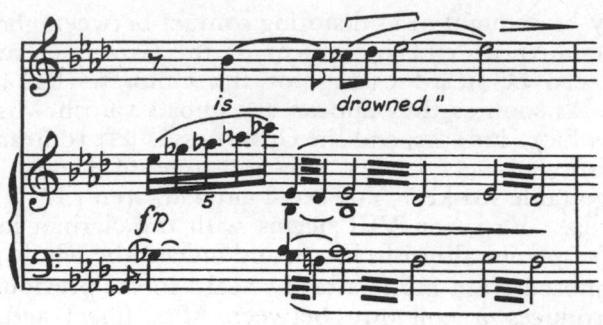

(The line is a quotation from Yeats, the theme derived from
Ex. 2), and it ends with a firm statement in octaves of the
theme, the first and only time in the opera that it appears in
the voice parts (Ex. 1). As the ghosts fade from sight (A flat
major to G sharp minor), the Governess can be heard in an
agony of meditation, her aria 'Lost in my labyrinth, I see no
truth', sung over a complicated ostinato bass.

The churchyard scene is heralded with an orchestral
invocation of church bells (variation IX) and the lights fade
in on the children as they sing a *Benedicite* which is half
straight, half parody ('O amnis, axis, caulis, collis . . . bless ye
the Lord.'). The Governess and Mrs. Grose are with them, but
stand a little apart, and Mrs. Grose does not realise the
implications until her attempts at comfort elicit from the
Governess all the horrors of the night before: 'Dear, good
Mrs. Grose, they are not playing, they are talking horrors'.
Mrs. Grose bustles Flora into church, but Miles hangs back
(as the percussion imitates a final peal or two) and asks when
he is going back to school. His final remark before going
inside—'You trust me, my dear, but you think and think . . .
of us, and of the others. Does my uncle think what you
think?'—elicits from the Governess a horrified 'It was a
challenge!' In despair, she decides that there is nothing for it
but for her to leave Bly, now, straightaway, while they are at
church. She runs out, and variation X (the theme in the bass)
is a postlude to the scene of her flight.

The moment she is inside her room the Governess can feel
Miss Jessel's presence and sees her sitting at the desk. In their
duet, Miss Jessel exudes calm and inexorability, Ex. 11:

but the Governess's nerves are screwed almost to breaking pitch (it is her nearest approach to the madness which in the story is a conceivable alternative to the haunting the Governess senses) and she now knows that she cannot after all bear the thought of abandoning the children. When Miss Jessel has gone, she cries 'I must write to him now', then, in one of the most beautiful passages of the whole opera given at first to the orchestra without the voice, sits at her desk and writes to ask the children's guardian if he will see her, as there are things she must tell him (Ex. 12) (Erwin Stein in a commentary felt the music had a faint resemblance to 'Malo').

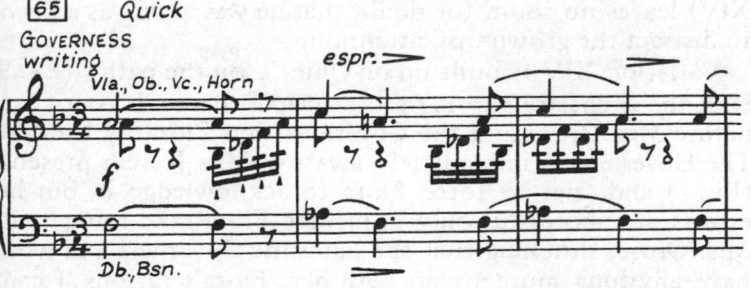

At variation XI's start, bass clarinet and bass flute have a
canon on the Theme, interrupted by Ex. 3, and, as the
curtain rises, the cor anglais adds Ex. 6 which the boy is
heard humming (tragically?) when the lights go up, and on
which the following scene is based, a scene where taut nerves
threaten at any moment to crack into the relief of tears. The
Governess tries to get him to tell her what happened at
school. Quint's voice is heard, Miles shrieks and the candle
goes out leaving the question still unanswered, the tear
unshed. The short variation XII has Quint's voice singing and
the theme in *pizzicato* strings. Quint tempts Miles to take the
letter the Governess has written: 'Take it! Take it!' He does
so. The scene ends with 'Malo' in the orchestra.

With the thirteenth variation the mood changes sharply
and the solo piano imitates a late eighteenth-century sonata
and nerves are seemingly under control again. Miles is seen
playing to an audience of the Governess and Mrs. Grose while
Flora, later joined by Mrs. Grose, plays at cat's cradle. The
Governess and Mrs. Grose sing in fourths; is this departure
from the conventional thirds the responsibility of the
Theme? Mrs. Grose nods—Flora's peremptory 'Go to sleep!'
from scene vii of Act I, has a sinister ring to it—and Flora
steals out. Her departure is soon noticed, but Miles'
triumphant attack on the piano (it reaches into variation
XIV) leaves no room for doubt that he was acting as a decoy
to distract the grown-ups' attention.

Variation XIV is built up on Quint's 'on the paths' (Ex. 9)
with the orchestra varying the principal theme. It is not long
before Mrs. Grose and the Governess find Flora by the lake.
The Governess is immediately aware of Miss Jessel's presence
(Ex. 7) and tries to force Flora to acknowledge it, but her
efforts are successful only in making Flora take refuge with
Mrs. Grose, shrieking that she hates the Governess and won't
have anything more to do with her: Flora's furious 'I can't

ee anybody, can't see anything' is sung to the theme of the
.rowning of innocence (Ex. 10) and she leads a quartet of
emale voices in which Miss Jessel rallies Flora to her side and
Mrs. Grose affirms that she can see nothing. With the
leparture of Mrs. Grose and Flora comes again the theme of
Mrs. Grose perplexed (Ex. 5) and the Governess's cadence,
lramatically transposed from Ex. 2, accompanies her
acknowledgement of failure, Ex. 13:

Variation XV begins with a 12-note chord, and is con
cerned mostly with the music of 'I can't see anybody
(piccolo and timpani). The last scene takes place out of
doors. Mrs. Grose takes Flora away (Ex. 4) and, as if to atone
for her own lack of support in the previous scene, reveals to
the Governess that her letter to the children's guardian must
have been stolen. Miles comes in alone and his entrance
coincides with the beginning of a loose passacaglia on the
first six notes of the theme, in whose course the other notes
are one by one added, the definition of the form being
gradually lost until, at the statement of the whole Theme, it
is abandoned. The melody in the upper parts, on strings when
Miles is concerned, on clarinet when it is the Governess
singing, is highly expressive and the whole scene one of great
tension. It remains for the Governess, almost as in a ritual, to
ask Miles to place his confidence in her and to tell her
whether he stole her letter. His attempts at being straight
forward are complicated by the admonitions of Quint (Exx. 2
and 9), but, when the Governess presses him to tell her who
it is that he can see (Ex. 1), the struggle for his soul reaches a
climax and he dies with a scream of 'Peter Quint! You
devil!', aimed, equivocal to the last, at one—or other—of his
tormentors. Quint's voice joins with the Governess's, and in
the end is heard at a distance with Ex. 3. The Governess is
left with the body of the little boy, and it is with pathetic
repetitions of his 'Malo' song that the opera comes to an end

H.

NOYE'S FLUDDE

The Chester Miracle Play[1] set to music by Benjamin Britten
Première, Orford Church during Aldeburgh Festival, June 18, 1958
with Gladys Parr, Owen Brannigan, Trevor Anthony, conductor Charle
Mackerras.

CHARACTERS

The Voice of God . . . . Speaking Part
Noye . . . . Bass Baritone
Mrs. Noye . . . . Contralto

[1] The text is from *English Miracle Plays, Moralities and Interludes*
edited by Alfred W. Pollard and published by the Clarendon Press
Oxford.

Sem, Ham and Jaffett . . . . Boy Trebles
Mrs. Sem, Mrs. Ham, Mrs. Jaffett . . . . Girl Sopranos
Mrs. Noye's gossips . . . . Girl Sopranos
Chorus of animals and birds . . . . Children
The Congregation

Britten's skilful writing for immature performers, in a way
that is within their scope and still meaningful for audiences,
is virtually unrivalled, as witness numerous examples in *The
Turn of the Screw, Albert Herring, Let's Make an Opera,* the
cantata *St. Nicholas, A Midsummer Night's Dream* and the
Church Parables. *Noye's Fludde* may contain nothing so
disturbingly apt as Miles's 'Malo' song, but it carries the
principle of adolescent participation further than in the other
operas. Noye and his wife are adult, as is the Voice of God,
and probably conductor and a few key musicians of the
orchestra, but the bulk of the cast consists of children: there
is a sizeable children's chorus, and children provide a full
string orchestra, groups of recorders and bugles, and a
number of percussion players, the last-named contributing
notably to the brilliant colouring of the score.

As Overture, Britten uses the hymn 'Lord Jesus, think on
me',[1] sung by the congregation, which is what the audience
becomes since the work is intended for church performance.
God's voice commands Noye to build the Ark, and Sem,
Ham, Jaffett and their wives enter to lively music, bringing
appropriate carpenters' tools. Mrs. Noye and her chorus of
gossips mock the preparations. Noye in solemn music leads
his family in the building of the Ark, which is accomplished
in a few minutes of music, but Mrs. Noye remains
vociferously sceptical and she and Noye quarrel.

God's voice commands Noye to take the animals into the
Ark and, heralded by bugles, a march leads them in two by
two and singing 'Kyrie eleison' as they go. Only Mrs. Noye
resists: 'I will not come theirin todaye . . . I have my
gossippes everyone, they shall not drowne, by Sante John!'
But in the end her children pick her up, more than a little
drunk, and carry her inside.

The great centrepiece of the opera is an extended
passacaglia in C, a favourite device of the composer's and

[1] Damon's Psalter, words by Bishop Synesius, translated by
Chatfield.

here used to depict the various phases of the flood's progress: rain, wind, lightning, thunder and the rising waves. Various instrumental colours are used to point up each aspect of the disaster, Noye and his family sing a prayer before committing themselves to the Ark, and the climax of the episode comes with the singing of the hymn 'Eternal Father, strong to save',[1] in whose second and third verses the congregation joins.

The flood music ends and there is a kind of postscript, an inversion of the raindrop figuration which has appeared earlier on, played now on tuned mugs and piano; during it I once experienced a torrential downpour in normally dry Mexico when the opera was given in the open air with local forces in Guadalajara at the time of the 1970 World Cup (Soccer)—a singularly inappropriate interruption of an otherwise enchanting performance.

Raven and dove are despatched according to tradition, Noye rejoices at the evidence of dry land, God's Voice commands disembarkation, and bugles cue the animals into an 'Alleluia' as they leave the Ark. The finale is built up on Tallis's *Canon*, 'The spacious firmament on high', the six verses differently treated and with the congregation joining in the last two to make the opera's climax.   H.

A MIDSUMMER NIGHT'S DREAM

Opera in three acts by Benjamin Britten, text after Shakespeare by the composer and Peter Pears. Première, Aldeburgh Festival, June 11, 1960, with Jennifer Vyvyan, April Cantelo, Marjorie Thomas, Johanna Peters, Alfred Deller, George Maran, Thomas Hemsley, Owen Brannigan, Peter Pears, conductor Britten. First produced Holland Festival with Joan Carlyle replacing April Cantelo as Helena, and Forbes Robinson singing Bottom, conductor George Malcolm; Covent Garden, 1961, with Joan Carlyle, Irene Salemka, Marjorie Thomas, Margreta Elkins, Russell Oberlin, André Turp, Louis Quilico, Geraint Evans, John Lanigan, conductor Georg Solti; Hamburg State Opera, 1961, produced by Rennert; Berlin, Komische Oper, 1961, produced by Felsenstein; la Scala, Milan, 1961; San Francisco, 1961; New York, City Centre, 1963.

---

[1] J. B. Dykes, words by W. Whiting.

CHARACTERS

Oberon, King of the Fairies. Counter-Tenor (or Contralto)
Tytania, Queen of the Fairies . . . . . Coloratura Soprano
Puck . . . . Speaking role (Acrobat)
Theseus, Duke of Athens . . . . Bass
Hippolyta, Queen of the Amazons, *betrothed to Theseus*
Contralto

Lysander ⎫ *in love with Hermia* . . . . ⎰ Tenor
Demetrius ⎭   ⎱ Baritone

Hermia, *in love with Lysander* . . . . . . .Mezzo-Soprano
Helena, *in love with Demetrius* . . . . Soprano
Bottom, *a weaver* . . . . Bass-Baritone
Quince, *a carpenter* . . . . Bass
Flute, *a bellows-maker* . . . . .Tenor
Snug, *a joiner* . . . . Bass
Snout, *a tinker* . . . . Tenor
Starveling, *a tailor* . . . . Baritone
Cobweb ⎫
Peaseblossom ⎬ *Fairies* .Trebles
Mustardseed ⎪
Moth ⎭
Chorus of Fairies . . . . Trebles or Sopranos

To turn a masterpiece in one medium into a work of
similar calibre in another is a vast undertaking and yet this is
what Benjamin Britten has succeeded in doing. His adaptation, with the perspicacious aid of Peter Pears caused David
Drew[1] to write à propos the première in 1960 of *A
Midsummer Night's Dream*, 'A corner of Shakespeare's Empire
has undergone a subtle change. It has not been ruthlessly
invaded, it has not even been quietly exploited. But for those
who were at Aldeburgh on June 11, and for those who will
follow them to Britten's new opera in the months and years
to come, Shakespeare's *A Midsummer Night's Dream* will
never be quite the same again.'

The opera elevates the fairies, and particularly Oberon, to
a position of prime influence and also, to become the
framework of the whole opera, places all except the final
scene in the wood, and relegates the question of anachronistic Athenian ambience very much to the background.

[1] *New Statesman*, June 18, 1960.

Britten's music moves on three sharply differentiated planes: fairies, mortals (lovers) and rustics.

I find the result, with its transparent orchestral textures adapted to fit children's voices and the use in a principal role of counter-tenor, one of Britten's most accessible and most attractive scores, as rich in invention as anything he had written before or after, and continually evoking in a movement or a single phrase a whole world of emotions. But its resonances go further than that, so that the snakes which infest Shakespeare's imagery are never far from the drama's surface, the fairies dispense a magic which is sure and purposeful but not inevitably benign, the equivocal figure of Oberon[1] flaunts the power to chill if he does not choose to warm, and only the wood—like Janáček's in *The Cunning Little Vixen*—is omnipresent, all-consoling. To me the opera is a source of inexhaustible pleasure and I have never yet heard the 5/4 'Now until the break of day', with its mesmeric Scotch snap, without a catch in the throat and the realisation that this is a supreme musical magician at work.

Act I.   The wood is represented by a slow-breathing string texture which rises and falls as the curtain goes up, and is heard again frequently throughout the opera, Ex. 1:

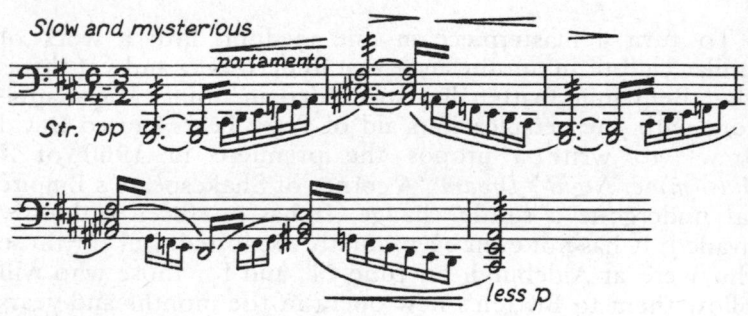

The fairies in two groups, led by Cobweb and Mustardseed, Peaseblossom and Moth, make their entrance with 'Over hill, over dale, thorough bush, thorough briar'. They are Tytania's instruments but are soon interrupted by Puck (trumpet and drum accompaniment throughout), of whom they are afraid.

[1] 'Whether intended or not', writes David Drew in the *New Statesman* 'Britten's Oberon is a more grimly effective horror than the Peter Quint who called from the Tower and had no Puck to help him.'

Puck announces Oberon and Tytania (slow march) who have quarrelled over an Indian page boy, Ex. 2:

in which 2(a) is particularly important.

Tytania departs and Oberon alone plots vengeance, summons Puck and sends him to fetch that herb whose juice 'will make or man or woman madly dote Upon the next live creature that it sees'. Celesta lends colour (eerie rather than sinister, as it was in *The Turn of the Screw*, points out Peter Evans[1]) in its *ostinato* accompaniment to the spell motif, Ex. 3:

Oberon, his plot in motion, disappears and the wood is left empty (Ex. 1).

---

[1] *Tempo*, Spring/Summer, 1960.

It is the turn of the lovers, whose themes throughout the opera are derived from Ex. 4:

We meet first Lysander and Hermia, eloping to avoid the forced betrothal of Hermia and Demetrius ('Compelling thee to marry with Demetrius' is the only line in the libretto not to be found in Shakespeare). If one senses at the start of the duet that they may not emerge from their predicament by their own efforts, the fire that has been wanting in them earlier starts to appear in the passage beginning 'I swear to thee'. They leave, the wood is empty again (Ex. 1), Oberon appears with schemes in his heart and music (Ex. 3), and the lovers, Lysander and Hermia, are succeeded by the quarrelling Demetrius and Helena, the latter breathlessly pursuing the former, who for his part wants nothing more than to be re-united with his betrothed Hermia. Helena has a short, character-revealing solo, 'I am your spaniel', and when they depart Oberon decides to put right the destinies of these star-crossed lovers. He sends for Puck who gives him the flower he demanded and lies at his feet. 'I know a bank where the wild thyme blows' is, for all its sinister undertones, an aria of exquisite sensibility, introduced by Ex. 3 with cellos supplying the vocal line and horns adding colour, and it marvellously rounds off the first half of the act.

Into the silent wood (Ex. 1) cautiously come six rustics, heralded by trombone *pianissimo*. Peter Quince calls the roll and, not without frequent interruptions from Bottom, assigns to each a part in the play which they plan to rehearse. Each is neatly characterised, from the swaggering Bottom through the shy but tenacious Francis Flute[1] to Snug the joiner, 'slow of study' and tending therefore to come in only on the weak beat of the bar. Bottom at one point offers to play Lion as well as his own Pyramus and believes that his performance

---

[1] Flute's hero-worshipping of Bottom is apparent from the moment he instinctively adopts Bottom's bouncy tune as he practises his lines, suggested David Cairns in *The Spectator* at the time of the opera's earliest performances.

would 'make the Duke say, Let him roar again', but Flute and the others think that the ladies would take fright, 'and that were enough to hang us all'. With promises to con their parts so that, according to Bottom, 'they may rehearse most obscenely and courageously', they whisper 'Adieu' and once more leave the wood empty (Ex. 1).

Hermia and Lysander are exhausted with their wanderings and they find a resting place and lie down together, only for Puck to discover them and mistakenly squeeze the juice of the magic flower on Lysander's eyes (celesta). Hermia sings in her sleep, and Helena and Demetrius, still quarrelling, enter in their turn to look for a resting place. Helena perceives Lysander, he wakes and declares love for her and hatred for Demetrius, in either instance to her considerable discomfiture. What has she done to be thus mocked? She runs out, followed by Lysander; Hermia wakes and distractedly follows where Lysander led.

Tytania can be heard in the distance and soon enters with her retinue whom she bids sing her to sleep before going to their respective nocturnal offices. They oblige with an astonishingly fresh setting of 'You spotted snakes with double tongue' without trace of archness, but Oberon moves invisibly past the single sentinel they have posted and (Ex. 3) squeezes the magic juice on to Tytania's eyes bidding her 'Wake when some vile thing is near'. The curtain falls (Ex. 1).

Act II is concerned with sleep, and the prelude is based on four chords, very differently scored, covering the twelve notes of the scale (there is little twelve-notish about the score but its gradual influence on Britten, even more than in *The Turn of the Screw*, is here apparent). The curtain rises immediately to disclose Tytania asleep at the back. After the prelude the six rustics enter for rehearsal. Bottom is full of suggestions to Peter Quince: ladies will like neither a killing on the stage nor the roaring of Lion—let there be a prologue to explain each. Quince himself has a couple of conundrums: How 'to bring the moonlight into the chamber' (the word 'moonshine' has a particular resonance for the rustics), and how to represent the wall. Rehearsal starts, watched now by Puck who follows Bottom at his exit and, when Flute has spoken his entire role without a pause, brings Bottom back with an ass's head on his shoulders, to the disgruntlement of the cast which runs off at top speed: 'Bless thee, Bottom, thou art translated'.

Bottom sings—or bellows—to keep his spirits up and Tytania wakes to love him. Her attendants are introduced to him one after another, detailed to attend his every want, and in their turn greet him ceremoniously ('Hail, mortal'). A languorous tune on A flat clarinet and flute expresses Tytania's infatuation and eventually she sets the fairies to play and sing to him[1] (sopranino recorders, cymbals and blocks). Bottom announces 'I have an exposition of sleep come upon me', Tytania sings ecstatically and then in her turn falls asleep.

A short interlude brings Puck on the scene and after him Oberon, who soon expresses his delight at Tytania's predicament. But Puck has been mistaken over the Athenians, and Demetrius and Hermia are clearly at cross-purposes. Puck is dispatched to find Helena, and Oberon squeezes more juice (Ex. 3) on to Demetrius's eyes, before Puck returns with Helena and Lysander. Helena upbraids Lysander for his faithlessness to Hermia, but Demetrius wakes up, sees Helena, and now she has two adoring swains. Hermia's re-entry adds a further complication, as Helena decides she is at the bottom of a plot against her. Helena's short aria ('O is all forgot?') describing her schooldays' friendship for Hermia starts off an ensemble of misunderstanding at the end of which the two girls quarrel bitterly (Hermia: 'She hath urg'd her height' . . . Helena: 'Get you gone, you dwarf') and all leave, the girls at odds, the men to fight a duel.

Oberon comes forward dragging Puck by the ear and complaining at what must either be incompetence or knavishness. He instructs him so to order the comings and goings of Demetrius and Lysander that their efforts to confront each other in mortal combat shall end in exhaustion before they contrive to come to blows. Puck carries out his instructions, imitating the voice of one to lead the other on, until curtain-fall finds the four lovers correctly lined up so that awakening may provide appropriate reconciliation. The fairies steal in to sing a benediction, 'Jack shall have Jill, Nought shall go ill'—their most involved musical intervention yet—Puck squeezes the juice on Lysander's eyes (Ex. 3) and the curtain falls.

Act III.   From the strings at the outset we sense reconciliation and resolution in the morning air and we are right—all

[1] To the tune of 'Boys and Girls come out to play'.

will be worked out in its own good time, and thoroughly. In the wood early next day can be seen lying asleep Tytania with Bottom, and the four lovers slightly apart. Oberon likes what he sees and, having acquired the Indian boy who was the cause of the trouble, is prepared to undo 'This hateful imperfection of her eyes'. To the sound of the celesta, he undoes the spell: 'Be as thou wast wont to be; See as thou wast wont to see' (Ex. 3). Tytania awakes (Ex. 2), is released from the spell and is reconciled (very slow; *quasi saraband*) with Oberon, who himself proposes to unite the pairs of lovers in wedded bliss to coincide with the marriage of Duke Theseus with Hippolyta.

Oberon, Tytania and the fairies disappear as the lovers, to the sounds of horns (Theseus's rather than the horns of Elfland), awake and are in their turn reconciled: 'And I have found Demetrius like a jewel. Mine own, and not mine own', Ex. 5 (page 1510); in a fine flowing ensemble of considerable beauty.

They leave, and Bottom, alone on the stage, starts to wake. Snatches of what has passed before go through his mind and he is indignant that his fellow mummers have abandoned him. He has dreamt—mysteries. But a ballad shall be made of his dream, 'And I will sing it in the latter end of the play before the Duke'. It is a key statement, not only musically and dramatically but because in it we have proof of the opera's mainspring, the omnipotent fairy power of Oberon; Bottom could not have *imagined* what he describes without their influence. As he walks away the others come in, still at a loss to explain Bottom's disappearance. Had it been possible to perform the play in front of the Duke and had Bottom been with them, he would surely have been granted sixpence a day for life for his playing of Pyramus! No sooner are they agreed on that than Bottom's voice is heard. All questioning is halted at the news that 'The Duke hath dined and our play is preferred'. In a flurry of ensemble marked 'very lively', they prepare to leave, the lights go down on the wood, and horns and woodwind carry the burden of a quick march as the scene changes to:

Theseus's palace. Theseus and Hippolyta enter with their court and in a few phrases voice their impatience that the wedding events of the day have not yet given way to the consummation of night. The four lovers enter to beg success-fully for the Duke's blessing, before Peter Quince comes in confidently with a playbill which he hands to Hippolyta: 'A

Ex. 5

tedious brief scene of young Pyramus, And his love Thisby

What follows is nothing less than a condensed comic opera occupying 36 pages of vocal and 40 of full score. Its introduction has all six rustics singing together in block harmony and marked *pomposo*: 'If we offend, it is with our good will'—but straightaway there is a sting in the tail when they attempt a canon on 'All for your delight' and the climactic top D proves too high for Flute. Prologue, in the person of Quince, introduces the characters, predictably failing to fit action to word as he pushes them out while reiterating the word 'Remain'.

Wall, played by Snout, introduces himself in *Sprechstimme*, before Bottom launches himself, in the character of Pyramus, into a short if full-blooded apostrophe to Night and to the obstacle between him and his love, in the manner of a big Italianate aria—indeed the whole thing is a satire on 19th-century romantic opera, as is plain from the rather timid flute tune introducing Flute in the character of Thisby and the overwrought if insubstantial duet for Thisby and Pyramus which follows it. Wall prepares to leave, still in *Sprechstimme*, and is succeeded by Snug as Lion and eventually Starveling as Moon. Thisby continues her *allegretto* flute-beset mood of before, but the music is quickly superseded by the roaring of Lion, who chases Thisby out. Pyramus enters, finds Thisby's mantle, assumes the worst and (without much changing of musical mood) plunges a sword into his bosom. Thisby finds the body of Pyramus and, at the end of her wits, enters upon a mad scene to which the flute does full justice, before embarking on an *adagio lamentoso* with full orchestral postlude. Bottom offers the assembled worthies an epilogue or a Bergomask dance and it is the dance which is chosen. It involves a maximum of misunderstanding between the players and is in two parts, the first hesitating between 6/8 and 9/8, and the second a very fast 2/4. Midnight sounds, the rustics stop dancing and Theseus and Hippolyta, followed by the four lovers, bid them and us 'Sweet friends, to bed'.

There is no change of scene but enter Cobweb, Mustardseed, Peaseblossom, and Moth to sing 'Now the hungry lion roars, And the wolf behowls the Moon'. Puck comes in with his broom, but the major musical statement is left to Oberon and the fairies with some help from Tytania. I have referred already to the uncannily cathartic effect 'Now until the break of day' can have on the listener. Not even Captain Vere with

is consolatory chords, not the return of the Borough's
orking chorus, not the reiteration of 'Malo' makes a greater
ffect, and for anything comparable one has perhaps to go
ack to *Gloriana*'s final orchestral Lute Song and 'Green
aves', Ex. 6:

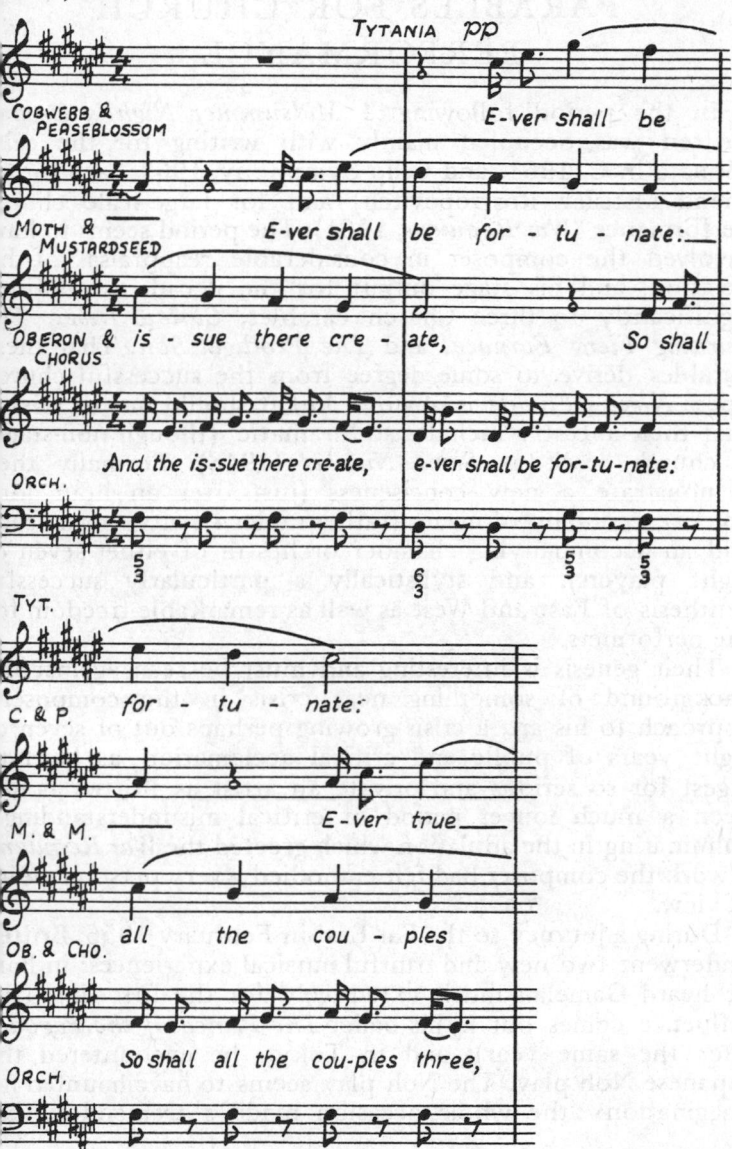

After this, who could gainsay Puck's valedictory 'Gentles, c
not reprehend'?' H.

PARABLES FOR CHURCH
PERFORMANCE

In the period following *A Midsummer Night's Dream*
Britten was occupied mainly with writing for the cell
(Sonata in C, 1961, and Cello Symphony, 1963, each for h
friend Mstislav Rostropovitch) and for large-scale churc
performance (*War Requiem*, 1961). The period seems to hav
involved the composer in considerable reappraisal of h
position, and his stage output for the decade is confine
significantly to three Church Parables, *Curlew River, Th
Burning Fiery Furnace*, and *The Prodigal Son*. That thes
parables derive to some degree from the successful churc
opera *Noye's Fludde* is obvious, but it should not be misse
that their ancestry includes so 'dramatic' (though non-stage
a church work as *Saint Nicolas* (1948). Formally the
demonstrate a new conciseness (just over an hour lor
apiece), economy of means (rather under twenty singers eac
and an accompanying chamber orchestra of either seven c
eight players), and stylistically a particularly successf
synthesis of East and West as well as remarkable freedom fc
the performers.

Their genesis is interesting and must be seen against th
background of something near crisis in the composer
approach to his art, a crisis growing perhaps out of seven c
eight years of public and critical acclamation—as hard t
digest for so serious and private an artist as Britten as ha
been a much longer period of critical misunderstanding
culminating in the adulation which greeted the *War Requien*
a work the composer had felt embodied a very personal poir
of view.

During a journey to the Far East in February 1956, Britte
underwent two new and fruitful musical experiences: in Bal
he heard Gamelan music extensively for the first time (th
influence comes out in his ballet *The Prince of the Pagod*
later the same year); and in Tokyo he encountered th
Japanese Noh play. The Noh play seems to have haunted h
imagination: 'the whole occasion made a tremendous in

ession upon me: the simple, touching story, the economy
the style, the intense slowness of the action, the marvel-
us skill and control of the performers, the beautiful
ostumes, the mixture of chanting, speech, singing which,
ith the three instruments, made up the strange music—it all
fered a totally new "operatic" experience'.[1]

Seven years later, it was the Noh play *Sumidagawa* which
asked William Plomer to transform into what became the
rst of his three 'Parables for church performance', and it
as *Curlew River* which provided the formal terms of
ference for the complete set. The story and its overtones
ere retained but the Japanese setting with its ancient
agaku music gave way to a modern version of the English
ediaeval liturgical drama with the music based on a plain-
ng hymn. So successful did the formula prove in *Curlew
iver* that composer and librettist retained it throughout the
t, each parable introduced by a different plainsong tune
id based upon it, each deemed to be taking place inside a
onastic community, which processes in, at the start of the
tion, and which provides from its male ranks all the
aracters of the drama, whether masculine or feminine.

Unlike say *Lucretia*, *Albert Herring* or *Les Mamelles de
résias*, which are miniature 'Grand' operas and where the
iall orchestra skilfully substitutes a big one, these Parables
e chamber operas of potentially seminal nature. Whether
e seed is finally proved fertile or sterile is a matter only
ne can resolve. These works will remain.

CURLEW RIVER

Parable for Church Performance by Benjamin Britten, libretto by
lliam Plomer. Première, Aldeburgh Festival, June 12, 1964, at Orford
iurch, with Peter Pears, John Shirley-Quirk, Bryan Drake, Don
arrard. First performed Holland Festival, 1964, and Tours, 1965, by
iglish Opera Group with substantially the above cast. First performed
enmark, Copenhagen, 1966; U.S.A., Caramoor, New York, 1966, with
idrea Velis; Mulhouse, 1968, with Michel Sénéchal; Australia at
lelaide Festival, 1970, with Peter Pears.

From the composer's sleeve-note to the recording of *Curlew River*.

CHARACTERS

The Abbot, eleven Monks, four Acolytes, seven Lay
Brothers who make up the cast of the Parable:

The Madwoman .... Tenor
The Ferryman .... Baritone
The Traveller .... Baritone
The Spirit of the Boy (*an Acolyte*) .... Treble
Leader of the Pilgrims (*the Abbot*) .... Bass
Chorus of pilgrims

Instrumentalists: Flute (doubling piccolo), Horn, Viola
Double Bass, Harp, Percussion, Chamber organ.

The story outline of *Curlew River* remains close to that o
Sumidagawa, as evidenced when the Prince of Hesse and th
Rhine, who went with Britten to Tokyo, described the No
play in his diary[1]: 'The ferryman is waiting in his boat,
traveller turns up and tells him about a woman who will soo
be coming to the river. The woman is mad, she is looking fo
her lost child. Then she appears and the ferryman does no
wish to take a mad person, but in the end he lets her into h
boat. On the way across the river the two passengers s
behind each other on the floor as if in a narrow boat, whil
the ferryman stands behind them, symbolically punting wit
a light stick. The ferryman tells the story of a little boy wh
came this way a year ago this very day. The child was ver
tired for he had escaped from robbers who had held him. H
crossed the river in this boat, but he died from exhaustion o
the other side. The woman starts crying. It was her son. Th
ferryman is sorry for her and takes her to the child's grave
The mother is acted by a tall man in woman's clothing with
small woman's mask on his face. Accessories help you t
understand what is going on ... The play ends in th
chanting of the chorus'.

It is precisely the 'plot' of *Curlew River*. To the thre
main characters already described in the Noh play, Britte
and Plomer add the Abbot of the monastery where th
performance is taking place, the voice of the dead child, an
nine pilgrims who act as chorus. In addition—and crucially-
the action and motivation are changed from mediaeva

[1] Printed in *Tribute to Benjamin Britten* (Faber, 1963).

apanese and Buddhist to mediaeval English and Christian, nd music and action start with ritual, the procession of nonks up the nave of the church singing the Compline Office ymn[1], Ex. 1:

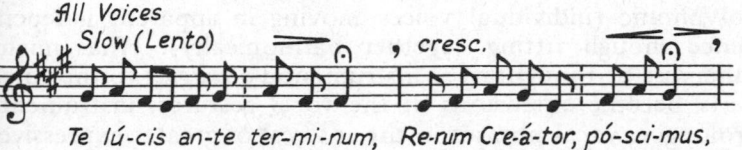

Te lú-cis an-te ter-mi-num, Re-rum Cre-á-tor, pó-sci-mus,

he Abbot leads the stylised action, in the sense that he sets he scene, after which the robing of the characters of the arable takes place in view of the audience, and the drama roper begins with the Ferryman's vigorous announcement of is role in the action.

Much has been written about *Curlew River* and the other :hurch Parables, each of which embodies the paradox of very ighly organised musical material (derived from the simple asis of plainchant) and a style of performance much freer han in Britten's other dramatic works. To take characterisaion of performance first, the composer dispenses with a onductor, and treats the singers as being as much a part of a hamber ensemble as the instrumental musicians, who themelves, exceptionally, form part of the stage action, walking 1 procession with the other brothers of the monastery and aking up dramatic stations on the stage (at least in the riginal performnces, which Colin Graham directed to maxium effect under the composer's eye).

Eric White[2] has drawn attention to 'an element of hapsody' in the vocal parts which is a consequence of the reedom allotted the performers, and the score specifies the eading voice at each moment as well as making liberal use of otted (as opposed to solid) barlines, in order to diminish his emphasis on regular pattern. Britten has invented a new ause mark, the 'curlew',[3] which, says Imogen Holst in her ntroduction to the published score, 'shows that the perormer must listen and wait till the other performers have

[1] Its intervals of seconds and thirds permeate the vocal line of Abbot nd monks when they sing *in propria persona* as opposed to in costume.

[2] In his invaluable *Benjamin Britten, his life and his operas* (Faber, 970).

[3] Used also in the other Church Parables.

reached the next barline or meeting-point, i.e. the note or
rest can be longer or shorter than its written value'.

Much of the writing is monophonic (confined to a single
part) or heterophonic (the simultaneous sounding of simple
and decorated versions of the same theme) rather than
polyphonic (individual voices moving in apparent independence though fitting together harmonically). What might
otherwise be thought of as instrumental *obbligati* to the voice
parts become extensions of the vocal gestures, instruments
prolonging vocal phrases in the interest of greater expressiveness, sometimes oddly and eerily as in the Madwoman's
scena after the communal recognition of her child's grave.
Monteverdi-like repetitions of notes are a feature of the vocal
style.

In *Curlew River*, each character is represented by certain
motifs and has associated with him his own instrument. The
Ferryman has an agitated version of Ex. 1 and his instruments are horn and to a lesser extent viola. The Traveller has

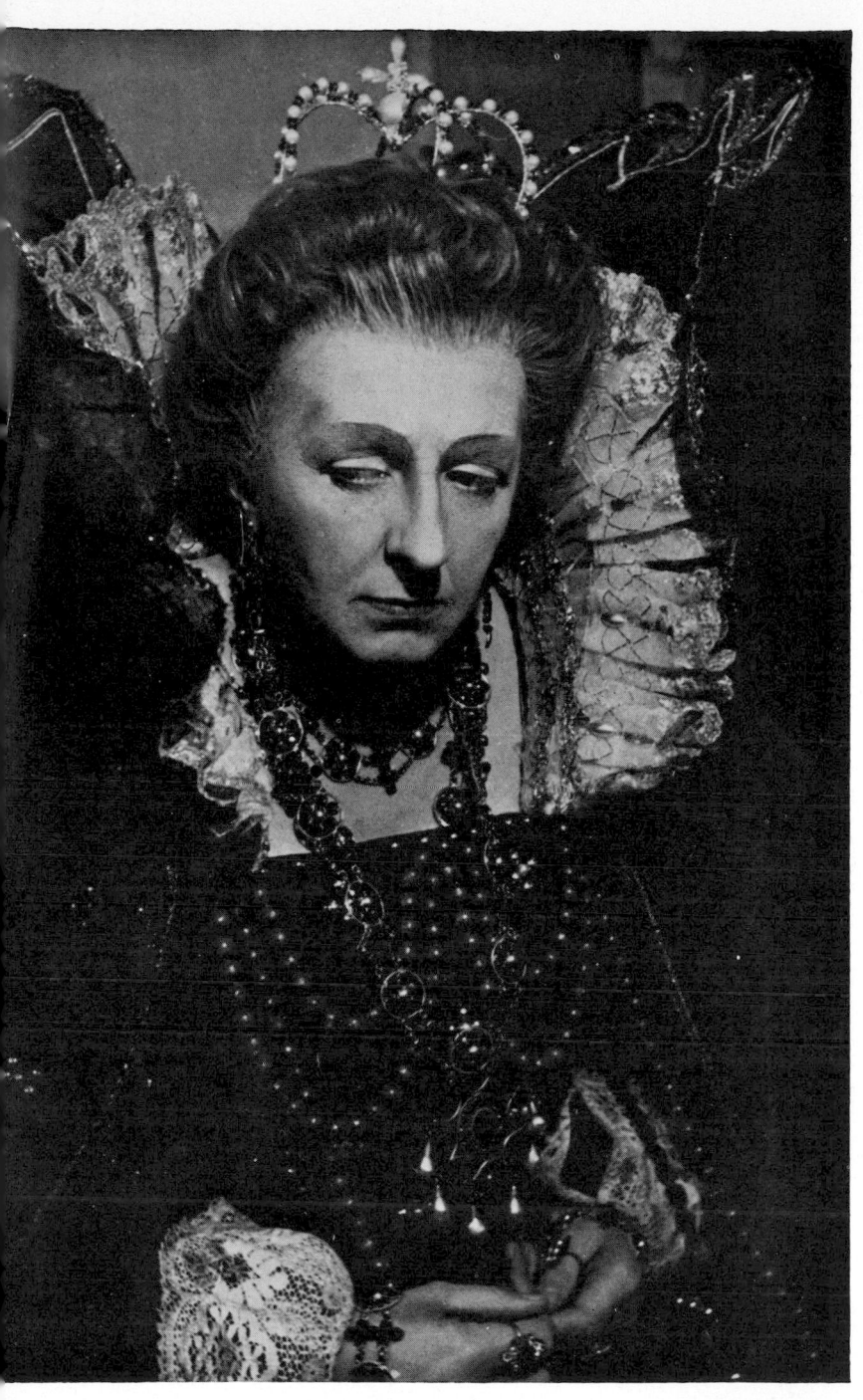

37 Joan Cross as Queen Elizabeth in *Gloriana*, 1953.

38 *Turn of the Screw*: Jennifer Vyvyan, the Governess, sees the ghost of Peter Quint (Peter Pears).

arp and double bass, playing arpeggios to his 'heavy, ʈrudging step'.[1] The Madwoman has flute, additionally flutter-tongued before her entry (Ex. 2) and later the Curlew theme (the curlew pause mark referred to above can be seen over the accompaniment's last bar), Ex. 3:

[1] Patricia Howard: *The Operas of Benjamin Britten* (Barrie and Rockliff, 1969).

The Madwoman's original motif, all fourths and sevenths, leads to an entrance scene modelled on the traditional operatic mad scene, the difference here being that *Curlew River*'s central figure starts insane and moves towards sanity rather than the more customary reverse. In her narrative aria, expression from an otherwise monotone line is achieved by means of the rising or falling of the final note by a tone or occasionally a semitone, upwards when she recalls her life or the child's loss, down when she refers to her grief.

The Parable moves through various stages of tension—notably the chorus's repeated enunciation of the Curlew River's Song of Separation, and an ensemble for Ferryman, Traveller, Chorus and flutes before the Madwoman is allowed to board the ferry—towards a climax as the Madwoman, now convinced that the grave on shore is that of her lost child whom the river people think of as a saint, prays with the travellers at the grave. Abbot and Chorus sing the hymn 'Custodes hominum' while Ferryman and Traveller pray in their turn, before, in a few phrases high in the treble (and followed by piccolo), the spirit of the boy releases his mother from her torment. At the final 'Amen' she has shed her madness, and the little drama of compassion can end as it began with the disrobing of the monks, an exhortation from the Abbot and the singing of the initial plainchant. It is a work of extraordinary tension and emotive power, which was hailed in the headline to Wilfrid Mellers's notice in the *New Statesman*,[1] punningly and appropriately, 'Britten's Yea-Play'.   H.

THE BURNING FIERY FURNACE

Parable for Church Performance by Benjamin Britten, libretto by William Plomer. Première, Aldeburgh Festival, June 9, 1966, at Orford Church, with Peter Pears, Bryan Drake, Robert Tear, Victor Godfrey, John Shirley-Quirk, Peter Leeming. First performed U.S.A., Caramoor, New York, 1967, with Andrea Velis; in Australia, at Adelaide Festival, 1970, with John Fryatt.

CHARACTERS

The Abbot, twelve Monks, five Acolytes and eight Lay Brothers who make up the cast of the Parable:

[1] July 3rd, 1964.

Nebuchadnezzar .... Tenor
The Astrologer (*Abbot*) .... Baritone
Ananias .... Baritone
Misael .... Tenor
Azarias .... Bass
The Herald and Leader of the Courtiers ...... Baritone
    Chorus of Courtiers; five attendants (treble)

Instrumentalists: Flute (doubling piccolo), Horn, Alto Trombone, Viola, Double Bass (doubling Babylonian drum), Harp, Percussion, Chamber organ (doubling small cymbals).

The story, much less esoteric than that of *Curlew River*, is drawn from the Old Testament and is concerned with the theme of steadfastness in the face of tyranny.

In sixth century B.C. Babylon, three young Israelites have been brought to the city as captives. On the advice of Daniel, they are appointed by King Nebuchadnezzar to rule over three provinces, their names changed to the Babylonian forms of Shadrach, Meshach and Abednego. When at a feast they refuse to betray the faith of their forefathers by eating and drinking with the courtiers, the Astrologer persuades the King that this is an insult to nation and faith. The Herald announces that all must bow down to a great golden image of the Babylonian god Merodak when the royal music sounds, but Shadrach, Meshach and Abednego refuse to worship. At Nebuchadnezzar's command, a furnace is prepared for their execution and they are thrown in, only for an angel to join them in the furnace, whose heat their faith successfully defies. When they reappear untouched by the fire, Nebuchadnezzar repudiates the Astrologer and is converted to their faith.

Instrumentation remains the same as in *Curlew River* except that alto trombone is added to the eight players of the first Church Parable. Once again, plainchant (the Advent sequence, 'Salus aeterna') provides the musical basis of the work, this time with a wider intervalic range than before, Ex. 1:

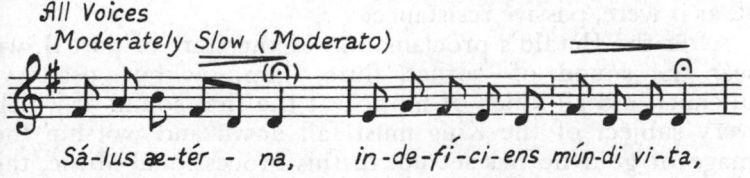

All Voices
Moderately Slow (*Moderato*)

Sá-lus æ-tér - na, in-de-fí-ci-ens mún-di ví-ta,

and is followed as in *Curlew River* by instrumental hetero-
phony (more Eastern-sounding than in *Curlew River*, and to
my ears Indian rather than Japanese) as the processing monks
robe for the drama. This is in two parts, each introduced by
an important announcement by the Herald. In the first part,
the main episode is the King's Feast; and in part II come the
Processional March and Hymn to Merodak, and the Furnace
and Conversion of the King.

Instrumental characteristics are associated with the Herald,
alto trombone; and with Nebuchadnezzar (and his *alter ego*,
the Astrologer—a role taken by the Abbot), flutter-tongued
flute over harp and horn with chords on double bass and
viola, Ex. 2:

Ananias, Misael and Azarias are more directly identified with
the plainchant theme than the Babylonians, who are characterised at the Abbot's first pronouncement, Ex. 3:

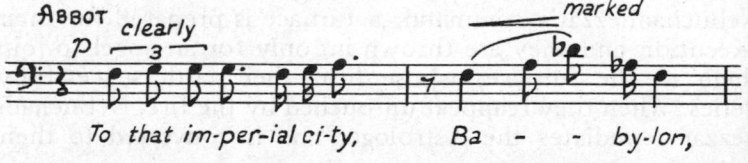

The Feast itself is distinguished by an Entertainment given
by three boys, two singers and a tumbler, the music deliberately in that simpler style regularly adopted by Britten in his
writing, dramatic or otherwise, for children's voices, the
words in the form of riddles, or at least question and answer.
By the end of the Feast, Shadrach, Meshach and Abednego
are isolated and in a touching scene reiterate their position
of, as it were, passive resistance.

After the Herald's proclamation at the start of part II, we
hear the sound of 'cornet, flute, harp, sackbut, psaltery,
dulcimer and all kinds of music', at the first sound of which
every subject of the King must fall down and worship the
image of gold he has set up. In this Processional Music, the

ight instruments have eight key phrases which they combine
.n ten different 'verses' of the march to astonishingly varied
effect, after which comes the Hymn to Merodak, god of the
Babylonians, already with its slurs suggested by the Herald
when he first mentions the Feast, and later by Nebuchadnezzar and the Astrologer before the isolation of the three in
part I, Ex. 4:

The final episode is that of the Furnace, with the solvent
of the Benedicite,[1] sung by the three with the addition of a
solo treble voice to symbolise the Angel of the Lord and
recalling the treble sound of the Spirit of the Boy in *Curlew
River*. Nebuchadnezzar's conversion comes as it were during a
pause in the psalm, to which he later joins his voice.   H.

THE PRODIGAL SON

Parable for Church Performance by Benjamin Britten, libretto by
William Plomer. Première, Aldeburgh Festival, June 10, 1968, at Orford
Church, with Peter Pears, John Shirley-Quirk, Bryan Drake, Robert
Tear. First performed in U.S.A., Caramoor, New York, 1969, with
Andrea Velis; Australia, Adelaide Festival, 1970, with Peter Pears.

CHARACTERS
The Abbot, eleven Monks, five Acolytes, eight Lay
    Brothers who make up the cast of the Parable:
Tempter (*Abbot*) . . . . .Tenor
Father . . . . .Bass Baritone
Elder Son . . . . .Baritone
Younger Son . . . . .Tenor
    Chorus of Servants, Parasites and Beggars;
    young Servants and distant voices (trebles)

[1] Also set in the first scene of *Peter Grimes*'s Act II and parodied in
The Turn of the Screw.

Instrumentalists: Alto flute (doubling piccolo), Trumpet (in D)
Horn, Viola, Double Bass, Harp, Chamber organ, Percussion.

The story of the Prodigal Son, with its emphasis on
repentance and forgiveness, is one of the best known and
most beautiful of all New Testament stories, and it appropriately furnishes out the trio of Noh play, Old Testament
legend and Christian parable which make up Britten's Triptych.

A family consisting of Father, Elder Son, Younger Son and
their Servants, lives by the fruit of its toil on the land. When
the Elder Son and the men go off to work in the fields, the
Younger Son hears a voice tempting him to unknown
delights, his 'most secret longings'. He asks for and obtains
his inheritance, but in the city, Parasites remove it from him
and he is left penniless and alone. He joins some Beggars,
shares the food of swine, and determines to return home to
ask his father's forgiveness. He is received with rejoicing,
orders are given that the fatted calf be killed, and even the
envious Elder Son is finally reconciled to the restored
situation.

The ground plan of *The Prodigal Son* is on lines made
familiar by the other Church Parables, starting with a plainchant theme, the Prime Office hymn, Ex. 1:

As the characteristic tone colour of *Curlew River* comes from
solo flute, associated with its principal character, so does that
of *The Burning Fiery Furnace* from alto trombone, and of
The Prodigal Son from trumpet and viola (alto flute,
doubling piccolo, and trumpet replace *The Burning Fiery
Furnace*'s flute and alto trombone). Alto flute is associated
with the Father, viola with the Younger Son, double bass
with the Elder Son, horn with pastoral toil and its workers.
The trumpet embodies the idea of Temptation and is therefore
frequently heard in connection with the Tempter himself.

Dramatic excitement is kindled from the moment the initial plainchant ends with the monks' 'Amen' echoed a third higher and then mocked a sixth higher as the Tempter introduces himself from the end of the nave in the garb of the as yet unseen Abbot, who in previous Church Parables has decorously, first as bass then as baritone, introduced the burden of the drama before robing to take part in it himself. Here we plunge *in medias res* from the start, and it is not until the Tempter has put forward himself and his motives that we hear with heightened effect the plainchant (Ex. 1) in heterophonic statement to accompany, as in the previous Parables, the robing of the principal characters.

'See how I break it up,' breathes Quint-like the Tempter over the idyllic family scene with which we are introduced to the drama, and this is musically speaking the liveliest character, working his wiles on the Younger Son as they walk, gourd-accompanied, towards the City of Sin in a splendid duet. With its two tenor voices, it recalls Monteverdi and Purcell in its outline just as it states Britten (and anticipates Tippett's Mel and Dov) in its melodic contours.

Choral writing is more prominent in *The Prodigal Son* than in its predecessors, and the quarter-hour sequence of the City and its temptations contains nine different choral sections as the Younger Son progresses from welcome by the Parasites to disintegration in face of the Beggars. The robe with which he was symbolically invested to represent his assumption of his inheritance is removed in sections as he loses a part of his patrimony.

Apart from perhaps the opening *arioso* statement of the Father to his Sons and Servants, the duet for Tempter and Younger Son, and the City sequence, there are no set pieces in *The Prodigal Son* to compare with those of *The Burning Fiery Furnace*, nor has this Church Parable the music or dramatic intensity of *Curlew River*, but the fact remains that there have been commentators to find it the best of the three.   H.

OWEN WINGRAVE

Opera in two acts by Benjamin Britten, libretto by Myfanwy Piper, based on the short story by Henry James. Commissioned for B.B.C. Television and first shown May 16, 1971, with Heather Harper, Jennifer Vyvyan, Sylvia Fisher, Janet Baker, Peter Pears, Nigel Douglas,

Benjamin Luxon, John Shirley-Quirk, conductor Britten. Stage première, Covent Garden, May 10, 1973, with the same cast apart from Janice Chapman as Mrs. Julian and Steuart Bedford conducting. First performed Santa Fé, 1973.

CHARACTERS

Owen Wingrave, *the last of the Wingraves* . . . . . Baritone
Spencer Coyle, *head of a military*
   cramming establishment . . . . Bass-Baritone
Lechmere, *a young student of Coyle's* . . . . Tenor
Miss Wingrave, *Owen's aunt* . . . . Soprano
Mrs. Coyle . . . . Soprano
Mrs. Julian, *a widow and dependant*
   at Paramore . . . . Soprano
Kate, *her daughter* . . . . Mezzo-Soprano
General Sir Philip Wingrave, *Owen's grandfather* . Tenor
Narrator, *the Ballad Singer* . . . . Tenor
Distant Chorus . . . . Trebles
Time: Late Nineteenth Century   *Place:* London; Paramore

Owen Wingrave was written for television, a fact which may have spurred the composer's creative dexterity, not least in transitional techniques already adumbrated in his earlier operas, but which should be taken to imply neither that it is unsuitable for stage nor that it makes very specific use of television techniques. When it was first mounted on the stage, in the large theatre of Covent Garden, one's regrets were not at all that the work had been transferred from one medium to another but rather that it should ideally have been in a different, smaller theatre—say, Glyndebourne or Sadler's Wells in Rosebery Avenue. Britten and Myfanwy Piper have together returned to Henry James for their subject (as with *The Turn of the Screw*), and the theme is the effort of the young scion of the military house of Wingrave to escape from the tyranny of the past and his family's warlike tradition and, more specifically, to make it possible for his pacifist conscience to prevail over the military instincts of his family. In a sense he wins, but at a cost.

The prelude to the opera consists of a dozen bars marked *marziale*, and ten instrumental 'portraits' of ten military forebears of Owen. Here is 'the sense of the past', as Henry James puts it, and in these few minutes Britten has set out the musical material of the opera. In the *marziale* section we

are introduced to a rhythmic idea, which later gives rise to
very many others in the course of the opera, and is always
associated with the percussion; Donald Mitchell, in his commentary accompanying the gramophone recording, has described it as 'this unforgettable pulsation, which is the heart-
beat of the opera'. In bar 4 of the *marziale* section occurs
Owen's theme which eventually provides the eleventh of the
portraits, Ex. 1:

The other ten 'portraits', each intended to go with a visual
realisation of some member of the family, constitute a great
orchestral cadenza, and are associated successively with
bassoon; oboe; horn; clarinet; trombone and piccolo (Colonel

and Boy); trumpet; woodwind; trombone; woodwind; all
wind (Owen's father).

Scene i, in the study at Mr. Coyle's military establishment.
Discussion between Mr. Coyle and his pupils, Owen Wingrave
and Lechmere, is initially accompanied by consolatory and
flowing triplets, but mention of casualties brings a bitter
reaction from Owen. With the triplets beneath the voice parts
again, Coyle refers to the conduct of war as a science while
Owen is inclined to condemn everyone who takes part in it.
Left alone with Coyle, Owen confesses that he cannot go
through with his military studies; he despises a soldier's life.
This is too much for Coyle who finishes the scene wondering
how he is either to set Owen's mind to rights or else contrive
to intercede with Miss Wingrave on his behalf.

The interlude is based on the *marziale* of the start as
regimental banners wave brilliantly to instrumental cadenzas,
most notably a dialogue for two trumpets.

The second scene has Owen in Hyde Park, Miss Wingrave
and Coyle in her London lodgings. There is cross-cutting
between the two scenes as Owen reiterates his determination
not to follow in his forefathers' footsteps, Miss Wingrave hers
that tradition shall be upheld. To one of the most positive of
the percussion rhythms of the opera, Owen is impressed by
the beauty of the Horse Guards trotting by, Miss Wingrave by
the military glory they represent. Coyle tries to persuade her
that Owen's is not a childish fancy, but she decides that he
shall be straightened out at Paramore.

The second interlude is subtitled 'A Sequence of Old,
Faded, Tattered Flags', and Owen recites from Shelley's
'Queen Mab' mostly to the accompaniment of solo instru-
ments.

The third scene finds Mr. and Mrs. Coyle at home drinking
sherry with Lechmere. The three discuss the predicament
Owen's decision seems to face them all with. Lechmere's
offer to 'tell him it's a shame'—or more particularly the last
word he uses—provokes a miniature ensemble, one of many
in the course of this opera which contrive to define the
attitudes of more than one character, bring the scene to a
musical climax and lead into the next episode within the
space of a few seconds; this one lasts 44 seconds. The
moment it is over Owen joins them and reiterates his
determination not to change his mind. He plainly dreads
facing his family and admits as much to Lechmere when the
others have gone out.

The third interlude is concerned with Paramore, musically a variation of Owen's theme punctuated with staccato muted trumpet semiquavers. The remainder of the act plays at Paramore.

Scene iv introduces us to Kate and Mrs. Julian, friends and dependants of the Wingraves who live at Paramore (Kate's uncle was Miss Wingrave's lover in the long distant past). They bemoan the latest turn of events, but both believe Owen will 'listen to the house', as does Miss Wingrave when she appears later.

Owen returns to the very reverse of a hero's welcome, Mrs. Julian resistant, Kate positively hostile, and the scene ends as Miss Wingrave ushers him peremptorily towards his grandfather's room, where he is received with a cry of 'Sirrah! how dare you'.

Scene v. In four bars of music and to reiterated cries from the family of 'How dare you!' a week passes. They accuse him of rejecting the family's tradition and insulting not only the memory of his ancestors but everyone present as well. It is the most extended ensemble of the opera and ends as it began with cries of 'How dare you!'

Mr. and Mrs. Coyle have arrived at Paramore and find the atmosphere eerie, the family gruesome. At mention of the possibility of the house being haunted, we hear the first adumbration of the Ballad theme (Ex. 2). Owen tries to welcome them nonchalantly, but Coyle admits he has come down to make one last attempt at persuading Owen to conform.

The seventh scene is preceded by an interlude as dinner is prepared, and consists of the family dinner party. Small talk continually threatens to grow and is at best uncomfortable. As the dishes are cleared, each character in turn betrays his or her thoughts, in close-up as it were and in characteristic music (the nearest to a use of specifically television technique in the opera). After a particularly barbed comment from Sir Philip, Mrs. Coyle is left pleading 'Ah! Sir Philip, Owen has his scruples'. A brilliant *scherzando* ensemble on this final word ensues for the family, and it goads Owen to the final insult: 'I'd make it a crime to draw your sword for your country, and a crime for governments to command it'. Sir Philip hobbles out in a fury and the Ballad theme (Ex. 2) is again heard in the orchestra (on the horn), a symbol no doubt of the inevitable clash between the head of the family and its rebellious son.

Act II.   The stage directions of the Prologue: 'A ballad-singer is heard alternating with the distant chorus and trumpet. The verses of the ballad are illustrated by the actions in slow motion.' The haunting melody, Ex. 2:

lies literally and figuratively at the heart of the work and the narrator tells the story of the young Wingrave from the past who, challenged by his friend at school to fight, refused, and was accused of cowardice by his father, only later to be struck down to his death in an upstairs room at Paramore. (The narrator, a tenor like Sir Philip, was in the original production[1] sung by the same singer.) A chorus of trebles sings a variation of Owen's motif (Ex. 1), and accompaniment

[1] And as in *The Turn of the Screw*.

is confined to solo trumpet until just before Owen's voice joins that of the narrator. Lechmere is walking below with the ladies and Owen contrives again to offend Kate; Mrs. Coyle pleads with her for patience, tolerance and trust, only to be rejected with some acerbity.

Suddenly Sir Philip shuffles out of his room and demands to see his grandson, whom he refers to as the traitor. Owen follows him in and the door is shut, but the drift of the interview can be heard outside and it is no surprise when Owen re-appears to say that he has been disinherited.

Mrs. Julian breaks down sobbing at this shattering blow to her hopes. Lechmere instinctively starts to make up to Kate, who plays up to him, to the indignation of the Coyles. He would do anything to prove his worth to Kate, even sleep in the haunted room! Miss Wingrave ushers them all to bed and refers to Owen in his presence as if he did not exist. Coyle as always tries to put the best face on things, consoling Mrs. Julian and making a special effort with Owen.

Owen is left alone. He turns away from the portraits and in what Donald Mitchell calls the climax of the opera, 'a radiant ecstatic avowal which surely foresees a peace a good deal more profound than the absence of war', sings, 'In peace I have found my image, I have found myself'. Percussion, associated so far with the symbols of war (the *marziale* of the opening), provides a quaver accompaniment into which are dropped what Mitchell calls 'chords of affirmation'.[1] Suddenly he sees the ghosts of the old man and the boy slowly walk up the stairs and for a moment he thinks his rejection by the family has in some way expiated all sins of the past. He sinks into a chair in the shadows.

Kate appears thinking she is alone and sings sadly of what might have been. It is the first sign of her affection for Owen and their encounter quickens into a duet as they remember innumerable shared impressions of the past. But Kate will not change to please Owen, and they start to wrangle, a quarrel culminating in Owen's rating her for flirting with Lechmere. Kate accuses him of being a coward, and demands he prove his courage by sleeping in the haunted room. There is a moment of stridency from the orchestra as, at Owen's injunction, she turns the key behind him in the lock of the

[1] Apart from the chordal association with *Billy Budd*, Donald Mitchell sees, rightly I think, a musical parallel with the quicker section of Billy's aria, following the passage known as 'Billy in the Darbies'.

haunted room, before the scene changes to the Coyles' bedroom later that evening.

Coyle tries to reassure his wife, who is full of indignation about Kate, but an hour later (only a few bars of music) she is still not asleep, and later still Lechmere knocks at the door saying he knows of Kate's 'dare' and is worried at its possible consequences for Owen. As they are about to go off to investigate, they hear Kate's agonised cry from the distance, 'Ah, Owen, Owen, you've gone!'. It might be the Governess with the dead Miles, it might even be Berlioz's Dido, but with her assumption of full responsibility she reaches toward tragic stature, as Sir Philip himself pushes open the door to disclose Owen lying dead on the floor. With a last *piano* reference to the ballad (narrator and chorus) the opera comes to an end.   H.

DEATH IN VENICE

Opera in two acts by Benjamin Britten, libretto by Myfanwy Piper after the story by Thomas Mann. Première at the Maltings during Aldeburgh Festival, June 16, 1973, with Peter Pears, John Shirley-Quirk, James Bowman, conductor Steuart Bedford, producer Colin Graham. First performed Covent Garden, 1973, and Metropolitan, New York, 1974, with same cast.

CHARACTERS

Gustav von Aschenbach, *a novelist* . . . . Tenor
The Traveller
The Elderly Fop
The Old Gondolier
The Hotel Manager   } . . . . Baritone
The Hotel Barber
The Leader of the Players
Dionysus
Voice of Apollo. . . . . Counter Tenor
The Polish Mother . . . . Dancer
Tadzio, *her son* . . . . Dancer
Her two Daughters . . . . Dancers
Their Governess . . . . Dancer
Jaschiu, *Tadzio's friend* . . . . Dancer
Hotel Porter . . . . Tenor

Lido Boatman .... Baritone
Hotel Waiter .... Baritone
Strawberry-seller .... Soprano
Guide .... Baritone
Glass-maker .... Tenor
Lace-seller .... Soprano
Beggar-woman .... Mezzo-Soprano
Newspaper-seller .... Soprano
Strolling Players .... Soprano, Tenor
English Clerk at the travel bureau .... Baritone
Two Acrobats .... Dancers
Russian Mother and Father .... Soprano, Bass
Russian Nanny .... Soprano
German Mother .... Mezzo-Soprano
Gondoliers .... Tenor, Baritone
Time: 1911   *Place:* Munich; Venice, and the Lido

After Shakespeare, Melville and two stories by Henry
James, Britten turned his attention to Thomas Mann, tackling
in *Death in Venice* what is in most ways a more intractable
problem precisely because Mann's story concerns itself so
unremittingly with the thoughts, aspirations and worries of a
single man. Britten and Myfanwy Piper have solved the problem
by making Aschenbach himself, the successful writer at the
centre of the story, serve additionally as narrator, so that his
monologues provide something of the detached, ironic
comment which is a feature of Mann's story. In place of the
nuances and cumulative impact of Mann's writing—inevitably
(and rightly) omitted from the libretto—Britten, wrote Peter
Evans in *Opera*[1] before the Aldeburgh première, 'offers ...
characteristic refinements of musical detail and a motivic
chain, more complex yet less obtrusive than in his previous
operas, that makes of the whole work his most sustained
study of festering obsession.'

Aschenbach is a solitary, and opposite him are ranged two
groups of characters. The main function of one group is to
propel Aschenbach towards his predestined end: Traveller,
Elderly Fop, Old Gondolier, Hotel Manager, Hotel Barber,
Leader of the Players, off-stage voice of Dionysus. They are
all played by the same baritone singer and they share the
same musical material, much of it related to Ex. 3. The

[1] *Opera*, June 1973.

function of the other group is to lure him towards self-destruction, towards the Dionysian upsetting of his Apollonian (and therefore classical) balance. This group, headed by Tadzio and his mother but including also the other children who play on the beach, are represented by dancers. Not only does this add the dimension of ballet and mime[1] to the opera's central means of expression (as opposed to using ballet as decoration or *divertissement*) but it emphasises the inability of Aschenbach to speak to Tadzio, the impossibility he, the most articulate of men, finds in formulating words for his thoughts, his basic failure in fact to communicate.

As Tadzio, his family and his companions are distinguished from the other dramatic characters by being danced and mimed rather than sung, so is the music associated with them generically different in that it is given to percussion. Tadzio's theme in fact is derived from the sounds of the Gamelan orchestra, a sound Britten used extensively years previously in his ballet *The Prince of the Pagodas* (1956), Ex. 1:

Its haunting, liquid A major (the key associated with Tadzio) suggests that it stands for the effect Tadzio has on Aschenbach[2] rather than for the healthy, vigorous youth himself, and it remains static throughout the opera, as does the beauty of Tadzio. The percussion music in *Death in Venice* embodies and symbolises everything strange, everything alien to Aschenbach's well ordered, rational world.

Aschenbach in contrast develops and changes musically just as he does morally and physically, and a number of themes are associated with him and his vision of his surroundings—the whole story in fact is seen through his eyes, in the same sort of way as a psycho-analyst sees events through the mind of his patient. Exx. 3 and 5 (and to a lesser extent Ex. 4a) are prominent exponents of Aschenbach's

[1] For the composer, a development of methods employed in the Church Parables.

[2] There is some kinship with Quint's celesta theme in *The Turn of the Screw*.

state of mind, changing as they do in the course of the action to show the changes within the mind of the central figure. Ex. 3, for example, starts as the purest of diatonic scales, but by the end of Act I, distorted and dissonantly thickened, accompanies that moment of self-knowledge when his cry of 'I love you' brings him to his own particular key of E major.

Act I, scene i. Munich. Aschenbach muses on his inability to work: 'My mind beats on . . .'; 'I . . . famous as a master-writer . . . self-discipline my strength, routine the order of my days', at a loss—literally—for words. Near the entrance to a cemetery, he is confronted by a Traveller, whose presence as much as his words conjure up an image, Ex. 2:

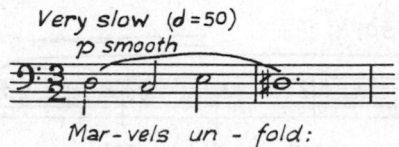

so that Aschenbach obeys his injunction 'Go, travel to the South'. Varied and played usually on tuba, this theme later symbolises the physical plague which itself parallels the canker eating into Aschenbach's mind.

For the first time are heard the urgent yet unworried scales of Ex. 3:

and it is not long before Aschenbach embarks on the first of several monologues in which he comments on the course of events and the motives which have led him to his current position. These piano-accompanied, prose monologues are a major feature of the score, with the singer's pitch indicated for him, but the duration of the notes and the 'shaping' of the phrases left to his imagination and discretion. As the orchestra breaks in, the music becomes more traditionally notated.

Scene ii: On the boat to Venice, youths shout to their girlfriends on shore (quiet chorus of 'Serenissima' underneath the banter), Ex. 4:

and are joined by an Elderly Fop, who has frequent recourse to a mincing falsetto and leads a vigorous song about the possibilities of life in Venice. He breaks off for an ironic greeting to Aschenbach ('Bound for Serenissima, I'm sure'), but Aschenbach finds him repulsive and starts to wonder why he ever decided to come to Venice (Ex. 4 in chorus and Ex. 3 in orchestra below his voice line).

An instrumental overture (Venice), marked *Lazily*, derived from Ex. 4 and consisting of barcarole-like gondola music of some tenderness (Ex. 4a):

(it even partly recalls the Lullaby in Act II of *Lucretia*)
precedes scene iii, the journey to the Lido. Aschenbach, by
now looking forward to his stay, is rowed against his will
(Ex. 4a) by the Old Gondolier to his hotel on the Lido (Ex. 4
in distant chorus). There he is greeted by a Boatman and the
Hotel Porter, but he finds when he turns to pay that the Old
Gondolier has disappeared. He recognises the black gondola
as a harbinger of death.

Scene iv. The first evening at the hotel. Aschenbach is
welcomed by the Hotel Manager, then shown his room with a
comment on the splendour of the view—to a typically
expansive Britten phrase, Ex. 5:

Aschenbach soliloquises on the prospect before him in
Venice (with Ex. 5 and its variants very much in evidence),
then watches the hotel guests assemble for dinner, discussing

the day's experiences in a variety of languages. Aschenbach sees the Polish family enter (Ex. 1 heard for the first time in the opera)—Governess, two girls and Tadzio—and comments on Tadzio: 'Surely the soul of Greece lies in that bright perfection, a golden look ... mortal child with more than mortal grace.' When the Polish family goes in to dinner, Aschenbach in a further monologue reflects on the relationship of form and content, on the discipline of the family and its beauty, and concludes, 'There is indeed in every artist's nature a wanton and treacherous proneness to side with beauty.'

Scene v. On the beach (Ex. 5). Aschenbach is not at his ease, but watches the children playing (rhythmical percussion). He buys fruit from a strawberry-seller, then decides that in spite of his misgivings he will stay by the sea. He watches Tadzio coming along the beach (Ex. 1), approves as Tadzio mimes dislike of the Russian family, listens as voices apparently call 'Adziù' from the distance (Ex. 5 varied), but finally catches the boy's true name as he continues in monologue to admire his grace and beauty.

Scene vi. The foiled departure. On a visit to the city (Ex. 4a), importunate guides, street-vendors and beggars together with the discomfort he feels from the sirocco prompt Aschenbach to leave Venice. He returns to the hotel (Ex. 4a) where the Manager remains courteous and understanding, but the sight of Tadzio crossing the lobby (Ex. 1) impels second thoughts on the way to the station (Ex. 4a), which are confirmed when he discovers his luggage has been put by mistake on the train to Como. He will return to the Lido (Ex. 4a) and his luggage must be sent to him there! 'I am become like one of my early heroes, passive in the face of fate' is the burden of his monologue. He is greeted by the Hotel Manager with the news that the wind is now from a healthier quarter, from the East in fact, and when he looks out of his window (Ex. 5) he sees Tadzio and the others playing on the beach. He begins to understand his relief at the foiled departure: 'Here I will stay, here dedicate my days to the sun and Apollo himself.'

Scene vii. The games of Apollo. Aschenbach from his chair allows his fancy to play with thoughts of ancient Greece. He seems to hear the voice of Apollo, in imagination turns the children's beach games into some sort of Olympiad with Tadzio crowned victor of the pentathlon. The music is a

series of choral dances, percussion-accompanied, linked by
the off-stage counter-tenor Voice of Apollo and coloured
(said Donald Mitchell, Britten's publisher, in an introduction
to the opera's first broadcast) by a fragment of an ancient
Greek hymn. Competitive running, long jump, discus, javelin-
throwing and wrestling leave Tadzio the winner, and
Aschenbach, after his impressive Hymn to Apollo (founded
on Ex. 1), with the realisation that through Tadzio he may
find inspiration to write again. At the very end, he tries
vainly to congratulate the winner of the games, Tadzio smiles
at him as he passes on his way to the hotel and Aschenbach
falls helplessly back on what he thinks of later as the supreme
cliché: 'I love you' (preceded by a distorted version of Ex. 3).

Act II sees an end of joy and the start of the process of
destruction through corruption to which Aschenbach is
inevitably committed. A slow orchestral introduction leads us
to Aschenbach, who has been writing but is hardly less
scornful of his inability to communicate with Tadzio than he
is of his guilty feelings for the boy. Nevertheless, he must
accept the situation.

Scene viii.   The Hotel Barber's shop (i). From the professional patter of the Barber, Aschenbach picks up a reference
to 'the sickness', which the Barber promptly plays down.

Scene ix.   The Pursuit. On his way to Venice (Ex. 4a),
Aschenbach starts to worry and subsequent events tend to
confirm his fears: the city is too quiet, people are reading
notices advising against eating shellfish, there is a smell of
disinfectant in the air, the German newspapers talk of
'rumours of cholera in Venice officially denied' (Ex. 4); and
yet, when he sees the Polish family, his one thought is to
keep the rumours from them in case they decide to leave
Venice. Here the Tadzio theme (Ex. 1) is conflated on the
top line, while beneath it can be seen and heard the yearning
theme (in crotchets) and at the bottom on the tuba (Ex. 2), in
the form in which it is connected with the plague, Ex. 6:

Restless ($\downarrow$=80)

Tuba, Db.

Aschenbach follows the Poles, sits near them in a café (café music), watches them pray in St. Mark's and comes to realise that Tadzio is conscious of his nearness. Suddenly he meets them face to face, raises his hat and turns away: 'O the joy I suffer!' He follows them back to the hotel (Ex. 4), then tries in soliloquy to justify his infatuation by reference to Greek examples.

Scene x.   The Strolling Players. Outside the hotel after dinner, a group of performers sing and dance, and their Leader sings a ditty before going round with his hat collecting from the guests. Aschenbach tries to pump him about the plague but he makes light of the whole affair and starts a laughing song before leading the players off.

Scene xi.   The Travel Bureau. A young English clerk is attempting to cope with a crowd of hotel guests frantically seeking reservations to leave the city. To Aschenbach, when they have left, he admits that Asiatic cholera has spread from India and was diagnosed in Venice earlier that year. The authorities deny it—but his advice is that Aschenbach should leave.

Scene xii.   The Lady of the Pearls. Aschenbach decides he must warn Tadzio's mother, the Lady of the Pearls, but, when she appears, he goes towards her, then turns into his room. He cannot understand himself, begins to wonder, 'what *is* self-possession? What is reason, moral sense? What is art itself compared to the rewards of chaos? . . . What if all were dead, and only we two left alive'. He sleeps.

Scene xiii.   The dream. He hears (Ex. 3) the Voices of Dionysus and Apollo and tries to reject the former's advice to 'stumble in the reeling dance', but finally in dream participates in a Dionysian orgy (Ex. 1 distorted and Ex. 2 in the orchestra). Awake, he is resigned to his fall: 'let the Gods do what they will with me'.

Scene xiv.   The empty beach. Tadzio and a few friends are playing on the nearly deserted beach, watched by Aschenbach.

Scene xv.   The Hotel Barber's shop (ii). Aschenbach in a frenzied search for youth allows his grey hair to be tinted, his cheeks rouged, not without ironical recall of the Elderly Fop of Scene ii.

Scene xvi.   The last visit to Venice. Aschenbach, in what the libretto describes as 'his new appearance', goes by gondola to Venice (Ex. 4), follows the Polish family, sees

Tadzio detach himself from his family and look full at him,
then turns away. He buys some fruit from a strawberry-seller,
finds it musty and over-ripe, and starts to take stock of his
situation. In spite of illness, his mind is clarity itself, and, in
the most sustained lyrical section of the opera, he recalls the
Socratic dilemma of the poet who perceives beauty only
through the senses: 'Does beauty lead to wisdom, Phaedrus?',
an inspired passage drawing on the reserves of the Donne
Sonnets and *Abraham and Isaac* from more than twenty years
before. I doubt if Britten set out to prove that the strands of
a drama can be drawn together and the work so revealed in a
cantilena melody with only a characteristic rhythmical snap
at the end of key lines, but in the event he did so.

Scene xvii. The departure (preceded by Ex. 5 as postlude
to the previous scene). Hotel Manager and Porter discuss the
weather and the departing guests, and it appears that the
Lady of the Pearls and her party are leaving. Aschenbach
comes in wearily and goes to the beach (Ex. 5 diminished so
that no exuberance or expansion is left in it). He watches
Tadzio and his friends playing at first listlessly, then more
roughly, until Tadzio's face is pressed into the sand. The
children cry out and run off, Aschenbach starts to protest,
but hears distant cries of 'Adziù' and is only able to answer
them gently with 'Tadzio' before slumping dead in his chair
(Ex. 1) as Tadzio walks slowly away. The final 20-bar
orchestral comment provides Aschenbach's threnody, with
Ex. 1 in percussion still plaintively, seductively, above the
orchestral comment. H.

19
Czech Opera

LEOŠ JANÁČEK
(1854–1928)

JEJÍ PASTORKYŇA
(JENŮFA)
Her Stepdaughter

OPERA in three acts by Leoš Janáček, text by the composer founded on a story by Gabriella Preissová. Première, Brno, January 21, 1904, with Marie Kabeláčová, Leopolda Svobodová, Staněk-Doubravský, Procházka; it was Janáček's first performed opera and scored a considerable local success. First performed Prague, 1916, with Ungrová, Horvátová, Schütz, Lebeda, when it immediately became a popular favourite. Translated into German by Max Brod (from whose version most other translations have been taken), and performed Vienna, 1918; Cologne, 1918; Berlin, 1924, with Jurjewskaya, Ober, Soot, Jöken, conductor Kleiber; Metropolitan, New York, 1924, with Jeritza, Matzenauer, Oehmann, Laubenthal, conductor Bodanzky; Venice, 1941, with Cigna; Stockholm, 1941, with Herzberg, Wettergren, Beyron, Svanholm; Berlin, 1942, with Müller, Marta Fuchs, Argyris, Anders; Vienna, 1948, with Welitsch, Helena Braun, Patzak, Treptow; Holland Festival, 1951, with Brouwenstijn, Vroons; Buenos Aires, 1951, with Lemnitz, Fischer, Ludwig, Fehenberger; Rome, 1952, with Caleva, Pederzini, Sinimberghi, Bergonzi; London, Covent Garden, 1956, with Shuard, Fisher, conductor Kubelik; Chicago, 1959, with Brouwenstijn, Fisher, Cassilly, Charlebois, conductor von Matacic; Vienna, 1964, with Jurinac, Höngen, Kmentt, Cox, conductor Krombholc; Edinburgh Festival, 1974, in Swedish Opera production by Götz Friedrich, with Söderström, Kjerstin Meyer, Höiseth, Johnny Blanc

CHARACTERS

Grandmother Buryja, *owner of the mill* . . . . . Contralto
Laca Klemeň ⎰ *stepbrothers, grandsons of* ⎱ . . . Tenors
Števa Buryja ⎱ *Grandmother Buryja* ⎰

1542

Kostelnička Buryjovka .... Soprano
Jenůfa, *her stepdaughter* .... Soprano
Foreman at the Mill .... Baritone
Mayor of the Village .... Bass
His Wife .... Mezzo-Soprano
Karolka, *his daughter* .... Mezzo-Soprano
A Maid .... Mezzo-Soprano
Barena, *servant at the mill* .... Soprano
Jano, *shepherd boy* .... Soprano
Aunt................................ Contralto

Musicians, Village People

Jenůfa, to give the opera the name by which it is known abroad, was the composer's first success, earned at the age of 50, and in the natural course of events it should have been given immediately in Prague. Unfortunately, some years earlier, Janáček had written woundingly about a composition by Karel Kovařovic, and Kovařovic was now head of the opera in Prague. He put off hearing the new work, and it was only after extraordinary efforts by the composer's friends and admirers that twelve years later he accepted *Jenůfa* for Prague, and then only with the stipulation that he should 'edit' the work. The editing consisted of some re-orchestration and a large number of small cuts, often only of a bar or two, but for this edition Kovařovic received a royalty and his widow after him. The opera triumphed nonetheless in Prague and 18 months later in Vienna, the latter a rather extraordinary success considering that Czechoslovakia had just declared its independence of the Austrian Empire.

Long before the opera begins, Grandmother Buryja has had two sons, each of them dead before the action starts. The elder, who owned the family mill, married the widow Klemeň, who already had a son Laca. Together she and the Miller had another son Števa, who is of course heir to his father and grandmother. The second son, Toma, had by his first wife a daughter named Jenůfa; after the death of Jenůfa's mother, he married Kostelnička (which means 'wife to the sexton').

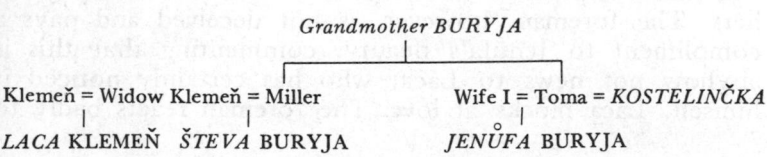

Act I.   A lonely mill in the mountains. Jenůfa, a pot of
rosemary in her arms, stands by the stream looking into the
distance. Old Grandmother Buryja sits in front of the mill
peeling potatoes. Laca is near her, shaping a whip-handle with
his knife. It is late afternoon. The prelude (in 6/4 time) has
running through it the tinkling sound of the mill at work
(xylophone). Jenůfa laments that Števa has not yet returned,
and wonders despairingly whether he has been taken as a
soldier by the recruiting officer. She is in love with him—in
fact, carries his child within her—and her heart will break if
he leaves her.

Laca makes sarcastic reference to his place in the household; he is only worth his food and lodging in return for the
work he can do, and Števa has always been the idol of old
Grandmother Buryja. At this point the orchestra shows the
pity for the foibles and misfortunes of his characters which is
one of Janáček's strongest and most lovable qualities and which
pervades his operas, but Laca's vocal line remains uncompromisingly bitter, and Jenůfa reproaches him for the way in
which he speaks to the old woman. Grandmother Buryja
affirms that she is mistress in her own house without respect
of kinship, but Laca wonders aloud what would be Jenůfa's
reaction if Števa were taken for the army. She is dismayed at
how he seems able to read her feelings, and tries to cover up
her embarrassment by assuring her grandmother she will
finish the housework.

Jano, the shepherd boy, is heard calling happily from the
mill. A new sense of joy comes into the music as he
announces that he really can read now. Jenůfa seems as
pleased as he, and, after he has run off, Grandmother Buryja
observes that Jenůfa is as much the teacher at heart as her
stepmother.

The foreman of the mill comes on to the scene, and asks
Laca what he is working at. A whip-handle—but his knife is
blunt, says Laca, and gives it to be ground (the xylophone is
heard again in the orchestra). Laca and Jenůfa quarrel for a
moment, and Laca taunts her with her love for Števa. She
goes off, and Laca remarks bitterly to the foreman that she
will make a splendid sister-in-law with those sweet ways of
hers. The foreman, however, is not deceived and pays a
compliment to Jenůfa's beauty, commenting that this is
anyhow not news to Laca, who has certainly noticed it
himself. Laca mocks at love. The foreman reacts badly to

what Laca says and warns him about his attitude towards
Jenůfa. What if Števa be taken for a soldier, says Laca; but
the foreman has heard that he has been passed over and is
free. Jenůfa and Grandmother Buryja are delighted at his
words, which they overhear, but Laca cannot conceal his
jealousy that Števa's luck should serve him even in this.
Kostelnička appears and goes into the mill, and Grandmother
Buryja suggests they follow her. Jenůfa, however, begs to be
left alone to meet Števa when he returns.

The jaunty song of the approaching recruits can be heard
in the distance, and they are followed by Števa, who is
extremely drunk. With an almost hysterical cry, Jenůfa tries
to bring Števa to his senses, but he answers crossly, boasting
of his prowess with the girls—look at the flowers he has had
from one of them—and throwing money to his companions,
whom he orders to sing and dance for the entertainment of
him and his Jenůfa. They start up a song, in which Števa
joins, and in between the verses the orchestra plays for the
dance, into which Števa drags the unwilling Jenůfa.

On the surface the scene is as gay as the dances in *The
Bartered Bride*, but Kostelnička interrupts it imperiously. She
is a formidable and authoritative—almost authoritarian—
character, and when she reads the company a lecture and
makes it apply particularly and unmistakably to her rich
nephew Števa, there is no gainsaying her. Until he can prove
that he has stopped drinking by a year of sobriety, there is to
be no more talk of a wedding with Jenůfa. Nobody tries to
contradict her, although the chorus comments that she is a
bit too severe.

Grandmother Buryja sends the musicians packing, and tells
Števa to go and sleep off his drunken condition. It is partly
the fault of his companions that he is so drunk, she says—this
causes an ironic comment from the said companions. The scene
comes to an end with a short *fugato* in which Grandmother
Buryja warns Jenůfa that life is full of sorrow, which must be
borne. In turn, she is joined by the foreman, Laca, the chorus
and finally Jenůfa herself, whose line soars up to C flat. The
xylophone makes a practical comment on the words that have
just been heard: the background to life, in this case the mill,
goes on regardless of the emotions of those in front of it.

Jenůfa and Števa are left alone, and Jenůfa pleads her love
for him and her fear that her secret should be found out. Her
music at this point is dominated by a recurrent figure:

The short phrase seems perfectly to characterise the situation: Jenůfa's confession of love and anxiety is dragged out of her, almost in spite of herself, with long pauses between phrases, yet the music never fails to convey the warmth of her nature. Števa answers crossly, and practically accuses Jenůfa and her stepmother of nagging at him, so that Jenůfa loses her patience and shakes him vigorously. Even when he partially pulls himself together, his answers have a conventional gallantry which in no way reassures Jenůfa. When Laca returns Jenůfa is alone in her misery; he makes derisive reference to Števa's hang-dog look just now when he felt the rough side of Kostelnička's tongue, but this only provokes Jenůfa to take Števa's side even more firmly than before. In a final effort to provoke some revulsion of feeling towards the lover he considers unworthy of her, Laca picks up the flowers which Števa has dropped and which were given him by some female admirer; let her pin *them* on her dress! Even this attempted insult Jenůfa accepts defiantly, for Števa's sake. Laca's comment is that Števa only looks at her because of her rosy-apple cheeks. He makes as if to embrace Jenůfa and slashes her across the cheek with the knife.

She runs into the house screaming, while Laca laments the horrible thing he has done. The servant Barena suggests that it happened accidentally, but, after Grandmother Buryja has gone to help Jenůfa, the foreman accuses Laca of having, for all his present remorse, committed the crime on purpose.

Act II is set in the living-room of Kostelnička's house. In it can be seen a big peasant stove, a bed, and furniture, and on the walls are holy pictures. A tense atmosphere is established in the music straightaway, and the curtain goes up to show Kostelnička and Jenůfa sewing, the latter's wound still visible. They are talking about Jenůfa's secret; the baby has been born, but Jenůfa has not seen his father for weeks now. Kostelnička is worried in case she has been too severe; but,

whatever her feelings for Jenůfa, she cannot find it in her
heart to forgive Števa for his behaviour. Jenůfa thinks she
hears her baby call, but she returns a moment later; he is
sleeping peacefully. Every utterance of Jenůfa's shows her joy
in her child, every one of Kostelnička's, the pride which has
been so cruelly hurt by the shame which has come to her
beloved stepchild and which has become an obsession with
her. Kostelnička gives Jenůfa a drink with a narcotic in it to
make her sleep, and Jenůfa goes into the inner room.

Kostelnička has sent for Števa. She admits to herself that
she has prayed that the child might die, but that, her prayers
being unanswered, she must steel herself to the thought of a
marriage between Jenůfa and Števa. When Števa comes, she
reproaches him for not having been to see them before; he
admits he did not even know that the child had been born.
He shrinks from going in to see Jenůfa and his son, and seems
half remorseful for what he has done to her, half resentful
that her beauty has been spoilt—for that at least he cannot be
blamed although it means the end of his love for her. He will
not grudge the child money—but no one must know that it is
his.

Kostelnička pleads with him; at least he must see his child.
As Števa says, her pleas would melt the heart of a stone:

They grow in intensity when Števa breaks down, but he still
persists in his refusal to marry Jenůfa, and eventually admits
that he is contracted to marry Karolka, the mayor's daughter.
Števa runs out and, as Kostelnička screams in horror, Jenůfa's
voice is heard coming from the inner room, calling in her
sleep. For a moment Kostelnička is afraid she has woken up,
but there is no further sound and she continues to brood on
the problem which seems now to be left to her, and her
alone, to solve, if solution be possible.

Laca comes in, angry that Števa was there but still anxious

above all things to win the love of Jenůfa. He asks
Kostelnička if Jenůfa is yet back from Vienna—it was given
out that she went away—and is delighted to hear that she has
returned. But Kostelnička has not the heart to hide the truth
from him any longer, and she tells him about the child. He is
horrified at the idea that marriage with Jenůfa involves taking
Števa's baby, and Kostelnička, who sees Jenůfa's last chance
slipping away from her, makes her decision and tells him that
the baby is dead. She sends him out to make enquiries about
the wedding of Števa and Karolka, and is left alone, face to
face with the facts as they are and the facts as she has represented them. For a moment she wonders whether she
can hide the baby. No, he would always bring bad luck on
Jenůfa; he is a true child of Števa. There is no other way but
to kill him. The music represents her agony and indecision,
and the scene is one of terrible power, particularly towards
its end, when Kostelnička yells her own name in horrible
reproach at her shadow. She goes into the bedroom and
brings the child out, wrapped in her shawl.

Jenůfa wakes, and calls for Kostelnička, tenderly at first,
then more urgently as she begins to realise, half-drugged by
the sleeping draught as she is, that Kostelnička is not there.
She draws the curtains and looks out at the stars, then
suddenly realises that her baby has gone too; Kostelnička must
have taken him to the mill to show to Števa, is her
explanation. She prays for his future, and the music is
suffused with sadness and tenderness, which is dispelled for a
moment when Kostelnička comes back in a state of extreme
agitation, but returns after Jenůfa has been told that her
child is dead and buried (Kostelnička explains this by saying
that Jenůfa has been unconscious and delirious for two days,
during which time his death and burial occurred).

Kostelnička tells Jenůfa that Števa has been there, and has
offered to give the child money, but steadfastly refused to
marry her, even admitting that he was engaged to Karolka.
Jenůfa must cast his memory from her mind. When Laca
comes in, his joy at seeing Jenůfa again is touching in its
sincerity. In response to Kostelnička's urgings, he asks Jenůfa
if they cannot finish their lives together. Jenůfa is at first
dignified and reserved, but she cannot hide her tender
feelings for Laca, and Kostelnička exclaims to herself that her
action has put everything right. Just then, the window blows
open, and the icy blast brings a horrible sense of foreboding

and disaster to Kostelnička who cries out in alarm, and clings desperately to Jenůfa and Laca.

Act III. The scene is the same as in Act II. Jenůfa, now looking much better, is preparing for the wedding, and Laca sits by her side. Near them is old Grandmother Buryja. Kostelnička, looking haggard and worn, paces up and down the room. The maid prattles away, but Kostelnička is obviously in a state of nervous exhaustion, and, when there is a knock at the door, she startles them all with her agitated reaction. It turns out to be only the mayor come to offer his congratulations, but even his equanimity cannot restore Kostelnička to calm. Eventually, she takes them all in to see the trousseau she has made for Jenůfa, and bride and bridegroom are left alone. Jenůfa is unhappy that her decision not to wear the customary wedding garland should have occasioned comment from the mayor's wife, but Laca gives her the flowers he has brought her, and she pins them to her dress. He cannot stop reproaching himself for what he has done to her; all his life must be spent making her amends, if that is ever possible. It transpires that it is at Jenůfa's insistence that Laca has been reconciled to Števa, even to the extent of asking him to the wedding, with his bride-to-be.

Karolka comes in with Števa to congratulate the happy couple. The visit looks likely to be completed without a word from Števa, but Laca asks him whether his own wedding-day is yet fixed. In two weeks' time, says Števa; but Karolka is determined to play the minx, and says she may yet change her mind. Števa is indignant at the idea that he might be jilted, but relapses into silence when Jenůfa expresses the hope that true love will never hurt him. The others return, and outside gathers a group of girls, headed by Barena and bringing flowers to offer to Jenůfa. They sing a little wedding song, and then bride and bridegroom are blessed by Grandmother Buryja.

Suddenly, cries are heard outside. The body of the murdered baby has been discovered in the mill-stream now that the ice has melted. Jano rushes in screaming out the news and goes out, taking the mayor with him, followed by the others except Števa, Kostelnička and Grandmother Buryja. Kostelnička becomes hysterical, but attention shifts from her when the voice of Jenůfa can be heard from outside crying that she recognises the baby as hers. In spite of Laca's efforts, she continues to ask why the baby was not properly buried, and feeling against her rises until the mob is ready to stone her for what they cannot but think is her crime. Laca is prepared to defend her, but silence falls on them all when Kostelnička raises her arms and tells them quite quietly that the guilt is hers. She tells the story, and for a moment Jenůfa turns from her in revulsion. But it is only too clear that her crime has been committed in an effort to do good, and Jenůfa's great act of forgiveness towards Kostelnička somehow redeems the crime from its sordid inplications. For a moment it looks as though Kostelnička will kill herself, then she remembers she will be needed as a witness if Jenůfa is not to suffer for something of which she is guiltless, and she goes quietly away with the mayor.

The others go, but Jenůfa and Laca remain behind. Sadly Jenůfa tells him to follow them. She must live out her life alone, though she is grateful to him for his greatness of spirit, and readily forgives him for the injury he did her; love for her was at the back of it, just as love was the cause of her own sin. Laca begs to be allowed to remain at her side, and his reward is Jenůfa's great cry of exultation as she understands that their sufferings have brought them a greater love than she has ever known. This is not just a conventional happy ending. The music has a freshness of its own, and the quality of Laca's devotion is pointed up by situation and music alike.

H.

THE ADVENTURES OF MR BROUČEK

Výlety Pànĕ Broučkovy

Opera in two parts by Leoš Janáček, libretto by V. Dyk and F. S. Procházka, after Svatopluk Čech. Première, Prague, April 23, 1920, with M. Stork, M. Jenik, E. Miriovská. V. Pivonková, V. Zitek, B. Novak, conductor Otakar Ostrčil.[1] Revived Brno, January, 1939. First performed Munich, 1959, with Lorenz Fehenberger, Wilma Lipp, Antonie Fahberg, Fritz Wunderlich, Kurt Böhme, Keith Engen, conductor Joseph Keilberth. Revived Prague, 1968, with Beno Blachut and Helena Tattermuschová, conductor Jaroslav Krombholc (this production seen at Holland and Edinburgh Festivals, 1970); Berlin, German Opera, 1969, with Martin Vantin; B.B.C. Broadcast, 1970, with John Winfield, conductor Mackerras.

[1] Ostrčil was second conductor in Prague at the time, newly engaged, and Janáček's old enemy Kovařovic was still musical director.

39 (*Above*) *Katya Kabanova* at English National Opera with Lorna
Haywood, Sylvia Fisher and Barbara Walker.

(*Below*) *The Cunning Little Vixen* at the Berlin Komische Oper.

40 Marie Collier as Emilia Marty in *The Makropulos Affair*,
Sadler's Wells, 1964.

CHARACTERS

Prague 1888	The Moon	Prague 1420	
Mathias Brouček,[1] *a landlord*		. . . .	Tenor
Mazal, *a painter*	Blankytný[2]	Petřik	Tenor
Sacristan	Lunobor[2]	Domšík	Bass-Baritone
Málinka	Etherea	Kunka	Soprano
Würfl	President[2]	A Magistrate	Bass
Pot-boy at the Inn	An Infant Prodigy	Student	Soprano
Mrs. Fanny Novak	–	Kedruta	Contralto
A guest at the Inn	Oblačny[2]	Vacek	Baritone
A Professor	Duhoslav, *the painter*	Vojta of the Peacocks	Tenor
A composer	Professor Harfoboj[2]	Miroslav, *the Goldsmith*	Tenor
		Apparition of the poet	Tenor or Baritone[3]

Time: The night of July 12/13, 1888   *Place:* Prague 1888; the Moon; Prague 1420

In the canon of Janáček's operas, *Jenůfa* (1904) is preceded by *Šarka* and the one-act, *Beginning of a Romance*, two early and unsuccessful works, *Šarka* not even reaching the stage until 1925. Between *Jenůfa* and the four great works of his maturity are two operas which have not achieved fame: *Osud* (Fate: 1903–4), a conversational piece, and the fantastic burlesque *The Adventures of Mr. Brouček* (written between 1908 and 1917). *Osud* is usually thought of as representing a transition between Janáček's early style, which reached its height in *Jenůfa*, and his later and more mature work. Its production in Brno during the International

[1] Brouček in Czech is a small beetle.
[2] Blankytný, Lunobor, President, Oblačny and Harfoboj are, in a translation provided with a Czech recording of the opera, rendered into English as Azurean, Lunigrove, Wonderglitter, Cloudy and Rainbow Glory.
[3] Written in the bass clef and sung by a high baritone, or even (as in the Prague recording) by a tenor.

Janáček Congress in 1958 was by no means a failure though the work has at most a toe-hold on even the Czech repertory. *Mr. Brouček* has however gradually gained ground and has even been produced successfully outside Czechoslovakia. For many years it was criticised, partly because the book is peculiar and some commentators have felt that the composer made an unhappy choice, and partly because it neither continues the 'folk' line of *Jenůfa* nor employs the concise and fully evolved style of the last four operas.

    The story is taken from two novels by the poet Svatopluk Čech chosen from several works in which he satirises a worldly but typical citizen of Prague—*The Excursion of Mr. Brouček to the Moon* (1887) and *New, Sensational Excursion of Mr. Brouček, this time into the 15th Century* (1888). No fewer than five different literary figures contributed something in the first part of the libretto, which was on the stocks between 1908 and 1917 and was finally edited and put into its present shape by Viktor Dyk. The second part was written by F. S. Procházka, and Janáček set it in a matter of seven months in 1917, spurred on no doubt by the war situation, the prospect of a better future for the Czech nation, and the parallel with events of 500 years earlier. In the figure of Mr. Brouček, Janáček satirises the philistinism of Bohemia's middle-class, as ridiculous on the unattainable Moon as in the equally remote past, and identifies his unimaginative hero firmly with the petit bourgeois of his own times.

    To look for motifs in Wagnerian terms is as useless, indeed harmful and futile, in the Janáček of this period as it would be to look for them in Verdi (or, in a different way, in Prokofiev, Britten, Shostakovich, Stravinsky); Roman Vlad was right when he made this point *à propos* the Italian première and talked of melodic motifs flowering incessantly during the development of events and parallel to the personalities and recurrent situations. He made, too, a neat point when he suggested that the opening scene's rhythmical alternation of 3/4 with 2/4 (waltz and polka) symbolises the frivolous bourgeoisie on the one hand and popular taste on the other—further, that each provides frequent chances for parody as well as obvious opportunity for local colour.

    Part I.   The Adventures of Mr. Brouček on the Moon. The prelude, in typically Janáček vein, alternates a matter-of-fact rapid staccato quaver figure associated with Brouček (first heard early on in bassoon), Ex. 1:

and a glorious and expansive lyrical phrase, Ex. 2:

associated with the love of Málinka and Mazal initially but
perhaps also with the idealism which a compassionate spirit
can find within us all. The two conflicting themes and their
variants permeate the music.

It is a moonlight night outside the Vikárka Inn below
Hradčany Castle in Prague. To the right is the Cathedral and
near it the home of the Sacristan. Málinka, the Sacristan's
daughter, is quarrelling with her lover, Mazal, whose quasi-
ecstatic phrases contrast throughout with the more
fragmentary sounds of the argument. Yesterday he was out
dancing with Fanny, Mr. Brouček's housekeeper—and she for
her part might as well marry Mr. Brouček! Their quarrel is
interrupted first by the Sacristan, then by carousing in the
Inn, and a moment later by Mr. Brouček, each of whom
contributes to further misunderstanding, the Sacristan by
supposing that he must defend his daughter's honour, Mr.
Brouček by his quarrelsome tipsiness and unfortunate
references to Fanny and by his insistence on the possibility
of life on the Moon. Mazal tries to divert his landlord's
attentions by references to the Moon and then goes back
inside the Inn. Brouček makes an absent-minded attempt to
comfort the distraught Málinka by telling her she is not bad-
looking and will certainly find a man, but provokes comment
from her father when he says that he for one would not be at
all averse to marrying her—but only on the Moon, he assures
them, as he staggers off into the distance.

Artists are drinking in the Inn and everyone shouts
something after the departing Mr. Brouček, some about the

sausages he has forgotten, Málinka about marriage, and Wür
the Innkeeper merely with his mechanical invitation to come
again soon. Initiated by Ex. 2, there is a short duet of
considerable tenderness for Mazal and Málinka at the end of
which, and heralded by laughter from them and from the
Inn's pot-boy, Mr. Brouček comes unsteadily back into sight,
staring at the Moon. At least up there he would have no
worries about tenants like Mazal who don't pay their rent.
Gradually, to the sound of hidden voices, Brouček seems to
rise towards this desirable dwelling place, everything is
covered in a white mist and we are conducted by an ecstatic
violin solo to the Moon itself.

In the background is a castle and in the foreground
Brouček lies asleep. A moonbeam, Blankytný by name but
wearing the aspect and voice of Mazal, arrives on a horse and
ties it to the stem of a flower. He is a poet and reacts with
astonishment and horror when Brouček addresses him as
Mazal and tries to shake him by the hand. Brouček is equally
angry that his tenant fails to recognise him and misunderstanding grows as Blankytný speaks with mounting lyrical
enthusiasm of beauty and the exalted nature of his lady love
(whom to touch would be to dissolve), only for Brouček's
answers to be as matter-of-fact as the sausages which fall out
of his pocket. Lunobor, a sort of Moon wizard-monster to
look at, an aesthete by outlook, announces the arrival of
the object of Blankytný's exaggerated affections, his
daughter Etherea, who sounds like Málinka and sings a pretty
waltz with her accompanying maidens. The sight of Brouček
has the strangest effect on them all, and the trio of Etherea,
Blankytný and Brouček ends with Etherea embracing
Brouček and flying off with him on the back of the horse on
which Blankytný arrived, just as Lunobor returns to read
them some chapters of Moon wisdom.

We move (with Ex. 2 to the fore in the orchestral
preamble) to the Temple of Arts, built in the shape of a star
with a staircase leading up to it in the foreground. Each ray
of the star is consecrated to a different branch of art. The
scene seems to be presided over by the President (Würfl),
who says he himself lacks all talent and might have decided
to become a critic had he not been kind-hearted by nature.
He corrects and praises the musicians, and describes himself
as a patron, regularly painted and sculpted by the artists and
the subject of their songs. The horse alights at the foot of the
staircase with Etherea and Brouček on board. She proclaims

em lovers and asks for the protection of the President, who
eacts with some mildness to the highly matter-of-fact
answers Brouček returns to his questioning. Blankytný
laments his lost love, but Lunobor, Etherea's father, catches
her and starts to take her away, while Brouček remains an
object of admiration and wonder to all the lunar dwellers.

Oblačny leads the artists in their attempts to welcome
Brouček, dancers perform in his honour, a child-prodigy
(with an ever-playing piccolo at its lips) joins the chorus of
admiration, until the President suggests a meal. The prodigy
sings the National Anthem[1], whose gist is that Moon
creatures smell their food instead of eating it, Etherea returns
to the scene and makes up to Brouček again, and all in
succession try to impress him to little avail; he finds Etherea
little more than a cobweb, will never kneel down when he is
asked to, and finally shocks them by falling asleep and in a
half-voice muttering, 'Waiter! Roast and two veg., please!'

The flowers which the child-prodigy waves under his nose
end by waking him up and he tells them that he has had sufficient delectation for his nose. The coarse word shocks them
again and they start to withdraw from him, Blankytný bursting
into tears at the affront to lunar society. Duhoslav the
painter insists that he admire the picture which he is
painting—such glorious colours! Brouček surreptitiously
covers his face and eats a sausage, deceiving the artists at first
into thinking that he is weeping only a moment later for the
horrible truth to emerge. They are sorry for him and are
astonished that he cannot feed on flowers like them. He tells
them in a matter-of-fact way that only vegetarians behave like
that on earth, sensible people preferring meat. This provokes
a fresh storm, and explanation of the sausage brings reference
to it as a murdered animal. Etherea makes a last attempt on
his virtue, dancing round him until Brouček blows furiously
at her and she subsides on the ground in a tangled cobwebby
mess. Brouček mounts Pegasus and flies away, leaving
Harfoboj and the child-prodigy to lead the musicians in
praising the President.

Fog starts to invade the scene and an ecstatic interlude
(Ex. 2 important again) takes us back to the Vikárka Inn,
with the artists about to leave and Mr. Würfl standing at the

---

[1] A verbal parody of the (in 1917) newly established Czech National
Anthem.

door. They thank him and say goodnight, the pot-bc announcing that Mr. Brouček is being carried helplessly hom (Ex. 1). The scene is left to Málinka and Mazal, the former returning home after a night of love with the latter; the music touchingly foreshadows the great double love duet of *Katya Kabanova*'s second act.

Part II.   The Excursion of Mr. Brouček into the Fifteenth Century. Act I. In the foreground, the Vikárka Inn; in the background, the Treasure Chamber of King Wenceslas IV. The period will shortly be that of the Hussite Wars,[1] 1420; jewels, helmets and armour in gold and silver, swords, shields, dishes, crowns and so on stand all around. The music at first is much less lyrical than that of Act I. Voices can be heard in the distance talking of subterranean passages and underground hideouts, and Brouček in an aside proclaims his belief in such a passage. Würfl is unkind enough to mention Brouček's excursion to the Moon and there is laughter, but when Würfl bids them all goodnight, Brouček is left calling for help and light and, in an extended monologue, wondering what on earth has happened for it to be so hard to get out of the Inn.

The portrait of King Wenceslas suddenly turns round and Brouček falls into the treasure chamber. He cannot think how he has got there and does his best to get out, but without success. Suddenly he is confronted with the apparition of the poet Svatopluk Čech,[2] from whose works the opera derives, in an unearthly light and explaining in a passage of measured solemnity,[3] Ex. 3:

---

[1] Jan Hus, burnt at the stake in 1415 for heresy, was influenced by the Englishman Wycliffe and like him advocated the printing of the Scriptures in the vernacular. His followers split into two, one group based on Prague, the other—the Taborites—adopting an extremist position and opposing much of the Church's ritual. In 1420, King Zikmund led an army against the Hussites, who, under Jan Žižka, defeated their opponents at the battle of Vikov Hill.

[2] In Brno's production of 1967 transferred (in this writer's view, not unsuccessfully) to form a prologue to Part II.

[3] Heard first at the rise of the curtain in the orchestra.

..hat the idealistic actions of the past necessarily, in view of
present circumstances, inspire him to celebrate freedom
with a certain irony. It is not just an old man longing for the
past, but the statement of a disappointed patriot,[1] and the
chorale-like music (not derived from subsequent chorale
quotations) colours the whole of the mediaeval section of the
opera.

Brouček now stands outside, wondering if he is in the
Jewish quarter and thinking he has found a short-cut to
remember in future. There is no proper light—he must write
to the press and complain—but he is very taken aback when a
moment later he is stopped by a citizen who at first does not
understand what he says and then takes him for a German,
moreover a spy for King Zikmund. The Magistrate (who
sings with the voice of Würfl) is astonished at Brouček's
reference to 'the late Žižka' and at his insistence that Žižka
beat King Zikmund in 1420 but that this is now history as
he speaks in 1888. In spite of his cries for help they take him
before the judge.

In front of his house, and as the voices of the armed
populace can be heard singing from the distance, Ex. 4:

the judge Domšík (Sacristan) asks Brouček who he is.
Brouček at last grasps the situation and, remembering the
Moon or at least half of it, says that he has come from the
land of the Turks, which explains why his Czech sounds so
strange to them. They agree to enroll him, as the Hussites, the
warriors of God, enter the square singing a chorale and going

---

[1] In Edinburgh in 1970, at the opera's first British performance, the
role of Svatopluk Čech was sung by the baritone Zdeněk Otava, who
had been the original Baron Prus at the première of *The Makropulos
Affair* in 1926—an opera many in the audience had been listening to the
night before. The poised intensity of his singing made an extraordinary
effect, as if the veteran baritone were embodying all that is best in the
Czech soul.

into church—a concise but splendid musical climax to the scene.

Act II. A room in Domšík's house. Through the window can be seen the Town Hall and the Square. Brouček sits on the bed and wonders what on earth has happened to him that he should find himself a Hussite—the music suggests his nervous state. At least he won't let himself be killed for no purpose! He is interrupted by the sight of Kedruta, whom he takes for his housekeeper Fanny (referred to but not visible in the first scene). Domšík comes in and tells him to put on some proper—medieval—clothes, which Brouček does with neither enthusiasm nor competence. The people can be heard coming from church, again singing, this time the Hussite chorale 'Hear ye, the warriors of God'[1]

Kunka (the daughter of Domšík and bearing as much resemblance to Málinka as her father does to the Sacristan) brings in guests for Domšík's table. In succession, Brouček is introduced to Vacek, Miroslav and Vojta. Kunka reports a militant sermon and all drink to the future, not least Brouček, who is congratulated on his prowess as a potman. When he says that abroad the Czechs are not much liked, all agree that this is a calumny which must be repudiated as soon as possible by victory over the oppressors. A student blames it all on the Taborite priests, to the anger of Vacek, but Brouček diverts attention by proclaiming that he is not interested in fighting Zikmund, who means nothing to him. Domšík is in process of rescuing him from an embarrassing situation when the voice of Petřík can be heard calling them to arms. Brouček cannot elude the distribution of arms and finishes by finding a pike in his hands. The music momentarily takes a lyrical turn as Kunka bids her father a tender farewell, kneeling at his departure and praying for victory for him and for the patriots (Ex. 3 in orchestra). As soon as they have gone she seizes a weapon and runs out in spite of the efforts of Kedruta to restrain her. Kedruta is left behind singing the Lord's Prayer while the Hussite chorale is heard outside. Suddenly Brouček appears, tears off his costume to put back his own clothes, lights a cigar and rushes out of the room.

The next scene is in the old Town Square. The sun is setting and the Square is full of people. The returning armies

---

[1] Used by Smetana in the finale of *Libuše*.

Praguers and Taborites, Jan Žižka at their head, enter after their victory over King Zikmund, to the acclamation of children and populace alike in a scene of considerable musical splendour. Brouček is noticed trying to escape from Domšík's house, and he spins an obviously false story to the questioning Taborites. Before Petřik can finish explaining what really happened, Kunka appears lamenting the death of her father and trying to take comfort from Petřik's presence amongst them. She goes into the house as Petřik recounts the story of Brouček's cowardice: he ran straight up to one of the German knights, knelt before him crying, 'My lord, I am yours! No Praguer, no Hussite! *Gnade!*' The Councillor, Vojta and the people demand his death, some by burning, others by burial alive in a barrel. Brouček's excuses—that he is a child of the future and not yet born—seem of little avail and Kedruta's voice is added to those demanding the supreme penalty.

As the barrel catches fire, the stage grows cloudy again, tension relaxes (music from the Moon) and the light of the fire turns into a candle in Würfl's hand outside the Vikárka Inn, where Mr. Brouček can be seen in a barrel (into which he fell drunk before going to sleep). His cries seem nearer to lamentation in his predicament than to rejoicing at his salvation, but safely outside his prison, he accepts Würfl's help up the stairs, assuring him that his adventures have indeed been strange—but let nobody be told about them! The opera ends, fast and gay, without even a glance at the idealistic Ex. 2, but with a sly reference in the harps to Ex. 3.

In the past, commentators in and out of Czechoslovakia used to describe the music as feeble and stress the savage nature of Janáček's attack on the shortcomings of his fellow-countrymen through the central figure of Brouček, preferring his musical mockery of Prague-1420 as compared with the Moon-1888. I am inclined to agree on only one count: the comparatively obvious target of the Hussite scenes is hit fairer and squarer than the more obliquely set scenes in the Moon, where aesthetes come under fire just as much as the bourgeois who does not appreciate them. Granted the sheer peculiarity of the stories Janáček has chosen—and even these read a degree less oddly in the age of Sputniks—the music to my mind remains engaging, moving, and above all original. With its kaleidoscopic mixture of satire and sentiment,

of genuine patriotic fervour (who can doubt the import of Ex.
3 and 4?) and relentless spoofing of aesthetic and chauvinistic
pretension, I believe it will yet win popular acclaim due to
the power of its musical invention, which seems to me each
time I meet it to create a sound world of its own, enveloping,
invigorating and wholly delightful.   H.

KATYA KABANOVA

Opera in three acts by Leoš Janáček, text by Cervinka, founded on
Ostrovsky's *The Storm*. Première, Brno, October 23, 1921, with Marie
Veselá, Karel Zavřel, conductor Neumann. First performed in Prague,
1922, conductor Ostrčil; in German, translated by Max Brod, at
Cologne, 1922, with Rose Pauly, Schröder, conductor Klemperer;
Berlin, 1926. Revived Munich, 1948, with Schech, Klarwein; Dresden,
1949, with Trötschel, Schindler. First performed in England, Sadler's
Wells, 1951, with Shuard, Rowland Jones, conductor Mackerras (later
Kubelik); in America, New York, 1960, with Shuard, Doree, Gari,
Petrak, conductor Halasz; Edinburgh Festival, 1964, by Prague Opera
with Domaninská; Florence (Italian première), 1957, by Belgrade
Opera; Paris, 1968, with Hélène Garetti, Berthe Monmart, Ion Piso.

CHARACTERS

Vanya Kudrjaš, *clerk to Dikoy* . . . . Tenor
Glasha, *a servant* . . . . Mezzo-Soprano
Dikoy, *a rich merchant* . . . . Bass
Boris Grigoryevich, *his nephew* . . . . Tenor
Feklusha, *a servant* . . . . Mezzo-Soprano
Marfa Kabanova, *a rich merchant's widow*
    (Kabanicha) . . . . Contralto
Tikhon Ivanich Kabanov, *her son* . . . . Tenor
Barbara, *foster-child in the Kabanov household*
                                        Mezzo-Soprano
Katerina Kabanova (Katya), *Tikhon's wife* . . . . Soprano
Kuligin, *friend of Vanya* . . . . Baritone
Time: About 1860   *Place:* The little town of Kalinov on
                                the banks of the Volga

Janáček's marriage in 1880 to a German-speaking girl from
Brno seems to have been a stormy affair from the start—within
a year, Zdenka had returned to her parents and the young
composer was attempting to woo her back by escorting her

to the door of the German-speaking theatre, which he would himself on principle not enter. In 1917, on holiday in Luhačovice, he met Kamila Stösslova, and at the age of 63 fell in love with this 25-year-old married woman in such a way as to revolutionise the remainder of his life. Two-thirds of his greatest music was written in his last dozen years, much of it explicitly inspired by Kamila, and nowhere else in musical history is there an instance of such late flowering on so prolific a scale, and for so romantic a reason. Czech musical historians are not charitable about Kamila, but the rest of the world has reason for gratitude for what she meant to the composer. Their association lasted to the end of Janáček's life, and its first musical fruit is *Katya*.

In *Katya Kabanova*, written between 1918 and 1921, Janáček contrasts the old and the new, the ancient Slavonic matriarchy (symbolised in Kabanicha) and the independent, enlightened modern generation (symbolised by Barbara and Vanya Kudrjaš). In between these two conflicting forces are found the unemancipated Katya and Boris; Katya is oppressed by Kabanicha and Boris by his uncle, Dikoy.

The prelude, with its *pp* B flat minor chords and its fateful drum figure against muted trombones, is concerned with setting the atmosphere which is to prevail throughout the opera, but at the same time it serves as an exposition of leading motifs. We are made acquainted soon after the opening with an agonised figure of three (later four) adjacent chromatic notes which, it has been suggested, symbolises the painful friction of people living too closely together; the first *allegro* passage has an important theme in the oboe (much used later in the opera) against a background of flute and sleigh-bells (Tikhon's departure); but most important of all is the tender

which dominates the prelude, and is heard, with its derivations, very frequently in the course of the opera.

The curtain rises to show the outside of the Kabanovs' house, which stands on the banks of the Volga and from which a broad view of the river can be seen. Kudrjaš is sitting on a bench exclaiming at the beauty of the river—a point of view with which Glasha, who works for Kabanicha, cannot sympathise. In the distance can be seen Dikoy, waving his arms about angrily as is his custom; Kudrjaš and Glasha retire out of sight in case he takes it into his head to give them a piece of his mind. Dikoy comes in, complaining at his nephew Boris's laziness—though what he is expected to work at on a Sunday morning Boris himself is unable to guess, nor does his uncle seem disposed to enlighten him. Dikoy makes no secret of his dislike of Boris, but he goes away when he has learned from Glasha that Kabanicha is still in church.

Kudrjaš listens sympathetically while Boris explains that he only stays with his tyrannical, loud-mouthed relation because of the terms of his grandmother's will; the money is to go to him and his sister when they come of age, provided they do what their uncle tells them. His sister has so far been kept away from Dikoy by their mother's family in Moscow, and if it were not for her, Boris himself would long ago have left Dikoy and given up his inheritance.

At that moment, the people are seen coming back from church, and Kudrjaš has to be restrained from going by the overwrought Boris. As Boris laments his rapidly-departing youth, Katya's theme is stated *dolce* and for the first time by the oboe.

At the same time, Glasha tells Feklusha that her employer, Kabanicha, is a hypocritical old tyrant. Boris gazes into the distance and his rapturous phrases tell the listener as plainly as his words that he is in love. To the accompaniment of repeated statements of Katya's theme, he admits to Kudrjaš that Katya is the object of his adoration—a married woman! The theme is heard in its most characteristic form as Katya comes into sight:

Kabanicha leads her little family party back from church. She pauses in front of the house to urge Tikhon, if he wants to please his mother, to go that very day to the market at Kazan. He immediately agrees, but Kabanicha makes a sneering reference to his wife Katya, and suggests that since his marriage he has paid his mother less than the respect and deference due to her. Tikhon hotly protests that he loves both, but when Katya also gently claims to love her mother-in-law, Kabanicha turns on her and insults her; who asked her opinion? Barbara is sarcastic: 'Oh, what a place to choose for a sermon!'[1] Katya goes into the house, and Kabanicha continues her abuse; Tikhon is too soft with Katya, and would make no protest even if she were to take a lover. Kabanicha goes, and Barbara vehemently abuses Tikhon for not taking Katya's part more firmly; she knows exactly what he will do now—drink to forget the scene. Barbara is alone as the curtain falls; 'Oh, how could anyone not love her?' is her comment on Katya's unhappiness.

The second scene is set inside the Kabanovs' house. Katya and Barbara are in conversation, and the former gradually pours out her heart to Barbara. She is unhappy in her present surroundings—a fact Barbara knows well. When she was young and unmarried, she was as free as the birds, and like them she wandered unhindered wherever she wished. She describes her girlhood. Even then, her mother treated her as a child and knew nothing of her fancies and longings. The music grows in intensity as she describes going to church alone; 'I felt as if I was entering Paradise,' she says. She saw visions of angels, lofty golden cathedrals high in the sky; she felt as if she were flying over the mountains and forests, surrounded by invisible choirs. For a moment she loses control of herself and reveals that strange desires fill her being, she is tempted to sin.

Barbara encourages her to describe her dreams. She says she feels that a voice is whispering in her ear, someone is embracing her and urging her to go with him—and she yields to his persuasion. Katya breaks off; how can Barbara, a child, understand what she means? But Barbara protests that she is not as innocent as Katya thinks; she has sins on her own conscience. Katya says that no sin can be worse than that of loving some other man than one's own husband, but Barbara asks why that should seem so dreadful; perhaps when Tikhon has gone, Katya will see this other man.

Katya protests vehemently, and at this moment, Tikhon appears saying that he must leave immediately for Kazan, as his mother wishes him to. In spite of Katya's protests, he can neither remain nor take her with him. Katya asks him to make

[1] Translation by Norman Tucker.

her swear a dreadful oath not to see or speak to a stranger while he is away, but he refuses to ask her to do such a thing. Katya starts to formulate an oath, but Kabanicha comes in and bids her son prepare for the journey. Before he leaves, he must give his orders to his wife—and in the presence of his mother, so that she may hear exactly what he says. He repeats in a milder form the injunctions of Kabanicha, and, in spite of his protests, they include a prohibition against seeing other men. It looks as though Katya will break down as she kisses her husband good-bye—Kabanicha's grim comment is 'Shameless girl! Is he your lover?'

Act II.   Living-room of the Kabanovs' house, later the same day. When the curtain rises, Kabanicha is obviously in the middle of a spate of nagging at Katya. Why can't she be like other wives—those that love their husbands, that's to say—and stay weeping in her room for the rest of the day when he goes away? She might at least pretend to weep; that would show people her word is to be trusted! Having vented some of her spleen, Kabanicha leaves the room.

Barbara says she feels hot; she will go into the garden, using the key which Kabanicha *thinks* she has hidden, but for which Barbara has substituted another key so that she will not know it has gone. If she should see 'him', says Barbara cryptically, she will tell him that Katya is waiting by the gate of the garden. Barbara goes out leaving the key. For a while Katya wrestles with temptation; she has the key to hand, should she use it? Suddenly, she can hear the voice of Kabanicha, but the danger passes, and the flood of relief which succeeds it tells her more certainly than could anything else that her love for Boris is too strong for her. Nothing could be more psychologically right than the musical portrayal of this sudden and involuntary crumbling away of resistance.

Katya goes out, to be succeeded by Kabanicha, who is followed by Dikoy. Straightaway he admits that he is a bit drunk, but he protests that he does not want to go home. 'Speak to me harshly' is the request he has come to make of Kabanicha—she alone dares do such a thing. Money is the thing that causes him to sin. The other day a peasant asked him to repay some money; he cursed him, all but thrashed him, and then went down on his knees to beg forgiveness. 'You should learn better manners' is Kabanicha's retort. The whole scene has a coarse and overblown erotic base, the very converse of what is to follow.

The scene changes to the garden below the house. The summer night is hot. Kudrjaš arrives first and sings a care-free peasant song to balalaika accompaniment. He is waiting for Barbara, and is surprised to see Boris, who explains that someone he passed in the dark told him to come there, and he felt that he should not ignore the suggestion. Kudrjaš tries to warn him, but Boris is plainly too much in love to benefit from warnings. Barbara signals her arrival by singing another snatch of folk-like melody, to which Kudrjaš makes appropriate answer. As she passes Boris, she tells him that Katya will not be long. He waits impatiently and with growing excitement as Katya comes into sight. In spite of herself, Katya admits her love for him and falls into his arms. There is apprehension as well as poignancy and yearning in their duet. The whole scene is saturated with the magic of the summer night, and a unique effect is produced by the blend and contrast of the characteristics of the two pairs of lovers, the one passionate and care-free, the other rapturous but guilty. The singing ends with a little folk-like duet for Barbara and Kudrjaš, but the shattering emotional climax comes in the orchestra, when Katya and Boris return to the stage and their pent-up feelings are expressed in three highly charged orchestral phrases, which are more revealing than might be a vocal section of ten times the length.

Act III.   Ten days later. The scene is laid in a tumble-down summer house on a terrace by the Volga. Kudrjaš and Kuligin, his friend, take shelter from the storm which threatens, and which bursts upon them with considerable violence. They look at the pictures on the walls; there is one of Ivan the Terrible, which elicits the sarcastic comment that Russia has never wanted for tyrants—there is one in every family. As if to match the words, Dikoy comes in, pushing everyone out of his way, and complaining that he sees far too much of Kudrjaš every day to want to see him again. Kudrjaš suggests that the frequent storms indicate the village should have lightning-conductors; he tries to explain what they are, but meets short shrift from the superstitious Dikoy, who takes each storm to be a warning from God to sinful mankind.

The rain stops and all leave the shelter, except Boris and Kudrjaš. Barbara appears, and whispers to Boris that Tikhon is back, and his return has driven Katya quite out of her senses, so that she seems ill with worry. Boris hides as Katya

comes in, supported by her husband and preceded b
Kabanicha. Thunder can be heard in the distance and the
storm starts all over again at just the moment when Katya
catches sight of Boris. In spite of the efforts of Barbara, who
tries to restrain her, she calls to Tikhon and Kabanicha at the
top of her voice, and confesses not only her adultery but
names the man with whom she has sinned. The scene has an
added horror in that it builds up with incredible rapidity
from comparative calm to climax and catastrophe. Tikhon at
first does not want to listen to Katya's confession, and is
beside himself with unhappiness, but Kabanicha's comment is
one of self-justification: 'Son, your mother warned you!'

The second scene re-introduces the great unifying
influence of the story, taking place as it does on the banks of
the Volga. Katya has fled from her family after her
confession, and they are looking for her. It is night, and
Tikhon's remarks to Glasha reveal that his mind is a turmoil
of doubt; women like that should not just be killed, he says,
but buried alive—and yet he still loves Katya, and how could
he harm her? He and Glasha continue their search, and
Barbara and Kudrjaš run in, the former explaining the
behaviour of Kabanicha. They agree that there is nothing for
it but to run away together, and their careless decision
accords well with what the music has told us about them
during the rest of the opera.

The voices of Tikhon and Glasha can be heard calling in
the distance. Katya comes slowly on to the empty stage,
hoping sadly to see Boris once again. Her experience has
obviously affected her very strongly, and she cannot think
coherently. How would Boris speak to her now? The thought
of the night overwhelms her with horror, but she reflects that
she will never see another night. Suddenly, remembrance of
her love fills her heart with longing; she calls for Boris, and,
as if in answer to her cry, he appears. Perhaps nothing in the
opera is sadder than the quiet way in which the two lovers
accept one another and each finds consolation in the
presence of the other. Boris tries to comfort her, but her
mind wanders and she cannot remember what she wants to
say to him. At first she wants to go away with him, then
changes her mind. Suicide is forgotten, and she pictures her
future life, perpetually tortured by Kabanicha. Sadly she asks
him to give alms to all the beggars he meets, with the request
that they pray for her. They say good-bye.

Katya is alone, and goes towards the bank of the river. She thinks of the birds and the flowers which have comforted her in life and will be with her in death, 'so peaceful, so lovely . . . and I must die'. She throws herself into the river. The voices of one or two men who have seen her fall are heard; Tikhon and Kabanicha rush to the spot, the latter restraining her son, Tikhon protesting that it is Kabanicha who has killed Katya. Her body is carried up on to the bank by Dikoy, and the last words of the opera are sardonically given to Kabanicha: 'Let me thank you, friends and neighbours, for your kindness.'

Katya is the logical development of *Jenůfa*. The extraordinarily tense atmosphere of the story is matched by a similar quality in the music, which has an economical, compressed quality that is hardly to be found to quite the same degree in operas by other composers. It is from this very close juxtaposition of the broadest of lyrical themes with the most insistent of dramatic, that Janáček derives his unusual power, and the concentrated nature of both music and drama in *Katya* makes it particularly in evidence in this work — which, to the present writer, seems one of the most remarkable of the twentieth century.   H.

THE CUNNING LITTLE VIXEN
Příhody Lišky Bystroušky

Opera in three acts by Leoš Janáček, text by the composer from R. Tešnohlídek's stories. Première, Brno, November 6,[1] 1924, with H. Hrdlicková, Flögl, conductor František Neumann. First performed Mainz, 1927, conductor Paul Breisach; Zagreb, 1939, conductor Milan Sachs; Leipzig, 1951, with Ingeborg Wengler, Theodor Horand, conductor Ernst Richter; Cologne, 1955, with Rota Bartos, Peter Nohl, conductor Ackermann; Zürich, 1955, with Inger Wallenstein, Willi Heyer, conductor Ackermann; Komische Oper, Berlin, 1956, in Felsenstein's production (in German), with Irmgard Arnold, Rudolf Asmus, conductor Václav Neumann (this production was subsequently seen at Wiesbaden and Paris); la Scala, Milan, 1958 (in Italian), with Mariella Adani, Dino Dondi, conductor Sanzogno; London, Sadler's

---

[1] Loewenberg gives November 16 but all Czech sources are agreed on November 6 as the proper date.

Wells, 1961, (in English) with June Bronhill, Neil Easton, conductor Colin Davis; Copenhagen, 1963, with Ellen Winther; U.S. première, Mannes College of Music at Hunter College, 1964; Munich, 1967, with June Card; Edinburgh Festival, 1970, by Prague Opera with Tattermuschová, conductor Gregor; Glyndebourne, 1975, with Norma Burrowes, Benjamin Luxon.

CHARACTERS[1]

Animals:

Bystrouška, *the Vixen* .... Soprano
The Fox .... Soprano
Lapák, *the Dachshund* .... Mezzo-Soprano
The Cock .... Soprano
Chocholka, *the Hen* .... Soprano
The Badger .... Bass
The Screech-owl .... Contralto
The Woodpecker .... Soprano

Humans:

The Forester .... Bass-Baritone
The Forester's wife .... Contralto
The Schoolmaster .... Tenor
The Parson .... Bass
Pásek, *the Innkeeper* .... Tenor
The Innkeeper's wife .... Soprano
Harašta, *the Pedlar* .... Bass
Birds, Flies, Insects, Cricket, Grasshopper, etc.

Few operas, even by Slavs, had an odder genesis than Janáček's *The Cunning Little Vixen*. The composer had read with growing pleasure a series of newspaper articles by the journalist Tešnohlídek, based on a Czech rural community and featuring a half-tame, half-wild vixen. He was particularly enthusiastic about the way the writer could jump naturally from the human to the animal worlds and, to the astonishment of Tešnohlídek himself, he asked if he might make an operatic text from the newspaper strips. 'Janáček's libretto', writes Erik Chisholm in his excellent *The Operas of Leoš Janáček* (Pergamon Press 1971), 'is written in the Líšeň (Brno) dialect and consequently is by no means easily

---

[1] In some productions, the Fox and the Dachshund have been sung by tenors. The score instructs that the following parts are to be doubled: Badger and Parson; Forester's Wife and Owl.

...essible to Prague singers and audiences, in much the same
...ay as the poems of Robert Burns in the Ayrshire dialect are
...uzzling to many English readers.'

The opera, with its juxtaposition of humans and animals,
has sometimes been thought unstageable, and in fact has
clearly been badly staged almost as often as it has been
attempted. But in 1956 at the Komische Oper, Berlin, came
complete vindication of Janáček's intentions in the wonderful production of Walter Felsenstein. Rumours of a lengthy
preparation period, varying from six to eighteen months
according to one's informants, heralded a performance that
quite startlingly combined realism and musicality. Its guest
visit to Paris a year after the Berlin première was a revelation
to those who saw the performances, and the work was
performed over 120 times in the four years following 1956,
with, to my mind, no diminution of the astonishing quality
of the early representations.

Act I, scene i.   The curtain rises in the first bar, Ex. 1:

to show a shady spot in the woods; the early afternoon
sunlight plays through the leaves of the trees. Animals and
insects dance in the heat, a badger smoking a pipe pokes his
head out of his earth, a blue dragon-fly hovers in a dance, Ex. 2:

The Forester comes from the wood looking for a place for
afternoon nap and sits down—he feels as tired as after h
wedding night! Only his gun, his true sweetheart, neithe
nags nor answers him back![1]

He goes to sleep, the insect noises begin again, there is an
enchanting waltz, Ex. 3:

as the flies dance round the Forester, and the tempo (now in 2
quickens as a frog chases a mosquito. A vixen cub, Ex. 4:

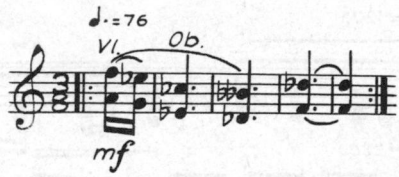

looks in amazement at the frog; can one eat it, she wonders
She pounces, the frog jumps quickly and lands cold and
slippery on the Forester's nose, much to his disgust. His eyes
meet the vixen's, and after a couple of feints he catches her
and goes away with her under his arm, Ex. 5:

[1] Just as Talich in his shortened orchestral arrangement of Act I of
The Cunning Little Vixen (brilliantly preserved in a Supraphon disc)
has pointed up the orchestration for the purposes of the suite, so
Janáček's friend Max Brod in his German translation has occasionally
gone further than the original libretto allows, underlining many points
Janáček no more than hinted at and greatly stressing the implied
symbolism. The glosses of this translation have until recently been
substantially accepted in German performances, even, to some extent
in Felstenstein's, but by no means in Czechoslovakia, though Brod was
a close friend of the composer's. When the Forester in the first scene
lies down for a nap, Brod introduces a first reference to a gypsy girl
Terinka, of whose beauty and love of freedom all the humans in the
opera are reminded when they meet the little vixen.

The dragon-fly darts towards the place where the vixen was playing, looks for her, and dances a touching little dirge for his lost friend to the tune of Ex. 2.

The interweaving forest motifs, the contrasting dance rhythms, the varying and unfailingly apt orchestral invention, above all the homogeneity of the themes and Janáček's skill and lightness of touch in putting the whole thing together contribute to a musical scene in its way unrivalled in operatic literature. The mixture of peaceful contemplation and feverish animal and insect activity which go to make up the atmosphere of a hot summer afternoon is a familiar enough country phenomenon but not one often portrayed in music.

The second scene is set outside the Forester's house on an autumn afternoon. From the very outset the music is pregnant with heartache and longing, Ex. 6:

The Forester's wife pours some milk into a saucer for the dachshund and the fox cub, which she and her husband are bringing up as a pet for their child. The little vixen is miserable (Ex. 6a) and the dog tries to preach resignation as a desirable state of mind—is he not head-over-heels in love at the appropriate time of year, but with no object for his affections—and he has learnt to make the best of a bad job. The vixen counters with chatter about the scandalous carrying-on of the starlings who nested over her home, but is quick to reject a rather half-hearted amorous approach on the part of the dachshund. When the Forester's son appears with a friend and teases the fox, he is rewarded with a sharp nip, and the Forester quickly ties her up, and she is left in a state of dejection (Ex. 6a) as the others go into the house.

As it gets dark, there begins an extraordinary musical episode, built up on Ex. 6. The vixen seems almost to change into a girl—perhaps the gypsy Terinka?—and provokes passionate orchestral love music starting in B flat, Ex. 7:

In Felsenstein's production in Berlin, the already highly charged situation was pointed up by having the Forester stare at the little vixen on her chain until what he saw merged with his memory of his free gypsy love. It is music of great intensity and one could think of Ex. 7, with its exhilarating leap, as contrasting with the pathetic Ex. 6, with its close intervals and repeated notes, in the same way as does an extraordinary experience with everyday life.

With the dawn, the Forester's wife throws out food for the chickens, who cluck to a parody of Ex. 7:

Mě - las   dě - lat   pod - li - vá   mně!
Nimm dir doch ein   Bei-spiel an   mir!

and strut around the yard until the fox starts a revolutionary
harangue. It is a brave new feminist world that she preaches,
no more to be dominated by such creatures as men or
cockerels. But the hens are unresponsive and in disgust the fox
digs itself a grave, lies down and shams dead. There is a
headlong orchestral *stretta* to the scene as the fox suddenly
springs up and bites off the heads of one chicken after
another. The Forester's wife runs out in alarm, and the fox
snaps its leash, trips up the Forester and escapes into the
woods.

Act II.   For the first scene, we are back again in the
sanctuary of the wood. The vixen teases the badger, enlists
the sympathy of the other animals, and when the badger goes
off in a huff, moves as she always intended into the badger's
vacated earth.

We arrive at the village inn by means of an interlude, which
suggests the bustling atmosphere inside. There we find the
Forester and the Schoolmaster playing cards, watched by the
village priest. In a song, the Forester mocks the Schoolmaster
for his backwardness in courting his sweetheart, but the
ribaldry is general, the Parson quotes Latin and it is not long
before they tease the Forester about the exploits of his pet
fox. The Innkeeper is worried at the quantity of noise
coming from the back room, the Parson takes comfort in his
Latin tag, "Non des mulieri corpus tuum" (Give not thy
body to a woman) and the Forester wonders if one can
describe a bag of bones like the Schoolmaster as a body. The
Innkeeper warns the Parson to leave if his drinking is not to

become a scandal with his new parishioners (German productions, but not Czech, have visible and audible choral interruptions at this point), and the Forester is left to wonder whether the Schoolmaster may not get married after all. He orders another beer, the Innkeeper says he will one of these days get him to tell the details of his adventures with the vixen, but the Forester reacts crossly and leaves the pub in a bad temper.[1]

The scene changes to the wood at night. The moonlight shows a bridge across the road; there are some sunflowers behind the fence. The Schoolmaster comes a little shakily down the road, lamenting his propensity to waste his time drinking. The vixen peeps out from behind a sunflower, to the joy of the Schoolmaster, who takes her for the gypsy Terinka, a past love, and in his ardour topples over the fence and lies prone. Next it is the turn of the Parson, who comes down the road trying to remember the source of a classical tag. He catches sight of the vixen, confuses her in his mind with Terinka, whom he also loved in student days and for whose pregnancy he was unjustly blamed. The appearance of the Forester puts an end to his moralising, and he and the Schoolmaster fall into each other's arms in their fear of where the Forester may shoot at this time of night. The Forester mutters that he is shooting at the vixen whom he has seen slinking through the woods—but the explanation seems scarcely sufficient to the frightened Parson and School-master.

The scene changes back to the vixen's earth. Moonlight. Behind the scene the voices of the forest sing a wordless chant, which will play a great part at the end of the scene,

---

[1] To give the Forester, as Max Brod does, a monologue here about the disruptive career of Terinka since she came into the village's life is to depart from the Czech libretto—but equally certainly there is an element of justification in Brod's repeated reference to Terinka in the second scene of this act, and it is not hard to argue that there is more than a likelihood of confusion when (as in Janáček's own libretto) two or three girls are named but none appears on the stage. To combine all in the person of the elusive but compulsively attractive Terinka has at least the merit of compression and stage logic.

Ex. 8:

The vixen meets a fox and tells him a romanticised story of her life. When the fox refers to her as beautiful, she starts to wonder about the significance of his remark; is she *really* beautiful? He brings her a rabbit he has killed, kisses her, and asks her if she has ever been in love. There is a full-scale love duet, at the end of which they go off together into the vixen's earth, leaving the dragon-fly—her guardian angel, surely—to rejoice to Ex. 2. The owl (suitably, the same singer as the Forester's wife) positively bubbles with joy with such a juicy bit of gossip. When the foxes emerge, the vixen whispers to the fox that she is now an expectant mother, and his reaction is to send for a priest, the woodpecker, who marries them as the wood voices celebrate the wedding in a paean of wordless joy (Ex. 8).

Act III. It is mid-day under a clear autumn sky. The quiet is disturbed by the singing of Harašta, out on a poaching foray with a pedlar's basket on his back. He comes on a dead hare lying where it has been killed by a fox, is about to pick it up when he catches sight of the Forester, who greets him sarcastically. Does he enjoy his lonely life? 'Lonely? I'm going to marry Terinka' is Harašta's answer. To cover his chagrin, the Forester sets a trap for the foxes near the hare they have killed and goes off, leaving Harašta to laugh at his discomfiture.

The vixen's family of cubs rush out and dance, watched by their parents, round the clumsily set trap, to a relaxed version of Ex. 8. The dog fox asks his vixen how many children they have had already and how many they will have in the future, but Harašta's song is heard in the distance and all hide except for the cunning little vixen herself. She attracts Harašta's attention as she limps away from him, and leads him a dance—'Do you want to kill me just because I am a fox?'—which finishes with him flat on the ground as he trips over a tree root and loses the skin off his nose. He gets up to see the fox cubs pulling the poultry out of his basket, shoots into the middle of them and by pure chance hits and kills the vixen, who lies dead on the ground as the curtain comes down.

The scene changes to the garden of the inn. The Inn-keeper's wife brings the Forester his beer. He is out of humour and tells the Schoolmaster that every time recently he has been to the fox's earth he has found it deserted; he will never get the muff he has promised his wife. Terinka gets married today, says the Schoolmaster; *and* gets a new muff, sniffs the Innkeeper's wife. The Forester is even more put out than before but he tries to console himself by telling the Schoolmaster that Terinka was wrong for either of them. They miss the Parson with his ready Latin tag: he writes sometimes, says the Innkeeper's wife, and sounds homesick—Janáček's few bars of orchestral comment exactly hit off their regret at this news of someone they liked, who through nothing but goodness of heart has been hurt. The Forester pays and goes, as he tells them, off to the wood.

The last scene takes us back to the clearing where the Forester caught the little vixen. He is looking for peace, but the scene's introduction is much more turbulent, more full of longing, than the music at the start of the opera. Again the Forester muses in music of movingly human character on the forest, where life provides never an ending, only a new beginning, and where men if they know how to look may find the happiness of eternal things. As he starts to fall asleep, he sees a fox cub playing on the edge of the clearing. 'I'll catch you like I did your mother, only this time I'll bring you up better, so that people won't talk about you and me in the newspapers'. He makes a move towards the cub, and finds a frog in his hand! The wheel has come full cycle, and with it the end of an opera that is a miniature of exquisite beauty, the product of a wise (and passionate) old age, a unique example of pantheism in music drama—in my view, one of the great masterpieces of opera, a work of outstanding genius.

                                                                    H.

THE MAKROPULOS AFFAIR

Věc Makropulos[1]

Opera in three acts by Leoš Janáček, libretto by the composer, founded on Karel Čapek's play of the same name. Première, Brno, December 18, 1926, with Čvanová, Zdeněk Otava, E. Olsovsky, conductor František Neumann. First performed Prague, 1928; Frankfurt, 1929, with Gentner-Fischer, Jean Stern, conductor Josef Krips. Revived Düsseldorf, 1957 (and the following year at the Holland Festival), with Hildegard Hillebrecht, Patzak, Wiener. First performed Sadler's Wells, 1964, in English, with Collier, Dempsey, Herincx, conductor Mackerras, the performance taken the following year to Zagreb; Edinburgh Festival, 1970, (by Prague Opera) with Kniplová, Hlavsa, Rudolf Jedlicka, conductor Bohumil Gregor; New York City Opera, 1970, with Maralin Niska, Harry Theyard, Chester Ludgin.

CHARACTERS

Emilia Marty, *a singer*	Dramatic Soprano
Albert Gregor	Tenor
Vítek, *a solicitor's clerk*	Tenor
Kristina, *his daughter*	Mezzo-Soprano
Jaroslav Prus, *a Hungarian nobleman*	Baritone
Janek, *his son*	Tenor
Dr. Kolenatý, *a barrister*	Bass-Baritone
A stage hand	Bass
A stage 'dresser'	Contralto
Count Hauk-Šendorf, *an old man-about-town*	Operetta Tenor
Chamber-maid	Contralto

Time: The 1920's   *Place:* Prague

For his penultimate opera (November 1923–December 1925), Janáček himself adapted Karel Čapek's *The Makropulos Secret*, using the play in spite of Čapek's offer to write him something round the figure of the 300-year-old woman, but more suitable for opera. The background to the

[1] The Czech word 'Věc' means 'thing', so that the title literally translated should be *The Makropulos Thing*, the object in question being the paper on which is written in Greek the secret of eternal life. Charles Mackerras, whose splendid conducting of the opera has been (and is) one of the glories of Sadler's Wells, suggests that *The Makropulos Secret* is both a more accurate and a more suggestive translation than the commoner *The Makropulos Case* or *The Makropulos Affair*.

story emerges gradually during the opera's action, but might be conveniently summarised beforehand. In 1565, Hieronymus Makropulos, court physician to the Habsburg Emperor Rudolph II, succeeded in finding an elixir of life. The Emperor refused to believe him and compelled his daughter Elina, a girl of sixteen, to drink it first. Makropulos died years later in prison, but Elina's life was prolonged through the potion. Every 60 or 70 years, she changes her identity to avoid suspicion, but throughout her 300 years and more of existence she has retained the initials 'E.M.'

As the Scottish singer Ellen MacGregor (in the opera, *Ellian*), early in the nineteenth century, she had a love affair in Prague with Baron 'Peppi' Prus, by whom she had a son, Ferdinand MacGregor, whom she entered under the name Makropulos in the parish register of the village in which he was born. In 1827,[1] Baron Prus died intestate, and the estate went to a cousin. It was not long before a new claimant appeared, one Ferdinand MacGregor, whose case was circumstantially plausible in spite of there being no written proof. All the same, Baron Prus conceded that there was reasonable evidence to suggest that a certain Gregor Mack should be a major beneficiary. Since no one could claim this identity, the case between the families of Prus and Gregor has continued for nearly a century. Interest in the opera revolves around Emilia Marty; sated with life so that her reaction to virtually everything is cold and negative, only two things rouse her interest: memories of the past and her fear of death.

The prelude contrasts, as is Janáček's habit (in for instance *Katya Kabanova*), lyrical themes like Ex. 1:

from which much later material derives, with orchestral ejaculations, and includes brilliant fanfares for brass and

---

[1] Norman Tucker in his translation for Sadler's Wells changed this date to 1817, having calculated that Čapek had miscalculated by ten years!

ttle drums, Ex. 2:

symbolising the Rudolphian period of Elina Makropulos's birth.

The curtain rises on the office of the lawyer Dr. Kolenatý, where the chief clerk Vítek is tidying away papers for the night. He is concerned with the case of Gregor v. Prus, Ex. 3:

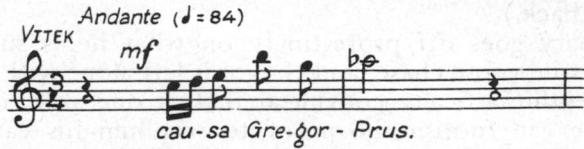

which has been going on for as long as anyone can remember, and which Albert Gregor now comes in to discuss. They are interrupted by the arrival of Vítek's daughter Krista, who is studying singing and is full of enthusiasm for the famous prima donna Emilia Marty, whose reputation greatly intrigues Gregor. Kolenatý's voice is heard and he introduces none other than the great Marty herself, with viola d'amore, to play her rather old-fashioned theme, Ex. 4:

She explains that she is interested in the Gregor-Prus case, and proceeds to show extraordinary knowledge of its details. Kolenatý, with frequent comments from Emilia Marty, goes through the case from its origins in 1827, when Baron Prus died apparently childless and intestate. Marty states categorically that the son of the Baron Prus in question was Ferdinand MacGregor (Ex. 4), his mother a singer at the

Hofoper, Ellian MacGregor. Her motif is, Ex. 5:

Questioned further, she reveals the probable hiding place of the paper which could furnish proof, and Gregor excitedly insists that Kolenatý examine this crucial evidence, even though it appears to be amongst some love letters (derivation of Ex. 1 on clarinet) in the archives of his adversary in the case, the present Baron Prus. (Ellian MacGregor had left the paper containing the elixir's secret in Prus's hands, perhaps as a kind of pledge that she would return, and Emilia badly wants it back.)

Kolenatý goes off protestingly on what he is sure will prove a wild-goose chase, and Gregor is left alone with Emilia Marty, enthusiastically convinced that at one and the same time she can furnish the proof to win him his case, the evidence he has so long sought about his ancestry (and particularly the mysterious Ellian MacGregor), and the love of his life (Ex. 5 in various manifestations). But Emilia will have none of him, and he is shocked to see her take on the look of an old woman. As she insists, apparently on the spur of the moment, that he give her some old Greek papers he will on inheriting find amongst his great-great-grandfather's effects, the scene is interrupted by the return of Kolenatý, who has found all exactly as Emilia Marty had described. Prus follows him and congratulates Gregor on having collected almost—but not quite—all the evidence he needs. Emilia offers to furnish written proof that the Ferdinand of the will and Ferdinand Gregor (No. 5) are the same person, but the curtain comes down with Kolenatý refusing to be persuaded to accept her assistance again.

Act II.   On to the empty stage of the opera house, where a stage-hand and a dresser are gossiping, comes Prus, looking for Emilia Marty. He is followed by his son, Janek, and Krista, who is mesmerised by Marty and tells Janek that their romance must take second place to her career. La Marty makes an entrance and Prus introduces to her Janek, who makes a poor showing. She is irritable and not in the mood

for compliments, reimbursing Gregor for the jewellery
hidden in a bunch of flowers which he brings her,
commenting that Strada used to sing out of tune, when Vítek
essays a comparison between her and the prima donna of the
past,[1] and asking Krista if she has yet slept with Janek.

There follows a curious episode as a stammering old roué,
Count Hauk-Šendorf, brings flowers for the diva in whom
he finds an uncanny resemblance to his one-time Spanish
mistress, Eugenia Montez. In the course of a short but
sharply-etched scene, it transpires to Hauk's amazement that
Marty is in fact the Andalusian singer to whom his heart was
given fifty years ago.

An autograph for Vítek, a wave of dismissal for Janek and
Krista, an evasion of Gregor's attempt to stay with her, and
Emilia Marty is alone with Prus. Immediately he questions
her about her special interest in Gregor, and goes on to ask
about the mysterious Ellian MacGregor,[2] from whose
illegitimate child by the Baron Prus of more than a hundred
years ago stems the present litigation. Prus is fascinated by
the mystery surrounding her; what was her real name? In her
letters to his ancestor, she signs only 'E.M.' (No. 5 dominates
the discussion), and this could equally stand for Ellian
MacGregor, Eugenia Montez, Emilia Marty—or even Elina
Makropulos.[3] He has discovered that it was in the last name
that the birth of a child, Ferdinand, was registered on the
appropriate day, which seems to dispose of Gregor's claim to
the estate. His archives contain one further packet, still
unopened; with the announcement of this new mystery, Prus
withdraws, refusing even to respond to Emilia Marty's offer
to buy the document.

Marty is sitting exhausted when Gregor returns and, in
spite of his presentiment that there is something unnatural
about her, renews his protestations of love. When she asks

[1] See page 48 (Handel's *Alcina*).

[2] Emilia has sent Dr. Kolenatý a paper signed by Ellian MacGregor
acknowledging Baron Prus as the father of her son Ferdinand.

[3] Janáček took immense pains to base his musical conversation on
the rhythms and stresses of spoken Czech, but when it came to setting
foreign languages (in this opera, Spanish for Hauk, some German for
Kolenatý and Greek for the heroine), he behaved as if the stresses were
Czech. Thus the word 'Makropulos', where the Greek stress would be on
the second syllable, is accented in the opera on the first, so that it tends
to emerge as *Mak*ropul*os*!

him to get back from Dr. Kolenatý the document he found in
the Prus archives, he threatens to kill her, at which she
shows him a scar on her neck where such an attempt has been
made in the past. When he renews his pleas, he is astonished
to find her fast asleep in her chair. He kisses her hand and
leaves, and, when she wakes, it is to find the tongue-tied
Janek gazing at her. Will he help her? His father has an old
letter addressed 'To my son Ferdinand' in a sealed packet;
will he steal it for her? He is about to agree when he is
shamed and put to flight by the appearance of his father.
Prus and Emilia Marty now face each other as adversaries but,
like the others, he succumbs to her beauty and agrees in
return for her favours to give her the unopened packet.

Act III.   Behind a curtain in Marty's hotel bedroom, two
people can be seen dressing. Emilia emerges and demands the
promised letter, which Prus silently gives her—due to her
coldness, it seems that the night together amounted to fraud.
She breaks the seal and agrees it is what she wanted. To Prus,
already depressed and disillusioned, is brought a message—his
only son Janek has committed suicide for love of Emilia.
Emilia for her part continues to arrange her hair and refuses
to accept any responsibility for his death. Hauk reappears to
invite Emilia to come to Spain with him, and in a short while
Gregor, Dr. Kolenatý, Vítek, Kristina, Prus and a doctor are
announced. The doctor removes the senile old man and
Kolenatý says he has some questions he must ask Emilia
Marty. To begin with, the autograph she gave Kristina and
the writing on the sealed packet found in Prus's house are the
same, indicating presumably that the old letter was forged by
her. She answers wearily that it was nobody but Ellian
MacGregor who wrote the letter and goes off into the
bedroom, while Kolenatý and the others start to search her
luggage. Finally, reeling from the effects of drinking half a
bottle of whisky but with her toilet complete, she starts to
answer Kolenatý's questions.

Her name is Elina Makropulos, and she was born in Crete
in 1549. Her father was Hieronymus Makropulos, physician
and alchemist to Emperor Rudolph II (Ex. 2), and she it was
who was made to drink the elixir of life her father had
brewed to convince the Emperor that it was not poisoned.
She was the Elina Makropulos who registered her son by
Baron Prus a hundred years ago as Ferdinand Makropulos.
Ellian MacGregor was her theatrical name, but she had at

various times used the names Ekaterina Myshkin and Elsa
Müller. To her son she left the most precious thing she
owned, the prescription for the elixir of life which her father
made for the Emperor and which was tried out on her,
causing her for 300 years to vindicate his alchemical skill.
Now the 300 years is up and she must renew life with the
elixir, or shrivel into old age and die.

In the course of the scene, Emilia Marty ages until at its
end she can hardly stand up. Her sceptical listeners begin to
wonder whether she has not been speaking the truth after all,
and carry her to bed. When she reappears, preceded by the
orchestra's insistence on a beautiful variant of No. 1, played
initially on solo violin, Ex. 6:

and perhaps denoting finally Marty's resignation to death and
therefore her salvation, she looks like a ghost. The former
hardness of manner has disappeared ('It is miraculous how
softly Death has touched me') and she has come to understand how desperately she has wanted to die (an unseen
chorus echoes her words). She gives the Makropulos 'secret'
(Ex. 2) to Kristina, the youngest, who throws it into the fire
as Marty sinks gratefully into death. With the understanding
that Elina Makropulos can—must—die, comes the end of a
splendid final scene, in which the music transcends the details
and carries the burden of Čapek's drama—that length of life is
far less important than man's fulfilment within it, that
mankind's fear of death must be replaced by an awareness of
what life would be without death.   H.

FROM THE HOUSE OF THE DEAD

Z Mrtvé ho Domu

Opera in three acts by Leoš Janáček; text by the composer from Dostoievsky's novel. Première, Brno, April 12, 1930, with F. Olšovsky (Filka Morosov), A. Pelc (Skuratov), G. Fischer (Shishkov), V. Sima (Goryanshikov), conductor Břetislav Bakala. First produced Mannheim, 1930, conductor Rosenstock; Berlin, Kroll Opera, 1931, with Soot, Cavara, Domgraf-Fassbaender, conductor Fritz Zweig (last première at Kroll before its closure); Düsseldorf, 1931, conductor Horenstein; Wiesbaden, 1954, with Kremer, Garen, Gschwend, conductor Elmendorff; Holland Festival, 1954, with van Mantgen, Wozniak, Broecheler, conductor Krannhals; Hanover, 1958, with Schneemann, Grobe, Alexander, conductor Schüler; Edinburgh Festival, 1964, with Blachut, Zidek, Přemysl Koci, conductor Gregor; London, Sadler's Wells, 1965, with Dowd, Dempsey, D. Bowman, conductor Mackerras; 1967, Milan, la Scala, with Bertocci, F. Ferrari, Piero Guelfi, conductor Smetaček; Stuttgart, 1967; New York (Television) with Rounseville, Lloyd, Reardon, conductor Adler; Hamburg, 1972, with Cassilly, W. Caron, Mittelman, conductor Kubelik.

CHARACTERS

Alexandr Petrovič Gorjančikov, *a political
   prisoner* .... Bass
Alyeya, *a young Tartar* .... Soprano (or Tenor)
Filka Morosov, *in prison under the name of
   Luka Kuzmič* .... Tenor
The Big Convict .... Tenor
The Small Convict .... Baritone
The Commandant .... Baritone
The Very Old Convict .... Tenor
Skuratov .... Tenor
Chekunov .... Baritone
The Drunken Convict .... Tenor
The Cook .... Baritone
The Smith .... Bass
The Priest .... Baritone
The Young Convict .... Tenor
A Whore .... Mezzo-Soprano
A Convict (*playing the roles of Don Juan and
   the Priest*) .... Baritone
Kedril .... Tenor
Shapkin .... Tenor
Shishkov .... Baritone

1584

Cherevin .... Tenor
A Guard .... Tenor
Chorus of convicts and guards; silent persons in the
play: a knight, Elvira, the cobbler's wife, the
priest's wife, the miller, the miller's wife, a scribe,
the devil

Time: Nineteenth Century   *Place:* Siberia

From February 1927 until the end of the year Janáček was
engaged on *From the House of the Dead*, finishing the score,
according to his letter to Kamila Stöslová on January 4,
having it copied out, and then, at the end of January, 1928,
starting to compose his second String Quartet. But later dates
(7.v.1928 at the end of Act II, 24.iv.1928 at the end of Act
III) appear on the score, and in point of fact the opera was
not truly finished at the time of the composer's death, some
of it existing only in short score. Orchestration and the filling of
whatever gaps remained was undertaken by the composer's
disciples, Břetislav Bakala, the conductor, and Osvald
Chlubna, the composer. The juxtaposition of the Glagolithic
Mass with the new opera contrasts the extremes of the Slav
mind, from the gentle but convinced exultation of the Mass
to the despair of some of the characters in the opera.

Janáček's art developed as time went on (one can hardly
write 'as he grew older' about a composer whose first *local*
success came when he was 50 and who was not known in the
capital of his native land until he was well over 60). Roman
Vlad's comment about *Brouček*—that melodic motifs flower
throughout the drama and are not employed in Wagnerian
fashion—becomes less true over the years. In *The Cunning
Little Vixen* he already weaves a motific tapestry in order to
create his forest, *The Makropulos Affair* carries the process a
stage further, and by the time of *From the House of the
Dead*, it is possible for Erik Chisholm to write with justice
'From even a casual study (of the music of Shishkov's story)
it should be clear that Janáček employs as highly complex a
system of leit-motif as any composer has attempted since the
death of Wagner.'

Act I. There is an extended prelude, moving and
evocative and derived from material originally intended for a
Violin Concerto to be called 'Wanderings of the Soul'. The
curtain rises on a penal settlement on the river Irtysh in
Siberia; it is winter and early morning. The prisoners waiting

about aimlessly outside their huts hear that a new prisoner is to arrive, a city man, perhaps an aristocrat. They argue and quarrel until Alexandr Petrovič Gorjančikov is brought in by the guard. The Camp Commandant reacts sarcastically to the prisoner's smart clothes, then orders him to behave while in prison. Questioned about the nature of his crime, Gorjančikov says he is a political prisoner, which answer produces a spasm of rage in the Commandant, who yells for him to be taken away and flogged. Nobody but Alyeya, a young Tartar prisoner, takes much notice when cries of pain are heard coming from behind the huts, but the music reacts in sympathy. The other prisoners occupy themselves with an eagle with a broken wing, which they keep in a cage. The eagle in his present condition clearly has symbolic significance for them, and an old man contrasts the eagle's pride with man's smallness of mind. The episode is interrupted by the Commandant, and the prisoners are forced to resume work by the guards, singing as they do so a lament for the homes they suspect they will never see again. Skuratov, the camp's self-appointed entertainer, joins the group and sings a folk song. There is clearly some tension between him and Luka Kuzmič, and Skuratov suddenly pours out his homesickness for Moscow, where he was happy in his work as a cobbler. He dances and collapses exhausted.

The remainder of the act is dominated by Luka's story of how he came to be in the camp. Baited by a brutal Commanding Officer, he first lulled him into a sense of security and then stabbed him to death. During the beating and torture which followed, he thought all the time that he would die. When he finishes his story, full of hideous detail, the old prisoner looks up and asks him, 'And did you die?', The characteristic speech of the prisoners is ejaculatory, as if they were forced to relieve nervous tension by their confessions.

Alexandr Petrovič is brought back after his flogging; all watch the gates close after him and eventually stop working. In the revisions which were made to the score after Janáček's death and before the première at Brno, a dramatic episode was here superimposed on the music, in which Gorjančikov makes a futile attempt to kill the Commandant, an addition which is at least questionable, since the music at this point is dominated by Skuratov's motif.

The second Act takes place on the banks of the River Irtysh.[1] The sun is shining and the steppes stretch away to the horizon (empty fifths of the flutes and then plaintive singing in the distance characterise the barren loneliness of the plain). Before the curtain rises, the working sound of hammers can be heard as the convicts break up an old boat. Gorjančikov asks Alyeya about his sister, but Alyeya is convinced she has died of grief at his disgrace, Gorjančikov tries to distract his attention and, much to Alyeya's delight, offers to teach him to read and write.

It is a holiday and the other prisoners have no patience with anything that distracts them from one of their few opportunities for rest and pleasure. They are going to have a theatrical performance of sorts, and a satirical march ushers into the camp the Commandant, the guards and the priest. The prisoners are given food, and Skuratov starts to describe the circumstances of his crime. It is a simple case of murder for jealousy, described with much of the conviction and agony which must have accompanied its commission. He was head over heels in love with a German girl, Luisa, who lived with her aunt. Unfortunately, though she had agreed to marry him, a richer compatriot asked for her hand in marriage and her aunt insisted that she make the better match. Skuratov shot him, was captured after escaping and condemned to prison for life. It is a touching narrative, and in its course Skuratov attacks and knocks to the ground a drunken man who has been continually interrupting with cries of 'It's lies!' Someone at the end asks what happened to Luisa, and Skuratov's cry of 'Oh, Luisa' remains to haunt the imagination.

It is time for the play to start and one may at first think it contradictory that, apart from dance tunes, Janáček employs similar musical language here as for the main action, his point being presumably that the fantasies of the prisoners are at least as real as their everyday thoughts and actions, in fact hardly to be distinguished from them. Don Juan and his servant Kedril are beset by devils, but Don Juan has three

---

[1] Janáček clearly wants contrast as a relief between the gloom of Act I and the grim horror of the hospital in Act III and in order to obtain it has not scrupled to put Dostoievsky's account of the play into the open air. To play this Act inside is wrong, and Max Brod, in his German translation, has underlined this by additionally placing it in summer.

adventures before he finally succumbs to them. He makes
love to Elvira and, when a knight appears to defend her, kills
him. He spurns a cobbler's wife introduced by Kedril, but
shows interest in the wife of a priest before the reappearance
of the devils heralds his end. After a good deal of general
laughter stylised in the music, Kedril announces that the next
piece will be the Tale of the Beautiful Miller's Wife. The
Miller says goodbye to his wife, who is satirised in a tune
with the bite of early Prokofiev in it and proceeds to take
advantage of his absence to receive a succession of lovers,
each one hiding when the next is about to appear. The last
is Don Juan, dressed as a priest; when the Miller returns, Don
Juan kills him and dances with the woman to the music of a
slow waltz of considerable intensity.

The play is over and the prisoners start to disperse, leaving
Alexandr Petrovič and Alyeya sitting together and drinking
tea. They watch a young prisoner make off with a
particularly unprepossessing whore and shortly afterwards one
of the other prisoners takes it into his head that they are
privileged in having tea and attacks Alyeya, leaving a gaping
wound in his head. The guards advance on the prisoners as
the curtain falls.

The third Act again takes place in winter, and the scene
shows the inside of the prison hospital. The Muslim, Alyeya,
lying in bed, tells Alexandr Petrovič that what has most
impressed him in the Bible—he can now read a bit—is the idea
that men should love their enemies. Luka mumbles away
from the bed in which he lies dying, Shapkin's story of how
he was caught poaching and had his ears pulled by the Chief
of Police is told against an accompaniment more than usually
consolatory, and Skuratov's feverish but heart-rending cries
of 'Oh, Luisa' eventually exasperate the other prisoners
who drag him back to his own bed.

Shishkov now embarks on what is to prove the longest of
the three major narratives of the opera. With a bitter irony,
his story is punctuated by the death agony of Luka, who
eventually turns out to have been the villain of Shishkov's
narrative. A young girl called Akulka is generally believed on
his evidence to have lost her honour to a certain Filka
Morosov. Her parents beat her but eventually Shishkov is
persuaded to marry her, and on his wedding night he
discovers that she is a virgin and has been grossly slandered.
When Filka is called up to the army, Akulka admits that she

1as been in love with him all along and that after her
marriage she has in fact been guilty of the sin of which she
was once falsely accused. Shishkov in his shame and agony
takes her out into the woods and cuts her throat. The story is
punctuated by the vain efforts of his listeners to hurry
Shishkov on to the point, by the heavy breathing of the sick
prisoners, and by the groans and sobs of Luka, who dies and is
carried out as the story comes to an end. As it passes, Shishkov
recognises the body as Filka Morosov's masquerading under
another name, and in spite of the forgiving comment of an
old prisoner, Shishkov curses the corpse all the way out to
the door. The scene ends as the guards call Alexandr
Petrovič Gorjančikov, Alyeya clutching despairingly at
him as he is taken out.

Wordless voices behind the curtain punctuate the interlude
before the curtain rises on the camp as in the first scene. The
sun is shining, the prisoners are at their work as the
Commandant addresses himself drunkenly to Gorjančikov
and asks his forgiveness for having had him flogged on his
arrival. He is to go free straightaway and his fetters are taken
off him. As Alexandr Petrovič tries to comfort the
despairing Alyeya, the music takes on the character almost of
optimism that lies somewhere at the heart of Dostoievsky's
masterpiece, the optimism that believes, in spite of the
evidence, that there is goodness in life, honesty and integrity
in man, a purpose behind it all. Petrovič leaves the camp and
the prisoners free the eagle, whose wings have now recovered
their strength, and the music is momentarily in the nature of
a hymn to freedom.

The end is controversial. In Janáček's original, after
Gorjančikov has left, the guard shouts at the remaining
prisoners 'March!', and with their chains clanking they are
herded back to their huts—after a glimpse of freedom, life in
the House of the Dead returns to stark normality. Only
Alyeya in his hospital nightgown and forgetful of everything
else now that he has lost Petrovič, remains behind, 'as a
symbol of God's spark in man'. At the suggestion of the
producer, Ota Zítek, Bakala the conductor and Janáček's
pupil, the composer Chlubna, omitted the intervention of the
guard and chose to maintain the optimism of the final
chorus, carrying it through to the end. Conductors
responsible for a revival of the opera must decide which of
the two versions to adopt; the vocal score contains only the

revision, but the original is reproduced in Jaroslav Vogel's *Leoš Janáček: His Life and Works*.

Perhaps no other composer than Janáček would have attempted to turn Dostoievsky's vast book into an opera. Certainly no one else could have compressed it into three acts of less than thirty minutes each, and still have preserved so magnificently the spirit of the original.   H.

JAROMIR WEINBERGER

(1896–1967)

SCHWANDA THE BAGPIPER

Švanda Dudák

OPERA in two acts by Jaromir Weinberger; text by M. Kareš. Première Prague, April 27, 1927, conductor Ostrčil. First performed Breslau, 1929; Berlin, 1929, with Müller, Branzell, Soot, Scheidl, Schützendorf, Helgers, conductor Kleiber; Vienna, 1930, with Angerer, Rünger, Piccaver, Hammes, Mayr, conductor Krauss; Metropolitan, New York, 1931, with Müller, Branzell, Laubenthal, Schorr, Andresen, Schützendorf, conductor Bodanzky; Covent Garden, 1934, with Ursuleac, Rünger, Kullmann, Schoeffler, Kipnis, Sterneck, conductor Krauss; Buenos Aires, 1935, with Fleischer, Kovaceva, Pataky, Gaudin, Baccaloni, conductor Panizza. Revived Sadler's Wells, 1948, with Shires, Gerald Davis, Roderick Jones, Glynne, conductor Robertson; Düsseldorf 1949, with Spletter, Gester.

CHARACTERS

Schwanda the Bagpiper ....Baritone
Dorotka, *his wife* ....Soprano
Babinsky, *a romantic robber* ....Tenor
The Queen ....Mezzo-Soprano
The Magician ....Bass
The Judge...............................Tenor
The Executioner.........................Tenor
The Devil ....Bass
The Devil's Familiar Spirit ....Tenor

The Captain of Hell's Guard ....Tenor
Two Forest Rangers ....Tenor, Bass

Act I.   Close to a forest is the cottage where Schwanda,
the piper of Strakonitz, dwells with his young wife, Dorotka.
As the curtain rises, two armed foresters hasten to the
cottage to enquire whether a suspicious stranger has been
seen in the neighbourhood. They are after the robber,
Babinsky. Dorotka, however, cannot help them; she has seen
no one and the foresters depart to try their luck elsewhere.

No sooner have they gone than Babinsky, who has been
hiding in the high branches of a tree, drops to the ground
before the astonished Dorotka. She questions Babinsky and
her astonishment grows when she learns that Babinsky has
never heard of her famous husband, Schwanda, the bagpiper
of Strakonitz. Why, the devil himself envies Schwanda his
gift. 'Are you the Devil?' asks the gentle Dorotka. Babinsky,
who obviously is struck by Dorotka's beauty, is rather hurt.
But Schwanda arrives from the fields where he has been
working, and courteously asks his unknown guest to share
their meal. In the course of the conversation Babinsky tells
the story of the great robber Babinsky, the friend of the
poor, the hero of a thousand adventures. The story makes an
impression on Schwanda, who would willingly go and see the
great world.

'A man gifted as you are,' replies Babinsky, 'could easily
make his way.' He tells of people who are wealthy and bored
and of the Queen whose heart is ice and who waits and waits
for someone who can melt it. Schwanda's ambition is on fire.
Dorotka would hold him back but, while she is out of sight,
Schwanda departs with Babinsky.

The second scene shows the chamber of Queen Iceheart,
who vainly hopes to find a cure in the tricks of the court
magician. Then, to the tune of the now famous polka,
Schwanda enters. His music is simply irresistible; the Queen's
maids-of-honour and pages dance. 'Who art thou, bringer of
jollity?' asks the Queen. 'I am Schwanda,' replies the piper in
a jovial aria, in which the chorus joins; 'I go where there is
bitterness and sorrow; I blow on my pipe and at once the
clouds melt and the whole world rejoices.' The Queen is so
much enamoured of the music that she decides to wed the
musician forthwith. Schwanda, fascinated by the prospect of
sharing a throne, agrees and kisses the Queen.

But if Schwanda can forget the faithful Dorotka, Dorotka, far from forgetting Schwanda, has followed him, and now overtakes him to tax him with infidelity. Schwanda's forgetfulness, however, was but a moment's aberration. The Queen, learning this, orders both to appear before the judge, who will condemn them to death.

In the third scene we see the scene of judgment when sentence is passed on Schwanda and Dorotka. They are to suffer the extreme penalty. But just as the execution is about to take place, the executioner discovers that his axe has been stolen. It is Babinsky who has come to the rescue of his friend, and now hands him the pipes. Schwanda plays and the public are helpless; they *must* dance while Schwanda and his friends move slowly towards the gate and go out of the town (Furiant).

Once they are well away Dorotka turns on him and taunts her errant husband. Schwanda denies everything. 'If I have given the queen a single kiss may the Devil take me,' he exclaims. The Devil does; and Schwanda disappears.

Act II. The scene represents Hell. The Devil is playing cards by himself; no one trusts his card-playing, and thus he is reduced to a lonely game of Patience. Schwanda is there too. But Schwanda need not obey the Devil, since he has not been sent there but came of his own free will, and the rules of Hell do not apply to him. The Devil is very bored, and begs Schwanda again and again to play for him. His requests meet with a blank refusal; Schwanda will not play to the Devil. The Father of Lies is at a loss for arguments, but he overhears Schwanda's lament for his lost earthly joys, above all for Dorotka, who made life pleasing to him. Here is his opportunity. He shows Schwanda the spectre of Dorotka and tells him he has but to sign a paper to get her. Schwanda signs quickly the paper giving away his soul. But instead of producing Dorotka, the Devil tells him that now, as his

...oject, he is bound to obey and, to begin with, he must play ..n his pipes.

The timely arrival of Babinsky saves Schwanda for the moment. The robber is, of course, well known to the Devil, who respects Babinsky's well-known skill. Moreover, he is only too pleased to welcome a man who is not afraid of having a game of cards with him. They gamble desperately, and in the end the Devil loses everything. The Devil is now a poor devil indeed. 'Be a man,' he is told, 'and bear your loss with courage.' He is sad; nothing is left him; he has gambled away his kingdom, his treasure, the soul of Schwanda, the insignia of his office; 'What sort of a devil am I now?' he asks full of self-pity.

Babinsky, however, is generous. He will leave the Devil his kingdom and his insignia; only Schwanda must be free to go with him. The servants of Hell cheer Babinsky, while the Devil thanks him and promises that should he ever return he will be welcomed as 'a son of the house'. To crown it all the piper will play them a tune so that they may learn what the playing of the great master Schwanda of Strakonitz is like. This is the ingenious fugue, which has become popular in the concert hall where it is played in conjunction with the polka.

The fifth and last scene takes us back to Schwanda's cottage. Babinsky makes a last attempt to divide the lovers. He tells Schwanda that, although he may not have known it, he has lived twenty years in Hell; that Dorotka is now an old peasant woman who, most likely, will not know him again, and invites him to go back to the great world where young queens and princesses live.

Schwanda has learnt his lesson. Never again will he depart from his beloved. 'Dorotka! Dorotka!' he calls at the door of the cottage, and Dorotka comes to him as young and beautiful as ever. Babinsky retires discomfited. Peasants passing see Schwanda and rush to congratulate him on his return.

F.B.

20
Polish Opera

KAROL
SZYMANOWSKI
(1882–1937)

KING ROGER

KRÓL ROGER

OPERA in three acts, music by Karol Szymanowski, libretto by J. Iwaszkiewicz. Première, Warsaw June 19, 1926, with Stanislava Korwin-Szymanowska (the composer's wife), Eugeniusz Mossakowski as King Roger, Adam Tobosz as the Shepherd, conducted by Emil Młynarski. First performed in German, Duisburg 1928; in Czech in Prague, 1932; in Italian, Palermo during ISCM Festival, 1949, with Clara Petrella, Annaloro, Inghilleri, conductor Mieczyslaw Mierzejewski; in English, 1955, (B.B.C. Broadcast), with Joyce Gartside, Rowland Jones, Redvers Llewellyn, conductor Stanford Robinson; London, New Opera Company, 1975, with Janet Gail, David Hillman, Peter Knapp, conductor Charles Mackerras.

CHARACTERS

Roger II, *King of Sicily* .... Baritone
Roxana, *his wife* .... Soprano
Edrisi, *an arab scholar* .... Tenor
The Shepherd .... Tenor
The Archbishop .... Bass
An Abbess .... Contralto
  Priests, monks, nuns, the King's guard, Norman knights, etc.

Time: Twelfth century   *Place:* Sicily

Karol Szymanowski in his lifetime occupied a curious position as the first Polish composer since Chopin to make an impact on the musical world, indeed the first since

Moniuszko to write his name in the history books at all. Born
of a land-owning family, after the Russian Revolution he led
a life of poverty, in spite of a considerable reputation as both
composer and pianist, and was repeatedly forced back on the
charity of his friends for sheer survival. His list of compositions includes two notable violin concertos; four
symphonies of which the fourth is the Symphonie concertante for piano and orchestra; a *Stabat Mater*; a ballet,
Harnasie; and a quantity of chamber and piano music. He was
a fairly extensive writer and his novel *Efebos* has a homosexual theme, an *apologia pro vita sua* according to those
who knew him.

King Roger is his second opera, the first, *Hagith* (1912–13;
performed 1922) is a one-acter with a lurid plot, modelled
according to his biographer B. M. Maciejewski on *Salome*.
Before 1914, Szymanowski travelled rather extensively in
Russia and Europe and even ventured as far as Algiers,
developing a strong taste for the Orient, sufficiently deep for
no lesser judge than Kaikhosru Sorabji, writing of the third
(choral) symphony, to say: 'Szymanowski has taken a poem
celebrating . . . the enigmatic and transcendental beauty of an
Eastern night, the like of which is to be found nowhere in
Europe except in Sicily, which belongs as much to the East as
it does to the West. Around this poem, Szymanowski has
written music . . . permeated with the very essence of . . .
Iranian art . . . that such a feat is unparalleled in Western
music. Here is no European in Eastern fancy-dress . . .'

The genesis of the opera seems to have come in conversations between the composer and his cousin Iwaszkiewicz,
during whose course Szymanowski made clear his enthusiasm
for the beauties of Sicily and particularly for the country's
unique mixture of Greek, Arabic, Byzantine and Latin
elements able to coexist in Sicily just as had, until the end of
the twelfth century, men of differing creeds. Intellectually,
the opera represents the conflict between Christian and pagan
ideals, or between the pulls of the Dionysian and the
Apollonian within each of us.[1] The voice of a new god
speaks through a mysterious shepherd who appears before
the Christian King Roger. He is rejected by all except Queen
Roxana, who is led by instinct rather than intellect to some
acceptance of the Shepherd and his message. After trying to
make him a prisoner, the King eventually comes to terms
with the challenge represented by the new phenomenon. The

[1] See Henze's *The Bassarids* page 1140.

music has something of the opulence and texture of Szymanowski's contemporaries Strauss and Scriabin, with occasionally the sharp insight of Debussy.

Act I.   The interior of a Byzantine cathedral, rich with characteristics of East and West. It is filled with worshippers and the Archbishop stands in front of the altar as the sound is heard of a great psalm of praise to God, boys' voices alternating with those of the congregation. The King and his court enter ceremoniously to a musical climax, and Archbishop and Abbess abjure him to protect the Church from her enemies and in particular from a new voice who corrupts men and women alike. Edrisi explains that they are speaking of a young shepherd boy, and Roxana raises her voice to beg the King at least to hear the boy in his own defence. The King commands that he be brought before him as the throng calls for his destruction.

To the King's questions, the Shepherd answers elliptically in a long, ecstatic utterance of considerable lyrical impact— his god is young, beautiful and full of life. Roxana's reaction to his words is favourable, to the King's obvious discomfiture, and for a moment he is disposed to order the Shepherd's instant death but relents and agrees to let him go free. Finally, to the fury of the worshippers, he orders his appearance that very night at the palace gate. The Shepherd leaves on the same note of ecstasy as had characterised the explanation of his philosophy.

Act II.   The inner courtyard of the King's Palace, where that night the King awaits his visitor. The gorgeous texture of the music perfectly conveys the hot Mediterranean night, as well as the tension in the King's mind, much of it, as Edrisi finds when he tries unavailingly to comfort him, on account of the sympathy he senses between his beloved Roxana and the Shepherd. In the distance they hear the sound of tamborines and zithers and immediately, on high A flat, Roxana starts to sing, wordlessly at first, but with rapt concentration and in a highly evocative manner. This is the score's best-known moment, more, unfortunately, from Pawel Kochanski's transcription for violin and piano than from performances of the opera.

The King is enraptured by the song but knows it is sung in honour of the Shepherd. Watchmen announce the Shepherd's appearance and, with a group of four followers carrying musical instruments, he advances towards the King's throne, in brightly coloured clothing and with his auburn hair flowing to his shoulders. He greets the King in the name of eternal love and tells him he comes from Benares on the banks of the Ganges in India. He proclaims that it is God who has sent him, from God that he derives his powers, and in another extended lyrical passage sings the praises of his faith, until the King stops him, horror-stricken at what he does not hesitate to brand as blasphemy. Immediately, Roxana's song starts again, arousing the Shepherd's evident delight and the King's no less evident jealousy.

Eventually, the Shepherd's followers start an arabic dance, initially in 7/8, and gradually all join in, until Roxana herself becomes visible in the gallery above the courtyard and in her turn starts to sing with the Shepherd and the others. Beside himself with rage, King Roger orders the guards to bind the Shepherd with chains, so that he stands fettered by Roxana's side. Angrily, the Shepherd breaks the bonds and casts them at the King's feet, then calls to Roxana and the people and leads them slowly from the King's presence into what he describes as the Kingdom of Light. The King is left alone in his grief with Edrisi, then suddenly throws aside crown, mantle and sword, announcing that he too will follow the Shepherd, as a pilgrim, no longer as King.

Act III. Among the ruins of a Greek Temple appear King Roger and the faithful Edrisi, the former still lamenting his powerless state in the face of his lost love, the latter begging him to call aloud to the echoes. At last he does so, and his cry of 'Roxana!' gets from the distance an immediate answer in the unmistakable voice of Roxana, only for his second attempt to receive a similar answer in the Shepherd's voice. The King's consternation is only partly assuaged by the Shepherd's admonition to leave his fear where he left his sword, and when a moment later Roxana reaches her hand towards him, he still cannot believe that the Shepherd is not playing a cruel joke. Roxana tries to persuade him that the Shepherd is in fact all round him, in every natural thing, and it is not long before Roxana and the King begin to throw great heaps of flowers on the fire which burns on the altar. The Shepherd has by now turned into the Greek god Dionysus and the members of his train into bacchants and maenads, and they whirl into a mad dance, in which Roxana joins, until gradually all disappear, leaving Roger alone with Edrisi. But through his trials the King has grown and it is

with confidence, indeed rapture, that he greets the rising of
the sun in a splendid paean of thanksgiving as the opera
comes to an end.   H.

KRZYSZTOF PENDERECKI

(b. 1933)

THE DEVILS OF LOUDUN

Die Teufel von Loudun

OPERA in three acts by Krzysztof Penderecki, libretto by the com-
poser, based on John Whiting's dramatisation of Aldous Huxley's *The
Devils of Loudun* (German translation by Erich Fried). Première,
Hamburg, June 20, 1969, with Tatiana Troyanos, Andre Hiölski,
Helmut Melchert, Bernard Ladysz, conductor Henrik Czyz, producer
Konrad Swinarski. First performed Stuttgart, 1969, with Colette
Lorand, Carlos Alexander, conductor Janos Kulka, producer Günther
Rennert; Santa Fé, 1969, with Joy Davidson, John Reardon, conductor
Stanislaw Skrowaczewski; Wuppertal, 1970; Graz, 1971, with Margarita
Kyriaki, Hans Laettgen, Dusan Popović. British première,
Sadler's Wells, 1973, with Josephine Barstow, Geoffrey Chard, Harold
Blackburn, produced John Dexter, conductor Nicholas Braithwaite.

CHARACTERS

Jeanne, *the Prioress of St. Ursula's*
   Convent .... Dramatic Soprano
Claire ⎫   ⎧ Mezzo-Soprano
Gabrielle ⎬ *Ursuline Sisters* .... ⎨   Soprano
Louise ⎭   ⎩   Contralto
Philippe, *a young girl* .... High Lyric Soprano
Ninon, *a young widow* .... Contralto
Grandier, *the Vicar of St. Peter's Church* ..... Baritone
Father Barré, *the Vicar of Chinon* .... Bass
de Laubardemont, *the King's Special Commissioner*
  .... Tenor

Father Rangier .... Basso Profondo
Father Mignon, *the Ursulines' father confessor* .. Tenor
Adam, *a chemist* .... Tenor
Mannoury, *a surgeon* .... Baritone
d'Armagnac, *the Mayor of Loudun* ..... Speaking part
de Cérisay, *Town Governor* .... Speaking part
Prince Henri de Condé, *the King's Special*
    Ambassador .... Baritone
Father Ambrose, *an old priest* .... Bass
Bontemps, *a gaoler* .... Bass-Baritone
Clerk of the Court .... Speaking part
Ursuline Nuns, Carmelites, people, children, guards, soldiers
Time: 1634   *Place:* Loudun

At the première of Penderecki's *The Devils of Loudun* in
Hamburg in June, 1969, I was vastly impressed by what the
composer had done, as it seemed to me, in wringing the last
drop out of the tensions of the original play, its inexorability
and its horrors—and expressing it all through music. His use
of musical colour, whether individual instruments or combinations, the not so common moments of full orchestra or
the frequently added chorus (live or amplified), struck me as
masterly and hard to parallel on such a scale in any opera I
have ever heard. Seldom is a texture or a musical movement
sustained for long at a stretch, much less developed, and the
solo voice—though every word is, exceptionally, audible—is
used either in declamation or in isolated expressive phrases,
seldom in the 'lyrical' manner developed in recent operas of
Stravinsky, Britten, Henze, or the concert works of Boulez.
And yet the *effectiveness* of what Penderecki has done is not
in doubt. With the precision of an acupuncturist and by
musical (*i.e.* not solely stage) means, he touches nerves
unerringly to produce a reaction, thus advancing the drama
and manipulating the emotions of his audience at one and the
same time.

The opera, commissioned by Rolf Liebermann for the
Hamburg Opera, was first heard at an ISCM Festival in 1969
and is based on John Whiting's dramatisation of Aldous
Huxley's novel, *The Devils of Loudun*. 'Huxley was
examining the phenomenon of the Ursuline nuns who
claimed to be possessed by devils as one manifestation of
mankind's innate urge for self-transcendence, others in-

cluding drink, drugs, and sexual adventure—though he also
compared the witch-hunting of Urbain Grandier with similar
persecutions in modern times. For Penderecki, whose earlier
works have proclaimed him a devout Christian, Grandier is a
Christ-like martyr, proudly set on the road to martyrdom
quite early on, and this is the Parson's passion that we are
witnessing in his opera.'[1] The personal tragedies of Grandier
and Mère Jeanne are set against a background of political
manoeuvrings in which Grandier, the vicar of St. Peter's
church in Loudun, comes to champion the independent spirit
of the town in opposition to Cardinal Richelieu and his
adherents. Grandier is falsely accused of being in league with
the devil, the most convincing of his traducers being Mère
Jeanne, whose invitation as Prioress to become confessor to
her order he had refused. Her dreams and sexual frustrations
start to centre on him and the suggestion is that her fixation
becomes indistinguishable from love, that she is used by
Grandier's enemies, political and social as well as spiritual (he
is a womaniser in a provincial society), to secure his downfall.

Act I.   Jeanne is lying on her bed in her cell at night
praying. The music, which plays throughout each act without
a break, steals in almost imperceptibly, worryingly, as, in her
vision, she sees Grandier[2] seated on a chair which has been
lashed to a litter and is carried by four soldiers. He wears a
heretic's shirt impregnated with sulphur, and there is a rope
round his neck. His broken legs dangle, he is a ridiculous,
hairless, shattered doll. The Clerk of the Court walks next to
him. De Laubardemont and soldiers follow. The Clerk of the
Court gives Grandier a two-pound taper to hold. During her
trance, Jeanne, who is a hunchback, prays to be made
straight. The vision fades and Jeanne is brought a letter; it is
from Grandier, regretting that he cannot accept her invitation
to become director of the Ursuline community. Her sick
imagination conjures up a vision of Grandier and Ninon lying
together, then she falls to her knees in convulsions. Bells.

Scene ii.   A corpse hangs from the municipal gallows of
Loudun as people leave St. Peter's church, among them
Adam, the chemist, and Mannoury, a surgeon. They
comment on the self-importance of the vicar, Grandier, on
the contented look of the young widow Ninon, which they

---

[1] William Mann, *The Times*, June 23, 1969.
[2] Throughout, I have quoted the vocal score's stage directions.

ay derives from Grandier's visits to her, and then on the new occupant of the gibbet.

Scene iii.   Grandier with Ninon in a tub.

Scene iv.   Adam and Mannoury have brought the human head from the gallows and they meet and greet Grandier, showing less than total enthusiasm.

Scene v.   Grandier kneels at the altar alone and prays to be shown the way to God's grace.

Scene vi.   Jeanne and the Ursuline nuns enter the church and Jeanne is overcome by a fit of coughing. When Grandier re-enters in full canonicals, Jeanne screams and runs from the church and the chorus mutters temporarily to a halt.

Scene vii.   Adam and Mannoury plot to draw up an indictment of Grandier.

Scene viii.   Grandier in a confessional, with Philippe outside. She confesses to unclean thoughts ... about him, and he draws her into the confessional and pulls the curtain.

Scene ix.   D'Armagnac, the town's Governor, confronts de Laubardemont and refuses to obey the latter's order to pull down the town's fortifications. Grandier supports d'Armagnac.

Scene x.   Adam and Mannoury prepare their indictment, referring to a small book containing a register of Grandier's movements. Mannoury finds the evidence very flimsy.

Scene xi.   Jeanne is walking with Father Mignon, a foolish old man who has accepted to become the Order's director. She tells him that she has lately suffered from terrible visions straight from the Devil and has recognised Grandier. Father Mignon asks her if she understands the gravity of her charge.

Scene xii.   In the pharmacy, Father Mignon, Adam and Mannoury are discussing the Prioress's visions, and Father Mignon says he has sent a message to Father Barré, the vicar of Chinon, an expert in exorcism. Suddenly there is a knock at the door and de Laubardemont enters, seeking information about Grandier. He seems to have come to the right place.

Scene xiii.   The first confrontation of Mère Jeanne with Barré and those who seek to support him in the exorcism. Jeanne is in private prayer and asks God to give her love; immediately she sees Grandier and Philippe walking by the town wall. De Laubardemont, Barré, Mignon, Mannoury, Adam and Father Rangier rush into the room and, as Barré attempts to communicate with the evil spirit, Jeanne throws

back her crooked head and peals of masculine laughter pour
from her distorted mouth. The scene draws to a climax as her
inarticulate cries form into a single word, 'Grandier!'

Act II, scene i.   The church. Jeanne kneels and facing her
are Barré, Rangier, Mignon and the Ursuline nuns. The scene
of exorcism proceeds but inarticulate whispers and laughter
interrupt and Asmodeus speaks in a deep voice through
Jeanne. Barré applies a small box to Jeanne's back, but the
Latin is interrupted when Jeanne demands that they should
speak about the sexual activities of priests. Barré diagnoses
that the Devil seems to be lodged deep in the lower bowel
and orders Adam and Mannoury to make appropriate preparations. Suddenly, and in spite of Jeanne's efforts to take
back what she has been saying, Barré and Rangier grab
Jeanne and carry her behind a curtain where apothecary and
chemist administer an enema to screams of protest and laughter.

Scene ii.   D'Armagnac and de Cérisay, Mayor and
Governor of Loudun, warn Grandier that the continual
mention of his name by the possessed Jeanne puts him in a
dangerous position. For his part, Grandier says he hopes God
will help her in her terror and unhappiness.

Scene iii.   Jeanne lies in her cell, while Barré and his
cronies continue to examine her, this time in the presence of
de Cérisay. Jeanne screams the name of Grandier and describes a kind of Black Mass, whispering occasionally into
Barré's ear, until Barré takes de Cérisay by the arm and draws
him aside. While Mignon and the nuns pray (for the first time
in the opera, 'normal' choral singing, but soon succeeded by
an amazing glissando effect), de Cérisay objects that the
whole thing is a product of Jeanne's imagination, speaking as
she does with her own voice and accusing Grandier as she has
of visiting her in the convent, where he swears he has never
set foot. Three of the sisters have, according to Barré,
testified that they have engaged in copulation with demons
and been deflowered, and Mannoury on examination has
found none of them intact. De Cérisay objects that everyone
knows about the sentimental attachments between the young
women of a convent, and orders the exorcism to cease
pending a thorough investigation of the case.

Scene iv.   Grandier is grateful to de Cérisay for his intervention, but d'Armagnac says that he has heard from Paris
that Grandier, because he has supported d'Armagnac against
de Laubardemont, now has a dedicated enemy in Richelieu,
and Grandier confesses that he feels himself forsaken.

Scene v. Philippe comes to Grandier in the church and tells him she is pregnant. Grandier, not without sympathy, says goodbye; how could he possibly own to being the child's father? He cannot help her.

Scene vi. In the pharmacy, Adam, Mannoury and Father Mignon are joined by Fathers Barré and Rangier. The Archbishop has issued an ordinance forbidding further exorcism and their 'mission' seems to be at an end. Their lament for a moment turns into a beautiful quintet, the most 'vocal' number in the score, and at its end Barré says that he must go back to his parish, to the regret of his co-agitators, but—'My friend, it needs but a whisper from Hell, and I'll be back again.'

Scene vii. The sisters ask Mère Jeanne why the Archbishop has forbidden Father Barré to see them any more, and why people are taking their children away from the nunnery, so that there is too much work left for the sisters to manage on their own. Suddenly, Jeanne laughs at them: 'Why don't you ask the devils to lend a hand?' But the sisters have the last word: 'We have mocked God!'

Scene viii. On the fortifications at night, during a storm Grandier hears from d'Armagnac and de Cérisay that the King has gone back on his word, to Richelieu's evident joy, and the town's fortifications are to be razed to the ground. Grandier paradoxically rejoices: 'Heavenly Father, You have restored strength to my enemies and hope to Your sinful child . . . You have made the way possible.'

Scenes ix and x. In the church, with its doors barred against the outside world, Mignon in the presence of de Laubardemont incites the sisters to go back on what they had told the Archbishop's doctor—that they were only playing parts and not truly possessed by the Devil—and reveal the truth: that the Devil had them in his power. Hysteria rises, the voices of Leviathan and Beherit start to speak through Jeanne, and only Sister Gabrielle sits still throughout the scene. De Laubardemont is galvanised into action, says he must depart for Paris but will leave Barré to prosecute the cause in Loudun.

The doors are opened and people of every kind and description rush in. The sisters perform their antics to the delight of the townspeople. Priests re-appear in full attire and the noise is only stilled by the arrival of the King's representative, Prince Henri de Condé. Relics are brought, Barré resumes his work, Leviathan speaks through Mère Jeanne, the sisters react to the name of Grandier, and pandemonium breaks loose, with lewd dancing, screaming and shouting. De Condé asks Beherit, concealed in the person of Mère Jeanne, what his opinion is of the King and his adviser the Cardinal. When Jeanne prevaricates, he congratulates Beherit. To have praised would have implied that the King's policy was hellish, to have disparaged could have resulted in a charge of treason! De Condé takes a small box from one of his pages, containing, he says, some true blood of the Saviour; let Barré exorcise the devils with it. Barré does his stuff and the devils leave Jeanne's body in a series of horrible screams. Barré is triumphant, but de Condé reveals that the box was empty and, when Barré declares that it was a cruel trick to play, de Condé suggests that he is not the only one to have been playing tricks.

Suddenly, Mignon and Rangier start to run in circles imitating the voices of Leviathan and Beherit, women in the crowd take up the cries, and Barré is once more in his element, plunging into the crowd and wielding his crucifix like a club. De Condé looks at Jeanne and tells her this act will cost her her immortal soul. Now the nuns gossip amongst themselves, the one delighted that her lovely legs have been so greatly admired, the other that her picture is on sale in the town. Grandier attempts to enter the church but finds his way barred by soldiers and by de Laubardemont, who arrests him. Leviathan speaks through Jeanne.

Act III, scene i.   It is night and the stage is divided into three, on one side Grandier in gaol, in a second section Jeanne and Father Mignon, and in a third, Mannoury. A crowd has gathered—Bontemps, the gaoler, tells Grandier that there are more than 30,000 people come to town to see the execution, and Grandier has to remind him that his trial has not even begun. Grandier prays that he will be able to bear the pain, and Father Ambrose attempts to comfort him. Grandier confesses that he has sinned, with women, in aiming for power, in his worldly attitude. Bontemps comes to say that from now on only Father Barré or Father Rangier may 'comfort' Grandier. As Grandier asks Father Ambrose to stay with him, Jeanne begs Father Mignon not to leave her as she is afraid. Adam and Mannoury meanwhile are preparing the tools of their respective trades. The chorus voices die away to nothing.

Scene ii.   De Laubardemont joins Mannoury and Adam

nd announces that Grandier is condemned and will shortly
be there. He made something of an impression in court, but
Father Barré explained it was the Devil's doing. Grandier
enters in full canonicals and bids surgeon and chemist 'Good
Morning'. Biretta and cape are removed and it is clear he is to
be shaved, a process accomplished to what *The Times*
described at the time of the première as 'a frenzied polyphonic *pizzicato*'. De Laubardemont reminds them not to
forget the eyebrows, and then instructs Mannoury to tear out
his fingernails. The surgeon jibs and de Laubardemont orders
Bontemps to complete the process, which he does to a
chatter and then a howl of orchestral pain.

Scene iii. A public place. A large number of people
watch the Clerk of the Court read out the sentence. At the
doors of St. Peter's and St. Ursula's, with a rope round his
neck and a two-pound taper in his hand, Grandier is to ask
pardon of God, the King and Justice. Next, he shall be tied to
a stake and burnt alive. Before sentence is carried out, he will
be subjected to the Question, both Ordinary and Extraordinary. Grandier himself is visible, his hands tied behind his
back and dressed in a nightgown and slippers but with a
skullcap and biretta on his head. De Laubardemont snatches
the hat and cap from Grandier's head and the priest is
revealed, shaven even to the eyebrows, a bald fool. There is a
hysterical giggle from the women who are watching and then
Grandier calls on God to witness that he has never been a
sorcerer and to allow his suffering to atone for his vain and
disordered life. Sympathy seems to be turning towards him
and de Laubardemont orders the Captain of the Guard to
clear the place. He abjures Grandier to confess his guilt and
sign a confession. Grandier refuses—how can he sign a lie? De
Laubardemont threatens him, and says that under torture he
will think, first, how can man do this to man; then, how can
God allow it; and then, there can be no God. Grandier still
refuses to sign. God has hardened his heart, says Barré.

Scene iv. Jeanne comes in, dressed in a simple white
undergarment and with a rope round her neck. Others
persuade her that it is too hot for her out-of-doors and take
the rope gently away from her.

Scene v. Grandier is bound, his legs, from the knees to
the feet, enclosed in a kind of box; movable boards within
the box, driven inwards by large wedges, crush his legs.
Bontemps is hammering the wedges home. Barré tries to

extract a confession, but Grandier asks him whether he thinks that a man, to save himself pain, should confess to a crime he has not committed. De Laubardemont joins in the attempt to get a confession, Barré himself takes a mallet to the wedges, and Grandier between screams prays to God. At the same time, Mother Jeanne, whose praying voice has been heard throughout, and the nuns sing a litany. Grandier faints, they take him out of the box and seat him on a stool while Bontemps covers his shattered legs with a blanket. Grandier stares down at himself. Barré says that the fact that there is no confession means that the Devil has made him quite insensible to pain, but Mannoury asks what the shouts and screams can have been about. De Laubardemont calls for the guard to take Grandier to the place of execution.

Scene vi. The procession. As in Jeanne's vision at the start, Grandier is seated on a chair which has been lashed to a litter and is carried by four soldiers. He wears a heretic's sulphur-impregnated shirt, there is a rope round his neck, and his broken legs dangle. He is a ridiculous, hairless, shattered doll.

Scene vii. Outside St. Peter's church, the procession stops and Ambrose attempts to console Grandier, who kisses his hand. The procession goes on to St. Ursula's convent where a soldier lifts him from the litter so that he collapses. When the Prioress and some other nuns emerge, de Laubardemont demands that Grandier shall ask their pardon but he says he can only ask that God shall forgive them their sins. The Prioress says that she has heard so often of Grandier's beauty which she can now behold with her own eyes, but Grandier answers: 'Look at this thing which I am and learn what love means.' The procession reaches the site of the execution and Grandier is bound to the stake. Monks sprinkle faggots, straw, executioners and victim with holy water, but when Grandier tries to address the crowd, his voice is drowned in the general excitement and Barré strikes him on the mouth with a crucifix to silence him. De Laubardemont and Barré still try vainly to get him to confess, and when Barré gives him the kiss of peace, there is a shout of 'Judas!' from the crowd. In his fury, Barré snatches up a torch and ignites the pile before the soldiers have had a chance of strangling the victim, a form of relative mercy customary at the time. As the opera ends, Jeanne can be seen in silent prayer.   H.

21
Hungarian Opera

BÉLA BARTÓK
(1881–1945)

DUKE BLUEBEARD'S CASTLE
A kékszakállú Herceg Vára

OPERA in one act by Béla Bartók, text by B. Balázs. Première, Budapest, May 24, 1918, with Olga Haselbeck, Oszkar Kalman. First performed Frankfort, 1922; Berlin, 1929. Revived Budapest, 1937; Florence Festival, 1938 (by Budapest company), with Ella di Nemethy, Szekely, conductor Failoni; Zürich, 1948, with Malaniuk, Pernerstorfer; Berlin, 1951, with Ilosvay, Hoffmann, conductor Fricsay; Naples, 1951, with Malaniuk, Petri, conductor Fricsay; New York City Centre, 1952, with Ayars, Pease, conductor Rosenstock; B.B.C., London, 1953, with Cross, Matters; Sadler's Wells, 1954, with Elliott, Ward; Paris, Opéra-Comique, 1960, with Monmart, Depraz; Rome, 1962, with Barbato, Rossi-Lemeni; Edinburgh Festival, 1963,[1] by Budapest Opera with Olga Szönyi, Andras Farago; Buenos Aires, 1965, with Christa Ludwig, Walter Berry, conductor Kertesz; Vienna Volksoper, 1966, with Seefried, Wiener, conductor Maag.

CHARACTERS
Duke Bluebeard .... Bass
Judith, *his wife* .... Mezzo-Soprano

Bartók's short opera (it lasts less than an hour) is one of the most impressive of his early works. Whatever it may owe in its conception to Debussy and to Maeterlinck, the music is

---

[1] The three Bartók stage works, this opera and the ballets *The Wooden Prince* and *The Miraculous Mandarin*, conducted by Janos Ferencsik, played together in one theatrical evening as the composer (retrospectively) wanted.

characteristic of its composer. Wrote Desmond Shawe-Taylor in 1972 in *The Sunday Times*: 'The fable can be understood on many levels: as a foreshortened process of mutual dis-covery between two persons such as in real life would take many years; as a conflict between rational, creative Man and emotional, inspiring, never fully comprehending Woman; more deeply still, as an allegory of the loneliness and solitude of all human creatures. Bartok, whose own need for inner solitude was imperious, and whose remoteness could be frightening, threw himself into the subject with an intensity which grips the listener.' The piece has almost no action, and yet the music is essentially dramatic, just as the orchestral colour retains life and vigour even in its most sombre moments.

A bard appears before the curtain to establish in spoken word that the action of the opera is legendary. When the curtain rises, it reveals a large round room, gothic in style.[1] On the left, a staircase leads up to a little iron door. To the right of this staircase can be seen seven larger doors. There are no windows or ornaments of any kind. The room is like a great, empty cavern.

Bluebeard enters, leading Judith by the hand. She has left her parents and her home to follow him, and is only just regaining her courage. She sees the doors and wants to open them to let light and air into the castle. She knocks at the first door, and hears a long sigh like that of the wind. With the key that Bluebeard gives her, she opens the door, from which immediately streams red light (violins *tremolo*, flutes *arpeggio*). It is the Torture Chamber, and Judith exclaims that the walls are wet with blood; but she is not afraid.

In succession she opens four more doors. A shaft of bronze-coloured light (solo trumpet, woodwind trills) comes from the Armoury; golden light (violin solo, three trumpets) pours from the Treasury, from which she takes a jewelled cloak and a crown; bluish light (harp *glissando*, strings *tremolo*, solo horn) comes from behind the door which conceals the Garden; and a dazzling white light (full orchestra, organ) blinds her as she opens the door which gives on to Bluebeard's Kingdom. Each time Judith sees signs of blood: on the weapons in the Armoury, on the jewels and robes in the Treasury, on the flowers in the Garden, even in the colour of the cloud over the Kingdom itself.

[1] Such are the stage directions now more honoured in the breach than the observance.

Judith will not heed Bluebeard's warning, but opens the
ixth door (harp, clarinet *arpeggios*). When she asks Blue-
)eard what is the significance of the water behind it, he
answers 'Tears'. He tries to turn her from completing her
ɔurpose and takes her lovingly in his arms. She asks him if he
ᴉas loved other women, and, when he tries to evade the
ꜰuestion, demands that he give her the seventh key so that
;he may find out what the door conceals. As he gives it her,
ᴉe tells her that it will show her all his former wives.

She opens the seventh door and immediately the sixth and
ꜰifth doors close; at the same time the light in the hall begins
:o grow dimmer. Three beautiful women emerge. Bluebeard
ᴋneels before them and assures them that they are not
ꜰorgotten, and even Judith is filled with awe at their beauty.
ᴉn his first wife Bluebeard sees the embodiment of the
norning of his existence, in the second of his noonday, in the
:hird of evening. One by one they disappear through the
ꓒoor, and the fourth door closes. Then he addresses Judith.
;he is the most beautiful of all, and her he met in the night;
ᴉfter her is eternal darkness. He goes slowly to fetch the
:rown and robe from the third door, which closes after him,
ᴉnd adorns Judith with them. For a moment she pleads with
ᴉim, then turns and goes through the seventh door which
;huts after her. Bluebeard is alone once more.   H.

ZOLTÁN KODÁLY
(1882–1967)
HÁRY JÁNOS

ꟻABLE in three acts, text by Béla Paulini and Zsolt Harsányi, music by
Zoltán Kodály. Première, Budapest, October 16, 1926, with Isabella
Nagy and Imre Palló, conductor Nador Rékai. First performed
Cologne, 1931; Zürich, 1950, with Malaniuk, Boehm, conductor
Reinshagen. New production Budapest, 1952, with Maria Matyas, Imre
Palló. New York, Juilliard School, 1960, in English; London, Camden
Town Hall, 1967, with Frank Olegario; Vienna Volksoper, 1967, with
Mirjana Irosch, Harald Serafin, conductor Carl Melles. Very successful
ᴉn Hungary.

CHARACTERS

Háry János .... Baritone
Ilka (Orzse), *his fiancée* .... Soprano
Empress of Austria .... Soprano
Emperor Napoleon .... Baritone
Marie-Louise, *his Austrian wife* ......Mezzo-Soprano
Old Marzci, *Marie-Louise's coachman* .... Baritone
Ritter von Ebelasztin, *Chamberlain to Empress*
    Marie-Louise .... Tenor
Kaiser Franz of Austria ....⎤
Countess Melusine ⎱ *Ladies-in-waiting* .⎟
Countess Estrella ⎰ *to Marie-Louise* ..⎟
Hungarian Sentry ....⎟
Russian Sentry ....⎟
General Blood-and-Thunder ....⎟
General Dufla ....⎬ Speaking roles
First and second Hussars ....⎟
First and Second Artillerymen ....⎟
Village Elder ....⎟
A Student ....⎟
Abraham, *an innkeeper* ....⎟
First and Second Peasants ....⎦
    Generals, Hungarian and French Soldiers, Peasant
      Women, Court Servants, People
Time: Beginning of nineteenth century   *Place:* Hungary

Háry János is less in the nature of a true opera than of a
play with a quantity of incidental music. Nevertheless its
home in Hungary is in the opera house, and it has been
successfully played abroad, notably in Switzerland. Only a
few of the large number of characters actually sing, but there
are no fewer than thirty musical numbers in the score,
varying from a full-dress operatic finale to a few bars of
incidental, atmospheric music. The play is conceived as a
fantastic adventure told to his cronies by an ignorant but
imaginative Hungarian peasant, and nothing that happens in
it bears any relation to reality, being based exclusively on
what Háry would expect it to be like. Kodály has clothed the
story in music of great charm and individuality, as will be
readily admitted by anyone who knows the attractive
orchestral suite drawn from the opera.

    Prologue.   The prelude (called *The story begins* in the
suite) aptly sets the 'once upon a time' atmosphere. The

ene is an Inn, on one of whose walls hangs a crude picture
f Napoleon. What sort of story is Háry János likely to tell
o-day, asks the village elder. When Háry appears, a student
points to the picture of Napoleon: that was a great hero. I
once took him prisoner with my own hands, is Háry's
rejoinder!

First adventure. The scene is the border of Galicia and
Russia. On the Russian side, it is deep winter; the sentry is
muffled in furs and stamps about, blowing on his hands, and
snow covers the scene. On the Hungarian side, the sun is
shining, the flowers are out, and the Hussar drips with sweat
and from time to time mops his forehead. They comment on
the weather. One's drink is too hot, the other's is frozen;
they exchange. As the curtain goes up and during the early
part of the conversation, a flute solo gives out the tune of the
big duet, which occurs later in the scene. A woman who tries
to cross from Hungary into Russia (she has a bit of music to
herself) is turned back and departs disconsolate. A Jewish
family, also introduced musically, comes from the Russian
side but is not allowed to leave.

Ilka appears, singing a little unaccompanied song. When
the sentry makes eyes at her, she warns him that she will set
Háry János on him if he does not stop immediately. She goes
out. Female voices are heard singing, and the Hungarian
sentry says that they are girls of the village; where they are,
Háry cannot be far away. He is right. Háry appears, asks for
Ilka, is told which way she went, and, shooing away his
female companions, goes off to find her.

Herr von Ebelasztin, Chamberlain at the French court,
puts his head out of the Russian side of the guardroom and
complains that his Empress has not been allowed to pass the
frontier. Háry and Ilka return and are soon in conversation
with Marczi, the Hungarian coachman employed at the
French court. Nothing will suit the French, he says, but to
de-Hungarianise him, a process he is strenuously resisting.
When he tells Háry that the Empress is being kept in the
Russian guardroom, Háry demands of the guard that she be
let through. 'No one in, no one out' is the Russian's answer.
There seems no solution until Háry takes hold of the
guardroom and pulls it bodily into Hungarian territory,
whereupon the ice and snow immediately begin to melt, and
the flowers to bloom.

Marczi compliments Háry and Ilka on their mutual

suitability, and, when he goes back into the house, they si
a beautiful duet: 'Tiszán innen, Dunán túl' (Rivers shinin
rivers twain, There's a drover with his horses on the plain[1]
The tune, of haunting, nostalgic beauty, occurs as the third
item in the orchestral suite.

Marczi returns and toasts the lovers in an attractive
drinking song, but Ebelasztin complains of the noise and they
are all ashamed at the thought that they may have disturbed
the Empress's rest. She, however, emerges and asks who i
was who sang so attractively. When told it was Háry, she ask:
him to come to Vienna with her, and offers to grant him
three wishes. He asks for double rations for his horse; for a
nice Hungarian livery for Marczi, and for permission for him
to retain his moustache; and to be allowed to take Ilka to
Vienna with him. All are granted.

The Russian re-appears, full of apprehension that he wil
be hanged if the guardroom's altered position is found
Ebelasztin tries to push it back but cannot, and it is not unti
Háry consents to do it that any progress is made. Back in
Russian territory, it immediately starts to freeze again.

Second adventure. This section is introduced by the
famous Intermezzo with its intoxicating rhythms. The scene
is the park of the Imperial Palace in Vienna, viewed strictly
through the eyes of Háry's imagination, i.e. the bushes have
blossoms in the shape of an Imperial crown, the trees are of
gold, the dovecot is inhabited by a two-headed eagle. In the
course of a conversation between Háry and Marczi, it appear
that all are conscious of the animosity with which Ebelasztin
regards Háry, although they are somewhat reassured when, a
moment later, the Empress Marie-Louise appears and tell
Háry to call on her for help if he is ever in need. Ebelasztin
sends Háry off to the riding-school, where—so Ilka tells us a
short time later—he is put on to the fiercest horse in the
stable, which immediately dashes on to the roof. But Háry
returns quite unconcerned, having put Lucifer quietly away
in his stall. Marie-Louise gives Háry a violet she has picked
much to the rage of Ebelasztin, who has asked for it fo
himself.

The Austrian Empress joins the group (she is knitting a
golden stocking), and Marie-Louise blushingly points out the
mighty Háry to her. Háry has an opportunity of advising the

---

[1] English translation by Edward Dent and Dennis Arundell.

Empress on an old recipé which he recommends for the
Emperor, who, he is told, is unwell. Ilka appears from the
kitchen with a dish of sweet-corn, whose seeds (of real gold)
she proceeds to feed to the two-headed eagle. Ebelasztin joins
her, and says he carries in his bag Napoleon's declaration of
war on Austria, to use when he thinks fit. Marie-Louise's gift
of the violet to a peasant bumpkin is quite sufficient
provocation, and he will use it forthwith. A moment later,
military noises are heard from the palace, and everyone rushes
in saying that war has been declared by France. Háry, by now
promoted Captain by the Emperor, kisses Ilka good-bye, and
the curtain falls as General Dufla wheels on an enormous
cannon.

Following the Intermezzo, the music of the Second Adventure consists of three songs and an extended orchestral
incident depicting the palace clocks striking midday, much to
the delight of the astonished Háry (this is included in the
suite). Marie-Louise sings a little song about a cuckoo as she
picks the violet which is to cause the ructions between
Ebelasztin and Háry and so to lead indirectly to the declaration of war. Ilka has two songs, one brief and almost pathetic
in character as she reflects on the danger Háry ran when he
rode the wild Lucifer, the other brisk and lively as she feeds
the Imperial fowls; this is one of the most charming pieces in
the score.

Third Adventure. The battlefield; in the background is the
fortress of Milan, and behind that the mountains. Cannon are
in evidence, and Hussars stand about, amongst them Háry, by
now promoted Colonel. A chorus of soldiers can be heard, at
first melancholy but gradually growing more animated as
they contrast the wonders of what they can now see with the
village life they knew back at home; there are even dragons in
the mountains here, says Háry. In richly comic terms, the
Hussars discuss the military situation with General Blood-and-
Thunder; shots are heard, and the General's immediate
reaction is to give the order: 'Withdraw according to plan.'
French soldiers appear, Háry draws his sabre and, by the
mere act of doing so, creates a draught which fells his
opponents to the ground. The music of the battle (included
in the suite) is in three distinct stages. First of all, the French
band can be heard off; when it comes on, Háry is laying low
the army with the wind of his sword, with the result that the
playing of the band becomes more and more confused. Very

soft percussion heralds the entry of Napoleon—in atmosphere it is rather like the accompaniment that would be given to the ogre in an English pantomime—but soon the brass enters *fortissimo*, with a hint of the 'Marseillaise' somewhere in the music. Napoleon falls on his knees and is taken prisoner by Háry, who declares the war over. There is a funeral march, dominated by a moaning little tune on the saxophone.

Marie-Louise comes on the scene and is contemptuous of the beaten Napoleon, who has a little song to the tune of the funeral march. Everyone congratulates Háry—he ought to be a General, says Blood-and-Thunder—and, to the accompaniment of gypsy music, a feast is prepared, Háry and Marie-Louise taking the opportunity of dancing together. Ebelasztin and Ilka come in, the latter admitting that the former's warnings seem to have had something behind them when she sees how Háry is behaving—Is this war's hardship? she asks bitterly.

There is an acrimonious exchange between Ilka and Marie-Louise, when the former dances with Háry—they are obviously very much in love. Marie-Louise announces she is going to marry Háry, and when the latter demurs, she rushes off threatening to commit suicide. Háry naturally manages to save the situation, and he leads a big marching ensemble as the episode comes to an end.

Fourth Adventure. Háry's elaborately furnished room in Vienna (the style is not at all Hungarian). The Empress and Marie-Louise sing a duet to the accompaniment of a chorus of attendants, Marie-Louise wondering which of her ten suitors she shall marry, her mother plumping for Háry. Marie-Louise's only doubts on the score are because she has already discovered that Háry will not always do as he is told; for instance, he has never yet kissed her.

To the accompaniment of outrageously noisy music, the Emperor leads in a procession in honour of Háry, who will in future, he announces, be endowed with half the Empire and half the Imperial Palace. At the feast Háry is not himself and will eat nothing; he is even cross when told that double-headed chickens are normal fare for the Imperial table. The Emperor toasts Háry in a speech, and then, to a march, in come the little archdukes to shake hands with the hero of the day.

Háry admits that he cannot marry Marie-Louise, not least because he has a sweetheart of his own—Ilka. If he is to have reward, says Háry, may he be let off half his military service, so that he can go home and get married. The Emperor grants his request, and Háry hands back his baton to General Blood-and-Thunder. Ilka comes in, knowing nothing of what has happened, and sings a melancholy and very beautiful song—perhaps, with the duet of the first adventure, the best sustained lyrical passage of the opera. Háry, now dressed as an infantryman, returns (for a Hussar, infantry uniform is practically the same as civilian clothes, he observes), and swears allegiance to the Emperor, whether he serves him as soldier or as farmer. There is only one more complication to clear up. Ebelasztin is sent in chains to Háry by the Emperor Napoleon, but Háry magnanimously pardons him and leads him over to his beloved Marie-Louise. The finale, for Háry, Ilka, and the chorus, makes use of material already used in the opera, notably the love duet and the intermezzo.

There is an epilogue, set in the same inn as the prologue. Háry János finishes his story: he and Ilka walked home and were married. Now, Ilka having died, there is no one to witness his story but he.   H.

22
Spanish Opera

ENRIQUE GRANADOS
(1867–1916)
GOYESCAS

OPERA in three scenes (one act) by Enrique Granados, text by
Fernando Periquet. Première, Metropolitan, New York, January 28,
1916, with Fitziu, Perini, Martinelli, de Luca, conductor Bavagnoli (in
Spanish). First performed Opéra, Paris, 1919; Buenos Aires, 1929; la
Scala, Milan, 1937, with Carbone, Elmo, Civil, Poli, conductor Capuana;
Royal College of Music, London, 1951; Florence, 1963, with Perez,
Companeez, Oncina, Cesari; London, Morley College, 1965.

CHARACTERS

Rosario, *a highborn young lady* . . . . Soprano
Fernando, *a young officer, her lover* . . . . Tenor
Paquiro, *a toreador* . . . . Baritone
Pepa, *a young girl of the people, Paquiro's*
    sweetheart . . . . Mezzo-Soprano
Majas and Majos

Time: About 1800   *Place:* Madrid

The characters and setting of the opera are suggested by
the work of the great Spanish painter Goya. The opera opens
with a crowd of majas and majos enjoying a holiday on the
outskirts of Madrid. Some of the majas are engaged in the
popular pastime of tossing the *pelele* (a man of straw) in a
blanket. Paquiro the toreador is paying compliments to the
women. Pepa, his sweetheart of the day, arrives in her
dogcart. Popular, she is warmly welcomed. Soon Rosario, a
lady of rank, arrives in her sedan-chair to keep a tryst with her
lover, Fernando, a captain in the Royal Spanish Guards.

Paquiro reminds her of a *baile de candil* (a ball given in a room lit by candlelight) which she once attended. He invites her to go again. Fernando overhears his remarks, and his jealousy is aroused. He informs Paquiro that Rosario shall go to the ball, but that he, Fernando, will escort her. He extracts Rosario's promise to go with him, while Pepa, enraged by Paquiro's neglect, vows vengeance upon her.

The second tableau shows the scene at the ball. Fernando appears with Rosario. His haughty bearing and disdainful speech anger all present. The two men arrange for a duel that evening, and when Rosario recovers from a swoon, Fernando takes her away.

The third tableau reveals Rosario's garden. She is discovered sitting by herself on a stone bench listening in pensive mood to the song of the nightingale. This is the famous aria called 'The Lover and the Nightingale' (La Maja y el Ruiseñor), one of the most beautiful and luxuriant nocturnes ever written for voice and orchestra.

Fernando visits Rosario before keeping his appointment with Paquiro. When a bell strikes the fatal hour, Fernando tears himself away. He is followed hesitatingly by Rosario. Soon the silence is broken by a cry from Fernando, followed by a shriek from Rosario. The lovers reappear. Rosario supports Fernando to a stone bench where he dies in her arms.

Granados adapted the music of his opera from a set of piano pieces (1911) inspired by the paintings of Goya:

1. Los Requiebros (Endearments)
2. Coloquio en la Reja (Conversation at the Window)
3. El Fandango del Candil (The Fandango by Moonlight)
4. Quejas o la Maja y el Ruiseñor (Complaints, or the Maiden and the Nightingale)
5. El Amor y la Muerte (Love and Death)
6. La Serenada del Espectro (The Spectre's Serenade)
7. El Pelele (The Straw-man)

The first tableau begins and ends with No. 7; No. 3 starts the second; and the third is almost entirely based on the music of Nos. 4, 2 and 5.   H.

MANUEL DE FALLA

(1876–1946)

LA VIDA BREVE

The Short Life

OPERA in two acts by Manuel de Falla, text by C. Fernandez Shaw; French version by P. Milliet. Première, Nice, April 1, 1913, with Lillian Grenville, David Devriès, Cotreuil, conductor Miranne. First performed Opéra-Comique, Paris, 1914, with Carré, Brohly, Francell, Vieuille, conductor Ruhlmann; Madrid, 1914; Buenos Aires, 1923, with Hina Spani; Metropolitan, 1926, with Bori, Tokatyan, d'Angelo, conductor Serafin; la Scala, Milan, 1934, with dalla Rizza, Castagna, Masini, Romito, conductor Votto. Revived Buenos Aires, 1946; San Carlo, Naples, 1951, with Arizmendi, Sinimberghi, conductor Fricsay; la Scala, Milan, 1952, with Araujo, Francesco Albanese, Beuf, conductor Giulini; Holland Festival, 1953, with de los Angeles, Vroons; Edinburgh Festival, 1958, with de los Angeles, Martinez.

CHARACTERS

Salud, *a gypsy* .... Soprano
Her grandmother .... Mezzo-Soprano
Carmela, *a young girl* .... Mezzo-Soprano
Paco .... Tenor
Uncle Sarvaor .... Bass
A Singer .... Baritone
Manuel, *Carmela's brother* .... Baritone
A Voice in the Forge ⎫
Voice of a Street-seller ⎬ .... Tenor
A Distant Voice ⎭

Time: The present   *Place:* Granada

La Vida Breve is the earliest of Falla's works which is still generally performed. It was written in 1904–5 and won a prize in Madrid, but was not immediately mounted on the stage. When Falla first went to Paris, he took the score with him, and the work was finally performed in 1913.

Act I.   The curtain rises after a dozen bars of introduction. Courtyard of a gypsy habitation. On one side of the stage, the house where the gypsies live, on the other the entrance to a smithy, from which can be heard a mysterious sound of singing. Salud's old grandmother is feeding some ɔirds in a cage. One is going to die, she thinks—perhaps of love, like Salud. The voices of street-sellers (off-stage, like that of the soloist in the smithy) can be heard.

Salud comes in from the street, looking unhappy. Her grandmother tries to reassure her; of course Paco will come. Salud is fearful that she may lose one of the two things she most values: the loves of Paco and of her grandmother. Alone Salud listens to the voices from the forge, and then sings a song with a sad philosophy—long live those who laugh, short life to those who cry: 'Vivan los que rien!' The poignant beauty of the music is like that of a folk-song, and indeed it is founded on the Andalusian style.

But her grandmother comes to tell Salud that Paco is on his way. Her joy is complete, and in their duet her sincerity and innocence contrasts with his more conventional utterances—Professor J. B. Trend, in his book on Falla, has suggested that the Massenet-like cast of Paco's music is intended to contrast with the characteristic folk style of Salud's. Salud's grandmother and her uncle observe the scene, and he mutters that he would gladly take revenge on Paco, whom he knows to be going to marry another girl the very next day. He is only playing with Salud.

The second scene is in the form of an intermezzo. A view of Granada from Sacro Monte can be seen.

Act II. A small street in Granada. Through the open railings can be seen the courtyard in which is being celebrated the betrothal of Paco and Carmela with song and dance. A professional singer has been engaged to entertain the company. He sings an Andalusian song, which is followed by a dance, made famous all over the world by generations of fiddlers who have appropriated it as an encore piece.

Just before the dance finishes, Salud appears and rushes to see what is going on. She is in despair when she finds her worst fears realised, and Paco laughing and talking with the girl who is separating him from her for ever. Her grief spills over in a terrible lament, and she longs for death. Her grandmother and uncle arrive, and the latter tries to relieve the situation by cursing Paco and everything to do with him. Salud hears Paco's voice and makes up her mind to speak to him once again. She repeats the sad song of the forge: 'The man that's born of a woman, is born in an evil day.' Salud is determined to enter.

During an interlude the scene changes to the courtyard of

the house. The guests are well dressed. Immediately the curtain rises there is a dance, hardly less well known than the previous one. Paco is ill-at-ease, having heard the voice of Salud. Manuel makes a speech to congratulate the happy pair, but Paco becomes more and more uncomfortable as Uncle Sarvaor comes into the patio, followed by Salud. Sarvaor offers their services to entertain the company, but Salud denounces Paco's treachery towards her in tones that would almost appear calm did they not so obviously conceal deep feeling. She falls dead of shock at Paco's feet, and her grandmother and Uncle Sarvaor curse Paco as the curtain falls.

H.

EL RETABLO DE MAESE PEDRO
Master Peter's Puppet Show

Opera in one act by Manuel de Falla, libretto by the composer from an episode in the 26th chapter of the second part of Cervantes's *Don Quixote de la Mancha*. Written for Princesse Edmond de Polignac, the première was in her drawing room, June 25, 1923, with Amparito Peris, Salignac, Dufranne, conductor Golschmann (publicly in Paris later the same year). First performed Seville in concert, March 23, 1923, with Redondo, Segura, Lledo, conductor Falla; Bristol, 1924 (in English), with Tannahill, Goody, Arthur Cranmer. Revived Ingestre Festival, England, 1957, with Adèle Leigh, conductor Pritchard.

CHARACTERS

Don Quixote . . . . Bass or Baritone
Master Peter . . . . Tenor
The Boy (El Trujamán) . . . . Boy Soprano
                                             or High Mezzo-Soprano

Sancho Panza
The Innkeeper
The Scholar   } . . . Silent roles
The page
The man with the lances and halberds

Charlemagne
Don Gayferos
Don Roland
Melisendra   } . . . Figures in the puppet show
King Marsilius
The enamoured Moor

Heralds, Knights, etc., at Court of Charlemagne; Moors

The little opera was originally intended to be performed entirely with puppets, double-sized when doing duty for human beings, ordinary-sized when representing puppets. The action takes place in the stable of an inn at la Mancha on the borders of Aragon. At the back of the stable is the puppet-show itself, standing on legs covered by curtains, behind which Master Peter works the puppets. The work, which lasts less than half an hour, introduces Master Peter and the stage audience, and then tells the story of the Deliverance of Melisendra, each episode being first introduced by the boy narrator in an extraordinary recitative style and afterwards mimed by the puppets. At the end Don Quixote interrupts the action. The grave beauty of much of the music, the irresistible liveliness of the boy's narration (when it is properly performed[1]), and Falla's fastidious orchestration (note the subtle use of muted trumpet throughout) and vivid sense of contrast as evidenced in the different sections, combine to make a work of peculiar distinction.

The wind section over a side drum plays a southern, *cornemuse* type of tune, a bell rings and Master Peter invites the guests at the inn to come to the show. While the orchestra plays Master Peter's Symphony, a combination of dignity and impudence in 6/8, the audience assembles, the last to appear being Don Quixote and Sancho Panza. The boy announces that they will see the story of the Deliverance of the fair Melisendra by her husband Don Gayferos from her captivity by the Moors. In the first scene, Don Gayferos is discovered playing chess with Don Roland. The Emperor Charlemagne, Melisendra's father, is furious that Don Gayferos prefers gaming to the rescue of his imprisoned wife. Gayferos overturns the chess board, tries unsuccessfully to borrow Roland's sword, then prepares to set out alone to rescue his wife.

The second scene shows the Moorish Tower of Saragossa, where Melisendra appears on a balcony. A Moor creeps up behind her and steals a kiss, whereupon Marsilius, king of the Moors, orders that he be whipped. In the third scene, he is to receive 200 strokes, a sentence carried out summarily, says the boy, and without legal proceedings. At this Don Quixote

[1] The boy's voice must be 'nasal and rather forced—the voice of a boy shouting in the street . . . exempt from all lyrical feeling. It should be sung by a boy soprano, but when this is not possible, a woman's voice (high mezzo-soprano) may be used.'

interrupts to complain about the boy's embroidery of the story: there must always be a legal weighing of the evidence—Master Peter agrees with him: 'Sing your proper plainsong and do not meddle with other voices, for much counterpoint ruins the lute strings.' The fourth scene shows Don Gayferos crossing the Pyrenees on horseback—a perfect piece of musical stylisation—from time to time sounding his hunting horn. In the fifth scene, Melisendra, who at first does not recognise her husband, is rescued and carried away to safety.

The sixth scene shows the pursuit by the Moors. The boy starts by wishing the couple happiness and long life in the most flowery terms, and is again pulled up by Master Peter for departing from the text. The alarm is given and the bells ring out from the mosques and minarets—Don Quixote objects: 'among Moors is no ringing of bells, but beating of drums and squealing hautboys'. Master Peter pleads stage licence, and the boy describes the Moorish horsemen setting out to overtake the fugitives. Don Quixote can bear the tension no longer, but sword in hand leaps into the puppet show and proceeds to attack the Moorish puppets, beheading some, knocking others over and dealing destruction all round, in spite of the protests of Master Peter. In some beautiful phrases Don Quixote invokes Dulcinea, praises the deeds of the knights errant, and the opera ends with him triumphant, and Master Peter sadly contemplating the ruin of his puppets.

H.

23
American Opera

VIRGIL THOMSON
(b. 1896)

FOUR SAINTS IN THREE ACTS

OPERA in four acts, text by Gertrude Stein (*an opera to be sung*). First given in concert form, Ann Arbor, Michigan, May 20, 1933; on the stage, at Hartford, Connecticut, February 8, 1934, by the Society of Friends and Enemies of Modern Music, conducted by Alexander Smallens, staged by Frederick Ashton, scenery and costumes by Florine Stettheimer. The opera was sung by negroes, including Edward Matthews as Saint Ignatius, Beatrice Robinson Wayne and Bruce Howard as Saint Teresa I and II, Embry Bonner as Saint Chavez, Bertha Fitzhugh Baker as Saint Settlement, and Abner Dorsey and Altonell Hines as Compère and Commère. First performance in New York, 44th Street Theatre, February 20, 1934. The work has since been heard in both concert and radio performances, and in May 1952 was presented by a negro company in Paris during the Festival of Twentieth Century Art, with Inez Matthews, Edward Matthews, conductor Virgil Thomson; February 1973, Mini-Met Forum, New York.

CHARACTERS

Compère .... Bass
Commère .... Mezzo-Soprano
Saint Teresa I .... Soprano
Saint Teresa II .... Contralto
Saint Ignatius Loyola .... Baritone
Saint Chavez .... Tenor
Saint Settlement .... Soprano
Double chorus of named and unnamed saints; six dancers

Gertrude Stein's text is partly evocative, partly satirical, and at no time lays any particular stress on meaning. Virgil Thomson, one of the best-known of American music critics, has written music for it which is the reverse of pretentious; he does not scorn the trivial (the work has been described as 'the opposite of epochal') and yet the relationship of unmeaning words and simple tunes is curiously rational. The straightforward tunes are simply harmonised—Thomson himself has said that 'the lack of the expected dissonance is the most striking characteristic of the score' (quoted in *American Opera* by Edward Ellsworth Hipsher)—and the music is always singable, and by no means devoid of that quality which makes it stick in the memory. The composer decided on the negro cast because of the clarity of their diction and because of their natural approach to religious subjects. A note in the score tells us that 'the precedent need not be considered binding', though for some years it was.

The surrealist nature of the work is emphasised by the fact that the scenario used for the original production was written (by Maurice Grosser) *after* the words and music had been completed. The original act headings (which are the only indications of 'story' the libretto contains) are given in italics in the following synopsis.

Prelude. *A narrative of Prepare for Saints*. The choral overture in waltz time on the following words:

To know to know to love her so.
Four saints prepare for Saints,
Four saints make it well fish.
Four saints prepare for saints it makes it well fish
it makes it well fish prepare for saints

leads to some conversation between the chorus, Compère, Commère, and various saints, and ends with the Commère and Compère reading out a lengthy list of saints, many of whom are not mentioned at any other point in the opera.

Act I. *Saint Teresa half indoors and half out of doors.* The scene is the steps of the Cathedral at Avila. Saint Teresa enacts for the instruction of saints and visitors seven scenes from her own life. The first has the Compère and Commère and two choruses singing antiphonally, then an aria for Saint Teresa with choral interjections. Saint Ignatius joins the guests just before the end of the first tableau, which gives way to the second, in which Saint Teresa, holding a dove in her hand, is photographed by Saint Settlement. In the third and fourth tableaux Saint Ignatius serenades Saint Teresa, and then offers her flowers. In tableau five Saint Ignatius and

Saint Teresa II admire the model of a Heavenly Mansion. In tableaux six and seven, Saint Teresa II is shown in an attitude of ecstasy, and rocking an unseen child.

Act II. *Might it be mountains if it were not Barcelona.* The scene is a garden party near Barcelona. The Compère and Commère sit at the side of an opera box from which they can watch the proceedings and where they are presently joined by both Saint Teresas and Saint Ignatius. A Dance of Angels is performed for their pleasure and there is a party game, after which everyone goes out except the Compère and Commère. There is a love scene between them, and the two Saint Teresas return in time to see it, and are pleased at what they see. A telescope is brought in and as the two Saint Teresas look through it a vision of a Heavenly Mansion appears. 'How many doors how many floors and how many windows are there in it?' ask the saints.

Act III. *Saint Ignatius and one of two literally.* The scene is a garden of a monastery on the sea coast. The men saints are mending a fish net. The introductory *allegro moderato* for the orchestra alone leads to a conversation about monastic life between Saint Ignatius, the two Saint Teresas and Saint Settlement, but the men stop their work and listen as Saint Ignatius describes to them his vision of the Holy Ghost. This is his well-known aria, 'Pigeons on the grass alas'; the vocal line is occasionally taken over by the chorus or the Compère, and there is an off-stage heavenly chorus to sing the words 'Let Lucy Lily Lily Lucy Lucy let Lucy Lucy Lily Lily Lily Lily Lily let Lily Lucy Lucy let Lily. Let Lucy Lily'. Saint Chavez lectures to the men, there is a dance in the Spanish style, a storm is quieted by Saint Ignatius, and Saint Ignatius predicts the Last Judgment. It grows dark, there is a devotional procession, and the Intermezzo recalls the opening of the Prelude.

Act IV. *The sisters and saints reassembled and re-enacting why they went away to stay.* The Compère and Commère discuss whether there shall be a fourth act, and when they have made up their minds, the curtain rises to show all the saints in heaven. They join in a hymn of communion 'When this you see remember me', the Compère announces 'Last Act', and the chorus and principals reply *fortissimo* 'Which is a fact'.   H.

GEORGE GERSHWIN

(1898–1937)

PORGY AND BESS

OPERA in three acts by George Gershwin; text by du Bose Heyward and Ira Gershwin. Première, Boston, September 30, 1935, with Todd Duncan (Porgy), Anne Brown (Bess), Warren Coleman (Crown), Eddie Matthews (Jake), Abbie Mitchell (Clara), Bubbles (Sporting Life), Eva Jessye Choir, produced by Rouben Mamoulian, conductor Alexander Smallens. First performed Zürich, 1945, with Cordy, Eftimiades, Kovacs, Boehm, Chabay, conductor Reinshagen; 1950, with Funk, Malaniuk, Jungwirth, Boehm, Wosniak, conductor Ackermann; Copenhagen, 1946, with Anne Brown and Einar Nørby. In 1952, an all-negro company set out from the States and toured with the opera through the capitals of Europe (notably Berlin and Vienna), ending up in London in the autumn at the Stoll Theatre, where they stayed until February 10, 1953, playing to packed houses. The cast included Leontyne Price, Thigpen, Warfield, Cab Calloway, conductor Smallens. Produced Vienna Volksoper, 1965, with Olive Moorefield, William Warfield, Robert Guillaume, conductor Lee Schaenen; Oslo, 1967.

CHARACTERS

Porgy, *a cripple*	. . . .	Bass-Baritone
Bess, *Crown's girl*	. . . .	Soprano
Crown, *a tough stevedore*	. . . .	Baritone
Serena, *Robbins's wife*	. . . .	Soprano
Clara, *Jake's wife*	. . . .	Soprano
Maria, *keeper of the cook-shop*	. . . .	Contralto
Jake, *a fisherman*	. . . .	Baritone
Sporting Life, *a dope pedlar*	. . . .	Tenor
Mingo	. . . .	Tenor
Robbins, *an inhabitant of Catfish Row*	. . . .	Tenor
Peter, *the honeyman*	. . . .	Tenor
Frazier, *a negro 'lawyer'*	. . . .	Baritone
Annie	. . . .	Mezzo-Soprano
Lily, *Peter's wife, strawberry woman*	. . .	Mezzo-Soprano
Jim, *a cotton picker*	. . . .	Baritone
Undertaker	. . . .	Baritone
Nelson	. . . .	Tenor
Crab man	. . . .	Tenor
Mr. Archdale, *a white man*	. . . .	Speaking Part

Detective
Policeman   } .... Speaking Parts
Coroner
Scipio, *a small boy*

Time: Recent past   *Place:* Charleston, South
                                       Carolina, U.S.A.

The scene is laid in Catfish Row, which is, according to the synopsis in the published score, 'a former mansion of the aristocracy, but now a negro tenement on the water front of Charleston, South Carolina'.

Act I, scene i, shows the inside of the court. After a short *allegro con brio* introduction, we are introduced to the variegated night life of the court. There is singing and dancing and presently a lazy Lullaby can be heard, sung by Clara, who nurses her baby. It is 'Summer time, an' the livin' is easy', and the song's lyric beauty has made it one of the most famous in the opera, and in fact of all Gershwin's songs. The lights fade from one group and come up on another where a crap game is seen to be in progress. The episodic music reflects the varied nature of the stage action, and the Lullaby is heard again as background to the game. Jake says he will take it on himself to send his and Clara's baby to sleep, and he sings 'A woman is a sometime thing', the bystanders joining in the refrain. A caterwaul from the baby brings this episode to an end.

The honeyman's call is heard before Porgy is spied coming towards the court. He is a cripple who cannot stand upright, and he gets about in a little goatcart. Everybody seems pleased to see him, and they twit him about Bess—'I think he's soft on Crown's Bess,' says Jake. Porgy defends Bess's reputation where it is attacked, and blames her present degradation on 'the Gawd fearin' ladies an' the Gawd damnin' men'. Porgy laments his crippled, lonely state, particularly with reference to women, but attention is diverted from him when Crown comes in with Bess, calling loudly for drink and going unsteadily to join the crap school. The play goes on, although Crown finds difficulty in reading the dice, a fact that does not escape the comment of the bystanders. Crown objects to losing his money when Robbins beats him in the game. He throws Robbins to the ground, attacking him with a cotton hook and killing him, to the horror of the inhabitants of Catfish Row. Bess gives Crown money and urges him to be off out of the way of the police; he says firmly that he will be back; any arrangement she may care to make in the meanwhile with another man will be with his permission—but strictly temporary.

Sporting Life approaches Bess and offers to take her to New York with him, but she spurns his offer, and tries to find shelter from someone in the court—unsuccessfully, until Porgy opens his door and lets her in, just as the police whistles can be heard blowing outside.

The scene changes to Serena's room, where Robbins's body lies on the bed, a saucer on its chest to receive any contributions which may be forthcoming against the expense of his burial. A large number of people are watching by the body, singing a spiritual as they mourn. Porgy and Bess enter and put money in the saucer, and the mourners exhort each other to follow their example. Porgy leads a rhythmic spiritual before a detective puts his head round the door and comes in. By accusing Peter of the murder, he gets the others to say that Crown did it—but he hauls off the protesting and inoffensive Peter (who is half deaf) as a 'material witness'.

Porgy reflects on the injustice of taking off an old man who never did anyone any harm, while a criminal like Crown wanders about scot-free, waiting to duplicate his crime. The wake goes on, and Serena, swaying to her words, begins a big lament, 'My man's gone now' in which the chorus supports her. The undertaker comes to see Serena and agrees to bury Robbins for the $15 which is all that is in the saucer. Bess leads the last of the spirituals, 'Oh, we're leavin' for the Promise' Land', and the scene comes to its end.

Act II takes place a month later. Jake and the fishermen are repairing their nets and preparing to put to sea, singing as they do so, 'It take a long pull to get there'. In spite of the warning that the time of year is coming round for the September storms, Jake and his friends are determined to set out. Porgy appears at his window, laughing and singing his Banjo song, 'Oh, I got plenty o' nuttin', an infectious and brilliant piece which causes the chorus to comment on the change for the better which has come over him since Bess has been living with him.

Sporting Life is sauntering around the court when Maria the cook sees that he has some dope with him. She gives him a piece of her mind, and when he suggests that they should be friends, catches him by the throat, bends him back over the table, and treats him to a lecture on what he has got coming to him from her. She only releases him when Lawyer Frazier comes in, looking for Porgy, to whom he sells a 'divorce' for Bess, clinching the bargain when he points out that it is naturally much more difficult (and expensive) to divorce somebody who has never even been married. The scene takes place to the accompaniment of choral comment on her age, and all the other details which Frazier asks her for.

There is another visitor, when Mr. Archdale appears, also asking for Porgy. At first everybody is too suspicious to tell him, but he wins them over, and informs Porgy that he will go bond for his friend Peter now in gaol. As he turns to leave, Porgy exclaims in horror at the sight of a buzzard flying over the court. If it alights, he explains to Mr. Archdale, it brings bad luck to everyone living in the house. Porgy's Buzzard song, with the chorus, is sometimes omitted,[1] seemingly at the suggestion of Gershwin himself, who thought the role of Porgy needed shortening if the singer were going to stand the strain of eight performances a week for a long run (one may be forgiven, too, if one thinks of it as only partially a loss; it is a long way from being the best number in the opera).

Sporting Life sidles up to Bess and again suggests they should team up and go off to New York, but she tells him she hates the sight of him—and she will have nothing more to do with the 'happy dust' he offers her. Porgy twigs what is going on and reaches round his door to catch hold of Sporting Life's wrist, making him cry out with the strength of his grip. He warns him to keep away from Bess.

It is the day of the organised picnic, and everybody disappears to get themselves ready, leaving Porgy alone with Bess, who tells him she does not want to go since he cannot. There is an extended love duet for the two of them, 'Bess, you is my woman now', at whose end the stage fills with life, a military band strikes up a *Tempo di Marcia giocoso*, and with a maximum of noise the picnickers start on their way. Maria persuades Bess that she must come along after all, and she takes a fond farewell of Porgy, who is left singing happily 'I got plenty o' nuttin'.

Scene ii is on Kittiwah Island, the evening of the same day. The picnickers dance riotously and Sporting Life treats them to a sermon in praise of the virtues of scepticism,

---

[1] In the 1952 London production it was transferred to the last act.

'It ain't necessarily so', whose jaunty tune and brilliant lyrics
have made it one of the most popular and also one of the
best numbers of the score. Two samples of its outrageous
rhymes:

> It ain't necessarily so,
> De t'ings dat yo' li'ble
> To read in de Bible,
> It ain't necessarily so;

and

> Oh, Jonah, he lived in de whale,
> Fo' he made his home in
> Dat fish's abdomen,
> Oh, Jonah, he lived in de whale.

Serena comes on the scene, sees the dancing, and
denounces the whole pack of them for sinners, also
reminding them, more prosaically, that the boat is leaving
soon and that they must hurry to get on board.

Bess waits behind a moment, and Crown appears in front
of her. He tells her that he will be back for her soon, but she
pleads to be allowed to stay in peace with Porgy, who has
taught her to live decently. Crown laughs at what she says,
and says he regards her living with Porgy as a temporary (but
permissible) arrangement, which will cease the moment he
comes back. Bess suggests he find some other woman ('Oh,
what you want wid Bess?'), but she cannot resist Crown's old
fascination, and when he takes her in his arms, she is too
weak to deny him anything. She stays behind with him and
the boat goes off without her.

Scene iii. Jake and the fishermen prepare to go off
fishing, singing a snatch of 'It take a long pull to get there'.
Peter is back from prison, and the sound of Bess's voice
coming in a delirium from Porgy's room indicates that she
too has returned from Kittiwah Island. She was lost for two
days and was incoherent when she finally got home. Serena
prays for her to get well, and at the end tells Porgy: 'Alright
now, Porgy. Doctor Jesus done take de case.' The cries of
respectively the strawberry woman, the honeyman, and the
crab man are heard, before Bess calls from off-stage,
evidently well on the way to recovery. She talks to Porgy,
who says that he knows she has been with Crown, but that it
makes no difference to his love for her. She admits that she
told Crown she would go with him when he came for her, but

pleads with Porgy to keep her for himself; she wants to stay but is afraid of the effect Crown's presence may have on her: 'I loves you, Porgy.' Porgy tells her he will take good care of Crown if he returns.

Clara is anxiously watching the sea, and presently her apprehension is confirmed, and the sound of the hurricane bell can be heard before the scene comes to an end.

The curtain for scene iv rises on Serena's room. Outside there is a terrific storm; inside the negroes are huddled in groups and sing. Every face is filled with fear as all pray that the danger, which threatens them and those they love, may be averted. 'I hear death knockin' at de do',' sings Peter—and almost immediately a real knock comes, and is answered with a hysterical rush to hold the door against whoever is trying to come in by it. It turns out to be Crown. The prayer stops with his entrance, and he orders Bess to him, throwing down Porgy who makes a move to come between them. Serena warns him against violent behaviour; at any moment the storm may get him. 'If God want to kill me,' he sings, 'He had plenty of chance 'tween here an' Kittiwah Island.'

The keening seems likely to go on indefinitely, but Crown stops it with his violent opposition, and in his turn he strikes up a cheerful jazz number, 'A red-headed woman makes a chow-chow jump its track'. Suddenly, Clara sees the boat, in which Jake put out to do his fishing, floating upside down in the river. She deposits her baby in Bess's arms while she goes off despairingly to learn the worst. Bess urges some man to follow her, but only Crown will venture out, which he does with the promise that he is coming back to get Bess. The act ends with a renewal of the prayer for mercy.

Act III, scene i, takes place inside the courtyard. The inhabitants are mourning Clara, Jake, and Crown, all of whom they think lost in the storm. When they reach the point of praying for Crown, they are interrupted by laughter from Sporting Life. His levity is promptly scolded by Maria, but he hints that he knows Crown is not dead, and he slyly wonders what will be the upshot of the rivalry between Crown and Porgy over Bess. Bess is heard singing Clara's Lullaby to the baby she left behind her when she rushed off into the storm, and the inhabitants of the court drift off to bed, leaving it empty.

Suddenly, Crown can be seen at the gate. He picks his way stealthily across the court, then crawls towards Porgy's door.

As he passes the window, the shutter opens silently and an arm is extended, grasping a long knife, which it plunges into Crown's back. Crown staggers into an upright position, and is seized round the neck in Porgy's iron grip and slowly throttled. Porgy exclaims: 'Bess, you got a man now, you got Porgy.'

Scene ii. Next afternoon. The police come to clear up the mystery of Crown's death. They question Serena, who it appears has been ill and knows nothing of the death of the man who—every inhabitant of Catfish Row is prepared to swear—was responsible for killing her husband, Robbins. Porgy is roped in to identify Crown's body, and is dragged away protesting that he won't have anything to do with Crown, his reluctance having been increased by Sporting Life's helpful suggestion that Crown's wound will begin to bleed the moment the man that killed him comes into the presence of his body.

Bess is left alone, and Sporting Life seizes the opportunity to offer her some 'happy dust' to tide over her nerves at the prospect of losing Porgy. She tries to refuse but cannot resist it, and Sporting Life sings a persuasive *Blues*, 'There's a boat dat's leavin' soon for New York', with the object of tempting her to come away with him. He goes out, leaving a second packet of dope behind him, and, after he is gone, Bess sneaks out of her room, and takes it inside with her.

The third scene plays again in Catfish Row, a week later. Normal life is going on, everyone says 'good morning' to everyone else, the children dance and sing, and Porgy is welcomed home after his week away—he would not look at Crown and was gaoled for contempt of court. Everyone is disconcerted by Porgy's arrival, but he distributes the presents he has bought them all (as a result of some successful crap-shooting in prison), and does not begin to notice that anything is wrong until he looks for Bess, whose present is the last and best. She is nowhere to be found, and he sees Serena looking after Clara's baby, which had been left in Bess's charge. 'Oh, Bess, oh where's my Bess?' he sings; Serena and Maria join in his song with explanations, the one excusing, the other condemning Bess for what she has done. Porgy's longing is admirably expressed in this trio, and in the final 'Oh Lord, I'm on my way', a spiritual with chorus, which Porgy sings as he starts off to follow Bess to New York, where he is told she has gone. He drives out of Catfish

Row in his goat-cart with his mind made up that, wherever she is, he will find her and bring her back.

Porgy and Bess is the first American opera to make a substantial success. It is also perhaps the only opera founded on the jazz of the nineteen-twenties and -thirties to survive the war which put an end to the period—which is perhaps partly due to the fact that most European composers (e.g. Křenek in *Jonny spielt auf*) used the medium satirically, and Gershwin was employing it as a folk basis for a story concerned with a community to which jazz was a natural means of expression.   H.

GIAN CARLO MENOTTI
(b. 1911)

GIAN Carlo Menotti continues to be America's most prolific operatic composer, though his meteoric success of the 1940's and early 1950's has not been sustained into the 1960's and 70's. His attempts at innovation, or at all events at a stylisation of traditional operatic form, in for instance *The Unicorn, the Dragon, the Manticore* (1958) were not widely successful, *Maria Golovin* (1957) met with a cold reception from critics, audiences and managements, and *The Saint of Bleecker Street*, for all its obvious appeal in Catholic countries, failed to duplicate the sensational success of the earlier *Medium* or *Consul*.

As a child in Italy, Menotti was taken by his nurse to a shrine, and a little later his crippled leg was found to be cured. It can be seen therefore that, just as *The Medium* stemmed from the vivid impressions of a real-life experience of a séance, so even the most successful of his recent operas, *Amahl* and *Bleecker Street*, owe a good deal to experiences towards which Menotti's attitude is, to say the least of it, ambivalent. Actuality, shown sometimes in a context of realism which is almost naive, has not goaded the composer to the sort of commitment which forced audiences to identify with Magda Sorel in a way they never have with Annina.

AMELIA AL BALLO
Amelia goes to the Ball

Opera in one act by Gian Carlo Menotti, text by the composer. Première (in English translation by G. Meade), April 1, 1937, in Philadelphia, conductor Reiner. First performed at Metropolitan Opera, New York (in English) in 1938, with Muriel Dickson, Chamlee, Brownlee, Cordon, conductor Panizza; San Remo, 1938 (in Italian), with Rosina Torri, Ugo Cantelmo, Luigi Borgonovo, Roberto Silva, conductor Votto; Berlin, 1947, with Irma Beilke, Kurt Rehm, Paul Schoeffler.

CHARACTERS

Amelia . . . . Soprano
Her husband . . . . Baritone
Her lover . . . . Tenor
Her Friend . . . . Contralto
The Commissioner of Police . . . . Bass
First maid . . . . Mezzo-Soprano
Second maid . . . . Mezzo-Soprano
Neighbours, Passers-by, Policeman

Time: Early Twentieth Century
Place: The luxurious bedroom of Amelia, wife of a wealthy, upper-middle-class citizen of a large European city.

A lively prelude, well suited to the frivolous nature of the piece, is dominated by a lyrical *andante* passage which refers to the trio in the second half of the work. The curtain rises as Amelia, described as 'a shapely young lady with red hair', is being dressed by her two maids for the first ball of the season, while her friend sits, threatening to leave without her if she does not hurry. The two women sing a duet ('La notte, la notte') in which they agree that nothing in the world, neither love nor honour, is of the slightest importance when a woman wants to go to a ball.

After a last-minute hitch as the maids frantically search for Amelia's precious fichu, she and her friend are on the point of leaving when Amelia's husband arrives and announces that they cannot go as he must discuss something privately with her. The others go off as Amelia furiously demands an explanation of such behaviour. The unhappy man tells her that he has found among her papers a love letter in passionate language, signed 'Bubu'. Amelia denies any knowledge of it, whereupon her husband, to a touching *andante* tune ('Amelia cara') reads the letter aloud to her. *Now* will she tell him her lover's name? 'What then?' asks Amelia anxiously, 'Shall we go to the ball?' Amelia gives a convincing performance as the loyal woman and at first vehemently refuses to betray her lover's name, until at last she says she will divulge it, provided her husband promises to take her to the ball. He agrees and, over the theme of the love letter, Amelia tells him it is the gentleman upstairs on the third floor—the one with a moustache. 'When do you see him?' demands the husband. 'Only at night', replies Amelia, and when reproached for her disloyalty to her sleeping husband retorts that, since sleeping is all he ever does do in bed, her infidelity is less than surprising.

Her husband puts on his top hat and coat and hurries to the door. Amelia is incredulous—what of his promise? He will keep it, says the husband, but first he would like to have a little chat with the gentleman on the third floor, assisted by his pistol; they can go dancing while her lover patches up his punctured skull.

Amelia reflects irritably that once the men begin to fight she will never get to the ball. She is beginning sadly to undress when a thought strikes her, and she runs out on to the balcony to call to her lover to climb down the lattice and thus avoid her husband. While she waits for him, she sings a *romanza*—men demand all kinds of impossible boons, but all she wants is to go to the ball, and she prays for time to stand still so that she may have her wish.

The lover arrives (by rope), full of ideas about defending Amelia against her husband until he hears about the pistol, when he suggests an immediate elopement. By the time they have finished arguing, it is too late for anything except concealment, and the husband comes in, furious at being balked of revenge. 'So, we can go now?' asks Amelia. 'Go where?' demands her husband, but, remembering the ball, agrees in the interests of peace to take her. While Amelia busies herself at her dressing table, he paces up and down

until he notices the rope on the balcony. It is the work of a
moment to find the hidden man; he aims and fires, only to be
rewarded by a loud but unlethal click. The lover advances
menacingly, but the husband reasons with him and the two
sit down to discuss the situation in a calm masculine manner,
leaving Amelia spluttering in the background.

The lover tells his story in an extremely sentimental
romanza ('Fu di notte'), after which discussion is renewed, to
the mounting fury of Amelia. There follows the trio referred
to in the prelude, in which action is interrupted for the three
to sing directly to the audience ('Chi può saper?—'Who knows
right from wrong?').

When Amelia, exasperated beyond measure, asks her
husband, 'For the last time, will you take me to the ball, yes
or no?' and he refuses, she snatches up a vase and hits him
over the head with it. He collapses and Amelia, horrified,
shouts for help.

To the sound of a short orchestral interlude, a crowd of
neighbours and passers-by gathers, intent on discovering what
has happened. Eventually the Chief of Police himself arrives.
Clearly realising that it is not dealing with the brightest of
men, the crowd takes pains to put the chief right as fast as he
gets the situation wrong. 'Well, who is this, anyway?' he
demands, only to jump to attention before the recumbent
'Excellency', the moment Amelia whispers her husband's
name into his ear. Amelia at her most bewitching flatters him
and tells him that her husband was assaulted by a robber—and
she points to her lover who, despite his protests, is dragged
off to prison. An ambulance takes away the husband, who,
the Police Chief assures the distracted Amelia, will soon
recover. 'I know,' says that single-minded lady. 'But who will
take me to the ball now?' As the chorus sings the moral—
when a women sets her heart on going to a ball, that's where
she'll go—the Chief of Police is preparing to transform
himself into a gallant escort, and so bring to its ordained end
one of Menotti's least pretentious but most sparkling and
appreciable scores.   H.

THE MEDIUM

Opera in two acts by Gian Carlo Menotti, text by the composer.
Première, Brander Matthews Theatre, Columbia University, May 8,

1946, with Evelyn Keller, Claramae Turner, conductor Luening. First performed New York (revised, and sponsored by Ballet Society), 1947, with Keller, Marie Powers, conducted by Barzin; London, Aldwych Theatre, 1948, with Powers, conductor Balaban; Genoa, 1950, with Pederzini, conductor Sanzogno; Venice, Bari, Palermo, Turin, 1951–2, each time with Pederzini; Paris, Opéra-Comique, 1968, with Eliane Lublin, Denise Scharley.

CHARACTERS

Monica, *daughter of Madame Flora* . . . . Soprano
Toby, *a mute* . . . . Dancer
Madame Flora (Baba), *a medium* . . . . Contralto
Mrs. Gobineau ⎫   ⎧   Soprano
Mr. Gobineau ⎬ *her clients* ⎨   Baritone
Mrs. Nolan   ⎭   ⎩ Mezzo-Soprano

Time: The present   *Place:* U.S.A.

Of *The Medium*, the composer himself has written (in notes to a complete gramophone recording published by Columbia Records in America): 'Despite its eerie setting and gruesome conclusions, *The Medium* is actually a play of ideas. It describes the tragedy of a woman caught between two worlds, a world of reality which she cannot wholly comprehend, and a supernatural world in which she cannot believe. Baba, the Medium, has no scruples in cheating her clients . . . until something happens which she herself has not prepared. This insignificant incident . . . shatters her self-assurance, and drives her almost insane with rage.' He goes on to explain that the idea for the opera came to him in 1936 when, staying near Salzburg, he was asked to go to a séance by some friends. It was not so much his own scepticism that struck him as the way his friends were pathetically anxious to believe that the spirit of their dead daughter was talking to them through the medium.

Act I.   Madame Flora's parlour. A puppet-theatre in one corner of the room. In a corner a tiny statue of the Virgin. No windows; the time of day is ambiguous throughout the play. When the curtain rises Toby is kneeling near a trunk from which he takes out bits of stuff and improvises a costume. Monica combs her hair and sings to herself. She tells him he is the King of Babylon, and they bow to each other. Then the sound of the door slamming down below frightens them, and they stand rigidly still. Madame Flora enters: 'How many times I've told you not to touch my things. . . . Is anything ready? Of course not.' Monica calms her mother, and they prepare for the séance, Monica putting on a white dress and veil, and Toby testing the various devices hidden in the puppet-theatre.

The clients arrive. One of them has not been before, but the others, who have been coming for two years, tell her how wonderful Madame Flora is. Mrs. Gobineau talks about her little child who was drowned in a fountain in their garden in France. The séance begins. All the lights, except the candle in front of the Madonna, are put out, and they sit round the table, their hands touching. Baba moans, and Monica slowly appears in a faint blue light, singing 'Mother, mother, are you there?' Mrs. Nolan is convinced it is her daughter, and she asks her various simple questions, which are answered to her satisfaction. Monica asks her about a gold locket, but it appears she has never had one, and immediately the apparition starts to disappear; Mrs. Nolan dashes towards the place where the figure appeared, but is restrained by the others.

Monica next imitates the sound of a child laughing, for the benefit of the Gobineaus. Suddenly, Baba shouts hysterically, and turns on the light. 'Who touched me?' They try to reassure her—Mr. Gobineau even says such things have often happened to him at her séances—but she sends them away. As they go they sing a trio: 'But why be afraid of our dead?'

Baba is in a paroxysm of fear, and she seizes Toby from the puppet-theatre, and tries to blame the whole phenomenon on him. Monica takes her away and soothes her with an extended melody, which Toby accompanies on a tambourine: 'O black swan, where, oh where, is my lover gone?' Baba suddenly thinks she can hear voices, and sends Toby round to see what is there; when he comes back to indicate there was nothing there, she falls on her knees and prays. Monica repeats a few phrases of the cradle song.

Act II takes place in the same setting as Act I; it is evening a few days later. Monica sits in front of the puppet-theatre watching a performance which Toby is giving. She applauds, and then sings while he dances barefoot round the room. The dance becomes a sort of love duet, in which Monica sings for both and Toby mimes his part. She has guessed his love for her, and tries to divert it into play-acting, which she knows he enjoys.

Baba drags herself up the stairs, and Toby retreats into a corner before she gets into the room, Monica having already left to go to her own room. Baba questions Toby about the incident of a few days back; did he touch her throat? Was he the one? She cannot get him to admit it, tries to keep her temper, then loses it hopelessly, seizes a whip and beats the unfortunate boy unmercifully. The doorbell rings, and the Gobineaus and Mrs. Nolan enter. Is it not the night of the séance? Yes, she says; but there will be no more—they were all frauds. She wants to give them their money back, but they will not admit they have been cheated; it has all been too real. Even the sight of the stage props and the sound of Monica imitating the children's voices does not convince them; those were not the voices they heard. Nothing will convince them, and they beg for another séance, until Madame Flora loses her temper suddenly and yells to them to get out. She tries to send Toby too, but Monica pleads for him, helpless as he is. Baba however is insistent, and Monica has only just time to say good-bye to Toby before he has run down the stairs and out into the street.

The voices come back to Baba. In desperation she goes to the cupboard and pours herself several drinks. She sits down at the table with the bottle in front of her. 'Afraid? Am I afraid?' she asks herself. She passes her life in review, and thinks of the horrible things she has known; then tries to comfort herself with the song of the black swan. Her scene dies away in hysterical laughter. For a moment she prays for forgiveness; then falls asleep, exhausted.

Toby comes up the stairwell, tiptoes across to Monica's room, finds the door locked, and hides behind the sofa when Baba stirring in her sleep knocks the bottle over. He starts to look in the trunk, but the lid falls with a bang, Baba wakes up with a start, and Toby hides behind the puppet-theatre. She yells 'Who's there?' but gets no answer, and taking out a revolver from a drawer shoots hysterically at the curtain. There is a moment of stillness, then a spot of blood appears on the white curtain. 'I've killed the ghost,' says Baba. Toby's hands clutch the side of the screen, which collapses with his weight, and he falls dead into the room. 'I've killed the ghost,' says Baba, as Monica pounds on the door and asks to be let in: 'I've killed the ghost.'

H.

THE TELEPHONE

Opera buffa in one act by Gian Carlo Menotti, text by the composer. Première, Heckscher Theatre, New York, February 18, 1947, with Marilyn Cotlow, Paul Kwartin, conductor Barzin. First performed Ethel Barrymore Theatre, New York, 1947, with Cotlow, Rogier, conductor Balaban; London, Aldwych Theatre, 1948, conductor Balaban; Zürich, 1949, with Oravez, Rehfuss; Hamburg, 1952, with Rothenberger, Günther; London, St. Pancras Town Hall, 1952, with Cantelo, Hemsley; Sadler's Wells, 1959, with Bronhill, Sharp, conductor Alexander Gibson; Paris, Opéra-Comique, 1968, with Berton, J. C. Benoit.

CHARACTERS

Lucy .... Soprano
Ben .... Baritone
Time: The present   *Place:* U.S.A.

Most performances of *The Medium*, at any rate those in English, have been preceded by performances of *The Telephone*, the little comedy Menotti wrote for the Ballet Society's first New York presentation of *The Medium*. But *The Telephone* would appear to have a life of its own, and it makes a capital curtain-raiser, a modern *intermezzo* as it were, in the style of Wolf-Ferrari's *Il Segreto di Susanna*.

The scene is Lucy's apartment. The opening music clearly indicates the *opera buffa* nature of the ensuing work. Lucy is busy opening a parcel which Ben has just handed her; 'Oh, just what I wanted,' she exclaims, as she unwraps a piece of abstract sculpture. Ben has something to tell her, he says, before his train goes in an hour's time. He seems to be reaching the point, when the telephone rings. Lucy answers it in a little *arietta* which seems to comprise all the things she always says to all her friends on the telephone. At one point in the conversation she dispenses with words altogether, then, much to Ben's dismay, seems to be about to go through the entire list of enquiries she has already made; but in the end she rings off.

Ben is about to start again, is again interrupted, but this time fortunately by a wrong number. An unfortunate mention of the time prompts Lucy to dial TIM, to discover that it is 'four-fifteen and three and a half seconds'. Another attempt is frustrated by another peal of the telephone bell. This time the conversation is fast and furious, and Lucy seems to quarrel with a boy friend. Ben comforts her, but she

goes off to her bedroom to get a handkerchief. Ben thinks
wryly of the impossible rival he has to face in the telephone,
with its 'hundreds of lives and miles of umbilical cord'. He is
about to cut the line when the telephone rings loudly and
desperately ('Like a child crying for help,' says the libretto),
and Lucy comes in and takes it protectively in her arms.

Lucy must make a call to tell her friend Pamela about the
quarrel with George. Again the conversation makes an *arietta*,
but this time Ben's voice joins in underneath Lucy's, complaining that he will never get the chance to say what he
wants to say. He goes out, much to Lucy's surprise ('I have a
feeling he had something on his mind'). At one side of the
stage Ben now becomes visible dialling in a telephone box.
Presently Lucy's bell rings, and she is confident it must be
him. This time he makes no mistake about it and gets the
proposal in early, and is immediately accepted. Lucy
demands only one thing: that he shall not forget. . . .
What? asks Ben; her hands, her eyes, her lips? No, her
number, exclaims Lucy, and the opera ends in a skittish waltz
tune, in which Ben promises never to forget her number. She
dictates it to him. . . .   H.

THE CONSUL

Opera in three acts by Gian Carlo Menotti; text by the composer.
Première, Philadelphia, March 1, 1950, with Neway, Powers, Lane,
Marlo, MacNeil, Lishner, McKinley, Jongeyans, conductor Lehman
Engel. First performed New York, 1951, by same cast; Cambridge
Theatre, London, 1951, with Neway, Powers, Lane, Lishner, Kelley,
conductor Schippers; Hamburg, 1951, with Mödl, Koegel, Wasserthal,
Ilosvay, Marschner, Meyer-Bremen; Zürich, 1951, with Schulz,
Malaniuk, conductor Reinshagen; la Scala, Milan, 1951, with Petrella,
Powers, Gardino, Guelfi, Campi, McKinley, Modesti, Cassinelli, con-
ductor Sanzogno; Vienna, 1951, with Zadek, Schürhoff, Rohs, Braun,
Jerger, Szemere, Rus, conductor Zallinger; Berlin, 1951, and Munich,
1952, with Borkh; Sadler's Wells, 1954, with Shuard; New York City
Opera, 1960, with Neway, Sarfaty, Joshua Hecht.

CHARACTERS

John Sorel . . . . Baritone
Magda Sorel, *his wife* . . . . Soprano
The Mother . . . . Contralto
Secret Police Agent . . . . Bass
First and Second Plain-clothes Men . . . . Silent

The Secretary		Mezzo-Soprano
Mr. Kofner		Bass-Baritone
The Foreign Woman	*waiting*	Soprano
Anna Gomez	*in the*	Soprano
Vera Boronel	*Consul's*	Contralto
The Magician (Nika	*office*	
Magadoff)		Tenor
Assan, *friend of John Sorel*		Baritone
Voice on the Record		Soprano

Time: After World War II   *Place:* Somewhere in Europe

Menotti's first full-length opera deals with a subject which was familiar to every member of every one of its early non-English-speaking audiences. Its immediate success was perhaps due in even greater measure to the grippingly theatrical nature of its story than to a corresponding power in its music.

The country in which the action takes place is not identified, any more than is the consulate whose secretary is the embodiment of every form-ridden bureaucrat in every big city in the world.

Act I.   The first scene takes place in the home of John Sorel. It is early morning, and the room is empty and dark. The sound of a gramophone record is heard as the curtain rises, coming from a café across the street: 'Tu reviendras. . . .' Suddenly the door is flung open and Sorel staggers into the room and throws himself into a chair. Magda hears the noise and runs to him, and immediately starts to bandage the wound which she sees in his leg. He tells her and the Mother, who has followed her into the room, the usual story: there was a secret meeting, the police had been tipped off about it and shot at them as they made their escape across the roofs, wounding him and killing another. Magda looks out of the window and sees the police. John is helped toward the window, and goes to what is obviously an agreed hiding-place, leaving his wife and mother to tidy up the room in preparation for the questioning which must inevitably follow in a few seconds.

As the secret police agents enter, the Mother is rocking the cradle, in which lies the little child of Magda and John. She sings a mournful song of lament for the peace which has vanished from their lives: 'Shall we ever see the end of all this?' The agent starts to question Magda, who answers non-committally. His threats are not just those of a bully, but carry potential danger in them: 'Courage is often a lack of imagination. We have strange ways to make people talk. Oh, not at all the way you think. . . . People like you can defy strength, but not the beat of your own heart.'

The agents leave, and Magda and the Mother watch as they arrest somebody opposite and drag him away. John comes down from his hiding-place; he must get away. He tells them that the signal which shall tell them that there is a message from him will be the breaking of their window by a stone. When this happens, they are to send for Assan, the glass-cutter, who will bring them news. Magda and John bid each other farewell ('Now, O lips, say good-bye'), and their duet becomes a trio when the Mother joins her voice with theirs before the end of the scene.

Scene ii.   The cheerless waiting-room of the Consulate, in one corner of which is the Secretary's desk, and behind it a door leading to the Consul's room. Mr. Kofner comes forward to renew his application for a visa; he has everything now . . . but the photographs turn out to be the wrong size. A 6/8 *allegretto* movement suggests the monotonous, automatic nature of the dealings between applicant and Secretary. As he moves away, the Foreign Woman comes up to the railing which separates the Secretary's desk from the rest of the room, and starts to make an enquiry. She does not know the Secretary's language, and another complication seems to have been introduced, but Mr. Kofner volunteers to act as interpreter. It appears that her daughter ran away with a soldier, who has now left her with a three-months-old baby. The daughter is ill and needs her mother's help; can she have a visa to visit her? Yes, says the Secretary; if she fills out the forms and her application is accepted, she may be able to leave in a couple of months' time. She is stunned by this information, but Mr. Kofner leads her away to fill in the forms.

More people come into the waiting-room, and Magda advances to the desk. The dialogue between her and the Secretary is typical of Menotti's style:

Magda: May I speak to the Consul?

Secretary: No one is allowed to speak to the Consul, the Consul is busy.

Magda: Tell him my name.

Secretary: Your name is a number.

Magda: But my name is Sorel, Magda Sorel. The wife of Sorel, the lover of freedom.

Secretary: Sorel is a name and a name is a number.

Magda: May I speak to the Consul?

Secretary: No one is allowed to speak to the Consul, the Consul is busy.

The duet gains in intensity: 'Explain to the Consul, explain . . . that the web of my life has worn down to one single thread . . .' But it is still a question of filling in forms and making applications in the customary manner, and Magda is handed a batch of forms as Nika Magadoff comes forward. He starts to do some simple conjuring tricks in an effort to impress the Secretary with his *bona fides*, but a slow ensemble begins ('In endless waiting-rooms'), and he joins in it. As the curtain falls, it has become a quintet in which Magda, Anna Gomez, Vera Boronel, the Magician and Mr. Kofner express the agony of frustration which their daily attendance at the Consulate entails.

Act II, scene i. Sorel's house, a month later. The same record is being played in the café opposite. Magda and her Mother are discussing the possibility of getting a visa. When Magda goes out, her Mother tries to cheer up the little baby. She sings him a lullaby, 'I shall find for you shells and stars,' and, after Magda has returned to the room and fallen asleep in a chair, goes out in her turn. Magda stirs in her sleep, and in her nightmare she sees John and the Secretary, whom he introduces to her as his sister. Magda is terrified of her, more particularly since John seems drawn to her. The nightmare comes to an end with a horrible vision of a dead child.

Magda wakes up with a scream, and is comforted by her mother. Suddenly, a stone shatters the glass of the window, and Magda rushes to the telephone to carry out John's instructions. She has no sooner finished talking to Assan than there is a knock at the door, which opens to reveal the Secret Police Agent. He starts to insinuate that there would be no obstacle to her joining her husband if she would only give him the little information about her husband's friends which he wants. She loses control and yells at him to get out, and threatens to kill him if he returns. He is by the door when Assan arrives to mend the window.

Assan tells Magda that John is still hiding in the mountains, and will not leave the country until he knows that his wife has a visa and can follow him. She says that he must be told that arrangements are complete; it is not true, but there is no other way of compelling him to save his own life. Assan agrees to do as he is asked, and leaves the room.

During the scene between Magda and Assan, the Mother suddenly realises that the little half-starved child has died quietly in his sleep. She gives no sign to Magda, but remains quite still by the cradle, not rocking it, not singing to the child. As soon as she looks at her, Magda knows what has happened. She stops her mother weeping ('It is too soon to cry'), but the Mother says she is thinking of John, 'who will never see his baby again'.

An interlude takes us to scene ii, in the Consulate, a few days later. The Secretary is standing by the filing-cabinet, looking for something; Anna Gomez is by the railing, and the Magician, Vera Boronel, Mr. Kofner, and the Foreign Woman are waiting in the room. The Secretary finds the card and reads: 'Three years in concentration camp. Husband, prisoner; whereabouts, unknown. No documents. I don't see what we can do for you.' It is only one case among many, and there is nothing to do but fill in forms, and try above all to avoid despair.

Magda comes in and asks to jump the queue, but the Magician explains in a kindly but firm way that he has been seven times to the Consulate, and always when his turn came it was time for the Consulate to close; he *must* take his turn now. There is a fairly long scene in which he again demonstrates his professional powers of conjuring and of hypnotism, much to the Secretary's dismay. He puts all the occupants of the waiting-room in a trance, and then makes them dance happily together, until the Secretary becomes quite desperate over the unaccustomed turn events have taken. She begs Magadoff to return everyone to normal, which done, he leaves the room.

The others allow Magda to go ahead of them. The Secretary does not remember her until she has looked her up in the card-index, and Magda is frantic with worry and near to despair. She demands to see the Consul but is again refused. Finally, she can bear it no more, and throws self-control to the winds, launching out into a denunciation of the bureaucratic system and the injustice it leads to. The rest of the act is given up to a *scena* for Magda, with interruptions from the Secretary and the others waiting at the Consulate: 'To this we've come: that men withhold the world from men.' Her outburst is at first directed at the useless questions upon which lives depend: 'What is your name? . . . My name is Woman. Age: Still young. Colour of hair: Grey. Colour of eyes: The colour of tears. Occupation: Waiting.' Her passionate indignation is finally summed up in a brave phrase: 'Oh, the day will come, I know, when our hearts aflame will burn your paper chains. Warn the Consul, Secretary . . . .'

The Secretary cannot conceal her own feelings, although she does her best: 'You're being very unreasonable, Mrs. Sorel.' She goes into the Consul's office, saying that she will ask if he can see her just a minute. The improbable happens when she comes out and informs Magda that she may go in when the important visitor who is with him has left. Anticipation rises as two shadows are seen on the glass panel of the door. The visitor shakes hands, but, when he turns into the room, he is seen to be the Secret Police Agent. Magda faints.

Act III, scene i.   The Consulate. Magda is waiting to see the Consul, in spite of the Secretary's warning that the place will be closed in ten minutes' time. Vera Boronel comes in, states her name, and is greeted with something like pleasure by the Secretary; at last there is somebody to whom she can give good news—her papers are through! Again there is an *allegretto* for the mechanical, trivial business of signing papers—even papers that represent the prospect of such happiness as these do—and the two women sing happily together: 'All the documents must be signed.'

Assan hurries in, looking for Magda, whom he tells that the news about John is bad; he has heard that his child and his mother are dead, and intends to come back over the frontier to fetch his wife. While the Secretary and Vera Boronel go on signing papers, Magda and Assan try to think of a way of convincing him that he must not come back. Magda thinks she knows one, and writes a note which she confides to Assan, refusing however to tell him what she has written.

Everyone leaves, and presently the Secretary too is ready to go. For a moment she seems to see the facts which have confronted her all day long on the benches in the waiting-room. 'One must not think,' she says. 'Why must there be so many names? Their cases are all alike.' She is about to leave when John rushes into the room, looking behind him to see that he is not being followed. He asks if Magda has been there, and is told he may still catch up with her if he hurries after her. But that he cannot do, he protests, since he was followed to the

Consulate by the police, who will not allow him to leave. At that moment, a confused noise is heard outside, and as John pulls out his gun, the Secret Police Agent comes in, followed by two plain-clothes men. John's gun is knocked out of his hand, and, when the Secretary protests that no arrest can be made in the Consulate, the Secret Agent says that Sorel will be coming with him of his own free will, not as an arrested man.

As they leave, the Secretary dials furiously, and when the curtain goes up again on scene ii, after an interlude based on a march rhythm, the telephone can be heard ringing in Mrs. Sorel's room, which she presently enters, though only after the bell is silent. She makes preparations to commit suicide, and turns on the gas.

As she bends over towards the stove with a shawl over her head, the walls dissolve and figures from the Consulate appear, looking exactly as Magda has known them there. Behind them are John and the Mother, the former in dark clothes, the latter in an old-fashioned wedding-dress. Magda talks to them, and the ghostly chorus sings the march tune of the interlude. Gradually the figures disappear and the music which has gone with them, and all that can be heard is the sound of Magda's deep breathing. Suddenly the telephone begins to ring. Magda stretches out her hand as if to answer it, but her reaction is feeble, and she falls inert over the chair, while the telephone bell continues to ring. The curtain falls as the orchestra gives out the tune associated with Magda's protest at the end of Act II.   H.

AMAHL AND
THE NIGHT VISITORS

Opera in one act by Gian Carlo Menotti, libretto by the composer. Originally written for Television, première, NBC studios, New York, December 24, 1951, with Rosemary Kuhlmann and Chet Allen, conductor Schippers. First stage performance, Indiana University, Bloomington, February 21, 1952, conductor Ernest Hoffmann. First performed City Center, New York, 1952; Florence Festival, 1953, with Simionato, Alvaro Cordova, Lazzari, Capecchi, Corena, conductor Stokowski. B.B.C. Television, 1967, with Cantelo; Hamburg State Opera, 1968–9, with Kjerstin Meyer; Geneva, 1971, with Kjerstin Meyer; Rome, 1971–2, with Giovanna Fioroni. Frequently performed in Italy and the United States.

CHARACTERS

Amahl, *a crippled boy of about 12* . . . . .Treble
His Mother . . . . Soprano
King Kaspar . . . . Tenor
King Melchior . . . . Baritone
King Balthazar . . . . Bass
The Page . . . . Baritone
Shepherds, Villagers, Dancers

After a few introductory bars the curtain rises to show the outside of a little shepherd's hut, where Amahl sits playing his pipe. Beside him on the ground is his home-made crutch. Inside the hut his mother listens to him for a bit, then calls him in. He makes one excuse after another to stay outside and even after his mother loses her patience he tries to persuade her to go out to look at the beautiful sky and the brilliant new star—'as large as a window and with a glorious tail'. She thinks it is another of his stories and scolds him for lying, but eventually breaks down in tears at the prospect of going out begging next day. They say goodnight and go to bed.

In the distance can be heard the voices of the three Kings. As they draw near, their way is lit by their black Page, bowed under the weight of rich-looking bundles, everything from a jewel box to a parrot in a cage. They stop at Amahl's home and King Melchior knocks. Amahl goes to the door and scurries back to his mother. Three times she thinks he is lying, but eventually she follows him to the door, the Kings bid her a grave good evening ('What did I tell you?'), and she for her part offers her meagre hospitality to the splendid visitors. They accept with gratitude, especially Kaspar who is inclined to get carried away and has to be restrained by his companions.

To a jaunty march, the Kings make their way into the hut and settle themselves on a bench. As the Page spreads out the treasures on a rug, the woman goes off to look for firewood, telling Amahl not to pester their visitors in her absence. As soon as she is out of the way, Amahl goes straight to the Nubian King Balthazar and bombards him with questions, meanwhile looking out of the corner of his eye at Kaspar, who is feeding his parrot with bits of food from his pocket. Amahl cannot resist Kaspar's eccentricity and soon it is his turn for cross-questioning. Kaspar however is deaf and things do not warm up until Amahl asks what is in the box, whereupon Kaspar becomes enthusiastic and shows Amahl the precious stones he keeps against all kinds of misfortune. When his mother returns and scolds him for being a nuisance, Amahl protests: 'It's not my fault; they kept asking me questions.'

Amahl goes off to fetch the other shepherds and the Kings tell his mother that they are looking for the Child, and in an *andante* describe their vision ('Have you seen a Child the colour of wheat, the colour of dawn?'). In her mind the mother identifies the Child with her own son.

They fall silent, and the sound of the shepherds' calling is heard. As they approach, led by Amahl, they sing a gay pastoral unaccompanied chorus. When they reach the door of the hut with their baskets of fruit and vegetables they are struck dumb by the splendour of the Kings, but the mother urges them to come in and shyly they present their humble gifts. The Kings thank them, and the mother asks the young people to dance for her guests. After some persuasion they do so, at first slowly and formally but gradually accelerating into a kind of *tarantella*.

Balthazar thanks the dancers and they file out, bowing to the Kings. As their song grows fainter, Amahl wistfully asks Kaspar if he has perhaps a magic stone to cure a crippled boy. But Kaspar, as usual, does not hear properly and Amahl goes sadly to his straw bed.

They all settle down for the night, the Kings sitting side by side on the bench and the Page lying at their feet, his arms round the precious gifts. The lights are lowered to indicate the passage of time and when they come up again, dawn is breaking. Everyone is asleep except the mother, who sings of the unfairness of all this wealth going to an unknown child while her own is starving. She takes hold of one of the bundles and the Page wakes up. The noise of their struggle disturbs Amahl who flings himself at the Page, beating him and pulling his hair in a desperate attempt to rescue his mother. Kaspar orders the Page to release the woman, and King Melchior says she may keep the gold as the Child they seek has no need of it.

The mother is enthralled with Melchior's glowing description and begs him to take back the gold—were she not so poor she would herself send a gift to the Child. Amahl wants to send his crutch. He lifts it and then, to everyone's amazement, takes a step without it. For a moment no one believes the miracle, then the Kings give thanks to God, as Amahl dances and leaps about the room until at last he falls down. One at a time the Kings ask Amahl to let them touch him. When the Page in his turn asks, Amahl, a little self-importantly, at first refuses but, at a sign from his mother, relents. Amahl begs to be allowed to go with the Kings to give the crutch to the Child and when the Kings join their voices to his, the mother gives her permission—whereupon they again have to quieten the now over-excited Kaspar. With a wealth of maternal advice to sustain him, Amahl sets off with the Kings and, as the procession moves away, he plays on his pipe the tune which began the opera.   H.

THE SAINT
OF BLEECKER STREET

Opera in three acts by Gian Carlo Menotti, text by the composer. Première, Broadway Theatre, New York, December 27, 1954, with Virginia Copeland, Gloria Lane, David Poleri, conductor Thomas Schippers. First performed la Scala, Milan, 1955, with Eugenia Ratti, Gloria Lane, David Poleri, conductor Schippers; Volksoper, Vienna, 1955, with Dorothea Siebert, Henny Herze, Josef Gostic, conductor Hollreiser; England, B.B.C. Television, 1957, with Virginia Copeland, Rosalind Elias, Raymond Nilsson; New York City Opera, 1964–5, with Joan Sena, Beverly Wolff, Muriel Greenspon, Enrico Di Giuseppe; Spoleto, 1968, with Maria Mirandara, Gloria Lane, Anna Assandri, Franco Bonisolli, conductor Schippers.

CHARACTERS

Assunta ....Mezzo-Soprano
Carmela .... Soprano
Maria Corona, *a newspaper-seller* .... Soprano
Her dumb, 16-year-old son
Don Marco, *a priest* .... Bass
Annina .... Soprano
Michele, *her brother* .... Tenor
Desideria, *Michele's mistress* ....Mezzo-Soprano
Salvatore .... Baritone
A young man .... Tenor
Neighbours, Wedding-Guests, etc.
Time: The Present   *Place:* A quarter of New York
known as Little Italy

An overture establishes the atmosphere of feverish religiosity and the rise of the curtain on the first scene of Act I shows a cold-water flat in Bleecker Street on Good Friday afternoon, with a crowd of neighbours waiting for Annina to emerge from her bedroom. She is a frail, deeply religious girl, subject to mysterious visions; signs of stigmata have appeared after her trances and she is reputed to have performed miraculous cures.

The crowd is impatient to be blessed by the girl, whom they consider a saint, and some of them are quarrelling about the uses to which her miraculous powers should be put; the hubbub is broken by the sudden appearance of the priest Don Marco, who announces that the vision has begun and that Annina is to be brought out. At first she lies motionless and hardly conscious, then suddenly cries out in pain, and begins a detailed description of the Crucifixion, falling back with a dreadful cry as she describes the driving of the last nail and on her hands appear the bleeding stigmata. Don Marco and Carmela try to fend off the hysterical neighbours struggling to touch the sick girl, but the crowd falls back at the sight of Michele, her brother, who is disgusted at their behaviour and drives them away. With Carmela's help, he carries Annina back into her room, then returns and reproaches the priest, saying her visions are mental delusions rather than the work of God. Don Marco warns Michele that his adversary is not a priest but God himself.

The second scene is set in an empty lot on Mulberry Street, flanked by tenement houses, from one of which can be heard the voice of Assunta singing a lullaby to her child. On the steps, Annina and her best friend Carmela are sewing gold paper stars on to the white gown of little Concettina, who is to be an angel in the forthcoming procession of San Gennaro, to which Annina says her brother will not let her go. When Carmela tells Annina that she is to be married and so they will not be able to take the veil together as they had planned, Annina says she will gladly go to Carmela's wedding if Carmela will come to hers when she becomes a nun. Assunta laughs at Carmela's dreams of happiness—once she has six children and a drunken husband, she will be sure to go to heaven. What is heaven like, they ask Annina. Saint Michael once, says Annina, took her in a dream to the gates of Paradise, and the three are singing in wonder at this splendid vision when Maria Corona rushes in with her dumb son, warning Annina that the Sons of Gennaro refuse to have their procession without their 'Little Saint' and are threatening to take her by force if necessary. Annina says she is not afraid and Carmela vows to defend her friend with her life if necessary. Maria Corona confesses that she once doubted Annina's miracles, but since she touched her son, dumb since birth, he has begun to speak—he is grunting pathetically when Michele enters and angrily sends the women away.

There is an extended scene for Annina and Michele. She is afraid for him, because he makes people hate him; he argues that he loves her and wants to protect her from their superstitious neighbours who mean to turn her into a saint. Why should God choose her of all people, when she was once mocked for her stupidity? Perhaps because she loves Him, answers Annina simply. His arguments seem useless and Michele grows desperate; she is the centre of his life, and he swears he will hide her away and that she shall never take the veil.

Suddenly the street lights up and the procession is heard approaching. Annina tries to persuade Michele to go inside with her but he refuses, and a group of young men sneak up and overpower him, leaving him tied up and helpless as they carry the frightened Annina off in triumph to head the procession. As the last stragglers vanish, Desideria appears and unbinds Michele who bursts out sobbing. She embraces him passionately.

Act II. The following May, Carmela's marriage to Salvatore is being celebrated in an Italian basement restaurant. At the climax of the revels, the bride is toasted in a rhapsodic song and before following the other guests into the next room, Annina begs Salvatore to be always kind to her friend. Desideria now comes looking for Michele, protesting that since she sleeps with him she is treated almost as an outcast; let him take her in with him to the wedding party and show he is not ashamed of her. When Michele refuses, because it will upset Annina, Desideria flies into a rage. Why can't Michele leave Annina alone? He is obsessed with her ('What does she ever do for you except light candles for your soul?'), whereas Desideria and he need each other.

Michele reluctantly agrees to go in with her, but at the door they find Don Marco, who begs Michele not to cause a scandal. Michele immediately swings over to Desideria's side, shouting that she is worth more than any woman there. Annina rushes to him but he pushes her away and sings bitterly of his treatment at the hands of those whom he wished to be his friends and of the impossibility of being accepted as an equal citizen in the New World ('You are ashamed to say: "I was Italian." . . .').

Annina is distressed at the upheaval and asks Michele to take her home. Desideria suddenly appears from a corner and accuses Michele of being in love with his sister. Michele cannot believe his ears but Desideria in a mounting rage insists that what she says is true. Michele suddenly seizes a knife from the bar and stabs her in the back. He runs out, leaving Annina praying with Desideria. She dies as the police sirens are heard in the distance.

Act III, scene i. In a deserted passage near a newspaper kiosk in a subway station, Annina and Maria Corona are waiting nervously for Michele. He comes in with Don Marco, and there is a tender reunion between brother and sister. Annina begs Michele to give himself up but he refuses and they comment on their terrible situation in a tragic duet. When she tells him that she is afraid of dying and is going into a nunnery, Michele is shocked and horrified. Nothing he can say affects her resolve, and the scene ends with Michele cursing her and rushing off, leaving her to be comforted by Maria Corona.

Scene ii. Annina's room, a week later. She is dying and wants to take the veil immediately if the Church will grant permission. She has no white dress to wear, but Carmela offers to lend her own wedding dress and Annina gratefully accepts it. A letter arrives for Don Marco—it is the Church's permission for Annina to become a nun. Annina is almost overcome with joy and excitement. She sends everyone out except Don Marco and Carmela, and prays that death will spare her long enough to attain her great wish. As Don Marco robes for the ceremony, neighbours crowd into the room and Assunta brings the news that Michele has been seen near by. The ceremony proceeds calmly until at the end Michele bursts in and begs his sister to reconsider. She appears not to hear him and the ritual continues as her hair is cut off and the black veil is put on. Michele watches incredulously as Annina collapses and Don Marco places the ring on her finger just before she dies. H.

24

Argentinian Opera

ALBERTO GINASTERA
(b. 1916)

BOMARZO

OPERA in two acts (fifteen scenes) by Alberto Ginastera, libretto by Manuel Mujica Lainez. Première, May 19, 1967, Washington, D.C., with Salvador Novoa, Isabel Penagos, Joanna Simon, Claramae Turner, Richard Torigi, conductor Julius Rudel. First performed City Opera, New York, 1968, with substantially the same cast. European première, Kiel, 1970 (in German), with Charles O'Neill; performed Buenos Aires, 1972, with Novoa.

CHARACTERS

Pier Francesco Orsini, *Duke of Bomarzo* .... Tenor
Silvio de Narni, *Astrologer* .... Baritone
Gian Corrado Orsini, *Father of Pier Francesco* .... Bass
Girolamo ⎫ *Brothers of Pier Francesco* ...... ⎧ Baritone
Maerbale ⎭ ⎩ Baritone
Nicolas Orsini, *Nephew of Pier Francesco* ...... Tenor
Julia Farnese, *Wife of Pier Francesco* .... Soprano
Pantasilea, *a Florentine Courtesan* ..... Mezzo-Soprano
Diana Orsini, *Grandmother of Pier Francesco* Contralto
Messenger .... Baritone
Shepherd boy ....Treble
Pier Francesco, Girolamo, Maerbale as children
Time: Sixteenth Century *Place:* Bomarzo, Florence and Rome

Born in Buenos Aires in 1916, Alberto Ginastera's rather prolific output had included music in every form, including a successful ballet (*Panambi:* 1939–40) and an even more successful opera, *Don Rodrigo* (1964), when he was commissioned to write a new opera for the Opera Society of

Washington. Over the years, his style has changed from something with a basically Argentinian flavour to an international professionalism that allowed him in the new work to range (in the words of Norman Fraser) 'from neo-organum in some of the chorales to serial variations and free-for-all pandemonium when they are required'.

His librettist is the Argentinian writer Manuel Mujica Lainez (born Buenos Aires 1910), who had published in 1962 a novel on the subject of the strange monsters in the gardens of Bomarzo, near Viterbo, north of Rome, and their creator in the sixteenth century, Pier Francesco Orsini. Lainez's programme notes (slightly shortened) are reproduced in italics at the beginning of each scene. Ginastera's comment on his hero: 'I see Bomarzo not as a man of the Renaissance, but as a man of our time. We live nowadays in an age of anxiety, an age of sex, an age of violence. Bomarzo struggles with violence, and is tormented by anxiety, the metaphysical anxiety of death.'

The opera is divided into two acts, with a prologue and an epilogue (actually a single divided scene) and thirteen scenes in between.

Slow, deep, preludial mutterings in the orchestra lead to the intervention of the chorus (confined, unamplified, to the pit throughout), sometimes precisely notated, sometimes aleatoric[1] —a portent of things to come.

Act I, Scene i.   The Potion. *I, Pier Francesco Orsini, Duke of Bomarzo, on the last day of my life went through the park until I reached a figure carved into the rock known as The Mouth of Hell. My astrologer, Silvio de Narni, carrying a luminous chalice, and Nicolas, my nephew, came with me. I remember we heard a shepherd boy sing that he would not change places with the Duke because I went through life dragging in my hump the burden of my sins. They left me there and, alone, I drank the mysterious potion that would make me immortal. I heard the voice of my beloved grandmother saying they had betrayed me and I was going to die. The shepherd boy appeared, but I couldn't make myself heard. Then I saw pass before my eyes all the events of my strange life, not the important ones, the Court, Battles and Wars—but the events of my secret life which, like the hump on my back, encumbered my soul.*

[1] Allowing a strong element of choice in the performer.

The music is concerned mainly with the innocent security of the boy's 'folk song', with its mediaeval overtones, and with Pier Francesco's two short solos, one bewailing the lack of peace and certainty in his life and the other a monologue when he confronts his fate alone in one of the monstrous carvings he has created. The first interlude, which uses the chorus, derives from the prelude and leads to:

Scene ii. Pier Francesco's Childhood. *I saw my brothers Girolamo and Maerbale, when they were children, playing in one of the rooms of the castle, amidst old clothes and jewellery that lay scattered about. They wanted me to join them in their play, but I knew that, as always, they would try to tease me. They put a dunce cap on my head but I didn't move. Angry at me, Girolamo decided that, since he was to be the Duke, I would be the Duchess of Bomarzo, and that Maerbale would marry us. They dressed me in an absurd female costume, but when my eldest brother tried to kiss me, I escaped. Suddenly, Girolamo fell upon me in a fury, pierced the lobe of my ear with an ear-ring which he picked up from the floor, saying that it was a present for the Duchess. My father heard my agonised cries, but instead of helping me, he said I was the disgrace of the family, and called me an effeminate hunchback. My brothers ran away and then my father, in mocking anger, reminded me that in a hidden room near by there lived a mysterious being nobody had ever seen but whom everyone dreaded. Opening a secret panel, he pushed me into the inner cell. Inside, I saw a skeleton crowned with rose-like rags. I know not whether I dreamt it, or if it really happened, but the skeleton stood up and started dancing.*

The Orsini children speak their roles, and the music supplies background to their sinister pantomime, until it assumes more importance at the entry of the warrior Duke himself, their father, characterised here and at his later appearance by the decisive tapping of his stick on the floor.

The dance of the skeleton is suggestively depicted by string *glissandi* and assorted percussion.

Scene iii. The Horoscope. *I next found myself as a young man in my study with the astrologer, who told me that I should be immortal, and consequently the most glorious of the Orsinis. I argued that my father hated me and that he wouldn't let me outlive him, but Silvio answered that he could avoid that by means of a magic spell. We heard peacocks scream in the park which surprised us, as there were none in Bomarzo, and my grandmother appeared on the terrace, filled with premonition. A messenger announced that my father, the* condottiere, *was returning to Bomarzo badly wounded. I realised that the astrologer's forecast was coming true.*

Silvio's incantation is rendered the more impressive by a whispered choral background, and the screams of the peacocks are heard from the orchestra. An extended interlude, depicting perhaps the mixed nature of Pier Francesco's reaction to the news of his father's serious wounds, leads to:

Scene iv.   Pantasilea. *The Duke wouldn't see me, and sent me to Florence to a famous courtesan, Pantasilea, perhaps to make fun of me. The courtesan was naturally disappointed when she saw a hunchback enter her chamber. I was attended by Abul, my slave, whom I loved dearly. I remember the terror I felt when I was left alone with Pantasilea in a room of mirrors peopled by my shameful image. I gave the voluptuous creature my sapphire necklace, and I asked her to let me go. She led me to a cupboard and I was revolted by the dreadful liquids used to fan the flame of failing love. I ran away, as the peacocks echoed the ominous cry I had heard in the castle.*

The scene opens with Pantasilea's mandoline-accompanied song of praise to Florence, a city to her synonymous with Love. Pier Francesco's horror of mirrors and their revelation to him of his crooked body is exposed for the first time, as also his homosexual security with the faithful, dumb Abul. The scene ends with a repetition of Pantasilea's song, as mournful and lonely as the profession she follows.

Scene v.   By the Tiber. *Memory then took me to a place in Bomarzo, near the Tiber, where my grandmother told me as she had often done the story of the marvellous Orsinis. Suddenly I saw Girolamo on top of the rock about to bathe in the river. He laughed at the promise of my horoscope, jeered at me and, as he stepped back, lost his footing and fell into the river. My grandmother wouldn't let me go to his assistance, though I realised he had hit his head on a rock and was dying.*

Musically, the scene is dominated by the powerful figure of Diana Orsini, whose biggest singing opportunity occurs in it. The interlude consists mainly of bells—on the whole festive for the proclamation of the new Duke rather than mournful for the death of the old.

Scene vi.   Pier Francesco Orsini, Duke of Bomarzo. *Soon*

after Girolamo's death, my father died, and I succeeded to the Dukedom. We held the traditional ceremony in the hall of the castle, where my grandmother introduced me to one of the guests, the beautiful Julia Farnese. Lords and vassals marched in procession before me. To my annoyance, Julia left the hall with my brother, Maerbale. I remained alone with Abul, and a hooded man approached, his face muffled, but I recognised—or thought to recognise—the ghost of my father.

The scene opens with a brilliant chorus, 'O Rex Gloriae', contains the disconcerting reappearance of Pier Francesco's father (accompanied by his stick-tapping), and ends with Diana Orsini's affirmation 'You are the Duke'.

Scene vii.   Fiesta at Bomarzo. *The courtiers were dancing and I, isolated by my terrible fate, hardly managed to mumble the love that I felt for Bomarzo, my Bomarzo, for I am Bomarzo. I passed from one dream to another, and I had the impression Abul, the slave, Julia Farnese and Pantasilea were dancing with me, trying to take possession of me. The masked dancers returned, and as they whirled away, the dream became a nightmare.*

A march and a musette precede Pier Francesco's soliloquy, in which he declares his identification with Bomarzo. This in turn is followed by two galliards and a masquerade, the latter in a maniacal *tempo di Saltarello* and the occasion for one of the scenes which has been most praised by critics as a successful fusion in operatic context of dance and opera.

Scene viii.   The portrait by Lorenzo Lotto. *I was back from the Picardy campaign, and I went to my study, my eyes eager for my portrait painted by Messer Lorenzo Lotto in Venice. I told Abul that the artist had reflected in it the best of myself. The slave withdrew and I noticed, by the portrait, a large mirror. In the clarity of its reflection I saw a version of my painful body in contrast with that in the lordly portrait. I realised I was both at the same time. From the depth of the mirror, there emerged the countenance of the Devil, as if invoked by the spirits of my father and of Girolamo. Blind with terror, I shattered the mirror with my helmet.*

While looking at the portrait with Abul, Pier Francesco speaks over orchestral background, regretting incidentally that Julia Farnese does not love him as does Abul. He breaks into song for an aria of longing for Julia, and, in a faster tempo, expression of his fear and loathing for the mirror and the demon which appears to him in it. The chorus at the end of the scene echoes his cries of horror as the act comes to an end.

Act II, Scene ix. Julia Farnese. *Julia Farnese was a constant obsession with me. I saw her in her father's palace in Rome, the evening she sang delicately about the graces of courtly love. Maerbale was singing with her and I, hidden, interpolated phrases of bitterness. When Maerbale and Julia were about to drink a glass of red wine, I could bear it no longer and involuntarily spilt the contents of the goblet on Julia's dress.*

In one of the main lyrical passages of the score, Julia's madrigal becomes a duet as Maerbale takes up the tune, and a trio when Pier Francesco, Otello-like, overhears it and in his jealousy interrupts the scene.

Scene x.   The bridal chamber. *Julia and I were married in Bomarzo. After the ceremony, we retired to the bridal chamber. I pointed out to Julia the mosaics that in heraldic design combined the roses of the Orsinis and the lilies of the Farneses. Suddenly I saw among the designs, one that represented the face of the Devil, invisible to Julia.*

A slow nuptial hymn from the chorus precedes Julia's *Canto triste de amor*, in which Pier Francesco, almost reluctantly it seems, finally joins. As the ladies-in-waiting finish undressing the Duchess, she hums to herself the song of the previous scene, until Pier Francesco screams in anguish at the apparition of the Devil, an apparition visible only to him. He orders the courtiers to leave him, and, clutching his bride by the wrist, seems to be trying to outstare the demon of the mosaics.

Scene xi.   The Dream. *I couldn't possess Julia that night and sank into despair, made worse by a dream. The painted figures of the men and women that people the Etruscan graves of Bomarzo came to life capturing Julia and myself in their dances, offering me through imagination what reality had denied me.*

Pier Francesco's fruitless attempts to consummate his marriage are symbolised by the momentary substitution of the figure of Pantasilea for that of Julia, and in between his soliloquy of frustration and a short, violent lament that it is only in dream that he can possess his wife, takes place an erotic ballet to aleatoric music. The G sharp of Pier Francesco's concluding cry of 'Dios mío' becomes the basis of an aleatoric choral interlude, intended to 'produce the sensation that Pier Francesco's shout is extended to the chorus and orchestra'.

Scene xii. The Minotaur. *Like a madman, I left the chamber and made my way along the corridor lined with the busts of the Roman emperors, until I came to the central sculpture, the Minotaur. I felt the proud Orsinis around me, and on recognising my fated brother in the dreadful image, the Minotaur, I kissed its marble lips. Bomarzo trembled with passion, yet I found solace only in that sweet brother.*

As Pier Francesco enters, he repeats the sustained G sharp of his lament, then sings to the Minotaur, subsequently in a final stanza, which comes after he has disturbed a half-naked pair of lovers, embracing the marble body as the only refuge of his lips, his passion, his doubts. The interlude is a beautiful, unaccompanied choral Villanella.

Scene xiii. Maerbale. *I couldn't erase from my feverish mind a suspicion that Julia and Maerbale were deceiving me. To ascertain whether it was true, Silvio de Narni convinced Maerbale that Julia was awaiting him on the loggia. Nicolas Orsini, my brother's son, was also watching. They kissed, and Nicolas, sensing the danger, warned his father to escape. Urged on by me, Abul pursued him with his naked dagger. Thus Maerbale met his end.*

There is a short duet for Maerbale and Julia, and the scene ends with Maerbale's murder and cries from Julia and Maerbale as Pier Francesco violently embraces his wife. The interlude provides savage comment on Pier Francesco's crime.

Scene xiv. The Alchemy. *Silvio de Narni devoted all those years to search in his laboratory for the formula that would win eternity for me and at last he found it. Around us, in Silvio's laboratory were the many-coloured statues of the famous alchemists and it seemed to me that those horrible shapes danced like furies around him. I didn't realise that Nicolas was watching us. He had sworn to avenge his father.*

As the scene of the invocation mounts in intensity the chorus joins its mouthings to the exhortations of Silvio, and the last section of the scene is preceded by the musical injunction: 'Each singer in the chorus has the choice of using given words in free order, shouting and articulating them with loose and discontinuous rhythms to create an atmosphere of chaos.' The last interlude is in the nature of a threnody for the dying Duke.

Scene xv. The Park of the Monsters. *And now, for Nicolas Orsini mixed the potion of immortality with poison, I know I am going to die. The monsters of Bomarzo keep watch by the Duke whose life is dying away. I will not die! I can't die! My eyes are closing. The shepherd boy has returned and he kisses my forehead. Bomarzo forgives me. My heart is not beating and yet I stand up and go, with open arms, towards my monsters—my immortality.*

The music recalls that of the first scene, as the chorus echoes the dying ravings of Pier Francesco. The little shepherd, who thinks the Duke may be asleep, finishes the opera as he had begun it.

'*Bomarzo*,' wrote the critic Robert Jacobson in the *Saturday Review*, 'is governed by a strict structure, beginning with the division of its fifteen scenes (separated by fourteen interludes), each of which is subdivided into three microstructures reproducing the classical Greek form of exposition, crisis and conclusion.' His partial employment of a post-Webern serialism avoids, says the same critic, the greyness which is often found in a 12-tone opera, and the result, wrote Irving Lowens in the Washington *Evening Star* at the time of the première, 'is the masterwork which *Don Rodrigo* foretold'. Such a laudatory press did not prevent a ban on its production in the composer's native Argentina, where it had been accepted for the Teatro Colón only to be thrown out by decree of the Mayor, who had apparently read the American notices! The whole episode seems not wholly unconnected with the official visit shortly before of President Ongario to a performance in the same theatre of the ballet *Sacre du Printemps*: 'If you show me anything dirty like that again, I'll close this place' was his reported reaction. H.

25

Danish Opera

CARL AUGUST NIELSEN
(1865–1931)

SAUL AND DAVID

OPERA in four acts by Carl August Nielsen; text by E. Christiansen. First produced at the Royal Theatre, Copenhagen, November 29, 1902, with Niels Juel Simonsen (Saul), Peter Cornelius (Jonathan), Helge Nissen (Samuel), Vilhelm Herold (David), Emilie Ulrich (Michal), Elisabeth Dons (Witch of Endor), conductor Nielsen. Revived Copenhagen, 1912, 1929; new production, 1934, with Holger Byrding, Tyge Tygesen, Einar Nørby, Marius Jacobsen, Else Schøtt, Ingeborg Steffensen, conductor Johan Hye-Knudsen; 1962, with Frans Andersson, Magnus Jonsson, Mogens Wedel, Otte Svendsen, Bonna Søndberg, Lilian Weber Hansen, conductor Hye-Knudsen. Also produced Göteborg, 1928, with Flagstad as Michal; Stockholm, 1930, with Einar Larson, Jussi Bjoerling, Ake Walgreen, Conrad Arnesen, Brita Hertzberg, conductor Armas Järnefelt; B.B.C., Glasgow, 1959 (English version by Geoffrey Dunn), with Stanislav Pieczora, Frans Vroons, Roger Stalman, John Mitchinson, Joyce Barker, conductor Ian Whyte; European Broadcasting Union, 1972 (in English), with Boris Christoff, Willy Hartmann, Michael Langdon, Alexander Young, Elisabeth Söderström, conductor Horenstein.

CHARACTERS

Saul, *King of Israel* . . . . Baritone
Jonathan, *his son* . . . . Tenor
Michal, *his daughter* . . . . Soprano
David, *a shepherd boy* . . . . Tenor
Samuel, *a prophet* . . . . Bass
Abner, *Captain of the King's Guard* . . . . Bass
The Witch of Endor . . . . Mezzo-Soprano

Abisay, *a follower of David's* ....Tenor
  Chorus, Maidens, Priests, Warriors, and People

From 1889 to the middle of June, 1905, Carl Nielsen
played second violin in the orchestra of the Royal Theatre in
Copenhagen and both his operas, with the exception of the
third act of *Maskarade*, were composed during this period, his
thirty-third to his forty-first year. In 1890, on a scholarship
to Germany, he went straight to Dresden where he steeped
himself in the music of Wagner. His first opera, *Saul and
David*, was written between 1898 and 1901, that is to say
just before his second symphony, *The Four Temperaments*,
which was published in 1902. He says that the subject of *Saul
and David* '... stirred and haunted me, so that for long
periods I could not free myself of it no matter where I
was—even when I was sitting in the orchestra with my second
violin, busy with ballets and vaudevilles.'

The composer and his librettist make Saul into a figure of
tragic stature, a man with the intelligence and courage to
question the accepted beliefs and superstitions of a primitive
society and in contrast to the more naturally representative
figure of David, who accepts the existing order and believes
in it.

A short, brilliant martial prelude takes us straight into the
action. In front of Saul's dwelling in Gilgal, priests and
Israelites together with the King and his son Jonathan wait
anxiously for the coming of Samuel, who alone may make
sacrifice to the Lord, in order that their stand against the
hosts of the Philistines may take place with the blessing of
the Almighty. Unable to bear the strain of waiting, Saul turns
impatiently on the priests, orders preparations to be
completed, and himself performs the priestly office. The
scene is one of great urgency, the voices of the soloists, now
almost incoherent with fear, now supplicatory to the King,
contrast with the choral background of prayer and
preparation from priests and people.

The voice of Samuel interrupts the sacrifice to upbraid the
King for his presumption, to pronounce him, in spite of his
protests of repentance, an outcast in God's sight and
unworthy of his kingdom. The people and Jonathan join
their voices to Saul's but Samuel is unrelenting: Saul's rule is
over, an evil spirit will possess him, but the kingdom of Israel
will flourish after he is gone. Jonathan alone tries to comfort
him, but Saul's spirit is cast down and in solitude he

communes with the Lord of Hosts, whom he treats now as his enemy to be defied and overcome. His fine, Iago-like monologue ends in a mood of submissiveness as Jonathan returns, bringing with him his friend, the shepherd boy David. David's singing charms the King and restores his spirit, so that his enthusiasm leads him to bid David stay with him as his guest.

Left alone, David tells Saul's daughter Michal that he has loved her since he saw her bathing in the brook with her attendants, and the curtain falls slowly on an idyllic scene of young love.

Act II starts with a martial prelude, more formal in character than that to the first Act. While David sings to King Saul, Abner forces his way past the guards to insist that the nearness of the Philistine host necessitates action on the King's part, in spite of his son Jonathan's recent victory over an enemy detachment. The Philistine champion Goliath, a giant of ferocious aspect, has challenged the Israelites to nominate a man to meet him in single combat, the loser's people to become subject to the winner's. Saul is reluctant to take up the challenge, but David undertakes to defeat him, refusing the King's sword and armour and relying instead on his sling and five smooth stones from the river. He bids farewell to Michal and leaves.

The progress of the fight is followed through the imaginations of Michal and her women, first their apprehension of bloody defeat, then the possibility of victory, until they see the reality of a messenger riding furiously across the valley—Jonathan, with the news of David's triumph over Goliath. A chorus of thanksgiving heralds the return of the Israelite warriors, David and Saul at their head, and the King joyfully gives David the hand of Michal in marriage. Rejoicing is general but when he hears the cry of 'Saul has slain his thousands and David his tens of thousands', Saul's happiness turns to bitterness, so that the act ends with the silencing of the crowd, David's effort to still the King's melancholy with his singing, Saul's hurling of the javelin at his prospective son-in-law and the latter's banishment, and David's defiance of the King.

Act III. A mournful nocturne in 12/8 introduces Saul's sleeping camp at night. Jonathan and Michal, in one of the score's most appealing lyrical passages, mourn the absence of David before they too fall asleep. Suddenly, David with his follower Abisay appear high up among the rocks above the camp, David comes down to stand over the defenceless Saul and then, as a sign that he has been there, takes the spear and the cruse of water which stand by Saul's pillow. David shouts to waken Abner and the King's Guard. Saul cannot remain hostile, faced with David's unrestrained loyalty, and takes him back to his arms. In an impressive and extended polyphonic choral ensemble, the people witness their renewed vows, but the arrival of Samuel fills Saul with new apprehension. Samuel relates his vision of God, telling him to proclaim David King of the Israelites, and solemnly anoints him before falling dead. Saul tries to reassert his sovereignty, bids his soldiers seize David and, when she defies him, Michal his daughter, only to have his authority flouted by his subjects and to be obliged to watch David and Michal walk away unharmed.

A rapid prelude takes us into the fourth Act and a viola solo introduces the scene where Saul and Abner come to consult the Witch of Endor. She insists that if Samuel's spirit is to be conjured from the dead, they must cover their faces and not see him. When he comes it is with accompaniment of trombones and to foretell the death of Saul and his sons at the hands of the Philistines. At the end of an impressive scene, soldiers come looking for Saul to lead them against the advancing enemy.

A vigorous battle interlude leads to the last scene, which takes place on Mount Gilboa. Jonathan enters wounded and dying and supported by Abner. They see on the mountainside the wounded Saul, and Jonathan recognises David behind him and proclaims him 'blest of the Lord' before he himself dies. Saul in a splendid *arioso* demands that Abner kill him so that he may not fall wounded into the hands of the enemy, then cursing God he turns his sword on himself. David arrives with Michal and some Israelite survivors, and together, in music of almost Handelian cast, they mourn Saul and Jonathan and proclaim David their King, chosen of God. H.

MASKARADE

Masquerade

Opera in three acts by Carl Nielsen, libretto by Vilhelm Andersen, after Ludvig Holberg's play. Première, Copenhagen, November 11, 1906, with Emilie Ulrich/Ingeborg Nørregaard-Hansen as Leonora, Ida Møller/Margrethe Lindrop as Pernille, Karl Mantzius as Jeronimus, Joanna Neiiendam as Magdelone, Hans Kierulf as Leander, Peter Jerndoff as Leonard, Helge Nissen as Henrik, Lars Knudsen as Arv, conductor Nielsen. Revived fairly frequently in Copenhagen, notably in 1918 when it was restudied, in 1936 when Edith Oldrup sang Leonora, in 1937 when Egisto Tango conducted, in 1943 when Tyge Tygesen sang Leander. Its hundredth performance took place in 1946, and in 1965 there was a new production with Ellen Winther, Else Margrete Gardelli, Willy Hartmann, Ib Hansen, Frans Andersson, conductor John Frandsen. American première, St. Paul, 1972.

CHARACTERS

Jeronimus, *a citizen of Copenhagen* . . . . Bass
Magdelone, *his wife* . . . . .Mezzo-Soprano
Leander, *their son* . . . . .Tenor
Henrik, *Leander's servant* . . . . Bass-Baritone
Arv, *Jeronimus's servant* . . . . .Tenor
Mr. Leonard, *a citizen of Copenhagen*. . .Tenor-Baritone
Leonora, *his daughter* . . . . Soprano
Pernille, *Leonora's maid* . . . . Soprano
A Nightwatchman . . . . Bass
A Constable . . . . Baritone
A Mask-seller . . . . Baritone
A Professor . . . . Bass
A Flower-seller . . . . Soprano
Master of ceremonies . . . . Bass-Baritone
A dancing master ⎫
His fiancée   ⎬ . . . . Dancers
                          ⎭
Students, Officers, Young Girls,
Maskers of both Sexes
Time: Spring 1723   *Place:* Copenhagen

In 1905 Nielsen set to work on *Maskarade*, an adaptation of Holberg's comedy of 1724. The influence of opéra-comique and a generally French style is apparent, says Jürgen Balzer in an essay published in connection with Nielsen's centenary in 1965, but it is hard when listening to the music not to believe that the composer must have heard—and loved—Verdi's *Falstaff* before setting to work on his own comedy. As it is, he is evidently more interested in the musical possibilities of situation than of character, but the result nonetheless is a work of charm and brilliance. To call it a Danish *Bartered Bride* would be too easy, not only because the subject is less than nationalistic but also because Nielsen is a leading composer in his own right. It is a comedy, thoroughly Danish, and (at least in my opinion) very many works are on the fringe of the international repertory with far lesser claims.

Act I. After a sparkling overture, whose opening arabesque becomes the Masquerade motif, the curtain rises to show us a room in Jeronimus's house, in afternoon. Leander, Jeronimus's son, has been to a masquerade[1] with his valet, Henrik, and neither finds it easy to wake up next day. Henrik is still dreaming of dancing and even motions to the orchestra to play a cotillon, but Leander in music of fine lyrical flow greets the light and recalls last night's adventure. He is in love, and they must go again to the Masquerade to meet this unknown girl! Unfortunately, there is a snag: his father long ago promised Leander's hand in marriage to Mr. Leonard's daughter, whom he has never seen, and in a spirited song Henrik points out that the law deals severely with breach of promise.

Their scene, high-spirited enough to contradict the hangovers they might be expected to be fighting, is interrupted by the entrance of Magdelone, Jeronimus's wife and Leander's mother, who is obviously more than a little envious of Leander's expedition to the Masquerade. She knows of its possibilities only at second hand but plainly would like to sample them, if we are to judge from the dancing in which she now indulges. The gavotte with which she starts is pleasant enough, but there is a change from duple to triple time with a *Folie d'Espagne*, and the combination makes for a charming scene.

The exhibition of Magdelone's prowess is abruptly interrupted by the entrance of Jeronimus himself. He suspects there is a plan to visit the Masquerade, and packs his wife off to her room. Henrik spills the beans about Leander having fallen in love, and Jeronimus, alone, in a monologue which is for the most part reminiscent rather than impassioned, yearns for the old God-fearing days when discipline was discipline and everyone in bed by nine o'clock. But he is not alone long as Mr. Leonard is announced and we find out almost immediately that his daughter is as unwilling to fall in with plans made for her as is Jeronimus's son. Together they plot

[1] A carnival ball open to all classes, to which all must go masked.

to prevent a scandal. Jeronimus instructs Arv, a particularly half-witted servant, to keep watch outside the house that night and prevent anyone leaving, then sends for Leander.

When ordered to give an explanation of the previous night's disgraceful behaviour, Henrik distinguishes himself by launching, in the jauntiest of songs, not only into a defence of their position but into a piece of special pleading for the few pleasures open to a servant that is so rebellious in its character and content as to be saved only by cheerfulness from being positively revolutionary. Mr. Leonard has some sympathy with the young, but Jeronimus demands that Leander make a full apology to Mr. Leonard and proceeds to dictate it to him. When it comes to promising to marry Mr. Leonard's daughter, Leander finally jibs, and the finale, a very lively male quintet, is concerned with Leander's reiterated refusal to toe the line, either in marriage or even in staying at home that night.

Act II takes place in the street between the brightly illuminated Playhouse and Mr. Jeronimus's home. Though this act is basically concerned with getting everyone to the Masquerade and identifying their costumes, the composer injects considerable lyrical force, beginning in the nocturne prelude with a most poetic evocation of eighteenth-century Copenhagen. There are songs for the night watchman and for Arv, the latter of whom is unexpectedly confronted, as it would appear, with a ghost, who bids him confess his sins since he must soon die. Arv clears his conscience of everything, from thefts of flour and wine to that of the cook's virginity, and it is only when the ghost starts to giggle that Arv understands it is Henrik in disguise. If all is not to be revealed, Arv must turn a blind eye when Henrik goes that night with his master to the Masquerade!

In effect, this seems to be the current destination of half the populace, amongst whom Arv recognises Mr. Leonard as he leaves Jeronimus's house. After him come Henrik and Leander, the latter ecstatic at the prospect before him, which indeed promptly materialises in the person of Leonora (of whose true identity he is of course still in ignorance); she appears in a sedan-chair accompanied by her maid Pernille. Nielsen worked many years in the opera house and his admiration for Wagner knew no bounds, but this ecstatic meeting of lovers, even if the composer had his tongue half in cheek, suggests that he was far from despising Puccini. The bustling of Henrik and Pernille round the two lovers and their attempts to parody what is going on by no means invalidate the ecstatic lyricism of the lovers as they sing in sixths.

Interruption comes in the shape of sounds from Mr. Jeronimus's house, as it becomes clear he has discovered the disappearance of Leander and Henrik. He is sure he knows where to find them, but for the Masquerade he must have a disguise and he goes with Arv to buy it (the mask-seller's song is one of many small cuts apparently sanctioned by the composer). Enter Mrs. Magdelone on pleasure bent, and Mr. Leonard equally in search of adventure. Disguised as they are, they meet and agree to go on to the Masquerade together. It remains only for Jeronimus and Arv, got up as Bacchus and Cupid respectively, to make their own way across the street before the nightwatchman, as in Wagner, pre-empts the last word.

Act III. The great hall of the Playhouse. We are plunged into the middle of the festivities with hardly a moment of preluding, and the brilliance and fun of the Masquerade is before us musically as well as visually right from the start. Here is an end of immediate cares and responsibility, here is release. Students seize girls and dance, lovers flirt, there is a charming female trio, and Leander sings happily with his Leonora, even to the extent of exchanging names. The duet[1] of Henrik and Pernille is a deliberate send-up of what their master and mistress have been singing, but warmth is by no means excluded. Soon it is the turn of Mrs. Magdelone and Mr. Leonard, the former of whom proclaims her unmarried state, though she refuses to unmask. Mr. Jeronimus, searching for Leander, interrupts their graceful flirtation, without of course knowing who either is.

There is some danger of a quarrel between students and soldiers, but the master of ceremonies announces the start of the evening's entertainment, and the first item is the very lively *Hanedansen* (Cock's dance), the best-known single number in the score. During its course, Henrik discovers that Jeronimus is there wearing a Bacchus mask, but he somehow persuades a professor who has come with a party of students to side with him and Leander, and together they make Jeronimus drunk.

The next item on the evening's bill has the dancing master

---

[1] Labelled in the score *Canzone Parodica*.

and his fiancée act the story of Mars and Venus to graceful waltz music. Jeronimus is inveigled into a round dance and the students sing a song, which does not conceal the intoxicated attempts of the old man to flirt with the dancing girl. The hour of general unmasking approaches and Nielsen perfectly captures in music the element of sadness implicit in this 'moment of truth'. The master of ceremonies (now dressed as Corporal Mors) calls on everyone present to throw their masks into a big urn placed in the middle of the floor. Mrs. Magdelone and Mr. Leonard recognise each other and Leonora and Leander, the chance lovers, are revealed as also the objects of the arranged marriage. Only Mr. Jeronimus does not at first comprehend that a happy ending seems to be in sight for everyone concerned, but explanations are swallowed up in a final gallop, during which Henrik, Puck-like, solicits the audience's applause.   H.

INDEX

A kékszakállú Herceg Vára. See *Duke Bluebeard's Castle*
Abandon d'Ariane, L', 1285, 1287–8
Abbey, Henry E., 664
Abraham, Gerald, 912, 924*n.*
Abraham and Isaac, 1307, 1541
Adam, Adolphe Charles, 654, 755–7
Adamberger, Josef Valentin, 75*n.*
Adami, G., 1187, 1190, 1200
Addison, Joseph, 29
Adenis, J., 830
Adriana Lecouvreur, 1205–9
Adventures of Mr Brouček, The, 1550–60, 1585
Aegyptische Helena, Die, 1004, 1033–6
Aeneid, 367, 767
Affe als Mensch, Der, 1149
Africaine, L' (*The African Maid*), 743–8
Agostini, Philippe, 1299
Aida, 91, 498, 515, 549, 591, 618, 628, 629–45, 646, 846, 847
Air and Variations (Rode), 408
Albert Herring, 1452–59, 1501, 1515
Albinoni, Tommaso, 48
Alboni, Marietta, 408, 409, 731
Alceste, 53, 64, 66–71, 77, 381
Alcina, 48–52, 1581*n.*
Alda, Frances, 846
Aldeburgh Festival, 1410, 1533
Alessandro Stradella, 183
Alfano, Franco, 1205
Algiers. As setting for opera, 388
All-of-a-sudden Carmen, 742
All's Well that Ends Well, 1429
Almaviva, ossia l'Inutile Precauzione (see also *Barbiere di Siviglia, Il*), 400, 405
Amahl and the Night Visitors, 1633, 1647–50

Amato, Pasquale, 529, 846
Ame en Peine, L', 176
Amelia al Ballo (*Amelia goes to the Ball*), 1634–6
America. As setting for opera, 602, 1102, 1155, 1183, 1292, 1627, 1637, 1640, 1650
   First performance in Italian, in, 410
American Opera (Hipsher), 1624
Amico, Fritz, L', 475, 695–8
Amore dei Tre Re, L', 1223–9
Ancelot, François, 462
Ancona, Mario, 846
Andersen, Hans Christian, 932, 1308
   Vilhelm, 1665
Andrea Chénier, 701–6
Anelli, A., 388
Ange de Feu, L'. See *Fiery Angel, The*
Anna Bolena (*Anne Boleyn*), 438–43, 451, 500
Annals of Opera, 27, 1305*n.*
Antropov, 921
Apollinaire, Guillaume, 1294, 1295
Arabella, 1036–41, 1042
Arabian Nights, 337
Araline, Mme., 152
Arden must Die, 114
Arditi, Luigi, 408, 409
Argentina: Teatro Cólon, 1661
Ariadne and Bluebeard. See *Ariane et Barbe-bleue*
Ariadne auf Naxos, 1018–24
Ariadne Deserted. See *Abandon d'Ariane, L'*
Ariane et Barbe-bleue, 1264–7
Arianna, 4, 9
Ariosto, Ludovico, 48, 49
Arlecchino, 1213–16
Arlésienne, L', 832
Armide, 77

Arnaud, Abbé, 76
Aroldo, 586–90
Arundell, Dennis, 1612n.
Ashton, Frederick, 739n.
Assedio di Haarlem, L'. See Battaglia di
  Legano
At the Boar's Head, 654
Attila, 531–4, 913
Auber, Daniel François, 408, 409, 602,
  603, 714–21, 864, 1368n.
Auden, W. H., 1134, 1135, 1140,
  1141, 1322
Aufstieg und Fall des Stadt
  Mahagonny, 1100–8, 1285
Aureliano in Palmira, 398, 407
Auric, Georges, 1295
Austin, Frederic, 30, 32, 35, 36
Austria. As setting for opera, 343,
  344n., 359, 680, 1009, 1029, 1037,
  1134

Babylon. As setting for opera, 428,
  513
Bacchae, The, 1140, 1141
Bach, Johann Sebastian, 766
Bache, 798
Bachmann, Ingeborg, 1130, 1131,
  1148
Bacio, Il (The Kiss), 408
Badoaro, G., 12
Baghdad. As setting for opera, 160, 337
Baglioni, Antonio, 104
Bakala, Břetislav, 1585, 1589
Baker, Theodore, 454
Bakhturin, K. A., 879
Balakirev, Mily Alexeievich, 883, 942
Balázs, B., 1607
Balfe, Michael William, 654, 954–6,
  960
Ballad Singer, The. See Gioconda, La
Ballo delle Ingrate, Il, 4
Ballo in Maschera, Un, 515, 602–9
Balzac, Honoré de, 421
Balzar, Jürgen, 1666
Barbaia, Domenica, 397, 398, 420,
  425n.
Barbarossa, Frederick, 543
Barber of Seville, The. See Barbiere di
  Siviglia, Il
Barbier, Auguste, 757
  Jules, 741, 778, 782, 783, 792,
  793, 809

Barbier de Seville, Le (Beaumarchais),
  401
Barbier von Baghdad, Der, 337–42
Barbiere di Siviglia, Il, 390, 398,
  400–10, 413, 414, 455, 864
  First called Almaviva, ossia
    l'Inutile Precauzione, 405
  Overture to, not the original, 407
Bardi, Count Giovanni, 3
Bardari, Giuseppe, 450
Barrett, Lawrence, 689
Bartered Bride, The, 963–9, 970, 975,
  976, 978, 979, 983, 985, 1545
Bartók, Béla, 1130, 1607–9
Bassarids, The, 1135, 1140–8, 1595n.
Bassi, Luigi, 104
Bastien and Bastienne, 90
Bat, The. See Fledermaus, Die
Bates, Blanche, 1181
Battaglia di Legnano, La (The Battle of
  Legnano), 543–6, 587
Battle, The. See Battaglia di Legnano,
  La
Bax, Sir Arnold, 997–8
Bayard, F., 465
Bayreuth–Wagner Theatre and Festival,
  194, 204, 254, 260, 326, 766
BBC Television, 1420n.
Bear, The, 1410–12
Beatrice di Tenda, 499–502
Béatrice et Bénédict, 774–8, 857
Beaumarchais, Pierre, 90, 400, 401
Bechi, Gino, 695
Bédier, Joseph, 217n.
Beecham, Sir Thomas, 938, 1020,
  1389n.
Beer, Jakob Liebmann. See Meyerbeer,
  Giacomo
Beethoven, Ludwig van, 103, 145–52,
  153, 184, 382, 438, 925, 1421n.,
  1432
Beggar's Opera, The, 28–37
Beggar Student, The. See Bettel-
  student, Der
Beginning of a Romance, 1551
Belasco, David, 1181, 1182
Belgium. As setting for opera, 203,
  1113
Belle Hélène, La, 801–5
Bellini, Giovanni, 438
Bellini, Vincenzo, 157, 399, 438, 439,
  475, 482–506, 695, 1149

Benedict, Julius, 957–9
Benelli, Sem, 1223, 1224
Benucci, Francesco, 93, 114
Benvenuto Cellini, 757–60, 775, 855
Berenstadt, Gaetano, 39n.
Berg, Alban, 1073–88, 1122, 1244, 1307
Bergmüller, Robert, 183
Berkshire Festival, Tanglewood, U.S.A., 79, 126
Berlin: Komische Oper, 1569
 Kroll Opera House, 1102
 Opera House, 1010, 1074
 Philharmonic, 173
Berlioz, Hector, 60, 64, 65n., 70, 71, 113, 431, 434, 749, 757–78, 855, 857, 858, 983, 1272, 1273, 1290, 1345, 1532
Bernanos, Georges, 1299, 1300
Bernasconi, Antonia, 75n.
Bernhardt, Sarah, 528, 579, 1174
Bertati, Giovanni, 103–4, 377
Berton, Pierre, 846
Bertoni, Ferdinando, 64
Bertram, or The Castle of St Aldobrando, 482
Betly, 451
Betrothal in a Monastery, 1348–53
Bettelstudent, Der, 368–71
Betz, Franz, 254
Beuckelszoon, Jan. See Leyden, John of
Bey, Mariette, 629, 631, 634
Bianca e Falliero, 428
Bianca e Gernando, 483
Bibliothèque Bleue, La, 160
Bielsky, V. I., 944, 947, 948
Billington, Mrs Elizabeth, 127
Billy Budd, 1406, 1464–77, 1531n.
'Billy in the Darbies', 1465, 1475, 1531n.
Binder, Carl, 798
Bing, Sir Rudolph, 1150n.
Biographical Dictionary of Musicians, 454
Bis, H. L. F., 434, 437
Bishop, Sir Henry Rowley, 410, 443n.
Bispham, David, 90
Bizet, Georges, 826–47, 1331
Bizet, His Life and Works, 833n.
Björling, Johan, 608
Blacher, Boris, 1108, 1109

Blau, Edouard, 816, 864
Blom, Eric, 66
'Blonda, Max', 1066
'Blue Danube, The', 347, 362
Boatswain's Mate, The, 1381–3
Boccaccio, Giovanni, 1276
Boccaccio, 333–6
Bodansky, Artur, 152, 167
Bohème, La, 1157–65, 1200
Bohemia. As setting for opera, 153, 964, 969, 976, 979, 982
Bohemian Girl, The, 954–6, 960
Boïeldieu, François Adrien, 711–14
Boito, Arrigo, 591, 595, 600, 601, 645, 646, 648, 649, 653, 663, 671–80
Bomarzo, 1654–61
Bonci, Alessandro, 504, 558, 559, 600, 608, 609
Bondini, Pasquale, 104
 Teresa, 104
Bonynge, Richard, 463
Booth, Edwin, 549
Boris Godounov, 888–900, 912, 925
Born, Ignaz von, 131
Borodin, Alekandr Porfyrevich, 881–8, 942
Borosini, Francesco, 39n.
Borough, The, 1435
Boucicault, D., 957
Boughton, Rutland, 1402–5
Bouhy, Jacques, 846
Bouilly, Jean Nicolas, 145, 146
Boulevard Solitude, 1121–5
Boulez, Pierre, 1310, 1599
Bourdin, 1258n.
Bourgeois Gentilhomme, Le, 1018, 1020, 1021
Boy, 630
Boyhood's End, 1432
Brandenburgers in Bohemia, The, 983
Brahms, Johannes, 1130
Brandt, Marianne, 152
Braun, Baron von, 146, 147
Breasts of Tiresias, The. See Mamelles de Tirésias, Les
Brecher, Gustav, 167
Brecht, Bertolt, 30, 1100, 1101, 1106
Bressler-Gianoli, Clotilde, 846, 847
Bretzner, 84
Breuning, Stephen von, 146
Brewster, Henry, 1378

Britten, Benjamin, 25, 30, 34, 35, 36, 37, 1129, 1434–1541, 1599
Britten, Benjamin, his life and his operas, 1517n.
The Operas of, 1519n.
Tribute to, 1516n.
Briusoff, Valery, 1340, 1342
Brod, Max, 1570n., 1574n., 1587n.
Browne, Rev. Marmaduke, 119n.
Bruckberger, Rev. Fr., 1299
Brunswick, L. L., 755
Büchner, Georg, 1073, 1074, 1108, 1109, 1114
Büchse der Pandora, Die, 1082
Bülow, Hans Guido von, 216, 254, 365
    Ulrich von, 365
Bunn, Alfred, 954, 955
Bunyan, John, 1395, 1397, 1399
Buondelmonte. See Maria Stuarda
Burani, Paul, 852
Burenin, V. P., 920
Burlador de Sevilla, El, 103
Burney, Charles, 29
Burning Fiery Furnace, The, 1514, 1520–3, 1524, 1525
Busch, Fritz, 541, 1089
Busenello, G. Francesco, 15, 17, 20
Busoni, Ferruccio, 1101, 1126, 1209–22
Busoni, Ferruccio (Dent), 1213, 1216, 1217n., 1218
Byron, Lord, 528, 529

Caccini, Giulio, 3, 4, 9
Cain, Henri, 875
Cairo: Italian Theatre, 629, 631
Cairns, David, 1413n., 1423, 1506n.
Calderón, Serafin Estébanez, 689
Callas, Maria, 49, 382, 440, 442, 486, 498, 572n., 581
Calvé, Emma, 846
Calvocoressi, M. D., 905
Calzabigi, Ranieri da, 60, 61, 66, 68, 71
'Camerata, The', 3, 4
Camille, 571
Cammarano, Salvatore, 453, 462, 543, 546, 561
Campanello, 451
Campanini, Cleofonte, 461
    Italo, 461, 469, 558, 559, 630, 734

'Campbells are Coming, The', 590
Campra, André, 78
Canon (Tallis), 1502
Cantata Profana, 1130
Canti di Prigionia, 1245, 1248
Čapek, Karel, 48n., 1577, 1578n., 1583
Capoul, Joseph, 793
Capriccio, 1051, 1054–9
Cardillac, 1088–93
Carestini, Giovanni, 49
Carmen, 723, 833, 834–47, 857
Carnaval Romain, 758
Carosse du Saint-Sacrement, La, 805, 806
Carpani, Giuseppe, 405
Carré, Michel, 741, 778, 782, 783, 790, 792, 793, 809, 826
Carreño, Teresa, 994
Carthage. As setting for opera, 26, 770
Caruso, Enrico, 445, 461, 549, 558, 559, 568, 614, 664, 846
Carvalho, Léon, 830
Cary, Annie Louise, 469, 630, 731, 734
Casella, Alfredo, 1126
Castelmary, 181
Castil-Blaze, F. H. J., 405, 406
Catalani, Alfredo, 680–3
Cavalieri, Katharina, 88, 112
Cavalleria Rusticana, 690–5
Cavalli, Francesco, 17
Čech, Svatopluk, 1550, 1552
Cendrillon, 410
Cenerentola, La, 396, 410–14, 415
Cervantes, Miguel de, 875, 1620
Cervinka, 1560
Cesarini, Duke, 405
Ceylon. As setting for opera, 827
Chabrier, Alexis Emmanuel, 848–58, 1295, 1297
Chaliapin, Fedor, 898
Chapuy, 846
Chasse royale et orage, 767, 771
Charpentier, Gustave, 1252–7
Chatfield, A. W., 1501n.
Chekhov, Anton, 1410
Chénier, André, 702
Cherubini, Luigi, 380–5, 387
Chezy, Helmine von, 157
Chicago Opera Company, 461, 550, 1341n.

Child and the Magic, The. See *Enfant et les Sortilèges, L'*
Child, Harold, 1387
China. As setting for opera, 1201, 1210
Chisolm, Erik, 1568, 1585
Chlubna, Osvald, 1585, 1589
Chopin, Frédéric François, 409, 497, 1594
Chorley, H. F., 382
Christiansen, E., 1662
Christmas Eve Revels, 938
Christophe Colomb, 1289–94
Cilea, Francesco, 1205–9
Cimarosa, Domenico, 377–80
Cinderella. See *Cenerentola, La*
Ciro in Babilonia (Cantata by Rossini), 407
Civinini, G., 1182
Clandestine Marriage, The, 377
Clari, 443n.
Claude (Claude Gellée), 771
Claudel, Paul, 1285, 1287, 1290
Clayton, Thomas, 29
Clemency of Titus, The. See *Clemenza di Tito, La*
Clément and Larousse, 63, 65
Clementi, Muzio, 131, 722
Clemenza di Tito, La, 126–9, 378, 601
Cloak, The. See *Tabarro, Il*
Coachman of Longjumeau, The, 755–7
Coates, Albert, 1330
Cocteau, Jean, 1283, 1318, 1342
Colautti, A., 706, 1205
Colbran, Isabella, 398, 399, 420, 425
Colette, 1277, 1278
Colleen Bawn, 957
Colman, George, 377
Cologne, Opera of, 1114
Columbia Records, 1637
    University, 689
Combattimento di Tancredi e Clorinda, Il, 4, 10–12
Comte de Comminges, Le, 468
Comte Ory, Le (Count Ory), 431–4
Congreve, William, 52, 53, 54
Conried, Heinrich, 846
Consul, The, 1633, 1641–7
Contes d'Hoffmann, Les, 809–15
Conversations with Klemperer, 1102n.
Copenhagen: Royal Theatre, 1663
Coq d'Or, Le, 938, 947–53

Cormon, 826
Cornelius, Peter, 337–42
Coronation of Poppaea, The. See *Incoronazione di Poppea, L'*
Correck, Joseph, 1030
Corregidor, Der, 374–6
Corsi, Jacopo, 3
Cosa Rara, Una, 113
Così fan tutte, 91, 115–26, 142, 396, 776, 973
Cours à l'abîme, 1345
Crabbe, George, 1434, 1435
Cramer, Heinz von, 1125
Crémieux, Hector, 797
Crete. As setting for opera, 79
Cristina, Queen Maria, of the Two Sicilies, 453
Crozier, Eric, 1452, 1459, 1464, 1465
Cruvelli, J. S. C., 580
Cuénod, Hugues, 1326
Cui, César Antonovich, 883, 890, 905
Cunning Little Vixen, The, 1504, 1567–76, 1585
Curlew River, 1514, 1515–20, 1521, 1522, 1523, 1524, 1525
Cuzzoni, Francesca, 45n.
Cymbeline, 160
Cyprus. As setting for opera, 645
Czechoslovakia. As setting for opera, 964, 969, 976, 979, 982, 1543, 1551

Dafne, 3
d'Albert, Eugen, 993–7
Dalibor, 969–73, 982, 983
Dallapiccola, Luigi, 12, 13, 1243–8
Dalmores, Charles, 847
Dame aux Camélias, La, 570, 571
Dame Blanche, La, 711–14
Damnation de Faust, La, 760–4
Damon's Psalter, 1501n.
Damrosch, Dr Leopold, 152, 255, 740, 763
'Dance of the Hours' (ballet suite), 669
Danchet, Antoine, 78
Daniélou, J., 1318
d'Annunzio, Gabriele, 606, 1239
Dante, 1196
Dantons Tod, 1108–11
Daphne, 1048–50, 1055
da Ponte, Lorenzo, 75, 90, 91, 102, 103, 104, 115, 116, 120

Dargomizhsky, A. S., 38, 1316
d'Arlincourt, Vicomte, 485
d'Arnaud, Baculard, 468
Daspuro, N., 695
Daughter of the Regiment, The. See
  Fille du Régiment, La
David, Félicien César, 409
Davis, Colin, 84
de Alarcon, P., 374
Dean, Winton, 39n., 830, 833
Deane, Basil, 1269n.
Death of Danton, The. See Dantons
  Tod
Death of Siegfried, The, 255
Death in Venice, 1532–41
Debussy, Claude, 1245, 1258–63,
  1401, 1596, 1607
de Caux, Marquise, 793. See also Patti,
  Adelina
de' Cavalieri, Emilio, 3
de Coster, Charles, 1243, 1245
Deep, Deep Sea, The, 152
Dehn, Paul, 1410
de Jouy, V. J. Etienne, 385, 434, 437
Delavigne, J. F. C., 714, 723
del Bene, Ferrarese, 120
Deldevez, Edouard, 183
Delestre-Poirson, 431
de Leuven, A., 755
Delibes, Léo, 821–6
de L'Isle-Adam, Villiers, 1243, 1245
Delius, Frederick, 1383–7
Délivrance de Thésée, La, 1285,
  1288–9
del Puente, Giuseppe, 734
de Lucia, Fernando, 914n.
de Molina, Tirso, 103
Demuth, Leopold, 175
de Najac, Emile, 852
de Nerval, Gérard, 760
Denmark. As setting for opera, 1665
Dent, Edward J., 62n., 81, 82, 92n.,
  96, 104, 105n., 111, 113, 117,
  132n., 147n., 764, 1213, 1216,
  1217, 1230, 1290, 1612n.
de Polignac, Princesse Edmond, 1314,
  1620
de Reszke, Edouard, 630, 731, 734,
  793
  Jean, 734, 793
Deschamps, Émile, 725, 726
de Troyes, Chrétien, 317

Deutsch, Otto Erich, 39n., 49n.
Devils of Loudun, The, 1598–1606
de Wailly, Léon, 757
Dexter, John, 583n.
Diaghilev, Serge, 1310, 1314, 1316
Dialogues and a Diary, 1305n.
Dialogues des Carmélites, 1296,
  1299–1304
Dictionnaire des Opéras, 63, 65, 446,
  744, 846
Didiée, Nantier, 182
Dido and Aeneas, 23–7
d'Indy, Vincent, 4, 5, 13, 15
Dinorah, ou le Pardon de Ploërmel,
  408, 475, 741–3
Discovery of America, The, 1289
Disney, Walt, 669
di Vernio, Count Giovanni Bardi, 3
Djamileh, 833–4
Dmitrij, 890
Doktor Faust, 1216–22
Don Alvaro o La Fuerza de Sino, 609,
  610
Don Carlos, 515, 538, 585, 606, 607,
  617–29, 631, 722n.
Don César de Bazan, 959
Don Giovanni, 91, 98, 102–15, 117,
  142, 551, 646, 811, 815, 1214
Don Giovanni Tenorio o sia il
  Dissoluto, 103
Donington, Robert, 1419n., 1421n.
Donizetti, Gaetano, 81, 146, 409–10,
  438–82, 486, 500, 506, 508, 515n.
Donna del Lago, La, 424–8
Donna Serpente, La, 1126
Donne, John, 1541
Don Pasquale, 439, 454, 477, 478–82,
  508, 515n., 1044
Don Procopio, 832n.
Don Quichotte, 875–6
Don Quichotte de la Mancha, 1620
Don Rodrigo, 1654, 1661
Dormoy, 481–2
Dostoievsky, Fedor, 1329, 1330, 1331,
  1584, 1587n., 1589, 1590
Douglas, Archibald, Earl of Angus, 426
Downes, Edward, 545n., 639n.,
  1357n., 1360n.
Drama Nuevo, 689
Dreigroschenoper, Die (The Beggar's
  Opera), 30, 1101
Dresden Opera House, 203, 1003

Drew, David, 1503, 1504n.
Dryden, John, 27, 63
Dschinnistan, 130
Due Foscari, I, (The Two Foscari),
528-31
Duenna, The, 1348, 1349
Dukas, Paul, 1264-7
Duke Bluebeard's Castle, 1607-9
du Locle, Camille, 617, 629, 631
Dumas, Alexandre, fils, 570, 571, 579
Dumb Girl of Portici, The. See Muette
de Portici, La
Dumilâtre, Adèle, 183
Duncan, Ronald, 1445
Duplessis, Marie, 579
Duprez, Gilbert, 437
Durastani, Margherita, 39n.
Durazzo, Count, 65
Durey, Louis, 1295
Durfey, Thomas, 29
du Roullet, Lebland, 71
Duse, Eleonora, 579, 691
Duveyrier, Charles, 579
Dvě Vdovy, 973-6
Dvořák, Antonín, 890, 987-90
Dyk, Viktor, 1550, 1552
Dykes, J. B., 1502n.
Dzerzhinsky, Ivan, 1376

Eames, Emma, 793
Ebert, Carl, 541
Echo et Narcisse, 64
Edinburgh Festival, 397n., 537, 604n.
Efebos, 1595
Egypt. As setting for opera, 40, 130,
420, 629, 869, 1034, 1276
Egyptian Helen, The. See Aegyptische
Helena, Die
1812 Overture, 925
Einem, Gottfried von, 1108-11
Einstein, Alfred, 65, 66, 79, 82, 85,
115, 130n., 136
Eisenstein, Sergei M., 1356
Elegy for Young Lovers, 1134-40
Elektra, 1002-8
Eliot, T. S., 1413
Elisir d'Amore, L' (The Elixir of Love),
439, 443-6, 451
Elisabeth d'Angleterre, 462
Elisabetta al Castello di Kenilworth,
451
Elisabetta, Regina d'Inghilterra, 397-
400, 405, 407

Enfant et les Sortilèges, L', 1277-82
England. As setting for opera, 28, 29,
173, 177, 216, 397, 439, 450, 462,
503, 587, 653, 1042, 1087, 1230,
1322, 1378, 1381, 1388, 1435,
1452, 1459, 1478, 1488, 1526
English Miracle Plays, Moralities and
Interludes, 1500n.
English Opera Group, 1452, 1453
Enlèvement d'Europe, L', 1285, 1286
Entführung aus dem Serail, Die, 75n.,
84-9, 135, 1150
Epicœne, or the Silent Woman, 1041
Erckmann-Chatrian, 695
Erdgeist, 1082
Ernani, 516, 521-8
Erwartung, 1065-6, 1067
Eschenbach, Wolfram von, 317
Escudier, Léon, 617n.
España, 857
Etienne, 410
Étoile, L', 848-52, 1297
Étoile du Nord, L', 722
Estrangère, L', 485
Eugene Onegin, 868, 908-17, 923,
928, 973, 1002n., 1359, 1361n.
Eugénie, Empress, 793
Euridice (Caccini), 4
(Peri), 3, 4
Euripides, 68, 380, 1140
Euryanthe, 157-60
Evans, Peter, 1505, 1533
Evening Star, Song of the, 201
Evenings on a Farm near Dekanka, 904
Evocations, 1268
Excursion of Mr Brouček to the Moon,
The, 1552
Expectation. See Erwartung
Expositions and Developments, 1305n.

Fair at Sorochintsy, The, 904-8
Fair Helen, The. See Belle Hélène, La
Fair Maid of Perth, The, 830-3
Fairy Queen, The, 27
Falla, Manuel de, 1618-22
Falstaff (Adam), 654
(Balfe), 654
(Salieri), 654
(Verdi), 608, 615, 653-62, 777,
1149, 1200, 1258
Fanciulla del West, La, 1182-7

Fantasia (film), 669
Farewell my Youth, 997–8
Farinelli, 49
Farrar, Geraldine, 846
Fauchois, René, 1249
Fauré, Gabriel, 1249–52
Faust (Busoni). See *Doktor Faust*
    (Goethe), 672, 783
    (Gounod), 672, 723, 762, 782–
    90, 793
    (puppet play), 1217
    (Spohr), 184
Favola d'Orfeo, La (Monteverdi). See
    Orfeo
Favorita, La (*The Favourite*), 439,
    468–74
Federico, G. A., 56
Fedora, 706–10
Feldlager in Schlesien, Ein, 722
Felsenstein, Walter, 811, 1569, 1570n.,
    1572
Femme de Tabarin, La, 690
Ferdinand, King, 397
Ferencsik, Janos, 1607n.
Fernando Cortez, 184, 185
Ferretti, Jacopo, 410
Ferrier, Kathleen, 1453
    Paul, 690
'Feste Burg, Ein', 726, 730, 733
Festin de l'Araingnée, Le (ballet), 1268
Festin de Pierre, Le, 103
Feuillère, Edwige, 806n.
Fidelio, 145–52, 759n., 970, 971
Fiery Angel, The, 1340–7
Figaro. See *Nozze di Figaro, Le*
*Fight between Tancredi and Clorinda,
    The*. See *Combattimento di
    Tancredi e Clorinda, Il*
Figlia dell'Aria, La. See *Semiramide*
Filippeschi, 436n.
Fille du Régiment, La (*La Figlia del
    Reggimento*), 465–8, 1214
Fille Mal Gardée, La, 400n.
Finta Giardiniera, La, 91
Fire Bird, The, 1310
Fischer, Ludwig, 75n.
Fitzball, Edward, 959, 960
Fledermaus, Die, 342–49
Fliegende Holländer, Der (*The Flying
    Dutchman*), 184, 188–94, 197,
    203, 316
Fliegende Holländer, Der. First Wagner

opera to be performed in London,
    188
Flood, The, 1305n., 1307
Florence: Festival, 185, 581
    Santa Croce, 421
Flotow, Friederich von, 176–83
Flying Dutchman, The. See *Fliegende
    Holländer, Der*
Fokine, Michael, 948
Fool's Revenge, The, 549, 557
Force of Destiny, The. See *Forza del
    Destino, La*
Forster, E. M., 1435, 1464, 1465
Fortner, Wolfgang, 1121
Forza del Destino, La, 453, 515, 606,
    608, 609–17, 642
Forzano, Gioacchino, 1194, 1195
Four Saints in Three Acts, 1623–5
Four Temperaments, The (symphony),
    1663
Fra due Litiganti, 113
Fra Diavolo, 718–21
Frail One, The. See *Traviata, La*
France. As setting for opera, 158, 415,
    431, 475, 486, 494, 507, 561, 571,
    610, 618, 696, 701, 706, 726, 741,
    755, 790, 859, 873, 918, 932,
    1055, 1087, 1089, 1109, 1122,
    1155, 1158, 1187, 1191, 1206,
    1253, 1278, 1295, 1300, 1599
France, Anatole, 869
Francesca da Rimini (Goetz), 365
    (Zandonai), 1239–43
Franc-Nohain, 1275
François I, King of France, 549n.
Fraser, Norman, 1655
Frau ohne Schatten, Die, 1024–9
Fräulein von Scuderi, 1088
Freemasonry. As subject for opera,
    131, 142
Freischütz, Der, 152–7, 165, 888, 1104
Fried, Erich, 1598
Friedenstag, 1045–7, 1055
Friedrich, W., 176
Friend Fritz. See *Amico Fritz, L'*
From One Day to the Next. See *Von
    Heute auf Morgen*
From the House of the Dead, 1584–90
Fursch-Madi, Emmy, 664

Galassi, Antonio, 461, 505, 549
Galilei, Vincenzo, 3

Gallet, Louis, 833, 869
Galli-Curci, Amelia, 409, 550, 864
Galli-Marié, 846
Gambler, The, 1329-34
Gandonnière, 760
Garcia, Manuel, 406, 407, 410, 430
Garden, Mary, 847, 1253, 1341n.
Garnett, Richard, 1390
Garrison, Mabel, 90
Gates, Lucy, 90
Gaveaux, Pierre, 146
Gay, John, 28, 29, 30
Gazza Ladra, La, 414-19
Gazzaniga, Giuseppe, 103
Geliot, Michael, 131n.
Genée, Richard, 333, 342, 350, 368
Gentele, Göran, 604n.
Gentle Shepherd, The, 29
Georgics, 63
Gérard, 760
Gerhard, Roberto, 1349n.
Germany. As setting for opera, 195,
    232, 261, 274, 290, 302, 372, 672,
    696, 734, 762, 779, 783, 810, 865,
    1082, 1094, 1131, 1149, 1217,
    1330, 1341
Gershwin, George, 1124, 1626-33
    Ira, 1626
Gerster, Etelka, 493, 505
Gerusalemme Liberata, 10
Geyer, Ludwig, 156
Gheradini, Giovanni, 414
Ghislanzoni, Antonio, 618, 629, 631
Giacosa, Giuseppe, 1157, 1165, 1175
Gianni Schicchi, 1191, 1195-1200
Gieseke, K. L., 130
Gigli, Beniamino, 695
Gilibert, Charles, 847
Gille, Philippe, 821, 858
Ginastera, Alberto, 1654-61
Gioconda, La, 663-71
Giojelli della Madonna, I, 1235-9
Giordano, Umberto, 695, 701-10
Giorgi-Righetti, Mme., 405, 406, 408,
    409
Giorno di Regno, Un, 507-12, 516
Gipsy, The, 954
Gipsy Baron, The. See Zigeunerbaron,
    Der
Girl of the Golden West, The. See
    Fanciulla del West, La
Giulio Cesare, 39-44

Glazunov, Alexander, 881, 882
Glinka, Michael Ivanovich, 877-81,
    1316
Gloriana, 1406, 1477-87
Gluck, Christoph Willibald, 60-77,
    107, 127, 381, 382, 387, 722n.,
    766, 801, 1286, 1453
Gluck: Preface to Alceste, 66-8
Glyndebourne Opera House, 17, 18,
    21n., 79, 537, 541, 1057n., 1453
Goehr, Alexander, 114
    Walter, 18
Goethe, Johann Wolfgang von, 205,
    672, 760, 763, 778, 783, 789, 793,
    864, 866, 1217
Goetz, Hermann, 365-8
Gogol, Nikolai, 904, 905, 937, 938
Gold, Didier, 1190
Golden Coach, The (film), 806n.
Golden Cockerel, The. See Coq d'Or,
    Le
Goldmark, Karl, 362-4
Goldoni, Carlo, 103, 1126, 1229
Golisciani, Enrico, 1233, 1235
Gondinet, Edmond, 821
Goossens, Eugene, 887
Goya, Francisco, 1616, 1617
Goyescas, 1616-17
Götterdämmerung (The Twilight of the
    Gods), 254, 255, 301-16, 498
Gounod, Charles François, 672, 762,
    782-97, 804
Gozzi, Carlo, 1125, 1126, 1200, 1209,
    1334, 1335
Graham, Colin, 811, 1517
Granados, Enrique, 1616-17
Grandi, Margherita, 537
Grau, Maurice, 730, 793, 846
Gray, Cecil, 1384
Graziani, Lodovico, 571
Great Exhibition of 1855, 580
Great Friendship, The, 1356
Greece. As setting for opera, 61, 72,
    381, 672, 801, 1003, 1141, 1286,
    1287, 1288, 1319
'Greensleeves', 36
Gregor, Hans, 810
    Joseph, 1045, 1048, 1050, 1051
Grétry, André, 930
Grisi, Giulietta, 408, 498
Grosser, Maurice, 1624
Grout, Donald, 6n., 766

Grove, Sir George, 39n., 694
Grün, Frau, 254
Grünewald, Mathias, 1089, 1094
Guadagni, Gaetano, 63, 64n, 65
Güden, Hilde, 347
Gueymard, Pauline, 621n.
Gui, Vittorio, 499n.
Guillard, François, 75
Guillaume Tell, 392, 399, 434–7, 805
Guimerà, Angel, 993
Guiraud, Ernest, 810
Gunsbourg, Raoul, 762
Gura, Eugen, 254
Gustave III, ou Le Bal Masqué, 602, 603
Gustavo III. See Ballo in Maschera, Un
Gustavus III, King of Sweden, 603, 604, 607
Gutiérrez, Antonio Garcia, 560, 590
Guy Mannering, 711
Gyrowetz, Adalbert, 507

Haffner, Carl, 342
Hagen, Oskar, 39n., 43
Hagith, 1595
Hahn, Reynaldo, 856
Halévy, Jacques François, 749–55
        Ludovic, 342, 797, 801, 805, 834
Hamburg Opera, 1599
Hamlet (Shakespeare), 769n.
        (Thomas), 654, 830
Hammerstein, Oscar, 846
Handel, George Frideric, 30, 33, 37–56, 65, 81, 486, 1581n.
Handel, A Documentary Biography, 39n., 49n.
Hanedansen (Cock's Dance), 1669
Hans Heiling, 184
Hänsel und Gretel, 371–3
Hanslick, Eduard, 224, 234, 235, 527, 734
Happy End, 1101
Harlequin. See Arlecchino
Harmonie der West, Die, 1089
Harnasie (ballet), 1595
Harper's Weekly, 689
Harsányi, Zsolt, 1609
Hartmann, Georges, 864
Háry János, 1609–15
Hassall, Christopher, 1405
Hauck, Minnie, 368, 846

Hauff, Wilhelm, 1148, 1149
Hawthorne, Nathaniel, 1390
Haydn, Franz Joseph, 404, 423n., 438
Haym, Nicola, 39, 44
Heartbreak House, 1416
Heart's Assurance, The, 1424, 1432
Heartz, Daniel, 81n.
Heine, Heinrich, 188, 376
Hell, Henri, 1300n.
Henderson, W. J., 238
Henry IV, 654
Henriette, ou La Servante de Greenwich, 176, 183
Henze, Hans Werner, 1120–53, 1595n., 1599
Her Stepdaughter. See Jeji Pastorkyňa (Jenůfa)
Hercules, 54
Herder, Johann Gottfried von, 205
Heritage of Music, The, 9n.
Hernani, 439, 528
Hesch, Wilhelm, 175
Hesse and the Rhine, Prince of, 1576
Heure Espagnole, L', 1258n., 1275–7
Heyward, du Bose, 1626
Heyworth, Peter, 1102n., 1141
Hill, Karl, 254
Hindemith, Paul, 1067, 1088–99, 1101, 1342
Hindu World, 1271
Hin und Zurück, 1285
Hipsher, Edward Ellsworth, 1624
Histoire de Gérard de Nevers, L', 157
Histoire d'un Soldat, L', 1305n., 1306, 1307, 1311–13, 1314, 1317
History of the Russian State, 888
Hofer, Josefa, 90, 132
Hoffmann, E. T. W., 115, 1088, 1089, 1091
        F. B., 380
Hoffnung der Frauen, 1089
Hofmannsthal, Hugo von, 1002, 1004, 1005, 1008, 1018, 1020, 1024, 1026, 1033, 1036, 1042, 1051
Holberg, Ludvig, 1665, 1666
Holland. As setting for opera, 169, 735
Holman, Miss, 410
Holst, Gustav, 654, 1400–1
'Home, Sweet Home', 408, 409, 443n.
Homer, Louise, 731
Honegger, Arthur, 1295
Hoppenot, Henri, 1285

Houppelande, La, 1190
Howard, Patricia, 1519*n.*
Howells, William Dean, 689
Hubička, 976–9
Hugh the Drover, 1387–90
Hugo Victor, 439, 447, 521, 527, 528, 548, 549, 556, 557
Huguenots, Les, 725–34, 747, 748
Humperdinck, Engelbert, 371–3
Hungary. As setting for opera, 355, 761, 1610
Huon de Bordeaux, 160
Hus, Jan, 1556*n.*
Hutchings, Arthur, 1384, 1387
Huxley, Aldous, 1598, 1599

Idomeneo, 74, 78–84, 85, 98, 119, 127, 722*n.*
Idylls of the King, 317
Igrok, 1329
Illica, Luigi, 680, 698, 701, 702, 1154, 1157, 1165, 1175
Immortal Hour, The, 1402–5
Impresario, The, 90
Incoronazione di Poppea, L', 4, 15–22
India. As setting for opera, 744, 822, 1268, 1400
Indigo, 343
Inferno, The, 1196
Instant Operas. See *Opéras-Minutes*
Intermezzo, 1029–33
Iolanta, 932–4
Iphigénie en Aulide, 71–5
Iphigénie en Tauride (Iphigenia in Tauris), (Gluck), 74, 75–7
(Piccini), 77
Ireland. As setting for opera, 957, 1393
Iris, 698–700
Ismail Pasha, Khedive of Egypt, 629, 631
Isouard, Nicolo, 410
Israel. As setting for opera, 363, 513, 517, 819, 998, 1663
Israelites in Egypt, The. See *Mosè in Egitto*
Italiana in Algeri, L' (The Italian Girl in Algiers), 388–93, 395, 413
Italy. As setting for opera, 16, 45, 116, 127, 185, 333, 350, 365, 377, 380, 386, 393, 444, 447, 479, 483, 499, 529, 532, 543, 546, 549, 580, 591,

603, 610, 664, 677, 683, 690, 715, 718, 723, 758, 775, 779, 793, 810, 1060, 1126, 1166, 1196, 1213, 1217, 1223, 1230, 1233, 1235, 1240, 1291, 1446, 1594, 1654
Ivan the Terrible. See *Pskovityanka* (film), 1356*n.*, 1367*n.*
Ivan Susanin. See *Life for the Tsar, A*
Ivanhoe, 184
Iwaszkiewicz, J., 1594, 1595

Jack the Ripper, 1087
Jacobs, W. W., 1381
Jacobson, Robert, 1661
Jadlowker, Hermann, 81
Jahnn, Hans-Henny, 1120
Jaide, Frau, 254
James V, King of Scotland, 426
James, Henry, 1487, 1489, 1495, 1525, 1526, 1533
Janáček Congress, International, 1551–2
Janáček, Leoš, 48*n.*, 1504, 1542–90
Janáček, Leoš, His Life and Works, 1590
The Operas of Leoš, 1568
Janáček, Zdenka, 1560
Japan. As setting for opera, 699, 1176
Jarnach, Philipp, 1222
Jasager, Der, 1101
Její Pastorkyňa. See *Jenůfa*
Jenůfa, 1542–50, 1551, 1552, 1567
Jessonda, 184
Jewels of the Madonna, The. See *Giojelli della Madonna, I*
Jewess, The. See *Juive, La*
Job, 1244
Jockisch, Walter, 1121
Jonny spielt auf, 1633
Jokai, M., 354
Jolie Fille de Perth, La, 830–3
Jongleur de Notre Dame, Le, 873–5
Jonson, Ben, 1041, 1042
Joseph II, Emperor of Austria, 68*n.*, 116, 131
Juive, La, 749–55
Julius Caesar, 40
Junge Lord, Der, 1148–53

Kabale und Liebe, 546
Kabalevsky, D. B., 1357
Kalbeck, Max, 1233

Kallman, Chester, 1134, 1135, 1140, 1141, 1322
Kammersymphonie, 1079
Karamzin, Nikolai, 888
Kareš, M., 1590
Karneval in Rom, Der, 343
Katerina Ismailova, 1371–7
Katschei the Immortal, 938
Katya Kabanova, 1556, 1560–7, 1578
Keller, Gottfried, 1383
Kelly, Michael, 93
Kemble, Adelaide, 498
Kepler, Johann, 1089
Khovansky, Prince Ivan, 901n.
Khovanshchina (*The Khovansky Rising*) (Moussorgsky), 900–4, 905, 912, 919, 922n.
  (Stravinsky), 1308
Khrennikov, 1356
Kind, Johann Friederich, 152
King, Martin Luther, 1432n.
King Arthur, 27
King for a Day. See *Giorno di Regno, Un*
King in Spite of Himself. See *Roi Malgré Lui, Le*
King of Ys, The, 816–19
King Priam, 1423–8, 1430
King Roger, 1594–8
King Stag. See *König Hirsch*
Kiss, The. See *Hubička*
Kitezh, 938
Kleiber, Erich, 1074
Kleist, Heinrich von, 1130, 1131
Klemperer, Otto, 1102n.
Knight of the Rose, The. See *Rosenkavalier, Der*
Knipperdölling, 739
Knot Garden, The, 1428–34
Kobbé, Gustave, 182–3, 742, 1003
Kochanska, Praxede Marcelline. See Sembrich, Marcella
Kochanski, Pawel, 1596
Kochno, Boris, 1316
Kodály, Zoltán, 1609–15
Koechlin, Charles, 1250
Kokoschka, Oskar, 1089
Kolisch, Gertrud ('Max Blonda'), 1066n.
König Hirsch (*Il Re Cervo*), 1125–30
Königin von Saba, Die, 362–4
Korngold, E. W., 352n.

Kotzebue, August von, 171
Koussevitzky, Serge, 1341, 1410, 1435
Kovařović, Karel, 979, 1543, 1550n.
Krasnohorská, Eliska, 976, 979
Kraus, Ernst, 1029n.
Krauss, Clemens, 1054, 1055
Krehbiel, Henry E., 90
Křenek, Ernst, 1633
Król Roger. See *King Roger*
Kurz, Selma, 609
Kvapil, S. J., 987

Lablache, Luigi, 482
Lachmann, Hedwig, 997
Lady Henriette, ou La Servante de Greenwich, 176
Lady of the Lake, The, 424–8
Lady of the Lake, The (poem), 424, 425, 426
Lady Macbeth of Mtsensk. See *Katerina Ismailova*
Lagunenwalzer, 350
Lainez, Manuel Mujica, 1654, 1655
Lakmé, 821–6
Lalo, Edouard, 816–19
Laloy, Louis, 1267, 1268
Lambert, Constant, 583
Lammert, Frl., 254
Lanari, 499
Large, Brian, 969n., 983
Larinov, 1314
'Last Rose of Summer, The', 179, 181, 409
Lauri-Volpi, Giacomo, 436n.
Lavery, Emmet, 1299
Lee, Sophia, 398
Leesugg, Miss, 410
Le Fort, Gertrude von, 1299
Legende d'Ulenspiegel et de Lamme Goedzak, La, 1243, 1245
Legouvé, G. E., 1205
Legros, Joseph, 64
Lehmann, Lilli, 152, 254, 255, 498, 847
  Marie, 254
Leigh, Adèle, 1420n.
Leila, 827
Le Lorrain, Jacques, 875
Lemaire, Ferdinand, 819
Lemeshev, Sergei, 914n.
Léna, Maurice, 873
Lenja, Lotte, 1101, 1102

Leningrad (St Petersburg): Maly Theatre, 1356
Maryinsky Theatre, 1330
Lenz, Jakob Michael, 1112, 1113, 1114
Leon, Viktor, 358, 359
Leoncavallo, Ruggiero, 683–90, 695
Leonore overtures, 147, 153, 759n.
Leopold II, Emperor of Bohemia, 68n., 127, 378
Leppard, Raymond, 10n., 17, 18, 19, 21n.
Leskov, N., 1371, 1372, 1376
'Les Six', 1342
Leszczyski, Stanislas, 508
Leterrier, E., 848
Let's Make an Opera!, 1459–64, 1501
Levi, Hermann, 338
Lewis, Richard, 1426
Leyden, John of, 726, 738–9
Lhérie, 846
Libertine, The, 103
Libuše, 981–6, 1558n.
Libuše's Judgement, 982
Liebe der Danae, Die, 1050–4, 1055
Liebe Farbe, Die, 1432
Liebermann, Rolf, 64n., 1599
Liebeskind, 130
Life for the Tsar, A, 877–9, 924n.
'Lilliburlero', 35, 1327
Lillo, George, 448
Lily of Killarney, The, 956, 957–9
Linda di Chamounix, 409, 440, 474–8
Lindberghflug, 1101
Lion, Ferdinand, 1088, 1089
Little House in the Forest, The, 1316
Liszt, Cosima (Frau Richard Wagner), 121, 204, 254
See also Wagner, Cosima
Franz, 192, 204, 205, 337, 338, 341
Lloyd-Jones, David, 1367n.
Lockspeiser, Edward, 1295
Loewenberg, Dr Alfred, 27, 715, 1305n., 1567n.
Lohengrin, 157, 184, 189, 202–16, 317, 324, 888
Lolli, Giuseppe, 104
Lombardi, I (The Lombards), 516–20
London: Coliseum, 561n., 1357n.
Covent Garden Company, 1406, 1408, 1413, 1423

Covent Garden Theatre, 30, 609, 617n., 758n., 887, 899, 956, 1121, 1182, 1429, 1433, 1434, 1526
Duke of York's Theatre, 1182
Lincoln's Inn Fields Theatre, 30
Royal College of Music, 1389n., 1393, 1398n.
Sadler's Wells Company, 561n., 739n., 1357n., 1359n., 1398n., 1422n., 1436, 1578n.
Sadler's Wells Theatre, 64n., 84, 601, 797n., 811, 815n., 899, 1230, 1233
Long, John Luther, 1181
Lortzing, Albert, 169–72, 175
Lothar, Rudolph, 993
Loti, Pierre, 821
Louise, 1252–7
Love for Three Oranges, The, 1126, 1334–40, 1341
Love of Danae, The. See *Liebe der Danae, Die*
Love of Three Kings, The. See *Amore dei Tre Re, L'*
Lowens, Irving, 1661
Lowlands, The. See *Tiefland*
Lucia di Lammermoor, 129, 409, 438, 439, 440, 451, 453–61, 550, 579
Lucio Silla, 98
Lucrezia Borgia, 447–50, 451
Ludwig II, King of Bavaria, 254, 766
Luisa Miller, 518, 546–8
Lully, Jean-Baptiste, 57, 722, 1089, 1290
Lulu, 1082–8
Lustigen Weiber von Windsor, Die, 173–6
Luther, Martin, 726, 733
Lytton, Bulwer, 185
Lyubov k trem Apelsinam. See *Love for Three Oranges*

Mabinogion, 317, 318
McAllister, Rita, 1355n., 1359n.
Macbeth, 516, 520, 533, 534–42, 601, 646, 654, 661n., 662
Maciejewski, B. M., 1595
Mackerras, Charles, 561n., 1577n.
Macleod, Fiona, 1402
Madama Butterfly, 1175–82
Madame Butterfly (play), 1181

Maddalena, 1330, 1341n.
Maeterlinck, Maurice, 1258, 1607
Maggio Musicale Fiorentino, 425
Magic Flute, The, 90, 91, 103, 127, 129–42, 146, 161, 168, 409, 1128. See also *Zauberflöte, Die*
Magistrate, The, 374–6
Magnani, Anna, 806n.
Mahā Bhārata, The, 1400
Mahagonny, 1285
Mahler, Gustav, 167–8, 810
Maid of Orleans, The, 917–20, 921
Maid of Pskov, The. See *Pskovityanka*
Maiden's Wish, 408
Maidservant turned Mistress, The. See *Serva Padrona, La*
Maiskaya Noch, 937–41
Makropulos Affair, The, 48n., 1557n., 1577–83, 1585
Malefille, P. J. F., 973
Malibran, Maria, 451, 498
Mamelles de Tirésias, Les, 1294–8, 1515
Mancinelli, Luigi, 609
Mann ist Mann, 1101
Mann, Thomas, 1532, 1533
    William, 1090, 1130, 1414n., 1422n., 1434, 1600n.
Manon, 408, 858–64, 871, 1124
Manon Lescaut (Auber), 408, 864
    (Puccini), 864, 1154–7
Mansfield Park, 1453
Manzoni Requiem, 646
Mapleson, Lionel, 460, 461
'Marche Hongroise', 858
Marchi, A., 48
Maresi, 734
Margarethe. See *Faust* (Gounod)
Maria Golovin, 1633
Maria Stuarda (*Mary Stuart*), 450–3, 515n.
Maria Theresa, Empress, 131
Mariage de Figaro, Le (Beaumarchais), 401
Mariage de Loti, Le, 821
Marie Antoinette, 65
    Theresa, 131
Marienleben, 1089n.
Mario, Giovanni, 448, 482, 549, 604
Maritana, 956, 959–62
Marouf, 1273–5
Marriage of Figaro, The, 90–102, 113, 117, 121, 142, 401, 410

Marschner, Heinrich, 184
Martha, 176–83
Martin, Frank, 217n.
    Vicente, 113
Martyn, Mrs. 152
Martyr de Saint Sébastien, Le, 1245
Mascagni, Pietro, 475, 690–700
Maskarade, 1663, 1665–70
Masked Ball, A. See *Ballo in Maschera, Un*
Massenet, Jules, 408, 409, 730, 858–76, 1124
Master Peter's Puppet Show. See *Retablo de Maese Pedro, El*
Materna, Amalia, 254, 255
Mathis der Maler (*Mathis the Painter*), 1089, 1093–9
Matrimonio Segreto, Il, 377–80
Mattinata, 409
Matullah, Alice, 90
Maturin, Rev. R. C., 482
Maugham, Somerset, 1018
Maupassant, Guy de, 1452
Maurel, Victor, 630, 734
Mavra, 1305n., 1306, 1313, 1314, 1316–18
May Night, A. See *Maiskaya Noch*
Mayr, Simone, 146
Mayreder-Obermayer, Rosa, 374
Mazaroff, 436n.
Mazeppa, 920–6
Mazzolà, Caterino, 126, 127, 128
Médée (*Medea*), 380–5
Méditation, 872
Medium, The, 1633, 1636–9
Mefistofele, 671–6, 677, 680
Mei, L. A., 934
Meilhac, Henri, 342, 801, 805, 834, 858
Meissonier, J. L. E., 572
Meistersinger von Nürnberg, Die, 232–53, 254, 258, 983
Melba, Nellie, 409, 549, 559, 734, 793
Mellers, Wilfrid, 1413, 1520
Melville, Herman, 1464, 1465, 1475, 1476, 1533
Memoirs of Herr von Schnabelewopski, 188
Menasci, G., 690
Mendelson, Mira, 1348, 1353, 1355
Mendelssohn, Felix, 165, 734
Mendès, Catulle, 689–90

Menotti, Gian Carlo, 1633–53
Merchant of Venice, The, 767
Mère Coupable, La (Beaumarchais), 401
Merelli, 508
Mérimée, Prosper, 805, 806, 834, 846, 847, 1330
Merle, J. T., 169
Merry Monarch, The, 848
Merry Widow, The, 359
Merry Wives of Windsor, The (Nicolai), 173–6, 654, 974
    (Shakespeare), 654
Méry, G., 617
Meser, 203
Mesmerism, introduced into opera, 121
Messiah, 65
Metastasio, Pietro, 126, 127, 128, 129
Metternich, Princess, 205
Meyer, Kerstin, 64n.
Meyerbeer, Giacomo, 184, 408, 475, 618, 630, 721–48, 750, 855, 920, 1290
Micelli, Catarina, 104
Midsummer Marriage, The, 133, 1406, 1412–23, 1424
Midsummer Night's Dream, A, 27, 165, 781, 1501, 1502–14
Mierzwiński, W., 437
Mignon, 778–82
Milan, La Scala, 415, 425, 440, 443, 483, 486, 508, 517, 572n., 630, 730n.
Milanov, Zinka, 550n.
Milhaud, Darius, 431, 1101, 1283–94, 1295
Military Band. First instance of employment of, in Italian opera, 429
Miller, Dr Frank E., 568
Milliet, Paul, 864, 1618
Millöcker, Karl, 368–71
Mingled Chime, A, 1020
Minotis, Alexis, 382
Miraculous Mandarin, The (ballet), 1607n.
Mireille, 790–2
Mireio, 790
Mistral, Frédéric, 790
Mitchell, Donald, 1527, 1531, 1539
Mitousoff, S., 1308
Mitridate, 79, 127

Moïse et Pharaon. See Mosè in Egitto
Molière, 103, 1018, 1020
Molotov, V. M., 1376
Monastery, The, 711
Moniuszko, Stanislaw, 1595
Montemezzi, Italo, 1223–9
Monteux, Pierre, 1341n.
Monteverdi, Claudio, 4–22, 129, 1244, 1288, 1321, 1525
Monteverdi (Schrade), 7n.
Moore, Tom, 181
Mörder, Hoffnung der Frauen, 1089
Mosca, L., 388
Moscow, Bolshoi Theatre, 1356, 1357n.
    Conservatory of Music, 909
    Free Theatre of, 1310
Mosè in Egitto (Moses in Egypt), 419–24, 431
Mosenthal, Hermann von, 173, 362
Moses und Aron, 1068–73
Mottl, Felix, 338
Moussorgsky, Modest Petrovich, 883, 887, 888–908, 919, 925, 1375
Moussorgsky (Calvocoressi), 905
Movements, 1307
Moving into Aquarius, 1413n.
Mozart, Wolfgang Amadeus, 75n., 78–142, 150, 166, 168, 378, 380, 399, 401, 410, 413, 434, 579, 601, 662, 722n., 1258
    First opera to be performed in London, 127
Mozart; his Character, his Work (Einstein), 85
Mozart and Salieri, 938
Much Ado About Nothing, 774, 778
Muette de Portici, La, 714–17, 805, 1368n.
Müller, Adolf, 359
    Wenzel, 131
Munich, Court Theatre, 754
Muradely, Vano, 1356
Music of Czechoslovakia, The, 970
Musical Poetics, 1316n.
Music and Musical Life in Soviet Russia 1917–1970, 1357n.
Music Review, The, 1419n.
Musician, The, 459

Nabucco, 512–16, 517, 520, 527, 540
Nacht in Venedig, Eine, 350–4

Nanneti, 630, 734
Naples, San Carlo Theatre, 397, 420, 425, 428, 543, 603
Napoleon III, 603
Nápravník, Eduard, 1330
Nash, Heddle, 832n.
Naufrageurs, Les, 1378
Naughty Anthony, 1181
Navarraise, La, 730, 827
Neitzel, O., 764
Népoty, Lucien, 1273
Nerone (Nero), 673n., 676–80
Neue Musik-Zeitung, 1075
Neues vom Tage, 1067
Newman, Ernest, 70, 71, 194, 338, 341, 347, 771, 884, 895, 896, 948, 1002n., 1196
Newmarch, Rosa, 915, 970
New, Sensational Excursion of Mr. Brouček, this time into the 15th Century, 1552
New Statesman and Nation, 539, 1413n., 1503n., 1504n., 1520
New York: Academy of Music, 408, 461, 469, 493, 505, 630, 734
    Ballet Society, 1640
    Casino, 846
    City Centre, 1340
    City Opera House, 888, 1150n.
    Empire Theatre, 90
    Herald Square Theatre, 1181
    Manhattan Opera House, 549, 559, 572, 846, 847
    Metropolitan Opera House, 64, 77, 152, 167, 181, 185, 238, 255, 445, 460, 461, 493, 549, 559, 583n., 604n., 630, 664, 730, 734, 740, 793, 846, 847, 1001, 1150n., 1307
    Park Theatre, 151, 410
New York Evening Post, 152, 410
New York Herald, 1181
New Yorker, The, 498
Nicolai, Otto, 173–6, 512, 654
Nicolini (Ernest Nicolas), 793
Nielsen, Carl August, 1662–70
    Francis, 1182
Niemann, Albert, 152, 254, 255
Night in Venice, A, 350–4
Night on the Bare Mountain, 907
Nightingale, The. See Rossignol, Le
Nijinska, Bronislava, 1314, 1317

Nilsson, Christine, 559, 572, 664, 734, 830
Noces, Les, 1306, 1307, 1314, 1317
Noni, Alda, 480
Nordica, Lillian, 734
Norma, 440, 494–8, 499, 504, 514
Norway. As setting for opera, 188
Nouritt, Adolphe, 64, 750
Noye's Fludde, 1500–2, 1514
Nozze di Figaro, Le, 90–102. See also Marriage of Figaro, The
Nusch Nuschi, Das, 1089
Nutcracker ballet, 932

Oberon, 160–8
    (Mahler's version of Weber's opera), 167–8
    (poem by Wieland), 160
Oberto, 508, 515, 526
Obey, André, 1445
Oca del Cairo, L', 91
Oedipus Rex, 1305n., 1306, 1307, 1317, 1318–22
Offenbach, Jacques, 797–815, 1286
Olimpia, 184, 185
Oliva, Domenico, 1154
Ondine, 1121
Opera, 908n., 1070n., 1076n., 1113n., 1533
Opera (Edward Dent), 1290
'Opéras Minutes', 1285–9
Opera Nights (Ernest Newman), 338, 771n., 948
Orchestra and Orchestral Music, The, 238
Orfeo (Monteverdi), 4–9, 17, 129, 1321
Orfeo ed Euridice (Orpheus and Eurydice), 60, 61–5, 77, 1453
Orlando Furioso, 48
Orleanskaya Dyeva. See Maid of Orleans, The
Orphée aux Enfers (Orpheus in the Underworld), 797–801, 804, 1286
Orpheus, The Legend of. See Orfeo
Orrey, Leslie, 486
Orsini, Felice, 603
Ostřeil, Otakar, 1551
Ostrovsky, Alexander Nicolaievich, 941, 1560
Osud, 1551
Otava, Zdeněk, 1557n.

Otello, 515, 588, 590, 591, 595, 608, 616, 645–52, 653, 654, 658, 662
Our Lady's Tumbler. See Jongleur de Notre Dame, Le
Owen Wingrave, 1525–32
Oxenford, J., 957

Padmavâtî, 1267–73
Paer, Ferdinando, 146, 407
Pagliacci, I, 683–90, 695
Paisiello, Giovanni, 405, 407
Palestrina, 1059–65
Palestrina, Giovanni da, 631
Panambi (ballet), 1654
Pan Voyevoda, 938
Panzacchi, 81
Pappenheim, Marie, 1065
'Parables for Church Performance', 1501, 1514–25, 1534n.
Parepa-Rosa, Euphrosyne, 734
Paris: Académie, 722
    Bouffes Parisiens, 798
    Comédie Française, 57, 798
    Exposition of 1855, 580
    Opéra-Comique, 631, 712, 764n., 810, 830, 845, 862n., 1295
    Opera House, 57, 64n., 630, 631, 715, 722, 723, 730, 757n., 764n., 783, 789, 793, 794, 796, 830, 1268, 1278
    Salle Louvois, 407
    Théâtre des Arts, 1268
    Théâtre des Italiens, 407, 630
    Théâtre Lyrique, 64, 160, 654, 766, 783, 793
    Théâtre National Populaire, 1131
Parsifal, 204, 207, 316–32
    (Poem by von Eschenbach), 317
Passion according to St Matthew, 766
Pasta, Giuditta, 439, 499
Patineurs, Les (ballet), 739n.
Patti, Adelina, 81, 408, 409, 428, 429, 461, 493, 549, 572, 742, 793, 864
Patzak, Julius, 347
Paulini, Béla, 1609
Pauvre Matelot, Le, 1283–5
Peace Day. See Friedenstag
Peace Jubilee, Boston, 408
Pearl, Cora, 798
Pears, Peter, 1494, 1502, 1503

Pêcheurs de Perles, Les (The Pearl Fishers), 826–9, 833
Pelléas et Mélisande, 1258–63
Penderecki, Krzysztof, 1598–1606
Pénélope, 1249–52
Pepoli, Count, 502
Pepusch, John Christopher, 28
Percival le Galois, 317
Performance of Othello, A, 68–9
Pergolesi, Giovanni, 56–9
Peri, Jacopo, 3, 4, 9
Périchole, La, 805–9
Périer, Jean, 1258n.
Perinet, 131
Periquet, Fernando, 1616
Perle du Brésil, La, 409
Perséphone, 1305n., 1307, 1317
Persia. As setting for opera, 337
Perti, Giacomo Antonio, 44
Peru. As setting for opera, 806
Peschka-Leutner, Minna, 408
Peter the Great, 901, 922n., 925
Peter Grimes, 1353n., 1408, 1434–45, 1446, 1523n.
Peters, Roberta, 956
Pfitzner, Hans, 1059–65
Phaeton, 1089
Phèdre, 1285, 1289
Philadelphia, Metropolitan Opera House, 549
Philippe, Gérard, 1131
Phillips, Thomas, 410
Piave, Francesco Maria, 521, 528, 534, 535, 548, 570, 571, 579, 586, 587, 590, 609
Piccinni, Nicola, 60, 77
Pierrot Lunaire, 1076
Pietro L'Eremita. See Mosè in Egitto
Pikovaya Dama (Pique Dame). See Queen of Spades, The
Pilgrim's Progress, The, 1395–9
Piper, Myfanwy, 1487, 1525, 1526, 1532, 1533
Pirata, Il (The Pirate), 482–5, 486
Pizzolato, G., 1229
Placide, Mr, 152
Planché, James Robertson, 160, 168
Plançon, Pol, 732, 734
Plomer, William, 1477, 1515, 1516, 1520, 1523
Poacher, The. See Wildschütz, Der
Poisoned Kiss, The, 1390–3

Poland. As setting for opera, 368, 853, 889, 955
Pollard, Alfred W., 1500n.
Polly, 30
Poltava, 920
Pomposo, or a Receipt for an Italian Song, 410
Ponchielli, Amilcare, 663–71
Ponselle, Rosa, 185, 498
Ponziani, Felice, 104
Poor Sailor, The. See Pauvre Matelot, Le
Pope, Alexander, 55n.
Porgy and Bess, 1626–33
Porter, Andrew, 397n., 498, 617n., 621n., 1121, 1131
Portugal. As setting for opera, 744
Postillon de Longjumeau, Le, 755–7
Poulenc, Francis, 1294–8
Poulenc, Francis, 1300n.
Pour et le Contre, Le, 49
Praga, Mario, 1154
Prague, National Theatre, 983
Pravda, 1376
Preis, A., 1371
Preissová, Gabriella, 1542
Prévost, Abbé, 49, 858, 864, 1330
Přibyl, Vilem, 75n.
Prigioniero Il (The Prisoner), 1243–8
Prigioniero Superbo, Il, 57
Příhody Lišky Bystroušky. See Cunning Little Vixen, The
Prince Igor, 881–8
Prince of the Pagodas, The (ballet), 1514, 1534
Prinz Friederich von Homburg, 1131
Prinz von Homburg, Der, 1130–4
Prinzessin auf der Erbse, Die, 1285
Prise de Troie, La, 764, 767–70
Proch, Heinrich, 408
Procházka, F. S., 1550, 1552
Prodaná Nevěsta. See Bartered Bride, The
Prodigal Son, The (Britten), 1514, 1523–5
        (Debussy), 1401
Prokofiev, Sergei, 1126, 1329–70, 1588
Prométhée, 1250
Prophète, Le, 583, 630, 726, 734–40, 744, 748
Proscritto, Il. See Ernani

Pskovityanka, 934–7, 938
Puccini, Giacomo, 695, 864, 1154–1205, 1210, 1211n., 1668
Pulcinella, 1317
Purcell, Henry, 23–7, 35, 36, 1525
Puritani, I, 440, 483, 486, 499, 502–6
Pushkin, Alexander, 879, 880, 888, 908, 909, 910, 914, 915, 920, 926, 927, 947, 948, 1316

Quattro Rusteghi, I, 1229–33
Queen of Sheba, The. See Königin von Saba, Die
Queen of Spades, The, 908, 913, 926–31
Quiet Flows the Don, And, 1376
Quintet (Mozart), 129n.

Raaff, Anton, 81
Rabaud, Henri, 1273–5
Racine, Jean, 1285, 1289
Rake's Progress, The, 114, 1305n., 1306, 1307, 1317, 1322–9
'Rákóczi March', 761
Rameau, Jean Philippe, 57, 1290
Ramsay, Allan, 29
Ramuz, C. F., 1311, 1313
Rape of Europa, The. See Enlèvement d'Europe, L'
Rape of Lucretia, The, 1445–52, 1453, 1458, 1515, 1537
Rasa, Lina Bruna, 695
Rasumovsky Quartet, second, 925
Ravel, Maurice, 1275–82
Recess, The, 398
Redlich, Hans, 6
Reich, Willi, 1075
Reicha, Antonín, 83
Reichert, H., 1187
Reinhardt, Max, 1020, 1209
Reiss, Albert, 90
Renard, 1305n., 1306, 1313–16
Renaud, Maurice, 549, 572
Rennert, Günther, 1114
Renoir, Jean, 806n.
Requiem (Mozart), 127
        (Verdi), 591
Resurrection, 1355
Retablo de Maese Pedro, El, 1620–2
Reveillon, Le, 342
Revue des deux Mondes, 439
Rheingold, Das (The Rhine Gold), 53,

254, 255, 260–73, 274, 290, 291, 293, 296, 303, 312, 1141
Rich, John, 30
Richard Cœur de Lion, 930
Richter, Hans, 254
Ricordi, Tito, 618*n*., 1239
Riders to the Sea, 1393–5
Rienzi, 185–8, 189, 190, 203, 386
Rigoletto, 453, 454, 516, 538, 548–60, 579, 587, 607, 762, 847
Rilke, Rainer Maria, 1089*n*.
Rimsky-Korsakov, Nicholai, 881, 882, 888, 889, 897, 899, 901, 925, 934–53, 1306, 1309
Rinaldo, 33
Ring of the Nibelung, The, 253–316, 341, 734, 766
Rinuccini, Ottavio, 4, 9
Rioton, Marthe, 1253
Rise and Fall of the City of Mahagonny. See *Aufstieg und Fall der Stadt Mahagonny*
Ritorno d'Ulisse in Patria, Il, 4, 12–15, 1245
Rivas, Duke of, 609, 610
Robert le Diable (Robert the Devil), 722, 723–5, 726
Roberto Devereux (Robert Devereux), 451, 462–5
'Robin Adair'. Used in opera, 410, 713, 714
Rode, Jacques, 408
Rodelinda, 44–8
Roi d'Ys, Le, 816–19
Roi malgré lui, Le, 852–8
Roi s'amuse, Le, 548, 549
Roller, Alfred, 167
Romani, Felice, 393, 438, 439, 443, 447, 482, 483, 485, 486, 489, 494, 499, 500, 507
Rome, Apollo Theatre, 603
    Argentine Theatre, 405
Romeo and Juliet (Shakespeare), 792, 794
    (Tchaikovsky), 921
Roméo et Juliette (Berlioz), 764
    (Gounod), 792–7
Ronconi, Giorgio, 549
Rondine, La, 1187–90
Ronsard, Pierre de, 1056*n*.
Rosamond, 29
Rosamunda d'Inghilterra, 463

Rosbaud, Hans, 1073
Rosenkavalier, Der, 1003, 1008–18, 1020, 1030, 1158*n*.
Rosier de Madame Husson, Le, 1452
Rossi, Gaetano, 428, 474
Rossignol, Le, 953, 1305*n*., 1306, 1308–10, 1317
Rossini, Gioacchino Antonio, 380, 388–437, 438, 508, 579, 722, 940, 1149, 1151, 1307
Rossini: a Study in Tragi-comedy, 434*n*.
Rossiniane, 405
Rostropovitch, Mstislav, 1514
Rouché, Jacques, 1268
Rousseau, Jean Jacques, 57
Roussel, Albert, 1267–73
Royer, Alphonse, 468
Rozen, G. F., 877
Ruffini, Giovanni, 478
Ruffo, Titta, 549
Ruins of Athens, The, 147
Rusalka, 987–90
Russia. As setting for opera, 706, 877, 882, 889, 901, 905, 909, 921, 926, 935, 938, 945, 1316, 1355, 1372, 1560, 1585
Russlan and Ludmila, 879–81
Rustic Chivalry. See *Cavalleria Rusticana*

Sabina, Karel, 963
Sachs, Hans, 234, 252, 258
Sacher, Paul, 1419*n*.
Sacre du Printemps (ballet), 1661
Sadie, Stanley, 81*n*.
Sadko, 938, 944–7, 951
Saffi, 354
Saint-Exupéry, Antoine de, 1244
Saint-Georges, J. H. Vernoy de, 176, 183, 465, 830, 885, 954
St Nicholas, 1501, 1504
Saint of Bleecker Street, The, 1633, 1650–3
St Paul (Oratorio), 734
Saint-Saëns, Camille, 64*n*., 819–21
Saléza, Albert, 793
Salieri, Antonio, 654
Sallé, Marie, 49
Salome, 997–1002, 1003, 1595
Salvi, A., 44
Salvini-Donatelli, 571

Samosud, 1356
Samson, 65
Samson et Dalila, 819–21
Sancta Susanna, 1089
Santley, Sir Charles, 734, 783, 784
Saporiti, Teresa, 104
'Saran Rose, Se', waltz, 409
Sardou, Victorien, 706, 1165, 1166n.
Šarka, 1551
Sarti, Giuseppe, 113
Sass, Marie, 621n.
Satie, Erik, 1295, 1342
Saturday Review, The, 1661
Sauget, Henri, 1283
Saul and David, 1662–5
Sāvitri, 1400–1
Sawallisch, Wolfgang, 1114
Scalchi, Sofia, 428, 429, 731, 734
Schaeffner, André, 1312
Schauspieldirektor, Der (The Impresario), 90, 91
Schefsky, Frl., 254
Scheik von Alexandria und seine Sklaven, Der, 1148
Scherchen, Hermann, 1069, 1073, 1074
Schikaneder, Emanuel Johann, 90, 129, 130–1, 141, 142, 146
Schiller, Johann Cristoph Friederich von, 434, 438, 451, 453, 546, 617, 618, 628, 917
Schipa, Tito, 482
Schirmer, G., Inc., 217, 235
Schlosser, 254
Schmidt, Giovanni, 397
Schnitzer, J., 354
Schoenberg, Arnold, 1065–73, 1075, 1076, 1078–9, 1121, 1222n., 1244, 1342
Schöffler, Paul, 1090
School for Fathers, The. See Quattro Rusteghi, I
Schrade, Leo, 7
Schreker, Franz, 1067n.
Schröder-Devrient, Wilhelmine, 147
Schubert, Franz, 55, 129, 146, 225, 369, 763, 1432
Schuh, Oscar Fritz, 1114
Schuller, Gunther, 1289
Schumann, Robert, 733, 734
Schumann-Heink, Ernestine, 447, 1003
Schwanda the Bagpiper, 1590–3

Schwarz, Boris, 1357n.
Vera, 347
Schweigsame Frau, Die, 1041–5
Scio, Madame, 381
Scolara, 630
Score, The, 1244n.
Scotland. As setting for opera, 425, 454, 535, 587, 711, 830
Scott, Sir Walter, 424, 425, 426, 438, 453, 711, 830, 833
Scotti, Antonio, 614
Scottish Opera, 766n.
Scriabin, A. N., 1596
Scribe, Augustin Eugène, 431, 579, 580, 585, 602, 603, 711, 714, 718, 723, 725, 726, 734, 743, 744, 747, 749, 751, 864, 1205
Seasons, The, 404
Secret, The. See Tajemství
Secret Marriage, The, 377–80
Segreto di Susanna, Il, 1233–5, 1640
Seidl, Anton, 152, 239
Sembrich, Marcella, 408, 409, 493, 572, 664
Semele, 52–6
Semiramide, 428–30
Serafin, Tullio, 425
Sermon, A Narrative, A Prayer, A, 1307
Serva Padrona, La, 56–9
Servilia, 938
Seven Deadly Sins, The, 1101
Shadwell, Thomas, 103
Shakespeare, William, 160, 173, 365, 535–6, 542, 645, 646, 647, 648, 649, 652, 654, 655n., 662, 767, 774, 775, 777, 778, 792, 793, 794, 891, 1502, 1503, 1504, 1506, 1533
Sharp, Evelyn, 1390
Shaw, C. Fernandez, 1618
        G. B., 1416
Shawe-Taylor, Desmond, 539, 908, 1608
Shepherds of the Delectable Mountains, The, 1398, 1399
Sheridan, Richard Brindsley, 1348, 1349
Shilovsky, K. S., 908
Shirkov, V. F., 879
Shirley, 1258n.
Sholokhov, Mikhail, 1376
Short History of Opera, A, 6n., 766

Short Life, The. See *Vida Breve, La*
Shostakovich, Dmitri Dmitrevich, 901, 1371–7
Sicilian Vespers, The, 408, 409, 630.
See also *Vêpres Siciliennes, Les*
Sicily. As setting for opera, 580, 690, 723, 775
Sieben Todsünen, Die, 1101
Siegfried, 254, 255, 290–301, 303, 1258n.
Siehr, 254
Siems, Margarethe, 1020n.
Silent Woman, The. See *Schweigsame Frau, Die*
Simionato, Giulietta, 428n.
Simon Boccanegra, 585, 590–601, 606
Simoni, R., 606, 1200
Simplizius, 352n.
Sir John in Love, 654
Sister Angelica. See *Suor Angelica*
Slater, Montagu, 1434, 1435
Sleeping Beauty, The (ballet), 1316
Sleepwalker, The. See *Sonnambula, La*
Smetana, Bedřich, 963–86, 1558n.
Smetana, 983n.
Smith, Patrick J., 769n.
Smyth, Dame Ethel, 1378–83
Snegurochka (The Snow Maiden), 938, 941–4
Society of American Singers, 90
Soldaten, Die (The Soldiers), 1112–20
Soldier's Bride, The, 410
Soldier's Tale, A. See *Histoire d'un Soldat, L'*
Solera, Temistocle, 512, 516, 531, 533
Sombrero de tres picos, El, 374
Somma, Antonio, 602
Songe d'une Nuit d'Eté, Le, 654
Sonnambula, La, 409, 439, 440, 475, 489–94, 504, 579
Sonnleithner, Georg Friedrich, 145
Joseph, 145, 146
Sophia, Empress, 901n.
Sophocles, 1002, 1318
Sorabji, Kaikhosru, 1595
Sorotchinski Fair, 904–8
Sotheby, William, 160
Soumet, L. A., 494
Souter, Josef, 75n.
Sousa, John Philip, 369
Spain. As setting for opera, 91, 103, 146, 317, 374, 401, 469, 521, 561,

610, 618, 835, 876, 960, 993, 1244, 1276, 1290, 1348, 1616, 1618, 1620, 1623
Spanish Hour, The. See *Heure Espagnole, L'*
Spectator, The, 1413n., 1506n.
Spindler, Erwin, 969, 981
Spohr, Ludwig, 184
Spontini, Gasparo, 184, 385–8, 1290
Sposo Deluso, Lo, 91
Stabat Mater, 57
Stabile, Mariano, 480
Stadler, Anton, 129
Stalin, 1356, 1376
Standard Operas, The, 151
Standrecht. See *Wreckers, The*
Star, The. See *Étoile, L'*
'Star Spangled Banner, The', 1177, 1181
Stassov, Vladimir, 881, 883, 900, 942
Stefan, Paul, 545n.
Stein, Erwin, 1070n., 1076n., 1081, 1087, 1497
Gertrude, 1623
Leo, 358, 359
Stendhal, 389, 398, 399, 400, 405, 415, 421, 422, 423n.
Stephanie, Gottlieb, 84
Sterbini, Cesare, 400, 405
Steuermann, Eduard, 1074
Stiffelio, 586, 587, 590
Stone Guest, 38
Storm, The, 1560
Stösslova, Kamila, 1561, 1585
Strada, Anna, 48n., 50n.
Strakosch, Max, 630
Straniera, La (The Stranger), 485–8
Stransky, Joseph, 1029
Strauss, Johann, 336, 342–62, 409, 800, 1219
Richard, 77, 156, 997–1059, 1089, 1121, 1122, 1342, 1596
Stravinsky, Igor, 114, 917, 940, 953, 1146, 1149, 1305–29, 1342, 1599
Stravinsky: A Critical Survey, 1312n.
Stravinsky in the Theatre, 1317n.
Striggio, Alessandro, 4, 9
Strolling Players, The. See *Pagliacci, I*
Suardon, P., 695
Sullivan, Sir Arthur, 465
Sumidagawa, 1515, 1516
Sunday Times, The, 1608

Suor Angelica, 1191, 1194–5
Suppé, Franz von, 333–6
Susanna's Secret. See Segreto di Susanna, Il
Süssmayer, Franz, 127
Sutcliffe, James Helme, 1113n.
Sutherland, Joan, 38, 49, 50, 51, 428n., 463
Sutter-Kottlar, 1074
Švanda Dudák. See Schwanda the Bagpiper
Swallow, The. See Rondine, La
Swarsenski, Hans, 1346n.
Sweden. As setting for opera, 602, 604
Swift, Jonathan, 29
Switzerland. As setting for opera, 435, 466, 489, 706, 749, 1384
Sydney Opera House, 1357n.
Synesius, Bishop, 1501n.
Synge, J. M., 1393
Szymanowski, Karol, 1594–8

Tabarin, 690
Tabarro, Il, 1190–4
Taglioni, Marie, 724
Tailleferre, Germaine, 1295
Tajemství, 979–81
Tales of Hoffmann, The. See Contes d'Hoffmann
Talich, Václav, 1570n.
Tallis, Thomas, 1502
Tamagno, Francesco, 436
Taming of the Shrew, The, 365–8
Tancridi, 408
Taneiev, Sergei Ivanovich, 921
Tannhäuser, 157, 184, 189, 195–202, 203, 207, 316, 386, 803
Tanzwalzer, 1219
Tapper, Thomas, 459
Targioni-Tozzetti, Giovanni, 690
Tasso, 10
Tate, Nahum, 23
Tauber, Richard, 347
Taylor, Tom, 549, 557
Tchaikovsky, Modest, 926, 932
  Peter Ilitsch, 908–34, 1359, 1370
Tcherepnin, Nicolas, 905, 906, 907, 908
Tebaldi, Renata, 185
Telephone, The, 1640–1
Tempest, The, 27, 1430, 1432

Templer und die Judin, Der (The Templar and the Jewess), 184
Tempo, 1346n., 1505n.
Tennyson, Alfred Lord, 317
Tenth Muse, The, 769n.
Tešnohlídek, R., 1567, 1568
Tetrazzini, Luisa, 493, 549
Teufel von Loudon, Die. See Devils of Loudon, The
Thackeray, W. M., 866
Thaïs, 869–72
Thieving Magpie, The, 414–19
Thill, Georges, 764n.
Thomas, Ambroise, 654, 778–82, 830
Thomas, Dylan, 1308
Thomson, Virgil, 1623–5
Tiefland, 993–7
Tierra Baixa, 993
Tietjens, Teresa, 382, 408
Times, The, 382, 1090, 1130, 1233, 1370, 1434n., 1434, 1600n., 1605
Tinker's Wedding, The, 1393
Tippett, Sir Michael, 133, 1129, 1412–34, 1525
Tippett, Michael: A Symposium on His 60th Birthday, 1421n., 1422n.
Tirsi e Clori, 4
Toch, Ernst, 1101, 1285
Tolstoy, Leo, 1353, 1355, 1370
Torriani, Mlle., 630
Torture par l'espérance, La, 1243, 1245
Torvaldo e Dorliska, 405
Tosca, 1165–75, 1191, 1200
Toscanini, Arturo, 64, 550n., 673n.
Tosti, Francesco, 409
Tottola, A. L., 419, 421, 424
Toye, Francis, 415, 421, 434, 542, 548, 580, 610, 615
Tracey, Edmund, 811
Traviata, La, 539, 545, 570–9, 808, 973
Trebelli, Zella, 731
Treitschke, Georg Friedrich, 147
Trend, J. B., 1619
Trentini, Emma, 847
Tristan und Isolde, 216–32, 245, 250, 254, 444, 646, 1258, 1456
Troilus and Cressida, 1405–9
Trojans, The. See Troyens, Les
Trojans in Carthage, The. See Troyens à Carthage, Les

Troubadour, The. See *Trovatore, Il*
Trovatore, Il, 357, 557, 561–70, 578, 579, 587, 846
Troy. As setting for opera, 764, 767, 1405, 1424
Troyens, Les, 764–74, 983, 1273
Troyens à Carthage, Les, 764, 766, 770–4
Tsar and Carpenter, 169–71
Tsar Saltan, 938
Tsar's Bride, The, 925, 938
Tsarouchis, John, 382
Tucker, Norman, 591, 592, 595, 596–7, 1563*n.,* 1578*n.*
Turandot (Busoni), 1126, 1209–13
   (Puccini), 1126, 1200–5, 1275
Turco in Italia, Il (The Turk in Italy), 393–7
Turina, Giuditta, 439
Turkey. As setting for opera, 84, 834
Turn of the Screw, The, 1487–1500, 1501, 1505, 1507, 1523*n.,* 1526, 1530*n.,* 1534*n*
Turner, W. J., 776
Tutankhamen, 639*n.*
Tuttifäntchen, 1089
Twilight of the Gods, The. See *Götterdämmerung*
Two Foscari, The. See *Due Foscari, I*
Two Widows, The. See *Dvě Vdovy*

Ugalde, Marguerite, 798
Ulisse, 1244
Ulysses' Return Home. See *Ritorno d'Ulisse in Patria, Il*
Unger, Georg, 254
Unicorn, the Dragon, the Manticore, The, 1633
Upton, George P., 151, 842

Vaez, Gustav, 468
Valkyrie, The. See *Walküre, Die*
Vampyr, Der (The Vampire), 184
Vandenburg, Howard, 1423*n.*
Vanloo, A., 848
Varesco, Abbé, 78
Varesi, Felice, 571
Velluti, Giovanni Battista, 398
Venice: Fenice Opera, 499
Vêpres Siciliennes, Les, 408, 409, 579–86, 630
Verdi, Giuseppe, 18, 75, 157, 399,

408, 413, 426, 438, 453, 469, 507–662, 722*n.,* 749, 772, 777, 913, 1149, 1200, 1666
Verdi: The Man in his Letters, 545*n.*
Verga, Giovanni, 690, 691
Vergil, 63, 764, 767, 771
Verona: Arena di Verona, 663*n.*
Vespri Siciliani, I. See *Vêpres Siciliennes, Les*
Vestale, La (The Vestal Virgin), 184, 185, 385–8
Viaggio a Reims, Il, 431
Viardot-Garcia, Pauline, 64*n.,* 65, 408
Victor Emanuel, King of Italy, 603
Vida Breve, La, 1618–20
Vie de Rossini, 405
Vienna, Imperial Theatre, 508
   Theater am Kärnthnerthor, 147
   Theater an der Wien, 146
Viennese Spirit, The, 358–62
Vigier, Baron, 580
Vilar, Jean, 1131
Village Romeo and Juliet, A, 1383–7
Vin Herbé, Le, 217*n.*
Viol de Lucrèce, Le, 1445
Visconti, Luchino, 440, 572*n.*
Vlad, Roman, 1244, 1245*n.,* 1246*n.,* 1552, 1585
Vocal Art Science, 568
'Voce di Primavera', waltz, 409
Vogel, Jaroslav, 1590
Vogler, Abbé, 722
Voina y Mir. See *War and Peace*
Vol de Nuit, 1244
Volo di Notte, 1244
Volpone, 1042
Voltaire, François Marie, 428
Von Heute auf Morgen, 1066–8
Voyage dans la Lune, Le, 810

Wachtel, Theodore, 734
Wagenseil, J. C., 239
Wagner, Cosima, 121, 204, 254
   Richard, 18, 53, 60, 71, 81, 155, 156, 157, 171, 184, 185–332, 341, 387, 438, 630, 730, 734, 749, 766, 964, 983, 1003, 1089, 1141, 1295, 1307, 1663, 1668, 1669
   Siegfried, 204
Wagner Nights (Ernest Newman), 194, 204

Wagner's Music-Dramas Analysed, 217, 235
Walker, Benjamin, 1271n.
Walküre, Die (The Valkyrie), 53, 254, 255, 259, 273–89, 290, 292, 293, 295, 298
Wallace, Vincent, 959–62
Wally, La, 680–3
Walpole, Sir Robert, 29
Walter, Bruno, 1341
Walton, Sir William, 1405–12
War and Peace, 1353–70
War Requiem, 1514
Warnéry, 1258n.
Washington, *Evening Star*, 1661
  Opera Society of, 1654–5
Weber, Carl Maria von, 150, 152–68, 184
Webern, Anton von, 1086
Weckerin, Frl., 254
Wedekind, Frank, 1082
Weil, Grete, 1121
Weill, Kurt, 30, 1100–8, 1285
Weimar, Opera House, 204–5
Weinberger, Jaromir, 1590–3
Welsh National Opera, 131n., 544
Wenzig, Josef, 969, 981
Werfel, Franz, 513, 545, 591
Werther, 864–9, 871
Westrup, Professor, 4, 9
Wette, Adelheid, 371
White, Eric, 1312, 1313, 1517
White Lady, The. See *Dame Blanche, La*
Whiting, John, 1598, 1599
  W., 1502n.
Widerspänstigen Zähmung, Der, 365–8
Widmann, J. V., 365
Wieland, Christoph Martin, 130, 160
Wienerblut, 358–62
Wilbye, John, 1481n.
Wilde, Oscar, 997
Wildschütz, Der, 169, 171–2

Wilhelm Meister, 778
Wilhelmj, T., 254
William Tell. See *Guillaume Tell*
Williams, Ralph Vaughan, 654, 1387–99
Willner, A. M., 1187
Wittich, Frau, 1001
Wolf, Hugo, 374–6
Wolf-Ferrari, Ermanno, 1229–39, 1640
Woman without a Shadow, The. See *Frau ohne Schatten, Die*
Wonders in the Sun, 29
Wood, Hugh, 1421n.
Wooden Prince, The (ballet), 1607n.
Wozzeck, 539, 1073–81, 1124, 1214, 1258, 1342
Wreckers, The, 1378–81

Yeats, W. B., 1496
Yevgeny Onyegin. See *Eugene Onegin*
Yorick's Love, 689
Young, Mrs, 50n.
Young Lord, The. See *Junge Lord, Der*

Zaccaria, Nicola, 382
Zaïde, 85
Zamboni, L., 406
Zandonai, Riccardo, 1239–43
Zangarini, C., 1182, 1235
Zar und Zimmermann, 169–71
Zauberflöte, Die (see *The Magic Flute*), 129–42, 1104
Zell, F., 333, 350, 368
Zhdanov, Andrei, 1356
Zhukovsky, V. A., 917
Zigeunerbaron, Der, 354–8
Zille, Moritz, 131n.
Zimmermann, Bernd Alois, 1112–20
Zítek, Ota, 1589
Zolotoy Pyetushok. See *Coq d'Or, Le*
Züngel, Emmanuel, 973
Zweig, Stefan, 1041, 1042